MURDOCH'S DICTIONARY OF IRISH LAW

(A Sourcebook)

Fourth Edition
by

Henry Murdoch

BE, C.Eng, F.IEI, MBA, FCGI.
Barrister

WITH A FOREWORD TO THE FIRST EDITION BY
The Hon. Thomas A. Finlay
Chief Justice from 1985 to 1994

LexisNexis™

Members of the LexisNexis Group worldwide

Ireland	LexisNexis 24–26 Upper Ormond Quay, DUBLIN 7
Argentina	LexisNexis Argentina, BUENOS AIRES
Australia	LexisNexis Butterworths, CHATSWOOD, New South Wales
Austria	LexisNexis Verlag ARD Orac GmbH & Co KG, VIENNA
Canada	LexisNexis Butterworths, MARKHAM, Ontario
Chile	LexisNexis Chile Ltda, SANTIAGO DE CHILE
Czech Republic	Nakladatelství Orac sro, PRAGUE
France	Editions du Juris-Classeur SA, PARIS
Germany	LexisNexis Deutschland GmbH, FRANKFURT and MUNSTER
Hong Kong	LexisNexis Butterworths, HONG KONG
Hungary	HVG-Orac, BUDAPEST
India	LexisNexis Butterworths, NEW DELHI
Italy	Giuffrè Editore, MILAN
Malaysia	Malayan Law Journal Sdn Bhd, KUALA LUMPUR
New Zealand	LexisNexis Butterworths, WELLINGTON
Poland	Wydawnictwo Prawnicze LexisNexis, WARSAW
Singapore	LexisNexis Butterworths, SINGAPORE
South Africa	LexisNexis Butterworths, DURBAN
Switzerland	Stämpfli Verlag AG, BERNE
United Kingdom	LexisNexis UK, LONDON and EDINBURGH
USA	LexisNexis, DAYTON, Ohio

A CIP Catalogue record for this book is available from the British Library.

ISBN 1 854 75362 2

Printed and bound in Great Britain by William Clowes Ltd, Beccles, Suffolk

Typeset by Columns Design Ltd, UK

Visit LexisNexis UK at www.lexisnexis.co.uk

MURDOCH'S DICTIONARY OF IRISH LAW

(A Sourcebook)

Also by Henry Murdoch:

Invention and the Irish Patent System (1971) published by the
Administrative Research Bureau, Dublin University.

Working Women, An International Survey (1984) - Chapter on
Ireland – published by John Wiley & Sons, London.

Building Society Law in Ireland – A Guide (1989) –published by
Topaz Publications, Dublin.

Murdoch's Irish Legal Companion (2004) – on CD-ROM and
online at http://milcnet.lendac.ie , published by Topaz
Publications and Lendac Data Systems Ltd, Dublin.

To my father Archie Murdoch from Dingle, Co Kerry, who passed away in 1995 in his 92nd year and to my mother Greta Murdoch (nee Lyons) from Ballyhaunis and Kilkelly, Co Mayo, who predeceased him in 1984, and both of whom throughout my life gave me tremendous encouragement, support and sound advice; and to my wife Davida who in a very practical way has made this dictionary a reality; and to my (now adult) children Maeve and Breffni for all their help.

About the Author

Henry Murdoch was born in Cavan in 1938 and was educated in University College Cork, Trinity College Dublin and Kings Inns Dublin. He is a barrister and a chartered engineer.

He was called to the Irish Bar in 1966 and practised in the Four Courts in the mid-1980s while on a career break, when he conceived and wrote the first edition of this dictionary.

He retired in 1999 from his position as Assistant Director General – Industry with FAS, the Training and Employment Authority of Ireland after a 40-year career in the private and public sectors, ranging from engineering, aviation, waste management, training, health services, banking, and vocational and medical rehabilitation.

He is currently Chairman of the National Rehabilitation Hospital, Dun Laoghaire, and a non-executive director of Skillnets Ltd. He is a member of the governing board in London of the City & Guilds Institute. In 2004 he was conferred with the highest award of City & Guilds – *Fellowship* of the Institute. He served for nine years as a non-executive director of First National Building Society/First Active plc.

He is married to Davida (nee Franklin) and they have two adult children – Maeve who works in the office of the President of the European Central Bank in Frankfurt, and Breffni who is a software engineer with CR2 Ltd in Dublin.

While at UCC, Henry Murdoch was the Irish Universities junior flyweight boxing champion and he represented the Irish Universities abroad. In the mid 1960s he was an international judge in water skiing. Now, in 2004, he is a keen but high handicap tennis player, golfer, sailor and occasional skier (snow).

FOREWORD TO FIRST EDITION

A dictionary of law is and has always been an intensely useful book. A dictionary of Irish law, the first as far as I am aware in anything like modern times, is particularly welcome.

This dictionary provides an excellent tool in the hands of lawyers both experienced and those less experienced as well. It will, I am certain, also provide an extremely convenient, if not indispensable, piece of equipment to persons of other disciplines who have, from time to time or consistently, recourse to the law or concern with the law or with legal documents.

The author has been most painstaking in the compilation of this dictionary and has been extremely conscientious in the accuracy of the information which he has provided. It seems to me a particularly attractive feature that this dictionary should bring the law up to a date so close to the time of its publication.

I warmly welcome this book and I have no doubt that it will attain the success and make the contribution to the understanding and administration of Irish law which it clearly deserves to do.

The 3rd day of November 1988.

Thomas A. Finlay
Chief Justice,
Four Courts,
Dublin 7.

PREFACE TO FIRST EDITION (1988)

I have written this book because, despite the development of our own legal system over the last sixty six years, there is no reference book available which gives to the reader a definition of the principal words and phrases which are encountered in Irish law. This book seeks to fill that gap by providing in one volume a definition of these key words, giving in most instances the legal source of such definition, whether statutory or judicial, and a brief introduction to the relevant law.

The book is designed primarily for busy practising lawyers, whether barrister or solicitor, who want an *aide memoire* or an introduction to an area of law with which they are not immediately familiar, and which will either fulfil their needs there and then, or point the correct direction for further information.

However, I hope that the book will prove useful also to the growing number of persons who are directly involved in or who encounter the law in their work, study, or otherwise eg students, company secretaries, accountants, auctioneers, bankers, journalists, engineers, architects, medical personnel, the Gardai, local and national politicians, trade union officials, employers and managers, and those involved in the public service, insurance, trade associations, or in law enforcement generally and of course the general public.

The book is extensively cross-referenced to increase its usefulness. ... Reference is made to the growing number of books on Irish law which can be consulted for further information. Included also are references to books on UK law where they are of relevance to Ireland and to those legal maxims in Latin which are in everyday use or which capture the essence or historical basis of our law.

I have endeavoured to cover all areas of law; however, because of limitations on the size of one volume, difficult choices had to be made on what to include and exclude. Inevitably, there may be omissions which some readers may consider should not have been made; these, and any errors which may have crept into the text, I would appreciate having pointed out to me.

I am most grateful to The Hon Thomas A. Finlay, Chief Justice, for so kindly writing the Foreword. His encouraging words have made the writing of this book all the more worthwhile.

I would also like to express my gratitude: to my colleagues in the Law Library, particularly Kieran Fleck BL and Vincent Landy SC; to the staff of the Central Office in the Four Courts; to the staff of the libraries of Trinity College Dublin, of Kings Inns, and of the Law Library, particularly Jennefer Aston and Pat Redmond; to Brendan Murphy for expert advice on my computer requirements; to Doreen McBride, Edie McGarry and Nuala Smith for the data input which was done with considerable skill; and to Michael Burke of Topaz Publications and Sarah Kelly and Peter Allman of Dublin University Press for translating the manuscript from 'floppy discs' to a book.

I particularly thank my father and my family to whom this book is dedicated.

The measure of success of this dictionary will be the extent to which it is used by those who buy it and the extent to which they find it helpful in such use. I hope it will be successful on both counts.

7 November 1988

PREFACE TO FOURTH EDITION (2004)

It is hard to believe that I have been writing this book for the last 18 years – since 1986! It has been a voyage of discovery for me. Every day I have come across new words which have a legal significance and which merit inclusion in the dictionary. This partly explains why the fourth edition is more than three times the size of the first edition.

Apart from updating the content of the dictionary to reflect changes in the law arising from new legislation, I have endeavoured over the years to widen the scope of the dictionary and deepen its content. Consequently, there is now more in-depth coverage of judicial decisions, rules of court, European law, medical ethics, codes of professional practice as regards lawyers, and relevant articles in the *Bar Review* and *Law Society Gazette*.

And with the explosion in the Internet as a great source of information, I have expanded the provision of relevant website addresses.

This fourth edition marks a major milestone. It is the first edition to be published by LexisNexis. In joining the stable of this international publisher, the dictionary is assured of a longevity beyond mine. In this respect I feel like a parent who has all his children happily settled down and married!

I would like to thank all the practitioners, judges, students and members of the public who have been kind enough to encourage me and help me over the last 18 years and particularly all those persons who supplied me with up-to-date information; the library staff in King's Inns and in Trinity College Dublin; the staff of the Law Society and the Bar Council; Eamonn Hayes of Lendac Data Systems whose assistance on my electronic needs has been invaluable, Kieran Fleck SC, Donal Egan BL, Lany Bacon BL and Mark McParland, Solicitor, for assistance on particular areas of law; and Louise Leavy, Sandra Mulvey and Ros Connell of LexisNexis for all their assistance in bringing this fourth edition into being.

I hope that this edition continues to make a contribution to an understanding of the law and is of some assistance. I have endeavoured to state the law as accurately as possible on the sources available to me, and as enacted, on 1 September 2004, unless otherwise stated.

Henry Murdoch
September 2004

GUIDE TO DICTIONARY

Consider this typical entry in conjunction with the notes below:

> **partnership.**[1] The relationship existing between two or more persons carrying on business in common with a view to profit: Partnership Act 1890, s 1.[2] There are rules for determining if a partnership exists (PA 1890, s 2).[3] ... There are two kinds of partnership, the ordinary partnership and the limited partnership (qv).[4] ... [Bibliography: Keane (1); Lindley UK].[5] See *Macken v Revenue Commissioners* (1962) IR 302.[6] See also RSC Ord 46, rr 3–4.[7] See FIRM.[8]

1. The entries are in alphabetical order in bold print. There may be further entries based on the key word eg **investment limited partnership; partnership, dissolution of; partnership, liability in;** and **partnership, number to form.**

2. A reference is usually given to the statutory basis for an entry with the section (s) of the Act identified. Where there is reference to draft legislation, the particular Bill under consideration by the Oireachtas at the time of writing, is identified. Care should be taken to compare the exact wording of these Bills, as the text of Bills is frequently changed during the course of their passage through the Dáil and Seanad. Note also that an Act or a section of an Act may require a Commencement Order to be made to bring the Act or the Section into force eg the different provisions of the Residential Tenancies Act 2004 come into operation on such days as are specified by Ministerial order.

3. Any further references to statutes use the appropriate acronym.

4. (qv) after a word or series of words indicates that there is a separate entry in the dictionary for that word or for the series of words. In the example, there is a separate entry under *limited partnership.*

5. Where a major topic of law is dealt with, for which there is a good book available which could be usefully consulted for further information, it is identified by the surname of the author after [Bibliography: ...]. If UK appears after the author's name, it indicates that the book deals with the law of the United Kingdom but is of some relevance to Irish Law. A list of authors and their publications is in Appendix 5.

6. Reference is made in many entries to the more significant or interesting case law which could be usefully consulted eg [1991] ITLR (21 January) HC; the date refers to the date of the Law Report and not the date the case was decided; in some instances the level of court eg HC (High Court) is indicated after the date. Cases are sometimes reversed on appeal. Consequently, care should be exercised with more recent cases, particularly those with 'under appeal' noted after them. The list of Law Reports and abbreviations is in Appendix 1.

7. Reference is also made in some entries to other sources eg the Rules of the Superior Courts (RSC) and the Order (Ord) and Rules (rr) applicable. A list of abbreviations is included below.

8. The final reference in capital letters directs the reader to another relevant or associated entry in the dictionary eg in this case to FIRM.

9. Where an email or website address flows from one line to another, disregard the hyphen which appears at the end of the first line of the address.

10. In many entries a reference is made to a function or power of a Minister but the Department is generally not indicated in view of the changes which take place from time to time in the allocation of these Departments to different Ministers.

11. Throughout the Dictionary, the male includes the female unless the context suggests otherwise.

Professional advice should be obtained before acting on the information contained in this book.

ABBREVIATIONS

A-G	=	Attorney General
App	=	appendix
art	=	article
CC	=	Circuit Court
CCC	=	Central Criminal Court
CCA	=	Court of Criminal Appeal
CFC	=	Circuit Family Court
CFI	=	Court of First Instance
C of A in NI	=	Court of Appeal in Northern Ireland
ch	=	chapter
CMAC	=	Courts Martial Appeal Court
DCR	=	District Court Rules 1997 - SI No 93 of 1997 as amended
DPP	=	Director of Public Prosecutions
ECJ	=	European Court of Justice
EC Pub	=	European Communities Publication
EO	=	Equality Officer
ET	=	Equality Tribunal
FL	=	First Law
Gov Pub	=	Government Publications
HC	=	High Court
LRC	=	Law Reform Commission
No	=	Number
Ord	=	Order Number
para	=	paragraph
PC	=	Privy Council
r	=	rule
rr	=	rules
RSC	=	Rules of the Superior Courts 1986, SI No 15 of 1986 as amended
regs	=	regulations
s	=	section
SC	=	Supreme Court
SCC	=	Special Criminal Court
Sch	=	schedule
SI	=	Statutory Instrument
SR & O	=	Statutory Rules and Orders
ss	=	sections

1922 Constitution = The Constitution of the Irish Free State (Saorstát Eireann) which came into operation on 6 December 1922.

1937 Constitution = The Constitution of Ireland enacted by the People on 1 July 1937 and which came into operation on 29 December 1937.

See   Appendix 1 – Abbreviations of Law Reports
Appendix 2 – Reports of Law Reform Commission
Appendix 3 – Amendments to the Constitution of Ireland
Appendix 4 – Irish Justice System 2004.
Appendix 5 – Bibliography.

A

a coelo usque ad centrum. [From heaven to the centre of the earth.] In principle, the extent of the ownership of property. See AIRSPACE, INTERFERENCE WITH; CUJUS EST SOLUM; LIGHT RAILWAY; SUBSTRATUM OF LAND.

a fortiori (rationale). [Much more; with or for a stronger reason.] See *Shelly v Mahon and DPP* [1990] ITLR (23 July).

a mensa et thoro. [From board and bed.] See DIVORCE A MENSA ET THORO.

a posteriori. [From the effect to the cause.] Inductive reasoning.

a priori. [From the cause to the effect.] Deductive reasoning.

a tempore cujus contrarii memoria non existet. [From a time of which there is no memory to the contrary.] See TIME IMMEMORIAL.

a verbis legis non est recedendum. [You must not vary the words of a statute.] See INTERPRETATION OF LEGISLATION.

a vinculo matrimonii. [From the bond of matrimony.] See DIVORCE.

A & B. See CONTRIBUTORY; TRADE MARK, REGISTERED.

ab antiquo. [From old times.]

ab extra. [From outside.]

ab initio. [From the beginning.] See TRESPASSER AB INITIO; MARRIAGE, NULLITY OF.

ab intestato. [From an intestate.] Succession *ab intestato* is succession to property of a person who has not disposed of it by will. See INTESTATE SUCCESSION.

Ab; Abr. Abridgment.

abandoned aircraft. Where an aircraft is left at a State airport and Aer Rianta, the State airport company, is of the opinion that it has been abandoned, the company is required to serve a notice on the registered owner or operator to remove the aircraft and, if they fail to do so, the company may remove, sell or otherwise dispose of the aircraft: Air Navigation and Transport (Amendment) Act 1998, s 41.

abandoned child. A person who finds an abandoned newborn child, or any person in whose charge the child is placed, has a duty to register the birth within three months of finding the child: Civil Registration Act 2004, s 21.

abandoned house. A house which has been abandoned by the person to whom a housing authority has made a housing loan and which has been or is in danger of being trespassed upon or damaged; the housing authority is empowered to take whatever measures it considers necessary to secure and protect the house: Housing (Miscellaneous Provisions) Act 1992, s 12.

abandoned vehicle. It is an offence to abandon a vehicle on any land; the offence is committed by the person who placed the vehicle and also the registered owner where the latter is not the person who so placed: Waste Management Act 1996, s 71. A local authority has power to enter any land to remove an abandoned vehicle; 24 hours' notice in writing must be given where entry is to a private dwelling (WMA 1996, s 71(4)). A *vehicle* includes part of a vehicle, an article designed as a vehicle, a skip, and a load on a vehicle (WMA 1996, s 5(1)).

abandonment. The relinquishment or surrender of an interest, claim or thing.

(1) A person will not be held to have surrendered or abandoned his constitutional rights unless it is shown that he is aware of what the rights are and of what he is doing, and that the action he has taken is such as could reasonably lead to the clear and unambiguous inference that such was his intention: *G v An Bord Uchtála [1980] IR 80.*

(2) An easement (qv) may be lost by abandonment; evidence of abandonment must be supported by evidence of conduct or intention adverse to the exercise of the right: *Carroll v Sheridan [1984] ILRM 451; O'Gara v Murray [1989] 7 ILT Dig 82.*

(3) In marine insurance, where there is a constructive total loss (qv), the insured may abandon the subject matter insured to the insurer or underwriter by giving notice of abandonment to him within a reasonable time. The insured then becomes entitled to the insurance moneys and the insurer or underwriter to the subject matter insured. See Marine Insurance Act 1906, ss 60–62.

(4) For abandonment of an option, see *Kearns v Dillon [1997] 3 IR 287, SC.*

(5) For abandonment of parental rights, see ADOPTION.

(6) For abandonment of children, see CRUELTY TO CHILDREN; FOSTER CHILD; WELFARE OF CHILDREN.

abandonment of claim. A plaintiff in District or Circuit Court proceedings may abandon any part of his claim in order to bring the claim within the jurisdiction of the court; such abandonment must be stated in the civil summons or civil bill, as the case may be: DCR 1997 Ord 39, r 12 and Ord 41, r 6; Circuit Court Rules 2001 Ord 5, r 5(c); O 10, r 4.

abatement. A reduction, allowance or rebate. An abatement *pro rata* refers to the proportionate reduction of the amount of each of a number of debts or claims eg where a fund or estate is insufficient to meet them all in full.

An action, proceeding or matter in the Circuit Court does not become abated by reason of the death or bankruptcy of any of the parties, if the cause of action survives: Circuit Court Rules 2001 Ord 22. See DAMAGES; DISABILITY PENSION.

abatement of action. A suspension or termination of proceedings in an action: RSC Ord 17, rr 12–13. A cause or matter is not abated by reason of death or bankruptcy if the cause of action survives: RSC Ord 17, r 1. See DEATH, EFFECT OF.

abatement of legacy. The reduction of a legacy due to an insufficiency of assets in the testator's estate. *Specific* legacies (qv) take priority over *general* legacies (qv) and are liable to abatement only if the assets are otherwise insufficient for the payment of debts. *Demonstrative* legacies (qv) only abate if the fund out of which payment is directed is insufficient or if otherwise the assets of the estate are insufficient to pay debts. *General* legacies abate proportionally between themselves except where a legacy has been given in payment of a debt. See Succession Act 1965, s 46 Sch 1. See ADMINISTRATION OF ESTATES; LEGACY.

abatement of nuisance. The right to remove or put an end to a nuisance (qv), as an alternative to taking an action. If a nuisance can only be abated by entry on the land of another, the person abating must give notice to the occupier of the lands on which it exists, except in the case of emergency. If no entry is required (eg to cut overhanging branches of a tree), no notice is required. Generally abatement is a remedy that the law does not favour. See SANITARY AUTHORITIES AND NUISANCE.

abattoir. Any premises used for or in connection with the slaughter of animals whose meat is intended for human consumption, and does not include a place situate on some farms: Abattoirs Act 1988. Abattoirs and knackeries are required to be licensed

annually, local authorities are responsible for veterinary control of the premises, and all meat intended for human consumption must be stamped with a health mark. The purpose of the 1988 Act is to provide the same standard at slaughtering premises as apply at export meat plants. See Abattoirs Act 1988 (Veterinary Examination) Regulations 1992, SI No 89 of 1992; (Amendment) Regulations 2002, SI No 165 of 2002; Abattoir (Health Mark) Regulations 1992, SI No 90 of 1992.

abbreviated accounts. Accounts of a company other than as part of the full accounts; abbreviated accounts must be distinguished from the full accounts filed with the Registrar of Companies: Companies Amendment Act 1986, s 19.

abdication. Voluntary renunciation of an office or responsibility.

abduction. The wrongful taking away of a person. It was an offence, without lawful authority or excuse to take out of the possession and against the will of any person having lawful care of her, an unmarried girl under the age of eighteen years with the intent that she would have unlawful sexual intercourse with men or a particular man: Criminal Law Amendment Act 1855, s 7 repealed by Criminal Justice Act 1951. See *The People (Attorney-General) v McCormack* [1944] Frewen 55. See LRC 12 of 1985. See also CHILD ABDUCTION; FALSE IMPRISONMENT.

abearance. Behaviour.

abet. To aid in the commission of a crime. See AID AND ABET.

abeyance. The condition of an inheritance which has no present owner; an estate is in abeyance when there is no person in whom it can vest.

abjuration. Renunciation by oath (qv).

abode. Habitation or place of residence. A man's residence, where he lives with his family and sleeps at night, is always his *place of abode* in the full sense of that expression: *R v Hammond* [1852] 17 QB 772. Possession by a person, when not in his *place of abode*, of any article intended to be used in a larceny or burglary, was an offence: Larceny Act 1990, s 2. *Place of abode* in similar UK legislation has been held to be a site in which the accused intends to reside: *R v Bundy* [1992] 2 All ER 382. *Place of abode* has been changed in the repealing Irish legislation to *place of residence*: Criminal Justice (Theft and Fraud Offences) Act 2001, s 15. See DOMICILE.

abolish. See REPEAL.

abominable crime. The expression used to describe the offences of sodomy (qv) and bestiality (qv): Offences Against the Person Act 1861, s 61. See BUGGERY.

abortion. Termination of pregnancy; the intentional procurement of miscarriage of a pregnant woman. It is an offence (formerly, a felony (qv)) to procure an abortion by means of any poison (qv), noxious substance, instrument or any other thing. It is also an offence for a woman, who is actually pregnant at the time, to procure or attempt to procure an abortion. See *The People (Attorney-General) v Coleman* [1945] IR 237; Offences Against the Person Act 1861, ss 58–59.

The right to life of the unborn, and consequently the general prohibition of abortion, is given constitutional recognition by art 40(3)(3), inserted by referendum. However, it has been held that termination of pregnancy is permissible under the Constitution where it is established as a matter of probability that there is a real and substantial risk to the life, as distinct from the health, of the mother, which can be avoided by the termination of her pregnancy: *A-G v X* [1992] ILRM 401, SC; 1937 Constitution art 40(3)(3). See *Kingston & Whelan (1992) 10 ILT & SJ 93*.

In a subsequent case a district court judge concluded that there was a real and substantial risk to the life, as distinct from the health, of 'C', which could only be avoided by the termination of her pregnancy, which termination was opposed by her parents, 'A' and 'B'. The High Court held that the termination of pregnancy which was authorised by the District Court judge was lawful under the Irish Constitution: *A & B V EASTERN HEALTH BOARD & C* [1998] 1 ILRM 460, HC and 1 IR 464.

As regards the legality of assisting pregnant women to travel abroad to obtain abortions, the European Court of Justice has held that medical termination of pregnancy, performed in accordance with the law of the State in which it is carried out, constitutes a *service* within the meaning of the Treaty of Rome 1957 art 60 (now, art 50 of the consolidated (2002) Treaty establishing the European Community); however, it also held that it is not contrary to Community law for a member state where medical termination of pregnancy is

forbidden, to prohibit the distribution of information about the identity and location of clinics in another member state where voluntary termination of pregnancy is lawfully carried out: *SPUC v Grogan [1992] ECJ ILRM 461.*

However in 1992, an amendment to the Constitution provided that art 40(3)(3) shall not limit freedom to obtain or make available, in the state, subject to such conditions as may be laid down by law, information relating to services lawfully available in another state: Fourteenth Amendment to the Constitution Act 1992. The subsequent Regulation of Information Act 1995 (which provides that it is not unlawful to publish certain information relating to services which are lawfully available in a particular place) has been found not to be repugnant to the Constitution: *[1995] 2 ILRM 81, SC* and *1 IR 1.*

It continues to be unlawful for a person to make an appointment or any other arrangement for or on behalf of a woman for the termination of pregnancy (Regulation of Information Act 1995 Act, s 8(1)). There is a prohibition on the EC Treaties affecting the application in Ireland of art 40(3)(3) of the Constitution: Maastricht Treaty 1992 (Abortion Protocol).

See also Health (Family Planning) Act 1979, s 10. The number of Irish women travelling to the UK to procure an abortion has been steadily increasing in recent decades, being less than 2,000 women in 1975 and reaching over 6,500 in 2002: *Primary Care for the Prevention and Management of Crisis Pregnancy* (April 2004). See *'Abortion and EC Law on Social Security'* in 11 ILT & SJ (1993) 244. See *'Abortion and Fathers' Rights: New Perspectives'* by Elaine Fahey in (2002) 10 ISLR 125. [Bibliography: Bacik, Kingston & Whelan.] See CRISIS PREGNANCY; PRIVATE PROSECUTION; MURDER; LIFE, RIGHT TO; SERVICES, PROVISION OF; TRAVEL, RIGHT TO.

abortion, green paper. In the *Green Paper on Abortion* published in September 1999, the Government put forward *seven* possible constitutional and legislative approaches for discussion, without recommending any one option: (i) an absolute constitutional ban on abortion; (ii) an amendment of the constitutional provisions so as to restrict the application of the *X* case; (iii) the retention of the status quo; (iv) the retention of the constitutional status quo with legislative restatement of the prohibition on abortion; (v) legislation to regulate abortion in circumstances defined by the X case; (vi) a reversion to the position as it pertained prior to 1983; (vii) permitting abortion on grounds beyond those specified in the X case.

This led to a referendum on 6 March 2002 which was rejected by the people: 25th Amendment of the Constitution Bill 2001. See ABORTION, REFERENDA REJECTED.

abortion, medical guidelines. The Medical Council issued guidelines on abortion in March 1993, stating that: 'Situations arise in medical practice where the life and/or health of the mother or of the unborn, or both, are endangered. In these situations, it is imperative ethically that doctors shall endeavour to preserve life and health'... 'it is unethical always to withhold treatment beneficial to a pregnant woman, by reason of her pregnancy.'

These guidelines were revised in 1998 to: 'The deliberate and intentional destruction of the *unborn child* is professional misconduct. Should a child in utero suffer or lose its life as a side effect of standard medical treatment of the mother, then this is not unethical. Refusal by a doctor to treat a woman with a serious illness because she is pregnant would be grounds for complaint and could be considered to be professional misconduct.': *A Guide to Ethical Conduct and Behaviour* (5th edn, 1998) para 26.5.

These guidelines were again changed in 2001 to: 'The Council recognises that termination of pregnancy can occur when there is real and substantial risk to the life of the mother.' The Council then states that it subscribes to the written views of the Institute of Obstetricians and Gynaecologists to an All-Party Oireachtas Committee on 29 February 2000. These views are: 'In current obstetrical practice rare complications can arise where therapeutic intervention is required at a stage in pregnancy when there will be little or no prospect for the survival of the baby, due to extreme immaturity. In these exceptional situations failure to intervene may result in the death of both mother and baby. We consider that there is a fundamental difference between abortion carried out with the intention of taking the life of the baby, for example for social reasons, and the unavoidable death of the baby resulting from essential treatment to protect the life of the mother. We

recognise our responsibility to provide aftercare for women who leave the State for termination of pregnancy. We recommend that full support and follow up services be made available for all women whose pregnancies have been terminated, whatever the circumstances.': Amendment No 1 to 5th Edition 1998 (2001), and now incorporated in *A Guide to Ethical Conduct and Behaviour* (6th edn, 2004) para 24.6 and Appendix C.

The Irish College of General Practitioners issued abortion guidelines in April 2004 stating that (a) a doctor must refrain from being, or appearing to be, judgmental, (b) it is important that the patient obtains reliable information about abortion clinics that have a good reputation, (c) the doctor cannot make an appointment with an abortion clinic but should write a medical record summary note and give this to the patient to take with her to the clinic, (d) a doctor with a conscientious objection may decide not to supply information about abortion clinics, but the doctor must never refuse treatment on the basis of moral disapproval, and should make the names of other doctors available to the patient, (e) the doctor's response to the initial consultation will have a profound influence on the patient's willingness after the abortion to attend for follow-up care, the importance of which is emphasised: *Primary Care for the Prevention and Management of Crisis Pregnancy* (2004). See website: *www.icgp.ie*. See CRISIS PREGNANCY.

abortion, referenda rejected. In 1992, the people, by referendum, rejected the Twelfth Amendment to the Constitution, which would have provided that: 'It shall be unlawful to terminate the life of an unborn unless such termination is necessary to save the life, as distinct from the health, of the mother where there is an illness or disorder of the mother, giving rise to a real and substantial risk to her life, not being a risk of self-destruction': Referendum (Amendment) (No 2) Act 1992.

In order to deal with the aftermath of the 'X' case (*A-G v X [1992] ILRM 401, SC*), the Government put a constitutional amendment to the people on 6 March 2002 to provide that the proposed Protection of Human Life in Pregnancy Act 2002 should be the law on abortion in the state: Twenty-Fifth Amendment of the Constitution Bill 2001. The amendment was rejected by a margin of less than 1%: 629,041 votes against (50.42%) and 618,485 for (49.58%).

The proposed text of art 40(3)(4) was that 'the life of the unborn in the womb shall be protected in accordance with the provisions of the Protection of Human Life in Pregnancy Act, 2002'.

In effect, the electorate was asked to approve a conditional amendment to the Constitution, which would have effect only if, subsequent to the referendum, the Oireachtas enacted the Protection of Human Life in Pregnancy Act 2002 exactly as contained in Sch 2 of that Act. The proposed text of art 40(3)(5) provided that any Bill containing provisions to amend the 2002 Act must be referred to the people in a further referendum.

The main features of the 2002 proposed legislation were:

(a) *Abortion* was defined as the intentional destruction by any means of unborn human life after implantation in the womb of a woman;

(b) *Abortion* did not include the carrying out of a medical procedure by a medical practitioner at an *approved* place in the course of which or as a result of which unborn human life is ended where that procedure is, in the *reasonable opinion* of the practitioner, necessary to prevent a real and substantive risk of loss of the woman's life other than by self-destruction;

(c) *Reasonable opinion* meant a reasonable opinion formed in good faith which has regard to the need to preserve unborn human life where practicable and of which a written record has been made and signed by the practitioner;

(d) It would be an offence to carry out or effect an abortion in the state or to attempt to or to aid, abet or procure any other person to do so;

(e) There was no restriction on a person travelling to another state to obtain an abortion or to obtain information relating to services lawfully available in another state.

The High Court rejected on 1 February 2002 a claim for a stay on the proposed referendum; the court held that the proposed referendum did not conflict with art 46 of the Constitution: *Morris & Ni Mhaoldomhnaigh v Minister for the Environment [2002] 1 IR 326, HC*. There was nothing in art 46 which expressly prohibited an amendment to the Constitution by reference to a document extraneous to it, nor was there a prohibition on the making of an amendment which was conditional upon some other event taking place.

abridged time bill. See BILL, ABRIDGED TIME.

abridgement of time. See TIME, COURT RULES.

abrogate. To repeal, cancel, annul or abolish. See REPEAL.

abscond. To go away secretly or to hide from the jurisdiction of the court. It may amount to an act of bankruptcy: Bankruptcy Act 1988, s 7(1)(c). An absconding debtor may be arrested by order of the court (BA 1988, s 9). An absconding bankrupt may also be arrested (BA 1988, s 23). It is an offence for a debtor to abscond with property to the value of £500 (€635) or more with the intent to defraud his creditors (BA 1988, s 124).

Also a person charged with an offence who has been admitted to bail, may be arrested and detained to await his trial, where he is about to abscond for the purpose of evading justice. See DCR 1997 Ord 20.

If, during the course of a trial and prior to final sentence, the accused absconds and the defending barrister's solicitor withdraws from the case, then a barrister acting for the accused must withdraw: *Code of Conduct for the Bar of Ireland* (December 2003), r 9.13. If, for any reason, the instructing solicitor does not withdraw from the case, a defending barrister retains an absolute discretion whether or not to continue to act. See BAIL; BANKRUPTCY, ACT OF.

absence. (1) Non-appearance by a party to a summons (qv) or a subpoena (qv).

(2) Absence of a spouse for seven years may be a conclusive defence to a charge of bigamy (qv).

(3) A person may be presumed to be dead if not heard of for seven years. See 'Body of Evidence' by barrister Tom Power in *Law Society Gazette* (April 2004) 18.

(4) A medical practitioner is required to ensure that his patients receive adequate care when alternative arrangements have to be made during his absence: Medical Council, *A Guide to Ethical Conduct and Behaviour* (6th edn, 2004) para 11.1.

(5) Where a defendant fails to appear in the District Court on the date specified in a valid summons duly served on him, the judge may proceed, in the absence of the defendant, to hear and determine the

charge described in the summons or may adjourn the hearing to a later date and may secure the attendance of the defendant by warrant or otherwise: *DPP v Roche [1988] ILRM 39, SC*. In relation to the absence of the prosecutor, see *DPP v Gill [1980] IR 263*.

Where an accused is not present in the District Court and is not represented to answer a complaint and it appears to the court that the summons was duly served, the court may proceed to deal with the complaint: DCR 1997 Ord 23, r 2; *Stewart v Patwell [2000] 1 ILRM 57, HC*. See DEATH, PRESUMPTION OF; JUDGMENT IN DEFAULT OF APPEARANCE; TÁNAISTE.

absent without leave. The offence committed by a person, subject to military law, who absents himself without authority eg leaving his unit or formation or the place where his duty requires him to be: Defence Act 1954, s 137. The penal sanction for a seaman being *absent without leave* has been repealed: Merchant Shipping (Miscellaneous Provisions) Act 1998, s 2. See DESERTER.

absenteeism. Absence without sufficient cause or in breach of a term or condition of employment may be a ground for dismissal from employment. Persistent absenteeism of a prison officer has been found to justify his dismissal: *Lang v Government of Ireland [1993] ELR 234, HC*. Failure of a crew member to notify his employer that he was not able to report for duty, knowing that a relief crew must be provided, was held to be sufficient ground to justify his dismissal: *Commissioners of Irish Lights v Sugg [1994] ELR 97, HC*.

The disciplinary procedures of a company were found to be arbitrary and unfair as they punished employees even when on certified sick leave: *Crawford v Donegal Meat Processors [2003] ELR 329, EAT*. See also *Ruane v Barrett [1990] ELR 28; Rigney v Offaly Co Council [1990] ELR 38; Hynes v GEC Distributors [1992] ELR 95, EAT; Flanagan v Emerson Electric Ltd [1997] ELR 29, EAT*. See UNFAIR DISMISSAL.

absente reo. [The defendant being absent.]

absoluta sententia expositore non indiget. [When you have plain words capable of only one interpretation, no explanation of them is required.] See INTERPRETATION OF LEGISLATION.

absolute. Complete and without conditions. An order of a court is absolute when it is complete and of full force and effect eg a garnishee order (qv) absolute. Contrast with NISI.

absolute discretion. The wide power given to a person of deciding a question where latitude of judgment is required. Trust deeds sometimes give to the trustee *absolute discretion* to deal with trust property as he deems fit; such an absolute discretion, however, would not necessarily relieve a trustee from his duty to exercise reasonable care and prudence: *Stacey v Branch [1995] 2 ILRM 136, HC*. Where a body is given statutory power in its absolute discretion, it must act fairly and reasonably: *Zockoll Group Ltd v Telecom Éireann [1998] 3 IR 287, HC*.

absolute liability. See STRICT LIABILITY.

absolve. To free from liability or guilt.

absorption capacity. In relation to the EU, usually means the ability of a country or organisation to receive aid and to use it effectively. Also called 'absorptive capacity'. Lack of infrastructure or trained personnel may adversely affect the absorptive capacity of a country.

absque impetitione vasti. [Without impeachment of waste (qv).]

absque tali causa. [Without the alleged cause.]

abstract of Act. Summary of the main provisions of a statute. Some statutes require a prescribed abstract of the Act to be displayed where it may be easily read by the target audience eg s 12 of the Protection of Young Persons (Employment) Act 1996.

abstract of title. A chronological statement of the instruments and events under which a person is entitled to land showing the links to his title. A vendor of land is bound to deliver an abstract to the purchaser, at the vendor's expense. See REQUISITIONS ON TITLE.

abundans cautela non nocet. [There is no harm done by great caution.] In order to ensure that there is no doubt, there is often expressed (eg in a contract) that which would otherwise be implied.

abuse. Words of insult, invective or vituperation; they do not generally afford a ground for defamation (qv): *Thorley v Kerry [1812] 4 Taunt 355*. See also *M'Gregor v Gregory [1843] 11 M & W 287*. See CHILD ABUSE; CHILD ABUSE, REPORTING OF; DISABILITY, PERSON UNDER; VULGAR ABUSE.

abuse of dominant position. See DOMINANT POSITION, ABUSE OF.

abuse of monopoly right. Formerly, the grounds upon which an application could be made to the Controller of Patents for a licence under a patent or for an endorsement of the patent *licences of right* (qv): Patents Act 1964, s 39. Although the 1964 Act has been repealed, a similar measure exists under the Patents Act 1992, s 70; the term 'abuse of monopoly right' however is not used. See LICENCES OF RIGHT, PATENTS.

abuse of process. A tort (qv) based on damage caused by use of a legal process for some purpose other than that for which it was designed. See *Cavern Systems Dublin Ltd v Clontarf Residents Association* [1984] ILRM 24. Also the defence to an action on the grounds that the action is frivolous, vexatious or is seeking to have litigated again a question already decided against the intending plaintiff. See *Kelly v Ireland* [1986] ILRM 318; *Re Bula Ltd (in receivership)* [1988] SC; *Olympia Productions Ltd v Cameron Mackintosh* [1992] ITLR (3 February), HC. See RSC Ord 19, r 19.

For a successful plea of *abuse of process*, it must be established that (a) the plaintiff had an ulterior motive in commencing the proceedings, and (b) the plaintiff seeks a collateral advantage for itself beyond what the law offers, and (c) the plaintiff has instituted the proceedings for a purpose which the law does not recognise as a legitimate use of the remedy which has been sought: *Seán Quinn Group v An Bord Pleanála* [2001] 2 ILRM 94, HC and 1 IR 505. In this case, the court held that the evidence adduced established conclusively that the plaintiff's sole motive in commencing proceedings was to achieve a commercial objective which was an advantage over a competitor and the infliction of damage on that competitor.

The adding of a party to proceedings in order to oust the jurisdiction of the English courts is technically an abuse of the processes of the court: Jurisdiction of Courts and Enforcement of Judgments Act 1988; *Gannon v B & I Steam Packet Co Ltd and Landliner Travel* [1993] ITLR (25 January), SC and 11 ILT Dig (1993) 144.

The inherent jurisdiction of the courts to strike out proceedings as an abuse of process should only be exercised with great caution: *McCauley v McDermot* [1997] 2 ILRM 486, SC. Given the constitutional right of access to the courts and the desirability of there being a judicial determination on the merits of every case, a claim could not be dismissed in its infancy unless the court was fully satisfied that it was bound to fail: *Magee v MGN Ltd* [2004] FL 8698, HC. See *Belton v Carlow County Council* [1997] 1 IR 172, SC; *Riordan v Ireland (No 4)* [2001] 3 IR 365, SC. See 'Fighting dirty' by solicitor Desmond Shiels in *Law Society Gazette* (November 2002) 14. [Bibliography: Shiels.] See BARRATRY; ISAAC WUNDER ORDER; ISSUE ESTOPPEL; MALICIOUS PROSECUTION; OPPRESSIVE PROCEEDINGS; PRIVILEGE, LEGAL PROFESSIONAL.

abuttals. The bounds of land; the parts where it abuts on other lands.

ac etiam. [And also.]

academic freedom. The freedom to question and test received wisdom, to put forward new ideas and to state controversial or unpopular opinions, without being disadvantaged, or subjected to less favourable treatment, for the exercise of that freedom: Universities Act 1997, s 14(2). *Academic staff* have academic freedom in teaching, research and any other activity, within the law, either in or outside the university.

academic staff. While not defined in the legislation, 'academic staff' has been held to include eligible part-time teachers: Dublin Institute of Technology Act 1992, s 6(4)(b); *Simon & Teachers Union of Ireland v DIT [1994] ELR 188, HC.*

ACC Bank. The necessary legislative provision has been made by the ACC Bank Act 2001 to facilitate the sale of the bank. Provision is made in the legislation for the establishment of an *Employee Share Ownership Trust* and for the disposal by the Minister for Finance of shares in the bank. The bank was acquired by the Dutch bank Rabobank Group in 2002. See website: *www.accbank.ie.*

acceding country. A *candidate* country which has met the Copenhagen criteria for joining the European Union and which has successfully completed negotiations for so joining. A country which has applied to join the EU, an *applicant* country, becomes a *candidate* country when its application has been officially accepted. See COPENHAGEN CRITERIA.

acceleration clause. A clause in a contract where a debtor repays sums of money in instalments whereby the whole balance becomes due immediately upon failure to pay any of the instalments. Such a clause will be upheld but will be policed carefully by the courts. See *Protector Loan Co v Grice* [1880] 5 QBD 529; *UTD Ltd v Patterson* [1973] NI 142; *Wadham Stringer Finance Ltd v Meaney* [1981] 1 WLR 39. See PENALTY.

acceptance. The act of assenting to an offer. Acceptance of an offer to create a contract, may be by words or by conduct. It must generally be communicated to the offeror and must be absolute and unqualified and must be made while the offer is in force, or before it has lapsed or been revoked or rejected. If the offer is one which is capable of being accepted by being acted upon, no communication to the offeror is necessary, unless stipulated for in the offer itself: *Carlill v Carbolic Smoke Ball Co* [1893] QB 256. See also *Tansey v College of Occupational Therapists* [1995] 2 ILRM 601 (1986) HC.

Where an acceptance (or offer) is couched in general terms and the parties contemplate the execution of a further contract between them, if the terms of such further contract were in existence and known to the parties, the offer and acceptance will be inclusive of the fuller terms. If the terms of the fuller contract were merely in contemplation, then the acceptance is too general to constitute a contract. See *Lowis v Wilson* [1949] IR 347; *Felthouse v Bindley* [1862] 31 LJCP 204; *Embourg Ltd v Tyler Group Ltd* [1996] 3 IR 480, SC. See ELECTRONIC CONTRACT; OFFER; WRITING, CONTRACTS REQUIRING.

acceptance of bill. Signing a bill of exchange by the *drawee* in such a way as to signify acceptance of liability to pay the sum of money stated in the bill: Bills of Exchange Act 1882, ss 17–19. Acceptance may be a *general* acceptance which is an acceptance without qualification or a *qualified* acceptance which can be *conditional, partial, local,* qualified as to *time* or qualified as to *parties.* Acceptance for honour *supra protest* is acceptance of a bill in order to safeguard the drawee's good name (BEA 1882, ss 65–68). See *Hazylake Fashions Ltd v Bank of Ireland* [1989] ILRM 698. See BILL OF EXCHANGE.

acceptance of goods. A buyer is deemed to have accepted goods when he intimates to the seller that he has accepted them, or, subject to the buyer's right of examining the goods, when the goods have been delivered to him and he does any act in relation to them which is inconsistent with the own-ership of the seller or when, without good and sufficient reason, he retains the goods without intimating to the seller that he has rejected them: Sale of Goods Act 1893, s 35; Sale of Goods and Supply of Services Act 1980, s 20. See *Gill v Heiton Co Ltd* [1943] Ir Jur Rep 67.

acceptance of service. Acceptance in writing of a summons (qv) by a solicitor on behalf of a defendant, undertaking to enter an appearance on his behalf: RSC Ord 9(1). See SUMMONS, SERVICE OF.

acceptance supra protest. [Acceptance for honour.] See ACCEPTANCE OF BILL.

access. Every employer has a duty to his employees to provide and maintain, as far as reasonably practicable, safe means of access to and egress from any place of work: Safety, Health and Welfare at Work Act 1989, s 6(2)(b). For former legislation, see Factories Act 1955, s 37, as amended by Safety in Industry Act 1980, s 12, and repealed by SI No 357 of 1995. See *Dunne v Honeywell Control* [1991] 9 ILT Dig 147, HC; *Daly v Avonmore Creameries Ltd* [1984] IR 131; *Kielty v Ascon Ltd* [1969] IR 122. See also NATIONAL QUALIFICATIONS AUTHORITY OF IRELAND.

Access Directive. Means Directive No 2002/19/EC of 7 March 2002 on access to, and interconnection of, electronic communications networks and associated facilities. See ELECTRONIC COMMUNICATIONS NETWORKS.

access programme of Law Society. The programme of the Law Society which supports students who, for financial reasons, could not otherwise consider becoming a solicitor. The access programme was introduced in 2001 and is open to students who complete a degree with the support of the university access system. See 'Access all areas' by Kathy Burke in *Law Society Gazette* (May 2004) 12.

access to children. See CHILD, ACCESS TO; CHILD, CUSTODY OF; CHILD IN CARE.

access to courts. There is a constitutional right of access to the courts. 'It is the right of the citizens under the Constitution to have access to the Courts for the resolution of justiciable controversies': *Bula Mines Ltd v Tara Mines Ltd (No 1)* [1987] IR 85 at 92, HC. Access to the courts may be curtailed by statute to the extent that the leave of the court may be required as a precondition to bringing a claim (e g proceedings under the Mental Treatment Act 1945, s 260). Such statutory limitation on right of access must be strictly construed: *Murphy v Greene [1991] ILRM 404, SC.*

It has not been definitively decided whether the levies imposed by the state on litigants (by way of stamp duty on legal documents and other charges) constitutes an unconstitutional restriction on the citizen's right of access to the courts: *MacGairbhith v A-G [1991] 2 IR 412.* See also *Boddie v Connecticut [1971] 401 US 371; Calor Teoranta v Colgan [1990] 8ILT & SJ (1990) 255.*

access to information. See INFORMATION, ACCESS TO.

access to road. See MOTORWAY; PUBLIC ROAD.

access to solicitor. See SOLICITOR, ACCESS TO.

accession. The process by which property belonging to a person becomes the property of another by reason of its having been affixed or annexed to the property of that other. See FIXTURES.

accessory. A person involved in the commission of an offence otherwise than as principal. Formerly, an accessory *before the fact* was a person who, being absent at the time of the felony, assisted, procured, counselled, commanded or instigated another to commit it: *The People (DPP) v Madden* [1977] IR 336; *People (DPP) v Egan* [1990] ILRM 780, SC. Now, a person who *aids and abets* the commission of an indictable offence is dealt with as a *principal* offender: Criminal Law Act 1997, s 7(1). See AID AND ABET.

An accessory *after the fact* was a person who, although not present at the crime, knowing that a felony had been committed, subsequently sheltered one of the felons in such a way as to enable him to evade justice; active assistance to the felon was required; mere passive connivance would be the misdemeanour of *misprision of felony* (qv). See *DPP v Diemling* [1993] 11 ILT Dig 185, CCA.

Now, where a person has committed an *arrestable offence* (qv), any other person who, knowing or believing him to be guilty of the offence or of some other arrestable offence, does, without reasonable excuse, any act with intent to impede his apprehension or prosecution is guilty of an offence (CLA 1997, s 7(2)). References to '*accessories before and after the fact*' in the Criminal Procedure Act 1967, ss 13(1) and 29(1)(f) are to be construed as references to *aiding and abetting* under CLA 1997, s 7(1) and to

the offence in s 7(2) of the 1997 Act (CLA 1997, s 7(6)). See Accessories and Abettors Act 1861, since repealed by Criminal Law Act 1997, s 16 and Sch 3. See FELONY; ARRESTABLE OFFENCE.

accident. An unlooked for mishap or an untoward event which is not expected or designed: *Fenton v Thorley Co [1903] AC 443.* Where something is under the management of a defendant and the accident is such that, in the ordinary course of things, it would not happen if those managing the item in question used proper care, in the absence of an explanation by the defendants this affords reasonable evidence that the accident arose from a want of care: *Merriman v Greenhill Foods Ltd [1997] 1 ILRM 46, SC,* applying *Scott v London & St Katherine Docks Co [1865] 3 H & C 596.*

Compensation for an *occupational* accident is available through the scheme pursuant to the Social Welfare (Consolidation) Act 1993, ss 48–77.

Accident insurance policies usually provide cover for *injury by accident* or *injury caused by accidental means.* If a deliberate act on the part of the assured brings about an injury which is an unexpected and unforeseeable result of that action, his injury is caused by accident.

The Minister has power to order an investigation into the causes of and the circumstances surrounding any accident or incident involving an energy infrastructure: Energy (Miscellaneous Provisions) Act 1995, s 12.

Formerly, a person could be appointed by the Minister to report upon the nature and causes of an accident at sea: Merchant Shipping Act 1894, s 728; where the Minister subsequently established a formal inquiry pursuant to s 466, a person represented at that inquiry was entitled to a copy of the report only if he established a right to the production of the report: *Haussman v Minister for the Marine [1991] ILRM 383, HC.*

Under the new arrangements for the investigation of marine accidents (now called *marine casualties*), provision is made for the publication of the report of the findings of the investigation, and for giving any person whose reputation might be adversely affected by the publication, a right of reply, which will be published in the report as an appendix: Merchant Shipping (Investigation of Marine Casualties)

Act 2000, ss 6, 34–36, repealing ss 466 and 728 of the 1894 Act. [Bibliography: White.] See DANGEROUS SUBSTANCE; NO FAULT COMPENSATION; PERSONAL INJURIES; SAFETY AT WORK; TRIBUNALS OF INQUIRY.

accident, inevitable. See INEVITABLE ACCIDENT.

accident, reporting of. (1) Where injury is caused to person or property in a public place and a vehicle is involved in the occurrence of the injury, whether the use of the vehicle was or was not the cause of the injury, various provisions apply regarding stopping the vehicle, keeping the vehicle at or near the place of the occurrence for a reasonable period, and giving appropriate information to a garda or to a person entitled to demand the information: Road Traffic Act 1961, s 106 as amended by the Schedule to the Road Traffic Act 1968.

(2) An accident at a place of work must be reported to the Health and Safety Authority (i) in the case of a death, by the quickest practicable means, with the name of the deceased, brief particulars and the location of the accident, and (ii) by way of written report in the approved form of the death, injury, condition, accident, or dangerous occurrence: Safety Health and Welfare at Work (General Application) Regulations 1993 (SI No 44 of 1993), reg 59. The accident must be reported if the person dies or is prevented from performing his normal work for more than three consecutive days or if he requires treatment from a registered medical practitioner or treatment in a hospital as an in-patient or out-patient. See MARINE CASUALTY INVESTIGATION BOARD; STATE CLAIMS AGENCY.

accidental omission. There are provisions in many statutes which ensure that proceedings or acts are not invalidated by the 'accidental omission' to do something eg omission to send a notice to a person entitled to receive one: Building Societies Act 1989, ss 68(6), 74(8), 75(6).

accommodation. See HOMELESS PERSON.

accommodation party. A person who has signed a bill of exchange (qv) as drawer, acceptor or indorser, without receiving value therefor and for the purpose of lending his name to some other person. An accommodation party is liable on a bill to a *holder for value* (qv), and it is immaterial when such holder took the bill, whether he knew such party to be an accommodation party or not: Bills of Exchange Act 1882, s 28.

accomplice. A person associated with another, whether as *principal* (qv) or *accessory* (qv) in the commission of an offence. The evidence of an accomplice is admissible but the judge must warn the jury of the danger of acting on the uncorroborated evidence of an accomplice. The purpose of pointing out the need for corroboration is not to confirm the accomplice's account of events, but to find whether the alleged corroborative evidence implicates the accused in the crime with which he is charged: *DPP v Hogan* [1994] 2 ILRM 74, CCA. It is for the judge to decide whether a witness is an accomplice and the jury must accept his ruling. See *People v Carney and Mulcahy* [1955] IR 324; *DPP v Murtagh* [1990] 8 ILT Dig 158; *DPP v Diemling* [1993] 11 ILT Dig 185, CCA; *DPP v Gilligan* [2003] FL 8123, CCA. [Bibliography: Charleton (4).] See WITNESS, COMPETENCE OF.

accord and satisfaction. The purchase of a release (qv) from an obligation (whether arising under contract or tort) by means of any valuable consideration (qv), not being the actual performance of the obligation itself. The *accord* is the agreement by which the obligation is discharged; the *satisfaction* is the consideration which makes the agreement operative: *British Russian Gazette v Associated Newspapers* [1933] 2 KB 616. If A owes B €100 for work done and B accepts a bicycle in full settlement, there is accord and satisfaction. If the satisfaction is executory (qv) and the other party has completely performed his part of the contract, it is ineffective unless under seal or there is consideration eg in the case where A has delivered corn to B and B has yet to pay for the goods, a promise by A not to sue B is ineffective unless under seal or consideration is given by B.

No satisfaction is needed for the renunciation of a debt owed to the holder of a bill of exchange or promissory note: Bills of Exchange Act 1882, s 62. See ESTOPPEL.

account, settled. A statement in writing of the account between two parties, one of whom is under a duty to account to the other, which both of them have agreed to and accepted as correct. It is a defence to a claim for an account. See *Re Webb* [1894] 1 Ch 83.

account payee. The addition of the words *account payee* on a cheque is an instruction to the collecting banker to collect only for the payee's account. The words put the bank on enquiry and it is negligence on the part of the banker should adequate enquiry not be made: *Home Property Co of London v London County and Westminster Bank* (1915) 84 LJ KB 1846.

account stated. An agreed balance between parties resulting from a series of transactions. An account stated with an infant is generally void: Infants Relief Act 1874, s 1. See *Joseph Evan Co v Heathcote* [1918] 1 KB 434.

accountability. The capacity or duty to account in an open, transparent manner for actions taken, or not taken, whether by an individual or an institution: *National Forum on Europe — Glossary of Terms* (2003). See CIVIL SERVANT; CORPORATE GOVERNANCE.

accountant. An accountant engaged for the purposes of preparing accounts for and representing a taxpayer at an appeal against an assessment for tax, is acting as an agent for the taxpayer. The taxpayer is entitled to obtain any documents prepared by the tax agent in drafting the accounts and, therefore, these documents are within the *power and possession* of the taxpayer and consequently can be required to be disclosed to the Revenue Commissioners: *QUIGLEY V BURKE* [1996] 1 ILRM 469, SC and [1995] 3 IR 278, SC; Income Tax Act 1967, s 174(1)(a), now Income Taxes Consolidation Act 1997, s 900(2)(b).

As regards claims in negligence and/or breach of contract against accountants, see *Sisk v Flynn* [1986] ILRM 128; *Golden Vale Co-operative Creameries v Barrett* [1987] HC; *Allied Pharmaceutical Distributors Ltd v Robert J Kidney Co* [1991] 2 IR 8. See *Geoghegan v Institute of Chartered Accountants in Ireland* [1995] 3 IR 86, HC & SC. See Institute of Chartered Accountants in Ireland (Charter Amendment) Act 1966 as amended by Companies (Auditing and Accounting) Act 2003, s 32, Sch 1, Pt 2. For the Institute of Chartered Accountants in Ireland, see website: *www.icai.ie*. See also AUDITOR; COMPANY, REGISTERED; MONEY LAUNDERING; PARTNERSHIP; PARTNERSHIP, NUMBER TO FORM.

accounting, false. See FALSE ACCOUNTING.

accounting principles. The principles governing the amounts to be included in the accounts of a company: Companies Amendment Act 1986, s 5; e g the company is presumed to be carrying on as a going concern (qv); the accounting policies are to be applied consistently from one year to the next; only realised profits at the balance sheet date are to be included in the profit and loss account; and all income and charges relating to the financial year are to be included in the accounts, irrespective of the date of payment. If there are special reasons for departing from these accounting principles, the directors of the company must state the particulars and reasons for departure in a note to the accounts (CAA 1986, s 6). For disclosure of accounting policies, see Companies Act 1990, s 205C inserted by Companies (Auditing and Accounting) Act 2003, s 43. See also Building Societies Act 1989, s 77(8)(c); Credit Union Act 1997, s 110.

Where an affidavit is made available to a jury, which is sworn by an accountant, he may be required to explain to the jury any relevant accounting procedures or principles: Criminal Justice (Theft and Fraud Offences) Act 2001, s 57.

accounting standards. Means: (a) statements of accounting standards, and (b) any written interpretation of those standards, issued by prescribed bodies: Companies Act 1990, s 205A inserted by Companies (Auditing and Accounting) Act 2003, s 41. Companies are required to ensure that their annual accounts have been prepared in accordance with applicable accounting standards, and to include a note in the accounts where there is any material departure from these standards.

accounts, company. Every company must keep proper books of accounts that (a) correctly record and explain the transactions of the company, (b) will at any time enable the financial position of the company to be determined with reasonable accuracy, (c) will enable any balance sheet, profit and loss account or income and expenditure account to comply with the Companies Acts, and (d) will enable the accounts to be readily and properly audited: Companies Act 1990, s 202.

Copies of the balance sheet, the profit and loss account and of the directors' and auditors' report must be sent to every shareholder and debenture holder and laid before the annual general meeting: Companies Act 1963, ss 148 and 159. The particular format of accounts to be used is specified in s 4 of the Companies Amendment Act 1986; a *small company* and a *medium-sized company* are exempted from many of the requirements of preparing and publishing a full set of accounts (CAA 1986, ss 10–12). A criminal offence may be committed by a director for failing to keep proper books of accounts (CA 1990, s 202(10)), or by officers where the company is wound up (CA 1990, s 203). Also, an officer may be ordered by the court to be personally liable for the debts of the company where proper books of accounts have not been kept (CA 1990, s 204). See *Healy v Healy Homes Ltd* [1973] IR 309; *Sinnot v O'Connor* [1991] 9 ILT Dig 266, SC; *Mehigan v Duignan* [1997] 1 IR 340, HC. See also Building Societies Act 1989, ss 76–77 as amended by Housing (Miscellaneous Provisions) Act 2002, s 23 and Sch 3. See *MacCann* in 9 ILT & SJ (1991) 177.

It is an offence for a relevant person (eg an auditor) to fail to report to the gardaí any suspected offence by a firm or a partner, director or manager of the firm, which is indicated by the firm's accounts: Criminal Justice (Theft and Fraud Offences) Act 2001, s 59. See also Companies (Auditing and Accounting) Act 2003, s 26. [Bibliography: Brennan & Hennessy; Kelleher S; Power.] See ACCOUNTING PRINCIPLES; BALANCE SHEET; FALSE ACCOUNTING; IRISH AUDITING AND ACCOUNTING SUPERVISORY AUTHORITY; PROFIT AND LOSS; SMALL COMPANY; MEDIUM-SIZED COMPANY.

accounts, solicitor. Where the Law Society is of the opinion that a solicitor, or a clerk or servant of a solicitor, has been guilty of dishonesty in connection with that solicitor's practice as a solicitor, or in connection with any trust of which that solicitor is a trustee, it may apply to the High Court, and the High Court may make an order directing either: (a) that no banking company shall, without leave of the High Court, make any payment out of a banking account in the name of the solicitor or his firm; or (b) that a specified banking company shall not, without leave of the High Court, make any payment out of a banking account kept by such company in the name of the solicitor or his firm: Solicitors (Amendment) Act 1960, s 20. It has been held that the purpose of s 20 was not alone to preserve the client account of a solicitor but the assets of a solicitor so that claims against the solicitor might be satisfied: *Law Society v Malocco* [2003 HC.] In this case the court refused to discharge a 1991 court order freezing bank accounts of Mr Elio Malocco.

The Law Society is empowered to make regulations, with the concurrence of the President of the High Court, governing the type of account which a solicitor may open arising from his practice as a solicitor: Solicitors Act 1954, s 66 as substituted by Solicitors (Amendment) Act 1994, s 76 and amended by Solicitors (Amendment) Act 2002, s 3.

The Regulations under s 66 prescribe the duties of the solicitor with regard to maintaining bank accounts for clients' money and the keeping of accounting records and provide for the appointment of authorised persons to inspect solicitor's accounts. The 2002 amendment is to obviate the need for the Society's authorised investigator to disclose to the solicitor, or any employee of the solicitor, the purpose of the investigator's attendance at the solicitor's offices, where the Society reasonably considers that to do so could prejudice the Society's functions.

See Solicitors' Accounts Regulations 2001, SI No 421 of 2001 which apply from 1 January 2002. There is a saver for continuation of the 1984 Regulations (SI No 304 of 1984) in certain circumstances. See also Solicitors' (Interest on Clients' Money) Regulations 1995, SI No 108 of 1995, and Regulations 2004, SI No 372 of 2004. See *A Guide to Professional Conduct of Solicitors in Ireland* (2002) ch 9.8. See CLIENT ACCOUNT; CLIENTS' MONEY; TEEMING AND LADING.

accredit. To furnish a diplomatic agent with papers, called credentials or letters of credit, which certify his public character. See AMBASSADOR.

accreditation. A process under which official recognition is given in a variety of circumstances eg to a diplomat, to a hospital which meets particular standards, or to skills acquired in the workplace, under a process called *accreditation of prior learning* (APL). The National Committee on Volunteering is required to examine and make recommendations on the possibilities for recognition and accreditation for voluntary work and for training undertaken as a volunteer: Comhairle Regulations 2000, SI No 369 of 2000. See also Environmental

Protection Agency Act 1992, s 66; Teaching Council Act 2001, s 23(2)(h). See ELECTRONIC COMMERCE; IRISH HEALTH SERVICES ACCREDITATION BOARD; NATIONAL QUALIFICATIONS AUTHORITY OF IRELAND; PRESIDENT OF IRELAND.

accretion. The act of growing on to a thing; usually applied to the gradual accumulation of land from out of the sea or a river. In the UK, if the accretion is imperceptible, it belongs to the owner of the land. If it is sudden and considerable, it belongs to the Crown. See *A-G for, s Nigeria v John Holt & Co* [1915] AC 613; *South Centre of Theosophy v State of, s Australia* [1982] AC 706.

Under the presumption of accretion, a tenant who encroaches on neighbouring land does so for the benefit of his landlord. There is no Irish authority on the presumption, but it does appear to form part of Irish law eg see *Meares v Collis & Hayes* [1927] IR 397. The Law Reform Commission has recommended that the presumption of accretion should remain: *Report on Title by Adverse Possession of Land,* LRC 67 (2002).

accrual of right. A right is said to *accrue* when it *vests* in a person, especially when it does so gradually over time or without his active intervention eg by lapse of time, or by determination of a preceding right. See CAUSE OF ACTION; LONG POSSESSION, TITLE BY.

accumulation. The process whereby there is a continual increase in principal by the investment of interest as it accrues. A person may not direct the accumulation of interest for any period longer than the life of the settlor, or 21 years from the settlor's death, or the minority of any person living at the death of the settlor, or the minority of the person entitled to the income: Accumulations Act 1800 (principles followed in Ireland) and 1892. A direction to accumulate for a period longer than the *perpetuity* period is void; but where the period is longer than the Acts allow but not longer than the perpetuity period, the direction is merely void in so far as it exceeds the former. See PERPETUITIES, RULE AGAINST.

accusare nemo se debet; accusare nemo se debet nisi coram Deo. [No one is bound to accuse himself except to God.] See INCRIMINATE.

accusatorial procedure. The legal procedure in common law (qv) countries whereby the responsibility of collecting and presenting evidence lies generally with the party who seeks to introduce that evidence. Contrast with INQUISITORIAL PROCEDURE. See also LIS INTER PARTES.

accused. A person charged with an offence. An accused has a fundamental constitutional right to be present at and to follow the proceedings against him; he must be present when his presence is required (eg to consent to be tried summarily) but in other cases the trial judge has a discretion to proceed with a trial where the accused has consciously decided to absent himself: *Lawlor v District Judge Hogan* [1993] ILRM 606, HC.

There is no such thing as the accused's version of events as presented by his counsel; if the accused wishes to put a version of events before the jury, he can only do so by calling evidence or by giving evidence himself: *The People (DPP) v Connolly* [2003] 2 IR 1, CCA.

accused, disclosure of name of. See PUBLIC JUSTICE.

acknowledgment. Avowal or assent to. As regards a will, if it is not signed by the testator in the presence of witnesses, he must acknowledge his signature in their presence: Succession Act 1965, s 78. As regards a right of action on a debt, an acknowledgment of the debt by the person liable, will result in the right of action being deemed to have accrued on and not before, the date of the acknowledgment: Statute of Limitations 1957, s 56. See *Smith v Ireland* [1983] ILRM 300. See Electronic Commerce Act 2000, s 20.

acquiescence. Consent which is expressed or implied from conduct. Acquiescence to the infringement of a right will normally result in the loss of equitable relief. See LACHES.

acquired rights, employees. The rights of employees which are safeguarded in the event of transfers of undertakings, businesses or parts of businesses. It includes obligations under the redundancy payments scheme. See *Premier Motors (Medway) Ltd v Total Oil of Great Britain Ltd* [1983] IRLR 471. See EC (Protection of Employees on Transfer of Undertakings) Regulations 2003 (SI No 131 of 2003) which gives effect to Directive 2001/23/EC. See *Barry* in 8 ILT & SJ (1991) 138. See 'All the right moves' by solicitor Ciaran O'Meara in *Law Society Gazette* (Aug/Sept 2003) 32. See REDUNDANCY; TRANSFER OF UNDERTAKINGS.

acquis. The entire body of EU law eg treaties, international agreements, directives, regulations and decisions, the judgments of the European Court of Justice, and actions taken by EU governments together in the area of justice and home affairs and on the Common Foreign and Security Policy. Candidate countries wishing to join the EU must accept the '*acquis*' and make EU law part of their own national legislation. *Acquis communitaire* means the EU as it is – in other words, the rights and obligations which EU member states share.

acquisition. There are rules governing acquisitions by *listed* companies; the rules specify the *classification* of the transaction (Classes 1, 2 and 3), the requirements for announcements and whether a circular and shareholder approval is required: Listing Rules 2000, paras 10.1–10.43. There are additional requirements for takeovers and mergers (para 10.45). See also Listing Rules 2000, para 4.27. See LISTING RULES; MAJOR SHAREHOLDER DIRECTIVE; MERGER; TAKEOVER.

acquisition notice. See OPEN SPACES.

acquisition of land. Acquiring, permanently or temporarily, by agreement or compulsorily, land or any easement, wayleave, water right, or other right over or in respect of land or water or any *substratum* of land: Planning and Development Act 2000, ss 2(1) and 213(2). It includes restricting or interfering with such easements, wayleave, water right or other right. A local authority has the right to acquire land and to restrict or interfere with it, for the purpose of performing its functions (PDA 2000, s 213(1)–(2)). See COMPULSORY PURCHASE ORDER; WAY, RIGHT OF.

acquittal. Discharge from prosecution following a verdict of not guilty or a successful plea in bar (qv). It has been held that a verdict of not guilty in respect of criminal charges is a certificate of a person's uninterrupted innocence: *McCarthy v Garda Commissioner* [1992] ELR 50, HC. However, the acquittal of an employee of criminal charges does not preclude his employer from considering whether he should or should not be dismissed because of the circumstances which gave rise to the charges: *Mooney v An Post* [1994] ELR 103, HC and [1998] ELR 238, SC.

When an accused is acquitted by the majority verdict of a jury, the fact that it was a majority verdict must not be disclosed: Criminal Justice Act 1984, s 25(4).

There is generally no appeal against acquittal. However, see APPEAL. Some statutes provide for an appeal by the prosecutor in the case of a dismissal; this is not unconstitutional eg see Fisheries (Consolidation) Act 1959, s 310; *Considine v Shannon Regional Fisheries Board* [1998] 1 ILRM 11, SC. Also where, on a question of law, a verdict in favour of an accused person is found *by direction* of the trial judge, the Director of Public Prosecutions may, without prejudice to the verdict in favour of the accused, refer the question of law to the Supreme Court: Criminal Procedure Act 1967, s 34. This also applies to an appeal from the Central Criminal Court to the Supreme Court, ie it is without prejudice to the verdict in favour of the accused: Courts and Court Officers Act 1995, s 44. [Bibliography: McDermott P A (2).] See APPEAL; AUTREFOIS ACQUIT; AUTREFOIS CONVICT.

acquittance. A written acknowledgment of the payment of a sum of money.

acronym, deceptive. See DECEPTIVE ACRONYM.

Act. Legislation which has passed, or deemed to have been passed by both Houses of the Oireachtas (qv) and has been signed by the President of Ireland (qv). The elements in an Act include: *number*, eg No 27 of 1965; *long title*, which describes the purpose of the Act; *short title*, by which the Act may be cited; *interpretation clause* with definitions; *commencement clause*, which specifies when or how the Act will come into operation; *transitional provisions*; *repealing clause*; and *schedules*. There will be a requirement by July 2006 for the texts of Acts to be printed and published simultaneously in each of the official languages of the State: Official Languages Act 2003, s 7.

Copyright in any Bill or enactment vests in the Houses of the Oireachtas and expires 50 years after it was first lawfully made available to the public: Copyright and Related Rights Act 2000, ss 192 and 194–195. For full text of Acts, see websites: *www.attorneygeneral.ie* and *www.irlgov.ie/oireachtas*. See BILL; ELECTRONIC COMMERCE; PASSING OF ACT; REPEAL; STATUTE LAW.

act of bankruptcy. See BANKRUPTCY, ACT OF.

Act of God. An event which happens independently of human intervention and due to natural causes (eg storm, earthquake, extraordinary rainfall, unusually bad weather at sea) which could not be foreseen and which could not be guarded against. It is a good defence in torts of *strict liability* (qv). See *Pandorf v Hamilton* [1886] 17 QBD 675. See INEVITABLE ACCIDENT.

act of law. The effect of the operation of law rather than as a result of the act of parties e g the legal right of a spouse in succession to property.

acta exteriora indicant interiora secreta. [External actions show internal secrets.] The maxim that intention may be inferred from a person's acts. See INFERENCE.

acta jure gestionis. [Acts of a commercial nature.] See *McElhinney v Williams* [1996] 1 ILRM 276, SC. Contrast with ACTA JURE IMPERII.

acta jure imperii. [Acts of government.] The basic principle that a foreign state is immune from the jurisdiction of the courts of the state: The *Cristina* [1938] AC 485; *Trendex Trading Corporation v Central Bank of Nigeria* [1977] QB 529. Originally, the immunity derived from the rules of public international law and was *absolute* in that the immunity was accorded to all activity, whether governmental or commercial. However, the increase in trade between states in the twentieth century led to a distinction, called the *restrictive* theory, between acts of government (*acta jure imperii*) which enjoyed immunity, and acts of a commercial nature (*acta jure gestionis*) which did not. The House of Lords has held that the restrictive theory of immunity applied at common law: The *I Congreso del Partido* [1983] 1 AC 244. See *Government of Canada v EAT* [1992] ELR 29, SC. See *McElhinney v Williams* [1996] 1 ILRM 276, SC. See IMMUNITY.

acting capacity. The appointment of a person in an acting capacity may give rise to a *legitimate expectation* of receiving a benefit or privilege which the court will protect: *Duggan & Ors v An Taoiseach* [1989] ILRM 710, HC. See LEGITIMATE EXPECTATION.

acting for oneself. When a solicitor acting for a client in any matter finds that the other party to the matter has decided to act for himself, the solicitor is not bound to actively assist the other party: *A Guide to Professional Conduct of Solicitors in Ireland* (2002) ch 6.3. However, when the solicitor forms the opinion that the other party is not competent to act for himself, the solicitor should recommend that the other party consult a solicitor. A barrister may not appear as counsel in any matter in which he

himself is a party or has a significant pecuniary interest: *Code of Conduct for the Bar of Ireland* (December 2003) r 3.12. For acting for oneself in court, see LAY LITIGANT. See also CONVEYANCE.

acting in concert. See CONCERT PARTY; FREEDOM OF INFORMATION.

actio personalis moritur cum persona. [A personal action dies with the person.] Formerly, a personal representative could not sue or be sued in respect of a tort committed against or by the deceased. However, since 1961, all causes of action survive for the benefit of a deceased's estate and also against the estate, other than excepted causes e g defamation, seduction: Civil Liability Act 1961, ss 6–10. See DEATH, EFFECT OF.

action. A civil proceeding commenced by summons or in such other manner as may be prescribed by the rules of court e g an administration action regarding a grant of representation.

Means a civil proceeding commenced by *civil bill* or such other procedure as is provided by these rules and includes a *cause* or matter: Circuit Court Rules, para 1. see CIVIL PROCEEDINGS.

actionable negligence. Arises where (a) a sufficient proximity exists between the wrongdoer and the person who has suffered damage, (b) the damage done is reasonably foreseeable, and (c) there is no compelling exemption based on public policy: *Ward v McMaster* [1988] IR 337, applied in *McShane Fruit v Johnston Haulage Co Ltd* [1997] 1 ILRM 86, HC. See NEGLIGENCE.

actions, consolidation of. See CONSOLIDATION OF ACTIONS.

active trust. A trust (qv) which requires the trustee to perform active duties e g collecting rents and transferring the proceeds to the beneficiaries. Contrast with BARE TRUST.

actuarial value. The equivalent cash value of a benefit, calculated in a manner as specified: Pensions Act 1990, s 2.

actuary. A person who is an expert on mortality and insurance statistics. The evidence of an actuary is not only desirable but is necessary to enable a jury to arrive at anything like a reasonably accurate figure for damages for *future loss of earnings*: *Long v O'Brien & Cronin Ltd* [1972] SC. Any insurer which has its head office in the State and which has an authorisation to undertake life assurance, is required to appoint an actuary: Insurance Act 1989, s 34 as amended by Central Bank and Financial Services Authority of Ireland Act 2003, s 35, Sch 1.

The Minister is empowered to prescribe the qualifications and experience of such actuary. For qualifications for appointment as an actuary to an occupational pensions scheme, see Pensions Act 1990, s 51. Any professional guidance issued by the Society of Actuaries in Ireland which is specified in regulations under the 1990 Act, cannot be altered or withdrawn without the prior consent of the Minister: PA 1990, s 7A inserted by Pensions (Amendment) Act 2002, s 12. See also PA 1990, s 119 inserted by P(A)A 2002, s 3. See also *Sexton v O'Keeffe* [1966] IR 204. See Actuary (Qualification) Regulations 1940, SR & Ord No 75 of 1940.

actus Dei nemini facit injuriam. [The act of God prejudices no one.] See ACT OF GOD.

actus legis nemini facit injuriam. [The act of the law injures no one.]

actus non facit reum, nisi mens sit rea. [An act does not of itself constitute guilt unless the mind is guilty.] A cardinal maxim of criminal law. See *Fowler v Padget* [1798] 7 TR 509. See ACTUS REUS; MENS REA.

actus reus. The elements of an offence excluding those which concern the mind of the accused; it consists of some act, or some omission, forbidden by law. The act must have been done voluntarily, and must be directly attributable to the accused and not to another person. See *Haughton v Smith* [1973] 3 All ER 1109. [Bibliography: McAuley & McCutcheon.] See MENS REA.

ad arbitrium. [At will.]

ad avizandum. [To be deliberated upon.]

ad colligenda bona. [To collect the goods.] A grant of administration of the estate of a deceased which is of a perishable or precarious nature, for the purpose of collecting and preserving it, but not for distributing it.

ad diem. [On the appointed day.]

adequate. See SUFFICIENT; WASTE COLLECTION.

ad eundem. [To the same class.]

ad hoc. [For this purpose.]

ad idem. [Of the same mind.] A contract, to be binding requires that there is *consensus ad idem* ie agreement as to the same thing: *Raffles v Wichelhaus* [1864] 2 H & C 906. See CONTRACT.

ad interim. [In the meantime.]

ad litem. [For the suit.]

(1) A *guardian ad litem* may be appointed by the court to defend an action on behalf of a minor (qv) or a person of unsound mind: RSC Ord 13, r 1; Ord 15, r 35; Ord 52, r 17(6,7); Ord 63, r 1(3); *Re Midland Health Board* [1988] ILRM 251. In care proceedings and proceedings regarding children in the care of a health board, the court may appoint a guardian ad litem for the child: Child Care Act 1991, s 26. In certain guardianship proceedings (eg under ss 6A, 11 or 11B of the Guardianship of Infants Act 1964) the court may appoint a guardian ad litem for the child, having regard to the special circumstances of the case (GIA 1964, s 28 as inserted by Children's Act 1997, s 11). See *Re A and B v Eastern Health Board & Attorney-General* [1998] 1 ILRM 460. See also DCR 1997 Ord 7.

The National Children's Office has undertaken, through consultants, a review of the guardian ad litem service, focusing on the organisation, management, extent and quality of the existing service, the need for guidelines and options for the future: *Review of the Guardian Ad Litem Service* (March 2004). The review was in June 2004 the subject of consultation with interested parties. The review contains six options: self-regulation for GALs, an independent national agency, regional panels, centrally-regulated service, GAL service plus independent advocacy, or volunteer/advocacy service. The review is available on the website: *www.nco.ie*. See also *A Guide to Professional Conduct of Solicitors in Ireland* (2002), App 4, para 21.

(2) A grant of *administration ad litem* may be made where it is necessary to appoint a personal representative to substantiate legal proceedings by or against an estate; it is a form of limited grant: Succession Act 1965, s 27(1).

ad medium filum viae (aquae). [To the middle line of the road (stream).] The normal boundary of lands separated by a road or a river. For example, see *Geraghty v Rohan Industrial Estates Ltd* [1988] IR 419. See PUBLIC ROAD.

ad referendum. [To further consideration.]

ad rem. [To the point.]

ad sectam; ads. [At the suit of.]

ad summam. [In conclusion.]

ad valorem. [According to the value.] An *ad valorem* tax is one which is proportionate to the value of the article taxed. See STAMP DUTIES.

adaptation. It is an infringement of copyright to make an *adaptation* of a *work* the subject of copyright without a licence from the copyright holder: Copyright and Related Rights Act 2000, s 37. An *adaptation* is made when it is recorded in writing or otherwise (CRRA 2000, s 43(1)). An *adaptation* eg of a musical work, includes a translation, arrangement of other alteration or transcription of the work (CRRA 2000, s 43(2)(b)). See COPYRIGHT; WORK; WRITING.

added defendant. See DEFENDANT.

additional charges. See INDICTMENT.

additional evidence. See FRESH EVIDENCE.

address. (1) If the *address* given by an applicant for planning permission is inadequate to afford the planning authority a choice of the full range of options for giving notice, then notwithstanding that the applicant had acted in good faith, such application is defective in law: *Walsh v Kildare County Council* [2001] 1 IR 483, HC.

(2) It is recommended that a solicitor keep the addresses of clients confidential; however, as a matter of courtesy, he may offer to forward correspondence to a client: *A Guide to Professional Conduct of Solicitors in Ireland* (2002) ch 4.2.

(3) The President of Ireland may, after consultation with the Council of State (qv), communicate with the Houses of the Oireachtas by message or *address* on any matter of national or public importance: 1937 Constitution, art 13(7). Each such message or address must have received the approval of the Government. Four such addresses have been made, in 1969 by President Eamon de Valera to commemorate the 50th anniversary of the first Dáil, in 1992 by President Mary Robinson on the topic *The Irish Identity in Europe*, again in 1995 by President Robinson on the theme of broadening and making as inclusive as possible the term '*the people of Ireland*', and in late 1999 by President Mary McAleese to mark the end of the second and the beginning of the third millennium.

address, mode of. See MODE OF ADDRESS.

adduce. To present or bring forward eg evidence in support of some proposition or statement already made in the course of a proceeding.

ademption. The complete or partial extinction or withholding of a legacy by some act of the testator during his life eg sale of the object comprising a *specific* legacy. Where a father or other person *in loco parentis* provides a *portion* by way of legacy in his will and subsequently provides a like or greater sum by a settlement on the marriage of that child, there is a presumption that the legacy is adeemed. See *Re Nolan* [1923] 58 ILTR 13.

adhesion, contract of. See CONTRACT OF ADHESION.

adjective law. The part of law dealing with practice and procedure in the courts as distinct from the actual law. See SUBSTANTIVE LAW.

adjoining. See ATTACHED AND ADJOINING.

adjournment. The postponement or suspension of the hearing of a trial to a future time or day; a judge may, if he thinks it expedient for the interest of justice, postpone or adjourn a trial for such time and upon such terms, as he thinks fit: RSC Ord 36, r 34. A judge may, if he thinks it expedient in the interests of justice, postpone or adjourn a trial for such time, and upon such terms, if any, as he thinks fit: Circuit Court Rules 2001 Ord 33, r 10. For adjournment in *commercial proceedings* (qv), see RSC Ord 63A, r 6(1)(xiii) inserted by Rules of the Superior Courts (Commercial Proceedings) 2004 (SI No 2 of 2004).

An adjournment *sine die* is a postponement for an indefinite time. An adjournment of a plaintiff's action in the District Court may be made pending the determination of the defendant's action in the High Court on the same issues: *Gay O'Driscoll Ltd v Kotsonouris* [1987] IR 265. Failure to grant an adjournment could constitute a breach of fair procedures to which an applicant has a constitutional right: *O'Reilly v Cassidy (No 2)* [1995] 1 ILRM 311, HC. A judge has jurisdiction to grant an adjournment to hear further evidence in forfeiture proceedings relating to the proceeds of drug trafficking: *England v Judge Dunne and DPP* [2003] FL 7003, HC. See also DCR 1997 Ord 2. See *Doyle v Hearne* [1988] ILRM 318; *Butler v Ruane* [1989] ILRM 159. See Residential Tenancies Act 2004, s 107.

adjudication. (1) Formal judgment or decision of a court eg the order declaring a debtor to be a bankrupt.

(2) The process under which the parties to a dispute hand over, either voluntarily or compulsorily, the assessment of the merits of a case, as presented by the disputing parties, to an independent third party (the *adjudicator*) who makes a determination

based on the facts. See BANKRUPTCY, ADJUDICATION OF.

adjudicators in tenancy disputes. Persons appointed by the *Private Residential Tenancies Board* to conduct an adjudication in relation to a dispute: Residential Tenancies Act 2004, ss 4(1), 97, 164(2). The adjudicator is required to inquire fully into each relevant aspect of the dispute concerned and provide to, and receive from, each party such information as is appropriate (RTA 2004, s 97). For that purpose, the adjudicator may require either party to furnish to him, within a specified period, such documents or other information as he considers appropriate. The adjudicator is required to determine the dispute by either: (a) reaching a decision himself in the matter, or (b) subject to s 98, declaring to the parties that he has adopted, as his determination of the dispute, a decision reached (through the adjudicator's assistance) by the parties themselves in resolution of the matter (RTA 2004, s 97(4)). Such agreement could arise on foot of a provisional conclusion indicated to both parties by the adjudicator.

The parties have a 21-day 'cooling off' period within which to indicate that an agreement, which the adjudicator proposes to reflect in his decision, no longer exists (as otherwise such an adjudication decision is binding) (RTA 2004, s 98). If either party indicates, within the time allowed, that the agreement no longer exists, the adjudicator is required to proceed to reach his own decision in the matter.

The adjudicator is required to prepare a report and furnish it to the Board, containing: (a) a statement of what matters, if any, relating to the dispute are agreed by the parties to be fact, (b) a summary of the matters (whether they go in whole or part to resolving the dispute or not) agreed to by the parties, (c) the terms of the determination made by the adjudicator, (d) in the case of a determination made by the adjudicator himself rather than reflecting an agreement between the parties, a summary of the reasons for the determination, and (e) relevant particulars in relation to the conduct of the adjudication (including particulars in relation to the number and duration of hearings held by the adjudicator, the persons who attended any such hearing and any documents submitted to the adjudicator) (RTA 2004, s 99).

A copy of the report is to be served by the Board on the parties together with a statement advising them that the adjudicator's decision will be the subject of a *determination order* of the Board unless a non-binding adjudication decision is appealed to the Tenancy Tribunal within 21 days in accordance with RTA 2004, s 100.

An adjudicator has a right not to deal with certain disputes eg which are statute-barred or trivial or vexatious (RTA 2004, s 85). Also an adjudicator must comply with certain requirements in relation to the disclosure of conflicts of interests, the manner in which he conduct himself and the maintenance of the absolute confidentiality of the proceedings (RTA 2004, ss 101 and 112). An adjudicator is empowered to enter and inspect any dwelling to which a dispute relates by giving at least 24 hours notice of that intention (RTA 2004, s 111).

An adjudicator is empowered to make one or more of the following declarations or directions: (a) a direction that a specified amount of rent or other charge be paid on, or on and from, or by a specified date, (b) a declaration as to whether or not an amount of rent set under a tenancy of a dwelling complies with s 19(1) ('market rent' and if the declaration is that that amount does not so comply, the declaration must be accompanied by an indication by the adjudicator as to what amount, in his opinion, would comply), (c) a direction as to the return or payment, in whole or in part, of the amount of a deposit, (d) a direction that a specified amount of damages or costs or both be paid, (e) a direction that a dwelling be quitted by a specified date, (f) a declaration as to the validity or otherwise of a notice of termination of a tenancy, (g) a declaration with regard to the right to return to, or continue in, occupation of a dwelling (and such a declaration may include provision to the effect that any period of interruption in possession that has occurred is to be disregarded for one or more purposes), (h) a declaration that a term of a lease or tenancy agreement is void by reason of s 184 (voidance provisions to facilitate terminations), (i) in the special circumstances of a dispute heard, a direction that the whole or part of the costs or expenses incurred by the adjudicator in dealing with the dispute be paid by one or more of the parties (RTA 2004, s 115).

The amount, other than costs or expenses of whatsoever kind, that an adjudicator may direct to be paid to a party must not exceed: (a) if solely of damages – €20,000, (b) if solely by way of arrears of rent or other charges €20,000 or an amount equal to twice the annual rent of the dwelling concerned, whichever is the higher, but subject to a maximum of €60,000 (RTA 2004, s 115(3)).

An adjudicator may give such directions as he thinks appropriate for the purpose of providing relief of an interim nature, while making clear that that relief may not necessarily be the relief provided for by the final determination (RTA 2004, s 117).

An adjudicator may be removed from the panel of adjudicators for stated misconduct by the District Court (RTA 2004, s 165(3)). *Misconduct* means any conduct likely to bring the procedures for determination by adjudicators into disrepute and includes (a) any demonstration by an adjudicator of bias towards the interests of a party before him, (b) gross discourtesy by an adjudicator to one or more of the parties before him, and (c) wilful failure by an adjudicator to attend to his duties as an adjudicator (RTA 2004, s 165(6)). The Board may appoint a person as both a mediator and an adjudicator (RTA 2004, s 164(3)). See COSTS IN CIVIL PROCEEDINGS; DETERMINATION ORDER; MEDIATION IN TENANCY DISPUTES; NOTICE TO QUIT; POSSESSION, ORDER FOR; RENT; RENT ARREARS; SUB-TENANCY; TENANCY DISPUTE; TITLE.

adjustment. The operation of ascertaining and settling the amount which an assured is entitled to receive under a policy of marine insurance, and of fixing the proportion which each underwriter (qv) is liable to pay. [Bibliography: Corrigan & Campbell.] See AVERAGE.

administration, grant of. See LETTERS OF ADMINISTRATION.

administration, revocation of. The revoking, cancelling or recalling of a grant of letters of administration (qv) which the High Court is empowered to do. See Succession Act 1965, ss 27(2) and 35.

administration of company. See COURT PROTECTION OF COMPANY.

administration of estates. The collection of the assets of a deceased person, payment of debts and distribution of the surplus to the persons beneficially entitled by the personal representatives (qv) of the deceased.

Where the estate is insolvent, ie the assets are insufficient for the payment of debts, the debts are paid as follows:
1. The funeral, testamentary and administration expenses.
2. As in bankruptcy. As from 1 January 1989, the estates of persons who die insolvent are wound up in bankruptcy: Bankruptcy Act 1988, ss 115–122.

Where the estate is solvent, the order in which the assets of the deceased are applied in payment of debts (subject to directions in the will and to charges on the property) is as follows:
1 Property undisposed of by will, subject to the retention of a fund sufficient to meet pecuniary legacies.
2. Property not specifically devised or bequeathed but included in a residuary gift.
3 Property specifically appropriated for payment of debts.
4. Property charged with payment of debts.
5. Fund retained to meet pecuniary legacies (qv).
6. Property specifically devised or bequeathed.
7. Property appointed by will under a general power.
8. Assets are applied in accordance with the value of devise or bequest at the death of the deceased.

See Succession Act 1965, s 46, Sch 1; Bankruptcy Act 1988, s 138. [Bibliography: Corrigan & Williams.] See INSOLVENT ESTATE; LETTERS OF ADMINISTRATION; PENAL SUM; PENDENTE LITE; PROBATE; PROBATE TAX; WILL.

administration of justice. See JUSTICE.

administration suit. An application requesting the court to administer the estate of a deceased where problems or disputes have arisen in the course of administration as between creditors, beneficiaries or personal representatives. It is instituted by a *special summons* in the High Court or by *succession law civil bill* in the Circuit Court. See RSC Ord 5, r 2(4)(a); Ord 15, r 8; Circuit Court Rules 2001 Ord 50. [Bibliography: Scanlon.]

administrative law. The law relating to the organisation, powers and duties of administrative authorities eg public and local authorities. [Bibliography: Hogan & Morgan; Stout.]

administrative tribunals. Tribunals concerned with administrative law or matters concerning large numbers of persons or concerns, where questions arise involving the conferring of rights, or the restriction or loss of rights of individuals. It has been held that when a court is reviewing (e g by judicial review (qv)) a decision of an administrative tribunal, the decision may be set aside where the decision plainly and unambiguously flies in the face of fundamental reason and common sense; the court may not substitute its own decision for that of the tribunal: *Stroker v Doherty* [1991] 1 IR 23, SC.

Allegations of criminal conduct may be aired before administrative tribunals or before inquiries which have a statutory basis: *Keady v Garda Commissioner* [1992] ILRM 312, SC. The Supreme Court has held that when reasons are required from administrative tribunals they should be required only to give the broad gist of the basis for their decisions: *Faulkner v Minister for Industry and Commerce* [1997] ELR 107, SC. See also *Matthews v Irish Coursing Club* [1992] ITLR (30 March), HC; *Rajah v Royal College of Surgeons in Ireland* [1994] 1 ILRM 233, HC. See TRIBUNALS.

administrator/administratrix. A person (male/female) appointed to manage the property of another. (1) The person to whom the grant of administration of the estate of a deceased person is made. An administrator of an estate has the same rights and liabilities as if he were the executor of the deceased: Succession Act 1965, s 27. He is required to enter into a bond called an *administration bond*: RSC Ord 79, rr 29–32; RSC, App Q, pt 11. An attorney, acting under a power of attorney, or a guardian, may be an administrator: RSC Ord 79, rr 23 and 25.

(2) An administrator may be appointed to take over management of the business of an insurer: Insurance (No 2) Act 1983 as amended by Central Bank and Financial Services Authority of Ireland Act 2003, s 35, Sch 1. See EXECUTOR; LETTERS OF ADMINISTRATION; ADMINISTRATOR OF INSURER; PROBATE TAX.

administrator of insurer. The taking over of the management of an insurer, on an order for administration made by the High Court, if the court considers (a) that the insurer has made inadequate provision for its debts or that the rights and interests of policy holders are being prejudiced or that the insurer is unable to comply with EC insurance regulations, and (b) that administration would be in the public interest:

Insurance (No 2) Act 1983 as amended by Central Bank and Financial Services Authority of Ireland Act 2003, s 35, Sch 1.

The administrator so appointed is required to carry on the business as a going concern with a view to placing it on a sound commercial and financial footing. There is provision for contribution from other insurers to an *Insurance Compensation Fund*. Under recent legislation, provision has been made to restore the right of the administrator to have access to that fund: Central Bank and Financial Services Authority of Ireland Act 2004, s 33, Sch 3. See *Re PMPA Insurance Co* [1986] ILRM 524 and [1988] ILRM 109. See also Credit Union Act 1997, s 137 as amended by CBFSAI Act 2003, s 35, Sch 1. [Bibliography: Forde (9).]

administrator pendente lite. When in the course of any proceedings it appears at any time to the judge that an administrator *pendente lite* (while litigation is pending) or a receiver should be appointed, such appointment may be made, whether or not the same be asked for as part of the relief in the *civil bill* or other originating document: Circuit Court Rules 2001 Ord 45, r 1. See PENDENTE LITE.

admiralty action. Proceedings for the determination of: a claim for the sale of a ship or any share therein; or a claim to prohibit any dealing with a ship or any share therein; or in respect of a mortgage of, or charge on, a ship or any share therein; or a claim arising out of bottomry (qv) or in the nature, or arising out, of pilotage or arising out of a general average act; or a claim for the forfeiture of any ship or her tackle. The High Court has jurisdiction in admiralty matters. The Cork Circuit Court traditionally had limited admiralty jurisdiction but its jurisdiction is now abolished: Jurisdiction of Courts (Maritime Conventions) Act 1989, s 14. See *Motokov v Fermoyle Investments Ltd* [1985] HC. See RSC Ord 64 as amended by SI No 143 of 1990. See the *Brussels I Regulation*, arts 7, 14, 64 on the recognition and enforcement of judgments in civil and commercial matters, as implemented by EC (Civil and Commercial Judgments) Regulations 2002, SI No 52 of 2002. See AVERAGE; CHARGE ON SHIP; COLLISION OF SHIP; DETENTION OF SHIP; MALICIOUS DAMAGE.

admissibility of evidence. Evidence may be received by a court only if it is both relevant and admissible. In general, all evidence relevant to *facts in issue* is admissible. Certain evidence is inadmissible e g evidence of privileged communications without the waiver of the person in whose favour the privilege exists. The admissibility of evidence is decided by the judge; the jury must be absent during arguments as to admissibility: *The State v Treanor* [1924] 2 IR 193; The People v Murray [1971] CCA; *The People v O'Brien* [1969] CCA.

It has been held that evidence, following a deliberate and conscious breach of a person's constitutional rights, must only be excluded if it has been obtained as a result of that breach and a causative link between the breach and the obtaining of the evidence is established: *The People (DPP) v O'Donnell* [1995] 3 IR 551, CCA.

Communications between spouses and a third party for the purposes of reconciliation or to reach agreement between them in respect of a separation or divorce, are inadmissible as evidence in any court: Family Law (Divorce) Act 1996, s 9.

Nothing in the rules of evidence applies so as to deny the admissibility in evidence of an electronic communication, an electronic form of a document, an electronic contract, writing in electronic form, or an electronic signature, on the sole ground that it is in *electronic form,* or on the ground that it is not in its original form, if it is the *best evidence* that the person adducing it could reasonably be expected to obtain: Electronic Commerce Act 2000, s 22. See also Companies Act 1990, s 22; Stock Exchange Act 1995, s 67; Competition Act 2002, s 13. [Bibliography: Walsh D (3).] See ELECTRONIC FORM; EVIDENCE; EVIDENCE AND CONSTITUTIONAL RIGHTS; FACT IN ISSUE; HEARSAY; PRIVILEGE, EVIDENTIAL; TRIBUNALS OF INQUIRY; VOIRE DIRE.

admission. An acknowledgment of fact, oral written or inferred from conduct, made by or on behalf of a party to a proceeding, which is admissible as against the party making it, as proof of the facts admitted. The admission may be formal or informal. A *formal* admission of a fact may arise in pleadings e g matters not denied in the defence are taken as admitted, or in answer to interrogatories (qv). An *informal* admission may arise by express or implied statement, by silence or by conduct, or in various documents such as wills, account books, or maps. Informal admissions are admissible if made by the parties themselves, their privies, partners or agents, and hearsay (qv) evidence of the admission may be admissible.

In criminal proceedings, admissions may be made by plea of guilt, by a statement of facts by the accused, or by a confession (qv). Silence after a legal caution is not an admission. See *Attorney-General v Durnan* [1934] IR 308. Provision is made for the formal admission in criminal proceedings of matters not in dispute in order to dispense with the need for formal proofs: Criminal Justice Act 1984, s 22.

In bankruptcy matters, a person who on examination, admits that he is indebted to a bankrupt or has property belonging to him, may be ordered by the court to pay it or deliver it to the Official Assignee (qv): Bankruptcy Act 1988, s 22. See INTERROGATORIES; NOTICE TO ADMIT.

admission directive. The EC Directive 79/279/EEC co-ordinating the conditions for the admission of securities to official stock exchange listing: Listing Rules 2000 (*definitions*). See LISTING RULES; STOCK EXCHANGE.

admission of guilt. Where a client admits to his solicitor, prior to the commencement or during the course of any criminal case, that he is guilty of the charge, the solicitor need only decline to act in such proceedings if the client is insistent on giving evidence to deny such guilt or requires the making of a statement asserting his innocence: *A Guide to Professional Conduct of Solicitors in Ireland* (2002) ch 5.1. The solicitor may advance any defences which obliges the prosecution to prove guilt, other than protesting the client's innocence.

In relation to a confession of guilt to a defence barrister made before the proceedings have started, the barrister may continue to act for the accused, only if the accused pleads guilty or subject to limitations if the accused pleads not guilty: *Code of Conduct for the Bar of Ireland* (December 2003) r 9.10. The limitations are that the barrister will not put forward on the accused's behalf any substantive defence involving an assertion of innocence. This should be explained to the accused who, if not satisfied, should be informed that he could seek other advice.

If the confession of guilt is made during the proceedings or in such circumstances that a barrister cannot withdraw without compromising the position of the accused, he should continue to act but subject to limitations on the conduct of the defence. These limitations are that the defence barrister may not set up an affirmative case inconsistent with the confession, such as, by asserting or suggesting that some other person committed the offence charged, or by calling evidence in support of an alibi, or by calling the accused to give evidence to deny the charges or support an alibi.

admission order. An order, known as an *involuntary admission order*, for the reception, detention and treatment of a person suffering from a *mental disorder* (qv): Mental Health Act 2001, s 14. The order is made by a consultant psychiatrist on the staff of an *approved centre*, having carried out an examination of the person and having previously received a recommendation from a registered medical practitioner for the involuntary admission of the patient.

An admission order remains in force for 21 days, may be renewed for a further three months, and further extended for a further six months, and thereafter for periods of twelve months (MHA 2001, s 15). The consultant psychiatrist must give notice in writing of the order or renewal order to the patient and to the Mental Health Commission (MHA 2001, s 16).

The Commission is required to refer such an order to a tribunal, assign a legal representative to the patient, and direct in writing that the patient be examined, to determine in the interest of the patient, whether the patient is suffering from a mental disorder (MHA 2001, s 17). A patient may appeal to the Circuit Court against a decision of the tribunal that he is suffering from a mental disorder (MHA 2001, s 19).

There are specific provisions governing the involuntary admission of children (MHA 2001, s 25). Such admission is subject to parental consent or an Order of the District Court. Where the parents cannot or will not give consent, a health board may apply to the court for an order permitting the involuntary admission of the child for psychiatric care and treatment. [Bibliography: Keys.] See MENTAL DISORDER.

admissions system. The Supreme Court has held that an *admissions system* in a hospital which allowed a junior hospital doctor to disregard the opinion of an experienced general practitioner, clearly suffered from an inherent defect: *Collins v Mid-Western Health Board* [2000] 2 IR 154, SC. 'When general practitioners refer patients to hospital they expect them to be seen during the course of their management by a doctor of consultant or equal status. It is not acceptable for patients to be cared for entirely by junior medical staff.': Medical Council, *A Guide to Ethical Conduct and Behaviour* (6th edn, 2004) para 12.6.

admit, notice to. See NOTICE TO ADMIT.

adoptable powers. Powers which must, in order to be exercised by a body, be 'adopted' by the body eg see Building Societies Act 1989, ss 2(1) and 36.

adopted child. See CHILD, ADOPTED.

adoption. The process by which the rights and duties of the natural parents of a child are extinguished by the making of an *adoption order*, while the equivalent rights and duties become vested in the adoptive parents to whom the child then stands in all respects as if born to them in lawful wedlock: Adoption Act 1952. There are specific requirements relating to the *consent* which is required before an adoption order may be made. A child must be under 18 years of age to be adopted: Adoption Act 1988, s 6. See also Adoption Acts 1964, 1974 and 1991; Adoption Rules 1984, SI No 134 of 1984; Adoption Rules 1988, SI No 304 of 1988; Adoption Rules 1990, SI No 170 of 1990.

It has been held that ss 34(4) and 34(4A) of the 1952 Act, as amended, were designed to outlaw both the giving and the receiving of a child for the purposes of adoption other than to or by a registered adoption society or a health board or to a relative of the child: *Eastern Health Board v E (No 1)* [2000] 1 IR 430.

While AA 1991 does not purport to define the word 'adoption', the concept of voluntarily taking a child into a relationship and treating him as one's own is known and practised throughout the world: *B & B v An Bord Uchtála* [1997] 1 ILRM 15, SC.

The consent of a mother to the *placement* of her child for adoption can never, in itself, lead to an extinguishment of her rights; it is only upon the making of an *adoption order* by the adoption board that her rights are finally extinguished: *MO'C v Sacred Heart Adoption Society* [1996] 1 ILRM 297, SC. In a particular case, the Court held that the custody of a baby by pregnancy counsellors, who intended to adopt the baby, was at all times unlawful, as the consent to the placing of the baby by the mother was not a free nor informed consent: *In the Matter of Baby A, an Infant* [1999] ITLR (20 September), HC.

The categories of children who may be legally adopted has been extended to include, in certain restricted and exceptional circumstances, children whose parents are married to each other and are alive, or where there is one parent alive: Adoption Act 1988. Such adoption is allowed only where the parents of a child have failed in their duty towards the child and the failure is likely to continue and it constitutes an *abandonment of their parental rights*. These provisions are not repugnant to the Constitution: Reference pursuant to art 26 of the Constitution: *Re Adoption (No 2) Bill 1987* [1989] IR 656, SC.

In relation to the *abandonment of parental rights* pursuant to s 3(1)(I)(C) of the 1988 Act, it has been held that the word 'abandonment' was used as a special legal term: *Southern Health Board v An Bord Uchtála* [2000] 1 IR 165, SC. The Court held that the section did not require that there be an intention to abandon; that parents may be said to have abandoned their child where, by their actions, they have failed in their duty so as to enable a court to deem that their failure constitutes an abandonment of parental rights. The Supreme Court has held that the test of abandonment is an objective one; opposition by a parent to adoption of her child in itself does not contradict the fact of abandonment: *Northern Area Health Board v An Bord Uchtála* [2003] 1 ILRM 481, SC.

Also, it has been held that AA 1988 applied to a child, born abroad of foreign parents, who is in the State: *TM and HM v An Bord Uchtála* [1993] ILRM 577, SC. Health boards are required to provide a service for the adoption of children: Child Care Act 1991, s 6. See *Eastern Health Board v An Bord Uachtála* [1994] 3 IR 207, SC. See *Woulfe* in 6 ILT & SJ (1988) 271. See also Rules of the Superior Courts (No 1) 1990, SI No 97 of 1990; Adoption Rules 1999, SI No 315 of 1999. [Bibliography: Kennedy & Maguire; O'Halloran; Shatter.] See ADOPTION, CONSENT TO; CHILD, ADOPTED; PARENTAL DUTIES; PHYSICAL REASONS.

adoption, application for. Applications from persons for an adoption order are made to the Adoption Board (qv). An applicant must be ordinarily resident in the State, must be of good moral character,

must have sufficient means to support the child and be a suitable person to have parental rights and duties: Adoption Act 1952, s 13(1). In addition the applicant, or applicants, must be: a married couple living together; or the natural mother; or the natural father; or a relative of the child; or a widow, or a widower: Adoption Act 1991, s 10(1).

Applicants must be at least 21 years of age, except where the applicants are a married couple and one of them is the mother, father or relative of the child when it suffices if one of them is 21 years of age (AA 1991, s 10(5)). There is no upper limit for applicants; guidelines issued by the Adoption Board in 1993 indicated that there was no embargo on or preventing persons over 40 years of age availing of their entitlement to an assessment for adoption; the test is the general suitability of the applicant to have parental rights and duties. Upper age limits for applicants applying to adopt foreign children, imposed by the Board in December 1999, were abolished in April 2000.

An adoption order must not be made where the applicant is married unless the applicant's spouse has consented, except in the case of divorce a *mensa et thoro*, judicial separation, separation by deed, or desertion (AA 1991, s 10(4)). See Adoption Acts 1952, 1964, 1974, 1998; Adoption Rules 1999, SI No 315 of 1999.

adoption, birth records. The decision as to whether to provide information to an adopted person to enable him to trace his natural parents is a matter for decision by the Adoption Board; the Board must decide on an application for such information on its individual merits: *CR v An Bord Uchtála* [1994] 1 ILRM 217, HC. See Dervla Browne, 'Family Law aspects of the European Convention on Human Rights Act 2003' by BL in *Bar Review* (April 2004) 39.

adoption, consent to. An adoption order cannot be made by the Adoption Board (qv) unless the consent of the natural mother or guardian (qv) or other person having control over the child, is given: Adoption Act 1952, s 14(1). The consent must be in writing and can be withdrawn before the adoption order is made; the consent must be a fully informed, free and willing surrender or abandonment of the consentor's rights: *G v An Bord Uchtála* [1980] IR 32. A consent is invalid if given before the child is six weeks old, or if given at any time before three months of the adoption application: Adoption Act 1974, s 8.

While the *consent* of the natural father is not required, he or a person who believes that he is the father, is required to be *consulted*, where it is reasonably practicable: Adoption Act 1998, ss 4–6. This provision was made in response to the European Court of Human Rights judgment in *Keegan v Ireland* [1994] 18 EHRR 342.

The failure of the natural father to perform his duty as a parent does not of itself amount to abandonment of all his parental rights in respect of his child: *Western Health Board v An Bord Uchtála* [1996] 1 ILRM 434, SC and [1995] 3 IR 178, SC.

There is prohibition on placing a child under the age of four weeks for adoption; this is to enable the natural father to notify the Adoption Board of his wish to be consulted. No consultation is required in particular circumstances e g father's identity unknown, inability to make contact with the father, and inappropriate to make contact with the father (e g rape, incest, holiday romance).

In cases of religious differences, an adoption order cannot be made unless every person whose consent is necessary knows the religion of the applicants: AA 1974, s 4; *M v An Bord Uchtála* [1975] IR 86. The Adoption Board (qv) may dispense with consent if it is satisfied that the person whose consent is required is mentally unfit or is unable to be found.

Where a child is placed for adoption and the appropriate person fails, neglects or refuses consent or withdraws a consent already given, the applicant for the adoption order may apply to the High Court for an order authorising the Adoption Board to dispense with such consent: Adoption Act 1974, s 3; *MO'C v Sacred Heart Adoption Society* [1995] 1 ILRM 229, HC. See *G v An Bord Uchtála* [1980] IR 32; McC v An Bord Uchtála [1982] ILRM 159. See ADOPTION.

adoption, foreign. An adoption of a child which was effected outside the State under and in accordance with the law of the place where it was effected: Adoption Act 1991, s 1 as amended by Adoption Act 1998, s 10. A foreign adoption is deemed, unless contrary to public policy, to have been effected by a valid Irish adoption order (AA 1991, ss 2–5 as amended by AA 1998, ss 11–13).

Certain conditions must be satisfied e g (a) that the adoption outside the State has, for as long as it is in force, substantially the same legal effect as regards guardianship of the child as an Irish adoption, (b) that the required consents have been obtained at the time or subsequently, (c) that the adoption was effected for the purpose of promoting the interests and welfare of the child, and (d) that payment or reward has not been made in consideration of the adoption. For adoptions effected after commencement of the AA 1991, the child must be under 18 years of age. An Bord Uachtála (Adoption Board (qv)) must maintain a *Register of Foreign Adoptions*. The 1998 Act was enacted to accommodate the Supreme Court ruling on the recognition of Chinese adoptions in *B & B v An Bord Uchtála* [1997] 1 ILRM 15, SC and to have regard for the adoption law practice in other countries, where a simple adoption is subsequently capable of being converted into a full adoption.

See reports on the *Recognition of Foreign Adoption Decrees* (LRC 29, 1989) and on *Protection of and Co-operation in respect of Intercountry Adoption of Children* (LRC 58, 1998). See *TM and AM v An Bord Uchtála* [1993] ILRM 577, SC; *McC & McD v Eastern Health Board* [1997] 1 ILRM 349, SC; *B & B v An Bord Uchtála* [1997] 1 ILRM 15, SC. [Bibliography: Rose.]

adoption, private. The placing of a child for adoption in an arrangement which does not involve *approved* bodies. In general, only a registered adoption society or a health board may place a child for adoption: Adoption Act 1952, s 34, Adoption Act 1974, s 6, Adoption Act 1998, s 7. The birth mother and/or the natural father have a right to make a direct placement of their child for the purpose of having the child adopted, but only to a *relative* of the child. *Relative* means a grandparent, brother, sister, uncle or aunt of the child, including the spouse of such persons, the relationship to the child being traced through the mother or father (AA 1998, s 2). Contravention of these provisions by the person placing or receiving the child is an offence.

In such an application for an adoption order by the mother or relative to the Adoption Board, where no adoption agency is involved, there is a general requirement for the natural father to be consulted where it is reasonably practicable (AA 1998, ss 5–6). See ADOPTION, CONSENT TO.

adoption, registration of. Provision has been made for the establishment and maintenance of a register of all adoptions and foreign adoptions under the Adoption Acts 1952 to 1998: Civil Registration Act 2004, ss 13(1)(c) and 31–35. The register is maintained by the Adoption Board. No information from the register may be given to any person except by order of the Board or the High Court (CRA 2004, s 35). For the particulars of adoptions to be entered in the register of adoptions, see CRA 2004, Sch 1, Part 3 (adoptions within the State) and Part 4 (foreign adoptions).

adoption and doctors. The Medical Council has issued guidelines for doctors: 'Adoption must occur only through the auspices of registered adoption agencies. Pregnant women who are considering adoption must be offered contact with a registered adoption agency (details of which may be obtained from the Adoption Board)': Medical Council, *A Guide to Ethical Conduct and Behaviour* (6th edn, 2004) para 24.7.

Adoption Board. The board set up for the purpose of making *adoption orders* (qv) and consisting of a chairman and eight ordinary members appointed by the Government (qv): Adoption Act 1952, s 8 as amended by Adoption Act 1991, s 11. The chairman must be a judge of the Supreme, High, Circuit or District Courts, or a barrister or solicitor of at least ten years' standing. An adoption society or a health board which wishes to process adoptions must be registered with the Adoption Board. An adoption society is not required to carry out its statutory tasks through its own servants or agents: *JP & SP v O'G* [1991] ITLR (24 June), SC.

Persons who wish to adopt a child must apply to the Board, which may at its discretion grant or refuse the application. When considering an adoption application, the Board must regard the welfare of the child as the first and paramount consideration: Adoption Act 1974. Privilege extends to all documents and records of the Adoption Board; where a *subpoena duces tecum* (qv) is served on an officer of the Board, it is entitled to have it set aside: Adoption Act 1976, s 8 and *PB v AL* [1996] 1 ILRM 154, HC. See also Adoptive Leave Act 1995, s 13. See also Justice (Transfer of Departmental Administration and Ministerial Functions) Order 1982, SI No 327 of 1982.

adoptive benefit. Social welfare benefit to which an adopter is entitled who is eligible for *adoptive leave* under the Adoptive Leave Act 1995: Social Welfare (Consolidation) Act 1993, ss 41G–41J inserted by Social Welfare Act 1995, s 11 and Social Welfare Act 1997, s 11. The duration of payment of *adoptive benefit* has been increased from 10 to 14 weeks: Social Welfare Act 2001, s 12. See also Social Welfare (Miscellaneous Provisions) Act 2002, s 9. Provision has been made to enable the Minister, by order, to increase adoptive benefit to 16 weeks: Social Welfare (Miscellaneous Provisions) Act 2004, s 9.

adoptive leave. The ten-week (originally) unpaid period of leave to which an employed adopting mother is entitled, but which attracts a social welfare payment, *adoptive benefit*: Adoptive Leave Act 1995, s 6. There is provision for optional additional leave which excludes welfare payment (ALA 1995, s 8). An adopting father is entitled to adoptive leave only where the adopting mother dies (ALA 1995, s 9). There is a general right to return to work on expiry of the leave (ALA 1995, s 18). The ten-week unpaid period of leave has been extended to 14 weeks (which period attracts social welfare payment *adoptive benefit*), and the optional four weeks additional unpaid leave, which excludes welfare payment, has been extended to eight weeks: Adoptive Leave (Extension of Periods of Leave) Order 2001, SI No 30 of 2001.

For rules governing applications to the court for the enforcement of decisions of a Rights Commissioner or determinations of the Employment Appeals Tribunal, pursuant to s 39 of the Adoptive Leave Act 1995, see Circuit Court Rules 2001 Ord 57, r 3.

The restriction of adoptive leave to women is not discrimination within the meaning of EC Directive 76/207: *Commission v Italy* [1993] ECR 3273; *Telecom Éireann v O'Grady* [1996] 2 ILRM 374, HC and [1998] 3 IR 432, SC and ELR 61. See also Organisation of Working Time Act 1997, s 15(4)(b). See also *Aer Rianta v Irish Distributive and Administrative Trade Union* DEE/1990 reported in *Doolan v City of Dublin VEC* [1994] EO ELR 193.

Under draft legislation, there is: (a) provision for a further increase in the duration of adoptive leave by two weeks, bringing the period of leave attracting payment/ benefit to 16 weeks; (b) provision of time off from work, without loss of pay, for employees to attend pre-adoption classes and meetings which they are obliged to attend; (c) provision for termination of additional adoptive leave in the event of the employee's illness (which would allow transfer onto paid sick leave from unpaid additional adoptive leave); (d) provision for an employee to split the period of adoptive leave and additional adoptive leave in the event of the hospitalisation of the child; and (e) provision that an employee's absence from work on additional adoptive leave will count for any employment rights associated with the employment (except remuneration, and superannuation benefits) such as annual leave and seniority: Adoptive Leave Bill 2004. See CHILDBIRTH; PARENTAL LEAVE.

ADR. The European Agreement concerning the international carriage of goods by road, done at Geneva in 1957 and amended in 1993. It was given effect in Ireland by the Carriage of Dangerous Goods by Road Act 1998. See also Carriage of Dangerous Goods by Road Regulations 2004, SI No 29 of 2004. See DANGEROUS GOODS.

adult. A person who attains *full age*. See AGE OF MAJORITY.

adultery. An act of voluntary sexual intercourse which takes place during the subsistence of a valid marriage with a person of the opposite sex who is not the spouse. It is a ground for a decree of judicial separation (qv), but may not be relied upon solely by an applicant for a decree, where the spouses have lived with each other for more than a year after the adultery became known to the applicant; the court may also refuse a decree where the respondent proves the adultery was committed with the connivance (qv) of the applicant: Judicial Separation and Family Law Reform Act 1989, ss 2(1)(a), 4(1) and 44(2). See JUDICIAL SEPARATION; CONNIVANCE; DIVORCE A MENSA ET THORO; MARRIAGE, NULLITY OF; RECRIMINATION.

advancement. A payment in anticipation of a limited portion of the share to which a beneficiary will ultimately be entitled for the beneficiary's benefit or advancement in life. It includes payments made out of the trust capital to a beneficiary before he becomes entitled to an interest under the trust: *Pilkington v IRS* [1964] AC 612 at 634. A power to make advancements out of

capital may be expressly conferred by the trust instrument. The court is empowered to sanction capital payments for the support of an infant beneficiary: Guardianship of Infants Act 1964, s 11.

advancement, child. A gift intended to make permanent provision for a child and includes *advancement* by way of portion or settlement: Succession Act 1965, s 63. Includes some permanent provision for the child of a deceased for the purpose of establishing the child in a profession, vocation, trade or business or a *marriage portion* (qv) or payments made for the education of a child to a standard higher than that provided for other children of the deceased (SA 1965, s 63(3)). Children must bring into *hotchpot* (qv) any money or property they received from the deceased in his lifetime by way of advancement if they wish to share in the distribution of the estate. See *Re Grimes* [1937] IR 470; *McCabe v Ulster Bank Ltd* [1939] IR 1. See DOUBLE PORTIONS, RULE AGAINST; RESULTING TRUST.

advancement, equitable doctrine of. The doctrine which presumes that advancement arises where a person advances money for the purchase of any property or right in the name of another for whom the purchaser is under a legal or moral obligation to provide. It may arise in the case of a spouse, a child or a person to whom the purchaser stands *in loco parentis*. The presumption of advancement arises where a husband transfers property to his wife or purchases it in her name: *Irwin v O'Connell* [1936] IR 44. The presumption can be rebutted by evidence of a contrary intention eg see *RF v MF* [1995] 2 ILRM 572, SC. See also *O'Brien v Sheil* [1873] IR 7 Eq 255; *Bennet v Bennet* [1879] 19 Ch D 474; *Fitzpatrick v Criminal Assets Bureau* [2000] 1 ILRM 299, SC.

adventure activities. A new legislative regime has been introduced to regulate the safe provision of adventure activities by way of a new statutory authority: Adventure Activities Standards Authority Act 2001. 'Adventure activity' means any one of the following: hill-walking or orienteering in areas more than 300 metres above sea level, caving, dinghy sailing, kayaking, canoeing, surfing with a surf board, wind-surfing, scuba-diving, snorkelling, abseiling, archery, rock climbing.

Provision has been made for: (a) the establishment of an independent *Adventure*

Activities Standards Authority; (b) a mandatory requirement for adventure activity operators to register with the Authority in respect of specified adventure activities; (c) the development of mandatory codes of practice by the Authority in respect of specified adventure activities; (d) the implementation by the Authority of a mandatory regulatory scheme; and (e) inspections.

The Authority may direct the suspension or cessation of a specified adventure activity for non-compliance with codes of practice.

adverse event. Means any untoward medical occurrence in a subject to whom a medicinal product has been administered, including occurrences that do not necessarily have a causal relationship with the treatment: EC (Clinical Trials on Medicinal Products for Human Use) Regulations 2004, SI No 190 of 2004, reg 4(1). An investigator must report any serious adverse event which occurs in a clinical trial immediately to the sponsor (reg 29). See ADVERSE REACTION; CLINICAL TRIALS, CONDUCT OF.

adversary procedure. Accusatory procedure (qv).

adverse possession, title by. See LONG POSSESSION, TITLE BY.

adverse reaction. Means any untoward and unintended response in a subject to an investigational medicinal product which is related to any dose administered to that subject: EC (Clinical Trials on Medicinal Products for Human Use) Regulations 2004, SI No 190 of 2004, reg 4(1). A sponsor of a clinical trial must ensure that a suspected, serious, unexpected adverse reaction which occurs during a clinical trial is reported as soon as possible to the Irish Medicines Board, the competent authorities of all EEA States, and to the relevant ethics committee (reg 30). See ADVERSE EVENT; CLINICAL TRIALS, CONDUCT OF.

adverse witness. A witness, adverse to the party calling him, who may be cross-examined by that party with the leave of the court. See HOSTILE WITNESS.

advertisement. An advertisement is a paid-for communication addressed to the public or a section of it, the purpose being to influence the opinions or behaviour of those to whom it is addressed: Advertising Standards Authority for Ireland Code of Advertising Standards, art 19.

The publisher of an advertisement can be compelled to disclose the name and address of the person or his agent who procured the publication of an advertisement in relation to the supply or provision of any goods, services, living accommodation or facilities. See Consumer Information Act 1978, s 13; Restrictive Practices (Amendment) Act 1987, s 30. Advertisement in this context includes a catalogue, a circular and a price list (CIA 1978, s 1).

See *Code of Ethics — The Institution of Engineers of Ireland* (Nov 2003), clause 1.4(i) and App 1. See also Indecent Advertisements Act 1889; Opticians Act 1956, s 52; Building Societies Act 1989, s 42(3)(a); Regulation of Information (Services outside the State for Termination of Pregnancies) Act 1995, s 14; Consumer Credit Act 1995, ss 2(1); Credit Union Act 1997, s 86 as amended by Central Bank and Financial Services Authority of Ireland Act 2003, s 35, Sch 1; Private Security Services Act 2004, s 37(1)(a). For the Advertising Standards Authority of Ireland, see website: *www.asai.ie*. For the Institute of Advertising Practitioners in Ireland, see website: *www.iapi.ie*. See EUROPEAN EXTRA-JUDICIAL NETWORK.

advertisement, misleading. An advertisement in relation to the supply or provision in the course or for the purpose of a trade, business or profession, of goods, services or facilities which in any way deceives or is likely to deceive the persons to whom it is addressed and is likely to affect their economic behaviour or which injures or is likely to injure a competitor: European Communities (Misleading Advertisements) Regulations 1988, SI No 134 of 1988; EC Directive 84/450/EEC, art 2(2).

It is an offence for a person to publish, or cause to be published, such an advertisement. The High Court may grant an order prohibiting the publication, or the further publication, of a misleading advertisement on the application of any person, including the Director of Consumer Affairs (reg 4).

The Supreme Court has ruled that an advertisement proposed to be published by a trade union which criticised the manner in which an employer treated its employees at Christmas, did not come within the category of advertisement from which the EC Directive sought to protect consumers, persons carrying on a trade, business, craft or profession, and the general public: *Dunnes Stores Ltd v Mandate* [1996] 1 ILRM 384, SC and ELR 56 and 1 IR 55. See Consumer Information Act 1978, s 8.

See 'Caught in the Web' by solicitor Sinead Morgan in *Law Society Gazette* (January/February 2004) 38. [Bibliography: Bird.]

advertisement, radio and television. The total daily time for advertising on independent radio and television services must not exceed: (a) 15% of the total daily broadcasting time; and (b) ten minutes in any hour: Radio and Television Act 1988, s 10(4). The limits on RTE were 7.5% of daily transmission time and five minutes in any hour: Broadcasting Act 1990, s 3. They are now such periods as are approved by the Minister: Broadcasting Authority (Amendment) Act 1993, s 2.

In construing the term 'advertisements' under s 10, regard should be had to the policy of the legislation to ensure a reasonable balance between advertising and the provision of news, entertainment and other programmes: *Radio Limerick One Ltd v IRTC* [1997] 2 ILRM 1, SC.

There is a prohibition on the broadcast of any advertisement which is directed towards any *religious* or *political end* or which has any relation to an industrial dispute: Radio and Television Act 1988, ss 10(3) and 18. An advertisement has a *political end* if it is directed towards furthering the interests of a particular political party or towards procuring or countering changes in the law: *Cregan v IRTC* [1999] 1 ILRM 22, HC.

The ban on advertisements directed towards any *religious end* does not constitute a discrimination or distinction on the grounds of religious profession, belief or status contrary to art 44(2)(3) of the 1937 Constitution: *Murphy v IRTC* [1998] 2 ILRM 360, SC. See *Murphy v IRTC* [1999] 1 IR 12, SC.

The Oireachtas was entitled to take the view that advertisements that were directed towards any religious end, which related to a matter which had proved extremely divisive in Irish society in the past, might lead to resentment and unrest (see *Murphy* case). It has been held that the objective of prohibiting the broadcast of advertisements in the sensitive areas of religion, politics and industrial disputes, so as to avoid giving proponents of any particular viewpoint an unfair advantage over anyone else, was an exercise in moderation in the common good: *Colgan v IRTC* [2000] 2 IR 490, HC.

The Minister announced in March 2003 a review of the legislative provisions which impose a ban on religious advertising. For submissions made to that review, see website: *www.dcmnr.gov.ie*. The Broadcasting Commission of Ireland outlined in July 2004 a new code governing advertisements as regards children, with the intention that the detailed code be published in October 2004 and implemented as from 1 January 2005. In response to concerns about obesity, the proposed code will require television advertising of fast food to carry an on-screen message that such food should be eaten in moderation and part of a balanced diet. See SOUND BROADCASTING SERVICE.

advertisement and airlines. Regulations have been made to provide transparency in airline advertising in order to give consumers accurate information about the full price of airline tickets and the availability of the airfares advertised: Consumer Information (Advertisements for Airfares) Order 2000, SI No 468 of 2000.

advertisement and barristers. A barrister may advertise by placing prescribed information concerning himself on the website of the Bar Council: *Code of Conduct for the Bar of Ireland* (Dec 2003), r 6.1. A barrister may arrange to be photographed as a barrister only in the following circumstances: on his call to the Bar or to the Inner Bar; and on becoming a judge (r 6.14). See BARRISTER; SOLICITOR AND ADVERTISING.

advertisement and discrimination. A person is prohibited from publishing an advertisement which indicates an intention to engage in *prohibited conduct* (i e discrimination, sexual harassment or harassment) or might reasonably be understood as indicating such an intention: Equal Status Act 2000, ss 12, 23(1)(b), 23(3)(b). See DISCRIMINATION.

advertisement and employment. Advertisements relating to employment must not contravene the Employment Equality Act 1998, s 10 as amended by Equality Act 2004, s 5. Advertisements must not indicate an intention to discriminate or reasonably be understood as indicating an intention to discriminate on nine different discriminatory grounds. As regards confining a post to a man or to a woman, the characteristic related to the gender ground must constitute a genuine and determining occupational requirement for the post, and the objective must be legitimate and the requirement proportionate e g for purposes of authenticity in entertainment (EEA 1998, s 25 amended by substitution by EA 2004, s 16). An Equality Officer has held that the use of the word 'young' in a recruitment advertisement indicated or might reasonably be regarded as indicating an intention to discriminate on the age ground: *Equality Authority v Ryanair* [2001] EO ELR 107. See *EEA v Cork Examiner* [1991] ELR 6. See also *Tipperary Sub-Contracting Ltd and Nenagh Guardian v EEA* (1993) EE 6. See *Flynn* in 11 ILT and SJ (1993) 157. See DISCRIMINATION.

advertisement and financial services. Advertisements in respect of investment services must comply with any conditions or requirements specified by the Central Bank: Stock Exchange Act 1995, s 31. See also Investment Intermediaries Act 1995, ss 23–24; Investment Compensation Act 1998, s 38.

Advertisements in respect of financial accommodation (credit or letting of goods) must comply with certain requirements: Consumer Credit Act 1995, s 26. The Central Bank may make regulations amending, ss 21–25 with respect to the form or content of advertisements relating to the availability or the cost or the provision of credit to consumers (CCA 1995, s 28 substituted by Central Bank and Financial Services Authority of Ireland Act 2003, s 35, Sch 1). See ANNUAL PERCENTAGE CHARGE; HOUSING LOAN.

advertisement and litter. There is a general prohibition on advertisements being exhibited on any structure, door, gate, window, tree, pole or post, in or visible from a public place: Litter Pollution Act 1997, s 19 as amended by Protection of the Environment Act 2003, s 56. There is an exception in respect of a notice required to be erected under any enactment, or relating to a public meeting, an election or a referendum, provided it is removed within seven days of the meeting, election or referendum (LPA 1997, s 19(7) as amended by PEA 2003, s 56(c)). See also LPA 1997, ss 20–21 as substituted by PEA 2003, s 57. See LITTER.

advertisement and medical practitioners. There are restrictions on advertisements by medical practitioners, on the Internet or other media eg they are permitted announcements in the national and/or local press, not measuring more than 100mm in any direction, concerning the commencement of practice: Medical Council, *A Guide to Ethical Conduct and Behaviour* (6th edn, 2004), para 6. Self advertisement, or publicity to enhance or promote a professional reputation for the purpose of attracting patients is unacceptable (para 14.3).

advertisement and planning. For the purposes of planning legislation, '*advertisement*' means any word, letter, model, balloon, kite, poster, notice, device or representation employed for the purpose of advertisement, announcement or direction: Planning and Development Act 2000, s 2(1). A refusal to grant planning permission for the use of land for the exhibition of any advertisement, does not attract compensation (PDA 2000, s 191, Sch 3, para 5). See Planning and Development Regulations 2001, SI No 600 of 2001, arts 5, 6, 201 and Sch 2. For previous legislation, see LG(P&D) Act 1963, ss 2(1) and 54, LG(P&D) Regulations 1994, Sch 2, Pt II, SI No 86 of 1994. See PLANNING PERMISSION; SIGN.

advertisement and takeovers. There are restrictions on the advertisements which may be published in connection with a company which is the subject of a takeover offer unless the advertisement falls into specified categories eg product advertisements not bearing on the offer or possible offer: Takeover Rules 2001, Pt B, r 19.4. The content, format and publication schedule of specified advertisements must have prior approval of the *Irish Takeover Panel* (qv).

advertisement and tobacco. An advertisement in relation to a tobacco product, means any form of commercial communications with the aim or direct or indirect effect of promoting a tobacco product: Public Health (Tobacco) Act 2002, s 2(1) inserted by Public Health (Tobacco) (Amendment) Act 2004, s 2 and EC Directive No 2003/33/EC. It is an offence to advertise a tobacco product in contravention of the Directive: PH(T)A 2002, s 33 as substituted by PH(T)(A)A 2004, s 5. This includes advertising in the printed media and information society services. There is an exception regarding advertisements directed at persons engaged in the sale of tobacco products (PH(T)A 2002, s 35 as substituted by PH(T)(A)A 2004, s 6). Prohibited also are advertisements in premises where tobacco products are sold (PH(T)A 2002, s 33A inserted by PH(T)(A)A 2004, s 5). See TOBACCO PRODUCT.

advertising order. An order which the Minister may make to compel inclusion of particular information in an advertisement of goods, services, living accommodation or facilities. It is an offence to publish an advertisement which fails to comply with the order. See Consumer Information Act 1978, s 11.

advertising structure. Means any structure which is a hoarding, scaffold, framework, pole, standard, device or sign and which is used or intended for use for exhibiting advertisements: Planning and Development Act 2000, s 2(1). A refusal to grant planning permission for the erection of any advertising structure does not attract compensation (PDA 2000, s 191, Sch 3, para 5).

advice on proofs. The directions given by counsel, at the close of pleading and prior to the trial of an action, as to the documents to be produced at the trial, the witnesses who are to be called and the notices which are to be served eg a notice to admit (qv).

advocacy services. See COMHAIRLE.

advocate. A person who pleads the cause of another in court eg a barrister (qv) or solicitor (qv). Formerly an advocate was a member of the College of Advocates which was abolished by the Court of Probate Act 1857. See 'Fast on your feet' in *Law Society Gazette* (December 2003) 23. [Bibliography: Finlay (2); O'Flaherty; Napley (UK).]

advocates-general. The independent persons who assist the judges of the European Court of Justice (qv). They are empowered to carry out their own personal examination of a case, including any related question not brought forward by the parties, and to express their opinion to the Court. Their reasoned oral submissions presented in open court, while not reflecting the Court's view, often contain the key reasoning behind the subsequent Court's decision. Their submissions are published with the Court's judgments in the reports of the Court. Provision has also been made for the Court of First Instance to be assisted by advocates-general. See Treaty establishing the European Community, arts 222 and 224 of the consolidated (2002) version.

Service as an advocate-general is deemed to be practice at the Bar for practice qualifying purposes for judicial appointment in the Irish court system: Courts and Court Officers Act 1995, s 28. An advocate-general who was a practising barrister or practising solicitor prior to their appointment is qualified for appointment as a judge of the Superior Courts of Ireland: Courts (Supplementary Provisions)

Act 1961, s 5(2) as substituted by Courts and Court Officers Act 2002, s 4. See FIRST INSTANCE, COURT OF.

aedificatum solo, solo cedit. [That which is built upon land becomes part of the land.] See FIXTURES.

aequitas sequitur legem. [Equity follows the law.] See EQUITY, MAXIMS OF.

Aer Lingus. A state-owned enterprise, originally incorporated in 1936, which was restructured and rationalised by the Air Companies (Amendment) Act 1993, with an injection of IR£175m of state funds. It carries over 6 million passengers annually and is a member, since 2000, of the *oneworld* global alliance, which includes American Airlines, British Airways, Finnair, Iberia, Cathay Pacific, Lan Chile and Qantas.

Provision has been made: (a) to give effect to the Employee Share Ownership Plan (ESOP) agreed by the Government and Aer Lingus unions; and (b) to provide a legal framework to facilitate any private sector investment process in the event that the Government embarks on such a process: Aer Lingus Act 2004. This Act also includes an enabling provision for the establishment of new pension schemes by Aer Lingus. See website: *www.aerlingus.com*.

Aer Rianta. See AIRPORT.

aerodrome. Includes an area of water intended for use for landing or taking off by aircraft (qv) and also includes an area, whether on land or water or on a building or other structure or elsewhere, intended for use for landing or taking off by aircraft capable of descending or climbing vertically: Irish Aviation Authority Act 1993, s 2(1). *State aerodromes* means Cork Airport, Dublin Airport and Shannon Airport: IAAA 1993, s 2(1). The Irish Aviation Authority is empowered to make orders for the licensing of aerodromes and for the regulation of aeronautical standards at aerodromes: IAAA 1993, s 60 as amended by Air Navigation and Transport (Amendment) Act 1998, s 61. It also has powers in relation to erecting and maintaining apparatus in the vicinity of aerodromes and to restrict the use of such land in the interest of safe air navigation (IAAA 1993, s 72(2)).

affidavit. A written (or printed bookwise) statement in the name of a person, called the *deponent*, by whom it is sworn: RSC Ord 40. It includes a *declaration* in the case of persons for the time being allowed by law to declare instead of swearing: Interpretation Act 1937, s 12, Sch.

An affidavit must be drawn up in the first person (RSC Ord 40, r 8) and must be confined to such facts as the deponent is able of his own knowledge to prove, and must state his means of knowledge thereof, except on *interlocutory* motions, on which statements as to his belief, with the grounds thereof, may be admitted (RSC Ord 40, r 4 and *Bula Ltd v Tara Mines Ltd* [1991] 9 ILT Dig 128, HC which permitted hearsay material in an interlocutory application). However, the High Court has held that an affidavit, grounding an application to amend a defence, may contain hearsay: *Walsh v Harrison* [2003] 2 ILRM 161, HC.

The facts relied upon must, in the absence of special procedures, be clearly deposed to in the affidavit itself and not by reference to any other written document: *Murphy v Greene* [1991] ILRM 404, SC. The court may order the attendance for cross-examination of a person making an affidavit (RSC Ord 40, r 1). Also, in proceedings commenced by *summary summons* and *special summons*, a party is entitled to cross-examine a deponent who has made an affidavit filed on behalf of the opposite party: RSC Ord 37, r 2; Ord 38, r 3.

The court has a discretion to permit any particular fact to be proved by affidavit where sufficient reason has been shown to so permit and justice so requires: *Phonographic Performance (Ireland) Ltd v Cody* [1998] 2 ILRM 21, SC.

In the Circuit Court all affidavits must be written or printed bookwise; expressed in the first person of the deponent; drawn up in numbered paragraphs; and entitled in the action or matter in which they are sworn: Circuit Court Rules 2001 Ord 25. For *affidavit of means*, see Ord 59, r 4(17)–(18). The District Court may, if it deems fit, permit facts to be proved by affidavit: DCR 1997 Ord 8, r 3(1).

An affidavit may be made also before a practising solicitor: District Court (Affidavit) Rules 1998, SI No 286 of 1999. However, an affidavit is not sufficient if sworn before the solicitor acting for the party on whose behalf the affidavit is to be used: DCR 1997 Ord 9, r 2.

Evidence in extradition proceedings may be given by affidavit, or by a statement in writing that purports to have been sworn by the deponent in a place outside the State: Extradition (European Union Convention) Act 2001, s 22. The High Court may direct that oral evidence be given, if it considers the interest of justice so requires. See also Arbitration Act 1954, s 22(1)(c). Discovery of documents will not be ordered where they are sought only to impugn the integrity of the deponent, in the absence of material suggesting that the averments were untrue: *Shortt v Dublin City Council* [2004] 1 ILRM 81, HC and [2003] 2 IR 69. Evidence may be given by affidavit in a personal injuries action, where the court so directs: Civil Liability and Courts Act 2004, s 19. Also an affidavit is required in a personal injuries action verifying the pleadings: CLCA 2004, s 14. See ARGUMENTATIVE AFFIDAVIT; DECLARATION BY DECEASED; OATH; PERSONAL INJURIES ACTION; ELECTRONIC FORM; JURAT; SUMMONS, HIGH COURT; THIRD PARTY NOTICE.

affidavit of discovery. A written document sworn or affirmed by a deponent disclosing all documents in his possession, custody or power, relating to matters in issue in an action. There are circumstances under which a court would wish to cross-examine a deponent of an affidavit of discovery, but such circumstances are rare: *Duncan v Governor of Portlaoise Prison* [1997] 2 ILRM 296, HC. This is because of the variety of other remedies available to test matters in such an affidavit eg orders for further and better discovery, delivery of interrogatories, and the inspection by the court itself of documents referred to in the affidavit. See RSC Ord 40, r 1. See DISCOVERY.

affidavit of service. An affidavit which states when, where, and how, and by whom, delivery of a document (eg a summons) was effected and in the case of delivery to any person, which states that the deponent was, at the time of such delivery, acquainted with the appearance of such person: RSC Ord 40, r 9.

In the Circuit Court, affidavits or declarations of service must state when, where, and how, and by whom, such service was effected: Circuit Court Rules 2001 Ord 25, r 15. See SUMMONS, SERVICE OF.

affiliation order. An order of the court which provided for the payment of a periodical or lump sum of money by the father of an illegitimate child as a contribution towards the maintenance of that child: Illegitimate Children (Affiliation Orders) Act 1930, s 2; Status of Children Act 1987, s 25. Formerly, the onus was on the applicant mother to prove to the satisfaction of the court that the person she alleged to be the father was the father; she had to give evidence herself and she had to produce corroborative evidence in support; and proceedings had to be brought within specified time limits: IC(AO)A 1930, s 2(2); Family Law (Maintenance of Spouses and Children) Act 1976, s 28(1)(b)).

However, a person may apply for a *maintenance order* (qv) for the support of a child whose parents are not married to each other, at any time during the child's dependency, and the court will have regard to the circumstances as if the application was one relating to a legitimate child; if there is any dispute as to paternity or parentage, the issue will be decided on the balance of probability, prior to any maintenance order being made: Status of Children Act 1987, ss 15–25. See *RB v HR* [1990] CC as reported in 8 ILT & SJ (1990) 295. See DEPENDENT CHILD; PARENTAGE, DECLARATION OF.

affinity. Relationship by marriage. The relationship between a husband and his wife's blood relations, and between a wife and her husband's blood relations. There is no affinity between a person and the relations by marriage of his or her spouse. See CONSANGUINITY; MARRIAGE.

affirm. (1) To elect to be bound by a voidable contract.

(2) To make a solemn declaration instead of an oath. See AFFIRMATION; VOIDABLE.

affirmanti non neganti incumbit probatio. [The burden of proof is on him who affirms, not on him who denies.] See PROOF.

affirmation. A solemn declaration which a person may make instead of taking an oath, where the person states that he has no religious belief or that an oath is contrary to his religious belief: Oaths Act 1888. See Arbitration (International Commercial) Act 1998, s 8; Taxes Consolidation Act 1997, s 1096A inserted by Finance Act 1999, s 30; Finance Act 2003, s 147. See Report on Oaths and Affirmations (LRC 34, 1990). See OATH.

affirmative order. An order made pursuant to a statute, a draft of which must be laid before each House of the Oireachtas and be approved by each such House eg an order conferring additional functions on An Foras Áiseanna Saothair: Labour Services Act 1987, s 5(3).

affordable housing. (1) Means houses or land made available for *eligible persons*: Planning and Development Act 2000, s 93(1). *Eligible person* means a person who is in need of accommodation and whose income would not be adequate to meet the payments on a mortgage for the purchase of a house because the payments would exceed 35% of that person's annual income, net of income tax and pay related social insurance (PDA 2000, s 93(1)). *Affordable housing* may be sold only to eligible persons who qualify in accordance with a scheme established by the planning authority (PDA 2000, s 98). There is provision for a clawback on any profits on a resale of affordable housing (PDA 2000, s 99).

The provisions relating to *housing supply* (PDA 2000, Pt V, ss 93 to 101) including *affordable housing* were referred by the President of Ireland to the Supreme Court under art 26 for a decision on the question as to whether they were repugnant to the Constitution. It held that the imposing of a condition to obtain planning permission whereby the owner was required to cede some part of the enhanced value of the land (deriving from its zoning for residential purposes and the grant of planning permission) in order to provide affordable housing, was an objective of sufficient importance to warrant interference with a constitutionally protected right and impaired that right as little as possible and was proportionate to the objective: *In the matter of The Planning and Development Bill 1999* [2000] 2 IR 321, SC and [2001] 2 ILRM 81 SC. See 'Social and Affordable' by James Macken SC in *Bar Review* (October 2000) 41. See 'Change of Plan' by solicitor John Gore-Grimes in *Law Society Gazette* (January/February 2003) 18.

(2) Means a house made available for sale by a housing authority at a price less than the market value ie the price which, in the opinion of the housing authority concerned, might reasonably be obtained if sold on the open market: Housing (Miscellaneous Provisions) Act 2002, s 5. A housing authority may acquire, build or cause to be built affordable houses for sale (H(MP)A 2002, s 6) and may pay a mortgage subsidy to eligible persons (H(MP)A 2002, s 7). Approved housing bodies may also provide affordable houses (H(MP)A

2002, s 6 as amended by Planning and Development (Amendment) Act 2002, s 19).

Every housing authority is required to establish a scheme that determines the order of priority to be accorded to persons to whom affordable houses are made available for sale (H(MP)A 2002, s 8). This is a *reserved function* of the housing authority (H(MP)A 2002, s 8(4)). There is control on the resale of affordable houses, including a formula-based clawback on any profit of a resale by the initial owners within 20 years of the date of purchase (H(MP)A 2002, s 9). See also Dublin Docklands Development Act 1997, s 25 as amended by PD(A)A 2002, s 22. See HOUSING STRATEGY.

afforestation. Initial afforestation has been removed from the planning control system to coincide with a separate statutory consent system under European Communities (Environmental Impact Assessment) (Amendment) Regulations 2001, SI No 538 of 2001: Local Government (Planning and Development) (Amendment) Regulations 2001, SI No 539 of 2001. See ENVIRONMENTAL IMPACT ASSESSMENT.

affray. Where: (a) two or more persons at any place use or threaten to use violence towards each other; and (b) the violence so used or threatened by one of those persons is unlawful; and (c) the conduct of those persons taken together is such as would cause a person of reasonable firmness present at that place to fear for his or another person's safety, then, each such person who uses or threatens to use unlawful violence is guilty of the offence of *affray*: Criminal Justice (Public Order) Act 1994, s 16. The place may be a public place, a private place or both. The common law offence of *affray* has been abolished: CJ(PO)A 1994, s 16(5).

Where two views are possible on the evidence, the jury should adopt that view which is favourable to the accused unless the State has established the other view beyond reasonable doubt: *DPP v Reid & Kirwan* (2004), Irish Times, 13 February. In this case the Court overturned the conviction of the accused of '*affray*', noting that the trial judge had failed to take account of a submission of the possibility that a person might be involved in a fight in exercise of a right to use lawful force to protect himself or another. See RIOT; VIOLENT DISORDER.

affreightment. A contract made by bill of lading (qv) or charterparty (qv), whereby a ship owner agrees to carry goods in his ship for reward. See FREIGHT.

after-acquired property. Property which is acquired by or devolves on a bankrupt before the discharge or annulment of the adjudication order by which he was declared a bankrupt. Such property vests in the Official Assignee (qv) if and when he claims it, except for damages recovered or recoverable by the bankrupt for personal injury or loss suffered by him: Bankruptcy Act 1988, ss 3 and 44(5). It is an offence for a bankrupt to fail to disclose to the Official Assignee any after-acquired property (BA 1988, s 127).

aftercare. The assistance which a health board (qv) is empowered to provide for a child who leaves the care of the board, where the board is satisfied as to his need for assistance: Child Care Act 1991, s 45. The aftercare may be provided until the person is 21 years of age, or beyond that age until the completion of the course of education in which he is engaged. See Health Act 1953, ss 55(4) and (5) which is repealed on the commencement of the 1991 Act. See CARE ORDER; WELFARE OF CHILDREN.

aftermath doctrine. See PSYCHIATRIC DAMAGE; RESCUER.

A-G Attorney-General (qv).

age. A person attains a particular age, expressed in years, on the commencement of the relevant anniversary of the date of his birth; this applies for the purpose of any rule of law or statutory provision, deed, will or other instrument: Age of Majority Act 1985, s 4. A person born on the 29 February attains a particular age on the 29 February in leap years and on 1 March in other years: *R v Roxby (Inhabitants)* [1829] 109 ER 370. At common law a person attained a particular age at the first moment of the day preceding the relevant anniversary of his birth. A person aged 65 or over is entitled to an *age allowance* in respect of his liability for income tax: Taxes Consolidation Act 1997, s 464 as amended by Finance Act 2000, s 8. Persons aged 65 or over are also entitled to an *age exemption* from liability for income tax; the limits for 2004 are €15,500 for single persons and €31,000 for married couples: Finance Act 2004, s 2. For previous limits, see Finance Act 2003, s 2; Finance Act 2002, s 4; Finance Act 1997, s 188 as amended by 2000 Act, s 2. See European Arrest Warrant Act 2003, s 43. See IDENTITY CARD; OLD AGE.

age and discrimination. An employer is prohibited from discriminating against an employee or prospective employee on age grounds: Employment Equality Act 1998, ss 8(1) and 6. Formerly, treating a person more or less favourably because he was under 18 years of age, or was 65 years of age or older, was not regarded as discrimination on age grounds (EEA 1998, s 6(3)). This provision has been replaced by a provision (a) which specifies that the *age ground* applies only in relation to persons above the maximum age at which a person is statutorily obliged to attend school and (b) which permits an employer (i) to set a minimum age, not exceeding 18 years of age, for recruitment, and (ii) to offer a fixed term contract to a person over the compulsory retirement age for that employment: Equality Act 2004, s 4(c) inserting a new s 6(3) in EEA 1998.

It is not discriminatory on age grounds to fix different ages for retirement, or to fix different rates of remuneration based on length of service, or to fix ages for admission to an occupational benefits scheme (EEA 1998, s 34 amended by EA 2004, s 23). Age discrimination provisions do not apply to employment in the defence forces, and may not apply to the garda síochána, the prison service or to an emergency service (EEA 1998, s 37(2) to 37(6) amended by substitution by EA 2004, s 25).

In a particular case, an Equality Officer held that a clear pattern had been established whereby the older candidates in a competition for promotion, had little chance of being appointed, regardless of the quality of their assessment, and consequently had been discriminated against on age grounds: *O'Mahony v Revenue Commissioners* [2002] EO ELR 215 upheld on appeal to Labour Court. Also the Labour Court, in awarding a civil servant €40,000, held that while statistical evidence showed that no candidate over 50 years of age was successful in competitions between 1999 and 2003, this evidence was not conclusive, but that consciously or unconsciously a bias had been created in favour of younger candidates: *Gillen v Department of Health and Children* [2004] Irish Times, 17 August, LC. Also it was held that the use of seniority for selection for promotion, based on date of birth, was discriminatory on age

grounds: *Dunbar v Good Counsel College* (2003) Irish Times, 12 December, EO. See also *A Firm of Solicitors v A Worker* [2002] ELR 305; *A Named Female v A Named Company* [2002] EO ELR 327; *Perry v Garda Commissioner* [2002] EO ELR 18.

A person must not discriminate on age grounds in disposing of goods or premises or in providing a service or accommodation; treating one person less favourably than another, in a comparable situation, because they are of different ages is discrimination: Equal Status Act 2000, ss 5, 6 and 3, amended by EA 2004, ss 48–49. However, except as regards the provision of motor insurance, treating a person under 18 years of age more or less favourably than another is not regarded as discrimination on age grounds (ESA 2000, s 3(3) inserted by EA 2004, s 48). Also, discrimination does not apply to an age requirement for a person to be an adoptive or foster parent (ESA 2000, s 5(2)(j)). Having a reasonable preferential charge for persons in a specific age group does not constitute discrimination (ESA 2000, s 16(1)(a)).

A 77 year-old man was awarded €2,000 compensation in respect of the refusal of an insurance company to offer him car insurance, the equality officer finding that there were grounds for quoting a higher premium, but not for refusing cover: *Ross v Royal and Sun Alliance Insurance Company* (2003) Irish Times, 4 October. Also an insurance company which had refused to provide a quotation for car insurance to a person on the sole ground that he was under 25 years of age, agreed in a settlement before the Equality Tribunal, to lift its age restriction and to pay compensation to the person: *Donoghue v First Call Direct* (2004) Irish Times, 2 September. A minimum age of 30 years for entry as a member of Aosdána, the body established by the Arts Council to honour outstanding artists, has been found to be discriminatory: *Clifford v Aosdána* (2004) Irish Times, 28 July. See also *O'Reilly v Q Bar* [2003] EO ELR 35. See *Re Employment Equality Bill 1996* [1997] 2 IR 321, SC and ELR 132. [Bibliography: Reid M.] See DISCRIMINATION; PENSION SCHEME AND DISCRIMINATION; PUBLIC SERVICE PENSION SCHEME.

age and pleasure craft. There are age restrictions on the operation or control of pleasure craft: Merchant Shipping (Pleasure Craft) (Lifejackets and Operation)

(Safety) Regulations 2004, SI No 259 of 2004, reg 4. The master or owner of a personal watercraft or a *fast power craft* must take all reasonable steps to ensure that a person under the age of 16 years does not operate or control the craft (SI No 259 of 2004, reg 4(1)). A *fast power craft* is one which can attain a speed through or over water equal to or exceeding 17 knots (SI No 259 of 2004, reg 2). Also the master or owner of a pleasure craft powered by an engine with a rating of more than 5 horse power or 3.7 kilowatts must take all reasonable steps to ensure that a person under 12 years of age does not operate or control the craft (SI No 259 of 2004, reg.4(2)). See LIFEJACKET.

age document. Means a document containing a photograph of the person and information that enables the age of the person to be determined: Intoxicating Liquor Act 1988, s 34A inserted by Intoxicating Liquor Act 2003, s 15. A person between the ages of 18 and 21 must not be in the bar of a licensed premises after 9pm without an age document. It is an offence also for the licence holder to permit such a person to be in the bar without an age document. An age document may be one of the following: a Garda age card, passport, identity card of a member state of the European Communities, driver's licence, or a document prescribed in regulations. The application form for a Garda age card may be downloaded from the Garda website: *www.garda.ie*. It must be accompanied by a birth certificate, at least one other document confirming identity, two recent identical passport-sized photographs, and the prescribed fee. A Northern Ireland Electoral Identity Card meets the requirements for an age document.

age for employment. See UNFAIR DISMISSAL; YOUNG PERSON.

age limit. The age at which a person is required by statute or by contract to cease to perform some function or to hold office e g trustees of a Trustee Savings Bank are required to retire at age 70 although there is no statutory age limit for company directors. Employees in the private and public sectors are generally required by their contract of employment to retire at age 65. See Trustee Savings Banks Act 1989, s 18.

age of child. See AGE OF MINOR.

age of consent. See CONSENT, AGE OF.

age of majority. The age at which a person attains *full age* i e when he attains the age of eighteen years, or, in case he marries before attaining that age, upon his marriage: Age of Majority Act 1985, s 2. The age of majority for all purposes of the Taxes Acts is also 18, except in the case of incapacitated children, where it remains 21 years: Finance Act 1986, s 112; now Taxes Consolidation Act 1997, s 7.

age of minor. When a *minor* sues as plaintiff, a certified extract from the register of births must be produced and proved on his behalf at the trial or hearing or on an application to have a proposed settlement approved by the court: RSC Ord 66, r 1.

In child care proceedings, the true age of a person to whom an application relates is deemed to be the age presumed or declared by the court following due inquiry, unless the contrary is proved: Child Care Act 1991, s 32.

Where a person who is charged with an offence is brought before the court and it appears to the Court that the person is a child, the Court must make due inquiry as to the age of the person: Children Act 2001, s 269. The age presumed or declared by the Court is deemed to be the true age of the person, and any order or judgment of the court is not invalidated by any subsequent proof that the age of the person had not been correctly stated to the court.

There is a general presumption in law that where an offence is alleged to have been committed against a child, and the person appears to the court to have been a child at the date of the alleged offence, then the person was a child at that date, unless the contrary is proved (CA 2001, s 256). See MINOR.

agency. See AGENT; EMPLOYMENT AGENCY.

agent. A person who is employed for the purpose of bringing his principal (qv) into contractual relations with third parties. An agent does not make contracts on his own behalf and consequently it is not necessary that he should have full contractual capacity. When the agent has brought his principal into contractual relations with another, he drops out and the principal sues or is sued on the contract.

An agent may be a *universal* agent, a *general* agent or a *special* agent. A *universal* agent has authority to act for the principal in all matters e g under a universal power of attorney (qv). A *general* agent has authority to act in transactions of a class e g a solicitor, a managing director of a company; the scope of authority is that usually possessed by such agents. A *special* agent is one who is appointed for a particular purpose and his authority is limited to that purpose e g an auctioneer. An act done by an agent within the scope of his authority binds his principal.

Agency may arise: (a) by express agreement, verbal or in writing, and will be limited by that agreement; (b) by implication or by conduct e g when a husband and wife are living together, the wife is presumed to have his authority to pledge his credit for necessaries suitable to their style of living; (c) by necessity (qv); (d) by ratification (qv) e g where a principal confirms and adopts a contract made by an agent who at the time of its making had no or insufficient authority.

An agency can be terminated by act of the parties (by agreement or by revocation) and by operation of law (death, bankruptcy or insanity of the principal or agent). See *Yonge v Toynbee* [1910] 1 KB 215.

A *perceived* relationship of principal and agent may lead to the *perceived* principal being liable in tort for the actions of the agent: *Irish Permanent Building Society v O'Sullivan and Collins* [1990] ILRM 598. See 'Special Agents' by barrister Murray Smith in *Law Society Gazette* (April 2003) 31. [Bibliography: Bowstead UK.] See COMMERCIAL PROCEEDINGS; COMMISSION; DELEGATUS NON POTEST DELEGARE; DUBLIN AGENT; ELECTION AGENT.

agent, duties of. An agent is required to use diligence and to display any special skill he may profess or be required to have. He must account for such property of his principal as comes into his hands. He must make no profit beyond his commission and may not become a principal against his own employer. He cannot enter into a transaction where his duty and his personal interest conflict, unless he makes a full disclosure. Also he must not delegate his authority unless justified by usage of the particular trade, by necessity or where the act is purely ministerial. See *Chariot Inns Ltd v Assicurazioni Generali SPA* [1981] ILRM 173.

agent, gratuitous. An agent who gives his services without any express or implied promise of remuneration. He is required to exercise the degree of care and skill which may reasonably be expected from him in all the circumstances of the case: *Chandhry v Prabhakar* [1988] 3 All ER 718 as discussed by *Gill* in 7 ILT & SJ (1989) 132.

agent, insurance. See INSURANCE AGENT.

agent, payment to. See PAYMENT TO AGENT.

agent of necessity. Agency of necessity arises where the law confers on a person the authority to act for and bind another (his principal) without requiring the consent of the principal. This may arise when: (a) the agent is unable to communicate with his principal; and (b) he acts under a definite commercial necessity; and (c) he acts *bona fide* in the interest of his principal e g the master of a ship may contract and bind the owner in an emergency: *Couturier v Hastie* [1852] 5 HLC 673. See also *Walsh v Bord Iascaigh Mhara* [1981] IR 470; *Flannery v Dean* [1995] 2 ILRM 393, HC.

agent provocateur. A person who entices another to commit an express breach of the law which he might not otherwise have committed and then proceeds to inform against him in respect of such offence. The evidence of a witness who acts as an *agent provocateur* in order to obtain the evidence tendered, may be accepted and evaluated on its merits, without as a matter of law requiring to be corroborated: *Dental Board v O'Callaghan* [1969] IR 181. For UK consideration of agent provocateur, see *R v Mealey and Sheridan* [1975] 60 Cr App R 150; *R v Sang* [1979] 3 WLR 263. See ENTRAPMENT.

aggravated assault. Formerly, an assault which was aggravated in respect of violence, not by reason of indecency: *R v Baker* [1876] 46 LJ Ex 75. The common law offence of *assault* was abolished by the Non-Fatal Offences against the Person Act 1997, s 28. See ASSAULT.

aggravated burglary. See BURGLARY, AGGRAVATED.

aggravated damages. A subset of compensatory damages that are directed to a plaintiff as additional compensation in recognition of the exceptional features that add to or exacerbate the plaintiff's injury: David McParland BL in *Bar Review* (April 2003) 55. Contrast with the term *exemplary damages* (qv), which shares some of the elements of aggravated damages. In a defamation (qv) action e g failure of a plea of justification (qv) may lead to an aggravation of damages e g the conduct of the defendant in repeating the defamation, in refusing to apologise, or in persisting in a charge known to be unfounded; or an inappropriate mode of publication.

'*Aggravated damages* are given for conduct which shocks the plaintiff, *exemplary damages* (qv) for conduct which shocks the jury': *Salmond on Torts* as cited in *McIntyre v Lewis & Dolan* [1991] ITLR (22 April), SC. See *Swaine v Commissioners of Public Works* [2003] 2 ILRM 252, SC and 1 IR 521 and *Law Society Gazette* (June 2003) 43 which cited with approval *Conway v INTO* [1991] 2 IR 305. See *Kennedy v Hearne* [1988] ILRM 52 and 531, HC & SC. See Law Reform Commission Consultation Paper on Aggravated, Exemplary and Restitutional Damages (LRC 60, 2000). See DAMAGES.

aggravated larceny. See LARCENY, AGGRAVATED.

aggravated murder. See MURDER, AGGRAVATED.

aggravated sexual assault. See SEXUAL ASSAULT.

aggravation of damages. See AGGRAVATED DAMAGES.

agistment. A licence to graze livestock on the land of another. The person on whose land the livestock graze is called the *agister*; he is a bailee (qv) for reward. See *Allingham v Atkinson* [1898] IR 239; *Carson v Jeffers* [1961] IR 44.

agm. See ANNUAL GENERAL MEETING.

agnates. Relations through males ie on the father's side, eg a father's son, brother or sister. See COGNATES.

agreement. A declared concurrence of will of two or more persons which affects or alters their rights and duties. A written agreement is to be construed in the factual matrix or surrounding circumstances in which the agreement was concluded: *Boyle v Whitvale Ltd & Hurley* [2003] ITLR (20 October). For *agreement to sell* see *Uniacke v Cassidy Electrical Supply Company* [1981] HC.

A planning authority is empowered to enter into an agreement with any person interested in land, for the purpose of restricting or regulating the development or use of the land, either permanently or during such period as may be specified by the agreement: Planning and Development Act 2000, s 47. See ACQUISITION OF LAND; CONTRACT; INTENTION; RETENTION OF TITLE; SALE OF GOODS.

agreement, closed shop. See CLOSED SHOP.

agreement, collective. See COLLECTIVE AGREEMENT.

agricultural land. See INTENSIVE AGRICULTURE; VALUATION.

agricultural land, leasing of. Provisions to facilitate the leasing of agricultural land are contained in the Land Act 1984.

agricultural products. Means meat, milk, eggs, cereal and other field crops, fish, poultry, rabbits, deer and horticultural produce: An Bord Bia Act 1994, s 2(1) as amended by An Bord Bia (Amendment) Act 2004, s 11(a). The definition of '*food*', which An Bord Bia is responsible for promoting, includes agricultural products. See BORD BIA; HORTICULTURE.

agricultural society. Any society or institution established for the purpose of promoting the interests of agriculture, horticulture, livestock breeding or forestry: Taxes Consolidation Act 1997, s 215. Profits or gains of such a society from a show or exhibition are exempt from income tax. For *agricultural co-operative society* see Industrial & Provident Societies Act 1978, s 4.

agricultural waste. The disposal of agricultural waste at a facility requires a *waste licence*: Waste Management Act 1996, s 39 as amended by Protection of the Environment Act 2003, s 33. A waste licence is not required for the spreading on land of natural agricultural waste and sludge, which is a widespread agricultural activity (WMA 1996, s 51(1)). However, the Minister may make regulations prohibiting, or limiting or controlling in a specified manner and to a specific extent, the injection of waste on land for the purpose of benefiting the carrying on of any agricultural or silvicultural activity or ecological system (WMA 1996, s 51(3)). Local authorities are empowered to require farmers to prepare *nutrient management plans* in respect of their farms (WMA 1996, s 66(3) inserting s 21A in the Local Government (Water Pollution) (Amendment) Act 1990). [Bibliography: Walsh E S.]

agriculture. Includes horticulture, fruit growing, seed growing, dairy farming, and breeding and keeping livestock, the training of horses and the rearing of bloodstock: Planning and Development Act 2000, s 2(1). Under previous legislation, *agriculture* included turbary and forestry uses and excluded bloodstock rearing. See EXEMPTED DEVELOPMENT.

agriculture appeals. Provision has been made for a statutory appeal mechanism to deal with appeals from farmers who wish to challenge a decision of a Departmental officer regarding their entitlement to benefit under any of certain specified schemes: Agriculture Appeals Act 2001.

Appeals are heard by *Appeals Officers* who are independent in the performance of their functions. The *Director of Agriculture Appeals*, who is the chief appeals officer, is empowered to overturn a decision of an appeals officer (AAA 2001, s 10(2)). An appeal lies to the High Court on a point of law (AAA 2001, s 11). Also the *Ombudsman* is empowered to investigate complaints from any person who is dissatisfied with a decision (AAA 2001, s 18). See Agriculture Appeals Regulations 2002, SI No 193 of 2002. The Schedule to the 2001 Act is amended by the Agriculture Appeals (Amendment of Schedule) Regulations 2002, SI No 558 of 2002.

aid and abet. Any person who aids, abets, counsels or procures the commission of an *indictable offence* (qv) is liable to be indicted, tried and punished as a principal offender: Criminal Law Act 1997, s 7(1). Previously, an *aider and abetter* was known as a *principal in the second degree*. 'The kernel of the matter is the establishing of an activity on the part of the accused from which his intentions may be inferred and the effect of which is to assist the principal (in the first degree) in the commission of the crime proved to have been committed by the principal': *The People (DPP) v Madden* [1977] IR 336. It is sufficient if the prosecution can show that the accused knew the nature of the crime intended; it is not necessary for the prosecution to show that the accused knew the means to be employed by the principal offender: *DPP v Egan* [1989] ITLR (27 November), CCA. See Accessories & Abettors Act 1861, since repealed by Criminal Law Act 1997, s 16 and Sch 3. See PROSTITUTE; SUICIDE.

aiel. A grandfather.

air, rules of the. The rules dealing with, *inter alia*, general flight rules, visual flight rules, instrument flight rules, signals, rules for lights, parachuting activities, and unmanned free balloons: Irish Aviation Authority (Rules of the Air) Order 2004, SI No 72 of 2004. The rules give effect to the Standards in Annex 2 and certain Standards in Annex 11 of the Chicago Convention.

air cargo security programme. A new security arrangement for air cargo based on the 'known/unknown' cargo principle. Cargo, courier and express shipments must be 'known' before being accepted for carriage on an aircraft. To be classified as known, the consignment must be: (a) security screened by an airline and/or approved freight forwarder; or (b) be received by an approved freight forwarder or airline from a designated 'known consignor'. To become a known consignor companies are required to apply to the independent validator for the Department of Transport: Crime Management Ltd, Regus House, Harcourt Road, Dublin 2; tel: (01) 805 8352; website: *www.cmg.ie/acsp* and email: *info@cmg.ie*.

air law. The body of law dealing with the flight and operation of aircraft, which is derived from common law, statutes and international agreements. The State is a party to the Chicago Agreements incorporating the Chicago Convention 1944, International Air Services (*two freedoms*) Agreement 1944 and the International Air Transport (*five freedoms*) Agreement 1944; the Warsaw Convention 1929 and the Hague Protocol 1955; the Guadalajara Convention 1961; the Paris Agreements of 1956, 1960 and 1967; the Brussels Protocols of 1970; 1978; 1981; the Tokyo Convention 1963; the Hague Convention 1970 (*unlawful seizure of aircraft*); the Montreal Convention 1971 (*unlawful acts against aviation safety*). See Air Navigation and Transport Acts 1936–1975; Air Navigation (Eurocontrol) Act 1983; Air Companies Act 1983; Air Transport Act 1986. For the replacement of the Warsaw Convention, see MONTREAL CONVENTION.

Further provisions for the promotion of security and safety of civil aviation and airports is contained in the Air Navigation and Transport Act 1988. Common rules in the field of aviation security have been established: EC (Civil Aviation Security) Regulations 2003, SI No 226 of 2003, implementing EU Regulation No 2320/2002. See also RSC Ord 111. For the Irish Aviation Authority, see website: *www.iaa.ie*. For the European Civil Aviation Conference, see website: *www.ecac-ceac.org*. [Bibliography: Forde (5); Kerr (2); Margo UK; Shawcross & Beaumont UK.] See FALSE ALARM; INDEMNITY TO AIR NAVIGATION UNDERTAKINGS; INTERCEPTION OF AIRCRAFT; IRISH AVIATION AUTHORITY; MONTREAL CONVENTION; PREINSPECTION; WARSAW CONVENTION.

air navigation. The Eurocontrol International Convention relating to co-operation for the Safety of Air Navigation has been given legal effect in the State by the Air Navigation (Eurocontrol) Acts 1963, 1971 and 1983. For procedure for recovery of sums due in respect of air navigation facilities and services, see DCR 1997 Ord 90; RSC Ord 111. See EC (Restriction of Civil Subsonic Jet Aeroplane Operations) Regulations 2003, SI No 195 of 2003 giving effect to Directive 98/20/EC and Directive 1999/28/EC.

air piracy/hijacking. Colloquial expression describing a range of offences involving the unlawful seizure or endangering the safety of an aircraft. See Air Navigation and Transport Act 1988, s 51.

air pollution. A condition of the atmosphere in which a *pollutant* (qv) is present in such a quantity as to be liable to: (a) be injurious to public health; or (b) have a deleterious effect on flora or fauna or damage property; or (c) impair or interfere with amenities or with the environment: Air Pollution Act 1987, s 4. The occupier of any premises, other than a private dwelling, must use the *best practicable means* to limit and, if possible, to prevent an *emission* from such premises; the occupier must not cause or permit an emission from such premises in such a quantity, or in such a manner, as to be a nuisance (APA 1987, s 24).

The Minister may, by regulation, prohibit either absolutely, or subject to exception, such emissions as may be specified or any substance which may cause air pollution (APA 1987, s 23). Local authorities have power to require measures to be taken to prevent or limit air pollution (APA 1987, s 26) and to declare or limit air pollution (APA 1987, s 26) and to declare an area to be a *special control area* (APA 1987, ss 39–45). The Minister may issue directions specifying the *best practical means* for preventing or limiting emissions (APA 1987, s 5(3)) and may make regulations (APA 1987, s 10). Contravention of any provision of the Act or of any regulation or any notice served under the Act is an offence (APA 1987, s 11).

There is provision for the licensing of industrial plant (APA 1987, ss 30–38 as amended by Environmental Protection Agency Act 1992, s 18(2) and Sch 3); for the specification of air quality standards and of emission limit values (APA 1987, ss 50–51); for the production of air quality management plans (APA 1987, s 46) and for monitoring of air quality and emissions (APA 1987, s 54).

In 1992 provision was made for civil remedies for air pollution by way of injunctive relief and damages, similar to that available under water pollution legislation (APA 1987, ss 28A and 28B inserted by EPAA 1992, s 18(2) and Sch 3, para 4). The Minister is empowered by regulation to extend any powers under the 1987 Act to the Environmental Protection Agency (EPAA 1992, s 101) and has so done: SI No 126 of 1996.

See DCR 1997 Ord 96 rr 1–3; RSC Ord 103A inserted by SI No 377 of 1996. See also SI Nos 201, 243, 244 of 1987; 265 of 1988, and 167 of 1989 and Municipal Waste Incineration Regulations 1993, SI No 347 of 1993. See also *Hanrahan v Merck Sharpe & Dohme (Ire) Ltd* [1988] ILRM 629, SC; *Cork County Council v Angus Fire Chemicals Ltd* [1991] ILRM 173, HC; *Truloc Ltd v McMenamin & Donegal Co Council* [1994] 1 ILRM 151, HC. See Protection of the Environment Act 2003, s 60. For 'real-time' figures on air pollution levels for various pollutants, including sulphur dioxide, nitrogen dioxide and particulate matter, see website: *www.epa.ie/air/monitoring*. [Bibliography: Duggan; Scannell; Maguire, O'Reilly & Roche.] See AIR QUALITY STANDARD; BEST AVAILABLE TECHNIQUES; COAL; SUSTAINABLE ENERGY IRELAND.

air quality standard. The standard prescribed by the Minister: Air Pollution Act 1987, s 50. Standards have been set on ambient air, with value limits set for a variety of pollutants: Environmental Protection Agency Act 1992 (Ambient Air Quality Assessment and Management) Regulations 1999, SI No 33 of 1999; Air Quality Standards Regulations 2002, SI No 271 of 2002. Some of these limit values come into effect in 2005 (eg sulphur dioxide) and others in 2010 (eg benzene). The Environmental Protection Agency, as the designated national competent authority, is required to disseminate public information routinely on ambient concentrations of all pollutants, and where there are exceedances of limit values and alert thresholds. The Regulations transpose into Irish law, European Directives 96/62/EC, 1999/30/EC and 2000/69/EC. See AIR POLLUTION.

air-raid shelter. Any premises, structure or excavation used or intended to be used to provide protection, otherwise than by war-like means or by any article of apparel, from attack from the air: Air-Raid Precautions Acts 1939, s 2. See also Air-Raid Precautions (Amendment) Act 1946. Provision has been made for the payment of compensation, medical and other expenses, in respect of death or personal injuries sustained by members of Air-Raid Precautions Services: SI No 104 of 1973 as amended by SI No 676 of 2003.

aircraft. A machine that can derive support in the atmosphere from the reactions of the air, other than reactions of the air against the earth's surface: Irish Aviation Authority Act 1993, s 2(1). Consequently, the definition includes power-driven aircraft, helicopters, non-power driven aircraft, balloons and gliders, but excludes hovercraft. *State aircraft* means aircraft of any state used in the military, customs or police service of that state (IAAA 1993, s 3).

Wide powers are given to the Irish Aviation Authority in relation to the registration of aircraft in the State, the inspection of aircraft, the licensing of personnel etc (IAAA 1993, ss 14 and 60) and these powers may, by ministerial order, apply to state aircraft (IAAA 1993, s 3(4)). An obligation is placed on both the operator and the pilot in command to comply with the legislation (IAAA 1993, s 74). For Obstacles to Aircraft in Flight Order 2002, see SI No 14 of 2002 and SI No 591 of 2002. See also Air Navigation and Transport (Amendment) Act 1998, ss 2(1) and 61–64; Equal Status Act 2000, s 46; Copyright and Related Rights Act 2000, s 185(b); Industrial Designs Act 2001, s 48(2). See *Bosphorus v Minister for Transport* [1997] 2 IR 1, SC. See COMMERCIAL PROCEEDINGS.

aircraft, unlawful seizure of. The Convention for the Suppression of Unlawful Seizure of Aircraft done at The Hague on 16 December 1970, is given effect in the State by the Air Navigation and Transport Act 1973. See AVIATION, UNLAWFUL ACTS AGAINST.

aircraft accident. Aircraft accident investigation is the responsibility of the Minister; however, the owner or operator of the aircraft may be required to pay all or part of the cost involved: Irish Aviation Authority Act 1993, s 64.

airport. The aggregate of the lands within an aerodrome and all land owned or occupied by an *airport authority*, including aircraft hangars, roads and car parks: Air Navigation and Transport (Amendment) Act 1998, s 2(1). An *airport authority* is the person owning or managing, either alone or jointly with another person, an airport. It is an offence for a person to interfere in any way with anything provided for the purpose of the operation, management or safety of an airport (ANT(A)A 1998, s 47). It is also an offence to bring certain specified dangerous articles within an airport eg a firearm, an explosive (ANT(A)A 1998, s 50). The 1998 Act also provided for the setting up of Aer Rianta as a normal commercial State body, to transfer all of the Minister's assets at Cork, Dublin and Shannon airports to Aer Rianta, and to assign to it certain functions previously undertaken by the Minister in relation to the management and development of the three State airports (ANT(A)A 1998, ss 1–38). See Airport (Amendment) Bye-Laws 2002, SI No 323 of 2002.

The High Court has held that the objective of preventing developments in the vicinity of airports, which might endanger or interfere with the safety of aircraft, is clearly a valid and appropriate one based on the common good and, therefore, an appropriate matter to be balanced against the constitutional rights in relation to private property: *Liddy v Aer Rianta* [2003] ITLR (10 March) HC, FL 6927 and [2004] 1 ILRM 9. This case concerned privately owned land, which was in a so-called 'red zone' around Shannon Airport, and in respect of which planning permission had been obtained from Clare County Council and subsequently overturned, on appeal by Aer Rianta, by An Bord Pleanála. The court held that if the plaintiff had suffered loss, it was by virtue of the operation of the planning legislation, which had not been shown to be discriminatory or unreasonable.

The question as to whether Aer Rianta was entitled to require Ryanair to pay rent in respect of its occupation of check-in-desks at Dublin Airport rests on the interpretation of Irish regulations implementing an EU Directive; the Supreme Court has referred the question of interpretation to the European Court of Justice: *Ryanair v Aer Rianta* [2003] 2 IR 143, SC.

For noise-related restrictions at airports, see European Communities (Air Navigation and Transport Rules and Procedures for Noise Related Operating Restrictions at Airports) Regulations 2003, SI No 645 of 2003 giving effect to EC Directive 2002/30/EC. Under recent legislation provision has been made for the restructuring of Aer Rianta and the establishment of Dublin, Cork and Shannon airports as independent airport authorities under State ownership: State Airports Act 2004. For report on the capacity of Dublin Airport, see website: *www.alanstratford.co.uk*. See also website: *www.aer-rianta.com*. See AERODROME; DISABLED PERSON AND AIR TRAVEL.

airspace. The atmosphere above ground or sea level through which aircraft (qv) can fly: Irish Aviation Authority Act 1993, s 2(1). *Irish airspace* means the airspace within the lateral limits of the Shannon Flight Information Region and the Shannon Upper Flight Information Region, established pursuant to the Chicago Convention (qv) (IAAA 1993, s 2(1)). One of the objectives of the Irish Aviation Authority is to ensure that Irish airspace and other airspace, for which it has responsibility by international agreement, are used in a safe and efficient manner and to facilitate their use (IAAA 1993, s 14(b)–(c)). The Authority is empowered to designate areas of Irish airspace for use only by the defence forces (IAAA 1993, s 68).

airspace, interference with. The owner of land is entitled to ownership and possession of a column of air above the surface. However, liability is avoided in respect of trespass or nuisance by reason only of the flight of aircraft over any property at a height above the ground, which having regard to wind, weather, and all the circumstances of the case is reasonable, or the ordinary incidents of the flight: Air Navigation and Transport Act 1936, s 55; Irish Aviation Authority Act 1993, s 72(1). Strict liability is provided for, where there is material damage or loss (ANTA 1936, s 21(1)).

alcohol, consumption of. Consumption of alcohol by an employee during working hours may be a ground for dismissal: *Lawless v RTV National Vision Ltd* [1990] ELR 46. The complaint that a doctor has been under the influence of alcohol or drugs is a grave charge, and may lead to a finding of professional misconduct: Medical Council, *A Guide to Ethical Conduct and Behaviour* (6th edn, 2004) para 5.1.

The master or owner of a pleasure craft must not, or must not allow another to, operate or control or attempt to operate or control the craft while he or the other is under the influence of alcohol or drugs, to such an extent as to be incapable of having proper control of the craft: Merchant Shipping (Pleasure Craft) (Lifejackets and Operation) (Safety) Regulations 2004, SI No 259 of 2004, reg 8. It is also an offence for a person on a pleasure craft to consume alcohol or drugs while on board the craft in circumstances which could affect the safety of persons or create a disturbance on board the craft, or affect the safety of other persons using Irish waters, or constitute a nuisance to such persons (SI No 259 of 2004, reg 9(1)). See DRUNKEN DRIVING; DRUNKENNESS; EXCLUSION ORDER; INTOXICATED; INTOXICATING LIQUOR.

alcohol strength. Bottles and cans containing a beverage with more than 1.2 % of alcohol are required to carry a label showing the actual alcoholic strength by volume: European Communities (Labelling, Presentation and Advertising of Foodstuffs) (Amendment) Regulations 1988, SI No 202 of 1988. See LABELLING OF ALCOHOL.

alcohol test. See BLOOD SPECIMEN.

alderman. The name borrowed from the Anglo-Saxon *ealdorman* (literally, an elder); an alderman is a member of the council which governs the municipal affairs of a borough (qv).

aleatory contract. A wagering contract (qv).

alias; alias dictus. [Otherwise called.] A false name; a second or assumed name.

alibi. [Elsewhere.] A defence of an accused that at the time of the commission of the offence, with which he is charged, he was elsewhere. Notice of intention to raise an alibi in a trial on indictment (qv) must be given to the prosecution: Criminal Justice Act 1984, s 20. See *The People (DPP) v Rawley* [1997] 2 IR 265, CCA.

Failure by an employer to conduct a full and fair inquiry into an employee's alibi, may lead to the employee's dismissal being held to be procedurally unfair: *Burke v Form Print Ltd* [1992] ELR 163, EAT. See WITNESS.

alien. A person who is not a citizen. There is substantial control given to the Minister over aliens eg to prohibit or restrict their entry or exit; to exclude or deport them; to require or prohibit residence in a particular area; and to regulate registration, travel and employment within the State: Aliens Act 1935 as amended.

It is in the interests of the common good of the State that it should have control over the entry of aliens, their departure, their activities within the State and the duration of their stay; the powers conferred on the Minister in this regard should be exercised in accordance with the requirements of the common good: *Tang v Minister for Justice* [1996] 2 ILRM 49, SC.

The right to expel or deport aliens is an aspect of the common good which inheres in the State by virtue of its nature as a sovereign state; the power is executive in nature and can be exercised in the absence of legislation: *Laurentiu v Minister for Justice* [2000] 1 ILRM 1, SC. In this case, the power given by s 5(1)(e) of the 1935 Act was found to be unconstitutional. See also *Leontjava & Chang v Minister for Justice* (22 January 2004, unreported), HC and (23 June 2004, unreported), SC.

However, only a grave and substantial reason associated with the *common good* would justify the removal of a family (constituting alien parents and children who are Irish citizens) against its will outside the State: *Fajujono v Minister for Justice* [1990] ILRM 234, SC.

There is freedom of movement for workers within the EC under the *Treaty establishing the European Community*, art 39 of the consolidated (2002) version. See also European Communities (Aliens) Orders 1977 to 1985; Air Navigation and Transport (Preinspection) Act 1986. See *Shum v Ireland* [1986] ILRM 593; *Osheku v Ireland* [1987] ILRM 330; *Ji Jao Lau v Ireland* [1993] ILRM 64, HC; *ANM (an infant) v An Bord Uchtála* [1992] ILRM 569, HC; *Gleeson v Chi Ho Cheung* [1997] 1 IR 521, HC.

The expression 'non-national' is now used in the context of *deportation* or *exclusion* orders: Immigration Act 1999, s 1(1). A *non-national* means an alien within the meaning of the 1935 Act, with the exception of citizens of particular countries who are exempt from the provisions of that Act.

'Non-national' is now also used instead of 'alien' in citizenship and naturalisation law: Irish Nationality and Citizenship Act 2001, ss 2(a) and 8. A *non-national*

means a person who is not an Irish citizen. See Alien (Visas) Order 2003, SI No 708 of 2003.

The sovereign power of the State to deport aliens is an executive power which can be exercised in the absence of legislation: *Kanaya v Minister for Justice* [2000] 2 ILRM 503, HC. See Immigration Act 2003, s 4. [Bibliography: Immigration Council.] See ASYLUM, CLAIM FOR; CITIZENSHIP; DEPORTATION; EUROPEAN CONVENTION ON HUMAN RIGHTS; EUROPEAN ECONOMIC COMMUNITY; VISA.

alienate. To exercise the power of disposing of or transferring property.

alienation. The power of an owner or tenant in property to dispose or transfer his interest. Alienation may be *voluntary* eg by conveyance or will; it may be *involuntary* eg sale by the court on the application of a judgment mortgagee. As regards covenants in leases against alienation, see Landlord and Tenant (Amendment) Act 1980, s 66. See Residential Tenancies Act 2004, s 193(d). See INALIENABILITY.

alienato rei preferturi juri accrescendi. [The law favours the alienation rather than the accumulation of property.] See INALIENABILITY.

alieni juris. [Of another's right.] Term used to refer to a person subject to the authority of another eg a minor (qv). Contrast with SUI JURIS.

alimentary trust. A protective trust (qv).

alimony. An allowance paid by a husband to his wife for her support in circumstances where they were judicially separated; the amount was determined by the court on consideration of the circumstances. It was called *alimony pendente lite* where ordered to be paid pending the court proceedings for the judicial separation, and *permanent alimony* when finally determined by the judge on making the judicial decree. A capital sum could not be awarded by a judge by way of alimony, since alimony was, by nature, a periodic payment which was subject to increase or decrease according to the income of the party paying it, or even to complete termination: *MB v RB* [1989] IR 412 and *Woulfe* in 7 ILT & SJ (1989) 296.

The Judicial Separation and Family Law Reform Act 1989 introduced new provisions for judicial separation and the maintenance of spouses; any alimony order made prior to the 1989 Act is deemed to be a *periodical payments order* under s 14(1)(a) and consequently can be varied (JSFLRA

1989, s 43). Provision is also made for *alimony pending suit* as such orders can still be made in nullity petitions (JSFLRA 1989, s 25). See also Defence Act 1954, s 98(1)(h) as amended by the JSFLRA 1989, s 27. See also Family Law (Divorce) Act 1996, s 29. See DIVORCE A MENSA ET THORO; MAINTENANCE ORDER.

alio intuitu. With a motive other than the ostensible and proper one.

aliquis non debetesse judex in propria causa quia non potest esse judex et pars. [No man ought to be a judge in his own cause, because he cannot act as a judge and at the same time be a party.] See NATURAL JUSTICE.

aliter. [Otherwise.]

aliud est celare, aliud tacere. [Silence is not the same thing as concealment.] However, active concealment may be equivalent to a positive statement that the fact does not exist and may amount to the tort of deceit (qv). See *Delany v Keogh* [1905] IR 267.

aliunde. [From elsewhere.] From another place or person.

allegation. A statement or assertion of fact in proceedings made by a party thereto; it particularly refers to a statement or charge which is not yet proven.

allegiance. In a monarchy, the natural and legal obedience which a subject owes to the monarch. A citizen of Ireland owes the fundamental political duties of fidelity to the nation and loyalty to the State: 1937 Constitution, art 9(2). See TREASON.

allocation. The appropriation (qv) of a fund to particular persons or purposes.

allocatur. [It is allowed.] In equity, the *allocator* rule directed that interest on costs ran from the date of taxation only. At common law, the *incipitur* rule directed that interest ran from the date of judgment. It has been held that costs are a liability from the date of judgment and when the costs are taxed, the liability relates back to the date of judgment with interest payable from that date: *Clarke v Garda Commissioner* [2002] 1 ILRM 450, SC and 1 IR 207. Under recent legislation, provision has been made for interest on costs to run from the date the parties agree the costs or, in the absence of agreement, from the date the costs are taxed or measured, and at a rate of interest specified from time to time: Civil Liability and Courts Act 2004, s 41. See INCIPITUR.

allocutus. The demand of a court to a person found guilty by jury of treason (qv) or of a felony (qv), asking whether he has cause to show why judgment should not be pronounced against him. See, however, MODE OF TRIAL.

allonge. [Make longer.] A piece of paper attached to a bill of exchange (qv) as a continuation sheet for endorsements where there is no further room for them on the bill: Bills of Exchange Act 1882, s 32(1). The last endorsement on the actual bill should be made partly on the bill and partly on the allonge.

allotted capital. See CAPITAL.

allotment, land. A piece of land, containing not more than one quarter of a statute acre, let or intended to be let for cultivation by an individual for the production of vegetables mainly for the consumption of himself and his family: Acquisition of Land (Allotments) Act 1926, s 1 and Acquisition of Land (Allotments) (Amendment) Act 1934. For recovery of possession of an allotment, see the AL(A)A 1926, s 14(1).

allotment, shares. The appropriation to a person of a certain number of shares in a company. Shares are said to have been allotted when a person acquires the unconditional right to be included in the company's register of members in respect of those shares: Companies Amendment Act 1983, s 2(2). A *public limited company* (plc) may not allot shares as fully or partly paid up otherwise than in cash, unless the consideration for the allotment has been valued by an expert (CAA 1983, s 30). Also a plc may not allot shares unless at least one quarter of their nominal value, together with any premium on them, is immediately payable to the company (CAA 1983, s 28); in other companies, at least 5% of the shares' nominal value must be payable on application: Companies Act 1963, ss 53(3) and 55, as amended by CAA 1983, Sch 1. A *return of allotments* must be made to the Registrar of Companies: CA 1963, s 58 as amended by the Companies Amendment Act 1982, s 19; CAA 1983, ss 31(2) and 55(1)(g).

Directors may not issue shares without express authority being given by the articles of association or by a resolution in general meeting. Such authority may be given for a specific allotment or generally, and must state the maximum amount of shares which may be issued; if authority is given by the articles, it cannot last for more than five years: CAA 1983, s 20. It is a criminal offence for a *private company* to offer shares or debentures in the company or to allot them for that purpose (CAA 1983, s 21). See also Building Societies Act 1989, s 106(7). See PRE-EMPTION; SHARES; UNDERSUBSCRIBED; VALUATION REPORT.

allowance to bankrupt. The High Court may make to the bankrupt out of his estate such allowances as the court thinks proper in the special circumstances of the case: Bankruptcy Act 1988, s 71. On adjudication as a bankrupt, the bankrupt is entitled to retain articles such as clothing, household furniture, bedding, tools or equipment of his trade or occupation or other like necessaries as he may select, not exceeding in value £2,500 (€3,174), or such further amount as the court may allow (BA 1988, s 45). See BANKRUPTCY.

alluvion. Land imperceptibly gained from the sea or a river by the washing up of sand and soil so as to form *terra firma*. See *Hindson v Ashby* [1896] 2 Ch 1. See AVULSION.

alteration. (1) A material alteration to an instrument without the consent of the other party generally invalidates it, except as against the person making the alteration eg the alteration of the date of a *bill of exchange* to accelerate payment, invalidates it. An alteration in a deed (qv) is presumed to have been made before or at the time of execution. Alterations, obliterations or interlineations in a *will* (qv) are presumed to have been made after execution and are invalid unless they existed in the will prior to its execution or, if made afterwards, unless they have been executed and attested or unless they have been rendered valid by re-execution of the will or by a codicil: Succession Act 1965, s 86; *Myles, Margaret Ismay, deceased* [1993] ILRM 36, HC; RSC Ord 79, rr 10–11; Ord 80 rr 12–13. It is a rebuttable presumption: *In the goods of Benn* [1938] IR 313. See *Re Rudd* [1945] IR 180; *Lombard & Ulster Banking v Bank of Ireland* [1987] HC. See DOCUMENTS, PRESUMPTIONS AS TO; WILL, REVOCATION OF.

(2) Includes: (a) plastering or painting or the removal of plaster or stucco; or (b) replacement of a door, window or roof, which materially alters the external appearance of a structure so as to render the appearance inconsistent with the character of the structure or of neighbouring structures: Planning and Development Act 2000, s 2(1). See ARCHITECTURAL CONSERVATION AREA; STRUCTURE; WORKS.

alternative, pleading in the. Including in pleadings (qv) of two or more inconsistent sets of material facts and claiming relief thereunder in the alternative.

alternative counts. Separate clauses in an indictment, each charging a separate offence, where the charges are based on the same facts or form part of a series of offences of the same or of a similar nature. See *The People (DPP) v Fowler* [1995] 1 IR 294, CCA; *The People (DPP) v Maughan* [1995] 1 IR 304, CCA. See INDICTMENT.

alternative directors. Substitute directors. See *Irish Civil Service Building Society v Registrar of Building Societies* [1985] IR 167.

alternative disputes resolution. Refers to systems for the resolution of disputes without recourse to formal legal proceedings eg arbitration (qv). In the UK, some 80% of cases referred to disputes resolution are settled without recourse to legal proceedings.

There are provisions for the use of alternative dispute resolution methods in relation to family law matters eg judicial separation, divorce and guardianship. In certain applications in guardianship, the solicitor to the applicant is obligated to discuss with the applicant the possibility of engaging in counselling, mediation, and negotiating a settlement by deed or in writing: Guardianship of Infants Act 1964, ss 20–22 as inserted by Children Act 1997, s 11. See 'New Resolution' and 'Finding the Middle Ground' by William Aylmer in *Law Society Gazette* (May 2003) 16 and (May 2004) 28 respectively. For *Centre for Effective Dispute Resolution*, see website: *www.cedr.co.uk*. See CONCILIATION; EUROPEAN EXTRA-JUDICIAL NETWORK; MEDIATION; SMALL CLAIM.

alternative employment. There is an obligation on an employer to look for an alternative to redundancy: *O'Connor v Power Securities Ltd* UD 344/89 as reported by Barry in 8 ILT & SJ (1990) 108.

alternative verdict. Where at a trial the evidence does not warrant a conviction for the offence specifically charged in the indictment, but the allegations in the indictment amount to or include an allegation of *another* offence (expressly or by implication), the accused may be found guilty of: (a) that *other* offence; or (b) of an offence of which he could be found guilty on an indictment specifically charging that *other* offence: Criminal Law Act 1997, s 9(4).

In addition, an allegation of an offence includes an allegation of *attempting* to commit that offence (CLA 1997, s 9(5)). An accused who is charged with attempting to commit an offence or of an assault or other act preliminary to an offence, may be convicted of the offence charged, notwithstanding that he is shown to be guilty of the completed offence (CLA 1997, s 9(5)). However, the court has discretion to discharge the jury with a view to the preferment of a new indictment for the completed offence.

A person charged with theft can be found guilty of *handling* or *possession* of stolen property if the facts so prove; also if charged with handling or possession of stolen property, the person can be found guilty of theft, if the facts prove theft: Criminal Justice (Theft and Fraud) Offences Act 2001, s 55.

The power to substitute verdicts is a matter of substantive jurisdiction and is not available to the Special Criminal Court: *DPP v Rice* [1979] IR 15. Also a person indicted for rape can be convicted of lesser offences eg if found guilty of rape under section 4, or of aggravated sexual assault, or of sexual assault: Criminal Law (Rape) (Amendment) Act 1990, s 8; or of attempted rape: *DPP v Riordan* [1992] ITLR (30 November), CCA. There are special provisions on alternative verdicts in relation to murder and aggravated murder; there is no alternative verdict in relation to treason. See ATTEMPT; MURDER; VERDICT.

allurement and children. See OCCUPIERS' LIABILITY TO CHILDREN.

amalgamation. The combination of two or more companies or bodies. See Companies Act 1963, ss 201–203 and 260; Trade Union Act 1975, s 15; Building Societies Act 1989, s 95; Trustee Savings Banks 1989, ss 47–48; Industrial Relations Act 1990, s 22; Credit Union Act 1997, s 128 as amended by Central Bank and Financial Services Authority of Ireland Act 2003, s 35, Sch 1. There is provision for exemption from stamp duty in relation to the transfer of property on the reconstruction or amalgamation of companies: Stamp Duties Consolidation Act 1999, s 80 as amended by Finance Act 2004, s 68. [Bibliography: O'Driscoll T.] See MERGER.

ambassador. Head of a diplomatic mission, representing his country, accredited to the Head of State in which he resides. See Diplomatic Relations and Immunities Acts 1967 and 1976. See DIPLOMATIC PRIVILEGE; TERRORISM.

ambiguitas verborum patens nulla verificatione excluditur. [A patent ambiguity in the words of a written instrument cannot be cleared up by evidence extrinsic to the instrument.] See AMBIGUITY.

ambiguity. Uncertain meaning. A *patent* ambiguity is one which is apparent on the face of an instrument eg a blank space in a deed. It cannot generally be resolved by oral evidence: *Watcham v A-G for E Africa* [1919] AC 533. A *latent* ambiguity is one not apparent on the face of the instrument (eg *my car I leave to my nephew Patrick* where the testator had two nephews of that name) and may be resolved by oral evidence. Extrinsic evidence (qv) is admissible to assist the court in construing ambiguity in a will: *Re Estate of Egan* [1990] 8 ILT Dig 108; *Rowe v Law* [1978] IR 55. See *B v Governor of Training Unit* [2002] 2 ILRM 161, SC. See CONSTRUCTION SUIT; CONTRA PROFERENTEM; EQUIVOCATION; UNAMBIGUOUS.

ambulatoria est voluntas defuncti usque ad vitae supremum exitum. [The will of a deceased person is ambulatory until the latest moment of death.] See WILL, REVOCATION OF.

ambulatory. Capable of being revoked. A person's will is ambulatory until death. See *Vynior's* case [1609] 8 Co Rep 81b. See CHATTEL MORTGAGE; WILL.

ameliorating waste. See WASTE.

amendment. The correction of a defect (eg an error or omission) in a summons or pleadings. See PLEADINGS, AMENDMENT OF; SLIP RULE; SUMMONS, AMENDMENT OF.

amendment of legislation. Primary legislation (ie a statute) is normally amended by subsequent primary legislation which repeals the earlier legislation in whole or in part, or which amends sections by substitution or insertion. Primary legislation may not be amended by a subsequent Ministerial regulation. The Supreme Court has ruled that delegated legislation cannot make, repeal or amend any law and to the extent that a parent Act purports to confer such a power, it will be constitutionally invalid: *Mulcreevy v Minister for the Environment & Dún Laoghaire – Rathdown County*

Council [2004] 1 ILRM 419, SC. Prior to this ruling, power has been given to a Minister in recent legislation for a limited period (of say three years) to modify any provision of the legislation by regulation in order to remove any difficulty which arises in bringing any provision into operation e g see Local Government Act 2001, s 232; Dormant Accounts Act 2001, s 4; Hepatitis C Compensation Tribunal (Amendment) Act 2002, s 9; Residential Institutions Redress Act 2002, s 36; Official Languages Act 2003, s 4(1)(c) and (d).

However, the Supreme Court has held that it could not accept that the framers of the Constitution intended to limit the power of the Oireachtas to legislate by prohibiting them from incorporating other instruments, such as secondary legislation and treaties, in an Act and give them the force of law without setting out the provisions in full: *Leontjava & Chang v Minister for Justice* (22 January 2004, unreported), HC and (23 June 2004, unreported) SC. [Bibliography: Hogan and Morgan.]

amends, offer of. See OFFER OF AMENDS.

amenity, loss of. The loss of a faculty (e g an eye or a leg) which may entitle a plaintiff to compensation. See *Roche v Kelly & Co* [1969] IR 100. See DAMAGES; PAIN AND SUFFERING.

amenity order, special. See SPECIAL AMENITY ORDER.

amicus curiae. [A friend of the court.] The Supreme Court has held that while there are no statutory provisions or rules of court providing for the appointment of an *amicus curiae*, save in the case of the Human Rights Commission, the court has an inherent right to appoint an *amicus curiae* where it appears that this might be of assistance in determining an issue before the court: *Iwuala v Minister for Justice* [2004] 1 ILRM 27, SC. The court also held that the jurisdiction to appoint an *amicus curiae* should be sparingly exercised. In this case the court allowed the application of the United Nations High Commissioner for Refugees (UNHCR) for leave to appear as an *amicus curiae* provided it bore its own costs of its appearance. See *O'R v B* [1995] 2 ILRM 57, HC. Contrast with INTERVENER. See HUMAN RIGHTS COMMISSION; LEGITIMUS CONTRADICTOR.

amnesty. The pardoning of certain past offences by enactment of the Houses of the Oireachtas; usually such amnesties are for taxation offences, conditional on the offender making a full disclosure by a specified date e g see Finance Act 1988, s 72 and Finance Act 1991, s 120; Waiver of Certain Tax, Interest and Penalties Act 1993. If a defendant wishes to set up the 1993 Act as a defence to an assessment of tax, he must produce the certificate referred to in s 6 of the Act: *Criminal Assets Bureau v Hutch* [1999] ITLR (21 June), HC.

The 1993 Act has been amended to ensure that enquiries by an inspector of taxes could continue where there are reasonable grounds to indicate that income declared by a person in the amnesty derived from an unlawful source (WCTIPA 1993, s 5 amended by Criminal Assets Bureau Act 1996, s 25). See *Comptroller and Auditor General v Ireland* [1997] 1 IR 248, HC.

Extradition cannot be granted where the person whose extradition is sought: (a) has been granted a pardon under art 13.6 of the Constitution of Ireland; or (b) has become immune by virtue of any *amnesty* or pardon in accordance with the law of the requesting Country; or (c) has, by virtue of any Act of the Oireachtas, become immune from prosecution or punishment for the act for which extradition is sought: Extradition (European Union Conventions) Act 2001, s 14. See Road Traffic Act 2002, s 9(6)(b); European Arrest Warrant Act 2003, s 39. See GENEVA CONVENTION; CHINESE WALL.

Amnesty International. An independent worldwide human rights movement which promotes the observance, throughout the world, of human rights pursuant to the Universal Declaration of Human Rights. See website: *www.amnesty.ie*.

amortisation. Provision for the payment of a debt by means of a sinking fund.

Amsterdam Treaty. The treaty signed in Amsterdam on 2 October 1997 amending the EC Treaty and ratified by referendum of the people on 22 May 1998 by 62% to 38%: Eighteenth Amendment to the Constitution Act 1998. Certain specified articles in the Amsterdam Treaty, which permit member states to exercise options or discretions, may only be exercised subject to prior approval of both Houses of the Oireachtas.

These are: (a) art 1.11 which provides for greater co-operation in criminal matters between police forces, custom authorities and judicial authorities, and, where necessary, the approximation of rules on criminal matters in the member states; (b) art 2.5

which provides for a group of member states (ie less than all members) to use the EU institutions to develop closer co-operation between themselves, subject to certain restrictions eg must not affect Community policies, actions or programmes, must not constitute a discrimination or restriction of trade between member states; (c) art 2.15 which deals with visas, asylum, immigration and other policies related to free movement and are bound up with the Second and Fourth Protocols as they relate to the *Schengen Agreement* which is brought within the framework of the Community. Articles 1.13 and 2 to 12 and annexed Protocols were given effect in the State by the European Communities (Amendment) Act 1998. For the consolidated (2002) version of the EC Treaty, see website: http://europa.eu.int/eur-lex/en/treaties/. See COMMUNITY LAW; FRAMEWORK DECISION; PROPORTIONALITY; SUBSIDIARITY, PRINCIPLE OF; SCHENGEN AGREEMENT; DEATH PENALTY.

amusement machine. A machine which: (a) is constructed or adapted for playing a game; and (b) the player pays to play the machine; (c) the outcome of the game is determined by the action of the machine; and (d) when played successfully, affords the player an opportunity to play again without paying: Finance Act 1992, s 120. Every amusement machine made available for play must be licensed and there must be a permit for the public place concerned (FA 1992, ss 120–129). Excise duty must be paid on the issue and renewal of a permit and the applicant must produce a tax clearance certificate: Finance Act 2002, ss 84–85. For previous legislation on excise duty, see Finance Act 1993, s 70. See *McKenna v Deery* [1998] 1 IR 62, SC

It has been clarified that a machine: (a) which allows a player to play again once more without paying; or (b) which awards a successful player the opportunity to win a non-monetary prize not greater than £5 in value, is an amusement machine and consequently must be licensed: Finance Act 2001, s 175. See also Finance Act 2003, ss 109–110.

ancestor. A relative from whom descent can be traced through the father or mother; the person prior to 1961 to whose property an heir succeeded on intestacy. See SUCCESSION.

ancient document. A document which is at least 30 years old and produced from proper custody. Execution of such a document does not have to be proved. See DOCUMENTS, PRESUMPTION AS TO.

ancient lights. The right to light which becomes absolute after 20 years of actual uninterrupted enjoyment of access to it, unless enjoyed by written consent: Prescription Act 1859, s 3. See LIGHT, RIGHT TO.

ancient monuments. See NATIONAL MONUMENTS.

ancipitus usus. [Of doubtful use.]

and. In a particular case, it was held that the word 'and' had to be given a conjunctive rather than a disjunctive meaning; it was not permissible to construe 'and' as if it were the word 'or': *Duggan v Dublin Corporation* [1991] ILRM 330, SC and Malicious Injuries Act 1981, s 6(1).

and company; & Co. The words marked on a cheque between two parallel traverse lines which have the effect of making the cheque payable only through a bank or building society: Bills of Exchange Act 1882, s 79(2) and Building Societies Act 1989, s 126. See CHEQUE, LIABILITY ON.

angling. Angling is to be construed as angling with rod and line: Fisheries (Consolidation) Act 1959, s 3(1). See TROUT.

Anglo-Irish Agreement. The agreement entered into in 1985 by the Governments of Ireland and the United Kingdom and lodged with the United Nations. It was an interstate treaty governed by the ordinary rules of international law ie the Vienna Convention on the Law of Treaties of 1969. The Agreement recognised the requirement for majority consent within Northern Ireland for any change in its status, established an intergovernmental ministerial conference and secretariat, set out the role of the conference in respect of security, policing, prison policy, law enforcement and extradition. The Agreement has been held not to be repugnant to the 1937 Constitution. See *Crotty v An Taoiseach* [1987] ILRM 400; *McGimpsey v A-G and Ireland* [1990] ILRM 440, SC. The Agreement constituted a recognition of the *de facto* situation in Northern Ireland but did so expressly without abandoning the constitutional claim to the integration of the national territory (qv): *McGimpsey* case. See also *Ex p Molyneux* [1986] 1 WLR 331.

The Anglo-Irish Agreement has been replaced by the British-Irish Agreement done at Belfast on 10 April 1998. [Bibliography: Hadden & Boyle.] See GOOD FRIDAY AGREEMENT; UNITED IRELAND.

Anglo-Irish Treaty. The treaty between Great Britain and Ireland, signed in London on 6 December 1921, under which Ireland was to have Dominion status within the British Empire and was to be styled and known as the *Irish Free State*. Although approved by the Dáil, the Treaty was to divide nationalist opinion and led to the civil war in 1922. See BOUNDARY COMMISSION.

animal product. Means any thing totally or in part derived from an animal, whether cooked or uncooked, processed or unprocessed: Diseases of Animals (Control of Animal Products) Order 2002, SI No 114 of 2003. This Order provides for certain controls on the import of animal products, including such products imported as personal baggage.

animal remedy. Any substance or combination of substances for the purpose of: (a) treating, preventing or modifying disease in animals; (b) making a medical or surgical diagnosis in animals; or (c) restoring, correcting or modifying physiological functions in animals: Animal Remedies Act 1993, s 1(1). A *prohibited animal remedy* is an animal remedy or ingredient for which a licence, authorisation or direction is required and has not been issued or has not been complied with (ARA 1993, s 1(1)).

Provision has been made in the 1993 Act for: (a) the regulation of the availability, possession and use of animal remedies and for the prescription of maximum permitted residues of animal remedies in foods of animal origin; (b) the control of animals, and food derived from animals, to which animal remedies are administered; and (c) the inspection and testing of substances, animals and food of animal origin. See Animal Remedies Regulations 1996, SI No 179 of 1996 and (Amendment) Regulations 2002, SI No 44 of 2002.

animal welfare. The European Union and its member states are required in formulating and implementing their policies to pay full regard to the welfare of animals, while respecting customs relating particularly to religious rites, cultural traditions and regional heritage: Amsterdam Treaty 1997 – protocol on protection and welfare of animals.

See also Protection of Animals kept for Farming Purposes Act 1984; EC (Protec-

tion of Animals kept for Farming Purposes) Regulations 2000, SI No 127 of 2000; EC (Welfare of Calves and Pigs) Regulations 2003, SI No 48 of 2003; EC (Welfare of Laying Hens) Regulations 2002, SI No 98 of 2002. For carriage of cattle and sheep by sea, see SI No 99 of 2002. For protection of animals during transport, see SI No 465 of 2003. For the Irish Society for the Prevention of Cruelty to Animals, see website: *www.ispca.ie.*

animals. Reasonable care must be taken by the owner, or controller, of animals which are brought onto the highway, to prevent them causing injury or damage: *Furlong v Curran* [1959] Ir Jur Rep 30. An owner of an animal which causes damage may be liable for: (a) negligence: *Howard v Bergin O'Connor & Co* [1925] 2 IR 110; (b) public nuisance: *Cunningham v Whelan* [1918] 52 ILTR 67; (c) private nuisance: *O'Gorman v O'Gorman* [1903] 2 IR 573, (d) trespass and (e) under the rule in *Rylands v Fletcher* (qqv).

Under the *scienter* (qv) action, the keeper of an animal is strictly liable if the animal which causes the damage is wild (*fera natura*), or if, being a tame or domesticated animal (*mansueta natura*), it had a vicious propensity known to the keeper. Formerly, no liability attached to the owner of domestic animals which strayed onto the highway and caused damage: *Searle v Wallbank* [1947] AC 341; *Gillick v O'Reilly* [1984] ILRM 402.

However, the Animals Act 1985, s 2(1) abolishes so much of the rules of the common law relating to liability for negligence as excludes or restricts the duty which a person might owe to others to take such care as is reasonable to see that damage is not caused by an animal straying onto a public road. There is an exemption for animals straying from unfenced land in certain circumstances (AA 1985, s 2(2)).

It has been held that s 2(1) created a *res ipsa loquitur* (qv) presumption and that it was necessary for the landowner to prove that he exercised reasonable care: *McCaffrey v Lundy* [1988] 6 ILT & SJ 245 as approved in *O'Reilly v Lavelle* [1990] 2 IR 372.

It is an offence for a taxi passenger to carry an animal in the vehicle, except with the permission of the driver, which permission may be withdrawn at any time: Taxi

Regulation Act 2003, s 40(2)(d). An exception is made for a guide dog in the company of a visually impaired passenger, and a domestic animal in need of urgent veterinary attention. See Malicious Damage Act 1861, ss 40–41 as amended by Criminal Damage Act 1991, s 14(2)(b). See Law Reform Commission Report on Civil Liability for Animals (LRC 2 of 1982). [Bibliography: Canny (2); Walsh E S.] See SCIENTER; DOGS; RYLANDS V FLETCHER, RULE IN; STRICT LIABILITY; HORSES; HOUSEHOLD CHATTELS; VIDEO RECORDING.

animals, diseases of. Provision has been made to increase significantly the powers which may be exercised where there is a risk of an outbreak of serious animal disease or during an outbreak: Diseases of Animals (Amendment) Act 2001. Provision has also been made for powers to regulate dealers and to control the resale of purchased animals. Penalties are increased and provision is made to deal with illegal tampering, switching and removal of ear-tags. Also provision is made for a court to ban a person from agriculture-related activities. Miscellaneous amendments are made to the Diseases of Animals Act 1966. See BSE.

animus. [Intention.]

animus cancellandi. [The intention of cancelling.]

animus dedicandi. [The intention of dedicating.] The owner of land beside a public road is presumed to be the owner of the soil of up to half of the road, having dedicated it to the public. See DEDICATION; PUBLIC ROAD.

animus et factum. [The combination of the intention with the act.]

animus furandi. [The intention of stealing.] See LARCENY.

animus manendi. [The intention of remaining.] An essential element in domicile (qv).

animus possidendi. [The intention of possessing.] See *Griffin v Bleithin* [1999] 2 ILRM 182, HC.

animus quo. [The intention with which.]

animus revertendi. [The intention of returning.]

animus revocandi. [The intention of revoking] eg a will.

animus testandi. [The intention of making a will.] See WILL.

anni nubiles. The marriageable age of a female. It is now the same age as that of a male ie 18 years of age. See MARRIAGE.

annotation. Addition of notes eg annotation of a statute usually consists of notes about each section or group of sections of an Act, explaining the reason for the section, giving the background to the previous law, both statutory and judicial, giving definitions of key words, giving any important links with other sections, and indicating if the section has been brought into force by a statutory instrument if applicable. See *Butterworths Annotated Irish Statutes* (2002).

A *restatement Act* may include annotations showing: (a) the derivation of its provisions; (b) the date of commencement of any provision; and (c) such notes or other information as the Attorney-General considers necessary or expedient: Statute Law (Restatement) Act 2002, s 3. [Bibliography: Butterworths (10).] See RESTATEMENT OF STATUTE.

annual general meeting; agm. Every company must hold an annual general meeting every year and not more than fifteen months may elapse between these meetings: Companies Act 1963, s 131.

In the event that a company fails to convene an annual general meeting, the Minister may direct the calling of a general meeting (CA 1963, s 131(3); *Phoenix Shannon plc v Purkey* [1997] 2 ILRM 381, HC).

The principal business to be transacted at an agm is consideration of the audited accounts and the directors' and auditors' reports, the election of directors, appointment of auditors and fixing their remuneration, and declaring a dividend (CA 1963, Table A, art 53).

The *ordinary business* of the agm of a *listed* company comprises: receiving and adopting accounts; declaring a dividend; appointing and re-appointing directors; re-appointing auditors; granting, renewing or varying authority for the allotment of shares or disapplying *pre-emption rights*; granting or renewing a general authority to purchase its own shares or to create treasury shares; and renewing or regranting an existing authority for a *script dividend* alternative: Listing Rules (*definitions* as amended by Irish Stock Exchange Ltd).

The agm must be held in the State unless the articles of association do not require the meeting to be so held. See also Building Societies Act 1989, s 67; Credit Union Act 1997, s 78 as amended by Central Bank and Financial Services Authority of

Ireland Act 2003, s 35, Sch 1. [Bibliography: Shaw & Smith UK.] See EXTRAORDINARY GENERAL MEETING; POLL; PROXY; QUORUM; RESOLUTION; VOTING AT MEETINGS.

annual leave. The period of annual holidays, in addition to public holidays (qv), to which employees are entitled by contract or by statute. The statutory entitlement is to four weeks holidays for each leave year (1 April to 31 March) in which the employee has worked at least 1,365 hours: Organisation of Working Time Act 1997, s 19. The entitlement is one-third of a working week for each month in the leave year in which the employee has worked at least 117 hours, or 8% of the hours he has worked in the leave year, subject to a maximum of four working weeks. Provision is made for an unbroken period of a certain length of leave; two working weeks in the case of employees who work eight or more months in a leave year. A *working week* is the number of days the employee usually works in a week. The 1997 Act implements EC Directive 93/104.

The times at which annual leave is granted is determined by the employer; however, he must take into account not only the opportunities for rest and recreation available to the employee, but also the need of the employee to reconcile work and family responsibilities (OWTA 1997, s 20(1)). In a particular case, it was held that dismissal was too severe a penalty for an employee taking holidays against the wishes of management: *Conroy v' Iggy Madden Transport Ltd* [1991] ELR 29, EAT. However, in another case it was held that the dismissal of four employees for taking leave outside the annual holiday period was not unfair: *Costello & Ors v May Roofing Ltd* [1994] ELR 19, EAT.

Pay for annual leave must be given to the employee in advance of that leave (OWTA 1997, s 20(2)). Any agreement or arrangement, the likely practical effect of which is that employees will not take holidays, is inconsistent with the result envisaged by the Directive which is to protect the health and safety of workers: *O'Donnell v Wolfe Security* [2001] LC ELR 136.

annual percentage charge; APR. The total cost of credit to the consumer, expressed as an annual percentage of the credit granted and calculated in a specified manner; it is required to be the equivalent, on an annual basis, of the present value of all commitments (loan, repayments and charges), future or existing, agreed by the creditor and the consumer, and calculated to the nearest rounded decimal place: Consumer Credit Act 1995, ss 2(1) and 9, as amended by Central Bank and Financial Services Authority of Ireland Act 2003, s 35, Sch 1. The Central Bank may make regulations amending the method of calculation of the APR.

The calculation of the APR must be complied with by the creditor in respect of a *credit agreement* (qv) (CCA 1995, s 10) and by a mortgage lender in respect of a *housing loan* (qv) (CCA 1995, s 122). Credit advertisements, which mention a rate of interest, must contain a clear and prominent statement of the APR, using a representative sample if no other means is practicable (CCA 1995, s 21).

Amendments have been made to the method of calculation of the annual percentage rate of charge for credit (APR): European Communities (Consumer Credit) Regulations 2000, SI No 294 of 2000. The SI contains additional direction and illustrative examples on how to apply the mathematical formula for calculating APR. The purpose of the SI is to give effect to EC Directive 98/7/EC, which amends certain provisions of ECl Directive 87/102/EEC.

annual report. A company listed on the stock exchange must issue an annual report and account which meets specified requirements eg an explanation must be given if the results for the period differ by 10% or more from any published forecast or estimate by the company: Listing Rules 2000, paras 12.41–12.43. A listed company must also prepare a report on its activities and profit or loss for the first six months of each financial year: Listing Rules 2000, paras 12.46–12.58.

For regulations on annual reports on occupational pension schemes, see SI No 233 of 2004. See also Local Government Act 2001, s 221 as amended by Civil Defence Act 2002, s 33. See INTERIM REPORTS DIRECTIVE.

annual results. A *listed* company must notify the stock exchange, without delay after board approval, of its preliminary statement of annual results: Listing Rules 2000, para 12.40. The results must have been agreed by the company's auditors.

annual return. See REGISTRAR OF COMPANIES.

annual value. The estimate of the net annual value of every tenement or rateable hereditament: Valuation (Ireland) Act 1852. See VALUATION.

annuity. (1) An annual payment of a certain sum of money; it may be perpetual or be for the life of the annuitant or be statutory. Connotes: (a) payments which are expected to continue over a period of more than one year; (b) a requirement that the payments are not mere gifts but are made and repeated by virtue of a commitment or obligation; and (c) are not made in return for goods supplied or services rendered: *McCabe v South City & County Investment Co Ltd* [1998] 1 ILRM 264, SC and [1997] 3 IR 300, SC.

(2) An 'annuity' given by a will is a *pecuniary* legacy (qv) payable by instalments.

(3) In pension law, an 'annuity' means a series of payments made at stated intervals until a particular event occurs. Usually, an annuity ends with the death of the holder but can be designed to be paid during the lives of more than one person. It is normally secured by payment of a single premium to an insurance company. It is not the same as a *Retirement Annuity Contract* (RAC). A *deferred* annuity is an annuity where the payment is postponed until some time after it is bought, usually to secure a preserved or deferred benefit for an individual who has left the service of an employer, or where a pension scheme is being wound up. See *A Guide to Annuities* (May 2004) at website: *www.pensionsboard.ie.*

(4) If an annuity is charged on land, it amounts to a rent-charge (qv): *Revenue Commissioners v Malone* [1951] IR 269. There are *statutory annuities* which are charged on land in repayment of sums advanced to tenant farmers under the Land Purchase Acts eg Land Law Act 1923, s 9; 1931, ss 4 and 7; Land Law Act 1953, s 4. Such annuities are burdens (qv) which affect registered land whether they are registered or not: Registration of Title Act 1964, s 72. See LAND ANNUITIES.

annuity mortgage. A mortgage (qv) wherein the principal sum advanced by the mortgagee (lender) is intended to be repaid by the mortgagor (borrower) in regular, usually monthly, instalments which comprise both principal and interest on the principal outstanding. Contrast with ENDOWMENT MORTGAGE.

annulment. (1) The declaration that judicial proceedings or their outcome are no longer of legal effect eg the annulment of adjudication of a person as a bankrupt: RSC Ord 76 as substituted by SI No 79 of 1989.

(2) The annulment of an act of the EC Council or Commission on appeal to the European Court of Justice (qv) on the grounds of lack of jurisdiction, or violation of an essential procedural matter, or infringement of the Treaty, or misuse of powers: Treaty establishing the European Community, arts 230–31 of the consolidated (2002) version.

annulment of bankruptcy. See BANKRUPTCY, ANNULMENT OF.

annulment of marriage. See MARRIAGE, NULLITY OF; CHURCH ANNULMENT.

annulment order. See COMPULSORY PURCHASE ORDER.

anonymity. The High Court in 2002 rejected the application of two persons to be allowed to proceed *anonymously* in an action to prevent the publication of their names in a report of court appointed inspectors into the affairs of Ansbacher (Cayman) Ltd. 'I have no hesitation whatever in saying that the right to have justice administered in public far exceeds any right to privacy, confidentiality or a good name': McCracken J in *Re Ansbacher (Cayman) Ltd* [2002] 2 IR 517, HC. The application to be allowed to proceed anonymously was heard *in camera* and the judge refused a request from the Attorney-General that the applicants' names be made public.

Provision is made for the identity of a Revenue official, who is a member of the Criminal Assets Bureau, not to be revealed eg he need not sign documents in the course of his duties, and he need not identify himself in any proceedings: Taxes Consolidation Act 1997, ss 859 and 908(5). See also Criminal Assets Bureau Act 1996, ss 10 and 23.

Provision is made for the anonymity of a child in any proceedings for an offence against a child or where a child is a witness in any such proceedings: Children Act 2001, s 252. Four national newspapers were fined a total of €45,000 for contempt of court in aspects of their coverage of a road accident which claimed the life of a taxi-driver and a youth; the court held that publication of the names and photographs of two youths, who had subsequently been charged in relation to the accident, and background information about them, indicating that they were awaiting trial on other charges, constituted contempt: *DPP v Independent Newspapers* [2003] 2 ILRM 260, HC. In this case the court held that publication made prior to the preferring of charges did not constitute contempt in Irish law. For proposals to provide anonymity for witnesses with a medical condition, see Criminal Justice Bill 2004, s 27. See CRIMINAL ASSETS BUREAU; INQUEST; FICTITIOUS NAME.

anonymous work. A *work* where the identity of the author is unknown or, in the case of a work of joint ownership, where the identity of the authors is unknown: Copyright and Related Rights Act 2000, s 2(1). Copyright in an *anonymous work* expires 70 years after the date on which the work is first lawfully made available to the public, or 70 years after the death of the author where his identity becomes known during that earlier period (CRRA 2000, s 24). This applies to literary, dramatic, musical, or artistic work or an original database. See also CRRA 2000, s 32. Provision is made for the protection of anonymous works of folklore (CRRA 2000, s 197). The copyright in an anonymous work is not infringed where it is not possible to ascertain the identity of the author by reasonable enquiry and it is reasonable to assume that the copyright has expired (CRRA 2000, s 88). See COPYRIGHT; WORK.

anorexia nervosa. A disorder characterised by a fear of becoming fat, resulting in loss of appetite and refusal of food, and leading to debility and even death. The Circuit Court has held that anorexia is a disability and persons suffering from it are entitled to the protection of equality legislation which prohibits discrimination on the grounds of disability: *Humphreys v West Wood Fitness Club* (2004) Irish Times, 17 February, CC. In this case, the defendant did not obtain any medical or psychiatric advice in relation to anorexia suffered by the plaintiff, which later developed into *bulimia*, and did not undertake any form of risk assessment. See BULIMIA NERVOSA; DISABILITY AND DISCRIMINATION.

answer. The reply to interrogatories (qv).

ante-date. The date which a document bears which is a date before the date on which it was drawn. A bill of exchange (qv) is not invalid by reason only that it is

ante-dated: Bills of Exchange Act 1882, s 13(2). See POST-DATE.

ante litem motam. [Before litigation was in contemplation.] See DECLARATION BY DECEASED.

ante-nuptial. Before marriage.

antecedent. An event which occurs before another event.

antecedent negotiations. In relation to a hire-purchase agreement, means any negotiations or arrangements with the hirer whereby he was induced to make the agreement or which otherwise promoted the transaction to which the agreement relates: Consumer Credit Act 1995, s 83. Where goods are let under a hire-purchase agreement to a hirer *dealing as consumer* (qv), the person by whom antecedent negotiations were conducted will be deemed to be a party to the agreement and that person and the owner, shall, *jointly and severally,* be answerable to the hirer for breach of the agreement and for any misrepresentations made by that person with respect to the goods in the course of the antecedent negotiations (CCA 1995, s 80). This provision extends liability to those persons such as dealers, salesmen or shopkeepers who carry out antecedent negotiations.

antenatus. A child born before the marriage of his parents.

anticipatory breach. The repudiation of a contract before the time for performance is due. The other party is not bound to wait until the actual time for performance has arrived, but may immediately treat the contract as discharged and sue for damages: *Hochster v De La Tour* [1853] 2 E & B 678; *Leeson v North British Oil & Candle Co* [1874] 8 IRCL 309.

anti-competitive. See COMPETITION, DISTORTION OF.

anti-discrimination. See DISCRIMINATION.

anti-social behaviour. Includes either or both of the following: (a) the manufacture, production, preparation, importation, exportation, sale, supply, possession for the purpose of sale or supply, or distribution of a controlled drug; (b) any behaviour which causes or is likely to cause any significant or persistent danger, injury, damage, loss or fear to any person living, working or otherwise lawfully in a house provided by a local authority: Housing (Miscellaneous Provisions) Act 1997, s 1(1). This includes violence, threats, intimidation, coercion, harassment or serious obstruction of any person.

The 1997 Act provides for a new *exclusion order* procedure to direct a tenant engaged in anti-social behaviour to quit a local authority house or to prohibit him from entering the house (H(MP)A 1997, s 3). There is also provision for an *interim* exclusion order where there is immediate risk of significant harm; such an order may be made *ex parte* in exceptional cases (H(MP)A 1997, s 4).

A housing authority can refuse or defer a letting where it considers the applicant is or has been engaged in anti-social behaviour (H(MP)A 1997, s 14). In 1998, ss 1, 3 and 14 of (H(MP)A 1997 were amended to extend the provisions to halting sites provided by housing authorities and approved bodies: Housing (Traveller Accommodation) Act 1998, ss 34–35. For further amendments to ss 1, 3, 3A, 4, 4A, 9 and 14 of the 1997 Act, see Residential Tenancies Act 2004, s 197. See DCR 1997 Ord 99A inserted by SI No 217 of 1999. See ESTATE MANAGEMENT; PART 4 TENANCY, TERMINATION OF; SQUATTER; TENANT, OBLIGATION OF.

anti-speculative property tax. A new tax of 2% of the *market value* of relevant *residential property* owned by an assessable person on 6 April in each of the years 2001, 2002 and 2003: Finance (No 2) Act 2000, ss 5–27. *Residential property* meant: (a) a building or part of a building situated in the State used or suitable for use as a dwelling; and (b) land which the occupier of such a building has for his occupation and enjoyment as its garden or grounds of an ornamental nature (F(No 2)A 2000, s 5).

Certain properties were excluded eg: (a) residential property of significant scientific, historical or aesthetic interest and to which reasonable access is afforded to the public; (b) rented residential properties under the various renewal schemes for urban, towns, seaside, rural, and islands; (c) listed holiday cottages and apartments; and (d) an individual's principal private residence.

Exempted also was: (a) property built after 14 June 2000 on land owned on that date, and (b) property purchased before 15 June 2000 but not conveyed until after that date, provided the relevant contract was evidenced in writing before 15 June 2000 (F(No 2)A 2000, s 8), (c) property taken by way of inheritance (F(No 2)A 2000, s 9), (d) property taken by way of a gift where the disponer already owned the property on 15 June 2000 (F(No 2)A 2000,

s 10); (e) property owned by charities, or a trust for permanently incapacitated individuals (F(No 2)A 2000, ss 11–12); (f) a property occupied by a person as their main residence following a decree of divorce or of judicial separation (F(No 2)A 2000, s 13).

The Government decided in February 2001 not to proceed with this new 2% tax. Legislative effect to the Government's decision is contained in Finance Act 2001, s 230.

anti-trust. Mainly US expression to describe the regulation or prohibition of trusts, monopolies, cartels or similar arrangements which have the intent or effect of restricting competition. The EU Commission has considerable powers to prohibit anti-competitive practices and to impose fines on firms found guilty of anti-competitive conduct. See COMPETITION LAW; COMPETITION, DISTORTION OF; COMPETITION, DISTORTION OF, EU.

Anton Piller order. A form of mandatory injunction (qv), normally granted *ex parte* without notice to the defendant, which requires the defendant to permit the plaintiff or his agents to enter his premises, to inspect documents or other articles and remove any that belong to the plaintiff. Its object is to prevent the defendant from removing or destroying pirated or stolen material before the action comes to trial: *Anton Piller K G v Manufacturing Process Ltd* [1976] Ch 55; *Rank Film Distributers Ltd v Video Information Centre* [1982] AC 380; *Bimeda Chemical Co v Brennan & Ruddy* [1989] HC. This form of injunction has been granted by the courts but has not yet been considered by the Supreme Court. See *Lynch* in (1994) 4 ISLR 67.

A form of statutory *Anton Piller* order is available on application by the owner of the copyright (eg of a video recording) to the District Court which can authorise a garda to seize without warrant infringing copies of the work: Copyright (Amendment) Act 1987, s 2. See Copyright and Related Rights Act 2000, s 132.

It is not of the essence that an *ex parte* application for an *Anton Piller* order should be held in camera: *Microsoft Corporation v Brightpoint Ireland* [2001] 1 ILRM 540, HC. In this case the court however ordered the parties not to make contact with the media and to erase forthwith any information in relation to the proceedings from the parties' websites. The court also held that:

(a) an affidavit in support of an application for an *Anton Piller* order should err on the side of excessive disclosure; and (b) it is essential for a solicitor executing an *Anton Piller* order at a defendant's premises to make a detailed record of the material removed from the premises. See BAYER INJUNCTION.

apartment. See FLAT.

apices juris non sunt jura. [Legal principles must not be carried to their most extreme consequences, regardless of equity and good sense.] See EQUITY.

apology. In a defamation (qv) action, an offer of apology from the defendant for having defamed the plaintiff was no defence at common law. However, an offer of apology is now admissible in mitigation of damages: Defamation Act 1961, s 17. In cases of *unintentional* defamation, an offer of amends may be made, which if rejected, is a good defence to defamation proceedings (DA 1961, s 21).

In a summary trial in the district court, a suggestion to an accused that the judge might apply the Probation of Offenders Act 1907 if the accused apologised for his actions, did not interfere with the accused's right to fair procedures: *Kelly v O'Sullivan* [1991] 9 ILT Dig 127, HC. See MITIGATION OF DAMAGES; OFFER OF AMENDS; PROBATION OF OFFENDERS.

apparent authority. See PRINCIPAL.

appeal. The transference of a case from an inferior to a higher tribunal in the hope of reversing or modifying the decision of the former: *Edlesten v LCC* [1918] 1 KB 81. There was no right to an appeal at common law. There can only be a right of appeal where one is provided for by statute, because the 1937 Constitution states that the right of appeal is 'as determined by law': art 34(3)(4) and *Todd v Murphy* [1999] 1 ILRM 261, SC and 2 IR 1.

However, where there is no provision in law for an appeal from the decision of a competent authority, the court nevertheless will set aside such a decision where it is shown to be unlawful because of the manner in which the decision was made, whether because: (a) the competent authority failed to consider the matter in a fair and impartial manner; or (b) because it took into account factors it should have excluded, or excluded factors it should have taken into account: *Carrigaline Co Ltd v Minister for Transport Energy and Communications* [1997] 1 ILRM 241, HC.

Where an appeal is provided for, generally only one appeal is allowable. However, the fact that one statute provides for a more extensive right of appeal than another statute, does not render it unconstitutional: *Dornan Research and Development Ltd v Labour Court* [2001] 1 IR 223, HC and [1998] ELR 256, HC. Where a statute provides for a *rehearing*, the general rule appears to be that there is a statutory right to an appeal *de novo*: *Orange v Director of Telecommunications* [1999] 2 ILRM 81, HC and [2000] 4 IR 136, HC.

The Supreme Court has appellate jurisdiction from decisions of the High Court, unless otherwise prescribed by law: 1937 Constitution art 34(4)(3); *Minister for Justice v Wang Zhu Jie* [1991] ILRM 823, SC. An exclusion or regulation of the right of appeal to the Supreme Court need not be express; it is a matter of construction of the relevant statutory provision in each case but there must not be any ambiguity or lack of clarity: *B v Governor of Training Unit* [2002] 2 ILRM 161, SC.

Matters occurring to a plaintiff after the making of a High Court order cannot provide grounds for an appeal to the Supreme Court: *Dalton v Minister for Finance* [1989] ILRM 519, SC. An appeal lies to the High Court from an order of the Circuit Court in a civil matter by way of a re-hearing (qv) and the decision is generally not appealable: Courts of Justice Act 1936, ss 3–839. See COURT; FINAL; FRESH EVIDENCE; MISCARRIAGE; REVIEW OF SENTENCE; STAY; TIME, COURT RULES.

appeal, crime. While the right of appeal in civil matters is generally evenly apportioned between the plaintiff and the defendant, subject to the principle of *finality in litigation* (qv), the situation is quite different in criminal law. In criminal matters, the defence has broad rights of appeal to a higher court. In addition, a new procedure has been established whereby a convicted person, who has exhausted the normal appeals procedure, may now seek leave to appeal again where a *new* or *newly-discovered* fact is alleged to show a miscarriage of justice: see MISCARRIAGE.

On the other hand, the rights of appeal of the prosecution are limited, as follows:

(a) an appeal from a decision of the Circuit Court and the Central Criminal Court to acquit a person, but 'without prejudice' to the verdict in favour of the accused, to clarify the law, where the acquittal was on the direction of the judge on a question of law: Criminal Procedure Act 1967, s 34; Courts and Court Officers Act 1995, s 44. There is no jurisdiction for the Supreme Court to overturn the acquittal. See *The People (DPP) v O'Shea* [1982] IR 384. See ACQUITTAL.

(b) a statutory right of appeal where so provided eg Fisheries (Consolidation) Act 1959, s 310. This statutory provision for an appeal to the Circuit Court against an acquittal in the District Court has been held not to be unconstitutional; the right of appeal was from a court of 'local and limited jurisdiction' as contemplated by the Constitution: *Considine v Shannon Regional Fisheries Board* [1994] 1 ILRM 499, HC and [1997] 2 IR 404, SC.

(c) a review of an *unduly lenient sentence* as provided by the Criminal Justice Act 1993, s 2. See REVIEW OF SENTENCE.

(d) there is no prosecution avenue of appeal from the Special Criminal Court.

Also a Circuit Court judge has the right to state a case to the Supreme Court on any question of law that arises before him and may adjourn pronouncement of his judgment or order pending determination of such case stated: Courts of Justice Act 1947, s 16.

It has been held that an *appeal* is a more appropriate remedy, rather than a *judicial review*, for an order of certiorari to quash a conviction, where there are allegations of unfair procedures in a criminal trial (eg non-attendance of witness and non-disclosure of documents favourable to an accused): *Maher v O'Donnell* [1996] 2 ILRM 321, HC.

See *Consultation Paper on Prosecution Appeals in cases brought on Indictment* (LRC CP 19, 2002. The paper considers whether reform is needed and, if so, whether prosecution appeals should be on a 'without prejudice' basis, or whether the current 'without prejudice' right of appeal should be expanded to encompass a wider range of trial rulings. See Report of Committee (Martin Committee) to *Enquire into certain Aspects of Criminal Procedure* (1990). For proposed changes in relation to appeals in certain criminal proceedings, see Criminal Justice Bill 2004, ss 20 – 23. See EUROPEAN CONVENTION ON HUMAN RIGHTS.

appeal, rules of court. For appeals to the Supreme Court, see RSC Ord 58. For appeals from the Central Criminal Court to the Supreme Court, see RSC Ord 87. For appeals from the Circuit Court, see RSC Ord 61.

For appeal provisions for civil and criminal cases from the District Court to the Circuit Court, see Circuit Court Rules 2001 Ord 41. In relation to an appeal from the Circuit Court to the Court of Criminal Appeal, application for a certificate required by s 63 of the Courts of Justice Act 1924 must be made to the Circuit Court immediately on termination of the trial or within three days thereof (CCR 2001 Ord 42).

For appeals *to* the District Court, see DCR 1997 Ord 100. For appeals *from* the District Court to the Circuit Court, see DCR 1997 Ord 101 as amended, in respect of the fixing of recognisances, by District Court (Appeals to the Circuit Court) Rules 2003, SI No 484 of 2003.

appeal and judicial review. It has been held that leave to apply for a judicial review should be refused where remedies of *appeal* and *judicial review* were both sought, and where an appeal was pending and not heard: *Buckley v Kirby* [2000] 3 IR 431, SC and [2001] 2 ILRM 395, SC. Where an appeal would clearly be the more appropriate remedy and that had not been brought, that did not mean that leave to apply for a judicial review should be granted. See also *Cremin v Smithwick* (27 June 2001, unreported), HC. See EMPLOYMENT APPEALS TRIBUNAL, APPEAL FROM.

appearance, entry of. The formal step taken by a defendant to a court action, after being served with a summons, which in the High Court, must be made within eight days of such service, exclusive of the day of service, unless the court orders otherwise; except that a defendant in proceedings commenced by *special* summons may enter an appearance at any time: RSC Ord 12.

If a defendant intends to defend a *civil bill* in the Circuit Court, he is required to enter an appearance in the prescribed form, to reach the office of the court not later than ten days from the service of the civil bill, exclusive of the day of service, or such further time as may be agreed between the parties unless the court otherwise directs: Circuit Court Rules 2001 Ord 15, rr 1 and 2. The defendant is required within a further ten days to deliver his defence to the plaintiff (CCR Ord 15, r 4). See also Ord 15, r 1; O 22; O 26, r 1; O 59, r 4(8).

Notice of *intention to defend* a civil summons in the District Court is required not later than four days before the date of sitting of the court to which the civil summons is returnable: DCR 1997 Ord 41, r 1.

Failure of an employer to enter an appearance to a claim of unfair dismissal to the Employment Appeals Tribunal (qv) does not prevent the Circuit Court from hearing an appeal from the employer against the decision of the Tribunal: *Mulvey v Kennedy & Fox* [1989] 7 ILT & SJ 28.

appellant. A person who appeals. See APPEAL.

appellate jurisdiction. See JURISDICTION.

appendant. Annexed to a hereditament. See POWER OF APPOINTMENT.

application of assets. See ADMINISTRATION OF ESTATES.

apply. When a court follows a previous decision in a current case, it is said to *apply* the previous decision. See RATIO DECIDENDI; DISTINGUISHING A CASE.

appointment, power of. See POWER OF APPOINTMENT.

apportionment. Division into parts which are proportionate to the interests and rights of the parties. See *Howe v Lord Dartmouth* [1802] 7 Ves 137. See AVERAGE CLAUSE; CONTRIBUTION; CONTRIBUTORY NEGLIGENCE.

appraisement. The valuation of goods or property; in particular the valuation of goods seized in execution, or by distraint, or by order of the court. A person who is authorised to conduct auctions may act as an *appraiser* within the meaning of the Appraisers Act 1806 without being licensed under that Act: Finance Act 1950, s 8. See AUCTIONEER.

appraiser. A valuer; a person who makes an appraisement. See AUCTIONEER.

apprentice. A person who binds himself for a definite time to serve and learn from an employer who undertakes to teach his trade or calling. An apprentice is also a person employed by way of apprenticeship in a *designated industrial activity*: Industrial Training Act 1967, s 2(1). 'In order to establish the relation of apprentice and master there must be a binding agreement on the part of the apprentice to serve for a definite period and, on the part of the master, a reciprocal agreement to teach the apprentice his trade or calling.': *Sister Dolores v Minister for Social Welfare* [1960] 2 IR 77 at p 92.

A *minor's* contract of apprenticeship is binding on him if it is substantially to his advantage. *Statutory apprenticeship* means an apprenticeship in a designated industrial activity within the meaning of the Industrial Training Act 1967. The Unfair Dismissals Act 1977 does not apply to a dismissal of a statutory apprentice if it takes place within six months of commencement of the apprenticeship or within one month of its completion (UDA 1977, s.4 and Unfair Dismissals (Amendment) Act 1993, s 14); *Boal v IMED Ireland Ltd* [1995] ELR 178, EAT. An apprenticeship stands suspended during absence of the apprentice on *protective leave* (qv): Maternity Protection Act 1994, s 25, as amended by Maternity Protection (Amendment) Act 2004, s 17, to clarify that this provision applies to both female and male employees.

There is no longer a preference given to the payment of apprentice fees from the property of a bankrupt: Bankruptcy Act 1988, s 81.

An Foras Áiseanna Saothair (FÁS) may make rules relating to the employment, education and training of apprentices: Labour Services Act 1987; Industrial Training Act 1967, ss 27–36. FÁS has made rules to underpin a new standards-based system of apprenticeship introduced in 1993/1994 (SI No 236 of 1993. SI No 198 of 1995). A payroll levy in certain sectors of industry was introduced in 1994 to fund partly the new standards-based apprenticeship system: Industrial Training (Apprenticeship Levy) Act 1994. This special payroll levy has now been replaced by a new *national training levy*, which finances a wider range of schemes and repeals the 1994 Act: National Training Fund Act 2000.

The power of the District Court to order an apprentice to perform his duties has been abolished: Age of Majority Act 1985, s 8(c). An apprentice is regarded as an employee for all provisions of the Safety, Health and Welfare at Work Act 1990 (s 2(1)). An apprentice who was dismissed for altering the date on a medical certificate, which he later admitted, was ordered to be re-engaged: *Parsons v Liffey Marine Ltd* [1992] ELR 136, EAT. See Private Security Services Act 2004, s 3(1)(f). See *Doyle v White City Stadium* [1935] KB 110; *Dempsey v Grant Shopfitting Ltd* [1990] ELR 43; *Redmond v EG Tew*

1971 Ltd [1992] ELR 7, EAT. See FIXED-TERM EMPLOYEE; WILFUL NEGLECT.

appreticii ad legem. [Apprentices to the law.]

approbate. To approve as valid; to sanction authoritatively. See *AMN v JPC* [1988] ILRM 170; JM and *GM v An Bord Uchtála* [1988] ILRM 203. Where there is no true consent to a marriage, there can be no question of approbation: *DB v O'R* [1991] ILRM 160, SC. See also *O'B v R* [2000] 1 ILRM 307, HC.

approbate and reprobate. Term used to describe that a person is not allowed to take a benefit under an instrument and to disclaim the liabilities imposed by the same instrument. See *Codrington v Codrington* [1875] 45 LJ Ch 660; *People (DPP) v Aylmer* [1995] 2 ILRM 624, SC. See ELECTION.

appropriation. Making a thing the property of a person. The setting apart of goods or moneys out of a larger quantity as the property of a particular person eg appropriating goods to a contract.

(1) Appropriation by a personal representative is the application of the property of the deceased in its actual condition towards satisfaction of any share in the estate: Succession Act 1965, s 55; also *H v O* [1978] IR 194. Where the estate includes the family dwelling, the surviving spouse may require the personal representative to appropriate the dwelling and household chattels (SA 1965, s 56; also *Hamilton v Armstrong* [1984] ILRM 306; *H v H* [1978] IR 194). The court is empowered to prohibit an appropriation but it may not modify the terms of an appropriation: *Messit v Henry* [2001] 3 IR 313, HC.

(2) Appropriation of payments made in respect of two or more agreements between a consumer and the same creditor or owner; in hire-purchase agreements, where one-third of the hire-purchase price has been paid on each agreement, the owner may, if the hirer has failed to do, appropriate the payment as he sees fit (eg to clear one of the agreements): Consumer Credit Act 1995, s 44.

(3) Where, in pursuance of a contract for the sale of goods, the seller delivers the goods to the buyer or to a carrier or other bailee (whether named by the buyer or not) for the purpose of transmission to the buyer, and does not reserve the right of disposal, he is deemed to have uncondition-

ally appropriated the goods to the contract: Sale of Goods Act 1893, s 18, r 5(2).

(4) In the EU context, appropriations relate to the budget and refer to amounts of money to be committed to be spent at some time in the next short period of years (*commitment appropriations*) or actually to be spent in the current or forthcoming financial year (*expenditure appropriations*): National Forum on Europe, *Glossary of Terms* (2003).

(5) For appropriation by the Official Assignee (qv) of a bankrupt's income see Bankruptcy Act 1988, s 65. See DISPOSAL OF GOODS; GOODS, PROPERTY IN.

Appropriation Act. This is an Act of the Oireachtas which is passed annually to enable the Government to pay out of the Central Fund the amounts needed to defray the charges for the public service incurred during the year in which the Act is passed into law eg Appropriation Act 2000. Provision has been made to permit the carry over from one year to another of any unspent Exchequer capital allocations, up to a maximum of 10% of the voted capital allocation: Finance Act 2004, s 91. This is to facilitate the rolling five-year multi-annual envelopes for capital expenditure announced in the 2004 Budget. Previously, any unspent moneys at the end of a year had to be surrendered to the Central Fund.

The Oireachtas in voting money to a body by means of the Appropriation Act does not empower the body to carry out works which are not authorised by its statutory constitution: *Howard & Ors v Commissioners of Public Works* (1993) Irish Times, 13 February, HC. See also Central Fund Permanent Provisions Act 1965; Appropriation Act 2001; Appropriation Act 2002; Appropriation Act 2003. See FINANCIAL RESOLUTIONS.

approval, sale on. When goods are delivered to a buyer *on approval,* or *sale and return,* the property therein passes to the buyer when he signifies his approval or acceptance to the seller, or does any other act adopting the transaction. If he does not signify his approval or acceptance but retains the goods without giving notice of rejection, the property therein passes to him on the expiration of the time fixed for the return of the goods, or, if no time has been fixed, on the expiration of a reasonable time. What is a reasonable time is a question of fact. See Sale of Goods Act 1893, s 18, r 4.

approximation of laws. The bringing about of a situation where the national law applying in certain areas of life in the different member states of the EU is more closely similar but not necessarily exactly the same: National Forum on Europe, *Glossary of Terms* (2003). The member states have agreed that the activities of the European Community includes 'the approximation of the laws on member states to the extent required for the functioning of the common market': Treaty establishing the European Community, art 3.1(h) of the consolidated (2002) version. The Council are empowered to issue directives for the approximation of such laws, regulations or administrative provisions of the member states as directly affect the establishment or functioning of the common market (consolidated arts 94–97). For example, EC Directive 77/143/EEC, as amended by 88/449/EEC, provides for the approximation of laws of the member states relating to roadworthiness tests for motor vehicles and their trailers. See COMMON POLICIES; FRAMEWORK DECISION; HARMONISATION OF LAWS.

appurtenant. Belonging to; necessary to the enjoyment of a thing; annexed to a hereditament eg a right of way. When land is conveyed or transferred, all appurtenant rights with the land are also transferred: Conveyancing Act 1881, s 6. See WAY, RIGHT OF.

APR. [Annual Percentage Charge (qv).]

aqua cedit solo. [Water passes with the soil.] Ownership of water generally goes with the ownership of the soil beneath the water. See *Tennant v Clancy* [1988] ILRM 214. See RIPARIAN.

aquaculture. The culture or farming of any species of fish, aquatic invertebrate animal of whatever habitat or aquatic plant, or any aquatic form of food suitable for the nutrition of fish: Fisheries (Amendment) Act 1997, s 3(1). The designation by the Minister of an area for which licences to engage in aquaculture may be granted, may be set aside by the High Court: *Courtney v Minister for the Marine* [1989] ILRM 605, HC. The 1997 Act establishes a new licensing and regulatory framework for aquaculture. *Aquaculture* involves the human intervention in the rearing of fish eg the farming and feeding of fin fish in cages or the propagation of shellfish which filter feed naturally in the waters where the feed is placed.

It is an offence for a person to engage in aquaculture except in accordance with a *licence* (F(A)A 1997, s 6). Aquaculture installations or structures on the foreshore remain subject to the Foreshore Acts and land-based facilities are subject to the planning laws. The Minister may grant *trial licences* authorising experimental investigations. Also there are provisions to deal with unauthorised developments and breaches of licence conditions. There is an independent *aquaculture licence appeals board* (F(A)A 1997, ss 22–60).

There is now an obligation on the Aquaculture Appeals Board to state the main reasons and considerations on which are based its determinations of appeals against Ministerial decisions to grant or refuse an aquaculture licence: F(A)A 1997, s 40 as amended by Fisheries (Amendment) Act 2001, s 10. The Board is given comprehensive inspection powers in relation to any land to which an appeal relates, whether or not the appeal is subject to an oral hearing (F(A)A 1997, s 57A inserted by F(A)A 2001, s 12). The 2001 Act contains other amendments to the 1997 Act e g regarding membership of the Board, employees, and advisers engaged by the Board.

To deter persons from engaging in aquaculture in anticipation of a licence, an application for a licence cannot be accepted from a person who commences engagement before a licence is granted: Fisheries and Foreshore (Amendment) Act 1998, s 4. See *Madden v Minister for the Marine* [1997] 1 ILRM 136, SC; *O'Sullivan v Aquaculture Licences Appeal Board* [2001] 1 IR 646, HC. See also British-Irish Agreement Act 1999, ss 31–34. See Aquaculture (Licence Application) Regulations 1998, SI No 236 of 1998 as amended by SI No 145 of 2001. See EC (Labelling of Fishery and Aquaculture Products) Regulations 2003, SI No 320 of 2003.

aquifer. Any stratum or combination of strata that stores or transmits groundwater: LG (Water Pollution) (Amendment) Act 1990, s 2. See also Environmental Protection Agency Act 1992, s 99I inserted by Protection of the Environment Act 2003, s 16. See GROUNDWATER; WATER POLLUTION.

arbitration. The determination of disputes by the decision of one or more persons called *arbitrators*. Differences between arbitrators are decided by an *umpire*. An agreement to refer a dispute to arbitration is called an *arbitration agreement* (qv). Most contracts of insurance, partnership agreements, travel and building contracts, include an *arbitration clause* requiring that disputes be determined by an arbitrator.

An *arbitration clause* in a contract is quite distinct from other clauses; even where there is repudiation of a contract (eg in an insurance contract for non-disclosure of a material fact), the arbitration clause will survive where it is worded to include 'all differences arising out of this policy': *Doyle v Irish National Insurance Co plc* [1998] 1 ILRM 502, HC.

The decision of an arbitrator is called an *award*. A court is empowered to grant interim relief pending determination of a dispute by arbitration: *Telenor AS v IIU Nominees & Esat Telecom* [1999] ITLR (11 October), HC.

There is now a dual arbitration regime in Ireland – international and domestic. *International arbitration* is governed by the Arbitration (International Commercial) Act 1998 and by the international arbitration conventions signed by Ireland eg the Geneva Convention, the New York Convention, and the Washington Convention, dealing with the enforcement and recognition of international awards. *Domestic arbitration* is governed by the Arbitration Acts of 1954 and 1980, as amended by the 1998 Act. Under *international* arbitration the role of the national court is to facilitate and support the arbitration, whereas under *domestic* arbitration there are greater possibilities for court intervention in the arbitration process.

The court has held that where a procedural mishap has occurred in an arbitration which has denied a person a fair hearing, the court should not set any permanent inflexible limits to the exercise of the wide power conferred in section 36(1) of the 1954 Act, which provided for the remission of matters by the court to the reconsideration of the arbitrator or umpire: *McCarrick v The Gaiety (Sligo) Ltd* [2001] 2 IR 266, HC and [2002] 1 ILRM 55, HC. For a critical appraisal of this case, see Rory White BL and Ercus Stewart SC in *Bar Review* (January/February 2002) 122. A barrister may be an arbitrator and may receive remuneration for such office: *Code of Conduct for the Bar of Ireland* (December 2003) r 2.10.

See *Tobin & Twomey Services Ltd v Kerry Foods Ltd* [1996] 2 ILRM 1, SC and [1999]

3 IR 483, HC. For the Chartered Institute of Arbitrators, see website: *www.arbitration .ie*. For the Chartered Institute of Arbitrators, see website: *www.arbitration.ie*. [Bibliography: Hutchinson (2); O'Reilly P; Stewart.] See COMMERCIAL PROCEEDINGS; EUROPEAN EXTRA-JUDICIAL NETWORK; TRIBUNAL AND ARBITRATION CENTRE.

arbitration, domestic. The determination of commercial domestic disputes. If legal proceedings are instituted in contravention of a domestic arbitration agreement or clause, they may be *stayed* by either party, but only after an appearance has been entered and before delivering pleadings or taking any other *steps in the proceedings*: Arbitration Act 1980, s 5. Any court before which an action has been commenced has the power to stay proceedings: *Mitchell v Budget Travel Ltd* [1990] ILRM 739, SC. However, a party cannot be prevented from commencing or dealing with a civil proceeding, provided by the rules of court, in respect of a *small claim* (AA 1980, s 5 amended by Arbitration (International Commercial) Act 1998, s 18).

A stay will not be placed on proceedings by a consumer where the damages recoverable in arbitration are limited under an arbitration clause unless: (a) the consumer's attention was specifically drawn to the arbitration term prior to contract: and (b) the arbitration term is fair and reasonable: *McCarthy v Joe Walsh Tours Ltd* [1991] ILRM 813, HC, also reported in [1991] 9 ILT & SJ 92.

An arbitrator has power to proceed despite the absence of a party where that party has been refused an adjournment: *Grangeford Structures Ltd v SH Ltd* [1990] ILRM 277, SC. See also *Williams v Artane Service Station Ltd* [1991] ITLR (14 October), HC. Unless otherwise agreed by the parties, the arbitrator may award interest, simple or compound, from the dates and at the rates which he considers meets the justice of the case (Arbitration Act 1954, s 34 as amended by A(IC)A 1998, s 17). This provision does not apply to property arbitrations pursuant to s 2 of the Property Values (Arbitration and Appeals) Act 1960.

The High Court has jurisdiction to *set aside* an arbitration award if there is an error in law on its face: *Church General Insurance Co v Connolly* [1981] HC. However, an arbitrator's decision on a point of law referred to him will not be set aside or remitted to him by a court by reason of the fact that it might be established to be erroneous: *McStay v Assicurazioni Generali SPA & Moore* [1991] ILRM 237, SC. See also *Stanbridge v Healy* [1985] ILRM 290; *Hogan v Saint Kevins Co* [1986] IR 80; *Childers Heights Housing v Molderings* [1987] ILRM 47; *Brenton Dewick (A Minor) v Falcon Group Overseas Ltd* [2001] HC; *Re Via Net Works (Ireland) Ltd* [2002] 2 IR 47, SC. See *Quinn* in 9 ILT & SJ (1991) 218. See 'Arbitration clauses and the infant plaintiff' by Derek Sheahan BL in *Bar Review* (December 2001) 74. See RSC Ord 56 and O 62(2). [Bibliography: Forde (11); Hutchinson (2); Bernstein UK; Russell UK.] See STEP IN PROCEEDINGS; SMALL CLAIMS; CONTRACT OF EMPLOYMENT.

arbitration, international. The determination of disputes regarding matters arising from all relationships of an international commercial nature, whether contractual or not: Arbitration (International Commercial) Act 1998 which gives effect in the State of the UNCITRAL Model Law on International Commercial Arbitration adopted by the UN Commission on International Trade Law on 21 June 1985. There is a wide definition of *international* in the Model Law (eg parties having their place of business in different states) and of *commercial* (eg trade transactions but not consumer contracts). An arbitral tribunal may award simple or compound interest from the dates and at the rates that it considers meets the justice of the case (A(IC)A 1998, s 10).

The High Court is the competent court to perform certain functions of arbitration assistance and supervision (A(IC)A 1998, s 6 and art 6 of Model Law). These include power to grant interim measures of protection (A(IC)A 1998, s 7 and art 9 of Model Law), to assist a party or the arbitral tribunal in taking evidence (A(IC)A 1998, s 7 and art 27 of Model Law), to set aside an award (A(IC)A 1998, s 13 and art 34 of Model Law), and to grant recognition and enforcement of awards (A(IC)A 1998, s 14 and arts 35–36 of Model Law). There is no provision for *stating a case* to the courts on issues of law as exists in domestic arbitration. An *interim* award is dealt with similarly as a *final* award as regards challenge, recognition and enforcement (A(IC)A 1998, s 3(1)). See New York Convention Order 2000, SI No 41 of 2000. See '*Ireland as a venue for International Arbitration; Five*

years on – where do we stand?' by Colm ÓhOisín BL in *Bar Review* (June 2003) 117. [Bibliography: Hutchinson (2).] See PATENT AGENT; TRADE MARK AGENT; SECURITY FOR COSTS, NON-RESIDENT PLAINTIFF.

arbitration agreement. A written agreement to refer present or future differences to arbitration whether an arbitrator is named therein or not: Arbitration Act 1954, s 2(1); an agreement in writing (including an agreement contained in an exchange of letters or telegrams) to submit to arbitration present or future differences capable of settlement by arbitration: Arbitration Act 1980, s 2.

The Court has a discretion to order that an arbitration agreement ceases to have effect where an allegation of fraud is made: *Administralia Asigurarilor de Stat v Insurance Corp of Ireland* [1990] 8 ILT Dig 190 and Arbitration Act 1954, s 39. See also *Sweeney v Mulcahy* [1993] ILRM 289, HC. An arbitration agreement also means an agreement concerning international commercial arbitration: Arbitration (International Commercial) Act 1998, s 3(1).

An arbitration agreement is not permitted to operate to preclude a dispute to which the agreement applies from being referred to the *Private Residential Tenancies Board* for resolution unless the tenant at or after the time the dispute arises consents to the dispute being referred to arbitration: Residential Tenancies Act 2004, s 90.

archaeological area. An area which the Commissioners of Public Works in Ireland consider to be of archaeological importance but does not include the area of a registered *historic monument* (qv): National Monuments (Amendment) Act 1987, s 1(1). The degree of protection afforded by legislation to an archaeological area is less than that afforded to an historic monument. See ALSO BORD NA MÓNA; COILLTE TEORANTA; NATIONAL MONUMENT; VALETTA CONVENTION; WRECK.

archaeological object. Means any chattel whether in a manufactured or partly manufactured or an unmanufactured state, which by reason of the archaeological interest attaching thereto or of its association with any Irish historical event or person, has a value substantially greater than its intrinsic (including artistic) value: National Monuments Act 1930, s 2 as amended by National Monuments (Amendment) Act 1994, s 14.

The expression includes treasure trove (qv) and ancient human, animal or plant remains. Ownership of any archaeological object vests in the State where the object has no known owner at the time it is found; the object may be disposed of by the State (NM(A)A 1994, s 2; National Cultural Institutions Act 1997, s 68).

Possession, control, purchase or sale of an archaeological object is an offence (NM(A)A 1994, s 4). The finder of an archaeological object, or the owner or occupier of the land, may be paid a reward where the object is retained by the State (NM(A)A 1994, s 10). The cleaning or restoring of such objects requires a licence (NM(A)A 1994, s 20). There are strict reporting requirements on a person who discovers an archaeological object (NM(A)A 1994, ss 5, 18, 19). It is an offence for a person to export or to attempt to export an archaeological object without a licence (NCIA 1997, ss 2(1) and 49(7)). See CULTURAL OBJECT; HERITAGE; PROTECTED STRUCTURE; VALLETTA CONVENTION.

architect. There is provision for the recognition by each member state of diplomas, certificates and other evidence of formal qualifications in architecture of other member states: EC Directive 85/384/EEC. There are no regulations in the State governing the taking up and practice of architecture under the professional title of architect and the Directive does not impose a duty on the Minister to make such regulations: *Scally v Minister for the Environment* [1996] 1 IR 367, HC. See EC (Establishment and Provision of Services in Architecture (Amendment) Regulations 2003, SI No 686 of 2003 implementing EC Directive 2001/19/EC. For the Royal Institute of the Architects of Ireland, see website: *www.riai.ie*.

architect's certificate. In a particular case, the court refused to stay a judgment sought by a building contractor for moneys due on an architect's interim certificate, notwithstanding a counterclaim for damages for defective work: *Rohan Construction Ltd v Antigen Ltd* [1989] ILRM 783, HC. See also *Rohcon Ltd v SIAC Architectural Ltd* [2003] FL 8221, HC. See FINAL CERTIFICATE; RIAI CONTRACT.

architectural conservation area. Means a place, area, group of structures or townscape, taking account of building lines and heights, that: (a) is of special architectural,

historical, archaeological, artistic, cultural, scientific, social or technical interest or value, or (b) contributes to the appreciation of *protected structures* (qv): Planning and Development Act 2000, s 2(1) and 81(1). A *development plan* must include an objective to preserve the character of an *architectural conservation area* if the planning authority is of the opinion that its inclusion is necessary (PDA 2000, s 81(1)). The carrying out of works to the exterior of a structure in such an area is exempted development, only if those works would not materially affect the character of the area (PDA 2000, s 82). Also the planning authority may acquire, by agreement or compulsorily, a structure or other land in such an area (PDA 2000, s 83).

A planning authority may, if it considers all or part of such an area to be of special importance, prepare a scheme setting out development objectives for the preservation and enhancement of the area (an *area of special planning control*) and vary and review the scheme (PDA 2000, ss 84–86). Any development within an area of special planning control shall not be exempted development, where it contravenes an approved scheme applying to that area (PDA 2000, s 87). The planning authority is empowered to compel the owner or occupier of land, to which an objective or provision of an approved scheme applies, to undertake work specified in a notice eg: (a) the restoration, demolition, removal, alteration, maintenance, repair or cleaning of any structure; or (b) the discontinuance of any *use* or the continuance of use subject to conditions) by order of the court if necessary (PDA 2000, ss 88–91). Such work does not require planning permission (PDA 2000, s 92). Refusal to grant planning permission because the proposed development would adversely affect an *architectural conservation area* is sufficient reason to rule out compensation (PDA 2000, s 191 and Sch 4, para 13).

In March 2003, Dublin City Council proposed a *special planning control scheme* for O'Connell Street in Dublin to 'guide private investment toward the creation of a busy, thriving commercial area that is in harmony with the street's architectural, cultural, civic and historic character'. See website: *www.dublincity.ie*. See SEX SHOP.

architectural heritage. Structures and buildings which are of architectural, historical, archaeological, artistic, cultural, scientific, social or technical interest; this includes sites, groups of buildings and structures, together with their settings and attendant grounds, fixtures and fittings: Architectural Heritage (National Inventory) and Historic Monuments (Miscellaneous Provisions) Act 1999. Provision has been made for the compiling of a national inventory of such buildings and structures, including the right to enter private property to enable the inventory to be established and maintained.

Provision has also been made for the better protection of *protected structures* ie of structures of special architectural, historical, archaeological, artistic, cultural, scientific, social or technical interest: Planning and Development Act 2000, ss 51–80. See Planning and Development Regulations 2001, Pt 6, arts 51–55, SI No 600 of 2001. For previous legislation, see Local Government (Planning and Development) Act 1999. See PROTECTED STRUCTURE; GRANADA CONVENTION.

architecture. See ARTISTIC WORK; SAFETY AT WORK.

archives. Includes records and documents held in the Public Records Office or the State Papers Office, Departmental records transferred to and accepted for preservation by the National Archives, other records or documents acquired permanently or on loan by the National Archives from public service organisations, institutions or private individuals, and other public records: National Archives Act 1986, s 2. Certain copying by *archivists* does not infringe copyright or related rights: Copyright and Related Rights Act 2000, ss 59–70 and 227–236. A reference to an archivist in the CRRA 2000 includes a reference to a *curator* (CRRA 2000, s 2(4)).

It is a function of local authorities to make arrangements for the proper management, custody, care and conservation of local records and local archives and for the inspection by the public of local archives: Local Government Act 1994, s 65, now Local Government Act 2001, s 80. See 'Treasures in your attic' by archivist Carol Quinn in *Law Society Gazette* (March 2004) 24. See NATIONAL ARCHIVES.

area of special planning control. An *architectural conservation area* (qv) to which a special planning control scheme has been approved: Planning and Development Act 2000, ss 2(1) and 85(8).

arguendo. [In the course of argument.]

argumentative affidavit. An affidavit (qv) which unnecessarily sets forth argumentative matter ie arguments as to the bearing of facts; the costs of such an affidavit will not be allowed: RSC 0 40, r 4.

argumentum ab inconvenienti plurimum valet in lege. [An argument based on inconvenience is of great weight in the law.]

armchair principle. The principle by which the court (in order to determine what was meant by the words used by a testator in his will) could *sit in the testator's armchair* and take account of all the circumstances surrounding the testator when he made his will: *Boyes v Cook* [1880] 14 Ch D 53; *Fitzgerald v Ryan* [1899] 2 IR 637; *Re Hall* [1944] IR 54. Extrinsic evidence is admissible to show the intention of a testator and to assist in the construction of, or to explain any contradiction in, a will: Succession Act 1965, s 90. See EVIDENCE, EXTRINSIC.

armed rebellion. See NATIONAL EMERGENCY.

arm's length, at. Removed from personal influence. *Articles of association* of a company usually require that a director is not to vote in respect of any contract in which he is interested, directly or indirectly. By statute, a director is required to disclose the nature of his interest in any contract between himself and the company; however, a general notice by the director will suffice stating that he is a member of a specified company or firm and that he is to be regarded as interested in any contract entered into by the company thereafter with that company or firm: Companies Act 1963, s 194, as amended by the Companies Act 1990, s 47. See also Finance Act 1991, s 31(1) now Taxes Consolidation Act 1997, s 110; Roads Act 1993, ss 37 and 40. See CONFLICT OF INTEREST; COUNCILLOR, DISCLOSURE OF INTEREST; ETHICS IN PUBLIC OFFICE; PURCHASER; QUALIFYING PATENT; UNDUE INFLUENCE.

army personnel, dismissal of. See GARDA, DISCIPLINE OF.

arraignment. The beginning of a criminal trial whereby the prisoner is called to the bar by naming him, the *indictment* (qv) is read to him and he is asked whether he is guilty or not. [Bibliography: Walsh D (3).] See PLEA.

Arramara Teoranta. A joint venture company between the government and a private sector partner in 1947 to produce seaweed-based products; the Minister may now expend a sum not exceeding €1.2 million in the acquisition of shares as part of a restructuring and capital development of the company: Alginate Industries (Ireland) Ltd (Acquisition of Shares) Act 1949 as amended by Arramara Teoranta (Acquisition of Shares) Act 2002. The company in 2002 was producing seaweed meal at its plant in Kilkieran, Co Galway.

arrangement. See ARRANGING DEBTOR; SCHEME OF ARRANGEMENT.

arrangement and reconstruction. See RECONSTRUCTION OF COMPANY.

arranging debtor. A debtor who has been granted an *order for protection* by the High Court: Bankruptcy Act 1988, ss 3 and 87–109. The debtor, seeking to effect an *arrangement* with his creditors under the control of the court, presents a petition setting out the reason for his inability to pay his debts and requests that his person and property be protected (BA 1988, s 87). An order for protection enables the debtor to continue to trade but he must not dispose of his property save in the ordinary course of trade (BA 1988, s 88).

The arranging debtor is required to file a *statement of affairs* containing his proposal for the future payment or *compromise* of his debts (BA 1988, s 91), which, if approved by three-fifths in number and value of the creditors voting at a private sitting of the court, and if approved by the court, will be binding on all persons who were creditors at the date of the petition and who had notice of the sitting (BA 1988, s 92). A creditor whose debt is less than £100 (€127) is not entitled to vote (BA 1988, s 92(2)).

The arranging debtor's proposal may provide for vesting of his property in the Official Assignee (qv) either as security of the offer or for the purpose of having the property realised and distributed by the Official Assignee (BA 1988, s 93). There is also provision for granting a *certificate* to an arranging debtor which will operate as a discharge to him from the claims of creditors who received notice of the arrangement (BA 1988, s 98). The court may, if it thinks fit, *adjudicate* an arranging debtor as bankrupt (BA 1988, ss 105–106). The court may refuse to grant protection to a debtor who is a member of a partnership, unless all the partners join in a petition (BA 1988, s 87(3) and *Re Love* [1889]

23 LR Ir 365). For procedure re an order for protection, see SI No 79 of 1989, Pt XXIII. See RECEIVER OF BANKRUPT'S PROPERTY.

arrears. Money not paid at the due date. A taxpayer may pay arrears of income tax, corporation tax, capital gains tax or capital acquisitions tax by making a gift of a *heritage item* for no consideration to an *approved body* eg the National Gallery: Taxes Consolidation Act 1997, s 1003 as amended by Finance Act 2004, s 85. See Revenue Leaflet HET1 'Relief for donation of heritage items'.

arrest. To deprive a person of his liberty by some lawful authority in order to compel his appearance to answer a criminal charge or as a method of execution. To constitute a valid arrest, the person must be told that he is being arrested; the physical act of taking a person into custody is insufficient, it must be accompanied by a form of words: *DPP v McCormack* [2000] 1 ILRM 241, HC and [1999] 4 IR 158, HC.

No person may be arrested (with or without a warrant) save for the purpose of bringing that person before a court at the earliest reasonable opportunity; arrest is simply a process of ensuring the attendance at court of the person so arrested: Walsh J in *The People v Shaw* [1982] IR 1. A person who is arrested pursuant to a warrant, or arrested without a warrant and charged with an offence, must be brought before a judge of the District Court as soon as practicable: Criminal Justice Act 1951, s 15 as amended by Criminal Justice (Miscellaneous Provisions) Act 1997, s 18. See DCR 1997 Ord 17 rr 2–3.

An arresting garda is entitled to use such force as is necessary to ensure that the arrest is maintained: *Dowman v Ireland* [1986] ILRM 111. It is lawful for a person to be arrested immediately at the cessation of an arrest under s 30 of the Offences Against the State Act 1939: *Finucane v McMahon* [1989] 7 ILT Dig 322. A garda may arrest a person on foot of a warrant or order of committal, even if the warrant or order is not in the garda's possession at the time; but the warrant must be shown to the arrested person as soon as practicable: Criminal Law Act 1997, s 5. See also *Madigan v Devally & DPP* [1999] 2 ILRM 141, SC.

A lawful arrest can follow an unlawful arrest and consequently, where a second set of extradition proceedings is launched, defects in the arrest warrants in the first set of proceedings having been corrected, there is no *estoppel* which prevents the re-initiation of the failed extradition proceedings: *Bolger v O'Toole* [2000] ITLR (3 July), HC.

The arrest without warrant provision of the Dublin Police Act 1842 is not unconditional; it is a reasonable inference that the difference in treatment between arrest in and outside Dublin related to the incidence of crime in Dublin, the difficulty in apprehending suspects in the area, and the need to do so speedily: *Molyneux v Ireland* [1997] 2 ILRM 241, HC. See *DPP v Forbes* [1995] 2 IR 542, SC; *The People (DPP) v O'Shea* [1996] 1 IR 556, CCA. See Treatment of Persons in Custody in Garda Síochána Stations Regulations 1987, SI No 119 of 1987, reg 7. [Bibliography: Walsh D (3).] See ARREST WITHOUT WARRANT; CIVIL ARREST; DETENTION OF SHIP; ESCAPE; EXTRADITION WARRANT; PRISONER, ARREST OF; PROVISIONAL ARREST.

arrest, resisting. It was an offence to resist a *lawful* arrest: Offences Against the Person Act 1861, s 38. This section has been repealed and replaced by an offence of resisting or wilfully obstructing a *peace officer* acting in the execution of his duty, which would include effecting a lawful arrest: Criminal Justice (Public Order) Act 1994, s 19(3). A *peace officer* means a garda, a prison officer or a member of the Defence Forces.

An *unlawful* arrest can be resisted but only with force which is reasonable; the use of lethal force will normally constitute manslaughter (qv): *The People v White* [1947] IR 247.

arrest of judgment. An accused at any time after conviction and before sentence may move the court to *arrest judgment* (eg for want of sufficient certainty in the indictment which has not been amended), which, if granted, has the effect of an acquittal (qv) but it does not bar a fresh indictment (qv).

arrest without warrant. There are wide powers given to various persons by statute to arrest another without a warrant, eg an officer of excise is entitled to arrest a person found in a place where illegal distillation is in progress: Illicit Distillation (Ireland) Act 1831, s 19; a pawnbroker is entitled to arrest a person offering to him stolen or lost property: Pawnbrokers Act 1964, s 35; an aircraft commander can arrest a person where he has reason to believe that the person has committed a serious offence aboard an aircraft: Air Navigation and Transport Act 1973, s 7; any person is entitled to arrest another on reasonable suspicion of a contravention of official secrets: Official Secrets Act 1963, s 15; a garda has wide powers of arrest eg when he is of the opinion that the person has committed the offence of dangerous driving and has caused death or serious bodily harm: Road Traffic Act 1961, s 53(6); also where he has reasonable grounds for believing that a person is committing or has committed certain specified offences: Transport Act 1987, s 11; Criminal Justice (Public Order) Act 1994, s 24; Domestic Violence Act 1996, s 18; Criminal Assets Bureau Act 1996, s 16; Criminal Justice (Public Order) Act 1994, s 19F inserted by Housing (Miscellaneous Provisions) Act 2002, s 24; Immigration Act 2004, s 13(2); Maritime Security Act 2004, s 4.

A garda in making an arrest does not have to use technical or precise language; provided the arrested person knows in substance why he is being arrested, the arrest is valid: *DPP (Cloughley) v Mooney* [1993] ILRM 214, HC. See also Criminal Damage Act 1991, s 12; Criminal Justice (Sexual Offences) Act 1993, s 13; Road Transport Act 1999, s 13; Criminal Justice (Theft and Fraud) Offences Act 2001, s 8(3)–(6); Road Traffic Act 1994, s 12(4) as substituted by Road Traffic Act 2003, s 2. For extensive list see Bibliography: Ryan & Magee. See INCAPABLE; UNLAWFUL ARREST.

arrestable offence. An offence for which a person may, under any enactment, be punished by imprisonment for a term of five years or by a more severe penalty; it includes an attempt to commit such an offence: Criminal Law Act 1997, s 2(1). Any person may *arrest without a warrant*, anyone who he, with reasonable cause, suspects: (a) to have committed an *arrestable* offence which has actually been committed: or (b) to be in the act of committing an *arrestable* offence (CLA 1997, s 4(1)–(2)). In the case of a garda arresting without a warrant, it is not necessary that the offence has been actually committed (CLA 1997, s 4(3)). These provisions were enacted to protect, in effect, the 'arrest without warrant' powers, which previously existed in relation to *felonies*; the 1997 Act abolished any distinctions between felonies and misdemeanours and applied the law and practice as regards misdemeanours to all offences. See Criminal Justice Bill 2004, s 7. See ACCESSORY; CONCEALING AN OFFENCE; ENTRY AND SEARCH.

arrested person, communications from. An arrested person is entitled to have reasonable access to a solicitor of his choice and to be enabled to communicate with him privately: Treatment of Persons in Custody in Garda Síochána Stations Regulations 1987, SI No 119 of 1987, reg 11(1). Where an arrested person has not had access to a solicitor in accordance with para (1) and a solicitor whose presence has not been requested by the arrested person presents himself at the station and informs the member in charge that he wishes to visit that person, the person must be asked if he wishes to consult the solicitor and, if he does so wish, he should be accommodated.

A consultation with a solicitor may take place in the sight, but out of hearing, of a garda (SI No 119 of 1987, reg 11(3)).

An arrested person may make a telephone call of reasonable duration free of charge to a person reasonably named by him or send a letter (for which purpose writing materials and, where necessary, postage stamps shall be supplied on request) provided that the member in charge is satisfied that it will not hinder or delay the investigation of crime (SI No 119 of 1987, reg 11(5)(a)). A garda may listen to any such telephone call and may terminate it if he is not so satisfied and may read any such letter and decline to send it if he is not so satisfied.

arrested person, information to. The member in charge of a garda station is required without delay to inform an arrested person, or cause him to be informed: (a) in ordinary language of the offence or other matter in respect of which he has been arrested; (b) that he is entitled to consult a solicitor; and (c) (i) in the case of a person not below the age of seventeen years, that he is entitled to have notification of his being in custody in the station concerned sent to another person reasonably named by him; or (ii) in the case of a person under the age of seventeen years, that a parent or guardian (or, if he is married, his spouse) is being given the information required and is being requested to attend at the station without delay: Treatment of Persons in Custody in Garda Síochána Stations Regulations 1987, SI No 119 of 1987, reg 8.

The information is to be given orally. The member in charge is required to explain or cause to be explained to the arrested person that, if he does not wish to exercise a right specified in subparagraph (b) or (c)(i) immediately, he will not be precluded thereby from doing so later. The member in charge is required to ask the arrested person, or cause him to be asked, to sign the custody record in acknowledgement of receipt of the notice. If he refuses to sign, the refusal shall be recorded (SI No 119 of 1987, reg.8(4)).

arrested person, visits to. An arrested person may receive a visit from a relative, friend or other person with an interest in his welfare provided that he so wishes and the member in charge is satisfied that the visit can be adequately supervised and that it will not hinder or delay the investigation of crime: Treatment of Persons in Custody in Garda Síochána Stations Regulations 1987, SI No 119 of 1987, reg.11(4).

arsehole. Means, when used to describe a person in an employment law context, 'a person obdurately marked by stubbornness or stolidity who tries to frustrate another': *Browne v Ventelo Telecommunications Ireland Ltd* [2001] UD 597/2001 (16 July 2002), EAT. See VULGAR ABUSE.

arson. The offence of *damaging property by fire* which must be charged as *arson*; the common law offence of arson has been abolished: Criminal Damage Act 1991, ss 2(4) and 14(1). Arson is now the offence of damaging by fire, without lawful excuse, any property belonging to another, intending to damage it or being *reckless* as to whether it would be damaged (CDA 1991, s 2(1)).

It also includes damage by fire to property, whether belonging to the accused or another, where there is an intention by the damage to endanger the life of another or being *reckless* as to whether the life of another would be thereby endangered (CDA 1991, s 2(2)). It also includes damage by fire of any property with intent to defraud (CDA 1991, s 2(3)). A person is *reckless* if he has foreseen the particular kind of damage that in fact was done might be done and yet has gone on to take the risk of it (CDA 1991, s 2(6)). See *Attorney-General v Kyle* [1933] IR 15. See CRIMINAL DAMAGE TO PROPERTY.

arterial drainage. The Commissioners of Public Works are empowered to execute *arterial drainage works* in any *river* catchment area where such work will prevent or reduce the prospect of flooding of lands: Arterial Drainage Act 1945. The powers of the Commissioners have been extended: (a) to any catchment area, not just rivers, so as to prevent or limit periodical flooding, or to improve the land by drainage; or (b) to any watercourse or part of a watercourse, for similar purposes: Arterial Drainage (Amendment) Act 1995, s 3.

articles. Clauses in a document e g articles in the 1937 Constitution of Ireland.

articles of association. See ASSOCIATION, ARTICLES OF.

artificial feeding. See DIE, RIGHT TO; HUNGER STRIKE.

artificial insemination. Introduction of semen into the uterus by other than natural means; a child is legitimate when born to a married couple as a result of artificial insemination whereby the husband's semen is used. The position is unclear if the husband's semen is used in his widow after his death e g from a sperm bank. A child is illegitimate (now – *a child whose parents are not married to each other*: Status of Children Act 1987) when born as a result of insemination by a third-party donor or born to a surrogate mother. See Law Reform Commission, *Report on Illegitimacy 1982* (LRC 4, 1982).

The Medical Council guidelines on *artificial insemination by donor* (*AID*) are: 'There is no objection to the preservation of sperm or ova to be used subsequently on behalf of those from whom they were originally taken. Doctors who consider assisting with donation to a third party must have regard to the biological difficulties involved, and pay meticulous attention to the source of the donated material. Doctors who fail to advise both donor and recipient about the potential implications of such measures and the possible consequences for the would-be parents and their baby could face disciplinary proceedings': *A Guide to Ethical Conduct and Behaviour* (6th edn, 2004) para 24.4.

As regards the control and practice of artificial insemination of cattle, sheep, goats, swine and horses, see Live Stock (Artificial Insemination) Act 1947. See *O'Neill v Minister for Agriculture* [1998] 1 IR 539, SC. [Bibliography: Shatter.] See ADOPTION; EMBRYO IMPLANTATION; HUMAN REPRODUCTION; SURROGATE MOTHER.

artificial person. A body which is invested by law with a personality having rights and duties e g a corporation (qv) or company (qv).

artist, tax exemption of. The exemption which may be claimed by a writer, dramatist, musical composer, painter, or sculptor, from income tax which would otherwise be payable on profits, arising from the publication, production or sale of *original* and *creative* works falling under the following headings: (a) a book or other writing; (b) a play; (c) a musical composition; (d) a painting or other like picture; or (e) a sculpture: Finance Act 1969, s 2, now Taxes Consolidation Act 1997, s 195. The exemption may be claimed only by an individual resident in the State, who is not resident in any other country as well, and only in respect of profits from works which have cultural or artistic merit.

It has been held that to qualify for the artist's tax exemption, a work must: (a) be an original and creative work; and (b) be determined by the Revenue Commissioners to be a work which actually has, in their opinion, cultural or artistic merit, or alternatively, to be a work generally recognised as having cultural or artistic merit: *Healy v Inspector of Taxes* [1986] IR 105. A work must comply with the Art Council's guidelines on what works are original and creative. A book published primarily for students or professionals or others as an aid to practice in a trade, profession, vocation or branch of learning, is not regarded as original and creative, overturning the decisions in *Revenue Commissioners v O'Loinsigh* [1994] ITR 199, [1995] 1 IR 509, HC, and *Forde v Revenue Commissioners* 4 ITR 348. There is a right of appeal to the Appeal Commissioners.

There is also an exemption from capital gains tax in respect of the disposal of certain items which have been loaned for public display for at least six years before their disposal; items qualifying are: a work of art, picture, print, book, manuscript, sculpture, or jewellery, with a market value of not less than £25,000 (€31,743) at the date of loan: Finance Act 1991, s 43, now Taxes Consolidation Act 1997, s 606.

artistic work. Includes *work* of any of the following descriptions: (a) photographs, paintings, drawings, diagrams, maps, charts, plans, engravings, etchings, lithographs, woodcuts, prints or similar works, collages or sculptures; (b) works of architecture, being either buildings or models for buildings, and (c) works of artistic craftsmanship: Copyright and Related Rights Act 2000, s 2(1). Included are any cast or model made for the purpose of a sculpture. Copyright subsists in an *original* artistic work (CRRA 2000, s 17(2)). The copyright expires 70 years after the death of the author irrespective of the date on which the work is first lawfully made available to the public (CRRA 2000, s 24(1)). For the provisions dealing with the effect of exploitation of a *design* derived from an *artistic work*, see Industrial Designs Act 2001, s 89, inserting new s 78B in the Copyright and Related Rights Act 2000. See COPYRIGHT; COPYRIGHT, QUALIFICATION FOR; PROCESSING; PROTECTED STRUCTURE.

arts. Means any creative or interpretative expression (whether traditional or contemporary) in whatever form and includes, in particular, visual arts, theatre, literature, music, dance, opera, film, circus and architecture, and includes any medium when used for those purposes: Arts Act 2003, s 2. The Minister is required to promote the arts both inside and outside the State (AA 2003, s 5). The Arts Council is a body corporate with perpetual succession, with general functions under the Act eg to stimulate public interest in the arts; to promote knowledge, appreciation and practice of the arts; to assist in improving standards in the arts; and to advise the Minister on artistic matters (AA 2003, ss 8–9). It may fund the arts out of moneys at its disposal and is independent in this respect (AA 2003, s 24). In other aspects of its functions it is required to comply with any written direction from the Minister (AA 2003, s 5(3)).

A local authority is required to prepare and implement plans for the development of the arts in its functional area and may provide financial and other assistance (AA 2003, s 6). The 2003 Act repeals the Arts Acts 1951 and 1973. See website: *www.artscouncil.ie.*

as soon as may be. The phrase '*as soon as may be*' should be construed as meaning as soon as may be reasonably practicable in all the circumstances: *McCarthy v Garda Síochána Complaints Tribunal* [2002] 2 ILRM 341, SC.

as soon as practicable. The phrase is not synonymous with '*as soon as possible*'. In construing the phrase, regard has to be paid to the context in which the words are used and all the surrounding circumstances and, in particular, the nature and purpose of the statutory obligation: *McC & McD v Eastern Health Board* [1997] 1 ILRM 349, SC; [1996] 2 IR 296, SC and Child Care Act 1991, s 8(1). In this case the Supreme Court held that the Eastern Health Board had not been carrying out assessments of potential adoptive parents '*as soon as practicable*'. See IMMEDIATELY.

asbestos. For amendments to the plan which must be prepared prior to any demolition work involving asbestos, see European Communities (Protection of Workers) (Exposure to Asbestos) Regulations 2000, SI No 74 of 2000.

In a case involving the exposure of a worker to significant quantities of asbestos dust while working in the basement of Leinster House in the 1980s, the Supreme Court has held that the law should not be extended by the courts to allow plaintiffs recover damages for psychiatric injury resulting from an irrational fear of contracting a disease, where the health risk is characterised by their medical advisers as very remote: *Fletcher v Commissioners of Public Works* [2003] SC, reported in *Law Society Gazette* (April 2003) 42 and [2003] 2 ILRM 94, SC; 1 IR 465; ELR 117. In this case the psychiatric illness was not accompanied by any physical injury.

However, the Supreme Court did allow an award of £45,000 (€57,138) for general damages to a plumber who was exposed to asbestos dust while working in Leinster House and who was suffering at the time of the trial from 'chronic reactive anxiety neurosis': *Swaine v Commissioners of Public Works* [2003] 2 ILRM 252, SC and 1 IR 521 and *Law Society Gazette* (June 2003) 43. In this case the defendants had withdrawn any plea denying liability to pay damages. However, the Supreme Court set aside an award of £15,000 for aggravated damages as the tests in *Conway v Irish National Teachers Organisation* [1991] 2 IR 305 had not been met. See also *Rafter v Attorney General* [2004] HC, reported in *Law Society Gazette* (June 2004) 47. See *Packenham v Irish Ferries Ltd* [2004] FL 8961, HC. See 'Damages for Exposure to Asbestos' by Anthony Moore BL in *Bar Review* (April 2003) 78.

ascertained goods. See UNASCERTAINED GOODS.

asportation. The *carrying away* with intention to steal, which is an essential element in the offence of larceny (qv).

assault. Formerly, the common law offence which consisted of an unlawful attempt to do with violence a corporal wrong to another person; a *battery* was such a wrong actually done in an angry, revengeful, rude or insolent manner. The offences of '*assault and battery*' and of '*assault occasioning actual bodily harm*' have been abolished: Non-Fatal Offences against the Person Act 1997, s 28(1)(a)–(b). See *Grealis v DPP* [2002] 1 ILRM 241, SC.

The statutory offences of *assault* are now: (a) assault under s 2 of the 1997 Act; (b) assault causing harm under s 3 of the 1997 Act; (c) assault under s 18 of the Criminal Justice (Public Order) Act 1994 with intent to cause bodily harm or to commit an indictable offence. In addition under NFOPA 1997 there are also new offences of: causing serious harm; threatening to kill or cause serious harm; injuring or threatening a person with a syringe; endangerment; false imprisonment; abduction of a child; coercion; and harassment (qqv).

The Director of Public Prosecutions is entitled to choose from the hierarchy of assault type charges, based on the evidence to establish such an offence: *DPP v Brennan* [1998] 2 ILRM 129, SC.

A person is guilty of assault of another person if he, without lawful excuse, intentionally or recklessly, and without the consent of that other person: (a) directly or indirectly applies *force* to or causes an impact on the body of that other person; or (b) causes that other person to believe on reasonable grounds that he is likely immediately to be subjected to such *force* or impact (NFOPA 1997, s 2(1)). *Force* in this context includes the application of various forms of energy eg heat, light, electric current, noise, liquid or gas (NFOPA 1997, s 2(2)). It is also an offence to assault or attempt to assault an officer or staff member (or a member of their family) of the Criminal Assets Bureau: Criminal Assets Bureau Act 1996, s 15.

A person is entitled to use force to protect himself from assault (NFOPA 1997, ss 18 and 20).

Dismissal of an employee for assaulting a fellow employee will generally be regarded as a *fair dismissal* but mitigating factors will usually be taken into account: *Treacy v Kilkenny Textile Mill BV* [1994] ELR 12, EAT. See *Mullins v Hartnett* [1998] 2 ILRM 304, HC. See also CAUSING SERIOUS HARM; PEACE OFFICER; ROBBERY; SEXUAL ASSAULT; TRESPASS TO THE PERSON.

assault causing harm. It is an offence for a person to assault another person causing him *harm*: Non-Fatal Offences against the Person Act 1997, s 3. *Harm* means harm to the body or mind and includes pain and unconsciousness (NFOPA 1997, s 1(1)).

assault, indecent. Any indecent touching of a female by a male or by another female, without her consent, is an offence and is punishable: Criminal Law (Rape) Act 1981, s 10. An indecent assault on a male person either by another male or by a female is an offence: CL(R)A 1981, s 10 and Offences Against the Person Act 1861, s 62. On a count for indecent assault, a person may be convicted of common assault: *R v Bostock* [1893] 17 Cox's CC 700. The offence of indecent assault upon a male or female person is now known as *sexual assault* and is an offence (formerly, a felony): Criminal Law (Rape) (Amendment) Act 1990, s 2. See *Doolan v DPP* [1993] ILRM 387, HC.

It has been held by the Supreme Court that the offence of *indecent assault* has not been abolished by s 28 of the Non-Fatal Against the Person Act 1997; also the effect of CL(R)(A)A 1990 was simply to change the name of the offence while leaving its nature and constituents unaltered: *O'C v Governor of Curragh Prison* [2002] 1 IR 66, SC. See SEXUAL ASSAULT.

assault in tort. See TRESPASS TO THE PERSON.

assault with intent to rob. See ROBBERY.

assay. The testing of the quality of an article. See HALLMARKING.

assay office. The office controlled by the Company of Goldsmiths of Dublin. See GOLDSMITHS OF DUBLIN; HALLMARKING.

Assembly, European. See EUROPEAN PARLIAMENT.

assembly, freedom of. The State guarantees, subject to public order and morality, liberty for the exercise of the right of citizens to assemble peaceably and without arms: 1937 Constitution, art 40(6)(1)(ii). Provision may be made by law, however, to prevent or control meetings calculated to cause a breach of the peace or to be a danger or nuisance to the general public and to prevent or control meetings in the vicinity of either Houses of the Oireachtas (qv). It is an offence to hold a meeting or procession in any public place within one-half mile of the Oireachtas in certain specified circumstances: Offences Against the State Act 1939, s 28. See CROWD CONTROL; EUROPEAN CONVENTION ON HUMAN RIGHTS; NUISANCE, PUBLIC.

assembly, riotous. See RIOTOUS ASSEMBLY.

assembly, unlawful. See UNLAWFUL ASSEMBLY.

assembly centre. Means a holding, collection centre or market at which animals from different holdings are grouped together to form consignments of animals intended for trade: European Communities (Assembly Centres) Regulations 2000, SI No 257 of 2000, as amended by Regulations 2004, SI No 200 of 2004. These regulations implement EC Directive 97/12/EC, as amended by EC Directive 98/99/EC, in so far as they concern assembly centres for animals being sent to EU countries.

assent. Agreement. The instrument or act whereby a personal representative effectuates a testamentary disposition by transferring the subject matter of the disposition to the person entitled to it. An assent to unregistered land must be in writing and to registered land must comply with s 61 of the Registration of Title Act 1964. See Succession Act 1965, ss 53–54.

assessment. The act of determining, apportioning or valuing e g assessment of damages, assessment of tax. See TAX ASSESSMENT. For assessment of *special educational needs*, see EDUCATION PLAN.

assessment, personal injuries. The mandatory assessment of the amount of damages the claimant is entitled to, in respect of a claim for personal injuries, on the assumption that the respondent is fully liable to the claimant: Personal Injuries Assessment Board Act 2003, s 20. The assessment is made by one or more 'assessors' employed by the Board, who may be assisted by 'retained experts', and is made on the same basis as an award of the courts, calculated by reference to the principles which govern the measure of damages in the law of tort and any relevant statutory provision. There is not an oral hearing; the assessment is made by reference to the information and documents provided and must be for a once-off lump sum (PIABA

2003, s 21). In addition to this sum, the Board may, in its discretion, direct that certain expenses of the claimant be paid (PIABA 2003, ss 44–45). Assessments must be made expeditiously (PIABA 2003, s 49).

There are provisions to assist the assessor to get to the true facts of the claim e g power to require additional information from the claimant and the respondent (PIABA 2003, s 23), medical examination of the claimant in certain circumstances (PIABA 2003, s 24), powers to request information from third parties (e g to verify an alleged loss) and enforcement of this power by the District Court (PIABA 2003, ss 26–27), limited power to require certain information from the Revenue Commissioners (PIABA 2003, s 28).

The assessment is served in writing on the claimant and on the respondent, who are required, within a specified timeframe, to indicate in writing if they accept it (PIABA 2003, s 30). If both parties accept the assessment, it is binding on them both (PIABA 2003, s 33). If the respondent fails to respond within the specified period, he is deemed to have accepted the assessment (s 31). The Board then issues an 'order to pay' on the respondent (s 38). This order to pay has the same legal effect as if it were a judgment of the court and is enforceable as such (s 40). Payment to the claimant on foot of the 'order to pay' operates as satisfaction of the claimant's claim (s 41).

If the assessment is not accepted by either of the parties, then the claimant will be authorised to take court proceedings (PIABA 2003, s 32). The respondent's agreement to have the assessment made in the first place does not constitute an admission of liability and must not be used to prejudice legal argument in court proceedings (PIABA 2003, s 16). Certain statements made in the course of the assessment procedure must not be used in evidence in the court proceedings; also the assessment is generally not admissible in evidence (PIABA 2003, ss 37 and 51). If the claimant does not have full legal capacity, any acceptance of an assessment is subject to the approval of the court (s 35). If that approval is not forthcoming, the claimant will be authorised to take court proceedings in respect of the claim (s 36). See FATAL INJURIES; LIMITATION OF ACTIONS; PERSONAL INJURIES ASSESSMENT BOARD.

assessor. (1) A person who investigates and assesses the amount of loss on behalf of an insurer.

(2) A person who assists the court in relation to scientific or technical matters. Trials with assessors take place in such manner and upon such terms as the court directs: RSC Ord 36, r 41. In any admiralty (qv) action, the judge may appoint assessors either at the insistence of any party or where he deems it requisite for the due administration of justice: RSC Ord 64, r 39. The court may call in the aid of an assessor to assist it in any action for infringement or revocation of a patent: Patents Act 1992, s 95; *Farbwerke Hoechst A-G v Intercontinental Pharmaceuticals (Eire)* [1968] FSR 187. See also *Martin v Irish Industrial Benefit Society* [1960] Ir Jur Rep 42.

There is provision for the President of the High Court to act as *judicial assessor* to the presidential returning officer in relation to ruling on the validity of a nomination as a candidate for a presidential election; the returning officer must have regard to the opinion of the assessor: Presidential Elections Act 1993, s 23. The Controller of Patents is empowered to appoint an assessor to assist him, at the request of all the parties to proceedings before him in relation to copyright and related rights: Copyright and Related Rights Act 2000, s 365. See MARINE CASUALTY; TRIBUNALS OF INQUIRY.

asset. As regards capital gains tax, means all forms of property, including options, debts and incorporeal property generally, foreign currency, and any form of property created by the person disposing of it, or otherwise becoming owned without being acquired: Taxes Consolidation Act 1997, s 532. See WASTING ASSET.

asset covered securities. Means *mortgaged covered securities* and *public credit covered securities* issued by designated credit institutions: Asset Covered Securities Act 2001, s 3 as amended by Central Bank and Financial Services Authority of Ireland Act 2003, s 35, Sch 1. The main aim of the 2001 Act is to facilitate the establishment and operation of a market in asset covered securities by Irish mortgage and public sector lenders, thereby enabling Irish lenders to finance their activities as efficiently as their European counterparts and to further develop the Irish capital markets and the IFSC.

The types of securities provided for by the Act are similar to German *Pfandbriefe*. These mortgage covered securities and public credit covered securities are secured on a pool of underlying assets (known as *cover assets*) held by the same financial institution. These cover assets are primarily mortgages or public sector loans respectively. Unlike the case in conventional *securitisation*, the assets remain the property of the institution issuing the securities and on that institution's balance sheet.

Public credit covered securities are, at all times, secured by a pool of assets of at least equal nominal value and yielding at least equal interest. *Mortgage covered securities* are similarly secured, but based on a very conservative valuation of the assets concerned. These asset pools are dynamic ie assets which disimprove in quality may be replaced by new assets. The key feature of the product is the enhanced security offered to the holders of the securities. In the event of the insolvency of the issuing institution, the assets in the pools must be used first to meet the claims of the holders of the securities. Ordinary creditors of the institution may not make a claim against these assets until the full obligation due to the investors in the securities has been discharged.

The enhanced security afforded by the legislatively guaranteed priority of claim in the event of issuer insolvency, the specification of strict matching of assets and liabilities and the regulatory environment for the product have made German *Pfandbriefe* an extremely popular investment. They are the largest single bond type in Europe. In recent years other European countries, including France, Spain and Luxembourg, have introduced enabling legislation to facilitate the issuance of similar securities. (Source*: Explanatory Memorandum to the Asset Covered Securities Bill 2001*).

The Central Bank has regulatory and supervisory powers under the 2001 Act (ACSA 2001, ss 9–11). The designated credit institutions are required to appoint *cover assets monitors* with responsibility for ensuring that the *cover assets pool* are sufficient to provide adequate security for any issued asset covered security (ACSA 2001, ss 59–70). Building societies are entitled to apply to issue securities under the Act to enhance their powers to fund through the issue of securities generally, while not affecting the rights of members: Building Societies Act 1989 as amended by ACSA

2001, Sch 2, Part 1. For regulations, see SIs No 382, 383, 384, 385, 386, 387 and 635 of 2002, and SIs 415, 416, 417, 418, 419, 420 and 421 of 2004. See 'Asset backed securities: Securitisation of the Irish mortgage and public credit markets' by Aillil O'Reilly BL in *Bar Review* (October/November 2002) 343. See SECURITISATION OF MORTGAGE.

asset stripping. See DEPRECIATORY TRANSACTION.

asset valuation. Fixed assets in a company must be valued at cost (or their valuation in the company's books) less the aggregate sum provided for or written off in respect of their depreciation: Companies Act 1963, Sch 6, reg 5; also see Companies Amendment Act 1983, s 45. This rule does not apply *inter alia* to goodwill, patents, trademarks, investments whose values are shown, and assets the replacement of which is provided for in a specified manner.

A company may treat as a realised profit any difference between the sum set aside for depreciation of a fixed asset which has been revalued and the amount of the unrealised profit thereby discovered: Companies Amendment Act 1983, s 45(6).

Where development costs are shown as an asset in the accounts, they must be properly written off: Companies Amendment Act 1986, s 20; they must be regarded as realised losses for the purposes of s 45 and s 47 of CAA 1983. See also CAA 1986, s 3(1). See SURPLUS ASSETS; VALUATION REPORT.

assets. Property available for the payment of debts. *Real* assets are real property and *personal* assets are personal property. Property is also classified as *legal* assets and *equitable* assets. The estate of a deceased person, both legal and equitable, together with estate disposed by will in pursuance of a general power, are assets for payment of debts, liabilities and any legal right (qv). See Succession Act 1965, s 45. See SURPLUS ASSETS.

assets, marshalling of. See MARSHALLING.

assign. To transfer property; an assignee (qv).

assignatus utitur jure auctoris. [An assignee is clothed with the right of his principal.]

assignee. The person to whom an assignment is made. See OFFICIAL ASSIGNEE.

assignment of contract. Generally liabilities under a contract cannot be assigned without the consent of the other party to the contract. Liabilities can be assigned by *novation* (qv). Some contractual rights in a contract cannot be assigned e g those involving contracts of service (qv) and some others must meet statutory requirements e g transfer of shares in a company.

Other rights may be assigned in a number of ways: (a) by operation of law e g death passes the rights and liabilities of the deceased to his personal representatives (qv); bankruptcy passes all rights and liabilities to the Official Assignee in bankruptcy; (b) under equity, but the assignee takes *subject to equities* and (c) under the Judicature Act 1877 which carries the advantage that the assignee can sue in his own name; the assignment must be absolute, in writing with notice also in writing to the debtor and the assignee still takes *subject to equities*.

The assignment of insurance contracts is generally limited to those of life insurance, which is effected either by an endorsement on the policy itself or by a separate document, and gives to the assignee the right to sue thereon in his own name. See also Marine Insurance Act 1906, ss 15 and 50.

assignment of lease. The transfer of the total interest of the lessee under a lease (qv) to a new lessee. The *assignee* or new lessee takes subject to all the rights and liabilities of the former lessee. See Deasy's Act 1860, ss 9, 12,13; Landlord and Tenant (Amendment) Act 1980, s 66. See Residential Tenancies Act 2004, s 193(d).

A lease often has a requirement that the consent of the landlord be obtained to an assignment, such consent not to be unreasonably withheld. In a particular case, it was held that a landlord was unreasonably withholding consent by requiring a guarantor of the lease to be jointly and severally liable for the performance of the covenants and conditions in the lease: *Gunne Estate Agents v Pembroke Estate Management Ltd* [2000] CC ITLR (12 June). See *Consultation Paper on General Law of Landlord and Tenant Law* (LRC CP 28, 2003) para 18.24 and 18.25. See PART 4 TENANCY, ASSIGNMENT OF; SUB-LETTING; TENANCY, FIXED TERM; TENANT, OBLIGATIONS OF.

assignment of trade mark. See TRADE MARK, ASSIGNMENT OF.

assignor. A person who assigns or transfers property to another.

assisa cadera. [A non-suit.]

assisting offenders. See ACCESSORY.

assize. [A sitting or session.] Formerly, there were courts of assize. See GRAND JURY.

associated trade mark. Formerly, a trade mark which was identical with another trade mark in the name of the same proprietor in respect of the same goods or description of goods, or so nearly resembled it as to be likely to deceive or cause confusion if used by a person other than the proprietor: Trade Marks Act 1963, s 31(2). Such trade marks could have been required by the Controller of Trade Marks at any time to be entered on the register as *associated* trade marks and this operated to prevent such marks from being assigned or transferred except as a whole (TMA 1963, s 31(1)). See *The Steel Nut and Joseph Hampton Ltd* [1964] Supp OJ No 956 p.23.

The concept of associated trade marks has been abolished; assignment of a registered trade mark may now be a partial assignment ie limited to some but not all of the goods or services or in relation to the use of the mark in a particular manner or locality: Trade Marks Act 1996, s 28(2).

association, articles of. The regulations by which a company is to be governed and managed. The articles must be printed, divided into paragraphs numbered sequentially, be stamped in the same way as a deed and be signed by each subscriber to the *memorandum of association* and attested: Companies Act 1963, ss 11–15. This Act contains a model set of articles in Table A, which apply to any company limited by shares unless excluded or modified in duly registered articles (CA 1963, s 13). A model set of articles for companies limited by guarantee and not having a share capital is contained in Table C, which applies to such a company registered after 1982 unless excluded or modified in duly registered articles: Companies Amendment Act 1982, s 14.

A company may by special resolution alter or add to its articles of association: Companies Act 1963, s 15 and Companies (Amendment) Act 1983, s 20(3). A circular to shareholders of a *listed* company with proposed amendments to its memorandum and articles of association must meet certain requirements eg inclusion of an explanation of the effect of the proposed amendments: Listing Rules 2000, paras 13.9 and 14.1. See also Building Societies Act 1989, s 102(2). See ASSOCIATION, MEMORANDUM OF.

association, freedom of. The State guarantees, subject to public order and morality, liberty for the exercise of the right of citizens to form associations and unions: 1937 Constitution, art 40(6)(1)(iii). The Garda Síochána may have to accept limitations in their right to form associations and unions which other citizens would not have to accept: *Aughey v Ireland* [1986] ILRM 207. See *Smartt* in (1993) 3 ISLR 116. See DEFENCE FORCES; EUROPEAN CONVENTION ON HUMAN RIGHTS; TRADE UNION.

association, memorandum of. A document which regulates a company's external activities and which must be drawn up on the formation of a company. Any seven or more persons associated for any lawful purpose may by subscribing their names to a memorandum of association and otherwise complying with the statutory requirements as to registration, form an incorporated company, with or without *limited liability;* two or more persons are only required where the company to be formed is to be a *private* company: Companies Act 1963, s 5(1). The memorandum must be printed, stamped as a deed, signed by each subscriber, witnessed and attested (CA 1963, s 7). It must state the company's name and the objects of the company (CA 1963, s 6 as amended by Companies (Amendment) Act 1983, Sch 1, para 2). The memorandum of a company limited by shares or by guarantee must state that the liability of its members is limited.

Where the company is *limited by guarantee,* the memorandum must state that each member undertakes to contribute to the assets of the company in the event of its being wound up (CA 1963, s 6(3)). If the company has a share capital, the memorandum must state its amount and each subscriber must write opposite to his name the number of shares he takes (CA 1963, s 6(4)).

The memorandum cannot be varied by the company itself except in specified circumstances (CA 1963, s 9). A circular to shareholders of a *listed* company with proposed amendments to its memorandum and articles of association must meet certain requirements eg inclusion of an explanation of the effect of the proposed amendments: Listing Rules 2000, paras 13.9 and 14.1.

The memorandum of association of a company, which is required to be delivered to the Registrar of Companies, must be accompanied by a statement in a prescribed form containing specified particulars e g the persons who are to be the first directors and secretary of the company and the situation of the company's registered office: Companies Amendment Act 1982, s 3 as amended by C(A)A 1983, Sch 2. If any of the persons named in the statement is disqualified under the law of another state, certain details must be supplied e g jurisdiction, date and period of disqualification: C(A)A 1983, s 3A inserted by Company Law Enforcement Act 2001, s 101. See ASSOCIATION, ARTICLES OF; NAME OF COMPANY; BUSINESS NAME; ULTRA VIRES.

association clause. The clause in a memorandum of association of a company in which the subscribers state that they desire to be formed into a company and agree to take the number of shares set opposite their names. See ASSOCIATION, MEMORANDUM OF.

assumed name. See FICTITIOUS NAME.

assumpsit. [He has undertaken.]

assurance. (1) The documentary evidence of the transfer of land. See Re Ray [1896] 1 Ch 468. (2) Insurance (qv).

assured. Insured (qv).

asylum. A refuge; a place of refuge and relative security; originally a place of safety from pursuit and later a place for reception and treatment of the insane. [Bibliography: Clarke & McMahon; Wallace UK.] See POLITICAL OFFENCE; PSYCHIATRIC DISORDER.

asylum, claim for. A claim by a nonnational to remain in the State. An alien claiming asylum must be given an adequate opportunity to put forward representations to show why his application should be acceded to; there is an obligation to follow fair procedures in dealing with the question of the removal of the applicant from the jurisdiction: Fakih v Minister for Justice [1993] ILRM 274, HC. Also fairness requires that an applicant for asylum is notified where the application is being dealt with under a new procedure: Dascalu v Minister for Justice [1999] ITLR (22 November), HC.

An asylum-seeker becomes a refugee on obtaining a declaration of refugee status. An application for asylum is not permitted to have the effect of preventing or postponing the surrender of a person under the International War Crimes Tribunals Act 1998, s 4(3).

Member states of the European Union (qv) are required to regard asylum policy as a matter of common interest: Maastricht Treaty 1992, art K.1 and Declaration. This requirement has resulted in the Dublin Convention 1990. There are restrictions on the right of a national of one member state of the European Union who seeks asylum in another member state: Amsterdam Treaty 1997, protocol on asylum.

The Council of Ministers is required, within five years of entry into force of the Amsterdam Treaty, to adopt measures on asylum (e g minimum standards on the reception of asylum seekers) and measures on refugees (e g minimum standards for giving temporary protection to displaced persons from third countries, and sharing a balance between the member states): Treaty establishing the European Community, art 63 of the consolidated (2002) version.

See Anisimova v Minister for Justice [1998] 1 ILRM 523, SC; Stefan v Minister for Justice [2002] 2 ILRM 134, SC and [2001] 4 IR 203, SC; L R v Minister for Justice [2002] 1 IR 260, HC. See also Refugee Act 1996, as amended by Immigration Act 2003, s 7. See 'The Illegal Immigrants (Trafficking) Act' by Kathy Skelly BL and Mary Feeney BL in Bar Review (December 2000) 170; 'Immigration and asylum law and policy' by solicitor John Handoll in Law Society Gazette (October 2003) 49 and (November 2003) 53; 'A Commentary on aspects of the Immigration Act 2003' by Phelim Molony BL in Bar Review (February 2004) 32. See website: www.justice.ie. [Bibliography: Cubie & Ryan; Fraser & Harvey.] See ALIEN; AMSTERDAM TREATY; BIOMETRICS; COMMON POLICIES; DEPORTATION ORDER; DUBLIN CONVENTION; EQUAL COMMUNITY INITIATIVE; EXTRADITION; ILLEGAL IMMIGRANT; INTERNAL PROTECTION ALTERNATIVE; JUDICIAL REVIEW, ASYLUM; REFUGEE; TRANSLATION; UNHCR.

ATM. [Automatic Teller Machine.] A local authority is empowered to serve notice on a financial institution, having automated equipment for withdrawals, deposits or payments located on an outside location at its premises, requiring the institution to take special measures to prevent or limit the creation of litter: Litter Pollution Act 1997, s 16.

The stamp duty on ATM and laser cards is now €10 per card per annum and €20 per annum for a combined card: Finance Act 2003, s 140. See IRISH PAYMENT SERVICES ORGANISATION.

atmosphere. Means the gaseous envelope surrounding the earth, and includes air: Environmental Protection Agency Act 1992, s 3 as substituted by Protection of the Environment Act 2003, s 5. See EMISSION.

ats; ad sectam. [At the suit of.]

attachiamenta bonorum. Distress (qv) of a person's goods and chattels for debt.

attached and adjoining. It has been held that the words '*attached and adjoining*' must be read disjunctively; '*attached*' requires physical connection, whereas '*adjoining*' does not: *In the matter of Hannigan Holdings Ltd* [2000] ITLR (10 July), SC and [2000] 2 ILRM 438, SC and 4 IR 369. In this case it was held that premises could not be said to be adjoining unless they are so close to one another as to be described aptly as adjoining. See Licensing (Ireland) Act 1902, s 6.

attachment. (1) An order which directs that a person be brought before the court to answer the contempt (qv) in respect of which the order is issued e g the failure of a witness without lawful excuse to attend court having been served with a sub-poena (qv) and having been paid or offered a reasonable sum for his expenses. For the High Court, see RSC Ord 44, r 1. In the Circuit Court, for attachment and committal of a person for failure to comply with the terms of a court order, see Circuit Court Rules 2001 Ord 37. For the District Court, see DCR 1997 Ord 44 and Ord 21; District Court (Attachment and Committal) Rules 1999, SI No 124 of 1999 and District Court (Attachment and Committal) Rules 2000, SI No 196 of 2000.

(2) The attachment of debts by way of garnishee (qv). For the attachment of debts by a *garnishee*, see Circuit Court Rules 2001 Ord 38. Attachment by way of garnishee proceedings or receiver by way of equitable execution can apply only to *present* debts due to a judgment debtor and cannot apply to *future* earnings; consequently attachment of a sum owing from the annual wages of an employee is not possible: *Shalvey v Telecom Éireann* (1992) HC reported in *Law Society Gazette* (March 1993).

(3) The enforcement of a direction to pay money. An *attachment of earnings order* is an order applied for by the person for whose benefit *maintenance* (qv) is to be paid; it is directed to the maintenance debtor's employer who is bound to make such periodical deductions from the debtor's earnings as specified by the order and to pay them over to the District Court clerk: Family Law (Maintenance of Spouses and Children) Act 1976 Act, s 10. There is a *normal deduction rate* and a *protected earnings rate* (s 11). A redundancy lump sum payment may not be so attached: *Byrne v Byrne* (76 *Gazette of Law Society* p.26). See also EC (Civil and Commercial Judgments) Regulations 2002, SI No 52 of 2002 reg 6(10)(b).

An attachment of earnings order may be sought to obtain a contribution towards a social welfare benefit or allowance from a person liable to maintain the recipient: Social Welfare (Consolidation) Act 1993, ss 285–297. For application procedure in the District Court, see DCR 1997 Ord 98. An attachment of earnings order may also be obtained to secure payments under a periodic payments order, made in connection with divorce proceedings: Family Law (Divorce) Act 1996, s 13(6). See also DCR 1997 Ord 56 as amended by District Court (Family Law) Rules 1998, SI No 42 of 1998. [Bibliography: Glanville.] See COMMITTAL, ORDER OF; COMPENSATION ORDER; NOTICE OF ATTACHMENT.

attachment of debt. The Revenue Commissioners may serve a notice of attachment, specifying the amount by which a taxpayer is in default, on a third party whom they have reason to believe has a debt due to the taxpayer; notice of attachment may now issue 14 days after default (it was previously a month): Finance Act 1988, s 73 now Taxes Consolidation Act 1997, s 1002, as amended by Finance Act 2001, s 238.

For the attachment of debts by a *garnishee*, see Circuit Court Rules 2001 Ord 38. See *Orange v Revenue Commissioners* [1995] 1 IR 517, HC.

attempt. The offence which arises from a proximate act towards the carrying out of an indictable (qv) offence; an act remotely leading to the commission of the offence will not be considered as an attempt to commit it. An attempt consists of an act done by the accused with a specific intent to commit a particular crime; it must go beyond mere preparation and must be a direct movement towards the commission after the preparations have been made: *The People (Attorney-General) v Thornton* [1952] IR 91.

There cannot be a conviction for the substantive offence and a conviction for an attempt to commit the same offence: *The People (Attorney-General) v Dermody* [1956] IR 307. See also *Attorney-General v Richmond* [1935] Frewen 28; *The People (Attorney-General) v England* [1947] CCA; *Devereaux v Kotsonouris* [1992] ILRM 140, HC. See ALTERNATIVE VERDICT.

attendant grounds. In relation to a structure, includes land lying outside the curtilage of the structure: Planning and Development Act 2000, s 2(1). See ARCHITECTURAL HERITAGE.

attest. To witness any act or event eg the signature or execution of a document or a will. If a document is required by law to be attested, it cannot be used as evidence until an attesting witness has proved its execution. If no such witness is alive, or procurable, it must be proved that the attestation of one attesting witness is in his handwriting and that the signature of the executing party is in his handwriting. In a document at least 30 years old produced from proper custody, the signature is presumed to be genuine. See DOCUMENTS, PRESUMPTION AS TO.

attestation clause. The statement in a deed or will or other document that it has been duly executed in the presence of witnesses eg in a will. The attestation clause is sometimes in the following form: *signed by the testator as his last will and testament in the presence of us who at his request and in his presence and in the presence of each other hereunto sign our names as witnesses.* See Solicitors (Amendment) Act 1994, s 72(4).

attorney. (1) A person appointed by another person to act in his place. (2) Prior to the Judicature Act 1873, there were attorneys as well as solicitors, the attorneys being those who conducted proceedings on behalf of clients in the common law courts, and solicitors, those who conducted them in the chancery courts. The 1873 Act abolished attorneys and made them all *solicitors of the supreme court.* [Bibliography: Hogan & Osborough.] See POWER OF ATTORNEY; TRADE MARK AGENT.

Attorney-General, A-G. The adviser to the government on all matters of law and legal opinion, who is appointed by the President of Ireland on the nomination of the Taoiseach: 1937 Constitution, art 30.

He also has the function of guardian of the public interest, which he exercises for the community independently of government, as *parens patriae* (qv), when he takes action to ensure that the law is enforced eg to vindicate and defend the right to life of the unborn: *A-G v Open Door Counselling Ltd* [1988] IR 393; *A-G v X* [1992] ILRM 401, SC. The nature of his office charges him with the duty to enforce the Constitution: *A-G v Tribunal of Inquiry into the Beef Industry* [1993] ILRM 81, SC.

The A-G is the only party who can bring civil proceedings to enforce a public right; no one other than the A-G can seek an injunction in the public interest to restrain an offence being committed in breach of a statute: *Law Society v Carroll* [1996] 2 ILRM 95, SC. However, see now Solicitors (Amendment) Act 2002, s 18.

There is an obligation on parties to certain proceedings to give notice of the proceedings to the A-G and the A-G is entitled to appear in any such proceedings eg European Convention on Human Rights Act 2003, s 6.

The A-G is not a member of the government and must retire from office on the resignation of the Taoiseach but may continue to carry out his duties until a successor to the Taoiseach has been appointed. He may be given additional functions and duties by law eg he is responsible for enforcing charitable trusts. If he is a practising barrister at the time of his appointment, he is deemed to continue to be a barrister in practice at the Bar: *Code of Conduct for the Bar of Ireland* (December 2003) r 2.1.

While serious criminal offences are prosecuted by the Director of Public Prosecutions, the A-G retains this function in respect of offences which may involve international and diplomatic complications eg prosecution of offences under the Sea Fisheries (Amendment) Act 1978, Sea Pollution Act 1991 and Dumping at Sea Act 1996, ss 11–12.

The A-G is immune from actions against him, arising from the performance of his functions, on public policy grounds; this denial of a right of action arises from the functions he is called upon to perform in the public interest and the consequences for his ability to perform them: *W v Ireland (No 2)* [1997] 2 IR 141, HC.

The A-G is entitled to seek election to the European Parliament but ceases to hold office as A-G on being so elected: European Parliament Elections Act 1997, s 11(4). See also Courts and Court Officers Act 1995, s 18.

The 28 Attorneys General since the establishment of the State have been: Rory Brady (2002– present); Michael McDowell (1999–2002); David Byrne (1997–99); Dermot Gleeson (1994–97); Eoghan Fitzsimons (1994); Harold Whelehan (1991–94); John Rogers (1984–87); John L Murray (1982–82 and 1987–91); Patrick Connolly (1982); Peter Sutherland (1981–82 and 1982–84); Anthony J Hederman (1977–81); John M Kelly (1977); Declan Costello (1973–77); Colm Condon (1965–73); Patrick McGilligan (1954–57); Aindrias O'Chaoimh (1954 and 1957–65); Thomas Teevan (1953–54); Charles Casey (1950–51); Cecil Lavery (1948–50); Cearbhall O'Dálaigh (1946–48 and 1951–53); Kevin Dixon (1942–46); Kevin Haugh (1940–42); Patrick Lynch (1936–40); James Geoghegan (1936); Conor Maguire (1932–36); John A Costello (1926–32); John O'Byrne (1924–26); Hugh Kennedy (1922–24).

Four A-Gs subsequently became Chief Justice: Hugh Kennedy (1925–36), Conor Maguire (1946–61), Cearbhall O'Dálaigh (1961–72), and John L Murray (2004 to present). One A-G also became President of Ireland, Cearbhall O'Dálaigh (1974–76) and one became Taoiseach, John A Costello (1948–51; 1954–57). Two A-Gs became EU Commissioners, Peter Sutherland (1985–88) and David Byrne (1999–2004). A number of A-Gs subsequently became High or Supreme Court judges. See 'The "political" role of the Attorney-General?' by Conleth Bradley BL in *Bar Review* (June/July 2001) 486.

See e-mail: *info@ag.irlgov.ie*. See website: *www.attorneygeneral.ie*. [Bibliography: Casey.] See CRIMINAL INFORMATION; DIRECTOR OF PUBLIC PROSECUTIONS; PARENS PATRIAE; RELATOR; STATE CLAIMS AGENCY.

Attorney-General's Scheme. The scheme to provide legal representation for persons who need it but cannot afford it and which is not covered by the civil or criminal aid schemes. The scheme applies only in certain types of litigation ie: (a) habeas corpus applications; (b) bail motions; (c) judicial reviews of certiorari, mandamus or prohibition.

The scheme is not based on statute or on contract; it is a voluntary assurance given by the Attorney-General to the courts that he will pay for the legal representation from funds at his disposal and he may expand or contract the scheme as he sees fit: *Byrne v Governor of Mountjoy Prison* [1999] 1 ILRM 386, HC. The scheme applies also to extradition cases in the district court (*Byrne* case).

An application must be made to the court at the commencement of the proceedings for a recommendation to the Attorney-General that the scheme be applied. See *Application of Michael Woods* [1970] IR 154. See *Law Society Gazette* (April1992) p 97. See website: *www.attorneygeneral.ie*. See LEGAL AID.

attorney, power of. See POWER OF ATTORNEY.

attornment. (1) An acknowledgment by a person in occupation of land to be the tenant of the owner thereof. A mortgage may contain an *attornment clause* whereby the mortgagor attorns himself tenant of the mortgagee so that possession of the land may be obtained by way of ejectment (qv). See Deasy's Act 1860, s 94; *Ulster Bank v Woolsey* [1890] 24 ILTR 65.

(2) The acknowledgment by a third person that he holds the seller's goods on behalf of the buyer: Sale of Goods Act 1893, s 29(3). Delivery of the goods to the buyer is not deemed to take place until this acknowledgment is made. See BAILMENT.

auction sales. A sale by auction is complete when the auctioneer announces its completion by the fall of a hammer or in other customary manner; until such announcement any bidder may retract his bid. A sale by auction may be notified to be subject to a *reserve* or *upset price* and a right to bid may also be reserved expressly by or on behalf of the seller. Where a sale by auction is not so notified, it is not lawful for the seller to bid himself or to employ any person (a *puffer*) to bid, or for the auctioneer knowingly to take any bid from the seller or any such person; a sale contravening this rule may be treated as fraudulent by the buyer. An *upset price* includes a price specifically named as the sum from which bidding may start.

Where goods are put up for sale by auction in lots, each lot is *prima facie* deemed to be the subject of a separate contract of sale. In a *dutch auction* (qv) the property is put up at an excessive price and is offered at decreasing prices until someone closes. See Sale of Goods Act 1893, s 58. [Bibliography: Mahon; Murdoch UK.] See SALE OF LAND.

auctioneer. A person who conducts sales by auction to the highest bidder. A person may not carry on or hold himself out or represent himself as carrying on the business of auctioneer except under and in accordance with a licence and no person may conduct an auction except with a licence or permit: Auctioneers and House Agents Act 1947, s 6. An auctioneer's licence is granted by the Revenue Commissioners on application accompanied by a *certificate of qualifications*, a certificate of maintenance by the applicant of a deposit in the High Court, and the excise duty payable (AHAA 1947, s 8). A certificate of qualifications is obtained on application to a judge of the district court (AHAA 1947, s 11; Auctioneers and House Agents Act 1967, s 12; DCR 1997 Ord 63). An auctioneer must keep a *client account* (AHAA 1967, s 5) and there are provisions governing proceedings in relation to deposits and banking accounts and bankruptcy (AHAA 1967, ss 7–11).

The auctioneer is the agent of the seller, but becomes an agent of the buyer and seller for the purposes of providing a memorandum (qv) under the Sale of Goods Act 1893 and the Statute of Frauds. A letter to a vendor of land, written and signed by an auctioneer who is acting on the vendor's behalf and who has authority to sign on his behalf, may be sufficient to satisfy the Statute of Frauds, and entitle the purchaser to a decree of *specific performance* for the sale of the land: *Keller v Crowe* [1999] ITLR (16 August), HC.

An auctioneer may owe a duty of care to the buyer in particular circumstances e g where he gives his opinion to the buyer on the purchase of the freehold interest which opinion amounts to a *negligent misstatement* (qv): *McAnarney v Hanrahan* [1994] 1 ILRM 210, HC. Also, while an auctioneer's advertisement and leaflet could not be regarded as part of the *contract of sale* of a house, they may amount to a misrepresentation, if inaccurate, inducing the purchaser to enter into the contract, and entitling him to repudiate the contract: *Peilow v Carroll* [1972] 106 ILTR 29, SC.

For the authority of an auctioneer as agent of the seller, see *Law v Roberts & Co* [1964] IR 292.

Any agreement in a contract relating to the sale, lease, or letting of property which makes the purchaser, lessee or tenant liable to pay the fees or expense of an auctioneer or house agent is void: Auctioneers and House Agents Act 1973, s 2. See *also Attorney-General v Manorhamilton Co-operative Livestock Mart Ltd* [1966] IR 192; *Ballyowen Castle Homes v Collins* [1986] HC. A Review Group to examine the regulatory framework for the auctioneering /estate agency profession was established in July 2004. For the Irish Auctioneers & Valuers Institute, see website: *www.iavi.ie*. [Bibliography: Mahon.] See APPRAISEMENT; BANKRUPTCY, ACT OF; COMMISSION; DEPOSIT; HOUSE AGENT; MONEY LAUNDERING; TAX CLEARANCE CERTIFICATE.

auctioneering service. Any business to which the Auctioneers and House Agents Act 1947 relates, including the business of a house agent (qv) within the meaning of that Act: Building Societies Act 1989, s 32(6)(a). A building society is, under certain circumstances, empowered to provide an *auctioneering service* and other *services relating to land* (BSA 1989, s 32(1)).

audi alteram partem. [Hear the other side.] One of the principles of *natural justice* (qv) that no judicial or quasi-judicial decision may be taken without giving the party affected an opportunity of stating his case and being heard in his own defence.

It has been held that *audi alteram partem* is a fundamental principle of procedural justice, both natural and constitutional, and requires the courts to ensure that judicial processes are conducted and seen to be conducted with scrupulous fairness to both sides: *Nevin v Crowley* [1999] 1 ILRM 376, HC and [2001] 1 IR 113, SC.

It was held by the Supreme Court that there was a *prima facie* breach of the *audi alteram partem* rule by virtue of the fact that counsel was not given the opportunity to argue his case fully before the High Court: *Brick v Burke* [2002] 2 ILRM 427, SC. A prison sentence imposed by the District Court in the absence of the accused, who did not know about the case, was a breach of the *audi alteram partem* rule: *Brennan v Judge Windle* [2003] ITLR (27 October) 2003, SC and FL 7856, and 2 ILRM 520.

See *The State (Ingle) v O'Brien* [1975] 109 ILTR 7; *The State (Gleeson) v Minister for Defence* [1976] IR 280; *Garvey v Ireland*

[1981] IR 75; *The State (IPU) v Employment Appeals Tribunal* [1986] ILRM 36; *Harte v Labour Court* [1996] 2 ILRM 450, HC and ELR 181; *Byrne v McDonnell* [1996] 1 ILRM 543, HC; *McSorley v Governor of Mountjoy Prison* [1997] 2 IR 258, SC; *Cassidy v Shannon Castle Banquets* [2000] ELR 248, HC.

audience, right of. The right to appear and conduct proceedings in court. Barristers (qv) and solicitors (qv) have such a right in all the courts. See DCR 1997 Ord 6. See LOCUS STANDI.

audit. A detailed inspection of the accounts of a body, usually by a person who is not employed by that body. A private company is exempted from having its accounts audited if its turnover does not exceed €1.5m, if its balance sheet total does not exceed £1.5m (€1.9m), if its average number of employees does not exceed 50, and if it is not a company in a certain specified class: Companies (Amendment) (No 2) Act 1999, ss 31–39 and Sch 2, as amended by Companies (Auditing and Accounting) Act 2003, s 53. The exemption is conditional on the timely filing of annual returns and comes into effect for financial years commencing on or after 1 July 2004: SI No 132 of 2004.

A specific statement must be included in the company's balance sheet that the exception is being availed of (C(A)(No 2)A 1999, s 33). A person holding one-tenth or more of voting rights may require the company not to avail of the exception (C(A)(No 2)A 1999, s 33(1)). A company which has availed of the exception, is also exempt from certain provisions of the Companies Acts, see list in Sch 1. The audit exception is also available to partnerships to which apply the EC (Accounts) Regulations 1993, SI No 396 of 1993 (C(A)(No 2)A 1999, s 38). See Taxes Consolidation Act 1997, s 904A inserted by Finance Act 2000, s 68. See AUDITOR, COMPANY; AUDITOR, LOCAL AUTHORITY; ENVIRONMENTAL AUDIT; REVENUE AUDIT.

audit committee. The committee of directors of a public limited company, whether listed or unlisted, which must be established and adequately resourced, and which has specified responsibilities eg reviewing the company's annual accounts, determining that the annual accounts comply with the applicable *accounting standards* (qv), determining that the company has kept proper books of accounts, advising in relation to the appointment of the company's auditor, monitoring the performance and quality of the auditor's work: Companies Act 1990, s 205B inserted by Companies (Auditing and Accounting) Act 2003, s 42. The board of directors of each large private company must decide to establish or not to establish an audit committee. The committee is required to have a minimum of two members and some directors are ineligible eg the chairman of the board. The committee must have written terms of reference prepared and approved by the board. See AUDITOR, COMPANY.

auditor, company. Every company must appoint an auditor or auditors at each annual general meeting. For exception, see AUDIT.

A firm is qualified for appointment as auditor of a company if at least one member of the firm holds a recognised practising certificate and details of such member have been forwarded to the registrar of companies. The auditor may not be a body corporate or a close family relative of, or a partner of, or in the employment of, an officer of the company: Companies Act 1990, s 187 as amended by Company Law Enforcement Act 2001, s 72 and by Companies (Auditing and Accounting) Act 2003, s 35.

Where qualification to act as an auditor is based on membership of a recognised accountancy body, then the auditor is required to hold a valid practising certificate from such body. It is an offence for an auditor to fail to produce evidence of qualification to the Director of Corporate Enforcement when so requested (CA 1990, s 187 (as amended)).

In relation to an accountancy firm which had audited the books of two companies when one of the directors was a director of the same two companies, the High Court has found that the issue was not who was appointed as auditor of the companies in question, but rather whether any person had acted as auditor when they were disqualified from acting as such: *Director of Corporate Enforcement v Gannon, Gilroy and Others* (2002) Irish Times, 20 November, HC.

An auditor's appointment lapses when he resigns, becomes ineligible to hold office or is removed from office or is replaced. An auditor, who is proposed to be removed, is entitled to have representations sent out before the meeting at which he is to be removed: Companies Act 1963, s 161 as amended by CA 1990, s 184. When an auditor resigns during his term of office, he must report to the members any circumstances connected with it which should be brought to their notice CA 1990, s 185).

See also Building Societies Act 1989, ss 83–88 as amended by Housing (Miscellaneous Provisions) Act 2002, s 23 and Sch 3; Pensions Act 1990, ss 2 and 56 as amended by Social Welfare Act 1993, ss 42 and 47 and Pensions (Amendment) Act 2002, s 38; Credit Union Act 1997, ss 113–123, as amended by Central Bank and Financial Services Authority of Ireland Act 2003, s 35, Sch 1; Investment Intermediaries Act 1995, ss 32–35 as amended by Investor Compensation Act 1998, s 62. See Companies Act 1963, s 160 *et seq* as amended; Companies Act 1990, ss 182–201. See *Re Kingston Cotton Mills (No 2)* [1896] 2 Ch 279; *Hedley Byrne v Heller* [1964] AC 465; *JEB Fastners Ltd v Marks Bloom Co* [1983] 1 All ER 583; *Sisk v Flynn* [1986] ILRM 128.

See Listing Rules 2000, para 6A.4. For the Institute of Chartered Accountants in Ireland, see website: *www.icai.ie*. For the Institute of Incorporated Public Accountants, see website: *www.iipa.ie*. For the Institute of Internal Auditors, see website: *www.iia.org.uk*. [Bibliography: Cahill N.] See ACCOUNTS, COMPANY; DISQUALIFICATION ORDER; IRISH AUDITING AND ACCOUNTING SUPERVISORY AUTHORITY; MONEY LAUNDERING; REGISTER OF AUDITORS.

auditor, company, duty of. The primary duty of the auditor is to ascertain and state the true financial position of the company by an examination of its books. The auditor must report to the members of the accounts examined by him and on every balance sheet and profit and loss account; the report must contain certain specified information: Companies Act 1990, s 193. The auditor is under a general duty to carry out the audit with professional integrity (CA 1990, s 193(6)) and to serve notice on the company if he forms the opinion that proper books of accounts are not being kept (CA 1990, s 194 as amended by Company Law Enforcement Act 2001, s 73 and Companies (Auditing and Accounting) Act 2003, s 37).

It is the duty of the auditor not only to report on the annual accounts but also to state whether the directors' annual report is consistent with the contents of the audited accounts, and if he considers them inconsistent, he must give particulars of the inconsistency: Companies Amendment Act 1986, s 15. See Prompt Payments of Accounts Act 1997, s 13. See DIRECTORS' REPORT.

auditor, company, reporting by. Auditors are required to report where they suspect breaches of the Companies Acts may have occurred in their client companies; there are also stricter rules governing their statutory obligations: Companies Act 1990, ss 187, 192 and 194 as amended by Company Law Enforcement Act 2001, ss 72–74 and Companies (Auditing and Accounting) Act 2003, ss 35 and 37.

Also auditors must also notify the Director of Corporate Enforcement, as well as the Registrar of Companies, where they form the opinion that a company is not keeping proper books of account, and must notify the Director if they, in the course of their audit, come into possession of information which may point to an indictable offence under the Companies Acts (CA 1990, amended s 194). The Director has issued 'guidance notes' in relation to this statutory reporting duty, as well as reporting by auditors in the public interest of suspected breaches of law or regulations going beyond the scope of s 194(5) of the CA 1990: Decision Notice D/2002/2 available on *www.odce.ie/publications*.

A recognised accountancy body must report to the Director whenever its disciplinary committee or tribunal has reasonable grounds for believing that an indictable offence has been committed by one of its members (CA 1990, s 192 as amended by CLEA 2001, s 73).

An auditor must also report to the gardaí any suspected offence by a firm or a partner or director or manager, indicated by the firm's accounts: Criminal Justice (Theft and Fraud Offences) Act 2001, s 59.

Auditors to an approved stock exchange and to authorised member firms are given a prominent role in policing the regulatory regime: Stock Exchange Act 1995, ss 33–35 as amended by Investor Compensation Act 1998, s 76. See also Investment Limited Partnerships Act 1994, s 16 as amended by Companies (Amendment) (No 2) Act 1999, s 40. Provision has been made for the imposition of additional obligations on auditors of regulated financial service providers: Central Bank and Financial Services Authority of Ireland Act 2004, s 26. See 'Accounting for Crime' by solicitor Emmet Scully in *Law Society Gazette* (April 2003) 24. See MONEY LAUNDERING.

auditor, company, supervision of. The recognition and supervision of bodies of accountants for the purposes of auditing is now the responsibility of the Irish Auditing and Accounting Supervisory Authority: Companies (Auditing and Accounting) Act 2003, s 32. This Act transposes the Companies Act 1990 (Auditors) Regulations 1992, SI No 259 of 1992 into primary legislation and implements recommendations of the *Review Group on Auditing* relating to accounting standards, the disciplinary procedures of the accountancy bodies, disclosure by companies of fees paid to auditors, enhanced corporate governance provisions and directors' compliance statements (C(AA)A 2003, ss 34–47, and 59). See IRISH AUDITING AND ACCOUNTING SUPERVISORY AUTHORITY.

auditor, local government. An auditor appointed by the Minister to investigate the accounts of a local authority: Local Government Act 1946, s 68. His duties include to examine into the matter of every account which is audited by him; to disallow all payments, charges and allowances which are contrary to law or which he deems to be unfounded; to *surcharge* (qv) any such payments upon the person making, or authorising the making of, the illegal payment: Local Government (Ireland) Act 1871, s 12 as amended by the Local Government (Ireland) Act 1902, ss 19–20. The auditor in carrying out the audit, is discharging a function of a judicial nature and is bound by the principles of *natural justice* (qv) and the doctrine of *res judicata* (qv). He is empowered to take evidence on oath and to require production of documents: LGA 1946, s 86. See *R (Butler) v Browne* [1909] 2 IR 333.

The auditor is also empowered to carry out a *value for money audit* ie whether and to what extent the resources of the local authority have been used economically and efficiently and whether any disposal of its resources has been effected upon the most favourable terms reasonably obtainable: Local Government (Financial Provisions) Act 1997, s 15.

Previously, the accounts of a health board (qv) were required to be audited by a local government auditor appointed by the Minister: Health Act 1970, ss 28–29. They are now audited by the Comptroller and Auditor General (qv): Comptroller and Auditor General (Amendment) Act 1993, s 6.

Significant reforms have been made in the area of local authority auditing, with provision for the establishment of the *Local Government Audit Service* and the *Director of Audit*: Local Government Act 2001, ss 114–126. There is provision for the establishment of an audit committee (LGA 2001, s 122). See also repeal of s 12 of Local Government Board (Ireland) Act 1872 (LGA 2001, s 5(1)). See Local Government (Financial Procedures and Audit) Regulations 2002, SI No 508 of 2002; Local Government (Audit Fees) Regulations 2003, SI No 622 of 2003. See FUNCTUS OFFICIO; SURCHARGE.

auditor independence. In order to enhance auditor independence, there is provision for the reporting in the notes to the annual accounts of companies, of the remuneration for audit, audit-related and non-audit work by the company's auditor and by any firm or affiliate of the auditor: Companies Act 1990, s 205D inserted by Companies (Auditing and Accounting) Act 2003, s 44. Where the remuneration for non-audit work exceeds the remuneration for audit and audit-related work, the directors (or the audit committee, if one is in place) are required to state in their report whether they are satisfied as regards the auditor's independence.

authentic instrument. A legal document which has been drawn up by a public official such as a public notary and which possesses, in some EU civil legal systems, a status comparable to that of a court judgment and which is directly enforceable as such. Such instruments are unknown in common law countries; they are mainly used in continental countries and generally without the need to have recourse to the courts. See Consumer Credit Act 1995, s 3(2)(b).

A document which has been formally drawn up or registered as an *authentic instrument* and is enforceable in one contracting state of the EU must, in another contracting state, have an order for its enforcement issued there, on application made in accordance with specified procedures, unless enforcement is contrary to public policy in the state in which enforcement is sought: Jurisdiction of Courts and

Enforcement of Judgments Act 1998, Sch 1, art 50. Applications for the recognition and enforcement of authentic instruments are made to the Master of the High Court (JCEJA 1998, s 7). As regards authentic instruments and EFTA countries, see JCEJA 1998, Sch 7, art 50. See SETTLEMENT.

The *Brussels I Regulation* on the recognition and enforcement of judgments in civil and commercial matters, replaces JCEJA 1998 as from 1 March 2002 for all EU states except Denmark: EC (Civil and Commercial Judgments) Regulations 2002, SI No 52 of 2002. For the purposes of the *Brussels I Regulation* a document that is duly authenticated and purports to be a copy of a judgment must, without further proof, be deemed to be such a copy, unless the contrary is shown (SI No 52 of 2002, reg 9(1)).

authenticate. To make valid and effective by proof or by appropriate formalities as required by law.

author. Means the person who creates the *work*: Copyright and Related Rights Act 2000, s 21. A *work of joint authorship* means a work produced by the collaboration of two or more authors in which the contribution of each author is not distinct from that of the other author or authors (CRRA 2000, s 22 (1)). Generally the author of a work is the *first owner* of the copyright (CRRA 2000, s 23(1)). Also the author has certain *moral rights* (qv). The author of a work is deemed to be known, where it is possible to ascertain his identity by reasonable inquiry (CRRA 2000, s 2(7)).

There is tax exemption for an author in respect of profits arising from original and creative works. See ARTIST, TAX EXEMPTION OF.

The *author* in relation to a design, means the person who creates the design: Industrial Designs Act 2001, s 17(1). In the case of a design which is *computer-generated*, 'author' means the person by whom the arrangements necessary for the creation of the design are undertaken (IDA 2001, s 17(2)). The author of a design is to be taken as the *first proprietor* of the design, unless the design is created by an employee in the course of employment, in which case the employer is to be treated as the first proprietor, subject to any agreement to the contrary (IDA 2001, s 19(1)).

'*Computer-generated*' means the design is generated by computer in circumstances where the author of the design is not an individual (IDA 2001, s 17(3)).

In competition law, when a document is retrieved from an electronic storage and retrieval system, there is a presumption, unless the contrary is shown, that the author of the document is the person who ordinarily uses that system in the course of his business: Competition Act 2002, s 12(4). See COPYRIGHT; JOINT AUTHORSHIP; LITERARY WORK; PERFORMERS' PROTECTION; PROPRIETOR OF NEW DESIGN; UNIVERSAL COPYRIGHT CONVENTION; WORK.

authorised trade union. See TRADE UNION, AUTHORISED.

authority. (1) The rights invested in a person or body by another allowing performance of an act. (2) A body exercising such rights eg a planning authority. (3) A decided case, judgment, textbook of repute or statute cited as a statement of the law. See AGENCY; ATTORNEY, POWER OF; DELEGATED LEGISLATION; STATE AUTHORITY.

authority, apparent. See PRINCIPAL.

authority, customary. See CUSTOMARY AUTHORITY.

authorship, false attribution of. A person has a right not to have a work falsely attributed to him as author: Copyright and Related Rights Act 2000, s 113. The right lasts for 20 years after the death of the author (CRRA 2000, s 115). See *Moore v News of the World* [1972] 1 QB 441.

authorship, joint. See JOINT AUTHORSHIP.

automated data. See DATA.

automated teller machine card; ATM. See ATM; CASH CARD.

automatism. In England, has been held to mean an act which is generally not punishable which is done by the muscles without any control by the mind, such as a spasm, a reflex action or a convulsion, or an act done by a person who is not conscious of what he is doing, such as an act done whilst suffering from concussion or whilst sleepwalking: *Bratty v A-G for Northern Ireland* [1963] AC 386. See *Donohue v Coyle* [1953–54] Ir Jur Rep 30.

In Ireland *automatism* is a defence in civil law within strict limits; there must be a total destruction of voluntary control on the defendant's part: *O'Brien v Parker* [1997] 2 ILRM 170, HC. Impaired, reduced or partial control is not sufficient to maintain the defence. [Bibliography: Charleton (4).] See IRRESISTIBLE IMPULSE.

autopsy. See POST-MORTEM.

autre droit, in. [In the right of another.] An executor or trustee holds property in right of the persons entitled thereto.

autre vie. [The life of another.] See LIFE ESTATE.

autrefois acquit. [Formerly acquitted.] A special *plea in bar* to a criminal prosecution that the accused has already been tried for the same offence before a court of competent jurisdiction and has been acquitted after a trial on the merits. An acquittal by direction of the judge on an insufficient indictment will not support a plea of autrefois acquit, nor will an *acquittal* arising from a conviction being quashed on certiorari (qv) proceedings: *The People (Attorney-General) v Marchel O'Brien* [1963] IR 92; *State (Tynan) v Keane* [1968] IR 348; *Grennan v Kirby* [1994] 2 ILRM 199, HC.

However, where a conviction is quashed on certiorari where there has been a breach of the fundamental tenets of constitutional justice, the defendant may plead *autrefois acquit*: *Sweeney v District Judge Brophy* [1993] ILRM 449, SC and 2 IR 202. See *The State (Keeney) v O'Malley* [1986] ILRM 31; *AA v Medical Council* [2002] 3 IR 1, HC; *Kelly v District Judge Anderson* [2004] FL 8697, SC and 1 ILRM 454. See DOUBLE JEOPARDY; AUTREFOIS CONVICT; GARDA, DISCIPLINE OF.

autrefois convict. [Formerly convicted.] A special *plea in bar* by which the accused alleges that he has already been tried and convicted for the same offence by a court of competent jurisdiction. If a court makes an order without jurisdiction, either because it never had jurisdiction or it subsequently lost jurisdiction, the principle of *autrefois convict* cannot apply to any order made by it: *Grennan v Kirby* [1994] 2 ILRM 199, HC. The principle of *autrefois convict* does not apply where a sentence is imposed in excess of permitted jurisdiction, because that judgment is void *ab initio*: *Gilmartin v Murphy* [2001] 2 ILRM 442, HC. See also *Singh v Ruane* [1990] ILRM 62, HC. See AUTREFOIS ACQUIT; EUROPEAN CONVENTION ON HUMAN RIGHTS.

aver. To allege or affirm, in pleadings (qv).

average. Apportionment of loss. In carriage of goods by sea, average can be *general* or *particular*. *General* average is the general loss which is caused by an act voluntarily incurred eg where goods are thrown over-

board in a storm to save the ship and the rest of the cargo; the loss is borne rateably by all those interested: Marine Insurance Act 1906, s 66. *Particular* average arises where the damage is not caused for the general benefit eg damage to goods by ingress of sea water; in which case the loss remains where it falls. See AVERAGE CLAUSE.

average clause. A term in a contract of insurance under which there is an apportionment of the loss between the insured and the insurer having regard to the extent to which the risk has been under-insured, eg in property insurance where the property is of greater value than the sum insured, the insured is in effect his own insurer of the difference and must bear a rateable share of any loss.

averia. Cattle.

averment. An allegation or affirmation in pleadings (qv). See INVESTIGATION OF COMPANY BY DIRECTOR OF CORPORATE ENFORCEMENT.

aviation. See AIR LAW; COMMISSION FOR AVIATION REGULATION.

aviation, unlawful acts against. The Convention for the Suppression of Unlawful Acts against the Safety of Civil Aviation, done at Montreal on 23 September 1971, is given effect in the State by the Air Navigation and Transport Act 1975. See AIRCRAFT, UNLAWFUL SEIZURE OF.

avoid. To make void. A person is said to avoid a contract when he repudiates it and sets up, as a defence in legal proceedings taken to enforce it, some defect which prevents it being enforceable.

avoidance. Setting aside; making null and void. See TAX AVOIDANCE.

avow. To admit or confess.

avulsion. Land torn off by an inundation or current of water from property to which it originally was joined, and gained by the land of another; also where a river or stream, flowing between two properties, changes course and thereby cuts off part of one property and joins it to the other property. Despite the separation, the property of the part separated continues in the ownership of the original owner. See ALLUVION.

award. The finding or decision of an arbitrator. Unless a contrary intention is expressed therein, every arbitration agreement (qv) is deemed to contain a provision that the award will be final and binding: Arbitration Act 1954, s 27. In international commercial arbitration, an award also includes an *interim* award: Arbitration (International Commercial) Act 1998, s 3(1).

Under the provisions of the Arbitration Act 1954, a court has no jurisdiction to set aside an award in the absence of any finding that an arbitrator had misconducted himself; at common law, the court has jurisdiction to set aside an award where an award shows on its face an error of law so fundamental that the courts cannot stand aside and allow it to remain unchallenged: *Doyle v Kildare County Council* [1996] 1 ILRM 252, SC and [1995] 2 IR 424, SC.

The courts should only in rare circumstances entertain applications to set aside awards or remit them to the arbitrator for further consideration: *Vogelaar v Callaghan* [1996] 2 ILRM 226, HC and 1 IR 88. In this case the arbitrator had awarded the defendant a lesser amount than the plaintiff had offered prior to the arbitration (and which the defendant had rejected) but despite this, the arbitrator had awarded costs against the plaintiff. The court remitted the award to the arbitrator because to allow the award to stand, with such a direction as to costs, would indicate a severe injustice.

Unless otherwise directed, money directed to be paid by a decision of an arbitrator carries interest as from the date of the decision and at the same rate as a judgment debt; the fact that the award has to be enforced by an order of the court does not prevent interest from running from the date of the award: *Horan v Quilter* [2004] FL 8906, SC.

An award is also an award which is conferred, granted or given by an awarding body and which records that a learner has acquired a standard of knowledge, skill or competence: Qualifications (Education and Training) Act 1999, s 2(1). See also Merchant Shipping (Salvage and Wreck) Act 1993, s 37. See *Tobin & Twomey Services Ltd v Kerry Foods Ltd* [1996] 2 ILRM 1, SC. See ARBITRATION, DOMESTIC; ARBITRATION, INTERNATIONAL; FUNCTUS OFFICIO; INTEREST ON JUDGMENTS.

B

baby, wrong. Damages of £35,000 (€44,440) were awarded to a mother who was given the wrong baby while in hospital: *Broomfield v Midland Health Board* (1990) Irish Times, 20 November, HC.

baby foods. Regulations have been made on processed cereal-based foods and baby foods for infants and young children: European Communities (Processed Cereal-Based Foods and Baby Foods for Infants and Young Children) Regulations 2000, SI No 142 of 2000. These regulations revoke Medicinal Products (Licensing and Sale) Regulations 1998, SI No 241 of 1998.

back injury. See MANUAL HANDLING OF LOADS.

back-up data. Data kept only for the purpose of replacing other data in the event of their being lost, destroyed or damaged: Data Protection Act 1988, s 1(1). Back-up data, which is necessarily inaccurate between updatings is exempted from the obligation to be accurate and up-to-date (DPA 1988, s 2(4)). See DATA PROTECTION.

backing of warrants. See RENDITION.

bad. Wrong in law; unsound; ineffectual; inoperative; void.

bad debt. A debt which seemingly cannot be recovered by a creditor. A trading debt is allowed to be written off as bad in the period in which it is irrecoverable. Debts previously written off as bad must, to the extent recovered in a subsequent period of account, be credited as a trading receipt.

As regards bad debts in respect of rental income, see Income Tax Act 1967, s 90, now Taxes Consolidation Act 1997, s 101.

bad reputation. See CHARACTER, EVIDENCE OF.

bail. The setting at liberty of an accused person upon others becoming sureties for the accused at his trial. The decision to admit a person to bail is a judicial matter and, consequently, the court cannot delegate the exercise of this judicial power to an administrative official: *DPP v Goulding* [2000] 1 ILRM 147, SC and [1999] 2 IR 398, SC. The accused is bailed into the custody of the sureties who must ensure the attendance of the accused at the trial or be liable to the State for the sums secured in the event of his non-appearance.

A person who has been convicted by the Circuit Court may be admitted to bail by the Court of Criminal Appeal pending the determination of his appeal: Courts of Justice Act 1924, s 32 as amended by Criminal Procedure Act 1993, s 3(6). However, bail can only be granted where some definite or discrete ground of appeal can be identified and isolated and is of such a nature that there is a strong chance of success on appeal: *People (DPP) v Corbally* [2001] 2 ILRM 102, SC and 1 IR 180.

A right to bail is not absolute; it must be balanced against the public interest in ensuring the protection of the integrity of the trial process: *DPP v Desmond* [2001] ITLR (28 May), HC.

Bail in extradition cases may be granted only by the High Court: Extradition (Amendment) Act 1994, s 5. The test for granting bail in extradition cases must not be different from that in ordinary criminal cases: *The People (Attorney-General) v Gilliland* [1986] ILRM 357.

A person may reapply for bail after a period of four months' detention: Bail Act 1997, s 3. The previous criminal record of the person must be considered by the court but must not be referred to in a manner which may prejudice the right to a fair trial; also there is a prohibition on the publication of such criminal record (BA 1997, ss 2(2)(d) and 4).

An enquiry under the *habeas corpus* provisions of the Constitution (art 40) will normally be refused where, at the time of the application, the applicant is on bail: *Bolger v Commissioner of Garda Síochána* [2000] 1 ILRM 136, HC & SC.

See Bail Act 1997, Sch, para 17 as amended by Criminal Justice (Theft and Fraud Offences) Act 2001, s 64. See also Criminal Justice (Safety of United Nations Workers) Act 2000, s 10; European Arrest Warrant Act 2003, ss 13(5)(a), 14(7)(a), 27(2); Maritime Security Act 2004, s 12. See RSC Ord 84 rr 15–17; DCR 1997 Ord 18. See Law Reform Commission, *Report on the Law of Bail* (LRC 50, 1995). [Bibliography: Walsh D (3).] See BAILPERSON; ILLEGAL IMMIGRANT; PREVENTATIVE DETENTION; STATION BAIL.

bail, conditions of. A person previously could not be released on bail until at least one third of the amount fixed for bail had been paid into court: Bail Act 1997, s 5. The court is now given a discretion as to the amount, having regard to the circumstances of the case, including the nature of the offence and the means of the person: Courts and Court Officers Act 2002, s 33 amending ss 5(1), 8(2), 9(1) and 9(7) of the BA 1997.

Mandatory conditions which must attach to bail are: (a) to appear before the court at the end of the remand period; (b) not to commit any offence; and (c) otherwise to be of good behaviour (BA 1997, s 6(1)(a)). Further conditions may be attached, at the discretion of the court, e g to report at a garda station at specific periods or to surrender one's passport (BA 1997, s 6(1)(b)). A copy of the *recognisance* (qv) must be given to the accused and the surety or sureties (BA 1997, s 6(2)).

bail, failure to surrender to. An offence of *failure to surrender to bail* has been created by the Criminal Justice Act 1984, s 13.

bail, indemnification of surety. It is unlawful for any person, including a solicitor, to be a party to a bargain to indemnify a surety for bail: *A Guide to Professional Conduct of Solicitors in Ireland* (2002) ch 5.8. A solicitor should not stand bail for a person for whom he or his firm acts.

bail, offences committed while on. Courts are required to pass a *consecutive* sentence for an offence committed by a person while on bail (qv) awaiting trial for a previous offence: Criminal Justice Act 1984, s 11. An offence committed on bail must be treated as an *aggravating factor* and the court must impose a sentence that is greater than in the absence of the factor (CJA 1984, s 11 as amended by Bail Act 1997, s 10).

bail, test for. The fundamental test in deciding whether to grant bail or not is the probability of the accused evading justice if released, either by the accused absconding, or interfering with witnesses, or by destroying, concealing or otherwise interfering with physical evidence: *The People v O'Callaghan* [1966] IR 501. Formerly, the likelihood that the accused might commit offences while awaiting trial was not an acceptable criterion for refusing bail: *DPP v Ryan* [1989] ITLR (27 February), SC.

However, provision has been made in the Bail Act 1997 for a further ground for refusing bail i e where the person is charged with a *serious offence* and the court is satisfied that such refusal is reasonably considered necessary to prevent the commission of a serious offence by that person (BA 1997, s 2).

A serious offence is an offence specified in the Schedule to BA 1997, for which a person of full capacity and not previously convicted, may be punished by a term of imprisonment for a term of five years or by a more severe penalty (BA 1997, s 1(1), Sch, as amended by Non-Fatal Offences against the Person Act 1997, s 30; Offences against the State (Amendment) Act 1998, s 16; Child Trafficking and Pornography Act 1998, s 12; Criminal Justice (United Nations Convention against Torture) Act 2000, s 10). The offence of *illegal immigrant trafficking* is covered by the provisions of the Bail Act 1997: Illegal Immigrants (Trafficking) Act 2000, s 8.

The s 2 provision of the BA 1997 was made possible by the 16th Amendment to the Constitution in 1996 which added art 40(4)(7) to the 1937 Constitution (now art 40(4)(6)): 'Provision may be made by law for the refusal of bail by a court to a person charged with a serious offence where it is reasonably considered necessary to prevent the commission of a serious offence by that person'. The s 2 provision came into operation on 15 May 2000.

bail and child. When releasing a child on bail the court may, in the interest of the child, make the release subject to one or more conditions e g that the child resides with his parents, that the child receives education or undergoes training, that the child does not associate with a specific individual or stays away from a specific place: Children Act 2001, s 90. Also when a child is arrested and brought to a garda station, the member in charge may release the child on bail (CA 2001, s 68). See also Bail Act 1997, s 5 as amended by 2001 Act, s 89.

bailee. A person to whom the possession of goods is entrusted by the owner (the *bailor*) but not with the intention of transferring ownership. The bailee must re-deliver the bail to the bailor on the determination of the bailment, unless he has a lien (qv) on the chattel.

Where a bailment is solely for the benefit of the bailor e g a gratuitous deposit, the bailee is liable only for gross negligence. Where the bailment is entirely for the benefit of the bailee e g a gratuitous loan, then the bailee is liable for slight negligence e g the omission of the care a vigilant person takes in his own goods. Where the bailment is for the mutual benefit of bailor and bailee e g hire for reward, the bailee is liable for ordinary negligence e g failure to take the care that an ordinary man would; the onus is on the bailee of the goods to show that loss did not occur through lack of reasonable care on his part: *Sheehy v Faughan* [1991] ILRM 719, HC.

When a bailee does an act so repugnant to the bailment as to show disclaimer, the bailment is automatically determined e g bailee selling a chattel hired under a hire-purchase agreement. Also if the bailee departs from the terms of the bailment, he will be liable for any loss or damage to the chattels due to such deviation: *Lilley v Doubleday* [1881] 7 QBD 510. A bailee is liable to account for any increase in profits accrued in respect of the chattel bailed e g a cow calving. Also a bailee must pay the ordinary expenses of maintaining the chattel and is estopped from denying the bailor's title. See BAILMENT; INTERPLEADER; TREASURE TROVE.

bailiff. A person employed by a sheriff (qv) to serve and execute writs and orders. A bailiff may plead the Statute of Limitations against a person beneficially entitled to a share in the estate of a deceased person: Succession Act 1965, s 124 overruling *Rice v Begley* [1920] 1 IR 243.

bailiwick.

The area under the jurisdiction of a sheriff (qv) or bailiff (qv).

bailment. The delivery of goods to another on the condition express or implied, that they shall be restored to the bailor, or according to his directions, as soon as the purpose for which they are bailed is answered: *Coggs v Bernard* [1703] 2 Ld Ray 909. The act of delivery is called a *bailment*, the person making the delivery is called a *bailor* and the person to whom it is made is called the *bailee*.

There are three classes of gratuitous bailment: (a) *depositum* (deposit) – delivery of goods to be taken care of by the bailee who receives no reward for his services; special kinds of deposit include *involuntary bailment* and *bailee by finding*; (b) *mandatum* (mandate) – delivery of goods to a bailee to do something to them or to carry them from place to place, with the bailee not receiving any reward; (c) *commodatum* (loan for use) – a gratuitous loan for the bailee's benefit.

There are two classes of bailment for valuable consideration: (a) *vadium*, pledge or pawn – delivery of goods to another as security for money borrowed by the bailor: see PAWNBROKER; (b) *locatio conductio* – delivery of goods for reward e g *locatio rei* – goods hired for reward; (c) *locatio operis faciendi* – goods to be carried or something to be done to them (e g repair) for reward;

and (d) *locatio custodiae* – goods deposited for reward.

Delivery may be *actual* (by handing over the article), *constructive* (by delivery of some instrument of dominion over the goods eg a key to a warehouse) or by *attornment* (qv). See *Webb & Webb v Ireland* [1988] IR 353. The mere permission to deposit cargo on the premises of Harbour Commissioners does not impute the necessary degree of control to create a bailment: *Doherty Timber Ltd v Drogheda Harbour Commissioners* [1993] ILRM 401, HC. See also Occupiers' Liability Act 1995, s 8(b)(ii). See APPROPRIATION; BAILEE; BAILOR; CONSUMER-HIRE AGREEMENT; CONVERSION; DETINUE; HIRE-PURCHASE.

bailment, involuntary. See INVOLUNTARY BAILMENT.

bailment by finding. See FINDING, BAILMENT BY.

bailor. A person who entrusts goods to another, called the bailee (qv). In a gratuitous loan of goods for the use of the bailee, the bailor must disclose details of defects which he knows would make the goods dangerous or unprofitable to the bailee. In bailment for hire and reward, the bailor must use reasonable care to ensure that the goods are reasonably fit for the purpose intended. See *Reed v Dean* [1949] 1 KB 188. See BAILMENT.

bailperson. A person accepted as a surety for the purpose of bail. The court must satisfy itself as to the *sufficiency* and *suitability* of such a person, having regard to his financial resources, his character and antecedents, his relationship to the accused, and any previous convictions he may have: Bail Act 1997, s 7. There is provision for the mandatory estreatment of the *recognisance* (qv) of any surety and the forfeiture of the amount paid into court (BA 1997, s 9).

Bain v Fothergill, Rule in. The rule which states that, where a breach of contract in the sale of land, relied upon by the purchaser, is the vendor's failure to show good title to the property in question, then, provided the vendor was not fraudulent and did not otherwise act in bad faith, the purchaser is not entitled to recover damages for loss of bargain, but is limited to recover his deposit with interest and any expenses incurred in the investigation of title: *Bain v Fothergill* [1874] LR 7 HL 158. The rule is followed in Ireland eg see *McQuaid v Lynam* [1965] IR 564. However, see *Fitzgerald v Browne* [1854] 4 ICLR 178; *Irish Leisure Industries Ltd v Gaiety Theatre Enterprises Ltd* (1975) unreported 1972/253P. [Bibliography: Wylie (2).]

balance. That which remains after something has been taken out of a fund: *Re Burke Irwin's Trusts* [1918] I IR 350.

balance of convenience. The test used by the court in deciding whether to grant an *interlocutory* injunction; it will grant such an injunction when the plaintiff has established a fair question to be tried, and the balance of convenience lies in granting the injunction, and where the recoverable damages would be an inadequate remedy. Where an interlocutory injunction is refused, the court may order the defendant to lodge certain moneys in a bank account (eg income from an alleged breach of copyright) to meet any claim which the plaintiff might establish at the hearing of the action eg see *Paramount Pictures Corp v Cablelink Ltd* [1991] 1 IR 521, HC. See *Campus Oil Ltd v Minister for Industry & Commerce (No 2)* [1983] IR 88; *Mantruck Services Ltd & Manton v Ballinlough Electrical* [1991] ITLR (23 December), SC. See INJUNCTION; STATUS QUO.

balance of probability. The concept in the law of evidence whereby a party, upon whom the burden of proving some matter rests, is entitled to a decision in his favour in that issue if he establishes the proof of the matter in the balance of probabilities. It is the normal standard of proof in civil proceedings. It applies in civil cases alleging breach of EC competition provisions: *Masterfoods Ltd t/a Mars v HB Ice Cream Ltd* [1992] ITLR (5 October), HC. It also applies to disciplinary hearings resulting in the dismissal of an employee: *Georgopoulus v Beaumont Hospital Board* [1994] 1 ILRM 58, HC. It is often explained to juries in court as: *Which story would you believe; which story is the more likely?*

A lapse of 23 years in a negligence action between the date of injury and the hearing of the action does not change the onus of proof from the 'balance of probability' to 'beyond reasonable doubt': *Maitland v Swan & Sligo Co Council* [1992] ITLR (6 July), HC. See *SEE Co Ltd v Public Lighting Services* [1988] ILRM 677, SC. See BEYOND REASONABLE DOUBT; RECTIFICATION; STANDARD OF PROOF.

balance sheet. The account required to be prepared by a company which shows its overall financial position at the end of the accounting period eg what its issued and actual capital is, what reserves it has, and its assets and liabilities: Companies Act 1963, Sch 6, regs 2–11. Banks, discount houses and assurance companies are exempted from many of the requirements (regs 23–26). The balance sheet must also give a true and fair view of the state of affairs of the company at the end of its financial year: Companies Amendment Act 1986, s 3. See also Building Societies Act 1989, ss 77 and 81 as amended by Housing (Miscellaneous Provisions) Act 2002, s 23 and Sch 3. See ACCOUNTS, COMPANY.

balloon lease. A lease which does not involve a broadly even spread of lease payments over the period under the lease. It is called 'balloon' because the lease payments increase or 'balloon' towards the end of the lease period. There are restrictions on the offset of capital allowances in the case of a lessor of machinery or plant under a balloon lease: Taxes Consolidation Act 1997, s 404. This is to avoid artificial losses being created by the capital allowances in the early years of the lease, giving a cash flow advantage as against the taxation authorities. This could be significant in the case of leases of ships and aircraft. The restrictions do not apply to small leases or to leases written by International Financial Services or Shannon based companies. It has been clarified that the restriction does not apply to such leases written before such a company's IFSC/Shannon certificate expires but which will extend beyond that time: Finance Act 2003, s 39.

ballot. Any system of secret voting. Voting in elections to Dáil Éireann, Seanad Éireann and for the President of Ireland must be by *secret* ballot, which has been held to mean secret to the voter: *McMahon v Attorney-General* [1972] IR 69. The ballot paper of a voter at a Dáil election must be in a specified form: Electoral Act 1992, s 88 and Sch 4. See also Electoral (Amendment) Act 2004, s 31.

Provision has been made for the inclusion of photographs and political party emblems on ballot papers in respect of both manual and electronic voting: Electoral (Amendment) Act 2001; Ballot Paper (Photographs and Emblems) Regulations 2002, SI No 16 of 2002. Candidates or their agents must not handle ballot papers during the counting of votes (EA 1992, s 117). Breach of secrecy of a ballot is an offence (EA 1992, s 137). A person cannot be required in legal proceedings to state how and for whom he voted (EA 1992, s 162).

Provision was made for the ballot papers from the 1999 European and local elections to be used for research into electronic methods of voting: Local Elections (Disclosure of Donations and Expenditure) Act 1999, s 25.

The selection of persons empanelled as jurors to serve on a particular jury is made by balloting in open court: Juries Act 1976, s 15. See also Building Societies Act 1989, ss 50–51; Presidential Elections Act 1993, ss 36–44, 48, 60. Referendum Act 1994, s 24; European Parliament Elections Act 1997, Sch 2, r 50. See also ELECTION; SPOILT VOTE; STRIKE.

Bangeman wave. The expression used to describe the waving by EC nationals of their unopened passports to gain entry to another EC State, named after Martin Bangeman, EC Internal Market Commissioner, who proposed it in 1992; introduced in Ireland on 1 March 1993.

banishment. Formerly, the compulsory quitting and expulsion from the realm.

bank. A financial institution engaged in the acceptance of deposits of money, the granting of credits by loan or overdraft or otherwise, and engaged in other financial transactions such as the collection and payment of cheques and other money transmission services, the discounting of bills and the dealing in foreign exchange. As regards bills of exchange (qv), a *banker* includes: (a) a body of persons, whether incorporated or not, which carries on the business of banking; (b) a building society; (c) ACC Bank plc; (d) ICC Bank plc: Bills of Exchange Act 1882, s 2 as amended by ICC Bank Act 1992, s 7.

Banking business, for which a licence is required from the Central Bank, means: (a) the business of accepting on own account, sums of money from the public in the form of deposits or other repayable funds, whether or not involving the issue of securities or other obligations, howsoever described; or (b) any other business normally carried out by a bank, which may include the granting of credits: Central Bank Act 1971, s 2 as amended by Central Bank Act 1989, s 29(a); Central Bank Act 1997, s 70(b) and Central Bank and Financial Services Authority of Ireland Act 2003, s 35, Sch 1.

No company, association or partnership consisting of more than ten persons may be formed for the purpose of carrying on the business of banking unless it is registered as a company or is formed in pursuance of some other statute: Companies Act 1963, s 372. A person must not carry on a banking business or hold himself out or represent himself as a banker unless he is the holder of a licence and maintains a deposit in the Central Bank: Central Bank Act 1971, s 7 (as amended by the Central Bank Act 1989, s 30). The Central Bank is empowered to seek an injunction to prevent an unauthorised banking business: Central Bank Act 1997, s 74.

Consumer protection in the Consumer Information Act 1978 applies to licensed banks (CIA 1978, s 23; Restrictive Practices (Amendment) Act 1987, s 3).

The Registrar of Companies is required to notify the Central Bank of the delivery to him of any memorandum of association or articles of any company, which would in his opinion, be holding itself out as a banker or have one of its objects the carrying out of banking business, and he may not issue a certificate of incorporation to such a company unless the Central Bank indicates its willingness to issue a licence to the company or to exempt it: Central Bank Act 1971, s 15. Only the Central Bank may present a petition to the court for the appointment of an examiner to a bank: Companies (Amendment) Act 1990, s 3 as amended by Companies (Amendment) (No 2) Act 1999, s 6.

It is prohibited for a building society, an industrial and provident society, a friendly society, a credit union, an investment trust company or a unit trust scheme (qv), to use in its name or description any of the words *bank, banker* or *banking* (CBA 1971, s 14). See also Central Bank Acts 1942 to 1989; Solicitors (Amendment) Act 1994, s 75; Central Bank and Financial Services Authority of Ireland Act 2004. For the Institute of Bankers in Ireland, see website: *www.instbank.ie* where the full text of current and back issues of more than 2,000 of the world's major banking, finance and business journals is available. For the Irish Banks' Information Service, see website: *www.ibis.ie*. For the Bank for International Settlements, see website: *www.bis.org*. [Bibliography: Breslin; Donnelly; Forde (5); Johnston; Johnston & O'Conor; Long; McGann; Holden UK; Paget UK.] See CENTRAL BANK; CREDIT INSTITUTION; IRISH FINANCIAL SERVICES REGULATORY AUTHORITY; MONEY LAUNDERING; OMBUDSMAN FOR THE CREDIT INSTITUTIONS.

bank, acquiring transaction. Acquisitions of shareholdings in banks over a specified percentage (10% or more) require the approval of the Central Bank, and the Minister for Finance in certain circumstances: Central Bank Act 1989, ss 74–88. The 1989 Act also covers acquisitions by banks of prescribed shareholdings in non-banks. The Central Bank and the Minister are empowered to attach conditions to their approval and these conditions must be complied with. A review group established by the Minister has recommended that the Minister for Finance should not have any role in the supervision of bank acquisitions: see Department of Finance, *The Banking Sector: Some Strategic Issues* (August 2000).

bank holiday. Formerly a day on which banks were closed by statute: Bank Holidays Acts 1871, 1875 and 1903, now repealed by the Central Bank Act 1989, s 4 and Sch. A bank holiday is now, in effect, a *public holiday* (qv) as defined in the Organisation of Working Time Act 1997, ss 21–22 and *second schedule*.

A public holiday is a *non-business* day, as are Saturdays and Sundays; a bill of exchange (qv) which is due and payable on a non-business day, is payable on the next succeeding business day: Central Bank Act 1989, s 132. Special provision is made for a Saturday where the drawee of the bill is a banker and the drawee is normally open for business on that day.

A person is not compellable to make any payment or do any act on a public holiday which he would not be compellable to make or do on Christmas Day or Good Friday by virtue of any rule of law (CBA 1989, s 135) or on a day in which the TARGET system is closed: Euro Changeover (Amounts) Act 2001, s 5. See PUBLIC HOLIDAY.

banker, duty of care. A bank owes no duty, contractual or otherwise, to consider the financial interests of a customer when deciding whether or not to engage in any financial transaction, such as whether or not to make a loan; the bank is entitled to make the decision exclusively on the basis of its own commercial interests: *Kennedy v Allied Irish Banks Ltd* [1998] 2 IR 48, SC.

The relationship between a banker and a customer who pays money into the bank is the ordinary relation between debtor and creditor, with a super-added obligation, arising out of the custom of bankers, to honour the customer's drafts: *Joachimson v Swiss Bank Corporation* [1912] 3 KB 110.

A banker owes a duty to pay all cheques properly drawn on the customer's account, provided the account is in credit or within an agreed overdraft limit. The duty and authority of a banker to pay a cheque drawn on him is terminated by a *counter-mand* from the customer, or by notice of death or mental disorder of the customer, or notice of the presentation of a bankruptcy petition in respect of the customer, or notice of presentation of a petition to wind-up a company customer. It has been held that the correction by a bank of an error in its procedures on a short notice to the plaintiff company, did not constitute a breach of the duty of care owed to the company: *Hazylake Fashions Ltd v Bank of Ireland* [1989] ILRM 698, HC. See also *Reade v Royal Bank of Ireland* [1922] 2 IR 46; *Dublin Port & Docks Board v Bank of Ireland* [1976] IR 118; *Towey v Ulster Bank Ltd* [1987] ILRM 142; *Banco Ambrosiano v Ansbacher & Co* [1987] ILRM 669; *Shield Life Insurance Co Ltd v Ulster Bank Ltd* [1995] 3 IR 225, HC. See BANKERS' BOOKS; CHEQUE; CHEQUE, DISHONOUR OF; BILL OF EXCHANGE; PARTNERSHIP, NUMBER TO FORM.

banker and confidentiality. The relationship between banker and customer is a confidential one, subject to certain statutory and other exceptions eg where the publication of this confidential information could be of assistance in defeating wrongdoing, then the public interest in such publication may outweigh the public interest in the maintenance of confidentiality: *National Irish Banks Ltd v RTE* [1998] 2 ILRM 196, SC and [1998] 2 IR 465, SC.

A court may make an order authorising a party to legal proceedings, to inspect, and take copies of, entries in the books of a bank: Bankers' Books Evidence Act 1879, s 7; RSC Ord 31, r 17; O 63, r 1(17). See *L'Amie v Wilson* [1907] 2 IR 130; *Chemical Bank v McCormack* [1983] ILRM 350.

A court may also order a *financial institution* to reveal the affairs of a customer and has power to freeze the account of a customer who is a taxpayer: Finance Act 1983, s 18, now Taxes Consolidation Act 1997,

s 908 as amended by Finance Act 2002, s 132. A financial institution is broadly defined to include a licensed bank, building society, friendly society, credit union, and industrial and provident society (FA 1983, s 18(1)). The court has construed s 18 restrictively eg see *O'C v D* [1985] ILRM 123. See also *Application of Liam Liston* [1996] 1 IR 501, SC.

In certain circumstances, the Revenue Commissioners can obtain from financial institutions, without court order, details of the accounts and certain auxiliary financial information on a taxpayer who is a resident of the State: Waiver of Certain Tax, Interest and Penalties Act 1993, s 13. In addition, the Commissioners are empowered to make an application to the High Court to require a financial institution to supply documents and information held by a non-resident associated institution over which it has control (TCA 1997, s 908B inserted by Finance Act 2004, s 87).

The Director of Consumer Affairs is empowered to examine the accounts maintained by a *financial institution* on the order of the High Court, which may so order if satisfied that it is reasonable to do so and is satisfied that the exigencies of the common good so warrant: Restrictive Practices (Amendment) Act 1987, s 41. *Financial institution* in this context is also widely defined in the Act to include licensed banks, building societies, industrial and provident societies, friendly societies and credit unions (s 41(4)(b)).

A court or judge is empowered to authorise a garda to inspect and take copies of any entries in a banker's book for the purposes of investigation of an indictable offence, where the court or judge is satisfied that there are reasonable grounds for believing that such an offence has been committed and that there is material in the possession of the bank which is likely to be of substantial value to the investigation: Bankers' Books Evidence Act 1879, s 7A, as inserted by the Central Bank Act 1989, s 131(2)(c).

In a particular defamation action, a bank was ordered to give to the defendant's legal team, details on 65 bank customers alleged to have benefited from an investment scheme introduced by the plaintiff: *Cooper-Flynn v RTE & Bird* [2000] ITLR (5 June), HC. See also Taxes Consolidation Act 1997, s 908A as amended by Finance Act 2000, s 68; Finance Act 2002, s 132; Finance Act 2004, s 88. [Bibliography:

Johnston.] See ATTACHMENT; CLIENT ACCOUNT; INVESTIGATION OF COMPANY.

bankers' books. A copy of an entry in a banker's book is *prima facie* evidence of the contents of the entry and of the matters recorded therein, on the copy being proved to be correct: Bankers' Books Evidence Act 1879, ss 3–5. See also Bankers' Books Evidence (Amendment) Act 1959; RSC Ord 31, r 17; O 63, r 1(17).

This provision is now extended to the books of a building society, of ACC Bank plc, and of ICC Bank plc: Building Societies Act 1989, s 126(1); ACC Bank Act 1992, s 10; ICC Bank Act 1992, s 7.

The definition of bankers' books and records which may be admissible in evidence in court proceedings has been extended to include computerised and other modern day recording media: Central Bank Act 1989, s 131 as amended by Disclosure of Certain Information for Taxation and other Purposes Act 1996, s 14. For access of Revenue Commissioners to bankers' books, see Taxes Consolidation Act 1997, ss 907–908 and 908A as amended by Finance Act 2000, s 68. See also DCR 1997 Ord 38, r 2; District Court (Bankers' Books Evidence) Rules 1998, SI No 170 of 1998. See *Blanchfield v Hartnett* [2001] 1 ILRM 193, HC and [2002] 2 ILRM 435, SC and 3 IR 207.

bankers' draft. An order for the payment of money drawn by a bank upon itself. Payment on such a draft is certain; however an injunction may be granted to restrain a bank from honouring its own draft where there is evidence that such honouring would aid and abet a fraudulent transaction: *Murphy v Allied Irish Banks and Deele Fuels* (1988) HC. See also Building Societies Act 1989, s 29(2)(q).

bankrupt. A debtor who has been adjudicated a bankrupt by the High Court. See AFTER-ACQUIRED PROPERTY; FRAUDULENT DEBTOR; RECEIVER OF BANKRUPT'S PROPERTY.

bankrupt, duties of. A bankrupt is required to deliver up to the Official Assignee (qv) his property and his books and accounts and other papers: Bankruptcy Act 1988, s 19. The bankrupt is required to make a *statement of affairs* in the prescribed form, to disclose any *after-acquired property* (qv), and to notify the Official Assignee of any change in his name or address (BA 1988, ss 19, 20, and 127). He cannot refuse to answer any question put to him on examination by the court on the ground that his answers might incriminate him (BA 1988, s 21(4)). For arrest of bankrupt and committal to prison, see BA 1988, ss 23–25. For format of statement of affairs, see Rules of the Superior Courts (No 3) 1989, SI No 79 of 1989, Part XX. See STATUTORY SITTING.

bankruptcy. Bankruptcy is a law for the benefit and the relief of creditors and their debtors, in cases where the latter are unable or unwilling to pay their debts: *Re Reiman* [1874] 20 Fed Cas 490. Its objective is to secure an equitable distribution of the property of the bankrupt: *Re Boyd* [1885–86] 15 LR Ir.

A person is *adjudicated* a bankrupt on the petition of the debtor himself or more usually on the petition of the creditor when the debtor has committed an *act of bankruptcy*. However, without becoming a bankrupt, a debtor may seek the protection of the court while he makes an *arrangement* with his creditors. This he does by petitioning the court to protect his property and person at the suit of creditors, until such time as he submits an offer of composition (qv). See ARRANGING DEBTOR.

New legislation to revise, update and consolidate bankruptcy law came into force on 1 January 1989, modelled on legislation drafted by the Bankruptcy Law Committee, which was established in 1962 and reported in 1972: Bankruptcy Act 1988 which repeals the Acts of 1857, 1872 and 1889. Under the 1988 Act: the unpaid debt which constitutes an act of bankruptcy is £1,500 (€1,900) (BA 1988, s 8(1)); the new legislation also provides for discharge of a bankrupt after 12 years in certain circumstances (BA 1988, s 85); the Official Assignee (qv) is given primary responsibility in bankruptcy administration similar to a *liquidator* of a company; bankruptcy law is more closely aligned to the law on the winding up of companies, particularly in regard to disclaimer of *onerous property* (qv), *fraudulent preferences* (qv) and *preferential payments* (qv); the jurisdiction of the Cork Circuit Court in bankruptcy is abolished; and provision is made for the winding up in bankruptcy of the estates of persons dying insolvent. Extremely compelling reasons are required to reverse the machinery of bankruptcy: *Gill v Philip O'Reilly & Co Ltd* [2003] 1 IR 434, SC. See Maternity Protection Act 1994, s 36; Adoptive Leave Act 1995, s 38(2); Employment Equality

Act 1998, s 103(2); National Minimum Wages Act 2000, s 49.

Provision has been made for the substitution with effect from 1 January 2002 of *convenient amounts* expressed in euros for the amounts expressed in Irish pounds in the provisions of the Bankruptcy Act 1988: Bankruptcy Act (Alteration of Monetary Limits) Order 2001, SI No 595 of 2001. The euro amounts expressed are: €3,100 in s 45(1); €1,900 in ss 8(1)(a), 11(1)(a) and s 15; €1,300 in ss 8(2) and 61(3)(h) – increased in respect of s 61(3)(h) to €7,000 by Courts and Court Officers Act 2002, s 34; €130 in ss 39(4), 61(3)(k), 92(2), 95(2) and 101. See also Euro Changeover (Amounts) Act 2001, s 7.

See RSC Ord 76 inserted by Rules of the Superior Courts (No 3) 1989, SI No 79 of 1989. For amendments to BA 1988, ss 3, 61, 69, 142 and new ss 140A, 140B, 140C, see EC (Personal Insolvency) Regulations 2002, SI No 334 of 2002. See *Lynch* in 7 ILT & SJ (1989) 138 and 300. [Bibliography: Forde (4); Glanville; Holohan & Sanfey; O'Reilly P; Robb; Gov Pub (2).] See BANKRUPTCY, ACT OF; BANKRUPTCY, PETITION FOR; FAMILY HOME AND BANKRUPTCY; INSOLVENT ESTATE; SUBSEQUENT BANKRUPTCY; WINDING UP BY TRUSTEE.

bankruptcy, act of. A debtor commits an *act of bankruptcy* if: (a) he conveys his property to a trustee for the benefit of his creditors generally; or (b) he makes a fraudulent conveyance of his property; or (c) he conveys his property or creates a charge on it which would be void as a fraudulent preference (qv) if he were adjudicated bankrupt; or (d) he leaves the State or departs from his dwellinghouse or otherwise absents himself or evades his creditors; or (e) he files in court a declaration of insolvency; or (f) if his goods have been seized under an order of the court or a return of no goods is made; or (g) if he fails to pay the sum referred to in a *bankruptcy summons* (qv) within 14 days after service or fails to compound for it to the satisfaction of the creditor: Bankruptcy Act 1988, s 7.

A transaction by a debtor is void as against the Official Assignee (qv) where it is entered into after an act of bankruptcy is committed and within three months of adjudication, if it is a sale at a substantial undervalue (BA 1988, s 58).

In addition, a banker and an auctioneer are deemed to have committed an act of bankruptcy in the circumstances as provided for under the Central Bank Act 1971, s 28(1) and the Auctioneers and House Agents Act 1967, ss 11(3) and 11(4) respectively. See BANKRUPTCY SUMMONS; DEBTOR'S SUMMONS.

bankruptcy, adjudication of. The adjudication by the court that a debtor is bankrupt where the court is satisfied that the requirements of the petition therefor are satisfied: Bankruptcy Act 1988, ss 14–15. A person adjudged bankrupt may show cause against the validity of the adjudication and it may be annulled: RSC Ord 76 inserted by Rules of the Superior Courts (No 3) 1989, SI No 79 of 1989; BA 1988 Act, s 16. See *Gill v Philip O'Reilly & Co Ltd* [2003] 1 IR 434, SC.

A certain degree of precision is required in the documentation grounding an application for bankruptcy as the bankruptcy code is *penal* in nature and the requirements of the statutes must be complied with strictly: *In the matter of Gerard Sherlock* [1995] 2 ILRM 493, HC.

Following adjudication, the bankrupt is required to surrender and conform and to make a full and true disclosure and discovery of his estate (BA 1988, s 19). A *composition* (qv) with creditors at this stage is still a possibility.

The court may summon before it a bankrupt, or anyone suspected of having possession or control of any property of the bankrupt, and may examine that person under oath and require him to produce any books of accounts or papers in his possession or control (BA 1988, s 21). This provision has been found to be constitutional, as there is no prohibition on the courts performing certain administrative functions for the purpose of discharging their own functions: *O'Donoghue v Ireland* [2000] 2 ILRM 145, HC and [2000] 2 IR 165, HC.

On adjudication as a bankrupt, all the debtor's property, real and personal, present and future, vested and contingent, vests in the Official Assignee (qv) (BA 1988, s 44). However, property of which a bankrupt is a trustee does not so vest, although bankruptcy will be a good ground for his removal as a trustee (BA 1998, s 44(4)(a)).

The creditors may appoint a creditor's assignee to act with the Official Assignee in realising the estate, by sale, public auction or private treaty; however from 1989, the role of the creditor's assignee is diminished and he no longer has a shared function with the Official Assignee in relation to the property of the bankrupt (BA 1988, ss 18 and 44). Following distribution to the creditors, the bankrupt could previously in certain circumstances, obtain a *certificate of conformity* from the court and this released him from all debts due at the date of bankruptcy and discharged him as a bankrupt: Bankruptcy Ireland (Amendment) Act 1872, s 56. From 1989, the certificate of conformity has been abolished; instead a certificate of *discharge* or *annulment* under the seal of the court may be issued (BA 1988, s 85(7)). For procedure for an order of adjudication, see SI No 79 of 1989, Pt VII. Property which is subject to certain court orders, made before the person in possession or control of the property is adjudicated bankrupt, is excluded from the property of the bankrupt for the purposes of the 1988 Act: Proceeds of Crime Act 1996, s 11. Also a debt, due as a personal liability pursuant to s 297(1) of the Companies Act 1963, is not provable in a debtor's bankruptcy: *In the matter of Matthew Kelly, a bankrupt* [2000] ITLR (27 March), HC. See also Criminal Justice Act 1994, s 28; Credit Union Act 1997, s 72. See ARRANGING DEBTOR; BANKRUPTCY, ANNULMENT OF; PROCEEDS OF CRIME; STATUTORY SITTING.

bankruptcy, annulment of. The order of annulment of adjudication which a bankrupt is entitled to, where he has shown cause against the validity of the adjudication or in any other case where, in the opinion of the High Court, he should not have been adjudicated bankrupt: Bankruptcy Act 1988, s 85(5); *Re M'G* 11 ILTR 93. An *order of annulment* will provide for any property then vested in the Official Assignee (qv) to be revested in the bankrupt and this will be deemed to be a conveyance, assignment or transfer, which may be registered where appropriate (BA 1988, s 85(6)). See *In the matter of Gerard Sherlock* [1995] 2 ILRM 493, HC.

bankruptcy, discharge from. A bankrupt is entitled to a discharge from bankruptcy: (a) where the adjudication took place before 1 January 1960; or (b) where provision has been made for the payment of all expenses as well as the preferential payments and he has either paid one pound in the pound (now one euro in the euro) or he has the consent of all his creditors; or (c)

where he has made a *composition* (qv) after bankruptcy and lodged with the Official Assignee (qv) cash or securities to meet the composition; or (d) where in the opinion of the High Court, his estate has been fully realised and certain specified conditions have been complied with e g where either 50 cents or more in the euro has been paid or the bankruptcy has subsisted for twelve years: Bankruptcy Act 1988, s 85.

An *order of discharge* is provided for any property then vested in the Official Assignee to be revested in the bankrupt and this is deemed to be a conveyance, assignment, or transfer, which may be registered where appropriate (BA 1988, s 85(6)). See also BA 1988, s 41. For procedural rules and forms, see Rules of the Superior Courts (No 3) 1989, SI 79 of 1989, Part XXXI. See UNDISCHARGED BANKRUPT.

bankruptcy, effect of. See UNDISCHARGED BANKRUPT.

bankruptcy, petition for. The petition which may be brought by a debtor or by a creditor for an *adjudication of bankruptcy* of the debtor. When a debtor cannot pay his debts, he may bring a *petition* to the High Court to be adjudged a bankrupt, if he can show that his assets are sufficient to produce a sum of £1,500 (€1,900): RSC 0 76 inserted by Rules of the Superior Courts (No 3) 1989, SI No 79 of 1989; Bankruptcy Act 1988, s 11(3). More usually the petition is brought by a creditor after the debtor has committed an *act of bankruptcy*.

The minimum debt to ground a petition by a creditor is £1,500 (€1,905); the period within which an act of bankruptcy is available for the purpose of obtaining an adjudication is three months; and the debtor must be domiciled or have resided or carried on business in the State within a year before the presentation of the petition (BA 1988, s 11). For format and procedure for petition, see SI No 79 of 1989, Part VI.

A petition for bankruptcy may be served by public advertisement where other modes of service have not proved feasible: RSC 0 76; *Re DH, a debtor* [2000] ITLR (24 April), HC. Notice of a bankruptcy petition by public advertisement may be ordered by the court, but this mode of service should only be resorted to if other modes have not proved feasible: *Bank of Ireland v DH* [2000] 3 IR 315 and 2 ILRM 408, HC. The Collector-General may take bankruptcy proceedings in his own name to collect taxes: Taxes Consolidation Act 1997, s 999. See also TCA 1997, ss 972, 976, 994 and 1000. See BANK-RUPTCY, ACT OF.

bankruptcy inspector. The new title given to the former Court Messenger: Bankruptcy Act 1988, ss 3 and 60(2) and (3). A bankruptcy inspector has power, acting under warrant from the High Court, to seize property of a bankrupt and for that purpose to enter and break open any house or place belonging to the bankrupt where any of his property is believed to be (BA 1988, ss 27–29). He has a duty to take an inventory and report on the bankrupt's property; to seize property of the bankrupt pursuant to a warrant issued by the court; and to take possession of an *arranging debtor's* (qv) property (BA 1988, s 62). It is an offence to obstruct an inspector (BA 1988, s 128).

bankruptcy summons. A summons which may be granted by the court to a creditor who proves that a *liquidated* debt of £1,500 (€1,900) or more is due to him by the person against whom the summons is sought and a notice in the prescribed form, requiring payment of the debt, has been served on the debtor: Bankruptcy Act 1988, s 8(1). Failure to comply with a bankruptcy summons within 14 days after service can constitute an *act of bankruptcy* (BA 1988, s 7(1)(g)). The court must dismiss the summons on the application of the debtor, who disputes the debt, if satisfied that an issue would arise for trial (BA 1988, s 8(5)). Also when the amount said to be due on foot of the *notice* requiring payment and on the *bankruptcy summons* is in excess of the amount owed, this constitutes a substantial defect, rendering the notice and the summons defective: *In the matter of Gerard Sherlock* [1995] 2 ILRM 493, HC.

For format and service of bankruptcy summons, see Rules of the Supreme Court (No 3) 1989, SI No 79 of 1989, Pt III. See DEBTOR'S SUMMONS.

banns. The proclamation in church in the form of a public notice of an intended marriage (qv).

bar. (1) A partition across a court of justice; only senior counsel, solicitors (as officers of the court) and the parties are allowed within the bar. Being *called to the Bar* means being admitted by the Chief Justice in the Supreme Court to practice as a barrister. *The Bar* is the collective name for the professional body of barristers. The Attorney-General is the Leader of the Irish Bar. See 'Competition in the Cab-rank and the Challenges to the Independent Bar' by John D Cooke, Judge of the Court of First Instance, in *Bar Review* (July 2003) 148 and (Nov 2003) 197.

(2) Any open bar or any part of a licensed premises exclusively or mainly used for the sale and consumption of intoxicating liquor and includes any counter or barrier across which drink is or can be served to the public: Intoxicating Liquor Act 1988, s 2(1). A restaurant in respect of which a special restaurant licence has been granted must not contain a bar (ILA 1988, s 16). It is an offence for the holder of a licence of any licensed premises to allow a person under the age of 18 years to be in the bar of the premises (ILA 1988, s 34 as substituted by Intoxicating Liquor Act 2003, s 14). However, it is permissible for: (a) a child aged 15–18 to be in the bar up to 9pm; or (b) for a child of any age, if accompanied by his parents or guardian, to be in the bar up to 9pm; or (c) on the occasion of a private function at which a 'substantial meal' is served, for a child of any age, if accompanied by his parent or guardian, or if at least 15 years old, to be in the bar. Other restrictions apply to persons under 18 years of age during extended hours or on an off-licensed premises (ILA 1988, ss 35–36). For the provisions on what constitutes a 'substantial meal', which must cost at least €9.00, see Intoxicating Liquor Act (section 9) Order 2003, SI No 442 of 2003. See also Equal Status Act 2000, s 15 as amended by ILA 2003, s 25.

(3) To bar a right is to destroy or end it eg a debt being barred by the Statute of Limitations.

(4) An impediment.

See DISBAR; INTOXICATING LIQUOR; LIMITATION OF ACTIONS.

Bar Council. The council, elected by members of the Law Library (qv), which deals with matters affecting the profession of barristers, eg etiquette and professional practice; relationship with the solicitors' profession and with the State and its civil service departments. The Law Library is situated in the Four Courts in Dublin; membership of the Library and practice at the Bar have become virtually synonymous. See website: *www.lawlibrary.ie*. See BARRISTER; COUNCIL OF THE EUROPEAN BARS AND LAW SOCIETIES.

bar, plea in. See PLEA.

Bar Review. The official journal of the Bar of Ireland containing articles written by barristers, academics and guest writers on a variety of legal topics. Editor, *The Bar Review*, Law Library, Four Courts, Dublin 7. Tel: +353-1-817 5505; fax: +353-1-872 0019; email: *eilisbrennan@hotmail.com*. [Bibliography: Brennan E.] See GAZETTE.

bare licence. A mere licence. A bare licensee is a person who has permission, which is not supported by consideration (qv), to enter land or premises for his own purposes, so as not to be a trespasser. A bare licence is always revocable. See LICENCE.

bare trust. A trust (qv) which merely requires the trustee to hold property on trust with no duty in relation thereto except to convey it when required. See *Christie v Ovington* [1875] 1 Ch D 279. See Companies Act 1990, s 55(1)(a). Contrast with ACTIVE TRUST.

bargain. A contract; an agreement.

barking, excessive. See DOGS.

barratry. The common law misdemeanour (now, offence) of inciting, promoting or maintaining a false or groundless action. It is very rarely prosecuted. Barratry also includes every wrongful act wilfully committed by the master or crew to the prejudice of the owner, or as the case may be, the charterer: Marine Insurance Act 1906, Sch 1, art 11.

barring order. An order preventing one spouse from entering the family home even if that spouse is the owner thereof, either wholly or in part: Family Law (Maintenance of Spouses and Children) Act 1976, s 2. The court may make such an order if it is of the opinion that there are reasonable grounds for believing that the safety and welfare of the other spouse, or of any child of the family, so requires it.

A *barring order* may also prohibit the respondent to the application from: (a) using or threatening to use violence against the applicant or any dependent person; (b) molesting or putting in fear the applicant or any dependent person; or (c) attending at or in the vicinity of, or watching and besetting a place where the applicant or dependent person resides: Domestic Violence Act 1996, s 3(3).

This widens the persons who may be protected, to include cohabitants and their children. Such a barring order may last for three years if granted by the District Court and may be renewed; a contravention of an order is a criminal offence (DVA 1996, ss 3(9) and 17).

The court may also grant an interim barring order if there is an immediate risk of significant harm and if a *protection order* would not give sufficient protection (DVA 1996, s 4). However, the Supreme Court has held that the procedure which permitted an interim barring order to be granted *ex parte* and without a time limit, was unconstitutional: *D K v Crowley* [2002] 2 IR 744, SC and [2003] 1 ILRM 88. This decision necessitated an amendment to s 4(3) which now provides that an *interim barring order* may be made *ex parte* where the court considers it necessary or expedient to do so in the interests of justice; however: (a) the application must be grounded on an affidavit or information sworn by the applicant; (b) a copy of the interim order, affidavit or information, and a note of the evidence given by the applicant must be served on the respondent as soon as practicable; and (c) the interim order has effect for a period, not exceeding eight working days, as specified in the order, unless on application by the applicant for the barring order and on notice to the respondent, the interim order is confirmed within that period by order of the court (DVA 1996, s 4(3) as substituted by Domestic Violence (Amendment) Act 2002, s 1(a)). See 'Interim Measures' by solicitor Alan Shatter in *Law Society Gazette* (January/February 2003) 24.

In divorce proceedings, the court may make a barring order, interim barring order or safety order: Family Law (Divorce) Act 1996, ss 11(a), 15(1)(d). A divorced person may apply for a barring order against a former spouse (FL(D)A 1996, s 51). See also Family Law (Miscellaneous Provisions) Act 1997, s 4.

A barring order may be made after an application for or on granting a decree of judicial separation (qv): Family Law Act 1995, s 6(a). See *O'B v O'B* [1984] ILRM 1. In the Circuit Court, an application for the making, varying or discharging of a barring order is instituted by the issuing of a *Domestic Violence Civil Bill*: Circuit Court Rules 2001 Ord 59, r 5. For the District Court, see DCR 1997 Ord 59, rr 5–6. [Bibliography: Duncan & Scully.] See EXCLUSION ORDER; MCKENZIE FRIEND; PROTECTION ORDER; SAFETY ORDER.

barring the entail. The conversion by the tenant in tail of an estate tail into a fee simple. The former methods of achieving such a conversion were by *suffering a recovery* or *levying a fine*. Since 1833 it is achieved by a *disentailing deed*. The Official Assignee (qv) in bankruptcy is empowered to bar the entail: Bankruptcy Act 1988, s 64. See FEE TAIL.

barrister. Counsel; a member of the Honourable Society of King's Inns who has been called to the Bar. A practising barrister is one who holds himself out as willing and obliged to appear in court on behalf of any client on the instructions of a solicitor and to give legal advice and other legal services to clients: *Code of Conduct for the Bar of Ireland* (December 2003) r 2.1. A barrister is required to uphold at all times the standards set out in the *Code* and must conduct himself in accordance with the standards of conduct expected of a barrister in his practice and it is his duty to be independent and free from any influence, especially such as may arise from his personal interests or external pressure, in the discharge of his professional duties as a barrister (r 1.1).

A barrister may not act in a professional capacity except upon the instructions of a solicitor or in appropriate cases a patent agent or trade mark agent (r 4.1) Exceptions may be authorised by the Bar Council, including access through the *Direct Professional Access Scheme*.

A barrister has a right of audience in every court. He appears in any court as of right and not by courtesy of the court (r 5.14). As a member of the Law Library (qv), a barrister intending to practise must spend twelve months as a pupil (previously called a *devil*) of an experienced barrister (called a *master*). After some years as a *junior counsel*, the barrister may take *silk* and become a *senior counsel* (equivalent to a Queen's Counsel in England) by applying to and obtaining the approval of the government.

A barrister is paid a fee, comprising a *brief fee* (qv) and a *refresher fee* (qv) where appropriate. The Taxing Master may review a barrister's fees; he is required to decide whether a reasonably prudent solicitor acting in a reasonable way would have offered such a fee: *Smyth v Tunney* [1991] 10 ILT Dig (1992) 267, HC. There is no rule to the effect that once fees have been marked by agreement between solicitor and counsel, they must be allowed; the appropriate test is what hypothetical counsel competent to do the case and not being in a position to expect a special or fashionable fee would be prepared to accept as his brief fee: *Best v Wellcome Foundation* [1996] 1 ILRM 34, HC. A barrister may not sue for his fees, which are deemed to be in the nature of an *honorarium*: *Wells v Wells* [1914] P 157.

The European Court of Justice has held that a national regulation which prohibits any multi-disciplinary partnerships between members of the Bar and accountants is not contrary to the Treaty of the European Community, since that regulation could reasonably be considered to be necessary for the proper practice of the legal profession, as organised in the country concerned: *Wouters, Savelbergh, Price Waterhouse Belastingadviseurs BV v Algemene Raad van de Nederlandse Orde van Advocaten* [2002] Case C-309/99.

However, since 1990 the Bar Council has authorised a number of approved organisations and institutions and their members to have *direct professional access* (i e without having to brief a solicitor) to practising barristers in non-contentious matters.

Law books purchased by a barrister are 'plant' within the meaning of Income Tax Act 1967, s 241(1), now Taxes Consolidation Act 1997, ss 284 and 300 as amended by Finance Act 2000, s 40, and qualify for wear and tear allowance: *Breathnach v McC* [1984] IR 340.

The Minister is empowered to specify by regulation, provided such regulation is approved by both Houses of the Oireachtas (qv), the maximum number of counsel in respect of whom costs may be allowed, on *taxation* by a Taxing Master, for payment by another party to certain actions e g actions which claim damages in respect of personal injuries caused by negligence, nuisance or breach of duty: Courts Act 1988, s 5. See also European Communities (Freedom to Provide Services) (Lawyers) Regulations 1979, SI No 58 of 1979; also European Communities (Freedom to Provide Services) (Lawyers) Regulations 1981, SI No 197 of 1981.

See websites: *www.lawlibrary.ie* and *www.kingsinns.ie.* [Bibliography: Comyn; Adamson UK.] See BRIEF; FRIEND, MY; IN CAMERA; LEADING BARRISTER; LITIGATION; PUPIL; SOLICITOR AND COUNSEL;

SOLICITOR, MUTUAL RECOGNITION; TAXATION OF COSTS.

barrister, disbarred. A barrister who has had his call to the Bar rescinded. A barrister who has procured himself to be disbarred, who has *practised* in the State as a barrister for a minimum period (up to three years), who is of good standing, and who has satisfied the Law Society that he is a fit and proper person to be admitted as a solicitor, is entitled to apply to be admitted and to be enrolled as a solicitor, having attended any courses and passed any examinations (other than examinations in substantive law subjects) prescribed by the Society: Solicitors (Amendment) Act 1994, s 51. Service by a person as a member of the judiciary, or as a barrister in the full-time service of the State or in employment in the provision of services of a legal nature is deemed to be *in practice* as a barrister. See Solicitors Acts (Apprenticeship and Education) (Amendment) Regulations 1991 and 1995, SIs No 9 of 1991 and 102 of 1995.

barrister, duty of. It is the duty of a barrister: (a) to comply with the provisions of the Code of Conduct; (b) not to engage in conduct which is dishonest or which may bring the barrister's profession into disrepute or which is prejudicial to the administration of justice; (c) to observe the ethics and etiquette of his profession; (d) to be competent in all his professional activities; (e) to conduct his profession as a barrister so as to ensure that there is no serious falling short, by omission or commission, of the standard expected of a barrister; (f) to be individually responsible for his own conduct; and (g) to co-operate with an investigation conducted by the Bar Council regarding his professional conduct: *Code of Conduct for the Bar of Ireland* (December 2003) r 1.2. There are particular duties specified for barristers in the conduct of a criminal case (r 9). See DEFENCE BARRISTER, DUTY OF; PROSECUTING BARRISTER, DUTY OF.

barrister, international practice. A barrister maintaining a principal place of practice outside of Ireland may, subject to such concessions as the rules of the local Bar may impose, practise there in association or share premises and facilities there with a 'foreign lawyer': *Code of Conduct for the Bar of Ireland* (December 2003) r 13.3. 'Foreign lawyer' means a 'lawyer' as defined in EC Directive 77/249/EC other than a barrister or advocate of the United Kingdom (r 13.1). A barrister who holds himself out as practising in Ireland while maintaining his principal place of practice abroad, must not practise as an employee of any foreign lawyers, person, undertaking or institution (r 13.4). A barrister may accept instructions directly from a lay client where the work involved originated or is to be performed wholly outside Ireland and the United Kingdom (r 13.6). A barrister may act on the instructions of a foreign lawyer without the intervention of an Irish solicitor where such instructions involve court work in Ireland (r 13.2). Nothing in these rules permits a barrister to undertake work outside of Ireland which if performed inside Ireland would involve an infringement of any other provision of this Code (r 13.5). For further provisions on the international practice of lawyers, see SOLICITOR, INTERNATIONAL PRACTICE.

barrister, misconduct of. It is professional misconduct for a barrister to fail to comply with the specified duties of a barrister; such misconduct may render the barrister liable to exclusion or suspension from membership of the Law Library or to be reported to the Benchers of the Honorable Society of King's Inns with a view to disbarment, or may render him liable to be admonished or suspended for a stated period from practice at the Bar of Ireland: *Code of Conduct for the Bar of Ireland* (December 2003) r 1.3. A failure to comply with the specified duties which does not amount to serious professional misconduct may be a breach of proper professional standards and may render the barrister liable to penalties including admonishment, imposition of a fine and the requirement to repay specified fees (r 1.4). Failure by a barrister to co-operate with an investigation into his professional conduct may be viewed as professional misconduct (r 1.5). See BARRISTERS' PROFESSIONAL CONDUCT TRIBUNAL.

barrister, negligence of. It had been held in England that a barrister was immune from actions for negligence in the performance of his professional duties: *Rondel v Worsley* [1969] 1 AC 191. However, that situation has changed in relation to claims in negligence in pre-trial work: *Saif Ali v Sydney Mitchell & Co* [1980] AC 198. In 2000, the House of Lords decided to abolish the immunity in respect of work as advocates in court and in respect of pre-trial work intimately connected with the conduct of cases in court: *Arthur J, s Hall & Co v Simons*. See 'The advocate's immunity from suit – protecting the difficult art' in *Bar Review* (October 2000) 3. See PROFESSIONAL INDEMNITY POLICY; PROFESSIONAL NEGLIGENCE.

barrister, withdrawal of. A barrister can withdraw from a case in particular circumstances, provided that his withdrawal will not have the effect of jeopardising his client's interests: *Code of Conduct for the Bar of Ireland* (December 2003) r 3.9. When a client behaves in an offensive manner towards his barrister, the barrister must nevertheless continue to act for that client; however he may withdraw from a case where he is justified in assuming that his professional conduct is being or is likely to be impugned or that the trust of the client in the barrister's professionalism has been thereby undermined. See ABSCOND; DEFENCE BARRISTER, DUTY OF; SOLICITOR, WITHDRAWAL OF; WITNESS.

barrister and client. A barrister must promote and protect fearlessly and by all proper and lawful means his client's best interests and do so without regard to his own interest or to any consequences to himself or to any other person including fellow members of the legal profession: *Code of Conduct for the Bar of Ireland* (December 2003) r 2.3. In a civil case, at any time before judgment is delivered, if a barrister is informed by his client that such client has lied to the court, or has procured another person to lie to the court, or has falsified, or procured another person to falsify, a document which has been tendered in evidence in any way, or he becomes aware that the client has otherwise been guilty of fraud upon the court, a barrister must: (a) refuse to take any further part in the case unless the client authorises the barrister to inform the court of the lie or falsification and, in that event; (b) promptly inform the court of the lie or falsification upon the client authorising the barrister to do so; but (c) not otherwise inform the court of the lie or falsification (r 5.9).

barrister and confidentiality. Confidentiality is a primary and fundamental right and duty of a barrister: *Code of Conduct for the Bar of Ireland* (December 2003) r 3.3. A barrister is under a duty not to communicate to any third-party information entrusted to him by or on behalf of his client and not to use such information to his client's detriment or to his own or another client's advantage. This duty continues at all times after the relation of barrister and client has ceased. Even when an accusation is made by a client against his solicitor, a barrister is bound to maintain confidentiality as to the matters coming to his knowledge as a barrister.

There is no breach of confidentiality in a barrister notifying and co-operating with his professional indemnifier, imparting information to his pupil, or disclosing information in the context of a complaint against that barrister or any other barrister. A barrister may not permit a member of the Garda Síochána, a Prison Officer, a Revenue Official or any other public officer, to read instructions confided in him as barrister, in any circumstances, without the authority of his client (r 3.4). A barrister may not make any public comment upon any case in which he has been briefed or instructed or upon any of the parties in the case (r 6.2). However he may speak and write on legal matters provided he does not breach confidentiality (rr.6.3–6.9). Also he may, at his discretion, show the pleadings to a news reporter in a matter which has been at hearing before a court, unless directed otherwise or there is an agreement not to do so (r 6.12). See also LAW LIBRARY.

barrister and court. A barrister has an overriding duty to the court to ensure in the public interest that the proper and efficient administration of justice is achieved and he must assist the court in the administration of justice and must not deceive or knowingly mislead the court: *Code of Conduct for the Bar of Ireland* (December 2003) r 2.2. He must maintain due respect and courtesy towards the court before which he is appearing (r 5.1). He must take appropriate steps to correct any misleading statement made by him as soon as possible after he becomes aware that the statement was misleading (r 5.3). He must not act as the mere spokesperson for the client or the instructing solicitor and must exercise an independent judgement (r 5.4). He must inform the court at once of a settlement or of an intention to apply for an adjournment (r 5.6). In a civil case, he must inform the court of any relevant decision on a point of law and, in particular, of any binding authority or of any applicable legislation of which he is aware and which he believes to be in point, whether it be for or against his contention (r 5.8). There is a prohibition on a barrister discussing a case with a trial judge unless the judge consents and the parties consent and are present or represented (rr 5.12 and 5.13).

barrister and fees. A barrister is entitled to charge for any work undertaken or to be undertaken by him (whether or not it involves an appearance in court) on any basis or by any method he thinks fit, provided that such basis or method is permitted by law, and a barrister is entitled to take into account when marking or nominating such fee, all features of the instructions which bear upon the commitment which is thereby undertaken or has been undertaken by him including: (a) the complexity of the issue or subject matter; (b) the length and venue of any trial or hearing; (c) the amount or value of any claim or subject matter at issue; (d) the time within which the work is or was required to be undertaken; (e) the other special feature of the case: *Code of Conduct for the Bar of Ireland* (December 2003) r 11.1(a).

Where a barrister has accepted a brief on the basis that his fee will be discharged before appearing for his client, such barrister is entitled to withdraw from the case in the event that such agreed fee is not paid by the agreed date (r 11.1(g)). Where a barrister is briefed but is unable to attend the hearing or contribute to the conduct of the case, he should forego his fee (r 11.4). See BRIEF FEE; SOLICITOR AND CLIENT COSTS.

barrister in employment. A practising barrister is required to keep his practice as his primary occupation and not to engage in any other occupation which is inconsistent with his practice at the Bar eg which is liable to interfere with his regular attendance at court or at the Law Library during term: *Code of Conduct for the Bar of Ireland* (December 2003) r 2.6. The following are regarded as compatible with practice at the Bar: membership of the Oireachtas or the European Parliament; the teaching of law at a university or other third-level establishment; the editorship of a learned legal journal; occasional journalism; and membership of a local authority or a subcommittee of a local authority (r 2.7).

A practising barrister may not be an executive director of a company or firm, but there is no prohibition on a barrister being a non-executive director (r 2.8). Also the rules do not preclude a barrister from being a member of any public body, board or council, whether or not an emolument is payable in respect of membership (r 2.12). There are certain restrictions on a barrister who, before his call to the Bar, has been a solicitor or has worked in a solicitor's office, eg he is required to give an undertaking prior to his entry to the Law Library not at any time to accept any work in which he may have been engaged when practising or working in a solicitor's office (r 8.11).

A barrister in the employment of the Personal Injuries Assessment Board may appear on behalf of the Board in an application to the courts to secure information which a party, not involved in a claim for personal injuries, is failing to supply to support the claimant's case: Personal Injuries Assessment Board Act 2003, ss 27 and 82. This provision applies notwithstanding: (a) any rule of law relating to the representation of bodies corporate; or (b) that the barrister would be prohibited from doing so by virtue of any rule of law or provision of any enactment or code of conduct imposing restrictions on employed barristers in relation to engaging in activity of that kind. See ARBITRATION; CORONER; FREE LEGAL ADVICE CENTRES; SOLICITOR'S OFFICE.

barristers, disputes between. It is the duty of a barrister to treat each of his colleagues with civility and respect and to treat each barrister with equality and not to discriminate in favour or against a barrister on any of the discriminatory grounds: *Code of Conduct for the Bar of Ireland* (December 2003) r 7.1. Where a barrister wishes to make a complaint against another barrister, the correct procedure in the first instance is to refer the matter to the Committee of the Bar Council dealing with such complaints (r 7.2).

barristers, partnership of. A barrister as an independent practitioner must not enter into any professional partnership or other form of unincorporated association or seek to practise his profession through a corporate entity and he must not enter into any professional partnership or relationship (including the sharing of briefs) with another barrister: *Code of Conduct for the Bar of Ireland* (December 2003) r 7.14. Barristers must not carry their practices as partners or as a group or as professional associates or in such a way as to lead solicitors or others to believe that they are partners or members of a group or associated in the conduct of their profession as barristers (r 8.6). Also no arrangements for the sharing of premises or facilities by two or more barristers may be made without the consent of the Bar Council (r 7.13). For European law on restrictions on multi-disciplinary partnerships between members of the Bar and accountants, see SOLICITOR.

barristers, precedence between. The order of precedence between barristers in court and in the conduct of professional business is: the Attorney-General; Senior Counsel in the order of their call to the Inner Bar; Junior Counsel in the order of their call to the Bar: *Code of Conduct for the Bar of Ireland* (December 2003) r 7.3. However, in the case of Junior Counsel called to the Bar after 2 July 1988 and who do not join the Law Library or commence practice within twelve months of their call, they are required to waive their precedence and to take their precedence in the order of their joining the Law Library.

In situations other than in court or in the conduct of professional business, the order of precedence is: the Father of the Bar who is the member of the Bar earliest in his initial call to the Bar; barristers whether Junior or Senior in the order of their initial call to the Bar; when dining at King's Inns the Benchers according to their order of precedence take precedence to all others; at Circuit Court functions, barristers take such precedence as the members of the Circuit determine.

The order of precedence applies *mutatis mutandis* to tribunals, inquiries, panels, boards, committees, arbitrators and such other bodies before whom a barrister appears (r 7.16). See JUDGES, PRECEDENCE BETWEEN.

Barristers' Professional Conduct Tribunal. The disciplinary tribunal with lay representation, established by the Bar Council, to consider complaints against barristers, whether from solicitors, members of the public or others. A range of penalties may be imposed, including fines and a recommendation to the Benchers of King's Inns that a barrister be disbarred. There is provision for appeal to the *Barristers' Professional Conduct Appeals Board*. The first case heard by the Tribunal and the Appeal Board was in 1993, when a barrister was found to have breached proper professional standards and was directed to pay £500 (€635) to the *Bar Benevolent Fund*. In 1995,

the tribunal admonished a barrister for accepting instructions directly from a client without the intervention of an instructing solicitor. See *Law Society Gazette* (April 1992) 98. In a particular court case, the court drew the attention of the Bar Council to the possible breaches of the code of conduct regarding the withdrawal of counsel: *DPP v McDonagh* [2001] 3 IR 411, CCA and [2002] 1 ILRM 225, CCA.

barter. The practice of exchanging goods for goods or services. See *Simpson v Connolly* [1953] 1 WLR 911. See *Miller* in 10 ILT & SJ (1992) 13.

base fee. A particular kind of determinable *fee simple*; it continues only so long as the original grantor or any heirs of his body are alive and there is a remainder (qv) or reversion (qv) after it. A base fee arises where a tenant in tail attempts to convey a fee simple without *barring the entail* or when the tenant in tail disentails without the consent of the *protector of the settlement* (qv). A base fee may be enlarged into a fee simple by a fresh disentailing deed by the former tenant in tail, or by the passage of time under the Statute of Limitations 1957, or by the owner of the base fee becoming the owner of the remainder or reversion in the fee simple immediately following the base fee.

bastard. A person born out of wedlock; an illegitimate person; now referred to as a person *whose parents are not married to each other*. See CHILD, ILLEGITIMATE; EVIDENCE TENDING TO BASTARDISE CHILDREN.

bather, liability to. The High Court has held that two defendants were responsible for an accident to a bather by failing to erect signs warning of the dangers of a rocky outcrop at the popular swimming area known as the Forty Foot: *McGowan v Dún Laoghaire-Rathdown County Council & Sandycove Bather's Association* (2004) 7 May 2004, HC (under appeal). The plaintiff sustained serious injuries as a result of striking a rock when he dived into the sea at the Forty Foot. The court held that the Council had a duty of care to bathers but had done nothing as regards following safety recommendations.

bathing waters. The EC Directive on bathing waters has as its objective that the quality of bathing water is maintained and, where necessary, improved so that it complies with specific standards designed to protect public health and amenity: EC

Directive 76/160/EEC. The Directive applies to water in which: (a) bathing is specifically authorised; or (b) bathing is not prohibited and is traditionally practised by a large number of bathers. See Quality of Bathing Water Regulations 1992, SI No 155 of 1992 and (Amendment) Regulations 1998, SI No 178 of 1998.

baths, public. A sanitary authority (qv) is empowered to provide and maintain: public baths; public swimming baths or public bathing places; conveniences for bathers; or public wash-houses: Local Government (Sanitary Services) Act 1948, s 5 and 35. In addition, the authority is entitled to make charges for their use, to employ lifeguards, and to arrange for the giving of instructions in swimming and life-saving (ss 36–40). The provision of swimming pools and other bathing places is a function of a local authority: Local Government Act 2001, s 67 and Sch 13.

BATNEEC. [Best available technology not entailing excessive costs.] See BEST AVAILABLE TECHNIQUES.

battery in crime. See ASSAULT.

battery in tort. See TRESPASS TO THE PERSON.

bawdy house. A brothel (qv).

Bayer injunction. An order of the court restraining a person from leaving the jurisdiction and requiring him to deliver up his passport. The term is derived from the decision in the English Court of Appeal of *Bayer A-G v Winter* [1986] 1 WLR 497, cited with approval in *O'Neill v O'Keeffe* [2002] 2 IR 1, HC. Such an injunction should be granted only where: (a) the court is satisfied that there is probable cause for believing that the defendant is about to absent himself from the jurisdiction *with the intention* of frustrating the administration of justice and/or an order of the court; (b) the jurisdiction should not be exercised for *punitive* reasons; a defendant's presence should be necessary to prevent a court hearing or process or existing order from being rendered nugatory; (c) the injunction should not be granted where a lesser remedy would suffice; (d) the injunction should be *interim* in nature and limited to the shortest possible period of time; (e) the defendant's right to travel should be outbalanced by those of the plaintiff and the proper and effective administration of justice; (f) the grant of the injunction should not be futile (*O'Neill* case). See *JN and*

C Ltd v TK [2003] 2 ILRM 40, HC. [Bibliography: Courtney (3).]

beach. See BATHS, PUBLIC.

beach material. Sand, clay, gravel, shingle, stones, rocks and mineral substances on the surface of the seashore (qv): Foreshore Act 1933, s 1. The Minister is empowered to grant a licence allowing a person to remove any beach material from, or disturb any beach material, in a foreshore (FoA 1933, s 3 as amended by Foreshore (Amendment) Act 1992, s 2). The Minister is also empowered by order to prohibit the removal of beach material from, or disturbance of beach material in, an area of seashore where he is of the opinion that such removal or disturbance had affected or is likely to affect any flora or fauna, or any amenities or public rights, or cause injury to land or any building, wall, pier or other structure (FoA 1933, s 6 amended by Fo(A)A 1992, s 3).

The High Court is empowered to prohibit continuance of contraventions of a licence, prohibitory order or notice, on the application of the Minister, a local authority or any other person (Fo(A)A 1992, s 5). Also application may be made to other courts (e g District – £5,000 (€6,349); Circuit – £30,000 (€38,092); High – no limit) to order a person to refrain from or cease removal or disturbance, or to mitigate or remedy any effects, or to reimburse the applicant for the costs in investigating, mitigating or remedying the effects of such removal or disturbance (Fo(A)A 1992, s 6). See FORESHORE.

bear. The term used to describe a person who sells stocks and shares before owning them, in the expectation that he will be able to buy in later when the price has fallen, and thereby make a profit. Contrast with bull. See SHARES, COMPANY.

bearer bill. A bill of exchange payable to bearer, or on which the only or last endorsement is an *endorsement in blank*. An *endorsement in blank* arises where the endorser merely signs his own name, or one which is payable to a fictitious or nonexistent person. See Bills of Exchange Act 1882, ss 8(3) and 34. See ORDER BILL; BILL OF EXCHANGE.

bed and breakfast. (1) Development consisting of the use of not more than four bedrooms in a house, where each bedroom is used for the accommodation of not more than four persons as overnight guest accommodation, e g bed and breakfast. It is *exempted development* (qv), provided that such development does not contravene a condition attached to the planning permission for the house or is inconsistent with any use specified or included in such permission: Planning and Development Regulations 2001, SI No 600 of 2001, art 10(4). For previous legislation, see Local Government (Planning and Development) Regulations 1994, SI No 86 of 1994. See DOMESTIC HEREDITAMENT.

(2) Colloquial expression describing an arrangement whereby the owner of shares in a company sells and repurchases sufficient shares to realise a capital gain which is within his annual capital gains tax allowance. The shares are sold and bought back at the same price. Where shares have increased in value from the price they were originally bought at, this *'bed and breakfast'* transaction enables the investor to retain his shareholding while increasing the base cost at which a future disposal of the shares will be reckoned for capital gains tax purposes. See CAPITAL GAINS TAX.

bedsit accommodation. Generally understood to mean a furnished sitting room containing sleeping accommodation and sometimes cooking and washing facilities. A *'self-contained residential unit'* includes the form of accommodation commonly known as 'bedsit' accommodation: Residential Tenancies Act 2004, s 4(1). See DWELLING.

beef. Provision has been made for the establishment of a *National Beef Assurance Scheme*, the purpose of which is: (a) to develop common *standards* for production, processing and trade in Irish cattle and beef for human consumption and the manufacture and trade of feedstuffs; (b) to apply these standards through a process of registration, inspection and approval, and (c) to enhance the animal identification and traceability system for Irish cattle: National Beef Assurance Scheme Act 2000. See also National Beef Assurance Scheme (Approval) Order 2002 and 2003, SI No 422 of 2002 and SI No 656 of 2003.

The aim of the 2000 Act is to underpin confidence in the domestic and export market in Irish beef, following the BSE scare and the possible link between BSE and a new variant in CJD in people. The *standards* are included in existing legislation and cover such matters as animal identification, animal health, animal remedies, hygiene and hygiene practices, production and

manufacturing practices, construction maintenance and operation of premises and equipment and the environment, including pollution and waste management.

The Act provides for mandatory inspection, approval and a registration process for all participants (e g farmers, manufacturers or traders in feedstuffs, dealers or exporters of live cattle, abattoirs, assembly centres, marts and meat plants). There is an appeal to the Circuit Court from a refusal or revocation by the Minister of a certificate of approval (NBASA 2000, s 17). Penalties have been increased under the Diseases of Animals Act 1966, the Livestock Marts Act 1967, and the Slaughter of Animals Act 1935 (NBASA 2000, ss 35–37). See also EC (Labelling of Beef and Beef Products) Regulations 2000 , SI No 435 of 2000 and (Amendment) Regulations 2002, SI No 485 of 2002.

beef carcase classification. Provision has been made for the dressing, classification, weighing and labelling of carcases of adult bovine animals slaughtered at export approved premises: EC (Beef Carcase Classification) Regulations 2004, SI No 45 of 2004 revoking SI No 8 of 1994. There is provision for on-the-spot fines, for mechanical classification (automated grading) and for price reporting by plants.

beg. It is an offence to cause or procure a child to be in any street or public place, or to make house-to-house visits, for the purpose of begging or receiving alms: Children Act 2001, s 247. There is a presumption that the person who has the custody, charge or care of the child, allowed the child to be in the street, place or house, unless the contrary is proved (CA 2001, s 247(2)). For previous legislation, see Children Act 1908, s 14.

beget. Procreate. There is a constitutional right to beget children within marriage, guaranteed by art 40 of the Constitution, which is suspended and placed in abeyance when one spouse is lawfully imprisoned: *Murray & Murray v Ireland & A-G* [1991] ILRM 465, SC.

begin, right to. See RIGHT TO BEGIN.

Belfast Agreement. See GOOD FRIDAY AGREEMENT.

Bell Houses clause. A clause in the objects of a company which permits the company, or the board of directors, to extend its activities into another business which would benefit the company's main business. There must be an honestly held belief that the extension will benefit the company: *Bell Houses Ltd v City Wall Properties Ltd* [1966] 2 QB 656. See *MacCann* in 10 ILT & SJ (1992) 81.

below cost selling. The selling, or advertising for sale, of grocery goods (including alcoholic beverages) below cost price; such selling or advertising is prohibited: Restrictive Practices (Groceries) Order 1987, SI No 142 of 1987; Restrictive Practices (Confirmation of Order) Act 1987. The Minister is empowered to amend or revoke the order: Competition Act 2002, s 49. The Order also contains provisions in relation to the withholding of supply of grocery goods, and the boycotting of any person in relation to grocery goods; it also prohibits the payment or receipt of *hello money* (qv). See also *Director of Consumer Affairs v Dunnes Stores* (1988) HC and (1992) HC.

A building society is prohibited from providing certain services at below cost e g services relating to land: Building Societies Act 1989, ss 31(12)(a) and 32(5)(a). [Bibliography: Lucey; O'Reilly M.]

bench. The judges in a court of law. Being *raised to the Bench* means being appointed a judge.

benchmarking. The technique by which something is measured against another thing, using some standard or reference e g the measurement of pay in the public sector by comparing with relevant pay in the private sector. In the context of the EU, a benchmark is the standard by which the performance of a country, business or industry is measured compared to others. Benchmarking is one of the techniques used in the '*Lisbon Process*' (qv).

bench warrant. An order of the court for the immediate arrest of a person e g for failure to surrender to bail. See Criminal Justice Act 1984, s 13(4) and (5). See WARRANT.

Benchers. The governing body of the Bar of Ireland. See KING'S INNS, THE HONOURABLE SOCIETY OF.

beneficial interest. The interest of a beneficial owner (qv) or beneficiary as contrasted with the estate or interest of a nominal or legal owner such as a trustee. See *Murray v Murray* [1996] 3 IR 251, HC.

beneficial owner. The person who enjoys or who is entitled to the benefit of property i e on his own right rather than on behalf of someone else. See INVESTIGATION OF COMPANY; REGISTER OF MEMBERS; TRUE PERSON.

beneficiary. A person for whose benefit property is held by a trustee or executor; a *cestui que trust* (qv); a person who receives a gift under a will.

beneficiary, remedies of. Where a trustee departs from the terms of the trust or is in breach of duties imposed by statute or by equity, the beneficiary of the trust may, in a suitable case, obtain an order for account, an injunction, damages, and a tracing order (qqv). See TRUSTEE, DUTY OF; TRACING.

benefit-in-kind. The provision of a benefit by an employer to an employee or a director e g the provision of a car for private use, or living accommodation; the benefit is chargeable to tax: Taxes Consolidation Act 1997, ss 116–122A as amended. Exempted from tax are certain benefits-in-kind: e g (a) mobile phones, computer and related equipment, and high speed Internet connections where the benefits are for business use and private use is incidental; (b) subscriptions to professional bodies where membership is relevant to the business of the employer; and (c) private use of a van in particular circumstances e g the van is necessary for the performance of the employee's duties and is kept at the employee's home, and he spends at least 80% of his time on duty away from the employer's premises: Finance Act 2004, s 8.

The provision of an annual or monthly bus or train pass in respect of a licensed passenger transport service is exempted from tax (TCA 1997, s 118(5A) as inserted by Finance Act 1999, s 33). This exemption has been extended to travel passes on the LUAS service (FA 2004, s 8). The taxation of the benefit of the availability of a company car for private use has been held not to be unconstitutional: *Browne & Ors v Attorney-General* [1991] 2 IR 58, HC.

The PAYE, PRSI, training and health levy systems have been extended to apply to benefits-in-kind as from 1 January 2004: Social Welfare (Miscellaneous Provisions) Act 2003, ss 16–18; Finance Act 2003, s 6; Social Welfare Act 2003, ss 13–15. The taxes are required to be deducted from cash remuneration at the same time as the benefit-in-kind is being provided. See also Finance Act 2004, s 9. See 'No such thing as a free lunch' by solicitor Richard Grogan in *Law Society Gazette* (April 2004) 26.

benignae faciendae sunt interpretationes et veba intentioni debent inservire. [Liberal interpretation should be the rule, and the words should be made to carry out the intention.] See CONSTRUCTION, RULES OF; INTERPRETATION OF LEGISLATION.

Benjamin order. An order of the court authorising the distribution of an estate on certain presumptions eg that certain beneficiaries are dead, where there is difficulty for the personal representative (qv) to so determine: *Re Benjamin, Neville v Benjamin* [1902] 1 Ch 723 applied *by Baker v Cohn-Vossen* [1986] ILRM 175.

bequeath. To give personal property by will eg a legacy.

bequest. A gift of personal property by will; a legacy. A *residuary bequest* is a gift of the residue of the testator's personal estate. A *specific bequest* is a gift of property of a certain kind eg *my large diamond ring.* See Copyright and Related Rights Act 2000, ss 123 and 296.

Where a client intends to confer a bequest under his will to the solicitor drafting the will and the bequest is of a significant amount, the solicitor should advise the client to obtain independent legal advise: *A Guide to Professional Conduct of Solicitors in Ireland* (2002) ch 3.5. This is not necessary where the amount is a token legacy of a nominal amount. See LEGACY.

bereavement grant. See DEATH, EFFECT OF.

Berne Copyright Union. The Copyright Convention which was signed at Berne in 1886. Most countries in the world, including Ireland, are members but not the USA or the former USSR. Under the Union, an author is given in countries other than the country of origin, not only the rights which are given by these countries' domestic laws but also the rights granted by the Union. Unlike the Universal Copyright Convention, there are no formalities required to be performed to obtain protection under the Union; the minimum term of protection is greater (generally 50 years); and the scope of protection is laid down in greater detail and is more extensive. Works published in any country of the Berne Union or of the Universal Copyright Convention are given the same protection in Ireland as if the works were first published within the State: Copyright (Foreign Countries) Order 1978, SIs No 132 and 133 of 1978. [Bibliography: Copinger UK; Laddie UK.] See UNIVERSAL COPYRIGHT CONVENTION.

BES. Business expansion scheme. See BUSINESS DEVELOPMENT SCHEME.

best available techniques. The Environmental Protection Agency must not grant a licence for an *activity* unless it is satisfied that the *best available techniques* will be used to prevent or eliminate or, where that is not practicable, generally to reduce an emission from the activity: Environmental Protection Agency Act 1992, ss 83(5)(a)(vi) and 5, as amended by Protection of the Environment Act 2003, ss 15 and 7. 'Best available techniques' is to be construed as a reference to the most effective and advanced stage in the development of an activity, and its methods of operation, so as to reduce an emission and its impact on the environment. 'Techniques' includes both the technology used and the way in which the installation is designed, built, managed, maintained, operated and decommissioned. 'Best available techniques' replaces BATNEEC (*best available technology not entailing excessive costs*) as the technical basis of the licensing system. See also Waste Management Act 1996, s 5(2) as substituted by PEA 2003, ss 20(3) and 21. See *Kimber and Maguire* in 11 ILT & SJ (1993) 196. See WASTE DISPOSAL.

best evidence rule. The rule that requires that the best and most direct evidence of a fact be adduced, or its absence accounted for eg the best evidence of the contents of a letter is its production in court. See *DPP v O'Donoghue* [1992] 10 ILT Dig 74, HC. See ADMISSIBILITY OF EVIDENCE; DOCUMENTARY EVIDENCE; EVIDENCE, PRIMARY.

bestiality. The crime of *buggery* (qv) committed with an animal. See Offences Against the Person Act 1861, ss 61–62 which are repealed by the Criminal Law (Sexual Offences) Act 1993 save in so far as they apply to buggery or attempted buggery with animals. See *R v Higson* [1984] 6 Cr App R (S) 20.

bet. A wager.

In 2002, the law on betting duties was consolidated and modernised, and a new collection system was provided for: Finance Act 2002, ss 64–83. An excise duty of 2% applies to bets, which becomes due when the bet is accepted (FA 2002, ss 67 and 69). The exemption from this duty continues to apply to bets placed *on course* at horse race courses and at greyhound tracks; there is a new exemption from duty for 'tote' bets placed in registered bookmaking premises (FA 2002, s 68).

There is a requirement on punters to pay the duty when placing bets; however the bookmaker may elect to pay the duty on specified classes of bets, and the previous penalties, which applied to bookmakers who offered tax-free betting, have been deleted (FA 2002, s 71). Failure to pay betting duty is an offence (FA 2002, s 67). For the arrangements for collection of betting duty and the records to be kept by bookmakers, see Betting Duty Regulations 2002, SI No 174 of 2002.

Under previous legislation, criminal prosecution for recovery of duty payable on a bet requires an order to be made by the Revenue Commissioners prior to commencement of the prosecution: Inland Revenue Regulations Act 1890, s 21(1) and *DPP v Cunningham* [1989] IR 481. The recovery of excise duty on a bet is a criminal matter within the meaning of the Prosecution of Offences Act 1974: *DPP v Boyle* [1993] ILRM 128, HC.

Also the prohibition on placing bets outside the State has been removed: Horse and Greyhound Racing Act 2001, s 18(3) repealing Betting Act 1931, ss 33–34. See also Betting Duty Regulations 2002, SI No 174 of 2002; Finance Act 2003, s 111. See BOOKMAKER; REVENUE OFFENCE; WAGERING CONTRACT.

betaghs. A class of unfree tenant found on Norman-Irish manors, drawn from the native Irish population, who owed labour services rather than rent, and were bound to the soil. *See Mac Niochaill* [1966] 1 Ir Jur (ns) 292.

better regulation. The objective of government to introduce 'lighter' regulation under a strategy to cut red tape: White Paper on Better Regulation (2004). The White Paper recommends the use of alternative means of enforcing legislation rather than pursuing offenders through the courts. It recommends greater use of measures such as the plastic bag tax, which helped to modify behaviour without the appointment of litter wardens or inspectors. On regulators, there is a commitment: (a) to assessing possibilities for consolidating or rationalising existing regulators; and (b) to creating new ones only if the case for them can be clearly demonstrated. For action plan on regulatory reform, see website: *www.betterregulation.ie*. The Minister for Finance said that the EU would prioritise regulatory reform in a con-

certed effort in 2004 and 2005 to seek more flexible European product, capital and labour markets: *Irish Times,* 27 January 2004. See COMMISSION FOR AVIATION REGULATION; COMMISSION FOR COMMUNICATIONS REGULATION; COMMISSION FOR ENERGY REGULATION; CONSUMER AFFAIRS, DIRECTOR OF; TAXI.

beware of dog sign. A Circuit Court judge is reported to have said that a defendant's *Beware of Dog* sign had 'no bearing in law': Martin J in *O'Sullivan v Delahunty* (1988) Irish Times, 19 September, CC. See GUARD DOG; SCIENTER.

beyond reasonable doubt. The concept in the law of evidence whereby an accused is entitled to an acquittal if the prosecution has not established his guilt beyond reasonable doubt. Contrast with balance of probability.

Generally in a criminal trial the judge, in instructing the jury on the need for the prosecution to establish the guilt of the accused *beyond reasonable doubt,* will say that if there is a doubt, the accused is entitled the *benefit of the doubt.* However, in a particular case, the Court of Criminal Appeal, while acknowledging that the trial judge had neglected to mention 'the benefit of the doubt', he had correctly instructed the jury with regard to the burden of proof: *DPP v Kiely* (2001) 21 March, CCA. See also *People (DPP) v LG* [2003] 2 IR 517, CCA. See INFERENCE; STANDARD OF PROOF.

bias. 'An inclination, leaning, tendency, bent, a preponderating disposition or propensity, predisposition, predilection, prejudice' *Oxford English Dictionary* quoted *in Dublin Wellwoman Centre Ltd v Ireland* [1995] 1 ILRM 408, SC at 418. A judge should discharge himself from a case where there is subjective or objective bias. 'Lack of bias in either form underpins the administration of justice': *Dublin Wellwoman* case.

The fact that a judge had, while a barrister, acted for a particular party was not sufficient to disqualify that judge from hearing a case in which that party was involved: *Bula Ltd v Tara Mines (No 6)* [2000] 4 IR 412, SC. The Supreme Court rejected allegations of bias in a case where a judge of the court had, while a member of the Bar acted for one of the parties to the proceedings: *Rooney v Minister for Agriculture* [2001] 2 ILRM 37, SC. The Chief Justice in this case said that the practice for judges, and other persons exercising quasi-judicial functions, to disclose the existence of any factor which either party might consider was capable of affecting the reality or the appearance of an impartial administration of justice, was an entirely proper one.

It has been held that the question of *bias* must be determined on the basis of what a right-minded person would think of the likelihood of prejudice and not on the basis of suspicion which might dwell in the mind of a person who is ill-informed: *Spin Communications Ltd v Independent Radio and Television Commission* [2000] ITLR (7 August), HC. A distinction must be drawn between those many factors such as education, religion, age and upbringing which may well be seen as influencing the decision of a judge and extraneous factors specific to a particular judge (*Rooney* case).

On appeal, the Supreme Court held that the test to be applied in determining what constitutes *objective bias* on the part of the decision-maker is whether there is a reasonable apprehension or suspicion that the decision-maker might have been biased ie whether, although there was no actual bias, there is an appearance of bias: *Spin Communications Ltd v Independent Radio and Television Commission* [2002] 1 ILRM 98, SC and [2001] 4 IR 411, SC. The court will set aside a decision of a tribunal or administrative body, exercising judicial or quasi-judicial functions, if there is reasonable apprehension of bias.

The fact that a judge had exercised jurisdiction pursuant to a particular Act on a previous occasion, did not disqualify him in relation to a similar occasion: *Blehein v St John of God's Hospital* (2001) 31 July, SC. In arbitration, any claim of perceived bias must be asserted during the course of the arbitration and not subsequent to the making of an award: *McCarthy v Keane* [2003] FL 7891, HC. See *McAuley v Keating* [1998] 4 IR 138, SC; *Orange v Director of Telecommunications* [2000] 4 IR 159, SC; *Curran v Finn* [2001] 4 IR 248, SC; *Allman v Minister for Justice* [2002] 3 IR 540, HC and [2003] ELR 7. See 'Bias and Legal Professional Independence' by Stephen Dodd BL in *Bar Review* (March 2001) 261. See JUDGES.

bid. An offer to buy at a stated price something which is being sold by auction. See AUCTION SALES.

bigamy. An offence committed by a person who has been previously married and has not since been legally divorced, and who goes through a legally recognised ceremony of marriage with another person, while the original spouse is still living: Offences Against the Person Act 1861, s 57. The remarriage of spouses of an existing marriage to each other is not bigamous: *B v R* [1995] 1 ILRM 491, HC and [1996] 3 IR 549, HC.

It is a conclusive defence to show that the accused's original spouse had been continually absent from the accused during the seven years preceding the second marriage and had never been heard of by the accused meanwhile. See *R v Tolson* [1889] 23 QBD 168.

A High Court judge has suggested that the legislative should consider seriously the abolition or restructuring of the crime of bigamy: Kinlen J, *Irish Times*, 21 July 1999. See DIVORCE.

bill. (1) An account sent by a creditor to a debtor.

(2) A written instrument eg a bill of exchange (qv).

(3) A draft legislative proposal, which when passed, or deemed to have been passed, by both Houses of the Oireachtas (qv), becomes an Act when signed by the President of Ireland: 1937 Constitution, art 13(3) and art 25(4)(1). A bill may be a *private* bill (eg referring to a particular person or town) or a *public* bill (applying to the State). A bill may also be classified as an *ordinary* bill, a *money* bill or an *abridged-time* bill, or a bill to amend the Constitution (qqv). A bill becomes law from the date of signature by the President unless a contrary intention appears; many Acts, or sections thereof, do not become operational until activated by a designated Minister. Copyright in any bill or enactment vests in the Houses of the Oireachtas and expires 50 years after it was first lawfully made available to the public: Copyright and Related Rights Act 2000, ss 192 and 194–195.

For the text of draft legislation from 1997 to date, in many cases supported by an Explanatory Memorandum, see *www.irlgov.ie/oireachtas*. The debate at each stage of a Bill is also available on this website.

bill, abridged-time. A bill, which the Taoiseach certifies in writing is, in the opinion of the government, urgent and immediately necessary for the preservation of the public peace and security: 1937 Constitution, art 24. The time for consideration of such a bill by the Seanad will be abridged, if Dáil Éireann so resolves and if the President of Ireland, after consultation with the Council of State (qv), concurs. Such legislation may remain in force for only ninety days unless both Houses prolong the period by resolution.

bill, money. A bill which contains only provisions dealing with all or any of the following matters, namely, the imposition, repeal, remission, alteration or regulation of taxation; the imposition for the payment of debt or other financial purposes of charges on public moneys or the variation or repeal of any such charges; supply; the appropriation, receipt, custody, issue or audit of accounts of public money; the raising or guarantee of any loan or the payment thereof; matters subordinate and incidental to these matters or any of them: 1937 Constitution, art 22(1)(1). A *money bill* can be initiated in Dáil Éireann only; the Seanad cannot amend or reject such a bill although it may make recommendations thereon, which the Dáil may accept or reject. An example of a money bill, certified as such, is the bill which was enacted as the Tourist Traffic Act 1987.

bill, ordinary. A bill other than a money bill or an abridged-time bill. An ordinary bill which is passed by Dáil Éireann and sent to Seanad Éireann and which is either rejected by the Seanad, or passed by the Seanad with amendments to which the Dáil does not agree, or is neither passed (with or without amendments) nor rejected by the Seanad within 90 days from first being sent to the Seanad, will be deemed to have been passed by both Houses of the Oireachtas (qv) if the Dáil so resolves within 180 days after the expiration of the 90-day period: 1937 Constitution, art 23.

bill, stages of. A bill is normally initiated by a Minister of the government in either Dáil Éireann or Seanad Éireann, except that a money bill must be initiated in the Dáil. The first stage of the bill is its introduction. During the second stage, the general principles of the bill are debated. At the third or *committee* stage, each section of the bill is considered and at the fourth or *report* stage, accepted amendments are incorporated, leading to the fifth or *final* stage when the bill is passed and sent for consideration to the other House. It is subsequently signed by the President of Ireland and is promulgated by notice in Iris Oifigiúil (qv). Bills, when enacted, are numbered in the order and year in which they are signed and promulgated as the law e g No 7 of 1988 is the seventh bill to become law in 1988. See COMMENCEMENT; MONEY; PRESIDENT OF IRELAND.

bill of costs. Includes any statement of account sent, or demand made, by a solicitor to a client for fees, charges, outlays, disbursements or expenses: Solicitors (Amendment) Act 1994, s 2. A solicitor is required to furnish a bill of costs to his client as soon as practicable after the conclusion of any *contentious business* (qv) carried out by him on behalf of that client (S(A)A 1994, s 68(6)). The bill of costs is required to include: (a) a summary of the legal services provided; (b) the total amount of damages or other moneys recovered; and (c) details of the charges recovered from any other party; (d) the amounts, shown separately, in respect of fees, outlays, disbursements and expenses.

Where a client disputes the amount of a bill of costs, the solicitor is required: (a) to take all appropriate steps to resolve the matter with the client; and (b) to inform the client in writing of the client's right: (i) to require the solicitor to submit the bill of costs to the Taxing Master (or County Registrar, as appropriate) for taxation; and (ii) to make a complaint to the Law Society (S(A)A 1994, s 68(8)). A solicitor cannot sue for payment for one month after delivery of such bill: Attorneys and Solicitors (Ireland) Act 1849, ss 2 and 6; *State (Shatter) v de Valera* [1986] ILRM 3. See COSTS AND CRIMINAL PROCEEDINGS; COSTS IN CIVIL PROCEEDINGS; SOLICITOR, COMPLAINT AGAINST; TAXATION OF COSTS.

bill of exchange. A form of negotiable instrument. An unconditional order in writing, addressed by one person to another, signed by the person giving it, requiring the person to whom it is addressed to pay on demand, or at a fixed or determinable future time, a sum certain in money, to, or to the order of, a specified person, or to bearer: Bills of Exchange Act 1882, s 3(1).

The person who gives the order to pay is the *drawer*; the person to whom the order to pay is made is the *drawee* and becomes the *acceptor* by writing his name across the face of the bill. The person to whom the payment is to be made is the *payee*; the payee must be named or indicated with reasonable certainty (BEA 1882, s 7(1)).

If the payee is a fictitious or non-existing person, the bill may be treated as payable to bearer (BEA 1882, s 7(3)). A non-existent person is one whom the drawer did not know existed when he signed, whereas a fictitious person is one who does exist but was not the person intended by the drawer to receive payment: *Clutton v Attenborough* [1897] AC 90; *Bank of England v Vagliano* [1891] AC 107. See Building Societies Act 1989, s 126; Credit Union Act 1997, s 39 as amended by Central Bank and Financial Services Authority of Ireland Act 2003, s 35, Sch 1; Stamp Duties Consolidation Act 1999, ss 22–28; Finance Act 2003, s 143(1)(a). See also *Gill* in 7 ILT & SJ (1989) 88. [Bibliography: Donnelly; O'Connor R; Byles UK; Paget UK; Richardson UK.] See NEGOTIABLE INSTRUMENT; CHEQUE; ENDORSEMENT; RENUNCIATION; HOLDER IN DUE COURSE.

bill of exchange, acceptance of. See ACCEPTANCE OF BILL.

bill of exchange, discharge of. See DISCHARGE OF BILL.

bill of exchange, dishonour of. See DISHONOUR OF BILL.

bill of exchange, payment of. A bill of exchange is *payable on demand* if it is expressed to be payable on demand, or at sight, or on presentation, or where no time for payment is expressed, or where it is accepted or endorsed when overdue: Bills of Exchange Act 1882, s 10. A bill which is not payable on demand must be payable at a fixed or determinable future time; i e it must be payable at a fixed period after date or sight, or on, or at a fixed period after, the occurrence of a specified event which is certain to happen, though the time of happening may be uncertain (BEA 1882, s 11).

bill of lading. A document, used in foreign trade, signed and delivered by the master of a ship to the shipper on goods being shipped. The bill of lading specifies: (a) the leading marks necessary for the identification of the goods; (b) the number of packages or pieces or the quantity or weight, as the case may be, as furnished in writing by the shipper; and (c) the apparent order and condition of the goods: Merchant Shipping (Liability of Shipowners and Others) Act 1996, s 33 and Sch 3 (art III(3)); International Convention for the Unification of Certain Rules of Law relating to Bills of Lading 1924, done at Brussels on 25 August 1924, as amended by Protocols in 1968 and 1979. Such a bill of lading is *prima facie* evidence of the receipt by the carrier as therein supplied (art III(4)). An absolute warranty of seaworthiness is not to be implied in contracts for the carriage of goods by sea (MS(LSO)A 1996, s 35). A bill of lading is a *document of title* transferable by endorsement and delivery, giving the holder the right to sue thereon but it is not a fully negotiable instrument (qv), in that the transferee obtains no better title than the transferor has. See *Vita Food Products v Unus Shipping Co* [1939] AC 277. See Merchant Shipping Act 1947, s 13, Sch 2.

bill of sale. A document given with respect to the transfer of chattels used in cases where possession is not intended to be given. There are two types of bills of sale: (a) *absolute*, purporting to be a complete transfer of the chattels by way of sale, gift or settlement; and (b) by way of *mortgage*, where there is a transfer for the purpose of creating a security, subject to a proviso for redemption on repayment of the money secured. Every bill of sale must be attested and registered within seven days of execution and must set forth the consideration for which it was given. A bill of sale of stock (whether including or not including any other chattels) is void and incapable of being registered under bill of sale legislation: Agricultural Credit Act 1978, s 36. Bills of Sale are now almost obsolete. See *Johnson v Diprose* [1893] 1 QB 512. See Bills of Sale (Ireland) Act 1879 and 1883; Central Bank Act 1971, s 36. [Bibliography: Forde (5).]

bill to amend constitution. See CONSTITUTION, BILL TO AMEND.

binding to the peace. An order, which may be made by a judge, binding a person to the peace or to good behaviour or to both the peace and good behaviour and requiring him to enter into a *recognizance* in that behalf: Courts (Supplemental Provisions) Act 1961, s 54. The jurisdiction to bind persons to the peace and to require sureties has an ancient history, originating from common law, and is not unconstitutional: *Gregory v Windle* [1995] 1 ILRM 131, HC. The power of the court to bind a person to the peace may be exercised without sentencing the person also to a fine or to imprisonment: Criminal Law Act 1997, s 10(4). A witness in a trial cannot be bound over to the peace without being warned that such an order might be made and without being given an opportunity to contest it: *Clarke v Judge Hogan* [1995] 1 IR

310, HC. See *Halpin v Rice* [1901] 1 IR 593. See PROBATION.

Bioethics, Irish Council for. The body established by the Royal Irish Academy and launched by the Tánaiste on 22 January 2003, with a wide remit to develop ethical standards for biological research. The Council is initially concentrating on three areas: (a) the handling, storage and disposal of human biological samples; (b) genetically modified organisms including food products; and (c) defining the bodies and organisations which should have ethical committees overseeing their activities. The Council published new ethical guidelines for research on 14 September 2004. See GENETICALLY MODIFIED ORGANISM; HUMAN TISSUE.

biofuel. Means any mineral oil which is produced from *biomass*: Finance Act 1999, s 94(1) as substituted by Finance Act 2004, s 49(a). *Biomass* means the biodegradable fraction of products, waste and residues from agriculture, forestry and related industries, as well as the biodegradable fraction of industrial and municipal waste (FA 2004, s 49(b)). The Revenue Commissioners are empowered to allow relief from mineral oil tax on biofuel used in pilot projects for either the production of biofuel, or the testing of the technical viability of biofuel for use as motor fuel (FA 1999, s 98A inserted by FA 2004, s 50).

biological diversity. Means the variability among living organisms from all sources, including terrestrial, marine and other aquatic ecosystems, and the ecological complexes of which they are part: Wildlife (Amendment) Act 2000, s 9. The Minister is responsible for promoting the conservation of *biological diversity* in the context of Ireland's ratification of the *UN Convention on Biological Diversity* in 1996, a landmark convention for the conservation of the diversity of natural life on earth.

biometrics. Automated methods of recognising a person based on the measurement of a physiological or behavioural characteristic. Features measured include face, fingerprints, hand geometry, handwriting, iris, retinal and voice. Biometrics are used by the Gardaí and the Office of the Refugee Applications Commissioner (ORAC) to monitor the movement of asylum seekers. Since September 2002, all new asylum seekers have had their right index fingers copied and stored on a computer chip on their *temporary residents cards*. The data is also stored in a central database at Garda headquarters and at the ORAC for cross-checking.

In the United States, their Enhanced Border Security Act 2002 removes from 24 October 2004 the visa waiver status, which Irish citizens currently enjoy with the US, unless they have a passport with biometric features. See government commissioned PA Consulting report 'Applying Biometrics to the Delivery of Public Services in Ireland' (2002). See GENETIC FINGERPRINTING.

biotechnological invention. Biotechnological inventions are patentable, in particular, if they concern: (a) biological material which is isolated from its natural environment or produced by means of a technical process even if it previously occurred in nature; (b) plants or animals if the technical feasibility of the invention is not confined to a particular plant or animal variety; or (c) a microbiological or other technical process, or a product obtained by means of such a process other than a plant or animal variety: European Communities (Legal Protection of Biotechnological Inventions) Regulations 2000, SI No 247 of 2000. These regulations give effect to EC Directive 98/44/EC. See 'Biotechnology and the ethical and moral concerns of European Patent Law' by Oliver Mills in *Bar Review* (Oct 2000) 46. See CLONING; MICRO-ORGANISM.

birching. See WHIPPING.

bird watching. See HUNT.

birds, wild. See WILD BIRDS, PROTECTED.

Birds Directive. Means EC Directive No 79/409/EEC of 2 April 1979 for the conservation of wild birds: Planning and Development Act 2000, s 2(1). See EUROPEAN SITE.

birth, concealment of. See CONCEALMENT OF BIRTH.

birth, home. See MIDWIFE.

birth, registration of. There is a requirement to establish and maintain a register: (a) of all births occurring in the State; and (b) of births outside the State of children of Irish citizens domiciled in the State where a system of registration does not exist; and (c) of certain other births occurring outside the State eg on board a ship or aircraft: Civil Registration Act 2004, ss 13(1)(a), and 26–27. When a child is born in the State, it is the duty of the parents of the child, or failing them a *qualified informant*, to attend before any registrar and to give to the registrar the required particulars of the birth within three months of the birth (CRA 2004, s 19). A *qualified informant* includes a guardian, a person present at the birth, an authorised person in a hospital where the birth took place, or a person in a dwelling when the birth took place in the dwelling, a person having charge of the child, or a man who makes a request to be registered as the father of the child (CRA 2004, s 19(6)).

There is provision for the registration of the father's details (or re-registration subsequently) where the parents are not married to each other at the date of birth or were not married to each other during the ten months prior to the birth of the child (CRA 2004, ss 22–23). Also re-registration is permitted in the case of a birth of a person legitimated by the parent's subsequent marriage (CRA 2004, s 24).

The particulars which are required to be registered are specified: (a) date, place and time of birth; (b) in respect of the child: forename(s) and surname; sex; personal public service number (PPSN); (c) in respect of the mother and father: forename(s), surname, former surname(s), birth surname, birth surname of mother's mother and father's mother, address and occupation; date of birth; marital status; PPSN; (d) in respect of the informant: forename(s), surname, qualification, address and signature of informant; (f) date of registration; (g) signature of registrar (CRA 2004, s 19 and Sch1, Pt 1).

Birth certificates are issued by an tArd Chláraitheoir (*Registrar General*), the superintendent registrars, and the local registrars. Two forms are available, the *full* certificate which is a true copy of the entry in the register, and the *short* certificate on which is shown only the name, surname, sex, date of birth, and district of registration. A new gender neutral format of birth certificate has been introduced for births registered from 1 October 1997.

A procedure for the identification of registration made pursuant to the Irish Nationality and Citizenship Act 1994 is provided for by the Foreign Births (Amendment) Regulations 1994, SI No 155 of 1994. The Minister for Foreign Affairs has been empowered to designate the Irish diplomatic and consular missions abroad which are required to maintain *foreign births entry books* ie to register the births to Irish citizens outside the island of Ireland: Irish Nationality and Citizenship Act 2001, s 7. The Department of Foreign Affairs also maintain a foreign births registry.

Provision has been made for the implementation of an *electronic register* of births: Social Welfare (Miscellaneous Provisions) Act 2002, s 16 and Sch. This also provided for in the 2004 legislation at s 13(3). See also Registration of Births Regulations 1988, SI No 123 of 1988; Registration of Births (Amendment) Regulations 2002, SI No 493 of 2002. For previous legislation, see Births and Deaths Registration (Ireland) Acts 1863 and 1880; Births and Deaths Registration Act 1972; Defence (No 2) Act 1960, s 6; Status of Children Act 1987, s 48; Defence (Amendment) Act 1993, s 3; Garda Síochána Act 1989, s 4; Registration of Births Act 1996. See ADOPTION, BIRTH RECORDS; NAME, CHANGE OF; PARENT; PATERNITY, PRESUMPTION OF; PARENTAGE, DECLARATION OF; STILLBORN CHILD; TRANSSEXUAL.

BL. Barrister-at-Law. See BARRISTER.

black leg. Generally understood to mean a person who continues, or attempts to continue, to work during a strike (qv).

blacklist. Generally understood to mean a list of persons, firms or companies with whom no dealings are to be made. See BELOW COST SELLING; BOYCOTT; UNFAIR PRACTICES.

blackmail. Popular name for offences involving extortion by menaces. See EXTORTION BY MENACES.

blank cheque. See FEE.

blank transfer. The transfer of fully paid shares in a company which need not specify the name of the transferee to be effective. See Stock Transfer Act 1963. See SHARES, EQUITABLE MORTGAGE OF.

Blaskets. The island group near Dingle in the Kerry Gaeltacht, the largest island of which is An Blascaod Mór. Provision has been made for the preservation of this island as a cultural centre and national park: An Blascaod Mór National Historic Park Act 1989. See also Gaeltacht Areas Order 1956, SI No 245 of 1956. The Supreme Court has held that the 1989 Act was invalid having regard to the Constitution as it classified persons whose land could be acquired compulsorily by *pedigree*, which appeared to have no place (outside the law of succession) in a democratic society committed to the principle of equality:

An Blascaod Mór v Minister for Arts [2000] 1 ILRM 401, SC.

blasphemous libel. A criminal prosecution for *blasphemous libel* may only be commenced by order of the High Court: Defamation Act 1961, s 8. See LIBEL.

blasphemy. The Constitution declares that the publication or utterance of *blasphemous matter* is an offence which shall be punishable in accordance with law: 1937 Constitution, art 40(6)(1)(i). Every person who composes, prints or publishes any *blasphemous libel* is guilty of an offence: Defamation Act 1961, s 13(1). However, blasphemy is not defined in the Constitution or in any Act of the Oireachtas and it is impossible to say of what the offence consists; neither the *actus reus* nor the *mens reus* is clear: *Corway v Independent Newspapers* [2000] 1 ILRM 426, SC and [1999] 4 IR 484, SC. It was for the legislature and not the courts to define the crime (*Corway* case). See LRC 41, 1991, The Crime of Libel.

It is an offence to be guilty of riotous, violent or indecent behaviour in a chapel or churchyard or burial ground, or to molest, disturb, vex or trouble a preacher or clergyman celebrating any sacrament or divine service or rite: Ecclesiastical Courts Jurisdiction Act 1860, s 2.

blind pension. The social welfare pension to which a blind person may be entitled, who has reached 18 years of age and is so blind that he either cannot perform any work for which eyesight is essential or cannot continue his ordinary occupation: Social Welfare (Consolidation) Act 1993, s 141 as amended eg Social Welfare Act 1998, s 19 and Social Welfare Act 2000, s 30. See also Taxes Consolidation Act 1997, s 468 as amended by Finance Act 2000, s 11. See also Social Welfare Act 2002, s 2

blind trust. A particular type of trust where the trust instrument expressly prevents the beneficiary from seeing trust accounts. This limitation on the normal duties of the trustees to account, stems from an agreement entered into between parties of full age and capacity. A blind trust may be used to protect a public person, such as a politician, from possible accusations of abuse of influence, by placing that person's wealth, or a substantial portion of it, with trustees who are prohibited from revealing their investment policy to the person. [Bibliography: Ford & Lee (UK)]

blocking. In relation to data, means so marking the data that it is not possible to process it for purposes in relation to which it is marked: Data Protection Act 1988, s 1(1) as inserted by Data Protection (Amendment) Act 2003, s 2(a)(i). The 2003 Act gives a data subject the right to have incorrect or inaccurate data blocked, in addition to the existing rights of erasure or rectification (DPA 1988, s 6 as amended by DP(A)A 2003, s 7). See INACCURATE DATA.

blood inspection. The Irish Medicines Board has responsibility for inspecting any service for the collection, screening, processing and quality control facilities and procedures in respect of human blood, blood components, blood products and plasma derivatives: Irish Medicines Board Act 1995, s 4(1)(l).

blood relationship. The quality or relationship which enables a person to take by descent, being descended from one or more common ancestors. A person is said to be of the *whole blood* to another where they are both descended from the same pair of ancestors eg two sisters who have the same father and mother. A person is said to be of the *half-blood* to another when they are descended from one common ancestor only eg two brothers who have the same father but different mothers. In an intestacy, relatives of the half-blood share equally with relatives of the whole blood in the same degree. See Succession Act 1965, ss 71–72. See BLOOD TEST; NEXT-OF-KIN; PARENTAGE, DECLARATION OF.

blood specimen. The specimen of blood which certain persons at a garda station are required to permit a designated doctor to take from them; it is an offence to *refuse or fail* to comply with this requirement: Road Traffic Act 1994, ss 13–15. Only one offence is created by the words '*refuses or fails*'; evidence of refusal and non-compliance is sufficient to establish '*failure*': *DPP v Doyle* [1997] 1 ILRM 379, HC and [1996] 3 IR 579, HC.

There is no requirement for a garda to refer specifically to s 13: *Brennan v DPP* [1996] 1 ILRM 267, SC. Also the omission of '1994' after 'Road Traffic Act' by the garda making the requirement of the person is immaterial: *DPP v Mangan* [2001] 1 IR 373, SC and [2002] 1 ILRM 417, SC.

The person has the option to provide a specimen of urine instead (RTA 1994, s 13(b)(ii) and *DPP v Swan* [1994] ILRM

314). However, the words '*blood* ' and '*urine*' are not on an equal footing; there is a legal requirement to permit the taking of a blood sample which can be discharged by the giving of a urine sample: *DPP v Corcoran* [1996] 1 ILRM 181, HC and [1995] 2 IR 259, HC. If a person opts to give a urine sample and is unable to do so, the obligation to permit the taking of a blood specimen revives. The reverse is not true; eg if through no fault of the person, the medical practitioner is unable to obtain a blood specimen, there is no legal obligation to furnish a specimen of urine (*Corcoran* case).

To escape the obligation of permitting a blood specimen to be taken, the person concerned must actually provide such a specimen of urine, not simply agree to provide such a specimen within a limited or reasonable time: *DPP (O'Driscoll) v O'Connor* [2000] 1 ILRM 61, SC.

A quantity of the blood specimen must be offered to the person (RTA 1994, s 18(2)). It is not necessary that the glass bottles into which the blood specimen is divided should themselves be sealed, only that the container in which they are placed is itself sealed: *DPP v Croom-Carroll* [2000] 1 ILRM 289, SC and [1999] 4 IR 126, SC.

Failure to allow a person access to a solicitor prior to obtaining a blood specimen does not render the evidence so obtained as inadmissible: *Walshe v O'Buachalla* [1991] 9 ILT Dig 226, HC. See *Director of Public Prosecutions v Smyth* [1987] ILRM 570; *Connolly v Sweeney* [1988] ILRM 35.

Under certain circumstances, a person may be required to provide a blood or urine specimen in a hospital eg where the driver or person in charge of the vehicle has been admitted to hospital (RTA 1994, s 15). Once an accused has arrived in hospital, a garda has a statutory right to require him to permit a specimen to be taken, which amounts to a right to require him to incriminate himself: *DPP v Elliot* [1997] 2 ILRM 156, HC.

If the defendant wishes to call as a witness the medical doctor who took the sample, he should be permitted by the judge so to do: *O'Regan v DPP* [2000] 2 ILRM 68, SC. *See DPP v Somers* [1999] 1 IR 115, SC. For power of a garda to have a blood sample taken in relation to other offences, see BODILY SAMPLE. [Bibliography: McGrath M (2).] See also BLOOD TEST; DESIGNATED; DRUNKEN DRIVING; IN CHARGE; MEDICAL BUREAU OF ROAD SAFETY; URINE SPECIMEN.

blood test. A test made with the object of ascertaining inheritable characteristics to assist the court in determining the question of *parentage*: Status of Children Act 1987, s 37. Statutory procedures for obtaining and giving blood test evidence in questions of parentage, arising in civil proceedings, are provided for in the SCA 1987, ss 37–43. Where an application is brought for an order directing that blood tests be used to determine parentage, judicial discretion is required to be exercised on matters touching on the welfare of the children: SCA 1987, s 38 and *JPD v MG* [1991] ILRM 217, SC. Where a person fails to comply with a direction by the court for the use of such blood tests, the court may draw whatever inferences it considers proper from the refusal (SCA 1987, s 42). For the rules of court governing an application for a direction for the use of blood tests where parentage is in issue, pursuant to s 38 of the Status of Children Act 1987, see Circuit Court Rules 2001 Ord 59, r 3 and DCR 1997 Ord 61. See GENETIC FINGERPRINTING; PARENTAGE, DECLARATION OF.

Blood Transfusion Service Board. See IRISH BLOOD TRANSFUSION SERVICE.

blot on title. A defect in title (qv) to land.

blue chip. Generally understood to mean the shares (qv) of a well established company which is highly regarded as an investment.

Blueshirts. The popular name given to members of the Army Comrades Association, an organisation of ex-Free State Army members, founded in 1932, who provided ex-ministers of the political party Cumann na nGaedheal (now, Fine Gael) with bodyguards at public meetings. In 1933, the blue shirt began to appear as the distinctive uniform of the movement.

board meeting. A meeting of the directors (qv) of a company (qv) at which decisions are made by majority vote, with the chairman having a casting vote. See Companies Act 1963, Table A, arts 100ff. See CHAIRMAN; MANAGING DIRECTOR; MINUTES.

board of conservators. See WATER POLLUTION.

board of directors. See DIRECTORS; RECKLESS TRADING.

boarding out. An arrangement by which a person becomes a resident in another person's private dwelling. A health board is empowered to board out a person with his consent, in a private dwelling and may pay for all or part of the cost; this applies to a person who, in the opinion of the board, ought having regard to his means and circumstances, be boarded out: Health (Nursing Homes) Act 1990, s 10. See FOSTER CHILD.

boards of guardians. Formerly, the bodies consisting of justices of the peace (qv) and members elected by ratepayers, with responsibility in their area, called the *Union*, for superintending the poor relief system including workhouses, the provision and maintenance of sewers and the enforcement of laws relating to public health generally, in addition to being the custodians of burial grounds and the construction of public water works, all of which were performed under the general supervision of the Poor Law Commissioners and later of the Local Government Board: Poor Relief (Ireland) Act 1838; Local Government Board (Ireland) Act 1872. The functions of the board of guardians were transferred initially to *rural district councils* (qv) which were themselves later abolished.

boat. Planning permission is not required for the keeping or storing of a boat within the curtilage of a house; however not more than one may be so stored: Planning and Development Regulations 2001, SI No 600 of 2001, Sch 2, class 8. Also it may not be kept or stored for more than nine months in any year or occupied as a dwelling while so kept or stored. See also ALCOHOL, CONSUMPTION; CAMPING.

bodily harm, grievous. It was a felony (qv) unlawfully and maliciously to *wound* or cause *grievous* bodily harm to any person or to shoot at him with intent to maim, disfigure or disable or do any other grievous bodily harm, or to resist arrest: Offences Against the Person Act 1861, s 18 repealed by the Non-Fatal Offences against the Person Act 1997, s 31. This offence is now replaced by the offence of *causing serious harm* (NFOPA 1997, s 4). See ASSAULT; POISON; BURGLARY.

bodily integrity, right to. There is a constitutional right to bodily integrity: *Ryan v Attorney-General* [1965] IR 294; THE STATE (*RICHARDSON*) V GOVERNOR OF MOUNTJOY [1980] HC. See 'The right to bodily integrity and the evolution of a right to a healthy environment' by Maria Colberts BL in *Bar Review* (January 2001) 248. See HUMAN TISSUE.

bodily restraint. A person is prohibited from placing a patient in seclusion or applying mechanical means of bodily restraint to the patient unless necessary for his treatment or to prevent him injuring himself or others and unless the seclusion or restraint complies with rules made by the *Mental Health Commission*: Mental Health Act 2001, s 69.

bodily sample. A sample of blood, hair, pubic hair, urine, saliva, nail or of any material found under a nail; a swab from a body orifice or a genital region or any other part of the body; a dental impression; a footprint or similar impression: Criminal Justice (Forensic Evidence) Act 1990, s 2.

A sample must not be taken of a person in custody in a garda station except with his written consent and, where he is under the age of 17 years, the written consent of an appropriate adult: Treatment of Persons in Custody in Garda Síochána Stations Regulations 1987, SI No 119 of 1987, reg 18. Consent is not required where the garda is otherwise empowered by law. A garda may take, or cause to be taken, such a bodily sample for the purpose of forensic testing from a person who is in custody under the provisions of s 30 of the Offences Against the State Act 1939 or s 4 of the Criminal Justice Act 1984 or in certain circumstances if the person is in prison (CJ(FE)A 1990, ss 2(1) and 2(2)); see DETENTION; OFFENCES AGAINST THE STATE).

This power enables the Gardaí to avail of developments in DNA (qv) profiling. Authorisation from a garda, not below the rank of superintendent, to take a bodily sample is required; the consent in writing of the person is also required if the sample is an intimate one (CJ(FE)A 1990, s 2(4)).

The court in determining whether a person is guilty of an offence may draw such inference as appears proper from a refusal to consent to taking a sample but cannot convict solely on the inference drawn (CJ(FE)A 1990, s 3 as amended by Criminal Justice Act 1999, s 17). There are particular protections for young persons regarding consent and inferences from a refusal (CJ(FE)A 1990, ss 2(10) and 3(4)). See Criminal Justice (Forensic Evidence) Act, 1990 Regulations 1992, SI No 130 of 1992.

The power of the gardaí to take bodily samples has been extended to persons detained under s 2 of the Criminal Justice (Drug Trafficking) Act 1996 (CJ(DT)A

1996, s 3). See BLOOD SPECIMEN; DNA; GENETIC FINGERPRINTING.

body. See DISSECTION.

body corporate. A succession or collection of persons having in the estimation of the law an existence and rights and duties distinct from the individual persons who form it from time to time eg a company registered under the Companies Acts, a local authority, a body established by charter. See CORPORATION.

bona fide. In good faith; honestly; without fraud, collusion, or participation in wrongdoing. See *O'Byrne v M50 Motors Ltd* [2003] 1 ILRM 275, HC.

bona vacantia. Goods without an apparent owner in which no one claims a property but the State eg shipwreck, treasure trove. The right of the State to forfeiture by way of *bona vacantia* in respect of personalty on an intestacy, has been replaced by the right of the State as ultimate intestate successor: Succession Act 1965, s 73. See also State Property Act 1954, ss 30–32. See TREASURE TROVE.

bond. (1) An agreement under seal whereby the *obligor* binds himself to the *obligee* to perform or refrain from an action. A *simple bond* is one without condition. A *common money bond* is one given to secure payment of money.

(2) An interest bearing document, securing long-term debt, usually issued by government or corporations. See Building Societies Act 1989, s 30; Package Holidays and Travel Trade Act 1995, ss 23–24. See EXCHEQUER BILLS; INSURANCE INTERMEDIARY; INVESTMENT BUSINESS FIRM; TOUR OPERATOR; TRAVEL AGENT; LAND BOND; PERFORMANCE BOND.

bond, engineering contract. Generally an agreement under seal whereby a *surety* and a *contractor* are jointly and severally bound unto an *employer* for the payment of a specified sum; it usually arises where the employer and the contractor have entered into a contract for the construction, completion and maintenance of certain works and provides that in default of such contract the surety shall satisfy and discharge the damages sustained by the employer up to the amount of the bond. [Bibliography: Abrahamson UK.]

bond washing. The term sometimes used to describe a transaction which has as its purpose the avoidance of tax by the sale and re-purchase of stocks, shares and other securities. The anti-avoidance rules governing such transactions are contained in the Income Tax Act 1967, ss 367–370 (purchase and sale *ex div* of securities); ITA 1967, ss 371–372 (purchase of shares by share dealers and exempted persons); ITA 1967, s 449 (transfer of right to receive interest etc from securities); Finance Act 1984, s 29 (sale of government securities cum div); Finance Act 1991, s 27 (sale of government securities ex div). Life assurance companies are relieved of the computational requirements imposed by Finance Act 1984, s 29, but are chargeable to corporation tax in respect of gains: Finance Act 1993, ss 21 and 11. See now Taxes Consolidation Act 1997, ss 748–753, 812, 815. [Bibliography: Judge.] See TAX AVOIDANCE.

bonded goods. Dutiable goods in respect of which a bond has been given to pay the duty. See *Patrick Monahan (Drogheda) Ltd v O'Connell* [1987] HC.]

bonded warehouse. A secure place approved by the Revenue Commissioners for the deposit of dutiable goods upon which duty has not been paid.

bonus shares. Shares in a company which are distributed free to existing members arising from the capitalisation by the company of undistributed profits in its reserves which are otherwise available for distribution as dividends. Sums capitalised in this way must be applied on behalf of the members who would have been entitled to receive the same if the same had been distributed by way of dividend and in the same proportions: Companies Act 1963, Table A, art 130. See also CA 1963, Table A, arts 130A and 131; Companies Amendment Act 1983, Sch 1, reg 24(f).

As regards a *listed* company, a *bonus issue* is an issue to existing holders of securities, in proportion to their holding, of further shares, credited as fully paid out of the issuer's reserves, in lieu of dividend or otherwise: Listing Rules 2000, paras 4.31–4.32. Also called a *capitalisation issue*. Contrast with RIGHTS ISSUE.

book. See PUBLISHED EDITION.

book and library. The publisher of any book *first* published in the State must, within a month after publication and at his own expense, deliver a copy of the book to the National Library of Ireland, University of Dublin (Trinity College), University of Limerick, Dublin City University, British Library Board, and four copies to the National University of Ireland for use in its constituent universities (Dublin, Cork, Galway and Maynooth): Copyright and Related Rights Act 2000, s 198. In addition, a book must be delivered, if so demanded, to an address in Dublin for the Bodleian Library Oxford, University Library Cambridge, National Library of Scotland, and National Library of Wales (CRRA 2000, s 198(5)). The publisher of any book published in the State (ie first published elsewhere) must deliver a copy of the book only to the National Library of Ireland (CRRA 2000, s 198(1)). See NATIONAL LIBRARY.

book debts. Any charges on the book debts of a company must be registered: Companies Act 1963, s 99 as amended by the Companies Act 1990, s 122. The Acts do not define a book debt. The assignment of a possible future refund from an insurance premium does not amount to a book debt: *Re Brian Tucker* [1989] 7 ILT Dig 259. See also *In re Keenan Bros Ltd* (1985) IR 40; *Re Wogan's (Drogheda) Ltd* [1993] 11 ILT Dig 67 and 1 IR 157, SC; *Re Holidair Ltd* [1994] 1 IR 416, SC. See *Fealy* in 11 ILT & SJ (1993) 133. See CHARGE, REGISTRATION OF.

book of evidence. The documents required to be given to an accused being sent forward for trial, namely a statement of the charges, a copy of any sworn information, a list of the witnesses proposed to be called at the trial, a statement of the evidence to be given by each such witness, certain documentary evidence, and a list of the exhibits (qv): Criminal Procedure Act 1967, ss 4B and 4C inserted by Criminal Justice Act 1999, s 9. The book of evidence must be served within 42 days after the accused first appears in the District Court, which period may be extended by the court. The book of evidence has been described as a component of the basic fairness of procedures which is implicit in the administration of justice: *The State (Williams) v Kelliher* [1983] IR 112, SC.

There is no requirement for the accused to disclose his defence except where he intends to raise the defence of *alibi* (qv). In an appeal, the book of evidence must not be given to the Court of Criminal Appeal (qv) as it may contain matters, highly prejudicial to the accused, which were not put in evidence at the trial: *DPP v McKeever* [1992] ITLR (24 August), CCA. The book of evidence is a record held or created by the DPP or the Office of the DPP: *Minister*

for Justice v Information Commissioner [2001] 3 IR 43, HC and [2002] 2 ILRM 1, HC. See also Criminal Evidence Act 1992, s 15(1). See *Smith v Judge O'Donnell & DPP* [2004] ITLR (28 June), HC. See DISCLOSURE IN CRIMINAL PROCEEDINGS; DOCUMENTARY EVIDENCE.

bookmaker, licensed. A person (not being a body corporate or an unincorporated body of persons) who is the holder of a bookmaker's licence: Betting Act 1931, s 1 as amended by the Irish Horseracing Industry Act 1994, s 64. The 1994 Act provides for a company of the Irish Horseracing Authority also to be a licensed bookmaker.

No person may carry on business or act as a bookmaker or hold himself out or represent himself as a bookmaker or a licensed bookmaker unless he holds a bookmaker's licence (BA 1931, s 2). A person to whom a *certificate of fitness* has been given may apply to the Revenue Commissioners for a licence (BA 1931, s 7); a person ordinarily resident in the State applies to a superintendent of the Garda Síochána for such certificate (BA 1931, s 4). An appeal against the refusal to issue a licence lies to the District Court which has a discretion to permit an objector to appear: *Cashman v Clifford* [1989] IR 121. See also *The State (Ledwidge) v Bray D J* [1944] IR 486; *The State (Bambury) v Walsh* [1977] HC; *McDonnell v Reid* [1987] IR 51, HC. See also Finance Act 1984, s 77; Finance Act 1998, s 85.

A *permit* is required by a bookmaker to conduct course-betting (IHIA 1994, ss 47–55 as amended by Horse and Greyhound Racing (Betting Charges and Levies) Act 1999, s 4). There is provision for appeal to the *Bookmaker Appeal Committee* (IHIA 1994, ss 56–58). See also Greyhound Industry Act 1958, s 32C as inserted by HGR(BCL)A 1999, s 10.

Duty is also payable for a *bookmaker's licence* and for a *registered bookmaking premises*: Finance Act 2002, ss 65–66. The Revenue Commissioners are empowered to deregister a bookmaker's premises for non-payment of betting duty (FA 2002, s 78).

In 1999, a new levy structure in respect of horse and greyhound racing was put in place: Horse and Greyhound Racing (Betting Charges and Levies) Act 1999. The on-course betting levy was reduced to zero, a new betting *turnover charge* (0.3%) on both on-course and off-course bets was introduced, and *flat rate charges* were introduced on on-course bookmakers and an *annual charge* on off-course bookmaker betting shops. Provision has been made to reduce to 0% the 0.3% turnover charge on off-course bookmakers introduced in 1999: Horse and Greyhound Racing Act 2001, s 19. The flat-rate charge on off-course bookmaker shops introduced also in 1999 was repealed from 31 August 2001 (HGRA 2001, s 20).

Further changes were introduced in 2004. Provision has been made to introduce a *pitch charge* for all bookmakers holding pitches at an authorised racecourse, to be collected with the monthly turnover charge: SI No 171 of 2004. Also the existing 0.3% turnover charge payable by on-course bookmakers was increased to 0.5%: SI No 172 of 2004. Betting offices at greyhound tracks and at race courses, in addition to opening during and up to two hours after racing, may now open for business for all hours that off-course bookmaker shops may open by law, including on non-race days (HGRA 2001, s 16 and Sch, para 14). See *Criminal Proceedings against Piergiorgio Gambelli* [2003] Case C-243/01, ECJ. See BET; TAX CLEARANCE CERTIFICATE; WAGERING CONTRACT.

Bord Bia, An. A body established to promote, assist and develop the marketing of Irish food and livestock: An Bord Bia Acts 1994, 1995 and 1996. Provision has been made for the amalgamation of An Bord Bia and An Bord Glas (the Horticultural Development Board) and to extend the functions of An Bord Bia to include promoting, assisting and developing the production, marketing and consumption of horticultural products: An Bord Bia (Amendment) Act 2004. Certain provisions of the 1994 Act are amended by the 2004 Act to take account of general developments in the intervening period since its enactment. See website: *www.bordbia.ie*. See AGRICULTURAL PRODUCTS; HORTICULTURE.

Bord Gáis. A body corporate with the duty to develop and maintain a system for the supply of natural gas, being a system which is both economical and efficient and which appears to the Board to be requisite for the time being: Gas Act 1976 as amended by Gas (Interim) (Regulation) Act 2002, s 11.

Provision has been made for *third party access* to the gas network, under which Bord Gáis may agree to transmit gas owned by other parties through its own network at an agreed price: Energy (Miscellaneous Provisions) Act 1995, s 2 as amended by G(I)(R)A 2002, s 14.

Also previously, Bord Gáis enjoyed a statutory monopoly as it had the right to have offered to it, on reasonable terms, all natural gas landed in the State or obtained within the jurisdiction of the State (GA 1976, s 37). This section was repealed in 1998, thereby enabling the State to meet its obligations in respect of open competition in the energy market, as provided for in the Energy Charter Treaty, the Energy Charter Protocol on Energy Efficiency and the EU Directive on Third Party Access to Gas Networks: Gas (Amendment) Act 1998.

Bord Gáis is now empowered to engage in any business activity, whether related to the production, transmission or distribution of energy or not, either alone or in conjunction with other persons, and either within or outside the State, that it considers to be advantageous: Gas (Amendment) Act 2000, s 17. However, ministerial approval is required.

Also the Minister retains the power to give Bord Gáis general directives concerning its financial objectives and on how its profits are applied (G(I)(R)A 2002, s 15). See also Gas (Amendment) Act 1987; Sustainable Energy Act 2002, s 31. See website: *www.bge.ie*. See COMMISSION FOR ENERGY REGULATION; GAS CAPACITY STATEMENT; SUSTAINABLE ENERGY IRELAND.

Bord na Gaeilge. A statutory semi-state body established to co-ordinate state policy and planning for the Irish language and to seek to ensure the survival of the Irish language as a spoken language. See Bord na Gaeilge Act 1978. See website: *www.bnag.ie*. Provision has been made for the dissolution of Bord na Gaeilge on the establishment of An Foras Teanga, arising from the Good Friday Agreement. See FORAS TEANGA, AN.

Bord na Móna. The statutory corporation established in 1946 with the responsibility of developing bogs to provide the State with an indigenous energy supply: Turf Development Act 1946. The company was reconstituted in 1998 as a public limited company under the Companies Acts: Turf Development Act 1998. It is required to form subsidiaries of its different business activities (TDA 1998, s 34). This was a requirement of the European Commission in the light of the Government's proposal to inject equity to deal with an unsustainable debt in the company, the objective being to prevent future cross-subsidisation, particularly in its horticulture division which actively competes with the private sector. The company and its subsidiaries are required to afford appropriate protection for the environment and the archaeological heritage (TDA 1998, s 56). See website: *www.bnm.ie.*

Bord Pleanála, An. A body corporate, consisting of a chairperson and seven other ordinary members, which is required to perform the functions set out in the Act: Planning and Development Act 2000, ss 102–104. There is provision for an independent committee to select three candidates for consideration by the government for the post of chairperson (PDA 2000, s 105). The Minister appoints the seven ordinary members as selected by prescribed organisations e g representing physical planning, engineering, architecture, construction industry, local government, rural and local communities, and persons concerned with the protection and preservation of the environment (PDA 2000, s 106).

It is an offence for a person to communicate with the chairperson, ordinary members, employees or consultants and advisors to the board for the purpose of influencing improperly the consideration of an appeal or referral or a decision of the board (PDA 2000, s 114).

The board may, in its absolute discretion, hold an oral hearing of an *appeal* or of a *referral* (PDA 2000, s 134). The board is required to have regard to the policies for the time being, of the Government, a State authority, the Minister, and planning authorities (PDA 2000, s 143). The board is empowered to direct that such sum as it considers proper is paid by an appellant or the person making the referral or by the planning authority (PDA 2000, s 145).

All matters which go before the board are either '*appeals*' or '*referrals*' (qv). Where a question of law arises on any appeal or referral, the board may refer the question to the High Court for decision (PDA 2000, s 50(1)).

The board is entitled to take into consideration the common good as envisaged by the government e g as evidenced by its entering into an international agreement concerning the 'Loran C' navigation system: *Keane v An Bord Pleanála* [1998] 2

ILRM 241, SC. Proceedings before planning authorities or before An Bord Pleanála are not *legal proceedings* within the meaning of s 22(1)(e) of the Interpretation Act 1937: *O'Flynn Construction Co Ltd v An Bord Pleanála* [2000] ITLR (3 January), HC.

Where the board grants planning permission in contravention of a development plan, it should give its reasons for so doing: *The Village Residents Association Ltd v An Bord Pleanála* [1999] ITLR (6 December), HC. It was held that the board had fulfilled its statutory obligation on the question of the adequacy of the reasons stated: *Village Residents Association v An Bord Pleanála (No 3)* [2001] 1 IR 441, HC. It has been held that where An Bord Pleanála had made available to each party the submissions of the other for comment, this fully satisfied the requirements of *natural justice*: *Fairyhouse Clubs Ltd v An Bord Pleanála* [2001] ITLR (15 October), HC.

See *Killiney and Ballybrack Development Association v Minister for Local Government* [1974] HC; *Geraghty v Minister for Local Government* [1976] IR 153; *O'Keeffe v An Bord Pleanála and Radio Tara* [1992] ILRM 237, SC and [1993] 1 IR 39, SC. See *Kimber* in 11 ILT & SJ (1993) 17. See Planning and Development Regulations 2001, SI No 600 of 2001, Pt 7, arts 56–78. See also Public Service Superannuation (Miscellaneous Provisions) Act 2004, Sch 2. See website: *www.pleanala.ie.* [Bibliography: Galligan (1).] See PLANNING APPEAL; CODE OF CONDUCT.

Bord Uchtála, An. [The Adoption Board (qv).]

border. The abolition of certain intra-Community border controls from the creation of the Single Market is given legal effect by the European Communities (Abolition of Intra-Community Border Controls) Regulations 1993, SI No 3 of 1993. See DUTY FREE; NORTHERN IRELAND.

borough. A *borough council* is now a local authority for a town as set out in Sch 6, Pt 1, Ch 1 of the Local Government Act 2001, s 11(4)(b)(i) ie in respect of Clonmel, Drogheda, Kilkenny, Sligo and Wexford.

Formerly, a borough was a town originally incorporated by royal charter with a common seal, the right to hold lands and to contract and to sue in the name of the *Mayor* (or *Lord Mayor*), *Aldermen and Burgesses of the Borough of* [...]

The boroughs of Dublin, Cork, Limerick and Waterford were originally established by royal charter; their corporate existence was confirmed as were their titles: Municipal Corporations (Ireland) Act 1840, s 12. Each of these boroughs was deemed to be an administrative county of itself, called a *county borough*, with the powers and duties of county councils: Local Government (Ireland) Act 1898, s 21.

The county borough councils of Dublin, Limerick and Waterford were each known as the *city council* and that of Cork, the *borough council*: Cork City Management Act 1929, s 1; Local Government (Dublin) Act 1930; Limerick City Management Act 1934; Waterford City Management Act 1939. Additional boroughs were created for Dún Laoghaire and Galway by the Local Government Act 1930, s 3 and Local Government (Galway) Act 1937 respectively; Galway achieved the status of a county borough by virtue of the Local Government (Reorganisation) Act 1985. See now LOCAL AUTHORITY. See also ALDERMAN; LORD MAYOR.

borrowing. A company may borrow money if expressly or impliedly authorised to do so by its *memorandum of association*; a trading company has an implied power to borrow as being incidental to the carrying on of its business. See *Re Bansha Woolen Mills* [1887] 21 LR Ir 181; *Northern Bank Finance Corp v Quinn* [1979] HC.

A building society with an 'authorisation' may raise funds to be used for the objects of the society by borrowing money: Building Societies Act 1989, s 18.

A solicitor should not borrow money from a client unless that client is independently advised in that transaction or it is part of the business of the client to lend money: *A Guide to Professional Conduct of Solicitors in Ireland* (2002) ch 3.7.

For the avoidance of doubt, following the UK House of Lord's decision in *Hazell v Hammersmith & Fulham London Borough Council* [1991] 1 All ER 545, legislation was introduced in 1992 to confirm that certain State bodies had the power to enter into *swap transactions* (qv). Similarly in 1996, legislation was enacted to confirm that State bodies have, and always have had, power to enter into a variety of financial transactions e g finance leases; securitisation of assets; debtor discounting facilities; discounting of bills of exchange; issue of notes, bonds, commercial paper or other debt instruments; letters of credit and guarantees: Borrowing Powers of Certain Bodies Act 1996. [Bibliography: Cahill D; Burgess UK.] See SWAP TRANSACTIONS.

borstal. The use of the term 'borstal' is required to be discontinued; reference in any statute or instrument to 'borstal' must be construed as a reference to St Patrick's Institution: Criminal Justice Act 1960, ss 12–13. See REFORMATORY SCHOOLS.

bottled water. See NATURAL MINERAL WATERS.

bottomry. A pledge of a ship and its freight as security for a loan of a sum of money. It is virtually obsolete in admiralty law. See ADMIRALTY ACTION.

boundary. See HEDGE AND DITCH RULE; PARTY WALL.

boundary alteration. A local authority may adopt a proposal to alter its boundary; a process of consultation with other local authorities and the public is prescribed, as is a report from the *Local Government Commission*: Local Government Act 2001, ss 55–62. The boundary alteration is made subsequently by Ministerial order following consideration of a report furnished by the Commission (LGA 2001, s 61). The procedure in the Act also deals with the alteration of the boundary of a city and a town. See also European Parliament Elections Act 1997, s 24. For previous legislation, see: Local Government Act 1991, s 31; Local Government Act 1994, ss 17 and 24; Local Government (Dublin) Act 1993, s 40. See Letterkenny Town Boundary Alteration Orders 2003, SIs No 679 and 680 of 2003. [Bibliography: Canny (2); Walsh E S.] See MARITIME BOUNDARIES; URBAN DISTRICT COUNCILS.

Boundary Commission. The commission provided for by the Anglo-Irish Treaty 1921, art 12, to review the boundary between Northern Ireland and the then Irish Free State. It first met in 1924. A subsequent leak to a newspaper forecasted that there was to be no substantial change to the border, except that an area of southern Co Armagh was to go to the Free State, and an important portion of east Donegal was to go to Northern Ireland, changes which were unacceptable both to the North and South. Consequently, under a tripartite agreement signed in London on 3 December 1925, the powers of the commission were revoked, and the boundary remained unchanged.

bovine animal. Provision has been made for holding a census of bovine animals: National Beef Assurance Scheme Act 2000, s 20. The Minister is empowered to make regulations in relation to the registration and identification of bovine animals, in particular, the possession of ear-tags and identity cards (NBASA 2000, s 19). There is also provision for *movement permits* in respect of animals, carcases, meat or feedingstuffs (NBASA 2000, s 22). See EC (Identification and Registration of Bovine Animals) (Amendment) Regulations 2002, SI No 83 of 2002. See BEEF.

bovine disease. Bovine tuberculosis or brucellosis in cattle: Bovine Diseases (Levies) Act 1979, s 1. The levy as from 1 January 2004 is: (a) as regards milk, 0.75 cents per gallon; and (b) as regards animals slaughtered or exported live, €3.80 per animal: Bovine Diseases (Levies) Regulations 2003, SI No 714 of 2003. See Brucellosis in Cattle (General Provisions) (Amendment) Order 2002, SI No 415 of 2002 and 2003, SI No 700 of 2003. See BSE.

boycott. A concerted refusal to have anything to do with another person or his goods or services, so called after Captain Boycott in the land agitation of the 1880s.

An injunction may be obtained to restrain a boycott of a company: *Talbot (Ireland) Ltd v Merrigan* [1981] SC. There are provisions governing the boycotting of any person in relation to grocery goods: Restrictive Practices (Groceries) Order 1987, SI No 142 of 1987 and Restrictive Practices (Confirmation of Order) Act 1987. The Minister is empowered to amend or revoke that SI: Competition Act 2002, s 49. [Bibliography: O'Reilly M.] See BELOW COST SELLING.

brain death. The term used to describe the death of a person when that person's brain has died, even though other organs of that person's body continue to function with mechanical or other assistance. In this State the concept of *brain death* has not been judicially determined or defined by statute, although one High Court judge has indicated that it was likely that the concept would be accepted by the courts if appropriate expert testimony established the validity of the criteria: Mr Justice Costello (1987). See also Costello J in 'The Terminally Ill – The Law's Concerns': 21 Ir Jur (1986) 35. For position in UK law, see *Airedale National Health Service Trust v Bland* (1992) *Times*, 10 December.

As regards organ transplantation, the Irish Medical Council has stipulated that brain death should be diagnosed, using currently accepted criteria, by at least two appropriately qualified clinicians, who are also independent of the transplant team: Medical Council, *A Guide to Ethical Conduct and Behaviour* (6th edn, 2004), para 21.1. See ORGAN TRANSPLANTATION.

brain injury. Injury to the part of the central nervous system enclosed by the skull. Acquired brain injury is caused mainly by: (a) road traffic accidents; (b) violent assaults; (c) falls; (d) suicide attempts involving hanging; and (e) successful cardiac resuscitation following heart attack which results in anoxic brain damage. For the *acquired brain injury service* of the National Rehabilitation Hospital, see website: *www.nrh.ie*. For Headway Ireland, see website: *www.headwayireland.ie*.

branch. See FOREIGN COMPANY; TREE.

breach. The invasion or violation of a right, duty or law.

breach of confidence. See CONFIDENCE, BREACH OF; CONFIDENTIAL COMMUNICATIONS; TRADE SECRETS.

breach of contract. The refusal or failure by a party to a contract to fulfil an obligation imposed by the contract. The breach may occur: (a) by repudiation of his liability to perform; (b) by his own act disabling himself from performing the contract; or (c) by failing to fulfil all his obligations during his performance of the contract.

Breach entitles the injured party to bring an action for damages. It may also entitle him to treat the contract as discharged if the breach is of the entire contract or is of some term which is so vital that it goes to the root of the contract. See ANTICIPATORY BREACH; FUNDAMENTAL BREACH; REPUDIATORY BREACH.

breach of duty. The phrase 'breach of duty', lying in juxtaposition with negligence and nuisance, carries with it the implication of a particular breach of duty not to cause personal injury, rather than an obligation not to infringe any legal right of another person; a breach of duty does not include a deliberate assault: *Devlin v Roche* [2002] 2 ILRM 192, SC and 2 IR 360. See DUTY OF CARE.

breach of promise. An agreement between two persons to marry each other has no effect as a contract and no action may be brought in the State for a breach of such agreement, whatever the law applicable to the agreement: Family Law Act 1981, s 2. However, where one party has incurred expenditure of a substantial nature on behalf of the other party, the court may make such order as appears to it just and equitable in the circumstances (FLA 1981, s 7). See Courts Act 1991, s 13. See LRC 1 of 1980. See *Ennis v Butterly* [1997] 1 ILRM 28, HC and [1996] 1 IR 426, HC. See ENGAGED COUPLE.

breach of statutory duty. See STATUTORY DUTY.

breach of the peace. Minor offences against the public peace which are common law misdemeanours (now, offences) eg affray (qv), challenge to fight, and creating a public nuisance.

Any act likely to cause reasonable alarm and apprehension to members of the public is a breach of the peace: *Attorney-General v Cunningham* [1932] IR 28. See BINDING TO THE PEACE; DISRUPTIVE BEHAVIOUR.

breach of trust. Some improper act, neglect or default of a trustee of which he is personally guilty; the measure of liability is the loss caused to the trust property: Trustee Act 1893, s 24. The trustee must replace misappropriated trust property with interest at 4%; if he has traded with the trust funds, the beneficiary can claim interest at 5% or the profits actually made.

In determining liability of a trustee for breach of trust, the court distinguishes between a breach of his duties, wherein utmost diligence is required (*exacta diligentia*), and a breach of a discretion, wherein he must act honestly and use the diligence of a prudent person.

A trustee is only liable for his own acts, but he must not sit passive while co-trustees commit a breach of trust.

There are certain circumstances where one trustee must indemnify his co-trustees. A beneficiary may be required to indemnify a trustee where the breach takes place at the instigation of the beneficiary: Trustee Act 1893, s 45; *Anketell Jones v Fitzgerald* [1931] 65 ILTR 185. Property acquired in breach of a trust can become subject to the trust: *Hortensius Ltd v Bishop* (*Trustees of TSB, Dublin*) [1989] ILRM 294, HC.

A *certificate of conformity* issued to a bankrupt trustee does not relieve him of liability for a breach of trust. See Statute of Limitations 1957, ss 2(2), 43–44 and 71, 72.

A 'breach of trust' by an employee has been held to warrant his dismissal: *Nolan v Assured Performance International Ltd* [1990] ELR 172. See BENEFICIARY, REMEDIES OF; FRAUDULENT CONVERSION; PLEADINGS; TRUST.

break clause. A clause in a lease, usually for a fixed term, conferring on the tenant an option to determine the lease before expiration of the term. Usually the option is made subject to various conditions eg that the tenant has complied with the terms of the lease up to the time of exercise of the option, or perhaps be confined to the happening of specified events: *Watters v Creagh* [1958] 92 ILTR 196. A break clause may also give the landlord a right to terminate a lease early eg in the event that the landlord gets planning permission for a development. [Bibliography: Wylie (4).]

breast implants. Provision has been made for the reclassification of breast implants to the higher classification of Class III medical devices: EC (Medical Devices) (Reclassification of Breast Implants) (Amendment) Regulations 2003, SI No 358 of 2003, implementing EC Directive 2003/12/EC. See MEDICAL DEVICE.

breathalyser. A challenge to the validity of the *Lion Intoxilyser*, a new device for measuring the presence of alcohol in alleged drunken driving cases, failed in the High Court: *Daly v DPP* [2002] 2 ILRM 290, HC.

However, in a case not to be seen as a test case, the Supreme Court has held that the garda guidelines, which stated that a person arrested on suspicion of drunken-driving should be observed for 20 minutes before a breath specimen was taken using the intoxilyser, have no basis in law: *DPP v Finn* [2003] FL 6904, SC and [2003] 2 ILRM 47 and 1 IR 372. The court held that the evidence obtained after that time was not admissible. If the procedure of observing an arrested person for 20 minutes was capable of being justified, the court held that it must be justified by a competent witness who could give appropriate evidence. There was no such evidence in this case. Also in a subsequent case, the High Court held that a garda does not have to ask a driver, before a breath test, when the driver had last consumed alcohol: *DPP v Quirke* (4 March 2003, unreported), HC. Unless the garda knew or had reason to suppose a suspect had consumed alcohol within the preceding 20 minutes, there was no need to wait 20 minutes before the garda could form a *bona fide* opinion on the condition of the suspect, based on the intoxilyser test.

In a subsequent Supreme Court case, the court held that it was lawful for a garda to detain a person for 20 minutes at a Garda station in order to observe him before requiring him to provide breath samples through a breathalyser: *DPP v McNiece* [2003] 2 IR 614, SC and FL 7712. Murray J said that he could not see anything unlawful or oppressive in adopting procedures to ensure that when the breath test was taken, it was effective or reliable.

The Supreme Court has held that a District Court judge was wrong not to have entertained the application of the accused to inspect an intoximeter in Dún Laoghaire Garda Station and to have properly considered the application: *Whelan v Judge Brian Kirby and DPP* [2004] 2 ILRM 1, SC. See also *DPP v Curry* [2002] 3 IR 131, HC. There is a presumption that the apparatus used to obtain a preliminary breath sample is an apparatus for indicating the presence of alcohol in the breath: Road Traffic Act 1994, s 12(5) as substituted by Road Traffic Act 2003, s 2. See BREATH SPECIMEN.

breath specimen. The *preliminary* specimen of his breath which a person, in charge of a mechanically propelled vehicle in a public place, is required by a garda to provide, by exhaling into an apparatus for indicating the presence of alcohol. A garda may so require whenever he is of the opinion that the person in charge of the vehicle: (a) has consumed intoxicating liquor; (b) is or has, with the vehicle, been involved in a collision; or (c) is committing or has committed a road traffic offence: Road Traffic Act 1994, s 12 as substituted by Road Traffic Act 2003, s 2.

Where the garda has formed the opinion that the person has consumed alcohol, he may require the person to provide a preliminary sample of their breath either at the scene or in a place or vehicle in the vicinity. If the garda does not have the appropriate equipment, he can require the person to remain for a period of not more than an hour at the location until a breathalyser can be brought to the scene.

Following arrest, a garda may require the person to provide two specimens of his breath or to submit to a blood or urine test (RTA 1994, s 13(1)(a) as amended by RTA 2003, s 3). Refusal or failure to comply forthwith with the requirement is an offence.

As regards the consumption of alcohol, before a garda may exercise his power to require a person to provide a breath specimen, he must first form the opinion that the person had consumed intoxicating liquor and the formation of that opinion, prior to the exercise of the power, must be proved by express evidence: *DPP v Duffy* [2000] 1 IR 393, HC.

It is a good defence to that charge if no evidence is adduced to show that the garda had formed the necessary opinion, but it is not a defence to a charge of exceeding the limit: *DPP v Brady* [1991] 1 IR 337, HC. However, where the garda had a reasonable and genuine opinion, which is adduced in evidence, it is no defence to show that his opinion was wrong eg that the vehicle was not a 'mechanically propelled vehicle': *DPP v Breheny* [1993] ITLR (31 May), SC. Also the garda, in requiring a person to submit to a breath test, does not have an obligation to inform the person of the particular statutory provision he is *invoking: DPP v Gaughran* [1993] ILRM 472, HC. See also *Director of Public Prosecutions v Joyce* [1985] ILRM 206; *Dougal v Mahon* [1989] 7 ILT Dig 229.

Under the 1994 Act, a new maximum permissible alcohol level of 35 microgrammes of alcohol per 100 millilitres of breath was introduced. The certificates produced by the intoxilyser are evidence of the facts stated on them unless the contrary is shown: *DPP v Syron* [2001] 2 IR 105, HC. For previous (now repealed) legislation, see Road Traffic Act 2002, s 10. [Bibliography: Hill & O'Keeffe; McGrath M (2).] See BLOOD SPECIMEN; BREATHALYSER; DRUNKEN DRIVING; IN CHARGE; PUBLIC PLACE; ROAD TRAFFIC CHECKS; SANCTUARY; URINE SPECIMEN.

Brehon Laws. The laws of Ireland which developed from before 250 AD until the seventeenth century when the *common law* (qv) of England was established throughout Ireland by proclamation of James I in 1606. The Brehon Laws were the laws of the clan (tribe), under the control of *brehons*, an hereditary caste of lawyers. The laws survived despite the arrival of the Danes in 790 AD and the Norman conquest. The Anglo-Norman nobles, who took the place of the Irish chieftains, chose to accommodate themselves to the *lex loci*, except in the

Pale (a small district, the extent of which varied with the fortunes of war and rarely exceeded four of the present Leinster counties). Under the Brehon system, land belonged to the clan, although the private ownership of copyright was recognised in the celebrated case of *Abbot Finnian v Columba* (561 AD) with the famous maxim: *'le gach bain a bainin, le gach leabhar a leabhran'* – '*to every cow its calf, to every book its copy*'. See also *Foyle and Bann Fisheries Ltd v Attorney-General* [1949] 83 ILTR 29. For information on the *Brehon Law Project*, see website: http:// ua.tuathal.tripod.com/testdefault.html. [Bibliography: Ginnel; Kelly; Hogan & Osborough.]

Bretton Woods Agreement. The agreement signed by the original contracting parties in New Hampshire USA in July 1944 and which established the *International Monetary Fund* (*qv*) and the *International Bank for Reconstruction and Development.* Ireland acceded to the agreement in 1957: Bretton Woods Agreement Acts 1957 and 1999. See also Central Bank Act 1997, s 65.

brevi manu. [A short cut.]

brewer, private. A brewer of beer, not being a brewer for sale within the meaning of the Inland Revenue Act 1880, s 19. A private brewer is not required to take out a brewer's licence; the beer brewed is not liable to excise duty provided it is solely for his own domestic use: Finance Act 1989, s 51. It is an offence for a private brewer to brew beer otherwise than for his own domestic use or for any person to offer such beer for sale.

bribe. See CONCEALING OFFENCE; SECRET PROFIT.

bribery and corruption. It is an indictable misdemeanour (now, an offence) at common law corruptly to solicit, promise, give, receive or agree to receive a bribe (ie a reward) in order that any public official should either: (a) act contrary to a duty he has to do something in which the public has an interest; or (b) show favour in the discharge of his duty and function. The offer of a bribe is an offence even though it is not accepted. See Prevention of Sale of Offices Act 1809; Public Bodies Corrupt Practices Act 1889; Prevention of Corruption Acts 1906 and 1916 as amended by Ethics in Public Office Act 1995, s 38.

It is an offence to give valuable consideration to induce a voter to vote at a Dáil election: Electoral Act 1992, s 135. See also CORRUPTION; CONCEALING OFFENCE; SECRET PROFIT.

bridewell. A prison.

bridge. The maintenance and construction of bridges is part of the duty of a local authority: Local Government Act 1925, ss 1 and 24.

The National Roads Authority is empowered to direct a roads authority to make an application to the Minister for a bridge order under the Local Government Act 1946: Roads Act 1993, s 20(1)(b). A road authority must not construct or reconstruct a bridge or viaduct, or a tunnel under a railway or any inland waterway or any navigable water, unless it has obtained the relevant Ministerial approval: RA 1993, s 15A as inserted by Local Government Act 2001, s 245. See also LGA 2001, s 227(2)(c).

In order to safeguard the validity of certain bridge orders, Pt IV of the LGA 1946 is deemed to continue to apply, notwithstanding its repeal: Local Government Act 2003, s 2. See *CIE v Carroll and Wexford County Council* [1986] ILRM 312. See NAVIGATION, RIGHT TO.

bridging loan. Generally a short-term advance made by a bank to a customer pending his receipt of funds from another source or by a building society to a member pending completion of his mortgage. See Building Societies Act 1989, s 23 as amended by Housing (Miscellaneous Provisions) Act 2002, s 23 and Sch 3. See UNSECURED LOANS.

brief. The written instructions furnished by a solicitor (qv) to a barrister (qv) to enable him to represent the client in legal proceedings. The term '*brief*' means instructions to appear before any court or tribunal, inquiry, board or other body (whether statutory or otherwise) on behalf of a client: *Code of Conduct for the Bar of Ireland* (December 2003) r 1.7(i). A brief usually contains a narrative of the facts; copies of material documents and correspondence; and the formal pleadings. Briefs are in general accepted on the understanding that the barrister concerned may be unavoidably prevented by a conflicting professional engagement from attending the case (r 4.5). A barrister having accepted a brief may not return it merely on the grounds that his client has no case or would not accept his advice on a settlement, but he must continue with the case if his client wishes it to be fought (r 3.6). See INSTRUCT; SOLICITOR AND COUNSEL.

brief fee. Formerly, it was the practice for a solicitor to mark a fee on the brief. It has been held that this practice, which has fallen into disuse, had the merit that the solicitor focused on the question of the appropriate fee for counsel, but that it was not the court's function to revive the practice: *Smyth v Tunney* [1992] 10 ILT Dig 267, HC.

The appropriate *brief fee* to be paid to counsel is the fee fixed with the approval of the client; the fee is 'what the market will bear': Kinlen J in *McGahan v Independent Newspapers* (1993) Irish Times, 21 October. However, the fact that a brief fee is agreed by a solicitor in advance of a hearing is not the only test; the test must be the objective one as to whether a reasonably careful and reasonably prudent solicitor would have agreed the fee: *Smyth v Tunney* [1999] 1 ILRM 211, HC. See *Commissioners of Irish Lights v Maxwell* [1998] 1 ILRM 421, SC and [1997] 3 IR 474, SC; *Best v Wellcome Foundation (No 3)* [1996] 3 IR 378, HC.

In a complex High Court action, the complexity should normally be reflected in the *brief fee* rather than in the *refresher*, as it was the brief fee which covered the preparation of the case: *Bloomer v Incorporated Law Society of Ireland (No 2)* [2000] 1 IR 383, HC. A barrister who does work, which is in reality solicitor's work, is not entitled to be remunerated for it (*Bloomer* case). See also *Bloomer v Incorporated Law Society of Ireland (No 3)* [2002] 1 IR 189, SC.

In an award of costs in the District Court a fee for counsel may not be included, unless the court certifies that the employment of such counsel was necessary, and only where the action is for a sum in excess of £500 (€635) or, in ejectment proceedings, the annual rent exceeds £500 (€635): DCR 1997 Ord 52.

A solicitor who instructs counsel should use his best endeavours to ensure that counsel receives fees that are due and owing to him at the earliest opportunity: *A Guide to Professional Conduct of Solicitors in Ireland* (2002) ch 8.4. However, a solicitor has no personal liability for counsel's fees. If he has reasonable grounds for believing that the client is unlikely to be in a position to pay counsel's fees in the event of the case being lost, counsel should be advised of this in the initial letter of instruction.

It is not proper conduct for a barrister to take over a case from another barrister unless and until he has satisfied himself, by direct contact with the original barrister, that the outstanding fees due to the original barrister have been discharged: *Code of Conduct for the Bar of Ireland* (December 2003) r 7.5. Where a barrister has nominated a fee in a case and it is not paid by a time fixed for it to be paid, there is no obligation on the barrister to act further in the matter (r 7.7). A barrister is required to report to the Bar Council any solicitor (or any person having direct professional access) from whom a fee is due and unpaid for a period in excess of twelve months, unless there is a reasonable explanation for the delay in payment (r 2.20). See BARRISTER AND FEES; RETAINER.

British citizen. A person who under the Act of the British Parliament entitled the British Nationality Act 1981 is a British citizen: Electoral Act 1992, s 8(7). Such a citizen is entitled to be registered as a Dáil elector if resident in Ireland and has reached 18 years of age. The Minister is empowered to amend the definition of British citizen to accommodate any changes in British legislation governing citizenship (EA 1992, s 8(4)(b)). British citizens may also vote at European and local elections. See DÁIL ELECTION.

British statute. An Act of the Parliament of the late United Kingdom of Great Britain and Ireland: Interpretation Act 1937, Sch, para 3. See LEGISLATION, CONSTITUTIONALITY OF; SAORSTÁT ÉIREANN; STATUTE LAW.

broadcast. A broadcast by wireless telegraphy of communications, sounds, signs or visual images or signals, whether such are actually received or not: Broadcasting and Wireless Telegraphy Act 1988, s 1. It is an offence to make a broadcast from any premises or vehicle in the State unless made pursuant to and in accordance with a licence (BWTA 1988, s 3).

It is also an offence to provide accommodation, equipment or programme material for unlicensed broadcasts, or to advertise by means of, or take part in broadcasts; the Minister is empowered to prohibit the provision of telephone or electricity services to premises in which illegal broadcasts are made (BWTA 1988). There is also a prohibition on the interception of services supplied by a licensee: Broadcasting Act 1990, ss 9–15.

Public sector broadcasting on radio and television is carried out by Radio Telefís Éireann and is regulated by the Broadcasting Authority Acts 1960 to 1979 and the Broadcasting Act 1990. Private sector broadcasting is carried out by sound broadcasting contractors under the *Broadcasting Commission of Ireland* (formerly called the Independent Radio and Television Commission) pursuant to the 1988 and 1990 Acts. The 1988 Act provides also for a private sector national television service under contract to the Commission.

Provision has been made to empower the Minister to designate a company which will be licensed by the *Director of Telecommunications Regulation* to construct and operate a digital terrestrial television infrastructure: Broadcasting Act 2001, ss 7–8.

This Act also provides for the name change to the *Broadcasting Commission of Ireland* with expanded powers and functions in relation to the regulation of digital broadcasting on all platforms (BA 2001, ss 10–11).

The powers of investigation of the *Broadcasting Complaints Commission* have been extended to cover all providers of broadcast content (BA 2001, s 24). Provision has also been made for the Minister to establish Teilifís na Gaeilge (now TG4) as a statutory corporate body (BA 2001, s 44). Additional clarity and detail is also provided as regards the *public service broadcasting* remit of RTÉ and TG4 (BA 2001, ss 28 and 45).

The Supreme Court has held that the power given to Radio Telefís Éireann to transmit political party broadcasts does not relieve it of its duty to 'be fair to all interests concerned' and 'objective and impartial': *Coughlan v Broadcasting Complaints Commission, RTE and the A-G* [2000] 3 IR 1, SC. The High Court, in this case, had held that a package of uncontested or partisan broadcasts, weighted on one side of the argument, was an interference with the referendum process and was undemocratic and a constitutionally unfair procedure.

The Green Party failed in its attempt to secure a court order compelling RTÉ to provide live television coverage of its árdfheis, the High Court holding that it was not for the courts to lay down the criteria for such broadcasts and that the criteria adopted by RTÉ could not be said to be illogical: *Green Party v RTÉ* [2003] 1 IR 558, HC. The High Court decided not to interfere with a decision by RTÉ to refuse

to accept an advertisement for a book of short stories written by the president of Sinn Féin: *Brandon Books v RTÉ* (1993) Irish Times, 17 July, HC.

The High Court has held that RTÉ does not have to reveal data in relation to coverage of the 2002 general election: *RTÉ v Information Commissioner* (unreported, 11 June 2004), HC. See also *Carrigaline Co Ltd v Minister for Transport Energy and Communications* [1997] 1 ILRM 241, HC; *Radio Limerick One Ltd v IRTC* [1997] 2 IR 291, SC; *Maigueside Communications Ltd v IRTC* [1998] 4 IR 115, HC.

See websites: *www.rte.ie*; *www.tg4.ie*; *www.bci.ie*. [Bibliography: Hall; McGonagle.] See COMMISSION FOR COMMUNICATIONS REGULATION; COPYRIGHT, QUALIFICATION FOR; EQUALITY BEFORE THE LAW; INDEPENDENT TELEVISION PROGRAMME; MAJOR EVENT.

broadcast and copyright. Broadcast, in the context of copyright law, means a transmission by wireless means, including by terrestrial or satellite means, for *direct public reception* or for presentation to members of the public of sounds images or data: Copyright and Related Rights Act 2000, s 2(1). It does not include the MMDS service. Copyright subsists in broadcasts (CRRA 2000, s 17(2)). Any reference in the 2000 Act to the *reception* of a broadcast, includes the reception of the broadcast by means of a telecommunications system (CRRA 2000, s 2(2)).

A broadcast that is *encrypted* is regarded as being broadcast for lawful *direct public reception* where the means required for decoding the signals for those broadcasts have been made available by, or with the authority of, the person making the broadcast (CRRA 2000, s 5).

The *author* of a broadcast includes the person making the broadcast (CRRA 2000, s 21(c)). A broadcast will be treated as a work of *joint authorship* (qv) if more than one person makes the broadcast and their contributions are not distinct (CRRA 2000, s 22(3)). The copyright in a broadcast expires 50 years after the broadcast is first lawfully transmitted; copyright in a repeat broadcast expires at the same time as the original broadcast (CRRA 2000, s 27). See CABLE PROGRAMME; COPYRIGHT; MEDIA MERGER; RETRANSMISSION.

broadcast and VAT. When radio and television broadcasting services are received for business purposes in this State from abroad, the place of supply is deemed to be in this State, and the recipient is liable for payment of Irish VAT; if such services are supplied from this State to business customers abroad, no Irish VAT arises: Finance Act 2003, s 131.

Broadcasting Commission of Ireland. The independent commission, appointed by the government, with the function to arrange for the provision of sound broadcasting services (including a national sound broadcasting service) and one television programme service additional to any broadcasting services provided by Radio Telefís Éireann: Radio and Television Act 1988, ss 3–4.

The Commission is required to enter into: (a) sound broadcasting contracts under which the contractors will have the right and duty to establish, maintain and operate sound broadcasting transmitters serving the areas specified in the contract and to provide a sound broadcasting service; and (b) a television programme service contract under which the contractor will have the right and duty to provide a television programme service (RTA 1988, s 4(2)).

The Commission is obliged to take every step reasonably open to it to ensure that its conclusions are reached in a manner, not merely free from bias, but also of apprehension of bias in the minds of reasonable people: *Radio Limerick One Ltd v IRTC* [1997] 2 IR 291 at 316, SC. See also *TV 3 Television Co Ltd v IRTC* [1993] 11 ILT Dig 187, HC and [1994] 2 IR 439, SC.

The Broadcasting Act 2001 provide for the name of the Commission to be changed from the *Independent Radio and Television Commission* (IRTC) to the *Broadcasting Commission of Ireland* with expanded powers and functions in relation to the regulation of digital broadcasting on all platforms (BA 2001, ss 10–11).

See website: *www.bci.ie*. See ADVERTISE-MENT, RADIO; BIAS; BROADCASTING FUNDING SCHEME; SOUND BROADCAST-ING SERVICE; TELEVISION PROGRAMME SERVICE.

Broadcasting Complaints Commission. The Commission established in 1976 to investigate and decide on complaints made to it by the public, provided the complaints fall within specified categories. The Commission has limited powers to provide relief. It must draw attention in its annual report, which is laid before the Houses of the Oireachtas, to any decision it has made which has not been accepted. RTÉ is required to broadcast the Commission's decisions where these decisions find in favour of the complainant, unless the Commission considers it inappropriate so to do. See Broadcasting Authority Act 1960, s 18 as inserted by the Broadcasting Authority (Amendment) Act 1976, s 4 and the Broadcasting Act 1990, s 8.

The Minister may, by regulation, direct complaints in respect of independent radio and television to the Commission (Radio and Television Act 1988, ss 11 and 18) and has done so (Radio and Television (Complaints by Members of the Public) Regulations 1992, SI No 329 of 1992). The power of investigation of the Commission has been extended to cover all providers of broadcast content: Broadcasting Act 2001, s 24.

broadcasting funding scheme. A grant scheme, funded by 5% of the net television licence fee revenue, administered by the Broadcasting Commission of Ireland, to support: (a) new television or radio programmes on Irish culture, heritage and experience; (b) new television or radio programmes to improve adult literacy; and (c) the development of archiving of programme material produced in the State: Broadcasting (Funding) Act 2003, s 2. Included are programmes on history; historical buildings; the natural environment; folk, rural and vernacular heritage; traditional and contemporary arts; the Irish language; and the Irish experience in European and international contexts (B(F)A 2003, s 2(1)(a)).

The objectives of the scheme in relation to programmes based on Irish culture, heritage and experience are (a) to develop high-quality programmes; (b) to develop these programmes in the Irish language; (c) to increase the availability of these programmes to audiences in the State; (d) to represent the diversity of Irish culture and heritage; (e) to record oral Irish heritage and aspects of Irish heritage which are disappearing, under threat, or have not been previously recorded; and (f) to develop local and community broadcasting (B(F)A 2003, s 3(1)).

The objective of the scheme in relation to the development of archiving of programme material is to develop an integrated approach to the archiving, including the development of suitable storage processes and formats and the accessing of material by interested parties (B(F)A 2003, s 3(2)).

brochure. A tour organiser or retailer is liable to compensate a consumer for any damage caused as a direct consequence of information in a brochure which is false or misleading: Package Holidays and Travel Trade Act 1995, s 11.

broker. A mercantile agent for the purchase and sale of stocks and shares, goods, insurance policies etc. He is an agent primarily to establish privity of contract between two other parties. A broker cannot sue or be sued on a contract unless he signs a written memorandum with his own name. For the Irish Brokers Association, see website: *www.irishbrokers.com*. See INSURANCE BROKER; AGENT.

brokerage. Payment or commission paid to a broker for his services.

brothel. A place resorted to by persons of both sexes for the purposes of prostitution: *Singleton v Ellison* [1895] 1 QB 607. It is an offence to keep or manage a brothel, or to permit a premises to be used as a brothel or to advertise a brothel: Criminal Law (Sexual Offences) Act 1993, s 11; Criminal Justice (Public Order) Act 1994, s 23.

A search warrant may be issued by the District Court where there are reasonable grounds for suspecting that a premises is a brothel; a garda may demand the name and address of every person found on the premises during the search: Criminal Law Amendment Act 1935, s 19 amended by CL(SO)A 1993, s 12.

It is an offence for a person, who has custody, charge or care of a child, to allow the child to reside in or frequent a brothel: Children Act 2001, s 248. See *DPP v Murphy* (1993) Irish Times, 6 February, CC.

Brussels Convention. Generally understood to mean the EC Convention on Jurisdiction and Enforcement of Judgments in Civil and Commercial Matters, given effect to by the Jurisdiction of Courts and Enforcement of Judgments (European Communities) Act 1988, as repealed and consolidated in 1998: Jurisdiction of Courts and Enforcement of Judgments Act 1998. The Brussels Convention has the aim of establishing the European Union as an area of free movement of national judgments as between the member states. The Convention sets out: (a) rules governing

the jurisdiction of the courts of the contracting states in civil litigation; and (b) rules and procedures for the recognition and enforcement in a contracting state of a judgment originating from another contracting state.

The *Brussels I Regulation* (qv) on the recognition and enforcement of judgments in civil and commercial matters, replaces the Brussels Convention for all EU States except Denmark: EC (Civil and Commercial Judgments) Regulations 2002, SI No 52 of 2002. See DCR 1997 Ord 62. See *Daly v Irish Travel Group Ltd* [2003] ITLR (30 June), HC. See JURISDICTION; DEFENDANTS, JOINT; EXCLUSIVE JURISDICTION; FOREIGN JUDGMENTS, ENFORCEMENT OF; TORT.

Brussels I Regulation. Means Council Regulation (EC) No 44/2001 of 22 December 2000 on the recognition and enforcement of judgments in civil and commercial matters, which replaces the Brussels Convention for all EU States except Denmark. Provision for the implementation of the Council Regulation in Ireland was made by EC (Civil and Commercial Judgments) Regulations 2002, SI No 52 of 2002. The Jurisdiction of Courts and Enforcement of Judgments Act 1998, except as provided in the Brussels I Regulation, art 68 and as regards Denmark, ceases to apply as between the State and other member states. See 'Judgment Calls' by T P Kennedy in *Law Society Gazette* (June 2002) 14. See DCR 1997 Ord 62. See JURISDICTION; DEFENDANTS, JOINT; EXCLUSIVE JURISDICTION; FOREIGN JUDGMENTS, ENFORCEMENT OF; TORT.

brutum fulmen. [An empty threat.] See THREAT.

BSE. [Bovine Spongiform Encephalopathy.] A disease of bovine animals with possible links to Creutz-Feld Jacob disease in humans. Council Regulation 96/1357/EEC provides for the payment to producers in the beef sector for losses arising from the BSE crisis and allotted funds to EU member states for this purpose. See also *Maxwell v Minister for Agriculture* [1999] 1 ILRM 161 and 2 IR 474, HC.

Regulations have been made regarding the removal, isolation and disposal of specified risk material for the purposes of the control of BSE: European Communities (Specified Risk Material) Regulations 2000, SI No 332 of 2000. See also Diseases of Animals (Bovine Spongiform

Encephalopathy) (Specified Risk Material) Order 2000, SI No 331 of 2000.

budget. An estimate of government expenditure and revenue for the ensuing year presented to Dáil Éireann by the Minister for Finance. It includes proposals for taxes which are necessary to raise the revenue required. These proposals, if accepted, are enacted as the Finance Act for that year. See 1937 Constitution, art 28(4)(4). See FINANCIAL RESOLUTION.

budgetary rules. Rules in the economic area to ensure the monetary stability of the EC, which become progressively applicable as the member states move towards *economic and monetary union* (qv): Treaty establishing the European Community, arts.101–104 of the consolidated (2002) version. The basic rules are: (a) no monetary financing e g by way of overdraft arrangements between governments and their central bank; (b) no bail-outs e g the EC will not step in to rescue a member state which defaults in its debt; (c) avoidance of excessive government deficits e g criteria are laid down (art 104(2) and the Protocol on the Excessive Deficit Procedure). Non-compliance with the budgetary rules may lead to the imposition of sanctions (art 104(11)). See EURO.

budgeting service. See MONEY ADVICE AND BUDGETING SERVICE.

bug. See PRIVACY.

buggery. Intercourse by penetration *per anum* upon a man, a woman, or an animal. It was a common law offence, the penalties for which were provided by the Offences against the Person Act 1861, ss 61–63. The European Court of Human Rights held in 1988 that the existence of legislation in Ireland penalising certain homosexual acts carried out in private by consenting adult males constituted a breach of rights under Art 8 of the European Convention on Human Rights: *Norris v Ireland* [1988] EHRR. See also *Attorney-General v Troy* 84 ILTR 193; *Norris v Attorney-General* [1984] IR 36, SC.

In 1993, the crime of buggery between adult persons was abolished: Criminal Law (Sexual Offences) Act 1993, s 2. However, a person is guilty of an offence who commits or attempts to commit an act of buggery with a person under 17 years of age or a person who is mentally impaired of any age (unless married to the person) (CL(SO)A 1993, ss 3 and 5). Also the crime of buggery with an animal (bestiality)

has been retained. See BESTIALITY; MENTALLY IMPAIRED; SOLICIT.

builder, duty of. A builder owes a duty of care in relation to hidden defects not discoverable by the kind of examination he could expect a purchaser to make; he also has a duty to avoid dangerous defects and to avoid defects in the quality of the work: *Ward v McMaster* [1985] IR 29.

Damages awarded may include economic loss, including the cost of alternative accommodation and a sum for inconvenience and discomfort. See *Quill* in 10 ILT & SJ (1992) 185 and 202.

building, dangerous. See FIRE SAFETY NOTICE; DANGEROUS STRUCTURE.

building bye-laws. The bye-laws which sanitary authorities were empowered to make with respect: to the structure and description of the substances used in buildings; to the sites and foundations of houses, buildings and other erections; to the sufficiency of space; and to the drainage: Public Health (Ireland) Act 1878, s 41. There is an obligation to obtain building bye-law approval for a development; the grant of planning permission does not of itself authorise development: *Carty v Fingal County Council* [2000] 1 ILRM 64, SC and [1999] 3 IR 577, SC. Building bye-laws have been replaced by building regulations: Building Control Act 1990, s 22 (except para 1 of s 41 of the Public Health (Ireland) Act 1878). See BUILDING REGULATIONS.

building contract. The High Court has held that where parties to a contract (in this case, a building contract) were in the same business and of equal bargaining power, then conditions which were habitually imposed in such contracts would be imposed into their contract on the basis of the common understanding of the parties that the usual conditions would apply: *Lynch Roofing Systems Ltd v Bennett & Son Ltd* [1999] 2 IR 450, HC. [Bibliography: Keane D (2).] See RIAI CONTRACT.

building control. See Fagan and Furlong in *Law Society Gazette* (May 1992) 137. See Building Control (Amendment) Regulations 2000, SI No 10 of 2000. [Bibliography: LexisNexis.] See BUILDING BYE LAWS; BUILDING REGULATIONS.

building construction. In an action for infringement of copyright in relation to the construction of a building, the court will not make an order which would prevent the building being completed or require the building to be demolished: Copyright and Related Rights Act 2000, s 124. See also MORAL RIGHT.

building law. [Bibliography: Keane D.] See ENGINEERING LAW.

building lease. A lease of land, situated in an urban area, or else demised for a term of at least 20 years, on which permanent buildings, which were not merely ancillary and subsidiary improvements, were erected by the lessee at the time of erection or under an agreement for the grant of the lease on their erection: Landlord and Tenant (Reversionary Leases) Act 1958, s 4; *Southern Health Board v Reeves Smith* [1980] IR 26. A building lease (although not now referred to as such), entitled to acquire the fee simple, is entitled to a reversionary lease (qv): Landlord and Tenant (Amendment) Act 1980, s 30. See PROPRIETARY LEASE.

building regulations. The regulations which the Minister is empowered to make in relation to: (a) the design and construction of buildings; (b) material alterations or extensions of buildings; (c) the provision of services, fittings and equipment in, or in connection with, buildings; and (d) buildings where a material change in use takes place: Building Control Act 1990, s 3.

The purposes for which building regulations may be made include not only public health and safety but also provisions for the special needs of disabled persons, energy conservation, the efficient use of resources and the encouragement of good building practice.

Every building to which building regulations apply must be designed and constructed in accordance with the regulations (BCA 1990, s 3(5)). Certain local authorities are the building control authorities (BCA 1990, s 2) with powers to grant dispensations or relaxations of the regulations (BCA 1990, s 4), to inspect buildings (BCA 1990, s 11) and to serve *enforcement notices* (BCA 1990, s 8). There is provision for self-regulation by way of *certificates of compliance* (BCA 1990, s 6(2)(a)(i)). A *fire safety certificate* from the building control authority is required in respect of buildings of a prescribed class (BCA 1990, s 6(2)(a)(ii)) and also a *certificate of approval* (BCA 1990, s 6(2)(a)(iii)) which indicates the opinion of the authority of compliance with the regulations. See Building Regulations 1997 to 2000, SI No. 497 of 1997; SI No 249 of 2000. See Building Control

Regulations 1997, SI No 496 of 1997 as amended by SI No 85 of 2004. See Building Regulations (Amendment) (No 3) Regulations 2000, SI No 441 of 2000; and Building Regulations (Amendment) (No 2) Regulations 2002, SI No 581 of 2002.

Provision has been made by building regulations for improved access to buildings for persons with a disability: Building Regulations 1997, SI No 497 of 1997; Building Regulations (Amendment) Regulations 2000, SI No 179 of 2000; Technical Guidance Document M (2000). For new energy efficiency requirements, see Building Regulations (Amendment) Regulations 2002, SI No 284 of 2002 amending Part L of the Building Regulations. See also Building Regulations Advisory Body Order 2002, SI No 2 of 2002 as amended by SI No 62 of 2003. [Bibliography: Keane D; OCofaigh.] See BUILDING BYE-LAWS; DISABLED PERSON AND BUILD ENVIRONMENT.

building society. A building society incorporated or deemed to be incorporated under the Building Societies Act 1989 (s 2(1) as amended by Central Bank and Financial Services Authority of Ireland Act 2003, s 35, Sch 1). Originally, a building society was a body established with the sole purpose of raising funds for making loans to its members to enable them to build a home. Now, while a building society must have one of its objects the raising of funds for making *housing loans* (qv), it may also engage in a wide range of financial and other services, provided it *adopts* the power to do so and obtains the approval of the Central Bank eg auctioneering, conveyancing, financial, and services relating to land. Societies are *mutual* societies but they may de-mutualise by converting to a public limited company.

A building society is a body corporate (with the name contained in its memorandum and rules) having perpetual succession and a seal (qv) and the power to hold land (BSA 1989, s 10(6)). A society must have a board of directors of at least three directors, a chairman, a chief executive and a secretary (BSA 1989, ss 48 and 49).

Where two or more building societies merge, a transfer of assets from one to the other does not give rise to a chargeable gain or allowable loss: Taxes Consolidation Act 1997, s 702. Where a building society converts from a mutual society to a limited company, the rules in Sch 16 apply eg both are treated as the same entity (TCA 1997, s 703). For amendments to ss 23, 25, 29, 34, 40(2), 53, 57, 59, 77, 81 and 88 of BSA 1989, see Housing (Miscellaneous Provisions) Act 2002, s 23 and Sch 3. For amendments to ss 10, 14, 40, 110, Sch 4 and Sch 5 of BSA 1989, see Central Bank and Financial Services Authority of Ireland Act 2004, Sch 1. A review group was established by the Department of the Environment and Local Government to consider possible further amendments to the 1989 Act; amending legislation was promised for 2004 but had not been introduced by September 2004. [Bibliography: Johnston & O'Conor; Murdoch (2); Ovey & Waters (UK); Wurtzburg & Mills (UK).] See BANKER AND CONFIDENTIALITY; CONVERSION; CONVEYANCING SERVICES; CREDIT INSTITUTION; DERIVATIVE ACTION; INSURANCE; IRISH FINANCIAL SERVICES REGULATORY AUTHORITY; LINKING SERVICES; MONEY LAUNDERING; MORTGAGEE, RIGHT OF; OMBUDSMAN FOR THE CREDIT INSTITUTIONS; PRIOR MORTGAGE; REDEMPTION FEE; SAVINGS PROTECTION SCHEME; SHARES, BUILDING SOCIETY; TIERED INTEREST RATE; VALUATION REPORT.

built-up area. Under proposed legislation, means the area of a city, a borough or a town within the meaning of the Local Government Act 2001: Road Traffic Bill 2004, s 2(1). The general speed limit in built up areas is proposed to be 50 kilometres per hour instead of 30 miles per hour (Road Traffic Bill 2004, s 5). This limit will not apply where a county or city manager makes a *road works speed limit* order or a local authority makes a *special speed limit* through bye-laws.

bulimia nervosa. A disorder characterised by compulsive over-eating followed by vomiting, sometimes associated with anxiety about gaining weight. See ANOREXIA NERVOSA.

bulk carrier. One of the following: (a) a ship constructed with single deck, top-side tanks and hopper-side tanks in cargo spaces and intended primarily to carry dry cargo in bulk; or (b) an ore carrier, meaning a sea-going single deck ship having two longitudinal bulkheads and a double bottom throughout the cargo region and intended for the carriage of ore cargoes in the centre holds only; or (c) a combination carrier: EC (Safe Loading and Unloading of Bulk Carriers) Regulations 2003, SI No 347 of 2003. These regulations give effect to EC Directive 2001/96/EC, as amended by EC Directive 2002/84/EC, the main purpose of which is to enhance the safety of bulk carriers calling at terminals in the member states, by reducing the risks of excessive stresses and physical damage to the structure of these ships.

bull. The term used to describe a person who buys stocks or shares with the intention of selling them at a higher price before the time for taking delivery of the shares. See BEAR.

bulls, control of. It is unlawful for a person to have in his possession an unregistered bull unless authorised by permit; a bull is an entire male of the bovine species over the the the age of nine months. See Control of Bulls for Breeding Act 1985. See also Control of Bulls for Breeding (Permits) Regulations 1986, SI No 333 of 1986; and Regulations, SI No 334 of 1986, SI No 166 of 1990, SI No 327 of 1994; No 280 of 1995 and SI No 447 of 2002.

bullying in the workplace. Repeated inappropriate behaviour, direct or indirect, whether verbal, physical or otherwise, conducted by one or more persons against another or others, at the place of work and/or in the course of employment, which could reasonably be regarded as undermining the individual's right to dignity at work: Industrial Relations Act 1990 (Code of Practice detailing Procedures for Addressing Bullying in the Workplace) (Declaration) Order 2002, SI No 17 of 2002. An isolated incident of the behaviour described in this definition may be an affront to dignity at work but, as a once-off incident, is not considered to be bullying.

One of the highest awards for bullying and harassment (£70,500/€89,517) was made in *LIZ ALLEN V INDEPENDENT NEWSPAPERS (IRELAND) LTD* [2002] ELR 84, EAT. Also a garda who was bullied by his colleagues when acting as a public service vehicle inspector was awarded €87,776: *McMahon v Garda Commissioner* (2003) Irish Times, 20 March, CC. See *Saehan Media Ireland Ltd v A Worker* [1999] ELR 41, LC; *Timmons v Oglesby & Butler Ltd* [1999] ELR 119, EAT; *Reyes v Print and Display Ltd* [1999] ELR 224, EAT; *O'Donoghue v South Eastern Health Board* [2000] ELR 189, HC. See 'The law of workplace stress, bullying and harassment' by Wesley Farrell BL and 'Workplace Bullying: internal investigation and fair procedures' by Murray Smith BL in *Bar Review* (June/July 2002) 252 and 271 respectively. See 'Psychiatric Injury and the Employment Appeals Tribunal: Double Bite at the Compensation Cherry?' by John Eardly BL in *Bar Review* (April 2003) 81. [Bibliography: Eardly (1).] See CODE OF PRACTICE; CONSTRUCTIVE DISMISSAL.

Bunreacht na hÉireann. [Constitution of Ireland (qv).]

burden. An encumbrance or liability affecting the ownership of land. The title of a registered owner of *registered land* is subject to: (a) the burdens which appear on the register as affecting the land: Registration of Title Act 1964, s 69; (b) the burdens, though not registered, which affect all registered land (RTA 1964, s 72 as amended by Gas (Amendment) Act 2000, s 22); (c) unregistered rights, which are enforceable personally against the registered owner who created them and against a volunteer (qv) transferee from the registered owner, but are not enforceable against a registered transferee for value.

There is provision for the registration of a *protected structure* (qv) as a burden affecting registered land: Planning and Development Act 2000, s 56. For previous legislation, see Local Government (Planning and Development) Act 1999, s 7.

The ownership of registered burdens is itself registered in the *register of leaseholds* where the burden is a lease, and in the *subsidiary register* for other burdens; except that a charge (qv) is usually registered in the register of the land on which the charge is a burden. See EC (Personal Insolvency) Regulations 2002, SI No 334 of 2002. [Bibliography: Charleton (5).] See CAUTION; DISCHARGE OF CHARGE; INHIBITIONS.

burden of proof. The obligation of proving facts. The obligation, in the sense of establishing a case, generally rests on the party who asserts the affirmative of the issue and it does not shift, being fixed at the beginning of the case eg in a criminal case, the burden of proving the guilt of the accused rests on the prosecution; in a negligence case, the onus of proving negligence rests on the plaintiff and of proving contributory negligence (qv) rests on the defendant.

The burden of proof, in the sense of adducing evidence, rests on the party who would fail if no evidence at all, or no more evidence, as the case may be, were given on either side. This burden will rest on the party substantially asserting the affirmative of the issue at the start of the case, but as evidence is presented, the burden may shift constantly throughout the case. The burden may shift because of the evidence, but also because of presumptions (qv) of the law, or statutory requirements which sometimes put proof of authority, consent or lawful excuse on the accused (eg Road Traffic Act 1961, s 38) or which put the onus of proof on the defendant (eg on an employer to justify a dismissal: Unfair Dismissals Act 1977). See also *Abbey Films v Attorney-General* [1981] IR 158; *O'Leary v A-G* [1991] 1 ILRM 454. See Refugee Act 1996, s 11A inserted by Immigration Act 2003, s 7(f); See Pensions Act 1990, s 76 as amended by substitution by Social Welfare (Miscellaneous Provisions) Act 2004, s 22(1). [Bibliography: Healy.] See DISCRIMINATION; GENDER GROUND; MATERNITY LEAVE; PROOF; RES IPSA LOQUITUR.

bureau de change. Any business which consists of the provision of foreign currency exchange services to the public but excluding the banks and other authorised credit institutions and insurance companies: Central Bank Act 1997, s 28. It is an offence for a person to carry on a *bureau de change* business without an authorisation from the Central Bank (CBA 1997, ss 29 and 34). A bureau must also comply with any requirements or conditions of the Central Bank to prevent *money laundering* (qv) (CBA 1997, s 30). Under recent legislation, new provisions have been made for the regulation of *bureaux de change* and money transmission businesses, replacing the 1997 provisions, with the aim of preventing money laundering and the financing of terrorism: Central Bank and Financial Services Authority of Ireland Act 2004, s 27.

burgess. Formerly, a special class of urban tenant who owed suit to the *hundred*, a court composed of fellow burgesses. Formerly, the council of any borough was empowered to elect any person, except a convicted felon, to be an honorary burgess of such borough: Municipal Privileges (Ireland) Act 1876, ss 11–12. The 1896 Act is now repealed and the power is replaced with a power to confer a *civic honour*: Local Government Act 1991, ss 4, 48 and Sch. See now Local Government Act 2001, s 74.

See *Lyons v Fitzgerald* [1825] Sm & Bat 405. See BOROUGH; CIVIC HONOUR.

burglary. The offence of burglary is committed by a person who enters a building as a trespasser intending to commit an *arrestable offence*, or being present as a trespasser, commits or attempts to commit such an offence: Criminal Justice (Theft and Fraud Offences) Act 2001, s 12. The reference to a *building* also applies to an inhabited vehicle or vessel and to any other inhabited temporary or moveable structure (CJ(T-FO)A 2001, s 12(2)). An *arrestable offence* means an offence carrying imprisonment of five years or more (CJ(TFO)A 2001, s 12(4)).

The previous *statutory* provision for the offence of burglary under the Larceny Act 1916, s 23A (as amended by Criminal Law (Jurisdiction) Act 1976, s 6) has been repealed, and any *common law* offence of burglary is abolished (CJ(TFO)A 2001, s 3 and Sch 1). [Bibliography: McGreal C.] See NIGHT; POSSESSION AND CRIME.

burglary, aggravated. The offence of *aggravated burglary* consists of burglary committed in circumstances where the perpetrator has with him at the time a firearm, imitation firearm, weapon of offence or explosive: Criminal Justice (Theft and Fraud Offences) Act 2001, s 13. An *imitation firearm* means anything which is not a firearm but has the appearance of being one (CJ(TFO)A 2001, s 13(2)). A *weapon of offence* includes e g an article with a blade or sharp point, or a weapon designed to discharge noxious liquid or gas (CJ(TFO)A 2001, s 13(2)).

A knife is an offensive weapon: *The People (Attorney-General) v O'Brien* [1969] 103 ILTR 109, CCA. The physical presence of the accused on or about the premises at which the burglary occurred is not required for him to be treated as a principal offender: *DPP v O'Reilly* [1991] 1 IR 77, HC.

The previous *statutory* provision for the offence of aggravated burglary under the Larceny Act 1916, s 23B (as amended by Criminal Law (Jurisdiction) Act 1976, s 7) has been repealed, and any *common law* offence of burglary is abolished (CJ(T-FO)A 2001, s 3 and Sch 1). [Bibliography: McGreal C.]

burial at sea. The Minister is empowered to make regulations in relation to the burial of human remains at sea: Merchant Shipping (Salvage and Wreck) Act 1993, s 66.

burial grounds. Land used for the burial of persons which may be vested in the legal incumbent of the parish or in the sanitary authority of the district as the *burial board* for such district: *Representative Church Body v Crawford* and *Crawford v Bradley* 74 ILTR 49; Public Health (Ireland) Act 1878, ss 160, 161, 174, 175. There are restrictions on the places in which a body may be buried; it is an offence to bury a body in a place which is not a burial ground: Local Government (Sanitary Services) Act 1948, s 44. Joint burial boards can be set up (LG(SS)A 1948, ss 12–13) and they have power to acquire land compulsorily: Local Government (Sanitary Services) (Joint Burial Boards) Act 1952. The Minister is empowered to make regulations in relation to the disposal of human remains otherwise than by burial e g by cremation (LG(SS)A 1948, s 47). Also a health board may arrange for the burial of a person who dies in an institution from an infectious disease: Health Act 1947, s 39 and Infectious Diseases Regulations 1981, SI No 390 of 1981, art 12. See *McCarthy v Johnson* [1989] ILRM 706, SC. See also Infectious Diseases (Amendment) Regulations 1996, SI No 384 of 1996. See also Local Government Act 2001, s 230. See EXHUMATION.

bus. See OMNIBUS.

bus pass. See BENEFIT IN KIND.

business. (1) 'Almost anything which is an occupation as distinguished from a pleasure – anything which is an occupation or duty which requires attention as a business': *Rolls v Miller* [1884] 27 Ch D 88 followed in *AE v Revenue Commissioners* [1984] ILRM 301.

(2) Any trade, profession or vocation: Finance Act 1989, s 86, now Taxes Consolidation Act 1997, s 811. [Bibliography: Nolan & Hollingsworth; Sheeran.] See COMMERCIAL PROCEEDINGS.

business associate. A person who provides relevant services to a building society e g conveyancing, advertising, public relations: Building Societies Act 1989, s 60. There are disclosure requirements regarding the fees paid to a business associate who is also an officer of the society.

business day. Any day which is not a Saturday, Sunday, Christmas Day, Good Friday or a bank holiday in Ireland: Listing Rules 2000 (*definitions*, as amended by Irish Stock Exchange Ltd).

business development scheme. The scheme whereby *qualified individuals* may claim tax relief for amounts subscribed for *eligible shares* in a *qualifying company*, which shares have been issued for the purpose of raising money for a *qualifying trade*: Finance Act 1984, ss 11–27; Finance Act 1986, s 13; 1987, ss 8–12; Finance Act 1988, s 7. Also known as the 'business expansion scheme' (BES). The shares must be new ordinary shares and they must not, for a period of five years from issue, carry any *preferential* right to receive dividends or to share in the company's assets on its winding up, or to be redeemed.

The shares must also be retained by the individual for more than five years from the date of issue. Extensions and restrictions on the scheme were made by Finance Act 1989, s 9; Finance Act 1990, s 10; Finance Act 1991, ss 14–17; Finance Act 1993, ss 25–27; Finance Act 1996, ss 16–24. See also Taxes Consolidation Act 1997, ss 488–508 as amended by Finance Act 1998; Finance Act 2000, s 19; Finance Act 2003, s 15. The BES company limit was increased in 2002 to €750,000: Finance Act 2002, s 16, and to €1m in 2004: Finance Act 2004, s 18.

Seed capital relief (SCS) is a special form of BES relief which allows a former employee (a *specified individual*) who takes up a *relevant employment* to obtain BES relief on a *relevant investment* in a start-up company that is to carry on a *relevant trading operation*: Taxes Consolidation Act 1997, s 497. Under this scheme, the individual can claim a refund of tax for the previous six years (was five years): Finance Act 2002, s 16. The BES and SCS were extended by FA 2004 to 31 December 2006. [Bibliography: Judge.]

business efficacy test. The test which may imply a term in a contract so as to give the contract the efficacy which both parties must have intended. See *The Moorcock* [1889] 14 PD 64; *Tridax (Ireland) Ltd v Irish Grain Board Ltd* [1984] IR 1.

business entertainment. Means entertainment (including food, drink, hospitality or accommodation) provided by a person, a member of his staff or a service-provider to him, in connection with his trade, business, profession or employment: Taxes Consolidation Act 1997, s 840. Business entertainment expenses are not tax deductible. See *Bentleys, Stokes and Lowless v Beeson* (1952) 33 TC 491; *Fleming v Associated Newspapers Ltd* 48 TC 382.

business expansion scheme, BES. See BUSINESS DEVELOPMENT SCHEME.

business name. The name or style under which any business is carried on, and in relation to a newspaper, includes the title of the newspaper: Registration of Business Names Act 1963, s 2. This Act requires registration of such name in the case of: (1) every individual or body corporate carrying on business under a name which does not consist of his true surname or corporate name respectively; and (2) every person carrying on the business of publishing a newspaper (RBNA 1963, s 3).

The Minister may refuse to permit the registration of any name which in his opinion is undesirable (RBNA 1963, s 14). The certificate of registration must be exhibited in a conspicuous position (RBNA 1963, s 8). An index of business names is maintained at the Companies Office which may be inspected by any person (RBNA 1963, ss 13 and 16). For rules of court, see RSC Ord 100. For consolidated regulations setting out the fees and forms in relation to the registration of business names, see Business Names Regulations 2002, SI No 291 of 2002 and Business Names Regulations 2003, SI No 188 of 2003.

It is an offence for a bankrupt (qv) or an arranging debtor (qv), without disclosure, to engage in any trade or business under a different name to that under which he was adjudicated a bankrupt or was granted protection: Bankruptcy Act 1988, s 129(b). See NAME OF COMPANY; NAME, CHANGE OF.

business premises. A local authority is empowered to make bye-laws requiring the owners or managers of specified businesses to wash, clean and brush down the public area outside their premises: Litter Pollution Act 1997, s 21(2)(e) substituted by Protection of the Environment Act 2003, s 57.

business relief. The provision under which the taxable value of any gift or inheritance of any relevant business property is reduced, thereby reducing liability to *capital acquisitions tax*: Finance Act 1994, ss 124–135. There is a requirement of a minimum period of ownership and provision for withdrawal of relief in certain circumstances. See also Finance Act 1995, s 161. For consolidated provisions, see Capital Acquisitions Tax Consolidation Act 2003, ss 90–102 as amended by Finance Act 2004, s 78.

business tenant. The tenant of a *tenement* (qv). The rights of *business* tenants have been extended as regards alienation of their interest, as to improvement and change of use of the leased premises, as to acquiring a new tenancy and to compensation for disturbance and improvements: Landlord and Tenant (Amendment) Act 1980.

For tenancies commencing prior to 10 August 1994, the tenant of a tenement has a right, subject to certain exceptions, to a new tenancy: (a) where the tenement was for *three* years continuously occupied by the tenant or his predecessors in title and *bona fide* used wholly or partly for the purpose of carrying on a *business*; a temporary break may be disregarded by the court if it considers it reasonable so to do; or (b) where the tenement was for the previous 20 years continuously in the occupation of the tenant or of his predecessors in title; or (c) where improvements have been made on the tenement so that they account for not less than half of the letting value of the tenement (LT(A)A 1980, s 13(1)). In a particular case, the tenant failed to show a *bona fide* business use as the user was in breach of an express term of the tenancy agreement: *O'Byrne v M50 Motors Ltd* [2003] 1 ILRM 275, HC.

Business includes trade, profession or business, whether or not carried on for gain or reward, and any activity for providing cultural, social or sporting services, for the public service, or for carrying out the functions of local authorities, health boards and harbour authorities.

It has been held that in relation to the *qualifying period* of business use to obtain a right to a new tenancy, the phrase 'at any time' was intended to relate to an inquiry as to whether a tenant had satisfied the requirements of the1980 Act to the termination of the tenancy; the relevant date was the date of expiry of the lease, the time from which a new tenancy can be granted: *Twil Ltd v Kearney* [2001] 4 IR 476, SC. The court held that to allow a tenant to 'crystallise' his rights at any time would run counter to the nature and purpose of business equity.

An indirect attempt to avoid the provisions of the LT(A)A 1980 will fail: *Bank of Ireland v Fitzmaurice* [1989] ILRM 452. The 1980 Act is restricted in its application to certain tenements in the Custom House Docks Area: Landlord and Tenant (Amendment) Act 1989. It also does not apply to a house leased under a shared ownership lease (qv) or to a house let by voluntary housing bodies: Housing (Miscellaneous Provisions) Act 1992, s 32. See also *Gatien Motor Co Ltd v The Continental Oil Co of Ireland* [1979] IR 406; *Irish Shell v John Costello Ltd* [1981] ILRM 66; *OHS Ltd v Green Property Co Ltd* [1986] ILRM 451; *Mealiffe v Walsh* [1987] ILRM 301.

For tenancies commencing from 10 August 1994, a tenant, or his predecessor in title, must have *five* years' continuous occupation before a right to a renewal will accrue, and in such instance, the lease can be renewed for a maximum of 20 years, or for a lesser term as the tenant may nominate, but not less than five years without the landlord's agreement: Landlord and Tenant (Amendment) Act 1994. Where the tenement is used wholly or exclusively as an *office*, the tenant can renounce his right to a renewal, provided the renunciation is executed prior to the commencement of the tenancy, and provided he has received independent legal advice in relation to the tenancy (LT(A)A 1994, s 4).

The Law Reform Commission, in a preliminary review of business tenancies, has identified as the most fundamental issue the question as to whether there is a continuing need for statutory protection of these tenancies: *Consultation Paper on Business Tenancies* (LRC CP 21, 2003). See Residential Tenancies Act 2004, s 3(2)(a). See IMPROVEMENTS, COMPENSATION FOR; DISTURBANCE, COMPENSATION FOR.

business to consumer rule; B2C. The new rule for electronically supplied services, other than radio and broadcasting, which determines the place of taxation. See ELECTRONICALLY SUPPLIED SERVICES.

busway. A public road (qv) or proposed public road specified to be a busway in a *busway scheme* approved by the Minister: Roads Act 1993, s 2(1) and 44. There is a prohibition on the use of a busway by pedestrians or pedal cyclists, and persons must not permit animals to be on a busway (RA 1993, s 44(4)). There is no right of direct access to a busway from land adjoining it and no such right may be granted (RA 1993, s 44(2)); this includes a prohibition on the granting of planning permission which would involve direct access (RA 1993, s 46). The Minister may prescribe the classes of vehicles which may use a busway (RA 1993, s 44(3)).

A road authority may submit a busway scheme to the Minister, having first notified the public and affected land owners/ occupiers (RA 1993, s 48). The Minister, before approving a scheme, must cause a public local inquiry to be held, must consider any objections, and the report and recommendations of the person conducting the inquiry (RA 1993, s 49). The road authority is required to prepare an environmental impact statement on the construction of the busway (RA 1993, s 50).

Similar provisions apply regarding compulsory purchase, compensation for disturbance and loss, and alternative access for adjoining landowners/occupiers as for a motorway scheme. See MOTORWAY.

buyer. A person who buys or agrees to buy goods: Sale of Goods Act 1893, s 62. The remedies available to a buyer include damages for non delivery of the goods, an order for specific performance of the contract, and damages for breach of warranty (SGA 1893, ss 51–53). Certain statements purporting to restrict the rights of buyers are prohibited: Sale of Goods and Supply of Services Act 1980, s 11.

bye-election. An election of a member of Dáil Éireann (qv) to fill a vacancy occasioned by a person having ceased to be a member of the Dáil otherwise than in consequence of a dissolution: Electoral Act 1992, s 2(1). A writ for a bye-election must be issued by the Clerk of the Dáil to the returning officer when he has been directed to do so by the Chairman of the Dáil; the Chairman must do so when directed by the Dáil (EA 1992, s 39(2)). A member of the Dáil, while still holding his seat, cannot be a candidate at a bye-election (EA 1992, s 43).

The High Court has refused to order that bye-elections be held to fill two vacant Dáil seats as to do so would be to interfere in the functions of the executive: *Grimes v Ireland* (1993) Irish Times, 27 June, HC. However, the High Court did grant leave to institute judicial review proceedings in another case, holding that there was an arguable case that there is a constitutional obligation to hold a bye-election within a reasonable time of a vacancy occurring: *Dudley v An Taoiseach* [1994] 2 ILRM 321, HC. See SEPARATION OF POWERS.

bye-law. 'An ordinance affecting the public or some portion of the public imposed by some authority clothed with statutory powers, ordering something to be done or not to be done and accompanied by some sanction or penalty for its non-observance ...it

has the force of law within the sphere of its legitimate operation': *Kruse v Johnson* [1898] 2 QB 91.

A bye-law must be reasonable: *Dún Laoghaire Corporation v Brock* [1952] Ir Jur Rep 37. It must not be repugnant to the general law; it can add to that law but cannot make lawful an act already made unlawful or vice versa. Generally, there is no obligation on a body charged with the introduction of bye-laws to consult with those affected in advance: *Ryanair v Aer Rianta* [2003] 2 IR 143, SC.

Local authorities are empowered to make bye-laws for the regulation of facilities and services provided or managed by them, or to regulate in the interest of the common good, matters of local concern or nuisance. Local Government Act 2001, ss 198–211. The power is a *reserved* function of the elected members. The Act sets out the procedure to be followed in making a bye-law, including the requirement to give public notice and to give consideration to any submission made in relation to a draft bye-law (LGA 2001, s 200). Bye-laws may include a provision for a system of 'on the spot' fines (LGA 2001, s 206). For previous legislation, see Local Government Act 1994, ss 37–42.

Local authorities are also empowered to make bye-laws for the control and welfare of horses: Control of Horses Act 1996, s 46; and for controlling the presentation of household waste for collection: Waste Management Act 1996, s 35 as amended by Protection of the Environment Act 2003, s 32; *O'Connell v Cork Corporation* [2001] 3 IR 602, SC. They also have power to make bye-laws for taxi stands and for bus stopping places: Road Traffic Act 2002, ss 15 and 16 respectively.

The Minister or the *Railway Procurement Agency* are empowered to make bye-laws for the management, control, operation and regulation of railways; it is an offence to contravene such a bye-law: Transport (Railway Infrastructure) Act 2001, s 66.

For power to make harbour and pilotage bye-laws, see Harbours Act 1996, ss 42, 71, 84. For power to make airport bye-laws, see Air Navigation and Transport (Amendment) Act 1998, s 42. For power to make litter bye-laws, see Litter Pollution Act 1997, s 21 as substituted by The Protection of the Environment Act 2003, s 57.

Bye-laws may be deemed to be statutory instruments (qv): Statutory Instruments

©

Act 1947, ss 1(1), 2(1)(b)(v) and (c)(i). Some bye-laws must be laid before the Oireachtas eg those made under Blascaod Mór National Historic Park Act 1989. See Solicitors (Amendment) Act 1994, s 5; British-Irish Agreement Act 1999, s 54. See Local Government Act 1994 (Bye-laws) Regulations 1999, SI No 78 of 1999. See BUILDING BYE-LAWS; FISHING.

C

©. [Copyright.] The symbol which some foreign countries require to be on all published copies of a work, accompanied by the name of the copyright proprietor and the year of first publication, in order to provide copyright protection to that work. For books, the copyright notice must appear on the title page or verso thereof. For periodicals, the notice must appear on the title page, the first page of text, or under the title heading. It is a requirement of the *Universal Copyright Convention* (qv).

cabinet. Popularly understood to mean the government (qv) but not named as such in the 1937 Constitution. The government is the executive organ of the State. See COLLECTIVE RESPONSIBILITY; CONFIDENCE, BREACH OF.

cabinet confidentiality. The confidentiality of discussions of meetings of the government must be respected in all circumstances, except where the High Court determines that disclosure should be made in respect of a particular matter: (a) in the interest of the administration of justice by a court; or (b) by virtue of an overriding public interest, pursuant to an application in that behalf by a tribunal appointed by the government or a Minister on the authority of the Houses of the Oireachtas to enquire into a matter stated by them to be of public importance: 1937 Constitution art 28(4)(3) as inserted by the Seventeenth Referendum in 1997. This provision overturned the Supreme Court decision in *A-G v Sole Member of the Beef Tribunal* [1993] ILRM 81 and 2 IR 250, SC, which held that discussions at meetings of the government were absolutely confidential as a constitutional right. See also *A-G for England & Wales v Brandon Books* [1987] ILRM 35. See Seventeenth Amendment to the Constitution Act 1997; RSC Ord 132 inserted

by Rules of the Superior Courts (No 2) (Applications pursuant to article 28.4.3 of the Constitution) 1998, SI No 281 of 1998.

Records of the government, or submissions to the government from a Minister or from the Attorney-General, were exempt from disclosure for a period of five years after being made: Freedom of Information Act 1997, s 19. The period has been extended to ten years and the exemption has been made mandatory: Freedom of Information (Amendment) Act 2003, s 14. The exemption has been extended: (a) to advice created for the primary purpose of government business; (b) to communications between Ministers dealing with matters under the consideration of government; and (c) to a committee of government and to a committee of officials. 'Officials' means two or more of the following: civil servant, special adviser, or a member of a prescribed class. The government decision to extend the period to ten years and to make the exemption mandatory was explained in the Dáil on 12 February 2003 by the Taoiseach Bertie Ahern as necessary, as the release of cabinet papers after five years would create 'major difficulties' for issues such as the Northern Ireland peace process. See OIREACHTAS COMMITTEES; INFORMATION, ACCESS TO.

cable programme. Means any item included in a *cable programme service*: Copyright and Related Rights Act 2000, s 2(1). A *cable programme service* means a service, including MMDS (qv), which consists of sending sounds, images or data by means of a telecommunication system: (a) for reception at two or more places; or (b) for presentation to members of the public (CRRA 2000, s 2(1)). Copyright subsists in a cable programme (CRRA 2000, s 17(2)). The copyright expires 50 years after the cable programme is first lawfully included in a cable programme service; copyright in a repeat cable programme expires at the same time as the original (CRRA 2000, s 28). The *author* of a cable programme includes the person providing the cable programme service in which the programme is included (CRRA 2000, s 21(d)). See BROADCAST; COPYRIGHT; COPYRIGHT, QUALIFICATION FOR; MMDS.

cableway installation. Provision has been made to regulate cableway installations which are designed to carry persons, giving effect to EC Directive 2000/9/EC: EC

(Cableway Installations Designed to Carry Persons) Regulations 2003, SI No 470 of 2003.

cabotage. [Coasting-trade.] A *cabotage authorisation* allows a haulier to carry goods from one point to another within any of the other member states of the EC; applicants must hold an *international road freight carrier's licence* as provided for by the Road Transport Act 1986. See CARRIER'S LICENCE.

cadit quaestio. [The matter admits of no further argument.]

caeteris paribus. [Other things being equal.] See CETERIS PARIBUS.

caeterorum. [Rest.] A *grant caeterorum* is a grant of representation in respect of the rest of the property of a deceased made to the person so entitled, where a grant of part only of the estate (*save and except*) has already been made. See PROBATE.

call. A demand on the holder of partly paid-up shares in a company for payment of the balance or part thereof. Companies whose articles of association so provide are allowed to differentiate between shareholders in the amounts of, and times for, paying calls, and to accept payments of unpaid amounts although they have not been called up: Companies Act 1963, s 66. See also: CA 1963, Table A, art 15; RSC 0rd 74, rr 92–94. See *Blackstaff Flax Spinning Weaving Co v Cameron* [1899] 1 IR 252. See OPTION.

call to the Bar. The formal ceremony whereby a member of the Honourable Society of King's Inns is admitted to take his place in court and to practice. See websites: *www.lawlibrary.ie* and *www.kingsinns.ie*. See 'The Call to the Bar in other Jurisdictions' by Arran Dowling Hussey BL in *Bar Review* (April 2004) 80. See BARRISTER.

call forwarding. Telephone calls forwarded to a subscriber's terminal. A telecommunications services provider must ensure that calls automatically forwarded to a subscriber's terminal as a result of action taken by a third party, are ceased to be so forwarded as soon as practicable after receipt of a request for such cessation: EC (Electronic Communications Networks and Services) (Data Protection and Privacy) Regulations 2003, SI No 535 of 2003, reg 11. See PRIVACY IN TELECOMMUNICATIONS.

camera. See ELECTRONIC APPARATUS.

camera, in. See IN CAMERA.

camping. The occupier of land cannot use it or permit it to be used for camping, on more than 18 consecutive days, or 36 days within a period of twelve consecutive months, without a licence from the sanitary authority and in accordance with the terms of that licence: Local Government (Sanitary Services) Act 1948, s 34. Planning permission is not required for the temporary use of land for camping: Planning and Development Regulations 2001, SI No 600 of 2001, Sch 2, class 1. However, a tent, campervan, caravan or vessel must not remain on the land for a period greater than ten days and there are other limitations e g location with respect to a public road or another tent or caravan. Also an *environmental impact assessment* (qv) is required in relation to an application for planning permission for permanent camp sites and caravan sites where the number of pitches would be greater than 100 (SI No 600 of 2001, Pt 10 and Sch 5).

canals. Ownership and responsibility for the Grand Canal and Royal Canal was transferred from CIE to the Commissioners for Public Works by the Canals Act 1986. It was the duty of the Commissioners to undertake the care, management and maintenance of the canals. The Commissioners were empowered to make bye-laws (qv) (CA 1986, s 7 and Canals Act 1986 (Byelaws) 1988, SI No 247 of 1988). Responsibility for canals has now passed to the Minister for Arts, Heritage, Gaeltacht and the Islands: Minister for Arts, keritage, Gaeltacht and the Islands (Powers and Functions) Act 1998. A road authority is prohibited from constructing or reconstructing a bridge or viaduct or a tunnel under any inland waterway or any navigable waterway, without the appropriate Ministerial consent: Roads Act 1993, s 15A inserted by Local Government Act 2001, s 245. See also LGA 2001, s 5(1), Sch 3, Pt 1. See INLAND WATERWAYS.

cancellation. The act of nullifying or invalidating an instrument e g by drawing lines across it with the intention of depriving it of its effect. For cancellation of a will, see WILL, REVOCATION OF.

cancer. A disorder of cell growth. Cancer occurs when there is an alteration in the behaviour of cells in response to various harmful factors, some known, many unknown. Substances which cause cancer are known as *carcinogens*. The most significant chemical carcinogen is tobacco smoke.

An award of €45,000 was made to a man who claimed that an eight-month delay in diagnosing that he suffered from prostrate cancer had reduced his life expectancy by several years, the High Court holding that the diagnosis of the consultant urologist was negligently wrong in the sense that it was a breach of the duty of care: *Philip v Bons Secour Hospital & Ryan* (2004) Irish Times, 12 March. See ASBESTOS; COMMISSION, EVIDENCE TO; DATA CONTROLLER; RADON; SMOKING.

candour, lack of. See CERTIORARI.

cannabis. The flowering or fruiting tops of any plant of the genus *cannabis* from which the resin has not been extracted, by whatever name they may be designated; *cannabis resin* means the separated resin, whether crude or purified obtained from any plant of the genus *cannabis*: Misuse of Drugs Act 1977, s 1; any plant of the genus *cannabis* or any part of such plant: Misuse of Drugs Act 1984, s 2. Every person who cultivates opium poppy or a plant of the genus cannabis, except in accordance with a licence issued in that behalf by the Minister, is guilty of an offence (MDA 1977, s 17). See also MDA 1977, s 19. See DRUGS, MISUSE OF.

canon. A rule of canon or ecclesiastical law. Sometimes used to mean a rule of the ordinary law eg the canons of descent; canons of construction.

canon law. The basic law of the Roman Catholic Church. It was codified in 1917 under Pope Benedict XV and was last promulgated on 25 January 1983 by Pope John Paul II. The Supreme Court has held that canon law is foreign law, which must be proved as a fact and by the testimony of expert witnesses according to the well-settled rules as to the proof of foreign law: *O'Callaghan v O'Sullivan* [1925] 1 IR 90 and [1926] IR 586, PC.

This case arose from the removal of a parish priest of Eyeries (Kilcatherine), Co Cork by his bishop, both parties accepting that the relationship between the priest and the bishop was subject to canon law. In commenting on this case in 2004, the Archbishop Emeritus of Dublin, Cardinal Desmond Connell, said that canon law enjoys the same status as foreign law, recognised as law enacted by a sovereign independent authority which resides in the Holy See: as reported in the *Irish Times*, 31 May 2004. However, in that reference, the Minister for Justice is reported as having said on 20 October 2002, that canon law is viewed by the civil law of the State 'as equivalent to the laws of, say, the Presbyterian Church, or the internal rules of a sporting organisation.'

The Bishop of Killaloe, Dr Willie Walsh, has said that confidentiality in the relationship between priest and bishop, though protected by canon law, does not take precedence over civil law: *Irish Times*, 6 September 2002. As regards the *incardination* (qv) of a curate under Canon 114 of the 1917 Code, the High Court of Justice in Northern Ireland held that the office of curate is to be distinguished from that of bishop or parish priest in that the powers of the curate are by direct grant of the bishop or parish priest and are not inherent in the office: *Buckley v Cathal Daly* [1991] ITLR (7 Jan), HC, NI. This case involved the interpretation by the court of canon law using expert evidence. [Bibliography: Veritas Publications.] See FOREIGN LAW.

canons of descent. See DESCENT.

canvassing. It is an offence to canvass voters at an election in any place within 100 metres of a polling station; included in the prohibition is loitering or congregating with other persons, displaying or distributing election literature, inducing an elector to vote or not to vote, or using any loudspeaker or public address system: Electoral Act 1992, s 147. In certain circumstances it is an offence for an employee of a building society to solicit support for a candidate for election as a director of the society: Building Societies Act 1989, s 51(8).

capacity of child in criminal law. See DOLI INCAPAX.

capacity to contract. The legal competency, power or fitness to enter and be bound by a contract. Generally a *minor* (qv) lacks contractual capacity. However an infant (ie a minor) or a person who by reason of mental incapacity or drunkenness is incompetent to contract, must pay a reasonable price for *necessaries* which are sold and delivered to him. Necessaries means goods suitable to the condition in life of such minor or other person, and to his actual requirements at the time of sale and delivery. See Sale of Goods Act 1893, s 2. See *Ryder v Wombwell* [1867] LR 4 Ex 32; *Davies v Beynon-Harris* [1931] 47 TLR 424; *Coutts & Co v Browne-Lecky* [1947] KB 104. See MINOR; INSANE PERSON; DRUNKEN PERSON.

capias. [That you take.]

capita. [Heads.] See PER CAPITA.

capital. The capital of a company is the amount of principal with which the company is formed to carry on business. The memorandum of association (qv) of a limited company with a share capital must state the amount of the share capital and the division of it into shares of a fixed amount: Companies Act 1963, s 6(4). This share capital is said to be the *nominal* or *authorised* capital ie the aggregate par value of shares the company is authorised to issue to its members. The *issued* or *allotted* capital is the total amount of capital issued in shares to members. It is prohibited to allot shares at less than their par value. Frequently, shares are issued at a premium (qv).

The *paid up* capital of a company is the amount in money or money's worth which has been paid to the company in return for shares allotted by it; it is the aggregate of the shares that have been allotted together with the total of any premiums paid on them. The *called-up* capital is the amount paid to a company where it does not require the entire amount to be paid over to it immediately; the *uncalled* capital is the remainder of such partly paid shares. The *reserve* capital is the portion of the uncalled capital which the company has by special resolution determined will not be called up except in the event of the company being wound up. *Working* capital is understood to mean the amount of money necessary for the company to trade or carry on business.

A public limited company (plc) must have a minimum authorised capital of £30,000 (€38,092): Companies (Amendment) Act 1983, ss 5(2), 17(1), 19(1).

Provision has been made for the *redenomination* of share capital from 1 January 2002 into euro; the nominal share value in *euro* is to be calculated as the total share capital value divided by the number of shares and that figure is not to be rounded: Economic and Monetary Union Act 1998, s 24. Companies have the period up to 30 June 2003 to *renominalise* ie to express share capital figures in amounts in euro if simple redenomination into euro leads to inappropriate (eg uneven) amounts, provided a resolution approving renominalisation is passed by shareholders (EMUA 1998, s 26). [Bibliography: O'Callaghan J M (1).] See REDUCTION OF CAPITAL; SHARES, COMPANY; THICK CAPITALISATION; UNDERSUBSCRIBED.

capital, serious loss of. Where the *net assets* of a registered company, public or private, are half or less of the amount of the company's called-up share capital; net assets are aggregate assets less total liabilities. When this fact is known to a director, there is an obligation within 28 days to convene an extraordinary general meeting of the company for the purpose of considering whether any, and if so what, measures are to be taken to deal with the situation. See Companies (Amendment) Act 1983, s 40.

capital acquisitions tax; CAT. A tax on *gifts* (ie taken during the donor's lifetime, the donee becoming beneficially entitled in possession otherwise than 'on a death') and on *inheritances* (ie taken following the disponer's death): Capital Acquisitions Tax Consolidation Act 2003 as amended by Finance Act 2003, ss 144–153 and Finance Act 2004, ss 76–79, 89 and Sch 3, para 2. The rate of tax is fixed at 20% of the taxable value of the gift or inheritance and is due and payable on the valuation date (CATCA 2003, ss 50–51 and Sch 2). The value of a limited interest (eg a life interest) is calculated from actuarial tables (CATCA 2003, Sch 1).

The Consolidation Act comprises twelve parts: preliminary (ss 1–3), gift tax (ss 4–8), inheritance tax (ss 9–25), value of property for tax (ss 26–30), provisions relating to gifts and inheritances (ss 31–44), returns and assessments (ss 45–50), payment and recovery of tax, interest and penalties (ss 51–65), appeals (ss 66–68), exemptions (ss 69–88), reliefs (ss 89–107), miscellaneous (ss 108–117), repeals (ss 118–120).

Exempt from tax are small gifts ie the first €3,000 in any year from 1 January 2003 (CATCA 2003, s 69 as amended). Also exempt are gifts or inheritances of any amount taken by one spouse from another (ss 70–71). There are many other exemptions eg: (a) the proceeds of special insurance policies taken out by the insured expressly for paying inheritance tax arising on his death or on the death of his spouse (s 72); (b) winnings from betting and lotteries (s 82); (c) certain transfers following the dissolution of a marriage (s 88). There are also reliefs against the tax – *agricultural relief* (s 89) and *business relief* (ss 90–102) – in either case a deduction of 90% of the market value may be allowable.

There are tax free *group threshold amounts* which vary depending on the relationship between the donee (or successor) and the donor (or disponer), and which amounts are index-linked to reflect inflation. The threshold for the tax year 1 January 2004 to 31 December 2004, are: (i) to a son or daughter – €456,438; (ii) to a parent, brother, sister, niece, nephew or grandchild – €45,644; and (iii) to other relationships to the disponer – €22,822. (CATCA 2003, Sch 2).

Transfers from a former spouse to the other spouse are exempt from CAT: Family Law (Divorce) Act 1996, s 34. This exemption from CAT has been extended in respect of certain transfers between former spouses, executed on foot of a foreign court order in consequence of a dissolution of marriage which is entitled to be recognised as valid in the State: Finance Act 2000, s 149.

If property is sold in the course of administration prior to the valuation date, the Revenue Commissioners will, on request, issue a letter discharging the property from the CAT charge and attaching the charge instead to whatever assets represent the sale of the property at the valuation date; a CAT clearance certificate is not required in such circumstances: 'Practice Note' in *Law Society Gazette* (November 2003) 42. For further information from Revenue Commissioners, phone locall 1890 201104. See 'The CAT's pyjamas' by Declan Rigney in *Law Society Gazette* (November 2003) 24. For former legislation, see Capital Acquisitions Tax Act 1976 as amended by annual Finance Acts. [Bibliography: Bohan; Boland; Condon & Muddiman; Clark & Smyth; Fitzpatrick T; O'Callaghan J M (1).] See CHILD, ADOPTED; DISPOSITION; FOSTER CHILD; HERITAGE; MARKET VALUE.

capital acquisitions tax, dwellinghouse. A gift or inheritance of a dwellinghouse taken on or after 1 December 1999, is exempt from capital acquisitions tax if certain specified conditions are met eg: (a) the recipient must have occupied the dwellinghouse continuously as his main residence for three years prior to the date of gift or inheritance; (b) the recipient at that date must not be beneficially entitled to any other dwellinghouse; and (c) the recipient must occupy the dwellinghouse as his main residence for a period of six years from that date: Capital Acquisitions Tax 1976, s 59C inserted by Finance Act 2000, s 151.

There are certain relaxations where the recipient is over 55 years of age, or is absent working abroad, or requires long-term medical care, or sells the dwellinghouse and reinvests in another dwellinghouse. Interest in respect of a *clawback* of tax applies from the date of the event giving rise to the clawback rather than from the date of the gift or inheritance: Finance Act 2002, s 118. For consolidated provision, see Capital Acquisitions Tax Consolidation Act 2003, s 86.

capital allowances. Relief from taxation permitted in respect of capital expenditure eg see Taxes Consolidation Act 1997, ss 268–321 as amended, eg as regards motor vehicles, plant and machinery, see Finance Act 2002, ss 28 and 31. The write off period for annual *wear and tear* allowances in respect of capital expenditure incurred on or after 4 December 2002 on plant and machinery has been increased from five years to eight years: Finance Act 2003, s 23. There are exceptions eg taxis and certain fishing boats. The annual rate for write off for capital expenditure on hotel buildings (including holiday camps) has been reduced to 4% ie giving a 25 year tax life (seven years previously); and the capital allowances for holiday homes has been abolished (FA 2003, s 23). A loophole relating to the effective transfer of capital allowances on buildings from companies to individual investors has been closed off (FA 2003, s 13). The scheme of capital allowances for hotels, holiday camps and holiday cottages has been extended to 31 July 2006: Finance Act 2004, s 25. [Bibliography: Connolly, Bradley & Purcell.] See HOSPITAL; NURSING HOME; SPORTS INJURIES CLINIC.

capital at risk. As regards life insurance, the amount payable on death less the mathematical reserve in respect of the relevant contracts: European Communities (Life Assurance) Regulations 1984, SI No 57 of 1984 as amended by Central Bank and Financial Services Authority of Ireland Act 2003, s 35, Sch 2 and by Central Bank and Financial Services Authority of Ireland Act 2004, s 10(3), Sch 2.

capital gains tax. A tax payable on the gains made on the disposal of an asset: Capital Gains Tax Act 1975; Capital Gains Tax (Amendment) Act 1978; as amended by annual Finance Acts, then consolidated in Taxes Consolidation Act 1997, ss 28–31 and ss 532–613 and amended by Finance Act 2000, ss 85–88; Finance Act 2002, ss 59–63; Finance Act 2003, ss 65–72.

Disposal includes sales, gifts and the transfer of assets into a *settlement*. Some gains are exempt eg the sale of a private residence, including grounds of up to one acre, which has been used as the main residence throughout the period of ownership.

There is provision for *indexation*, ie an adjustment is made for inflation as measured by the *consumer price index* in calculating the chargeable gain, up to 31 December 2002. There are also special reliefs eg on the disposal of a business or farm within the family or on retirement. The sale of shares of the same class in a company are deemed to be on a *first in, first out* basis ie the shares held longest are deemed to be the ones sold.

Capital gains tax is not payable on the disposal of a debt but may be chargeable on a 'debt on a security': CGTA 1975, s 46. A 'debt on a security' is not a synonym for a secured debt; it is a debt with added characteristics such as may enable it to be realised or dealt with at a profit: *Mooney v Sweeney* [1997] 2 ILRM 429 and 3 IR 424, HC.

Capital gains tax has been brought within the self-assessment system: Finance Act 1991, ss 45–53, now Taxes Consolidation Act 1997, ss 950–959.

Certain disposals between one former spouse and the other, made pursuant to a court order, are treated for capital gains tax purposes on a *no gain/no loss* basis: Family Law (Divorce) Act 1996, s 35, now Taxes Consolidation Act 1997, s 1031(1)–(4).

A number of amendments to capital gains tax are contained in the Finance Act 2001, ss 92–95. No capital gains applies to the transfer of land valued at no more than £200,000 (€254,000) by a parent to a child to enable the child to build a principal private residence (FA 2001, s 93). Also such a transfer does not attract stamp duty (FA 2001, s 206). The 60% rate applied to the disposal of certain residential development land (which was introduced by the Finance (No 2) Act 1998) has been reduced to 20% for disposals on or after 6 April (FA 2001, s 94).

Significant changes to capital gains tax were introduced in 2003 eg: (a) indexation is allowed only up to 31 December 2002; (b) no rollover relief arising from disposals made on and from 4 December 2002; (c) no deferral of capital gains tax by taking the proceeds in the form of loan notes; (d)

capital gains tax in respect of deemed disposal of certain assets that an individual owns when taxable within the State, prior to becoming taxable elsewhere; and (e) preliminary tax is payable by 31 October each year in respect of gains made up to September in that tax year, with the tax due on gains made over the remainder of the tax year being payable by the following 31 January: Finance Act 2003, ss 42, 65–67, 69.

Certain bodies are exempt from capital gains tax eg local authorities and health boards: Taxes Consolidation Act 1997, s 610. The list of exempt bodies has been extended to include certain sports bodies and registered trade unions, subject to certain conditions being fulfilled: Finance Act 2003, s 72.

See Capital Gains Tax (Multipliers) (2000–01) Regulations 2000, SI No 76 of 2000; Capital Gains Tax (Multipliers) (2001) Regulations 2001, SI No 125 of 2001; Capital Gains Tax (Multipliers) (2002) Regulations 2002, SI No 1 of 2002; Capital Gains Tax (Multipliers) (2003) Regulations 2003, SI No 12 of 2003. See Electronic Transmission of Returns Regulations 2003, SI No 443 of 2003. See *Dilleen (Inspector of Taxes) v Kearns* [1994] 1 ILRM 503, HC. See *O'Connell v Keleghan* [2001] 2 IR 490, SC. [Bibliography: Appleby & O'Hanlon; Gaffney M; O'Callaghan J M (1).] See BED AND BREAKFAST; ROLLOVER RELIEF; VALUATION.

capital liberalisation. The prohibition on restrictions on the movement of capital and payments between member States of the EC: Treaty establishing the European Community, arts 56–60 of the consolidated (2002) version. Capital liberalisation also affects movement of capital and payments between member states and third countries as from 1 January 1994. The rights of member states however are not prejudiced in relation to taxation, to prudential supervision of financial institutions, or to issues of public policy or public security. See EXCHANGE CONTROL.

capital money. Money arising by way of exercise of the powers given by the Settled Land Acts 1882 and 1890. See SETTLEMENT.

capital murder. Formerly was the murder of a member of the Garda Síochána or a prison officer acting in the course of his duty; or murder done in the course or furtherance of specified offences created by the Offences Against the State Act 1939; or murder committed within the State for a political motive of the head of a foreign State or of a member of its government or of its diplomatic officer; or the commission by a person subject to military law of a number of offences created by the Defence Act 1954: Criminal Justice Act 1964, s 1. Now, with the abolition of the death penalty, capital murder is replaced by the offence of *aggravated murder*: Criminal Justice Act 1990, s 3.

The death penalty was mandatory in a conviction of capital murder: CJA 1964, s 3(2). See also *The People (DPP) v Murray* [1977] IR 360. See MURDER; MURDER, AGGRAVATED; PARDON.

capital punishment. Death by hanging (qv). Commutation or remission of capital punishment is vested solely in the President of Ireland: 1937 Constitution art 13.6. However, the death penalty has now been abolished. See DEATH PENALTY; HANGING.

capital reconstruction. Changes to the share capital clause of the memorandum of association may be made in general meeting by a company, provided that the articles of association (qv) authorise the changes: Companies Act 1963, ss 68–70. It may increase its share capital by the issue of new shares; consolidate its shares into ones of larger amounts; convert any paid up shares into stock; reconvert stock into shares; and subdivide any of its shares into smaller amounts.

However a proposed reduction of capital must be approved by special resolution of the members, by creditors and by the court (CA 1963, ss 72–77 as amended by the Companies Act 1990, s 231(c); RSC 0.75, r 17). Accounting rules have been prescribed to prohibit paying dividends from capital: Companies (Amendment) Act 1983, Part IV, ss 45–51 as amended by Companies Act 1986, s 20 and Companies Act 1990, s 232(d).

Any limited company having a share capital is prohibited from acquiring its own shares, whether by purchase, subscription or otherwise; there are some important exceptions eg redemption of preference shares or redeemable shares, forfeiture of shares, or authorised capital reduction (C(A)A 1983, s 41 as amended by CA 1990, s 232(a)). Also a limited company may acquire its own fully paid shares other-

wise than for valuable consideration (C(A)A 1983, s 41(2)). See *In re Irish Provident Assurance Co* [1913] IR 352. See CLASS RIGHTS; REDEEMABLE SHARES; REDUCTION OF CAPITAL; SHARES, COMPANY; STOCK; SURPLUS ASSETS.

capitalisation issue. An issue to existing holders of securities, in proportion to their holding, of further shares, credited as fully paid out of the issuer's reserves, in lieu of dividend or otherwise: Listing Rules 2000, paras 4.31–4.32. Also called a *bonus issue*. See BONUS SHARES.

caption. The formal heading of a legal instrument.

car testing. Testing for roadworthiness of motor vehicles became compulsory on a phased basis as from 4 January 2000; the tests are carried out by the National Car Testing Service (NCTS) Ltd as the designated issuing authority: Road Traffic (National Car Test) Regulations 1999, SI No 395 of 1999, giving effect to EC Directive 96/96/EC. The regulations were consolidated in 2003: Road Traffic (National Car Test) Regulations 2003, SI No 405 of 2003.

Cars must be tested on the fourth anniversary of first registration and thereafter at each biennial (SI No 405 of 2003, reg 3). Exempted from testing are cars: (a) first registered 30 or more years prior to their test due date; (b) which are used solely on an offshore island; or (c) which are owned by the Garda Síochána or the Defence Forces (SI No 405 of 2003, reg 3(5)).

A test certificate ceases to be in force on the test date which occurs after the certificate to which it relates was issued (SI No 405 of 2003, reg 5(1)). However, a test certificate which is issued prior to the test due date, continues in force until the subsequent test due date (SI No 405 of 2003, reg 5(2)). This can be up to 180 days before a first test due date and up to 90 days before other test due dates. A test disc which is in force must be displayed on the front windscreen of the car (SI No 405 of 2003, reg 6). There is provision for an appeal to the District Court (SI No 405 of 2003, reg 13).

A 'small public service vehicle' (ie a hackney, limousine, taxi or wheelchair accessible taxi) must be tested from the date of application for a small public service vehicle licence and from each licence renewal date (SI No 405 of 2003, reg 3(4)).

The NCTS may issue a *certificate of suitability* in respect of such vehicles (SI No 405 of 2003, reg 15).

See also Road Traffic Act 1961, s 18. For previous regulations which now are revoked, see Road Traffic (National Car Test) (No 3) Regulations 2001, SI No 550 of 2001 which revoked SI No 395 of 1999; and Road Traffic (National Car Test) (Amendment) Regulations 2002, SIs No 55 and 500 of 2002.

carat. A measure to denote the fineness of gold; pure gold is said to be 24 carats fine. See HALLMARKING.

caravan. Any structure designed or adapted for human habitation which is capable of being moved from one place to another, whether by towing or transport on a vehicle or trailer, and includes a motor vehicle so designed or adapted and a mobile home, but does not include a tent: Housing Act 1988, s 13(7) as amended by Housing (Traveller Accommodation) Act 1998, s 29.

It is an offence to place a caravan on a public road, without lawful authority or consent, for the purposes of advertising, the sale of goods, the provision of services, or other similar purpose; the caravan may be removed by an authorised person: Roads Act 1993, s 71.

Planning permission is not required for the keeping or storing of a caravan or campervan within the curtilage of a house; however not more than one may be so stored: Planning and Development Regulations 2001, SI No 600 of 2001, Sch 2, class 8. Also it may not be kept or stored for more than nine months in any year or occupied as a dwelling while so kept or stored. See CAMPING; TRAVELLER.

carcinogens. Employers are required to carry out an assessment of the risks associated with the use of a *carcinogen* or *mutagen* in the workplace and to take steps to control such risks by eliminating or minimising exposure: Safety, Health and Welfare at Work (Carcinogens) Regulations 2001, SI No 78 of 2001.

care, duty of. See DUTY OF CARE.

care of child. See CHILD, CARE OF.

care order. An order which the District Court is empowered to make, committing a child (qv) to the care of a health board (qv) for so long as he remains a child or for such shorter period as the court may determine: Child Care Act 1991, s 18. The effect of a *care order* is to suspend the parent's right to custody of the child and to place him in the control of the health board as if it were his parent (CCA 1991, s 18(3)(a)). A health board has a duty to apply for a care order or supervision order (qv) in respect of a child who requires care or protection (CCA 1991, s 16). See SPECIAL CARE ORDER.

The court may make a care order when it is satisfied that the child requires care or protection which he is unlikely to receive unless a care order is made and that: (a) the child has been or is being assaulted, ill-treated, neglected or sexually abused; or (b) the child's health, development or welfare has been or is being avoidably impaired or neglected; or (c) the child's health, development or welfare is likely to be avoidably impaired or neglected (CCA 1991, s 18(1)).

The court is required to have regard to the rights and duties of the parents, whether under the 1937 Constitution or otherwise, but must regard the welfare of the child as the first and paramount consideration and must give due consideration, in so far as is practical, to the wishes of the child (CCA 1991, s 24). A care order ceases to have effect where the child becomes adopted (s 44(2)). There is also provision for the court to make an *interim care order* (s 17), an *emergency care order* (s 13) or a *supervision order* (qv).

The court has a wide jurisdiction, on its own motion or on the application of any person, in relation to the care of a child, not only in proceedings before the court but also where a child is already in the care of a health board: *Eastern Health Board v McDonnell* [1999] 2 ILRM 382, HC. See also Childrens Act 1997, s 17; Domestic Violence Act 1996, s 7. A child over whom a care order is in place can be allowed abroad for a limited period only ie for a holiday; to interpret otherwise would be to allow the health board to abandon its control under the care order: *Western Health Board v K M* [2001] 1 IR 729, HC. The Supreme Court held that such an order must be made rarely and with considerable caution, and the health board would continue to have responsibility for the welfare of the child: *Western Health Board v M* [2001] (FL5016), SC and [2002] 2 IR 493, SC.

See *Southern Health Board v CH and CH* [1996] 2 ILRM 142, SC. For a district court procedure in relation to care orders, see DCR 1997 Ord 84. See also School Attendance Act 1926, s 17 (as substituted by Child Care Act 1991, s 75); DCR 1997 Ord 84, r 33. See 'Age of Innocents' by solicitor Geoffrey Shannon in *LAW SOCIETY GAZETTE* (April 2004) 12. [Bibliography: Ward.] See AFTERCARE; CHILD, EMERGENCY CARE OF; CHILD, CARE OF; SPECIAL CARE ORDER; WARD OF COURT; WELFARE OF CHILDREN.

careless driving. The offence committed by a person who drives a vehicle in a public place (qv) without due care and attention: Road Traffic Act 1961, s 52 as substituted by Road Traffic Act 1968, s 50. Where a person is tried on indictment (qv) or summarily for the offence of *dangerous driving* (qv) and the jury (or the court in a summary trial) is of the opinion that he was not guilty of that offence, he may be found guilty of the offence of careless driving. An acquittal on a charge of dangerous driving affords a *plea in bar* to a charge of careless driving, arising out of the same facts: *Attorney-General v Power* [1964] IR 458. Endorsement on the defendant's licence is mandatory in the event of a third conviction: *DPP v O'Brien* [1989] 7 ILT Dig 260. See also *The People (Attorney-General) v O'Neill* [1964] Ir Jur Rep 1; *The Queen v Megaw* [1993] ITLR (1 February) CA NI. [Bibliography: Hill & O'Keeffe.] See PLEASURE CRAFT.

carer. A person who resides with and provides full-time care and attention to a *relevant person*, ie a person who is so incapacitated as to require full-time care and attention: Social Welfare (Consolidation) Act 1993, ss 163–169 as amended eg Social Welfare Act 1999, s 10. The relevant person must be 16 years of age or older or, if under 16, is a handicapped child. The carer need not reside with the relevant person if the carer still provides full-time care and attention. An *allowance* is payable to a carer. A *respite care grant* may also be payable (SWA 1999, s 11). See Social Welfare Act 2000, ss 22 and 28; Social Welfare (Miscellaneous Provisions) Act 2002, s 3; Social Welfare (Miscellaneous Provisions) Act 2003, s 4; SI No 121 of 2003; Social Welfare (Miscellaneous Provisions) Act 2004, s 4. From 1 June 2004 the grant is €835 for the care of one person and €1,670 for carers who provide care to two or more persons.

The annual allowance for income tax purposes for employing a carer to look after an incapacitated relative was increased in 2001 to €12,700: Finance Act 2001, s 7 and to €30,000 in 2002: Finance Act 2002, s 5.

carer's benefit. A new scheme which commenced in October 2000, designed to facilitate and support persons who wish to leave the workforce temporarily to care for older persons or persons with disabilities in need of full-time care and attention: Social Welfare Act 2000, ss 10–12. The benefit is payable for a period of 65 weeks in respect of the same care recipient. The new scheme is closely linked to the means-tested *Carer's Allowance*. See also Social Welfare (Miscellaneous Provisions) Act 2002, s 15; Social Welfare Act 2003, s 2(2)(c); Social Welfare (Consolidated Payments Provisions) (Amendment) (Carers) Regulations 2003, SI No 121 of 2003.

carer's leave. A new entitlement of employees to temporary *unpaid* leave to enable them to care personally for persons who require full-time care and attention: Carer's Leave Act 2001. The employee must have been in the continuous employment of the employer, from whose employment the leave is to be taken, for at least 12 months before the leave (CLA 2001, s 6). The entitlement is for a maximum period of 65 weeks leave. Carer's leave is unpaid but reckonable for the purpose of employment rights, other than superannuation and certain public holidays.

An employer may refuse, on reasonable grounds, carer's leave for a period of less than 13 weeks (CLA 2001, s 8(2)). Disputes can be heard by a Rights Commissioner, with a right of appeal to the Employment Appeals Tribunal (CLA 2001, ss 19–20). For social welfare benefits, see Social Welfare Act 2001, ss 14 and 26.

caretaker. A person who has been put into possession of any lands or premises by the owner thereof and who agrees to give up possession when requested by the landlord. So long as the relationship of caretaker exists, the caretaker cannot acquire a title under the Statute of Limitations: *Musgrave v McAvey* [1907] 41 ILTR 230. A caretaker is estopped from disputing or disclaiming his landlord's title: *Gowrie Park Utility Society Ltd v Fitzgerald* [1963] IR 436. See also Deasy's Act 1860, s 86. See OCCUPATION.

carltona principle. The principle that recognises that the duties imposed upon Ministers and the powers given to them are normally exercised under the authority of the Ministers by responsible officials of their departments and that, constitutionally, the decisions of the officials are the decisions of their respective Ministers: *Carltona Ltd v Commissioners of Works* [1943] 2 All ER 560 endorsed in *Tang v Minister for Justice* [1996] 2 ILRM 46, SC; *DEVANNEY V SHIELDS* [1998] 1 ILRM 81, SC and [1998] 1 IR 230, SC. See *Tang v Minister for Justice* [1996] 2 ILRM 49, SC. See DELEGATION BY MINISTER.

carnal knowledge, unlawful. The offence of sexual intercourse with a female under the age of fifteen years which was a felony (qv) (now, an offence); or with a female under the age of seventeen, which was a misdemeanour (now, also an offence): Criminal Law Amendment Act 1935, ss 1–3 as amended by Criminal Law Act 1997, s 13 and Sch 1, para 7. These offences are *statutory rape* in that intercourse is essential to constitute the offence but the element of consent is removed. There cannot be a conviction of rape and unlawful carnal knowledge in relation to the same incident: *The People (Attorney-General) v Dermody* [1956] IR 307.

To prove carnal knowledge it is not necessary 'to prove the actual emission of seed in order to constitute a carnal knowledge, but the carnal knowledge shall be deemed complete upon proof of penetration only': Offences against the Person Act 1861, s 63. It is also an offence for a person to have *sexual intercourse* with a person who is mentally impaired (qv); sexual intercourse is construed as a reference to carnal knowledge as defined in the 1861 Act, s 63: Criminal Law (Sexual Offences) Act 1993, ss 1(3) and 5(1). See SEXUAL INTERCOURSE; SEXUAL OFFENCES.

carriage by air. See AIR LAW; WARSAW CONVENTION.

carriage by rail. See LIABILITY, STATUTORY EXEMPTION FROM; CMR.

carriage by sea. For liability for carriage of passengers and goods by sea, see MARITIME CLAIMS. See also PASSENGER BOAT; PASSENGER SHIP.

carriage contracts. See COMMERCIAL PROCEEDINGS; LIABILITY, STATUTORY EXEMPTION FROM.

carriage of goods. See CMR; COMMERCIAL PROCEEDINGS; DANGEROUS GOODS.

carriage of passengers. See CARRIER'S LICENCE; WARSAW CONVENTION.

carrier. A person who carries goods for reward. A carrier is either a *private* carrier (a bailee for reward) or a *common* carrier

(qv). A licence is not required for a person to carry his own goods, or to deliver goods supplied by him to a customer in the course of his business, or to deliver goods repaired, cleaned, laundered or dyed by him.

A person whose principal business is the provision of transport by land, sea or air on aircraft, vessels or other modes of transport owned and operated by such persons: Transport (Tour Operator and Travel Agents) Act 1982, s 2(1) as amended by Package Holidays and Travel Trade Act 1995, s 27. See Dangerous Substances Act 1972, s 51. [Bibliography: Chitty UK; Clarke UK.] See BULK CARRIER; CARRIER'S LICENCE; NON-NATIONAL.

carrier, common. A person who holds himself out to the public, expressly or by conduct, as ready and willing to carry all goods of a certain kind, offered to him for carriage to and from specified places for reward. At common law, a common carrier is bound to carry between the places he professes to carry, all goods offered to him in respect of which he professes to carry; to deliver the goods within a reasonable time; to be an insurer of the goods entrusted to him while *in transit* except caused by an Act of God, the consignor's fault, or an inherent defect in the goods carried. The carrier has a lien (qv) on the goods carried for the cost of carriage.

A common carrier by land is not liable for loss or injury to certain articles contained in a package delivered to him for carriage when the value of the package exceeds £10 (€12.70) unless the nature and value is declared and any increased charge paid which the carrier may demand: Carriers Act 1830, s 1; Transport Act 1944, s 87(1), Sch 9. The articles specified include gold or silver articles, precious stones, jewellery, clocks, bank notes or securities, stamps, maps, title deeds, engravings, pictures, glass, china or furs. A carrier may make a special contract with the consignor (CA 1830, s 6). See *Belfast Ropework Co v Bushell* [1918] 1 KB 210.

A common carrier is liable for loss of property arising from theft, embezzlement or forgery of his servants (CA 1830, s 8 as amended by Criminal Law Act 1997, s 13 and Sch 1, para 2). See CARRIER'S LICENCE; CONSIGNMENT.

carrier, delivery of goods to. Delivery of goods to a carrier, whether named by the buyer or not, for the purpose of transmission to the buyer, is *prima facie* deemed to be delivery of the goods to the buyer: Sale of Goods Act 1893, s 32. If the carrier is the agent of the seller, delivery to the carrier is not deemed to be delivery to the buyer. The seller is obligated to make a contract with the carrier on behalf of the buyer as may be reasonable having regard to the nature of the goods and the other circumstances of the case; if the seller omits to do so and the goods are lost or damaged in the course of transit, the buyer may decline to treat delivery to the carrier as a delivery to himself, or hold the seller responsible in damages (SGA 1893, s 32(2)). See *Michel Freres Societe Anonyme v Kilkenny Woolen Mills Ltd* [1959] IR 157; *Spicer-Cowan Ireland Ltd v Play Print Ltd* [1980] HC.

carrier, private. A carrier who is not a common carrier (qv) ie he does not hold himself out as ready and willing to carry for all persons without discrimination, either all goods or certain classes of goods; he is free to enter into such transactions as he so wishes. He is liable at common law for his negligence. See *Barnfield v Goole and Sheffield Transport Co* [1910] 2 KB 94. See also Transport Act 1958, s 8(8); European Communities (International Carriage of Passengers) Regulations 1974, SI No 133 of 1974, reg 3; Transport (Reorganisation of Córas Iompair Éireann) Act 1986. See CARRIER'S LICENCE; PASSENGER ROAD SERVICE.

carrier's licence. A licence for the carriage of passengers or freight for reward. The categories of licence are: (a) a *Community* licence for the international carriage of passengers by road for hire or reward; (b) a *road passenger* transport operator's licence which may be *international* or *national*; or (c) a *road freight* carrier's licence which may be *international* or *national*. An *international* licence entitles the holder to carry for reward within the State as well as qualifies the holder to carry for reward outside the State. See Road Transport Acts 1935, 1978, 1986, 1999; EC Regulation 684/92/EEC art 3a as inserted by EC Regulation 11/98/EC.

A licence holder is entitled to have issued to him a *transport disc* in respect of each vehicle operated under the licence (RTA 1999, s 4). It is an offence to operate a vehicle for carriage without such a disc visibly displayed (RTA 1999, s 5). A licence holder is required to have adequate parking spaces and operating premises in the State for the vehicles operated or intended to be operated under the licence (RTA 1999, s 11).

A person must not engage or use the services of any undertaking for the carriage by road for reward of merchandise in a vehicle unless: (a) the undertaking is the holder of a road freight carrier's licence; or (b) the carriage is one in respect of which a licence is not required by law (RTA 1999, s 9). Licences are issued for a period of up to five years, although there is provision for the issue of restricted road freight licences (RTA 1999, ss 2–3). [Bibliography: Canny (1).] See CABOTAGE; WEIGHBRIDGE.

carrier's lien. The common law lien (qv) by which a carrier is entitled to keep possession of the goods consigned until he has been paid the *freight* owing to him for their carriage: *Skinner v Upshaw* [1702] 2 Ld Raym 752.

carry over. The postponement of the completion of a contract to buy or sell shares from one account period of the Stock Exchange (qv) to the other.

cartel. An association with the objective on maintaining higher prices for goods than would otherwise obtain. See 'US and Them' by Terry Calvani in *Law Society Gazette* (April 2003) 28. [Bibliography: Power V.] See DOMINANT POSITION, ABUSE OF; UNFAIR PRACTICES.

case. Means any matter in which a barrister is asked to advise, draft pleadings or other legal documents or to represent a client: Code of Conduct for the Bar of Ireland (December 2003) r 1.7(1).

case booklet. The booklet which the judge may direct to be prepared in *commercial proceedings* (qv) which are subject to 'case management': RSC Ord 63A, r 14 inserted by Rules of the Superior Courts (Commercial Proceedings) 2004, SI No 2 of 2004. The case booklet is required to contain: (a) a case summary, comprising: (i) an agreed outline of the case and sequence of relevant events not in dispute; (ii) a list of those issues which are not in dispute; (iii) an agreed statement of those issues that are in dispute; and (b) pre-trial documentation in chronological sequence, including (where appropriate) copies of pleadings exchanged, affidavits filed (other than affidavits of service), statements of issues, orders made or directions given, and any correspondence between the parties, not being expressed to be 'without prejudice', relating to the preparation of the case for trial (r 14(10)).

The plaintiff, applicant or other party prosecuting the proceedings must, in consultation with the other party or parties, prepare the case booklet to be lodged with the registrar and served on the other party or parties not later than four clear days prior to the first date fixed for the case management conference (r 14(9)).

The case booklet must be produced and maintained in such form, including electronic form as the judge may direct and, where the judge so directs, must be lodged or served by electronic means, and on such conditions and subject to such exceptions as he may prescribe (r 14(11)). The party preparing the case booklet must, in consultation with the other party or parties, revise or add to its contents from time to time as necessary (r 14(12)).

case management conference. The conference which is ordered where in *commercial proceedings* (qv), the judge has directed that the proceedings be subject to case management due to their complexity, the number of issues or parties, the volume of evidence, or for other special reasons: RSC Ord 63A rr 6(1)(xii) and 14–15 inserted by Rules of the Superior Courts (Commercial Proceedings) 2004, SI No 2 of 2004. The judge may direct the preparation of a *case booklet* (qv).

The purpose of the case management conference is to ensure that the proceedings are prepared for trial in a manner which is just, expeditious and likely to minimise the costs of the proceedings, and in particular that, as soon as may be in advance of the trial: (a) the issues, whether as to fact or law, are defined as clearly, as precisely and as concisely, as possible; (b) all pleadings, affidavits and statements of issues are served; (c) any applications by letter for particulars and replies thereto, any admissions, or requests for admissions, notices to admit documents or facts and replies thereto, and any affidavits made in pursuance of any notices to admit facts or documents, are served or delivered, as the case may be; (d) all applications for relief of an interlocutory nature intended to be made by any of the parties are made; (e) any directions given or orders made at the initial directions hearing, or in the course of a case management conference have been complied with (r 14(7)).

case stated. A statement of the facts in a case submitted for the opinion of a higher court, clearly identifying the point of law upon which opinion is sought. It is consultative in that the lower court seeks the assistance of the higher court. The procedure normally contemplates that the case will return to the same judge, as the case stated arises from a particular view which that judge has taken of the law. Consequently, a District Court judge cannot sign a case stated after his promotion as a judge of the Circuit Court: *DPP v Galvin* [1999] 2 ILRM 277, HC and 4 IR 18.

A Circuit Court judge may refer any question of law to the Supreme Court by way of case stated and may adjourn the pronouncement of his judgment or order pending the determination of such case stated: Courts of Justice Act 1947, s 16; *Doyle v Hearne* [1988] ILRM 318. For the rules of court governing a *case stated* from the Circuit to the Supreme Court, including special rules governing a *Revenue case stated*, see Circuit Court Rules 2001 Ord 62. See also *Irish Refining plc v Commissioner of Valuations* [1990] 1 IR 568.

A case may be stated on a question of law by the High Court to the Supreme Court: Courts of Justice Act 1936.

A case may be stated on a question of law from the District Court to the High Court, before or after the determination of the proceedings in the District Court: Courts (Supplemental Provisions) Act 1961, ss 51–52; Summary Jurisdiction Act 1857; *DPP (Whelan) v Delaney* [1996] 1 ILRM 70, HC. No appeal is allowed to the Supreme Court except by leave of the High Court: C(SP)A 1961, s 52(2) and *Minister for Justice v Wang Zhu Jie* [1991] ILRM 823, SC. An exception, is that a case may be stated from the District Court to the Supreme Court in relation to the Malicious Injuries Act 1981, s 18. See DCR 1997 Ord 102, rr 1–6.

A District Court judge is not entitled to state a case to the High Court on a question concerning the validity of a statutory provision having regard to the constitution: 1937 Constitution art 34(3)(2); *DPP v Dougan* [1997] 1 ILRM 550, HC.

A judge of the District Court must not refuse to state a case where the application is made to him by or under the direction of a Minister, the Director of Public Prosecutions, or the Revenue Commissioners; the only ground for refusing in other cases is where he is of opinion that the application is frivolous: Summary Jurisdiction Act 1857, s 4; *Sport Arena Ltd v O'Reilly* [1987] IR 185, HC. Section 4 of the SJA 1857 is not unconstitutional: *Fitzgerald v DPP* [2003] FL 7966, SC and 2 ILRM 537. However, the District Court cannot refer a consultative case stated in relation to an indictable offence which is not being dealt with summarily by the District Court: [1995] 2 IR 511, HC. Also the jurisdiction to entertain a case stated by way of appeal against acquittal must be strictly construed, given that an otherwise acquitted person is exposed to potentially serious adverse consequences (*Fitzgerald* case).

Service in relation to a case stated on the solicitor who acted as a party in the District Court may be sufficient: *Crowley v McVeigh* [1989] IR 73. Also, the court has jurisdiction to enlarge the time limit fixed for transmission of a case stated to the High Court but only in appropriate circumstances: *DPP v Regan* [1993] ILRM 335, HC. See *DPP v Brennan* [1998] 2 ILRM 129, SC; *Eastern Health Board v Ballagh* [1999] 1 ILRM 544, HC; *DPP (Gannon) v Conlon* [2001] 4 IR 376, HC. See also RSC Ord 59 Ord 62, r 1 and O 122, r 7. [Bibliography: Collins & O'Reilly.] See SUPREME COURT; PRELIMINARY RULINGS; VALUATION.

case stated, principles applied. When a court has before it a *case stated* seeking its opinion as to whether a particular decision was correct in law, the following principles should be applied: (a) findings of *primary fact* (qv) by the judge should not be disturbed unless there is no evidence to support them; (b) *inferences* from primary facts are mixed questions of fact and law; (c) if the judge's conclusions show that he has adopted a wrong view of the law, they should be set aside; (d) if the judge's conclusions are not based on a mistaken view of the law, they should not be set aside unless the inferences he drew were ones which no reasonable judge could draw; (e) while some evidence will point to one conclusion and other evidence will point to the opposite conclusion, these are essentially a matter of degree and the judge's conclusions should not be disturbed, even if the court does not agree with them, unless they are such that a reasonable judge could not have arrived at them or they are based on a

mistaken view of the law: *O'Culachain v McMullan Brothers Ltd* [1995] 2 ILRM 498, SC.

It is preferable that a case stated should set out the relevant principles of law accepted by the trial judge: *per curiam* in *Brosnan v Mutual Enterprises Ltd* [1995] 2 ILRM 304, HC.

case summary. In *commercial proceedings* (qv), the summary comprising: (i) an agreed outline of the case and sequence of relevant events not in dispute; (ii) a list of those issues which are not in dispute; (iii) a list of the persons principally involved in the matters or events the subject of the proceedings; and (iv) where appropriate, a glossary of technical terms which are likely to be used in the course of the trial: RSC Ord 63A, r 21(1)(b) inserted by Rules of the Superior Courts (Commercial Proceedings) 2004, SI No 2 of 2004. Unless otherwise directed by the judge chairing the pre-trial conference, the plaintiff is required, in consultation with the other parties, to prepare and lodge with the registrar, not less than four days prior to the date fixed for the trial, a case summary and a *trial booklet* (qv).

cash. Cash that is *legal tender* (qv): Payment of Wages Act 1991, s 1(1).

cash card. A card issued by a bank or building society to a person having an address in the State by means of which cash may be obtained in the State by the person from an automated teller machine: Finance Act 1992, s 203 as amended by Finance Act 1993, s 102. Stamp duty is payable in respect of cash cards: Stamp Duties Consolidation Act 1999, s 123. The stamp duty on cash cards (ATM cards) is now €10 per card per annum, or €20 for a combined card ie an ATM card with a laser function: Finance Act 2003, s 140. The Laser card attracts stamp duty of €10 per card per annum.

casting vote. The second and deciding vote which a chairman may have power to give when there is an equality of votes.

In a *tribunal of inquiry* of more than one member, decisions or determinations are made by a majority of the members; however in the case of an equal division, the chairperson decides: Tribunals of Inquiry (Evidence) Act 1979, s 2(4) as added by Tribunals of Inquiry (Evidence) (Amendment) Act 2002, s 4. See also Competition Act 2002, s 37(3). See CHAIRMAN; FOSS V HARBOTTLE, RULE IN.

casual trading. Selling goods at a place (including a public road) to which the public have access as of right or at any other place that is a *casual trading area:* Casual Trading Act 1995, s 2. It does not include a number of selling transactions e g selling by auction, other than by *Dutch auction* (qv), selling to a person at the place he resides or carries on business, or selling for charitable purposes (CTA 1995, s 2(2) as amended by SI No 191 of 2004 to exclude the selling of certain fruit and vegetables e g strawberries and potatoes having loose skins and which have been harvested prior to maturity). The onus of showing that the activity is excluded is on the defendant: *Crosby v Delap* [1992] ILRM 564.

It is an offence for a person to engage in casual trading unless he holds a casual trading *licence* and the casual trading is in accordance with the licence (CTA 1995, s 3). A local authority cannot grant a casual trading licence to a person with two or more convictions for specified offences, if two at least of the convictions occurred less than three years before the day casual trading is proposed to commence (CTA 1995, s 4(7)). A five-year period in the 1980 (repealed) legislation has been found not to be repugnant to the Constitution: *Hand v Dublin Corporation* [1991] ILRM 556, SC.

A local authority has power to designate casual trading areas (CTA 1995, s 6). Regulations made by Limerick Corporation of casual trading have been held not to be in breach of the Limerick Markets Act 1852: *Bridgeman v Limerick Corporation* [2001] 2 IR 517, SC. See also *Skibbereen UDC v Quill* [1986] IR 123 ILRM 170; *Comerford v O'Malley* [1987] ILRM 595; *Lyons v Corporation of Kilkenny* [1987] HC; *Shanley v Galway Corporation* [1995] 1 IR 396, HC.

In 2003, the Tánaiste published a report on the implementation of the 1995 Act; the report confirms the economic importance of casual trading, particularly for local markets. For the report, see website: *www.entemp.ie.* [Bibliography: Canny (2).] Contrast with OCCASIONAL TRADING.

casual vacancy. A vacancy in the European Parliament caused by an elected member no longer being entitled to be a member or who ceases to be a member otherwise than by the effluxion of time; it is filled by the *replacement candidate* whose name stands highest on the replacement candidate list of the political party or non-party candidate concerned: European Parliament Elections Act 1997, s 19 and Sch 2, rr 96–101.

For provisions on casual vacancies in local authorities, see Local Government Act 2001, s 19.

casus belli. [A case for war.] An event which is used to justify a war.

casus omissus. [An omitted case.] A matter which has not been, but should have been provided for by statute or by statutory rule or regulation.

catalogue. See ADVERTISEMENT.

catching bargain. See UNCONSCIONABLE BARGAIN.

category licence. See EXCLUSIVE DISTRIBUTION AGREEMENT; FRANCHISE; SOLUS AGREEMENT.

cattle trespass. See ANIMALS.

causa causans. The immediate cause; the last link in the chain of causation. The real effective cause of damage: *Pandorf v Hamilton* [1886] 17 QBD 675. *Causa causans* is to be distinguished from *causa sina qua non* which means some preceding link but for which the *causa causans* could not have become operative: see *Kehoe & Haythornwaite v Cullimore* (1991), CC as reported by *Boyle* in 10 ILT & SJ (1992) 50. See also *Fitzsimmons v Bord Telecom and ESB* [1991] ILRM 277, HC. See CAUSATION.

causa mortis. [Because of death.] See DONATIO MORTIS CAUSA.

causa proxima non remota spectatur. [The immediate, not the remote cause, is to be considered.] See CAUSATION.

causa remota. [The remote cause.] See NOVUS ACTUS INTERVENIENS.

causa sine qua non. See CAUSA CAUSANS.

causation. The relation of cause and effect. A defendant in an action in tort is liable only if the chain of causation between himself and the plaintiff is unbroken. See NOVUS ACTUS INTERVENIENS.

cause. (1) Includes any action, suit or other original proceeding between a plaintiff and defendant and any criminal proceedings: RSC Ord 125, r 1. The definition of *cause* as including criminal proceedings is ousted in the context of the rules pertaining to *discovery: People* (*DPP*) *v Sweeney* [2002] 1 ILRM 532, SC. See also *KA v Minister for Justice* [2003] 2 IR 93, HC. See DISCOVERY RE CRIMINAL CASES.

(2) Includes any suit or other original proceeding: Circuit Court Rules 2001, Interpretation of Terms, para 2.

cause of action. The facts which give rise to a right of action in a court of law. Every fact which is material to be proved to entitle the plaintiff to succeed, and every fact which the defendant would have a right to traverse: *Cooke v Gill* [1873] LR 8 CP 107.

A cause of action runs from the time a wrongful act is committed when the act is actionable *per se* without proof of damage eg as in libel; however when the wrong is not actionable without actual damage (eg as in negligence (qv)), the cause of action is not complete until that damage happens, eg time runs when a provable personal injury, capable of attracting compensation, occurs to the plaintiff: *Hegarty v O'Loughran* [1990] ITLR (2 April), SC.

In a particular case involving the presence of excess of iron pyrites in concrete blocks, used in the construction of a house, it was held that the cause of action did not accrue until cracks came into existence in the walls: *O'Donnell v Kilsaran Concrete Ltd* [2002] 1 ILRM 531, HC and [2001] 4 IR 183, HC.

However, in personal injuries cases the then three-year limitation period, within which an action may be taken, now runs from the date of accrual of the cause of action or from the *date of knowledge* if later: Statute of Limitations (Amendment) Act 1991. The *date of knowledge* is the date the person first had knowledge that he had been 'injured' and that the injury had been *significant*: SL(A)A 1991, s 3(1) and *Maitland v Swan & Sligo County Council* [1992] ITLR (6 July), HC. '*Knowledge*' does not mean a vague suspicion but rather a reasonable belief in a particular set of circumstances such as would justify a person in issuing legal proceedings: *Gallagher v Minister for Defence* [1998] 4 IR 457, HC. In a particular case involving a patient plaintiff and a consultant obstetrician, the court held that that the then three-year limit began to run when the plaintiff had knowledge that the operation to remove her ovary was unnecessary, as alleged: *Cunningham v Neary* (2003) Irish Times, 29 October. However, the Supreme Court held that the plaintiff had such knowledge in 1998 when she made a complaint to the Medical Council and consequently her action was statute-barred (20 July 2004, unreported), SC. The Supreme Court has also held that it is not helpful to try to equate the word 'injury' in s 3 with harm: *Gough v Neary* [2004] 1 ILRM 35, SC. Under recent legislation, provision has been made to reduce the three-year period to two years: Civil Liability and Courts Act 2004, s 7.

In a particular case, it was held that the date when the plaintiff first had knowledge that his injury was significant, was the date when the plaintiff knew or reasonably ought to have known from facts observable or ascertainable by him that he had a significant injury: *Bolger v O'Brien & Ors* [1999] 2 ILRM 372, SC and 2 IR 431. In a hearing loss claim, it was held that time began from the date on which the person first obtained knowledge that his injury was significant: *Keogh v Minister for Defence* [2004] ITLR (22 March), HC. See also *O'Driscoll v Dublin Corporation* [1999] 1 ILRM 106, HC.

In determining whether an injury is '*significant*', a primarily *subjective* test should be applied, taking into account the state of mind of the particular plaintiff at the particular time having regard to his particular circumstances at that time; a certain degree of *objectivity* is also required by the 1991 Act, as it requires consideration of the knowledge which a particular plaintiff ought to have acquired either from facts observable or ascertainable by him, or from facts ascertainable by him with help of medical or other expert advice: *Whitely v Minister for Defence* [1997] 2 ILRM 416, HC and [1998] 4 IR 442, HC. See also *Gough v Neary & Cronin* [2002] FL 6895, HC and (2002) *Law Society Gazette* (November 2003), SC. See 'The Statute of Limitations and Discoverability' by William Abrahamson BL in *Bar Review* (April 2004) 48.

Also in an action for breach of contract, the limitation period commences on the date of the breach and not on the date of the damage caused. In an action in negligence, other than personal injuries, the question of discoverability is irrelevant to the appropriate commencement date eg alleged negligence in the design of a building: *Irish Equine Foundation Ltd v Robinson & Ors* [1999] 2 ILRM 289, HC and 2 IR 442. See *Boylan v Motor Distributors Ltd* [1994] 1 ILRM 115, HC. See also Liability of Defective Products Act 1991, s 7(4). See DEATH, EFFECT OF; DISABILITY, PERSON UNDER; DISCOVERABILITY TEST; LIMITATION OF ACTIONS; UNSOUND MIND.

cause of action estoppel. See RES JUDICATA.

causes books. The books in the Central Office (qv) in which all proceedings commenced by originating summons, issued out of the office, must be entered. See RSC Ord 5, r 7.

causing serious harm. It is an offence for a person, intentionally or recklessly, to cause serious harm to another person: Non-Fatal Offences against the Person Act 1997, s 4. An assault is not required; it is sufficient if the serious harm is caused by the accused. *Serious harm* means injury which creates a substantial risk of death, or which causes serious disfigurement or substantial loss or impairment of the mobility of the body as a whole or of the function of any particular bodily member or organ (NFOPA 1997, s 1(1)). It is also an offence for a person to *threaten* by any means, without lawful excuse, to cause serious harm to another person (NFOPA 1997, s 5). The sentence appropriate to serious bodily injury does not necessarily have to be less than that appropriate to manslaughter if death had resulted from the same crime: *obiter dictum* in *People (DPP) v Osborne* [2003] FL 7503, CCA. See ENDANGERMENT.

caution. A warning.

(1) An entry in the register of the Land Registry to protect unregistered rights on registered land from being defeated by the registration of a subsequent transferee for value: Registration of Title Act 1964, ss 97–98. It is a requisition to the Registrar requiring notice to be given to the *cautioner* before registration of any dealing by the registered owner of specified land.

(2) The *judge's rules* (qv) provide that when a police officer has made up his mind to charge a person with a crime, he should first *caution* such person before asking any questions or any further questions as the case may be. The caution to a prisoner when he is formally charged should be in the following words: '*Do you wish to say anything in answer to the charge? You are not obliged to say anything unless you wish to do so, but whatever you say will be taken down in writing and may be given in evidence*'.

Everything said by an accused during an interview with a garda is not required to be reduced to writing; however, anything of consequence should be recorded: *DPP v McKeever* [1994] 2 ILRM 186, CCA.

(3) There is now provision for the administration of a *formal* or *informal* caution to a child admitted to the *diversion programme* (qv) – formerly known as the juvenile liaison office scheme – in respect of the child's criminal behaviour: Children Act 2001, s 25. A victim may be invited to be present at the administration of a formal caution and the child may be invited to apologise to the victim and, where appropriate, to make financial or other reparation to the victim (CA 2001, s 26).

See BURDEN.

CAV. See CUR ADV VULT.

caveat. A warning. An entry made in the books of the offices of a registry or court to prevent a certain step being taken without previous notice to the person entering the caveat (who is called the *caveator*). Any person having, or claiming, an interest in the estate of a deceased person may enter a caveat at the Probate Office and so prevent a grant of representation issuing in respect of that estate without reference to him. See RSC Ord 79 rr 41–51; O 80 rr 48–55. [Bibliography: Keating.]

caveat actor. [Let the doer beware.]

caveat emptor. [Let the buyer beware.] At common law, a buyer was expected to look after his own interest. However statute law now imposes *implied conditions* (qv) and *warranties* (qv) to protect the buyer in many instances eg where the seller acts in the course of a business and also where the buyer deals as consumer. See *Wallis v Russell* [1902] 2 IR 585; *Riordan v Carroll t/a Wyvern Gallery* [1996] 2 ILRM 263, HC. See CONSUMER, DEALING AS; PRODUCT LIABILITY.

caveat venditor. [Let the seller beware.]

CD-ROM. [Compact disc read-only memory.] An individual compact disc designed for use with a computer and capable of storing up to 650 megabytes of data. Increasingly books on legal matters are being published in CD-ROM versions, making for ease of access to data and providing excellent search capability eg see Bibliography: Butterworths (3), Killen & Williams.

CE Mark. Means the EC *mark of conformity* consisting of the symbol 'CE'. In order for a device to bear the CE marking, its manufacturer must have followed the EC declaration of conformity procedure of the EC type-examination procedure. For example, see SI No 253 of 1994, Sch 9. See website: *www.nsai.ie/cemark.htm*. See MEDICAL DEVICE; NATIONAL STANDARDS AUTHORITY OF IRELAND.

Ceann Comhairle. The chairman of Dáil Éireann elected from its members: 1937

Constitution, art 15(9)(1). Provision may be made by law for the outgoing Ceann Comhairle to be deemed to be elected at the ensuing general election without actually contesting the election (1937 Constitution, art 16(6)). Such provision has been made by the Electoral Act 1992, s 36. See also EA 1992, s 63. It has been held that it would be inappropriate for the court to intervene in a matter concerning the internal working of Dáil Éireann except in very extreme circumstances; in this case the manner in which questions are framed for answer by Ministers: *O'Malley v An Ceann Comhairle* [1997] 1 IR 427, SC.

cement. A company was not permitted to manufacture cement in the State without a Ministerial licence: Cement Acts 1933 to 1962. This legislation facilitated the establishment of an indigenous manufacturing base for the production of cement. However, a licensing regime is no longer seen as necessary and may have had the effect of discouraging competition. Consequently, these Acts have now been repealed: Cement (Repeal of Enactments) Act 2000.

censorship. The prohibition on exhibiting in public, cinematograph pictures which have not been certified as fit for such exhibition by the *official censor;* the prohibition on publishing material which is indecent or obscene or which advocates abortion (qv); the prohibition on the sale of indecent pictures. See *Irish Planning Association v Judge Ryan* [1979] IR 295. Provision has been made for the appointment of assistant censors and for the refund of fees in the event that an appeal is successful: Censorship of Films (Amendment) Act 1992. See also Censorship of Films Acts 1923 to 1970; Censorship of Publications Acts 1929 to 1967; Health (Family Planning) Act 1979, s 12(3). See VIDEO RECORDING.

censorship of books. The Censorship of Publication Board has power to prohibit the sale and distribution in the State of books which it has examined and where the Board is of opinion that the books are indecent or obscene: Censorship of Publications Act 1946, ss 6 and 7; Health (Family Planning) Act 1979, s 12.

census. (1) The enumeration of the inhabitants of the State. The last census of population was taken on 28 April 2002. Provision has been made to permit access to the records of a census of population after 100 years: Statistics Act 1993, s 35. (2) Compilation of statistics in relation to any specified matter eg census of production (SI No 81 of 1993). See STATISTICS.

Central Bank. A body corporate, named the *Central Bank and Financial Services Authority of Ireland,* which is managed and controlled by a board of directors, consisting of a Governor (qv) and other directors: Central Bank Act 1942, ss 5 and 18B as substituted or inserted by the Central Bank and Financial Services Authority of Ireland Act 2003, ss 4 and 13.

The bank has the general function of promoting the development within the State of the financial services industry, but in such a way as not to affect the objective of the bank in contributing to the stability of the State's financial system (CBA 1942, ss 5A and 5B, as inserted by CBFSAIA 2003, s 5). The bank has power to do whatever is necessary for the performance of its functions.

The bank is required to perform the functions of the European System of Central Banks through its Governor (CBA 1942, s 6 as substituted by CBFSAIA 2003, s 6). In discharging this function, the primary objective is to maintain price stability; while also contributing to the stability of the European financial system and promoting the efficient and effective operation of the payment and settlement systems (CBA 1942, s 6A as inserted by CBFSAIA 2003, s 7). The Governor is required to keep his board of directors informed of his activities in this regard. The bank is independent of political control and influence.

The bank has been given similar powers as the Director of Consumer Affairs in respect of many designated provisions of the Consumer Credit Act 1995 eg Pt III (requirements relating to credit agreements and the form and content there of), Pt IV (matters arising during currency of agreements), Pt V (matters arising on termination of agreements or on default), Pt VI (hire-purchase agreements), Pt VII (consumer-hire agreements), Pt VIII (provisions relating to moneylending), Pt IX (housing loans made by mortgage lenders), and Pt XII (obligation on credit institutions to notify Director of all customer charges): CCA 1995, s 8G inserted by CBFSAIA 2003, s 35, Sch 1. The 2003 Act established the *Irish Financial Services Regulatory Authority* (IFSRA) which operates generally under the Central Bank but with a degree of independence, and which took over these former functions of the Director of Consumer Affairs.

See also Central Bank Act 1971; Central Bank Act 1989; Central Bank Act 1997; Central Bank Act 1998, all as amended by CBFSAIA 2003 Act, s 35, Sch 1. For amendments to CBA 1942 and CBA 1997, see Central Bank and Financial Services Authority of Ireland Act 2004, ss 2–32. See *Central Bank of Ireland v Gildea* [1997] 1 IR 160, SC and ELR 238. [Bibliography: Johnston & O'Conor.] See BUREAU DE CHANGE; CONSUMER AFFAIRS, DIRECTOR OF; EUROPEAN CENTRAL BANK; GOVERNOR OF CENTRAL BANK; IRISH FINANCIAL SERVICES REGULATORY AUTHORITY.

Central Criminal Court. See HIGH COURT.

central office. The administrative office, situated in the Four Courts (qv), established by the Courts (Supplemental Provisions) Act 1961, s 55(1), Sch 8.

centrebinding. The practice which took its name from the case *In re Centrebind Ltd* [1967] 1 WLR 377 whereby a liquidator (qv) appointed at a shareholders' meeting could dissipate the assets of the company prior to the creditors' meeting e g by selling the assets of the company at a very low price to another company closely connected to the existing shareholders. The practice has been countered by limitations put on the liquidator's powers to dispose of assets in the period prior to a creditors' meeting: Companies Act 1990, s 131.

certificate. A statement in writing by a person with a public or official status, concerning some matter within his own knowledge or authority. See DOCUMENTARY EVIDENCE.

certificate of conformity. See BANKRUPTCY, PETITION FOR.

certificate of evidence. See EVIDENCE, CERTIFICATE OF.

certificate of fitness. See BOOKMAKER, LICENSED.

certification, trial by. See TRIAL BY CERTIFICATION.

certification mark. A mark indicating that the goods or services, in connection with which it is used, are certified by the proprietor of the mark in respect of certain *characteristics*: Trade Marks Act 1996, s 55. The *characteristics* are origin, material, mode of manufacture of goods or performance of services, quality, accuracy or other characteristics. A certification mark cannot be registered if the proprietor carries on a business involving the supply of goods and services of the kind certified (TMA 1996, Sch 2, para 4). A certification mark differs from an ordinary trade mark, which is intended to identify the goods or services of a particular proprietor from those of his competitors.

certification service provider. Means a person or public body who issues *certificates* or provides other services related to *electronic signatures* (qv): Electronic Commerce Act 2000, s 2(1). A *certificate* means an electronic attestation which links signature verification data to a person or public body, and confirms the identity of the person or public body (ECA 2000, s 2(1)). There is no requirement for licensing of service providers; however, the Minister is required to prescribe a scheme of supervision of service providers established in the State, who issue *qualified certificates* to the public i e certificates which meet the requirements set out in Annex I (ECA 2000, s 29(3) and Sch). A certification service provider is liable for any damage caused to a person who (or a public body which) relies on a certificate issued by the service provider (ECA 2000, s 30). See ELECTRONIC SIGNATURE.

certified copy. A copy of a public document, signed and certified as a true copy by the officer to whose custody the original is entrusted, and admissible as evidence when the original would be admissible. Attested copies of all documents filed in the High Court are admissible in evidence in all causes and matters and between all persons and parties to the same extent as the originals would be admissible: RSC Ord 39, r 3. See DOCUMENTARY EVIDENCE.

certified trade union. See TRADE UNION, CERTIFIED.

certiorari. An order of the High Court granted in exercise of its general superintending and corrective jurisdiction over orders of inferior courts for the purpose of bringing up orders for review: *The State (Hunt) v C J Midland Circuit* [1934] IR 196. The grounds for an order of certiorari include where there is: want or excess of jurisdiction; error apparent on the face of an order of an inferior court; disregard of the essentials of justice; bias or disqualification of the court or tribunal; fraud: *R (Martin) v Mahony* [1910] 2 IR 695; *Lennon v Clifford* [1993] ILRM 77, HC.

Certiorari is also the appropriate remedy where a court or tribunal apparently acts within jurisdiction but where the proceedings are so fundamentally flawed as to deprive an accused of a trial in due course of law: *Sweeney v District Judge Brophy* [1993] ILRM 449, SC.

Certiorari however must not be used as a method of appealing decisions of inferior courts: *The State (Daly) v Ruane* [1988] ILRM 117. An *appeal* is a more appropriate remedy, rather than a *judicial review* for an order of certiorari to quash a conviction, where there are allegations of unfair procedures in a criminal trial (eg non-attendance of witness and non-disclosure of documents favourable to an accused): *Maher v O'Donnell* [1996] 2 ILRM 321, HC. However, the presence of an appeal does not bar the court exercising its discretion having considered the requirements of justice: *Stefan v Minister for Justice* [2002] 2 ILRM 134, SC and [2001] 4 IR 203, SC.

Certiorari is also not available to correct an error in respect of the discrepancy between a written order and an oral order of a court: *The State (Wilson) v D J Nealon* [1987] ILRM 118. However, it may be available where there is an adequate remedy which has been inadequately prosecuted: *Duff v D J Mangan & Judge Gleeson* [1994] 1 ILRM 91, SC.

An order of certiorari is frequently used to review and to quash decisions of bodies which, or of persons who, have exceeded their legal powers. Delay or lack of candour does not, of itself, disentitle a person to an order of certiorari where it can be shown that a public wrong has been done to him and that the wrong continues to mark his life: *The State (Furey) v Minister for Justice and Attorney-General* [1988] ILRM 89.

Certiorari is a discretionary remedy; if an order would confer no practical benefit to an applicant, relief will be refused: *Ryan v Compensation Tribunal* [1997] 1 ILRM 194, HC. See also *The State (Gleeson) v Minister for Defence* [1976] IR 280; *The State (Keeney) v O'Malley* [1986] ILRM 31; *McGirl v McArdle* [1989] IR 596; *O'Neill v Iarnród Éireann* [1991] ELR 1, SC; *Matthews v Irish Coursing Club* [1992] ITLR (30 March), HC; *Bannon v Employment Appeals Tribunal* [1992] ELR 203, HC; *Harte v Labour Court* [1996] 2 ILRM 450, HC and ELR 181; *Bane v Garda Representative Association* [1997] 2 IR 449, HC; *de Roiste v Minister for Defence* [2001] 2 ILRM 241, SC; 1 IR 190 and ELR 33. See

CONVICTION; JUDICIAL REVIEW; PROHIBITION; STATE SIDE ORDERS.

certitudine indigent sunt referenda. [Subsequent words, added for the purpose of certainty, are to be referred to preceding words which need certainty.]

certum est quod certum reddi potest. [That which is capable of being made certain is to be treated as certain.] See *Duncombe v Brighton Club and Norfolk Hotel Company* [1875] LR 10 QB 371.

cess. See GRAND JURY.

cessante causa, cessat effectus. [When the cause ceases, the effect ceases.]

cessante ratione legis, cessat ipsa lex. [When the reason of the law ceases, the law itself ceases.] This maxim may apply to common law, but not generally to statute law.

cessante statu primitivio cessat derivativus. [The original estate ceasing, that which derived from it ceases.]

cessat executio. [Suspending execution.]

cessate grant. A grant of administration of a deceased's estate which is given to a minor, named as an executor, on attaining his majority; it has the effect of terminating the powers of an administrator *durante minore aetate* (qv).

cessation notice. See INDOOR EVENT.

cesser. Ending or determination. Where an executor renounces probate, there is cesser of his right to prove the will.

cestui que trust. [He for whom is the trust.] A beneficiary of a trust.

cestui que use. See USE.

cestui que vie. The person for whose lifetime another holds an estate or interest in land. See LIFE ESTATE.

cestuis que trust. Beneficiaries of a trust (qv).

ceteris paribus. [Other things being equal.]

cf, confer. Compare.

chain of representation. See EXECUTORSHIP BY REPRESENTATION.

chain of title. The instruments which show the successive conveyances from the original source to the present owner. See MARKETABLE TITLE.

chairman. Person who regulates the proceedings of a meeting. At a general meeting of a company, the chairman has the duty of ensuring that the business before the meeting is properly conducted. His rulings on points of order and related matters are deemed *prima facie* to be correct (see *John v Rees* [1970] Ch 345). He normally has a casting vote where there is an equality of votes: Companies Act 1963, Table A, art 61. It has been held that the casting vote of a chairman who has been invalidly appointed is void: *Clark v Workman* [1920] 1 IR 107.

challenge to jurors. See JUROR, CHALLENGE TO.

chambers. The rooms of judges. A judge sitting in chambers can exercise the full jurisdiction of the court. Applications which in the opinion of the judge would be more conveniently and expeditiously disposed of in chambers than in open court, may be made to and heard by the judge in chambers: Circuit Court Rules 2001 Ord 20.

Some statutes require proceedings to be in chambers for reasons of confidentiality eg proceedings regarding the legal right of a testator's spouse; making provision for children; and excluding persons from succession as being unworthy to succeed: Succession Act 1965, ss 119 and 122.

The Supreme Court has acknowledged that it has long been the practice for a trial judge occasionally to invite the legal representatives of the parties to come to his chambers in the absence of clients, with a view to facilitating the resolution of issues; the judge must ensure that the rights of the parties to the proceedings are not affected by such a course: *Shannon v McCartan* [2002] 2 IR 377, SC. See PUBLIC JUSTICE.

champerty. The maintenance and finance by a person, not necessarily a solicitor, of an action or litigation in order to make a gain; it is a common law misdemeanour (qv) (now, offence). Where a person undertakes actively to assist in the recovery of shares of an estate to which other persons are entitled, an agreement whereby the former will receive a percentage of the shares of the latter savours of champerty and is void: *McElroy (t/a Irish Genealogical Services) v Flynn* [1991] ILRM 294, HC.

The law of maintenance and champerty has not undergone any change since the nineteenth century: *Fraser v Buckle* [1996] 2 ILRM 34 and 1 IR 1, SC.

The law of champerty condemns, as contrary to Irish public policy, any agreement where a person *maintains* an action in consideration of a promise to give the maintainer a share in the subject matter or proceeds thereof; *maintenance* is defined as giving of assistance or encouragement to one of the parties to an action by a person who has neither an interest in the action

nor any other motive, recognised by law, as justifying his interference: *Fraser v Buckle* [1994] 1 ILRM 276, HC.

The law relating to champerty must not be extended so as to deprive a person of their constitutional right of access to the courts; consequently, it is doubtful whether the fact that an action is being maintained in an unlawful and champertous manner is in itself a defence to an action: *O'Keeffe v Scales* [1998] 1 ILRM 393 and 1 IR 290, SC.

It is not illegal for solicitors taking action on behalf of persons of little or no means to charge a solicitor/client fee estimated at 10% of the moneys recoverable, particularly where the solicitor had paid all the expenses in relation to the case out of his own pocket: *obiter dictum* in *Kennedy v Nolan* [1990] ITLR (23 October), HC. See also *Rees v De Bernardy* [1896] 2 Ch 437. See Twomey A F, *Competition, Compassion and Champerty* (1994) 4 ISLR 1. See CONTINGENCY FEE; HEIR-LOCATOR; NO FOAL NO FEE.

chancery. The court of chancery was a court of *equity* (qv), presided over by the Lord Chancellor, which was merged in the High Court by the Judicature Act 1873.

chance-medley. The killing of an aggressor in self-defence in the course of a sudden brawl or quarrel. It has been held in England that the doctrine of chance-medley has no longer any place in the law of *homicide* and that each case must now be decided on the principles of self-defence (qv) or provocation (qv): *R v Semini* [1949] 1 KB 405.

change of parties. The change permitted in the parties to an action after proceedings have commenced eg because of death or bankruptcy or where there is misjoinder (qv) or non-joinder (qv). For rules of court governing the change in parties in proceedings, see High Court, RSC Ord 17, r 4; RSC Ord 15; Circuit Court, Circuit Court Rules 2001 Ord 22.

change of user. See PLANNING PERMISSION.

character. Reputation and disposition: *Selvey v DPP* [1970] AC 304.

character, evidence of. Evidence as to the character of a person is generally inadmissible in proceedings, unless character is in issue or is relevant. In civil cases, the character of the plaintiff is in issue in defamation (qv) cases eg where the defence claims justification (qv). In criminal cases, evidence of the good character of the accused is always relevant and admissible. Evidence of the bad character of the accused is admissible in the following instances: (a) where the accused seeks to establish his good character, the prosecution may rebut it by giving evidence of his bad character including previous convictions; and (b) an accused person, who gives evidence, may be cross-examined as to his bad character and previous convictions in specified circumstances: Criminal Justice (Evidence) Act 1924, s 1(f).

However, claims that the gardaí fabricated a confession by the accused does not put his character in issue: *DPP v McGrail* [1990] ITLR (19 February), CCA. Also evidence of bad reputation should never found a view that an accused had been guilty of offences: *DPP v Martin* [1991] ITLR (4 November), CCA.

The character of the person prosecuting may be relevant in rape and similar offences e g Criminal Law (Rape) Act 1981, s 3 as amended by the Criminal Law (Rape) Amendment Act 1990, s 13. The character of a witness is always relevant as to his credit (qv). See *Attorney-General v O'Leary* [1926] IR 445; *Attorney-General v O'Sullivan* [1930] IR 552. *See Hill v Cork Examiner Publications Ltd* [2001] 4 IR 219, SC; *The People (DPP) v Shortt* [2002] 2 IR 686, CCA. In the event that a court puts any question to the solicitor for the accused as to the character of the accused, whether his character is or is not in issue, the solicitor's reply should be that the question is not one for him to answer: *A Guide to Professional Conduct of Solicitors in Ireland* (2002) ch 5.1. See CONVICTION, EVIDENCE OF; CROSS-EXAMINATION.

character or quality of goods. Formerly, words which had no direct reference to the character or quality of goods, could be registered as a trade mark (qv) under Part A of the register. *See Fry-Cadbury (Ireland) Ltd v Synott* [1935] IR 700; *Bulmers Ltd v Showerings Ltd* [1962] IR 189. See PART A.

charge. (1) A criminal accusation. (2) A judge's instructions to a jury. See CHARGE SHEET; LIEN; FIXED CHARGE; FLOATING CHARGE; CHARGE, REGISTRATION OF; SURCHARGE.

charge, registration of. The systems which exist to register charges on a person's property to enable others to determine the assets which are mortgaged. The systems often impute notice of the existence and the

content of the charges registered. Special procedures exist for registering mortgages on land, mortgages on ships, farmers' chattel mortgages, and company charges. See Registration of Title Act 1964; Mercantile Marine Act 1955, s 50; Agricultural Credit Act 1978, s 26. Gift tax and inheritance tax is a charge on registered land whether or not the charge is registered: Capital Acquisitions Tax Consolidation Act 2003, s 113(2).

As regards companies, a wide category of charges must be registered at the Registry of Companies within 21 days of their creation. A registered charge takes priority over an unregistered one, even if the owner of the registered charge knew of the other's existence, and an unregistered charge cannot be enforced in a liquidation; there is provision, however, for the court to extend the time for registration. See Companies Act 1963, ss 99–106. See *In re Manning Furniture* [1996] 1 ILRM 13, HC.

A company is required to register charges it creates on ships or aircraft or any part of an aircraft: Companies Act 1990, s 122 amending s 99 of the CA 1963. Also the Minister may by regulation amend the list of charges requiring registration.

As regards the registration of charges created by a foreign company where the property comprised in the charge is situate in Ireland, see Courtney in *Law Society Gazette* (May 1992) 151. See also *Bank of Ireland Finance v Daly Ltd* [1978] IR 79; *In re Telford Motors Ltd* [1978] HC. See BOOK DEBTS; CHARGE ON LAND; DISCHARGE OF CHARGE; FIXED CHARGE; FLOATING CHARGE; SEARCHES.

charge, take in. A local authority *takes in charge* a road when it declares the road to be a public road and takes over responsibility for its maintenance. A planning authority is required to *take in charge* a housing estate when it is completed, when so requested by the developer or by a majority of qualified electors who are owners or occupiers: Planning and Development Act 2000, s 180(1). The planning authority is empowered to hold a plebiscite to ascertain the wishes of the qualified electors (PDA 2000, s 180(3)). When a housing estate is not completed, the obligation of the planning authority to take it in charge does not arise during the seven-year period during which time the planning authority may take enforcement action to compel the developer to complete the estate (PDA 2000, s 180(2)). See PUBLIC ROAD.

charge card. A card issued by a promoter to an individual having an address in the State by means of which goods, services or cash may be obtained by the individual, and amounts in respect of the goods, services or cash may be charged to the individual's account: Finance (No 2) Act 1981, s 17(2)(a).

charge d'affaires. The subordinate head of a diplomatic mission accredited to the Minister for Foreign Affairs. If the sending state accredits the head of mission to more than one state, it may establish a diplomatic mission headed by a charge d'affaires *ad interim* in each state where the head of mission has not his permanent seat: Diplomatic Relations and Immunities Act 1967, Sch 1, art 5(2). See DIPLOMATIC PRIVILEGE.

charge on land. A charge which the registered owner of land can create to secure an advance of money; the charge must be registered as a charge on the land and the chargeant must be registered as the owner of the charge. The registered owner of the charge has all the powers of a mortgagee (qv) by deed within the meaning of the Conveyancing Acts: Registration of Title Act 1964, s 62.

It has been held that a provision in a deed of charge permitting the registered owner to take possession in the event of certain defaults of the chargor need not be registered on the folio separately from the deed of charge: *Gale & Gale v First National Building Society* [1985] IR 609.

The deposit of a certificate of charge, or of a land certificate (qv) has the same effect as the deposit of title deeds of unregistered land. Money charged on land in the State must be construed, unless otherwise described, as being in the currency of the State: *Northern Bank v Edwards* [1986] ILRM 167. [Bibliography: Johnston.] See DEPOSIT OF TITLE DEEDS; DISCHARGE OF CHARGE.

charge on public funds. The terms of any international agreement involving a charge on public funds, must be approved by Dáil Éireann, otherwise the State is not bound thereby: 1937 Constitution, art 29(5)(2). See *The State (McCaud) v Governor of Mountjoy Prison* [1986] ILRM 129; *The State (Gilliland) v Governor of Mountjoy Prison* [1987] ILRM 278. For example, see Multilateral Investment Guarantee Agency Act 1988.

charge on ship. A charge on a ship in the form of a legal mortgage must comply with the requirements of the Mercantile Marine Act 1955. A yacht is not a ship in this context: *In re South Coast Boatyard, Barbour v Burke* [1980] SC. See CHARGE, REGISTRATION OF.

charge sheet. Whenever a person is arrested and brought to a garda station and is being charged with an offence, particulars of the offence alleged against the person must be set out on a *charge sheet*, a copy of the particulars furnished to the accused, and the charge sheet lodged with the district court clerk: DCR 1997 Ord 17, r 1. See also Treatment of Persons in Custody in Garda Síochána Stations Regulations 1987, SI No 119 of 1987, reg 15.

charge to jury. See SUMMING UP.

charging order. An order of the court made on the application of a judgment-creditor to charge the amount of his judgment upon stocks (qv) or shares (qv) belonging to the judgment-debtor, or upon his interest in funds in court, which application is made ex-parte and grounded on an affidavit of facts: RSC Ord 46, r 1. An order of the court may be obtained subsequently, by motion on notice to the defendant, to have the stocks and shares transferred to the sheriff (qv) to be realised to satisfy the judgment debt (r 2). See also RSC Ord 77, rr 84 and 95.

A solicitor may obtain a *charging order* on property or costs recovered or preserved as a result of his efforts; the charging order is made by the same court which made the original order under which the claim to costs arose: Legal Practitioners Act 1876, s 3; *Lismore Buildings Ltd v Bank of Ireland Finance Ltd (No 2)* [2000] 2 IR 316, SC. [Bibliography: Glanville.] See STOP ORDER.

charitable devise or bequest. Where a will contains a charitable devise or bequest, the Commissioners of Charitable Donations and Bequests (qv) may, in their discretion, require the personal representative: (a) to deliver to them evidence to show that the gift has been transferred to the charity or the trustees of the charity are aware of the gift; or (b) to publish such particulars of the gift as the Commissioners (the *Board*) may require: Charities Act 1973, s 16. The probate officer is required to notify the

Commissioners as to all charitable gifts in wills entered in the probate office (qv).

charitable gift. A gift for charitable purposes: Charities Act 1961. See CHARITIES.

charitable trust. See CHARITIES.

charities. Trusts (qv) in favour of legally *charitable objects*. Such trusts, unlike private trusts, are not subject to the rule against perpetuities (qv) and they do not fail for uncertainty.

A charity must confer a benefit on the public or on a sufficiently wide section of the public. Charitable objects are classified into *four* main divisions: *Income Tax Special Purposes Commissioners v Pemsel* [1891] AC 531; *Barrington's Hospital v Commissioner of Valuations* [1957] IR 299. These are: (a) *relief of poverty* – a public element is essential; (b) *advancement of education* – contrast *University College Cork v Commissioner of Valuations* [1911] 2 IR 593 and *Wesley College v Commissioner of Valuations* [1984] ILRM 17; (c) *advancement of religion* – *religion* includes all religions tolerated by law; a gift for Masses is a charitable purpose: *O'Hanlon v Cardinal Logue* [1906] 1 IR 247; *Halpin v Hannon* [1948] ILTR 75; *In re Greene* [1914] 1 IR 242; (d) *other charitable purposes* – the gift must not only be for the benefit of the community but must be beneficial in a way the law regards as charitable eg *National Anti-vivisection Society v IRC* [1948] AC 31; *In re MacCarthy's Will Trust* [1958] IR 311.

Any body of persons or trust, *established* for charitable purposes only, is exempted from income tax: Income Tax Act 1967, ss 333–334 (now Taxes Consolidation Act 1997, ss 207–208). *Established* means established in the State: *Revenue Commissioners v Sisters of Charity of the Incarnate Word* [1998] 2 IR 552, HC.

Charities are also exempt from tax on capital gains applied for charitable purposes (TCA 1997, s 609); they are exempt from deposit interest retention tax (ss 256 and 266); corporate donations to charities are a trading or management expense of the company making the donation (s 486A); and charities concerned with aid to third world countries may claim repayment of tax in respect of donations received (s 848): Taxes Consolidation Act 1997 as amended by Finance Act 1998, s 61. An upper limit is placed on the tax relief which may be claimed by an individual in respect of a donation to a charity with which the individual is associated: Finance Act 2003,

s 21. A gift or inheritance which is taken for public or charitable purposes is exempt from tax: Capital Acquisitions Tax Consolidation Act 2003, s 76.

The general administration of charities is the responsibility of the Commissioners of Charitable Donations and Bequests for Ireland (qv), a statutory body, appointed by the government. See Charities Acts 1961 and 1973. See also Courts and Court Officers Act 1995, s 52 amending CA 1961, s 29. See Stamp Duties Consolidation Act 1999, s 82. See *Report of the Committee ('Costello Committee') on Fundraising Activities for Charitable and other Purposes* (1990). See also Consultation Paper on *Establishing a Modern Statutory Framework for Charities* (Febuary 2004), available on website: *www.pobail.ie*. See *Law Society Gazette* (January/February 2004) 7. [Bibliography: Delany; Keane (2); Kiely; O'Callaghan J M (2); O'Halloran (2); O'Halloran & Cormacain; Snell UK.] See CY-PRES.

charter. A deed; a constitution; an instrument from the State (formerly, the Crown) conferring rights and privileges. See Adaptation of Charters Act 1926.

A recognised institution which has authority to make awards, delegated to it by the National Qualifications Authority of Ireland, is required to have a charter: Qualifications (Education and Training) Act 1999, s 31. The charter may be required, by Ministerial regulation, to have included eg: (a) its arrangements for consulting with the local community, including commercial and industrial interests; (b) its policy in respect of adult and continuing education; (c) its arrangements for access, transfer and progression; and (d) its procedures in relation to quality assurance. See COMPANY, CHARTERED; ROYAL CHARTER.

Charter of Fundamental Rights. The Charter which sets out in a single text, civil, political, economic and social rights and freedoms of European citizens and all persons resident in the EU: *National Forum on Europe – Glossary of Terms* (2003). The Charter has been incorporated as Part II of the proposed Treaty establishing a Constitution for Europe, agreed on 18 June 2004, but not yet ratified. The Charter would apply to the institutions of the Union and to the governments of the member states only when they were implementing Union law. See EUROPEAN UNION CONSTITUTION; FUNDAMENTAL RIGHTS.

Chartered Accountants in Ireland, Institute of. The professional body established by Royal Charter in 1888 as amended by the Chartered Accountants in Ireland Act 1966, s 6. See *Geoghegan v Institute of Chartered Accountants in Ireland* [1995] 3 IR 86, SC. For the Institute of Chartered Accountants in Ireland, see website: *www.icai.ie*. See ACCOUNTANT.

chartered company. See COMPANY, CHARTERED.

charterparty. A contract between a shipowner and a charterer whereby the shipowner lets the ship to the charterer for the conveyance of goods. The contract must be in writing but need not be sealed. The charterparty may operate as a demise or lease of the ship with or without the services of the master and crew. A *time* charterer of a ship has an interest in the ship which he can enforce against a purchaser of the ship with notice of the charterparty: *Strathcona v Dominion Coal Co* [1926] AC 108; *Port Line Ltd v Ben Line Steamers Ltd* [1958] QB 146. See *The MV 'Turquoise Bleu'* [1996] 1 ILRM 406, HC. See DEMURRAGE.

chattel mortgage. When used without qualification, it means an instrument under seal made between a recognised borrower of the one part and a recognised lender of the other part which is: (a) a floating chattel mortgage; or (b) a specific chattel mortgage; or (c) both a floating and specific chattel mortgage: Agricultural Credit Act 1978, s 23(1). A *floating chattel mortgage* is an instrument under seal whereby the borrower charges stock from time to time on the borrower's land with the payment of any money advanced or to be advanced to the borrower. A *specific chattel mortgage* is one which charges specific stock (wherever situate). A register of chattel mortgages must be kept and maintained in every Circuit Court office (ACA 1978, s 26).

A registered specific chattel mortgage operates and has the effect of prohibiting the mortgagor from selling or otherwise transferring ownership or possession of the stock without giving notice in writing to the mortgagee, and of prohibiting the mortgagor from selling at less than a fair and reasonable price (ACA 1978, s 27). A registered floating chattel mortgage creates an ambulatory and shifting charge on all stock the property of the mortgagor, from time to time on the land to which the chattel mortgage relates (s 30). Priority of chattel mortgages is in accordance with the times at which they are respectively registered (s 34). See also Chattel Mortgages (Registration) Order 1928, SR & O No 40 of 1928. [Bibliography: Forde (5).] See BILL OF SALE.

chattels. Generally property other than freehold. *Chattels real* are leasehold and other interests in land which are less than freehold. *Chattels personal* are movable tangible articles of property eg goods (qv) and choses in possession (qv). It has been held that on the purchase of a chattel, the title to it passes to the person who paid for it: *Fitzpatrick v Criminal Assets Bureau* [2000] 1 IR 217, SC. See CHOSE; HOUSEHOLD CHATTELS; WASTING ASSET.

cheating. Any *common law* offence of cheating, except in relation to the public revenue, is abolished: Criminal Justice (Theft and Fraud Offences) Act 2001, s 3(2). A similar abolition was made in the UK by the Theft Act 1968, s 32. However, the Supreme Court has held that as regards extradition, there is no corresponding common law offence of '*cheating the public revenue*': *Hilton v DPP* (30 July 2004, unreported), SC. See also *R v Sinclair* [1968] 3 All ER 241. For previous legislation, see Gaming and Lotteries Act 1956, s 11, repealed by CJ(TFO)A 2001, s 3 and Sch 1. See now DECEPTION. See also GAMING.

chemical agent. Employers have obligations to protect their employees as regards exposure to chemical agents: Safety, Health and Welfare at Work (Chemical Agents) Regulations 2001, SI No 619 of 2001.

chemical weapon. Means: (a) toxic chemicals except where intended for peaceful purposes or for law enforcement purposes within the State, (b) munitions and devices designed to cause death or otherwise harm through the toxic properties released on their deployment: Chemical Weapons Act 1997, s 2(1) implementing the United Nations Convention on the Prohibition of the Development, Stockpiling and Use of Chemical Weapons and their Destruction, signed by Ireland on 13 January 1993 and ratified on 13 June 1996. The 1997 Act provides a framework for verification and inspection to monitor chemical industries, and for the prevention and destruction of chemical weapons, the objective being to keep Ireland free of chemical weapons and their production facilities.

A licensing scheme has been established relating to the production, use, acquisition or possession of toxic chemicals or precursors listed in the CWA 1997, Sch 1: Chemical Weapons (Licensing of Scheduled Toxic Chemicals and Precursors) Regulations 2001, SI No 54 of 2001. For the Organisation for the Prohibition of Chemical Weapons (OPCW), see website: *www.opcw.org*.

cheque. A bill of exchange (qv) drawn on a banker, payable on demand: Bills of Exchange Act 1882, s 73. The person making the cheque is the *drawer* and the person to whom it is payable is the *payee*. When a cheque bears across its face the words *and company*, or any abbreviation thereof, between two parallel traverse lines, it is said to be *crossed generally*, and when it bears across its face the name of a banker, it is said to be *crossed specially* (BEA 1882, s 76). A generally crossed cheque can be paid only through a bank and a specially crossed cheque only through the bank so specified. A cheque which is crossed *not negotiable* cannot give to the transferee a better title than the holder of the cheque had (BEA 1882, s 81).

It is not open to a drawer of a cheque to question the value of his own cheque; the endorsement by the defendant of a cheque to the plaintiff amounted to an absolute discharge of any indebtedness: *Private Motorists Provident Society v Moore* [1988] ILRM 526, HC. See *Shield Life Insurance Co Ltd v Ulster Bank Ltd* [1995] 3 IR 225, HC. See also Cheques Act 1959; Building Societies Act 1989, ss 29(2)(f) and 126.

The stamp duty on cheques has been increased from midnight on 4 December 2002 to €0.15 per cheque: Finance Act 2003, s 143. [Bibliography: Donnelly; Johnston; McGann; O'Connor; Paget UK; Richardson UK.] See ACCOUNT PAYEE; DAYS OF GRACE; ENDORSEMENT; IRISH PAYMENT SERVICES ORGANISATION; KITING.

cheque, blank. See FEE.

cheque, countermand of payment. Revocation by the drawer of the authority to pay a cheque. *Stopping* a cheque is dishonour by non-payment: *Gaynor v McDyer* [1968] IR 295. A cheque in general is a conditional payment which suspends but does not extinguish a debt; the debt revives if the cheque is countermanded. A banker is liable if he wrongly pays a countermanded cheque. See Bills of Exchange Act 1882, s 75. See *Reade v Royal Bank of Ireland* [1922] 2 IR 22. See *Doyle* in 9 ILT & SJ (1991) 255. See DISHONOUR OF BILL.

cheque, dishonour of. The refusal by the drawee of a cheque (eg a bank) to accept the cheque or having accepted it fails to pay it: Bills of Exchange Act 1882, s 47. With the exception of claims arising on cheques not presented for payment within a reasonable time (s 74) or on specially crossed cheques (s 79(2)) or on cheques marked good by the paying bank, the general principle is that a payee named in a cheque has no right of action against the bank on which the cheque is drawn if the cheque is dishonoured: *Dublin Port & Docks Board v Bank of Ireland* [1976] IR 118. However, this is subject to qualification if the bank, without lawful justification, embarks on a course of conduct which is calculated to deceive the payee in a manner which may result in financial loss to such payee: *TE Potterton Ltd v Northern Bank Ltd* [1993] ILRM 225, HC. See also *Curtis v Kenny* [2001] 2 IR 96, HC. See BANKER, DUTY OF CARE.

cheque, drawing of. Drawing a cheque implies three statements: (a) that the drawer has an account with that bank; (b) that he has authority to draw on it for that amount; and (c) that the cheque, as drawn, is a valid order for that amount (ie that the present state of affairs is such that, in the ordinary course of events, the cheque will on its future presentation be duly honoured). The drawing of a cheque by a company does not itself operate as a disposition of the funds in the accounts of a company; the disposition occurs when the cheque is paid: *In re Ashmark Ltd (in liquidation) v Nitra Ltd* [1990] ITLR (5 March), HC.

cheque, issue. A cheque is *issued* at the time of its first delivery complete in form to the person who takes it as a holder: Bills of Exchange Act 1882, s 2.

cheque, liability on. A banker who pays a cheque drawn on him in good faith and in the ordinary course of business, is not liable to the true owner if an endorsement is forged: Bills of Exchange Act 1882, s 60. Also, where a banker pays the holder of a cheque, in good faith and without notice that the holder's title is defective, the payment is valid and the banker is entitled to debit the customer's account (BEA 1882, s 59).

In order to obviate the long established practice by which bankers refused to pay a cheque unless it was endorsed at the bank by the party presenting it, the law was changed in 1959 to provide that, 'where a banker in good faith and in the ordinary course of business pays a cheque drawn on him which is not endorsed, or is irregularly endorsed, he does not in doing so, incur any liability by reason only of the absence of, or irregularity in, endorsement, and he is deemed to have paid it in due course': Cheques Act 1959, s 1.

A collecting banker is protected from liability to the true owner of a cheque where the banker receives payment of the cheque for a *customer*, who has no title, or a defective title to the cheque, provided the banker acts in good faith and without negligence: Cheques Act 1959, s 4. A collecting banker is also protected if he becomes a *holder for value* (qv) or a *holder in due course* (qv).

cheque, overdue. A cheque which has been in circulation for an unreasonable time. It can only be negotiated subject to any defect of title affecting it at its maturity. See Bills of Exchange Act 1882, s 36(2) and(3). See MATURITY.

cheque, post-dated. A cheque which bears a date subsequent to the actual date on which it was drawn, and issued before the date it bears. A cheque is not invalid by reason only that it is post-dated: Bills of Exchange Act 1882, s 13(2). See *Royal Bank of Scotland v Tottenham* [1894] 71 LT 168.

cheque, presentation by notification. Provision has been made for presentation for payment by a collecting banker of a cheque *by notification* to the drawee banker of the *essential features of the cheque* other than by its physical presentation: Bills of Exchange Act 1882, s 45A, as inserted by the Central Bank Act 1989, s 132(1)(c). Presentation by notification includes presentation by the transmission of an electronic message.

A cheque paid on presentation by notification is deemed to have been paid in the *ordinary course of business* but this does not relieve the collecting banker or the drawee banker from the liability they would have been subject to if the cheque had been physically presented for payment. The drawee banker can request the physical presentation of the cheque and this does not constitute *dishonour* of the cheque for non-payment.

The *essential features of the cheque* include: the serial number, the identification code number of the drawee banker, the account number of the drawer of the cheque, and the amount of the cheque.

cheque, stale. A cheque which is *out of date* ie one bearing a date of twelve (or, in some cases, six) months prior to presentation. See *London County Banking Co v Groome* [1881] 8 QBD 288.

cheque, stopping of. See CHEQUE, COUNTERMAND OF PAYMENT.

cheque, unendorsed. A solicitor is prohibited from lodging to his own account an unendorsed cheque or other negotiable or non-negotiable instrument drawn in favour of another person: Solicitors Act 1954, s 66(17) as amended by Solicitors (Amendment) Act 1994, s 76.

cheque card. A card issued by a bank (or building society) and presented with a cheque to a supplier of goods or services, who as a consequence is assured of payment by the bank to a stated maximum amount. The drawer of the cheque represents that he has authority from the bank to use the card so as to oblige the bank to honour the cheque. See *Metropolitan Police Comr v Charles* [1977] AC 177. See IRISH PAYMENT SERVICES ORGANISATION.

cheque clearing system. The system established in 1845 by the main banks, which then became known as the *associated banks*, and which involved the physical exchange between the banks of cheques drawn upon each other, with a settlement of the difference in value being made on a daily basis. In time, a central clearing house was established in London and the main UK provincial cities, including Dublin. The cheque clearing system and other type of payment and settlement systems have been brought under the control of the Central Bank: Central Bank Act 1997, ss 5–21 as amended by Central Bank and Financial Services Authority of Ireland Act 2003, s 35, Sch 1. See also Central Bank Act 1989, s 132. See Australian case *Riedel v Commercial Bank of Australia Ltd* [1931] VLR 382. See IRISH PAYMENT SERVICES ORGANISATION.

Chicago Convention. The Convention on International Civil Aviation opened for signature at Chicago on 7 December 1944 and Annexes thereto. Under the Convention, Ireland has responsibility for a substantial area of airspace known as the

Stanwick (Shannon and Prestwick) Oceanic CTA of the North Atlantic in co-operation with the UK. The Irish Aviation Authority is empowered to make orders to give effect to the Annexes and to apply the Annexes to aircraft which are in or over Ireland: Irish Aviation Authority Act 1993, s 59. Under an agreement reached by the Irish Aviation Authority (IAA) with the UK authorities in 2003, the IAA will from January 2005 control an additional area known as NOTA – Northern Oceanic Transition Area.

Chief Herald of Ireland. A member of the staff of the National Library of Ireland designated to perform the duty of researching, granting and confirming *coats of arms*: National Cultural Institutions Act 1997, s 13(2). The Register which is controlled by the Chief Herald and which may be inspected by the public at his discretion, contains grants, certificates and confirmations. *Certificates* are given to recognise arms originally given by another heraldic authority. *Confirmations* maintain the practice of the Ulster Kings of Arms who recognised arms by the grant of *letters patent* on the basis of use over 100 years or three generations. *Grants* are made to Irish citizens, to persons domiciled in Ireland, as well as to schools, colleges, associations and bodies in Ireland. Grants are also made to persons who are domiciled outside Ireland but who can prove descent from a known Irish ancestor. See COLLECTIVE MARK; NATIONAL LIBRARY OF IRELAND.

Chief Justice. The presiding judge of the Supreme Court (qv); he is also ex officio an additional judge of the High Court (qv): 1937 Constitution, art 34(4)(2); Courts (Establishment and Constitution) Act 1961, ss 1(2) and 2(3). The Chief Justice is an ex officio member of the Council of State (qv) and of the Presidential Commission (qv). He is empowered to appoint notaries public and commissioners to administer oaths. The Chief Justice arranges the distribution and allocation of the business of the Supreme Court: Courts and Court Officers Act 1995, s 8.

Where the Chief Justice is of opinion that the conduct of a judge of the District Court has been such as to bring the administration of justice into disrepute, he may interview the judge privately and inform him of such opinion (C(EC)A 1961, s 10(4)). If the Chief Justice is unable, owing to illness or any other reason, to transact the business of his office, his powers may be exercised by the President of the High Court (C(EC)A 1961, s 10(2)).

The appointment of Chief Justice is now for a seven- year non-renewable period: Courts (No 2) Act 1997, s 4. The Chief Justices since the establishment of the State have been: The Hon Mr Justice John Murray (July 2004 – present); Ronan Keane (2000 to July 2004); Liam Hamilton (1994–2000); Thomas A Finlay (1985–94): Thomas F O'Higgins (1974–85); William O'Brien Fitzgerald (1973–74); Cearbhall O'Dalaigh (1961–72); Conor A Maguire (1946–61); Timothy Sullivan (1936–46); Hugh Kennedy (1925–36). See JUDGES; NOTARY PUBLIC.

chief office. A building society is required to have an office in the State (to be known as its chief office) to which all communications and notices (qv) may be addressed: Building Societies Act 1989, s 15. See BUILDING SOCIETY.

Chief Prosecution Solicitor. The *Chief Prosecution Solicitor* is solicitor to the Director of Public Prosecutions. The office of the CPS was formally launched on 11 May 2002 with the objective of achieving greater cohesion of the prosecution service under the DPP and was one of the central recommendations of the report of the *Public Prosecution Systems Study Group* available on website: *www.dppireland.ie*. Formerly the prosecution service was provided by the criminal division of the Chief State Solicitor's office. The change was given legal effect by providing that the *Chief State Solicitor* means the Chief Prosecution Solicitor where the Director of Public Prosecutions is a party or intended party to proceedings or in respect of functions conferred on the DPP by s 3 of the Prosecution of Offences Act 1974 or otherwise: RSC Ord 125, r 1 as amended by insertion by Rules of the Superior Courts (No 4) (Chief Prosecution Solicitor) 2001, SI No 535 of 2001. See 'Hail to the Chief' in *Law Society Gazette* (July/August 2002) 35.

Chief State Solicitor. The current functions of the Chief State Solicitor are to act as solicitor to Ireland, the Attorney-General and government departments and offices. These functions include: (a) carrying out all conveyancing of State property, including Landlord and Tenant and other land law matters; (b) furnishing of legal advice on the various matters that are submitted by government departments and offices and the drafting of the necessary accompanying legal documents; (c) preparing and presenting all prosecutions initiated by Ministers or Government Departments; (d) acting as agent of the Government before the European Court of Justice; (e) acting for the State in enquiries under the Tribunals of Enquiry (Evidence) Acts 1921–1998, and supplying legal staff to act for the tribunals, the public interest and other relevant State authorities; (f) providing a solicitor service in all civil courts and tribunals in which the State or any State authority is involved; (g) discharging functions under the 1965 Hague Convention on the Service Abroad of Judicial and Extrajudicial Documents in Civil or Commercial Matters; (h) representing the State and State Authorities including the Director of Public Prosecutions in taxation of costs before the Taxing Masters.

There are also 32 local State Solicitors who undertake State work on a contract basis for areas outside of Dublin. The bulk of this work relates to criminal matters for which the Office of the *Chief Prosecution Solicitor* (qv) is responsible. See STATE SOLICITOR.

child. A person under the age of 18 years other than a person who is or has been married: Child Care Act 1991, s 2(1). A person under the age of 18 years: Children Act 2001, s 3(1). For tax purposes, a *child* includes a stepchild and an adopted child; an adopted child is regarded as the child of the adopted parents and not of the biological parents: Taxes Consolidation Act 1997, s 6; Capital Acquisitions Tax Consolidation Act 2003, s 2. For the purposes of sexual offences committed outside the State, a *child* is a person under the age of 17 years: Sexual Offences (Jurisdiction) Act 1996, s 1(1). For the purposes of the investigation of complaints regarding administrative functions of certain bodies, a *child* means a person under the age of 18 years: Ombudsman for Children Act 2002, s 2(1). Under recent legislation, a child means a person not more than 18 years of age: Education for Persons with Special Educational Needs Act 2004, s 1(1).

For rules of the district court relating to proceedings involving children and young persons, see DCR 1997 Ord 37. See also *A Guide to Professional Conduct of Solicitors in Ireland* (2002), App 4, paras 18–31. See 'Children and the Welfare Principle' by Alma Clissman and 'Age of Innocents' by

Geoffrey Shannon in *Law Society Gazette* (April 2004) 7 and 12 respectively. [Bibliography: Kilkelly (1); McDermott & Robinson; Power C; Shannon.] See AGE; MINOR; OMBUDSMAN FOR CHILDREN; SEX TOURISM; SPECIAL EDUCATIONAL NEEDS.

child, access to. The right of the non-custodial parent to see and share the company of children of the family. Access to children is a basic right of parents but it may be lost by the misbehaviour of a parent. The courts will usually grant the right to access to take place at particular times. A person who is a relative of a child, or has acted *in loco parentis* to a child, may apply to the court for an order giving that person access to the child on such terms and conditions as the court may order: Guardianship of Infants Act 1964, s 11B as inserted by Children Act 1997, s 9.

When a court grants a decree of divorce, it may give such directions as it considers proper regarding access to any dependent member of the family concerned who is a child: Family Law (Divorce) Act 1996, ss 5(2) and 15(1)(f).

A health board is required to facilitate reasonable access to a child in its care by his parents, any person acting *in loco parentis*, or any other person who has a *bona fide* interest in the child; the court may make an order refusing to allow a named person access to such a child in order to safeguard or promote the child's welfare: Child Care Act 1991, s 37. See also Guardianship of Infants Act 1964, s 11 and Judicial Separation and Family Reform Act 1989, s 11(b); Domestic Violence Act 1996, s 20. For district court procedure in relation to access to a child, see DCR 1997 Ord 84, rr 25–30. See CARE ORDER; CHILD, CUSTODY OF; GUARDIAN.

child, adopted. A child in respect of whom an *adoption order* has been made. In general, adoption is restricted to orphans and children whose parents are not married to each other; such children must be at least six weeks old and if over the age of seven years be consulted, and must be under the age of eighteen years (previously 21). In 1988, the categories of children who could be adopted was extended and the age was reduced to under eighteen years: Adoption Act 1988.

An adopted child has the same property and succession rights after the making of an adoption order as a child of the adopter or adopters born in lawful wedlock: Adoption

Act 1952, s 26; Succession Act 1965, s 110; this does not infringe the rights under the Constitution of natural born children of a marriage: *The State (Nicolaou) v An Bord Uchtála* [1966] IR 567. A reference in a will or other disposition is to be interpreted as including a child adopted subsequent to the making of the will or disposition: Status of Children Act 1987, s 27(4).

This provision reverses the previous law in that regard by providing that an adopted person, unless a contrary intention appears, is entitled to take under a disposition in the same manner as he would have been entitled to take if, at the date of the adoption order, he had been born in lawful wedlock to the person or persons who adopted him. See Taxes Consolidation Act 1997, s 6. See also Capital Acquisitions Tax Consolidation Act 2003, s 2 where a 'child' is defined as including an adopted child.

Also a gift or inheritance taken by an adopted child from a natural parent, is entitled to the benefit of the group threshold for a child of the donor or disponer before it attracts *capital acquisitions tax*: Finance Act 2001, s 222; now consolidated by CATCA 2003, Sch 2, Pt 1(1). See ADOPTION; ADOPTION, BIRTH RECORDS; ISSUE.

child, advancement. See ADVANCEMENT, CHILD.

child, begetting of. See BEGET.

child, born out of wedlock. See CHILD, ILLEGITIMATE.

child, care of. The High Court has held that the State has an obligation under the Constitution to provide appropriate care facilities for children in special difficulty; if the State fails to so provide, the court ought to exercise its right and duty to protect those rights, even if to do so would be to interfere with the activities of the executive: *TD (a minor) v Minister for Education, Ireland, A-G, Minister for Health* [2000] ITLR (3 April), HC. This decision was overturned in the Supreme Court, holding that in so far as the order of the High Court purported to force the government to implement a particular policy, that court was in breach of the doctrine of the *separation of powers* (qv): *TD (a minor) v Minister for Education* [2001] 4 IR 259, SC. See *Eastern Health Board Board v McDonnell* [1999] 1 IR 174, HC. [Bibliography: Nestor; O'Halloran (3); Ward.] See AFTER-CARE; CARE ORDER; CHILD, EMERGENCY

CARE OF; CHILD IN CARE; MOOT; WARD OF COURT; WELFARE OF CHILDREN.

child, confidentiality and. See ANONYMITY; PARENTAGE, DECLARATION OF; PUBLIC JUSTICE.

child, crime and. The court may now order that compensation be paid by the parent or guardian of a child who has been found guilty of an offence, where it is satisfied that a wilful failure of the parent or guardian to take care of or to control the child, contributed to the child's criminal behaviour: Children Act 2001, s 113. See DCR 1997 Ord 33. For previous legislation, see Children's Act 1908, s 99.

In relation to sexual offences alleged to have been committed by a 14 year old child, it was held by the Supreme Court that there should be no delay, so that the trial would take place when memories were fresh and while the accused was reasonably close to the age at which he was alleged to have committed the offences: *B F v Director of Public Prosecutions* [2001] 1 IR 656, SC. See 'Babes in the hood' by solicitor Geoffrey Shannon in *Law Society Gazette* (November 2003) 12. [Bibliography: Shannon (2).] See also ANONYMITY; COMPENSATION ORDER; DEPRAVED; DOLI INCAPAX; FAMILY CONFERENCE; SPECIAL CARE ORDER; PUNISHMENT OF CHILD; REFORMATORY SCHOOLS.

child, cruelty to. See CRUELTY TO CHILDREN.

child, custody of. In deciding on the question of custody and access to children, the courts must have regard to their welfare as the first and paramount consideration; welfare comprises their religious and moral, intellectual, physical and social welfare: *S v S* [1992] ILRM 732, SC, Judicial Separation and Family Law Reform Act 1989, s 3 and Guardianship of Infants Act 1964, s 11.

When a court grants a decree of divorce, it may give such directions under GIA 1964, s 11 as it considers proper, as regarding custody and welfare of any dependent member of the family concerned who is a child: Family Law (Divorce) Act 1996, ss 5(2) and 15(1)(f). The court is empowered to declare either of the spouses to be unfit to have custody of any dependent member of the family (FL(D)A 1996, s 41).

It has been held that an unmarried mother has a constitutional right to the custody and control of her child: *G v An*

Bord Uchtála [1980] IR 32. It has also been held not to be unconstitutional to allow the adoption of an illegitimate child without the consent of the father: *The State (Nicolaou) v An Bord Uchtála* [1966] IR 567. However, for consultation requirements, see ADOPTION.

All matters concerning the guardianship and custody of children must be decided on the basis of the welfare of the child and to the constitutional principle that parents have equal rights to, and are joint guardians of, their children: Guardianship of Infants Act 1964, ss 3 and 6.

In disputes relating to the custody of children, in general, young children will be given into the custody of their mother; parents or a parent will be given custody as against a stranger or the State: (GIA 1964, s 10). However, see *S v S* [1992] ILRM 732, SC where custody was given to the father.

Previously, in relation to an illegitimate child, the natural mother had a constitutional right to the custody of the child, while the natural father could apply to the court for an order for custody of the child (GIA 1964, s 6(4) and 11(4)); the natural father and mother may now agree custody by way of a statutory declaration (GIA 1964, s 2 as inserted by Children Act 1997, s 4). The court in making an order under s 11 may grant custody to the father and mother jointly (GIA 1964, s 11A as inserted by CA 1997, s 9). See also *In re O'Brien* [1954] IR 1; *The State (McP) v G* [1965] HC; *B v B* [1975] IR 54.

Where a court grants a decree of judicial separation or a decree of nullity, it may declare either spouse to be unfit to have custody of any dependent child of the family; if that spouse is the parent of the child, he will not, on the death of the other spouse, be entitled as of right to the custody of that child: Judicial Separation and Family Law Reform Act 1989, s 41; Family Law Act 1995, s 46. See also JSFLRA 1989, s 11(b). See DCR 1997 Ord 58; District Court (Custody and Guardianship of Children) Rules 1999, SI No 125 of 1999. See 'Family Law aspects of the European Convention on Human Rights Act 2003' by Dervla Browne BL in *Bar Review* (April 2004) 39. See CARE ORDER; CHILD ABDUCTION; CHILD IN CARE; GUARDIAN; MOOT; NATURAL PARENTS.

child, disturbed. The jurisdiction of the High Court to detain a child in a penal institution must be exercised in extreme and rare occasions, and only when the court is satisfied that it is required for a short period in the interest of the welfare of the child and there is no other suitable facility: *DG v Eastern Health Board* [1998] 1 ILRM 241 and [1997] 3 IR 511, SC.

The State is under a constitutional obligation to establish as soon as reasonably practical, suitable arrangements of containment with treatment for disturbed young offenders: *F N v Minister for Health* [1995] 2 ILRM 297, HC; *DB v Minister for Justice* [1999] 1 ILRM 93, HC. See Greene v Governor of Mountjoy Prison [1996] SC 2 ILRM 16 and [1995] SC 3 IR 541. See also 'Age of Innocents' by solicitor Geoffrey Shannon in *Law Society Gazette* (April 2004) 12. See CHILD OFFENDER, DISTURBED.

child, emergency care of. An emergency care order placing a child in the care of the health board for eight or lesser days may be made by a judge of the District Court on application of the health board if he is of the opinion that there is a reasonable cause to believe that: (a) there is an immediate and serious risk to the health or welfare of the child; or (b) there is likely to be such risk if the child is removed from the place where he is for the time being: Child Care Act 1991, s 13.

A garda may enter, by force if need be, a house or other place and remove a child to safety if he has reasonable grounds for believing that: (a) there is an immediate and serious risk to the health or welfare of the child; and (b) it would not be sufficient to await the making of an application for an emergency care order (CCA 1991, s 12). An appeal from an emergency care order does not stay the order (CCA 1991, s 13(5)). It is not necessary to name the child in an application or order if such name is unknown (CCA 1991, s 13(6)). A health board may also obtain a *care order* or *interim* care order. See Child Care Regulations 1995 – residential care, foster care, placement with relative, SIs No 259, 260 and 261 of 1995 respectively. [Bibliography: Ward.] See CARE ORDER; fosterchild; welfare of children.

child, employment of. For the purposes of employment, a child is a person who is under 16 years of age or the school-leaving age (qv), whichever is the higher: Protection of Young Persons (Employment) Act 1996, s 1(1). It is an offence for an employer to employ a child to do work, except that an employer may employ a child over the age of 14 years to do light work *outside the school term*, provided that: (a) the work is not harmful to the safety, health and development of the child; (b) the work hours do not exceed seven hours in a day or 35 hours in any week; and (c) the child does not do any work for a period of at least 21 days during the summer holidays (PYP(E)A 1996, s 3(4)). Also an employer may employ a child over 15 years of age to do *light* work *during the school term*, provided that the hours of work do not exceed eight hours in any week (PYP(E)A 1996, s 3(5)).

There are also provisions which permit the employment of a child, by Ministerial licence or regulation, in specified circumstances e g in cultural, artistic, sports or advertising activities (PYP(E)A 1996, ss 3(2)–(3)).There are also provisions setting minimum rest periods (PYP(E)A 1996, s 4). *Light work* is work which is not industrial work and which is not likely to be harmful to children and their school attendance (PYP(E)A 1996, s 1(1)). An employer may employ a child over the age of fifteen to participate in training or work experience, not greater than eight hours per day or 40 hours per week (PYP(E)A 1996, s 3(8)). An employer, prior to employing a child, must have satisfactory evidence of the child's age and the written permission of the parent or guardian (PYP(E)A 1996, s 5). See also Organisation of Working Time Act 1997, s 36; Intoxicating Liquor Act 1988, s 38. See YOUNG PERSON; DOUBLE EMPLOYMENT.

child, evacuation of. A party to an armed conflict must not arrange the evacuation of children, other than their own nationals, to a foreign country: (a) except for a temporary evacuation where compelling reasons of the health or medical treatment of the children so requires: or (b) except in occupied territory where their safety so requires: Geneva Conventions (Amendment) Act 1998, Sch 5, art 78. To facilitate the return of evacuated children to their families and country, the Minister may establish an information card in respect of each child (GC(A)A 1998, s 12).

child, evidence of. In *civil* cases, the unsworn evidence of a child under 14 years of age may be received in evidence if the court is satisfied that the child is capable of giving an intelligible account of events

which are relevant to the proceedings: Children Act 1997, s 28. This also applies to a person with a mental disability of any age (CA 1997, s 28(3)). The unsworn evidence may corroborate sworn or unsworn evidence given by any other person (CA 1997, s 28(4)). Previously, it had been held that a child's unsworn evidence in a civil case could not be accepted even if both parties to the action agreed to such a course: *Mapp v Gilhooley* [1991] ILRM 695, SC.

In *criminal* proceedings, the unsworn evidence of a child under 14 years of age may be received in evidence if the court is satisfied that he is capable of giving an intelligible account of events which are relevant to the proceedings: Criminal Evidence Act 1992, s 27. The Childrens Act 1908, s 30 required that the unsworn evidence of a child of tender years be corroborated; this requirement has been abolished (CEA 1992, s 28(1)). Also there is no longer a requirement for a judge to warn a jury on the danger of convicting an accused on the uncorroborated evidence of a child (CEA 1992, s 28(2)(a)). A judge may in his discretion give such a warning (CEA 1992, s 28(2)(b)). Unsworn evidence of a child may corroborate evidence (sworn or unsworn) given by any person (CEA 1992, s 28(3)). *See Attorney-General v Sullivan* [1930] IR 552.

A judge of the District Court may take the evidence of a child, in respect of whom an offence is alleged to have been committed: (a) by way of sworn deposition; or (b) by way of live television link, where the judge is satisfied on the evidence of a registered medical practitioner, that the attendance before the court of a child, would involve serious danger to the safety, health or wellbeing of the child: Children Act 2001, s 255. [Bibliography: Spenser & Flin UK.] See HEARSAY; OATH; TELEVISION LINK.

child, illegitimate. A child born to parents who are not validly married to each other. Previously, a child born to a void marriage (qv) was illegitimate: *N otherwise K v K* [1986] 6 ILRM 75, while children born of a voidable marriage were illegitimate from the granting of an annulment. An illegitimate child had no succession rights on the death of her father intestate: *In the Goods of Walker* [1985] ILRM 86; an illegitimate child had rights to succeed to the estate of his mother: Legitimacy Act 1931, s 9. However, legislation in 1987 provided that relationships were to be deduced for the purposes of the Succession Act 1965 irrespective of the marital status of a person's parents: Status of Children Act 1987, s 29. Illegitimate children are now *children whose parents are not married to each other.*

The new provisions will not retrospectively affect any rights under the intestacy of a person who died before commencement of Pt V of SCA 1987. In addition, the rule is now abrogated which rendered void, as contrary to public policy, a provision in a disposition for the benefit of an illegitimate child not in being when the disposition takes effect (SCA 1987, s 27(5)).

The 1987 Act has enabled the State to ratify the European Convention on the Status of Children Born out of Wedlock, which came into force for Ireland on 6 January 1989. Children born out of wedlock have the same legal status as regards income tax, capital gains tax, capital acquisitions tax and stamp duty, as children born in wedlock: Taxes Consolidation Act 1997, s 8. The expression *'my children'* in a will creating a discretionary trust, was held to include the daughter of the testator's wife, the product of another union, as the testator, when alive, had habitually referred to her as his daughter: *Crawford v Lawless* (6 November 2002, unreported). See LRC 4 of 1982. See AFFILIATION ORDER; CONSTRUCTION OF DISPOSITIONS; PATERNITY, PRESUMPTION OF.

child, legitimate. The status of a child arising where his parents were married to each other at the time of his conception or at the time of his birth. There is a presumption that a child born in wedlock is legitimate until the contrary is proven beyond reasonable doubt. Legitimate children are now known as *children whose parents are married to each other:* Status of Children Act 1987. See CHILD, LEGITIMATED; MARITAL STATUS.

child, legitimated. A child was legitimated upon the subsequent marriage of his parents, provided the father was domiciled in the State at the time of such marriage, and both he and the mother could have been lawfully married to each other at the time of the birth or at some time during the period of ten months preceding the birth: Legitimacy Act 1931, s 1. The child was legitimated from the date of the marriage.

However, under legislation enacted in 1987, the subsequent marriage of the parents of a child born outside marriage, who remains unadopted, will always render that child legitimate, irrespective of the marital situation of the parents at the time of the birth: Status of Children Act 1987, s 7.

A legitimated child had most of the succession rights of a legitimate child; however he could only share in a distribution on intestacy where he was legitimated at the date of death of the intestate and he could not take by descent under an entailed interest created before the date of his legitimation. See Succession Act 1965, s 110; also *In re P* [1945] Ir Jur Rep 17.

Under the Status of Children Act 1987, s 29, provision is made that relationships shall be deduced for the purposes of the Succession Act 1965 irrespective of the marital status of a person's parents. The new provisions will not retrospectively affect any rights under the intestacy of a person who died before commencement of Pt V of the SCA 1987. See BIRTH, REGISTRATION OF; CONSTRUCTION OF DISPOSITIONS.

child, liability relating to. See OCCUPIERS' LIABILITY TO CHILDREN; NEGLIGENCE.

child, medical treatment of. A child must give his consent to medical treatment; however such consent may be given by the parent or guardian of the child where the medical procedure is in the best interest of the child where the child is incapable of consenting on his own behalf. The doctor is required to give the child's parent or guardian information about the child's condition, the effects (including side effects) of the treatment, including where appropriate, alternative forms of treatment. A minor who had attained the age of sixteen can give effective consent to surgical, medical or dental treatment which, without consent, would constitute trespass to the person: Non-Fatal Offences against the Person Act 1997, s 23. In England, the House of Lords has held that a parent can give a legally effective consent to any procedure to which a *reasonable* parent would give consent: *S v McC; W v W* [1972] AC 24. For example, no battery is committed by a doctor who, with parental consent, vaccinates a protesting 4-year old against measles.

In the UK, a child can give a valid consent if he fully comprehends the nature and consequences of the proposed medical treatment eg contraceptive advice to an under 16 year old: *Gillick v West Norfolk and*

Wisbech Area Health Authority [1985] 3 All ER 402.

As regards the court intervening to order the medical treatment of a child to which the parents object, the Supreme Court has held that the State can intervene to supply the place of the parents in exceptional circumstances, in the interest of the common good or where parents, for physical or moral reasons, have failed in their duty: Constitution art 42.5 and *North Western Health Board v H W* [2001] 3 IR 622, SC. In this case the court refused to order a PKU screening test on an infant child to which the parents objected.

'If the doctor feels that a child will understand a proposed medical procedure, information and advice, this should be explained fully to the child. Where the consent of parents or guardians is normally required in respect of a child for whom they are responsible, due regard must be had to the wishes of the child. The doctor must never assume that it is safe to ignore the parental/guardian interest': Medical Council, *A Guide to Ethical Conduct and Behaviour* (6th edn, 2004), para 18.3. [Bibliography: Donnelly (2); Tomkin & Hanafin.] See PATIENT, CONSENT OF; SURGICAL OPERATION.

child, protection of. For guidance on the promotion of child welfare and the development of safe practices in work with children, including how to recognise signs of child abuse, see publication *Our Duty to Care – The principles of good practice for the protection of children and young people* issued by the Department of Health and Children in 2002. See also 'Age of Innocents' by solicitor Geoffrey Shannon in *Law Society Gazette* (April 2004) 12. See CARE ORDER.

child, provision for. Where the court is of the opinion that a *testator* has failed in his moral duty to make proper provision for a child in accordance with his means, the court may order that suitable provision be made out of the estate, provided it does not diminish a gift by will to the surviving spouse or her *legal right* (qv). See Succession Act 1965, s 117; also *FM v TAM* [1970] 106 ILTR 82; *L v L* [1978] IR 288; *MH and NMcG v NM and CM* [1983] ILRM 519; *In b.GM* [1972] 106 ILTR 82; *McDonald v Norris* [1999] 1 ILRM 270, HC.

There is a relatively high onus of proof on the applicant which requires that a posi-tive failure of moral duty be established: *C & F v WC & TC* [1989] ILRM 815, SC.

In 1987, s 117 of the SA 1965 was amended to ensure that in any case where a testator had not married the other parent of his child, the child had a right to apply for proper provision out of the estate, irrespective of whether the will was made before or after commencement of the 1987 Act: Status of Children Act 1987, s 31. In 1996, s 117 was further amended to reduce from twelve months to six months, the period within which an application is to be made by the child of the testator: Family Law (Divorce) Act 1996, s 46.

The fact that a testator has simply treated all his children equally is not an answer to an application under s 117; the maxim *'equality is equity'* has no application where a testator disregards the special needs of a child eg due to the physical or mental disability of that child: *EB v SS* [1998] 2 ILRM 141 and 4 IR 527, SC.

Also the moral obligation recognised by s 117 is an obligation which flows from the relationship between the parties and is one which is continuous from the date of birth of the child until the date of death of the parent, unless in the meantime it has been satisfied or extinguished: *McDonald v Norris* [2000] 1 ILRM 382, SC and [1999] 4 IR 303, SC. The bad behaviour of a child could be taken into account either to extinguish or diminish the moral obligation of the parent (*McDonald* case).

The moral duty of the parent is assessed by the court as of the date of death of the testator: *In the estate of ABC, deceased* [2003] ITLR (12 May), HC and FL 7270 and 2 ILRM 340 and 2 IR 250. Where the testator by his will set up a *discretionary trust* (qv), the court will consider whether he discharged his moral duty, having regard to the circumstances in which he found himself when making his will and to the requirement that the moral duty be assessed as of the date of death (*ABC* case). The report of this case sets out the principles governing SA 1965, s 117 arising from previous judicial decisions and in particular, the implications for a 'discretionary trust'. See also JUDICIAL SEPARATION.

child, removal from the State. See CHILD ABDUCTION; PASSPORT.

child, rights of. The United Nation's Convention on the Rights of the Child was adopted by the UN General Assembly on 20 November 1989 and entered into force for Ireland on 28 October 1992 (Iris Oifigiúil, 15 March 1994, p.321). The Convention treats the child as a juristic person with a special status needing special care and attention. The rights which are recognised are survival, development and protection rights. See *Blake* in 9 ILT & SJ (1991) 114 and *Horgan* in 9 ILT & SJ (1991) 161.

child, special needs of. Where a child has very special needs which cannot be provided for by the parents or guardian, there is a constitutional obligation on the State under the 1937 Constitution, art 42(5), to cater for those needs in order to vindicate the constitutional rights of the child: *FN v Minister for Education* [1995] 2 ILRM 297, HC and 1 IR 409. The High Court granted injunctive relief to a number of children with special education needs, requiring the Minister to adhere to time limits and plans he had already made: *TD v Minister for Education* [2000] 2 ILRM 321. This was subsequently overturned in the Supreme Court which held that to grant such injunctions relief would breach the concept of the separation of powers, as between the judiciary and the executive: *TD (a minor) v Minister for Education* [2001] 4 IR 259, SC.

child, sexual exploitation of. It is an offence for a person to take or use a child, under the age of 17 years, for sexual exploitation or to facilitate the sexual exploitation of a child: Child Trafficking and Pornography Act 1998, s 3. *Sexual exploitation* includes inducing or coercing the child to engage in prostitution (qv) or to participate in any unlawful sexual activity or the production of child pornography. See CHILD PORNOGRAPHY; CHILD TRAFFICKING.

child, status of. The relationship of every person is now determined, unless a contrary intention appears, irrespective of whether his father or mother are or have been married to each other: Status of Children Act 1987, s 3. This now also applies to taxation legislation: Finance Act 1988, s 74, now Taxes Consolidation Act 1997, s 8. See District Court (Status of Children Act 1987) Rules 1988, SI No 152 of 1988 and Circuit Court Rules, SI No 152 of 1990.

child abduction. It is an offence for a parent or guardian to take, send or keep a child out of the State or cause a child to be so taken: (a) in defiance of a court order; or (b) without the consent of each person who is a parent or guardian: Non-Fatal Offences against the Person Act 1997, s 16. A child

for the purpose of this offence is a child under 16 years of age. It is a defence to the charge that the defendant has been unable to communicate with the other parent or guardian but believes that they would consent if they were aware of the relevant circumstances. It is also an offence for other persons not covered by s 16, to abduct a child; it is a defence that the defendant believed the child had attained the age of 16 (NFOPA 1997, ss 1(2) and 17).

Measures have been introduced to secure the return of a child who has been removed to any *Contracting State* in defiance of a court order or against the wishes of a parent with custody rights: Child Abduction and Enforcement of Custody Orders Act 1991. A child for the purposes of the Conventions, given force by this Act, is a person under 16 years of age.

The fact that the central authority (Minister for Justice) is required to take action or cause action to be taken, when it receives an application to which the Hague Convention applies, does not mean that the central authority is required to be an applicant in any court proceedings: *DGH and Minister for Justice v TCH* [2003] FL 8084, HC.

The Department of Justice will initiate steps to trace a child who has been abducted into the State and seek a child's return where a child has been abducted from the State. The Department will assist the wronged party in seeking return of the child. Applicants are entitled to legal aid and no charge is imposed for the services. The Convention envisaged a summary process to ensure the prompt return of a child wrongfully removed from the country of his *habitual residence*: *P v B* [1999] 4 IR 185, SC.

Provision was made in 2000 to give force in law in the State to the Convention which was signed at the Hague on 19 October 1996: Protection of Children (Hague Convention) Act 2000. The Convention deals with jurisdiction, applicable law, recognition, enforcement and co-operation in respect of parental responsibility, and measures for the protection of children. The Act amends ss 14 and 30 of the Child Abduction and Enforcement of Custody Orders Act 1991. See Rules of the Superior Courts (No 1) (Child Abduction and Enforcement of Orders) 2001, SI No 94 of 2001. See also Child Abduction (Section 4) (Hague Convention) Order 2001, SI

No 507 of 2001; Child Abduction (Section 18) (Luxembourg Convention) Order 2001, SI No 508 of 2001. See Appointment of Central Authorities Order 1993, SI No 121 of 1993. See also SIs No 476, 477, 478 of 1998.

The High Court has held in a particular case that while the applicant father of a child did not have custody of the child under the Convention, he was a guardian of the child and was entitled to be consulted on all matters affecting the welfare of the child eg where the child should be educated and where the child should live: *C(R) v S(I)* [2003] FL 8643, HC. The court held that the removal of the child from Ireland to Belgium by the mother, who had custody of the child, was a wrongful removal under the Convention as was the subsequent retention of the child. See also *Northampton County Council v ABF and MBF* [1982] ILRM 164; *Kent Co Council v CS* [1984] ILRM 292; *Wadda v Ireland* [1994] 1 ILRM 126, HC; *RJ v MR* [1994] 1 IR 271, SC; *SD v RS* [1996] 3 IR 524, HC; *HI v MG* [1999] 2 ILRM 1, HC & SC and [2000] 1 IR 110, SC; *In the Matter of CM* [1999] 2 ILRM 103 and 2 IR 363, HC; *AS v PS* [1998] 2 IR 244, SC; *WPP v SRW* [2001] 1 ILRM 371, SC and [2000] 4 IR 401, SC; *MSH v LH* [2001] 1 ILRM 448, SC and [2000] 3 IR 390, SC. See *Corrigan* in 9 ILT & SJ (1991) 273 & 10 ILT & SJ (1992) 4. See 'The hand that robs the cradle' by solicitor Geoffrey Shannon in *Law Society Gazette* (April 2003) 8. See CHILDREN, CUSTODY OF; HABITUAL RESIDENCE.

child abduction, defences. The main defences to child abduction are: (a) acquiescence to the removal of the child; (b) the child's objection to being returned; and (c) a grave risk that the child would be exposed to physical or psychological harm if returned.

The court is not bound to return the child, where the person seeking the return has consented to or acquiesced in the removal of the child; *acquiescence* means acceptance of the removal and retention of the child: *P v B* [1995] 1 ILRM 201, SC and [1994] 3 IR 507, SC. *Acquiescence* under the Hague Convention means acceptance of the removal or retention of the child; whether or not there has been acquiescence must be considered on a survey of all the relevant circumstances: *RK v JK* [2000] 2 IR 416, SC. See also *London Borough of Sutton v M(R), M(J) and J(M)* [2002] FL 7220, HC.

It has been held that as regards a child's *objection* to being returned, there was no requirement to interpret '*object*' to mean anything stronger than its literal meaning: *TMM v MD* (*Child Abduction: Article 13*) [2000] 1 IR 149, SC. The welfare of the child is the paramount consideration: *BB v JB* [1998] 1 ILRM 136, SC and 1 IR 299, SC. It was also held that the conduct of the abducting parent was in most cases crucial but that the court might look past that conduct to the manifest needs of the child: *P v B* [1999] 4 IR 185, SC.

The expression '*rights of custody*' in the Hague Convention does not extend to inchoate rights which a father of a child born out of lawful wedlock could be said to have: *AS v EH* [1999] 4 IR 504, HC. In this case the removal of the child to Ireland from England by the Irish relatives, was held to be lawful as the plaintiff father had no custody rights unless and until he obtained such rights from a court.

However, a child will not be returned to another jurisdiction where there would be a grave risk that the child would be exposed to physical or psychological harm: Hague Convention 1980, art 13(b) and *RG v BG* [1993] ITLR (1 February), HC; *M v M* [2002] FL 7046, HC. Such a risk must be weighty and in regard to psychological harm, it must be substantial and not trivial: *CK v CK* [1993] ILRM 534, HC.

The grave risk exception should be strictly applied in the narrow context in which it arises: *M(E) ex parte v M(J)* [2003] FL 7668, SC. Also, the court which makes a decision relating to the custody of a child who has been removed from the State, must be the same court to make a declaration that the removal of the child from the State was unlawful: *C v B* [1996] 1 ILRM 63, SC and 2 IR 83, and s 34(1) of Child Abduction and Enforcement of Custody Orders Act 1991.

child abuse. A Commission was established in 2000, to inquire into *child abuse*, with four primary functions: (a) to provide for persons, who suffered abuse in childhood in institutions, a forum in which they can tell of that abuse; (b) to inquire into allegations of abuse and to determine its nature, the circumstances under which it occurred and its extent; (c) to establish the extent to which institutions, management and regulatory authorities had responsibility for the abuse; and (d) to publish a report to the public: Commission to Inquire into Child Abuse Act 2000.

'*Abuse*' is broadly defined and includes causing physical injury to a child; using a child for sexual arousal or gratification; failure to care for a child; and any other act or omission which results in serious impairment to the health, development, behaviour or welfare of a child (CICAA 2000, s 1). '*Child*' is a person who has not attained the age of 18 at the time the abuse was committed (CICAA 2000 s 1).

The Commission has two committees: (a) a *Confidential Committee* – which hears abuse victims who do not wish to have that abuse inquired into and which is therapeutic in nature, although it will make general findings; and (b) an *Investigation Committee* – which hears abuse victims, investigates the abuse, determines the nature of the abuse and why it happened, determines the extent to which the institutions contributed to the abuse, and reports to the Commission. The first public sitting of the Commission took place on 29 June 2000 under the chairmanship of the Hon Justice Mary Laffoy.

The functions of the *Commission to Inquire into Child Abuse* were extended in 2001 to empower it to inquire into the circumstances, legality, conduct, ethical propriety and effects on the subjects thereof of clinical trial of vaccines on children: Commission to Inquire into Child Abuse (Additional Functions) Order 2001, SI No 280 of 2001. However, the High Court has held that the 2001 Order is invalid: *Hillary v Commission to Inquire into Child Abuse* (11 June 2004, unreported), HC. The court held that even though 'abuse' was widely defined in the Act, it was clear that none of the issues raised in the Chief Medical Officer's report on clinical trials even suggested the existence of abuse as so defined.

The High Court has held that the *Investigation Committee* can make findings against deceased, elderly, infirm or untraceable members of the Christian Brothers or those unable to give instructions: *Congregation of the Christian Brothers v Commission to Inquire into Child Abuse* (2003) Irish Times, 18 October, HC (under appeal). The Supreme Court held that the Commission had not adhered to fair procedures in requiring a witness to appear before it, in that it had declined to consider medical reports about the witness's health and, if necessary, arrange for an independent medical examination of him: *Meenan v Commission* [2003] FL 7866, SC. The court held that s 14(1) of CICAA 2000 gave power to the Commission to issue a direction to attend at its public hearings for the purpose of giving evidence to it, not for the purposes of investigating his ability to give evidence.

The non-statutory '*Ferns Inquiry*' into how allegations of clerical child abuse were handled by Church and State authorities in the diocese of Ferns commenced oral hearings in Dublin on 15 September 2003 under retired Supreme Court judge Frank Murphy.

For amendments to ss 20 and 23 of CICAA 2000, see Residential Institutions Redress Act 2002, s 32. See Law Reform Commission consultation paper on the *Limitation of Actions arising from the Non-Sexual Abuse of Children*, LRC CP16 of September 2000; Law Reform Commission *Consultation Paper on Public Inquiries including Tribunals of Inquiry*, LRC CP 22, 2003. See *MQ v Gleeson* [1999] 4 IR 85, HC; *Re Commission to Inquire into Child Abuse* [2002] 3 IR 459, HC; *McD v Commission to Inquire into Child Abuse* [2003] 2 ILRM 503 and 2 IR 348, HC. See website: *www.childabusecommission.ie*. See CRUELTY TO CHILDREN; DISABILITY, PERSON UNDER; SEX OFFENDER.

child abuse, future of Commission. The first Chairman of the Commission announced on 7 September 2003 her decision to resign for a number of reasons, including her contention that the Commission had never been properly established by the government to fulfil satisfactorily the functions conferred on it by the Oireachtas. Her final interim report was published on 30 January 2004, stating that the Commission has been 'devoid of any real independent capacity to perform its statutory functions'. Her place has been taken by the Hon Mr Justice Seán Ryan SC.

In May 2004, he made a number of recommendations, including that the Commission to Inquire into Child Abuse Act 2000 be amended to delete the requirement for the Commission to exercise its discretion in relation to the identification of individuals. The ending of the policy of '*naming and shaming*' would speed up the work of the Commission and it would mean that individuals would not be entitled to insist on their rights to be represented and cross-examine. The emphasis of the Commission would be to find out what happened and why, on the malfunction of the system rather than on the individual wrongdoer. Not all of the 1,712 complainants would be heard by the *Investigation Committee*.

In June 2004, the Commission announced that it was to seek changes in the legislation to allow it to address the role of the courts in placing children in the residential institutions it is inquiring into, indicating that it would be unsatisfactory for the Commission to ignore this part of the history.

child abuse, recognition of. For information on how to recognise signs of child abuse and on the correct steps to take within organisations if it is suspected, witnessed or disclosed, see publication *Our Duty to Care – The principles of good practice for the protection of children and young people* issued by the Department of Health and Children (2002). The process of reporting suspected or actual child abuse to the appropriate health board is described step by step, and guidance is given on how to handle sensitive issues.

child abuse, redress. A structure has been put in place for the making of financial awards to assist the recovery of persons who as children, were resident in *institutions* in the State and who suffered *injuries* consistent with child *abuse* received while so resident: Residential Institutions Redress Act 2002. The Act provides for the establishment of an independent *Residential Institutions Redress Board* to make financial awards which are fair and reasonable and without regard to any issue of fault or negligence (RIRA 2002, s 5) and a *Residential Institutions Redress Committee* to hear appeals against decisions of the Board (RIRA 2002, s 14).

An applicant for an award must make an application within 3 years from the establishment of the Board, which period may be extended by the Board at its discretion (RIRA 2002, s 8).

'Abuse' is given a wide definition covering sexual and physical abuse, neglect or any other act or failure to act which results in injury (RIRA 2002, s 1). 'Injury' includes physical or psychological injury and injury which has occurred in the past (RIRA 2002, s 1). 'Institution' means an institution that is specified in the Sch

(RIRA 2002, s 1) or any industrial or reformatory school, orphanage, children's home or special school specified by Ministerial order (RIRA 2002, s 4).

There is provision for the awards and the costs of the Board to be met from a *special account*, funded from public moneys and from persons who contribute with Ministerial agreement (RIRA 2002, s 23). An applicant for redress, on accepting an award must waive, in writing, any right of action against a public body or a person who has made a contribution under s 23 (RIRA 2002, s 13(6)). An award is not subject to income tax (RIRA 2002, s 22). However, an award is regarded in the assessment of means for social assistance or supplementary welfare allowance purposes in the same way as is compensation awarded to persons who have contracted hepatitis C or HIV or to persons who have disabilities caused by thalidomide: Social Welfare (Consolidated Supplementary Welfare Allowance) (Amendment) (No1) Regulations 2003, SI No 426 of 2003; Social Welfare (Consolidated Payments Provisions (Amendment) (No 5) (Compensation Payments) Regulations 2003, SI No 427 of 2003.

child abuse, reporting. A person is provided with immunity from civil liability who, reasonably and in good faith, reports child abuse to a designated officer of a health board or to any member of the garda síochána: Protection of Persons Reporting Child Abuse Act 1998, s 3. *Child abuse* is where: (a) a child has been or is being assaulted, ill-treated, neglected or sexually abused; or (b) a child's health, development or welfare has been or is being avoidably impaired or neglected (PPRCAA 1998, s 3(1)). A *designated officer* of a health board is any one of 17 designated categories of health board employees, including eg consultants, nurses, social workers, and child care workers (PPRCAA 1998, s 2).

There is also protection for employees against dismissal or penalisation for reporting child abuse, provided the employee acted reasonably and in good faith, which is presumed unless the contrary is proven (PPRCAA 1998, s 4). A new offence of false reporting of child abuse has been created; the accused however must be shown to have known that the report was false (PPRCAA 1998, s 5). A person who reports child abuse to someone other than the gardaí or health board personnel, may still be able to claim that the report was made on an occasion of qualified privilege, if the person receiving the report has a duty to receive it eg if the report is made to a sports organisation in respect of a member or participant, or if made to the Irish Society for the Prevention of Cruelty to Children (PPRCAA 1998, s 6).

A solicitor may waive the confidentiality which he owes to a client where the client is a child who reveals information which indicates continuing sexual or other physical abuse but refuses to allow disclosure of such information: *A Guide to Professional Conduct of Solicitors in Ireland* (2002) ch 4.2. See also Residential Institutions Redress Act 2002, s 28(5)(b). See *Kilkenny Incest Investigation Report 1993*; *Report of the Committee of Inquiry into the Death of Kelly Fitzgerald 1996*.

child and parent. See PARENTAGE, DECLARATION OF.

child benefit. The non-means-tested social welfare payment which is payable to the person with whom a qualified child normally resides: Social Welfare (Consolidation) Act 1993, ss 192–196 as amended. See Social Welfare Act 2000, s 6; Social Welfare (Miscellaneous Provisions) Act 2002, s 2; Social Welfare (Miscellaneous Provisions) Act 2003, ss 3; Social Welfare (Miscellaneous Provisions) Act 2004, s 3. Where a person is in receipt of child benefit, the Minister may provide for the award of child benefit to that person in respect of a second or subsequent child on receipt of the information that may be prescribed, and verified in the manner that may be prescribed (SW(MP)A 2003, s 11 and SI No 417 of 1994 as amended by SI No 396 of 2003). The monthly amount specified from 1 April 2004 is €131.60 for each of the first two children, and €165.30 for each child in excess of two.

child in care. Where a child is *in the care* of a health board, the board must provide care for him: (a) by placing him with a foster parent; or (b) by placing him in residential care; or (c) by placing him with a suitable person with a view to his adoption; or (d) by making other suitable arrangements: Child Care Act 1991, s 36. The board must facilitate reasonable access to the child by his parents; such access may include allowing the child to reside with his parents (CCA 1991, s 37). See DCR 1997 Ord 84, r 25.

The board may remove a child in its care from the custody of any person with whom he has been placed under s 36 (CCA 1991, s 43(1)). The Minister is required to make regulations governing the placement of children with relatives (CCA 1991, s 41). See also Report on Child Sexual Abuse (LRC 32, 1990). See AFTERCARE; CARE ORDER; CHILDREN'S RESIDENTIAL CENTRE; WELFARE OF CHILDREN.

child offender, disturbed. See CHILD, DISTURBED.

child pornography. Any visual representation: (a) that shows a child engaged in explicit sexual activity or witnessing such activity; or (b) whose dominant characteristic is the depiction, for sexual purpose, of the genital or anal region of a child: Child Trafficking and Pornography Act 1998, s 2(1). The definition is drawn widely to capture offensive material, no matter how it is represented, including an audio representation, or how it is made. Included is any figure generated or modified by computer-graphics if the predominant impression conveyed is that the figure shown is a child (CTPA 1998, s 2(2)). A child is a person under the age of 17; this is the age at which a person may lawfully consent to sexual relations (CTPA 1998, s 2(1)).

It is an offence for a person who, having custody, charge or care of a child, allows the child to be used for the production of child pornography (CTPA 1998, s 4). It is also an offence knowingly to possess any child pornography (CTPA 1998, s 6) or knowingly to produce, distribute, print or publish child pornography (CTPA 1998, s 5). See District Court (Child Trafficking and Pornography Act 1998) Rules 1999, SI No 216 of 1999.

The 1998 Act was amended in 2004 to ensure that nothing in the Act prevents the possession, distribution, printing, publication or showing of child pornography by the Houses of the Oireachtas, or of a committee, or any person, for the purposes of any function conferred by the Constitution or by law on the Houses, or conferred by a resolution of the Houses: CTPA 1998, s 13 inserted by Child Trafficking and Pornography (Amendment) Act 2004, s 1. The amendment also provided that nothing in CTPA 1998 prevents the giving of or compliance with a direction under s 3 of the Committees of the Oireachtas (Compellability, Privileges and Immunity of Witnesses) Act 1997. The amendments were deemed necessary to enable the Houses of the Oireachtas to enquire into the behaviour or capacity of Circuit Court Judge Brian Curtin. See CYBERCRIME.

child stealing. Formerly, the offence committed by any person who unlawfully, either by force or fraud, led or took away any child under the age of fourteen years or who harboured such a child: Offences Against the Person Act 1861, s 56.

child suspect. The gardaí are required, in any investigation of an offence by children, to act with due respect for the rights of children and their dignity as human persons, for their vulnerability owing to their age and level of maturity and for the special needs of any of them who may be under a physical or mental disability: Children Act 2001, s 55.

When a child is arrested and brought to a garda station, the member in charge must inform the parent or guardian of the child as soon as practicable: (a) that the child is in custody; (b) in ordinary language of the nature of the offence; and (c) that the child is entitled to consult a solicitor and as to how this entitlement can be availed of (CA 2001, s 58). There are provisions regarding the notification of a solicitor (CA 2001, s 60).

Also, generally, a child cannot be questioned, or asked to make a written statement except in the presence of a parent or guardian or (in their absence) another adult, nominated by the member-in-charge (CA 2001, s 61).

The Treatment of Persons in Custody in Garda Síochána Stations Regulations 1987, SI No 119 of 1987, reg 13, provides that, except with the authority of the member in charge, an arrested person who is under the age of 17 years must not be questioned in relation to an offence or asked to make a written statement unless a parent or guardian is present, which authority must not be given unless: (a) it has not been possible to communicate with a parent or guardian; (b) no parent or guardian has attended at the station concerned within a reasonable time of being informed that the person was in custody and of being requested so to attend; (c) it is not practicable for a parent or guardian to attend within a reasonable time; or (d) the member in charge has reasonable grounds for believing that to delay questioning the person would involve a risk of injury to persons or serious loss of or damage to property, destruction of or interference with evidence or escape of accomplices. See INTERVIEW.

child trafficking. It is an offence, punishable by life imprisonment, for a person to organise or knowingly facilitate: (a) the entry into, transit through or exit from the State of a child under 17 years of age for the purpose of his or her sexual exploitation; or (b) the provision of accommodation for a child for such a purpose while in the State: Child Trafficking and Pornography Act 1998, s 3). See District Court (Child Trafficking and Pornography Act 1998) Rules 1999, SI No 216 of 1999. [Bibliography: Kelleher & Murray.] See CHILD, SEXUAL EXPLOITATION OF; JOINT INVESTIGATION TEAMS.

childbirth, attendance at. It is an offence for a person to attend a woman in childbirth unless that person is a midwife, a registered medical practitioner, or a student undergoing professional training, except in a case of sudden or urgent necessity: Nurses Act 1985, s 58. See MIDWIFE.

childcare facilities. A new scheme of accelerated capital allowances has been introduced in respect of expenditure on the construction, refurbishment or extension of childcare premises that meet the required standards under the Child Care Act 1991: Taxes Consolidation Act 1997, s 843A as amended by Finance Act 2000, s 63. See *Kelly v Department of Social, Community and Family Affairs* [2002] ELR 293, EO.

Children Court. (1) Under the Courts of Justice Act 1924 provision was made for a justice of the District Court to sit in a special court in the cities of Dublin, Cork, Limerick and Waterford to be called 'The Children's Court' to deal with all charges against children (CJA 1924, s 80).

(2) The District Court is known as the *Children Court* when hearing charges against children, or when hearing applications for orders relating to a child at which the attendance of the child is required, or when exercising any other jurisdiction conferred on the Children Court: Children Act 2001, ss 71–76. There is provision for the Court when sitting to be held on different days from other courts, and as far as practicable, that persons attending are not brought into contact with persons in attendance at other courts. A judge is required to participate in any relevant course of training or education, which may be required by the President of the District Court, before transacting business in the

Children Court (CA 2001, s 72). [Bibliography: McDermott & Robinson.]

See FAMILY COURT; TELEVISION LINK.

children detention schools. Schools for the detention of children under the age of 16 years who have been referred to them by the courts on being found guilty of offences: Children Act 2001, ss 157–224. These schools replace *reformatory* and *industrial* schools. The objective of the children detention schools is to provide appropriate educational and training programmes for children referred to them (CA 2001, s 158).

The schools are managed by a board of management appointed by the Minister (CA 2001, ss 164–179).

There is provision for the appointment of inspectors to the schools (CA 2001, ss 185–189), for visiting panels (CA 2001, ss 190–191), and for visits by judges of the Children Court (CA 2001, s 192). There is also provision for the establishment of a *special residential services board* for the purpose of ensuring the efficient and co-ordinated delivery of services to children detained in these schools and in *special care units* (CA 2001, ss 225–244). It is an offence to escape from a children detention school, to help a child escape, or to harbour an escaped child (CA 2001, ss 215–217). [Bibliography: McDermott & Robinson.]

children's residential centre. Any home or other institution for the residential care of children in the care of health boards or other children who are not receiving adequate care and protection: Child Care Act 1991, s 59. Health boards (qv) are required to establish and maintain a register of children's residential centres; it is an offence to carry on such a centre unless it is registered (CCA 1991, ss 60–64). For district court procedure for an appeal by a proprietor of a centre against a decision of the health board, see DCR 1997 Ord 84, r 32.

Health Boards are also required to make arrangements to ensure the provision of an adequate number of residential places for children in care (CCA 1991, s 38). The Minister is required to make regulations for the purpose of ensuring proper standards (CCA 1991, s 63) and in relation to the placing of children in residential care (CCA 1991, s 40).

When Pt VIII of CCA 1991 has come into operation, every institution which was an industrial school certified under the Children's Act 1908 or was a school approved under the Health Act 1953, s 55, will be deemed to be registered as a children's residential centre. [Bibliography: McDermott & Robinson; Ward.] See CARE ORDER.

chimney fire. It is an offence wilfully to set or cause to be set a chimney fire: Town Police Clauses Act 1847 as amended by Criminal Law Act 1997, s 13 and Sch 1, para 3.

chinese wall. A metaphor to describe a set of internal rules and procedures established by an organisation for the purpose of preventing certain types of information in the possession of one part of the organisation from being communicated to other parts of the same organisation. A chinese wall will sometimes be provided eg to prevent insider dealing (qv) or to protect the confidentiality of a tax amnesty. See Companies Act 1990, s 108(7); Waiver of Certain Tax, Interest and Penalties Act 1993, ss 7–8.

chirograph. Formerly, a deed was written in two parts on the same paper or parchment, with the word *chirographum* (ie autograph) written in capital letters between the two parts; it was then cut through the middle of the letters and a part given to each party. When the cutting was indented, the deed was known as an *indenture* (qv).

chirographum apud debitorum repertum praesumitur solutum. [A deed or bond found with the debtor is presumed to be paid.]

chocolate products. Provision has been made for prescribing, and harmonising within the European Union, standards for the composition and labelling of cocoa and chocolate products: EC (Marketing of Cocoa and Chocolate Products) Regulations 2003, SI No 236 of 2003. The sales designation 'milk chocolate' may be used within the State to describe a designated product provided the amount of dry milk solids is indicated in the form 'milk solids ... % minimum'. It is an offence to fail to comply with the regulations. The regulations give effect to EC Directive 2000/36/EC. See *Commission v Spain and Italy* [2003] C-12/00 and C-14/00, ECJ.

chose. A thing. A *chose in possession* is a movable chattel in the custody or control of the owner or the right to which can be enforced by taking physical possession eg of one's own goods. A *chose in action* is a right of proceeding in law to procure the payment of a sum of money or to recover pecuniary damages for a wrong inflicted or the non-performance of a contract. A *legal chose in action* is a right of action which could be enforced in a court of law eg debts; an *equitable chose in action* is a right which formerly could only be enforced in a court of chancery eg an interest in a trust. See Patents Act 1992, s 79. See *Lynch v Burke* [1996] 1 ILRM 114, SC.

Christian name. Includes any forename: Registration of Business Names Act 1963, s 2. See FORENAME; NAME, CHANGE OF.

Church annulment. Refers generally to a decree of nullity of marriage granted by an Ecclesiastical Tribunal of the Catholic Church; it cannot be a factor bearing on the decision of the courts whether to grant a nullity decree: *N (otherwise K) v K* [1986] ILRM 75. See MARRIAGE, NULLITY OF.

Church holidays. Days which an employer may substitute for a public holiday (qv) by giving the employee notice of the substitution at least 14 days beforehand. They are Ascension Thursday, Feast of Corpus Christi, and the following except when they fall on a Sunday: 6 January, 15 August, 1 November, 8 December. See Organisation of Working Time Act 1997, Sch 2.

c.i.f. [Cost, insurance, freight.] If a seller agrees to sell goods to a buyer at a price *c.i.f. Dublin Docks*, the price includes the price of the goods, the insurance premium and freight payable as far as Dublin Docks. See *Michel Freres Societe Anonyme v Kilkenny Woolen Mills Ltd* [1959] IR 157.

cigarettes. See TOBACCO PRODUCT.

cinematograph film. See FILM; CENSORSHIP; COPYRIGHT; INFRINGEMENT OF COPYRIGHT; VIDEO.

Circuit Court. The court above the District Court (qv) in the hierarchical system of courts. The country is divided into a number of circuits; a Circuit Court judge is assigned to each circuit and travels to several towns in that circuit to hear cases, sitting alone in civil cases and with a jury in criminal cases when the accused is so entitled. There are permanent Circuit Courts in Dublin and Cork. Circuit judges hold office by the same tenure as the judges of the High Court and the Supreme Court: Courts of Justice Act 1924, s 39.

On civil matters, the Circuit Court can award damages of up to £30,000 (€38,092). It can deal with proceedings relating to the execution of trusts where the trust estate (in so far as it relates to land),

does not exceed £200 (€253.95) rateable valuation. Failure to give formal proof of rateable valuation does not deprive the Circuit Court of jurisdiction: *Harrington v Murphy* [1989] IR 207. It can also deal with matters relating to registered land with a similar valuation.

Under recent legislation, the Circuit Court is empowered to award damages up to €100,000; this provision will come into effect on a date to be determined by the Minister: Courts and Court Officers Act 2002, s 13. As of 1 September 2004, the Minister had decided to await the experience of the recently established Personal Injuries Assessment Board and to assess the proposed increase in the light of that experience. The final report of the Motor Insurance Advisory Board recommended that the current limit not be increased, other than to express the figure in a convenient euro amount. Also under recent legislation, provision has been made to change the 'rateable valuation' jurisdiction of the Circuit Court to a 'market value' (qv) of €3m to reflect the new valuation system introduced by the Valuation Act 2001: Civil Liability and Courts Act 2004, ss 45–48, 50–53.

On criminal matters the Circuit Court hears *indictable* (qv) offences sent to it by the District Court. The judge may impose whatever punishment is permitted by statute or common law. An appeal lies from the decision of the Circuit Court to the High Court in civil cases and to the Court of Criminal Appeal (in future, the Supreme Court) in criminal cases. See RSC Ord 61 as amended by Rules of the Superior Courts 1989 (No 2) 1989, SI No 20 of 1989.

The Circuit Court also hears appeals from the District Court, both civil and criminal, which appeal consists of a rehearing of the case and the substitution of the court's decision for the District Court's decision, but limited to the jurisdiction in that regard of the lower court.

The Circuit Court is empowered to enforce *final* decisions of the Director of the Equality Tribunal, *final* determinations of the Labour Court, and the terms of *mediated settlements* in relation to discrimination in employment and in disposing of goods or in providing a service: Employment Equality Act 1998, s 91 amended by Equality Act 2004, s 39; Equal Status Act 2000, s 31 amended by EA 2004, s 62.

The jurisdiction of the Circuit Court is conferred on that court and upon its judges collectively, and accordingly the jurisdiction of the court is capable of being transferred from one individual of the several circuit judges to another: *The State (Boyle) v Nealon Ors* [1986] ILRM 337.

The President of the District Court is an ex officio judge of the Circuit Court: Courts and Court Officers Act 1995, s 33. For the first consolidation of the rules of the Circuit Court in 51 years, see Circuit Court Rules 2001, SI No 510 of 2001. These rules came into operation on 3 December 2001. Where there is no rule provided by these rules to govern practice and procedure, the practice and procedure in the High Court may be followed (Ord 67, r 16).

See also CCOA 1995, ss 4–5. See Courts (Supplemental Provisions) Act 1961; Courts Act 1981 and 1991; Jurisdiction of Courts and Enforcement of Judgments Act 1998, s 16; Companies (Amendment) Act 1990, s 3(9). The county of Sligo has been removed from the Northern Circuit and added to the Midland Circuit: Circuit Court (Alteration of Circuits) Order 2002, SI No 134 of 2002. The *Brussels I Regulation* on the recognition and enforcement of judgments in civil and commercial matters, replaces the 1998 Act as from 1 March 2002 for all EU States except Denmark: EC (Civil and Commercial Judgments) Regulations 2002, SI No 52 of 2002. For fees charged in Circuit Court offices from 10 March 2003, see Circuit Court (Fees) Order 2003, SI No 88 of 2003. [Bibliography: Cordial; Lee.] See DISCRIMINATION; ENLARGEMENT OF JURISDICTION; FAMILY COURT; FAMILY LAW PROCEEDINGS; REMITTAL OF ACTION; RULES OF COURT.

circuits. The division of the State for judicial business. See CIRCUIT COURT.

circular. There are rules governing circulars sent by a *listed* company to its shareholders e g in relation to the content, approval and lodging of circulars: Listing Rules 2000, ch 14. There is no requirement for approval of circulars of a routine nature e g script dividend alternative, notices of meetings (para 14.5). See ADVERTISEMENT.

circumcision. Surgical removal of part of the foreskin (prepuce) of the penis. The Department of Health announced in January 2004 that hospitals will be issued with guidelines in 2004 for carrying out circumcisions on cultural or religious grounds.

This followed the death of a four-week-old baby in Waterford after a home circumcision.

circumstantial evidence. Evidence of a fact relevant to a fact in issue (qv), from which the fact in issue may be inferred. Before an accused person may be found guilty on circumstantial evidence, the court must be satisfied not only that the circumstances are consistent with his guilt but also that they are inconsistent with any other rational conclusion that he is the guilty person. In cases of manslaughter and murder, the fact of death can be proved by circumstantial rather than by direct evidence; death can be inferred from such strong and unequivocal circumstances of presumption as to render it morally certain and leaves no room for reasonable doubt: *The People (Attorney-General) v Thomas* [1954] IR 319. See also *R v Exall* [1886] 4 F F 922.

citation. (1) The calling upon a person who is not a party to an action or proceedings to appear before the court e g a person interested in the estate of a deceased may issue a citation requiring the executor to prove the will where he has failed to do so: RSC Ord 79, rr 52–57; Ord 80 rr 56–57.

(2) The quotation of a decided case in legal argument as an authority supporting the argument.

citator. Reference material which typically gives information on where statutes and statutory instruments have been amended by primary or secondary legislation. References may also be given as to where statutes or statutory instruments have been judicially considered, thus allowing the user to see how a particular part of legislation has been applied in practice e g see 'Irish Current Law Statutes Annotated' which include a '*Statute Citator*' and a '*Statutory Instrument Citator*'.

citizenship. The civil status which determines the rights and obligations of a person under the domestic law of the State. Fidelity to the nation and loyalty to the State are fundamental political duties of all citizens: 1937 Constitution, art 9(3). No person may be excluded from Irish citizenship by reason of the sex of that person (art 9(1)(3)). Citizenship can be acquired by birth, by marriage, by grant as a token of honour, and by naturalisation (qv): Irish Nationality and Citizenship Act 1956.

Under the *Good Friday Agreement*, the UK and Irish Governments recognise the birthright of all the people of Northern Ireland to identify themselves and be accepted as Irish or British, or both, as they may choose, and accordingly confirm that their right to hold both British and Irish citizenship is accepted by both governments and would not be affected by any future change in the status of Northern Ireland (art 1(vi)).

Citizens of the State who are part of a family unit are entitled to exercise their right to the company, care and parentage of their parents within the State: *Fajujonu v Minister for Justice* [1990] ILRM 234, SC. However, this right is not absolute and unqualified; the Irish citizenship of a minor child does not give rise to an absolute right to have his family, parents or siblings, reside in Ireland: *AO and DL v Minister for Justice* [2003] 1 IR 1, SC. However, unsuccessful asylum applicants are entitled to appeal to the Minister for leave to remain in the State on humanitarian grounds, which could include their parentage of Irish born children; each case is dealt with on an individual basis. See 'Guests of the Nation' by solicitor Aisling Ryan in *Law Society Gazette* (January/February 2004) 21.

The expression '*every citizen*' in the 1937 Constitution, art 40(3)(2) is not confined to citizens in their individual capacity as human persons; artificial legal entities must also be protected by the laws of the State against unjust attacks on their property rights: *Iarnród Éireann v Ireland* [1995] 2 ILRM 161, HC and [1996] 3 IR 321, SC.

For the regulations which prescribe the procedures to be followed and the forms to be used by persons who make declarations for the purposes of the 1956–2001 Acts, see Irish Nationality and Citizenship Regulations 2002, SI No 567 of 2002. A *restatement* of citizenship legislation is available at website: *www.justice.ie.* [Bibliography: Cubie & Ryan; Fraser & Harvey.] See GOOD FRIDAY AGREEMENT; NATION; PASSPORT; PETITION; TITLE OF NOBILITY.

citizenship, European. Provision has been made for the establishment of *European citizenship.* Every person holding the nationality of a member state is a citizen of the European Union (qv) with rights and duties eg to move and reside freely within the territory of the member states of the Union; to vote and stand as a candidate at municipal (local) and European Parliament elections in the member state in which he resides; to petition the European Parlia-

ment; to make complaints to the European Ombudsman; and the right to consular protection outside the Community from the embassy of any member state: *Treaty establishing the European Community,* arts 17–22 of the consolidated (2002) version. Citizenship of the Union complements but does not replace national citizenship (art 17(1)).

citizenship as honour. The President of Ireland may grant citizenship as a token of honour to a person, or his child or grandchild, who in the opinion of the government has rendered signal honour to the nation: Irish Nationality and Citizenship Act 1956, s 12. The first honorary Irish citizen was Sir Alfred Chester Beatty in 1957; he bequeathed his famous library in Dublin for the use and enjoyment of the public on his death in 1968. See Chester Beatty Library Acts 1968 and 1986.

citizenship by birth. Significant changes to citizenship law were introduced in 2001 primarily to reflect the Good Friday Agreement and the 19th Amendment to the Constitution of Ireland (to arts 2 and 3) by providing that every person *born in the island of Ireland,* which includes its islands and seas, is entitled to be an Irish citizen: Irish Nationality and Citizenship Act 2001, s 3 substituting new s 6 in the Irish Nationality and Citizenship Act 1956.

Such a person is an Irish citizen *from birth* if he does any act which only an Irish citizen is entitled to do (eg apply for a passport): INCA 1956, new s 6(2)(a). Consequently, the previous declaration required by a person born in Northern Ireland to become an Irish citizen is abolished. To remove any doubt, the new law states that a person, born in the island of Ireland, is also an Irish citizen from birth if he is not entitled to citizenship of any other country (INCA 1956, new s 6(3)). This would not apply to a person born in Northern Ireland, who is entitled to British citizenship (or Irish citizenship or both).

As the Constitution (art 2) declares that everyone, without exception, born in the island of Ireland is part of the Irish nation, provision is made for certain persons (eg born in Ireland of foreign diplomats or born to non-national parents in a foreign aircraft or vessel in Irish airspace or waters) to exercise their rights to Irish citizenship by declaration (INCA 1956, new s 6(4)).

Because of the constitutional entitlement and birthright to be part of the Irish nation, an entitlement which cannot be renounced, provision has been made to enable a person who has made a *declaration of alienage* to continue to be entitled to be an Irish citizen, which entitlement the person can exercise by a declaration in a prescribed manner (INCA 1956, new s 6(5)).

The Advocate General of the European Court of Justice has ruled that a Chinese mother and her Belfast-born daughter are entitled to live in any EU country on account of the child's Irish citizenship and the fact that the family had enough resources to ensure that she would not be a burden on the state: *Chen v UK* (2004) Irish Times, 19 May. See 'The Chen decision: striking a blow for human rights?' by Conor Quigley QC in *Law Society Gazette* (June 2004) 12.

Under a referendum in June 2004, carried by 79.2% to 20.8%, the previous automatic right to Irish citizenship from the Irish-born children of non-nationals was removed. The referendum approved that art 9 be amended by the insertion of:

'9(2)1 Notwithstanding any other provision of this Constitution, a person born in the island of Ireland, which includes its islands and seas, who does not have, at the time of the birth of that person, at least one parent who is an Irish citizen or entitled to be an Irish citizen is not entitled to Irish citizenship or nationality, unless provided for by law.

9(2)2 This section shall not apply to persons born before the date of the enactment of this section'.

The government has indicated that the law will lay down a requirement for one of the non-national parents to be legally resident in Ireland for between three and five years for the child to qualify for citizenship. See Twenty-seventh Amendment to the Constitution Act 2004.

As regards *citizenship by descent* the law is restated that a person is an Irish citizen from birth if at the time of birth, either parent was an Irish citizen, or would if alive have been an Irish citizen (INCA 2001, s 3 inserting new s 7(1) in INCA 1956). The fact that the parent had not done an act which only an Irish citizen is entitled to do (eg apply for a passport) does not exclude the person from their entitlement (INCA 1956, new s 7(2)).

The fact that a person's parents have not married each other is not a bar to Irish citizenship: Status of Children Act 1987,

s 5. As a consequence, a person born abroad whose parents have not married each other is an Irish citizen if either of his parents was an Irish citizen at the time of the person's birth. There are also provisions regarding persons born outside Ireland if the parent from whom they derive citizenship was also born outside the island of Ireland (INCA 2001 inserting new INCA 1956, s 7(3)).

citizenship by marriage. Formerly every woman, if not already a citizen, acquired Irish citizenship from the date of her marriage to a citizen; a man did not so acquire: *Somjee v Minister for Justice* [1981] ILRM 324. This was changed so that the acquisition of Irish citizenship by post-nuptial declaration was available to the alien spouse, whether male or female, of a person Irish by birth or descent, at any time after a three-year period following marriage (or acquisition of citizenship by the Irish spouse if later) provided the marriage was still subsisting in law and fact: Irish Nationality and Citizenship Acts 1986, s 3.

This system has now been replaced by a *naturalisation* procedure for the *non-national* (new term instead of *alien*): Irish Nationality and Citizenship Act 2001. See NATURALISATION BY MARRIAGE.

citizen's arrest. Popular expression meaning the power of an individual person to arrest another in certain circumstances. See ARREST WITHOUT WARRANT.

city code. The *self-regulatory* code which operates under the London Panel on Takeovers and Mergers in the UK (and which operated in Ireland up to 1997) to ensure fair and equal treatment of all shareholders in relation to takeovers and which provides an orderly framework within which takeovers may be conducted. Since 1997 a *statutory scheme* is in operation in Ireland pursuant to the Irish Takeover Panel Act 1997. See IRISH TAKEOVER PANEL; TAKEOVER. See also MERGERS.

city council. A *city council* means a local authority to which section 11(3)(b) relates ie the primary unit of local government of a city set out in Sch 5, Pt 2 of Local Government Act 2001, s 2(1). A city council is a body corporate with perpetual succession, with power to sue and be sued in its corporate name, and with a seal which must be judicially noticed (LGA 2001, s 11(7)). See also BOROUGH.

civic honour. One of the ceremonial functions of a local authority is its power to confer a *civic honour* on a distinguished person, as it may determine, including the *honorary freedom* of its administrative area: Local Government Act 2001, s 74. The decision is a *reserved* function of the elected members. For previous legislation. see Municipal Privileges (Ireland) Act 1876, ss 11–12. Local Government Act 1991, s 48. See BURGESS; HONOUR; TITLE OF NOBILITY.

civil. As opposed to criminal, ecclesiastical, or military. See CIVIL LAW.

civil arrest. The arrest of a person by order of the court in connection with a civil matter eg: (a) the arrest of a contributory of a company about to quit the State or otherwise to abscond: Companies Act 1963, s 247; *In re Ulster Land, Building & Investment Company* [1887] 17 LR Ir 591; *In re Central Trust Investments Society* [1982]; *In re O'Shea's (Dublin) Ltd* [1984] HC; (b) an arrest in relation to bankruptcy: Bankruptcy Act 1988, ss 9 and 23; *In re O'M, a bankrupt* [1988] HC; (c) the arrest of a debtor about to quit Ireland under the Debtors Act (Ireland) 1872, s 7 and RSC Ord 69. See *Courtney* in 8 ILT & SJ (1990) 200. See also ARRESTABLE OFFENCE.

civil bill. Where the context so requires, the term *civil bill* includes all other forms of originating document: Circuit Court Rules 2001, Interpretation of Terms, para 1. A *civil bill* is deemed to be issued when it is presented to the Office of the Circuit Court, sealed, and marked with a record number: Circuit Court Rules 2001 Ord 11, r 3. However, in an anomalous position, where a civil bill was served by registered post, it was deemed to be issued as of the time of posting: Courts Act 1964, s 7(6)(a)(ii). The *Circuit Court Rules Committee* recommended the repeal of this provision in order to have similar procedures in the Circuit Court as apply in the High Court and to provide certainty, particularly as regards the Statute of Limitations 1957 (Circuit Court Rules 2001, *Memorandum from Rules Committee*, page 329). Section 7 has now been amended and s 7(6)(a)(ii) has been repealed in so far as it relates to a document by which proceedings in the Circuit Court are instituted: Courts and Court Officers Act 2002, ss 3, 25 and Sch 1. See *Murphy v McNamara* [2003] 2 ILRM 333, HC and 2 IR 243. See APPEARANCE; CIVIL PROCEEDINGS; PLEADINGS; SUMMONS, SERVICE OF.

civil custody. The custody of the Garda Síochána or other lawful civil authority authorised to retain in custody civil prisoners and includes confinement in a public prison: Defence Act 1954, s 2(1).

civil defence. Means the performance of some or all of the specified humanitarian tasks intended to protect the civilian population against the dangers, and to help it to recover from the immediate effects, of hostilities or disasters and also to provide the conditions necessary for its survival: Civil Defence Act 2002, Sch 1.

The specified tasks include warning, evacuation, management of shelters and of blackout measures, rescue, fire-fighting, detection and marking of danger areas, decontamination, provision of emergency accommodation and supplies, emergency disposal of the dead, and medical services, including first aid, and religious assistance.

The main purpose of the CDA 2002 is: (a) to update civil defence legislation, which is currently governed by the Air Raid Precautions Acts 1939 and 1946; and (b) to provide for the establishment of a *Civil Defence Board* to promote, develop and maintain civil defence as an effective voluntary service in support of the emergency services. See AIR-RAID SHELTER.

civil law. The body of law dealing with the resolution of disputes between individuals; it provides a remedy, usually a financial one, to the aggrieved party against the wrongdoer by way of compensation rather than as punishment.

civil liability. Legal obligation or duty enforced by a civil court. [Bibliography: Kerr (2).] See LIABILITY.

civil power, in aid of. A reservist may be called out in aid of the civil power, on the direction of the Minister, in the maintenance or restoration of the public peace: Defence Act 1954, s 90.

civil proceedings. Proceedings in the civil courts which are commenced in the High Court by originating summons or by petition, in the Circuit Court by civil bill, and in the District Court by civil summons. See RSC Ord 1, r 1; Circuit Court Rules 2001; DCR 1997, r 39. There is no general rule that civil proceedings should be postponed until the conclusion of criminal proceedings relating to the same matter; there is no basis for *staying* a civil action where criminal proceedings are not pending or threatened: *O'Keeffe v Ferris* [1994] 1 ILRM 425, HC.

Civil proceedings in the Circuit Court are normally instituted by the issue of a *civil bill* in the appropriate form: Circuit Court Rules Ord 5, r 1. The civil bill has to be endorsed with particulars of the plaintiff's demand, stating the nature, extent and grounds thereof, full particulars of special damage being claimed and the relief sought: Circuit Court Rules 2001 Ord 5, r 5.

For issue of the civil bill, service, and acceptance of service, see (CCR Ord 11). A civil bill expires after twelve months but may be renewed (CCR Ord 12).

No civil proceedings may be instituted in respect of an act relating to the Mental Health Act 2001 except by leave of the High Court: Mental Health Act 2001, s 73. The court must not refuse such leave unless it is satisfied: (a) that the grounds are frivolous or vexatious; or (b) that there are no *reasonable grounds* for contending that the person against whom the proceedings are brought acted in bad faith or without reasonable care. Under the repealed Mental Treatment Act 1945, s 260, the court had to be satisfied that that there were *substantial grounds*. See *Blehein v Murphy (No 2)* [2000] 3 IR 357, SC and [2000] 2 ILRM 481, SC. See *O'Flynn & O'Regan v Mid-Western Health Board* [1991] 2 IR 223, SC.

Where the State or a public body is party to civil proceedings before a court, the State or the public body is required to use the official language chosen by the other party: Official Languages Act 2003, s 8(4). Where there are two or more other parties who cannot agree on the official language to be used, the State or the public body is required to use the official language which appears to be reasonable, having regard to the circumstances. [Bibliography: Buckley, Melody; Collins & O'Reilly; Zuckerman.] See CIVIL SUMMONS; COSTS IN CIVIL PROCEEDINGS; PLEADINGS; SUMMONS, SERVICE OF; TORT.

civil registration. The official recording of certain specified life events: births, stillbirths, adoptions, marriages and deaths: Civil Registration Act 2004. There are approximately 111,000 events registered each year, 500,000 certificates produced and 1.2m searches or enquiries carried out each year: *Explanatory Memorandum* to the Bill. Civil registration records: (a) serve the need for evidence which has a bearing on rights, liabilities, status and nationality; (b) are used with other data for many purposes e g planning of hospitals, schools and housing, and for medical research into the causes of and prevention of disease; (c) provide information for persons tracing their family history.

The objectives of the CRA 2004 are: (a) to rationalise the procedures for registering births, stillbirths and deaths; (b) to streamline the existing procedures governing the registration of adoptions; (c) to reform the procedures governing the registration of marriages; (d) to establish new registers of divorce and nullity of marriage; (e) to give to an tArd-Chláraitheoir (Registrar General) responsibility for overall policy for the Civil Registration Service, including maintaining standards of service; and (f) to assign responsibility for the management, control and administration of the Service at local level to health boards.

There is provision for appeals of decisions made by a registrar (CRA 2004, s 60), for searches, subject to certain conditions (CRA 2004, ss 61–62), for correction of errors (CRA 2004, ss 63–64), and for charging fees (CRA 2004, s 67). See BIRTH, REGISTRATION OF; DEATH, REGISTRATION OF; MARRIAGE, REGISTRATION OF; STILLBORN CHILD.

civil remedy. The remedy available to an aggrieved person following civil proceedings by way of compensation rather than punishment of the wrongdoer e g damages, specific performance, injunction, judicial review (qqv). [Bibliography: Kerr (2).]

civil servant. A servant of the State, other than the holder of political or judicial office, who is employed in a civil capacity and whose remuneration is paid wholly and directly out of moneys voted by the Oireachtas. Civil servants who are *established* (ie permanent) hold office at the will and pleasure of the government whereas *unestablished* (ie temporary) officers may have their services terminated by the appropriate authority: Civil Service Regulation Act 1956, ss 5–6. Other conditions of employment are fixed by the Minister (CSRA 1956, s 17).

However, since 1997 the Secretary General of a Department has the authority, responsibility and accountability for managing all matters pertaining to the appointment, performance, discipline or dismissal of civil servants below the grade of Principal: Public Service Management (No 2) Act 1997, s 4. The Secretary General is required to prepare and submit to the Minister for approval a strategy statement which contains the key objectives, outputs and related strategies of the Department (PSM(No 2)A, s 5). The Secretary General is accountable to the Minister and must appear before a committee of either or of both Houses of the Oireachtas when so requested in writing (PSM(No 2)A, ss 6 and 10).

It has been held that the power of termination of a civil servant (during, or at the end of, a probationary period) is not one which can be exercised arbitrarily: *The State (Daly) v Minister for Agriculture* [1988] ILRM 173. Also an extension of a probationary period must be explicit and the appropriate authority must have been satisfied during the period of probation of a failure of the civil servant to fulfil a condition of the probation: *Whelan v Minister for Justice* [1991] 2 IR 241, HC: see *Barry* in 9 ILT & SJ (1991) 2 and 9 ILT Dig (1991) 73. See also Civil Service Regulations (Amendment) Act 1958; Houses of the Oireachtas Commission Act 2003, ss 19–20. See *Flynn v An Post* [1987] IR 68, SC; *Reidy v Minister for Agriculture* [1989] ITLR (4 Septmeber), HC; *O'Reilly v Minister for Industry and Commerce* [1993] HC; *O'Leary v Minister for Finance* [1998] 2 ILRM 321, HC; *Gilheaney v Revenue Commissioners* [1998] 4 IR 150, HC. See also Public Service Superannuation (Miscellaneous Provisions) Act 2004, Sch 2. For the Office of the Civil Service and Local Appointments Commission, see website: *www.publicjobs.ie*. See INCITEMENT; MARRIAGE BAR; PUBLIC SERVICE PENSION SCHEME; PUBLIC SERVICE RECRUITMENT; VICARIOUS LIABILITY.

civil society. In terms of the EU, means all kinds of organisations and associations which are not part of government but which represent professions, interest groups or sections of society, including trade unions, employers' associations, environmental lobbies and groups representing women, farmers, and people with disabilities. In EU policymaking there is regular consultation with civil society.

civil summons. Means a summons issued under Ord 39, 42, 49 and 62: DCR 1997, Interpretation of Terms. The summons the issue of which commences civil proceedings in the district court, in respect of proceedings founded on contract, tort, or in ejectment proceedings: DCR 1997 Ord 39. The summons must set out concisely the nature

of the plaintiff's claim and the grounds therefor, the costs if the plaintiff's claim is paid within ten days, the date in which the summons is returnable, two detachable notices of defence, the consequences if the defendant fails to act, signature and date of issue, and stamped in accordance with law (Ord 39, rr 4–6). The proceedings are *stayed* if the defendant pays the amount sued for and the ten-day costs (Ord 39, r 8). See APPEARANCE; PLEADINGS; SUMMONS, SERVICE OF.

civil wrong. A tort (qv).

civilian. A person who is not a member of the defence forces.

claim. The assertion of a right. For *letter of claim* in personal injuries proceedings, see Civil Liability and Courts Act 2004, s 8. See INDORSEMENT OF CLAIM; PERSONAL INJURIES ACTION; STATE CLAIMS AGENCY; STATEMENT OF CLAIM.

clam vi, aut precario. [By stealth, violence or entreaty.] See PRESCRIPTION.

class action. An action brought by a member of a class of persons on behalf of himself and the other members of the class. Where there are numerous persons having the same interest in one cause or matter, one or more such persons may sue or be sued, or may be authorised by the Court to defend, on behalf of or for the benefit, of all persons so interested: RSC Ord 15, r 9. See *Moore and Others v Attorney-General for Saorstát Éireann (No 2)* [1930] IR 471; *Turner & Ors v Hospital Trust (1940) Ltd* [1994] ELR 35, HC.

Where there are numerous persons having the same interest in one action or matter, one or more of such persons may sue or be sued, or may be authorised by the judge to defend, in such action or matter, on behalf of or for the benefit of all persons so interested: Circuit Court Rules 2001 Ord 6, r 10. This does not apply in actions founded on *tort*.

In the District Court, where several persons have the same interest in one action or matter, one or more such persons may sue or be sued or may be authorised by the court to defend such action or matter on behalf of or for the benefit of all persons so interested: DCR 1997 Ord 39, r 10.

The Law Reform Commission has recommended the introduction of a class actions procedure, under which the judge issuing an order certifying a class action would be required to be satisfied that: (a) the pleadings disclose a cause of action; (b) there is an identifiable class of ten or more persons at the time of certification; (c) the claims or defences of the class raise common issues of fact or law; (d) there is a class representative who will fairly and adequately represent the interest of the class; and (e) the class action is an appropriate, fair and efficient procedure: Consultation Paper on *Multi-Party Litigation (Class Actions)* (LRC CP 25, 2003).

In *equal pay* (qv) cases there cannot be a class action, but there can always be a number of claims. In such cases, only two persons are dealt with – the claimant is one and the comparator is the other: *Verbatim Ltd v Duffy* [1994] ELR 159, HC and Anti-Discrimination (Pay) Act 1974, s 3 (now repealed and replaced by Employment Equality Act 1998 and Equality Act 2004). See however, COLLECTIVE AGREEMENT.

class gift. A gratuitous grant to a number of persons of the same description e g *to X's brothers*. A class gift in a will, speaks from the date of death of the testator. If any member of the class is alive at the testator's death, membership of the class is fixed at that moment. If no member of the class is alive at the testator's death, then *prima facie*, the gift includes all members born at any future date. If a life interest precedes the class gift, then all those of the class alive when the life interest ceases are entitled to share in the gift. See Succession Act 1965, ss 91 and 98. See LAPSE.

class rights. The special rights attaching to different classes of shares in a company. In certain circumstances, class rights are not *ipso facto* deemed to vary in two major kinds of change to the capital structure, in the absence of some provision to the contrary, e g the issue of additional shares ranking *pari passu* with the existing ones, and the issue of new shares carrying preferential rights as regards voting, dividend, return of capital or otherwise: Companies Act 1963, Table A.

For variation of class rights see Companies Amendment Act 1983, s 38. Class rights may not be varied in a capital reduction without the requisite class approval (s 38(3)). Where a proposed variation of class rights obtains the requisite approval of the class affected, dissenting shareholders representing 10% in value of the class may apply to the court to stop the proposal being put into effect: Companies Act 1963, s 78. See *In re Holders Investment Trust*

[1971] 2 All ER 289. See RECONSTRUCTION OF COMPANY; TAKE-OUT MERGER.

clause. A sub-division of a document.

clausulae inconsuetae semper inducunt suspicionem. [Unusual clauses always excite suspicion.]

clausum fregit. [He broke the close.]

Clayton's case. The rule that in a running account in the absence of special agreement a creditor may treat the earliest credit as being in repayment of the earliest debt: Clayton's Case (*Devaynes v Noble* [1816]1 Mer 572). However, see Companies Act 1963, s 288 as amended by Companies Act 1990, s 136 and *Smurfit Paribas Bank Ltd v AAB Export Finance Ltd* [1991] 2 IR 19, HC.

clean hands. A maxim of equity (qv): *he who comes to equity must come with clean hands*. In remitting a case back to the High Court, the Supreme Court held that the finding by the High Court that the plaintiff had not come to court with *clean hands* was not supported by the evidence and no such claim had been advanced before that court: *Professor Conall Fanning v University College Cork* (2003) Irish Times, 31 January 2003. The Supreme Court also restored an injunction restraining UCC from publishing the findings of its disciplinary inquiry concerning Prof Fanning, whose claims will have to be considered by the High Court i e claims that the disciplinary procedure was unlawful, was in excess of UCC's powers, and did not apply to him given his statutory appointment. See *Ardent Fisheries v Minister for Tourism and Forestry* [1987] ILRM 528; *Curust Financial Services Ltd v Loewe-Lack-Werk* [1994] 1 IR 450, SC and [1993] ILRM 723, SC.

clear days. Complete days. Days prescribed in the Rules of the Superior Courts which are not expressed to be clear days, are to be reckoned exclusively of the first day and inclusively of the last day: RSC Ord 122, r 10. See TIME, COURT RULES.

cleared site value. The value of land as a site cleared of buildings, less such sum as the arbitrator determines to be the cost of clearing and levelling the land, to which the owner of a house is entitled as compensation in relation to a *compulsory purchase* (qv) effected under the provisions of the Housing Act 1966 and where the acquired property includes the house which, in the opinion of the housing authority (qv), is unfit for human habitation and not capable of being rendered fit for human habitation at reasonable expense (HA 1966, s 84(1)). See also Housing Act 1966 (Acquisition of Land) Regulations 1966, SI No 278 of 1966. See COMPENSATION AND COMPULSORY PURCHASE.

clergy expenses. A minister of a religious denomination is entitled, in calculating his income for tax purposes, to deduct any expenses incurred wholly, exclusively and necessarily in the performance of his profession: Taxes Consolidation Act 1997, s 837. He is also permitted to deduct up to one-eight of the rent paid for a residence used for his ministerial duties. See *Mitchell v Child* (1942) 24 TC 511.

clerical error. A mistake made in a mechanical process such as writing or copying as opposed to the intellectual process of drafting: *Maere's Application* [1962] RPC 182. See Waste Management Act 1996, s 42B inserted by Protection of the Environment Act 2003, s 38. See ORDER; SLIP RULE; TYPOGRAPHICAL ERROR.

client account. Means an account opened and kept by a solicitor, arising from his practice as a solicitor, for clients' money: Solicitors (Amendment) Act 1994, s 2. Money in a client account is held by a solicitor in trust for his clients; he is not beneficially entitled to it and he is not entitled to draw a cheque on the account for the purposes of discharging an amount due by him to an other person: *Incorporated Law Society v Owens* [1990] 8 ILT Dig 64. See Solicitors' Accounts Regulations 2001, SI No 421 of 2001; Solicitors' (Interest on Clients' Money) Regulations 1995, SI No 108 of 1995, and Regulations 2004, SI No 372 of 2004.

In 2004, a solicitor lost her High Court challenge to a District Court judge's direction permitting the Minister for Justice to inspect and take copies of the solicitor's client account: *Gavin v District Judge Haughton* (2004) Irish Times, 28 May, HC. The judge was acting in response to a *letter of request* (qv) from the Italian authorities. See also ACCOUNTS, SOLICITOR; AUCTIONEER; INSURANCE BROKER; SOLICITOR; SOLICITOR'S LIEN.

client file. The file maintained by a solicitor in respect of his client. An employee leaving a firm of solicitors cannot, without formal authority, take the files of clients, even files of clients introduced by the employee: *A Guide to Professional Conduct of Solicitors in Ireland* (2002) ch 7.6. If a partner leaves a firm, or if the partnership is dissolved, there should be prompt notification to the clients of the firm, explaining to them that they may choose to instruct whomsoever they wish. Files should never be a pawn in disputes between solicitors. In certain circumstances the client file belongs to the client, but it may be the subject of a lien by the solicitor. Solicitors are required to ensure that all files, documents and other records are retained for appropriate periods (*Guide to Professional Conduct*, ch 9.13). See SOLICITOR, CHANGE OF; SOLICITOR'S LIEN.

clients' money. (1) Means money received, held or controlled by a solicitor, arising from his practice as a solicitor, for or on account of a client, whether as agent, bailee, stakeholder, trustee or in any other capacity: Solicitors (Amendment) Act 1994, s 2. It is an offence for a solicitor to fail to lodge clients' moneys in a bank account or to lodge it in an unapproved account, or to fail to record the receipt of clients' moneys or to fail to record the lodgement of clients' moneys to a bank account: Solicitors Act 1954, s 66 as substituted by S(A)A 1994, s 76 and amended by Solicitors (Amendment) Act 2002, s 3.

The Law Society is required to make regulations governing the requirement of a solicitor either to maintain clients' moneys in deposit accounts for the benefit of clients or to pay to clients a sum equivalent to the interest which would have accrued if the money had been kept on deposit (S(A)A 1994, s 73). See Solicitors' Accounts Regulations 2001, SI No 421 of 2001; Solicitors' (Interest on Clients' Money) Regulations 1995, SI No 108 of 1995, and Regulations 2004, SI No 372 of 2004.

Moneys handled by a solicitor acting for a client under a power of attorney are clients' moneys within the meaning of the Solicitors Accounts Regulations: *A Guide to Professional Conduct of Solicitors in Ireland* (2002) ch 9.8. All moneys received by a solicitor for or on behalf of a client from a financial institution or insurance company are deemed to be the client's money (*Guide to Professional Conduct*, ch 10.5).

A barrister is prohibited from directly or indirectly administering or handling the funds or assets of any client and a barrister is prohibited from giving any financial advice or assistance to a client or his solicitor on the investment of such funds or assets: *Code of Conduct for the Bar of Ireland*

(December 2003), r 2.22. See ACCOUNTS, SOLICITOR.

(2) The Supreme Court has held that funds in the client bank account of a stockbroker was *clients' money* within the meaning of the Stock Exchange Act 1995, s 52(5)(a) and were trust funds held in a fiduciary capacity to meet in full those clients' proper claims: *Re Money Markets International Ltd* [2000] 3 IR 437, SC and *Re Money Markets International Ltd (No 2)* [2001] 2 IR 17, HC. See TEEMING AND LADING.

clinical claim. A claim connected with the provision of, or failure to provide, a '*professional medical service*': National Treasury Management Agency (Delegation of Functions) Order 2003, SI No 63 of 2003. A '*professional medical service*' means: (a) services provided by registered medical practitioners or registered dentists of a diagnostic or palliative nature, or consisting of the provision of treatment in respect of any illness, disease, injury or other medical condition; (b) services provided by other health professionals in the performance of their duties, including pharmacists, nurses, midwives, paramedics, ambulance personnel, laboratory technicians; or (c) services connected with the provision of health or medical care provided by persons acting under the direction of a person to whom (a) or (b) applies. The regulation provides for the delegation of the management of certain clinical claims (i e claims against the Minister for Health and Children, or against specified bodies i e health boards and voluntary hospitals) to the Agency. See STATE CLAIMS AGENCY.

clinical trials, conduct of. The conducting of a systematic investigation or series of investigations for the purpose of ascertaining the effects (including kinetic effects) of the administration of one or more substances or preparations on persons where such administration may have a pharmacological or harmful effect: Control of Clinical Trials Act 1987, s 6(2) and Control of Clinical Trials Act 1990, s 2.

Excluded from clinical trials are the administration of substances or preparations in the ordinary course of medical or dental practice where the principal purpose is to prevent disease in, or to save the life, restore the health, alleviate the condition or relieve the suffering of, the patient (CCTA 1990, s 2).

A person must not conduct a clinical trial unless: (a) he is a registered medical practitioner or a registered dentist; and (b) there is a subsisting permission granted by the Irish Medicines Board in respect of the trial; and (c) an *ethics committee* has given its approval (CCTA 1987, s 6(1) as amended by Irish Medicines Board Act 1995, s 35). These provisions do not apply in specified circumstances to a clinical trial of a substance or preparation which has been granted a *product authorisation* under the Medical Preparations (Licensing, Advertisement and Sale) Regulations 1984, SI No 210 of 1984 (CCTA 1987, s 2).

Consent in writing to participation in a clinical trial is required (CCTA 1987, s 9). Prior to a clinical trial being arranged or conducted, the Irish Medicines Board must be satisfied on the adequacy of security to compensate participants who may suffer injury, loss or damage (CCTA 1990, s 3). See Control of Clinical Trials Act, 1987 (Commencement) Order 1988, SI No 321 of 1988. A person who is suffering from a *mental disorder* (qv), who has been admitted to an approved centre, must not be a participant in a clinical trial: Mental Health Act 2001, s 70.

The 1987 and 1990 Acts do not apply to clinical trials that are subject to the EC (Clinical Trials on Medicinal Products for Human Use) Regulations 2004, SI No 190 of 2004. In the context of these regulations, a *clinical trial* means any investigation in human subjects, other than a non-interventional trial, intended: (a) to discover or verify the clinical, pharmacological or other pharmacodynamic effects of one or more investigational medicinal products; or (b) to identify any adverse reaction to one or more investigational medicinal products; or (c) to study absorption, distribution, metabolism and excretion of one or more such investigational medicinal products; or (d) to discover, verify, identify or study any combination of the matters referred to at (a), (b), and (c) (reg 4(1)). The purpose of the regulations is to implement EC Directive 2001/20/EC on the approximation of the laws, regulations and administrative provisions of the member states relating to good clinical practice in the conduct of clinical trials on medicinal products for human use.

'Informed, written consent must be obtained if patients are to be involved in clinical trials or any form of research. The aims and methods of the proposed research, together with any potential hazards or discomfort, should be explained to the patient': Medical Council, *A Guide to Ethical Conduct and Behaviour* (6th edn, 2004), para 20.1. Doctors engaged in research have a duty to be truthful to patients about all aspects of the study (para 4.14). [Bibliography: Keys; Tomkin & Hanafin.] See ADVERSE EVENT; ADVERSE REACTION; DRUG TRIALS; ETHICS COMMITTEE.

clog on equity of redemption. The equitable doctrine which does not permit the *equity of redemption* (qv) to be fettered or unreasonably restricted by any provision which would make it difficult for the mortgagor (qv) to redeem a mortgage after the date for repayment of the mortgage debt.

cloning. The copying of genes by asexual reproduction; a clone will be genetically identical to the cloned. There are two types of cloning – *reproductive* cloning and *therapeutic* cloning. Human *reproductive* cloning involves creating genetically identical foetuses or babies, while *therapeutic* cloning involves cloning human embryo cells under two weeks old for the purpose of research into diseases such as Parkinson's disease, cancers, and stroke: 'Human genetics and the need for regulation' by Stephen Dodd BL in *Bar Review* (May 2001) 418.

Cloning processes are in general excluded from patentability under the EU Directive on the legal protection of Biological Inventions 1998 (implemented in Ireland by European Communities (Legal Protection of Biotechnological Inventions) Regulations 2000, SI No 247 of 2000). Specifically excluded under art 6(2) of the Directive are process for cloning human beings. The reason for this exclusion is 'because the social and ethical ramifications of cloning remain unexplored in the EU': Oliver Mills in 'Biotechnology and the ethical and moral concerns of European Patent Law', *Bar Review* (October 2000) 46. See 'Cell Division' by solicitor Niamh Pollak in *Law Society Gazette* (June 2004) 36. See BIOTECHNOLOGICAL INVENTION; EMBRYO IMPLANTATION; GENE THERAPY; HUMAN REPRODUCTION; IN-VITRO FERTILISATION.

close. (1) The termination of pleadings, as in *close of pleadings*. (2) Enclosed land. See WAY, RIGHT OF.

close company. A company which, for the purposes of corporation tax, is considered as under the control of five or fewer partici-pators or by any number of participators who are directors. A *participator* is one who owns share capital and has voting rights in the company: Corporation Tax Act 1976, Pt X; ss 94–104, now Taxes Consolidation Act 1997, ss 430–441. Excluded from the definition of *close company* are companies owned by the State (TCA 1997, s 430(1)(d)). Also excluded are companies owned by an EU member state or owned by a country with which Ireland has a double taxation treaty: Finance Act 2003, s 63. The amount of a loan made by a close company to a participator in that close company is treated as a net payment, after deduction of standard rate income tax i e it is grossed up; this does not apply to loans made by a close company to companies resident outside the EU (TCA 1997, s 438 as amended by FA 2003, s 45). A dividend or other distribution by a company in respect of shares in that company will not be regarded as 'investment income' for the purposes of the close company surcharge of 20% in certain circumstances (TCA 1997, s 434 as amended by Finance Act 2004, s 36). See *Rahinstown Estates v Hughes* [1987] ILRM 599.

close period. See DIRECTORS AND SHARE DEALING.

close season. The varying periods of the year during which it is unlawful to hunt game. See OPEN SEASON.

closed shop. The term used to describe agreements between employers and trade unions whereby jobs are only to be obtained or retained if the employee is, or becomes and remains, a member of a specified union. They can be *pre-entry* agreements where the individual must be a trade union member before he can be employed, or *post-entry* where the employer is entitled to employ a non-trade unionist provided he agrees to join the union immediately or shortly after employment.

It has been held that the imposition of a closed shop on existing employees, being a restriction on their right to disassociate, is unconstitutional: *Educational Co of Ireland Ltd v Fitzpatrick (No 2)* [1961] IR 345; *Meshell v CIE* [1973] IR 121. The practice of requiring potential employees to join specific trade unions as a pre-condition to obtaining employment may be unconstitutional and contrary to art 11 of the European Convention on Human Rights: *Young, James Wester v UK* [1981] IRLR 408; 75 Gazette Law Society 237. See *Nathan v*

Bailey Gibson Ltd [1996] ELR 114, SC and [1998] 2 IR 162, SC.

closing order. See UNFIT HOUSE.

closing speeches. In a trial on indictment, the prosecution has the right to a closing speech, except where the accused is unrepresented and does not call a witness other than a witness of character only: Criminal Justice Act 1984, s 24. The defence has a right to a closing speech in all cases; the closing speech of the defence is made after that for the prosecution. The purpose of s 24 is to give the prosecution the right to a closing speech where the accused has been professionally represented by advocates who may have exposed weaknesses or lacunae in the prosecution case: *The People (DPP) v Byrne* [1998] 2 IR 417, CCA. See LEADING BARRISTER; SUMMING UP.

closure notice. A notice which an 'authorised person' is empowered to serve on a person who owns, occupies or is in control of a building, when he is of the opinion that a building or premises poses or is likely to pose a serious and immediate risk, including a risk of fire, to the safety of persons on or in such building: Fire Services Act 1981, s 20A inserted by Licensing of Indoor Events Act 2003, s 30. The closure notice will direct that the activities to which the notice relates must be discontinued by any persons unless the matters posing the risk are remedied. The notice takes effect immediately on service, if it so declares. An appeal, within seven days of service of the notice, lies to the District Court but such appeal does not have the effect of suspending an immediate closure notice. An 'authorised person' is a person so authorised by a fire authority, by an order to this effect made by a county or city manager as the case may be.

closure order. (1) An order, served on the proprietor or person in charge of a *premises*, directing that the premises be closed, where in the opinion of an authorised officer there is or is likely to be a grave and immediate danger to public health: Food Safety Authority Act 1998, s 53. The order must specify the matters which give rise to the risk and, if there is a contravention of food legislation, specify the provision. *Premises* affected are those involved in the production, preparation, processing, manufacture, exportation, importation, storage, distribution or sale of food (FSAA 1998, s 2(1)). An appeal against a closure order may be made to the District Court within seven days from service of the order (FSAA 1998, s 53(5)). See IMPROVEMENT NOTICE, FOOD.

(2) An order of the District Court requiring the temporary closure of a licensed premises, in addition to any other penalty imposed, where the licensee has been convicted of certain specified offences e g supplying a drunken person with alcoholic liquor or permitting drunkenness: Intoxicating Liquor Act 2003, s 9. The closure order is mandatory on conviction, but the judge is given some discretion on the closure period. It must not exceed seven days for a first offence; and for subsequent offences, not more than 30 days and not less than seven days. There is provision for an appeal against a closure order. It is an offence not to affix a conspicuous notice giving details of the closure order (ILA 2003, s 16(c)).

(3) An order of the District Court under which certain specified premises may be restricted from opening for business for certain times and periods, as the court may determine, where there has been disorder either on the premises or in the vicinity of, and involving persons who were on, the premises, and such disorder is likely to recur: Criminal Justice (Public Disorder) Act 2003, ss 4–5. The premises include: public houses, off-licences, dance venues of all types, amusement arcades, night clubs, premises providing food (whether fixed or mobile e g mobile food vans).

A closure order may also be made if there has been loud or persistent noise from the premises, or in the vicinity of the premises, and caused by persons who were on the premises. The noise must be so loud, so continuous, so repeated, of such duration or pitch or occurring at such times as to give reasonable cause for annoyance to persons in that vicinity and such noise is likely to recur (CJ(PD)A 2003, s 4(1)). 'Vicinity' means land within a reasonable distance, not exceeding 100 metres, of the premises (CJ(PD)A 2003, s 2(1)).

An application for a closure order is made by a garda, not below the rank of inspector, to the District Court, following notice in writing to the licensee of the premises concerned. A closure order may be for a period up to seven days for a first order, or seven to 30 days for a second or subsequent order.

A notice must be affixed by the licensee to the exterior of the premises concerned in a conspicuous place, specifying the closure times or the period of closure under the order and the grounds for making it (CJ(PD)A 2003, s 5(6)). An appeal against a closure order lies to the Circuit Court (CJ(PD)A 2003, s 6). A person who permits a premises to open in contravention of a closure order commits an offence, as does a person who is on the premises unless he can show that the requirement regarding the affixing of a notice had not been complied with (CJ(PD)A 2003, s 8). It is also an offence for a person not to leave a premises when so requested, to enable compliance with a closure order (CJ(PD)A 2003, s 8(3)).

club. A voluntary association of persons combined for purposes other than carrying on business. It is not a partnership. A club sues and is sued in the names of the members of its committee, or the officers, on behalf of themselves and all other members of the club. A club is founded on the contract between the members; in the absence of a contrary provision, members are liable only to the extent of their subscriptions, and payments by members become the property of all the members and cannot be the subject of a resulting trust if the club is wound up, in which case any surplus assets are distributed to the members for the time being per capita.

The property of a club is usually vested in trustees who hold it on behalf of the members. A club often has no legal persona apart from that derived from all the members and consequently cannot incur liability from wrongs at the suit of a member of that body: *Murphy v Roche* [1987] IR 106, HC. Also failure to comply with the rules regarding the election of members, prevents a person becoming a member of a club: *Walsh v Butler (Bandon Rugby Club)* [1997] 2 ILRM 81, HC.

Frequently clubs are registered under the Registration of Clubs (Ireland) Acts 1904 to 2003 in order to avail of the provisions to supply their members with excisable liquors without a licence: see *In re Parnell GAA Club Ltd* [1984] ILRM 246. For the steps to be taken for a club to apply for and hold a Certificate of Registration, see *Cassidy* in 7 ILT & SJ (1989) 112. See also DCR 1997 Ord 83. The extended permitted hours for consuming intoxicating liquor in licensed premises, introduced in 2000, and the exemption of one hour permitted to hotels and restaurants is also applied to clubs: Intoxicating Liquor Act 2000, s 7 and Intoxicating Liquor Act 2003, s 23.

Registered clubs are restricted on advertising functions to be held by the club, except in relation to events where intoxicating liquor is not provided in conjunction with the event: Intoxicating Liquor Act 1988, s 45 as amended by ILA 2000, s 31; *DPP (Barron) v Wexford Farmers Club* [1994] 2 ILRM 295, HC. The 2000 Act also clarifies the position regarding the holding of functions in a registered club; such functions must be for the benefit of the club as a whole, organised by the club and be related to the club's objects and be attended only by members and their guests (ILA 2000, s 29). There are exemptions for functions which are for the benefit of the community or for private functions for a member and his guests. The 2000 Act also extends to clubs the provisions relating to underage persons and intoxicating liquor (ILA 2000, s 16 and ILA 2003, s 23).

Some clubs are *proprietary clubs* wherein the property of the club is owned by the proprietor who bears the expenses but who also receives the subscriptions of the members; such a club cannot be registered under Registration of Clubs (Ireland) Acts 1904. Alternatively, some clubs incorporate themselves as companies usually *limited by guarantee*.

Any proposal to expel a member from a club must comply with the principles of *natural justice*; he must be informed of the complaint against him and be given an opportunity to be heard in his own defence. See *Rochford v Storey* [1982] HC. However, the rules of a club, association or union, form the contract between the officers and the members and set down how the affairs of the body should be conducted; consequently, its affairs are not in general susceptible to judicial review in the absence of *mala fides* or disregard of the rules: *McEvoy v Prison Officers Association* [1999] 1 ILRM 445 and ELR 129, SC. See also Courts (No 2) Act 1986, s 9; Intoxicating Liquor Act 1988, ss 42–46; Taxes Consolidation Act 1997, s 1044. [Bibliography: Woods (2); Palmer UK; Warburton UK.] See UNINCORPORATED ASSOCIATION; WILD-LIFE DEALING.

club, discriminating. A club may be a *discriminating club* or a *non-discriminating club*: Equal Status Act 2000, ss 8–10. A certificate of registration under the Registration of Clubs Acts 1904 to 1999, which permits the sale of intoxicating liquor, will not be granted or renewed in respect of a discriminating club (ESA 2000, s 10). A *club* means a club that has applied for or holds a certificate of registration (ESA 2000, s 8(1)). A club is considered to be a *discriminating club* if (a) it has any rule, policy or practice which discriminates against a member or an applicant for membership; or (b) a person involved in its management discriminates against a member or an applicant for membership in relation to the affairs of the club (ESA 2000, s 8(2)(a)).

The following acts are evidence that a club is a discriminatory club if done on *discriminatory grounds* eg: (a) refusing to admit a person to membership; (b) providing different terms and conditions of membership for members or applicants; (c) terminating membership or subjecting a member to any other sanction; or (d) refusing or failing to do all that is reasonable to accommodate the needs of a member, or an applicant, with a disability (ESA 2000, s 8(2)(b)).

However, having a reasonable preferential charge for persons together with their children, married couples, persons in a specific age group, or persons with a disability does not constitute a discriminatory rule, policy or practice for the purposes of s 8(2)(a): see ESA 2000, s 16(1)(b).

Any person, including the Equality Authority, may apply to the District Court and request the court to make a determination as to whether a club is a discriminating club (ESA 2000, s 8(3)). The determination may be appealed to the Circuit Court within 42 days after the order (ESA 2000, s 8(8)). See 'Sex equality and the Equal Status Act' by Cliona Kimber BL and Marguerite Bolger BL in *Bar Review* (January 2001) 198. [Bibliography: Reid M.] For the ten *discriminatory grounds*, see DISCRIMINATION.

club, non-discriminating. A club is not considered to be a *discriminating club* by reason only that its principal purpose is to cater only for the needs of particular persons and it refuses membership to other persons eg the particular persons can be: (a) persons of a particular gender, marital status, family status, sexual orientation, religious belief, age, disability, nationality or ethnic or national origin; (b) persons who are of the Traveller community; or (c) persons who have no religious belief: Equal

Status Act 2000, s 9(1)(a). The District Court has held that as the principal purpose of Portmarnock Golf Club was the playing of golf, not the playing of men's golf (as women played golf there but could not become members) it was a discriminating club and could not avail of the exemption under s 9(1)(a): *Equality Authority v Portmarnock Golf Club* (2004) Irish Times, 21 February, DC. The District Court subsequently suspended the club's liquor licence for seven days, with enforcement of the suspension depending on the outcome of proceedings being taken by the club in the High Court: *Equality Authority v Portmarnock Golf Club* (2004) Irish Times, 19 May, DC.

A club is not considered a discriminating club by reason only that it has different types of membership, access to which is not based on any *discriminatory ground* (ESA 2000, s 9(1)(c). Also a club may confine access to a membership benefit or privilege to members within the category of a particular gender or age, where it is not practicable for members outside and within the category to enjoy the privilege or benefit *at the same time*, and arrangements have been made by the club to offer the same or reasonably equivalent benefit or privilege both to members outside and within the category (ESA 2000, s 9(1)(b)).

A club may provide different treatment to members in relation to sporting facilities and events, where the different treatment is relevant to the purpose of the facility or events and is reasonably necessary (ESA 2000, s 9(1)(e)). Reserving places on its board or committees in order to promote equality will not make a club discriminating (ESA 2000, s 9(2)). See also Employment Equality Act 1998, s 67 as amended by ESA 2000, s 39 and Sch. [Bibliography: Reid M.] For the ten *discriminatory grounds*, see DISCRIMINATION.

CMR. [*Convention relative au contrat de transport international de merchandises par route.*] The Convention on the Contract for the International Carriage of Goods by Road as given effect in Ireland by the International Carriage of Goods by Road Act 1990. The Convention lays down standard conditions of contract for the international carriage of goods. It defines the rights and obligations of the consignor, carrier and the consignee eg the carrier is generally liable for loss, damage or delay to the goods, but the liability is limited unless there has been wilful misconduct or a special value for the goods has been declared. Limits set on liability in the Canals Act 1830, the Railway and Canal Traffic Act 1854, s 7, or the Sale of Goods Acts 1893 to 1980 do not apply to contracts for the carriage of goods governed by the Convention (ICGRA 1990, s 3(3)). The Statute of Limitations 1957, Pt III (which allows for exceptions for fraud, mistake and disability) applies to actions under the CMR. See CMR Contracting Parties Order 1991, SI No 160 of 1991.

co. Abbreviation of *company* (qv).

co-authors. See JOINT AUTHORSHIP.

co-defendants. See DEFENDANT, JOINT.

co-operatives. As a general rule, co-operatives are commercial enterprises which tend to do business principally with their own members with the object of providing a product or service at minimal cost; while a dividend may be payable to members, its maximisation is not necessarily the primary objective. Co-operatives are usually registered as companies under the Companies Acts 1963 as amended or as societies under the Industrial and Provident Societies Acts 1893 to 1978. Special legislation exists for building societies and credit unions: Building Societies Act 1989 and Credit Union Act 1997. A disciplinary hearing of a co-operative must observe the requirements of natural justice (qv): *Ryan v VIP Taxi Co-operative Society Ltd* [1989] ITLR (10 April). See *In re Belfast Tailors' Co-Partnership* [1909] 1 IR 49.

co-opted director. A director appointed to the board of a company by the other directors, instead of by the members at an annual general meeting, usually to fill a casual vacancy. A *listed* company must ensure that at all times not more than one third of its board is composed of persons who have been co-opted to the Board: Listing Rules 2000, para 16.20. A company which breaches this requirement, must convene an EGM for the election of the relevant director and make an immediate announcement to the stock exchange (para 16.20(b)(i)). Failure to comply will lead to suspension of the company (para 16.20(d)). See *Phoenix Shannon plc v Parkay* [1998] 4 IR 597, HC.

co-ownership. The concurrent ownership of two or more persons in the same property. See JOINT TENANCY; TENANCY IN COMMON.

coal. In 1990 regulations were introduced which prohibited the marketing, sale and distribution of bituminous coals within the restricted area of Dublin and set standards for allowable fuels in that area: Air Pollution Act 1987 (Marketing, Sale and Distribution of Fuels) Regulations 1990, SI No 123 of 1990. The ban was extended to Cork in 1994 (SI No 403 of 1994), to Arklow, Drogheda, Dundalk, Limerick and Wexford in 1998 (SI No 118 of 1998), and to Bray, Kilkenny, Sligo and Tralee in 2003 (SI No 111 of 2003). It is proposed to extend the ban to Athlone, Carlow, Clonmel and Ennis in the future. The Department for the Environment has claimed in 2004 that independent medical research has shown that the ban has resulted in some 116 fewer respiratory deaths and 243 fewer cardiovascular deaths per year in Dublin alone. See AIR POLLUTION.

coarse fish. Any freshwater fish or the spawn or fry thereof other than salmon, trout (including rainbow trout and char) or eels or their spawn or fry: Fisheries (Amendment) (No 2) Act 1987, s 2. See FISHING LICENCE; TROUT.

coat of arms. See CHIEF HERALD; COLLECTIVE MARK; NATIONAL LIBRARY OF IRELAND.

cockfight. 'A fight between two gamecocks fitted with sharp metal spurs': *Collins English Dictionary*. It is a crime to cause, procure or assist at a cockfight. If any person shall cause, procure or assist at the fighting or baiting of any animal, such person is guilty of an offence of cruelty: Protection of Animals Act 1911, s 1(1)(c). Persons commit the offence also if they keep, use, manage, or act or assist in the management of any premises for the purpose of fighting or baiting any animal.

code. A systematic collection in comprehensive form of laws or a branch of law eg the Sale of Goods Act 1893 and the Bills of Exchange Act 1882 were statutes collecting and stating the whole of the law, as it stood at the time they were enacted, including not only statute law but also judicial decisions. Contrast with CONSOLIDATION ACT. See also RESTATEMENT OF STATUTE.

code of behaviour. See SCHOOL DISCIPLINE.

code of conduct. Rules for practical guidance in relation to practices to be followed eg under the Insurance Act 1989, the Minister may by order prescribe the practices to be followed by insurance brokers (qv) or insurance agents (qv) in their dealings with their clients or undertakings or with other persons (IA 1989, s 56). See also Stock Exchange Act 1995, s 38; Investment Intermediaries Act 1995, s 37.

Every planning authority and An Bord Pleanála are required to adopt a *code of conduct* for dealing with conflicts of interest and for promoting public confidence in the integrity of the conduct of its business: Planning and Development Act 2000, s 150. It will be a condition of employment of a member or employee of An Bord Pleanála or an officer of a planning authority to comply with the code, and a condition of taking up and holding office by a member of a planning authority (PDA 2000, s 150(4)).

Provision has been made for the development of codes of conduct which will apply to Ministers, other office holders, members of the Oireachtas and employees of public bodies: Standards in Public Office Act 2001, s 10. The Government drew up a code in 2003 which applies to the Taoiseach, Tánaiste, Ministers, Ministers of State and chairs of Oireachtas committees. See also Gas (Interim) (Regulation) Act 2002, s 8; Digital Hub Development Agency Act 2003, s 23. See BARRISTER; COUNCILLOR, DISCLOSURE OF INTEREST; ETHICS IN PUBLIC OFFICE; MODEL CODE.

code of practice. Rules for practical guidance with respect to the requirements of some statute or with respect to the manner in which business is conducted.

Failure to observe a code may not of itself generally render a person liable to legal proceedings, but it may be admissible in evidence eg see Safety, Health and Welfare at Work Act 1989, ss 2, 30 and 31; Industrial Relations Act 1990, ss 42–43; Environmental Protection Agency Act 1992, ss 76–77; Employment Equality Act 1998, s 56 as amended by Equal Status Act 2000, s 39 and Sch.

Provision however has been made that any code of practice prepared by bodies representing data controllers (qv) or data processors (qv) will have the force of law where approved by a resolution of each House of the Oireachtas, and be taken into account by any court or tribunal: Data Protection Act 1988, s 13 as amended by Data Protection (Amendment) Act 2003, s 14. Also the Central Bank can compel compliance with a code of practice it draws up: Central Bank Act 1989, s 117. The Director of Consumer Affairs is empowered to publish codes of practice to secure transparency and fairness in consumer agreements: Consumer Credit Act 1995, s 5(1)(f) as substituted by Central Bank and Financial Services Authority of Ireland Act 2003, s 35, Sch 1.

Forfás (formerly Eolas) is empowered to issue codes of recommended practice: Industrial Research & Standards Act 1961; Science and Technology Act 1987; Industrial Development Act 1993, ss 9 and 18, as amended by Industrial Development (Science Foundation Ireland) Act 2003, s 35(c). The Labour Court is empowered to investigate a complaint that there has been a breach of a code of practice concerning industrial relations: Industrial Relations Act 1990, s 43. See Organisation of Working Time Act 1997, s 33; National Disability Authority Act 1999, ss 8(2)(d), 10, 15(4). See Code of Practice on Disciplinary Procedures Order 1996, SI No 117 of 1996. See also Industrial Relations Act 1990, Code of Practice on Employee Representatives (Declaration) Order 1993, SI No 169 of 1993; Organisation of Working Time (Code of Practice on Compensatory Rest and Related Matters) (Declaration) Order 1998, SI No 44 of 1998. See Enhanced Code of Practice on Voluntary Dispute Resolution (Declaration) Order 2004, SI No 76 of 2004; Code of Practice on Grievance and Disciplinary Procedures (Declaration) Order 2000, SI No 146 of 2000; Code of Practice detailing Procedures for Addressing Bullying in the Workplace, SI No 17 of 2002; Code of Practice (Harassment) Order 2002, SI No 78 of 2002. See also Licensing of Indoor Events Act 2003, ss 9 and 31.

Banks, building societies and finance houses, jointly adopted in 2000 a new *Code of Practice on Transparency in Credit Charges for Personal Customers*; it can be obtained on various banking websites, including *www.ibis.ie*. For code of practice for solicitors in relation to family law, see *A Guide to Professional Conduct of Solicitors in Ireland* (2002), App 4. See BULLYING IN THE WORKPLACE; UNFAIR DISMISSAL; WORKER PARTICIPATION.

codicil. An instrument executed by a testator for adding to, altering, explaining or confirming a will previously made by him. A codicil must be executed with the same formalities as a will, as a will is defined as including a codicil: Succession Act 1965, s 3(1). The effect of the codicil is to bring the will down to the date of the codicil and both instruments are read together, with the original dispositions as altered by the codicil. See *Earl of Mountcashell v Smyth* [1895] 1 IR 346. See RSC Ord 79, r 85; Ord 80, r 84. See ELECTRONIC FORM; SUPPLEMENTAL PROBATE, GRANT OF.

coercion. It is an offence for a person to take specified actions, without lawful authority, with a view to compelling another person to abstain from doing or to do any act which that other person has a right to do or to abstain from doing: Non-Fatal Offences against the Person Act 1997, s 9. The specified actions include: (a) using violence to or intimidating that person; (b) injuring his property; (c) persistently following him from place to place, (d) watching or besetting where he works or resides (NFOPA 1997, s 9(1)). See DURESS; MARITAL COERCION.

cogitationis poenam nemo patitur. [The thoughts and intents of men are not punishable.] See INTENTION.

cognates. Those persons who are related on the mother's side. See AGNATES.

cognisance, judicial. Judicial notice (qv) or knowledge.

cohabitation. Living together as or as if husband and wife. The guarantees in the 1937 Constitution relating to the family are confined to families based on marriage: *The State (Nicolaou) v An Bord Uchtála* [1966] IR 567. See also *Mulhern v Clery* [1930] IR 649. The favourable treatment that cohabiting claimants enjoyed, as regards social welfare, over their married counterparts was removed by the Social Welfare (No 2) Act 1989.

Contracts, express or implied, the consideration for which is cohabitation, are incapable of being enforced as a matter of public policy as that would give such agreements a status similar to that of marriage contracts: *Ennis v Butterly* [1997] 1 ILRM 28, HC and [1996] 1 IR 426, HC. Non-marital cohabitation cannot have the same constitutional status as marriage (*Ennis* case).

Cohabitation disqualifies a claimant from receiving a deserted wife's benefit (now called a one-parent family payment) or a survivor's pension (now called a widow's or widower's pension): Social Welfare (Consolidation) Act 1993, ss 101(3) and 110(3). See also *Foley v Moulton* [1989] ILRM 169.

There are 77,600 cohabiting couples in Ireland, making up 1 in 12 of all family units; one third of births in 2002 were outside marriage and 52,000 children live with cohabiting couples: solicitor Geoffrey Shannon in *Law Society Gazette* (August/September 2003) 7. [Bibliography: Murtagh B; Walpole.] See CONJUGAL RIGHTS, RESTITUTION OF; DIVORCE A MENSA ET THORO; FAMILY INCOME SUPPLEMENT; PART 4 TENANCY, TERMINATION OF; SPOUSE.

cohabitation, law reform. The Law Reform Commission issued in April 2004 a consultation paper on the rights and duties of cohabitees, in which it made substantial recommendations for reform of the law concerning cohabitees: LRC CP 32, 2004. The reforms proposed are confined to 'qualified cohabitees', who are defined as persons who live together in a 'marriage like' relationship for a continuous period of three years or, where there is a child of the relationship, for two years. This includes relationships between same sex or opposite sex couples, neither of whom are married to each other or to any other person.

The consultation paper deals with the rights and duties of cohabitees under a number of headings, including property rights, succession, maintenance, social welfare, pensions, taxation, health care and domestic violence, and recommends that cohabitees should be encouraged to regulate their financial and property affairs by means of co-ownership agreements. The paper also proposes that cohabitees should be given the right to apply to court for certain rights and financial reliefs following the termination of the cohabiting relationship eg for relief where provision has not been made in the will of the deceased or under intestacy rules.

cohaeredes sunt quasi unum corpus, propter unitatem juris quod habent. [Co-heirs are regarded as one person on account of the unity of title which they possess.] See COPARCENARY.

cohesion. Term used to describe the process whereby economic and social disparities between the richer and the less well-off regions of the European Community are to be reduced progressively: Treaty of Rome 1957. The Maastricht Treaty 1992 reinforced the objective of *economic and social cohesion* in the Treaty of Rome and specified many of the means to be used to achieve it eg the principles of cohesion were included and actions to strengthen cohesion were specified, including the establishment of a *Cohesion Fund,* and there was a specific Protocol on cohesion which contained several important commitments on funding. For consolidated provisions, see Treaty establishing the European Community, arts 2, 3(1)(k), 158–162 of the consolidated (2002) version.

cohesion fund. Provision has been made for the establishment of a new EC *Cohesion Fund* before the end of 1993 to provide financial contributions towards projects in the environment and *trans-European networks* in the area of transport infrastructure: *Treaty establishing the European Community,* art 161 of the consolidated (2002) version. The Fund is for the benefit of member States with a GNP per capita of less than 90% of the EC average, which have a programme leading to the fulfilment of the conditions of *economic convergence*: Protocol on Economic and Social Cohesion 1992.

coif. A white silk cap which serjeants-at-law (qv) wore in court.

Coillte Teoranta. The company established to manage public forests commercially: Forestry Act 1988. It owns and manages some 440,000 hectares of forest land, including 11 forest parks and 180 recreational facilities around the country. In 2002 Coillte agreed a *code of practice* which allows it to manage its forests without compromising the importance of the archaeological heritage. See website: *www.coillte.ie.*

Coimisineir Teanga, An. The Official Languages Commissioner, appointed by the President on the advice of the government, independent in the performance of the functions of the office, which includes to monitor compliance by public bodies of their duties as regards the official languages of the State: Official Languages Act 2003, ss 20–21 and Sch 2, as amended by Public Service Superannuation (Miscellaneous Provisions) Act 2004, Sch 2. Any investigation by the Commissioner is required to be conducted in private (OLA 2003, s 23). A party to an investigation may appeal to the High Court on a point of law from a decision of the Commissioner (OLA 2003, s 28). This also applies to any other person affected by the findings and recommendations of the Commissioner. See PUBLIC BODY.

coins, coinage. The Minister is empowered to provide coins denominated in euro and cent: Economic and Monetary Union Act 1998, s 11. There are one hundred cent in a euro. There are eight euro coins in denominations of 1, 2, 5, 10, 20 and 50 cent and in 1 and 2 euro. It is an offence to melt down coins; this includes euro coins circulating in the State (EMUA 1998, s 17 amending Decimal Currency Act 1969, s 15).

The Minister for Finance is empowered to direct the Central Bank to pay into the Exchequer the accrued net proceeds arising from the issue of coins: Finance Act 2002, s 137. See also Central Bank Act 1997, s 85; Organisation of Working Time Act 1997, ss 4(5) and 15(5); Pensions (Amendment) Act 1996, s 32.

As regards European legislation, member states are empowered to issue coins subject to approval by the European Central Bank (qv) of the volume of the issue: *Treaty establishing the European Community,* art 106(2) of the consolidated (2002) version. The EC Council adopted measures to harmonise the denominations and technical specification to permit smooth circulation within the Community: EC Resolution (EC) No 974/98 of 3 May 1998 on the introduction of the *euro.*

Under previous domestic legislation, there was provision for coins of 1p, 2p, 5p, 10p, 20p, 50p and £1: Decimal Currency Acts 1969 to 1990; New Coinage (Twenty Pence) Order 1986, SI No 52 of 1986; Coinage (Dimensions and Design) (One Pound Coin) Regulations 1990, SI No 83 of 1990. See COMMEMORATIVE COINAGE; COUNTERFEIT; EURO; LEGAL TENDER.

cold-calling. Popularly understood to mean unsolicited approaches made by a person on a potential customer without making an appointment. The Law Society is empowered to prohibit, by regulation, advertising by a solicitor which comprises or includes unsolicited approaches to any person with a view to obtaining instructions in any legal matter: Solicitors Act 1954, s 71(5)(d) as amended by Solicitors (Amendment) Act 2002, s 4. See also Solicitors (Advertising) Regulations 2002, SI No 518 of 2002. See SOLICITOR AND ADVERTISING.

collaborative law. Term used to describe a 'court-free' process for marital breakdown cases which shifts the lawyer's traditional role from 'warrior' to 'facilitator' and where the main emphasis is to help the spouses reach an agreement. See 'Marital breakdown with minimum heartache' in *Law Society Gazette* (March 2004) 7.

collateral. [By the side of.] An additional contract, agreement, or assurance, which is independent of, but subordinate to, the main contract, agreement, or assurance affecting the same subject-matter. A collateral security is one given in addition to the main security. See *McCullough Sales Ltd v Chetham Timber Co Ltd* [1983] HC; *Namlooze Venootschap De Faam v Dorset Manufacturing Co* [1949] IR 203.

In assessing damages in a personal injuries action, account must not be taken of any sum payable under any contract of insurance or any pension, gratuity or other like benefit payable under statute or otherwise in consequence of the injury: Civil Liability (Amendment) Act 1964, s 2, as amended by Civil Liability and Courts Act 2004, s 27(2), which provides for the deductibility of a charitable gift made by the defendant if the latter specifies in advance that he is making the donation on that basis. There is a similar provision in respect of a gift to a plaintiff in respect of the death of a deceased: Civil Liability Act 1961, s 50 as amended by CLCA 2004 s 27(1).

The Law Reform Commission was requested in 1997 by the Attorney-General to address the question of repealing or amending this provision 'with a view to ensuring that a plaintiff does not receive double compensation in respect of the same loss'. See *Consultation Paper on the Deductibility of Collateral Benefits from Awards of Damages* (LRC: CP15, 1999).

collection. A collection of money from the public in any public place or places or by house-to-house visits or both in such place or places and by such visits for the benefit (actual, alleged or implied) of a particular object, whether charitable or not charitable, and whether any badge, emblem or other token is or is not exchanged or offered in exchange for money so collected: Street and House to House Collection Act 1962. A *collection permit* is required; otherwise such a collection by a person will constitute an offence. For appeal procedure in the District Court against a refusal by the gardaí to grant a collection permit, see DCR 1997 Ord 88. See also House to House Collection Order 1972, SI No 75 of 1972. See also PUBLIC APPEAL, MONEY COLLECTED IN.

collective agreement. An agreement between an employer and a body or bodies representative of the employees to which the agreement relates: Employment Equality Act 1998, s 2(1) inserted by Equality Act 2004, s 3. Nothing in these Acts invalidates any term in a collective agreement to the effect that seniority in a particular post may be determined by reference to the relative ages of employees on their entry to that post (EEA 1998, s 34(7A) inserted by EA 2004, s 23). See also EEA 1998, s 9 and EA 2004, s 38.

A collective agreement may be incorporated into a contract of employment; enforceability of such an agreement may depend on whether it was intended to create legal relations. See *Allied Irish Banks Ltd v Lupton* [1985] ILRM 170; *Kenny & Ors v An Post* [1988] IR 285; *O'Cearbhaill v Bord Telecom Éireann* [1994] ELR 54, SC.

A rule in a collective agreement which does not comply with the principle of equal treatment is null and void: Pensions Act 1990, s 74. A provision in a collective agreement is null and void where: (a) it provides for differences in rates of remuneration based on specified discriminatory grounds; and (b) it conflicts with an equal remuneration term in a person's contract of employment (EEA 1998, s 9). A person affected by such a provision in a collective agreement and who claims that it is null and void, may refer the matter to the *Director of the Equality Tribunal* (qv); the Equality Authority may also refer the matter to the Director (EEA 1998, ss 86–87). See Protection of Employees (Fixed-Term Work) Act 2003, ss 2(1) and 5(1)(b); Pensions Act 1990, s 81C as amended by substitution by Social Welfare (Miscellaneous Provisions) Act 2004, s 22(1). See CUSTOM AND PRACTICE; REST PERIOD; WORKING HOURS.

collective mark. A mark distinguishing the goods and services of members of an association, which is the proprietor of the mark, from those of other undertakings: Trade Marks Act 1996, s 54 and Sch 1. This new concept permits associations to register their *logos* or *coats of arms* as trade marks. See CHIEF HERALD; TRADE MARK.

collective responsibility. The government (qv) is *collectively responsible* to Dáil Éireann for the Departments of State administered by the members of the government: 1937 Constitution, art 28(4). This involves an obligation to accept collective responsibility for decisions, and the non-disclosure of dissenting or different views of members of the government prior to the making of decisions: *Attorney-General v The Sole Member of the Tribunal of Inquiry into the Beef Processing Industry* [1993] ILRM 81, SC. See EUROPEAN COMMISSION; RECKLESS TRADING.

colligenda bona. See AD COLLIGENDA BONA.

collision of ship. Civil jurisdiction in relation to the physical collision of ships (and also where a ship has suffered damage due to evasive action to avoid a collision) has been agreed in a 1952 international Convention which is given domestic effect in Ireland by the Jurisdiction of Courts (Maritime Conventions) Act 1989. Jurisdiction may be in the courts: where the defendant has his place of business or residence; where the defendant's ship has been arrested; where the collision took place if in a port or inland waters; or where the parties agree. The choice is normally at the option of the plaintiff.

The expression '*an action for collision*' in art 1(1) of the 1952 Collision Convention is sufficiently wide to cover an action for damages brought by the estate of a deceased person whose death was caused by a collision between two seagoing vessels: *Doran v Power* [1996] 1 ILRM 55, SC and [1995] 2 IR 402, SC. See ASSESSOR.

collop. The unit, under the *common* (qv) of pasture, by which the right to graze animals upon a common grazing was measured; a cow was the equivalent of two collop, a horse was a collop and a half. In the Land Registry (qv) a collop has been registered as appurtenant to the land. [Bibliography: Healy.]

collusion. An agreement, usually secret, for some deceitful or unlawful purpose. It may amount to the crime or tort of conspiracy (qv). See also PRINCIPAL IN CRIME.

colore officii. [By virtue of a person's office.] See *Steele v Williams* [1853] 8 Exch 625.

colour. The European Court of Justice has held that for a colour to constitute a trademark, it must satisfy three conditions: (a) it must be a sign; (b) it must be capable of graphic representation; and (c) it must be capable of distinguishing the goods or services of one undertaking from those of others: *Libertel Groep BV v Benelux Merkenbureau* [2003] Case C-104/01, ECJ. The court also held that there was a public interest in not unduly restricting the availability of other colours for other operators.

See TRADE MARK. See also HATRED, INCITEMENT TO; RACE.

colourable. Term to indicate that which is pretended. See *McCartaigh v Daly* [1986] ILRM 116.

colourable device. The term sometimes referred to in relation to an arrest under the Offences Against the State Act 1939, s 30 where the arresting garda has no *bona fide* suspicion that the person arrested has committed an offence under that Act, but wishes to detain and question him in respect of another offence. See *The People (DPP) v Quilligan* [1987] ILRM 606. See SCHEDULED OFFENCE.

colouring agent. See E-NUMBER.

combatant. See PRISONER OF WAR.

comfort, letter of. See LETTER OF COMFORT.

Combined Code. The principles of good governance and code of best practice, appended to, but not forming part of the *Listing Rules* (qv). A new Code was introduced in 2003 which was derived from a review of the role and effectiveness of non-executive directors by Derek Higgs, and a review of audit committees by a group led by Sir Robert Smith. The new Code applies to companies for reporting years beginning on or after 1 November 2003, and replaces the previous Code issued by the Hampel Committee on Corporate Governance in 1998. The new Code contains main and supporting principles and provisions. It introduces a wider definition of 'independence' eg a non-executive director will not be considered to be sufficiently independent when he has served on the board for more than nine years, or is a member of the company's pension scheme, or represents a significant shareholder.

A *listed* company is required to include in its annual report and accounts, a narrative statement on how it has applied the principles of the Combined Code, and a statement as to whether it has complied with the Code's provisions, giving reasons for any non-compliance: Listing Rules 2000, para 12.43A (a) and (b).

For the full text of the new Combined Code, see website: *www.ecgi.de/codes/country_documents/uk/combined_code_final.pdf*. For the *Higgs Report* (2003), see website: *www.dti.gov.uk/cld/non_exec_review*. For the *Smith Report* (2003), see website: *www.frc.org.uk/publications/content/ACReport.pdf*. For previous reports eg *Cadbury* (1992), *Greenbury* (1995) and *Hampel*

(1998), see website: *www.ecgi.org/codes/ country_pages/codes_uk.htm*. See CORPORATE GOVERNANCE.

combined drain. A drainage pipe, or a system of such pipes, that is not vested or controlled by a sanitary authority and is used to convey trade effluent or other matter (other than storm water) from two or more premises to any waters or to a sewer: Local Government (Water Pollution) (Amendment) Act 1990, s 2. A local authority is empowered to declare a specified combined drain to be a *sewer*; this enables the authority to treat each discharge into a private drain as a discharge to a sewer and thereby exercise greater control on the effluent (s 22).

Comhairle. A body corporate established in 2000, merging the National Social Services Board and certain functions of the National Rehabilitation Board: Comhairle Act 2000. Its primary function is to ensure that individuals have access to accurate, comprehensive and clear information relating to social services and are referred to the relevant services (CA 2000, s 7). It is enabled to provide directly, or support the provision of, independent information, advice and *advocacy services*.

Advocacy services include services in which the interests of a person seeking a social service are represented in order to assist the person in securing entitlements to such service, but does not include legal representation (CA 2000, s 2(1)). Comhairle has responsibility for assisting and supporting individuals, in particular those with disabilities, in identifying and understanding their needs and options (CA 2000, s 7(1)(b)).

Provision has been made to specify the legal relationship as between the *National Committee on Volunteering* and the Board of Comhairle: Comhairle Regulations 2000, SI No 369 of 2000. The Minister has specified that the National Committee is a body to which the provisions of paragraph (h) of section 7(1) of the Comhairle Act 2000 applies. For website, see *www.comhairle.ie*. See NATIONAL DISABILITY AUTHORITY.

Comhairle na n-Ospideal. The statutory body with power to regulate the number and type of consultant medical appointments in hospitals taking patients under the Health Acts and to specify the qualifications for such appointments: Health Act 1970, s 41. See website: *www.comh-n-osp.ie*.

comitology. The term often used to describe the '*committee procedure*' under which the European Commission, when implementing EU law, is required to consult special advisory committees made up of experts from the EU member states.

comity. Courtesy. The *comity of nations* is the friendly recognition of each other's laws. Under the principle of the *comity of nations*, the Irish courts are slow to refuse an order sought by way of *letter of request* (qv), from a court of another jurisdiction, for the examination on oath of a person and for production of documents: *Novelle Inc v MCB Enterprises* [2001] 1 IR 608, SC. For example of recognition of the laws of other states, see Investment Limited Partnerships Act 1994, s 43. See *Mallows v Governor of Mountjoy Prison* [2002] 2 IR 385, SC. See LETTER OF REQUEST.

comma. A comma inserted in error in legislation can give a different meaning from that intended e g '*waste, water ...*' instead of '*waste water*': see Planning and Development Act 2000, s 49(7)(c) as corrected by Planning and Development (Amendment) Act 2002, s 11.

commemorative coinage. The Minister may provide coins of a commemorative nature, which coins are legal tender; these coins may be put on sale at a price, not less than the face value of the coins, as determined by the Central Bank of Ireland: Economic and Monetary Union Act 1998, ss 30–32. See EURO; LEGAL TENDER.

commencement. The time at which an Act, regulation, statutory instrument, or section or part thereof, comes into operation. A Bill becomes law on and from the day it is signed by the President of Ireland and, unless the contrary intention appears, comes into operation on that day: 1937 Constitution, art 25(4)(1). A *commencement order* is an order made, usually by a Minister under a statutory power, specifying a commencement date, where such an order is required. See Interpretation Act 1937, s 12 sch. See REPEAL.

commentaries. The Official Languages Commissioner may prepare and publish *commentaries* on the practical application and operation of the Act, including commentaries on the experience of holders of the office of Commissioner: Official Languages Act 2003, s 29. See also Freedom of Information Act 1997, s 39. The most famous commentaries are probably *Black-stone's Commentaries on the Laws of England* (1765).

commercial agent. Means a self-appointed intermediary who has continuing authority to negotiate the sale or purchase of goods on behalf of another person (the *principal*) or to negotiate and conclude such transactions on behalf of and in the name of the principal: European Community (Commercial Agents) Regulations 1994, SI No 33 of 1994. These regulations give effect to EC Directive 86/653/EEC which deals with the relationship between commercial agents and their principals and their respective rights and obligations eg the regulations deal with the drawing up of a written contract between principal and agent, the conditions of the contract, the obligation of the agent to look after his principal's interest and to act honestly, the obligation of the principal to act dutifully towards his agent, and rules about payment of salaries and commission. See 'Commercial Agents and Compensation' by Imelda Higgins BL in *Bar Review* (July 2004) 145.

Commercial Court. The High Court dealing with the Commercial List. The court was established in January 2004 with Mr Justice Peter Kelly designated as the judge having charge of the High Court 'Commercial List'. A pilot Commercial Court was recommended to be developed in the High Court which would be accessible electronically and which could develop links with arbitration centres: *Report from the Committee on Court Practice and Procedure* (February 2002). The committee, chaired by Mrs Justice Susan Denham of the Supreme Court, proposed that e-Courts should be developed throughout the courts system and that the development of an e-Commercial Court would underpin and reinforce Ireland's position as an e-commerce hub. See 'The Commercial Court' by Mr Justice Kelly in *Bar Review* (February 2004) 4. For article by barrister Denis Kelleher 'justice@e-court.ie?' which argues for an e-court specialising in IT and intellectual property, see *Law Society Gazette* (December 2002) 35. [Bibliography: Forde (5).] See COMMERCIAL PROCEEDINGS.

commercial credit. See LETTER OF CREDIT.

commercial law. The body of law dealing with contracts, (eg sale of goods and supply of services), intellectual property, bankruptcy, banking, insurance, agency, companies and partnership (qqv). [Bibliography: Byrne R (1); Courtney; Doolan (5); Forde (5); O'Reilly P; Sheeran; White F.]

commercial proceedings. Means: (a) proceedings in respect of any claim or counterclaim, not being a claim or counterclaim for damages for personal injuries, arising from or relating to any one or more of the following: (i) a business document, business contract or business dispute where the value of the claim or counterclaim is not less than €1m; (ii) the determination of any question of construction arising in respect of a business document or business contract where the value of the transaction the subject matter thereof is not less than €1m; (iii) the purchase or sale of commodities where the value of the claim or counterclaim is not less than €1m; (iv) the export or import of goods where the value of the claim or counterclaim is not less than €1m; (v) the carriage of goods by land, sea, air or pipeline where the value of the claim or counterclaim is not less than €1m; (vi) the exploitation of oil or gas reserves or any other natural resource where the value of the claim or counterclaim is not less than €1m; (vii) insurance or re-insurance where the value of the claim or counterclaim is not less than €1m; (viii) the provision of services (not including medical, quasi-medical or dental services or any service provided under a contract of employment) where the value of the claim or counterclaim is not less than €1m; (ix) the operation of markets or exchanges in stocks, shares or other financial or investment instruments, or in commodities where the value of the claim or counterclaim is not less than €1m; (x) the construction of any vehicle, vessel or aircraft where the value of the claim or counterclaim is not less than €1m; (xi) business agency where the value of the claim or counterclaim is not less than €1m;

(b) proceedings in respect of any other claim or counterclaim, not being a claim or counterclaim for damages for personal injuries, which the Judge of the Commercial List, having regard to the commercial and any other aspect thereof, considers appropriate for entry in the Commercial List;

(c) any application or proceedings under the Arbitration Acts 1954 to 1998 (other than an application in pursuance of s 5 of the Arbitration Act 1980 to stay proceedings in respect of a matter referred to arbitration) where the value of the claim or any counterclaim is not less than €1m;

(d) any proceedings instituted or any application or reference made or appeal lodged under the provisions of the Patents Act 1992, not including an application under s 108(4) of that Act;

(e) any proceedings instituted, application made or appeal lodged under: (i) the Trade Marks Act, 1996; (ii) the Copyright and Related Rights Act, 2000; (iii) the Industrial Designs Act, 2001;

(f) any proceedings instituted for relief in respect of passing off;

(g) any appeal from, or application for judicial review of, a decision or determination made or a direction given by a person or body authorised by statute to make such decision or determination or give such direction, where the Judge of the Commercial List considers that the appeal or application is, having regard to the commercial or any other aspect thereof, appropriate for entry in the Commercial List: RSC Ord 63A inserted by Rules of the Superior Courts (Commercial Proceedings) 2004, SI No 2 of 2004.

A party to commercial proceedings may, at any time prior to: (a) the close of pleadings, in the case of plenary proceedings; or (b) completion of the filing of affidavits, in the case of summary proceedings or any other proceedings to be heard on affidavit without pleadings, by motion on notice to the other party or parties to those proceedings, apply to the Judge of the Commercial List for an order entering the proceedings in the Commercial List. The notice of motion shall have appended thereto a certificate of the solicitor for the applicant to the effect that the proceedings are appropriate to be treated as commercial proceedings within the meaning of rule 1 of this Order, and setting out such facts relating to the proceedings as shall demonstrate this (RSC Ord 63A, r 4(2)).

The Order provides for a pre-trial procedure (initial directions, motions and applications, interrogatories, case management, including a case booklet, preparation for trial, pre-trial conference); evidence by live video link or other means; trial venue; functions of Registrar; costs; and electronic service, exchange and lodgement of documents. In addition, forms are specified for: interrogatories, answer to interrogatories,

pre-trial questionnaire dealing with pre-trial procedures, trial, expert and other witnesses (RSC Ord 63A, App X).

Unless otherwise directed by the judge chairing the pre-trial conference, the plaintiff is required, in consultation with the other parties, to prepare and lodge with the registrar, not less than four days prior to the date fixed for the trial, a *trial booklet* (qv) and a '*case summary*' (qv) (RSC Ord 63A, r 21(1)). See also *Practice Direction on the High Court Commercial List* issued by Courts Service in January 2004, available on website: *www.courts.ie/press.nsf*. See CASE BOOKLET; CASE MANAGEMENT CONFERENCE; ELECTRONIC TRANSMISSION OF DOCUMENTS; ORAL EVIDENCE; PRE-TRIAL CONFERENCE.

commercial tenancy. See BUSINESS TENANT.

commercial waste. See WASTE; WASTE MANAGEMENT PLAN.

commercially sensitive information. Means (a) Trade secrets; (b) financial, commercial, scientific or technical or other information whose disclosure could reasonably be expected to result in a material financial loss or gain to the person to whom the information relates; or (c) information whose disclosure would prejudice the conduct or outcome of contractual or other negotiations of the person to whom the information relates: Freedom of Information Act 1988, s 27. A request for access to a record which contains commercially sensitive information may be permitted subject to certain conditions being met eg where the information relates only to the requester, provided his identity has been satisfactorily established (FOIA 1988, s 27(2) as amended by Freedom of Information (Amendment) Act 2003, s 22).

commission. (1) An order or authority to do an act or exercise a power eg an authority to an agent to enter into a contract. (2) A body charged with a commission eg the proposed *Commission for Public Service Appointments*. (3) The remuneration of an agent or an employee.

As regards companies, it is not permissible for a company to apply any of its shares or capital money in payment of any commission to any person, in consideration of the subscription for any shares in the company, except where permitted by its *articles of association* and the commission does not exceed 10% of the issued price of the shares: Companies Act 1963, s 59.

As regards auctioneer's commission, the test applied by the court in relation to a dispute over commission is whether the event contracted for by the principal actually happened and whether the agent was the cause of the happening. It has been held that a *sole agent* is not entitled to commission where the exertions of the sole agent had not played any part in effecting a sale and the agency agreement did not contain any express term prohibiting the principal from negotiating a sale during the continuance of the agency: *Murphy, Buckley Keogh Ltd v Pye (Ireland) Ltd* [1971] IR 57. See also *Cusack v Bothwell* [1943] 77 ILTR 18; *Stokes Quirke Ltd v Clohessy* [1957] IR 84; *Henehan v Courtney* [1967] 101 ILTR 25; *Walkin v Murphy* [1991] 9 ILT & SJ 247, DC; *Kehoe & Haythornwaite* [1991] 10 ILT & SJ (1992) 50, CC. [Bibliography: Mahon; Murdoch UK.]

As regards insurance, the Minister is empowered to reduce the commission payments to insurance intermediaries (qv), where he is of the opinion that these are excessive: Insurance Act 1989, s 37 as amended by Central Bank and Financial Services Authority of Ireland Act 2003, s 35, Sch 1. He is also empowered to prohibit commission payments in the form of benefits-in-kind or loans (IA 1989, s 38 as amended by CBFSAIA 2003, s 35). A life assurance policy which is in contravention of these provisions is voidable at the instance of the policyholder within one month of conviction of the insurer and the premium will be refunded together with interest (IA 1989, s 42 as amended by CBFSAIA 2003, s 35). Commission paid on life assurance to an intermediary must be disclosed: Life Assurance (Provision of Information) Regulations 2001, SI No 15 of 2001 and Life Assurance (Provision of Information) Regulations 2002, SI No 161 of 2002.

As regards building societies, a commission includes any gift, bonus, fee, payment or other benefit: Building Societies Act 1989, s 2(1). There are prohibitions on the acceptance of commissions eg by a person authorising the making of a loan (BSA 1989, s 25). See AUCTIONEER; EUROPEAN COMMISSION; HUMAN RIGHTS COMMISSION; OVERRIDE COMMISSION; UNDERSUBSCRIBED; UNDERWRITER; WRONGFUL DISMISSAL.

commission, evidence to. The taking of evidence on oath from a witness whose attendance at court ought for some sufficient reason be dispensed with: RSC Ord 39. Before making an order for the taking of evidence on commission, a court must be satisfied that it is necessary for the proper determination of the issues between the parties and the onus of so satisfying the court rests on the party seeking such an order: *Henry & Henry v Allied Irish Banks plc* [2003] ITLR 17 November 2003, HC. In this case the High Court ordered the taking of evidence on commission of the first named plaintiff who was suffering from prostate cancer and who had been medically advised to minimise avoidable stress.

commission agent. An incomplete form of agency by indirect representation e g where a principal appoints a person to deal (especially to buy) on his behalf, on the understanding that when dealing with any third party, the agent will deal in his own name as principal; he is normally remunerated by commission; he is a fiduciary also and consequently may not without disclosure take a commission from the third party. See *Montgomerie v UK Mutual, ss Assn* [1891] 1 QB 370.

commission de lunatico inquirendo. An enquiry carried out pursuant to the Lunacy Regulations (Ireland) Act 1871. See RSC Ord 67, r 10–16. See INQUISITION.

Commission for Aviation Regulation. The Commission established on a statutory basis by the Aviation Regulation Act 2001. The Commission provides an independent regulation of airport charges, including charges for aviation terminal services provided by the *Irish Aviation Authority*.

In addition, the Commission is responsible for: (a) the granting of operating licences to air carriers established in the EU; (b) the designation, where necessary, of Irish airports as co-ordinated airports under the relevant EU regulations; (c) the approval of ground handling service providers at airports; and (d) the licensing and bonding of tour operators and travel agents. Also ARA 2001 corrects a typographical error in s 7(4) of the Air Navigation and Transport (Amendment) Act 1998. See Aviation Regulation (Levy) Regulations 2002, SIs No 439, 482 and 612 of 2002. See website: *www.aviationreg.ie*.

Commission for Communications Regulation. A body corporate with specified functions: (a) to ensure compliance by undertakings with obligations in relation to the supply of and access to electronic communication services, networks and associated facilities; (b) to manage the radio frequency sprectrum; (c) to ensure compliance by providers of postal services with relevant obligations; (d) to investigate complaints regarding the supply of and access to electronic communication services and networks; and (e) to ensure compliance in relation to the placing on the market of communications and radio equipment: Communications Regulation Act 2002, s 10.

The Commission, known as *ComReg*, replaces the office of the *Director of Telecommunications Regulation* previously established by the Telecommunications (Miscellaneous Provisions) Act 1996. See TELECOMMUNICATIONS REGULATOR.

The Commission, in exercising its functions, has specified objectives e g to promote competition in electronic communication networks, to promote the development of the postal service and to have the service available at affordable prices, and to ensure the efficient management and use of the radio frequency sprectrum (CRA 2002, s 12). While the Commission is independent in the exercise of its functions, it must comply with policy directions given to it by the Minister (CRA 2002, s 13).

Where the Commission has reasonable grounds for believing that a person has committed a specified offence, the Commission may, by notice in a prescribed form, give the person an opportunity to remedy the default that constitutes the offence and pay the Commission €1,000, and thereby avoid prosecution: Communications Regulation (Notice of Intention to Prosecute) Regulations 2003, SI No 318 of 2003.

See Broadcasting Act 2001, ss 7–8. For amendments to the CRA 2002, see Digital Hub Development Agency Act 2003, s 45. For *ComReg*, see website: *www.comreg.ie*. For *International Telecommunication Union*, see website: *www.itu.int*. See DOMAIN NAME; ELECTRONIC COMMUNICATIONS NETWORKS; LEVY; PRIVACY IN TELECOMMUNICATIONS.

Commission for Energy Regulation. The body established for the independent regulation of the electricity and natural gas sectors in Ireland; it was formerly called the *Commission for Electricity Regulation*: Electricity Regulation Act 1999 as amended by Gas (Interim) (Regulation) Act 2002.

The Commission has the function of advising the Minister on the development of the electricity and natural gas industries, to promote competition in both these industries, to exercise its functions in a non-discriminatory manner and which protects the interests of customers, to promote security and continuity of supply, and to ensure adequate supply capacity to meet demand (ERA 1999, s 9 as amended by G(I)(R)A 2002, s 6).

The Commission has power to grant licences to generate and supply electricity, to grant authorisations to construct generating stations, and to provide access to the transmission or distribution system. It also takes over the Minister's powers regarding the construction of gas pipelines, compulsory acquisition orders, the granting of orders to acquire land or rights over land and the extinguishment of rights of way (G(I)(R)A 2002, s 7 and Sch).

The Commission also has the power to grant licences to gas undertakings involved in the supply of natural gas, the operation of transmission and distribution pipelines, the storage of natural gas, and the prosecution of persons operating without a licence (G(I)(R)A 2002, s 16). It is the duty of the Commission to take account of the protection of the environment; to take account of the needs of rural customers, the disadvantaged and the elderly; and to require priority to be given to renewable, sustainable or alternative energy sources (ERA 1999, s 9(5)).

The Commission is empowered to select persons, to whom will be allocated a certain amount of the capacity of the *natural gas network* for the generation of electricity: Gas (Amendment) Act 2000, ss 1–11. In selecting persons, the Commission is required to have regard to the need to promote competition in the market for the generation and supply of electricity; however, it is required to give priority to the need for the demand for electricity to be met (G(A)A 2000, s 4(b)–(c)). The Commission is entitled to give Bord Gáis directions with regard to the use or management of the natural gas network for the purpose of securing the enjoyment of the selected persons of their rights (G(A)A 2000, s 8).

There is a prohibition on Bord Gáis supplying natural gas for new generating stations for the purpose of generating electricity before 30 September 2004, except with the prior written consent of the Commission, except to the selected persons (G(A)A 2000, ss 9–10). For amendments to the ERA 1999, see G(A)A 2000, ss 12–15 and Sustainable Energy Act 2002, ss 32–33.

Profits arising to the Commission are exempt from corporation tax: Taxes Consolidation Act 1997, s 220 as amended by Finance Act 2000, s 84. The qualifying period for tax relief has been extended to 31 December 2004: Finance Act 2002, s 43.

A new system of trading in electricity has been established: Market Arrangements for Electricity Regulations 2003, SI No 304 of 2003. All generators and suppliers, unless exempted, are required to buy and sell electricity through a mandatory centralised pool. This replaces the previous arrangement in Electricity Regulation Act, 1999 (Trading Arrangements in Electricity) Regulations 2000, SI No 49 of 2000. See also European Communities (Internal Market in Electricity) Regulations 2000, SI No 445 of 2000, (Amendment) Regulations 2002, SI No 145 of 2002, and (Amendment) Regulations 2003, SI No 328 of 2003; Electricity Regulation – Public Service Obligations Order 2002, SI No 217 of 2002, as amended by SI No 174 of 2004; Electricity Regulation Levy Order 2000, SI No 447 of 2000. See also Electricity Regulation Act 1999 (Eligible Customer) (Consumption of Electricity) Order 2003, SI No 632 of 2003. See EC Directive 96/92/EC of 19 December 1996. See website: *www.cer.ie*. See ELECTRICAL CONTRACTING; ELECTRICITY; GAS CAPACITY STATEMENT; PUBLIC SERVICE OBLIGATION.

Commission for Taxi Regulation. A body corporate, independent in the exercise of its functions, the principal one being the development and maintenance of a regulatory framework for the control and operation of *small* public service vehicles and their drivers: Taxi Regulation Act 2003, ss 6–9. In exercising its functions, the Commission is required to seek to achieve certain objectives e g to promote the provision and maintenance of quality services by small public service vehicles and their drivers, that is professional, safe, efficient and customer-friendly (TRA 2003, s 9). The Minister may give general policy directions

to the Commission, with which it must comply (TRA 2003, s 10).

The Commission may make regulations in relation to the licensing, ownership, control and operation of small public service vehicles, the licensing and control of their drivers, and the standards to be applied to such vehicles and drivers (TRA 2003, s 34). It may also make regulations in relation to the conduct, general behaviour, deportment and duties of these drivers (TRA 2003, s 39). There is provision for appeal to the District Court against a refusal to grant, or a suspension or revocation of a licence (TRA 2003, s 35).

There is automatic disqualification from holding a licence in the event of conviction of certain serious offences (TRA 2003, s 36 as proposed to be amended by Road Traffic Bill 2004, s 26). The Commission is required to set up a procedure to consider complaints e g regarding the condition and cleanliness of the vehicle, the conduct and behaviour of the driver, and overcharging (TRA 2003, s 51). There is also an Advisory Council to advise the Commission or the Minister in relation to issues relevant to small public service vehicles and their drivers (TRA 2003, ss 53–55). The 18-member Advisory Council met for the first time on 17 November 2003, under the chairmanship of the former Garda Commissioner Pat Byrne. See TAXI.

Commission of EC. See EUROPEAN COMMISSION.

commission of inquiry. A body established with specified functions to inquire into some matter e g the Commission to inquire into child abuse established in 2000: Commission to Inquire into Child Abuse Act 2000. Such a commission obtains its powers from the specific legislation establishing it. Contrast with a *tribunal of inquiry* which derives its powers from the Tribunals of Inquiry Acts 1921 to 1998. See CHILD ABUSE; TRIBUNALS OF INQUIRY.

commission of investigation. An independent Commission established from time-to-time by government order, with the approval of the Oireachtas, to investigate into and report on a matter considered to be of significant public concern: Commissions of Investigation Act 2004, s 3. The primary function of a Commission is to establish the facts in relation to the matter of concern.

While the focus is on seeking and facilitating the voluntary co-operation of witnesseses, a Commission has a wide range of coercive powers, eg giving directions to attend, to answer questions, to disclose and to produce documents, powers of entry (on foot of a warrant in the case of private dwellings) and to seize documents and equipment, and powers to make determinations and give directions where privilege is claimed over documents.

Evidence is generally to be received by a Commission in private and may be submitted orally, by affidavit, or in any form that is acceptable to the Commission, including by live video link, video recording, or sound recording (CIA 2004, ss 11 and 14). Persons are required to be informed of matters arising in evidence that affect them and about which they may wish to comment.

The Act includes a number of provisions aimed at the tighter control of costs, including competitive tendering (CIA 2004, s 8). The terms of reference of a Commission must be accompanied by statements relating to costs (including legal costs) and time frames (CIA 2004, s 5). Before it takes evidence, a Commission is required to issue the relevant Ministerial guidelines as to the limitations on the legal costs that witnesses may recover (CIA 2004, s 23). Each application for such costs is to be considered by the Commission in accordance with those guidelines and the detailed statutory criteria (CIA 2004, s 24). Persons who are found to have obstructed or delayed the work of a Commission may be held liable for any additional costs the Commission or other witnesses have incurred as a result (CIA 2004, s 17).

A written report must be submitted at the conclusion of the investigation, setting out the facts established by the Commission (CIA 2004, s 32). If for any reason (eg insufficient, conflicting or inconsistent evidence) the Commission considers that the facts on an issue have not been established, it must identify the issue, and indicate its opinion as to the quality and weight of any evidence relating to the issue (CIA 2004, s 32(2)). A draft of the report must be sent in advance to any person who is identified in the report, and such person may request alterations: (a) on the basis of a belief that fair procedures have not have been observed; and/or (b) to preserve confidentiality of sensitive commercial information (CIA 2004, ss 34–36). Evidence presented to a Commission or its reports may not be used in any criminal or other legal proceedings (CIA 2004, s 19).

Provision is made for the possibility that an investigation may be followed by a Tribunal of Inquiry, under the Tribunals of Inquiry (Evidence) Acts 1921–2002, into a matter within a Commission's terms of reference (CIA 2004, s 44). This could happen, for example, where there is a sharp divergence in the evidence and an adjudication is required. In these circumstances, the government may terminate the investigation or alter its terms of reference to reflect the establishment of the Tribunal. Evidence presented to the Commission will be available to the Tribunal, which should facilitate reducing the cost and time required by the Tribunal (CIA 2004, s 45).

In July 2004, the government announced that a commission of investigation would be established to examine the Garda investigation of the 1974 Dublin and Monaghan bombings and the disappearance of security files from the Department of Justice and Garda intelligence. See FALSE STATEMENT; TRIBUNALS OF INQUIRY.

Commission on Electronic Voting. An independent body of five members (a judge of the High Court who is chairman, the clerk of the Dáil, the clerk of the Seanad, and two other persons with knowledge or experience in the field of information technology) with the function of preparing reports to the Chairman of the Dáil as required by its terms of reference: Electoral (Amendment) Act 2004, ss 17–29, and Sch 5. Its primary function is to prepare reports on the secrecy and accuracy of the chosen electronic voting and counting system – the *Powervote/Nedap* system. Provision is made in the legislation for the *interim* Commission which was appointed pending the legislation. As a result of the reservations expressed in the *interim* Commission's first report, electronic voting was not introduced in the local and European Parliament elections in 2004. See website: *www.cev.ie*. See ELECTRONIC VOTING.

Commission on Liquor Licensing. A Commission established in 2000 with the remit of reviewing the liquor licensing system. It submitted four reports with over 130 recommendations and completed its work in March 2003. Many of its recommendations were recognised and adopted in the Intoxicating Liquor Act 2003. See website: *www.justice.ie*.

commission rogatoire. See LETTER OF REQUEST.

commissioner for oaths. A person appointed to administer oaths and to take affidavits for the purpose of any court or matter: Commissioners for Oaths Act 1889, s 1; Supreme Court of Judicature Act (Ireland) 1877, s 72. Oaths include affirmations and declarations (COA 1889, s 11). Judicial and official notice must be taken of the seal or signature of a commissioner for oaths (COA 1889, s 3(2)). A statutory declaration may be taken and received by a commissioner for oaths: Statutory Declarations Act 1938, s 1(1). Every solicitor who holds a current practising certificate has all the powers of a Commissioner for Oaths: Solicitors (Amendment) Act 1994, s 72. See also Diplomatic and Consular Officers (Provision of Services) Act 1993. For fees payable to a Commissioner, see SI No 616 of 2003.

Commissioner of Garda Síochána. See GARDA SÍOCHÁNA; TRAFFIC MANAGEMENT.

commissioners, town. See TOWN COMMISSIONERS.

Commissioners of Charitable Donations and Bequests. The statutory body, appointed by the government, with responsibility for the general administration of charities in the State. They act as trustees of some charitable trusts and hold funds on behalf of others. They are empowered to invest, and authorise charity trustees to invest, in securities outside the ordinary range of trustee securities. Their functions also include the appointment of new trustees and the authorisation of sale of charity property. See Charities Act 1961 and 1973 wherein the Commissioners are referred to as *the Board*.

The Commissioners have power to authorise or make sale, exchange, certain other dispositions of, or mortgages of charity land (CA 1961, s 34 as substituted by CA 1973, s 11). The definition of 'disposition' has been widened to include the leasing of land; the Commissioners can require that the lease contain covenants, conditions or other provisions (CA 1961, s 34 as amended by Social Welfare (Miscellaneous Provisions) Act 2002, s 16 and Sch, Pt 2). See CHARITIES; CHARITABLE DEVISE OR BEQUEST.

Commissioners of Irish Lights. The all-Ireland body with power to provide lighthouses, buoys and beacons, to acquire land, to supervise generally local lighthouses, buoys and beacons, and to mark and remove dangerous wrecks when a local harbour authority has no such power: Merchant Shipping Acts 1894 to 1993. The Commissioners have, and are deemed always to have had, power to provide radio navigation systems: Merchant Shipping (Commissioners of Irish Lights) Act 1997, s 3 which was necessitated by the decision in *Keane v An Bord Pleánala and Commissioners of Irish Lights* [1997] 1 IR 184, SC dealing with the controversial 'Loran C' installation in West Clare. The power of the Commissioners to borrow money was extended by the Merchant Shipping (Miscellaneous Provisions) Act 1998, s 5. Apart from the Commissioners of Irish Lights, there are two other general lighthouse authorities listed in s 634 of MSA 1894, *Trinity House Lighthouse* (responsible for the waters around England and Wales) and the *Commissioners of Northern Lighthouses* (responsible for the waters around Scotland and the Isle of Man). Provision has been made to dissolve the Commissioners of Irish Lights and to transfer its functions to the cross-border body, the *Foyle Carlingford and Irish Lights Commission*: British-Irish Agreement Act 1999, ss 31–38. See website: *www.cil.ie*. See FOYLE CARLINGFORD; GOOD FRIDAY AGREEMENT.

Commissioners of Public Works. Commissioners with a wide range of functions for the State including: (a) providing and maintaining property used by government departments; (b) designing and supervising the construction of new buildings; (c) designing and executing arterial drainage schemes; (d) procurement and supply of goods through the Government Supplies Agency; and (e) advising the government in relation to Dublin Zoo. Certain powers were conferred on the Commissioners by the Public Works Ireland Act 1831 but the powers were exercisable only for the purposes of specific statutes, which inadequacy came to light in *Howard v Commissioners of Public Works* [1994] IR 101, necessitating the State Authorities (Development and Management) Act 1993, which retrospectively conferred on the Commissioners a general power to develop, maintain, repair and manage public buildings.

Further provision is made in relation to the functions and powers of the Commissioners, which are applied retrospectively, by the Commissioners of Public Works

(Functions and Powers) Act 1996. These functions include making schemes to assist persons who suffer undue hardship by reason of flooding, including the payment of money or provision of living accommodation (CPW(FP)A 1996, s 2(1)(c)). See *MacPharthalain v Commissioners of Public Works* [1994] 3 IR 353, SC. See Finance Act 2004, s 81. See website: *www.opw.ie*. See ARTERIAL DRAINAGE; STATE AUTHORITY.

committal, order of. An order which directs that a person upon his arrest be lodged in prison until he purges his contempt (qv) and is discharged pursuant to further order of the court: RSC Ord 44, r 2. For attachment and committal of a person for failure to comply with the terms of a Circuit Court order, see Circuit Court Rules 2001 Ord 37. For the District Court, see DCR 1997 Ord 25, r 5; District Court (Attachment and Committal) Rules 1999, SI No 124 of 1999 and 2000, SI No 196 of 2000.

committal warrant. (1) The order which the court makes for the committal of a person to prison where he has been sentenced to imprisonment: DCR 1997 Ord 25, r 1. Once issued, it must be executed as soon as reasonably possible, as the date of commencement of a sentence is as important as the term of the sentence: *Dalton v Governor of the Training Unit* [1999] 1 ILRM 439, HC.

(2) An order of committal to imprisonment for the non-payment of a fine or the non-performance of a condition imposed on a person convicted of an offence in a summary jurisdiction; the order may be made by a district court judge within six months from the date fixed for the payment of the fine or the performance of the condition: Petty Sessions (Ireland) Act 1851, s 23 as amended by the Courts (No 2) Act 1991; DCR 1997 Ord 25, rr 2–4. A committal warrant will not issue for a failure to pay compensation, costs or expenses, unless a fine has also been imposed: DCR 1997 Ord 25, r 6. See also Ord 27, r 6(2). For committal warrant in relation to default in payment of a periodic payment (eg maintenance), see Enforcement of Court Orders Act 1940, s 8; DCR 1997 Ord 57.

committee. A person to whom the custody of another person of unsound mind or the estate of that other person is committed by

order of the High Court. See RSC Ord 67, rr 57–69. See Personal Injuries Assessment Board Act 2003, s 4(1). See OIREACHTAS COMMITTEES.

committee of inquiry. See OIREACHTAS COMMITTEES; TRIBUNALS OF INQUIRY.

committee of inspection. See WINDING UP BY TRUSTEE; WINDING UP, VOLUNTARY.

committee of the regions. A consultative body of 222 members (in 2004) which is asked for its opinion in the areas of education, culture, public health, trans-European networks and economic and social cohesion (qqv); it is appointed by the EU Council on the basis of nominations from the member states; Ireland has nine members: Treaty establishing the European Community, arts 263–265 of the consolidated (2002) version. The Nice Treaty (qv) provides for the committee to have a maximum of 350 members when the EU has expanded to 27 member states; Ireland will continue to have nine members on the committee.

commodatum. [Loan for use.] See BAILMENT.

common. A right of *common* is the right to take some part of any natural product of the land or water belonging to another. It may be created by grant or claimed by prescription (qv). The principal rights of common are: pasture, piscary, estovers and turbary (qqv). See also Wildlife Act 1976, s 55(1).

The *Commonage Framework Plans* are expert assessments of the environmental status of commonages, which include recommendations, where necessary, for the reduction in sheep numbers to allow vegetation to recover from overgrazing. The Minister for Agriculture announced in December 2002 a special appeals procedure for sheep farmers who feel that they have been unfairly treated by such plans. See LANDSCAPE CONSERVATION AREA.

common, tenancy in. See TENANCY IN COMMON.

common agricultural policy; CAP. The main instrument through which EC support is channelled to agriculture: Treaty establishing the European Community, arts 32–38 of the consolidated (2002) version. Its main objectives are: to increase agricultural productivity, to ensure a fair standard of living for the agricultural community, to stabilise agricultural markets, to assure the availability of supplies, and to ensure reasonable prices for consumers (art 33). The CAP operates through various instruments which vary from commodity to commodity. These include: guaranteed prices with intervention purchasing of commodities in surplus supply; quotas, levies and tariffs on imports to prevent external supplies undercutting EC produced commodities; support for Community exports mainly by way of refunds to allow them to compete on world markets and a range of direct supports to producers or processors.

The EU agreed further reforms of the CAP in 2003, with the emphasis on high quality farm produce and animal-friendly farming practices that respect the environment and preserve the countryside. The reforms include a planned reduction on direct subsidies to farmers.

common assault. An assault at common law, not amounting to an aggravated assault; now abolished by the Non-Fatal Offences against the Person Act 1997, s 28. See ASSAULT.

common carrier. See CARRIER, COMMON.

common commercial policy. The policy of the EC which is required to be based on uniform principles, particularly in regard to tariff rates, the conclusion of tariff and trade agreements, the achievement of uniformity in measures of liberalisation, export policy and measures to protect trade such as those to be taken in the event of dumping or subsidies: Treaty establishing the European Community, art 133 of the consolidated (2002) version.

common contract. Generally understood to mean the nationally negotiated contract, regulated by Comhairle na nOspidéal, under which medical hospital consultants are employed. It has been held that as this contract has statutory provisions in its disciplinary procedures, it has a sufficient public law content to make matters under it justiciable by way of judicial review: *O'Donoghue v South Eastern Health Board* [2000] ELR 189, HC. Under the common contract, a hospital is entitled to initiate disciplinary proceedings against a consultant, not only on the basis of complaints received, but also, *inter alia*, on the basis of its own concerns: *Traynor v Ryan* [2003] 2 IR 564 and ITLR (28 July), SC. See also *McKay v Adelaide and Meath Hospital Dublin* [2003] ELR 237, HC.

common control. See MONOPOLY.

common defence. There is a constitutional ban on Ireland joining an EU common defence. This was inserted by referendum on 19 October 2002, linked to a provision to enable the Nice Treaty to be ratified. See Twenty-sixth Amendment of the Constitution Act 2002. See 1937 Constitution art 29(4)(9).

common employment. The common law rule that a master was not liable to his servant for injuries resulting from the negligence of a fellow servant in the course of their common employment. The doctrine was eroded by successive judicial decisions and eventually by the Law Reform (Personal Injuries) Act 1958. See also *Doyle v Flemings Coal Mines Ltd* [1955] SC.

common foreign and security policy; CFSP. The policy of the European Union (qv) the objectives of which are: (a) to safeguard the common values, fundamental interests, independence and integrity of the Union in conformity with the principles of the United Nations Charter; (b) to strengthen the security of the Union in all ways; (c) to preserve peace and international security; (d) to promote international co-operation; and (e) to develop and consolidate democracy, and the rule of law, and respect for human rights and fundamental freedoms: Treaty on European Union, art 11 of the consolidated (2002) version. The Union is required to pursue these objectives by: defining the principles and general guidelines for the CFSP; deciding on common strategies; adopting joint actions; adopting common positions; and strengthening systematic cooperation between member states in the conduct of policy (consolidated arts 12–28). The powers of the European Court of Justice do not apply to the provisions on the CFSP.

The policy provisions in the Maastricht Treaty 1992 replaced the provisions on European Political Co-operation in the Single European Act 1987. The Amsterdam Treaty (qv) and the Nice Treaty (qv) give greater capacity to the EU to carry out humanitarian and crisis management tasks. The Nice Treaty also establishes the *Political and Security Committee* as a permanent institution of the EU, with the responsibility of monitoring the international situation in the areas covered by the CFSP and contributing to the definition of policies (consolidated art 25). The committee is composed of representatives of each of the member states. See COMMUNITY LAW; PETERSBERG TASKS.

common form. See WILL, PROOF OF.

common informer. A member of the public capable of giving information in respect of the commission of an offence: *The State (Cronin) v CJ Western Circuit* [1936] 71 ILTR 3. The person need not be an eyewitness of the event: *McCormac v Carroll* [1910] 45 ILTR 7. It has been held that a common informer has a common law right of access to the courts to lay a complaint and to prosecute for an offence in a court of summary jurisdiction and any restrictions upon such a right would require clear statutory expression: *The State (Collins) v Ruane* [1984] IR 105; *O'Donnell v DPP* [1988] HC.

A body corporate cannot, at common law, prosecute as a common informer; it requires a specific power granting a right to prosecute by statute: *Cumann Lúthchleas Gael Teo v Windle & Dublin Corporation* [1993] ITLR (27 September), SC and [1994] 1 IR 525, SC. See also *The People v Roddy* [1977] IR 177. See DIRECTOR OF PUBLIC PROSECUTIONS; INFORMATION; PROSECUTOR; INDICTABLE OFFENCE.

common law. Originally the ancient unwritten law of England, so called because it became common to the whole of England and Wales after the Norman Conquest in 1066. In time it came to mean judge-made law as opposed to statute law. Common law rules are judge made rules and may be modified in accordance with the current policy of the court: *G McG v DW & AR* [2000] 1 ILRM 107, HC. [Bibliography: O'Higgins & McEldowney; Milson UK.]

common law marriage/wife/husband. (1) Colloquial terms sometimes used to denote the relationship of a man and a woman who live together as if man and wife but without having gone through a legal ceremony of marriage; the terms have no legal significance in the terms as stated. (2) The essential conditions for a valid marriage at common law are: contracting parties, intending there and then to get married, interchanging their mutual consent, one to be husband, the other to be wife, in the presence of a priest in holy orders: *Ussher v Ussher* [1912] 2 IR 482. The existence of a common law marriage must be determined by the nature of the ceremony and the intention of the parties to that ceremony and not as to their belief as to its effects: *Conlan v Mohamed* [1987] ILRM 172. See COHABITATION; FAMILY INCOME SUPPLEMENT; MARRIAGE; SPOUSE.

Common Market. Formerly, the popular name for the European Economic Community (qv) when its focus was primarily to create a *common market* for goods and services and before its development in the social, economic, monetary and political fields. By the end of 1992, the *Single Market*, as it became known, was in place. See CUSTOMS DUTIES; ECONOMIC AND MONETARY UNION; HARMONISATION OF LAWS.

common policies. The European Community is required to have *common policies* in the following spheres – commercial, agriculture and fisheries, and transport: Treaty establishing the European Community, art 3 of the consolidated (2002) version. In addition the Community is entitled to have *common rules* applying to such areas as transport, competition, taxation and approximation of laws (arts 81–97). The European Union (qv) has an objective of providing citizens with a high level of safety by developing *common action* among the member states in the fields of police and judicial co-operation, with the objective of preventing and combating crime, in particular terrorism, trafficking in persons and offences against children, illicit drug trafficking and illicit arms trafficking, corruption and fraud: Treaty on European Union, art 29 of the consolidated (2002) version.

common travel area. The area within which there is freedom to travel without documentation, such as a passport. The area comprises Ireland, and the United Kingdom of Great Britain and Northern Ireland, the Channel Islands and the Isle of Man. See SOCIAL WELFARE LAW; SCHENGEN AGREEMENTS.

commonage. Something held in *common* such as land. See COMMON.

commorientes. Persons dying together on the same occasion where it cannot be ascertained by clear evidence who died first. See DEATH, SIMULTANEOUS.

communicable diseases. See INFECTIOUS DISEASES.

communicate, right to. See EXPRESSION, FREEDOM OF; INFLUENCE, IMPROPER; PRISON.

communications, privileged. See PRIVILEGE, EVIDENTIAL.

communications regulation. See COMMISSION FOR COMMUNICATIONS REGULATION.

communis error facit jus. [Common mistake sometimes makes law.] See MISTAKE; RESCISSION.

community and local authorities. A local authority may take such steps as it considers appropriate to consult with and promote effective participation by the local community in local government: Local Government Act 2001, s 127.

Community bridge. The term used to describe the procedure for transferring certain matters from the third 'pillar' of the EU to the first 'pillar', in order that they may be dealt with using the *Community method* (qv). Any decision to use the bridge must be taken by the European Council, unanimously, and be ratified by each member state. See PILLARS OF THE EU.

Community design. A design which complies with the conditions contained in the Community Design Regulation (EC Regulation (EC 6/2002), art 1(1)). A '*registered Community design*' means a design protected as a result of being registered in the manner provided for in the Community Design Regulation: EC (Community Designs) Regulations 2003, SI No 27 of 2003. A design is protected as a Community design to the extent that it is *new* and has *individual character* (Council Regulation (EC 6/2002), art 4). It is considered to be *new* if no identical design has been made available to the public (Council Regulation (EC 6/2002), art 5). It is considered to have *individual character* if the overall impression it produces on the informed user differs from the overall impression produced on such user by any design which has been made available to the public (Council Regulation (EC 6/2002), art 6).

The Council Regulation establishes a system for the registration of industrial designs, providing protection throughout the Community in the same manner as the Community trade mark system currently does for trade marks. The system came into operation in 2003 and is administered by the *Office for Harmonisation in the Internal Market* (*Trade Marks and Designs*) in Alicante, Spain. See website: *www.oami.eu.int*. See DESIGN.

community employment scheme. See SOCIAL EMPLOYMENT SCHEME.

Community law. The body of law arising from membership of the EC. It arises from the treaties of the Community with their annexes and protocols; conventions between member states; legislation; and judicial determinations of the European Court of Justice (qv). It takes precedence over the domestic law of Ireland in the event of conflict. The courts are required to give precedence to community law over national law, and in construing national legislation the court has to interpret the legislation in a manner consistent with the provisions of community law: *Murphy v Minister for the Marine* [1997] 2 ILRM 523, HC.

Legislation of the Community consists of: (a) *regulations* – which have a general application and are binding in their entirety and directly applicable in all member states; (b) *directives* – which state an objective which the member state must realise within a stated period; (c) *decisions* – which are binding on those to whom they are addressed. There are also *recommendations* and *opinions* which do not have any legal effect.

In general, there is no obligation on member states to promulgate EC law; it takes effect from the date of its publication in the Official Journal of the European Communities: *Campbell v Minister for Agriculture* [1999] 1 ILRM 517, SC and 2 IR 245.

However, provision has been made for greater scrutiny by the Houses of the Oireachtas of proposed European measures ie: (a) regulations or directives of the EC Treaty; (b) a *joint action* or a *common position* adopted under arts 14 and 15 respectively of the EC Treaty, or (c) the exercise of *options* and *discretions* under the EC Treaty pursuant to art 29.4.6 of the Constitution of Ireland: European Union (Scrutiny) Act 2002 as amended by European Communities (Amendment) Act 2002, s 2. Under these Acts, proposed measures must be laid before the Oireachtas by the relevant Minister, with a statement outlining the content, purpose and likely implications for Ireland of the proposed measure; the Minister is required to have regard to any recommendations made (EC(A)A 2002, s 2).

See http://europa.eu.int/eur-lex/html. [Bibliography: Butterworths (1); Collins & O'Reilly; Curtin & O'Keeffe; Griffin; Keville & Lucy; McDonald M (3); McMahon & Murphy; Phelan; O'Reilly & Collins; EC Pub (1).] See EUROPEAN ECONOMIC COMMUNITY; DIRECTIVE, EC; EUR-LEX; EUROPEAN DECISION; EUROPEAN UNION; INFRINGEMENT OF EC LAW; PRELIMINARY RULINGS; REGULATION, EC; SINGLE EUROPEAN ACT.

Community method. The method which describes the institutional set-up, brought into being by the Treaty of Rome, which invented a unique way of defining relations between sovereign states of unequal size who agree to pool sovereignty: *National Forum on Europe – Glossary of Terms* (2003). In practice the Community method involves: (a) pooling sovereignty; (b) an ongoing dialogue to identify the common interest; (c) majority decisions usually; (d) negotiations taking place within a strict institutional structure where the European Commission alone has the right to propose European legislation and where decisions are taken in a number of different ways; and (e) decisions being open to challenge before a supranational court whose judgments override national law in the domain covered by the EU. See COMMUNITY BRIDGE.

Community Patent Agreement. The Agreement of 1989 which has as its objective the creation of a Community patent system for the European Community (EC) (qv) with a view to ensuring the free movement within the EC of goods protected by patents. It amends and supersedes the original Community Patent Convention of 1975. It constitutes a special agreement within the meaning of Part IX of the European Patent Convention (qv) and it is one of the measures identified by the EC Commission as necessary for completion of the internal market.

The Agreement provides for the grant by the European Patent Office of *unitary patents* valid for, and having equivalent effect in, the member states of the EC. These Community patents may be transferred, revoked, allowed to lapse etc, in respect of the whole of the EC. In contrast, a European patent designating a member state has the effect of a national patent in that State and is subject to the national law.

The Agreement creates a centralised litigation procedure for Community patents, involving a common *patent appeal court* to be set up under the Agreement; it will have jurisdiction to determine certain matters concerning Community patents raised on appeal from decisions of national courts in domestic litigation concerning such patents.

The Agreement will enter into force upon ratification by all member states of the EC. A perceived constitutional problem in ratifying the Agreement in Ireland led to an amendment to the Constitution in 1992 to permit ratification which was approved by the people: 1937 Constitution art 29(4)(11).

EU Ministers agreed in 2003 to the introduction by 2010 of a *community-wide patent*, with an *EU patent court* in Luxembourg to adjudicate on disputes. Mr Frits Bolkestein, the EU Internal Market Commissioner, is quoted as saying that companies using the new patent system would not have 'to run the risk of potential legal action before national courts in each and every member state, with all the legal uncertainty, inconvenience and cost that would have entailed' *Irish Times,* 19 March 2003. Only the part of the patent document which describes use and function will be translated into all EU official languages; the rest of the document will be translated into English, German and French. However in May 2004, the Agreement was in difficulties due to objections from Germany, France, Portugal and Spain. See PATENT; EUROPEAN PATENT CONVENTION.

community sanction. Means the following orders which may be made by a court on being satisfied that a child is guilty of an offence: a community service order under the Criminal Justice (Community Service) Act 1983, a day care centre order, a probation order, a training or activities order, an intensive supervision order, a residential supervision order, a care and supervision order, a family support order, a restriction on movement order, and a dual order: Children Act 2001, ss 115 and 116–141.

community service order. An order under which an offender is obliged to complete between 40 and 240 hours of unpaid work under the supervision of a probation officer; the order may be made by any court, other than the Special Criminal Court, in respect of any offender over 16 years of age who has been convicted of an offence for which the appropriate sentence would otherwise be one of imprisonment: Criminal Justice (Community Service) Act 1983. When the court is of opinion that the offender is at risk of a custodial sentence, he must be informed of his right to legal representation: *Clarke v Kirby* [1998] 2 ILRM 31, HC.

The court may only make a community service order if the offender consents and if it is satisfied, having considered the offender's circumstances, the offender is suitable to perform work under the order. It is an offence to fail to perform the community work under such an order (CJ(CS)A 1983, s 7). See DCR 1997 Ord 30. See *O'Malley* in 11 ILT & SJ (1993) 201. See PROBATION AND WELFARE OFFICER; PUNISHMENT.

Community trade mark. A registered trade mark which is protected in the 15 States of the European Union: Community Trade Mark Regulation (EC) No 40/94 of 20 December 1993: Trade Mark Act 1996, s 56. The Regulation governs the registration and enforcement of a Community trade mark. Applications are submitted directly to the *Office for the Harmonisation of the Internal Market* (OHIM) in Alicante (Spain), or they can be lodged in the Irish Patents Office for onward transmission to Spain, thereby obtaining the Irish lodgment date. See Community Trade Mark Regulations 2000, SI No 229 of 2000.

Provision has been made to enable certain details regarding the seniority of *community trade marks* to be recorded in the Register of Trade Marks: Trade Marks (Section 66) Regulations 2001, SI No 9 of 2001. See *Consten and Grundig v Commission* [1966] CMLR 418; *Toltee v Dorcets* [1985] FSR 533. The OHIM refused to register 'TDI', standing for 'turbo diesel injection' or 'turbo direct injection', as a community trade mark, on the basis that the mark was devoid of any distinct character. The Court of First Instance held that such a mark could be capable of being registered if it had become distinctive through use in the entire EC, but that Audi had produced no evidence enabling the court to find that the mark had become distinctive in this way: *Audi A-G v OHIM* [2003] CaseT-16/02, CFI. See *Doyle* 'Unifying Europe – The EC Trademark Harmonisation Directive and Irish Law' in 11 ILT & SJ (1993) 76. For the *Office for Harmonization in the Internal Market (Trade Marks and Designs)*, see website: *www.oami.eu.int*. See PARIS CONVENTION; TRADE MARK; SOUND.

commutation. The conversion of the right to receive a variable or periodic payment into the right to receive a fixed or gross payment eg the commutation of a pension.

commute. To substitute one punishment for another. For restriction on power to commute punishment for treason (qv) and aggravated murder (qv), see Criminal Justice Act 1990, s 5. See CAPITAL PUNISHMENT; PARDON.

companies office. See REGISTRAR OF COMPANIES.

company. An association of persons formed for the purpose of some business or undertaking, carried on in the name of the association, each member having the right to assign his shares to any other person, subject to the regulations of the company. Companies are either incorporated or unincorporated. An *unincorporated* company has no existence separate from its members who are individually liable for its debts without limit eg a partnership. An *incorporated* company is a legal entity distinct from its members. Companies are incorporated: (1) by charter; (2) by statute; and (3) by registration.

Companies are limited or unlimited, depending on whether the liabilities of their shareholders are limited or not. A *limited* company may be either a *private* company or a *public* company. A private limited company must include *limited* or *teoranta* in its name. A public limited company must include *public limited company* or *cuideachta phoibli teoranta* in its name. The transferability of the shares of a private limited company is restricted but is not restricted in the case of a public limited company. A private company must have at least two members whereas the minimum number in a public company is seven.

The statute law relating to companies is mainly contained in the Companies Act 1963 and the Companies Acts 1977, 1982, 1983, 1986, 1990 (two Acts, No 27 and No 33) and 1999 (two Acts, No 8 and No 30); Stock Transfer Act 1963; Registration of Business Names Act 1963; Irish Takeover Panel Act 1997; Company Law Enforcement Act 2001; Competition Act 2002; Companies (Auditing and Accounting) Act 2003. For amendments to 1963 and 1990 Acts, see EC (Corporate Insolvency) Regulations 2002, SI No 333 of 2002. For repealed legislation, see Mergers, Take-Overs and Monopolies Control Act 1978; Competition Act 1991; Competition (Amendment) Act 1996. For consolidated company legislation, see bibliography: Round Hall. The Company Law Review Group in April 2004 had reached an advanced stage in determining the shape of the proposed Companies Consolidation Bill, see website: *www.clrg. ie*. [Bibliography: Egan; Cahill; Ford (1);

Keane (1); Laragy; Lucey; MacCann; McGahon; Phelan; McConville; McCormack; McGrath S; Round Hall; Ussher; Dine (UK); Palmer (UK).] See COMPANY, LIMITED; COMPANY, UNLIMITED; COMPANY, REGISTERED; COMPANY, PUBLIC LIMITED; EUROPEAN ECONOMIC INTEREST GROUPING; NAME OF COMPANY; ONE-MAN COMPANY; REGISTERED OFFICE.

company, chartered. A corporation established by *charter* with a legal identity separate from its members; originally granted by the Crown in exercise of the royal prerogative. In earlier times, trading companies were created by royal charter (see *In re Commercial Buildings Co of Dublin* [1938] IR 477) but later charters were mainly granted to non-trading corporations eg Law Society of Ireland. Charters may now be granted by the State: Adaptation of Charters Act 1926; Executive Powers (Consequential Provisions) Act 1937.

company, division of. See DIVISION OF COMPANY.

company, European. See EUROPEAN COMPANY.

company, inspection of. See INVESTIGATION OF COMPANY.

company, limited. An incorporated company with limited liability. The liability of members of such a company may be limited to the amount, if any, unpaid on the shares respectively held by them, in which case it is known as a *company limited by shares*. Alternatively, liability may be limited to the amount which the members respectively undertake to contribute to the assets of the company in the event that the company is wound up, in which case it is known as a *company limited by guarantee*. In practice, companies limited by guarantee are generally non-profit type companies.

Limited companies may be registered as private or public; however, a *company limited by guarantee having a share capital*, which is a hybrid type company, cannot be formed as or become a public limited company (plc).

Limitation of liability may be lost where the number of members falls below the minimum amount and the company continues to carry on business for more than six months at the reduced membership. It can also be lost in the event of *fraudulent trading*. See Companies Act 1963, ss 5(2)(a), 5(2)(b), 26(2), 207(1)(d), 207(1)(e) and 207(3); Companies Amendment Act 1983, ss 7 and 53(7)(a).

It is an offence for a person to trade or carry on business under the name or title of '*limited*' or '*teoranta*' unless duly incorporated: Companies Act 1963, s 381 repealed and substituted by Company Law Enforcement Act 2001, s 98. The *Director of Law Enforcement* may apply to the court for an injunction to prevent the continued use of the name or title, and the costs of the application must be borne by the person against whom it is made.

A limited company may be exempted from the requirement to use the word '*limited*' or '*teoranta*' as part of its name: CA 1963, s 24 as inserted by CLEA 2001, s 88. The form of *Statutory Declaration of Compliance* which is required is specified in the Companies Act (Section 24) Regulations 2001, SI No 571 of 2001. [Bibliography: O'Kane.] See COMPANY, PRIVATE; COMPANY, PUBLIC; COMPANY, PUBLIC LIMITED; FRAUDULENT TRADING; PERSONAL LIABILITY; SINGLE MEMBER COMPANY.

company, merger of. See MERGER OF COMPANY.

company, migration of. See MIGRATION OF COMPANY.

company, non-resident. A company incorporated but not resident in the State: Finance Act 1999, s 83. Such a company is required to identify the territory in which it is resident and to give certain information to the Revenue Commissioners which will identify ownership. Also all companies incorporated in the State are treated as resident in the State for tax purposes, except where: (a) the company is regarded as not resident in the State under a tax treaty between Ireland and another country; or (b) the company carries on a trade in the State and either: (i) the company is ultimately controlled by persons resident in EU member states or in countries with which Ireland has a tax treaty; or (ii) the company is a quoted company (FA 1999, s 82). For provisions introduced to tackle the problems created by Irish registered non-resident companies, see COMPANY, REGISTERED. See also FOREIGN COMPANY.

company, private. An incorporated company which has been registered as a private company; such registration is permitted provided certain criteria are met. See, however, SINGLE MEMBER COMPANY.

A private company must have a minimum of two members and its *articles of association* (qv) must require that: (1) its membership will not exceed 50, apart from worker shareholders; (2) the transferability of its shares is restricted; and (3) the public are not to be invited to subscribe for shares or debentures in the company. A private company becomes a public company when any of these three requirements is removed from the articles of association. When a private company contravenes any of the three requirements eg by offering its shares or debentures to the public, it loses the legal privilege of private status and a criminal offence will have been committed.

Formerly, the principal advantage of a private company was that it was not required to disclose its financial and trading position to the public via the registry of companies and many EC directives did not apply to it. This has changed since the enactment of the Companies Amendment Act 1986, which implements the Fourth EC Directive on Company Law, and which specifies new disclosure requirements for all companies. However, there are important reliefs for a private *small company* (qv) and a private *medium-sized company* (qv), which are not required to prepare and publish a full set of accounts, and certain small private companies are exempt from having their accounts audited. See AUDIT.

A person with a financial interest in a private company can obtain a court order (a *disclosure order*) compelling disclosure of interest in shares and debentures in the company in certain circumstances: Companies Act 1990, ss 97–104. See Companies Act 1963, s 5(1), 33, 34(1), 34(2), 35; Companies Amendment Act 1983, s 21 and Sch 1, para 6; Companies Amendment Act 1986, ss 8–11. [Bibliography: Courtney.] See DISCLOSURE ORDER; SHARES, VALUE OF.

company, public. A company which is not a private company: Companies Amendment Act 1983, s 2(1). Since 1983, it has been possible to create a new type of public company called a *public limited company* (qv) or plc. An old public company with limited liability had to become a plc or else reregister under some other form (CAA 1983, s 13). See COMPANY, PRIVATE; ASSOCIATION, ARTICLES OF.

company, public limited; plc. A public company limited by shares with a minimum of seven members, which complies with specific requirements of the Companies Acts. To become and remain a plc, the company must have a minimum authorised share capital of at least £30,000 (€38,092); at least one-quarter of the nominal amount must have been paid up on its issued share capital, together with any premium on its shares; it must not have allocated any shares it offered for subscription when the offer was under-subscribed; it must not have allocated shares for service contracts, or for contracts that can be performed more than five years from the allotment date; an independent valuation must have been made of non-cash consideration transferred in order to acquire shares in it, and of major transactions between it and its first members during its first two years' commercial existence; shares taken by its subscribers must have been paid for in cash; any lien or other charge on its own shares is void; and it may not pay a dividend if it is insolvent in that its net assets are less than its called up share capital and its undistributed reserves: Companies Amendment Act 1983, ss 5(2), 17(1), 19(1), 22, 26(2), 28–35, 44 and 46.

A *company limited by guarantee and having a share capital* cannot be formed as or become a plc (CAA 1983, s 7). A building society may convert itself into a public limited company: Building Societies Act 1989, s 101. See VALUATION REPORT.

company, registered. A company registered in the registry of companies: Companies Act 1963, s 18. It may be registered with either *limited* or *unlimited* liability, and it may be registered as a *private* or as a *public limited company*. A company, association or partnership must be registered as a company if it consists of more than 20 persons formed for the purpose of carrying on any business that has as its object the acquisition of gain; in the case of a bank it must be registered if it consists of more than ten persons (CA 1963, ss 372 and 376). Partnerships of solicitors and accountants are excluded from these requirements: Companies Amendment Act 1982, s 13, as amended by Companies (Auditing and Accounting) Act 2003, s 55.

A company must not be formed and registered unless it appears to the Registrar of Companies that the company will, when registered, carry on an activity in the State, which is an activity mentioned in its memorandum: Companies (Amendment) (No 2) Act 1999, s 42. Also the company must have a director resident in the State or alternatively: (a) provide a bond to the value of £20,000 (€25,395); or (b) obtain a certificate that it has a real and continuous link with one or more economic activities in the State (C(A)(No2)A 1999, ss 43–44 as amended by C(AA)A 2003, s 54). These provisions, with a limitation on the number of directorships any one person can hold, were introduced to tackle the problems created by Irish registered non-resident companies.

A registered company has perpetual succession and has legal rights and duties separate from its owners' own entitlements and duties; in law the company and its owners are separate and distinct entities. See *Salomon v Salomon Co* [1897] AC 22; *Roundabout Ltd v Beirne* [1959] IR 423; *Irish Permanent Building Society v Registrar of Building Societies* [1981] ILRM 242.

Certain limited information on every company registered in the companies office is available free on *www.irion.ie*. See REGISTRAR OF COMPANIES.

company, sham. See LIFTING THE CORPORATE VEIL.

company, statutory. A statutory corporation, colloquially known as a *state sponsored* or *semi-state* body; a company established by special legislation. Many of the state sponsored organisations are statutory companies eg the ESB by the Electricity (Supply) Act 1927. In the last century, special general enactments established public utilities eg Companies Clauses Acts.

Statutory companies are restricted to the statutory purposes of their establishment and cannot apply funds to purposes not authorised by their constituting statute. They are subject to the *ultra vires* (qv) doctrine. They may have extensive powers including, in many cases, the power to acquire land compulsorily eg E(S)A 1927, s 45. See *Linnane* in 8 ILT & SJ (1990) 144. See EQUALITY BEFORE THE LAW; PRIVATISATION.

company, unlimited. An incorporated association, the members of which wish to engage in business in common but for one reason or another, do not wish their liability to be limited. Because of the numerical limit on the size of partnerships (other than solicitors or accountants), an unlimited company is registered where there are more than 20 such members, or more than ten in the case of bankers.

The advantages of an unlimited company are that it is exempted from many of the Companies Acts disclosure requirements, it is relatively easy to return contributed capital to its members, and it enjoys certain fiscal and tax advantages. Unlike a partnership, unpaid creditors of an unlimited company have no direct claim against the members and must secure the winding up of the company, and the liquidator will then attempt to recover outstanding amounts from the members with unlimited liability. See Companies Act 1963, ss 372 and 376; Companies Amendment Act 1982, s 13; Companies (Auditing and Accounting) Act 2003, s 55.

However, from 1994, unlimited companies or partnerships in which the members are themselves limited companies, are subject to the same reporting requirements as limited companies: European Communities (Accounts) Regulations 1993, SI No 396 of 1993. See PARTNERSHIP; COMPANY, REGISTERED.

company formation service. A service provided by the Law Society of Ireland to solicitors through which it forms private companies limited by shares, single member companies, guarantee companies, charitable status companies, and unlimited companies. See website: *www.lawsociety.ie*; email: *companyformation@lawsociety.ie*.

company forms. For recent prescribed forms for the purposes of certain provisions of the Companies Acts, see Companies (Forms) Order 2000, SI No 62 of 2000; Companies (Forms) Order 2001, SI No 466 of 2001; SIs Nos 38, 39, 54 and 114 of 2002; Companies (Forms) Order 2003, SI No 189 of 2003 and Companies (Forms) Order 2004, SI No 133 of 2004. Forms can be obtained from the Companies Office website: *www.cro.ie*.

company law enforcement. The office of the *Director of Corporate Enforcement* (qv) was established in 2001 to enforce and ensure compliance with company law: Company Law Enforcement Act 2001. This Act also established a statutory *Company Law Review Group* to ensure that company law is updated on a continuous basis. The Act also amended company law eg as regards investigation of companies, restriction and disqualification of directors, winding up and insolvency, filing obligations, auditors, transactions involving directors, and increased penalties. See also Companies (Auditing and Accounting) Act 2003. [Bibliography: Cahill N; Courtney; MacCann; McGrath S; O'Connell; Power.] See AUDITOR, COMPANY.

company law review group. The group with the functions of monitoring, reviewing and advising the Minister concerning: (a) the implementation, amendment and consolidation of the Companies Acts; (b) the introduction of new legislation; (c) the Rules of the Superior Courts; (d) the approach to issues on company law arising from EU membership; (e) international developments in company law: Company Law Enforcement Act 2001, ss 67–71. The group is required to make an annual report of its activities to the Minister (CLEA 2001, s 71).

The group published their first report on 28 February 2002 containing 195 recommendations. Some of the radical measures proposed as regards private companies are: (a) allowing private companies limited by shares to dispense with holding an annual general meeting; (b) abolishing the memorandum and articles of association and replacing them with a simple constitution; (c) permitting private companies limited by shares to have only one director; (d) abolishing the doctrine of *ultra vires*; and (e) codifying what the courts have held to be the fiduciary duties of directors so as to make them more accessible to the users of company law. The group's second report is due in 2004.

By August 2004, nine parts of a new companies consolidation and reform Bill had been drafted and posted on the website *www.clrg.ie*, dealing with the following issues as they apply to private companies: incorporation, share capital, corporate governance, duties of directors, debentures and charges, receivers, reconstructions, dissolution and reinstatement and compliance, investigation and enforcement. See also website: *www.entemp.ie*.

company secretary. See SECRETARY.

comparative advertisement. An advertisement which purports to compare the level of repayments or cost under one or more forms of *financial accommodation*; such advertisements must contain the relevant terms of each of the forms of financial accommodation; *financial accommodation* includes credit and letting of goods: Consumer Credit Act 1995, ss 2(1) and 24. The use of a competitor's registered trade mark in a comparative advertisement could amount to an infringement of the competitor's property rights; however, if such use is in accordance with 'honest practices in industrial or commercial matters' this will be a good defence to infringement proceedings: Trade Marks Act 1996, s 14(6).

compellable witness. See OIREACHTAS COMMITTEES; SUBPOENA; WITNESS, COMPETENCE OF.

compensation. A payment to make amends for loss or injury to person or property, or to compensate for some deprivation. See CRIMINAL INJURIES COMPENSATION TRIBUNAL; HOUSING STRATEGY; MOTORWAY; PATENT; PROCEEDS OF CRIME; WAYLEAVE.

compensation and compulsory purchase. The compensation to which the owner in land is entitled where his land is compulsorily acquired; he is entitled to get for his land precisely what it is worth to him in money terms immediately before the acquisition and in deciding how much it is worth, both its advantages and disadvantages have to be taken into account: *In re Lucas and Chesterfield Gas and Water Board* [1909] 1 KB 16; Acquisition of Land (Assessment of Compensation) Act 1919 as amended by the Local Government (Planning and Development) Act 1963, s 69(1) and Planning and Development Act 2000, s 265(3). These Acts set out rules for determining compensation; these rules do not affect the assessment of compensation for *disturbance* or for *severances and injurious affection* (qv). See *Manning v Shackleton* [1994] 1 ILRM 346, HC.

Interest on a compulsory purchase award is payable at the *local loans fund rate* where there is entry on the land following service of a notice of entry: Housing of the Working Classes Act 1890, Sch 2, art 24 and *Murphy v Dublin Corporation* [1972] IR 215. Where there is no entry before compensation is agreed or assessed, the local authority is obliged to pay interest on the award at the rate appropriate to an ordinary contract for sale of land from the time a good title is shown: *In re Piggot and Great Western Railway* [1881] 18 Ch D 146.

An arbitrator's award of compensation is not required to incorporate a reasoned judgment, but he may be required to specify the amount awarded in respect of any particular heading; the request for this may be made during the course of the hearing or after publication of the award: *Manning v Shackleton* [1997] 2 ILRM 26, SC. Also an unconditional offer under s 5(1) of Acquisition of Land (Assessment of Compensation) Act 1919 must be in writing and must be unconditional (*MANNING* case).

The assessment of compensation is in the nature of an award of damages for the expropriation of property against the wishes of the owner: *Dublin Corporation v Building & Allied Trade Union* [1996] 2 ILRM 547, SC. Where the arbitrator is satisfied that the owner intends to reinstate a building on some other site, the *'equivalent reinstatement'* basis of compensation provides machinery for compensating the owner in full where he would not be fully compensated by being awarded the open market value. The owner on being awarded compensation on the basis of *equivalent reinstatement* is entitled to treat the litigation as being at an end and cannot be called to account in the event that the building is not reinstated (*Dublin Corporation* case).

No additional compensation will be paid in respect of a compulsory acquisition where land is used for a purpose other than that for which it was acquired: Planning and Development Act 2000, s 210.

Compensation is statutorily provided for when the ESB exercises its power to acquire land compulsorily: Electricity Supply (Amendment) Act 1985. As regards compensation on compulsory purchase of protected structures (qv), see Planning and Development Act 2000, s 28. See *Dublin Corporation v Gemmata NV* [1995] 1 IR 204, HC; *Doyle v Kildare County Council* [1996] 1 ILRM 252, SC. See also Housing (Miscellaneous Provisions) Act 1992, s 35; Roads Act 1993, s 52; Minister for Community, Rural and Gaeltacht Affairs (Powers and Functions) Act 2003, s 3(3)(d)(ii). [Bibliography: McDermott & Woulfe.] See ARBITRATION; CLEARED SITE VALUE; COMPULSORY PURCHASE ORDER; HOUSING STRATEGY; NOTICE TO TREAT; OPEN MARKET VALUE.

compensation and planning permission. A person who is refused planning permission (qv) to develop land or is granted permission subject to conditions, has a right to be paid by the planning authority by way of compensation, the amount of the reduction in value of his interest in the land *at the time of the decision* and in the case of the occupier of the land, the damage (if any) to his trade, business or profession carried out on the land: Planning and Development Act 2000, s 190. No statutory right to compensation can arise until a decision is made: *Wood v Wicklow Co Council* [1995] 1 ILRM 51, HC.

However, there are significant restrictions on the right to compensation eg compensation is not payable in respect of: (a) a *refusal* of permission for any development described in Sch 3 eg demolition of a habitable house; (b) a refusal of permission where the *reason* for the refusal is a reason set out in Sch 4 eg premature development by reference to constraints eg sewerage facilities; (c) a *condition* imposed on a permission as set out in Sch 5 eg requiring payment of a contribution for public infrastructure benefiting the development; (d) a refusal of permission or conditions imposed for retention of unauthorised structures; (e) refusal of permission based on a change in zoning of land as a result of the making of a new development plan (PDA 2000, s 191).

Also compensation is not payable in respect of any condition specified for the protection of a *protected structure* (qv) or in respect of any development which would affect a protected structure (PDA 2000, s 191 and Sch 3, para 3). Compensation is also not payable where the refusal of permission, or a condition imposed, relates to specified matters concerning motorways, busways and protected roads: Roads Act 1993, s 46(3). See also RA 1993, s 52(6).

A planning authority can avoid paying compensation by serving a notice on the claimant stating that, in their opinion, the land is capable of other development for which planning permission ought to be granted (PDA 2000, s 192). This notice is not invalidated by reason of the fact that the planning permission it proposed could be granted only after the pursuit of a material contravention procedure: *Ballymac Designer v Louth County Council* [2002] 2 ILRM 481, SC and 3 IR 247.

Compensation may be payable where by notice a planning permission is revoked or modified; where by notice there is removal or alteration of an authorised structure; where by notice there is discontinuance of use of land or where use is subjected to conditions, or refusal to grant permission for the erection of a new structure substantially replacing a structure demolished or destroyed by fire (PDA 2000, ss 193, 195–197).

There is also provision for compensation in relation to damage caused in the course of authorised entry to land; in relation to reduced value arising in an area of *special planning control*; in relation to placing cables, wires and pipelines; and in relation to the creation of rights of way (PDA 2000, ss 198–201).

There is provision for the repayment of compensation where development is carried out on land on which compensation has been paid (PDA 2000, s 192). There is also a prohibition on the assignment of prospective compensation to any other person (PDA 2000, s 194).

Compensation claims must be made within six months (PDA 2000, s 183) and are determined, in the absence of agreement, by arbitration under the Acquisition of Land (Assessment of Compensation) Act 1919 subject to the proviso that the arbitrator may make a nil award and the Rules for Determination of the Amount of Compensation (PDA 2000, s 184 and Sch 2). See Planning and Development Regulations 2001, SI No 600 of 2001, Pt 13, arts173–178. See *Arthur v Kerry County Council* [2000] 3 IR 407, HC and [2000] 2 ILRM 414, HC. [Bibliography: LexisNexis.] See ARBITRATION; HOUSING STRATEGY; PARKS, PUBLIC; PURCHASE NOTICE; SPECIAL AMENITY ORDER.

compensation for criminal injuries. See COMPENSATION ORDER; CRIMINAL INJURIES COMPENSATION TRIBUNAL.

compensation for disturbance. See DISTURBANCE, COMPENSATION FOR.

compensation for improvements. See IMPROVEMENTS, COMPENSATION FOR.

compensation for miscarriage of justice. See MISCARRIAGE.

Compensation Fund. The fund maintained by the Law Society pursuant to the Solicitors Act 1960, ss 21–22 as amended by Solicitors (Amendment) Act 1994, ss 2, 29, 30 (as amended by Solicitors (Amendment) Act 2002, s 16) and S(A)A 1994, s 30A inserted by Investor Compensation Act 1998, s 46.

The Society is empowered to make a grant, of up to €700,000 to the client of a solicitor from the fund, where it is proved to the satisfaction of the Society that the client has sustained loss in consequence of dishonesty on the part of the solicitor or any clerk or servant of the solicitor (S(A)A 1994, s 29). A grant of a larger amount, at the discretion of the Society, may be made in cases of grave hardship. A solicitor is required to pay an annual contribution to the fund as a precondition to being issued a practising certificate (S(A)A 1994, s 30 as amended S(A)A 2002, s 16(b)).

The Society is empowered to require solicitors who are authorised *investment business firms* or *insurance intermediaries* to have a form of indemnity in place to protect clients similar to the professional indemnity in s 26 of S(A)A 1994 or similar to the Compensation Fund (S(A)A 1994, new s 30A). It has been held that compensation from the fund is not confined to clients of the dishonest solicitor: *Trustee Savings Bank v Incorporated Law Society* [1989] ILRM 665, SC. See Solicitors (Compensation Fund) Regulations 1963, SI No 115 of 1963. [Bibliography: O'Callaghan P.] See SOLE PRACTITIONER.

compensation order. An order which a court may make on conviction of any person of an offence, requiring him to pay *compensation* in respect of any *personal injury* or *loss* resulting from the offence to any person who suffered such injury or loss (the *injured party*): Criminal Justice Act 1993, s 6. The compensation order may be in addition to any other sentence or fine which the court may impose but the amount of the compensation: (a) must not exceed the amount of damages which, in the opinion of the court, the injured party would be entitled to recover in a civil action; and (b) must have regard to the means, including financial commitments, of the convicted person (or his parent or guardian where applicable).

There are restrictions in respect of injury or loss that results from the use of a mechanically propelled vehicle (CJA 1993, s 6(4)). Where death has resulted from the offence, *loss* means any matter for which damages could be awarded in respect of the death, and *injured party* includes a dependant of the deceased (CJA 1993, s 6(12)(a)). Also provision has been made for payment to a district court clerk for transmission to the injured party and for payment by way of attachment of earnings (CJA 1993, s 7). For compensation in relation to drug trafficking offences, see Criminal Justice Act 1994, ss 65–66.

The court may now order that compensation be paid by the parent or guardian of a child who has been found guilty of an offence, where it is satisfied that a wilful failure of the parent or guardian to take care of or to control the child, contributed to the child's criminal behaviour: Children Act 2001, s 113. See DCR 1997 Ord 33. See DAMAGE TO PROPERTY.

compensatory damages. Damages (qv) awarded as compensation for and measured by the material loss suffered by a plaintiff. *Aggravated damages* may be awarded when the motives and conduct of the defendant aggravate the injury to the plaintiff. *Exemplary damages* may be awarded to reflect the proper indignation of the public and to reflect disapproval. See *McIntyre v Lewis & Dolan* [1991] 1 IR 121, SC. See DAMAGES.

competence. There are many references in legislation to the requirement that a function be carried out by a 'competent person' or 'competent persons' but there is no definition on what constitutes 'competence'. There are exceptions. A competent person is a chartered engineer who has specified experience: Local Government (Multi-Storey Buildings) Act 1988, s 1(1). A competent person means a competent individual person possessing adequate knowledge, training and ability to perform his duties or work in such a manner as to prevent, as far as practicable, risk of injury: Carriage of Dangerous Goods by Road Regulations 2001 (SI No 492 of 2001), now repealed and replaced by Carriage of Dangerous Goods by Road Regulations 2004, SI No 29 of 2004.

'Competence' in relation to any director or manager of an investment business firm or a member firm of a stock exchange, means competence in respect of which such director or manager would be expected to be competent in the discharge of his professional responsibilities: Stock Exchange Act 1995, s 3(3); Investment Intermediaries Act 1995, ss 2(3) and 36. Equality legislation does not require an employer to employ a person who is not fully competent and fully capable to carry out the duties of the job: Employment Equality Act 1998, s 16 as amended by Equality Act 2004, s 9.

Where a barrister receives instructions which he believes to be beyond his competence he should decline to act in the matter and must so inform the instructing solicitor without delay: *Code of Conduct for the Bar of Ireland* (December 2003) r 4.4. Chartered engineers are required to accept and perform only work for which they are qualified and competent and must obtain whatever advice and assistance is necessary to discharge this responsibility: *Code of Ethics – The Institution of Engineers of Ireland* (November 2003) clause 3.3.

One of the objects of the National Qualifications Authority of Ireland is to establish and maintain a framework of qualifications based on standards of knowledge, skill or competence to be acquired by learners: Qualifications (Education and Training) Act 1999, s 7. See also Sustainable Energy Act 2002, s 10; Air Navigation (Notification and Investigation of Accidents and Incidents) Regulations 1997, SI No 205 of 1997; Safety, Health and Welfare at Work (Construction) Regulations, 2001, SI No 481 of 2001.

In relation to EU Treaties, 'competence' means the legal capacity or ability to legislate or to take other action: National Forum on Europe, *Glossary of Terms* (2003). The principle of *conferral of competences* means that the Union does not have general competences in its own right, but only those that are specifically conferred upon it by the member states by treaty. See also CONTINUING PROFESSIONAL DEVELOPMENT; DISQUALIFICATION ORDER, DRIVING; FLEXIBILITY CLAUSE; NATIONAL QUALIFICATIONS AUTHORITY OF IRELAND.

competence of witnesses. See WITNESS, COMPETENCE OF.

competition, common detriment. The 1937 Constitution provides that the operation of free competition will not be allowed so to develop as to result in the concentration of the ownership or control of essential commodities in a few individuals to the common detriment (art 45(2)(3)). See MONOPOLY.

competition, distortion of. All agreements between undertakings, decisions by associations of undertakings and concerted practices which have as their object or effect the prevention, restriction or distortion of competition in trade in any goods or services in the State or in any part of the State are prohibited and void: Competition Act 2002, s 4(1). Included are agreements which: fix purchase or selling prices; limit or control markets, production, technical development or investment; share markets or sources of supply; apply dissimilar terms to similar transactions, or require supplemental obligations which have no connection with the contract. Exempted are arrangements which meet certain efficiency conditions (CA 2002, s 4(2)).

It is a criminal offence for an undertaking to enter into such an agreement, or to make or implement such a decision or to engage in a *concerted practice* (CA 2002, s 6(1)). There is a presumption that the object or effect was to prevent, restrict or distort competition unless the defendant proves otherwise (CA 2002, s 6(2)).

The Competition Authority (qv) has expressed its view that the prohibition in s 4(1) only applies to a current or continuing contractual commitment or one entered into subsequent to the coming into force of the (now repealed) Competition Act 1991: *Iris Oifigiúil*, 14 May 1993, p 367.

Previously, the Competition Authority could grant a certificate or a licence in respect of an agreement, decision or concerted action; this in effect gave an exemption. This provision has been abolished. However, the Authority may declare that a specified category of agreements, decisions or concerted practices complies with certain efficiency conditions, which in effect gives an exemption (CA 2002, s 4(3)). An appeal against such a declaration may be made to the High Court within 28 days of publication (s 15).

A person who is aggrieved in consequence of any prohibited agreement, decision or concerted practice has a right of action for relief against any undertaking which has been a party to such; the Competition Authority also has a right to take civil action (CA 2002, s 14). The action may be brought in the Circuit or High Court (CA 2002, s 14(3)). There is also provision for appeal to the High Court against a determination of the Competition Authority and for an appeal to the Supreme Court on a point of law only (CA 2002, s 24).

In ordering disclosure of certain documents, the court remarked that competition cases have the special feature that any documents relating to anti-competitive behaviour are likely to be in the possession of the party engaged in that behaviour: *Ryanair v Aer Rianta* [2004] 1 ILRM 241, SC. Provision has been made for open competition in public works and public supply contracts in the EC: SIs Nos 36, 37 and 38 of 1992. See also *RGDATA v Tara Publishing Co Ltd* [1995] 1 ILRM 453, HC and 1 IR 89; *Chanelle Veterinary Ltd v Pfizer Ltd* [1999] 2 ILRM 55, SC; *M & J Gleeson v Competition Authority* [1999] 1 ILRM 401, HC. For repealed legislation, see Competition Act 1991, s 4(1); Competition (Amendment) Act 1996. See also Meade in *Law Society Gazette* (January/February 1992) 7. See 'Awarding damages to a party to an anti-competitive agreement' by Brian Kennedy BL in *Bar Review* (January/February 2002) 171. See 'Criminalising Anti-Competitive Practices' by P A McDermott BL in *Bar Review* (February 2003) 11. [Bibliography: Brown; Competition Authority; Forde (5); ICEL; Lucey; McCarthy & Power; Maher; Massey & O'Hare; O'Connor T; Power V; Jones (UK).] See BELOW COST SELLING; CONCERTED PRACTICE; DOMINANT POSITION, ABUSE OF; EXCLUSIVE DISTRIBUTION AGREEMENT; HELLO MONEY; MERGER OF COMPANY, EC REGULATIONS; RESTRAINT OF TRADE, CONTRACT IN; SOLUS AGREEMENT; STATE AID; VERTICAL AGREEMENTS.

competition, distortion of, EU. The EC Treaty prohibits as incompatible with the common market all agreements between undertakings and concerted practices which may affect trade between member states and which have as their object or effect the prevention, restriction or distortion of competition within the common market (EC Treaty art 81 of the consolidated 2002 version). Any agreement or decision prohibited by this Article is void. Any abuse by one or more undertakings of a *dominant* position within the common market or in a substantial part of it, is prohibited as incompatible with the common market in so far as it affects trade between member states (art 82). It is not sufficient however to prove that the undertaking is in a dominant position, the practice complained of must also constitute an abuse of that position: *Masterfoods Ltd v H B Ice Cream Ltd* [1993] ILRM 145, HC. It is now an offence for an undertaking to engage in activity which is prohibited by consolidated arts 81 or 82: Competition Act 2002, ss 6(1) and 7(1). An *undertaking* is a body which carries on an economic activity; bodies whose functions are purely social, which are founded on the principle of solidarity and have no profit motive, are not undertakings: *FENIN v Commission* [2003] case T-319/99, CFI.

For procedures on the application of EC rules on competition relating to restrictive practices between undertakings which affect trade between member states and abuses of dominant positions with respect to consolidated arts 81–82, see EC (Rules on Competition) Regulations 1993, SI No 124 of 1993.

Provision has been made for a radical change in the manner in which EC competition law is enforced as from 1 May 2004;

a key element will be the abolition of the existing notification and exemption system: Commission Regulation (EC) 1/2003 on the *Implementation of the Rules on Competition* laid down in arts 81 and 82 of the Treaty. See EC (Implementation of the Rules on Competition laid down in Articles 81 and 82 of the Treaty) Regulations 2004, SI No 195 of 2004. Undertakings will be entitled to argue that the exemption in art 81(3) is directly applicable to their agreement or arrangement and can therefore be relied on without any prior decision by the European Commission. The new regime will allow the Commission to concentrate its resources on matters other than the review of notified agreements in particular, the pursuit of more serious EC competition law infringements eg price fixing and other cartel arrangements. See 'Enforcement of EC Competition Law: radical changes for practitioners' by solicitor Lynn Sheehan in *Law Society Gazette* (January/February) 57. [Bibliography: Lucey.] See MERGER OF COMPANY, EC REGULATIONS; STATE AID.

Competition Authority. The independent corporate body originally established by Competition Act 1991, s 10 and continued in being by the Competition Act 2002, s 29. The Competition Authority comprises a chairperson and from two to four other whole-time members as determined and appointed by the Minister (CA 2002, s 35).

The functions of the Authority include: the investigation of anti-competitive agreements, decisions and concerted practices; the investigation of the abuse of a dominant position; the determination of whether mergers or acquisitions can be put into effect; the study and analysis of any practice or method of competition affecting the supply of goods or the provision of services (CA 2002, s 30). The Authority in discharge of its functions, has power to summon witnesses before it, to examine witnesses on oath, and to require them to produce documents under their power or control (CA 2002, s 31). The Authority is also required to produce a strategic plan for the ensuing three-year period (CA 2002, s 33).

There is provision for the enforcement by the courts of determinations of the Authority and of commitments made by undertakings (CA 2002, s 26). There is also provision for co-operation between the Authority and other statutory bodies eg to avoid duplication of activities (CA 2002, s 34 and Competition Act 2002 (Section 34(11))(Director of Consumer Affairs) Order 2003, SI No 130 of 2003) and for the exchange of information with foreign competition bodies (CA 2002, s 46).

An authorised officer of the Authority, with a search warrant, has wide powers of entering and inspecting premises or vehicles, and of seizing and retaining books and records (CA 2002, s 45).

In reviewing a decision of the Authority, the appropriate standard adopted by the courts is that of *reasonableness*, which is a standard between that of *correctness* and *patent unreasonableness*: *M & J Gleeson v Competition Authority* [1999] 1 ILRM 401, HC. See *Cronin v Competition Authority* [1998] 2 ILRM and 1 IR 265, SC.

The Authority announced in 2002 its decision to carry out a study of competition issues in the provision of banking services, excluding investment banking, in the State under s 30(1)(a) of the 2002 Act. For preliminary consultation document for the purpose of the study, see *www.tca.ie/banking.html*. For decisions of the Competition Authority, see *www.bailii.org*. See also *www.tca.ie*. See also 'Representing clients before the Competition Authority' by solicitor Vincent Power in *Law Society Gazette* (April 2004) 44. For previous repealed legislation, see Competition Act 1991, s 10 and Sch and Competition (Amendment) Act 1996. See GUN JUMPING; MERGER OF COMPANY, LOCAL PROVISIONS; TAKEOVER.

competition law. The body of law dealing with such matters as monopolies, abuse of dominant position, mergers and acquisitions, restraint of trade, trade regulation, and restriction and distortion of competition.

Significant changes have been made to competition and merger law, including:(a) transfer of responsibility for examining and deciding on mergers and takeovers to the Competition Authority (from the Minister) but with the Minister empowered to overrule the Authority in the case of the merger of media companies; (b) increase in the threshold at which a non-media merger can be investigated from a minimum turnover to €40m; (c) more severe punishment, including imprisonment, in respect of offences such as price fixing, bid rigging or market sharing: Competition Act 2002.

The Act also consolidates and modernises the existing enactments relating to competition, mergers and acquisitions and repeals the Mergers, Takeovers and Monopolies (Control) Act 1978, the Competition Act 1991 and the Competition (Amendment) Act 1996. The High Court has held that the 1991 Act was an autonomous Act of the Oireachtas and not one implementing a directive of the European Union; it had its own machinery for implementing its rules on competition which was different from those of the EC Treaty: *Blemings v David Patton Ltd* [2001] 1 IR 385, HC.

Provision has been made for a radical change in the manner in which EC competition law will be enforced as from 1 May 2004: see COMPETITION, DISTORTION OF. See 'Competition Law and the Internet' by Stephen Dodd BL in *Bar Review* (December 2000) 133; 'Competition Act 2002' by Mark O'Connell BL in *Bar Review* (December 2002) 382. [Bibliography: Brown; Lucey; McCarthy & Power; Maher; O'Connor T; Power; Travers & Byrne; Whish UK.] See MERGER OF COMPANY; TAKEOVER; WHISTLE BLOWER.

competitive tender. See CONSUMER, DEALING AS.

compilation. A collection into serviceable form of, for example, facts, statistics, tables, and quotations. *Copyright* can exist in compilations; the copyright of a work of compilation is infringed where another person, relying on the efforts and the compilation of the copyright owner, reproduces all or part of such a work in any material form without any or only minimal input of his own: *Allied Discount Card Ltd v Bord Fáilte Éireann* [1990] ITLR (6 August). See also *Private Research Ltd v Brosnan* [1996] 1 ILRM 27, HC. See DATABASE; LITERARY WORK.

complainant. The person who makes a complaint. See DCR 1997 Ord 15, r 1. See COMPLAINT; COMMON INFORMER.

complaint. (1) The issue of a *summons* alleging an offence may be grounded on the making of a *complaint* to either a district court judge or a district court clerk: DCR 1997 Ord 15; Petty Sessions (Ireland) Act 1851, s 10; Courts (No 3) Act 1986, s 1(4), as amended by Civil Liability and Courts Act 2004, s 49. There is no form prescribed for making a complaint: *Irish Insurance Commissioners v Trench* [1913] 47 ILTR 115. However, when a complaint is made on oath, it must be made by sworn information: Form 15.3, Sch B: DCR 1997 Ord 15, r 1(2).

A complaint may be made either with or without an oath and in writing or not, but must be communicated to a person duly authorised to receive it: *Murray v McArdle* [1999] 2 ILRM 283, HC. However, a complaint must be made by information on oath and in writing where a warrant is sought for the arrest of a person *charging* him with having committed an indictable offence: DCR 1997 Ord 16, r 1.

A party in any proceedings is entitled to obtain from the district court clerk, a copy of any written complaint in his custody, on payment of the prescribed fee, if any: DCR 1997 Ord 35, r 2.

In a summons *alleging* an offence contrary to a statute, it is sufficient to state the substance of the offence in ordinary language, with such particulars as may be necessary to give reasonable information as to the nature of the complaint: DCR 1997 Ord 15, r 9.

In general a complaint must be made within six months from the time when the cause of complaint has arisen: Petty Sessions (Ireland) Act 1851, s 10; *Minister for Agriculture v Norgro Limited* [1980] IR 155.

Where there is a variation between the evidence and the complaint, the court is empowered to amend the summons, warrant or other document: DCR 1997 Ord 38, r 1(1). Also where the complaint discloses no offence at law it may be struck out: Ord 38, r 1(4).

For other ways of initiating a summons, see Courts (No 3) Act 1986 and summons. See also CHARGE SHEET.

(2) A statement made to a third party by a female against whom a sexual offence is alleged to have been committed. To be admissible, the complaint must have been made at the first opportunity which reasonably offers itself and it must be voluntary and spontaneous, and must not be elicited by leading, intimidating or inducing questions. It should be explained to the jury that evidence of a complaint does not constitute corroboration, in the legal sense of that word, of the evidence of the complainant: *The People (DPP) v MA* [2002] 2 IR 601, CCA. It should be made clear to the jury that such evidence was not evidence of the facts on which the complaint was based but could be considered by the jury as showing that the victim's conduct in so complaining

was consistent with her testimony (*MA* case). See also *R v Lillyman* [1896] 2 QB 167; *R v Osborne* [1905] 1 KB 551; *People (DPP) v Brophy* [1992] ILRM 709, CCA; *The People (DPP) v G* [1993] 11 ILT Dig 186, CCA.

(3) In relation to a complaint about services, see CREDIT UNION; OMBUDSMAN FOR THE CREDIT INSTITUTIONS; OMBUDSMAN; OMBUDSMAN, EUROPEAN; INSURANCE OMBUDSMAN; SOLICITORS' DISCIPLINARY TRIBUNAL.

complementary medicine. 'Alternative medicine; the treatment, alleviation or prevention of disease by techniques such as osteopathy and acupuncture allied with attention to factors such as diet and emotional stability, which affect a person's general wellbeing': *Collins English Dictionary*. 'Complementary medicine should only be used where there is evidence that it will benefit the patient. Doctors who practise or refer patients for complementary medicine must be aware of the efficacy and potential side effects of those treatments and advise patients accordingly': Medical Council, *A Guide to Ethical Conduct and Behaviour* (6th edn, 2004) para 4.5.

complete specification. Formerly, the full description of an invention which was required to be filed before action towards granting a patent could be taken: Patents Act 1964, ss 8–11. An application for a patent could be accompanied by a *provisional specification* initially, the advantage being that the applicant could, at minimal cost, protect his priority while he determined whether there was a prospect of using the invention profitable. Provisional patent protection has been abolished and replaced by a system of claiming priority from earlier applications. Also a less costly *short-term* patent has been introduced. See RSC Ord 94, rr 15–22. See PATENT, APPLICATION FOR; SHORT-TERM PATENT.

completed offence. See ALTERNATIVE VERDICT; PUNISHMENT.

completion. Final stages in a contract for the sale of land which is effected by the delivery up by the vendor of a good title and of the actual possession or enjoyment thereof to the purchaser and by the purchaser in accepting such title, and paying the agreed purchase price. A purchaser is not obliged to complete in advance of the resolution of a question as to whether he is entitled to compensation for loss suffered by him as a result of error eg due to

possibility of a right of way existing over the land: *O'Brien v Kearney* [1995] 2 ILRM 232, HC.

The High Court has held that: (a) the giver of a notice to complete a sale under which time is made of the essence, is as equally bound by it as is the recipient of the notice; and (b) the party giving the notice must be ready and willing at the time to fulfil its own outstanding contractual obligations: *Tyndarious v Nicholls*, (11 January 2002, unreported), HC. See 'Completion Notices: A Word of Warning' by solicitor Patrick Mullins in *Law Society Gazette* (January/February 2003) 30. See *Report on Conveyancing Law – Service of Completion Notices* (LRC 40, 1991).

completion rate. Means the number of learners who complete a programme of education and training expressed as a percentage of the number of learners who commenced: Qualifications (Education and Training) Act 1999, s 2(1). Bodies seeking validation of their programmes are required to supply information in respect of their completion rates (Q(ET)A 1999, ss 15(5)(d) and 25(5)(d)). Also any new universities and the Dublin Institute of Technology are required to provide such information to the National Qualifications Authority of Ireland (Q(ET)A 1999, ss 38(2)(c) and 41(2)(c)).

compliance statement. See DIRECTORS' REPORT.

complicity. The fact or condition of being an accomplice (qv). [Bibliography: Charleton (4).]

compos mentis. [Of sound mind.]

composition. A sum of money accepted by creditors in satisfaction of debts. A debtor may propose to his creditors a composition in satisfaction of his liabilities as an alternative to *bankruptcy*. A debtor following adjudication as a bankrupt may, with the consent of the majority of creditors and despite opposition from the minority, offer and carry a composition after bankruptcy.

The court has now got full control over a composition ie it must approve of it before it is binding, which it will do where three fifths in number and value of creditors accept the offer of composition; any creditor whose debt is less than £100 (€126.97) will not be entitled to vote: Bankruptcy Act 1988, s 39. However, an instalment in the payment of a composition may not be secured by a bill, note or other security signed by or enforceable against the bankrupt alone (BA 1988, s 40(2)). Also, the court has a discretion to refuse an offer of composition if the final offer is not payable within two years (BA 1988, s 40(3)).

The court is empowered to discharge the bankruptcy *adjudication order* on the application of the bankrupt and on the report of the Official Assignee (qv) after lodgment with him of cash or specified securities to satisfy the composition (BA 1988, s 41). See BANKRUPTCY; BANKRUPTCY, DISCHARGE FROM; CORRUPT AGREEMENT WITH CREDITOR.

compound. To settle or adjust by agreement e g to agree to accept a composition (qv).

compound interest. Interest calculated on both the principal and its accrued interest.

(1) The law does not permit compound interest except on commercial or mercantile accounts which are still running. The relationship between banker and customer is mercantile in nature so as to permit charging of compound interest even without express agreement, it being taken that the customer acquiesces in the compounding. Demand for repayment brings the banker/customer relationship to an end and the automatic right to charge compound interest ceases as the relationship is now of creditor and debtor.

The practice in the Master's (High) Court is to allow compounding of interest only to issue of summons and simple interest thereafter. See *Yourrell v Hibernian Bank* [1918] AC 372; *Allied Irish Bank v The George Ltd* [1975] HC; *National Bank of Greece v Pinios Shipping Co* [1989] 1 All ER 213 & [1990] 1 All ER 78. See *Doyle* in 7 ILT & SJ (1989) 215; 8 ILT & SJ (1990) 94; and 10 ILT & SJ (1992) 66. However, in a particular case, the court held that a bank had no implied right to charge compound interest or interest at a specially high default rate: *Trustee Savings Bank v Maughan* [1991] in 10 ILT & SJ (1992) 66 and 265, HC. It is likely that the law now leans against a presumption of compounding interest unless by agreement, express or implied, whether by custom or otherwise.

(2) As regard building societies, for compound interest to be chargeable, provision for such interest must be provided for in the mortgage deed: *Eastern Counties Building Society v Russell* [1947] 1 All ER 500. It has been general practice in the past for building societies to carry forward annually, the total outstanding indebtedness of the borrower in one sum (which may include arrears in accrued interest) and to charge the borrower with interest on that one sum for the ensuing account period, which arrangement may include an element of compound interest.

(3) Compound interest is allowable in relation to salvage awards: Merchant Shipping (Salvage and Wreck) Act 1993, s 37. See ARBITRATION, DOMESTIC; ARBITRATION, INTERNATIONAL.

compound settlement. A settlement constituted by more than one document e g deeds or wills over a period of time. See SETTLEMENT.

compounding a felony. Formerly, a common law misdemeanour, committed by a person who bargained for value to abstain from prosecuting an offender. Now replaced by the offence of *concealing an offence* (qv): Criminal Law Act 1997, s 8(3).

compromise. A settlement; an agreement between parties to a dispute to settle it out of court. In general, a compromise must satisfy these conditions: (a) the initial claim must have been reasonable and not vexatious and frivolous; (b) the plaintiff must have had an honest belief in the chances of its success; (c) the party contending that the compromise is valid must not have withheld or suppressed facts that would have shown the claim in a truer light.

It has been held that a defendant was not bound by a settlement where counsel were not *ad idem* because of mutual mistake regarding a compromise: *Mespil Ltd v Capaldi* [1986] ILRM 373. A plaintiff can be estopped from asserting in proceedings that which he has abandoned in a compromise to previous proceedings: *Hennerty v Bank of Ireland* [1989] 7 ILT Dig 24. A dependant is not entitled to maintain an action where her deceased husband had compromised the action prior to his death: Civil Liability Act 1961, ss 7, 48 & 49; *Mahon v Burke* [1991] ILRM 59, HC.

In a particular case, the court held that the trial judge should acquiesce to the wishes of the parties to a settlement ie to extend the time for acceptance of a lodgment of money in court by one of the defendants and for the payment of the moneys lodged to the plaintiff: *Superwood Holdings plc v Sun Alliance plc (No 2)* [1999] 4 IR 531, SC. A pre-hearing settlement precludes the Employment Appeals Tribunal from hearing a claim for unfair dismissal: *Duffy-Finn v Lundbeck Ltd* [1990] ELR 224.

The 'judicial review' procedure is not the appropriate procedure to be used to resolve a dispute as to the terms of settlement of litigation: *Ainsworth v Minister for Defence* [2003] ITLR (21 July 2003). A compromised appeal against assessment to tax may properly be the subject of a subsequent additional assessment: *Hammond Lane Metal Co Ltd v O'Culachain* [1990] ILRM 249, HC.

As it is the policy of the courts to encourage settlements, documents obtained during settlement negotiations are privileged: *Hogan v Murray* [1999] 1 ILRM 257, HC. *Structured* settlements are settlements whereby the plaintiff is paid an annual monetary amount, usually index-linked and paid for life with a minimum payment period; they are becoming more common in the UK.

In relation to claims by infants or persons of unsound mind, no settlement or compromise or payment or acceptance of money paid into court, either before or at or after trial, is valid without the approval of the court (RSC Ord 22, r 10 and Civil Liability Act 1961, s 63). See also SI No 99 of 1990.

A barrister must not for the purposes of procuring a settlement of a case, discuss the merits of the case with the parties and witnesses on the other side without the consent of his own solicitor and the consent of the solicitor and/or barrister for the other side: *Code of Conduct for the Bar of Ireland* (December 2003) r 4.10. He may negotiate only with the barrister or solicitor retained by the other party (r 11.8). It is the duty of a barrister who concludes or rules a settlement to endorse the terms of or the effect of the same on his brief or otherwise record them in writing (r 4.17). Where in the course of settlement negotiations an offer is made to a barrister and/or solicitor, it is the duty of the barrister to inform the solicitor that all the terms of the settlement be imparted to the client, and in the event of the solicitor refusing to do so, the barrister must cease to accept any further instructions from that solicitor in the case (r 3.16).

Also during settlement negotiations, a solicitor should explain matters fully to the client, including legitimate deductions which will be made, so that the client will know the net amount he will receive: *A Guide to Professional Conduct of Solicitors in Ireland* (2002) ch 10.1. An undertaking should not be given by a solicitor in relation to funds to be recovered on behalf of children, as the court has exclusive jurisdiction (ch 6.5). A barrister is entitled to charge a brief fee where there is a settlement resulting from negotiations (*Bar Code*, r 11.2).

See also *Leonard v Leonard* [1812] 2 Ball B 171; *O'Donnell v O'Sullivan* [1913] ILTR 253; *O'Neill v Ryan, Ryan O'Brien* [1991] ITLR (2 September), HC. See Residential Institutions Redress Act 2002, s 12; Personal Injuries Assessment Board Act 2003, s 6(3)–(4). See Credit Union Act 1997, s 161 as amended by Central Bank and Financial Services Authority of Ireland Act 2003, s 35, Sch 1. See RSC Ord 22, r 10; Ord 75, r 4(k). See PERSONAL INJURIES; LODGMENT IN COURT; RECONSTRUCTION OF COMPANY; SETTLEMENT, EU; WITHOUT PREJUDICE.

Comptroller and Auditor General. The office holder, appointed by the President of Ireland on the nomination of the Dáil, to control on behalf of the State all disbursements and to audit all accounts of moneys administered by or under the authority of the Oireachtas: 1937 Constitution, art 33.

In 1993, the nature of the audit process carried out by the C & A G was extended to cover, at his discretion, statutory examinations of economy, efficiency in the use of resources and management effectiveness; the range of bodies covered by his audit and examination processes was also extended to include Vocational Education Committees, third-level educational bodies and health boards: Comptroller and Auditor General (Amendment) Act 1993. In addition, he was empowered at his discretion to carry out inspections of the accounts of harbour authorities, regional tourism organisations, and bodies which receive the bulk of their receipts from public funds, to check that public moneys have been spent for the purposes for which they were provided (CAG(A)A 1993, s 8). The C & A G must not question or express an opinion on the merits of policy or of policy objectives in any of his reports (CAG(A)A 1993, s 11(5)). He is ineligible to stand as a candidate for election to the European Parliament: European Parliament Elections Act 1997, s 11(2)(b).

See also Central Bank Act 1997, s 77 as amended by Central Bank and Financial Services Authority of Ireland Act 2004, s 31; Comptroller etc and Committees of the Houses of the Oireachtas (Special Provisions) Act 1998; Communications Regulation Act 2002, s 32; Competition Act 2002, s 41(5); Houses of the Oireachtas Commission Act 2003, s 14(2); Personal Injuries Assessment Board Act 2003, s 77(3); Public Service Superannuation (Miscellaneous Provisions) Act 2004, Sch 2; Residential Tenancies Act 2004, s 178(3). See *Comptroller and Auditor General v Ireland* [1997] 1 IR 248, HC. See website: *www.irlgov.ie/audgen*; Email: *postmaster@audgen.irlgov.ie*. See DIRT.

compulsory licence. See LICENCES OF RIGHT.

compulsory purchase of shares. See SHARES, COMPULSORY PURCHASE OF.

compulsory purchase order (CPO). The order which certain bodies are empowered by statute to make, which enables them to acquire land compulsorily. In the case of local authorities, the power is contained in many statutes, but now must be construed as giving the local authority power, for the purpose of performing any of its functions, to acquire by way of purchase, lease, exchange or otherwise, land, any easement, wayleave, water right, or other right over or in respect of land or water or any *substratum* of land, inside or outside its functional area: Planning and Development Act 2000, s 213(1)–(2). The power to acquire may be in respect of land not immediately required for a particular purpose or even where the planning authority has not determined the purpose, but is of the opinion that it will require the land in the future (PDA 2000, s 213(3)).

A local authority has power to acquire land by *compulsory purchase order* under the following enactments: Public Health (Ireland) Act 1878, Local Government (Ireland) Act 1898; Local Government Act 1925, Water Supplies Act 1942; Local Government (No 2) Act 1960, Local Government (Sanitary Services) Act 1964; Housing Act 1966; Derelict Sites Act 1990, Roads Acts 1993 and 1998, and Dublin Docklands Development Authority Act 1997.

When a CPO is made by a local authority under the listed enactments and there are no objections, An Bord Pleanála advises the local authority and the local authority confirms the order, with or without modification, or may refuse to confirm the order: (PDA 2000, s 216). Where there is an objection, An Bord Pleanála may hold an oral hearing (PDA 2000, s 218). It may hear matters in relation to an *environmental impact statement* in parallel with the hearing of the CPO (PDA 2000, s 220).

A CPO becomes operative on final determination of the proceedings if it is challenged or, if no challenge is made, within a period of three weeks, following which, the local authority is entitled to serve a *notice to treat* (qv) on the persons interested in the land. The relevant date for assessing the value of the land is the date of the first notice to treat: HA 1966, s 84(1); *Murphy v Dublin Corporation* [1972] IR 215. Fourteen days *notice of entry* by the local authority on the land may be given after service of the notice to treat: HA 1966, s 80.

A planning authority is empowered to acquire compulsorily a *protected structure* (qv): (PDA 2000, ss 71–77). Additional compulsory purchase powers are contained in the 2000 Act eg a local authority's powers of compulsory acquisition now extends to the foreshore (PDA 2000, s 227) and to a structure in an architectural conservation area (PDA 2000, s 83).

Certain other bodies are given power by statute to acquire land compulsorily eg: (a) the Custom House Docks Development Authority under the Urban Renewal (Amendment) Act 1987; (b) health boards (qv) for their own use and for voluntary bodies by virtue of the Health Act 1947 Part VIII and Health Act 1970, s 40; (c) the Minister in relation to an aerodrome or to ensure that land near an aerodrome is not used in a way which would be a danger to aircraft: Air Navigation and Transport Acts 1936 and 1950; Irish Aviation Authority Act 1993, s 42.

Failure of such bodies to exercise this power within a reasonable time from the date of giving notice may result in their losing the right to enforce the notice: *Van Nierop v Commissioners for Public Works* [1990] 2 IR 189.

For *capital gains tax* provisions on the disposal of assets under a CPO, see Taxes Consolidation Act 1997, ss 605 and 542 as amended by Finance Act 2002, ss 61 and 62 respectively. See Harbours Act 1996, s 16 and Sch 4; Roads (Amendment) Act 1998, ss 2, 5, 7; Air Navigation and Transport (Amendment) Act 1998, ss 17 and 62; Electricity Regulation Act 1999, s 47; Gas Act 1976, s 26 as amended by Gas (Amendment) Act 2000, s 20; Minister for Community, Rural and Gaeltacht

Affairs (Powers and Functions) Act 2003, s 3(1)(a). [Bibliography: Bland (2); McDermott & Woulfe.] See BLASKETS; COMPENSATION AND COMPULSORY PURCHASE; FORESHORE; OPEN SPACES; MOTORWAY; SUBSTRATUM OF LAND; URBAN RENEWAL; WAY, RIGHT OF.

compulsory winding up. See WINDING UP, COMPULSORY.

computer. Any machine which accepts structured input, processes it to prescribed rules, and produces the results as outputs: Microsoft Press, *Computer Dictionary* (1997). Computers are either: (a) *analogue* which represent values by continuously variable signals; or (b) *digital* which represent values by discrete signals, the bits representing the binary digits 0 and 1.

The unauthorised operation of a computer with intent to access *data*, whether or not any data accessed are modified, is an offence: Criminal Damage Act 1991, s 5. Any modification of data after access has been obtained constitutes *damage* to the data and is also an offence (CDA 1991, s 2). To *damage* in relation to data is to add to, alter, corrupt, erase or move to another storage medium or to do any act that contributes towards causing this (CDA 1991, s 1(b)). *Data* means information in a form in which it can be accessed by means of a computer and includes a program.

It is an offence to operate or cause to be operated, dishonestly, a computer with the intention of making a gain for oneself or for another or causing a loss to another: Criminal Justice (Theft and Fraud Offences) Act 2001, s 9. For the offence to be committed the person may be within or outside the State at the time he operates or causes to operate the computer, but the computer must be within the State.

It is sufficient to prove that the accused did the act charged dishonestly with the intention of causing loss or making a gain; it is not necessary to prove an intention dishonestly to cause such loss or gain at the expense of a particular person (CJ(TFO)A 2001, s 54(1)).

The books and records of a company may be kept on computer: Companies Acts 1977, s 4 and 1990, s 202(1) and (7). Also the Minister is empowered to make regulations to enable the title to shares in companies to be transferred without a written instrument (CA 1990, s 239). A cheque can be presented electronically eg by computer or fax: Central Bank Act 1989, ss 132

and 133. Schedules and maps of public roads can be kept on computer: Roads Act 1993, s 10(5)(d).

Where an officer of the Revenue Commissioners has power to inspect records and those records are kept on computer, the officer is entitled access to the data equipment and any associated software and to be afforded reasonable assistance: Finance Act 1992, s 237, now Taxes Consolidation Act 1997, s 912. The register of solicitors may be kept in an electronic or other non-written form: Solicitors Act 1954, s 47(4)(a) as amended by Solicitors (Amendment) Act 1994, s 54.

See also Building Societies Act 1989, s 117(2); Finance Act 1986, s 113 as amended by Finance Act 1993, s 99, now Taxes Consolidation Act 1997, s 887; Stock Exchange Act 1995, s 8(4); Local Government (Delimitation of Water Supply Disconnection Powers) Act 1995, s 6; Child Trafficking and Pornography Act 1998, s 2(2); Finance Act 1997, s 81; Finance Act 2002, ss 119–120. See *Dwyer* in 9 ILT & SJ (1991) 192. See LRC Working Paper 9 of 1980 and LRC No 25 of 1988. [Bibliography: Kelleher & Murray; Microsoft Press.] See BANKERS' BOOKS; BENEFIT-IN-KIND; CD-ROM; CHEQUE, PRESENTATION BY NOTIFICATION; CRIMINAL DAMAGE TO PROPERTY; DATA PROTECTION; DIGITAL SIGNATURE; FAX; HACKING; INTERNET; MEDICAL PRACTITIONER; PATENTABLE INVENTION; RAM; TRADING HOUSE, SPECIAL; WORKSTATION.

computer evidence. Computer printouts may be admissible if they constitute 'real evidence' ie if tendered to show what is recorded without human intervention eg printout of a machine monitoring guests' phone calls in an hotel. But they may infringe the hearsay (qv) rule. Foundation testimony may be required to authenticate that the computer and its programme was operating properly eg a copy record of a register kept in computer by the Environmental Protection Agency may be given in evidence and is *prima facie* evidence of any fact therein stated, provided that the court is satisfied of the reliability of the system used to make the copy record and the original entry on which it was based: Environmental Protection Agency Act 1992, s 112(4).

In criminal proceedings, information contained in a document is *prima facie* admissible in evidence of any fact contained in it, where the information has been compiled in the ordinary course of business on computer; information in the computer printout, however, must have been reproduced in the course of the normal operation of the reproduction system concerned: Criminal Evidence Act 1992, s 5. Statutory provision is made for the admissibility of certain computer records eg bankers' books and records: Central Bank Act 1989, s 131(a); social welfare records: Social Welfare Act 1989, s 20. See DOCUMENTARY EVIDENCE.

computer-generated. In relation to a *work*, means that the work is generated by computer in circumstances where the author of the work is not an individual: Copyright and Related Rights Act 2000, s 2(1). The *author* of a work which is computer-generated includes the person by whom the arrangements necessary for the creation of the work are undertaken (CRRA 2000, s 21(f)). Copyright in a computer-generated work expires 70 years after the date on which it was first lawfully made available to the public (CRRA 2000, s 30).

Computer-generated in relation to a design, means the design is generated by computer in circumstances where the author of the design is not an individual: Industrial Designs Act 2001, s 17(3). See AUTHOR; COMPUTER PROGRAM; WORK.

computer program. Means a program which is *original* in that it is the author's own intellectual creation and includes any design materials used for the preparation of the program: Copyright and Related Rights Act 2000, s 2(1). The *author* of an original computer program includes the individual or group who made it (CRRA 2000, s 21(g)). Copyright subsists in an *original* computer program (CRRA 2000, s 17(2)). The copyright expires 70 years after the death of the author, irrespective of the date on which the work is first lawfully made available to the public (CRRA 2000, s 24(1)).

An *adaptation* of a computer program includes a *translation*, arrangement or other alteration of the program; a *translation* includes making a version in which the program is converted into or out of a computer language or code or into a different language or code (CRRA 2000, s 43). The making of an *adaptation* of a computer program without a licence of the copyright holder constitutes an infringement of copyright (CRRA 2000, s 37(2)). It is not an infringement of copyright for a lawful user of a computer program to make a back-up copy of the program (CRRA 2000, ss 80–82). As computer programs are included in the definition of a *literary work*, for copyright provisions, see LITERARY WORK. A computer program used in the making or generation of databases is not regarded as a database (CRRA 2000, s 2(6)). Where a computer program performs the same function as another program, this does not constitute direct evidence that there is a similarity in the programs themselves: *News Datacom Ltd v Lyons* [1994] 1 ILRM 450, HC. [Bibliography: Forde (13); Kelleher & Murray.] See COMPUTER-GENERATED; COPYRIGHT, OWNERSHIP OF; CRIMINAL DAMAGE TO PROPERTY; PATENTABLE INVENTION; TRADE SECRET; TRADING HOUSE, SPECIAL.

conacre. A licence to enter land and to till the land, sow crops and reap the harvest, generally for an eleven-month period. Such a licence does not create the relationship of landlord and tenant. A *conacre* tenant has a *special possession* only, a mere right of use for a strictly limited purpose, the general possession remaining with the landlord: *Winters v Owens* [1950] IR 225.

The Land Act 1984 was introduced to facilitate the leasing of agricultural land without creating rights in the lessee eg of automatic renewal or compensation for disturbance, the lessor and lessee being treated as of equal status. See OCCUPATION; POSSESSION.

concealed danger. The source of danger concerning which an occupier may have a duty of care to warn another. See *Shelton v Crean* [1987] HC. See OCCUPIER'S LIABILITY.

concealing an offence. It is an offence for a person to accept or agree to accept any *consideration* for not disclosing information which might be of material assistance in securing the prosecution or conviction of an offender ie a person who has committed an *arrestable offence* (qv): Criminal Law Act 1997, s 8(1). An arrestable offence must have been committed and the person concealing the offence must know or believe that the offence, or some other arrestable offence, has been committed. No offence is committed where the *consideration* consists of making good the loss or injury caused by the offence or the making of reasonable compensation for the loss or injury. In effect the offence is one of accepting a *bribe* for concealing information. It replaces the former offence of *compounding a felony*.

concealment. Suppression of, or neglect to communicate, a material fact. If it is fraudulent, it may provide grounds for rescission of a contract. Even if not fraudulent, concealment may be fatal to a contract *uberrimae fidei* eg a contract of insurance. See UBERRIMAE FIDEI; MISREPRESENTATION.

concealment of birth. The offence committed by the secret disposition by any person, of the dead body of a child, whether such child dies before, at, or after, birth, in an endeavour to conceal the birth of the child: Offences Against the Person Act 1861, s 60.

concentrations, control of. See MERGER OF COMPANY, EC REGULATIONS.

concert party. As regards a public limited company (plc), a group of persons acting together so as to avoid the object of legislation on disclosure of shareholding of the notifiable percentage (5%), the interest of none of them reaching that percentage, but that of all of them together amounting to a substantial or even controlling interest: Companies Act 1990, ss 73–75.

All the persons involved in a concert party are attributed with the interests of all the others in the shares of the target company as regards the obligation to notify that company of the amount of shares they are able to control acting in concert (CA 1990, s 74).

As regards a takeover, two or more persons are deemed to be *acting in concert* if, pursuant to an agreement or understanding (whether formal or informal) between them, they actively co-operate in the acquisition of securities in a relevant company: Irish Takeover Panel Act 1997, s 1(3). There is a rebuttable presumption that certain specified persons are concert parties eg a company, its subsidiaries, its holding company and its subsidiaries: Takeover Rules 2001, Part A, r 3.3. See also Takeover Rules 2001, Part B, r 9.1. See IRISH TAKEOVER PANEL; MONOPOLY.

concerted practice. A form of co-ordination between undertakings which, without having reached the stage where an agreement so-called has been concluded, knowingly substitutes practical co-operation between them for the risks of competition: *ICI v Commission* [1972] ECR 619. A con-*certed practice* which has as its object or effect the prevention, restriction or distortion of competition in trade in any goods or services in the State or in any part of the State, is prohibited: Competition Act 2002, s 4(1). It is also an offence (CA 2002, s 6).

A concerted practice can exist between parties who do not appear to have been *ad idem* and very little evidence is required to justify the inference of concerted practices: *Chanelle Veterinary Ltd v Pfizer Ltd* [1999] 2 ILRM 55, SC and 1 IR 365. For previous (now repealed) legislation, see Competition Act 1991, s 4(1). [Bibliography: Lucey.] See COMPETITION, DISTORTION OF.

concession. The Director of Public Prosecutions is not bound by a concession made in a previous case: *Grealis v DPP* [2002] 1 ILRM 241, SC. The DPP discharges his function by retaining counsel and solicitors to act on his behalf. The fact that counsel in a particular case may have made a concession which was erroneous in law, does not have the effect of estopping the DPP from canvassing the point in subsequent proceedings.

conciliation. A voluntary informal process of dispute resolution, whereby an independent third party assists the parties to a dispute to clarify the points of disagreement and attempts to promote a settlement. A binding award is not made. Any agreement reached is the responsibility of the parties. Conciliation frequently takes place between employees and employers. For examples, see INDUSTRIAL RELATIONS OFFICER; LABOUR RELATIONS COMMISSION. Contrast with ARBITRATION and MEDIATION.

The Royal Institute of the Architects of Ireland (RIAI) and the Institution of Engineers of Ireland (IEI) have *Conciliation Rules* applicable to their own contracts, which provide, where no agreement is reached, for the conciliator to issue a recommendation, which becomes final and binding on the parties if neither party rejects it in writing within a specified time period. See 'Friendly Persuasion' by solicitor Denis O'Driscoll in *Law Society Gazette* (June 2002) 20.

conciliation and arbitration schemes. The schemes for dealing with claims relating to pay and conditions of employment in parts of the public service eg civil service, local authorities. They are non-statutory and have been described as merely contracts. See *Inspector of Taxes Association v Minister for the Public Service* [1983] HC & [1986] ILRM 296.

concurrent ownership. The co-ownership of two or more persons in the same property. See COPYRIGHT, LICENSING OF; JOINT TENANCY; PERFORMERS' RIGHTS, LICENSING OF; TENANCY IN COMMON.

concurrent sentences. When an accused is convicted of several offences at the same trial, the court, in general, is empowered to impose separate sentences to be served concurrently ie together and at the same time. See *The People (DPP) v TB* [1996] 3 IR 294, CCA. Contrast with consecutive sentences. See BAIL, OFFENCES COMMITTED ON.

concurrent wrongdoers. Persons who are responsible to an injured party for the *same damage*: Civil Liability Act 1961, s 11. This may arise as a result of vicarious liability (qv), breach of joint duty, conspiracy, concerted action to a common end or independent acts causing the same damage. The wrong may be a tort, breach of contract or breach of trust.

Each concurrent wrongdoer is liable for the whole of the damage done to the injured party (CLA 1961, s 12); this provision is not unconstitutional. The 1961 legislation marked an amelioration and rationalisation of the liability of concurrent wrongdoers *inter se* from what had been there before; the solution established by the Oireachtas, far from being irrational or disproportionate, it was in fact fair and just: *Iarnród Éireann & Irish Rail v Ireland* [1996] 2 ILRM 500, SC and 3 IR 321. An unfortunate aspect of litigation is that one of a number of defendants may be insolvent and unable to meet a liability. A solution which is in harmony with the core principles underlying civil liability is that the risks should fall on the other solvent defendants who are concurrent wrongdoers, because their independent acts caused the same damage (*Iarnród Éireann* case).

Satisfaction by any concurrent wrongdoer will discharge the other (CLA 1961, s 16) as will a release which indicates such intention (CLA 1961, s 17); however, settlement of a personal injuries action with one co-defendant does not constitute 'satisfaction' as against all the defendants: *Murphy & Murphy (infants) v Donohue Ltd & Ors* [1992] ILRM 378, SC. Judgment against a wrongdoer is not a bar to an action against another concurrent wrongdoer (CLA 1961, s 18).

A third-party notice to join an alleged concurrent wrongdoer cannot be issued after conclusion of the trial of the action: *Kelly v St Laurence's Hospital* [1989] ITLR (20 November), SC. Independently of a third-party notice, a concurrent wrongdoer may sue any other for a *contribution* to the extent of that wrongdoer's responsibility for the injury (CLA 1961, s 21). Where persons cause independent items of damage, they are not concurrent wrongdoers. See also Personal Injuries Assessment Board Act 2003, ss 42–43; Liability for Defective Products Act 1991, s 8. See *Crowley v Allied Irish Banks* [1988] ILRM 225; *Cowan v Faghaile, Cumann Lúthchleas Gael Teo, McInerney* [1991] 1 IR 389, HC; *Hussey v Plunkett Dillon* [1995] 1 ILRM 496, SC and 1 IR 111; *Staunton v Toyota (Ireland) Ltd* [1996] 1 ILRM 171, SC; *R L v Minister for Health* [2001] 1 IR 744, HC. [Bibliography: Kerr (2).] See NEXT FRIEND; THIRD-PARTY NOTICE.

condemnation. The process by which things are *condemned as forfeited*: Finance Act 1995, s 92. Any goods or vehicles that are liable to forfeiture under excise law may be seized (FA 1995, s 89). Notice of the seizure is given to the owner and he is advised that the thing is liable to forfeiture (FA 1995, s 90). If he does not give notice disputing this within one month of the seizure, the thing is deemed to have been duly condemned as forfeited (FA 1995, ss 91–92). Where notice disputing the condemnation is given, the High Court or the District Court (value of thing not exceeding £5,000 (€6,349)) has civil jurisdiction to condemn the thing as forfeited or may order its release to its owner (FA 1995, ss 92–93). See FORFEITURE.

condemnation of will. Refusal to grant probate of a purported will where the statutory provisions are not complied with. See RSC Ord 79, r 7; Ord 80, r 9. See *Glynn v Glynn* [1987] ILRM 589.

condition. An assurance or guarantee. A provision which makes the existence of a right dependent on the happening of an event; the right is then *conditional* as opposed to an *absolute* right. An *express* condition is one set out as a term in a contract or a deed. An *implied* condition is one derived from law on the presumed intention of the parties. A *condition precedent* is one which delays the vesting of a right until the occurrence of a particular event; a *condition subsequent* is one which provides for the defeat of an interest on the occurrence or non-occurrence of a particular event. A *condition concurrent* is one under which performance by one party is rendered dependent on performance by the other at the same time.

A condition providing that a contract for the sale of land is subject to planning permission is a condition subsequent and not a condition precedent; the purchaser is entitled to waive the condition: *O'Connor v Coady* [2003] ITLR (15 December) and FL 8589, HC.

A condition in a contract of sale of goods is a stipulation which goes to the root of the contract, the breach of which gives rise to a right to treat the contract as repudiated. A stipulation may be a condition, though called a warranty in such a contract; and a condition may in certain instances be treated as a warranty eg where the contract is not *severable* and the buyer has accepted part of the goods. See Sale of Goods Act 1893, s 11; Sale of Goods and Supply of Services Act 1980, s 10.

Where a buyer *deals as a consumer* and there is a breach of a condition by the seller, which the buyer would be compelled to treat as a breach of warranty, the buyer is entitled to reject the goods and repudiate the contract, or, to have the defect constituting the breach remedied elsewhere and to maintain an action against the seller for the cost thereby incurred by him; provided that the buyer, promptly, upon discovering the breach, makes a request to the seller that he either remedy the breach or replace any goods which are not in conformity with the condition, and the seller refuses to comply with the request or fails to do so within a reasonable time. See Sale of Goods Act 1893, s 53; SGSSA 1980, s 21.

In a contract of sale of goods, there is an implied condition that the seller has a right to sell the goods or, in the case of an *agreement to sell,* that he will have a right to sell the goods at the time the property is to pass (SGA 1893, s 12; SGSSA 1980, s 10).

There are similar provisions concerning implied conditions in hire-purchase agreements (SGSSA 1980, s 26).

Contrast with WARRANTY. See CONSUMER, DEALING AS; DESCRIPTION, SALE BY; FAIR AND REASONABLE TERMS; IMPLIED TERM; QUALITY OF GOODS.

conditional access. Means any technical measure or arrangement whereby access to the *protected service* in intelligible form is made conditional upon prior individual authorisation; *protected service* means a service provided for remuneration eg television or radio broadcasting or information society services: European Communities (Conditional Access) Regulations 2000, SI No 357 of 2000. The regulations give legal protection to these services and implements EC Directive 98/84/EC.

conditions of employment. See CONTRACT OF EMPLOYMENT.

conditions of sale. (1) The terms under which a purchaser is to take property sold by auction. The usual terms state: the number of years title to be shown; the title which is to be a good *root of title* (qv); the time within which *requisitions on title* are to be made; the rescission by the vendor on onerous conditions being made; the deposit and conditions for forfeiture; the compensation for misdescription; the payment of the purchase money and the interest thereon. It is usual to adopt the standard form of conditions issued by the Law Society of Ireland (qv). See *Report on Conveyancing Law – Passing of Risk from Vendor to Purchaser* (LRC 40 of 1991). [Bibliography: Wylie (2).] See AUCTION SALES; SALE OF LAND.

(2) The court has power to determine the conditions upon which property is to be sold. See RSC Ord 51, r 4 (pursuant to a judgment or order); Ord 76, r 123 (bankruptcy); Ord 74, r 124 (company); and Ord 67, r 81 (e,f) (wards of court).

condominium. Joint sovereignty over territory eg: (a) the territory of Andorra administered by Spain and France; (b) arises where title over a block of apartments is vested in a company and each apartment owner possesses a transferable share in the company which represents his interest. See FLAT; MANAGEMENT COMPANY.

condom. Colloquial term to describe a contraceptive sheath (qv).

condonation. The voluntary forgiveness and re-instatement of the erring party to a marriage by the wronged spouse with knowledge of the offence of the former. It was a complete defence to a charge of cruelty or adultery (qv) by a petitioner for a *divorce a mensa et thoro* (qv). Condonation could be express or implied, eg the latter in the case of the continuance or resumption of sexual intercourse. See *O'Reardon v*

O'Reardon [1975] HC. However, condonation on the part of an applicant is no longer a bar to the grant of a decree of *judicial separation*: Judicial Separation and Family Reform Act 1989, s 44. However see s 4 which seems to retain it in a modified form. See CONNIVANCE.

conduct. The *conduct* of each of the spouses is a matter which the court will have regard to in making ancillary orders in or after proceeding for divorce, where the conduct is such that it would, in all the circumstances, be unjust to disregard it; however, the conduct of the spouses must be disregarded in relation to orders for the benefit of dependent members of the family: Family Law (Divorce) Act 1996, ss 20(2)(i) and 23. See PREVIOUS CONDUCT.

conference. A meeting between counsel and solicitor and sometimes the client, to discuss a case. See also CONSULTATION.

confession. An admission of guilt made to another by a person charged with a crime. A confession may be in writing, signed or acknowledged by the accused, or it may be verbal or by conduct. A confession is admissible as evidence of the facts stated therein, but only if the prosecution establish that it was *voluntarily* made; a confession induced by any promise or threat in relation to the charge, made by or with the sanction of any *person in authority*, or in breach of the accused's constitutional rights, is deemed not to be voluntary. See *A-G v M'Cabe* [1927] IR 129; *DPP v Shaw* [1982] IR 1. It is immaterial whether the compulsion or inducement used to extract an involuntary confession comes from the executive or from the legislature: *In the matter of National Irish Bank Ltd* [1999] 1 ILRM 321 and 3 IR 145, SC.

An appeal to the accused on moral or religious grounds is not an inducement which will render a confession inadmissible. A *person in authority* is someone engaged in the arrest, detention, examination or prosecution of the accused; one who is in a position to press for punishment or to plead for leniency. An incriminating statement made by an accused when his detention is unlawful, is not admissible in evidence: *The People (DPP) v Coffey* [1987] ILRM 727.

Even where a confession is made voluntarily, a trial judge retains a residual discretion to exclude it where it is made to a garda otherwise than in accordance with certain procedures accepted in Ireland as being embodied in the Judges' Rules: *People*

v Buck [2002] 2 ILRM 454 and 2 IR 268, SC. It is open to a jury to convict solely on an uncorroborated confession: *The People (DPP) v Quilligan & O'Reilly (No 3)* [1993] 2 IR 305. However, the judge must advise the jury to have *due regard* to the absence of corroboration: Criminal Procedure Act 1993, s 10; *Lindsay v DPP* (23 February 2004, unreported) CCA. The phrase '*due regard*' was intended to connote an objective, normative standard of regard or attention to be paid in the absence of corroboration: *The People (DPP) v Connolly* [2003] 2 IR 1, CCA. See also *The People (Attorney-General) v Galvin* [1964] IR 325; *The People (Attorney-General) v O'Brien* [1965] IR 142; *The People (DPP) v Byrne* [1987] IR 363, SC; *The People (DPP) v Hoey* [1988] ILRM 666, SC. [Bibliography: Charleton (5); Healy.] See ADMISSION OF GUILT; CORROBORATION; DUE REGARD; INCRIMINATE; JUDGES' RULES; SOLICITOR, ACCESS TO.

confidence, breach of. Disclosure of confidential information may amount to a breach of contract where so provided in such a contract. The obligation to respect confidentiality is not confined to the parties to the contract, but extends to any third party to whom the information is communicated: *Oblique Financial Services Ltd v The Promise Production Co* [1994] 1 ILRM 74, HC. In the absence of contract, the donee of confidential information may be under a duty, in equity, not to use that information to the donor's detriment.

To succeed in an action for *breach of confidence*, the plaintiff must establish: (a) that the information he seeks to protect is of a confidential nature, (b) that the information was communicated in circumstances importing an obligation of confidence, and (c) that the defendant has made, or is about to make, an unauthorised disclosure or use of that information: *Coppinger and Skone on Copyright*, cited in *Private Research Ltd v Brosnan* [1996] 1 ILRM 27, HC.

There is no absolute confidentiality where the parties concerned are a government and a private individual: *The A-G for England and Wales v Brandon Books* [1987] ILRM 135.

Disclosure of confidential information obtained by way of discovery (qv) can amount to contempt of court eg the use of the discovered material for any purpose extraneous to the proceedings: *Ambiorix Ltd v Minister for the Environment* [1992] ILRM 209, SC. There may be special circumstances which would permit the use of material in an action which was discovered in another action: *Smyth v Tunney* [2004] 1 ILRM 464, HC. It has been held in relation to the discovery of confidential bank documents, that where discovery would confer a litigious advantage on one party, it should be made, notwithstanding the fact that the documents were of a confidential nature: *Cooper Flynn v Radio Telefís Éireann* [2000] 3 IR 344, HC.

See also *Prince Albert v Strange* [1841] 1 Mac G 25; *Seager v Copydex Ltd* [1967] 2 All ER 415; *Aksjeselskapet Jutul v Waterford Ironfounders Ltd* [1977] HC; *House of Spring Gardens v Point Blank* [1984] IR 611; *Kennedy & Arnold v Ireland* [1988] ILRM 472. See 'Recent developments in Privacy and Breach of Confidence' by Patrick Leonard BL in *Bar Review* (December 2001) 102. [Bibliography: Clark & Smyth; Lavery; Clarke (UK); Gurry (UK).] See BANKER AND CONFIDENTIALITY; CABINET CONFIDENTIALITY; EMPLOYEE; EMPLOYER, DUTY OF; INFORMATION, ACCESS TO; JURY; OFFICIAL SECRET; SPRING BOARD; TRADE SECRETS; UTTERANCE.

confidential communications. Communications which are privileged from disclosure or discovery eg professional communications between counsel or solicitor and client, between parishioner and parish priest, matrimonial communications, and discussions at meetings of the government. See CANON LAW; PRIVILEGE, EVIDENTIAL; UTTERANCE.

confidential information. In order to succeed in obtaining an injunction restraining the disclosure by a former employee of confidential information, it would have to be shown that it could reasonably be anticipated that the employee would be required to or would disclose information: *Norbrook Laboratories v Mountford* [2001] ELR 189, HC. This case involved an employee who had signed a confidentiality and ownership of invention agreement and who had left to join a competitor company. The court held that undertakings given by the employee had shifted the balance of convenience in favour of refusing the injunction.

Attempts by an employee to access confidential computer data has been held to justify the dismissal of the employee: *Mullins v Digital Equipment International BV* [1990] ELR 139. See also *McDermott v Kemek Ltd* [1996] ELR 233, EAT.

Where a financial institution transfers moneys to the *Dormant Accounts Fund*, the institution is prohibited from identifying the account holder; a similar prohibition applies where a claim for a repayment is made: Dormant Accounts Act 2001, s 48(1). A similar prohibition applies in the movement of moneys to the Fund from the *Intestate Estates Fund Deposit Account*: the identity of a deceased person or a person rightfully claiming money must not be identified (DAA 2001, s 48(2)).

A request for access to the record of a public body may be refused where the record concerned contains confidential information, given to the body on the understanding that it would be treated as confidential: Freedom of Information Act 1988, s 26. The body is permitted to refuse to confirm or deny the existence of such a record: Freedom of Information (Amendment) Act 2003, s 21. See also Unclaimed Life Assurance Policies Act 2003, s 26; Digital Hub Development Agency Act 2003, s 27; European Union (Scrutiny) Act 2002, s 3; Competition Act 2002, s 32; National Development Finance Agency Act 2002, s 18; Companies (Auditing and Accounting) Act 2003, s 31; Personal Injuries Assessment Board Act 2003, s 73; Private Security Services Act 2004, s 18. See ENGINEER AND CONFIDENTIALITY; INFORMATION, ACCESS TO; MEDICAL PRACTITIONER AND CONFIDENTIALITY; SOLICITOR AND CONFIDENTIALITY.

confined space. Means any place which, by virtue of its enclosed nature creates conditions which give rise to a likelihood of an accident, harm or injury of such a nature as to require emergency action due to: (a) the presence or the reasonably foreseeable presence of eg excessive high temperature, or (b) the lack or reasonably foreseeable lack of oxygen: Safety, Health and Welfare at Work (Confined Spaces) Regulations 2001, SI No 218 of 2001. These regulations impose requirements and prohibitions with respect to the safety and health of persons carrying out work in confined spaces.

confinement. Labour resulting in the issue of a living child, or labour after 24 weeks of pregnancy resulting in the issue of a child, whether alive or dead: Social Welfare (Consolidation) Act 1993, s 41; Maternity Protection Act 1994, s 2(1). See MATERNITY LEAVE.

confirmation order. See COMPULSORY PURCHASE ORDER.

confiscate. To deprive of property by seizure. A *confiscation order* may be obtained against a person for the recovery of the proceeds of drug trafficking and other offences: Criminal Justice Act 1994, ss 4 and 9. The standard of proof as to whether the person has benefited from the offence and the amount to be recovered is that applicable to civil proceedings ie on the balance of probability (CJA 1994, ss 4(6) and 9(7)). A confiscation order may be enforced as if it were a judgment of the High Court (CJA 1994, s 19(1)). There is also provision for the execution in the State of an *external confiscation order* from a designated country (CJA 1994, s 46 and SI No 177 of 2003 which designates the State of Israel, the Rwandese Republic, and the Kingdom of Thailand). Jurisdiction to make a confiscation order no longer requires an application to the court by the Director of Public Prosecutions; it is now a matter for the court: Criminal Justice Act 1999, ss 25–28 amending CJA 1994, ss 4, 7, 10, 11.

An interlocutory injunction to prevent the Special Criminal Court conducting an inquiry into whether the plaintiff had benefited from drug trafficking was refused on the basis that the consequences of the inquiry were not unremediable if it transpired that the legislation allowing for the inquiry was unconstitutional: CJA 1994, s 4 as amended by CJA 1999, s 25; *Gilligan v Special Criminal Court* [2001] 4 IR 655, SC. See *Walsh v United Kingdom* (9 February 1995) ECHR. See *Report on Confiscation of the Proceeds of Crime* (LRC 35, 1991). See DRUG TRAFFICKING.

conflict of interest. (1) A company director has a duty to avoid placing himself in a position where his personal interests conflict with those of his principal, the company. Substantial property transactions between a company and its directors must be approved at a general meeting of the company: Companies Act 1990, s 29. The non-cash asset must exceed in value either £50,000 (€63,487) or 10% of the company's assets, with a minimum threshold of £1,000 (€1,270). See *MacCann* in 9 ILT & SJ (1991) 81. See also Building Societies

Act 1989, s 56; Credit Union Act 1997, s 69; Taxi Regulation Act 2003, s 22; Industrial Development (Science Foundation Ireland) Act 2003, s 16; Companies (Auditing and Accounting) Act 2003, s 18; Personal Injuries Assessment Board Act 2003, ss 71–72; Private Security Services Act 2004, s 17; Residential Tenancies Act 2004, ss 170 – 171.

(2) Where a conflict of interest exists between the interests of a solicitor and those of his client, the solicitor must not act for the client: *A Guide to Professional Conduct of Solicitors in Ireland* (2002) ch 3.1. If a conflict of interest arises between two clients in a matter in which the firm is acting, the firm must cease to act for either client in the matter (ch 3.2). In exceptional circumstances, one of the clients may consent to the other client remaining. As a general principle, a solicitor should not act for both the vendor and purchaser in a transfer of property for value at arm's length (ch 3.3). There are exceptions e g where the vendor and the purchaser are related by blood, adoption or marriage. However, where a solicitor acts for both parties to a voluntary transfer of property or a transfer of property at a consideration other than full market value, the transferor should be advised to obtain independent advice.

Where a number of purchasers' solicitor's fee is paid by the vendor (e g a builder of an estate paying the fees of one solicitor representing all purchasers), such an arrangement does not contravene any regulation but it may be difficult for the solicitor to argue against a conclusion that a conflict of interest existed to the extent that the interests of the clients were compromised: Practice Note in *Law Society Gazette* (July 2004) 40.

(3) A barrister must promote and protect his client's best interests and do so without regard to his own interest, and he may be justified in refusing instructions where a conflict of interest arises or is likely to arise: *Code of Conduct for the Bar of Ireland* (December 2003) rr 2.3 and 2.17. He must not accept any instructions or a brief on behalf of a company of which he is a director (r 2.8). He also must not appear as counsel: (a) either for or against any local authority of which he is a member, or (b) either for or against any company, firm or other organisation of which he is an officer, director or partner or in which he has

directly or indirectly a significant pecuniary interest (r 3.12).

If, by reason of negligence of his instructing solicitor or otherwise, a barrister forms the view that there is a conflict of interest between his client and his instructing solicitor, he should advise that it would be in the client's best interest to instruct another solicitor (r 3.2). In cases involving several parties, a barrister is required to advise the solicitor as to whether, on grounds of conflict of interest, any of the clients should be separately advised and represented by a barrister or solicitor (r 3.15). A barrister may appear for more than one defendant in a criminal trial provided he has satisfied himself that there is no conflict of interest (r 9.9). See *Prince Jefri v KPMG* [1999] 1 All ER 517.

(4) The Competition Authority published guidelines in August 2004 to resolve potential conflicts of interest in relation to legal representation of those attending before the Authority. Specifically, where the Authority is of the opinion that the integrity of its investigative process may be compromised by the fact that the same lawyer represents more than one person in any particular matter, the Authority will permit that lawyer to appear before it on behalf of only one of those persons. Such a conflict of interest could arise where an employee of a company under investigation wishes to offer information (e g a whistleblower) and is represented by the same lawyer as other employees or directors. See ARM'S LENGTH, AT; COMBINED CODE; COUNCILLOR, DISCLOSURE OF INTEREST; DIRECTORS AND SHARE DEALING; ETHICS IN PUBLIC OFFICE; GOVERNMENT; MODEL CODE; RESIDENTIAL UNIT.

conflict of laws. An alternative name for private international law (qv). [Bibliography: Binchy (1); Phelan.]

conformity, certificate of. See BANKRUPTCY, PETITION FOR.

confusion of goods. See INTERMIXTURE OF CHATTELS.

congested district. A district within which it was estimated that the population could not be adequately supported on the arable land which was available: Purchase of Land (Ireland) Act 1891, s 36. The Congested District Boards set up by this Act had the power to purchase estates and sell them to tenants under the land purchase schemes. Certain counties were designated as congested. See LAND COMMISSION.

conglomerate merger. A merger between firms which do not have a pre-existing competitive relationship, either as direct competitors or as suppliers and customers. Conglomerate mergers do not give rise to true horizontal overlaps between the activities of the parties to the merger or to a vertical relationship between the parties. Conglomerate mergers are generally not presumed to produce anti-competitive effects, but they may do so in particular instances e g where the merged entity would have market power in one or more complementary products. See *Tetra Laval BV v Commission of the European Communities* (2002) Case T-5/02, CFI as reported in *Law Society Gazette* (April 2003) 53.

conjugal rights. The right of a married person to the society and cohabitation of his or her spouse. It is not an unqualified right e g it is placed in suspense if and when one or both of the spouses is imprisoned and thereby deprived of personal liberty in accordance with law: *Noel & Marie Murray v Ireland & the A-G* [1991] ILRM 465, SC. See BEGET; CONSORTIUM.

conjugal rights, restitution of. Formerly a decree which a party to a marriage could obtain to compel the other party to resume cohabitation. To obtain the decree, the petitioner had to prove that the respondent had refused to comply with a written demand to resume cohabitation; it was a good defence to prove that the petitioner had committed a matrimonial offence sufficient to ground an action for a *divorce a mensa et thoro*. It was a rarely sought remedy and the Law Reform Commission had recommended its abolition: LRC Report No 6, 1983. Actions for restitution of conjugal rights were abolished as from 22 November 1988: Family Law Act 1988. See *Molloy v Molloy* [1871] IR 5 Eq 367; *Bell v Bell* [1922] IR 103; *Hood v Hood* [1959] IR 225; RSC Ord 70, r 4.

connected person. The spouse, parent, brother, sister or child of a director of a company; a partner of the director; a trustee of a trust the principal beneficiaries of which are the director, his spouse, or any of his children or any body corporate which he controls: Companies Act 1990, s 26. There are restrictions on loans by a company to *connected persons*. See also Building Societies Act 1989, s 52.

As regards the disclosure of interests in shares and the Model Code, a connected person is deemed not to include a parent, brother, sister or adult child of a director or company secretary: Listing Rules 2000 (*Definitions*, as amended by Irish Stock Exchange Ltd). See LOAN TO DIRECTOR; FRAUDULENT PREFERENCE; MODEL CODE.

connemara voting. Popularly understood to mean 'public voting' whereby a person declares his voting preference before a returning officer. It was originally introduced to facilitate voting by illiterate persons. See DISABLED VOTER; VOTERS, SPECIAL.

connivance. The intentional active or passive acquiescence by the petitioner for a decree of *divorce a mensa et thoro* (qv) in the adultery of the respondent. When connivance was proved it could act as a complete bar to the petitioner alleging adultery (qv) as a ground for such a decree. See *Harris v Harris* [1829] 162 ER 894; *Huckerby v Elliott* [1970] 1 All ER 189 at 194. Now, where an application for a decree of *judicial separation* is made on the ground of adultery and the respondent proves that the adultery was committed with the connivance of the applicant, the court may refuse the application: Judicial Separation and Family Law Reform Act 1989, s 44(2). See also Food Safety Authority of Ireland Act 1998, s 7(1). See CONDONATION.

consanguinity. [Of the same blood.] Relationship by descent. The relationship may be *lineally* e g as between father and son; or *collaterally* e g as between cousins where descent is from a common ancestor. See AFFINITY; MARRIAGE.

conscientious objection. Generally understood to mean a refusal to carry out some act on the grounds of conscience. Because there are persons who would have a conscientious objection to giving information to others on abortion services provided outside the State, statutory recognition to this is given by providing that there is no obligation on any person to give such information: Regulation of Information (Services outside the State for Termination of Pregnancies) Act 1995, s 13.

'If a doctor has a conscientious objection to a course of action this should be explained and the names of other doctors made available to the patient': Medical Council, *A Guide to Ethical Conduct and Behaviour* (6th edn, 2004) para 2.6. A conscientious objection to abortion does not permit a doctor to discourage a patient from seeking an abortion, by unprofessional means: Irish College of General Practitioners, *Primary Care for the Prevention and Management of Crisis Pregnancy* (April 2004) p 18. See ABORTION, MEDICAL GUIDELINES; EUROPEAN CONVENTION ON HUMAN RIGHTS.

conscription. Compulsory military service. There is no provision for conscription in Ireland. Under the Emergency Powers Act 1939, during the Second World War, the government was given power to make by order (referred to as *emergency orders*) such provisions as were, in the opinion of the government, necessary or expedient for securing the public safety or the preservation of the State, or for the maintenance of public order, or for the provision and control of supplies and services essential to the life of the community (EPA 1939, s 2(1)). However, such orders could not authorise the imposition of any form of compulsory military service or any form of industrial *conscription* (EPA 1939, s 2(5)).

As regards the legislation of Austria, the following periods are accepted as insurance periods for Irish nationals who were Austrian nationals immediately before 13 March 1938; with regard to the Second World War, periods of war service in the armed forces of the German Reich or in the forces of any state allied to it, periõds of *conscription* in the forces or the labour service as well as periods of duty in the emergency services and air-raid services, and periods of captivity as a prisoner of war (civil internee) and the return therefrom, which are similarly treated: Social Welfare (Agreement with the Republic of Austria on Social Security) Order 1989, SI No 307 of 1989, Sch, art 4(4)(b). See also European Convention on Human Rights, art 4(3)(b).

The European Court of Justice has held that EC law does not govern the member states' choice of military organisation for the defence of their territory; consequently Germany's decision to ensure its defence in part by compulsory military service is such a choice of military organisation to which EC law is not applicable: *Dory v Federal Republic of Germany* [2003] Case C-186/01, ECJ. In this case the plaintiff argued in vain that as military service in Germany was compulsory for men only and as there were no objective reasons justifying the exemption of women from the requirement, it was discriminatory under EC law.

consecutive sentences. The sentences which a court generally is empowered to impose on an accused, who has been found guilty of several offences at the same trial, which sentences are to follow one another in time of service. The District Court is not prohibited by statute from imposing consecutive periods of *detention* exceeding twelve months: *The State (Clinch) v Connellan* [1986] ILRM 455; *Meagher v O'Leary* [1998] 2 ILRM 481, SC. See BAIL, OFFENCES COMMITTED WHILE ON; INDICTABLE OFFENCE.

consensus ad idem. [Agreement as to the same thing.] The common consent necessary for a binding contract. See *Mespil Ltd v Capaldi* [1986] ILRM 373; *Minister for Education v North Star Ltd* [1987] HC; *Boyle & Boyle v Lee & Goyns* [1992] ILRM 65, SC; *Brennan v Religious of the Sacred Heart* [2000] ELR 297, EAT. See AD IDEM.

consensus facit legem. [Consent makes law.] Parties to a contract are legally bound to do what they agree to do. See SPECIFIC PERFORMANCE.

consensus non concubitus facit matrimonium. [Consent and not cohabitation constitutes a valid marriage.] See MARRIAGE; COMMON LAW MARRIAGE.

consensus tollit errorem. [Consent takes away error.] See ACQUIESCENCE.

consent. Acquiescence or compliance with or deliberate approval of or agreement to a course of action. Consent is inoperative if obtained by coercion, fraud or undue influence (qqv). Consent is a good defence to charges of offences against the person, except in the case of homicide, an assault which is a breach of the peace or is carelessly dangerous, or certain indecent offences created by the Criminal Law Amendment Act 1935. Failure or omission by a person to offer resistance to a criminal act done to that person does not of itself constitute consent to the act: Criminal Law (Rape) (Amendment) Act 1990, s 9.

In a rape trial, the jury has to consider whether the accused believed that the woman was consenting to sexual intercourse; the presence or absence of reasonable grounds for such belief is a matter to which the jury must have regard: Criminal Law (Rape) Act 1981, s 2(2). It has been held that for greater safety in charging the jury in certain rape cases, it may be necessary for the judge to link any particular evidence which would constitute potential reasonable grounds for that belief: *DPP v F* [1993] ITLR (30 August), CCA.

It has been held that if a man knew that consent to sexual intercourse was given because the woman concerned believed him to be another person, then he knew there was no consent by the woman to having sexual intercourse with him: *The People (DPP) v C* [2001] 3 IR 345, CCA. See also *DPP v Creighton* [1994] 1 ILRM 551. See Gourdon, *Consent in Rape – A comparative analysis* (1994) 4 ISLR 117.

Inability to give a true consent to marriage is a ground for nullity: *DB v O'R* [1991] ILRM 160, SC. [Bibliography: McAuley & McCutcheon.] See ADOPTION, CONSENT TO; CHILD, MEDICAL TREATMENT OF; CLINICAL TRIALS, CONDUCT OF; PATIENT, CONSENT OF; SURGICAL OPERATION.

consent, age of. Usually refers to the age, currently 17 years, at which a person is legally competent to consent to sexual intercourse. See SEXUAL OFFENCES; RAPE.

conservation. The Minister is empowered to make grants to local authorities or any other body concerned with the conservation of buildings, to defray expenses incurred in: (a) promoting urban and village renewal; or (b) the conservation of buildings or structures of artistic, architectural or historical interest: Urban Renewal Act 1998, s 17. See also *Minister for Arts v Kennedy* [2002] 2 ILRM 94, HC.

conservation of fish stocks. Provision has been made to give effect to the UN Convention on the Law of the Sea 1982 relating to the conservation and management of *straddling fish stocks* (eg stocks occurring within the exclusive economic zones of two or more coastal States) and *highly migratory fish stock* (eg albacore tuna), done at New York on 4 August 1995 and signed by Ireland on 27 June 1996: Fisheries (Amendment) Act 2003, ss 22–31 and Schs 2 and 3. For the States which are parties to the Convention, see SI No 46 of 2004.

conservation order. The order which a planning authority was empowered to make to preserve from extinction or otherwise any flora or fauna in an area to which a *special amenity area* (qv) order related; the conservation order could prohibit the taking, killing or destroying of such flora or fauna: Local Government (Planning and Development) Act 1963, s 46(1) as inserted by the LG(P&D) Act 1976, s 40(b). See also Local Government (Planning and Development) Regulations 1977, SI No 65 of 1977, art 64.

These provisions have not been re-enacted in the consolidating Planning and Development Act 2000, as the power to make *conservation orders* was never used and more appropriate powers are available under specialised legislation. See HABITATS DIRECTIVE.

conservatory. Planning permission is not required for the building or erection of a conservatory to the rear of a dwellinghouse, provided certain conditions and limitations are complied with. For details, see EXTENSION OF HOUSE.

consideration. Some valuable benefit received by a party who gives a promise (*promisor*) or performs an act, or some detriment suffered by a party who receives a promise (*promisee*). *Some right, interest, profit or benefit accruing to one party, or some forbearance, detriment, loss, or responsibility given, suffered or undertaken by the other*: *Currie v Misa* [1875] 10 Ex 153. Consideration is necessary to the validity of every *simple contract* (qv), including those in writing. Consideration must be *real*; it need not be adequate to the promise, but it must have some ascertainable value. Consideration must be *legal*. Consideration must move from the promisee. A person may be a party to a contract but a stranger to the consideration.

Consideration may be *executed* or *executory* but not *past*. Consideration is *executed* when the act constituting the consideration is performed; consideration is *executory* when it is in the form of a promise to be performed at a future date. A *past* consideration is one which is wholly executed and finished before the promise is made.

In 1988 the defendant designated the plaintiff as its one millionth passenger and awarded her free flights for life and in return the plaintiff engaged in publicity for the defendant: *O'Keeffe v Ryanair Holdings plc* [2002] 3 IR 228, HC and [2003] 1 ILRM 14. The High Court held in this case that *valuable consideration* sufficient to support a valid contract passed from the plaintiff to the defendant in the form of the surrender by her of her anonymity and privacy and participation in the publicity generated.

For consideration to support a bill of exchange, see HOLDER FOR VALUE. See CONTRACT; EQUAL PAY; STRANGER TO CONSIDERATION; UNCONSCIONABLE BARGAIN; VALUABLE CONSIDERATION.

consignment. Goods delivered by a carrier (qv) to a consignee at the instance of the consignor. The consignor has a duty to pre-pay a reasonable charge for the carriage of the goods and impliedly warrants that the goods rendered for carriage are fit to be carried in the ordinary way and that they are not dangerous. See *Farrant v Barnes* [1862] ii CB (ns) 553.

consignor. See CONSIGNMENT.

Consolidation Act. An Act of the Oireachtas which repeals or re-enacts or collects in a single statute previous enactments and amendments relating to a particular topic eg the Social Welfare (Consolidation) Act 1993. Such an Act is subject to a rebuttable presumption that no change in the pre-existing law was intended: *Harvey v Minister for Social Welfare* [1989] ITLR (7 August).

The Attorney-General certifies that a Bill is a consolidating Bill.

Substantial amendments of the statute law are not permissible; the only permissible amendments are those designed to remove ambiguities or inconsistencies, substitute modern for archaic language and to achieve uniformity of expression: Explanatory Memorandum to Social Welfare (Consolidation) Bill 1993. See 'As clear as mud?' by barrister Edward Donelan in *Law Society Gazette* (May 2003) 28. Contrast with CODE. See also RESTATEMENT OF STATUTE.

consolidated accounts. See HOLDING COMPANY.

consolidation of actions. Causes or matters pending in the court may be ordered to be tried together on the application of any party and whether or not all the parties consent to the order: RSC Ord 49, r 6. The court has an inherent jurisdiction to order that proceeding be heard together, taking account of the possibility of substantial saving of expense or inconvenience even though otherwise it would not be appropriate to have the proceedings consolidated: *O'Neill v Ryan, Ryanair Ltd & Ors* [1990] ILRM 140. HC.

The tests applied are: (a) is there a common question of law or fact of sufficient importance; (b) is there a substantial saving of expense or inconvenience; (c) is there a likelihood of confusion or miscarriage of justice?: *Duffy v Newsgroup Newspapers Ltd* [1992] ILRM 835, SC. Defamation actions will not be consolidated where there is a likelihood of confusion (*Duffy* case). For consolidation of actions in *commercial proceedings* (qv), see RSC Ord 63A, r 6(1)(iii) inserted by Rules of the Superior Courts (Commercial Proceedings) 2004, SI No 2 of 2004. See also Arbitration (International Commercial) Act 1998, s 9. See DEFENDANTS, JOINT.

consolidation of mortgages. The equitable doctrine that a mortgagee (qv) who holds two or more mortgages made by the same mortgagor (qv) on different properties, can consolidate them into one and refuse to be redeemed as to one without payment of what is due to him on all. The time for repayment on the mortgages being consolidated must have passed and at least one of the mortgage deeds must contain a clause permitting consolidation: Conveyancing Act 1881, s 17.

consortium. (1) A business combination. A company is regarded as being owned by a consortium if 75% of its ordinary share capital is owned by five or fewer companies: Taxes Consolidation Act 1997, s 411 as amended by Finance Act 2000, s 79. The relaxation of the definition (previously it required all the share capital to be so owned) is intended to facilitate the participation of non-EU companies in consortia which may be formed as part of future Public Private Partnership projects. Where a company which is owned by a consortium incurs trading losses, those losses can be surrendered to the members of the consortium in proportion to their interests in the consortium, and they in turn can offset these losses against their profits for tax purposes.

(2) The common law right of one spouse to the companionship and affection of the other. The sum total of the benefits which a wife may be expected to confer on her husband by their living together: help, comfort, companionship, services and all the amenities of family and marriage: *O'Haran v Divine* [1966] 100 ILTR 53. Damages may be recovered for the total loss of a wife's society or consortium as a result of the negligence of another but not for an impairment of consortium: *Spaight v Dundon* [1961] IR 201.

There is now an analogous right in a wife to sue for the loss of her husband's society or companionship: *McKinley v Minister for Justice* [1990] ITLR (7 May), HC and [1993] 11 ILT Dig 115, SC. Damages for loss of consortium are to be related to the damages recoverable for the death of a spouse (*McKinley* case). See also *McKinley v Minister for Defence (No 2)* [1997] 2 IR 176, HC.

An action for loss of consortium is not a derivative action but an independent action for a different type of damage eg as a result of a car accident; and the damages recoverable cannot be reduced by reason of the husband's contributory negligence: *Coppinger v Waterford County Council* [1996] 2 ILRM 427, HC in which damages of £60,000 (€76,184) was awarded for loss of consortium. See also *Coppinger v Waterford County Council* [1998] 4 IR 243, HC. See Civil Liability Act 1961, s 35; LRC 1 of 1980. See CONJUGAL RIGHTS; PER QUOD SERVITIUM AMISIT.

conspiracy, crime of. The crime of conspiracy involves the agreement of two or more persons to effect an *unlawful purpose*; it is an offence (formerly, a misdemeanour (qv)). An unlawful purpose includes an agreement to commit a crime, or a tort which is malicious or fraudulent, or other acts which are extremely injurious to the public while not being a breach of law. It has been held that conspiracy to commit an offence should not be charged where the substantive offence can be laid: *The People (Attorney-General) v Singer* [1975] IR 408; *The People (Attorney-General) v Keane* [1975] 109 ILTR 1.

The combination of a conspiracy charge with the substantive offence might be regarded as leading to the possibility of unfair procedures: Walsh J in *Ellis v O'Dea & Shields* [1990] ITLR (8 January), SC. It is a fundamental principle of Irish *common law* (qv) that a person joining in a conspiracy or a joint venture outside the State, in furtherance of which an overt criminal act is committed within the State, will be amenable to the jurisdiction of the Irish courts even where he has not committed an overt act within the State: *Ellis v O'Dea and Governor of Portlaoise Prison* [1991] ITLR (14 January), SC.

See also *The State (McCaud) v Governor of Mountjoy Prison* [1986] ILRM 129; *McDonald v McMahon* [1990] 8 ILT Dig 60. See also Industrial Relations Act 1990, s 10.

conspiracy, tort of. The tort (qv) of conspiracy involves the combination of two or more persons with intent to injure another in his trade or business, without lawful justification, thereby causing damage or to perform an unlawful act thereby causing damage. Persons are given immunity from actions in conspiracy in respect of acts done in combination, in contemplation or furtherance of a *trade dispute*, which would not be actionable if done by one person alone: Industrial Relations Act 1990, s 10. See *Crofter Hand Woven Harris Tweed Co v Veitch* [1842] AC 435; *Connolly v Loughney* 87 ILTR 49; *Taylor v Smyth* [1990] ILRM 377.

In a particular case, the plaintiff was permitted to change the proceedings from judicial review to a plenary summons, and to include a new and distinct claim of conspiracy: *O'Leary v Minister for Transport* [2001] 1 ILRM 132, SC.

conspiracy and companies. A company can in appropriate circumstances commit the crime and tort of conspiracy. See *Taylor v Smyth* [1990] 8 ILT & SJ 298, SC; *Belmont Finance Corporation Ltd v Williams Furnituire Ltd* [1979] 1 All ER 118; and *MacCann* in 8 ILT & SJ (1990) 197.

conspirator. A person who commits the offence of conspiracy (qv). Everything said, done or written by one conspirator is relevant against each of them, provided it was in the execution of their common purpose: *R v Blake* [1844] 6 QB 126.

constat. [It appears.] It follows; it is clear beyond argument.

constituency. A geographic area for parliamentary and local government elections. The number of constituencies for the *Dáil Éireann* elections is as determined by law: 1937 Constitution, art 16(2). However, no law may be enacted whereby the number of Dáil members to be returned by any constituency, may be less than three. Also the Oireachtas is required to revise the constituencies every twelve years, with due regard to changes in distribution of the population. When a census return discloses major changes in the distribution of the population, there is a constitutional obligation on the Oireachtas to revise the constituencies: *O'Malley v An Taoiseach* [1990] ILRM 460. The recommendation on this revision is made by the *Constituency Commission*. See Electoral (Amendment) Act 1995; Electoral Act 1992, ss 19 and 29 and Electoral Act 1997, s 5.

The Minister is required to submit proposals to the Oireachtas for the review of the *European Parliament* constituencies by 1 December 2003 and at least every ten

years thereafter: European Parliament Elections Act 1997, s 15. A *presidential* election is normally conducted by reference to Dáil constituencies, but the Minister is empowered to order it to be conducted by reference to counties and county boroughs e g to facilitate the holding of *local government* elections and a presidential election at the same time: Presidential Elections Act 1993, s 12. See also Referendum Act 1994, s 18. See DÁIL ÉIREANN; RESIDENCE.

constituency commission. The independent commission which makes recommendations in relation to Dáil and European Parliament election constituencies: Electoral Act 1997, ss 5–15. The commission is required to have regard to certain specified matters e g constitutional provisions, geographic considerations, contiguous areas, continuity of arrangements, and avoidance of the breach of county boundaries as far as practicable (EA 1997, s 6). The commission is established by Ministerial order following publication of the Census Report setting out the population of the State (EA 1997, s 5). The commission comprises the Chief Justice, the Ombudsman, the Clerks of the Dáil and Seanad, the Secretary General of the Department of the Environment, and either a Supreme or High Court judge (EA 1997, s 7). The number of Dáil constituencies has been increased from 41 to 42, implementing the Commission Report of Mr Justice Richard Johnson: Electoral (Amendment) (No 2) Act 1998, s 3. There is a convention that the Oireachtas does not modify the recommendations of the constituency commission.

Constitution, bill to amend. A bill to amend the Constitution must be initiated in Dáil Éireann and must be submitted by referendum (qv) to the decision of the people, having been passed or deemed to have been passed by the two Houses of the Oireachtas (qv): 1937 Constitution, art 46. It has been held that a bill which contains an amendment to the Constitution and which has been passed by the people in a referendum, could not be unconstitutional, because it has been passed by the people; the courts and the President of Ireland have no function in relation to the content of such legislation as this is a matter exclusively for the people: *Riordan v Taoiseach (No 1)* [1999] 4 IR 321, SC. Such a bill, having been passed by the people and promulgated by the President as a law, no longer exists as a separate entity: *Riordan v Taoiseach (No 2)* [1999] 4 IR 343, SC

Constitution of Ireland. The written Constitution which was enacted by the people in a referendum on 1 July 1937 and came into effect on 29 December 1937: Interpretation Act 1937, s 12, Sch, para 7.

It continued in force the laws in Saorstát Éireann prior to its adoption, except in so far as they were inconsistent with the Constitution. Notice must be served on the Attorney-General (qv), if the court so directs, where in any proceedings a question as to the interpretation of the Constitution arises: RSC Ord 60, rr 1–2.

The Constitution must not be read in an uncompromisingly literal fashion if the result would violate the Constitution read as a harmonious whole: *Considine v Shannon Regional Fisheries Board* [1997] 2 IR 404, SC.

The Constitution may be amended by a majority of votes in a referendum (qv). It has been amended a number of times e g to reduce the voting age, to remove the special position of some churches, to alter the Seanad representation from universities, to remove doubts as to certain adoptions, to protect the life of the unborn, to extend the Dáil franchise to non-citizens, to provide for the State to join the European Economic Community, to ratify the Single European Act (qv), the Maastricht Treaty (qv), the Amsterdam Treaty (qv), and the British-Irish Agreement, to restrict bail, to permit divorce, to regulate confidentiality of cabinet discussions, to ensure that freedom to travel and to information is not restricted by the right of the unborn to life, and to give constitutional recognition to the role of local government. Constitutional amendments were rejected which sought to provide for the removal of the prohibition on divorce (qv), the removal of proportional representation (qv) as the election system, and to amend the provision dealing with the life of the unborn.

See APPENDIX 3. See *Report of the Constitution Review Group* (May 1996). [Bibliography: Beytagh; Casey; Doolan (3); Curtin & O'Keeffe; Finlay (1); Forde (2); Hogan & Whyte; Kelly; Litton; Mackey N; Morgan; O'Cearuil; O'Reilly & Redmond; Ryan; Ward..] See LANGUAGE; LEGISLATION, CONSTITUTIONALITY OF; SUPREME COURT.

constitutional right. Rights which derive from the 1937 Constitution; they may be express or implied. The Constitution sets out certain *fundamental rights* (qv) e g personal rights, the family, education, private property, and religion (arts 40–44). There is a hierarchy of constitutional rights and when conflict arises between them, that which ranks higher must prevail: *DPP v Delaney* [1998] 1 ILRM 507, SC; *People (DPP) v Shaw* [1982] IR 1.

An action for damages for the breach of a constitutional right is subject to the time limit imposed by the Statute of Limitations 1957, s 11(2) ie as an action founded in *tort* which is statute barred after the expiration of six years from the date on which the cause of action accrued, except in respect of personal injuries: *McDonnell v Ireland* [1996] 2 ILRM 222, HC. See also *Murphy v Ireland* [1996] 2 ILRM 461, HC. See ABANDONMENT; EVIDENCE AND CONSTITUTIONAL RIGHTS; PRIVATE PROSECUTION; SOLICITOR, ACCESS TO; UNLAWFUL INTERFERENCE WITH CONSTITUTIONAL RIGHT.

constitutionality of legislation. The Oireachtas must not enact any law which is in any respect repugnant to the Constitution and any law which is so repugnant is invalid to the extent of the repugnancy: 1937 Constitution, art 15(4). The Constitution continued in force the laws in Saorstát Éireann prior to its adoption, except in so far as they were inconsistent with the Constitution (art 50).

A law passed by the Oireachtas is presumed to be constitutional unless and until the contrary is clearly established; all laws in force prior to the coming into operation of the Constitution do not enjoy such a presumption but remain part of the legislative framework until found to be inconsistent with the Constitution. See *F v Supt of B Garda Station* [1991] 1 IR 189; *TF v Ireland* [1995] 2 ILRM 321, SC.

The burden of proving that legislation is unconstitutional is particularly formidable where the legislation concerns economic matters, as views on such matters could change from generation to generation, making it difficult to reconcile the exercise of personal rights with the claim of the common good: *Louth v Minister for Social Welfare* [1998] 4 IR 321, SC.

As regards the constitutionality of a *Money Bill*, the court will not enter into the area of taxation policy or concern itself with the effectiveness of the choices made by government or the Oireachtas; the court will confine itself to whether there is an adverse effect on constitutional rights, obligations and guarantees: *MacMahuna v A-G* [1995] 1 IR 484, SC. The constitutionality of an Act which has not yet commenced can be challenged, where an order could be made commencing it at any time: Land Commission (Dissolution) Act 1992; *O'Cleirigh v Minister for Agriculture* [1998] 2 ILRM 263, SC.

In determining the constitutionality of legislation, the courts have no power to consider the discussions and interviews which Ministers might have had with members of the Oireachtas prior to introducing legislation through either houses of the Oireachtas: *Controller of Patents v Ireland* [2001] 4 IR 229, SC. Also of no relevance to proceedings challenging the constitutionality of an Act is documentation in relation to the preparation, drafting, advice, changes, amendments, discussions with and briefings of Dáil deputies and members of the Seanad (*Controller* case).

There is a constitutional prohibition on the enactment of laws applicable in the counties of Northern Ireland (qv) pending the re-integration of the national territory: *McGimpsey v Ireland* [1990] ILRM 440, SC. However, see 1937 Constitution, new art 3 and GOOD FRIDAY AGREEMENT.

Notice must be served on the Attorney-General in any proceedings wherein any question arises as to the validity of a law, having regard to the provisions of the Constitution: RSC Ord 60, rr 1–2. See also *Re The Equal Status Bill 1997* [1997] 2 IR 387, SC and ELR 185. [Bibliography: Collins & O'Reilly (1); O'Cearuil (2).] See DOUBLE CONSTRUCTION; NATIONAL EMERGENCY; RESOLUTION; RETROSPECTIVE LEGISLATION; SEVERANCE; SUPREME COURT.

constitutionality of legislation, jurisdiction. The High Court has jurisdiction to decide on the validity of any law having regard to the provisions of the Constitution: 1937 Constitution, art 34(3)). An appeal lies to the Supreme Court. Also the Supreme Court deals with a referral by the President of Ireland of a Bill under art 26 in which event the Court may deliver only one decision (art 34(4)(5)). There is also a presumption of constitutionality of a Bill so referred: *In the matter of the Matrimonial Home Bill 1993* [1994] 1 ILRM 241, SC.

A citizen may only challenge the constitutionality of legislation where his interests have been adversely affected, or they stand in real or imminent danger of being adversely affected by the operation of the legislation: *Cahill v Sutton* [1980] IR 269. The Supreme Court will not pronounce on the constitutional validity of a statutory provision where such pronouncement can be of no conceivable interest or benefit to the applicant; the court will avoid dealing with a constitutional issue where a case can be decided on some other ground: *McDaid v Judge Sheehy* [1991] ILRM 250, SC; *Re Application of Tivoli Cinema Ltd* [1992] ILRM 522, HC.

Generally the Supreme Court has no power to determine the constitutionality of a law which has not been the subject of an adjudication in the High Court: *Dunnes Stores v Minister for Enterprise* (2000) Irish Times, 9 February 2000, SC. See also *Dunnes Stores Ireland Company v Ryan & Minister for Enterprise* [2002] 2 IR 60, SC. It is only in exceptional circumstances that the Supreme Court will consider issues of constitutional law which have not been argued in the High Court: *Blehein v Murphy* [2000] 2 IR 231, SC and 2 ILRM 481.

The Circuit Court does not have jurisdiction to determine the constitutionality of legislation or of common law: *DPP v MS* [2003] 1 IR 606, SC.

construction, rules of. Rules laid down by statute or by the courts for the interpretation of documents or of legislation. Every power conferred by an Act of the Oireachtas (qv) to make any regulations, rules or bye-laws is to be construed as including the power to revoke or amend any regulation, rule or bye-law made under such power: Interpretation Act 1937, s 15(3). It would appear that this rule of construction does not apply to *resolutions* unless specifically provided for in particular legislation relating to such resolutions. See SECTION 4 RESOLUTION; CONTRA PROFERENTEM; CONTRACT, INTERPRETATION OF; EJUSDEM GENERIS; INTERPRETATION OF LEGISLATION; PUNCTUATION; TRANSPOSING OF WORDS.

construction of dispositions. Words denoting *family relationships* when used in wills, deeds and other instruments, are in future to be interpreted in respect of dispositions after the commencement of Pt V of the Status of Children Act 1987, without regard to whether the parents of any person involved are or were married to each other (SCA 1987, s 27). If a disposition is expressed to be *to the children of X*, then X's legitimate, legitimated and illegitimate children are entitled to benefit. However, if the disposition is *to the legitimate children of X*, legitimated children will be entitled to benefit as if born legitimate (SCA 1987, s 27(2)). See ARMCHAIR PRINCIPLE; CONSTRUCTION SUIT; ISSUE.

construction law. Law dealing with building contracts e g variations, liquidated damages, prolongation and disruption claims. [Bibliography: Lyden & MacGrath; Powell-Smith UK.] See ENGINEERING LAW.

construction of written instrument. See CONSTRUCTION SUIT.

construction safety. Regulations have been made which prescribe the main requirements for the protection of the safety, health and welfare of persons working on construction sites: Safety, Health and Welfare at Work (Construction) Regulations 2001, SI No 481 of 2001 as amended by SI No 277 of 2003. For discussion on the 2001 Regulations, see 'Building Confidence' by solicitor Geoffrey Shannon in *Law Society Gazette* (September 2002) 24. [Bibliography: Canny (3); Shannon.]

construction suit. A procedure to discover the meaning of a deed, will or other written instrument where the sense or intention is not clear. It is instituted by *special summons* in the High Court. The court will determine any question of construction arising under the instrument and will give a declaration of the rights of the person interested. The courts will construe a will to give effect to the intention of the testator but will not make a will for the testator: *Curtin v O'Mahony & A-G* [1992] ILRM 7, SC. See RSC Ord 83; Ord 125, r 1; Ord 4, r 2 (App B, Pt II); Circuit Court Rules 2001 Ord 50. See COMMERCIAL PROCEEDINGS; DECLARATORY JUDGMENT.

constructive. Inferred; not directly expressed.

constructive desertion. See DESERTION.

constructive dismissal. A dismissal which is inferred where it is reasonable for the employee to terminate the contract of employment because of the employer's conduct: Unfair Dismissals Act 1977, s 1. The Employment Appeals Tribunal has recognised two forms of constructive dismissal: (1) where the employee is *entitled* to terminate the contract of employment and does so; this entitlement is not conferred by the 1977 Act, but rather recognised by it; and (2) where it is *reasonable* for the employee to terminate the contract of employment

and he does so: *Fitzgerald v Pat the Baker* [1999] ELR 227, EAT.

The resignation of a manager whose position has been undermined may amount to a constructive dismissal: *O'Beirne v Carmine Contractors* [1990] ELR 232. A constructive dismissal may arise where an employee leaves because the employer: (a) fails to relieve a bad atmosphere in the workplace: *Smith v Tobin* [1992] ELR 253, EAT; (b) fails to comply with a requirement of the Health & Safety Authority: *Burke & Ors v Victor Collins Enterprises Ltd* [1993] ELR 37, EAT; or (c) deals inadequately with complaints of bullying and harassment: *Allen v Independent Newspapers* [2002] ELR 84, EAT; *Monaghan v Sherry Brothers Ltd* [2003] ELR 293, EAT.

A constructive dismissal may also arise where actions amounting to sexual harassment justifies the employee terminating her employment: *O'Doherty v Hennessy & Harrow Holdings Ltd* [1993] ELR 161, EAT. However, a court will not hold that there is a constructive dismissal in circumstances where an employer has drawn an employee's attention to legitimate concerns that he may have about their work, as long as this falls within the bounds of acceptable criticism: *Leeson v Glaxo Wellcome Ltd* [1999] ELR 170, CC.

The referral of a complaint of constructive dismissal under the Employment Equality Act 1998, s 77(2) does not create an obstacle to an Equality Officer investigating a complaint of discriminatory treatment referred under s 77(1) of that Act: *O'Hanlon v Educational Building Society* [2002] ELR 107, EO. There is no entitlement to notice in the case of a constructive dismissal: *Halal Meat Packers Ltd v Employment Appeals Tribunal* [1990] ELR 49; *Holmes v O'Driscoll* [1991] ELR 80, EAT. See *McKeon v Murphy Plastics (Dublin) Ltd* (1980) UD 142/1980; *White v Aluset Ltd* (1988) UD 259/88, [1989] ILT & SJ 207; *O'Connor v Garvey* [1990] ELR 228; *Lee v Transirish Lines Ltd* [1992] ELR 150, EAT; *Anne-Marie Kennedy v Foxfield Inns Ltd* [1995] ELR 216, EAT; *Battles v Walls Timber Contractors Ltd* [1996] ELR 191, EAT; *McConville v Electricity Supply Board* [1997] ELR 46, CC; *Kiely v Moriarty Holdings Ltd* [1999] ELR 177, EAT; *Maclehose v R & G Taverns Ltd* [1999] ELR 180, EAT; *Magee v Ideal Cleaning Services Ltd* [1999] ELR 218, EAT; *May v Moog Ltd* [2002] ELR

261, EAT. [Bibliography: Redmond (1).] See UNFAIR DISMISSAL.

constructive notice. See NOTICE.

constructive total loss. In marine insurance where the subject matter insured is reasonably abandoned on account of its actual total loss appearing to be unavoidable, or because it could not be preserved from actual total loss without an expenditure which would exceed its value when the expenditure has been incurred: Marine Insurance Act 1906, s 60. Where there has been a constructive total loss, the assured may either treat the loss as a partial loss, or abandon the subject-matter insured to the insurer and treat the loss as if it were an actual total loss (MIA 1906, s 61). See *Assicurazioni Generali v Bessie Morris SS Co* [1892] 1 QB 571. See ABANDONMENT.

constructive trust. A trust imposed by equity (qv) in the interest of justice, without any reference to the presumed or express intention of the parties, e g a trustee who makes a profit from his position, holds the profit as constructive trustee for the benefit of the beneficiaries. The law will impose a *constructive trust* in all circumstances where it would be unjust and unconscionable not to do so: *Murray v Murray* [1996] 3 IR 251, HC. See *Keech v Sandford* [1726] Sel Cas Ch 261; *Re Frederick Inns Ltd* [1994] 1 ILRM 389, SC.

A constructive trust is a form of equitable remedy by which the court can restore property to a person to whom in justice it should belong. In its traditional form, it arises because of equity's refusal to countenance any form of fraud; in its modern guise, the *new model constructive trust,* it is imposed by law whenever justice and good conscience require it: *Kelly v Cahill* [2001] 2 ILRM 205, HC and [2001] 1 IR 56, HC which followed *Hussey v Palmer* [1972] 1 WLR 1286. It is not possible to impose a constructive trust on the ground of *unjust enrichment* (qv): *Re Money Markets International Ltd (No 2)* [2001] 2 IR 17, HC. [Bibliography: Delaney H.] See GRAFT, DOCTRINE OF; TRUST.

construe. To discover and apply the meaning of a written instrument. See CONSTRUCTION, RULES OF; CONTEMPORANEA EXPOSITO.

construed as one. Term frequently found in the collective citation of an Act with previous Acts e g the Merchant Shipping Act 1992, s 1(3) requires that the Act 'be *construed as one* with the Merchant Shipping Acts 1894 to 1983, and may be cited together therewith as the Merchant Shipping Acts 1894 to 1992'. This means that each and every part of each of the Acts has to be construed as if it had been contained in one Act, unless there is some manifest discrepancy, making it necessary to hold that the later Act has to some extent modified something found in the earlier Act: *Canada Southern Railway Co v International Bridge Co* [1883] 8 App Cas 727.

consuetudo est altera lex. [A custom has the force of law.] See CUSTOM AND PRACTICE.

consuetudo est optimus interpres legum. [Custom is the best interpreter of the laws.]

consuetudo et communis assuetudo vincit legem non scriptam, si sit specialis; et interpretatur legem scriptam, si lex sit generalis. [Custom and common usage overcome the unwritten law, if it be special; and interpret the written law, if it be general.] See CUSTOM AND PRACTICE.

consul. An agent appointed to protect the interests of the state or its nationals in another country and to further the development of commercial, economic, cultural, scientific and friendly relations between the two states. The duties and privileges of consular officers are set out in the Diplomatic Relations and Immunities Act 1967, Sch 2. Consuls are divided into four classes: consuls-general, consuls, vice-consuls, and consular agents. The severance of diplomatic relations does not *ipso facto* involve the severance of consular relations.

Consular officers and employees are not amenable to the jurisdiction of the judicial or administrative authorities of the receiving state in respect of acts performed in the exercise of consular functions, except in respect of a civil action: (a) by a third party for damages arising from an accident caused by a vehicle, vessel or aircraft; or (b) arising from a contract not on behalf of the sending state (DRIA 1967, Sch 2, art 43). Privileges and immunities may be waived by the sending state and must be communicated in writing (DRIA 1967, Sch 2, art 45).

There is provision for the examination of witnesses before Irish consuls in a foreign country and also for the taking of affidavits: RSC Ord 39, r 5(3); Ord 40, r 7. See also Rules of the Superior Courts (No 1), (Proof of Foreign Diplomatic, Consular and Public Documents) 1999, SI No 3 of

1999. See Diplomatic and Consular Officers (Provision of Services) Act 1993. See DIPLOMATIC PRIVILEGE; TERRORISM.

consular officer. A person in the civil service of Ireland who is a consul-general, a consul, or a vice-consul: Interpretation Act 1937, Sch, para 6.

consultancy referral scheme. A scheme, facilitated from time to time by the Law Society, under which a register is maintained of solicitors with a particular expertise. This enables a solicitor, who does not have the necessary expertise in a particular area of law, to contact a solicitor on the register with a view to referring his client to that solicitor for the particular expert task. A solicitor, so referred to, should not take advantage of the trust placed on him by his colleague, by agreeing to take on further instructions, for a period of twelve months, from the client of a type which the referring practitioner could carry out himself: *A Guide to Professional Conduct of Solicitors in Ireland* (2002) ch 7.9.

consultant referral. A consultant normally should not accept a patient without referral from a general practitioner: Medical Council, *A Guide to Ethical Conduct and Behaviour* (6 edn, 2004) para 12.2. 'Referring doctors should supply appropriate information for the consultation. Irrespective of the mode of referral, consultants have a duty to inform the patient's general practitioner as well as the referring doctor of the findings and recommendations' (para 12.3). See COMMON CONTRACT; FEE SPLITTING.

consultation. A meeting between counsel and solicitor and sometimes the client, to discuss a case. A barrister must not charge a fee in respect of a consultation which he has not attended: *Code of Conduct for the Bar of Ireland* (December 2003) r 11.7.

consultative case stated. See CASE STATED.

consultative jurisdiction. See JURISDICTION.

consumer. A natural person acting outside his trade, business or profession: Consumer Credit Act 1995, s 2(1). Wide-ranging provisions for the protection of consumers are contained in this Act covering eg consumer-hire agreements, credit agreements, credit-sale agreements, hire-purchase agreements, housing loans and moneylending agreements (qqv). See Consumer Credit Act 1995 (Section 2) Regulations 2000, SI No 113 of 2000. Under recent legislation, provision has been made to amend the 1995 Act by way of an enabling provision to allow the Minister to extend some or all of the provisions of that Act to lending to non-personal consumers: Central Bank and Financial Services Authority of Ireland Act 2004, s 33, Sch 3.

For multilingual website dedicated to the interests of European consumers, see *www.europa.eu.int/comm/consumers*. For Consumers' Association of Ireland, see website: *www.consumerassociation.ie*. For Consumers International, see website: *www.consumersinternational.org*. [Bibliography: Bird; Johnston & O'Conor; Long; McHugh; O'Reilly P.] See EUROPEAN EXTRA-JUDICIAL NETWORK; IRISH FINANCIAL SERVICES REGULATORY AUTHORITY.

consumer, dealing as. A party to a contract is said to *deal as a consumer* in relation to another party if: (a) he neither makes the contract in the course of a business nor holds himself out as doing so, and (b) the other party does make the contract in the course of a business, and (c) the goods or services supplied under or in pursuance of the contract are of a type ordinarily supplied for private use or consumption: Sale of Goods and Supply of Services Act 1980, s 3. A buyer dealing as a consumer is given the protection of certain implied conditions which cannot be excluded.

A buyer is not regarded as dealing as consumer on a sale by competitive tender, or a sale by auction of goods of a type or by or on behalf of a person of a class, defined by the Minister. It is for those claiming that a party does not deal as consumer to show that he does not (Sale of Goods and Supply of Services Act 1980, s 3(3)). See *Rasbora Ltd v JCL Marine Ltd* [1977] 1 Lloyd's Reports 645; *O'Callaghan v Hamilton Leasing (Ireland) Ltd* [1984] ILRM 146; *Cunningham v Woodchester Investment Ltd* [1984] HC. See also Consumer Credit Act 1995, s 152. See QUALITY OF GOODS; EXCLUSION CLAUSES, RESTRICTION OF.

Consumer Affairs, Director of. A statutory officer, appointed by the Minister, who is independent in the performance of her functions: Consumer Information Act 1978, s 9 amended by Company Law Enforcement Act 2001, s 114. Under the 1978 Act, the Director is required: (a) to keep under general review practices in relation to the advertising of, and the provision to members of the public, of information in relation to and description of goods, services, accommodation and facilities; (b) to carry out examination of such practices; and (c) to seek, voluntarily or by court order, the discontinuation of such practices which are, or are likely to be, misleading to members of the public in a material matter (CIA 1978, s 9(6)).

Under the Consumer Credit Act 1995 the Director is given additional functions which include: (a) keeping under general review practices in relation to *designated* provisions; (b) carrying out investigations of such practices requested by the Minister or which she, the Director, considers should be carried out in the public interest; (c) requesting persons to discontinue or refrain from such practices that are contrary to the obligations imposed on them; (d) instituting proceedings in the High Court to prevent such practices; (e) investigating complaints concerning possible breaches of any of the designated provisions; (f) publishing codes of practice in order to secure transparency and fairness in consumer agreements (CCA 1995, s 5 as substituted by Central Bank and Financial Services Authority of Ireland Act 2003, s 35, Sch 1). The designated provisions are Pt XI (credit intermediaries) and other parts in so far as they deal with credit intermediaries. The Director continues to be responsible for the licensing and regulation of pawnbrokers under CCA 1995, Pt XV.

The Director has extensive powers in respect of investigations eg to require a person in possession of information to provide that information (CCA 1995, s 7 as substituted by CBFSAIA 2003, s 35, Sch 1). The Director may, in the interests of better informing consumers, give directions as to the location and size of any statement or notice required under the designated provisions (CCA 1995, s 8 as substituted by CBFSAIA 2003, s 35, Sch 1). Authorised officers have also extensive powers in carrying out an investigation.

The Director is generally not required to permit inspection of documents which have come into her possession as part of a complaint made to her by a member of the public: *Director of Consumer Affairs and Fair Trade v Sugar Distributors Ltd* [1991] ILRM 395, HC.

The functions of the Director have changed substantially since 1978. The functions formerly vested in the Examiner of Restrictive Practices were vested in 1987 in the Director whose title was changed to Director of Consumer Affairs and Fair Trade: Restrictive Practices (Amendment) Act 1987, s 6(1); SI No 2 of 1988; since repealed by the Competition Act 1991, s 22. The Director's functions were widened further under the 1995 Act and the Central Bank Act 1997. The Director became the regulator of consumer charges made by credit institutions (CCA 1995, ss 149–150) and by *bureau de change* (CBA 1997, s 36). In a particular case, the Director was held to have the right to issue directions regarding such charges and to indicate the basis on which she would approve them; she was quite entitled to adopt that procedure as it telescoped in a sensible way the more cumbersome statutory procedure: *Director of Consumer Affairs v Bank of Ireland* [2003] 2 IR 217, HC.

The Central Bank (through IFSRA) is now the regulator of these charges and it has taken over the functions of the Director of Consumer Affairs in relation to many of the provisions of CCA 1995.

See also Sale of Goods and Supply of Services Act 1980, s 55; National Standards Authority of Ireland Act 1996, s 32; Personal Injuries Assessment Board Act 2003, s 56(6). See SI No 130 of 2003. See RSC Ord 104. See email: *odca@entemp.ie* and website: *www.odca.ie*. [Bibliography: Bird.] See ADVERTISING, MISLEADING; BANKER AND CONFIDENTIALITY; CENTRAL BANK; CONSUMER DIRECTOR; ELECTRONIC CONTRACT; IRISH FINANCIAL SERVICES REGULATORY AUTHORITY; MONOPOLY; PRODUCT PRICES.

consumer contract. A contract concluded by a person for a purpose which can be regarded as outside his trade or profession, which is a contract for the sale of goods on instalment credit terms, or a contract for a loan payable by instalments, or for any other form of credit, made to finance the sale of goods, or any other contract for the supply of goods or a contract for the supply of services and which meets particular requirements: Jurisdiction of Courts and Enforcement of Judgments Act 1998, Sch 1, arts 13–15; however, from 2002 see below.

A consumer may bring proceedings against the other party to such a contract either in the courts of the *contracting states* of the EU in which that party is domiciled or in the courts of the contracting state in which the consumer is domiciled (JCEJA

1998, Sch 1, art 14). As regards EFTA countries, see JCEJA 1998, Sch 2, art 14.

The *Brussels I Regulation* on the recognition and enforcement of judgments in civil and commercial matters, replaces the JCEJA 1998 as from 1 March 2002 for all EU states except Denmark: EC (Civil and Commercial Judgments) Regulations 2002, SI No 52 of 2002. The scope of the consumer contract provision has been extended to give consumers better protection. The limitation to other contracts for the supply of goods or for the supply of services which met particular requirements has been deleted. Consumer contracts now also include a contract which has been concluded with a person who pursues commercial or professional activities in the member state of the consumer's domicile or, by any means, directs such activities to that member state or to several countries including that member state, and the contract falls within the scope of such activities (*Brussels I Regulation*, art 15(1)(c)). This provision is intended to capture contracts concluded through an interactive website accessible in the place of the consumer's domicile. See SMALL CLAIMS; SUMMONS, SERVICE OUT OF JURISDICTION; UNFAIR TERMS.

consumer debt. Under draft legislation, a debt owing by an individual which that individual has or may have difficulty managing, reducing or discharging; this includes the personal representatives of an individual who is deceased: Money Advice and Budgeting Service Bill 2002, s 1(1). See MONEY ADVICE AND BUDGETING SERVICE.

Consumer Director. The person appointed by the Irish Financial Services Regulatory Authority (IFSRA) with responsibility: (a) for monitoring the provision of financial services to consumers, having regard to the public interest and to the interests of those consumers, and (b) for exercising important consumer protection powers under the Consumer Credit Act 1995, the Investment Intermediaries Act 1995, the Stock Exchange Act 1995, the Insurance Act 1989 and under Central Bank legislation: Central Bank Act 1942, ss 33Q–33S, inserted by Central Bank and Financial Services Authority of Ireland Act 2003, s 26. The Consumer Director is required to operate in a way that is consistent with the orderly and proper functioning of the financial markets, and the prudential supervision

of providers of financial services. Telephone no for consumer enquiries to the Regulatory Authority is lo-call 1890–777-777. See websites: *www.ifsra.ie*; *www.itsyourmoney.ie*. See IRISH FINANCIAL SERVICES REGULATORY AUTHORITY.

consumer goods. Any tangible moveable item, other than: (a) goods sold by way of execution or otherwise by authority of law; (b) water or gas where it is not put up for sale in a limited volume or set quantity; and (c) electricity: EC (Certain Aspects of the Sale of Consumer Goods and Associated Guarantees) Regulations, SI No 11 of 2003, reg 2(1). Consumer goods delivered under a contract of sale must be in conformity with that contract (reg 5(1)). They are presumed to be in conformity if they eg comply with the description given by the seller and possess the qualities which the seller held out to the consumer, are fit for the purposes for which goods of the same type are normally used, and are fit for any particular purpose made known to the seller (reg 5(2)).

The seller is liable to the consumer for any lack of conformity and the consumer is entitled to have: (a) the goods brought back into conformity free of charge by repair or replacement, or (b) an appropriate reduction made in the price, or (c) the contract rescinded with respect to those goods (SI No 11 of 2003, reg 7(2)). 'Free of charge' includes the cost of carriage, post, labour and materials (reg 7(6)). A 'consumer' is a natural person who is acting outside his trade, business or profession; a 'seller' is any natural or legal person, who, under a contract, sells consumer goods in the course of his trade, business or profession (reg 2(1)).

These Regulations, which give effect to EC Directive 1999/44/EC, give protection to the consumer in addition to, and not in substitution for, protection given by other enactments eg the Sale of Goods Act 1893 and the Sale of Goods and Supply of Services Act 1980 and the EC (Unfair Terms in Consumer Contracts) Regulations 1995, SI No 27 of 1995. The consumer can opt for the measure which gives the most protection. See GUARANTEE, SALE OF GOODS.

consumer-hire agreement. An agreement of more than three months' duration for the bailment of goods to a hirer under which the property of the goods remains with the owner: Consumer Credit Act 1995, s 2(1). An advertisement offering the letting of goods under such an agreement must state that it is such a letting, that ownership remains with the owner, and the amount payable by the hirer (CCA 1995, s 23). The agreement must contain certain statements (eg cash price, number of instalments, total amount payable, costs of early termination, and that the goods remain the property of the owner) and a copy must be handed personally to the hirer upon making the agreement or delivered or sent to him within ten days (CCA 1995, s 84). The hirer is required to take reasonable care of the goods (CCA 1995, s 90). Protections which are given to a hire-purchase hirer, also apply to a hirer under a consumer-hire agreement eg implied warranty that the goods are free from any charge (CCA 1995, s 88). [Bibliography: Bird.] Contrast with CREDIT-SALE AGREEMENT. See also COOLING OFF PERIOD.

consumer law. The general area of law dealing with the sale of goods and supply of services, hire purchase, consumer credit, information and protection. A civil summons in a proceeding brought pursuant to the Consumer Credit Act 1995 must contain a statement that the appropriate provisions of the Act have been complied with: DCR 1997 Ord 40. See 'Aspects of Post-Sale Consumer Protection' by Brendan Kirwan BL in (2003) 11 ISLR 42. [Bibliography: Bird; Cassidy (2); Forde (5); Grogan, King & Donelan; O'Reilly P; Round Hall.] See CONSUMER DIRECTOR; ELECTRONIC CONTRACT.

consumer price index number. The All Items Consumer Price Number Index compiled by the Central Statistics Office: Broadcasting Authority (Amendment) Act 1993, s 1(1). The consumer price index in a CSO publication or in a document signed by the director general of the CSO must be accepted as *prima facie* evidence of that statistic in any legal proceedings: Statistics Act 1993, s 45. See INTEREST AND SOCIAL WELFARE.

consumer protection. The EC is required to contribute to a high level of consumer protection through: (a) measures adopted pursuant to EC Treaty, art 95 in the context of the completion of the internal market (ie by adopting measures which have as their objective the establishment and functioning of the internal market); (b) measures which support, supplement and monitor the policy pursued by the member states: EC Treaty, art 153 of the consolidated (2002) version. In this way, the Community contributes to protecting the health, safety and economic interests of consumers, as well as promoting their right to information and education.

consumers' interests. *Qualified entities* are now entitled to apply to the Circuit Court for an order requiring the cessation or prohibition of an infringement of the national law implementing specified directives on misleading advertisements, contracts negotiated away from business premises, consumer credit, television broadcasting activities, packaged travel, advertising of medicinal products, unfair terms in consumer contracts, timeshare, and distance contracts: European Communities (Protection of Consumers' Collective Interests) Regulations 2001, SI No 449 of 2001. This Regulation implements EC Directive 98/27/EC on injunctions for the protection of consumers' interests. See DISTANCE CONTRACTS; LIFE ASSURANCE; TIME SHARING; UNFAIR TERMS.

consummated. Completed eg a marriage is consummated when completed by ordinary and complete sexual intercourse. If either party is impotent (qv) or refuses to consummate the marriage, such marriage is voidable by *decree of nullity*. See *R (otherwise W) v W* [1980] HC; *AMN v JPC* [1988] ILRM 170. See MARRIAGE, NULLITY OF; VIRGO INTACTO.

contemporanea exposito est optima et fortissima in lege. [The best way to construe a document is to read it as it would have read when made.] Contemporaneous interpretation. See ARMCHAIR PRINCIPLE; CONSTRUCTION, RULES OF; INTERPRETATION OF LEGISLATION.

contempt of court. A failure to comply with an order of the court or an act of resistance to the court or its judges; also conduct liable to prejudice the fair trial of an accused person. *Criminal* contempt is punitive, to punish for the offence; *civil* contempt is coercive, to compel compliance.

A charge of *criminal* contempt amounts to a criminal offence; it entitles, *prima facie*, the defendant to a trial with a jury where it consists of a major such offence: *de Rossa v Independent Newspapers Ltd* [1998] 2 ILRM 293, HC. However, where the issue is simply whether articles published amounted to contempt of court, this was a matter primarily of law to be decided by a judge and did not entitle the defendant to a trial by jury (*de Rossa* case).

A contempt committed in the face of the court can be punished immediately: *Re Kevin O'Kelly* [1974] 108 ILTR 97. In the District Court, contempt must be committed in the face of the court for sanctions to apply: Petty Sessions (Ireland) Act 1851, s 9. See DCR 1997 Ord 25, r 5. A newspaper article concerning an accused, found guilty of an offence but not yet sentenced, may amount to *criminal contempt*: *Kelly v O'Neill & Brady* [2000] 1 ILRM 507, SC and [2000] 1 IR 354, SC. The law of *criminal contempt* is founded not only on the interests of the parties to litigation, which in a criminal trial, includes the constitutional right of an accused to a trial in due course of law, but upon the wider public interest in the administration of justice (*Kelly* case). Three newspapers were fined for *criminal contempt* in their coverage of a manslaughter trial, two for reporting on arguments that took place in the absence of the jury, and one for publishing an article during the trial detailing and commenting on the fact that two of the four defendants were on free legal aid: *DPP v The Star on Sunday, The Examiner, and the College Tribune* (10 May 2004, Dublin Circuit Court).

As regards tribunals of inquiry, the Supreme Court has held that the machinery available for dealing with contempt is there to advance the public interest in the proper and expedition of the matters within the remit of the tribunal so as to ensure that all persons complied with their obligations, fully and without qualification: *Flood v Lawlor* [2002] 3 IR 67, SC.

A High Court judge has supported the view that the law on contempt is uncertain in many respects and in need of clarification by legislation: *Kelly J in DPP v Independent Newspapers Ltd* [2003] FL 7148, HC and 2 ILRM 260 and 2 IR 367. He said that the publication of prejudicial material where charges are 'imminent' does not constitute a contempt of court; however publication that arrested youths were already before the courts and awaiting trial on other charges was a contempt of court. He held that there was no such thing in common law as 'contingent contempt'.

It is an offence for a person to be in contempt of a court-martial, even where the person is not subject to military law: Defence (Amendment) Act 1987, s 12; *Re Haughey* [1971] IR 217. There are separate rules governing how contempt of court prisoners are treated in prison eg the general rules relating to remission of sentence do not apply to them: Rules for the Government of Prisons 1947, r 270.

See also *Keegan v de Burca* [1973] IR 223; *The State (DPP) v Walsh* [1981] IR 294; *Weeland v Radio Telefís Éireann* [1987] IR 662; *Desmond & Dedeir v Glackin & Minister for Industry & Commerce* [1992] ILRM 489, HC; *Bar Council v Sun Newspapers* [1993] HC; *MP v AP* [1996] 1 IR 144, HC; *Curtis v Kenny* [2001] 2 IR 96, HC. See also Offences Against the State (Amendment) Act 1972, s 4; Companies Act 1990, s 10(5) except the words 'punish in like manner as if he had been guilty of contempt of court' which words have been found to be unconstitutional (*Desmond* case). See also Energy (Miscellaneous Provisions) Act 1995, s 5; Private Security Services Act 2004, s 13(5); Commissions of Investigation Act 2004, s 16(9); Residential Tenancies Act 2004, s 105(5)(c). See Law Reform Commission, Consultation Paper of 1991, *Report on Contempt of Court* (LRC 47, 1994). See 'Contempt for failure to make discovery following The Sole Member v Lawlor' by Cathal Murphy BL in *Bar Review* (January/February 2002) 160; 'Contempt of court and the media' by Hugh Mohan SC in *Bar Review* (December 2002) 384. [Bibliography: McGonagle; Murphy.] See EUROPEAN COURT OF HUMAN RIGHTS; SCANDALISING THE COURT; SUB JUDICE; SUBPOENA; WITNESS SUMMONS; WITNESS ORDER.

contentious business. Means business done by a solicitor in or for the purposes of or in contemplation of proceedings before a court, tribunal or arbitrator: Solicitors (Amendment) Act 1994, s 2. On taking instructions from a client to provide legal services involving *contentious business*, a solicitor is required to provide the client with particulars in writing of: (a) the actual charges or, where this is not possible, an estimate, or if neither is possible, the basis of the charges for legal services, and (b) the circumstances in which the client may be required to pay costs to the another party and the circumstances, if any, where costs recovered from another party may not discharge the client's liability to the solicitor (S(A)A 1994, s 68). A solicitor is prohibited from charging a client on the basis of a percentage or proportion of any damages awarded to the client, except in the case of recovery of a debt or liquidated demand (S(A)A 1994, s 68(2)). See *A Guide to Professional Conduct of Solicitors in Ireland* (2002) ch 10.3. See Solicitors (Advertising) Regulations 2002, SI No 518 of 2002, reg 8. See LEGAL CHARGES; PARTY AND PARTY COSTS; SOLICITOR; SOLICITOR AND CLIENT COSTS.

continental shelf. The sea bed and subsoil outside the seaward limits of the territorial waters; any rights of the State outside territorial waters over the sea bed and subsoil for the purpose of exploring such sea bed and subsoil and exploiting their natural resources are vested in and exercisable by the Minister: Continental Shelf Act 1968, s 2. The government may by order designate any area as an area within which these rights are exercisable (CSA 1968, s 2(3)) and any offence taking place on an installation in a designated area or within 500 metres of such installation will be deemed to have taken place in the State (CSA 1968, s 3). An agreement between Ireland and the UK concerning the continental shelf between the two countries came into force on 11 January 1990 (Iris Oifigiúil, 10 Apr 1990).

The European Court of Justice recognises the sovereignty of a coastal state over its continental shelf; consequently work carried out on an installation above the continental shelf could be regarded as work carried out in the territory of that state: *Hebert Weber v Universal Ogden Services Ltd* [2002] Case C-37/00, ECJ. See Continental Shelf (Protection of Installations) Order 2003, SI No 6 of 2003. [Bibliography: Symmons.] See PETROLEUM, EXPLORATION FOR; MARITIME JURISDICTION.

contingency fee. A fee for a legal service which depends on the result of litigation. A barrister may not accept instructions on condition that payment will be subsequently fixed as a percentage or other proportion of the amount awarded: *Code of Conduct for the Bar of Ireland* (December 2003) r 11.1(e). A solicitor is prohibited from charging a client on the basis of a percentage or proportion of any damages awarded to the client, except in the case of recovery of a debt or liquidated demand: Solicitors (Amendment) Act 1994, s 68(2) and Solicitors (Advertising) Regulations 2002, SI No 518 of 2002, reg 8. See *A Guide to Professional Conduct of Solicitors in Ireland* (2002) ch 10.3. See Twomey AF

'The Contingent Fee in Profile' (1994) 4 ISLR 1. See also CHAMPERTY; NO FOAL NO FEE.

contingent. Something which awaits or depends on the happening of an event. See JOINT ACCOUNT; LIABILITY.

contingent liability. A future unascertained obligation. In relation to calculating *capital gains tax* liability, no deduction is allowed in respect of a contingent liability until it crystallises eg: (a) a contingent liability of a person who assigns a leasehold interest in land, while retaining a liability to the assignee in relation to the lease; (b) a contingent liability of a seller of land, a lessor, or a person who grants an option binding himself to sell land; (c) a contingent liability arising from a warranty given on a sale or lease of property other than land: Taxes Consolidation Act 1997, s 562 (1) and *Randall v Plumb* [1975] STC 191. In the event that a contingent liability is subsequently enforced against the person who disposed of the property, his tax liability will be adjusted to reflect the cost involved and he will be entitled to a refund of tax overpaid (TCA 1997, s 562(2)).

contingent remainder. A remainder (qv) where the grantee is unascertained or where the title depends on the occurrence of a specified event e g *to A (a bachelor) for life, remainder to his first child to reach 21 years.* A contingent remainder is saved if it is one which can be treated as a legal remainder and if it does not offend against the rule against perpetuities: Contingent Remainders Act 1877. Contingent remainders are alienable *inter vivos* by deed: Real Property Act 1845, s 6; and are devisable by will: Succession Act 1965, s 76. See PERPETUITIES, RULE AGAINST.

continuance, presumption of. See PRESUMPTION OF CONTINUANCE.

continue. In considering a letter written by a company to its employees as follows: 'In the unlikely event of TEAM getting into difficulty existing employees will continue to maintain the Aer Lingus fleet as a minimum', the word 'continue', in the context of a volatile labour market, did not mean indefinitely but at a minimum, meant such work or its equivalent, or compensation in lieu thereof, would be available for some reasonable time: *King v Aer Lingus plc* [2002] 3 IR 481, HC and [2003] ELR 173.

continuing professional development; CPD. The term used to describe the regular updating of the professional knowledge, skill and ability of persons in certain regulated professions. It is often a mandatory requirement eg for solicitors from 2003. Doctors must maintain competence; this is best achieved by taking part in Continuing Professional Development, peer review and audit: Medical Council, *A Guide to Ethical Conduct and Behaviour* (6th edn, 2004) para 4.11. The Medical Council regards the maintenance of up-to-date knowledge and competence as a professional responsibility for every doctor. As regards chartered accountants, they are required to sustain their professional competence by keeping themselves informed of, and having regard to, developments in professional standards in all functions in which they practice, or are relied upon because of their calling: *Rules of Professional Conduct of the Institute of Chartered Accountants in Ireland*, r 202. See website: *www.cpd.ie*. See COMPETENCE; SOLICITOR, CONTINUING PROFESSIONAL DEVELOPMENT OF.

continuing risk policy. Means a policy which has acquired a *surrender value (qv)* and continues, by the imposition of charges on the policy without reference to the policy holder, to assure an amount which will become payable by the insurance undertaking in the event of death or disability: Unclaimed Life Assurance Policies Act 2003, s 2(1). Where such a policy is an 'unclaimed policy' and the net encashment value of the policy is being transferred to the Dormant Accounts Fund, the amount transferred is required to be exclusive of the charges (if any) to maintain the policy in force until the life assured has reached 100 years of age (ULAPA 2003, s 2(4)(c)). See UNCLAIMED LIFE ASSURANCE POLICY.

continuity of employment. See REDUNDANCY; UNFAIR DISMISSAL.

contra. [Against; opposite.]

contra bonos mores. [Against good morals.] See also EXPRESSION, FREEDOM OF.

contra formam statuti. [Against the form of the statute.] A necessary ending to an indictment charging a statutory offence. See *BH v DPP* [2003] 2 IR 43, SC.

contra proferentem. The doctrine that the construction least favourable to the person putting forward an instrument should be adopted against him, provided that this works no wrong. This doctrine has been used in contracts of insurance to lighten the effects of a non-disclosure of material facts; ambiguous expressions will be held against those using them: *Re Sweeney Kennedy Arbi-*

tration [1950] IR 85. See also *Brady v Irish National Insurance* [1986] ILRM 669; *Capemel Ltd v Lister* [1989] IR 319 and 323.

contraceptive. Any appliance, or instrument, excluding contraceptive sheaths (ie condoms), prepared or intended to prevent pregnancy resulting from sexual intercourse between human beings: Health (Family Planning) Act 1979, s 1 as amended by Health (Family Planning) (Amendment) Act 1993, s 2. Only certain persons were authorised to sell contraceptives eg chemists, medical doctors, health board employees, and only in respect of a prescription or authorisation of a registered medical practitioner; in addition the person to whom the contraceptive was sold had to be over 17 years of age or married: Health (Family Planning) (Amendment) Act 1992, s 4 as amended by H(FP)(A)A 1993, s 5.

The former licensing requirement for importers and manufacturers of contraceptives has been repealed (H(FP)(A)A 1993, s 8). See *McGee v Attorney-General* [1974] IR 284; *Director of Public Prosecutions v McCutcheon* [1986] ILRM 433. See *Primary Care for the Prevention and Management of Crisis Pregnancy* (April 2004), issued by ICGP and Crisis Pregnancy Agency. See CONTRACEPTIVE SHEATH; FAMILY PLANNING SERVICE; MARITAL PRIVACY; MEDICAL PREPARATIONS.

contraceptive sheath. Includes a contraceptive sheath designed and intended for use by a male person and a contraceptive sheath designed and intended for use by a female person: Health (Family Planning) (Amendment) Act 1993, s 1. The only control over contraceptive sheaths are the power of the Minister to prescribe standards for them (H(FP)(A)A 1993, s 4) and to prohibit their sale by vending machines at a place of a class specified in regulations (H(FP)(A)A 1993, s 3).

contract. A legally binding agreement. A *specialty contract (qv)* is one which is in writing and is sealed and delivered; it is also known as a *deed* or a *contract under seal*. A *simple contract (qv)* is one which is not under seal; all simple contracts require *consideration (qv)* to support them. An *implied contract* arises from the assumed intention of the parties. A *quasi-contract* arises by operation of law, irrespective of the intention of the parties. A *contract of record* arises from obligations imposed by a court of record eg a recognisance.

In general, for a contract to be valid and legally enforceable, there must be (1) an offer and unqualified acceptance; (2) an intention to create legal relations; (3) *consensus ad idem*; (4) legality of purpose; (5) contractual capacity of the parties; (6) possibility of performance; (7) sufficient certainty of terms; (8) valuable consideration. In some cases, a contract or evidence of it must be in a prescribed form ie in writing or by deed. A contract by deed does not require consideration to support it. A valid binding agreement can be found to exist notwithstanding that the full terms of the contract are not set out precisely: *Mackey v Wilde* [1998] 1 ILRM 449, SC.

A contract may be enforceable by way of judicial review (qv), in which case the court will make the appropriate order unless it would be unfair to do so: *Browne v Dundalk UDC* [1993] ILRM 328, HC.

See *O'Keeffe v Ryanair Holdings plc* [2002] 3 IR 228, HC and [2003] 1 ILRM 14. See Law Reform Commission report, *Statute of Limitations: Claims in Contract and Tort in respect of Latent Damage (other than Personal Injury)* (LRC 64, 2001). [Bibliography: Clark (1); Doolan (4); Fitsimons & Mulcahy; Friel; Haigh; McDermott; Cheshire, Fifoot & Furmston UK; Chitty UK.] See CONSUMER CONTRACT; ELECTRONIC CONTRACT; JURISDICTION; POST, CONTRACTS BY; PROPER LAW OF A CONTRACT; STATUTE OF FRAUDS; SUBJECT TO CONTRACT; SUMMONS, SERVICE OUT OF JURISDICTION.

contract, assignment of. See ASSIGNMENT OF CONTRACT.

contract, breach of. See BREACH OF CONTRACT.

contract, discharge of. See DISCHARGE OF CONTRACT.

contract, EU jurisdiction. A person domiciled in a *contracting* state of the EC may, in another contracting state, be sued in matters relating to a contract, in the courts for the place of performance of the obligation in question or the domicile of the defendant: Jurisdiction of Courts and Enforcement of Judgments Act 1998, Sch 1, art 5. However, from 2002, see below. The place of performance of the obligation is the place where the right which corresponds to it is to be taken: *Carl Stuart Ltd v Biotrace Ltd* [1993] ILRM 633, HC. See also *Hanbridge Services Ltd v Aerospace Communications Ltd* [1994] 1 ILRM 39,

SC. As regards contracts and EFTA countries, see JCEJA 1998, Sch 7, art 5. Regulation of the *choice of law* in contract is provided by the Contractual Obligations (Applicable Law) Act 1991. The basic rule is that the parties to a contract are free to select the applicable law to govern the contract; there are rules to determine the applicable law in the absence of an express or implied choice. See *McIlwraith v Seitz Filtration (GB) Ltd* [1998] ELR 105, LC.

The *Brussels I Regulation* on the recognition and enforcement of judgments in civil and commercial matters, replaces the JCEJA 1998 as from 1 March 2002 for all EU states except Denmark: EC (Civil and Commercial Judgments) Regulations 2002, SI No 52 of 2002. The *Regulation* retains a similar provision as in JCEJA 1998, however the *place of performance* is specified in relation to contracts for the *sale of goods* (the place where the goods were or should have been delivered) and *supply of services* (the place where the contract provided that the services were or should have been provided) (*Brussels I Regulation*, art 5(1)(b)).

contract, interpretation of. It is an important principle for the interpretation of all contracts that it is not legitimate to use as an aid in the construction of a contract, anything said or done by the parties after the contract was made: *Re Wogan's (Drogheda) Ltd* [1993] 11 ILT Dig 67, SC and 1 IR 157. See CONSTRUCTION, RULES OF; INTENTION.

contract, naked. See NUDUM PACTUM.

contract, printed. See TYPE, SIZE OF.

contract, privity of. See PRIVITY OF CONTRACT.

contract, standard form of. See CONTRACT OF ADHESION; STANDARD FORM OF CONTRACT.

contract, subject to. See SUBJECT TO CONTRACT.

contract, time of essence of. See TIME OF ESSENCE OF A CONTRACT.

contract, tripartite. See TRIPARTITE CONTRACT.

contract, unconstitutional. See UNCONSTITUTIONAL CONTRACT.

contract for services. A contract with an independent contractor. It has been held that it is not possible to devise any hard and fast rule as to what constitutes a servant and what constitutes an independent contractor; each case has to be considered on its own facts in the light of the broad guidelines provided by case law: *McAuliffe v*

Minister for Social Welfare [1995] 1 ILRM 189, HC and [1995] 2 IR 238, HC.

Although the degree of control exercised over a person is always a factor to be considered in determining whether the person was employed under a contract *of* service or a contract *for* services, it is not the only factor to be taken into account: *Tierney v An Post* [2000] 1 IR 536, SC; 2 ILRM 214; and [1999] ELR 293, SC. Although the maxims associated with *natural justice* were not necessarily capable of application to a contract *for* services, in the *Tierney* case it was held that, as there was a contractual disciplinary procedure set out, there was an implied term that any inquiry held would be conducted fairly. See *An Foras Áiseanna Saothair v Minister for Social Welfare & Ryan* [1991] No 653 Sp, HC; *Kane v McCann* [1995] ELR 175, EAT; *Denny & Sons v Minister for Social Welfare* [1996] 1 ILRM 418 and ELR 43, HC and [1998] ELR 36, SC; *O'Hara v Radio 2000 Ltd* [1997] ELR 61, EAT; *Dower v Radio Ireland Ltd* [2001] ELR 1, HC. See Consumer Credit Act 1995, s 34. See INDEPENDENT CONTRACTOR.

contract for the sale of land. See CONDITIONS OF SALE; STATUTE OF FRAUDS.

contract of adhesion. A standardised form of contract which the customer must accept or reject, but which the supplier may vary unilaterally as it may think fit. Where it involves a monopoly supplier of a vital public utility, its terms may have to be construed not simply as contractual elements but as component pieces of delegated legislation: *McCord v ESB* [1980] ILRM 153.

contract of employment. A contract of service or of apprenticeship whether it is express or implied and (if it is express) whether it is oral or in writing: Unfair Dismissals Act 1977. A contract of employment may be created by deed, be in writing or be verbal. See also Employment Equality Act 1998, s 2(1) as amended by Equality Act 2004, s 3.

In certain employments, the employer is required to give to each employee a written statement setting out the conditions under which he is employed: Terms of Employment (Information) Act 1994. It is inadequate that revised conditions of service be displayed only on a notice board; they should be sent directly to the personnel concerned: *Hayes v Longford Co Council* [1990] ELR 93, EAT. The imposition of revised conditions of employment may amount to the *constructive dismissal* of an employee: *Pender & Ors v Trinity Sports & Leisure Club* [1990] ELR 106.

A contract of employment in restraint of trade (qv) is generally void. While an individual contract of employment may include an arbitration clause, the staying by a court of legal proceedings in contravention of the clause generally does not apply: Arbitration Act 1980, s 5. However legal proceedings may be stayed in the case of an arbitration clause in a contract for services: *Williams v Artane Service Station Ltd* [1991] ELR 126, HC.

An employer cannot generally deprive an employee of the protection given by Irish law by choosing another law to apply to the contract of employment: Contractual Obligations (Applicable Law) Act 1991, Sch 1, art 6. There are also provisions to prevent abuses in connection with employment, of the right of access which persons have to personal data held on them by a data controller eg a bank or the gardaí. It is an offence for a person (eg an employer) to require another person (eg an employee or potential employee) to require that other person to make an access request or to require him to supply the data resulting from the request: Data Protection Act 1988, s 4(13) inserted by Data Protection (Amendment) Act 2003, s 5.

See also Adoptive Leave Act 1995, s 15; Redundancy Payments Act 2003, s 3; Protection of Employees (Fixed-Term Work) Act 2003, s 2(1); Pensions Act 1990, s 81D as amended by substitution by Social Welfare (Miscellaneous Provisions) Act 2004, s 22(1). See *McIlwraith v Seitz Filtration (GB) Ltd* [1998] ELR 105, LC; *Coonan v Attorney-General* [2002] 1 ILRM 295, SC and [2001] ELR 305, SC; *King v Aer Lingus plc* [2002] 3 IR 481, HC and [2003] ELR 173. See COMPETITION, DISTORTION OF; EMPLOYEE; SPECIFIC PERFORMANCE; TERMS OF EMPLOYMENT.

contract of guarantee. Generally, a contract whereby the guarantor, in consideration of the creditor making a loan to the principal debtor, agrees that in the event of the default of the principal debtor, payment shall be made by the guarantor within a certain time of all moneys due: *International Commercial Bank plc v Insurance Corporation of Ireland* [1990] ITLR (3 December), HC.

See also *Hong Kong and Shanghai Banking Corp v Icarom plc* [1993] 11 ILT Dig 142, SC.

A contract of guarantee relating to a credit agreement (qv), a hire-purchase agreement (qv), or a consumer-hire agreement (qv) is not enforceable where the requirements of the Consumer Credit Act 1995 relating to these agreements have not been complied with, unless the court decides that it would be just and equitable to dispense therewith (CCA 1995, ss 38, 59, 85 respectively). See CREDIT GUARANTEE; GUARANTEE; LETTER OF CREDIT; TYPE, SIZE OF.

contract of record. Judgments and recognisances of courts of record. A *judgment* imposes an obligation to pay the sum awarded; a *recognisance* imposes an obligation or bond on an offender e g to be of good behaviour subject to a money penalty if the obligation is broken.

contract of sale. See SALE.

contract of service. A contract of employment. See *Henry Denny & Son (Ireland) Ltd v Minister for Social Welfare* [1998] ELR 36, SC; *Walker v Department of Social, Community and Family Affairs* [1999] ELR 260; *McMahon v Securicor Omega Express* [2002] ELR 317, EAT; *Duijne v Irish Chamber Orchestra* [2002] ELR 255, EAT appealed to Circuit Court and appeal upheld by consent. Contrast with a CONTRACT FOR SERVICES. See EMPLOYEE.

contracts, doorstep. See DOORSTEP CONTRACTS.

contracts, evidenced in writing. See SIMPLE CONTRACTS; STATUTE OF FRAUDS.

contracts, illegal. See ILLEGAL CONTRACTS.

contracts, quasi-. See QUASI-CONTRACTS.

contracts, required to be in writing. See DEED; ELECTRONIC CONTRACT; SALE OF GOODS; SIMPLE CONTRACTS; STATUTE OF FRAUDS.

contracts, void. See VOID CONTRACTS.

contracts for differences. An agreement between two persons who agree that they will ascertain the difference in price of certain shares on one day and their price at a later date, with no intention that the shares will be purchased, and with payment being made from one to the other based on the difference. Such an agreement is void as a wager. See *Byers v Beattie* [1867] IR ICL 209 (Exch).

contractual obligations. Contractual obligations derive from an agreement made between two or more parties, under which one promises or undertakes with the other, the performance of some action: *Tansey v College of Occupational Therapists* [1995] 2 ILRM 601, HC. See CONTRACT.

contradictor. A person who puts an opposing point of view. It is a feature of the adversarial legal system. When the President of Ireland refers a Bill to the Supreme Court under art 26 of the 1937 Constitution for a decision on its constitutionality, the court hears arguments by or on behalf of the Attorney-General in favour of constitutionality and by counsel assigned by the Court who argue against its constitutionality. Such counsel are *contradictors* in this respect. See also LEGITIMUS CONTRADICTOR; MARITAL STATUS; REFERENDUM COMMISSION.

contravention. Includes failure to comply: Building Societies Act 1989, s 2(1).

contribution. (1) Payment made by or imposed on some person.

(2) Payment of a proportionate share of a liability which has been borne by one, or some only, of a number of persons liable e g where there are a number of insurance policies in respect of a particular risk and one insurer pays out on that risk, he may bring an action against the other insurers for a rateable contribution. Also an employee who has been unfairly dismissed may have an award of compensation abated to have regard to the contribution he made to his dismissal e g see *Pritchard v Oracle* [1992] ELR 24, EAT. See Residential Institutions Redress Act 2002, s 24. See CONTRIBUTORY NEGLIGENCE.

contributory. Every person liable to contribute to the assets of a company in the event of the company being wound up. The present and past members are liable to contribute to the assets to an amount sufficient for the payment of its debts and liabilities and the costs of the winding up, and for an adjustment of the rights of the contributories between them: Companies Act 1963, s 207.

The list of contributories is made out by the *liquidator* in two parts: *A* contributories consisting of present members who are primarily liable and *B* contributories consisting of past members within the year preceding the winding up. *B* contributories are liable to contribute only after the *A* contributories are exhausted, and are not liable for debts contracted since they ceased to be members.

In the case of a company *limited by guarantee*, a contributory's liability is limited to the amount he undertook to contribute in the event of a winding up. In a company *limited by shares*, a contributory's liability is limited to the amount, if any, unpaid on his shares. See RSC Ord 74, rr 50–83, 86–89. See SHARES; PERSONAL LIABILITY; WINDING UP.

contributory negligence. Negligence or want of care on the part of the plaintiff to an action or of one for whose acts he is responsible: Civil Liability Act 1961, s 34. Where there is contributory negligence on the part of the plaintiff, his damages are reduced by such amount as the court thinks just and equitable having regard to the degrees of fault of the parties (CLA 1961, s 34); if it is not possible to establish different degrees of fault, the liability is apportioned equally. The onus on establishing contributory negligence is on the defendant: *Clancy v Commissioners of Public Works* [1991] ILRM 567, SC. See *O'Leary v O'Connell* [1968] IR 149; *Sinnott v Quinnsworth Ltd* [1984] ILRM 523; *Conley v Stram* [1988] HC.

The negligence of the plaintiff in an action for breach of contract may be pleaded and result in a reduction of damages for such breach; this arises because a *wrong* is defined in the Civil Liability Act 1961, s 2, as including *a tort, breach of contract* or *breach of trust*. See *Lyons v Thomas* [1985] HC; *Curley v Dublin Corporation* [2003] in *Law Society Gazette* (May 2004) 46, *Lyons v Thomas* [1985] HC. See also Health (Amendment) Act 1986, s 2(2)(a). See CONCURRENT WRONGDOERS; PLEADINGS; SAFETY BELT.

control. (1) Means the holding, whether directly or indirectly, of securities carrying not less than 30% of the voting rights of the company: Irish Takeover Panel Act 1997, s 1(1). See TAKEOVER.

(2) A person who involves himself so closely with the operation of a company so as to be effectively in control, may be personally liable for acts of negligence which injure an employee of the company which he supervised: *Shinkwin v Quin-Con Ltd and Nicholas Quinlan* [2001] 1 IR 514, SC. In this case, the first named defendant company was uninsured. The criteria of control (e g nature and degree) is not an addition to the test for the existence of *proximity* (qv).

control, common. See MONOPOLY.

control of monopoly. See MONOPOLY, CONTROL OF.

controlled drugs. Any substance, product or preparation specified or declared to be a controlled drug; possession of a controlled drug may be an offence: Misuse of Drugs Act 1977, ss 2–3, Sch. See SI No 78 of 2004. [Bibliography: Charleton.] See DRUGS, MISUSE OF.

controlled dwelling. A house which is subject to statutory rent control, let as a separate dwelling, or a part so let, of any house, whether or not the tenant shares with any other persons any portion thereof or any accommodation, amenity or facility in connection therewith: Housing (Private Rented Dwellings) Act 1982.

For such a dwelling to be subject to control, there must be a letting of not greater than year to year. There is no control where the rateable valuation exceeds certain limits; where the dwelling is erected on or after 7 May 1941 or let by local authorities or furnished; or is subject to a service letting, or where let *bona fide* for *temporary convenience* or to meet a temporary necessity; or in certain cases where it is a separate and self-contained flat. See also Housing (Private Rented Dwellings) Act 1983.

A tenant or spouse of the original tenant of a controlled dwelling is entitled to retain possession during their lifetime; a member of the tenant's family, if *bona fide* residing with the tenant or spouse of the tenant, is entitled to retain possession from the date of death of the tenant or spouse to the expiration of the '*relevant period*' ie 26 July 2002, 20 years from commencement of H(PRD)A 1982: H(PRD)A 1982, s 9 and Housing (Private Rented Dwellings) Act 1982 (Commencement) Order, 1982, SI No 216 of 1982.

Provision has been made to enable an allowance to be paid to persons who on 25 July 2002 were tenants of dwellings, whose entitlement to retain possession subsists after 25 July 2002 by operation of law or otherwise, and who otherwise suffer hardship by reason of increases in rent (H(PRD)A 1982, s 28 inserted by Housing (Miscellaneous Provisions) Act 2002, s 20).

It has been held that the amount of the landlord's income is only a relevant factor in determining the tenant's rent if the landlord seeks to make it so: *Quirke v Folio Homes* [1988] ILRM 496, SC. A determination of the Rent Tribunal was quashed as the Tribunal had failed to furnish adequate reasons for its determination: *Beatty and Beatty v Rent Tribunal* (25 July 2001, unreported), HC. The plaintiffs were subsequently awarded damages for the breach by the Tribunal of the duty of care which it owed to the plaintiffs: *Beatty and Beatty v Rent Tribunal* [2003] FL 7989, HC. See *Foley v Johnson* [1988] IR 7, HC.

For District and High Court proceedings under the 1982 and 1983 Acts, see respectively DCR 1997 Ord 93 and RSC Ord 112. See Housing (Rent Tribunal) Regulations 1983 and 1988 (SI No 222 of 1983 and SI No 140 of 1988). For discussion on whether the State is bound by the H(PRD)A 1983, see *de Blacam* in 7 ILT & SJ (1989) 33. See also Housing (Miscellaneous Provisions) Act 1992, ss 17, 18, 20; Residential Tenancies Act 2004, s 3(2)(b). See also 7 ILT & SJ (1989) 209. [Bibliography: de Blacam (1).] See RENT CONTROL.

Controller of Patents. The office, being a corporate sole with perpetual succession and an official seal, known as the Controller of Patents, Designs and Trade Marks: Patents Act 1992, ss 6 and 97 as amended by Intellectual Property (Miscellaneous Provisions) Act 1998, s 5. The Controller, who is appointed by the government for a five-year term, may sue and be sued in that name, and has a wide range of functions, powers and authority under PA 1992 in respect of patents (qv), under the Trade Marks Act 1996 in respect of trade marks (qv), formerly under the Industrial and Commercial Property (Protection) Act 1927 and now under the Industrial Designs Act 2001 in respect of designs (qv), and under the Copyright and Related Rights Act 2000 in relation to copyright, performers' rights, and database rights. The Controller is required to act under the general supervision of the Minister (PA 1992, s 6 as amended by IP(MP)A 1998, s 4).

Under the Patents Act 1964 (since repealed) the Controller did not have the authority and power to direct his Examiners to dispense with statutory investigations in the course of examination of certain patent applications for registration: *The State (Rajan) v Minister for Industry and Commerce* [1988] ILRM 231. It has also been held that the Controller is required, having been requested so to do, to give in writing his reasons for dismissing an appli-

cation for removal of a trade mark: *Anheuser Busch v Controller of Trade Marks* [1988] ILRM 247. The Controller is required to prepare an annual report: Patents Act 1992, s 103; Trade Marks Act 1996, s 75.

Under the Copyright and Related Rights Act 2000, the Controller is required to determine within a reasonable time, disputes arising under the Act; he may order costs against a party; he may also refer a dispute to an arbitrator; he may appoint assessors, and he may consult with the Attorney-General (CRRA 2000, ss 362–368). An appeal on a point of law lies to the High Court from a decision of the Controller (CRRA 2000, s 366). In any reference to the Controller relating to a licence or a licensing scheme, the Controller is required to exercise his powers to ensure that there is no unreasonable discrimination between licensees or prospective licensees (CRRA 2000, ss 162 and 278). Under a new regime for the registration of designs, the Controller has wide powers in relation to the registration of *design rights*: Industrial Designs Act 2001. See *Controller of Patents v Ireland* [2001] 4 IR 229, SC. See DESIGN; IMMUNITY; PATENTS OFFICE JOURNAL.

Controller of Trade Marks. See CONTROLLER OF PATENTS.

convalescent home. See NURSING HOME.

convenience, balance of. See BALANCE OF CONVENIENCE.

convention. (1) Agreed usage and practice.

(2) A treaty between states. The Oireachtas is entitled to give effect in domestic law to a convention which confers jurisdiction in cases with an international dimension to foreign courts with the object of protecting children: *Wadda v Ireland* [1994] 1 ILRM 126, HC. In interpreting legislation giving effect to a convention, the courts, recognising that the convention is an international treaty to which the State is a party, will give it a construction which accords with its expressed objectives and the *travaux preparatoires* which accompanied its adoption may be legitimately used as an aid to its construction: *HI v MG* [1999] 2 ILRM 1, HC & SC. See TREATY.

convention application. An application for a patent from an applicant in a country that is a member of the Paris Convention (qv) to another convention country for protection in that other country. See Patents Act 1992, s 25. See PATENT.

Convention on the future of Europe. A body established following the *Declaration on the Future of the Union,* attached to the Nice Treaty (qv), to address three basic challenges: (a) how to bring citizens, and primarily the young, closer to the EU, (b) how the EU should be better organised, (c) how the EU can most effectively play a positive role in the wider world. It was chaired by a former President of France, Valery Giscard d'Estaing. See *www.european-convention.eu.int.* The Convention proposed in 2003 a draft *Constitutional Treaty for the European Union. See* 'Irish Criminal Law and the Convention on the Future of Europe' by Eugene Regan BL in *Bar Review* (July 2003) 161. See EUROPEAN UNION CONSTITUTION.

convergence. Becoming more alike or closer together in terms of various characteristics or capabilities: *National Forum on Europe – Glossary of Terms* (2003).

convergence criteria. The conditions which are required to be met by member states of the EC in order to achieve *economic and monetary union* (qv). The criteria are: achievement of a high degree of price stability, absence of excessive budget deficit, observance of exchange rate mechanism of the European Monetary System, and durability of convergence as reflected in long-term interest rates: EC Treaty, art 121 of the consolidated (2002) version. See also Protocol on Convergence Criteria 1992. See also COHESION FUND; EUROPEAN COMMUNITY.

conversion. A building society may convert itself into a public limited company by approving a *conversion scheme*: Building Societies Act 1989, s 101. The successor company is protected from being taken over for a period of five years (BSA 1989, s 102). Also only the Central Bank may present a petition to the court for the appointment of an examiner to such a company: Companies (Amendment) Act 1990, s 3 as amended by Companies (Amendment) (No 2) Act 1999, s 6.

The Irish Permanent Building Society converted in 1994 into Irish Permanent plc (now, since 1999, Irish Life & Permanent plc, see website: *www.irishlifepermanent.ie*) and First National Building Society converted in 1998 into First Active plc (website: *www.firstactive.com*). See also TRUSTEE SAVINGS BANK.

conversion, fraudulent. See FRAUDULENT CONVERSION.

conversion grant. See LEASE FOR LIVES RENEWABLE FOREVER.

conversion in equity. In equity, conversion is the notional change of realty into personalty, or personalty into money, which arises as soon as the duty to convert arises.

Conversion may arise: (a) under a trust eg where a testator or settlor directs trustees to convert realty into personalty or vice versa, the property will be treated as having been converted from the time the instrument containing the direction came into operation; (b) under the Partnership Act 1890 where freehold land has become partnership land, it is treated as between the partners as personalty (PA 1890, s 22); (c) under a sale by court order, conversion takes place from the date of the order, provided the order is final and conclusive; (d) under a specifically enforceable contract for sale of realty, the vendor's interest is converted to personalty and the purchaser's into realty as from the date of the contract.

In the event of total failure of the objects for which the conversion was directed in a deed or will, no conversion takes place. There are other rules for partial failure. [Bibliography: Keane (2); Wylie (3).] See RECONVERSION; FRAUDULENT CONVERSION; INFRINGEMENT OF COPYRIGHT.

conversion in tort. A tort (qv) committed by a person who deals with chattels not belonging to him in a manner inconsistent with the rights of the owner. There must be *dealing* with the goods and there must be the *intention* to deny the right of ownership on the part of the wrongdoer. As to goods the subject of a hire-purchase agreement, see the Consumer Credit Act 1995, ss 71 and 73. See *British Wagon Co Ltd v Shortt* [1961] IR 164; *Morgan v Maurer Son* [1964] Ir Jur Rep 31.

conversion rate. Means the irrevocably fixed conversion rate adopted for the currency of each participating EU member state by the Council according to the first sentence of the EC Treaty, art 109(1)(4): Economic and Monetary Union Act 1998, s 5(1). The conversion rate of the Irish pound was set at IR£0.787564 = 1 euro. See now EC Treaty, art 111 of the consolidated (2002) version.

convertible security. See DEBENTURE.

conveyance. The transfer of the ownership of property; the instrument effecting the transfer. The deed of conveyance will contain the date, names of the parties, narrative recitals or introductory recitals, testatum, operative clause, parcels, habendum, and testimonium (qqv). Conveyancing for any fee, gain or reward is primarily restricted to solicitors (qv): Solicitors Act 1954, s 58 as amended by Solicitors (Amendment) Act 1994, s 77.

If it can be shown that the necessary and probable result of a conveyancing agreement is to defeat or delay creditors, it can be avoided; it is not necessary that the agreement was motivated by fraud: Conveyancing Act (Ireland) 1634; *McQuillan v Maguire* [1996] 1 ILRM 394, HC.

If a purchaser's solicitor makes amendments to the terms of a conveyancing contract, or a map which forms part of that contract, he should alert the vendor's solicitor to this fact in the covering letter returning the contracts: *A Guide to Professional Conduct of Solicitors in Ireland* (2002) ch 7.1. When dealing with a lay conveyancer, a solicitor should explain to his own client the difficulties which may be encountered e g inability to accept undertakings from that person, undesirability of handing over a deposit to a lay vendor (ch 6.3).

The Law Reform Commission has proposed changes in the law to simplify conveyancing, including reducing the period of title which has to be investigated from 40 to 20 years: Ninth Report of LRC (LRC 87, 1986). See also *Report on Land Law and Conveyancing Law – General Proposals* (LRC 30, 1989); Restrictive Practices Commission Report, *Solicitors – Conveyancing and Advertising* (1982). See also Stamp Duties Consolidation Act 1999, ss 29–49, 91–98. See 'Avoiding professional negligence in Conveyancing' by solicitor Brian Gallagher in *Law Society Gazette* (December 2002) 10. [Bibliography: Bland (2); Buckley J F; Laffoy & Wheeler; Linehan; Wylie (2).] See MARKETABLE TITLE; OVERREACHING CONVEYANCE; RESIDENTIAL UNIT; SOLICITOR; VOLUNTARY CONVEYANCE.

conveyancing services. The Minister is empowered to make regulations authorising building societies to provide conveyancing services: Building Societies Act 1989, s 31(1). *Conveyancing services* are the preparation of transfers, conveyances, contracts, leases or other assurances in connection with the disposition or acquisition of estates or interests in land (BSA 1989, s 31(13)).

convict. A person sentenced to death or penal servitude (qv) for treason (qv) or a felony (qv): Forfeiture Act 1870, s 6. A convict was incapable of making any con-

tract, express or implied (FA 1870, s 8; *O'Connor v Coleman* [1947] 81 ILTR 42). The 1870 Act has been repealed and any distinction between a felony and a misdemeanour has been abolished: Criminal Law Act 1997, ss 3 and 16. See also Statute of Limitations 1957, s 48(1)(c) repealed by the CLA 1997, s 16 and Sch 3.

conviction. The finding of a person guilty of an offence after trial. Dismissal of an employee convicted of a serious offence unconnected with his work, may be an *unfair* dismissal: *Brady v An Post* [1992] ELR 227, EAT. A conviction, quashed on certiorari (qv) on the ground that the sentence pronounced is in excess of the jurisdiction of the court, is null and void *ab initio* and consequently the accused may be put on trial again for the same charge: *State (Tynan) v Keane* [1968] IR 348 cited in *Sheehan v District Judge O'Reilly* [1993] ITLR (15 March), SC.

Convictions in a court of criminal jurisdiction of any registered medical practitioner are notified to the Medical Council which will investigate the circumstances involved: Medical Council, *A Guide to Ethical Conduct and Behaviour* (6th edn, 2004) para 1.6. A doctor may not be able to avoid an inquiry by claiming that he was not on duty at the time of the alleged offence. A barrister must forthwith report to the Bar Council the fact that he has been convicted of a criminal offence involving dishonesty or of a criminal offence which might bring the profession into disrepute: *Code of Conduct for the Bar of Ireland* (December 2003) r 2.16. A licensee for security services, or an applicant for a licence, must inform the Private Security Authority if he is convicted of an offence or if proceedings for an offence are pending: Private Security Services Act 2004, s 36. See SUMMARY OFFENCE; SUMMARY PROCEEDINGS; PROVISIONAL CONVICTION.

conviction, evidence of. Evidence of previous conviction of a crime is admissible in civil cases where the fact that a party has been convicted is in issue e g malicious prosecution (qv). Such evidence is also admissible in both civil and criminal cases, where a witness denies his conviction when cross-examined as to credit: Criminal Procedures Act 1865. In criminal cases, evidence of a previous conviction is admissible: (a) on any charge to which a previous conviction is essential to the charge e g formerly, being a habitual criminal: Prevention of Crime Act 1908; (b) formerly, evidence of conviction of fraud or dishonesty in the previous five years, to show guilty knowledge on the former charge of receiving stolen goods: Larceny Act 1916; (c) after conviction to assist the judge in imposing a proper sentence; (d) in circumstances where evidence of the bad character of the accused is admissible. See *The People (Attorney-General) v Kirwan* [1943] IR 279.

Where an accused gives evidence to the court and, in so doing, accepts a list of previous convictions given to the court and which list is to the knowledge of his solicitor incorrect, that solicitor must then cease his representation of the accused: *A Guide to Professional Conduct of Solicitors in Ireland* (2002) ch 5.1. If asked by the court to comment on the accused's previous convictions outlined by the prosecution, which the defendant's solicitor knows to be incorrect or incomplete, the defendant's solicitor should decline to comment. If after a finding of guilty, the prosecution is asked if there are any previous convictions and informs the court that there are none and a defence barrister knows that there are previous convictions, he is under no duty to so inform the court: *Code of Conduct for the Bar of Ireland* (December 2003) r 9.16. See BAIL; CHARACTER, EVIDENCE OF; HABITUAL CRIMINAL.

conviction, proof of. A previous conviction may be proved against any person by production of a certificate of conviction: Prevention of Crimes Act 1871, s 18; or in the case of proof for the purpose of discrediting a witness by a certificate: Criminal Procedure Act 1865, s 6; or to assist the judge in imposing a proper sentence by oral recitation by a garda witness of previous convictions from a list already acknowledged by the accused as correct.

convictions, freedom to express. See EXPRESSION, FREEDOM OF.

cooling-off period. The period during which a consumer may withdraw from an agreement; it is ten days from the date of receiving the agreement or a copy thereof: Consumer Credit Act 1995, s 50. A consumer can forego the right to a cooling-off period by signing a separate statement to this effect (CCA 1995, s 50(2)). Excluded agreements are housing loans and credit availed of by a credit card or an overdraft facility (CCA 1995, s 50(4)). Specific

requirements for the insertion of 'cooling-off' statements in credit agreements, hire-purchase agreements and consumer-hire agreements are contained in CCA 1995, ss 30, 58(5) and 84(5) respectively. See also ADJUDICATORS IN TENANCY DISPUTES; CODE OF PRACTICE; DOORSTEP CONTRACTS; LIFE ASSURANCE; MEDIATION IN TENANCY DISPUTES.

coparcenary. The ownership in land which formerly arose on an *intestacy* where no sons survived the deceased and the nearest relatives were females, those relatives collectively constituted the heir and took the realty as coparceners. It was a hybrid form of *co-ownership;* there was no right of survivorship and the interests of each coparcener passed under her will or on an intestacy; each coparcener held an undivided share in the property and union in a sole tenant destroyed the coparcenary. Effectively abolished by the Succession Act 1965, ss 10(1) and 11(1) except in relation to the descent to an unbarred entail. See *Re Matson* [1897] Ch 509. See BARRING THE ENTAIL; JOINT TENANCY.

Copenhagen criteria. The criteria, agreed in Copenhagen in 1993, which must be met by a *candidate* country for entry into the European Union: (a) the country must have stable institutions guaranteeing democracy, the rule of law, human rights and respect for minorities; (b) the country must have a functioning market economy; and (c) the country must take on board all the *acquis* of the EU and support its aims. The EU reserves the right to decide when a candidate country has met these criteria and when the EU is ready to accept the new member. See ACQUIS; ENLARGEMENT OF EU.

Copenhagen Declaration. The Declaration signed in Copenhagen by the Education Ministers of 31 European countries in November 2002, in which the Ministers agreed on a set of priorities which has as its aim 'to increase voluntary co-operation in vocational education and training, in order to promote mutual trust, transparency and recognition of competencies and qualifications, and thereby establish a basis for increasing mobility and facilitating access to lifelong learning'. The Declaration is part of a strategy objective for the EU to become the world's most dynamic knowledge-based economy. See website: *www.europa.eu.int/education/copenhagen/index_*

en.html. See LISBON PROCESS; NATIONAL REFERENCE POINT.

copy. See DOCUMENTARY EVIDENCE; OFFICE COPY.

copyright. Copyright is a *property right* whereby the owner of the copyright in any *work* may undertake or authorise certain acts in the State, referred to as *acts restricted by copyright*: Copyright and Related Rights Act 2000, ss 17 and 37. Copyright is presumed to exist in a work until the contrary is proved; this presumption applies in any proceedings, civil or criminal, for infringement of the copyright in any work (CRRA 2000, s 139).

It has been held that the intention of parliament in enacting copyright legislation was to reward the skill involved in producing an original work and not to reward the good memory, verbal acuity and gift of articulation of a bright child who entertainingly recounted a story the child had been told: *Gormley v EMI Records (Ireland) Ltd* [2000] 1 IR 74.

Copyright subsists in: (a) *original* literary, dramatic, musical or artistic works, including computer programs, (b) sound recordings, films, broadcasts or cable programmes, (c) the typographical arrangement of published editions, and (d) *original* databases (CRRA 2000, s 17(2)). It is the creativity and not the language which creates the copyright; *originality* does not require the work to be unique, but merely that there should have been original thought: *Gormley v EMI Records (Ireland) Ltd* [1999] 1 ILRM 178, SC.

Copyright protection does not extend to the ideas and principles which underlie any element of a work (CRRA 2000, s 17(3)). Copyright does not subsist in a literary, dramatic or musical work until the work is recorded in *writing* or otherwise, by or with the consent of the author (CRRA 2000, s 18) or in sound recordings until the first *fixation* of the sound recording is made (CRRA 2000, s 19).

The *acts restricted by copyright* are the copying of the work, the making of the work available to the public, and the making of an *adaptation* of the work (CRRA 2000, s 37(1)). The author of a work is the first owner of the copyright, but there are exceptions eg where the work is made by an employee in the course of employment (CRRA 2000, s 23). The previous *commissioner* exception has been abolished.

The copyright in a work is transmissible by assignment, by testamentary disposition or by operation of law, as *personal* or *moveable* property (CRRA 2000, s 120(1)). An assignment of copyright is not effective unless it is in writing and signed by or on behalf of the assignor (CRRA 2000, s 120(3)). The government may restrict copyright protection for authors from non-convention countries where Irish works are not adequately protected in those other countries (CRRA 2000, s 190). There are specific provisions in the Act dealing with *database rights*, which subsist independent of copyright (CRRA 2000, ss 320–361). International protection of copyright is obtained via the Berne Copyright Union (qv) and the Universal Copyright Convention (qv).

The Controller of Patents, Designs and Trade Marks has jurisdiction in relation to copyright licensing, licensing schemes, registration of licensing bodies and the determination of disputes between licensing bodies and persons with or requiring licences (CRRA 2000, ss 149–181). A licence scheme is in the nature of a standing *invitation to treat*: *Phonographic Performance (Irl) Ltd v Controller of Industrial and Commercial Property* [1993] 11 ILT Dig 162, HC. See also *Allibert SA v O'Connor* [1982] ILRM 40; *Phonographic Performance (Ire) Ltd v Chariot Inns Ltd* [1993] 11 ILT Dig 162, HC; *Phonographic Performance (Ireland) Ltd v Controller of Industrial and Commercial Property* [1996] 1 ILRM 1, SC.

Many regulations have been made in relation to the Copyright and Related Rights Act 2000 eg SI No 404 of 2000 (commencement of certain Parts/sections); SI No 405 of 2000 (recording of broadcasts and cable programmes for archival purposes); SI No 406 of 2000 (provision of modified works); SI No 407 of 2000 (recording for purposes of time-shifting); SI No 408 of 2000 (works of folklore); SIs Nos 409 and 410 of 2000 (educational establishments); SI No 411 of 2000 (material open for public inspection – international organisations); and SI No 427 of 2000 (librarians and archivists – copying of protected materials).

See 'The Copyright and Related Rights Act 2000' by Terence Coghlan BL in *Bar Review* (March 2001) 294. For amendment to the CRRA 2000 to complete the implementation into Irish law of EC Directive

2001/29/EC, see SI No 16 of 2004. [Bibliography: Clark & Smyth; Kelly & Murphy; Copinger UK; Laddie UK; Oppenheim UK.] See BREHON LAWS; COMMERCIAL PROCEEDINGS; DATABASE; DATABASE RIGHT; DESIGN; FAIR DEALING; INFRINGEMENT OF COPYRIGHT; INTERNET; IRISH COPYRIGHT LICENSING AGENCY; LICENCE TO RIGHT; MORAL RIGHTS; PERFORMERS' RIGHTS; RECORDING RIGHT; RIGHTS PROTECTION MEASURE; WRITING.

copyright, design document. The copyright in a *design document* or model recording or embodying a design for anything other than an artistic work or a typeface, is not infringed by the making of a product to the design or the copying of a product made to the design: Industrial Designs Act 2001, s 89 inserting new s 78A in the Copyright and Related Rights Act 2000. In this context, *design* means the design of any aspect of the shape or contours (whether internal or external) of the whole or part of a product, other than surface decoration. Also *design document* means any record of a design, whether in the form of a drawing, a written description, a photograph, storing the work in any medium or otherwise.

copyright, duration of. The duration of copyright is the author's life plus 70 years; however in the case of sound recordings, broadcasts, cable programmes, and typographical arrangements of a published edition, the copyright term is 50 years from the date the work was lawfully made available to the public: Copyright and Related Rights Act 2000, ss 24–36. Where a work is made available to the public in volumes, parts, instalments, issues or episodes, and where the copyright subsists from the date on which the work is so made available, the copyright subsists in respect of each separate item (CRRA 2000, s 31).

Where copyright is not calculated from the death of the author and the work is not lawfully made available to the public within 70 years of its creation, the copyright expires on the expiration of that period (CRRA 2000, s 33). However, a person who lawfully makes available to the public a work, which previously had not been made available and the copyright on which has expired, will be entitled to 25 years' protection (CRRA 2000, s 34).

Duration of copyright is calculated from 1 January of the year following the event which gave rise to the term of copyright (CRRA 2000, s 35). There are special provisions dealing with *anonymous* or *pseudonymous* works (qv) (CRRA 2000, ss 24 and 32). The rules specified for duration of copyright in ss 24–35 do not apply to government or Oireachtas copyright or to the copyright of prescribed international organisations (CRRA 2000, s 36). Also a perpetual copyright subsists in *legal tender*.

Copyright subsists in a *design* registered under the Industrial Designs Act 2001 and its duration is: (a) 25 years after the filing date for registration of the design; or (b) on the date of expiration of the copyright under the Copyright and Related Rights Act 2000, whichever is the sooner: Industrial Designs Act 2001, s 89 inserting new s 31A in CRRA 2000.

For details on duration of copyright, see individual entries eg ARTISTIC WORK; COMPUTER PROGRAM; LITERARY WORK; PUBLISHED EDITION.

copyright, exemptions. A wide variety of acts, in relation to a work in which copyright subsists, do not infringe any copyright: Copyright and Related Rights Act 2000, ss 49–106. Provision is made for a number of permitted acts or 'exceptions' to copyright protection; these are divided into different categories and limited to certain situations.

These categories include: (a) fair dealing with a work for the purposes of research, private study, criticism or review; incidental inclusion of a work in another work (CRRA 2000, ss 50–52); (b) exceptions for the purposes of education (CRRA 2000, ss 53–58); (c) exceptions for the purposes of prescribed libraries and prescribed archives (CRRA 2000, ss 59–70); (d) exceptions for the purpose of public administration (CRRA 2000, ss 71–77); (e) designs; computer programs; original databases; typefaces; works in electronic form (CRRA 2000, ss 78–86); (f) transient and incidental copies; anonymous and pseudonymous works; use of notes or recordings of spoken words in certain cases; public reading or recitation of works; abstracts of scientific or technical articles; fixations (eg recordings) of works of folklore; representation of certain artistic works on public display; advertisement of sale of artistic works; making of subsequent works by the same author (CRRA 2000, ss 87–95); (g) reconstruction of buildings (CRRA 2000, s 96); (h) playing or showing sound recordings and broadcasts in certain premises; playing of sound recordings for clubs and societies;

copying for purpose of broadcast or cable programme; recording for purposes of supervision and control of broadcasts and cable programmes; recording for purposes of time shifting (CRRA 2000, s 97–101); (i) photographs of television broadcast or cable programmes; reception and transmission of broadcasts in cable programme services; provision of modified works; recording for archival purposes and adaptations of a work (CRRA 2000, ss 98–106).

copyright, infringement of. The High Court in granting an injunction prohibiting the publication of extracts of the work of James Joyce, held that the courts cannot, by failing to recognise and uphold the right to copyright, condemn the owner of the right to be content until the hearing of the action, to permit the breach of the right in respect of which there is a statutory presumption: *Sweeney v NUI Cork t/a Cork University Press* [2001] 1 ILRM 310, HC and 2 IR 6. See INFRINGEMENT OF COPYRIGHT; PUBLIC EXHIBITION OF CERTAIN WORKS.

copyright, international. See BERNE COPYRIGHT UNION; UNIVERSAL COPYRIGHT CONVENTION.

copyright, licensing of. A *copyright licence* means a licence to undertake or authorise the undertaking of any of the acts restricted by copyright: Copyright and Related Rights Act 2000, s 149(1). A licence granted by a copyright owner is binding on every successor in title to his interest in the copyright, except a purchaser in good faith for valuable consideration and without notice (actual or constructive) of the licence (CRRA 2000, s 120(4)).

An *exclusive licence* is a licence in writing signed by or on behalf of the owner, which authorises the licensee, to the exclusion of all other persons, including the person granting the licence, to exercise all the rights otherwise exclusively exercisable by the copyright owner (CRRA 2000, s 122). An exclusive licensee has the same rights and remedies as if the licence had been an assignment and his rights are concurrent with those of the copyright owner (CRRA 2000, s 135). In any action for an infringement of copyright brought by either the copyright owner or the exclusive licensee, the other must be joined as a plaintiff or defendant, unless the court directs otherwise (CRRA 2000, s 136).

Provision is made for the registration of licensing bodies (CRRA 2000, s 175–180).

There is an obligation on *collecting societies* (ie a society which collects royalties on behalf of copyright owners) to register and remain registered (CRRA 2000, s 181). Provision is also made for the reference of disputes between licensees and licensing bodies (in relation to licences and licensing schemes) to the Controller of Patents for adjudication (CRRA 2000, ss 149–173). See Copyright and Related Rights (Register of Copyright Licencing Bodies) Regulations 2002, SI No 463 of 2002.

The European Court of Justice has held that in exceptional circumstances, the refusal of the exclusive owner of a copyright to grant a licence can give rise to abusive conduct: Case C-418/01 *IMS Health GmbH v NDC Health GmbC* [2004] EJC. Three conditions must be be fulfilled: (a) the undertaking requesting the licence must intend to offer new products or services not offered by the owner of the copyright for which there is a potential consumer demand; (b) the refusal cannot be justified by objective considerations; and (c) the refusal must be such as to reserve to the undertaking which owns the copyright the relevant market by eliminating all competition from that market.

copyright, ownership of. The author of a work is the *first owner* of the copyright, unless: (a) the work is made by an employee in the course of employment, in which case the employer is the first owner, subject to any agreement to the contrary; (b) the work is the subject of government or Oireachtas copyright or of a prescribed international organisation; or (c) the copyright is conferred on some other person by an enactment: Copyright and Related Rights Act 2000, s 23(1). In the case of a work made by an author in the course of employment in a newspaper or periodical, the author may use the work without infringing the copyright; this does not apply to a computer program (CRRA 2000, s 23(2)).

Formerly, where a person commissioned the taking of a photograph, or the printing or drawing of a portrait, or the making of an engraving and paid, or agreed to pay, for it in money or money's worth and the work was made in pursuance of that commission, that person and not the author was entitled to the copyright: Copyright Act 1963, s 10(3). The 2000 Act is silent in relation to works which have been commissioned;

consequently, in the absence of a contractual arrangement otherwise, the author is the first owner of a commissioned work. See PHOTOGRAPH.

copyright, perpetual. See PERPETUAL COPYRIGHT.

copyright, qualification for. Certain works qualify for copyright protection *where* they are *first* lawfully made available to the public in the State, or in any country, territory, state or area to which Part II of the Act applies: Copyright and Related Rights Act 2000, s 184. The works are a literary, dramatic, musical or artistic work, a sound recording, film, typographical arrangement of a published edition, or an original database (CRRA 2000, s 184(1)). A work is deemed to be *first* made available to the public in an area even if it is *simultaneously* made available elsewhere; *simultaneously* in this case means within the previous 30 days (CRRA 2000, s 184(2)).

A *broadcast* qualifies for copyright protection *where* it is lawfully made from (CRRA 2000, s 186). A *cable programme* qualifies for copyright protection *where* it is first sent from a place (a) in the State, or (b) in any country, territory, state or area to which Part II of the Act applies (CRRA 2000, s 186) For list of the agreements, treaties and conventions which are reckonable for the purpose of extension of qualification of copyright protection to works, see CRRA 2000, s 188 and Sch 3.

copyright offences. Apart from the civil liability which may arise where a person infringes the copyright of another, such infringement may give rise to a criminal offence. It is an offence in relation to a copy of a *work*, which the person knows (or has reason to believe) is an *infringing copy*, and without the consent of the copyright owner: (a) to make a copy for sale, rental or loan; or (b) to sell, rent offer or expose for sale, rental or loan; or (c) to import into the State otherwise than for private and domestic use; or (d) to have in possession, custody or control in the course of a business trade or profession: Copyright and Related Rights Act 2000, s 140(1).

There are other offences specified in relation to articles specifically designed or adapted for making copies, and in relation to protection-defeating devices (CRRA 2000, s 140(3)–(4)). It is also an offence for a person to cause a *work* to be performed, played, broadcast or shown where the person knew, or had reason to believe, that the

copyright would be infringed (CRRA 2000, s 140(5)). It is also an offence for a person, for financial gain, to make a false claim of copyright (CRRA 2000, s 141). There are provisions for *search warrants* and *seizure* and for orders for delivery up of infringing copies in criminal proceedings (CRRA 2000, ss 142–143). See PROHIBITED GOODS.

copyright owner, rights of. The exclusive rights of a copyright owner are: (a) a *reproduction right* ie a right to store the work in any medium and to make copies of the work; (b) a *making available right* ie a right to make the work available to the public eg by performing, broadcasting, displaying, or exhibiting the work; (c) a *distribution right* ie a right to make the work available to the public or to authorise others to do so; and (d) a *rental and lending right*: Copyright and Related Rights Act 2000, ss 37–42. See FILM; PROSPECTIVE OWNER; MORAL RIGHTS.

copyright royalty. See ROYALTY.

coram judice. [In the presence of the judge.]

cor; coram. [In the presence of.]

coram non judice. [Before a person who is not a judge.]

Coras Iompair Éireann; CIÉ. CIÉ may now, with the consent of the Minister, acquire or form and establish one or more subsidiary companies pursuant to the Companies Act 1963: Transport (Railway Infrastructure) Act 2001, s 71. Provision has also been made: (a) to increase the number of board members on the existing subsidiaries – Bus Átha Cliath, Iarnród Éireann and Bus Éireann; and (b) to remove the need for common membership of the boards of Iarnród Éireann and Bus Éireann (T(RI)A 2001, s 72). See website: *www.cie.ie*.

coroner. An office holder, appointed by the local authority in whose area the coroner's district is situated, with the general duty to hold inquests (qv) or to cause a post-mortem examination to be made in lieu of an inquest in respect of certain deaths in his district: Coroners Act 1962, ss 8, 17–19. A coroner has jurisdiction to enquire into the finding of treasure trove (qv) (CA 1962, s 49). See also Dangerous Substances Act 1972, s 28; Criminal Justice (Location of Victims' Remains) Act 1999, ss 10–11. A coroner enjoys *absolute* privilege in respect of anything he says while he is performing his duties as coroner in the holding of an inquest under s 30 of CA 1962. However, once he strays outside the functions which he is required to perform (ie to ascertain the identity of the person in respect of whose death the inquest is being held, and how, when and where the death occurred) he ceases to enjoy immunity from suit in respect of anything he says: *Desmond v Riordan* [2000] 1 ILRM 502 and 1 IR 505, HC.

At the conclusion of criminal proceedings in the District Court in relation to the death of a person, the clerk of the court is required to inform the coroner holding the inquest, of the result of the proceedings: DCR 1997 Ord 38, r 3. A coroner is empowered, in certain circumstances, to authorise the disposal by burial, cremation or other means, of the body of a deceased person before the registration of the death: Civil Registration Act 2004, s 44. A barrister may be a coroner and may be remunerated for such office: *Code of Conduct for the Bar of Ireland* (December 2003) r 2.9. See *Report of the Review Group on the Review of the Coroner Service*. Arising from that review, see *Report on the Coroner's Rules Committee* (November 2003), available on website: *www.justice.ie*. [Bibliography: Farrell.] See EXHUMATION; INQUEST; SUICIDE.

corporal punishment. Physical force against a person which was permitted by law (eg whipping) or could amount to a crime (eg assault) or a tort (eg trespass to the person). Parents have a broad discretion as to how they maintain discipline among their children; physical force or confinement is permissible, provided it is not excessive. School teachers also had such a discretion previously (*McCann v Mannion* 66 ILTR 161); however, corporal punishment in schools has been forbidden by the Minister since 1982; a teacher who uses corporal punishment is 'regarded as guilty of conduct unbefitting a teacher and will be subject to severe disciplinary action' (Department of Education Circular 9/82, January 1982).

'Teachers have most unwisely been deprived of the power of inflicting reasonable corporal punishment which could deal with disobedience': Carrol J in *Walsh v St Joseph's National School* (1990) Irish Times, 11 Oct 1990, CC.

The common law rule which gave immunity to teachers from criminal liability in respect of physical chastisement of pupils has been abolished: Non-Fatal Offences against the Person Act 1997, s 24. See DISCIPLINE IN SCHOOL; WHIPPING.

corporate crime. A wide range of crimes relating mainly to companies and the manner in which they are operated eg fraudulent trading, insider dealing, regulatory offences, and competition offences eg abusing a dominant position. In statutes creating new offences, provision is being increasingly made for an officer of the body corporate to be guilty of the offence, where the offence is committed by the body corporate, but with the consent or connivance or due to the neglect of the officer or by a person purporting to act in that capacity eg Immigration Act 2003, s 6; Containment of Nuclear Weapons Act 2003, s 14(2). [Bibliography: Charleton (4).] See CORPORATE KILLING.

corporate enforcement. See DIRECTOR OF CORPORATE ENFORCEMENT.

corporate governance. The system by which companies are directed and controlled and made accountable to shareholders and other stakeholders. Increasingly, other stakeholders include creditors and employees and indeed the general community (eg via the environment, product safety and reliability, mis-selling of products). The principles of corporate governance may also apply to organisations in general and not be confined to companies.

Examples of practices adopted to underpin good corporate governance are: a majority of independent non-executive directors on the board; separation of posts of chairman and chief executive; audit committee independent of management; independent remuneration committee; nomination committee to consider new appointments to the board; particular focus by the board on risk management and strategy; closed period for directors dealing with shares.

In exercising her powers under s 19(2)(a) of the Companies Act 1990 to give directions on the production of books and documents by companies, the Minister can take into account breaches of standards of *corporate governance* as laid down or reinforced by the Companies Acts, but an expression of general concern with breaches of such standards would not constitute a sufficient statement of reasons for exercising such powers: *Dunnes Stores Ireland Company v Ryan & Minister for Enterprise* [2002] 2 IR 60, SC. In 2001, s 19 of the CA 1990 was repealed and new ss 19 and 19A substituted: Company Law Enforcement Act 2001, s 29.

In 2002, a *Centre for Corporate Governance* was established in University College, Dublin in a joint initiative with the Institute of Directors in Ireland (email: *info@iodireland.ie*). The Centre runs courses for company directors covering all aspects of corporate governance; in addition it is intended to act as a hub, promoting research in the area of corporate governance and publishing papers and reports. For the European Corporate Governance Institute and the corporate governance codes of many countries, see website: *www.ecgi.org/codes/*. See also website: *www.corporategovernance.ie*. [Bibliography: Cahill N; Gee Publishing (2); O'Connell M (1).] See ACCOUNTABILITY; AUDIT COMMITTEE; AUDITOR INDEPENDENCE; COMBINED CODE; DIRECTOR OF CORPORATE ENFORCEMENT; IRISH AUDITING AND ACCOUNTING SUPERVISORY AUTHORITY.

corporate homicide. The unlawful killing of a human person caused by a corporate wrong or wrongs. See CORPORATE KILLING.

corporate insolvency. See INSOLVENT COMPANY.

corporate killing. The Law Reform Commission has recommended the establishment of a statutory offence of 'corporate killing' equivalent to 'gross negligence manslaughter' which would be prosecuted on indictment: *Consultation Paper on Corporate Killing* (LRC CP 26, 2003). The negligence required would have to be of a very high degree and would have to involve a serious risk of substantial personal injury risk to others. The Commission has recommended that vicarious criminal liability should not be imposed on corporations for crimes of homicide. For the test for 'gross negligence manslaughter', see *The People (A-G) v Dunleavy* [1948] IR 95. See MANSLAUGHTER.

corporate trades, investment in. The relief from income tax in respect of the investment by individuals in corporate trades, known generally as the *business development scheme; BES* (qv) or the *business expansion scheme*.

corporate veil. See LIFTING THE CORPORATE VEIL.

corporation. A body of persons having in law an existence and rights and duties distinct from those of the individual persons who from time to time form it. A corporation *sole* consists of only one member at a time in succession eg a bishop. A corporation *aggregate* consists of a number of persons eg an incorporated company and a municipal corporation. A partnership has no legal personality of its own and consequently a partnership firm is not a corporation. See CORPORATION AGGREGATE; CORPORATION SOLE.

corporation aggregate. A corporation consisting of more than one member eg a company registered under the Companies Acts. A corporation aggregate must have at least two members, although one may be the nominee of the other. See Powers of Attorney Act 1996, ss 17(2)–(3). See COMPANY; CORPORATION SOLE.

corporation sole. A corporation consisting of a single person whose corporate status arises from an office or function. The object of a corporation sole is to make it possible to distinguish the holder of the office or function in his official and in his private capacity eg a bishop, a minister of State. The property of a corporation sole is treated for the purposes of the Act as belonging to the corporation notwithstanding a vacancy in it: Criminal Damage Act 1991, s 1(5). See also Public Service Management (No 2) Act 1997, s 13; Powers of Attorney Act 1996, s 17(2).

corporation tax. A tax charged on the profits of companies: Taxes Consolidation Act 1997, ss 21–27, as amended by annual Finance Acts. The general rate of corporation tax has been reduced each year from 32% for the financial year 1998, to 20% for 2001, to 16% for 2002, and to 12.5% for the financial year 2003 and subsequent years (TCA 1997, s 21 as amended by Finance Act 1999, s 71). As regards a higher rate of corporation tax, see TCA 1997, s 21A inserted by FA 1999, s 73 and amended by Finance Act 2000, s 75. For further provisions and amendments, see Finance Act 2001, ss 82–91; Finance Act 2002, ss 53–58; Finance Act 2003, ss 59–64.

It has been held that corporation tax in respect of interest earned by moneys kept on deposit by the liquidator of a company is a liability properly incurred: Companies Act 1963, s 281; *Burns v Hearne* [1987] ILRM 508. Also money spent on tax and accountancy advice on possible investment opportunities does not constitute management expenses and therefore is not tax deductible: *Hibernian Group plc v Inspector of Taxes* (2000) Irish Times, 21 January. See Taxes Consolidation (Date for Payment of Preliminary Corporation Tax) Order 2002, SI No 394 of 2002. For original legislation, see Corporation Tax Act 1976.

[Bibliography: Brennan, Moore, O'Sullivan & Clarke; Williams.] See EXPENSES OF MANAGEMENT; MANUFACTURED GOODS; PROFIT AND LOSS; TRADING HOUSE, SPECIAL.

corporeal property. Property which is visible or tangible e g land and goods. See OWNERSHIP.

corpus delicti. The body of an offence; the facts which constitute an offence. The prosecution must first prove that the offence has been committed by someone; in murder cases this is usually proved by production of a dead body, though this is not necessary: *Attorney-General v Edwards* [1935] IR 500.

correction. Many statutes provide for corrections to be made to ensure that records are accurate e g a planning authority is empowered to make corrections in the planning register: Planning and Development Act 2000, s 7(3). For other examples, see DATA PROTECTION; DEFECT; ERROR; FREEDOM OF INFORMATION LEGISLATION; SLIP RULE.

corresponding law. Means a law stated in a certificate to be a law providing for the control or regulation in that country of various activities relating to dangerous or otherwise harmful drugs e g manufacture, production, supply: Misuse of Drugs Act 1977, s 20(2). It is an offence in the State for a person to aid, abet, counsel or induce the commission outside the State of an offence punishable under a corresponding law in force in that place (MDA 1977, s 20(1)).

corresponding offence. (1) For the purposes of the European Arrest Warrant Act 2003: (a) an offence under the law of the issuing state corresponds to an offence under the law of the State, where the *act* or *omission* that constitutes the offence under the law of the issuing state would, if committed in the State, constitute an offence under the law of the State, and (b) an offence under the law of the State corresponds to an offence under the law of the issuing state, where the *act* or *omission* that constitutes the offence under the law of the State would, if committed in the issuing state, constitute an offence under the law of the issuing state (EAWA, s 5). The European arrest warrant replaces the existing extradition arrangements between Ireland and other EU member states as from 1 January 2004. See EUROPEAN ARREST WARRANT.

(2) In relation to extradition which is not between member states of the EU, the offence specified in an extradition warrant must *correspond* with an offence under Irish law which is an indictable offence or is punishable on summary conviction by imprisonment for a period of at least twelve months: Extradition Act 1965, s 10(1), and European Convention on Extradition (Extradition Act, 1965 (Part II) (No 23) Order 1989, SI No 9 of 1989). The judge must satisfy himself before ordering the extradition of the accused whether there is a sufficient statement of the ingredients of the alleged offence to enable him to determine whether the acts alleged would constitute an offence under Irish law: *The State (Furlong) v Kelly* [1971] IR 132.

In extradition law and the *backing of warrants* arrangement with the UK, *correspondence* existed where the act constituting the offence in the UK would, if done in the State, constitute an offence under the law of the State, being an offence which was punishable on indictment or punishable on summary conviction by imprisonment for a maximum term of not less than six months or a more severe penalty: Extradition (European Union Conventions) Act 2001, s 26. This meant that while an offence in the State might not be in the same category or of the same description as the offence in the UK, it would still be an offence for which a person could be extradited, provided the act constituting the offence would, if done in the State, constitute an offence of the same gravity in Ireland. The warrant must contain such essential factual material as may be necessary to recognise whether or not the acts complained of are ones which, if committed in this country, would amount to a criminal offence: *A-G v Scott Dyer* [2004] ITLR (1 March), SC and [2004] 1 ILRM 542.

Prior to the 2001 Act, the following were the significant cases on corresponding offences: (i) It was insufficient that the offence charged has the same name as an offence under Irish law; the specification of the offence on the warrant must identify the offence by reference to the factual components relied upon, the words used being given their ordinary or popular meaning: *O'Shea v Conroy* [1995] 2 ILRM 527, HC.

(ii) It was preferable that a judge of the District Court, making an order for extradition, should specify the nature of the offences which he considered to be *corresponding*, but failure to do so is not fatal once correspondence was in fact established in the High Court: *Sey v Johnston* [1989] IR 516. Use of the phrase 'grievous bodily harm' in a warrant without factual details, does not satisfy the correspondence requirements: *A-G v Heywood* [2004] FL 8919, HC. See *Long v O'Toole* [2001] 3 IR 548, HC; *Myles v Sreenan* [1999] 4 IR 294, HC; *A-G v Fay* [2003] FL 7988, HC; *Newell v O'Toole* [2003] 1 ILRM 1, HC. See ROB; STOLE.

corroboration. Independent evidence which tends to show that the principal evidence is true; independent evidence of material circumstances tending to implicate the accused in the commission of the crime with which he is charged: *Attorney-General v Williams* [1940] IR 195; *People (A-G) v Trayers* [1956] IR 110; *DPP v PJ* [2003] FL 8155, CCA and [2004] 1 ILRM 220, CCA. Evidence of a feature which is so commonplace that it is not of sufficient particularity is not corroboration: *The People (DPP) v PC* [2002] 2 IR 285, CCA.

The general rule of law is that a court can act on the testimony of one witness. However, corroboration of another witness is required by law for: perjury; treason: Treason Act 1939; affiliation orders: Illegitimate Childrens Act 1930 (now repealed); offence of procuring defilement of a girl by threats or fraud or administering drugs: Criminal Law (Amendment) Act 1885.

Corroboration is required as a rule of practice to support the evidence of an *accomplice* (qv) and formerly of the injured party in a sexual assault; the jury could convict on the uncorroborated evidence of one witness in these cases, but the judge had to warn the jury of the danger of acting on such evidence. A warning is no longer a requirement in relation to offences of a sexual nature but the judge retains a discretion, having regard to all the evidence given, to decide whether the jury should be given a warning; no particular form of words is required: Criminal Law (Rape) (Amendment) Act 1990, s 7; *DPP v Riordan* [1992] ITLR (30 November), CCA.

In a particular rape case, the Court of Criminal Appeal held that the trial judge had acted correctly and within his discretion not to give a warning with regard to corroboration: *DPP v C* [2001] 3 IR 345, CCA. In another case of alleged indecent assault, the court quashed the conviction of the accused because of the failure of the trial judge to warn the jury: *DPP v Farrell* (2003) Irish Times, 26 November. See also *The People (DPP) v J E M* [2001] 4 IR 385, CCA.

The Supreme Court has held that where the prosecution seeks to rely upon confession evidence, it should if possible be corroborated, due to the risks associated with excessive reliance on confession evidence: *Braddish v DPP* [2001] 3 IR 127, SC and [2002] 1 ILRM 151, SC. See *People (DPP) v RB* [2003] FL 7079, CCA; *People (DPP) v LG* [2003] 2 IR 517, CCA; *DPP v Gavin* [2000] 4 IR 557, CCA; *The People v Cradden* [1955] IR 130; *DPP v Reid* [1991] as reported by Whelan in 9 ILT & SJ (1991) 109 and 266, CCA. [Bibliography: Healy.] See ACCOMPLICE; CHILD, EVIDENCE OF; CONFESSION; DNA.

corrupt agreement with creditor. A creditor commits an offence who accepts property from a bankrupt (qv) or an arranging debtor (qv) or any other person as an inducement for forbearing to oppose or for accepting a proposal or an offer of composition (qv). The person offering the inducement also commits an offence and the claim of the creditor will be void and irrecoverable: Bankruptcy Act 1988, s 125.

corruption. An inducement by means of an improper consideration to violate some duty. If it is proven that any money, gift or other consideration has been given to or received by an office holder, employee or director of a public body by a person holding or seeking a contract from the public body, it will be deemed to have been given and received corruptly unless the contrary is proved: Ethics in Public Office Act 1995, s 38 amending the Public Bodies Corrupt Practices Act 1889, Prevention of Corruption Acts 1906 and 1916. See also Criminal Law Act 1997, s 16 and Sch 3.

Provision has been made to strengthen the law on corruption and to enable Ireland to ratify three international agreements regarding corruption: Prevention of Corruption (Amendment) Act 2001. Section 1 of the Prevention of Corruption Act 1906 is amended by substitution of a new section which introduces three changes: (i) the offence of *corruption* is revised to apply not only, as previously, to corruption of or by an agent, but also to corruption of or by a third party (eg a spouse of an agent) with a view to influencing the conduct of the agent; (ii) the definition of '*agent*' is extended to cover categories of office holders and officials, both national and foreign, not covered previously by PCA 1906; and (iii) the maximum penalty is increased to ten years' imprisonment and/or an unlimited fine (PC(A)A 2001, s 2).

There is a presumption of corruption in relation to a person elected to public office (or a candidate) where the person has received a political donation in excess of the permitted amount (PC(A)A 2001, s 3). There is also a presumption of corruption where there is proof that a domestic office holder has received money or benefit from a person who has an interest in the way the office holder's functions are exercised (PC(A)A 2001, s 4). Jurisdiction is extended to corruption abroad involving Irish office holders and officials (PC(A)A 2001, s 7).

A new offence of corruption in office is created, covering any act or omission by an Irish office holder or official, done with the intention of corruptly obtaining a gift, consideration or advantage for that office holder or official or any other person (PC(A)A 2001, s 8). Offences by a corporate body can be attributed also to certain of its officers (PC(A)A 2001, s 9). The former Dublin assistant county manager, George Redmond, was found guilty of corruption by a jury in the Dublin Criminal Circuit Court in November 2003. He was given permission by the Court of Criminal Appeal on 6 July 2004 to call new evidence in his appeal against that conviction, the court holding that bank records of the prosecution's core witness were admissible and relevant. That court on 28 July 2004 quashed his conviction, holding that the conviction was unsafe and unsatisfactory. See BRIBERY AND CORRUPTION; EUROPEAN COMMUNITIES FINANCIAL INTERESTS; ILLEGAL CONTRACTS; INFLUENCE, IMPROPER; PERFORMANCE, INDECENT OR PROFANE.

cosmetic product. Any substance or preparation intended to be placed in contact with the various external parts of the human body or with teeth with a view to cleaning them, perfuming them, changing their appearance and/or correcting body odours and/or protecting them or keeping them in good condition: EC Directive No 93/35/EEC of 14 June 1993. The Minister may make regulations in relation to *cosmetic products* eg concerning their manufacture, production, importation, distribution, sale, supply, placing on market, advertisement, or promotion: Irish Medicines Board Act 1995, s 32. See European Communities (Cosmetic Products) (Amendment No 4) Regulations, 2000, SI No 227 of 2000; SI No 553 of 2003. See MEDICINAL PRODUCT.

costs and criminal proceedings. The court has jurisdiction to award costs to an accused person who is acquitted of a criminal charge, but as legal aid will have been granted in most of such cases, the issue does not normally arise: *The People v Bell* [1969] IR 24. The Court of Criminal Appeal no longer has jurisdiction to award costs in respect of proceedings for which a legal aid certificate has been granted: Criminal Justice (Legal Aid) Act 1962, s 8.

Where that court reverses a conviction and orders the appellant to be re-tried for the same offence, it may order the costs of the re-trial (in the absence of a legal aid certificate) to be paid by the State unless the court is of the opinion that the cause of the new trial has been caused or contributed to by the defence: Court of Justice Act 1928, s 5 and CJ(LA)A 1962, s 8; *The People v Moran* [1974] Frewen 380. Also the Court of Criminal Appeal has jurisdiction to award costs in cases where a sentence is being reviewed on grounds of undue leniency: RSC Ord 99 and *The People (DPP) v Redmond* [2001] 3 IR 390, CCA.

Where an offender is released on probation (qv), the court may order the offender to pay the costs of the proceedings: Probation of Offenders Act 1907, s 1(3). Also a person convicted of an offence under the Environmental Protection Agency Act 1992 will be ordered to pay to the Agency its costs in relation to the investigation, detection and prosecution of the offence unless the court is satisfied that there are special and substantial reasons for not so doing (EPAA 1992, s 12). There is a similar provision in the Residential Tenancies Act 2004, s 9(5). See Merchant Shipping Act 1992, s 37 inserted by Merchant Shipping (Investigation of Marine Casualties) Act 2000, s 44(11). See *Redmond v DPP* (30 July 2004, unreported), CCA.

costs in civil proceedings. The court has a discretion in awarding costs in civil proceedings; however, the general practice is that the costs follow the event, ie the successful litigant is generally entitled to his costs: RSC Ord 99, r 1(4). It would require very substantial reasons of an unusual kind before the Court would depart from that principle: *SPUC v Coogan & Ors* [1990] 8 ILT Dig 156.

A plaintiff who failed to prove an actionable defamation nonetheless had costs awarded in his favour, where the newspaper defendant acknowledged a serious misstatement in the newspaper article only at the appeal hearing: *Harkin v Irish Times* (1993) Irish Times, 2 April. Also, in a particular case, involving for the first time consideration by the courts of the extent of the State's obligation to provide *for* free primary education in the context of the guarantee of parental freedom of choice, the court awarded costs to the unsuccessful plaintiff: *Coolenbridge School (Steiner) v Minister for Education* [1999] Irish Times, 11 May1999, HC.

A litigant who unsuccessfully challenged the right of the government to permit the use of Shannon Airport by US military aircraft during the Iraq war was awarded 50% of his costs as he had raised public law issues of general importance: *Horgan v An Taoiseach* [2003] 2 ILRM 357, HC and 2 IR 468.

There is no longer a justification for allowing a wife her costs against her husband in matrimonial proceedings: *F v L* [1990] ILRM 886, HC.

Also, costs will not be awarded against a judge of the District or Circuit court in respect of a successful overruling by a higher court of his decision, where there is no question of impropriety or *mala fides* on the part of the judge concerned, and where he had not opposed the proceedings: *McIlwraith v His Hon Judge Fawsitt* [1990] 1 IR 343 cited with approval in *O'Connor v Carroll* [1999] 2 IR 160, SC. A taxpayer successfully appealing a determination of the Appeals Commissioners to the Circuit Court is entitled to an award of costs: *Inspector of Taxes v Arida Ltd* [1995] 2 IR 230, SC.

Costs in interlocutory proceedings will normally be reserved to be dealt with by the trial judge. However, costs may be awarded at the interlocutory stage, where that hearing dealt with a discrete issue which would have no further relevance at the trial of the action: *Davis v Walshe* [2003] 2 IR 152, SC.

Costs may be payable on: (a) a *party and party* basis, ie all cost which were necessary and proper for the attainment of justice or for enforcing or defending the rights of the party whose costs are being *taxed*; and (b) a *solicitor and client* basis, ie the costs normally associated between a solicitor and his own client.

For costs in winding up of a company, see *MacCann* in 8 ILT & SJ (1990) 245. See also *O'Neill v Adidas Sportschuhfabriken* [1992] ITLR (17 August), SC; *Re Hibernian Transport Companies Ltd (in liquidation)* [1992] ITLR (20 April), SC.

The Labour Court or the Director of the Equality Tribunal may order a person who is obstructing an investigation or an appeal under employment equality legislation, to pay to another person, travelling and other expenses reasonably incurred by that other person in connection with the investigation or appeal: Employment Equality Act 1998, s 99A inserted by Equality Act 2004, s 41. There is a similar provision for the Director in relation to a person who is obstructing an investigation on discrimination in relation to disposing of goods or to providing a service: Equal Status Act 2000, s 37A inserted by EA 2004, s 63.

Only in exceptional circumstance may legal or other professional costs and expenses be awarded in matters dealt with by the *Private Residential Tenancies Board* (qv), its Tenancy Tribunal, adjudicators or mediators: Residential Tenancies Act 2004, s 5(3). For costs in *commercial proceedings* (qv), see RSC Ord 63A, rr 3(1), 14(6), 15(d), 15(e), 28–30, inserted by Rules of the Superior Courts (Commercial Proceedings) 2004, SI No 2 of 2004.

[Bibliography: O'Callaghan P.] See BRIEF; INTEREST ON COSTS; LODGMENT IN COURT; PRE-EMPTIVE COSTS ORDER; REPETITIVE LEGAL WORK; SECURITY FOR COSTS; TAX APPEAL; TAXATION OF COSTS.

costs in civil proceedings, amount of. There are limitations on the amount of costs which may be recovered by a plaintiff in particular circumstances. If a plaintiff is awarded damages which could have been awarded in a lower court, the plaintiff will be entitled to the costs appropriate to the lower court: Courts Act 1991, s 14 inserting a new s 17 to the Courts Act 1981.

In the High Court: (a) if an award is made between £25,000 (€31,743) and

£30,000 (€38,092), the plaintiff will be entitled to Circuit Court costs except where the trial judge grants a special certificate; (b) if the award is between £15,000 (€19,046) and £25,000 (€31,743), the plaintiff will be entitled to Circuit Court costs; (c) if the award is between £5,000 (€6,349) and £15,000 (€19,046), the plaintiff will be entitled to the lesser of Circuit Court costs or costs equivalent to the damages awarded. The judge has a discretion to order the plaintiff to pay the additional costs incurred by the defendant in defending in a higher court than was necessary (CA 1981, s 17(5)). If, and when, Courts and Court Officers Act 2002, s 17 comes into operation with the enlargement of the jurisdiction of the Circuit Court, £5,000 will become €20,000, £15,000 will become €50,000, £25,000 will become €85,000, and £30,000 will become €100,000.

In a case where a High Court jury awarded a District Court judge €25,000 in damages for libel, the Supreme Court held that the High Court had correctly limited the plaintiff's costs to Circuit Court costs for the action and preceding aborted action, and had correctly exercised discretion in refusing to speculate on the length of a Circuit Court hearing and in view of the time taken up by unjustifiable defences: *Judge Mangan v Independent Newspapers Ltd* [2003] ITLR (3rd March), SC and [2003] 2 ILRM 33 and 1 IR 442.

A plaintiff who institutes proceedings in the High Court and subsequently accepts a sum lodged which is within the jurisdiction of the Circuit Court, is still entitled to have his costs taxed on the High Court level: *Cronin v Astra Business Systems Ltd* [2003] 2 IR 603, HC and [2004] ITLR 5 July, SC. See also *O'Connor v Bus Átha Cliath* [2003] SC reported in *Law Society Gazette* (January/February 2004) 60.

In defended proceedings in the Circuit Court, if the relief granted could have been obtained in the District Court, the costs which will be allowed to a successful plaintiff are those which would have been recoverable in that court, except that the judge may withhold costs if he is of opinion that the case was one proper to have been prosecuted in that court: Circuit Court Rules 2001 Ord 66, r 11.

In the District Court, there is a *scale of costs*; where a person represents himself he may be allowed only his actual or necessary outlay: DCR 1997 Ord 51. For interest on costs, see *Lambert v Lambert* [1987] ILRM 390.

costs in civil proceedings, recovery of. There are three requirements to enable costs to be recovered by a party to litigation: (a) an order for costs had to be made in his favour; (b) the matters claimed as costs must have been properly incurred in the course of litigation; and (c) he must be under a legal liability to pay costs in the action: *A-G v Sligo Co Council* [1989] ILRM 785.

cottier. A letting by agreement or memorandum in writing of a dwelling-house or cottage without land or with any portion of land not exceeding half an acre, at a rent not exceeding £5 (€6.35) per year for one month or from month to month or for any lesser period and under which the landlord is bound to keep and maintain the dwelling-house or cottage in tenantable condition and repair: Deasy's Act 1860, s 81; Cottier Tenant (Ireland) Act 1856. Such tenancies have now become obsolete. See also Deasy's Act, s 84. See *Murphy v Kenny* [1930] 64 ILTR 179. The Law Reform Commission has recommended that ss 81–83 of Deasy's Act be repealed without replacement: *Consultation Paper on General Law of Landlord and Tenant Law* (LRC CP 28, 2003) para 18.45.

couchant. Cattle lying down.

council. See COUNTY COUNCIL; URBAN DISTRICT COUNCIL; BOROUGH.

Council of Europe. An international body, comprising 45 European parliamentary democracies, including Ireland, which promotes European co-operation in a number of fields, except defence, with particular emphasis on the safeguarding of human rights, improving the quality of life and strengthening democratic institutions. One of its early achievements was the drawing up of the European Convention on Human Rights. In 2004, there was one applicant country (Monaco) and five countries with observer status (Canada, Holy See, Japan, Mexico, and the United States). See website: *www.coe.int*. See COVENANT, DEED OF; CYBERCRIME; DATA PROTECTION CONVENTION; EUROPEAN CONVENTION ON HUMAN RIGHTS; PRISONER TRANSFER OF.

Council of Europe Development Bank. A bank, attached to the Council of Europe and administered under its supreme authority. It was previously known as the

'Resettlement Fund' but changed its name in 1999. The primary purpose of the bank is to help in solving the social problems with which European countries are or may be faced as a result of the presence of refugees, displaced persons or migrants consequent upon movements of refugees or other forced movements of populations and as a result of the presence of victims of natural or ecological disasters. The investment projects to which the Bank contributes may be intended either to help such people in the country in which they find themselves or to enable them to return to their countries of origin when the conditions for return are met or, where applicable, to settle in another host country.

The bank may also contribute to the realisation of approved investment projects which enable jobs to be created in disadvantaged regions, people in low income groups to be housed or social infrastructure to be created. Under draft legislation, provision is made for the approval of the terms of agreement establishing the bank: Council of Europe Development Bank Bill 2004.

Council of Ministers. The main decision-making institution of the European Community (qv), represented by one member from each member state, presided over by a President which office rotates every six months: EC Treaty, arts 202–210 of the consolidated (2002) version. The members must be at Ministerial level and be authorised to commit their government. The Council is sometimes referred to as the (a) *European Council* when the members are the heads of government, meeting 4 times a year to agree overall EU policy and to review progress, and (b) *Council of the European Union* when the members are government ministers, meeting regularly to take detailed decisions and to pass EU laws.

Decisions of the Council are taken either: unanimously, by a simple majority; or by *qualified majority* depending on the issue. Decisions in most areas are by qualified majority, in which case the votes of its members are weighed eg Ireland has three votes and the UK has ten votes out of the total weighed votes of 87. For a proposal to be carried, 62 votes out of the 87 are required (EC Treaty, art 205). Under the Nice Treaty (qv), when the EU comprises 27 member states, Ireland will have seven votes out of a total 345 and the UK will have 29. For a proposal to be carried, it will require 255 of the 345 votes, and also the

support of a majority of member states, representing 62% of the EU population. With 25 member states from 1 May 2004, the requirement is 232 out of 321 votes and the 62% population provision: draft Constitutional Treaty for the European Union (2003). This was changed in the proposed Treaty establishing a Constitution for Europe, agreed on 18 June 2004 but not yet ratified, to 55% of member states, representing 65% of the population. This Treaty also provides for a 'presidential team' of three persons for an 18-month period.

Qualified majority voting (QMV) has been in use since the EC was founded. The Nice Treaty provided for an expansion of areas requiring QMV eg areas such as trade in services, the appointment and members of the European Commission. Certain other areas still require unanimity eg taxation. For Council, see website: *www.ue.eu.int*. For Ireland's EU Presidency, see website: *www.eu2004.ie*. See COMMUNITY LAW; SINGLE EUROPEAN ACT.

Council of State. The advisory body established by the 1937 Constitution to aid and counsel the President of Ireland (qv) on all matters relating to the exercise and performance by her of her powers and functions (art 31). Its ex-officio members are: the Taoiseach, the Tánaiste, the Chief Justice, the Chairman of Dáil Éireann, the Chairman of Seanad Éireann, and the Attorney-General. In addition, the President may appoint not more than seven persons to be members; also every *former* President, Taoiseach and Chief Justice, able and willing to act is a member.

Council of the European Bars and Law Societies; CCBE. The membership organisation which represents the Bar and Law Societies of the member states in their dealings with the European institutions eg with the European Commission, the European Court of Justice and the Court of First Instance, the European Parliament and the European Court of Human Rights. See 'The man with Eurovision' by solicitor John Fish in *Law Society Gazette* (March 2002) 18. See BAR COUNCIL; LAW SOCIETY OF IRELAND.

Council of the Isles. The popular name given to the *British-Irish Council* provided for under the *Good Friday Agreement* (qv). The Council has the objective of promoting harmonious and mutually beneficial development of the totality of relationships among the people of the islands of the UK and Ireland. Membership comprises representatives of the British and Irish governments, the devolved institutions of Northern Ireland, Scotland and Wales, and the Isle of Man and the Channel Islands. The establishment of the Council was the subject of a supplemental agreement between the governments of Ireland and the UK, done at Dublin on 8 March 1999. The first meeting of the Council took place in 1999. See website: *www.british-irishcouncil.org*.

councillor. An elected or co-opted member of a local government body; there is no residence or property ownership requirement to be eligible: Electoral Act 1963. Persons are disqualified from being a member of a local authority in a variety of circumstances eg undergoing a prison sentence exceeding six months, convicted of corrupt practice, convicted of fraudulent or dishonest dealings affecting a local authority, being a Minister or a Minister of State: Local Government Act 1994, s 6 as amended by Local Elections (Disclosure of Donations and Expenditure) Act 1999, s 24. A person is also disqualified who fails to furnish statements of donations and election expenses, or who furnishes statements which are, to his knowledge, false or misleading (LE(DDE)A 1999, s 20). See also Local Government Act 2001, s 16(1).

councillor, disclosure of interest. A councillor who is a member of a planning authority is required to make a declaration in a prescribed form, at least once a year, of any estate or interest in land (except his private residence), and of any business and any occupation which relates to land: Planning and Development Act 2000, s 147. A councillor who has a pecuniary or other beneficial interest in a matter before the planning authority, is required to declare his interest before discussion of the matter commences, and he must withdraw from the meeting (PDA 2000, s 148(2)). It is an offence not to comply with these provisions. On conviction of an offence under ss 147 or 148, a councillor stands disqualified from being a member of the authority (PDA 2000, s 149). See Planning and Development Regulations 2001, SI No 600 of 2001, Pt 15, arts180–181. For previous

legislation, see Local Government (Planning and Development) Act 1976, ss 32 and 33(3).

There is also a prohibition on persons voting as members of a housing authority, or of certain committees, on resolutions or questions relating to any house or any land in which they are beneficially interested: Housing Act 1966, s 115. See CODE OF CONDUCT; LOCAL ELECTION.

councillor, retirement of. A special scheme was introduced in 1998, colloquially called the '*scrappage scheme*', under which long-serving councillors who retired before the 1999 local elections were paid a gratuity: Local Government Act 1998, s 12. The scheme was intended to give due recognition to the service of these councillors and to create openings for new councillors. For new scheme, see Local Authority Members (Gratuity) Regulations 2002, SI No 281 of 2002, (Amendment) Regulations 2002, SI No 378 of 2002 and (Amendment) Regulations 2003, SI No 302 of 2003.

counsel. See BARRISTER; SENIOR COUNSEL.

count. Sections in an *indictment*, each containing and charging a different offence. The test as to whether several counts should be heard together is whether the evidence in each count would be admissible on each of the other counts: *The People (DPP) v BK* [2000] 2 IR 199, CCA. To be so admissible, it is necessary for the probative value of such evidence to outweigh its prejudicial effect. See INDICTMENT; RECOUNT.

counter-offer. See OFFER.

counterclaim. A claim by a defendant for relief or remedy against a plaintiff and maintained in the same action. Where a defendant seeks to rely upon any grounds as supporting a counterclaim, he must in his defence, state specifically that he does so by counterclaim; if such counterclaim raises questions as between himself and the plaintiff along with any other person, he is required to add a title setting forth the names of the defendants to such cross-action: RSC Ord 21, rr 9–16.

For procedure dealing with counterclaims in the Circuit Court, see Circuit Court Rules 2001 Ord 15, rr 7 and 19; Ord 29, r 8; Ord 33, r 7; Ord 59, r 4(20); Ord 66, r 16. For provisions dealing with counterclaims in the District Court, see DCR 1997 Ord 41, rr 5–8; Ord 46, r 3. See also *Murphy v Hennessy* [1985] ILRM 100; *Re MV Anton Lopatin* [1995] 3 IR 503, HC.

A counterclaim in a personal injuries action is required to contain specified information, similar to that required in a personal injuries summons: Civil Liability and Courts Act 2004, s 12. See DEFENCE; PLEADINGS; SET OFF.

counterfeit. A *counterfeit* includes things which resemble currency notes and coins, on one side only or on both, to such an extent as to be reasonably capable of passing for a currency note or coin: Criminal Justice (Theft and Fraud Offences) Act 2001, s 32. It is an offence to make a counterfeit currency note or coin intending to pass it as genuine in the State or in any member state of the EU, to have possession or control of such counterfeits, or materials or implements for making counterfeits, or to import or export counterfeits (CJ(T-FO)A 2001, 33–38). A designated body (eg banks and building societies) is required to transmit to the Central Bank any notes or coins received by it which it suspects are counterfeit (CJ(TFO)A 2001, s 39).

The making or issuing of any piece of metal or mixed metal of any value whatsoever as a coin or token for money or purporting that the holder thereof is entitled to demand any value denoted thereon, is an indictable offence (qv): Decimal Currency Act 1969, s 14 as amended by Economic and Monetary Union Act 1998, s 12 to prohibit counterfeiting of *euro* coins of the State or of participating member states. For counterfeiting currency notes or postal stamps, see Central Bank Act 1942, s 56; Post Office Act 1908, s 65. Where the intent is to deceive or defraud, the offence is that of forgery.

Previously, the making of false or counterfeit coins was a felony: Coinage Act 1861; Currency Act 1927, s 11. The possession of any false or counterfeit coins was a *misdemeanour*, as was the uttering of such coins (CA 1861, since repealed by the CJ(TFO)A 2001, s 3 and Sch 1). [Bibliography: McGreal C.] See CURRENCY, FOREIGN; FORGERY.

counterpart. A lease is generally prepared in two identical forms, one called a lease and the other a counterpart, the lease being signed by the lessor and the counterpart by the lessee and then exchanged and signed. The contents of a lease may be proved by its counterpart: Deasy's Act 1860, s 23. See *Jagoe v Harrington* [1882] 10 LR Ir 335. See *Consultation Paper on General Law of Landlord and Tenant Law* (LRC CP 28, 2003) para 18.15.

county borough. See BOROUGH.

county charge. A charge levied by a county council on a *town council*, which is a rating authority, in respect of services provided or functions carried out by the county council in relation to the town: Local Government Act 2001, s100.

county council. A county council means a local authority to which Local Government Act 2001, s 11(3)(a) relates ie the primary unit of local government of a county set out in Part I of Schedule 5: Local Government Act 2001, s 2(1). A county council is a body corporate with perpetual succession, with power to sue and to be sued in its corporate name, and with a seal which must be judicially noticed (LGA 2001, s 11(7)).

County Councils are *housing authorities* under the Housing Acts 1966 to 1988; *planning authorities* under the Planning and Development Act 2000, s 2(1); *fire authorities* under the Fire Services Act 1981. They are also *sanitary authorities* in respect of sewers, water supply, dangerous buildings, abatement of nuisances, refuse collection and street cleaning, baths, wash-houses, bathing places, sanitary conveniences, offensive trades, burial grounds, temporary dwellings, building bye-laws, street lighting, markets and slaughterhouses (qqv).

Many important functions relating to health matters, formerly the responsibility of county councils, were transferred to the health boards under the Health Act 1970. See LOCAL AUTHORITY; LOCAL GOVERNMENT, ELECTION OF; GRAND JURY; BOARDS OF GUARDIANS; BOROUGH; HEALTH BOARD.

county development board. Provision has been made for the establishment on a statutory basis of *County or City Development Boards*, whose function is to develop a strategy for the economic, social and cultural development of their areas: Local Government Act 2001, s 129.

county enterprise boards. Bodies established for the purpose of promoting and assisting economic development within their areas of operation and incorporated as companies limited by guarantee under the

Companies Act 1963: Industrial Development Act 1995, s 10 as amended by Industrial Development (Science Foundation Ireland) Act 2003, s 36. Provision has been made for the establishment of 35 such bodies: IDA 1995, Sch.

county manager. The person responsible for the efficient and effective operation of the local authorities for which he has responsibility and for ensuring the implementation, without due delay, of the decisions of the elected councils: Local Government Act 2001, s 144–154. Each county and city is required to have a manager, the county manager also being the manager of every *town council* in his administrative area (LGA 2001, s 144).

The manager is an employee of the council and has the duty to carry into effect all lawful directions of the council in relation to their *reserved* functions (LGA 2001, s 132). Every function of a local authority which is not a reserved function, is an *executive* function; it is the duty of the manager to exercise and perform the executive functions (LGA 2001, s 149).

The position of manager is, subject to s 145, an office to which the Local Authorities (Officers and Employees) Act 1926 applies (LGA 2001, s 144(8)).

For previous legislation, see County Management Act 1940, s 1; Local Government Act 1941, s 23(1)); Local Government Act 1991, s 47 and Local Government (Tenure of Office) Order 1991, SI No 128 of 1991; Local Government Act 2000, s 1; Local Government (Tenure of Office of Manager) Regulations 2003, SI No 47 of 2003; Local Government Act 1994, s 51. See *East Wicklow Conservation Community Ltd v Wicklow County Council* [1996] 3 IR 175, SC.

[Bibliography: Canny (2); Collins N.] See SECTION 3 AND 4 RESOLUTION; EMERGENCY.

county registrar. (1) An officer of the court attached to the Circuit Court office in each county: Court Officers Act 1926, s 35 as amended by Courts and Court Officers Act 1995, s 51.

(2) Means the Registrar in any County attached to the Circuit Court under the Court Officers Act 1926, and any Act amending or extending the same, and includes any deputy County Registrar and any person appointed to act as such Registrar: Circuit Court Rules 2001, *Interpretation of Terms*, para 5. The Orders which the County Registrar is empowered to make are set out in Ord 18.

The County Registrar sits as registrar to the Circuit Court judge assigned to the county. Apart from controlling and managing the Circuit Court office, he is responsible, outside the Counties of Dublin and Cork, as sheriff, for executing all orders of the court lodged with him for execution and for elections and referenda; these specific functions are the responsibility of independent sheriffs in Counties Dublin and Cork.

A county registrar may make a wide range of orders, and may even try an issue of fact with the consent of all the parties concerned (CCOA 1995, s 34 and Sch 2). There is provision to extend the powers of the county registrar even further on a date to be determined by the Minister: Courts and Court Officers Act 2002, s 22. It is now legally possible for a county registrar to carry out the duties of another county registrar (CCOA 2002, s 23). County registrars are answerable to the Board of the Courts Service through the Chief Executive but only in so far as their court-related administrative functions are concerned: Courts Service Act 1998, ss 9, 20 and 31.

A solicitor or barrister of not less than eight years' standing may be appointed county registrar. Provision is made for the poundage fees of a county registrar or sheriff in relation to the execution of an order of the court: Finance Act 1988, s 71. See now Taxes Consolidation Act 1997, s 1006. The certificate from the Collector-General to the county registrar, certifying the amount of an outstanding tax liability in default for collection, may now be issued in an electronic format (TCA 1997, s 962 as amended by Finance Act 2004, s 84). For warrant of county registrar, see DCR 1997 Ord 48, r 1(2). See Civil Liability and Courts Act 2004, s 44. See DISTRICT PROBATE; RETURNING OFFICER; SIDE-BAR ORDERS; SUBPOENA; TAXATION OF COSTS.

county road. See PUBLIC ROAD.

course of trade. The term which is of significance in relation to trade marks and any infringement thereof. See *Bank of Ireland v Controller of Trade Marks* [1987] HC. See also *Gallagher (Dublin) Ltd v Health Education Bureau* [1982] ILRM 240; *ITT World Directories Inc v Controller of Patents, Designs and Trade Marks* [1985] ILRM 30; *Eurocard International v Controller of Trade Marks* [1987] HC.

The term 'course of trade' is also important as regards income tax. See *Browne v Bank of Ireland Finance Ltd* [1991] 9 ILT Dig 268, SC. See TRADE MARK.

court. A place where justice is administered; the judge or judges who sit in court. Justice is required to be administered in courts established by law by judges appointed in the manner provided by the Constitution: 1937 Constitution, art 34. The *superior* courts are the High Court and the Supreme Court as required by the Constitution; other courts, known as *inferior* courts, of a limited and local nature, are established by statute eg District Court and Circuit Court: Courts (Establishment and Constitution) Act 1961. These *ordinary* courts also include the Central Criminal Court and the Court of Criminal Appeal. There are also *special* courts (qv) which may be established under the Constitution. A person may use either of the official languages of the State in any court: Official Languages Act 2003, s 8. The court has a duty to ensure that any person appearing in or giving evidence before it, may be heard in the official language of his choice, and the court may provide for simultaneous or consecutive interpretation to ensure that no person is placed at a disadvantage. [Bibliography: Daly B D (4); Delaney H; Kotsonouris (2).] See RULES OF COURT; TIME, COURT RULES.

court costume. See DRESS IN COURT.

court fees. It has been held that the imposition of charges for and in respect of court services is not unconstitutional provided such charges are reasonable: *Murphy v Minister for Justice* [2001] 2 ILRM 144, SC and 1 IR 95. In this case the relevant constitutional right was the right to have access to the courts to defend or vindicate a right. Responsibility for the collection of court fees has been transferred to the Courts Service as from 23 January 2004: Courts Service Act 1998, Sch 2 as amended by SI No 35 of 2004.

court forms. Many court forms (eg a *plenary summons*) are now available for download from the Courts Service's website: *www.courts.ie*.

court jurisdiction. See JURISDICTION.

court system, review of. The Chief Justice announced on 10 January 2002, the setting up of a working group to carry out a root-and-branch examination of the organisation of the court system and to recommend any necessary changes to allow for the fair, expeditious and economic administration of justice. The working group, which is chaired by Supreme Court Judge Mr Justice Fennelly, is broadly representative of bodies, both public and private, interested in or affected by the functioning of the courts. The first recommendations of the group on the criminal courts were published on 15 July 2003. See *Report of the Working Group on the Criminal Jurisdiction of the Courts* (2003), available on website: *www.courts.ie*. See 'What is coming down the tracks in Ireland' by Mr Justice Paul Carney in *Bar Review* (April 2003) 76.

courthouse. Formerly, every local authority was required to provide and maintain in its functional area courthouse accommodation for the sitting of any court which was held in its area, as the Minister directed either generally or in any particular case: Courthouse (Provision and Maintenance) Act 1935. See *Hoey v Minister for Justice* [1994] 1 ILRM 334, HC. This is now the function of the new *Courts Service*, the 1935 Act having been repealed: Courts Service Act 1998, s 26. Responsibility for the *Four Courts* in Dublin remains with the Office of Public Works (OPW). See COURTS SERVICE; FOUR COURTS.

Court of Criminal Appeal. The court which hears appeals from the judgments of the Central Criminal Court, the Circuit Criminal Court and the Special Criminal Court: Courts (Establishment and Constitution) Act 1961. The court consists of one Supreme Court judge and two judges of the High Court. Provision has been made for the powers, jurisdiction and functions of the *Court of Criminal Appeal* and of the *Courts-Martial Appeal Court* to be vested in the *Supreme Court*: Courts and Court Officers Act 1995, ss 4–5. An order to bring this into operation had not been made by 1 September 2004 and there were no plans to make such an order.

An appeal to the Court of Criminal Appeal is not a rehearing of the case but is based on a transcript (qv) of the evidence and is usually confined to points of law or that the verdict was against the weight of the evidence. The Court, however, cannot substitute its own subjective view of evidence for the verdict of a jury: *DPP v Egan* [1990] ITLR (8 October), SC. The court can consider grounds of appeal which are contradictory to the trial submission: *DPP v Hardy* [1992] ITLR (16 November), SC.

The decision of the court is by a majority and only one judgment is given.

It has been held that the fundamental principle underlying the jurisdiction of the Court of Criminal appeal was that it had the power and jurisdiction to do justice in the case before it: *The People (DPP) v MS* [2000] 2 IR 592, CCA and [2000] 2 ILRM 311, CCA.

A determination by the court is final (qv), except that an appeal can lie to the Supreme Court on a point of law of exceptional public importance: Courts of Justice Act 1924, s 29; *Pringle v Ireland* [1994] 1 ILRM 467, HC; *The People (DPP) v D K* [2002] 3 IR 534, CCA. The Supreme Court has held that while the wording of s 29 of the 1924 Act was obscure and ambiguous, the intention of the Oireachtas was not to confer a right of appeal on the Attorney-General in addition to the the right of appeal conferred on accused persons: *People (DPP) v O'Callaghan* [2004] FL 8706, SC and 1 ILRM 431.

When hearing an appeal from the Special Criminal Court, the Court of Criminal Appeal considers whether any inference of fact drawn by that court could properly be supported by the evidence: *People v Madden* [1977] IR 336 cited in *People (DPP) v Farrell* [1993] ILRM 743, CCA. When hearing appeals from courts martial, the court is known as the *Courts-Martial Appeal Court*.

The Court of Criminal Appeal was given a new role in 1993 of reviewing the sentence imposed by a court which appears to the DPP to be unduly lenient: Criminal Justice Act 1993, s 2. See RSC Ord 86 as amended by Rules of the Superior Courts (No 2) of 1993, SI No 265 of 1993, para 5.

Also provision was made for the use by the Court of a sound recording or videotape of the proceedings of the trial court in addition to the transcript verified by the trial judge: Criminal Justice (Miscellaneous Provisions) Act 1997, s 7. See BOOK OF EVIDENCE; MISCARRIAGE; REVIEW OF SENTENCE.

court of first instance. See FIRST INSTANCE, COURT OF.

court of justice. See EUROPEAN COURT OF JUSTICE.

court of last resort. A court from which there is no appeal.

court of record. A court which has the records of its acts and judicial proceedings maintained and preserved and which has power to fine and imprison for contempt (qv) of its authority. The Supreme, High and Circuit Courts are courts of record as is the District Court: Courts (Supplemental Provisions) Act 1961, ss 7, 8 and 21; Courts Act 1971, s 13 respectively.

court poor box. The non-statutory procedure adopted by the courts over many years, particularly in the District Court, whereby the defendant is not convicted of the offence charged, even though the prosecution has proved its case, on the basis that a contribution is made to the 'court poor box', the contents of which are given to various charities. This procedure is adopted where the judge takes the view that it is not appropriate to enter a conviction, particularly against a young person, and particularly where the judge anticipates that the defendant will not commit another offence. Some concern has been expressed on the need to ensure equal treatment for offenders from different economic backgrounds and the need for accountability on the use of the funds generated. The Law Reform Commission has published a Consultation Paper which proposes to replace the present scheme with a 'Court Charity Fund' to be placed on a statutory basis: *Consultation Paper on the Court Poor Box* (LRC CP 31, 2004). See also 'The Court Poor Box' by Charles Lysaght BL in *Bar Review* (July 2004) 124. See PROBATION OF OFFENDERS.

court protection of company. A legal mechanism for the rescue or reconstruction of ailing but potentially viable companies: Companies (Amendment) Act 1990 as amended by Companies (Amendment) (No 2) Act 1999. The central feature of the provision is the appointment by the court of an *examiner* and the placing of the company concerned under the protection of the court for 70 days. While the company is so protected, it may not be wound up, a receiver may not be appointed, and generally debts or securities may not be executed against it except with the consent of the examiner.

If the examiner considers it appropriate and if it is possible, the company should be maintained as a going concern during the period of protection: *ReHolidair Ltd* [1994] 1 ILRM 481, SC and 1 IR 416. Also pre-petition debts may be paid where so recommended by the independent accountant (C(A)(No 2)A 1999, s 15).

The appointment of the examiner does not automatically suspend the directors' management powers, although the examiner can apply to the court to have all or any of the directors' functions or powers exercised or performed only by him (C(A)A 1990, s 9). A duty is imposed on the examiner, on appointment and after his investigation, to disclose to the court if misleading information in relation to assets or liabilities had led to his appointment: *Re Wogans (Drogheda) Ltd* [1992] HC. Also, where the court, having considered the independent accountant's report, is of the opinion that there are serious irregularities in the company's affairs, the court is required to hold a hearing to consider the matter (C(A)(No 2)A 1999, s 21)

Priority is given to the costs, remuneration and expenses of the examiner which have been sanctioned by the court; however, liabilities incurred by the company during the protection period rank after any claim secured by mortgage, charge, lien or other encumbrance of a fixed nature (C(A)A 1990, s 29 as amended by C(A)(No 2)A 1999, s 28).

See *Re Don Bluth Entertainment Ltd* [1994] 2 ILRM 436, SC and 3 IR 141; *In the Matter of Springline Ltd* [1998] 1 ILRM 301, HC and [1999] 1 ILRM 15, SC and 1 IR 467; *Re Cavan Crystal Ltd* [1998] 3 IR 570, SC. See also Companies Act 1990, ss 180–181; Companies (Forms) Order 1990, SI No 224 of 1990. See RSC Ord 75A inserted by Rules of Superior Courts (No 3) 1991, SI No 147 of 1991 for rules governing the procedures to be followed. See also Credit Union Act 1997, ss 142–158, as amended by Central Bank and Financial Services Authority of Ireland Act 2003, s 25. [Bibliography: Forde (9); O'Donnell.] See DISQUALIFICATION ORDER; EXAMINATION RE COMPANY; FLOATING CHARGE; GUARANTEE; OPPRESSION OF SHAREHOLDER; RECEIVER, COMPANY; REPUDIATION.

court protection of company, petition for. A petition to appoint an examiner must be accompanied by a report (a *pre-petition* report) of an independent accountant containing specified information: Companies (Amendment) Act 1990, s 3 as amended by Companies (Amendment) (No 2) Act 1999, s 7. In exceptional circumstances the court is empowered to give protection to the company for ten days pending the submission of the report (C(A)(No 2)A 1999, s 9). The court will not give a hearing to a petition until security for costs has been given as the court considers reasonable (C(A)(No 2)A 1999, s 8). Creditors must be given an opportunity to be heard (C(A)(No 2)A 1999, s 9).

An examiner may be appointed by the court where: (a) the company is or is likely to be unable to pay its debts, and (b) no order has been made and no resolution subsists for its winding up, and (c) the court is satisfied that there is a reasonable prospect of the survival of the company or part of it as a *going concern* (C(A)A 1990, s 2 as amended by C(A)(No 2)A 1999, s 5). See *Re Tuskar Resources plc* [2001] 1 IR 668, HC. Previously, the petitioner did not have to establish as a matter of probability that the company was capable of surviving as a going concern: *Re Atlantic Magnetics Ltd* [1992] ITLR (16 March), SC and [1993] 2 IR 561, SC. See also *Re Jetmara Teo* [1992] 10 ILT Dig 197, HC. See 'Oil in Trouble Waters – Tuskar Resources and the 1999 Act' by John O'Donnell SC in *Bar Review* (March/April 2002).

court protection of company, scheme of arrangement. If the examiner appointed by the court, in relation to a company under protection, considers that the company, or part of it, can be saved and that this would be more advantageous than a winding up, the examiner is required to formulate proposals for a *compromise* or *scheme of arrangement* within 35 days of appointment: Companies (Amendment) Act 1990, s 18 as amended by Companies (Amendment) (No 2) Act 1999, s 22. This must be put to appropriate meetings of members and creditors for information. If the court confirms the proposal, it becomes binding on those concerned and the examiner's appointment will be terminated. While the court has the power to make modifications to a *scheme of arrangement*, it will not make modifications which would require new creditors' meetings: *Re Antigen Holdings Ltd* [2001] 4 IR 600, HC.

It has been held that where the examiner's proposal is rejected by the court because it contains defects which are not remediable, the examiner's costs and expenses will be refused: *Re Wogan (Drogheda)* (1993) Irish Times, 10th February.

court sittings. See SITTINGS OF COURT.

courts-martial. A military tribunal for the trial of a member of the defence forces on active service. It has been held that the failure to provide a member of the defence forces with *legal representation* at the preliminary stages of an investigation, did not imperil a fair hearing or fair result or cause injustice to the accused, because he was not put in peril until the hearing of the courts-martial, at which he would have legal representation, and the sworn evidence obtained during the investigation would not be placed before the courts-martial where the accused pleaded not guilty: Rules of Procedure (Defence Forces) 1954, SI No 243 of 1954; *Scariff v Taylor* [1996] 2 ILRM 278, SC and 1 IR 242.

The choice by an accused of an alternative representative does not breach court-martial rules: *Private William Murphy (appellant)* [1993] ITLR (1 March) and 11 ILT Dig [1993] 187. The court review of an alleged *miscarriage* of justice or excessive sentence also applies in the case of a conviction by a courts-martial: Criminal Procedure Act 1993, s 6. See *Re Gunner Buckley* [1998] 2 IR 454, CMAC.

See 1937 Constitution, art 38(4); Courts-Martial Appeals Act 1983; Courts-Martial (Legal Aid) Regulations 1987, SI No 46 of 1987. See Rules of the Superior Courts (No 2) 2000, SI No 105 of 2000 as amended by SI No 646 of 2003. See Criminal Law (Insanity) Bill 2002, s 16. See Criminal Justice (Safety of United Nations Workers) Act 2000, s 6. [Reports: Frewen.] See CONTEMPT OF COURT; MISCARRIAGE.

courts-martial appeal court. See COURT OF CRIMINAL APPEAL.

Courts Service. A corporate body, independent in the performance of its functions, which are: (a) to manage the courts, (b) to provide support services for the judges, (c) to provide information on the courts system to the public, (d) to provide, manage and maintain court buildings, and (e) to provide facilities for users of the courts: Courts Service Act 1998, ss 4–5. The judicial independence of judges and of persons carrying out quasi-judicial functions (eg county registrars) is protected (CSA 1998, s 9).

The Board of the Courts Service comprises 17 persons, including nine judges, the Chief Executive Officer and seven others, including a practising solicitor and barrister. The CEO's primary function is to manage and control generally the staff, administration and business of the court

service and he is responsible to the Board for the performance of his functions and the implementation of the policies of the Board (CSA 1998, s 20 as amended by Courts and Court Officers Act 2002, s 43).

The 2002 Act restores the exemption which the Court Service enjoys from certain planning permission requirements, and which, inadvertently, was not carried forward in the Planning and Development Act 2000; the Court Service is deemed to be a State Authority for the purposes of s 181(1) of PDA 2000 (CCOA 2002, s 44). The 2002 Act also made a number of amendments of an administrative nature to CSA 1998 (CCOA 2002, ss 38–42). See also website: *www.courts.ie*. [Bibliography: Delaney H (1).] See COUNTY REGISTRAR; COURTHOUSE; RESERVED JUDGMENT.

covenant. (1) An international agreement providing for binding legal obligations. See HUMAN RIGHTS, COVENANTS ON.

(2) A clause, usually in a deed, which binds a party to do some act or to refrain from doing some act. No technical words are necessary to constitute a covenant: *Lant v Norris* [1757] 1 Burr 287.

Usual covenants in a lease refer to the covenant of the landlord that the tenant will have quiet enjoyment; and refer to the covenants of the tenant to pay the rent and rates; to keep the premises in repair and to deliver them up at the end of the tenancy in good repair; to permit the landlord to enter and inspect the premises from time to time.

Restrictive covenants in certain leases, absolutely prohibiting a change in use or improvements, are to be construed as prohibiting same without the licence or consent of the lessor, which shall not be unreasonably withheld: Landlord and Tenant (Amendment) Act 1980, ss 64–69. There may be a refusal of consent based on valid estate management grounds: *OHS Ltd v Green Property Co Ltd* [1986] ILRM 451. A restrictive covenant (eg not to build a structure in excess of a certain height) is enforceable by a tenant against the assignee of the landlord: *Tulk v Moxhay* [1848] 2 Ph 774; *Whelan v Cork Corporation* [1991] ILRM 19, HC.

A *restrictive covenant* in relation to the sale of land is not in the nature of a *restraint of trade*, as in a restraint of trade a person gives up a freedom he previously had. In the case of a restrictive covenant, since a purchaser had no previous right to be there at all, when he takes up possession of newly purchased land subject to a restrictive covenant, he gives up no right or freedom which he previously had: *Sibra Building Co Ltd v Ladgrove Stores Ltd* [1998] 2 IR 590, SC.

For discussion on how restrictive covenants might be discharged, see *Lyall* in 9 ILT & SJ (1991) 156.

A covenant is said to *run with the land* when the advantage or liability of it passes to the assignee of the land. Covenants may be registered as burdens affecting registered land: Registration of Title Act 1964, s 69. See also Deasy's Act 1860, ss 41–42. See *Hampshire v Wickens* [1878] 7 Ch D 555; *White v Carlisle Trust Ltd* [1977] HC; *Green Property Co Ltd v Shalame Modes Ltd* [1978] HC; *Belmont Securities Ltd v Crean* [1989] 7 ILT Dig 22. See Residential Tenancies Act 2004, s 193(d). For Law Reform Commission proposals on the enforceability of freehold covenants, see Report on *Positive Covenants over freehold land and other proposals* (LRC 70, 2003). See also *Consultation Paper on General Law of Landlord and Tenant Law* (LRC CP 28, 2003) paras 18.42–18.44. [Bibliography: Pearce & Mee; Power A.] See FREEHOLD COVENANT; GROUND RENT; PRIVITY OF CONTRACT; RESTRAINT OF TRADE; SET OFF.

covenant, deed of. A person may covenant to make annual payments to a relevant beneficiary for a minimum period whereby his own total income for tax purposes is reduced and the beneficiary's income is thereby increased: Income Tax Act 1967, s 439 as amended. See now Taxes Consolidation Act 1997, s 792. The minimum period is three years where the beneficiary is a university or college in the State for research or a body having consultative status with the United Nations (qv) or the Council of Europe (qv) which promotes human rights. The period in the case of an individual beneficiary must exceed six years and the beneficiary must be aged 65 or over, or permanently mentally or physically incapacitated. In general the maximum part of the donor's income which may be covenanted, and therefore be treated as income of the covenantee, is 5%. This limit and the time periods do not apply to a payment entirely given to the covenantee which arises from capital. See Revenue Leaflet IT7, Covenants to Individuals; and Revenue Leaflets CHY5 and CHY6, Deeds of covenant for the conduct of Research. [Bibliography: Judge.]

covenant to insure. A lease will often have a covenant requiring the lessee to reimburse the lessor in respect of the cost of insuring the demised premises. There is a heavy onus of proof on a lessee who challenges the lessor's insurance charges; it is not sufficient for the lessee to show that a quotation for a smaller figure could be obtained elsewhere: *Sepes Establishment v KSK Enterprises Ltd* [1993] ILRM 46, HC. In relation to tenancies of dwellings, see LANDLORD, OBLIGATIONS OF.

cover note. A document issued by an insurer to the insured covering risks until issue of a policy of insurance. It is a separate contract distinct from the policy and is operative for a specific period. In marine insurance, the contract is deemed to be concluded when the proposal of the assured is accepted by the insurer, whether the policy is issued or not; for the purposes of showing when the proposal was accepted, reference may be made to the slip or covering note or other customary memorandum of the contract: Marine Insurance Act 1906, s 21. See *Mackie v European Assurance Society* [1869] 21 LT 102.

covert take-over. An EC directive, aimed at identifying any person launching a covert take-over bid for a company, requires obligatory disclosure by a person who acquires or sells a large number of shares in a company: Directive 88/627/EEC. This directive is given effect in the State by the Companies Act 1990 which requires any person who acquires or disposes of shares of a public limited company, which is officially listed on the Irish Stock Exchange, to notify the Exchange when, following such acquisition or disposal, his shareholding exceeds or falls below the 10%, 25%, 50% or 75% disclosure thresholds (CA 1990, ss 89–96).

The Exchange must publish this information unless it considers that this would be contrary to the public interest or seriously detrimental to the company or companies concerned. The disclosure requirements continue to operate even during *price stabilising* activity: Companies (Amendment) Act 1999, s 3(2).

There is now a duty on the Stock Exchange to advise the Director of Corporate Enforcement whenever it appears to the Exchange that there has been a failure by a person to notify the Exchange on the acquisition and disposal of shares which exceeds or falls below the reporting thresholds: CA 1990, s 92 as amended by Company Law Enforcement Act 2001, s 36. See IRISH TAKE-OVER PANEL; PRICE STABILISING; SHARES, DISCLOSURE OF; TAKE-OVER.

coverture. The condition of being a married woman.

cpt. See PUBLIC LIMITED COMPANY.

crash helmet. The driver of a motor cycle and a passenger carried on a motorcycle must each wear a crash helmet while the motor cycle is used in a public place: Road Traffic (Construction, Equipment and use of Vehicles) (Amendment) (No 2) Regulations, 1978, SI No 360 of 1978.

creche. See PRE-SCHOOL SERVICE.

credibility. Worthy of belief. It has been held that it would be an injustice if the Supreme Court, on appeal, were to reject the determination of a court of trial as to the *credibility* of witnesses who gave evidence before it except in cases of manifest perversity: *People v Mulligan 2 Frewen 16* cited in *DPP v Egan* [1990] ILRM 780, SC. See also dictum (qv) in *Northern Bank Finance Corporation Ltd v Charlton* [1979] IR 172 at 181. See *DPP v McDonagh and Cawley* [1991] 9 ILT Dig 171, CCA. See Children Act 1997, s 25; Refugee Act 1996, s 11B inserted by Immigration Act 2003, s 7(f). [Bibliography: Healy.] See DOCUMENTARY EVIDENCE; PREVIOUS STATEMENT, INCONSISTENT.

credit. (1) The time which a creditor allows his debtor to pay a debt; the total amount he permits the debtor to borrow or to owe. *Credit* includes a deferred payment, cash loan, or any other form of financial accommodation: Consumer Credit Act 1995, s 2(1); Money Advice and Budgeting Service Bill 2002, s 1(1). See MONEY ADVICE AND BUDGETING SERVICE.

(2) Cross-examination *as to credit* means asking questions of a witness with the objective of testing his credibility. See CONVICTION, EVIDENCE OF; EXAMINATION.

credit, letter of. See LETTER OF CREDIT.

credit agreement. An agreement whereby a creditor grants or promises to grant to a consumer a credit in the form of a deferred payment, a cash loan or other similar financial accommodation: Consumer Credit Act 1995, s 2(1). A credit agreement must provide for a *cooling-off period* (qv) (CCA 1995, s 30) and where for a cash loan, must contain a *statement* of specified matters e g interest charged and Annual Percentage Charge (APR), number of instalments,

total amount payable and termination conditions (CCA 1995, s 31). See also CCA 1995, Sch 3, Pt I. [Bibliography: Bird; Long.] See ANNUAL PERCENTAGE CHARGE; COOLING-OFF PERIOD.

credit by fraud, obtaining. It is an offence for a bankrupt (qv) or arranging debtor (qv), to obtain credit without disclosing the fact that he is a bankrupt or arranging debtor: Bankruptcy Act 1988, s 129.

It was an offence for a person, in incurring any debt or liability, to obtain credit under false pretences, or by means of any other fraud: Debtors (Ireland) Act 1872, s 13(1), since repealed by the Criminal Justice (Theft and Fraud Offences) Act 2001, s 3 and Sch 1. See now DECEPTION.

credit card. A credit instrument issued to an individual by a bank (qv) or other body by means of which cash, goods or services may be obtained by the individual on credit on production of the instrument, the issuer undertaking to pay the supplier of the cash, goods or services in return for payment to him (the issuer) by the individual. A credit card is also defined in a number of statutes e g it is a card issued by a credit institution by means of which goods, services or cash may be obtained by an individual on credit and amounts in respect of the goods, services or cash may be charged to the credit card account of the individual: Consumer Credit Act 1995, s 2(1). A *credit agreement* operated by means of a credit card must contain certain specified information e g the credit limit if any, the interest charged and the APR, terms of use and repayment, and means and cost of termination (CCA 1995, s 31(2)). See also *Diners Club Ltd v Revenue Commissioners* [1988] IR 158, HC; *Eurocard International v Controller of Trade Marks* [1987] HC.

The stamp duty on credit cards and charge cards is now €40 per card per annum: Finance Act 2003, s 140. See also Stamp Duties Consolidation Act 1999, s 124. [Bibliography: Donnelly.] See IRISH PAYMENT SERVICES ORGANISATION.

credit guarantee insurance. In a particular case it was held that a credit guarantee insurance agreement was a *contract of guarantee* and not a contract of insurance: *International Commercial Bank plc v Insurance Corp of Ireland* [1990] ITLR (3 December), HC. In that case, the indemnifier agreed in the event of default of the principal debtor repaying a loan from the creditor, the indemnifier would pay all moneys due, the principal debtor having paid the indemnifier a premium for such indemnity. See CONTRACT OF GUARANTEE.

credit institution. (1) An undertaking, other than a credit union or friendly society, whose business it is to receive deposits or other repayable funds from the public and to grant credit on its own account: EC (Licensing and Supervision of Credit Institutions) Regulations 1992, SI No 395 of 1992 as amended, to correct an error, by SI No 86 of 2003. These regulations, implementing EC Directive 89/646/EEC, lay down common Community-wide provisions for the licensing and supervision of credit institutions and the provision of banking services in the EC. See also Central Bank and Financial Services Authority of Ireland Act 2004, s 10(3), Sch 2.

(2) A holder of a licence under the Central Bank Act 1971, a building society, a trustee savings bank, any other deposit-taking institution supervised by the Central Bank or a credit institution authorised in a member state of the Community: EC (Consolidated Supervision of Credit Institutions) Regulations 1992, SI No 396 of 1992 as amended by Central Bank and Financial Services Authority of Ireland Act 2003, s 35, Sch 2 and Central Bank and Financial Services Authority of Ireland Act 2004, s 34, Sch 4. These regulations, implementing EC Directive 92/30/EEC, require the Central Bank to supervise credit institutions and their subsidiary and associated companies on a consolidated basis ie taking account of the entire group activity and relationships rather than on a single company basis. See also Stock Exchange Act 1995, s 3(1); Consumer Credit Act 1995, s 2(1), both Acts as amended by CBFSAIA 2003, s 35, Sch 1.

The definition of credit institution now includes Arnotts plc, Asgard Financial Services Ltd, Irish Permanent (IOM) Ltd, Lombard & Ulster Banking Ltd, Vodaphone Ireland plc, FAI Finance Corporation Ltd, and CIT Group Finance (Ireland) Ltd: Consumer Credit Act 1995 (Section 2) Regulations 2001, SI No 432 of 2001 and Regulations 2002, SIs Nos 142 and 339 of 2002 and Regulations 2004, SIs Nos 93 and 414 of 2004. See EC (Credit Institutions: Accounts) Regulations 1992, SI No 294 of 1992, as amended by SI No 84 of 2003 to enable credit institutions to include in their accounts, interest from

trading activity either in the institution's net interest line, or its dealing profits line. See EC (Electronic Money) Regulations 2002, SI No 221 of 2002 as amended by CBFSAIA 2003, s 35, Sch 2 and CBFSAIA 2004, s 10(3), Sch 2. See EC (Reorganisation and Winding-Up of Credit Institutions) Regulations 2004, SI No 198 of 2004. [Bibliography: Bird; Donnelly.] See INVESTOR COMPENSATION SCHEME; OMBUDSMAN FOR THE CREDIT INSTITUTIONS.

credit intermediary. A person, who in the course of his business, arranges or offers to arrange for a consumer the provision of credit or the letting of goods in return for a commission, payment or consideration of any kind from the provider of the credit or the owner of the goods, as the case may be: Consumer Credit Act 1995, s 2(1). A credit intermediary is required to have an *authorisation* from the Director of Consumer Affairs and a *letter of recognition* from each undertaking for which he is a credit intermediary (CCA 1995, s 144 as amended by Central Bank and Financial Services Authority of Ireland Act 2003, s 35, Sch 1.) Alternatively, he must hold a *mortgage intermediary's* authorisation. A credit intermediary is required to explain to the consumer the nature of the finance arranged (CCA 1995, s 148). See MORTGAGE INTERMEDIARY.

credit-sale agreement. A *credit agreement* for the sale of goods under which the purchase price, or part of it, is payable in instalments and the property in the goods passes to the buyer immediately upon the making of the agreement: Consumer Credit Act 1995, s 2(1). A credit-sale agreement must contain a statement of certain specified information eg total cost of credit, cash price of goods, details on instalments and interest (if any), and a description sufficient to identify the goods (CCA 1995, s 32).Unlike a hire-purchase agreement, ownership passes in a credit-sales agreement immediately and is not dependent on payment of the purchase price.

An agreement not coming within the definition of a credit-sale or hire-purchase agreement may still be subject to the Factors Act 1889. See *Leavy v Butler* [1893] 2 QB 318; *Helby v Matthews* [1895] AC 471. See Courts Act 1991, s 6(2). See RSC Ord 4, r 13; Ord 13, rr 3, 15; Ord 27, rr 2, 16. See ANNUAL PERCENTAGE CHARGE; PRICE CONTROL.

credit union. A society, consisting of at least 15 members with a *common bond,* which has as its objects: (a) the promotion of thrift among its members by the accumulation of their savings, (b) the creation of sources of credit for the mutual benefit of its members at a fair and reasonable rate of interest; and (c) the use and control of members' savings for their mutual benefit: Credit Union Act 1997, s 6 as amended by Central Bank and Financial Services Authority of Ireland Act 2003, s 35, Sch 1. The *common bond* includes those of association, employment, residence, and membership.

The 1997 Act consolidates credit union legislation and provides an updated framework for the development and regulation of the credit union movement. Limits have been set eg £30,000 (€38,092) on loans, £20,000 (€25,395) on deposits, £50,000 (€63,487) on shares including deposits.

The Minister is empowered to make regulations authorising credit unions to provide *will-making* and *probate* services and to have a scheme for the investigation of complaints in respect of such services: Solicitors (Amendment) Act 1994, ss 78–79, as amended by CBFSAIA 2003, s 35, Sch 1.

Dividends paid by credit unions are not *distributions* for tax purposes and consequently do not attract *dividend withholding tax*: Taxes Consolidation Act 1997, s 700 as amended by Finance Act 2000, s 32.

Under new tax arrangements however, a credit union member: (a) is liable to pay Deposit Interest Retention Tax (DIRT) on deposit interest at the standard rate of tax, (b) may opt to hold shares in a special share account, the dividends from which are liable to DIRT at 20%, and (c) may, as an individual, opt to hold shares in a *special term share account* for a term of three or five years, which terms attract a tax exemption in respect of dividends of the first €480 and €635 respectively, with dividends in excess of these amounts attracting DIRT at 20%: Finance Act 2001, s 57. Equivalent tax exemptions apply to interest on deposits held in special three and five-year term accounts with other relevant deposit-taking financial institutions. An individual may not hold a special term deposit account and a special term share account at the same time: Finance Act 2002, s 21. Also there is an exemption from DIRT in respect of dividends paid on shares in a credit union where the shares are held in a special share account within a *Special Saving Incentive Account* (qv): FA 2002, s 49. See also Euro Changeover (Amounts) Act 2001, s 6.

Since 2003, credit unions have come under the regulatory control of the Central Bank (IFSRA). For further amendments to CUA 1997, see Central Bank and Financial Services Authority of Ireland Act 2004, Sch 1 and 3. For regulations on the services which credit unions may offer which are exempt from specified additional service requirements, see SI No 223 of 2004. See *Prison Credit Union v Registrar of Friendly Societies* [1987] ILRM 367. For Irish League of Credit Unions, see website: *www.creditunion.ie.* [Bibliography: Quinn A.] See INCAPACITY; IRISH FINANCIAL SERVICES REGULATORY AUTHORITY; DEATH, EFFECT OF; PASSBOOK; SAVINGS PROTECTION SCHEME; REGISTRAR OF CREDIT UNIONS; REGISTRAR OF FRIENDLY SOCIETIES.

creditor. A person to whom a debt is owing. A *secured creditor* is one who holds a mortgage (qv), or charge (qv), or lien (qv) on the debtor's property eg Bankruptcy Act 1988, s 3. An *unsecured creditor* is one who does not so hold. A *judgment creditor* is a person in whose favour a judgment for a sum of money has been entered against the debtor. A *maintenance creditor* is the applicant spouse for a maintenance order.

A secured creditor of a bankrupt debtor has a right to realise his security outside of the bankruptcy: Bankruptcy Act 1988, s 136(2). See also BA 1988, Sch 1, para 24. Company directors have a duty to consider the interests of creditors of the company. See *McCann* in 9 ILT & SJ (1991) 30. However, any conveyance or assignment by a company of all its property to trustees for the benefit of its creditors is void: Companies Act 1963, s 286(2) as amended by the Companies Act 1990, s 135.

A 'creditor' within the meaning of s 12B(9) of the Companies (Amendment) Act 1982, inserted by s 46 of the Companies (Amendment) (No 2) Act 1999, in relation to an application to restore a company to the register of companies, must be interpreted so as to include prospective or contingent creditors: *In the matter of Deauville Communications Worldwide Ltd* [2002] 2 ILRM 388, SC and 2 IR 32. See BANKRUPTCY; CORRUPT AGREEMENT WITH CREDITOR; MAINTENANCE ORDER; WINDING UP.

creditor, statutory notice to. The statutory notice given by a personal representative (qv) to creditors with claims against the estate of a deceased, usually in practice by advertising twice at intervals of one week in a newspaper, with a time limit for receipt of claims expiring four weeks after the last insertion. Such notice gives statutory protection to the personal representative but does not prevent a creditor following the assets into the hands of any person who has received them. See Succession Act 1965, s 49.

creditors' assignee. See BANKRUPTCY, ADJUDICATION OF.

creditors' meeting. A meeting in relation to a company whereby a *voluntary winding up* of the company may be achieved: Companies Act 1963, ss 266–267. The court is not empowered to extend the time for holding a creditors' meeting: *Walsh v Registrar of Companies* [1987] HC. See also ARRANGING DEBTOR; COMPOSITION; WINDING UP BY TRUSTEE; WINDING UP, VOLUNTARY.

creditors' winding up. See WINDING UP, VOLUNTARY.

cremation. The burning of a dead body in a crematorium. See BURIAL GROUNDS.

crest system. The system operated by CRESTCo Ltd, which provides for the holding and transferring of securities in an electronic format, pursuant to the Companies Act 1990, s 239; Companies Act (Uncertified Securities) Regulations 1996, SI No 68 of 1996. Title to securities may be evidenced and transferred without a written instrument, provided such title is evidenced and transferred in accordance with these regulations. These regulations provide a framework under which these securities may be transferred under a computer-based system and procedure by an *approved operator*. The CREST company is such an operator.

Companies which wish to have their securities within the system have to ensure that their registrars meet certain technical and service standards. When a company's shares have been admitted to CREST, the register of members will include uncertified accounts for CREST members. An operator-instruction in CREST is deemed to be an instrument of conveyance or transfer for stamp duty purposes: Finance Act 2003, s 135. However, exempt from stamp duty is an operator-instruction effecting a transfer of rights to securities, where that transfer is a renunciation of those rights under a letter of allotment: Finance Act 2004, s 67. See Electronic Commerce Act 2000, s 11(b); Finance Act 2002, s 112. See Listing Rules 2000, paras 3.27, 9.39. See SHARES, COMPANY.

crime. An unlawful act or default which is an offence against the public and renders the person guilty of the act or default liable to legal punishment. Whether there is a crime against the community can only arise if an offence is clearly established: *McLoughlin v Tuite* [1986] ILRM 304. Crimes are either *minor* (summary) or *indictable* (qv) depending on whether the offence entitles the accused to a trial with a jury or not; minor offences are tried by courts of summary jurisdiction: 1937 Constitution, art 38.2.

The common law divided crimes into *treason, felonies* and *misdemeanours* (qqv). Formerly a felon was liable to lose his life and forfeit his property. All distinctions between felonies and misdemeanours have been abolished; crimes are now either *offences* or *arrestable offences*: Criminal Law Act 1997, s 3(1). See District Court (Criminal Justice) Rules 1998, SI No 41 of 1998. For links between crime and poverty, see Bibliography: Bacik & O'Connell. [Bibliography: Carroll; Fennell (2); McCullagh; McDermott P A; O'Donnell & McAuley; O'Higgins; Ó Síocháin; Ryan & Magee; Watson; Archibald UK.] See DEFENCE; INJUNCTION, CRIMINAL; JOINT INVESTIGATION TEAMS.

crime prevention directory. A directory which lists crime prevention measures in operation in the State, ranging from the *national age card* to various *youth diversion* and *anger management* programmes. The directory gives in respect of each measure the name and address of the organisation responsible, funding sources, description of work and methodology, and work evaluation. The directory, which was launched on on 27 March 2003, is available on website: *www.justice.ie*. See DIVERSION PROGRAMME; IDENTITY CARD.

crimen laesae majestatis. [The crime of injured majesty.] For example, treason (qv).

criminal. (1) A person found guilty of an indictable offence. (2) Pertaining to a crime. See INDICTABLE OFFENCE.

Criminal Assets Bureau. A body corporate established with the following objectives: (a) the identification of criminal assets or suspected criminal assets wherever situated, (b) the taking of appropriate steps under the law to deprive the holders of such assets of their use or benefit, and (c) the pursuit of any investigation or doing of preparatory work in relation to any proceedings arising from the objectives: Criminal Assets Bureau Act 1996, ss 3–4.

The Bureau, acting through its officers (who are members of the Garda Síochána, officers of the Revenue Commissioners, and officers of the Minister for Social Welfare) is empowered to use the powers vested in those persons under various statutes in respect of the proceeds of criminal activity and the assets derived from such activity (CABA 1996, s 5).

Provision is made for the *anonymity* of Bureau officers and staff (CABA, s 10). It is an offence to identify by publication a Revenue or Social Welfare officer (or a member of his family) who is or was a Bureau officer (CABA, s 11). It is also an offence to intimidate in any way a Bureau officer or staff member or a member of their family (CABA, s 13); or to obstruct such officer, or staff member accompanying or assisting the officer (CABA, s 12).

When the Bureau raises tax assessments, it is bound by the elaborate procedures for the determination of a taxpayer's liability by assessment and appeal to the Appeals Commissioners, accompanied by a right of appeal to the Circuit Court, and to the High Court on a point of law: *Criminal Assets Bureau v Hunt* [2003] 2 ILRM 481 and 2 IR 168, SC. The Supreme Court held that the CAB were not entitled to obtain a High Court judgment in respect of alleged unpaid taxes, when the tax assessments in relation to the defendant were not final and conclusive under the tax legislation. The Chief Justice said that it was clearly the intention of the Oireachtas 'to provide an exclusive machinery for the ascertainment of a taxpayer's liability'.

Civil proceedings under the Social Welfare Acts may be brought by or against the Bureau: Social Welfare Act 1999, s 28(2). See *M v D* [1998] 3 IR 175, HC; *Gilligan v Criminal Assets Bureau* [1998] 3 IR 185, HC; *Criminal Assets Bureau v Hutch* [1999] ITLR (21 June), HC. See 'Asset Forfeiture & the European Convention on Human Rights' by Claire Hamilton BL in *Bar Review* (May 2001) 414. [Bibliography: Ashe & Reid; McCutcheon & Walsh.] See AMNESTY; ASSAULT; GARDA COMPENSATION; PROCEEDS OF CRIME.

criminal contempt. See CONTEMPT OF COURT.

criminal conversation. The common law remedy by which a man had a right of action for damages against a person who had sexual intercourse with his wife; the consent of the wife to the act of intercourse did not affect the issue. Abolished by the Family Law Act 1981, s 1. See LRC 1, 1980.

criminal damage to property. The offences committed by a person who: (a) without lawful excuse damages the property of another intending to damage it or being reckless as to whether it would be damaged; (b) without lawful excuse damages any property intending to endanger the life of another or being reckless in that regard; (c) damages any property with intent to defraud: Criminal Damage Act 1991, s 2. A person is *reckless* if he has foreseen that the particular kind of damage that in fact was done might be done and yet has gone on to take the risk of it (CDA 1991, s 2(6)). An offence committed under s 2 by damaging property by fire must be charged as arson (qv).

It is also an offence to threaten damage to property and to have possession of any thing with intent to damage property (CDA 1991, ss 3–4). *Property* means: (a) property of a tangible nature, whether real or personal, including money and animals that are capable of being stolen; and (b) data ie information in a form in which it can be accessed by means of a computer and includes a program (CDA 1991, s 1(1)). To *damage* includes to destroy, deface, dismantle or, whether temporarily or otherwise, render inoperable or unfit for use or prevent or impair the operation of property (CDA 1991, s 1(1)). For commencement of s 14(4), see SI No 226 of 1992. See also Non-Fatal Offences against the Person Act 1997, s 21; Family Law (Divorce) Act 1996, s 48. See COMPUTER; DAMAGE TO PROPERTY; MALICIOUS INJURIES SCHEME.

criminal information. A written complaint made *ex officio* by the Attorney-General and filed in the High Court; it is limited to offences (formerly, *misdemeanours*) of a public nature eg libel on judges, and is tried on the civil side of the court. No criminal information has been filed in recent years; the modern practice is to proceed by way of indictment (qv).

criminal injuries. See MALICIOUS INJURIES SCHEME.

Criminal Injuries Compensation Tribunal. A tribunal established in 1974 to deal, on an *ex gratia* basis, with applications for compensation from persons injured (or from their dependants in fatal cases) in the course of crimes of violence or in the course of assisting the prevention of crime or the saving of human life. The injury must be serious enough to justify an award of at least £50 (€63.49). It is an extra-statutory scheme and was revised as from 1 April 1986, from which date claims for pain and suffering are excluded; only *special damages* are now claimable.

The chairman and six ordinary members of the tribunal, who are appointed by the Minister for Justice, must be practising barristers or solicitors.

While there is no provision in the scheme for an appeal against or review of a final decision of the tribunal, a person who is dissatisfied with a decision given by one member, may have his claim heard by a panel of three members, the member who gave the initial decision not being one of the three (*Scheme of Compensation*, para 25).

Despite the absence of an appeal mechanism from a final decision of the tribunal, such decisions have been the subject of review by the courts: *O'Toole v CICT* [1988] HC; *State (Creedon) v CICT* [1989] ILRM 104; *Hill v CICT* [1990] ILRM 36, HC. However, the courts are reluctant to intervene where there is no final determination by the tribunal: *Tomlinson v CICT* [2004] ITLR 24 May 2004, HC, and FL 9020 (under appeal). See also *Garavan v CICT* (20 July 1993, unreported), SC.

Where the tribunal rejects a claim, it is required to advise the applicant in general terms of the grounds on which his application has failed: *Gavin v Criminal Injuries Compensation Tribunal* [1997] 1 IR 133, HC. Also the requirement under the scheme that the applicant's injuries be 'directly attributable' to a crime of violence does not mean that it must be the sole cause; if the injury is directly attributable, in whole or in part, to the events complained of, the applicant is entitled to compensation (*Gavin* case). See *Scheme of Compensation for Personal Injuries Criminally Inflicted* (PI 3920) as laid by the Minister for Justice before each House of the Oireachtas (March 1986). [CICT, 13 Lower Hatch Street, Dublin 2. Tel: (01) 661 0604; Fax: (01) 661 0598.] See GARDA COMPENSATION.

criminal jurisdiction, place. Generally the jurisdiction of our courts extends only to criminal activity in the State, its land, islands and waters. The main exceptions are: (a) certain *specified offences* which are committed in Northern Ireland: Criminal Law (Jurisdiction) Act 1976; Non-Fatal Offences against the Person Act 1997, ss 26 and 28(2); (b) *larceny* (now *theft* or *robbery*) committed in any part of the United Kingdom: Larceny Act 1916; Criminal Justice (Theft and Fraud Offences) Act 2001, s 65(5); (c) certain offences committed by Irish *seamen* abroad: Merchant Shipping Act 1894; *The People (Attorney-General) v Thomas* [1954] IR 168; (d) *treason* committed by an Irish citizen: Treason Act 1939; (e) *murder, manslaughter,* and *bigamy*: Offences Against the Person Act 1861; (f) *forgery*: Forgery Act 1913; Criminal Justice (Theft and Fraud Offences) Act 2001, s 65(5); (g) *drug trafficking* offences at sea: Criminal Justice Act 1994, ss 33–37; (h) *child sexual offences*: Sexual Offences (Jurisdiction) Act 1996; Child Trafficking and Pornography Act 1998, s 11.

See also Criminal Damage Act 1991, s 7(1); Criminal Justice Bill 2004, ss 25–26. See CONFISCATE; FORFEITURE; JURISDICTION.

criminal jurisdiction, time. There is generally no time limit for commencing proceedings for *indictable* (qv) offences, although some statutes prescribe a time limit. For *summary* offences (qv), unless a time limit is specified in the statute governing the offence, an *information* (qv) must be laid or a *complaint* (qv) must be made within six months from the time when the matter of such information or complaint arose: Petty Sessions (Ireland) Act 1851. See Criminal Justice Bill 2004, s 24. See SUMMARY JURISDICTION.

criminal law. The body of law which defines the variety of actions (or omissions) which are forbidden by the State and which provides punishment as a sanction. In January 2003, the Minister for Justice, Michael McDowell SC, appointed a group to advise on the scope of a proposed codification of the criminal law. The Minister said that the challenge facing the group was to devise an approach to codification which would bring greater clarity and consistency to criminal law. However, he said that at the same time it should be sufficiently adaptable so as to facilitate ongoing amendments necessary to keep abreast of advances in criminology, both domestically and on a European basis. The group is chaired by Professor Finbar McAuley, University College Dublin. See 'The European Convention on Human Rights and the Irish Criminal Justice System' by Una Ní Raifeartaigh BL in *Bar Review* (December 2001) 111. [Bibliography: Bacik; Carroll; Charleton (1–3); Goldberg; Ó Síocháin; McAuley & McCutcheon; McDermott P A; McIntyre & McMullin; O'Donnell & McAuley; O'Mahony; Ryan & Magee; Walsh D. Reports: Frewen; Casey; *Irish Criminal Law Journal*.]

criminal law, proposed amendments. Under draft legislation, it is proposed *inter alia*: (a) to strengthen powers in relation to the investigation of offences eg to provide for photographing arrested persons and a statutory basis for the designation of a place as a crime scene; (b) to increase the power of detention from the current maximum of twelve hours by an extension of a further twelve hours; (c) to provide that samples of mouth swabs and saliva may be taken without consent; (d) to provide for the admissibility of prior inconsistent witness statements; (e) to broaden the basis under which the prosecution may appeal in criminal proceedings; and (f) to provide for anonymity of witnesses with a medical condition so that they cannot be identified as having that condition: Criminal Justice Bill 2004.

criminal libel. See LIBEL.

criminal lunatic. Generally understood to be a person who has been found to be insane in any of the following circumstances: (a) while on remand or awaiting trial; (b) while undergoing sentence; (c) while awaiting the pleasure of the government, having been found to be insane on arraignment; (d) while awaiting the pleasure of the government, having been found *guilty but insane* (ie guilty of the act charged against him but insane at the time; it is a verdict of acquittal on the charge). Criminal lunatics are confined in the Central Mental Hospital, Dundrum or in a district mental hospital. See SPECIAL VERDICT.

criminal responsibility. There is now: (a) a *conclusive presumption* that no child under the age of 12 years is capable of committing an offence, and (b) a *rebuttable presumption* that a child who is not less than 12 but under 14 years of age is incapable of committing an offence, because the child did not have the capacity to know that the act or omission concerned was wrong: Children Act 2001, s 52.

A person who aid, abets, counsels or procures an under-age child to commit an offence is himself guilty of that offence and may be tried as a principal offender (CA 2001, s 54).

A garda has certain duties in relation to an underage child offender eg to inform the health board where the garda has reasonable grounds for believing that the child is not receiving adequate care or protection (CA 2001, s 53). See CHILD, CRIME AND; DOLI INCAPAX; GUILTY BUT INSANE.

criminating questions. See INCRIMINATE.

crisis pregnancy. Means a pregnancy which is neither planned nor desired by the woman concerned, and which represents a personal crisis for her: Crisis Pregnancy Agency (Establishment) Order 2001, SI No 446 of 2001. A *Crisis Pregnancy Agency* has been established with the function of preparing a strategy to address the issue of crisis pregnancy in order to provide for: (a) a reduction in the number of crisis pregnancies by the provision of education, advice and contraceptive services; (b) a reduction in the number of women with crisis pregnancies who opt for abortion by offering services and supports which make other options more attractive; (c) the provision of counselling and medical services after crisis pregnancy.

See Agency publication, in association with the Irish College of General Practitioners, *Primary Care for the Prevention and Management of Crisis Pregnancy* (April 2004). For list of agencies for women with unplanned pregnancies, see website: *www.positiveoptions.ie*. See also website: *www.crisispregnancy.ie*. See ABORTION, MEDICAL GUIDELINES.

cross-action. An action by a defendant against the plaintiff in respect of the same subject matter. See COUNTERCLAIM.

cross-appeals. Appeals by both plaintiff and defendant against judgment in a case eg see *Clancy v Commissioners of Public Works* [1991] ILRM 567, SC.

cross-border bodies. See GOOD FRIDAY AGREEMENT.

cross-border credit transfer. A transaction carried out on the initiative of an originator via an institution in an EU member state with a view to making available an amount of money to a beneficiary at an institution in another member state: Central Bank Act 1997, s 22. The Minister may make regulations governing cross-border credit transfers as regards eg transparency. See EC (Cross Border Credit Transfers) Regulations 1999, SI No 231 of 1999, and Regulations 2003, SI No 231 of 2003, as amended by Central Bank and Financial Services Authority of Ireland Act 2004, s 34, Sch 4.

See Commission Notice on the Application of EU Competition Rules to Cross-Border Credit Transfers (1995) OJ 251/3. See EC (Cross Border Payments in Euro) Regulations 2002, SI No 335 of 2002 as amended by Central Bank and Financial Services Authority of Ireland Act 2003, s 35, Sch 2. See IRISH PAYMENT SERVICES ORGANISATION; OMBUDSMAN FOR CREDIT INSTITUTIONS.

cross-border insolvency. Insolvency in one member state involving assets in another member state. Regulations on insolvency proceedings have been made which permit the law of one member state to apply to insolvency proceedings which take or involve assets in another member state: Council Regulation (EEC) 1346/2000. It allows for EU-wide recognition for judgments in cross-border insolvencies and judgments which are delivered directly on the basis of such proceedings. See 'The cross border insolvency regulation' by Aillil O'Reilly BL in *Bar Review* (December 2001) 97.

cross-border shopping. See DUTY FREE.

cross-examination. *Cross-examination* is the examination of a witness by the opposite party with a view to diminishing the effect of his evidence. It has been held that cross-examination as to previous actions for defamation brought by the plaintiff in respect of other unrelated publications was not relevant to the issues of justification, fair comment, the meaning to be attributed to the words complained of, or the identification of the plaintiff: *Browne v Tribune Newspapers plc* [2001] 2 ILRM 424, SC and 1 IR 521. The only relevance of such cross-examination could be in relation to the issue of damages. See also *Kavanagh v The Leader* [2001] 1 IR 538, SC.

In an employment disciplinary hearing, it was held that the employee had been given an opportunity to respond to the allegations and that the absence of an opportunity to cross-examine the witnesses did not preju-

dice the employee's case: *Massey v Western Health Board* [2000] ELR 142, EAT. [Bibliography: Healy.] See EXAMINATION; TENANCY TRIBUNAL.

crossing of cheque. See CHEQUE.

crowd control. The gardaí have been given power to erect barriers on any road, street, lane or alley not more than one mile from where an event, which is likely to attract a large assembly of persons, is taking place: Criminal Justice (Public Order) Act 1994, s 21. A garda in uniform may direct persons and, where possession of a ticket is required for entry to the event, may prohibit persons who have no ticket from crossing or passing the barrier. The gardaí also have power to search a person going to an event, and to seize intoxicating liquour or a disposable container or any article which could be used to cause injury (CJ(PO)A 1994, s 22).

cruelty. Conduct which causes danger to life or health, physical or mental, of the other party; it is a ground for a *judicial separation* (qv). See DIVORCE A MENSA ET THORO.

cruelty to animals. It is an offence cruelly to beat, kick, ill-treat, over-ride, overdrive, overload, torture, infuriate, or terrify any animal, or to abandon it in circumstances likely to cause it unnecessary suffering: Protection of Animals Act 1911, s 1 and Protection of Animals Act 1965, s 4; Control of Dogs Act 1986, s 20. A person convicted of the offence of cruelty to a dog may be disqualified from keeping a dog (CDA 1986, s 18). Also protection is given to animals used for experimental and other scientific purposes: Cruelty to Animals Act 1876 as amended by EC (Amendment to Cruelty to Animals Act 1876) Regulations 2002, SI No 566 of 2002. See ANIMALS; COCKFIGHT.

cruelty to children. A person who has the custody, charge or care of a child is guilty of an offence if the person wilfully assaults, ill-treats, neglects, abandons or exposes the child, in a manner likely to cause unnecessary suffering or injury to the child's health or seriously to effect his wellbeing: Children Act 2001, s 246. The offence is also committed where the person causes or procures or allows the child to be so treated. The 'child's health' or 'wellbeing' includes the child's physical, mental or emotional health or wellbeing. The expression 'ill-treat' includes any frightening, bullying or threatening of the child.

For previous legislation, see Children Act 1908, s 12; Children (Amendment) Act 1957, s 4. For the Irish Society for the Prevention of Cruelty to Children, see website: *www.ispcc.ie*. See CARE ORDER.

crystallisation. See FLOATING CHARGE.

cuideachta phoiblí theoranta; cpt. [Public limited company (qv).]

cujus est dare ejus est disponere. [He who gives anything can also direct how the gift is to be used.] See PRECATORY TRUST.

cujus est instituere ejus est abrogare. [He who institutes may also abrogate.]

cujus est solum ejus est usque ad coelum et ad inferos. [Whose is the soil, his is even to the heaven and the depths of the earth.] However, there can be separate ownership of the airspace above the surface of land just as there can be such ownership of the subterranean area below the surface: *Humphreys v Brogden* [1850] 12 QB 739. See AIRSPACE, INTERFERENCE WITH; FLAT; LIGHT RAILWAY; PLANNING PERMISSION; PRIVATE PROPERTY; SUBSTRATUM OF LAND; WAY-LEAVE.

culpable. Blameworthy; being responsible for a breach of legal duty.

cultural object. Includes museum heritage objects, library material, and any other object or thing considered appropriate to be exhibited or kept by a specified institution: National Cultural Institutions Act 1997, s 42. The Minister is required to establish a *register of cultural objects* whose export from the State would constitute a serious loss to the heritage of Ireland (NCIA 1997, s 48(1)).

It is an offence to export, or to attempt to export a registered cultural object (NCIA 1997, s 49). The restriction on exporting without a licence also applies to documents not less than 70 years old and paintings not less than 25 years old where the value exceeds a specified amount, and certain objects (eg furniture, pottery, antique objects) not less than 70 years old where the value is not less than £35,000 (€44,441) (NCIA 1997, s 49 and Sch 3). See LRC *Report on Unidroit Convention on Stolen or Illegally Exported Cultural Objects* (LRC 55, 1997). See EC (Return of Cultural Objects) (Amendment) Regulations 2002, SI No 498 of 2002.

culture. The EC is required to contribute to the flowering of the cultures of the member states, while respecting their national and regional diversity and at the same time bringing the common cultural heritage to the fore: EC Treaty, arts 87(3)(d) and 151 of the consolidated (2002) version. Every year a number of European cities are designated as 'cultural capitals'. Genoa and Lille have been chosen for 2004. See websites: *www.genova-2004.it* and *www.lille2004.fr*. See ARTIST, TAX EXEMPTION OF; COMMITTEE OF THE REGIONS; EDUCATION; PROTECTED STRUCTURE.

cum. [With.]

cum div. [With dividend.] Stock exchange quotation relating to stocks and shares, indicating that the price includes dividends accrued to date. See BOND WASHING; EX DIV.

cum testamento annexo. [With the will annexed.] See LETTERS OF ADMINISTRATION; PROBATE.

cur adv vult. [Curia advisari vult (qv).]

curator. See ARCHIVES; LIBRARIES.

curia advisari vult. [The court wishes to be advised.] Indicates in a law report (qv) that the judgment of the court was not delivered immediately, but given later after further deliberation.

currency, decimal. See COINS, COINAGE; EURO; POUND.

currency, foreign. A plaintiff may sue for amounts expressed in a foreign currency when the proper law of the contract is that of the foreign country or when a term of the contract so provides. Judgment may be given in the foreign currency or the Irish currency equivalent thereto at the time when the order is made or, in summary judgment proceedings, when judgment is entered in the office: *Damen v O'Shea* [1977] HC.

In relation to the enforcement of *maintenance orders* of other contracting EC states where the amount stated therein is in a currency other than that of the State, payment must be made on the basis of the exchange rate prevailing, on the date of making of an *enforcement order*, between that currency and the currency of the State: Jurisdiction of Courts and Enforcement of Judgments (European Communities) Act 1998, s 11. The *Brussels I Regulation* on the recognition and enforcement of judgments in civil and commercial matters, replaces the 1998 Act as from 1 March 2002 for all EU States except Denmark: EC (Civil and Commercial Judgments) Regulations 2002, SI No 52 of 2002, reg 8 which contains a similar provision.

Foreign currency notes are bank notes within the meaning of the Forgery

Act 1916: Central Bank Act 1942, s 53. A building society may make loans or raise funds in foreign currency: Building Societies Act 1989, ss 18, 22(1), 23 as amended by Housing (Miscellaneous Provisions) Act 2002, s 23 and Sch 3. See also *Northern Bank v Edwards* [1986] ILRM 167. See EURO; POUND.

currency, functional. The computation of capital allowances and trading losses of a company since 1994 is made in the company's functional currency; its *functional currency* is the currency of the *primary economic environment*: (a) in which the company operates if the company is resident in the State; or (b) in which the company carries on trading activities in the State if the company is non-resident: Taxes Consolidation Act 1997, s 402. If the accounts of either such company are prepared in Euro, the functional currency is Euro. The primary economic environment of the company is generally determined by the currency in which the company's net cash flows are generated.

current account. A running account kept between parties with debits and credits e g a current banking account. Money paid into a current account which is then in credit, becomes the property of the bank, which then becomes a debtor of the account holder: *Re Ashmark Ltd (in liquidation)* [1994] 1 ILRM 223, HC. See Building Societies Act 1989, s 29(2)(f). See OVERDRAFT.

current cost accounting convention; CCA. The convention by which accounts are prepared having regard to replacement costs rather than historic or actual costs. It has been held that, in the light of the judicial meaning consistently given to profits, the CCA method was not an appropriate method for calculating profit for tax purposes: *Carroll Industries plc v O'Culachain* [1989] ILRM 552, HC.

curtesy. The life estate which a husband who survived his wife had in her heritable freeholds ie fee simple and fee tail, provided that his wife died intestate and a child of the marriage was born alive capable of inheriting the freehold. Abolished for registered land by the Registration of Title Act 1964 and abolished entirely by the Succession Act 1965, s 11. See DOWER.

curtilage. A courtyard, garden, yard, field, or piece of ground lying near and belonging to a dwellinghouse. See DRUNKEN DRIVING; EXTENSION OF HOUSE.

custody. (1) Confinement or imprisonment of a person. (2) Control and possession of some person or thing. See DETENTION; ESCAPE; PUNISHMENT.

custody in garda station. Gardaí are required to act with due respect for the personal rights of persons in custody in garda stations and their dignity as human persons, and must have regard for the special needs of any of them who may be under a physical or mental disability, while complying with the obligation to prevent escapes from custody and continuing to act with diligence and determination in the investigation of crime and the protection and vindication of the personal rights of other persons: Treatment of Persons in Custody in Garda Síochána Stations Regulations 1987, SI No 119 of 1987, reg 3. There must be no unnecessary delay in dealing with persons in custody.

The regulations deal, *inter alia*, with custody record, record of arrest and detention, notification to solicitor or other persons, enquiries, visits and communications, interviews, foreign nationals, charge sheets, searches, fingerprints, conditions of custody, no ill-treatment, medical treatment, mentally handicapped persons, other matters to be recorded, preservation of custody records.

custody of children. See CHILD ABDUCTION; CHILD, CUSTODY OF.

custom and practice (or usage). A rule of conduct established by long usage, which if valid, has the force of law. A valid custom must have been exercised from *time immemorial* (qv); it must be certain, reasonable, and not be contrary to statute law. Custom may be proved by the direct evidence of witnesses of their personal knowledge of its existence; by evidence of a similar custom in an analogous trade or in another locality; by the declaration of a person, now deceased, of competent knowledge. See *Mills v Mayor of Colchester* [1867] LR 2 CP 567.

Customs and practices may be implied as terms of an employment contract where they are so universal that 'no workman would be supposed to have entered into the service without looking to it as part of the contract': *Devonald v Rosser & Sons* [1906] 2 KB 728. The immunity given to authorised trade unions and their members as regards acts done in furtherance of a trade dispute, is only available where agreed procedures availed of by custom and practice, or in a collective agreement, have been resorted to and exhausted: Industrial Relations Act 1990, s 9.

An employer's right to lay off an employee without pay may be established through custom or general usage; however such custom must be reasonable, certain and notorious: *Lawe v Irish Country Meats Ltd* [1998] ELR 266, CC. See INTERNATIONAL LAW; LAY OFF.

custom house docks development authority. See URBAN RENEWAL.

customary authority. The implied authority which an *agent* has, who carries on a particular trade, profession or calling, to perform such acts as are usual in that trade, profession or calling e g a stockbroker on the Stock Exchange (qv).

customs duties. Taxes on imports and exports. The government is empowered to impose, vary or terminate customs duties by order: Imposition of Duties Act 1957, provided the order is confirmed by the Oireachtas. Customs officers are given wide powers of detention of goods reasonably suspected of being imported without payment of duty, including detention of the means of conveyance of the goods (e g ship, car), and of forfeiture of goods where they were imported without payment of duty: Customs Consolidation Act 1876, s 177 and Customs and Excise (Miscellaneous Provisions) Act 1988, ss 7–8. See also *Mc Daid v Sheehy* [1991] ILRM 250, SC. The Community Customs Code and its implementing Regulation, comprising over 1180 Articles and 115 Annexes, came into being on 1 January 1994.

The Customs and Excise (Mutual Assistance) Act 2001 enables Ireland to adopt a number of EU Conventions on Mutual Assistance and Co-operation between Customs Administrations and on the use of Information Technology for Customs purposes. Co-operation between EU customs administrations has centred mainly on a flow of intelligence and exchange of information to combat international smuggling, including drugs smuggling. This co-operation has been made more important with the abolition of internal Community frontier controls on the completion of the Single Market. See European Communities (Mutual Assistance for the Recovery of Claims relating to Certain Levies, Duties, Taxes and Other Measures) Regulations 2002, SI No 462 of 2002 as amended by SIs Nos 344 of 2003 and 711

of 2003. For protection of manual data, see SI No 254 of 2004. For *World Customs Organisation,* see website: *www.wcoomd.org.* [Bibliography: Walsh & McCarthy.]

cyber cafe. A coffee shop or restaurant which offers access to computer terminals connected to the Internet usually at a charge per hour or per minute. See INTERNET.

cyber libel. Libel by publication via the Internet e g by a webpage or an email. 'Irish employers sued for defamation committed by employees may wish to consider the tactical merits of joining the ISP (*Internet Service Provider*) as a third party in such proceedings': Ann Power BL in 'Employers' liability in the electronic workplace' in *Bar Review* (October 2000) 14 at 20. See also 'Libel on the Internet' by Patrick O'Callaghan BL in *Bar Review* (February 2003) 15. See INTERNET.

cyber squatter. Colloquial term to describe a person who registers another person's or a company's name as a *domain name* and then endeavours to sell that domain name to them. The names of Irish politicians were registered as domain names in 1999/2000 by US cyber squatters. See 'The protection of trade marks against cyber-squatters' by Anne Bateman BL in *Bar Review* (March 2001) 298. For provisions to deal with cyber squatters, see DOMAIN NAME.

cybercrime. Crimes committed via the Internet and other computer networks. Ireland became a party to the Council of Europe Convention on Cybercrime on 28 February 2002. The main object of the Convention is to protect society against new types of serious crime, as well as against traditional types of crime using new technologies. The Convention aims principally at: (a) harmonising the domestic criminal substantive law elements of offences in the areas of cybercrime; (b) providing for the powers to investigate and prosecute such offences; and (c) setting up a fast and effective regime of international co-operation.

'The Convention will be an important element in tackling crimes such as fraud and child pornography using the new technologies, and crimes such as hacking or virus creation which impact on the legitimate use of information communications': Minister for Justice at the signing of the Convention. See INTERNET.

cycleway. A public road (qv) or proposed public road reserved for the exclusive use of pedal cyclists or pedal cyclists and pedestrians: Roads Act 1993, s 68. A road authority may construct (or otherwise provide) and maintain a cycleway (RA 1993, s 68(2)(a)).

cy-pres. [As near.] The doctrine by which a trust, which discloses a general charitable intention, will not be permitted to fail because the particular mode of application specified by the testator cannot be carried out; the law will substitute another mode *cy-pres*, that is, as near as possible to the mode specified by the testator.

Failure of purposes justifying recourse to cy-pres include where: the purposes are fulfilled; or the purposes cannot be carried out in the spirit of the gift; or the gift is too large; or the purposes are adequately provided for by other means; or the purposes are no longer charitable; or the purposes are not providing a suitable and effective application of the gift: Charities Act 1961, s 47; *Royal Kilmainham Hospital* [1966] IR 451. The *cy-pres* doctrine may also apply where a conjuncture of funds would result in the gift being more effectively used (CA 1961, s 47).

Where the purposes fail or where difficulty arises in applying the charity property so that it is available to return to the donor, there are provisions by which it will be applied *cy-pres* to charitable purposes where the donor cannot be found or in other particular circumstances (CA 1961, s 48). The court should not attempt to envisage how the particular donor would now dispose of his property; instead the court has to consider how a hypothetical benefactor of the present day with the same background and interests as the donor and a charitable disposition would act: *Re the Worth Library* [1994] 1 ILRM 161, HC and [1995] 2 IR 301, HC.

Provision has been made in the case of charities established by statute, to have their property applied *cy-pres* if the objects are no longer relevant: Charities Act 1973, s 4(2)(dd) inserted by Courts and Court Officers Act 2002, s 32.

The Commissioners of Charitable Donations and Bequests had power to frame charitable schemes of up to £250,000 (€317,435) in value (CA 1961, s 29 as amended by Courts and Court Officers Act 1995, s 52). This financial limit has now been abolished, thus eliminating the necessity to apply to the High Court and consequently providing a low-cost means of applying a gift to an alternative charitable purpose: Social Welfare (Miscellaneous Provisions) Act 2002, s 16 and Sch, Pt 2. See also *Governors of Erasmus Smith School v A-G* [1932] 66 ILTR 57. See CHARITIES; PUBLIC APPEAL, MONEY COLLECTED IN; SIGN MANUAL.

D

Dáil Éireann. The house of representatives of the national parliament (the Oireachtas): 1937 Constitution, art 15. The sole and exclusive power of making laws for the State (otherwise than by the EC) is vested in the Oireachtas. The number of members of the Dáil is fixed from time to time by law but must not be fixed at less than one member for each thirty thousand of the population, or at not more than one member for each twenty thousand of the population. There must be, as far as practicable, uniformity of representation (art 16(2)(3) and *O'Donovan v A-G* [1961] IR 114). The Dáil currently consists of 166 members: Electoral (Amendment) (No 2) Act 1998 s 2. The same Dáil must not continue for more than seven years, although a shorter period may be fixed by law (Constitution art 16(5)); a five-year period has been fixed: Electoral Act 1992 s 33. A member of the Dáil is generally known by the title *TD*. See CONSTITUENCY; COMMUNITY LAW; DISSOLUTION; FRANCHISE; TD; UTTERANCE.

Dáil election. An election of a member or members to serve in the Dáil and includes a bye-election as well as a general election: Electoral Act 1992 s 2(1). A person is entitled to be registered as a Dáil elector if he has reached the age of 18, is a citizen of Ireland, and is ordinarily resident in the constituency (EA 1992, s 8(1)). In addition: (a) a British citizen, and (b) a national of an EC member state which permits Irish citizens to vote in their national parliaments, are entitled to be registered as Dáil electors (EA 1992, s 8(2)). Election is by proportional representation (qv) with each elector having one transferable vote (EA 1992, s 37).

damage. Loss or harm, physical or economic, resulting from a wrongful act or default and generally leading to an award of a measure of compensation. Generally a wrong to be actionable must result in damage, except that some wrongs (eg libel, trespass) are actionable *per se*.

damage, malicious. See MALICIOUS DAMAGE.

damage, remoteness of. See REMOTENESS OF DAMAGE.

damage-feasant. [Doing damage.] See DISTRESS DAMAGE-FEASANT.

damage to property. Compensation for loss due to damage to property may be recovered by the party suffering the loss (the *injured party*) by way of a *compensation order* (qv) made against a convicted person. Where the commission of the offence by the convicted person involved the taking of property out of the possession of the injured party and the property has been recovered, any loss occurring to the injured party by reason of the property being damaged while out of his possession is treated as having resulted from the offence, irrespective of how the damage was caused or who caused it: Criminal Justice Act 1993, s 6(3). This applies to loss resulting from the use of a mechanically propelled vehicle (CJA 1993, s 6(4)(b)). See also CRIMINAL DAMAGE TO PROPERTY; MALICIOUS INJURIES SCHEME; STATE CLAIMS AGENCY.

damages. The compensation in money for loss suffered by a person owing to the tort, breach of contract, or breach of statutory duty of another person. The test by which the amount of damages is ascertained is known as the *measure of damages* (qv). The general principle is that the injured or aggrieved person should be put as nearly as possible in the same position, so far as money can do it, as if he had not suffered injury or loss: *Robinson v Harman* [1848] 1 Exch 850.

Damages may be *general* or *special* (qqv). Damages can be classified as: (a) *nominal* – where there has been no loss, and the damages recognise that the plaintiff has had a legal right infringed; (b) *contemptuous* – where the amount awarded is derisory: *Dering v Uris* [1964] 2 QB 669; (c) *ordinary* – consisting of general and special damages; (d) *aggravated* – where additional compensation is awarded in recognition of the exceptional features which add to or exacerbate the plaintiff's injury: *Kennedy v Hearne* [1988] ILRM 52 and 531, HC & SC; (e) *vindictive, punitive* or *exemplary* – where awarded to punish the defendant: *Garvey v Ireland* [1979] 113 ILTR 61;

McIntyre v Lewis & Dolan [1991] 1 IR 121, SC; (f) *speculative* – calculated having regard to events which may happen in the future: *Hickey & Co Ltd v Roches Stores (Dublin) Ltd (No 2)* [1980] ILRM 107; (g) *liquidated* – where fixed or ascertained by the parties in the contract; (h) *unliquidated* – dependant on the circumstances of the case to be determined by the court.

It is not strictly necessary for the court to assess damages under separate headings so long as the judge makes clear findings of fact; it is for the trial judge to decide the extent to which assessment under separate headings was likely to be of assistance to a court of appeal: *Rossiter v Dún Laoghaire Rathdown County Council* [2001] 3 IR 578. Where a plaintiff is entitled to succeed in a claim against a defendant under a number of headings, he is not entitled to recover damages under all headings where the claim arises from the same set of circumstances and cause of action: *Carey v Independent Newspapers (Ireland) Ltd* [2003] ITLR (3 November) and [2004] ELR 45.

Where an accident is due mainly to the plaintiff's default, damages will be reduced accordingly: *Hogan v ESB* [2000] ITLR (6 March), HC.

The assessment of damages is not an exact science and does not admit of mathematical certainty (*Furlong* case). A High Court judge has held that the difficulty in assessment of damages for *personal injuries* lies mainly in the determination of the injuries sustained rather than in identifying their financial consequences: Barron J in *Best v Wellcome Foundation Ltd* [1996] 1 ILRM 34.

In a particular personal injuries case, the court held that the plaintiff was entitled to compensation in respect of suffering due to the injury, but also in respect of suffering due to the aggravation of an existing condition (in this case, progressive multiple sclerosis): *Curran v Finn* [2001] ITLR (16 April).

It is unusual for damages to be assessed in the first instance by the Supreme Court; however that court can assess and award damages where finality is desirable and where the cost of referring a case back to the High Court is out of all proportion to the amount of damages likely to be awarded: *Bakht v The Medical Council* [1990] ILRM 840, SC.

See 'Recent developments in the law of damages' by John Healy BL in *Bar Review*

(November 2000) 69. In relation to the control of excessive damage awards, see Law Reform Commission report, *Aggravated, Exemplary and Restitutionary Damages*: (LRC 60, 2000 of August 2000). See AGGRAVATED DAMAGES; COMPENSATORY DAMAGES; DISABILITY PENSION; EXEMPLARY DAMAGES; PAIN AND SUFFERING, DAMAGES FOR; PENAL DAMAGES; QUANTUM; REMOTENESS OF DAMAGE; STAY OF EXECUTION.

damages, aggravation of. See AGGRAVATED DAMAGES.

damages, appeal of. An appellate court may overturn an award of damages where no reasonable proportion exists between what was awarded and what the appellate court would have awarded: *McGrath v Bourne* [1876] IR 10 CL 160; *Foley v Thermocement Products Ltd* [1954] 90 ILTR 92; *McKevitt v Ireland* [1987] ILRM 542.

The Supreme Court will adjust an award of damages by the High Court only where the award it might have fixed differs substantially: *Sheriff v Dowling* [1993] ITLR (13 September), SC; or is outside the scale of appropriate damages: *Furlong v Waterford Co-op Society Ltd* [1995] 1 ILRM 148, SC.

damages, exemplary. See EXEMPLARY DAMAGES.

damages, general. See GENERAL DAMAGES.

damages, measure of. See MEASURE OF DAMAGES.

damages, mitigation of. See MITIGATION OF DAMAGES.

damages, personal injuries. A court, in assessing damages in personal injuries actions, is required to have regard to: (a) the Book of Quantum prepared by the *Personal Injuries Assessment Board*; (b) prescribed *actuarial tables* in respect of future financial loss; and (c) a prescribed *discount rate* to determine the current value of any future financial loss: Civil Liability and Courts Act 2004, ss 22–24. Account must be made by the court for certain collateral benefits and for income undeclared for tax purposes: CLCA 2004, ss 27–28. See COLLATERAL; PERSONAL INJURIES ACTION; PERSONAL INJURIES ASSESSMENT BOARD.

damages, special. See SPECIAL DAMAGES.

damages and social welfare. Certain payments under the Social Welfare Acts are to be taken into account in assessing damages for personal injuries arising out of a mechanically propelled vehicle being used in respect of which liability is required to be covered by an approved policy of insurance: Social Welfare (Consolidation) Act 1993, s 237; *O'Loughlin v Teeling* [1988] ILRM 617.

damages and solicitor. A solicitor is prohibited from deducting any sum in respect of costs from the amount of any damages awarded to his client, except by agreement with the client: Solicitors (Amendment) Act 1994, s 68. Such agreement must be in writing to be enforceable against the client, and it must contain an estimate of the costs recoverable from the other party in the event of the client recovering damages.

damnum absque injuria. [Loss without wrong.] See DAMNUM SINE INJURIA.

damnum sine injuria. [Damage without wrong.] The phrase used to indicate that damage may be caused without any infringement of a legal right of another eg by a person exercising rights over his own property: *Mayor of Bradford v Pickles* [1895] AC 587. See INJURIA SINE DAMNUM.

dangerous building, potentially. See FIRE SAFETY NOTICE.

dangerous building notice. See DANGEROUS STRUCTURE.

dangerous chemicals. For the enforcement provisions regarding the export and import of dangerous chemicals, see EC (Export and Import of certain Dangerous Chemicals) (Industrial Chemicals) (Enforcement) Regulations 2002, SI No 395 of 2002. These regulations implement the enforcement provisions of EC Regulation 2455/92/EC as amended by EC Regulation 3135/94/EC.

dangerous conditions and practices. See PROHIBITION NOTICE, WORK.

dangerous dogs. Although not described as 'dangerous', restrictions have been placed on certain dogs: Control of Dogs (Restriction of Certain Dogs) Regulations 1991, SI No 123 of 1991 as amended by SI No 146 of 1991). The restrictions include the requirement that certain breeds be securely muzzled in a public place and be on a strong chain or leash held by a person over 16 years of age. The breeds specified include bulldogs, rottweilers, and certain bull terriers. The courts have power to order the destruction of 'dangerous' dogs: Control of Dogs Act 1986 s 22. See DOGS.

dangerous driving. The offence committed by a person who drives a vehicle in a public place in a manner (including speed) which, having regard to all the circumstances of the case (including the condition of the vehicle, the nature, condition and use of the place and the amount of traffic which then actually is or might reasonably be expected then to be therein) is *dangerous to the public*: Road Traffic Act 1961, s 53(1) as amended by the Road Traffic Act 1968, s 51(a), and as proposed to be amended by Road Traffic Bill 2004, s 14.

The prosecution does not have to prove intent; whether a person has driven in a manner *dangerous to the public* is a question of fact to be decided by the court in each particular case. There are higher penalties where dangerous driving is prosecuted on indictment (qv) where the contravention causes death or serious bodily harm to another person (RTA 1961, s 53(2)(a)). See also Road Traffic Acts 1994 and 1995. See *The People (Attorney General) v Gallagher* [1972] IR 365; *Attorney General v Dunleavy* [1947] ILTR 71; *Kelly v DPP* [1997] 1 ILRM 69, SC; *DPP v O'Buachalla & Mulhall* [1999] 1 ILRM 362, HC. [Bibliography: O'Keeffe & Hill.] See CARELESS DRIVING; FURIOUS DRIVING; PLEASURE CRAFT.

dangerous goods. Those substances and articles, the carriage by road of which is prohibited, or authorised only in certain circumstances, and includes wastes which are being transported for reprocessing, dumping, elimination by incineration or other method of disposal: Carriage of Dangerous Goods by Road Act 1998, s 1(1). The purpose of the Act is to put in place enabling powers which allow the State to accede to the European Agreement concerning the international carriage of dangerous goods by road, known as the ADR.

It is an offence for a person who engages in the carriage of dangerous goods by road if he does not take all practicable steps to prevent risk or injury to persons or damage to property (CDGRA 1998, s 11(1)). Any breaches of regulations adopted from EC Directives 94/55/EC and 95/50/EC can be prosecuted against out-of-state carriers in the course of a journey within this State (CDGRA 1998, s 9 as amended by Road Transport Act 1999, s 21).

The transport of dangerous goods by air is forbidden, except as permitted by the Convention on International Civil Aviation, Annex 18. See Air Navigation (Carriage of Munitions of War, Weapons and Dangerous Goods) Order 1973, SI No 224 of 1973. See ICOA publication DOC 9284-AN/905.

Regulations have been made which apply to the carriage, both in bulk and in packages, of dangerous goods by road, including the loading and unloading of the dangerous goods: Carriage of Dangerous Goods by Road Regulations 2001, SI No 492 of 2001, now revoked and replaced by SI No 29 of 2004. The regulations impose duties on the consignor and on the carrier of the dangerous goods and on the driver of the vehicle carrying the goods. The regulations replace existing regulations, revoking nine Statutory Instruments from 1979 to 1997. See also Carriage of Dangerous Goods by Rail (Fees) Regulations 2001, SI No 494 of 2001; European Communities (Transport of Dangerous Goods by Rail) Regulations 2003, SI No 701 of 2003. See also SIs Nos 6 and 493 of 2001. See DANGEROUS SUBSTANCE.

dangerous place. An excavation, quarry, pit, well, reservoir, pond, stream, dam, bank, dump, shaft or land that, in the opinion of the sanitary authority (qv) in whose sanitary district it is situate, is or is likely to be dangerous to any person: Local Government (Sanitary Services) Act 1964, s 1. A sanitary authority is empowered to carry out such works as will, in the opinion of the authority, prevent the place from being a dangerous place (LG(SS)A 1964, s 2). There is provision for *notice* to be given by the authority and for an appeal to the District Court to annul the notice (LG(SS)A 1964, s 5).

dangerous occurrence. A specified occurrence which occurs at any place of work eg the collapse or failure of a crane, the escape of a substance which might be liable to cause serious injury, an unintentional ignition of explosives, an incident during the conveying of a dangerous substance by road: Safety Health and Welfare at Work (General Application) Regulations 1993, SI No 44 of 1993, reg 58. There is a requirement to send a written report to the Health & Safety Authority of a dangerous occurrence (SI No 44 of 1993, reg 59 (1)(ii)) and to keep records (reg 60).

dangerous premises. The liability to compensate persons injured on premises due to their dangerous state is generally upon the occupier and not the owner. If the owner has a duty to repair, liability may fall on him. An independent contractor may be liable: *Haseldine v Daw* [1941] 2 KB 243. See OCCUPIER'S LIABILITY.

dangerous preparations. Regulations have been made which require persons placing a dangerous preparation on the market, to classify and label it according to the inherent hazards: EC (Classification, Packaging and Labelling of Dangerous Preparations) Regulations 2004, SI No 62 of 2004.

dangerous structure. Any building, wall or other structure of any kind, or any part of, or anything attached to, a building, wall or other structure of any kind, that, in the opinion of the sanitary authority (qv) in whose sanitary district it is situate, is or is likely to be dangerous to any person or property: Local Government (Sanitary Services) Act 1964, s 1. A sanitary authority may give notice (generally referred to as a *dangerous building notice*) requiring the carrying out of such works, including demolition, as will prevent the building from being a dangerous structure and to terminate or modify any use of the structure. The sanitary authority may carry out the works necessary itself. It may also obtain an order of the District Court requiring compliance with the notice (LG(SS)A 1964, s 3(5)–(6)). See *The State (McGuinness) v Maguire* [1967] IR 348.

Where a *protected structure* (qv) is concerned, the sanitary authority is required to consider whether an *endangerment notice* (qv) would be more appropriate or an order under the Derelict Sites Act 1990, s 11: Planning and Development Act 2000, s 79. For previous legislation, see Local Government (Planning and Development) Act 1999, s 30.

Also the owner or occupier of any structure must take all reasonable steps to ensure that it is not a hazard or potential hazard to persons using a public road: Roads Act 1993, s 70(1). The road authority may serve a notice on the owner or occupier of a hazardous structure to remove, modify or carry out specified works to the structure (RA 1993, s 70(1)(b)). An appeal lies to the District Court (RA 1993, s 70(3)(a)). See SUPPORT, RIGHT TO.

dangerous substance. (1) A substance which the Minister by order declares to be such on the ground that in his opinion it constitutes a potential source of danger to person or property: Dangerous Substances Act 1972, s 24. A person engaged in the storage, labelling, packing or conveyance of any dangerous substance must take all practical steps to prevent risk of injury to person or property (DSA 1972, s 25). The Minister may make regulations for the protection of persons against risk of injury caused by any dangerous substance (DSA 1972, s 26). Certain other sections of DSA 1972 were repealed when particular sections of the Safety, Health and Welfare at Work Act 1989 came into force eg see SI No 357 of 1995 repealing s 27.

Regulations have been made to protect man and the environment from the harmful effects of new and existing dangerous substances: European Communities (Classification, Packaging, Labelling and Notification of Dangerous Substances) Regulations 2003, SI No 116 of 2003 which revokes SI No 393 of 2000. The regulations apply to all substances which are intended to be placed on the market on their own or in a preparation, with exceptions for certain categories of substances (such as medicinal, cosmetic, pesticide, and waste products, which are covered by other Directives).

Other regulations have been made on the control of major accident hazards involving dangerous substances, implementing EC Directive 96/82/EC: European Communities (Control of Major Accident Hazards Involving Dangerous Substances) Regulations 2000, SI No 476 of 2000, as amended by SI No 402 of 2003.

Regulations also lay down the restrictions and conditions which must be observed in the marketing and use of specified dangerous substances and preparations: EC (Dangerous Substances and Preparations) (Marketing and Use) Regulations 2003, SI No 220 of 2003 as amended by SI No 503 of 2003. See also SI No 584 of 2001 (Retail and Private Petroleum Stores). See DANGEROUS GOODS; HAZARDOUS WASTE.

(2) Has the meaning assigned to it by the Major Accidents Directive: Planning and Development Act 2000, s 2(1). The *development plan* of a planning authority must include the control of establishments (or development in the vicinity of establishments) for the purpose of reducing the risk, or limiting the consequences, of a major accident (PDA 2000, s 10(2)(k)). The Major Accident Directive means EC Directive 96/82/EC of 9 December 1996 on the control of major accident hazards involving dangerous substances. See also Planning and Development Regulations 2001, SI

No 600 of 2001, Pt 11, arts 133–155. See DEVELOPMENT PLAN.

dangerous things. See PRODUCT LIABILITY; RYLANDS & FLETCHER, RULE IN.

dangerous tree. See TREE.

dangerous waste. See HAZARDOUS WASTE.

data. Means 'automated data' and 'manual data': Data Protection Act 1988, s 1(1) as amended by substitution by Data Protection (Amendment) Act 2003, s 2(a)(ii). 'Automated data' means data that: (a) is being processed by means of equipment operating automatically in response to instructions given for that purpose, or (b) is recorded with the intention that it should be processed by means of such equipment. 'Manual data' means information that is recorded as part of a 'relevant filing system' or with the intention that it should form part of a relevant filing system. A 'relevant filing system' means any set of information relating to individuals, structured in such a way that specific information relating to a particular individual is readily accessible.

The data protection legislation does not apply to data kept solely for historical research or other data consisting of archives (DP(A)A 2003, s 2(b)). See Education (Welfare) Act 2000 s 28. See also CRIMINAL DAMAGE TO PROPERTY; PERSONAL DATA; PERSONAL PUBLIC SERVICE NUMBER.

data, inaccurate. See INACCURATE DATA.

data, personal. See PERSONAL DATA.

data controller. A person who, either alone or with others, controls the contents and use of *personal data* (qv): Data Protection Act 1988 s 1(1). A data controller has an obligation in relation to the collection, accuracy, adequacy, relevance, storage and security of personal data kept by him. He must ensure that the data is not used or disclosed in a manner incompatible with the specified and lawful purposes for which they are kept (DPA 1988, s 2 as amended by Data Protection (Amendment) Act 2003, s 4). The 2003 Act imposes on the data controller a requirement for a level of security appropriate to the risks presented by the processing and the nature of the data to be protected (DPA 1988, s 2C inserted by DP(A)A 2003). Additional obligations are also placed on the controller for the fair processing of personal data (DPA 1988, s 2D inserted by DP(A)A 2003, s 4).

Provision has been made to permit certain specified bodies, participating in a cancer screening programme, to request information from any person and such information may be supplied, notwithstanding the data protection legislation: Health (Provision of Information) Act 1997.

A data controller also has to comply with an *enforcement notice* (qv) issued by the Data Protection Commissioner (DPA 1988, s 10 as amended by DP(A)A 2003, s 11). All data controllers and data processors are required to be registered except: (a) those who carry out processing whose sole purpose is the keeping of a register which is open to consultation by the public; (b) those who carry out processing of manual data unless provided for by regulation; (c) processing by any non-profit-making body in relation to the members of the body; and (d) data controllers and data processors specifically excluded by regulation (DPA 1988, s 16(1) as substituted by DP(A)A 2003, s 16). See Data Protection Act 1988 (Section 5(1)(d)) (Specification) Regulations 1993, SI No 95 of 1993. See PERSONAL DATA.

data processing equipment. See TRADING HOUSE, SPECIAL.

data processor. A person who processes personal data on behalf of a data controller (qv) but does not include an employee of a data controller who processes such data in the course of his employment: Data Protection Act 1988, s 1(1). He is required to ensure that appropriate security measures are taken to protect the data (DPA 1988, s 2(2) as amended by Data Protection (Amendment) Act 2003, s 4).

data protection. The statutory protection provided to protect the privacy of individuals with regard to personal data; it entitles individuals to establish the existence of *personal data* kept in relation to them, to have access to the data (with some exceptions); and to have inaccurate data rectified or erased: Data Protection Act 1988, ss 3–6 as amended by Data Protection (Amendment) Act 2003. The 2003 Act extended the provisions of data protection to include manual data, partly now and fully from 24 October 2007.

Various obligations are imposed on persons who keep personal data e g that the data must be accurate, be kept for lawful purposes, not be disclosed in any manner incompatible with those purposes and be protected by adequate security measures (DPA 1988, s 2 amended by DP(A)A

2003, s 3). Persons keeping such data, ie data controllers (qv) and data processors (qv), owe a *duty of care* to the data subjects (qv) concerned to the extent that the law of torts (qv) does not already provide (DPA 1988, s 7).

The legislation provides for the appointment of a Data Protection Commissioner (qv). Certain categories of persons and bodies who keep personal data are required to register with the Commissioner eg those who keep particularly sensitive data (political opinions, health, criminal convictions etc), the public sector and financial institutions (DPA 1988, s 16 as amended by DP(A)A 2003, s 16; SIs Nos 350 and 351 of 1988).

The legislation does not apply to: (a) personal data kept for State security purposes, (b) personal data which is required by law to be made available to the public, (c) personal data kept by an individual only for recreational purposes, or (d) personal data kept by an individual and concerned only with the management of his personal, family or household affairs (DPA 1988, s 1(4)). Various regulations: (a) prohibit the supply of data to a person where it could cause serious harm to his health, (b) restrict access to data which would prejudice the performance of certain functions eg by the Central Bank, and (c) continue in force certain existing statutory restrictions to data eg information obtained by the Ombudsman: (SIs Nos 81, 82, 83 and 84 of 1989). See also SI No 95 of 1993.

There are various restrictions on the transfer of personal data outside the State. A transfer to a country outside the European Economic Area may not take place unless that country ensures an adequate level of protection of a person's privacy rights (DPA 1988, s 11 substituted by DP(A)A 2003, s 12). These restrictions do not apply where eg the transfer is provided for by law, the data subject has given consent, or the transfer is necessary for the performance of a contract.

For the rules governing appeals to the court for the reliefs set out in s 26 of the Data Protection Act 1988 (eg an appeal against a refusal or a decision of the Data Commissioner), see Circuit Court Rules 2001 Ord 60.

The 1988 Act applies to the cross-border implementation bodies in certain circumstances eg where the data controller or processor is established in the State only: British-Irish Agreement Act 1999, s 51.

For regulations giving effect to Council Directive (EC) 58/02 concerning the processing of personal data and the protection of privacy in the electronic communications sector, see EC (Electronic Communications Networks and Services) (Data Protection and Privacy) Regulations 2003, SI No 535 of 2003 which revokes SI No 192 of 2002.

See Commission to Inquire into Child Abuse Act 2000, s 33. See Residential Institutions Redress Act 2002, s 30. The 2001 regulations, SI No 626 of 2001, have been repealed by DP(A)A 2003. See 'Secure in the knowledge' by Denis Kelleher BL in *Law Society Gazette* (April 2002) 8; 'The changing face of data protection' by Karen Murray BL in *Bar Review* (March/April 2002); 'Data Protection: the implication for Solicitors' by solicitor Paul Lavery in *Law Society Gazette* (December 2002) 26. See *www.dataprivacy.ie*. [Bibliography: A & L Goodbody (1); Clark (2); Kelleher & Murray; Oppenheim UK.] See CRIMINAL DAMAGE TO PROPERTY; DATA; PERSONAL DATA; PRIVACY IN TELECOMMUNICATIONS.

Data Protection Commissioner. A body corporate appointed by the government; the Commissioner is independent in the exercise of his function and is empowered to enforce compliance with the statutory provisions dealing with the protection of personal data (qv), either on his own initiative or following complaints from data subjects (qv): Data Protection Act 1988, ss 9–15 and Sch 2, as amended by Data Protection (Amendment) Act 2003 and Public Service Superannuation (Miscellaneous Provisions) Act 2004, Sch 2.

The Commissioner's functions include the maintenance of a register of data controllers (qv) and data processors (qv), the encouragement of preparation and dissemination of codes of practice, the issuing of enforcement notices (qv); prohibition notices (qv) and information notices (qv), and he is also the *designated officer* for the purpose of the *mutual assistance* provisions of the Data Protection Convention (qv). The Commissioner was given additional functions by the DP(A)A 2003 eg a monitoring role in relation Eurodac, established for the comparison of fingerprints; dissemination of Community findings in relation to transfers of personal data outside the

European Economic Area; and the Commissioner is the supervisory authority in the State for the purposes of Directive (EC) 46/95 on the protection of individuals with regard to the processing of personal data and on the free movement of such data (DPA 1998, s 9 amended by DP(A)A 2003, s 10).

The Commissioner is entitled to obtain data on a data subject from the Revenue Commissioners to enable him to determine whether he should serve an enforcement notice on the Revenue Commissioners to make the data available to the data subject: *Data Protection Commissioner v Revenue Commissioners* (1992) Irish Times, 8 December. email: *info@dataprivacy.ie*. See DATA PROTECTION; EUROPEAN POLICE OFFICE.

Data Protection Convention. The Convention of the Council of Europe done at Strasbourg on the 28 January 1981, which has as its purpose to secure in the territory of each party to the Convention, for every individual, whatever his nationality or residence, respect for his rights and fundamental freedoms, and particularly his right to privacy, with regard to automatic processing of personal data relating to him (*data protection*): art 1. The Convention has been given effect within this State by the Data Protection Act 1988 and is printed in full in Sch 1 to the Act.

data subject. A person who is the subject of *personal data* (qv): Data Protection Act 1988, s 1(1). A data subject was given additional rights and protections in 2003 eg: (a) the right to object to the processing of personal data likely to cause substantial damage or distress, and (b) a ban on decision making, based on processing by automatic means of personal data, intended to evaluate certain personal matters relating to the data subject eg relating to performance at work, creditworthiness, reliability or conduct (DPA 1988, ss 6A and 6B inserted by Data Protection (Amendment) Act 2003, s 8). See Case C-101/01 *Bodil Lindqvist* [2003] ECJ.

database. Means a collection of independent *works*, data or other materials, arranged in a systematic or methodical way and individually accessible by any means : Copyright and Related Rights Act 2000 s 2(1). While *work* includes a computer program, a computer program used in the making or operation of a database is not a *database*. An *original database* means a database in any form which, by reason of the selection or arrangement of its contents, constitutes the original intellectual creation of the author (CRRA 2000, s 2(1)). Copyright subsists in an *original database* (CRRA 2000, s 17(2)).

The author of an original database includes the individual or group who made it (CRRA 2000, s 21(g)). The copyright expires 70 years after the death of the author, irrespective of the date on which the work is first lawfully made available to the public (CRRA 2000, s 24(1)). However, see PUBLISHED EDITION. See Personal Injuries Assessment Board Act 2003, s 86. See also COPYRIGHT; COPYRIGHT, QUALIFICATION FOR.

database right. A recently created right which subsists in a *database* where there has been a *substantial investment* in obtaining, verifying or presenting the contents of the database: Copyright and Related Rights Act 2000 s 321(1). It is immaterial whether the database, or any of its contents, is a copyright work or not (CRRA 2000, s 321(3)). The owner of a database right has the right to undertake, or authorise others to undertake: (a) *extraction* ie the transfer of the contents of the database to another medium; or (b) *re-utilisation* ie making the contents available to the public by any means (CRRA 2000, ss 324(1) and 320(1)).

Substantial investment means substantial in terms of quantity or quality or a combination of both in terms of investment, whether of financial, human or technical resources (CRRA 2000, s 320(1)).

A database right expires 15 years from the end of the calendar year in which the making of the database was completed (CRRA 2000, s 325). The *maker* of the database is the first owner (CRRA 2000, s 323). The person who takes the initiative in obtaining, verifying or presenting the contents of the database and assumes the risk of investing is regarded as the *maker*; however, where this is an employee who made it in the course of his employment, the employer is the first owner (CRRA 2000, s 322).

Remedies for infringement of a database right are the same as for copyright (CRRA 2000, s 338).

Certain acts are permitted and are not infringement eg there are exemptions in respect of research and private study, education, public administration, anonymous and pseudonymous works (CRRA 2000, ss 328–337). There are also provisions dealing with the registration of licensing bodies and for the reference of disputes between licensees and licensing bodies to the Controller of Patents (CRRA 2000, ss 340–360). There is an obligation on collecting agencies (ie agencies collecting royalties in relation to database rights) to register (CRRA 2000, s 361). The provisions on database rights implement EU Directive on the Legal Protection of Databases 96/9/EC.

date of. It has been held that the *date of* an Equality Officer's recommendations can only mean the date appearing on the recommendation, and not the date of receipt of the recommendation: *Hegarty & Hogan v Labour Court* [1999] ELR 198, HC.

day. A period of 24 consecutive hours commencing at midnight: Protection of Young Persons (Employment) Act 1996, s 1(1). 'Days' when not expressed to be 'clear days' shall be exclusive of the first and inclusive of the last of such days: Circuit Court Rules 2001, Interpretation of Terms, para 7. There are provisions dealing with Saturdays and Sundays in the computation of time. See CLEAR DAY; TIME; TIME, COURT RULES.

day nursery. See PRE-SCHOOL SERVICE.

days of grace. Days allowed for making a payment or doing some other act after the time limited for same has expired. Formerly, three days of grace were added to the period in which a *bill of exchange* had to be paid, unless the bill provided to the contrary eg where it was payable on demand or was a fixed dated bill: Bills of Exchange Act 1882, s 14. As a *cheque* is a bill payable on demand, the drawer thereof was not entitled to any days of grace (BEA 1882, ss 14 and 73; *M'Lean v Clydesdale Banking Co* [1883] 9 App Cas 95). Days of grace as regards bills of exchange have been abolished: Central Bank Act 1989, s 132. See BANK HOLIDAY; BILL OF EXCHANGE.

DCM. Developing companies market. A DCM company is a company, any of whose securities have been admitted to trading on the DCM: Listing Rules 2000 (*definitions* as amended by Irish Stock Exchange Ltd). DCM replaces AIM, *alternative investment market*, in the Listing Rules of the London Stock Exchange. See Listing Rules 2000, paras 8.9(1), 12.11(c).

de bene esse. [Of well being.] Anticipating a future occasion. In a particular case, the decision of a court to hear the evidence *de bene esse*, was held to result in an unfair process: *In the Matter of MK, SK and WK* [1999] 2 ILRM 321, SC. See PERPETUATING TESTIMONY.

de bonis asportasis. [Of goods carried away.]

de bonis non. [Of goods not administered.] An administrator appointed to succeed a deceased administrator or executor to complete the administration of an estate. See *In b. Stuart* [1944] Ir Jur Rep 62. See Succession Act 1965, s 19.

de bonis propriis. [From one's own goods.]

de die in diem. [From day to day.]

de facto. [In fact.]

de facto director. A person who is deemed to be a director when in fact occupying the position of director, irrespective of the name of the position: Companies Act 1990, s 27. The High Court has held that a person could be regarded as a *de facto* director where there is clear evidence that he was: (a) the sole person directing the affairs of the company, or (b) directing the affairs of the company with others equally lacking in valid appointment, or (c) acting on an equal or more influential footing in directing the affairs of the company with the people who had been appointed formally as directors: *Re Lynrowan Enterprises Ltd* [2002] FL 8565, HC. See DIRECTORS; SHADOW DIRECTOR.

de jure. [By right.]

de lunatico inquirendo. [Inquiry into the condition of a person's mind.] See COMMISSION LUNATICO INQUIRENDO.

de minimis non curat lex. [The law does not concern itself with trifles.] See *Molloy & Walsh v Dublin Co Council* [1989] ILRM 633, HC. See PLANNING PERMISSION, DECISION ON.

de non apparentibus, et non existentibus, eadem est ratio. [Of things which do not appear and things which do not exist, the rule in legal proceedings is the same.]

de novo. [Anew.] There is a hearing of a case *de novo* when an appeal is made to the Circuit Court to challenge an order of the District Court on the merits. All questions of law and fact are open to review and either party may call fresh evidence.

de sont tort. [Of his own wrong.] See EXECUTOR DE SON TORT.

dealer, general. See GENERAL DEALER.

dealing as consumer. See CONSUMER, DEALING AS.

dealing in securities. Acquiring, disposing of, subscribing for or underwriting securities, or making or offering to make, an agreement to do any of the foregoing: Companies Act 1990, s 107. See EXCHEQUER BILLS; INSIDER DEALING.

Deasy's Act. [Landlord and Tenant Amendment Act Ireland 1860.] The consolidating Act, which introduced the notion that the relationship of landlord and tenant is one of contract; so called after Serjeant Deasy, then Attorney-General for Ireland, who piloted the Act through parliament. It continued up to 2004 as the foundation of the law of landlord and tenant in Ireland. See Residential Tenancies Act 2004, s 193(a). For proposals to amend Deasy's Act, see Law Reform Commission, *Consultation Paper on General Law of Landlord and Tenant Law* (LRC CP 28, 2003). [Bibliography: Deale; Wylie (1).] See PRIVATE RESIDENTIAL TENANCIES BOARD.

death, effect of. On the death of any person, all causes of action vesting in him or subsisting against him survive for the benefit of his estate or against it, as the case may be: Civil Liability Act 1961, ss 7–8. However, no action against the estate of a deceased person may be maintained unless: (a) the proceedings against the deceased person were commenced within the relevant *limitation* period and were pending at the date of death, or (b) the proceedings were commenced within the relevant limitation period, or within the period of two years after the death, whichever period expires first (CLA 1961, s 9(2)). See *McCullough v Ireland* [1990] 8 ILT Dig 83.

An action in respect of personal injuries to a person now deceased, may be brought for the benefit of his estate within two years from the date of his death, or the date of his personal representative's knowledge of the cause of action, whichever is the later: Statute of Limitations (Amendment) Act 1991, s 4, as amended from three to two years by Civil Liability and Courts Act 2004, s 7. In the case of criminal libel involving a deceased person, the mere vilifying of the deceased is not enough; there must be a vilifying with a view to injuring his posterity: *R v Ensor* [1887] 3 TLR 366 cited in *Hilliard v Penfield Enterprises Ltd* [1990] 1 IR 138.

A High Court judge has said that he was unable to find any legal authority in the history of the common law asserting the right of a deceased to a good name or to any property rights; additionally there was no place in the Constitution from which the rights of a deceased could be rationally inferred: Abbott J in *Congregation of the Christian Brothers v Commission to Inquire into Child Abuse* (2003) Irish Times, 18 October 2003.

The authority of an agent is terminated by his or his principal's death. As regards contracts, an offer lapses on the death of the offeror or offeree before acceptance. Death may also terminate a contractual obligation through the doctrine of frustration (qv). If a bankrupt should die after his adjudication as a bankrupt, the court may proceed in the bankruptcy as if the bankrupt were living: Bankruptcy Act 1988, s 42.

For the liabilities of an air carrier in respect of the death of a passenger, and the specified persons who are entitled to claim compensation, see Air Navigation and Transport (International Conventions) Act 2004, s 7.

A *death grant* was payable on the death of insured persons: Social Welfare (Consolidation) Act 1993, ss 114–116. This has been replaced by a *bereavement grant* in relation to deaths on or after 6 April 1999: Social Welfare Act 1999, s 19. See also Social Welfare Act 2000, s 25; Social Welfare Act 2003, s 2(2)(d). Certain social welfare payments were payable for six weeks after the death of the recipient; this payment continues even where the spouse of the deceased is already receiving a social welfare payment in their own right, thereby removing an anomaly: Social Welfare (Miscellaneous Provisions) Act 2003, s 7. From 1 June 2004, all social welfare payments continue after death for six weeks: Social Welfare (Miscellaneous Provisions) Act 2004, s 5.

A building society is empowered to pay to such person who appears to the society to be entitled to receive it, the funds of a deceased shareholder, up to such amount as is fixed from time to time by the Central Bank: Building Societies Act 1989, s 19. The maximum amount fixed in 2004 was €10,000. In the case of a credit union, the maximum amount has been specified as €6,400: Credit Union Act 1997, s 23 as amended by Euro Changeover (Amounts) Act 2001, s 6(d). See Residential Institutions Redress Act 2002, s 9. See *Moynihan v Greensmith* [1977] IR 55. [Bibliography:

Kerr (2).] See CAUSE OF ACTION; COMPENSATION ORDER; COMPROMISE; CORONER; FATAL INJURIES; JOINT ACCOUNT; LIMITATION OF ACTIONS; MEDICAL RECORDS.

death, on a. The meaning of the expression 'on a death' determines the distinction between a gift (qv) and an inheritance: Capital Acquisitions Tax Consolidation Act 2003, s 3. If a benefit is taken in connection with a death, the benefit is an *inheritance* taken by a *successor*. If it is not taken in connection with a death, the benefit is a *gift* taken by a *donee*.

death, presumption of. The presumption in law that a person is dead arises when it is proved: (a) that the person has not been heard of for seven years by persons who would be likely to have heard of him, and (b) that all appropriate enquiries have been made. There is no presumption as to the time the person died or the age at which he died; the burden of proving his death at a particular time rests on the person who asserts it. The court is empowered to make an order after a lesser period than seven years in an appropriate case eg as it did in the case of a person believed to have died ten months earlier on a mountaineering expedition in the Andes mountains: *Re Donegan* (2000) Irish Times, 16 May 2000. See *McMahon v McElroy* [1869] Ir R 5 Eq 1; *Re Lavelle* [1940] Ir Jur Rep 8; *Re Doherty* [1961] IR 219. See 'Body of Evidence' by barrister Tom Power in *Law Society Gazette* (April 2004) 18. See DEATH, SIMULTANEOUS.

death, proof of. The establishment of death in evidence by: production of a death certificate and proof of identity; or identification of the corpse; or identification of the person at the time of death; or presumption of death. See BRAIN DEATH; DEATH, PRESUMPTION OF.

death, registration of. There is a requirement to establish and maintain a register of all deaths occurring in the State, and of deaths occurring outside the State of Irish citizens domiciled in the State, and of certain other deaths occurring outside the State eg on board an Irish aircraft or ship: Civil Registration Act 2004, ss 13(1)(d) and 38–39. Where a death occurs in the State, it is the duty of a relative of the deceased who has knowledge of the required particulars to give them to any registrar within three months from the date of the death (CRA 2004, s 37). If there is

no such relative, the duty of giving the required particulars falls on a *qualified informant*, which includes a person present at the death, any other person who has knowledge of the required particulars, a person who found the body, a person who took charge of the body, the person who procured the disposal of the body, an authorised person where the death took place in a hospital or institution, any person in a dwelling where the death occurred, or any other person who has knowledge of the death (CRA 2004, s 37(5)).

A coroner is required to give to the appropriate registrar the required particulars for registration, where he: (a) holds an inquest, or (b) adjourns an inquest at which evidence of identification as to the cause of death has been given, or (c) decides, as a result of a post-mortem examination, not to hold an inquest (CRA 2004, s 41). A certificate of the cause of death, signed by a registered medical practitioner, must be given to the registrar where that doctor attended the person in his last illness (CRA 2004, s 42).

The particulars which must be registered are specified: (a) date and place of death; (b) in respect of the deceased person: forename(s), surname, birth surname and address, date of birth or age, sex, profession or occupation, personal public service number, marital status, profession or occupation of person's spouse, occupation of person's parent(s) or guardian(s) if deceased under 18 years of age, forename(s) and birth surname of mother and father, certificated cause of death; (c) in relation to the registered medical practitioner who certified the death: forename, surname, place of business, daytime telephone number and qualification; (d) in relation to the informant: forename(s), surname, qualification, address and signature; (e) date of registration; (f) signature of registrar (CRA 2004, s 37 and Sch 1, Pt 5). See *O'Connell v An tArd Chláraitheoir* [1997] 1 IR 377, HC. See FOETAL DEATH.

death, simultaneous. The presumption in law which deems that two or more persons died simultaneously, where they died in circumstances which render it *uncertain* (qv) which of them survived the other; the presumption is only for the purposes of distribution of the estate of any of them: Succession Act 1965, s 5. See *In the goods of Murphy* [1973] ILT & SJ 267.

The presumption of simultaneous death can only be rebutted where there is clear and cogent evidence to establish and prove positively the order of death, even if the time interval is a matter of only seconds: *Re Kennedy* [2000] 2 IR 571, HC. The onus of establishing that one deceased survived another, rests with the party so asserting.

The courts have held that where *joint tenants* perish by one blow, the estate will remain in joint tenancy in their respective successors, who may be numerous, and the right of *survivorship* will operate between them, even though they may have little or nothing to do with each other e g *Bradshaw v Toulmin* (1784) Dick 633. The Law Reform Commission has recommended that in such circumstances of the simultaneous death of joint tenants, their joint tenancy property should pass to their respective successors under a *tenancy in common*: Law Reform Commission Report, *Positive Covenants over freehold land and other proposals* (LRC 70, 2003). See JOINT TENANCY; TENANCY IN COMMON.

death benefit. Means a superannuation benefit payable under a public service pension scheme on the death of a member: Public Service Superannuation (Miscellaneous Provisions) Act 2004, s 1(1). For the *death benefit pension*, see Social Welfare (Consolidation) Act 1993, s 60, as amended by Social Welfare (Miscellaneous Provisions) Act 2004' s 6. See PUBLIC SERVICE PENSION SCHEME.

death duty. Generally, where a provision in a document refers to any 'death duty' it is to be taken as referring to 'inheritance tax' (qv): Capital Acquisitions Tax Consolidation Act 2003, s 112. See PUBLIC SERVICE PENSION SCHEME.

death of candidate. If a candidate in a Dáil election dies between the period of 48 hours before the latest time for receipt of nominations and the commencement of the poll, a new election is required, with the proceedings for the election starting afresh: Electoral Act 1992, s 62. There are similar provisions regarding elections to the European Parliament: European Parliament Elections Act 1997, Sch 2, r 27. If a candidate dies more than 48 hours before the close of nominations, the returning officer is required to give public notice to that effect and the candidature of the deceased candidate is deemed to have been withdrawn.

death penalty. The sentence that a person shall suffer death for an offence. The death penalty was retained until 1990 but only for capital murder (qv) and treason (qv) and certain offences by a person subject to military law under the Defence Act 1954, ss 124, 125, 127 or 128. See Criminal Justice Act 1964, s 1. The death penalty was abolished in 1990: *no person shall suffer death for an offence*: Criminal Justice Act 1990, s 1. In 2001, a constitutional ban on the death penalty was carried in a referendum of the people in the following terms, '*The Oireachtas shall not enact any law providing for the imposition of the death penalty.*' (1937 Constitution, art 15(5)(2)).

The Conference which agreed the Treaty of Amsterdam 1997, noted that since 1983 the death penalty had been abolished in most EU member states and had not been applied in any of them: Treaty of Amsterdam 1997, Declaration No 1.

The Minister must refuse to surrender to a Convention state, a person arrested on suspicion of drug trafficking by sea, where the offence for which the person is sought is punishable by a death sentence in that country, unless the Minister receives satisfactory assurances that the death penalty will not be carried out: Criminal Justice (Illicit Traffic by Sea) Act 2003, s 22. See EUROPEAN CONVENTION ON HUMAN RIGHTS; HANGING; PARDON.

debenture. An instrument, often but not necessarily under seal, issued by a company or public body as evidence of a debt or as security for a loan of a fixed sum of money upon which interest is payable. It is usually called a *debenture* on the face of it and it contains a promise to pay the amount mentioned on it. *Debenture* includes debenture stock, bonds and any other security of a company whether constituting a charge on the assets of the company or not: Companies Act 1963, s 2(1). Debentures do not form part of the capital of a company; debenture holders are creditors of the company not shareholders.

A debenture usually gives a charge over the company's assets or some form of security. Power to issue debentures is usually stated in express terms in the memorandum of association. A *convertible* debenture is one that the holder can at some stage convert into shares in the company. Debentures can be made redeemable on the remotest of contingencies, or even be irredeemable or perpetual (CA 1963, s 94).

A company may issue *debenture stock* which is transferrable, registered, and changes hands in much the same way as shares. When a company issues such stock in a series ranking *pari passu,* a register must be kept which is open to inspection by any person (CA 1963, ss 91 and 92).

When debenture stock is issued to a large number of persons, it is usual to appoint a trustee to act on the stockholders' behalf, with the function of ensuring that the loan agreement is adhered to and to protect the lenders and their successors' interests. Any provision in the trust deed, relieving the trustees of liability for breach of trust where they fail to show the 'degree of care and diligence' required of them, is void (CA 1963, Act s 93). See also *Re Dorman Long & Co* [1934] Ch 635.

A debenture holder who has neglected to cash cheques for interest before the winding up of a company, does not lose his right to be paid arrears of interest: *Re Defries & Sons* [1909] 2 Ch 423.

The Minister is empowered to obtain information on the ownership of shares and debentures of a company and to impose restrictions on them: Companies Act 1990, ss 15–16 eg restrictions imposed by the Minister on debentures issued by Siuicre Éireann cpt to Talmino Ltd (Iris Oifigiúil, 25 October 1991). See also Companies Act 1963, ss 93 and 200. See *Platt v Casey's Drogheda Brewery Co* [1912] 1 IR 279; *Daly v Allied Irish Banks* [1987] HC; *Re Tullow Engineering (Holdings) Ltd (in receivership)* [1990] 1 IR 452; *Bula Ltd and Others v Crowley and Others* [2002] FL 5044, HC and [2003] 1 ILRM 55. See SHARES; FLOATING CHARGE; INTEREST; MAREVA INJUNCTION; OPTION; RECEIVER, COMPANY.

debitor non praesumitur donare. [A debtor is not presumed to give.]

debitum in praesenti, solvendum in futuro. [Owed at the present time, payable in the future.]

debt. A sum of money which one person is bound to pay to another. Debts are: (a) *simple* contract debts; (b) *specialty* debts, created by a document under seal; (c) debts of *record* eg recognisances and judgment debts; (d) *secured* debts, for which security has been given; (e) *preferential* debts. A contract by way of guarantee to pay for the debts of another must be evidenced in writing: Statute of Frauds (Ireland) 1695, s 2.

It is an offence for a person to demand payment of a debt where the demands, by reason of their frequency, are calculated to subject the debtor, or a member of his family, to alarm, distress or humiliation: Non-Fatal Offences against the Person Act 1997, s 11. It is also an offence for a person to represent falsely that criminal proceedings lie for non payment or that he is authorised in some official capacity to enforce payment (NFOPA 1997, s 11(b)–(c)).

Where a solicitor is instructed to collect a simple debt, it is improper to demand the costs of the letter which he sends to the debtor, as the costs of that letter are not part of the debt: *A Guide to Professional Conduct of Solicitors in Ireland* (2002) ch 6.4. It is also improper to imply in that letter that the debtor will have to pay the costs of litigation, if any, which may follow, as that will be a matter for the court. However, the solicitor may say that the letter will be used as evidence in an application for costs to be awarded against the debtor.

As regards debts provable and proof of debts in bankruptcy, see Bankruptcy Act 1988, ss 75, 76 and 79. As regards extending the time for a creditor to prove a debt in bankruptcy, see: *Re M Kelly* [2000] 2 IR 219, HC. As regards infants and debts, see ACCOUNT STATED; RATIFICATION. See also BOOK DEBTS; CLAYTON'S CASE; HARASSMENT; PREFERENTIAL PAYMENTS.

debt management service. Means a service provided to individuals relating to the management of *consumer debt* (qv) and budgetary and financial matters: Money Advice and Budgeting Service Bill 2002, s 1(1). See MONEY ADVICE AND BUDGETING SERVICE.

debtor. One who owes a debt. A *judgment debtor* is a person against whom a judgment for a sum of money has been made. A *maintenance debtor* is a spouse ordered to pay maintenance. See BANKRUPTCY; EXAMINATION OF DEBTOR; FRAUDULENT DEBTOR; MAINTENANCE ORDER; MAREVA INJUNCTION.

debtor, imprisonment of. A debtor may be imprisoned for failure to obey a court order directing him to pay a debt either in one payment or by instalments: Enforcement of Court Orders Act 1940, s 6. See DCR 1997 Ord 53, r 8. Delay in exercising a warrant for the debtor's arrest may render the imprisonment invalid: *Berryman v Governor of Loughan House* [1993] 11 ILT Dig 212, HC.

If a bankrupt is in prison by virtue of that section in respect of a debt incurred before he was adjudicated a bankrupt, the court may order his release: Bankruptcy Act 1988, s 26. The traditional protection from imprisonment for debt for non-commissioned personnel of the defence forces is now restricted to personnel on active service: Defence (Amendment) Act 1987, s 10. There are separate rules governing how debtor prisoners are treated in prison eg remission of sentence does not apply to them: Rules for the Government of Prisons 1947, r 270. See also BA 1988, s 87(6).

A person must not be deprived of his liberty merely on the ground of inability to fulfil a contractual obligation: art 1 of the Fourth Protocol to the *European Convention on Human Rights*: European Convention on Human Rights Act 2003 s 1 and Sch 3. A report published in 2003 by the Free Legal Advice Centres (FLAC), called for an urgent overhaul of how the legal system deals with people in financial trouble: *An End Based on Means?*. The report recommends that committal for non-payment of fines should be replaced by 'attachment', where money would be deducted at source from a person's wages or social welfare payments. It also recommends that imprisonment for non-payment of civil debt is an anachronism and should be replaced by a civil-enforcement remedy. See EUROPEAN CONVENTION ON HUMAN RIGHTS.

debtor's summons. (1) A summons requiring the attendance of a debtor before the district court for examination as to the debtor's means: DCR 1997 Ord 53, r 3. Whenever a debt is due on foot of a judgment of a competent court and the creditor wishes to enforce that judgment, the creditor may prepare and lodge with the court clerk a *debtor's summons* together with a statutory declaration.

(2) Formerly, a summons served by a creditor on a debtor in bankruptcy proceedings, requiring payment of the debt of not less than £20. Failure to comply with the summons was deemed to constitute an *act of bankruptcy*. A debtor's summons has being replaced by a *bankruptcy summons* (qv) and the minimum amount of debt has been increased to £1,500 (€1,905): Bank-

ruptcy Act 1988, ss 3 and 8. See also s 7(2). See *O'Maoileoin v Official Assignee* [1989] IR 647. See BANKRUPTCY, ACT OF; EXAMINATION OF DEBTOR.

decedent. A deceased person.

deceit. A tort (qv) arising from a false statement of fact made by a person, knowingly or recklessly, with the intent that it be acted on by another, who as a result suffers damage. Also known as *fraud* (qv). It has been held that while the standard of proof in fraud is that of the balance of probability, where such proof is largely a matter of inference, such inference must not be drawn lightly: *Banco Ambrosiano v Ansbacher Co* [1987] ILRM 669.

To establish a cause of action in deceit for damages in relation to the acquisition of securities in a company, it is necessary to show that the defendant made, or authorised the making of, a false statement of fact so as to induce the plaintiff to acquire the securities in question, and that the inducement worked. As regards agency, a principal is not liable for the deceit of his agent: *United Dominions Trust (Ireland) Ltd v Shannon Caravans Ltd* [1976] IR 225. See INJURIOUS FALSEHOOD; MISREPRESENTATION; PLEADINGS.

deception. It is an offence to *obtain services* from another by any deception, where the person dishonestly, obtains services, with the intention of making a gain for himself or another, or of causing loss to another: Criminal Justice (Theft and Fraud Offences) Act 2001, s 7. A person *obtains services* from another where the other is induced to confer a benefit on some person by doing some act, or causing or permitting some act to be done, on the understanding that the benefit has been or will be paid for (CJ(TFO)A 2001, s 7(2)).

Similarly, it is an offence to induce another dishonestly by any deception to do or refrain from doing an act with a view to making a gain or causing loss. 'Gain' and 'loss' are to be construed as extending only to gain or loss of money or other property, whether any such gain or loss is temporary or permanent (CJ(TFO)A 2001, s 2(3)).

It is sufficient to prove that the accused did the act charged dishonestly with the intention of causing loss or making a gain; it is not necessary to prove an intention dishonestly to cause such loss or gain at the expense of a particular person (CJ(TFO)A 2001, s 54(1)). See District Court (Theft and Fraud Offences) Rules 2003, SI

No 412 of 2003. [Bibliography: McGreal C.] See MAKING OFF WITHOUT PAYMENT.

deceptive acronym. An acronym which is identical with the acronym of another will be refused registration as a trade mark eg *ANCO* was refused registration as it would indicate, contrary to the facts, a connection between goods thus marked with those produced in connection with the activities of An Chomhairle Oiliuna (AnCO). See also *The Anderson Company Application* [1972] Supp OJ No 1159 p.1.

deciding officer. A person appointed to determine a variety of claims and disputes arising under social welfare law eg under the Redundancy Payments Act 1967 (ss 37–38) and Social Welfare (Consolidation) Act 1993, ss 246–249. A deciding officer is entitled to take into account an applicant's personal circumstances: *Corcoran v Minister for Social Welfare* [1992] 10 ILT Dig 268, HC. Provision has been made to allow certain awards of *child benefit* in certain defined circumstances to be made without recourse to a deciding officer: Social Welfare (Miscellaneous Provisions) Act 2003, s 11.

decision. 'The action of deciding (a contest, controversy, question etc), settlement, determination': *Oxford English Dictionary* as quoted in *Dublin Wellwoman Centre Ltd v Ireland* [1995] 1 ILRM 1 ILRM 408 at 417, SC. The Supreme Court has appellate jurisdiction from all *decisions* of the High Court: 1937 Constitution art 34(4)(3). This includes all determinations of the High Court which have the characteristics of a decision, even in the absence of formal words: *SPUC (Ireland) Ltd v Grogan* [1989] IR 753. See also *B v Governor of Training Unit* [2002] 2 ILRM 161, SC.

decision of EC. See COMMUNITY LAW; EUROPEAN DECISION.

declaration, statutory. See STATUTORY DECLARATION.

declaration by deceased. Declarations by a deceased person are admissible in evidence, as an exception to the *hearsay* rule, as follows: (a) a declaration which was opposed to his pecuniary or proprietary interest, in a matter that he had peculiar means of knowledge and no interest to misrepresent the declaration; (b) a declaration made in the course of duty, made contemporaneously with the facts stated, and with no interest to misrepresent the facts; (c) a declaration made as to public or general rights, made *ante litem motam* by

some person having competent means of knowledge; (d) a declaration as to pedigree, where pedigree is in issue, made *ante litem motam* by a person related by blood or marriage; (e) a declaration by a testator as to his will, where the will has been lost, or where the question is whether a will is genuine or was improperly obtained, or where the question is whether which of several documents constitute the will; (f) dying declarations. See ANTE LITEM MOTAM; DYING DECLARATIONS; PEDIGREE.

declaration of incompatibility. See EUROPEAN CONVENTION ON HUMAN RIGHTS.

declaration of intention. A declaration by a person that he intends that an offer will be made or invited in the future. It does not mean that an offer is made now and consequently it gives no right of action to another who suffers loss because he does not carry out his intention. See *Harris v Nickerson* [1873] LR 8 QB 286. See OFFER.

declaration of interest. See ARM'S LENGTH; CONFLICT OF INTEREST.

declaration of marital status. See MARITAL STATUS.

declaration of parentage. See PARENTAGE, DECLARATION OF.

declaration of solvency. See WINDING UP.

declaration statute. A statute which declares or formally states the existing law in order to remove any doubts.

declaratory judgment. A declaration by the High Court of the rights of a person eg having regard to the determination of any question of construction of any deed or will or other written instrument; the proceedings are commenced by *special summons*: RSC Ord 3, r 7. The court may make binding declarations of right, whether any consequential relief is or could be claimed or not: RSC Ord 19, r 29.

A plaintiff may be entitled to declaratory relief only and not to damages: *Greene v Minister for Agriculture* [1990] 2 IR 17. It has been held that Order 84 RSC (ie regarding judicial review) is not to be construed as providing an exclusive procedure for persons seeking declaratory relief in matters of public law: *O'Donnell v Corp of Dún Laoghaire* [1991] ILRM 301, HC. The jurisdiction of the courts to grant declaratory relief was conferred by the Chancery (Ireland) Act 1867, s 155. See *Grianan an Aileach Interpretative Centre Company Ltd v Donegal County Council*

[2003] FL 8100, HC, overturned by the Supreme Court on 15 July 2004.

As regards patents, the proprietor or exclusive licensee may be entitled to a declaration from the court: (a) that his patent is valid and has been infringed; (b) that threats of infringement proceedings are unjustified; (c) that the use by a person of a process or product would not constitute an infringement: Patents Act 1992, ss 47, 53 and 54. See CONSTRUCTION SUIT; INFRINGEMENT OF PATENT; JUDICIAL REVIEW; PARENTAGE, DECLARATION OF.

decommissioning. In relation to arms, means: (a) destroying the arms, or (b) transferring to, or doing an act leading to the collection and destruction of the arms by or on behalf of, the *Independent International Commission on Decommissioning*: Decommissioning Act 1997, s 1(1). *Destruction* includes making permanently inaccessible or unusable. The International Commission was established pursuant to an agreement between the governments of Ireland and of the United Kingdom on 26 August 1997.

Under the Good Friday (Belfast) Agreement in 1998, all the participants reaffirmed their commitment to the *total disarmament* of all paramilitary organisations and they confirmed their intention to continue to work constructively and in good faith with the Commission, and to use any influence they may have, to achieve the decommissioning of all paramilitary arms within two years.

The 1997 Act mirrors the UK Northern Ireland Decommissioning Act 1997 and provides for the encouragement of decommissioning by prohibiting criminal proceedings arising from the decommissioning process and prohibiting forensic examination or testing of decommissioned arms (DA 1997, ss 5–6). The Commission is chaired by General John de Chastelain of Canada. See Decommissioning (Amendment) Regulations 2000, SI No 134 of 2000; (Amendment) Regulations 2001, SI No 211 of 2001 and SI No 379 of 2001; (Amendment) Regulations 2002, SIs Nos 41 and 42 of 2002; (Amendment) Regulations 2003, SIs Nos 69 and 70 of 2003; and (Amendment) Regulations 2004, SIs Nos 79 and 80 of 2004. See GOOD FRIDAY AGREEMENT.

decree. Means the order of the Circuit Court embodying its judgment: Circuit Court Rules 2001, Interpretation of Terms,

para 8. Every decree of the court has full force and effect for a period of twelve years from the date thereof (Ord 36, r 9).

The term is also used to indicate an order (decree) of nullity of marriage and to indicate an order of the District Court (DCR 1997 Ord 46, r 1).

A decree (or dismiss) of the District Court remains in full force and effect for twelve years, but the leave of the court is required for an execution of the order after six years: DCR 1997 Ord 48, r 4.

In District Court proceedings, *cross-decrees* between the same parties may be set-off against each other: DCR 1997 Ord 46, r 10. Also a decree of the District Court may be registered as a judgment mortgage (qv) and may also be registered in the Central Office (qv) of the High Court: Courts Act 1981, s 24–25; DCR 1997 Ord 53, rr 15–17. See JUDGMENT; MARRIAGE, NULLITY OF.

decree absolute. A final and conclusive decree.

decree nisi. A conditional decree. See NISI.

dedication. Formerly, the creation of a public road by dedication and acceptance. See PUBLIC ROAD.

deed. An instrument which is in writing, sealed and delivered, to prove and testify the agreement of the parties whose deed it is, as to its contents. It is usually signed. The seal is usually fixed to the deed before execution. The deed is sealed by placing a finger on the seal with the intention of sealing it; delivery is effected by handing the deed to the other party or by words indicating an intention to deliver it. A deed takes effect from the date of delivery. It is known as an *escrow* (qv) when it is delivered subject to a condition.

Certain contracts must be made under seal eg contracts made without consideration; authorisation of an agent to execute a deed; the transfer of a ship; contracts made by corporations (with exceptions). A right of action on a contract made under seal is statute barred after twelve years, while it is six years for a similar right under a simple contract. [Bibliography: Madden.] See ESCROW; NON EST FACTUM; ORAL AGREEMENT, MODIFICATION OF CONTRACT BY.

deed of conveyance. The deed to effect the transfer of property. It often includes: recitals; testatum; parcels; operative words; habendum; tenendum; reddendum; conditions; powers; covenants; testimonium (qqv). See Law Reform Commission

Report on *Further General Proposals including the Execution of Deeds* (LRC 56, 1998). [Bibliography: Bland (2).]

deed of retirement. See TRUSTEE, RETIREMENT OF.

Deed of Settlement company. Formerly an unincorporated company established by promoters who attempted, by using devices of contract and trust, to endow the company with many of the privileges and advantages normally reserved to corporations, which in those days could only be obtained by royal charter or special act of parliament. It is virtually extinct today.

deed poll. A deed which is *polled* or smooth ie not indented; a unilateral deed eg a declaration by a party of his intention to change his name. See INDENTURE; NAME, CHANGE OF.

deeds, registration of. The system which provides for the registration of deeds, conveyances and wills at the Registry of Deeds situated in Dublin: Registration of Deeds (Ireland) Act 1707. The document registered continues to be the evidence of title, unlike the system of registration of title. Registration is voluntary and a wide variety of documents dealing with interest in land may be registered. Failure to register may mean a *loss of priority* against other interests charged against the land.

A search in the Registry of Deeds will inform a purchaser of certain transactions affecting the title of the *unregistered* land, with the assurance that all transactions which were capable of being registered but which were not registered, will be treated as fraudulent and void, unless actual notice of them was brought to the attention of the purchaser. See *Fullerton v Provincial Bank of Ireland* [1903] IR 483. For information on the conversion to electronic format of information on deeds, see ITRIS. [Bibliography: Ellis & Eustace.] See LAND REGISTRATION; MEMORIAL; OFFICIAL SEARCH.

deemed. To be treated as; supposed; eg the law deems the dismissal of an employee to be an unfair dismissal (qv) unless there are substantial grounds justifying the dismissal: Unfair Dismissals Act 1977, s 6.

deer. See WILD ANIMALS, PROTECTED.

defamation. The tort (qv) consisting of the publication of a *defamatory* statement concerning another without just cause or excuse, whereby he suffers injury to his reputation. A *defamatory statement* is a false statement which exposes the person to hatred, ridicule or contempt, or which causes him to be shunned or avoided, or which tends to injure him in his office, calling or business. The test is whether the words tend to lower the person in the estimation of right-thinking members of society. Defamation may be a *libel* (qv) or a *slander* (qv).

To establish an action for defamation, the plaintiff must prove: (a) that the words complained of are defamatory; (b) that they refer to the plaintiff; (c) that they were *published* by the defendant; and (d) in the case of slander, *special damage* (ie some definite material loss) was suffered by the plaintiff or that the slander comes within a category which is actionable without proof of special damage. *Publication* means making known the defamatory matter to some person other than the person of whom it is made: see *Berry v Irish Times Ltd* [1973] IR 368.

A plaintiff who alleges that he has been defamed must set forth in his pleadings the details of his complaint with some particularity and not hope by *discovery* to make his case: *Galvin v Graham-Twomey* [1994] 2 ILRM 315, HC.

The words complained of must be defamatory in their ordinary meaning or by *innuendo* (qv). It is for the judge to say whether the words are capable of bearing a defamatory meaning and for the jury (or the judge where there is no jury) to decide if the words in the circumstances of the case in fact bear that meaning. Appellate courts are extremely slow to interfere with the assessment of damages in defamation cases, either on the basis of excess or inadequacy: *Barrett v Independent Newspapers* [1986] IR 13; *McDonagh v News Group Newspapers Ltd* [1993] ITLR (27 December), HC. The Supreme Court has held that a special status attaches to an award for damages for defamation as determined by a jury: *Hill v Cork Examiner Publications Ltd* [2001] 4 IR 219, SC.

The defences to a defamation action are: (a) consent by the plaintiff; (b) privilege, absolute or qualified; (c) fair comment; (d) apology; (e) offer of amends; (f) fair and accurate report; (g) justification (qqv). See Defamation Act 1961; Committees of the Houses of the Oireachtas (Compellability, Privileges and Immunities of Witnesses) Act 1997, s 11(2). See *Duffy v News Group Newspapers Ltd (No 2)* [1994] 3 IR 63.

All provisions of existing defamation law applies to all *electronic communications* within the State, including the retention of information electronically: Electronic Commerce Act 2000, s 23.

The Law Reform Commission has made recommendations for major changes in the law of defamation: LRC 38, 1991; also see O'Dell in 9 ILT & SJ (1991) 181. The report of the *Legal Advisory Group on Defamation*, established by the Minister for Justice in 2002 and chaired by Hugh Mohan SC, was published in June 2003. The report can be accessed on website: *www.justice.ie*. A public consultation process on the report was initiated with a cut-off point of end 2003 for receipt of submissions. See Eoin McCullough SC in *Bar Review* (July 2003) 140. See 'Defamation: which court to choose' and 'Publish and be damned?' by solicitor Pamela Cassidy in *Law Society Gazette* (April 2002) 22 and (August/September 2003) 18, respectively. See 'Defamation, Isolation and the Ordinary Reader – *McGrath v Independent Newspapers* (21 April 2004, unreported)' by Brendan Kirwan BL in *Bar Review* (July 2004) 130. [Bibliography: Burke & Corbett; McDonald (1); McGonagle; McHugh; Murphy; Duncan & O'Neill UK; Gatley UK.]

See CYBER LIBEL; ELECTRONIC COMMERCE; INJURIOUS FALSEHOOD; LODGMENT IN COURT; MALICE; MITIGATION OF DAMAGES; NAME, RIGHT TO GOOD; NEWSPAPER RULE; OFFENSIVE WORDS; PRELIMINARY ISSUE; PUBLICATION.

default. To fail to do something required by law eg non-payment of a sum by the due date; failure to deliver a defence to an action within the prescribed time. See eg JUDGMENT IN DEFAULT OF DEFENCE; PLEADINGS.

default judgment. A judgment of a court in default of appearance or defence on the part of the defendant. There is provision for the courts to review and set aside a default judgment; for the High Court, see RSC Ord 27, r 14, as amended by SI No 63 of 2004. For the District Court, see DCR 1997 Ord 45, r 3.

For the Circuit Court, see Circuit Court Rules 2001 Ord 26 and Ord 27. For review of such judgment, see Ord 30. A judgment has full force and effect for a period of twelve years from the date thereof (Ord 36, r 9). See 'Practice Notes' in *Law Society Gazette* (May 2004) 39. See DISMISSAL FOR WANT OF PROSECUTION; LIQUIDATED DEMAND; JUDGMENT IN DEFAULT OF APPEARANCE.

default permission. Generally understood to mean the grant of planning permission (qv) which is deemed to have been given where the planning authority fails to give its decision within the appropriate period. See PLANNING PERMISSION, DEFAULT.

defeasible. Capable of being annulled.

defect. An irregularity or fault. A *patent* defect is one which ought to be discovered by ordinary vigilance; a *latent* defect is one which could not be discovered by reasonable examination. See *Ashburner v Sewell* [1891] 3 Ch 405; *Re Flanagan & McGarvey & Thompson's Contract* [1945] NI 32. There must be a connecting factor between a *known* defect in an object and an *unknown* defect (in the object which caused injury to an employee) to put the owner on notice of the unknown defect therein: *Everett v Thorsman Ireland Ltd* [2000] 1 IR 256, HC. A vendor of real estate is obliged to disclose only latent defects of which he is aware or of which he should be aware: *Molphy v Coyne* [1919] 53 ILTR 177. See Law Reform Commission report, *Statute of Limitations: Claims in Contract and Tort in respect of Latent Damage (other than Personal Injury)* (LRC 64, 2001).

The District Court has jurisdiction to amend a summons, warrant or other document to remedy a defect in it: DCR 1997 Ord 38, r 1(2).

Once an accused appears in the District Court, his presence cures any procedural defect and once the *charge sheet* is laid before the court, then the court has seisin of the case and can proceed to the next stage: *DPP (Ivers) v Murphy* [1999] 1 ILRM 46, SC.

Where an accused has been sent forward for trial, the trial court may correct any *defect* in a charge against the accused, unless it considers that the correction would result in injustice: Criminal Procedure Act 1967, s 40 as inserted by Criminal Justice Act 1999, s 9. See SLIP RULE.

defective building. See BUILDER, DUTY OF; CAUSE OF ACTION.

defective goods/products. See MERCHANTABLE QUALITY; PRODUCT LIABILITY; QUALITY OF GOODS.

defective motor vehicle. See MOTOR VEHICLE, SALE OF.

defective product. See MERCHANTABLE QUALITY; PRODUCT LIABILITY; QUALITY OF GOODS.

defectum sanguinis. [Failure of issue.] See ESCHEAT.

defence. (1) The opposition or denial by a defendant of the prosecutor's case. (2) A written statement in reply to a *statement of claim* (qv) in a High Court action which must be served within 28 days of delivery of the statement of claim or from the time limited for appearance, whichever be later: RSC Ord 21, r 1. Facts not denied specifically or by necessary implication are taken to be admitted; a mere denial of a debt or liquidated demand in money is inadmissible; in some other actions it is necessary to deny some matter of fact (RSC Ord 21, rr 3–8). In default of defence, the plaintiff may be permitted to *enter judgment.*

As regards the *amendment* to a defence, it has been held that the courts decide matters in controversy and therefore as soon as it appears that the way in which a party has framed his case, will not lead to a decision on the matters in controversy, that party has a right to have it corrected if this can be done without injustice to the other party: RSC Ord 28, r 1; *Aer Rianta v Walsh Western International Ltd* [1997] 2 ILRM 45, SC: this case involved amendment to the defence denying the existence of a contractual relationship, the existence of which had been admitted in the original defence.

In Circuit Court civil proceedings, a defendant is required to deliver his defence to the plaintiff within ten days of entering an appearance: Circuit Court Rules 2001, Ord 15, r 4. In the District Court, *notice of intention to defend* a civil summons must be given not later than four days before the date of the sitting of the court to which the summons is returnable: DCR 1997 Ord 41, r 1. A defence in a personal injuries action must specify those elements of the claim of which the defendant does not require proof, the elements of the claim of which the defendant requires proof and the grounds on which the defendant claims he is not liable for any injuries suffered by the plaintiff: Civil Liability and Courts Act 2004, s 12. See COUNTERCLAIM; DEFEND, RIGHT TO; JUDGMENT IN DEFAULT OF DEFENCE.

defence, self. See SELF-DEFENCE.

defence barrister, duty of. It is improper for a barrister to conduct a criminal defence unless the following requirements have been met by his solicitor: (a) that he receives his instructions within a reasonable period of time in advance of the date of trial, which instructions include the book of evidence, a statement of the accused taken by the solicitor, a copy of the indictment, and the statements of any witnesses to be called on behalf of the accused; and (b) that any proofs advised have been carried out: *Code of Conduct for the Bar of Ireland* (December 2003) r 9.4. An exception is provided for circumstances which would result in the accused not being represented by any barrister during his trial. A barrister who has undertaken to defend a person charged with a criminal offence should not undertake any commitment which conflicts with his duty to that person (*Code of Conduct*, r 9.1).

A barrister is under a duty to defend any accused person on whose behalf he is instructed irrespective of any belief or opinion he may have formed as to the guilt or innocence of that person (*Code of Conduct*, r 9.14). So long as the accused maintains his innocence a barrister's duty lies in advising the accused on the law appropriate to his case and the conduct thereof (*Code of Conduct*, r 9.11). He should not put pressure on the accused to tender a plea of guilty whether to a restricted charge or not. He should always consider very carefully whether it is in the interest of justice to accept instructions to enter a plea of guilty. He should ensure that the accused is fully aware of all of the consequences of such a plea and have it recorded by his instructing solicitor and in his presence.

A barrister may properly advise the accused on the issue of the right of the accused to give evidence in his own defence, but the accused himself must make the decision (*Code of Conduct*, r 9.12). Also a barrister should not withdraw from a criminal case and leave the accused unrepresented because of the conduct of or anything said by the trial judge, unless the barrister considers that by doing so he is acting in the best interests of his client (*Code of Conduct*, r 9.15). It is the duty of a defence barrister to appear for the accused in any appeal against conviction or sentence if instructed to do so, unless such barrister has advised that he has no reasonable prospect of success on appeal (*Code of Conduct*, r 9.18). In normal circumstances it is the duty of the defence barrister to see the accused after conviction and sentence and if he is unable to do so, to ensure that his instructing solicitor does so (*Code of Conduct*, r 9.17). See ADMISSION OF GUILT.

defence forces. The right to raise and maintain military or armed forces is vested exclusively in the Oireachtas (qv): 1937 Constitution, art 15(6). The President of Ireland is the supreme commander of the defence forces and all officers hold their commission from her (art 13(5)(2)). Overall control of the defence forces rests with the Minister: Defence Act 1954. The discretion given to a commanding officer by DA 1954, s 64 when deciding on whether to re-engage a member of the forces does not restrict the officer as to the matters to which he should have regard: *Byrne v Minister for Defence* [2004] ITLR (17 May), HC.

There is no immunity at common law from suit by, or the negation of any duty of care to, a serving soldier, in respect of operations consisting of armed conflict or hostilities; superior officers owe a duty of care to serving soldiers: *Ryan v Ireland* [1989] 7 ILT & SJ 118 & 204 and [1990] ITLR (3 April).

Representative bodies may be established in the defence forces to deal with such non-operational matters as remuneration; such bodies must not be constituted as trade unions: Defence (Amendment) Act 1990.

Defence Act 1954, s 289 was amended to allow the recruitment of men, as well as women, to the army nursing service: Employment Equality Act 1998, s 24(2). There is provision for deductions from pay of members of the defence forces who have children in care: Child Care Act 1991, s 78.

The minimum pensionable age for *new entrants* to the defence forces has been set at 50 years of age; it is 65 for new members of the army nursing service: Public Service Superannuation (Miscellaneous Provisions) Act 2004, ss 7–10(2). See *Re Employment Equality Bill 1996* [1997] 2 IR 321 and ELR 132, SC. See Criminal Justice (United Nations Convention against Torture) Act 2000, s 6; Protection of Employees (Fixed-Term Work) Act 2003, s 17(a); See Pensions Act 1990, ss 77 and 81F as amended by substitution by Social Welfare (Miscellaneous Provisions) Act 2004, s 22(1); Private Security Services Act 2004, s 3(1)(b). For the Department of Defence, see website: *www.defence.ie*. For An Cosantoir, see website: *www.military.ie*. For representative body for the defence forces, see website: *www.pdforra.ie*. See COMMON DEFENCE; PART-TIME WORKER; PEACE OFFICER; MILITARY LAW; RETIREMENT, EARLY; UNITED NATIONS.

defence forces, reorganisation of. Provision was made in 1998 for the reorganisation of the defence forces under a single command structure, the *Defence Force Headquarters*, headed by a Chief of Staff, and supported by two Deputy Chiefs of Staff, (Operations) and (Support), who report to the Chief of Staff but are appointed by the government: Defence (Amendment) Act 1998. The previous quasi-independent offices of Adjutant-General and Quartermaster General are abolished and their functions are assigned to the Chiefs of Staff, who is appointed or removed from office by the President of Ireland, but is responsible to the Minister for such duties as are assigned to him.

defence forces and discipline. Particular respect has to be accorded to the fundamental importance under the 1937 Constitution and society of the disciplinary machinery and disciplinary code of the defence forces; consequently the courts will not intervene except where necessary to do justice to a member of the defence forces: *Scariff v Taylor* [1996] 2 ILRM 278 and 1 IR 242, SC. Procedural flaws in a decision to discharge a member of the defence forces which amount to a breach of justice, will entitle the member to have the decision quashed by the court: *O'Toole v Minister for Defence* [1999] ITLR (26 July).

The discharge of a member of the Naval Services for smoking cannabis while aboard a naval vessel, was upheld by the Court of Criminal Appeal: *Hackett v Department of Defence* (2003) Irish Times, 25 November. The court held that the Naval Service was a disciplined force and had to have strict rules and requirements concerning illicit drugs. Also the discharge of a recruit from the defence forces because she was a coeliac was upheld: *Fitzgerald v Minister for Defence* [2003] ITLR, 1 December. See COURTS-MARTIAL; HOMOSEXUAL CONDUCT.

defence forces and offences. The Defence Act 1954 was amended in 1997: (a) to keep military law in line with the ordinary criminal law by incorporating in DA 1954 such amendments as flow from the abolition of the distinction between a *felony* and a *misdemeanour*, and the abolition of *penal servitude* and *hard labour*, and (b) to provide that where a sentence of imprisonment is passed by a courts-martial, the military prisoner will serve the sentence: (i) in a public prison if the sentence is for a term exceeding two years; or (ii) in a military prison, detention barracks or public prison (or a mixture) if the sentence is for a term not exceeding two years: Criminal Law Act 1997, s 14 and Sch 2.

It is an offence, triable by court-martial, for a person subject to military law, to steal or handle or possess stolen property belonging to a person subject also to military law, or any public service property: Defence Act 1954, s 156 as amended by substitution by Criminal Justice (Theft and Fraud Offences) Act 2001, s 63. See COURTS-MARTIAL; DESERTER; MILITARY COURT OF INQUIRY; MILITARY TRIBUNALS; MILITARY PRISONER.

defence forces and UN. Certain members of the defence forces are liable for service with an International United Nations Force; such a force, being a force established by the Security Council or the General Assembly of the UN, is no longer required to be of a police character only and may be engaged in peace *enforcement* as well as peace *keeping*: Defence (Amendment) (No 2) Act 1960 as amended and extended by Defence (Amendment) Act 1993. See Kimber in (1993) 3 ISLR 48 on *UN Enforcing the Peace.*

defence policy. See COMMON FOREIGN AND SECURITY POLICY.

defences, criminal. The defences which may be relevant to answer a criminal charge include: insanity, infancy, consent, obedience to orders, self-defence, duress, mistake, drunkenness, immunity, and absence of *mens rea* (qqv).

defend, right to. The right to defend an action has been recognised as part of the constitutional right of access to the courts: *Calor Teoranta v Colgan* [22 June1990, unreported] SC. See Doyle in 8 ILT & SJ (1990) 255.

defendant. The person against whom an action, information or other civil proceeding is brought; also a person charged with an offence. Where a defendant has been *added* to proceedings, the proceedings are deemed against the added defendant to have begun on the making of the order adding the defendant, thereby treating the added defendant in a like manner as the original defendant as regards the Statute of Limitations: RSC Ord 15, r 13. See *McMeel v Minister for Health* [1986] HC; *Fincorig SAS v Ansbacher Co* [1987] HC.

All persons may be joined as defendants against whom the right to any relief is alleged to exist, whether jointly, severally,

or in the alternative: Circuit Court Rules 2001 Ord 6, r 2.

The person against whom a petition (qv) is presented is known as a respondent (qv). See also RSC Ord 15, r 4; DCR 1997 Ord 41. See O'BYRNE LETTER.

defendants, joint. Co-defendants; persons charged jointly with the same offence. Several persons may be joined in the same indictment (qv); one or more counts may charge several persons with the same crime eg where they are concerned, albeit in different capacities, in say robbing a bank.

In general two or more persons who are charged with the same offence, are tried together. They are not entitled, as of right, to separate trials; it is a matter of discretion for the judge: *The People (Attorney-General) v Carney & Mulcahy* [1955] IR 324. The judge will order separate trials where an accused would be prejudiced by being tried with another eg where one accused has made a statement implicating the other, or where the prosecution or the defence wishes to call a witness who could not be called if the accused were tried with others.

A joint defendant is a competent (qv) but not compellable witness for the prosecution against the other co-defendant: *Attorney-General (Ryan) v Egan* [1948] IR 433. However, once a co-defendant offers himself as a witness on his own behalf, he is bound by the terms of his oath to tell the truth and he may be cross-examined by his co-accused, and his evidence is admissible against his co-accused: *Attorney-General v Joyce & Walsh* [1929] IR 526. See Criminal Evidence Act 1992, s 24.

Where persons are charged on separate summonses or charge sheets with similar offences arising out of the same set of facts, in the absence of their consent to being tried together, they are entitled to separate trials: *Aldas & Anor v Watson* [1973] RTR 466. See also *The People v Murtagh* [1966] IR 361. It is desirable, if at all possible, for all co-accused to be sentenced at the same time, or in any event, by the same judge: *semble* in *The People (DPP) v Duffy and O'Toole* [2003] 2 IR 192, CCA.

As regards certain civil matters involving defendants in different EC states, a connection must exist between the different actions brought by a plaintiff against the defendants which is such as makes it expedient to have the actions tried together to avoid the risk of irreconcilable judgments arising from separate proceedings:

Case-189/87 *Kalfelis v Banque Schroder* [1988] ECR 5565. See CONSOLIDATION OF ACTIONS; JOINDER OF DEFENDANTS.

deferred shares. See FOUNDERS SHARES.

defilement. Unlawful carnal knowledge. It is an offence for a householder to permit the defilement of a girl under the age of 17 years on his premises: Criminal Law Amendment Act 1885, s 6 as amended by Criminal Law Act 1997, s 13 and Sch 1, para 5. See SEXUAL OFFENCES.

definition order. An order which the Minister may make to assign meanings to words or expressions used as, or as part of, a trade description applied to goods, services, living accommodation or facilities, of that description. See Consumer Information Act 1978, s 12.

deforcement. The wrongful holding of the land of another.

defraud. See FRAUD; ILLEGAL CONTRACTS.

degree. A step in the line of descent (qv) or consanguinity (qv). See MARRIAGE.

degressively proportional. Refers to a system of representation of EU member states in the European Parliament, whereby the number of seats a country has is broadly proportional to the size of its population, but with the ratio between the number of seats and the population size being progressively more favourable the smaller the size of a country's population: National Forum on Europe, *Glossary of Terms* (2003).

dehors. [Without.] Irrelevant; outside the scope of.

del credere agent. [Of belief.] An agent for the sale of goods, who in consideration of a higher rate of commission than is usual, guarantees that his principal will receive due payment for the price of all goods sold by him. The contract of agency is not required to be evidenced in writing under the Statute of Frauds, as the guarantee given is only incidental to the larger contract of agency. See *Hamburg India Rubber Comb Co v Martin* [1902] 1 KB 778.

delay. Negligent or unreasonable delay will defeat an action to enforce one's rights; *equity aids the vigilant and not the indolent.*

An accused has a constitutional right to reasonable expedition in the prosecution of an offence. The test which applies in all cases involving delay in criminal proceedings is whether or not it is shown that the delay is prejudicial to a fair trial of the accused: *Maguire v DPP and Kirby* [1988] ILRM 166; *O'Connor v DPP* [1987] ILRM 723; *O'Flynn & Hannigan v Clifford* [1989]

7 ILT Dig 124 & [1990] 8 ILT Dig 160; *Fitzpatrick v Shields* [1989] ILRM 243, HC; *DPP v Ryan* [1989] ITLR (3 April), CCA.

Where there is no real risk of unfairness to the accused, the trial will not be prohibited in spite of the delay: *McKenna v Presiding Judge of District Court and DPP* [2000] ITLR (7 February), HC relying on *DPP v Byrne* [1994] 2 IR 236 and *DPP v B* [1997] 3 IR 140. However, where there is blameworthy delay on the part of the prosecuting authorities, the court will not allow the case to proceed against the accused and additional actual prejudice to the accused need not be proved: *PP v DPP* [1999] ITLR (1 November).

Where delay between the date of an alleged offence and the date of a proposed trial may be a ground to prohibit the trial, the overall period of the delay must be broken down and examined in some detail: *Mulready v DPP* [2001] 1 ILRM 382, HC.

Also the court must inquire as to the reasons for the delay and whether it is satisfied, as a matter of probability, that the failure of the victim to complain of the offending conduct (in this case, alleged indecent assault of a pupil by a teacher) was the result of the conduct itself: *PO'C v DPP* [2000] 3 IR 87, SC. If there is a real risk that an accused would not receive a fair trial, the accused's right to a fair trial would prevail: *JL v DPP* [2000] 3 IR 122, SC. See also *P C v DPP* [1999] 2 IR 25, SC; *J O'C v DPP* [2000] 3 IR 478, SC; *PP v DPP* [2000] 1 IR 403, HC.

Extremely long delay, without cogent explanation and justification, may in itself constitute a ground for refusing relief: *de Roiste v Minister for Defence* [2001] 2 ILRM 241, SC and 1 IR 190 and ELR 33. In dismissing the plaintiff's action, the court held in another case that a delay of 50 years was inordinate and that no evidence had been adduced seeking to explain or excuse the delay: *Kelly v O'Leary* [2001] 2 IR 526, HC. See also *SF v DPP* [1999] 3 IR 235, SC; *DPP v Arthurs* [2000] 2 ILRM 363, HC; *DPP v Rice* [2000] 2 ILRM 393, HC.

In relation to whether an accused is entitled to have extradition (qv) refused on the ground of excessive delay, see *Harte v Fanning* [1988] ILRM 70. Delay in a county registrar or sheriff in executing certificates issued by the Collector General pursuant to s 485 of the Income Tax Act 1967 (see now Taxes Consolidation Act 1997, s 962) does not invalidate the certificates: *Weekes v Revenue Commissioners* [1989] ILRM 165, HC. Where a valid summons is before the court, the onus is on the defendant, if he seeks to have it dismissed because of delay, to satisfy the court that there are grounds for doing so; the onus is not on the prosecution to explain or justify the delay: *DPP v Byrne* [1994] 2 ILRM 91, SC. There also can be no objection to differing periods between the offence, the application for the summons, the service, and the trial: *DPP (Finn) v Hayes* [1993] 11 ILT Dig 211, HC. However, once charged a person is entitled to be tried within a reasonable time; there is no definitive time limit: *DPP (Harrington) v Kilbride* [1999] ILRM 452, HC.

See also *Sweeney v Horan's (Tralee)* [1987] ILRM 240; *The State (Brennan) v Connellan* [1986] HC; *DPP v Carlton* [1991] ITLR (4 November), HC; *Hogan v President of the Circuit Court* [1994] 2 IR 513, SC; *Cahalane v Murphy* [1994] 2 ILRM 383, SC and 2 IR 236; *Southern Mineral Oil Ltd (in liquidation) v Cooney* [1997] 3 IR 549, SC; *DO'R v DPP* [1997] 2 IR 273, HC; *DPP (Coleman) v McNeill* [1999] 1 IR 91, SC; *BJ v DPP* [2002] FL 6812, HC; *PM v Malone* [2002] 2 IR 560, SC; *M(J) v DPP* [2003] FL 7845, HC; *Minister for Social etc Affairs v Lawlor* [2003] FL 7292, HC; *Grendon v DPP* [2003] FL 7268, HC; *Dr James M Barry v DPP* (17 December 2003, unreported); *Carey Finn v DPP* [2003] 1 ILRM 217, HC. See LACHES; LIMITATION OF ACTIONS; STRIKE OUT.

delay and sexual abuse. Delay in cases relating to allegations of sexual abuse of children and young persons fall into a special category; the interpersonal relationship between the accused and the complainant has to be considered including any dominance of the accused over the complainants. The onus is on the accused to prove on the balance of probability that there is a real risk that he would not obtain a fair trial: *B v DPP* [1997] 2 ILRM 118, SC. See also *EO'R v DPP* [1996] 2 ILRM 128, HC.

The trial of a person in respect of sexual offences allegedly committed 20 years earlier was not prevented from proceeding: *JL v DPP* [1999] ITLR (9 August), HC. However, the Supreme Court in 2000 granted orders preventing the further prosecution of two men on sexual abuse charges relating to events which allegedly took place 18 to 20 years beforehand, upholding a High Court decision that the accused had established, as a matter of probability, that there was a real and serious risk of an unfair trial: *Irish Times*, 7 July 2000. See *W(D) v DPP* [2003] FL 8364, SC.

delay in civil cases. Where delay in a civil case has been both *inordinate and inexcusable*, the court will decide whether the balance of justice is in favour of, or against, the proceeding of the case; where the delay is not both inordinate and inexcusable, it would appear that there are no real grounds for dismissing the proceedings; also while a party acting through a solicitor is to an extent vicariously liable for the activity or inactivity of the solicitor, the court must consider the litigants' personal blameworthiness for the delay: *O'Domhnaill v Merrick* [1984] IR 151 cited in *Guerin v Guerin & McGrath* [1993] ILRM 243, HC. See also *Rainsford v Limerick Corporation* [1995] 561, HC. See 'Slow Motion' by Edmond Honohan, Master of the High Court, in *Law Society Gazette* (January/February 2004) 30.

delegated legislation. Subordinate legislation; rules or law as laid down by some person or body under authority delegated by legislation. Examples are: (a) *orders* permitted to be made by the government under legislation e g the government may by order activate part of the Offences Against the State Act 1939 which established the Special Criminal Court; (b) *statutory instruments* which designated Ministers are permitted to make under various statutes e g the Minister for the Environment may make orders dealing with a wide range of matters in the area of planning and development under the Planning and Development Act 2000; (c) *bye-laws* which local authorities and other bodies are empowered to make e g the Garda Commissioner is empowered to make bye-laws in relation to stands and stopping places for buses and taxis and for the general control of traffic and pedestrians under the Road Traffic Act 1961; (d) *autonomous* regulations e g the power given to the Law Society by the Solicitors Acts 1954 to 1994 to make regulations governing the conduct of its members.

Delegated legislation must in its method of enactment apply basic fairness of procedures; it must be reasonable, i e it must not be arbitrary, unjust or partial; and it must not be *ultra vires* (qv). See *Cassidy v Minister for Industry Commerce* [1978] IR 297; *Burke v Minister for Labour* [1979] IR 354; *Cityview Press v An Chomhairle Oiliuna* [1980] IR 381; *Cooke v Walsh* [1984] ILRM 208. See PLANNING REGULATIONS.

delegated regulation. Under the proposals of the draft European Constitutional Treaty, where there are non-essential elements to a European law or a European framework law, these laws may delegate to the European Commission the power to enact detailed regulations to supplement or amend these elements: National Forum on Europe, *Glossary of Terms* (2003). See proposed Treaty establishing a Constitution for Europe. See EUROPEAN UNION CONSTITUTION; REGULATION OF EC.

delegation by minister. It has been held that in the case of a function which could legitimately be exercised by an official on behalf of a Minister (provided the established practice within a department ensured that a particular function was performed by an appropriate official in the department), it must be presumed that the Minister authorised the performance of the function by the official and no express act of delegation is necessary: *McM v Manager of Trinity House* [1995] 2 ILRM 546, HC. The authority of officials to act in the name of their Minister derives from a general rule of law and not from any particular act of delegation: *Devanney v Shields* [1998] 1 ILRM 81, SC. See *Tang v Minister for Justice* [1996] 2 ILRM 49, SC. See CARLTONA PRINCIPLE.

delegatus non potest delegare. [A delegate cannot delegate.] A person to whom powers have been delegated cannot delegate them to another. An agent cannot delegate his authority without the express or implied authority of the principal. However authority to delegate may be implied: (a) where justified by usage of a particular trade; (b) where unforeseen emergencies arise which render it necessary for the agent to delegate; or (c) where the act done is purely ministerial and does not involve confidence or discretion. For delegation by company directors, see MacCann in 9 ILT & SJ (1991) 60. See *De Bussche v Alt* [1878] 8 Ch D 286. See AGENT OF NECESSITY; TRUSTEE, DUTY OF.

delict. A wrongful act. See TORT.

deliverable state. See GOODS, DELIVERABLE STATE.

delivery of deed. See DEED.

delivery of goods. The voluntary transfer of possession of goods from one person to another: Sale of Goods Act 1893, s 62. Delivery may take place by physical transfer of the goods; by physical transfer of a document of title eg a bill of lading; by physical transfer of the means of control eg a key to a warehouse with the goods therein; by attornment (qv); or by the seller becoming a bailee for the buyer. Whether it is for the buyer to take possession of the goods or for the seller to send them to the buyer is a question depending in each case on the contract, express or implied, between the parties (SGA 1893, s 29). Delivery of goods to a carrier is deemed prima facie to be a delivery to the buyer (SGA 1893, s 32). See *Board of Ordnance v Lewis* [1855] 7 Ir Jur (os) 17; *Bonner v Whelan* [1905] 39 ILTR 24. See CARRIER, DELIVERY OF GOODS TO; INSTALMENT DELIVERIES; WRONG QUANTITY.

delusion. Self-deception relating to some matter. In relation to delusions and wills, see SOUND DISPOSING MIND. In relation to insane delusions, see MCNAGHTEN RULES.

demand of debt. See DEBT.

demanding with menaces. See EXTORTION WITH MENACES.

demesne. [Own.] The part of the manor occupied by the lord.

demise. (1) The grant of a tenancy or lease; to let or lease land. Land which is let or leased is often referred to as *demised premises*. (2) A person's death.

democracy. See ELECTION; WORKER PARTICIPATION.

demolition. See DANGEROUS STRUCTURE; UNFIT HOUSE; HABITABLE HOUSE.

demonstrative legacy. A gift of personal property by will which is general in nature but which is directed to be paid out of a specific fund or part of the testator's property eg *£1000 to X to be paid out of my Irish Permanent Building Society shares*: *McCoy v Jacob* [1919] IR 134.

demurrage. An agreed sum fixed by a charterparty (qv) payable to the shipowner for the detention of a ship beyond the number of days allowed for loading and unloading. [Bibliography: Tiberg (UK).]

demurrer. Legal objection to an indictment (qv) on the basis that it is not sufficient in law and that the accused is not bound to answer it. See INDICTMENT; PLEA.

denature Means to mix an alcohol product with any substance so as to render the mixture unfit for human consumption:

Finance Act 2003, s 73. It includes to methylate and cognate words must be construed accordingly. There is provision for relief from alcohol products tax where the alcohol product has been denatured (FA 2003, s 77). Alcohol products which have been completely denatured are still subject to the rules and procedures for intra-Community movement of excisable products (FA 2003, s 89). See also Finance Act 2004, s 43.

dental health service. Means: (a) a dental health screening service, (b) a preventative dental treatment service, and (c) a primary care dental treatment service in respect of defects noted during a screening examination: Health (Dental Services for Children) Regulations 2000, SI No 248 of 2000. These regulations extend eligibility for health board dental services to children up to their 16th birthday.

dental insurance. Tax relief, at the standard rate, is now available in respect of dental insurance policies for non-routine dental treatment from insurers who provide dental insurance only: Taxes Consolidation Act 1997, s 470 as amended by Finance Act 2004, s 11. Tax relief continues to be available for medical insurance policies which may include cover for non-routine dental treatment.

dentistry, practice of. The performance of any operation and the giving of any treatment, advice, opinion or attendance which is usually performed or given by a dentist and includes the performance of any operation or the giving of any treatment, advice or attendance on or to any person preparatory to, for the purpose of, or in connection with, the fitting, insertion or fixing of artificial teeth: Dentists Act 1985, s 2. A person who is not a *registered dentist* is prohibited from using the title of dentist, dental surgeon or dental practitioner or from practising dentistry (DA 1985, ss 50–51).

The High Court has held that it would be a breach of the constitutional separation of powers for the court to order the Dental Council to introduce a scheme for *denturists* ie dentures fitters: *Kenny v Dental Council & Minister for Health* (2004) Irish Times, 28 February, HC. See *Hennan & Co Ltd v Duckworth* [1904] 90 LT 546; *McNamara v South Western Area Health Board* [2001] ELR 317, HC. See also Public Service Superannuation (Miscellaneous Provisions) Act 2004, Sch 2.

dependant. See FATAL INJURIES; CHILD, PROVISION FOR.

dependant in fatal injury cases. See FATAL INJURIES.

dependent child. For the purposes of a claim for a *maintenance order* (qv), a child under the age of sixteen years who is the natural child of the spouses, or an adopted child, or a child in whom the spouses stand *in loco parentis* (qv), or a child of one spouse who is known by the other spouse not to be his child but who is treated as a member of the family and includes a child whose parents are not married to each other: Family Law (Maintenance of Spouses and Children) Act 1976, s 3(1), as amended by the Status of Children Act 1987, s 16.

A child over the age of sixteen is dependent if receiving full-time education and is under the age of twenty-one years, or if suffering from some mental or physical handicap which prevents the child from maintaining himself fully. Any income of the dependent children will be taken into consideration by the court in determining whether a maintenance order should be made and how much should be awarded. See DISABLED PERSON AND SEPARATION; JUDICIAL SEPARATION; MAINTENANCE ORDERS; SEPARATION AGREEMENT; SUCCESSION, LAW OF.

dependent relative allowance. See Taxes Consolidation Act 1997, s 466 as amended by Finance Act 2000, s 10.

dependent relative revocation. A conditional revocation of a will where revocation is relative to another will and intended to be dependent on the validity of that will; the revocation is ineffective unless the other will takes effect. See Brady, 'A case of dependent relative revocation' (1981) 75 *Law Society Gazette* 5.

deponent. A person who makes an *affidavit* (qv) or *deposition* (qv).

deportation order. An order requiring any *non-national* specified in the order to leave the State within such period as may be specified in the order and to remain thereafter out of the State: Immigration Act 1999, ss 1(1) and 3(1).

A person, the subject of a deportation order, may be required to present himself to a garda or to an immigration officer, to produce travel documents and passport, to reside in a particular place pending removal from the State, and to notify any change in address. A garda or immigration officer is empowered to arrest and detain such a person without a warrant, if they have reasonable cause to suspect that the person has failed to comply with any of these requirements, or has destroyed his identity documents, or is in possession of forged identity documents, or intends to avoid removal from the State (IA 1999, s 5 as amended by Illegal Immigrants (Trafficking) Act 2000, s 10).

A deportation order may be made against a wide range of persons eg a person whose application for asylum has been refused, a person whose deportation has been recommended by a Court, a person whose deportation would, in the opinion of the Minister, be conducive to the common good (IA 1999, s 3(2)).

The Minister must have regard to a number of factors, including the age of the person, the duration of residence in the State, family and domestic circumstances, employment, character and conduct, humanitarian considerations, representations made, common good, national security and public policy (IA 1999, s 3(6)). The word 'reasons' in s 3 embraces the singular reason; also the 'common good' includes the control of aliens: *P v Minister for Justice* [2002] 1 ILRM 16, SC and 1 IR 164. It is an offence for a person to contravene a deportation order (IA 1999, s 3(10)). The 1999 legislation was necessitated by the decision in *Laurentiu v Minister for Justice* [2000] 1 ILRM 1, SC and [1999] 4 IR 26, SC.

It has been held that the true effect of a deportation order, which has not been revoked, was that if the person returned to the State following deportation, he must forthwith leave the State: *DP v Governor of the Training Unit* [2001] 1 IR 492, HC.

An applicant for asylum was refused leave to challenge the procedures which had been adopted by the Minister in handling his application, notifying him of the outcome and the Minister's intention to deport him, and the legality of the deportation order: *DPP v Popa* (2000) Irish Times, 19 August 2000.

A judge is entitled to impose a condition on the suspension of a person's sentence for a criminal offence that he leave the State; this does not encroach on the deportation powers of the Minister: *DPP v Alexiou* (2003) Irish Times, 1 August. See Immigration Act (Deportation) Regulations 2002, SI No 103 of 2002. See Criminal Justice (United Nations Convention against Torture) Act 2000, s 4. For the removal from the State of non-nationals who have been refused leave to land or who entered the State in contravention of the Aliens Order 1946, see Immigration Act 2003, s 5 as amended by Immigration Act 2004, s 16(8). See Removal Places of Detention Order 2003, SI No 444 of 2003; Removal Direction Regulations 2003, SI No 446 of 2003. See *Caldaras v Minister for Justice* [2003] FL 8563, HC; *Singeorzan v Minister for Justice* [2004] FL 9100, HC. See ALIEN; ASYLUM, CLAIM FOR; DUBLIN CONVENTION; EXPULSION; ILLEGAL IMMIGRANT; NON-NATIONAL.

deportation order and detention. A person, the subject of a *deportation order*, may be detained for the purpose of ensuring his departure from the State: Immigration Act 1999, s 3 as amended by Illegal Immigrants (Trafficking) Act 2000, s 10. The provisions relating to detention were referred by the President of Ireland to the Supreme Court under art 26 for a decision on the question as to whether they were repugnant to the Constitution; the Supreme Court held that the provisions were constitutional, holding that the aggregate detention period of eight weeks was a relatively narrow time-limit: *In the matter of art 26 and the Illegal Immigrants (Trafficking) Bill 1999* [2000] 2 IR 360, SC. See 'Sections 5 and 10 of the Illegal Immigrants (Trafficking) Act 2000' by Mary Rogan in (2002) 10 ISLR 3.

deportation order and Irish citizenship. The Irish citizenship of a minor child does not give rise to an absolute right to have his family, parents or siblings, reside in Ireland: *AO & DL v Minister for Justice* [2003] 1 IR 1, SC. Reasons for deporting 'the family of an Irish citizen of tender years will depend on the circumstances of each case but may include (a) the length of time the family has been in the State; (b) the application of the Dublin Convention; and (c) the overriding need to preserve respect for and the integrity of the asylum and immigration system': Denham J in *AO & DL* case, distinguishing *Fajujonu v Minister for Justice* [1990] 2 IR 151, SC. Following this judgment, the government decided that each outstanding claim to reside in the State on the basis of parentage of an Irish-born child would be examined and decided individually, with factors such as the person's individual family and domestic circumstances and humanitarian considerations being taken into account. See 'Guests of the Nation' by solicitor Aisling Ryan in *Law Society Gazette* (January February 2004) 21.

depose. To make a deposition or statement on oath (qv).

deposit. (1) In a contract for the sale of land, a part-payment of the purchase price; it is a usual condition of such sale that where the purchaser makes default, the vendor may forfeit the deposit and resell the land, and recover any deficiency and expenses on resale from the purchaser, being allowed this amount or the deposit, whichever is the greater. In auction sales, the conditions usually require the deposit to be paid to the auctioneer, who holds as stakeholder (qv). In the absence of agreement to the contrary, a deposit paid to the vendor's solicitor is treated as paid to him as the vendor's agent rather than as a stakeholder. See *Leemac Overseas Investments Ltd v Harvey* [1973] IR 160; *Desmond and Boyle v Brophy* [1986] ILRM 547.

(2) In a contract for the sale of goods, a deposit is a guarantee that the purchaser means business: *Soper v Arnold* [1889] 61 LT 702.

(3) As regards financial institutions, a deposit is generally understood to be a sum of money paid on terms whereby it will be returned with or without interest. 'There is no definition in Irish law as to what is or is not a deposit': *Re Irish Commercial Society Group Ltd (in receivership and in liquidation)* (1987, unreported) HC Vol 3, p 828. A building society is empowered to accept deposits: Building Societies Act 1989, s 18(1). Small deposits of a deceased depositor in savings banks and building societies may be paid to the beneficiaries without the necessity for *probate* (qv) or *letters of administration* (qv): Building Societies Act 1989, s 19 and Trustee Savings Banks Act 1989, s 60. See also HIRE-PURCHASE PRICE; INDUSTRIAL AND PROVIDENT SOCIETY; INVESTMENT TRUST COMPANY; SAVINGS PROTECTION SCHEME.

deposit interest retention tax; DIRT. The taxation at source of interest paid or credited on *relevant deposits* with banks, building societies and certain other bodies: Finance Act 1986, ss 31–40. A relevant deposit is any deposit other than an *exempted deposit*; an exempted deposit includes eg a deposit in respect of which no person ordinarily resident in the State is beneficially entitled to any interest (FA 1986, s 31(1)). Apart from companies chargeable to corporation

tax, only three classes of persons may claim repayment of retention tax: incapacitated persons, persons aged 65 or over, and charities (FA 1986, s 39). Taxation is now at the standard rate: Finance Act 1992, s 22; and for all taxpayers this deduction is regarded as the individual's full liability to income tax in respect of the interest: Finance Act 1993, s 15. There are now provisions for *three rates* of DIRT: Taxes Consolidation Act 1997, ss 256 and 257 amended by Finance Act 2000, s 28. See also Finance Act 2002, s 20.

The Comptroller and Auditor General was given special powers to enable him to investigate bogus *non-resident* accounts held in financial institutions in which DIRT had not been paid: Comptroller & Auditor General and Committees of the Houses of the Oireachtas (Special Provisions) Act 1998. The Revenue Commissioners are empowered to report to the Public Accounts Committee on the results of the 'look back' audit of financial institutions in relation to DIRT as was recommended by the Parliamentary Inquiry into DIRT in 1999: Taxes Consolidation Act 1997, s 904B inserted by Finance Act 2000, s 68. Also tax-geared penalties, rather than a fixed penalty, now apply for fraudulently or negligently making an incorrect return in respect of DIRT: Finance Act 2002, s 128. See *In the matter of NIB (No 2)* [1999] 2 ILRM 443, HC. See SPECIAL SAVINGS ACCOUNT.

deposit of goods. See BAILMENT.

deposit of title deeds. The delivery of title deeds to lands which creates an *equitable mortgage* (qv) thereon. The title deeds may be deposited to secure a debt antecedently due, or a sum then advanced or future advances; the depositee acquires a right to hold the deeds until the debt is paid and also acquires an equitable interest in the lands. Where the title deeds are accompanied by a memorandum of deposit signed by the mortgagor (qv), the mortgagee (qv) can protect his interest by registering the memorandum in the Registry of Deeds (qv). The mortgagee's remedy to obtain repayment of debt and interest is by way of mortgage suit (qv). See CHARGE, REGISTERED; FAMILY HOME; GUARANTEE; LAND CERTIFICATE; TITLE DEEDS.

deposition. A statement on oath of a witness in a judicial proceeding eg the statement of witnesses in criminal matters before the committing justice: RSC

Ord 86, r 15. Generally a deposition may not be given in evidence at a trial without the consent of the party against whom it may be offered, unless the deponent is dead, or beyond the jurisdiction of the court, or unable from sickness or other infirmity to attend the trial: RSC Ord 39, r 17. If the deponent refuses to sign the deposition, it must be signed by the examiner: RSC Ord 39, rr 11, 15. For examination of a witness in *commercial proceedings* (qv), see RSC Ord 63A, r 6(1)(xi) inserted by Rules of the Superior Courts (Commercial Proceedings) 2004, SI No 2 of 2004.

In criminal proceedings, at any time after an accused has been sent forward for trial, the prosecutor or the accused may apply to have a person's evidence taken by way of sworn deposition; that evidence may be admitted in evidence at the trial if the witness is dead, or unable to attend, or is prevented from attending or does not give evidence at the trial through fear or intimidation: Criminal Procedure Act 1967, ss 4F and 4G inserted by Criminal Justice Act 1999, s 9. The accused must have been present and afforded the opportunity to cross-examine and re-examine the witness. This provision also includes evidence given by live television link. Also where the above procedure is not possible or practicable, a document will be admissible which contains information compiled in the presence of a district judge from a non-resident victim of an offence where the victim has died or where it is not reasonably practicable to secure the victim's attendance at the trial: Criminal Evidence Act 1992, s 5(4).

An order was made in the Circuit Criminal Court under CPA 1967, s 4F requiring the referee of a Gaelic football match, involving an alleged assault on a player, to give evidence on deposition to the District Court; an official of the Louth GAA had told the court that it was policy not to co-operate with investigations of such incidents unless directed to do so by the court: *DPP (Segrave) v King* [2003] Irish Times, 20 March 2003, CC.

An accused before the Central Criminal Court is entitled to have supplied to him the depositions relating to the offences with which he is charged: RSC Ord 85, r 5. See *R v O'Loughlen* [1988] 3 All ER 431. See Bankruptcy Act 1988, s 140. See DOCUMENTARY EVIDENCE; FRESH EVIDENCE; LETTER OF REQUEST; PERPETUATING TESTIMONY; SHIP PROTEST; TELEVISION LINK.

depositum. [Deposit.] See BAILMENT.

deprave. To corrupt. See PERFORMANCE, INDECENT OR PROFANE.

depraved. A judge of the District Court was empowered to certify that a young person was so *depraved* a character that he serve his sentence in a prison rather than in an institution for young offenders: 'depraved' was not defined: Children's Act 1908, s 102 (now repealed) and *G & McD v Governor of Mountjoy Prison* [1991] 9 ILT Dig 266, HC. See DICTIONARY.

depreciation. Depreciation in the value of property in the vicinity is a valid reason for refusing planning permission: *Maher v An Bord Pleanála* [1993] ILRM 359, HC. See ASSET VALUATION; PROVISION; RESERVE.

depreciatory transaction. A transaction whereby assets are disposed of, other than at market value, by one group member company to another group member company: Taxes Consolidation Act 1997, s 621. A loss, on the ultimate disposal of shares, created by a depreciatory transaction will be reduced by an inspector of taxes to an amount which appears just and reasonable. This is an anti-avoidance provision to prevent 'asset stripping' which creates an artificial capital loss within a group. There is a similar provision to deal with 'dividend stripping' (TCA 1997, s 622).

derelict site. Any land which detracts, or is likely to detract, to a material degree from the amenity, character or appearance of land in the neighbourhood of the land in question because of: (a) the existence on the land of structures which are in a ruinous, derelict or dangerous condition, or (b) the neglected, unsightly or objectionable condition of the land or any structures, or (c) the presence, deposit or collection on the land of any litter, rubbish, debris or waste: Derelict Sites Act 1990, s 3.

There is a general duty on owners and occupiers of land to prevent land from becoming or continuing to be a derelict site (DSA 1990, s 9). There is also a duty on a local authority to prevent land in its functional area becoming or continuing to be a derelict site (DSA 1990, s 10) and a duty to establish and maintain a *derelict site register* (DSA 1990, s 8). An annual *derelict site levy* in respect of urban land on the register, is payable by the owner; the levy is fixed at 3% of the market value in the first year and a maximum of 10% is stipulated and is a charge (qv) on the land (DSA 1990, ss 21–26).

A local authority may acquire by agreement or compulsorily any derelict site situate in their functional area (DSA 1990, s 14). They may also require the owner by notice to carry out such works as are necessary to prevent the land from continuing to be a derelict site (DSA 1990, s 11). They may also enter on the site themselves, carry out the works and recover the expenses of so doing from the owner (DSA 1990, s 11). See Derelict Sites (Urban Areas) Regulations 1993, SI No 392 of 1993; Planning and Development Act 2000, s 79 (formerly Local Government (Planning and Development) Act 1999, s 30).

Areas in the counties of Tipperary NR, Louth, Meath, Clare, Laoighis; Dún Laoghaire-Rathdown and Kilkenny have been prescribed as *urban areas* for the purposes of the Derelict Sites Act 1990: Derelict Sites (Urban Areas) Regulations 2000, 2001, and 2003, SI No 440 of 2000, SI No 578 of 2001 and SI No 621 of 2003. Procedural matters have been prescribed to take account of the transfer to An Bord Pleanála of Ministerial powers in relation to the compulsory acquisition of derelict sites: Derelict Sites Regulations 2000, SI No 455 of 2000. See VESTING ORDER.

dereliction. The act of abandoning.

derivative. Includes any financial product the value of which in whole or in part is determined directly or indirectly by reference to the price of an underlying security but which does not include the possibility of delivery of such underlying securities: Takeover Rules 2001, Part A, r 2.1 (a). Unless the context otherwise requires, a reference in these Rules to 'relevant securities' of a company' includes references to a derivative (Takeover Rules 2001, r 8.9). See 'Know when to hold 'em' by Cedric Heather in *Law Society Gazette* (April 2003) 36. See TAKE-OVER.

derivative action. A company's action, the right to which is derived from the company, brought by a *minority shareholder* or shareholders. It is an exception to the rule that the proper plaintiff in respect of a wrong alleged to be done to a company is, *prima facie*, the company. It arises where the company is controlled by the defendant and the only way in which the wrong can be remedied is to allow any member to bring suit on the company's behalf. See *Prudential Assurance Co v Newman Industries Ltd* [1981] 1 Ch 229.

The Central Bank may bring proceedings in the name of a building society in respect of any fraud (qv), misfeasance (qv) or other misconduct in connection with the management of its affairs: Building Societies Act 1989, s 47(6). See also *MacCann* in 8 ILT & SJ (1990) 71. See FOSS V HARBOTTLE, RULE IN.

derogate. To destroy, prejudice, restrict or evade a right or obligation. Under the doctrine of *derogation from grant*, a person cannot avoid the consequences of their grant of title to another. The grantor must not seek to take away with one hand what he has given with the other. No man may derogate from his own grant: *Wheeldon v Burrows* [1879] 12 Ch 31. However, for the doctrine to apply where the owner of land disposes of part of it while retaining the balance, it is essential to show that the *easement* (qv) at issue was in existence and was being used at the time of the grant by the grantor for the benefit of the property which was granted over the property which was retained: *William Bennett Construction v Greene and Greene* [2004] ITLR 26 April 2004, SC.

EC Directives often contain provisions on *derogations* which may be availed of by member states e g Article 17 of the Council Directive (EC) 104/93: Organisation of Working Time Act 1997, Sch 6. See GENERALIA SPECIALIBUS NON DEROGANT; TRANSBORDER DATA FLOWS.

descendant. A person descended from an ancestor (qv). '*Descendants*' include issue of every degree of remoteness in descent; accordingly, a gift to descendants, if not otherwise qualified expressly or by implication, includes all children of children indefinitely and without limit: *O'Byrne v Davoren* [1994] 2 ILRM 276, HC.

descent. The devolution of an interest in land upon the death intestate of the owner to a person or persons by virtue of consanguinity with the deceased. Under the *Canons of Descent*, applicable to deaths prior to 1 January 1967, *realty* (except freehold registered land: Registration of Title Act 1891, Pt IV) went to the heir-at-law traced as follows: (a) inheritance descended lineally to issue of the last purchaser; (b) males took before females; (c) elder males took before a younger male in the same degree but females took equally as coparceners (qv); (d) lineal descendants represented their ancestor e g eldest son's son took before the younger son of the purchaser; (e) nearest lineal ancestor took on failure of lineal descendants; (f) relatives of the half-blood were admitted by the Inheritance Act 1833; (g) where there was a total failure of heirs of the last purchaser, the descent was traced to the last person entitled as if he had been the purchaser; (h) escheat (qv) then occurred but if the widow of the last person entitled survived, she took instead under the Intestate's Estates Act 1954.

Canons of Descent were abolished by the Succession Act 1965, s 11 except in so far as they apply to the descent of an *estate tail*; new rules for intestate succession were introduced under which realty and personalty devolve in the same way. See INTESTATE SUCCESSION.

description, sale by. Where there is a sale of goods by *description*, there is an implied condition (qv) that the goods will correspond with the description. A sale of goods is not prevented from being a sale by description by reason only that, being exposed for sale, they are selected by the buyer. A reference to goods on a label or other descriptive matter accompanying goods exposed for sale may constitute or form part of a description. See Sale of Goods Act 1893, s 13; Sale of Goods and Supply of Services Act 1980, s 10. Similar provisions apply as regards goods let by description under a hire-purchase agreement (SGSSA 1980, s 27). See *Arcos Ltd v Ronaasen* [1933] AC 470; *Goff v Walsh* [1940] Ir Jur Rep 49; *Egan v McSweeney* [1956] 90 ILTR 40; *Reardon-Smith v Hansen-Tangen* [1976] 1 WLR 989; *T O'Regan & Sons Ltd v Micro-Bio (Ireland) Ltd* [1980] HC. See SELF-SERVICE; TRADE MARK.

deserted wife's benefit. Formerly, the social welfare *benefit* to which a woman could be entitled where she has been deserted by her husband, was less than 40 years of age and had at least one qualified child residing with her: Social Welfare (Consolidation) Act 1993, ss 110–113. Cohabitation with any person as man and wife disqualified the person (SW(C)A 1993, s 110(3)). A deserted wife's *allowance* could be payable (SW(C)A 1993, ss 152–154). See also Social Welfare (No 2) Act 1995, ss 4 and 6.

It was held that there were ample grounds for the Oireachtas to conclude that deserted wives were in general likely to have greater needs than deserted husbands so as to justify legislation to meet such needs:

Lowth v Minister for Social Welfare [1999] 1 ILRM 5, SC.

The deserted wife's benefit and allowance was replaced in 1996 by the *one-parent family payment*: Social Welfare Act 1996, ss 17–21. See also Social Welfare Act 2002, s 2.

deserter. A person, subject to military law, who deserts or attempts to desert the defence forces is guilty of an offence against military law.

The offence is committed by a member of the defence forces if he absents himself from his unit *with the intention of not returning* to it; a person is presumed to have the intention of not returning to his unit if he has been absent without authority for a continuous period of six months or more: Defence Act 1954, s 135. It has been held that where a matter is presumed against an accused person unless the contrary is proved, a tribunal of fact (in this case a *courts-martial*) should be directed: (a) that it is for them to decide whether the contrary is proved, (b) that the burden of proof required is less than that at the hands of the prosecution in proving the case beyond reasonable doubt, and (c) that the burden may be discharged by evidence satisfying the tribunal of the probability of that which the accused is called upon to establish: *Convening Authority v Doyle* [1996] 2 ILRM 213, CMAC.

desertion. (1) Cessation of cohabitation (qv) which may be a ground for refusing a *maintenance order* (qv) to an applicant spouse who has deserted: Family Law (Maintenance of Spouses and Children) Act 1976, s 5(2). *Desertion* requires actual separation and an intention to desert. The definition of 'desertion' clearly and unambiguously envisages constructive desertion: *K v K* [1992] ITLR (4 May), SC. The spouse who physically leaves the matrimonial home is not necessarily the deserter; the spouse who intends to bring the cohabitation to an end and whose conduct causes its termination, commits the act of desertion. See *RK v MK* [1978] HC. Constructive desertion is normally a bar to a claim for maintenance (FL(MSC)A 1976, s 5(2)) unless it would be repugnant to justice not to make a maintenance order (Judicial Separation and Family Law Act 1989 s 38).

Desertion is a ground for a decree of *judicial separation* in marriage; desertion in this case includes conduct by one spouse that results in the other spouse, with just cause, leaving and living apart from the other spouse (JSFLA 1989, s 2(3)(b)). The court will not normally make an order for the support of a spouse who has deserted (JSFLA 1989, s 20(3)).

Compulsory deductions from the pay of a member of the Defence Forces may be made where he has deserted his wife and left her in destitute circumstances: Defence Act 1954, s 99; Status of Children Act 1987, s 24(2). See ATTACHMENT; JUDICIAL SEPARATION; UNWORTHINESS TO SUCCEED.

(2) As regards the desertion of children, see ADOPTION; CRUELTY TO CHILDREN; FOSTER PARENTS.

(3) As regards seamen, the penal sanction for desertion and for other disciplinary offences has been repealed: Merchant Shipping (Miscellaneous Provisions) Act 1998, s 2.

design. Means the appearance of the whole or a part of a *product* resulting from the features of, in particular, the lines, contours, colour, shape, texture or materials of the product itself or of its ornamentation: Industrial Designs Act 2001, s 2(1). A design which is *new* and has *individual character* is registrable by the proprietor of the design (IDA 2001, s 11). A *design right* subsists in a registered design from the date of registration (which is the filing date) and is owned by the registered proprietor (IDA 2001, s 42 and 29).

The design right is a *property right* and confers on its owner the *exclusive right* to use the design or to authorise others to use it (IDA 2001, s 42(4)). The design right expires five years after registration but is renewable for four further periods, giving a maximum of 25 years exclusive use (IDA 2001, s 43).

A design is considered *new* where no design identical to it has been previously made available to the public before the filing date for registration, or where priority is claimed, before the date of priority (IDA 2001, s 12). A design is deemed to have *individual character* if the overall impression it produces on the informed user differs from the overall impression produced on such user by a design which has been made available to the public (IDA 2001, s 13). The features of appearance of a product which are solely dictated by its technical function is not registrable (IDA 2001, s 16).

Product means any industrial or handicraft item, including parts intended to be assembled into a *complex product*, packaging, get-up, graphic symbols and typographical typefaces, but not including computer programs (IDA 2001, s 2(1)). A *complex product* is a product composed of multiple components, which can be replaced, permitting disassembly and reassembly of the product (IDA 2001, s 2(1)).

The State may use a registered design for the service of the State on terms to be agreed or, in default of agreement, on terms to be decided by the High Court (IDA 2001, s 86).

Copyright subsists in a registered design and generally has a term of 25 years from the filing date (IDA 2001, s 89(a) inserting new s 31A in the Copyright and Related Rights Act 2000). The making of an object which is in *three dimensions* will not be taken as an infringement of the copyright in a work in *two dimensions*, if the object would not appear to a non-expert to be a reproduction of the work (CRRA 2000, s 79(1)). [Note that s 79(2) of CRRA 2000 is repealed by IDA 2001, s 89(g); s 89(b) is redundant and will not be commenced.] The 2001 Act is intended to give effect in Irish law to EU Directive 98/71/EC on the legal protection of designs and to provide for future ratification and implementation of the Hague Agreement on the international registration of industrial designs.

For the *European Institute of Design and Disability*, see website: *www.design-for-all.org*. For the *Office for Harmonization in the Internal Market (Trade Marks and Designs)*, see website: *www.oami.eu.int*. For previous legislation see Industrial and Commercial Property (Protection) Act 1927, s 3; Industrial and Commercial Property (Protection) (Amendment) Act 1957, s 5; Copyright Act 1963, s 59. See also *Allibert SA v O'Connor* [1981] FSR 613 and [1982] ILRM 40. [Bibliography: Clark R; Clark & Smyth; Kelleher & Murray.] See AUTHOR; COMMERCIAL PROCEEDINGS; COMMUNITY DESIGN; COMPULSORY LICENCE; COPYRIGHT, DESIGN DOCUMENT; EXHAUSTION PRINCIPLE; HAGUE AGREEMENT; LICENCES OF RIGHT; PRIORITY DATE.

design, proprietor of new or original. See PROPRIETOR OF NEW OR ORIGINAL DESIGN.

design, registration of. Applications for registration of designs are made to the

Controller of Patents, Designs and Trade Marks, who has a wide range of powers. The Controller may refuse registration on the grounds that: (a) the design is contrary to public policy or to accepted principles of morality, or (b) the design constitutes an infringement of a copyright work, or (c) the design consists of or includes anything which would not be registered under certain sections of the Trade Marks Act 1996: Industrial Designs Act 2001, s 21. The Controller is required to maintain a *register of designs* which is available for public inspection (IDA 2001, ss 30 and 38). There is also provision for the registration of assignments and other interests in design rights (IDA 2001, s 41).

For the regulations which prescribe the fees payable, the forms to be used and the procedures to be observed in connection with the registration of designs, see Industrial Designs Regulations 2002, SI No 280 of 2002. See DESIGN.

design right, assignment of. A *design right* is transmissible by assignment, testamentary disposition, or operation of law, as personal or moveable property: Industrial Designs Act 2001, s 76. An assignment, mortgage or vesting assent of a design right must be in writing and signed by the assignor, mortgagor, or the party giving the assent (IDA 2001, s 76(3)). Provision is made for the registration of a variety of interests in a design right eg whether by way of assignment, transmission by law, mortgage or licence (IDA 2001, s 41).

Failure to register an assignment does not affect the validity of the assignment as between the assignor and assignee. However, the legal right to sue third parties (eg for infringement of the design right) will remain with the registered proprietor and consequently, if the assignment is not registered, the registered proprietor will have to be made a party to the action. Also a transfer of a design right is ineffective as against a person acquiring a conflicting interest, in ignorance of the transfer, until an application to register the transfer has been made under s 41 (IDA 2001, s 76(4)).

design right, infringement of. A design right is infringed by a person who, without a licence of the registered proprietor of the design, undertakes any act which is the exclusive right of the registered proprietor: Industrial Designs Act 2001, s 51(1). Such *infringement* includes authorising another person to take such an act. An infringement only occurs when the design right is in force and does not apply to acts done privately and for non-commercial purposes, acts done for experimental purposes, or acts of reproduction for the purposes of making citations or teaching (IDA 2001, s 48(1)). *Secondary infringement* takes place where a person, without a licence, sells, rents or offers for sale or rent: (a) a product which he knows, or has reason to believe is, an *infringing product* (qv), or (b) an article designed to make infringing products (IDA 2001, ss 52–53).

Infringement of a design right is actionable by the registered proprietor of the design (IDA 2001, s 57). The court may award aggravated or exemplary damages or both for infringement, but no damages may be awarded in the case of innocent infringement, although an account for profits may be ordered (IDA 2001, ss 58–59). An infringement of a design right may also constitute a criminal offence (IDA 2001, ss 66–68).

Provision is made for delivery up of infringing products and infringing articles, for their seizure and disposal (IDA 2001, ss 61–62, 69–72), and for preventing their importation as *prohibited goods* (qv) (IDA 2001, ss 73–74). See INFRINGING ARTICLE; INFRINGING PRODUCT.

design right, licence of. A licence of a design right, including an *exclusive licence*, is not effective unless it is in writing and signed by the grantor: Industrial Designs Act 2001 s 78(3). An *exclusive licence* means a licence authorising the licensee, to the exclusion of all other persons (including the person granting the licence), to use a registered design in the matter authorised by the licence (IDA 2001, s 77(1)). There is provision for the registration by the Controller of Patents of a licence (IDA 2001, s 41). A licence is ineffective as against a person acquiring a conflicting interest in ignorance of the licence, until an application to register the licence has been made under s 41 (IDA 2001, s 78(1)).

A licensee is entitled to invite the registered proprietor of a design to take infringement proceedings in respect of any matter which affects the licensee's interests, and if he refuses or fails to do so, to bring such proceedings himself as licensee (IDA 2001, s 65). An *exclusive licensee* however, except as against the registered proprietor of the design, has the same rights and remedies as if the licence had been an assignment, i e the rights and remedies are concurrent with those of the proprietor (IDA 2001, ss 63–64).

designated. When considered in its Latin etymological sense relates to a sign or a mark of approval; the formal introduction to an accused renders a doctor a *designated* registered medical practitioner under the Road Traffic Acts: *DPP v Hyland* [1991] ITLR (28 January), HC. See Road Traffic Act 1994, s 9(1). See BLOOD SPECIMEN; URINE SPECIMEN.

destructive insect. See INSECT.

detain. See DETENTION.

detection devices. See METAL DETECTORS.

detention. (1) A sentence of detention e g in St Patrick's Institution, which is distinct from a sentence of imprisonment: *The State (Clinch) v Connellan* [1986] ILRM 460; *The State (White) v Martin* [1976] 111 ILTR 21. See CHILD SUSPECT; DETENTION OF CHILD.

(2) The Garda Síochána are empowered to detain a person following arrest on reasonable suspicion of having committed an *indictable offence* (qv) attracting a penalty of five years or more imprisonment: Criminal Justice Act 1984, ss 4–10 as amended by Criminal Justice (Miscellaneous Provisions) Act 1997, s 2. Detention is for a maximum of six hours, which is renewable up to a maximum of twelve hours; time spent overnight is not normally reckonable, nor is time while being taken to court, and the maximum time a person may be in custody before release is twenty hours. The purpose of CJ(MP)A 1997, s 4 is to give the gardaí effecting an arrest adequate time, but no more, to progress to a position where a garda could prefer charges for the offence in question: *DPP v Cleary* [2001] FL 4878, HC. The person may be removed from the garda station to a hospital or to the court for a legitimate purpose; the period of lawful detention continues during this absence: *Clarke v Member in Charge of Terenure Garda Station* [2002] 2 ILRM 11, SC and [2001] 4 IR 171, SC. The gardaí have a duty to arrange access to a solicitor (qv) and to notify a parent or guardian (qv) in the case of a juvenile. See Criminal Justice Bill 2004, s 8.

(3) The powers of detention have been extended in relation to persons suspected of having committed a drug trafficking offence; a period of detention for up to 168 hours is provided for: Criminal Justice (Drug Trafficking) Act 1996, s 2. The approvals required are: up to six hours (garda), next 18 hours (chief superintendent), next 24 hours (chief superintendent), next 72 hours (court), next 48 hours (court). The continued operation of CJ(DT)A 1996, ss 2–6, requires a resolution of both Houses of the Oireachtas. See Criminal Justice Bill 2004, s 9.

(4) The period of 48 hours detention permitted under s 30 of the Offences against the State Act 1939 can be extended by a further 12 hours in certain circumstances e g if the district court judge is satisfied that it is necessary for the proper investigation of the offence concerned and that the investigation is being conducted diligently and expeditiously: Offences against the State (Amendment) Act 1998, ss 10 and 18 as amended by Criminal Justice Act 1999, s 37. A re-arrest, following release without charge, is permitted by district court warrant, for a further period not exceeding 24 hours (OS(A)A 1998, ss 11 and 18).

It has been held that it would be an unwarranted and unlawful usurpation of the constitutional role of the High Court for any inferior court to embark on an enquiry under Article 40 of the 1937 Constitution with a view to holding that a person is being unlawfully detained: *Keating v Governor of Mountjoy Prison* [1990] ILRM 850, SC. Also the restriction of movement of a person, by virtue of the surrender of his passport, does not constitute detention: *Bolger v Commissioner of Garda Síochána* [2000] 1 ILRM 136, HC and SC

(5) The master of a ship and the pilot of an aircraft are empowered to detain on board the ship or aircraft any non-national until he is examined or landed for examination by an immigration officer or a garda: Immigration Act 2004, s 7. For places of detention of persons the subject of a deportation order, see DEPORTATION ORDER. See Treatment of Persons in Custody in Garda Síochána Stations Regulations 1987, SI No 119 of 1987, reg 7. See DCR 1997 Ord 20. See also Maritime Security Act 2004, s 4. [Bibliography: Walsh D (3).] See BODILY SAMPLE; CUSTODY IN GARDA STATION; DEPORTATION ORDER; EUROPEAN ARREST WARRANT; HABEAS CORPUS; IDENTIFICATION PARADE; INTERNMENT; OFFENCES AGAINST THE STATE; PREVENTATIVE DETENTION; PUNISHMENT;

REFUGEE; SOLICITOR, ACCESS TO; SPECIAL VERDICT; UNFIT TO PLEAD.

detention of aircraft. Provision has been made for the detention of an aircraft in specified circumstances e g where air navigation and aeronautical communication services charges are unpaid: Irish Aviation Authority Act 1993, s 67; Air Navigation and Transport Act 1998, s 64. The 1998 Act also gave power to Aer Rianta to detain an aircraft where airport charges are unpaid (ANTA 1998, s 40). See ILLEGAL IMMIGRANT.

detention of boat. For provisions regarding obtaining an order from the District Court for the detention of a boat and persons on board under fisheries legislation, see DCR 1997 Ord 65. See ILLEGAL IMMIGRANT.

detention of child. A court may by order impose on a child a period of detention either (a) in a children detention school provided by the Minister for Education for child offenders under 16 years of age; and (b) in a children detention centre provided by the Minister for Justice for 16 and 17 year olds: Children Act 2001, ss 142–156.

For the purposes of the Minister's powers to order temporary release, a person serving a sentence of imprisonment is to be construed as including a person serving a sentence of detention in St Patrick's Institution, and a person detained in a place provided under s 2 of the Prisons Act 1970: Criminal Justice Act 1960, s 2(11) as substituted by Criminal Justice (Temporary Release of Prisoners) Act 2003, s 1. See CHILD SUSPECT; CHILDREN DETENTION SCHOOLS; PUNISHMENT OF CHILD; REFORMATORY SCHOOLS.

detention of patient. A chief medical officer, with the agreement of a second medical practitioner, may order the detention of a person who is a probable source of certain infections in a hospital or other place: Health Act 1947, s 38 as amended by Health Act 1953, s 35; Infectious Diseases Regulations 1981, SI No 390 of 1981, art 8.

Where a person, who is being treated in an approved centre as a *voluntary patient,* indicates that he wishes to leave the centre, he may be detained for 24 hours if a consultant psychiatrist, registered medical practitioner or registered nurse on the staff of the approved centre is of the opinion that the person is suffering from a *mental disorder* (qv): Mental Health Act 2001, s 23. See *Croke v Smith* [1998] 1 IR 101, SC; C-

33267/96 *Croke v Ireland* [2000] ECHR 671. See 'Involuntary psychiatric treatment and detention' by Simon Mills BL in *Bar Review* (February 2003) 42. [Bibliography: Keys.]

detention of ship. The *arrest* of ships within the jurisdiction of the State in respect of *maritime claims* is authorised by the Jurisdiction of Courts (Maritime Conventions) Act 1989 which gives effect to the International Convention on the Arrest of Seagoing Ships 1952. Maritime claims include claims arising out of salvage, loss of life or personal injury in connection with the operation of the ship, agreements relating to carriage of goods or use or hire of the ship by charterparty or otherwise, the mortgage (qv) or hypothecation (qv) of the ship (1952 Convention, art 1). Arrest means the detention of a ship by judicial process but not seizure in execution or satisfaction of a judgment. The High Court has jurisdiction in these admiralty proceedings (JC(MC)A 1989, s 5).

The Convention applies to any vessel flying the flag of a contacting state; however, a ship flying the flag of a non-contacting state may be arrested in respect of claims against that ship but not a sister ship: In the matter of *MV Kapitan Labunets* [1995] 1 ILRM 430, SC and 1 IR 164. See also Fisheries (Amendment) Act 1994, ss 10–12.

A dredger can constitute a 'ship'; to come within the category of a ship, it is not necessary that the purpose of a craft is to go from one place to another: *The Von Rocks* [1998] 1 ILRM 481, SC.

An inspector or a harbour master is empowered to stop and detain a ship, or to take it to such place in the State as he considers appropriate and there detain it, in certain circumstances e g where he has reasonable cause to believe that it may cause or has caused pollution: Sea Pollution Act 1991, s 24 as amended by Sea Pollution (Amendment) Act 1999, s 14. See *The Marshall Gelovani* [1995] 1 IR 159, HC.

A ship can also be arrested where it is suspected of carrying drugs. When the ship is on the high seas, the Irish authorities, with the permission of the flag state (ie the country where the ship is registered) are entitled to stop, board, search the ship, and if drugs are found, to take and detain the ship in an Irish port, and arrest, charge and prosecute the crew: Criminal Justice (Illicit

Traffic by Sea) Act 2003, which implements the Council of Europe Agreement on Illicit Traffic by Sea. Alternatively, the flag state, exercising *preferential jurisdiction,* could insist on prosecuting the crew, and could, through the Agreement, require the crew, the ship and any evidence found on board to be surrendered to it by the Irish authorities. See also DRUG TRAFFICKING; ILLEGAL IMMIGRANT.

detention of vehicle. The Minister is empowered to make regulations authorising the detention of a mechanically propelled vehicle where a garda is of the opinion that it is not insured or taxed or that the driver, by reason of his age, is ineligible to hold a driving licence: Road Traffic Act 1994, s 41. See ILLEGAL IMMIGRANT.

deterioration, medical. The Supreme Court will not consider facts concerning an alleged medical deterioration of a plaintiff subsequent to the trial of an action in the High Court. 'To allow the plaintiff to appeal by reference to facts which had come to light after the hearing of the claim in the High Court would undermine the finality of legal proceedings ... ': *Dalton v Minister for Finance* [1989] ILT Dig 230.

determinable fee. See FEE SIMPLE.

determination. See DECISION.

determination order. A written record prepared by the *Private Residential Tenancies Board* of: (a) an agreement mentioned in a report of a mediator; (b) a determination in a report of an adjudicator; (c) a determination of the Tenancy Tribunal; or (d) a direction given by an adjudicator or the Tribunal: Residential Tenancies Act 2004, s 121. A *determination order* may be expressed in a different manner in order to remove any ambiguity in, or to help clarify, the agreement, determination or direction. Also the Board may seek a fresh determination of the Tribunal when it is of the opinion that the earlier determination is not consistent with previous determinations in relation to disputes of a similar nature (RTA 2004, s 122).

A *determination order* which embodies the terms of an agreement reached at mediation or adjudication is binding on the parties when it is issued (RTA 2004, s 123(1)). A *determination order* which embodies a determination of the Tribunal is binding, unless within 21 days of its issue to the parties, it is appealed on a point of law to the High Court (RTA 2004, s 123(2)–(8)).

The High Court judgment is final and conclusive.

There is provision for a *determination order* to be enforced by the Circuit Court on the application of the Board or a person mentioned in the determination order (RTA 2004, s 124). The court is required to make an order unless it considers that there are substantial reasons for not making the order eg: (a) a requirement of procedural fairness was not complied with in the relevant proceedings; (b) a material consideration was not taken account of in those proceedings or account was taken in those proceedings of a consideration that was not material; (c) a manifestly erroneous decision in relation to a legal issue was made in those proceedings; or (d) the determination made by the adjudicator or the Tribunal, as the case may be, on the evidence before the adjudicator or Tribunal, was manifestly erroneous. There is also provision for the cancellation by the Board or by the Court of a *determination order* and the ordering of a rehearing and a fresh determination, in cases of non-appearance by a party for good and substantial reasons (RTA 2004, s 125).

A person who fails to comply with one or more terms of a *determination order* is guilty of an offence (RTA 2004, s 126). However, a person convicted of such an offence must not be sentenced to any term of imprisonment in respect of that offence if he shows that the failure to comply with the term or terms concerned was due to his limited financial means (RTA 2004, s 126(3)). See ADJUDICATORS IN TENANCY DISPUTES; MEDIATION IN TENANCY DISPUTES; PRIVATE RESIDENTIAL TENANCIES BOARD; TENANCY DISPUTE; TENANCY TRIBUNAL.

determine. To come to an end or to bring to an end. A creditor cannot *determine* an agreement with a consumer, despite a breach by the consumer, unless he has served notice on the consumer specifying the nature of the alleged breach: Consumer Credit Act 1995, s 54.

detinue. A tort (qv) which consists of the withholding of goods from the person who is immediately entitled to their possession. An *action in detinue* is one by which a person claims the specific return of goods wrongfully detained or their value and damages for detention. Detinue is proven by evidence that a demand for the return of the goods was made by the plaintiff and yet the defendant failed to deliver them up. As to goods the subject of a hire-purchase agreement, see the Consumer Credit Act 1995, ss 64 and 66. See *Poole v Burns* [1944] Ir Jur Rep 20; *Treasure Island v Zebedee Enterprises* [1987] HC; *McCrystal Oil Co Ltd v Revenue Commissioners* [1993] ILRM 69, HC. See Courts Act 1991, s 7. See BAILMENT.

Deus solus haeredem facere potest non homo. [God alone, and not man, can make an heir.] See SUCCESSION.

devastavit. [He has wasted.] The wasting or converting to his own use by a personal representative (qv) of any part of the estate of a deceased. *Devastavit* may be by *misfeasance* eg by the personal representative using the estate for his own benefit; or by *non-feasance* eg by the personal representative neglecting to invest funds in his hands for the benefit of the estate. The personal representative is liable for such waste and his own estate is similarly liable in the event that he dies: Succession Act 1965, s 24. This provision also applies to an *executor de son tort* (qv): *Ennis v Rochford* [1884] 14 LR Ir 285. See WASTE.

development. The carrying out of any works on, in, over or under land or the making of any material change in the use of any structures or other land: Planning and Development Act 2000, s 3(1). See *Flanagan v Galway City and County Manager* [1990] 2 IR 66; *Hoburn Homes Ltd v An Bord Pleanála* [1993] ILRM 368, HC; *Butler v Dublin Corporation* [1999] 1 IR 565, SC. For control of development, see Planning and Development Regulations 2001, SI No 600 of 2001, Pt IV, arts 16–47 as amended by Planning and Development Regulations 2002, SI No 70 of 2002. See also Environmental Protection Agency Act 1992, s 3(1) as amended by Protection of the Environment Act 2003, s 5. [Bibliography: LexisNexis.] See PLANNING PERMISSION; EXEMPTED DEVELOPMENT.

development costs. See ASSET VALUATION.

development land. (1) Land with a 'hope' value ie the owner 'hopes' it will be rezoned: *Morgan v Gibson* [1989] STC 568.

(2) Land in the State, the consideration for the disposal of, or the *market value* of which at the time the disposal is made, exceeds the *current use value* of the land at the time the disposal is made: Taxes Consolidation Act 1997, s 648. The *current use value* is the market value on the basis that it would be unlawful to carry out any development of the land ie before rezoning.

Development land gains are subject to capital gains tax (TCA 1997, s 649). The rates were 20% for small disposals, 40% for disposals other than small disposals, and 60% from 6 April 2002 in respect of land zoned for residential purposes (TCA 1997, s 649A inserted by Finance (No 2) Act 1998, s 3).This measure was subsequently dropped in favour of a 20% rate: Finance Act 2001, s 94.

As regards VAT and development land and buildings, all costs associated with the acquisition and development of such land and buildings, including professional fees, are included in the '*economic value*' test: Value Added Tax Act 1972, s 4, as amended by Finance Act 2003, s 114. *Economic value* means the cost of acquisition and development of the property. See LEASEHOLD.

development plan. The plan, which every planning authority is required to prepare every six years, and which sets out the overall strategy for the proper planning and sustainable development of the area of the plan: Planning and Development Act 2000, ss 2(1), 9–10.

It has been held that a development plan, founded upon and justified by the common good and answerable to public confidence, is a representation in solemn form, binding on all affected or touched by it, that the planning authority will discharge its statutory function strictly in accordance with the published plan: *Byrne v Fingal County Council* [2002] 2 ILRM 32, HC and [2001] 4 IR 565, HC. The owners and occupiers of land and the residents in the district were entitled to assume that the council would honour the unconditional and unambiguous undertaking and commitment given in the development plan, and if necessary enforce them (*Byrne* case). A planning authority enjoys no statutory discretion in interpreting its development plan: *Jeffers v Louth County Council* [2003] FL 8804, HC.

Where An Bord Pleanála grants planning permission in contravention of a development plan, it should give its reasons for so doing: *The Village Residents Association Ltd v An Bord Pleanála* [1999] ITLR (6 December), HC. It was held that the board had fulfilled its statutory obligation on the question of the adequacy of the reasons stated: *Village Residents Association v An Bord Pleanála (No 3)* [2001] 1 IR 441, HC.

A planning authority has a duty to take steps to secure the objectives in the development plan; the manager is required to give a report to the members on the progress achieved not more than two years after the making of the plan (PDA 2000, s 15). Copies of the plan must be available for public inspection and purchase (PDA 2000, s 16). A planning authority is required to *have regard to* any regional planning guidelines when making or adopting a development plan (PDA 2000, s 27(1)). The phrase 'have regard to' is permissive in nature and creates an obligation to consider something rather than follow or slavishly adhere to something: *McEvoy v Meath County Council* [2003] 1 ILRM 431 and 1 IR 208, HC.

See Planning and Development (Regional Planning Guidelines) Regulations 2003, SI No 175 of 2003 which: (a) set out certain procedural requirements in relation to the preparation of *regional planning guidelines* by regional authorities, and (b) specify the *National Spatial Strategy 2002-2020* as being of relevance to the determination of strategic planning policies. See website: *www.irishspatialstrategy.ie*.

Also, the Minister may direct a planning authority, for stated reasons, to amend a development plan where he considers that the plan fails to set out an overall strategy for the proper planning and sustainable development of the area (PDA 2000, s 31).

A planning authority is required to include in its development plan a record of *protected structures* (qv) in its functional area (PDA 2000, ss 51–55). See also Local Government (Planning and Development) Regulations 1977, SI No 65 of 1977. See Housing (Traveller Accommodation) Act 1998, s 26. See *An Taisce v Dublin Corporation* [1973] HC; *O'Leary v Dublin Co Council* [1988] IR 150, HC; *Sharpe v Dublin City & County Manager* [1989] ILRM 565, SC; *A-G v Sligo Co Council* [1989] ILRM 768, SC; *Hoburn Homes Ltd v An Bord Pleanála* [1993] ILRM 368, HC; *Malahide Community Council Ltd v Fingal County Council* [1997] 3 IR 383, SC; *Blessington Heritage Trust Ltd v Wicklow County Council* [1999] 4 IR 571, HC. [Bibliography: Galligan (1).] See HOUSING STRATEGY; IRISH LANGUAGE; PLANNING PERMISSION; PROTECTED STRUCTURE; REGIONAL AUTHORITY; TRAVELLER.

development plan, consultation on. Procedures are specified for the preparation of the *draft* development plan, including extensive public notification and consultation: Planning and Development Act 2000, s 11. Procedures are also specified for the public display, consideration and adoption of the development plan (PDA 2000, s 12 as amended by Planning and Development (Amendment) Act 2002, s 7). If the members of the planning authority decide to make a *material alteration* to the draft plan, a further public notification and consultation procedure must be followed (PDA 2000, s 12(7)). If the members fail to make the plan by the specified time period, the manager must make the plan (PDA 2000, s 12(14)).

Under the previous legislation, it was held that this consultation process is mandatory: *Keogh v Galway Co Council* [1995] 1 ILRM 141, HC and [1995] 2 ILRM 312, HC. The Oireachtas did not intend that there should be only one shot at amending a draft development plan; the planning authority must give consideration to any representations for a further amendment and if it adopts any such amendment which involves a material alteration, the public consultation procedures have to be repeated: *Raggett v Athy UDC* [2000] 1 ILRM 375, HC and 1 IR 469. A failure to fulfil the public consultation requirements would constitute a material contravention of the development plan: *Jeffers v Louth County Council* [2003] FL 8804, HC.

When considering an application for planning permission, the planning authority must have regard for the relevant development plan for the area; it cannot have regard to a *draft* of a proposed development plan: *Ebonwood Ltd v Meath County Council* [2003] FL 7911, HC and [2004] 1 ILRM 305. In a particular case, the acceptance by a planning authority of a financial contribution to help preparatory work for the review of a development plan, did not lead to the conclusion that the whole review procedure was tainted and invalid: *Huntsgrove Developments Ltd v Meath Co Council* [1994] 2 ILRM 36, HC.

Provision is also made for the *variation* of a plan after it is adopted, involving also public notification and consultation (PDA 2000, s 13).

development plan, objectives of. A development plan is required to include objectives for: (a) the *zoning* of land for use solely or primarily of particular areas for particular purposes, (b) the provision of infrastructure, including transport, energy, communications, water supplies, waste recovery and disposal, (c) the conservation and protection of the environment, (d) the protection of structures of architectural interest and of *architectural conservation areas*, (e) the development of areas which need regeneration, (f) the provision of accommodation for travellers, (g) the provision of amenities and recreational amenities, (h) the control of establishments to reduce the risk of major accidents, (i) the provision of facilities for the community, including schools, creches and childcare facilities, (j) the protection of the linguistic and cultural heritage of the Gaeltacht: Planning and Development Act 2000, s 10(2). It is doubtful whether development objectives must be positive in character: Keane CJ in *Glencar Exploration plc v Mayo County Council* [2002] 1 ILRM 481, SC and 1 IR 84.

Other objectives which the planning authority may include in the development plan are set out in PDA 2000, Sch 1. There is now no distinction as between *urban* and *rural* areas in relation to the objectives in the development plan. The reduction or prevention of noise may be included as an objective in a development plan: Environmental Protection Agency Act 1992, s 106(3).

deviation. In marine insurance, where a ship, without lawful excuse, deviates from the voyage contemplated by the policy, the insurer is discharged from liability as from the time of the deviation, and it is immaterial that the ship may have regained her route before any loss occurs: Marine Insurance Act 1906, s 46.

devil. See BARRISTER.

devise. A gift of real property by will, either specific or residuary; to make such a gift. The recipient is the *devisee*. An *executory* devise is one limited to take effect in the future on fulfilment of a condition eg marriage. See LAPSE.

devolution. The passing of property or rights from one person to another eg on death.

diagnosis, incorrect. An incorrect diagnosis has been held not to be in itself evidence of bad faith or want of reasonable care: *Murphy v Greene* [1991] ILRM 404, SC. A doctor however was found to be in breach of duty in failing to take account of information in a general practitioner's referral letter and in failing to consult the log book

notes concerning the plaintiff's previous tendencies: *Armstrong v Eastern Health Board* [1991] 9 ILT Dig 199 & 227, HC.

DIBOR. [Dublin Interbank Offered Rate.] This has been replaced by the EURIBOR [Euro Interbank Offered Rate.] See Economic and Monetary Union Act 1998, s 22.

dictionary, use of. A dictionary may be used by the court to ascertain the meaning of words to which no particular legal interpretation attaches.

A High Court judge has said that there is a time lag between a new word being used in common parlance and being listed in a dictionary: Smith J in *Sealed Air Corporation v Patents Office* (2003) Irish Times, 3 August.

For examples of the use of a dictionary in court, see *R v Peters* [1866] 16 QBD 636; *McCann v O'Culachain* [1986] ILRM 229; *G & McD v Governor of Mountjoy Prison* [1991] 9 ILT Dig 266, HC; *DPP v Cafolla* [1992] ITLR (22 June), SC; *Trustees of Kinsale Yacht Club v Commissioner of Valuations* [1993] ILRM 393, HC; *Hoburn Homes Ltd v An Bord Pleanála* [1993] ILRM 368, HC; *Madden v Minister for the Marine* [1993] ILRM 446, HC; *An Post v Irish Permanent plc* [1995] 1 ILRM 336, HC.

For a recent reference to *Murdoch's Dictionary of Irish Law*, see *Corway v Independent Newspapers Ltd* [2000] 1 ILRM 426 at 430, SC and [1999] 4 IR 484 at 495, SC; *The People (DPP) v Cunningham* [2002] 2 IR 712, SC and [2003] 1 ILRM 124 at 138. [Bibliography: Microsoft Press; Byrne UK; Burke UK; O'Connor P; Stroud UK; Wharton UK.]

dictum. See OBITER DICTUM.

dictum meum pactum. [My word is my bond.] See ORAL AGREEMENT.

die, right to. The right to life necessarily implies the right to have nature take its course and to die a natural and dignified death and, unless the individual so wishes, not to have life artificially maintained by the provision of nourishment by abnormal artificial means, which has no curative effect and which is intended merely to prolong life; a competent adult has the right to forego or discontinue life-saving medical treatment: *In the matter of a Ward of Court* [1995] 2 ILRM 401, SC and [1996] 2 IR 79, SC. It was held in this case that the provision of nourishment to a patient through a tube surgically implanted in her stomach, constituted medical treatment which was intrusive and an interference with the integrity of her body. It was further held that it was in her best interest that the artificial nourishment should be terminated, and that she be allowed to die with all such palliative care and medication as was necessary to ensure a peaceful and pain-free death. See also *Airedale NHS Trust v Bland* [1933] AC 789. See LIFE, RIGHT TO.

die without issue. The phrase which in a devise or bequest of real or personal property, is to be construed to mean a want or failure of issue during the lifetime of the person or at the time of his death, and not an indefinite failure of issue, unless a contrary intention appears: Succession Act 1965, s 96. See *Re Mooney* [1925] 29 ILTR 57. See ISSUE.

dietary foods. Regulations have been made which lay down compositional and labelling requirements, and general provisions for the sale in Ireland, of *dietary foods* for special medical purposes: European Communities (Dietary Foods for Special Medical Purposes) Regulations 2001, SI No 64 of 2001 and (Amendment) Regulations 2002, SI No 150 of 2002.

differences, contracts for. See CONTRACTS FOR DIFFERENCES.

digest. A summary of the main points of cases, arranged by branch of law in an alphabetical order e g *The Irish Digest*, the *Irish Law Times Digest* (ILT Dig). See Appendix 1, Law Reports.

digital broadcasting. See BROADCASTING COMMISSION OF IRELAND; TELECOMMUNICATIONS REGULATOR.

Digital Hub Development Agency. A body corporate, established with the main function of promoting and facilitating the development of the *digital hub* as a location for digital enterprises and related activities: Digital Hub Development Agency Act 2003, s 8. It is required to formulate strategies to encourage individuals and enterprises engaged in *digital content* to locate in the digital hub. *Digital hub* means the geographical area set out in the Schedule to DHDAA 2003, which area may be extended or varied by the Minister (DHDAA 2003, ss 2(1) and 3). *Digital content* means content which can be created, manipulated and exchanged electronically, and which is stored in a digital format, or electronically in a format which is not digital (DHDAA 2003, s 2(1)).

Digital Media Development Ltd. A company established by the government in 2000 to: (a) manage the development of the *Digital Media District*, and (b) to relate to *MediaLabEurope* on behalf of the Irish government. The *Digital Media District* is a district in Dublin to be developed as a creative centre for digital industries, such as multimedia, Internet and electronic commerce content and applications. *MediaLabEurope* is located in the district. It is a high-tech research and development institute developed in partnership between the government and the Massachusetts Institute of Technology (MIT). The company was dissolved on the establishment of the *Digital Hub Development Agency* (qv): Digital Hub Development Agency Act 2003, s 39.

digital signature. Means the transformation of a message by an approved person using an approved *asymmetric crytosystem*, such that the Revenue Commissioners can determine: (a) whether the transformation was created using the *private key* which corresponds to the *public key* they have in respect of the approved person, and (b) whether the message has been altered since the transformation was made: Taxes Consolidation Act 1997, s 917I as inserted by Finance Act 1999, s 209.

Asymmetric crytosystem means an algorithm or series of algorithms which provide a secure key pair. *Key pair* means a private key and its corresponding key in such a system such that the public key verifies a digital signature that the private key creates. A *private key* means the key of the key pair used by an approved person to create a digital signature. A *public key* means the key of a key pair used by the Revenue Commissioners to verify a digital signature. See 'Signed, sealed and delivered' by Eamonn Keenan and Tony Brady in *Law Society Gazette* (March 2003) 27. See ELECTRONIC SIGNATURE; ELECTRONIC TAX RETURN.

diminished responsibility. The defence allowed in England to a charge of murder (qv) which if proved reduces the offence to manslaughter (qv). It has been held that such a defence cannot exist in this State side by side with a defence of insanity: *The People (DPP) v O'Mahony* [1986] ILRM 244.

However, under a major reform of the law on insanity, provision is made for a person who is tried for murder to be found guilty of manslaughter on the ground of *diminished responsibility*, where it is found that the person: (a) committed the act alleged, (b) was at the time suffering from a *mental disorder* (qv), and (c) the mental disorder was not such as to justify finding him not guilty by reason of insanity, but was such as to diminish substantially his responsibility for the act: Criminal Law (Insanity) Bill 2002, s 5. This provision on diminished responsibility is applied only in the case of murder because murder carries a mandatory life sentence; in other cases the judge is able to take into account the mental condition of the accused when considering what sentence to impose. See 'Crazy Situation' by solicitor Dara Robinson in *Law Society Gazette* (January/February 2003) 12. [Bibliography: McAuley.]

diplomatic privilege. The exemption of a diplomatic agent of a foreign state from the ordinary law of the state to which he is accredited. A diplomatic agent enjoys immunity from the criminal jurisdiction of the receiving state. He also enjoys *immunity* from its civil and administrative jurisdiction except in cases, not involving his mission, of a real action to private immovable property or an action relating to succession or relating to any professional or commercial activity by the agent.

A diplomatic agent is not obliged to give evidence as a witness and his person and his private and official residence is inviolable. He is not liable to any form of arrest or detention. Members of his family, if they are not nationals of the receiving state, enjoy the privileges and immunities of the agent.

The immunity from jurisdiction may be waived by the sending state but it must be express; the initiation of proceedings by a diplomatic agent precludes him from invoking immunity in respect of any counter claim. See Diplomatic Relations and Immunities Acts 1967 and 1976. See *McMahon v McDonald* [1988] HC & SC; *O'Brien v Ireland* [1995] 1 IR 568, HC. See AMBASSADOR; CONSUL; IMMUNITY; PERSONA NON GRATA; TERRORISM.

direct applicability. The term used to describe EC law which enters into force in each member state without any national act of reception or incorporation. A provision of the EC Treaty is *directly applicable* in the domestic law of a member state if it is: (a) clear and precise, (b) unconditional, and (c) of such a kind that it requires no further action on the part of the Community institutions or the member states or, if the measure requires execution, that it leaves no discretion to the member state in the execution of the measure: *Van Gend en Loos v Netherlandse Belastingsadministratie* [1963] ECR 1; [1963] LMLR 105.

In a case dealing with the rights, under an EC Directive, of persons of different sexes to receive the same social welfare benefits, the court held that the wrong committed by the State in continuing the discrimination by failing to fully implement the Directive was a wrong arising from Community law which had *direct effect: Robinson v Minister for Social Welfare* [1995] ELR 86, HC. See DIRECTIVE, EC; REGULATION, EC.

direct effect. See DIRECT APPLICABILITY; DIRECTIVE; EC; FRAMEWORK DECISION.

direct evidence. See EVIDENCE.

direct examination. Examination-in-chief. See EXAMINATION.

direct mailing list. See DIRECT MARKETING.

direct marketing. Includes *direct mailing* other than *direct mailing* carried out in the course of political activities by a political party or its members, or a body established by or under statute or a candidate for election to, or a holder of, elective political office: Data Protection Act 1988, s 1(1) as amended by substitution by Data Protection (Amendment) Act 2003, s 2(a)(iii). A data subject (qv) is entitled to have his name removed from a direct marketing or direct mailing list, by requesting the data controller (qv) in writing not to process the data for that purpose or to cease using the data for that purpose (DPA 1988, s 2(7) as amended by substitution by DP(A)A 2003, s 3(d)). See DATA PROTECTION.

direct universal suffrage. Election directly under a system where all persons of voting age are eligible to vote: National Forum on Europe, *Glossary of Terms* (2003).

direction. An instruction from the court e g an instruction given by a judge to a jury on a relevant point of law to be applied to the facts they are considering.

In a criminal trial, a direction may be given by the judge to the jury to find the accused not guilty at the close of the prosecution case. When an application for a direction is made, it is the function of the judge to consider whether there is evidence which a jury might reasonably accept as establishing the guilt of the accused; it is not his function to make any finding on the alleged facts: *DPP v Gilligan* [1992] ITLR (30 March), CCA. A judge must not direct a jury to enter a verdict of guilty in a case where he felt that to be the only proper verdict: *DPP v Davis* [1993] ILRM 407, SC and 2 IR 1.

In civil proceedings, a direction may be sought by a defendant at the end of the plaintiff's case for a non-suit ie a dismissal of the plaintiff's action. Where the trial is *before a jury*, a direction will be given to the jury to dismiss the action where the judge, assuming that all matters in controversy will be resolved according to the evidence in favour of the plaintiff, nevertheless holds that even in those circumstances there is not sufficient evidence to support the plaintiff's case.

Where the judge is sitting *without a jury*, he should enquire if the defendant intends, if refused the direction, to go into evidence. If the defendant intends to present evidence, the judge must decide whether the plaintiff has made out a *prima facie* case; if the judge decides in the affirmative, a direction to dismiss the action will be denied. However, if the defendant does not intend to present evidence on liability, the judge must decide if the plaintiff has established as a matter of *probability* the facts necessary to support a verdict in his favour; if the plaintiff has, then the judge will give judgment for the plaintiff; if the plaintiff has not, then the judge will dismiss the action: *O'Toole v Heavey* [1993] ILRM 343, SC expanding and clarifying *Hetherington v Ultra Tyre Service Ltd* [1991] ITLR (22 July), SC and [1993] ILRM 353.

Also where more than one defendant is sued, the judge should decide on an application for a non-suit by a defendant only where he is completely satisfied that another defendant could not escape liability by affixing blame in evidence on the defendant applying for the direction to be dismissed from the action (*O'Toole* case). See MISDIRECTION; SUMMING-UP; SUPREME COURT.

directions, summons for. The receiver of a company may apply by special summons to the court for directions in relation to any particular matter arising in connection with the performance of his function: Companies Act 1963, s 316 as amended by the Companies Act 1990, s 171. See *Re Tullow Engineering (Holdings) Ltd (in receivership)* [1988] HC; *In the matter of Bula Ltd* [2002] 2 ILRM 513, HC. See RECEIVER, COMPANY.

directive, EC. Legislation of the EC which states an objective which each member state must realise within a prescribed period. 'A directive shall be binding, as to the result to be achieved, upon each member state to which it is addressed, but shall leave to the national authorities the choice of form and methods': EC Treaty, art 249 of the consolidated (2002) version.

The principles contained in an EC Directive do not normally have the direct force of law in the member states and will usually require a legislative process to be legally binding, although in some instances the directive can have direct effect between the member state and its citizens, by which the member state will be *estopped* from denying the effect of the directive and will be bound by the law not as it is but as it should be: *Browne v An Bord Pleanála* [1989] ILRM 865, HC.

Where the provisions of a directive appear, as far as their subject matter is concerned, to be unconditional and precise, individuals may rely on those provisions in the absence of implementing measures adopted within the prescribed period as against a national provision incompatible with the directive: *McDermott & Cotter v Minister for Social Welfare* [1987] ILRM 324. See also *Greene v Minister for Agriculture* [1989] ILRM 364, HC; *Carberry v Minister for Social Welfare* [1989] ITLR (5 June); *Robinson v Minister for Social Welfare* [1995] ELR 86, HC.

If a directive leaves the determination of matters of principle or policy to the national authority, the enactment of Irish legislation is necessary; however, if the principles and policies have been determined by the directive, it is permissible to effect implementation by means of delegated legislation eg by regulations/statutory instruments: *Meagher v Minister for Agriculture* [1994] 1 ILRM 1, SC.

It has been held that it was well established that legal provisions, enacted by a member state to implement a Council Directive, were to be interpreted in order to achieve the results envisaged by the Directive: *Watson v Environmental Protection Agency* [2000] 2 IR 454, HC. The Supreme Court has held that in implementing directives, Irish law should be construed in the light of the obligations on the State by the provisions of the directive and with a view to giving effect to European Community law and that it was a matter for the national court to decide how that result was best achieved: *O'Connell v EPA* [2003] 1 IR 532, SC.

An actionable breach of a directive is a tort and therefore a wrong within the meaning of the Civil Liability Act 1961: *Dermot Coppinger v Waterford County Council* [1998] 4 IR 220, HC. See also *Tate v Minister for Social Welfare* [1995] 1 ILRM 507, HC and 1 IR 418; *Scally v Minister for the Environment* [1996] 1 IR 367, HC. See COMMUNITY LAW; EUROPEAN FRAME-WORK LAW; FRAMEWORK DECISION; INTERPRETATION OF LEGISLATION, EURO-PEAN; REGULATION.

director. See DIRECTORS.

director, managing. See MANAGING DIRECTOR.

Director of Consumer Affairs. See CON-SUMER AFFAIRS, DIRECTOR OF; CON-SUMER DIRECTOR.

Director of Corporate Enforcement. The independent corporation sole with func-tions: (a) to enforce the Companies Acts, including the prosecution of offences by way of *summary* proceedings; (b) to encour-age compliance with the Companies Acts; (c) to investigate instances of suspected offences; (d) to refer cases of suspected *indictable* offences to the Director of Public Prosecutions; and (e) to exercise a supervi-sory role over the activities of liquidators and receivers: Company Law Enforcement Act 2001, ss 7 and 12, as amended by Companies (Auditing and Accounting) Act 2003, s 51.

Provision has been made to transfer to the Director certain specified functions and powers previously vested in the Minister (CLEA 2001, s 14 and Sch).

The Director is indemnified against losses in respect of any thing done or omit-ted to be done in good faith by him (CLEA 2001, s 15). He is required to account to an appropriately established Committee of the Oireachtas for the performance of his func-tions (CLEA 2001, s 16). He is empowered to levy a fine in lieu of a prosecution for an alleged offence (CLEA 2001, s 109). He also has many other powers, including a power to obtain a court order for the pro-duction of certain documentation from a bank (CLEA 2001, s 113. See also s 97).

The Director may disclose to the Compe-tition Authority (qv) information which, in his opinion, may relate to the commission of a competition law offence: Competition Act 2002, s 47. See District Court (Com-pany Law Enforcement) Rules 2002, SI No 207 of 2002. See website: *www.odce.ie*. [Bibliography: Cahill N.] See DIRECTORS' RESTRICTION ORDER; DISQUALIFICATION ORDER, COMPANY; INSIDER DEALING; INVESTIGATION OF COMPANY; IRISH AUDITING AND ACCOUNTING SUPERVI-SORY AUTHORITY; LIQUIDATOR; RECEIVER, COMPANY; SHARES, DISCLOSURE OF; WIND-ING UP, COMPULSORY.

Director of Public Prosecutions; DPP. The independent office established by statute by which all serious crimes are prosecuted in the name of the People: Prosecution of Offences Act 1974. The holder of the office is a civil servant and is independent in the exercise of his function.

The function of the DPP in deciding whether or not to prosecute an individual for the alleged commission of a criminal offence is an executive one, and it is only reviewable by the courts if it is demon-strated that he reached a decision *mala fides* or was influenced by an improper motive or improper policy: *H v DPP* [1994] 2 ILRM 285, SC and 2 IR 589; or had abdicated his functions: *O'Sullivan v District Judge Wal-lace* [1999] ITLR (5th July), HC. See also *Shannon v McGuinness* [1999] 3 IR 274, HC.

A decision by the DPP to reverse his original decision not to prosecute may be subject to review by the courts: *Eviston v DPP* [2001] ITLR (2 April), HC and [2002] 1 ILRM 134, HC. The Supreme Court has held that the DPP is entitled to review an earlier decision not to prosecute and to arrive at a different decision even in the absence of new evidence and is not obligated in either instance to give reasons for his decision: *Eviston v DPP* [2002] 3 IR 260, SC and [2003] 1ILRM 178. However in this case, the court held that Eviston was not given fair procedures as the DPP had already decided not to prosecute her, had communicated that decision to her and had then reversed it without any change of circumstances or any new evidence coming to light.

A person is not entitled to get from the DPP the reasons why he has decided to embark on a prosecution: *obiter dictum* in *Deely v Information Commissioner* [2001] 3

IR 439, HC. See also *The State (McCormack) v Curran* [1987] ILRM 225. It is not part of the function of the DPP to institute proceedings in the hope or expectation of an acquittal: *Landers v Garda Síochána Complaints Board* [1997] 3 IR 347, HC.

The DPP performs most of the functions formerly capable of being prosecuted by the Attorney-General in relation to criminal matters. He is not confined in his nomination or appointment of a solicitor to conduct a charge on an indictable offence (qv) to solicitors employed in the public service: *Flynn v DPP* [1986] ILRM 290.

Privilege applies to communications between the DPP and professional officers in his office, solicitors and counsel relating to prosecutions which are in being or contemplated: however it does not extend to documents submitted by an investigating garda to the DPP: *Logue v Redmond* [1999] 2 ILRM 498, HC. Once a *prima facie* claim of privilege has been established, the court should proceed to inspect the documents; those which would reasonably assist the accused should be discovered, unless their discovery was counter-balanced by the public interest in ensuring the free communications between the DPP, the gardaí and the State solicitors: *Corbett v DPP* [1999] 2 IR 179, HC.

The DPP will examine a request for a *review* of a decision not to prosecute and in appropriate cases will have an independent internal review carried out, *Victim's Charter 1999*, available on website: *www.dppireland.ie*. In 2003 the DPP said that he was investigating ways of giving explanations to crime victims in cases where his office decides not to prosecute the suspected perpetrators: *Law Society Gazette* (August/September 2003) 6. See 1937 Constitution, art 30(3). See RSC Ord 97. [Bibliography: Casey J.] See CHIEF PROSECUTION SOLICITOR; COMMON INFORMER; INDICTMENT; LOCUS STANDI; PROSECUTOR; SPECIAL COURTS.

Director of the Equality Tribunal. The person, appointed by the Minister, who is independent in the exercise of his functions; these functions include investigating claims of discrimination in employment: Employment Equality Act 1998, s 75 amended by Equality Act 2004, s 30. Previously, called the *Director of Equality Investigations*, the office of the Director is now known as the *Equality Tribunal*. The role of the Director has been expanded to encompass investigations into *prohibited conduct* (ie discrimination, sexual harassment and harassment) outside employment under the Equal Status Act 2000, except in respect of prohibited conduct on entry to licensed premises: Intoxicating Liquor Act 2003, s 19.

In employment, discrimination claims comprise: (a) a claim to have been discriminated against in contravention of EEA 1998, (b) a claim not to be receiving remuneration in accordance with an equal pay term, (c) a claim not to be receiving a benefit under an equality clause, and (d) a claim to have been penalised in circumstances amounting to victimisation (EEA 1998, s 77 amended by EA 2004, s 32). The Director may dismiss a claim if of opinion that it has been made in bad faith or is frivolous, vexatious or misconceived or relates to a trivial matter (EEA 1998, s 77A inserted by EA 2004, s 33).

The Director is assisted by *equality officers* and *equality mediation officers*. The Director may refer a case to an equality mediation officer where it appears that the case could be resolved by mediation and neither party objects (EEA 1998, s 78 amended by EA 2004, s 34).

Following investigation of a case, the Director is required to issue a *decision* in the matter in writing and, if he thinks fit or if any of the parties so requests, he must include a statement of the reasons why he reached that decision (EEA 1998, s 79 amended by EA 2004, s 35, and EEA 1998, s 88). An appeal against a decision of the Director lies to the Labour Court (EEA 1998, s 83). The Labour Court may require the Director to investigate or further investigate a case and the Equality Authority may also refer certain cases to the Director for investigation (EEA 1998, ss 84–85 amended by EA 2004, s 37). The Circuit Court may request the Director, in relation to a case before the court, to appoint an equality officer to investigate and report to it on any question specified by it (EEA 1998, s 80).

Provision has been made to clarify that all or any of the equality officers who are staff of the Director of the Equality Tribunal have jurisdiction to decide disputes under Pt VII of the Pensions Act 1990 ie dealing with equal treatment for men and women in occupational benefit schemes: Social Welfare (Miscellaneous Provisions) Act 2003, s 24, Sch, paras 6, 7 and 8; Pensions Act 1990, ss 81E, 81F and 81I as amended by substitution by Social Welfare (Miscellaneous Provisions) Act 2004, s 22(1).

See *Re Employment Equality Bill 1996* [1997] 2 IR 321, SC and ELR 132; *New Era Packaging v A Worker* [2001] ELR 122, LC; *Fitzsimons-Markey v Gaelscoil Thulach na nOg* [2004] ELR 110. LC. See 'Office of the Director of Equality Investigations 2001 – Legal Review and Case Summaries' by Madeleine Reid, available free of charge from ODEI. See 'Last chance saloon' by barrister Cliona Kimber in *Law Society Gazette* (August/September 2003) 12. [Bibliography: Reid M.] See DISCRIMINATION; EQUALITY AUTHORITY.

directors. The persons with powers and duties to manage the business of a company: Companies Act 1963, Table A, arts 80–90. They are agents of the company, trustees of its money and property. In general, they do not owe a fiduciary duty, merely by virtue of their offices, to individual shareholders, except in particular circumstance, where mutual confidence and trust existed between the parties: *Crindle Investments v Wymes* [1998] 4 IR 567, SC. However, see FIDUCIARY.

Their powers and duties are governed by the *articles of association* of the company. Every company must have at least two directors (CA 1963, s 174). A body corporate may not be a director nor may a director be an undischarged bankrupt nor any person convicted on indictment of either an offence in connection with their involvement with a company or any offence involving fraud or dishonesty (CA 1963, ss 176, 183 and Sch 1, para 91, and Companies Act 1990, ss 149–169).

A person is deemed to be a director if the directors are accustomed to act on his directions or instructions (CA 1990, s 27). A director is an officer of the company; whether or not a director is an employee of the company depends on the facts (eg see *Stakelum v Canning* [1976] IR 314).

Subject to certain exceptions, a person must not be a director or *shadow* director of more than 25 companies at the same time: Companies (Amendment) (No 2) Act 1999, s 45.

Service contracts of directors lasting for more than five years must be approved at a general meeting of the company (CA 1990, s 28). The names of directors must be shown on all business letters of the company and their nationality if not Irish (CA 1963, s 196) and a register of the directors, including other directorships held, must be kept at the registered office of the company (CA 1963, s 195 as inserted by CA 1990, s 51).

It is the duty of each director and secretary of a company to ensure that the requirements of the Companies Acts are complied with by the company: Companies Act 1963, s 383(3) as substituted by Company Law Enforcement Act 2001, s 100.

Shareholders may by ordinary resolution remove a director from the board before his period of office expires (CA 1963, s 182). The office of director is normally deemed vacated if the director is adjudged bankrupt, makes an arrangement or composition with his creditors generally, becomes of unsound mind, or is absent for more than six months from board meetings without the board's consent (CA 1963, Table A, art 91). See *Glover v BLN Ltd* [1973] IR 388; *Carvill v Irish Industrial Bank Ltd* [1968] IR 325; *Healy v Healy Homes Ltd* [1973] IR 309; *Re City Equitable Fire Insurance Co* [1925] Ch 407; *Feigherty v Feigherty* [1999] 1 IR 321, HC; *McGilligan v O'Grady* [1999] 1 IR 346, SC.

The Irish Stock Exchange in 1999 introduced a new *listing rule* requiring public quoted companies to reveal *individual* director's remuneration (instead of aggregated) in their annual reports, commencing with the annual reports for 2000.

Directors have a duty to have regard to the interests of the company's employees (CA 1990, s 52(1)). There is no statutory age limit for appointment as a director. The government announced in March 2003 its intention to prohibit the appointment as directors of persons under 18 years of age. For duty of directors to their company, shareholders, creditors and employees, see MacCann in 9 ILT & SJ (1991) 3, 30, 56, 80. For article on directors' remuneration and loans, see MacCann in 9 ILT & SJ (1991) 250 and 276. See also Building Societies Act 1989, ss 48–49; Stock Exchange Act 1995, s 3(1) as amended by Central Bank and Financial Services Authority of Ireland Act 2003, s 35, Sch 1; Credit Union Act 1997, ss 53–57 as amended by CBFSAIA 2003, s 35. See *Mehigan v Duignan* [1997] 1 ILRM 171, HC. For the Institute of Directors in Ireland, see website: *www.iod.ie*. For the UK Institute, see website: *www.iod.com*. For the

Tyson Report on the Recruitment and Development of Non-Executive Directors (2003), see website: *www.london.edu/tysonreport/Tyson_Report_June_2003.pdf*.
[Bibliography: Doyle; McGrath S; O'Connell M (2); Round Hall.] See COMBINED CODE; DE FACTO DIRECTOR; DISQUALIFICATION ORDER, COMPANY; FIDUCIARY; LOAN TO DIRECTOR; MODEL CODE; PROSPECTUS; REMUNERATION OF DIRECTORS; RESTRICTION ORDER; SHADOW DIRECTOR; WORKER PARTICIPATION.

directors, offences by. Where an offence under the Criminal Justice (Theft and Fraud Offences) Act 2001 is committed by a body corporate or unincorporated, with the consent or connivance of a director, manager, secretary or other officer, that person as well as the body is guilty of the offence: Criminal Justice (Theft and Fraud Offences) Act 2001, s 58. A similar provision is included in the Local Government Act 2001, s 234 and the Communications Regulation Act 2002, s 42.

In competition law offences, a director of an undertaking is presumed to have consented to the doing of the prohibited acts if his duties included making decisions that, to a significant extent, could have affected the management of the undertaking: Competition Act 2002, s 8(7). See also Commissions of Investigation Act 2004, s 48. See CORPORATE CRIME; INSIDER DEALING.

directors' report. The report that directors are required to make on the state of the company's affairs, the dividend they recommend and the amount they propose to carry to reserves; the report, which must be attached to the balance sheet laid before the annual general meeting, must be signed by two directors: Companies Act 1963, s 158.

In addition, the report must give a fair view of the development of the company's business, an indication of any important events which have occurred, of likely future developments in broad terms and of research and development undertaken by the company: Companies (Amendment) Act 1986, s 13. The report must also include particulars of the acquisition by the company of its own shares, or of the acquisition by other persons with financial assistance given by the company, and also of the forfeiture (qv) and surrender of shares and of shares being made subject to a lien (qv) or a charge (C(A)A 1986, s 14).

The directors' report must now be expanded to include a statement of the measures taken by the directors to keep proper books of account and to state precisely the location of the books of account: Companies Act 1963, s 158 as amended by the Company Law Enforcement Act 2001, s 90.

The directors' report under CA 1963, s 158 must also include a statement acknowledging their responsibility for securing compliance by the company with its *relevant obligations*, confirming that the company has in place internal financial and any other necessary procedures designed to achieve compliance, and confirming that the directors have reviewed the effectiveness of these procedures during the financial year to which the report relates: Companies Act 1990, s 205E inserted by Companies (Auditing and Accounting) Act 2003, s 45. *Relevant obligations* means the company's obligations under: (i) the Companies Acts, (ii) tax law, and (iii) any other enactments that provide a legal framework within which the company operates and that may materially affect the company's financial statements. In addition, the company's auditor is required to review the directors' compliance statement (CA 1990, s 205F inserted by C(AA)A 2003, s 45).

directors' restriction order. Where a company is *insolvent* in its winding up, the court must declare that any person who was a director at the commencement of the winding up or within the previous 12 months, must not be appointed as a director or secretary or take part in the promotion or formation of any company for five years, unless that company has a share capital of £250,000 (€317,435) if it is a public limited company (plc), or £50,000 (€63,487) if it is a private company, fully paid up in cash in each case: Companies Act 1990, s 150 as amended by Company Law Enforcement Act 2001, s 41; *USIT Ireland Ltd (In Liquidation)* [2003] 2 IR 635 and FL 8079, HC and [2004] 1 ILRM 296, HC.

The 2001 Act also: (a) gives the Director of Corporate Enforcement, a liquidator or a receiver a right to apply for a restriction order, and (b) provides for the person, against whom the order is made, to bear the cost of the application. However, the liquidator or creditors of an insolvent company are obliged to bear the costs of an unsuccessful application by a liquidator under

CA 1990, s 150: *Re GMT Engineering* [2004] 1 ILRM 343, HC.

There are some exceptions e g that the person acted honestly and responsibly in relation to the conduct of the affairs of the company (CA 1990, s 150(2)). Similar provisions apply where a company is in *receivership* (CA 1990, s 154). The onus is on the director to show that he had acted honestly and responsibly in order to avoid the mandatory restriction order: *Re Newcastle Timber Ltd (in liquidation)* [2001] 4 IR 586, HC. A person may apply to the court for relief from the restrictions placed on him and the court has a wide jurisdiction in the matter (CA 1990, s 152; *Robinson v Forrest* [1999] 2 ILRM 169 and 1 IR 426, HC).

A restriction order under s 150 of the Companies Act 1990 is prospective in that any restriction dates from the date of the relevant court order: *Duignan v Carway* [2001] 4 IR 550, SC. The failure by a director to fulfil his statutory obligations, to file a statement of affairs, and to explain such non-compliance was sufficient reason to make a declaration under s 150: *In the Matter of Dunleckney Ltd* [1999] ITLR (19 April). Factors to trigger an order under s 150 include the extent to which the company has complied with its statutory obligations, the director's general competency and commercial probity, and the extent to which he has been responsible for the insolvency of the company; the court should look at the entire tenure of the director and not simply the few months prior to liquidation: *Re Squash (Ireland) Ltd* [2001] 3 IR 35, SC. The size of a deficit does not preclude the court from finding that the directors had acted responsibly: *Kavanagh v Cummins* [2004] 2 ILRM 37, HC.

The persons entitled to bring an application under CA 1990, s 150 are the persons authorised by CA 1990, s 160(4)(b) to apply for a disqualification order: *Re Steamline Ltd (In liquidation)* [2001] 1 IR 103, HC. The primary purpose of s 150 is the protection of the public from persons who, by their conduct, have shown themselves unfit to hold the office of, and discharge the duties of, a director of a company, and, in consequence, represent a danger to potential investors and traders dealing with such companies: *La Moselle Clothing Ltd v Soualhi* [1998] 2 ILRM 345, HC. A director who needs access to the books of a company to prepare his answer to a s 150

application can apply to the courts if he is obstructed by the liquidator: *Carway v Attorney-General* [1997] 1 ILRM 110, HC and [1996] 3 IR 300, HC.

In addition, the provisions concerning the disqualification of directors and other officers is widened (CA 1990, s 160). See 'Restriction & Disqualification of Directors' by Brian Kennedy BL in *Bar Review* (June/July 2002) 241. [Bibliography: Cahill N.]

See DISQUALIFICATION ORDER, COMPANY; WINDING UP, COMPULSORY.

directors' service contract. A copy of the contract of service of every director, or a written memorandum thereof setting out the terms of the contract, must be kept by the company and be available for inspection by members during business hours; excluded are contracts with less than three years to run or terminable without compensation within three years: Companies Act 1990, s 50. In the case of *listed* companies, the specified three years is to be interpreted as 12 months: Listing Rules (*Definitions*, as amended by Irish Stock Exchange Ltd).

directors and share dealing. A director of a *listed* company must not deal in any securities of the listed company at any time when he is in possession of unpublished *price-sensitive information* or otherwise where clearance from the Chairman (normally) to deal has not been given: Listing Rules 2000, Chapter 16, Appendix, para 4 as amended by Irish Stock Exchange Ltd. A director must not be given clearance to deal during a *prohibited period*, which means: (a) any *close period*, or (b) any period where there exists any matter which constitutes unpublished *price-sensitive information*, or (c) any period where the person giving the clearance has reason to believe that the proposed dealing is in breach of the *model code* (qv) (para 7).

The *close period* is generally the two-month period preceding the preliminary announcement of the company's annual results or half-yearly results (para 3). It is a criminal offence for an individual who has information as an *insider* to deal on a recognised stock exchange in securities whose price would be likely to be materially affected if the information were generally available: Companies Act 1990, Pt V. A director must also not deal in any securities of the listed company on considerations of a short-term nature (para 2). An employee who is likely to be in possession of unpublished price-sensitive information must comply with the code as though he were a director (para 21). See INSIDER DEALING; MODEL CODE.

directory entries. A person is not liable for any payment by way of charge for inclusion in a directory of an entry relating to that person or his trade or business if the entry is unsolicited. It is an offence to make a demand for payment therefor. See Sale of Goods and Supply of Services Act 1980, s 48. In relation to *invoices* see s 49.

DIRT. Deposit interest retention tax (qv).

disability. (1) A lack of legal capacity. Persons deemed to be *under a disability* are given special protection. See DISABILITY, PERSON UNDER.

(2) In relation to a person, means a substantial restriction in the capacity of a person to participate in economic, social or cultural life on account of an enduring physical, sensory, learning, mental health or emotional impairment: National Disability Authority Act 1999, s 2(1).

The Disability Bill 2001 was withdrawn by the government following objections from organisations representing persons with disabilities. The objections related mainly to the fact that the Bill was 'duty' based rather than 'rights' based. See 'Disabilities Legislation: All bark and no bite?' by Henry Murdoch BL in *Law Society Gazette* (October 2001) 12; 'The Disability Bill 2001' by barrister Shivaun Quinlivan in *Bar Review* (March/April 2002). The year 2003 was the European Year of Disabled Persons. See also Education for Persons with Special Educational Needs Act 2004, s 52. See DISABLED PERSON AND EDUCATION; INTEGRATED EDUCATION; NATIONAL DISABILITY AUTHORITY.

disability, person under. A person who lacks legal capacity eg a minor (qv) or a person of unsound mind (qv): Statute of Limitations 1957, s 48 as amended by Criminal Law Act 1997, s 16 and Sch 3. Where a person is under a disability *on the date when a right of action accrued*, time does not run as regards the Statute, until the person ceases to be under a disability (1957 Statute, s 49; Statute of Limitations (Amendment) Act 1991, s 5, as amended by Civil Liability and Courts Act 2004, s 7). *On the date* means at any time on such date; it is immaterial whether the plaintiff was at the date of the accident of unsound mind or immediately as a result thereof

became of unsound mind: *Rohan v Bord na Móna* [1990] 2 IR 425 at 430. See also Trade Marks Act 1996, s 22(2). See DCR 1997 Ord 7.

A person is under a disability for the purpose of bringing an action while he is suffering from any *psychological injury* that: (i) is caused by *an act of sexual abuse* committed against him when he had not reached *full age*; and (ii) is of such significance that his ability to make a reasoned decision to bring such action is substantially impaired: Statute of Limitations 1957, s 48A(1) inserted by Statute of Limitations (Amendment) Act 2000, s 2. This applies in relation to an act of sexual abuse, both to: (a) an action in tort, or (b) an action claiming damages against another person for negligence or breach of duty in respect of personal injuries caused by the act of sexual abuse.

This is made retrospective to a limited extent, where such action had become statute barred before the passing of SL(A)A 2000 (21 June 2000). Such an action could be brought not later than 21 June 2001, provided that between the time the action would have otherwise been statute barred and 30 March 2000, a complaint had been made to the gardaí in respect of the act of sexual abuse, or the person had received professional advice which caused him to believe that the action was statute barred (SL 1957, s 48A(3)). The rights given by s 48A are in SL 1957, s 48A(5)). See LIMITATION OF ACTIONS; SEXUAL ABUSE.

disability allowance. The social welfare allowance payable to a person who is substantially handicapped, by reason of a specified disability, in undertaking employment: Social Welfare Act 1996, ss 13–16 as amended eg Social Welfare Act 1999, s 20. See also Social Welfare Act 2000, s 21; Social Welfare Act 2003, s 3(2)(c). The allowance replaced the DPMA (disabled persons maintenance allowance) which was administered by the health boards under the Health Act 1970, s 69. See *O'Connell v Ireland* [1996] 1 ILRM 187, HC and 2 IR 522 and ELR 19.

disability and discrimination. Disability in this context means: (a) the total or partial absence of a person's bodily or mental functions, including the absence of a part of a person's body, or (b) the presence in the body of organisms causing, or likely to cause, chronic disease or illness, or (c) the malfunction, malformation or disfigurement of a part of a person's body, or (d) a condition or malfunction which results in a person learning differently from a person without the condition or malfunction, or (e) a condition, illness or disease which affects a person's thought processes, perception of reality, emotions or judgement or which results in disturbed behaviour: Employment Equality Act 1998, s 2(1); Equal Status Act 2000, s 2(1).

An employer is prohibited from discriminating against an employee or prospective employee on the grounds of disability (EEA 1998, ss 8(1) and 6; *An Employee v Bus Éireann* [2003] ELR 351, EO). However, an employer is not required to recruit or retain any person who is not fully competent and capable to undertake the duties of the job position (EEA 1998, s 16(1)). A person with a disability is considered fully competent and capable, if he could undertake the duties on reasonable accommodation (*appropriate measures*) being provided by the person's employer (EEA 1998, s 16(3) amended by substitution by Equality Act 2004, s 9). An employer is required to take *appropriate measures* to enable a disabled person to have access to employment, to participate or advance in employment, or to undergo training, unless the measures would impose a *disproportionate burden* on the employer. Under the previous legislation, an employer was required to do all that was reasonable to provide special treatment or facilities, but only if the cost was *nominal* in nature.

An employer was found to have discriminated against an employee on disability grounds, because the employer had failed to examine the options available to accommodate the needs of the employee given his disability: *Kehoe v Convertec Ltd* [2002] ELR 236, EO. A temporary injury constitutes a disability: *Customer Perception Ltd v Leydon* [2004] ELR 101, LC. In this case the Labour Court clarified that where facts are established by the employee from which discrimination may be inferred, the obligation falls on the employer to prove the contrary on the balance of probability. See also *Gorry v Manpower* [2001] ELR 275, EO; *An Employee v A Local Authority* [2002] ELR 159, EO; *A Computer Component Company v A Worker* [2002] ELR 124, LC; *Tannam v An Post* [2003] ELR 53, HC.

It is not unlawful for an employer to pay an employee with a disability a rate of remuneration which is less than that paid to an employee without a disability, by reason of the output of the former being less than that of the latter, provided the rate is not below the rate of the national minimum wage (EEA 1998, s 35 amended by EA 2004, s 24). It is also not discriminatory to have measures to protect the health and safety of persons with a disability or to promote their integration into the working environment (EEA 1998, s 33 amended by substitution by EA 2004, s 22). Disability discrimination provisions do not apply to employment in the defence forces and may not apply in the Garda Síochána, the prison service and in any emergency service (EEA 1998, s 37(2)–(6) amended by substitution by EA 2004, s 25).

A person must not discriminate on *disability* grounds in disposing of goods or premises or in providing a service or accommodation; treating one person less favourably than another person, in a comparable situation, because one is a person with a disability and the other either is not, or is a person with a different disability, is discrimination: Equal Status Act 2000, ss 5, 6 and 3, amended by EA 2004, ss 48–49.

In addition, discrimination includes a refusal or failure by the *provider of the service* to do all that is reasonable to accommodate the needs of a person with a disability by providing special treatment or facilities, if without such special treatment or facilities, it would be impossible or unduly difficult for the person to avail himself of the service (ESA 2000, s 4). It is not discrimination if the cost involved is more than a nominal cost. Also in s 4, *provider of a service* is widely defined to include a person disposing of goods or an estate or interest in premises, a person responsible for the provision of accommodation, an educational establishment, and a club (ESA 2000, s 4(6)). Having a reasonable preferential charge for persons with a disability does not constitute discrimination (ESA 2000, s 16(1)(a)).

An Equality Officer has found that a company, by refusing to allow a guide dog into a pub, failed to do all that was reasonable to provide the complainant, who was visually impaired, with special treatment or facilities contrary to s 4 of the ESA 2000: *Roche v Alabaster Associates Ltd* [2002] ELR 343, EO. See also Communications Regulation Act 2002, s 12(2)(a)(i). See 'Equality

& Disability' by barrister Cliona Kimber in *Bar Review* (September 2001) 494 and (December 2001) 66. [Bibliography: Reid M.] See ANOREXIA NERVOSA; CLUB; DISCRIMINATION; PENSION SCHEME AND DISCRIMINATION; PHYSICAL REASONS.

disability benefit. The social welfare benefit to which a person is entitled in respect of any day of *incapacity for work* which forms part of a period of interruption of employment: Social Welfare (Consolidation) Act 1993, ss 31–36. Provision has been made to change the rules which were seen as creating a disincentive to persons, on benefit for a long period, returning to work; under the new provisions, such persons who have returned to work and subsequently, after a short period, find themselves unfit to continue working, will be able to revert to the original benefit to which they were entitled without the need to requalify: Social Welfare (Miscellaneous Provisions) Act 2002, s 5. See also Social Welfare 1998, s 21. See Social Welfare Act 2003, s 2(2)(b), 8 and 9. See OCCUPATIONAL INJURIES BENEFIT.

disability pension. The Minister cannot, without considering all relevant factors, abate the disability pension of a person who has received damages: *Breen v Minister for Defence* [1990] ITLR (5 November), SC.

disabled driver. There is provision for repayment of excise duty, value added tax and remission of road tax in respect of a motor vehicle (and hydrocarbon oil) used by a severely and permanently disabled person where he could not drive the vehicle unless it was specially constructed or adapted to take account of the disablement: Finance Act 1989, s 92; FA 1991, s 124; F(No 2)A 1992, s 17. There are also tax concessions for a disabled person as a passenger. See *Wiley v Revenue Commissioners* [1993] ILRM 482, SC and [1994] 2 IR 160, SC. See SI No 353 of 1994. See SAFETY BELT.

disabled person and air travel. All airlines, service providers and other agencies conducting business at Aer Rianta airports are required to do all that is reasonable to accommodate the needs of persons with a disability, by providing special treatment or facilities, if without such special treatment or facilities it would be impossible or unduly difficult for these persons to avail themselves of the service: SI No 469 of 1999.

disabled person and build environment. Provision has been made by the building regulations for improved access to buildings for persons with a disability: SI 179 of 2000 inserting new Part M in SI No 497 of 1997. The provisions are: (a) adequate provision must be made to enable *people with disabilities* to safely and independently access and use a building; (b) if sanitary conveniences are provided in a building, adequate provision must be made for such persons; (c) if a building contains fixed seating for audience or spectators, adequate provision must be made for such persons. 'People with disabilities' means people who have an impairment of hearing or sight or an impairment which limits their ability to walk, or which restricts them to a wheelchair. Part M of the building regulations does not apply to works in connection with extensions to and the material alterations of existing dwellings, provided that such works do not create a new dwelling. See BUILDING REGULATIONS.

disabled person and education. It has been established, on a worldwide basis, that children suffering from profound mental handicap would benefit from formal education; accordingly there is a constitutional obligation upon the State to provide *for* free primary education for profoundly handicapped children in as full and positive a manner as it had done for other members of the community: *O'Donoghue v Minister for Health* [1996] 2 IR 20, HC.

The Supreme Court has held that the constitutional obligation of the State to provide *for* free primary education was owed to children and not to adults and consequently the obligation stopped at the age of 18: *Sinnott v Minister for Education* [2001] 2 IR 545, SC. The court held in this case that the plaintiff was entitled to a declaration that the Minister had deprived a severely autistic child of his constitutional rights by failing to provide for free primary education for him up to 18 years of age. The High Court ordered, at interlocutory stage, that a 4-year-old autistic child be provided with 29 hours home tuition each week: *Cronin v Minister for Education* [6 July 2004, unreported] HC. However, the High Court rejected the claim of a boy suffering from Attention Deficit Hyperactivity Disorder that the State had failed to provide early and appropriate education and therapies for him: *Clare v Minister for Education* [30 July

2004, unreported] HC. See also *Downey v Minister for Education* [2001] 2 IR 727, HC.

Recent legislation, makes further provision, having regard to the common good and in a manner that is informed by best international practice, for the education of people with *special educational needs* (qv): Education for Persons with Special Educational Needs Act 2004. The aims of the Act are: (a) to provide that the education of people with such needs, wherever possible, takes place in an inclusive environment, with those who do not have such needs; (b) to provide that people with special educational needs have the same right to avail of, and benefit from, appropriate education as do their peers who do not have such needs; (c) to assist children with special educational needs to leave school with the skills necessary to participate, to the level of their capacity, in an inclusive way in the social and economic activities of society and to live independent and fulfilled lives; (d) to provide for greater involvement of parents of children with special educational needs in the education of their children; (e) for those purposes to establish a body to be known as the National Council for Special Education and to define its functions; (f) to confer certain functions on health boards in relation to the education of people with special educational needs; and (g) to enable certain decisions made in relation to the education of people with such needs to be the subject of an appeal to an appeals board: long title of the Act. The Bill originally had the title of 'Education for Persons with Disabilities Bill 2003'.

The 2004 Act sets out a range of services which must be provided, including assessments, individual education plans and support services and provides for a process of appeals, including mediation, where needs are not met. While the Act is primarily concerned with the education of persons who are 18 years and younger, there is provision for the planning of a person's education, while that person is still a child, after the age of 18 (EPSENA 2004, ss 1(1) and 15).

See also *AHEAD – Association for Higher Education Access and Disability* at website: *www.ahead.ie*. See 'The Duration of Primary Education' by Oran Doyle BL in (2002) 10 ISLR 222. [Bibliography: Glendenning.] See DEPENDENT CHILD; EDUCATION; EDUCATION PLAN; INTE-GRATED EDUCATION; SCHOOL; SPECIAL EDUCATIONAL NEEDS.

disabled person and employment. See DISABILITY AND DISCRIMINATION; REHABILITATION.

disabled person and housing. Planning permission is not required for a development consisting of a *change of use* of a house, to use as a residence for persons with an intellectual or physical disability or mental illness and for persons providing care for such persons: Planning and Development Regulations 2001, SI No 600 of 2001, Sch 2, class 14. The number of such disabled persons living in the residence must not exceed six and the number of resident carers must not exceed two. For previous legislation, see Local Government (Planning and Development) Regulations 1994, SI No 86 of 1994.

Provision has been made for grants for the adaptation of houses for disabled persons and the carrying out of essential repairs to certain unfit houses: Housing (Disabled Persons and Essential Repair Grants) Regulations 2001, SI No 607 of 2001. See also BUILDING REGULATIONS; HOUSING.

disabled person and human rights. The interpretative incorporation of the European Convention on Human Rights into Irish law could have significance for persons with a disability. 'In particular, article 8, the right to private and family life, is wide ranging in its scope, applying to such matters as the freedom to express one's sexuality, to consent to medical treatment, to have access to one's children, to form and to keep social relationships, and to protect one's reputation.': 'Human Rights for disabled people' by Alma Clissmann in *Law Society Gazette* (March 2004) 9. See European Convention on Human Rights Act 2003.

disabled person and information. A public body has a duty to give reasonable assistance to a person with a disability who is seeking a record of a public body, so as to facilitate the exercise by that person of his rights under the Freedom of Information Act 1997 (FOIA 1997, s 6(2)). See FREEDOM OF INFORMATION; INFORMATION, ACCESS TO.

disabled person and medical treatment. 'Patients with disabilities are entitled to the same treatment options and respect for autonomy as any other patient. Disability does not necessarily mean lack of capacity.'

Medical Council, *A Guide to Ethical Conduct and Behaviour* (6th edn, 2004) para 2.2. See PATIENT, CONSENT OF.

disabled person and mobility. See KERB RAMPS; TRANSPORT ACCESSIBILITY.

disabled person and qualifications. One of the objects of the Qualifications (Education and Training) Act 1999 is to facilitate lifelong learning through the promotion of access and opportunities for learners, including learners with a disability (Q(ET)A 1999, ss 2(1) and 4(1)(e)). Bodies and persons are required to have regard for this in exercising their functions under the Act (Q(ET)A 1999, s 4(2)).

disabled person and separation. The physical or mental disability of a spouse or any dependent child of the family is a consideration which the court must have regard for in providing for that spouse and/or child arising from the granting by the court of a decree of judicial separation (qv): Judicial Separation and Family Law Reform Act 1989, s 20(2)(e) and 20(4)(c).

disabled person and severance. A severance payment made to an employee on account of his disability is exempt from income tax: Income Tax Act 1967, s 115 and *Cahill (Inspector of Taxes) v Harding* [1991] 9 ILT Dig 147, HC. An *ex-gratia* payment to an employee who resigned on ill-health was treated as a disability payment: *O'Shea v Mulqueen* [1995] 1 IR 504. See Taxes Consolidation Act 1997, s 201.

disabled person and social services. See COMHAIRLE.

disabled person and tax. See DISABLED DRIVER; INCOME TAX.

disabled person's welfare. See CHILD, EVIDENCE OF; HEARSAY; TELEVISION LINK.

disabled vehicle. A vehicle which stands so substantially disabled (either through accident, break down or the removal of the engine or other such vital part) as to be no longer capable of being propelled mechanically; it is regarded as not being a *mechanically propelled vehicle* (qv): Road Traffic Act 1961, s 3(2).

disabled voter. A disabled person is entitled to vote from his home in elections if he is qualified as a *special voter* (qv). A disabled person who does not so qualify, may be authorised to vote at another polling station where it would be more convenient for the elector because of his disability. See Electoral Act 1992, s 100.

A disabled person (ie a person with a physical illness or physical disability who is unable to go in person to vote) is now entitled to vote by post: Electoral (Amendment) Act 1996, s 4. Also polling stations and counting places must be, where practicable, accessible to wheelchairs (E(A)A 1996, ss 2 and 5). See also Electoral Act 1997, s 82; European Parliament Elections Act 1997, Sch 2, rr 41–47.

A blind or otherwise physically handicapped person may have his ballot paper marked for him by either a companion or the presiding officer; an illiterate person may also have his ballot paper marked for him by the presiding officer: EA 1992, s 103. See also Referendum Act 1994, s 29. See REGISTER OF ELECTORS; VOTERS, SPECIAL.

disabling statute. Legislation which restricts a pre-existing right. See ENABLING ACT.

disbar. To expel a barrister from the Honorable Society of King's Inns. A barrister may apply to have himself disbarred e g in order to become a solicitor. See BARRISTER; BARRISTER, DISBARRED; JUDGES, QUALIFICATION OF; KING'S INNS, HONORABLE SOCIETY OF.

discharge. To release from an obligation; to release a person from prison.

discharge from bankruptcy. See BANKRUPTCY, DISCHARGE FROM.

discharge of bill. Release from the obligations of a *bill of exchange* which occurs when all the rights and obligations attached to it are released, in one of the following ways: by payment in due course; by remuneration; by cancellation; by material alteration; by delivery up. See Bills of Exchange Act 1882 ,ss 59 and 61–64. See PAYMENT IN DUE COURSE.

discharge of charge. It is the view of the Conveyancing Committee of the Law Society that when a vendor's solicitor gives an undertaking on the closing of a sale to furnish a discharge of a charge or other burden on the vendor's folio or a vacated mortgage/charge, that this undertaking, by implication, extends to and includes the certificate of charge, if one has issued in respect of any such charge, and any other document necessary for the removal of the charge or burden from the folio: *Law Society Gazette* (April 2004) 36 and (May 2004) 40.

discharge of contract. The release from the obligations of a contract which may arise by performance, agreement, release, rescission, accord and satisfaction, breach, impossibility of performance, frustration, merger, judgment of a court, or bankruptcy (qqv).

disciplinary proceedings. Disciplinary hearings must observe the requirements of natural justice: *Ryan v VIP Taxi Co-Operative* [1989] ITLR (10 April). In a particular case, it was held that to deny the person the opportunity to cross-examine witnesses as to the facts central to the establishment of the charges against him, amounted to a failure to afford him fair procedures and constituted a breach of the requirement of natural justice to *audi alterem partem*: *Gallagher v Revenue Commissioners* [1995] 1 IR 55, SC and ELR 108.

Where the High Court is reviewing disciplinary proceedings in which the issues on review are direct issues of fact, it must itself decide those contested issues of fact; it may not merely endorse the findings of fact of the disciplinary body: *Kerrigan v An Bord Altranais* [1990] ITLR (30 July), SC. An employee is entitled to know the nature and extent of any proposed disciplinary action against him: *Deegan & Ors v Dunnes Stores* [1992] ELR 184, EAT. Also where there are *disciplinary procedures* agreed between an employer and a trade union, a dismissal in breach of the procedures is an unfair dismissal: *Mellett v Tara Mines Ltd* [1997] ELR 79, EAT.

There is provision for the intervention of the *Irish Auditing and Accounting Supervisory Authority* (qv) in relation to the investigation and disciplinary process of a prescribed accountancy body to ensure that it has complied with approved procedures: Companies (Auditing and Accounting) Act 2003, s 23. Provision is also made for statutory backing for the disciplinary procedures of these bodies (s 36). See *Bane v Garda Representative Association* [1997] 2 IR 449, HC; *Walsh v Irish Red Cross Society* [1997] 2 IR 479, SC; *Vogel v Cheeverstown House Ltd* [1998] 2 IR 496, HC. See ADMINISTRATIVE TRIBUNAL; GARDA, DISCIPLINE OF; LEGAL REPRESENTATION; PROFESSIONAL DISCIPLINARY BODIES; SOLICITOR'S DISCIPLINARY TRIBUNAL.

discipline in school. See CORPORAL PUNISHMENT; SCHOOL DISCIPLINE.

disclaimed estate. An interest in an estate which is renounced. Where a person disclaims an interest in the estate of a deceased who has not made a will (*intestate succession* (qv)) and there are other possible successors of the estate, they will take prec-

edence over the State for the purposes of intestate succession: Succession Act 1965, s 72A inserted by Family Law (Miscellaneous Provisions) Act 1997, s 6. This also applies in the case of *testate succession* eg where there is a residuary beneficiary who disclaims, thereby causing a partial intestacy. The 1997 amendment was enacted to codify and confirm existing practice and for the avoidance of doubt. There is no tax liability where a person disclaims a benefit under a will or under an intestacy, or disclaims an entitlement to an interest in settled property: Capital Acquisitions Tax Consolidation Act 2003, s 12. See 'Carved in Stone? – post-death planning' by solicitor Anne Stephenson in *Law Society Gazette* (October 2003) 20.

In a disclaimer by a number of beneficiaries, it is considered good practice to have one disclaimer signed by all of them, and to provide that it will take effect only when it is signed by all of them, and from the date on which it is signed by the last person to sign: practice note in *Law Society Gazette* (December 2003) 41, which includes a precedent. See FAMILY ARRANGEMENT.

disclaimer. A renunciation.

A disclaimer of an *unregistered* enduring power of attorney, is not valid unless and until the attorney gives notice of it to the donor; also a disclaimer of a *registered* enduring power of attorney is not valid except on notice to the donor and with the consent of the court: Powers of Attorney Act 1996, ss 5(10) and 11(1)(b). See DISCLAIMED ESTATE; ONEROUS PROPERTY.

disclaimer clause. See EXCLUSION CLAUSE.

disclosure in civil proceedings. See DISCOVERY; EXPERT REPORT; NEWSPAPER RULE; PERSONAL INJURIES.

disclosure in criminal proceedings. In the UK, it has been held that there is a common law duty on the prosecution to disclose relevant evidence, which duty exists irrespective of any request by the defence and which continues throughout the trial: *Judith Ward* [1992] 142 NLJ 859. See ALIBI; BOOK OF EVIDENCE.

disclosure of information. See INFORMATION, ACCESS TO.

disclosure of interest. See ARM'S LENGTH, AT; CONFLICT OF INTEREST; COUNCILLOR, ETHICS IN PUBLIC OFFICE.

disclosure of invention. An essential element in an application for a patent; a failure to *disclose* the invention is also a ground for the revocation of a patent which has been granted: Patents Act 1992, ss 19 and 57–58. See PATENT, APPLICATION FOR.

disclosure of material fact. See UBERRIMAE FIDEI.

disclosure order. The order which a court may make to oblige any person whom the court believes to have relevant information about share or debenture ownership in a private company, to give such information to the court: Companies Act 1990, ss 99–104. A person with a defined *financial interest* in a company may apply to the court for such an order. The court will only make a *disclosure order* if it deems it just and equitable to do so and if it is of the opinion that the financial interest of the applicant is or will be prejudiced by the non-disclosure. See SHARES, COMPANY.

discontinuance. The voluntary putting to an end of an action by a plaintiff. The plaintiff may at any time before the receipt of the defendant's defence, or after receipt thereof before taking any other proceeding in the action, discontinue his action by producing to the proper officer a consent signed by all the parties: RSC Ord 26. The court has an inferred jurisdiction to permit the withdrawal of a notice of discontinuance: *Smyth v Tunney* [2004] 1 ILRM 464, HC.

For provisions governing the discontinuance by a plaintiff of an action in the Circuit Court, see Circuit Court Rules 2001 Ord 21. There are no particular rules for discontinuing an action in the District Court. See also Residential Tenancies Act 2004, s 89.

discount, issue of shares at a. The allotment of shares in a registered company at less than their *par* value. Such allotment is not permitted otherwise than for brokerage and commissions authorised by the Companies Act 1963, s 59: Companies Amendment Act 1983, s 27.

discoverability test. The concept that a *cause of action* in respect of a wrong, accrues on the date of discovery of damage caused by the wrong, rather that on the date of occurrence of the damage. This concept had not been incorporated into Irish law until 1991. The Law Reform Commission had recommended a discoverability test in respect of personal injuries: LRC 21, 1987. See Statute of Limitations (Amendment) Act 1991. See CAUSE OF ACTION.

discovert. A woman who is unmarried or a widow.

discovery. The process whereby the parties to an action disclose to each other on *affidavit* all documents in their possession, custody or power, relating to matters in issue in the action. Final documents which have been approved by a professional adviser for the sight of his client (but remaining in the possession of the adviser) are documents within the *power* of the client and are discoverable in a party/party discovery: *Bula Ltd v Tara Mines Ltd* [1994] 1 ILRM 111, SC. In exceptional circumstances, a judge may order a party to discover a document, notwithstanding that the document is not in its power ie the party has no enforceable legal right to obtain the document: *Johnson v Church of Scientology* [2001] 2 ILRM 110, SC.

In High Court actions, discovery is obtained by application by one party to the other in writing requesting that discovery be made *voluntarily*; the court will only order discovery where the other party has failed, refused or neglected to make such discovery or has ignored such request: RSC Ord 31, r 12 as substituted by Rules of the Superior Courts (No 2) (Discovery) 1999, SI No 233 of 1999.

The High Court has held that this rule imposes a clearly defined obligation on a party who is seeking discovery, to pinpoint the documents or category of documents required and to give the reasons why they are required: *Swords v Western Protein Ltd* [2001] 1 ILRM 481, HC and 1 IR 324. The Supreme Court has held that the applicant for discovery must discharge the *prima facie* burden of proving that the discovery sought 'is necessary for disposing fairly of the cause or matter' and that the applicant's affidavit must, in addition, 'furnish the reasons why each category of document is required': *Ryanair plc v Aer Rianta cpt'* [2004] ITLR (12 January 2004) and 1 ILRM 241.

Any discovery sought and agreed between the parties must be made in like manner and form as if directed by order of the court. Where the parties have consented to an order for discovery, the Court has jurisdiction to order the discovery: *Greene v Instruelec Services Ltd* [2001] 1 IR 653, HC and [2002] 1 ILRM 237, HC. An application for discovery must not be made later than 28 days after the action has been set down or 28 days after is has been listed for trial.

Failure to comply with an order for discovery may lead to the action being dismissed or the defence being struck out: RSC Ord 31, r 21. This rule exists to ensure that parties to litigation comply with orders for discovery. It does not exist to punish a defaulter, but to facilitate the administration of justice by ensuring compliance with the order of the court: *Murphy v J Donohoe Ltd* [1996] 1 ILRM 481, SC. An order for discovery is complied with by an affidavit of discovery. There is no rule in Irish law that an *affidavit of discovery* was to be considered as conclusive and incapable of ever being the subject of cross-examination: *Duncan v Governor of Portlaoise Prison* [1997] 1 IR 558, HC. To hold otherwise would mean that the court would be prevented from investigating the accuracy or adequacy of an affidavit of discovery and would have to accept at face value whatever was averred therein (*Duncan* case). See RSC Ord 40, r 1.

Also in civil proceedings, documents may be discovered which were brought into being in the course of investigations by the gardaí of the incident which gave rise to the civil proceedings: *Walsh v Peters* [1993] 11 ILT & SJ 182, CC applying *DPP v Holly* [1984] ILRM 149. A person is entitled to discovery of any correspondence which had come into being subsequent to his dismissal from employment, provided that such correspondence is relevant to the matters in issue: *Tobin v Cashell* [1998] ELR 277, SC. It is not necessary in a discovery application for the court to adjudicate on the admissibility of the proposed evidence: *Von Gordon v Helaba Dublin Landes Bank Hessen* [2003] FL 8407, HC.

In Northern Ireland, it has been held that there is a distinction made between discovery in judicial review (qv) and in plenary actions: *Re Glór na nGael* [1991] ITLR (19 August), HC of J.

For discovery and inspection of documents in *commercial proceedings* (qv), see RSC Ord 63A, r 6(1)(vi) inserted by Rules of the Superior Courts (Commercial Proceedings) 2004, SI No 2 of 2004. See *McKenna v Best Travel Ltd* [1995] 2 ILRM 471, HC; *Brooks Thomas Ltd v Impac Ltd* [1999] 1 ILRM 171, SC; *F McK v F C (Proceeds of Crime)* [2001] 4 IR 521, SC. See 'Discovery and the need for strict com-

pliance with the 1999 Rules' by Ian Kavanagh BL in *Bar Review* (March 2001) 273; 'Discovery in the Master's Court' by William Abrahamson BL in *Bar Review* (December 2002) 360; 'Discovery Channels' in *Law Society Gazette* (December 2003) 18. See 'Voyage of Discovery' by solicitor Eoin Dee in *Law Society Gazette* (March 2002) 16. For draft letter of discovery, notice of motion, and affidavit, see 'The changing face of discovery' by barrister Andrew Fitzpatrick in *Law Society Gazette* (April 2003) 14. See Commissions of Investigation Act 2004, s 16(4). [Bibliography: Barron; Cahill E; Dee; Glanville.] See CONSUMER AFFAIRS, DIRECTOR OF; JOURNALIST, COMMUNICATIONS WITH; EXPERT REPORT; NEWSPAPER RULE; NOTICE TO PRODUCE; PRE-TRIAL DISCOVERY; PUBLIC POLICY; RELEVANCY TEST; SOLE DISCOVERY; STAY OF EXECUTION.

discovery, fishing for. Discovery is not allowed for the purpose of *fishing* out a case eg *Galvin v Graham-Twomey* [1994] 2 ILRM 315. A *fishing expedition* is one where there is no stated objective by reference to the pleadings: *McDonnell v Sunday Business Post Ltd* [2000] ITLR (13 March), HC. Consequently, discovery will be ordered only after delivery of a statement of claim, unless there are exceptional circumstances: *Law Society v Rawlinson* [1997] 3 IR 592, HC. 'Discovery in respect of non-specific pleas is the classic example of '*fishing*' – plead in general terms, then hope something turns up on discovery!': the Master of the High Court in *Kelly v Mona (Ireland) Ltd* [1999/833P] reported in *Law Society Gazette* (December 2003) 20.

However, discovery is available as a substantive remedy against a defendant where that person has become inadvertently involved in a tortious activity and is in possession of information which will assist the plaintiff obtain justice; however this jurisdiction of the court must be used sparingly and only to seek the identity of the wrongdoer rather than factual information concerning the commission of the wrong: *Megaleasing UK Ltd v Barrett (No 2)* [1993] ILRM 497, SC. See also *Shortt v Dublin City Council* [2004] 1 ILRM 81, HC and [2003] 2 IR 69.

discovery, further. There is no principle of continuing automatic obligation for discovery of documents created *after* the filing of an affidavit of discovery: *Bula Ltd v Tara Mines* [1993] ITLR (20 December), SC.

Also the court will not order *further and better discovery* unless a document has been excluded in the affidavit of discovery which was clearly identified as specially relevant to the issues in the action (*Bula* case).

In order to obtain further and better discovery, evidence should be adduced to show that there are additional relevant documents in the possession of the respondent or that he misunderstood the issues in the action: *Phelan v Goodman* [2000] 2 ILRM 378, SC. In a particular case the court decided that a further inspection of documents was not necessary where the case had not materially altered: *Barry v DPP* [2001] ITLR (21 May), HC.

discovery, resisting. Discovery can be resisted on a number of grounds: (a) that the documents are protected by privilege (qv): eg *Incorporated Law Society v Minister for Justice* [1987] ILRM 42; *PMPS Ltd v PMPA Insurance plc* [1989] ITLR (11 December), HC; or (b) that the documents do not pass the *relevancy test* (qv); or (c) that discovery is prohibited by statute eg the Adoption Act 1976, s 8 prohibits any order for discovery in respect of documents generated for adoptions or related matters: *DC v DM (Adoption)* [1999] 2 IR 150, HC.

Where privilege (qv) is claimed, the deponent in the affidavit of discovery, should list and briefly describe each document over which privilege is claimed, specifying in respect of each such document the precise basis or ground of privilege relied on: *Bula Ltd v Tara Mines Ltd* [1990] ITLR (20 August), SC; *Bula Ltd v Crowley* [1990] ILRM 756, SC. Also there are restrictions on discovery which can be made against the Commission: Commission to Inquire into Child Abuse Act 2000, s 31.

discovery, use of documents. A party obtaining the production of documents by discovery in an action is prohibited from making any use of the documents or the information contained in them otherwise than for the purpose of the action: *Greencore Group plc v Murphy* [1996] 1 ILRM 210, HC and [1995] 3 IR 520, HC. However, the court has a discretion to permit such use in special circumstance and where the release would not occasion injustice to the person making discovery: *Roussel v Forchepro Ltd* [2000] 1 ILRM 321, HC and [1999] 3 IR 567, HC (under appeal).

Discovery on terms that only lawyers for the plaintiff would have access to the docu-ments will not be permitted by the courts: *Burke v Central Independent Television plc* [1994] 2 ILRM 161 and 2 IR 63, SC.

discovery and judicial review. While discovery of documents is rare in judicial review proceedings, it is available: *Shortt v Dublin City Council* [2004] 1 ILRM 81, HC and [2003] 2 IR 69. The circumstances in which discovery will be granted in judicial review proceedings are much narrower than in a plenary action: *Kilkenny Community Communications v Broadcasting Commission of Ireland* [2004] 1 ILRM 170, SC. Discovery will not normally be regarded as necessary if the application for judicial review is based on procedural impropriety, as ordinarily that can be established without the benefit of discovery: *Carlow/Kilkenny Radio Ltd v Broadcasting Commission of Ireland* [2004] 1 ILRM 161, SC. Where discovery will be necessary is: (a) where there is a clear factual dispute on the affidavits that would have to be resolved in order to adjudicate properly on the application; or (b) where there is *prima facie* evidence to the effect either: (i) that a document which ought to have been before the deciding body was not before it, or (ii) that a document which ought not to have been before the deciding body was before it (*Carlow* case).

discovery in Circuit Court. For the provisions on *discovery* and *inspection* of documents in the Circuit Court, see Circuit Court Rules 2001 Ord 32. An application to the Court for discovery may only take place following a failure of a request for voluntary discovery. Failure to comply with an order of discovery can lead to a dismissal of the action or a striking out of the defence (Order 32, r 6).

discovery in District Court. In the District Court up to recent times, there were no specific provisions dealing with the discovery of documents, although the judge was and is empowered to order further and better particulars of any matter: DCR 1997 Ord 40, r 3. However, provision has now been made for discovery of documents in civil proceedings in the District Court; the order is to make discovery on oath of the documents which are or have been in a person's possession, power or procurement relating to any matter in question in those proceedings: DCR 1997 Ord 46A inserted by District Court (Discovery of Documents) Rules 1998, SI No 285 of 1999.

discovery re criminal cases. While the Rules of the Superior Court 1986 (Ord 31, r 29) leave open the possibility of ordering discovery in criminal cases, there is no authority which would support the making of such an order: *People (DPP) v Flynn* [1996] 1 ILRM 317, CCC. The principle that each party should be entitled to know from the other, in advance, any information which would enhance his own case or destroy his adversary's case, was less applicable in criminal proceedings where the burden of proof rests with the prosecution. Also discovery is intended to be mutual between the parties; it could not be mutual in a criminal case as it would not be ordered against an accused (*Flynn* case).

The Supreme Court has ruled that there is no jurisdiction for making an order of discovery in criminal proceedings, approving the *Flynn* case: *People (DPP) v Sweeney* [2002] 1 ILRM 532, SC and [2001] 4 IR 102, SC. It would be clearly repugnant to treat the word 'cause' in the Rules dealing with discovery, as extending to criminal proceedings: *obiter dictum* in *D H v Groarke* [2002] 3 IR 522, SC.

However, the Supreme Court did order discovery of documents sought by an applicant in judicial review proceedings, for the purpose of prohibiting a criminal trial for fraudulent trading on the grounds of delay: *Burke v DPP* [2001] 1 IR 760, SC and RSC Ord 31, r 12 as substituted by Rules of the Superior Courts (No 2) (Discovery) 1999, SI No 233 of 1999. Also in a rape case, the Supreme Court ordered discovery of a document listed in a schedule to an affidavit; the court held that the status of a document, from the point of view of privilege or immunity from disclosure, changes once it has been referred to in pleadings or in an affidavit: *T H v DPP* [2002] 1 ILRM 48, SC. In an assault case, the High Court held that where conflict arose between the public interest involved in the production of evidence and the public interest in the confidentiality of the exercise of the executive powers of the State, the judicial power should decide which public interest should prevail: *Corbett v DPP* [1999] 2 IR 179, HC.

discovery re foreign states. A foreign state must be prepared to make discovery where it has submitted itself to the jurisdiction of the Irish courts eg where it is the plaintiff; however, discovery will not be allowed in any other circumstances, as this would undermine the principle that foreign states are generally immune from the jurisdiction of the courts of another state: *Fusco v O'Dea* [1994] 2 ILRM 389, SC

discovery re third parties. Discovery is also permitted to be made against a *third party* (a stranger) not involved in the proceedings, in respect of relevant documents; the party seeking such order must indemnify the third party in respect of any costs reasonably incurred: RSC Ord 31, r 29. This rule does not give the court power to make an order which would permit a party to search the files of a stranger to the action for the purpose of finding relevant documents; the party seeking the order must also serve notice of his motion on all parties to the action: *Holloway v Belenos Publications* [1987] ILRM 791 and IR 405.

Also the court must be satisfied that the third party is likely to have the documents in its possession, that they are relevant to the issues in the case, and that discovery is not unduly oppressive: *Allied Irish Banks plc v Ernst & Whinney* [1993] 1 IR 375, SC.

Non-party discovery, with all the inconvenience which it involves, should only be ordered where there is no realistic alternative available: *Chambers v Times Newspapers Ltd* [1999] 1 ILRM 504, HC and 2 IR 424. Non-party confidential documents are discoverable if necessary for the fair disposal of an action: *Beverly Cooper-Flynn v RTE, Charlie Bird & James Howard* [2000] ITLR (5 June), HC and [2000] 3 IR 343. In this case the judge ordered inspection by a limited number of persons of confidential documents in the possession of National Irish Bank. See also *Von Gordon v Helaba Dublin Landes Bank Hessen* [2003] FL 8407, HC.

A non-party to an action against whom discovery is made is entitled to all costs reasonably incurred in consequence of the order: *Dunne v Fox* [1999] 1 IR 283, HC. See also *Silver Hill Duckling v Minister for Agriculture* [1987] ILRM 516; *Fitzpatrick v Independent Newspapers Ltd* [1988] IR 132, HC; *Fusco v O'Dea* [1994] 2 ILRM 389, SC. See also RSC Ord 63, r 1(6).

discretion. The power given to a person of deciding a question where latitude of judgement is allowed. A discretionary remedy is consequently one which may or may not be granted. In the UK it has been held that a person entrusted with a discretion must direct himself properly in law, must call his own attention to matters which he is bound to consider and exclude irrelevant matters: *Associated Picture Houses Ltd v Wednesday Corporation* [1947] 2 All ER 680. See ABSOLUTE DISCRETION.

discretion to prosecute. It is for the Director of Public Prosecution (qv) to decide whether or not to prosecute an individual for an alleged indictable offence (qv). Such a decision is reviewable by the courts in only very limited circumstances. See DIRECTOR OF PUBLIC PROSECUTIONS.

discretionary trust. A trust where property is vested in trustees who have a discretion as to which members of a specified class, such as the children of the settlor or testator, they will pay the income of the trust property or transfer the capital to and in what proportions. It is a trust whereby a beneficiary has no right to any part of the income of the trust property and where the trustees have discretionary power to pay him such income as they deem fit, eg a conveyance to trustees of land to apply the rents and profits *for the benefit of X in the absolute discretion of the trustees.*

Provision has been made by the courts for an adult child, who was seriously mentally ill, by means of a discretionary trust of which all the testator's children would be beneficiaries: *Re FF, HL v Bank of Ireland* [1978] HC. See also *MPD v MD* [1981] ILRM 179; *L v L* [1984] ILRM 607.

Where property has become subject to a discretionary trust, the trust is deemed to have taken an inheritance: Capital Acquisitions Tax Consolidation Act 2003, s 15. A charge to tax however does not arise, in certain circumstances, until the disponer is dead. See CHILD, PROVISION FOR; TRUST.

discriminating club. See CLUB, DISCRIMINATING.

discrimination. The Constitution provides that all citizens shall, as human persons, be held equal before the law: 1937 Constitution, art 40(1). Statute law provides that it is unlawful for an employer to *discriminate* against an employee or prospective employee in relation to employment; also a person must not *discriminate* in disposing of goods or premises or in providing a service or accommodation: Employment Equality Act 1998; Equal Status Act 2000. See 'A level Playing Field?' by solicitor Dr Mary Redmond in *Law Society Gazette* (September 2002) 18.

The Equality Act 2004 amends the 1998 and 2000 Acts: (a) to give effect to Directive (EC) 43/2000 implementing the principle of equal treatment between persons irrespective of racial or ethnic origin, Directive (EC) 78/2000 establishing a general framework for equal treatment in employment and occupation, and Directive (EC) 2002/73 amending Directive (EEC) 207/76 on the implementation of the principle of equal treatment for men and women as regards access to employment, vocational training and promotion, and working conditions; and (b) to revoke in part European Communities (Burden of Proof in Gender Discrimination Cases) Regulations 2001, SI No 337 of 2001, and to enact its provisions for proceedings under equality legislation. See 'Equal Partners' by solicitor Ciaran O'Mara in *Law Society Gazette* (April 2004) 30. [Bibliography: Bolger & Kimber; Reid M.] See DISCRIMINATION IN EMPLOYMENT; DISCRIMINATION IN GOODS AND SERVICES; EUROPEAN CONVENTION ON HUMAN RIGHTS; PENSION SCHEME AND DISCRIMINATION.

discrimination in employment. It is unlawful for an employer to *discriminate* against an employee or prospective employee in relation to access to employment, conditions of employment, training or work experience, promotion or regrading, or classification of posts: Employment Equality Act 1998, s 8(1). Also a provider of agency work must not discriminate against an agency worker.

Discrimination is taken to occur where one person is treated less favourably than another person is (has been or would be) treated, on any of *nine* grounds (called, *discriminatory grounds*) ie gender, marital status, family status, sexual orientation, religion, age, disability, race, or membership of the Traveller community (qqv).

Equality legislation does not require an employer to recruit or retain a person who is not fully competent, fully capable and available to carry out the duties of the job (EEA 1998, s 16 amended by Equality Act 2004, s 9). Also certain posts in the Garda Síochána, the defence forces and the prison service are excluded from parts of the legislation (EEA 1998, ss 27 and 37(6) amended by EA 2004, ss 18 and 27).

It is not discriminatory to confine a job to a particular sex, where the characteristic relating to gender constitutes a genuine and determining occupational requirement for the post eg in entertainment (EEA 1998, s 25 amended by substitution by EA 2004, s 16). There is an exemption in respect of non-gender discrimination in relation to employment to maintain the religious ethos of an institution (EEA 1998, s 37(1)). As regards equality provisions on access to employment, an 'employee' does not include a person employed in another person's home for the provision of personal services for persons residing in that home where the services affect the private or family life of those persons (EEA 1998, s 2(1) inserted by EA 2004, s 3).

Certain bodies must not discriminate as regards admission to membership or benefits eg trade unions, employer organisations, and professional organisations (EEA 1998, s 13). Candidates for employment in the State and Local Authorities have a right to pursue complaints of discrimination; to deny them this right would be wholly inconsistent with the EC Directive: *Southern Health Board v A Worker* [1999] ELR 322, LC. For other amendments to the 1998 Act, see EA 2004, Sch, and Equal Status Act 2000, Sch.

See also UN Convention on the Elimination of all Forms of Discrimination Against Women 1979 acceded to by Ireland in 1985 with some reservations: see *Mullally* in 10 ILT & SJ (1992) 6. See 'Last chance saloon' by barrister Cliona Kimber in *Law Society Gazette* (August/September 2003) 12. See also Pensions Act 1990, ss 65–81 as amended by Pensions (Amendment) Act 2002, s 45. [Bibliography: Bolger & Kimber; Curtin; Eardly (2); Reid M.] See ADVERTISEMENT; DISABILITY AND DISCRIMINATION; EQUAL COMMUNITY INITIATIVE; EQUALITY AUTHORITY; EQUALITY BEFORE THE LAW; EQUAL PAY; INDIRECT DISCRIMINATION; INTERVIEW BOARD; NON-DISCRIMINATION NOTICE; OMBUDSMAN; PENSION SCHEME AND DISCRIMINATION; PROCURE; SEXUAL HARASSMENT; VICTIMISATION; VICARIOUS LIABILITY.

discrimination in employment, redress for. A claim for redress of *discrimination* or *victimisation* (qv) is taken to the *Director of the Equality Tribunal* (qv), or to the *Circuit Court* (qv) in the case of discrimination on grounds of gender if compensation in excess of that permitted under Employment Equality Act 1998, s 82 is in issue (EEA 1998, s 77 amended by Equality Act 2004, ss 32–33 and 36). The 1998 Act provides no apparent obstacle to the simultaneous referral of a complaint of discrimi-

natory treatment to the Director of the Equality Tribunal and a complaint of discriminatory dismissal to the Labour Court: *A Complainant v A Company* [2002] ELR 230, EO. However, the initial jurisdiction which the Labour Court (qv) previously had, where dismissal was involved, has now been assigned to the Director (EA 2004, s 46).

A claim for redress must be brought within 6 months from the date of the last occurrence of discrimination or victimisation; this may be extended to 12 months for 'reasonable cause' (EEA 1998, s 77(5)–(6) amended by EA 2004, s 32). Prior to this amendment, the circumstance required to justify an extension was required to be 'exceptional'. It was held that to be 'exceptional', a circumstance did not need to be unique or unprecedented or very rare, but it could not be one which was regularly or routinely or normally encountered: *Fitzsimons-Markey v Gaelscoil Thulach na nOg* [2004] ELR 110, LC. The 2004 amendment also provides that where a delay in referring a case is due to a misrepresentation by the respondent, the date of the occurrence of the alleged discrimination or victimisation is taken to be the date the misrepresentation came to the notice of the complainant.

For an allegation of discrimination to be upheld under EEA 1998, a claimant must first show *prima facie* evidence of discrimination; the burden of proof then moves to the employer to rebut the presumption of discrimination by demonstrating the existence of objective, non-discriminatory reasons for its actions: *Nevin v The Plaza Hotel* [2002] ELR 177, EO. Now, where in any employment equality proceedings, facts are established by or on behalf of a complainant from which it may be presumed that there has been discrimination in relation to him, it is for the respondent to prove the contrary (EEA 1998, s 85A inserted by EA 2004, s 38).

In relation to equality legislation prior to the 1998 Act, see *Murphy v Attorney General* [1980] SC; *The State (Aer Lingus) v The Labour Court* [1987] ILRM 373 & [1990] 8 ILT Dig 238; *Aer Lingus Teo v Labour Court* [1990] ELR 113; *Vavasour v EEA* [1991] ELR 199, LC; *North Western Health Board v Martyn* [1988] ILRM 519, SC; *Cadwell v Labour Court* [1989] IR 280; *Natham v Bailey Gibson Ltd* [1992] HC reported by Flynn in 11 ILT & SJ (1993) 96; *Fennelly v*

Midland Health Board [1998] 28, EAT. See DIRECTOR OF THE EQUALITY TRIBUNAL.

discrimination in goods and services. A person must not discriminate in disposing of *goods* to the public or in providing a *service*; treating one person less favourably than another person, in a comparable situation, on any of ten *discriminatory grounds* is discrimination: Equal Status Act 2000, s 3, as amended by Equality Act 2004, s 48. The ten *discriminatory grounds* are gender, marital status, family status, sexual orientation, religion, age, disability, race, victimisation, membership of the Traveller community (qv) (ESA 2000, s 3(2)). The discriminatory ground must exist at present, or have previously existed but no longer exists, or may exist in the future, or is imputed to the person concerned. Treating a person who is associated with another person less favourably, by virtue of that association, is also discrimination.

Goods means any articles of moveable property (ESA 2000, 2(1)). *Service* means a service or facility of any nature which is available to the public generally, and includes: (a) access to and the use of any place; (b) facilities for: (i) banking, insurance, grants, loans, credit or financing, (ii) entertainment, recreation or refreshment, (iii) cultural activities, or (iv) transport or travel; (c) a service or facility provided by a club which is available to the public generally; and (d) a professional or trade service (ESA 2000, s 2(1)). The disposal or provision does not require consideration (ESA 2000, s 5(1)). Discrimination does not apply to a disposal of goods by will or gift, or to a disposal or provision which can reasonably be regarded as suitable only to the needs of certain persons (ESA 2000, s 5(2)(k)–(l)).

Discrimination does not apply to the difference in treatment of persons in connection with a dramatic performance or other entertainment where reasonably required for reasons of authenticity, aesthetics, tradition or custom (ESA 2000, s 5(2)(i)).

Also, a person must not discriminate in the disposal of premises and the provision of accommodation (ESA 2000, s 6 amended by EA 2004, s 49, to provide for the removal of the exclusion for 'small premises' and to provide an exception for accommodation in a part of a person's home). There are other exceptions eg (a) accommodation reserved for the use of persons in a particular category for a religious purpose, or as a refuge, nursing home, retirement home, home for persons with a disability, or hostel for homeless persons, and (b) certain differences in treatment by housing authorities eg Traveller accommodation. There are also specific provisions dealing with educational establishments (ESA 2000, s 7 amended by EA 2004, s 50), clubs (ESA 2000, ss 8–10), vehicle and station equipment (ESA 2000, s 17–18), kerbs (ESA 2000, s 19), prohibited advertising (ESA 2000, s 12).

Certain measures or activities are not prohibited eg (a) positive measures which are *bona fide* intended to promote equality of opportunity for disadvantaged persons or to cater for the special needs of persons requiring special facilities, services or assistance (ESA 2000, s 14 amended by EA 2004, s 52), and (b) a reasonable preferential charge for persons together with their children, married couples, persons in a specific age group, or persons with a disability (ESA 2000, s 16(1)). See Residential Tenancies Act 2004, s 196.

A solicitor should avoid discrimination against any person whether clients, counsel, professional witnesses, opposing clients or witnesses because of their sex, race, colour, religion, sexual persuasion, creed, ethnic origin or membership of any social grouping: *A Guide to Professional Conduct of Solicitors in Ireland* (2002) ch 6.9. A barrister must not discriminate in favour of or against any person availing, or seeking to avail, of the services of the barrister on the grounds of race, colour, sex, sexual orientation, language, politics, religion, nationality, national or social origin, national minority, birth or other status and it must be the professional duty of a barrister to comply with all laws intended to prevent discrimination on any grounds: *Code of Conduct for the Bar of Ireland* (December 2003) r 3.1(b). [Bibliography: Bolger & Kimber.] See CLUB, DISCRIMINATING; INDIRECT DISCRIMINATION; DISABILITY AND DISCRIMINATION; DISABILITY EQUALITY AUTHORITY; EDUCATIONAL ESTABLISHMENT; SEXUAL HARASSMENT.

discrimination in goods and services, redress for. To seek redress for *prohibited conduct* (ie discrimination, sexual or other harassment), the complainant must first notify the person who is alleged to have engaged in prohibited conduct (the *respondent*) within 2 months of the last occurrence, in writing, of: (a) the nature of the allegation, (b) the complainant's intention, if not satisfied with the respondent's response, to seek redress by referring the case to the Director of the Equality Tribunal: Equal Status Act 2000, ss 20–21 amended by Equality Act 2004, ss 53–54). The two-month period may be extended to four months on application for 'reasonable cause' replacing the previous 'exceptional circumstances' for such extension. Further extensions are available 'exceptionally'.

The Director may, if both parties agree, refer the matter for mediation to an equality mediation officer (ESA 2000, s 24 amended by EA 2004, s 58). There is now provision for the Circuit Court to enforce a mediated settlement (ESA 2000, s 31 amended by EA 2004, s 62).

Where in proceedings under the 2000 Act, facts are established by or on behalf of a person from which it may be presumed that prohibited conduct has occurred in relation to him, it is for the respondent to prove the contrary (ESA 2000, s 38A inserted by EA 2004, s 64).

Where the Director investigates a claim, the Director may dismiss the claim or order redress which may be: (a) an order for compensation to the maximum civil jurisdiction of the District Court (£5,000; €6,349 at present), or (b) an order that persons specified in the order take specified action (ESA 2000, s 27 amended by EA 2004, s 61). The maximum award applies to the claim even if the conduct constitutes a number of discriminatory grounds, with the exception of victimisation where a separate additional award may be made. The Director's decision may be appealed to the Circuit Court by either party within 42 days from the date of the decision; a further appeal lies to the High Court on a point of law (ESA 2000, s 28). The Circuit Court has jurisdiction to award costs: *Joyce v Madden* [2004] ELR 78, HC and 1 ILRM 277.

Redress for prohibited conduct as regards entry to licensed premises has been moved from the Director to the District Court: Intoxicating Liquor Act 2003, s 19. The court is entitled not only to make an order of compensation, but also to order a temporary closure of the premises. See DIRECTOR OF THE EQUALITY TRIBUNAL.

disentailing deed. See FEE TAIL.

disfigurement. A ground for damages in respect of injuries where suffered as a result of the negligence of another. A plaintiff is entitled to damages for the embarrassment she would suffer in the future as a woman with a major disfigurement and her inability to wear without major embarrassment various quite ordinary types of clothing: *Rooney v Connolly* [1987] ILRM 768. See CAUSING SERIOUS HARM; FACIAL INJURIES.

disfranchise. To deprive of a right. See FRANCHISE; FELONY.

disherison. Disinheriting. See DISINHERITING DISPOSITION.

dishonesty. The Law Reform Commission has recommended that a range of larceny (qv) offences be replaced by one offence of dishonest appropriation or theft. See *The Law Relating to Dishonesty* (LRC 43, 1992). See also *Report of the Government Advisory Committee on Fraud* (1993).

The Criminal Justice (Theft and Fraud Offences) Act 2001 brings the law up-to-date and consolidates the law relating to dishonesty, deception, theft and fraud. The Act also deals with the offences of forgery, counterfeiting, computer offences and measures designed to protect the European Communities' *financial interests* from fraud and corruption. For discussion on the 2001 Act, see 'Stolen Moments' by barrister Byron Wade in *Law Society Gazette* (October 2002) 10. See District Court (Theft and Fraud Offences) Rules 2003, SI No 412 of 2003. [Bibliography: McGreal C.] See DISQUALIFICATION ORDER, COMPANY; THEFT.

dishonour of bill. A *bill of exchange* is dishonoured if the drawee refuses to accept it or having accepted it fails to pay it: Bills of Exchange Act 1882, s 47. *Dishonour* gives the holder an immediate right of recourse against the drawer and endorsers of the bill; but notice of such dishonour must be given to those whom the holder wishes to hold liable. Where a *foreign bill* is dishonoured, formal notice of dishonour must be given by the process of *noting and protesting* (qv).

Where a bank has been repaid after a bill of exchange (which was discounted to it) was dishonoured, the drawer/payee effecting payment cannot rely on his being a holder in due course (qv) in order to claim payment if he is guilty of fraud in the course of the transaction giving rise to the bill: *Terex Equipment Ltd v Truck and Machinery Sales Ltd* [1994] 1 ILRM 557, HC. See *Walex & Co v Seafield Gentex Ltd* [1978] IR 167; *Spicer-Cowan Ireland Ltd v*

Play Print Ltd [1980] HC. See CHEQUE, COUNTERMAND OF; CHEQUE, DISHONOUR OF.

disinheriting disposition. A voluntary disposition by a deceased within three years before his death of his property for the purpose of defeating the share of his spouse, as a legal right (qv) or on intestacy, or of leaving his children insufficiently provided for. It includes a *donatio mortis causa* (qv). The court may order that such a disposition be deemed to be a gift made by will and to form part of the estate of the deceased. See Succession Act 1965, s 121; also *MPD v MD* [1981] ILRM 179.

dismissal, constructive. See CONSTRUCTIVE DISMISSAL.

dismissal, summary. See SUMMARY DISMISSAL.

dismissal, unfair. See UNFAIR DISMISSAL.

dismissal, wrongful. See WRONGFUL DISMISSAL.

dismissal for want of prosecution. The dismissal of an action, which the defendant may apply to the court for, where there has been no proceedings for two years; or where the plaintiff in a *plenary* summons has failed to deliver a statement of claim (qv) within the specified time; or where the plaintiff fails to comply with any order to answer interrogatories or for discovery or inspection of documents; or where the plaintiff fails to serve notice of trial after the close of pleadings; or where there is no attendance of the plaintiff at the trial.

The court will only grant a dismissal where the delay is both inordinate and inexcusable, and then only where the balance of justice so requires; the court will have regard for the extent of the litigant's personal blameworthiness for the delay and any failure to apply for a dismissal at an earlier stage: *Hogan v Jones* [1994] 1 ILRM 512, HC; *Sweeney v Horan's (Tralee) Ltd* [1987] ILRM 240. See also *Toal v Duignan* [1991] ILRM 135,140; *Celtic Ceramics Ltd v IDA* [1993] ILRM 248, HC and [1993], SC; *Murray v Devil's Glen Equestrian Centre* [2001] 4 IR 34, SC; *Anglo Irish Beef Processors Ltd v Montgomery* [2002] 3 IR 510, SC; *Ewins v Independent Newspapers (Ireland) Ltd* [2003] 1 IR 583, SC. See RSC Ord 31, r 21; Ord 36, rr 12, 13, 32; Ord 122, r 11.

In a Circuit Court action, other than a probate action, if the plaintiff does not within ten days after the delivery of the Defence serve notice of trial, the defendant,

in lieu of serving notice of trial himself, may apply to the Court to dismiss the action for want of prosecution: Circuit Court Rules 2001 Ord 33, r 5. When a case is called in Court, and the plaintiff does not appear, the defendant is entitled to judgment dismissing the action; however, if the defendant has a *counterclaim*, he may prove such counterclaim, in so far as the burden of proof lies on him (Ord 33, r 12).

It has been held that in deciding whether to dismiss proceedings for want of prosecution, the court is required to inquire whether the delay is inordinate and, even if inordinate, whether it has been inexcusable: *Silverdale Ltd v Italiatour Ltd* [2001] 1 ILRM 464, HC. In a particular case, the court held that the delay of some 12 months between the issuing and service of the plenary summons and the further delay of some three years and ten months in delivering the statement of claim was inordinate and inexcusable: *A Smoker v John Player and Sons Ltd & Others* (2004) Irish Times, 13 March, HC.

A dismissal for want of prosecution is not a bar to a future action on the same cause of action. The Supreme Court has specified the principles of law relevant to an application to dismiss an action for want of prosecution: *Primor plc v Stokes Kennedy Crowley* [1996] 2 IR 459, SC. See DELAY; LIMITATION OF ACTIONS.

dismissal of action. The dismissal of proceedings to which a defendant may be entitled to e g where the *statement of claim* (qv) discloses no cause of action, or the proceedings constitute an *abuse* of the process of the court. The High Court has an inherent jurisdiction to dismiss an action on the basis that, on the admitted facts, it could not succeed: *Barry v Buckley* [1981] IR 306. However, the court should be slow to dismiss such an action and should not do so where the statement of claim admits of an amendment which might save the action: *Sun Fat Chan v Osseus Ltd* [1991] ITLR (9 December), SC. See Supreme Court of Judicature (Ireland) Act 1877, s 27(5).

In the District Court, a *dismiss* is the dismissal of an action by civil summons e g an *ejectment dismiss* for recovery of possession of premises: DCR 1997 Ord 47, r 13. For execution of dismisses, see DCR 1997 Ord 48. See also ABUSE OF PROCESS; DIRECTION; DISMISSAL FOR WANT OF PROSECUTION.

dismissal of employee. Some act brought about by one party, contrary to the wishes of the other party, which renders the contract of employment to cease to exist and all the duties and obligations thereunder are no longer binding and as such the employment relationship has plainly come to an end: *Casey v Dunnes Stores* [2003] ELR 313, EAT. Termination of an employee's contract of employment by the employer.

At common law, an employer is entitled to dismiss an employee for any reason or for no reason, on giving reasonable notice: *Sheehy v Ryan and Moriarty* [2004] ELR 87, HC. An employee may be entitled to a specified, minimum or reasonable period of notice. However, a summary dismissal, ie without notice, may be justified. A dismissal may amount to an *unfair dismissal* (qv) or a *wrongful dismissal* (qv). An employer conducting an enquiry into whether conduct of an employee justifies his dismissal must comply with the requirements of *natural justice* (qv); the standard of proof is the *balance of probability*: *Georgopoulos v Beaumont Hospital Board* [1994] 1 ILRM 58, HC and [1998] 3 IR 132, SC.

An employee found not guilty of criminal charges, may be dismissed from employment following fair procedures. It has been held that it would be absurd, if a party who had failed to establish a proposition beyond reasonable doubt should, by that fact alone, be debarred from attempting to establish the same proposition on the balance of probability: *Mooney v An Post* [1998] 4 IR 288, SC and ELR 238.

Where an employee has been dismissed and he takes an action against his employer for unfair dismissal and where trust has irretrievably broken down between them, his likely remedy, if successful in the action, will be in damages rather than re-instatement: *Doyle v Grangeford Precast Concrete Ltd* [1998] ELR 260, HC. See *Fitzgerald v Regsimm Ltd* [1997] ELR 65, EAT; *Maher v Irish Permanent plc* [1998] 4 IR 302, HC. [Bibliography: Barry J.] See CONSTRUCTIVE DISMISSAL; INCOMPETENCE; NOTICE, EMPLOYMENT; REASONABLENESS; SPECIFIC PERFORMANCE; SUMMARY DISMISSAL; TERMINATION OF EMPLOYMENT; UNFAIR DISMISSAL; WRONGFUL DISMISSAL.

dismissal of garda. See GARDA, DISCIPLINE OF.

disorderly conduct. (1) Means any unreasonable behaviour by a person on licensed premises which, having regard to all the circumstances, is likely to cause injury, fear or distress to any other person on the premises: Intoxicating Liquor Act 2003, s 2(1). It includes, but is not limited to: (a) violent, threatening, abusive, quarrelsome or insulting behaviour, (b) conduct causing damage to property, (c) conduct constituting certain offences, (d) conduct in breach of a duty imposed by the Fire Services Act 1981, s 18(3), or (e) conduct likely to constitute a risk to the health, safety or welfare of any person. It is an offence to engage in disorderly conduct on a licensed premises (ILA 2003, s 8).

A person who engages in disorderly conduct is required to leave the premises on being requested to do so and must not re-enter the bar of the premises within a period of 24 hours (ILA 2003, s 8(2)). The request to leave may be made by the licensee or a garda. 'Bar' means any open bar or part of a licensed premises exclusively or mainly used for the sale and consumption of intoxicating liquor. It is an offence for a licensee to permit disorderly conduct to take place on the licensed premises (ILA 2003, s 7). A licensee can refuse admission to a person convicted of disorderly conduct (ILA 2003, s 8(5)).

(2) It is an offence for any person in a public place to engage in *offensive conduct* between midnight and 7am, or at any other time after being requested by a garda to desist: Criminal Justice (Public Order) Act 1994, s 5. *Offensive conduct* means any unreasonable behaviour which is likely to cause serious offence or serious annoyance to any person. It is also an offence for a person to use or engage in any threatening, abusive or insulting words or behaviour in a public place (CJ(PO)A 1994, s 6) or to distribute or display material in a public place which is threatening, abusive, insulting or obscene (CJ(PO)A 1994, s 7). A garda is empowered to give a direction to a person to desist from acting and to leave immediately the vicinity of the place concerned (CJ(PO)A 1994, s 8). See DISRUPTIVE BEHAVIOUR; VIOLENT DISORDER.

disorderly house. Any house, room, garden or place kept or used for any of the purposes of public music, singing or other public entertainment of a like kind, without a licence: Public Health Acts Amendment Acts 1890, s 51(5).

disparagement of property. See SLANDER OF TITLE.

display screen equipment. Any alphanumeric or graphic display screen, regardless of the display process involved: Safety, Health and Welfare at Work (General Application) Regulations 1993, SI No 44 of 1993) reg 29. See WORKSTATION.

disponer. In relation to a disposition (qv), *disponer* means the person who directly or indirectly provided the property comprised in the disposition ie the person who provided the property which is the subject of a gift or inheritance: Capital Acquisitions Tax Consolidation Act 2003, s 2.

disposal. (1) In relation to capital gains tax, a disposal of an asset includes a part disposal: Taxes Consolidation Act 1997, s 534. A disposal generally involves a transfer of ownership of an asset by one person to another: *Kirby v Thorn EMI plc* [1987] STC 625.

(2) In relation to waste, disposal includes any of the activities specified in Sch 3: Waste Management Act 1996, s 4(3). See also Environmental Protection Agency Act 1992, s 3(1) as amended by Protection of the Environment Act 2003, s 5.

(3) There are rules governing disposals by *listed* companies; the rules specify the *classification* of the transaction (Classes 1, 2, and 3), the requirements for announcements and whether a circular and shareholder approval is required: Listing Rules 2000, paras 10.1–10.43. There are additional requirements for takeovers and mergers (para 10.45). See EMISSION; LISTING RULES; MAJOR SHAREHOLDER DIRECTIVE; PROCEEDS OF CRIME; WASTE DISPOSAL/RECOVERY.

disposal of goods. There are wide powers under intellectual property law for the disposal of *infringing* articles, copies, materials and products eg see Patents Act 1992, s 47; Copyright and Related Rights Act 2000, ss 144–145. As to reservation of the right of disposal of goods by the seller, see Sale of Goods Act 1893, s 19. See INFRINGING ARTICLE; INFRINGING COPY; INFRINGING MATERIAL; INFRINGEMENT OF PATENT; PROHIBITED GOODS.

disposition. The passing of property, whether by act of parties or act of law.

(1) For capital acquisitions tax purposes, a disposition is an act or instrument by which a gift or inheritance is made; it includes the payment of money, a will, an intestacy, a *donatio mortis causa* (qv): Capital Acquisitions Tax Consolidation Act 2003, s 2. As regards settlements, a disposition includes any trust, covenant, agreement or arrangement: Taxes Consolidation Act 1997, s 791. A disposition for a short period is commonly known as a covenant. A *testamentary disposition* is a will or other testamentary instrument or act: Succession Act 1965, s 101.

(2) It has been held that once a winding up of a company had commenced, all payments made either into or out of the bank account of that company are *dispositions* within the meaning of s 218 of the Companies Act 1963, and were consequently invalid: *In the matter of Industrial Services Company (Dublin) Ltd (in liquidation)* [2001] 2 IR 118, HC. This was so notwithstanding that the payments in this case were paid into an account which was largely in credit. For examination of the implications of this case, see Micheal O'Connell BL in *Bar Review* (June/July 2001) 441.

(3) As regards divorce proceedings, means any disposition of property howsoever made, other than a disposition by a will or codicil: Family Law (Divorce) Act 1996, s 37. The court is given broad power to restrain a person from attempting to prevent or limit the financial relief which the court would otherwise be able to grant, arising from the divorce proceedings; it may restrain the disposal of property or set aside a disposition of property. A disposition made less than three years before the application for relief is presumed, unless the contrary is shown, to have been intended to defeat the applicant's claim for relief (FL(D)A 1996, s 37(4)). However, a disposition will not be set aside if made for valuable consideration (other than marriage) to a third party acting in good faith and without notice of the other spouse's intention to defeat the relief being claimed (FL(D)A 1996, s 37(1)). It has been held that shares in companies, in which the applicant for a divorce had an interest, constituted personal property, the disposition of which was encompassed by s 37: *L O'M v N O'M (Reviewable disposition)* [2002] 3 IR 237, HC and [2003] 1 ILRM 401.

A disposal of an asset from one legally separated spouse to another, is treated as having been made for a consideration which gives rise to no gain or no loss: Taxes Consolidation Act 1997, s 1030. This provision is extended to property disposition orders made by foreign courts on foot of foreign divorces or foreign judicial separations which are recognised as valid in the State, and which are analogous to those which would be made by an Irish Court in similar circumstances (s 1030 amended by FA 2000, s 88). See CONSTRUCTION OF DISPOSITION; COVENANT, DEED OF; ISSUE.

dispute. A conflict of claims or rights. See ALTERNATIVE DISPUTES RESOLUTION.

dispute, trade. See TRADE DISPUTE.

disqualification. A deprivation of a right, power or privilege. Disqualification from holding a driving licence is mandatory in the case of certain offences: Road Traffic Act 1961, ss 26–27; Road Traffic (Licensing of Drivers) Regulations 1999, SI No 352 of 1999. Conviction of certain offences may disqualify a person from serving on a jury: Juries Act 1976, s 8. Conviction of treason (qv) (and formerly of a felony) can result in disqualification from certain public offices. Conviction of offences can also lead to disqualification from being a director of a company or of a building society or from pursuing a particular profession eg Companies Act 1990. ss 149–169; Unit Trust Act 1972, s 16; Auctioneers and House Agents Act 1947, s 18; Solicitors Act 1954, s 34; Health (Nursing Homes) Act 1990, s 6(4); Electoral Act 1992, s 41(j). See DISQUALIFICATION ORDER, DRIVING; SCHEDULED OFFENCE.

disqualification order, company. An order that a person shall not be appointed or act as an auditor, director or other officer, receiver, liquidator or examiner or be in any way, directly or indirectly, concerned or take part in the promotion, formation or management of any company: Companies Act 1990, s 159. The order will be made by the court where it is satisfied that the person has been guilty of any fraud or breach of duty in relation to a company or has been made personally liable for the company's debts or his conduct is such as to make him unfit to be concerned in the management of the company or where the person has been persistently in default in relation to certain reporting requirements of the Companies Acts (CA 1990, s 160(2)).

A person is deemed to be subject to a disqualification order for five years where he is convicted on indictment of any indictable offence in relation to the company, or involving fraud or dishonesty (CA 1990,

s 160(1)). A person who is subject to a disqualification order may apply to the court for relief (CA 1990, s 160(8)). See also CA 1990, s 144. There are penalties and civil consequences for breaching a disqualification order or for acting under the direction of a disqualified person (CA 1990, ss 161, 163–165). See also Building Societies Act 1989, s 64. See also RSC Ord 75B inserted by SI No 278 of 1991.

Under recent legislation: (a) the grounds under which a person may be disqualified from being a director of a company have been extended; (b) the Director of Corporate Enforcement is empowered to apply to the court for a *disqualification order*; (c) a *restriction order* pursuant to to s 150 of the Companies Act 1990 may be imposed by the court where a disqualification order is not justified; and (d) costs may be recovered from the person disqualified or restricted: CA 1990, s 160 as amended by Company Law Enforcement Act 2001, s 42.

See 'Restriction & Disqualification of Directors' by Brian Kennedy BL in *Bar Review* (June/July 2002) 241. [Bibliography: Cahill N.] For other provisions on disqualification of directors, see DIRECTORS' RESTRICTION ORDER. See also UNDISCHARGED BANKRUPT; WINDING UP, COMPULSORY.

disqualification order, driving. An order disqualifying a person from driving a motor vehicle which is either a *consequential* disqualification or an *ancillary* disqualification or an *exceptional* disqualification: Road Traffic Act 1961 ss 26 and 29 as amended by the Road Traffic Acts 1968 s 19; 1994 ss 26–27, 1995 s 2.

Disqualification is not a primary punishment but an adjudication on the person's fitness to drive: *Conroy v A-G* [1965] IR 411; consequently, in an application for removal of a disqualification, the court will consider the applicant's fitness to drive, the nature of the offence and his conduct since the original conviction: *DPP v O'Byrne* [1989] ITLR (19 June). Before imposing a disqualification, there must be evidence before the district judge as to the defendant's fitness to drive and the judge must be apprised of the circumstances in order to allow him to reach a conclusion as to fitness to drive: *Glynn v Hussey* [1996] 1 ILRM 234, SC. See also *People (A-G) v Poyning* [1972] IR 402.

However, under the 1994 and 1995 legislation, a person found guilty of certain specified drink driving and other road traffic offences is automatically disqualified from holding a driving licence for a minimum period and also, exceptionally, until a certificate of competency (driving test) or a certificate of fitness, or both, is obtained. Also the minimum period which must pass before an application may be made to the court to review a disqualification order has been increased. The 1995 Act introduced graded length of disqualification from three months to four years, depending on the concentration of alcohol involved and whether a first or subsequent offence, and also reduced the exceptional cases to '*hit and run*' offences. For endorsement of certain convictions and disqualifications, see RTA 1961, s 36 as amended by Road Traffic Act 2002, s 8. See DCR 1997 Ord 97. See Road Traffic (Licensing of Drivers) Regulations 1999, SI No 352 of 1999.

Provision has been made to permit a disqualification from driving imposed on a person who is normally resident in this State (by a competent authority in another EU member state for a specified offence in that state) to lead to a disqualification order in this State: Road Traffic Act 2002, s 9. The judge may refuse to make such an order if the specific conduct does not constitute an offence in this State or does not constitute an offence for which disqualification can be ordered by the court (RTA 2002, s 9(7)). This provision implements the *European Convention on Driving Disqualification* done at Brussels on 17 June 1998. For proposed amendment to RTA 2002, s 9, see Road Traffic Bill 2004, s 19.

Disqualification from driving can now occur automatically under a new *penalty points* system introduced in 2002. [Bibliography: Hill & O'Keeffe; McGrath M (2).] See PENALTY POINTS.

disregard clause. Generally understood to mean a clause in a lease (qv) whereby the review of rent provided for in the lease must not take into consideration any future rent reviews, notwithstanding that provision may have been made for such reviews to be carried out on a regular basis. See RENT REVIEW CLAUSE.

disruptive behaviour. It is an offence for a person on board an aircraft in flight to engage in behaviour: (a) of a threatening, abusive or insulting nature with intent to cause a breach of the peace; or (b) which is likely to cause serious offence or annoyance, after having been requested by a crew member to cease such behaviour: Air Navigation and Transport (Amendment) Act 1998, s 65. It is also an offence to be so intoxicated as to give rise to a reasonable expectation that he is likely to endanger his own or other's safety.

diss; dissentiente. Delivering a dissenting judgment. See NEM DIS.

dissection. Dissection of the human corpse was originally a punishment for the crime of murder: Geo.3, c.17 (1791). It was abolished as a punishment by the Anatomy Act 1832 (2 & 3 Will.4, c.75). Bodies can be handed over for dissection unless the deceased or a surviving spouse objects: 1832 Act and 1871 Act (34 & 35 Vict, c.16). There is provision for the appointment of an Inspector of Anatomy to whom anatomists are accountable for bodies in their possession. See SI No 256 of 1949, Sch, Pt 1. See also *Doherty* in (1992) 2 ISLR 84. See HUMAN TISSUE.

disseisin. The wrongful putting out of a person seised of a freehold. See SEISIN.

dissolution. Breaking up; bringing to an end; eg dissolution of a partnership under the Partnership Act 1890, ss 32–35 or of a company under the Companies Act 1963. The dissolution of Dáil Éireann is performed by the President of Ireland on the advice of the Taoiseach: 1937 Constitution, art 13(2). A general election for the Dáil must be held within thirty days of the dissolution (1937 Constitution, art 16(3)(2)). The clerk of the Dáil is required immediately on dissolution to issue a writ to each returning officer (qv) directing him to cause an election to be held of the full number of members of the Dáil: Electoral Act 1992, s 39(1) and Sch 4.

The Seanad is not dissolved with the dissolution of the Dáil; members of the Seanad hold office until the day before the polling day for the panels for the new Seanad (1937 Constitution, art 18(9)). It has been held that the Courts have no jurisdiction to place any impediment between the President and the Taoiseach in relation to the dissolution of the Dáil: *O'Malley v An Taoiseach* [1990] ILRM 460, HC. See Houses of the Oireachtas Commission Act 2003, s 9.

Where a Minister has dissolved a statutory body (in this case, the National Rehabilitation Board, SIs No 170 and 171 of 2000) and has not transferred liability for any claims against it to other statutory bodies, the residual liability must lie with the Minister: *O'Briain v National Rehabilitation Board* [2002] ELR 210, EAT. See FINANCIAL RESOLUTIONS; PRESIDENT OF IRELAND; PRESIDENTIAL COMMISSION; SEANAD ÉIREANN; WINDING UP.

distance. Every word or expression in an Act of the Oireachtas, or in any instrument made under any such Act, relating to the distance between two points and every reference to the distance from or to a point shall, unless the contrary intention appears, be construed as relating or referring to such distance measured in a straight line on a horizontal plane: Interpretation Act 1937, s 11(e).

distance contracts. Provision has been made by regulation for the protection of consumers in respect of *distance contracts*; the regulations apply to contracts for goods and services (other than financial services) to be supplied to a consumer where the contract is made exclusively by means of *distance communications* i e without the simultaneous physical presence of the supplier and the consumer: European Commission (Protection of Consumers in respect of Contracts made by means of Distance Communications) Regulations 2001, SI No 207 of 2001.

Key provisions include the information which a consumer must be given before entering into a contract, subsequent written confirmation of that information, and a cooling-off period within which the consumer may cancel the contract. The regulations implement Directive (EC) 7/97. See 'A safe distance?' by solicitor Edward Madden in *Law Society Gazette* (May 2002) 14.

distinctive mark. Formerly, for the purposes of registration of a mark in Part A (qv) of the register of trade marks, a mark was *distinctive* if it was *adapted* to distinguish the goods with which the proprietor of the trade mark was or could be connected in the *course of trade*, from goods in the case of which no such connection subsists: Trade Marks Act 1963, s 17(2). Registration of *Dunlop Weather coat, Mothercare, Bond Street* as marks were refused on the ground that the words were not adapted to distinguish the goods to which they referred from the goods of others.

Marks which were refused registration in Part A could be registered in Part B (qv) if they met the lesser requirement of being *capable* of distinguishing the applicant's goods from the goods of others (TMA 1963, s 25(3)). See *British Colloids v Controller of Industrial Property* [1943] IR 56; *Ideal Weatherproofs Ltd v Irish Dunlop Ltd* [1938] IR 295; *Re Mothercare Ltd* [1968] IR 359; *Philip Morris Inc* [1970] IR 82; *Waterford Glass Ltd v Controller of Patents, Designs and Trade Marks* [1984] ILRM 565. See TRADE MARK.

distinguishing a case. Where a court does not follow a previous decision and does not overrule it, (because it considers that there are important differences between that the decision and the case on which it was based and the case it is now considering), the previous case is said to be *distinguished*. See PRECEDENT.

distortion of competition. See COMPETITION, DISTORTION OF.

distrain. To seize goods by way of *distress* (qv).

distress. (1) A ground for damages in fatal injury cases. The law in general does not provide a remedy for annoyance, upset or distress in the absence of a recognised psychiatric illness being pleaded: *Packenham v Irish Ferries Ltd* [2004] FL 8961, HC. See MENTAL DISTRESS; FATAL INJURIES.

(2) The act of taking movable property out of the possession of a wrongdoer, to compel the performance of an obligation, or to procure satisfaction for a wrong committed. As to goods the subject of a hire-purchase agreement, see Consumer Credit Act 1995, s 64. Distress may not be levied on the goods of a bankrupt (qv) or an arranging debtor (qv) after the date of adjudication or order for protection: Bankruptcy Act 1988, s 139. Distress is a form of legal *self-help* e g distress for rent due. However, a landlord is now prohibited from using distress as a means of enforcing payment of rent due on a premises let solely as a dwelling: Housing (Miscellaneous Provisions) Act 1992, s 19. Distress also refers to the goods seized. Generally the law does not look favourably on distress. For *distress warrants* for revenue offences, see *Murphy v D J Wallace* [1990] ITLR (24 December), HC. See DCR 1997 Ord 25, r 7; Ord 27, r 6; Ord 57, r 8.

distress damage-feasant. The seizure and detention of animals or other chattels which are unlawfully on a person's land by the occupier thereof and which have caused damage thereto, in order to compel the owner to make reasonable compensation for the damage done. The right of *distress damage feasant* is no longer available for animals as the Summary Jurisdiction (Ireland) Act 1851 provided that animals are to be returned to their owner where known, or taken to a local pound where unknown, and compensation in the former case claimed on a scale specified in the Act. Pounds are regulated by the Pounds Act 1935. See also Animals Act 1985, ss 5 and 7; Control of Horses Act 1996, ss 2(1), 49, 50. See Pounds (Amendment) Regulations 1990, SI No 4 of 1990. See POUNDS.

distribute. In a share subscription agreement, the word 'distribute' has been held to suggest the payment of a dividend which the defendant was obliged to distribute when profits were available for that purpose and did not suggest the discharge of a particular commercial indebtedness: *Igote Ltd v Badsey Ltd* [2001] 4 IR 511, SC.

distribution. The division of the personal property of an *intestate* among his next-of-kin, the rules for which were laid down in the Statute of Distribution 1695, now replaced by the Succession Act 1965. See INTESTATE SUCCESSION.

distribution, company. Includes not only dividends but also any other method by which the profits of a company are paid to its shareholders: Taxes Consolidation Act 1997, s 130 as amended by Finance Act 2002, s 39. A distribution also includes a scrip dividend (qv). See DISTRIBUTE; DIVIDEND; SCRIP DIVIDEND.

District Court. The lowest court in the hierarchical system of courts, with *original* jurisdiction in civil matters and jurisdiction to hear *summary* offences (qv) and, in certain instances, *indictable* offences (qv). The country is divided into over 200 District Court areas. Cases are heard by a judge sitting alone without a jury. District Court judges hold office by the same tenure as the judges of the High Court and the Supreme Court: Courts of Justice (District Court) Act 1946, s 20.

On civil matters, the court can award damages of up to £5,000 (€6,349); it has jurisdiction over a wide range of matters but has no jurisdiction in actions in tort for defamation, slander of title, malicious prosecution or false imprisonment only. Where the parties consent in civil matters the

District Court has unlimited jurisdiction: Courts Act 1991, s 4(c); DCR 1997 Ord 39, r 14. Under recent legislation, the District Court is empowered to award damages up to €20,000; this provision will come into effect on a date to be determined by the Minister: Courts and Court Officers Act 2002, s 14. As of 1st September 2004, the Minister had decided to await the experience of the recently established *Personal Injuries Assessment Board* and to assess the proposed increase in the light of that experience. The final report of the Motor Insurance Advisory Board recommended that the current limit not be increased, other than to express the figure in a convenient euro amount.

An appeal from the District Court lies to the Circuit Court (qv). A District Court judge is not entitled to state a case to the High Court on a question concerning the validity of a statutory provision having regard to the constitution: 1937 Constitution, art 34(3)(2); *DPP v Dougan* [1997] 1 ILRM 550, HC and [1996] 1 IR 544, HC. However, the District Court can consider the constitutionality of a pre-1937 law but not of any post-1937 law: *DPP (Stratford) v O'Neill* [1998] 2 IR 383, HC.

There is provision for the forwarding of an action from the District Court to the Circuit Court or to the High Court, where the court is of opinion that the action is one fit to be tried in the higher court: Courts (Supplemental Provisions) Act 1961, s 22(8)(b) inserted by Courts Act 1971, s 21; DCR 1997 Ord 50.

The High Court has jurisdiction to interfere in the middle of a trial in the District Court and prohibit its continuing, but will only do so in exceptional circumstances: *Landers v District Judge Patwell* (2003) Irish Times, 3 May 2003.

See Jurisdiction of Courts and Enforcement of Judgments (European Communities) Act 1998, ss 9 and 16. The *Brussels I Regulation* on the recognition and enforcement of judgments in civil and commercial matters, replaces the 1998 Act as from 1 March 2002 for all EU States except Denmark: EC (Civil and Commercial Judgments) Regulations 2002, SI No 52 of 2002. See District Court Rules 1997, SI No 93 of 1997 as amended. See also District Court (Criminal Justice) Rules 2001, SIs No 194 and 448 of 2001. For fees charged in District Court offices from 10 March 2003, see SI No 87 of 2003.

[Bibliography: Woods.] See CIVIL SUMMONS; REMITTAL OF ACTION; SMALL CLAIMS PROCEDURE; TORT.

District Court, preliminary examination. Formerly, in criminal matters, where a defendant was entitled to elect for trial by jury, the District Court conducted a *preliminary examination* to determine if there was sufficient evidence to return the defendant for trial by jury to a higher court. If the judge was not satisfied he *discharged* the defendant. A defective preliminary examination in the District Court invalidated the entire criminal proceedings against an accused: *Glavin v Governor of Mountjoy Prison* [1991] ITLR (25 March). The preliminary examination was abolished in 2001: Criminal Justice Act 1999 (Part III) (Commencement Order) 2001, SI No 193 of 2001. See INDICTABLE OFFENCE.

District Judge, inquiry re. A judicial inquiry into the health or conduct of a district judge must take place whenever the Minister requests the Chief Justice to appoint either a judge of the Supreme Court or, with the consent of the president of the High Court, a judge of the High Court to conduct an *investigation* into the condition of health, either physical or mental, or to conduct an *inquiry* into the conduct (either in the execution of his office or otherwise) of a district judge and to report the result thereof to the Minister: Courts of Justice (District Court) Act 1946. The judge so appointed has all the powers, rights and privileges in conducting the investigation or inquiry as are vested in a judge of the High Court.

An inquiry into the conduct of a district court judge, pursuant to the provisions of CJ(DC)A 1946, s 21, was ordered by the government in 2000. The inquiry was held before Supreme Court judge, Mr Justice Francis D Murphy. See also CHIEF JUSTICE; JUDGES, COMPLAINTS ABOUT.

District Justice. The former name of a judge of the district court, now called a 'judge': Courts Act 1991, s 21 amending the Courts (Establishment and Constitution) Act 1961. See CHIEF JUSTICE; JUDGES.

district probate registry. A registry with authority to issue *grants of representation* in the name of the High Court, where the deceased had a fixed place of abode within the district where the application for the grant is made. There are currently 14 such registries controlled by County Registrars. See Succession Act 1965, ss 36 and 129. See RSC Ord 80 as amended by SI No 20 of 1989. See PROBATE.

distringas notice. The name formerly given to the notice which a person, who claims to be interested in any stock (which includes shares, securities or dividends) of a company, may give to that company, whereupon it is not lawful for the company to permit the stock specified in the notice to be transferred or to pay the dividends, as long as the notice remains operative. The notice is now governed by RSC Ord 46, rr 5–13 which provides that the person must serve on the company an attested copy of an affidavit, which has been filed in the Central Office (qv), and a duplicate notice in a prescribed form. See STOP ORDER.

disturbance. Interference with the existence or exercise of a right eg by trespass or nuisance. See *Fitzgerald v Forbank* [1897] 2 Ch 96.

disturbance, compensation for. The compensation payable to a *business tenant* (qv) with a business equity of renewal, who is not entitled to a new tenancy in certain specified circumstances eg where the landlord is to pull down and rebuild or reconstruct the property or where the landlord requires vacant possession to carry out a scheme of development for which he has planning permission: Landlord and Tenant (Amendment) Act 1980. The amount of compensation will usually be the pecuniary loss, damage or expense which the tenant sustains or incurs or will sustain or incur by reason of his quitting the tenement (LT(A)A 1980, s 58). Provision has been made for compensation to be available for *residential* as well as *business* lettings: Residential Tenancies Act 2004, s 199.

ditch. See HEDGE AND DITCH RULE.

diversion programme. A programme for a child who accepts responsibility for his criminal behaviour, which has the objective to divert him from committing further offences: Children Act 2001, ss 17–51. The objective is to be achieved primarily by administering a *caution* (qv) to the child and, where appropriate, placing him under the supervision of a juvenile liaison officer, and by convening a conference to be attended by the child, family members and other concerned persons (CA 2001, s 19(2)). There is a bar on prosecution for the criminal behaviour (CA 2001, s 49), privilege in respect of matters disclosed during the conference (CA 2001, s 50), and protection of the identity of a child on the programme (CA 2001, s 51). See Criminal Justice Bill 2004, s 31. See CRIME PREVENTION DIRECTORY.

divest. To take away an estate or interest which had already vested.

dividend. (1) The amount payable upon each pound of a bankrupt's liabilities or of a company's liabilities to creditors in a winding up of the company. See RSC Ord 74, rr 112–116.

(2) Also in a company, the payment made out of profits to its shareholders. Also called a *distribution*. The directors' report to the annual general meeting must state the amount, if any, which the board recommends should be paid in dividends and how much is to be retained in the reserves: Companies Act 1963, s 158. The shareholders decide the dividend at the AGM but it must not exceed the amount recommended by the directors (CA 1963, Table A, art 116). Special classes of shareholder, such as those owning preference shares, may be entitled to be paid in priority to other classes, such as *ordinary* or *deferred* shareholders.

In all *registered* companies, distributions may only be made from the company's accumulated realised profits, so far as not previously utilised by distribution or capitalisation, less its accumulated realised losses, so far as not previously written-off in a reduction or reorganisation of capital ie current profits and any profits carried forward, less current losses and any losses carried forward: Companies Amendment Act 1983, s 45.

In a *public limited company* (plc), there is an additional safeguard requiring a balance sheet surplus, as distributions may only be made when the amount of the company's net assets is not less than the aggregate of its called-up share capital and its undistributable reserves ie the value of the company's assets less its liabilities must exceed its called-up share capital together with any undistributable reserves (CAA 1983, s 46). A *listed* company is obliged to notify the stock exchange, without delay after board approval, of any decision to pay a dividend, with details thereof: Listing Rules 2000, para 12.40.

As regards income tax and corporation tax, a dividend includes interest, annuities and shares from annuities: Taxes Consoli-

dation Act 1997, s 32. A shareholder who exercises an option to receive additional shares in a company instead of a cash dividend is taxed as if he had received the cash dividend: TCA 1997 as amended by Finance Act 1998, s 43(1)(a). This affects shares issued on or after 3 December 1997. See DISTRINGAS NOTICE.

dividend withholding tax; DWT. A tax at the standard rate of income tax which must be deducted at source in respect of dividends paid or other profit distributions made from 6 April 1999 by companies resident in the State: Taxes Consolidation Act 1997, ss 172A–172M inserted by Finance Act 1999, s 27. Certain shareholders are exempted eg Irish registered companies, charities, pension funds, certain collective investment funds, certain employee share ownership trusts, certain residents of EU member states or tax treaty countries. The obligation to withhold tax is placed on the company paying the dividend or an authorised agent acting for the company. An Irish registered company which makes a distribution to its parent company which is resident in another EU state is not required to withhold tax (TCA 1997, s 831 amended by FA 1999, s 29 and implementing the EU Parent/Subsidiaries Directive No 90/435/EEC).

Substantial changes to DWT have been provided in the Finance Act 2000, ss 30–33. These include exemption from DWT in respect of: distributions which are exempt from income tax; distributions to amateur and sporting bodies and to special portfolio investment accounts; distributions to companies in a *relevant* territory and not controlled by Irish residents; distributions to non-resident companies which are wholly-owned by quoted companies. Also provision is made to allow Irish unlimited companies to pay dividends to their parent company in another EU member state without deducting DWT, putting them in the same position as Irish limited companies (TCA 1997, s 831 as amended by FA 2000, s 33). Further amendments to s 831 were made in 2004 to implement Directive (EC) 123/2003 which amended the earlier Directive, eg to reduce from 25% to 5% the shareholding threshold for a company to be considered as a parent company: Finance Act 2004, s 34.

DWT is no longer deductible in respect of distributions: (a) to thalidomide victims, and (b) to permanently incapacitated persons who are exempt from income tax from the investment of compensation payments in respect of personal injuries: Finance Act 2001, s 43.

Also tax-geared penalties, rather than a fixed penalty, now apply for fraudulently or negligently making an incorrect return in respect of DWT: Finance Act 2002, s 128.

divisible contract. A contract which is made up of a series of separate obligations e g where the contract provides that payment is to be made during the process of the contract. An *entire* or *indivisible* contract is one where neither party may demand performance until he is ready to fulfil, or has fulfilled, his obligation. See *Verolme Cork Dockyards Ltd v Shannon Atlantic Fisheries Ltd* [1978] HC.

division of company. The dissolution of a company by the acquisition of its assets and liabilities by more than one other company; such division may be a division by acquisition or by formation of new companies. A *division by acquisition* is an operation whereby two or more companies (the acquiring companies) of which one or more but not all may be a new company, acquire between them all the assets and liabilities of another company in exchange for the issue to the shareholders of that company of shares in one or more of the acquiring companies with or without any cash payment and with a view to the dissolution of the company being acquired.

A *division by formation of new companies* means a similar operation whereby the acquiring companies have been formed for the purposes of such acquisitions. Regulations now govern such divisions of companies since 1987 in respect of plcs and some specified unregistered companies: European Communities (Mergers and Divisions of Companies) Regulations 1987. See also MERGER, COMPANY; IRISH TAKEOVER PANEL.

divisional court. See HIGH COURT.

divorce. The termination of a valid marriage (qv) otherwise than by death or annulment.

The Family Law (Divorce) Act 1996 provides that the court, in exercise of the jurisdiction conferred by article 41(3)(2) of the Constitution, may grant a decree of divorce if it is satisfied that certain criteria are complied with ie the constitutional requirements (FL(D)A 1996, s 5). The Act contains safeguards to ensure that the parties are aware of the alternatives to divorce

proceedings and to assist attempts at reconciliation (FL(D)A 1996, ss 6–8).

The phrase 'lived apart' in FL(D)A 1996, s 5(1) must be construed as meaning more than mere physical separation; the mental and intellectual attitude of the parties is of considerable relevance: *M.McA v X.McA* [2000] 2 ILRM 48, HC and [2000] 1 IR 457, HC. In that case, it was held that a couple who had resided under the same roof, but had separate bedrooms, complied with the *living apart* requirement.

The court is empowered to make preliminary and ancillary orders in or after proceedings for divorce, including giving directions regarding the welfare, custody of or right of access to any dependent member of the family who is an infant (FL(D)A 1996, s 5(2)); and making certain orders e g maintenance order pending suit (s 12); periodic and lump sum orders (s 13); property adjustment orders (s 14); financial compensation orders (s 16); and pension adjustment orders (s 17) (qqv). In making these orders, the court is required to endeavour to ensure that such provision as the court considers is proper, exists or will be made for the spouses and for any dependent family members (FL(D)A 1996, s 20). These orders may be varied or discharged having regard to changes in circumstances or to any new evidence tendered (FL(D)A 1996, s 22). There are provisions for the voidance of transactions intended to prevent or reduce the relief which the court would otherwise be able to grant (FL(D)A 1996, s 37).

Where one party to a divorce dies, the other party may, unless that party has remarried, apply to the court for financial provision from the deceased spouse's estate; however, the person cannot obtain more, when other payments are taken into account, than they would have been entitled to if the marriage had not been dissolved (FL(D)A 1996, s 18).

The Circuit Family Court has jurisdiction to hear and determine proceedings under the Act; it is required to transfer the proceedings to the High Court, on application by any person with an interest in the proceedings, where the rateable valuation of any land exceeds £200 (€253.95) (FL(D)A 1996, s 38). The court may grant a decree of divorce only where, on the date of the institution of the proceedings, either of the spouses concerned was: (a) *domiciled* in the State on that date, or (b) was *ordinarily resident* in the State throughout the period of one year ending on that date (FL(D)A 1996, s 39(1)).

The effect of a decree of divorce is that the marriage is dissolved and a party to that marriage may marry again (FL(D)A 1996, s 10).

Provision has been made for the establishment and maintenance by the Courts Service of a register of all decrees of divorce: Civil Registration Act 2004, ss 13(1)(f) and 59(1). For the particulars to be entered in the *register of decrees of divorce*, see CRA 2004, Sch 1, Pt VI. For the rules of the High Court, see RSC Ord 70A inserted by SI No 343 of 1997. For the rules governing a *Family Law Civil Bill* seeking a decree of divorce in the Circuit Court, see Circuit Court Rules 2001, Ord 59, r 4(4)(a). See also Taxes Consolidation Act 1997, ss 1026(3), 1027 and 1031(1)–(4). See 'Financial Non-Disclosure in Judicial and Divorce Cases' by Inge Clissmann SC and Mary Fay BL in *Bar Review* (February 2003) 3. [Bibliography: Amory Solicitors; Brown; Coggans & Jackson; Kennedy & Maguire; Martin & McCarthy; McCormack M; Murtagh B; Power C; Shannon; Shatter; Walls & Bergin; Walpole; Wood & O'Shea.] See BIGAMY; DIVORCE A MENSA ET THORO; FAMILY HOME AND DIVORCE; JUDICIAL SEPARATION; MARRIAGE, NULLITY OF.

divorce, clean break. The Supreme Court has held that the principles of Irish law regarding the division of assets between spouses were based on the principles of fairness and not equality, with credit being given for the wife's contribution in the family home, although a 'clean break' was neither permissible or possible: *MK v JP (otherwise SK) (Divorce: ancillary relief)* [2001] 3 IR 371, SC.

The Chief Justice however has said that while Irish legislation was careful to avoid going as far as English legislation in adopting the 'clean break' approach, not least because of constitutional constraints, it was not correct to say that the legislation went so far as virtually to prevent financial finality: *D T v C T (Divorce: Ample resources)* [2002] 3 IR 334, SC and [2003] 1 ILRM 321. In this Supreme Court divorce case, involving assets of some £14m, the court awarded the wife a lump sum payment of £5m without any provision for periodic payments by way of maintenance and 55%

of the husband's pension benefit. See 'Split Decisions' by solicitor Ann FitzGerald in *Law Society Gazette* (April 2003) 18; see 'Family Values' by solicitor Keith Walsh in *Law Society Gazette* (May 2004) 16.

In another case, the High Court held that a separation agreement entered into in 1982, fell far short of providing proper provision for the applicant, and that, as there were ample resources available, the wife should be put in a position akin to that which she would probably now be enjoying had she not foregone the opportunity of a remunerative career in order to rear the children of the marriage: *K v K* [2003] ITLR (24 February) and 1 IR 326. In this case the judge ordered the husband to pay the wife a lump sum of €450,000 plus €40,000 a year in pension and maintenance payments, and that the wife retain the family home. See 'What price a 'clean break' divorce now' by solicitor Geoffrey Shannon in *Law Society Gazette* (December 2002) 20.

divorce, constitutional change. Prior to 1995, no law could be enacted providing for the grant of a dissolution of marriage. However, this constitutional prohibition did not prevent the courts from granting a *decree of nullity* which is a declaration that no valid marriage ever existed, or from granting a *judicial separation* (qv), or from upholding *separation agreements* (qv), or from recognising foreign divorces. However, only in the case of a decree of nullity or a recognised foreign divorce could the parties remarry.

In 1995, the people by the narrowest of margins (818,842 in favour, 809,728 against) approved an amendment to the Constitution, which provided that a Court designated by law may grant a dissolution of marriage where, but only where, it is satisfied that: (i) at the date of the institution of the proceedings, the spouses have *lived apart* from one another for a period of, or periods amounting to, at least four years during the previous five years, (ii) there is no reasonable prospect of a reconciliation between the spouses, (iii) such provision as the Court considers proper, having regard to the circumstances, exists or will be made for the spouses, any children of either or both of them and any other person prescribed by law, and (iv) any further conditions prescribed by law are complied with: Fifteenth Amendment to the Constitution

Act 1995. See 1937 Constitution, art 41(3)(2).

The jurisdiction of the High Court to grant a decree of dissolution of marriage derives from the Constitution and not from the Family Law (Divorce) Act 1996: *RC v CC* [1997] 1 ILRM 401, HC and 1 IR 334. In this case the High Court granted an order for the dissolution of a marriage in proceedings which had been instituted before the 1996 Act had come into force.

divorce, foreign, recognition of. A foreign divorce is recognised in the State if the parties were *domiciled* (qv) in the place where the divorce was granted: *Bank of Ireland v Caffin* [1971] IR 123. Formerly, a married woman's domicile was deemed to be that of her husband, but now she is entitled to an independent domicile: Domicile and Recognition of Foreign Divorces Act 1986, ss 1–3. The former presumption was held to be unconstitutional: *CM v TM* [1991] ILRM 268; *W v W* [1993] ILRM 294, SC.

A foreign decree of divorce is recognised in the State if either spouse is domiciled within the jurisdiction of the foreign court which grants the divorce decree, at the date of the institution of the divorce proceedings (DRFDA 1986, s 5; see also *GMcG v DW & AR* [2000] 1 ILRM 107, HC and [2000] 1 IR 96, HC). In determining whether one's domicile of origin has been replaced by a domicile or choice, there must be an intention to abandon one's former domicile: *D T v F L* [2003] FL 8350, SC and [2004] 1 ILRM 509, SC. The Irish courts will not recognise a foreign divorce decree made when the parties were both resident in Ireland at the time: *MEC v JAC* [2001] 2 IR 399, HC. All aspects of recognition of foreign divorces are governed by the 1986 Act and not by the *common law*: *D T v F L* [2002] 2 ILRM 152, HC.

Provision has been made for the automatic recognition of divorces (and separations and nullities) granted in the courts of other EU member states: Brussels II Regulations (EC No 1347/2000) which came into force on 1 March 2001 and applies to all EU member states, except Denmark. The 1986 Act does not apply to such divorces. There are now different rules applying to the recognition of: (a) foreign divorces obtained before 2 October 1986, (b) foreign divorces obtained on or after 2 October 1986, and (c) foreign divorces obtained on or after 1 March 2001 in an EU state, other than Denmark. See 'Break for the Border' by solicitor Eugene Davy in *Law Society Gazette* (January/February 2004) 34.

Various relief orders may be made by the court where spouses are legally divorced outside the State and the divorce is recognised as valid in the State: Family Law Act 1995, ss 23–28. For the rules governing a *Family Law Civil Bill* seeking relief after a foreign divorce or separation, see Circuit Court Rules 2001 Ord 59, r 4(4)(c). See LRC 10 and 20 of 1985. See also 1937 Constitution, art 41(3)(3). See *W v W* [1993] 2 IR 476, SC; *G McG v DW and AR* [2000] 4 IR 1, SC.

divorce, registration of. Provision has been made for the establishment and maintenance of a register of all decrees of divorce: Civil Registration Act 2004, s 13(1)(f).

divorce a mensa et thoro. [Judicial separation from table and board.] Formerly, a judicial separation which did not dissolve a marriage (qv) but relieved the parties thereto of the obligation to cohabit with each other. Such a judicial separation was granted on the ground of *adultery* (qv) or of unnatural practices or of the *legal cruelty* of the other party. Legal cruelty was conduct which caused danger to the life or health, physical or mental, of the other party. See *McA v McA* [1981] ILRM 361.

The decree of divorce *a mensa et thoro* has been abolished; it has been replaced by a decree of *judicial separation*: Judicial Separation and Family Law Reform Act 1989. See LRC 8 of 1983. See ALIMONY; CONDONATION; CONNIVANCE; DIVORCE; JUDICIAL SEPARATION; MARRIAGE, NULLITY OF; RECRIMINATION; SEPARATION AGREEMENT; UNWORTHINESS TO SUCCEED.

divorce a vinculo matrimonii. [Divorce from the bond of matrimony.] See DIVORCE.

DNA. [Deoxyribo nucleic acid.] The basic genetic material, made up of long chains of amino acids, found in all animal cells, the precise configuration and formation of which controls the development and functioning of most living things. A genetic profile of a person is obtainable by the examination of his skin, hair or bodily fluids. For example of the use of DNA in a paternity suit, see *JPD v MG* [1991] ILRM 212.

In a murder case it appears that DNA evidence alone, in the absence of corroborative evidence, will result in a direction to the jury to acquit: *DPP v Howe* (2003) Irish Times, 15 October, CCC. A retrial was ordered in a case where the accused had at least one brother with a criminal record and in the absence of any statistical evidence at the trial of the probability of similarity of DNA evidence between siblings: *DPP v Allen* [2003] Irish Times, 19 December. See *R v Cramer* [1988] 10 Cr App 485; *DPP v Barr (No 2)* [1993] 11 ILT Dig 185, CCA; *Z v DPP* [1994] 2 ILRM 481, SC and 2 IR 476. See Fennell in 8 ILT & SJ (1990) 227. See 'Blood, sweat and tears' by Paula Scollan in *Law Society Gazette* (July 2004) 28. See Law Reform Commission, *Consultation Paper on the Establishment of a DNA Database* (LRC CP 29, 2004). [Bibliography: Healy.] See BODILY SAMPLE; GENETIC FINGERPRINTING.

dock identification. The identification by a witness of an accused in court. Such identification is undesirable and unsatisfactory as the identification of the accused for the first time takes place when he is sitting in the place normally reserved for the accused and usually flanked by prison officers and consequently is of little probative value. The appropriate procedure, where the identity of the accused is at issue, is the holding of an *identification parade*.

However, where this is not possible (eg due to the refusal of the accused), *dock identification* evidence may be admitted at the discretion of the trial judge, but he must warn the jury as to the dangers involved in acting on such evidence: *People (DPP) v Cooney* [1997] 3 IR 205, SC and [1998] 1 ILRM 321, SC. Also, where a witness gives evidence through a live *television link* (qv) in criminal cases of physical or sexual abuse, the witness may not be required to identify the accused at the trial, if evidence is given that the accused was known to the witness before the offence is alleged to have been committed: Criminal Evidence Act 1992, s 18. See *The State (Daly) v Ruane* [1988] ILRM 117.

In the District Court, before being entitled to enter a conviction against the accused of a criminal offence, the court must be satisfied that there is evidence identifying the accused as the perpetrator of the offence, but this evidence need not necessarily consist of a physical identifica-

tion of the accused in court: *DPP v Crimmins* [2000] ITLR (21 August), HC. See VISUAL IDENTIFICATION.

doctrines of equity. See EQUITY, DOCTRINES OF.

document. Something upon which there is writing, printing or inscriptions and which gives information. Includes deeds, wills, papers, books of account, records, vouchers, correspondence and files and is construed to include any document stored in an electronic or other non-written form or on film or otherwise: Solicitors (Amendment) Act 1960 as amended by Solicitors (Amendment) Act 1994, s 3(3).

It has been held that section 30 of the Criminal Evidence Act 1992 confers a very wide discretion on a judge to accept *copies* of documents as admissible evidence in the course of criminal proceedings: *Carey v Hussey* [2000] 2 ILRM 401, HC. See also *People (DPP) v Byrne* [2001] 2 ILRM 134, CCA. See Criminal Justice (Theft and Fraud Offences) Act 2001, s 52. See AUTHOR; FAX; SOLICITOR AND DOCUMENTS; SUPPRESSION OF DOCUMENT; VALUABLE SECURITY.

document, unstamped. See UNSTAMPED DOCUMENT.

document of title. A document which enables the possessor to deal with the property described in it as if he were the owner eg a bill of lading: Factors Act 1889, s 1(4).

documentary evidence. In an exception to the hearsay rule, information contained in a document is *prima facie* admissible in criminal proceedings as evidence of any facts contained in it; the information must have been compiled, whether on computer or otherwise, in the course of a *business* and must have been supplied, either directly or indirectly, by someone who had, or may reasonably be supposed to have had, personal knowledge of the matters dealt with in the document recording the information: Criminal Evidence Act 1992, s 5. 'Business' is very widely defined eg trade, profession, or other occupation, performance of functions by persons or bodies paid or financed out of public funds and by EC and international institutions (CEA 1992, s 4).

A certificate is required stating that the conditions for admissibility have been fulfilled (CEA 1992, s 6); advance notice must be given to the other party (s 7); evidence may be given as to the credibility of the supplier of the information (s 9); and the court may exclude the evidence or, if included, estimate the weight to be given to it (s 8).

Certain documents are inadmissible such as those covered by legal professional privilege or containing information supplied by a person who is not compellable to give evidence (CEA 1992, s 5(3)). All documents which are admissible (not just under s 5) may be given in evidence by producing an authenticated copy; this includes films, sound recordings, video recordings, and a fax copy (CEA 1992, s 30).

Where information in a document is admissible in evidence, in civil proceedings concerning the welfare of a child, a copy will be admissible, irrespective of how many removes there are between the copy and the original and by what means it was produced eg by facsimile transmission: Children Act 1997, s 26. *Document* in this context, includes a sound recording and a video-recording.

In competition law proceedings, criminal or civil, there are presumptions regarding documents eg that a document purported to have been created by a person is presumed, unless the contrary is shown, to have been created by that person: Competition Act 2002, s 12. See also CA 2002, ss 13 and 31. See LRC Report, *The Hague Convention on Abolishing the Requirement of Legislation for Foreign Public Documents* (LRC 48, 1995). See MEDICAL PRACTITIONER.

documents, construction of. Rules are laid down by statute and by the courts for the interpretation of documents eg planning documents are to be construed in their ordinary meaning as it would be understood by a member of the public, unless such documents read as a whole indicate some other meaning: *Re JS Investments* [1987] ILRM 659.

In the construction of documents, the court will look at the reality of what has been done and the labels of the parties will not be accepted blindly: *McCabe v South City & County Investment Co Ltd* [1998] 1 ILRM 264, SC. See CONSTRUCTION, RULES OF; CONSTRUCTION SUIT; CONTRA PROFERENTUM; PUNCTUATION; TRANSPOSING OF WORDS.

documents, discovery of. See DISCOVERY.

documents, joinder of. See JOINDER OF DOCUMENTS.

documents, presumptions as to. Where a document, which is at least 30 years old, is produced from proper custody, there is a presumption in law that the signature and handwriting thereon is genuine; attestation (qv) or execution need not be proved. Where a deed has been proved to have been signed and attested, it is presumed to have been sealed and delivered, even though no impression of seal appears thereon. An alteration in a deed is presumed to have been made prior to execution, and in a will is presumed to have been made after execution. There is no presumption about documents not under seal, except the presumption of legality ie that they were made so as not to commit an offence.

documents intended for another. A solicitor should desist from opening letters not addressed to him or his firm; however, if the contents of documents come to his knowledge in another way, he is entitled, and may have a duty, to use the information obtained for the benefit of his client: *A Guide to Professional Conduct of Solicitors in Ireland* (2002) ch 4.3. Where information of a privileged nature inadvertently comes to the notice of the opposing party, although the documents remain privileged, the opposing party is not precluded on the grounds of privilege from giving secondary evidence of their contents.

dogs. Under the Control of Dogs Act 1986 responsibility for the control of dogs is delegated to the local authorities; they are required to employ dog wardens and erect dog shelters. Dogs are required to be kept under effectual control and dog wardens are empowered to seize stray dogs.

It is unlawful for a person to keep a dog without a licence (CDA 1986, s 2). There is provision for dealing with dangerous dogs (CDA 1986, s 22; DCR 1997 Ord 91, r 3). It is a good defence to an action for shooting a dog if the defendant proves that the dog was worrying, or was about to worry livestock (CDA 1986, s 23). There is provision for the District Court to deal with the nuisance of excessive barking of a dog (CDA 1986, s 25; DCR 1997 Ord 91, r 4).

There is also *strict liability* (qv) in damages for any damage caused by a dog and it is no longer necessary to show a previous *mischievous propensity* in the dog (CDA 1986, s 21(1)). Apart from this statutory remedy, the owner or keeper of a dog may be liable in negligence (qv): see *Kavanagh v Stokes* [1942] IR 596; or in trespass (eg if he commanded the dog to attack). See SIs Nos 30 and 59 of 1987 and 255 of 1988.

The 1986 Act was amended in 1992 to provide additional powers to deal more effectively with dangerous dogs, to increase licence fees, and to amend the earlier Act where it had been found to be deficient: Control of Dogs (Amendment) Act 1992. For prosecution of offences in the District Court, see DCR 1997 Ord 91.

It is an offence if a person in charge of a dog, fails to remove immediately the faeces deposited by the dog in specified places or fails to ensure that the faeces is properly disposed of in a suitable sanitary manner: Litter Pollution Act 1997, s 22. The places specified include a public road, beach, shopping centre, school ground, sports ground, playing field or recreational or leisure area, and the curtilage of a dwelling whose occupier has not consented to the presence of the dog (LPA 1997, s 22(2)). See also Control of Horses Act 1996, s 48. See Importation of Dogs and Cats Regulations 2003, SI No 192 of 2003.

A local authority may make *bye-laws* relating to the control of dogs in its functional area: Local Government Act 2001, s 211. The 2001 Act also amends the 1986 Act. See ANIMALS; BEWARE OF DOG SIGN; DANGEROUS DOGS; GUARD DOG; PET DOG AND CAT; SCIENTER; STRAY DOG.

dole. A share; the popular name given to unemployment benefit and assistance. See SOCIAL WELFARE LAW.

doli capax. [Capable of crime.] See CRIMINAL RESPONSIBILITY; DOLI INCAPAX.

doli incapax. [Incapable of crime.] There is an irrebuttable presumption that a child under the age of seven years is incapable of committing a crime. A minor between the age of seven and 14 years is presumed to be *doli incapax*, but the presumption is rebuttable by evidence of *mischievous discretion* ie knowledge that what was done was morally wrong. A child under 14 years of age is capable of committing the offence of perjury if he makes an unsworn statement, material to the proceedings, which he knows to be false or which he does not believe to be true: Children Act 1997, s 28(2). Formerly, a boy under 14 years of age was irrebuttably presumed incapable of rape or of an attempt thereat. Now the rule of law which treated a male person by reason of his age as being physically incapable of committing an offence of a sexual nature is abolished: Criminal Law (Rape) (Amendment) Act 1990, s 6. A minor on reaching his fourteenth birthday becomes

fully responsible for his criminal behaviour. See *Cashman v Cork County Council* [1950] Ir Jur Rep 7; *Goodbody v Waterford Corporation* [1953] Ir Jur Rep 39; *Monagle v Donegal Co Co* [1961] Ir Jur Rep 47. See CHILD, CRIME AND; CRIMINAL RESPONSIBILITY.

domain. (1) The territory over which authority is exercised. (2) The highest subdivision of a *domain name* in an Internet address which identifies: (a) the type of entity owning the address (eg *.com* for commercial users and *.edu* for educational institutions); or (b) the geographical location of the address (eg *.ie* for Ireland and *.fr* for France).

domain name. The address of an Internet connection that identifies the owner of the address in a hierarchical format: *server. organisation.type.* For example *www.irlgov. ie/ag* identifies the web server at the Attorney-General's office in the Irish government.

The Irish Domain Registry (IEDR – *www.domainregistry.ie* or *www.iedr.ie*) is an independent not-for-profit organisation that manages the ie *domain name* as a service to the public. It maintains the database of *.ie* registered Internet names. It is not a governing or regulatory body. It is a member of CENTR, the Council of European National Top-Level Domain Registries.

The 'ie domain name' means the top level of the global domain name system assigned to Ireland according to the two-letter code in the international Standard ISO 3166-1 (Codes for Representation of Names of Countries and their Subdivision) of the International Organisation for Standardisation: Electronic Commerce Act 2000, s 31(4). The Minister is empowered by regulation to place the registration and use of ie domain names' in the State on a statutory basis (ECA 2000, s 31(1)). The Minister in making regulations may consult with such bodies as the Minister deems fit, including the *Internet Corporation for Assigned Names and Numbers.* In April 2004, the Minister for Communications announced that proposed legislation would transfer regulation and control of the ie domain name to the Commission for Communications Regulation (ComReg).

The World Intellectual Property Organisation (WIPO) operates a dispute resolution process called ICANN (Internet Corporation for Assigned Names and

Numbers – *www.icann.net*) to resolve disputes concerning domain names. All domain name registrars are affiliated to ICANN and those with registered domain names have agreed to be bound by the ICANN procedures.

In May 2000, ICANN ruled that the actress Julia Roberts had a common law trade mark in her name and ordered that the domain name www.juliaroberts.com be returned to her. In August 2000, the UK budget airline EasyJet failed in its attempt to take the domain name www.easy-jet.com from the holder, who was a person selling refills for printer cartridges, as it failed to prove that the holder of the site was using it in bad faith or had no legitimate interest in it. For similar reasons, France Telecom failed in its attempt to take www.pagesjaunes.com or www.pagesjaunes.net from the first registered holder. In Ireland, solicitors L K Shields in a settlement to a High Court action recovered ownership of the domain name www.lkshields.com in May 2000: *Shields v Mulcahy* [2000] HC (unreported). Also in September 2003, ICANN ruled that Irish 007 star Pierce Brosnan should have transferred to him the domain name www.piercebrosnan as the then registered Canadian owner was using it in bad faith. See *Local Ireland Ltd v Local Ireland-Online Ltd* [2000] 4 IR 567, HC.

In August 2004, EUR*id* was in negotiation with the European Commission, having been chosen to manage the new internet domain name *.eu*. See website: *www.eurid.org*. See 'The protection of trade marks against cybersquatters' by Anne Bateman BL in *Bar Review* (March 2001) 298. See 'Domain Name Disputes: A Review of the Case Law' by Eleanor Keogan in *Bar Review* (September 2001) 502. See 'Troubled Times at the IEDR' by J Rossa McMahon in (2002) 10 ISLR 94. [Bibliography: Oppenheim UK.] See COMMISSION FOR COMMUNICATIONS REGULATION; ELECTRONIC COMMERCE.

domestic agreements. Agreements made in the course of family life and which are not intended to create legal relations. See *Balfour v Balfour* [1919] 2 KB 571. See LEGAL RELATIONS, INTENTION TO CREATE.

domestic and private use. It is not an infringement of *copyright* or an infringement of a *performer's right* for a person to make for private and domestic use a *fixation* of a broadcast or cable programme solely for the purpose of enabling it to be viewed or listened to at another time or place: Copyright and Related Rights Act 2000, ss 101 and 250. *Fixation* means the embodiment of sounds or images from which they can be perceived, reproduced or communicated through a device (CRRA 2000, s 2(1)). See also FAIR DEALING.

domestic animals. See ANIMALS.

domestic extension. See EXTENSION OF HOUSE.

domestic hereditament. Any hereditament which consists wholly or partly of premises used as a dwelling and which is not a mixed hereditament: Local Government (Financial Provisions) Act 1978, s 1(1). A domestic hereditament enjoys relief from rates. A partial use of a premises to provide lodgings ('bed and breakfast'), where there is a multiplicity of other uses, will not in itself render the premises a 'mixed hereditament': *Slattery v Flynn* [2003] 1 ILRM 450, HC. In this case the owner and her family resided in the house and offered 'bed and breakfast' to paying guests; the court held that the dwelling house was a 'domestic hereditament' and consequently entitled to relief from rates.

Also holiday chalets have been found to be within the definition of a domestic hereditament; the definition did not require the occupier to make private use of the dwelling, nor did it preclude him from using it for commercial advantage: *Kerry County Council v Kerins* [1996] 3 IR 493, SC.

domestic refuse. See HOUSEHOLD REFUSE.

domestic sewage. See SEWAGE CHARGES.

domestic violence. Provision has been made for the protection of any spouse and any children or other dependent persons, and of persons in other domestic relationships, whose safety or welfare requires it, because of the conduct of another person in the domestic relationship concerned: Domestic Violence Act 1996. The legislation provides for *barring orders* (qv) and *safety orders* (qv) to protect persons against domestic violence; it provides new powers to health boards to apply for such orders; and it gives the gardaí new powers of arrest to deal with cases of domestic violence. See also Family Law (Divorce) Act 1996, ss 11(a), 15(d); Family Law (Miscellaneous Provisions) Act 1997, s 4. For applications to the court for reliefs (eg barring orders) pursuant to the Domestic Violence Act 1996, see Circuit Court Rules 2001

Ord 59, r 5. For District Court procedure in relation to domestic violence, see DCR 1997 Ord 59. The Law Reform Commission has recommended a number of changes to the 1996 Act: *Consultation Paper on the Rights and Duties of Cohabitees*: (LRC CP 32, 2004). [Bibliography: Shannon.]

domestic water. See WATER CHARGES.

domicile. The place in which a person has a fixed and permanent home, and to which, whenever he is absent, he has the intention of returning. It depends on the physical fact of residence in addition to the intention of remaining.

Every person receives at birth a *domicile of origin*. However, each person may acquire a *domicile of choice* by the combination of residence and an intention of permanent or indefinite residence. The domicile of choice may be lost by abandonment and then either a new domicile of choice is acquired or the domicile of origin revives: *Proes v Revenue Commissioners* [1998] 1 ILRM 333, HC and 4 IR 174.

The domicile of a married woman was deemed to be that of her husband notwithstanding that she was permanently resident abroad: see *Gaffney v Gaffney* [1975] IR 133; this common law rule was held to be unconstitutional: *CM v TM* [1991] ILRM 268; *W v W* [1993] ILRM 294, SC. A married woman's domicile is now determined by the same factors as applied in the case of any person capable of having an independent domicile: Domicile and Recognition of Foreign Divorces Act 1986. See *W v S* [1987] HC; *Re Fleming, deceased* [1987] ILRM 638; *Rowan v Rowan* [1988] ILRM 65.

As regards the recognition of a foreign divorce, an uncontradicted declaration of intention to reside in a particular country, which is consistent with a person's actions, may be regarded as evidence of an acquisition of a domicile of choice: *PL v An tArd Chláraitheoir* [1995] 2 ILRM 241, HC. In determining whether one's domicile of origin has been replaced by a domicile of choice, there must be an intention to abandon one's former domicile: *D T v F L* [2003] FL 8350, SC and [2004] 1 ILRM 509. The onus of proof that a person (who seeks recognition of a foreign divorce) had relinquished his domicile of origin and had acquired a domicile of choice, rests with that person: *D T v F L* [2002] 2 ILRM 152, HC. See also *PK (otherwise C) v TK* [2002] 2 IR 186, SC; *RB v AS (Nullity: domicile)* [2002] 2 IR 428, SC.

The domicile of a minor at common law was that of his father; but where the child was born after the father's death or where the parents were not married to each other, the domicile was that of the mother. The common law rules were amended by the DRFDA 1986 to provide that the domicile of the minor is that of the mother where the mother and father are living apart and the minor has a home with the mother and not with the father (DRFDA 1986, s 3(1)).

An individual is domiciled in the State, or in a state other than a *contracting* state if, but only if, he is *ordinarily resident* in the State or in that other state: Jurisdiction of Courts and Enforcement of Foreign Judgments Act 1998, s 15(1) and Sch 9, Pt I. The *Brussels I Regulation* on the recognition and enforcement of judgments in civil and commercial matters, replaces the 1998 Act as from 1 March 2002 for all EU states except Denmark: EC (Civil and Commercial Judgments) Regulations 2002, SI No 52 of 2002. An individual is domiciled in a place in the State only if he is domiciled in the State and is *ordinarily resident* or carries on any profession, business or occupation in that place (reg 11). Domicile questions are decided by the Circuit Court (reg 12). See LRC 7, 1983. The words 'ordinarily resident' are given their ordinary meaning in the light of the intention of the legislation: *Deutche Bank v Murtagh* [1995] 1 ILRM 381, HC. See DIVORCE; DIVORCE, FOREIGN, RECOGNITION OF; SEAT OF CORPORATION; WILL, INTERNATIONAL.

domiciliary childbirth. 'There is considerable evidence of a strong divergence of professional opinion on the merits of domiciliary childbirth as opposed to childbirth in hospital. The court has no role in the resolution of this debate.' Hardiman J in *O Ceallaigh v An Bord Altranais* (2000) Irish Times, 18 May 2000. See MIDWIFE.

dominant position, abuse of. Any *abuse* by one or more undertakings of a dominant position in trade for any goods or services in the State, or in any part of the State, is prohibited: Competition Act 2002, s 5(1). 'Abuse' may consist in: imposing unfair purchase or selling prices or other unfair trading conditions; limiting production, markets or technical development to the prejudice of consumers; applying dissimilar conditions to equivalent transactions with other trading parties; or requiring supplemental obligations which have no connection with the contract (CA 2002, s 5(2)).

Any person who is aggrieved in consequence of any prohibited abuse has a right of action for relief against any undertaking which has been a party to the abuse; the Competition Authority also has a right of action (CA 2002, s 14). Relief is by way of an injunction, a declaration, and damages including exemplary damages (qv). An action in respect of a prohibited abuse may be brought in the Circuit or High Court (CA 2002, s 14(3)). It is also an offence for an undertaking to act in a manner prohibited by s 5(1) (CA 2002, s 7).

Dominance in EC law is a position of strength enjoyed by an undertaking which enables it to prevent effective competition being maintained on the relevant market by affording it the power to behave to an appreciable extent independently of its competitors, its customers and ultimately of the consumers: Case 85/76 *Hoffman-La Roche v EC Commission* [1979] ECR 461 cited in *Master Foods Ltd t/a Mars Ireland v HB Ice Cream* [1993] ILRM 145, HC. The Court of First Instance has held that HB had abused its dominance through its exclusivity clause relating to the use of its freezer cabinets: Case T-65/98 *Van den Bergh Foods Ltd v Commission of the EC* [2003], CFI.

The Court has held that abuse of a dominant position can consist of applying dissimilar conditions to equivalent transactions with other trading parties: Case T-219/99 *British Airways plc v Commission of the European Communities* [2003], CFI. The Court has also upheld a fine of €19.76m on tyre maker Michelin for abusing its dominant position through a system of discounts, refunds and financial advantage with its dealers: Case T-203/01 *Manufacture Francaise des Pneumatiques Michelin v Commission of the European Communities* [2003] CFI. See *Donovan v Electricity Supply Board* [1994] 2 ILRM 325, HC and [1997] 3 IR 573, SC; *Blemings v David Patton Ltd* [2001] 1 IR 385, HC; *Meridian Communications Ltd v Eircell Ltd* [2002] 1 IR 17, HC. See 'Abuse of Dominance in Meridian v Eircell' by Stephen Dodd BL in *Bar Review* (October/November 2001) 12. For previous (now repealed) legislation, see Competition Act 1991, s 5; Competition (Amendment) Act 1996, s 7. [Bibliography: Lucey; Power V.] See ABUSE OF MONOPOLY RIGHT; COMPETITION, DISTORTION OF; TRADE ASSOCIATION.

dominant tenement. See EASEMENT.

dominium. Ownership.

domitae naturae. [Of tame disposition.] See ANIMALS.

domus sua cuique est tutissimum refugium. [To every person his house is his surest refuge.] See *Seymayne's Case* [1604] 5 Co Rep 91. See INVIOLABILITY OF DWELLING.

dona clandestina sunt semper suspiciosa. [Clandestine gifts are always to be regarded with suspicion.]

donatio mortis causa. A gift of personal property in anticipation of death. To be a valid gift it must be made in contemplation of the donor's death, be intended to take effect from his existing illness (unless the donor indicates otherwise) and be completed by delivery at the time to the donee. See *Re Beaumont* [1902] 1 Ch 889. See also Judicial Separation and Family Law Reform Act 1989, ss 10 and 29. See DISINHERITING DISPOSITION.

donation. A new uniform scheme of tax relief for donations has been introduced, merging the existing reliefs under the umbrella of a single scheme but with different arrangements for individual and corporate donations, as well as introducing new reliefs for donations to domestic charities and educational institutions: Finance Act 2001, s 45. See Finance Act 2003, s 21. See GIFT; HERITAGE; POLITICAL DONATION; SPORTS BODY.

donee. A gratuitous recipient; a person who takes a gift (qv); a person who is given a power of appointment (qv).

donor. A giver; a person who makes a gift (qv); a person who makes a power of appointment (qv).

doom; dome. A judgment (qv).

door supervisor. Means a person who for remuneration, as part of his duties, performs any of the following functions at, in or in the vicinity of any premises or any other place where a public or private event or function is taking place or is about to take place: (a) controlling, supervising, regulating or restricting entry to the premises or place, (b) controlling or monitoring the behaviour of persons therein, (c) removing persons therefrom because of their behaviour: Private Security Service Act 2004, s 2(1). See PRIVATE SECURITY AUTHORITY.

doorstep contracts. Contracts between a consumer and trader when negotiations have been initiated away from business premises. An EC Directive has been adopted on doorstep contracts: Directive (EEC) 577/85 and implemented in the State by the European Communities (Cancellation of Contracts Negotiated Away from Business Premises) Regulations 1989, SI No 224 of 1989. See also *Dunn* in 7 ILT & SJ (1989) 309. See COOLING-OFF PERIOD.

dormant account. An account where, during the *dormancy period* no transaction has been effected by the account holder: Dormant Accounts Act 2001, s 7. The *dormancy period* means: (a) a period of not less than 15 years ending on: (i) 31 March 2002, and (ii) 30 September in each subsequent year commencing on 30 September 2003, or (b) any other period prescribed under s 9 which empowers the Minister to extend the application of the Act (DAA 2001, s 2).

An *account* includes a very wide range of deposit accounts, saving certificates and savings bonds; an *account holder* is also broadly defined to include a person who holds an account and also a person who is authorised to act as agent of such person (DAA 2001, s 2).

The purpose of the 2001 Act is to provide for a scheme to transfer *dormant* funds in banks, building societies and the Post Office Savings Bank to the care of the State, while guaranteeing a right of reclaim of those funds. It also provides for the introduction of a scheme for the disbursement for charitable purposes or for purposes of societal and community benefit, of funds which are not likely to be reclaimed. Provision is made for a *Dormant Accounts Fund* to be established by the National Treasury Management Agency (NTMA) (DAA 2001, s 17) and for a *Dormant Accounts Disbursement Board* (DAA 2001, s 30).

Financial institutions are required to maintain a '*Register of Dormant Accounts*' (DAA 2001, s 14), to notify holders of dormant accounts (DAA 2001, s 10), to transfer moneys to the Dormant Accounts Fund not later than 30 April each year, commencing 2003 (DAA 2001, s 12), and to provide an annual '*certificate of compliance*' (DAA 2001, s 20). See Dormant Accounts (Certificate of Compliance) Regulations 2002, SI No 105 of 2002.

A procedure is specified under which the holder of a dormant account may make a claim on the financial institution for repayment of moneys transferred to the Dormant Accounts Fund, and for the institution on being satisfied that he or she is the holder, to notify the NTMA of the amount transferred and the accrued interest and for payment thereof to the claimant within specified time periods (DAA 2001, s 19).

For amendments to the 2001 Act, see Unclaimed Life Assurance Policies Act 2003, s 27 and Sch 2; Central Bank and Financial Services Authority of Ireland Act 2003, s 35, Sch 1. Under draft legislation, it is proposed that there will be a two-stage process whereby decisions on spending from the Dormant Accounts Fund will be made by government, following a transparent process of inviting applications for programmes or types of projects: Dormant Accounts (Amendment) Bill 2004. It is proposed that a list of all successful applications as approved by government will be published along with the amounts involved in each case. See website: *www.dormantaccounts.ie*. See UNCLAIMED LIFE ASSURANCE POLICY.

dormant partner. A sleeping partner. See LIMITED PARTNERSHIP.

dosage. The court will not decide the appropriate level of dosage for a patient plaintiff where his doctor had acted *bona fide* and in the best interest of the patient and where the dosage was within an appropriate range advised in accordance with a practice approved by a reputable body of medical opinion: *Hughes v Staunton* [1991] 9 ILT Dig 52, HC. See MEDICAL NEGLIGENCE.

double construction. The term used to describe the situation where in the interpretation by the court of the constitutionality of a provision of an Act, there are two or more constructions reasonably open, one of which is constitutional and the other or others are unconstitutional, it must be presumed by the court that the Oireachtas intended only the constitutional construction, and the court must uphold the constitutionality of the statutory provision: *Kelly v Minister for the Environment* [2003] 2 ILRM 81, SC. See LEGISLATION, CONSTITUTIONALITY OF.

double employment. Where an employee works for two or more employers on the same day. It is an offence for an employer to permit an employee to work for him on a day on which the employee has worked for another employer, where the aggregate hours worked for both employers exceeds the lawful maximum that the employee could work for the one employer. A young person can commit an offence in such a circumstance, as can a parent or guardian who aids or abets an employer. See Protection of Young Persons (Employment) Act 1996, s 10; Organisation of Working Time Act 1997, s 33. See *Martin v Galbraith Ltd* [1942] IR 37. See WORKING HOURS; CHILD, EMPLOYMENT OF; YOUNG PERSON.

double insurance. Insurance by the insured, with more than one insurer, of the one risk on the same interest in the same subject-matter. Provisions for dealing with double marine insurance is provided for by s 32 of the Marine Insurance Act 1906. See *Zurich Insurance v Shield Insurance* [1987] SC.

double jeopardy. The common law doctrine that a person should not face repeated prosecution for the same offence. However, he may be charged with different offences arising out of the same act, whether of commission or omission, but usually cannot be punished twice for the same offence: Interpretation Act 1937, s 14; *O'B v Pattwell* [1994] 2 ILRM 465, SC. The doctrine applies to the bringing of identical or similar charges, and not the prosecution of charges which may have similar or identical evidence involved: *In the matter of NIB (No 2)* [1999] 2 ILRM 443, HC.

A person who has been acquitted or convicted outside the State of a sexual offence against a child, cannot be prosecuted in the State in respect of the act which constituted the offence: Sexual Offences (Jurisdiction) Act 1996, s 9. See *In the matter of National Irish Bank Ltd* [1999] 3 IR 190, HC; *AA v Medical Council* [2002] 3 IR 1, HC. See Criminal Justice (Safety of United Nations Workers) Act 2000, s 10; European Arrest Warrant Act 2003, s 41; Maritime Security Act 2004, s 9. [Bibliography: McDermott P A (2).] See APPEAL; AUTREFOIS ACQUIT.

double portions, rule against. The rule that where a father (or other person *in loco parentis*) makes provision for his child by will, and subsequently provides a portion (qv) inter vivos for the child, the portion is presumed to take the place of the legacy in whole or in part. Equity leans against dou-

ble portions. See Succession Act 1965, s 63(9). See ADEMPTION; HOTCHPOT.

double probate, grant of. A grant of representation to another executor, whose rights had been reserved by the first executor, who is still alive and who has already extracted a grant of probate.

double taxation agreement. A tax treaty or convention; a bilateral agreement between the State and another state containing rules aimed at avoiding the taxation twice of income flowing from sources in one of the countries to residents of the other and vice versa, thereby facilitating the movement of capital, labour and commercial activity between the two states. The agreement may also provide for the relief or prevention of double taxation of capital gains or of capital. The government is empowered to make such agreements and has made agreements with more than 33 countries: Taxes Consolidation Act 1997, s 826.

Double taxation is the imposition of comparable taxes in two or more states on the same taxpayer in respect of the same subject matter and for identical purposes: OECD Model Double Taxation Covenant on Income and Capital (1997) page 7, para 3. Irish treaties generally follow the OECD Model and its classification of income e g business profits, dividends, interest, royalties, rent, salaries and wages, and pensions.

There are three basic methods of relieving double taxation: (a) the tax paid in the foreign country may be *deducted*, as if it were a business expense, when calculating the income which is liable to Irish tax, or (b) the tax paid in the foreign country may be *credited* against the Irish tax payable on the same income, or (c) the income arising in the foreign country is *exempt* from Irish tax.

All Irish tax treaties contain the OECD provision on *mutual assistance* i e the provision under which each State to a tax treaty agrees to exchange information obtained in the normal course of administration of tax law. EU member states have also agreed to exchange information which may be useful in combating tax evasion: SI No 334 of 1978 and SI No 407 of 1980, now both revoked and replaced by SI No 711 of 2003. Also the EU has introduced a common tax system for mergers, divisions and transfers of corporate assets (90/434/EEC) and a limitation on withholding tax on distributions in the case of parent companies with subsidiaries in another member state (90/435/EEC). For continuation of relief from double taxation in connection with the adjustment of profits of associated enterprises, see SIs Nos 40 and 41 of 2004.

Sea and air transport agreements have been agreed with Spain and South Africa (SIs No 26 of 1977 and No 210 of 1959 respectively, and TCA 1997, s 835). For conflict between a Double Taxation Agreement and domestic legislation, see *Murphy v Asahi Synthetic Fibres Ltd* 3 ITR 246.

Member states of the EC are required, so far as is necessary, to enter negotiations with each other with a view to securing, for the benefit of their nationals, the abolition of double taxation within the Community: EC Treaty, art 90 of the consolidated (2002) version. See also Finance Act 2004 s 31. [Bibliography: Haccius & O'Brien; Moore (3); Walsh M.] See TAX INFORMATION EXCHANGE AGREEMENT; TRANSFER PRICING; TREATY SHOPPING.

doubt, beyond reasonable. See BEYOND REASONABLE DOUBT.

doubt, for the avoidance of. See FOR THE AVOIDANCE OF DOUBT.

doubt, letter of expression of. A person who has a doubt about the application of *value added tax* to a transaction is entitled to lodge with his VAT return, a *letter of expression of doubt* with supporting documentation: Finance Act 2002, s 107. This prevents the application of interest to any additional liability, subject to certain conditions. An *expression of doubt* facility has been extended to 'capital acquisition tax' returns: Finance Act 2003, s 146.

dower. The right which a widow had to a life estate in one third of her deceased husband's heritable freeholds, ie fee simple and fee tail, provided her husband died intestate, birth of heritable issue was possible, and the husband had not defeated the widow's right to dower under the Dower Act 1833. Abolished for registered land by the Registration of Title Act 1964 and abolished entirely by the Succession Act 1965, s 11. See CURTESY.

DPP. Director of Public Prosecutions (qv).

draft. (1) An order for the payment of a sum of money. (2) A rough copy of a document. See BANKERS' DRAFT.

drain. A road authority may construct and maintain drains in, on, under, through or to any land for the purpose of draining water from, or preventing water flowing onto, a public road (qv): Roads Act 1993, s 76(1)(a). See also Local Government Act 2001, s 231. See ARTERIAL DRAINAGE; COMBINED DRAIN; SEWERS; TRADE EFFLUENT.

dramatic work. Includes a choreographic work or a work of mime: Copyright and Related Rights Act 2000, s 2(1). Copyright subsists in an *original* dramatic work (CRRA 2000, s 17(2)). It expires 70 years after the death of the author irrespective of the date on which the work is first lawfully made available to the public (CRRA 2000, s 24(1)). However, see PUBLISHED EDITION. It is an offence to make a dramatic work with the intent that it may comprise or be included in an illegal broadcast: Broadcasting and Wireless Telegraphy Act 1988, s 5(2)(b). See ARTIST, TAX EXEMPTION OF; COPYRIGHT; COPYRIGHT, QUALIFICATION FOR.

drawback. The refund of duty made on the exportation of goods for which customs duties have been paid on importation. It is an offence to claim drawback unlawfully: Customs Consolidation Act 1876, s 108 as amended by the Finance Act 1963, s 34(4) and Finance Act 1976, s 44.

drawee. The person to whom a *bill of exchange* (qv) is addressed eg a bank.

drawer. The person who signs a bill of exchange (qv) as the maker thereof.

drawing of cheque. See CHEQUE, DRAWING OF.

dress code. The requirement that employees wear particular type of clothes at work. Such codes are often intended to ensure that staff who interact with the public present an acceptable standard of neatness and grooming. Such code may also be justified on grounds of safety or hygiene; however if a code differentiates between male and female employees in its requirements, such differentiation may amount to discrimination on the grounds of gender. In a particular case the Labour Court held that the dress code of the respondent company restricted the complainant's freedom to determine his own appearance to a greater degree than it did women, and constituted unfavourable treatment on the grounds of gender: *O'Byrne v Dunnes Stores* [2004] ELR 96, LC.

In this case, the dress code banned facial hair, other than moustaches, and when the employee refused to remove his goatee beard, he was required to wear a form of facemask at work. The Labour Court stated that dress codes by their nature apply different rules to men and women and that it would be absurd to suggest that they would do otherwise. The court said that anti-discrimination law does not require that men and women be treated the same in every circumstance; what it requires is that they be treated equally. See also UNIFORM, WEARING OF.

dress in court. The costume which judges and counsel are ordinarily required to wear in the superior courts during sittings: RSC Ord 119. For judges, it is a black coat and vest of uniform make and material of the kind worn by senior counsel (qv), a black Irish poplin gown of uniform make and material, white bands, and a wig of the kind known as the small or bobbed wig. Formerly, counsel would not be heard in any case during *sittings* unless wearing the prescribed costume.

Judges of the Circuit Court are required, except where otherwise provided, to wear a black coat and vest of uniform nature and material, of the kind heretofore worn by Senior Counsel; a black gown of uniform make; white bands as heretofore worn; and a wig of the kind known as the small or bobbed wig: Circuit Court Rules 2001 Ord 3, r 1.

However, in family law proceedings in the Circuit and High Courts, judges, barristers and solicitors are prohibited from appearing with wig and gown: Judicial Separation and Family Law Reform Act 1989, ss 33 and 45. It has been clarified that the rule of court which dispensed with the wearing of a wig and gown by the Judge or Senior and Junior Counsel in family law proceedings, applies only to the wig and gown. The requirement for the Judge to wear a black coat and vest, and for Counsel to be habited in a dark colour remains. See Rules of the Superior Courts (No 4) (Amendment of Order 70A) 2000, SI No 327 of 2000.

Also, since 1995, a barrister or solicitor cannot be required to wear a wig in any court: Courts and Court Officers Act 1995, s 49. However, the Chief Justice published a notice in the Legal Diary of 4 April 2000 which stated that in the ceremony where counsel are being called to the Inner Bar as Senior Counsel, they 'must wear on that occasion the coat, vest and bands referred to in Order 119 of the Rules of the Superior Court and a ceremonial or full-bottomed wig'.

In the district court the judge wears a black coat and gown of uniform nature and material and white bands, except he does not wear such gown or bands when hearing such proceedings as are referred to in the JSFLA 1989, s 45, or proceedings involving a child or young person within the meaning of the Children Acts 1908 to 1989: DCR 1997 Ord 5. The President of the District Court clarified in 2003 that counsel are expected to robe in all district courts, except: (a) where there is statutory provision to the contrary, as in family law and children courts, and (b) where there is no robing room for counsel, as is frequently the case in small rural venues.

A solicitor appearing in court should always dress in a manner which shows respect for the dignity and formality of the court: *A Guide to Professional Conduct of Solicitors in Ireland* (2002) ch 5.9. See FAMILY COURT; TELEVISION LINK.

driftnet. A wall of netting used in fishing, which is free to move according to tide and wind conditions: Sea Fisheries (Driftnets) Order 1998, SI No 267 of 1998. The Order, implementing an EU Council Regulation, prohibits the keeping on board of a vessel or the use for fishing of one or more driftnets whose individual or total length is more than 2.5 kilometres. It also prohibits the use of driftnets for the capture of a specified number of species.

The High Court has ruled that the purported transposition of the EU Regulation was in excess of the Minister's powers in that the SI, which defined a 'driftnet', infringed the exclusive lawmaking powers of the Oireachtas: *Browne v Minister for the Marine* (2002) Irish Times, 7 March. This ruling was upheld by the Supreme Court: *Irish Times*, 18 July 2003.

drinking up time. Colloquial expression describing the time permitted after closing time in a licensed premises for the consumption of intoxicating liquor supplied during permitted hours; it was increased from 10 to 30 minutes: Intoxicating Liquor Act 1988, s 27. See INTOXICATING LIQUOR.

drinking water. A sanitary authority has a duty to take the necessary measures to ensure that water intended for human consumption is wholesome and clean: European Communities (Drinking Water) Regulations 2000, SI No 439 of 2000. The regulations give effect to Directive (EC) 98/83 on the quality of water intended for human consumption and revoke SI No 81 of 1988 as from 1 January 2004. The regulations prescribe the quality standards to be applied in relation to certain supplies of drinking water, including requirements as to sampling, frequency, methods of analysis and the provision of information to consumers.

The Environmental Protection Agency may require a sanitary authority to submit to it information on such monitoring; the Agency is required however to carry out its own monitoring and to prepare a public annual report on such monitoring: Environmental Protection Agency Act 1992, s 58. See SEWAGE EFFLUENT; WATER FRAMEWORK DIRECTIVE.

driver, uninsured. See MOTOR INSURER'S BUREAU OF IRELAND; UNTRACED DRIVER.

driving, careless. See CARELESS DRIVING.

driving, furious. See FURIOUS DRIVING.

driving, dangerous. See DANGEROUS DRIVING.

driving instruction. Instruction given for reward in or in respect of the driving of a mechanically propelled vehicle: Road Traffic Act 1968, s 18(1A)(a) as inserted by Road Traffic Act 2002, s 19. The Minister is empowered to approve bodies for the purposes of operating quality control of driving instructors and to exempt from the requirements of direct licensing, driving instructors who hold certificates issued by such approved bodies. Under the RTA 1968, s 18, the Minister is empowered to make regulations in relation to the control of driving instruction eg the licensing of instructors, their qualifications, conduct, duties, records. For regulations regarding the vehicles used in driving instruction, see SIs Nos 392 and 393 of 1986.

driving licence. It is an offence for a person to drive a *mechanically propelled vehicle* (qv) in a public place unless he holds a driving licence for the time being having effect and licensing him to drive the vehicle: Road Traffic Act 1961, s 38. See *Joyce v Esmonde* [1987] ILRM 316.

A person commits an offence if he refuses or fails to produce a driving licence there and then when so requested by a garda (RTA 1961, s 40 as inserted by Road Traffic Act 1994, s 25 and amended by Road Traffic Act 2002, s 18). It is also an offence to refuse or fail to produce a licence at a garda station within 10 days of the demand. There is also provision for the inspection by an officer of the Court Serv-

ice of driving licences of persons charged with certain offences (RTA 2002, s 22, as proposed to be amended by Road Traffic Bill 2004, s 18).

Under a mutual recognition directive, the member states of the EU are required to recognise the driving licences of each other. The European Court of Justice has held that the Dutch requirement for registration by holders of a licence from another member state was disproportionate and ran counter to the directive; failure to register had the effect of rendering the licence of the other state, valid for one year from establishment in the Netherlands: Case C-246/00 *Commission v Kingdom of the Netherlands* [2003] ECJ. [Bibliography: Pierce (2).]

Provision has been made to facilitate the application for a driving licence online at website: *www.motortax.ie*: SI No 486 of 2003. See DANGEROUS DRIVING; DISQUALIFICATION ORDER, DRIVING; DRUNKEN DRIVING; FURIOUS DRIVING; PENALTY POINTS; PROVISIONAL DRIVING LICENCE.

driving test. For the regulations governing the *practical test* to obtain a driving licence, see Road Traffic (Licensing of Drivers) Regulations, SI No 352 of 1999 as amended by SI No 169 of 2001. In 2001, provision was made for the introduction of a driver *theory test* in accordance with the requirements of Directive (EEC) 91/439: EC (Licensing of Drivers) Regulations 2001, SI 168 of 2001, now revoked and replaced by EC (Driving Theoretical Tests) Regulations 2003, SI No 52 of 2003. In April 2004 it was announced that a new statutory body would be established under proposed legislation to overhaul the current system of testing drivers, to set standards for driving instructors, and to monitor general driving standards in the State: Driver Testing and Standards Authority Bill 2004. In August 2004, there were about 120,000 persons on the driving test waiting list.

driving without reasonable consideration. The offence committed by a person who drives a vehicle in a public place without reasonable consideration for other persons using the place: Road Traffic Act 1961, s 51A as inserted by the Road Traffic Act 1968, s 49.

drug, presence of. See MEDICAL BUREAU OF ROAD SAFETY.

drug trafficking. Producing or supplying, transporting or storing, importing or exporting a controlled drug or using any ship for illicit traffic in controlled drugs, where prohibited: Criminal Justice Act 1994, s 3(1). A *confiscation order* can be obtained to recover the proceeds of drug trafficking (CJA 1994, s 4 as amended by Criminal Justice Act 1999, s 25). The 1999 Act introduced a mandatory minimum sentence of 10 years in the case of possession of a controlled drug for the purposes of selling or supply, where the value of the drug exceeds £10,000 (€12,698) (CJA 1999, ss 4–7). The Court of Criminal Appeal has no jurisdiction to make a determination under s 4 of the CJA 1994: *Gilligan v Special Criminal Court* [2002] FL 7010, HC.

There is also provision for the seizure and forfeiture of cash related to drug trafficking which is being imported or exported from the State (CJA 1994, ss 38–45). Section 39 of CJA 1994 provides for a forfeiture proceeding which is *in rem* and does not provide for a criminal offence: *England v Judge Dunne and DPP* [2003] FL 7003, HC.

There are new offences created in relation to drug trafficking at sea (CJA 1994, ss 33–37 as amended by Criminal Justice (Illicit Traffic by Sea) Act 2003, s 28). Under the amended provision, a person is guilty of a drug trafficking offence if the person does, on an Irish ship, a ship registered in a Convention state or a ship not registered in any country or territory, any act which, if done in the State, would constitute such an offence. The consent of the flag state is no longer required to arrest a ship on suspicion of drug trafficking where the ship is in Irish territorial water.

It is an offence for a person to handle any property knowing or believing that such property, directly or indirectly, represents another person's proceeds of drug trafficking or other criminal activity (CJA 1994, s 31(3)). The prosecution must prove, as a fact, the criminal origin of the property as well as the knowledge or belief of the accused: *The People (DPP) v McHugh* [2002] 1 IR 352, CCA. See also *The People (DPP) v Meehan* [2002] 3 IR 139, CCA.

The gardaí have been given extra powers to combat drug trafficking e g powers of detention of up to 168 hours, power to take bodily samples, and powers of arrest; also inferences may be drawn by the failure of the accused to mention particular facts on being questioned or when being charged:

Criminal Justice (Drug Trafficking) Act 1996 as amended by CJA 1999, s 35. See DETENTION. Also provision has been made for disqualification, forfeiture, suspension and revocation of liquor, dance or public entertainment licences for drug trafficking offences and for permitting premises to be used for drug-related activities: Licensing (Combating Drug Abuse) Act 1997.

See *O'Donoghue v McDonnell* [2000] 1 ILRM 185, HC; *DPP v Galligan* [2003] FL 8022, CCA. See SIs Nos 152, 153 and 154 of 2002. See SIs Nos 177, 178, and 179 of 2003. See SI No 78 of 2004. See 'Mandatory Minimum Sentences in Drug Cases' by Kiwana Ennis BL in *Bar Review* (February 2003) 30. See BODILY SAMPLE; CONFISCATE; CRIMINAL ASSETS BUREAU; DETENTION OF SHIP; JOINT INVESTIGATION TEAMS; MONEY LAUNDERING; PUBLIC DANCE LICENCE; PROCEEDS OF CRIME; SILENCE, RIGHT TO; STUFFERS AND SWALLOWERS.

drug trials. 'Drug trials must conform to the Declaration of Helsinki. Trials must be managed well, data must be collected accurately and doctors appropriately remunerated. Doctors are reminded that data collection represents participation in drug trials and attention must be paid to the interpretation and dissemination of the data.': Medical Council, *A Guide to Ethical Conduct and Behaviour* (6th edn, 2004) para 4.13. See CLINICAL TRIALS, CONDUCT OF.

drugs, misuse of. To prevent the misuse of drugs, various statutory provisions have been made including: powers of search of persons, vehicles, vessels and aircraft; powers of inspection and arrest; procedures for investigation and dealing with irresponsible prescribing of drugs by practitioners; provisions governing the production and supply of drugs; and prohibition on printing of publications which encourage drug abuse: Misuse of Drugs Act 1977 and 1984.

Additional powers have been given to officers of customs and excise to deal with drug smuggling, including powers to detain and search, without warrant, persons and vehicles: Customs and Excise (Miscellaneous Provisions) Act 1988. See *O'Callaghan v Ireland* [1994] 1 IR 555, SC; *DPP v Yamanoha* [1994] 1 IR 565, CCA; *People (DPP) v Van Onzen* [1996] 2 ILRM 387, CCA; *Farrelly v Devally* [1998] 4 IR 76, HC; *DPP v Early* [1998] 3 IR 158, HC;

The People (DPP) v Byrne [1998] 2 IR 417, CCA. See DCR 1997 Ord 32.

The complaint that a doctor has been under the influence of alcohol or drugs is a grave charge, and may lead to a finding of professional misconduct: Medical Council, *A Guide to Ethical Conduct and Behaviour* (6th edn, 2004) para 5.1. Also doctors should only treat drug-misusing patients if they have the proper training and facilities and the support of the statutory and voluntary services (para 10.4). For the *European Monitoring Centre for Drugs and Drug Addiction*, see website: *www.emcdda.org*. [Bibliography: Charleton (1); Murphy T.] See CLINICAL TRIALS; DEFENCE FORCES AND DISCIPLINE; FORFEITURE; MEDICAL PREPARATIONS; POLICE CO-OPERATION; PUBLIC HEALTH; RAVE DANCE; SPORT.

drunken driving. There are *four* separate offences of drunken driving: Road Traffic Act 1961, s 49 as inserted by the Road Traffic Act 1994, s 10. It is an offence for a person to drive or attempt to drive a mechanically propelled vehicle in a public place: (a) while under the influence of an *intoxicant* to such an extent as to be *incapable* of having proper control of the vehicle, or (b) while there is in his body a quantity of *alcohol* such that, within three hours after so driving or attempting to drive, (i) the concentration of alcohol in his blood exceeds a concentration of 80 milligrammes of alcohol per 100 millilitres of blood, or (ii) the concentration of alcohol in his urine exceeds a concentration of 107 milligrammes of alcohol per 100 millilitres of urine, or (iii) the concentration of alcohol in his breath exceeds a concentration of 35 microgrammes per 100 millilitres of breath. Failure to prove compliance with the three-hour requirement will lead to an acquittal: *DPP v Doyle* [1992] HC.

The description of *drunk driving* may be applied equally to the offences under s 49(2) and (3) of the RTA 1961 as amended; the use of the phrase 'drunk driving' is sufficient communication by a garda of the reason for an arrest; a technical explanation is not required: *DPP (Cloughley) v Mooney* [1993] ILRM 214, HC.

An *intoxicant* includes alcohol and drugs and any combination of them. The alcohol level or presence of a drug may be proved by the production of a certificate of analysis from the Bureau of Road Safety. It is also an offence to be *in charge* of a mechanically propelled vehicle in a public place, with intent to drive or attempt to drive, while under the influence of an intoxicant (RTA 1961, s 50 as inserted by RTA 1994, s 11).

The decision to prosecute for drunken driving where there is a fatality has, since 1991, been taken by the Director of Public Prosecutions rather than by the gardaí. A garda is empowered to arrest a person without a warrant who, in the garda's opinion, was committing or had committed an offence of drink or drug-related driving (RTA 1961, s 49). See *A-G (Ruddy) v Kenny* [1959] 94 ILTR 185.

The garda must inform the accused at the time of the arrest that he has formed such opinion: *DPP v Lynch* [1991] 1 IR 43, HC. A garda may enter without a warrant any place, including the curtilage of a dwelling (but not the dwelling itself), to secure an arrest (RTA 1994, s 39 and *DPP v Delany* [2003] 1 IR 363, HC). Also a designated doctor may enter a hospital to take a blood or urine sample (RTA 1994, ss 15 and 39(4)). An intoxicated driver may be detained where he is a danger to himself or others (RTA 1994, s 16). An admission by a person, drunk or sober, that he had been driving the vehicle, is *prima facie* admissible evidence: *DPP v McCormack* [1999] 1 ILRM 398, SC.

A person can be charged with the offence of being drunk in charge of a carriage (Licensing Act 1872, s 12) but not in respect of the same occurrence if liable to be charged under the 1994 Act (RTA 1994, s 11(9)). [Bibliography: de Blacam (2); Hill & O'Keeffe; McGrath M (2).] For penalties for drunken driving, see DISQUALIFICATION ORDER, DRIVING. See also ALCOHOL, CONSUMPTION OF; BREATH SPECIMEN; BLOOD SPECIMEN; HIP FLASK DEFENCE; INCAPABLE; IN CHARGE; INTENTION; ROAD TRAFFIC CHECK; STOP, OBLIGATION TO; URINE SPECIMEN.

drunken person. (1) Means a person who is intoxicated to such an extent as would give rise to a reasonable apprehension that the person might endanger himself or any other person, and 'drunk' and 'drunkenness' are to be construed accordingly: Intoxicating Liquor Act 2003, s 2(1). A drunken person is required to leave a licensed premises on being requested to do so by the licensee or a garda (ILA 2003, s 6(1)). Also, it is an offence for a drunken person to seek entry to the bar of a licensed premises (ILA 2003, s 6(2)). It is an offence for a licensee: (a) to supply intoxicating liquor to a drunken person; (b) to permit a drunken person to consume intoxicating liquor; (c) to permit drunkenness to take place in the bar; or (d) to admit any drunken person to the bar (ILA 2003, s 4(1)). It is also an offence for a non-licensee to supply intoxicating liquor to a drunken person in a licensed premises or to purchase liquor for the drunken person (ILA 2003, s 5).

(2) A drunken person in custody in a garda station is required to be visited and spoken to and if necessary aroused for this purpose at intervals of approximately a quarter of an hour for a period of two hours or longer if his condition warrants it: Treatment of Persons in Custody in Garda Síochána Stations Regulations 1987, SI No 119 of 1987, reg 19(6). This requirement also applies to a person under the influence of drugs.

(3) Where a contract is made by a person who is so drunk at the time as not to understand what he is doing, such contract is *voidable* (qv) at the option of the drunken person, provided the other party knew of his condition. The burden of proof is on the person suffering the incapacity to prove the knowledge of the other party. A contract made by a drunken person can be *ratified* when he is sober. A drunken person is liable for *necessaries* (qv) supplied to him: Sale of Goods Act 1893, s 2. See CAPACITY TO CONTRACT; INTOXICATED.

drunkenness. Intoxication. Drunkenness may be a constituent part of an offence eg driving a motor vehicle while under the influence of alcoholic drink. Drunkenness generally is not a defence to a crime; merely to establish that a person's mind was so affected by drink that he more readily gave way to some violent passion, forms no excuse. However if actual *insanity* (qv) in fact supervenes, even as a result of alcoholic excess, it furnishes as complete an answer to a criminal charge as insanity induced by any other cause. Drunkenness which renders the accused incapable of forming the specific intent essential to constitute the crime should be taken into consideration, with the other facts proved, in order to determine whether or not he had this intent: *DPP v Beard* [1920] AC 479. See also *R v Gamlen* [1858] 1 F F 90; *A-G for Northern Ireland v Gallagher* [1963] AC 359; *The People (Attorney General) v Regan*

[1975] IR 367; *People (DPP) v McBride* [1997] 1 ILRM 233, CCA.

The behaviour of an employee while drunk on duty can be sufficiently serious to warrant dismissal: *Quinn v B & I Line* [1990] ELR 175. See LRC Report on Intoxication as a Defence to a Criminal Offence (LRC 51, 1995). [Bibliography: Charleton (4).] See ALCOHOL, CONSUMPTION OF; INTOXICATED; MENS REA; MCNAGHTEN RULES.

dry rent. See RENT SECK.

dual carriageway. A road the roadway of which is divided centrally so as to provide two separate carriageways, on each of which traffic is required by road regulation to proceed in one direction only: Road Traffic (Signs) Regulations 1962, SI No 181 of 1997, art 3.

dual mandate. Expression to describe membership by a person at different levels of government at the same time eg at local government, national government and at European government. Dual mandate at local and national government is prohibited in respect of a Minister of the government or a Minister of State or the Chairman of Dáil Éireann or of Seanad Éireann: Local Government Act 1994, s 6 as amended by Local Elections (Disclosure of Donations and Expenditure) Act 1999, s 24.

The dual mandate limitation also prohibits a person being a member of a local authority who is also a member of the EU Commission, or a representative of the European Parliament, or a Minister or Minister of State or Chairman of the Dáil or Seanad, and also a member of another local authority: Local Government Act 2001, ss 13–14.

From the local elections in 2004 and thereafter, a member of the Dáil or Seanad is disqualified from being elected, or co-opted, or from being a member of a local authority (LGA 2001, s 13A inserted by Local Government (No 2) Act 2003 s 2). A similar provision in s 14 of the Local Government Bill 2000 was dropped during the passage of the Bill through the Oireachtas. In order to keep members of the Dáil and Seanad in touch with what is happening at local level, local authorities are required to conduct their dealings with members of either House of the Oireachtas in accordance with regulations made by the Minister eg requiring the supply of notice, agenda and minutes of local authority meetings to members of the Dáil and Seanad (LGA 2001, s 237A inserted by LGA 2003, s 3 and SI No 274 of 2003).

The High Court in upholding this ban on the dual mandate, has held that there is no constitutionally guaranteed right to stand for election to a local authority; the powers and functions of a local authority, including who is eligible to be members of such authorities, are matters to be decided by the Oireachtas: *Ring v Attorney General* (2004) 20 February, HC and ITLR (15 March). In the constitutional provision dealing with local government, it is stated that the powers and functions were 'conferred by law': 1937 Constitution art 28A(1).

Provision has been made for the termination of the dual mandate for a person who is a member of the Houses of the Oireachtas and the European Parliament, with a once-off derogation for a member of either House who is elected to the European Parliament in June 2004 until the next general election: European Parliament Elections (Amendment) Act 2004, s 2(c).

dual-use product. A product which can be used for both civil and military purposes. There is control on the use of and export of such products. The Tánaiste announced in April 2004 the intention of the government to introduce primary legislation for arms control to bring Ireland into line with best practices internationally. See EXPORTS, CONTROL OF; NUCLEAR WEAPONS.

dubitante. [Doubting.]

Dublin agent. A solicitor in the City of Dublin near the Four Courts who acts for another solicitor situated elsewhere. Formerly, a solicitor wishing to undertake work in the Dublin High Court was required to have a registered office within a radius of two miles from the Four Courts e g for the service of documents. This led to the practice of solicitors outside Dublin having a Dublin agent. Although no longer a requirement, the practice continues for convenience and efficiency.

When a solicitor employs a legal or other agent to carry out work related to a client's business, he should endeavour to ensure that the work will be carried out in a competent manner: *A Guide to Professional Conduct of Solicitors in Ireland* (2002) ch 2.2. See LAW AGENT.

Dublin Convention. The Convention determining the State responsible for examining applications for asylum, lodged in one of the member states of the European Communities 1990: Refugee Act 1996, Sch 4. The Minister is empowered to make orders to give effect to the principles set out in the Convention (RA 1996, s 22 as substituted by Immigration Act 2003, s 7(l)). An application for refugee status cannot be transferred to another Convention country unless that country has agreed to accept responsibility for its examination. A person may be deported from the State, whose application has been transferred to a convention country: Immigration Act 1999, s 3(2)(e).

The Supreme Court had held that it was clearly the intention of the framers of the Convention that where an application for asylum, made in another Member State, had been rejected in that State, and the person then arrives illegally in this State, he should be taken back to the State which has already dealt with his application: *D Y v Minister for Justice* [2004 SC] 1 ILRM 481.

Regulations have been made to give effect to the State's obligation as a party to the Dublin Convention: Dublin Convention (Implementation) Order 2000, SI No 343 of 2000. This Order, which revokes SI No 360 of 1997, puts in place procedures for the *Refugee Applications Commissioner* to determine whether an application for asylum should, in accordance with the Dublin Convention, be dealt with in the State or in another Convention country. However, new rules and procedures have been agreed for determining which member state of the European Union is responsible for dealing with an asylum application made in one of them: SI No 423 of 2003 giving effect to Regulation (EC) 343/2003, which applies also to Iceland and Norway, but not to Denmark which continues to be governed by the Dublin Convention. See *R v Secretary of State (ex parte Adan & others)* [1999] 4 All ER 774. *DL, JL and Others v Minister for Justice* (2003) 23 January, Case ref 109/02 and 108/02. See REFUGEE.

Dublin Docks Development Authority. See URBAN RENEWAL.

Dublin Institute of Technology. An institute of education and training with the function to provide vocational and technical education and training for the economic, technological, scientific, commercial, industrial, social and cultural development of the State: Dublin Institute of Technology Act 1992. It is required: (a) to facilitate the National Qualifications Authority of Ireland in carrying out its functions, (b) to implement procedures for access, transfer and progression determined by the Authority, and (c) to provide such information as required by the Authority, including information in respect of *completion rates*: Qualifications (Education and Training) Act 1999, s 38.

The DIT is an awarding body in its own right (DITA 1992, ss 5(1)(b) and 5(2)) but it may apply to the new awards councils to have one or more of its programmes validated (Q(ET)A 1999, s 38(3)). It is required to establish procedures for *quality assurance* and must agree them with the Authority (Q(ET)A 1999, s 39). See *Grennan v DIT* [1995] ELR 188, HC and [1997] 3 IR 415, HC.

The Institute is now entitled, with the consent of the Minister, to acquire or to form subsidiaries registered under the Companies Acts, to perform such of its functions as it considers appropriate: Vocational Education (Amendment) Act 2001, s 38. See website: *www.dit.ie*. See COMPLETION RATE; EDUCATIONAL ESTABLISHMENT; GRANGEGORMAN DEVELOPMENT AGENCY; NATIONAL QUALIFICATIONS AUTHORITY OF IRELAND; EDUCATION AWARD.

Dublin light rail. See LIGHT RAILWAY.

duces tecum. [Bring with you.] See SUBPOENA.

duck. See GAME.

due. Owed eg a debt.

due course of law. No person shall be tried on any criminal charge save in *due course of law*: 1937 Constitution, art 38(1). The phrase 'due course of law' requires a fair and just balance between the exercise of individual freedoms and the requirements of an ordered society: O'Higgins CJ in *Re Criminal Law (Jurisdiction) Bill 1975* [1977] IR 129 cited in *O'Callaghan v A-G & DPP* [1993] ILRM 267, HC.

Where an issue is raised in a criminal trial that the accused will not be tried 'in due course of law' if the trial proceeds, the accused should be given the opportunity to seek an order of prohibition to prevent the trial proceeding: *DPP v Judge Cyril Kelly* [1997] 1 ILRM 497, HC.

The phrase *in due course of law* denotes no more than fair and just procedures in the conduct of a trial and the due application of the relevant law; it does not mean

that an acquittal by a jury cannot be appealed: *Consodine v Shannon Regional Fisheries Board* [1998] 1 ILRM 11, SC. The essential purpose of trial by jury in *due course of law*, does not include a requirement of unanimity in the jury: *O'Callaghan v A-G* [1993] ILRM 765, SC and 2 IR 17.

due process of law. The term used to describe the regular application of the law through the courts. See *Gill v Connellan* [1988] ILRM 448, HC.

due regard. The Court of Criminal Appeal has held that in order for a judge to advise a jury meaningfully that 'due regard' be paid to the absence of corroboration, the term was to be properly and not merely technically, explained: *The People (DPP) v Connolly* [2003] 2 IR 1, CCA. It held that phrase 'something you should bear in mind' as used by the trial judge was vague and less forceful than the statutory phrase 'to have due regard' in Criminal Procedure Act 1993, s 10. See CONFESSION.

dum bene se gesserit. [During good conduct.]

dum casta clause. A clause which is sometimes included in a *separation agreement* (qv) whereby a spouse's obligation to maintain the other terminates upon the other committing adultery or ceasing to lead a chaste life. In the absence of such a term the courts will not imply such a term: *Lewis v Lewis* [1940] IR 42; *Ormsby v Ormsby* [1945] 79 ILTR 97.

dum casta vixerit. [While she lives chastely.]

dum fuit infra aetatem. [While he was within age.]

dum sola. [While single or unmarried.]

dump. Popularly understood to mean a landfill site for the disposal of waste; a *permit* is required for such a site if operated by a person other than a *public waste collector* (qv). Dumping near aerodromes may be restricted: Air Navigation and Transport Act 1988, s 23. See HOUSEHOLD REFUSE; LANDFILL SITE; WASTE.

dumping. The selling of products in a national market at a price below the price commanded by the same products in their country of origin; it can also include price discrimination as between national markets. Dumping is regulated by Regulation (EC) 3017/79 amended by Regulation (EC) 2176/84; penalties are determined by the *dumping margin*, which is the amount by which the *normal value* of the product exceeds the *export price*. See *NTN Toyo*

Bearing Co v Council [1989] 2 CMLR 76. See also *Friel* in 8 ILT & SJ (1990) 96. See COMMON COMMERCIAL POLICY.

dumping at sea. It is an offence to dump any vessel, aircraft, substance or material in the *maritime area*, or anywhere in the sea from an Irish vessel or aircraft, except in accordance with a *permit*: Dumping at Sea Act 1996, ss 2(1) and 5. It is also an offence to dispose deliberately in the maritime area of an offshore installation; or of radioactive substances or material; or of toxic, harmful or noxious substances (DSA 1996, s 4). The *maritime area* comprises: (a) the territorial seas of the State, and the seabed and subsoil, (b) the Continental Shelf which extends up to 350 miles off the Irish coast, and (c) 200 nautical miles from the baselines of the Maritime Jurisdiction Acts 1959 to 1988 (DSA 1996, s 1(1)).

Under draft legislation, it is proposed to improve the Dumping at Sea Act 1996 by: (a) updating the definition of *harbour authority*, (b) requiring applicants for *dumping permits* to advertise their application in a newspaper circulating in the approximate area, and (c) requiring consideration to be given to any likelihood of interference with important natural or archaeological heritage before a decision on an application is made: Dumping at Sea (Amendment) Bill 2000. See OIL POLLUTION; SEA POLLUTION; WASTE.

durable. See MERCHANTABLE QUALITY.

durante absentia. [During absence.] Special administration *durante absentia* may be granted during the absence abroad of a personal representative. See Succession Act 1965, s 31; also *In the Goods of Cassidy* [1832] 4 Hag 360.

durante bene placito. [During the pleasure of the Crown.]

durante minore aetate. [During minority.] The High Court has power to appoint an administrator *durante minore aetate* where a minor is the sole executor. See Succession Act 1965, s 32; also *Re Thompson and McWilliams Contract* [1896] 1 IR 356. See CESSATE GRANT.

durante viduitate. [During widowhood.]

durante vita. [During life.]

duress. Actual or threatened physical violence or unlawful imprisonment or threat of criminal proceedings. An act done under duress is generally not valid. A contract entered into under duress is voidable at the option of the party coerced. The person threatened need not be the actual contract-ing party, but may be the husband or wife or near relative of that party: *Kaufman v Gerson* [1904] 1 KB 591.

A threat of imprisonment and dishonour has been held to be sufficient to render void a contract of marriage for duress, as has extreme pressure from parents which drove the parties unwillingly into a union which neither party desired: *Griffith v Griffith* [1944] IR 35; *M K (McC) v McC* [1982] ILRM 277. See also *Smelter Corporation of Ireland v O'Driscoll* [1977] IR 305. [Bibliography: Charleton (4); McAuley & McCutcheon.] See INEQUALITY OF POSITION; INSTRUCT; MARRIAGE, NULLITY OF; UNDUE INFLUENCE.

duress in crime. Duress *per minas* may be a good defence to some crimes. Threat of immediate death or serious personal violence which is so great as to overbear the ordinary power of human resistance will be accepted as a justification for acts which would otherwise be criminal, but not for murder, no matter how great the duress: *Attorney General v Whelan* [1934] IR 526. The defendant to succeed in this defence must show clearly that the overpowering of the will was operative at the time the crime was actually committed. If there was reasonable opportunity for the will to reassert itself, no justification can be found in antecedent threats.

Where duress is pleaded and evidence adduced in support, there is a burden of proof on the prosecution to prove that the accused was not acting under duress and this should be explained to the jury: *The People (DPP) v Dickey* [2003] FL 7195, CCA. A judge should take into account the factor of duress when sentencing an accused who has been found guilty: *DPP v O'Toole* [2003] FL 7365, CCA.

It has been held in Northern Ireland that it is open to a person accused of murder as a principal (qv) *in the second degree* to plead duress: *Lynch v DPP for Northern Ireland* [1975] AC 653.

duress of goods. Doctrine whereby a transaction is voidable where a person in legal possession of goods (e g pawner) demands more than is justifiably due because of his stronger bargaining position; any excess paid is recoverable: *Lloyds Bank v Bundy* [1975] QB 326. See INEQUALITY OF POSITION.

dutch auction. A sale of goods by auction in which the price is reduced by the auctioneer until a purchaser is found: Casual Trading Act 1995, s 1. See AUCTION SALES.

duty. (1) An act which is required as a result of a legal obligation; the correlative of a right. Every *duty* imposed by an Act of the Oireachtas or by an instrument made wholly or partly under any such Act shall, unless the contrary intention in such Act or instrument, be performed from time to time as occasion requires: Interpretation Act 1937, s 16(1). Contrast with POWER.

(2) A tax levied. See DUTY OF CARE; DRAWBACK.

duty-free. Generally understood to mean the freedom from liability to pay a tax on goods imported from another state. There is a personal limit on the importation of certain goods. Duty-free purchases for passengers travelling between EU countries ceased as from 1 July 1999. However, provision has been made for the continuation for a transitional period of the duty free arrangements for tobacco products in respect of some of the new EU accession States, SI No 201 of 2004. See Directive (EEC) 12/92 of 25 February 1992.

duty of care. 'You must take reasonable care to avoid acts or omissions which you can reasonably foresee would be likely to injure your neighbour. The answer seems to be – persons who are so closely and directly affected by my act that I ought reasonably to have them in contemplation as being affected when I am directing my mind to the acts or omission which are called in question': *Donoghue v Stevenson* [1932] AC 562.

It has been held that the person whose negligence has caused injuries to another, does not owe a duty of care to that other's children not to deprive them of the non-pecuniary benefits derived from the parent-child relationship: *Hosford v John Murphy & Sons* [1988] ILRM 300. See also *Ward v McMaster* [1989] ILRM 400, SC; *McEleney v McCarron* [1992] SC; *McCann v Brinks Allied Ltd* [1997] 1 ILRM 461, SC. See BREACH OF DUTY; DEFENCE FORCES; MEDICAL NEGLIGENCE; NEGLIGENCE; NEIGHBOUR PRINCIPLE; ROAD USER'S DUTY; SCHOOL AUTHORITY'S DUTY.

dwelling. In relation to the Residential Tenancies Act 2004, a '*dwelling*' means a property let for rent or valuable consideration as a *self-contained residential unit* and includes any building or part of a building used as a dwelling and any out office, yard, garden or other land appurtenant to it or usually enjoyed with it and, where the context so admits, includes a property available for letting but excludes a structure that is not permanently attached to the ground and a vessel, whether mobile or not (RTA 2004, s 4(1)). The 2004 Act applies to dwellings which are subject to a tenancy, including tenancies created before the passing of the Act (RTA 2004, s 3(1)). However the Act does not apply to dwellings which are subject to certain tenancies or leases eg rent controlled and long occupation leases; holiday, employment related or business lettings; owner-occupied or social housing (RTA 2004, s 3(2)). It applies however to rented dwellings where the landlord's spouse, child or parent is a resident if a lease or written tenancy agreement has been entered into. See CONTROLLED DWELLING; INVIOLABILITY OF DWELLING.

dwellinghouse. The Supreme Court has held that the meaning of *dwellinghouse*, within the exemption provided for in the Local Government (Planning and Development) Regulations 1994, did not require the house to be lived in prior to work being carried out: *Smyth v Colgan* [1999] 1 IR 548, SC. See EXTENSION TO HOUSE; INVIOLABILITY OF DWELLING.

dying. In a will, a reference to the contingency of a person dying, refers only to that person dying during the lifetime of the testator, unless the contrary was clearly indicated: *Mulhern v Brennan* [1999] 3 IR 528, HC. In this case the contingency was if any of his sons died 'without issue'.

dying declaration. A statement made by a person, since deceased, as to the cause of death, made in the settled hopeless expectation of imminent death. Such a declaration is admissible in trials for murder and manslaughter of the deceased, as an exception to the hearsay rule. The declarant victim must have realised that he was in actual danger of death and had given up all hope of recovery. See *R v Woodcock* [1789] 1 Leach 500; *Q v Jenkins* [1869] 20 LT 178.

dying patient. 'Where death is imminent, it is the responsibility of the doctor to take care that the sick person dies with dignity, in comfort, and with as little suffering as possible. In these circumstances a doctor is not obliged to initiate or maintain a treatment which is futile or disproportionately burdensome. Deliberately causing death of a patient is professional misconduct': Medical Council, *A Guide to Ethical Conduct and Behaviour* (6th edn, 2004) para 23.1. See DIE, RIGHT TO; EUTHANASIA; HUNGER STRIKE; SERIOUSLY ILL PATIENT.

E

E & OE. [Errors and omissions excepted.] Often noted on commercial documents with the intention of protecting the maker thereof from mistakes.

e converso. [Conversely.]

e-court. See COMMERCIAL COURT.

e-Government. The use of Information Society technologies for the delivery of government services. The government has adopted a three-stranded approach to online delivery of public services: (i) ensuring that all public service information is available online through the websites of departments and agencies, and at the same time as it is delivered through traditional channels; (ii) delivery of public services online, enabling complete transactions to be conducted through electronic channels; (iii) rearrangement of information and service delivery around user needs, and availability in an integrated manner through a single point of contact with government. See Report of Information Society Commission, *E-government: More than an Automation of Government Services* (2003). See website: *www.reach.ie*. See INFORMATION SOCIETY COMMISSION.

e-Learning. Learning assisted by technology. 'This includes computer-based learning which can utilise the richness and capacity of the Internet, multimedia technologies including video and audio, mobile phones with text messaging and CD-ROMs to enable learning': Dr Kenney-Wallace, City and Guilds of London Institute, June 2002. The Minister for Education had under consideration, in January 2003, the allocation of financial support for a service to enhance *higher* and *further* education and training in Ireland through the implementation of an e-learning service. The process of selecting a service provider is being managed by the Higher Education Authority (qv).

e-mark. A mark prescribed in accordance with the Packaged Goods (Quality Control) Act 1980. See PACKAGE.

e-money. See ELECTRONIC MONEY.

e-working. Generally understood to mean working from home for an employer, using technology such as computers and email to communicate and often to deliver work output. For the issues involved in e-working, see 'Getting the balance right' by Colleen Cleary and Wendy Doyle in *Law Society Gazette* (May 2004) 22.

earnest. A nominal sum given to bind a bargain.

easement. A right enjoyed by the owner of land over the lands of another e g a right of way, right to water, right to light, right of support. Includes a *profit a prendre* (qv) and any right in or over water: Fisheries Act 1980, s 2(1).

An easement cannot exist *in gross* ie independently of property, otherwise it may amount to a mere licence; it is a right which is annexed to property, *in alieno solo* (qv), rather than to an individual. The *dominant* tenement is the land owned by the possessor of the easement, and the *servient* tenement is the land over which the right is enjoyed.

An easement may be created by statute; by deed; by an implied grant; by presumed grant under the doctrine of the *lost modern grant* (qv), by *prescription* (qv) including by the Prescription Act 1832 (applied to Ireland in 1859 by the Prescription (Ireland) Act 1858).

An easement of *necessity* can include a user in excess of that which has been enjoyed prior to the grant of the dominant tenement: *Dwyer Nolan Ltd v Kingscroft Ltd* [1999] 1 ILRM, HC.

An easement may be lost by abandonment, or by release expressly or by implication by the non-user of the easement over a long period of time. See *Gaw v CIE* [1953] IR 232; *Carroll v Sheridan* [1984] ILRM 451. See Conveyancing Act 1881, s 6(1). See Law Reform Commission, *Report on the Acquisition of Easements and Profit A Prendre by Prescription* (LRC 66, 2002). [Bibliography: Bland (1); Lyall; Power A; Walsh E S.] See APPURTENANT; DEROGATE; QUASI-EASEMENT.

Easter. A sitting of the court. See SITTINGS OF COURT.

Eastern Regional Health Authority (ERHA). A body corporate with responsibility for planning, arranging for and overseeing the provision of health and personal social services in its functional area of the county borough of Dublin and the administrative counties of South Dublin, Fingal, Dún Laoghaire-Rathdown, Kildare and Wicklow: Health (Eastern Regional Health Authority) Act 1999. The provision and funding of services is required to be based on written agreements between the Authority and service providers. There is recognition of the right of voluntary bodies to manage their own affairs in accordance with their independent ethos and traditions (H(ERHA)A 1999, s 8(3)(f)).

In 2004, provision was made to abolish the membership of the Eastern Regional Health Authority and its three area health boards, and to assign the functions of the Authority and the area boards to their respective chief executive officers: Health (Amendment) Act 2004, ss 16–25 and 27. The Act abolishes the distinction between *reserved* and *executive* functions and assigns what were *reserved* functions to the chief executive officer of the Authority, or to the Minister for Health in certain circumstances (eg appointment of chief executive officer). The consent of the Minister for Health is now required for the acquisition or disposal of land: Health Act 1947, ss 78 and 89 as amended by H(A)A 2004, s 15.

The 2004 legislation is part of a major overhaul of the health services, including the abolition of the membership of the other seven health boards and the establishment of the *Health Service Executive*. See website: *www.erha.ie*. See also Public Service Superannuation (Miscellaneous Provisions) Act 2004, Sch 2. See GRANGEGORMAN DEVELOPMENT AGENCY; HEALTH BOARD; HEALTH BOARDS EXECUTIVE; HEALTH SERVICE EXECUTIVE.

eat inde sine die. [Let him go without a day.]

EC. European Economic Community (qv).

eco-labelling scheme. A voluntary EC-wide voluntary labelling scheme introduced for products and services (eg tourism) which meet strict ecological and performance criteria. The scheme does not apply to food, drink or pharmaceuticals, but applies to a wide range of products eg batteries, refrigerators, gardening products, bedding, footwear, household appliances, cleaning, furniture, electrical equipment, textiles, paper and services. The scheme is administered by the European Eco-labelling Board (EUEB) supported by independent certifying bodies in each member state.

The Environmental Protection Agency must, if it considers it necessary or desirable to do so, establish or arrange for the establishment of the eco-labelling scheme: Environmental Protection Agency Act 1992, s 78. It is an offence to use a symbol provided for in such a scheme in respect of a product or service which has not been approved under the scheme (EPAA 1992, s 78(4)). The symbol is a 'flower'. The independent certifying body in Ireland is now the National Standards Authority of Ireland (qv). See Regulation (EEC) 880/92. For an interactive catalogue that has been specifically designed for consumers to find eco-labelled products throughout Europe, see website: *www.eco-label.com*. For details on the eco-label for tourism, see website: *www.eco-label-tourism.com/frameset/frameset.html*. See CE MARK; ENERGY LABELLING.

ecommerce. See ELECTRONIC COMMERCE; ELECTRONICALLY SUPPLIED SERVICES.

economic and monetary union; EMU. The Maastricht Treaty 1992 provides the legal base and sets out a procedure for moving to full *economic and monetary union* in the EC by 1999 at the latest and, subsequently, replacing the national currencies with a single currency. There is a three-stage process; the *first* stage which began in July 1990 completes the Single Market; the *second* stage began on 1 January 1994 during which the process of policy co-ordination intensified with the assistance of the European Monetary Institute which was the forerunner of the European Central Bank; the *third* stage began on 1 January 1999, at which stage the *ECU*, now called the *euro*, became the single currency of the participating member states. At that stage also the European System of Central Banks, consisting of the European Central Bank (ECB) and the central banks of the member states came fully into operation. See EC Treaty, arts 98–111 of the consolidated (2002) version. See also Economic and Monetary Union Act 1998 as amended by Euro Changeover (Amounts) Act 2001, s 4. See BUDGETARY RULES; CONVERGENCE CRITERIA; EURO.

economic and social cohesion. See COHESION; COMMITTEE OF THE REGIONS.

economic and social committee. The EU advisory committee to the Commission and the Council, with 222 members in 2004, representative of employers, workers and other economic interests, which is consulted on a broad range of economic and social aspects of EU policy: EC Treaty, arts 257–262 of the consolidated (2002) version. Ireland has nine members on this committee. The Nice Treaty (qv) provides for the committee to have a maximum of

350 members when the EU has expanded to 27 member states; Ireland will continue to have nine members on the committee. See website: *www.esc.eu.int.*

economic duress. Concept by which consent (eg in a contract) is treated in law as revocable where the apparent consent is induced by illegitimate pressure (eg threatened breach of contract unless the contract is renegotiated). See *Universal Tankerships v International Transport Workers Federation* [1983] 1 AC 366; *Atlas Express Ltd v Kafco* [1989] 1 All ER 641. See also *Smelter Corp of Ireland v O'Driscoll* [1977] IR 305 where 'fundamental unfairness' negatived valid consent.

economic relations. See UNLAWFUL INTERFERENCE IN ECONOMIC RELATIONS.

economic loss. Damages may be recovered where a negligent act has caused economic loss: *McShane Fruit v Johnston Haulage Co Ltd* [1997] 1 ILRM 86, HC. The quality of damage is immaterial in Irish law; damage may be to property, to the person, financial or economic – the fact that damage is economic is not itself a bar to recovery (*McShane* case).

It has been held that it is foreseeable that there will be economic loss and possible loss of profits if property in a warehouse is damaged: *Egan v Sisk* [1986] ILRM 283. It has also been held that where economic loss flows directly from the failure of the Rent Tribunal to comply with natural and constitutional justice, then damages may be recoverable by an injured party: *Beatty & Beatty v Rent Tribunal* [2003] ITLR (2 June), HC.

See 'Pure economic loss – can defendants avoid paying for it?' by Byron Wade BL in *Bar Review* (November 2000) 115.

ecu. European currency unit. The Minister is empowered to issue coins denominated in ecu but they are not legal tender for the payment of any amount; they are intended to be *commemorative coins* eg to mark the Irish Presidency of the EC: Decimal Currency Act 1990, s 2.

A company was entitled to file its accounts in ecus as well as the currency in which they were drawn up: EC (Accounts) Regulations 1993, SI No 396 of 1993. The ecu has been replaced by the euro. All references to the ecu in any legal instrument, including legislative and statutory provisions, are to be interpreted as references to the euro, at the rate of one euro to one ecu: art 2 of Regulation (EC) 1103/97

of 17 June 1997. See ECONOMIC AND MONETARY UNION; EURO; EXCHANGE RATE POLICY.

education. Education essentially is the teaching and training of a child to make the best possible use of his inherent and potential capacities, physical, mental and moral: *Ryan v Attorney-General* [1965] IR 294.

Prior to the Education Act 1998, it was held that many important decisions relating to educational policy had no foundation in the State's laws; they had no statutory force and the sanction which ensured compliance with them was not a legal one but the undeclared understanding that the Department of Education would withhold financial assistance in the event of non-compliance: Costello J in *Callaghan v Co Meath Vocational Education Committee* (1990) Irish Times, 21 November, HC.

Primary education derived its legal status from the Stanley Letter of 1831, and from Royal Charters in 1845 and 1861. Secondary education was governed by the Intermediate Education (Ireland) Acts 1878 and 1924. The system of technical education was co-ordinated by the Vocational Education Act 1930, while higher education relies on royal charters, university legislation (eg University of Limerick Act 1989; Universities Act 1997) and the Higher Education Authority Act 1971, and the National Council for Educational Awards Act 1979. The Dublin Institute of Technology has been established on a statutory basis and given greater independence and authority, as have the Institutes of Technology (formerly called Regional Technical Colleges): Dublin Institute of Technology Acts 1992 and 1994; Regional Technical Colleges Acts 1992, 1994 and 1999.

Under the Education Act 1998, the functions of the Minister are: (a) to determine national education policy, (b) to ensure that there is available to every person resident in the State, support services and a level and quality of education appropriate to meeting the needs and ability of that person, and (c) to plan and co-ordinate the provision of education in recognised schools (EA 1998, s 7(1)). Persons include persons with a disability or who have special educational needs.

Parents may be restrained from leaving their children at a school where they had not been enrolled: *Fr Carmody (Scoil Mochna) v Meehan & Cullen* (1993) Irish Times, 15 September, HC. See *Minister for*

Education v Letterkenny RTC [1995] 1 ILRM 438, SC; *FN v Minister for Education* [1995] 1 IR 409, HC; *Greally v Minister for Education* [1999] 1 IR 1, HC and ELR 106. See 'The Duration of Primary Education' by Oran Doyle BL in (2002) 10 ISLR 222. See website: *www.education.ie*. [Bibliography: Farry; Glendenning.] See ACADEMIC FREEDOM; COMMITTEE OF THE REGIONS; COMPTROLLER AND AUDITOR GENERAL; COPENHAGEN DECLARATION; CORPORAL PUNISHMENT; EXAMINATION RESULTS; EXEMPLARY DAMAGES; EUROPEAN CONVENTION ON HUMAN RIGHTS; MATURE STUDENT; SCHOOL; SCHOOL AUTHORITY'S DUTY; STATE EXAMINATIONS COMMISSION; SUSPENSION; UNIVERSITY.

education, advancement of. See CHARITIES.

education and EU. The EC is required to contribute to the development of quality education by encouraging co-operation between member states and, if necessary, supporting and supplementing their action, while fully respecting the responsibility of the member states for the content of teaching and the organisation of education systems and their cultural and linguistic diversity: EC Treaty, art 149 of the consolidated (2002) version. See COPENHAGEN DECLARATION.

education and taxation. Tax relief is available in respect of fees paid to private colleges for full-time, third-level education and for fees paid for part-time, third-level education: Taxes Consolidation Act 1997, ss 474 and 475 as amended by Finance Act 2000, s 21. Tax relief is now also allowable in respect of *postgraduate fees* paid in publicly funded colleges in this State and in the EU, as well as in private colleges in the State; approved courses must be at least one year's duration and must lead to a postgraduate award based on a thesis or examination (TCA 1997, s 475A inserted by FA 2000, s 21). Some previous restrictions have been removed eg on repeat years, on individuals taking more than one course, on individuals already holding a third level qualification, and on certain courses previously excluded eg medicine, veterinary medicine and teacher training: Finance Act 2001, s 29.

Capital allowances are available in relation to capital expenditure incurred on certain buildings used for third-level education, provided that at least 50% of the qualifying expenditure is provided from private sources; the scheme is extended to 31 July 2006: Taxes Consolidation Act 1997, s 843 as amended by Finance Act 2002, s 35 and Finance Act 2004, s 27.

education and the Constitution. The State acknowledges that the primary and natural educator of the child is the family and guarantees to respect the inalienable right and duty of parents to provide, according to their means, for the religious and moral, intellectual, physical and social education of their children: 1937 Constitution, art 42(1). Parents are free to provide this education in their homes or in private schools or in schools recognised or established by the State (1937 Constitution, art 42(2)).

The State shall, however, as guardian of the common good, require in view of actual conditions that children receive a *certain minimum education*, moral, intellectual and social (1937 Constitution, art 42(3)(2)). The State has the power to define the minimum standard: *Re School Attendance Bill 1942* [1943] IR 334. The fact that the legislature had not defined what constituted a *certain minimum education* did not prevent a district judge from pronouncing a formal order of conviction or acquittal as the case may be: School Attendance Act 1926; *DPP v Best* [1999] Irish Times, 28 July, SC overturning *DPP v Best* [1998] 2 ILRM 549, HC. For new provisions regarding a *certain minimum education*, see NATIONAL EDUCATIONAL WELFARE BOARD.

The duty of the State is to provide *for* free primary education and does not have a duty to provide it: 1937 Constitution, art 42(4); *Crowley v Ireland* [1980] IR 102. Where a child has special educational needs which cannot be provided by the parents or guardian, the State is obliged by virtue of art 42(5) of the Constitution to cater for the special needs in order to vindicate the child's constitutional rights: *Comerford v Minister for Education* [1997] 2 ILRM 134, HC.

There is a constitutional obligation upon the State to provide *for* free primary education for profoundly handicapped children in as full and positive a manner as it had done for other members of the community: *O'Donoghue v Minister for Health* [1996] 2 IR 20, HC. The Supreme Court has held that the constitutional obligation of the State to provide *for* free primary education was owed to children and not to adults and consequently the obligation stopped at the age of 18: *Sinnott v Minister for Education* [2001] 2 IR 545, SC. See also *Downey v Minister for Education* [2001] 2 IR 727, HC.

It has been held that art 42 of the Constitution is a complex provision embodying several elements and the court must adopt a global approach in construing it: *O'Sheil v Minister for Education* [1999] 2 ILRM 241, HC.

Damages may be awarded for unlawful interference with the constitutional right to free primary education pursuant to the 1937 Constitution, art 42(4): *Hayes v Ireland & INTO* [1987] ILRM 651; *Conway v Ireland & INTO* [1991] ILRM 497, SC.

See DISABLED PERSON AND EDUCATION; EXEMPLARY DAMAGES.

education awards. Awards of certificates, diplomas, degrees and post-graduate degrees awarded by educational bodies relying on powers they possess themselves (eg universities) or relying on powers of other bodies.

Prior to the establishment of the National Qualifications Authority of Ireland: (a) the National Council for Educational Awards had wide powers as regards higher educational awards outside the universities: National Council for Educational Awards Act 1979 repealed by the Qualifications (Education and Training) Act 1999, s 37; (b) the National Council for Vocational Awards which was established in 1991 on a non-statutory basis, made vocational awards; its work and that of the NCEA is subsumed into the new bodies established under Q(ET)A 1999; (c) An Foras Áiseanna Saothair (FÁS) had authority to award certificates of the attainment of standards recommended by FÁS: Industrial Training Act 1967, s 9(2)(d); Labour Services Act 1987, and it may continue to do so if it obtains the delegation provided for under the 1999 Act; (d) the Dublin Institute of Technology continues to have power to confer diplomas, certificates or other educational awards; it may also confer degrees, postgraduate degrees and honorary awards by order of the Minister: Dublin Institute of Technology Act 1992, ss 5(1)(b) and 5(2); (e) the universities continue to have wide power to award diplomas, certificates and degrees. For FÁS, see website: *www.fas.ie.* For the new arrangements for educational and training awards, see NATIONAL QUALIFICATIONS AUTHORITY OF IRELAND.

education fees. See EDUCATION AND TAXATION.

education plan. A plan for the appropriate education of a student with special educational needs (qv), prepared following an assessment of the student: Education for Persons with Special Educational Needs Act 2004, ss 3 and 8. Prior to the assessment being carried out, the principal of the school is required to consult with the parents of the student. Where the arrangement of an assessment is not practicable, the principal must request the National Council for Special Education to arrange for an assessment.

The content of an education plan must contain: (a) the nature and degree of the child's abilities, skills and talents; (b) the nature and degree of the child's special educational needs and how those needs affect his educational development; (c) the present level of educational performance of the child; (d) the special educational needs of the child; (e) the special education and related support services to be provided to the child to enable the child to benefit from education and to participate in the life of the school; (f) where appropriate, the special education and related services to be provided to the child to enable the child to effectively make the transition from pre-school education to primary school education; (g) where appropriate, the special education and related support services to be provided to the child to enable the child to effectively make the transition from primary school education to post-primary school education, and (h) the goals which the child is to achieve over a period not exceeding 12 months (EPSENA 2004, s 9).

There is provision for regular reviews of the education plan (EPSENA 2004, s 11). The person preparing or reviewing the plan, must, at the appropriate time, have regard to the provision which will need to be made to assist the child to continue his education or training on becoming an adult (EPSENA 2004, s 15). See DISABLED PERSON AND EDUCATION; SPECIAL EDUCATIONAL NEEDS.

educational establishment. Means a pre-school service, a primary or post-primary school, an institution providing adult continuing or further education, or a university or any other third-level or higher-level institution, whether or not supported by public funds: Equal Status Act 2000, s 7(1). An educational establishment must not discriminate on any *discriminatory ground* in relation to: (a) admission or conditions of admission, (b) access to any course, facility or benefit, (c) any other term or condition of participation, (d) expulsion of a student or any sanction against a student (ESA 2000, s 7(2)).

There are exceptions eg primary and post-primary schools are not regarded as discriminatory just because they are single-gender, and a seminary may restrict admission to students of one gender or religious belief (ESA 2000, s 7(3)). As regards grants and discrimination, see ESA 2000, s 7(5) inserted by Equality Act 2004, s 50. For the ten discriminatory grounds, see DISCRIMINATION. [Bibliography: Reid M.] See also SEXUAL HARASSMENT.

educational grants. 'Non-promotional educational grants represent the only acceptable mechanism for financial support by the pharmaceutical and medical manufacturing industries to individual doctors.': Medical Council, *A Guide to Ethical Conduct and Behaviour* (6th edn, 2004) para 10.1.

educational welfare officer. A person employed by the National Educational Welfare Board with a variety of functions: Education (Welfare) Act 2000, ss 11 and 30, eg see SCHOOL DISCIPLINE; NATIONAL EDUCATIONAL WELFARE BOARD; YOUNG PERSONS IN EMPLOYMENT REGISTER.

EEA Agreement. The Agreement on the *European Economic Area*: European Communities (Amendment) Act 1993, s 1(1). This is an agreement between the EEC and EFTA and extends the EC Treaty concerning the internal market to EFTA contracting states. The European Economic Area in April 2004 comprised the then 15 EU States and Norway, Iceland and Liechtenstein. The agreement enables these three latter States to have the benefits of the EU's single market without the full privileges and responsibilities of EU membership. Ratification of the EEA Agreement by this State is effected by the EC(A)A 1993, ss 3 and 4. See Copyright and Related Rights Act 2000, ss 2(1), 41, 187, 206 and 326. See EXHAUSTION PRINCIPLE; EFTA; REGULATION.

EEC. [European Economic Community (qv).]

EEIG. [European Economic Interest Grouping (qv).]

EEJ-Net. [European Extra-Judicial Network (qv).]

eel. Legal regulation of eel fishing is provided for in the Fisheries (Amendment) Act 1994, Pt III. Provision has been made for responsibility for issuing eel fishery authorisations to be transferred from the Minister to regional fisheries boards: Fisheries (Amendment) Act 1999, s 27. See SALMON DEALER'S LICENCE.

effects. A person's property. See *Mitchell v Mitchell* [1820] 5 Madd 69.

effluent. See SEWAGE EFFLUENT; TRADE EFFLUENT.

EFTA. [European Free Trade Association.] The trade association established in 1960 to eliminate trade tariffs on industrial products between certain countries. Originally comprised of Austria, Denmark, Norway, Portugal, Sweden, Switzerland, and the UK. The UK, Denmark, Portugal, Austria, Finland and Sweden left EFTA on joining the EC. EFTA now comprises of Iceland, Liechtenstein, Norway and Switzerland.

See website: *www.efta.int.* See EEA AGREEMENT; EXECUTION OF JUDGMENT; FOREIGN JUDGMENTS, ENFORCEMENT OF; JURISDICTION; LUGANO CONVENTION.

eg. See EXEMPLI GRATIA.

egm. See EXTRAORDINARY GENERAL MEETING.

ei incumbit probatio qui dicet, non qui negat. [The burden of proof is on him who alleges, and not on him who denies.] See BURDEN OF PROOF.

ei qui affirmat, non ei qui negat, incumbit probatio. [The burden of proof lies on him who affirms a fact, not on him who denies it.] See BURDEN OF PROOF.

Éire. The name of the State in the Irish language: 1937 Constitution, art 4. The name of the State in the English language is *Ireland.* See STATE.

ejectment. The recovery of possession of land. In proceedings for ejectment for non-payment of rent or overholding, the *civil bill* is required to specify certain matters eg names of landlord and lessor, and tenant or tenants respectively, the nature of the tenancy, and the rent: Circuit Court Rules 2001 Ord 51, r 1(2). See also Ord 5, r 2.

Similar provisions for ejectment apply in the District Court which has jurisdiction where the rent does not exceed £5,000 (€6,349) per annum. See Deasy's Act 1860, ss 52 and 72; Courts Act 1991, s 4. See DCR 1997 Ord 47 as amended by District

Court (Ejectment) Rules 1999, SI No 218 of 1999 allowing renewal of a warrant of possession if not issued within six months of the order. However, as regards rent disputes in tenancies of dwellings under recent legislation, see PART 4 TENANCY, TERMINATION OF; RENT; RENT ARREARS; TENANCY DISPUTE.

An action by a personal representative to recover land in succession to the owner is not statute barred (qv) for twelve years: *Gleeson v Feehan & O'Meara* [1991] ILRM 783, SC. See WRIT.

ejusdem generis. [Of the same kind or nature.] The maxim that where particular words are followed by general words, the general words are limited to the same kind or genus, as the particular words eg *offensive trades* are particularly defined in the Public Health (Ireland) Act 1878, s 128 and all involve the collection of large quantities of animal matter; such trades are also generally defined as consisting of *any other noxious or offensive trade, business or manufacture*; a trade to come within the general category would have to have the features of the particular definition. See *Re Miller* [1889] 61 LT 365. See also *Cronin v Lunham Brothers Ltd* [1986] ILRM 415; *C W Shipping Ltd v Limerick Harbour Commissioners* [1989] ILRM 416, HC; *RDS v Revenue Commissioners* [1998] 2 ILRM 487, HC and [2000] 1 IR 270, SC. See INTERPRETATION OF LEGISLATION.

elderly law. See OLD AGE.

election. Choice.

(1) The equitable doctrine of election by which a person who takes a benefit under an instrument must accept or reject the instrument as a whole eg if there is in the will of X *a gift of A's property to B and a gift to A*, A can only take the gift by giving his own property or its value to B. Alternatively he can *elect* to keep his own property and reject the gift. See *Re Sullivan* [1917] IR 38. [Bibliography: Wylie (3).]

(2) In a will where there is a devise or bequest to a spouse, the spouse may *elect* to take either that gift or the share to which she is entitled as a legal right (qv). In default of election the spouse is entitled under the will only. See Succession Act 1965, s 115; also *Reilly v McEntee* [1984] ILRM 572.

(3) The right of an accused to chose to be tried summarily or on indictment. Unless the statute provides for election by the accused, it is the sole right of the

prosecutor to determine whether the charge should be prosecuted summarily or on indictment: *DPP v O'Donnell* [2003] 1 ILRM 71, HC. A district judge, however, must decline jurisdiction to try summarily if he forms the opinion that the offence is of a non-minor nature. See INDICTABLE OFFENCE; SUMMARY OFFENCE; SUMMARY PROCEEDINGS.

(4) The system by which the choice of the people is determined in contests for vacancies in parliament and in local government. It has been held that the system by which candidates names are placed in an alphabetical order on the ballot paper, constitutes a reasonable regulation of elections to Dáil Éireann: *O'Reilly v Minister for the Environment* [1987] ILRM 290. Elections for the Dáil and European Parliament, Presidential elections, referenda, local elections and elections to Údarás na Gaeltachta can all be held on the same day: Electoral Act 1992, s 165; Regulations 2004, SI No 237 of 2004.

The conduct of elections and referenda is the responsibility of the county registrars (qv) outside the Counties of Dublin and Cork; in these latter counties it is the responsibility of the sheriff. RTÉ has a duty to maintain a fair balance in respect of its coverage of elections and candidates ie to be fair to all interests concerned, to be objective and to be impartial: *Madigan v Radio Telefís Éireann* [1994] 2 ILRM 472, HC.

Failure to allow a person to vote at an election due to a mistaken identity, does not give rise to an actionable negligence: *Graham v Ireland* [1998] 2 IR 88, HC. See RSC Ord 97. See Electoral Regulations 1992 and 1999, SI No 314 of 1999. See ADVERTISEMENT; CONSTITUENCY; DÁIL ELECTION; ISLAND, POLLING ON; PRESIDENT OF IRELAND; FRANCHISE; EUROPEAN CONVENTION ON HUMAN RIGHTS; EUROPEAN ELECTION; LOCAL ELECTION; PROPORTIONAL REPRESENTATION; RECOUNT; SIGN; SPOILT VOTE.

election agent. A candidate may appoint one election agent to assist him generally in relation to a Dáil election: Electoral Act 1992, s 59. The candidate or his election agent may appoint agents to be present on the candidate's behalf in polling stations and at the counting of votes (EA 1992, s 60); they may also appoint *personation agents* (qv). See also Presidential Elections Act 1993, ss 33–35; Referendum Act 1994, ss 26–27; European Parliament Elections Act 1997, Sch 2, rr 24–26. See PERSONATION AGENT.

election deposit. The High Court has held that the requirement for candidates to pay deposits in Dáil and European elections is unconstitutional, being repugnant to art 40.1 of the Constitution: *Redmond v Minister for the Environment* [2001] 4 IR 61, HC.

As an alternative to election deposits, there is now a requirement for a candidate at a Dáil election, who is not in possession of a certificate of political affiliation (ie confirmation that the candidate is a candidate of a registered political party) to have their nomination paper assented to by 30 electors (excluding the candidate or proposer) who are registered Dáil electors in the relevant constituency: Electoral Act 1992, s 46 (4A) inserted by Electoral (Amendment) Act 2002, s 1.

There are similar requirements for nomination papers in European Parliament and local elections, except that the number of assentors is 60 and 15 respectively (E(A)A 2002, ss 2 and 3, inserting respectively s 12(1A) in the European Parliament Elections Act 1997, and inserting art 14(6A) in the Local Elections Regulations 1995, SI No 297 of 1995).

An application by three aspiring non-party Dáil candidates for an order directing Returning Officers to include their names on the ballot papers in their constituencies without meeting the 30 assentor requirement failed in the High Court on the grounds of convenience and on jurisdictional issues, although the judge said that the applicants' challenge to the new requirements had 'considerable merits': *King, Stack and Riordan v Ireland and A-G* (2002) Irish Times, 3 May, HC. The applicants' case was that the new assentor requirement was discriminatory, unconstitutional and a barrier to entry to the electoral process.

election documents. Every notice, bill, poster or similar document having reference to an election, except those published by the returning officer, must bear on its face the name and address of the printer and of the publisher thereof: Electoral Act 1992, s 140 and ss 166–170.

election expenses. There is provision for the reimbursement out of public funds of the *election expenses* (up to a limit of £5,000/€6,349) of all candidates at Dáil elections, successful or unsuccessful, who have either been elected or have received at least one quarter of the *quota* (qv): Electoral Act 1997, s 21. The Minister may make regulations for the reimbursement of election expenses of candidates for the European Parliament (EA 1997, s 21(2)). There are specified limits placed on the *campaign expenses* of candidates and of political parties; there is provision for candidates to allocate any proportion of their limit to their political party (EA 1997, ss 27–32, 34–44). There are similar provisions for the limitation of expenditure at European and Presidential elections (EA 1997, s 33, 42, 45–46, 50–62). For amendments to EA 1997, see Electoral (Amendment) Act 1998; Electoral (Amendment) Act 2002, s 4 and Electoral (Amendment) (No 2) Act 2002.

There is no limit imposed on expenditure at *local elections* and no provision for reimbursement of election expenses; however, there is a requirement for channelling the expenditure through designated individuals and for disclosure of election expenses, with disqualification being one sanction for failing to comply with the requirement: Local Elections (Disclosure of Donations and Election Expenses) Act 1999. The disclosure must be by way of a statement in a prescribed form (LE(DDEE)A 1999, s 13 and SI No 689 of 2003).

Members of the public may inspect *Expenditure Statements* provided by qualified political parties showing how they used funding which they received from the Exchequer, and the *statement of expenditure* incurred by candidates and political parties at Dáil bye-elections and the European Parliament election, at the Standards in Public Office Commission, 18 Lower Leeson Street, Dublin 2. See website: *www.sipo.ie*.

It has been held by the High Court that that the exemption of publicly funded facilities for outgoing members of the Dáil for the purposes of election expenses control is unconstitutional: *Kelly v Minister for the Environment* [2002] IEHC 38. The court held that such facilities (eg postage, telephone, fax, photocopying etc) could be said to be unfair and discriminatory to other candidates. The decision of the High Court has been upheld by the Supreme Court: *Kelly v Minister for the Environment* [2003] 2 ILRM 81, SC.

The High Court upheld the claim made by the Minister for Health that as neither the constituency unit in his Department nor his special advisors were engaged in electoral work, their cost did not require to be included in his statement of expenditure: *Sinnott v Martin* (2004) Irish Times, 31 January, HC.

The Electoral (Amendment) (No 2) Act 2002 extends the time for furnishing election expenses statements only for the 2002 general election until after the Supreme Court has made its pronouncement. See EUROPEAN ELECTION; POLITICAL DONATION.

election of local government. See LOCAL ELECTION.

election petition, European. A European election may be questioned only by a petition to the High Court; leave to present the petition must be sought from the court not later than seven days after the declaration of the result and, if leave is granted, the petition must be lodged not later than three days thereafter: European Parliament Elections Act 1997, s 21 and Sch 2 rr 130–146. An application for leave to present a petition may be made by any person registered as a European elector in the constituency or by the Director of Public Prosecutions (EPEA 1997, s 21(2)(c) and Sch 2, r 130). The court may require a lodgment of up to £5,000 (€6,349) as security for costs (EPEA 1997, s 21(5)). See also Electoral (Amendment) Act 2004, ss 15–16.

election petition, local. The procedure by which the validity of a local election may be questioned; the petition must be presented to the Circuit Court: Local Elections (Petitions and Disqualifications) Act 1974 as amended by Local Elections (Disclosure of Donations and Expenditure) Act 1999, s 23.

The petition may be presented by any person who has reached the age of eighteen years, or by the Director of Public Prosecutions (qv) where it appears to him that a local election may have been affected by the commission of electoral offences (LE(PD)A 1974, ss 2 and 4). See also *Cowan v Attorney-General* [1961] IR 411. For the rules governing a petition to the court to question a local election, pursuant to LE(PD)A 1974, see Circuit Court Rules 2001 Ord 58. See also Electoral (Amendment) Act 2004, ss 15–16.

election petition, parliamentary. A petition to the High Court questioning a Dáil election: Electoral Act 1992, s 132 and Sch 3 as amended by Electoral Act 1997, s 44. The petition may be presented by a person registered as a Dáil elector or the DPP; however, leave of the court must first be obtained to present a petition (EA 1997, s 44(b)). The Dáil election may be questioned on the grounds of want of eligibility, the commission of an electoral offence, obstruction of or interference with or other hindrance to the conduct of the election or mistake or other irregularity which is likely to have affected the result of the election (EA 1992, s 132(5)). The court must either: (a) dismiss the petition, (b) declare the correct result, or (c) declare that the election or a specified part is void in which event a fresh election must take place. It is an offence to withdraw a petition corruptly (EA 1992, s 155). As regards petitions in European elections, see European Parliament Elections Act 1997, ss 130–146 as amended by Electoral Act 1997, s 45. See also Electoral (Amendment) Act 2004, ss 15–16. See RSC Ord 97. See REFERENDUM PETITION.

election petition, presidential. A person is able to question the result of a presidential election by way of petition to the High Court: Presidential Elections Act 1993, ss 57–58. Leave of the Court to present a petition may be sought by the DPP or a candidate or his agent (PEA 1993, s 57(6)). The procedures are similar to those applying to Dáil election petitions (PEA 1993, s 58).

electoral law. Reforming legislation enacted in 2001 provides for: (a) improvements in the process of registration of electors, (b) the inclusion of photographs and political party emblems on ballot papers, (c) changes in the conditions for the registration of political parties, and (d) the use of voting machines and electronic vote counting at elections: Electoral (Amendment) Act 2001. Provision has been made for the use of voting machines and electronic vote counting in designated constituencies at a referendum: SI No 460 of 2002.

Also the Electoral Act 1997 is amended to improve its operation for candidates, election agents, political parties and the *Standards in Public Office Commission*. The European Parliament Elections Act 1997 is also amended, and there are consequential amendments to other election legislation. See also Electoral Regulations 2002, SI No 144 of 2002, as amended by SI No 175 of 2004. Provision was made in 2004 for the introduction of electronic voting by primary legislation, rather than by Ministerial order under s 48 of E(A)A 2001, see ELECTRONIC VOTING.

electoral offences. A variety of offences including personation, bribery, undue influence, interfering with ballot boxes, disorderly conduct at election meetings, breach of secrecy, voting when not entitled to be registered, handling of ballot paper by candidate, canvassing in the vicinity of a polling station: Electoral Act 1992, ss 133–160. See also EA 1992, ss 166–170; Presidential Elections Act 1993, s 59; European Parliament Elections Act 1997, Sch 2, rr 102–129.

electrical contracting. Under draft legislation, it is proposed to provide for a system of regulation, in the interests of public safety, of the electrical contracting sector in Ireland: Electricity Regulation (Amendment) Bill 2003. The main provisions proposed are: (a) an extension of the functions for the *Commission for Energy Regulation* (qv) to oversee safety and technical standards in the electrical contracting sector in Ireland; and (b) imposition of an obligation on electrical contractors, electricians and employers of electricians operating in factory environments, to register with an *Electrical Contracting Supervisory Body* which will supervise electricians, electrical contractors and registered employers and ensure adherence with appropriate technical codes.

electricity. Provision had been made for a 5% *employee shareholding scheme* in the Electricity Supply Board without having to wait for the passage of legislation to change the status of the company from a statutory corporation to a plc under the Companies Acts: Electricity (Supply) (Amendment) Act 2001. The break-even mandate enshrined in the Electricity Supply Act 1927, s 21 is also repealed in order that the ESB can make profits and pay dividends (E(S)(A)A 2001, s 10).

Provision has been made to impose on the ESB certain *public service obligations* (*PSO*); these require ESB to purchase until 31 December 2019, the output of certain peat and renewable, sustainable or alternative electricity generating stations, in the interests of security of supply and environmental protection: Electricity Regulation – Public Service Obligations Order 2002, SIs Nos 217 and 614 of 2002. Provision is made for the introduction of a PSO levy to compensate ESB for the additional cost incurred. The statutory borrowing limit of the ESB has been increased from IR£1.6 billion to €6 billion to fund its extensive capital expenditure programme: Electricity (Supply) (Amendment) Act 2004.

Regulations have been made which apply to the generation, transformation, conversion, switching, controlling, regulating, rectification, storage, transmission, distribution; provision, measurement or use of electrical energy in every place of work: Safety Health and Welfare at Work (General Application) Regulations 1993, SI No 44 of 1993, reg 33. There are separate requirements for mines and quarries: Mines and Quarries Act 1965. For Electricity Supply Board, see website: *www.esb.ie*. See ELECTRICAL CONTRACTING; SUSTAINABLE ENERGY IRELAND.

electricity regulation. Market liberalisation of the electricity industry was provided for in 1999, giving effect to Directive (EC) 96/92: Electricity Regulation Act 1999. Under the 1999 Act, a *Commission for Electricity Regulation* was established. It was renamed the *Commission for Energy Regulation* in 2002 with extended powers to regulate also the natural gas sector: Gas (Interim) (Regulation) Act 2002. See SI No 632 of 2003. See BORD GÁIS; COMMISSION FOR ENERGY REGULATION; ELECTRICAL CONTRACTING.

electricity supply. It is an offence unlawfully and maliciously to cut or injure any electric line or work with intent to cut off or diminish any *supply of electricity*: Electricity (Supply) Act 1927, s 111. The relay of cable television and radio signals to domestic householders, transmitted by means of electric current, does not constitute the *supply of electricity*: *Brosnan v Cork Communications* [1992] 10 ILT Dig 268, HC. A person who steals electricity is guilty of an offence; the offence is committed by interference with a meter or having in one's possession anything designed to interfere with a meter, or by dishonestly using any electricity: Energy (Miscellaneous Provisions) Act 1995, s 15. See LIABILITY, STATUTORY EXEMPTION FROM.

electronic apparatus. Increasingly, electronic and other equipment, including cameras have an important role in establishing factual evidence in relation to offences. In proving specified road traffic offences (e g exceeding the speed limit, dangerous driving, parking in a dangerous position) it is not necessary to prove that the electronic apparatus (including a camera) was accurate or in good working order; it suffices to tender evidence from which the constituent of the offence can be inferred, by measurements or other indications which were given by the apparatus and contained in the record produced by the apparatus: Road Traffic Act 2002, s 21. See VIDEO RECORDING.

electronic commerce. [e-commerce; e-business.] Commercial activity which takes place by means of connected computers. Electronic commerce can take place between a user and a vendor through an online information service or via the Internet.

The Electronic Commerce Act 2000 was enacted with the objective of creating a legal framework for electronic commerce in order to facilitate the growth of e-business and electronic transactions. The Act also transposes into domestic law the European Union's *Electronic Signatures Directive 1999/93/EC* which has the aim of harmonising the legal acceptance of certain *electronic signatures* throughout the EU. Many sections of the Act are based on the UN Model Law on Electronic Commerce and on certain articles of the EU draft Electronic Commerce Directive.

The Act provides for legal recognition of electronic signatures, electronic originals, electronic contracts, retention of electronic documents, admissibility of electronic evidence in court, prohibition of fraud in electronic signatures, consumer law and defamation law to apply, accreditation and supervision of certification service providers, and domain name registration.

The legislation was signed into law on 10 July 2000 when President Mary McAleese used an *electronic signature* to sign the Bill, having first signed the Bill with a pen. It is the first Bill signed electronically. The government announced in July 2000 a campaign to target small businesses with financial incentives and assistance to help them to prepare and to implement 'e-commerce' strategies and to develop Internet sites; see website: *www.empower.ie*. A survey conducted by the Central Statistics Office in 2003, revealed that 1 in 6 computer users in the Republic of Ireland have bought goods over the web. The most popular purchases were travel, holiday accommodation, books, magazines, videos and DVDs.

See *E-Commerce Legislation: Facilitating Requirements for Export Expansion*, McCann Fitzgerald Solicitors and Institute of International Trade in Ireland (July 2000). See 'Competition Law and the Internet' by Stephen Dodd BL in *Bar Review* (December 2000) 133. See website: *www.lawreform.ie/lawunderreview/*. [Bibliography: Haigh; Kelleher & Murray.] See ADMISSIBILITY OF EVIDENCE; CERTIFICATION SERVICE PROVIDER; COMMERCIAL COURT; CONSUMER CONTRACT; DIGITAL MEDIA DEVELOPMENT LTD; DISTANCE CONTRACTS; ELECTRONIC CONTRACT; ELECTRONIC FORM; ELECTRONIC SIGNATURE; ELECTRONIC ORIGINAL; ELECTRONICALLY SUPPLIED SERVICES; FRAUD; INFORMATION SOCIETY SERVICES; INTERNET; M-COMMERCE; RESIDENCE; WRITING.

electronic communications networks. Regulations have been made governing access to, and interconnection of, electronic communications networks and associated facilities: SI No 305 of 2003. These implement Directive (EC) 2002/19, the Access Directive. The aim of the Regulations is to establish a regulatory framework for the relationship between suppliers of networks and services that will result in sustainable competition, interoperability of electronic communications services and consumer benefits. Provision is also made for: (a) the authorisation of these networks and services, SI No 306 of 2003, implementing Directive (EC) 2002/20, the Authorisation Directive; (b) a common regulatory framework, SI No 307 of 2003, implementing Directive (EC) 2002/21; and (c) universal service and users' rights, SI No 308 of 2003, implementing Directive (EC) 2002/22. See also SI No 80 of 2003. See COMMISSION FOR COMMUNICATIONS REGULATION.

electronic contract. Means a contract concluded wholly or partly by means of an *electronic communication*: Electronic Commerce Act 2000, s 2(1). *Electronic communication* is widely defined to include communications in electronic form, excluding speech unless the speech is processed at its destination by an automatic voice recognition system (ECA 2000, s 2(1)).

An electronic contract will not be denied legal effect, validity or enforceability, solely on the grounds that is, wholly or partly, in electronic form or has been concluded, wholly or partly, by way of electronic communication (ECA 2000, s 19(1)). In the formation of a contract, an offer, acceptance of an offer or any related communication, may be communicated by electronic means (ECA 2000, s 19(2)). Unless the parties agree otherwise, an electronic communication is taken to have been *sent* when it enters an information system outside the control of the originator, and to have been *received* when it enters the information system designated by the addressee, and is taken also to have been sent and received where the originator and addressee have their place of business or where they reside, if they do not have a place of business (ECA 2000, s 21).

If a signature is required, an *electronic signature* may be used (ECA 2000, s 13). Where a signature requires to be witnessed, an *advanced electronic signature* is required (ECA 2000, s 14). If a *seal* is required, this requirement can be met by the use of an advanced electronic signature of the person by whom it is required to be sealed (ECA 2000, s 16).

All electronic contracts within the State are subject to all existing consumer law, and the role of the Director of Consumer Affairs applies equally to consumer transactions, whether conducted electronically or non-electronically (ECA 2000, s 15). See CONSUMER CONTRACT; DISTANCE CONTRACTS; ELECTRONIC FORM; FRAUD; INTERNET; SIGNATURE; WRITING.

electronic court. See COMMERCIAL COURT.

electronic form. *Information* must not be denied legal effect, validity or enforceability solely on the grounds that it is wholly or partly in electronic form, whether as an *electronic communication* or otherwise: Electronic Commerce Act 2000, s 9.

Excluded from this provision is: (a) the law governing the creation, execution, amendment, variation or revocation of a will or codicil or a trust, or an enduring power of attorney, (b) the law governing the manner in which an interest in real property may be created, acquired, disposed of or registered, other than a contract for the creation, acquisition or disposal of such interests, (c) the law governing the making of an affidavit or a statutory or sworn declaration, (d) the rules, practices or procedures of a court or tribunal (ECA 2000, s 10). *Information*

includes data, all forms of writing and other text, images (including maps and cartographic material), sound, codes, computer programmes, software, databases and speech (ECA 2000, s 2(1)) Information which is required to be retained or produced, may be retained or produced in electronic form (ECA 2000, s 18). See Copyright and Related Rights Act 2000, s 86.

Any document or other information required or permitted to be given in writing, may be given in *electronic form*: (a) if at the time it was given it was reasonable to expect it would be readily accessible, and (b) the body receiving it has given its consent: Planning and Development Act 2000, s 248.

It is now possible to apply for and obtain a tax clearance certificate by electronic means: Finance Act 2002, s 127. See also Residential Tenancies Act 2004, s 130. See PLANNING REGISTER.

electronic mail. See EMAIL.

electronic money. Means monetary value as represented by a claim against the issuer of it, that is: (a) stored on an electronic device, (b) issued on receipt of funds of an amount not less in value than the monetary value issued, and (c) accepted as a means of payment by undertakings other than that issuer: EC (Electronic Money) Regulations 2002, SI No 221 of 2002 as amended by Central Bank and Financial Services Authority of Ireland Act 2003, s 35, Sch 2, and by Central Bank and Financial Services Authority of Ireland Act 2004, s 10(3), Sch 2.

Reference to 'e-money' means electronic money (SI No 221 of 2002, reg.2). Only the following may issue e-money: a credit institution or an electronic money institution; it is an offence for any other person to issue e-money (reg 6). An electronic money institution must not issue e-money if it receives funds in respect of the transaction which has a value which is less than the value of the e-money (reg 8). The maximum storage capacity of each issued electronic device must not exceed €5,000 (reg 10).

In a measure to prevent money laundering, certain designated bodies are required to take measures to establish the identity of any person for whom it proposes to provide a service: Criminal Justice Act 1994, s 31.

Electronic money institutions are now designated bodies under s 32(1) of the 1994 Act: SI No 216 of 2003.

electronic original. If by law or otherwise, information is required or permitted to be presented or retained in its original form, then the information may be presented or retained, as the case may be, in electronic form: Electronic Commerce Act 2000, s 17(1). There are requirements laid down eg there must exist a reliable assurance as to the integrity of the information from the time it was generated in its final form.

electronic record. The Revenue Commissioners are empowered to store records (eg taxpayer returns) electronically while preserving the value of such records so stored as evidence in legal proceedings: Taxes Consolidation Act 1997, s 1096B inserted by Finance Act 2002, s 135. The original records can be destroyed subject to compliance with the National Archives Act 1986.

electronic settlement. See CREST SYSTEM.

electronic signature. Means data in electronic form attached to, incorporated in or logically associated with other electronic data and which serves as a method of authenticating the purported originator; it includes an *advanced electronic signature*: Electronic Commerce Act 2000, s 2(1). Where by law or otherwise, the signature of a person or or of a public body is required or permitted, then an electronic signature may be used, if the person to whom it is to be given consents, and in the case of a public body if its information technology and procedural requirements are met (ECA 2000, s 13).

An *advanced electronic signature* means an electronic signature: (a) uniquely linked to the *signatory*, (b) capable of identifying the signatory, (c) created under means that are capable of being maintained by the signatory under his sole control, and (d) linked to the data to which it relates in such a manner that any subsequent change in the data is detectable (ECA 2000, s 2(1)).

A *signatory* means a person who holds a *signature creation device*, which is a device, such as configured software or hardware, used to generate *signature creation data*, which in turn means data, such as codes, passwords, algorithms or public cryptographic keys, used by a signatory in generating an electronic signature (ECA 2000, s 2(1)). A *signature verification data* means data used for the purpose of verifying an electronic signature (ECA 2000, s 2(1)).

For provisions dealing with signatures, witnessing of signatures, and documents under seal, see ELECTRONIC CONTRACT. For provisions dealing with signature verification, see CERTIFICATE SERVICE PROVIDER. See also DIGITAL SIGNATURE.

electronic tax return. Provision has been made for making electronic tax returns; the electronic transmission of information in response to an obligation to make a tax return will be treated as fulfilment of that obligation: Taxes Consolidation Act 1997, ss 917D–917N inserted by Finance Act 1999, s 209. Certain conditions must be met eg: (a) the transmission must be by a person approved by the Revenue Commissioners, (b) the transmission must comply with certain procedures and processes, (c) the transmission must incorporate the *digital signature* of the person making the transmission and (d) the receipt of the transmission must be acknowledged by the Revenue. See Taxes (Electronic Transmission of Certain Tax Returns) Order 2000, SI No 289 of 2000.

The legislation which permits the electronic filing of tax returns has been amended so that the Revenue's system can be used to receive most other types of information which a person is required to send to the Revenue: Finance Act 2001, s 235. See Taxes (Electronic Transmission of Certain Revenue Returns) Order 2001, SI No 112 of 2001; Taxes (Electronic Transmission of Income Tax and Capital Gains Tax) Order 2001, SI No 441 of 2001. See also SI No 194 of 2002.

The Revenue Commissioners are empowered to make regulations to require those taxpayers, specified in the regulations, to file their tax returns and to pay their tax liability electronically: Finance Act 2003, s 164. There is a requirement on the Revenue to exclude those taxpayers who cannot reasonably be expected to have the capacity to meet this obligation. See COMPUTERS; DIGITAL SIGNATURE; FAX; FINGERPRINTS; INTERNET.

electronic transaction. Provision has been made for electronic transactions of Irish Government Bonds: Central Bank Act 1997, s 63 as amended by Finance Act 2000, s 158. See STOCK EXCHANGE.

electronic transmission of documents. Provision has been made for the transmission of documents or information electronically in *commercial proceedings* (qv) on such terms as the judge may direct: RSC Ord 63A, r 6(1)(x) inserted by Rules of the Superior Courts (Commercial Proceedings) 2004, SI No 2 of 2004. The service or exchange of documents under these rules may be served or exchanged electronically where so specified by the President of the High Court by practice direction (r 31).

Such a practice direction may prescribe requirements as to: (a) the hardware and other equipment, diskettes or CD-ROMs and communications protocol or protocols to be employed by parties filing, serving or exchanging documents electronically; (b) the use of passwords, electronic signatures, digital signatures or other means of authenticating documents filed, served or exchanged electronically; (c) the use of firewalls, anti-virus tools or other devices or applications for the purpose of avoiding damage to the information system of the Courts Service or of any party or their solicitor or counsel; (d) compliance with practices or protocols for the purpose of ensuring that harmful, deleterious or offensive material does not enter the information system of the Courts Service or of any party or their solicitor or counsel; (e) the formatting, organising, identifying, coding and indexing of documents to be filed, served or exchanged electronically; (f) the manner in which documents filed, served or exchanged electronically, or copies of such documents, may be presented or otherwise used in Court (r 31(3)). See CASE BOOKLET; TRIAL BOOKLET.

electronic voting. In 2002, the government announced that it intended to extend electronic voting throughout the State for all elections by 2004, following the successful trial of electronic voting in several constituencies in the general election and Nice referendum in 2002. Statutory provision for electronic voting was proposed in the Electoral (Amendment) Bill 2004, which also provided for the establishment of an independent *Commission on Electronic Voting*.

The *interim* Commission, appointed pending enactment of the legislation, concluded in a report issued on 30 April 2004 that, having regard to the issues of secrecy, accuracy and testing as set out in its terms of reference, it was unable to recommend the use of the proposed system at the local and European elections and, by extension, at the referendum on citizenship which was

due to be held on 11 June 2004. The government deferred the replacement of the paper ballot by electronic voting to a later unspecified date.

Provision for the general introduction of electronic voting in primary legislation was subsequently enacted as the Electoral (Amendment) Act 2004. The Act, apart from establishing the Commission, provides for offences in relation to the unlawful interference with any voting system equipment (E(A)A 2004, s 2) or being in unlawful possession of a polling information card (E(A)A 2004, s 35). An *electronic voting system* means a voting system in which the votes are recorded and automatically counted and the results automatically tabulated by use of electronically operated apparatus (E(A)A 2004, s 4(1)). See BALLOT; COMMISSION ON ELECTRONIC VOTING; ELECTORAL LAW.

electronically supplied services. Includes: (a) website supply, web-hosting, distance maintenance of programmes and equipment, (b) supply of software and updating of it, (c) supply of images, text and information, and making databases available, (d) supply of music, films and games, including games of chance and gambling games, and of political, cultural, artistic, sporting, scientific and entertainment broadcasts and events, and (e) supply of distance teaching: Finance Act 2003, s 113. Communication between the supplier and the customer by electronic mail does not of itself mean that the service performed is an electronic service. This provision is part of a package of measures transposing Directive (EC) 2002/38 concerning VAT on e-commerce into national law.

Where e-services are supplied by non-EU businesses to private consumers in the State, then the place of taxation is the State (FA 2003, s 115(c)). This is known as the *business to consumer* (B2C) rule. There is provision for an optional scheme under which the non-EU trader would register in one EU country, make electronic supplies to each member state at the VAT rate applicable in each such member state and remit the VAT to the country of registration, which would in turn remit the VAT to the country of consumption (FA 2003, s 116).

When electronically supplied services are received for business purposes in this State from abroad, the place of supply is deemed to be in this State, and the recipient will be liable for payment of Irish VAT; if such services are supplied from this State to business customers abroad, no Irish VAT will arise (FA 2003, s 131).

elegit. [He has chosen.]

email. [Also Email or e-mail.] (1) An electronic text message. (2) The exchange of electronic text messages and computer files over a communications network, such as a local area network or the Internet, usually between computers or terminals. Increasingly, legislation is including references to *email*, eg an application to have a car test may be made by email: Road Traffic (National Car Test) Regulations 1999, SI No 395 of 1999, art 8(2). See Takeover Rules 2001, Part B, r 19.8.

The Employment Appeals Tribunal has stressed that it was highly desirable for employers to include in their email/Internet policy, a statement that the sending of offensive emails was prohibited and would be dealt with in accordance with the company's disciplinary procedures: *Mehigan v Dyflin Publications Ltd* (2003) Irish Times, 8 February, EAT.

The Tribunal found as unfair the dismissal of an employee for abuse of emails, holding that the dismissal was inordinately disproportionate to the offence complained of, and that there was inconsistency of treatment of the employee versus others who actively participated in the offence to a similar degree: *O'Leary v Eagle Star Life Assurance Co* [2003] ELR 223, EAT. In another case, the Tribunal held that an employee had contributed 100% to his dismissal: *Coleman v Ove Arup* [2004] ELR 11, EAT.

It is desirable that a barrister, when providing advice or draft documents to a solicitor by email or by the forwarding of software, either keep a hard copy of such documents or forward such a copy to his instructing solicitor as soon as reasonably practicable: *Code of Conduct for the Bar of Ireland* (December 2003) r 4.18. All such communications should be expressed to be confidential and privileged.

Guidelines on the use of email in a solicitor's office are available to solicitors on the Law Society website under *Technology Committee*: *www.lawsociety.ie*. 'In the employment context, the virtual world must be regarded as the real world, because it is': Ann Power BL in 'Employers' liability in the electronic workplace' in *Bar Review* (October 2000) 14 and (Nov 2000) 120.

See also 'Sticking it to the spammers' by solicitor Paul Lambert in *Law Society Gazette* (Mar 2002) 21. [Bibliography: Hall.] See INTERNET.

emanation of the State. Flowing or issuing from the State. If a body is held to be an *emanation of the State*, then its obligations towards a private individual are no different than if it were the State itself: *Dermot Coppinger v Waterford County Council* [1998] 4 IR 220, HC. In this case, a county council was held to be an 'emanation of the State'.

embarrassment. A possible ground for damages arising from injuries caused by the negligence of another. See DISFIGUREMENT.

embassy, employee of. See AMBASSADOR; IMMUNITY.

embezzlement. The *felony* (qv)) committed by a clerk or servant, who *fraudulently* appropriated to his own use property delivered to or taken into possession by him on account of his master or employer: Larceny Act 1916, s 17. Property included chattels, money, or valuable securities. Fraudulent appropriation could be shown eg by the accused having absconded with money or by his wilful omission to pay it over to his employer. See *The People (Attorney-General) v Warren* [1945] IR 24. The 1916 Act has been repealed by the Criminal Justice (Theft and Fraud Offences) Act 2001, s 3 and Sch 1. See now THEFT. See also FALSE ACCOUNTING; FRAUDULENT CONVERSION.

emblements. The profits from sown land; the crops or products as are the result of agricultural labour. The personal representative (qv) of a tenant for life is entitled to take the year's crops when the tenancy determines between seed sowing and harvest time. The right to emblements is lost where a tenancy is ended by the tenant's own act. See GOODS.

embracery. The common law offence of any improper endeavour or attempt corruptly to influence or instruct a jury by money, promises, threats, or by other persuasions or fraudulent devices, other than the strength of evidence and the arguments of counsel in open court. See INTIMIDATION, CRIME OF.

embryo implantation. A child born as a result of the test tube fertilisation of a wife's ova by her husband's semen and borne by the wife following embryo implantation, is legitimate (or now, a child whose parents are married to each other: Status of Children Act 1987). If a third party's semen is used, the child is illegitimate (or now, a child whose parents are not married to each other), although if the wife is living with her husband at the time, there may be a presumption that the child is a marital child unless rebutted in court proceedings. See ARTIFICIAL INSEMINATION; CLONING; GENE THERAPY; HUMAN REPRODUCTION; REPRODUCTIVE MEDICINE.

emergency. (1) The Minister is empowered, in the interest of the State or of the public, during any emergency, to give directions as to the use, or possession of any aircraft or aerodrome, or any facilities at an aerodrome; failure to comply with a direction is an offence: Air Navigation and Transport Act 1988, s 22.

(2) A local authority manager is empowered to deal with an *emergency situation* calling for immediate action without having first to inform the elected members: Local Government Act 2001, s 138(4). An *emergency situation* is deemed to include a situation where, in the opinion of the manager, the works concerned are urgent and necessary (having regard to personal health, public health and safety considerations) in order to provide a reasonable standard of accommodation for any person (LGA 2001, s 138(5)). See also Housing (Traveller Accommodation) Act 1998, s 24 as amended by LGA 2001, Sch 4. For previous legislation, see City and County Management (Amendment) Act 1955, s 2 as amended by Housing Act 1988, s 27. See also *O'Reilly v Sullivan* [1997] 1996 No 226, SC.

(3) 'Doctors should provide care in emergencies unless they are satisfied that alternative arrangements have been made. They should also consider what assistance they can give in the event of a major incident, a road traffic accident, fire, drowning or other similar occurrences': Medical Council, *A Guide to Ethical Conduct and Behaviour* (6th edn, 2004) para 2.3. See NATIONAL EMERGENCY; PATIENT, CONSENT OF.

emergency vehicle. Under draft legislation it is proposed that, with certain exceptions, the requirements under the Road Traffic Acts relating to vehicles and requirements, restrictions and prohibitions relating to the driving and use of vehicles, do not apply to a driver of a fire brigade vehicle, an ambulance or the use by a member of the garda

of a vehicle in the performance of the duties of that member or a person driving or using a vehicle under the direction of a member of the garda, where such use does not endanger the safety of road users: Road Traffic Bill 2004, s 21.

emission. Means a release of substances, heat or noise into the atmosphere, water or land, and includes: (a) an emission into the atmosphere of a pollutant within the meaning of the Air Pollution Act 1987; (b) the release of a greenhouse gas into the atmosphere; (c) a discharge of polluting matter, sewage effluent or trade effluent within the meaning of the Local Government (Water Pollution) Act 1977, to waters or sewers within the meaning of that Act; or (d) waste: Environmental Protection Agency Act 1992, s 3(1) as amended by Protection of the Environment Act 2003, s 5.

A licence issued by the Agency must include *emission limit values* for environmental pollutants likely to be emitted in significant quantities (EPAA 1992, s 86 inserted by PEA 2003, s 15). See Emissions of Volatile Organic Compounds from Organic Solvents Regulations 2002, SI No 543 of 2002 implementing Directive (EC) 1999/13. See AIR POLLUTION; INJUNCTION, ENVIRONMENT.

emission ceilings. National emission ceilings have been specified for certain atmospheric pollutants: sulphur dioxide, nitrogen oxides, volatile organic compounds and ammonia, to be achieved by 2010: EC (National Emission Ceilings) Regulations 2004, SI No 10 of 2004. The regulations, which transpose Directive (EC) 2001/81 into Irish law, also provide for the preparation of a national strategy with the aim of complying with the ceilings and the preparation and reporting of annual national emission inventories and projections.

emissions trading. An EU initiative to reduce greenhouse gas emissions under which emission allowances are traded. There is an incentive for a company to reduce emissions as allowances which are not used by a company may be traded, and companies which need to increase their limit may purchase allowances. There are stringent penalties in place to ensure that companies do not exceed their limits. The overall allocation to the emissions trading sector in Ireland is designed to be consistent with achieving our national obligations under the Kyoto Protocol, which is to limit annual emissions in the period 2008 to 2012 to 13% above 1990 levels. See GREENHOUSE GAS.

emolument. (1) Some profit or advantage: *R v Postmaster General* [1878] 3 QBD 428; remuneration.

(2) Anything assessable to income tax under Schedule E: Income Tax Act 1967, s 124. It includes all payments of salaries, fees, wages, and perquisites, whether taxable directly under the main Schedule E charging section (ITA 1967, s 110) or by virtue of any other provision in the Income Tax Acts which requires the particular payment to be taxed under Schedule E. The payment of emoluments are subject to the PAYE system of taxation unless the payments are excluded by virtue of s 125 of ITA 1967 as amended by the Finance Act 1985, s 6. See now Taxes Consolidation Act 1997, ss 112, 983, 984.

(3) The amount of the remuneration and other payments to company directors must be disclosed in the annual accounts: Companies Act 1963, ss 191–193. See PAY AS YOU EARN.

emotional immaturity. The incapacity to enter into and to sustain a normal, functional lifelong marital relationship by reason of a lack of *emotional maturity* and of psychological weakness and disturbance, affecting both parties to a marriage is a ground for nullity in Irish law: *PC v JC* [1989] ITLR (2 October). See MARRIAGE, NULLITY OF.

emotional upset. Damages may be payable for emotional upset: *Sullivan v Southern Health Board* [1997] 3 IR 123, SC.

employee. (1) A person who is under a *contract of service* to another person, called the employer, under which the employer has the right to direct the employee not only as to what is to be done but as to how it is to be done: *Roche v Patrick Kelly & Co Ltd* [1969] IR 100. See also Employment Equality Act 1998, s 2(1) as amended by Equality Act 2004, s 3.

(2) Any person in receipt of emoluments (qv): Income Tax Act 1967, s 124 (now Taxes Consolidation Act 1997, s 983). The parties cannot alter the truth of the employer/employee relationship by putting a different label on it: *Lamb Bros Dublin Ltd v Davidson* [1979] HC, unreported; *Massey v Crown Life Insurance Co* [1978] 2 All ER 576. The fact that a person is not paying income tax under the PAYE system is not, of itself, a bar to his being an employee:

McCurdy v Bayer Diagnostics Manufacturing Ltd [1993] ELR 83, EAT. The issuance of a P60 form and the description 'employer' and 'employee' on the P60 form do not determine the relationship of employer/employee: *Millen v Presbyterian Church in Ireland* [2000] ELR 292, EAT. See also *Young v Bounty Services (Ireland) Ltd* [1993] ELR 224, EAT. An employee generally has access to employment protection legislation.

There is a duty on an employee to do his work with reasonable care and skill; he must be honest and diligent, he must generally obey instructions provided they are reasonable and lawful and he must not wilfully disrupt the employer's business or other activities. He must not disclose confidential information or trade secrets: *Faccenda Chicken Ltd v Fowler* [1984] IRLR 61. He also has a duty to take care for his own safety and health and that of any other persons who might be affected by his acts or omissions at work: Safety in Industry Act 1980, s 8(1)(a). See also *Minister for Labour v PMPA Insurance* [1986] HC, unreported; *Cervi v Atlas Staff Bureau* UD 616/85, 26 November 1987, EAT; *Redmond v South Eastern Health Board* [1996] ELR 228, EAT; *Bank of Ireland v Kavanagh* [1987] HC, unreported. See Directive (EC) 91/533. See Redundancy Payments Act 2003, s 3; Protection of Employees (Fixed-Term Work) Act 2003, s 2(1). [Bibliography: Forde (8); Higgins & Keher.] See EQUAL PAY; UNFAIR DISMISSAL; OFFICE HOLDER; EMPLOYER, DUTY OF; INDEPENDENT CONTRACTOR; PROTECTIVE EQUIPMENT; WORKERS, FREEDOM OF MOVEMENT OF.

employee tax credit. See INCOME TAX.

employees and inventions. See INVENTOR.

employees' share scheme. A scheme designed to encourage or facilitate a company's employees to acquire its shares or debentures. The holders of such shares must be offered a proportionate amount of any further equity which is issued. See Companies Amendment Act 1983, ss 2(1) and 23(1)(a). There is provision for income tax relief for an employee who buys new ordinary shares in his employing company; the overall limit has been increased to £5,000 (€6,349): Finance Act 1986, s 12 as amended. See now Taxes Consolidation Act 1997, s 479. For *profit sharing schemes* and *employee share ownership trusts*, see TCA 1997, ss 509–519; FA 1998, s 36, FA 1999, s 69; FA 2000, s 24; TCA 1997, Sch 11 amended by FA 2000 s 25; Sch 12 amended by FA 2000, s 26 and by FA 2004, s 15. For *savings-related share option schemes* (SAYE schemes) see TCA 1997, ss 12A; 519A–519C; FA 1999, s 68 and FA 2000, s 51. See also FA 2002, s 13.

Provision has been made for employee profit sharing schemes in Aer Lingus plc, not exceeding 5% of the total issued share capital: Air Companies (Amendment) Act 1993, s 5. See Listing Rules 2000, para 13.13–13.17, ch 16 (*appendix*, para 20). [Bibliography: Ferguson, Gilvarry & Langford.] See also PRE-EMPTION.

employer. (1) The master of a servant. (2) The person by whom an employee is or was employed. (3) A person for whom one or more workers work or have worked or normally work or seek to work having previously worked for that person: Industrial Relations Act 1990, s 8. (4) Any person paying emoluments (qv) Income Tax Act 1967, s 124 (now Taxes Consolidation Act 1997, s 983).

It has been held that a skipper is not the employer of crew on a trawler for the purposes of income tax regulations: *DPP v McLoughlin* [1986] ILRM 493.

Where there is doubt as to who is the employer of an employee, a major test used is the 'control test': *Walsh v Oliver Freeney & Co* [1995] ELR 209, EAT. See *Performing Rights Society v Mitchell and Booker* [1924] 1 KB 762; *Lynch v Palgrave Murphy* [1964] IR 150; *Minister for Social Welfare v Griffith* [1992] ELR 44, HC. See also Redundancy Payments Act 2003, s 3; Protection of Employees (Fixed-Term Work) Act 2003, s 2(1). For Irish Business and Employers' Confederation (IBEC), see website: *www.ibec.ie*. For Union of Industrial and Employers' Confederations of Europe, see website: *www.unice.org*. See EMPLOYMENT AGENCY; EMPLOYMENT LAW; EMPLOYER, DUTY OF; EMPLOYEE; INSOLVENCY OF EMPLOYER.

employer, duty of. An employer has a duty to provide a safe place of work, proper equipment and processes, and a safe system of work: *Burke v John Paul & Co Ltd* [1967] IR 277; *O'Hanlon v ESB* [1969] IR 75; *Kielthy v Ascon Ltd* [1970] IR 122. He must provide adequate training and instruction and he must not require the employee to do anything unreasonable or illegal. He must pay wages or other remuneration but he is generally not required to provide any actual

work, except where the employee requires work to develop and maintain special skills relevant to the job (see *Nethermere (St Neots) Ltd v Taverna* [1984] IRLR 240).

An employer is vicariously liable for the torts of his employee if they are committed within the scope of his employment: *Kiely v McCrea Sons Ltd* [1940] Ir Jur Rep 1; *Byrne v Maguire* 60 ILTR 11. An employer may be under a duty not to disclose confidential information concerning its employees: *Dagleish v Lothian & Borders Police Board* [1991] IRLR 422 as reported by *Barry* in 10 ILT & SJ (1992) 30. Directors of a company must have regard to the interests of the company's employees generally, as well as to the shareholders (members): Companies Act 1990, s 52. [Bibliography: Meenan; White.] See EMPLOYEE; FIRST AID; HEALTH SURVEILLANCE; PROTECTIVE EQUIPMENT; SAFETY AT WORK; RESTRAINT OF TRADE.

employment, contract of. See CONTRACT OF EMPLOYMENT; TERMS OF EMPLOYMENT.

employment, minimum age for. The minimum age for employment is 14 years although employment under the age of 16 or the school leaving age, whichever is the higher, is generally restricted. See Protection of Young Persons (Employment) Act 1996. See CHILD, EMPLOYMENT OF; YOUNG PERSON.

employment, protection of. The Protection of Employment Act 1977 has been amended: (a) to provide for representation of, and consultation with, employees in the absence of a trade union, staff association or excepted body; (b) to provide for a right of complaint to a Rights Commissioner where an employer contravenes ss 9 or 10 (information and consultation of employees); and (c) to provide for increases in fines: European Communities (Protection of Employment) Regulations 2000, SI No 488 of 2000. For other amendments to the 1977 Act, see SI No 370 of 1996. [Bibliography: Forde; Kerr.] See PROTECTIVE LEAVE; TRANSFER OF UNDERTAKINGS.

employment agency. A business involved in seeking, whether for reward or otherwise, on behalf of others, persons who will give or accept employment. A licence is required. See Employment Agency Act 1971; Employment Agency Regulations 1993, SI No 49 of 1993; Protection of Employees (Fixed-Term Work) Act 2003, s 19(1).

For the purposes of *unfair dismissal* legislation, the person hiring an individual from an employment agency is deemed to be the employer of that individual, irrespective of whether or not the person pays his wages or salary: Unfair Dismissals (Amendment) Act 1993, s 13. Any redress for unfair dismissal will be awarded against the person who hired the individual from the agency (UD(A)A 1993, s 13(c)).

An employment agency, as an employer, must not discriminate against an agency worker; it also must not discriminate against those who seek the services of the agency to obtain employment with another person: Employment Equality Act 1998, ss 8(1) and 11. There is an exception made for agencies which provide services exclusively for persons with disabilities (EEA 1998, s 11(5)). As regards claims for *equal pay*, the comparator for establishing that there is *like work* (qv) must be another agency worker (EEA 1998, s 7(2)). See *O'Rourke v Cauldwell* [1998] ELR 287, HC; *Diageo Global Supply v Rooney* [2004] ELR 133, LC. See Social Welfare (Miscellaneous Provisions) Act 2003, s 19. For Discussion Paper (May 2004) on a review of the EAA 1971, see website: *www.entemp. ie/employment/rights/agencies.htm*. See DISCRIMINATION; UNFAIR DISMISSAL.

employment agreement. An agreement relating to the remuneration or the conditions of employment which is registered pursuant to the Industrial Relations Act 1946, ss 25–33. An agreement so registered applies to all workers of the class to which the agreement relates; their employers are bound to grant such workers rates of pay and conditions of employment not less favourable than those fixed by the agreement whether or not they are a party to the agreement. For registration to be valid, fair procedures must be followed and the statutory prerequisites must be complied with: *National Union of Security Employers v The Labour Court & Ors* [1992] HC as reported by *Barry* in 11 ILT & SJ (1993) 50. The Labour Court cannot widen the category of employers to whom the agreement applies, thereby including workers not already included, contrary to the express provisions of s 28 of IRA 1946: *Serco Services Ireland Ltd v Labour Court* [2002] ELR 1, HC. See also Industrial Relations Act 1990, ss 51–55; Pensions Act 1990, s 81C as amended by substitution by Social Welfare (Miscellaneous Provisions) Act 2004,

s 22(1). See 'Riding the coat tails' by solicitor Anthony Fay in Law Society Gazette (June 2004) 28. See JOINT LABOUR COMMITTEE.

Employment Appeals Tribunal. The tribunal which hears appeals, claims and disputes in relation to a wide range of employment legislation e g redundancy, maternity protection, adoptive leave, and unfair dismissal. Established by the Redundancy Payments Act 1967, s 39 as the Redundancy Appeals Tribunal, it was renamed by the Unfair Dismissals Act 1977, s 18 and its procedures are governed by the various Acts under which it has jurisdiction, as well as by SI No 24 of 1968 (redundancy) and SI No 286 of 1977 (unfair dismissal).

The tribunal has a chairman who must be a practising barrister or solicitor of at least seven years' standing and seven vice-chairmen. It sits in divisions, each division consisting of a chairman (or vice-chairman) and one member each from the nominees of both sides of industry. An objection to the composition of the tribunal was overruled in a particular case: *Wexford Council of Trade Unions v Malone* [1997] ELR 235, EAT.

The tribunal can only exercise its discretion to exclude a party in exceptional circumstances e g failure to furnish Notice of Appearance within the prescribed time would not be an exceptional circumstance: *Halal Meat Packers (Ballyhaunis) Ltd v EAT* [1990] ELR 49, SC.

The tribunal does not award costs against any party unless a party has acted frivolously or vexatiously (regulation 19(2) of SI No 24 of 1968): *Sherry v Panther Security Ltd* [1991] ELR 239, EAT. Also the tribunal has held that the Oireachtas did not intend to give it power to make any compensatory award to an employer: *Leopard Security Ltd v Campbell* [1997] ELR 225, EAT.

There are provisions for the enforcement by the Circuit Court of determinations made by the tribunal or of orders made by the Court, including interest on any financial compensation awarded, compensation for any delay in implementing re-instatement or re-engagement; the Court may also change an award from re-engagement or re-instatement to financial compensation: Unfair Dismissals (Amendment) Act 1993, s 11.

The tribunal does not have jurisdiction to strike out a claim or appeal on the application of the respondent; the only way in which a claim or appeal can be removed from the tribunal is by way of a withdrawal of the claim or by a determination of the tribunal: *Concannon v St Grellan's National School* [1994] ELR 229, EAT and [1995] ELR 162, EAT. The tribunal may, however, adjourn a matter to a definite time in the future.

See also *IBM Ireland Ltd v Employment Appeals Tribunal* [1983] ILRM 50; *The State (IPU) v Employment Appeals Tribunal* [1987] ILRM 36. See Adoptive Leave Act 1995, s 35; Redundancy Payments Act 2003, s 9. See RSC Ord 105. See APPEARANCE, ENTRY OF; RIGHTS COMMISSIONER.

Employment Appeals Tribunal, appeal from. An appeal from the tribunal lies either to the High Court or to the Circuit Court depending on the matter in dispute. In unfair dismissal an appeal lies to the Circuit Court within six weeks from the date on which the tribunal determination is communicated to the parties: Unfair Dismissals (Amendment) Act 1993, s 11(1); *Amber Ltd v Donnelly* [1993] ELR 170, CC; SI No 279 of 1994. Also an appeal lies from the Circuit Court to the High Court: *McCabe v Lisney & Son* [1981] ILRM 289; *Commissioners of Irish Lights v Sugg* [1994] ELR 97, HC; an appeal to the Circuit Court is within the time limit if the jurisdiction of the court is invoked within the limitation period: *Norris v Power Security Ltd* [1990] ELR 181, HC.

An appeal on a point of law should state the decision being appealed against, the question of law which is suggested to be in error, and the grounds of appeal; this summons should be supported by an affidavit which exhibits the determination of the tribunal, including any findings of fact or recital of evidence made by it: *Bates v Model Bakery Ltd* [1992] ELR 193, SC. The facts as stated by the Tribunal must be accepted by the High Court: *An Post v McNeill* [1998] ELR 19, HC.

It would appear that relief by way of judicial review (certiorari) of the tribunal's decision will be refused where appeal to Circuit and High Court has not been pursued: *Memorex v Employment Appeals Tribunal* [1989] 7 ILT & SJ 154 & 204.

employment awards. There is an obligation on an employer to deduct income tax at source from any awards or settlements made in respect of an employment dispute: Taxes Consolidation Act 1997, ss 123, 201 and Sch 3; Finance Act 2002, s 15. However, there is an exemption from income tax of compensation paid, on or after 4 February 2004, under employment law in respect of the infringement of employees' rights and entitlements under that law (TCA 1997, s 192A inserted by Finance Act 2004, s 7). The exemption does not apply to payments which are in respect of earnings, changes in working conditions or the termination of an employment.

Where there is termination of employment, there are certain exemptions from tax and, as an alternative, the taxpayer may claim an amount known as SCSB – *standard capital superannuation benefit*. If the award or settlement includes payments made by the employer in respect of the employee's legal costs, such payments do not attract tax in the hands of the employee, provided: (a) the payment is made by the former employer directly to the former employee's solicitor, (b) the payment is in full or partial discharge of the *bill of costs* incurred by the employee only in connection with the termination of his employment, and (c) the payment is under a specific term in the settlement agreement: Practice Note in *Law Society Gazette* (June 2003) 41. See REDUNDANCY PAYMENT.

Employment Equality Agency. Formerly, the body with the following general functions: (a) to work towards the elimination of discrimination in relation to employment; (b) to promote equality of opportunity between men and women in relation to employment; (c) to keep under review the working of equality and anti-discrimination legislation: Employment Equality Act 1977, ss 34–35. The Agency was replaced by the *Equality Authority* which has a much broader remit: Employment Equality Act 1998, ss 38–67. See EQUALITY AUTHORITY; DISCRIMINATION.

employment injunction. See INTERLOCUTORY INJUNCTION.

employment interview. See INTERVIEW BOARD.

employment law. The body of law dealing with the relationship between employer (master) and employee (servant) and organisations representing them. Also known as labour law. Originally the relationship between master and servant was based on contract as between two equal parties; and also trade unions were illegal in so far as their operations were in restraint of trade. Significant changes have taken place in the last two centuries, with trade unions being given statutory recognition in 1871 and immunity from many liabilities in 1906; the Constitution in 1937 recognised the right to work and the right to form associations, and a whole range of employee protection legislation was introduced in the 1960s and 1970s e g equal pay, anti-discrimination, unfair dismissal, maternity protection, holidays, minimum notice and redundancy. In the 1990s came further provisions on adoptive leave, parental leave, working time, protection of young persons, sexual harassment, victimisation, and equality. [Bibliography: Barry J; Conlan; Curtin; Forde (8); Garvey & Macaulay; Higgins & Keher; Kerr (3); Kerr & Whyte; Kimber; Maguire C (2); O'Mara; von Prondznski; Redmond (1); Bercussen UK.] See COMMON EMPLOYMENT; EMPLOYEE; TRADE UNION.

employment notice. See NOTICE, EMPLOYMENT.

employment permit. A permit granted by the Minister which is a prerequisite for a *non-national* (qv) to be in employment in the State: Employment Permits Act 2003, s 2. It is an offence: (i) for a person to employ a non-national in the State except in accordance with an employment permit, and (ii) for a non-national to enter the service of an employer in the State, or to be in employment in the State, except in accordance with an employment permit (EPA 2003, s 2(3)). This does not apply to a person who is entitled to enter the State and to be in employment in the State pursuant to the treaties governing the European Communities (EPA 2003, s 2(10)(c)).

The requirement for employment permits does not apply to nationals of EU Accession States after enlargement. However, the Minister is empowered to re-impose the requirement for such permits in respect of the relevant new EU member states after accession, if the labour market is experiencing, or is likely to experience, a disturbance (EPA 2003, s 3).

In February 2004 the government announced a scheme under which employment permits are automatically granted under a fast-track process to the spouses of non-nationals working in the State in healthcare, information technology, construction and research. At that time there were 10,000 such persons working in the State. See websites: *www.entemp.ie* and *www.fas.ie*. See ENLARGEMENT OF EU; SOCIAL WELFARE LAW; WORK PERMIT.

employment regulation order. See JOINT LABOUR COMMITTEE; REST PERIOD.

ems. European monetary system. See *Northern Bank v Edwards* [1986] ILRM 167.

emu. Economic and monetary union (qv).

E-number. Generally understood to mean the serial number applying to a particular *colouring agent* in food. A person may not import, distribute, sell or expose for sale any colouring agent other than a permitted colouring agent, for use in the manufacture or preparation of food, or may not import, distribute, sell or expose for sale specified foods which have in or on them any colouring agent other than a permitted agent: SI No 149 of 1973; SI No 140 of 1978; SI No 336 of 1981; SI No 68 of 1992.

en autre droit. [In the right of another.]

en ventre sa mère. [In the womb of his mother.] An unborn child. Descendents and relatives of a deceased person begotten before his death but born alive thereafter are regarded for the purposes of succession as having been born in the lifetime of the deceased and as having survived him: Succession Act 1965, s 3(2). See also Status of Children Act 1987, s 27(5). See CHILD, ILLEGITIMATE; CLASS GIFT; ISSUE; GESTATION PERIOD.

enabling Act. A statute legalising that which was previously illegal or incompetent; a statute giving obligatory or discretionary powers. For example, see Turf Development Act 1990 which enables Bord na Móna to establish and acquire companies. See also NONFEASANCE.

enactment. Legislation (qv). See ACT; BILL.

enceinte. [Pregnant.] See PREGNANCY.

encrypted broadcast. See BROADCAST.

encroachment. Unauthorised extension of the boundaries of land; unauthorised entrance upon another's rights or possessions. An encroachment by a tenant on another person's land generally enures for the landlord's benefit, unless the conduct of the landlord or the tenant indicates a contrary intention: *Meares v Collis* [1927] IR 397. See Law Reform Commission, *Report on Title by Adverse Possession of Land* (LRC 67, 2002). See LONG POSSESSION, TITLE BY; TRESPASS.

encumbrance. A charge or liability which burdens property eg a mortgage, lease, easement, restrictive covenant (qqv). An *encumbrancer* is a person who has the right to enforce an encumbrance.

end-of-life vehicle. Means a specified vehicle which is discarded or is to be discarded by its registered owner as waste: Waste Management Act 1996, s 53B inserted by Protection of the Environment Act 2003, s 44. The Minister is empowered to make regulations placing an obligation on the producer of such vehicles to ensure that the registered owner can deposit the vehicle at an authorised treatment facility without any cost being incurred by the owner in respect of such deposit, treatment or recovery (WMA 1996, new s 53C). The registered owner will be required to deposit the vehicle at an authorised treatment facility when he decides to discard the vehicle as waste (WMA 1996, new s 53D).

endangered. Means exposed to harm, decay or damage, whether immediately or over a period of time, through neglect or through direct or indirect means: Planning and Development Act 2000, s 2(1). See PRO-TECTED STRUCTURE.

endangering traffic. It is an offence for a person to place or throw, intentionally, any dangerous obstruction upon a railway, road, street, waterway or public place, where the person is aware that injury to a person or damage to property may be caused thereby, or is reckless in that regard: Non-Fatal Offences against the Person Act 1997, s 14. Similarly, it is an offence to throw anything at a *conveyance* or to interfere with traffic control or regulation equipment.

endangerment. It is an offence for a person to engage in conduct, intentionally or recklessly, which creates a substantial risk of death or serious harm to another person: Non-Fatal Offences against the Person Act 1997, s 13. *Serious harm* means injury which creates a substantial risk of death or which causes serious disfigurement or substantial loss or impairment of the body (NFOPA 1997, s 1(1)). See CAUSING SERIOUS HARM.

endangerment notice. The notice which a planning authority is empowered to serve on the owner or occupier of a *protected structure* (qv) requiring the person served to carry out specified works which it considers necessary to prevent the structure from becoming or continuing to be endangered: Planning and Development Act 2000, s 59. The planning authority can give assistance in having the work carried out; it is also empowered to carry out the work itself in the event of a default (PDA 2000, ss 59(2) and 69). It is an offence not to comply with an endangerment notice (PDA 2000, s 63). An appeal lies to the District Court against an endangerment notice (PDA 2000, s 61). See also PDA 2000, s 67. For previous legislation, see Local Government (Planning and Development) Act 1999, ss 10, 12, 14, 18, 20. See PROTECTED STRUCTURE; RESTORATION NOTICE.

endorsement. A signature, usually on the reverse side of a document, generally operating as a transfer of rights arising from the document. Endorsement is a mode of transferring bills of exchange and bills of lading. An *endorsement in blank* is an endorsement by the endorser of his own signature without specifying the name of the transferee, under which the bill becomes payable to the bearer. A *special endorsement* is one which specifies the name of the person to whom or to whose order the bill is to be made payable. A *conditional endorsement* is one which is subject to the fulfilment of a specific condition. A *restrictive endorsement* prohibits further transferability (eg *pay John Murphy only*, signed [...]).

An endorser of a bill agrees to compensate the holder or any endorser subsequent to his own endorsement who is compelled to pay it if the bill is dishonoured when duly presented for payment. See Bills of Exchange Act 1882, ss 32–35.

Where a solicitor receives a cheque payable to a client which cannot be lodged to the solicitor's account because the necessary endorsement has not been made by the client and the solicitor has no written authority to make the endorsement, the solicitor can only exercise a lien over the uncashed cheque: *A Guide to Professional Conduct of Solicitors in Ireland* (2002) ch 9.11. See BILL OF EXCHANGE; CHEQUE; SOLICITOR'S LIEN.

endorsement of claim. See INDORSEMENT OF CLAIM.

endorsement of driving licence. A person convicted of certain offences under the Road Traffic Acts 1961 to 1995 will have particulars of the offence endorsed on his driving licence. See Road Traffic (Licensing of Drivers) Regulations 1999, SI No 352 of 1999. See DRIVING LICENCE.

endowment. (1) Provision for a charity. (2) Formerly, giving a woman a right to dower (qv). See CHARITIES.

endowment loan. A housing loan which is to be repaid out of the proceeds of an insurance policy on its maturity; it does not include a mortgage protection policy: Consumer Credit Act 1995, s 115(2) as amended by Central Bank and Financial Services Authority of Ireland Act 2003, s 35, Sch 1. There is provision for a *warning notice* in respect of such a loan on specified documents (eg information documents, application forms, approval documents): 'Warning. There is no guarantee that the proceeds of the insurance policy will be sufficient to repay the loan in full when it becomes due for repayment' (CCA 1995, s 133). The insurance company is required every five years to supply a statement to the borrower setting out the value of the policy and a revised estimate of its valuation at maturity (CCA 1995, s 133(6)).

endowment mortgage. A mortgage wherein the principal sum advanced by the mortgagee (lender) is intended to be repaid by means of a *life-endowment insurance policy* effected by the mortgagor (borrower). The endowment policy from an insurance company will typically provide for the payment of the principal sum at a specified date or on the mortgagor's death, whichever is earlier. If the policy is a *with profits* one, it will provide for the mortgagor to participate in the profitability of the insurance company. The mortgagor pays a regular premium to the insurance company, and interest to the mortgagee on the principal sum advanced. The mortgage deed usually provides that the monthly repayments of the principal sum advanced by the mortgagee are suspended, so long as the endowment policy is kept up and the mortgagor continues to pay interest on that principal sum. An endowment mortgage may also be a *unit-linked* mortgage wherein the premiums are invested in unit trusts whose value may fluctuate. See ENDOWMENT LOAN; MORTGAGE.

enduring power. See POWER OF ATTORNEY, ENDURING.

enemy. Includes armed mutineers, armed rebels, armed rioters and pirates: Defence Act 1954, s 2(1). For *enemy aliens*, see Prisoners of War and Enemy Aliens Act 1956, s 1(3).

enemy of state. See ILLEGAL CONTRACTS.

energy labelling. A person may not place on the market, for sale, hire or reward, household air conditioners unless accompanied by information relating to the consumption of electrical energy, in addition to certain supplementary information: EC (Energy Labelling of Household Air-Conditioners) Regulations 2002, SI No 578 of 2002. Similar provisions apply to household electric ovens, see SI No 579 of 2002.

enforcement notice. A notice issued by a planning authority to a person carrying out an *unauthorised development*, requiring the unauthorised development to end, or not to commence, or for the developer to comply with the terms and conditions of a planning permission: Planning and Development Act 2000, s 2(1) and 154. The authority can require rectifying measures to be taken, including the demolition of a structure and the restoration of land to its previous state. It can also require the person served with the notice to pay to the planning authority the costs incurred by the authority in investigating the unauthorised development. If the notice is not complied with after a specified time, the authority may enter on the land to carry out the work itself, with the costs recoverable from the person served with the notice (PDA 2000, s 154(6)–(7)).

A person who fails to comply with the notice, or knowingly assists or permits another to fail to comply, is guilty of an offence, which may be prosecuted summarily or on indictment (PDA 2000, ss 154(8)–(9) and 156). An enforcement notice, unlike those which could be served under the Local Government (Planning and Development) Act 1963, ss 31–35 as amended by LG (P&D) Act 1992, s 19(1) and (2), applies in all instances where there is unauthorised development.

An enforcement notice may also be served by a *building control authority* to ensure compliance with building regulations (qv): Building Control Act 1990, s 8. See *Dublin Co Council v Hill* [1992] ILRM 397, SC. For the enforcement provisions of the 2000 Act, see 'The best laid plans' by barrister Stephen Dodd in *Law Society Gazette* (March 2004) 20. [Bibliography: LexisNexis.] See WARNING LETTER.

enforcement notice, data. The notice in writing, served on a data controller (qv) or data processor (qv) by which the Data Protection Commissioner (qv) may require such person to take such steps as are specified in the notice within such time as may be so specified, to comply with the data protection legislation: Data Protection Act 1988, s 10(2) as amended by Data Protection (Amendment) Act 2003, s 11. This will arise where the Commissioner is of opinion that the person has contravened or is contravening the statutory provisions, other than a provision the contravention of which is an offence. An enforcement notice may be appealed to the Circuit Court. See DATA PROTECTION.

enforcement of judgment. Proceedings for the enforcement of a judgment under the Enforcement of Court Orders Acts 1926 to 1940 may be brought, heard and determined at any sitting of the district court for the court area wherein the debtor is ordinarily resident: DCR 1997 Ord 53, r 2. See also EC (Personal Insolvency) Regulations 2002, SI No 334 of 2002. [Bibliography: Glanville.] See DEBTOR, IMPRISONMENT OF; DEBTOR'S SUMMONS; EXECUTION OF JUDGMENT; FOREIGN JUDGMENTS, ENFORCEMENT OF.

enfranchise. Conferring the right to vote. See FRANCHISE.

engaged couple. Two persons who have agreed to marry each other. In the absence of evidence to the contrary, it is presumed that a gift of property given by another person, is given to them as *joint owners* and subject to a condition that it be returned to the donor if the marriage does not take place: Family Law Act 1981, s 3. A gift of property, including an engagement ring, is presumed to be given subject to a condition that it will be returned if the marriage does not take place, or given unconditionally if on account of the death of the donor, the marriage does not take place (FLA 1981, s 4). The rights of spouses in relation to property apply where an agreement to marry is terminated (FLA 1981, s 5). Any disputes in relation to property in which either or both of the persons had a beneficial interest while they were engaged may be resolved in a summary manner by the court pursuant to s 36 of the Family Law Act 1995: Family Law (Divorce) Act 1996, s 44. See BREACH OF PROMISE; MATRIMONIAL PROPERTY.

engineer, professional negligence. It has been held that an engineer who certifies that a house has been erected above the flood level for the area is guilty of negligence if he does not satisfy himself in an appropriate professional manner that the crucial measurements have been observed: *Moran v Duleek Developments Ltd & Hanley*

[1991] ITLR (14 October), HC. See COMPETENCE.

engineer and confidentiality. Chartered engineers must not divulge any confidential information regarding the business affairs, technical processes or financial standing of their clients or employers without their consent: *Code of Ethics – The Institution of Engineers of Ireland* (November 2003), clause 1.8.

engineer in employment. Chartered engineers in full-time employment must not undertake part-time work where this is in conflict with their terms of employment: *Code of Ethics – The Institution of Engineers of Ireland* (November 2003), clause 1.5. They must not undertake part-time work which they might subsequently have to review, or in which they could influence a decision, in the course of their salaried employment.

engineering law. Generally understood to refer to the body of law dealing with the forms of construction contracts used for engineering works, including matters such as tender and agreement; liability and insurance; sub-contracting; the bond; delay, disruption and acceleration claims; price fluctuation; disputes, arbitration and litigation. [Bibliography: Keane D; Lyden & MacGrath; Abrahamson UK.] See BOND, ENGINEERING CONTRACT; RIAI CONTRACT.

engraving. See ARTISTIC WORK.

engross. To prepare the text of a document.

engrossment. A deed prior to execution. An engrossment of a will must be written in a legible hand or printed or typewritten or, in suitable cases, photocopied and certified as a true copy of the original will. See RSC Ord 79, r 69.

enhanced co-operation. Expression used to describe the process in the EU which permits a sub-group of member states to choose to co-operate on a specific matter. Enhanced co-operation was provided for by the Amsterdam Treaty (qv) but had not been used, allegedly because the rules were too restrictive. The rules have been modified by the Nice Treaty (qv). Enhanced co-operation in a project can now take place where at least eight member states agree to participate in a group; all member states must have a right to join the group, either at the start or later. Also the project must be authorised by the Council of Ministers by qualified majority votes, except in the area of *Common Foreign and Security Policy* when unanimous approval by the

Council is required. Enhanced co-operation must not undermine the common market, it must not be a barrier to trade, and it must not distort competition between member states. See Treaty on European Union, arts 43–45 of the consolidated (2002) version.

Enhanced co-operation between member states must not undermine the *internal market* (qv) of the EC (art 43).

enjoyment. The exercise of a right.

enlarge. To free; to extend a limit; to extend a period of time.

enlargement. Increasing an estate eg the enlargement of a base fee (qv) into a fee simple (qv).

enlargement of EU. Any European State may apply to become a member of the European Union: Maastricht Treaty 1992, art O; Treaty on European Union, art 49 of the consolidated (2002) version. The applicant state must address its application to the Council, which is required to act unanimously, after consulting with the Commission and after receiving the assent of the European Parliament. From 1992 to 2003, three further countries have joined: Austria, Finland and Sweden, bringing the number of EU members in April 2004 to 15.

Ratification of the Nice Treaty in 2002 by Ireland has paved the way for the further enlargement of the EU, with a further ten countries joining on 1 May 2004: Cyprus, Czech Republic, Estonia, Hungary, Latvia, Lithuania, Malta, Poland, Slovakia, and Slovenia. See Accession Treaty done at Athens on 16 April 2003; European Communities (Amendment) Act 2003.

Planning to join in 2007 are two countries: Bulgaria and Romania. A date for joining the EU has not been indicated yet for Turkey; however it was indicated at a meeting of EU leaders in Copenhagen on 13 December 2002 that if Turkey fulfils the political conditions for EU membership by December 2004, it can then commence accession negotiations. See Protocol on the Enlargement of the European Union, adopted at Nice in 2001. See 'Ireland and Europe's Future Integration' by Michael McDowell SC (then Attorney-General) in *Bar Review* (June/July) 480. See 'Ireland and Europe's Future Integration: A Response to the Attorney General' by Eugene Regan BL in *Bar Review* (September 2001) 525. See 'All together now' by solicitor Wendy Hederman in *Law Society Gazette* (May 2004) 8. See COPENHAGEN

CRITERIA; NICE TREATY; TOBACCO PRODUCT; WORK PERMIT.

enlargement of jurisdiction. The parties to proceedings before the Circuit Court may consent to the court having jurisdiction in the action or matter without any limit: Courts of Justice Act 1924, s 48(1); Circuit Court Rules 2001, Form 1A. The consent to enlargement must be lodged with the County Registrar either before or at any time during the hearing: Circuit Court Rules 2001 Ord 5, r 8. See also DISTRICT COURT.

enquiry. See INQUIRY.

enrolment. The registration or recording on an official record of an act or document.

ens legis. A legal being or entity.

entail. See FEE TAIL.

enter. (1) To go onto land so as to assert some right. (2) To record in an account. See also BURGLARY.

Enterprise Ireland. A body corporate with the following functions: (a) to develop industry and enterprise in the State, (b) to promote, assist and develop the marketing of goods, (c) to promote, assist and develop the marketing of service industries, (d) to assist enterprises in strategy assessment and formulation, (e) to develop the technological base and the capacity of enterprises to innovate and undertake research, development and design, (f) to strengthen the skills base in industry, (g) to provide services which support such development, (h) to make investments in and provide supports to industrial undertakings which comply with the requirements of the enactments for the time being in force, (i) to administer such schemes, grants and other financial facilities requiring the disbursement of European Union and other funds, (j) to apply for and receive, in the State or elsewhere, any trade marks, licences, protections or concessions in connection with trade or the marketing of goods or services, and in relation thereto, to do all such things as the body considers necessary or desirable for the purposes of its functions: Industrial Development (Enterprise Ireland) Act 1998. See website: *www.enterprise-ireland. com*. See INDUSTRIAL DEVELOPMENT.

entertainment. Where an entertainment for children is provided, or any entertainment at which the majority of persons attending are children, it is the duty of the person providing the entertainment to take reasonable precautions for the safety of the children, including the stationing of trained adult attendants and control of the movement of the children: Children Act 2001, s 270.

enticement of spouse. Formerly an actionable tort whereby a spouse was wrongfully enticed away from another. Abolished by the Family Law Act 1981, s 1. See LRC 1 of 1980.

entrapment. The enticing of a person into committing a crime in order to prosecute him. [Bibliography: Charleton (4).] See AGENT PROVOCATEUR.

entry, right of. Many statutes give a right of entry to premises to the gardaí or to authorised or specified officers. The right of a local authority to enter upon and take possession of land (eg following a notice of entry served pursuant to the Housing Act 1966, s 80) which the authority can enforce by issuing a warrant to the sheriff (qv) to deliver possession of the land to the person appointed in the warrant to receive possession: Land Clauses Act 1845, s 91. An authorised office may enter any premises at all reasonable times provided he has reasonable grounds for believing that a trade, business or activity is or has been carried out there; he may not enter a private dwelling unless he has the consent of the occupier or a court warrant: Consumer Credit Act 1995, s 8B inserted by Central Bank and Financial Services Authority of Ireland Act 2003, s 35, Sch 1. See also Energy (Miscellaneous Provisions) Act 1995, s 16; Commissions of Investigation Act 2004, s 28.

An authorised person is empowered, on giving notice, to enter on any lands at all reasonable times between the hours of 9am and 6pm, or during business hours in respect of a premises which is normally open outside these hours, for any purpose connected with planning legislation: Planning and Development Act 2000, s 252(1). The person may also enter without notice where this is required in relation to enforcement powers; however, entry into a private house must not be made unless not less than 24 hours' notice is given or the occupier consents (PDA 2000, s 253). There is also a right of entry on land by the owner in relation to complying with an endangerment or restoration notice in respect of a *protected structure*; or by the planning authority in the event of failure by the owner to comply (PDA 2000, ss 64 and 69). See also ENTRY AND SEARCH; FORCIBLE ENTRY AND OCCUPATION; MORTGA-

GEE, RIGHTS OF; PRIVATE RESIDENTIAL TENANCIES BOARD.

entry and search. For the purpose of arresting a person, a garda is empowered to *enter* (if need be, by use of reasonable force) and *search* any premises (including a dwelling) where the person is or where the garda, with reasonable cause, suspects the person to be: (a) with a warrant of arrest or an order of committal, or (b) without a warrant for an *arrestable offence* (qv) but in this case may only enter a dwelling with consent, or without consent: (i) where the garda has observed the person within or entering the dwelling, or (ii) the person ordinarily resides in the dwelling, or (iii) the garda suspects that the person will abscond or obstruct the course of justice or will commit an arrestable offence before a warrant could be obtained: Criminal Law Act 1997, s 6.

For Revenue officers' powers of search and entry of premises for excise purposes, see Finance Act 2002, s 87 and Finance Act 2003, s 90. See also Aliens Act 1935, s 7 as substituted by Immigration Act 2003, s 4; Intoxicating Liquor Act 2003, s 18; European Arrest Warrant Act 2003, s 25; Immigration Act 2004, s 15; Private Security Services Act 2004, s 15. [Bibliography: Walsh D (3).] See INVIOLABILITY OF DWELLING.

entry of appearance. See APPEARANCE, ENTRY OF.

entry of judgment. See JUDGMENT; SUMMARY SUMMONS.

enure. To take effect; to operate.

environment assessment directive. The Directive (EEC) 85/337, done at Luxembourg on 27 June 1985, which requires developers to produce *environment impact assessments* of a wide range of projects. The assessment is required to identify the direct and indirect effects of a *project* on human beings, fauna, and flora; soil, water, air, climate and landscape; the interaction between these factors; material assets and the cultural heritage (art 3). A *project* means the execution of construction works or of other installation or schemes, or other interventions in the natural surroundings and landscape including those involving the extraction of mineral resources (art 2).

Subject to certain exemption provisions, an environment impact assessment is mandatory for projects of the class listed in Annex 1 (Directive (EEC) 85/337, art 4); these projects include crude oil refineries, power stations, integrated chemical installations and waste disposal installations. Member states were required to implement the directive by 3 July 1988; it was implemented by the European Communities (Environmental Assessment) Regulations 1989, SI No 349 of 1989 as amended by Local Government (Planning and Development) Act 1992, ss 22(2) and 3. See also Amendment Regulations SI No 84 of 1994 (Part III of which is revoked by Protection of the Environment Act 2003, s 3 and Sch 2, Pt II). The earlier Department Circular of 1 July 1988 to local authorities was held not to have had the force of law: *Browne v An Bord Pleanála* [1989] ILRM 865, HC.

A person who is required to submit an environmental impact statement can now request the competent authority concerned to provide an opinion on the information to be contained in the Statement: EC (Environmental Impact Assessment) (Amendment) Regulations 1999, SI No 93 of 1999. These Regulations transpose Directive (EC) 97/11 of 3 March 1997 into Irish law. See also SI No 92 of 1999. The Regulations dealing with environmental impact statements are now contained in the Planning and Development Act 2000. [Bibliography: Duggan; Galligan (1); O'Sullivan & Shepherd; Scannell.] See BUSWAY; ENVIRONMENTAL IMPACT STATEMENT; PROTECTED ROAD; MOTORWAY; WASTE DISPOSAL.

Environment Fund. Provision has been made for the establishment of an Environment Fund, into which revenues from the *Environmental Levy* (eg levy on plastic bags) and the *Landfill Levy* may be paid: Waste Management (Amendment) Act 2001, ss 9–12. The Minister may pay money from the Fund for a range of measures, including programmes or schemes to prevent or reduce waste, operation of waste recovery activities, litter prevention, environment partnership projects and environmental awareness, education and training. Moneys from the Fund may also be used for initiatives undertaken in the State, or on an international or trans-national basis relating to the protection of the environment or to sustainable development: Environment Fund Prescribed Payments Regulations 2003, SI No 478 of 2003.

environmental audit. In relation to any process, development or operation, means a systematic, documented and objective periodic assessment of the organisation structure, management systems, processes and equipment pertaining to, or incidental to, that process, development or operation, for the purposes of environmental protection: Environmental Protection Agency Act 1992, s 74(1). The Agency may promote the carrying out of environmental audits and publish guidelines (EPAA 1992, s 74(2)).

environmental impact assessment. Regulations have been made to reduce the *environmental impact assessment* thresholds in relation to initial afforestation (from 70 hectares to 50 hectares) and peat extraction (from 50 hectares to 30 hectares) to facilitate compliance with the European Court of Justice ruling on 21 September 1999 (Case C-392/96) which held that the thresholds adopted by Ireland exceeded the discretion available under Directive (EEC) 85/337 in that they did not take account of the nature, location or cumulative effect of projects below the original thresholds set: European Communities (Environmental Impact Assessment) (Amendment) Regulations 2001, SI No 538 of 2001. These regulations also introduce amendments to the Wildlife (Amendment) Act 2000 and to the EC (Natural Habitats) Regulations 1997 to provide for the possibility of *environmental impact assessment* for peat extraction below the 10 hectare planning thresholds in certain cases.

The function of certifying an *environmental impact assessment* of a local authority's own development has been transferred from the Minister to An Bord Pleanála as from 1 January 2001: European Communities (Environmental Impact Assessment) (Amendment) Regulations 2000, SI No 450 of 2000.

For consolidating regulations on *environmental impact assessments* under the Planning and Development Acts, see Planning and Development Regulations 2001, Pt X, arts 92–132: SI No 600 of 2001.

environmental impact statement; EIS. Means a statement of the effects, if any, which proposed *development*, if carried out, would have on the environment: Planning and Development Act 2000, s 2(1). A planning application must be accompanied by an EIS where it is in respect of a development or class of development referred to in regulations made by the Minister (PDA 2000, s 172(1) and 176). The Minister is empowered to make EIA (*Environmental*

Impact Assessment) regulations: (a) identifying developments which may have significant effects on the environment, and (b) specifying the manner in which the likelihood that such development would have significant effects on the environment is to be determined (PDA 2000, s 176(1)). The Minister is also empowered to prescribe the information which is required to be contained in an EIS (PDA 2000, s 177). An Bord Pleanála is empowered to grant an exemption from the requirement to prepare an EIS in exceptional circumstances (PDA 2000, s 172(3)).

A planning authority, and An Bord Pleanála on appeal, must have regard to the EIS when considering a planning application (PDA 2000, s 173(1)). A planning authority is also required to give a person, on request, a written opinion on the information to be contained in an EIS, before that person submits an application for planning permission – this is a process known as 'scoping' (PDA 2000, s 173(2)).

There is special provision requiring the approval of An Bord Pleanála to any development of a local authority that is a planning authority (or in partnership with a local authority) where the development is in the class requiring an EIS (PDA 2000, s 175). There are also provisions regarding developments which are likely to have a significant effect on the environment of other states.

The Environmental Protection Agency may, and must if requested by the Minister, prepare guidelines on the information to be contained in the environment impact statements in respect of developments: Environmental Protection Agency Act 1992, s 72. The Agency has a right to comment on all environment impact statements and must be consulted before a decision is made to exempt a project from a statutory requirement to prepare such a statement. See also Waste Management Act 1996, s 40 amended by Protection of the Environment Act 2003, s 35.

The Conference, which agreed the Amsterdam Treaty, noted that the European Commission undertakes to prepare *environmental impact assessment studies* when making proposals which may have significant environmental implications: Amsterdam Treaty 1997, Declaration 10, p 133.

The proposal for the construction of the millennium 'Spike' in O'Connell Street, Dublin did not proceed as planned in 1999 because an environmental impact statement had not been carried out: *O Nuallain v Dublin Corporation* [1999] 4 IR 137, HC. The 'Spike' or the 'Spire of Dublin', to give it its official name, was finally erected in 2003. See *O'Connell v EPA* [2003] 1 IR 532, SC. See Roads Act 1993, ss 50–51. [Bibliography: Duggan; Galligan (1); O'Sullivan & Shepherd; Scannell.] See BUSWAY; PROTECTED ROAD; MOTORWAY; TRANSBOUNDARY CONVENTION; WASTE DISPOSAL.

environmental information, access to. The public must be given access to information relating to the environment ie any available information in written, visual, aural or data base form on the state of water, atmosphere, soil, fauna, flora, land and natural sites, and on actions or measures affecting or likely to affect these, including administrative measures and environmental management programmes: Directive (EEC) 90/313: Environmental Protection Agency Act 1992, s 110. This information must be made available by public authorities. Also the public must be given access to information on monitoring which the Agency considers appropriate (EPAA 1992, s 67). See Access to Information Regulations, SI No 185 of 1996.

environmental law. The law of planetary housekeeping, concerned with protecting the planet and its people from activities that upset the earth and its life-sustaining capacities: Rodgers, *Environmental Law* (1977, USA). Environmental law in Ireland is primarily concerned with pollution of the air and water, noise pollution, waste disposal and resource recovery, pesticides and toxic substances.

EC policy on the environment is required to contribute to pursuit of the following objectives: (a) preserving, protecting and improving the quality of the environment; (b) protecting human health; (c) prudent and rational utilisation of natural resources; and (d) promoting measures at international level to deal with regional or worldwide environmental problems: EC Treaty, art 174 of the consolidated (2002) version.

Persons, natural and legal, are entitled to access to information on the environment from public authorities: Directive (EEC) 90/313; Environmental Protection Agency Act 1992, s 110. See also O'Leary in *Law Society Gazette* (January/February 1993) 23. For the Department of Environment, see website: *www.environ.ie*. For all recent

EU Environmental Council conclusions, see *www.europa. eu.int/pol/env/index_en.htm*. For promotion of environmental awareness in Irish industry, see website: *www.envirocentre.ie*. For the Environmental Information Service, see website: *www.enfo.ie*. [Bibliography: Comerford & Fogarty; Duggan; Galligan; Gore Grimes; Maguire, O'Reilly & Roche; Matheson Ormsby Prentice; Scannell.] See EUROPEAN ENVIRONMENT AGENCY; PRECAUTIONARY PRINCIPLE.

environmental medium. Includes the atmosphere, waters and land: Environmental Protection Agency Act 1992, s 4(3) as substituted by Protection of the Environment Act 2003, s 6.

environmental pollution. (1) In relation to waste, means the holding, transport, recovery or disposal of waste in a manner which would, to a significant extent, endanger human health or harm the environment, and in particular: (a) create a risk to waters, the atmosphere, land, soil, plants or animals, or (b) create a nuisance through noise, odours or litter, or (c) adversely affect the countryside or places of special interest: Waste Management Act 1996, s 5(1).

(2) Air pollution (qv); the condition of waters after entry of polluting matter; the handling of waste in a manner which would endanger human health or harm the environment; noise which is a nuisance, or would endanger human health or damage property or harm the environment: Environmental Protection Agency Act 1992, s 4(2) as substituted by Protection of the Environment Act 2003, s 6. See INTEGRATED POLLUTION CONTROL.

environmental protection. Includes: (a) the prevention, limitation, elimination, abatement or reduction of environmental pollution (qv), and (b) the preservation of the quality of the environment as a whole: Environmental Protection Agency Act 1992, s 4(1) as substituted by Protection of the Environment Act 2003, s 6.

The Minister is empowered to make regulations to protect the environment against damage caused by the use of mechanically propelled vehicles; this includes the reduction of emissions and noise and the protection of persons and animals from harmful emissions and excessive noise: Road Traffic Act 2002, s 13.

Chartered engineers are required to strive to accomplish the objectives of their work with the most efficient consumption of natural resources which is practicable economically, including the maximum reduction in energy usage, waste and pollution: see *Code of Ethics – The Institution of Engineers of Ireland* (November 2003), clause 2.4. For Earthwatch – Friends of the Earth Ireland, see website *www.iol.ie/~foeeire/*. [Bibliography: Canny (2); LexisNexis.] See PRECAUTIONARY PRINCIPLE.

Environmental Protection Agency. A body corporate, consisting of a director general and four other directors, with perpetual succession: Environmental Protection Agency Act 1992, ss 19–20. The functions of the Agency include (a) the licensing, regulation and control of activities for the purposes of environmental protection, (b) the monitoring of the quality of the environment, (c) the provision of support and advisory services, (d) the promotion and co-ordination of environmental research, (e) liaison with the European Environment Agency provided for by Council Regulation (EEC) 90/1210 (EPAA 1992, s 52). The Agency may be assigned additional functions and powers and may have certain functions of public authorities transferred to it (EPAA 1992, ss 53–54; 100–101).

The agency is empowered to delegate functions to any person and to public authorities (EPAA 1992, ss 25(6) and 45). It is also required to establish regional environmental units (EPAA 1992, s 43), to make an annual report (EPAA 1992, s 51) and a report every five years on the quality and condition of the environment in the State (EPAA 1992, s 70). It has power to supervise the performance of statutory functions of local authorities in relation to environmental protection and to give them directions (EPAA 1992, s 68 and s 63 as substituted by Protection of the Environment Act 2003, s 13).

The Agency has a major function in relation to *integrated pollution control* (qv) by the issue of licences (EPAA 1992, ss 82–99H, as substituted by PEA 2003, s 15). It also may arrange for an inquiry to be held into any incident of environmental pollution and may be directed by the Minister to hold such an inquiry (EPAA 1992, s 105).

The Agency also has a major function in relation to waste management, hazardous waste, and waste licences: Waste Management Act 1996. See also Waste Management (Amendment) Act 2001, s 13;

Minister for the Environment and Local Government (Performance of Certain Functions) Act 2002. See EPA (Extension of Powers) Orders 1994 and 1996, SI No 206 of 1994; SI No 126 of 1996. See DCR 1997 Ord 96, rr 7–8. See *Kimber & Maguire* in 11 ILT & SJ (1993) 196. See also Public Service Superannuation (Miscellaneous Provisions) Act 2004, Sch 2. [Bibliography: Maguire, O'Reilly & Roche; Scannell.] See AIR POLLUTION; BEST AVAILABLE TECHNIQUES; COSTS AND CRIMINAL PROCEEDINGS; DRINKING WATER; ENVIRONMENT ASSESSMENT DIRECTIVE; HAZARDOUS WASTE; INFLUENCE, IMPROPER; INTEGRATED POLLUTION CONTROL; NOISE; SEWAGE EFFLUENT; WASTE.

eo instanti. [At that instant.]

eo nomine. [In that name.]

eodem modo quo oritur, eodem modo dissolvitur. [What has been effected by agreement can be undone by agreement.]

eodem modo quo quid constituitur, eodem modo destruitor. [A thing is made and is destroyed by one and the same means.]

Equal Community Initiative. An initiative, part funded by the European Social Fund, which supports organisations working in partnership and transnationally, to promote new means of combating all forms of discrimination and inequalities in connection with the labour market. It also takes account of the social and vocational needs of asylum seekers. See website: *www.equal-ci.ie.*

equal pay. Every member state is required to ensure that the principle of equal pay for male and female workers for equal work or work of equal value is applied: EC Treaty, art 141 of the consolidated (2002) version. 'Pay' means the ordinary basic or minimum wage or salary and any other consideration, whether in cash or kind, which the worker receives directly or indirectly, in respect of his employment from his employer.

A woman is entitled to the same rate of remuneration as a man who is employed by the same employer if both are employed in *like work* (qv) and any difference in remuneration cannot be justified on objective factors unrelated to the sex of the person; a man is similarly entitled in relation to his remuneration relative to that of a woman: Employment Equality Act 1998, s 19 as amended by Equality Act 2004, s 12. *Remuneration* includes any consideration,

whether in cash or in kind, which an employee receives directly or indirectly from the employer in respect of employment, but excludes pension rights (EEA 1998, s 2(1)). Provision of a uniform to female members of staff and not to males has been held not to be remuneration (*Male Employees v Educational Building* Society EP9/1987), whereas the provision of a taxi service for female shift workers and not to male workers was held to be remuneration: *Field v Irish Carton Printers* [1994] ELR 129, EO.

There is also an entitlement to *equal pay* for persons employed to do *like work*, where any difference in pay is related to the person's gender, marital status, family status, sexual orientation, religion, age, disability, race, or membership of the Traveller community (qqv) (EEA 1998, s 29 amended by EA 2004, s 19). An employer may pay different rates of pay to different employees who are employed on like work, provided the differences are not based on any of the *discriminatory grounds* (EEA 1998, ss 19(5) and 29(5)).

A claim for equal pay is heard by the *Director of the Equality Tribunal* (qv) who may award equal pay and arrears of up to three years (EEA 1998, s 82 amended by EA 2004, s 36).

See *PMPA Insurance Co Ltd v Keenan* [1983] SC, unreported; *Dept of Public Service v Robinson* EP 36/ 78; *The State (Polymark) v ITGWU* [1987] ILRM 357; *Sales and Clerical Assistants v Pennys Ltd* [1996] ELR 78, EO; *24 Female Employees v Spring Grove Services* [1996] ELR 147, EO; *IMPACT v Department of Agriculture* [1996] ELR 155, LC; *Penneys Ltd v Mandate* [1998] ELR 94, LC; *Brides v Minister for Agriculture* [1999] 4 IR 250, HC and [1998] ELR 125, HC; *Flynn v Primark* [1997] ELR 218, HC and [1999] ELR 91, HC; *IMPACT v Irish Aviation Authority* [2000] 29, LC. [Bibliography: Bolger & Kimber; Reid M.] See CLASS ACTION; DISCRIMINATION; LIKE WORK; LABOUR COURT; RED-CIRCLING; SOCIAL POLICY; VICTIMISATION.

equality action plan. A programme of actions to be undertaken in employment in a business to further the promotion of equality of opportunity in that employment: Employment Equality Act 1998, s 69(2). The Equality Authority is empowered to carry out an *equality review* (qv) and prepare an *equality action plan* or may invite a business or group of businesses to so do (EEA 1998, s 69(3)–(4)). An equality action plan can be enforced by a *substantive notice* (qv). Equality action plans may now be prepared in relation to *equal status* matters (EEA 1998, s 69 as amended by Equal Status Act 2000, s 39 and Sch). [Bibliography: Reid M.]

Equality Authority. A corporate body with the following general functions: (a) to work towards the elimination of discrimination in employment, (b) to promote equality of opportunity, (c) to provide information to the public on equality, and (d) to keep equality legislation under review and other statutory provisions regarding maternity leave, adoptive leave, and equal treatment in pensions: Employment Equality Act 1998, s 39. The Authority may draft *codes of practice* (qv) and may conduct an *inquiry*, with power to obtain information, summon and examine witnesses (EEA 1998, ss 56, 58–61). It is also empowered to serve a *non-discrimination notice* (qv) during the course of or following such inquiry (EEA 1998, s 62). It may also issue a *substantive notice* (qv) in relation to an *equality review* and *action plan* (EEA 1998, s 70). See also Equality Act 2004, ss 26–28.

The functions of the Authority have been expanded to include: (a) working towards the elimination of *prohibited conduct* (ie discrimination, sexual harassment and harassment outside of employment), (b) promotion of equality of opportunity in equal status matters, (c) providing information to the public on equal status matters; (d) reviewing and making proposals for amendment of the equal status legislation: Equal Status Act 2000, s 39.

The Authority may refer cases to the *Director of the Equality Tribunal* for investigation where it appears that prohibited conduct is generally directed against persons, or where prohibited conduct is being directed against a person who has not made a claim and it would not be reasonable to expect him to do so, or where a person has contravened or is contravening ESA 2000, s 12(1) (prohibited advertising), s 19 (provision of kerb ramps) or regulations made under ss 17 or 18 (transport accessibility) ESA 2000, s 23). Following a decision by the Director, the Authority may apply to the High or Circuit Court for an injunction to prevent further occurrence of prohibited conduct (ESA 2000, s 23(3)). For the application of the 1998 Act to pension law,

see Pensions Act 1990, s 81J as amended by substitution by Social Welfare (Miscellaneous Provisions) Act 2004, s 22(1). The Labour Court no longer has jurisdiction, in the first instance, in cases of dismissal in circumstances amounting to discrimination or victimisation: Equality Act 2004 s.66. See website: *www.equality.ie*. [Text: Fullerton & Kandola; Reid M.] See DIRECTOR OF THE EQUALITY TRIBUNAL; DISCRIMINATION.

equality before the law. All citizens are required to be held equal before the law: 1937 Constitution, art 40(1). However, the State may in its laws have due regard to differences of capacity, physical and moral, and of social function. The guarantee of equality prohibits the State from causing unjustified advantage to a third party or class of persons in its electoral law: *Ring v Attorney General* [2004] 20 February 2004, HC and ITLR (15 March 2004).

The constitutional guarantee of equality is not absolute. There is no unfair discrimination provided every person in the same class is treated in the same way; the classification must, however, be for a legitimate legislative purpose and each class must be treated fairly: *An Blascaod Mór v Minister for Arts* [2000] 1 ILRM 401, SC, approving *Quinn's Supermarket v Attorney-General* [1972] IR 1, and *Brennan v Attorney-General* [1983] ILRM 449. Also it has been held that the most expansive construction of art 40(1) could not support the proposition that the guarantee of equality required the executive to inform the public of the availability of any public service post, before it indicated a preference as to how that post might be filled: *Riordan v Ireland* [2000] 4 IR 537, SC.

A legislative inequality will not be set aside as being repugnant to the Constitution unless the court considers that the law is based on a distinction between men and women which cannot be justified by the factual circumstances: *Lowth v Minister for Social Welfare* [1994] 1 ILRM 378, HC. See *Landers v Attorney-General* [1975] 109 ILTR 1; *de Burca v Attorney-General* [1976] IR 38. See DISCRIMINATION; MARITAL COERCION.

equality clause. A clause which is deemed to be included as a term in a contract of employment to provide for not less favourable terms for an employee, where the work done by that person is not materially different from that being done by a person of the other sex in the same employment: Employment Equality Act 1998, s 21. A *non-discriminatory equality clause* is also deemed to be included in a contract of employment, entitling a person to be treated as favourably as a person with a different characteristic, in the same employment, whose work is not materially different (EEA 1998, s 30). In a claim for *equal treatment* (other than equal pay), the *Director of the Equality Tribunal* may award equal treatment and compensation of up to two years' pay, or up to £10,000 (€12,697) where the person is not an employee (EEA 1998, s 82(4)). [Bibliography: Reid M.] See DISCRIMINATION; EQUAL PAY; LIKE WORK.

equality officer. See DIRECTOR OF THE EQUALITY TRIBUNAL.

equality review. An audit of the *level of equality of opportunity* which exists in employment and an examination of the practices, procedures and other relevant factors: Employment Equality Act 1998, s 69(1). The Equality Authority is empowered to carry out an *equality review* and prepare an *equality action plan* (qv) or may invite a business or group of businesses to so do (EEA 1998, s 69(3)–(4)). Equality reviews may now be carried out in relation to *equal status* matters (EEA 1998, s 69 as amended by Equal Status Act 2000, s 39 and Schedule). [Bibliography: Reid M.] See SUBSTANTIVE NOTICE.

Equality Tribunal. See DIRECTOR OF THE EQUALITY TRIBUNAL.

equitable assignment. An assignment purporting to assign a future debt, operates only as a contract to assign; it remains a purely *equitable assignment* which will be enforced like any other contract but only if given for valuable consideration: *Law Society v O'Malley* [1998] 2 ILRM 531, SC.

equitable charge. See EQUITABLE MORTGAGE.

equitable doctrines. The doctrines of advancement, election, performance, satisfaction, conversion and reconversion (qqv). A person who comes to court seeking the benefit of an equitable doctrine will be denied that benefit if the grant of it would amount to reward for unfair, unconscionable or inequitable conduct: *RF v MF* [1995] 2 ILRM 572, SC. [Bibliography: Delaney H (2).] See EQUITY, MAXIMS OF.

equitable estoppel. A person, who by his words or conduct, wilfully causes another to believe in the existence of a certain state of things, and induces him to act on that belief to his detriment, is estopped from denying that state of things in any subsequent litigation between the parties: *Pickard v Sears* [1837] 6 A E 469; *Doran v Thompson* [1978] IR 223. Equitable estoppel may be classified as *promissory* and *proprietary*.

Promissory estoppel or quasi-estoppel, arises where one party says to another that their existing legal relations are modified in some way, with the intent and result that the other acts on the supposed change of relationship; he is not then permitted, except on reasonable notice to the other party, to revert to their previous relationship: *Central London Property Trust Ltd v High Trees House Ltd* [1947] KB 130. It has been held that it would be inequitable to allow a party to compensation proceedings to dispute the assumptions on which they were based: *Conroy v Commissioner of Garda Síochána* [1989] IR 140, HC. To establish promissory estoppel, a person has to prove detrimental reliance upon the promise or representation in question: *Daly v Minister for the Marine* [2001] 3 IR 513, SC.

Proprietary estoppel arises where the owner of land has encouraged, or acquiesced in, the infringement of his title to the land by another in circumstances which, in the view of the law, renders it inequitable for the owner to assert his legal title to the land in an unqualified manner: *Willmot v Barber* [1880] 15 Ch D 96; *McMahon v Kerry County Council* [1981] ILRM 419; *Smith v Ireland* [1983] ILRM 300; *Haughan v Rutledge* [1988] IR 295, HC.

It has been held that where the subject matter of the representation is land, no right or interest in the land results from this estoppel; instead, a personal right is vested in the representee which will preclude the representor from enforcing a title to the land: *In the matter of JR, a Ward of Court* [1993] ILRM 657, HC. See *Hinde Livestock Exports Ltd v Pandora Ltd* [1998] 2 IR 203, HC. [Bibliography: Delaney H (2); Lyall; McDermott P A (2).] See ISSUE ESTOPPEL; LEGITIMATE EXPECTATION.

equitable execution. The procedure by which the rights of a *judgment creditor* may be enforced by the appointment of a *receiver*. In general a receiver by way of equitable execution will not be appointed over payments to be made in the future: *Ahern v O'Brien* [1991] 1 IR 421. For exception, see GROUND RENT. [Bibliography: Glanville.] See also ATTACHMENT;

JUDGMENT MORTGAGE; RECEIVER, COMPANY; RECEIVER BY WAY OF EQUITABLE EXECUTION; RECEIVER OF MORTGAGED PROPERTY.

equitable lien. A lien (qv) which exists independently of possession and which is binding on all who acquire the property with notice of the lien eg a vendor's lien for unpaid purchase money; a purchaser's lien for prematurely paid purchase money. See PURCHASER'S EQUITY.

equitable mortgage. The mortgage which arises in equity (qv) by: (a) the agreement to execute a legal mortgage; or (b) the formal mortgage of the *equity of redemption*; or (c) the deposit of title deeds, with or without a memorandum of deposit. A legal mortgage takes priority over an equitable one, even if created after the equitable one, under the equitable maxim *where the equities are equal, the law prevails*. See *ACC Bank plc v Malocco* [2000] 3 IR 191, HC. See DEPOSIT OF TITLE DEEDS; EQUITY OF REDEMPTION; MORTGAGE.

equitable mortgage of shares. See SHARES, EQUITABLE MORTGAGE OF.

equitable remedies. The discretionary remedies that evolved from equity (qv) eg rescission, specific performance, injunction, appointment of receiver (qqv).

equitable remuneration. See FILM; PERFORMERS' RIGHTS; REMUNERATION; SOUND RECORDING.

equitable waste. See WASTE.

equities. See ORDINARY SHARES.

equity. (1) Fairness, impartiality, natural justice.

(2) The doctrines and procedures which developed alongside the common law (qv) and statute law, administered originally by the Court of Chancery to remedy some of the defects of the common law, and which became fused together by the amalgamation of the courts by the Judicature (Ireland) Act 1877. This Act provided that where there is any conflict between the rules of law and equity, equity is to prevail.

(3) The issued share capital of a company.

(4) Any financial interest resulting from the purchase of shares for a consideration: National Development Finance Agency Act 2002, s 1(1). [Bibliography: Bell; Delaney H (2); Keane (2); Kiely; Wylie (3); Snell UK.] See CAPITAL.

equity, maxims of. Principles which state the fundamental principles of equity eg equity acts *in personam*; equity follows the law; equity will not suffer a wrong to go without a remedy; equity acts on the conscience; equity looks on the intent rather than on the form; where the equities are equal, the law prevails; where the equities are equal, the first in time prevails; he who seeks equity must do equity; he who comes to equity must come with clean hands; equity aids the vigilant and not the indolent; delay defeats equity; equity regards the balance of convenience; equity regards as done that which ought to be done; equity imputes an intention to fulfil an obligation; equality is equity; equity will not assist a volunteer; equity never lacks a trustee. [Bibliography: Delaney H (2); Wylie (3).]

equity civil bill. See CIVIL BILL.

equity of redemption. The sum total of the mortgagor's rights in equity; it is an equitable estate which can be assigned, devised or mortgaged again. It exists from the moment the mortgage is made. It includes the equitable right to redeem the mortgage when the legal right has been lost by failure to pay the mortgage debt by the due date. There must be no *clogs* (qv) on the equity of redemption. A formal mortgage of the equity of redemption creates an equitable mortgage.

The equity of redemption is lost by: (a) sale by a court in lieu of foreclosure; (b) sale out of court by a mortgagee under an express power of sale given in the mortgage deed or by statutory power of sale given by the Conveyancing Act 1881, s 19; (c) lapse of time under the Statute of Limitations 1957. See *Allied Irish Banks v Finnegan* [1996] 1 ILRM 401, HC. See FORECLOSURE; MORTGAGE; PUISNE MORTGAGE; REDEMPTION.

equity release schemes. Schemes offered by lending and other institutions to persons usually aged over 65 or 70, whereby these persons raise capital on their residences either by way of loans or sales of a share therein, with a right of residence till death. The Conveyancing Committee of the Law Society has warned that the schemes being offered are complicated and difficult for the lay person to comprehend fully without effective and clear advice: *Law Society Gazette* (May 2001) 33. The Committee advises practitioners to take particular care to advise their clients of all the conditions therein, many of which differ from those in the usual standard residential loan documentation, including those relating to the interest rate charged, the involvement of executors and beneficiaries, and the events which will allow the lender/investor to call in the loan and sell the property. The Committee believes that equity release schemes can be a useful method of releasing 'dead capital' which is tied up in residential property. However, the Committee warns that, since all such schemes involve the elderly in disposing of some interest in their homes, it is critical that the procedures involved are fair and reasonable and that solicitors are able to advise their clients accordingly: *Law Society Gazette* (June 2003) 42.

equity securities. See PRE-EMPTION.

equity suit. *Equity suit* and *equity proceedings* include any proceedings of the nature set forth in section 33 of the County Officers and Courts (Ireland) Act 1877, or any Act extending or amending the same: Circuit Court Rules 2001, Interpretation of Terms, para 11. Proceedings under COC(I)A 1877, s 33 and under the Settled Land Acts, the Trustee Relief Acts or the Trustee Acts are taken by a *civil bill* which is then entitled, an '*Equity Civil Bill*': Circuit Court Rules 2001 Ord 46.

equivocation. An ambiguity in a document. Where the language of a document, though intended to apply to one person or thing only, applies equally to two or more, and it is impossible to gather from the context which was intended, the document may be interpreted by oral evidence as to the surrounding circumstances of the writer as well as to his direct declaration of intention. Extrinsic evidence is admissible to assist in the construction of a will: Succession Act 1965, s 90. See *Richardson v Watson* [1833] 4 B Ad 787. See AMBIGUITY.

Erasmus. An EU-supported education programme which commenced in 1987 and has enabled over 1 million young Europeans to spend time studying in another EU country. Named after the great Dutch scholar (1466–1536) of the Renaissance of northern Europe.

erasure. Erasures or obliterations in a will do not prevail unless proved to have existed in the will prior to its execution, or unless the alterations are duly executed and attested, or unless rendered valid by re-execution or by a codicil: RSC Ord 79, r 12. See ALTERATION; WILL, REVOCATION OF.

error. A person who makes an error or mistake in a tax return as a result of which he is excessively assessed to tax, is entitled, within six years of the end of the tax year in which the mistake was made, to apply to the Revenue Commissioners to have the appropriate relief or repayment made to him: Taxes Consolidation Act 1997, s 930. See also CORRECTION; PLEADINGS, AMENDMENT OF; SLIP RULE.

escape. It is an indictable offence (qv) to aid an escape or attempt to escape from lawful custody: Criminal Law Act 1976, s 6. It is an offence for a person, while under lawful arrest or in lawful custody, to regain his liberty either by himself or by the voluntary act of his custodian. Prison breaking (qv) is also an offence. See also Convict Prisons (Ireland) Act 1854; Offences Against the State Act 1939, s 32(2); Firearms Act 1964, s 27.

escape clause. See EXCLUSION CLAUSE.

escape of dangerous things. See RYLANDS V FLETCHER, RULE IN.

escheat. The *reversion* of land to the lord of the fee or the State on failure of heirs of the owner. It derived from the feudal rule that where an estate in fee simple came to an end, the land reverted to the lord by whose ancestors or predecessors the estate was originally created. Abolished by the Succession Act 1965, s 11. In default of next-of-kin, the State takes the estate as ultimate intestate successor (SA 1965, s 73). See also State Property Act 1954, ss 30–32.

escrow. A deed delivered to a person who is not a party to it, to be held by that party until certain conditions are performed eg the payment of money, after which it is delivered and takes effect as a deed. See *Bank of Ireland v Smyth* [1993] ILRM 790, HC. See DEED.

essence of a contract. The essential conditions of a contract without which agreement would not have been entered into. See CONDITION; TIME OF ESSENCE OF CONTRACT.

establishment, right of. See RIGHT OF ESTABLISHMENT.

estate. An interest in land. An estate may be of *freehold* or less than freehold. Freehold estates are those of fee simple, fee tail and a life estate; less than freehold estates are leases and tenancies (qqv).

estate agent. See AUCTIONEER; HOUSE AGENT.

estate duty. A tax imposed on property which passed on death. Now replaced for deaths on or after 1 April 1975 by a new capital acquisitions tax called *inheritance tax* and, in addition, from 18 June 1993 to

5 December 2000 by a *probate tax* (qv). See Capital Acquisitions Tax Act 1976; Finance Act 1993, ss 109–119; Capital Acquisitions Tax Consolidation Act 2003. [Bibliography: O'Callaghan J M (1).] See INHERITANCE TAX; PROBATE TAX.

estate management. (1) The refusal of consent by a landlord to an assignment of a lease may be upheld where it is based on valid *estate management* grounds and is not unreasonable: *OHS Ltd v Green Property Co Ltd* [1986] ILRM 451.

(2) Includes: (a) the securing or promotion of the interests of any tenants, lessees, owners or occupiers, whether individually or generally, in the enjoyment of any house, building or land provided by a housing authority, (b) the avoidance, prevention or abatement of *anti-social behaviour* in any housing estate in which is situate a house provided by a housing authority: Housing (Miscellaneous Provisions) Act 1997, s 1(1).

A housing authority may refuse to make or defer the making of a letting of a dwelling to a person where the authority considers that the person is or has been engaged in anti-social behaviour or that the letting to that person would not be in the interest of good *estate management* (H(MP)A 1997, s 14(1)(a)).

The housing authority may refuse to sell a dwelling to a tenant or refuse consent to sell to a purchaser on similar grounds. In 1998, ss 1 and 14 of H(MP)A 1997 were amended to extend the provisions to halting sites provided by local authorities and approved bodies: Housing (Traveller Accommodation) Act 1998, ss 34 and 35. For further amendments to ss 1, 3, 3A, 4, 4A, 9 and 14 of H(MP)A 1997, see Residential Tenancies Act 2004, s 197. See ANTI-SOCIAL BEHAVIOUR; BUSINESS TENANT; COVENANT; SQUATTER.

estate tail. See FEE TAIL.

estimates. The annual statement of the government's proposals for public expenditure in the ensuing year. See BUDGET.

estimates meeting. Formerly, the statutory meeting, which a local authority (qv) was required to hold, to consider an estimate of expenses and rate in the pound to be levied for the several purposes in the estimate: City and County Management (Amendment) Act 1955, s 10 and s 10A as inserted by Local Government Act 1994, s 44. See *Ahern v Kerry County Council* [1988] ILRM 392.

The meeting is now known as a *budget meeting* which a local authority must hold, and at which it must adopt a budget by resolution and must, if it is a rating authority, determine the annual rate on valuation to be levied: Local Government Act 2001, ss 2(1) and 103. See RATES.

estoppel. A rule of evidence which precludes a person from asserting or denying a fact, which he has by words or conduct led others to believe in. If a person by a representation induces another to change his position on the faith of the representation, he cannot afterwards deny the truth of his representation. Estoppel must be pleaded to be taken advantage of; it provides a shield not a sword and consequently it cannot create a cause of action.

Estoppel can arise under four headings: (1) estoppel by *record:* a party cannot deny the facts upon which a judgment against him was based; the matter is *res judicata;* (2) estoppel by *deed:* a party to a deed cannot deny the facts recited in the deed unless the deed is tainted by illegality or fraud; (3) estoppel by *conduct* (or in pais) eg a tenant who has accepted a lease cannot dispute the lessor's title; (4) *equitable* estoppel (qv).

Although a representation, promise or assurance must be clear and unambiguous to found a claim of *estoppel*, it is unnecessary for it to be incapable of more than one possible interpretation: *Ryan v Connolly* [2001] 2 ILRM 174, SC and 1 IR 627.

In a particular case, the court held that the plaintiff's claim for personal injuries in the High Court (subsequent to District Court proceedings where the plaintiff recovered a sum of money in respect to damage to her motor vehicle) was not barred by *cause of action estoppel* and that the defendant was not entitled to plead *accord and satisfaction*: *Hayes v Callanan* [2000] 1 IR 321, HC.

A party who took part in a reference to a Rights Commissioner and in a subsequent appeal to the Labour Court without challenging their jurisdiction, is estopped from so challenging in an appeal to the High Court: *Furey & Ors v Robert Clarke* [1994] ELR 41, HC. However, the doctrine of estoppel may not be used to prevent a person from relying on his marital status as a defence to a claim for judicial separation: *CK v JK & FMcG* [2004] ITLR (3 May), SC. In this case the person was not prevented from relying on his own misconduct to impugn the validity of his marriage.

The doctrines of *estoppel* and *legitimate expectation* do not apply where an applicant has not suffered any damage and where the right being claimed is one to which he is not statutorily entitled: *Gavin v Appeals Officer* [1997] 3 IR 240, HC. See *Boyce v McBride* [1987] ILRM 95; *Kenny v Kelly* [1988] IR 457; *Friends Provident v Doherty* [1992] ILRM 372; *Amstrad plc v Walker* [1993] ELR 173, HC. See 'Estoppel and the right to plead a defence under the Statute of Limitations' by Anthony Barr BL in *Bar Review* (June/July 2001) 445. See ARREST; ISSUE ESTOPPEL; LEGITIMATE EXPECTATION; RES JUDICATA.

estovers, common of. The right to cut wood, gorse or furze on the lands of another. [Bibliography: Bland (1).] See PROFIT A PRENDRE.

estreat. [Extract.] A true copy of a court record, relating to recognisances (qv) and fines (qv). The estreat of a recognisance involves enforcing the record of a recognisance which had become forfeited. For estreatment of recognisances where charges are struck out and subsequently re-entered, see *Supt Kennelly v Cronin* [2002] FL 6919, SC and [2003] 1 ILRM 505. See Criminal Procedure Act 1967, s 32; Bail Act 1997, s 9. See also *Tynan v Attorney-General* 96 ILTR 144: *A-G v Sheehy* [1990] 8 ILT Dig 239, SC. See DCR 1997 Ord 25, r 8, Ord 27. See new Form 27.6B and revised Forms 27.7 and 27.8: Estreatment of Recognisances Rules 2003, SI No 411 of 2003. See BAILPERSON.

et al; et aliae; et alia. [And others.]

et al; et alibi. [And elsewhere.] See ALIBI.

et seq; et sequentes. [And those which follow.]

etching. See ARTISTIC WORK.

ethical conduct. One of the functions of the Medical Council is to give guidance to the medical profession generally on all matters relating to ethical conduct and behaviour: Medical Practitioners Act 1978, s 69(2). The Council has issued guidance in such areas as: (a) conduct and behaviour; (b) doctors and patients e g responsibility to patients, behaviour towards patients; (c) professional responsibilities e g continuing medical education, drug trials, research, health problems; (d) doctors in practice e g practice announcements, practice premises, medical reports, certification, prescribing and irresponsible prescribing, deputising and locum

arrangements, consultant referral, centres of health care, the media and advertising, change of practice, retirement, incapacity or death; (e) confidentiality and consent e g confidentiality, informed consent, special situations and consent, teaching and consent, research and consent, organ transplantation and consent, inability to communicate and consent, the dying patient; (f) genetic testing and reproductive medicine e g gene therapy, genetic testing, frozen sperm and ova, AIDs, in-vitro fertilisation, the child in utero, adoption: *A Guide to Ethical Conduct and Behaviour* (6th edn, 2004).

For the International Bar Association, International Code of Ethics, see *A Guide to Professional Conduct of Solicitors in Ireland* (2002), App 3. As regards chartered engineers, see *Code of Ethics – The Institution of Engineers of Ireland* (November 2003). [Bibliography: Madden D; Mills S.] See ABORTION; ABORTION, MEDICAL GUIDELINES; ADOPTION; ARTIFICIAL INSEMINATION; GENE THERAPY; IN-VITRO FERTILISATION; LIFE, RIGHT TO; REPRODUCTIVE MEDICINE.

ethics committee. As regards the conducting of a *clinical trial* (qv), the committee, approved by the Minister, which is required to consider the justification for conducting the proposed trial and the circumstances under which it is proposed to be conducted; it must not consider the proposed trial to be justified unless it is satisfied that the risks to be incurred by the participants would be commensurate with the objectives of the trial: Control of Clinical Trials Act 1987, s 8. The committee is required to consider specified matters, including details of any proposed inducements or rewards, whether monetary or otherwise to be made for becoming a participant (CCTA 1987, s 8(4)). See also EC (Clinical Trials on Medicinal Products for Human Use) Regulations 2004, SI No 190 of 2004. [Bibliography: Cusack; Mills; Sheikh.] See ETHICAL CONDUCT.

ethics in public office. Provision has been made for the disclosure of the personal and business interests of holders of public office, and of directors and employees of certain public bodies, where these interests could give rise to a possible conflict of interest between private interests and the public good: Ethics in Public Office Act 1995. Disclosures are: (a) an annual written statement, which is published in relation to Oireachtas members, and available to the *Public Office Commission* in relation to public and civil servants and directors and employees; and (b) *ad hoc* – whenever a potential conflict of interest becomes apparent in the performance of official duties or functions.

An ethics framework has been provided for in respect of members of local authorities, their managers and employees: Local Government Act 2001, ss 166–182. It includes a new duty on members and staff to maintain proper standards of conduct, and a provision for the Minister to issue codes of conduct for the guidance of members and staff. Provision has been made for a *public register of interests* and designation by the manager of a person to be the *ethics registrar*. For the classes of local authority employees to whom the ethical framework applies, and for the annual declaration form to be furnished, see Local Government Act (Part 15) Regulations 2002, SI No 582 of 2002 and Regulations 2003, SI No 73 of 2003. See GIFT; STANDARDS IN PUBLIC OFFICE COMMISSION.

ethos. The distinctive character, spirits and attitudes of a group of people. In education, the *ethos of a school* is called the characteristic spirit of the school as determined by the cultural, educational, moral, religious, social, linguistic and spiritual values and traditions which inform and are characteristic of the objectives and conduct of the school: Education Act 1998, s 15(2)(b). There is an exemption from employment equality legislation in respect of more favourable treatment to maintain or protect the *religious ethos* of an institution: Employment Equality Act 1998, s 37(1). See DISCRIMINATION; RELIGIOUS BELIEF; RELIGIOUS ETHOS; SCHOOL; TALLAGHT HOSPITAL.

EUR-LEX. EUR-LEX is the European Union law webpage: see *www.europa.eu.int/ eur-lex/en/index.html*. Access is available to the text of European *directives*, *regulations* or *decisions*, as well as to proposals therefor, by using the link to the Official Journal. Also access is available by link to recent case law involving the European Court of Justice.

EURIBOR. [Euro Interbank Offered Rate.] The interest rate which has replaced DIBOR – Dublin Interbank Offered Rate. See Economic and Monetary Union Act 1998, s 22.

euro. The currency unit referred to in the second sentence of art 2 of the Council Resolution (EC) 98/974 of 3 May 1998. The currency of the State from 1 January 1999 is the *euro*, and the Irish pound unit was a subdivision of the euro in the transition period: Economic and Monetary Union Act 1998, s 6. The euro is also the currency of the 12 participating member states from 2002 ie Austria, Belgium, France, Germany, Greece, Finland, Ireland, Italy, Luxembourg, Netherlands, Portugal and Spain, unofficially referred to as *Euroland*.

The three non-participating member states in May 2004 are Denmark, Sweden and the UK. The Danish people decided by referendum in September 2000 not to participate, as did the Swedish people by referendum in September 2003.

The accession states, which joined the EU on 1 May 2004, are required to adopt the euro as their legal currency when they meet the economic criteria ie Cyprus, Czech Republic, Estonia, Hungary, Latvia, Lithuania, Malta, Poland, Slovakia, and Slovenia. Lithuania plans to adopt the euro by January 2007, Hungary by January 2008, and Slovakia by January 2009.

Irrevocably fixed conversion rates between the euro and the then currencies of the participating member states were fixed (eg €1 = IR£0.787564). Legislation provided that Irish pounds would no longer be legal tender from 30 June 2002 or such earlier date as the Minister might specify by order (EMUA 1998, s 9). The Minister specified that Irish pound notes and coins would be withdrawn from 1 January 2002 in a six-week transition period to midnight 9 February 2002 when the Irish currency would no longer be legal tender.

See Euro Changeover (Amounts) Act 2001 which amends the Economic and Monetary Union Act 1998, the Credit Union Act 1997 and the Heritage Act 1995. See also Finance Act 2001, s 240 and Sch 5; Courts and Court Officers Act 2002, s 31. See the Solicitors Acts (Euro Changeover) Regulations 2001, SIs Nos 460 and 504 of 2001; Rules of the Superior Courts (No 4) (Euro Changeover) 2001, SI No 585 of 2001; Supreme Court and High Court (Fees) (No 2) Order 2001, SI No 488 of 2001. See also SIs Nos 310, 311, 313, 582, 583 of 2001.

The Euro Changeover Board was established in 1998 to oversee the detailed implementation of the euro and to provide public and consumer information. See websites: *www.irlgov.ie/ecbi-euro* and *www. emuaware.forfas.ie*. See also *www. europa.eu.int/euro*. See CONVERSION RATE; CAPITAL; LEGAL TENDER; COINS; COUNTERFEIT.

euro, banknotes and coins. There are *seven* euro banknotes, in denominations of 5, 10, 20, 50, 100, 200 and 500 euro. There are one hundred *cent* to the euro. There are *eight* euro coins, in denominations of 1, 2, 5, 10, 20 and 50 cent and of 1 and 2 euro.

No person is obliged to accept more than 50 coins in euro or in *cent* in any single transaction: Economic and Monetary Union Act 1998, s 10.

Provision has been made for the Irish design of the *national face* of the euro and cent coins and for the 'edge lettering' design of the 2 euro coin: Economic and Monetary Union (Design of Coins) Order 2001, SI No 347 of 2001. The description agreed at EU level for the designs of the *common faces* of the coins is repeated in the Schedule to the Order. See COINS; COMMEMORATIVE COINAGE; LEGAL TENDER.

euro, convenient amounts. Provision has been made to replace Irish pound (IR£) amounts which are set down by law, with *convenient* amounts in euro with effect from 1 January 2002: Euro Changeover (Amounts) Act 2001. The amounts being replaced relate to certain fees or charges levied by government departments or bodies. Where *fees* are involved, they are reduced to the nearest convenient euro amount below the exact equivalent (eg inspection of a public file of a credit union – £5 becomes the convenient €6). Where the amount is a *threshold amount*, it is increased to the nearest equivalent euro amount above the exact equivalent (eg the maximum amount which may be released without probate to a spouse of a deceased member of the Civil Service, £15,000, becomes the convenient €20,000). The objective in all cases is to favour members of the public. See BANKRUPTCY; DISTRICT COURT; CIRCUIT COURT.

euro, copyright in. Copyright subsists in euro notes and coins: Economic and Monetary Union Act 1998, ss 20 and 34; Copyright and Related Rights Act 2000, s 189.

Euro Info Centre. Centres established by the European Commission Representation in Ireland with existing organisations to provide information to small and medium-sized firms on all aspects of EU affairs, and located in Dublin (with Enterprise Ireland), Limerick (with Shannon Development) and in Cork, Galway, Sligo and Waterford (with the local Chambers of Commerce).

Euro-Jus. A network of legal experts on Community law, one in each member state of the European Community, whose function is to answer practical questions on Community law, addressed to them by individuals, on matters which affect their everyday life eg right to work and to social security in another member state. The service is provided free of charge to the individual. The Irish *Euro-Jus* is located at the EC Office in Ireland, European Union House, 18 Dawson Street, Dublin 2. Tel (01) 6625113; Fax (01) 6625118. Email: *frank.meates@cec.ecc.int*; website: *www. euireland.ie*.

Eurobarometer. A European Commission service, established in 1973, which measures and analyses trends in public opinion in all the member states and in the candidate countries. It produces about 100 reports every year. See website: *www. europa.eu.int/comm/public_ opinion/*.

Eurocontrol. The European Organisation for the Safety of Air Navigation established by the Eurocontrol Convention ie the International Convention relating to Co-operation for the Safety of Air Navigation signed at Brussels on 13 December 1960 and amended in 1970, 1978 and 1981: Irish Aviation Authority Act 1993, ss 2(1) and 46–57. See Irish Aviation Authority (Eurocontrol Safety Regulatory Requirements) Order 2003, SI No 387 of 2003. See website: *www.eurocontrol.int*. See AIR NAVIGATION.

Eurocrat. A colloquial term which refers to a person who works for one of the EU institutions. It is a pun on the word 'bureaucrat'.

Eurojust. [European Judicial Co-operation Unit.] The body established by Council Decision of 28 February 2002, under the Nice Treaty, with a view to reinforcing the fight against serious crime: European Arrest Warrant Act 2003, s 2(1); OJ No L63 of 6 March 2002, p 1. If the High Court has not made a decision on surrender of a person named in a European arrest warrant within 60–90 days from the arrest of the person, or has decided not to make an order, it must direct the Minister for Justice to inform the issuing judicial authority and, where appropriate, *Eurojust* in relation thereto and of the reasons therefor (EAWA 2003, s 16(10)–(11)). The executing judicial authority may seek the advice of *Eurojust* when making a choice between warrants issued by two or more member states for the same person (EAWA 2003, Sch, Pt B, art 16(2)). See EUROPEAN ARREST WARRANT.

Europe Day. The 9th of May, designated as the day to celebrate the birthday of the EU. It was on 9 May 1950 that Robert Schuman, then Foreign Minister of France, made his famous speech proposing European integration as the way to secure peace and build prosperity in post-war Europe. See FOUNDING FATHERS OF THE EU; SYMBOLS OF THE EU.

European Agency for the Evaluation of Medicinal Products (EMEA). The agency of the European Union, located in London, with responsibility for co-ordinating scientific resources existing in member states with a view to evaluating and supervising medicinal products for both human and veterinary use.

See website: *www.eudra.org/emea.html.* See MEDICINAL PRODUCT.

European Armaments Agency. Under the draft Treaty establishing a Constitution for Europe it is proposed to establish a *European Armaments, Research and Military Capabilities Agency* to identify operational requirements, to promote measures to satisfy those requirements, to contribute to identifying and, where appropriate, implementing any measure needed to strengthen the industrial and technological base of the defence sector, to participate in defining a European capabilities and armaments policy, and to assist the Council in evaluating the improvement of military capabilities. See EUROPEAN UNION CONSTITUTION.

European arrest warrant, general. Means a warrant, order or decision of a judicial authority of a member state, issued under such laws as give effect to the Framework Decision in that member state, for the arrest and surrender by the state to that member state of a person in respect of an offence committed or alleged to have been committed by him under the law of that member state: European Arrest Warrant Act 2003, s 2(1). The Framework Decision means the decision of the Council of 13 June 2002 on the European arrest warrant and the surrender procedures between member states, the text of which is set out

in Irish and English in Pt A and Pt B of the Schedule of the EAWA 2003.

The Framework Decision is based on the concept of mutual recognition and respect for the judicial processes of the member states of the EU. It seeks to simplify procedures for the surrender of wanted persons, in particular by replacing the inter-state aspects of extradition with an inter-court system. The EU member states that have been designated by 1 September 2004 as having given effect to the Framework Decision under their respective national laws are: Austria, Belgium, Cyprus, Denmark, Finland, France, Hungary, Lithuania, Luxembourg, Malta, Poland, Portugal, Slovenia, Spain, Sweden, the Netherlands and the UK: SIs Nos 4, 130, 206 and 400 of 2004.

The first person to be extradited to Ireland under the European arrest warrant is believed to be Laurence Andrew McMillan, who was charged with and convicted of stealing a yacht from Crosshaven, Co Cork: *Irish Times*, 21 May 2004. See CORRESPONDING OFFENCE; EXTRADITION; EUROJUST; JUDICIAL AUTHORITY; SCHENGEN ALERT; SPECIALTY RULE.

European arrest warrant, execution of. Where a judicial authority in an issuing state duly issues a European arrest warrant in respect of a specified person, that person must be arrested and surrendered to the issuing state: European Arrest Warrant Act 2003, s 10. The specified person is a person: (a) against whom that state intends to bring proceedings for the offence to which the warrant relates, or (b) on whom a sentence of imprisonment or detention has been imposed and who fled from the issuing state before he commenced serving that sentence, or before he completed serving that sentence.

An application must be made to the High Court for an endorsement of the warrant in order that it may be executed (EAWA 2003, s 13). A person arrested must be brought before the High Court as soon as may be, and may be remanded in custody or granted bail (EAWA 2003, s 13(5)). A garda may arrest a person without a warrant, where a *Schengen alert* has been issued by a judicial authority in a member state and the garda believes, on reasonable grounds, that the person is likely to leave the State before the warrant is received in the State (EAWA 2003, s 14).

There are provisions in the 2003 Act dealing with consent to surrender, postponement of surrender on humanitarian grounds, and conditional surrender (EAWA 2003, ss 15, 18, 19), committal (s 16), surrender by issuing state to another member state or to a third state (ss 23–24), handing over of property (s 26), remand (s 27), and transit (s 28). See SCHENGEN ALERT.

European arrest warrant, issue of. An Irish court may issue a European arrest warrant in respect of a person: (a) where it is satisfied upon reasonable grounds that: (i) a domestic warrant was issued for the arrest of that person but was not executed, and (ii) the person is not in the State, and (b) where the person would, if convicted of the offence concerned, be liable to a term of imprisonment of 12 months or more, or (ii) a term of imprisonment of not less than four months has been imposed on the person and the person is required to serve all or part of that term of imprisonment: European Arrest Warrant Act 2003, s 33(1). The application must be made by or on behalf of the DPP and the court may be the District, Circuit Criminal, Central Criminal or Special Criminal Court.

A European arrest warrant is transmitted to a member state by the Minister for Justice (EAWA 2003, s 34). Where a person is surrendered to the State pursuant to such a warrant, a garda may execute the domestic warrant notwithstanding that it is not in his possession (EAWA 2003, s 35). There is provision for a deduction from the sentence imposed in respect of the offence specified in the European arrest warrant, of any period of detention in the executing state prior to surrender (EAWA 2003, s 36).

European arrest warrant, prohibition on surrender. A person must not be surrendered, pursuant to a European arrest warrant, to the issuing state: (a) if the surrender would be incompatible with the State's obligations under the European Convention on Human Rights; (b) if the surrender would constitute a contravention of any provision of the Constitution of Ireland; or (c) if there are reasonable grounds for believing: (i) that the warrant was issued for the purposes of facilitating his prosecution or punishment in the issuing state for reasons connected with his sex, race, religion, ethnic origin, nationality, language, political opinion or sexual orientation, or (ii) that he would be tortured or subjected to other inhuman or degrading treatment or liable to the imposition of the death penalty: European Arrest Warrant Act 2003, s 37(1).

Surrender must not take place unless: (a) the offence corresponds to an offence of the State and is punishable under the law of the issuing state by a maximum period of at least 12 months, or the person has already been sentenced to imprisonment or detention of at least four months, or (b) the offence is a specified offence punishable in the issuing state by imprisonment for a maximum period of not less than three years (EAWA 2003, s 38(1)). There are 32 specified serious offences, including hijacking, terrorism, murder, rape, arson, laundering the proceeds of crime, child pornography, illicit trafficking in drugs and radioactive material, and trafficking in human beings (EAWA 2003, Sch, Pt B, art 2(2)).

There are also provisions preventing surrender under a number of other grounds eg where there has been a pardon or amnesty (EAWA 2003, s 39); passage of time from commission of offence (s 40), double jeopardy (s 41), proceedings in the State for the offence (s 42), age (s 43), commission of offence outside issuing state (s 44), person convicted *in absentia* (s 45), and immunity from prosecution (s 46). See POLITICAL OFFENCE; REVENUE OFFENCE.

European Bank for Reconstruction and Development. The bank established with the object of fostering and promoting the transition of the former command economies of Central and Eastern Europe towards a market-based economic system. See European Bank for Reconstruction and Development Act 1991 as amended by Central Bank Act 1997, s 68. See SI No 65 of 1991 for privileges and immunities in Irish law. For the *European Agency for Reconstruction,* see website: *www.ear.eu.int.*

European Bureau for Lesser Used Languages. The body established in 1982, with offices in Brussels and Dublin, with the role of promoting and defending the regional and minority languages of the European Union and the linguistic rights of those that speak them. The bureau endeavours to ensure that all citizens belonging to a linguistic minority, obtain all the services they need in order to develop and use their language in everyday life. There are some 40 different such languages in the EU, spoken by about 50 million persons. See website: *www.eblul.org*. See LANGUAGE.

European Centre for the Development of Vocational Training (CEDEFOP). The body established in 1975 by the Council of the European Communities with responsibility for promoting and developing vocational training and continuing education at EU level. Located in Thessaloniki, Greece, it has taken a lead role in promoting transparency in vocational qualifications. See websites: *www.cedefop.eu.int* and *www.training village.gr*.

European Central Bank. Provision has been made for the establishment of a European Central Bank (ECB) and a European System of Central Banks (ESCB): EC Treaty, art 8 of the consolidated (2002) version. They are both required to act within the limits of the powers conferred on them by the Treaty and their individual Statutes. The ESCB is composed of the national central banks of the member states and the ECB. See European Parliament Elections (Amendment) Act 2004, s 2. See website: *www.ecb.int*. See CENTRAL BANK; LEGAL TENDER; MONETARY POLICY.

European citizenship. See CITIZENSHIP, EUROPEAN.

European Commission. The civil service of the European Community (qv). Prior to the enlargement of the EU in 2004, the Commission consisted of 20 members (a President, two Vice-Presidents and 17 Commissioners). Each Commissioner is assigned a particular portfolio and the Commissioners are collectively responsible. Each member state must have a national on the Commission but not more than two. A Commissioner represents the Commission and not his own State. Following the Maastricht Treaty (qv) the Commission retains, with a few exceptions, the sole right to initiate legislation. The term of office of the Commission however is five years (from 1995) to run more closely with the term of the European Parliament which must approve the appointment of the Commission. See EC Treaty, arts 211–219 of the consolidated (2002) version.

Under the Nice Treaty (qv), the following changes will take place: (a) regardless of size, each member state will nominate one Commissioner from 2005; (b) when the EU reaches 27 member states, the Council of Ministers will unanimously decide the size of the Commission which will be fewer than 27 Commissioners, with a system of rotating the right to nominate a Commissioner rotated among the member states on a strictly equal and fair basis. Under the proposed Treaty establishing a Constitution for Europe, agreed on 18 June 2004, but not yet ratified, there will be one Commissioner per member state until 2014, after which the Commission will consist of a number of members corresponding to two-thirds of the number of member states, ie 20 Commissioners when there are 30 member states, with rotation on a strictly equal basis. See websites: *www.europa.eu.int* and *www.euireland.ie*. See COMITOLOGY; EUROPEAN UNION CONSTITUTION; SINGLE EUROPEAN ACT.

European Commission Food and Veterinary Office (FVO). The EU office, located in Grange, Co Meath, with responsibility for monitoring the observance of food hygiene, veterinary and plant health legislation and contributing towards the maintenance of confidence in the safety of food offered to the European consumer. See PHYTOSANITARY.

European Communities' Financial Interests. Recent legislation gives effect in Irish law to the *Convention on the Protection of the European Communities Financial Interests* done at Brussels on 26 July 1995 and subsequent Protocols: Criminal Justice (Theft and Fraud Offences) Act 2001, ss 40–47. It is an offence to commit, participate in or obtain benefit or pecuniary advantage from a fraud affecting the Communities' financial interests (CJ(TFO)A 2001, s 42).

Also *active corruption* (ie a deliberate action of giving an advantage to an official for him to act or refrain from acting in accordance with his duty) and *passive corruption* (ie a deliberate action of an official who requests or receives an advantage to act or refrain from acting in accordance with his duty) are both offences (CJ(TFO)A 2001, ss 43–44). See also CJ(TFO)A 2001, s 60. [Bibliography: McGreal C.] See EXTRA-TERRITORIAL JURISDICTION; REVENUE OFFENCE.

European Community; EC. The Community, established by the Treaty signed at Rome on the 25th day of March 1957. The fourth amendment to the Constitution in 1972 provided for the State to join the Community. By the amendment, no provision of the Constitution invalidates laws enacted, acts done or measures adopted by the State *necessitated by the obligations of* *membership* or prevents laws enacted, acts done or measures adopted by the Community, or institutions thereof, from having the force of law in the State: 1937 Constitution, art 29(4)(3). The Constitution was further amended in 1987, 1992, 1998 and 2002 by the 10th, 11th, 18th and 26th referenda to enable the State to ratify the *Single European Act* (qv), the *Maastricht Treaty* (qv); the *Amsterdam Treaty* (qv) and the *Nice Treaty* (qv) respectively, the four main revisions of the Treaty of Rome (1937 Constitution, art 29(4)(3)–(11)).

The Treaty of Rome became binding in the State from 1 January 1973 and provision was made for all existing and future acts adopted by the institutions of the Community to be binding on the State and to be part of the domestic law thereof under the conditions laid down in the Treaty: European Communities Act 1972, s 2, European Communities Acts 1992 and 1993. A Minister of State may make regulations for enabling s 2 to have full effect (ECA 1972, s 3). Provision has been made to amend the 1972 Act in order to provide that certain parts of the Treaty of Nice shall form part of the domestic law of the State on ratification by Ireland of the Treaty: European Communities (Amendment) Act 2002. The 1972 Act was further amended in 2003 to provide for enlargement of the EC by a further ten countries in 2004: European Communities (Amendment) Act 2003.

The European Community has a legal personality, and in each of the member states must enjoy the most extensive legal capacity accorded to legal persons under their laws: EC Treaty, arts 281–282 of the consolidated (2002) version.

The European Community has as its task, by establishing a common market and an economic and monetary union and by implementing common policies or activities, to promote throughout the community a harmonious and balanced development of economic activities, sustainable and non-inflationary growth respecting the environment, a high degree of convergence of economic performance, a high level of employment and of social protection, the raising of the standard of living and quality of life, and economic and social cohesion and solidarity among member states (EC Treaty, art 2).

The tasks entrusted to the Community are carried out by the following institutions:

European Parliament, Council, Commission, Court of Justice, Court of Auditors (EC Treaty, art 7). The Council and Commission are assisted by an *Economic and Social Committee* (*qv*) and a *Committee of the Regions* (*qv*) acting in an advisory capacity.

The government is obligated to make a report each year, beginning with the year 2003, to each House of the Oireachtas on developments in the European Communities and the European Union: European Union (Scrutiny) Act 2002 as amended by European Communities (Amendment) Act 2002, s 2.

The 15 members of the European Community in April 2004 were: Austria, Belgium, Denmark, France, Germany, Greece, Finland, Ireland, Italy, Luxembourg, Netherlands, Portugal, Spain, Sweden, United Kingdom. A further ten countries joined on 1 May 2004: Cyprus, Czech Republic, Estonia, Hungary, Latvia, Lithuania, Malta, Poland, Slovakia, and Slovenia.

Provision was made in Irish legislation for accession to membership of Austria, Finland, Sweden and Norway, although Norway voted by referendum not to join: European Communities (Amendment) Act 1994. See *Greene v Minister for Agriculture* [1989] ITLR (12 June), HC. See website: *www.euireland.ie*. For the consolidated (2002) EC Treaty, see *www.europa.eu.int/eur-lex/en/treaties/index.html*

[Bibliography: Phelan.] See COMMUNITY LAW; COUNCIL OF MINISTERS; ENLARGEMENT OF EU; EUROPEAN COMMISSION; EUROPEAN UNION; INTERNAL MARKET.

European Company. A company created under EC law and known as a SE (*Societas Europaea*), as proposed in 1988. The *European Company Statute*, which comes into force on 8 October 2004, will give companies which are established in more than one member state, the option of merging into one company, a European company, and operating throughout the EU on the basis of a single set of company law rules instead of having a network of subsidiaries governed by different national laws. The minimum capital requirement has been set at €120,000. See Regulation (EC) 2001/2157 of 8 October 2001 on the Statute for a European company (SE); Directive (EC) 2001/86 of 8 October 2001 supplementing the Statute for a European company with regard to the involvement of employees. See 'The European company statute' by solicitor Gerald FitzGerald in *Law Society Gazette* (March 2002) 36. See *Quinn* in 8 ILT & SJ (1990) 231; Buttimore, *Societas Europaea and Worker Participation* (1994) 4 ISLR 17.

European Consumer Centre. The centre in Dublin, jointly funded by the European Commission and the Director of Consumer Affairs, which provides a free information and advice service to the public on their consumer rights and entitlements in Ireland and throughout the European Union. It is part of a European network of consumer centres – *Euroguichets*. It also provides an outreach programme and a free *litigation advice service* to members of the public who are involved in Small Claims proceedings. See email: *ecic@indigo.ie*, website: *www.ecic.ie*. See SMALL CLAIMS.

European contract law. There have been many moves towards the harmonisation of European contract law eg directives on consumer goods and guarantees, on unfair contract terms in consumer goods, on package holidays, distance contracts, doorstep contracts, consumer credit, timeshare contracts, direct marketing and privacy, and electronic commerce. However, the obstacles to the realisation of a modern European common law of contract is probably due to the constraints imposed by the principles of subsidiarity and proportionality. See *The Communication from the Commission and the European Parliament on European Contract Law* COM (2001 398 Final). See 'Irish Contract Law Reform and the European Commission's Agenda' by Prof Robert Clark in *Bar Review* (January/February 2001) 126.

European Convention on Human Rights. A Convention of the Council of Europe which was ratified by Ireland in 1953 and which seeks to protect human rights and fundamental freedoms and to maintain and promote the ideals and values of a democratic society. The Convention protects the right to life; the right to freedom from torture and inhuman or degrading treatment or punishment; the right to freedom from slavery, servitude and forced or compulsory labour; the right to liberty and security of the person; the right to a fair and public trial within a reasonable time; the right to freedom from retrospective criminal law and no punishment without law; the right to respect for private and family life, home and correspondence; the right to freedom of thought, conscience and religion; the right to freedom of expression; the right to freedom of assembly and association; the right to marry and found a family; the right to an effective remedy; and the prohibition of discrimination in the enjoyment of the rights as set out under the Convention.

The operational Protocols to the Convention are: (a) the 1952 Protocol which deals with property, educational and electoral rights; (b) the Fourth Protocol of 1963 which prohibits imprisonment for inability to pay a debt, contains the right of freedom of movement, and prohibits the individual or collective expulsion of nationals; (c) the Sixth Protocol of 1983 which provides for the abolition of the death penalty except in time of war; and (d) the Seventh Protocol of 1984 which provides for the right of appeal in criminal matters, compensation for wrongful conviction involving a miscarriage of justice, the right not to be punished twice for the same offence, equality between spouses, and procedural safeguards concerning the expulsion of lawfully resident aliens.

Rights under the Convention are now enforceable in Irish Courts: European Convention on Human Rights Act 2003. The Schedules to the Act contain the full text of the Convention and the operational Protocols.

Under the *Good Friday Agreement* (qv), the British government was required to incorporate the Convention into Northern Ireland law, whereas the Irish government was required only to examine the incorporation of the Convention. The Irish government subsequently decided to provide for an 'interpretative incorporation' of the Convention into domestic law and not 'direct incorporation'. Interpretative incorporation, as permitted under the Convention, allows for interpretation of the Convention in accordance with the political and legal culture of a state.

The 2003 Act is intended to ensure that there are two complementary systems in place in Ireland for the protection of fundamental rights and freedoms, with the superior rules under the Irish Constitution taking precedence.

Under the Act, any *statutory provision* and any *rule of law* must be interpreted, in so far as possible, in a manner compatible with the State's obligation under the Convention, retrospectively and prospectively (ECHRA 2003, s 2). 'Statutory provision' is widely defined to include any provision of an Act, or any order, regulation, rule, licence, bye-law created thereunder (ECHRA 2003, s 1(1)). 'Rule of law' includes common law (qv) ECHRA 2003, s 1(1). Where the court decides that a statutory provision or a rule of law is incompatible with the State's obligation under the Convention, and there is no other adequate or available remedy, it may make a 'declaration of incompatibility' (ECHRA 2003, s 5). If any issue as to the making of a 'declaration of incompatibility' arises in any proceedings, the party having carriage of the proceedings must serve notice on the Attorney-General and the Human Rights Commissioner: RSC Ord 60A inserted by SI No 211 of 2004.

The declaration does not affect the validity of the statutory provision or the rule of law, but it must be laid before each of the Houses of the Oireachtas, and it enables the party to the proceedings to apply to the Attorney-General for an *ex-gratia* payment of compensation in respect of any injury or loss or damage suffered by him as a result of the incompatibility concerned.

Where a person suffers injury, loss or damage because of a breach by an organ of the State (of its duty to perform its functions in a manner compatible with the Convention), the person may institute proceedings in the Circuit or High Court to recover damages (ECHRA 2003, s 3).

Under the Convention, the *European Commission of Human Rights* and the *European Court of Human Rights* were created. The European Commission operates in a conciliatory manner, receiving petitions alleging non-compliance with the Convention and initiating investigations. A 'declaration of incompatibility' under ECHRA 2003 does not prevent a party from initiating proceedings in the European Court (ECHRA 2003, s 5(2)(b)).

The European Union (qv) is required to respect human rights, as guaranteed by the Convention, and as they result from the constitutional traditions common to the member states, as general principles of Community law: Maastricht Treaty 1992, art F.2; now, Treaty on European Union, art 6 of the consolidated (2002) version. See *Re O'Laighleis* [1960] IR 93; *Norris v Attorney-General* [1982] HC (unreported) and [1984] IR 36, SC; *Doyle v Commissioner of Garda* [1999] 1 IR 249, SC; *MFM v MC (Proceeds of Crime)* [2001] 2 IR 385, HC;

Quinn v Ireland [2004] HC, *Law Society Gazette* (June 2004) 7.

See 'One step forward, two steps back?' by solicitor John Moher in *Law Society Gazette* (April 2002) 12; 'From Ireland to Strasbourg: Form and Substance of the Convention System' by Anna Austin in *Bar Review* (March 2001) 303; 'The European Convention on Human Rights and Irish Incorporation – Adopting a Minimalist Approach' by Ray Murphy and Siobhán Wills in *Bar Review* (September 2001) 541 and (October/November 2001) 41; 'The European Convention on Human Rights and the Irish Criminal Justice System' by Una Ní Raifeartaigh BL in *Bar Review* (December 2001) 111. For key procedural differences between the UK and Ireland, see 'An unconventional approach' by Barry O'Halloran in *Law Society Gazette* (January/February 2003) 26. See 'Practice and Procedure' by Anthony Lowry BL in *Bar Review* (November 2003) 183. See 'UK court sets benchmark for ECHR' in *Law Society Gazette* (January/February 2004) 5. For full text of the European Convention on Human Rights, see website: *www.echr.coe.int*. See Practice Direction HC 32 in *Law Society Gazette* (May 2004) 5. [Bibliography: Clark & McMahon; Collins & O'Reilly; Heffernan; Kilkelly (2); Harris O'Boyle & Warwick UK; Lester & Pannick UK.] See EUROPEAN COURT OF HUMAN RIGHTS; HUMAN RIGHTS COMMISSION.

European Convention on Torture. See TORTURE.

European Council. See COUNCIL OF MINISTERS.

European Court of Auditors. The body responsible for the audit of the legality and regularity, as well as the sound financial management, of the resources managed by the institutions and bodies of the European Union. It is located in Luxembourg and comprises 15 members who are appointed for a six year term by the Council of Ministers, following consultation with the European Parliament. See arts 246–248 of the consolidated EC Treaty. See European Parliament Elections (Amendment) Act 2004, s 2. See website: *www.eca.eu.int*.

European Court of Human Rights. The judicial body of the Council of Europe in Strasbourg which hears cases involving basic rights and freedoms under the *European Convention on Human Rights* (qv). Irish courts are now required to take judicial notice of the Convention and of any declaration, decision, advisory opinion or judgment of the European Court and of any decision or opinion of the *European Commission of Human Rights*: European Convention on Human Rights Act 2003, s 4.

Formerly, it was held that member states were not obliged to accept the jurisdiction of the European Court and its decisions did not bind our courts: *Re O'Laighléis* [1960] IR 93. However, it was held that a judgment of the Court might have a persuasive effect in Ireland in relation to contempt of court: *Desmond & Dedeir v Glackin & Minister for Industry & Commerce* [1992] ITLR (17 February), HC.

The European Court has held:

(a) that internment without trial in Ireland did not breach the Convention on Human Rights as the government had derogated from the terms of the Convention in times of national emergency: *Lawless v Ireland* [1961] 1 EHRR 15;

(b) that inhuman and degrading treatment had been inflicted on certain persons who had been in custody in Northern Ireland: *Ireland v United Kingdom* [1978] 2 EHRR 25;

(c) that the non-availability of state-funded legal aid in matrimonial matters was a breach of the Convention: *Airey v Ireland* [1979] 2 EHRR 305;

(d) that the Convention on Human Rights had been violated as the applicants had not been brought promptly before a judge or other judicial officer following their arrest: *Brogan & Ors v United Kingdom*: 7 ILT & SJ [1989] 16;

(e) that a company and an individual had their right to peaceful enjoyment of their possessions interfered with: *Healy Holdings Ltd & Healy v Ireland* (1991) Irish Times, 30 November;

(f) that there was an inadequate investigation into the circumstance of the death in 1989 of Belfast solicitor Patrick Finucane: *Finucane v United Kingdom* (2003) Case no 29178/95;

(g) that two articles of the Convention were violated due to the extent of the court delays in a case involving the purchase of a site by a Co Wicklow couple: *Doran v Ireland* (2003) Irish Times, 1 August 2003.

A judge of the European Court of Human Rights who was a practising barrister or practising solicitor prior to their appointment, is qualified for appointment as a judge of the Superior Courts of Ireland: Courts (Supplementary Provisions) Act 1961, s 5(2) as substituted by Courts and Court Officers Act 2002, s 4. For full text of the Rules of Court 2002, European Convention on Human Rights, see website: *www.echr.coe.int*. [Bibliography: Berger; Clark & McMahon; Collins & O'Reilly.] See BUGGERY; EUROPEAN CONVENTION ON HUMAN RIGHTS; HUMAN RIGHTS COMMISSION; LEGAL AID.

European Court of Justice. The institution of the EC, consisting of one judge per member state assisted by eight advocates-general. The court adjudicates on issues between an individual and his government, between member states of the Community, or between institutions of the Community: EC Treaty, arts 220–245 of the consolidated (2002) version. Each member state is entitled to nominate a national to the court. Courts of the member states may *refer* matters relating to the treaties establishing the European Community to the European Court for determination. These treaties are: Treaty of Rome 1957, Single European Act 1986, Maastricht Treaty 1992, Amsterdam Treaty 1997, and Nice Treaty 2001 (qqv).

The issue as to what stage a *reference* should be made to the Court of Justice is a matter exclusively for the national courts to determine; the Supreme Court has jurisdiction to grant an interlocutory injunction notwithstanding a reference of separate issues to the Court of Justice: *SPUC v Grogan* [1990] 8 ILT Dig 156 and Treaty of Rome, art 177 (now, consolidated art 234). A ruling of the European Court may be relied upon retrospectively where that Court, on a question of interpretation of Community law, does not within the same judgment, limit its retrospective effect: *Carberry v Minister for Social Welfare* [1989] ITLR (5 June).

If the Court of Justice finds that a member state has not complied with its judgment, it may impose a lump sum or penalty on it (EC Treaty, art 228). The Court has no jurisdiction over certain aspects of the European Union (qv) eg over the common foreign and security policy, or over the common provisions: Treaty on European Union, art 46 of the consolidated (2002) version.

A judge of the European Court of Justice who was a practising barrister or practising solicitor prior to their appointment is qualified for appointment as a judge of the

Superior Courts of Ireland: Courts (Supplementary Provisions) Act 1961, s 5(2) as substituted by Courts and Court Officers Act 2002, s 4. See also *Portion Foods Ltd v Minister for Agriculture* [1981] ILRM 161; *McNamara v An Bord Pleanála* [1998] 3 IR 453, SC. See Protocol on the Statute of the Court of Justice, adopted at Nice in 2001. See website: *www.curia.eu.int*. See 'The Treaty of Nice and Reform of the Community Courts' by Liz Heffernan BL in *Bar Review* (June/July 2001) 474. [Bibliography: Lasok UK.] See ADVOCATES-GENERAL; EUROPEAN COMMUNITY; FIRST INSTANCE, COURT OF; FRAMEWORK DECISION; PERJURY; PRELIMINARY RULINGS.

European decision. The name proposed in the draft European Constitutional Treaty for an EU non-legislative act, which is binding in its entirety: National Forum on Europe, *Glossary of Terms* (2003). See proposed Treaty establishing a Constitution for Europe. A decision which specifies those to whom it is addressed is binding only on them. See EUROPEAN UNION CONSTITUTION.

European Economic Area. See EEA AGREEMENT.

European Economic Community; EEC. Term in the Treaty of Rome 1957; it is replaced by the term European Community: Maastricht Treaty 1992, art G.A(1), now art 1 of the EC Treaty, consolidated (2002) version. See EUROPEAN COMMUNITY.

European Economic Interest Grouping (EEIG). A form of international association which enables its members to combine part of their activities while retaining their economic and legal independence: Regulation (EEC) 85/2137: OJ 1985 L119 p 1 and SI No 191 of 1989. See Linnane in 7 ILT & SJ (1989) 213, 9 ILT & SJ (1991) 36, 10 ILT & SJ (1992) 163; Power in 8 ILT & SJ (1990) 19. See also Finance Act 1990, s 29, now Taxes Consolidation Act 1997, s 1014. [Bibliography: Anderson UK.]

European election. An election in the State of members to the European Parliament by European electors; *European elector* means a person entitled to vote at such election: Electoral Act 1992, s 2(1); European Parliament Election Act 1997, s 2(1). A person is entitled to be registered as a *European elector* in a constituency if he has reached the age of 18 years, is ordinarily resident in that constituency and is either: (a) a citizen of Ireland, or (b) a national of another EU member state (EA 1992, s 9).

A national of another EU member state, other than the UK, is required to produce a statutory declaration to be so registered (EPEA 1997, s 6). Voting is by secret ballot, with each elector having a single transferable vote, counted by the principles of proportional representation (EPEA 1997, s 7).

A *candidate* for election, or for nomination as a *replacement candidate*, must have reached the age of 21 and must be either: (a) a citizen of Ireland, or (b) a national of another EU member state and normally resident in Ireland, and not be disqualified from being a candidate eg of unsound mind, or an undischarged bankrupt (EPEA 1997, s 11; EA 1992, s 41). For elections held after 1 January 2004, there are *four constituencies* returning 13 Members of the European Parliament (MEP): Dublin (4), East (3), North-West (3), and South (3): European Parliament Elections (Amendment) Act 2004, s 4. The 2004 Act: (a) extends the number of office holders who are ineligible for election, (b) provides for the termination of the dual mandate, and (c) prohibits the declaration of the result of the poll until polling has closed in the member state whose electors are the last to vote. A limit of €230,000 has been set for the aggregate election expenses for a candidate in any European Parliament constituency: SI No 87 of 2004. Also provision has been made for the inclusion of photographs of candidates and the emblems of political parties on the ballot paper: SI No 204 of 2004. For election forms, see SI No 203 of 2004. See CASUAL VACANCY; DEATH OF CANDIDATE; ELECTION DEPOSIT; EUROPEAN PARLIAMENT; ELECTION PETITION, EUROPEAN; PROPORTIONAL REPRESENTATION.

European Employees' Forum. A forum established in accordance with an agreement for the establishment of arrangements for the information and consultation of employees of *large undertakings*, operating across *two* or more European countries: Transnational Information and Consultation of Employees Act 1996, ss 3(1) and 11(1). The undertakings must have at least 1,000 employees within the member states and at least 150 employees in each of at least two member states, called a

'*Community-Scale Undertaking*'. If agreement for establishing a European Employees' Forum is not reached, there is provision for the establishment of a standard *European Works Council* with a specified composition, role, operation and set of rights (TICEA 1996, s 13). There is an exemption from these requirements for any undertaking which had an agreement in force by 22 September 1996 covering their entire workforce, providing for the transnational information and consultation of employees (TICEA 1996, s 6).

European Environment Agency. The body located in Denmark which has the aim of producing objective, reliable and comparable information for those concerned with European environmental policy. See website: *www.eea.eu.int*.

European Extra-Judicial Network; EEJ-Net. The network established in October 2001 by the European Commission to assist consumers resolve their cross-border disputes regarding goods and services through alternative dispute resolution (ADR) schemes. The EEJ-Net aims to provide a communications and support structure to facilitate the work of the ADR bodies across borders. The six nominated ADR bodies in Ireland are: ELCOM, the Electricity Supply Board; Chartered Institute of Arbitrators (arbitration scheme for tour operators); Ombudsman for Credit Institutions; Centre for Dispute Resolution; Insurance Ombudsman of Ireland; and the Advertising Standards Authority of Ireland. For the list of ADR bodies in the EU, see website: *www.europa.eu.int/comm/consumers/redress*. See also *www.eej-net.org* and *www.eccdublin.ie*. See 'Alternative Remedies' by Susan Reilly in *Law Society Gazette* (November 2003) 32.

European Foundation for the Improvement of Living and Working Conditions. The EU body located in Dublin with the role of contributing to the planning and establishment of a better quality of life through an improvement in living and working conditions. See websites: *www.eurofound.ie* and *www.eurofound.eu.int*.

European framework law. The term proposed to be used in the draft European Constitutional Treaty for a 'directive' ie a legislative act which is binding as to the result to be achieved on the member state to which it is addressed, but leaves national authorities free to decide the forms and means to achieve that result: National Forum on Europe, *Glossary of Terms* (2003). See proposed Treaty establishing a Constitution for Europe. See DIRECTIVE, EC; EUROPEN UNION CONSTITUTION.

European Health Insurance Card. An electronic health card proposed to be introduced for all EU citizens in 2004; it will replace the E111 Form which enables a person to access subsidised medical care in another EU member state when travelling abroad. It is proposed that the card will eventually carry details of the person's medical history and essential information eg the person's blood type. The card will eventually replace other paper-based forms, such as the E112 and E128, which entitle citizens to treatment in other member states, which they are unable to avail of in their own country. For details on applying for a card and to download an Application Form, visit website: *www.ehic.ie*.

European Investment Bank. The non-profit making bank, comprising the member states of the EC, which has the task of granting loans and giving guarantees which facilitate the financing of a range of projects eg projects for developing less developed regions; projects for modernising or converting undertakings; projects of common interest to several member states: EC Treaty, arts 266–267 of the consolidated (2002) version.

The governors of the bank are empowered to establish a European Investment Fund; ratification by the State of the agreement to so empower the governors has been effected by adding the agreement to the list of Treaties governing the EC as they appear in s 1(1) of the European Communities Act 1972: European Communities (Amendment) Act 1993, s 2.

The Supreme Court held that the putting forward of the name of former Supreme Court judge Hugh O'Flaherty for vice-president of the Bank and the announcement to that effect by the Minister for Finance was not in breach of the Constitution; it held that the 'purported nomination' had no legal effect and was no more than an expression of the wish of one of the Bank's shareholders (the Irish government) that a particular candidate should be appointed: *Riordan v Ireland & Attorney-General* [2000] 4 IR 537, SC.

See European Parliament Elections (Amendment) Act 2004, s 2. For European Investment Bank, see website: *www.eib.org*.

European law. Under the proposed Treaty establishing a Constitution for Europe, a legislative act of general application. It is binding in its entirety and directly applicable in all member states. See COMMUNITY LAW; EUR-LEX; EUROPEAN FRAMEWORK LAW; REGULATION OF EC.

European ombudsman. See OMBUDSMAN, EUROPEAN.

European opinion. Under the draft European Constitutional Treaty, the name for a form of non-binding legal act of the European Union: National Forum on Europe, *Glossary of Terms* (2003). See proposed Treaty establishing a Constitution for Europe. See EUROPEAN UNION CONSTITUTION.

European Parliament. The institution of the European Economic Community (qv) which is elected by direct universal suffrage every five years, presided over by a President: EC Treaty, arts 189–201 of the consolidated (2002) version. It has a right to be consulted on all politically important measures; it also has advisory and supervisory powers. It participates in the process leading up to the adoption of Community acts by exercising its powers under the procedures laid down in arts 251 and 252 and by giving its assent or delivering advisory opinions (EC Treaty, consolidated art 192). The parliament may, by *Motion of Censure*, force the resignation of the Commission (EC Treaty, art 201).

The role of the parliament has been strengthened by the Maastricht Treaty 1992 eg: (a) the parliament has the right to reject legislation in a number of areas; (b) parliament approval is required in a number of areas including the appointment of the Commission; and (c) the parliament has extended rights of involvement in the detailed operation of the Community eg a right of enquiry, a right to receive petitions, a right to call on the Commission to initiate legislation, and the right to appoint the European Ombudsman.

Election in Ireland to the parliament is by proportional representation with a form of democratic endorsement for substitutes for the elected member who retires, dies or otherwise relinquishes his seat. In April 2004 the parliament had 626 members and Ireland elected 15 of these. Under the Nice Treaty (qv) an upper limit of 732 members has been set to cater for the enlargement of the EU. When there are 27 member states, Ireland will be entitled to elect 12 members of the parliament. With 25 member states from 1 May 2004, Ireland is entitled to 13 members: Protocol on the Enlargement of the European Union.

Under the proposed *Treaty establishing a Constitution for Europe*, agreed on 18 June 2004, but not yet ratified, there is provision for a minimum of 6 MEPs per member state and a maximum of 96. This proposed Treaty also provides for the national parliaments to receive draft proposals at the same time as the European Parliament, with a view to enhancing their capacity to review and debate proposals at the earliest possible date. See websites: *www.europarl.eu.int* and *www.europarl.ie*. See CITIZENSHIP, EUROPEAN; COMMUNITY LAW; CONSTITUENCY; EUROPEAN ELECTION; EUROPEAN UNION CONSTITUTION; SINGLE EUROPEAN ACT; MAASTRICHT TREATY; NICE TREATY.

European patent. A patent granted under the European Patent Convention (qv): Patents Act 1992, s 2(1). See also COMMUNITY PATENT AGREEMENT.

European Patent Convention; EPC. The Convention of 1973 which established a European patent organisation with its own European Patent Office situated in Munich for the granting of *European patents* under the system of law as set out in the Convention. The Convention is expressed to be a special agreement within the Paris Convention (qv). Ireland ratified the Convention on 1 May 1992.

An application under the EPC must designate in which of the contracting States patent protection is desired, and if the application is accepted, a European patent is granted for each of the designated States, which patent must be treated in the State as having the same effect of and subject to the same conditions as are national patents granted by that State (EPC, art 2). This is given effect in Ireland by the Patents Act 1992, s 119.

If the language of the specification of the European patent is not English, a translation in English must be filed with the Irish Patents Office for the patent to have effect in Ireland (PA 1992, s 119(6)–(7)). There is provision for the conversion of an application for a European patent into an application for an Irish patent (PA 1992, s 120) and for the High Court to determine questions as to the right to a European patent (PA 1992, s 121). See also PA 1992, ss 122–132. For proposed amendments to ss 119 and 120 of PA 1992, see Patents

(Amendment) Bill 1999. See also EPC Protocol on Recognition. See COMMUNITY PATENT AGREEMENT.

European Police Office; EUROPOL. A body corporate with a range of powers, duties and privileges and having as its over-all objective to improve the effectiveness of member states in preventing and combating terrorism, unlawful drug trafficking and other forms of international crime, where there are factual indications that an organised criminal structure is involved and two or more member states are affected by the forms of crime in question: Europol Convention adopted by the EU member states on 26 July 1995 and given effect in Ireland by the Europol Act 1997.

Provision is made in the 1997 Act: (a) for the establishment, composition and management of a *national unit* in Ireland, (b) for sending persons from the unit to be *liaison officers* at Europol in the Hague, (c) for the *Data Protection Commissioner* to be the national supervisory body in data protection matters, and (d) for the application of the Official Secrets Act 1963 to information or facts which come to the knowledge of Europol officers or employees. See Europol Act 1997 (Designation of National Unit) Order 1998, SI No 368 of 1998. For *common action* in the EU in the field of police co-operation, see Treaty on European Union, art 30 of the consolidated (2002) version. See website: *www.europol. eu.int*. See COMMON POLICIES; POLICE CO-OPERATION.

European Prison Rules. Rules governing prisons, which comprise recommendations of the Committee of Ministers of the Council of Europe to which Ireland is a party. The Rules are an international agreement but are not part of the domestic law of the State: *McAlister v Minister for Justice* [2003] 1 ILRM 161, HC. See PRISON.

European Public Information Centre. [EPIC.] The one-stop shop for a variety of information on Europe located at European Union House, 18 Dawson Street, Dublin 2. The centre provides comprehensive information through databases, multimedia facilities and satellite links to Europe. Email: *eu@carrcomm.iol.ie*.

European recommendation. Under the draft European Constitutional Treaty, the name for a form of non-binding legal act of the European Union: National Forum on Europe, *Glossary of Terms* (2003). See proposed Treaty establishing a Constitution for Europe. See COMMUNITY LAW; EUROPEAN UNION CONSTITUTION.

European regulation. Under the proposed *Treaty establishing a Constitution for Europe* a non-legislative act of general application for the implementation of legislative acts and of certain specific provisions of the Constitution. It may either be binding in its entirety and directly applicable in all member states, or be binding, as to the result to be achieved, upon each member state to which it is addressed, but shall leave to the national authorities the choice of form and methods. See EUROPEAN UNION CONSTITUTION; REGULATION OF EC.

European site. Means a special area of conservation under the EC (Natural Habitats) Regulations, SI No 94 of 1997, a site of Community importance in the Habitats Directive, or an area classified under the Birds Directive: Planning and Development Act 2000, s 2(1). It is mandatory that these sites be recorded in the *development plan* of the planning authority and that their status be taken into account when the authority decides on a planning application (PDA 2000, s 10(2)(c)). If a proposed development would contravene materially a development objective indicated in the development plan for the conservation and preservation of a European Site, this will justify refusal of planning permission without compensation (PDA 2000, s 191 and Sch 4, para 19). See PLANNING PERMISSION, DECISION ON.

European Transparency Directive. The directive which lays down the procedure for the provision of information in the field of technical standards and regulations: Directive (EC) 98/34 and Directive (EC) 98/48. There is a requirement on member states to inform the Commission on certain draft legislation and regulations and must not adopt them for three months from the date of receipt of the draft by the Commission. The introduction of the banning of smoking in the workplace in 2004 was delayed by the need to comply with the directive. See TOBACCO PRODUCT.

European Union. The Union, founded on the European Communities (qv), established by the member states of the EC by the Maastricht Treaty 1992, art A; now, Treaty on European Union, art 1 of the consolidated (2002) version. The Union includes the European Community together with separate provisions on common foreign and security policy and on judicial co-operation. The task of the Union is to organise, in a manner demonstrating consistency and solidarity, relations between the member states and between their peoples. The Union has a number of objectives eg: (a) to promote economic and social progress, (b) to assert its identity on the international scene, (c) to strengthen the protection of the rights and interests of the nationals of its member states, (d) to develop close co-operation on justice and home affairs (Treaty on European Union, consolidated art 2).

The Union must respect the national identities of its member states and fundamental rights (Treaty on European Union, consolidated art 6). Ireland is empowered to be a member of the Union: 1937 Constitution, art 29(4)(4). No provision of the Constitution invalidates laws enacted, acts done or measures adopted by the State which are necessitated by the obligations of membership of the Union (Treaty on European Union, art 29(4)(10)).

The government is obligated to make a report each year, beginning with the year 2003, to each House of the Oireachtas on developments in the European Communities and the European Union: European Union (Scrutiny) Act 2002 as amended by European Communities (Amendment) Act 2002.

Under the proposed Treaty establishing a Constitution for Europe, agreed on 18 June 2004, but not yet ratified, the European Community and Euratom would be replaced by the European Union, which would have a legal personality and have treaty-making powers. See 'Balance of power shifts in new European Treaty' by Conor Quigley QC in *Law Society Gazette* (July 2003) 8. See websites: *www.euireland.ie* and *www.europa.eu.int*. For the consolidated (2002) version of the Treaty on European Union, see: *www.europa.eu.int/eur-lex/en/treaties/index.html*. For the Institute of European Affairs, see website: *www.iiea.com*. For European Movement – Ireland, see website: *www.europeanmovement.ie*. [Bibliography: Lucey M C & Keville C.] See COMMON POLICIES; ENHANCED COOPERATION; ENLARGEMENT OF EU; MAASTRICHT TREATY; SYMBOLS OF THE EUROPEAN UNION.

European Union Constitution. A proposed *Treaty establishing a Constitution for Europe*, to replace all the existing treaties, was agreed by the Intergovernmental Conference of the 25 EU member states on 18 June 2004. It requires to be ratified by each member state, either by their parliaments or by referendum, depending on their legal arrangements or commitments. The proposed Constitution is divided into four parts, introduced by a preamble.

Part I deals with the definition and objectives of the Union, fundamental rights and citizenship of the Union, Union competencies, the Union's institutions and bodies, exercise of Union competence, the democratic life of the Union, the Union's finances, the Union and its immediate environment and Union membership.

Part II incorporates the *Charter of Fundamental Rights*, dealing with dignity, freedoms, equality, solidarity, citizens' rights and justice.

Part III consolidates the Articles from previous treaties dealing with all the policies and functioning of the Union. It also contains more details regarding the institutions of the Union, the policy in the area of justice and home affairs, foreign policy, the financial arrangements and decision making.

Part IV is a general part, including transitional arrangements, and sets out how member states may go about ratifying and amending the Treaty. See 'Draft EU constitution fails the test of liberal-democracy' by David Mangan in *Law Society Gazette* (January/February 2004) 14. See CHARTER OF FUNDAMENTAL RIGHTS; DELEGATED REGULATION; EUROPEAN ARMAMENTS AGENCY; EUROPEAN DECISION; EUROPEAN FRAMEWORK LAW; EUROPEAN OPINION; EUROPEAN RECOMMENDATION; EUROPEAN REGULATION; FLEXIBILITY CLAUSE; LEGAL BASE; PETERSBERG TASKS.

European Works Council. See EUROPEAN EMPLOYEES' FORUM.

European Year of ... A year designated by the EU to draw public attention to a particular European issue by organising a series of special events in connection with the issue. The year 2004 is the *European Year of Education through Sport*. See DISABILITY.

euthanasia. The term used to describe the painless killing of a person; it is unlawful. 'Deliberately causing the death of a patient is professional misconduct': Medical Council, *A Guide to Ethical Conduct and Behaviour* (6th edn, 2004) para 23.1. For a seriously ill patient, the Council has reiterated its view that access to nutrition and hydration remain one of the basic needs of human beings, and all reasonable and practical efforts should be made to maintain both (para 22.1). [Bibliography: Hanafin.] See DYING PATIENT; MURDER; SERIOUSLY ILL PATIENT; SUICIDE.

event. A public performance which takes place, wholly or mainly, in the open air or in a structure with no roof or a partial, temporary or retractable roof, a tent or similar temporary structure and which comprises music, dancing, displays of public entertainment or any activity of a like kind: Planning and Development Act 2000, s 229.

It is an offence to hold an event without a licence from the local authority or to be in control of land when an unlicensed event is held (PDA 2000, s 230). A licence, which is only granted following a process of public notice and application, can be granted subject to conditions concerning, for example, the safety of persons at the event, insurance cover, provision of transport, and minimisation of disruption of the area in which the event is held (PDA 2000, s 231).

An event holder has a statutory duty to have regard for safety, as has every person attending the event (PDA 2000, s 234). The gardaí have powers of inspection in connection with events (PDA 2000, s 235). There are special provisions dealing with the approval of the holding by a local authority itself of an event (PDA 2000, s 238). The holding of an event, or *works* relating to an event, is not development and consequently does not require planning permission (PDA 2000, s 240).

Regulations have been made setting out the type of events for which a licence is required under the Planning and Development Act 2000, Pt XVI: Planning and Development Regulations 2001, Part 16, arts 182–199: SI No 600 of 2001. For previous regulations, see Planning and Development (Licensing of Outdoor Events) Regulations 2001, SI No 154 of 2001.

A local authority is empowered to make bye-laws requiring the promoters or organisers of events at which large numbers of persons are likely to be present to take measures to prevent or limit the creation of litter at the events and provide for its removal: Litter Pollution Act 1997, s 21(2)(d) substituted by Protection of the Environment Act 2003, s 57. See INDOOR EVENT.

eviction. Dispossession; recovery of land by due process of law. See EJECTMENT. See also PART 4 TENANCY, TERMINATION OF; RENT; RENT ARREARS; TENANCY DISPUTE.

evidence. The testimony of witnesses and the production of documents and things which may be used for the purposes of proof in legal proceedings. The law of evidence comprises the rules which govern the presentation of facts and proof in proceedings before a court. Evidence may be direct or circumstantial. *Direct* evidence is evidence of a fact in issue (qv); it may be the statement of someone who observed with his senses. *Circumstantial* evidence is evidence of a fact relevant to the *fact in issue;* it is evidence from which the fact in issue may be inferred.

It has been held that the rules of evidence should not be allowed to offend common sense: *The People (DPP) v BK* [2000] 2 IR 199, CCA. [Bibliography: Cannon & Neligan; Charleton (5); Cole; Fennell; Healy; Ó Síocháin; Cross UK; Phibson UK.] See VIVA VOCE.

evidence, adducing. See BURDEN OF PROOF.

evidence, book of. See BOOK OF EVIDENCE.

evidence, certificate of. Certain matters stated in a certificate are admissible in evidence eg a certificate signed by a garda stating that he, at a specific time and place, arrested a person, charged the person, and cautioned the person in respect of a specified offence: Criminal Justice (Miscellaneous Provisions) Act 1997, s 6. This provision was introduced to make more efficient use of garda time. The court may require oral evidence if the interests of justice so require (CJ(MP)A 1997, s 6(4)). The certificate relates to a preliminary process and is a justifiable way of proving matters of a technical nature: DPP *(Ivers) v Murphy* [1999] 1 ILRM 46, SC. See also Company Law Enforcement Act 2001, s 110A inserted by Companies (Auditing and Accounting) Act 2003, s 52.

evidence, circumstantial. See CIRCUMSTANTIAL EVIDENCE.

evidence, extrinsic. Evidence of statements or circumstances or facts not referred to in a document which may explain or vary its meaning. Such evidence is generally inadmissible except to show the intention of a testator and to assist in the construction of or to explain any contradiction in a will. It must be capable of showing what the intention of the testator was in the particular context: *O'Connell v Bank of Ireland* [1998] 2 ILRM 465, SC. See Succession Act 1965, s 90; also *Rowe v Law* [1978] IR 55; *Clinton, deceased: O'Sullivan v Dunne* [1988] ILRM 80. See AMBIGUITY.

evidence, false. See PERJURY; PERVERTING THE COURSE OF JUSTICE.

evidence, fresh. See FRESH EVIDENCE.

evidence, hearsay. See HEARSAY.

evidence, new. See FRESH EVIDENCE.

evidence, preservation of. Evidence relevant to guilt or innocence must so far as is necessary and practicable be kept until the conclusion of a trial; also articles which may give rise to the reasonable possibility of securing relevant evidence must be preserved also: *Murphy v DPP* [1989] ILRM 71; 7 ILT & SJ [1989] 158. The gardaí are under a duty, arising from their unique investigative role, to seek out and preserve all evidence having a bearing or potential bearing on the issue of guilt or innocence: *Braddish v DPP* [2001] 3 IR 127, SC and [2002] 1 ILRM 151, SC approved in *Dunne v DPP* [2002] 2 ILRM 241, SC and 2 IR 305. The Supreme Court has said that there was a need for a more cohesive practice among the gardai regarding the preservation of pre-trial evidence: *Bowes v DPP* [2003] FL 7119, SC and 2 IR 25. See also *Connolly v DPP* [2003] FL 7603, HC. See Commissions of Investigation Act 2004, s 31; Criminal Justice Bill 2004 s.6. See 'The obligation to seek out and preserve evidence' by George Birmingham SC in *Bar Review* (June 2004) 86.

evidence, primary. Primary evidence is the best evidence available eg primary evidence of a document is the document itself or a duplicate of the original. See BEST EVIDENCE; DOCUMENTARY EVIDENCE; EVIDENCE, SECONDARY.

evidence, secondary. Evidence which suggests the existence of better evidence and which may be rejected if that better evidence is available eg a copy of a document or oral evidence of the contents of a lost will. See DOCUMENTARY EVIDENCE; OFFICE COPY.

evidence and constitutional rights. The courts will rule as inadmissible, evidence obtained in violation of constitutional rights unless the act constituting the breach was committed unintentionally or accidently or there are extraordinary excusing circumstances justifying its admissibility:

People (DPP) v Kenny [1990] ILRM 569, SC. [Bibliography: Healy.]

evidence for use outside State. See LETTER OF REQUEST.

evidence in previous proceedings. As an exception to the hearsay (qv) rule, the evidence of a witness in previous proceedings is admissible where the witness is dead, or unable to travel, or is otherwise unprocurable, provided that: (a) the person against whom the evidence is tendered had on the former occasion an opportunity of examining the witness; (b) the question in issue is substantially the same; (c) the proceedings are between the same parties. See DEPOSITION; HOSTILE WITNESS; PREVIOUS STATEMENT, INCONSISTENT.

evidence in rebuttal. See REBUTTAL, EVIDENCE IN.

evidence obtained illegally. Evidence obtained illegally is not necessarily inadmissible. It has been held that it is admissible if it is relevant, the illegality being merely ignored although not condoned; however, the trial judge has a discretion to exclude it, if it appears to him that public policy, based on a balancing of public interests, requires such exclusion. In a criminal trial, the question as to whether illegally obtained evidence should be admitted must be decided by the trial judge: *Blanchfield v Hartnett* [2001] 1 ILRM 193, HC and [2002] 435, SC and 3 IR 207. See *The People (Attorney-General) and O'Brien v McGrath* [1964] 99 ILTR 59; *The People v O'Brien and O'Brien* [1965] IR 142; *The People v Madden* [1977] 111 ILTR 117; *DPP v McMahon* [1987] ILRM 87. [Bibliography: Healy.] See CONFESSION; EVIDENCE AND CONSTITUTIONAL RIGHTS.

evidence of character. See CHARACTER, EVIDENCE OF.

evidence of conviction. See CONVICTION, EVIDENCE OF.

evidence tending to bastardise children. The rule of law, known as the *rule in Russell v Russell,* under which neither spouse could give evidence which would tend towards rendering a child of their marriage illegitimate, ceased to have legal effect in the State after the enactment of the 1937 Constitution: *S v S* [1983] IR 68. Statutory recognition of this is given by the Status of Children Act 1987, s 47 which provides that the evidence of a husband or wife is admissible in any proceedings to prove that marital intercourse did or did not take place between them during any period.

ex abundanti cautela. [From excess of caution.] Sometimes a provision will be included in a statute for the avoidance or removal of doubt eg that the terms and conditions of employment of existing members of University staff are not affected by the Universities Act 1997 (UA 1997, s 25(8)).

ex aequo et bono. [In justice and good faith.]

ex cathedra. [From the chair.] With official authority.

ex contractu. [Arising out of contract.]

ex curia. [Out of Court.]

ex debito justitiae. [Arising as a matter of right.] A remedy which the applicant obtains as of right, in contrast with a discretionary right eg in the case of an order of *habeas corpus* (qv). A petitioning creditor who is unable to have his debt paid by a company is entitled to a winding up order *ex debito justitiae*: *Bowes v Hope Life Insurance and Guarantee Co* [1865] 11 HLC 389. See also *Re Downs & Co* [1943] IR 420; *Devereaux v Kotsonouris* [1992] ILRM 140, HC; *de Roiste v Minister for Defence* [2001] 2 ILRM 241, SC and 1 IR 190 and ELR 33.

ex delicto. [Arising out of wrongs.] See TORT.

ex diuturnitae temporis omnia praesumuntur esse rite et solemnitur acta. [From lapse of time, all things are presumed to have been done rightly and regularly.] See ANCIENT DOCUMENT.

ex div. Ex dividend; indicates that the price of stocks and shares does not include dividends or interest to date. See BOND WASHING; CUM DIV.

ex dolo malo non oritur actio. [No right of action can have its origin in fraud.]

ex gratia. [As a favour.] Not arising pursuant to a legal liability. A local authority was empowered to make an *ex gratia* payment to an officer who was suspended: Local Government Act 1994, s 49. This provision has been repealed by the Local Government Act 2001, s 5(1), Sch 3, Pt 1, and not re-enacted. See European Convention on Human Rights Act 2003, s 5(4). See CRIMINAL INJURIES COMPENSATION TRIBUNAL; SWEEPSTAKE; UNTRACED DRIVER.

ex informata conscientia. [From an informed conscience.] A district court judge cannot have regard to such matters *ex informata conscientia* in dismissing a charge under the Probation of Offenders Act 1907 where there is no such evidence before the court. He must have (in the nature of the offence or the facts established in evidence before him), the materials entitling him to apply the Act: *McClellan v Brady* [1918] 2 IR 63. See INTERPRETATION OF LEGISLATION; JUDICIAL NOTICE.

ex maleficio non oritur contractus. [A contract cannot arise out of an illegal act.] See ILLEGAL CONTRACTS.

ex mero motu. [Of one's own free will.]

ex nudo pacto non oritur actio. [No action arises from a nude contract.] See NUDUM PACTUM.

ex officio. [By virtue of office.]

ex parte. [On behalf of.] An application made in a judicial proceedings made by a party to the proceedings in the absence of and without notice to the other party or parties or by a person who has an interest but is not a party thereto. See RSC Ord 40, r 20.

The High Court has jurisdiction to set aside leave previously granted in *ex parte* judicial review proceedings, if it is satisfied on *inter partes* argument that leave plainly should not have been granted: *Adam v Minister for Justice* [2001] 2 ILRM 452, SC and 3 IR 53. It is not appropriate to appeal to the Supreme Court against such orders made *ex parte*, as this would involve the Supreme Court acting as a *court of first instance* in considering argument and perhaps evidence never considered by the High Court.

In the Circuit Court, there are a number of applications which may be made to the judge by any party, without notice to the other party, on lodging with the County Registrar a copy of the *civil bill*, an *ex parte* docket in accordance with Form 27 of the *Schedule of Forms*, and filing an affidavit in support of the application: Circuit Court Rules 2001 Ord 20, r 2. Examples of orders are service out of the jurisdiction; receiving a consent and making same a rule of court; the production of any deed; and liberty to effect service in a special manner.

For District Court *ex parte* applications, see DCR 1997 Ord 11, r 3; Ord 12, r 5; Ord 101, r 3 as amended by District Court (Appeals to the Circuit Court) Rules 2003, SI No 484 of 2003. For contrasting examples of *ex parte* applications, see JUDICIAL REVIEW; LABOUR INJUNCTION; INJUNCTION. See also LETTER OF REQUEST.

ex post facto. [By a subsequent act.] Retrospectively. See RETROSPECTIVE LEGISLATION; ULTRA VIRES.

ex proprio motu. [Of his own accord.] Refers to an action taken by the court on its own initiative.

ex relatione; ex rel. [From a narrative or information.]

ex tempore judgment. See EXTEMPORE JUDGMENT.

ex turpi causa non oritur actio. [An action does not arise from a base cause.] An illegal contract is unenforceable as it is void. See *Scott v Doering* [1892] 2 QB 724; *Brady v Flood* [1841] 6 Circuit Cases 309. See ILLEGAL CONTRACTS.

exacta diligentia. [Utmost diligence.] See BREACH OF TRUST.

exaggerated claim. The Supreme Court has ruled that a falsehood in one aspect of a claim, made in order to exaggerate the claim, could at worst lead to that part of the claim being reduced or disallowed: *Shelly-Morris v Bus Átha Cliath* [2002] FL 6849, SC. Deliberate exaggeration of a claim may be such as to be an abuse of process of the court. The courts had the power and duty to protect their own processes from being made the vehicle of *unjustified recovery*; in a proper case this can be done by staying or striking out the plaintiff's proceedings. If there had been a finding in this case of an abuse of process by the plaintiff (there was not) it could have affected the determination of costs: *Shelly-Morris v Bus Átha Cliath* [2003] 2 ILRM 12, SC and 1 IR 232.

In another case the judge held that the plaintiff had a tendency to 'gild the lily' in relation to aspects of her claim: *Wall v Raleigh* [2003] FL 6826, HC. See *O'Connor v Bus Átha Cliath* [2003], SC reported in *Law Society Gazette* (January/February 2004) 60. See also *Law Society Gazette* (March 2003) 37. See PERSONAL INJURIES ACTION; SUMMONS, PERSONAL INJURIES.

examination. Interrogation of a person on oath. *Examination-in-chief* (or direct examination) is the examination of a witness by the party who has called him. *Cross-examination* is the examination of that witness by the opposite party with a view to diminishing the effect of his evidence. *Re-examination* is the further examination of the witness by the party who called him, with a view to explaining or contradicting any false impression created by the cross-examination; re-examination must be confined to matters arising out of the cross-examination. *Leading questions* (qv) must

not be asked in the examination-in-chief or re-examination; they may be asked in cross-examination. A judge may disallow any question put in cross-examination which may appear to him to be vexatious and not relevant: RSC Ord 36, r 37. For examination in *commercial proceedings* (qv), see RSC Ord 63A, r 6(1)(xi) inserted by Rules of the Superior Courts (Commercial Proceedings) 2004, SI No 2 of 2004.

In the district court, it is part of a judge's function to decide what sort of examination-in-chief and cross-examination may be pursued; if his error in refusing cross-examination is so gross, it may oust his jurisdiction: *O'Broin v D J Ruane* [1989 HC] ILRM 732. As a general rule, the prosecution are not bound to inform the defence of matters which they may put in cross-examination to witnesses for the defence: *People (DPP) v James Ryan* [1993 CCA] ITLR (19 Apr). See also CONVICTION, EVIDENCE OF; DISTRICT COURT; HOSTILE WITNESS.

examination of goods. Where goods are delivered to a buyer which he has not previously examined, he is not deemed to have accepted them unless and until he has had a reasonable opportunity of examining them for the purpose of ascertaining whether they are in conformity with the contract: Sale of Goods Act 1893, s 34; Sale of Goods and Supply of Services Act 1980, s 20. See *White Sewing Machine v Fitzgerald* [1895] 29 ILTR 37; *Marry v Merville Dairy Ltd* [1954] 88 ILTR 129.

examination of debtor. The examination in the district court of a debtor's means which the creditor can compel whenever a debt is due on foot of a judgment of a competent court: Enforcement of Court Orders Act 1926, s 15 as amended by the Courts (No 2) Act 1986, ss 1 and 3. The examination is compelled by the issue of a summons requiring the attendance of the debtor in court and the completion beforehand by him of a *statement of means*, setting forth his assets and liabilities, his income, and the means by which it is earned or the source from which it is derived, and the persons for whose support he is legally or morally liable: DCR 1997 Ord 53, r 3.

Following examination, the judge may make an *instalment order* requiring the debt to be repaid by instalments, in default of which the debtor may be imprisoned by order: Ord 53 rr 6–8. See DEBTOR'S SUMMONS; INSTALMENT ORDER.

examination paper. Includes any paper, plan, map, drawing, diagram, pictorial or graphic work or other document and any photograph, film or recording in which questions are set for answer by candidates: Education Act 1998, s 49. It is an offence, without lawful authority, to publish an examination paper or to have such a paper in one's possession prior to the holding of an examination (EA 1998, s 52). The Minister has wide powers to prescribe examinations (EA 1998, s 50). See NATIONAL QUALIFICATIONS AUTHORITY OF IRELAND.

examination re bankrupt. The court may summons a bankrupt or any person who is known or suspected to have property of the bankrupt; a person is not entitled to refuse to answer on the grounds that his answer might incriminate him but his answers will not be admissible in evidence against him in other proceedings: Bankruptcy Act 1988, s 21. This provision has been found to be constitutional, as there is no prohibition on the courts performing certain administrative functions for the purpose of discharging their own functions: *O'Donoghue v Ireland* [2000] 2 ILRM 145, HC. See also *Re Wilson ex p Nicholson* [1880] 14 Ch D 243.

examination re company. As regards a company which is compulsorily or voluntarily being wound up, the court has extensive power to examine persons on oath and they may not refuse to answer any question on the grounds that they may be incriminating themselves; however, any answers given will not be admissible in evidence in any other proceedings, except in regard to perjury in respect of the answers.

The court has power to order a person being examined to pay his debt owed to the company or to return to the liquidator any money, property or books and papers of the company on such terms as the court directs. See Companies Act 1963, ss 245 and 245A as amended or inserted by the Companies Act 1990, ss 126–127.

The power of the High Court to order an examination under s 245 of the 1963 Act is discretionary and the application for the examination may be made by the creditors to the company: *Re Comet Food Machinery Ltd (in liquidation)* [1999] 1 IR 485, SC. See RSC Ord 74, r 125; Ord 39, r 4. See *Re Aluminium Fabricators Ltd* [1983]; *Alba Radio Ltd v Haltone (Cork) Ltd* [1995] 2 ILRM 466, HC and 2 IR 170. See COURT

PROTECTION OF COMPANY; INVESTIGATION OF COMPANY.

examination results. Special provisions have been made concerning the right of individuals to personal data (qv) regarding examination results; examination authorities are required to comply with a request for a copy of any such personal data within 60 days from the date of the request or from the date of first publication of the results whichever is the later: Data Protection Act 1988, s 4(6). See STATE EXAMINATIONS COMMISSION.

examiner of company. See COURT PROTECTION OF COMPANY.

Examiner of Restrictive Practices. Formerly, the person appointed by the Minister with many functions relating to restrictive practices in the supply or distribution of goods or of the provision of a service: Restrictive Practices Acts 1972 and 1987, now repealed. See Competition Act 1991, ss 2(2) and 22. See now COMPETITION AUTHORITY.

examinership. See COURT PROTECTION OF COMPANY.

excardination. See INCARDINATION.

exception. (1) In proceedings, an objection to an answer. (2) In a deed, a *saving clause* to prevent the passing of something which otherwise would pass.

excess clause. A clause in an insurance policy whereby the insured is to bear the first specified amount of any loss. See INSURANCE.

exchange. (1) Reciprocal transfer of ownership or possession. (2) A place for the purchase and sale of, for example, stocks and shares. (3) A transfer of settled land for other land. See SETTLEMENT; STOCK EXCHANGE.

exchange, bill of. See BILL OF EXCHANGE.

exchange control. The restricting of certain outward movement of funds from the State and ensuring that funds accruing to Irish residents from external sources are not withheld from the country's external reserves: Exchange Control Acts 1954 to 1990. Breach of an exchange control regulation constituted an offence; however, as regards civil proceedings, the courts would enforce a contract even if the consequences of so doing would involve a breach of exchange control regulations: *Fibretex v Belier Ltd* [1954] 89 ILTR 141; *Shelley v Pollock* [1980] QB 348. There was nothing illegal or improper in an inspector, validly appointed to investigate a company pursuant to the Companies Act 1990, obtaining through the Minister information from the Central Bank concerning exchange control transactions: *Desmond & Dedeir Ltd v Glackin & Minister for Industry and Commerce* [1992] ITLR (7 December), SC.

Full liberalisation of capital investment within the EC is the objective of the EC Treaty, arts 14 and 56–60 of the consolidated (2002) version. In accordance with this objective, exchange controls with all countries were abolished as from 1 January 1993 as the 1990 Act lapsed on 31 December 1992.

However, the Minister may by regulation impose restrictions on *financial transfers* involving specified States: Financial Transfers Act 1992. 'Financial transfers', without prejudice to the generality of the expression, includes all transfers which could be movement of capital or payments within the meaning of the treaties governing the EC if made between member states of the Community (FTA 1992, s 3). Restrictions were imposed in 1992 on financial transfers involving Iraq and the Federal Republic of Yugoslavia as part of UN agreed sanctions: SIs No 414 and 415 of 1992. See Financial Transfers (Zimbabwe) (Prohibition) Order 2002, SI No 283 of 2002; Financial Transfers (Counter Terrorism) Order 2004, SI No 458 of 2004; Financial Transfers (Usama Bin Laden, Al-Qaida and Taliban of Afghanistan) (Prohibition) Order 2004, SI No 456 of 2004. See also *Luisi and Carbone v Ministero de Tesero* [1984] ECR 377. See CAPITAL LIBERALISATION.

exchange rate. See CONVERGENCE CRITERIA; RATE OF EXCHANGE.

exchange rate policy. The Council of Ministers are empowered to conclude formal agreements on the exchange rate system for the *ECU* in relation to non-Community currencies: EC Treaty, art 111 of the consolidated (2002) version. See now EURO; CONVERSION RATE.

exchequer bills and notes. Bills and notes of credit issued by government under the authority of parliament; they are for various sums and bear interest according to the usual rate at the time. The Minister is empowered to create and issue securities bearing interest at such rate and subject to such conditions as to repayment, redemption or any other matter as he thinks fit: Finance Act 1970, s 54 as amended by Finance (No 2) Act 1970, s 6, National

Development Finance Agency Act 2002, s 23 and Housing (Miscellaneous Provisions) Act 2002, s 18.

The National Treasury Management Agency previously offered for sale on behalf of the Irish government *exchequer bills,* which were bearer instruments sold by tender every week and had a maturity of 91 or 182 days. Now, the NTMA offer for sale *exchequer notes,* which are short-term transferrable instruments sold daily on behalf of the government, with a range of maturity dates, not more than one year. See also National Treasury Management Agency Act 1990.

excise duty. A duty chargeable on certain goods eg intoxicating liquors and tobacco. The government is empowered to impose, vary or terminate excise duties by order, provided the order is validated by confirmation by the Oireachtas (qv): Imposition of Duties Act 1957; *McDaid v Judge Sheehy* [1989] ILRM 342, HC and [1991] ILRM 250, SC. The Director of Public Prosecutions has a year to apply for a summons in certain excise matters: *DPP v Howard* [1990] ITLR (26 February), HC.

As regards the EC, the general principle is that excise duty becomes payable at the time of production of the product within or its entry into the Community in the relevant member state: Directive (EEC) 92/12 of 25 February 1992. It is in the member state of consumption where excise duty is to be paid, except products acquired by private individuals for their own use and transported by them, in which case duty is charged in the member state where they are acquired. See Control of Excisable Products Regulations 1992, SI No 430 of 1992. See Finance Act 2004, ss 43–53. See *Travers* in 10 ILT & SJ (1992) 254. See BET.

excise law. General excise law has been consolidated and modernised, existing provisions have been streamlined, and the level of penalties which apply to comparable excise offences has been standardised: Finance Act 2001, ss 96–153 as amended by SI No 711 of 2003. In addition: (a) the time limit for the institution of summary proceedings in excise offences has been harmonised with that in customs law, (b) a presumption in relation to proceedings for tobacco offences has been introduced, (c) a garda is now empowered to detain unstamped tobacco products, and (d) a Revenue officer is empowered to have a vehicle kept stationary or removed to a suitable place for excise control purposes. Excise law relating to alcohol products has been consolidated, modernised, and its structure brought more into line with EU law relating to alcohol products which is set down in Directive (EEC) 92/83: Finance Act 2003, ss 73–86.

Regulations have been made which prescribe the obligations on and the procedures to be complied with by persons engaged in the intra-Community movement of excisable products under the provisions of Directive (EEC) 92/12: Control of Excisable Product Regulations 2001, SI No 443 of 2001. See Finance Act 2004, ss 43–53. See INTOXICATING LIQUOR LICENCE.

exclusion clause. A clause in a contract which excludes or modifies an obligation, whether primary, general secondary or anticipatory secondary, that would otherwise arise under the contract by implication of law: *Photo Productions Ltd v Securicor Transport Ltd* [1980] AC 827. It has been held that an exclusion clause in a loan application form which stated 'no responsibility can be accepted by the Society for the condition of the property', absolved the Society from any liability in respect of the condition of the property and the clause was binding: *O'Connor v First National Building Society* [1991] ILRM 208, HC. See EXCLUSION CLAUSES, RESTRICTION OF.

exclusion clauses, restriction of. Any term which exempts a seller from certain implied conditions in a contract for the sale of goods is void where the buyer *deals as a consumer* (qv) and, in any other case, is not enforceable unless it is shown that it is *fair and reasonable*: Sale of Goods Act 1893, s 55; Sale of Goods and Supply of Services Act 1980, s 22. Similar provisions apply also in relation to a term of a hire-purchase agreement (SGSSA 1980, s 31). A condition or warranty is not negatived except by clear words (SGA 1893, s 55(2)) and an exclusion clause may also be ineffective under the doctrine of fundamental breach eg where the performance is totally different from that which the contract contemplated or there is some other breach going to the root of the contract (SGA 1893, s 55(5)).

A producer of a *defective product* cannot limit or exclude his liability, contractually, by notice or by any other provision: Liability for Defective Products Act 1991, s 10. See *Clayton Love v B & I Steamship Co Ltd* [1970] 104 ILTR 157; *Tokn Grass Products Ltd v Sexton Co Ltd* [1983] HC. See CONSUMER, DEALING AS; FAIR AND REASONABLE TERMS.

exclusion order. (1) An order excluding a spouse from occupation of the family home (qv) which may be made following the grant of a decree of judicial separation: Judicial Separation and Family Law Reform Act 1989, s 16(a). Contrast with a *barring order* (qv), the breach of which may lead to a criminal sanction whereas breach of s 16(a) does not. See Domestic Violence Act 1996, s 20. See ANTI-SOCIAL BEHAVIOUR.

(2) An order by the Minister excluding from the State any *non-national* specified in the order: Immigration Act 1999, s 4(1). The Minister may make such an order if he considers it necessary in the interest of national security or public policy. It is an offence to contravene a provision of an exclusion order (IA 1999, s 4(2)). Every exclusion order must be laid before each of the Houses of the Oireachtas as soon as possible after it is made and may be annulled or overturned (IA 1999, s 12). The 1999 Act was necessitated by the decision in *Laurentiu v Minister for Justice* [1999] 1 ILRM 1, SC and [1999] 4 IR 26, SC.

(3) An order prohibiting a person from entering or being in the vicinity of certain specified premises eg public houses, off-licences, dance venues of all types, amusement arcades, night clubs, premises providing food (whether fixed or mobile eg mobile food vans): Criminal Justice (Public Order) Act 2003, s 3. Being in the 'vicinity' means being within 100 metres of the premises (CJ(PO)A 2003, s 2(1)).The exclusion order applies for such times, and during such a period not exceeding 12 months, as the District Court may specify. The order is an additional penalty which may be imposed on a person on conviction for a public order offence under the Criminal Justice (Public Order) Act 1994, ie under s 4 (intoxication in a public place), s 5 (disorderly conduct), s 6 (threatening, abusive, insulting behaviour), s 7 (distribution or display of offensive material), s 8 (failure to comply with a garda direction), or s 9 (wilful obstruction).

An appeal lies to the Circuit Court from an exclusion order (CJ(PO)A 2003, s 3(5)).

A person who, without reasonable cause, does not comply with an exclusion order is guilty of an offence (CJ(PO)A 2003, s 3(4)). The purpose of the 2003 Act is to deal more effectively with late night public disorder and disturbance which mainly has its origins in alcohol abuse.

exclusionary rule. The rule whereby otherwise admissible evidence is excluded because of the constitutional imperative of protecting the personal rights of the citizen as far as possible eg evidence obtained pursuant to an invalid search warrant. See *DPP v Kenny* [1990] ILRM 569. See O'Gorman in 9 ILT & SJ (1991) 142. See EVIDENCE AND CONSTITUTIONAL RIGHTS.

exclusive. In a particular case, the Supreme Court refused to require that machinery be used *exclusively* in a designated area to qualify for an investment allowance, where the legislation did not include this restriction: *McNally v O'Maoldomhnaigh* [1990] ITLR (22 October), SC.

exclusive dealing. A term in a contract which restricts a party to dealing only with the other party; it may constitute a restraint of trade (qv) and thereby render it void: *McEllistrem v Ballymacelligott Co-operative Agricultural and Dairy Society* [1919] AC 548. See SOLUS AGREEMENT.

exclusive distribution agreement. The Competition Authority (qv) considered that exclusive distribution agreements constitute agreements which have the object and effect of preventing, restricting or distorting competition and that this offended against the Competition Act 1991, s 4(1) now Competition Act 2002, s 4(1). The Authority granted a licence in 1993 to specified categories of such agreements, subject to a specified period and specified conditions: see Iris Oifigiúil, 19 November 1993. Under the 2002 Act, the Competition Authority does not have power to issue licences. [Bibliography: Forde (13); Lucey; Power V.] See COMPETITION, DISTORTION OF.

exclusive jurisdiction. (1) As regards the EC, the courts of the State have *exclusive jurisdiction* regardless of domicile of the parties in certain specified proceedings eg proceedings which have as their object rights *in rem* in, or tenancies of, immovable property situated in the State; proceedings which have as their object the constitution, nullity or dissolution of a company which has its *seat* in the State; certain specified proceedings regarding validity of public registers, the registration or validity of patents, trade marks or designs, and the enforcement of judgments: Jurisdiction of Courts and Enforcement of Judgments (European Communities) Act 1998, Sch 1, art 16; however, from 2002 see below. As regards EFTA countries, see JCEJ(EC)A 1998, Sch 7, art 16.

The *Brussels I Regulation* on the recognition and enforcement of judgments in civil and commercial matters, replaces the 1998 Act as from 1 March 2002 for all EU States except Denmark: EC (Civil and Commercial Judgments) Regulations 2002, SI No 52 of 2002. For similar provisions on 'exclusive jurisdiction', see SI No 52 of 2002, art 22.

(2) The *exclusive jurisdiction* given to the courts of one State, agreed between parties, where one or more of them is domiciled in a contracting State, to settle disputes between them if and when they arise (JCEJ(EC)A 1998, Sch 1, art 17); however, from 2002 see below. The agreement conferring jurisdiction must either be in writing or evidenced in writing or, in international trade or commerce, in a form which accords with the practices in that trade or commerce of which the parties are or ought to be aware. The provisions of art 17 must be strictly applied and interpreted in accordance with European Community law in order to be effective in granting exclusive jurisdiction to the courts of a particular State: *Clare Taverns t/a Durty Nelly's v Charles Gill & Ors* [2000] 2 ILRM 98, HC. In this case, it was decided that the English courts had jurisdiction and the Irish courts had not. As regards EFTA countries, see JCEJ(EC)A 1998, Sch 7, art 17.

The *Brussels I Regulation* on the recognition and enforcement of judgments in civil and commercial matters, replaces JCEJ(EC)A 1998 as from 1 March 2002 for all EU states except Denmark: EC (Civil and Commercial Judgments) Regulations 2002, SI No 52 of 2002. This retains the right of parties to choose the jurisdiction of a certain court, which gives that court exclusive jurisdiction, provided the evidential requirements are met (SI No 52 of 2002, art 23). It also provides that any communication by electronic means which can provide a durable record of the agreement is deemed to be in writing (SI No 52 of 2002, art 23(2)). See SEAT OF CORPORATION.

exclusive licence. In respect of patents of invention, means a licence from a proprietor of or applicant for a patent which confers on the licensee and persons authorised by him, to the exclusion of all other persons (including the proprietor or applicant for the patent), any right in respect of the invention: Patents Act 1992, s 2(1). The holder of an exclusive licence has the like right as the proprietor of the patent to take proceedings in respect of any infringement of the patent (PA 1992, s 51). Contrast with *sole* licence which does not exclude the proprietor himself; a sole licensee cannot sue for infringement. An exclusive licence may be partially written and partially oral: *Morton-Norwich v United Chemicals* [1981] FSR 337. See COPYRIGHT, LICENSING OF; INFRINGEMENT OF PATENT; LICENCES OF RIGHT, PATENTS; PERFORMERS' RIGHTS, LICENSING OF.

exclusive user. See RESTRICTED USER CLAUSE.

exeat. [Let him go.] Permission to leave.

executed. That which is done or completed. Contrast with EXECUTORY. See DEATH PENALTY.

execution. (1) The act of completing or carrying into effect, particularly of a judgment.

(2) The execution of deeds is accomplished by the signing sealing and delivery of them by the parties as their own acts and deeds in the presence of witnesses.

(3) Formerly, the carrying out of a court's sentence of death. 'Doctors should not assist in judicial execution': Medical Council. *A Guide to Ethical Conduct and Behaviour* (6th edn, 2004) para 2.8. See DEATH PENALTY; DEED; STAY OF EXECUTION; WILL.

execution debtor. A person against whom judgment has been given for a sum of money, whose property is taken in execution. See FIERI FACIAS.

execution of judgment. The act of completing or carrying into effect the judgment of a court, which is usually done by *fieri facias*, by attachment, by order of garnishee, by appointment of a receiver by way of equitable execution, by a stop order, by a charging order, by examination order and instalment order, or by judgment mortgage (qqv). Execution of a judgment may issue at any time within six years from judgment: RSC Ord 42, r 23. Application to the court for liberty to issue execution is necessary: (a) where six years has elapsed; or (b) where a change has taken place in the parties by death or otherwise; or (c) where judgment is upon assets *in futuro* (r 24).

An action on a judgment is statute barred after twelve years from the date on which the judgment became enforceable: Statute of Limitations 1957, s 11.

For the rules governing the enforcement of a judgment or order of the Circuit Court, see Circuit Court Rules 2001 Ord 36. For details on an *execution order,* see Ord 36, rr 12–22. For execution of decrees in the District Court, see DCR 1997 Ord 48. See also Enforcement of Court Orders Acts 1926 and 1940; Courts of Justice Act 1936, s 61; Bankruptcy Act 1988, s 50. See *Minister for Social Welfare v Riordan* [1966] IR 556.

There is reciprocal recognition and enforcement of judgments in civil and commercial matters between EC States and, since 1993, between EC States and EFTA countries (ie now, Iceland, Liechtenstein, Norway and Switzerland) and vice versa: Jurisdiction of Courts and Enforcement of Judgments Acts 1998. [Bibliography: Glanville.] See JUDGMENT; FOREIGN JUDGMENTS, ENFORCEMENT OF; RECEIVER OF MORTGAGED PROPERTY; STAY OF EXECUTION.

execution order. An order which includes an order of *fieri facias*, of *sequestration*, or of *attachment* (qqv): RSC Ord 42, r 8. An *execution order* in respect of High Court matters may not issue without the filing of a *praecipe* for that purpose (RSC Ord 42, r 11); if unexecuted, such an order remains in force for one year from the date of issue but it may be renewed (r 20). For the rules governing an *execution order* of the Circuit Court, see Circuit Court Rules 2001 Ord 36, rr 12–22. For execution of decrees in the District Court, see DCR 1997 Ord 48. See DECREE.

executive. See SEPARATION OF POWERS.

executive functions. Every function of a local authority which is not a *reserved function* is an *executive function* of the local authority and is required to be exercised and performed by the manager: Local Government Act 2001, ss 2(1) and 149. For previous legislation, see: County Management Act 1940, s 17. See COUNTY MANAGER; HEALTH BOARD; RESERVED FUNCTIONS; SECTION 4 RESOLUTION.

executor. An *executor* is the person to whom the execution of a will, ie the duty of carrying its provisions into effect, is confided by the testator. The duties of an executor are: to bury the deceased; to prove the will; to collect the estate and, as necessary, to convert it into money; to pay the debts in their proper order; to pay the legacies and to distribute the residue among the persons entitled. The executor may bring actions against persons who are indebted to the testator or are in possession of property belonging to the estate.

When several executors are appointed and only some of them prove the will, they are called the *proving* or *acting executors.* A testator may appoint an *alternative* executor, but the substituted executor may obtain probate only where others entitled before him have renounced: *In the Matter of the estate of Clare Bernadette Doran* [2000] 4 IR 551, HC and ITLR (9 October).

It is the duty of an executor to notify a spouse in writing of the right of election between the spouse's *legal right* (qv) and any rights under the will: Succession Act 1965, s 115. Once an executor has proven a will and thus has accepted the duty of administering the testator's estate, he can be removed only if there are serious grounds or weighty reasons for overruling the wishes of the testator: *Dunne v Heffernan* [1997] 3 IR 431, SC.

The removal of an executor is only justified where there is serious misconduct on the part of the executor and/or some other serious circumstances: *Flood v Flood* [1999] 2 IR 234, HC. In this case the court removed the defendant from his position as trustee.

On the death of a client who is a testator, the solicitor of the testator should not, without the consent of the executor, disclose any information other than to the executor about the testator's affairs: *A Guide to Professional Conduct of Solicitors in Ireland* (2002) ch 4.2. It is recommended as desirable for a solicitor who is a sole practitioner or sole principal, to nominate a solicitor as one of his executors: (ch 9.16).

Executorship is a *financial service* which a building society may be empowered to provide: Building Societies Act 1989, s 29(2)(n). See ADMINISTRATOR; MURDER; PERSONAL REPRESENTATIVE; PROBATE; PROBATE TAX; STATUTE OF FRAUDS.

executor according to the tenor. A person named in a will, wherein no executor is named, whose duties are described in terms sufficient to constitute him executor; a grant of probate may be given to such a person: RSC Ord 79, r 5(8)(c). See TENOR.

executor de son tort. A person who in defraud of creditors or without full valuable consideration, obtains, receives or holds any part of a deceased's estate or effects the release of any debt or liability due to the estate; he is chargeable as executor in his own wrong (*de son tort*). See Succession Act 1965, s 23; *In b. Leeson* [1937] 71 ILTR 82.

executor's year. The period allowed for the personal representative of a deceased to distribute the estate. An action for failure to distribute within this year is not permissible without leave of the court. This does not affect the right of creditors to bring proceedings. See Succession Act 1965, s 62.

executorship by representation. Doctrine under which an executor of a sole or last surviving executor of a testator became the executor of that testator without the need for a new grant. Abolished by the Succession Act 1965, s 19.

executory. That which remains to be done. See TRUST.

executory interest. A future interest in land which is not a reversion (qv) or a remainder (qv). Legal executory interests can arise under the Statute of Uses 1634 and under the Statute of Wills 1540, namely springing and shifting uses and devises.

executrix. The feminine form of executor (qv).

exemplary damages. Damages awarded by way of punishment of the defendant for a breach of contract or a statutory or constitutional right or duty or a tort. *Punitive* and *exemplary* damages are recognised as constituting the same element in that awarding damages for the purposes of making an example of a defendant to some extent punishes the person and vice versa: *Conway v INTO* [1991] ILRM 497, SC.

One of the ways in which the rights of citizens is vindicated, when subjected to oppressive conduct by employees of the State, is by an award of exemplary damages; exemplary damages do not have to be pleaded under the rules of court, but it is desirable that defendants be put on notice of an intention to claim such damages: *McIntyre v Lewis & Dolan* [1991] ITLR (22 April), SC. In a defamation action, the Supreme Court held that as there was no evidence to indicate that the defendants had intended to defame the plaintiff or knew that the article was untrue, the trial judge had been correct not to allow the issue of exemplary damages be considered by the jury: *O'Brien v Mirror Group Newspapers* [2001] 1 IR 1, SC. See *Kinlan v Ulster Bank* [1928] IR 171; *Rookes v Barnard* [1964] AC 1129 as applied by *Garvey v Ireland* [1979] 113 ILTR 61; *Kennedy v Hearne* [1988] ILRM 52; *Crofter Properties Ltd v Genport Ltd* [2002] HC (unreported).

While exemplary damages may be awarded to mark the court's disapproval of the conduct of the defendant, the corollary does not apply ie a court is not entitled to reduce or extinguish the damages to which the court considered the plaintiff to be entitled, in order to mark the court's disapproval of sustained dishonesty which characterised the plaintiff's prosecution of his claim: *Vesey v Bus Éireann* [2001] 4 IR 192, SC. Contrast with 'aggravated damages' (qv).

Some statutes provide for exemplary damages eg Competition Act 2002, ss 14(4) and 14(5)(b) – exemplary damages; Industrial Designs Act 2001, s 59, and Copyright and Related Rights Act 2000, s 128(1) and (3) and s 304(3) – aggravated or exemplary damages or both; Landlord and Tenant (Amendment) Act 1980, s 17(4) – punitive damages; Hepatitis C Compensation Tribunal Act 1997, s 5(3) – aggravated or exemplary damages. Some statutes exclude the recovery of exemplary or punitive damages eg See also Civil Liability Act 1961, ss 7(2) and 14(4).

See 'Exemplary Damages; Teaching wrongdoers that tort does not pay' by David McParland BL in *Bar Review* (April 2003) 55. See LRC Consultation Paper on *Aggravated, Exemplary and Restitutionary Damages* (1998); LRC Report on *Aggravated, Exemplary and Restitutionary Damages* (2000). See DAMAGES; PENAL DAMAGES; UNLAWFUL INTERFERENCE WITH CONSTITUTIONAL RIGHTS.

exempli gratia. [For example.] Usually abbreviated to eg.

exempted development. The carrying out of any *works* on, in, over or under land which is exempted from the requirement of planning permission; this includes the making of any material change in the *use* of any structures or other lands: Planning and Development Act 2000, ss 2(1) and 4. Examples of exempted development are: development for the purpose of agriculture;

development by a local authority or statutory undertaker in relation to sewers, mains, pipes, cables, overhead wires, including excavation; interior development which does not materially affect the external appearance of a structure; use of any structure or other land within the curtilage of a house incidental to the enjoyment of the house; development for the purposes of a casual trading area or in relation to land reclamation; thinning, felling and replanting of trees, forests and woodlands.

Also development by a planning authority in its functional area is exempted development; however such development is subject to the requirements of public notification (PDA 2000, s 4(1)). This includes development carried out on behalf of, or in partnership with a local authority (PDA 2000, s 4(1)(f)). Provision has been made for prescribing classes of development, which would normally be exempt, not to be exempt where the environmental impacts of the development must be assessed under Pt X (PDA 2000, ss 172–177) (PDA 2000, s 4(4)–(5)).

A person may seek a declaration from the planning authority on the question of what, in any particular case, is or is not development or is or is not exempted development (PDA 2000, s 5). The person, or the planning authority, may refer the question to An Bord Pleanála for a decision on the matter. See *Esat Digiphone v South Dublin County Council* [2002] 2 ILRM 547, HC and 3 IR 585.

For regulations dealing with exempted development, see Planning and Development Regulations 2001, Part II, arts 5–11: SI No 600 of 2001. For previous legislation, see Local Government (Planning and Development) Act 1963, s 4 and s 78 as amended by LG(PD)A 1993, s 3; LG(PD)A 1976, ss 43(1)(c)) and 14(9)(b); LG(PD)A 1999, s 19. See LOCAL AUTHORITY, DEVELOPMENT BY; PLANNING PERMISSION.

exemption clauses. See EXCLUSION CLAUSES, RESTRICTION OF.

exequator. The authorisation from a receiving state to the head of a consular post, admitting him to the exercise of his functions: Diplomatic Relations and Immunities Act 1967, Sch 2, art 12.

exhaustion principle. The principle that once a copy of a work has been put into circulation in the European Economic Area by or with the consent of the copyright owner, the subsequent distribution of the work within the EEA cannot be prohibited: Copyright and Related Rights Act 2000, s 41. This is a limitation on the *distribution rights* of the copyright owner. A similar limitation applies in the case of the distribution rights of *performers* in relation to copies of recordings (CRRA 2001, s 206).

A *design right* is not infringed by the doing of anything in relation to the products to which the design has been applied or is incorporated, where such products have been put on the market in a member state of the EEA by or with the consent of the registered proprietor: Industrial Designs Act 2001, s 75. The *design right* is exhausted in relation to the products. This measure gives effect to Directive (EC) 98/71 art 15 on the legal protection of designs and is intended to give effect to the single market in the EU. See DESIGN.

exhibit. A document or thing produced for the inspection of the judge or jury, or to be shown to a witness who is giving evidence, or referred to in an affidavit. In a criminal trial, the accused is entitled to be given a list of the exhibits and an opportunity to inspect the exhibits: Criminal Procedure Act 1967, ss 4B and 4D as inserted by Criminal Justice Act 1999, s 9. A statutory means of proof of garda custody of an exhibit was provided for in 1999 to remedy the problem sometimes caused in prosecutions through the inability to demonstrate continuity of possession (CJA 1999, s 30). See *The State (Pletzer) v Magee* [1986] ILRM 441.

exhumation. The disinterring of a buried corpse; it is an unlawful act unless authorised. The Minister may order the exhumation by the Garda Síochána of a body on being requested so to do by a coroner (qv): Coroners Act 1962, s 47(2). Where a coroner is informed by a member of the Garda Síochána not below the rank of inspector that, in his opinion, the death of any person whose body has been buried in the coroner's district may have occurred in a violent or unnatural manner, the coroner may request the Minister to order the exhumation of the body by the Garda Síochána (CA 1962, s 47(1)). Following exhumation, the coroner has like powers and duties as if the body had not been buried (CA 1962, s 47(4)). Also, a local authority has power to exhume the body of a person if the burial appears to threaten public health: Public Health (Ireland) Act 1878.

exitum. [The will of the testator is ambulatory down to the very end of his life.] See WILL, REVOCATION OF.

exoneration. To relieve from liability; to clear from an accusation.

exor. An executor.

expectation, legitimate. See LEGITIMATE EXPECTATION.

expectation of life, loss of. In an action for damages for personal injuries, compensation may be recovered for shortening of life arising therefrom, but the compensation must be moderate: *McMorrow v Knott* [1959] SC; *O'Sullivan v Dwyer* [1971] IR 275. Where a cause of action survives for the benefit of a deceased person's estate, damages for loss or diminution of expectation of life are not recoverable: Civil Liability Act 1961, s 7(2). See FATAL INJURIES.

expedient. Where an Act is expressed to come into operation on a day subsequent to the date of the passing of the Act, and the Act confers a power to make or do any instrument, act or thing, which is necessary or *expedient* to enable the Act to have full force and effect, such power may be exercised at any time after the passing of the Act: Interpretation Act 1937, s 10(1)(b). *Expedient* has been held to mean 'conducive to advantage in general or to a definite purpose': *McInerney v Minister for Agriculture* [1995] 3 IR 449, HC.

expenses of management. It has been held by the Supreme Court that expenditure by an investment company relating to the appraisal of existing investments or the scope of new investments is 'expenses of management' and consequently deductible from profits for the purposes of corporation tax: *Hibernian Insurance Co Ltd v Mac Uimis* [2000] 2 IR 263, SC and [2000] 2 ILRM 196, SC. However, once an appraisal becomes specific, in the sense of relating to a particular investment, this is not 'expenses of management' but expenses of possible acquisition or disposal, as the case may be.

expert evidence. Means evidence of fact or opinion given by a person who would not be competent to give such evidence unless he had a special skill or expertise: Civil Liability and Courts Act 2004, s 2(1). In a personal injuries action, the court may appoint such approved persons as it considers appropriate to carry out investigations into, and give expert evidence in relation to, such matters as the court directs: CLCA 2004, s 20. A party to a personal injuries action is required to cooperate with such appointed expert.

expert opinion. The opinion of experts is admissible in evidence whenever the subject is one upon which competency to form an opinion can only be acquired by special study or experience eg in science, art, trade, handwriting, fingerprints, ballistics, or foreign law. See *McFadden v Murdock* [1867] IR 1 CL 211; *Poynton v Poynton* [1903] 37 ILTR 54. See Competition Act 2002, s 9; Civil Liability and Courts Act 2004, s 54. A barrister must not practise and be an expert witness in the same court but this rule does not apply to expert evidence on foreign law: *Code of Conduct for the Bar of Ireland* (December 2003) r 5.11.

In *commercial proceedings* (qv), the judge may, as part of the pre-trial procedure direct any expert witnesses to consult with each other for the purposes of: (a) identifying the issues in respect of which they intend to give evidence, (b) where possible, reaching agreement on the evidence that they intend to give in respect of those issues, and (c) considering any matter which the judge may direct them to consider, and requiring that such witnesses record in a memorandum to be jointly submitted by them to the Registrar and delivered by them to the parties, particulars of the outcome of their consultations: provided that any such outcome shall not be in any way binding on the parties: RSC Ord 63A, r 6(1)(ix) inserted by Rules of the Superior Courts (Commercial Proceedings) 2004, SI No 2 of 2004. See 'In the know' by Paul Jacobs and Tim Roulston in *Law Society Gazette* (May 2004) 25. See *A Guide to Professional Conduct of Solicitors in Ireland* (2002) App 4, para 31. [Bibliography: Daly B D (5); Healy; O'Flaherty; Gee Publishing.] See CANON LAW; PROFESSIONAL WITNESS; REFRESHING MEMORY; STANDBY FEE; WITNESS, PRIVILEGE OF.

expert report. A party to proceedings for damages for *personal injuries* may only rely on a statement or report during the course of the trial of the action, where that statement or report has been disclosed in accordance with RSC Ord 39, rr 45–51 inserted by the Rules of the Superior Courts (No 6) (Disclosure of Reports and Statements) 1998, SI No 391 of 1998. A report means a report or statement from accountants, actuaries, architects, dentists, doctors, engineers, occupational therapists, psychologists, psychiatrists, scientists, or any other expert whatsoever intended to be called.

A party who has indicated an intention to call an expert witness and has already delivered the report of that witness, may withdraw reliance upon such by confirming in writing that he does not now intend to call the author of the report as a witness; in this event the report has the same privilege, if any, which it previously enjoyed before the delivery: RSC Ord 46(6). There is no obligation to deliver the report to the other side, where the intention to call the witness has been communicated, and the party then changes his mind before delivery of the report: *Kincaid v Aer Lingus* [2003] 2 IR 314, SC and *Law Society Gazette* (October 2003) 39.

The Supreme Court has held that an *expert* may be defined as a person whose qualifications or expertise give an added authority to opinions or statements given or made by him within the area of his expertise: *Galvin v Murray* [2001 SC] 2 ILRM 234 and 1 IR 331. The court held that an engineer was such an expert and identified as such in the rules of court. The fact that an engineer was employed by one or other of the parties may affect his independence with a consequent reduction in the weight to be attached to his evidence, but it did not deprive him of his status as an expert.

In a personal injuries action, the right of the defendant to have the plaintiff medically examined and to interview his treating doctors, is not dependant on the pleadings having been closed; a medical examination may be sought at any stage: *McGrory v Electricity Supply Board* [2003] ITLR (13 October), SC; also reported in *Law Society Gazette* (August/September 2003) 48. In general, pre-accident medical reports are discoverable only on a limited basis; however where the earlier reports are significant they will be discoverable: *McCord v Dunnes Stores* [2000/1409P] reported in *Law Society Gazette* (December 2003) 18. See MEDICAL REPORT.

expert tribunal. See TRIBUNALS.

expert witness. See EXPERT OPINION; EXPERT REPORT.

explanatory memorandum. A memorandum which sometimes accompanies a Bill with the purpose of explaining the proposed legislation. It may be examined by the court to discover the purpose of an enactment: *McLoughlin & Ors v Minister for* *the Public Service* [1986] ILRM 28. The annual Finance Acts are now accompanied by an explanatory memorandum and it is intended to extend this practice, over time, to all Acts.

exploration for petroleum. See COMMERCIAL PROCEEDINGS; PETROLEUM, EXPLORATION FOR.

explosive. A substance of a kind used to produce a practical effect by explosion or a pyrotechnic effect or anything of which that substance is an integral part; a *licence* is required to import, manufacture, keep, sell or purchase any explosive: Dangerous Substances Act 1972, ss 9–15. The Minister may regulate the manufacture, storage, marking, packing, conveyance, purchase, sale and keeping of fireworks, safety, signalling and rescue devices and other prescribed articles and substances (DSA 1972, s 19). Ammunition is governed by the Firearms Act 1925. Sodium chlorate is an explosive substance within s 9 of the Explosive Substances Act 1883, as are mercury tilt switches: *DPP v Hardy* [1992] ITLR (16 November), SC. See Classification and Labelling of Explosives Order 1994; Carriage of Dangerous Goods by Road Act 1998, s 16.

It is an offence to make, or knowingly have possession or control of any *explosive substance* under such circumstances as to give rise to a reasonable suspicion that it is without a lawful object: Explosive Substances Act 1883, s 4. It is also an offence, unlawfully and maliciously, to cause by an explosive substance an explosion likely to endanger life or cause serious injury to property or to do any act with intent to cause such an explosion (ESA 1883, ss 2 and 3 inserted by Criminal Law (Jurisdiction) Act 1976, s 4).

The courts are now empowered to impose a fine as well as a custodial sentence for such offences: Offences against the State (Amendment) Act 1998, ss 15 and 18. Also, having possession or control of any article which could give rise to a reasonable suspicion that it was for a purpose connected with the commission, preparation or instigation of a scheduled explosives offence, is itself an offence (OS(A)A 1998, ss 7 and 18). An *explosive substance* includes any materials for making an explosion or any apparatus, machine, implement or material, intended to be used, or adapted for causing any explosion. See Criminal Justice Act 1999, ss 36 and 37 for amendments to

ss 15 and 18 of OS(A)A 1998 respectively. See Explosives Act 1875 as amended by Dangerous Substances Act 1972, s 7, Schedule; Carriage of Dangerous Goods by Road Act 1998, s 16. See *Hardy v Ireland* [1994] 2 IR 550, SC. See Stores for Explosives Order 1955, SI No 42 of 1955 as amended by SI No 71 of 2003. See PROPERTIES.

explosive atmosphere. Where an explosive atmosphere is or is likely to be present in a workplace, the employer is required to make a suitable and appropriate assessment of the risk to his employees: Safety, Health and Welfare at Work (Explosive Atmosphere) Regulations 2003, SI No 258 of 2003. He is required to take technical and organisational measures: (a) to prevent the formation of explosive atmospheres, (b) to avoid the ignition of explosive atmospheres, and (c) to mitigate the detrimental effects of an explosion so as to ensure the health and safety of workers. The Regulations give effect to Directive (EC) 99/92.

exports, control of. The Minister is empowered by order to prohibit the export of certain specified goods, except where a licence is obtained: Control of Exports Act 1983. Examples are: rifles, guns, weapons, and flame throwers: Control of Exports Order 2000, SI No 300 of 2000. These regulations have been extended to the customs-free airport: SI No 430 of 2000. See also European Communities (Control of Exports of Dual-Use Items) Regulations 2000 and 2002, SI No 317 of 2000 and SI No 512 of 2002. See COMMERCIAL PROCEEDINGS; DUAL-USE PRODUCT.

exposure, indecent. The deliberate exposure of the person which may amount to the offence of an act of an indecent nature, if committed at or near or in the sight of any place along which the public habitually pass: Criminal Law Amendment Act 1935, s 18. See INDECENCY.

express. Directly and distinctly stated, rather than implied e g an express trust.

express trust. See trust, express.

expressio unius est exclusio alterius. [An express provision excludes another; the mention of one thing is the exclusion of another.] In a particular case, it was held that a specific provision introduced in aid of the prosecution has replaced the common law in this area: *Brennan v Judge*

Windle [2003] FL 7856, SC, and 2 ILRM 520. See also *Joyce v Madden* [2004] ELR 78, HC.

expressio unius personae vel rei, est exclusio alterius. [The express mention of one person or thing is the exclusion of another.] A maxim sometimes used in the interpretation of a document or statute but has to be handled with caution. See *Wavin Pipes Ltd v Hepworth Iron Co Ltd* [1981] HC; *Doyle v Hearne* [1988] ILRM 318.

expression, freedom of. The State guarantees, subject to public order and morality, liberty for the exercise of the right of citizens to express freely their convictions and opinions: 1937 Constitution, art 40(6)(1)(1). The State however must endeavour that the organs of public opinion, such as the radio, the press, the cinema, while preserving their rightful liberty of expression, including criticism of government policy, are not used to undermine public order or morality or the authority of the State. The publication or utterance of blasphemous, seditious, or indecent matter is stated by the Constitution to be an offence which is punishable in accordance with law. Also the right of freedom of expression may be restricted as necessary to maintain the authority and impartiality of the judiciary: *Desmond & Dedeir v Glackin & Minister for Industry* [1992] ILRM 489, HC.

But the freedom of expression enjoyed by the media will not be interfered with merely to avoid the distress which would be caused by publication of matters which would show a parent in a sordid or unfavourable light: *Maguire v Drury* [1995] 1 ILRM 108, HC. See *The State (Lynch) v Cooney* [1983] ILRM 89; *The A-G for England and Wales v Brandon Books* [1987] ILRM 135; *Weeland v Radio Telefís Éireann* [1987] IR 662, HC; *Kelly v O'Neill & Brady* [2000] 1 ILRM 507, SC. [Bibliography: MacDonagh.] See CENSORSHIP; DEFAMATION; EUROPEAN CONVENTION ON HUMAN RIGHTS; FAIR COMMENT; FREEDOM OF THE PRESS; LIBEL; SECTION 31.

expression of doubt. See DOUBT, LETTER OF EXPRESSION OF.

expressum facit cessare tacitum. [When there is express mention of certain things, then anything not mentioned is excluded.] See EXPRESSIO UNIUS.

expulsion. A person must not be expelled, by means either of an individual or of a collective measure, from the territory of the State of which he is a national: art 3 to the Fourth Protocol to the European Convention on Human Rights: European Convention on Human Rights Act 2003, s 1 and Sch 3. See DEPORTATION ORDER.

extempore judgment. The formal decision of a court made immediately at the conclusion of the trial of an action. Where there are no *primary facts* relevant to an issue which have not previously been decided, it is not necessary for the trial judge to set out in an *extempore judgment* the precise findings of primary fact on which he reaches his conclusion: *K v K* [1992] ITLR (4 May), SC. However, it has been held that where it is not possible to identify clear findings of fact from the note of the *extempore* judgment of the High Court, the best course is to remit the case for rehearing on all issues: *Kelly v Bus Átha Cliath* [2000] ITLR (8 May), SC. Contrast with RESERVED JUDGMENT. See JUDGMENT.

extension of house. Planning permission is not required for certain extensions within the *curtilage* of a house, by the construction or erection of an extension (including a conservatory) to the rear of the house or by the conversion for use as part of the house of any garage, store, shed or similar structure attached to the rear or to the side of the house: Planning and Development Regulations 2001 SI No 600 of 2001, Sch 1, class 1.

The floor area however must not exceed 40 square metres and the floor area of the first floor, if any, must not exceed: (a) 12 square metres in the case of a terraced or semi-detached house, or (b) 20 square metres in the case of a detached house. The floor area of previous extensions is taken into consideration. There are other requirements in the Regulations eg the roof of the extension must not be used as a balcony or roof garden. For previous legislation, see Local Government (Planning and Development) Regulations 1994, SI No 86 of 1994 as amended by Local Government (Planning and Development) Regulations 2000, SI No 181 of 2000.

extension of time. See TIME, COURT RULES; RENEWAL.

extinguishment. The ceasing of a right or obligation eg an easement (qv) is extinguished when the *dominant* and *servient* tenements are united in the same person. [Bibliography: Bland (1).] See also CONSOLIDATION; MERGER.

extortion. Any offence at common law of extortion under colour of office is abolished: Criminal Justice (Theft and Fraud Offences) Act 2001, s 3(2). See DECEPTION.

extortion with menaces. The offence committed by a person who, with a view to gain for himself or another or with the intent to cause loss to another, makes any *unwarranted* demand with menaces: Criminal Justice (Public Order) Act 1994, s 17. The demand is not unwarranted if the person making it, does so in the belief that he has reasonable grounds and if the use of the menaces is a proper means of reinforcing the demand (CJ(PO)A 1994, s 17(2) and *R v Harvey, Ulyett and Plummer* [1980] 72 Cr App R 139). Any offence at common law of extortion under colour of office is abolished: Criminal Justice (Theft and Fraud Offences) Act 2001, s 3(2). See MENACE; POSSESSION, CRIME.

extradition. The formal surrender, based upon reciprocating arrangements by one nation with another, of an individual, accused or convicted of an offence, who is within the jurisdiction of the requested country when the requesting country, being competent to try and punish him, demands his surrender: *Wyatt v McLoughlin* [1974] IR 378. The formal arrangements by which this may be secured and the principles of reciprocity enshrined are either by way of treaties or by reciprocal legislation. The term *extradition* is often used to embrace the term *rendition* (qv) which is the backing of warrants as between states. For extradition between EU member states from 2004, see EUROPEAN ARREST WARRANT.

Extradition cannot be granted for an offence which is a *political offence* or an offence connected with a *political offence*: Extradition Act 1965, s 11; Extradition (Amendment) Act 1994, ss 2–3. Also extradition cannot be granted for offences under *military law* which are not offences under criminal law (EA 1965, s 12). This restriction however, does not apply to offences under the *Geneva Convention* (qv) dealing with armed conflict: Geneva Conventions (Amendment) Act 1998, s 15. The Extradition (Amendment) Act 1994 further restricted the political offence exception, centralised all extradition proceedings, restricted the grant of bail to the High Court, and extended powers of arrest.

Also, a warrant for the arrest of a person must not be endorsed for execution if the Attorney-General (qv) so directs; such a direction not to endorse must be given unless the Attorney-General having considered such information as he deems appropriate, is of opinion that: (a) there is a clear intention to prosecute the person, and (b) such intention is founded on the existence of sufficient evidence: Extradition (Amendment) Act 1987. These functions of the A-G are procedural and not judicial in nature: *Wheeler v Culligan* [1989] IR 344.

A claim to be entitled to early release under the Good Friday Agreement is not sufficient to refuse extradition: *Quinlivan v DPP* (2000) Irish Times, 15 April. Extradition must be refused where the court is satisfied that there is a real danger that the person whose extradition is sought will suffer ill-treatment in breach of his constitutional rights if delivered out of the jurisdiction: *Finucane v McMahon* [1990] ILRM 505, SC; or if the extradition would give effect to an unconditional act: *Larkin v O'Dea* [1995] 2 ILRM 1, SC and 2 IR 485. Also the court cannot properly undertake an investigation into the validity of a conviction recorded in a requesting state: *Clarke v Mc Mahon* [1990] ILRM 648, SC.

If the evidence before the court gives rise to a reasonable doubt as to the intention of the police to prosecute the accused in respect of the offences specified in the warrant, the district judge should refuse to make the extradition order: *Brien v King* [1997] 1 ILRM 338, HC. It was held that there can be no estoppel to prevent the restart of failed extradition proceedings after the correction of the defects: *Bolger v O'Toole* [2000] ITLR (3 July), HC. A person who absconds from the jurisdiction may have his claim (that he will be unable to have a fair trial because of delay) rejected, because by absconding he has contributed to the delay: *Coleman v O'Toole* [2002] FL 7594, HC and [2004] 1 ILRM 389, SC.

A request by an *international tribunal* for the surrender of a person has primacy over an extradition request: International War Crimes Tribunals Act 1998, s 7. Judicial co-operation in the EU includes facilitating extradition between member states: Treaty on European Union, art 31 of the consolidated (2002) version. Inter-state communications in connection with extradition may be disclosed in the public interest for the purpose of litigation: *Walker v Ireland* [1997] 1 ILRM 363, HC.

In 2000, all the extradition arrangements of the State, made pursuant to international agreements, were set out in a single consolidated Order which replaced all previous Orders made under s 8(1) of the Extradition Act 1965: Extradition Act 1965 (Application of Part II) Order 2000, SI No 474 of 2000. This Order has now been amended by SI No 173 of 2002; also SI No 479 of 2003 and SI No 649 of 2003. See also European Arrest Warrant Act 2003, s 49.

Changes were made to the law on extradition in 2001: (a) to enable the State to ratify two EU Conventions on extradition which simplify extradition, and (b) to make some substantive and procedural changes to general extradition law: Extradition (European Union Conventions) Act 2001, as amended by EAWA 2003, s 52.

The main changes introduced by the 2001 Act were: (a) a person may consent to the High Court to being surrendered to a Convention country, and may then be extradited provided the High Court is satisfied that the consent is given voluntarily, and in the case of an Irish citizen, the Minister for Justice consents also (E(EUC)A 2001, s 6); (b) a person so consenting may waive his rights under the *specialty rule* (E(EUC)A 2001, ss 7 and 15); (c) the Minister for Justice is the *central authority* in Ireland for the transmission and reception of extradition requests and necessary supporting documents (E(EUC)A 2001, s 9); (d) offences are extraditable if they are punishable by six months' imprisonment or detention in the requested State and twelve months in the requesting State (E(EUC)A 2001, s 11); (e) the previous bar on *revenue offences* which prevented extradition in the case of such offences is removed (E(EUC)A 2001, s 13); (e) extradition cannot be granted where a person has been granted a pardon or amnesty (E(EUC)A 2001, s 14); (f) the formal requirements in relation to authentication of documents has been simplified (E(EUC)A 2001, s 17); (g) the facsimile of documents is permitted (E(EUC)A 2001, s 18); (h) evidence may be given by affidavit and through a television link by a person outside the State (E(EUC)A 2001, ss 22 and 24); (i) a new definition of what constitutes a *corresponding offence* (qv) is provided (E(EUC)A 2001, s 26); and (j) all extradition proceedings must now take place in

the High Court (E(EUC)A 2001, s 20). See also EAWA 2003, s 47.

See Criminal Procedure Act 1967, ss 35–38; Criminal Law (Jurisdiction) Act 1976, s 20; Air Navigation and Transport Acts 1973 and 1975; Non-Fatal Offences against the Person Act 1997, s 27; Criminal Justice Act 1999, ss 31–33; Criminal Justice (Safety of United Nations Workers) Act 2000, ss 5(2) and 8. For amendments to the 1965 and 1994 Acts, see Criminal Justice (United Nations Convention against Torture) Act 2000, ss 7 and 9 respectively. See also Maritime Security Act 2004, s 11.

See *Long v O'Toole* [2001] 3 IR 548, HC; *Martin v Conroy* [2002] 1 ILRM 461, HC; *McMahon v McDonald* [1988] 6 ILT 263, HC; *Fusco v O'Dea (No 2)* [1998] 3 IR 470, SC; *Smithers v Governor of Mountjoy Prison* [1998] 2 IR 392, HC; *Kwok Ming Wan v Conroy* [1998] 3 IR 527, SC; *Quinlivan v Conroy* [1999] 1 IR 271, SC; *MB v Asst Commissioner Conroy* [2001] 2 ILRM 311, SC; *Lynch v A-G* [2003] FL 8104, HC and [2004] 1 ILRM 129, SC. See DCR 1997 Ord 29; District Court (Extradition) Rules 1998, SI No 89 of 1998. See RSC Ord 98. [Bibliography: Forde (3); Forde UK.]

See ARREST; AMNESTY; CORRESPONDING OFFENCE; EUROPEAN ARREST WARRANT; FAX; PARDON; POLITICAL OFFENCE; RENDITION; REVENUE OFFENCE; SPECIALTY RULE.

extradition, deliver up. A person on whom an extradition order has been made under Extradition Act 1965, s 47 must be delivered up within one month of the making of the order: EA 1965, s 53(1). The Supreme Court has held that there is a public policy discernable from the Extradition Acts that persons subject to extradition should, subject to certain savings in respect of the initiation of court proceedings, have their cases dealt with expeditiously and at least within one month of the making of an order under s 47, unless reasonable cause is shown for the delay: *Mallows v Governor of Mountjoy Prison* [2002] 2 IR 385, SC. The Supreme Court has also held that it would be unjust and oppressive to deliver up the defendant who had suffered a stroke, as his extradition was being sought for a complex trial in the England and he now had mental impairment and physical difficulties as a consequence of the stroke (EA 1965, s 50 and *DPP v Armstrong* [2004] Irish Times, 11 February, SC. The European Arrest

Warrant Act 2003, s 50 repeals ss 41–55 of EA 1965. See EUROPEAN ARREST WARRANT.

extradition between EU member states. Extradition arrangements between Ireland and all EU member states from 1 January 2004 is governed by the European Arrest Warrant Act 2003. A European arrest warrant is a court decision in one member state, addressed to a court in another member state, for the purpose of conducting a criminal prosecution or the execution of a custodial sentence in the member state issuing the warrant. See EUROPEAN ARREST WARRANT.

extradition warrant. The words in an extradition warrant, by which the factual content of the specified offence is identified, should *prima facie* be given their ordinary or popular meaning, unless they are used in a context which suggests they have a special significance: *Stanton v O'Toole* [2000] ITLR (18 December), SC. In refusing extradition, the High Court criticised the unsatisfactory nature of information furnished by the Lithuanian authorities with their request for extradition, holding that the translation of the documents was not sufficiently clear to understand precisely the procedures and the sequence of events prior to and subsequent to the application: *Musinskas v A-G* [2004] Irish Times, 18 August, HC. See EUROPEAN ARREST WARRANT.

extradition with Spain. Provision has been made to give effect to an international agreement between Ireland and Spain in relation to the extradition of own nationals whereby each State will not refuse a request for extradition on the basis that the person whose extradition is being sought is a national of the requested State: SI No 649 of 2003.

extradition with USA. The Washington Treaty 1983 contains provisions relating to extraditable offences between Ireland and the United States: Washington Treaty on Extradition (SI No 33 of 1987). Under the Treaty, before an offence becomes extraditable, the offence in question must be punishable by imprisonment for more than one year: *A-G v Oldridge* [2000] 2 ILRM 233, HC. The Supreme Court held in this case that the Washington Treaty threshold had been met as the *corresponding offence* in Ireland, conspiracy to defraud, was a common law offence punishable by imprisonment for life or any lesser term: *A-G v Oldridge* [2001] 2 ILRM 125, SC and [2000] 4 IR 593, SC.

extraordinary general meeting; egm. As regards companies, a meeting other than an annual general meeting: Companies Act 1963, Table A, art 49. Where members of a company representing at least one tenth of the paid-up capital with voting rights request the board to call an extraordinary general meeting and it does not do so for 21 days, the meeting may be convened by at least half of those requisitionists (CA 1963, s 132). An extraordinary general meeting of every registered company must be convened whenever a director knows that the net assets of the company are half or less of the company's called-up share capital, for the purpose of considering the measures to be taken to deal with the situation: Companies Amendment Act 1983, s 40. See ANNUAL GENERAL MEETING; RESOLUTION; VOTING AT MEETINGS.

extra-territorial jurisdiction. A person who outside the State commits the offence of counterfeiting of currencies notes and coins (and related offences) is guilty of an offence and liable to conviction on indictment to the penalty attached to the offence as if committed in Ireland: Criminal Justice (Theft and Fraud Offences) Act 2001, s 38. It is an offence in the State also for a person to commit outside the State *active* or *passive* corruption if the person is an Irish citizen (CJ(TFO)A 2001, s 45). An offence committed on a vessel or on a hovercraft or on an installation in the territorial seas (or in a designated area) is to be treated as an offence committed in the State (CJ(TFO)A 2001, s 61). See also Maritime Security Act 2004, s 3. [Bibliography: McGreal C.] See also COMPUTER; JURISDICTION; TERRORISM.

extra-territoriality. The legal fiction by which certain persons and things are deemed for the purpose of jurisdiction and control to be outside the territory of the state in which they really are and within that of another state eg ambassadors and other diplomatic agents while in the country to which they are accredited. See UNITED NATIONS WORKERS, OFFENCES AGAINST.

extrinsic evidence. See EVIDENCE, EXTRINSIC.

F

facial injuries. The courts regard facial injuries as more important for women than for men when considering compensation for such injuries. See *Foley v Thermocement Products Ltd* (1954) 90 ILTR 92; *Ronayne v Ronayne* [1970] SC. See DISFIGUREMENT; CAUSING SERIOUS HARM.

facsimile. See FAX.

fact. That which is in actual existence; an event or circumstance which is in issue between parties to a dispute before a court. In general, questions of fact are decided by a jury in jury trials and questions of law by the judge. Findings of facts, for the purposes of an appellate review thereof, are either *primary* or *secondary*; the Supreme Court is entitled to reject a trial judge's finding of a secondary fact: *JM and GM v An Bord Uchtála* [1988] ILRM 203; *Hanrahan v Merck Sharpe & Dohme (Ire) Ltd* [1988] ILRM 629, SC. The state of a person's mind at a relevant time is necessarily a matter of inference or opinion ie a secondary fact rather than a primary fact, and it is open to the Supreme Court to decide whether the inference drawn by the trial judge was correct. The Supreme Court will not set aside findings of fact made by a trial judge which were based on credible evidence: *Scott v Victoria House* [2003] FL 8309, SC. See *Metropolitan Railway v Jackson* [1887] 7 App Cas 193; *Coleman v Clarke* [1991] ILRM 841, SC; *Hay v O'Grady* [1992] ILRM 689, SC. See INFERENCE; MOOT; PRIMARY FACTS; SECONDARY FACTS.

fact in issue. In civil cases, that which is alleged by one party and denied by the other in the pleadings (qv). In criminal cases, it is the constituents of the offence alleged by the prosecution and the facts alleged by the defence and denied by the prosecution e g an alibi (qv). See RELEVANT.

factor. A mercantile agent; a person who, in the customary course of his business has possession of goods of his principal, or the documents of title to such goods, with authority to sell, pledge, or raise money on the security of same: Factors Act 1889,

s 1(1). The principal is bound by such sale or pledge even though he has forbidden it, unless there is notice of such prohibition (FaA 1889, s 2). As regards the rights of an owner of goods in the case of the bankruptcy of a mercantile agent to whom they have been entrusted, see s 12(2) and Bankruptcy Act 1988, s 77. [Bibliography: Cahill D.] See CREDIT-SALE AGREEMENT; AGENT.

factory. A premises or workplace in which persons are employed in manual labour in any process for or incidental to: (a) the making of any article or part of an article, or (b) the altering, repairing, ornamenting, finishing, cleaning or washing, or breaking up or demolition, of any article, or (c) the adapting for sale of any article. It also includes a wide range of specifically defined premises e g a laundry, fish net making or mending, printing works, docks, wharfs, quays, warehouses, electrical stations and certain institutions and training establishments. See Factories Act 1955, s 3; Safety in Industry Act 1980, s 3. Certain other sections of the 1955 Act are repealed when particular sections of the Safety, Health and Welfare at Work Act 1989 come into force e g see SI No 357 of 1995. See AIR POLLUTION; DANGEROUS CONDITIONS AND PRACTICES; SAFE SYSTEM OF WORK.

factual information. Includes information of a statistical, econometric or empirical nature, together with any analysis thereof: Freedom of Information (Amendment) Act 2003, s 2(c). The confidentiality of meetings of the government does not extend to a record which contains factual information relating to a decision of the government that has been published to the general public (FOI(A)A 2003, s 14). See also s 15. See FREEDOM OF INFORMATION.

factum. An act or deed.

factum probanda. Facts which have to be proved.

factum probantia. Facts which are given in evidence to prove those other facts which are in issue.

Fáilte Ireland. The operational name of the *National Tourism Development Authority* (qv).

fair and accurate report. A fair and accurate report, published in any newspaper, or broadcast of court proceedings is *privileged* if published or broadcast contemporaneously; the privilege does not cover blasphemous or obscene matter: Defamation

Act 1961, s 18. Privilege extends to reporting of litigation only where a judge becomes involved in some substantive way, not to the preliminary administrative or office stage of litigation: *Stringer & Murray v Irish Times Ltd* (1993) Irish Times, 4 April, HC

Qualified privilege is given to newspapers and broadcasts in respect of fair and accurate reports, without obligation to publish explanation or contradiction, concerning public proceedings of foreign legislatures, or of international conferences to which the government sends a representative, or proceedings before foreign courts, or an extract from a register open to public inspection or a court notice (DA 1961, s 24(1); *malice* will destroy the privilege.

Qualified privilege is also given, but subject to the obligation to publish a reasonable explanation, in respect of fair and accurate reports concerning: (a) findings of associations for science or learning, or for professional interests or for sport; (b) a public meeting, being a meeting *bona fide* and lawfully held for discussion on any matter of public concern, whether admission is general or restricted; (c) meetings of a local authority, commission of inquiry or statutory board; (d) general meeting of any company (other than a private company); or (e) a government notice or garda notice (DA 1961, s 24(2)). See *Nevin v Roddy Carthy* [1935] IR 392. See MALICE; PRIVILEGE.

fair and reasonable terms. In determining whether a term in a contract for the sale of goods or supply of services is *fair and reasonable* regard will be had to the following: (a) the strength of the bargaining position of the parties to each other, (b) whether the customer received an inducement to agree to the term, (c) whether the customer knew or ought reasonably to have known of the existence and extent of the term, (d) whether compliance with a condition imposed would be practicable, (e) whether the goods were manufactured, processed or adapted to the special order of the customer: Sale of Goods and Supply of Services Act 1980, Sch. See EXCLUSION CLAUSES, RESTRICTION OF; UNFAIR TERMS.

fair comment. The defence which may be pleaded in an action for *defamation* (qv). To succeed it must be proved that the comment is based on true facts, the comment must be on some matter of general public interest, and the comment must be fairly and honestly made: *Lefroy v Burnside* [1879] 4 LR Ir 556; *McQuire v Western Morning News* [1903] 2 KB 100. *Malice* will destroy the defence of fair comment. The defence of fair comment will also fail if the defendant omits from the statement of facts on which his comment purports to be based, some important fact which would alter the complexion of the facts which have been stated: *Foley v Independent Newspapers* [1994] 2 ILRM 61, HC. Before a plea of fair comment is included in a defence, the defendant should have reasonable evidence to support that plea or reasonable grounds for supposing that sufficient evidence will be available at the trial: *McDonnell v Sunday Business Post Ltd* [2000] ITLR (13 March), HC. The law as to fair comment should be construed liberally to afford a proportionate right to freedom of expression of opinion, even when such expressions could give offence: *Hunter & Callaghan v Duckworth & Cooper* [2003] ITLR (8 December), HC. See MALICE; ROLLED-UP PLEA.

fair dealing. *Fair dealing* is an *act* permitted in relation to works protected by copyright or in relation to a performance or in respect of a database right: Copyright and Related Rights Act 2000, ss 50–51, 221 and 329. As regards a performance or a recording, *fair dealing* means making use of a performance or a recording for a purpose and to an extent which will not unreasonably prejudice the interests of the rightsowner (CRRA 2000, s 221(2)). Fair dealing with a performance or recording for the purposes of criticism or review, or for the purpose of reporting current events, does not infringe a performer's property rights (CRRA 2000, s 221(1)).

A similar definition applies to the making use of literary, dramatic, musical or artistic work, film, sound recording, non-electronic database, or a typographical arrangement of a published edition etc (CRRA 2000, s 50(4)); in this case *fair dealing* for the purpose of research or private study does not infringe any copyright where the dealing does not unreasonably prejudice the interests of the rightsowner (CRRA 2000, s 50(1)). Also fair dealing for the purposes of criticism or review does not infringe copyright (CRRA 2000, s 51). However, *fair dealing* does not include converting a computer program from a low-level computer language to a higher-level language (CRRA 2000, s 50(5)).

Fair dealing in relation to a *database right* is limited to research or private study of a non-electronic database to an extent which will not unreasonably prejudice the interests of the rightsowner (CRRA 2000, s 329). See DOMESTIC AND PRIVATE USE.

fair dismissal. The dismissal of an employee where there are substantial grounds justifying the dismissal; the onus of proof is on the employer: Unfair Dismissals Act 1977, s 6. See UNFAIR DISMISSAL.

fair practice rules. Rules which, in the opinion of the Fair Trade Commission, represented fair practice conditions with regard to the supply and distribution of goods or the provision of services: Restrictive Practices Act 1972, s 4, since repealed. See Competition Act 1991, ss 2(2) and 22, since repealed also by Competition Act 2002, s 48. See now COMPETITION, DISTORTION OF; DOMINANT POSITION, ABUSE OF.

fair procedures. The rules and procedures which must be followed by all persons and bodies making decisions affecting the individual and which must be fair and seen to be fair. The courts will protect the right of its citizens to fair procedures. The court will intervene where a procedure is unfair and oppressive, eg see *McGrath v Garda Commissioner* [1990] ILRM 817. The rules of fair procedure do not necessarily apply to decisions made by a religious superior about a member of her community: *Sister O'Dea v O'Briain* [1992] ILRM 364, HC. The absence of an appeal against the test findings of a veterinary surgeon in the TB eradication scheme did not amount to an unfair procedure: *Carroll v Minister for Agriculture* [1991] 1 IR 230, HC.

An accused's right to fair procedures is superior to the community's right to have crimes prosecuted: *Z v DPP* [1994] 2 ILRM 481 and 2 IR 476; *Larkin v O'Dea* [1995] 2 ILRM 1, SC. In employment dismissal cases, the test for fairness of procedures is objective; the function of the Employment Appeals Tribunal is to determine what a reasonable, prudent and wise employer would have done having regard to the nature of the case: *Pacelli v Irish Distillers Ltd* [2004] ELR 25, EAT. See also *Ryan v VIP Taxi Co-operative* [1989] ITLR (10 April); *Clancy v Irish Rugby Football Union* [1995] 1 ILRM 193, HC; *Gallagher*

v Revenue Commissioners [1995] 1 ILRM 241, SC and ELR 108. See NATURAL JUSTICE; VOW.

Fair Trade Commission. Formerly, the Commission which had a number of functions relating to the supply and distribution of goods or the provision of service: Restrictive Practices Acts 1972 and 1987, now repealed. See Competition Act 1991, ss 2(2) and 22, since repealed also by Competition Act 2002, s 48. See now COMPETITION AUTHORITY.

fair trial. Every accused is entitled to a fair trial; the right is of fundamental constitutional importance: *D v DPP* [1994] 1 ILRM 435, SC. The appropriate burden of proof in establishing the likelihood of an unfair trial is for the applicant to show that there is a real or serious risk that there will be an unfair trial (*D* case). See also *Magee v O'Dea* [1994] 1 ILRM 540, HC; *Z v DPP* [1994] 2 ILRM 481 and 2 IR 476, SC; *Nolan v DPP* [1994] 3 IR 626, SC. See 'Article 6 of the European Convention on Human Rights, Administrative Tribunals and Judicial Review' by William McKechnie in *Bar Review* (October/November) 333 and (December 2002) 364. See EUROPEAN CONVENTION ON HUMAN RIGHTS; PUBLICITY; SUB JUDICE.

fairground equipment. See FUNFAIR.

fait. [A deed.]

falconry. See *Devlin v Minister for Arts* [1999] 1 IR 47, SC.

falsa demonstratio non nocet cum de corpore constat. [A false description does not vitiate a document when the thing is described with certainty.] The maxim was held not to be applicable to the use by the plaintiffs of the phrase 'Cost of Living Index' (which did not then exist) as they had chosen the phrase and it was not open to them now to substitute an alternative phrase: *Bank of Ireland v Fitzmaurice* [1989] ILRM 452, HC. See also *Pratt v Mathew* [1856] 22 Beav 328; *Boyle v Mulholland* [1860] 10 ICLR 150.

false accounting. An offence of *false accounting* is committed by a person if he dishonestly with the intention of making a gain for himself or another or of causing loss to another: (a) destroys, defaces, conceals or falsifies any account or any document made or required for any accounting purpose, (b) fails to make or complete any account or any such document, or (c) furnishes accounts or documents which to his knowledge are or may be misleading, false or deceptive in a material particular: Criminal Justice (Theft and Fraud) Offences Act 2001, s 10(1). A *document* includes: (a) a map, plan, graph, drawing, photograph or record or (b) a reproduction by a computer or other means (CJ(TF)OA 2001, s 2(1)).

It is sufficient to prove that the accused did the act charged dishonestly with the intention of causing loss or making a gain; it is not necessary to prove an intention dishonestly to cause such loss or gain at the expense of a particular person (CJ(TF)OA 2001, s 54 (1)). See District Court (Theft and Fraud Offences) Rules 2003, SI No 412 of 2003. [Bibliography: McGreal C.] See ACCOUNTS, COMPANY; EMBEZZLEMENT.

false alarm. It is an offence to give knowingly, or to cause to be given, a false alarm which interferes with the operation of any aircraft, aerodrome or air navigation installation: Air Navigation and Transport Act 1988, s 43.

false attribution. See AUTHORSHIP, FALSE ATTRIBUTION OF; MORAL RIGHT.

false evidence. It is an offence for a person to give or dishonestly to cause to be given, or to adduce or dishonestly cause to be adduced, evidence in a personal injuries action that: (a) is false or misleading in any material respect, and (b) he knows to be false or misleading: Civil Liability and Courts Act 2004, s 25. There is a similar offence in relation to the act of giving false or misleading instructions or information to a solicitor or to an expert appointed by the court. An act is done dishonestly by a person if done with the intention of misleading the court: CLCA 2004, s 25(3). For penalties see CLCA 2004, s 29. See PERJURY; PERVERTING THE COURSE OF JUSTICE.

false imprisonment. Formerly, the common law offence comprising the total and unlawful restraint of the personal liberty of another whether by constraining or compelling him to go to a particular place, confining him in a prison or police station, or private place, or detaining him against his will in a public place; abolished by the Non-Fatal Offences against the Person Act 1997, s 28(1)(d).

False imprisonment is now committed when a person, intentionally or recklessly: (a) takes or detains, or (b) causes to be taken or detained, or (c) otherwise restricts the personal liberty of, another without that other's consent (NFOPA 1997, s 15(1)).

Without consent means also where consent is obtained by force or threat of force or by deception (s 15(2)). See *Mee v Cruickshank* [1902] 20 Cox 210; *Kane v Governor of Mountjoy Prison* [1988] ILRM 724; *The People (DPP) v Prunty* [1985] ILRM 716. For the *tort* of false imprisonment, see TRESPASS TO THE PERSON. See also KIDNAPPING.

false or misleading information. A person who knowingly and recklessly gives information which is false or misleading in a material way may be guilty of an offence eg see Containment of Nuclear Weapons Act 2003, s 12; Residential Tenancies Act 2004, s 113. For other examples, see BROCHURE; COUNCILLOR; FALSE ACCOUNTING; FALSE TRADE DESCRIPTION; PRICE, FALSE OR MISLEADING INDICATION OF; SERVICES, FALSE OR MISLEADING STATEMENT AS TO; SOLICITOR AND ADVERTISING; STATUTORY DECLARATION; UNLAWFUL ORGANISATION.

false pretences. Formerly, the offence committed by a person who by a false *statement* of fact, knowing it to be false, obtains from another any chattel, money or valuable security, with the *intention* to cheat or defraud that other: Larceny Act 1916, s 32. There had to be an intention to defraud; where money is obtained by false pretences there is a *prima facie* case of intent to defraud: *The People (Attorney-General) v Thompson* (1960) Frewen 201, CCA.

It was also an offence to obtain from any person by any false pretence anything capable of being stolen with intent to defraud: Criminal Justice Act 1951, s 10. See also *The People (Attorney General) v Finkel* [1951] CCA. The 1916 Act and the CJA 1951, s 10 have been repealed by the Criminal Justice (Theft and Fraud Offences) Act 2001, s 3 and Sch 1. See now DECEPTION. See also CREDIT BY FRAUD, OBTAINING; POSSESSION, CRIME.

false statement. A person who, while giving evidence to a Commission of Investigation, makes a statement, material in the investigation concerned, that the person knows to be false or does not believe to be true, is guilty of an offence: Commissions of Investigation Act 2004, s 18. See also s 30.

false trade description. A trade description (qv) which is false in a material respect as regards the *goods* to which it is applied, and includes every alteration of a trade description, whether by way of addition, effacement, or otherwise, where that alteration makes the description false in a material respect, and the fact that a trade description is a trade mark, or part of a trade mark, shall not prevent such trade description being a false trade description: Merchandise Marks Act 1887, s 3(1).

Goods include vehicles, ships and aircraft, land, things attached to land and growing crops: Consumer Information Act 1978, s 2(1). *False in a material respect* is to be construed as false to a material degree and is to include being misleading to a material degree (CIA 1978, s 2(2)). The definition of false trade description is further extended by including anything which is not a trade description but is likely to be taken for an indication of any of the matters specified in the 1887 Act (CIA 1978, s 2(2)).

Every person is guilty of an offence who in the course of any trade, business or profession, *applies* any false trade description to goods, or sells or exposes for sale, or has in his possession for sale, any goods or things to which any false trade description is applied (MMA 1887, s 2; CIA 1978, s 4(1)–(2)). A wide definition is given to *applies* including an oral statement (CIA 1978, s 4(3)). See *Lemy v Watson* [1915] 32 RPC 508; *R v Hammertons Cars Ltd* [1976] 1 WLR 1243; *Donnelly v Rowlands* [1970] 1 WLR 1600; *O'Neill & Co v Adidas* [1992] ITLR (17 August), SC; *Director of Consumer Affairs & Fair Trade v Barden* [1991] HC (unreported). See UNLAWFUL INTERFERENCE IN ECONOMIC RELATIONS.

falsification. It is an offence for an officer of a company to destroy, mutilate or falsify any document affecting or relating to the property or affairs of the company: Companies Act 1990, s 243. See also Building Societies Act 1989, s 120(3); Credit Union Act 1997, s 174.

family. The natural primary and fundamental unit group of society, and a moral institution possessing inalienable and imprescriptible rights, antecedent and superior to all positive law, and recognised by the State as such: 1937 Constitution, art 41(1)(1). The State is required to guarantee to protect the family in its constitution and authority, as the necessary basis of social order and as indispensable to the welfare of the Nation and the State (art 41(1)(2)). See *North Western Health Board v H W* [2001] 3 IR 622, SC.

The family is based on the institution of marriage: *The State (Nicolaou) v An Bord Uchtála* [1966] IR 567. Family rights include such matters as succession, maintenance, family home, adoption, guardianship, education, and marital privacy (qqv). See also *Re J an infant* [1966] IR 295. A person is liable to maintain their spouse and their child: Social Welfare (Consolidation) Act 1993, s 285. The High Court has held that the fact that the word 'family' was not defined in the Immigration Act 1999, did not mean that its meaning should be extended to include grandparents as distinct from parents and children: *Caldaras v Minister for Justice* [2003] FL 8563, HC. For constitutional protection for the married family, see *Whyte* in 7 ILT & SJ(1989) 115. It is not considered advisable for doctors to treat or to issue prescriptions or certificates for themselves or for members of their families: Medical Council, *A Guide to Ethical Conduct and Behaviour* (6th edn, 2004) para 5.5. See ALIEN; EDUCATION; EUROPEAN CONVENTION ON HUMAN RIGHTS; MARRIAGE; WELFARE OF CHILDREN.

family arrangement. A phrase used to describe a situation, in the administration of an estate, where the beneficiaries under the will or the parties entitled on intestacy, decide amongst themselves how the property is to be vested. This may arise where a testator leaves the family home to his four sons as tenants-in-common, one of whom wishes to sell his share to the others and another who wishes to release his share voluntarily to the two remaining. Such an arrangement would necessitate a *deed of family arrangement* involving a sale by one beneficiary of his share and a voluntary disposition by another beneficiary of his share to the remaining two beneficiaries. For the legal and tax implications of deeds of family arrangements, see 'Keeping it in the Family' by solicitor Anne Stephenson in *Law Society Gazette* (November 2003) 28 and (December 2003) 26. For example of 'deed of family arrangement', see *Irish Conveyancing Precedents* (precedent J24) by Mary Laffoy. [Bibliography: Buckley J F; Laffoy & Wheeler.] See DISCLAIMED ESTATE.

family company. A company in which a person either has at least 25% of the voting rights or he together with his family have 75% of the voting rights and he has at least 10%: Taxes Consolidation Act 1997, s 598 as amended by Finance Act 2002, s 59. If the person is over 55 years of age and he disposes of the family company, he may be entitled to *retirement relief*. Provision is being made to extend the scheme to include disposals of land which have been leased under the EU *Early Retirement from Farming* Scheme introduced in 2000: Finance Act 2003, s 68. The limit to the consideration, for the disposal of assets eligible for relief, has been rounded up to €500,000.

family conference. A conference called by a probation and welfare office, on the direction of the court, to formulate an action plan for a child who is before the court charged with an offence: Children Act 2001, s 79. The court will so direct, where the child accepts responsibility for his criminal behaviour, the child and his parents or guardian agree to attend such a conference, and it appears to the court to be desirable that an action plan be formulated by the family conference (CA 2001, s 78). The conference must be called not later than 28 days after the court direction (CA 2001, s 79). Where the court has ordered the child to comply with the action plan, and he fails, the court may resume the proceedings in respect of the offence (CA 2001, s 84). See 'Babes in the hood' by solicitor Geoffrey Shannon in *Law Society Gazette* (November 2003) 12. [Bibliography: Shannon (2).]

Family Court. The Circuit Court is known as the Circuit Family Court when dealing with *family law proceedings* (qv): Judicial Separation and Family Law Reform Act 1989, s 31, as amended by Civil Liability and Courts Act 2004, s 50. Its proceedings must be as informal as practicable and consistent with the administration of justice; no wigs and gowns are allowed (JSFLRA 1989, s 33). It must sit in a different place or time from ordinary sittings of the Circuit Court (JSFLRA 1989, s 32, as amended by Courts and Court Officers Act 1995, s 54). In judicial separation applications involving land with a 'market value' exceeding €3m, the matter must be transferred to the High Court if the respondent so requires (JSFLRA 1989, s 31(3), as amended by CLCA 2004, s 50(a)). See Circuit Court Rules (No 1 of 1991), SI No 159 of 1991. See also Family Law Act 1995, s 38, as amended by Family Law (Miscellaneous Provisions) Act 1997, s 2(2) and CLCA 2004, s 51; Family Law

(Divorce) Act 1996, s 38, as amended by CLCA 2004, s 52. See also LRC Consultation Paper (1994) and Report on Family Courts (LRC 52, 1996). See DIVORCE; FAMILY LAW PROCEEDINGS.

family home. Primarily, a *dwelling* in which a married couple ordinarily reside; it includes a dwelling in which a spouse whose protection is in issue ordinarily resides, or if that spouse has left the other spouse, ordinarily resided before so leaving: Family Home Protection Act 1976; Judicial Separation and Family Law Reform Act 1989, s 10. A *dwelling* means any building or part of a building and includes a garden and a structure and a vehicle, or vessel, whether mobile or not, occupied as a separate dwelling (FHPA 1976, s 2(2) as amended by Family Law Act 1995, s 54).

If a spouse conveys any *interest* in the family home to a person other than the other spouse, such conveyance is void unless the prior consent in writing of that other spouse has been obtained (FHPA 1976, s 3(1)). The purpose of s 3 of FHPA 1976 is to enable a spouse to protect the family home; the spouse giving consent to a charge on the family home must know to what his consent pertains: *Bank of Ireland v Smyth* [1996] 1 ILRM 241, SC and [1995 SC] 2 IR 459. In this case the court held that the plaintiff had *constructive notice* of the spouse's lack of knowledge by virtue of s 3 of the Conveyancing Act 1882, because if the plaintiff had enquired as to the knowledge of the defendant, he would have discovered that she believed the consent did not apply to the family home. The Supreme Court also held that the plaintiff did not owe a duty to the spouse to explain the charge to her or to suggest that she get independent advice.

However, proceedings by a spouse to have such a conveyance declared void cannot be instituted any later than six years after the conveyance, unless that spouse is then in occupation; also a conveyance is not void unless so declared by the court (FHPA 1976, s 3 as amended by FLA 1995, s 54).

If both spouses join in the sale of the family home, one spouse cannot subsequently object to the sale on the ground that a consent in writing of that spouse had not been obtained: *Nestor v Murphy* [1979] IR 326. A consent by a spouse to the property being security to a loan should be contemporaneous with the making of the loan: *Standard Life Assurance Co Ltd v Satchwell* [1990] HC (unreported).

If a spouse omits or refuses to consent to a disposal of the family home, the court may order the dispensing of such consent eg where the non-owning spouse has deserted the other spouse (FHPA 1976, s 4; *R v R* [1978] HC). Also, the court may make such order as is just and equitable, where it appears to the court on the application of a spouse, that the other spouse is engaging in such conduct as may lead to the loss of any interest in the family home, or may render it unsuitable for habitation as a family home with the intention of depriving the applicant spouse or a dependent child of his residence in the family home: FHPA 1976, s 5(1) and *S v S* [1983] ILRM 387.

The provisions of the 1976 Act apply only where one spouse has any estate, right, title or other interest, legal or equitable in the family home (FHPA 1976, s 1(1)). It has been held that a house, owned by a company in which the husband was the major shareholder, was a family home: *LB v HB* [1980] HC; *C v C* [1983] HC.

Also, the deposit of title deeds of a family home in 1975 did not provide a lender with security for the repayment of advances made after the passing of the FHPA 1976: *Bank of Ireland v Purcell* [1988] ILRM 480, HC; [1990] ILRM 106, SC.

For provisions in the district court regarding removal or disposition of household chattels in the family home, see FHPA 1976, s 9; DCR 1997 Ord 60 as amended by SI No 42 of 1998. See also *Friends Provident v Doherty* [1992] ILRM 372, HC; *National Irish Bank Ltd v Graham* [1994] 2 ILRM 109, SC and [1995] 2 IR 244, SC; *Allied Irish Banks v O'Neill* [1995] 2 IR 473, HC; *Bank of Ireland v Slevin* [1995] 2 IR 454, HC; *Allied Irish Banks v Finnegan* [1996] 1 ILRM 401, HC. See *Mee* in 10 ILT & SJ (1992) 213. See also Family Law Act 1981, s 10; Criminal Damage Act 1991, s 1(3); Civil Liability and Courts Act 2004, s 48. [Bibliography: Holohan & Sanfey; Shatter; Wylie (1); Wylie (2).] See MATRIMONIAL HOME; MATRIMONIAL PROPERTY; MORTGAGEE, RIGHTS OF; PRIMARILY.

family home and bankruptcy. Any disposition of the property of a bankrupt (qv), an arranging debtor (qv), or a person dying insolvent, which comprises a family home without the prior sanction of the court, is void: Bankruptcy Act 1988, s 61(4) and 61(5).

family home and divorce. In *divorce* (qv) proceedings, the court may make orders concerning the protection of the family home and contents: Family Home Protection Act 1976, ss 5, 9; Family Law (Divorce) Act 1996, s 11(c)). It may also, on granting a decree of divorce or at any time thereafter, make similar orders in respect of the family home as in *judicial separation* proceedings having regard to similar considerations (FL(D)A 1996, s 15(1)).

family home and judgment mortgage. A spouse's prior consent is not required to render a *judgment mortgage* (qv) effective against a family home: *Containercare (Ireland) Ltd. v Wycherley* [1982] IR 143; *Murray v Diamond* [1982] 2 ILRM 113. However, conduct of a wife which resulted in the registration of a judgment mortgage has been held to entitle the husband to an order under s 5(1) of the Family Home Protection Act 1976; the order made was to transfer the wife's interest to trustees to protect the family home for the husband and children: *O'N v O'N* [1989] ITLR (4 December), HC, also reported by *Woulfe* in 8 ILT & SJ (1990) 165. The Law Reform Commission has recommended that there should not be an order for sale of a family home pursuant to a judgment mortgage unless the court so orders, having considered legislative guidelines: *Consultation Paper on Judgment Mortgages* (LRC CP 30, 2004).

family home and judicial separation. Following the granting of a decree of *judicial separation* (qv), the court may make a number of orders relating to the family home, including an order for its sale, an order conferring on one spouse the right to occupy the family home to the exclusion of the other spouse; the court must take into consideration that proper and secure accommodation be provided for a dependent spouse and any dependent children: Judicial Separation and Family Law Reform Act 1989, ss 16(a) and (b), and 19). See *MK v PK* in 9 ILT & SJ [1991] 176.

family home and property rights. An order granting the right of one spouse to occupy the family home to the exclusion of the other spouse does not constitute an unjust attack on the property rights of the other spouse: *TF v Ireland* [1995] 2 ILRM 321, SC.

family income supplement. A statutory scheme designed to provide financial assistance to families where one or more of the *spouses* are in full-time employment but net family income falls below the level prescribed in the legislation. *Spouse* was extended in 1991 to include a man and a woman who are not married to each other but are cohabiting as man and wife and extended further in 1995 to cater for divorced persons. See *Healy v Minister for Social Welfare* [1999] 1 ILRM 72, HC. See Social Welfare (Consolidation) Act 1993, ss 197–203; Social Welfare (No 2) Act 1995, s 9; Social Welfare Acts 1997, s 6 and 2000, s 7. See also Social Welfare Act 2001, s 7; Social Welfare (No 2) Act 2001, s 4; Social Welfare Act 2002, s 4.

The weekly net income thresholds used to determine entitlement to *family income supplement* have been increased to €407 in the case of a family with one child, and to €584 in the case of a family with eight or more children as from 1 January 2004: Social Welfare Act 2003, s 4.

family law. The body of laws dealing with marriage, divorce, separation, guardianship, adoption, maintenance of spouse and children, custody of and access to children, and matrimonial property including the family home (qqv).

It is important that matrimonial disputes are heard as soon as possible and that the final decision is based upon a full disclosure of all the relevant facts: *MW v DW* [2000] 1 ILRM 416, SC. While the Family Law Act 1995 allows for the joining of the Attorney-General as a party to proceedings, it is not mandatory: *McG v DW* [2000] 2 ILRM 451, SC.

See RSC Ord 70A inserted by SI No 343 of 1997. For the rules of court governing: (a) the appointment of the registered father as guardian of an infant, (b) declaration of parentage, (c) blood test where parentage is in issue, (d) other family law matters eg guardianship, maintenance of spouses and children, family home protection, judicial separation, and divorce, see Circuit Court Rules 2001 Ord 59.

The practice of family law requires a special approach and the development of skills which enable the practitioner to assist the parties reach a constructive settlement of their differences: *A Guide to Professional Conduct of Solicitors in Ireland* (2002) ch 2.2. The *Guide* recommends that the welfare of children should be a first priority and that solicitors should encourage a conciliatory approach. For code of practice for solicitors in relation to family law, see (*Guide* App 4).

For the District Court, see DCR 1997 Ord 54–Ord 62; District Court (Family Law) Rules 1998, SI No 42 of 1998; District Court (Maintenance) Rules 2003, SI No 614 of 2003. See 'Family Matters' and 'Family Fortunes' by solicitor Keith Walsh in *Law Society Gazette* (May 2002) 26 and (July 2003) 18, respectively. See 'Family Law aspects of the European Convention on Human Rights Act 2003' by barrister Dervla Browne in *Bar Review* (April 2004) 39. See 'Modern Love' by solicitor Geoffrey Shannon in *Law Society Gazette* (June 2004) 18. [Bibliography: Kennedy & Maguire; Power; Shannon; Shatter; Ward & Byrne.] See MCKENZIE FRIEND.

family law proceedings. Proceedings before a court of competent jurisdiction under the following enactments: Judicial Separation and Family Reform Act 1989; Adoption Acts 1952–1988; Family Home Protection Act 1976; Family Law (Maintenance of Spouses and Children) Act 1976; Family Law (Protection of Spouses and Children) Act 1981 (repealed by Domestic Violence Act 1996, s 23); Family Law Act 1981; Guardianship of Infants Act 1964; Legitimacy Declaration Act (Ireland) 1868; Married Women Status Act 1957; Status of Children Act 1987: FRA 1989, s 30 as amended by Courts and Court Officers Act 1995, s 53.

Also included are proceedings between spouses under the Partition Acts 1868 and 1876 where the fact that they are married to each other is of relevance to the proceedings. See RSC Ord 70A inserted by SI No 343 of 1997; Circuit Court Rules 2001 Ord 59; DCR 1997 Ord 54–Ord 62; District Court (Family Law) Rules 1998, SI No 42 of 1998; District Court (Maintenance) Rules 2003, SI No 614 of 2003. See 'The Family Law Reporting Project' by Siobhan Flockton BL in *Bar Review* (July 2003) 174. There are special rules governing family law proceedings eg see DRESS IN COURT; FAMILY COURT; IN CAMERA; PUBLIC JUSTICE.

family planning service. A service for the provision of information, instruction, advice, or consultation in relation to one or more of the following: family planning, contraception, contraceptives (qv); it does not include the provision or supply of contraceptives: Health (Family Planning) Act 1979, s 1.

The Minister is required to secure the orderly organisation of comprehensive family planning services; he may make regulations for the making available of a comprehensive family planning service by a health board or by other persons: Health (Family Planning) (Amendment) Act 1992, s 8. The former requirement regarding a *natural* family planning service has been repealed. See Health (Family Planning) Regulations 1992, SI No 312 of 1992.

family status. (1) Means responsibility: (a) as a parent or as a person in *loco parentis* in relation to a person who has not attained 18 years, or (b) as a parent or resident primary carer of a person with a disability: Employment Equality Act 1998, s 2(1). An employer is prohibited from discriminating against an employee or prospective employee on the grounds of *family status* (EEA 1998, ss 8(1) and 6). *Harassment* on the grounds of family status is also prohibited (EEA 1998, s 14A inserted by Equality Act 2004, s 8). It is not discrimination to provide a benefit to an employee with a family status to assist the employee in caring for the person for whom they have responsibility (EEA 1998, s 34(1)).

(2) Means: (a) being pregnant, or (b) having responsibility: (i) as a parent or as a person in *loco parentis* in relation to a person who has not attained the age of 18 years, or (ii) as a parent or resident primary carer of a person with a disability: Equal Status Act 2000, s 2(1). A person must not discriminate on *family status* grounds in disposing of goods or property or in providing a service or accommodation; treating one person less favourably than the other, in a comparable situation, because one has family status and the other does not (or that one has a different family status from the other) is discrimination: ESA 2000, ss 5, 6 and 3, amended by Equality Act 2004, ss 48–49. Having a reasonable preferential charge for persons together with their children, or for married couples, does not constitute discrimination (ESA 2000, s 16(1)(a)). [Bibliography: Reid M.] See DISCRIMINATION; HARASSMENT; PENSION SCHEME AND DISCRIMINATION.

Family Support Agency. A new statutory body which brings together the main pro-grammes designed to help prevent marital breakdown, to support ongoing parenting relationships for children, and to promote local support for families: Family Support Agency Act 2001.

The functions of the new Agency are: (a) to provide a *family mediation service* either directly or, where the Agency considers it is necessary, to provide a family mediation service and training in family mediation through support for others providing these services; (b) to support, promote and develop the provision of marriage and relationship counselling and family support services; (c) to support, promote and develop the *Family and Community Services Resource Centre* programme; (d) to provide, subject to the consent of the Minister, financial assistance to voluntary bodies providing these services and to administer for the purpose such schemes, grants and other facilities for financial assistance as are authorised by the Minister; (e) to promote and disseminate information about issues relating to family mediation, marriage and relationships education, parenting and family responsibilities; (f) to undertake and commission research and to have an information and assistance function to the Minister (FSAA 2001, s 4).

family welfare conference. Means a conference called for the purpose of deciding if a child, in respect of whom the conference is being convened, is in need of special care or protection: Children Act 2001, s 8. It is intended as an early intervention mechanism at an inter-agency level for children at risk, and can be triggered by: (a) the court where it considers that a child before it on a criminal charge may be in need of special care or protection, or (b) where it appears to a health board that a child in its area may be in need of special care or protection (CA 2001, s 7).

On receipt of the recommendations of the family welfare conference, the health board may: (a) apply for a *special care order* under the Child Care Act 1991; (b) apply for a *care order* or *supervision order* under CCA 1991, or (c) provide any service or assistance to the child or his family (CA 2001, s 13). See also CA 2001, s 78. [Bibliography: McDermott & Robinson.]

famosus libellus. [A scandalous libel.] See LIBEL.

farm assist scheme. A social welfare scheme to assist farming families on low income to continue in farming: Social Welfare Act 1999, ss 15–18. See also Social Welfare Act 2000, s 18; Social Welfare Act 2003, s 3(2)(a).

farm tax. Farming profits are taxed as trading profits under Schedule D, Case 1: Taxes Consolidation Act 1997, s 655. Farming means *occupying* farm land in the State, wholly or mainly for husbandry (TCA 1997, s 654). The *occupation of land* means having the right to use the land and graze livestock on the land (s 654). See *Purcell v Attorney-General* [1995] 3 IR 287, SC.

FÁS. [An Foras Áiseanna Saothair.] The Training and Employment Authority established by the Labour Services Act 1987. Its functions include the operation of training and employment programmes, the provision of an employment and recruitment service, an advisory and support service for business, and support for co-operative and community-based enterprise.

Where a person applies to FÁS for a certificate in respect of a *relevant activity* which has been pursued in the State, FÁS is required to issue such certificate, provided it is satisfied that the applicant has the relevant qualifications and experience gained in the State: EC (Recognition of Qualifications and Experience) Regulations 2003, SI No 372 of 2003, implementing Directive (EC) 99/42. A *relevant activity* is an activity which falls within the list of activities set out in *Annex A* to the Directive. See also Industrial Training Act 1967; Qualifications (Education and Training) Act 1999. See website: *www.fas.ie*. See EDUCATION AWARDS; INDUSTRIAL DEVELOPMENT; TRAINING.

fatal injuries. At common law, dependants had no right to sue in respect of a death from fatal injuries. Under the Civil Liability Act 1961, as amended by Civil Liability (Amendment) Act 1996, a *dependant* of a deceased, whose death was caused by a wrongful act (which includes a crime) may recover damages. A *dependant* means a spouse, parent, grandparent, step-parent, child, grandchild, step-child, brother, sister, half-brother or half-sister of the deceased. A *dependant* also includes: (a) a person though not married to the deceased, had been living with the deceased as man and wife for at least three years before the date of death, and (b) a person whose marriage to the deceased has been dissolved by a decree of divorce (CL(A)A 1996, s 1). See also Courts Act 1981.

The damages which may be awarded are under *three* headings: (a) loss of pecuniary benefits which could have been reasonably expected but for the wrongful act of the defendant; (b) reasonable compensation for mental distress as determined by the judge, subject to a maximum award of £20,000 (€25,395); (c) funeral and other expenses actually incurred by reason of the wrongful act (CLA 1961, s 49; CA 1981, s 28(1); CL(A)A 1996, s 2). However, a divorced spouse is not entitled to claim for mental distress (CL(A)A 1996, s 3).

The basis of assessment of damages for fatal injuries is the balancing of losses and benefits accruing to dependants; this can include the effect of remarriage of a widow the likelihood of which is to be calculated at the time of death: *Fitzsimons v Bord Telecom & ESB* [1991] ILRM 277. The failure of the deceased to declare his income for income tax purposes does not prevent the court from making an award for loss of dependancy: *Downing v O'Flynn* [2000] 4 IR 383, SC.

The assessment of a claim in respect of fatal injuries under CLA 1961, s 48, which comes within the remit of the Personal Injuries Assessment Board, must specify the proportion of damages to which each of the dependants is entitled: Personal Injuries Assessment Board Act 2003, s 21(3).

An action must be brought within two years of the date of death or the date of knowledge of the person for whose benefit the action is brought, whichever is the later: Statute of Limitations (Amendment) Act 1991, s 6, as amended from 3 to 2 years by Civil Liability and Courts Act 2004, s 7. See *Wates v Cruickshank* [1967] IR 378; *O'Sullivan v CIE* [1978] IR 407. See also Air Navigation and Transport Act 1936 (as amended) and as further amended by CL(A)A 1996, s 4. [Bibliography: Kerr (2).] See ASSESSMENT; PERSONAL INJURIES; DAMAGES; MENTAL DISTRESS.

father. See PARENTAGE, DECLARATION OF; PATERNITY, PRESUMPTION OF.

Father of the Bar. The member of the Bar of Ireland earliest in his initial call to the Bar. In 2004, the Father of the Bar is Mr Richard Cooke SC who was called to the Bar in 1938 and to the Inner Bar in 1959. See BARRISTERS, PRECEDENCE BETWEEN.

fauces terrae. A narrow inlet of the sea; a gulf.

fault liability. See STRICT LIABILITY.

fax. Transmission of documents by fax has been held in the District Court to be good service of the documents: *ICDS Recruitment Consultants Ltd v Gillespie* [1992] DC as reported in *Law Society Gazette* (January/February 1993) 10. Where a document is admissible in criminal proceedings, it may be given in evidence by producing an authenticated copy of it, including a fax copy: Criminal Evidence Act 1992, s 30.

The Minister for Justice, as the *central authority* in Ireland for extradition, is empowered to receive extradition requests and documents by fax: Extradition (European Union Conventions) Act 2001, s 18. The central authority of a requesting member state must state that it certifies that the documents transmitted correspond to the originals; and must make use of cryptographic devices to ensure confidentiality and authenticity. See also European Arrest Warrant Act 2003, s 12(5) and (6).

Provision has also been made to facilitate the use of faxed *stock transfer forms* in order to provide a speedier mechanism for the transfer of securities: Stock Transfer (Forms) Regulations 2000, SI No 206 of 2000.

However, it has been held that service by fax of a notice under Companies Act 1963, s 214 was not valid: *Re WMG (Toughening) Ltd* [2001] 3 IR 113, HC. See Criminal Justice (Illicit Traffic by Sea) Act 2003, s 28(c)(ii); Private Security Services Act 2004, s 49(1)(e). See also BENEFIT-IN-KIND; COMPUTERS; DOCUMENTARY EVIDENCE; UNSOLICITED CALL.

feadhmannaigh shíochána. [Peace Commissioners (qv).]

fee. (1) The term used in land law to denote that an estate is capable of being inherited. A fee was originally a feudal benefice of land granted to a man and his heirs in return for services to be rendered to the grantor. (2) A financial charge made for a privilege eg a certificate or licence. The Public Offices Fees Act 1879 provides for the collection of fees payable in any public office by means of stamps. Its provisions are often excluded eg Merchant Shipping Act 1992, s 31(4); Radiological Protection (Amendment) Act 2002, s 2(e); Immigration Act 2004, s 19(6).

Where a fee is paid by cheque, it is received when it is delivered provided it is subsequently honoured in the normal way; acceptance of a blank cheque for a fee implies an agreement to act on an inferred authority to fill in the amount of the prescribed fee: *Maher v An Bord Pleanála* [1993] ILRM 359, HC. See BARRISTER AND FEES; BRIEF FEE.

fee farm grant. A *fee simple* estate with a rent reserved to the grantor. Since the Renewable Leasehold Conversion Act 1849, a *lease for lives renewable forever* (qv) operates as a fee farm grant if the lessor is capable of making such a grant. A fee farm grant creates the relationship of landlord and tenant between the parties: Deasy's Act 1860. A fee farm rent, whether rent seck (qv) or rent charge (qv) may be recovered by various remedies: Conveyancing Act 1881, s 44. See FEE SIMPLE.

fee simple. An estate of freehold being the most extensive that a person can have. A fee simple estate may be: (a) a *fee simple absolute*, which is an estate which continues forever; (b) a *determinable fee*, which is a fee simple which will automatically determine on the occurrence of some specified event which may never occur; (c) a *fee simple upon condition*, which may be upon a condition precedent or a condition subsequent; (d) a *base fee*, which is a particular kind of determinable fee; and (e) a *fee farm grant* which is a fee simple with a rent reserved to the grantor.

To convey a fee simple estate it is essential to use the correct words of limitation: *to A and his heirs* or *to A in fee simple*; or *to A and successors* in the case of a grant to a corporation sole. No words of limitation are required in a devise by will or a grant to a corporation aggregate (eg a limited company). For determination of the purchase price of the fee simple, see Landlord Tenant (Amendment) Act 1984, s 7. See also Conveyancing Act 1881, s 51. See BASE FEE; FLYING FREEHOLD; SHELLEY'S CASE, RULE IN; GROUND RENT.

fee splitting. An arrangement under which the fee for a service is shared between the persons providing the service. Such a practice as between medical practitioners is deemed to be against the interest of patients: Medical Council, *A Guide to Ethical Conduct and Behaviour* (6th edn, 2004) para 12.7. See also SOLICITOR.

fee tail. An entail; an estate tail; a freehold estate which continues for as long as the original tenant and any of his descendants survive. It is created by the words of limitation *heir* followed by some words of procreation e g *To A and the heirs of his body*, or *to A in tail* since the Conveyancing Act 1881. An estate tail may be created by will only by the same words of limitation as those required in a deed: Succession Act 1965, s 95.

The owner of the estate tail is known as the *tenant-in-tail*. A *tail male* or a *tail female* are entails where the property descended to males or females exclusively. In order to *bar* the entail and create a fee simple (qv) estate, it is necessary for the tenant-in-tail to execute a *disentailing deed* which must be enrolled in the Central Office (qv) within six months of execution: Fines and Recoveries Act 1833. An entail cannot be barred by will. See *Re Fallon* [1956] IR 268; *Bank of Ireland v Domville* [1956] IR 37.

Canons of descent (qv) have been abolished except in so far as they apply to the descent of an estate tail: Succession Act 1965, s 11. See BARRING THE ENTAIL; PROTECTOR OF THE SETTLEMENT.

felo de se. [Felon of himself.] Formerly, a person who committed suicide (qv).

felon. Formerly, a person who committed a felony (qv).

felony. A crime which at common law carried the penalty of death and forfeiture of the land and goods of the offender. All other crimes were *misdemeanours*. Many crimes were made felonies by statute. Forfeiture generally was abolished by the Forfeiture Act 1870. The distinction between felonies and misdemeanours became blurred over time, although felonies generally carried heavier penalties; also a person could be arrested without penalty when suspected of committing a felony, whereas an arrest warrant was required for a misdemeanour unless the offender was caught actually committing the misdemeanour. Additionally, only in felonies was the distinction drawn between principals (qv) and accessories (qv).

As from 1997, all distinctions between felonies and misdemeanours are abolished: Criminal Law Act 1997, s 3(1). The effect of this Act is that the existing law relating to misdemeanours is applied to all offences, although the power of arrest without warrant, which applied to felonies, is effectively retained by the designation of a new class of serious offences called '*arrestable offences*' (qv). See also COMPOUNDING A FELONY;

MISPRISION OF FELONY; TORT; TRANSPORTATION.

feme covert. A married woman.

feme sole. An unmarried woman.

feminine gender. Every word in an Act of the Oireachtas, passed on or after 22 December 1993, importing the *feminine gender* is to construed, unless the contrary intention appears, as if it also imported the *masculine gender*: Interpretation (Amendment) Act 1993.

fence. Includes a hoarding or similar structure but excludes any bank, wall or similar structure composed wholly or mainly of earth or stone: Planning and Development Act 2000, s 2(1). See LANDSCAPE CONSERVATION AREA.

Fennelly Order. An interlocutory order directing an employer to continue to pay an employee's salary and restraining the employer from dismissing the employee, so called after *Fennelly v Assicurazioni Generali Spa* [1985] 3 ILTR 73. While it has traditionally been a fundamental principle of employment law that courts would not normally order specific performance of an employment contract, in recent years these *Fennelly Orders* have become more usual, at least at the interlocutory stage. See also *Lonergan v Salter-Townshend* [2000] ELR 15, HC. For more examples, see INTERLOCUTORY INJUNCTION.

feodum. A *fee* (qv).

feoffee to uses. See USE.

ferae naturae. [Of a wild nature.] See ANIMALS.

FETAC. [Further Education and Training Awards Council (qv).]

feudal system. The system under which the king was lord of all land; he granted land to his lords in return for military and other services. The lords in turn granted land to others, the process being known as *subinfeudation*. The unit of land in the system was the *manor*, each of which had a lord; he exercised jurisdiction over the servile tenants of the manor and all owed allegiance to the king.

fi fa. See FIERI FACIAS.

fiat. [Let it be done.] A decree, an order, a warrant.

fiat justitia, ruat coelum. [Let justice be done, though the heavens fall.] However, see FINALITY IN LITIGATION.

fictio legis non operatur damnum vel injuriam. [A legal fiction does not work loss or injustice.] See FINE.

fictitious name. There is nothing in the law or the Rules of the Superior Courts 1986 which would permit a plaintiff to prosecute proceedings using a fictitious name; the court has no jurisdiction to allow a plaintiff to prosecute proceedings using an assumed name and to purport to do so would contravene art 34 of the Constitution: *Roe v Blood Transfusion Service Board* [1996] 1 ILRM 555, HC and 3 IR 67. In this case the plaintiff, whose real name and address had been disclosed to the defendants, wished to prosecute her case using an *alias*, as she wished to protect her privacy and avoid any public discrimination which might arise from the disclosure that she had contracted hepatitis C as a result of the alleged negligence of the defendants. See also *Re R Ltd* [1989] IR 126. See HEPATITIS.

fiduciary. A person who has been entrusted with powers for the benefit of others but who in the exercise of those powers is not subject to the direct and immediate control of those others eg company directors, trustees, liquidators, executors and court appointed receivers (qqv). The general rule is that a person in a fiduciary position is not entitled to make a profit and he is not allowed to put himself in a position where his interest and his duty conflict.

Any provisions in a company's regulations are proscribed which exempt or indemnify an officer of the company in respect of any liability which attaches to him in respect of his negligence, default, breach of duty or breach of trust: Companies Act 1963, s 200 as amended by Companies Amendment Act 1983, Sch 1, para 16, and Companies (Auditing and Accounting) Act 2003, s 56. The court may excuse an officer from such liability if he acted reasonably and honestly (CA 1963, s 391). The 2003 Act provides that, notwithstanding s 200(1), a company may purchase and maintain for any of its officers or auditors, insurance in respect of any liability referred to in that subsection. See *Jackson v Munster Bank* [1885] 15 LR Ir 356; *Cockburn v Newbridge Sanitary Steam Laundry Co* [1915] 1 IR 249; *Nash v Lancegaye Safety Glass (Ireland) Ltd* [1958] 92 ILTR 1; *Clark v Workman* [1920] 1 IR 107; *Irish Microforms v Browne* [1987] HC. See also Building Societies Act 1989, s 114(1). For fiduciary duties of company directors, see MacCann in 9 ILT & SJ (1991) 30 & 104.

For fiduciary duties of partners, see Bibliography: Twomey. See DIRECTOR; RETENTION OF TITLE CLAUSE.

fieri facias; fi fa. [Cause to be made.] An order of *execution* directing the sheriff (qv) to whom it is addressed to levy from the goods and chattels of the debtor a sum equal to the amount of the judgment debt, interest, and costs of execution. The sheriff seizes the goods and sells them by auction. An order of *fieri facias* is not invalidated by an incorrect statement of the person's description and place of abode: RSC Ord 42, r 16 and *Mehigan v Duignan* [1999] 2 ILRM 216, HC and 2 IR 593. See *Incorporated Law Society v Owens* [1990] 8 ILT Dig 64. See RSC Ord 42–43. See VENDITIONI EXPONAS.

fieri feci. [I have caused to be made.] The return of a sheriff (qv) to an order of *fieri facias*. An order binds the property in the goods of the execution debtor as from the delivery of the order to the sheriff: Sale of Goods Act 1893, s 26. See RSC Ord 42, r 35.

filius nullius. [Son of nobody.] An illegitimate child; a bastard; now referred to as *a child whose parents are not married to each other*: Status of Children Act 1987. See CHILD, ILLEGITIMATE.

film. Means a *fixation* on any medium from which a moving image may, by any means, be produced, perceived or communicated through a device: Copyright and Related Rights Act 2000, s 2(1). *Fixation* means the embodiment of sounds or images (CRRA 2000, s 2(1)). Consequently, a film for the purposes of the Act includes a video. The *author* of a film includes the producer and the principal director; a film will be treated as a work of *joint authorship* unless the producer and principal director are the same person (CRRA 2000, ss 21(b) and 22(2)).

Copyright subsists in a film (CRRA 2000, s 17(2)). The copyright expires 70 years after the last of the following persons die: the principal director, the author of either the screenplay, dialogue or music (CRRA 2000, s 25(1)).

There is a presumption in any film production agreement that the author transfers to the film producer any *rental rights*; there is provision for *equitable remuneration* of the author where the rental right is transferred, and in default of agreement, the remuneration to be determined by the Controller for Patents (CRRA 2000, ss 124–126). There is a similar presumption as regards a *performer* and a film producer and film rental rights (CRRA 2000, ss 297–299).

The Irish Film Board has responsibility for promoting the film and audio-visual industry: Irish Film Board Acts 1980 and (Amendment) Act 1993. The *tax relief* on investment in films has been extended to investments made up to 5 April 2005, the maximum funding eligible for tax relief has been increased by 10%, and some other changes have been made to address concerns expressed by the European Commission: Taxes Consolidation Act 1997, s 481 as amended by Finance Act 2000, s 48. In 2003, the end of the scheme was brought forward to 31 December 2004 and a number of technical changes were made to s 481 of TCA 1997: Finance Act 2003, s 58. In 2004, the scheme was extended to 31 December 2008, the limit on funding for any one film was increased to €15m, and measures were introduced to address certain abuses of the tax relief: Finance Act 2004, s 28.

See *Universal City Studios v Mulligan* [1998] 1 ILRM 438 and [1999] 3 IR 381, HC. For Irish Film Board, see website: *www.filmboard.ie*. For the Film Institute of Ireland, see website: *www. fii.ie*. For Cybercinema, see website: *www.eif.ie*. See AUTHOR; COPYRIGHT; COPYRIGHT, QUALIFICATION FOR; DOCUMENTARY EVIDENCE; PERFORMERS' RIGHTS.

final. The decision of the Supreme Court is final and conclusive: 1937 Constitution, art 34(4)(6). The determination of the Court of Criminal Appeal is final: Courts of Justice Act 1924, s 29. The word 'final' puts the decision of these courts beyond review by any other judicial body: *Pringle v Ireland* [1994]1 ILRM 467, HC. However, see APPEAL; EUROPEAN COURT OF JUSTICE; FINALITY IN LITIGATION; MISCARRIAGE.

final certificate. Often refers to the certificate of an architect pursuant to a standard building contract, which provides that the certificate is conclusive evidence that the works have been properly carried out and completed in accordance with the contract. See *Elliot & Co v Minister for Education* [1987] ILRM 710. See RIAI CONTRACT.

final judgment. Judgment awarded when an action is ended. The fact that no formal order was drawn up, does not affect the nature of a judge's ruling, where that ruling was accepted by the parties at that time: *Carroll v Ryan* [2003] 2 ILRM 1, SC.

final order. The Supreme Court has held that the grounds upon which a *final order* might be challenged were limited to correcting the final judgment to ensure that it reflected the intention of the court which made it and to set aside an order that was obtained by fraud: *L P v M P* [2002 SC] 1 IR 219.

A *final order* of the Supreme Court which is made and perfected, can only be interfered with: (i) in special and unusual circumstances, (ii) where there has been an accidental slip in the judgment as drawn up, or (iii) where the court itself finds that the judgment as drawn up does not correctly state what the court actually decided and intended: *Re Greendale Development (No 3)* [2000] 2 IR 514, SC. See also *G McG v DW and AR* [2000 SC] 4 IR 1; *In the matter of Greendale Developments Ltd (in liquidation)* [2001] 1 ILRM 161, SC.

finality in litigation. It is of the essence of litigation that, subject to a proper right of appeal, the judgment of a court should be a final one: *Dalton v Minister for Finance* [1989] ILRM 519, SC. Decisions of the Supreme Court are final and conclusive; however a decision can be set aside for fraud, pleaded with particularity and established on the balance of probability: 1937 Constitution, art 34(4)(6); *Bruno Tassan Din v Banco Ambrosiano SPA* [1991] 1 IR 569, HC. Even if a decision of the Supreme Court on a matter of law is established to have been wrong by a subsequent decision of the Supreme Court, such a correction is not a valid ground for upsetting the original judgment: *A-G v Ryans Car Hire Ltd* [1965] IR 642 and *Bruno Tassan Din* case. See *Blackall v Grehan* [1995] 3 IR 208, SC. See FRESH EVIDENCE; GENERAL DAMAGES; FOREIGN LAW; SET ASIDE.

finance house, liability of. A finance house is deemed to be a party to the sale of goods to a buyer *dealing as consumer*, and the finance house and the seller of the goods are *jointly and severally* answerable to the buyer for any breach of contract and for any misrepresentation made by the seller with respect to the goods, where the buyer has entered into an agreement with the finance house for the repayment to the finance house of money paid by the finance house to the seller in respect of the price of goods. See Supply of Goods and Supply of

Services Act 1980, s 14. See CONSUMER, DEALING AS.

financial accommodation. Includes credit and the letting of goods: Consumer Credit Act 1995, s 2(1). An advertisement of *financial accommodation* related to goods and services must comply with certain requirements eg nature of accommodation, cash price, total cost of credit or hire-purchase price, deposit payable, and details on instalments (number, amount, duration of intervals, number before delivery) (CCA 1995, s 22).

financial collateral. Means cash or financial instruments provided under a *financial collateral arrangement*, but does not include shares in a company whose exclusive purpose is: (a) to own means of production that are essential for the collateral provider's business, or (b) to own real property: EC (Financial Collateral Arrangements) Regulations 2004, SI No 1 of 2004 as amended by SI No 89 of 2004. The regulations give effect to Directive (EC) 2002/47, the aim of which is to create a Community-wide regime for the provision of financial instruments (mainly securities) and cash (not banknotes, but rather money credited to an account) as collateral and where possession or control of the collateral passes to the collateral taker. The regime does not apply to non-financial forms of collateral, such as real estate, plant and machinery, or book debts.

financial compensation order. An order of the court: (a) requiring the assignment of a spouse's interest in a life insurance policy in favour of the other spouse or dependent child, or (b) requiring a spouse to take out a life insurance policy in favour of the other spouse or dependent child, or (c) requiring a spouse to make the necessary payments required under the terms of the insurance policy: Family Law Act 1995, s 11. Such an order may be made on granting a decree of *judicial separation* (qv) or at any time thereafter (FLA 1995, s 11(1)). A similar order is provided for, which may be made by the court, in favour of a spouse or dependent family member on granting a decree of *divorce* or at any time thereafter: Family Law (Divorce) Act 1996, s 16.

financial institution. See BANKER AND CONFIDENTIALITY; CREDIT INSTITUTION; IRISH FINANCIAL SERVICES REGULATORY AUTHORITY; IRISH PAYMENT SERVICES ORGANISATION; MONEY LAUNDERING.

financial perspective. The term used to describe the spending plan of the European Union over a number of years. The *financial perspective* states the maximum amount that the institutions of the EU may spend and on what. *Perspective* essentially means *plan*.

financial resolutions. Resolutions of Dáil Éireann, sitting as a committee of the whole House, to give temporary effect to certain tax measures announced in the government's budget statement: Provisional Collection of Taxes Act 1927. The resolutions may increase, reduce, vary or abolish a specified permanent tax, or renew a specified temporary tax, which was in force immediately before the end of the previous financial year, or may create a new tax. The effect of the financial resolutions is to amend the tax and the related law as it stands immediately before the financial resolutions take effect: Finance Act 2002, s 139.

The maximum period for which a Dáil financial resolution can have statutory force is four months unless enacted into law (PCTA 1927, s 4) (eg by the subsequent Finance Act). However, any period of dissolution of the Dáil after the resolution is passed is disregarded: Finance Act 1992, s 250.

In recent years, with the alignment of the financial year with the calendar year, the practice has been to include the financial resolutions in the *Appropriation Act* (qv) at the end of the calendar year eg the Appropriation Act 2002, s 2 provides that legislation to give effect to the financial resolutions passed by the Dáil on 4 December 2002 may be enacted in 2003, subject to the time period specified in s 4 of the PCTA 1927. See also Appropriation Act 2003, s 2.

financial services action plan. An EU plan, launched in 1999, which has the aim of integrating European financial markets, enabling capital and financial services to flow freely throughout the EU, while at the same time providing proper prudential safeguards and investor protection. Key strategic objectives include: (a) the creation of a single wholesale market in financial services, (b) the establishment of an open and secure retail market for consumers, and (c) increasing co-ordination between supervisory authorities and implementing state-of-the-art prudential rules. See 'No Pain, No Gain' by solicitors David Dillon and Peter

Stapleton in *Law Society Gazette* (Mar 2004) 30. See SAVINGS DIRECTIVE.

Financial Services Appeal Tribunal. See IRISH FINANCIAL SERVICES REGULATORY AUTHORITY.

Financial Services Ombudsman. Under recent legislation, provision has been made for the establishment of an independent statutory Financial Services Ombudsman scheme to deal with consumer complaints against financial service providers: Central Bank and Financial Services Authority of Ireland Act 2004, s 16. The main features of the scheme are: (a) comprehensive coverage of complaints from personal consumers against financial services providers, including banks, building societies, insurance companies, credit unions and intermediaries (brokers), with provision for extension of the scheme to complaints from non-personal consumers; (b) a Council, composed of persons with appropriate consumer and industry backgrounds, to appoint the Ombudsman and Deputy Ombudsmen and to make detailed regulations governing the scheme; (c) the Ombudsman to be fully independent in making decisions on individual complaints: (d) the scheme to be funded by levies/charges on financial service providers; (e) the scheme to be independent of the Irish Financial Services Regulatory Authority, but with provision for close co-operation; (f) determinations of Ombudsman to be binding on financial institutions, subject to their right to appeal to the High Court; (g) transparency in operations, including regular published reports and accountability to Oireachtas committee; (h) enabling provision for the existing non-statutory Insurance and Credit Institutions Ombudsmen, and their staff and systems to be absorbed into the statutory scheme, with the current Ombudsmen being designated by the Minister as Deputy Ombudsmen-designate under the statutory scheme. See INSURANCE OMBUDSMAN; IRISH FINANCIAL SERVICES REGULATORY AUTHORITY; OMBUDSMAN FOR CREDIT INSTITUTIONS.

financial standing. Where a consumer is refused an agreement by a creditor (or owner) and the refusal was influenced by information concerning the *financial standing* of the consumer, the creditor is required to supply to the consumer, the name and address of the person from whom the information was sought: Consumer Credit Act 1995, s 142, as amended by Central Bank and Financial Services Authority of Ireland Act 2003, s 35, Sch 1. This does not apply to information which comes within the scope of the Data Protection Act 1988, as that Act will provide the consumer with a like remedy. See DATA PROTECTION.

financial transfer. See EXCHANGE CONTROL.

finding. (1) The conclusions of an enquiry of fact. (2) The finder of goods has a better title to them against everyone except the true owner. If the finder is under a duty to hand over found property to another, and if the true owner is not found, the goods belong to that other. See *Quin v Coleman* [1898] 32 ILTR 79; *Crinion v Minister for Justice* [1959] Ir Jur Rep 433. See TREASURE TROVE.

finding, bailment by. The custody of a lost chattel, found in a public place, which gives to the finder all the rights which belong to a bailee by virtue of his possession. The finder has the obligations of a depository to the true owner, including the obligation to return the chattel to him on demand. The finder does no wrong to the true owner, unless he takes it, meaning to appropriate it to himself, knowing or having reasonable grounds for believing that the owner can be found, in which case the taking would be a *trespass* and the finder would be guilty of *larceny* (qv). See *Bridges v Hawkesworth* [1851] 21 LJ QB 15; *Webb & Webb v Ireland & The A-G* [1988] IR 353, SC.

finding, larceny by. See LARCENY BY FINDING.

finding is keeping. Popular misconception that the finder of property acquires a title as against all others, including the rightful owner. See LARCENY BY FINDING.

fine. (1) A lump sum payment for the grant of a lease (qv).

(2) A fictitious collusive action which resulted in an agreement to convey land being entered in the court records as a compromise to an action. It was used to *bar an entail*. It was abolished by the Fines and Recoveries Act 1833 which substituted a simple disentailing assurance.

(3) A monetary penalty payable on conviction. Where a fine is unlimited, care and restraint must be used in the exercise of the power to fine: *People (DPP) v Oran Precast Ltd* [2003] FL 9058, CCA. The court held in this case, involving a fatal accident at work, that the actual level of fault is the principal consideration, and the financial

state of the company to which the fine relates cannot be irrelevant and cannot be ignored. The court reduced the fine from €500,000 to €100,000.

The Law Reform Commission has recommended that fines be indexed against inflation and they should vary to take account of the offender's ability to pay, in order to convey 'the principle of equality of impact upon offenders of different means': *Report on the Indexation of Fines: A Review of Recent Developments* (LRC 65, 2002). For previous Report, see LRC 37 of 1991. See BARRING THE ENTAIL; PENALTY.

fine, on-the-spot. See ON-THE-SPOT FINE.

fineness, standard of. The standard of fineness, known as the *Irish Standard of Fineness*, which the Minister may by regulation prescribe for articles of precious metal and for solders of such articles: Hallmarking Act 1981, s 7.

fingerprints. The clear prints of the external filaments of the skin surface which are obtained by pressing the fingers and thumbs of both hands on paper or cardboard, having first pressed them upon an inked plate: Regulations as to the Measuring and Photographing of Prisoners 1955, SI No 114 of 1955; Penal Servitude Act 1891,s 8 as amended by Criminal Law Act 1997, s 16 and Sch 3. These regulations permit the photographing, measuring and fingerprinting, which includes the taking of palm prints, of a convicted person at any time during his imprisonment, and of an untried person if he does not object or with the authority of the Minister if the prisoner objects.

Good practice requires twelve points of comparison in fingerprints as regards an accused, but a lesser amount will be admissible as regards a witness: *People (DPP) v James Ryan* [1993] ITLR (19 April), CCA and 11 ILT Dig [1993] 185.

Fingerprints must not be taken of a person in custody except with his written consent and, where he is under the age of 17 years, the written consent of an appropriate adult: Treatment of Persons in Custody in Garda Síochána Stations Regulations 1987, SI No 119 of 1987, reg.18. Consent is not required where the garda is otherwise empowered by law.

There are further powers given to the gardaí in relation to fingerprinting of persons detained under the Offences Against the State Act 1939, s 30: Criminal Law Act 1976, s 7(1). Also provision has been made for fingerprinting of persons who are prosecuted for an indictable offence, or convicted, or who are detained under powers of *detention* (qv) contained in the Criminal Justice Act 1984 (CJA 1984, ss 6 and 28 as amended by Criminal Justice (Miscellaneous Provisions) Act 1997, s 12). For application in connection with the preservation of fingerprints, palm prints and photographs pursuant to CJA 1984,s 8(7), see DCR 1997 Ord 31. The power to take fingerprints and palmprints includes the power to record them by electronic means: Criminal Justice (Miscellaneous Provisions) Act 1997, s 11. See BIOMETRICS; GENETIC FINGERPRINTING.

finis finem litibus imponit. [A fine puts an end to legal proceedings.]

fire, liability for. At common law, a person was liable for damage caused by fire escaping from his premises. However, by statute there is no liability if the fire accidentally occurs on land or in buildings and escapes without negligence: Accidental Fires Act 1943, s 1. An occupier is liable if he or his servant negligently started the fire, or negligently allows it to escape after being started without negligence. The 1943 Act does not apply to any claims for damages under the Hotel Proprietors Act 1963.

A tenant is generally required to give up possession of premises on determination of a lease in good and substantial repair, except in the case of accidents by fire without the tenant's default: *Kiernan v O'Connell* [1938] 72 ILTR 205. See also *Bradley v Donegal Co Council* [1990] ITLR (29 January), HC. See RYLANDS V FLETCHER, RULE IN.

fire authority. The council of a county, the corporation of a county borough, the corporation of Dún Laoghaire and any other borough corporation or urban district council which has established and is maintaining a fire brigade at the commencement of this section: Fire Services Act 1981, s 9(1). A duty is imposed on fire authorities: (a) to make provision for the prompt and efficient extinguishing of fires occurring in buildings and other places of all kinds in their functional areas and for the protection and rescue of persons and property from injury by fire; (b) to establish and maintain a fire brigade; (c) to make adequate provision for the reception of and response for the assistance of the fire brigade. For amendments to ss 2, 5, 6, 13, 16, 18, 19, 20, 21, and 38 of FSA 1981, see

Licensing of Indoor Events Act 2003, ss 24–34. A minimum pensionable age of 55 years of age has been set for *new entrants* as specified fire brigade employees: Public Service Superannuation (Miscellaneous Provisions) Act 2004, ss 6 and 10(5). See FIRE SAFETY NOTICE; CLOSURE NOTICE.

fire warning label. A 'keep away from fire' warning label on a child's clothing is a sufficiently clear warning to carers that a child wearing the garment to which the warning was attached, should be kept away from unprotected fire: *Cassells (a minor) v Marks and Spencer plc* [2002] 1 IR 179, SC. The High Court has ruled that a fire warning on a tag in the side seam of a child's dress was an adequate warning: *Rodgers (a minor) v Adams Childrenswear Ltd* (2003) Irish Times, 12 February.

fire brigade. See FIRE AUTHORITY.

fire safety. See Bibliography: McMahon M.

fire safety notice. The notice which a fire authority may serve on the owner or occupier of any building which appears to the authority to be a *potentially dangerous building* ie a building which would, in the event of a fire occurring therein, constitute a serious danger to life for any one of specified reasons: Fire Services Act 1981, ss 19–20 as amended by Licensing of Indoor Events Act 2003, ss 30 and 34.

A *fire safety notice* imposes on the owner or the occupier certain specified requirements eg the provision and maintenance of exit signs. An appeal lies against such a notice (FSA 1981, s 21 and DCR 1997 Ord 92, r 4). The fire safety notice provisions are extended to factories and other premises covered in the Safety in Industry Act 1955 and 1980: Safety, Health and Welfare at Work Act 1989, s 55. See CLOSURE NOTICE.

firearm. A *lethal* (qv) firearm or other lethal weapon of any description from which any shot, bullet, or other missile can be discharged: Firearms and Offensive Weapons Act 1990, s 4. A firearm also includes a crossbow, a stun gun, and an air gun (which expression includes an air rifle and an air pistol and any other weapon incorporating a barrel from which metal or other slugs can be discharged), a defective firearm, and a prohibited weapon (qv) (FOWA 1990, s 4(1)). Generally it is not lawful for a person to have in his possession, use, or carry any firearm or ammunition save in so far as such possession, use, or carriage is authorised by a *firearms certificate*: Firearms

Act 1925, s 2. See also Firearms (Proofing) Act 1968; Firearms Act 1964 and 1971; Firearms Regulations 1976.

It is an offence to have possession of a firearm *with intent* to endanger life; pointing a loaded gun at a person establishes the required intent; there is a distinction between an intent to kill and an intent to endanger life: Firearms Act 1925, s 14(a) as amended; *People (DPP) v Farrell* [1993] ILRM 743, CCA.

Using or producing a firearm or an imitation firearm for the purpose of, or while, resisting arrest by a member of the Garda Síochána, or in the course of aiding or abetting an escape or rescue from lawful custody is an indictable offence (qv): Firearms Act 1964, s 27. The 1990 Act extended the definition of *firearm*, introduced strict controls on silencers and *offensive weapons*. It also introduced a new offence of reckless discharge of a firearm (FOWA 1990, s 8).

In 1998, the courts were empowered to impose a fine as well as a custodial sentence for certain offences relating to the possession of a firearm or ammunition: Offences against the State (Amendment) Act 1998, s 15. A new offence was created of training persons in the making or use of firearms without lawful authority or reasonable excuse (OS(A)A 1998, ss 12 and 18). Also having possession or control of any article which could give rise to a reasonable suspicion that it was for a purpose connected with the commission, preparation or instigation of a scheduled firearm offence, is itself an offence (OS(A)A 1998, ss 7 and 18). OS(A)A 1998, ss 15 and 18 were amended by Criminal Justice Act 1999, ss 36 and 37 respectively. See BURGLARY, AGGRAVATED; HUNT; LETHAL; OFFENSIVE WEAPON; WITHHOLDING INFORMATION.

firearms certificate. A certificate issued by a superintendent of the Garda Síochána to a person residing in his district or by the Minister to a person not ordinarily resident in the State: Firearms Act 1925, s 3; Wildlife Act 1976 s 62.

In 2000, the gardaí introduced new security requirements for holders of licensed firearms. These requirements were struck down by the Supreme Court in 2002, the court holding that a garda superintendent would be acting beyond his statutory powers if he imposed as a pre-condition (that a gun safe be installed) in relation to all applications for the granting or renewal of firearms certificates: *Dunne v Donohoe* [2002] 2 ILRM 200 and 2 IR 533, SC.

A licence to hunt game with firearms in open season, is required, and is effected by way of endorsement on the firearms certificate or otherwise as provided: WA 1976, ss 20 and 29. Revocation of a certificate by a garda superintendent must not be made without the holder being given an opportunity to state his case: *Hourigan v Supt Kelly* [1992] 10 ILT Dig 266, HC.

The holder of a firearms certificate is entitled to a *European Firearms Pass* issued by a Garda Superintendent: EC (Acquisition and Possession of Weapons and Ammunition) Regulations 1993, SI No 362 of 1993); EC (Acquisition and Possession of Weapons and Ammunition) (Amendment) Regulations 2002, SI No 49 of 2002.

Temporary measures were introduced to enable the respective Ministers to continue to grant firearms certificates and hunting licences to persons not ordinarily resident in the State, provided they fulfilled certain conditions; this was necessitated by the decision in *National Association of Regional Games Councils v Minister for Justice* [1998] HC: Firearms (Temporary Provisions) Act 1998.

In 2000, amendments were made to the provisions governing the limitations and restrictions for the granting of firearm certificates under s 3 of Firearms Act 1925 in respect of persons not ordinarily resident in the State and for the granting and renewal of hunting licences under s 29 of the 1976 Act: Firearms (Firearm Certificates for Non-Residents) Act 2000. The gardaí grant these certificates as from 1 March 2002: Firearm Certificates for Non-Residents Order 2002, SI No 48 of 2002. For a proposed further condition to be met before the granting of a firearms certificate, see Criminal Justice Bill 2004, s 30.

fireplace. See COAL; FUEL.

fireworks. It is an offence for any person to throw or cast any fireworks in or into, or to ignite any fireworks in, any highway, street, thoroughfare or public place: Dangerous Substances Act 1972, s 61. It is an offence to throw or set fire to any fireworks: Dublin Police Act 1842, s 14(15). See also Explosives Act 1875 as amended; DSA 1972, s 7, Sch; and Explosive Substances Act 1883.

For regulations on the prohibition of fireworks in parks, see SR & O No 6 of 1926, reg 9(12) – Phoenix Park; SI No 175 of 1962, reg 3(v) – St Stephens Green; SI No 234 of 1971, reg 7(13) – Bourn Vincent Memorial Park. See Keeping of Fireworks Order 1984, SI No 129 of 1984. See *Report on Offences under the Dublin Police Acts and Related Offences* (LRC 14, 1985), ch 5.13. See EXPLOSIVE.

firm. Persons who have entered into partnership with one another; the name under which their business is carried on is called the firm name: Partnership Act 1890, s 4. In the event that partners trade under names other than their own, they must comply with the Registration of Business Names Act 1963. An action may be brought by or against a firm in the name of the firm.

For rules governing actions in the High Court and Circuit Court by or against firms and persons carrying on business in names other than their own, see RSC Ord 14 and Circuit Court Rules 2001 Ord 8 respectively. See BUSINESS NAME.

first aid. Treatment of an injury which does not need treatment by a registered medical practitioner or registered general nurse, or otherwise treatment for the purpose of preserving life or minimising the consequences of injury or illness until the services of such a practitioner or nurse are obtained: Safety Health and Welfare at Work (General Application) Regulations 1993, SI No 44 of 1993, reg 54. It is the duty of every employer to provide where required first aid equipment, suitably marked and easily accessible, and to provide occupational first-aiders as are necessary (reg 56).

first instance, court of. (1) A court in which proceedings are initiated. Under the Constitution of Ireland, there is provision for *Courts of First Instance* (which include the High Court with full original jurisdiction in and power to determine all matters and questions whether of law or fact, civil or criminal) and a Court of Final Appeal called the Supreme Court). See 1937 Constitution, arts 34(2); 34(3)(1); 34(3)(4). See COURT.

(2) The Single European Act (qv) has provided for the creation of a *Court of First Instance* to supplement the European Court of Justice (qv): EC Treaty, art 225 of the consolidated (2002) version. Both of these courts are required, each within its jurisdiction, to ensure that in the interpretation and application of the Treaty, the law is observed. The Court of First Instance comprises at least one judge per member state (art 224).

The *Court of First Instance* has jurisdiction to hear and determine, subject to a right of appeal to the European Court of Justice on points of law only, certain classes of action or proceedings brought by natural or legal persons eg: (a) disputes between the EU institutions and its servants, (b) actions brought by undertakings against the Commission regarding levies, production, prices and agreements and concentrations, (c) actions brought against an institution relating to EU competition rules applicable to undertakings, (d) actions for damages caused by an institution through an act or a failure to act, (e) preliminary rulings in specific areas, and (f) appeals from judicial panels (EC Treaty, art 225). The role of the court has been broadened by the Nice Treaty (qv); this is to enable the European Court of Justice to deal with the more important cases.

Service as a judge of the *Court of First Instance* is deemed as practice at the Bar for the purpose of qualifying for judicial appointments in Ireland: Courts and Court Officers Act 1995, s 28. A judge of the *Court of First Instance* who was a practising barrister or practising solicitor prior to their appointment, is qualified for appointment as a judge of the Superior Courts of Ireland: Courts (Supplementary Provisions) Act 1961, s 5(2) as substituted by Courts and Court Officers Act 2002, s 4. See website: *www.curia. eu.int*. See European Parliament Elections (Amendment) Act 2004, s 2. See 'The Treaty of Nice and Reform of the Community Courts' by Liz Heffernan BL in *Bar Review* (June/July 2001) 474. See JUDICIAL PANEL.

first refusal. An option (qv) to purchase any property on the same terms as offered by another party. A right of first refusal must be supported by consideration (qv) to be enforceable. Where the property is land, the right of first refusal does not constitute an interest in that land: *Aga Khan v Firestone* [1992] ILRM 31, HC.

fiscal nullity, doctrine of. The UK doctrine which treats as a nullity for tax purposes a series of transactions taken together and intended from the outset to produce neither a gain nor a loss, in other words to be self-cancelling: *W T Ramsay Ltd v Inland Revenue Commissioners* [1982] AC 300. The doctrine did not apply in Ireland as the courts did not look at the substance or financial results of a transaction but at the actual legal effect and legal rights of the

parties: *McGrath v McDermott* [1988] ILRM 181 and 647, HC & SC. However, under s 86 of the Finance Act 1989, if a transaction is a tax avoidance transaction as defined, it is ineffective to avoid tax. For a transaction to be struck down, the Revenue Commissioners must first form an opinion that it is a tax avoidance transaction, they must send notice of that opinion to the taxpayer who can appeal to the Appeal Commissioners.

fiscal prosecutor. A person who, on behalf of the State, prosecutes offences relating to taxes, duties, customs or exchange control. The Law Reform Commission has recommended that the Revenue Commissioners continue to prosecute summarily under a delegation from the DPP, rather than under an independent statutory authorisation: LRC Consultation Paper on *A Fiscal Prosecutor and a Revenue Court* (LRC CP 24, 2003).

fish. The phrase 'use a net for the capture of fish' means only that the accused must have embarked on the action of fishing, by means of a net, in circumstances where that was forbidden by law; it does not require that fish actually be caught: *Southwest Regional Fisheries Board v O'Leary & Cremin* [1999] 2 ILRM 368, HC and 2 IR 577. See *Slevin v Shannon Regional Fisheries* [1995] 1 IR 460, HC. See SHARE FISHERMAN.

fisheries board. See REGIONAL FISHERIES BOARD.

fishery harbour centre. A harbour or the land adjoining it, or both, declared by Ministerial order to be a fishery harbour centre: Fishery Harbour Centres Act 1968, ss 1–2 and 1980. Howth and Dunmore East Harbours were declared to be fishery harbour centres in 1989; their ownership and management was transferred from the Commissioners of Public Works to the Minister: SIs No 336 and 337 of 1989. The seaward limits of Castletownbere harbour have been defined so as to include Berehaven Sound within its limits and consequently facilitate the collection of harbour dues from foreign factory ships anchored in the Sound: Fisheries Harbour Centres (Amendment) Act 1992.

Provision has been made for the designation by Ministerial order of Dingle Harbour as a fisheries harbour centre: Harbours Act 1996, s 86. Also the Minister has been given wide powers in relation to how fishery harbour property may be used, leased, let or sold: Fisheries and Foreshore (Amendment) Act 1998, s 6.

fishery limits, exclusive. The exclusive fishery limits of the State comprise all sea areas which lie within the line every point of which is at a distance of twelve nautical miles (qv) from the nearest point of the *base line*: Maritime Jurisdiction Act 1959, s 6 as amended by the Maritime Jurisdiction Act 1964, s 2. See MARITIME JURISDICTION.

fishery rights. Interference in public rights of fishery must not take place without notice or without access to the courts where the Oireachtas (qv) so provides: *Madden v Minister for the Marine* [1993] ILRM 436, HC. A person entitled to a *several fishery* in non-tidal waters is presumed to be the owner of the bed and soil of the river over which the right was exercised, subject to proof to the contrary: *Gannon v Walsh* [1998] 3 IR 245, HC. See also *O'Sullivan v Aquaculture Licences Appeal Board* [2001] 1 IR 646, HC.

fishery society. For *fishing co-operative society* see Industrial and Provident Societies Act 1978, s 4; Fisheries (Amendment) Act 1991 as amended by Fisheries (Amendment) Act 1999, s 28; Fisheries Co-operative Societies Order and Rules 1992, SIs Nos 126 and 127 of 1992 and Amendment Rules 1994, SI No 54 of 1994. See also TROUT.

fishing. The main purpose of the Fisheries (Amendment) Act 2000 is: (a) to provide for on-the-spot fines in relation to offences under the Fisheries Acts and (b) to provide for offences in respect of the wild salmon and sea trout carcass tagging scheme, by amending the Fisheries (Amendment) Act 1999 and the Fisheries (Consolidation) Act 1959. See also Fisheries (Payment in Lieu of Prosecution) Regulations 2003, SI No 297 of 2003, as amended by SI No 207 of 2004; Wild Salmon and Sea Trout Tagging Scheme Regulations 2004, SI No 136 of 2004. For Central Fisheries Board, see website: *www.cfb.ie.*

The court has held that a bye-law made by the Minister was expedient for the management and protection of eel fisheries; it was unfortunate that it interfered with the plaintiffs' (eel fishermen's') livelihoods but regard had to be had for the greater good and for the preservation of fish for the future: *Maxwell v Minister for the Marine* [2001] ITLR (12 February), HC. [Bibliography: Comerford (2).]

fishing interrogatories. See INTERROGATORIES, FISHING.

fishing licence. The licence required to angle for salmon; or which may be required, by way of a share certificate in a Fisheries Co-operative Society, to angle for trout or coarse fish: Fisheries (Amendment) Act 1991. See *Re Beara Fisheries and Shipping Ltd* [1988] ILRM 221. See TROUT; SALMON ROD LICENCE; COARSE FISH.

fishing rights. See RIPARIAN OWNER.

fishing vessel. A vessel designed, equipped or used commercially for catching or taking fish or other living resources of the sea (including the sea bed) or freshwater: Merchant Shipping Act 1992, s 2(1) as amended by Merchant Shipping (Investigation of Marine Casualties) Act 2000, s 44(1)(a). The Minister is empowered to make regulations for the purpose of ensuring: (a) the safety of fishing vessels, their crews, and other persons, or (b) that the use of a fishing vessel does not create a disturbance or constitute a nuisance (MSA 1992, s 19 as amended by MS(IMC)A 2000, s 44(6)). See Merchant Shipping (Musters) (Fishing Vessels) Regulations 1993 (SI No 48 of 1993).

Amendments to the law on the *licensing* and *registration* of sea-fishing ships and improvements in the procedures governing the *detention* of ships infringing the law and increased penalties were made by the Fisheries (Amendment) Act 1994 and Fisheries (Amendment) Act 2003 s 30. Equal treatment for EU nationals is also provided for (F(A)A 2003, ss 3 and 6). See *Irish Fisheries Companies, Re: EC Commission v Ireland* [1991] 3 CMLR 697.

Regulations have been made requiring all crew members of a fishing vessel to undergo basic safety training before going to sea for the first time and also requiring all serving crew members to undertake basic safety training on a phased basis between 2003 and 2008: Fishing Vessel (Basic Safety Training) Regulations 2001, SI No 587 of 2001.

Also all crew members of a fishing vessel are required to wear a personal flotation device at all times when on the deck of any fishing vessel: Fishing Vessel (Personal Flotation Devices) Regulations 2001, SI No 586 of 2001. For regulations giving effect to a harmonised safety regime and setting down safety standards for fishing vessels of 24 metres in length and over, see respectively: EC (Safety of Fishing Vessels) Regulations 2002, SI No 417 of 2002, (Amendment) Regulations 2003, SIs No 72 and 633 of 2003; Fishing Vessels (Safety Provisions) Regulations 2002, SI No 418 of 2002 as amended by SI No 634 of 2003. See CONSERVATION OF FISH STOCKS; QUOTA HOPPING; SEA-FISHING BOAT LICENCE.

fitness for purpose. See QUALITY OF GOODS.

fitness to be tried. See UNFIT TO BE TRIED.

fitness to plead. See UNFIT TO PLEAD; UNFIT TO BE TRIED.

fitness to teach. The *Investigating Committee* of the Teaching Council is empowered to hold an inquiry into the *fitness to teach* of a registered teacher on all or any of the following grounds: (a) he has failed to comply with or has contravened specified legislation; (b) his behaviour constitutes professional misconduct; (c) his registration is erroneous due to a false or fraudulent declaration or misrepresentation; (d) he is medically unfit to teach: Teaching Council Act 2001, ss 41–47.

There is provision for an inquiry by the *Disciplinary Committee* following the Investigating Committee inquiry, and in the event of a finding of *unfitness to teach*, there is provision for removal or suspension from the register, or retention subject to conditions, and for confirmation of decisions by the High Court.

fixed charge. A specific charge on specific property of say a company, e g on land and buildings of the company, as security for a loan, as contrasted with a *floating charge*. A *fixed charge* invariably involves the vesting of a legal interest in the vendor of the loan at the time of the transaction. See DEBENTURE; FLOATING CHARGE; CHARGE, REGISTRATION OF.

fixed-purpose contract. A contract under which an employee is employed for a specified purpose, being a purpose of such a kind that the duration of the contract was limited but was, at the time of its making, incapable of precise ascertainment: Redundancy Payments Act 1967, s 9(1)(b) as substituted by Redundancy Payments Act 2003, s 6. When a fixed-purpose contract ceases, a redundancy situation exists. See REDUNDANCY.

fixed-term contract. Unfair dismissal legislation does not apply to fixed-term contracts of employment where the dismissal consists only of the expiry of the term or cesser of the purpose: Unfair Dismissals Act 1977, s 2(2)(b).

However, s 2(2)(b) only applies where the fixed-term contract specifically states that the 1977 Act shall not apply to a dismissal consisting of an expiry or cesser: *Sheehan v Dublin Tribune Ltd* [1992] ELR 239, EAT. Also an amendment in 1993 to s 2(2)(b) provides for the application of the Act to a dismissal where the employee is re-employed within three months of the dismissal and it is found that the entry by the employer into the subsequent contract was wholly or partly for the purpose of avoiding liability under the Act: Unfair Dismissals (Amendment) Act 1993, s 3(b). Also re-employment by the same employer not later than 26 weeks after the dismissal will not operate to break continuity of service (UD(A)A 1993, s 3(c)).

A right to terminate a contract during its currency does not destroy the fixed-term nature of the contract: *O'Mahony v Trinity College* [1998] ELR 159, EAT. See *Cahill v Teagasc* [1996] ELR 215, EAT; *Earlie v Aer Rianta International CPT* [1997] ELR 69, EAT. See Redundancy Payments Act 2003, s 6. See FIXED-TERM EMPLOYEE.

fixed-term employee. Means a person having a contract of employment entered directly with an employer where the end of the contract of employment concerned is determined by an objective condition such as arriving at a specific date, completing a specific task or the occurrence of a specific event: Protection of Employees (Fixed-Term Work) Act 2003, s 2(1). It does not include: (a) employees in initial vocational training relationships or apprenticeship schemes, or (b) employees within a framework of a specific public or publicly-supported training, integration or vocational retraining programme. The Act does not apply to members of the Defence Forces, trainee gardaí or nurses in training (PE(FTW)A 2003, s 17). The Act implements Directive (EC) 1999/70.

A fixed-term employee must not be treated less favourably, in respect of conditions of employment, than a 'comparable permanent employee' (PE(FTW)A 2003, s 6). Less favourable treatment is permissible if the treatment is based on objective grounds e g different length of service, or for the purpose of achieving a legitimate objective of the employer, which treatment is appropriate and necessary for that purpose (PE(FTW)A 2003, ss 6(2) and 7). When a fixed-term employee has completed a third year of continuous employment, only one further fixed-term renewal of the contract is permissible and is limited to a fixed term of one year (PE(FTW)A 2003, s 9).

Fixed-term employees are given other protections eg: (a) they must be informed in writing as soon as practicable of the objective condition determining the contract (PE(FTW)A 2003, s 8); (b) they must be informed of vacancies so as to have the same opportunity as other employees to secure a permanent position (s 10); (c) they are protected from being penalised by the employer for invoking their rights under the Act (s 13); (d) a provision in an agreement is void if it purports to exclude or limit the application of the Act (s 12).

There is provision for a complaint to a Rights Commissioner, with a right to appeal his decision to the Labour Court within six weeks of the date on which the decision was communicated to the party, and a further appeal, on a point of law, to the High Court (PE(FTW)A 2003, ss 14–15). The Circuit Court has enforcement powers in the event that an employer fails to implement a determination of the Labour Court (s 16).

A *fixed-term employee* also means an employee whose employment is governed by a contract of employment for a fixed term or for a specified purpose: Safety Health and Welfare at Work (General Application) Regulations 1993, SI No 44 of 1993, reg 2(1). These regulations apply to employers of fixed-term employees, temporary employees, as well as of permanent employees (reg 4(2)). See Pensions Act 1990, s 5 as amended by Social Welfare (Miscellaneous Provisions) Act 2004, s 23 and Sch 2. See 'Fixed-term workers' by solicitor Michelle Ní Longain in *Law Society Gazette* (June 2003) 49.

fixtures. (1) Personal chattels annexed to the freehold by a temporary occupier and which are removable by him. A chattel which, judging from the mode in which it is affixed and all the surrounding circumstances, was affixed by the occupier to be enjoyed as a chattel is removable. If it was affixed to constitute an improvement to the house or land, it is not. See Deasy's Act 1860, s 17.

The Law Reform Commission has recommended that the law relating to tenant's fixtures should be replaced by a new statutory provision to replace entirely the common law and all existing statutory provisions: *Consultation Paper on General Law of Landlord and Tenant Law* (LRC CP 28, 2003) para 18.40.

(2) Television aerials are *fixtures* within the meaning of the Value Added Tax 1972, s 10(8): *Maye v The Revenue Commissioners* [1986] ILRM 377.

FLAC. Free Legal Advice Centres (qv).

flag. The national flag is the tricolour of green, white and orange: 1937 Constitution, art 7. A trade mark which consists of or contains the flag of a country, which is a party to the Paris Convention, must not be registered without the authorisation of the competent authority of that country: Trade Marks Act 1996, s 62(1). In the case of the national flag of this State, such a trade mark must not be registered if it appears to the Controller of Trade Marks that the use of the trade mark would be misleading or grossly offensive (TMA 1996, s 9(2)). See SYMBOLS OF THE EUROPEAN UNION.

flag officer. An officer holding the commissioned naval rank of commodore: Defence Act 1954, s 2(1).

flagrante delicto. [In the commission of the offence.]

flat. Colloquially, a suite of rooms in a building, usually on one floor of a building which has a number of floors. A leasehold or freehold interest may be created in a flat; there is no reason at common law why the owner of land cannot convey horizontal slices of the air space above it to others, whether by way of lease or freehold interest: *Humphries v Broghen* [1850] 12 QB 739.

A flat is entitled to vertical support from the lower part of the building and to the benefit of such lateral support as may be of right enjoyed by the building itself: *Dalton v Angus* [1881] 6 App Cas 740. There is provision for the registration of land which is a *flat or floor, or part of a flat or floor, of a house*: Land Registration Rules 1972, SI No 230 of 1972, r 30(1)(a).

A housing authority is empowered to sell a flat in like manner as a house, except that it may make a management charge in respect of areas common to two or more such flats; alternatively it may transfer responsibility for such areas to a company or other body: Housing Act 1966, s 90(6) as inserted by Housing (Miscellaneous Provisions) Act 1992, s 26(1). See also s 90(11)(a). See CONDOMINIUM; FLOOR AREA CERTIFICATE; FLYING FREEHOLD; MANAGEMENT COMPANY; MULTI-STOREY BUILDINGS.

flexibility clause. The clause within the draft European Constitutional Treaty which allows flexible adjustments of EU competence within the defined remit of the Union, and not confined as heretofore to the common market only: National Forum on Europe, *Glossary of Terms* (2003). See proposed Treaty establishing a Constitution for Europe. See EUROPEAN UNION CONSTITUTION.

floatation. The offer of a large block of shares in a public company either to the public at large or to clients of an issuing house ie a merchant bank or similar financial institution specialising in this business. A company may be *floated*: (a) by a *direct offer* of shares to the public by prospectus; or (b) by *an offer for sale* by which the entire issue is sold to an issuing house which then offers the shares to the public by prospectus; or (c) by an allotment of shares to an issuing house which *places* them with its clients; or (d) by an offer of shares by *tender* with the shares going to the highest bidder. See ALLOTMENT; PROSPECTUS; SHARES, COMPANY.

floating charge. An equitable charge or mortgage on the assets for the time being of a going concern. It attaches to the subject charged in the varying conditions it happens to be in from time to time. The charge remains dormant or floats over the assets until the undertaking ceases to be a going concern, or until the person in whose favour the charge is created (the *chargee*) intervenes.

A floating charge becomes a fixed charge, and is said to *crystalise*, when a receiver is appointed, or a winding up commences, or if the chargee intervenes when entitled so to do. An *automatic crystallisation clause* is one stipulating that a floating charge will crystalise on some specific event occurring. Debentures issued by a company are often secured by a floating charge on the property, present and future, of the company. A floating charge which has crystallised upon the appointment of a receiver, becomes *de-crystallised* and floating on the appointment by the court of an examiner to protect the company for a period: *Re Holidair Ltd* [1994] 1 ILRM 481 and 1 IR 416, SC.

A floating charge given within twelve months of a company being wound up is invalid if the company was insolvent at the time it created the charge; there is an exception for *cash paid*: Companies Act 1963, s 288 as amended by the Companies Act 1990, s 136. The test of solvency is whether immediately after the floating charge was given, the company was able to pay its debts as they became due: *Re Creation Printing Company Ltd* [1981] IR 353. The onus of proof lies on the person who asserts the validity of the floating charge: *Crowley v Northern Bank Finance Corp* [1981] IR 353. See also *Evans v Rival Granite Quarries Ltd* [1910] 2 KB 979; *Re Bushmills Distillery Co* [1896] 1 IR 301; *Welch v Bowmaker (Ireland) Ltd* [1980] IR 251; *Re Keenan Bros Ltd* [1984] HC; *Re Tullow Engineering (Holdings) Ltd (in receivership)* [1990] 1 IR 452; *Re Manning Furniture* [1996] 1 ILRM 13, HC.

The 1990 Act amended s 288 of CA 1963 to include goods and services sold or supplied to the company as an exception on the same basis as *cash paid*; also it provided that a floating charge is invalid if given to a person *connected* with a company up to two years before the company went into liquidation, unless it could be shown that the company was solvent after the creation of the charge. [Bibliography: Johnston.] See COURT PROTECTION OF COMPANY; FIXED CHARGE.

floating policy. A policy of marine insurance (qv) which describes the insurance in general terms, and leaves the name of the ship or ships and other particulars to be defined by subsequent declaration: Marine Insurance Act 1906, s 29.

flooding. See ARTERIAL DRAINAGE; COMMISSIONERS OF PUBLIC WORKS.

floor area certificate. The certificate required in order to qualify for a new house grant: Housing (Miscellaneous Provisions) Act 1979, s 4(2)(b); Housing Regulations 1980, SI No 296 of 1980, art 8. Section 4 of the 1979 Act has been repealed with the introduction of a more flexible approach to new house grants: Housing (Miscellaneous Provisions) Act 2002, ss 4 and 11, and Sch 1.

For exemption from stamp duty for an owner occupier of a new house or apartment, with or without a floor area certificate, see Stamp Duties Consolidation Act 1999, ss 91, 91A, and 92, as amended or inserted by Finance Act 2004, ss 71–73.

Where there is a certificate, the total floor area of the dwellinghouse or apartment must not exceed 125 square metres or be less than 38 square metres and must comply with conditions set down in regulations made by the Minister eg in relation to standards of construction and the provision of water, sewerage and other services therein (FA 2004, s 72). For the exemption to apply, there must be a statement inserted in the instrument of transfer that there is in existence, at the date of execution of the instrument, a floor area certificate, certifying compliance. For the manner of measurement of the floor area and the quality standards to be applied for eligibility for stamp duty concessions, see SI No 128 of 2004. See HOUSING GRANT.

flora and fauna. See CONSERVATION ORDER; NATURE RESERVE; RESERVE.

flotsam. Goods of a shipwreck which remain floating on the sea. See JETSAM; LAGAN.

fluoridation. The addition of fluorine in any form to water supplied to the public by sanitary authorities through pipes, which a health authority is required to arrange pursuant to regulation: Health (Fluoridation of Water Supplies) Act 1960. The amount of fluorine must not exceed one part by weight of fluorine per million parts of water (H(FWS)A 1960, s 2(3)(a)). See also SI No 69 of 1987.

In September 2002, a *Report of the Forum on Fluoridation* concluded that fluoridation was not only harmless to health, but had been very effective in improving the oral health of children and adults in Ireland. For Report, see *www. fluoridationforum.ie*. See also *Ryan v Attorney-General* [1965] IR 294.

flying freehold. Colloquial expression used to describe freehold land which is held in separate horizontal layers, each being a separate fee simple estate eg in practice a flat or apartment. See *Metropolitan Properties Ltd v O'Brien* [1995] 2 ILRM 383, SC.

foal. A horse not exceeding one year of age which is being suckled by its dam or foster-mother; a horse licence in a control area is not required for a foal: Control of Horses Act 1996, ss 2(1) and 19(1)(i). The Irish Horseracing Authority is authorised to introduce a *thoroughbred foal registration levy* to finance the development of the thoroughbred breeding sector: Horse and Greyhound Racing (Betting Charges and Levies) Act 1999, s 5. See *Thoroughbred*

Foal Levy Regulations 2000, SI No 178 of 2000, as amended by SI No 173 of 2004.

f.o.b. Free on board. A price for goods which is quoted f.o.b. includes the cost of placing the goods on board ship.

foetal death. The death of a human embryo. See STILLBORN CHILD.

FOI. [Freedom of Information (qv).]

folio. In relation to taxation of costs, a folio comprises 72 words, every figure contained in a column or authorised to be used being counted as one word: RSC Ord 99, r 37(9). See also LAND REGISTRATION.

folklore. See ANONYMOUS WORK; PERFORMERS' RIGHTS.

food. Includes: (a) any substance used, available to be used or intended to be used, for food or drink by human persons, and (b) any substance which enters into or is used in the production, composition or preparation of these substances: Food Safety Authority of Ireland Act 1998, s 2(1).

It is an offence to mix into foodstuffs any ingredient or material which thus renders the article injurious to health with the intention that the article will be sold: Sale of Food and Drugs Acts 1875 to 1936. The extent to which chemical substances and drugs may be used in foodstuffs is also controlled or prevented eg control of chemical and antibiotic residues in meat and dairy products (SI No 236 of 1986).

Minimum standards are laid down by the Food Standards Act 1974 and the regulations which may be made thereunder. Potato growers and packers are required to register and to identify themselves on packages sold by them: Potato Growers and Packers Act 1984. See also *Hinde v Allmand* [1918] 87 LJ KB 893. See also Health Act 1947, s 56 as amended by Health Act 1953, s 38. For Food Safety Authority of Ireland, see website: *www.fsai.ie*. For An Bord Bia, see website: *www.bordbia.ie*. See ANIMAL REMEDY; BORD BIA; EUROPEAN COMMISSION FOOD AND VETERINARY OFFICE.

food, standard of. Provisions for the establishment and enforcement of standards for food or drink used by human beings are contained in the Food Standards Act 1974. The Minister is empowered to make regulations in relation to food, regarding: name; description; composition and quality; method of manufacture and preparation; additives; contaminants (including pesticide residues); hygiene; time limits for consumption; packaging, labelling and presentation; transportation, storage and distribution; weights and measures (FSA 1974, s 2). See also Food Safety Authority of Ireland Act 1998, s 2(1). See PESTICIDES.

food additives. For prohibition on the use of food additive E 425 konjac in the manufacture of jelly confectionary, see SI No 442 of 2002. See also EC (Purity Criteria on Food Additives other than colours and sweeteners) Regulations 1998, SI No 541 of 1998; (Amendment) Regulations 2002, SI 260 of 2002; and (Amendment) Regulations 2003, SI No 488 of 2003; EC (Additives, Colours and Sweeteners in Foodstuffs), SI No 437 of 2000 and (Amendment) Regulations 2002, SIs No 344 and 380 of 2002; EC (Food Additives other than Colours and Sweeteners) Regulations 2004, SI No 58 of 2004.

food and medicines, patents for. Where the Controller of Patents makes an order to grant a *compulsory* licence relating to a patent for food and medicine, he must, in settling the terms, endeavour to secure that food and medicine will be available to the public at the lowest prices consistent with the proprietors of patents deriving reasonable remuneration having regard to the nature of the inventions: Patents Act 1992, s 70(3)(f). See *Pfizer Corporation v Minister for Health* [1965] 1 AE 450. See LICENCES OF RIGHT, PATENTS.

food business, suspension of. Whenever, as respects any food premises or any food stall or food vehicle used in connection with a food business, the Minister is of opinion that there is a grave and immediate danger that food intended for sale for human consumption is liable to cause serious illness if consumed, he may by order direct that such premises, stall or vehicle not be used in connection with a food business: Food Hygiene Regulations 1950, SI No 205 of 1950, art 34. An appeal lies to the District Court (qv). See CLOSURE ORDER.

food inspection. Means the system of inspection carried out in order to ascertain whether certain specified matters/ substances comply with food legislation aimed at preventing risks to public health eg the food, the process, the physical environment, the skills training and competence of people, food additives, materials intended to come into contact with the food, and products of the soil, produce of stock farming, aquaculture and of fisheries and game: Food Safety Authority of Ireland Act 1998, s 2(1). The Authority is required to keep under review the efficacy of the food inspection services (FSAI 1998, s 17) and it may contract out those services (s 48) or carry them out itself (s 46).

food legislation. The Acts, statutory instruments, and EC Regulations with which the Food Safety Authority must take all reasonable steps to ensure that food complies: Food Safety Authority of Ireland Act 1998, ss 2(1) and 11. These are set out in Sch 1 to the 1998 Act as amended by SI No 210 of 2004. The Acts include: Abattoirs Act 1988, Agricultural Produce (Fresh Meat) Acts 1930 to 1988, Agricultural Produce (Meat) Acts 1954 and 1978, Butter and Margarine Act 1907, Food Standards Act 1974, Health Act 1947, Margarine Act 1887, Pigs and Bacon Acts 1935 to 1988, Poisons Act 1961, and Sale of Food and Drugs Acts 1875 to 1936. See FSAI 1998, Sch 2, as amended by SI No 735 of 2003, for list of *official agencies*.

food safety. Means the steps taken to avoid risks to public health arising from food intended for human consumption: Food Safety Authority of Ireland Act 1998, s 2(1). This legislation established the Authority which has as its principal function to take all reasonable steps to ensure that: (a) food produced in the State (whether or not distributed or marketed in the State), and (b) food distributed in the State, meets the highest standards of *food safety* and *hygiene* reasonably available (FSAI 1998, s 11). By *hygiene* is meant the observance of standards of good practice aimed at the avoidance of contamination of food (FSAI 1998, s 2(1)).

The Authority also must take all reasonable steps to ensure that food complies with *food legislation* (qv) in respect of food safety and hygiene standards (FSAI 1998, s 11). It is also required to foster, encourage and promote high *standards* at all levels in the human food chain, from primary production to final use by the consumer eg in the home (s 12). The Authority is empowered to establish *food safety assurance schemes* and it may provide a *certification system* for food for sale (ss 13 and 19). It is empowered to enter into *service contracts* with a variety of agencies in respect of its functions (s 48); it can carry out *food inspections* (qv), issue *improvement* notices and orders (qv), *closure orders* (qv), and *prohibition orders* (qv).

As regards plastic materials and articles intended to come into contact with foodstuffs, see SI No 307 of 1991 as amended, including: (a) SI No 542 of 2002 which gives legal effect to Commission Directives (EC) 2001/62 and (EC) 2002/17, and (b) SI No 76 of 2003 which gives legal effect to Directive (EC) 2002/16 on the use of certain epoxy derivatives. For amendment to FSAI 1998, Sch 2, see SI No 735 of 2003. For *Food Safety Authority of Ireland*, see website: *www.fsai.ie*. [Bibliography: Gallagher, Ellard & Langan.] See BEEF; EUROPEAN COMMISSION FOOD AND VETERINARY OFFICE; HYGIENE OF FOODSTUFFS.

Food Safety Promotions Board. The cross-border body with functions of promoting food safety, research into food safety, communication of food alerts, surveillance of food-borne diseases, promotion of scientific co-operation, and development of cost-effective facilities for specialised laboratory testing: British-Irish Agreement Act 1999, ss 14–17. It operates under the name *Safefood*. See website: *www.safefoodonline.com*. See GOOD FRIDAY AGREEMENT.

food supplements. Means foodstuffs the purpose of which is to supplement the normal diet and which are concentrated sources of nutrients or other substances with a nutritional or physiological effect eg vitamins: EC (Food Supplements) Regulations 2003, SI No 539 of 2003 implementing Directive (EC) 2002/46. The regulations set certain requirements in respect of the content and packaging of food supplement products; the packaging must bear certain particulars and be free from certain claims or statements.

food unfit for human consumption. Food which is or is suspected by an *authorised officer* to be diseased, contaminated or otherwise unfit for human consumption; the authorised officer may seize, remove and detain any such article of food intended for sale for human consumption and destroy it in specified circumstances: Food Hygiene Regulations 1950, SI No 205 of 1950, art 11. An authorised officer is defined as health officer, a veterinary officer, an officer of the Minister for Agriculture, or a garda authorised by the Minister (SI No 205 of 1950, art 2). The local chief medical officer may make a *prohibition order* in respect of food which has been or is about to be imported into the State (art 13). See also SI

No 322 of 1971; SI No 62 of 1989. See PROHIBITION ORDER.

foot-and-mouth disease. Every person who has or had in his possession or under his charge an animal or carcase infected, or suspected of being infected, with foot-and-mouth disease must immediately give notice of the infection or suspicion of infection to a member of the Garda Síochána at the nearest garda station, who must immediately inform the Secretary of the Department of Agriculture in Dublin and the secretary of the local authority: Foot-and-Mouth Disease Order 1956, SI No 324 of 1956 as amended by SI No 412 of 2004.

Over 75 regulations were made in 2001 relating to the foot-and-mouth disease crisis, largely relating to restricting the movement of animals, restricting artificial insemination, and restricting the import of animals. One example is the Diseases of Animals (Foot-and-Mouth Disease) (Import Restrictions) Order 2001, SI No 82 of 2001.

footpath. A road over which there is a public right of way for pedestrians only, not being a footway (qv): Roads Act 1993, s 2(1). See ROAD.

footway. The portion of any road which is provided primarily for the use of pedestrians: Road Traffic Act 1961, s 3. That portion of any road associated with a roadway (qv) which is provided primarily for use by pedestrians: Roads Act 1993, s 2(1). See ROAD.

for the avoidance of doubt. The expression which is frequently employed in statutes when the legislature is expressly refraining from altering the law in any way and seeks to make it clear beyond doubt that the existing law remains unaltered: *Kelly v Minister for the Environment* [2003] 2 ILRM 81, SC.

Foras Teanga, An. The cross-border corporate body with functions of promoting the Irish language and Ullans: British-Irish Agreement Act 1999, ss 24–30. The Act provides for the dissolution of Bord na Gaeilge and the transfer of its functions and certain Irish language functions of Ministers to the new body eg the development of terminology and vocabulary of An Coiste Tearmaíochta.

The new body is composed of two separate and largely autonomous agencies: (a) the *Irish Language Agency* (Foras na Gaeilge) which has taken over the functions of Bord na Gaeilge and has responsibility for the promotion of the Irish language on an all-island basis, and (b) the *Ulster-Scots Agency* (Tha Boord o Ulstèr-Scotch) which has responsibility for the promotion of Ullans and Ulster-Scots cultural issues. See websites: *www.forasnagaeilge.ie* and *www. ulsterscotsagency.com*. See COIMISINÉIR TEANGA, AN; GOOD FRIDAY AGREEMENT; ULLANS.

forbearance. Refraining from enforcing a right eg for a debt. A forbearance to sue may be adequate consideration (qv) to support a contract. See *Fullerton v Bank of Ireland* [1903] AC 309.

forbidden degrees. The prohibited degrees of relationship in relation to marriage; there are 28 such degrees. See PROHIBITED DEGREES.

force. Violent action; it is generally unlawful to use force on another. Under common law, a person who is attacked is entitled to use *proportionate* force in retaliation to protect himself and his family and anyone attacked in his presence: *The People v Keatley* [1954] IR 12.

Statutory provision on the *use of force* is contained in the Non-Fatal Offences against the Person Act 1997, ss 18 to 20. The *use of force* by a person is not an offence, if only such as is reasonable in the circumstances as he believes them to be, for the following purposes: (a) to protect himself or his family from injury, assault or detention caused by a criminal act; or (b) to protect himself or another from trespass to the person; or (c) to protect his or another's property from appropriation, destruction or damage caused by a criminal act, or (d) to prevent crime or a breach of the peace (NFOPA 1997, s 18).

The use of force by a person in effecting or assisting in a lawful arrest, is also not an offence (NFOPA 1997, s 19). A person is treated as using force if he threatens its use or if he detains a person without using it (NFOPA 1997, s 20). A *threat of force* may be reasonable although the actual use of force may not be (s 20(3)). Also the fact that a person had an opportunity to *retreat* before using force must be taken into account to determine if the use of force was reasonable (s 20(4)).

Some statutes authorise specified persons to use *force* if necessary in specified circumstances eg to enter premises with a warrant: Consumer Credit Act 1995, s 8C(3) as inserted by Central Bank and Financial

Services Authority of Ireland Act 2003, s 35, Sch 1. See also ENTRY AND SEARCH.

It has been held in the UK that if a person meets an obstacle, he uses force if he applies any energy to the obstacle with a view to removing it: *Swales v Cox* [1981] QB 849. The Law Reform Commission plans to publish a Consultation Paper on the legitimate force which may be used in homicide. See website: *www. lawreform.ie*. [Bibliography: Charleton (4).] See SELF-DEFENCE.

force-feeding. See HUNGER STRIKE.

force majeure. An overpowering event which could not be anticipated or controlled eg an Act of God (qv). Contracts often contain a *force majeure clause*. A force majeure may amount to a frustration (qv) of the contract.

force majeure leave. The special *leave with pay* to which an employee is entitled where, for urgent family reasons, owing to an injury to or illness of a *family member*, his immediate presence at home or elsewhere is indispensable: Parental Leave Act 1998, s 13. The *family member* must be a parent, adoptive parent, a spouse, a person with whom the employee is living as husband and wife, a brother or sister, a parent or grandparent, or a person to whom the employee is *in loco parentis*. Force majeure leave must not exceed three days in any twelve consecutive months or five days in any 36 consecutive months. See SI No 454 of 1998.

The urgency of a family situation could not be judged in hindsight, nor could the question as to whether the employee's presence was indispensable; the matter should be looked at from the employee's point of view at the time the decision was made not to go to work: *Carey v Penn Racquet Sports Ltd* [2001] 3 IR 32 and ELR 27, HC. The fact that an illness subsequently transpired to be non-serious is not relevant. Whether or not an employee's presence is indispensable is a question of fact and not a question of law: *McGaley v Liebherr Container Cranes Ltd* [2001] 3 IR 563, HC and ELR 350. See *Quinn v J Higgins Engineering Galway Ltd* [2000] ELR 102, EAT. See 'Recent developments in Force Majeure Leave' by Wesley Farrell BL in *Bar Review* (March 2001) 300.

forcible entry and occupation. A person who forcibly enters land (which includes houses or other buildings or structures) or a vehicle or who remains in forcible occupation thereof is guilty of an offence, except where the person does not interfere with the use and enjoyment of the land or vehicle by the owner and leaves when requested to do so: Prohibition of Forcible Entry and Occupation Act 1971. *Forcibly* is defined as using or threatening to use force in relation to person and property. The Act also defines *forcible occupation*. It is a good defence to prove that the accused is the owner, or *bona fide* claimant of the property. Evidence obtained as a result of a forcible entry on foot of an invalid search warrant is not admissible: *People (DPP) v Kenny* [1990] ILRM 569, SC. See *Ross Co Ltd v Swan* [1981] ILRM 416. See ENTRY AND SEARCH; SIT-IN.

foreclosure. The forfeiture by a mortgagor (qv) of his *equity of redemption* (qv). The mortgagee's right to foreclosure is the right to apply to the court for an order directing the mortgagor to redeem his mortgage within a certain time or in default to be deprived of his right to redeem forever. See MORTGAGE SUIT.

foreign adoption. See ADOPTION, FOREIGN.

foreign bill. See INLAND BILL.

foreign company. A company which is incorporated outside Ireland but which establishes a place of business in the State, is required to provide the Registrar of Companies with particular information e g the address of the company's principal place of business in the State and the name and address of one or more persons resident in the State authorised to accept service on behalf of the company: Companies Act 1963, s 352.

There are particular disclosure requirements in respect of branches opened in a member state of the EU by certain types of companies governed by the law of another State: SIs Nos 395 and 396 of 1993 which give effect to Directive (EEC) 89/666.

Where a foreign company has no place of business within the State, the court will not make any order which would amount to regulating the internal affairs of a company not amenable to its jurisdiction: *Balkanbank v Naser Taher & Ors* [1992] ITLR (13 April), HC. See also Gill in 7 ILT & SJ (1989) 264.

A foreign company is also a non-resident company which is controlled by a person resident in a country with which Ireland has a double tax treaty: Taxes Consolidation Act 1997, s 44. A foreign company which carries on a relevant trade through a branch or agency in the State may be exempt from corporation tax on certain securities issued by the Minister for Finance. See also COMPANY, NON-RESIDENT.

foreign currency. See CURRENCY, FOREIGN.

foreign divorce. For the rules governing a *Family Law Civil Bill* seeking relief after a foreign divorce or separation, see Circuit Court Rules 2001 Ord 59, r 4(4)(c). See DIVORCE, FOREIGN, RECOGNITION OF.

foreign earnings. An employee is entitled to tax relief in respect of income earned outside the State, when he works outside the State for 90 days or more in a tax year or a continuous twelve-month relevant period, part of which is comprised in a tax year. The relief applies only to private sector employment and does not apply to employment exercised in the UK or Northern Ireland. A cap is set of £25,000 (€31,743) and the minimum period of absence must be at least 11 consecutive days at a time: Taxes Consolidation Act 1997, s 823 as amended by Finance Act 2000, s 47.

foreign judgments, enforcement of. A foreign judgment is generally enforceable in Ireland if it has been rendered by a court of competent jurisdiction, is final and conclusive and is for a fixed sum of money. It is not necessary for a notice of enforcement to cite every element of the foreign judgment being enforced: *Paper Properties Ltd v Power Corporation plc* [1996] 1 ILRM 475, HC.

Relation to judgments of *contracting* states of the EC, the jurisdiction of the court of the state giving judgment may not be reviewed; there is also provision for enforcement of judgments of periodic payments (e g maintenance orders) as well as fixed sums, and of non-money judgments: Jurisdiction of Courts and Enforcement of Judgments Act 1988, repealed and consolidated in 1998.

The 1988 Act enabled the State to ratify the 1968 EC ('Brussels') Convention in that regard, which Convention dealt with civil and commercial matters only; excluded are judgments concerning status, matrimonial property, wills, succession, bankruptcy, arbitration, social security, revenue, customs and administrative matters.

The High Court is bound to grant protective measures (eg a *Mareva* injunction) where an *enforcement order* under the 1968 Convention is granted; such protective measures include eg an injunction to prevent the defendant reducing his assets below the judgment sum pending enforcement: *Elwyn (Cottons) Ltd v Master of the High Court* [1989] ITLR (6 March and 22 May). The law of the state in which enforcement is sought governs the entire procedure: *Rhatigan v Textiles y Confecciones Europeas SA* [1990] ILRM 825, SC. The question to be answered is whether it would be inexpedient to make the order: *Credit Suisse Fides Trust v Cuoghi* [1998] QB 818.

Strict compliance with the order of the Master of the High Court is required in relation to service of an enforcement order: it is not feasible for the court to 'deem good' at a subsequent date a form of service which did not comply with that prescribed by the Master: *Barnaby (London) Ltd v Mullen* [1997] 2 ILRM 341, SC.

The 1988 Act was amended in 1993 to take account of the accession of Spain and Portugal (the 1989 Accession Convention) and also to bring the 1968 EC Convention into line with the Lugano Convention, which governs the enforcement of judgments between EC and EFTA member states: Jurisdiction of Courts and Enforcement of Judgments Act 1993.

Both the 1988 and 1993 Acts were repealed and consolidated by the Jurisdiction of Courts and Enforcement of Judgments Act 1998 which has the following objectives: (a) to consolidate Irish law as regards the Brussels and Lugano Conventions, (b) to utilise similar procedures for the recognition and enforcement of *authentic instruments* and court settlements as were available for judgments, and (c) to cater for the accession of Austria, Finland and Sweden to the EU.

The *Brussels I Regulation* on the recognition and enforcement of judgments in civil and commercial matters, replaces the 1998 Act as from 1 March 2002 for all EU States except Denmark: EC (Civil and Commercial Judgments) Regulations 2002, SI No 52 of 2002. An application for recognition or enforcement of a judgment under the *Brussels I Regulation* is made to the Master of the High Court who, as regards enforcement, must be declared immediately enforceable on completion of the formalities and without any review under arts 34 and 35 (unenforceability due to conflict with public policy, breach of the special jurisdiction rules for insurance and consumer contracts and reserved areas) (SI No 52 of 2002, reg 4). An enforcement order has the same force and effect as a judgment of the High Court (reg 5). However, in 2004 the High Court held that judgments obtained in other EU member states could not be enforced by an order of the Master of the High Court, as had been the practice; enforcement required an order of the Court: *Society of Lloyds v Monaghan* (2004) Irish Times, 11 March.

The *Brussels I Regulation* makes the recognition and enforcement mechanism for foreign judgments faster: see 'Judgment Calls' by T P Kennedy in *Law Society Gazette* (June 2002) 14. See *United Meat Packers v Nordstern Allgemeine Versicherungs* [1997] 2 ILRM 553; *Society Lacoste S A v Keely Group Ltd* [1999] 1 ILRM 510, HC and 3 IR 534 (under appeal). See SI No 101 of 1994; SI No 3 of 1999; SI No 40 of 2000. See RSC Ord 11A inserted by SI No 14 of 1989; Circuit Court Rules 2001 Ord 14; Ord 27; Ord 61; DCR 1997 Ord 62. See EC (Personal Insolvency) Regulations 2002, SI No 334 of 2002; EC (Corporate Insolvency) Regulations 2002, SI No 333 of 2002. [Bibliography: Barron; Byrne P; Glanville.] See MAREVA INJUNCTION; SET ASIDE; SUMMONS, SERVICE OUT OF JURISDICTION.

foreign law. The law of a foreign country which must be proved as a matter of *fact* in Irish courts, if a question depending on that law is in dispute: *McNamara v Owners of SS Hatteras* [1933] IR 675. *Canon* law is foreign law in this context: *O'Callaghan v O'Sullivan* [1925] 1 IR 90. The opinion of an expert as to the foreign law is admissible and generally required. When a dispute arises between experts as to how a foreign statute should be construed, then the Irish court may resolve the dispute by itself construing the instrument: *McC v McC* [1994] 1 ILRM 101, HC. The decision of an Irish court adjudicating on a question of foreign law is on the basis of the evidence presented to it and its decision thereon is final: *Tassan Din v Banco* Ambrosiano [1991] 1 IR 569, HC. See also *The State (Griffin) v Bell* [1962] IR 355. See CANON LAW; EXPERT OPINION.

foreign tribunal, evidence for. See LETTER OF REQUEST.

foreign trust. Formerly a trust in respect of which the settlor and the beneficiaries were not resident, ordinarily resident or domiciled in the State; the assets were situated outside the State; the income arose from sources outside the State; and the trustees, other than certain Irish resident trustees, were not resident, ordinarily resident or domiciled in the State: Finance Act 1993, s 49 repealed by Finance Act 1997 s 146(2).

foreman of jury. The member of a jury (qv) who is chosen to be their chairman and who announces their verdict. See ISSUE PAPER; VERDICT.

forename. First as distinct from family or surname. The forename(s) of a child must be registered in the register of births: Civil Registration Act 2004, s 19 and Sch 1. There is provision for altering the registered forename on application of the parents (s 25).

forensic. Relating to legal matters.

forensic accounting. The application of accounting and financial knowledge and expertise to the purposes of the law. *Forensic* means related to legal matters. Consequently, *forensic accounting* involves expert specialist accounting work performed for litigation, disputes, legal problems, conflict resolution and investigations, including tribunals of inquiry. The specialty of *forensic accounting* involves the integration of skills in accounting, auditing and financial investigation.

In his evidence to the Moriarty Tribunal on 25 September 2000, former Taoiseach Mr Charles J Haughey, said ' … I engaged the services of a very expert forensic accountant to help the Tribunal in unravelling these figures'. See 'Forensic Accounting and the Calculation of Damages – Personal Injuries and Commercial Damages' by Prof Niamh Brennan and John Hennessy BL in *Bar Review* (September 2001) 533 and (October/November 2001). [Bibliography: Brennan & Hennessy.]

forensic examination. Where stolen property becomes the subject matter of criminal proceedings, any forensic examination (whether by the prosecution or by the defence) should take place within a reasonable time, having regard to all the circumstances, so that the property can then be returned as expeditiously as possible to its true owner: *Rogers v DPP* [1993] 11 ILT Dig 164, HC.

forensic evidence. The Criminal Justice (Forensic Evidence) Act 1990 empowers the gardaí to take a variety of bodily samples for forensic testing from persons detained under the s 30 of the Offences Against the State Act 1939 or s 4 of the Criminal Justice Act 1984. Records and samples may be retained by order of the court (CJ(FE)A 1990, s 4(5)). See DCR 1997 Ord 31. See 'Weird Science' by Barry O'Halloran in *Law Society Gazette* (June 2003) 19.

forensic medicine. Medical jurisprudence; the application of medical knowledge to the purposes of the law.

Forensic Science Laboratory. The central laboratory, under the aegis of the Department of Justice, which provides a scientific analytical service to the Garda Síochána and the courts in criminal investigations. A certificate purported to be signed by an officer of the laboratory relating to a controlled drug or other substance, is evidence of any fact thereby certified without proof of any signature thereon, unless the contrary is proved: Misuse of Drugs Act 1984, s 10. A person in charge of, or employed in, a forensic science laboratory is ineligible to serve on a jury: Juries Act 1976, ss 7, 9, 31 and Sch 1, Pt I. See also SI No 6 of 1993; SI No 338 of 1993 as amended by SI No 92 of 2004; SI No 91 of 2004; SI No 43 of 2003.

Under draft legislation it is proposed to specify that documentary evidence in the receipt, handling, transmission and storage of anything by the laboratory can be admitted in court: Criminal Evidence Act 1992, s 5, as proposed to be amended by Criminal Justice Bill 2004, s 33. See MEDICAL BUREAU OF ROAD SAFETY; STATE LABORATORY.

forensic testing. See BODILY SAMPLE.

foreseeable damage. See REMOTENESS OF DAMAGE; RESCUER.

foreshore. (1) The bed and shore, below the line of high water of ordinary or medium tides, of the sea and of every tidal river and tidal estuary and of every channel, creek, and bay of the sea or of any such river or estuary: Foreshore Act 1933, s 1. The foreshore belongs to the State: 1937 Constitution, art 10(2). The Minister is empowered to make leases and licences of the foreshore (FoA 1933, 2–3 as amended by Foreshore (Amendment) Act 1992, s 2) and to prescribe fees for applications, approvals and consents (Fisheries (Amendment) Act 2003, s 32). No registration of land which appears to comprise the foreshore may be made without sending prior notice to the Minister: Registration of Title Act 1964, s 125. See *Attorney-General v McCarthy* [1911] 2 IR 260; *Madden v Minister for the Marine* [1993] ILRM 436, HC.

In 1998, the Minister's power to remove unauthorised structures on State land was increased, and provision was made for increased fines for unauthorised dumping on the foreshore and for dumping of harmful material beside or into the sea: Fisheries and Foreshore (Amendment) Act 1998, s 5. See also Foreshore (Environmental Impact Assessment) Regulations 1990, SI No 220 of 1990; Fisheries (Amendment) Act 1997, s 82. See BEACH MATERIAL; SEAWEED.

(2) *Foreshore* has the meaning assigned to it by the Foreshore Act 1933, but includes land between the line of high water of ordinary or medium tides and land within the functional area of the planning authority concerned that adjoins the first-mentioned land: Planning and Development Act 2000, s 224. There is an obligation to obtain permission in respect of *development* on the foreshore; development in this context includes reclamation of any land on the foreshore (PDA 2000, ss 224–225). A local authority has power to acquire compulsorily land on the foreshore; it may also carry out development itself, or in partnership with others, in which case it requires the approval of An Bord Pleanála (PDA 2000, ss 226–227). See SEASHORE; SHORE.

foresight. Looking forward. A person has a duty of care to avoid acts or omissions which he can reasonably foresee. Also in relation to murder, the accused is presumed to have intended the natural and probable consequences of his conduct. See DUTY OF CARE; ECONOMIC LOSS; MURDER; RESCUER.

forestry. A commercial company to implement the afforestation programme of the State is provided for in the Forestry Act 1988. The Act also amends the penalties for certain offences, mostly relating to tree felling. See also VESTING ORDER.

Forfás. A body established to advise the Minister on matters relating to the development of industry in the State and to advise and co-ordinate Enterprise Ireland (qv) and IDA Ireland in relation to their func-

tions: Industrial Development Act 1993, ss 5–6. It also has the function of advising on policy for these two bodies and such other bodies as the Minister may designate; the Minister has designated FÁS as such a body (IDA 1993, s 6, as amended by Industrial Development (Science Foundation Ireland) Act 2003, s 35(b)). See also Industrial Development Act 1995; Industrial Development (Enterprise Ireland) Act 1998. See website: *www.forfas.ie*. See INDUSTRIAL DEVELOPMENT; SCIENCE FOUNDATION IRELAND.

forfeiture. The deprivation of a person of his property as a penalty for some act or omission. Forfeiture may take place by agreement or by operation of law eg a forfeiture clause in a lease may enable the lessor to determine the lease; the government is empowered to order the forfeiture of the property of an unlawful organisation. Fishing gear and catch may be forfeited pursuant to the Fisheries (Consolidation) Act 1959 but not summarily: *Kostan v A-G* [1978] HC. A forfeiture order may be made in relation to a drug offence but only where the property to be forfeited is related to the particular offence: Misuse of Drugs Acts 1977 and 1984; *Bowes v Devally* [1995] 2 ILRM 149, HC and 1 IR 315; Criminal Justice Act 1994, s 62.

The forfeiture of the lands and goods of a felon was abolished by the Forfeiture Act 1870; however, some forfeitures and disabilities survived, but all these have now been abolished as the distinction between a felony and a misdemeanour was abolished in 1997 and the 1870 Act repealed: Criminal Law Act 1997, ss 3, 16 and Sch 3.

An offensive weapon may be forfeited by order of the court: Firearms and Offensive Weapons Act 1990, s 13. A covenant for the forfeiture of a lease on the bankruptcy (qv) of the lessee is void as against the Official Assignee (qv): Bankruptcy Act 1988, s 49(1). A vessel may be forfeited on a second conviction on indictment of certain offences under the Merchant Shipping Act 1992 (MSA 1992, s 22) and Fisheries (Amendment) Act 1994, s 14. Provision has also been made for the forfeiture of sea-fishing boats in certain circumstances: Fisheries (Amendment) Act 2003, ss 25(3), 27(5) and 28. The sale or use of a product forfeited under the Customs Acts does not constitute an infringement of a patent: Patents Act 1992, s 116.

In 1994, a general *discretionary* power of forfeiture was introduced: (a) of property for the purpose of committing an offence, or facilitating the commission of an offence, or (b) where the offence itself is defined as involving the possession of some property, and that property is in the defendant's possession when he was apprehended: Criminal Justice Act 1994, s 61. This section was amended in 1998 to remove the discretionary nature of the power of forfeiture in the case of certain firearm and explosive substance offences and to make forfeiture *mandatory*: Offences against the State (Amendment) Act 1998, ss 17 and 18.

There is also provision for the execution of *external forfeiture orders* from a designated country (CJA 1994, s 47). The State of Israel, the Rwandese Republic, and the Kingdom of Thailand have been so designated: SI No 178 of 2003.

There is provision for the forfeiture of seized property eg counterfeit currency notes and coins, and false instruments: Criminal Justice (Theft and Fraud Offences) Act 2001, s 50. See also Regulation of Information (Services outside the State for Termination of Pregnancies) Act 1995, s 12; Control of Horses Act 1996, s 8; Child Trafficking and Pornography Act 1998, s 8; Public Health (Tobacco) Act 2002, s 5(6); Containment of Nuclear Weapons Act 2003, s 15. See 'Asset Forfeiture & the European Convention on Human Rights' by Claire Hamilton BL in *Bar Review* (May 2001) 414. See CONDEMNATION; CRIMINAL ASSETS BUREAU; FELONY; LEASE, DETERMINATION OF; POSSESSION AND CRIME; PRESERVED BENEFIT; PROCEEDS OF CRIME; SCHEDULED OFFENCE; UNLAWFUL ORGANISATION.

forfeiture of shares. In a company, the shares of a member may be forfeited by resolution of the directors if such power is given in the company's *articles of association:* Companies Act 1963, Table A, art 35. However, a power claimed by a company to forfeit its own shares is invalid as an unauthorised return of capital, unless it is for non-payment of calls: *Hopkinson v Mortimer, Harley Co* [1917] 1 Ch 646. The courts interpret the power to forfeit very strictly. The prescribed detail must be followed scrupulously; *mala fides* or abusive exercise by the directors of their fiduciary power will cause the forfeiture to be struck down. See *Ward v Dublin North City Milling Co* [1919] 1 IR 5. See SURRENDER OF SHARES; SHARES.

forged endorsement. See CHEQUE, LIABILITY ON.

forgery. A person is guilty of *forgery* if he makes a *false instrument* with the intention that it be used to induce another person to accept it as genuine and, by reason of so accepting it, to do some act, or to make some omission, to the *prejudice* of that person or any other person: Criminal Justice (Theft and Fraud Offences) Act 2001, s 25(1).

An *instrument* means any document, whether formal or informal, includes any disk, tape, soundtrack or other device, money order, postal order, postage stamps, revenue stamp, share certificate, insurance certificate, marriage, death or birth certificates, public service card, charge card, credit card, cheque card or debit card (CJ(TFO)A 2001, s 24 as amended by Immigration Act 2004, s 16(7)). An instrument is *false* if it purports to be something it is not because, for example, its terms were not authorised (CJ(TFO)A 2001, s 30).

A person *makes* a false instrument if he alters an instrument so as to make it false in any respect (CJ(TFO)A 2001, s 30(2)). Also an act or omission intended to be induced is to a person's *prejudice* if it is one: (a) which in respect of that person, will result in loss of property or deprivation of an opportunity to earn remuneration or financial advantage or (b) which will give another person an opportunity to earn remuneration or gain financial advantage, or (c) which will be accepted as genuine in connection with his performance of a duty (CJ(TFO)A 2001, s 31(1)).

It is an offence to use a *copy* of a false instrument with the intention of inducing another person to accept it as a copy of a genuine instrument (CJ(TFO)A 2001, s 28). It is also an offence to have custody or control of certain false instruments (s 29). The *common law* offence of forgery is abolished (CJ(TFO)A 2001, s 3(2)).

See District Court (Theft and Fraud Offences) Rules 2003, SI No 412 of 2003. For previous legislation, see Forgery Act 1913; Forgery Act 1861 as amended by Criminal Law Act 1997 s 16 and Sch 3. A carrier licensing document is deemed to be a public document for the purposes of the Forgery Act 1913: Road Transport

Act 1999, s 12(3). See also Dangerous Substances Act 1972, s 50; Hallmarking Act 1981, s 13; Metrology Act 1996, s 23; Stamp Duties Consolidation Act 1999, ss 140, 142; Public Health (Tobacco) Act 2002, s 53. See also *DPP v Harrington* [1991] 9 ILT Dig 171, CCA. [Bibliography: McGreal C.] See COUNTERFEIT; UTTER.

forinsecus. [Outside.]

forma pauperis. See IN FORMA PAUPERIS.

forms, legal. See PRECEDENT.

formula bid. (1) An offer to purchase (eg shares of a company) which is expressed in terms of a formula eg 15% more than the highest monetary bid by any other bidder. See *Howberry Lane v Telecom Éireann, RTÉ & NTL Inc* [1999] 2 ILRM 232, HC.

(2) An offer for the share capital of an investment trust where the consideration under the offer is to be calculated by reference to a formula related to the net assets of the offeree: Takeover Rules 2001, Pt B, App.2.

fortuna. [Treasure trove (qv).]

fortune telling. Telling of fortunes for money may amount to the offence of false pretences (qv).

forum non conveniens. Common law doctrine whereby the court refuses to exercise its right of jurisdiction because, for the convenience of the parties and in the interest of justice, an action should be brought elsewhere. Where a dispute arises as to the appropriate forum for litigation and a party seeks a stay in the proceedings, the test to be applied is whether or not justice requires that the action be stayed: *Doe v Armour Pharmaceutical Co Inc* [1994] 1 ILRM 416, SC and 3 IR 78. The court will only grant a stay on the ground of *forum non conveniens* where it is satisfied that there is some other available *forum*, having competent jurisdiction, which is the appropriate *forum* for the trial of the action: *Jahwar v Betta Livestock 17* [2001] 4 IR 42, HC. See Jurisdiction of Courts and Enforcement of Judgments Act 1998 which incorporates the Brussels Convention 1968.

The High Court has held that the discretion of the court to stay proceedings on the basis of the doctrine of *forum non conveniens* had not survived the incorporation of the Brussels Convention into Irish law and consequently the court had no jurisdiction under this doctrine to stay proceeding where both the plaintiff and the defendant were domiciled in Ireland: *D C v W O C* [2001] 2 IR 1, HC. In this case the plaintiff had issued High Court proceedings in Ireland claiming damages against the defendant in respect of rape and sexual assault alleged to have been committed in Sweden. See also *In the matter of Intercare Ltd* [2004] 1 ILRM 351, HC.

The *Brussels I Regulation* on the recognition and enforcement of judgments in civil and commercial matters, replaces the 1998 Act as from 1 March 2002 for all EU States except Denmark: EC (Civil and Commercial Judgments) Regulations 2002, SI No 52 of 2002.

See 'Staying proceedings on the grounds of Forum Non Conveniens' by Patrick McEvoy BL in *Bar Review* (January 2001) 235. See Case C-351/89 *Overseas Union Insurance Ltd v New Hampshire Insurance Co Ltd – Court of Justice of EC*; *Kelly v Cruise Catering Ltd* [1994] 2 ILRM 394, SC; *Edwins v Carlton* [1997] 2 ILRM 223, HC; *Intermetal Group Ltd v Worslade Trading Ltd* [1998] 2 IR 1, HC; *Analogue Devices v Zurich Insurance* [2002] 1 IR 272, HC; *McCarthy v Pillay* [2003] 2 ILRM 284, SC and 1 IR 592. See *Byrne* in 10 ILT & SJ (1992) 230 and 11 ILT & SJ (1993) 63. See JURISDICTION.

Foss v Harbottle, rule in. The rule in company law that only a company can maintain proceedings in respect of wrongs done to it: *Foss v Harbottle* [1843] 2 Hare 461. The exceptions to the rule include the right of an individual shareholder to bring proceedings in respect of an act done on behalf of the company which is illegal or *ultra vires* (qv) the company or where there is *oppression of a shareholder* (qv). It has been held that a 50% shareholder outvoted by the casting vote of a chairman to the detriment of the company is a minority shareholder entitled to sue for the purposes of the rule: *Balkanbank v Naser Taher & Ors* [1992] ITLR (13 April), HC.

In a particular case where a member of a trade union sought an injunction against her trade union, it was argued that the court could not entertain her grievance as it was excluded by the operation of the rule in *Foss v Harbottle*. However, the court held that it would be inequitable to apply the rule as the union's rules were deficient to provide her with an adequate remedy: *McNamara v Civil and Public Service Union* [1996] ELR 160, HC. See *Moylan v Irish*

Whiting Manufacturers Ltd [1980] HC; *Duggan v Bourke & Bank of Ireland* [1986] HC; *O'Neill v Ryan* [1993] ILRM 557, SC; *Murray v Times Newspapers Ltd* [1997] 3 IR 97, SC; *Crindle Investments v Wymes* [1998] 2 ILRM 275, SC and 4 IR 567; *Re Via Net Works (Ireland) Ltd* [2002] 2 IR 47, SC. See MacCann in 8 ILT & SJ (1990) 68–74. See DERIVATIVE ACTION; OPPRESSION OF SHAREHOLDER.

foster care, private. A *private foster care arrangement* means any arrangement or undertaking whereby a child is for more than 14 days in the full-time care, for reward or otherwise, of a person other than his parent, guardian or a relative: Child Care Act 1991, Pt IVB, s 230 as inserted by Children Act 2001, s 16. There are exceptions eg where the child is in a boarding school and receiving full-time education.

A person arranging or undertaking a private foster care arrangement: (a) is required to have regard to the child's welfare as the first and paramount consideration and to take all reasonable measures to safeguard the health, safety and welfare of the child; (b) is required to give notice to the health board in a specified manner; (c) cannot do so for the purpose of adopting the child; (d) cannot apply for adoption unless the child is eligible for adoption and the health board has consented to the continuation of the foster care arrangement pending the completion of an assessment under the Adoption Acts.

foster child. Prior to commencement of Part VI of the Child Care Act 1991, a child taken into care by a health board (qv) by the *boarding out* of the child to foster parents: Health Act 1953, s 55; Boarding Out of Children Regulations 1983, SI No 67 of 1983. The child had to be under 16 years of age and either be: (a) a legitimate child (now, a child *whose parents are married to each other*) whose parents were dead or who was deserted by his parents or (where one of them was dead) by the surviving parent, or (b) an illegitimate child (now, a child *whose parents are not married to each other*) whose mother was dead or who was deserted by his mother. However, a health board could continue to support such a child beyond 16 years of age until the completion of his education.

On commencement of Part VI of the CCA 1991, a child boarded out by a health board is deemed to have been placed in *foster care* under an arrangement made

under section 36 (CCA 1991, s 6). A foster child is now a person under the age of 18 years (CCA 1991, s 2(1)). See Child Care (Placement of Children in Foster Care) Regulations 1995, SI No 260 of 1995. Two brothers were awarded their foster parents' farm under the doctrine of *legitimate expectation*: *O'Rourke v Gallagher* (2000) Irish Times, 18 February 2000.

A foster child is now to be treated in the same way as other children as regards *capital acquisitions tax* ie the foster child is entitled to the benefit of the group threshold for a child in respect of a gift or inheritance before it attracts capital acquisitions tax: Finance Act 2001, s 221. This applies to gifts or inheritances taken on or after 6 December 2000. The child must have resided with the disponer (foster parent) for a successive period of five years, except where formally fostered under the relevant Child Care Regulations. See *DC v DM (Adoption)* [1999] 2 IR 150, HC. For consolidated provision, see Capital Acquisitions Tax Consolidation Act 2003, Sch 2, Pt 1(9)). See CHILD; FOSTER PARENTS; WELFARE OF CHILDREN.

foster parent. Prior to commencement of Part VI of the Child Care Act 1991, a *foster parent* was a person into whose foster care a health board (qv) placed a child, where such care was paid for by the board: Health Act 1953, s 55; Boarding Out of Children Regulations 1983, SI No 67 of 1983. Foster parents had to be properly assessed by the board and their suitability and the suitability of their home determined (reg 7). A foster parent could not be of a different religion to the child unless: (a) each of the child's parents, or (b) where the child's parents were not married to each other, the mother, or (c) the child's guardians, knew the religion of the foster parent and consented (reg 8). In the case of desertion of the child or death of the parents, it sufficed if the foster parent undertook to bring up the child in the religion to which the child belonged.

On commencement of Part VI of CCA 1991, *foster parent* means a person other than a relative of a child who is taking care of the child on behalf of a health board in accordance with regulations made under CCA 1991, s 39 and *foster care* is construed accordingly (CCA 1991, s 36(2)). These regulations may fix the conditions under which children may be placed in foster care, prescribe the form of contract to be entered into by a health board with foster parents, and provide for supervision and visiting (CCA 1991, s 39(2)). Also where a foster child is *adopted* by the foster parent, the health board may continue to contribute to the maintenance of the child as if he continued to be in foster care (CCA 1991, s 44(1)).

There is no limitation on the District Court in relation to its powers to place a child outside the State with a foster parent or relatives; it is within the court's discretion to order that the period be a limited one or unlimited: *Western Health Board v K M* [2001] 1 IR 729, HC upheld by the Supreme Court in [2002] 2 IR 493, SC. See Child Care (Placement of Children in Foster Care) Regulations 1995, SI No 260 of 1995. See FOSTER-CHILD; ORPHAN.

founders' shares. Deferred shares which do not receive a dividend until other shareholders have been paid a dividend. Founders' shares sometimes entitle the holders to the whole or a substantial part of the distributable profits but are now rarely issued. See Listing Rules 2000, para 6F.1. See SHARES, COMPANY.

founding fathers of the EU. The persons generally recognised as being the persons with the dream of uniting the peoples of Europe in lasting peace and friendship, following the Second World War, and whose dream became a reality with the creation of the European Community and the European Union. They were Jean Monnet and Robert Schuman. See EUROPE DAY.

foundling. An abandoned infant whose parents are not known. Such a child may be adopted. See Adoption Act 1988. See ADOPTION.

Four Courts. The buildings in Dublin, designed by Gandon, opened in 1796; the *four* courts leading from the round hall were originally Exchequer, Chancery, King's Bench and Common Pleas. The buildings, as extended, now comprise courts from the District to the Supreme Court, the Law Library (qv), consultation rooms of the Law Society (qv), the Central Office (qv) and other court offices. The bicentennial anniversary of the first sitting at the Four Courts was celebrated on 8 November 1996 at a ceremony attended by President Mary Robinson.

The burning of the Four Courts in 1922 destroyed many legal records which in many cases barred persons from making claims to moneys paid into the court to which they may have been entitled; this is one reason for the accumulation of unclaimed assets in the *funds of suitors*. See SUITORS, FUNDS OF.

four freedoms. The term sometimes used to describe the frontier-free area in the EU within which people, goods, services and money, can move around freely. See FINANCIAL SERVICES ACTION PLAN; RIGHT OF ESTABLISHMENT; SERVICES, PROVISION OF; WORKERS, FREEDOM OF MOVEMENT.

four unities. See JOINT TENANCY.

Foyle Carlingford and Irish Lights Commission. The cross-border corporate body with functions in relation to Lough Foyle, Carlingford Lough, the development and licensing of aquaculture, the development of marine tourism, and the existing functions of the Commissioners of Irish Lights in respect of providing and maintaining aids to navigation along the coast of the whole island of Ireland and its adjacent seas and islands: British-Irish Agreement Act 1999, ss 31–38. Consequent on the establishment of the new Commission, provision was made for the exclusion of the Carlingford Area from the Dundalk Fisheries District: Fisheries (Amendment) Act 1999, s 31.

It was intended that the Commission would operate through two agencies: (1) the *Loughs Agency*, which is operational and has replaced the Foyle Fisheries Commission, and (2) the *Lights Agency*. A number of complexities have arisen in relation to the transfer of functions from the Commissioners of Irish Lights to the Lights Agency and the matter is under review. See website: *www.loughs-agency.org*. See GOOD FRIDAY AGREEMENT.

fractionem diei non recipit lex. [The law does not recognise any fraction of a day.] See CLEAR DAYS; GALE DAY.

framework decision. A new type of European Union legislative act which corresponds to an EC *directive* (qv) in that it is binding on member states as to the result to be achieved, but leaves to the national authorities the choice of form and method: Treaty on European Union, art 34 of the consolidated (2002) version. The doctrine of *direct effect* is specifically excluded. Framework decisions are for the purpose of approximation of the laws and regulations of the member states. The Court of Justice may be permitted to give preliminary rulings on the validity and interpretation of a framework decision, if a member state accepts its jurisdiction to so do (art 35). See APPROXIMATION OF LAWS; DIRECT APPLICABILITY; DIRECTIVE, EC; EUROPEAN FRAMEWORK LAW.

franchise. (1) The right to vote in a parliamentary or local authority election. All citizens of the State who have reached the age of eighteen years and who are not disqualified by law have the right to vote in an election for members of Dáil Éireann: 1937 Constitution, art 16(1)(2). This also includes, apart from citizens, such other persons in the State as may be determined by law, as a result of a constitutional amendment in 1984 to permit the extension of the franchise by statute law to non-citizens. The franchise was extended to British citizens resident in the State by the Electoral (Amendment) Act 1985; similar voting rights may be extended by order to nationals of member states of the EC resident in Ireland, provided reciprocal voting rights are extended to Irish citizens. Only *presidential electors* are entitled to vote in a referendum (qv) or presidential election. The constitutional ban on double voting did not forbid double registration: 1937 Constitution, art 16(1)(4); *Quinn v Mayor of City of Waterford* [1991] ILRM 433, SC. Now, a person must not be registered as an elector more than once in any registration area nor in more than one such area: Electoral Act 1992, s 11(1). See also CITIZENSHIP; LOCAL GOVERNMENT, ELECTION OF; PERSONATION; PRESIDENT OF IRELAND; PROPORTIONAL REPRESENTATION; VOTERS, SPECIAL.

(2) A liberty or privilege e g to hold fairs and markets. At common law a franchise was a royal privilege which not only authorised something to be done, but gave the owner the right to prevent others from interfering with the right. The 1937 Constitution provides that all royalties and franchises in the State belong to the State subject to all estates and interests therein for the time being lawfully vested in any person or body (art 10(1)). Franchises are burdens (qv) which can affect registered land without registration: Registration of Title Act 1964, s 72(1). See *Skibbereen UDC v Quill* [1986] ILRM 170.

(3) A right to trade under the name of another. See *Dunlea v Nissan* [1991] 9 ILT Dig 74, HC. [Bibliography: AIB; McGarry S.]

(4) A package of industrial or intellectual property rights relating to trade marks, trade names, shop signs, utility models, designs, copyrights, know-how or patents, to be exploited for the resale of goods or the provision of services to end users: Category Licence in respect of *franchise agreements* (giving a right to exploit a franchise) granted by the Competition Authority (Iris Oifigiúil, 9 December 1994).

fraud. (1) The crime which may involve a false pretence, false accounting, forgery, embezzlement or fraudulent conversion (qqv). For previous legislation, see Larceny Act 1861, s 84; Debtors (Ireland) Act 1872, s 13, since repealed by Criminal Justice (Theft and Fraud Offences) Act 2001, s 3. See District Court (Theft and Fraud Offences) Rules 2003, SI No 412 of 2003. [Bibliography: McGreal C.]

(2) A number of new offences of *electronic fraud* have been created eg the fraudulent use of electronic signatures, signature creation devices and electronic certificates: Electronic Commerce Act 2000, s 25. These provisions extend also to activities which take place partly outside the State (ECA 2000, s 26). There is provision for a judge of the District Court to issue a search warrant, which will include a requirement for disclosure in intelligible form of anything which contains information which cannot be readily accessed (ECA 2000, s 27). However, the confidentiality of deciphering data is protected, as disclosure is not required of unique data, such as codes, passwords, algorithms or private cryptographic keys (ECA 2000, s 28).

(3) Fraud is also the tort of *deceit* (qv). The Supreme Court has held that fraud must be pleaded with the most particularity; it would not be inferred from the circumstances pleaded, at all events if those circumstances were consistent with innocence: *Superwood Holdings plc v Sun Alliance* [1995] 3 IR 303, SC.

A barrister must not settle a pleading claiming fraud without express instructions: *Code of Conduct for the Bar of Ireland* (December 2003) r 5.16. For fraud as a ground for setting aside the judgment of a court, see SET ASIDE. For fraud on court, see BARRISTER AND CLIENT. See Credit Union Act 1997, s 173. See Maguire Committee, *Report of the Government Advisory Committee on Fraud* (1992). [Bibliography:

Spollen.] See CONSPIRACY, CRIME OF; CYBERCRIME; DECEPTION; DISHONESTY; FALSE ACCOUNTING; FORGERY; INJUNCTION, PLANNING; INSURANCE, CONTRACT OF; PLEADINGS; STATUTE OF FRAUDS; VOIDABLE; UBERRIMAE FIDEI.

fraud, international. See POLICE CO-OPERATION.

fraudulent action. If a plaintiff in a personal injuries action gives or adduces, or dishonestly causes to be given or adduced, evidence that: (a) is false or misleading, in any material respect, and (b) he knows to be false or misleading, the court is required to dismiss the plaintiff's action unless, for reasons that the court must state in its decision, the dismissal of the action would result in injustice being done: Civil Liability and Courts Act 2004, s 26(1). There is a similar provision in respect of the verifying affidavit required under s 14: CLCA 2004, s 26(2)). An act is done dishonestly by a person if done with the intention of misleading the court: CLCA 2004, s 26(3). For penalties, see CLCA 2004, s 29.

fraudulent conversion. Formerly, the offence committed by a person who *fraudulently converted* to his own use any property with which he has been entrusted to keep in safe custody or to deliver to another or which he has received for, or on account of, any other person: Larceny Act 1916, s 20. In relation to trusts, it was an offence for a person with intent to defraud, to convert or appropriate to any purpose other than that of his trust, any property given to him on an express trust (qv) created in writing (LA 1916, s 20).

When money is received by a person under circumstances which impose on him a definite legal obligation to pay it over to another person, it is money *received for, or on account of, any other person*: Attorney-General v Lawless [1930] IR 247; The People (Attorney-General) v Heald [1954] IR 58. See also The People (Attorney-General) v Murphy [1947] IR 236; The People (Attorney-General) v Cowan [1957] CCA; The People (Attorney-General) v Singer [1975] IR 408.

The 1916 Act has been repealed by the Criminal Justice (Theft and Fraud Offences) Act 2001, s 3 and Sch 1. See THEFT.

fraudulent debtor. A wide range of offences which a bankrupt (qv) or an *arranging debtor* (qv) may commit e g concealing or fraudulently removing any part

of his property to the value of £500 (€635) or upwards: Bankruptcy Act 1988, s 123. It is also an offence for a person, including persons who subsequently become bankrupts or arranging debtors, to do certain acts with intent to defraud their creditors; there is a rebuttable presumption that the act constituting the offence was done with that intent if it occurred within twelve months before *adjudication* of the person as a bankrupt or of the granting of an *order for protection* to the person (BA1988, s 123(3)).

fraudulent misrepresentation. See MISREPRESENTATION.

fraudulent preference. Any conveyance, mortgage, delivery of goods, payment, execution or other act relating to property, by a company (within six months of being wound up) in favour of any creditor, with the view to giving such creditor, or any surety or guarantor for the debt due to such creditor, a preference over other creditors. A fraudulent preference is invalid. However, for a transfer of property to be caught by this prohibition, the company must have been unable to pay its debts as they fell due at the time the preference was made. See Companies Act 1963, s 286 as amended by the Companies Act 1990, s 135.

The six-month period has been extended to two years in the case of transactions in favour of persons *connected* with the company eg directors, shadow directors, close relatives, and related companies. The onus of establishing the legitimacy of the transaction is placed on the connected person. See Re John Daly Co Ltd [1886] 19 LR Ir 83; Re Olderfleet Shipbuilding Co Ltd [1922] 1 IR 26; Eddison v Allied Irish Banks [1987] HC.

It has been held that the giving of security by a third party to a creditor of an insolvent company in circumstances where the payment would constitute a fraudulent preference if made by the insolvent company, cannot amount to a fraudulent preference: Parkes & Sons Ltd v Hong Kong & Shanghai Banking Corporation [1990] ILRM 341, HC. For provisions governing fraudulent preference by a person who is unable to pay his debts as they become due, see Bankruptcy Act 1988, s 57.

fraudulent trading. The offence committed by a person who is knowingly a party to the carrying on of the business of a company with intent to defraud creditors of the company or creditors of any other person or for any fraudulent purpose: Companies

Act 1963, s 297 as amended by the Companies Act 1990, s 137.

Such a person may also be declared by the court to be personally responsible without limitation of liability for the debts or other liabilities of the company, on the application of the receiver, examiner, liquidator or any creditor or contributory of the company: CA 1963, s 297A inserted by CA 1990, s 138. See RSC Ord 74, r 49. See also *Re Aluminium Fabricators Ltd (No 2)* [1984] ILRM 399; *Re Kelly's Carpetdrome Ltd* [1983 & 1984] HC; *Re Hunting Lodges Ltd* [1985] ILRM 75, HC; *Southern Mineral Oil Ltd v Cooney* [1998] 2 ILRM 375, HC and [1999] 1 IR 237, HC. See RECKLESS TRADING.

fraus omnia vitiat. [Fraud (qv) vitiates everything.]

Free Legal Advice Centres; FLAC. A non-governmental organisation which: (a) campaigns for full and equal access to justice for all, (b) promotes the use of innovative methods to meet the legal needs of persons living in poverty, and (c) operates a range of services designed to achieve those aims. A barrister may be a member or officer of a law centre established by FLAC and may accept non-paying briefs from such centre, provided he is instructed and attended by a solicitor in court: *Code of Conduct for the Bar of Ireland* (December 2003) r 2.11. See 'Northside Community Law Centre – its place in the legal landscape' by barrister Rory White in *Bar Review* (December 2003) 263. [Free Legal Advice Centre, Head Office, 13 Lower Dorset Street, Dublin 1.] See website: *www.flac.ie*. [Bibliography: O'Morain P.] See also EUROPEAN CONSUMER CENTRE ; EURO-JUS.

free movement. The phrase used in the Treaty of Rome 1957 in relation to the movement of persons, services and capital within the EC. See now EC Treaty, arts 39–60 of the consolidated (2002) version. The European Court of Justice has held that the free movement of goods is one of the fundamental principles of the EU and that a member state may be held liable if it fails to take measures required to deal with obstacles to intra-Community trade, even if the obstacles arise from actions taken by private individuals: Case C-112/00 *Eugen Schmidberger, Internationale Transporte and Planzüge* [2003] ECJ. In this case it found that the failure of Austria to ban a demonstration which blocked a main motorway and interfered with the free movement of goods, was reasonable in all the circumstances. See also *Masterson v DPP* [2002] 3 IR 193, HC; Case C-469/00 *Ravil SARL v Bellon Import SARL*; Case C-325/00 *Commission v Federal Republic of Germany* [2002] ECJ; Case C-109/01 *Secretary of State for the Home Department/Hacene Akrich* [2003] ECJ. See ALIEN; EXCHANGE CONTROL; EUROPEAN CONVENTION ON HUMAN RIGHTS; INTERNAL MARKET; SOLICITOR, INTERNATIONAL PRACTICE; SOLICITOR; MUTUAL RECOGNITION; RIGHT OF ESTABLISHMENT; WORKERS, FREEDOM OF MOVEMENT.

free of tax. Where a gift or inheritance is given 'free of tax', the benefit is deemed to include the amount of tax chargeable, in other words, it is grossed up: Capital Acquisitions Tax Consolidation Act 2003, s 87. The meaning of the expression 'free of income tax' is clear; the same cannot be said for the expression of 'net of income tax': *MP v AP* [2001] 1 ILRM 51, SC.

free port. The land enclosed within the limits defined by an order made by the Minister: Free Ports Act 1986, s 2. The principal benefits of free port status are the deferral of payments of custom duties and value added tax on imports and simplified customs documentation and procedures. See Ringaskiddy Free Port (Establishment) Order 1988, SI No 113 of 1988.

free trade area. Generally means an area where a group of countries have removed barriers to trade between them, such as import tariffs and quotas. Examples of free trade areas are: Mercosur in South America, Nafta in North America, and EFTA in Europe. The European Union is also a free trade area, but it is more than that because it is built on a process of economic and political integration. See FOUR FREEDOMS.

freedom, honorary. See CIVIC HONOUR.

freedom of assembly. See ASSEMBLY, FREEDOM OF.

freedom of association. The right of citizens guaranteed by the State under the Constitution to form associations and unions, subject to public order and morality (art 40.6.1). Laws regulating the right must not contain political, religious or class discrimination (art 40.6.2). See TRADE UNION.

freedom of establishment. Every EU citizen, through freedom of establishment, is allowed to set up a business in any EU country in the same way and on the same legal basis as a national of that country: National Forum on Europe, *Glossary of Terms* (2003). See RIGHT OF ESTABLISHMENT.

freedom of expression. See EXPRESSION, FREEDOM OF.

freedom of information. Legislation which has as its aim, greater openness and transparency in relation to government and public bodies, consistent with the public interest and the right to privacy.

The Freedom of Information Act 1997 provides for: (a) a right of access to records of public bodies following the making of a request, (b) the right to require amendment of incorrect, incomplete or misleading personal information in the possession of a public body, (c) the right to be given reasons for administrative decisions, and (d) the requirement of publication by public bodies of a reference book setting out details of the structure, organisation and functions of the public body, and of the services they provide. It has been held that the onus on a body, to justify a refusal to grant access to records sought from it, is a heavy one: *Minister for Agriculture v Information Commissioner* [2001] 1 ILRM 40, HC and [2000] 1 IR 309, HC.

Records created under the Companies Acts by the *Director of Corporate Enforcement* are excluded from the provisions of the Freedom of Information Act 1997: Company Law Enforcement Act 2001, s 112. This provision is to ensure the secrecy of this information, which information may lead to criminal proceedings against individuals or companies. A similar exemption is in place in respect of the Director of Public Prosecutions.

The 1997 Act has been amended: (a) to ensure the efficient operation of the Act, (b) to extend additional protection to certain sensitive government records, and (c) to clarify certain technical procedures under the Act: Freedom of Information (Amendment) Act 2003. The refusal on administrative grounds to grant a request for access to records has been strengthened, by allowing the behaviour of the requester in relation to previous manifestly unreasonable requests to be taken into account, including the behaviour of requesters who appear to be acting in concert (FOIA 1997, s 10 as amended by FOI(A)A 2003, Act s 7).

See also Public Service Management Act 1997, s 5; Criminal Justice (Location of Victims' Remains) Act 1999, s 9; Electricity Regulation Act 1999, s 46; Commission to Inquire into Child Abuse Act 2000, s 34; Sustainable Energy Act 2002, s 19(5); Ombudsman for Children Act 2002, s 20; Gas (Interim) (Regulation) Act 2002, s 23(5); Residential Institutions Redress Act 2002, s 31; Houses of the Oireachtas Commission Act 2003, ss 16(4)(d) and 17; Commissions of Investigation Act 2004, s 40. See RSC Ord 130 inserted by Rules of the Superior Courts (Freedom of Information Act 1997) 1998 (SI No 325 of 1998). See Prescribed Bodies Regulations 2000, SIs No 67 and 115 of 2000. [Bibliography: McDonagh.] See INFORMATION, ACCESS TO; INFORMATION NOTICE, DATA; NATIONAL ARCHIVES; PERSONAL INFORMATION; PERSONNEL RECORD; PROCEEDINGS; PUBLIC BODY; TRANSCRIPT.

freedom of the press. The constitutional guarantee of freedom of expression is not confined to mere expressions of convictions and opinions but includes the right to impart facts and information; the *freedom of the press* guaranteed by this provision includes the right to report and comment on proceedings in courts of law: 1937 Constitution, art 40(6)(1)(1); *Irish Times Ltd v Murphy* [1998] 2 ILRM 161, SC.

A court may interfere with the right of the media to publish contemporaneous reports of proceedings before it, where this is necessary to protect the right of an accused to a fair trial; however the trial judge must be satisfied (a) that there is a real risk of an unfair trial if contemporaneous reporting is permitted, and (b) that the damage caused by any improper reporting could not be remedied by appropriate directions to the jury or otherwise (*Irish Times* case).

The constitutionally guaranteed right of freedom of expression should not be curtailed save to the extent necessary to protect the administration of justice: *Kelly v O'Neill & Brady* [2000] 1 ILRM 507, SC. See FAIR COMMENT; PRIVILEGE.

freehold. An interest in land being either a fee simple, a fee tail or a life estate (qqv). Interests which are less than freehold are leases and tenancies (qqv). See FLYING FREEHOLD.

freehold covenant. A clause in a conveyance of freehold land which binds the purchaser to do some act or to refrain from doing some act. Such covenants are usually entered into when the freehold owner sells off part only of his lands. If the vendor is concerned about the use and development of what is becoming neighbouring land, he will require the purchaser to enter into various covenants to protect the vendor in his and his successors' continuing enjoyment of the retained land.

There is generally little problem about the enforceability of leasehold covenants, whereas there is a major problem in this respect about freehold covenants eg: (a) only 'restrictive' or 'negative' covenants of freehold land pass to successors in title to the original covenantor eg a positive covenant to pay money, such as service charges, or to carry out works, would not pass to successors; (b) the rule in *Tulk & Moxhay* (qv) is based on equitable principles, so there is no certainty that a court will grant an injunction to enforce a covenant; and (c) difficulty may arise where the covenanted land is subsequently sold off in parts eg for a housing scheme where there may be some question as to whether the benefit is annexed to each and every part.

The Law Reform Commission has proposed that freehold covenants acquire the status of legal rights, enforceable against successive owners of the 'servient' land, just like easements: Report on *Positive Covenants over freehold land and other proposals* (LRC 70, 2003). See COVENANT.

freeman. A person who possesses the *freedom* of a city or borough with its rights and privileges. Honorary freedom can be conferred by a local authority. See CIVIC HONOUR.

freeze assets. The colloquial term to describe an order of the court which prevents any dealing in assets to which the order relates eg an order to prevent monies leaving a bank account under powers conferred by the Finance Act 1983, s 18. See now Taxes Consolidation Act 1997, s 908 as amended by Finance Act 2002, s 132. See ATTACHMENT; BANKER AND CONFIDENTIALITY; INJUNCTION; STOP ORDER.

freight. The consideration (qv) paid to a carrier for the carriage of goods.

fresh evidence. New or additional evidence which an appellant (qv) in an appeal may call with the leave of the court. In order for fresh evidence to be admitted on appeal, it must be shown that: (a) the evidence sought to be adduced was in existence at the time of the trial but could not have been obtained with the use of reasonable diligence for use at the trial, (b) the evidence is such that if given it probably would have had an important influence on the result of the case, though it need not be decisive, and (c) the evidence must be apparently credible, though it need not be incontrovertible: *Murphy v Minister for Defence* [1991] 2 IR 161; *Smyth v Tunney* [1996] 1 ILRM 219, SC.

Although it is desirable to have *finality in litigation* (qv), a court should exercise its discretion and admit fresh evidence where a serious injustice would be suffered by a plaintiff such as where, for example, basic assumptions, common to both sides, have clearly been falsified by subsequent events, and when to refuse fresh evidence (eg plaintiff's loss of employment) would be an affront to common sense or a sense of justice: *Fitzgerald v Kenny* [1994] 2 ILRM 8, SC and 2 IR 383.

If leave is given, the evidence will normally be heard by the Court, although it may order that it be taken on deposition (qv). A witness, however, will not be permitted to give evidence at the appeal which recants his earlier sworn evidence and supports a different case: *Smyth & Ors v Tunney & Ors* [1992] ITLR (7 September), SC.

In certain circumstances the need for finality in litigation would be outweighed by the need to do justice: *O'Connor v O'Shea* [1989] ITLR (18 September), SC. Fresh evidence which was available but was not used will only be admitted in the most exceptional cases; however regard will be had to one of the principal objects of a criminal trial, being to ensure that an innocent person is not convicted: *Attorney-General v Kelly* [1937] IR 315.

Further evidence may be allowed in a case at the judge's discretion after the close of the case for the prosecution and the case for the defence: *The People v O'Brien* [1969] Frewen 343. However, a judge of the district court acted in excess of jurisdiction in re-opening a case to hear fresh evidence at an adjourned hearing, in the absence of the accused's counsel of choice, the counsel having previously been excused from appearing: *Dawson v Hamill* [1990] ILRM 257.

The decision of the Supreme Court cannot, in the absence of fraud, be challenged in subsequent proceedings on the basis of new evidence: *Tassan Din v Banco Ambrosiano* [1991] 1 IR 569, HC. See also *DPP v Quirke* [1991] CCA; *Riordan v Carroll t/a Wyvern Gallery* [1996] 2 ILRM 263, HC; *Gill v Philip O'Reilly & Co Ltd* [2003] 1 IR 434, SC. See also RSC Ord 86, r 24. See DE NOVO; FINALITY IN LITIGATION; SET ASIDE.

friend, my. The term used by counsel in a case to refer to counsel on the opposing side.

friend in court. See MCKENZIE FRIEND; NEXT FRIEND.

friendly society. A society established for the purpose of providing by voluntary subscription of its members for the relief or maintenance of its members and their families during sickness or other infirmity or in old age or in widowhood or for the relief or maintenance of their orphan children during minority: Friendly Societies Act 1896, s 8. It also includes a society providing for life and endowment insurance, or established for a social educational or recreational purpose and includes working-men's clubs.

A friendly society may be registered with the Registrar of Friendly Societies; certain privileges apply to registered societies (FSA 1896, s 32–37). A friendly society is not a corporation; consequently its property is vested in its trustees (FSA 1896, s 49). See also Registry of Friendly Societies Acts 1936 and 1977. An arranging debtor (qv) or a bankrupt (qv) who is a treasurer of a friendly society, must pay the full amount of his debt to the society before paying his other creditors a composition (qv) or dividend (FSA 1896; Bankruptcy Act 1988, s 81(10)).

New rules governing the qualification for appointment as auditors to friendly societies have been enacted: Companies Act 1990, s 187. Additionally, insurance activities permitted to be carried on by friendly societies are now limited to mutual, self-help and small-scale activities: Insurance Act 1989, s 28. See Friendly Societies Regulations 1988, SI No 74 of 1988; Friendly Societies Regulations 1992, SI No 59 of 1992; Friendly Societies (Amendment) Regulations 2002, SI No 143 of 2002. See also Taxes Consolidation Act 1997, s 211. Compare with INDUSTRIAL AND PROVIDENT SOCIETY. See also IRISH FINANCIAL SERVICES REGULATORY AUTHORITY.

frivolous action. See ABUSE OF PROCESS.

frontier workers. Workers who cross a border of an EU state when going to and from work; if they become unemployed, they are entitled under community regulations to social security benefits in the State in which they reside as though they were employed in that State: Case C-311/01 *Commission v Kingdom of the Netherlands* [2003] ECJ.

frozen sperm and ova. See ARTIFICIAL INSEMINATION.

fructus industriales. [Fruits of industry.]

fructus naturales. [Fruits of nature.]

fruit juices. Provision has been made for prescribing, and harmonising within the European Union, standards for the composition and labelling of fruit juices and certain similar products: EC (Marketing of Fruit Juices and Certain Similar Products) Regulations 2003, SI No 240 of 2003. It is an offence to fail to comply with the regulations. The regulations give effect to Directive (EC) 2001/112.

frusta legis auxilium quaerit qui in legem committit. [He who offends against the law vainly seeks the help of the law.] He who comes to equity must come with clean hands. See EQUITY, MAXIMS OF.

frustration, self-induced. Frustration of a contract as a result of a person's own conduct or the conduct of other persons for whom he is responsible. Self-induced frustration will not relieve that party from liability under the contract. The party pleading frustration must show that he took all reasonable steps to prevent the contract being frustrated. See *Herman v Owners of SS Vicia* [1942] IR 304; *Byrne v Limerick Steamship Co Ltd* [1946] IR 138; *Shindler v Northern Raincoat Co* [1960] 2 All ER 239.

frustration of contract. Impossibility of performance of a contract which excuses the parties from performance. Frustration is the premature determination of an agreement between parties, lawfully entered into and in course of operation at the time of its premature determination, owing to the occurrence of an intervening event or change or circumstances so fundamental as to be regarded by the law both as striking at the root of the agreement and as entirely beyond what was contemplated by the parties when they entered into the agreement: *Cricklewood Property and Investment Trust v Leightons Investment Trust* [1945] AC 221.

Frustration takes place when a supervening event occurs without the default of either party and for which the contract makes no sufficient provision; the event must so significantly change the nature of the contractual rights and obligations that it would be unjust to hold the parties to the stipulations of the contract: *Neville & Sons Ltd v Guardian Builders Ltd* [1995] 1 ILRM 1, SC.

The basis of the doctrine of frustration is that there is a supervening event which must be so unexpected and beyond the contemplation of the parties, even as a possibility, that neither party can be said to have accepted the risk of the event taking place when contracting it: *Zuphen & Others v Kelly Technical Services (Ireland) Ltd* [2000] ELR 277, HC.

Frustration may arise: (a) by statutory interference: *Baily v De Crespigny* [1869] LR 4 QB 180; (b) the destruction of a specific object necessary for the performance of the contract: *Taylor v Caldwell* [1863] 2 B S 836; (c) the non-existence of a state of things, the continued existence of which formed the basis of the contract: *Herne Bay SS v Hutton* [1903] 2 KB 123; (d) personal incapacity in contracts where the personal qualifications of one of the parties are important: *Robinson v Davison* [1871] LR 6 Ex 269; (e) frustration of the adventure or of the commercial or practical object of the contract: *Metropolitan Water Board v Dick Kerr & Co Ltd* [1918] AC 119.

The Employment Appeals Tribunal has held that the doctrine of frustration automatically terminates a contract of employment and therefore there is no onus on the employer to inform the employee that his contract of employment is at an end: *Boyle v Marathon Petroleum (Ireland) Ltd* [1995] ELR 2000, EAT.

On frustration, a contract is automatically discharged from the time of the event and cannot give rise to liabilities subsequent to the time of discharge. However a contract cannot normally be discharged through the doctrine of frustration if a contract term covers the events which are alleged to constitute frustration: *Mulligan v Browne* [1976] SC. See also *Fibrosa Spolka Cheyjna v Fairbairn, Lawson, Combe Barbour Ltd* [1943] AC 32; *Kearney v Saorstát Continental Shipping* [1943] Ir Jur Rep 8; *Herman v Owners of SS Vicia* [1942] IR 304; *Mc Guill v Aer Lingus & United Airlines* [1983] HC.

In relation to a lease (qv), in the absence of any express covenants to repair, a tenant may surrender his tenancy if the premises are destroyed or rendered uninhabitable by fire or some other inevitable accident: Landlord and Tenant Law Amendment Act (Ireland) 1860 (Deasy's Act), s 40. See also *Irish Leisure Industries Ltd v Gaiety Enterprises Ltd* [1975] HC; *National Carriers Ltd v Panalpina (Northern) Ltd* [1981] AC 675. See FRUSTRATION, SELF-INDUCED.

fuel. The Minister, for the purpose of preventing or limiting air pollution, is empowered to make regulations in relation to the standard, specification, composition and contents of fuel which is used in mechanically propelled vehicles or which is burnt in fireplaces: Air Pollution Act 1987, s 53. See COAL.

fugam fecit. [He has made flight.]

full age. See AGE OF MAJORITY.

functions. Term often used to describe powers and duties eg functions of the chief executive officer of a health board: Health Act 1970, s 17(4). See also Patents Act 1992, s 2(1). See STATUTORY DUTY.

functus officio. [Having discharged his duty.] Refers to a person who has exercised his authority and brought it to an end in a particular case. When a local government auditor has made a decision in relation to his functions, he is a *functus officio* and cannot alter or vary his decision: *R (Bridgeman) v Drury* [1894] 2 IR 489. Once an arbitrator makes an award, he is *functus officio*: *McStay v Assicurazioni Generali Spa* [1990] 8 ILT Dig 105. A judge of the district court having granted a public music or dance licence is *functus officio*; he is not entitled to grant, in effect, a reviewable licence: *Sheehan v Reilly* [1992] 10 ILT Dig 267, HC.

fundamental breach. A breach of contract which goes to the root of the contract entitling the innocent party to treat the contract as terminated and to sue for damages. To determine if a breach is fundamental, consideration is given to the seriousness of the breach, the effect of the breach and the likelihood of it recurring. See *Dundalk Shipping Centre Ltd v Roof Spray Ltd* [1979] HC. See also *Robb v James* [1881] 15 ILTR 59. See BREACH OF CONTRACT; EXCLUSION CLAUSES, RESTRICTION OF.

fundamental rights. Interests recognised and protected by the courts, which are superior to the law, the respect of which is a duty and the disregard of which is a wrong. Certain fundamental rights are *declared* in the constitution eg personal rights and rights relating to the family, education, private property and religion: 1937 Constitution, arts 40–44. It has been held that fundamental rights declared in the Constitution are not created by it; they are an acknowledgement that the individual has an inalienable possession of them: *McGee v Attorney-General* [1974] IR 101.

Not all fundamental rights are declared; there are many *implied* rights which the courts will declare as the occasion arises: *Ryan v Attorney-General* [1965] IR 294. These rights are not absolute rights, as their exercise may be regulated by the Oireachtas (qv) for the common good. Some fundamental rights are declared to attach to *citizens* and some to *persons*.

Examples of fundamental rights are: right to life; right to bodily integrity; equality before the law; inviolability of dwelling; personal liberty; freedom of expression; freedom to communicate; freedom to publish information; freedom of assembly; freedom to form associations and unions; freedom to travel; religious freedom; right to the private ownership of property; rights in relation to the family, marriage and education (qqv). See European Arrest Warrant Act 2003, s 37. See CHARTER OF FUNDAMENTAL RIGHTS; PERSONAL RIGHTS.

funds in court. When money in court is directed to be invested, it must be held in the name of the Accountant or his nominee, or in the case of funds standing to the credit of a *ward of court*, in the name of a nominee of the Accountant or of the *Registrar of Wards of Court*: RSC Ord 77, r 43(1) and (2) as amended by substitution by Rules of the Superior Courts (No 1) (Amendment to Order 77) 2001, SI No 268 of 2001.

funds of suitors. See SUITORS, FUNDS OF.

funeral expenses. Priority in payment out of a deceased's estate is given to funeral and testamentary expenses. See Succession Act 1965, ss 45–46; Sch 1. See ADMINISTRATION OF ESTATES; INSOLVENT ESTATE.

funfair. Means an entertainment where *fairground equipment* is used: Planning and Development Act 2000, s 239(1). *Fairground equipment* includes a wide variety of equipment eg a funfair ride which is designed to be in motion for entertainment, swings, dodgems, and equipment designed to be used as a slide or for bouncing on (PDA 2000, s 239(1)). An organiser of a funfair must not make available to the pub-

lic funfair equipment unless such equipment has a valid *safety certificate* in accordance with regulations (PDA 2000, s 239(4)). The organiser has a statutory duty of care to persons attending the funfair (PDA 2000, s 239(4)). The holding of a funfair, or works relating to a funfair, is not development and consequently does not require planning permission (PDA 2000, s 240). See also Planning and Development (Amendment) Act 2002, s 15. For procedure, administration and control in relation to applications for, and grant of, certificates of safety for funfair equipment, see Certification of Fairground Equipment Regulations 2003, SI No 449 of 2003.

furious driving. The offence committed by a person who, having the charge of any carriage or vehicle, does or causes to be done any bodily harm to any person, by wanton or furious driving or racing or other wilful misconduct: Offences Against the Person Act 1861, s 35. See also Defence Act 1954, s 159.

Further Education and Training Awards Council; FETAC. A body corporate with functions in the area of *further* education and training, *inter alia*: (a) to establish and publish policies and criteria for the making of awards and the *validation* of programmes, (b) to determine the standards of knowledge, skill or competence to be acquired by learners, (c) to make or recognise awards, (d) to ensure that providers have procedures for the assessment of learners which are fair and consistent: Qualifications (Education and Training) Act 1999, ss 12 and 14.

The Council may delegate to a 'relevant provider' (eg FÁS, CERT or Teagasc) the authority to make further education and training awards (Q(ET)A 1999, s 19). The National Qualifications Authority of Ireland may determine whether any particular programme of education and training is *further* or *higher* education and training (Q(ET)A 1999, s 10). See websites: *www.fetac.ie*; *www.hetac.ie* and *www.nqai.ie*. See HIGHER EDUCATION AND TRAINING AWARDS COUNCIL; NATIONAL QUALIFICATIONS AUTHORITY OF IRELAND.

future goods. See GOODS.

future interest. An interest limited to come into existence at some time in the future. A future interest in land is an interest which confers a right to the enjoyment of the land at a future time eg the right to land after the death of a living person. A future interest may be *vested* or *contingent*. A *vested* future interest is where the persons entitled to the interest are ascertained and the interest in ready to take effect on the determination of all the preceding interests; a *contingent* interest arises where either of these conditions is absent. Future interests can be classified also as reversions, legal remainders, future trusts and legal executory interests (qqv). [Bibliography: Pearce & Mee.]

future trust. A trust limited to come into existence at some time in the future. Future trusts are classified as: (a) *equitable remainders*, which, at the time of their creation, are capable of complying with rules governing legal remainders and (b) *equitable executory interests*, which at the outset infringe one or more of these rules eg springing trusts and shifting trusts.

G

Gaeltacht. [Irish speaking district.] An area designated as an area for the preservation and usage of the Irish language as the vernacular language. See Gaeltacht Areas Order 1956; Ministers and Secretaries (Amendment) Act 1956, s 2(2); Official Languages Act 2003, s 2(1). The Gaeltacht area in Rathcarn in Co Meath was created in 1935 by the migration of 27 families from Connemara, as part of the work of the Land Commission (qv) in the enlargement and rearrangement of small holdings and the relief of congestion.

Recognised schools in a Gaeltacht area are required to use their available resources, *inter alia*, to contribute to the maintenance of Irish as the primary community language: Education Act 1998, s 9(h). See also SI No 192 of 1974.

Provision has been made to revise and update legislation regarding housing in Gaeltacht areas to make the legislation more relevant to present needs: Housing (Gaeltacht) (Amendment) Act 2001. Topics covered include: the extent of the Gaeltacht, grants in relation to dwelling-houses, general provisions as to grants, increased grants in respect of work on off-shore islands, and recovery of grants and loans. Income received by persons in Gaeltacht areas under the Irish language student scheme known as *Scéim na bhFoghlaimeoirí*, is exempt from income tax: Finance Act 2004, s 12. For Údarás na Gaeltachta, see website: *www.udaras. ie.* See also COIMISINEIR TEANGA, AN; DEVELOPMENT PLAN; IRISH LANGUAGE; PLACENAME.

gage. A pledge or pawn. See MORTGAGE.

gain. Acquisition; something obtained or acquired; it is not limited to pecuniary gain nor to commercial profit: *Re Arthur Association for British and Colonial Ships* [1875] LR 10 Ch App 542 as cited in *Deane v VHI* [1992] ITLR (31 August), SC. *For gain* denotes an activity carried on, or a service supplied, which was done for a charge or payment (*Deane* case). See VOLUNTARY HEALTH INSURANCE.

gale. A rent or duty; a periodic payment of rent.

gale day. A rent day. Every tenancy from year to year is presumed to have commenced on the last *gale day* of the calendar year on which rent has become due and payable in respect of the premises, unless a contrary intention appears: Deasy's Act 1860, s 6. It has been held that the consistent and regular recognition by parties to a tenancy of a particular day of each month as the gale day, is *prima facie* evidence of the commencement of the tenancy on that day of some month, and of its being a monthly tenancy: *White v Mitchell* [1962] IR 348. The Law Reform Commission has recommended that s 6 should be repealed and replaced by a comprehensive set of statutory provisions governing the determination of periodic tenancies: *Consultation Paper on General Law of Landlord and Tenant Law* (LRC CP 28, 2003), para 18.18.

game. Wild birds, the hunting of which, the Minister may declare open season (qv) by order: Wildlife Act 1976, s 24. They include grouse, cock pheasant, woodcock, partridge, wild duck, mallard and certain species of wild goose and plover.

gaming. Playing a game (whether of skill or chance or partly of skill and partly of chance) for stakes hazarded by the players: Gaming and Lotteries Act 1956, s 2. Gaming is unlawful if: (a) the chances of all of the players, including the banker, are not equal; or (b) if a portion of the stakes are retained by the banker otherwise than as winnings; or (c) gaming is conducted by way of slot machines (GLA 1956, s 4). Gaming is lawful in specific instances at a circus, travelling show, carnival, public house, amusement hall and funfair. The winner of a lawful game can sue for the prize provided it is not a stake (GLA 1956, s 36(4)).

Part III of the 1956 Act dealing with the licensing of amusement halls and funfairs, does not have effect in any area unless there is for the time being in force a resolution by the local authority under GLA 1956, s 13 adopting it for its area: *The State (Divito) v Arklow* [1986] ILRM 123. It has been held that before a District Court grants a certificate authorising the issue of such a licence to permit gaming, it must be satisfied that the local authority had adopted such a resolution allowing gaming in its area; unless such a resolution is in force, neither the District Court nor the Circuit Court has jurisdiction to grant a certificate or the Revenue Commissioners to issue a licence: *Camillo v O'Reilly* [1988] ILRM 738, SC. See also *Cafolla v Ireland* [1986] ILRM 177; *DPP v Olympic Amusements* [1987] ILRM 320; *DPP v Cafolla* [1994] 1 IR 571, SC. For application provisions in relation to a certificate authorising a licence to permit gaming at an amusement hall or funfair, see DCR 1997 Ord 66, r 2.

For provisions on gaming machine licence duty, see Finance Act 1975, s 43 as amended by Finance Act 1993, s 71 and Finance Act 2003, ss 107–108. See *McKenna v Commissioner of An Garda* [1993] 3 IR 543, SC; *McKenna v Deery* [1998] 1 IR 62, SC.

The activity of operating gaming machines is a service within the meaning of art 50 of the consolidated (2002) EC Treaty; however restrictions on providing such a service which was imposed by national law, which confined gaming machines to casinos, was justified as it had the objective of protecting consumers and maintaining order in society: Case C-6/01 *Associacno Nacional de Operadores de Máquinas Recreativas (Anomar) v Portuguese State* [2003] ECJ. See AMUSEMENT MACHINE; CHEATING; LOTTERY; WAGERING CONTRACT.

garage. See EXTENSION OF HOUSE.

garbage. All kinds of victual, domestic and operational waste and any other substance generated during the normal operation of a ship; a harbour master is empowered to take samples of such garbage, as well as any oil, oily mixtures, noxious liquid substances, harmful substances or sewage from a ship: Sea Pollution Act 1991, s 3(1) and

s 25 as amended by Sea Pollution (Amendment) Act 1999, s 5. See HARBOUR AUTHORITIES; SEA POLLUTION.

garda, complaints against. A system of investigation and adjudication of complaints made by the public about the conduct of members of the (other than the Commission of the garda) is provided for in the Garda Síochána (Complaints) Act 1986. The legislation creates a civilian majority *Garda Síochána Complaints Board* which is charged with overseeing the investigation of complaints. The Board adjudicates on disciplinary charges through a *Tribunal* made up of three members of the Board. There is provision for an appeal from the *Tribunal* to the Garda Síochána Complaints *Appeal Board* but not from a decision of the Complaints Board itself.

The Complaints Board does not carry out a quasi-judicial function; its function is to reach an opinion on questions of fact after assessing evidence and considering the recommendations of its Chief Executive: *McCormack v Garda Complaints Board* [1997] 2 ILRM 321, HC and 2 IR 489. The Board does not give reasons for its decisions. As there is no appeal, the reasons for its decisions are not required to make effective a statutory right of appeal (*McCormack* case).

The exercise by the Complaints Board of its functions cannot be challenged on the ground that it formed the wrong opinion, as the merits of a decision cannot be challenged; the failure of the Board to state the reasons for its decision is not unjust or unfair: *Stanley v Garda Síochána Complaints Board* [2000] 2 ILRM 121, HC.

A complaint may be made orally or in writing at a garda station, to the Complaints Board, or to Garda Headquarters. The complaint is recorded and sent to the Chief Executive of the Complaints Board who decides whether the complaint is *admissible* or *inadmissible* (eg frivolous or vexatious) (GS(C)A 1986, s 4). If a complaint is vexatious, it remains vexatious whether there is an opposing statement or not: *Kelly v Garda Síochána Complaints Board* [2002] FL 4918, HC.

If admissible, the Garda Commissioner decides whether the complaint is suitable for informal resolution (GS(C)A 1986, s 5). If it is not suitable, the Commissioner must appoint an *investigating officer* to conduct an investigation into the complaint and to furnish a report to the Chief Executive (GS(C)A 1986, s 6).

If the report discloses a criminal offence, the Board must refer the matter to the Director of Public Prosecutions. If it discloses a disciplinary breach of a minor nature, the Board may refer the matter to the Commissioner to be dealt with informally (GS(C)A 1986, s 7). If the matter is not suitable for informal treatment, the Board must refer the matter to the *Tribunal* for adjudication. The *Tribunal* has a range of penalties available to it from a caution to dismissal (GS(C)A 1986, s 9) and its finding may be appealed by the garda to the *Appeal Board* (GS(C)A 1986, ss 10–11).

Natural justice requires that the text of a complaint, or an accurate statement thereof and any material made available to the decision maker, must also be made available to the garda and that he be given an opportunity to respond to same: *Dooner v Garda Síochána Complaints Board* [2000] ITLR (14 August), HC. In a particular case, it was held that the complainant was not prejudiced by procedural irregularities in a garda investigation of his complaint: *Trent v Commissioner of Garda Síochána* [1999] ITLR (5 April), HC. Also remarks made by the chairman of the Board, relating to the investigation stage of a complaint, were held not to disclose bias or prejudgment in relation to the adjudication stage which had not yet begun: *Corcoran v Garda Síochána Complaints Board* (2004) Irish Times, 6 February. See *Skeffington v Rooney* [1997] 2 ILRM 56, v and 1 IR 22; *Flood v Garda Síochána Complaints Board* [1997] 3 IR 321, HC and [1999] 4 IR 560, SC; *Landers v Garda Síochána Complaints Board* [1997] 3 IR 347, HC; *McCarthy v Garda Síochána Complaints Tribunal* [2002] 2 ILRM 341, SC. See Garda Síochána (Complaints) (Tribunal Procedure) Rules 1988, SI No 96 of 1988; Appeal Board Procedure Rules 1988, SI No 192 of 1988.

See 'Sed quis custodiet ipsos custodies' by Caroline Carney SC in *Bar Review* (October/November 2002) 335. For proposed new complaints scheme, see GARDA SÍOCHÁNA OMBUDSMAN COMMISSION.

garda, discipline of. Special considerations apply to the power of the State to dispense with the services of members of the armed forces, of the Garda Síochána, and of the prison service, because it is of vital concern to the community as a whole that the members of these services should be completely trustworthy: *The State (Jordan) v Commissioner of Garda Síochána* [1987] ILRM 107. Any alleged breaches of discipline should be dealt with expeditiously and as a matter of urgency: *McNeill v Commissioner of An Garda Síochána* [1997] 1 IR 469, SC.

An inquiry under the Garda Síochána (Discipline) Regulations is one which must be conducted judicially in accordance with the procedures laid down, but this does not constitute the exercise of judicial power: *Keady v Garda Commissioner* [1989] 7 ILT Dig 260. It has also been held that to allow a garda disciplinary inquiry to proceed after the accused member had been acquitted of identical criminal charges would be unfair and oppressive: *McGrath v Garda Commissioner* [1990] ILRM 817, SC, and Regulation 38 of Garda Síochána (Discipline) Regulations 1989, SI No 94 of 1989. See also *Stroker v Doherty* [1991] 1 IR 23, SC; *Ryan v Commissioner* [1992] HC. However, allegations of criminal conduct, which have been the subject of a *nolle prosequi* (qv) before a court, may be aired before a garda disciplinary inquiry: *Keady v Garda Commissioner* [1992] ILRM 312, SC. The 1989 Regulations cannot be applied to conduct or events occurring before they were brought into force: *Healy v Garda Commissioner* (1993) Irish Times, 14 July.

In a particular case, it was held that evidence of a relationship between the complainant and a witness could not be said to constitute new evidence: *Cahill v Garda Commissioner* [2000] ITLR (31 July), HC.

A garda accused of 'discreditable conduct' is entitled to know precisely what is alleged against him: *Deasy v Garda Commissioner* [1999] ELR 84, HC. It is not essential that misconduct be established before a probationer garda could be discharged: *Duffy v Commissioner* [1999] 2 IR 81, HC. See also *O'Shea v Garda Commissioner* [1993] ELR 229, HC; *Mc Neill v Garda Commissioner* [1995] 1 ILRM 321, HC; *Fitzpatrick v Commissioner of an Garda Síochána* [1996] ELR 244, HC; *McAuley v Commissioner* [1996] 3 IR 208, SC. See also Garda Síochána (Police Co-operation) Act 2003, ss 5–6. See ACQUITTAL; ADMINISTRATIVE TRIBUNAL; POLICE CO-OPERATION.

garda, identification of. In relation to road traffic matters, a person is not bound to comply with a request, demand or requirement of a garda unless he is either in uniform or produces, if requested, an official identification or such other evidence of his identity as may be prescribed: Road Traffic Act 1961, s 111.

garda as prosecutor. See PROSECUTOR.

garda associations. Provision has been made for the establishment of representative associations for various ranks in the Garda Síochána: Garda Síochána Act 1924, s 13 inserted by Garda Síochána Act 1977, s 1(1); Police Forces Amalgamation Act 1925, s 14. See also Garda Síochána (Associations) Regulations 1978, SI No 135 of 1978 as amended by SI No 151 of 1983, SI No 366 of 1994, and SI No 706 of 2003.

garda compensation. The scheme whereby compensation is paid out of public moneys in respect of death from injury of, or personal injuries (not causing death) to, a garda which injury was maliciously inflicted on him in the course of or in relation to the performance by him of his duties as a member of the Garda Siochána: Garda Síochána (Compensation) Act 1941.

An application for compensation is made to the Minister who will authorise the applicant to apply to the High Court, unless the Minister is of opinion that the injuries are of a minor character (GS(C)A 1941, s 6).

The phrase 'personal injuries not causing death' suggests that the minimum level of injury required is considerably above that of a nosebleed and associated bleeding: *McGee v Minister for Finance* [1997] 1 ILRM 301, HC and [1996] 3 IR 234, HC. The certification by the Minister authorising the applicant to apply to the High Court (GS(C)A 1941, s 6(1)(b)) cannot be set aside by the court (*McGee* case).

The High Court is empowered to fix the amount of compensation in accordance with the Act: GS(C)A 1941, ss 8 and 10 as amended by the Garda Síochána (Compensation) (Amendment) Act 1945, s 2. See *McLoughlin & Ors v Minister for the Public Service* [1986] ILRM 28; *Conroy v Commissioner of Garda Síochána* [1988] HC.

The garda compensation scheme also applies to the officers and staff of the *Criminal Assets Bureau*; it also applies to solicitors employed in the office of the Chief State Solicitor in respect of injuries maliciously inflicted on them because of anything done by them in a professional capacity on behalf of the Bureau: Criminal Assets Bureau Act 1996, s 18(3).

Garda Inspectorate. The Minister for Justice announced on 5 August 2004 the intention of the government to establish a Garda Inspectorate, staffed by civilians, which would act as an audit and inspection body, reporting directly to the Minister. The Inspectorate would examine procedures, mechanisms and methods within the Garda Síochána to ensure that they are working well, that they provide value for money and that they comply with best international standards. The Inspectorate will be independent of the proposed Garda Síochána Ombudsman Commission.

Garda Síochána. The national police force, the general direction and control of which is vested in the Commissioner of the Garda Síochána, who is appointed by and may be removed by the government: Police Force Amalgamation Act 1925, ss 6 and 8. He is responsible to the Minister for Justice. The Commissioner is authorised to enrol and appoint women to be members of the force by the Garda Síochána Act 1958.

Provision has been made for the admission of persons as *trainees*, who may subsequently be appointed as gardaí; such subsequent appointment must be on *probation* (qv) for a period of two years: Garda Síochána (Admissions and Appointments) Regulations 1988, SI No 164 of 1988. The Commissioner exercising the power to dismiss a trainee must observe the rules of natural justice and fair procedures; his decision is one which comes within the ambit of decisions which are subject to judicial review: *Beirne v Garda Commissioner* [1993] ILRM 1, SC. See Admission and Appointment (Amendment) Regulations 2000, SI No 164 of 2000.

Regulations have been made providing for: (i) the introduction of a pre-entry physical competence test and the abolition of the height requirement for entry to the garda síochána, and (ii) the extension of the probationary period of garda trainees in certain circumstances: Garda Síochána (Admissions and Appointments) (Amendment) Regulations 2001, SI No 498 of 2001. See Protection of Employees (Fixed-Term Work) Act 2003, s 17(a).

The selection procedure for promotion to the rank of Assistant Commissioner has also been changed: Garda Síochána (Promotion) (Amendment) Regulations 2001, SI No 392 of 2001.

Members of the garda may serve outside the State with the peace-keeping forces of the United Nations: Garda Síochána Act 1989. A compulsory retirement age for *new entrants* to the gardaí has been set at 55 years of age, with the possibility of extension to 60 subject to meeting certain health, fitness and competence criteria: Public Service Superannuation (Miscellaneous Provisions) Act 2004, ss 4 and 10(3). See *Garvey v Ireland* [1979] 113 ILTR 61; *DPP (Lenihan) v McGuire* [1996] 3 IR 586, HC. See also Garda Síochána Act 1924. See Garda Síochána (Retirement) Regulations 2003, SI No 273 of 2003; Garda Síochána (Ranks) Order 2004, SI No 222 of 2004. See *Re Employment Equality Bill 1996* [1997] 2 IR 321, SC and ELR 132. See Private Security Services Act 2004, s 34.

Under draft legislation, it is proposed to reform the law relating to the administration and management of the Garda, including in particular the respective roles of the Garda Commissioner and the Minister for Justice: Garda Síochána Bill 2004. The Bill also provides for the establishment of an independent body to be known as the Garda Ombudsman Commission. See also Road Traffic Bill 2004, s 21. See 'Is there something offbeat about An Garda Síochána?' by solicitor Pat Igoe in *Law Society Gazette* (April 2004) 10. See *Report on Performance and Accountability for the Garda Síochána* (September 2002). See website: *www.garda.ie*. [Bibliography: O'Sullivan D J; Walsh D.] See COMMON POLICIES; EUROPEAN POLICE OFFICE; JOINT INVESTIGATION TEAMS; NON-UNIFORMED GARDA; PEACE OFFICER; POLICE CO-OPERATION; PROSECUTOR; SED QUIS CUSTODIET IPSOS CUSTODIES.

Garda Síochána Ombudsman Commission. Under draft legislation, an independent body proposed to be established, with the primary function of investigating complaints by members of the public against members of the Garda Síochána and in that respect it will replace the existing Garda Síochána Complaints Board, which was established under the Garda Síochána (Complaints) Act 1986: Garda Síochána Bill 2004. The agreed *Programme for Government* contains a commitment to establish an independent Garda Inspectorate, which will have the power to investigate complaints, and will have the powers of an Ombudsman. The Complaints Board has itself acknowledged that there are problems with the present arrangements regarding Garda accountability in this area and that they must be addressed. The government has therefore decided that a new mechanism is needed to ensure openness and transparency in dealing with complaints against members of the Garda Síochána.

The Commission will have comprehensive powers of investigation to deal with complaints and it will have ultimate control and oversight of all complaints processed in accordance with the provisions of the Bill. It will also have the power to investigate of its own motion, ie without a complaint having to be made, any case involving the Garda Síochána where death or serious harm to a person has occurred where it is desirable in the public interest or, any matter that appears to it to indicate that a member of the Garda Síochána may have committed an offence, or behaved in a manner that would justify disciplinary proceedings. The Commission will also be charged with examining practices, policies and procedures within the Garda Síochána which may give rise to complaints.

garnish. To warn.

garnishee. A debtor in whose hands a debt has been attached by a court. Garnishee proceedings enable a judgment creditor (qv) to have assigned to him the benefit of any debt owed by the garnishee to the judgment debtor (qv). A *garnishee order* is an order, served on a garnishee, attaching a debt in his hands. See *Fitzpatrick v Daf Sales & Allied Irish Finance Ltd* [1989] ILRM 777. For the rules governing the *attachment of debts* by garnishee, See RSC Ord 45, rr 1–8; see also Circuit Court Rules 2001 Ord 38. [Bibliography: Glanville.] See ATTACHMENT; NOTICE OF ATTACHMENT.

gas. See BORD GÁIS; COMMERCIAL PROCEEDINGS; COMMISSION FOR ENERGY REGULATION.

gas capacity statement. A statement of forecasts for the following period of seven years in respect of capacity, forecast flows and customer demand on each part of the natural gas system, which the Commission for Energy Regulation is required to publish annually: Gas (Interim) (Regulation) Act 2002, s 19.

gay. See HOMOSEXUAL.

Gazette. The official magazine of the Law Society of Ireland providing news and relevant information for the solicitors' profession. It was relaunched as a full-colour,

56-page magazine in 1997 and went on to win top prizes in Ireland's leading magazine awards. The magazine has a circulation of 8,000 copies. For archive copies, see website: *www.lawsociety.ie/Gazargen.htm.* [Editor, Law Society Gazette, Law Society of Ireland, Blackhall Place, Dublin 7. Tel: +353–1–672 4828; fax: +353–1–672 4801; email: *c.oboyle@lawsociety.ie.*] See BAR REVIEW.

gazumping. Popularly understood to describe the situation in which a vendor of a house which is sold *subject to contract*, withdraws from the sale or threatens to do so, in expectation of receiving a higher price elsewhere. A Supreme Court judge has expressed the view that he would prefer that the occasional gazumper go unbound rather than that people be involved in needless uncertainty leading often to long drawn out litigation: O'Flaherty J in *Boyle & Boyle v Lee & Goyns* [1992] ILRM 65, SC.

The Law Reform Commission has made recommendations to control gazumping. One recommendation was that advertisements of houses in new developments should specify the number of houses offered for sale at each price level and the period for which this price is fixed. See LRC, *Report on Gazumping* (LRC 59, 1999). See subject to contract.

gearing. The ratio between a company's debt and its equity. A company is said to be highly geared where it has borrowed heavily in relation to its share capital.

gelatine. 'A colourless or yellowish water-soluble protein prepared by boiling animal hides and bones, used in foods, glue and photographic emulsions': *Collins English Dictionary.* Gelatine intended for human consumption must be produced from the following raw material: bones; hides and skins of farmed ruminant animals; pig skins; poultry skin, tendons and sinews; wild game hides and skins; fish skin and bones: EC (Gelatine) Regulations 2002, SI No 4 of 2002. It is an offence to produce, place on the market or import gelatine intended for human consumption other than in compliance with these regulations, which implement Decision (EC)1999/724 of 28 October 1999.

gender balance. Balance of representation on gender grounds. The first statute to provide for *equality in representation* as regards men and women on the board of a state-sponsored organisation was the Broadcasting Authority (Amendment)

Act 1993, s 7 which provided, *inter alia*, that where the number of members of the RTE Authority is seven, not less than three of them must be men and not less than three of them must be women.

Also Vocational Education Committees are required to ensure gender balance when recommending members for appointment to the governing bodies of an Institute of Technology: Regional Technical Colleges (Amendment) Act 1994, s 4(2) and Dublin Institute of Technology Act 1994, s 4(2). It has been held that there are no constitutional or statutory difficulties about ballot procedures that are intended to produce fair gender balances in elected bodies: *Grennan v DIT* [1997] 3 IR 415, HC and [1995] ELR 188, HC.

At least 40% of the solicitor members and of the lay members of the *Solicitor's Disciplinary Tribunal* (qv) are required to be men and at least 40% to be women: Solicitors (Amendment) Act 1960, s 6 as substituted by Solicitors (Amendment) Act 1994, s 16 and amended by Solicitors (Amendment) Act 2002, s 8. For other references to gender balance, see Courts Services Act 1998, s 11(2); Qualifications (Education and Training) Act 1999, ss 66, 6(6), 13(6), 22(6); National Disability Authority Act 1999, s 20(3)(b); Sustainable Energy Act 2002, s 10(19); Taxi Regulation Act 2003, s 54(9)(a); State Examination Commission (Establishment) Order 2003, art 7(4), SI No 373 of 2003; Personal Injuries Assessment Board Act 2003, s 56(7). See EQUALITY BEFORE THE LAW; GENDER GROUND; INTERVIEW BOARD.

gender ground. An employer is prohibited from discriminating against an employee or a prospective employee on *gender grounds* i e treating one person less favourably than the other on the grounds that one is a woman and the other is a man: Employment Equality Act 1998, ss 8(1) and 6, as amended by Equality Act 2004 s 4, in order to include as discrimination on gender grounds of less favourable treatment on grounds of pregnancy or maternity leave. However, these prohibitions are without prejudice to positive action on equal opportunities i e any measures (a) maintained or adopted with a view to ensuring full equality in practice between men and women in their employments, and (b) providing for specific advantages so as (i) to make it easier for an under-represented sex to pursue a vocational activity, or (ii) to prevent or compensate for disadvantages in professional careers (EEA 1998, s 24(1) amended by substitution by EA 2004, s 15). Also it is not unlawful for an employer to confer benefits on women in connection with pregnancy, maternity (including breastfeeding) or adoption (EEA 1998, s 26(1)).

The Equality Tribunal awarded a female school teacher, who it held was discriminated against because of her gender in an interview for the position of school principal and was subsequently victimised when she complained about the matter, compensation of €10,000 in relation to the discrimination and €110,000, the equivalent of two years' salary, in relation to the victimisation: *McGinn v St Anthony's Boys National School* (2004) Irish Times, 20 August, ET (under appeal).

A person must not discriminate on *gender grounds* in disposing of goods or premises or in providing a service or accommodation; treating one person less favourably than another person, in a comparable situation, because one is a male and the other is female is discrimination: Equal Status Act 2000, ss 3, 5 and 6, amended by EA 2004, ss 48–49. This does not apply where embarrassment or infringement of privacy can reasonably be expected to result from the presence of a person of another gender (ESA 2000, s 5(2)(g)).

Where, in any proceedings, facts are established by, or on behalf of, a person from which it may be presumed that there has been direct or indirect gender *discrimination* in relation to that person, it shall be for the other party concerned to prove the contrary: European Communities (Burden of Proof in Gender Discrimination Cases) Regulations 2001, SI No 337 of 2001. The Equality Act 2004 revokes this SI in part and enacts similar provisions in respect of proceedings on gender and other discriminatory grounds (EA 2004, ss 38 and 64).

See 'Sex equality and the Equal Status Act' by Cliona Kimber BL and Marguerite Bolger BL in *Bar Review* (January 2001) 198. See 'Gender InJustice – A Report on Women Lawyers in Ireland' by Ivana Bacik BL in *Bar Review* (December 2003) 260; and 'Ascent of a Woman' by Ivana Bacik BL in *Law Society Gazette* (July 2004) 16. See *Fox v National Council of the Blind* [1995] ELR 74, EO; *Flynn v Garda Commissioner* [1995] ELR 129, EO; *Kearney v Monkstown Park CBC* [1995] ELR 193, LC; *Duberry v Monkstown Park CBC*

[1995] ELR 196, LC; *Nathan v Bailey Gibson Ltd* [1996] ELR 114, SC and [1998] 2 IR 162, SC; *SIPTU v Peamount Hospital* [1999] ELR 39, LC; *Gleeson v Rotunda Hospital* [2000] ELR 206, LC; *Nelson v Boxing Union of Ireland* [2001] ELR 289, EO; *161 Named Female Employees v University of Dublin, Trinity College* [2002] ELR 30, EO; *Mid-Western Health Board v Fitzgerald* [2003] FL 8752, HC. [Bibliography: Eardly (2); Reid M.] See DISCRIMINATION; EQUALITY CLAUSE; PENSION SCHEME AND DISCRIMINATION; SEX DISCRIMINATION; UNIFORM, WEARING OF.

gene therapy. 'It is ethical to use gene therapy to modify the genome of human somatic cells provided that the risk is not disproportionate to the benefit. Gene therapy of gametes (sperm or ova) though not yet considered safe for use in humans, may become so with advancing technology. If it then has as its aim the improvement of health it may be ethical': Medical Council, *A Guide to Ethical Conduct and Behaviour* (6th edn, 2004) para 24.2. See 'Human genetics and the need for regulation' by Stephen Dodd BL in *Bar Review* (May 2001) 418. See EMBRYO IMPLANTATION; GENETIC TESTING; HUMAN REPRODUCTION; REPRODUCTIVE MEDICINE.

genealogy. The study of the descent and relationship of persons. See NATIONAL LIBRARY OF IRELAND.

general agent. See AGENT.

general average. See AVERAGE.

General Council of the Bar of Ireland. See BAR COUNCIL.

general damages. The damages which the law presumes to flow from the defendant's act eg damages for pain and suffering in the case of personal injury. Because of the need for *finality in litigation*, the damages must be assessed once and for all, so the plaintiff is entitled to *prospective damages* to compensate him for future suffering or future loss of earnings. A plaintiff cannot seek a variation of damages based on matters occurring after a trial eg where he has suffered more damages than appeared probable on the evidence given at the trial: *Dalton v Minister for Finance* [1989] ILRM 519. However, where a dramatic alteration has taken place it may be proper to consider evidence of that alteration: *O'Connor v O'Shea* [1989] ITLR (18 September), SC.

The poverty of the plaintiff is not to be taken into account in assessing damages. Also the bad impression which the plaintiff makes in court is not a relevant factor in the assessment of damages: *Deans v Sheridan* [1994] ITLR (1 January), SC. No account is to be taken of any sum payable by way of insurance or pension or gratuity in consequence of an injury sustained by the plaintiff: Civil Liability (Amendment) Act 1964, s 2.

The Supreme Court will only interfere with an award of general damages in a personal injuries action where the court is of the view that the award is an entirely erroneous estimate of the damage or is plainly unreasonable: *Dunne v Honeywell Control Systems Ltd* [1993] ITLR (15 November), SC. See *Fitzgerald v Treacy* [2001] 4 IR 405, SC. See DAMAGES; FRESH EVIDENCE; KINLEN ORDER; SPECIAL DAMAGES.

general dealer. Any person buying otherwise than at a public auction held by a licensed auctioneer (qv), or selling old metal, scrap metal, broken metal or partly manufactured metal goods in specified quantities: General Dealers (Ireland) Act 1903, s 12. It is an offence to act as a general dealer without a licence (s 1). For application for a licence, see DCR 1997 Ord 67. See *Dunne v Lee* [1913] 2 IR 205.

general election. A general election for members of Dáil Éireann (qv) held in accordance with the 1937 Constitution, art 16(3)(2): Electoral Act 1992, s 2(1).

general legacy. See LEGACY.

general medical services. The Health (Miscellaneous Provisions) Act 2001, s 1(1)(b) updates the statutory basis for the supply of drugs, medicines and medical and surgical appliances under the general medical services and community drugs schemes, promoting as it does a more equitable and accountable service in this regard and making better provision for the delivery of community pharmacy services, amending by substitution s 59 of the Health Act 1970.

general meeting. See ANNUAL GENERAL MEETING; EXTRAORDINARY GENERAL MEETING.

general power. See POWER OF APPOINTMENT.

generalia specialia derogant. [Special things derogate from general things.]

generalia specialibus non derogant. [General things do not derogate from special things.] General statutes do not affect particular statutes unless the contrary intention appears. 'Where there are general words in a later Act capable of reasonable and sensible application without extending them to subjects specially dealt with by earlier legislation, you are not to hold that earlier and special legislation indirectly repealed, altered or derogated from merely by force of such particular words, without any indication of a particular intention to do so': *Seward v Vera Cruz* [1884] 10 App Cas 59 at 68, cited with approval in *Hatch v Governor of Wheatfield Prison* [1993] ITLR (29 March), SC and 11 ILT Dig 142.

The maxim is often given statutory recognition eg the exemptions from liability conferred by statute are unaffected by the Sale of Goods and Supply of Services Act 1980, s 4(2). See also *Welch v Bowmaker (Ireland) Ltd* [1980] IR 251; *National Authority for Occupational Safety and Health v Fingal Co Council* [1997] 1 ILRM 128, HC. See INTERPRETATION OF LEGISLATION.

generalia verba sunt generaliter intelligenda. [General words are to be understood generally.]

genetic engineering. See MICROORGANISM.

genetic fingerprinting. The production of a genetic profile of a person through the examination of his skin, hair or bodily fluids. It is claimed that the likelihood of two persons having the same DNA genetic code are less than one in five billion and that DNA fingerprinting will consequently have an important role to play in cases involving murder, rape, assault and in declarations of parentage (qqv). The *blood test* which can be ordered to determine parentage includes genetic fingerprinting carried out with the objective of ascertaining inheritable characteristics: Status of Children Act 1987, s 38 and *JPD v MG* [1991] 1 IR 47, SC. Genetic fingerprinting can also be utilised in particular instances where the taking of *bodily samples* is permitted. See Fennell in 8 ILT & SJ (1990) 227. See BODILY SAMPLES; BIOMETRICS; DNA.

genetic testing. 'Genetic testing may be of benefit in diagnosing an illness or predicting its development in the future. Individuals who undergo such testing should be counselled regarding the consequences of their actions and testing should not be done without their informed consent': Medical Council, *A Guide to Ethical Conduct and Behaviour* (6th edn, 2004) para 24.3. The

Irish Insurance Federation operates a voluntary code of practice under which information on genetic tests is not sought for life insurance policies below the value of €381,000. See EMBRYO IMPLANTATION; GENE THERAPY; HUMAN REPRODUCTION; REPRODUCTIVE MEDICINE.

genetically modified organism. An *organism* derived from the formation of a combination of genetic material by artificial techniques, or an organism inheriting such combination of genetic material: Environmental Protection Agency Act 1992, s 111(7). Organism means any multicellular, unicellular, subcellular or a cellular entity capable of replication or of transferring genetic material whether by natural or artificial processes (EPAA 1992, s 111(7)). The Minister may make regulations for the control, management, regulation or prohibition of any process or action involving a genetically modified organism (giving full effect to Directives (EEC) 90/219 and (EEC) 90/220): (EPAA 1992, s 111(1) as substituted by Protection of the Environment Act 2003, s 17(a)) and has done so: Genetically Modified Organism Regulations 1994, SI No 345 of 1994 as amended in 1996 and 1997, SIs Nos 348 of 1996, and 332 of 1997 and now substantially revoked by Genetically Modified Organisms (Deliberate Release) Regulations 2003, SI No 500 of 2003 which give effect to Directive (EC) 2001/18. The main objective of the 2003 regulations is to protect people and the environment from the deliberate release into the environment or marketing of such organisms.

Regulations have also been made which seek to protect people and the environment from any adverse effects arising from the *contained use* of genetically modified organisms: Genetically Modified Organism (Contained Use) Regulations 2001, SI No 73 of 2001 as amended by the 2003 regulations. With limited exceptions, all contained uses must comply with the regulations; proposed uses must be subjected to an environmental risk assessment which must be submitted, or otherwise made available, to the Environmental Protection Agency (EPA).

The definition of *contained use* depends on whether it relates to genetically modified *micro-organisms* (Part II) or genetically modified *organisms* (Part III). Subject to limited confidentiality requirements, a register of all contained use must be maintained by the EPA and made available to the general public. The regulations give effect to Directive (EC) 98/81 and replace Part II of the Genetically Modified Organism Regulations 1994.

There is now a framework to enable detailed rules to be introduced in respect of genetically modified plant varieties and plant genetic resources: European Communities (Beet Seed) Regulations 2001, SI No 142 of 2001. For regulations on the transboundary movement of genetically modified organisms, see SI No 54 of 2004. For regulations on genetically modified feedingstuffs, see SI No 424 of 2004. See EPAA 1992, s 99A (1)(m) inserted by PEA 2003, s 15. See also *Watson v Environmental Protection Agency* [2000] 2 IR 454, HC. See BIOETHICS, IRISH COUNCIL FOR; HARMFUL ORGANISMS.

Geneva Conventions. The four Conventions of 1949 dealing with the *laws of war*, aimed at protecting a number of specific categories of persons, largely in relation to *international armed conflicts* e g the wounded and sick during land and sea warfare, prisoners-of-war, and civilian populations under military occupation. These Conventions were given legal effect in this State by the Geneva Conventions Act 1962.

Two protocols to the Conventions were adopted in 1977 and given effect in Ireland by the Geneva Conventions (Amendment) Act 1998.

The *first protocol*: (a) extended the definition of armed conflict to include wars of national liberation, (b) entrenched the principle of proportionality to military operations to minimise the risk to civilians, (c) extended the category of *grave breaches* to include combat offences causing excessive loss of civilian life, (d) provided for the establishment of an *International Fact-Finding Commission*, and (e) provided for human rights standards e g in relation to the right to a fair trial.

The *second protocol*, which deals with non-international armed conflicts which meet a relatively high threshold, (a) provides for greater protection of civilians, with a specific prohibition on acts or threats of violence the primary purpose of which is to spread terror among the civilian population, (b) provides for an amnesty at the end of the conflict, and (c) provides a number of safeguards for detainees and internees.

See HORS DE COMBAT; MERCENARY; PER-
FIDY; PRISONER-OF-WAR; RED CROSS; SPY-
ING; WAR.

genocide. The offence committed by a person who commits certain acts with intent to
destroy, in whole or in part, a national,
ethnical, racial or religious group, by: (a)
killing members of the group, or (b) causing serious bodily or mental harm to members of the group, or (c) deliberately
inflicting on the group, conditions of life
calculated to bring about its destruction in
whole or in part, or (d) imposing measures
intended to prevent births within the
group, or (e) forcibly transferring children
of the group to another group: Genocide
Convention, art 2 (United Nations,
9 December 1948); Genocide Act 1973 as
amended by Criminal Justice Act 1994,
s 51(8). See also International War Crimes
Tribunals Act 1998, Sch 3, art 4, and
Sch 4, art 2. See WAR CRIMES.

gentleman's agreement. Popularly understood to mean an agreement, the performance of which rests on the honour of the
parties and is not intended to create legal
relations between the parties or to be
enforceable in a court of law. See LEGAL
RELATIONS.

geographical indications. The names of
food products which are given protection
under European law. There are two classes
of geographical indications: *protected designations of origin* (PDOs) and *protected geographical indications* (PGIs). For a PDO the
foodstuff must be produced, processed and
prepared in a fixed geographical area using
recognised skills and techniques and where
the quality is essentially or exclusively due
to the particular geographic environment,
with its inherent natural or human factors.
PGIs, on the other hand, require that only
part of the production, processing or
preparation takes place in the defined geographical area, so long as they comply with
registered specifications. Any direct or indirect use of the name of a PDO or PGI,
once registered, is prohibited, as well as any
misuse, imitation or evocation of the name,
even if the true origin of the product is
indicated. In 2004 the only products from
Ireland which had protection were Clare
Island Salmon, Imokilly Regato and
Timoleague Brown Pudding, while Irish
whiskey and Irish cream liqueur were protected under parallel rules for the protection of wines and spirits. See Case
C-216/01   *Budejovicky   Budvar   v*

Ammersin GmbH [2003] ECJ. See 'Food for
thought – protecting Irish brands' by Bernard O'Connor in *Law Society Gazette*
(March 2004) 14.

geographical name as trade mark. Under
previous legislation, it was possible to register a prominent geographical name as a
trade mark in Part B (qv) of the register of
trade marks if there was very compelling
evidence of *distinctiveness* (qv). See *Waterford Glass Ltd v Controller of Trade Marks*
[1984] ILRM 565. See TRADE MARK,
REGISTERED.

George Mitchell Scholarship. The scholarship scheme, established to honour US
Senator George Mitchell's contribution to
the cause of peace in Ireland and particularly to the Good Friday Agreement (qv),
under which scheme US citizens and
nationals, who are students or research
scholars with a high level of academic
achievement, will be able to study or carry
out research at certain designated Irish
third-level educational institutions, including institutions in Northern Ireland:
George Mitchell Scholarship Fund
Act 1998.

gestation period. The extension to the perpetuity period which is permitted to take
account of children *en ventre sa mere* (qv),
where the gestation period actually exists
and where the subsequent birth is relevant
to the perpetuity period eg a gift *to the first
son of A to reach the age of 21* is valid if A is
alive at the time of the gift and dies subsequently leaving his wife pregnant with their
first child, who is subsequently born a son
and attains 21. See PERPETUITIES, RULE
AGAINST.

gift. A gratuitous grant or transfer of property. The person giving the gift is the *donor*
and the recipient is the *donee*. For a valid
gift there must be an intention to give and
such acts as are necessary to give effect to
the intention. See *AIB Finance Ltd v
Sligo Co Council* [1995] 1 ILRM 81, HC. A
gift in a will is a *devise* (real property) or a
bequest (personal property). A gift may be
subject to taxation: Capital Acquisitions
Tax Consolidation Act 2003, ss 4–8.

Gifts, the value of which exceed £500 (€
635), given to certain office holders
(eg Minister of government, Attorney-
General) or to the spouse or child of the
office holder, are deemed to be gifts to the
State: Ethics in Public Office Act 1995,

s 15. Donations ie contributions for political purposes, are excluded. However, see CORRUPTION.

Under an *enduring power of attorney*, the attorney may, if specific provision is made to that effect in the instrument creating the power, dispose of the property of the donor by way of gift, but limited to: (a) gifts of a seasonal nature or on birthdays or marriage anniversaries of person related or connected to the donor, and (b) gifts to any charity to which the donor made or might be expected to make gifts: Powers of Attorney Act 1996, s 6(5). The gifts must not be unreasonable having regard to all the circumstances and in particular the extent of the donor's assets.

A person who donates money to the Minister for Finance for use towards public expenditure, may deduct the donation, if the Minister accepts it, from his income for the year in which the gift is made: Taxes Consolidation Act 1997, s 483. It has been clarified that a similar donation from a company is regarded as a trading loss by the company: Finance Act 2002, s 56. See also State Property Act 1954, s 19.

Where a client intends to confer a gift by deed to the solicitor drafting the deed and the gift is of a significant amount, the solicitor should advise the client to obtain independent legal advise: *A Guide to Professional Conduct of Solicitors in Ireland* (2002) ch 3.5. This is not necessary where the amount is a token gift of a nominal amount. See CLASS GIFTS; DONATIO MORTIS CAUSA; JOINT ACCOUNT; LAPSE; POLITICAL DONATION; UNSOLICITED GOODS.

gift tax. A tax applicable to gifts *inter vivos* introduced by the Capital Acquisitions Tax Act 1976 and now consolidated by the Capital Acquisitions Tax Consolidation Act 2003. Charged to tax is property to which a donee becomes beneficially entitled in possession otherwise than 'on a death' (CTCA 2003, s 5). [Bibliography: Condon J & Muddiman J.] See BUSINESS RELIEF; CAPITAL ACQUISITIONS TAX; SELF-ASSESSMENT.

given. It was held in a particular case that the date on which a planning decision was *given* was the date stated upon the order which gave effect to the decision, unless the contrary were proved: *Keelgrove Properties Ltd v An Bord Pleanála* [2000] 1 IR 47, HC.

In a subsequent decision, the Court held that a distinction must be made between the *decision* of a planning authority to grant a planning permission and the *grant* itself; the day upon which a planning decision is '*given*' is the date on which the planning authority decides to grant permission and not the date of the grant itself: *Henry v Cavan County Council* [2001] 2 ILRM 161, HC and 4 IR 1.

global maritime distress and safety system; GMDSS. The radio communications equipment required to be carried on cargo ships of 300 tons or more and on passenger ships registered in the State and on other such ships registered outside the State while they are in a port in the State: Merchant Shipping (Radio) Rules 1992, SI No 224 of 1992.

global system mobile; GSM. Certain frequency bands are designated for the co-ordinated introduction of a public pan-European cellular digital land-based mobile communication system in the European Union. See Directive (EEC) No 87/372; SI No 416 of 1994. See also Wireless Telegraphy (Third Generation and GSM Mobile Telephony Licence) Regulations 2002, SI No 345 of 2002 and 2003, SI No 340 of 2003. See M-COMMERCE; MOBILE PHONE; THIRD GENERATION.

global valuation. The valuation (qv) of properties taken as a whole, wherever situated, of a specified *public utility undertaking* or such undertakings of a specified description, which the Minister may by order direct the Commissioner of Valuations to provide for the determination of: Valuation Act 1988, s 4. This provides a special method of establishing the valuation of such undertakings (eg ESB, Bord Gáis) and is an exception to the Valuation Act 1852, s 11. See SI No 268 of 1988 and SI No 281 of 2003. See Valuation Act 2001, ss 53–54.

glue-sniffing. See SOLVENTS, SALE OF.

go-slow. See WORKING TO RULE.

going concern. The concept concerning a company which implies that the enterprise will continue in operational existence for the foreseeable future; in particular that the profit and loss account and balance sheet assume no intention or necessity to liquidate or curtail significantly the scale of the operation: Standard Accounting Practice as cited in *Re Clubman Shirts Ltd* [1991] ILRM 43, HC. In determining the value of shares of an oppressed minority share-holder of a company which cannot be regarded to be a going concern, the assets of the company should be valued on a break up basis.

In a particular case, the court held that as the petitioner's only undertaking was the holding *of shares in its subsidiary, the peti-tioner was not a 'going concern'*: Re Tuskar Resources plc [2001] 1 IR 668, HC. See ACCOUNTING PRINCIPLES; SHARES, COM-PULSORY PURCHASE OF.

gold directive. The EU directive dealing with *investment gold* whether in physical form or represented by payer transactions, such as securities: Directive (EC) 98/80 of 12 October 1998; Value Added Tax Act 1972, s 6A inserted by Finance Act 1999 and amended by Finance Act 2000, s 109.

golden handcuff. Colloquial expression to describe a restrictive covenant in an employment contract for which the employee may be given a substantial sum of money (hence 'golden'), with the objective of preventing him setting up in competition with his employer for a period of time in the event that he should terminate his employment. Such a covenant may be void as being in restraint of trade and a restric-tion on competition. See RESTRAINT OF TRADE.

golden handshake. Popularly understood to mean payments made as compensation for loss of office or as consideration for or in connection with retirement from office: Companies Act 1963, ss 186–189. These payments must not be paid tax-free, except for the first £6,000 (€7,618), and the aggregate amount of them in any year must be disclosed in or along with the annual accounts (CA 1963, ss 185 and 191(1)(c) and (4)). See REDUNDANCY.

golden rule. The rule of construction for interpreting a statute which is utilised where the literal interpretation of the words would lead to such an absurdity that it is self-evident that the legislature could not have meant what is stated. Under the rule the grammatical and ordinary sense of the words may be modified so as to avoid an absurdity, repugnancy or inconsistency. See *Grey v Pearson* [1857] 6 HLC 61. See INTERPRETATION OF LEGISLATION.

golden share. Popularly understood to refer to a special share arrangement, combined with provisions of a company's memoran-dum, whereby one shareholder can effec-tively prevent the takeover of a company eg by limiting the size of shareholding of any one shareholder or consortium of shareholders. It is sometimes utilised in the privatisation of a state owned company where the government wishes to prevent foreign ownership eg in the case of the privatisation of Irish Life Assurance plc.

golden umbrella. Popularly understood to mean service contracts made with company directors which are for a long duration and at high remuneration, often with the objec-tive of deterring shareholders from remov-ing them due to the prohibitive damages which might ensue. Also known as a *golden parachute*. Service contracts of longer than five years are prohibited unless approved by the members of the company in meeting by ordinary resolution: Companies Act 1990, s 28. See REMUNERATION OF DIRECTORS.

Goldsmiths of Dublin, Company of. The company, established and incorporated by royal charter of Charles I on 22 December 1637, with power of enforcing prescribed minimum standards of *fineness* for the qual-ity of gold, silver and platinum to be used in manufacture, and the assay and hall-marking of all gold, silver and platinum wares submitted to it. It also has power to make bye-laws, and the powers of search seizure and destruction of sub-standard wares. The company controls the assay office and is described in the charter as the *Wardens and Commonality of Goldsmiths of the city of Dublin*. See Hallmarking Act 1981. See HALLMARKING.

golf. A golf course need not be constructed so that greens and tees are not close to one another for safety reasons; such a rule would impose serious limitations on where golf could be played: *Potter v Carlisle & Cliftonville Golf Club Ltd* [1939] NI 114, CA. In this case a golf player while putting on a green was struck by a ball driven by a player from an adjoining tee and lost the sight of an eye. The court held that when the plaintiff paid his green fee and received his ticket, he impliedly agreed to take the course as he found it, provided it was free from unusual dangers or traps, and to accept the risks of the game as between himself and the Club, and that the injury he received was due to a risk of the game and not to any negligent design or construction of the course. The court held that 'if the (defendants) are guilty of actionable negligence, then all the well-known clubs such as St Andrews, are also guilty of actionable negligence.'

A person who goes on to a golf course, just as a person who crosses the street, takes certain risks inherent to the place where he is: *Cleghorn v Oldham* 43 TLR 465. However, a golfer who was struck on the head by a ball after a 'viciously hooking' shot was awarded £5,250 (€6,666) damages on the basis that a net or fence would have protected him from injury and the golf club was in fault in not erecting same: *Gray v Leopardstown Golf Centre* (1999) Irish Times, 21 July 1999.

A golf spectator at the 1990 Irish Open, who was struck on the head by a golf ball, had her action dismissed, the judge finding that the defendants did not have a duty to provide against improbable or unlikely happenings: *Dalton v Portmarnock Golf Club and PJ Carroll & Co plc* [1992] CC.

In other cases:

(a) the plaintiff struck a golf ball onto the wrong fairway and in recovering it, was stuck by a ball driven by another golfer from the tee of that fairway. It was held that had the other golfer seen the plaintiff, the plaintiff would have been 25% contributory negligent for failing to check on the actions of golfers on that tee: *Feeny v Lyall* 1991 SLT 156; [1991] CLY 5298 (OH);

(b) the defendant, a 24-handicap golfer, mis-hit a ball from the tee and struck the plaintiff on an adjacent green. It was held that the defendant was liable as all he had to do was wait for the plaintiff to finish putting. The risk of a golfer of the defendant's level of skill mis-hitting the ball was not so small that a reasonable man would disregard it. There was no basis for a plea of *volenti non fit injuria* (qv): *Lewis v Blackpool Golf Club* [1993] SLT (Sh Ct) 43; [1992] CLY 6076.

The 'exempted development' (qv) status of golf courses has been abolished: Planning and Development Regulations 2001, SI No 600 of 2001, art 9. However, exempted are works incidental to the maintenance and management of a golf course, including alterations to the layout thereof, excluding any extension of the area of the golf course (Sch 2, class 34). For previous legislation which abolished the exempted status, see Local Government (Planning and Development) Regulations 1994, SI No 86 of 1994. See also *Castle v St Augustine's Links Ltd* 38 TLR 615. For the Golf-

ing Union of Ireland, see website: *www.gui.ie*. As regards the finding of golf balls, see LARCENY BY FINDING. See 'Tigerland: Golf and the Law' by Henry Murdoch BL in *Law Society Gazette* (May 2003) 8. See also CLUB; OCCUPIERS' LIABILITY TO VISITORS; PLANNING PERMISSION, CONDITIONS OF; SPORTING LEASE; SPORTS BODY; SPORTS INJURY CLINIC; SPORTSPERSON'S TAX RELIEF; STANDARD OF CARE.

good consideration. Consideration founded on generosity, natural affection or love or relationship. It is not regarded as *valuable consideration* (money or money's worth). See CONSIDERATION.

good faith. In relation to contracts for the sale of goods, *good faith* means done honestly, whether negligent or not: Sale of Goods Act 1893, s 62(2). See Consumer Credit Act 1995, s 70. See MARKET OVERT; PURCHASER; STOPPAGE IN TRANSITU; VOIDABLE TITLE, SALE UNDER.

Good Friday Agreement. The agreement reached in the multi-party negotiations in Belfast on 10 April 1998 and annexed to the agreement between the government of the United Kingdom of Great Britain and Northern Ireland and the government of Ireland and done on the same date. Also known as the *Belfast Agreement* or the *British-Irish Agreement*.

The agreement covers constitutional issues, human rights, issues of culture and economics, social issues, decommissioning, security, policing and justice, and prisoners.

It also comprises *three strands* as regard the creation of institutions: (a) *strand one* – the creation of an assembly of 108 members for Northern Ireland, elected by proportional representation, and with authority to pass primary legislation; (b) *strand two* – the establishment of a North-South Ministerial Council to develop consultation, co-operation and action within the island of Ireland on matters of mutual interest; (c) *strand three* – (i) the establishment of a British-Irish Council (also known as the Council of the Isles) to promote the harmonious and mutually beneficial development of the totality of relationships among the people of the islands of the UK and Ireland, and (ii) the establishment of a British-Irish Governmental Conference to promote bilateral co-operation at all levels on all matters of mutual interest.

There is provision for the creation of *implementation bodies* on a cross-border or all-island level. The agreement provides for the dropping of the Irish constitutional territorial claim to Northern Ireland and the reinforcement of the previously agreed position that a united Ireland can only happen if agreed by a majority of the people of Northern Ireland and, if so agreed, both governments will give legislative effect to that decision.

Four supplemental agreements between the UK and Ireland were done in Dublin on 8 March 1999 in relation to the establishment of the North-South Council, the British-Irish Intergovernmental Conference, the British-Irish Council, and the Implementation Bodies.

These Implementation Bodies were established in 1999 to implement, on an all-island basis and cross-border basis, policies agreed by the North-South Council. The bodies are: Waterways Ireland; Food Safety Promotions Board; Trade and Business Body; Special EU Programme Body; An Foras Teanga (the North-South Language Body); the Foyle Carlingford and Irish Lights Commission: British-Irish Agreement Acts 1999 and (Amendment) 1999.

The Good Friday Agreement was endorsed by the people in referenda held in both parts of the island of Ireland on 22 May 1998. The amendments to the Irish Constitution arising from the Agreement were contingent on a declaration by the Government that the State had become obliged to give effect to the amendments; this was delayed due to the delay in establishing the Assembly Executive, thereby necessitating the Declaration under art 29.7 of the Constitution (Extension of Time) Act 1999. The declaration was made on 2 December 1999: Iris Oifigiúil, 7 December 1999.

All the institutions under the Good Friday Agreement were subsequently established. However, the Northern Ireland Assembly and Assembly Executive was temporarily suspended on 11 February 2000, pending a review, and in the meantime direct rule of Northern Ireland from London was re-imposed as from that date. The Assembly was subsequently restored as from 30 May 2000 following an IRA commitment to put its arms completely and verifiably beyond use.

Following a further suspension on 11 August 2001 and a restoration on 6 November 2001, the Northern Ireland Assembly and the power-sharing Executive were again suspended on 14 October 2002 and direct rule re-imposed because of a political crisis blamed on doubts about the republican movement's commitment to exclusively democratic and non-violent means. This necessitated the British-Irish Agreement (Amendment) Act 2002 which enables the work of the North/South Implementation Bodies to continue, pending the restoration of the Northern Ireland Assembly. As of 1 September 2004 the Assembly remained suspended.

For the Northern Ireland Assembly, see website: *www.ni-assembly.gov.uk*. [Bibliography: Morgan A.] See ANGLO-IRISH AGREEMENT; DECOMMISSIONING; GEORGE MITCHELL SCHOLARSHIP; HUMAN RIGHTS COMMISSION; INDEPENDENT MONITORING COMMISSION; JURISDICTION; NATION; NATIONAL TERRITORY; NORTHERN IRELAND; NORTH-SOUTH MINISTERIAL COUNCIL; POLICE CO-OPERATION; PRISONER, RELEASE OF; REMEMBRANCE FUND; UNITED IRELAND; VICTIM OF VIOLENCE.

good name. See NAME, RIGHT TO GOOD; TRIBUNALS OF INQUIRY.

good title. See MARKETABLE TITLE.

goods. The term includes all *chattels personal* other than things in action and money; it also includes emblements, industrial growing crops, and things attached to and forming part of the land which are agreed to be severed before sale or under the contract of sale. *Things in action* include debts, cheques, bills of exchange, shares and patents. *Future goods* means goods to be manufactured or acquired by the seller after the making of the contract of sale. *Specific goods* means goods identified and agreed upon at the time a contract of sale is made. See Sale of Goods Act 1893, ss 5 and 62. See DISCRIMINATION, GOODS AND SERVICES; MANUFACTURED GOODS; UNASCERTAINED GOODS; UNSOLICITED GOODS.

goods, acceptance of. See ACCEPTANCE OF GOODS.

goods, carriage by sea. See BILLS OF LADING; MARITIME CLAIMS.

goods, character and quality of. See CHARACTER OR QUALITY OF GOODS.

goods, deliverable state. Goods are in a deliverable state when they are in such a state that the buyer would under the contract be bound to take delivery of them: Sale of Goods Act 1893, s 62. See DELIVERY OF GOODS; GOODS, PROPERTY IN.

goods, examination of. See EXAMINATION OF GOODS.

goods, international classification of. See INTERNATIONAL CLASSIFICATION OF GOODS.

goods, property in. In a contract for the sale of goods, unless a different intention appears, the following are rules for ascertaining the intention of the parties as to the time at which the *property* in the goods is to pass to the buyer:

Rule 1 – Where there is an unconditional contract for the sale of specific goods, in a deliverable state, the property in the goods passes to the buyer when the contract is made, and it is immaterial whether the time of payment or the time of delivery, or both, be postponed. See *Clarke v Reilly* [1962] 96 ILTR 96.

Rule 2 – Where there is a contract for the sale of specific goods and the seller is bound to do something to the goods, for the purpose of putting them into a deliverable state, the property does not pass until such thing be done, and the buyer has notice thereof.

Rule 3 – Where there is a contract for sale of specific goods in a deliverable state, but the seller is bound to weigh, measure, test, or do some other act or thing with reference to the goods for the purpose of ascertaining the price, the property does not pass until such act or thing be done, and the buyer has notice thereof.

Rule 4 – See APPROVAL, SALE ON.

Rule 5 – Where there is a contract for the sale of unascertained or future goods by description, and goods of that description and in a deliverable state are unconditionally appropriated to the contract, either by the seller with the assent of the buyer, or by the buyer with the assent of the seller, the property in the goods thereupon passes to the buyer. Such assent may be express or implied, and may be given either before or after the appropriation is made.

Property in goods means the ownership of them rather than the mere physical possession. See *Re Interview Ltd* [1975] IR 382; *Cronin v IMP Midleton Ltd* [1986] HC. See Sale of Goods Act 1893, s 18. See APPROPRIATION; RETENTION OF TITLE.

goods, receiving stolen. See HANDLING STOLEN PROPERTY; RECEIVING STOLEN GOODS.

goods, recovery of. See RECOVERY OF GOODS.

goods, rejected. See REJECTED GOODS.

goods, sale of. See SALE OF GOODS.

goods, title to. See TITLE TO GOODS.

goods, unlawful possession of. See UNLAWFUL POSSESSION OF GOODS.

goodwill. An intangible asset of a business arising from the advantage the business derives from its past reputation and its connection with its customers. It has been described as the attractive force which brings in custom: *Inland Revenue v Muller* [1901] AC 224. The sale of a business usually includes the sale of the goodwill, in which circumstance the vendor may be restrained from soliciting his former customers: *Trego v Hunt* [1896] AC 7. A charge (qv) on goodwill of a company must be registered under s 99 of the Companies Act 1963 (as amended by Companies Act 1990, s 122) to prevent the security being void as against a liquidator or creditor of the company. See ASSET VALUATION, PASSING OFF.

goose. See GAME.

government. The body through which the executive power of the State is exercised; it consists of not less than seven and not more than fifteen members appointed by the President of Ireland: 1937 Constitution, art 28. The head of the government is the Taoiseach (qv). The government meets and acts as a *collective authority* and is responsible to Dáil Éireann.

The Taoiseach, the Tánaiste (qv) and the member of the government in charge of the Department of Finance must be members of the Dáil. The other members of the government must be members of the Dáil or the Seanad (qv) but not more than two may be members of the Seanad.

The Taoiseach may at any time, for reasons which to him seem sufficient, request a member of the government to resign; should the member concerned fail to comply with the request, his appointment will be terminated by the President if the Taoiseach so advises (1937 Constitution, art 28(9)(4)). See *Treoracha Faoi Nós Imeachta an Rialtais* (Government Procedure Instructions) which sets out the rules for day-to-day operations of government, including submission of memoranda, government appointments, and conflicts of interest. See CABINET CONFIDENTIALITY; ETHICS IN GOVERNMENT; SEPARATION OF POWERS; OBSTRUCTION OF GOVERNMENT; TREASON; USURPATION OF GOVERNMENT.

government copyright. The copyright which subsists in any *work* made by an officer or employee of the government or of the State in the course of his duties; the government is the first copyright owner: Copyright and Related Rights Act 2000, s 191. The copyright expires 50 years from the end of the calendar year in which the work was made (CRRA 2000, s 191(4)). See COPYRIGHT.

government services. A new website has been launched, aimed primarily at business, which permits access to government services from a single point of access: *www.basis.ie*. It offers a cross-agency view of all services, available from the public sector, from a single point of access. See also *www.reach.ie*.

Governor-General. Formerly, the official representative of the British Crown in the *Irish Free State* under the provisions of the Anglo-Irish Treaty 1921. It was a controversial symbolic office, eventually abolished by the Executive Authority (External Relations) Act 1936.

Governor of Central Bank. The person appointed as Governor of the Central Bank and Financial Services Authority of Ireland by the President of Ireland on the advice of the Government: Central Bank Act 1942, s 19 as amended by Central Bank and Financial Services Authority of Ireland Act 2003, s 14. His term of office is for seven years. He is disqualified from being a director of a credit institution, financial institution or insurance undertaking.

The Governor is responsible for: (a) holding and managing by the Central Bank of the foreign reserves of the State, and (b) promoting the efficient and effective operation of payment and settlement systems (CBA 1942, s 19A(1) inserted by CBFSAIA 2003, s 15). He has sole responsibility for the exercise of the powers in relation to the European System of Central Banks (CBA 1942, s 19A(2) inserted by CBFSAIA 2003, s 15). Any decision to remove the Governor may be subject to a referral to the European Court of Justice (CBA 1942, s 21(4) as substituted by CBFSAIA 2003, s 16). The Governor is required to attend before a committee of the Oireachtas when so requested (CBA 1942, s 33AM inserted by CBFSAIA 2003, s 26).

The Director General of the bank is empowered to carry out certain functions of the Governor in certain circumstances eg due to his absence or ill-health (CBA 1942, s 22A inserted by CBFSAIA 2003,

s 18). See also Central Bank and Financial Services Authority of Ireland Act 2004, ss 5 and 26. See CENTRAL BANK.

grace, days of. See DAYS OF GRACE.

graft, doctrine of. The equitable doctrine whereby in a constructive trust (qv) the profit or accretion (eg obtained by a person in a fiduciary position) is deemed to be *engrafted* upon the original trust property and thereby held upon the same trusts. See *Dempsey v Ward* [1899] I IR 463. For an example of a statutory provision on grafting, see Land Law (Ireland) Act 1887, s 14(3).

Granada Convention. The Convention for the Protection of the Architectural Heritage of Europe done at Granada on 3 October 1985 and ratified by Ireland on 20 January 1997. The legislative response is contained in: (a) the Architectural Heritage (National Inventory) and Historic Monuments (Miscellaneous Provisions) Act 1999 which set up, on a statutory footing, a *national inventory* of buildings and structures of architectural and other importance and (b) the Planning and Development Act 2000, ss 51–80 which provides better protection for *protected structures*. For previous legislation, see Local Government (Planning and Development) Act 1999. See ARCHITECTURAL HERITAGE; PROTECTED STRUCTURES.

grand jury. Formerly, the jury with no corporate or continuous existence, appointed by the Lord Lieutenant, with responsibility for making and repairing roads and bridges and the construction and maintenance of court houses and the support of lunatic asylums, county infirmaries, industrial schools and coroners (qv), financed by a local revenue known as a *county cess* or *grand jury cess*: Grand Jury (Ireland) Act 1836. Its expenditure proposals, known as *presentments* had to be submitted to the judge of the assizes for approval; when its work was completed, it was discharged by the judge and ceased to exist for any purpose. Its local government functions were transferred to the county councils (qv): Local Government (Ireland) Act 1898, s 4. See *The State (Feeley) v O'Dea* [1986] HC. See Local Government Act 2001, s 5(1), Sch 3, Pt 1.

grandfather clause. Colloquial expression to describe a provision exempting certain persons from new requirements, eg in the introduction of new minimum levels of qualifications, persons are deemed to meet the qualification requirement on the basis of practice, experience and expertise e g Companies Act 1990, s 188 regarding qualifications of company auditors. The expression comes from a clause in the constitutions of several states in the US that waived electoral literacy requirements for lineal descendants of persons voting before 1867, thus ensuring the franchise of illiterate white voters; the clause was declared unconstitutional in 1915. See UNDERTAKINGS FOR COLLECTIVE INVESTMENT IN TRANSFERABLE SECURITIES.

Grangegorman Development Agency. Under draft legislation, the new statutory body proposed to be established to facilitate the development of the Grangegorman site in Dublin as a modern campus for the Dublin Institute of Technology (DIT) and to provide the Eastern Regional Health Authority (ERHA) with upgraded facilities: Grangegorman Development Agency Bill 2004. The Agency will be established to project manage the development in an integrated and sustainable manner. The Agency will have functions of promoting the development of the Grangegorman site as a location for education, health and other facilities; entering into arrangements to exploit any research, development or consultancy work undertaken by the Agency; accepting the vesting of the Grangegorman site and property vacated by the ERHA or DIT; carrying out or facilitating renewal or conservation of land on the site; applying for permission for development of land to facilitate the site's future development; deciding on the appropriate procurement strategy for individual elements of the site; and arranging for a communications strategy to facilitate consultation with local residents, health and education sectors, and representatives of trade unions, employers and the public.

grant. The allocation of rights and powers by an authority to a particular person or persons and for particular purposes e g grant of letters of administration, grant of probate, grant of a patent. A conveyance is a deed of grant. See PATENT, GRANT OF.

gratis. [Free.] Without recompense or charge.

gratis dictum. [Mere assertion.]

gratuitous agent. See AGENT, GRATUITOUS.

gratuitous bailment. See BAILMENT.

Great Britain. Does not include the Channel Islands or the Isle of Man: Interpretation Act 1937, Sch, para 12. See BRITISH CITIZEN; COUNCIL OF THE ISLES.

greenhouse gas. In so far as the emission of any such gas contributes to global climate change, means: (a) carbon dioxide, methane, nitrous oxide, sulphur hexafluoride, any hydrofluorocarbon or any perfluorocarbon (i e the gases specified in the Kyoto Protocol), and (b) such other gases as may be prescribed: Environmental Protection Agency Act 1992, s 3 as substituted by Protection of the Environment Act 2003, s 5. A licence issued by the Agency must include *emission limit values* for environmental pollutants, including greenhouse gases, likely to be emitted in significant quantities (EPAA 1992, s 86 inserted by PEA 2003, s 15). See EMISSION; EMISSIONS TRADING.

greyhounds. Greyhounds must be led by a chain or leash in any public place and one person must not lead more than four greyhounds: Control of Dogs Act 1986, s 10.

The controlling authority for *greyhound racing* is Bord na gCon and for greyhound breeding and coursing is the Irish Coursing Club (subject to the overall supervision of Bord na gCon): Greyhound Industry Act 1958. The Minister is empowered to make regulations providing for the muzzling of greyhounds at coursing meetings: Greyhound Industry (Amendment) Act 1993, s 3.

Betting offices at greyhound race tracks are now controlled by Bord na gCon; there is provision for the payment of a *levy* by bookmakers on on-course bets (zero at present), a *turnover charge* on bets wherever placed, and a *flat rate charge* in respect of operating at a greyhound race track: Horse and Greyhound Racing (Betting Charges and Levies) Act 1999, ss 9 to 15. See also Irish Horseracing Industry Act 1994, s 54F as inserted by HGR(BCL)A 1999, s 4. See Greyhound Race Track (Racing) (Amendment) Regulations 2002, SI No 77 of 2002.

There is provision for the licensing of the sale for consumption of intoxicating liquor at authorised events at greyhound race tracks: Intoxicating Liquor Act 2000, s 23. The permitted time for such sale begins at the time the public are admitted to the event (but not before 10.30 am) and ending 30 minutes after the conclusion of the event.

See also Taxes Consolidation Act 1997, s 140.

See BET; STALLION.

grievous bodily harm. See BODILY HARM, GRIEVOUS.

Griffith's valuation. The valuation (qv), called after the first Commissioner of Valuation, carried out of the entire country under the Valuation (Ireland) Act 1852, which is still the valuation in force today, except where a re-valuation has been carried out under s 34 of V(I)A 1852 or s 65 of the Local Government (Ireland) Act 1898. See VALUATION.

gross. Entire; exclusive of deductions. See IN GROSS.

gross indecency. Acts of a gross nature and purpose between male persons which fall short of buggery (qv) and which are an offence. It is an offence for a male person to commit an act of gross indecency with another male person under the age of 17 years or with a mentally impaired male person of any age: Criminal Law (Sexual Offences) Act 1993, ss 4 and 5(2). An attempt is also an offence, as is soliciting or importuning for the purposes of gross indecency (CL(SO)A 1993, s 6). See BUGGERY; MENTALLY IMPAIRED; SOLICIT.

gross misconduct. A ground for dismissal from employment. What constitutes *gross misconduct* can vary depending on the circumstance and how such conduct is perceived in employment; and how a particular employer reacts to such conduct and what is reasonable: *Horan v Glanbia Meats plc* [2002] ELR 205, EAT. See MISCONDUCT.

gross negligence. Colloquial phrase referring to a very high degree of negligence. The gross negligence of an employee may be a ground for dismissal: *O'Brien v Heinz Pollmeier* [1991] ELR 157. See MANSLAUGHTER.

ground. A reason, a basis, a justification, a matter for consideration or enquiry, a position, viewpoint or contention. Where a party is aware of the existence of grounds or contentions that could be raised and chose not to raise them at that stage, to allow him to include them at a later stage would be oppressive towards the defendant and would interfere gravely with the public and private interest in the efficient conduct of litigation: *Carroll v Ryan* [2003] 2 ILRM 1, SC and 1 IR 309. However, see PLEADINGS, AMENDMENT OF.

ground rent. A lease may determine by enlargement by *buying out the ground rent*, whereby the lessee can require the ground landlord to transfer the *fee simple* to the lessee. A wide category of lessees are enti-

tled to acquire the fee simple, including persons holding under building (qv) and proprietary (qv) leases, under long leases with low rent, and under certain local authority leases: Landlord and Tenant (Ground Rents) (No 2) Act 1978, ss 8–15 as amended by the Landlord and Tenant (Amendment) Act 1980, ss 70–73. The 1978 Act does not apply to a shared ownership lease (qv): Housing (Miscellaneous Provisions) Act 1992, s 2(3). The creation of new ground rents is prohibited. See also Landlord and Tenant (Ground Rents) Acts 1984 and 1987.

Unless the fee simple in the land can be acquired, s 8 of LT(GR)(No 2)A 1978 does not give a person, who satisfies the relevant criteria, the right to acquire intermediate interests in the land: *Metropolitan Properties Ltd v O'Brien* [1995] 2 ILRM 383, SC and 1 IR 467.

When a lessee enlarges his interest into a fee simple pursuant to the LT(GR)(No 2)A 1978, s 8, all covenants subject to which he held the land, including those for the benefit of third parties, cease to have effect: *Whelan & Whelan v Cork Corporation* [1991] ILRM 19, HC and [1994] 3 IR 367, SC.

Landlord and Tenant (Ground Rents) Act 1984, s 7 enacted new provisions regarding the determination of the purchase price by arbitration, particularly to deal with the case of a lease with less than 15 years to run, following the ruling in *Gilsenan v Foundary House Investments Ltd and Rathmines Property Ltd* [1980] ILRM 273. The County Registrar determines the purchase price of the fee simple estate in the absence of agreement: *Heatons Wholesale Ltd v McCormack* [1994] 2 ILRM 83, HC.

Landlord and Tenant (Ground Rents) Act 1987 extended indefinitely the period of operation of Part III of LT(GR)A 1978; this provides ground rent tenants of domestic dwellinghouses with a cheap and expeditious method of buying out the ground rent, with the Registrar of Titles having the same power as the County Registrar. A receiver by way of equitable execution may be appointed over ground rents in certain circumstances: *Ahern v O'Brien* [1991] 1 IR 421. See also *Bank of Ireland v Gleeson* [2000] ITLR (15 May), SC.

For the court rules governing an appeal under s 22(1) of the Landlord and Tenant (Ground Rent) Act 1967, see Circuit Court

Rules 2001 Ord 51, r 3. For buying out the ground rent, see website: *www.landregistry. ie*. See Residential Tenancies Act 2004, s 3(2)(d). See SPORTING LEASE.

groundwater. Statutory provision has been made for the implementation of the Groundwater Directive ((EEC) 80/68) which deals with the control of emissions of hazardous substances to aquifers: Environmental Protection Agency Act 1992, s 99I inserted by Protection of the Environment Act 2003, s 16. In addition, to the prevention or limitation of the entry into groundwater of certain hazardous substances, there is a requirement to review within four years a licence granted in relation to a discharge to groundwater. Also when the Agency grants a licence in relation to an emission, it is required to attach a condition, if necessary, to protect groundwater (EPAA 1992, s 86(1)(a)(iii) inserted by PEA 2003, s 15). See AQUIFER.

group accounts. See HOLDING COMPANY.

grouse. See GAME.

guarantee. A collateral promise to answer for the debt, default or miscarriage of another person. It is a contract by which a person (known as the *surety*) becomes bound to another (the *creditor*) for the fulfilment or performance of a promise or engagement or other duty of a third party (the *principal*). Although guarantees most often relate to a debt, they can pertain to any type of duty or obligation. Contrast with *warranty* which generally bears no obligations to third parties.

A bank obtaining a guarantee or a deposit of title deeds in respect of money advanced to another, may be required to advise the surety to seek independent legal advice: *Allied Irish Banks plc v English* [1992] reported in 11 ILT & SJ [1993] 108, CC. See *Lombard & Ulster Banking v Murray* [1987] ILRM 522, HC.

Where a third party (a surety or guarantor) becomes liable in respect of the debt of a company to which an examiner has been appointed, the creditor can enforce the guarantee, and the guarantor becomes entitled to the creditor's vote and any right of recovery under any *scheme of arrangement* approved by the court: Companies (Amendment) Act 1990, s 25 as amended by Companies (Amendment) (No 2) Act 1999, s 25.

The Minister for Finance is empowered to guarantee the due payment by a *scheduled body* of the principal (and/or interest on the principal) of all moneys, including foreign currency, borrowed by such body with the consent of the Minister: State Guarantees Acts 1954, s 2 and 1964, s 2. See also Building Societies Act 1989, ss 29(2)(b), 36(11)(f), 57(1)(d) as amended by Housing (Miscellaneous Provisions) Act 2002, s 23 and Sch 3. [Bibliography: Johnston; Rowlatt UK; Salter UK.] See CONTRACT OF GUARANTEE; DEBT; MEMORANDUM, STATUTE OF FRAUDS; PERFORMANCE BOND; SURETY.

guarantee, contract of. See CONTRACT OF GUARANTEE.

guarantee, sale of goods. (1) Any document, notice or other written statement, however described, supplied by a manufacturer or other supplier, other than a retailer, in connection with the supply of any goods, and indicating that the manufacturer or other supplier will service, repair or otherwise deal with the goods following purchase: Sale of Goods and Supply of Services Act 1980, s 15. A guarantee must comply with a particular format (SGSSA 1980, s 16). The seller of goods who delivers a guarantee to a buyer is liable to the buyer for the observance of its terms (SGSSA 1980, s 17).

Rights under a guarantee may not in any way exclude or limit the rights of the buyer at common law or pursuant to statute and every provision in a guarantee which imposes obligations on the buyer which are additional to his obligation under the contract is void (SGSSA 1980, s 18). A buyer of goods may maintain an action against a manufacturer or importer or other supplier who fails to observe the terms of a guarantee; a buyer in this context includes all persons who acquire title to the goods within the duration of the guarantee. See *Tokn Grass Products Ltd v Sexton Co Ltd* [1983] HC.

(2) Any undertaking by a seller or producer to the consumer, given without extra charge, to reimburse the price paid or to replace, repair or handle consumer goods in any way if they do not meet the specification set out in the guarantee statement or in the relevant advertising: EC (Certain Aspects of the Sale of Consumer Goods and Associated Guarantees) Regulations 2003, SI No 11 of 2003, reg 2(1). Such a guarantee is legally binding on the offerer under the conditions laid down in the guarantee statement and the associated advertising (reg 9(1)).

The guarantee is required to: (a) state that the consumer has legal rights under these regulations and the other enactments governing the sale of consumer goods and make clear that those rights are not affected by the guarantee, and (b) set out in plain intelligible language the contents of the guarantee and the essential particulars necessary for making claims under the guarantee, including the duration and territorial scope of the guarantee as well as the name and address of the guarantor (SI No 11 of 2003, reg 9(2)).

These Regulations give protection to the consumer in addition to, and not is substitution for protection given by other enactments e g the Sale of Goods Act 1893 and SGSSA 1980 and the EC (Unfair Terms in Consumer Contracts) Regulations 1995, SI No 27 of 1995. The consumer can opt for the measure which gives the most protection. See CONSUMER GOODS; CONTRACT OF GUARANTEE.

guarantee company. See COMPANY, LIMITED.

guarantor. A person who binds himself by a guarantee; a person who promises to answer for another; a surety (qv).

guard dog. A dog which is being used: (a) to protect premises, or (b) to protect goods or property kept on premises, or (c) to protect a person guarding premises or such goods or property: Control of Dogs Act 1986, s 19 as substituted by Control of Dogs (Amendment) Act 1992, s 8(1) and (Guard Dogs) Regulations SI No 255 of 1988 and No 329 of 1989. Controls on the use of guard dogs include an identification system consisting of a collar and a skin implanted electronic encoded device, registration by local authorities, and standards for operation of kennels. Notices must be placed on buildings where guard dogs are present.

guardian. A person having the right and duty of protecting the person, property or rights of another who has not full legal capacity or is otherwise incapable of managing his own affairs e g the parent of a minor (qv). All matters concerning guardianship and custody of children have to be decided on the basis of the welfare of the child and to the constitutional principle that parents have equal rights to, and are joint guardians, of their children: Guardianship of Infants Act 1964, ss 3 and 6. The grant of a decree of divorce does not affect the right of the father or mother of a child

to be joint guardians: Family Law (Divorce) Act 1996, s 10(2). Custody and guardianship are not synonymous; a parent deprived of custody of a child is not deprived of the rights of guardian: *B v B* [1975] IR 54.

The mother of an illegitimate child (now a child whose parents have not married each other) is its guardian and consequently may abandon the right by placing the child for adoption: GIA 1964, s 6(4); *G v An Bord Uchtála* [1980] IR 32. Under the Status of Children Act 1987, ss 11–12 the father of a child whose parents have not married each other, could become guardian of the child jointly with the mother on application to the court; the mother was the sole guardian of the child unless the father has been appointed guardian jointly with her. The SCA 1987 did not give the natural father a right to be appointed guardian but only a right to apply to be appointed; he has no constitutional right to guardianship; the welfare of the child is the first and paramount consideration: *K v W* [1990] ILRM 121, SC. See also *PQ v CL* [1990] 8 ILT & SJ [1990] 269, CC; *WO'R v EH* [1996] 2 IR 248, SC.

The Children Act 1997, s 4 provides a simpler procedure for the father to be appointed guardian; the father and mother make a statutory declaration agreeing that the father be appointed guardian and setting out the arrangements regarding custody of, and, as the case may be, access to the child; there is now no requirement to apply to the court. See Guardianship of Children (Statutory Declaration) Regulations 1998, SI No 5 of 1998. See Circuit Court Rules 2001 Ord 59, r 1.

A parent in whose custody a child is, can apply to the courts for a *maintenance order* (qv) requiring the other parent to provide financial support for the child: GIA 1964, s 11(2); Family Law (Maintenance of Spouses and Children) Act 1976, s 5(1). See also Child Care Act 1991, ss 20, 76–77; Domestic Violence Act 1996, s 13(2); Courts and Court Officers Act 2002, s 21. See also *Cosgrove v Ireland* [1982] ILRM 48. See also DCR 1997 Ord 58 and District Court (Custody and Guardianship of Children) Rules 1999, SI No 125 of 1999. [Bibliography: Shatter.] See TESTAMENTARY GUARDIAN; UNDUE INFLUENCE; UNSOUND MIND; WARD.

guardian ad litem. [Guardian for the suit.] An infant and a person of unsound mind may defend proceedings by his *guardian ad litem*: Circuit Court Rules 2001 Ord 6, rr 6–8. See *A Guide to Professional Conduct of Solicitors in Ireland* (2002), App 4, para 21. See DCR 1997 Ord 7. See AD LITEM.

guardians, boards of. See BOARDS OF GUARDIANS.

guilty. (1) The finding after trial that the accused committed the offence with which he is charged. (2) A plea by an accused that he committed the offence. The court in determining what sentence to pass on a person who has pleaded guilty must take into account the stage in the proceedings at which he pleaded guilty and the circumstances; this requirement, however, does not preclude the court from passing the maximum sentence prescribed by law, if the court is satisfied that there are exceptional circumstances which so warrant: Criminal Justice Act 1999, s 29 overruling *DPP v G* [1992] IR 587.

Also if an accused pleads guilty to an *indictable* offence in the District Court, the court, with the consent of the prosecutor, may deal with the offence summarily or send him forward to the trial court for sentence: Criminal Procedure Act 1967, s 13 amended by CJA 1999, s 10, and by Maritime Security Act 2004, s 10(a). Where he is sent forward to the trial court, he may be dealt with as if he had been convicted on indictment by the trial court: Criminal Law Act 1997, s 10(5).

An accused who had entered a guilty plea to a number of sexual offences was permitted to set aside his guilty plea, as he and his senior counsel were unaware of certain documents, including a form of diary kept by the complainant, which if they had been seen, the accused might have pleaded not guilty and might have been acquitted: *The People (DPP) v B* [2002] 2 IR 246, CCA. The court set aside the convictions and ordered a retrial on the count of rape. See ADMISSION OF GUILT; ALTERNATIVE VERDICT; DEFENCE BARRISTER, DUTY OF; SPECIAL VERDICT.

guilty but insane. See SPECIAL VERDICT.

guilty mind. See MENS REA.

gun jumping. Colloquial expression which means starting before the starting signal is given. The Competition Authority in May 2003 warned companies not to jump the gun on mergers. 'If the parties are found to have breached the pre-merger waiting period ie *gun jumping*, then the transaction will be deemed void'. The Authority said that a 'dramatic' example of gun jumping would be if a company took control of another company prior to the expiry date. But it warned against even exchanging sensitive information or implementing 'co-ordinated strategies'. The Authority stressed that it is important that companies maintain separate and independent operations until the Authority had made its determination.

H

habeas corpus. [That you have the body.] An order of the High Court to compel a person in whose custody another person is detained to produce the body of that other person before the court and to certify in writing the grounds of his detention; the court having given the person in whose custody he is detained an opportunity of justifying the detention, will order the release of the person from detention unless satisfied that he is being detained in accordance with law: 1937 Constitution, art 40(4)(2).

It is open to any person, citizen or non-citizen, to make an application for *habeas corpus*: *The State (Kugan) v O'Rourke* [1985] IR 658. However, the *habeas corpus* procedure cannot be used as a fast-track procedure where the appropriate remedies are by way of *judicial review* or *plenary proceedings*: *Bolger v Commissioner of Garda Síochána* [2000] 1 ILRM 136, HC & SC.

Applications which clearly raise an issue as to the legality of the detention of a person must be treated as applications under art 40 no matter how they are described eg as judicial review or otherwise: *Sheehan v District Judge O'Reilly* [1993] ILRM 427, SC. The Supreme Court has confirmed that it has no power to put a *stay* on an order for release made by the High Court: *The State (Trimbole) v Governor of Mountjoy Prison* [1985] IR 550. See also *McSorley v Governor of Mountjoy Prison* [1996] 2 ILRM 331, HC and [1997] 2 ILRM 315, SC.

See Habeas Corpus Act 1781 as amended by Criminal Law Act 1997, s 16 and Sch 3. See RSC Ord 84, rr 2–13. [Bibliography: Collins & O'Reilly (1).] See

ATTORNEY-GENERAL'S SCHEME; BAIL; DETENTION.

habendum. [To have.] The clause in a conveyance which defines the estate to be taken by the purchaser e g *To have and to hold in fee simple.*

habitable house. (1) A building or part of a building which is used as a dwelling; or which is not used as a dwelling but which, when last used, was used as a dwelling: Housing Act 1969, s 1. The demolition of a habitable house was prohibited, as was the use otherwise than for human habitation, save under and in accordance with permission from the housing authority, which could either grant the permission, subject to or without conditions, or could refuse permission (HA 1969, s 4). Two separate permissions had to be obtained for *change of use* of a habitable house; planning permission (qv) had to be obtained but only after permission had already been obtained under the 1969 Act (HA 1969, s 10).

If the housing authority was of the opinion that a person had, for the purpose of avoiding the provisions of the Act, caused or permitted a house to deteriorate to such an extent that it ceased to be a habitable house, they could, if they thought fit, serve on the owner of the house a *reinstatement notice*, requiring him to execute such works as might be necessary to make the house fit for human habitation (HA 1969, s 5).

The Act, which was intended to be temporary in nature, expired on 31 December 1984 (HA 1969, s 13), and now stands repealed: Housing Act 1988, s 30. See *State (MacGauran) v Dublin Corporation* [1979] HC; *Dublin County Council v Baily Holdings Ltd* [1978] SC; *Creedon v Dublin Corporation* [1978] HC. See OVERCROWDED HOUSE.

(2) The letting of a house by a housing authority includes an implied term that the house is fit for human habitation: Housing Act 1966, s 66; *Burke v Dublin Corporation* [1991] 1 IR 341, SC. A housing authority had a duty to ensure by a proper valuation that a house, offered as a security for a loan, was a good security for that loan and it owed a duty of care in that regard to the person seeking the loan: HA 1966, s 39; *Ward v McMaster* [1986] ILRM 43 and 400, HC & SC. However, the granting of assistance by a housing authority e g by way of grant, loan or subsidy does not imply any warranty as to the condition of the house or

its fitness for habitation: Housing (Miscellaneous Provisions) Act 1992, s 22.

(3) A *habitable house* means a house which: (a) is used as a dwelling, or (b) is not in use but when last used was used, disregarding any unauthorised use, as a dwelling and is not derelict, or (c) was provided for use as a dwelling but has not been occupied: Planning and Development Act 2000, s 2(1). A refusal of planning permission to demolish a habitable house, does not attract compensation (PDA 2000, s 191 and Sch 3, para 2). See HOUSING STRATEGY.

Habitats Directive. Means Council Directive (EEC) No 92/43 of 21 May 1992 on the conservation of natural habitats and of wild fauna and flora: Planning and Development Act 2000, s 2(1). Three conditions are required in order for the Minister to apply to the Court to prohibit an operation or activity on a site under the EC (Natural Habitats) Regulations, SI No 94 of 1997: (a) the site must have been placed on the appropriate list, (b) the Minister must consider that an operation or activity is being carried out or may be carried out which is likely to have significant effect on the site, and (c) an appropriate assessment must have been undertaken of the implications for the site in view of the site's conservation objectives: *Minister for Arts v Kennedy* [2002] 2 ILRM 94, HC. See EUROPEAN SITE.

habitual criminal. Formerly, a person could be pronounced a *habitual criminal* where the court had sentenced that person to penal servitude (qv) for having committed a felony, the person having had at least three previous serious convictions since the age of sixteen: Prevention of Crime Act 1908, s 10, now repealed by Criminal Law Act 1997, s 16 and Sch 3. See PREVENTATIVE DETENTION.

habitual residence. The *habitual residence* of a child is a matter of fact to be decided in each particular case; it is not governed by the rigid rules of dependency: *In the Matter of CM* [1999] 2 ILRM 103 and 2 IR 363, HC. Where a child is residing in the lawful custody of its parent, the child's habitual residence is that of the parent. In a particular case the Supreme Court held that a more detailed explanation was required in relation to a High Court finding that the habitual residence of a child had not changed: *Minister for Justice (ex parte G(P)) v C(V)* [2002] FL 4912, SC. For '*habitually* *resident*', see SOCIAL WELFARE LAW. See also CHILD ABDUCTION.

habitually work. The place where an employee *habitually* carries out his work, can be defined as the base of the worker's operations, where the worker receives his instructions from his employer, from where he communicates with his clients and to which he returns after each trip: *A Retail Company v A Worker* [2002] ELR 366, LC. An employer may be sued in the State where the employee habitually carries out his work: Jurisdiction and the Enforcement of Judgments Act 1998, Sch 1, art 5(1). Where an employee performs the obligations under his contract of employment in several States, the place where he habitually works is the place where, or from which, he performs the essential part of his duties vis-à-vis his employer: Case C-37/00 *Hebert Weber v Universal Ogden Services Ltd* [2002] (27 February 2002), ECJ. See also *A Retail Company v A Worker* [2001] ELR 358, LC.

An Equality Officer has held in a particular case that the fact that an employee spent 60% of his working time in the State was not sufficient to find that he habitually carried out his work in this State: *A Complainant v A Company* [2003] ELR 333, EO. Other factors had to be taken into account, including that he had his home and his office in Northern Ireland.

The *Brussels I Regulation* on the recognition and enforcement of judgments in civil and commercial matters, replaces JEJA 1998 as from 1 March 2002 for all EU States except Denmark: EC (Civil and Commercial Judgments) Regulations 2002, SI No 52 of 2002. Under this *Regulation* an employer may be sued in the courts of the member State where the employer is domiciled, or in the courts for the place where the employee *habitually* carries out his work or in the courts for the last place where he did so (*Regulation*, art 19). If the employee does not or did not *habitually* carry out his work in any one country, he can sue the employer in the courts for the place where the business which engaged the employee is or was situated (art 19(2)(b)).

hacking. Generally understood to mean the unauthorised access to or acquisition of information automatically processed on computers. It is an offence for a person who obtains personal data without the prior authority of the data controller (qv) or data processor (qv) by whom the data are kept, and *discloses* the data to another person:

Data Protection Act 1988, s 22. [Bibliography: Kelleher & Murray.] See COMPUTERS; CYBERCRIME; DATA PROTECTION; FRAUD.

hackney. A public service vehicle which is defined by references to types of uses other than the category of uses of a taxi: Road Traffic (Public Service Vehicles) Regulations 1963, as amended. It has been held that the fact that hackney licences were regulated in a different manner to taxi licences, with the result that there were dissimilar side effects in the market, did not in any way render the regulatory scheme discriminatory as there was no legal obligation on the Minister to create or maintain such a side effect: *O'Dwyer v Minister for the Environment* [2001] 1 IR 255, HC. See Taxi Regulation Act 2003, s 43. See CAR TESTING; TAXI.

Hague Agreement. Means the Geneva Act of the Hague Agreement concerning the International Registration of Industrial Designs adopted at Geneva on 2 July 1999. The Hague Agreement, which is administered by the World Intellectual Property Organisation (WIPO), is an international system of design registration which enables applicants from member countries to obtain protection for their designs (*international designs*) in all other member countries with a single application.

An applicant for registration of an *international design* under the international system who designates Ireland in the application, has the same rights, remedies and conditions as an applicant under the domestic Irish legislation: Industrial Designs Act 2001, s 79(3). The Minister is empowered to introduce measures, by secondary legislation, to enable the ratification and implementation in Ireland of the Hague Agreement (IDA 2001, s 79(2)).

See DESIGN.

Hague Convention. The Hague Convention of 1965 on the Service Abroad of Judicial and Extrajudicial Documents in Civil or Commercial Matters. See RSC Ord 11B inserted by Rules of the Superior Courts (No 3) 1994, SI No 101 of 1994; DCR 1997 Ord 45, r 5(2), Ord 62 and Ord 11, rr 7–12.

hair-length. It has been held that whereas an employer is entitled to set standards of appearance for its employees, which may differ between male and female employees for business reasons allied to public perception, different requirements for hair-lengths of male and female employees cannot be justified today: *Pantry Franchise (Ireland) Ltd v A Worker* [1994] ELR 8, LC.

half-blood. See BLOOD.

hallmarking. The marking of articles of the precious metals of gold, silver and platinum by a sponsor's mark (qv), indicating the distinctive mark of the sponsor, or assay mark, indicating standard of fineness and place where assay took place. An *approved* hallmark is: (a) a mark lawfully struck by the assay master; or (b) a mark struck in an assay office of the United Kingdom before the 21st day of February 1927; or (c) a mark, to be known as an *international hallmark* which is prescribed by regulations: Hallmarking Act 1981, ss 2–4. Permissible descriptions of unhallmarked articles are specified (HA 1981, s 6). See SIs No 327 and 328 of 1983.

Provision has been made by which articles consisting of or containing gold, silver or platinum marketed in Ireland, do not require further assay or hallmark in Ireland where certain conditions are met eg the articles have hallmarks lawfully applied in another member state, with a sponsor's or maker's mark, applied by a body which offers a guarantee of independence, and which provides the consumer with information which is intelligible to consumers in Ireland, and the hallmarks are equivalent to the marks referred to in the Hallmarking Act 1981: European Communities (Hallmarking of Articles imported from other Member States) Regulations 2001, SI No 579 of 2001.

For the prescribed *hallmarks* and *fineness marks* which can be applied by the Dublin Assay Office to articles of precious metal consisting of gold, silver and platinum, see Hallmarking (Approved Hallmarks) Regulations 2001, SI No 560 of 2001. For the *standards of fineness* for such articles, see Hallmarking (Irish Standards of Fineness) Regulations 2001, SI No 561 of 2001. These two regulations revoke SIs Nos 327 and 328 of 1983; SIs Nos 138 and 139 of 1990. See GOLDSMITHS OF DUBLIN, COMPANY OF.

halting site. A site for caravans for persons belonging to the class of persons who traditionally pursue or have pursued a nomadic way of life: Housing Act 1988, s 13 as amended by Housing (Traveller Accommodation) Act 1998, s 29. It is also a site provided or managed under s 6 of the Housing (Miscellaneous Provisions) Act 1992 or any other site for caravans for travellers provided or managed with or without the assistance of a housing authority (H(TA)A 1998, s 2(1)).

In a particular case, it was held that a local authority had breached its own traveller accommodation programme in considering only one of a list of 26 potential sites for a halting site: *Jeffers v Louth County Council* [2003] FL 8804, HC. See *Keogh v Galway Corporation* [1995] 3 IR 457, HC; *Ward v South Dublin County Council* [1996] 3 IR 195, HC; *County Meath VEC v Joyce* [1997] 3 IR 402, HC; *Byrne v Fingal County Council* [2002] 2 ILRM 321, HC and [2001] 4 IR 565, HC. [Bibliography: Canny (2).] See TRAVELLER.

handcuffs. The Court of Criminal Appeal has warned that it views seriously the presentation in handcuffs of a defendant in areas of the courts where they may be seen by jurors or the photographing of defendants in handcuffs: *McCowen v DPP* (2003) Irish Times, 1 April. The court in this case quashed the conviction of the accused on a number of grounds, including that he was seen by potential jurors in handcuffs and this could be prejudicial. In another case, the High Court warned television station TV3 that it was in clear contempt of court in showing an accused in handcuffs: Carney J in *DPP v Collinson* (2004) Irish Times, 28 January. See PUBLICITY.

handling stolen property. A person is guilty of the offence of handling stolen property if (otherwise than in the course of stealing) he *knows* that the property was stolen or being *reckless* as to whether it was stolen, dishonestly: (a) receives or arranges to receive it, or (b) undertakes, or assists in, its retention, removal, disposal or realisation by or for the benefit of another person, or arranges to do so: Criminal Justice (Theft and Fraud Offences) Act 2001, s 17(1).

A person is *reckless* if he disregards a *substantial risk* that the property handled is stolen; *substantial risk* means a risk of such a nature and degree that its disregard involves culpability of a high degree (CJ(TFO)A 2001, s 16(2)).

Under previous legislation, a person committed the offence of handling stolen property if, *knowing or believing* it to be stolen property, he *dishonestly*: (a) received it, or (b) retained, removed, disposed or realised it by or for the benefit of another person, or (c) arranged to do any of these things: Larceny Act 1916, s 33 as inserted by Larceny Act 1990, s 3. The *mens rea* (qv) for the crime consisted of 'knowing or believing' and 'dishonestly': see *Hanlon v Fleming* [1981] IR 489 and *R v Feely* [1973] QB 530. It is permissible to direct a jury that they may infer knowledge or belief from the accused's conduct and *The People v Oglesby* [1966] IR 163.

See *People (DPP) v Fowler* [1995] 1 ILRM 546, CCA; *People (DPP) v Byrne* [2001] 2 ILRM 134, CCA. [Bibliography: McGreal C.] See ALTERNATIVE VERDICT; DRUG TRAFFICKING; RECEIVING STOLEN PROPERTY; UNLAWFUL POSSESSION OF GOODS.

hanging. The Ordinary way in which the death penalty (qv) was carried out: *The People v Pringle* [1981] CCA. The sentence was required to be carried out within the walls of the prison in which the prisoner was confined up to the time of execution: Capital Punishment Amendment Act 1868, s 2. *If at the first attempt the criminal is not thoroughly hanged, and is afterwards revived, he shall be hanged again, for the former hanging was not an execution of the sentence which implies a completion of the punishment*: 2 Hale 412. The last hanging in Ireland took place in 1954. Prior to the abolition of the death penalty in 1990, the practice has been to commute the death sentence to imprisonment for 40 years. [Bibliography: Henry.] See DEATH PENALTY.

happy hour. Colloquial expression to describe a time, usually in the early evening, when licensed premises sold intoxicating liquor at reduced prices. It is now an offence for a licensee to so supply at a reduced price during a limited period on any day: Intoxicating Liquor Act 2003, s 20. 'Reduced price' means a price less than that regularly being charged during an earlier part of the day.

harassment. It is an offence for a person, without lawful authority or reasonable excuse, to *harass* another person by persistently following, watching, pestering, besetting or communicating with him, by any means, including by use of the telephone: Non-Fatal Offence against the Person Act 1997, s 10. Popularly known as *stalking*. A person *harasses* another where he seriously interferes with the other's peace and privacy, or causes alarm, distress or harm to the other, by acts which are intentional or reckless and which a reasonable person would realise would have that effect

(NFOPA 1997, s 10(2)). See DEBT; SEXUAL HARASSMENT.

harassment in employment. Any form of *unwanted conduct* related to any of the *discriminatory grounds*: Employment Equality Act 1998, s 14A inserted by Equality Act 2004, s 8. Such *unwanted conduct* may consist of acts, requests, spoken words, gestures or the production, display or circulation of written words, pictures or other material. Harassment constitutes discrimination by the victim's employer in relation to the victim's conditions of employment. The *discriminatory grounds* are: gender, marital status, family status, sexual orientation, religion, age, disability, race, or membership of the Traveller community (qqv). See Code of Practice (Harassment) Ord 2002, SI No 78 of 2002. See 'The law of workplace stress, bullying and harassment' by Wesley Farrell BL in *Bar Review* (June/July 2002) 252. For previous legislation, see EEA 1998, s 32 repealed by EA 2004, s 21. [Bibliography: Eardly (1).] See also SEXUAL HARASSMENT.

harassment in general. Harassment is any form of *unwanted conduct* related to any of the *discriminatory grounds*: Equal Status Act 2000, s 11(5), as amended by substitution by Equality Act 2004, s 51. Such *unwanted conduct* may consist of acts, requests, spoken words, gestures or the production, display or circulation of written words, pictures or other material. The *discriminatory grounds* are: gender, marital status, family status, sexual orientation, religion, age, disability, race, or membership of the Traveller community (qqv). A person in authority in an educational establishment, a person providing services or accommodation or disposing of goods or premises, is prohibited from harassing another person (ESA 2000, s 11(1)). [Bibliography: Reid M.] See DISCRIMINATION; SEXUAL HARASSMENT.

harassment in litigation. Repeated action concerning the same subject matter. Such harassment can arise whether or not a set of proceedings was pursued to judgment or settlement. A defendant is protected against harassment in litigation, as a litigant is not allowed to make the same contention in legal proceedings which might have been, but was not, brought forward in previous litigation: *Carroll v Ryan* [2003] 2 ILRM 1, SC and 1 IR 309 which followed *Henderson v Henderson* [1843] 3 Hare 10.

harbour authorities. Statutory bodies established to operate and maintain specified harbours, the members of which are elected and are representative of users of the harbours, local authorities, commercial and labour interests, with some members being nominated by the Minister: Harbours Acts 1946 to 1976. Rosslare Harbour is managed by Córas Iompair Éireann; fishing harbours not specified by the Harbour Acts are the responsibility of the Minister.

Provision was made in 1996 for State commercial companies to manage and operate the ports of Arklow, Cork, Drogheda, Dublin, Dundalk, Dún Laoghaire, Foynes, Galway, New Ross, Shannon, Waterford and Wicklow: Harbours Act 1996. This Act provides a framework under which small harbours may: (a) continue to operate under the 1946 legislation, or (b) be set up as State commercial companies, or (c) be transferred to local authorities.

A harbour authority is empowered to remove any obstruction which is within the limits of its harbour or in the seaward approaches thereto: HA 1946, s 57 as amended by the Merchant Shipping (Salvage and Wreck) Act 1993, s 54. See also Sea Pollution (Amendment) Act 1999, ss 2, 3, 5.

The primary duty of care for cargo stored on an unenclosed quay, where damage is foreseeable, rests with the owner and not the harbour authority: *John C Doherty Timber Co Ltd v Drogheda Harbour Commissioners* [1993] ILRM 401, HC. See *C W Shipping Ltd v Limerick Harbour Commissioners* [1989] ILRM 416, HC; *MPGWU v Pandora Ltd* [1994] ELR 244, HC. See also Oil Pollution of the Sea (Civil Liability and Compensation) Act 1988, s 3(1). See also State Harbours Act 1924.

In 2000, provision was made: (a) for the establishment of a new company, resulting in the amalgamation of existing companies, whenever the Minister is of the opinion that this would be more efficient and cost effective; (b) for the injection of moneys to finance capital works or for equity; and (c) to enable the amalgamation of the functions of the Foynes Port Company and the Shannon Estuary Ports Company: Harbours (Amendment) Act 2000. See COMPTROLLER AND AUDITOR GENERAL; FISHERY HARBOUR CENTRE; PILOTAGE; OIL POLLUTION.

harbour police. Persons so appointed by the Dublin Port Company and the Dún Laoghaire Harbour Company to police their respective harbours; such persons have the power of arrest without warrant, but must forthwith deliver the person arrested to a garda to be dealt with in accordance with law: Harbours Act 1996, s 54. See Private Security Services Act 2004, s 3(1)(c).

harbouring of spouse. Formerly an actionable tort (qv) whereby a person harboured another man's wife after notice that she had left that other without his consent. Abolished by the Family Law Act 1981, s 1.

hard labour. Formerly, the punishment of imprisonment with hard labour to which a person could be sentenced. See *The People v Giles* [1974] IR 422. For many years, there has been no distinction in the treatment of prisoners sentenced to imprisonment with hard labour and those sentenced to imprisonment only. Now, a person cannot be sentenced to imprisonment with hard labour: Criminal Law Act 1997, s 11(3). The expressions in statutes 'with or without hard labour', 'with hard labour' and 'without hard labour' are repealed. See PUNISHMENT.

hardware. The physical components of a computer system, including any peripheral equipment such as printers, modems and mouse devices. Compare with SOFTWARE.

hare. See WILD ANIMALS, PROTECTED.

harm. See ASSAULT; CAUSING SERIOUS HARM; ENDANGERMENT.

harmful organisms. Provision has been made on protection measures against the introduction of organisms harmful to plants and plant products and to prevent the spread of harmful organisms: SI No 125 of 1980, as amended by SI No 197 of 2002, SI No 117 of 2004, implementing Directive (EC) 2003/116, and SI No 224 of 2004. See GENETICALLY MODIFIED ORGANISM.

harmonisation. Means co-ordinating national policies, rules and technical standards so closely that products and services, capital and labour can move freely throughout the EU: National Forum on Europe, *Glossary of Terms* (2003). See CE MARK; EUROPEAN TRANSPARENCY DIRECTIVE; MUTUAL RECOGNITION; STANDARD MARK.

harmonisation of laws. The approximation of the laws of the member states of the EC to the extent required for the functioning of the common market; this is a required activity of the Community: EC Treaty, art 3(h) of the consolidated (2002) version. The Council of Ministers, acting unanimously, has power to issue directives for the approximation of such laws, regulations or administrative provisions of the member states as directly affect the establishment and functioning of the common market (EC Treaty, consolidated art 94 and arts 95–97).

See *Cassis de Dijon* Case 120/78 [1979] ECR 649. See *Travers* in 11 ILT & SJ (1993) 4. See 'Subsidiarity, Federalism and the Internal Market' by Mr Justice Nial Fennelly in *Bar Review* (November 2000) 75. The Irish EU Commissioner David Byrne has favoured the approximation of criminal law provided it is limited to a few specified offences, such as money laundering, drug trafficking and people trafficking that have a clear cross-border element: Irish Times, 25 January 2003. See COMMUNITY DESIGN; COMMUNITY TRADE MARK; EUROPEAN CONTRACT LAW; EUROPEAN ECONOMIC COMMUNITY; FRAMEWORK DECISION; MUTUAL RECOGNITION.

hatred, incitement to. It is an offence to incite hatred of persons in the State or elsewhere on account of their race, colour, nationality, religion, ethnic or national origins, membership of the Travelling community or sexual orientation: Prohibition of Incitement to Hatred Act 1989. The first conviction under the 1989 Act is believed to be *DPP v O'Grady* (2000) Irish Times, 15 September 2000. The Minister for Justice announced in September 2000 that a review of the legislation was to take place. See 'The Prohibition of Incitement to Hatred Act – a Paper Tiger?' by Conor Keogh BL in *Bar Review* (December 2000) 178. See also VIDEO RECORDING.

have regard to. In many statutes there is a requirement for a body or an individual to *have regard to* some matter when performing a specified function eg a planning authority is required to *have regard to* any regional planning guidelines when making or adopting a development plan: Planning and Development Act 2000, s 27(1). In this particular provision, the phrase '*have regard to*' has been held to be permissive in nature and to create an obligation to consider something rather than follow or slavishly adhere to something: *McEvoy v Meath County Council* [2003] 1 ILRM 431, HC and 1 IR 208. 'The statutory obligation to "have regard to" means precisely that, no

more and no less.': Quirke J in *McEvoy* case. An Bord Pleanála is required to *have regard to* the policies for the time being, of the government, a State authority, the Minister, and planning authorities (PDA 2000, s 143). See ASSESSOR; DEPORTATION ORDER; DEVELOPMENT PLAN; IRISH LANGUAGE; SOUND BROADCASTING SERVICE.

hawker. A travelling seller of goods: Hawkers Act 1888, s 1 since repealed by Finance Act 1989, s 49. However, there is still an offence of *hawking stamps*: Management Act 1891, s 6 amended by Finance Act 1999, s 151, now Stamp Duties Consolidation Act 1999, s 149.

hazardous waste. The Environmental Protection Agency is required to make a *national* plan called the *hazardous waste management plan* with regard to: the prevention, minimisation, recovery, collection and movement of hazardous waste, and also the disposal of such hazardous waste as cannot be prevented or recovered: Waste Management Act 1996, s 26. The plan must be reviewed at least once every five years (WMA 1996, s 26(3)). Local authorities must comply with recommendations made by the EPA as regards hazardous waste (WMA 1996, s 26(6)). There is no obligation on the EPA to provide waste facilities or other resources (s 26(8)). See Waste Management (Hazardous Waste) (Amendment) Regulations 2000, SI No 73 of 2000; Exposure to Asbestos (Amendment) Regulations 2000, SI No 75 of 2000. See WASTE; WASTE MANAGEMENT PLAN.

head lease. The lease from which lesser interests (ie subleases) have been created. See LEASE.

headings. Words in an Act placed at the head or beginning of a part, section or provision. Such words must not be considered or judicially noticed in relation to the construction or interpretation of the Act: Interpretation Act 1937, s 11(g). See MARGINAL NOTES.

headnote. A summary of the points decided in a case, which is found at the commencement or head of a law report.

health and EC. See PUBLIC HEALTH.

health and safety. See SAFETY AT WORK.

health board. A body corporate with perpetual succession, established by the Minister, to perform functions conferred on it and other functions in its functional area which, before its establishment, were performed by a local authority (other than as a sanitary authority) in relation to the operation of services provided under various specified enactments: Health Act 1970, ss 6 and 4(1), as amended by Health (Amendment) Act 2004, s 4. The Minister for Health is empowered to establish the number of health boards as may appear to him to be appropriate and to define the functional area of each board so established.

Under the 2004 Act, provision was made: (a) to abolish the membership of the seven health boards, the Eastern Regional Health Authority and its three area health boards; (b) to abolish the distinction between *reserved* and *executive* functions and to assign what were *reserved* functions to the chief executive officers of the boards and the Authority, or to the Minister for Health in certain circumstances (eg appointment of chief executive officer): H(A)A 2004, ss 4–14, and 27. The consent of the Minister for Health is now required for the acquisition or disposal of land by a health board: Health Act 1947, ss 78 and 89 as amended by H(A)A 2004, s 15. The 2004 legislation which came into operation on 15 June 2004 (SI No 378 of 2004) is part of a major overhaul of the health services, including the establishment of the *Health Service Executive*.

Health boards are required in carrying out their functions: (a) to secure the most beneficial, effective and efficient use of resources, (b) to co-operate and co-ordinate their activities with other bodies in their area, including voluntary bodies, and (c) to give due consideration to the policies and objectives of Ministers and the government: Health (Amendment) (No 3) Act 1996, s 2. The functions of a health board are now required to be performed by its chief executive officer (H(A)(No 3)A 1996, s 3 as substituted by H(A)A 2004, s 9).

The Minister is required to specify the maximum amount of net expenditure (the 'determination') which may be incurred by a health board in any one year and the board is required to monitor this expenditure to ensure that it does not exceed the determination (H(A)(No 3)A 1996, ss 5–10, as amended by H(A)A 2004 Act s 11). The Minister may give a direction to a health board and the board is required to comply with the direction (H(A)(No 3)A 1996, s 13).

The High Court has held that a health board is not restricted in relation to discontinuing services in a particular hospital provided it maintained the hospital as a hospital: *Tierney and Others v North Eastern Health Board* (2004) Irish Times, 30 July, HC. In this case the court held that the 1970 Act did not preclude the health board from taking its decision to suspend the maternity services at Monaghan General Hospital.

See Health Board Regulations 1970, SI No 170 of 1970 and H(A)A 2004, s 3(2). For other amendments to 1996 Act, see Health (Eastern Regional Health Authority) Act 1999, s 24 and H(A)A 2004, ss 9–14). See also Child Care Act 1991, s 72; Health (Amendment) Act 1994; Domestic Violence Act 1996, s 6; Public Service Superannuation (Miscellaneous Provisions) Act 2004, Sch 2; Education for Persons with Special Educational Needs Act 2004, ss 16 and 39. See also *O'Flynn & O'Regan v Mid-Western Health Board & Ors* [1991] 2 IR 223; *Rajpal v North Eastern Health Board* (7 May 2004, unreported), HC. [Bibliography: Canny (2); Hensey.] See COMPTROLLER AND AUDITOR GENERAL; EASTERN REGIONAL HEALTH AUTHORITY; HEALTH SERVICE EXECUTIVE; HEALTH SERVICES; AUDITOR, LOCAL GOVERNMENT; NATURAL JUSTICE; PATIENT CHARGES.

Health Boards Executive. A body corporate which was established to perform, on behalf of health boards, *functions* of health boards as may be specified or directed: Health (Eastern Regional Health Authority) Act 1999, s 21 as amended by Health (Amendment) Act 2004, s 24. The members of the Executive are the chief executive officers of the health boards and the area chief executives. The Executive acts as a central agency for the health boards through which the chief executive officers can jointly pursue some of their common objectives eg health promotion. See website: *www.hebe.ie.* See HEALTH SERVICE EXECUTIVE.

health contributions. The levy which individuals over the age of 16 years with reckonable earnings, or with emoluments other than reckonable earnings, or with income other than emoluments, must pay towards the cost of the provision of services under the Health Acts: Health Contributions Act 1979. Provision has been made to ensure that from 1 January 2004 the health contribution levy is payable in respect of non-pecuniary emoluments received by individuals who are not in insurable employment eg directors: SI No 719 of 2003. See also Social Welfare (Miscellaneous Provisions) Act 2002, s 16; Social Welfare (Miscellaneous Provisions) Act 2004, s 20.

health expenses. Includes the cost of fees of a qualified practitioner, diagnostic procedures, treatment in hospital, prescribed drugs and medicines, prescribed physiotherapy or orthoptic treatment, prescribed medical, dental or nursing appliance, and ambulance support: Taxes Consolidation Act 1997, s 469. A person who has *defrayed* more than €125 in health expenses (ie expenses on *health care* for a tax year) is entitled to income tax relief at the marginal rate for the excess. *Health care* means the diagnosis, prevention or treatment of illness, injury or old age; it includes non-routine maternity care. Where a family claim is made, the excess is €250. *Defrayed* means that the health care expenses must be borne by the person at some time; they need not be actually paid in the tax year.

In 2002, TCA 1997, s 469 was amended to permit health expenses to be claimed against tax in respect of a wider range of 'relatives': Finance Act 2002, s 9. See Revenue Leaflet IT6, *Medical Expenses Relief* and Revenue Leaflet IT46, *Dependant Relative Allowance*.

health insurance. A contract of insurance which provides for the making of payments specifically for the reimbursement or discharge of fees or charges in respect of the provision of hospital in-patient or ancillary health services; it does not include a contract of insurance which provides for payments calculated by reference only to the duration of a sickness, injury or disease: Health Insurance Act 1994, s 2(1).

All health insurance undertakings are required to be registered before they can engage in the business of health insurance in the State. The 1994 legislation allowed for competition in the private health insurance market for the first time, implementing Directive (EC) 92/49. Health insurance contracts must provide for: *open enrolment* (ie open to all under 65 years of age), *community rating* (ie charge the same premium for a given level of benefits irrespective of age, sex or health status), and *lifetime cover* (ie the undertaking may not refuse to renew the health cover). There is provision

for a *risk equalisation scheme* to provide for the sharing of certain adverse risk factors between health insurance undertakings. See Risk Equalisation Scheme 2003, SI No 261 of 2003 as amended by SI No 710 of 2003. See also SI No 359 of 1994, as amended by Central Bank and Financial Services Authority of Ireland Act 2003, s 35, Sch 2.

The Health Insurance (Amendment) Act 2001: (a) provides for the removal of *ancillary health services* from the scope of legislative control eg out-patient services, general practitioner services and dental services, (b) allows insurers to apply *late entry premium loadings* in specified circumstances, (c) extends the enrolment provisions of the Health Insurance Act 1994 to persons of, or over 65 years of age, in certain circumstances, (d) permits new insurers to the market the option of not participating in *risk equalisation arrangements* for a specified period, (e) empowers the Minister to give the Health Insurance Authority a significant role in relation to the commencement of risk equalisation, and (f) gives additional powers to the Voluntary Health Insurance Board to carry out schemes for the provision of services in respect of health care, health insurance, illness-related insurance, personal care or related services.

As regards the conditions for prior authorisation which may be required in order for medical treatment in another member state to be paid from an insurance sickness fund, the European Court of Justice has held that: (a) a condition that the treatment must be regarded as 'normal' should be interpreted so that authorisation cannot be refused on that ground where the treatment is sufficiently tried and tested by international medical science, and (b) a condition that the insured person must require that treatment should be interpreted so that authorisation can be refused only if the same or equally effective treatment can be obtained without undue delay at an establishment having a contractual arrangement with the insured's sickness insurance fund: Case C-157/99 *Geraets-Smits v Stichting Ziekfonds VGZ and Peerbooms v Stichting CZ Groep Zorgverzekeringen* [2001] ECR 1–5473. See also Health Insurance Levy Regulations 2001, SI No 255 of 2001.

Amendments have been made to the provisions concerning application of the limited exemption from *risk equalisation* for new entrant insurers to the market: Health Insurance (Amendment) Act 2003, s 5. See websites: *www.vhi.ie* and *www.bupa.ie*. See PERMANENT HEALTH INSURANCE; VOLUNTARY HEALTH INSURANCE.

health mark. See ABATTOIR.

health professional. Includes a registered medical practitioner, a registered dentist, or a member of a class of health worker or social worker specified in Ministerial regulations: Data Protection Act 1988, s 2B inserted by Data Protection (Amendment) Act 2003, s 4. There is no prohibition on a data controller in processing *sensitive personal data* where the processing is necessary for *medical purposes* and is undertaken by a health professional or another person subject to a duty of confidentiality. 'Medical purposes' includes the purposes of preventative medicine, medical diagnosis, medical research, the provision of care and treatment and the management of healthcare services. See MEDICAL RECORDS; SENSITIVE PERSONAL DATA.

health research board. The body established under the Health (Corporate Bodies) Act 1961 to promote, assist, commission or conduct medical, health, epidemiological and health services research: SI No 279 of 1986 as amended by SI No 205 of 2002. The purpose of the 2002 amendment is to achieve greater congruence between the composition and work of the Board and the National Strategy for Health Research and to comply with the code of practice for the governance of State bodies. See website: *www.hrb.ie*.

The Irish Medical Council has stipulated that (a) research results must always preserve patient anonymity, (b) refusal to participate in research must not influence the care of a patient in any way, (c) consent to take part in research may be unobtainable in the case of those who are not competent, and (d) all institutions which undertake research should have Research Ethics Committees to whom proposals for research should be submitted: Medical Council, *A Guide to Ethical Conduct and Behaviour* (6th edn, 2004) para 20.1–20.5. See CLINICAL TRIALS, CONDUCT OF.

Health Service Executive. A body to be established to plan and provide, or arrange to be provided, health services which are presently provided by or on behalf of the health boards: Interim Health Service Executive (Establishment) Order 2004, SI No 90 of 2004. The interim Executive will plan for the establishment of a Heath Service Executive and the incorporation within it of the management and administrative and service delivery structures of the heath boards. The intention is to provide a national unified and administrative structure for the promotion and delivery of health services. See HEALTH BOARD.

health services. Persons who are entitled to *full eligibility* for health services are those adults who are ordinarily resident in the State and who are unable without undue hardship to arrange general practitioner medical and surgical services for themselves and their dependants; and also the spouses of such adults: Health Act 1970, s 45 as amended by the Health (Amendment) Act 1991, s 2. A person ordinarily resident in the State who is without full eligibility, has *limited eligibility* ie entitled to public consultant care in public hospitals free of charge (H(A)A 1991, s 3). Persons lose their eligibility if and when they opt for private treatment (H(A)A 1991, s 5).

These provisions are without prejudice to the operation of the EC Regulations in relation to the provision of health services to residents of other EC states who are temporarily resident in Ireland (H(A)A 1991, ss 6 and 9). See also Health Services Regulations 1991, SI No 135 of 1991 and SI No 136 of 1991.

A person who is at least 70 years of age and is ordinarily resident in the State is now entitled to full eligibility for health services ie they are entitled to a medical card regardless of income: Health (Miscellaneous Provisions) Act 2001, s 1(1)(b) amending Health Act 1970, s 45.

Provision has been made for a refund to be made to a person of the amount by which their expenditure exceeds IR£42 (€53.33) in any month on prescribed medicines and surgical appliances: Health Services Regulations 2001, SI No 66 of 2001. This threshold has been increased to €65 as from 1 August 2002, to €70 as from 1 January 2003, and to €78 as from 1 January 2004: Health Services Regulations 2002 and 2004, SI No 368 of 2002, SI No 603 of 2002 and SI No 658 of 2003.

For the Department of Health and Children, see website: *www.doh.ie*. For the Office for Health Management, see website: *www.tohm.ie*. For Health Service Employers Agency, see website: *www.hsea.ie*. For independent health information in a joint Irish Medical Organisation/Department of

Health project, see website: *www.myGP.ie*. See HEALTH BOARD.

health surveillance. The periodic review, for the purpose of protecting health and preventing occupationally related disease, of the health of employees, so that any adverse variations in their health which may be related to working conditions are identified as early as possible: Health, Safety and Welfare at Work (General Application) Regulations 1993, SI No 44 of 1993, reg 15(3). It is the duty of every employer to ensure that health surveillance is made available for every employee. See MATERNITY LEAVE.

hearing. (1) The trial of a cause or action. (2) Proceedings before a court, arbitrator or tribunal. See TRIAL.

hearing injury. Includes *hearing loss* caused by injury and *tinnitus*: Civil Liability (Assessment of Hearing Injury) Act 1998, s 1. The courts are required, in all proceedings claiming damages for personal injury arising from a hearing injury to take *judicial notice* (qv) of the Report of an Expert Hearing Group, entitled 'Hearing Disability Assessment' (CL(AHI)A 1998, s 3) and to have regard to certain matters in the Report (CL(AHI)A 1998, s 4). It is a matter for the courts to determine what weight they will attach to the Report.

Although this legislation was prompted by the large number of claims from Army personnel in respect of hearing injury, it is not confined to such claims. In a particular case, it was held that where audiogram results differ, damages for hearing loss are to be based on the average figure: *Kinlan v Minister for Defence and A-G* [2000] ITLR (10 April), HC.

The Supreme Court has approved an alternative scale for the calculation of damages for hearing loss: *Hanley v Minister for Defence* [2000] 2 ILRM 276, SC and [1999] 4 IR 392, SC. The High Court has held that a hearing loss claim of an employee was not statute-barred where adverse hearing test results had not been disclosed by the employer: *Keogh v Minister for Defence* [2004] ITLR (22 March), HC. See also *Greene v Minister for Defence* [1998] 4 IR 464, HC.

hearsay. Evidence of a fact not perceived by a witness with his own senses, but asserted by him to have been stated by another person; *what someone else has been heard to say*. It is hearsay evidence if it is offered to prove the truth of the facts stated therein

and generally will not be admissible; however hearsay evidence is admissible if its purpose is to show that the statement was made (eg to explain the mental state or conduct of the witness) rather than to prove the truth of the facts therein.

Exceptions to the general rule are: informal admissions; confessions; declarations of deceased persons; evidence in former proceedings; statements in public documents (qqv). Hearsay evidence cannot establish the truth of the answer given: *Mullen v Quinnsworth Ltd* [1991] ILRM 439, SC. However, hearsay evidence (eg medical records) is admissible on consent of the parties: *Hughes v Staunton* [1991] 9 ILT Dig 52, HC. See *Cullen v Clarke* [1963] IR 368. For exceptions in criminal proceedings regarding documents, see DOCUMENTARY EVIDENCE. The Law Reform Commission has recommended that generally hearsay evidence should be allowed in civil cases: (LRC 25, 1988).

In general, assertions made by persons who are not called as witnesses are inadmissible to prove the truth of the matters stated therein. They are inadmissible to protect the fair trial process because: (a) the author was not on oath when he made it, (b) it was made in private and not in public, (c) the court has not had an opportunity of observing his demeanour when making the assertion, and (d) there is no opportunity to test the assertion on cross-examination: *In the matter of MK, SK and WK* [1999] 2 ILRM 321, SC. 'It is doubtful whether evidence adduced by means of a tape recording is properly described as hearsay evidence' per Barrington J in *MK case*. There are many exceptions to the rule eg in wardship proceedings where the judge has a discretion: *Eastern Health Board v MK* [1999] 2 IR 99, SC. Also a court is entitled to admit hearsay evidence in an application for bail in certain circumstances: *People v McGinley* [1998] 2 ILRM 233 and 2 IR 408, SC.

Provision has been made for the admission of hearsay evidence of a child (ie a *statement*) in civil proceedings concerning the welfare of a child where the court considers that: (a) the child is unable to give evidence by reason of age, or (b) the giving of oral evidence by the child, either in person or by live television link, would not be in the interest of the welfare of the child: Children Act 1997, s 23. A *statement*, in this context, means any representation of fact or opinion however made (CA 1997, s 19(1)). The civil proceedings may also be concerning a person of full age who has a mental disability. It is a matter for the court to assess what weight is to be given to the hearsay evidence (CA 1997, s 24). Evidence as to the child's credibility is admissible (CA 1997, s 25). See *Re M, S, W (Infants)* [1996] 1 ILRM 370; *Southern Health Board v CH* [1996] 2 ILRM 142; *Criminal Assets Bureau v Hunt* [2003] 2 ILRM 481 and 2 IR 168, SC. [Bibliography: Charleton (5); Healy.] See CHILD, EVIDENCE OF; DYING DECLARATIONS; EVIDENCE IN PREVIOUS PROCEEDINGS.

hedge. (1) To reduce by contract the risk of loss arising from changes in interest rates, currency exchange rates or other similar factors affecting one's business. See Building Societies Act 1989, s 34 as amended by Housing (Miscellaneous Provisions) Act 2002, s 23 and Sch 3. See SWAP TRANSACTION.

(2) The former provisions which provided for the removal or alteration of hedges and for compensation to be payable, have not been re-enacted in the consolidating Planning and Development Act 2000, as sufficient powers are available under the Roads Act 1993, s 70 in relation to hazardous road-side trees and hedges. See formerly Local Government (Planning and Development) Act 1963, s 44 and LG(PD)A 1990, s 20. See TREE.

hedge and ditch rule. The common law rule or presumption that the boundary between adjoining lands, runs along the edge of the ditch away from a bank or hedge: *Vawles v Miller* [1810] 3 Taunt 137. This rule arose from the assumption that a bank of earth separating two parcels of land would be created by digging up the soil and throwing it onto the bank. The presumption only arises where there is an actual bank and not where there is a natural hedge or ditch, or where there is evidence to the contrary eg where a map describing the boundary clearly indicates the boundary along the centre of the hedge. The general rule was applied in *Walsh v McGauran* (1977, unreported), HC. Caution needs to be exercised in the definition of '*ditch*', as in parts of Ireland it means an excavation in the ground and elsewhere it means a bank extending from the ground upwards. [Bibliography: Wylie (2).]

heir. A person who succeeds to property by descent (qv); now *heirs* for the purpose of devolution mean the persons entitled to succeed on intestacy under Part VI of the Succession Act 1965. When the word *heirs* is used in any enactment or deed passed or executed after the 1 January 1967 as a *word of purchase* (qv), it is to be construed to mean those entitled under the Succession Act 1965, Pt VI, and when used as a *word of limitation* (qv) to have the same effect as if the Act had not been passed: Succession Act 1965, s 15. See *Re McIntyre, Crawford v Ruttledge* [1970] HC.

heir apparent. A person who, if he survived his ancestor, would be his heir. He was not the heir until after death as nobody could be the heir of a living person – *nemo est heres viventis*.

heir locator. A person carrying on a commercial enterprise of seeking to locate beneficiaries of estates or the apparent owners of unclaimed property. An *heir locator agreement* is typically one in which the located beneficiary agrees to assign a share of the value of the property to which the beneficiary may become entitled, in return for the heir locator revealing details of the claim. Such an agreement infringes the law of *champerty* (qv) and is contrary to Irish public policy, notwithstanding that the claim is in another jurisdiction, and as such is unenforceable: *Fraser v Buckle* [1994] 1 ILRM 276, HC.

In the Supreme Court it was held that if an arrangement is not merely that information will be given, but that the person who gives it and who is to share in what may be recovered, will himself recover the property, or actively assist in the recovery of it by procuring evidence, the arrangement is contrary to the policy of law and void: *Frazer v Buckle* [1996] 2 ILRM 34, SC.

heirloom. (1) *Such goods and personal chattels as shall go by special custom to the heir along with the inheritance*: Blackstone, *Commentaries on the Laws of England*, Vol ll. (2) Personal chattels (qv) settled so as to devolve with the land, such as family pictures, tapestries, antiques and furniture: Settled Land Act 1882, s 37. See *Gormanstown v Gormanstown* [1923] 1 IR 137.

hello money. Popularly understood to mean money paid by a supplier of grocery goods to a wholesaler or retailer in consideration of: (a) the carrying out by that person of advertising of such goods or (b) the making available of selling space on the opening of a new retail outlet or the extension of an existing outlet, or after the change of ownership of an existing outlet.

The payment of such money or the making of an allowance or the giving of a reduction of or discount on the price of grocery goods or the giving of any other benefit is prohibited, as is the receipt of such benefit: Restrictive Practices (Groceries) Order 1987, SI No 142 of 1987; Restrictive Practices (Confirmation of Order) Act 1987. The Minister is empowered to amend or revoke the Order: Competition Act 2002, s 49. [Bibliography: O'Reilly M.]

hepatitis. Inflammation of the liver. The Tribunal of Inquiry into the Blood Transfusion Service Board, chaired by Mr Justice Finlay, found in 1997 that the primary source for the infection of Anti-D produced by the Board was through the taking of plasma from a patient X in 1976 and 1977, and the use of that plasma to form pools from which the product was manufactured.

The Minister for Health established in 1997 a statutory compensation tribunal to replace a non-statutory one which had certain limitations e g the non-statutory tribunal could not award exemplary or aggravated damages and there was no right of appeal to the High Court: Hepatitis C Compensation Tribunal Act 1997. The Act was amended in 2002 in order to enable the Tribunal to award compensation also to persons who contracted HIV (*human immunodeficiency virus*) within the State from certain blood products and to rename the Tribunal accordingly: Hepatitis C Compensation Tribunal (Amendment) Act 2002.

It has been held by the Supreme Court that the tribunal has the power to award interest on foot of an award as would the High Court on a subsequent appeal from the Tribunal: *M O'C v Minister for Health* [2002] 1 IR 234, SC.

While an appeal lies to the High Court against an award of the tribunal, the Supreme Court has held that an appeal is barred: (a) after the time specified in the 1997 Act, or (b) after a claimant has accepted an award of the tribunal: *Mr A v Minister for Health* (2003) Irish Times, 27 March 2003. The High Court had previously held that a person who had accepted an award of compensation from the tribunal, was still entitled to appeal the award to the High Court and that the court had jurisdiction to extend the time for

bringing such an appeal: *Mr A v Minister for Health* (2002) Irish Times, 1 August 2002. See *B(D) V Minister for Health* [2003] FL 7130, SC.

For appeals against the decisions (including awards) of that tribunal, see RSC Ord 105A as inserted by SI No 392 of 1998. See also SIs Nos 417 and 432 of 1998. Compensation payments are exempt from income tax: Finance Act 1996, s 9, now Taxes Consolidation Act 1997, s 191. Certain persons who contracted hepatitis C are entitled to a free primary health care service: Health (Amendment) Act 1996, and are exempt from in-patient or out-patient charges: SI No 116 of 1987 as amended by SI No 348 of 2003; SI No 37 of 1994 as amended by SI No 349 of 2003. Also moneys received by way of compensation are disregarded in the assessment of means for social assistance purposes: SI No 417 of 1994 as amended by SI No 323 of 2003. In relation to supplementary welfare allowance, see SI No 324 of 2003.

The Minister for Health established a Tribunal of Inquiry in September 1999 into the infection with HIV and Hepatitis C of persons with Haemophilia, under Her Honour Judge Alison Lindsay. *The Report of the Lindsay Tribunal* was published on 5 September 2002. See *Ryan v Compensation Tribunal* [1997] 1 ILRM 194, HC; *Kealy v Minister for Health* [1999] 2 IR 456, HC; *R L v Minister for Health* [2001] 1 IR 744, HC. See FICTITIOUS NAME.

heraldry. The science and art of designing coats of arms. See CHIEF HERALD; NATIONAL LIBRARY OF IRELAND.

hereditament. Real property which on the death intestate of the owner devolved on an heir. *Corporeal* hereditaments are visible and tangible property e g land and structures thereon. *Incorporeal* hereditaments are intangible property e g easements (qv) and profits a prendre (qv). See DOMESTIC HEREDITAMENT; TOLL.

heritage. *Heritage objects* means objects over 25 years old which are works of art or of industry of cultural importance; they include books, documents and other records, including genealogical records: Heritage Act 1995, s 2(1). *Heritage buildings* includes any building which is of significance because of its intrinsic architectural or artistic quality (HA 1995, s 2(1)). There is provision for the protection and preservation of heritage buildings owned by a public authority (HA 1995, s 10 as amended by Minister for Arts Act 1998, s 6).

There is also provision for the establishment of a *Heritage Council* whose function it is to propose policies and priorities for the identification, protection, preservation and enhancement of the national heritage, including monuments, archaeological objects, wrecks, heritage objects, architectural heritage, heritage gardens and parks (HA 1995, ss 5 and 6). See also Euro Changeover (Amounts) Act 2001, s 8.

To qualify for exemption from capital acquisitions tax, a *heritage house* or *garden* must be open to the public for 60 days in the year (including not less than 40 days during the period 1 May to 30September, of which ten days must be on a Saturday or Sunday): Capital Acquisitions Tax Consolidation Act 2003, s 77. A taxpayer is entitled to tax relief in respect of the donation to national collections of important heritage items; the annual cap on tax relief was increased in 2000 to £3m (€3.8m): Taxes Consolidation Act, s 1003 as amended by Finance Act 2000, s 161. The cap was increased in 2002 to €6 million on an annual basis: Finance Act 2002, s 124. See also Finance Act 2002, s 118; Finance Act 2004, ss 81 and 85. See NATIONAL MONUMENT.

heritage fund. A fund established to enable the principal State collecting cultural institutions to acquire *heritage objects* eg such artifacts as manuscripts, books and works of art that are rare, costly (minimum fair market value of at least €317,435), of national importance and otherwise could not be acquired: Heritage Fund Act 2001. The collecting (*eligible*) institutions are the National Museum, National Library, National Gallery, National Archives, and the Irish Museum of Modern Art (HFA 2001, s 2(1)).

Decisions on acquisitions using the fund are made by the Minister for Arts on the recommendation of the *Council of National Cultural Institutions*, which Council is representative of the collecting institutions as well as the Chester Beatty Library, the National Concert Hall, Abbey Theatre, the Arts Council and Heritage Council (HFA 2001, s 9). Provision is made for the fund to receive £10m (€12.7m) from the Exchequer over a five-year period, as well as private funds from individuals and companies (HFA 2001, s 4). See also Euro Changeover (Amounts) Act 2001, s 8.

HETAC. [Higher Education and Training Awards Council (qv).]

High Court. The court above the Circuit Court (qv) in the hierarchical system of courts, which is invested with full *original* jurisdiction in and power to determine all matters and questions whether of law or fact, civil or criminal: 1937 Constitution, art 34(3)(1). It sits in Dublin and at other locations in the State as required.

In civil matters the High Court can award unlimited damages; in criminal matters it is known as the *Central Criminal Court* and hears only very serious crimes such as treason, murder, attempted murder, conspiracy to murder, rape, or certain offences against the State (qqv): Courts (Supplementary Provision) Act 1961, s 25(2); *DPP v Hamill & Deighan* [2000] 1 ILRM 150, HC (under appeal). Also a person indicted for a competition law offence is tried in the Central Criminal Court: Competition Act 2002, s 11. See ACQUITTAL.

The judge sits alone except: (a) in criminal cases and in certain civil actions eg defamation, false imprisonment or intentional trespass to the person, when he sits with a jury, and (b) in cases of importance at the direction of the President of the High Court, when three judges sit as a *divisional court*, and may give separate judgments, although the decision of the court is the majority.

The High Court exercises considerable supervisory jurisdiction over inferior courts, administrative bodies and individuals by way of *judicial review* (qv). An appeal from the High Court lies to the Supreme Court (qv). Previously, an appeal from the *Central Criminal Court* lay only to the Court of Criminal Appeal (qv), except that an appeal directly to the Supreme Court was retained in respect of: (a) the constitutionality of any law, and (b) the reference of a verdict of not guilty by direction of the trial judge pursuant to s 34 of the Criminal Procedure Act 1967: Criminal Procedure Act 1993, s 11. When the Court of Criminal Appeal is subsumed into the Supreme Court, an appeal will lay only to the Supreme Court: Courts and Court Officers Act 1995, s 4–5.

See Rules of the Superior Courts 1986, SI No 15 of 1986 as amended. See Supreme Court and High Court (Fees) Order 2003, SI No 89 of 2003. [Bibliography: Goldberg; O'Floinn; Wood K.] See

COMMERCIAL PROCEEDINGS; JUDGES; JURY, ABOLITION OF; REMITTAL OF ACTION; STATE SIDE ORDERS.

High Court on Circuit. The High Court when sitting in an appeal town; twice a year the court is required to sit in every county and county borough to hear appeals from the Circuit Court and to transact other business: Courts and Court Officers Act 1995, s 42.

Higher Education and Training Awards Council; HETAC. A body corporate with functions in the area of *higher* education and training, *inter alia*: (a) to establish and publish policies and criteria for the making of awards and the *validation* of programmes, (b) to determine the standards of knowledge, skill or competence to be acquired by learners, (c) to make or recognise awards, (d) to ensure that providers have procedures for the assessment of learners which are fair and consistent: Qualifications (Education and Training) Act 1999, ss 21 and 23.

The Council may delegate to a 'recognised institution' the authority to make higher education and training awards (Q(ET)A 1999, s 29). A recognised institution with this delegated power must have a charter (qv) (Q(ET)A 1999, s 31). The National Qualifications Authority of Ireland may determine whether any particular programme of education and training is *'higher'* or *'further'* education and training (Q(ET)A 1999, s 10). See websites: *www.hetac.ie*; *www.fetac.ie*; and *www.nqai.ie*. See FURTHER EDUCATION AND TRAINING AWARDS COUNCIL; NATIONAL QUALIFICATIONS AUTHORITY OF IRELAND.

Higher Education Authority. A statutory body responsible for the funding of universities and designated third-level education institutions; its functions include the development of third-level education: Higher Education Authority Act 1971. As regards reviews by the Authority, guidelines to the universities, and information on staffing which universities must provide to the Authority, see Universities Act 1997, ss 49–51. See also Qualifications (Education and Training) Act 1999. See website: *www.hea.ie*. See E-LEARNING; UNIVERSITY; NATIONAL QUALIFICATIONS AUTHORITY OF IRELAND.

highway. *Prima facie* the space between the fences and not merely the metalled part of the road and includes the footpath: *McKee v McGrath* [1892] 30 LRI 41; *Collen v Ellis*

[1893] 32 LRI 491; *Attorney-General v Mayo County Council* [1902] 1 IR 13. See PUBLIC ROAD; ROAD.

hijacking. A person is guilty of an offence who unlawfully by force or threat or by other form of intimidation, seizes or exercises control of or otherwise interferes with the control of, or compels or induces some other person to use for an unlawful purpose, any vehicle (whether mechanically propelled or not) or any ship or hovercraft: Criminal Law (Jurisdiction) Act 1976, s 10(1). See AIR PIRACY.

Hilary. A sitting of the court. See SITTINGS OF COURT.

hip flask defence. Refers to where a person takes or attempts to take any action, including the consumption of alcohol, with the intention of frustrating a prosecution for driving a vehicle (or being *in charge* of) a vehicle while under the influence of an intoxicant; it is an offence: Road Traffic Act 1994, s 20.

In addition, the court is required to disregard any evidence of having consumed alcohol between the time of the alleged offence and the giving of a specimen (RTA 1994, s 18(2)). See IN CHARGE.

hire. Payment for the temporary use of something. See CONSUMER-HIRE AGREEMENT; HIRE-PURCHASE AGREEMENT; and contrast with CREDIT-SALE AGREEMENT. See HIRER.

hire-purchase agreement. An agreement for the bailment of goods under which the hirer may buy the goods or under which the property in the goods will, if the terms of the agreement are complied with, pass to the hirer in return for periodic payments: Consumer Credit Act 1995, s 2(1). Consequently, a bailment of goods *with an option to buy* them, constitutes a hire-purchase agreement, as does a bailment where the property in the goods passes to the hirer (bailee) by operation of the agreement, provided the periodic payments are made.

In practice, the hirer selects goods which the seller sells to a finance house (then, the owner), which then enters into a hire-purchase agreement with the hirer. The seller, however, is deemed to be a party to the agreement and with the owner is *jointly and severally* answerable to the hirer for breach of the agreement and for any misrepresentations made by the seller (CCA 1995, s 80). The hirer (bailee) has an option to buy the goods on fulfilment of certain conditions, or he may return the goods to the owner on payment of the sum stated in the agreement.

A hire-purchase agreement must meet particular statutory requirements eg it must be in writing and must contain the *hire-purchase price* (qv), the *cash price* of the goods; the amount of each instalment and date payable; and a statutory notice on the rights of the hirer to terminate the agreement and on the restrictions on the owner's right to recover the goods (CCA 1995, s 58 and Sch 5).

A copy of the agreement must be handed personally to the hirer upon the making of the agreement or delivered or sent to the hirer within ten days, and there must be a *cooling-off period* (qv) (CCA 1995, ss 58(1) and 58(5)). Certain provisions in hire-purchase agreements are void eg any restriction or exclusion of the right of the hirer to determine the agreement (CCA 1995, s 62).

In a hire-purchase agreement there is an implied condition (qv) on the part of the owner that he will have the right to sell the goods at the time the property is to pass and an implied warranty that the goods are free from any charge or encumbrance not disclosed to the hirer and that the hirer will enjoy quiet possession (CCA 1995, s 74). There is also an implied condition that the goods are of merchantable quality and, if let by description, that the goods will correspond with the description (CCA 1995, ss 76 and 75).

Parties to an agreement are entitled to arrange the relationship between themselves such as not to constitute in law a hiring: *O'Grady (Inspector of Taxes) v Laragan Quarries Ltd* [1991] 1 IR 237, HC. Leasing of aircraft or spare parts of aircraft are excluded from the scope of the hire-purchase legislation: Air Navigation and Transport Act 1988, s 48.

For provisions on costs in the District Court in relation to hire-purchase claims, see DCR 1997 Ord 51, r 9. See *United Dominions Trust (Commercial) Ltd v Nestor* [1962] IR 140; *British Wagon Credit Company Ltd v John Henebry* 97 ILTR 123; *McMullan Brothers Ltd v James J Ryan* [1958] IR 94; *Mercantile Credit Company of Ireland v Cahill* 98 ILTR 79; *Henry Ford & Son Finance v Forde* [1986] HC. See also Building Societies Act 1989, s 29(2)(j); Courts Act 1991, s 6. [Bibliography: Bird; Forde (5).] Contrast with CREDIT-SALE AGREEMEN. See ANTECEDENT NEGOTIA-

TIONS; COOLING OFF PERIOD; HIRER, HIRE-PURCHASE; PRICE CONTROL; RECOVERY OF GOODS; SMALL CLAIMS.

hire-purchase price. The total sum payable by the hirer under a hire-purchase agreement in order to complete the purchase of the goods to which the agreement relates, exclusive of any sum payable as a *penalty* or as compensation for a breach of the agreement: Consumer Credit Act 1995, s 65. It includes any sum payable by the hirer by way of deposit or other initial payment (eg by a trade-in of goods). As regards *penalty* see *Lamdon Trust Ltd v Hurrell* [1955] 1 WLR 391. An inaccuracy in the hire-purchase price known to the hirer but not to the owner will not invalidate the agreement: *AIF Ltd v Hunt & Hunt* [1992] 10 ILT Dig 199, HC. See PENALTY.

hirer. A consumer who takes, intends to take or has taken goods from an owner under a *hire-purchase agreement* (qv) or a *consumer-hire agreement* (qv) in return for periodic payments: Consumer Credit Act 1995, s 2(1). A hirer must take reasonable care of the goods (CCA 1995, ss 67 and 90).

A hirer under a hire-purchase agreement is entitled to determine such agreement by notice in writing and by paying the amount, if any, by which one-half of the *hire-purchase price* (qv) exceeds the total sums paid and due immediately before termination, without prejudice to any liability which has accrued before the termination and to any damage for failure to take reasonable care of the goods (CCA 1995, s 63). Alternatively, the hirer is entitled to purchase the goods by paying the difference between the amounts already paid and the hire-purchase price (qv) after the latter has been reduced in accordance with CCA 1995, s 52 or s 53. In either case, if a lesser amount on termination is specified in the agreement, then that will be the amount.

Certain provisions or statements purporting to restrict the rights of hirers are prohibited (CCA 1995, ss 62 and 78, 79). A clause providing for the termination of a hire-purchase agreement on the bankruptcy (qv) of the hirer is void as against the Official Assignee (qv): Bankruptcy Act 1988, s 49. See *Lamdon Trust Ltd v Hurrell* [1955] 1 WLR 391; *Halpin v Rothwell & United Dominions Trust (Ireland) Ltd* [1984] ILRM 613.

hirer-dealer. A hirer of goods of any class or description who is a dealer in goods of that class or description; a sale by such a person of goods of which he is the hirer when ostensibly acting in the ordinary course of his business as such dealer, shall be as valid as if he were expressly authorised by the owner to make the sale: Consumer Credit Act 1995, s 70. However, the buyer must act in *good faith* and not have notice that the dealer has no authority to make the sale.

historic building. Tax relief is available in respect of the cost of maintenance and restoration of approved buildings, and their gardens, which are of significant scientific, historical, architectural interest and to which *reasonable access* is afforded to the public: Finance Act 1982, s 19. *Reasonable access* means open to the public for at least 60 days a year (40 days of which are to be during the period 1 May to 30 September) for at least four hours daily, access which is reasonably priced, and access is to a substantial part of the property. The relief has been extended to the cost of maintenance or restoration of gardens that are not attached to such buildings but which are of significant horticultural, scientific, architectural or aesthetic interest: Finance Act 1993, s 29. A requirement was introduced in 2000 that ten of the 40 days in the period May to September must be at weekends. See Taxes Consolidation Act 1997, s 482 as amended by Finance Act 1998, s 33 and Finance Act 2000, s 49 and Finance Act 2002, s 42. Also provision has been made to restrict the use by passive investors of the tax relief: Finance Act 2002, s 14 inserting new s 409C into the Taxes Consolidation Act 1997.

historic cost accounting. See CURRENT COST ACCOUNTING.

historic monument. Includes a prehistoric monument, and any monument associated with the commercial, cultural, economic, industrial, military, religious or social history of the place where it is situated or of the country and includes all monuments in existence before 1700 AD or such later date as the Minister may appoint by regulations: National Monuments (Amendment) Act 1987, s 1(1). All *national monuments* (qv) are historic monuments but historic monuments, being more broadly defined, are not necessarily national monuments. There is provision for the establishment of a national body, the Historic Monuments Council (NM(A)A 1987, s 4). A sanitary authority which carries out work on an

historic monument is required, as far as possible, to preserve the monument: Architectural Heritage (National Inventory) and Historic Monuments (Miscellaneous Provisions) Act 1999, s 5.

historic wreck. See WRECK.

hit and run. See MOTOR INSURERS' BUREAU OF IRELAND; UNTRACED DRIVER.

HIV. [Human Immunodeficiency Virus.] See HEPATITIS.

hoax call. Popular expression which, if it involves: (a) the reporting of a bogus crime to the garda whereby the gardaí waste time in investigation, will amount to a *public mischief* (qv), or (b) the sending of a message by telephone which is known to be false for the purpose of causing annoyance, inconvenience or needless anxiety to any other person, may be an offence: Post Office (Amendment) Act 1951, s 13.

holder for value. A person who takes a bill of exchange (qv) and who has given, or is deemed to have given, valuable consideration for the bill. Valuable consideration for a bill may be constituted by any consideration sufficient to support a simple contact or any antecedent debt or liability. A holder for value obtains no better title to the bill than the transferor had. See Bills of Exchange Act 1882, s 27.

holder in due course. A person who takes a *bill of exchange* (qv), complete and regular on the face of it, before it is overdue and without notice of dishonour (qv), in good faith and for value, without notice of any defect of title of the transferor; such a person holds the bill free from any defect of title of prior parties: Bills of Exchange Act 1882, s 29.

However, where a bill of exchange is given to a creditor by a consumer in connection with a *credit agreement* (qv) and is negotiated by the creditor to a third party, the creditor can plead, against the third party, any defence available to him against the creditor, in any proceedings for enforcement of the bill: Consumer Credit Act 1995, s 41(2). See *Shield Life Insurance Co Ltd v Ulster Bank Ltd* [1995] 3 IR 225, HC. See DISHONOUR OF BILL.

holding company. A company which has a subsidiary e g where the holding company is a member of the subsidiary and controls the composition of its board of directors, or holds more than half in nominal value of its equity share capital or of its shares carrying voting rights; a holding company/subsidiary relationship arises also where one company is a subsidiary of another's subsidiary: Companies Act 1963, s 155. Group or consolidated accounts must be laid before the annual general meeting of the holding company (CA 1963, ss 150–154).

Particulars regarding a company's holding in subsidiary and associated companies must be disclosed in the notes to the company's accounts e g name, registered office, details of share capital and reserves, details of profit and loss of the latest financial accounts: Companies Amendment Act 1986, s 16.

A subsidiary may, subject to certain conditions, acquire and hold shares in its holding company: Companies Act 1990, ss 224–225. A subsidiary to a building society has the same meaning as it has in the Companies Acts: Building Societies Act 1989, s 2(1).

Where a holding company enters into a transaction not for its own benefit but instead to facilitate one of its subsidiary companies in the group or the group as a whole, then the transaction may be *ultra vires*. See *Charterbridge Corp v Lloyds Bank* [1970] 1 Ch 74; *Power Supermarkets Ltd v Crumlin Investments Ltd* [1981] HC. See also Companies Act 1990, ss 41(1) and 43(2). See RELATED COMPANY.

holding over. Where a tenant continues in possession of land on termination of his tenancy. See MESNE RATES.

holidays. See ANNUAL LEAVE; PUBLIC HOLIDAYS.

holograph. A deed or will written entirely in the grantor's or testator's own hand.

holy hour. Popularly understood to mean the period between 2pm and 4pm on a Sunday when licensed premises (intoxicating liquor) were required to be closed; this is no longer a requirement: Intoxicating Liquor Act 2000, s 3.

home. See FAMILY HOME; INVIOLABILITY OF DWELLING; MOTHER; NURSING HOME.

home birth. The birth of a child in the home. If a registered medical practitioner is present at the birth or stillbirth or examines the child in a place other than a hospital or institution, he has a duty to inform the registration authority: Civil Registration Act 2004, s 30(2). If a doctor is not present, but a midwife is, then the duty is on the midwife. See MIDWIFE.

home brew. Colloquial expression meaning beer brewed by a private brewer. See BREWER, PRIVATE.

home carer's allowance. A new tax allowance of £3,000 (€3,809) was introduced in 2000 for families where one spouse works at home to care for children, the aged and incapacitated persons: Finance Act 2000, s 12. See CARER.

home loan. See MORTGAGE.

home nursing service. A service to give eligible persons advice and assistance on matters relating to their health and to assist them if they are sick: Health Act 1970, s 60. Public health nurses provide the service.

homeless person. A person must be regarded by a housing authority as being *homeless* if: (a) there is no accommodation available which, in the opinion of the authority, he, together with any other person who normally resides with him or who might reasonably be expected to reside with him, can reasonably occupy or remain in occupation of; or (b) he is living in a hospital, county home, night shelter or other such institution, and is so living because he has no accommodation; and he is, in the opinion of the authority, unable to provide accommodation from his own resources: Housing Act 1988, s 2. A housing authority is required specifically to have regard for the needs of homeless persons in making an annual assessment of housing needs (HA 1988, s 9) and is given additional powers to meet those needs (HA 1998, s 10). A housing authority has a duty to provide accommodation for homeless persons: *County Meath VEC v Joyce* [1994] 2 ILRM 210, HC. A health board is required to make available suitable accommodation for a child in its area who is homeless: Child Care Act 1991, s 5. For Threshold, see website: *www. threshold.ie* and for Focus Ireland, see website: *www.focusireland.ie*. See HOUSING.

homicide. The killing of a human being. Homicides are either *justifiable, excusable* or *felonious. Justifiable* homicides are killings without blame in the execution of a legal duty or in the furtherance of a legal purpose e g formerly, the putting to death of a person pursuant to a legal judicial sentence; or the killing of a doer of an offence (formerly, a felony) of violence if he cannot otherwise be prevented from escaping. *Excusable* homicides are killings which the law excuses e g by misadventure, in self-defence, or by chance-medley (qqv). *Felonious* homicides are killings resulting from murder, manslaughter, infanticide, and aiding and abetting the suicide of another (qqv). [Bibliography: Charleton.] See CORPORATE HOMICIDE; FELONY; YEAR AND A DAY.

homosexual. A person who is sexually attracted to members of their own sex. Although homosexual activity amongst consenting adults is no longer prohibited by the criminal law, allegations of homosexual activity are nevertheless capable of being defamatory; eg numerous references in an article to a person as a 'gay bachelor' were, by reason of the secondary meaning which nowadays attaches to the word 'gay', clear references to homosexuality and capable of being defamatory: *Reynolds v Malocco* [1999] 1 ILRM 289, HC and 2 IR 203. See BUGGERY.

homosexual conduct. Sexual activity with a member of one's own sex. It may amount to the offence of buggery (qv). A homosexual relationship by a man prior to his marriage may not be sufficient reason to annul the marriage; however, if a person at the time of marriage is, by reason of homosexuality, incapable of entering into and sustaining the relationship which should exist between married couples if a lifelong union is to be possible, this would entitle the other party to a decree of nullity of that marriage: *MF McD (otherwise M O'R) v W O'R* [1986] ILRM 336.

Inherent and unalterable homosexuality may be a ground for marriage annulment, at least in a case where the petitioner had no knowledge of the existence of the homosexuality of the respondent at the time of the marriage ceremony: *UF v JC* [1991] 2 IR 330, SC. See also *F v F* [1990] 1 IR 348.

The prohibition, under an army code, of consensual sexual activity between members of the defence forces even in the private home of the member, is not an unlawful or unconstitutional invasion of any alleged right of privacy: *Re C.* [1998] 2 IR 447, CMAC. See *Woulfe* in 8 ILT & SJ (1990) 242. See BUGGERY; GROSS INDECENCY; HATRED, INCITEMENT TO; MARRIAGE, NULLITY OF; SEXUAL ORIENTATION; VIDEO RECORDING.

hon. The Honourable. The title of District, Circuit and Superior Court judges. See MODE OF ADDRESS.

honey. It is an offence for a person to place honey on the market which does not comply with specified standards: EC (Market-ing of Honey) Regulations 2003, SI No 367 of 2003, implementing Directive (EC) 2001/110. New standards apply from 1 August 2004.

honorary freedom. See CIVIC HONOUR.

honorary position, termination of. It has been held by the High Court that the principles of natural justice apply to the termination of a prestigious and responsible honorary position because of the importance of the post and the effect of termination on the office holder: *McEvoy v Prison Officers Association* [1998] ELR 250, HC. In this case the President of the Prison Officers Association was awarded £10,000 in respect of a *motion of no confidence* which had been passed in breach of the requirements of fair procedures and natural and constitutional justice. However, on appeal to the Supreme Court, it was held that the *motion of no confidence* related to the internal policy of the association and therefore the procedural safeguards required when, for example, an allegation of misconduct is made, were not necessary: *McEvoy v Prison Officers Association* [1999] 1 ILRM 445, SC and ELR 129.

honorarium. A voluntary, or honorary, payment or reward eg a barrister's fee. A Trustee Savings Bank may pay its trustees *honoraria* as approved by the Central Bank: Trustee Savings Banks Act 1989, s 20. See BARRISTER; BRIEF FEE.

honour. A title of honour may not be accepted by a citizen except with the prior approval of the government; 1937 Constitution, art 40(2)(2). The President of Ireland may grant citizenship as a token of honour to a person. Also the Minister is empowered to award 'The Distinguished Service Medal' to members of the defence forces: Defence Force Regulations (A19 Part V). See CITIZENSHIP AS HONOUR; CIVIC HONOUR; TITLE OF NOBILITY.

hors de combat. [Out of the fight.] In an armed conflict, a person is *hors de combat* if: (a) he is in the power of an adverse party, or (b) he clearly expresses an intention to surrender, or (c) he has been rendered unconscious or is otherwise incapacitated by wounds or sickness and therefore incapable of defending himself: Geneva Conventions (Amendment) Act 1998, Sch 5, art 41. A person who is recognised to be *hors de combat* must not be made the object of an attack; he must not, however, attempt to escape or engage in any hostile act.

horseplay. Rough or boisterous play. Dismissal of an employee for engaging in *horseplay* in a factory may be unfair where the horseplay has been an on-going problem and not brought under control by management: *Dunphy v Largo Food Exports Ltd* [1992] ELR 179, EAT.

horseracing. A significant restructuring of the organisation and administration of horseracing, including increased permanent funding for the horse and greyhound racing industries, is provided for in the Horse and Greyhound Racing Act 2001. The Act provides for the establishment of a new State body, *Horse Racing Ireland* (HRI) to replace the Irish Horseracing Authority (IHA) and to take over certain functions of the *Racing Regulatory Body* (the Turf Club and the National Hunt Steeplechase Committee).

The functions of the HRI include: (a) the overall administration of racing e g the authorisation of racecourses, the setting of fixtures, control of on-course bookmakers, the development and promotion of the industry, the negotiation of media rights to racing pictures and information, the provision of support towards the improvement of the health status of the Irish horse and the specialised education and training requirements of the sector, and (b) also the *Registry Office* functions heretofore carried out by the Racing Regulatory Body e g horseracing passports, race entries and declarations, stakeholding of race entry funds and prize money, and registration of racehorse owners (HGRA 2001, s 8).

HRI is required to establish a special *Racegoers Consultative Forum* for the purposes of consultations relating to the operations of the HRI (HGRA 2001, s 9) and a *Media Rights Committee* to negotiate broadcasting or photographing or sound recording for commercial purposes of a race fixture (HGRA 2001, s 10). There is also provision for a *Horse and Greyhound Racing Fund* to provide from 2001 onwards permanent funding for HRI and Bord na gCon (HGRA 2001, s 12).

The functions which remain with the Racing Regulatory Body include: (a) the sole and independent responsibility for the making and enforcing of the *Rules of Racing*, (b) employing, licensing, monitoring and controlling on-course officials responsible for the integrity of racing, and (c) making all decisions on doping control,

forensics and handicapping (HGRA 2001, Sch, para 6).

The number of ordinary members of the *board of HRI* has been increased from 12 to 13, with the additional member being appointed directly by the Minister, having regard to creating a balance among the different interests in the horseracing industry: Horse Racing Ireland (Membership) Act 2001. In addition, this later 2001 Act removes the election requirement for the nominees to represent employee interests and interests of horseracing in Northern Ireland. Paragraph 16 of the Schedule to the Horse and Greyhound Racing Act 2001 is repealed.

There is provision for the licensing of the sale for consumption of intoxicating liquor at authorised events at racecourses: Intoxicating Liquor Act 2000, s 23. The permitted time for such sale begins at the time the public are admitted to the event (but not before 10.30 am) and ends 30 minutes after the conclusion of the event. See Thoroughbred Foal Levy Regulations 2000, SI No 178 of 2000, as amended by SI No 173 of 2004. For previous legislation, see Irish Horseracing Industry Act 1994, s 10. See website: *www.horseracingireland.ie*. See BET; BOOKMAKER, LICENSED; FOAL; STALLION.

horseracing, 'run on its merits'. The High Court has held that it was central to the sport of racing that a horse should be *run on its merits* in a race; the disqualification of a horse was not a punishment imposed on the owner but was a consequence arising out of the actions of the trainer and/or jockey: *Moran & Lynch v Irish Turf Club* (2003) Irish Times, 19 March 2003. In another case, the court overturned a decision of the Turf Club Appeal Board which had imposed a fine on a trainer on the allegation that the horse he had trained did not *run on its merits*: *Bolger v Osborne* [2000] 1 ILRM 250, HC. In this case it was held that the failure of the Turf Club to disclose the facts upon which the liability of the trainer was based, was a breach of his constitutional right to a fair and proper hearing. See also *Madden v Irish Turf Club* [1997] 2 ILRM 148, SC and 2 IR 184.

horses. All horses in certain designated areas (*control* areas) must be licensed; a local authority may declare certain areas to be control areas: Control of Horses Act 1996, ss 17–18. This Act was introduced to deal with two main issues: (a) the welfare of horses, and (b) the protection of persons and property from the dangers of wandering horses. A horse includes a donkey, mule and hinny (CHA 1996, s 2(1)).

It is an offence to sell or to offer to sell a horse to a person 'apparently' under the age of 16 (CHA 1996, s 43). Also, where the owner of a horse is under 16 years of age, the head of that person's household is deemed to own the horse (CHA 1996, s 2(2)). Horses in certain circumstances may be seized by authorised persons (including the gardaí) and detained in a *pound* (CHA 1996, s 37). It is an offence for the owner of a horse, wilfully or recklessly, to permit the horse to pose a danger or cause injury to a person; the offence is also committed by the keeper or person in charge or control of the horse (CHA 1996, s 45).

It is lawful for a local authority to seize an unlicensed horse within its functional area and detain it in a pound outside its functional area: *Mongan v South Dublin County Council* [2000] ITLR (20 November).

A person leading horses, whether mounted or on foot, is required to do so with his left hand keeping the led animals between himself and the lefthand side of the road: Road Traffic General Bye Laws (Amendment) Regulations 1993. The previous requirement that stallions be licensed has been abolished: Horse Breeding Act 1990 repealing the 1934 Act. See Control of Horses Regulations, SI No 171 of 1997. See FOAL; STALLION; STRAY HORSE.

horticulture. That branch of agriculture that relates to the cultivation of plants used for food or for the production of food or ornament: An Bord Bia Act 1994, s 2(1) as amended by An Bord Bia (Amendment) Act 2004, s 11. Horticulture includes fruit, vegetables including potatoes, herbs, fungi, nuts, cut flowers, dried flowers, hops, decorative foliage, sports turf, honey, pot plants, bedding plants and herbaceous plants, shrubs and trees, fruit trees, fruit bushes and fruit plants, seeds, bulbs, corms and tubers. Formerly, An Bord Glas (the Horticultural Development Board) had the general functions of developing and promoting the production, marketing and consumption of horticultural products: Bord Glas Act 1990, s 4. Provision has now been made for An Bord Glas to be dissolved and its functions amalgamated with An Bord

Bia (ABB(A)A 2004, ss 3 and 12). See AGRICULTURAL PRODUCTS; BORD BIA.

hospital. Capital allowances are available for the construction or refurbishment of buildings used as private hospitals: Finance Act 2001, s 64. There are certain specified conditions e g previously there had to be a minimum of 100 in-patient beds, 20% to be available for public patients at a discount price to the State of 10%, and the hospital had to be operated by a body with a charitable status for tax purposes. In 2002, the minimum number of beds was reduced to 70 and the condition on charitable status of the operating body was removed: Finance Act 2002, s 32. The allowances are subject to the usual £25,000 limit (€31,743) for a passive investor.

Capital allowances have been extended to hospitals providing acute services on a day-case basis; there is a requirement of a minimum of 40 day-case beds: Finance Act 2003, s 24. Previously, where an investor fell into any of the excluded categories, all the investors were denied relief; now relief will be denied only to the excluded investor: Finance Act 2004, s 24.

A doctor who has a financial interest in a private clinic, hospital, pharmacy or any institution to which he is referring patients for investigation or therapy, has a duty to declare such an interest to patients: Medical Council, *A Guide to Ethical Conduct and Behaviour* (6th edn, 2004) para 13.1. Such doctors must take exceptional care to prevent their financial interests influencing their management of patients. See ADMISSIONS SYSTEM; CONSULTANT REFERRAL; IN-PATIENT SERVICES.

hospital charges. The Supreme Court has held that the assessment of hospital charges under s 2 of the Health (Amendment) Act 1986 can be made by reference to the *average daily cost* of hospital beds: *Crilly v Farrington* [2001] 3 IR 251, SC and [2002] 1 ILRM 161, SC. See EUROPEAN HEALTH INSURANCE CARD; KINLEN ORDER.

hostage. See TERRORISM.

hostile witness. A witness whose mind discloses a bias hostile to the party examining him and who may, with the leave of the court, be cross-examined by the party who called him. A witness may be found to be hostile for a number of reasons, including a refusal to answer questions or an obvious disregard of the witness's duty to the proper administration of justice; this is a matter for the discretion of the judge: *Price v Manning*

[1889] 42 Ch D 372; *O'Flynn v District Judge Smithwick* [1993] ILRM 627, HC. Where a witness gives evidence which is inconsistent with a previous statement of his, he may be cross-examined with the leave of the judge: Criminal Procedure Act 1865; *The People (Attorney-General) v Hannigan* [1941] IR 252. It has been held that the trial judge should explain to the jury that in such a case, the written statement is only evidence against the credibility of the witness and not evidence of the truth of the matters contained in it: *People v Taylor* [1974] IR 97.

hotchpot. [Hocher: to share together.] A blending of properties for the purpose of securing an equal division. Where a fund is appointed to be divided amongst a class and one of the class has already received a special share, that person may be required to add his special share to the fund, for the purpose of computing the share of each beneficiary, before it is distributed and he is then said to bring his special share into hotchpot. See Succession Act 1965, s 63. See ADVANCEMENT.

hotel. An establishment which provides sleeping accommodation, food and drink for reward for all comers without special contract and includes every establishment registered as a hotel with Bord Fáilte Éireann: Hotel Proprietors Act 1963, s 1. An hotel proprietor has a duty to receive all comers, unless he has reasonable grounds for refusal, and to take reasonable care for the safety of his guests (HPA 1963, ss 3–4). See *Duggan v Armstrong & Tighe* [1993] ILRM 222, SC.

In respect of guests who engage sleeping accommodation, the hotel proprietor is liable for damage to, or loss of, property received from guests (HPA 1963, ss 5–6). He can limit his liability to £100 (€126.97) for any one guest by displaying a notice in a specified form, but this limitation does not apply to a motor vehicle, to property which was deposited for safe custody, or property damaged or lost through the default of the proprietor or his servant (HPA 1963, s 7). The proprietor has a lien (qv) on property brought by a guest in respect of a debt due for sleeping accommodation, food or drink (HPA 1963, s 8).

The National Tourism Development Authority is empowered to exercise its powers regarding the registration and grading of hotels by or through contractors: Tourist Traffic Act 1995. A hotel is not regarded as an industrial building or structure for capital allowances in the tax system, if any part of the capital expenditure is met by way of grant assistance: Finance Act 2001, s 81. This provision is further strengthened by a requirement for certification regarding compliance with EU rules on State aids, before capital allowances will apply: Finance Act 2002, s 27.

It is the duty of keepers of hotels (or other places in which lodging or sleeping accommodation is provided on a commercial basis) to keep a register in the prescribed form of all non-nationals staying at the premises: Immigration Act 2004, s 10. See Safety, Health and Welfare at Work Act 1989; Courts Act 1991, s 9. [Bibliography: Cassidy; Dempsey; McDonald.] See CAPITAL ALLOWANCES; FIRE, LIABILITY FOR; NATIONAL TOURISM DEVELOPMENT AUTHORITY; WILDLIFE DEALING.

hours of work. See WORKING HOURS.

house. (1) Includes any building or part of a building used or suitable for use as a dwelling and any out-office, yard, garden or other land appurtenant thereto or usually enjoyed therewith and *housing* shall be construed accordingly: Housing (Miscellaneous Provisions) Act 1992, s 1(1). See also Consumer Credit Act 1995, s 2(1).

(2) A building or part of a building occupied as a dwelling or built for use as a dwelling; it includes apartments and flats: Planning and Development Act 2000, s 2(1). The use of two or more dwellings of any house, previously used as a single dwelling, constitutes a *material change* of use and consequently requires planning permission (PDA 2000, s 3(3)). [Bibliography: Canny (4); McDonald T.] See AFFORDABLE HOUSING; HOUSING STRATEGY; OVERCROWDED HOUSE.

house, disorderly. See DISORDERLY HOUSE.

house agent. A person who, as agent for another person and for or in expectation of reward, purchases, sells, lets or offers for sale or letting, or invites offers to purchase or take a letting of, or negotiates for the purchase, sale or letting of a house otherwise than by auction or attempts to effect such purchase, sale or letting: Auctioneers and House Agents Act 1947, s 2. A person may not carry on or hold himself out or represent himself as carrying on the business of house agent except under and in accordance with a *licence* (AHAA 1947, s 7).

Any agreement in a contract relating to the sale, lease, or letting of property which makes the purchaser, lessee or tenant liable to pay the fees or expense of an auctioneer or house agent is void: Auctioneers and House Agents Act 1973, s 2. See *Law v Roberts Co* [1964] IR 292. A Review Group to examine the regulatory framework for the auctioneering / estate agency profession was established in July 2004. [Bibliography: Mahon.] See AUCTIONEER; MONEY LAUNDERING; TAX CLEARANCE CERTIFICATE.

house to house collection. See COLLECTION.

household chattels. Furniture, bedding, linen, china, earthenware, glass, books and other chattels of ordinary household use or ornament and also consumable stores, garden effects and domestic animals but does not include any chattels used by either spouse for business or professional purposes or money or security for money: Judicial Separation and Family Law Reform Act 1989, s 10. The court may make an order for the protection of household chattels (JSFLRA 1989, s 11(d)). See also Family Home Protection Act 1976, s 10 as amended by the Courts Act 1991, s 8, and by Civil Liability and Courts Act 2004, s 48; Domestic Violence Act 1996, ss 8 and 20. See MATRIMONIAL HOME.

household waste. See BYE-LAW; WASTE; WASTE COLLECTION.

Houses of the Oireachtas. See OIREACHTAS.

Houses of the Oireachtas Commission. A body corporate with the function of providing for the running of the Houses of the Oireachtas and of administering the Office of the Houses: Houses of the Oireachtas Commission Act 2003. The Act provides for the establishment of an independent permanent Commission with responsibility for overseeing and controlling the funding, staffing and organisation of the Office. The Chairman of Dáil Éireann is the chairperson of the Commission and is required to ensure that it performs its functions efficiently (HOCA 2003, s 7(1)). See also Staff of the Houses of the Oireachtas Act 1959 as amended by HOCA 2003, s 21. See OIREACHTAS.

housing. Housing authorities have an express statutory duty imposed on them to assess the adequacy of the supply and condition of housing in their areas and to draw up programmes, known as *building pro-*

grammes to meet the needs of the area: Housing Act 1966, ss 53–55. They are required to adopt a written statement of policy for the effective carrying out of their function as regards the management and control of their housing stock: Housing (Miscellaneous Provisions) Act 1992, s 9. They are empowered to provide dwellings and works, services and building sites and amenities (HA 1966, s 56–57). Housing authorities are also empowered to take account of the needs of persons resident outside their functional area and to build and let houses to such persons: Housing Act 1984. This Act was necessitated by the decision in *McNamee v Buncrana UDC* [1984] ILRM 77.

Legislation in 1988: (a) sought to ensure that the housing needs of categories of persons such as the homeless, the aged, the disabled and travellers obtain due priority, and (b) provided a simplified procedure for discharging mortgages in certain cases: Housing Act 1988. A housing authority is required to draw up a scheme of priorities for letting housing accommodation (HA 1988, s 11). The court will not interfere with a decision of the authority in relation to the granting of accommodation pursuant to such a scheme unless the decision flew in the face of reason or was defective on grounds of failure to observe the rules of natural justice or was illegal or *ultra vires*: *Carton v Dublin Corporation* [1993] ILRM 467, HC.

Legislation in 1992: (a) provided a statutory basis for shared ownership, (b) permitted housing authorities to carry out improvements to privately owned houses, (c) provided for a rental subsidy scheme in respect of houses of approved bodies, (d) required measures to counteract social segregation, (e) provided for increased participation by tenants in the maintenance and management of their housing, and (f) added safeguards for tenants in the private rented sector through the use of rent books, minimum notice to quit, minimum physical standards, and abolition of distress for rent: Housing (Miscellaneous Provisions) Act 1992.

Legislation in 2002: (a) provided for the increase of resources for housing, (b) sought to improve the delivery and management of affordable and social housing, (c) made a number of technical changes to the law governing building societies: Housing (Miscellaneous Provisions) Act 2002.

Grants may be paid to a housing co-operative or a voluntary group or association or to a body that provides advice or conducts research in housing needs (H(MP)A 2002, s 12). See also *O'Reilly v Limerick Corporation* [1988] ILRM 181, HC; *Kerry Co Council v McCarthy* [1997] 2 ILRM 481, SC.

For the rules of procedure governing: (a) an appeal under s 72 of the Housing Act 1966 (eg against a repair order), (b) an application for an order determining a lease under s 73 of the Housing Act 1966, and (c) an appeal under s 18(5) of the Housing (Miscellaneous Provisions) Act 1979 (eg against a refusal of the Minister to grant a *certificate of reasonable value*), see Circuit Court Rules 2001 Ord 54–55. See Housing (Traveller Accommodation) Act 1998; Housing (Miscellaneous Provisions) (Amendment) Regulations 1993, SI No 157 of 1993. See Building Societies Act 1989, s 38(3). [Bibliography: Bland (2); Canny (2).] See AFFORDABLE HOUSING; ANTI-SOCIAL BEHAVIOUR; FLOOR AREA CERTIFICATE; ESTATE MANAGEMENT; HABITABLE HOUSE; HOMELESS; OVERCROWDED HOUSE; PLANNING AUTHORITY; TENANT PURCHASE SCHEME; TRAVELLER; UNFIT HOUSE.

housing, repossession of. A housing authority is entitled to recover possession of dwellings or buildings; if a demand for possession is *duly made*, the district judge is required to issue a warrant for possession: Housing Act 1966, s 62 as amended by Housing Act 1970, s 13. This rapid method of recovering possession without having to give reasons for so doing, is both reasonable and constitutional: *Dublin Corporation v Hamilton* [1998] 2 ILRM 542, HC and [1999] 2 IR 486, HC. See ANTI-SOCIAL BEHAVIOUR.

housing and compulsory purchase. Regulations have been made to prescribe the forms to be used by local authorities in connection with the compulsory purchase of land under s 76 of the Housing Act 1966: Housing (Acquisition of Land) Regulations 2000 and 2001, SI No 454 of 2000. Forms 4 and 9 in these regulations have been replaced: SI No 320 of 2001. See Housing Regulations (Amendment) Regulations, SI No 608 of 2001. All tenants are now entitled to notice in connection with a compulsory purchase order affecting their dwelling: Housing Act 1966,

s 79(1) and Sch 3, amended by Residential Tenancies Act 2004, s 198).

housing and energy. Higher energy efficiency standards for *new* houses have been set, which come into effect on 1 January 2003: SI No 284 of 2002 amending Part L of the Building Regulations. The regulations also set new thermal performance standards for replacement external doors, windows and rooflights in *existing* houses where work commences on or after 1 July 2003. For the revised Technical Guidance Document L, see *www.environ.ie/planning/construct.html*.

housing authority. A county council, a city council, and specified borough and town councils (except for certain functions under the Housing Acts). Housing (Miscellaneous Provisions) Act 1992, s 23 as amended by Housing (Miscellaneous Provisions) Act 2002, s 16. For the new names of local authorities, see LOCAL AUTHORITY. See also SEGREGATION.

housing body, approved. A body approved of by the Minister for the purposes of s 5 of the Housing Act 1988, or a society registered under the Industrial and Provident Societies Acts 1893 to 1978, or under the Friendly Societies Acts 1896 to 1977, or a voluntary group: Building Societies Act 1989, s 28(5); Housing (Miscellaneous Provisions) Act 1992, s 6(10). A building society may, subject to the *adoption* of the power and the approval of the Central Bank, support *approved housing bodies* by means of loans, grants, guarantees and the provision of services and property (BSA 1989, s 28(1)(b)). See also BSA 1989, Sch 2, Pt I, para 3.

A housing authority is empowered to provide assistance to another housing authority or to an approved voluntary housing body in respect of the provision or management by them of housing; assistance may take the form of a loan, grant, subsidy, periodic contribution, guarantee or assistance in kind (H(MP)A 1992, s 6). See Housing (Accommodation provided by Approved Bodies) Regulations 1992 and 2002, SI No 86 of 1992; SI No 106 of 2002. See ADOPTABLE POWERS.

Housing Finance Agency. A limited company with objects: (a) to provide, by way of mortgage or charge, loans for the construction of houses, (b) to provide moneys to enable such loans to be made by *housing authorities*, and (c) to borrow money for the aforesaid purposes: Housing Finance

Agency Act 1981. The Agency was established to lend money to housing authorities for their functions under the Housing Acts. The borrowing capacity of the Agency was increased from £1,500 million to €6,000 million: Housing (Miscellaneous Provisions) Act 2002, s 17. See H(MP)A 2002, s 18; Planning and Development (Amendment) Act 2002, s 20. See also Housing Finance Agency (Amendment) Acts 1982, 1985 and 1988. See SI No 23 of 2003.

housing grant. There is provision for the payment of a grant to persons in respect of a new house; the Minister is empowered to make regulations setting out the classes of persons to whom a grant may be paid and the amount: Housing (Miscellaneous Provisions) Act 2002, s 11. This provision enables a more flexible approach to be taken in relation to new house grants than heretofore. The grant for 'first time' occupiers of new houses has been abolished as from 14 November 2002; however the grant is payable: (a) where a contract to purchase or a contract to build had been entered into on or before 14 November 2002, or (b) in the case of a 'self-build' house where the foundations had been poured on or before 14 November 2002. See Housing (New House Grant) (Amendment) Regulations 2002 and 2003, SI No 517 of 2002 and SI No 502 of 2003. For further information, telephone Housing Grants Section, Lo-Call 1890 30 50 30.

housing loan. (1) A loan on the security of a mortgage (qv) of a freehold or leasehold estate or interest in a *house* (qv) for the purpose of enabling a member of a building society to provide or improve the house or to purchase the said estate or interest: Building Societies Act 1989, s 22. A society is empowered to make *housing loans* to members, including, with the approval of the Central Bank, housing loans in a foreign currency.

(2) An agreement for credit on the security of the mortgage of a freehold or leasehold estate or interest in a house (qv), where the loan is made for the purpose of enabling the borrower to provide or improve the house or to purchase the said estate or interest: Consumer Credit Act 1995, s 2(1). The loan may also be for the purpose of refinancing a housing loan.

Certain documents in relation to a housing loan must include a warning: 'Warning. Your home is at risk if you do not keep up payments on a mortgage or any other loan

secured on it'; and where the interest rate is variable: 'The payment rates on this housing loan may be adjusted by the lender from time to time' (CCA 1995, s 128).

An agreement for a housing loan must contain certain specified information on the front page (CCA 1995, s 129 and Sch 3, Pt II). There are provisions in the Act in relation to regulations on the disclosure of fees; disclosure of interest rates and penalties applied to arrears; advertising of housing loans; protection of the borrower in the event of the lender being wound up (CCA 1995, ss 132, 134, 135, 136).

Under recent legislation, the 1995 Act is amended to provide that all institutions who lend on the security of a borrower's principal home are made subject to Part IX of that Act, in order to protect the borrower by imposing various obligations on housing loan lenders e g disclosure of charges: Central Bank and Financial Services Authority of Ireland Act 2004, s 33, Sch 3.

(3) A loan for: (a) the acquisition of estates or interests in or the construction of houses; (b) the carrying out of improvement works to houses; (c) the acquisition of buildings or other land for the purpose of providing housing; (d) the conversion of a building; (e) the provision of hostel accommodation; (f) the payment of a deposit for the purchase of property: Housing (Miscellaneous Provisions) Act 1992, s 11. Housing loans may be made by a housing authority (H(MP)A 1992, s 11(4)). Where the terms of the loan have been breached, the housing authority may recover possession by order of the District Court pursuant to the Landlord and Tenant Amendment Act, Ireland, 1860, ss 84–89 (H(MP)A 1992, s 11(5)). [Bibliography: Bird.] See ABANDONED HOUSE; ANNUAL PERCENTAGE CHARGE; ENDOWMENT LOAN; LEGAL INVESTIGATION OF TITLE; MORTGAGE INTERMEDIARY; MORTGAGE LENDER; MORTGAGE PROTECTION INSURANCE; REDEMPTION FEE; VALUATION REPORT.

housing strategy. Each planning authority is required to include in their *development plan* a strategy for the purpose of ensuring the provision of housing of the existing and future population of the area in the manner set out in the strategy: Planning and Development Act 2000, s 94(1). The housing strategy must take into account: (a) the existing and the likely future needs for housing, (b) the need to ensure that housing is available for persons who have different levels of income (c) the need to ensure a mixture of house types to match reasonably the requirements of different categories of households, including the elderly and persons with disabilities, and (d) the need to counteract undue segregation in housing between persons of different social backgrounds (PDA 2000, s 94(3)). The housing strategy must estimate the amount of housing required and must provide that up to 20% of land to be used for residential purposes is provided for *social* and *affordable* housing (PDA 2000, s 94(4)).

A planning authority must attach a condition to a planning permission in relation to land to which a social or affordable housing objective applies, requiring the developer to enter into an agreement with the authority (PDA 2000, s 96(2) as inserted by Planning and Development (Amendment) Act 2002, s 3). The agreement may provide for: (i) the transfer of land required to be reserved for social and affordable housing, or (ii) the transfer on completion of a number of houses, or (iii) the transfer of fully or partially serviced sites, or (iv) the transfer of other land or the provision of houses or sites at another location, or (v) the payment of money to the local authority, or (vi) a combination of these options (PDA 2000, s 96(3) as inserted by PD(A)A 2002, s 3). The 2002 Act introduced alternative ways (iv), (v) and (vi) in which the developer could meet the requirements; the alternative must however be of an equivalent monetary value.

Compensation is payable at the existing use value of the land ie the value of the land prior to its being zoned for residential use, rather than the market value, unless it can be shown that the land was purchased at a higher price before the Act was published as a Bill – 25 August 1999 (PDA 2000, s 96(6) as inserted by PD(A)A 2002, s 3). Where land was acquired by the applicant for permission by way of gift or inheritance, the compensation payable is the market value of the land when acquired (PDA 2000, s 96(6)(a)(ii)).

A person may, before applying for permission in respect of a development (a) consisting of the provision of four or fewer houses, or (b) for housing on land of 0.1 hectares or less, apply to the planning authority for a certificate that s 96 shall not apply to a grant of planning permission of the development concerned (PDA 2000, s 97 as amended by PD(A)A 2002, s 5 and Local Government (No 2) Act 2003 s 5). In relation to any planning application or appeal, compliance with the housing strategy must be a consideration material to the proper planning and sustainable development of the area (PDA 2000, s 93(4)).

Provision has been made to reverse the impact of s 96(15) of the 2000 Act (which limited planning permission on residential development to 31 December 2002 or two years from planning permission, whichever longer, sometimes called a *withering permission*) by applying the normal rules on planning duration to such development, while also introducing a levy which cannot be passed on to the purchaser (PDA 2000, ss 96A and 96B inserted by PD(A)A 2002, s 4).

See Planning and Development Regulations 2001, Pt V, arts 48–50: SI No 600 of 2001 as amended by SI No 90 of 2003. See 'Social and Affordable' by James Macken SC in *Bar Review* (October 2000) 41. See 'Change of Plan' by solicitor John Gore-Grimes in Law Society Gazette (January/February 2003) 18. See AFFORDABLE HOUSING; DEVELOPMENT PLAN.

housing strategy, constitutionality of. The provisions relating to *housing supply* (Part V, ss 93 to 101 of Planning and Development Act 2000) which include *housing strategy* and *affordable housing* were referred by the President of Ireland to the Supreme Court under art 26 for a decision on the question as to whether they were repugnant to the Constitution. The court held on 28 August 2000 that the provisions were constitutional and that Part V was rationally connected to an objective of sufficient importance to warrant interference with a constitutionally protected right: *In the matter of art 26 and the Planning and Development Bill 1999* [2000] 2 IR 321, SC and [2001] 2 ILRM 81, SC. The court also found that an unjust attack on the right to private property was not envisaged and that the greater good was served by Part V. The court held that while the principle of compensation at least at the level of market value was well established, there was no absolute right to market value compensation.

housing supply. See HOUSING STRATEGY.

hue and cry. An ancient common law procedure for pursuit of a felon with horn and voice. See MISPRISION OF FELONY.

human body. See DISSECTION.

human habitation, fit for. See UNFIT HOUSE.

human reproduction. The Minister for Health established in 2002 a *Commission on Assisted Human Reproduction* to prepare a report on the possible approaches to the regulation of all aspects of assisted human reproduction and the social, ethical and legal factors to be taken into account in determining public policy in this area. See 'Human genetics and the need for regulation' by Stephen Dodd BL in *Bar Review* (May 2001) 418. See ARTIFICIAL INSEMINATION; EMBRYO IMPLANTATION; GENE THERAPY; REPRODUCTIVE MEDICINE.

human rights. The Irish Centre for the Study of Human Rights is located in the Law Faculty of University College, Galway. See also O'Flaherty in 9 ILT & SJ (1991) 285. For the Irish Council for Civil Liberties, see website: *www.iccl.ie*. [Bibliography: Bacik & Livingstone; O'Reilly.] See NATURAL RIGHTS.

human rights, covenants on. The covenants of the United Nations called the International Covenant on Civil and Political Rights (ICCPR) and the International Covenant on Economic and Social Rights (ICESR) which were unanimously adopted by the UN General Assembly on 16 December 1966. Ireland signed the covenants on 1 October 1973 and announced its intention to ratify the conventions in December 1987. The Covenants are legally binding *in se* and are supported by an integrated enforcement machinery; they are formal international agreements which restate the provisions of the Universal Declaration on Human Rights (qv) as binding legal obligations. See Power & Gill in 7 ILT & SJ (1989) 36 and 69; O'Flaherty in 10 ILT & SJ (1992) 109 and 128.

human rights, European Convention on. See EUROPEAN CONVENTION ON HUMAN RIGHTS.

human rights, European Court of. See EUROPEAN COURT OF HUMAN RIGHTS.

Human Rights Commission. A body corporate consisting of a President and 14 other members, with the functions which include: (a) keeping under review the adequacy and effectiveness of law and practice in the State relating to the protection of human rights, (b) instituting proceedings for the purpose of obtaining relief of a declaratory nature in respect of any matter concerning the human rights of any person

or class of persons, (c) conducting enquiries on its own volition or at the request of any person, (d) appearing, on application, in an informative role as a friend of the court (*amicus curiae*) in proceedings before the High Court or Supreme Court that involve or are concerned with human rights, (e) providing legal advice, legal representation or other assistance to individuals relating to human rights: Human Rights Commission Act 2000, ss 4, 5, 8. The number of ordinary members of the Commission was increased from 8 to 14: Human Rights Commission (Amendment) Act 2001, s 1 amending s 5 of HRCA 2000.

The establishment of the Commission meets an obligation under the *Good Friday Agreement* (qv) and matches a similar Commission in Northern Ireland.

Human rights is defined for all purposes of the Act other than s 11 (which deals with the institution of legal proceedings by the Commission) as: the rights, liberties and freedoms conferred on, or guaranteed to persons: (a) by the Constitution, and (b) by any agreement, treaty or convention to which the State is a party (HRCA 2000, s 2).

The definition of human rights as regards s 11 is restricted as regards any agreement, treaty or convention to which the State is a party by including only those (or a provision thereof) *which have been given the force of law in the State* (HRCA 2000, s 11(3)). This restriction is required because of the dualistic principle relating to the effect in Irish law of international agreements; such agreements to which the State is a party may not necessarily be part of the law of the State and consequently may not be relied on in cases before the Irish courts. However, s 11(3) has been amended to enable the Commission to institute proceedings to obtain relief in respect of the human rights of a person under the *European Convention on Human Rights*: European Convention on Human Rights Act 2003, s 7.

The Commission has other functions, including consulting with national and international human rights bodies, making recommendations to government, promoting awareness and understanding of human rights issues, participating in the joint North/South committee as provided for in the *Good Friday Agreement*, and publishing reports (ECHRA 2003, s 8). See 'Human

Rights Commissions: North & South Compared' by solicitor Mary Johnson in *Bar Review* (June/July 2002) 251. [Bibliography: Binchy & Sarkin; Driscoll.] See PARIS PRINCIPLES.

human tissue. A generic name for bodily materials; human tissue comprises the basic unit of cells, with the human body being made up of some 100 million million cells. Tissues are structured to form complex organs such as brain and kidneys. At common law and under statute a person must consent to the removal of human tissue: Non-Fatal Offences Against the Person Act 1997. For article on the law relating to the protection of bodily organs and human tissues, see 'Property in the Living Body' by Crionna Creagh BL in *Bar Review* (January 2001) 209. See BIOETHICS, IRISH COUNCIL FOR; BODILY INTEGRITY, RIGHT TO; POST-MORTEM; UNBORN, RIGHT TO LIFE OF THE.

hung jury. A jury (qv) unable to agree on any verdict. See VERDICT.

hunger strike. 'A voluntary fast undertaken, usually by a prisoner, as a means of protest': *Collins English Dictionary*. Hunger strikes have been used as a form of passive resistance in recent Irish history eg by Terence McSwiney, Lord Mayor of Cork, who died in Brixton Prison on 25 October 1920 after a fast of 74 days, and who said that 'it is not those who can inflict the most but those who can suffer the most who will conquer'. Hunger strikes have also been a feature of the political turmoil in Northern Ireland in the 1980s eg the death on hunger strike of 12 persons, including that of Bobby Sands who died with nine others in the 'H Block', and Michael Gaughan and Frank Stagg who died in jail in England.

'Where a prisoner refuses nourishment and is considered by the doctor as capable of forming an unimpaired and rational judgement concerning the consequences of such a voluntary refusal of nourishment, he or she shall not be fed artificially. The decision as to the capacity of the prisoner to form such a judgement should be confirmed by at least one other independent doctor. The consequences of the refusal of nourishment shall be explained by the doctor to the prisoner.' Medical Council, *A Guide to Ethical Conduct and Behaviour* (6th edn, 2004) para 2.8, endorsing the Declaration of Tokyo 1975, para 5.

hunt. In relation to any wild bird or wild animal, whether it be of a protected species or not, means to stalk, pursue, chase, drive, flush, capture, course, attract, follow, search for, lie in wait for, take, trap or shoot by any means whether with or without dogs, and includes killing in the course of hunting: Wildlife Act 1976, s 44(1). It does not include bird watching, wildlife photography, sketching or painting (WA 1976, s 2). A *licence* is required to hunt game (qv) with firearms and only permitted in open season (qv) (WA 1976, ss 20 and 29). For District Court appeal procedure against a refusal of the Minister to grant or renew a licence to hunt with firearms, see DCR 1997 Ord 89. See FIREARMS CERTIFICATE.

husband and wife. At common law a husband and wife were the one person and the wife had limited contractual and property rights; also she was deemed to have the domicile of her husband. A wife is now capable of having an independent domicile, her contractual capacity is unchanged on marriage, the family home cannot be sold without her consent and she cannot be disinherited by her husband. See DOMICILE; FAMILY HOME; MARRIED WOMAN; MATRIMONIAL HOME; LEGAL RIGHT OF SPOUSE.

hydrometric data. Information on the levels, volumes and flows of water in rivers, lakes and groundwaters in the State: Environmental Protection Agency Act 1992, s 64(1). The Agency is required to prepare a national programme for the collection, analysis and publication of this information.

hygiene of foodstuffs. Regulations have been made on the hygiene of foodstuffs, covering all stages after primary production and setting down the obligation of proprietors of food businesses, including the requirement that such business is operated in a hygienic way: European Communities (Hygiene of Foodstuffs) Regulations 2000, SI No 165 of 2000. The regulations give effect to Council Directive (EEC) 93/43. See FOOD SAFETY.

hypothecation. The pledging by bottomry bond of a ship or her freight or cargo for the payment of money borrowed by the master. See BOTTOMRY; DETENTION OF SHIP.

hypothetical arguments. A plaintiff has no *locus standi* (qv) to advance hypothetical arguments and is limited to showing how he himself is affected: *Madigan v Attorney-General Ors* [1986] ILRM 136. A court cannot take into account assumptions or hypotheses outside the facts or circumstances of the action before the court: *MhicMhathuna v Ireland* [1990] 8 ILT Dig 59. Also a court must determine the actual and not any hypothetical facts surrounding an alleged offence: *Carron v McMahon* [1990] ILRM 802, SC. See, however, MOOT.

I

ibid, ib, ibidem. [In the same place.] From the same source.

ICC Bank. The ICC Bank Act 2000 was enacted, primarily, to increase the authorised share capital of the bank and to make provision for the Minister for Finance to dispose of shares in the bank. The bank was subsequently acquired by, and is now part of, the Bank of Scotland group. See also Finance Act 2001, s 17.

id certain est quod certum reddi potest. [That is certain which can be made certain.]

id est. [That is.] Usually abbreviated to ie.

IDA. Industrial Development Authority, which operates under the name 'IDA Ireland'. A body corporate with the following functions: (a) to promote the establishment and development, in the State, of industrial undertakings from outside the State, (b) to make investments in and provide supports to industrial undertakings which comply with the requirements of the enactments for the time being in force, (c) to administer such schemes, grants and other financial facilities as may from time to time be authorised by the Minister: Industrial Development Act 1993. See website: *www.idaireland.com.* See INDUSTRIAL DEVELOPMENT; FORFÁS.

idem. [The same.]

identification. As to whether a person has been sufficiently identified as the person named in a warrant, the High Court has authority to reach a different conclusion from that in the District Court as regards uncontested evidence; a person who answers the description in a warrant of name, address and former address, it can be concluded that the person is the person named in the warrant: *Crowley v McVeigh* [1990] ILRM 220. See also *The People (DPP) v Duff* [1995] 3 IR 296, CCA. See DOCK IDENTIFICATION.

identification, visual. See VISUAL IDENTIFICATION; DOCK IDENTIFICATION; PHOTOGRAPHS, USE OF IN IDENTIFICATION.

identification parade. A formal procedure whereby persons, including an arrested suspect, are viewed by a witness for the purpose of identification. An accused has a right not to participate in a formal identification parade: *The People v Martin* [1956] IR 22. In a particular case, it was held that the accused should have been given the option of submitting to an identification parade; the holding of an identity parade had not outlived its usefulness: *DPP v O'Reilly* [1990] ITLR (9 July).

Also, an identity parade which consisted of six, instead of the recommended eight, persons and at which the defendant's solicitor was not present was ruled to have breached fair procedures: *DPP v Bates* [1992] CCC. A direction by a District Court judge, requiring an accused to attend an identity parade to pick out the supplier of cannabis, the possession of which the accused had been charged with, was quashed by the High Court as exceeding the judge's jurisdiction: *O'Dea v Mangan* (2002) Irish Times, 26 February.

The conducting officer, who should be a garda unconnected with the offence under investigation, must record the proceedings meticulously, and should say to each witness: '*This is an identification parade. I want you to look very carefully at this line of men (or women) and see if you can recognise the person (who etc). Do not say anything until I ask you a question*'.

When a witness indicates that he has made an identification, he should normally be asked to touch the person whom he purports to identify on the shoulder; however where the witness is a child or an old person or is frightened, it will suffice to point at and describe the person identified. Where a witness gives evidence by means of a live television link in cases of physical or sexual abuse, evidence by a person other than the witness that the witness identified the accused at an identification parade is admissible as evidence that the accused was so identified: Criminal Evidence Act 1992, s 18(b)(ii).

The result of an identification is not conclusive and a warning is required in relation to the dangers of visual identification (*O'Reilly* case). It is a matter for the jury (where trial is by jury) to determine whether the conduct of an identification parade was fair: *People (DPP) v O'Toole* [2003] FL 7502, CCA. The gardaí are entitled to extend a period of detention (qv) of a person under the Criminal Justice Act 1984, s 4 for the purposes of facilitating an identity parade: *DPP v O'Toole & Hickey* [1990] 8 ILT Dig 298, CCA. An *informal* identification parade is proper where a suspect refuses to take part in a formal parade; its acceptability depends on the circumstances of the case: *DPP v Cahill and Costello* [2001] 3 IR 494, CCA. See also *The People v Hughes* 92 ILTR 179; *DPP v McDonagh* [2001] 3 IR 411, CCA and [2002] 1 ILRM 225, CCA. A practising barrister must not attend identification parades: *Code of Conduct for the Bar of Ireland* (December 2003) r 9.8. [Bibliography: Healy; Ryan & Magee.] See TELEVISION LINK; VISUAL IDENTIFICATION.

identity badge. As regards the badge which a member of a prescribed category of licensees must wear when providing a *security service* (qv), means a badge: (a) which clearly indicates the licence number of the licensee concerned, (b) whose form, content and size are as prescribed, and (c) which, when worn, is clearly visible: Private Security Services Act 2004, s 30. See PRIVATE SECURITY AUTHORITY.

identity card. (1) An individual providing a *security service* (qv) is required to have an identity card, issued by the Private Security Authority, in his possession: Private Security Services Act 2004, s 29. A garda may arrest without warrant an individual who refuses to produce such an identity card. See IDENTITY BADGE; PRIVATE SECURITY AUTHORITY.

(2) Provision has been made for the introduction of a voluntary identity card scheme for young persons aged 18 years and over, in an effort to curb underage drinking of alcohol: Intoxicating Liquor Act 1988, ss 40–41 and 41A as inserted by Intoxicating Liquor Act 2000, s 15. See Age Card Regulations 1999, SI No 4 of 1999. A voluntary *age identity card scheme*, was introduced in September 2000 by the Minister for Justice: Irish Times, 7 September 2000. See AGE DOCUMENT; CHILD, EVACUATION OF; CRIME PREVENTION DIRECTORY; JOURNALIST IN ARMED CONFLICT; PERSONAL PUBLIC SERVICE NUMBER.

identity of parties. See PUBLIC JUSTICE.

ignorantia eorum quae qui scire tenetur non excusat. [Ignorance of those things which everyone is bound to know does not constitute an excuse.]

ignorantia facti excusat; ignorantia juris neminen excusat. [Ignorance of the fact excuses; ignorance of the law does not excuse.] See IGNORANTIA JURIS NEMINEN EXCUSAT.

ignorantia juris neminen excusat. [Ignorance of the law does not excuse.] Every person is presumed to know the law. See *O'Loghlen v O'Callaghan* [1874] IR 8 CL 116. Whether this applies to matrimonial cases is yet to be argued: *O'R v B* [1995] 2 ILRM 57, HC. See MISTAKE.

ill-health. See SICKNESS.

illegal. Unlawful; contrary to law; in violation of a law or a rule which has the force of law.

illegal contracts. Contracts which are forbidden by statute or are contrary to common law or to the Constitution; such contracts are void and collateral contracts are also vitiated. Contracts which are illegal at common law include: (1) a contract to commit a criminal offence or a civil wrong: *Fibretex (Societe Personnes Responsabilite Limite) v Beleir Ltd* [1958] 89 ILTR 141; (2) a contract prejudicial to the administration of justice: *Nolan v Shiels* [1926] 60 ILTR 143; (3) a contract which serves to corrupt public officials: *Lord Mayor of Dublin v Hayes* [1876] 10 IRCL 226; (4) a contract tending to encourage immorality: *Pearce v Brooks* [1867] 11 WR 834; *Seidler v Schallhofer* [1982] 2 NSWSR 80; (5) a contract to trade with the enemies of the State: *Ross v Shaw* [1917] 2 IR 367; (6) a contract that is illegal according to the law where it is to be performed: *Stanhope v Hospital Trust Ltd* [1936] Ir Jur Rep 25: (7) a contract which serves to defraud the Revenue: *Lewis v Squash Ireland Ltd* [1983] ILRM 363; *Winters v Vital Security Ltd* UD 852/1987; *McCarthy v Alan Hair Studios Ltd* [1990] ELR 148; *O'Dowd v Crowley* [1991] ELR 97, EAT; *Tracey v Cheadle Investments* [1991] ELR 130, EAT; *Aspel v Fame Clothing Co Ltd* [1993] ELR 42, EAT; *Hayden v Seán Quinn Properties Ltd* [1994] ELR 45, HC.

A contract which is illegal on its face is illegal at its inception and unenforceable: *Murphy Co Ltd v Crean* [1915] 1 IR 111; *Macklin & McDonald v Greacen & Co* [1983] IR 61. Where a contract is lawful on its face but one party intends to perform it unlawfully, it will be enforceable: *Whitecross Potatoes v Coyle* [1978] HC. See TRADE; UNFAIR DISMISSAL; VOID CONTRACTS.

illegal earnings. See TRADE.

illegal immigrant. Means a non-national who enters or seeks to enter or has entered the State unlawfully: Illegal Immigrants (Trafficking) Act 2000, s 1. *Trafficking in illegal immigrants* is an offence ie a person who organises or knowingly facilitates the entry into the State of a person whom he knows, or has reasonable cause to believe, to be an illegal immigrant, or a person who intends to seek asylum, is guilty of an offence (II(T)A 2000, s 2). This applies to acts done or omissions made outside, as well as to acts done or omissions made, in the State. However, the provision does not apply to anything done by a person otherwise than for gain, or to anything done to assist an asylum seeker, where the person assisting is employed by a *bona fide* organisation assisting asylum seekers.

There is provision for the detention by the gardaí of certain vehicles and for the forfeiture of a boat, ship, aircraft or other vehicle (II(T)A 2000, ss 3–4), for the stopping and searching of a vehicle and persons in the vehicle (II(T)A 2000, s 6), and for the issue by the District Court of a warrant for entry, search and seizure (II(T)A 2000, s 7). For amendments to the Refugee Act 1996, see II(T)A 2000, s 9; Immigration Act 2003, s 7; Immigration Act 2004, s 16(4). See 'Sections 5 and 10 of the Illegal Immigrants (Trafficking) Act 2000' by Mary Rogan in (2002) 10 ISLR 3. See also ASYLUM, CLAIM FOR; BAIL; DEPORTATION ORDER.

illegal means, evidence obtained by. See EVIDENCE OBTAINED ILLEGALLY.

illegitimacy, presumption of. The presumption of illegitimacy arising out of a *divorce a mensa et thoro* (qv) has been abolished and replaced by a presumption of non-paternity. See PATERNITY, PRESUMPTION OF.

illegitimate. See CHILD, ILLEGITIMATE; PATERNITY, PRESUMPTION OF.

illicit distillation. See POITIN.

illicit recording. A recording which is made without the consent of the performer or which constitutes an infringement of the performer's rights: Copyright and Related Rights Act 2000, s 210. Where a copy made by a librarian or archivist, which would otherwise be an illicit recording, is subsequently sold or otherwise made available to the public, it is to be treated as an *illicit recording* (CRRA 2000, s 236). See ARCHIVES; LIBRARIES; PERFORMERS' RIGHTS, INFRINGEMENT OF.

illiterate person. See CONNEMARA VOTING; SIGNATURE.

illness. See SICKNESS.

illusory appointment. See POWER OF APPOINTMENT.

illusory trust. A trust whereby a debtor vests property in trustees on trust to pay his debts; it is *illusory* because the creditors do not always have the right to compel the trustee to carry out the trust. Such a trust may be irrevocable in certain circumstances: *Simmonds v Pallas* [1846] I Eq r. An assignment to a trustee for the benefit of creditors generally is an *act of bankruptcy* and is void unless registered within seven days of execution: Deed of Arrangements Act 1887; Bankruptcy Act 1988, ss 7(1)(a) and 57.

imitation. It is an offence for a person to issue any document not *issued under lawful authority* which by its form, contents, or appearance is calculated or is reasonably likely to lead the person receiving it to believe that it is issued under lawful authority: Courts of Justice Act 1936, s 81. *Issued by lawful authority* means issued by, from, or by order of any court of justice or any judge or justice of any such court or by or from any officer of or office attached to any such court. See COPYRIGHT; FIREARM; FORGERY.

imitation firearm. See FIREARMS.

immediately. In a particular case, where a deposit was required to be paid *immediately* the purchase price had been agreed between the parties or had been determined by a valuer, the court held that *immediately* envisaged that the deposit would be paid *as soon as practicable*: *Kramer v Arnold* [1997] 3 IR 43, SC.

immemorial. See TIME IMMEMORIAL.

immigration. A non-national coming by air or sea from a place outside the State is required to present himself on arrival in the State to an immigration officer and apply for permission to land or be in the State: Immigration Act 2004, s 4(2). An immigration officer is empowered to refuse to give permission to a non-national to land or to be in the State for a variety of reasons e g the non-national is not in a position to support himself and any accompanying dependants, the non-national intends to take up employment but does not have a valid employment permit, the non-national suffers from a specified condition, the non-national is not in possession of a valid Irish visa and a valid passport (IA 2004, s 4(3)).

The Council of Ministers is required to adopt measures on *immigration policy* within the following areas: (a) conditions of entry and residence, and standards on procedures for the issue by member states of long-term visas and residence permits, including those for the purpose of family reunion, (b) illegal immigration and illegal residence, including repatriation of illegal residents: art 63(3) of the consolidated EC Treaty. There are over 19 million immigrants in EU countries, of whom 6 million are from other EU countries, including Ireland, and this number will grow after enlargement of the EU from 15 to 25 member states: statement by Minister Mary Coughlan TD on 2 April 2004. See 'Immigration and asylum law and policy' by solicitor John Handoll in *Law Society Gazette* (October 2003) 49 and (November 2003) 53. [Bibliography: Cubie & Ryan; Immigrant Council.] See ALIEN; PASSPORT; PREINSPECTION; VISA.

immoral contracts. Agreements which tend to encourage immorality are generally void. See ILLEGAL CONTRACTS.

immunisation schemes. Health board prophylactic campaigns have concentrated on diphtheria, poliomyelitis, whooping cough, rubella (german measles) and measles. See Health Act 1947, s 29; Infectious Diseases Regulations 1981 and 1985, SI No 390 of 1981; No 268 of 1985. See VACCINE, CARE INVOLVING.

immunity. The condition of being exempt from some liability to which others are subject eg:

(a) immunity of a judge when performing his judicial functions: *Macauley & Co Ltd v Wyse-Power* [1943] 77 ILTR 61; *Deighan v Ireland* [1995] 1 ILRM 88, HC and 2 IR 56. However, once a judge ceases to exercise his judicial functions, he ceases to enjoy immunity: *Desmond v Riordan* [2000] 1 ILRM 502, HC. See also *Flynn v Minister for Justice & District Judge Connellan* [2003] FL 7298, HC. See CORONER.

(b) immunity of a trade union from tortious liability: Industrial Relations Act 1990, ss 9–13.

(c) immunity of foreign diplomats: Diplomatic Relations and Immunities Acts 1967 and 1976; *Saorstát & Continental Steamship Co v de las Morenas* [1945] IR 291; *McMahon v McDonald* [1988] SC. See SOVEREIGN IMMUNITY.

(d) immunity of the President of Ireland for the exercise and performance of the powers and functions of her office: 1937 Constitution, art 13(8).

(e) immunity of members of the Houses of the Oireachtas in respect of any utterances in either House: 1937 Constitution, art 15(13); *A-G v The Sole Member of the Tribunal of Inquiry into the Beef Processing Industry* [1992] ITLR (23 November), SC.

(f) immunity of Minister and the Controller of Patents as regards their official acts in respect of patent validity or searches: Patents Act 1992, s 118.

(g) immunity of the Environmental Protection Agency and the National Roads Authority in respect of action for damages alleged to have been caused by their failure to perform or comply with any functions conferred on them: Environmental Protection Agency Act 1992, s 15; Roads Act 1993, s 19(4).

(h) immunity from liability in respect of disclosures made in good faith in relation to drug trafficking offences: Criminal Justice Act 1994, s 57, as amended by Central Bank and Financial Services Authority of Ireland Act 2003, s 35, Sch 1.

(i) immunity of the Director of Consumer Affairs or the Central Bank in respect of either of their failure to perform their functions: Consumer Credit Act 1995, s 16 as substituted by Central Bank and Financial Services Authority of Ireland Act 2003, s 35, Sch 1.

(j) immunity of persons giving evidence to an Oireachtas Committee: Committees of the Houses of the Oireachtas (Compellability, Privileges and Immunity of Witnesses) Act 1997; RSC Ord 131 inserted by SI No 381 of 1998.

(k) immunity of banks and financial institutions in respect of acts or omissions in complying with orders made under the Proceeds of Crime Act 1996, s 14.

(l) immunity of witnesses to the Commission: Commission to Inquire into Child Abuse Act 2000, s 18.

(m) immunity in respect of the conduct of investigations into marine casualties and reports of such investigations: Merchant Shipping (Investigation of Marine Casualties) Act 2000, s 37.

See also *McMahon v Ireland and Registrar of Friendly Societies* [1988] ILRM 610, HC. See also Irish Takeover Panel Act 1997, s 20; Planning and Development Act 2000, s 236; Radiological Protection (Amendment) Act 2002, s 10; Health Insurance (Amendment) Act 2003, s 3; Criminal Justice (Illicit Traffic by Sea) Act 2003, s 12; Central Bank Act 1942, s 57AT inserted by Central Bank and Financial Services Authority of Ireland Act 2003, s 28; Digital Hub Development Agency Act 2003, s 38; Containment of Nuclear Weapons Act 2003, s 5(1)(b); Independent Monitoring Commission Act 2003, s 5; European Arrest Warrant Act 2003, s 46. See ACTA JURE IMPERII; CHILD ABUSE, REPORTING; DEFENCE FORCES; DIPLOMATIC PRIVILEGE; IMPEACHMENT; OIREACHTAS; PRIVILEGE; TRADE UNION; UNLAWFUL INTERFERENCE WITH CONSTITUTIONAL RIGHTS; UTTERANCE; WITNESS, PRIVILEGE OF.

impeachment. The solemn charge which may be preferred by either of the Houses of the Oireachtas against the President of Ireland, for stated misbehaviour: 1937 Constitution, art 12(10). See PRESIDENT OF IRELAND.

impeachment of waste. Liability of a person for *waste* (qv).

imperitia culpae adnumeratur. [Inexperience is counted a fault.]

impersonation. False personation. See PERSONATION.

implead. To prosecute or to take proceedings against another.

implied conditions. See IMPLIED TERM.

implied term. A term in a contract which has not been expressly stated but which must be implied to give effect to the law or to the presumed intention of the parties. See *The Moorcock* [1889] 14 PD 64. A term to be implied in a contract: (a) must be one which the parties must have intended to be a term, (b) would have been adopted by the parties as reasonable men if it had been suggested to them, and (c) must have been one to give business efficacy to the contract: *Carna Foods Ltd v Eagle Star Insurance* [1997] 2 ILRM 499, SC and 2 IR 193.

An implied term may be a condition (qv) or a warranty (qv). In contracts for the sale of goods, certain conditions and warranties are implied by statute eg an implied condition that goods are of *merchantable quality* and implied conditions in relation to *description* and *samples* and to the sale of motor vehicles. Terms are also implied in contracts for the supply of services where the supplier is acting in the course of a business. A term will not be implied: (a) where it is not necessary to give efficacy to the terms of a contract: *Grehan v North Eastern Health Board* [1989] IR 422; or (b) where it would have the effect of defeating the contract: *Aga Khan v Firestone* [1992] ILRM 31, HC.

The courts will not imply a term into a contract where it would have the consequences of contradicting the express terms of the contract and where the implied term could not be formulated with reasonable precision: *Jestdale Ltd v Millennium Theatre Co Ltd* [2001] 3 IR 337, HC.

Subject to certain limited statutory exceptions, the law does not normally imply terms into leases relating to the quality of premises; the principle *caveat emptor* applies and so it is incumbent on the lessee to ensure that he is protected by express provisions in the lease: *Riordan v Carroll t/a Wyvern Gallery* [1996] 2 ILRM 263, HC. See *Sweeney v Duggan* [1997] 2 ILRM 211, SC and 2 IR 531; *Sullivan v Southern Health Board* [1997] 3 IR 123, SC. See Animal Remedies Act 1993, s 7. See BUSINESS EFFICACY TEST; OFFICIOUS BYSTANDER TEST; SERVICE, SUPPLY OF; SPARE PARTS; TITLE OF GOODS.

implied trust. See TRUST, IMPLIED.

importune. See PROSTITUTE; SOLICIT.

impossibility of performance. As regards contractual obligations, impossibility of performance does not as a general rule, excuse performance: *Paradine v Jane* [1647] Aleyn 26. However, in certain cases, impossibility will excuse the parties from performance under the doctrine of *frustration*. See FRUSTRATION OF CONTRACT.

impossibilium nulla obligato est. [Impossibility is an excuse for the non-performance of an obligation.] See FRUSTRATION OF CONTRACT.

impost. Any tax or tribute imposed by authority, particularly a tax or duty imposed by government on goods imported. See Electronic Commerce Act 2000, s 11(a).

impotence. The inability to perform the act of sexual intercourse. Impotence, caused by the wrongful act of another, can lead to damages for *loss of consortium* (qv). Impotence is a ground for annulment of a marriage. The impotence however must have existed at the time of the marriage and must be incurable; impotence accruing after marriage is not a ground for nullity. Qualified impotence, ie inability to have sexual intercourse with the partner of the purported marriage but not with another, may be a ground for nullity: *S v S* [1976] SC; *R (otherwise W) v W* [1980] HC. See *AB v EB* [1997] 1 IR 305, HC; *JS v CS* [1997] 2 IR 506, HC. See MARRIAGE, NULLITY OF.

impound. To seize. A grant of representation is said to be *impounded* where the sole executor or administrator becomes insane. Provision has been made for the Minister to empower the gardaí, by regulation, to detain a mechanically propelled vehicle for motor tax or motor insurance offences or where the driver is too young to hold a driving licence: Road Traffic Act 1994, s 41. See ILLEGAL IMMIGRANT.

imprescriptible. That which cannot be rightfully taken away, lost or revoked; inviolable. See CARE ORDER.

imprimatur. [Let it be printed.] A licence to publish or print a book.

imprisonment. The restraint of a person's liberty by another. See BEGET; FALSE IMPRISONMENT; HABEAS CORPUS; PUNISHMENT.

improvement notice, food. A notice stating that an authorised officer is of the opinion that any activity involving the preparation, handling, processing, manufacturing, distribution, storage or selling of food (or the condition of any premises in which such activity is carried out), is of such a nature that if it persists, it will or is likely to pose a risk to public health: Food Safety Authority Act 1998, s 52. The notice is required to identify the problem and specify the remedial action to be taken and the time limit by which it is to be completed.

Where the notice is not complied with, the District Court is empowered to issue an *improvement order* which will provide for a *closure order* to be served in the event of further non-compliance (FSAA 1998, ss 52(4) and 52(5)). See CLOSURE ORDER.

improvement notice, lease. The notice which a business tenant (qv) serves on his landlord when he proposes to carry out improvements to the *tenement* (qv). The landlord may within a month serve the tenant with an *improvement consent*, or an *improvement undertaking* where he undertakes to carry out the work himself, or an *improvement objection*. A landlord has only limited grounds upon which he may object to an improvement. A landlord who carries out the improvement himself is entitled to increase the rent; a tenant who carries out improvements may be entitled to compensation when he quits the tenement. See Landlord and Tenant (Amendment) Act 1980. See IMPROVEMENTS, COMPENSATION FOR.

improvement notice, work. A notice, signed by an inspector, stating his opinion that a person has contravened or is contravening a statutory provision regarding safety, health or welfare at work and directing that the alleged contravention be remedied by a specified date: Safety, Health and Welfare at Work Act 1989, s 36. The notice may include directions as to the remedial measures required. An improvement notice may also be founded on a failure by a person to submit or implement an *improvement plan* (qv). An appeal lies to the District Court. Contravention of an improvement notice is an offence (SHWWA 1989, s 48(5)).

improvement plan. A plan regarding an activity at work, which is required to be submitted to an inspector, specifying remedial action which it is proposed will be taken to rectify matters regarding that activity; the plan may be requested by the inspector when he is of the opinion that the activity involves, or is likely to involve, risk to the safety or health of persons: Safety, Health and Welfare at Work Act 1989, s 35. Failure to submit an improvement plan is an offence (SHWWA 1989, s 48(4)). Implementation of an improvement plan is enforceable by the issue of an *improvement notice* (qv).

improvements, compensation for. A business tenant (qv) who quits his *tenement* (qv) is entitled to compensation by the landlord for every improvement made which adds to the letting value of the tenement on the termination date, and which is suitable to the character of the tenement: Landlord and Tenant (Amendment) Act 1980, Pt IV. A business tenant who quits by surrender or because of non-payment of rent is not so entitled.

The amount of compensation may be agreed upon by the landlord and tenant or in the absence of agreement, it will be an amount determined by the court, as the *capitalised value* of such addition to the letting value of the tenement at the termination as the court determines to be attributable to the improvement (LT(A)A 1980, s 47(1)). The maximum capitalised value which the court may determine is 15 times the annual amount of addition to the letting value. See IMPROVEMENT NOTICE, LEASE.

in absentia. [In the absence of.] See European Arrest Warrant Act 2003, s 45. See ABSENCE; AUDI ALTERAM PARTEM.

in aequali jure melior est conditio possidentis. [Where the rights of the parties are equal, the claim of the actual possessor is strongest.] See *Bailey v Barnes* [1894] 1 Ch 25.

in alieno solo. On another's land. See EASEMENT.

in ambiguis orationibus maxime sententia est ejus qui eas protelisset. [In dealing with ambiguous words the intention of him who used them should especially be regarded.]

in articulo mortis. [At the point of death.]

in autre droit. [In the right of another.] An executor holds property in the right of his testator.

in bonis, in b. [In the goods of.]

in camera. The hearing of a case in private e g in court but with the public excluded or in a judge's private room. Justice is required to be administered in public, save in such special and limited cases as may be prescribed by law: 1937 Constitution, art 34(1).

Where a case is heard *in camera*, the public must be excluded; the only persons permitted to be present are the parties directly concerned, their legal representatives and officers of the court. Where the law requires that proceedings be held *otherwise than in public*, the public will be excluded but certain specified persons may be entitled to be present e g *bona fide* representatives of the press in rape and incest proceedings; or a parent, relative or friend of the complainant or of a minor accused in rape proceedings: Criminal Law (Rape) Amendment Act 1990, s 11; Criminal Law (Incest Proceedings) Act 1995. See *The People (DPP) v DR* [1998] 2 IR 106, CCA.

The law prescribes that justice may be administered *otherwise than in public* in the case of eg: (a) urgent applications for relief by way of *habeas corpus*, bail, prohibition or injunction; (b) matrimonial cases; (c) lunacy and cases involving minors; (d) cases involving the disclosure of a secret manufacturing process: Courts (Supplemental Provisions) Act 1961, s 45; (e) proceedings under the Data Protection Act 1988, s 28; (f) cases involving rape offences: Criminal Law (Rape) (Amend-

ment) Act 1990, s 11; (g) proceedings for the appointment of an examiner to a company: Companies (Amendment) Act 1990, s 31.

Before ordering that proceedings be heard *in camera*, the Court has to be satisfied that a public hearing of all or part of the proceedings would fall short of the doing of justice, it being a fundamental principle of the administration of justice in a democratic state that justice be administered in public: *Re R* [1989] IR 126.

There is no specific provision in Irish law which provides for an absolute embargo on the publication of information derived from *in camera* proceedings: *Eastern Health Board v Fitness to Practise Committee of the Medical Council* [1998] 3 IR 399, HC. However, the law implies an absolute embargo on the production of information which derived from, or was introduced in, proceedings protected by s 34 of the Judicial Separation and Family Law Reform Act 1989; such information could not therefore be the subject matter of investigation in an inquiry by a professional body without the consent of the court: *RM v DM (Practice: in camera)* [2000] 3 IR 373, HC and [2001] 2 ILRM 369, HC. In this case the court held that the public interest in the resolution of family disputes, outweighed the public right that justice be administered in public and outweighed the public interest in maintaining trust in the professional services of barristers. A solicitor must not disclose the contents of a family law file which is subject to the *in camera* rule to any third party, even if he has his own client's consent: *A Guide to Professional Conduct of Solicitors in Ireland* (2002) ch 4.5.

'In the hierarchy of rights, ... the privacy rights and the welfare of children in *in camera* proceedings will normally come ahead of the right to freedom of expression and the right to have justice done in public': Horgan, Gallagher and Shannon in 'Camera Angles' *Law Society Gazette* (July/ August 2002) 26 and *Bar Review* (June/July 2002) 278. See *Re Kennedy & McCann* [1976] IR 382; *Irish Press plc v Ingersoll Irish Publications Ltd* [1993] ILRM 747; *Z v DPP* [1994] 2 IR 476, SC; *MP v AP* [1996] 1 IR 144, HC; *Re Greendale Developments Ltd (in liquidation)* [1997] 3 IR 540, HC; *de Gortari v District Judge Smithwick* [1999] 4 IR 223, SC; *In Re Ansbacher (Cayman) Ltd* [2002] 2 ILRM 491, HC.

See Companies Act 1963, s 205(7); Criminal Procedure Act 1967, s 4I as inserted by Criminal Justice Act 1999, s 9.

Under recent legislation, provision has been made to change the 'in camera' rule as regards family law, so as to allow the preparation by a barrister or solicitor and publication of a report of such proceedings, or the publication of a court decision, provided that the report or decision does not contain any information which would identify the parties or any child to which the proceedings relate: Civil Liability and Courts Act 2004, s 40. The Act further provides that nothing in any enactment prohibiting proceedings from being heard in public, will prevent the production of a document or the giving of information or evidence relating to such proceedings to a body or person conducting a hearing or inquiry pursuant to statute. See 'Family Law aspects of the European Convention on Human Rights Act 2003' by Dervla Browne BL in *Bar Review* (April 2004) 39. See ANTON PILLER ORDER; CHAMBERS; MCKENZIE FRIEND; OPPRESSION OF SHAREHOLDER; PUBLIC JUSTICE.

in casu extremae necessitatis omnia sunt communia. [In cases of extreme necessity, everything is in common.]

in commendam. [In trust.]

in consimili casu, consimile debet esse remedium. [In similar cases the remedy should be similar.]

in contemplation of death. See DONATIO MORTIS CAUSA.

in contractis tacite insunt quae sunt moris et consuetudinis. [The clauses which are in accordance with custom and usage are an implied part of every contract.]

in conventionibus contrahentium voluntas potius quam verba spectari placuit. [In construing agreements the intention of the parties, rather than the words actually used, should be considered.]

in curia. [In open court.]

in custodia legis. [In the custody of the law.]

in esse. [In being.] Actually existing.

in extenso. [At full length.] The reporting of a case in full rather than a summary.

in extremis. [In last extremity.] Final illness.

in facie curiae. [In the face of the court.] See CONTEMPT OF COURT.

in flagrante delicto. [With the crime still blazing.] While committing the offence. See MITIGATING FACTORS.

in forma pauperis. [In the character of a pauper.] See *Salomon v Salomon & Co* [1897] AC 22. See LEGAL AID.

in futuro. [In the future.]

in gremio legis. [In the bosom of the law.]

in gross. A right which is not appendant, appurtenant, or otherwise annexed to land. See EASEMENT.

in invitum. [Against a reluctant person.]

in jure non remota causa, sed proxima spectatur. [In law the proximate, and not the remote, cause is to be regarded.]

in lieu. [In place of.]

in limine. [On the threshold.] Preliminary. See *Comhlucht Paipéar Riomhaireachta Teo v Údarás na Gaeltachta* [1990] ITLR (19 February), SC; *Dekra Erin v Minister for the Environment* [2002] 2 ILRM 30, HC and [2003] 2 ILRM 210, SC and 2 IR 270 See POSTLIMINIUM.

in loco parentis. [In the place of a parent.] A person who is not the parent of a particular child but takes on himself parental offices and duties in relation to the child. 'Any situation where one person assumes moral responsibility, not binding in law, to provide for the material needs of another': O'Hanlon J. in *Hollywood v Cork Harbour Commissioners* [1992] 2 IR 457 at 465. The court does not require the assumption of a clear and definite obligation to provide financially for the person in question: *Waters v Cruickshank* [1967] IR 378. See CHILD, ACCESS TO; FORCE MAJEURE LEAVE; SATISFACTION; SUPERVISION ORDER; TRESPASS; TRESPASS TO PERSON; WELFARE OF CHILDREN.

in media res. [In the midst of the matter.]

in misericordia. [At mercy.] See *The People (DPP) v Cunningham* [2002] 2 IR 712, SC and [2003] 1 ILRM 124. See MERCY.

in nomine. [In the name of.]

in pais. [In the country.] As contrasted with *in the court*. Refers to that which happens without legal proceedings eg estoppel *in pais* or estoppel by conduct eg a tenant, having accepted a lease, cannot dispute his lessor's title.

in pari causa potior est conditio possidentis. [Everyone may keep what he has got, unless and until someone else can prove a better title.]

in pari delicto, potior est conditio possidentis. [Where both parties are equally to blame, the condition of the possessor is the best.] See *Daly v Daly* [1870] IR 5 CL 108.

in pari materia. [In an analogous case.] See INTERPRETATION OF LEGISLATION.

in-patient services. Institutional services provided for persons while maintained in a hospital, convalescent home or home for persons suffering from physical or mental disability or in accommodation ancillary thereto: Health Act 1970, s 51. See also Health (Amendment) Act 1986; SI No 116 of 1987 as amended by SI No 348 of 2003. The Supreme Court has held that the obligations of the health board to provide certain services in a 'home' referred to an institutional home and not an individual's home: *K(C) v Northern Area Health Board* [2003] 2 IR 544 and FL 7622, SC.

The daily charge for in-patient services has been increased from 1 January 2004 to €45 and the maximum payable in any period of 12 consecutive months to €450: Health (In-Patient Charges) (Amendment) Regulations 2003, SI No 654 of 2003. The usual exemptions, which include medical card holders and hardship provisions, continue to apply. See EUROPEAN HEALTH INSURANCE CARD; OUT-PATIENT SERVICES.

in perpetuum. [For ever.]

in personam. [Against a person.] An expression to indicate an action against a specific person, as distinct from *in rem* (qv). Equity acts *in personam* e g by imprisoning a person for disobeying a judgment. A mareva injunction is an *in personam* order restraining the defendant from dealing with assets in which the plaintiff claims no right whatsoever: *O'Mahony v Horgan* [1996] 1 ILRM 161, SC.

in pleno. [In full.]

in posse. [Potentially existing.] Contrast with actually existing, see IN ESSE.

in praesenti. [At the present time.]

in propria persona. [In his own proper person.]

in re. [In the matter of.]

in rem. [Against a thing.] An expression to indicate an action *against the world*, as distinct from an action against a specific person e g an action to assert a right to property. A judgment *in rem* is a judgment of a court of competent jurisdiction determining the status of a person or thing. A decision *in rem* is one which determines once and for all the status of a particular *res* or thing: *Abrahamson v Law Society of Ireland* [1996 HC] 2 ILRM 481. A decree of divorce must be addressed to the public at large and is a decision *in rem*: McGuinness

J in *CK v JK & FMcG* [2004] ITLR (3 May 2004), SC. See *Bruno Tassan Din v Banco Ambrosiano SPA* [1991] 1 IR 569, HC; *Lazarus-Barlow v Regan Estates* [1949] 2 KB 465. See IN PERSONAM.

in situ. [In its original or natural position.]

in specie. In its own form and essence, and not in its equivalent. See MUTUUM.

in statu quo. [In the former position.]

in terrorum. [By way of terror] e g a penalty in a contract. See PENALTY.

in totidem verbis. [In so many words.]

in toto. [Entirely; wholly.]

in transitu. [In course of transit.] See STOPPAGE IN TRANSITU.

in vitro diagnostic medical device. Means a medical device intended to be used *in vitro* for the examination of specimens, including blood and tissue donations, derived from the human body, solely or principally for the purpose of providing specified information e g concerning a physiological or pathological state or a congenital abnormality: European Communities (*In Vitro* Diagnostic Medical Devices) Regulations 2001, SI No 304 of 2001. All such devices placed on the market or put into service must comply with the relevant essential requirements.

in-vitro fertilisation; IVF. Technique enabling some women, who are unable to conceive, to bear children. Egg cells removed from a woman's ovary are fertilised by sperm *in-vitro* (ie outside the body); some of the resulting fertilised egg cells are incubated until the blastocyst stage and then implanted into her uterus. The Medical Council has issued guidelines on in-vitro fertilisation: 'Techniques such as IVF should only be used after thorough investigation has failed to reveal a treatable cause for the infertility. Prior to fertilisation of an ovum, extensive discussion and counselling is essential. Any fertilised ovum must be used for normal implantation and must not be deliberately destroyed. If couples have validly decided they do not wish to make use of their own fertilised ova, the potential for voluntary donation to other recipients may be considered.' Medical Council, *A Guide to Ethical Conduct and Behaviour* (6th edn, 2004) para 24.5. See HUMAN REPRODUCTION.

inaccurate data. Personal data (qv) which are incorrect or misleading as to any matter of fact, as distinct from opinion: Data Protection Act 1988, s 1(2). There is provision for rectification, blockage or erasure of inaccurate data (DPA 1988, s 6 as amended by Data Protection (Amendment) Act 2003, s 7). See BLOCKING; DATA PROTECTION; SENSITIVE PERSONAL DATA.

inalienability. Not transferable. The general rule of law is that land must not be rendered inalienable; however, no gift for charitable purposes is void merely because it renders land inalienable in *perpetuity*. A condition in a testator's will which prohibited the sale of land to members of a particular family, was held to be void as contrary to public policy: *Re Dunne* [1988] IR 155. However, a devise in a will which was conditional on the plaintiff being the beneficial owner of land, which the testator had transferred to the plaintiff during his lifetime, was not void; it did not render the land inalienable: *Fitzsimons v Fitzsimons* [1993] ILRM 478, HC.

Social welfare benefits or assistance or children's allowances are inalienable, as are documents upon which they are payable: Social Welfare (Consolidation) Act 1993, ss 226–229.

Generally leases of premises contain a covenant prohibiting alienation. This has the intended effect of preventing the tenant from assigning his interest in the lease to another person. However, in certain leases, such a covenant must be interpreted to mean that the tenant is not permitted to alienate his interest without the consent of the landlord, *which consent must not be unreasonably withheld*: Landlord and Tenant (Amendment) Act 1980, s 66. See Residential Tenancies Act 2004, s 193(d). See CHARITIES; MORTMAIN.

incapable. As regards the opinion of a garda that a person is *incapable* of driving a motor vehicle, 'incapable' connotes that a person is no longer capable of having proper control, whereas 'unfit' connotes that he is not suitable or not qualified to drive: *DPP v Fanagan* [1991] HC. See DRUNKEN DRIVING.

incapacitated child. A parent of a child who is permanently incapacitated, mentally or physically, is entitled to claim for each such child an allowance in computing his income tax liability for 1998–99 and later tax years: Taxes Consolidation Act 1997, s 465 as amended by Finance Act 2000, s 9.

incapacity. Lack of legal power or competence e g due to being a minor (qv) or being of unsound mind (qv). The incapacity of an employee may be a ground for dismissal

eg see *Gurr v Office of Public Works* [1990] ELR 42; *Caulfield v Waterford Foundry Ltd* [1991] ELR 137, EAT. A credit union may make to any person, whom they judge proper to receive it, a payment of any property held on behalf of a member who is *incapable* by reason of mental condition to manage and administer his own property: Credit Union Act 1997, s 24. See CAPACITY TO CONTRACT; DISABILITY, PERSON UNDER; INCOME TAX; INCOMPETENCE; SICKNESS; UNFAIR DISMISSAL.

incardination. The act by which a bishop permanently attaches a cleric to his diocese in the Roman Catholic Church. *Excardination* means the act by which a bishop permanently allows one of his own clergy to leave the diocese in order to belong to another. See *Buckley v Cahal Daly* [1991 NI] ITLR (7 January), HC.

incest. The offence committed by a male person who has sexual intercourse with a female who is, to his knowledge, his mother, sister, daughter or granddaughter; or by a female over the age of sixteen years who permits her father, brother, grandfather or son to have sexual intercourse with her, knowing him to be so related: Punishment of Incest Act 1908. Since 1988, a spouse is a competent and compellable witness against the other spouse charged with the offence of incest: *DPP v JT* [1988] CCA (see O'Connor in 7 ILT & SJ (1989) 95 and Charlton in 8 ILT & SJ (1990) 140). For statutory provision, see Criminal Evidence Act 1992, ss 20–26. A male convicted of incest is now liable to imprisonment for life: PIA 1908, s 1 as amended by Criminal Law (Incest Proceedings) Act 1995, s 5. See PARENT; WITNESS, COMPETENCE OF.

inchoate. Begun, or in an early stage, but not complete. See INCHOATE BILL.

inchoate bill. A bill of exchange (qv) which arises when a person signs a blank stamped paper with the intention that it may be converted into a bill; this operates as an authority to fill it up as a complete bill for any amount the stamp will cover, using the signature already on it: Bills of Exchange Act 1882, s 20. Also, where a bill is wanting in any material particular, the holder of it has authority to fill up the omission in any way he thinks fit (BEA 1882, s 20). A promissory note (qv) is inchoate and incomplete until delivery to the payee or bearer (BEA 1882, s 84).

inchoate crime. An offence which is committed even though the substantive crime with which it is connected is not committed eg incitement, conspiracy, attempt (qqv). [Bibliography: Charleton (4).]

incineration. A licence is required for a waste disposal activity which involves incineration on land or sea: Waste Management Act 1996, Sch 3, as substituted by Protection of the Environment Act 2003, s 54 and Sch 3. See also WMA 1996, s 2 as amended by PEA 2003, s 19. More stringent standards have been specified with the objective of preventing pollution by emissions from incinerators into air, soil, surface water, and the resulting risk to human health: EC (Incineration of Waste) Regulations 2003, SI No 275 of 2003, implementing Directive (EC) 2000/76. The Directive applies to new plants from 28 December 2002 and to existing plants from 28 December 2005. See *Martin v An Bord Pleanála* [2002] 2 IR 655, HC and [2003] 1 ILRM 257. See AIR POLLUTION; DANGEROUS GOODS.

incipitur. [It is begun.] This was the technical commencement of a declaration or judgment. See ALLOCATUR.

incitement. The offence of soliciting some other person to commit a crime. Formerly, if the crime solicited was actually committed, the inciter would be liable as an *accessory* (qv) *before the fact* if the crime solicited was a felony, and liable as a *principal* offender if it was a misdemeanour. See now AID AND ABET. It is an offence to incite or encourage any civil servant to refuse, neglect, or omit to perform his duties: Offences Against the State Act 1939, s 9. See *The People (Attorney-General) v Capaldi* [1949] CCA. See HATRED, INCITEMENT TO.

include. The word *include* has been held to be a word of extension when used in a statutory definition: *Attorney-General (McGrath) v Healy* [1972] IR 393. A word in a statute will have its ordinary meaning in addition to that included by the extension where the extension *include* is given in its definition. The word *include* has the function of enlarging the meaning of the words or phrase with which it is associated: *Dilworth v Stamp Commissioner* [1899] AC 99. Contrast with MEANS.

inclusio unius est exclusio alterius. [The inclusion of one is the exclusion of the other.]

inclusive education. The education of a child with special educational needs in an inclusive environment with children who do not have such needs. Under recent legislation, inclusive education must be provided for such a child unless it is inconsistent with: (a) the best interest of the child as determined by any assessment carried out under the legislation, or (b) the effective provision of education for children with whom the child is to be educated: Education for Persons with Special Educational Needs Act 2004, s 2. See DISABLED PERSON AND EDUCATION; INTEGRATED EDUCATION; SPECIAL EDUCATIONAL NEEDS.

income averaging. The provision in relation to farmer taxation which permits the farmer's profits for a tax year to be taken as the average annual profits over three years ie over the current tax year and the two immediately preceding tax years: Taxes Consolidation Act 1997, s 657.

income tax. The tax on income or profits comprising income tax, corporation tax and capital gains tax. Individuals are liable in principle to pay income tax on their income and capital gains tax on chargeable gains realised on the disposal of assets; companies and other bodies of persons with corporate status do not in general pay income tax or capital gains tax, but are chargeable to a separate corporation tax levied on their income and chargeable gains.

Income tax was originally designed as a temporary tax which had to be renewed every year: *Bowles v Attorney-General* [1912] 1 Ch 123. It was finally made a permanent tax in 1972: Finance Act 1972.

Income tax is levied on income from sources classified as follows: A – arising from the ownership of land prior to 6 April 1969; B – arising from the occupation of land prior to 6 April 1969; C – collection of tax at source from interest, annuities, dividends or shares of annuities payable in the State out of any public revenue; D – arising from trade (case 1), profession (case II) etc; E – income from other offices and employments; F – company distributions and dividends etc.

There is an exemption from income tax on the income from the proceeds of a court action for compensation for personal injuries where the recipient is *permanently and totally incapacitated* by reason of mental or physical infirmity from maintaining himself: Finance Act 1990, s 5, now Taxes

Consolidation Act 1997, s 189. This provision also applies to payments made following an assessment made by the Personal Injuries Assessment Board of claims for damages in similar circumstances: Finance Act 2004, s 6. The tax exemption applies from 2004 to both the income and gains derived from the investment of the compensation, and the rules requiring that this be the sole or main income of the individual have been relaxed; they now must represent more that 50% of the individual's total income and gains for the year concerned (FA 2004, s 17).

Income tax is managed by the Revenue Commissioners; there is provision for appeal. The income tax year previously ran from 6 April to 5 April; it is now aligned with the calendar year as from 1 January 2002: Finance Act 2001, s 77. A system of *self-assessment* for the self-employed has been introduced: Finance Act 1988, ss 9–21, now Taxes Consolidation Act 1997, ss 950–959. Provision was made in 2000 for the introduction of individual standard rate bands, known as *individualisation*: Finance Act 2000, s 3.

The State must not by its taxation legislation breach its pledge to guard with special care the institution of marriage and protect it from attack: *Murphy v Attorney-General* [1982] IR 241. The provisions under the 1967 Act for the assessment and collection of income tax in default of the making of a return by a taxpayer are not unconstitutional: *Deighan v Hearne & Ors* [1990] 1 IR 499, SC.

Payments made to an employee, by a person other than his employer, might be liable to income tax under Schedule E: *O'Connell v Keleghan* [2001] 2 IR 490, SC.

The completion of the move to a *tax credit system* was made in 2001 by converting the various fixed standard rated allowances into formal tax credits: Finance Act 2001, s 2; Finance Act 2002, s 3. The standard rate of tax was reduced from 22% to 20% and the higher rate from 44% to 42% (FA 2001, s 3). For the standard tax bands for 2002, 2003 and 2004, see Finance Act 2002, s 2. The *employee tax credit* (formerly known as the PAYE allowance) was raised from €660 to €800 for the income tax year 2003: Finance Act 2003, s 3, and to €1,040 for 2004. [Bibliography: Judge; McAteer, Reddin, & Deegan; O'Brien & Trueick; O'Reilly & Carroll.]

See EMPLOYMENT AWARDS; FINANCIAL RESOLUTIONS; QUALIFYING PATENT.

income tax penalties. It has been held that the recovery of a penalty imposed by the Income Tax Act 1967, s 128, now Taxes Consolidation Act 1997, s 987, is not a criminal matter within the meaning of the Prosecution of Offences Act 1974, s 3 and that the Director of Public Prosecutions (qv) has no *locus standi* (qv) in relation thereto: *Downes v DPP* [1987] ILRM 665. Certain penalties under the income tax code are not criminal in character and may be recovered in civil proceedings: *McLoughlin v Tuite* [1989] IR 82, SC.

A prior demand is required before the commencement of proceedings for the recovery of income tax: *Criminal Assets Bureau v Craft and McWatt* [2001] 1 IR 121, HC. See *Gilligan v Criminal Assets Bureau* [1997] 1 IR 526, HC.

It has also been held that publication of an *enforcement notice* in respect of PAYE can constitute a libel (qv): *Kennedy v Hearne & Ors* [1988] ILRM 52. See REVENUE OFFENCE; REVENUE PENALTY.

income tax regulations. Regulations have been made which revise and consolidate, subject to certain changes, the existing regulatory provisions, which prescribe the manner in which the deduction of tax from salaries and wages under the *pay as you earn system* operates: Income Tax (Employments) (Consolidated) Regulations 2001, SI No 559 of 2001, as amended by SI No 511 of 2002, and SI No 613 of 2003.

The main changes are: (i) the system for casual employees has been abolished; (ii) there is an obligation on employers paying their liability by direct debit to review the adequacy of the payment from time to time; (iii) with effect from 1 January 2003, employees who do not supply their employer with a *personal public service number* (PPS Number) will be subject to tax under the emergency system at the higher rate of tax; (iv) employers have an obligation to take reasonable steps to ensure that the PPS Number provided by the employee does, in fact, refer to that employee; (v) the extension of the PAYE 'net pay' arrangements to PRSA and RAC contributions; and (vi) the extension of PAYE from 1 January 2004 to non-cash remuneration of employees in the form of perquisites and other benefits.

incompetence. A ground for dismissal of an employee: Unfair Dismissals Act 1977;

O'Neill v Bus Éireann [1990] ELR 135, CC. The test to be used has two elements: (a) the employer's honest belief of incompetence, and (b) reasonable grounds for that belief: *McDonnell v Spar Supermarket* [1992] ELR 214, EAT.

inconsistent previous statement. See PREVIOUS STATEMENT, INCONSISTENT.

inconvenience. A court will not award damages for *inconvenience* caused by a local authority which acts *bona fide* in the *ultra vires* exercise of its statutory powers (eg disconnecting a water supply): *O'Donnell v Dún Laoghaire Corporation (No 2)* [1991] 9 ILT Dig 199 & 227, HC.

Incorporated Law Society of Ireland. The former name of the Law Society of Ireland: Solicitors (Amendment) Act 1994, s 4. See LAW SOCIETY OF IRELAND; SOLICITOR.

incorporation. Merging together to form a whole; conferring legal personality on an association of persons eg registration of a company: Companies Act 1963, s 18; or incorporation of a building society: Building Societies Act 1989, s 10. See COMPANY; ASSOCIATION, MEMORANDUM OF; BUILDING SOCIETY.

incorporeal hereditaments. Intangible property eg easements (qv) and profits a prendre (qv). See OWNERSHIP.

incriminate. To involve oneself or another in the possibility of being prosecuted for a criminal offence. Generally a witness, on grounds of *privilege,* need not answer any question which exposes him to any criminal charge, perjury (qv) or forfeiture (qv). The witness must say on oath that he honestly believes that the answer may tend to incriminate him.

The privilege does not arise if there are no reasonable grounds for his fears, the time for prosecution has passed, he has been prosecuted previously or has been pardoned, or a statute provides for full disclosure. An accused person giving evidence under the Criminal Justice (Evidence) Act 1924 may be asked questions in cross-examination notwithstanding that they would tend to criminate him as to the offence charged. See *R v Boyes* [1861] 1 B S 311; *Re Reynolds* [1882] 20 Ch D 294; *The State (Magee) v O'Rourke* [1971] IR 205. See also Companies Act 1963, s 245(6) as amended by Companies Act 1990, s 126.

There is no rule of law requiring a judge to instruct a jury that, where the only evidence consists of an incriminating statement by an accused, there was a danger of convicting without corroborative evidence; any such warning could involve the implication that the gardaí involved in obtaining such a statement were to be treated in the same way as accomplices: *People (DPP) v Quilligan & O'Reilly (No 3)* [1993] 11 ILT Dig 88, SC. As regards spouses, see WITNESS, COMPETENCE OF.

A person is not entitled to refuse to answer a question or to refuse to hand over a document to the Commission on the ground that the answer or the document might incriminate him; however a statement or admission made by a person will not be admissible against that person in any criminal proceedings: Commission to Inquire into Child Abuse Act 2000, s 21. See BANKRUPT, DUTIES OF; BLOOD SPECIMEN; EXAMINATION RE COMPANY; SILENCE, RIGHT TO; TRIBUNALS OF INQUIRY.

incumbrance. Encumbrance (qv).

indecency. Any act which offends modesty, causes scandal or injures the morals of the community. A person commits an offence who at, or near, or in sight of any place along which the public habitually pass, commits any indecent act: Criminal Law Amendment Act 1935, s 18 as amended by Criminal Law (Rape) (Amendment) Act 1990, s 18. The publication or utterance of indecent matter is an offence and is required to be punishable by law: 1937 Constitution, art 40(6)(1)(1).

Any public sale, or exposure for sale, or exposure to public view of any indecent book, or print is an offence: Censorship of Publications Act 1946. The Supreme Court has held that the Censorship of Publications Board has no obligation to disclose the identity of persons who make complaints to the Board; to do so would discourage the public from making complaints: *Melton Enterprises Ltd v Censorship of Publications Board* [2004] 1 ILRM 260, SC. See *Melton Enterprises Ltd v Censorship of Publications Board* [2003] 2 ILRM 18, HC. See also Indecent Advertisements Act 1889; Regulation of Information (Services outside the State for Termination of Pregnancies) Act 1995, s 14. See CENSORSHIP OF BOOKS; EXPOSURE, INDECENT; PERFORMANCE, INDECENT OR PROFANE.

indecency, gross. See GROSS INDECENCY.

indecent assault. See ASSAULT, INDECENT.

indecent exposure. See EXPOSURE, INDECENT.

indemnify. To make good a loss which one person has suffered in consequence of the act or default of another. Normally an employer will be held to have indemnified an employee against all liabilities and expenses incurred by the employee in the proper performance of his employment.

Any provisions in a company's regulations are void if they exempt or indemnify an officer of the company in respect of any liability which attaches to him in respect of his negligence, default, breach of duty or breach of trust: Companies Act 1963, ss 200 and 391. Similar provisions apply to officers of building societies: Building Societies Act 1989, ss 114–115.

A contract of insurance usually indemnifies the insured, in consideration of a premium, against loss he has suffered. See *Rohan Construction v Insurance Corporation of Ireland* [1986] ILRM 419 and [1988] ILRM 373, SC. See also *Hong Kong and Shanghai Banking Corp v Icarom plc* [1993] 11 ILT Dig 142, SC.

Payment on a policy of insurance to a company which is being wound up, may be applied only in discharging valid claims and not towards the payment of its debts: Civil Liability Act 1961, s 62 and *McKenna v Best Travel Ltd* [1995] 2 ILRM 471, HC.

There may be circumstances which would require the executive to indemnify the judiciary in relation to costs which are properly awarded against them: *McIlwraith v Fawsett* [1989] 7 ILT Dig 326. However, see *McIlwraith v His Hon Judge Fawsitt* [1990] 1 IR 343 cited with approval in *O'Connor v Carroll* [1999] 2 IR 160, SC. See Roads Act 1993, s 33; Local Government (Planning and Development) Act 1998, s 2; Food Safety Authority of Ireland Act 1998, s 55; Communications Regulation Act 2002, s 41; Public Health (Tobacco) Act 2002, s 49; Residential Institutions Redress Act 2002, s 24; Digital Hub Development Agency Act 2003, s 37; Companies (Auditing and Accounting) Act 2003, s 33; Personal Injuries Assessment Board Act 2003, s 69; Electoral (Amendment) Act 2004, s 29; Residential Tenancies Act 2004 s.168. See Takeover Rules 2001, Pt B, r 8.7. See also CONTRACT OF GUARANTEE; INNOCENT MISREPRESENTATION; INSURANCE; PROFESSIONAL INDEMNITY POLICY; VICARIOUS LIABILITY.

indemnity to air navigation undertakings. Under a temporary measure, the Minister for Public Enterprise is empowered, with the consent of the Minister for Finance, to grant or renew an indemnity to an *air navigation undertaking* (airline, airport and essential service providers) in respect of specified risks: Air Navigation and Transport (Indemnities) Act 2001.

The measure was introduced in the wake of the withdrawal by the worldwide insurance market of third-party cover in respect of acts of war, terrorism and allied perils, following the terrorist acts in the United States on 11 September 2001.

The government is empowered to make or renew an Order, declaring that a *state of difficulty* exists affecting the supply of insurance relating to air navigation undertakings, and during the course of such Order, the Minister is empowered, but not obliged, to grant an indemnity. The 2001 Act ceases to be in operation 12 months after coming into operation, unless continued by resolution of the Oireachtas (ANT(I)A 2001, s 19) eg see SI No 458 of 2002.

indenture. (1) Originally a document written in duplicate on the same parchment or paper and divided in two by cutting through it in a wavy line; the genuineness of the indenture was proved by fitting the two parts (known as *counterparts*) together. (2) Means an indenture of apprenticeship: Solicitors (Amendment) Act 1994, s 2.

indentures of apprenticeship. Includes any form of agreement as may be prescribed whereunder solicitors provide training for persons seeking to be admitted as solicitors: Solicitors (Amendment) Act 1994, s 2. There are provisions governing the assignment of indentures on the death of a solicitor and also governing the discharge of indentures (S(A)A 1994, ss 45–46). See APPRENTICE; SOLICITOR'S APPRENTICE.

independent contractor. A person who contracts to perform a particular task for another and is not under the other person's control as to the manner in which the task is performed. An employer is not normally liable for the torts of an independent contractor, unless the employer has been negligent himself eg in supervising the work. The distinction between an employee (qv) and an independent contractor is important in relation to taxation, social welfare and employment protection legislation.

An occupier of premises is protected from liability for the negligence of an independent contractor, but not if the occupier had or ought to have known that the work was not properly done: Occupiers' Liability Act 1995, s 7.

Records in the possession of an independent contractor, who is or was providing a service for a public body, are covered by the provisions of the Freedom of Information Act 1997 to the extent that they relate to the service being provided (FIA 1997, s 6(9)). See *Walshe v Baileboro Co-operative* [1939] 73 ILTR 232; *Lynch v Palgrave Murphy* [1964] IR 150; *Ryan v Shamrock Marine* [1992] ELR 19, EAT; *Connolly v Dundalk UDC* [1993] 11 ILT Dig 144, SC; *Duncan v O'Driscoll* [1997] ELR 38, EAT; *Denny & Sons v Minister for Social Welfare* [1996] 1 ILRM 418, HC and ELR 43 and [1998] ELR 36, SC. See VICARIOUS LIABILITY.

Independent Monitoring Commission. An independent corporate body established pursuant to an Agreement between the Irish and British governments, done at Dublin on 25 November 2003: Independent Monitoring Commission Act 2003. The objective of the Commission is to carry out specified functions with a view to promoting the transition to a peaceful society and stable and inclusive government in Northern Ireland (IMCA 2003, s 3 and art 3).

The functions of the Commission include: (a) monitoring any continuing activity by paramilitary groups, (b) assessing whether the leaderships of such organisations are directing such incidents or seeking to prevent them, (c) assessing trends in security incidents, (d) monitoring whether commitments made with respect to security normalisation measures are being fully implemented by the British government, and (e) reporting on any claim by any party represented in the Northern Ireland Assembly: (i) that a Minister, or another party in the Assembly, is not committed to non-violence and exclusively peaceful and democratic means, or (ii) that a Minister has failed to observe any other terms of the pledge of office (IMCA 2003, s 3 and arts 4–7). The Commission consists of four members, two appointed by the British government, one appointed by the Irish government, and one appointed by both governments having been nominated by the USA government (art 10).

The Commission issued its first report on 20 April 2004 in which it found, *inter alia*, that: (a) some senior members of Sinn Féin are also senior members of the Provisional IRA, and (b) that loyalists were responsible for eight of eleven murders carried out in the North since 1 January 2003, while republicans were responsible for three. See GOOD FRIDAY AGREEMENT.

Independent Radio and Television Commission. Renamed the *Broadcasting Commission of Ireland* in 2001 with a wider remit. See website: *www.bci.ie*. See BROADCASTING COMMISSION OF IRELAND.

independent television programme. A programme made by a person who: (a) has control of the participants, the persons involved in making the programme, and the equipment and facilities used in making the programme, and (b) is neither a subsidiary nor a holding company of a broadcaster: Broadcasting Authority (Amendment) Act 1993, s 5. The RTÉ Authority is required to keep a special account (termed the 'independent television programme account') into which specified amounts of moneys are to be made available by RTÉ for programmes to be commissioned from the independent sector (BA(A)A 1993, s 4). For amendments to the 1993 Act, see Broadcasting Act 2001, ss 33 and 35.

indicia. Signs; marks; criteria. In relation to whether a tenancy exists, the courts will look at the document relied upon as a whole and see if the *indicia* exist to constitute a tenancy or other relationship: *Gatien Motor Company v Continental Oil Co of Ireland Ltd* [1979] IR 406. See also *McLoughlin v Tuite* [1986] ILRM 304.

indictable offence. An offence which the accused is entitled as of right to a trial by jury. An accused charged with an indictable offence before the District Court must be sent forward for trial to the trial court where the prosecutor consents and where the accused has been served with the book of evidence, unless the case is being tried summarily, or the accused is unfit to plead: Criminal Procedure Act 1967, s 4A inserted by Criminal Justice Act 1999, s 9. At that stage, only the fact that proceedings were brought against a named person and any decision resulting from the proceedings may be broadcast or published (CPA 1967, s 4J as inserted).

The 1999 Act provides for the abolition of the previous practice of a *preliminary examination* (qv); such an examination was abolished in 2001: Criminal Justice Act 1999 (Part III) (Commencement Order) 2001, SI No 193 of 2001.

A judicial review by the trial court is permitted to determine whether there is a sufficient case to put the accused on trial; a *prima facie* case is enough (CPA 1967, s 4E as inserted; *The State (Sherry) v Wine* [1985] ILRM 196; *DPP v Killeen* [1998] 1 ILRM 1). An appeal lies to the Central Criminal Court in respect of a decision by the trial court that there is not a sufficient case to put the accused on trial (CPA 1967, s 4E(7) as inserted). The accused may request the broadcast or publication of information in relation to an application for a pre-trial dismissal (CPA 1967, s 4J(b) and *Irish Times v Murphy* [1998] ILRM 161, SC).

With the consent of the DPP, the District Court has power to deal with an indictable offence e g where there is a guilty plea in which event the maximum punishment is twelve months imprisonment and/or a fine. However, a District Court is empowered to impose consecutive sentences up to a maximum of two years' imprisonment: Criminal Justice Act 1984, s 12. Also, the District Court may try summarily a person charged with specified offences if the court is of the opinion that the offence is a minor one, the accused does not object and the DPP consents: Criminal Justice Act 1951, s 2(2) as amended by Criminal Justice (Miscellaneous Provisions) Act 1997, s 8. See also Criminal Law Act 1997, ss 7(6) and 7(7).

In a trial on indictment, a trial judge has no jurisdiction to direct a jury to find the accused not guilty, where the prosecution has not been allowed open its case or to adduce any evidence: *DPP v Judge Cyril Kelly* [1997] 1 ILRM 497, HC.

Provision has been made for the transfer of the trial of a person charged with an indictable offence from the Circuit Court before which the person is triable to the Dublin Circuit Court: Courts Act 1981, s 31; *The State (Boyle) v Nealon* [1987] ILRM 535. As regards the prosecution of an indictable offence by a private citizen, he can only go as far as securing a return for trial, after which the DPP, if he so chooses, must prosecute: *State (Ennis) v Farrell* [1966] IR 107. See also *Gilligan v DPP* [1987] HC; *The State (Daly) v Ruane* [1988] ILRM 117; *DPP v Doyle* [1994] 2 IR 286, SC; *DPP v Logan* [1994] 3 IR 254, SC; *B H v DPP* [2003] 2 IR 43, SC.

[Bibliography: Walsh D (3).] See AID AND ABET; COMMON INFORMER; GUILTY; INDICTMENT; MINOR OFFENCE; SUMMARY OFFENCE.

indictment. A written accusation of a crime made against one or more persons and preferred to a jury; formerly it was made by *The People at the suit of the Attorney General*: 1937 Constitution, art 30(3). An indictment is now brought in the name of *The People at the suit of the Director of Public Prosecutions*: Prosecution of Offences Act 1974. For the rules governing the form of an indictment, see Criminal Justice (Administration) Act 1924; Indictment Rules 1924. For prosecution of a company on indictment, see the Companies Act 1963, s 382.

Any change in an indictment, once it has been preferred, requires statutory authority; the only power to amend an indictment is contained in s 6(1) of the Criminal Justice (Administration) Act 1924. It has been held that this section confers no jurisdiction on the Circuit Court to consolidate, into one indictment, two independent indictments based on separate returns for trial: *Conlon v Kelly* [2001] 2 ILRM 198, SC; [2002] 1 IR 10.

The prosecution may include new charges in an indictment, either in substitution for, or in addition to, the charges on which the accused has been sent forward for trial: Criminal Procedure Act 1967, s 4M inserted by Criminal Justice Act 1999, s 9. The new charges must be founded on the documents served on the accused, and must be of a type which could lawfully have been joined on the same indictment e g founded on the same facts or are part of a series of offences of the same character e g see *People v Wallace* [1981] 2 Frewen 125. The additional charges must not be of such a nature as would be unfair to the accused: *Walsh v DPP* [1989] ILRM 325.

It has been held that the inclusion of different additional charges in an indictment at the behest of the DPP following the return by a district court judge of an accused for trial is not unconstitutional: *O'Shea v DPP* [1989] ILRM 309. The DPP is entitled to add counts based on the documents and exhibits considered by the district court judge: *O'Donnell v DPP* [1994] 2 ILRM 21, SC. A judge is entitled to add a new count to an indictment if satisfied that evidential material put before him justified him in so doing; there is no requirement that it be in substitution for an existing charge: *O'Brien v Patwell* [1994] 2 ILRM 465, SC. It is not necessary for counsel (qv) to sign an indictment (*Walsh* case). Where two procedures are available, one to prosecute summarily, and the other to prosecute by way of indictment, only one may proceed to trial: *Kelly v DPP* [1996] 2 IR 596, SC and [1997] 1 ILRM 69, SC. See also *Costello v DPP* [1984] IR 436; *O'Connell v DPP* [1994] 3 IR 554, SC.

Any number of persons may be charged on the one indictment with reference to the same theft: Criminal Justice (Theft and Fraud Offences) Act 2001, s 54(2). See *Consultation Paper on Prosecution Appeals in cases brought on Indictment* (LRC CP 19, 2002). [Bibliography: Walsh D (3).] See DEFECT; INDICTABLE OFFENCE; JOINDER OF UNRELATED CHARGES.

indirect discrimination. *Direct* discrimination occurs where on any *discriminatory ground* a person is treated less favourably than another person: Employment Equality Act 1998, s 6, amended by Equality Act 2004, s 4; Equal Status Act 2000, s 3. *Indirect* discrimination on *gender* grounds occurs where a provision (eg a requirement) is such that the proportion of persons who are disadvantaged by the provision is substantially higher in the case of persons of one sex than of the other and the provision cannot be justified by objective factors unrelated to sex (EEA 1998, s 22 amended by EA 2004, s 13). A similar provision applies in the case of other *discriminatory grounds* (eg marital status, family status, sexual orientation, religion, age, disability, race, or membership of the travelling community) where the provision cannot be justified as being reasonable in all the circumstances of the case (EEA 1998, s 31 amended by EA 2004, s 20).

Under the previous employment equality legislation (Employment Equality Act 1977, applying only to sex and marital status) it was held that to determine whether discrimination has occurred, the following questions need to be addressed: (a) what is the requirement with which the claimant is obliged to comply; (b) is the requirement such that either a higher proportion of males than females (or single females than married females) can comply with it; (c) if the answer is yes, is that fact an attribute of their sex or marital status; (d) is the requirement essential for such

employment: *Vavasour v Northside Centre for the Unemployed Ltd & FÁS* [1993] ELR 112, HC. See also *Civil and Public Service Union v FÁS* [1994] determination DEE 794, LC; *Conlon v University of Limerick* [1999] ELR 155, HC. See *Bolger* in (1993) 3 ISLR 1; *Cousins* in 11 ILT & SJ (1993) 147.

Under other equality legislation, indirect discrimination is defined as taking place where an apparently neutral provision puts a person (referred to in the discriminatory grounds listed in s 3(2) of Equal Status Act 2000) at a particular disadvantage compared with other persons, unless the provision is objectively justified by a legitimate aim and the means of achieving that aim are appropriate and necessary: ESA 2000, s 3(1)(c) amended by substitution by EA 2004, s 48. See Pensions Act 1990, s 68 as amended by substitution by Social Welfare (Miscellaneous Provisions) Act 2004, s 22(1). [Bibliography: Reid M.] See DISCRIMINATION.

indirect evidence. Hearsay or circumstantial evidence. See EVIDENCE.

individualisation. See INCOME TAX.

indivisible contract. See DIVISIBLE CONTRACT.

indoor event. Means: (a) a performance which takes place wholly or mainly in a building and comprises music, singing, dancing, displays of entertainment or any similar activity and in respect of which members of the public may or may not attend, or (b) an event which takes place wholly or mainly in a building and is prescribed by Ministerial regulation: Licensing of Indoor Events Act 2003, s 2(1). 'Building' means any building, structure or erection (whether permanent or temporary).

It is an offence to organise, promote or hold or otherwise be materially involved in the organisation of an indoor event without, or not in accordance with, a licence from the appropriate fire authority (LIEA 2003, s 5(11)). The purpose of the licensing system under the Act is to provide for the safe holding, particularly as regards public safety and crowd control, of indoor events in buildings which will already have been granted planning permission to use the building for that purpose. There is provision for an appeal to the District Court within four weeks against a decision of the fire authority (LIEA 2003, s 8). There is also provision to revoke a licence where the licensee has been convicted of an offence under the Act (LIEA 2003, s 14).

A statutory requirement to take reasonable care is placed on persons organising or attending an indoor event (LIEA 2003, s 10). There is a prohibition on civil proceedings against the Minister, local authorities, health boards or the Gardaí, for injury or loss alleged to have been caused by a failure to exercise any function under the Act (LIEA 2003, s 13). Also a fire authority is empowered to issue a *cessation notice* in respect of an event; failure to comply with such a notice is an offence (LIEA 2003, s 11). There are special provisions regarding the holding of an indoor event by a local authority (LIEA 2003, s 23).

An 'indoor event' does not include an event for which a licence is required under the Planning and Development Act 2000. See EVENT.

indorsement. See ENDORSEMENT.

indorsement of claim. An indorsement of the relief claimed and the grounds thereof expressed in general terms; in High Court proceedings it is called a *general indorsement of claim* on a plenary summons, and a *special indorsement of claim* on a summary or special summons: RSC Ord 4. For the rules governing the indorsement of claim on a *civil bill* in the Circuit Court, see Circuit Court Rules 2001 Ord 10. For amendment of indorsement of claim in *commercial proceedings* (qv), see RSC Ord 63A, r 6(1)(v) inserted by Rules of the Superior Courts (Commercial Proceedings) 2004, SI No 2 of 2004.

inducement. (1) Persuasion by promise or threat to a course of action. An improper inducement will render a confession (qv) inadmissible. See *The People (DPP) v Hoey* [1988] ILRM 666, SC. See ANTECEDENT NEGOTIATIONS; CORRUPT AGREEMENT WITH CREDITOR; FAIR AND REASONABLE TERMS; DURESS; UNDUE INFLUENCE.

(2) As regards inducement fees or break fees which are part of a frustrating action in respect of a proposed takeover, contingent upon an offer lapsing or not being made, see Takeover Rules 2001, Pt B, r 21.2.

(3) A solicitor should not actively encourage or offer inducements to any third party with a view to obtaining instructions from any person: *A Guide to Professional Conduct of Solicitors in Ireland* (2002) ch 6.2. See SOLICITOR AND ADVERTISING.

inducing breach of contract. The tort (qv) at common law whereby a person knowingly and without lawful justification induces another to break a subsisting contract with a third person whereby that third person suffers damage: *Lumley v Gye* [1853] 2 E B 216. See also *Cooper v Millea* [1938] IR 749; *Hynes v Conlon* [1939] Ir Jur Rep; *B & I Steampacket Co Ltd v Branigan* [1958] IR 128; *Flogas Ltd v Ergas Ltd* [1985] ILRM 221.

industrial accident. See ACCIDENT.

industrial action. Any action which affects, or is likely to affect, the terms or conditions, whether express or implied, of a contract and which is taken by any number or body of workers acting in combination or under a common understanding as a means of compelling their employer, or to aid other workers in compelling their employer, to accept or not to accept terms or conditions of or affecting employment: Industrial Relations Act 1990, s 8. See *Tuke v Coillte Teo* [1998] ELR 324, EAT. See LABOUR INJUNCTION; STRIKE.

industrial and provident society. A society for carrying on any industry, business or trade specified in or authorised by its rules, whether wholesale or retail and including dealings of any description with land and the business of banking: Industrial and Provident Societies Act 1893, s 4. Registration of such a society renders it a body corporate with perpetual succession and limited liability (IPSA 1893, s 21). Farmers' and other co-operative societies are often registered as industrial and provident societies; registration is with the Registrar of Friendly Societies. See also Industrial and Provident Societies (Amendment) Act 1978. A society may not accept deposits (IPS(A)A 1978, s 5(1)). As regards *special resolutions*, see IPSA 1893, s 51 as amended by Competition Act 2002, s 51.

The members of a society are virtually free to manage the affairs of their society as they see fit; the majority however may not abuse the power to alter the share capital; no shareholder has a legal right to any specific portion of the assets of a society; rules of a society which benefit members who trade with that society over those who prefer not to do so are reasonable and not in restraint of trade: *Kerry Co-Operative Creameries Ltd & O'Connell v An Bord Bainne Co-Operative Ltd* [1992] 10 ILT Dig 28, SC. The view has been expressed that a shareholding in a society is not intended primarily as an investment but merely as an 'entrance fee' (*Kerry Co-op* case).

New rules governing the qualification for appointment as auditors to industrial and provident societies are contained in the Companies Act 1990, ss 182 and 187. See *PMPS Ltd & Moore v Attorney General* [1983] IR 339; *PMPS Ltd v Moore (No 2)* [1989] 7 ILT Dig 123; *Re Irish Commercial Society Group* [1987] HC; *McMahon v Ireland* [1988] ILRM 610. See also RSC Ord 109.

industrial democracy. See WORKER PARTICIPATION.

industrial design. See DESIGN.

industrial development. Provision has been made for the development of industry and technology and for the stimulation and encouragement of investment in industrial undertakings from sources whether within or outside the State: Industrial Development Act 1993. This Act provides for the establishment of Forfás, which had the function of advising on the development and co-ordination of policy for Forbairt (development of indigenous industry), IDA (attraction of overseas firms and their development in Ireland) and An Bord Trachtála (development of exports).

In 1998, both Forbairt and An Bord Trachtála were dissolved and their functions, including certain elements of the Services to Business functions of FÁS, were taken over by the newly created Enterprise Ireland: Industrial Development (Enterprise Ireland) Act 1998. The Minister is required to prepare every three years a review of national industrial performance and of national industrial policy (IDA 1993, s 13). See also Industrial Development Acts 1986 and 1991; Science and Technology Act 1987 and Industrial Research and Standards Act 1961 as amended. See also Údarás na Gaeltachta Acts 1979 to 1999. See also Industrial Development (Science Foundation Ireland) Act 2003, ss 28–37. For UNIDO (*United Nations Industrial Development Organisation*) see website: *www.unido.org*. See FÁS; FOR-FÁS; INDUSTRY; SERVICE INDUSTRY.

industrial dispute. See TRADE DISPUTE.

industrial plant. See AIR POLLUTION; VALUATION, INDUSTRIAL PLANT.

industrial property. See INTELLECTUAL PROPERTY; PARIS CONVENTION.

industrial relations inquiry. In a particular case, where the applicant sought a declaration that a report (into an industrial relations dispute prepared by persons appointed by the Minister pursuant to the Industrial Relations Act 1990, s 38(2)) was *ultra vires* and should be quashed, the court held that the matter was not justiciable, because there was no decision susceptible to being quashed and, even if there was, there was no legal right of the applicant which could be affected by a fact-finding report: *Ryanair Ltd v Flynn* [2001] 1 ILRM 283, HC and [2000] 3 IR 240, HC.

industrial relations law. The branch of law dealing with, *inter alia*, industrial action (strikes, lockouts, picketing, 'blacking'), collective bargaining, and trade unions (qqv). [Bibliography: Forde (6); Kerr.]

industrial relations officer. An officer of the Labour Relations Commission (qv) whose main function under the Industrial Relations Act 1990 is to conciliate in industrial disputes (IRA 1990, s 33).

industrial school. A school for the industrial training of children, in which children were lodged, clothed and fed, as well as taught: Childrens Act 1908, s 44 (now repealed); *McM v Manager of Trinity House* [1995] 2 ILRM 546, HC. See now CHILDREN DETENTION SCHOOL. See also CHILDRENS' RESIDENTIAL CENTRE; REFORMATORY.

industrial waste. See WASTE; WASTE MANAGEMENT PLAN.

industry. The EC and the member states are required to ensure that the conditions necessary for the competitiveness of the Community's industry exist: EC Treaty, art 157 of the consolidated (2002) version. Their action is required to be aimed at: (a) speeding up the adjustment of industry to structural change; (b) encouraging an environment favourable to initiative and to the development of undertakings throughout the community, particularly small and medium-sized undertakings; (c) encouraging an environment favourable to co-operation between undertakings; (d) fostering better exploitation of the industrial potential of policies of innovation, research and technological development. See INDUSTRIAL DEVELOPMENT; SERVICE INDUSTRY.

inequality of position. The UK doctrine which attempts to fuse into one concept, five areas of law where the normal rules of freedom to contract are waived on the grounds of inequality of the position of the parties viz salvage, duress of goods, coercion, undue influence, and unconscionable bargain (qqv): *Lloyds Bank v Bundy* [1975]

QB 326; *National Westminster Bank v Morgan* [1985] AC 686. For discussion on whether Irish courts might approve such a doctrine, see Doyle in 8 ILT & SJ (1990) 282. See also Vail in 9 ILT & SJ (1991) 258. See UNFAIR TERMS.

inertia selling provision. A provision in an agreement or in any proposal or application form, which requires the consumer to indicate positively that he does not wish to obtain credit, purchase or hire goods or avail of any service: Consumer Credit Act 1995, s 138. Such a provision is prohibited.

inevitable accident. An unforeseen and unlooked for event which could not be avoided by the exercise of reasonable care and skill. It is a good defence in negligence and in actions for trespass to chattels and to persons. See *Stanley v Powell* [1891] QB 86. An *Act of God* (qv) is a special form of inevitable accident which can provide a good defence in torts of strict liability (qv).

infant. A minor (qv). See Age of Majority Act 1985, s 3.

infant and crime. See DOLI INCAPAX.

infant formulae. Means foodstuffs intended for particular nutritional use by infants during the first four to six months of life and satisfying by themselves the nutritional requirements of this category of persons: EC (Infant Formulae and Follow-on Formulae) Regulations 2004, SI No 242 of 2004. 'Follow-on formulae' means foodstuffs intended for particular nutritional use by infants aged over four months and constituting the principal liquid element in a progressively diversified diet of this category of person. 'Infants' means children under the age of twelve months. These regulations give effect to EC Directives on compositional, labelling, marketing and informational requirements for such foodstuffs intended for infants in good health.

infanticide. The killing of a newly born child. It is a statutory offence with the same punishment as for manslaughter. It arises where a woman by wilful act or omission causes the death of her child under the age of twelve months, at a time when the balance of her mind was disturbed by reason of her not having fully recovered from the effect of giving birth to the child, and where the circumstances are such but for this Act it would be murder: Infanticide Act 1949. See 'A Woman's Crime' by Alexis Guilbride (1995) *Irish Times*, 30/31 October. See YEAR AND A DAY RULE.

infectious diseases. Diseases which the Minister by regulation specifies to be infectious diseases: Health Act 1947, s 29. There is a general duty on persons with an infectious disease to take precautions against infecting others (HA 1947, s 30). See also Health Act 1953, ss 34–37. A medical practitioner is required to send written notification to the medical officer of health as soon as he becomes aware or suspects that a person on whom he is in professional attendance is suffering from or is the carrier of an infectious disease: SI No 390 of 1981.

The notifiable infectious diseases specified in the 1981 regulations are: Acute anterior poliomyelitis, Acute encephalitis, Acute viral meningitis, Anthrax, Bacillary dysentery, Bacterial meningitis (including meningococcal septicaemia), Brucellosis, Cholera, Diphtheria, Food poisoning (bacterial other than salmonella), Gastro enteritis (when contracted by children under two years of age), Infectious mononucleosis, Influenzal pneumonia, Legionnaires Disease, Leptospirosis, Malaria, Measles, Ornithosis, Plague, Rabies, Rubella, Salmonellosis (other than typhoid or paratyphoid), Smallpox, Tetanus, Tuberculosis, Typhoid and Paratyphoid, Typhus, Venereal diseases ie gonococcal infections: syphilis, other (including non-specific urethritis, chancroid, granuloma inguinale, and lympho-granuloma venereum), Viral haemorrhagic diseases (including lassa fever and marburg disease), Viral hepatitis: Type A, Type B, Type unspecified, Whooping cough, Yellow fever.

The 1981 regulations have been amended: (a) to include a number of additional non-specific sexually transmissible diseases: SI No 268 of 1985; (b) to designate mumps as an infectious disease: SI No 288 of 1988; (c) to designate CJD and nvCJD as infectious diseases; (d) to designate Severe Acute Respiratory Syndrome (SARS) as an infectious disease: SI No 115 of 2003 and SI No 180 of 2003; (e) to enable health boards to furnish to the Director of the National Disease Surveillance Centre, rather than to the Minister, weekly returns of cases of infectious diseases notified to them: SI No 151 of 2000; (f) to update the list of infectious diseases and their causative pathogens, to require the clinical directors of diagnostic laboratories to report infectious diseases, to require the reporting of unusual clusters or changing pattern of illness, and to make the National Disease Surveillance Centre responsible for the maintenance, updating and circulation of case definitions in relation to infectious diseases: SI No 707 of 2003. In relation to aircraft and shipping, see SIs No 136 of 1948; No 170 of 1948.

The infectious diseases for which maintenance allowances from the State are payable are: acute anterior poliomyelitis, diphtheria, dysentery, salmonellosis, tuberculosis, typhoid and paratyphoid fevers, typhus and viral haemorrhagic diseases (including lassa fever and marburg disease): Infectious Diseases (Maintenance) Regulations 1988, SI No 151 of 1988. Provision has been made to increase the maximum rates of maintenance allowances as from 1 January 2004: Infectious Diseases (Maintenance Allowances) Regulations 2003, SI No 734 of 2003. See BURIAL GROUNDS; DETENTION OF PATIENT; NON-NATIONAL, EXCLUSION ON MEDICAL GROUNDS; SARS.

infectious diseases and doctors. 'Acceptance of the risk of treating patients with communicable diseases is a time-honoured tradition of the medical profession. Failure to do so may be unethical': Medical Council, *A Guide to Ethical Conduct and Behaviour* (6th edn, 2004) para 2.4. 'Certain communicable diseases are notifiable by statute. Such notifications should preferably be made with the informed consent of the patient. In cases where informed consent is not provided, reporting should be to the relevant authority but should observe the patient's confidentiality in all other respects. Where others may be at serious risk if not aware that a patient has a communicable infection, a doctor should do his/her best to obtain permission from the patient to tell them, so that appropriate safeguards can be put in place. If the patient refuses to consent to disclosure, those who might be at risk of infection should be informed of the risk to themselves (para 16.8).

It is unethical for doctors who believe that they might be infected with a serious communicable disease not to seek appropriate medical advice (para 5.3).

inference. A conclusion that a court or a jury may properly draw arising from particular evidence eg appropriate inferences may be drawn from the failure or refusal of an arrested person to account to a garda for his presence in a particular place at or about the time an offence was committed, or to account for particular objects or marks: Criminal Justice Act 1984, ss 18–19 as amended by Criminal Justice Act 1999, s 16. These provisions are not unconstitutional as: (a) an inference could not form the basis for a conviction in the absence of other evidence and (b) only inferences as appear proper to the court could be drawn: *Rock v Ireland* [1998] 2 ILRM 35, SC.

It has been held that where the circumstances of an accident are to be established by inference as well as from direct but limited evidence, the plaintiff must establish facts from which negligence may reasonably be inferred; it is not sufficient that the plaintiff establish merely that negligence could be inferred, but that it ought to be inferred: *Clancy v Dublin Corporation* [1989] 7 ILT Dig 83. See also *Clancy v Commissioner for Public Works* [1991] ILRM 567, SC.

It has been held that in criminal proceedings where different inferences can be drawn from certain facts, the court is obliged to draw the inference most favourable to the accused: *The People (DPP) v Clare O'Hare* [1988] SC. If several inferences were possible, one of which was innocent, then the innocent inference is the one to be drawn and the jury must be so directed: *The People (DPP) v BK* [2000] 2 IR 199, CCA.

An appellate court has a discretion to reverse inferences of fact drawn by the trial judge from circumstantial evidence (qv): *Best v Wellcome Foundation Ltd* [1992] ILRM 609, SC. See *The People (DPP) v O'Neill* [1997] 1 IR 365, CCA. See BODILY SAMPLE; DECEIT; FACT; OPINION; SECONDARY FACTS.

inferior courts. Courts with a jurisdiction which is limited geographically and as to the value of the matter in dispute, and which are subject to the supervision of the superior courts eg the District Court (qv) and the Circuit Court (qv).

inflation. There is no constitutional right that social welfare allowances keep pace with inflation: *Mhic Mhathuna v Ireland* [1990] 8 ILT Dig 59. See CURRENT COST ACCOUNTING CONVENTION; INTEREST AND SOCIAL WELFARE.

influence, improper. There is a prohibition on communications with a director, employee, or person connected with the Environmental Protection Agency for the purpose of influencing improperly his consideration of any matter which falls to be considered or decided by the Agency: Environmental Protection Agency Act 1992, s 40. There is a similar prohibition as regards the National Roads Authority: Roads Act 1993, s 39. There is also a prohibition on certain communications to the DPP or Attorney-General or to the gardaí for the purpose of influencing the making of a decision in relation to: (a) the initiation or withdrawal of criminal proceedings, or (b) an application for review of a sentence: Prosecution of Offences Act 1974, s 6; Criminal Justice Act 1993, s 2(4). See also National Development Finance Agency Act 2002, s 19. See BORD PLEANÁLA, AN.

influence, undue. See UNDUE INFLUENCE.

Info Points Europe. Centres established to provide information on a wide range of European affairs to the general public. One is located in Mullingar and it is planned to open others. See EURO INFO CENTRES; EUROPEAN PUBLIC INFORMATION CENTRE.

informal. Without formality. Certain statutes require proceedings to be informal eg proceedings in the High Court regarding the care of children are required to be as informal as is practicable, consistent with the administration of justice: Child Care Act 1991, s 29(4). See also FAMILY COURT.

information. A statement concerning an offence for which a summons or warrant is required. It has been held that the failure to provide or cause to be provided to a person whose extradition (qv) is sought, copies of the sworn *informations* grounding a warrant for his extradition, did not amount to a denial of fair procedures: *Ellis v O'Dea & Shiels* [1990] ILRM 87, SC.

A garda is required to disclose to his superior officers the identity of an informant on being so requested: *Church v Commissioner of an Garda* [1997] 3 IR 231, HC. See COMMON INFORMER; COMPLAINT; INFORMER'S PRIVILEGE.

Information Commissioner. The independent office holder, appointed by the President on the advice of the government, who reviews, on written request, decisions made by public bodies denying a person access to public records: Freedom of Information Act 1997, ss 33–34 as amended by Freedom of Information (Amendment) Act 2003, ss 25–26. The Commissioner has wide powers of access to information in relation to her reviews. She is required to keep the operation of the Act under review and to publish an annual report (FIA 1997, ss 36 and 40). She has extensive discretion as to the procedures to be adopted in conducting a review or an investigation under the Act: *Deely v Information Commissioner* [2001] 3 IR 439, HC. See also FIA 1997, Sch 2.

An appeal lies to the High Court on a point of law against a decision of the Commissioner; on a subsequent appeal to the Supreme Court, it is empowered to order that the costs of a person be paid by a public body where the appeal involved a point of law of exceptional importance (FIA 1997, s 42 as amended by FI(A)A 2003, s 27). The precedents developed in *judicial review* apply to an appeal under s 42; the courts will only interfere with a decision of the Commissioner if the decision flies in the face of reason, or common sense or is so irrational or unreasonable that no reasonable Commissioner could have reached that decision: *Killilea v Information Commissioner* [2003] 2 IR 402, HC.

The office of the *Ombudsman* (qv) and Information Commission are combined. See email: *foi@ombudsman.irlgov.ie* and website: *www.oic.ie*. For decisions of the Information Commissioner, see website: *www.bailii.org*. See INFORMATION, ACCESS TO.

information, access to. A person has a right of access to records held by a public body; the right exists regardless of any interest or need on the part of the requester to access the record concerned: Freedom of Information Act 1997, s 6 as amended by Freedom of Information (Amendment) Act 2003, s 4.

The right is not absolute as: (a) not all public bodies are covered by the legislation; (b) only records created after the coming into operation of the Act are covered (21 April 1998) except in respect of: (i) *personal information* (qv) of the requester where prior records are included or (ii) where the prior records are necessary to understand the current records; (c) certain records are *excluded* eg records of courts or tribunals, and records revealing the source of information relating to criminal law enforcement; (d) certain records are *exempted* as balancing other rights as against the right to information.

Access to records created prior to 21 April 1998 is permitted where it is shown that access is necessary or expedient to understand records created after that date (FIA 1997, s 6(5)(a) as amended by FI(A)A 2003, s 4). It has been held that the test is whether these prior records are necessary to understand the substance or gist of the documents created after the date: *Salve Marine Ltd v Commission for Information* (2000) Irish Times, 20 July.

The *twelve* grounds for *exemption* under (d) above are: meetings of the government; deliberations of public bodies; functions and negotiations of public bodies; parliamentary, court and certain other matters; law enforcement and public safety; security, defence and international relations; information obtained in confidence; commercially sensitive information; personal information regarding a person other than the requester; research and natural resources; financial and economic interests of the State and public bodies; and enactments relating to non-disclosure of records (FIA 1997, ss 19–32 as amended by FI(A)A 2003, ss 14–24). Also excluded are the drafts of a strategy statement of a government department or a Ministerial direction in relation thereto: Public Service Management (No 2) Act 1997, s 5(3).

A refusal to grant access to records is subject to appeal by way of an internal review within the public body and subsequently, if still refused, a review by the Information Commissioner (FIA 1997, ss 14 and 34 as amended by FI(A)A 2003, ss 9 and 26 respectively).

A refusal is required if the record concerned is such that its disclosure would constitute a *contempt of court* (FIA 1997, s 22(1)(b) as now amended by FI(A)A 2003, s 17). The purpose of this provision is to prevent the 1997 Act from interfering with the administration of justice eg obtaining documents via the 1997 Act, the disclosure of which had been prohibited by the court or made subject to certain conditions; the word 'disclosure' in FIA 1997 had to be interpreted in the widest sense: *E H v Information Commissioner* [2001] 2 IR 463, HC. There is no jurisdiction under the 1997 Act to impose conditions on the type or extent of disclosure or the use of the documents after disclosure (*E H* case). [Bibliography: McDonagh.] See ABORTION; CABINET CONFIDENTIALITY; DISABLED PERSON AND INFORMA-

TION; ENVIRONMENTAL INFORMATION, ACCESS TO; INFORMATION COMMISSIONER; INDEPENDENT CONTRACTOR; PERSONAL INFORMATION; NATIONAL ARCHIVES; PUBLIC BODY.

information, disclosure of. Various statutes and rules of court impose a requirement to disclose information eg lodgment by a debtor of a statement setting forth his assets and liabilities on foot of an order therefor.

A county manager is required, when requested, to afford to the council of which he is manager or to the chairman of the council, all such *information* which is in his possession or procurement, if it concerns any business or transaction of the council: County Management Act 1940, s 27. The use of the word 'information' in s 27 without any express limitation, gives it a very wide and general meaning; it is not confined to the written word but embraces any knowledge, however gained or held: *Cullen v Wicklow County Manager* [1997] 1 ILRM 41, HC and [1996] 3 IR 474, HC. The 1940 Act has been repealed; however, the s 27 provision has been re-enacted with minor amendments as s 136 of the Local Government Act 2001. See DISCOVERY; EXAMINATION RE COMPANY; EXAMINATION OF DEBTOR; SILENCE, RIGHT TO.

information, withholding. See WITHHOLDING INFORMATION.

information notice, data. The notice in writing, served on a person, by which the Data Protection Commissioner (qv) may require that person to furnish to him such information in relation to matters specified in the notice as is necessary or expedient for the performance by the Commissioner of his functions: Data Protection Act 1988, s 12. An appeal against the requirements in the notice lies to the Circuit Court. See DATA PROTECTION.

Information Society Commission. An independent advisory body to government, reporting directly to the Taoiseach, with a key role in shaping the evolving public policy framework for the Information Society in Ireland. 'Information Society' is the term used to capture the increasing contemporary influence of information and communication technologies (ICTs). The Commission has representatives from the business community, the social partners and from government itself.

The Commission contributes to the formulation of Government policy by: (a) highlighting the challenges and opportunities presented by Information Society developments; (b) monitoring Ireland's performance in its evolution as an Information Society, both nationally and internationally; (c) identifying areas of co-operation with other jurisdictions, including establishment of links with the Northern Ireland Information Age Initiative; (d) establishing advisory groups, as required, to provide expert advice on specific areas of public policy development. See website: *www.isc.ie*. See EGOVERNMENT; SCIENCE FOUNDATION IRELAND.

information society services. Services provided 'online'. Regulations have been made which lay down a framework for the supply of Information Society (IS) services between one member state of the European Economic Area (the EU, Iceland, Liechtenstein and Norway) and another: EC (Directive 2000/31/EC) Regulations 2003, SI No 68 of 2003, as amended by SI No 490 of 2004. These regulations transpose into Irish law the essential requirements of the Directive on certain legal aspects of IS services, in particular electronic commerce, in the internal market.

The framework lays down that IS services provided by an Irish service provider to a person in another member state must comply with the applicable Irish law for that service. The regulations empower each member State to take measures against incoming IS services, including to prevent crimes relating to public policy or to protect consumers, including investors. Persons sending unsolicited commercial emails are required to ensure that they are clearly identifiable on receipt. Also members of the regulated professions are entitled to engage in IS services, provided they respect the rules of their profession. Failure to comply with certain provisions of the regulations constitute an offence, prosecutable by the Director of Consumer Affairs or the Data Protection Commissioner in respect of unsolicited commercial communications, reg 9. See ELECTRONIC COMMERCE.

information technology law. The law dealing with the technology of the production, storage, and communication of information using computers and microelectronics. [Bibliography: Kelleher & Murray; Norfolk & Bannister.] See COMPUTER.

informer. See COMMON INFORMER.

informer's privilege. The privilege preventing disclosure which protects the anonymity of police informers. The privilege is essential for the prevention and detection of crime; however it is subject to the *innocence at stake* exception, where the disclosure of the identity of the informant is necessary or right to show the innocence of the accused: *Ward v Special Criminal Court* [1998] 2 ILRM 493, SC and [1999] 1 IR 60, SC. See INFORMATION.

infortunium, per. [Misadventure (qv).]

infra. [Below.]

infringement. Interference with, or the violation of, the right of another. The remedy is an injunction to restrain future infringements, and an action for the recovery of the damage caused or profits made by the past infringements. See INFRINGEMENT OF COPYRIGHT; INFRINGEMENT OF PATENTS; INFRINGEMENT OF TRADE MARK.

infringement of copyright. The copyright in a *work* is infringed by a person who, without the licence of the copyright holder, undertakes or authorises another to undertake, any of the *acts restricted by copyright* ie to copy a work, to make the work available to the public, or to make an *adaptation* of the work: Copyright and Related Rights Act 2000, s 37. This includes copying an adaptation or making available an adaptation.

A *secondary infringement* of copyright can occur in relation to infringing copies (qv).

Infringement of copyright is actionable by the copyright owner, and all relief by way of damages, injunction, account of profits or otherwise, is available to the plaintiff as is available in respect of the infringement of any other *property right* (CRRA 2000, s 127). In awarding damages, no damages will be awarded where it is shown that the defendant did not know, and had no reason to believe, that copyright subsisted in the work, but the plaintiff will be entitled to an account of profits in respect of the infringement (CRRA 2000, s 128(2)). In other cases, the court may award damages as it considers just; it may in addition, or as an alternative to compensating the plaintiff for financial loss, award aggravated or exemplary damages or both (CRRA 2000, s 128 (1) and (3)).

However, no order will be made which would prevent a building from being completed or require a building to be demolished (CRRA 2000, s 129). A court may also award damages for *conversion* in respect of infringing copies (CRRA 2000, s 134).

In infringement proceedings, copyright is presumed to exist in a work until the contrary is proved, and the plaintiff is presumed to be the owner, or as the case may be, the exclusive licensee, until the contrary is proved (CRRA 2000, s 139). Also infringement of copyright in respect of a video recording can lead to forfeiture of a licence to sell or hire such recordings or to disqualification: Video Recordings Act 1989, s 24. See RSC Ord 94, r 3. See *DPP v Irwin* [1985] HC; *House of Spring Gardens v Point Blank* [1985] ILRM 107, SC; *Private Research Ltd v Brosnan* [1995] 1 IR 534, HC. See COPYRIGHT; COPYRIGHT OFFENCES; DOMESTIC AND PRIVATE USE; FAIR DEALING; INFRINGING COPY; LICENCES OF RIGHT, COPYRIGHT; PROHIBITED GOODS.

infringement of EC law. The right to recover damages from a member state for the breach of an obligation imposed on it by community law has been clearly recognised by the European Court of Justice: *Emerald Meats Ltd v Minister for Agriculture (No 2)* [1997] 1 IR 1, SC. It is a principle of community law that member states are obliged to make good, any loss and damage caused to individuals by breaches of community law for which they can be held responsible: *Tate v Minister for Social Welfare* [1995] 1 ILRM 507, HC.

The European Court of Justice has held that member states are obliged to make good damage caused to individuals by infringements of EC law attributable to national courts adjudicating at last instance: Case C-224/01 *Gerhard Kobler v Republic of Austria* [2003] ECJ. There are three conditions necessary to make the State liable for infringements of EC law attributable to it: (a) the rule of law must be intended to confer rights on individuals, (b) the breach must be sufficiently serious, and (c) there must be a direct causal link between the breach of the obligation incumbent on the State and the loss or damage sustained. See 'Suing the State for breaches of Community law by the Supreme Court' by Anthony Lowry BL in *Bar Review* (June 2004) 107. See COMMUNITY LAW; DIRECTIVE, EC; REGULATION, EC.

infringement of patent. The violation of the rights of the proprietor of a patent (qv) of invention; he can enforce his rights by civil proceedings: Patents Act 1992, ss 40–41, 47–56. The proprietor may seek: (a) an injunction to restrain further infringement; (b) delivery up or destruction of infringing products; (c) damages or an account of the profits derived by the defendant; (d) a declaration that the patent is valid and has been infringed (PA 1992, s 47). As regards a patented process for obtaining a new product, there is a presumption that where the same product is produced, it has been produced by the patented process and the onus of proof of non-infringement passes to the defendant (PA 1992, s 46).

Damages will not be awarded against a defendant who proves that he was not aware that the patent existed, and had no reasonable grounds for supposing it existed; the words *patent* or *patented* on a product without the number of the patent is ineffective to make the defendant aware that a patent had been obtained for the product (PA 1992, s 49(1)). See *Lancer Bros v Henley Forklift Co and H M Sideloaders* [1974] FSR 14.

A person threatened with an action of infringement may institute proceedings himself for a *declaration* that the threats were unjustifiable and for an injunction and damages, if he has suffered any (PA 1992, s 53). A general warning not directed to any person in particular is not actionable: *Speedcranes v Thompson* [1978] RPC 221. The validity of a patent may be raised by way of defence in proceedings for infringement (PA 1992, s 61).

Infringement proceedings are taken in the High Court in respect of *normal* patents (PA 1992, s 47) and in the Circuit Court in respect of *short-term* patents; there are also special provisions governing infringement proceedings in respect of short-term patents (PA 1992, s 66). An injunction to prevent the marketing of goods, alleged to be an infringement of a patent, will not be granted where the commercial loss suffered by the plaintiff can be compensated by the award of damages following trial of the action: *Smithkline Beecham plc v Genthorn BV and Synthon BV* [2003] FL 7231, HC. See RSC Ord 94, rr 4–14. See DECLARATORY JUDGMENT; PATENT RIGHTS; SECRET PRIOR USE; SHORT-TERM PATENT.

infringement of trade mark. A person infringes a *registered* trade mark if the person *uses* in the *course of trade* a sign which is identical with the trade mark in relation to goods or services which are *identical* with those for which it is registered: Trade Marks Act 1996, s 14(1). Also, use of a sign which is *similar* to the registered trade mark and there is a likelihood of confusion, including the likelihood of association of the sign with the trade mark, may amount to infringement. *Use of a sign* includes affixing it to goods or packaging, offering for sale under the sign, or using on business papers or in advertising (TMA 1996, s 14(4)).

There is a similarity between a trade mark and a sign when each looked on as a whole and in relation to each other, demonstrate such auditive, visual or conceptual resemblance, that associations between sign and trade mark are evoked merely on the basis of this resemblance: *Smithkline v Antigen Pharmaceuticals* [1999] 2 ILRM 190, HC. The European Court of Justice has held that the essential function of a trade mark is to guarantee to consumers the real origin of goods or services by enabling them to distinguish them from those of different origin: Case C-206/01 *Arsenal Football Club v Matthew Reed* [2002] ECJ. Arsenal were entitled to prevent an infringement of their trade mark by identical goods; it was immaterial that these goods were perceived by the public as a badge of support or loyalty to the Club. The ECJ also held that it is sufficient if the relevant section of the public establishes a link between the sign and a mark with a reputation even if it does not confuse them: Case C-408/01 *Addidas-Salomon AG v Finesseworld Trading Ltd* [2003] ECJ.

An infringement is actionable by the proprietor of the trade mark or by an exclusive licensee (TMA 1996, ss 18 and 35(2)). Relief is the same as available for the infringement of any other property right eg damages, injunction, accounts, erasure of offending sign, order for delivery up or disposal of goods.

For *course of trade*, see *Gallagher (Dublin) Ltd v Health Education Bureau* [1982] ILRM 240; *Bank of Ireland v Controller of Trade Marks* [1987] HC.

It is usual in an action for infringement of a registered trade mark, to combine in one set of pleadings (qv), the common law remedy of *passing off* (qv) as well, for example see *United Biscuits Ltd v Irish Biscuits Ltd* [1971] IR 16.

A party threatened with infringement proceedings may seek a declaration that the threats are unjustifiable (TMA 1996, s 24). However once the threat burgeons into an action against the party threatened, the jurisdiction conferred by s 24 is spent: *Symonds Cider v Showerings (Ireland) Ltd* [1997] 1 ILRM 481, HC. See *IBP Industrie Buitoni Perugina Spa v Dowdall O'Mahony Co Ltd* [1977] HC; *Hennessy Co v Keating* [1908] 1 IR 43. See also RSC Ord 94, rr 4–14 and rr 46–53. See COMPARATIVE ADVERTISING; COURSE OF TRADE; PASSING OFF; TRADE MARK.

infringing articles. In relation to a registered *trade mark*, means articles: (a) which are specifically designed for making copies of a *sign* identical or similar to that mark, and (b) which are in the possession, control or custody of a person who knows that they are to be used or have been used to produce *infringing goods* or *infringing material*: Trade Marks Act 1996, s 21(5). There are provisions for the delivery up of *infringing articles* and for their disposal (TMA 1996, ss 20, 22 and 23 as amended by Copyright and Related Rights Act 2000, s 146).

In relation to a registered *design*, an *infringing article* is an article which is specifically designed or adapted for applying to products, and a person makes, sells or rents, or offers or exposes for sale or rent, or imports such an article: Industrial Designs Act 2001, s 54(3). It also includes such an article which a person has in his possession, custody or control, knowing or having reason to believe, that it has been or is to be used to make *infringing products*. See DESIGN RIGHT, INFRINGEMENT OF; INFRINGING PRODUCT; INFRINGEMENT OF TRADE MARK.

infringing copy. In relation to copyright, a copy is an *infringing copy*: (a) where the making of it constitutes an infringement of the copyright in the work concerned, or (b) where it has been or is to be imported into the State, and its making in the State would have constituted an infringement of the copyright in the work concerned, or the breach of an exclusive licence agreement relating to the work: Copyright and Related Rights Act 2000, s 44(2).

Where a copy is made by a librarian or archivist, which would otherwise be an infringing copy, and is subsequently sold or otherwise made available to the public, it is to be treated as an *infringing copy* (CRRA 2000, s 70).

A *secondary infringement* of copyright may occur in dealing with an infringing copy, providing means for making infringing copies, permitting use of premises for infringing performances, and permitting use of apparatus for infringing performances (CRRA 2000, ss 45–48). A court order may be obtained requiring delivery up to the copyright owner of infringing copies (CRRA 2000, s 131) or for the seizure of infringing copies, articles or protection-defeating devices (CRRA 2000, s 132). A copyright owner also has a right to seize infringing copies, articles or devices where it would be impracticable to apply to the court (CRRA 2000, s 133). For further provisions on delivery up and disposal of infringing copies, see CRRA 2000, s 144–145. See *Roche v District Justice Martin* [1993] ILRM 651, HC. See INFRINGEMENT OF COPYRIGHT; COPYRIGHT OFFENCES; PROHIBITED GOODS.

infringing goods. Goods, in relation to a registered trade mark, where their packaging bears a sign identical or similar to that of that mark and either: (a) the application of the sign was an infringement of the mark, or (b) the sign has otherwise been used so as to infringe the mark: Trade Marks Act 1996, s 21(2). There are provisions for the delivery up of *infringing goods* and for their disposal (TMA 1996, ss 20, 22 and 23 as amended by Copyright and Related Rights Act 2000, s 146). See INFRINGEMENT OF TRADE MARK.

infringing material. Material, in relation to a registered trade mark, which bears a *sign* identical or similar to that mark and either: (a) it is used in such a way as to infringe the mark (e g for labelling or packaging goods), or (b) it is intended to be so used: Trade Marks Act 1996, s 21(4). There are provisions for the delivery up of *infringing material* and for its disposal (TMA 1996, ss 20, 22 and 23 as amended by Copyright and Related Rights Act 2000, s 146). See INFRINGEMENT OF TRADE MARK.

infringing product. In relation to a registered design, an *infringing product* is a product which infringes the *design right* in the design by the use of the product or by the application of the design in the product: Industrial Designs Act 2001, s 54(1). See DESIGN RIGHT, INFRINGEMENT OF; INFRINGING ARTICLE.

ingross. See ENGROSS.

inhabitant. In relation to liquor licensing law, means an occupier; in relation to local government law, means a rate payer or occupier: *Re Whitesheet Inn Ltd* [2003] 2 ILRM 177, HC and 2 IR 156. In order to qualify as an objector to an application under the Licensing (Ireland) Act 1833, Intoxicating Liquor Act 1960, and Intoxicating Liquor Act 2000, the person must be an inhabitant of the civil parish. See INTOXICATING LIQUOR.

inheritance. An estate in land which descended from a man to his heirs.

For capital acquisitions tax purposes, a person is deemed to have taken an *inheritance*, when the person becomes beneficially entitled in possession on a death to any benefit otherwise than for full consideration in money or money's worth paid by such person: Capital Acquisitions Tax Consolidation Act 2003, s 10. See BUSINESS RELIEF; CAPITAL ACQUISITIONS TAX.

inheritance tax. A capital acquisitions tax levied and paid upon the taxable value of every taxable inheritance taken by a successor where the date of inheritance is on or after 1 April 1975; it replaced estate duty: Capital Acquisitions Tax Act 1976, as amended and as now consolidated by the Capital Acquisitions Tax Consolidation Act 2003. [Bibliography: Condon J & Muddiman J.] See CAPITAL ACQUISITIONS TAX; PROBATE TAX; SELF-ASSESSMENT.

inhibition. An entry in the register of the Land Registry in respect of registered land in the form of a restriction on registration; the restriction will prevent all registrations except those made in compliance with the inhibition. It imposes on a subsequent applicant for registration the onus of ensuring that the registration he applies for complies with the inhibition. Inhibitions are used to protect interests which are not permitted to be registered as *burdens* (qv). See Registration of Title Act 1964, ss 96–98.

injunction. An order of the court directing a party to an action to do, or to refrain from doing, a particular thing. An injunction is enforced by committal for contempt of court in respect of any breach. An injunction is either: (a) *prohibitory* (restrictive/preventative) – forbidding continuance of a wrongful act, or (b) *mandatory* (compulsive) – directing direct performance of a positive act: *Bula Ltd v Tara Mines* [1988] ILRM 157; e g payment of wages: *Doyle & Ors v An Post* [1992 HC] 10 ILT & SJ 150.

As regards time, an injunction is either:

(a) *perpetual* – a permanent injunction after hearing of the action;

(b) *interim* – restraining the defendant until some specified time; or

(c) *interlocutory* – a temporary injunction pending trial of the action, only granted where the balance of convenience lies in so granting it and where the recoverable damages would be an inadequate remedy: *Campus Oil Ltd v Minister for Industry & Energy (No 2)* [1983] IR 88; *Westman Holdings Ltd v McCormack & Ors* [1991] ILRM 833, SC. Difficulty in assessment of damages is not a ground for characterising the awarding of damages as an inadequate remedy: *Curust v Loewe GmbH* [1993] ILRM 723, SC and [1994] 1 IR 450, SC. See *Premier Dairies Ltd v Doyle* [1996] 1 ILRM 363, SC and 1 IR 37; *Study Group International v Miller t/a High Schools International* [2002] FL 7346, HC. See INTERLOCUTORY INJUNCTION.

A *Mareva injunction* (qv) is a particular type of interim injunction granted on an *ex parte* application. A *quia timet* (qv) injunction is one to prevent or restrain some act, merely feared or threatened.

The courts are slow to grant mandatory relief on an interlocutory application but will do so in a suitable case: *Barrington v Bank of Ireland* [1993] ITLR (19 April), HC; *Charlton v H H The Aga Khan Studs* [1999] ELR 136, HC; *Martin v Nationwide Building Society* [1999] ELR 241, HC; *Donohue v Bus Éireann* [1999] ELR 306, HC.

An injunction may be granted to enforce a negative stipulation in a contract, even if it is only inferred from the contract: *Metropolitan Electric Supply Co v Ginder* [1901] 2 Ch 799. In a contract for personal services, an express negative stipulation (but not an inferred one) may be enforced by an injunction in a suitable case: *Lumney v Wagner* [1852] 90 RR 125.

See Supreme Court of Judicature Act (Ireland) 1877. See RSC Ord 50, rr 2 and 12. [Bibliography: Delaney H (2); Keane (2); Wylie (3); Bean UK.] See ANTON PILLER ORDER; BALANCE OF CONVENIENCE; BAYER INJUNCTION; INFRINGEMENT OF COPYRIGHT; LIVELIHOOD; MAREVA INJUNCTION; QUIA TIMET; STATUTORY POWER, RESTRAINT OF.

injunction, constitutional right. Where an injunction is sought to protect a constitutional right, the only matter which could properly be capable of being weighed against the grant of such protection, is another competing constitutional right: *SPUC v Grogan* [1990] ILRM 350, SC.

injunction, criminal. An order which the High Court is empowered to make to prohibit a criminal act; however, it will make such an order only in exceptional cases and will consider the alternative statutory remedy: *Attorney-General v Paperlink* [1984] ILRM 373.

There is no general right for a person to injunct the commission of a criminal offence: *O'Connor v Williams* [1996] 2 ILRM 382, HC and [2001] 1 IR 248, HC. In this case, the court held that the criminal law was sufficiently strong to prevent damage being caused to the plaintiff taxi drivers by the defendant hackney drivers who were acting as taxi drivers.

The postponement of a trial for a criminal offence, committed by a breach of a licence, is not a bar to the granting of an injunction, but a factor to be considered in weighing the balance of convenience: *Re Beara Fisheries and Shipping Ltd* [1988] ILRM 221. Where an existing statute renders an activity illegal, the court will not restrain the imposition of preventative measures authorised by the statute: *Cooke v Minister for Communications* [1989] ITLR (20 February). See also *Campus Oil v Minister for Industry (No 2)* [1983] IR 88.

The High Court is empowered to make an order prohibiting a solicitor, or any other person concerned, from contravening any provision of the Solicitors Acts 1954 to 2002 or any provision of regulations made under those Acts, notwithstanding that such contravention may constitute an offence: Solicitors (Amendment) Act 2002, s 18. The order is made on the application of the Law Society. It was necessitated by the decision in *Law Society v Carroll* [1996] 2 ILRM 95, SC and [1995] 3 IR 145, SC wherein it was held that the Law Society occupies a unique role in regard to the solicitors' profession and therefore it has an interest in stopping the activities of unqualified persons who appear to be holding themselves out as solicitors; but that it did not have an exclusive right to prosecute in respect of offences to protect the public.

injunction, environment. An order of the High Court or Circuit Court which requires the person in charge of an activity, which is being carried out in contravention of this Act, to refrain from or cease doing any specified act: Environmental Protection

Agency Act 1992, s 99H inserted by Protection of the Environment Act 2003, s 15. This includes to refrain from or cease making an emission. The application may be made by any person by motion and the Court may make such interim or interlocutory order as it considers appropriate (EPAA 1992, s 99H(2)). The Circuit Court has jurisdiction when it is satisfied it is appropriate for it to deal with, as a court of local and limited jurisdiction, having regard to the nature and extent of the environmental pollution alleged and the estimated cost of complying with the order to which the application relates (EPAA 1992, s 99H(3)).

injunction, labour. See LABOUR INJUNCTION.

injunction, planning. An order which the High Court or Circuit Court may make to ensure: (a) that an *unauthorised development* is not carried out or continued; (b) in so far as is practicable, that any land is restored to its condition prior to the commencement of any unauthorised development; (c) that any development is carried out in conformity with the permission pertaining to that development or any *condition* to which the permission is subject: Planning and Development Act 2000, s 160(1). The order may be made on the application of a planning authority or any other person, whether or not the person has an interest in the land. The order of the Court may require a person to do or not to do, or to cease to do, as the case may be, anything that the Court considers necessary and specifies in the order to ensure, as appropriate (a), (b) or (c) above. Section 160 is a re-enactment, with modifications, of the s 27 injunction provisions of the Local Government (Planning and Development) Act 1976 as inserted by LG(PD)A 1992, s 19(4)(g). See *Ampleforth Ltd t/a Fitzwilliam Hotel v Cherating Ltd* [2003] FL 7319, SC.

An injunction may not be sought after seven years from the date of commencement of a development for which there is no permission, or from the expiry of the planning permission where there was permission, except in the case of an injunction relating to a condition regarding the *use* of the land (PDA 2000, s 160(6)). When an injunction is sought, any other enforcement action may be commenced or continued eg an *enforcement notice* (PDA 2000, s 160(7)). When the Court grants a planning injunction, it must order also that the costs and expenses of the action be paid to

the planning authority or any other person (eg the applicant), as appropriate, unless it is satisfied that there are special or substantial reasons for not doing so (PDA 2000, s 161(1)). Provision has been made to change the 'rateable valuation' jurisdiction of the Circuit Court to a 'market value' (qv) of €3m (PDA 2000, s 160(5) as amended by Civil Liability and Courts Act 2004, s 53).

Orders made by the court are discretionary: *White v McInerney Construction Ltd* [1995] 1 ILRM 374, SC.

The injunction procedure is not to be used to determine serious allegations of fraud or misapplication of moneys by directors of companies: *Dublin County Council v O'Riordan* [1986] ILRM 104; *Corp of Dún Laoghaire v Park Hill Developments Ltd* [1989] ILRM 235. In addition, the planning injunction has been held to be in essence a *fire brigade* section, intended to deal with an urgent situation and not to deal with an unauthorised development which had been completed a number of years ago: *Dublin Corp v McGowan* [1993] 11 ILT Dig 212, HC. Also, it is not the function of the court to determine what constitutes good planning for the environment of an area; such function is reserved for the relevant planning authority: *Furlong v McConnell Ltd & Ors* [1990] ILRM 48, HC. See *Mahon v Butler* [1997] 3 IR 369, SC; *Westport UDC v Golden* [2002] 1 ILRM 439, HC.

See RSC Ord 103 as amended by SI No 5 of 1996, which provided for a s 27 order in the High Court against unknown persons carrying out unauthorised development. For Circuit Court procedure to obtain a planning injunction, see Circuit Court Rules 2001, Form 35C. See Grist in 11 ILT & SJ (1993) 79. See UNAUTHORISED DEVELOPMENT.

injuria. [A legal wrong.]

injuria non excusat injuriam. [One wrong does not justify another.]

injuria sine damnum. [A wrong without damage.] The phrase used in the law of torts (qv) to refer to where there is an infringement of a legal right which is actionable without proving any actual damage eg trespass which is actionable *per se*. See DAMNUM SINE INJURIA.

injurious affection. See SEVERANCE AND INJURIOUS AFFECTION.

injurious falsehood. A tort (qv) consisting of maliciously making a false statement respecting any person or his property with the result that other persons deceived thereby are induced to act in a manner which causes loss to him. It is different from deceit (qv) in that the falsehood in deceit is addressed to the plaintiff who acts on it to his loss, whereas in injurious falsehood, the falsehood is addressed to other persons who act on it and cause loss to the plaintiff.

It is not necessary to prove *special damage*, if the words are calculated to cause pecuniary damage to the plaintiff and are published in permanent form, or if the words are calculated to cause pecuniary damage to his office, profession or calling, trade or business, carried on at the time of publication: Defamation Act 1961, s 20(1). See *Ratcliffe v Evans* [1892] 2 QB 254; *Royal Baking Powder Co v Wright Crossley Co* [1901] RPC 95; *Irish Toys and Utilities Ltd v The Irish Times Ltd* [1937] IR 298. See DEFAMATION; SLANDER OF GOODS; SLANDER OF TITLE.

injury. (1) A violation of a legal right. (2) A disease or impairment of the physical or mental condition of a person. It has been held that the word *injured* is synonymous with *harmed*: Statute of Limitations (Amendment) Act 1991, s 2; *Maitland v Swan and Sligo Co Council* [1992] ITLR (6 July), HC. (3) An actionable wrong. See ASSAULT; CAUSE OF ACTION; CAUSING SERIOUS HARM.

injury, personal. See PERSONAL INJURIES.

inland bill. A bill of exchange both drawn and payable within Ireland and Britain. A *foreign* bill is any other bill of exchange. See Bills of Exchange Act 1882, s 4. See BILL OF EXCHANGE.

inland waters. The internal or inland waters of the State extending to all sea areas which lie on the landward side of the baseline of the *territorial seas*: Maritime Jurisdiction Act 1959, s 5. [Bibliography: O'Laoghaire.] See MARITIME JURISDICTION.

inland waterways. Any river or lake (including canalised sections), navigation or canal as specified, and includes a part thereof, any land comprised in the description thereof, and its associated navigational features: Minister for Arts etc Act 1998, s 1 and Sch. The Minister has certain functions and powers in relation to inland waterways, including their management and development (MAA 1998, s 3). [Bibli-

ography: Comerford (2).] See CANALS; WATERWAYS.

inn. An inn was defined at common law as a house the occupier of which held himself out to the public as willing to receive all travellers provided that they were willing to pay a price adequate to the sort of accommodation given, they came in a proper condition, and the innkeeper had room for them. The term has been replaced by the term *hotel* and the Innkeepers Acts of 1863 and 1878 repealed by the Hotel Proprietors Act 1963. See HOTEL.

inner bar. See BAR; SENIOR COUNSEL.

innocence, presumption of. See PRESUMPTION OF INNOCENCE.

innocent misrepresentation. A false statement which is neither negligent or fraudulent, which is of fact, intended to be acted upon, actually misleads and induces a contract. It generally does not entitle the person induced to rescind the contract but does entitle him to an indemnify (qv).

However, since 1980, where a person has entered into a certain type of contract after a misrepresentation has been made to him, and (a) the misrepresentation has become a term of the contract, or (b) the contract has been performed, or both, then, if otherwise he would be entitled to rescind the contract without alleging fraud, he will be so entitled notwithstanding the matters mentioned in (a) and (b): Sale of Goods and Supply of Services Act 1980, s 44. This provision applies to contracts of sale of goods, hire-purchase agreements, agreements for letting of goods, and contracts for the supply of service. Provisions in such agreements excluding liability for misrepresentation are not enforceable unless they are shown to be *fair and reasonable* (qv) (SGSSA 1980, s 46). See *Pearson v Dublin Corporation* [1907] AC 351.

As regards shares in a company, a person who by a material misrepresentation made innocently and not negligently, induces another to acquire shares, is generally not thereby liable in damages. If, however, the misrepresentation amounts to a warranty, then the party making it may be liable in damages for breach of contract. See *Bank of Ireland v Smith* [1966] IR 646. See MISREPRESENTATION.

innovative high growth companies. Provision has been made to enable innovative high growth companies, without the normal three-year trading record, to raise finance by listing their securities, provided they meet certain criteria: Listing Rules 2000, Ch 25. The company must be able to demonstrate that the company's business is innovative in nature, whether through the development of new products and/or services or new methods of business, and whose activities can be expected to generate significant organic growth in revenues. See listing rules.

innuendo. The claim by the plaintiff in a defamation action that, although the words complained of are not defamatory in themselves, they have a *secondary* meaning which is defamatory. A defamatory innuendo may be drawn from the circumstances of the publication rather than from the published words or picture: *Tolley v J S Fry and Sons Ltd* [1931] AC 333. In this case, the defendants by way of advertisement for their chocolate product, issued a caricature of the plaintiff, a well-known amateur golfer, without his knowledge or permission, depicting him playing golf with a packet of their chocolate protruding from his pocket. The House of Lords held that the caricature was capable of bearing the defamatory innuendo that the plaintiff had agreed to promote the defendant's products for reward and had thereby prostituted his reputation as an amateur golfer. See also *Campbell v Irish Press Ltd* [1955] 90 ILTR 105; *Fullam v Associated Newspapers Ltd* [1956] Ir Jur Rep 45. See also REFER TO DRAWER.

inoperative provisions. Provisions of a statute which no longer have effect eg it has been held that the provisions of, s 8(1) of the Petty Sessions (Ireland) Act 1851 are inoperative due to the disappearance of Grand Juries (qv) and county presentments (qv): *The State (Feely) v O'Dea* [1986] HC.

inops consilii. [Without advice.] Eg without legal advice.

inquest. An enquiry in relation to the death of a person which a coroner has a duty to hold, upon being informed that the body of a deceased person is lying within his district, if he is of opinion that the death may have occurred in a violent or unnatural manner or suddenly and from unknown causes or in a place or in circumstances which, under provisions in that behalf contained in any other enactment, require that an inquest should be held: Coroners Act 1962, s 17. The question of a *post-mortem* is for the discretion of the coroner: *Hanley v Coroner for Co Kildare* (1999) Irish Times, 11 June.

Questions of civil or criminal liability must not be considered or investigated at an inquest and accordingly every inquest must be confined to ascertaining the identity of the dead person *and how, when, and where the death occurred* (CA 1962, s 30; *The State (McKeown) v Scully* [1986] ILRM 133). A coroner's concern ought to be the proximate medical cause of death ie what is the real and actual cause of death: *Eastern Health Board v Farrell* [2000] 1 ILRM 447, HC, upheld on appeal: *Eastern Health Board v Farrell* [2001] 4 IR 627, SC. An inquest jury is permitted to reach a verdict of murder, manslaughter or infanticide, but this is confined to third-party involvement in a death; in all other instances the jury is prohibited from reaching a verdict which involves attaching criminal liability eg formerly suicide: CA 1962, s 40 and *Green v McLoughlin* [1991] 1 IR 309, HC.

The verdict or any *rider* (qv) to the verdict at an inquest must not contain a censure or exoneration of any person; however, recommendations of a general character designed to prevent further fatalities may be appended to the verdict (CA 1962, s 31).

A coroner must sit with a jury in certain circumstances eg if either before or during the inquest, he becomes of opinion that the deceased person came to his death by murder, infanticide or manslaughter (qqv) (CA 1962, s 40).

In relation to an inquest into the death of a patient in a hospital, to which the health board objected, it was held that a coroner must have a certain amount of latitude and discretion in investigating the cause of death: *Northern Area Health Board v Geraghty* [2001] 3 IR 321, HC and 1 ILRM 367. In this case, the court held that a coroner was entitled to hold an inquest to serve any of the following purposes: to determine the medical cause of death; to allay rumours or suspicion; to draw attention to the existence of circumstances which, if unremedied might lead to further deaths; to advance medical knowledge; to preserve the legal interests of the deceased person's family, heirs or other interested parties.

A coroner's jury consists of not less than six and not more than twelve persons (CA 1962, s 41). Every citizen of age eighteen and upwards and under the age of 65 residing in a coroner's district is qualified and liable to serve on the jury at a coroner's inquest: Juries Act 1976, ss 31–32. A judicial review (qv) has been permitted of the decision of a coroner to hold an inquest in the absence of the next-of-kin: *Boyle v Farrelly* [1992] HC.

The Attorney-General is empowered to order a new inquest; this power is not limited to situations where the first inquest is quashed by the High Court: CA 1962, s 24(1); *Farrell v Attorney-General* [1998] 1 ILRM 364, SC and 1 IR 203.

There are special provisions in relation to an inquest into a death arising from a workplace injury or disease: Safety, Health and Welfare at Work Act 1989, s 56. See also Carriage of Dangerous Goods by Road Act 1998, s 13. See *O'Connell v An tArd Chláraitheoir* [1997] 1 IR 377, HC. [Bibliography: Farrell.] See CORONER; INSANITY.

inquest and witnesses. A coroner may, at any time before the conclusion of an inquest held by him, cause a summons in the prescribed form to attend and give evidence at the inquest to be served on any person (including in particular any registered medical practitioner) whose evidence would, in the opinion of the coroner, be of assistance at the inquest: Coroners Act 1962, s 26.

The holding by a coroner of an inquest is a purely fact-finding exercise which has no legal consequences other than the provisions as to the registration of death under s 50(1) of the Coroners Act 1962 (now s 41 of the Civil Registration Act 2004): *Morris v Dublin City Coroner* [2001] 1 ILRM 125, SC and [2000] 3 IR 592. In this case the Supreme Court held that the coroner was clearly entitled to adopt the course which he did of preserving the anonymity of the gardaí witnesses.

The Supreme Court has held that while the courts have the power to grant an injunction to enforce the law where other remedies are inadequate and where it is just and convenient to do so, this jurisdiction should be exercised only in exceptional circumstances: *Attorney-General v Lee* [2001] 1 ILRM 553, SC and [2000] 4 IR 298, SC. In this case the Supreme Court refused to order a defendant to attend an inquest in response to a witness summons, who had declined to attend, as there was no indication in the plaintiff's affidavit as to the reason why the defendant was an essential witness at the inquest. The Chief Justice described the 1962 Act as 'defective'.

See 'Refusals to attend and give evidence at Inquests' by Jim O'Callaghan BL in *Bar Review* (March 2001) 310.

inquiry. The court may, at any stage of a proceedings, direct any necessary inquiries to be made or accounts to be taken: RSC Ord 33, r 2. See also COMMISSION OF INQUIRY; ENVIRONMENTAL PROTECTION AGENCY; INVESTIGATION OF COMPANY; PUBLIC LOCAL INQUIRY; TRIBUNALS OF INQUIRY.

inquisition. An inquiry held before a jury to determine whether a person is of unsound mind and incapable of managing his own affairs: Lunacy Regulation (Ireland) Act 1871 and *Re Anne Hobson* (1995) Irish Times, 9 December. See RSC Ord 67, rr 10–16. See WARD OF COURT.

inquisitorial procedure. The system in force in countries whose legal systems originate in Roman or Civil Law and under which the judge initiates the investigation, and summons and examines witnesses and in which the trial is an inquiry by the court. The right of silence by an accused at his trial is based on the law's rejection of an inquisitorial system: *Heaney v Ireland* [1994] 2 ILRM 420, HC. See 'Protecting the Interests of the Accused in France and Ireland' by Genevieve Coonan in (2003) 11 ISLR 95.

However, the approach adopted by the assessors of claims before the Personal Injuries Assessment Board is inquisitorial ie getting to the true facts of the extent of the allowable claim, to ensure that claimants get that to which they are entitled – no more and no less: Personal Injuries Assessment Board Act 2003, ss 19–38. See also Civil Liability and Courts Act 2004, s 20. Contrast with ACCUSATORIAL PROCEDURE. See ASSESSMENT, PERSONAL INJURIES.

insane person. A person of unsound mind. Contracts made by an insane person are valid, but if the other party knew he was contracting with a person, who by reason of the unsoundness of his mind, could not understand the nature of the contract, the contract is *voidable* (qv) at the option of the insane party. An insane person is liable for *necessaries* (qv) supplied to him: Sale of Goods Act 1893, s 2. See *Imperial Loan Co v Stone* [1892] 1 QB 559. See CAPACITY TO CONTRACT; UNSOUND MIND.

insanity. Unsoundness of mind; mental disease. It is a defence to the charge of a criminal offence; the defence is largely governed by the McNaghten Rules (qv) but these are not the sole rules. It has been accepted that *irresistible impulse* (qv) may be a defence in appropriate cases: *Attorney-General v O'Brien* [1936] IR 263. Mental abnormality does not amount to legal insanity: *Attorney-General v O'Shea* [1931] IR 728. However, insanity as a defence was widened in 1974 to include cases where the defendant is unable to control his actions as a result of illness or disease: *Doyle v Wicklow Co Council* [1974] IR 55.

Insanity as a defence must be proved on the balance of probability (qv). When the defence succeeds, the accused is found *guilty but insane* and is ordered to be kept in custody until his release is ordered by the Executive: Trial of Lunatics Act 1883; *DPP v Gallagher* [1991] ILRM 339, SC. The Minister for Justice has established an advisory committee to advise him in relation to applications for release made by persons found guilty but insane.

In relation to standing for trial, the test is whether the accused has sufficient intellect to comprehend the course of the proceedings of trial, so as to make a proper defence, to challenge a juror and to understand the details of the evidence: *The State (Coughlan) v Minister for Justice* [1968] ILTR 177. See also *The People (DPP) v O'Mahony* [1986] ILRM 244.

In 1991 it was held that in an inquest, a coroner must not allow medical evidence as to the deceased's state of mind since it would bring up for the jury the question of criminal liability in respect of a possible suicide: *Green v McLoughlin* [1991] 1 IR 309, HC.

Under draft legislation, a major reform of the law on insanity is proposed: Criminal Law (Insanity) Bill 2002. For details on proposals, see DIMINISHED RESPONSIBILITY; SPECIAL VERDICT; SURPRISE; UNFIT TO BE TRIED. See also 'Crazy Situation' by solicitor Dara Robinson in *Law Society Gazette* (January/February 2003) 12; 'Putting the sanity back into insanity?' by Simon Mills BL in *Bar Review* (June 2003) 101. [Bibliography: Charleton (4); McAuley; Robbins.] See MUTE; PSYCHIATRIC DISORDER; SUICIDE; UNFIT TO PLEAD; UNSOUND MIND; WARD OF COURT.

insect, destructive. Destructive insects or pests are to be construed as: (a) insects fungi or other pests destructive to crops, (b) bacteria or agents causative of a trans-

missible crop disease: Destructive Insects and Pests (Consolidation) Act 1958, s 1. The Act empowers the making of orders preventing the import of any insect, fungus, or other pest destructive to agriculture or horticulture crops or to trees and bushes. It also provides for the service on a cropowner of a *spraying notice*. The offence provisions of the 1958 Act were extended by the Destructive Insects and Pests (Amendment) Act 1991.

insider dealing. It is unlawful for a person *connected* with a public limited company to deal in its quoted securities, if he has *inside* information related to the company ie information which is not generally available but, if it were, would be likely materially to affect the price of those securities: Companies Act 1990, s 108.

A *connected* person is a natural person: (a) who is an officer or shareholder of the company or of a related company, or (b) who occupies a position that may reasonably be expected to give him access to such information (CA 1990, s 108(11)). Such a person is also precluded from dealing in the securities of any other company if he has *inside information* related to a transaction involving both companies (CA 1990, s 108(2)). A person who receives inside information from a connected person is also precluded from dealing (CA 1990, s 108(3)). *Price stabilising* activity in relation to the issue or sale of securities does not constitute insider trading: Companies (Amendment) Act 1999, s 2.

Insider dealing is both a civil wrong and a criminal offence (CA 1990, ss 109–112). The civil wrong creates a liability to compensate any party to the transaction who was not in possession of the information and with liability to account to the company for any profit in the transaction (CA 1990, s 109). A person convicted of insider dealing is prohibited from dealing for twelve months from conviction (CA 1990, s 112). See also s 223 of CA 1990 regarding the dealings of a company in its own securities. A policing role is given to the Stock Exchange (CA 1990, s 115).

The Stock Exchange is now required to report to the *Director of Corporate Enforcement* apparent breaches of the provisions dealing with insider dealing: Companies Act 1990, s 115 as amended by Company Law Enforcement Act 2001, s 37. This provision reflects the role of the Director in the investigation and prosecution of offences under the Companies Acts.

In the first *criminal prosecution* in the State alleging insider dealing, the trial judge directed the jury that to bring in a guilty verdict it had to be satisfied, beyond reasonable doubt: (a) that the defendant was in possession of price-sensitive information at the time he sold the shares, and (b) that he knew he was selling the shares, and (c) that he was intending to profit by using the price-sensitive information: *DPP v Byrne* [2001] CCC. The defendant was found not guilty.

In January 2002, the first *civil proceedings* involving alleged insider dealing was commenced by Fyffes plc against DCC plc, followed shortly thereafter by actions by Hibernian Investment Managers Ltd and Eagle Star Assurance Company against DCC plc.

Insider trading is also prohibited by the Stock Exchange: Listing Rules 2000, ch 16, Appendix, paras 2–12. See also *Securities Trust v Associated Properties* [1980] HC; Ryan in 7 ILT & SJ (1989) 6; MacCann in 9 ILT & SJ (1991) 130 & 151. See also SI No 131 of 1992. [Bibliography: Cahill D; Murphy & Ashe; ICEL.] See DIRECTORS AND SHARE DEALING; PRICE STABILISING.

insolvency. As regards the sale of goods, a person is deemed to be insolvent who either has ceased to pay his debts in the ordinary course of business, or cannot pay his debts as they become due, whether he has committed an *act of bankruptcy* (qv) or not: Sale of Goods Act 1893, s 62. See STOPPAGE IN TRANSITU; UNPAID SELLER.

insolvency, declaration of. See BANK-RUPTCY, ACT OF.

insolvency judgment. Means a judgment referred to in article 25 of the Insolvency Regulations: EC (Personal Insolvency) Regulations 2002, SI No 334 of 2002.

insolvency of employer. An employer is taken to be insolvent if he has been adjudicated bankrupt, or he has died and his estate is insolvent, or, being a company, a winding-up order has been made or a receiver appointed, or he is an employer as specified in regulations: Protection of Employees (Employers' Insolvency) Act 1984, s 1(3). Employees may claim payment of debts from the Redundancy and Employers' Insolvency Fund, where such debts arise from the employment relationship and have not been paid because of the employer's insolvency (PE(EI)A 1984,

s 6). In addition, the Minister may use the Fund to make payments into the assets of an occupational pension scheme to cover contributions not paid on the employer's insolvency (PE(EI)A 1984, s 7). As regards trade union dues deducted from remuneration of employees, see *Re Solus Teoranta* [1990] ELR 64, HC.

An order has been made which rectifies an anomaly in the 1984 Act which denied access to the Fund to employees over the age of 66 because their age prevented them being fully insurable: Protection of Employees (Employers' Insolvency) Act 1984 (Amendment Order) Order 1988, SI No 48 of 1988.

The moneys in the fund have been transferred to the Social Insurance Fund: Social Welfare Act 1990, ss 24 and 28. Part-time employees now have the same protection as full-time employees: Worker Protection (Regular Part-time Employees) Act 1991, s 1. Employees of an insolvent firm who have not received statutory notice, can now submit claims directly to the liquidator or receiver without having to go to the Employment Appeals Tribunal: Redundancy Payments Act 2003, s 15; SI No 197 of 2003. See also Maternity Protection Act 1994, s 41; Employment Equality Act 1998, s 103(4); National Minimum Wages Act 2000, s 47; Industrial Relations (Miscellaneous Provisions) Act 2004, s 15. See *Re Cavan Rubber Ltd* [1992] 79, EAT.

Revised forms have been specified in connection with the submission of claims under the Protection of Employees legislation: Protection of Employees (Employers' Insolvency) (Forms and Procedure) (Amendment) Regulations 2001, SI No 581 of 2001. [Bibliography: Barrett; Forde (9).]

insolvent. A person who is unable to pay his debts as they become due. See also ADMINISTRATION OF ESTATES; BANKRUPTCY; INSOLVENCY; STOPPAGE IN TRANSITU.

insolvent company. A company which is unable to pay its debts as they fall due. A company is deemed to be unable to pay its debts in a variety of circumstances e g failure to comply with a demand by a creditor for payment: Companies Act 1963, s 214. However, a petition to wind up a company on such a ground will be refused where the petition is not being presented for the benefit of all its members and creditors: *Re WMG (Toughening) Ltd* [2001] 3 IR 113, HC.

A company which was thought to have been insolvent at the date of liquidation (qv) but whose assets when realised are sufficient to pay its debts, is not and never was insolvent: *Re Lines Bros Ltd* [1984] BCLC 215. The only relevant criterion is whether the liquidation produced a surplus, irrespective of whether this arose from the realisation of its assets or from interest earned in any other way: *Re Hibernian Transport Companies Ltd* [1994] 1 ILRM 48, SC and [1995] 3 IR 217. See EC (Corporate Insolvency) Regulations 2002, SI No 333 of 2002. [Bibliography: Forde (7); Forde (9); Lynch.] See FLOATING CHARGE; FRAUDULENT PREFERENCE; WINDING UP, COMPULSORY.

insolvent estate. Provision has been made for the administration of the estates of persons who die insolvent to be wound up in bankruptcy: Bankruptcy Act 1988, ss 115–122. The petition in the High Court for the administration in bankruptcy may be made by the personal representative (qv) or by a creditor whose debt would have supported a *bankruptcy petition* against the deceased had he been alive (BA 1988, s 115(1)).

A petition may not be presented when proceedings have already begun in the Circuit Court for the administration of the deceased's estate; however that court may, when satisfied that the estate is insolvent, transfer the proceedings to the High Court (BA 1988, s 115(4)). When an order is made by the court for the administration in bankruptcy of the deceased's estate, his property will vest in the Official Assignee (qv) for realisation and distribution (BA 1988, s 118). Priority in payment is given to funeral and testamentary expenses (BA 1988, s 119).

inspection. The word 'inspection' has a wide connotation and includes interview, although any invasive test procedures or treatment are excluded: *JS v CS* (*Nullity*) [1997] 2 IR 506, HC.

inspection of company. See INVESTIGATION OF COMPANY.

inspection of documents. See DISCOVERY.

inspection of property. The court may order that an applicant be allowed carry out an inspection of a defendant's property (eg re mining activities) in order to ascertain whether a trespass of the applicant's property has taken place: *Bula Ltd & Ors v Tara Mines Ors* [1988] ILRM 149. See RSC Ord 50, r 4. See ANTON PILLER

ORDER; SOLICITOR, PROFESSIONAL NEGLIGENCE.

instalment. A part or portion of the total sum or quantity due, arranged to be taken on account of the total sum or quantity due.

instalment decree. An order of the District Court requiring a person to pay such money instalments and at such time as the court appoints; the court may make such an order as a condition to granting a stay of execution of a decree for the payment of money by way of debt or damages. The court must be satisfied that: (a) the person is unable to discharge the full sum of money by an immediate payment, (b) such inability is not occasioned by the person's own conduct, and (c) there are reasonable grounds to extend the time for payment: DCR 1997 Ord 46, r 7(2). Contrast with INSTALMENT ORDER.

instalment deliveries. Unless otherwise agreed, the buyer of goods is not bound to accept delivery thereof by instalments: Sale of Goods Act 1893, s 31. See *Wilkinson v McCann Verdon & Co* [1901] 35 ILTR 115; *Norwell v Black* [1931] 65 ILTR 104. See WRONG QUANTITY.

instalment order. An order which the District Court may make, compelling a debtor to pay the debt and costs which are due on foot of a judgment of a competent court. The instalment order is made following the examination of the debtor as to his means: Enforcement of Court Orders Act 1940, s 5; DCR 1997 Ord 53, r 7. Contrast with INSTALMENT DECREE. See also DEBTOR'S SUMMONS; EXAMINATION OF DEBTOR.

instance, court of first. See FIRST INSTANCE, COURT OF.

Institute of Technology. The former Regional Technical Colleges which were redesignated as Institutes of Technology and the Dublin Institute of Technology. There are 14 institutes of technology, located in: Athlone, Blanchardstown, Carlow, Cork, Dublin, Dún Laoghaire, Dundalk, Galway-Mayo, Letterkenny, Limerick, Sligo, Tallaght, Tralee and Waterford. See Dublin Institute of Technology Acts 1992 and 1994; Regional Technical Colleges Acts 1992, 1994 and 1999.

A person must not use the words 'institute of technology' to describe a provider of a programme of education and training, without the approval of the Minister: Qualifications (Education and Training) Act 1999, s 65. Also a new institute of technology may be established only where an independent review and the Higher Education Authority both support the proposal: Regional Technical Colleges Act 1992, s 3 as amended by Q(ET)A 1999, s 32.

The former Regional Technical Colleges became Institutes of Technology as follows: Waterford on 7 May 1997, SI No 199 of 1997; Cork on 18 December 1997, SI No 512 of 1997; and the other RTCs on 28 January 1998, SI No 19 of 1998. The Dún Laoghaire College of Art and Design became the Dún Laoghaire Institute of Art, Design and Technology, SI No 149 of 1997; SI No 19 of 1998. The Institute of Technology, Blanchardstown, was established by the 1999 Act.

These Institutes are now entitled, with the consent of the Minister, to acquire or to form subsidiaries registered under the Companies Acts, to perform such of their functions as they consider appropriate: Vocational Education (Amendment) Act 2001, s 37. See *Minister for Education v Letterkenny RTC* [1997] 1 IR 433, SC. See EDUCATION; EDUCATION AWARDS; EDUCATIONAL ESTABLISHMENT; NATIONAL QUALIFICATIONS AUTHORITY OF IRELAND.

instruct. (1) When a client authorises a solicitor to act on his behalf, he is said to *instruct* the solicitor. The decision by a solicitor to accept instructions in any particular case is a matter for the discretion of the individual solicitor; however he must not discriminate unfairly between members of the public or accept instructions which would involve himself in the furtherance of a crime: *A Guide to Professional Conduct of Solicitors in Ireland* (2002) ch 2.1. A solicitor should not accept instructions where he does not have sufficient expertise or time. He is entitled to refuse to act for a client unless the client pays all fees due in advance or as they fall due. He should not take instructions which he suspects have been given by a client under duress or undue influence. Also he should cease to act for a client where the client refuses or fails to give the solicitor further instructions (para 2.3).

Where a solicitor on the legal aid panel in criminal matters is instructed by the defendant (or nominated by the court), he is under a duty to comply with those instructions unless he has reasonable grounds for refusing to act in that particu-

lar case for that particular client, subject to the agreement of the court, where this is necessary (para 2.1).

When a solicitor communicates information to counsel in relation to proceedings or authorises him to act, he is said to *instruct* counsel. He is known as the *instructing* solicitor.

(2) The term *instructions* includes a request (whether or not accompanied by documents) to advise, to draft proceedings or other legal documents, and/or to appear in court or before any tribunal or other body: *Code of Conduct for the Bar of Ireland* (December 2003) r 1.7(f). A barrister may not accept so many instructions that he cannot reasonably expect to give adequate attention to all of it within a reasonable time (r 2.19). He owes a duty to his instructing solicitor to inform him promptly if it becomes apparent that he is unlikely to be able to attend to his instructions or if there is likely to be a substantial delay in attending to them.

A barrister is bound to accept instructions in any field in which he professes to practice, unless there is a conflict of interest or special circumstances arise (r 2.17). In contentious matters a barrister should not take instructions directly from a client (r 3.7). If a client contacts a barrister initially and asks him to act, the barrister should do nothing unless and until he is contacted by the solicitor, but if it is a matter of urgency, the barrister may contact the client's solicitor (r 3.8). A barrister ought not to accept instructions if he would be embarrassed in the discharge of his duties because he had previously advised on or drawn pleadings for another client on the same matter or appeared for another person who is or was connected with the same matter (r 3.10). Also a barrister may not accept instructions in any case where by reason of his connection with the client or the subject matter it would be difficult for him to maintain his professional independence (r 3.11). See BARRISTER, INTERNATIONAL PRACTICE; BRIEF; SOLICITOR AND COUNSEL.

instruction fee. The fee charged by a solicitor for instructing counsel in legal proceedings. The Taxing Master is entitled to determine whether an instruction fee sought by a solicitor is the correct fee. There are only three criteria upon which the amount of a solicitor's instruction fee can be determined: the special expertise of the solicitor, the amount of work done, and the degree of responsibility borne by him: RSC Ord 99, r 37(22)(ii) and *Best v Wellcome Foundation Ltd* [1996] 1 ILRM 34, HC and 3 IR 378. The appropriate principle is that the higher the award, the lower the percentage of such award can be allowed by way of instruction fee (*Best* case). The instruction fee cannot be used to compensate the solicitor for the low level of fees allowable for other expenses: *Smyth v Tunney* [1992] 10 ILT Dig 267, HC. See TAXATION OF COSTS.

instrument. A formal legal document in writing which evidences rights and duties eg a deed (qv) or a will (qv). It is also defined as an order, regulation, rule, byelaw, warrant, licence, certificate or other like document: Interpretation Act 1937, s 3.

insurable employment. It has been held that *insurable employment* must be defined with reference to the qualifying characteristics of the employment and not by reference to the status of the employee: *Kenny v Minister for Trade and Employment* [2000] 1 IR 249, HC and [1999] ELR 163, HC.

insurable interest. An interest giving an insured person a right to enforce a contract of insurance. An insurance contract is void unless the assured has some *insurable interest* in the life or property which is the subject of the insurance at the time the contract is entered into. The interest exists if the insured is liable to sustain some monetary loss, or if he may be claimed against following a loss to another. In life insurance, no contract of insurance may be made by a person on the life of another unless he has an interest in the life of that other: Life Assurance Act 1774, s 1; Life Assurance Act 1886.

A person has an unlimited interest in his own life. A father may not necessarily have an insurable interest in his son's life: *Halford v Kymer* [1830] 10 B & C 724; a husband may insure his wife and vice versa: *Griffiths v Fleming* [1909] 1 KB 805; a trustee may insure in respect of an interest of which he is trustee: *Tidswell v Ankerstein* [1792] Peake 151; tenants-at-will may insure a premises which they occupy and are required to maintain: *Church & General Insurance Co v Connolly* [1981] HC.

Statutory provisions prevent insurance being used as a means of gaming and wagering: Gaming and Lotteries Act 1956; Marine Insurance Act 1906, s 4. See also *Coen v Employers Liability Assurance Corporation* [1962] 104 ILTR 157; *P J Carrigan Ltd v Norwich Union Fire Society* [1987] IR 619, HC. See INSURANCE, CONTRACT OF.

insurable value. The measure of insurable value in marine insurance, in the absence of any express provision in the policy, is provided for by s 16 of the Marine Insurance Act 1906.

insurance. A contract whereby a person called the *insurer* agrees in consideration of money paid to him, called the *premium*, by another person called the *assured*, to indemnify the latter against loss resulting to him on the happening of certain events. An obligation to pay on the happening of a specified event is essential to the existence of a contract of insurance: *Rafter v Solicitors Mutual Defence Fund Ltd* [1999] 2 ILRM 305, HC and [2002] 3 IR 621. The event must constitute an *insurable interest* (qv). The *policy* is the document in which is contained the terms of the contract.

Insurance is a contract *uberrimae fidei* (of the utmost good faith) and of indemnity only, except in the case of life and accident insurance, when an agreed sum is often payable.

An insurance company is not required to give reasons as to why it cancels an insurance policy or why it declines to enter into or renew an insurance policy: *Carna Foods Ltd v Eagle Star Insurance* [1997] 2 ILRM 499, SC and 2 IR 193.

For information on the single insurance market of the EC, see Ping-Fat in 11 ILT & SJ (1993) 43. See Insurance Acts 1909 to 1990.

Provision was made in 2000: (a) to allocate regulatory responsibility for insurance intermediaries to the Central Bank of Ireland, (b) to enable the Minister to make *disclosure regulations* requiring insurance undertakings and intermediaries to make information of a specified nature available to insurance consumers, (c) to strengthen the existing system of notification by re-insurance undertakings, and (d) to update existing provisions for offences and penalties: Insurance Act 2000. The Act also gives full effect in the State to Council Directive (EEC) 92/96 of 10 November 1992.

See Stamp Duties Consolidation Act 1999, ss 59–62; Unclaimed Life Assurance Policies Act 2003. For the Insurance Institute of Ireland, see website:

www.insurance-institute.ie. For the Irish Insurance Federation, see website: *www.iif.ie.* [Bibliography: Corrigan & Campbell; O'Regan Cazabon; Forde (5); Hill UK; Ivamy UK; MacGillivray & Parkington UK; Cameron Markby & Hewitt UK.] See COMMERCIAL PROCEEDINGS; INDEMNIFY; INSURANCE BUSINESS; INSURANCE, CONTRACT OF; INSURANCE OMBUDSMAN; IRISH FINANCIAL SERVICES REGULATORY AUTHORITY; LIFE ASSURANCE; SUBROGATION; ULTRA VIRES; UNCLAIMED LIFE ASSURANCE POLICY.

insurance, contract of. Insurance policies fall into two broad categories: *life assurance* which insures against an event which must happen and *liability insurance* which insures against events which may happen. A contract of insurance does not come into effect and the insurer put on risk until the precise time specified in the contract or, if not stated, when the parties intended. Often, this is at the time the first premium is paid: *Harney v Century Insurance Co Ltd* [1983] HC. Unless provided for in the contract, there is no obligation on an insurance company to give reasons for its decision to cancel or refuse insurance: *Carna Foods Ltd v Eagle Star* [1995] 1 ILRM 474, HC and 1 IR 526. However, see HEALTH INSURANCE.

Most contracts of insurance provide that disputes between the parties be resolved by arbitration (qv). The High Court has jurisdiction to set aside an arbitration award if there is an error in law on its face: *Church & General Insurance Co v Connolly* [1981] HC. See also *Stanbridge v Healy* [1985] ILRM 290.

An insurer domiciled in a contracting EU state may be sued: (a) in the courts of the State in which he is domiciled, or (b) in another contracting state in the courts for the place where the policy holder is domiciled: Jurisdiction of Courts and Enforcement of Judgments Act 1998, Sch 1, art 8. As regard EFTA countries, see JCEJA 1998, Sch 7, art 8. The *Brussels I Regulation* on the recognition and enforcement of judgments in civil and commercial matters, replaces JCEJA 1998 as from 1 March 2002 for all EU states except Denmark: EC (Civil and Commercial Judgments) Regulations 2002, SI No 52 of 2002. The right to sue an insurance company in the place of one's own domicile is now extended to the insured person and the beneficiary when they are the plaintiffs (*Regulation*, art 9(1)(b)). See COVER NOTE; CREDIT GUARANTEE INSURANCE; FRIENDLY SOCIETY; PRIVATE INTERNATIONAL LAW; UBERRIMAE FIDEI.

insurance, double. See DOUBLE INSURANCE.

insurance, over-. See OVER-INSURANCE.

insurance, vehicle. It is an offence for a person to use in a public place a *mechanically propelled vehicle* (qv) unless either a vehicle insurer, or an exempted person would be liable for injury caused by the negligent use of the vehicle by him: Road Traffic Act 1961, s 56 as amended by the Road Traffic Act 1968, Pt IV and by the Road Traffic Act 2002, s 17; and the European Communities (Road Traffic) (Compulsory Insurance) Regulations 1975 to 1995, SIs Nos 178 of 1975, 322 of 1987, 347 of 1992, and 353 of 1995. The 2002 Act increases the minimum cover for property damage to €200,000.

A demand for production of a certificate of insurance or a certificate of exemption may be made by a garda: RTA 1961, s 69. Failure to produce a certificate creates a presumption that the vehicle was being driven without insurance. In order for the burden of proof to pass to the defendant that the vehicle was not being used in contravention of the legislation, there must be evidence both that a demand was made under s 69 of RTA 1961 and that the person on whom the demand was made, failed to produce a genuine certificate of insurance as defined in s 66 of RTA 1961: *Stokes v O'Donnell* [1996] 2 ILRM 538, HC and [1999] 3 IR 218, HC. See *Greaney v Scully* [1981] ILRM 340; *Boyce v McBride* [1987] ILRM 95.

The gardaí are permitted to check for insurance cover of motor vehicles normally based in another member state, provided the checks are random or in the course of a routine investigation of an accident or mishap or of a suspected offence relating to the user of the motor vehicle: Council Directives (EEC) 72/166 and 84/5; *DPP v O'Connor* [2000] 2 ILRM 137, SC.

Where a person uses a mechanically propelled vehicle with the consent of the owner, he is deemed to use it as the servant of the owner as regards injury caused by negligent use of the vehicle by the user (RTA 1961, s 118). It is against the policy of s 118 to permit a leasing company who lets out vehicles on the road, as owners, to claim that the driving of the vehicle by the lessee was not with their consent because no insurance had been obtained by the lessee: *Homan v Kiernan* [1997] 1 ILRM 384, SC and 1 IR 55.

It has been held that dismissal of a driver employee because the employer was unable to get insurance cover for the employee due to accidents he had, was fair: *Brennan v Bluegas Ltd* [1994] ELR 94, EAT.

Regulations have been made to extend compulsory third-party insurance cover to Irish registered vehicles being driven abroad in EC member states or other designated territories on or after 31 December 1995, up to: (a) the minimum legal cover required in the EC member state or other designated territory, or (b) the minimum legal cover required in Ireland, whichever is the more beneficial to the injured party: Road Traffic (Compulsory Insurance) (Amendment) Regulations 1992, SI No 346 of 1992. See also SI No 347 of 1992; SI No 359 of 1994 as amended by Central Bank and Financial Services Authority of Ireland Act 2003, s 35, Sch 2.

An insurer is now required to notify a client in writing of certain specified information, not less than 15 working days before the date of renewal of the motor insurance policy eg the terms of the policy, including restrictions or limitations, and any discount applied to the policy: Motor Insurance (Provision of Information) (Renewal of Policy of Insurance) Regulations 2002, SI No 389 of 2002. See *Fairbrother v Motor Insurers Bureau of Ireland* [1995] 1 IR 581, HC; *Bus Éireann v Insurance Corporation of Ireland plc* [1995] 1 IR 105, HC; *Lynch v Lynch* [1996] 1 ILRM 311, HC; *Scanlon v McCabe* [1997] 2 ILRM 337, SC and 1 IR 63. See MOTOR INSURANCE, EC; MOTOR VEHICLE, NEGLIGENT DRIVING OF; MOTOR INSURER'S BUREAU OF IRELAND; UNTRACED DRIVER; VEHICLE INSURER, PROCEEDING AGAINST.

insurance agent. Any person who holds an appointment in writing from an insurer enabling him to place insurance business with that insurer, but does not include an *insurance broker* or an employee of an insurer when the employee is acting for that insurer: Insurance Act 1989, s 2(1). Certain conditions are specified for insurance agents eg that an agent must hold appointment from not more than four authorised insurers (IA 1989, s 49). An insurance agent is an *insurance intermediary* (qv) and is governed by the provisions in IA 1989 concerning such intermediaries.

It has been held that where an insurance agent's authority is confined to submitting proposal forms (and not to completing the forms), the insurer is not bound by any statement or representation by the agent: *Connors v London & Provincial Assurance Co* [1913] 47 ILTR 148. Under the 1989 legislation, an insurance agent is deemed to be acting as the agent of the insurer when he completes in his own hand or helps the proposer of an insurance policy to complete a proposal (IA 1989, s 51). An insurance agent must comply with the Investor Compensation Act 1998 (IA 1989, s 49). See EC (Insurance Agents and Brokers) Regulations, SI No 178 of 1978 as amended by Central Bank and Financial Services Authority of Ireland Act 2003, s 35, Schedule 2. See INSURANCE BROKER; INSURANCE INTERMEDIARY; INSURANCE OMBUDSMAN; PAYMENT TO AN AGENT; PREMIUM; TIED INSURANCE AGENT.

insurance and building societies. Insurance is a *financial service* which a building society may be empowered to provide: Building Societies Act 1989, s 29(2)(g). However, a society must not carry on insurance business otherwise than by a subsidiary or other associated body of the society except where it acts as an insurance intermediary (qv) (BSA 1989, s 29(4) as inserted by Housing (Miscellaneous Provisions) Act 1992, s 30).

insurance and mortgaged property. A *building society* is prohibited from requiring a member to effect insurance on any security for a loan with an insurer directed by the society or through the agency of the society or of any intermediary directed by the society: Building Societies Act 1986, s 6(1)(c); SI No 27 of 1987; SI No 339 of 1987. Notwithstanding the repeal of BSA 1986, this provision continues in force: Building Societies Act 1989, s 6. Any dispute between a member and the society in relation to this matter is to be determined by the Central Bank.

Similarly, any insurance which a *mortgage lender* (qv) may require a borrower to effect, may be effected by the borrower with any insurer: Consumer Credit Act 1995, s 124. See MORTGAGE PROTECTION INSURANCE.

insurance bond. See INSURANCE COMPANY; INSURANCE BROKER.

insurance broker. A person who, acting with freedom of choice (ie being in a position to arrange insurance contracts with at least five insurance undertakings) brings together, with a view to the insurance of risks, persons seeking insurance and insurance undertakings, and carries out work preparatory to the conclusion of contracts of insurance, but does not include an *insurance agent* or an employee of an insurer when the employee is acting for that insurer: Insurance Act 1989, ss 2(1) and 44. Insurance brokers are required to meet certain qualifications eg membership of a recognised body (IA 1989, s 44).

Insurance brokers as *insurance intermediaries* (qv) are governed by the provisions of the 1989 Act regarding such intermediaries. An insurance broker may be negligent in not advising his client to disclose material information to the insurance company: *Latham v Hibernian Insurance Co and Sheridan & Co* [1992] 10 ILT Dig 266, HC. See *Chariot Inns Ltd v Assicurazioni Generali SPA* [1981] ILRM 173. An insurance broker must comply with the Investor Compensation Act 1998 (ICA 1998, s 49). See EC (Insurance Agents and Brokers) Regulations 1978, SI No 178 of 1978 as amended by Central Bank and Financial Services Authority of Ireland Act 2003, s 35, Sch 2. A practising barrister must not act as an insurance broker or as an official of an insurance company: *Code of Conduct for the Bar of Ireland* (December 2003) r 7.10. [Bibliography: Ellis.] Contrast with INSURANCE AGENT. See INSURANCE INTERMEDIARY.

insurance business. Insurance business is carried out by insurance companies which are governed by the Insurance Acts 1909 to 1989, and by registered friendly societies which are governed by the Friendly Societies Act 1896 to 1977, and by subsidiaries or other associated bodies of building societies which are governed by the Building Societies Act 1989. These Acts and regulations made under the European Communities Act 1972, provide the statutory base for supervision by the State in the interest of policy holders. Insurance companies must hold an *authorisation*, maintain a *bond* with the High Court and make annual returns.

The supervising powers of the Minister have been updated and clarified, a system of regulation of insurance brokers and agents has been introduced, and the Minister has been given power to regulate commission payments to insurance intermediaries (qv): Insurance Act 1989. See also European Communities (Non-Life Insurance) Regulations 1976, SI No 115 of 1976 as amended by Central Bank and Financial Services Authority of Ireland Act 2003, s 35, Sch 2, and by Central Bank and Financial Services Authority of Ireland Act 2004, s 10(3), Sch 2.; European Communities (Life Assurance) Regulations 1984, SI No 57 of 1984 as amended CBFSAI 2003, s 35, Sch 2 and by CBFSAI 2004, s 10(3), Sch. See also RSC Ord 113. See COMMISSION; INSURANCE AGENT; INSURANCE BROKER.

insurance compensation fund. The fund established by the Insurance Act 1964 as amended by Central Bank and Financial Services Authority of Ireland Act 2003, s 35, Sch 1. The right to compensation via the fund, for refunds of premiums or payment of unsatisfied claims to policyholders or claimants of an insurance company being wound up, is restricted to 65% of unsatisfied claims or £650,000 (€825,330) per claim, whichever is the lesser: Insurance Act 1989, s 31.

insurance intermediary. An insurance broker or an insurance agent: Insurance Act 1989, s 2(1). Insurance intermediaries are required to keep a separate client bank account (IA 1989, s 48). Previously they were required to hold a bond in a specified form to a value of not less than £25,000 (€31,743) which, in the event that the intermediary failed to meet his financial obligations, would be available for the benefit of his clients who had thereby suffered loss (IA 1989, s 47 now repealed by the Investor Compensation Act 1998, s 7 as they are now required to comply with the latter Act (ICA 1998, s 46)).

The Minister may provide by regulation that a person must not act or hold himself out to be an insurance agent or broker unless he effects a policy of *professional indemnity insurance* as the Minister may prescribe (IA 1989, s 45).

Also an insurance intermediary is disqualified from acting as such if adjudged bankrupt (qv); or if convicted of an offence involving fraud (qv) or dishonesty, whether connected with insurance or not; or if he is or was a director in a company involved in insurance which has been wound up (IA 1989, ss 54–55).

Every insurance undertaking is required to keep a register of its appointed insurance intermediaries (IA 1989, s 50). Regulatory responsibility for insurance intermediaries is now allocated to the Central Bank: Insurance Act 2000. The Act also empowers the

Minister to require insurance intermediaries, by regulation, to make relevant information of a specified nature available to insurance customers. See INSURANCE AGENT; INSURANCE AND BUILDING SOCIETIES; INSURANCE BROKER; INSURANCE OMBUDSMAN; INVESTOR COMPENSATION.

insurance of unnamed persons. See UNNAMED PERSONS, INSURANCE OF.

insurance ombudsman. An independent and impartial arbitrator of unresolved disputes or claims between a personal policy holder and his insurance company in respect of any insurance taken out in Ireland. The ombudsman can deal with such matters where the amount in dispute is €160,000 or less, or, where the policy concerns permanent health, the basic benefits insured are €26,000 or less per annum.

The Ombudsman cannot deal with: (a) any dispute about life assurance which concerns the actuarial standards, tables and principles which the insurance company applies, including the method of calculating surrender values and paid up policy values, and the bonus system and bonus rates applicable; (b) disputes relating to acts or omissions of insurance intermediaries other than those for which the insurance company bears full legal responsibility (eg tied insurance agents); (c) time barred matters; (d) matters more appropriate to a court of law.

The insurance ombudsman is empowered to make a judgment against an insurance company of up to €160,000 which is binding on the company but not on the policy holder. This non-statutory scheme was established in 1992. See: Insurance Ombudsman of Ireland, 32 Upper Merrion Street, Dublin 2. Tel: 6620899; fax 6620890. See email: *enquiries@ombudsman-insurance.ie* and website: *www.ombudsman-insurance.ie.*

Under recent legislation, provision is made for the establishment of an independent statutory *Financial Services Ombudsman* scheme: Central Bank and Financial Services Authority of Ireland Act 2004, s 16. The Act contains an enabling provision for the existing non-statutory Insurance Ombudsman, and her staff and systems to be absorbed into the statutory scheme, with the current Ombudsman being designated by the Minister as a Deputy Ombudsman-designate under the statutory scheme. [Bibliography: O'Regan Cazabon.] See

EUROPEAN EXTRA-JUDICIAL NETWORK; FINANCIAL SERVICES OMBUDSMAN.

insured. Includes a person who is indemnified by another (the insurer) against loss resulting to him on the happening of an event.

insurer. The person who indemnifies another (the insured) against loss, in consideration of a premium (qv). See INSURANCE, CONTRACT OF; VEHICLE INSURER, PROCEEDING AGAINST.

insurer, administrator of. See ADMINISTRATOR OF INSURANCE.

intangible property. A *chose* in action as compared with corporeal property, such as goods. [Bibliography: Power A.] See CHOSE.

integrated area plan. See URBAN RENEWAL.

integrated education. Term often used to describe the education of persons with special educational needs in an inclusive environment with persons who do not have such needs. Now referred to as 'inclusive education'. See DISABLED PERSON AND EDUCATION; INCLUSIVE EDUCATION; SPECIAL EDUCATIONAL NEEDS.

integrated pollution control. A single system of licensing to replace separate air and water pollution licensing systems: Environmental Protection Agency Act 1992, Pt IV, ss 82–99H, as substituted by Protection of the Environment Act 2003, s 15. The 2003 Act provided for the replacement of the 'integrated pollution control' (IPC) licensing system by a Community-wide system of 'integrated pollution prevention and control' (IPPC).

A person who carries out an activity listed in the EPAA 1992, Sch 1 (now Sch 1 to PEA 2003) may only do so pursuant to a licence issued by the Agency (EPAA 1992, s 82). The activities listed include activities relating to minerals, energy, metals, mineral fibres and glass, chemicals, intensive agriculture, food and drink, wood, paper, textiles, leather, fossil fuels, cement, waste, surface coatings, testing of engines, production of lime, and manufacture of printed circuit boards.

There are certain mandatory conditions which the Agency must attach to a licence eg concerning emission limit values, pollution minimisation, soil and groundwater protection, waste management, monitoring, plant breakdown, responses to incidents and accidents, and the ceasing of the activity (EPAA 1992, s 86(1)(a)). There are certain discretionary conditions which the Agency may specify eg the periods during which an emission may or may not be made (EPAA 1992, s 86(1)(b)).

Procedures for the processing of applications for licences are specified, with provision for notification of the relevant planning authority and for objections, time limits, and possible oral hearings (EPAA 1992, ss 87–89). There is also provision for review, amendment, time limit, transfer, surrender, revocation or suspension, and registration of licences (EPAA 1992, ss 90–97). A charge may be imposed by the Agency in respect of emissions (EPAA 1992, s 99).

The Agency must obtain the consent of the relevant sanitary authority in relation to a licence, which it proposes to grant, which involves a discharge of any trade effluent or other matter (other than domestic sewage or storm water) to a sewer (EPAA 1992, s 99E). See *Ní Eile v EPA* [1997] 2 ILRM 458, HC; *O'Connell v Environmental Protection Agency* [2003] FL 7019, SC and 2 ILRM 297. See also Taxes Consolidation Act 1997, s 681 as amended by Finance Act 1998, s 41. See EPA (Licensing) Regulations 1994, SI No 85 of 1994, as amended by SI No 394 of 2004. See JUDICIAL REVIEW; JUDICIAL REVIEW, POLLUTION CONTROL; PLANNING PERMISSION, DECISION ON.

integrated ticketing system. Means a system of ticketing which enables a passenger to use a single ticket on one or more public transport services by road or rail: Transport (Railway Infrastructure) (Additional Functions) (Integrated Ticketing) Order 2002, SI No 84 of 2002. The *Railway Procurement Agency* (qv) has the function of providing such a system or of securing its provision. It has been clarified that an integrated ticket provided by an employer to an employee is exempted from tax as a benefit-in-kind: Finance Act 2004, s 8.

integrity right. See MORAL RIGHT.

intellectual property. Personal property which is given limited protection by the law eg *patents, designs, trade marks, copyright,* and *know-how* (qqv). The law attempts to balance the need to reward human ingenuity and inventiveness on the one hand, with the promotion of the public good on the other hand. There is provision for exemption from stamp duty on the sale, transfer or other disposition of intellectual property, as defined in the provision: Stamp Duties

Consolidation Act 1999, s 101 as substituted by Finance Act 2004, s 74. See 'Intellectual property licensing in Europe – proposed new EU competition rules' by solicitor Conor Maguire in *Law Society Gazette* (December 2003) 57. [Bibliography: Clark & Smyth; Forde (5); Kelleher & Murray; ICEL; Groves UK; von Lewinski UK; Oppenheim UK.] See TOPOGRAPHY RIGHT; TRADE SECRET.

intensive agriculture. The rearing: (a) of poultry in installations where the capacity exceeds 40,000 places, (b) of pigs in installations where the capacity exceeds 750 places for sows in a breeding unit, or 285 places for sows in an integrated unit, or 2,000 places for production pigs: Environmental Protection Agency Act 1992, Sch 1, as substituted by Protection of the Environment Act 2003, s 18 and Sch 1, para 6. Intensive agriculture is an activity to which Part IV of EPAA 1992 applies ie it is subject to *integrated pollution control* (qv).

In a particular case it was held the grant of planning permission was fatally flawed as *weaners* and *finishers* should have been regarded as being pigs for the purposes of calculating the capacity of the proposed development: *Maher v Bord Pleanála* [1999] 2 ILRM 198, HC.

intensification of use. See PLANNING PERMISSION.

intention. 'Intention is a sense of purpose as to future action': *DPP v Byrne* [2002] 2 ILRM 68, SC and 2 IR 397. It is an offence to be *in charge* of a mechanically propelled vehicle in a public place, with *intent to drive* or attempt to drive, while under the influence of an intoxicant: Road Traffic Act 1961, s 50 as inserted by Road Traffic Act 1994, s 11. Whether a person had an 'intent to drive' a car depends on the circumstances of each case. The fact that a person who is in charge of a car, falls asleep, even involuntarily, does not mean that the purpose for which he is in the car has been abandoned and that an intention to drive has ceased to exist (*Byrne* case). The trial judge is entitled to consider the intentions of the person before he went to sleep. See DRUNKEN DRIVING; IN CHARGE.

The general rule of law is that a person is presumed to intend the natural reasonable and probable consequences of his acts, whether in fact he intended them or not. See *People (DPP) v Farrell* [1993] ILRM 743, CCA.

The intention of the parties to an agreement may be ascertained only from the document concluded by them and the actual words used therein, which document could be construed in the context of the general surrounding circumstances; the task of the court was not to ascertain the subjective intention of the parties from the surrounding circumstances: *Igote Ltd v Badsey Ltd* [2001] 4 IR 511, SC.

For ascertaining the intention of parties to a contract for the sale of goods, as to the time at which property in the goods passes to the buyer, see rules in GOODS, PROPERTY IN. See also FIREARM; MALICE; MENS REA; MURDER.

inter alia. [Among other things.]

inter alios. [Among other persons.]

inter arma leges silent. [Between armies the law is silent.] See WAR CRIMES.

inter partes. [Between parties.] See LIS INTER PARTES.

inter se. [Among themselves.]

inter vivos. [During life; between living persons.] [Bibliography: Pearce & Mee.]

interception of aircraft. There are detailed provisions for the interception (including required landing) of civil aircraft flying without authority or being used for any purpose inconsistent with the 1944 Chicago Convention on International Civil Aviation: Air Navigation (Interception of Aircraft) Order 1990, SI No 12 of 1990. See Air Navigation and Transport Act 1988, ss 38–39.

intercourse, sexual. See SEXUAL INTERCOURSE.

interesse termini. [Interest of a term.]

interest. (1) A right in property.

(2) Rights, titles, advantages, duties and liabilities connected with a thing, whether present or future, ascertained or potential.

(3) Interest on judgment debts under the Debtors (Ireland) Act 1840, s 26 has been reduced from 11% to 8% as from 23 January 1989: Courts Act 1981 (Interest on Judgment Debts) Order 1989, SI No 12 of 1989.

(4) Interest on a dishonoured cheque may be claimed from the time of its presentment for payment: Bills of Exchange Act 1882, s 57(1).

(5) Interest at 6% per annum may be recovered on any debt or sum certain, payable at a certain time or otherwise, in respect of which interest is not provided for: (a) if the sum certain is payable by virtue of a written instrument, or (b) if the sum is not so payable but a written demand is made including a demand for interest: RSC Ord 74, r 107. See *Re Car Replacements Ltd (In Liquidation)* [1995] 3 IR 473, SC.

(6) Where an order for costs is made and the order is merely expressed as an order 'for costs', interest accrues thereon from the date of the order and not from the date of taxation, notwithstanding the fact that costs are of necessity unascertained until taxation: *Best v Wellcome Foundation (No 2)* [1995] 2 IR 393, HC. See also *Clarke v Garda Commissioner* [2002] 1 ILRM 450, SC and 1 IR 207.

(7) A sum of money payable in respect of the use of another sum of money called the principal. The interest charged by a building society on a mortgage loan provides the cover for the interest paid by the society to its shareholders and depositors.

In a company which is being wound up, interest upon debts of the company which carry interest, ceases to run from the date of commencement of the winding up, unless the assets are sufficient to pay all the debts in full: *Re International Contract Company Ltd Hughes Claim* [1872] LR 13 Eq 623. See also *Daly v Allied Irish Banks* [1987] HC; *McCairns (PMPA) (In Liquidation)* [1992] ILRM 19, SC. See Taxes Consolidation Act 1997, s 244 as amended by Finance Act 2000, s 17. See ARBITRATION, DOMESTIC; COMPENSATION AND COMPULSORY PURCHASE; INSOLVENT COMPANY; INTEREST ON JUDGMENTS; PROMPT PAYMENT.

interest, disclosure of. The duty imposed by law on certain persons to disclose their interest in a matter eg the duty of a director of a company to disclose the nature of his interest in any contract between himself and his company. See ARMS LENGTH, AT; COUNCILLOR, DISCLOSURE OF INTEREST.

interest, excessive. A consumer may apply to the Circuit Court for a declaration that the total cost of credit provided for in an agreement is excessive; the court will have regard for a number of factors in making the decision eg prevailing interest rates, degree of risk, creditor's costs, extent of competition for type of credit, and the age, business competence and level of literacy and numeracy of the consumer: Consumer Credit Act 1995, ss 47–48 as amended by Central Bank and Financial Services Authority of Ireland Act 2003, s 35, Sch 1. This protection does not apply to any credit agreement with a credit institution (eg associated banks, building societies, TSB) or a mortgage lender. The Central Bank must be given an opportunity to be heard at the court hearing.

interest and bankruptcy. Where interest is reserved or agreed for on a debt which is overdue at the date of adjudication of a bankrupt, the creditor is entitled to prove or be admitted as a creditor for such interest up to the date of the adjudication: Bankruptcy Act 1988, s 75(2). See also EC (Personal Insolvency) Regulations 2002, SI No 334 of 2002. See BANKRUPTCY.

interest and social welfare. By agreement with the Ombudsman (qv), compensation based on the consumer price index is paid in respect of social welfare payments which are over two years late: Annual Report of Ombudsman 1986, pp 16 and 36.

interest and tax. There is now a general right to interest on repayments of *overpaid* tax: Finance Act 2003, s 17. This section deals with income tax, corporation tax and capital gains tax. Where the repayment arises because of a mistaken assumption by the tax authorities in the application of the law, interest will be paid from the date the tax was paid until the repayment is made. In all other cases, interest will be paid from the end of six months after a valid claim for repayment has been made until the repayment is made. The interest at 0.011% per day is not itself taxable in the hands of the recipient.

As regards interest on repayments of excise duty, VAT, stamp duty and residential property tax, see Finance Act 2003, ss 98, 125, 142 and 155 respectively. As regards interest on 'capital acquisitions tax', see Capital Acquisitions Tax Consolidation Act 2003, ss 51 and 57, as amended by Finance Act 2003, s 145.

Interest is also payable to the Revenue Commissioners on *overdue* tax: Taxes Consolidation Act 1997, ss 1080–1083, 1089. Interest paid by a person may be allowable to reduce his tax liability eg TCA 1997, ss 244–245. Interest charged on unpaid taxes and paid on overpaid taxes is now calculated, with effect from 1 September 2002, on a daily basis rather than a monthly basis: Finance Act 2002, s 129.

Prior to the 2003 statutory provisions, some judicial decisions had recognised the right to receive interest on tax overpayments eg it was held that interest was payable on VAT overpayments: *Bank of Ireland Trust Services Ltd v Revenue Commissioners* [2003] 2 ILRM 241, HC. Interest may be awarded on overpaid tax: *Navan Carpets v O'Culachain* [1988] IR 164, SC. It was also held that interest on an overpayment of tax (based on an assessment to tax which is reduced by the High or Supreme Court) was to be calculated by applying the rate applicable under the Courts Act 1981: *Texaco (Ireland) Ltd v Murray* [1992] ILRM 304, SC.

While a capital sum borrowed by a company to finance the redemption of redeemable shares is not a deductible expense in computing the company's profits, the ongoing interest arising thereon is expenditure wholly and exclusively laid out for the purposes of the company's trade and is a deductible expense: *MacAonghusa v Ringmahon Company* [2001] 2 IR 507, SC. Interest received by a company on advance payments on the sale of goods abroad is not *income from the sale of goods* so exported: *Kerrane v Hanlon (Ir) Ltd* [1987] HC.

Statutory provision has been made to make, on a discretionary basis, payments for loss of purchasing power to some 1,000 widows affected by a High Court judgment: *O'Coindealbhain v O'Carroll*, as recommended by the Ombudsman in his Report of November 2002 entitled *Redress for Taxpayers* (FA 2003, s 166). See DEPOSIT INTEREST RETENTION TAX; RENTED RESIDENTIAL ACCOMMODATION; SAVINGS DIRECTIVE; TAX, REPAYMENT OF.

interest on awards. See ARBITRATION, DOMESTIC; ARBITRATION, INTERNATIONAL.

interest on costs. An award simpliciter of the costs of an action carries with it interest at the rates fixed pursuant to the provisions of the Debtors (Ireland) Act 1840, s 25 from the date of the order and not from the date of taxation; the addition of the words 'when taxed' or 'when taxed and ascertained' to the order for costs, does not impose an element of futurity or impose a condition precedent: *Best v Wellcome Foundation Ltd* [1995] 1 ILRM 554, SC. A litigant who succeeds in reversing a High Court decision in the Supreme Court and is entitled to the costs of the High Court action, is entitled to interest on the costs as from the date of the High Court order which ought to have been awarded to him (*Best* case). See also *Clarke v Garda Commissioner* [2002] 1 ILRM 450, SC and 1 IR 207.

Interest on the amount of the cost, charges or expenses awarded to a party in a court to which s 27 of the Debtors (Ireland) Act 1840 applies (ie judgment debts) is now calculated as follows: (a) a nominal interest rate of 2% per annum applies from the date the judgment is given to the date: (i) when the parties agree costs as between themselves, or (ii) to the date a certificate of taxation issues, or (iii) to the date a county registrar measures the amount, whichever is appropriate; and (b) thereafter, the interest rate applicable to judgment debts specified in s 26 of D(I)A 1840 applies until the outstanding costs are paid: Courts and Court Officers Act 2002, s 30. Under recent legislation, provision has been made for interest on costs to run from the date the parties agree the costs or, in the absence of agreement, from the date the costs are taxed or measured, and at a rate of interest specified from time to time: Civil Liability and Courts Act 2004, s 41, amending CCOA 2002, s 30. See Courts Act 1981 (Interest on Judgment Debts) Order 1989, SI No 12 of 1989).

However, an award of costs in respect of a person appearing and being legally represented at a tribunal, does not carry interest: Tribunals of Inquiry (Evidence) Act 1979, s 6 and Goodman v Minister for Finance [1999] 3 IR 356, HC. Under draft legislation, it is proposed that interest on costs will run from the date the parties agree the costs or, in the absence of agreement, from the date the costs are taxed or measured, and at a rate of interest specified from time to time: Civil Liability and Courts Bill 2004, s 32. See COSTS IN CIVIL LITIGATION.

interest on judgments. A court may award interest at 8% from the date of entering up judgment until satisfaction of the judgment: Debtors (Ireland) Act 1840, s 26; Courts Act 1981, s 19(1); SI No 12 of 1989. It has been held that s 26 of the Debtors (Ireland) Act 1840 gave a right to interest from the date of entering judgment; interest is also payable on costs from the date of the judgment which awarded them: Clark & McCarthy v Garda Commissioner (31 July 2001, unreported)

Judgments on amounts not exceeding £150 (€190.46) do not carry interest (CA 1981, s 23). The rate of interest may be changed by the Minister (s 20(1)). A judge is empowered to award interest between the date the cause of action accrued and the date of judgment (CA 1981, s 22). Formerly, only a *judge* could order the payment of such interest and not the Master of the High Court: *Mellowhide Products Ltd v Barry Agencies Ltd* [1983] ILRM 152. However, such interest can now be awarded in a claim for a debt or liquidated sum, in default of defence or appearance, by the Master of the High Court, the Registrar in the Central Office, or the County Registrar as specified: Courts and Court Officers Act 1995, s 50.

Interest may also be awarded for the period between a breach of contract and the date of judgment; however the sum must be a *liquidated* or certain amount and the creditor must have served notice in writing of intention to claim interest. Interest on a dishonoured cheque may be claimed from the time of its presentment for payment: Bills of Exchange Act 1882, s 57(1). Interest has been awarded on the recoupment of capital outlay at the average of the overdraft and deposit rates: *Dwyer Nolan Developments v Dublin County Council* [1986] IR 130.

A decree of the District Court which exceeds £150 (€190.46) carries interest calculated from the date of the decree, unless the court directs a different date: DCR 1997 Ord 46, r.15. For interest on judgments obtained in other *contracting* EC states being enforced in this State, see Jurisdiction of Courts and Enforcement of Judgments Act 1998, s 10. The *Brussels I Regulation* on the recognition and enforcement of judgments in civil and commercial matters, replaces the 1998 Act as from 1 March 2002 for all EU states except Denmark: EC (Civil and Commercial Judgments) Regulations 2002, SI No 52 of 2002, reg 7 which provides for interest on judgments and reasonable cost and interest on costs.

In relation to interest on legal costs, see *Lambert v Lambert* [1987] ILRM 390. See D(I)A 1840, s 53 and CA 1981, s 22. See *East Cork Foods v O'Dwyer Steel Co* [1978] IR 103; *Incorporated Food Products Ltd v Minister for Agriculture* [1984] HC; *Turner & Ors v Hospital Trust (1940) Ltd* [1994] ELR 35, HC. See also Employment Equality Act 1998, ss 92(2) and 82(5).

For interest on insolvency judgments, see EC (Personal Insolvency) Regulations 2002, SI No 334 of 2002; EC (Corporate Insolvency) Regulations 2002, SI No 333 of 2002. See ACCUMULATION;

BREACH OF TRUST; COMPOUND INTEREST; HEPATITIS; MONEYLENDER; PREJUDGMENT INTEREST.

interest reipublicae ne maleficia remaneant impunita. [It is a matter of public concern that wrongdoings are not left unpunished.]

interest reipublicae ne sua re quis male utatur. [It concerns the state that no one should make a wrongful use of his property.]

interest reipublicae ut sit finis litium. [It concerns the state that litigation be not protracted.] See *Belton v Carlow Co Council* [1997] 2 ILRM 405, SC and 1 IR 172. See FINALITY IN LITIGATION.

interference. It is an offence to interfere with the military or police force by violence, with the intent of undermining public order, or the authority of the State: Offences Against the State Act 1939, s 9. See also INTIMIDATION.

interference with goods. See CONVERSION; DETINUE; TRESPASS TO GOODS.

Intergovernmental Conference (IGC). Term used to describe the only arena in which, through negotiations between the governments of the EU member states, amendments to the treaties may be agreed: National Forum on Europe, *Glossary of Terms* (2003). See EUROPEAN UNION CONSTITUTION.

interim. In the meantime.

interim injunction. See INJUNCTION.

interim order. An order of the Court, made in the course of proceedings, pending further directions from the Court.

Interim Reports Directive. The Directive (EC) 82/121 on the information to be published on a regular basis by companies, the shares of which have been admitted to official stock exchange listing: Listing Rules 2000 (*definitions*). See ANNUAL REPORT; LISTING RULES.

interlineation. See ALTERATION.

interlocutory. [Interloqui = to speak between.] Not final (i e during the course of an action).

interlocutory applications. Applications to the court, made during the course of an action between entry of appearance and close of pleadings for orders, with a view to assisting either party in the prosecution of his case e g orders for discovery of documents, interpleader, and security for costs (qqv). An *interlocutory application* is one which is purely procedural in nature and an *interlocutory order* is an order made on foot

of an interlocutory application: *Minister for Agriculture v Alte Leipziger* [2001] 1 ILRM 519, SC and [2000] 4 IR 32, SC.

The right of a litigant to seek and obtain an order of inspection is in no way dependent upon the court being satisfied as to the strength of his case: *Bula Ltd v Tara Mines* [1987] IR 85. For interlocutory applications in the Circuit Court, see Circuit Court Rules 2001 Ord 16, Ord 32, Ord 40. See Residential Institutions Redress Act 2002, s 7(7). [Bibliography: Buckley, Melody.] See also INJUNCTION.

interlocutory injunction. A temporary injunction pending trial of an action. An interlocutory injunction is not normally granted where damages would be an adequate remedy: *Ryanair Ltd v Aer Rianta cpt* [2001 HC] ITLR (19 March). However, the Supreme Court has held that it will, where there is a serious issue to be tried, grant a short-term mandatory interlocutory injunction, even if damages are an adequate remedy, and will exercise its equitable jurisdiction to restrain the presentation of a winding up petition for the duration of that injunction, where proceedings have already been determined by the High Court: *Meridian Communications Ltd v Eircell Ltd* [2001] ITLR (18 June), SC.

Where *interlocutory* relief is sought, the court should not attempt to decide any disputed question of fact or any difficult issue of law: *Ferris v Ward* [1998] 2 IR 194, SC.

Termination of employment may be restrained by *interlocutory* injunction in a case: (a) involving alleged oppressive conduct: *Irish Press Ltd v Ingersoll Irish Publications* (1993) Irish Times, 6 April, or (b) where the plaintiff has made out a fair issue to be tried as to the legality of the purported termination and the balance of convenience was in favour: *Shortt v Data Packaging Ltd* [1994] ELR 251, HC.

Increasingly, the courts are finding that the balance of convenience often justifies the granting of interlocutory relief to prevent the dismissal of senior employees e g see *Boland v Phoenix Shannon plc* [1997] ELR 113, HC, or to require that the employee be paid his full salary pending the trial of the action: e g see *Harte v Kelly* [1997] ELR 125, HC; *Lonergan v Salter-Townshend* [2000] ELR 15, HC; *Gee v Irish Times Ltd* [2001] ELR 249, HC. While loss of reputation was compensatable by damages, that did not mean that in all cases damages were an adequate remedy: *Garrahy v Bord na gCon* [2002] 3 IR 566, HC and [2003] ELR 274. An interlocutory order was made restraining University College Cork from removing a professor as head of the German Department or appointing anyone else to the post, as the court held that if it subsequently transpired that her removal was unlawful, it would prove extremely difficult for the trial judge to assess a sum to compensate her adequately for the harm suffered: *Howard v UCC* [2000] ITLR (4 September), HC and [2001] ELR 8, HC.

Also it was held that damages were an inadequate remedy where the plaintiff had a family to support and a trial date would be months away: *O'Donnell v Chief State Solicitor* [2003] ELR 268, HC. See also *Keane v Swim Ireland* [2004] ELR 6, HC; *McNamara v Civil and Public Service Union* [1996] ELR 160, HC; *Fitzpatrick v Commissioner of an Garda Síochána* [1996] ELR 244, HC; *Courtenay v Radio 2000 Ltd* [1997] ELR 198, HC; *A Worker v A Hospital* [1997] ELR 214, HC; *Harkins v Shannon Foynes Port Company* [2001] ELR 75, HC; *Rooney v Kilkenny* [2001] ELR 129, HC; *McNamara v South Western Area Health Board* [2001] ELR 317, HC; *Moore v Xnet Information Systems Ltd* [2002] 2 ILRM 278, HC and ELR 65.

However, in *Foley v Aer Lingus* [2001] ELR 193, HC, the court, in refusing to grant an interlocutory injunction, held that the damage to a company left without a CEO indefinitely would outweigh the potential damage to an employee. Also two senior credit union executives were refused an interlocutory injunction seeking to prevent the filling of their positions pending a full hearing of their case: *Good & O'Neill v Gurranabraher Credit Union* (2003) Irish Times, 17 July, HC. If a plaintiff denies that he has been dismissed, then he has no right to injunctive relief: *Davis v Walshe* [2003] ELR 1, HC. See *Miss World Ltd v Miss Ireland Beauty Pageants Ltd* [2004] ITLR (10 May), HC. See 'Developments in the Employment Injunction' by Donal O'Sullivan BL in *Bar Review* (October/November 2002) 303.

For interlocutory relief in *commercial proceedings* (qv), see RSC Ord 63A, r 6(3) inserted by Rules of the Superior Courts (Commercial Proceedings) 2004, SI No 2 of 2004. See Personal Injuries Assessment Board Act 2003, s 12(3). See also FENNELLY ORDER; INJUNCTION; SUSPENSION.

intermediary. See BROKER; CREDIT INTERMEDIARY; INVESTMENT INTERMEDIARY; INSURANCE INTERMEDIARY; MORTGAGE INTERMEDIARY; STOCKBROKER; THIRD-PARTY INFORMATION.

intermixture of chattels. The intermingling of chattels so that the several portions are no longer distinguishable. Where, by agreement, the chattels of two persons are intermixed, they become *tenants-in-common* in proportion to their respective shares. This also occurs where a bailee intermixes bailed chattels with his own, except that the bailee will be liable for any costs associated with separating the chattels into shares. See TENANCY IN COMMON.

internal market. Means an area without internal frontiers in which the free movement of goods, persons, services and capital is ensured in accordance with the provisions of the Treaty: EC Treaty, art 14(2) of the consolidated (2002) version. The Community was required to adopt measures with the aim of progressively establishing the *internal market* over a period which expired on 31 December 1992 (EC Treaty, art 14(1)). See SINGLE EUROPEAN ACT.

internal protection alternative. The concept that an asylum seeker should not be recognised as a refugee if protection is available to him in some part of his country of origin. The UN High Commissioner for Refugees (UNHCR) holds the view that the IPA concept 'rests on understandings which are basically at odds with those underlying the fundamental refugee protection principles'. From research carried out, it would seem that an IPA inquiry is frequently relied on by assessors to justify negative recommendations on asylum application in Ireland: 'The Internal Protection Alternative in the Irish asylum process' by solicitor Sheila McGovern in *Bar Review* (February 2003) 36.

international agreements. Every international agreement to which the State becomes a party must be laid before Dáil Éireann; the State is not bound by any such agreement involving a *charge on public funds* unless the term of the agreement has been approved by the Dáil: 1937 Constitution, art 29(5). This does not apply to agreements or conventions of a technical or administrative character (1937 Constitution, art 29(5)(3)). See *State (Gilliland) v Governor of Mountjoy Prison* [1987] ILRM 278.

An international agreement should be given a purposive interpretation and should be applied by the courts of a contracting state in accordance with national procedural rules and the rules of evidence: *APH Manufacturing BV v DHL* [2001] 4 IR 531, SC. The court could have regard to common law principles, but terms in a convention should receive, as far as practicable, an autonomous convention meaning. See DOUBLE TAXATION AGREEMENTS.

international carriage of goods. See CARRIER'S LICENCE; CMR.

international carriage of passengers. See CARRIER'S LICENCE; MARITIME CLAIMS; PACKAGE HOLIDAY; PASSENGER SHIP; WARSAW CONVENTION.

international carriage of perishable foodstuffs. There is legislative provision for: (a) the laying down of technical standards for the thermal efficiency of insulated, refrigerated, mechanically refrigerated or heated equipment used in the international carriage of perishable foodstuffs; (b) the testing of such equipment and its certification; and (c) the requirement that only equipment complying with specified standards will be used in the international carriage of perishable foodstuffs: International Carriage of Perishable Foodstuffs Act 1987. See Consolidated Regulations 1993, SI No 188 of 1993.

international classification of goods. The classification of goods in the International Classification adopted under the Nice Agreement of 15 June 1957 as revised at Stockholm on 14 July 1967 and at Geneva on 13 May 1977. A single application may be made for registration of a trade mark in respect of one or more classes of the Nice Agreement; every application must specify the class or classes to which it relates and must specify the goods or services relating to that class in respect of which registration is sought: Trade Marks Act 1996, s 39; Trade Mark Rules 1996, SI No 199 of 1996, r 14. See TRADE MARK, REGISTERED.

international convention. No international agreement can be part of domestic law save as may be determined by the Oireachtas; the sole and exclusive power of making laws in the State is vested in the Oireachtas: arts 29.6 and 15.2.1 of the Constitution of Ireland. It has been held by the High Court that the development of the *common law* must not be used as a device to circumvent these provisions: *Kavanagh v Governor of Mountjoy Prison* (29 October 2001, unreported). On appeal, the Supreme Court held that art 29 of the Constitution conferred no rights on individuals, capable of being invoked by individuals; if the government wished the terms of an international agreement to have effect in domestic law, it could ask the Oireachtas to pass the necessary legislation: *Kavanagh v Governor of Mountjoy Prison* [2002] 2 ILRM 81, SC and 3 IR 97.

International Convention on Civil and Political Rights. [ICCPR.] The international convention which came into effect in 1976 and which was ratified by Ireland in 1989. It protects a wide range of civil and political rights. Each state which is a party to the convention undertakes to respect the rights in the convention and to ensure to all individuals these rights, without distinction of any kind, such as race, colour, sex, language, religion, political or other opinion, national or social origin, property, birth or other status (ICCPR, art 2). See O'Flaherty in 11 ILT & SJ (1993) 225. See also *Kavanagh v Governor of Mountjoy Prison* [2002] 2 ILRM 81, SC and 3 IR 97.

international copyright. See BERNE COPYRIGHT UNION; UNIVERSAL COPYRIGHT CONVENTION.

International Court of Justice. The principal judicial organ of the United Nations: UN Charter, art 92. The court, sometimes called the *World Court*, is composed of fifteen members sitting at The Hague, no two of whom may be nationals of the same state; they are to be independent and are elected regardless of nationality by the General Assembly and Security Council of the UN. The Court has jurisdiction over all matters specifically provided for in the UN Charter or in treaties and conventions in force, and over all cases which the parties refer to it. Although the court has no power to impose sanctions or to enforce its judgments, it is understood that all of its decisions have been followed, the exception being *Corfu Channel Case (United Kingdom v Albania)* [1949] ICJ 4.

A judge of the International Court of Justice who was a practising barrister or practising solicitor prior to their appointment, is qualified for appointment as a judge of the Superior Courts of Ireland:

Courts (Supplementary Provisions) Act 1961, s 5(2) as substituted by Courts and Court Officers Act 2002, s 4. For the *Statute of the International Court of Justice*, see website: *www.un.org*. See UNITED NATIONS.

International Criminal Court. An international court with power to try persons accused of genocide, crimes against humanity and war crimes, where national courts are unwilling to do so. The *Statute of the International Criminal Court* was concluded at Rome on 17 July 1998 and was signed, subject to ratification, by Ireland on 7 October 1998. The Statute enters into force internationally two months after 60 states have become a party to it. In June 2001, art 29 of the Constitution of Ireland was amended by referendum of the people to enable the State to ratify the Statute. A total of 64% of those voting in the referendum voted in favour. Legal effect is proposed to be given to the Statute by draft legislation: International Criminal Court Bill 2003.

Justice Maureen Harding Clark, formerly of the Irish Bar, was one of 18 judges sworn in to the new court on 11 March 2003 in the Knights Hall of the Dutch Parliament in The Hague. As of that date a total of 89 states had joined, but not USA, China, Israel, India, Japan and Russia.

A judge of the International Criminal Court who was a practising barrister or practising solicitor prior to their appointment, is qualified for appointment as a judge of the Superior Courts of Ireland: Courts (Supplementary Provisions) Act 1961, s 5(2) as substituted by Courts and Court Officers Act 2002, s 4. See 'The International Criminal Court' by Siobhán Ni Chulacháin BL and Ercus Stewart SC in *Bar Review* (May 2001) 425. See *Challenges to the International Criminal Process* by Sara Siebert in (2003) 11 ISLR 29.

International Development Association. An affiliate of the World Bank which provides loans to the world's poorest countries at low or zero rates of interest. The three main aims of the Association are poverty reduction, economic adjustment, and environmental protection. Under recent legislation, the government is empowered to make a total payment of €50m to the *Thirteenth Replenishment* of the IDA: International Development Association Act 2004. See International Development Association

Acts 1960 to 2000; Central Bank Act 1997, s 66. See website: *www.worldbank.org/ida/*.

International Covenants of UN. See HUMAN RIGHTS COVENANTS.

international hallmark. See HALLMARK.

international haulage. See CARRIER'S LICENCE.

international hire-purchase agreement. See INTERNATIONAL SALE OF GOODS.

International Labour Organisation; ILO. The specialised agency of the United Nations, founded in 1919, which seeks the promotion of justice and internationally recognised human and labour rights. It is the only surviving major creation of the *Treaty of Versailles*, which brought the *League of Nations* into being. The ILO became the first specialised agency of the UN in 1946. See website: *www.ilo.org*.

international law. The body of legal rules applying between states. Ireland accepts the generally recognised principles of international law as its rule of conduct in its relations with other States: 1937 Constitution, art 29(3). This refers only to *public* international law: *Hederman J in W v W* [1993] ILRM 294, SC.

The principles of international law enter domestic law only to the extent that no constitutional, statutory or other judge-made law was inconsistent with the principle in question: *Horgan v An Taoiseach* [2003] 2 ILRM 357, HC and 2 IR 468. Article 29(1)(3) of the Constitution contains statements of principles or guidelines rather than binding rules on the Executive towards its own citizens (*Horgan* case). This case involved an unsuccessful challenge to the government's decision to allow Shannon Airport to be used by US aircraft involved in the Iraq war.

The Constitution has established an unmistakable distinction between domestic and international law; if the government wishes the terms of an international agreement to have effect in domestic law, it can ask the Oireachtas to pass the necessary legislation: *Kavanagh v Governor of Mountjoy Prison* [2002] 2 ILRM 81, SC and 3 IR 97.

Established principles of customary international law may become part of Irish municipal law through established usage, provided they are not contrary to the provisions of the Constitution, statute law or common law: *ACT Shipping Ltd v Minister for the Marine* [1995] 2 ILRM 30, HC and 3 IR 406.

However, principles set forth in individual state legislation cannot be regarded as establishing public international law; statutes are evidence of the domestic law in individual states and not evidence of international law generally: *McElhinney v Williams* [1996] 1 ILRM 276, SC and [1995] 3 IR 382, SC.

The State may also exercise *extraterritorial jurisdiction* in accordance with the generally recognised principles of international law: 1937 Constitution, new art 29(8) inserted by referendum in 1998: Nineteenth Amendment to the Constitution Act 1998 to enable the State to be bound by the *Good Friday Agreement* (qv).

The rules which define the rights and duties as between the citizens of different states is known as *private international law* (qv) or *conflict of laws*.

International Maritime Organisation. The specialised agency of the United Nations which has the objective of providing machinery for the co-operation amongst governments in relation to regulations and practices regarding shipping, maritime safety, efficiency of navigation and prevention and control of marine pollution from ships. See website: *www.imo.org*. See OIL POLLUTION.

International Monetary Fund. The international organisation of 184 member countries, established as a specialised agency of the United Nations, to promote international monetary co-operation, exchange stability, and orderly exchange relationships; to foster economic growth and high levels of employment; and to provide temporary financial assistance to countries to ease balance of payment adjustments. See website: *www.imf.org*. See BRETTON WOODS AGREEMENT.

international road freight licence. See CARRIER'S LICENCE.

international sale of goods. A contract for the international sale of goods is a contract made by parties whose place of business (or, if they have none, habitual residences) are in territories of different states and one of three other conditions are satisfied. Such a contract may negative or vary any right or duty or liability which would otherwise arise by implication of law. See Sale of Goods Act 1893, s 61(6) and Sale of Goods and Supply of Services Act 1980, s 24. A similar provision exists for international hire-purchase agreements (SGSSA 1980, s 37).

international trade mark. A trade mark which is entitled to protection in the State under the Madrid Protocol: Trade Marks Act 1996, s 58. Under the Protocol, a person who has applied for national registration but who seeks international registration of a trade mark, makes a single application to WIPO (World Intellectual Property Organisation) in Geneva, designating those other contracting countries in which registration is required. The Patents Office in these countries are notified and, if no objection is raised within 18 months, the applicant obtains registration in the designated countries. For procedures to be followed, see Trade Marks (Madrid Protocol) Regulations 2001, SI No 346 of 2001. See 'Ireland in Madrid – a new trade mark system for Ireland' by Niamh Hall in *Irish Business Law* [2001] 134. See TRADE MARK.

Internet. Also called the Net. The worldwide collection of networks and gateways which use a suite of protocols to communicate with one another. The genesis of the Internet was a decentralised network called ARPANET created by the US Department of Defence in 1969 to facilitate communications in the event of a nuclear attack.

A number of other networks were connected over time, so that now the Internet offers a range of services to users, including email, the World Wide Web, Usenet news, Gopher, telnet and others.

A copyright owner of a *work* has the right to make it available to the public; this includes making copies (including the original) of the work available to the public by wire or wireless means, in such a way that members of the public may access the work from a place and at a time chosen by them (including the making available of copies of the work through the *Internet*): Copyright and Related Rights Act 2000, s 40(1)(a). A similar provision applies in relation to recordings of a performance (CRRA 2000, s 205(5)(a)).

The first statutory reference to the *Internet* is believed to be the Dublin Docklands Development Authority Act 1997 which made provision for making a draft masterplan available on the World Wide Web (DDDAA 1997, s 18(4)). Also an initial legal framework to enable the Minister to process online motor tax applications has been provided for: Motor Vehicles (Duties and Licences) Act 2003, s 8.

Many companies have policies in place for their employees regarding the use of the Internet at the workplace. Such policies were brought sharply into focus when the group chief executive of the Bank of Ireland resigned from his post on 29 May 2004: 'This arises from access by me on my PC to Internet sites that contain content that infringed the group's policy on these matters. The content accessed was not illegal but did contain links to material of an adult nature. I now understand and accept that in doing this I breached the policies of the Bank of Ireland': resignation statement of Michael Soden in *Irish Times*, 31 May 2004. As he said subsequently, 'it was a case of curiosity killed the cat'.

The Medical Council has recognised that the Internet and practice websites can provide valuable services to patients. However, it warns that the content of a website must be non-promotional, evidence based and compatible with advertising restrictions: Medical Council, *A Guide to Ethical Conduct and Behaviour* (6th edn, 2004) para 6.2.

The *Irish Internet Association* established in 1997 has a charter with the objective to promote and assist the development of the Internet as a medium for business in Ireland and beyond. [Irish Internet Association, 70 Amiens Street, Dublin1. email: *info@iia.ie*, website: *www.iia.ie*].

A survey conducted by the Central Statistics Office in 2003 revealed that 458,700 households in the Republic of Ireland had computers with Internet access in June 2003, an increase of 75% on November 2000. Almost 10% of the population use the Internet every day. Access to the Internet is available free of charge at public libraries throughout the State.

For legal material sources relevant to Ireland on the Internet, see websites: Irish Government: *www.irlgov.ie*; OASIS: *www.oasis.ie*; BASIS: *www.basis.ie*; Revenue Commissioners: *www.revenue.ie*; Houses of the Oireachtas: *www.irlgov.ie/oireachtas*; BAILII: *www.bailii.org*; IRLII: *www.irlii.org*; Irish Law Page: *www.irish-law.org*; Murdoch's Irish Legal Companion: *www.milcnet.lendac.ie*; Courts Service: *www.courts.ie*; Companies Registration Office: *www.cro.ie*; Land Registry: *www.landregistry.ie*; Delia Venables: *www.venables.co.uk*; FirstLaw: *www.firstlaw.ie*.

For government campaign to assist small companies to use the Internet, see websites: *www.empower.ie* and *www.openup.ie*. See also 'Legal Sources on the Web; Useful sites for Practitioners' by Nuala Byrne in *Bar Review* (February 2004) 28. See 'Competition Law and the Internet' by Stephen Dodd BL in *Bar Review* (December 2000) 133. See 'Is there such a thing as Cyberlaw?' by Rory McIntyre-O'Brien in (2003) 11 ISLR 118. [Bibliography: Butterworths (2); Kelleher & Murray; Reed UK; Oppenheim UK.] See CHILD PORNOGRAPHY; COMPUTERS; CYBER LIBEL; DIGITAL MEDIA DEVELOPMENT LTD; E-MAIL; WORLD WIDE WEB.

internet access provider. Means a person whose business consists wholly or partly in the connection of persons to the Internet, and who holds personal data relating to such persons: Data Protection (Registration) Regulations 2001, SI No 2 of 2001. These regulations provide for the registration under the Data Protection Act 1988, s 16 (as amended by Data Protection (Amendment) Act 2003, s 16) of persons who provide Internet services or telecommunication services and who keep such personal data.

internment. Deprivation of liberty without trial. Internment has been upheld as not infringing the Constitution: art 26 and the Offences Against the State (Amendment) Bill 1940 [1940] IR 470. Following proclamation by the government that specified powers are necessary to secure the preservation of public peace and order, a Minister may order for arrest and detention of a person, if he is of opinion that that person is engaged in activities prejudicial to the preservation of public peace and order or to the security of the State: Offences Against the State (Amendment) Act 1940.

It would appear now that the courts will look behind the exercise of the administrative power and that any opinion formed by the Minister must be one which is *bona fide* held and factually sustainable and not unreasonable: *The State (Lynch) v Cooney* [1983] ILRM 89. Also discovery (qv) may be ordered of documents, relating to the internment of a person, which could be regarded as confidential and sensitive but not as involving national security: *Gormley v Ireland* [1992 HC] 10 ILT Dig 200.

A government-appointed committee, under the chairmanship of Mr Justice Anthony Hederman, concluded that the possibility of internment should be retained and that it should not be ruled out as a matter of principle: *Report of the Committee to Review the Offences Against the State Acts 1939–1998* (2002). See EUROPEAN COURT OF HUMAN RIGHTS; PREVENTATIVE DETENTION; PRISONER OF WAR.

internship registration. Registration of a person, with a primary qualification, in the *Register of Medical Practitioners* as an intern: Medical Practitioners Act 1978, s 28 as inserted by Medical Practitioners (Amendment) Act 2002, ss 2(d) and 6. Such registration was previously called 'provisional' registration in contrast with 'full' and 'temporary' registration. The 2002 Act was introduced to enable medical graduates of EU member state colleges to undertake medical internships in Ireland and also to provide for internship to be undertaken in a variety of health care settings, rather than solely in hospital work (MP(A)A 2002, ss 6, 8 and 9).

An Equality Officer has held that a period of internship in a hospital does not constitute vocational training for the purposes of the Employment Equality Act 1998; an intern is an employee and therefore entitled to equal pay for equal work: *Eng v St James's Hospital* [2002] ELR 143, EO.

interpleader. A procedure whereby a person (who is sued, or expects to be sued, by rival claimants to property which is in his possession and in which he claims no interest and he knows not to whom he can safely give it up), can compel the claimants to *interplead* ie to take proceedings between themselves to determine who is entitled to it. This is a *stakeholder's interpleader* eg where a bank holds money to which there are opposing claims eg see *AIB Finance Ltd v Sligo Co Council* [1995] 1 ILRM 81, HC; *Bank of Ireland v Meeneghan* [1995] 1 ILRM 96, HC. Similarly, a *sheriff's interpleader* arises where goods, taken by the sheriff under an order of *fi fa* (qv), are claimed by a third party. For interpleader provisions in the High Court, see RSC Ord 57; in the Circuit Court, see Circuit Court Rules 2001 Ord 40; and in the District Court, see DCR 1997 Ord 49. See *Fitzpatrick v Criminal Assets Bureau* [2000] 1 ILRM 299, SC. See also Courts Act 1991, s 5.

interpretatio chartarum benigne facienda est ut res magis valeat quam pereat. [The construction of deeds is to be made liberally, that the thing may rather avail than perish.]

interpretation clause. A clause, eg in a statute or deed, which provides that certain specified words and phrases used therein have certain meanings eg *In this Act, except where the context otherwise requires, 'valuable consideration' means consideration in money or money's worth*: Succession Act 1965, s 3(1).

interpretation of legislation. Statutes are interpreted by the literal rule, the golden rule, the mischief rule, the purposive rule, or by the maxims, *ejusdem generis*, and *generalia specialibus non derogant* (qqv). See also Interpretation Act 1937; Interpretation (Amendment) Act 1993; Interpretation (Amendment) Act 1997.

The Supreme Court has held that there are three basic rules of interpretation: (a) if the statute is directed to the public at large, a word or expression should be given its ordinary or colloquial meaning; (b) when a word or expression creates a penal or taxation liability, it should be construed strictly; (c) when a word is a simple word which has widespread and unambiguous currency, the judge's own experience of its use should be drawn on to construe it: *Inspector of Taxes v Kiernan* [1981] IR 117 and [1982] ILRM 13. When interpreting a *taxing statute*, the court will give it only the meaning which can be gleaned from the literal words of it; the court may not look to the intention of the legislature in order to read in or imply any additional meaning to the words used: *Saatchi & Saatchi Advertising Ltd v McGarry* [1998] 2 IR 562, SC.

There is a presumption that words in a statute were not used without a meaning and were not tautologous or superfluous; effect must be given, if possible, to all the words used, for the legislature must be deemed not to waste words or to say anything in vain: Egan J in *Cork County Council v Whillock* [1993] 1 IR 231, SC.

The court has no function to add to or delete from express statutory provisions so as to achieve objectives which to the court appear desirable: *McCabe v South City & County Investment Co Ltd* [1998] 1 ILRM 264, SC. Also words or phrases must not be inserted into a statutory provision in order to interpret it: *McDonagh v County Borough of Galway* [1993] ITLR (23 August), SC. However, where the intention of the legislature is plain on the construction of a statute as a whole, the court is entitled to transpose, interpolate or otherwise alter words to give effect to the statute and avoid manifest absurdity or injustice: *Re Employment Equality Bill 1996* [1997] 2 IR 321, SC and ELR 132.

There is no principle which presumes that a general statute does not apply to the State or State agencies; no rule exists whereby the executive enjoys a special position in regard to legislation: *Howard v Commissioners for Public Works* [1993] 665, SC.

In construing a particular Irish statutory provision, no provision of another statute may be used as an aid or a guide unless that other statutory provision is *in pari materia,* that is forming part of the same statutory context: *The State (Sheehan) v Ireland* [1988] ILRM 437, SC. The *long title* of an Act is only relevant to the issue of interpretation where the text of a statutory provision is ambiguous or equivocal: *The People (DPP) v Quilligan* [1987] ILRM 606.

See also *Cooke v Walsh* [1984] ILRM 208; *DPP v Go Travel Ltd* [1991] ILRM 577, SC; *McCann v O'Culachain* [1986] ILRM 229; *Texaco v Murphy* [1992] ILRM 304, SC; *Irish Bank of Commerce v O'Hara* [1992] ITLR (10 August), SC; *Ó Síocháin v Neenan* [1997] 2 ILRM 451, HC and [1998] 2 ILRM 444, SC; *DPP (Ivers) v Murphy* [1999] 1 IR 115, SC. See CONSTRUE AS ONE; CONVENTION; DIRECTIVE, EC; EXPLANATORY MEMORANDUM; FEMININE GENDER; INTERNATIONAL AGREEMENTS; MARGINAL NOTES; NOSCITUR A SOCIIS; PREAMBLE; REPEAL.

interpretation of legislation, European. The fundamental principle of interpretation to be applied to EC *regulations* and *directives* is the schematic and teleological approach e g looking at the purpose rather than the cause: *Bosphorus Hava v Minister for Transport* [1994] 2 ILRM 551, HC. In construing domestic legislation which implements European law, the court is required to adopt a *teleological* approach to interpreting the former so as to achieve and implement the true scheme and purpose of the latter: *Coastal Line Container Terminal Ltd v SIPTU* [2000] 1 IR 549, HC at 559, and ELR 1 at 11.

Particular legislation may require that its provisions be construed to give effect to an EU Directive and for the court to have regard to the provisions of the Directive and its preamble e g Package Holidays and Travel Trade Act 1995, s 2(7). The Waste Management Act 1996 must be interpreted in a way that achieves the objective of the Act: *Wicklow County Council v Fenton* [2003] 1 ILRM 279, HC.

interpretation of legislation, parliamentary history. A court may, as an aid to the construction of a statute or one of its provisions, consider its *legislative history*, a term which includes the legislative antecedents of the provisions under construction, as well as pre-parliamentary and parliamentary material relating to it: *People (DPP) v McDonagh* [1996] 2 ILRM 468, SC and 1 IR 565. But a statute cannot be interpreted on the basis of either speculation or information obtained with regard to the belief of statutory draftsmen or legislators: *Howard v Commissioners for Public Works* [1993] 665, SC. Even though it might be argued that Irish legislation was a copy of English legislation, it was a doubtful exercise to take into account English legislative history: *Devlin v Roche* [2002] 2 ILRM 192, SC and 2 IR 360.

Generally a Bill, as it was introduced in the Oireachtas, will not be admitted in evidence to assist the court as to the meaning of words contained in the ultimate Act. However, the High Court has held that while it was clear that, in general, statutes should be interpreted solely by their express wording, in circumstances where the validity of a statute under the Constitution was in issue, the court should consider admitting the Bill in evidence for the protection of constitutional rights, the presumption of constitutionality, and the double construction rule which gives effect to that presumption: *An Blascaod Mór Teo v Commissioners of Public Works (No 2)* [2000] 1 IR 1. The court is entitled to consider pre-parliamentary materials, including a Law Reform Commission Report, as an aid to the construction of an enactment: *S O'C v Governor of Curragh Prison* [2000] 2 ILRM 76, HC.

While it has been held that the court cannot rely on the expression of a Minister, given in the Dáil, when interpreting an Act: *Conaty v Tipperary (NR) Co Council* [1989] 7 ILT & SJ 222; it has also been held that a court may, in certain circumstances, get legitimate assistance in construing a statutory provision from a statement or explanation made by the Minister who piloted the relevant Bill through the Oireachtas; however the other side should be given prior notice that such statements are intended to be relied upon: *Crilly v T & J Farrington Ltd* [2000] 1 ILRM 548, HC.

Also, Dáil and Seanad debates may be admissible as an aid to understanding what motivated the legislature in framing a statute: *Wavin Pipes Ltd v Hepsworth Iron Co Ltd* [1982] FSR 32. However, the Supreme Court has recently sounded a note of caution regarding the use of Ministerial statements in construing and interpreting statutes: *Crilly v T & J Farrington Ltd* [2001] 3 IR 251, SC and [2002] 1 ILRM 161, SC. The Supreme Court has now stated firmly that the courts would not entertain the citation of passages from debates in the Oireachtas with a view to ascertaining the intention behind the passing of legislation by the Oireachtas: *Controller of Patents v Ireland* [2001] 4 IR 229, SC. The Supreme Court also held that it would not be justified in having regard to what was said during the passing of a Bill in the Oireachtas: *Baby O v Minister for Justice* [2002] 2 IR 169, SC and [2003] 1 ILRM 241. See Kerr, *Parliamentary History as an Aid to the Interpretation of Statutes* in 11 ILT & SJ (1993) 72.

interpretation of legislation, reform. Under draft legislation, it is proposed to replace and update all former Interpretation Acts, with the exception of the Interpretation (Amendment) Act 1997 which is being left as a stand-alone Act: Interpretation Bill 2000. The language of the previous Acts is proposed to be updated and in some cases expanded to have broader application. Also a new provision will enable Acts, Regulations and other subordinate legislation to be enacted without the need for *interpretation provisions,* dealing with such matters as references to enactments, including amendments to those enactments.

See LRC Consultation Paper, *Statutory Drafting and Interpretation: Plain language and the Law* (LRC CP 14, 1999). See also Law Reform Commission Report on *Statutory Drafting and Interpretation: Plain Language and the Law*: (LRC 61, 2000 of December 2000). See 'Plain language: the end of the road for recondite legislation' by Brain Hunt in *Bar Review* (October/November 2001) 47. See also website: *www.plainlanguage.gov/library/kimble.htm*.

interpreters. See IRISH LANGUAGE; OATH, INTERPRETER'S.

interrogation. Questioning of suspects. As a matter of law, there is no impropriety in questioning a suspect with only one garda present: *The People (DPP) v Connolly* [2003] 2 IR 1, CCA. The Minister may provide by regulations for the electronic recording of questioning of persons in police custody: Criminal Justice Act 1984, s 27. Regulations have been made to provide for the electronic recording of interviews with suspects, detained under certain specified Acts, in Garda stations where equipment has been provided and installed for this purpose: Electronic Recording of Interviews Regulations 1997, SI No 74 of 1997. The first time that such an electronic recording was produced in an Irish court and viewed by a jury was in 2002: *DPP v John Reilly* (2002) Irish Times, 2 May 2002. See 'Video Recording of Accused Persons in Custody' by Mary Rose Gearty BL in *Bar Review* (April 2004) 65. See JUDGES' RULES; EXAMINATION; SOLICITOR, ACCESS TO.

interrogatories. Written questions, answerable on affidavit, which a party may, with leave, put to the other party to an action: RSC Ord 31. Their purpose is to obtain admissions and to limit the scope of an opponent's case. Interrogatories are also intended to avoid injustice where one party has the knowledge and ability to prove facts which are important to the opposing party's case and that party does not have the knowledge or ability to prove these facts: *Bula Ltd v Tara Mines Ltd* [1995] 1 ILRM 401. Answers to interrogatories are binding.

No party to litigation is entitled *as of right* to have interrogatories delivered and answered. Leave to deliver interrogatories will be granted where it is established that delivery would serve a clear litigious purpose by saving costs or promoting the fair and efficient conduct of the action in question. Interrogatories as to opinions on matters of law, such as the meaning or effect of documents or statements are not permissible: *Woodfab Ltd v Coillte Teoranta* [1998] 1 ILRM 381, HC and [2000] 1 IR 20, HC. An order requiring a party to answer interrogatories will be refused if a fair hearing of the issues between the parties might be prejudiced by it. See also *Heaton v Goldney* [1910] 1 KB 758.

Interrogatories may be delivered either to obtain information from the interrogated party about the issues that arise in an action or to obtain admissions; if they seek information, they must relate to the issues raised in the pleadings and not to the evidence which a party wishes to adduce in order to establish his case: *Mercantile Credit Co Ltd v Heelan* [1994] 1 ILRM 406, HC.

If information sought by interrogatories can be said to be properly at the disposal of the party interrogated, then the party cannot avoid giving an answer merely on the grounds that the subject matter is not within his personal knowledge: *Money Markets International Stock Brokers Ltd (in liquidation) v Fanning & Ors* [2001] 1 ILRM 1, HC and [2000] 3 IR 215, HC. For the Circuit Court, see Circuit Court Rules 2001 Ord 32. For interrogatories in *commercial proceedings* (qv), see RSC Ord 63A, rr 6(1)(vi), 9–13, and App X, inserted by Rules of the Superior Courts (Commercial Proceedings) 2004, SI No 2 of 2004. [Bibliography: Barron.] See NEWSPAPER RULE.

interrogatories, fishing. Written questions to elicit answers to support a case which is lacking in substance; a party will not be required to answer such questions. See *Pankhurst v Hamilton* [1886] 2 TLR 682. See RSC Ord 31.

InterTradeIreland. See TRADE AND BUSINESS BODY.

intervener. A person who voluntarily intervenes in an action with the leave of the court or the Master of the High Court: RSC Ord 63, r 1(13). It may occur in actions for recovery of land (RSC Ord 12, r 20), in matrimonial causes (RSC Ord 70, r 19), in probate actions (RSC Ord 12, r 14) and in Admiralty actions *in rem* (RSC Ord 64, r 14). The Supreme Court has held that the position of an *amicus curiae* is quite different from that of an intervener, as the *amicus curiae*, unlike an intervener, has no right of appeal and is not normally entitled to adduce evidence: *Iwuala v Minister for Justice* [2004] 1 ILRM 27, SC. Contrast with AMICUS CURIAE.

intervening act. See CAUSATION; NOVUS ACTUS INTERVENIENS.

interview. (1) Before an arrested person is interviewed, the garda conducting the interview must identify himself and any other garda present by name and rank to the arrested person: Treatment of Persons in Custody in Garda Síochána Stations Regulations 1987, SI No 119 of 1987, reg 12. The interview must be conducted in a fair and humane manner. Not more than two gardaí may question the arrested person at any one time and not more than four gardaí may be present at any one time during the interview. If an interview has

lasted for four hours, it should be either terminated or adjourned for a reasonable time. As far as practicable, interviews should take place in rooms set aside for that purpose. Where an arrested person asks for a solicitor, he should not be asked to make a written statement in relation to an offence until a reasonable time for the attendance of the solicitor has elapsed.

Except with the authority of the member in charge, an arrested person should not be questioned between midnight and 8am in relation to an offence, which authority shall not be given unless: (i) he has been taken to the station during that period, (ii) in the case of a person detained under s 4 of the Criminal Justice Act 1984, he has not consented in writing to the suspension of questioning in accordance with subsection (6) of that section, or (iii) the member in charge has reasonable grounds for believing that to delay questioning the person would involve a risk of injury to persons, serious loss of or damage to property, destruction of or interference with evidence or escape of accomplices.

Where an arrested person is deaf or there is doubt about his hearing ability, he should not be questioned in relation to an offence in the absence of an interpreter, if one is reasonably available, without his written consent.

An arrested person who is under the influence of intoxicating liquor or drugs to the extent that he is unable to appreciate the significance of questions put to him or his answers should not be questioned in relation to an offence while he is in that condition except with the authority of the member in charge.

A record must be made of each interview either by the garda conducting it or by another garda who is present. It must include particulars of the time the interview began and ended, any breaks in it, the place of the interview and the names and ranks of the members present.

Where an interview is not recorded by electronic or other similar means, the record must: (i) be made in the notebook of the garda concerned or in a separate document and must be as complete as practicable, (ii) if it is practicable to do so and the garda concerned is of opinion that it will not interfere with the conduct of the interview, be made while the interview is in progress or otherwise as soon as practicable afterwards, and (iii) be signed by the member making it and include the date and time of signature. A record should be made of the times during which an arrested person is interviewed and the members present at each interview. [Bibliography: Walsh D (3).]

(2) It is not permissible to convert, unannounced, an interview into a disciplinary hearing: *O'Scanaill v Minister for Agriculture* [1993] ELR 176, HC. See CAUTION; CHILD SUSPECT; INTERROGATION; MARRIAGE, NULLITY OF; OFFENCES AGAINST THE STATE; VIDEO RECORDING.

interview board. Gender imbalance on an employment interview board, although highly undesirable, does not, in itself, lead to a *prima facie* finding of discrimination in every case; nonetheless, such a practice is potentially discriminatory and can form part of the evidential chain on which a claim of discrimination could be made out: *Mitchell v Southern Health Board* [2001] ELR 201, LC. In a particular case the Labour Court held that it was a matter of concern that there was a lack of notes, a lack of transparency in the selection process and an absence of predetermined criteria for the assessment of applicants: *Gleeson v Rotunda Hospital* [2000] ELR 206, LC.

There is no obligation on a selection board, who conduct an employment interview process, to give reasons for its decision; the giving of such reasons would be gratuitously unfair, perhaps offensive, and would serve no useful purpose: *O'Dwyer v McDonagh* [1997] ELR 91, HC. In this case it was held that it was not for the Court to decide whether the procedure adopted by the board was the best one; the Court had no function in the matter unless the procedure was so flawed as to vitiate the validity of the selection process.

Remarks made at interview which identified an applicant by her sex could give rise to a *prima facie* finding of discrimination, particularly as the questions were not put to the male applicants (*Gleeson* case). Questions asked at interview concerning *marital status* can constitute discrimination contrary to the Employment Equality Act 1977, s 2(a) and 3: Medical *Council & Barrington* EE9/1988; *Trinity College Dublin & McGhee* EE1/1988 in 7 ILT & SJ (1989) 126; *Corrib Airport Ltd v A Worker* [1995] ELR 81, LC; *Phelan v Michael Stein Travel* [1999] ELR 59, EO. See Employment Equality Act 1998, repealing 1977 Act and

widening discrimination grounds. See 'Discriminating Questions in Job Interviews' by Flynn in 11 ILT & SJ (1993) 221. See DISCRIMINATION.

intestacy. Dying intestate ie without making a valid will. Partial intestacy is the leaving of a will which validly disposes of part only of the property of the deceased, so that the rest goes on an intestacy. *Equity* (qv) leans against an intestacy: *Re Estate of Egan* [1990] 8 ILT Dig 168.

The Law Reform Commission has recommended, in relation to the Succession Act 1965, s 126, that the operative date on intestacy should be the same as where there is a will, ie from the date of death where the property was vested in the deceased at that time: Report on *Positive Covenants over freehold land and other proposals* (LRC 70, 2003). [Bibliography: Keating.] See SUCCESSION, LAW OF; INTESTATE SUCCESSION.

Intestate Estates Fund Deposit Account. This deposit account which is under the control of the Minister for Finance was established pursuant to the State Property Act 1954. The Minister is authorised to make payment out of the account in connection with the administration of the estates of deceased persons and such other payments as the Minister thinks proper (SPA 1954, s 36). Section 36 has now been amended to empower the Minister to make payments from the account to the *Dormant Accounts Fund*: Dormant Accounts Act 2001, s 28.

intestate succession. The residuary estate of an intestate devolves according to the Succession Act 1965, ss 66 to 73 (as amended by Family Law (Miscellaneous Provisions) Act 1997, s 6) under rules which apply to both real and personal property:

(1) If there is a surviving spouse and issue, then the spouse takes two-thirds and the issue take one-third.

(2) If there is a surviving spouse and no issue, the spouse takes all.

(3) If there are issue and no spouse, the issue take all; if they are in equal relationship to the deceased, the distribution is in equal shares among them; if they are not, it is *per stirpes* (qv).

(4) If there are no surviving issue or spouse, the parents of the deceased take all in equal shares; if only one parent survives, that parent takes all.

(5) In the event that there are no such survivors, the estate is distributed among brothers and sisters in equal shares. If a brother or sister does not survive the intestate, the children of that brother or sister (where any other brother or sister survive) represent their parent and divide his or her share. If the intestate leaves no surviving brothers or sisters, his estate is distributed in equal shares among the children of his brothers and sisters and not *per stirpes*.

(6) In all other cases, the estate is distributed in equal shares among the next-of-kin.

(7) In default of next-of-kin, the estate passes to the State as ultimate intestate successor. See DISCLAIMED ESTATE; LETTERS OF ADMINISTRATION; NEXT-OF-KIN.

intimate examination. 'Any intimate examination (of a patient) should be accompanied by an explanation. The patient, irrespective of age or gender, should be offered a chaperone': Medical Council, *A Guide to Ethical Conduct and Behaviour* (6th edn, 2004) para 3.9.

intimidation, crime of. A person commits an offence who harms or threatens, menaces or in any other way intimidates or puts in fear another person, with the intention of causing the investigation of an offence or the course of justice to be obstructed, perverted or interfered with: Criminal Justice Act 1999, s 41. The person intimidated must be a person assisting the gardaí in the investigation, or a witness, or a juror or potential juror, or a member of his family. See CRIMINAL ASSETS BUREAU; DEPOSITION; RELOCATED WITNESS; TELEVISION LINK.

intimidation, tort of. Arises where harm is inflicted by the use of *unlawful threats* whereby the lawful liberty of others to do as they please is interfered with. It may arise by intimidation of other persons which results in injury to the plaintiff. To constitute the tort there must be a threat, the threat must be to do an unlawful act, and there must be a submission to the threat. See *Rookes v Barnard* [1964] AC 1129; *Whelan v Madigan* [1978] HC. See also ANTI-SOCIAL BEHAVIOUR.

intoxicated. Means under the intoxicating influence of any alcoholic drink, drug, solvent or other substance or a combination of substances: Criminal Justice (Public Order) Act 1994, s 4. It is an offence for a person to be present in any public place while being intoxicated to such an extent as to give rise to a reasonable apprehension that he might endanger himself or any other person in his vicinity (CJ(PO)A 1994, s 4(1)). [Bibliography: McAuley & McCutcheon.] See also DRUNKENNESS; DRUNKEN PERSON; DRUNKEN DRIVING; SAFETY AT WORK.

intoxicating liquor. The sale and consumption of intoxicating liquor is controlled by the Licensing Acts 1833 to 2003 and by the Registration of Clubs Acts 1904 to 2003. The Intoxicating Liquor Act 2000 made extensive changes to the law, particularly in relation to: (a) a relaxation in relation to the hours during which it is lawful to sell intoxicating liquor in licensed premises and registered clubs, (b) a strengthening of the law relating to underage drinking, (c) a new system for the grant of licences for premises never before registered, (d) an extension of the scope of licences for greyhound race tracks and racecourses, and (e) new and increased penalties for breaches of the law. The Intoxicating Liquor Act 2003 made further changes, aimed mainly at combating drunkenness and disorderly conduct, as well as underage and binge drinking.

Closing times are: Sunday (11pm), Monday–Thursday (11.30pm), Friday–Saturday (12.30am of following day), eve of public holiday (12.30am of following day), St Patrick's Day (12.30am of following day), Christmas Day and Good Friday (closed): (ILA 2000, s 3 as amended by ILA 2003, s 10). Thirty minutes *drinking-up time* is also permitted; however, there is a prohibition on the provision of entertainment during this time (ILA 2003, s 12).

Restaurants which have a *wine on-licence* are now permitted to supply beer with a meal (ILA 2000, s 26). There is a relaxation of the conditions relating to *Special Restaurant Licences* (ILA 2000, s 27). See *Ampleforth Ltd t/a Fitzwilliam Hotel v Cherating Ltd* [2003] FL 7319, SC. There is also a relaxation in the conditions under which a wine retailer's and beer retailer's off-licence may be obtained (ILA 2000, ss 36–37).

There is provision for increased and new penalties where alcohol is served to underage persons (under 18) including increased fines, temporary closure of the premises, and abolition of the *reasonable belief* defence in relation to the sale of intoxicating liquor to an underage person (ILA 2000, ss 13–16). A person who is under 18 (but not under 16) must not be permitted to work behind the bar in a licensed premises but may be permitted to work at serving at tables (ILA 2000, s 14).

The 2000 Act also rationalises the manner in which a licence may be acquired for a premises never before licensed; a new licence may be issued anywhere in the State for one existing licence, subject to certain conditions (ILA 2000, s 18). There is also provision for the upgrading of restricted and other licences (ILA 2000, ss 19–20).

Discrimination is prohibited by law; however, actions taken in good faith for the sole purpose of ensuring compliance with the provisions of licensing legislation, will not constitute discrimination: Equal Status Act 2000, s 15(2). A licensee may set a minimum age for the sale of intoxicating liquor above the statutory minimum age of 18 and this is not discriminatory on age grounds, if implemented in good faith and a notice setting out the policy is displayed in a conspicuous place (ESA 2000, s 15 as amended by ILA 2003, s 25).

The 2003 Act also, *inter alia*, provides for: (a) the elimination of the 'happy hour', (b) mandatory temporary closure of licensed premises, (c) non-uniformed gardaí to have powers to enforce the licensing laws, (d) regulations to prohibit or restrict licensees from engaging in practices to encourage persons to consume alcohol to an excessive extent, and (e) the District Court to have jurisdiction for redress for prohibited conduct regarding entry to licensed premises. See *DPP v Joyce* [2003] FL 8078, HC and [2004] 1 ILRM 300; *Re Whitesheet Inn Ltd* [2003] 2 ILRM 177, HC. See Constance Cassidy SC in *Bar Review* (July 2003) 146.

There were indications in June 2004 that a major overhaul of the liquor licensing laws was planned by the Minister for Justice, including the issuing of new licences for small pubs and cafés, a cap on the size allowed for a licensed premises to curb the increase of 'superpubs', a streamlining of the licensing application and renewal system, and greater power for the gardaí in respect of breaches of the terms of licences. [Bibliography: Cassidy; McDonald M (3); McGrath M (1); Woods (2).] See BAR; COMMISSION ON LIQUOR LICENSING; CLOSURE ORDER; DRUG TRAFFICKING; EXCISE LAW; EXCLUSION ORDER; OFF-LICENCE; SHADOW LICENCE HOLDER; THEATRE.

intoxicating liquor licence. For intoxicating liquor licensing procedure, see DCR

1997 e g off-licence (Ord 68, r 1); restaurant (Ord 69); wine retails on-licence (Ord 70); special exemption orders (Ord 71); general exemption order (Ord 72); exemption for special events (Ord 73); exemptions for licensed business on Sunday afternoons and St. Patrick's Day (Ord 74); exemptions for unlicensed business on Sunday mornings and St. Patrick's Day (Ord 75); occasional licences (Ord 76); ad-interim transfers of licences (Ord 77); transfer of licences held by nominees (Ord 78); certificate of transfer (Ord 79); objections to renewal of licences (Ord 80); annual licensing court (Ord 81); register of licences (Ord 82); registration of clubs (Ord 83).

Every application to the Circuit Court in respect of an excise licence for the sale of intoxicating liquor must be made at the court held in the town nearest the premises to which the application relates, and in the country in which such premises are situate: Circuit Court Rules 2001 Ord 49.

See *O'Rourke v Grittar* [1995] 1 ILRM 532, SC and 1 IR 541; *Application of Thank God It's Friday Ltd* [1990] ILRM 228; *Perfect Pies Ltd v Doran* [1993] ILRM 737, HC; *Re an Application by Tivoli Cinema Ltd* [1992] ILRM 522, HC; *Jaggers Restaurant Ltd v Aherne* [1988] IR 308, SC. [Bibliography: Cassidy; McDonald; McGrath M(1); Woods (2).] See BAR; DRUG TRAFFICKING; OFF-LICENCE; SHADOW LICENCE HOLDER; SPECIAL EXEMPTION ORDER; THEATRE.

intoxicating liquor licence renewal. Revised procedures for the renewal of intoxicating liquor licences and registered club certificates have been in operation since 1988. It is no longer necessary to produce a certificate of the District Court to the Revenue Commissioners, except in specified circumstances e g where a notice of objection has been lodged. Club certificates are renewable at the annual licensing District Court in September and not, as heretofore from the date of issue or date of last renewal. Also a *tax clearance certificate* is now required before a licence will be renewed at the annual licensing: Finance Act 1992, s 242, now Taxes Consolidation Act 1997, s 1094 as amended by Intoxicating Liquor Act 2003, s 21(7).

An application for a licence, or a renewal or transfer of a licence will be refused by the Revenue Commissioners unless accompanied by: (a) a *certificate of incorporation*, if the applicant is a company, or (b) a *certificate of registration*, if the applicant is carrying on business under a name that is not his own: Intoxicating Liquor Act 2000, s 38. See Courts (No 2) Act 1986 as amended by Licensing (Combating Drug Abuse) Act 1997, s 19. See DCR 1997 Ord 81 and Ord 68 to Ord 83.

intra vires. [Within the power of.] See ULTRA VIRES.

intrinsic. Essential to, or inherent in, something.

inure. Enure; to take effect.

invalidity pension. The social welfare pension to which a person may be entitled who is *permanently incapable of work*; a person may be disqualified if he fails, without due cause, to observe any prescribed rule of behaviour e g to submit to a medical examination: Social Welfare (Consolidation) Act 1993, ss 95–99. See Social Welfare Act 2003, s 2(2)(c).

invasion. The government is empowered to take whatever steps they consider may be necessary for the protection of the State in the case of an actual invasion: 1937 Constitution, art 28(3)(2).

invented word. Formerly, for the purpose of registration of a trade mark in Part A of the register, a word which was new, which was pronounceable and which had no obvious meaning for an Irishman: *Re ACEC (Ireland) Ltd* [1964] IR 201. It has been held that the time to be considered as to whether a word was an invented word or not, was the date of the application to register the word and not the date of the hearing: *Willys-Overland Motors Inc v Controller of Industrial Property* [1947] IR 344. Words such as *cosco, SAF, Jeep,* and *Zing* have been held to be invented words, whereas *Gramaphone* and *cellular* have not been so held. See also *Re Hamilton Cosco Inc* [1966] IR 266; *La Soudure Autogene Francaise v Controller of Patents, Designs and Trade Marks* [1982] ILRM 207; *Application of Schweppes (Overseas) Ltd* [1970] IR 209. See DISTINCTIVE MARK; PART A; TRADE MARK.

invention. An invention is not defined in the Patents Act 1992, although certain matters are excluded (e g an aesthetic creation) and certain requirements are specified for an invention to be patentable e g *new*, involving an *inventive step*, and being susceptible of *industrial application*. Micro-organisms produced by genetic engineering are not excluded from patent protection: *National Research Development Corporation's Application* [1986] FSR 620, distinguishing *Ranks Hovis McDougall Ltd v Controller of Patents* [1979] IR 142. See INVENTOR; PATENTABLE INVENTION; MICRO-ORGANISMS; SIMULTANEOUS INVENTION.

inventive step. See PATENTABLE INVENTION.

inventor. The actual deviser of an invention: Patents Act 1992, s 2(1). The right to a patent belongs to the inventor or his successor in title; where the inventor is an employee, the right to a patent depends on the law of the State where the employee is employed e g in Ireland in the absence of any express term to the contrary, the employee is presumed to be a trustee for his employer in any invention made in the course of his duty as an employee (PA 1992, s 16). The inventor is entitled to be mentioned as such in any patent granted for the invention (PA 1992, s 17).

investigation. Employees have a duty to assist their employer in any investigation carried out by the employer into suspected unusual conduct amounting to malpractice, criminal activity or unacceptable behaviour and this duty may be an implied term of a contract of service: *Pacelli v Irish Distillers Ltd* [2004] ELR 25, EAT. See ACCIDENT; COMMISSION OF INVESTIGATION.

investigation of company. There are three main investigations which may be made of a company: (a) an investigation of the affairs of a company ordered by the court; (b) an investigation of the true ownership of a company ordered by the Director of Corporate Enforcement (formerly, the Minister), and (c) an examination of company documents without an inspector being appointed: Companies Act 1990, ss 7–24; Company Law Enforcement Act 2001, s 19–35. See RSC Ord 75B inserted by SI No 278 of 1991.

See also Building Societies Act 1989, ss 45–47; Stock Exchange Act 1995, ss 57 and 64; Investment Intermediaries Act 1995, s 66; Irish Takeover Panel Act 1997, s 21; Credit Union Act 1997, s 92 as amended by Central Bank and Financial Services Authority of Ireland Act 2003, s 35, Sch 1; Companies (Amendment) (No 2) Act 1999, s 53. See 'Investigations under the Companies Act 1990' by McGrath in 11 ILT & SJ (1993) 264. See Law Reform Commission, *Consultation Paper on Public Inquiries including Tribunals of Inquiry* (LRC CP 22, 2003).

[Bibliography: Cahill N.] See EXAMINATION RE COMPANY.

investigation of company by Court. The High Court is empowered to appoint inspectors to investigate the affairs of a company on the application of the company, a director, a creditor, or a certain minimum number of members: Companies Act 1990, s 7. In addition, the court may, on the application of the Director of Corporate Enforcement (formerly, the Minister), appoint inspectors if it is satisfied that there are circumstances suggesting illegality or fraud or of some members being unfairly prejudiced (CA 1990, s 8). The inspectors have wide powers regarding the production of books relating to the company, directors' private bank accounts, and attendance before the inspectors for examination on oath (CA 1990, ss 9–10).

The powers given to the inspectors under s 10 are no greater than the public interest requires; accordingly, bank officials are not entitled to refuse to answer questions properly posed to them by the inspectors: *In the Matter of National Irish Bank Ltd* [1999] 1 ILRM 321, SC and 3 IR 145.

The court having considered the inspectors' report, may make such order as it deems fit, including the winding up of a body corporate or the remedying of any disability; the Director (formerly, the Minister) may also present a winding-up petition (CA 1990, s 12). In giving access to the Revenue Commissioners to confidential information accumulated by inspectors investigating Ansbacher Bank, the High Court held that the public interest in the assessment and collection of taxes outweighed the contractual right to confidentiality and the constitutional right to privacy of the individuals and companies mentioned in the inspectors' report: *Revenue Commissioners v Ansbacher Bank* [2004] (26 May), HC.

The investigation of a company by an inspector is not the administration of justice and consequently is not required to be dealt with in public: *In the matter of County Glen plc* [1995] 1 ILRM 213, HC. See also *In the Matter of NIB (No 2)* [1999] 2 ILRM 443, HC. For amendments to 1990 Act, see Company Law Enforcement Act 2001, ss 19–35. The final report of the court-appointed inspectors into the affairs of National Irish Bank Ltd was presented to the High Court on 12 July 2004 and published on 30 July 2004. The report is available on website: *www.odce.ie*. [Bibliography: Cahill N.]

investigation of company by Director of Corporate Enforcement. The Director of Corporate Enforcement (formerly, the Minister) may appoint *inspectors* to investigate the membership of any company for the purpose of determining the *true persons* (qv) who are financially interested in the success or failure of the company or able to control or materially to influence the policy of the company: Companies Act 1990, s 14. The inspectors appointed have similar powers to those appointed by the court, except in respect of access to private bank accounts. An inspector can compel production of documents which pre-date the 1990 Act: *Chestervale Properties & Hoddle Investments v Glackin & Ors* [1992] ILRM 221, HC. An inspector is entitled to 'tear the veil of secrecy of ownership from the company' and identify those financially interested in its success or failure, even where the company was registered outside the State: *Desmond & Dedeir Ltd v Glackin* [1993] 3 IR 67, SC.

An inspector is not required to accept averments (made by a person he wishes to examine on oath) as *prima facie* evidence of their truth: *Probets & Freezone Investments Ltd v Glackin* [1993] 3 IR 134, SC. A financial institution must comply with a request for information made by an inspector and does not have to consult with its client; the 1990 Act overrides any question of confidentiality: *Glackin v Trustee Savings Bank* [1993] 11 ILT Dig 114, HC. The interim and final report of an inspector are admissible to give all findings of primary facts, clearly expressed as such, the status of proven facts, unless disproved: *Countyglen plc v Carway* [1998] 2 IR 540, HC. See also *Lyons v Curran* [1993] ILRM 375, HC; *Minister for Justice v Siuicre Éireann cpt* [1993] 11 ILT Dig 114, HC; *Countyglen plc v Carway* [1995] 1 IR 208, HC.

The Director (formerly, the Minister), without the appointment of inspectors, can compel a wide variety of companies to produce to an *authorised officer* the documents he specifies (CA 1990, ss 19–20). He can also compel disclosure of information as to the persons interested in shares or debentures (CA 1990, s 15).

He is required to give reasons for the decision to appoint an authorised officer;

failure to do so is a breach of the requirements of fair procedures: *Dunnes Stores Ireland Co v Maloney & Minister for Enterprise* [1999 HC] 1 ILRM 119. It is a matter exclusively for him to form the required opinion, which is necessarily a subjective one but for a purpose contemplated by the 1990 Act and the decision had to be rational and neither arbitrary nor disproportionate: *Dunnes Stores Ireland Company v Ryan & Minister for Enterprise* [2002] 2 IR 60, SC. In this case the High Court subsequently held that s 19(6) was unconstitutional (since repealed, see below).

Provision was made in 2001 for the investigation of a company to be made by the Director of Corporate Enforcement in place of the Minister: Company Law Enforcement Act 2001, ss 19–35. An officer appointed by the Minister under s 19 of CA 1990 is entitled to continue the investigation of a company and to make demands on the company, using delegated powers from the Director: *Dunne v Minister for Enterprise* (2003) Irish Times, 10 May, HC.

In addition amendments in the 2001 Act to the Companies Act 1990, ss 7–11, 13–14, 16, 18–21, 23, 23A and 79, CLEA 2001: (a) increases the security for the costs of an investigation; (b) amends the term '*related company*' to include a company with which the company under investigation has a commercial relationship; (c) protects the *lien* which may exist on company books; (d) extends the list of persons to whom the court may furnish a copy of an inspector's report; (e) creates an offence of destroying or concealing a document relating to an offence which the person knows or suspects the Director is investigating; (f) extends the grounds on which a search warrant may be sought; and (g) empowers the Director to use his powers to respond to a request from a company law authority in another jurisdiction.

A statement made by an individual may be used in evidence against him in any proceedings except proceedings for an offence (other than the offence of failing to produce a book or document or providing a false statement which is false or misleading in a material respect): CLEA 2001, s 29 repealing s 19 of CA 1990. [Bibliography: Cahill N.] See SILENCE, RIGHT TO.

investigator, tribunal. A person appointed by a *tribunal of inquiry* to assist it in the performance of its functions, by carrying out a preliminary investigation into matters relevant to the inquiry: Tribunals of Inquiry (Evidence) (Amendment) Act 2002, s 6. The investigator is empowered to require persons to give information, to produce documents and to answer questions. The High Court may be requested to order a person, who refuses to comply with such requirement, to so comply. Failure to comply with an order of the court constitutes a *contempt of court*. The person has the same privileges and immunities as a witness before the High Court. Importantly, a statement or an admission made to an investigator, cannot be used against the person making it, in any criminal proceedings (TI(E)(A)A 2002, s 8). Also it is an offence for a person not to comply with a requirement of an investigator or to obstruct or hinder the investigator (TI(E)(A)A 2002, s 7).

investment business firm. Any person who provides one or more *investment business services* or *investment advice* to third parties on a professional basis: Investment Intermediaries Act 1995, s 2(1) as amended by Investor Compensation Act 1998, s 52. Excluded are certain bodies already regulated e g banks, stock exchange members, insurance companies, and practising solicitors whose investment business is incidental (IIA 1995, ss 2(6) and 2(7) as amended by ICA 1998, s 44). It is an offence for any company registered in the State or any person operating in the State to act as an investment business firm without an appropriate authorisation (IIA 1995, s 9 as amended by ICA 1998, s 53). Previously, a bond of £25,000 (€31,743) or 25% of turnover, whichever was the greater, was required of the firm for the benefit of its clients in the event of its failure or inability to meet its financial obligations (IIA 1995, s 51 repealed by ICA 1998, s 7). [Bibliography: Clarke B (2).] See INVESTOR COMPENSATION; MONEY LAUNDERING.

investment funds, designated. Funds in a scheme whereby each participant owns a particular share in a particular company, and in which all subscriptions must be paid up by a specific date, after which no new entrants may join. See Designated Funds Act 1985.

investment company. A company limited by shares, the sole object of which is the collective investment of its funds in property with the aim of spreading investment risk and giving members of the company the benefit of the management of its funds: Companies Act 1990, s 253(2). The shareholders may call for the shares to be bought in by the company at any time. A company which falls within the definition of a UCITS is excluded but certain of the UCITS regulations apply to an investment company. To facilitate the operation of these investment companies with variable capital, certain provisions of company law do not apply; however, such companies must be authorised by the Central Bank and are subject to constant supervision by the Bank. See CA 1990, Pt XIII, ss 252–262 as amended by Companies (Amendment) (No 2) Act 1999, s 54. See UNDERTAKINGS FOR COLLECTIVE INVESTMENT IN TRANSFERABLE SECURITIES.

investment entities. Investment companies, investment trusts and unit trusts: Listing Rules 2000, Chs 21 and 26. The rules set out requirements for *listing* on the stock exchange of such entities. See also Irish Stock Exchange publication: *Investment Funds – Listing Requirements and Procedures.*

investment in corporate trades. See BUSINESS DEVELOPMENT SCHEME.

investment incentive scheme. A scheme introduced in 1993 to encourage the start-up of new businesses by providing tax relief of £25,000 (€31,743) per year on a retrospective basis against income of any three of the preceding five years to a person who leaves employment (or an unemployed person) to start his own business: Finance Act 1993, s 25. This in practice allows immediate relief by way of a tax refund on investments up to £75,000 (€95,230). See now Taxes Consolidation Act 1997, s 494. See also BUSINESS DEVELOPMENT SCHEME.

investment intermediary. In 1995 provision was made for the authorisation and supervision of *investment business firms* and *investment product intermediaries* by the Central Bank: Investment Intermediaries Act 1995 as amended by Central Bank and Financial Services Authority of Ireland Act 2003, s 35, Sch 1, and by Central Bank and Financial Services Authority of Ireland Act 2004, Sch 1 and 3. Other investment intermediaries are regulated under different legislation eg banks, insurance companies, building societies, stockbrokers. [Bibliography: Clarke B (2); Johnston & O'Conor; O'Reilly P.] See INVESTMENT BUSINESS FIRM; INVESTOR COMPENSATION; IRISH FINANCIAL SERVICES REGULATORY AUTHORITY.

investment limited partnership. A partnership of two or more persons, the principal business of which, is the investment of its funds in property, and which holds a certificate of authorisation in accordance with the Investment Limited Partnership Act 1994, s 3 as amended by Central Bank and Financial Services Authority of Ireland Act 2003, s 35, Sch 1. The 1994 legislation is intended to allow fund managers in Ireland to offer collective investment opportunities to North American investors, by overcoming the difficulties in utilising the Limited Partnership Act 1907 for such partnerships. These difficulties related to the maximum permissible number of partners, the involvement of the partners in fund management, the withdrawal of funds, and the possibility of judgments being levied against the limited partners. The 1994 Act corrects these difficulties and provides for the establishment, authorisation and regulation of investment limited partnerships by the Central Bank. See also Stock Exchange Act 1995, s 3(1) as amended by CBFSAIA 2003, s 35, Sch 1; Companies (Amendment) (No 2) Act 1999, s 40. [Bibliography: Clarke B (2); Twomey.] See LIMITED PARTNERSHIP; UNDERTAKINGS FOR COLLECTIVE SECURITIES.

investment trust company. A company whose main business consists of the investment of its funds in securities: Central Bank Act 1971, s 2 as amended by Central Bank and Financial Services Authority of Ireland Act 2003, s 35, Sch 1. An investment trust company may not accept or hold deposits: Industrial & Provident Societies (Amendment) Act 1978, s 36. See *Re Irish Commercial Society Group* [1987] HC.

investment undertaking. A unit trust, a UCITS, an authorised investment company, and an investment limited partnership: Taxes Consolidation Act 1997, ss 739B–739G inserted by Finance Act 2000, s 58. Provision has been made for tax to be levied on the occasion of the payment of an investment return to a unit holder who is resident or ordinarily resident in the State. See also TCA 1997, s 904D as inserted by FA 2000, s 68; Finance Act 2002, ss 44 and 45; Finance Act 2003, ss 53 and 56; Finance Act 2004, s 29.

investment services directive. The directive of the EC which has as its objective the creation of a single market in financial services: Directive (EEC) 93/22 of 10 May 1993. See Investor Compensation Act 1998, s 2(1). See 'The future of European Securities Markets: Rewriting the Investment Services Directive' by Norman Ali in *Bar Review* (November 2003) 211.

investments, trustee. See TRUSTEE INVESTMENTS.

investor compensation. The compensation, to which an *eligible* investor may be entitled, amounting to 90% of the amount of the investor's net loss or 20,000 ECU (now, euro) whichever is the lesser: Investor Compensation Act 1998, s 30. Compensation is not payable under this Act just because an investment did not succeed or because the investor obtained bad or negligent advice. It only applies to clients of *investment firms* who are unable to meet their financial obligations ie: (a) an authorised investment business firm, (b) an authorised stock exchange member firm, (c) a credit institution, or (d) an insurance intermediary (ICA 1998, s 2(1).

Certain losses are excluded eg money laundering investments (ICA 1998, s 30). Certain investors are excluded eg professional or institutional clients, local authorities, close relatives, and large companies (ICA 1998, s 2(1)). Payment of compensation is made either by the *Investor Compensation Company Ltd* or pursuant to an approved investor compensation scheme of a professional body (eg accountants) (ICA 1998, ss 10–26 as amended by Central Bank and Financial Services Authority of Ireland Act 2003, s 35, Sch 1).

A practising solicitor providing investment business services in an incidental manner, is not required to obtain an authorisation as an investment business firm, but the services he gives are deemed to be 'legal services' for which he is accountable to his client (ICA 1998, ss 44–47). The supervisory authority for the investor compensation regime is the Central Bank.

The Central Bank, the Irish Stock Exchange Ltd and the Irish Association of Investment Managers were appointed as members of the Investor Compensation Company Ltd: SI No 352 of 1998. For the procedure in relation to an application under the 1998 Act, see RSC Ord 75C inserted by the Rules of the Superior Courts (No 3) (Investor Compensation Act 1998) 2001, SI No 270 of 2001. See also Investor Compensation (Prescription

of Bodies) Regulations, SI No 130 of 2002; and (Prescription of Body and Individuals) Regulations 2002, SI No 147 of 2002. The 1998 Act implements the EU Investment Compensation Directive, Directive No (EC) 97/9. For further amendments to 1998 Act, see Central Bank and Financial Services Authority of Ireland Act 2004, Sch 1 and 3. See SAVINGS PROTECTION SCHEME.

inviolability of dwelling. The *dwelling* of every citizen is inviolable and must not be forcibly entered save in accordance with law: 1937 Constitution, art 40(5). In a case where members of a family live together in the family home, the house as a whole is the *dwelling* of each member of the family; however, if a member of a family occupies a clearly defined portion of the house apart from the other members of the family, then it may well be that the part not so occupied is no longer his dwelling and that the part he separately occupies is his dwelling, as would be the case where a person not a member of the family occupied or was in possession of a clearly defined portion of the house: *The People (A-G) v O'Brien* [1965] IR 142.

Safeguarding of life and limb is more important than the inviolability of the dwelling of a citizen, especially when it is under attack: *DPP v Delaney* [1996] 1 ILRM 536, HC and 3 IR 556; [1998] 1 ILRM 507, SC and [1997] 3 IR 453, SC. See also *DPP v Gaffney* [1988] ILRM 39; *McCormack v ICS Building Society* [1989] HC; *People (DPP) v Kenny* [1990] ILRM 569, SC; *Freeman v DPP* [1996] 3 IR 565, HC; *The People (DPP) v McCann* [1998] 4 IR 397, CCA; *DPP (Dooley) v Lynch* [1998] 4 IR 437, HC; *Hanahoe v Hussey* [1998] 3 IR 69, HC.

See also Road Transport Act 1986, s 16 as amended by Road Transport Act 1999, s 14; Containment of Nuclear Weapons Act 2003, s 7(3); European Arrest Warrant Act 2003, s 25(4); Private Security Services Act 2004, s 15(2); Commissions of Investigation Act 2004, ss 28(2) and 29. See *Re Employment Equality Bill 1996* [1997] 2 IR 321, SC and ELR 132. See ENTRY AND SEARCH. See also DIPLOMATIC PRIVILEGE; DRUNKEN DRIVING; PRIVATE RESIDENTIAL TENANCIES BOARD; RECOVERY OF MOTOR VEHICLE.

invitation to treat. An offer to receive an offer eg an advertisement to receive tenders. An advertisement or an invitation to make an offer is not an offer which is capable of being turned into a contract by acceptance. A shopkeeper who displays goods in his window with a ticket on them stating a price, does not make an offer for sale, the acceptance of which constitutes a contract; he merely invites the public to make an offer to buy the goods at the price stated. See *Fisher v Bell* [1961] 1 QB 394; *Minister for Industry and Commerce v Pim* [1966] IR 154. See COPYRIGHT; OFFER; TENDER.

invitee. Under common law, a person who entered premises with the express or implied invitation of the occupier in a matter in which they both had a common interest eg a customer in a shop. For statutory provision, see OCCUPIER'S LIABILITY TO VISITORS.

invoice. A written document or electronic transmission provided by a supplier requesting payment for goods or services, provided to or on the direction of a purchaser: Prompt Payment of Accounts Act 1997, s 1(1).

In a particular case, it was held that the printing of *general conditions of sale* on the reverse side of *invoices*, with a reference on the face of the invoice to the conditions, was in conformity with common commercial practice in international trade and commerce: *Clare Taverns t/a Durty Nellly's v Charles Gill & Ors* [2000] 2 ILRM 98, HC. In that case the party receiving the invoices over a period of time was bound by the *jurisdiction clause* contained therein. See DIRECTORY ENTRIES; EXCLUSIVE JURISDICTION; PROMPT PAYMENT; UNSOLICITED GOODS.

involuntary bailment. Where a person takes possession of a chattel involuntarily (eg a parcel left mistakenly at one's residence), he is the *bailee* of that chattel for the owner. He will be liable to the owner for wilful damage thereto. See *Lethbridge v Phillips* [1819] 2 Stark 544. See BAILMENT.

ionising radiation. Means radiation consisting of photons or particles capable of producing ions, either directly or indirectly, and includes x-rays and gamma rays, alpha particles, beta particles, electrons, positrons, protons, neutrons and heavy particles: Radiological Protection Act 1991, s 2.

Licensing as regards ionising radiation rests with the Radiological Protection Institute of Ireland under the 1991 Act, s 30 as amended by the Radiological Protection (Amendment) Act 2002, s 2.

Basic safety standards for the protection of health workers and the general public against the dangers arising from ionising radiation are provided for in Council Directive 96/29 of Euratom, implemented by SI No 125 of 2000. Also a person is not permitted to carry out a medical or dental treatment involving ionising radiation unless the person is a medical practitioner or a dentist deemed by the Medical Council or the Dental Council, as the case may be, to have the required competence in terms of radiation protection and radiation techniques: SI No 189 of 1988.

Regulations have been made to give effect to Council Directive (Euratom) 97/43 on health protection of individuals against the dangers of ionising radiation in relation to medical exposures: EC (Medical Ionising Radiation Protection) Regulations 2002, SI No 478 of 2002. 'Doctors who undertake radiation procedures for patients and who are not radiologists or nuclear medicine physicians are required to complete a course of training in radiation safety and techniques recognised by the Medical Council': Medical Council, *A Guide to Ethical Conduct and Behaviour* (6th edn, 2004) para 10.5.

Regulations have been made laying down general provisions for the treatment of foodstuffs with ionising radiation, and for the approval and control of irradiation facilities, and for rules on labelling: European Communities (Foodstuffs Treated with Ionising Radiation) Regulations 2000, SI No 297 of 2000. These regulations give effect to Directives (EC) 99/2 and 99/3. See RADIOACTIVE SUBSTANCE.

IOU. [I owe you.] A written admission of a debt with an implied undertaking that the debt will be repaid sometime. It is not a negotiable instrument (qv). If it contains a written undertaking to repay at some date, it could amount to a promissory note (qv).

ipse dixit. [He himself said it.]

ipsissima verba. [The identical words.]

ipso facto. [By the mere fact.] By the nature of the case.

ipso jure. [By the law itself.] By operation of the law.

Ireland. The name of the State in the English language: 1937 Constitution, art 4; *Ellis v O'Dea & Shiels* [1990] ITLR (8 January), SC. An injunction cannot issue against the entity *Ireland*: *Pesca Valentia Ltd v Minister for Fisheries* [1986] ILRM 68. See STATE.

Iris Oifigiuil. The official organ of the government for announcing appointments to public offices and publishing proclamations, statutory instruments, appointment of receivers to companies etc. It is usually published every Tuesday and Friday. *Prima facie* evidence of any proclamation, order, rule, regulation, bye-law, or other official document may be given in any legal proceedings by production of a copy of the Iris purported to contain such matter: Documentary Evidence Act 1925, ss 3–4. Notices in relation to many matters concerning companies must be published in the Iris within six weeks of the delivery to the Registrar of Companies: SI No 163 of 1973; Companies Amendment Act 1983, s 55. Iris Oifigiúil replaced the Dublin Gazette in 1922: Adaptation of Enactments Act 1922, s 3.

Irish Auditing and Accounting Supervisory Authority. A company limited by guarantee, with principal objects: (a) to supervise how the prescribed accountancy bodies regulate and monitor their members; (b) to promote adherence to high professional standards in the auditing and accountancy profession, (c) to monitor compliance with the Companies Acts of accounts of certain classes of companies and other undertakings, and (d) to provide specialist advice to the Minister on auditing and accounting matters: Companies (Auditing and Accounting) Act 2003, ss 5 and 8.

The Supervisory Authority is required to do all things necessary and reasonable to further its objects (C(AA)A 2003, s 9). It also has the function of: (i) granting recognition to bodies of accountants for the purposes of s 187 of the Companies Act 1990; (ii) co-operating with recognised accounting bodies in developing standards relating to the independence of auditors and monitoring the effectiveness of these standards; (iii) supervising the effectiveness and disciplinary procedures of each prescribed accountancy body; (iv) conducting enquiries and investigations and imposing sanctions on prescribed accountancy bodies; and (v) arranging for the regulation and supervision of individually authorised auditors by recognised accountancy bodies (C(AA)A 2003, ss 9, 23–25). It may adopt rules and issue guidelines and may apply to the High Court for an order compelling compliance (C(AA)A 2003, ss 10 and 29(7)).

The Supervisory Authority has been given important powers in relation to the annual accounts of certain companies and undertakings (C(AA)A 2003, s 26). If it appears to the Authority that there is a question surrounding the compliance of these annual accounts with the Companies Acts, it may send a notice to the directors, requiring an explanation or the preparation of revised accounts which do comply. There is provision for application to the High Court to compel compliance (C(AA)A 2003, s 26(8)). See ACCOUNTING STANDARDS; ACCOUNTS, COMPANY; AUDITOR INDEPENDENCE; DIRECTOR OF CORPORATE ENFORCEMENT; DIRECTORS' REPORT.

Irish Aviation Authority. A State owned limited company which has the following functions: (a) the management of Irish airspace, (b) the operation of air navigation services and aeronautical communication services, (c) the regulation of safety aspects of civil aviation, and (d) the implementation of certain international agreements in relation to the safety of civil aviation: Irish Aviation Authority Act 1993.

Matters which come within its remit include: personnel licensing, rules of the air, aeronautical charts, units of measurement, operation of aircraft, aircraft nationality and registration marks, airworthiness of aircraft, aeronautical telecommunications, air traffic services, aerodromes, aeronautical information services, and safe transport of dangerous goods by air. Matters retained by the Minister include: meteorological services, security, facilitation of international air travel, search and rescue, and aircraft accident investigation. The Authority is the competent authority in the State for the purposes of the European Aviation Safety Agency Regulations: SI No 469 of 2003.

For amendments to the 1993 Act, see Air Navigation and Transport (Amendment) Act 1998, ss 61–65. See Operations Order 2002, SI No 437 of 2002 and SI No 592 of 2002 and Order 2003, SI No 388 of 2003; Rules of the Air Order 1999, SI No 20 of 1999; Rules of the Air (Amendment) Order 2002, SI No 76 of 2002; Designated Area Order 2002, SI No 140 of 2002; Air Traffic Control Standards Order 2002, SI No 220 of 2002. See website: *www.iaa.ie.* See AIR LAW; AIRCRAFT; AIRSPACE, CHICAGO CONVENTION.

Irish Blood Transfusion Service. A body established pursuant to the Health (Corporate Bodies) Act 1961 with functions: (a) to organise and administer a blood transfusion service including the processing or supply of blood derivatives or other blood products, (b) to make available blood and blood products and clotting factor concentrates, (c) to organise and administer an eye banking service, (d) to organise a service for assessing reports of unexpected or undesirable effects of transfusion: Blood Transfusion Service Board (Establishment) Order 1965, SI No 78 of 1965, as amended by SI No 209 of 1988, SI No 22 of 2000, and SI No 268 of 2003. Prior to 2000, it was called the Blood Transfusion Service Board.

Irish Centre for European Law; ICEL. A charitable company established in May 1988 which has the following objectives: (a) evaluation of the effects of EC law on Irish law; (b) preparing Irish lawyers and other professional advisers to be more competitive in EC law; (c) liaison with EC and Council of Europe institutions; (d) providing a forum for examining practical legal issues between EC and EFTA countries. [ICEL, Trinity College, Dublin 2.]

Irish Copyright Licensing Agency. A non-profit making company, limited by guarantee, representative of publishers and authors, incorporated with the objective of acting as a clearing centre between owners and users of copyright material. The ICLA grants licences to educational establishments for the reprographic copying of literary works. The licensing scheme operated by ICLA has been certified as a licensing scheme for the purposes of s 57 of the Copyright and Related Rights Act 2000 as from 13 January 2003: SI No 514 of 2002. It provides users such as schools and third-level institutions with an easy means of obtaining permission to copy. ICLA passes on the fees collected to publishers and authors. Under the scheme the annual fee is €2 per student per annum in schools and €6 per student per annum in third-level colleges (plus VAT) and is subject to limits on the number of copies permitted. See Quinn AP in *Law Society Gazette* (April 1993). email: *icla@esatlink.com*. See PERFORMING RIGHTS SOCIETY LTD.

Irish Film Board. The body established in 1980 to assist and encourage the making of films in the State and the promotion of the film and audio-visual industry: Irish Film Board Acts 1980, 1993 and 1997. Also known as Bord Scannán na hÉireann. The limit of expenditure which may be incurred by the Irish Film Board has been increased to £80 million: Irish Film Board (Amendment) Act 2000. See websites: *www.filmboard.ie*; and *www.filmmakersireland.ie*. See FILM.

Irish Financial Services Regulatory Authority; IFSRA. A body, established as a constituent part of the Central Bank and Financial Services Authority of Ireland, with specific responsibility for the financial services supervisory functions of the bank: Central Bank Act 1942, s 33A inserted by Central Bank and Financial Services Authority of Ireland Act 2003, s 26. In performing its functions and in exercising its powers, the Regulatory Authority is required to promote the best interests of users of financial services in a way that is consistent with the orderly and proper functioning of financial markets and prudential supervision of providers (CBA 1942, s 33C(3)). The Governor or the board of the bank may issue guidelines to the Authority as to policies and principles and it is required to comply with the guidelines (CBA 1942, s 33D).

There is provision for the appointment of a *Consumer Director* (qv) with responsibility: (a) for monitoring the provision of financial services to consumers and (b) for exercising important consumer protection powers under the Consumer Credit Act 1995, the Investment Intermediaries Act 1995, the Stock Exchange Act 1995, the Insurance Act 1989 and under Central Bank legislation (CBA 1942, ss 33Q and 33S).

There is provision for the appointment of a *Registrar of Credit Unions* (qv) to take over the functions of the *Registrar of Friendly Societies* in relation to the supervision of credit unions (CBA 1942, ss 33W to 33AF). There is also provision for the establishment of a *Financial Services Appeals Tribunal* to hear appeals from appealable decisions of the Authority under certain legislation, and for appeals from the Tribunal to the High Court on points of law (CBA 1942, ss 57A–57AZ inserted by CBFSAIA 2003, s 28).

The Regulatory Authority was established on an interim basis in 2002 and on a statutory basis in 2003. Unusually for a State body, the interim Authority made a submission on the Bill establishing itself. For a full listing of the 29 enactments and

35 regulations under which the Regulatory Authority is to perform functions of the Central Bank, see CBFSAIA 2003, s 31, Sch 2.

Under recent legislation, provision is made for: (a) the establishment of a *Financial Services Ombudsman*, to deal with consumer complaints about financial institutions; (b) the establishment of *Consumer and Industry Consultative Panels* to advise the Regulatory Authority; (c) new reporting and auditing obligations for financial institutions; (d) power for the Regulatory Authority to impose sanctions directly on financial institutions for failure to comply with regulatory requirements, subject to a right of appeal to the Appeals Tribunal; (e) right of appeal to the Appeals Tribunal in relation to certain supervisory decisions of the Authority; (f) new regulatory requirements for money transmission and bureau de change businesses; and (g) miscellaneous other amendments to financial services legislation: Central Bank and Financial Services Authority of Ireland Act 2004.

Telephone for consumer enquiries to the Regulatory Authority is lo-call 1890–777-777. See also website: *www.ifsra.ie*; *www.itsyourmoney.ie*. [Bibliography: Johnston & O'Conor.] See CENTRAL BANK; FINANCIAL SERVICES OMBUDSMAN.

Irish Free State. See SAORSTÁT ÉIREANN; TREATY, THE.

Irish Health Services Accreditation Board. A body corporate with functions of operating hospital *accreditation* programmes and to grant accreditation to hospitals meeting standards set or recognised by the Board: Irish Health Services Accreditation Board (Establishment) Order 2002, SI No 160 of 2002. *Accreditation* means a process involving measurement against a set of standards predetermined by the Board (reg 2).

Irish language. The Irish language as the national language is the first official language; the English language is recognised as a second official language: 1937 Constitution, art 8. In the event of conflict between the text of the Constitution, or of a law enrolled in accordance with the Constitution, in both the official languages, the text in Irish will prevail (arts 25(4)(6) and 25(5)(4)). However, in interpreting the Constitution, where there appears to be a conflict between terms used in the two texts, search must first be made for a common meaning before the Irish language text is permitted to prevail: *The State (Guilland) v Governor of Mountjoy Prison* [1986] ILRM 381 applying *O'Donovan v Attorney-General* [1961] IR 114.

A litigant has a constitutional right to conduct his case in the Irish language: *R (O'Coileain) v D J Crotty* [1927] 61 ILTR 81. He has a similar right in respect of the English language: The *State (Buchan) v Coyne* [1936] 70 ILTR 185. He has no right to insist on only Irish being spoken in a proceedings: *O'Monachain v An Taoiseach* [1982] SC. Either the national language or the English language may be used in any court document or at the hearing of any cause or matter: DCR 1997 Ord 3 and Circuit Court Rules 2001 Ord 1, r 6.

In a case conducted in the Irish language, there is no requirement for the jury to have the capacity to understand the Irish language without the assistance of an interpreter: *MacCarthaigh v Eire* [1999] 1 IR 186, SC.

The Minister is empowered to make arrangements as he thinks proper for the preparation and publication of forms and precedents in the Irish language of legal instruments and documents: Irish Legal Terms Act 1945, s 4. A person has a constitutional right to Irish language copies of documents required under the Companies Act 1963: *O'Murchu v Registrar of Companies* [1989] 7 ILT Dig 24. There is also a constitutional obligation on the State to make available the Rules of Court (qv) in the Irish language: *Delap v An tAire Dli agus Cirt Éire agus An tÁrd Aighne* [1990] ITLR (24 December), HC; *O Beolain v Fahy* [2001] 2 IR 279, SC. There is a constitutional obligation to make available an official translation of the Acts of the Oireachtas in Irish in general when the President signs the text of a Bill in English (*O Beolain* case).

There is provision for interpreters in the courts and for the translation of any affidavit, summons, petition or notice from English into Irish and from Irish into English: RSC Ord 120.

The basic records of a company must be kept in an official language of the State: Companies Act 1990, s 202(7). See Place Names (Irish Forms) Act 1973. In Northern Ireland, restrictions on the use of the Irish language by prisoners at the Maze Prison was held not to be unlawful: *MacCormaic & Pickering v Governor of HM*

Prison [1991] ITLR (29 April), HC(NI). See *Attorney-General v Joyce* [1929] IR 526. See Tearmaí Dlí, Oifig an tSolathair. For law reports in the Irish language, Tuairisci Speisialta 1980–98 (Irish Reports as gaeilge) by O'Tuathail & Ní Chulachain (2000). See 'Legislation in Irish – a lot done, more to do' by John Smith BL in *Bar Review* (June 2004) 91.

[Bibliography: Kelly A; Mac Unfraidh; O'Cearuil.] See COIMISINÉIR TEANGA, AN; DEVELOPMENT PLAN; FORAS TEANGA; GAELTACHT; LANGUAGE; LEGAL TERMS ORDER; PLACENAME; TEACHER; ULLANS; WILL, PROOF OF.

Irish language and EU. See LANGUAGE.

Irish language and planning. The *development plan* (qv) of a local authority is required to include objectives for the protection of the linguistic and cultural heritage of the Gaeltacht (qv) including the promotion of Irish as the community language: Planning and Development Act 2000, s 10(2)(m). The draft development plan for Co Galway in 2002 has a requirement on the applicant for planning permission in the Connemara Gaeltacht to have a proven ability to converse in Irish; the standard of spoken Irish will be set by a *language impact statement*: *Irish Times*, 18 December 2002.

Irish language and promotion. Provision has been made by legislation: (a) for promoting the use of the Irish language for official purposes in the State; (b) for the use of both official languages in parliamentary proceedings, in Acts of the Oireachtas, in the administration of justice, in communicating with or providing services to the public and in carrying out the work of public bodies; (c) for the duties of such bodies with respect to the official languages of the State to be set out; and (d) for the establishment of Oifig Choimisinéar na dTeangacha Oifigiula: Official Languages Act 2003. This Act comes into operation on such day or days by Ministerial order, but not later than three years after the passing of the Act ie not later than 14 July 2006.

The Courts Service in its strategic plan is required to have regard to the government policy on bilingualism and, in particular, to the need to ensure that an adequate number of staff are competent in the Irish language, so as to be able to provide service through Irish as well as English: Courts Service Act 1998, s 7(2)(d).

One of the objects of the Qualifications (Education and Training) Act 1999 is to contribute to the extension of bilingualism in Irish society and, in particular, the achievement of a greater use of the Irish language and to contribute to the promotion of the distinctive cultures of Ireland (Q(ET)A 1999, ss 4(1)(k) and 31(1)(e)). See also Education Act 1998, s 31.

A local authority may, in performing its functions, take such steps as it considers appropriate, to encourage the use of the Irish language: Local Government Act 2001, s 68. The Minister may issue guidelines in relation to the use of the Irish language in local government and the local authority must have regard to such guidance in the performance of its functions. See COIMISINÉIR TEANGA, AN; FORAS TEANGA.

Irish language and schools. *Recognised* schools are required to use their resources, *inter alia*, to promote the development of the Irish language and traditions, Irish literature, the arts and other cultural matters: Education Act 1998, s 9(f).

The *study* of the Irish language at primary and second-level schools is compulsory under regulations made by the Minister for Education: Department of Education: Circulars M10/94 and 12/96; Rules and Programme for Secondary Schools 2002/03, rr 21(1)(1)(e), 45 and 46. Exemptions apply to certain pupils: (a) who have spent part of their education outside the State (eg whose primary education up to 11 years of age was outside the State, or, having been previously enrolled, who left the Irish school system for an absence of at least three years, and the student is at least 11 years of age on re-enrolment); or (b) who have a general learning disability due to serious or sensory impairment; or (c) who have a specific learning disability; or (d) who are from abroad and have no understanding of English (such students are required to study either English or Irish); or (e) who are children of foreign diplomatic or consular representatives; or (f) who are political refugees. A *Certificate of Exemption* is required.

Irish language and work. Any requirement for proficiency in the Irish language for certain posts in the public sector does not infringe equality legislation and is not discriminatory: Employment Equality Act 1998, s 36(2)(c). A rule which requires teachers in recognised primary schools to have a proficiency in Irish is constitutional: *O'Shiel v Minister for Education* [1999] 2 ILRM 241, HC and 2 IR 321.

Proficiency in the Irish language is a prerequisite to qualifying as a solicitor or barrister; solicitors must pass the examination of the Law Society under the Solicitors Act 1954, s 40(3) and barristers must pass the examination prescribed by the Chief Justice under the Legal Practitioners (Qualification) Act 1929, s 3.

Irish Medicines Board. A body corporate established as the licensing authority for both human and veterinary medicines; it also grants permissions to conduct clinical trials: Irish Medicines Board Act 1995. See CLINICAL TRIALS, CONDUCT OF; MEDICINAL PRODUCT.

Irish music rights. See PERFORMING RIGHTS SOCIETY LTD.

Irish National Petroleum. The Irish National Petroleum Corporation Act 2001 provides for the sale of the Minister's shares in the Corporation and/or the disposal of certain assets and liabilities of the corporation, including the sale of certain of its subsidiaries.

Irish Payment Services Organisation; IPSO. An umbrella body, established in 1997 for payment services for financial institutions in Ireland. It provides strategic and technical support to the payments industry in Ireland, a forum for consultation among participants, and represents the payments industry at national and international levels. There are currently five autonomous payment system companies, called the *Clearing Companies*, operating under the umbrella of IPSO, each responsible for its own rules, settlement procedures, standards and access criteria. The payments system deals with a wide variety of payments eg cheque payments and credit transfers, debit card payments via Laser, credit card payments, cross-border payments, and ATMs. See website: *www.ipso.ie*.

Irish Stock Exchange. Originally, the market in Dublin which facilitated the purchase and sale of stock or securities on commission and which required the person dealing (a *stockbroker*) to have a licence from the Lord Lieutenant (qv): Stockbrokers (Ireland) Acts 1799 and 1918. Now the body known as the Irish Stock Exchange Ltd: Stock Exchange Act 1995, s 3(1) as amended by Central Bank and Financial Services Authority of Ireland Act 2003,

s 35, Sch 1. [Bibliography: Cahill D; Clarke B (2).] See website: *www.ise.ie*. See IRISH FINANCIAL SERVICES REGULATORY AUTHORITY; STOCK EXCHANGE.

Irish Takeover Panel. A public company, limited by guarantee, with responsibility for making rules in relation to *take-overs* (qv) and other *relevant transactions* and for monitoring and supervising these take-overs and relevant transactions to ensure compliance with the Act and the Rules: Irish Takeover Panel Act 1997, ss 3, 5, 7; Takeover Rules 2001; Substantial Acquisition Rules 2001.

A *relevant transaction* means any offer, agreement or transaction which the Panel specifies (ITPA 1997, s 1(1)). The Panel has specified these: Takeover Rules 2001, Part A, r 2.1(a) and r 3.1. The Panel has also specified the circumstances in which a person is to be presumed as *acting in concert* with another person (ITPA 1997, s 1(1) and Rules, Pt A, r 3.3).

The Takeover Rules include provisions covering the following areas: (a) the approach, announcements and independent advice (Pt B, rr 1–3); (b) dealings and restrictions on the acquisition of securities and rights over securities (rr 4–8); (c) the mandatory offer and its terms (r 9); (d) offer terms – general (rr 10–13); (e) provisions applicable to all offers (rr 14–18); (f) conduct during the offer (rr 19–22); (g) documents from the offeror and the offeree board (rr 23–27); (h) forecasts and valuations (rr 28–29); (i) timing and revision (rr 30–34); (j) miscellaneous eg partial offers, scheme of arrangement (rr 35–41); (k) procedures for receiving agents (App 1); (l) procedures for formula offers (App 2); (m) disclosure forms (App 3). The Panel has issued very helpful guidance notes to these rules.

The Panel is empowered to grant derogations from and waivers in respect of any rules in exceptional circumstances (ITPA 1997, s 8(7)). It is also empowered to give directions, and to advise, admonish or censure a person in relation to his conduct, to conduct a hearing, and to apply to the court for an *enforcement order* where it believes that a *ruling* or *direction* is unlikely to be complied with or has not been complied with (ITPA 1997, ss 9–12).

The *Schedule* to the Act sets out *12 principles* which are applicable to the conduct of take-overs eg all shareholders of the same class are to be treated similarly; directors of the offeree to act in disregard of personal interest; no oppression of minority; ability of offerer to implement the offer; offeree not to be disrupted in conduct of his affairs; equal information and accurate and timely advice to shareholders; prevent false market in shares; offeree not to frustrate offer or deprive shareholders of opportunity to consider the offer on its merits.

Where transactions in relation to a takeover have been completed, the provisions ITPA 1997 cannot be used to have them unwound; this provision gives certainty to parties to a takeover (ITPA 1997, s 15). See website: *www.irishtakeoverpanel.ie*. See CONCERT PARTY; MANDATORY OFFER; MERGER; SUBSTANTIAL ACQUISITION; TAKE-OVER; TENDER OFFER.

irrationality, test of. The test which the court may apply in a judicial review (qv) of the decision of administrative action. Also referred to as the *test of unreasonableness*. The test lies in considering whether the impugned administrative decision: (a) is fundamentally at variance with reason and common sense; (b) is indefensible for being in the teeth of plain reason and common sense, and that the court is satisfied; (c) that the decision-maker has breached his obligation whereby he must not flagrantly reject or disregard fundamental reason or common sense in reaching his decision: *The State (Keegan) v Stardust Victims Tribunal* [1986] IR 642.

In order for the court to intervene and quash the decision, the applicant must establish that the decision-making authority had before it no relevant material which would support its decision: *O'Keeffe v An Bord Pleanála & Radio Tara* [1992] ILRM 237, SC; *Faulkner v Minister for Industry and Commerce* [1993] ELR 187, HC. A regulation made under an Act may be held to be *ultra vires* the Act for unreasonableness where it lacks any logical basis: *McHugh v AB* [1993] 11 ILT Dig 28, SC. See also *Fairleigh Ltd v Temple Bar Renewal Ltd* [1999] 2 IR 508. See 'If not O'Keefe, Then What?' by Imelda Higgins BL in *Bar Review* (June 2003) 123. See WEDNESDAY TEST.

irrebuttable presumptions. Inferences which cannot be rebutted as evidence to contradict them is not allowed eg the presumption that a child under the age of seven is incapable of committing a crime. See PRESUMPTION.

irresistible impulse. A person is said to act under an *irresistible impulse* to do an act when, from disease of mind, he is incapable of restraining himself from doing it, although he may know at the time of committing it that the act was wrong: *Attorney-General v O'Brien* [1936] IR 263. It is a defence of insanity which must be proved on the balance of probability. See AUTOMATISM; INSANITY.

irrevocable. Incapable of being revoked. See POWER OF ATTORNEY.

irrevocable letter of credit. See LETTER OF CREDIT.

Isaac Wunder order. An order which requires a litigant, who is found to have initiated proceedings which are an *abuse of process* against another party, to apply to the court for its prior consent before that litigant can issue fresh proceedings against that same party: *Wunder v Hospitals Trust* (24 January 1967, unreported), SC. The making of a restriction on the right of access to the courts has to be examined in the context of a constitutional right and a right under art 6(1) of the European Convention on Human Rights to such access: *Riordan v Ireland (No 5)* [2001] 4 IR 463, HC. See ABUSE OF PROCESS.

Islam. The religion of Muslims, having the Koran as its sacred scripture and teaching that there is only one God and that Mohammed is his prophet. The main areas of conflict between Islamic family law and family law in common law jurisdictions is in relation to: (a) the original validity of the Islamic marriage contract, (b) the legal status of Islamic polygamy, and (c) Islamic divorces and the legal status of the *mahr* or dowry. See *Islamic Family Law Principles in Common Law Jurisdictions* by Mark O'Connor in (2003) 11 ISLR 141.

island, designated. Certain tax reliefs were available for renewal and improvement of designated islands: Taxes Consolidation Act 1997, ss 360 to 365. The percentage of the total cost of a project which had to be incurred by 31 July 1999 in order to qualify for the termination date of 31 December 1999 was reduced from 50% to 15% (TCA 1997, s 360 as amended by Finance Act 2000, s 43).

island, polling on. Provision has been made for taking an election poll on an island on any of the five days before the polling day if the returning officer considers it desirable to do so because of weather or transport problems: Electoral Act 1992, ss 85–86. See also Presidential Elections Act 1993, s 42; Referendum Act 1994, s 30; European Parliament Elections Act 1997, Sch 2, r 48.

island, transport to. The Minister is empowered to finance the building, acquisition, overhaul or repair of vessels suitable for the operation of ferry services to inhabited islands of the State and to subsidise the operation of such services and the operation of bus services provided in conjunction with a ferry service or an air service: Minister for Community, Rural and Gaeltacht Affairs (Powers and Functions) Act 2003, s 2. The Minister also has the power: (a) to acquire, by agreement or compulsorily, any existing aerodromes or any land for the purpose of the construction, improvement, extension or development of aerodromes and ancillary facilities on the islands, or as the case may be, the mainland, (b) to finance the construction, maintenance, restoration, repair or improvement of such aerodromes and ancillary facilities, and (c) to manage and operate them (MCRGA(PF)A 2003, s 3). For previous, now repealed legislation, see Aran Islands Transport Act 1946; Minister for Arts etc Act 1998, s 4.

island allowance. A new allowance is paid to certain social welfare recipients who ordinarily reside on an island off the coast of Ireland: Social Welfare Act 2001, s 15. The allowance has been extended to further social welfare recipients: Social Welfare (Miscellaneous Provisions) Act 2003, s 6.

issue. (1) In pleadings (qv), a matter which is claimed by one party and denied by the other, is said to be *at issue*.

(2) Offspring. A person's issue consists of his children, grandchildren and other lineal descendants. A gift *to A and his issue* confers a life estate only because of the failure to use the appropriate word *heirs*. The words *die without issue* are to be construed in a will as meaning a want or failure in the lifetime or at the death of the party and not an indefinite failure of issue, unless a contrary intention appears from the will: Succession Act 1965, s 96, re-enacting the Wills Act 1837, s 29.

Issue has been held to mean only legitimate issue and consequently illegitimate children had no succession rights on the death of their father: *In the Goods of Walker dec'd* [1985] ILRM 86. However, legislation in 1987 provided that relationships shall be deduced for the purposes of the Succession Act 1965 irrespective of the marital status of a person's parents: Status of Children Act 1987, s 29. It has been held however that the word *issue* used in a will, does not include adopted children; the testator died in 1954: *Re John Stamp* [1993 HC] ILRM 383. See CHILD, ILLEGITIMATE; CONSTRUCTION OF DISPOSITIONS.

issue estoppel. For a successful plea of issue estoppel it must be established that: (a) the same question has been decided in earlier proceedings; (b) the judicial decision which is said to create the estoppel is final; and (c) the parties to that decision or their privies are the same persons as the parties to the proceedings in which the estoppel is raised or their privies: *McCauley v McDermot* [1997] 2 ILRM 486, SC cited in *Sweeney v Bus Átha Cliath/Dublin Bus* [2004] ITLR (23 February), HC.

In order for issue estoppel to arise there must be mutuality; the same parties must have been involved in the earlier proceedings and there must be reciprocity: *Clare County Council v Mahon* [1996] 1 ILRM 521, HC and [1995] 3 IR 193, HC.

'Where a clearly identifiable issue has been decided against a party in a criminal trial, by means of a judgment explaining how the decision was reached, such decision may give rise to issue estoppel in subsequent civil proceedings in which that party is involved and in the absence of special circumstances, an effort by a party to challenge by means of civil proceedings a decision made against him by a court of competent jurisdiction is an abuse of the process of court': *Kelly v Ireland* [1986] ILRM 318.

The Court of Criminal Appeal has ruled that issue estoppel as between one criminal trial and another should be regarded as available in Ireland: *People (DPP) v O'Callaghan* [2001] 2 ILRM 184, CCA and 1 IR 584. In this case, certain evidence was ruled inadmissible at the first trial, but ruled admissible at a retrial. The second ruling was not permissible under the principle of issue estoppel.

See also *Meath County Council v Daly* [1987] IR 391, HC; *Breathnach v Ireland* [1990] 8 ILT Dig 192; *Lawless v Bus Éireann* [1994] 1 IR 474, SC; *McGuinness v Motor Distributors Ltd* [1997] 2 IR 171, HC; *Belton v Carlow Co Council* [1997] 2 ILRM 405, SC and 1 IR 172; *Rhatigan v*

Gill [1999] 2 ILRM 427, HC. See ESTOPPEL; RES JUDICATA.

issue paper. A formulation of the charges and indication of the issues to be determined in a trial which is given to the foreman of the jury (qv); a list of questions may be sufficient. See *The People v McCormack* [1944] Frewen 55.

issued capital. See CAPITAL.

ITRIS. [Integrated Title Registration Information System.] The new electronic system, commenced in 1999, which involves the conversion of documents held by both the Land Registry and the Registry of Deeds into electronic format, and making them available to *account holders*. The project involves the scanning, digitising and cataloguing of old property folios, and merging this information with the ongoing influx of newly created electronic folios. It is planned to have all of the 1.8 million folios in electronic format by 2004. When fully operational, it will be possible for account holders to search electronically for deed and title information covering property throughout the whole State and to request a certified copy for official transactions. In 2004, there were over 6,600 account holders. See *www.landregistry.ie*. See LAND REGISTRY ELECTRONIC ACCESS SERVICE.

J

jactitation of marriage. [Jactitare – to boast.] A procedure by which a person (the respondent) could be prevented by court order from making false assertions of being married to another person (the petitioner). It is not a declaration of nullity and consequently cannot bind third parties. See *Duchess of Kingston's case* [1776] 168 ER 175. The right to petition for jactitation of marriage has been abolished: Family Law Act 1995, s 34. See also Law Reform Commission Report (LRC 6,1983).

jam. Regulations have been made to prescribe and harmonise within the European Union, standards for the composition and labelling of fruit jams, jellies, marmalades and sweetened chestnut puree products: SI No 294 of 2003, implementing Directive (EC) 2001/113.

jeopardy, in. In danger of being convicted of a criminal charge. See DOUBLE JEOPARDY.

jet skis. Regulations came into operation on 1 April 1993 which enable local authorities, regional fisheries boards, the Commissioners of Public Works and harbour authorities to propose areas as being unsuitable for the operation of jet skis and fast power boats, in the interest of safety of pleasure craft and their occupants: Merchant Shipping (Jet Skis and Fast Power Boats) Regulations 1992. Under draft legislation, it is proposed to introduce new controls on the use of jet skis in inland and coastal waters, including provision for on-the-spot fines: Maritime Safety Bill 2004. See PERSONAL WATERCRAFT; PLEASURE CRAFT.

jetsam. Goods of a ship which are cast overboard and sink. See Larceny Act 1916, s 15, now repealed by Criminal Justice (Theft and Fraud Offences) Act 2001, s 3 and Sch 1. See FLOTSAM; LAGAN.

jettison. To throw overboard a ship's goods from necessity to lighten the vessel. See *Milward v Hibbert* [1842] 3 QB 120.

job-sharing. The division of a job between two or more persons, such that each covers the same job for complementary parts of the day, week or month. There is no statutory entitlement to job-sharing. Also the existence of a job-sharing scheme within an organisation does not mean that every employee has an automatic entitlement to such a post: *Burke v NUI* [2001] ELR 181, EOrd.

It has been held that a job-sharer is entitled to be on the point of an incremental scale she would have been on if she had not job-shared: *Hill v Revenue Commissioners* [1994] ELR 65, EOrd Issues arising in this case were referred by the Labour Court to the European Court of Justice which held that to grant workers who convert to full-time employment the same scale point as they had under their job-sharing contract does not constitute discrimination in favour of female workers: *Hill v Revenue Commissioners* [1998] ELR 225, ECJ.

Job sharers who are on maternity leave are entitled to be paid at the same rate as if they had not been on maternity leave; they are not entitled to the rate of pay of full-time workers: *Ormond v Department of Finance* [1999] ELR 25, LC. See *Flood v Revenue Commissioners* [1999] ELR 31, LC; *Weir v St Patrick's Hospital* [2001] ELR 228, Eord.

jobsearch course. It has been held that decisions to disallow unemployment assistance payments for failure to attend a jobsearch course must be based on the rules in the Social Welfare (Consolidation) Act 1981 and the requirements of natural justice: *Thompson v Minister for Social Welfare* [1989] IR 618.

joinder of a party. There is no bar to joining a party to proceedings at the appeal stage: *TDI Metro Ltd (No 1) v District Judge Delap* [2001] 1 ILRM 321, SC and [2000] 4 IR 337, SC. In this case, the Supreme Court held that the Attorney-General may be permitted to join proceedings if the court decides that it is appropriate; he has no right to join proceedings on his own decision and his intervention, if permitted, does not permit additional grounds to be added to the appeal.

joinder of claims. Two or more claims may be made in one originating document, either alternatively or otherwise, so long as the claims are not mutually inconsistent or based on inconsistent allegations of fact: Circuit Court Rules 2001 Ord 9, r 1. If it appears to the judge that claims joined in any action or matter cannot be conveniently tried together, he may order separate trials or may exclude any claim. No claim is permitted to be joined with one for the recovery of land, except in respect of *mesne profits* or arrears of rent (Ord 9 r 2). For joinder of plaintiffs in one action, see Ord 6 r 1.

In the High Court, the plaintiff may unite in the same action, several causes of action: RSC Ord 18. However, if it appears to the court that any such causes of action cannot be conveniently tried or disposed of together, the court may order separate trials. There are similar provisions as in the Circuit Court regarding actions for the recovery of land.

In the District Court, the court may, if it considers it desirable, order that two or more actions be tried together: DCR 1997 Ord 46, r 2.

joinder of defendants. The adding of a defendant to proceedings. The court will not permit a person to be made a defendant to an action at a time when that defendant could rely on the Statute of Limitations as barring a fresh action against him: RSC Ord 15, r 13; *Allied Irish Coal v Powell Duffryn* [1998] 2 ILRM 61, SC. The court is entitled to join as a defendant a party situate outside the jurisdiction where the party could have been named as a co-defendant if the party had been situate within the jurisdiction: RSC Ord 11, r 1(h); *Tromso Sparebank v Byrne & Ors* [1990] ITLR (5 March), SC.

Exceptional circumstances are required to exist to justify the joinder of a defendant against the plaintiff's wishes, eg if the defendant's presence is required for the court to effectually and completely adjudicate upon all issues arising during the hearing of the cause or matter: *Barlow v Fanning and UCC* [2002] 2 IR 593, SC and [2003] 1 ILRM 29. For the rules in the Circuit Court governing the joinder of defendants, and the misjoinder or non-joinder of parties, see Circuit Court Rules 2001 Ord 6, rr 2 and 4. See DEFENDANT; DEFENDANTS, JOINT; MULTIPLE DEFENDANTS.

joinder of documents. The joining of two or more documents to be read together, so as to satisfy the requirements of the Statute of Frauds (Ireland) 1695. If one of the documents is signed, it must refer to the other document, and the other document must have existed at the time of signature. See *McQuaid v Lynam* [1965] IR 564; *Kelly v Ross & Ross* [1980] HC.

joinder of unrelated charges. Charges which are not founded on documents served on an accused may, with the consent of the accused, who has been sent forward for trial, be added to the indictment: Criminal Procedure Act 1967, s 4N inserted by Criminal Justice Act 1999, s 9.

joint account. A banking account which can be operated either singly or collectively by the parties to the account, as arranged and agreed.

Money is frequently placed in a bank or other account in the joint names of two persons, often the depositor ('A') and another person ('B'). Where it is held that A had intended that B should be entitled to the beneficial interest in the money in the joint account on the death of A, then the survivor B has a legal interest in the money by reason of the contractual relationship which had arisen between B and A with the bank; alternatively, the survivor B's legal interest arose by reason of the gift being a contingent gift subject to the death of the donor A: *Lynch v Burke & AIB* [1996] 1 ILRM 114, SC and [1995] 2 IR 159, SC, reversing *Owens v Greene* [1932] IR 225.

Generally, parties to a joint account are entitled to share the funds in the account equally and not in proportion to their contributions to it: *Jones v Maynard* [1951] Ch 572. Where a joint account is in the name of a husband and wife and the husband only has contributed to it, the doctrine of *advancement* (qv) may arise. See also *Murray v Murray & Anor* [1939] IR 317.

Whenever the amount in a joint deposit account exceeds €31,750 and one of the parties to the account dies, the financial institution must not pay the money, or any part of it, to the survivor until the institution has an *inheritance tax certificate*: Finance Act 2001, s 223. This does not apply where the person who dies is the spouse of the surviving joint account holder. For consolidated provision, see Capital Acquisitions Tax Consolidation Act 2003, s 109. See also Investor Compensation Act 1998, s 37. See DOUBLE PORTIONS; RESULTING TRUST.

joint and several obligation. An obligation entered into by two or more persons, jointly and severally, so that each is liable separately, and all liable jointly, and an action may be taken against one or more separately or all jointly. The obligation may arise by agreement of the parties or by operation of law. See Powers of Attorney Act 1996, s 14. See ANTECEDENT NEGOTIATIONS; FINANCE HOUSE, LIABILITY OF.

joint authorship. A work of *joint authorship* means a work produced by the collaboration of two or more authors in which the contribution of each author is not distinct from that of the other author or authors: Copyright and Related Rights Act 2000, s 22(1). Such authors are deemed to be known, where it is possible for a person to identify one or more of them by reasonable enquiry (CRRA 2000, s 2(8)). As regards the duration of copyright where it is calculated from the death of the author, in joint authorship it is calculated from the death of the last joint authors (CRRA 2000, s 32(4)).

Joint authors or *co-authors* hold the copyright as *tenants in common* (qv) rather than as joint tenants (qv): *Lauri v Renad* [1892] 3 Ch 402. In the absence of agreement to the contrary, it has been held that they hold the copyright in equal undivided shares: *Redwood Music Ltd v B Feldman & Co Ltd* [1979] RPC 1. An author may obtain an injunction to restrain his co-author for

infringing their copyright: *Cescinsky v George Routledge & Sons Ltd* [1916] KB 325.

A *design of joint authorship* means a design of two or more authors in which the contribution of each author is not distinct from that of the other author or authors: Industrial Designs Act 2001, s 18(1). References in the 2001 Act to the author of a design are to be construed in relation to a design of joint authorship as references to all the authors (IDA 2001, s 18(2)). See AUTHOR; BROADCAST; COPYRIGHT; DESIGN.

joint defendants. See DEFENDANTS, JOINT.

Joint Industrial Council. [JIC.] An association of employers and employees for a particular industry, having as its objective the promotion of harmonious relations. Provided the association fulfils certain conditions, it may be registered as a JIC by the Labour Court. See Industrial Relations Act 1946, ss 59–65.

joint investigation teams. Investigation teams which may be set up for a specific purpose and limited period, by mutual agreement of the competent authorities of two or more member states in order to carry out criminal investigations with a cross-border dimension in one or more of the member states setting up the team: Criminal Justice (Joint Investigation Teams) Act 2004. The purpose of the Act is to enable effect to be given in Irish law to the EU Council Framework Decision of 13 June 2002 on Joint Investigation Teams. The European Council held in Tampere in 1999 called for joint investigation teams, as foreseen in Article 30 of the Treaty on European Union, to be set up without delay, as a first step, to combat trafficking in drugs and human beings as well as terrorism. The Act provides that the Commissioner of An Garda Síochána will be the competent authority in Ireland for the purposes of the Framework Decision.

Joint Labour Committee. [JLC.] A committee established by the Labour Court under the Industrial Relations Act 1946, ss 35–41 to determine minimum wages and conditions of employment for all workers covered by it. It consists of an equal number of employer and trade union representatives and of independent persons nominated by the Minister: Industrial Relations Act 1990, s 44 and Sch 5. The committee formulates proposals for an *employment regulation order* which when agreed by the Labour Court has the effect of automatically amending the contracts of employment of all workers covered by it (IRA 1990, s 48). The committee must seriously consider objections put forward by any dissenting members or the resulting order will be invalidated: *Burke v Minister for Labour* [1979] IR 354. The Labour Relations Commission is required to carry out a periodic review of joint labour committees (IRA 1990, s 39). The High Court has held that the delay of contract cleaning companies in bringing judicial review proceedings to challenge two employment regulation orders, was fatal to their case: *Irish Times*, 26 February 2004 p 4. See also *Minister for Labour v Costello* [1989] ILRM 485. For an example of an *employment regulation order*, see SI No 137 of 2002. See Pensions Act 1990, s 81C as amended by substitution by Social Welfare (Miscellaneous Provisions) Act 2004, s 22(1). See EMPLOYMENT AGREEMENT; REST PERIOD.

joint stock company. See COMPANY; STOCK.

joint tenancy. The ownership of land by two or more persons where there is a *right of survivorship* ie when a joint tenant dies his interest passes to the remaining joint tenants. For this reason it is usual to make trustees joint tenants. The *four unities* of *possession, interest, title* and *time*, must exist or otherwise the ownership will be a *tenancy in common* (qv).

The joint tenants must have a unity of possession by which they have equal rights to possession of the whole land; they must have the identical share or interest in the land; they must have the same title by taking it from the same instrument; and their interest must have come into existence at the same time, with some exceptions.

Severance of a joint tenancy may be legal or equitable; when severance is legal, the joint tenancy is at an end; when equitable, only the beneficial interest is severed, the legal estate remaining unaffected.

A joint tenancy may be created by grant or devise *to A and B* or *to A and B jointly*, ie without words which indicate that they are to hold separate and distinct shares. A corporation, because its perpetual existence prevented the right of survivorship, originally could not be a joint tenant until the Bodies Corporate (Joint Tenancy) Act 1899. See *Maher v Maher* [1987] ILRM 582.

Where persons become beneficially entitled to a gift (qv) as joint tenants, their liability to tax is the same as if they took the property as tenants in common in equal shares: Capital Acquisitions Tax Consolidation Act 2003, s 7.

The Law Reform Commission has recommended that a joint tenant should not be able to sever the joint tenancy by acquiring another interest, without first obtaining the consent of all the other joint tenants to the acquisition and therefore to the severance: Report on *Positive Covenants over freehold land and other proposals* (LRC 70, 2003). The Commission has also recommended that the effect of a judgment mortgage on a joint tenancy, should be the same whether the property is registered or unregistered: *Consultation Paper on Judgment Mortgages* (LRC CP 30, 2004). See DEATH, SIMULTANEOUS; MATRIMONIAL HOME; PER MY ET PER TOUT; TENANCY IN COMMON.

joint tortfeasors. [Joint wrongdoers.] See CONCURRENT WRONGDOERS.

joint venture. A special, institutionally fixed form of co-operation between undertakings: EC Commission Notice concerning the assessment of co-operative joint ventures (JV) to Art 85 EEC, OJ [1993] C 43/2. A JV may infringe competition rules. See Competition Authority Decision No 24 on Cambridge/Imari (25 June 1993). See *Travers* in 11 ILT & SJ (1993) 172. [Bibliography: Power V.] See MERGER/TAKEOVER.

jointress. A woman entitled to jointure (qv).

jointure. A provision made by a husband for the support of his wife after his death eg an annual income during widowhood. See STRICT SETTLEMENT.

journalist, communications with. There is no privilege (qv) attaching to communications with a journalist: *O'Brennan v Tully* [1935] 69 ILTR 115; *Re Kevin O'Kelly* [1974] ILTR 97. However, in a particular defamation case, discovery of a TV programme journalist's notebook naming persons in Northern Ireland was refused, as their lives might be put in risk; however, in order to do justice between the parties, the defence of fair comment was struck out and the plea of justification allowed: *Burke v Central Independent Television plc* [1994] 2 ILRM 161, SC and 2 IR 63.

A tribunal of inquiry is empowered to order a journalist to reveal the source of information on which articles published in his newspaper were based: *Kiberd v Tribunal of Inquiry into the Beef Industry* [1992]

ILRM 574, HC. It has been held that it is improper for a judge presiding at a criminal trial to discuss in any way the trial or any aspect of it with representatives of the media, including vetting in any way the newspaper reports of the trial: *DPP v Barr (No 2)* [1993] 11 ILT Dig 185, CCA. [Bibliography: McGonagle; Murphy.] See NEWSPAPER RULE.

journalist in armed conflict. A journalist engaged in dangerous professional missions in areas of armed conflict must be considered as a civilian and protected against dangers arising from military operations: Geneva Conventions (Amendment) Act 1998, Sch 5, art 79. The journalist may be entitled to obtain an *identity card* issued on behalf of the government (GC(A)A 1998, s 11).

joyriding. Colloquial expression which may constitute the crime of taking possession of a mechanically propelled vehicle without the consent of the owner and also dangerous driving (qv): Road Traffic Act 1961, ss 53 and 112, Road Traffic Act 1968, s 51.

judge's declaration. The declaration which every judge appointed under the Constitution must make and subscribe: 'In the presence of Almighty God I do solemnly and sincerely promise and declare that I will duly and faithfully and to the best of my knowledge and power execute the office of ... without fear or favour, affection or ill-will towards any man, and that I will uphold the Constitution and the laws. May God direct and sustain me': 1937 Constitution, art 34(5)(1).

judge's intervention. A judge may intervene at a trial to maintain an even balance between the parties, but must not (eg by criticism of a witness) take over the function of counsel. See *Donnelly v Timber Factors Ltd* [1991] 1 IR 553, SC.

judge's robes. See DRESS IN COURT.

judges. Judges are appointed by the President of Ireland, on the advice of the government, to administer justice in courts: 1937 Constitution, arts 35(1) and 34(1). The *Judicial Appointments Advisory Board* (JAAB) has the function of identifying persons and informing the government on the suitability of those persons for appointment to judicial office; it recommends at least seven persons in respect of each vacancy: Courts and Court Officers Act 1995, s 16 as amended by Courts and Court Officers Act 2002, s 8. The JAAB is required to

make an annual report to the Minister (CCOA 2002, s 11).

As regards the offices of Chief Justice or President of the High, Circuit or District Court, the government must have regard first to already serving judges (CCOA 1995, s 23).

Judges are independent in the exercise of their judicial functions; they may not be members of the Oireachtas or hold any other office or position of emolument (1937 Constitution, art 35). However, the appointment of judges to appointments outside the courts is valid eg to chair a tribunal or a commission of inquiry: *Riordan v Taoiseach (No 1)* [1999 SC] 4 IR 321. Judges are ineligible to stand for election to the European Parliament: European Parliament Elections Act 1997, s 11(2)(b).

They may not be removed from office except for stated misbehaviour and then only upon resolutions passed by both Houses of the Oireachtas. Their remuneration cannot be reduced during their continuance in office. An inequity in the manner of dealing with the reduction in pension to fund a retirement gratuity, highlighted in *McMenamin v Ireland* [1997] 2 ILRM 177, SC and [1996] 3 IR 100, SC, was corrected by the Oireachtas (Allowances to Members) Act 1998, ss 24–30. Judges enjoy immunity (qv) from action when performing their judicial functions: *Macauley & Co Ltd v Wyse-Power* [1943] 77 ILTR 61. No action is maintainable in respect of anything said or done by a trial judge in exercise of a jurisdiction which belongs to and is exercisable by him: *Deighan v Ireland* [1995] 1 ILRM 88, HC and 2 IR 56.

The conviction of an accused by a person who was not a judge appointed in accordance with the Constitution cannot be retrospectively validated by legislation: Courts (No 2) Act 1988 and *Shelly v Mahon* [1990] ITLR (23 July). It is unusual, but not unheard of, for a judge to visit the actual scene of a dispute eg Mr Justice Kearns visited the Glen of the Downs after legal submissions had concluded in the hearing of a challenge to the proposed dual carriageway through the glen; the judge was accompanied by solicitors representing each party: *Irish Times*, 13 March 1999 – see *Murphy v Wicklow County Council* [1999] IEHC.

There is provision to ensure that a judge who is appointed to a higher court may complete any partly heard cases which that judge may have been hearing in the lower court: Courts (Establishment and Constitution) Act 1961, s 6A inserted by Courts and Court Officers Act 2002, s 12. This has been a long-standing practice in respect of judges appointed to the Supreme Court: *McMullen v Clancy* [2002] 3 IR 493, SC at 508. See *O'Byrne v Minister for Finance* [1959] IR 1; *The State (Walshe) v Murphy* [1981] IR 275; *Coates v Judge O'Donnell* [1997] 1 IR 417, HC. See also Courts Act 1985 and Courts of Justice (District Courts) Act 1946, s 20. [Bibliography: Ball.] See CHIEF JUSTICE; DRESS IN COURT; JUDICIAL NOTICE; LOCUS IN QUO; MODE OF ADDRESS.

judges, complaints about. A judge of the Supreme Court or the High Court may not be removed from office except for stated misbehaviour or incapacity, and then only upon resolutions passed by the Dáil and by the Seanad calling for his removal: 1937 Constitution, art 35(4). District Court and Circuit Court judges hold office by the same tenure as judges of the High Court and the Supreme Court: Courts of Justice (District Court) Act 1946, s 20 and Courts of Justice Act 1924, s 39 respectively. There is provision for a judicial inquiry into the conduct or health of a District Court judge (CJ(DC)A 1946, s 21).

On 2 June 2004, the Houses of the Oireachtas adopted Standing Order (SO 63A) to provide a framework under which a resolution under art 35(4) could be moved and a Select Committee could be established to enquire into the behaviour or capacity of Circuit Court Judge Brian Curtin. On 3 June 2004, such a committee was established by the Houses. Also amendments were made to two Acts to facilitate such an inquiry. Judge Curtin has denied any wrongdoing. See CHILD PORNOGRAPHY; OIREACHTAS COMMITTEES.

A judicial committee, established by the Chief Justice in 1999, reported in 2000 with a recommendation for the establishment of a *Judicial Conduct and Ethics Committee* which would investigate complaints against members of the judiciary. If a complaint were found to have substance, the complaint would be heard by a *Panel of Inquiry*, which would include a lay representative appointed by the Attorney-General. The Panel would be able to recommend a number of sanctions, ranging from a reprimand to a recommendation for

dismissal. The government has indicated that legislation to implement the recommendations would be introduced in 2004.

In 2001 a Bill was withdrawn, which would have provided for an amendment to the Constitution to provide for the establishment by law of a body to investigate whether a judge engaged in conduct constituting misbehaviour or was affected by incapacity: Twenty Second Amendment to the Constitution Bill 2001. See DISTRICT JUDGE, INQUIRY RE.

judges, number of. The number of judges in each court is as follows: Supreme Court – 8; High Court – not more than 31; Circuit Court – not more than 33; District Court – not more than 54 in addition to the President of the District Court: Courts and Court Officers Act 1995, ss 6, 9–11; Courts Act 1996; Courts (No 2) Act 1997; Courts and Court Officers Act 2002, ss 26–28; Courts and Court Officers Act 2003, s 2; Civil Liability and Courts Act 2004, s 56. See also Human Rights Commission Act 2000, ss 5–6.

Supreme Court judge Mrs Susan Denham has said that that Ireland has fewer judges per head of population than many other states eg Ireland has one judge per 32,700 persons: *Irish Times*, 3 March 2004. She said that the comparable figures for other countries were: Northern Ireland – 29,056; Scotland – 19,773; England and Wales – 15,562; Denmark – 16,072; Spain – 10,135; Slovenia – 2,484; average for other EU member states (prior to enlargement in May 2004) – 6,000 to 7,000.

judges, potential bias. It has been held that it is essential to the administration of justice that there should not be actual bias (a *subjective* test) or no reasonable apprehension of bias (the *objective* test): *Dublin Wellwoman Centre Ltd v Ireland* [1995] 1 ILRM 408, SC. A barrister must not habitually practice in any court of which his parent, spouse or near blood relative is a presiding judge; the fact of the relationship should be made known to the opposing party: *Code of Conduct for the Bar of Ireland* (December 2003) r 5.10. It has been held that where there exists a relationship between an advocate and a judge and no objection is made, there is no impropriety in the judge continuing to hear the case: *O'Reilly v Cassidy* [1995] 1 ILRM 306, SC. However, where complaint is made about the relationship (eg a judge's daughter briefed before him), it could give rise to fear that the outcome could be affected by the relationship: *O'Reilly v Cassidy* [1995] (No 2) 1 ILRM 311, HC.

judges, precedence between. The ranking of judges is in the following order: Chief Justice, President of the High Court, former Chief Justices, other Supreme Court judges, former Presidents of the High Court, other judges of the High Court, President of the Circuit Court, former presidents of the Circuit Court: Courts of Justice Act 1924, s 9 as amended by Courts (No 2) Act 1997, s 9. The amendment was necessitated by the provision in 1997 for the appointment of *presiding judges* for a specified period. See BARRISTERS, PRECEDENCE BETWEEN.

judges, presiding. The *presiding judges* are the Chief Justice and the Presidents of the High, Circuit and District Courts: Courts (No 2) Act 1997, s 1. For all appointments of presiding judges from 18 December 1997, the appointment is for a non-renewable period of seven years or until retirement age, whichever first occurs (C(No 2)A 1997, s 4). At the end of the seven-year term, the former presiding judge becomes an ordinary judge but with his remuneration maintained at the former level until retirement. The President of the District Court is an *ex officio* additional judge of the Circuit Court; the President of the Circuit Court is an *ex officio* additional judge of the High Court; and the President of the High Court is an *ex officio* additional judge of the Supreme Court.

judges, qualification of. For appointment to the Superior Courts (ie High and Supreme Courts), practising barristers and solicitors of not less than 12 years' standing are eligible, as are Circuit Court judges of two years' standing (was four years) and judges of certain international courts eg European Court of Human Rights: Courts (Supplementary Provisions) Act 1961, s 5 as amended by Courts and Court Officers Act 2002, s 4. Practising barristers and solicitors must have practised for a continuous period of not less than two years immediately before first-time appointment to judicial office.

For appointment to the Circuit Court, practising barristers and solicitors of not less than 10 years standing are eligible, as are judges of the District Court, and County Registrars who practised as a barrister or solicitor for not less than 10 years prior to their appointment: Courts of Jus-

tice Act 1924, s 43; Courts of Justice Act 1936, s 14(1); Courts Act 1961, s 17; Courts Act 1973, s 2 as amended by Courts and Court Officers Act 1995, ss 29–31 and by CCOA 2002, s 5.

For appointment to the District Court, practising barristers and solicitors of not less than ten years standing are eligible, as are County Registrars: Courts of Justice Act 1924, s 69 and Courts of Justice (District Court) Act 1946, s 14 as amended by Courts of Justice Act 1953, s 24.

Periods of practice as both a barrister and solicitor may be aggregated and reckoned to satisfy the minimum practice requirements for appointment (CCOA 2002, s 6).

judges, retirement of. Judges of the Supreme and High Courts appointed since 1995 must retire at 70 years of age; existing judges at that date must retire at 72 years: Courts and Court Officers Act 1995, s 47. A judge of the Irish courts, following retirement or resignation, who returns to the Bar may not practice in a court of equal or lesser jurisdiction than the court of which he was a judge: *Code of Conduct for the Bar of Ireland* (December 2003) r 5.21. Also it has been suggested that a retired judge of the superior courts should not exercise the personal right of audience in the courts since he 'would still be regarded as laying down the law with judicial authority, and he would tend to overbear inferior courts, while it would be a scandal were he to explain his own judgments for the purpose of advancing a client's cause', *obiter* by Kennedy CJ in *Re the Solicitors Act and Sir James O'Connor* [1930] IR 623. See 'The Return of Retired Judges: A Case for Change' by Brian Conroy in *Bar Review* (February 2004) 23.

Provision was made for pension payments to a Supreme Court judge, a High Court judge, and a County Registrar, who resigned in April 1999 over the *Philip Sheedy* case: Courts (Supplemental Provisions) (Amendment) Act 1999. Also, provision was made for the grant of full pension rights to a High Court judge who would otherwise not have accumulated the necessary 15 years' service as a judge to entitle him to a full pension: Courts (Supplemental Provisions) (Amendment) Act 2000. Provision was also made for enhanced pension arrangements for Mr Justice Frederick

Morris who chaired the Morris Tribunal: Courts and Court Officers Act 2002, s 29.

judges' rules. Code of guidance for police officers, drawn up by English judges in 1912 relating to questioning and charging a person suspected of having committed a crime. Five more rules were added in 1918. The rules were framed with the object of preventing confessions being improperly elicited from suspects by police officers. They do not have the force of law; a statement obtained from an accused in breach of a provision of the judges' rules is admissible provided it is a voluntary one: *McCarrick v Leavy* [1964] IR 225. An admission may be admissible – where a previous admission made after caution was ruled inadmissible due to breach of the Judges' Rules: *DPP v Buckley* [1990] 1 IR 14. See also *The People (Attorney-General) v Cummins* [1974] 108 ILTR 5; *People (DPP) v Reddan* [1995] 3 IR 560, CCA; *People (DPP) v Van Onzen* [1996] 2 ILRM 387, CCA; *DPP (Higgins) v Byrne* [1999] 1 ILRM 500, HC. See CAUTION.

judges, temporary. It has been held that the appointment of judges of the District Court for fixed short periods is not inconsistent with any provision of the 1937 Constitution nor does it in any way interfere with or limit their constitutionally guaranteed independence: *Magee v Culligan* [1992] ILRM 186, SC. See Courts (Supplemental Provisions) Act 1961, s 48; Courts and Court Officers Act 1995, ss 37–41.

judgment. (1) The formal decision or sentence pronounced by a court in legal proceedings; also the reasoning of the judge or judges which leads him or them to the decision. (2) Means, as the context permits or requires, the decision or order of the court or of a judge in any proceedings: Circuit Court Rules 2001, *Interpretation of Terms*, para 12.

A judge may, at or after a trial, direct that judgment be entered for any or either party; no judgment may be entered after a trial without the order of the judge: RSC Ord 36, r 38. A judgment for the payment of money and/or costs may be registered in the Central Office (qv) within twenty-one days after the entry of the judgment.

District Court decrees may be registered in like manner as a similar judgment of the High Court: Courts Act 1981, s 25. See also Circuit Court (Registration of Judg-

ments) Act 1937 as amended by the Courts Act 1981, s 27.

In civil proceedings in the High Court (qv), judgment *after trial* may be appealed to the Supreme Court within twenty-one days from the perfection of the judgment: RSC Ord 58, r 3. It is the duty of a barrister who takes judgment to endorse the terms of or the effect of the same on his brief or otherwise record them in writing: *Code of Conduct for the Bar of Ireland* (December 2003) r 4.17. Judgment may also arise *in default of appearance* and *in default of defence* (qqv). See websites: Irish Legal Information Initiative (*www.irlii.org*); BAILII (*www.bailii.org*), and the Courts Service (*www.courts.ie*). [Bibliography: Glanville.] See DECREE; DECLARATORY JUDGMENT; DIRECTION; EXECUTION OF JUDGMENT; FOREIGN JUDGMENTS, ENFORCEMENT OF; OBITER DICTUM; ORDER; RATIO DECIDENDI; RESERVED JUDGMENT; SUMMARY SUMMONS.

judgment, liberty to enter. See SUMMARY SUMMONS.

judgment by consent. Provision is made for a defendant to civil proceedings in the Circuit Court to consent to judgment being entered against him; the judgment may be entered without reference to the court, only where certain conditions are met eg the parties to the consent are *sui juris*: Circuit Court Rules 2001 Ord 29.

judgment creditor. One in whose favour a judgment for a sum of money is given against a judgment debtor. In relation to a company which is being wound up, a creditor who has issued execution against the company's property or attached a debt due to it is not entitled to retain the benefit of the process unless it was completed before the winding up commenced or before the creditor received notice of the meeting at which it was proposed to wind it up: Companies Act 1963, ss 291, 292 and 219. See CREDITOR; EXECUTION OF JUDGMENT.

judgment debtor. A person against whom a judgment (qv) has been given for a sum of money in favour of a judgment creditor. See EXECUTION OF JUDGMENT; INTEREST ON COSTS.

judgment in default of appearance. Judgment to which a plaintiff is entitled where the defendant fails to enter an appearance to a summons duly served: RSC Ord 13. Where the originating summons (whether plenary or summary) is for a liquidated (qv) sum, final judgment may be entered in the Central Office (qv) without an order of the court, except in the case of hire purchase and moneylending matters when the plaintiff must seek liberty to enter such judgment from the Master (qv) or the court (RSC Ord 13, r 3).

Where the summons is a *plenary* one for an unliquidated sum, the plaintiff must deliver a statement of claim (qv) to the Central Office in lieu of delivery to the defendant and then apply to the court for judgment which, if granted, will be that the plaintiff do recover against the defendant damages (qv) to be assessed by a judge with or without a jury, as the case may be (RSC Ord 13, r 6). A defendant may subsequently apply to have such a judgment set aside on the grounds that there is a defence: *Maher v Dixon* [1995] 1 ILRM 218, HC.

For Circuit Court rules governing obtaining judgment where the defendant fails to enter an appearance to a *civil bill*, see Circuit Court Rules 2001 Ord 26 and Ord 27. For review of such judgment, see Ord 30. A judgment has full force and effect for a period of twelve years from the date thereof (RSC Ord 36, r 9). Where a defendant in the District Court fails to give notice of intention to defend a civil summons, the plaintiff may obtain judgment: DCR 1997 Ord 45, rr 2 and 5.

For pre-judgment interest, see INTEREST ON JUDGMENTS. See APPEARANCE.

judgment in default of defence. Judgment to which a plaintiff is entitled where the defendant fails to deliver a defence to a *plenary* summons: RSC Ord 27, as amended by SI No 63 of 2004. In the case of a claim for a debt or liquidated demand, the plaintiff may have final judgment entered in the Central Office without an order of the court, except in the case of hire-purchase and money lending matters wherein such final judgment may not be entered until after twelve months from the issue of the summons, unless the leave of the court is first obtained by motion on notice on the defendant (RSC Ord 27, rr 2, 15–16).

In claims for unliquidated damages in tort or contract, judgment is obtained by *notice of motion* (qv) to the court, served on the defendant. However, the plaintiff must first serve a 21 days warning letter on the defendant, warning of intention to serve a notice of motion for judgment, and consenting to a further 21 days late delivery of defence; he then allows the defendant

deliver his defence even after service of notice of motion for judgment, but not later than six days before the return date; in which event if the defence is delivered, the motion is not put in the judge's list and the plaintiff is entitled to a fixed sum of €750 for costs (RSC Ord 27, r 9 as amended by SI No 63 of 2004). However, in continuing default of defence, the court may then order judgment that the plaintiff do recover against the defendant damages (qv) to be assessed by a judge with or without a jury, as the case may be. See *Practice Notes* in *Law Society Gazette* (May 2004) 39.

For Circuit Court rules governing obtaining judgment where the defendant fails to deliver a defence to a *civil bill*, see Circuit Court Rules 2001 Ord 26 and Ord 27. For review of such judgment, see Ord 30. A judgment has full force and effect for a period of twelve years from the date thereof (Ord 36, r 9). Where a defendant in the District Court fails to give notice of intention to defend a civil summons, the plaintiff may obtain judgment: DCR 1997 Ord 45, rr 2 and 5.

There is a prohibition on the recognition in an EC state of a default judgment given in another EC state when the document instituting the proceedings was not properly served on the defendant who did not contest the proceedings: (Case-123/91 ECJ) *Minalmet GmbH v Brandeis Ltd* reported by *Byrne* in 11 ILT & SJ (1993) 136. See DEFENCE.

judgment mortgage. A mortgage created by the registration as a mortgage, by a judgment creditor against the lands of the judgment debtor, of a judgment of a court for the payment of a sum of money: Judgment Mortgage Acts 1850 and 1858. Judgments which may be registered are such money judgments of the Supreme, High, Circuit and District Courts: Circuit Court (Registration of Judgments) Act 1937; Courts Act 1981, s 24.

A judgment may be registered against all legal and equitable interests of the judgment debtor in freehold and in leasehold property; a judgment mortgage is rarely registered against leaseholds as the judgment mortgagee then becomes liable for rent and covenants therein.

When a judgment is validly registered as a mortgage, the registration has the effect of a mortgage by deed over the debtor's beneficial interest at the time of registration in the lands set out in the *judgment mortgage affidavit* which is sworn by the judgment creditor: Judgment Mortgage Act 1850, s 7.

If the affidavit filed achieves the purpose which the legislature sought to achieve, strict compliance with the statutory provisions will not be required; the mere omission of a requirement of s 6 of the 1850 Act which does not affect the question of the identity of the property or the debtor could not of itself invalidate the charge on the property: *Irish Bank of Commerce Ltd v O'Hara* [1993] 11 ILT Dig 68, SC – see *Doyle* in 7 ILT & SJ (1989) 304 and 11 ILT & SJ (1993) 52. The statutory requirements are to be construed purposively and the judgment mortgage is not to be invalidated by technical flaws which do not mislead: *Ulster Bank Ltd v Crawford* [2000] ITLR (28 February). However, the affidavit must comply with the relevant Rules of Court and content of affidavits generally: *Credit Finance Ltd v Hennessy* [1979] as reported by *Doyle* in 8 ILT & SJ (1990) 51.

A judgment mortgage is subject to all equitable interests affecting the land at the date of its registration: *MaQuillan v Maguire* [1996] 1 ILRM 394, HC. A judgment mortgage does not obtain priority over a prior unregistered mortgage: *Eyre v McDowell* [1861] 9 HLC 620, unless the judgment mortgage is carried on the back of a subsequent registered mortgage: *Re Scott's Estate* [1862] 14 Ir Ch R 57.

The remedy of the judgment mortgagee is to seek a sale by the court by instituting a *mortgage suit* (qv). For *priority* of a judgment mortgage in the event of the judgment debtor becoming bankrupt (qv), see Bankruptcy Act 1988, s 51. See Registration of Title Act 1964, s 71. See Law Reform Commission, *Consultation Paper on Judgment Mortgages* (LRC CP 30, 2004). [Bibliography: Babington; Bland (2); Glanville; Madden; Scanlon.] See FAMILY HOME AND JUDGMENT MORTGAGE; LAW AGENT; LIS PENDENS; SATISFACTION; WIDOW.

judici officium suum excedenti non paretur. [Effect is not given to the decision of a judge in excess of his jurisdiction.] See CERTIORARI; JUDICIAL REVIEW.

judicial authority. As regards the requirement that an extradition warrant be signed by a judicial authority, it has been held that the term *judicial authority* as used in the Extradition Act 1965 falls to be tested by the law of the place requesting extradition and that there are no grounds for suggesting that a person lacking legal training or security of tenure cannot be a judicial authority: *Russell v Fanning* [1988] ILRM 333. For arrangements concerning the endorsement of such warrants, see EXTRADITION. See also EUROPEAN ARREST WARRANT.

judicial conduct. See JUDGES, COMPLAINTS ABOUT.

judicial co-operation. It is an objective of the European Union (qv) to provide citizens with a high level of safety by developing *common action* among the member states in the fields of police and judicial co-operation in criminal matters; this is directed at preventing and combating crime, in particular terrorism, trafficking in persons and offences against children, illicit drug trafficking and illegal arms trafficking, corruption and fraud: arts 29–42 of the consolidated EC Treaty.

judicial notice. Judicial cognisance. Matters which a judge takes notice or cognisance of, without formal proof, because they are matters of common knowledge and everyday life, or because he is required to take notice of them without proof e g Acts of the Oireachtas. 'A judge is entitled to take judicial notice of the making of regulations when their making was so notorious, well established, embedded in judicial decisions, and susceptible to incontrovertible proof': DPP v Collins [1981] ILRM 447. When a court takes judicial notice of a fact, it declares that the fact exists, although the existence of the fact has not been established in evidence.

Judicial notice is required to be taken of the EEC Treaties, of the Official Journal and of any decision of, or expression of opinion by, the European Court on any question in respect of which that Court has jurisdiction: European Communities (Judicial Notice and Documentary Evidence) Regulations 1972, SI No 341 of 1972. See also Irish Takeover Panel Act 1997, s 23; Civil Liability (Assessment of Hearing Injury) Act 1998, s 3; European Convention on Human Rights Act 2003, s 4. See *Byrne v Londonderry Tram Co* [1902] 2 IR 457; *The State (William Taylor) v Circuit Court Judge for Wicklow* [1951] IR 311; *Waters v Cruickshank* [1967] IR 378; *Greene v Minister for Defence* [1998] 4 IR 464, HC; *Hanley v Minister for Defence* [1998] 4 IR

496, HC. See EX INFORMATA CONSCIENTIA; HEARING INJURY; PRELIMINARY RULINGS.

judicial panel. A panel of independent persons which the Council of Ministers may create to hear and determine at first instance, certain classes of action or proceedings brought in specific areas: EC Treaty, art 225a of the consolidated (2002) version. This provision was inserted by the Nice Treaty (qv). Members of these panels must possess the ability required for appointment to judicial office. Decisions given by judicial panels may be subject to appeal to the Court of First Instance. See FIRST INSTANCE, COURT OF.

judicial power. See SEPARATION OF POWERS.

judicial review. A 'legal remedy available in situations where a body or tribunal with legal authority to determine rights or impose liabilities, and with a duty to act judicially, has acted in excess of legal authority or contrary to its duty': *Murtagh & Murtagh v Board of Management of St Emer's National School* [1991] ILRM 549, SC. Judicial review is generally concerned not with the decision of a body or tribunal but with the decision-making process: *O'Keeffe v An Bord Pleanála & Radio Tara* [1991] ILRM 237, SC. Judicial review is a review and not an appeal: *Garda Representative Association v Ireland, A-G and Minister for Justice* [1994] 1 ILRM 81, SC.

An application for judicial review is an application to the High Court for orders of certiorari, prohibition, mandamus or quo warranto (qqv): RSC Ord 84, r 18. An application for a declaration (qv) or for an injunction (qv) may also be made by an application for judicial review.

Judicial review is now the uniform system for the High Court to exercise its supervisory function over inferior courts, administrative bodies and individuals. The Law Reform Commission has stated that there are probably more applications for judicial review, per head of population, in Ireland than in any other jurisdiction in the world: website: *www.lawreform.ie/lawunderreview/*.

Where a *notice party* would be seriously affected by the outcome of judicial review proceedings, then that notice party has a sufficient *locus standi* to maintain an application to strike out those proceedings, even though the notice party had not been joined as a respondent and could have applied to the court to be added as such:

O'Connell v Environment Protection Agency [2001] ITLR (22 October).

For judicial review of a motorway scheme, see Roads Act 1993, s 55A as inserted by Roads (Amendment) Act 1998, s 6. For judicial review and employment dismissal cases, see *Barry* in 9 ILT & SJ (1991) 54 and *O'Neill v Iarnród Éireann* [1991] ELR 1, SC. See *An Post v Brady* [1993] ELR 46, HC; *G v DPP* [1994] 1 IR 374, SC; *Lancefort Ltd v An Bord Pleanála* [1997] 2 ILRM 508, HC; *Rafferty v Bus Éireann* [1997] 2 IR 424, HC; *Solan v DPP* [1989] ILRM 491; *DPP v McDonnell* [1991] 9 ILT Dig 128, HC; *Dooner v Garda Síochána Complaints Board* [2000] ITLR (14 August); *Z v Minister for Justice* [2002] 2 ILRM 215, SC; *McD v Commission to Inquire into Child Abuse* [2003] 2 ILRM 503, HC and 2 IR 348. See also RSC Ord 124. See also Delaney in 11 ILT & SJ (1993) 12. For practice and procedure where the State is a party, see Bibliography: Collins & O'Reilly (1). See LRC Working Paper 8 of 1979. See also *Consultation Paper on Judicial Review Procedure* (LRC CP 20, 2003); *Report on Judicial Review Procedure* (LRC 71, 2004). [Bibliography: Bradley; De Blacam (3); Delaney (4); Hadfield.] See APPEAL AND JUDICIAL REVIEW; COMMERCIAL PROCEEDINGS; DECLARATORY JUDGMENT; DISCOVERY; EX-PARTE; MINISTERIAL DECISION; RAILWAY ORDER.

judicial review, application for. An application for judicial review may not be made unless the leave of the court is first obtained, which leave is sought by way of a motion made *ex parte*, grounded upon a supporting statement and verifying affidavit: (RSC Ord 84, r 20).

If leave is granted, the application for judicial review is then made by originating notice of motion unless the court directs that it be made by plenary summons (Ord 84, r.22(1)). The respondent is allowed seven days from service of the notice of motion within which to serve his statement and affidavit (Ord 84, r 22(4)).

An application for leave to apply for a judicial review must be made promptly and in any event within *three months* from the date when grounds for the application first arose, or *six months* when the relief sought is certiorari (qv): RSC Ord 84, r 21(1)). There is a duty on an applicant for a judicial review, not only to apply within the specified time limits, but also to act promptly: *O'Connor v Minister for the*

Marine [1999] ITLR (15 November), HC. See also *Gilligan v Ireland* [2000] 4 IR 579, SC.

An application for judicial review which is out of time, will still be permitted where the issue is too important to permit the application being considered on a point of time only: *Eastern Health Board v Farrell* [2000] 1 ILRM 446, HC.

The court may allow an applicant for judicial review to amend a statement of claim at any time; the applicant must however give notice to all other parties: *Molloy v Governor of Limerick Prison* [1991] ITLR (2 December), SC. However, the test for an application to amend the grounds under which leave for a judicial review has been granted is much more stringent than that which applies to the amendment of a statement of claim under RSC Ord 28, r 1; only in exceptional circumstances will liberty to amend a grounding statement for a judicial review be allowed: *O'Leary v Minister for Transport* [2000] 1 ILRM 391, HC: *McCormack v Garda Síochána Complaints Board* [1997] 2 IR 489.

There are special rules applying to applications for judicial review as regards asylum, pollution control, planning, and the take-over of companies. See JUDICIAL REVIEW, POLLUTION CONTROL; JUDICIAL REVIEW, PLANNING; JUDICIAL REVIEW, TAKE-OVER.

judicial review, asylum. The validity of a range of matters relating to asylum seekers cannot be questioned by a person otherwise than by way of judicial review under RSC Ord 84, SI No 15 of 1986: Illegal Immigrants (Trafficking) Act 2000, s 5(1) as amended by Immigration Act 2003, s 10 and Immigration Act 2004, s 16(6). The matters include: notifications, recommendations, determinations, decisions, refusals, and exclusion and deportation orders. An application for leave to apply for a judicial review must be made within a period of 14 days commencing on the date on which the person was notified of the matter and there is limitation on the right to appeal to the Supreme Court (II(T)A 2000, s 5(2)).

This provision (s 5) was referred to the Supreme Court by the President of Ireland under art 26 of the Constitution for a decision on whether it was repugnant to the Constitution. The Supreme Court held on 28 August 2000 that it was not unconstitutional: *In the matter of art 26 and the Illegal Immigrants (Trafficking) Bill 1999*

[2000 SC.] The court held that the limitation period was not unreasonable and that the discretion of the High Court to extend the 14-day period was sufficiently wide to enable persons who, having regard to all the circumstances of the case including language difficulties, communication difficulties, difficulties with regard to legal advice or otherwise, have shown reasonable diligence, to have sufficient access to the courts for the purpose of seeking judicial review in accordance with their constitutional rights.

The time for applying for judicial review can only be extended where the High Court considers that there is good and sufficient reason for extending the period; the substantive claim must be an arguable one: *G K v Minister for Justice* [2002] 1 ILRM 401, SC and 2 IR 418. It has been held that leave is not required to appeal against a decision to extend the 14-day period: *B v Governor of Training Unit* [2002] 2 ILRM 161, SC; *AB v Minister for Justice* [2002] 1 IR 296, SC. See also *S v Minister for Justice* [2002] 2 IR 163, SC.

The courts are slow to interfere with the decision of a specialist statutory tribunal (in this case the *Refugee Appeals Authority*) by means of judicial review on the grounds of irrationality: *Camara v Minister for Justice* [2000] ITLR (25 September). See 'Caselaw on Judicial Review Applications in Asylum Law' by Stephen O'Sullivan BL in *Bar Review* (October/November 2002) 312; 'Sections 5 and 10 of the Illegal Immigrants (Trafficking) Act 2000' by Mary Rogan in (2002) 10 ISLR 3. [Bibliography: Fraser & Harvey.] See ASYLUM, CLAIM FOR.

judicial review, crime. Judicial review is a remedy which permits challenge to decisions made in the course of a criminal trial but only in the most exceptional cases: *Blanchfield v Harnett* [2002] 2 ILRM 435, SC and 3 IR 207.

judicial review, damages. Damages may be awarded on an application for judicial review if: (a) the applicant has included a claim for such relief in his supporting statement, and (b) if the court is satisfied that the applicant would have been awarded damages if the claim had been made in a civil action: RSC Ord 84, r 24(1).

The High Court has a discretion to require an *undertaking* as to damages as a condition to the grant or continuance of an application for a judicial review: RSC

Ord 84, r 20(6). Even though the threshold to obtain leave to apply for a judicial review on planning matters was higher than in other applications, there is no basis for drawing a distinction between applications as regards an undertaking as to damages: *Seery v An Bord Pleanála* [2001] 2 ILRM 151, HC.

judicial review, European Court of Justice. The test for judicial review adopted by the European Court of Justice is whether the decision maker has made a clear or manifest error: *SIAC v Mayo County Council* [2002] 2 ILRM 401, SC and 3 IR 148.

judicial review, pollution control. As regards an integrated pollution control licence, an application for leave to apply for a judicial review must be made within eight weeks of the decision of the EPA: Environmental Protection Agency Act 1992; s 87(10) inserted by Protection of the Environment Act 2003, s 15; RSC Ord 84, r 23(2). The eight-week time period is absolute. While this section imposes a non-expandable upper time limit, it does not in any way suspend or lessen the requirement under RSC Ord 84, r 21 that every application for a judicial review must be made promptly: *O'Connell v EPA* [2002] 1 ILRM 1, HC and [2001] 4 IR 494, HC.

An applicant for a judicial review within the time limit is not permitted to change the grounds of the challenge outside the statutory time limit; to allow amendments would run counter to the statute, negative its intent, and, in effect, permit of no time bar at all in respect of additional reliefs sought: *Ní Eile v EPA* [1997] 2 ILRM 458, HC.

judicial review, planning. A person can question the validity of a decision of a planning authority or of An Bord Pleanála only by way of an application to the courts for a *judicial review* under RSC Ord 84, SI No 15 of 1986: Planning and Development Act 2000, s 50(2) as amended by Planning and Development (Amendment) Act 2002, s 12. The decisions which may be questioned are: (a) a decision of a planning authority on an application for planning permission, or on its own development under s 179 of PDA 2000, and (b) a decision of An Bord Pleanála on any appeal or referral, or on the approval of a local authority development which requires an environmental impact assessment under s 175, or under Part XIV on the acquisition of land. PD(A)A 2002 extends the applica-

tion of s 50 to decisions by local authorities to confirm compulsory acquisitions to which no objection has been made or sustained.

An application for leave to apply for a judicial review must be made within eight weeks of the grant of permission or the decision, as appropriate, and the court will not extend this period unless there is good and sufficient reason to do so (PDA 2000, s 50(4) as amended by PD(A)A 2002, s 12).

The application for leave to apply for judicial review must be made by the filing in court of the notice of motion and its service on the mandatory parties within the time limit: *KSK Enterprises Ltd v An Bord Pleanála* [1994] 2 ILRM 1, SC. The applicant must specify the relief claimed within the time limit, but when doing so must also specify the grounds upon which relief is sought: *McNamara v An Bord Pleanála* [1996] 2 ILRM 339, HC. The onus is on the applicant to demonstrate good and sufficient reason for a failure to issue proceedings at the earliest opportunity: *Casey v An Bord Pleanála* [2003] ITLR (24 November); FL 8189, HC.

The court is required not to grant leave unless it is satisfied that there are *substantial grounds* for contending that the decision is invalid or ought to be quashed, and that the applicant has a *substantial interest* (not limited to an interest in land or other financial interest) in the matter (PDA 2000, s 50(4)(b) and (d)). Under the previous legislation, *substantial grounds* were held to mean *reasonable grounds*: *Blessington & District v Wicklow County Council* [1997] 1 IR 273, HC. In order for a ground to be *substantial*, it must be reasonable, it must be arguable, and it must be weighty: *Evans v An Bord Pleanála* [2004] ITLR (26 January) SC. Rejection by An Bord Pleanála of an inspector's recommendation and failure to explain this rejection is not a substantial ground, but failure to explain what was wrong with the proposed development is a *substantial* ground: *Stack v An Bord Pleanála* [2000] ITLR (28 August) HC citing *Save Britain's Heritage v The Secretary of State for the Environment* [1991] 2 All ER 10. See also *Sloan v An Bord Pleanála* [2003] 2 ILRM 61, HC.

There are also restrictions on any appeal to the Supreme Court (PDA 2000, s 50(4)(f)). The Oireachtas has the competence to exclude certain decisions of the

High Court from the appellate jurisdiction of the Supreme Court; such exceptions can only be made by law and such law must be clear and unambiguous: *Irish Asphalt Ltd v An Bord Pleanála* [1997] 1 ILRM 81, SC and [1996] 2 IR 180, SC; *Ní Ghruagáin v An Bord Pleanála* [2003] FL 8033, HC.

No appeal lies to the Supreme Court from a refusal of the High Court to grant a certificate permitting such an appeal; the High Court will only grant such a certificate where its decision regarding a planning judicial review involves a point of law of exceptional public importance: *Irish Hardware v South Dublin County Council* [2001] 2 ILRM 291, SC. There has to be a point of law of exceptional public importance that at least transcends beyond the individual facts and parties of any given case: *Kenny v An Bord Pleanála (No 2)* [2001] 1 IR 704, HC and [2002] 1 ILRM 68, HC.

Where a condition, attached to a planning permission, requires a developer to submit certain details to the planning authority for agreement, an order made by the authority signifying its agreement with the details submitted is not a 'decision' given on approval, and an application for leave to apply for a judicial review in respect of the order is governed by RSC Ord 84 and not s 82 of the Local Government (Planning and Development) Act 1963: *O'Connor v Dublin Corporation & Borg Developments* [2000] ITLR (19 June), HC.

An Bord Pleanála or any party to an appeal or referral which is currently before the board, may apply to the High Court to stay the proceedings pending a decision by the board on the appeal or referral (PDA 2000, s 50(3)).

In a particular case, the Supreme Court held that the two-month time period to apply for a judicial review under previous legislation was unconstitutional, as the applicants were deprived of any genuine opportunity to challenge the legality of the planning decision due to the unlawful act of the decision-maker: *White v Dublin City Council* (10 June 2004, unreported). The court held that the council's decision that there was no requirement to notify the public of revised plans, the subject of the planning application, was based on the council's incorrect interpretation of its discretionary powers.

See *KSK Enterprises Ltd v An Bord Pleanála* [1994] 2 ILRM 1, SC; *Scott & Ors v An Bord Pleanála* [1995] 1 ILRM 424, SC; *McNamara v An Bord Pleanála* [1998] 2 ILRM 313, SC; *Lancefort Ltd v An Bord Pleanála* [1998] 2 ILRM 401, SC and [1999] 2 IR 270, SC; *Maire de Faoite v An Bord Pleanála* [2000] ITLR (29 May), HC; *Murray v An Bord Pleanála* [2000] 1 IR 58, HC; *Kenny v An Bord Pleanála (No 1)* [2001] 1 IR 565, HC; *Brick v Burke* [2002] 2 ILRM 427, SC; *Martin v An Bord Pleanála* [2002] 2 IR 655, HC and [2003] 1 ILRM 257. See 'Judicial Review of Planning Decisions – Section 50 Practice Procedure' by Garret Simons BL in *Bar Review* (June/July 2001) 449. See INJUNCTION, PLANNING; PLANNING PERMISSION, CONDITIONS ON.

judicial review, private law. Excluded from judicial review are decisions made in the realm of private law where the duty being performed by the decision making authority is manifestly a private duty derived solely from contract or solely from consent or agreement of the parties affected: Finlay CJ in *Beirne v Commissioner of Garda Síochána* [1993] ILRM 1, SC. See also *Rajah v RCSI* [1994] 1 ILRM 233, HC.

Judicial review extends to bodies which exercise functions of a public nature but not a domestic tribunal: *Murphy v The Turf Club* [1989] IR 171. The factors relevant to whether judicial review extends to a particular body are: the source of power of the body, the nature of its powers, and the effect of the sanctions it can impose: see *Taylor* in 9 ILT & SJ (1991) 14. See CLUB; COMMON CONTRACT; COMPROMISE; CONTRACT.

judicial review, take-over. As regards the take-over of companies, an application for leave to apply for a judicial review, must be made within *seven days* of a rule, ruling, derogation, waiver, or direction of the Irish Takeover Panel and leave will not be granted unless the court is satisfied that there are *substantial* grounds for its quashing; there are also restrictions on any appeal to the Supreme Court: Irish Takeover Panel Act 1997, s 13. See *In R. v Panel on Takeovers and Mergers, ex parte Datafin plc* [1987] 1 All ER 564. See IRISH TAKEOVER PANEL.

judicial review, tribunals. It has been held that the proper purpose of the remedy of judicial review of administrative action is to ensure that a decision reached by a tribunal has been open to it upon the evidence before it; it is not the function of the court to substitute its opinion for that of the authority constituted by law to decide such matters: *The State (Keegan) v Stardust Victims Tribunal* [1987] ILRM 292. See TRIBUNALS OF INQUIRY.

judicial separation. The decree granted by the court which relieves the spouses to a marriage of the obligation to cohabit; the marriage however is not dissolved: Judicial Separation and Family Law Reform Act 1989. The 1989 Act as a whole constituted an attempt by the Oireachtas to deal with the unfortunate situation created by the breakdown of a marriage and the inability of one of the spouses to cohabit with the other, while providing various safeguards for the rights of the persons involved: *TF v Ireland* [1995] 2 ILRM 321, SC and 1 IR 321.

A decree may be awarded to an applicant on one or more of a number of grounds eg: (a) adultery of the respondent: (b) unreasonable behaviour of respondent; (c) desertion by respondent for at least one year; (d) spouses have lived apart for at least one year and respondent consents to the decree; (e) spouses have lived apart for at least three years; (f) marriage has broken down to such extent that normal marital relationship has not existed for at least one year (JSFLRA 1989, s 2(1)).

It has been held that s 2(1)(f) could not be interpreted as referring to non-continuous periods of time totalling one year: *TF v Ireland* [1995] 2 ILRM 321, SC. It is not necessary for the court to identify how, when and for what reason the marriage has broken down; the court must be satisfied on the balance of probability that it has broken down: *F v F* [1994] 2 ILRM 401, HC.

There are safeguards to ensure the applicant and respondent are aware of the alternatives to separation proceedings and to assist attempts at reconciliation (JSFLRA 1989, ss 5–7). Also the court will not grant a decree unless satisfied that proper provision is made for the *welfare* of dependent children of the family; 'welfare' comprises the religious and moral, intellectual, physical and social welfare of the children (JSFLRA 1989, s 3).

The court is empowered to make ancillary financial, property, custody and other orders, including orders in relation to the *family home* (qv), succession rights and any pension entitlements: Family Law Act 1995, ss 5–22 (Pt II). It will generally seek to ensure that provision is made for the spouses and any dependent child of the family as is adequate and reasonable having regard to all the circumstances. There is also provision for the voidance of transactions intended to prevent or reduce the provision of financial relief of a spouse or child (FLA 1995, s 35). Where a court extinguishes succession rights and one of the spouses dies, the other spouse may apply to the court for provision to be made out of the estate of the deceased spouse (FLA 1995, s 15A inserted by Family Law (Divorce) Act 1996, s 52).

The Circuit Court is established as a *Circuit Family Court* (JSFLRA 1989, s 31).

There is no jurisdiction to grant a decree of judicial separation where a deed of separation already existed which relieved the parties of the duty to cohabit and where they had lived apart since the conclusion of the agreement: *PO'D v AO'D* [1998] 2 IR 225, SC. Also the Supreme Court has held that earlier proceedings for a divorce *a mensa et thoro* which had been settled by the parties, precluded the institution of separate proceedings for judicial separation under the 1989 Act: *F v F* [1995] 2 IR 354, SC.

See *O'H v O'H* [1990] 2 IR 558, HC reported in 9 ILT & SJ (1991) 28; *MK v PK* [1990] HC reported by Corrigan in 9 ILT & SJ (1991) 176; *VS v RS* [1991] ITLR (11 November), HC; *JD v DD* [1997] 3 IR 64, HC; *BD v JD* [2003] FL 8851, HC. For the High Court rules, see RSC Ord 70A inserted by SI No 343 of 1997. For the rules governing a *Family Law Civil Bill* seeking a decree of judicial separation, see Circuit Court Rules 2001 Ord 59, r 4(4)(b). See also Child Care Act 1991, s 20; Children Act 1997, s 16; Domestic Violence Act 1996, ss 20–21; Family Law (Divorce) Act 1996, s 45; Civil Liability and Courts Act 2004, s 50.

See 'Financial Non-Disclosure in Judicial and Divorce Cases' by Inge Clissmann SC and Mary Fay BL in *Bar Review* (February 2003) 3. [Bibliography: Browne; Duncan & Scully; Kennedy & Maguire; McLoughlin; Murtagh B; Power; Shannon; Walpole.] See DIVORCE A MENSA ET THORO; PROPERTY ADJUSTMENT ORDER; RESIDENCE, RIGHT OF; SEPARATION AGREEMENT; SUCCESSION, LAW OF.

Judicial Studies Institute. An institute located at the Four Courts in Dublin, which was established in 1996 for the training and ongoing education of the judiciary. It is chaired by the Chief Justice.

judiciary. The collective name for judges (qv). Expense allowances paid to a member of the judiciary are exempt from income tax: Taxes Consolidation Act 1997, s 196. See 'Benchmark: judicial activism Irish-style' by Prof David Gwynn Morgan in *Law Society Gazette* (October 2003) 14. See 'Stepping into the breach: judicial activism revisited' by solicitor Pat Igoe in *Law Society Gazette* (November 2003) 9. [Bibliography: Gwynn Morgan.]

junior counsel. See BARRISTER.

jura eodem modo destituuntur quo constituuntur. [Laws are abrogated by the same means by which they were made.]

jura publica anteterenda privatis. [Public rights are to be preferred to private.]

jurat. A certificate at the end of an affidavit, stating where and when the affidavit was sworn, with the signature and description of the person before whom it was sworn. The jurat must contain a certificate by the person taking the affidavit that he knows the deponent himself, or some person named in the jurat who certifies his knowledge of the deponent: RSC Ord 40, r 14. See Solicitors (Amendment) Act 1994, s 72(4).

juratores sunt judices facti. [Juries are the judges of fact.]

jure imperii. The right inherent in sovereignty. See *McElhinney v Williams* [1996] 1 ILRM 276, SC and [1995] 3 IR 382, SC. See ACTA JURE IMPERII.

juris et de jure. [Of law and from law.]

jurisdiction. (1) The power of a court or a judge to hear and decide an action, petition or other proceeding.

(2) The territorial limits within which legal authority may be exercised.

(3) The district or limits within which the judgments or orders of a court can be enforced or executed. The reference to the 'jurisdiction' of the justices in s 86 of the Landlord and Tenant Law Amendment Act Ireland 1860 was merely to the justices' territorial jurisdiction and not to the exercise of their judicial duties: *Kerry Co Council v McCarthy* [1997] 2 ILRM 481, SC.

The High Court is already empowered to act in aid of the United Kingdom in bankruptcy (qv) matters, and the government may by order extend this aid to other jurisdictions: Bankruptcy Act 1988, s 142; *Re*

Gibson, A Bankrupt in England, ex parte Walter [1960] Ir Jur Rep 60.

A judge of the High Court does not have jurisdiction to overrule an earlier order of the same court: *R v Minister for Justice* [2001] FL 5092, HC. Civil penalties in tax matters can now be pursued in the District, Circuit and High Courts depending on the level of penalty: Taxes Consolidation Act 1997, s 1061 amended by Finance Act 2003, s 162. For specific jurisdiction of each court, see separate entry under each court and App 4.

See *The State (McCormack) v Curran* [1987] ILRM 225; *Handbridge Ltd v British Aerospace Communications Ltd* [1993] 3 IR 343, SC; *Devrajan v District Judge Ballagh* [1993] 3 IR 377, SC; *Ferndale Films Ltd v Granada Television Ltd* [1993] 3 IR 362, SC; *Hanley v Someport-Walon* [1995] 2 IR 132, HC; *Re MV 'Turquoise Bleu'* [1995] 3 IR 437, HC; *Short v Ireland* [1996] 2 IR 188, SC; *Papamicolaou v Thielen* [1998] 2 IR 42, HC; *McIlwraith v Seitz Filtration (GB) Ltd* [1998] ELR 105, LC; *Zimmerman v Der Deutsche Schuliverein Ltd* [1999] ELR 211, EAT; *Clare Taverns v Gill* [2000] 1 IR 286, HC; *Minister for Agriculture v Alte Leipziger* [2001] 2 IR 83, SC and [2002] 1 ILRM 306, SC. See also Gill in 7 ILT & SJ (1989) 2 and 8 ILT (1990 179. [Bibliography: Byrne P.] See also CIRCUIT COURT; CRIMINAL JURISDICTION; ENLARGEMENT OF JURISDICTION; EXCLUSIVE JURISDICTION; FOREIGN JUDGMENTS, ENFORCEMENT OF; MARITIME JURISDICTION; PREFERENTIAL JURISDICTION; SPLITTING OF ACTION; SUMMONS, SERVICE OUT OF JURISDICTION.

jurisdiction, civil and commercial, EU. The jurisdiction of Irish courts has been extended further in civil and commercial matters by the Jurisdiction of Courts and Enforcement of Judgments Act 1998: however, see below for changes since 2002. Persons domiciled in a 'contracting state' must be sued in the courts of that state; however: (a) in matters relating to a contract they may be sued in the place of performance of the obligation, and (b) in matters relating to tort in the place where the harmful event occurred (JCEJA 1998, Sch 1, arts 2, 5 and 6; *Gannon v B & I and Landliner Travel Merseyside Ltd* [1993] 2 IR 359, SC.

Where a plaintiff has a choice of jurisdictions, he is entitled to choose that which he perceives to be most advantageous to him: *Ewins v Carlton* [1997] 2 ILRM 223, HC.

The Irish court has jurisdiction where there is a plausible cause of action against an Irish co-defendant; it is not open to one of a number of defendants from a contracting State to admit liability so as to deprive the plaintiff of the right to pursue a claim in a court in which jurisdiction has been established: *Kelly v McCarthy & Ors* [1993] ITLR (12 April), HC.

A defendant may raise the issue of jurisdiction at any time before serving his defence: *Campbell International Trading House Ltd v Peter van Aart and Natur Pur gmbh* [1992] ILRM 663, SC. The Irish courts do not have jurisdiction as regards a contractual obligation which is to be performed in another EC state: *Olympia Productions Ltd v Cameron Mackintosh* [1992] ILRM 204, HC.

It is not sufficient to show that the obligation which it is claimed has been breached *could* have been performed in Ireland: *Hanbridge Services Ltd v Aerospace Communications* [1994] 1 ILRM 39, SC.

A plaintiff who seeks to have his claim tried in the jurisdiction of a contracting state, other than the contracting state in which the defendant is domiciled, must establish that his claim unequivocally comes within the relevant derogation from the rule provided in art 5 of the Brussels Convention: *Bio-Medical Research v Delatex SA* [2001] 2 ILRM 51, SC and [2000] 4 IR 307, SC.

The 1998 Act gives force of law to the Lugano Convention on jurisdiction and enforcement of judgments between EU member states and EFTA countries. See SIs No 39 and 40 of 2000. See Contractual Obligations (Applicable Law) Act 1991. For the rules of court governing the provision of documentation pursuant to s 14 of the Jurisdiction of Courts and Enforcement of Judgements (European Communities) Act 1998, see Circuit Court Rules 2001 Ord 61.

The *Brussels I Regulation* on the recognition and enforcement of judgments in civil and commercial matters, replaces the Brussels Convention and the 1998 Act for all EU states except Denmark: EC (Civil and Commercial Judgments) Regulations 2002, SI No 52 of 2002. See 'Judgment Calls' by T P Kennedy in *Law Society Gazette* (June 2002) 14. See BRUSSELS I REGULATION.

jurisdiction, criminal. See CRIMINAL JURISDICTION.

jurisdiction, monetary. There are monetary limits set on the jurisdiction of the hierarchy of courts; however, where the parties consent in civil matters the Circuit Court has unlimited jurisdiction (Courts (Supplemental Provisions) Act 1961, s 22(1)(b)), as has the District Court (Courts) Act 1991, s 4(c)). For specific jurisdiction of each court, see separate entry under each court and Appendix 4.

jurisdiction, territorial. Up to 1998, the 1937 Constitution, art 3, stated that, without prejudice to the right claimed to exercise jurisdiction over the whole of the *national territory* (qv), the laws of the State have the like area and extent of application as the laws of *Saorstát Éireann* (qv) and the like extra-territorial effect. However, since the Nineteenth Amendment to the Constitution, approved by the people in 1998, new art 3 states that until a united Ireland has been brought about by the consent of the people, the laws enacted by the parliament established by the Constitution, have the like area and extent of application as the laws enacted by the previous parliament. Also under this article, institutions with executive powers and functions shared with Northern Ireland may exercise their powers and functions in respect of all or part of the island of Ireland. The State may also exercise extra-territorial jurisdiction in accordance with generally recognised principles of international law: 1937 Constitution, new art 29(8). See CRIMINAL JURISDICTION, PLACE.

jurisprudence. The science, philosophy or theory of law. The study of the principles of law. [Bibliography: Murphy T (2).]

juror. A member of a jury (qv).

juror, challenge to. In criminal cases, the prosecution and each accused may challenge without cause shown (called a *peremptory challenge*) up to seven jurors, and jurors so challenged are not included in the jury. The prosecution and each accused may challenge for cause shown any number of jurors; the cause must be shown immediately on the challenge being made and the judge will then rule on the challenge; if the challenge is allowed, the juror is not included in the jury. In civil cases, each party may similarly challenge jurors. See Juries Act 1976, ss 20–21. See JURY, SELECTION OF.

juror, intimidation of. See INTIMIDATION, CRIME OF.

juror's oath. See OATH, FORM OF.

jury. A body of persons selected according to law and sworn to give a verdict on some matter according to the evidence. A jury is chosen from panels which are drawn from citizens aged between eighteen and seventy years of age who are registered on the register of electors of Dáil Éireann: Juries Act 1976. Certain categories of persons are ineligible, excused or disqualified.

A jury comprises twelve persons; however, if a juror dies or is discharged by the judge (eg due to illness), the jury will remain properly constituted unless the judge directs otherwise or the number of jurors is reduced below ten (JA 1976, s 23). Jurors in criminal matters are provided with meals and other facilities; jurors in civil cases generally are not. However, since July 2000, jurors in High Court civil actions get lunch vouchers of £10 (€12.70): *Irish Times*, 7 July 2000.

The deliberations of a jury must always be regarded as completely confidential and must not be published after a trial; it is a well-established principle that the deliberations of a jury in a criminal case must not be revealed or inquired into: *O'Callaghan v A-G* [1993 SC] ILRM 764. Juries should be warned by the judge not to discuss the case with any person other than another member of the jury: *DPP v McKeever* [1994] 2 ILRM 186, CCA. A jury in a murder trial was discharged when it came to the judge's attention that the jury could be overheard: *DPP v Nevin* (2000) Irish Times, 27 January 2000, CCC.

The purpose of sending a jury to a hotel for the night is so that they can rest and recuperate from their deliberations; a judge's direction to a jury at the trial to deliberate further that night at their hotel was incorrect and rendered the trial unsatisfactory: *DPP v Gavin* [2000] 4 IR 557, CCA. A retrial of a murder case was ordered when the court held that the behaviour of two gardaí acting as a jury-keeper at a hotel rendered the trial unsatisfactory; the gardaí had been drinking with some jurors in the hotel bar until about 2am: *McDonagh v DPP* (2003) Irish Times, 14 October.

It is too late to raise, on appeal, a suggestion that a juror had been asleep at the trial, when no application had been made at the trial that the jury be discharged: *The People*

(*DPP*) *v O'Regan* [1999] ITLR (7 June), CCA. See RSC Ord 36, rr 5, 10, 34, 35, 42; Ord 22, r 7; Ord 76, r 91. See 'A Representative and Impartial Jury' by barrister Tom O'Malley in *Bar Review* (December 2003) 232. See EMBRACERY; GRAND JURY; HUNG JURY; INQUEST; INTIMIDATION, CRIME OF; JUROR, CHALLENGE TO; TRIAL BY JURY, CRIMINAL OFFENCES; TRIAL BY JURY, CIVIL MATTERS; VERDICT; WAGES.

jury, abolition of. Juries were abolished for civil actions in the Circuit Court by the Courts Act 1971. Juries were abolished for certain *actions* in the High Court for recovery of damages for *personal injuries* from 1 August 1988: Courts Act 1988, s 1(1). *Personal injuries* include any disease and any impairment of a person's physical or mental condition (CA 1988, s 1(7)).

Actions include: (a) actions where the personal injuries were caused by negligence, nuisance or breach of duty; (b) actions under the Civil Liability Act 1961, s 48 ie actions brought where death is caused by wrongful act, neglect or default; or (c) actions under the Air Navigation and Transport Act 1936, s 18 (as inserted by the Air Navigation and Transport Act 1965, s 4) ie liability of a carrier in the event of death of a passenger. Such actions do not include actions where the damages claimed consists only of damages for false imprisonment or for intentional trespass to the person or both (CA 1988, s 1(3)). See RSC Ord 36 and Ord 49 both as amended by SI No 20 of 1989 to take account of the abolition of juries.

jury, discharge of. A trial judge is empowered to dismiss or discharge a jury if there is an unavoidable risk of a fair trial. The judge must however consider whether any unfairness could be avoided with appropriate directions being given to the jury as to matters they could or could not take into account. See *Murtagh v Ireland & A-G* [2004] FL 8680, SC. See ALTERNATIVE VERDICT.

jury, information to. The judge has a wide discretion in a trial on indictment under the Criminal Justice (Theft and Fraud Offences) Act 2001 on what copies he may direct be given to the jury eg: (a) any document admitted in evidence at the trial, (b) the transcript of the opening speeches of counsel, (c) any charts, diagrams, graphics, schedules or summaries of evidence produced at the trial, (d) the transcript of the whole or part of the evidence given at the trial, (e) the transcript of the judge's charge to the jury, (f) any other document that in the opinion of the judge would be of assistance to the jury in its deliberations, including, where appropriate, an affidavit by an accountant summarising, in a form which is likely to be comprehended by the jury, any transaction by the accused or other person relevant to the offence: (CJ(TFO)A 2001, s 57).

As regards the affidavit by an accountant, such affidavit must be given in advance of the trial to the accused. Also the judge must take into account any representations made by the accused in relation to it, and may require the accountant to explain to the jury any relevant accounting procedure or principles. See also Company Law Enforcement Act 2001, s 110; Competition Act 2002, s 10; Finance Act 2003, s 161. See OFFENCES UNDER COMPANIES ACTS, TRIAL OF.

jury, selection of. The selection of person as jurors from a panel to serve on a particular jury is made by balloting in open court: Juries Act 1976, s 15. Before the selection is begun, the judge must warn the jurors present that they must not serve if they are ineligible or disqualified; and the judge must also invite any person selected to communicate to the judge if he has an interest in or connection with the case (JA 1976, s 15(3)). The final filter to eliminate disqualified, ineligible or biased jurors is provided for in s 15(3) of the JA 1976.

A trial judge does not have statutory power, either express or implied, to circulate a letter or questionnaire to a member of the jury panel; the Juries Act 1976 does not make provision for members of the jury panel to be questioned before they attended in open court: *DPP v Haugh, Charles J Haughey and A-G* [2000] 1 IR 184, HC. See JUROR, CHALLENGE TO.

jury, trial by. See TRIAL BY JURY, CIVIL MATTERS; TRIAL BY JURY, CRIMINAL OFFENCES.

jury, voting by. See TRIAL BY JURY, CIVIL MATTERS; TRIAL BY JURY, CRIMINAL OFFENCES.

jury bias. The appropriate test to be applied to a challenge of jury bias is whether a reasonable person in the circumstances would have a reasonable apprehension that the accused would not receive a fair trial: *DPP v Tobin* [2001] 3 IR 469, CCA and [2002] 1 ILRM 428, CCA.

jus. [A right.] See EURO-JUS.

jus accrescendi. [The right of survivorship.] See JOINT TENANCY.

jus canonicum. [Canon law.]

jus ex injuria non oritur. [A right does not arise out of a wrong.]

jus in personam. [A right against a specific person.]

jus mariti. [The right of a husband.]

jus publicum privatorem pactis mutari non potest. [Public law is not to be superseded by private agreements.]

jus quaesitum tertio. [Rights on account of third parties.] Generally, a contract cannot confer rights on a third party; only a party to a contract can sue on it. However, rights may be conferred on third parties by way of trust. See *O'Leary v Irish National Insurance Co Ltd* [1958] Ir Jur Rep 1; *Cadbury Ireland Ltd v Kerry Co-op Creameries Ltd* [1982] ILRM 77; *Rooney v Trustees of Textile Operatives Society of Ireland* [1913] 47 ILTR 303. See PRIVITY OF CONTRACT.

jus spatiendi. The right to stray; the right of perambulation. The law does not recognise a right in the nature of a *jus spatiendi*: *Smeltzer v Fingal County Council* [1999] 1 ILRM 24, HC. There is no common law right in the public or any customary right in inhabitants of any particular place to stray over open space; the only right may be a right by the public to pass and repass from one point to another across an open space: *Murphy v Wicklow Co Council* [1999] IEHC 225. The only right which may be claimed by the inhabitants of a particular place is to use a green for exercise and recreation, including the playing of lawful games. See WAY, RIGHT OF.

jus tertii. [The right of a third person.] A defendant cannot, unless he has the consent of the true owner, claim as a defence that the plaintiff is not entitled to possession, because a third party is the true owner. See *Webb & Webb v Ireland & A-G* [1988] ILRM 565; *O'Beirne v Fox* [1990] ELR 151.

Jus tertii fails as a defence for a trespasser only if it is a mere *jus tertii*; if the claim of the third party is coupled with a further claim that the alleged trespasser is in occupation on the authority of the third party, then the defence does not fail on the grounds of *jus tertii*: *Rhatigan v Gill* [1999] 2 ILRM 427, HC.

just and equitable. The phrase sometimes used in statutes conferring power to a judge to make an order where the court is of opinion that it would be *just and equitable* to do so eg in company law, a company may be wound up if the court is of the opinion that it would be just and equitable. See Companies Act 1963, s 213; Consumer Credit Act 1995, s 59. See *Re Murph's Restaurant Ltd* [1979] HC; *Re Vehicle Building* [1986] ILRM 239.

justice. The impartial resolution of disputes, the upholding of rights, and the punishment of wrongs, by the law. Justice is required to be administered in courts established by law by judges appointed in the manner provided in the Constitution: 1937 Constitution, art 34(1). Certain articles of the Constitution indicate that *justice is placed above the law and acknowledge that natural rights, or human rights, are not created by law but that the Constitution confirms their existence and gives them protection*: *McGee v Attorney-General* [1974] IR 101.

For characteristics of the *administration of justice*, see *McDonald v Bord na gCon* [1965] IR 217 as cited in *Goodman v Mr Justice Hamilton* [1992] ILRM 145, HC & SC. Two essential ingredients are that there is a contest between parties and that some form of liability or penalty should be imposed on one of the parties: *Keady v Commissioner of Garda Síochána* [1992] ILRM 312, SC. See also *The People (DPP) v Cunningham* [2002] 2 IR 712, SC and [2003] 1 ILRM 124 at 138. [Bibliography: O'Flaherty.]

Justice, Department of. The civil service department with responsibility for law enforcement, counter-terrorism, treatment of offenders, human rights, courts policy, prisons policy, immigration and asylum issues, elimination of discrimination and promotion of equality of treatment of disadvantaged groups, and aspects of the Northern Ireland peace process. A number of agencies operate under the aegis of the department, on a statutory or administrative basis eg the Garda Síochána, the Courts Service, the Probation and Welfare Service, the Irish Prison Service, the Interim Parole Board, the State Pathology Service, the Film Censor's Office, the Censorship of Films Appeal Board, the Censorship of Publications Board, the Censorship of Publications Appeal Board, the Criminal Injuries Compensation Tribunal, the Land Registry and Registry of Deeds, the Legal Aid Board, the Equality Authority, the Office of the Director of the Equality Tribunal, the Refugee Applications Commissioner, the Refugee Appeals Tribunal, and

the Reception and Integration Agency. For website, see *www.justice.ie*.

justice, district. See DISTRICT JUSTICE.

justice, natural. See NATURAL JUSTICE.

justice, public. See PUBLIC JUSTICE.

justice of the peace. Replaced by Peace Commissioners who have all the powers and authorities which immediately before 6 December 1922 were vested in a Justice of the Peace: Courts of Justice Act 1924, s 88. See PEACE COMMISSIONER.

justiciable. Capable of being reviewed or determined by a court of law. The High Court has held that matters raised by the plaintiff regarding a report of an inquiry team, into an industrial relations dispute which closed Dublin Airport in March 1998, were not justiciable, because there was no decision of the inquiry team capable of being quashed in the sense that no legal rights of the plaintiff were affected by what was a mere fact-finding report: *Ryanair v Flynn & McAuley* [2000] ELR 161, HC.

justifiable homicide. See HOMICIDE.

justification. A plea in a defamation (qv) action that the statement complained of made by the defendant is substantially true, ie true not only in its allegations of fact but also in any comments made therein. It is a dangerous plea as the onus of proving justification rests on the defendant and if it fails, *exemplary* damages may be awarded.

Before a plea of justification is included in a defence, the defendant should have reasonable evidence to support that plea or reasonable grounds for supposing that sufficient evidence to prove the allegations will be available at the trial: *McDonnell v Sunday Business Post Ltd* [2000] ITLR (13 March), HC. A defendant pleading justification may be entitled to discovery of documents in the power or possession of the plaintiff, but only if the plea of justification is clear: *Harris v Fagan & Burgess* [1999] ITLR (22 March) SC.

In a particular case the Supreme Court held that the defence of justification was concerned with the quality of the plaintiffs as human beings, whereas the plea in mitigation of damages was concerned with the plaintiff's reputation or standing within the community, and that evidence that would support the conclusion that a man had a bad reputation in the community, would not necessarily support, or even be admissible to support a plea of justification: *Murphy v Times Newspapers Ltd* [1996] 1 IR 169, SC.

In defamation proceedings, it is permissible to plead *partial justification* where the words complained of are capable of containing more than one meaning or are otherwise severable; the defendant is entitled to justify part of the defamatory words and remain liable to pay damages on the remainder: *Murphy v Times Newspapers Ltd* [2000] 1 IR 522, SC and [2000] 2 ILRM 491, SC. *Partial justification* could be a full defence where the remaining words did not materially injure the plaintiff's reputation. See Defamation Act 1961, s 22. See AGGRAVATED DAMAGES.

justis celex. The official data base of the European Union, containing information on all aspects of EU law, including EU treaties, enacted and preparatory legislation, case law, national law implementing EU legislation, and European parliamentary questions. Other EU databases are *justis scad* which is a bibliographic database and *justis spicers* which contains abstracts from over 100 EU sources.

K

kangaroo court. Colloquial expression to describe a hearing in which the elementary and generally accepted norms of justice have not been observed.

keeping the peace. See BINDING TO THE PEACE.

kerb-crawling. Colloquial expression to describe soliciting or importuning from or in a motor vehicle for the purposes of prostitution; it is a criminal offence: Criminal Law (Sexual Offences) Act 1993, ss 1(1) and 7. See PROSTITUTE.

kerb ramps. Road authorities are required when constructing or altering public footpaths or pavements to provide ramps, dished kerbs or other sloped areas for the purpose of facilitating the mobility of persons with a disability: Equal Status Act 2000, s 19.

kidnapping. Formerly, the common law offence of stealing and carrying away, or secreting of some person against his will; it was the most aggravated form of false imprisonment. See *The People (Attorney-General) v Edge* [1943] IR 115. The offence was abolished by the Non-Fatal Offences against the Person Act 1997, s 28(c), which created new statutory offences of *false*

imprisonment (NFOPA 1997, s 15) and *child abduction* (NFOPA 1997, ss 16–17). See CHILD ABDUCTION; FALSE IMPRISONMENT.

kill. To cause the death of another. It is an offence, without lawful excuse, to make a threat by any means to kill another person, intending that other person to believe it will be carried out: Non-Fatal Offences against the Person Act 1997, s 5. See also Maritime Security Act 2004, ss 2(1) and 10. See HOMICIDE; MURDER.

kin. Relationship by blood.

King's Inns, Honorable Society of. The society, the Benchers of which constitute the governing body of the Bar of Ireland. The Society, founded in 1541, provides a course of education and training which when successfully completed leads to admission of the student by the Benchers to the degree of barrister-at-law and to being called to the Bar by the Chief Justice and thereby to being admitted to practise in the courts.

The High Court has dismissed a challenge by a Trinity College honours law graduate to a decision of the Society refusing her entry to the course of education and training leading to the barrister-at-law degree: *Quinn v King's Inns* (15 June 2004, unreported). The plaintiff had claimed that the 25% mark which she obtained in the company law entrance examination was not consistent with her average of 68% in four other subjects. However, the court held that it was satisfied that fair procedures had been followed by the Society.

The *McCarthy Bursary* was established in 2002 to assist one person, every two years, to study law at the King's Inns. It was established by the McCarthy family in memory of the late Supreme Court judge Niall McCarthy and his wife Barbara who were killed in a car crash in Spain ten years previously. Email: *mccarthy.bursary@ kingsinns.ie.*

King's Inns is empowered to sell or exchange any of the books of the King's Inns Library: Copyright and Related Rights Act 2000, s 201. See also King's Inns Library Act 1945; Finance Act 2003, s 165. See also 'King's Inns and the Battle of the Books, 1972' in *Bar Review* (December 2002) 394. See Kenny in 10 ILT & SJ (1992) 172. See website: *www.kingsinns.ie.* [Bibliography: Hogan & Osborough;

Kenny]. See BARRISTER; BARRISTER, MIS-CONDUCT OF; LAW LIBRARY; SUITORS FUNDS OF.

Kinlen Order. Generally known as an order in respect of the amount which a health board may charge for in-patient or out-patient services upon a person who received or is entitled to receive damages or compensation for injuries caused to the person by the negligent use of a motor vehicle in a public place; so named after Kinlen J in *O'Rourke v Scott* (1993, unreported). See Health (Amendment) Act 1986, s 2(1).

Mr Justice Kinlen fixed the amount at a maximum of £100 (€126.97) per day which by 1999, with updating, had increased to £150 (€190.46) per day. The matter was reviewed in *Crilly v T & J Farrington Ltd* [2000] 1 ILRM 548, HC where Mr Justice Geoghegan held that s 2(1) could not be interpreted as permitting a fixed charge. He held that the charge must be a reasonable one, assessed on a *quantum meruit* basis and must, therefore, be one in respect of services which the plaintiff has received. However, the matter was finally put to rest when the Supreme Court held that the assessment of hospital charges under s 2 could be made by reference to the *average daily costs* of hospital beds: *Crilly v Farrington* [2001] 3 IR 251, SC and [2002] 1 ILRM 161, SC.

Where the patient services have been provided by a voluntary hospital on behalf of the health board under an arrangement entered into pursuant to s 26 of the Health Act 1970, the legal power to raise the appropriate charges lies with the relevant health board, although in practice the bills will be issued by the voluntary hospital on behalf of the health board.

Mr Justice Kinlen retired from the bench on 23 April 2002 and became the State's first *Inspector-General of Prisons and Places of Detention.*

kiting. A fraudulent scheme whereby a party with two accounts with different financial institutions, passes cheques between them in such a way that, although he has no money to meet them, they will be met by further cheques also unsupported by funds. Such a scheme enables the perpetrator to run an overdraft without it being disclosed. 'Kiting is a term used with regard to obtaining money by cheques passed through banks without value being deposited against the cheques – that is, kiting is

an effort to obtain the use of money during the process of a cheque passing through one bank or through a clearing house to another, and perhaps through many more': Lord Wrenbury in *Corporation Agencies Ltd v Home Banking of Canada* [1927] AC 318, Privy Council.

For example, company 'A', which has an account with bank 'B', issues cheques on this account in favour of one of its directors, who has an account with building society 'C'. These cheques are lodged to the director's account with 'C'. At the director's request, 'C' issues there and then cheques payable to 'A' drawn on 'C's' account with its own bank 'D'. The cheques so issued are then lodged by company 'A' to its account with bank 'B' with the intention of meeting cheques issued earlier in the cycle by 'A' on its account with 'B'.

The scheme relies on the delay in clearing cheques through the clearing system and on permission to withdraw against uncleared cheques. See *Bank of Ireland v EBS* [1998] 2 ILRM 451, SC and [1999] 1 IR 220, SC.

knackery. Any premises used for and in connection with the collection, delivery, supply, slaughter, storage, skinning or cutting up of animals or parts of animals which are not intended for human consumption: Abattoirs Act 1988. Knackeries require annual licensing, the objective being to regulate such activities where animal carcasses and offals are handled for industrial and other purposes. See ABATTOIR.

knock for knock. Phrase used eg to describe an agreement whereby insurance companies pay their own insured on the basis that there will be no action brought by one insured against the other. It also refers to agreements between companies in relation to their employee pension funds, whereby pension liabilities in respect of an employee moving from one company to the other, are borne by the receiving company's fund.

know-how. Industrial information and techniques likely to assist in the manufacture or processing of goods or materials, or in carrying out any agricultural, forestry, fishing, mining, or other extractive operations: Finance Act 1968, s 2, now Taxes Consolidation Act 1997, s 768(1). A trader may deduct as a trading expense any expenditure including capital expenditure in acquiring know-how for use in his trade, if it would not otherwise be deductible. However, no deduction is given for capital expenditure where: (a) the know-how is acquired as part of the acquisition of the whole or part of a trade from another person, or (b) an element of *control* arises as regards the buyer and/or seller within the definition of control in the Income Tax Act 1967, s 299(6), now Taxes Consolidation Act 1997, s 312(1). See TRADE SECRET.

knowledge. Awareness of, or acquaintance with, fact or truth. The law can presume knowledge of facts under the *doctrine of notice* where a person would have known if he had made proper enquiries. Everyone is presumed also to know the law. See CAUSE OF ACTION; IGNORANTIA FACTI EXCUSAT; NOTICE.

L

l.s. *Locus sigilli* (qv).

labelling of alcohol. Regulations may be made by the Minister requiring particulars be affixed to any container in which intoxicating liquor is sold for consumption off licensed premises, which are adequate to enable the licensee and licensed premises to be identified: Intoxicating Liquor Act 2003, s 22(1)(b). See also ALCOHOL STRENGTH.

labelling of foodstuffs. For consolidated regulations on the approximation of the laws of the Member Sates on the labelling, presentation and advertising of foodstuffs, giving effect to Directive (EC) 2000/13, see European Communities (Labelling, Presentation and Advertising of Foodstuffs) Regulations 2002, SI No 483 of 2002, and amending Regulations 2003, SIs No 257 of 2003 and No 451 of 2003. See also BEEF; CHOCOLATE PRODUCTS; FOOD, STANDARD OF; FRUIT JUICES; IONISING RADIATION; JAM; POULTRYMEAT.

labelling of products and services. There are specific labelling requirements in relation to a range of products and services eg aquaculture, dangerous substances, dietary foods, explosives, medicinal products, poisons, and prescription drugs (qqv). There is an *eco-labelling scheme* (qv) for environmentally friendly products and a *CE-Mark* scheme for products which meet certain conformity requirements. See CE

MARK; CHOCOLATE PRODUCTS; ENERGY LABELLING.

Labour Court. A tribunal established by the Industrial Relations Act 1946, s 10 with the role of promoting collective bargaining and of resolving industrial conflict. It is a tripartite tribunal, consisting of a chairman, three deputy chairmen, as well as four members nominated by trade unions and four nominated by employers' organisations; formal legal qualifications are not required.

The Labour Court may not investigate a trade dispute unless the parties to the dispute have requested it to do so and the Labour Relations Commission has either: (a) waived its functions of conciliation, or (b) has given it a report stating that no further efforts on its part will resolve the dispute: Industrial Relations Act 1990, s 26. However, the Labour Court may intervene in exceptional circumstances (IRA 1990, s 26(5)) or where there is specific provision for the direct reference of trade disputes to the Court (IRA 1990, s 25(3)). Also the Court is required to endeavour to resolve a dispute affecting the public interest, referred to it by the Minister (IRA 1990, s 38).

The court is bound by few procedural rules other than the general principles of law and of *natural justice*. It may not use expert evidence without disclosing the substance of that evidence to the parties and allowing them to make submissions on it: *State (Cole) v Labour Court* [1983] HC. The court should in an unambiguous fashion, state the facts which it has found and the evidence upon which it has found them; however, failure by the court to so do, does not invalidate its order: *North Western Health Board v Martyn* [1987] IR 565; *Faulkner v Minister for Industry & Commerce* [1993] ELR 187, HC. However, on appeal, the Supreme Court has held that when reasons are required from administrative tribunals they should be required only to give the broad gist of the basis for their decisions: *Faulkner v Minister for Industry and Commerce* [1997] ELR 107, SC. Also, the court in its determination must contain an indication of the reasons for the determination, sufficient to enable a party to ascertain whether a point of law exists which would allow that party to appeal to the High Court: *Golding v Labour Court* [1994] ELR 153, HC.

The court hears appeals from decisions of the *Director of the Equality Tribunal* (qv). Previously, the court, in the first instance, heard claims on *discrimination* (qv) and *victimisation* (qv) involving dismissal: Employment Equality Act 1998, s 77. This jurisdiction is now with the Director in the first instance: Equality Act 2004, s 46.

The High Court will only interfere with a finding of the Labour Court when it involves a clear breach of legal principle or a conclusion of fact so irrational as to be unsustainable: *Mulcahy v Minister for Justice* [2002] ELR 12, HC; *Thompson v Tesco Ireland* [2003] ELR 21, HC. In a particular case, the High Court held that the Labour Court had erred in law in reaching a decision, based on a misunderstanding for which there was no evidential basis: *Doran v Minister for Finance* [2001] 2 IR 452, HC and ELR 330. See *The State (Polymark) v ITGWU* [1987] ILRM 357. See RSC Ord 106. See DISCRIMINATION.

labour injunction. An injunction (qv) in a labour dispute, restraining a strike or other industrial action (qv). Where the strike or other industrial action is in accordance with a secret ballot and the trade union has given notice to the employer, the employer cannot seek an injunction unless he gives notice to the trade union and its members (ie no *ex parte* injunction): Industrial Relations Act 1990, s 19.

Where an injunction is sought, the onus is on the person resisting the injunction to establish that the provisions governing the secret ballot (IRA 1990, s 14) have been complied with: *Daru Bricklaying Ltd v BATU* [2002] 2 IR 619, HC; [2003] 1 ILRM 227 and ELR 244. The court cannot grant an injunction where the union establishes a fair case that it was acting in contemplation or furtherance of a *trade dispute* (IRA 1990, s 19(2)). If it does not so establish, the court will decide, as it does in other injunction applications, where the balance of convenience lies. In a particular case, the Supreme Court held that the trial judge was entitled to conclude that damages would be an inadequate remedy if an injunction were refused: *G & T Crampton v BATU* [1998] ELR 7, SC and 1 ILRM 430. See *Allied Irish Banks plc v Irish Bank Officials Association* [1991] HC; *Molloy, Enright & McCarty v IBOA* [1992] HC; *Draycar Ltd v Whelan* [1993] ELR 119, HC; *Bus Éireann v SIPTU* [1993] HC; *Iarnród Éireann v NBRWU* [1993]; *Malin-*

cross Ltd v BATU [2002] ELR 78, HC and 3 IR 607. See Barry in 11 ILT & SJ (1993) 146. See INJUNCTION; TRADE DISPUTE.

labour law. See EMPLOYMENT LAW.

Labour Relations Commission. The Commission with the general responsibility of promoting the improvement of industrial relations: Industrial Relations Act 1990, ss 24–42. The Commission also provides conciliation and advisory services, prepares and offers guidance on codes of practice; provides a rights commissioner service; conducts or commissions research into matters relevant to industrial relations; assists joint labour committees and industrial councils in the exercise of their functions (IRA 1990, s 25).

Trade disputes must be referred to the Commission first, except where there is a specific provision for the direct reference of a dispute to the Labour Court (IRA 1990, s 25(3)) eg as provided for in the Industrial Relations Act 1969, s 20, or the Labour Court intervenes as it is empowered to do (IRA 1990, s 26). The Commission must endeavour to resolve a trade dispute affecting the public interest, referred to it by the Minister (IRA 1990, s 38). See email: *info@lrc.ie* and website: *www.lrc.ie*. See LABOUR COURT.

laches. Negligent or unreasonable delay in asserting or enforcing a right; the equitable doctrine that delay defeats equity, or that equity aids the vigilant and not the indolent. 'A court of equity has always refused its aid to stale demands where a party has slept upon his rights and acquiesced for a great length of time. Nothing can call forth this court into activity but conscience, good faith and reasonable diligence.' *Smith v Clay* [1767] Amb 645. A dismissal from employment which is affected by laches is unfair: *Sheehan v M Keating & Son Ltd* [1993] ELR 12, EAT. See also *Re Sharpe* [1892] 1 Ch 154; *Murphy v Minister for the Marine* [1996] 3 IR 517, HC. See DELAY; LIMITATION OF ACTIONS.

lading, bill of. See BILL OF LADING.

lagan. Goods which have been cast from a ship in danger but where they are marked with a buoy or other means to facilitate recovery. See FLOTSAM; JETSAM.

laissez-passer. [Let pass]. The travel documents issued to officials of the United Nations or of its specialised agencies which are accorded recognition as valid travel documents by the Diplomatic Relations and Immunities Act 1967, Sch 2.

land. As regards the law of real property or land law, *land* includes things attached to the land, such as buildings and other structures. As regards Acts of the Oireachtas (qv), *land* includes messuages, tenements and hereditaments, houses and buildings of any tenure: Interpretation Act 1937, ss 4 and 12, Sch, para 14. A general devise of *land* is to be construed as including leasehold land as well as freehold land, unless a contrary intention appears from the will: Succession Act 1965, s 92.

As regards planning permission, *land* includes any structure and any land covered with water, whether inland or coastal: Planning and Development Act 2000, s 2(1). In relation to the *acquisition* of land, by a local authority, includes any interest or right in or over land or in any substratum of land (PDA 2000, s 213).

As regards the Rules of the Superior Courts, *land* includes messuages, tenements, hereditaments, houses and buildings of any tenure: RSC Ord 125, r 1. In bankruptcy matters, *land* includes any estate or interest in or charge over land: Bankruptcy Act 1988, s 3.

In landlord and tenant matters, *land* includes houses, messuages, and tenements of every tenure, whether corporeal or incorporeal: Deasy's Act 1860, s 1. The words *all lands* are to be taken literally and include land comprising the seabed: *Trustees of Kinsale Yacht Club v Commissioner of Valuations* [1993] ILRM 393. As regards pre-1922 statutes, see Interpretation Act 1889, s 3. See Law Reform Commission, *Report on Land Law and Conveyancing Law – General Proposals* (LRC 30, 1989). [Bibliography: Cannon; Conway H; Coughlan; Lyall; Pearce & Mee; Wylie (1)]. See ACQUISITION OF LAND; COMPULSORY PURCHASE ORDER; CONVEYANCE; ELECTRONIC FORM; PLANNING PERMISSION; SALE OF LAND.

land, compulsory acquisition of. See COMPULSORY PURCHASE ORDER.

land, planning and control. See PLANNING PERMISSION.

land, recovery of. See EJECTMENT.

land, sale of. See SALE BY COURT; SALE OF LAND.

land annuities. Formerly, payments in respect of British government loans to tenants to enable them to purchase land from their Ascendancy class landlords under a series of Land Acts. On the establishment of the *Irish Free State* in 1922, the land annuities were collected by the Department of Finance in Dublin and forwarded to London. The new Fianna Fáil government in 1932 withheld the annuity payments, leading to the 'economic war' between Ireland and the UK, which was eventually settled in 1938, with a once-off payment of £10 million to the UK in full settlement of land annuities and other claims. In 2003 there were an estimated 7,000 farmers paying land annuities.

The government in August 2003 announced its intention to introduce a new Land Bill which would facilitate the buy-out of land annuities, as well as other reforming measures eg the transfer of title of former Land Commission land to sporting clubs and community groups, and the removal of the need for Ministerial consent for non-nationals to purchase agricultural land. No new legislation had been initiated in the Houses of the Oireachtas by 1 September 2004.

land bond. An interest-bearing bond issued by the Land Commission (qv) to effect the compulsory purchase of land, as part of the scheme commenced in the late nineteenth century for the transfer of land from landlords to tenant farmers: Purchase of Land (Ireland) Act 1891; Land Act 1923. All remaining land bonds were redeemed in 1989 and the Land Bond Fund dissolved in 1992: Land Bond Act 1992. Payments of annuities by tenant-farmers are now used for the benefit of the Exchequer.

land certificate. The certificate of title to which the person registered as owner of *registered* land is entitled: Registration of Title Act 1964, s 28. The land certificate must be produced to the Registrar of the Land Registry for alteration, before any subsequent transaction can be noted on the register (RTA 1964, s 105).

A lien (qv) is created when a land certificate is deposited to secure an advance of money; the depositee protects his rights by refusing to produce the certificate. However a solicitor holding a land certificate as security for costs due by a client may be required by the Registrar to produce the certificate for the purpose of any dealings with the land. The production of the certificate does not alter the right to the custody of the certificate or affect the solicitor's lien: *A Guide to Professional Conduct of Solicitors in Ireland* (2002) ch 2.4 and RTA 1964, s 105.

The safe storage of land certificates has been a problem for the legal profession and financial institutions. To help overcome the problem and to simplify conveyancing and mortgage transactions, the following actions have been initiated: (a) Instead of having a new paper land certificate issued for the first time, or an existing land certificate re-issued on completion of a dealing, it is possible since 2003 to have the land certificate stored in the Land Registry: *Law Society Gazette* (March 2003) 6; and (b) In respect of applications for registration of transfers or transmissions on death (assents) lodged on or after 1 September 2004, the land certificate, where it has already been issued, will not be reissued in respect of the new ownership and will, instead, be cancelled: *Law Society Gazette* (July 2004) 30. The Irish Mortgage Council has confirmed that lending institutions no longer have an automatic requirement that land certificates be bespoken in respect of property taken as security by way of legal mortgage. The Law Society has confirmed that practitioners should no longer bespeak a land certificate, unless they have specific instructions from their clients to do so. See Land Registry's *Application for registration (incorporating form 17)* in electronic or paper form. See LAND REGISTRATION; LAND REGISTRY ELECTRONIC ACCESS SERVICE; SOLICITOR'S LIEN.

Land Commission. The Commission, originally established in 1881, with power: (a) to acquire land for distribution among small farmers to relieve congestion, and (b) to advance money for the purchase by tenants of landlords' estates: Land Law (Ireland) Act 1881. By 1992, the Commission had overseen the purchase by tenants of approximately 87% of the agricultural land on the whole island (largely achieved prior to independence in 1921) and the structural distribution of about 20% of the agricultural land in the State (largely achieved since 1921).

With the decline in the number of large estates available for acquisition, the rise in land prices and the unacceptability of land bonds (qv) as a means of payment of owners, the Commission ceased to acquire land in 1983. Provision for the Commission to be dissolved was made in 1992; there is provision that the jurisdiction of the Judicial Commissioner and the Appeal Tribunal be vested in the High Court; that any power or duty vested in the Commission or the Lay Commissioners be exercised by the

Minister; and that Commission land be vested in the Minister or the Central Fisheries Board: Irish Land Commission (Dissolution) Act 1992. See also Land Law (Commission) Act 1923; Land Act 1933, s 9; Land Act 1950, ss 12 and 14. The Land Commission was eventually abolished in 1999, see SI No 75 of 1999. See *O'Cleirigh v Minister for Agriculture* [1998] 2 ILRM 263, SC.

land registration. There are two mutually exclusive systems of land registration, the *registration of title* and the *registration of deeds*. Under the registration of deeds, the existence of a deed, will or conveyance may be registered; the document remains itself the evidence of title. Under the registration of title, the document ceases to be evidence of title, being replaced by the register which is conclusive evidence of title of the person whose name appears therein. However, the description of the land in the register or on maps, is not conclusive as to the boundaries or extent of the land: *Persian Properties Ltd v Registrar of Titles* [2003] 1 IR 450, SC.

The registry of title was established by the Registration of Title Act 1891 and continued by the Registration of Title Act 1964. There are three registers, one each for registering the ownership of freehold land, leasehold land, and subsidiary interests (RTA 1964, s 8). The register is kept in *folios*, and each folio is in three parts: the first part has a description of the property; the second part describes the owner of the property, including cautions (qv) and inhibitions (qv) restricting the registration of dispositions of the property; the third part contains burdens (qv) and charges (qv), such as mortgages (qv). The register is prepared and maintained in the Land Registry which has a central office in Dublin and other constituent offices as designated elsewhere; Waterford was designated in 1997: Registration of Title (Amendment) Act 1997 and SI No 340 of 1997. Each registered holding is marked on the *registry map* by a plan number corresponding to the register.

Registration is compulsory for: (a) all freehold and leasehold property acquired by local authorities and state sponsored bodies; (b) freehold property purchased under the various Land Purchase Acts; (c) acquisition on sale of property in areas designated as *compulsory registration areas*. Currently the counties of Carlow, Laois, and Meath have been so designated; in

2004 there were no immediate plans for other such designations.

There is provision for the entry of an *inhibition* in respect of registered land in the Land Registry and the registration of a notice in the Registry of Deeds in respect of unregistered land, where the land is the subject of an interim or interlocutory order for its preservation: Proceeds of Crime Act 1996, s 10.

An application for the registration of title to land which is based on possession must be accompanied by a *capital acquisitions tax clearance certificate*: Capital Acquisitions Tax Consolidation Act 2003, s 62. A system of self-certification is available as an option for solicitors in particular circumstances.

For Law Reform Commission recommendations on the registration of interest which arise pursuant to the Irish Church Act 1869, see Law Reform Commission, *Report on Positive Covenants over freehold land and other proposals*' (LRC 70, 2003). For information on the conversion to electronic format of information on deeds and folios, see ITRIS; LAND REGISTRY ELECTRONIC ACCESS SERVICE. See Land Registration Rules 1972 to 2000, SI No 230 of 1972, SI No 258 of 1981; SI No 310 of 1986, and SI No 175 of 2000. See Courts Act 1991, s 3; Civil Liability and Courts Act 2004, s 46. See also Public Service Superannuation (Miscellaneous Provisions) Act 2004, Sch 2. See website: *www.landregistry.ie*. [Bibliography: Fitzgerald; McAllister; Wylie (2)]. See DEEDS, REGISTRATION OF; BURDEN; CAUTION; INHIBITION; MEMORIAL; NOTICE; OVERRIDING INTERESTS; QUALIFIED TITLE; QUIT RENT.

Land Registry. The registry which maintains registers in which entries may be made of the ownership of land and of the incumbrances, called *burdens* (qv), affecting ownership. For Land Registry *practice notes* covering all aspects of registry procedures, see website: *www.landregistry.ie*. See ITRIS; LAND REGISTRATION.

Land Registry Electronic Access Service (EAS). The pre-payment subscription service which allows authorised users to conduct online searches (*www.landregistry.ie*) of the electronically available register of the Land Registry by reference to one or more criteria, e g name of the registered owner and plan number. The user can print any located folio. Also 'dealings pending' on a particular folio can be checked. By end

2004 it is planned to have all folios and filed plans available electronically for the entire country. There is provision for electronic lodgement of applications for registration – Form 17. In 2003, more than 1,200 dealings were being lodged electronically every month. Also there were more than 5,500 users registered for EAS, with over 2,000 electronic transactions being undertaken every day. See 'The paper chase' by Michael Treacy in *Law Society Gazette* (January/February 2003) 29. See ITRIS.

landfill site. A waste disposal facility used for the deposit of waste onto or under land: Waste Management Act 1996, s 5(1). A person must not dispose of or recover waste at a facility (a site or premises) except in accordance with a *waste licence* (qv).

The Environmental Protection Agency is required to specify and publish criteria and procedures for the selection, management, operation and termination of the use of landfill sites for the disposal of domestic and other wastes: Environmental Protection Agency Act 1992, s 62(1). The specified criteria and procedures may relate to e g site selection; design and bringing into operation of sites; impacts on the environment; leachate management, treatment and control; control and recovery of landfill gas; operational guidelines; fire, pest and litter control; appropriate recovery, reuse and recycling facilities; co-disposal of industrial and other wastes; monitoring of leachate, other effluents and emissions; termination of use and subsequent monitoring (EPAA 1992, s 62(2)).

A landfill site managed or operated by a local authority must comply with the specified criteria and procedures (EPAA 1992, s 62(5)). Provision has been made to require a landfill operator to levy landfill charges so as to ensure recovery of the full costs of the facility concerned (EPAA 1992, s 53A inserted by Protection of the Environment Act 2003, s 43).

A new levy of €15 per tonne was imposed from 1 June 2002 on waste disposed of at landfill sites: Waste Management (Landfill Levy) Regulations 2002, SI No 86 of 2002. Revenues raised by the levy are ring fenced, and placed in an Environment Fund, to be used in support of waste minimisation and certain recycling initiatives. The levy applies to local authority landfill sites, to private sites and to unauthorised sites.

There are certain disposal exemptions, e g the disposal of street cleaning waste. See also *East Coast Conservation Ltd v Wicklow Co Council* [1995] 2 ILRM 16, HC and [1996] 3 IR 175, SC; *Boyne Valley v EPA* [2002] FL 7843, HC; *Rooney, Curley and Coady v Galway County Council* [2003] FL 8838, HC. [Bibliography: Scannell]. See LEACHATE; LITTER; WASTE.

landlocked. See CLOSE; EASEMENT.

landlord. A lessor; the owner or holder of land leased to another called the tenant or lessee. The relationship of landlord and tenant arises *in all cases in which there shall be an agreement by one party to hold land from or under another in consideration of any rent*: Deasy's Act 1860, s 4. A landlord is also defined as the person for the time being entitled to receive (otherwise than as agent for another) the rent paid in respect of premises by the tenant thereof: Landlord and Tenant (Amendment) Act 1980, s 3(1); Residential Tenancies Act 2004, s 5(1).

For the rules dealing with proceedings for the recovery of land or ejectment from land, see Circuit Court Rules 2001 Ord 51. The Law Reform Commission has made wide-ranging provisional recommendations on reform and updating of landlord and tenant law: *Consultation Paper on General Law of Landlord and Tenant Law* (LRC CP 28, 2003). [Bibliography: Bland (2); Deale; Wylie (4)]. For reform of landlord and tenant law in relation to the private rented sector, see PRIVATE RESIDENTIAL TENANCIES BOARD. See also COVENANT; GROUND RENT; IMPROVEMENT NOTICE, LEASE; LANDLORD, OBLIGATIONS OF; RENTED HOUSE, STANDARD OF.

landlord, obligations of. The landlord of a dwelling is required (a) to allow the tenant to enjoy peaceful and exclusive occupation, (b) to carry out repairs to the structure and to the interior of the dwelling, (c) to effect and maintain a policy of insurance in respect of the structure, (d) to return or repay any deposit paid by the tenant, (e) to provide contact details for the tenant so that the landlord may be contacted at all reasonable times, (f) to reimburse the tenant in certain circumstances for vouched expenses incurred by the tenant on repairs for which the landlord is responsible: Residential Tenancies Act 2004, s 12.

A landlord is prohibited from penalising a tenant for referring any dispute to the *Private Residential Tenancies Board* for reso-lution, or for giving evidence, or for reporting a complaint to the gardai or a public authority (RTA 2004, s 14). A tenant is penalised if subjected to any action that adversely affects his peaceful enjoyment of the dwelling. This includes steps taken by the landlord in the exercise of his rights, having regard to the frequency of such exercise. Also a landlord owes to third parties, who could be potentially affected, a duty to enforce the obligations of the tenant; the third party is entitled to make a complaint to the Board (RTA 2004, s 15).

No provision of any lease, tenancy agreement, contract or other agreement may operate to vary, modify or restrict in any way the obligations under s 12 (RTA 2004, s 18). This does not prevent more favourable terms for the tenant being imposed on the landlord in the lease or tenancy agreement. See MANAGEMENT COMPANY; PRIVATE RESIDENTIAL TENANCIES BOARD; RENT DEPOSIT; RENT REVIEW; TENANT, OBLIGATIONS OF.

landscape conservation area. Any area or place within the functional area of a planning authority designated by it by *order* for the preservation of the landscape: Planning and Development Act 2000, s 204. The Minister may prescribe development which will not be *exempted development* in such an area (PDA 2000, s 204(2)). This new type of *order* will enable a planning authority to apply planning control in respect of developments which would normally be exempted developments e g the removal of hedges and ditches, the division of commonage, afforestation and land reclamation.

language. The Irish language as the national language is the first official language; the English language is recognised as a second official language: 1937 Constitution, art 8; Official Languages Act 2003, s 2(1).

There were 11 official languages in the EU in 2003: Danish, Dutch, English, Finnish, French, German, Greek, Italian, Portuguese, Spanish, Swedish. With the enlargement of the EU in 2004, an additional nine official languages were added: Estonian, Latvian, Lithuanian, Polish, Czech, Slovak, Hungarian, Slovene and Maltese. Two languages have a special status: Irish and Letzeburgesch. There are some 40 *lesser used* languages in the EU, the promotion of which is the responsibility of the *European Bureau for Lesser Used Languages*, 10 Hatch Street, Dublin 2. (Tel: 661 2205).

The Maastricht Treaty 1992 was drawn up in the Danish, Dutch, English, French, German, Greek, Irish, Italian, Portuguese and Spanish languages, the texts in each of these languages being equally authentic: Maastricht Treaty 1992, art S; now, Treaty on European Union, art 53 of the consolidated (2002) version. Subsequent to the accession of Finland and Sweden in 1994, the Finnish and Swedish versions are also authentic.

The languages of the European Patents Office are English, French and German: see Patents Act 1992, ss 119 and 121. If there is an inconsistency between the English and French texts of the Warsaw Convention (on air travel), the French text prevails: Air Navigation and Transport (International Conventions) Act 2004, s 5. See COIMISINÉIR TEANGA, AN; IRISH LANGUAGE; FORAS TEANGA; PLACENAME; ULLANS; WILL, PROOF OF.

lapse. (1) Generally when a person to whom property has been devised or bequeathed dies before the testator, the devise or bequest fails or *lapses* and the property falls into residue; a lapsed share of residue however does not fall into residue, but devolves upon an intestacy. A lapse does not occur if land is given to a person *in tail* who predeceases the testator and who leaves issue living at the testator's death capable of inheriting the entail: Succession Act 1965, s 97.

Also there is no lapse where property is given to issue of the testator and such descendant dies leaving issue living at the testator's death (SA 1965, s 98). See Capital Acquisitions Tax Consolidation Act 2003, s 42. See *Moorehead v Tilikainen* [1999] 2 ILRM 471, HC.

Another exception to the doctrine of lapse is where the gift is charitable and the property can be applied *cy-pres* (qv). In the case of a devise to persons as joint tenants (qv), if one dies before the testator, the others take his share; whereas if two persons hold as tenants in common (qv), the share of the deceased tenant lapses.

(2) Proceedings lapse in the event of the death of a defendant in criminal proceedings. See DEATH, EFFECT OF.

lapse of offer. A lapse of an offer occurs: (a) on the death of the offeror or offeree before acceptance; or (b) by non-acceptance within the time prescribed; or (c) by non-acceptance within a reasonable time where no time is prescribed. See *Ramsgate Hotel v Montefiore* [1866] LR 1 Ex 109. See OFFER.

larceny. The *statutory* offence of larceny, created by the Larceny Act 1916, s 1, has been abolished and replaced by statutory offences of *theft* and *robbery*; also any offence at *common law* of larceny has been abolished: Criminal Justice (Theft and Fraud Offences) Act 2001, s 3 and Sch 1.

The 1916 Act (as amended by the Criminal Law Act 1997, s 13 and Sch 1, para 6), has been repealed by the CJ(TFO)A 2001, s 3. See also *DPP v Keating* [1989] ILRM 561, HC; *People (DPP) v Rock* [1994] 1 ILRM 66, SC; *The People (Attorney-General) v Mill* [1955] CCA; *The People (DPP) v O'Loughlin* [1979] IR 85. [Bibliography: McCutcheon]. See RESTITUTION OF POSSESSION; ROBBERY; THEFT. See also HANDLING STOLEN PROPERTY; REWARD; STOLE.

larceny, aggravated. Larceny which carried more severe penalties than simple larceny: Larceny Act 1916. *Aggravated larceny* arose in the case of: (a) the particular type of property stolen eg cattle (LA 1916, s 3) or a will (LA 1916, s 6); (b) the manner in which the larceny was committed eg stealing from the person (LA 1916, s 14); (c) the place where it was committed eg a ship (LA 1916, s 15); and (d) the person who committed it eg larceny by a tenant (LA 1916, s 16). The 1916 Act has been repealed by the Criminal Justice (Theft and Fraud Offences) Act 2001, s 3 and Sch 1. See now ROBBERY.

larceny by finding. The larceny which occurred where a person found goods which had been lost and appropriated them to his own use in circumstances where he believed that the owner could be found by taking reasonable steps. There could be *larceny by finding* of a golf ball, even though abandoned by its owner; this was particularly the case where the finding was by a trespasser: *Hibbert v McKiernan* [1948] 1 All ER 860. A person was convicted of *larceny by finding* who had found £2,890 at Coolmine Woods, Blanchardstown: *The People v O'Mara* (2000) Irish Times, 5 Jul, DC. For modern legislation, see THEFT.

larceny by trick. The larceny which occurred when a person, with the necessary intent, obtained possession of goods, by means of some trick, from the owner who did not intend to part with the entire right to the property but only to the possession. On conviction, the stolen property revested in the true owner. See *R v Edmundson* [1912] 8 C App R 107. For modern legislation, see DECEPTION; MAKING OFF WITHOUT PAYMENT; RESTITUTION IN POSSESSION; THEFT.

laser. See ATM; IRISH PAYMENT SERVICES ORGANISATION.

last resort, court of. See COURT OF LAST RESORT.

last straw. Colloquial expression meaning the final irritation or problem that stretches a person's endurance or patience beyond the limit. For there to be a 'last straw' dismissal of an employee, there must be a blameworthy act by the employee, judged by standards of belief by the employer of misconduct by the employee which is sustained by evidence establishing the facts on the balance of probabilities and ascertained by a full and fair investigation: *Donnelly v Arklow Pottery Ltd* [1992] ELR 240, EAT.

lateness for work. Lateness in arriving for work may not be a valid ground for dismissal of an employee if it has been tolerated in the past by the employer: *O'Connell v Garde* [1991] ELR 105, EAT.

latent ambiguity. See AMBIGUITY.

latent damage. Damage which is not obvious or explicit. The Law Reform Commission was requested to review the Statutes of Limitation in cases where the loss is *latent* ie in circumstances where a person was not or could not have been aware of the accrual of a right of action until after the expiration of the relevant limitation period. The Commission has concluded that the current law does not adequately protect the plaintiff in such circumstances: see Law Reform Commission, *Report on Statute of Limitations: Claims in Contract and Tort in respect of Latent Damage (other than Personal Injury)*: (LRC 64, 2001). See CAUSE OF ACTION.

latent defect. See DEFECT.

late payment. See PROMPT PAYMENT.

laundering. See MONEY LAUNDERING.

law. The written and unwritten body of rules, derived from custom, formal enactment or judicial decision, which are recognised as binding on persons who constitute a community or state, so that they will be imposed upon and enforced among those persons by appropriate sanctions. The law can be classified as municipal (domestic) or international, public or private, criminal or civil. [Bibliography: Byrne & McCutcheon;

Dawson Greer & Ingram; Doolan (1); O'Brien; O'Flaherty; O'Higgins; and see Appendix 5]. See RULE OF LAW.

law, EC. See COMMUNITY LAW.

law agent. A person who is qualified and authorised to conduct the legal business of another; the solicitor employed by a corporate body eg the Law Agent of Dublin Corporation. A judgment mortgage affidavit may be made by the law agent of any corporate body: Judgment Mortgage Amendment Act 1858, s 3.

A full-time solicitor employed by a county borough is known as a *law agent* whilst the corresponding post in a county council is also known as a *county solicitor*.

It has been held that the files of the law agent of a county council, containing information concerning a transaction of the county council, was 'within the possession or procurement of the county manager' and consequently would have to be given to the chairman of the council, when so requested: County Management Act 1940, s 27; *Cullen v Wicklow County Manager* [1997] 1 ILRM 41, HC and [1996] 3 IR 474, HC. The 1940 Act has been repealed; however, the s 27 provision has been re-enacted with minor amendments as s 136 of the Local Government Act 2001.

The first law agent to Dublin Corporation was Edward Scriven who undertook legal work for the Corporation on a commission basis from 1756 until his death in 1794; he prepared a translation of the seventeenth-century Recorder's Book from the original Latin and French.

As regards costs and expenses of a law agent allowed in taxation (qv), see *Joan O'Reilly v Dublin Corporation* [1963] HC. See DUBLIN AGENT.

law and equity, fusion of. See EQUITY.

law and fact. *Law* is a conceived principle, a rule of duty; *fact* is actual, an event which is according to or in contravention of the rule.

Law Library. The central location(s) of practice from which a barrister is entitled to conduct his practice: *Code of Conduct for the Bar of Ireland* (December 2003) r 1.7(k). It is the central and primary place of practice for the Bar of Ireland and includes the Law Libraries in Dublin and Cork and the Law Library Buildings at Church Street, Dublin 7 (r 8.1). The *Code* states that it is desirable that all practising barristers be members of the Law Library (r 8.2). Subject to certain exceptions, membership of the Law Library is confined to full-time practising barristers (r 8.3).

All conversations and communications between barristers in the Law Library are, unless otherwise expressly agreed, strictly private, confidential and without prejudice (r 8.12). This obligation of confidentiality applies also to any barrister who is not a party to any such conversations or communications but who overhears them. A barrister must not use for any professional or private purpose or otherwise disclose any information obtained accidentally or otherwise from observation of documents or from conversation with or between colleagues in or outside of the Law Library (r 8.14). Any infringement of these rules on confidentiality may render the barrister concerned liable to exclusion from the Law Library (r 8.15).

As of May 2004, there were 1,474 members of the Library, 1,211 *junior counsel* and 263 *senior counsel*. The Library is governed by a committee which is elected by the Bar Council (qv) which is itself elected by members of the Library. Prior to the founding of the Law Library, it was customary for Irish barristers to get many of the books they required on loan from private booksellers who conducted lending libraries. In the early eighteenth century, one of these book lenders went bankrupt and the Bar decided to set up its own Library. See website: *www.lawlibrary.ie*. See BARRISTER; LIBRARY.

law merchant. The custom of merchants which when proved became part of the common law. It is nothing more or less than the usages of merchants and traders in the different departments of trade, ratified by decisions of courts of law: *Goodwin v Robarts* [1875] LR 10 Ex 337. See also Sale of Goods Act 1893, s 61(2).

law of nations. International law or private international law (qqv).

Law Reform Commission. An independent statutory body corporate with functions: to keep the national law of the State under review and to undertake examinations and conduct research with a view to reforming the law and to formulate proposals for law reform: Law Reform Commission Act 1975 as amended by Courts (No 2) Act 1997, s 3. The Commission also examines a particular branch of the law when requested to do so by the Attorney-General (qv) (LRCA 1975, s 4(2)(c)).

There is a President and four Commissioners all appointed by the government. The current President is The Hon Mr Justice Declan Budd, Judge of the High Court. See also Human Rights Commission Act 2000, s 5.

Service by a barrister or solicitor as a whole-time Law Reform Commissioner, or officer, is reckonable towards the length of practice required to be eligible for appointment as a judge; however the person must have two years continuous practice prior to appointment to judicial office (LRCA 1975, s 14 as amended by Courts and Court Officers Act 2002, s 7).

For the reports of the Commission, listed by subject area, with links to the full text, see App 2. The reports of the Commission, its publications and information on its current programme of work are also available on website: *www.lawreform.ie*.

law report. A published account of legal proceedings which gives a statement of the facts and the reasons given by the court for its decision. Law reports commenced in the thirteenth century with the Year Books (c.1270–1530) which were written in Anglo-French and Latin. The Incorporated Council of Law Reporting was established in the mid-nineteenth century and produced reports which were written by barristers.

It has been enacted for the avoidance of doubt that a report of a case made by a solicitor has the same authority as if it had been made by a barrister: Solicitors (Amendment) Act 2002, s 21.

The current Irish law reports are contained in the Irish Reports of the Incorporated Council of Law Reporting (IR); the Irish Law Reports Monthly (ILRM); the reports on the Court of Criminal Appeal (Frewen; Casey); the Irish Times Law Reports (ITLR); the Student Law Reporter; Employment Law Reports (ELR); Irish Criminal Law Journal (ICLJ); Family Law Journal (Fam L J); Irish Journal of European Law (IJEL) and the unreported judgments.

A website offering a data-base of British and Irish law, organised by the British and Irish Legal Information Institute (BAILII) was launched in 2000. Free web access is afforded to primary legal materials from Ireland, Northern Ireland, England, Scotland and Wales; see *www.bailii.org*. The Irish Legal Information Initiative (*www.irlii.org*), a sister site of BAILII, currently provides, amongst other free services, an index of decisions of the High Court, Supreme Court and Court of Criminal Appeal from 1997 to present, including citations of reported cases and links to the full text of decisions which are available on BAILII. See also *www.irish-law.or*; *www.lexis-nexis.com*; *www.firstlaw.ie*. Other electronic reports are: Electronic Irish Weekly Law Reports (eIWLR); Irish Reports on *www.justis.com*; Westlaw.IE. It is intended that court judgments will be available on the website of the Courts Service, see website: *www.courts.ie*. See 'The Family Law Reporting Project' by Siobhan Flockton BL in *Bar Review* (July 2003) 174. [Bibliography: Cox & Heffernan]. See APPENDIX 1; PRECEDENT; RESERVED JUDGMENT.

Law Society of Ireland. The representative body for solicitors with statutory powers and duties under the Solicitors Acts 1954, 1960, 1994 and 2002, in relation to the education, admission, enrolment, discipline and regulation of the profession. It is a defence to an action for damages in relation to the exercise of these statutory powers, for the Society to prove that it acted in good faith and reasonably in all the circumstances: Solicitors (Amendment) Act 1994, s 36.

The Society is required to investigate any complaint which it receives from a solicitor's clients alleging: (a) that the *legal services* provided were inadequate and were not of a quality that could reasonably have been expected of a solicitor, or (b) that the *bill of costs* issued by the solicitor is excessive in respect of the legal services provided (S(A)A 1994, ss 8–14 as amended by Solicitors (Amendment) Act 2002, s 13). The Society is empowered to impose sanctions on the solicitor and may order that the solicitor make a contribution to the cost of the investigation; the solicitor may appeal to the High Court against determinations, directions or requirements of the Society (S(A)A 1994, s 11).

The Minister may by regulation, require the Society to establish, maintain and fund a scheme for the independent adjudication of complaints concerning the handling by the Society of a complaint about a solicitor (S(A)A 1994, s 15). The Society is required to publish annually information on complaints (S(A)A 1994, s 22).

The Society is empowered to require the production of documents from a solicitor where it is of the opinion that the solicitor

has been guilty of dishonesty; it may also seek a High Court order to control his bank accounts (S(A)A 1994, ss 27–28).

The Society is required to maintain a register of solicitors who are prepared to act for a person in civil proceedings against another solicitor, arising from the conduct of that other solicitor while acting for that person (S(A)A 1994, s 67). See 'Law Society of Ireland 1852–2002' by Dr Eamonn Hall and Daire Hogan in *Law Society Gazette* (October 2002) 26. See email: *k.murphy@lawsociety.ie* and website: *www.lawsociety.ie*. [Bibliography: Hogan & Hall]. See COUNCIL OF THE EUROPEAN BARS AND LAW SOCIETIES; GAZETTE; SOLICITOR; SOLICITOR, COMPLAINT AGAINST.

law terms. See SITTINGS OF COURT.

lawful. Authorised or permitted by the law.

lawful homicide. Excusable or justifiable homicide (qv).

lawsuit. Contentious litigation.

lawyer. A legal practitioner; a barrister (qv) or solicitor (qv).

lay days. The days allowed by a charterparty (qv) for loading and unloading a ship.

lay litigant. A person who represents himself in legal proceedings. Such a person is entitled to appear in court and to be heard. The trial of cases involving lay litigants require that trial judges ensure on the one hand that justice is not put at risk by the absence of expert legal representation, while also bearing in mind that the party with legal representation is not unfairly penalised because of that absence: *RB v AS (Nullity: domicile)* [2002] 2 IR 428, SC.

The Supreme Court has held that private expenditure of labour and trouble by lay litigants is not recoverable and cannot be measured by the courts; only legal costs can be measured and only of solicitors who are *on record* for the litigant: *Dawson v Irish Brokers Association* [2002] 2 ILRM 210, SC.

Also, save as otherwise provided by statute or by rules of court, the father, mother, son, daughter, husband, wife, brother or sister of any party may appear on behalf of that party in the District Court, provided such person has the leave of the court to appear and be heard, and that the court is satisfied that the party is, from infirmity or other unavoidable cause, unable to appear: DCR 1997 Ord 6, r 2.

Where an accused represents himself in a criminal trial and where during the trial proceedings, he is totally incompetent to defend himself, there is an even greater burden on the trial judge to ensure that the trial is in all respects above reproach: *The People (DPP) v Ramachchandran* [2000] 2 IR 307, CCA. See ACTING FOR ONESELF; LEGAL AID; LOCUS STANDI; MCKENZIE FRIEND; SOLICITOR, ACCESS TO.

lay-off. A cessation of employment caused by the employer's inability to provide work but where the employer believes that this is temporary and he gives the employee notice to that effect before the cessation: Redundancy Payments Act 1967, s 11(1). Lay-off may give an entitlement to redundancy payment. There is no general right at common law to lay off without pay: *Lawe v Irish Country Meats Ltd* [1998] ELR 266, CC. A lay-off can exceed 26 weeks: An *Post v McNeill* [1998] ELR 19, HC. An employee who claims and receives redundancy payment in respect of lay-off or short-time is deemed to have voluntarily left his employment: Unfair Dismissals Act 1977, s 20; *Scott & Ors v Irish Printed Circuits Ltd* [1990] ELR 167; *Connolly v McInerney & Sons Ltd* [1990] ELR 26. See *Industrial Yarns Ltd v Greene* [1984] ILRM 15. See Redundancy Payments Act 2003, s 3. See CUSTOM AND PRACTICE; SHORT-TIME.

laying an information. See COMMON INFORMER.

leachate. Any liquid percolating through deposited waste and emitted from or contained within a landfill (qv): Waste Management Act 1996, s 5(1). See WASTE.

leading barrister. Means a barrister who is first in point of call to the outer Bar or the inner Bar as the case may be: *Code of Conduct for the Bar of Ireland* (December 2003) r 1.7(q). Where more than one barrister is briefed, it is for the leader to determine when and to what extent any of them may be absent from the hearing and the consent of the consulting solicitor is also necessary for such absence permitted by the leader (r 7.4). It is also for the leading barrister to decide which barrister will make the closing address, but he should ensure that such barrister has been present during a substantial part of the case and has heard the submissions to which he is to reply (r 5.17). See BARRISTER.

leading case. An important case which settles the principles in a particular branch of law and which is cited in court. See PRECEDENT.

leading question. A question put to a witness which directly or indirectly suggests the desired answer or one which may be answered simply *yes* or *no*. Leading questions may not be asked of a witness by the party who called him except: in introductory or undisputed matters; to lead a witness's mind to a particular topic; to identify a person or thing already described; to establish a contradiction to what was said by another witness; where the witness is hostile (qv). See EXAMINATION.

leap year. See AGE.

learner. Means a person who is acquiring or who has acquired knowledge, skill or competence: Qualifications (Education and Training) Act 1999, s 2(1). There are provisions in place for the protection of learners in the event of the insolvency of a commercial provider of training or education eg return of fees, transfer to a similar programme, or assistance in finding an alternative programme (Q(ET)A 1999, ss 43–45). All providers are required, before accepting from a learner, or before commencement of the programme, to inform the learner of the name of the awarding body which will make an award if the learner is successful and the provisions for access, transfer or progression (Q(ET)A 1999, s 46). There is provision for the representation of learners on the National Qualifications Authority of Ireland and the two awards councils (Q(ET)A 1999, ss 6,13, 22). See NATIONAL QUALIFICATIONS AUTHORITY OF IRELAND.

lease. A conveyance or grant by a *lessor* to a *lessee* of possession of property, to last for a certain period of time; it must be for a period less than the estate or interest of the lessor as otherwise it is a conveyance or assignment and not a lease. A lease is usually made in consideration of a *fine* (which is a payment from the lessee to the lessor on the creation of the interest) and on the payment of *rent*. The expression *lease* is usually used to denote an interest for a long period of time, whereas *tenancy* is used to denote a relatively short period. A *sub-lease* or *under-lease* is a lease created by a person who himself is a lessee, for a shorter term than he himself holds.

A tenancy or letting may be *periodic* eg week to week or month to month; it may be expressly created or arise by reference to the payment by the tenant to the landlord of rent.

The main differences between *leases* and *periodic tenancies* are: (a) they are brought to an end (*determined*) in different ways; (b) leases are of a fixed and agreed duration, whereas periodic tenancies are indefinite in duration; (c) leases generally contain detailed conditions and covenants, whereas periodic tenancies may not be as specific, except as regards basic obligations; (d) certain statutory provisions apply where nothing specific has been agreed by the parties and consequently these statutory provisions are more likely to apply in relation to periodic tenancies; (e) certain statutory provisions apply only in the case of leases (eg in relation to restrictive covenants). See *Davies v Hilliard* [1967] 101 ILTR 50.

The Law Reform Commission has recommended that the expressions 'lessor', 'lessee' and 'lease' should be confined to situations where the tenancy has been created by a written document, and has reiterated that confusion would be avoided if the expressions 'landlord', 'tenant' and 'tenancy' were regarded as generic terms: Law Reform Commission, *Consultation Paper on General Law of Landlord and Tenant Law* (LRC CP 28, 2003) para 18.10.

A *'lease'* means an instrument in writing, whether or not under seal, containing a contract of tenancy in respect of a dwelling: Residential Tenancies Act 2004, s 5(1). See Stamp Duties Consolidation Act 1999, ss 50–56, 67. See Leases Acts 1849 and 1850, and Deasy's Act 1860. [Bibliography: Deale; Wylie (1)]. See ASSIGNMENT OF LEASE; QUIET ENJOYMENT, COVENANT FOR; MODEL LEASE; RESIDENTIAL TENANCIES; TENANCY, TERMINATION NOTICE; TENANCY AT WILL; TENANCY BY SUFFERANCE; UNAMBIGUOUS.

lease, creation of. A lease may be created orally where it is for year certain, from year to year or lesser period: Deasy's Act (qv) 1860; for any other period, writing is required and certain statutes require particular leases to be under seal eg Settled Land Act leases. Also letting, sub-letting or subdividing of agricultural holdings requires the consent of the Land Commission: Land Act 1965, s 12. For the purposes of the Landlord and Tenant (Amendment) Act 1980, a lease is an instrument in writing, whether under or not under seal, containing a contract of tenancy in respect of any land in consideration of a rent or return and includes a *fee farm grant* (qv) (LT(A)A 1980, s 3(1)). For arrangements following the dissolution of

the Land Commission in 1999, see LAND COMMISSION. For leases of dwellings, see Residential Tenancies Act 2004, s 5(1) and RESIDENTIAL TENANCIES.

lease, determination of. The ending of a lease or tenancy. It may happen by efflux of time, by surrender, merger, forfeiture or by notice to quit. Where a lease is for a fixed period of time, it automatically expires when the fixed period ends; however certain lessees may have a statutory right to a new lease eg Landlord and Tenant (Amendment) Act 1980 for business leases (qv).

A lease is *surrendered* when the lessee gives up to the lessor the residue of the term still to run; this may arise by express act of the lessee or by operation of law. *Merger* takes place where the lessee acquires the reversion (qv); the lease is absorbed by the reversion. *Forfeiture* can occur for a breach of a condition in a lease, with or without a forfeiture clause, or a breach of a covenant (qv) with a forfeiture clause (sometimes called a *proviso for re-entry*). Forfeiture is strictly construed against the lessor or landlord: *Bennett v Kidd* [1926] NI 50.

Where a landlord proposes to forfeit a lease in reliance on a proviso giving a right of re-entry for non-payment of rent or breach of other covenants in the lease, the re-entry may only be effected either by physical possession or by the issue and service of proceedings for recovery of possession of the premises: *Bank of Ireland v Lady Lisa Ireland Ltd* [1993] ILRM 235, HC. It has been held that there are no restrictions on *discovery* in the case of actions for the forfeiture of a lease: *Dublin Port Company v Bond Road Container Storage and Transport Ltd* [2002] 3 IR 321, SC and [2003] 1 ILRM 426.

A yearly, monthly, weekly or other periodic tenancy may be determined by a *notice to quit* but not a lease or tenancy for a fixed period of time unless expressly reserved in the lease. See also Deasy's Act (qv) 1860; Conveyancing Act 1881, s 14; Landlord and Tenant (Ground Rent) Act 1967; Landlord and Tenant (Amendment) Act 1980, s 60.

However, under recent legislation, a tenancy of a dwelling may not be terminated by the landlord or the tenant by means of a notice of forfeiture, a re-entry or any other process or procedure not provided by

Part 5: Residential Tenancies Act 2004, s 58. See also RTA 2004, s 193(b). See COVENANT; GROUND RENT; NOTICE TO QUIT; PART 4 TENANCY; TENANCY, TERMINATION NOTICE.

lease, short-term. An alternative taxing mechanism has been introduced for short-term leases of plant and machinery, which does not change the amount of tax paid but allows for a more even spread of the tax over the lease period: Taxes Consolidation Act 1997, s 80A inserted by Finance Act 2004, s 35. Under the previous legislation, where lease payments were received on a short-life asset over, say, a three-year period but capital allowances were given over an eight-year period, a timing mismatch occurred for the lessor.

lease for lives renewable for ever. A lease granted for the term of lives, usually three, which contained a provision that when any of the lives dropped out, the grantor would grant a renewal of the lease for a new life on the payment of a sum of money called a renewable fine. A *conversion grant* enabled either party to convert the lease into a fee farm grant (qv); also such a lease, if made for the first time since 1849, operates as a fee farm grant if the lessor is capable of making such a grant: Renewable Leasehold Conversion Act 1849.

Surviving *leases for lives renewable for ever* have been converted into *fee simple* estates: Landlord and Tenant (Amendment) Act 1980, s 74.

leasehold. The interest created by a lease (qv). See Value Added Tax Act 1972, s 4, as amended by Finance Act 2003, s 114. See 'VAT and Leasehold Interests' by solicitor Michael O'Connor in *Law Society Gazette* (May 2003) 18.

leasehold, mortgage of. In order to prevent the mortgagee (lender) becoming liable to pay the rent and perform the covenants in a lease, it is usual to create a mortgage of a lease, by way of a sub-demise of the residue of the mortgagor's interest in the term, less one day, and by way of a declaration by the mortgagor to hold the nominal reversion of one day as trustee for the mortgagee in order that the mortgagee will be able to sell the whole leasehold interest on exercising his power of sale, should this arise. See REVERSION.

leave to apply. Refers to where a plaintiff must seek and obtain the permission of the court before he is permitted to apply for a relief eg the permission of the court is required before an application for a judicial review is applied for: RSC Ord 84, r 20. Contrast with LIBERTY TO APPLY.

leave to defend. The permission given to a defendant to a summary summons to defend the proceedings, which permission may be unconditional or subject to such terms as to security, or time and mode of trial, or otherwise as the court may think fit: RSC Ord 37, r 10. In relation to third parties, see RSC Ord 16, r 8(1)(c).

leave year. As regards the statutory entitlement to annual leave (qv), the year beginning on 1 April: Organisation of Working Time Act 1997, s 2(1). See ANNUAL LEAVE; ADOPTIVE LEAVE; FORCE MAJEURE LEAVE; MATERNITY LEAVE; PARENTAL LEAVE; PROTECTIVE LEAVE; SICK PAY.

legacy. A gift of personal property by will; a bequest. The person to whom the property is given is called the *legatee* and the gift or property is called a *bequest*. A *general* legacy is a piece of personal estate which has not been distinguished from personal property of the same kind eg a bequest of a 'horse' of which the testator has several. A *specific* legacy is a bequest of a special part of the testator's personal estate eg 'my horse which won the Irish Sweep's Derby in 1974.' Legacies are also classified as *pecuniary* (qv) and *demonstrative* (qv). See ABATEMENT OF LEGACY; LAPSE.

legal. (1) In accordance with the law. (2) In accordance with the common law (qv) as distinct from equity (qv).

legal advice. The right of a claimant to seek legal advice must not be affected and no rule may be made which affects that right: Personal Injuries Assessment Board Act 2003, s 7. See PRIVILEGE, LEGAL PROFESSIONAL; SOLICITOR, ACCESS TO.

legal aid. (1) *Criminal legal aid.* The assistance of a qualified lawyer which a person, accused of a serious charge, is entitled to in the preparation and conduct of his defence, the cost of which is to be borne by the State from public funds: *The State (Healy) v Donoghue* [1976] IR 325.

When the circumstances are such that if, in the event of a conviction, or on a plea of guilty, a sentence of imprisonment is likely, the judge is required to inform an indigent defendant of his right to legal aid under the provisions of the Criminal Justice (Legal Aid) Act 1962. The failure of a judge, proposing to impose a custodial sentence, to advise an accused appearing before him without representation, of his constitutional right to legal aid, is such a denial of justice as to render a conviction void: *McSorley v Governor of Mountjoy Prison* [1996] 2 ILRM 331, HC.

Legal aid may be available to an accused in the District Court where evidence will be given through a live television link (qv): CJ(LA)A 1962, s 2A as inserted by Criminal Evidence Act 1992, s 15(4). See *Cahill v DJ Reilly & DPP* [1992] ITLR (13 July), HC.

A District Court judge should choose a solicitor for a defendant only where he has not nominated one himself, or where any nominated by him are not acceptable to the judge for good and sufficient reasons: *The State (Freeman) v DJ Connellan* [1987] ILRM 470. See *Kirwan v Minister for Justice* [1994] 1 ILRM 444, HC. See SI No 76 of 1998; SI No 713 of 2003. See *Final Report of the Criminal Legal Aid Review Committee* (July 2002).

(2) *Civil legal aid.* The State was held to have been in breach of the Convention on Human Rights (qv) because of the non-availability of state-funded legal aid in matrimonial matters: *Airey v Ireland* [1979] 2 EHRR 305. A non-statutory legal aid scheme for civil matters was established in December 1979 under the Legal Aid Board, the purpose of which was to make the services of solicitors and, if necessary, barristers available to persons of modest means at little cost; certain matters were excluded e g land disputes.

It has been held that there is no constitutional duty on the State to provide for any form of financial support for civil litigation among citizens; the Board was required however to consider an application for civil legal aid and advice within a reasonable time: *Cosgrove v Legal Aid Board* [1990] ITLR (19 November), HC. See also *MF v Legal Aid Board* [1993] ILRM 797, SC.

In 1995, statutory provision was made for a civil legal aid scheme operated by the Legal Aid Board: Civil Legal Aid Act 1995. Under the scheme, *legal aid* and *legal advice* is provided to persons who satisfy the financial eligibility requirements and who pay to the Board a contribution towards the cost (CLAA 1995, s 29). *Legal advice* means oral or written advice on the application of the law to the particular circumstances and the steps which might be appropriate to take (CLAA 1995, s 25). *Legal aid* means representation by a solicitor or barrister in civil proceedings (CLAA 1995, s 27).

A *legal aid certificate* is a requirement to obtain legal aid and will be granted where an applicant meets the financial eligibility requirements, has reasonable grounds in law, is reasonably likely to succeed, the proceedings are the most satisfactory means available, and it is reasonable to grant the certificate (CLAA 1995, s 28).

Legal aid or advice is not available in respect of certain designated matters e g defamation, disputes over land, licensing, conveyancing, or group actions to establish a legal precedent; however, aid or advice may be available in relation to disputes on title or possession of property between spouses, or persons who are living together or have lived together or were engaged to be married (CLAA 1995, s 28(9)). See Civil Legal Aid Regulations, SI No 8 of 2002. See also Children Act 1997, s 13. The Law Society in a report launched on 29 June 2000 has recommended that civil legal aid be extended to all persons on social welfare: *Irish Times*, 30 June 2000.

In Northern Ireland it has been held that the fact that a party to a civil action is legally assisted may be a relevant factor to be considered by the judge in deciding whether to dismiss the action due to the failure of the party to attend at court: *In the matter of Patricia Murphy* [1992] ITLR (24 February), HC NI.

A *tax clearance certificate* must be produced by a barrister or solicitor willing to act for persons to whom legal aid certificates are granted: Finance Act 1998, s 132. An applicant under the *ad hoc* legal aid scheme (Criminal Assets Bureau) must show to the satisfaction of the court that his means are insufficient and that it is essential in the interest of justice that he should have legal aid in the preparation or conduct of his case: *MM v GM* [2001] ITLR (7 May), SC.

A practising barrister must not have his name placed on a Legal Aid Panel until he has completed six months pupillage or until he has been a member of the Law Library for one year: *Code of Conduct for the Bar of Ireland* (December 2003) r 7.9. See also *The State (O'Connor) v Clifford* [1987] HC; *DP v Governor of the Training Unit* [2001] 1 IR 492, HC. See Criminal Procedure Act 1967, s 4H inserted by Criminal Justice Act 1999, s 9. See Courts-Martial (Legal Aid) Regulations 1987, SI No 46 of 1987; Refugee Civil Legal Aid Regulations 1999,

SIs No 74 , 262 and 385 of 1999; Criminal Justice (Legal Aid) (Amendment) Regulations 2002, SI No 575 of 2002. See European Agreement on the Transmission of Applications for Legal Aid entered into force for Ireland on 15 December 1988. See Cousins in 10 ILT & SJ (1992) 41. [Bibliography: Gov Pub (4) & (5)]. See ATTORNEY-GENERAL'S SCHEME; EUROJUS; FREE LEGAL ADVICE CENTRES; HUMAN RIGHTS COMMISSION; MENTAL HEALTH COMMISSION.

legal base. In order for the EU to have power to act in any area, that area must have what is known as a *'legal base'* in the treaty structure; any areas where the EU is to have such power must be recognised formally and explicitly in the legal structure of the treaties: National Forum on Europe, *Glossary of Terms* (2003). The proposed Treaty establishing a Constitution for Europe maintains all areas where there were legal bases previously and creates legal bases in some further limited areas. See EUROPEAN UNION CONSTITUTION.

legal charges. On taking instructions from a client to provide *legal services*, a solicitor is required to provide the client with particulars in writing of the actual charges or, where this is not possible, an estimate, or if neither is possible, the basis of the charges for legal services: Solicitors (Amendment) Act 1994, s 68. 'The law now requires that clients are made fully aware of the charges which they will have to pay for the provision of any legal services provided by their solicitors': *A Guide to Professional Conduct of Solicitors in Ireland* (2002) ch 10.1. The information must be given in writing and applies to both contentious and non-contentious business. Included in the definition of 'charges' are fees, outlays, disbursements and expenses. The Law Society is required to investigate complaints of excessive charging. The Society is empowered to impose sanctions on a solicitor where it finds that the solicitor has issued a bill of costs which is excessive (S(A)A 1994, s 9). The European Court of Justice has held in a case before a German court, between German and Austrian parties in which the Austrian party was successful, that the German court was within its rights to limit the level of fees payable to a lawyer appearing before it: Case C-289/02 *AMOK Verlags GmbH v A & R Gastronomie GmbH* [2003] (11 December), ECJ. See BARRISTER AND FEES; BRIEF FEE;

COSTS IN CIVIL PROCEEDINGS; CONTENTIOUS BUSINESS; LEGAL COSTS ACCOUNTANT; LEGAL SERVICES; SOLICITOR AND CLIENT COSTS; TAXATION OF COSTS.

legal costs accountant. An accountant often engaged by a solicitor to draw, prepare and submit a bill of costs in legal proceedings. It has been held that the cost of using a legal costs accountant is not a cost properly incurred by the official liquidator in a winding up of a company: *Re Castle Brand Ltd (in liquidation)* [1990] ILRM 97, HC. It has also been held that the liability of the other party for costs cannot be dependant on how a solicitor makes a choice as between preparing his own bills, employing a cost accountant within his own office or going to an outside cost accountant: *Best v Wellcome Foundation Ltd* [1996] 1 ILRM 34, HC. See TAXATION OF COSTS.

legal costs, investigation of title. A *building society* is precluded from requiring a member to pay its costs of legal investigation of title to any property offered as security for a loan: Building Societies Amendment Act 1986, s 6(1)(d); SI No 27 of 1987, first schedule (iv); SI No 339 of 1987 art 6. Notwithstanding the repeal of BSAA 1986, this provision continues in force as if made by the Central Bank: Building Societies Act 1989, s 6. See also BSA 1989, s 11(2)(b)(iv)). Also, any costs incurred by a *mortgage lender* (qv) in the legal investigation of title to any property offered as security by a borrower must be paid by the lender and is not recoverable from the borrower: Consumer Credit Act 1995, s 125. See COSTS IN CIVIL PROCEEDINGS; SOLICITOR AND CLIENT COSTS.

legal executive. An executive in a law firm who carries out a variety of tasks under the supervision and guidance of a qualified solicitor. In the United Kingdom, legal executives have a right of audience in chambers (ie not in open court) and a limited right of audience in open court in the county court. They do not enjoy such rights in Ireland. A *Legal Executive Professional Legal Studies* course is now available in Ireland, leading to a *certificate* after one year and a *diploma* after two years. The *Irish Institute of Legal Executives* (ILEX) was formed in 1987 and incorporated in 1992. Its main purpose is to represent, promote and encourage persons identified as legal executives practising in all legal areas of employment. In 2003 it launched its Continuing Professional Development (CPD) courses.

A *Managing Clerk* is a legal assistant (not being a solicitor) who is fully experienced in all branches of a solicitor's work conducted in the office in which he is employed and who is able to, and habitually does, conduct legal cases including the interviewing of clients, in that office, without constant supervision: Employment Regulation Order (Law Clerks Joint Labour Committee) 2002, SI Nos 88 of 2002; and SIs No 154 and 543 of 2003. See 'Executive Class' in *Law Society Gazette* (December 2003) 30. [Irish Institute of Legal Executives, 22/24 Lower Mount Street, Dublin 2. Tel/fax (01) – 890 4278, email: *info@irishinstituteoflegalexecutives.com*. See website: *www.irishinstituteoflegalexecutives.com*.

legal memory. See TIME IMMEMORIAL.

legal metrology. See METROLOGY.

legal mortgage. See MORTGAGE.

legal privilege. See PRIVILEGE, LEGAL PROFESSIONAL.

legal profession. Barristers (qv) and solicitors (qv). See Fair Trade Commission Report of *Study into Restrictive Practices in the Legal Profession* (1990).

legal professional privilege. See PRIVILEGE, LEGAL PROFESSIONAL.

legal relations, intention to create. An essential element in the creation of a valid and legally enforceable contract. In business dealings an intention to create legal relations will be presumed. In social arrangements it will not be so assumed unless the contrary is shown. A condition in a contract expressly excluding legal relations is binding and is not contrary to public policy. In a particular case, the High Court has held that as the parties had only agreed the price at which they were prepared to deal, there was no intention at that time to create a contractual relationship: *McGill Construction Ltd v McKeon & Others* (19 May 2004, unreported). See *Appleson v Littlewoood Ltd* [1939] 1 All ER 464; *Balfour v Balfour* [1919] 2 KB 571. See GENTLEMAN'S AGREEMENT.

legal representation. A person is entitled to be represented in court by a solicitor (qv) or barrister (qv). It has been held that a judge of the District Court was wrong not to allow an adjournment sought by an accused in order that he might secure legal representation: *Flynn v DJ Ruane* [1989] ILRM 690, HC. A person may not be entitled to legal representation where such entitlement is not provided for eg in an appeal hearing under social welfare law: *Corcoran v Minister for Social Welfare* [1992] ILRM 133, HC.

An employee may be entitled to have legal representation at a disciplinary hearing, particularly where the charges are serious: *Gallagher v Revenue Commissioners* [1991] ILRM 632, HC. In a subsequent case, it was held that there is no general right to legal representation at a quasi-judicial disciplinary hearing: *Aziz v Midland Health Board* [1995] ELR 48, HC. In this case it was held that there was no entitlement to formal legal representation as the issues investigated raised simple questions of fact and that it was not intended that any party would have legal representation.

A determination of an inquisitorial inquiry to limit parties to be represented by one solicitor and one counsel was not approved by the High Court, as the determination was an interference with the extent to which the team selected by the client was permitted to act on behalf of the client, and the inquiry did not have jurisdiction to make the determination: *Re Commission to Inquire into Child Abuse* [2002] 3 IR 459, HC. [Bibliography: Walsh D (3)]. See also LEGAL AID; NATURAL JUSTICE; REPRESENTATIVE; SENTENCE REVIEW GROUP; SOLICITOR, ACCESS TO.

legal right of spouse. See SPOUSE, LEGAL RIGHT OF.

legal separation. See DIVORCE A MENSA ET THORO; JUDICIAL SEPARATION; SEPARATION AGREEMENT.

legal services. Services of a legal or financial nature provided by a solicitor, arising from that solicitor's practice as a solicitor; it also includes any investment business services provided by a solicitor who is not an authorised investment business firm: Solicitors (Amendment) Act 1994, s 2 as amended by Investor Compensation Act 1998, s 45. A solicitor is deemed to practise as a solicitor if he engages in the provision of legal services (S(A)A 1994, s 56(2)). A solicitor must not practice as a solicitor without a current practising certificate (S(A)A 1994, s 56(1)). See CONTENTIOUS BUSINESS; SOLICITOR.

legal tender. Tender or offer of payment in a form which a creditor is bound to accept. Prior to the full introduction of the *euro* in

2002, a tender of money in the Irish pound unit in coins was legal tender for 20 times the face value of each denomination of coin tendered: Central Bank Act 1989, s 127. Also notes issued by the Central Bank are legal tender in the State for the payment of any amount (CBA 1989, s 118). Perpetual copyright subsists in Irish legal tender notes, euro notes, consolidated bank notes and in Irish and euro coins: Copyright and Related Rights Act 2000, s 200.

The only euro banknotes which have the status of legal tender within the participating member states are euro banknotes issued by the European Central Bank (qv) and the participating national central banks: EC Treaty, art 106 of the consolidated (2002) version. The ECB has the exclusive right to *authorise* the issue of euro banknotes within the Community.

As from 30 June 2002, the euro has been the legal tender in the then twelve participating member states to the exclusion of the previous local currency.

A perpetual copyright exists in legal tender; it belongs to the ECB in respect of euro notes, and belongs to the Minister in respect of any *national face* of coins issued by the Central Bank of Ireland: Copyright Act 1963, s 57 as amended by Economic and Monetary Union Act 1998, ss 20 and 34. See now Copyright and Related Rights Act 2000, s 200. See COINS; COMMEMORATIVE COINAGE; EURO; TENDER.

legal tender note fund. The fund which was wound up by the Central Bank of Ireland with effect from the close of business on 27 July 1989 pursuant to the Central Bank Act 1989, s 22. The assets of the fund have been transferred to the General Fund of the bank; legal tender notes on issue at any time from 28 July 1989 are a liability on the General Fund (Iris Oifigiúil, 1 August 1989).

legal terms order. The order which the Minister is empowered to make, declaring that the equivalent in the Irish language of any specified term shall be such word or words as he thinks fit and which he specifies in the order: Irish Legal Terms Act 1945, s 3. See IRISH LANGUAGE.

legal unit of measurement. See MEASUREMENT, LEGAL UNIT OF.

legal year. The annual period of time constituted by the four sittings of the courts, being Michaelmas, Hilary, Easter and Trinity. See SITTINGS OF COURT.

legality, presumption of. See OMNIA PRAESUMUNTUR RITA ESSE ACTA.

legatee. A person to whom a legacy is left. See LEGACY.

leges posteriores priores contrarias abrogant. [Later laws abrogate prior contrary laws].

legislation. (1) The making of laws. (2) The body of enactments or statutes of the legislature. Legislation is either *superior* or *subordinate*. Superior legislation is law as enacted by the legislature ie by the Oireachtas (qv); subordinate legislation is the rules or law as laid down by some person or body under authority delegated by the legislature. See ACT; BILL; DELEGATED LEGISLATION; JURISDICTION.

legislation, amendment of. See AMENDMENT OF LEGISLATION.

legislation, constitutionality of. See CONSTITUTIONALITY OF LEGISLATION.

legislation, delegated. See DELEGATED LEGISLATION.

legislation, interpretation of. See INTERPRETATION OF LEGISLATION.

legislation, retrospective. See RETROSPECTIVE LEGISLATION.

legislative. See SEPARATION OF POWERS.

Legislative Act. Under the draft European Constitutional Treaty, an act making primary law for or within the EU; this includes *European law* (qv) and *European framework law* (qv): National Forum on Europe, *Glossary of Terms* (2003). See proposed *Treaty establishing a Constitution for Europe.* See EUROPEAN UNION CONSTITUTION.

legitimacy. This is a political concept, relating to whether, or how far, a political system or a set of political arrangements or institutions is regarded as being valid and worthy of acceptance or support by the people who are governed under such arrangements or whose lives are affected by what is done by the institutions: National Forum on Europe, *Glossary of Terms* (2003). See proposed *Treaty establishing a Constitution for Europe.* See EUROPEAN UNION CONSTITUTION.

legitimacy, presumption of. The presumption of legitimacy arising out of marriage has been abolished and replaced by a *presumption of paternity:* Status of Children Act 1987, s 44 and 46. See *Russell v Russel* [1924] AC 687; *AS v RB* [1984] ILRM 66. See PATERNITY, PRESUMPTION OF.

legitimate. See CHILD, LEGITIMATE.

legitimate expectation. The doctrine by which a person may obtain a remedy where he has had a *legitimate expectation* regarding some representations made to him eg an undertaking to be consulted in relation to a change in the law: *Pesca Valentia Ltd v Minister for Fisheries & Forestry* [1989] 7 ILT Dig 324; *Wiley v Revenue Commissioners* [1989] IR 350 and [1994 SC] 2 IR 160; *Nolan v Minister for the Environment* [1989] 7 ILT Dig 325.

The plea of legitimate expectation is merely an aspect of the well recognised equitable concept of *promissory estoppel*, whereby a promise or representation as to intention may in certain circumstances be held to be binding on the representor or promisor: *Re 'La Lavia'* [1996] 1 ILRM 194, SC and [1999] 3 IR 413, SC; *Webb v Ireland* [1988] IR 353. It is sometimes described as *reasonable expectation*.

The test to be applied is whether in all the circumstances it would be unfair or unjust to allow a party to resile from a position created or adopted by that party which at that time gave rise to a legitimate expectation in the mind of another person that that situation might continue and might be acted on by that other person to their advantage: *Cannon v Minister for the Marine* [1991] ILRM 261, HC.

There cannot be a legitimate expectation which has the effect of fettering the exercise of a statutory discretion imposed by statute on a particular decision maker: *Smith v Judge O'Donnell & DPP* [2004] ITLR (28 June) HC. As regards the exercise of a discretionary statutory power, the only legitimate expectation relating to the conferring of a benefit that can be inferred from words and conduct is a conditional one: *Tara Prospecting v Minister for Energy* [1993] ILRM 771, HC. Also the doctrine of legitimate expectation cannot create any new cause of action where none existed before, so that where a promise is made which is not supported by any consideration, the promisee cannot bring an action: *Association of GPs v Minister for Health* [1995] 2 ILRM 481, HC.

The doctrines of *estoppel* and *legitimate expectation* do not apply where an applicant has not suffered any damage and where the right being claimed is one to which he is not statutorily entitled: *Gavin v Appeals Officer* [1997] 3 IR 240, HC.

A prisoner who has been granted regular periods of temporary release may develop a legitimate expectation to a renewal or, if not, to an explanation: *Sherlock v Governor of Mountjoy Prison* [1991] 1 IR 451, HC.

The court will not extend the boundaries of legitimate expectation in a way which would result: (a) in the court ordering a statutory body to act *ultra vires* its powers: *Wiley v Revenue Commissioners* [1993] ILRM 482, SC and [1994] 2 IR 160, SC; or (b) in the fettering of the exercise of a statutory power: *Dempsey v Minister for Justice* [1994] 1 ILRM 401, HC. The doctrine of legitimate expectation cannot be invoked to limit the exercise of the discretionary power of a Minister when exercised in the public interest: *Gilheany v Revenue Commissioners* [1996] ELR 25, HC.

A person cannot base a claim for breach of legitimate expectation on the legitimate expectation of a second person, as it is at one remove from the first person: *Gulyas v Minister for Justice* [2001] 3 IR 216, HC. The doctrines of legitimate expectation and legal certainty, as recognised by the jurisprudence of the European Court of Justice, have no application to the interpretation of statutes in Irish domestic law: *McKone Estates Ltd v Dublin Co Council* [1995] 2 ILRM 283, SC. In a particular case, the court held that a university professor did not have a legitimate expectation to continue in office after 65 years of age: *Eogan v University College Dublin* [1996] 2 ILRM 303, HC and 1 IR 390.

See also *Donegal Co Council v Porter* [1993] ELR 101, HC and [1992] ELR 222, EAT; *Kavanagh v Government of Ireland* [1996] 1 ILRM 133, HC; *Abrahamson v Law Society* [1996] 1 IR 403, HC; *O'Leary v Minister for Finance* [1998] 2 ILRM 321, HC; *Gilheaney v Revenue Commissioners* [1998] 4 IR 150, HC; *Hinde Livestock Exports Ltd v Pandora Ltd* [1998] 2 IR 203, HC; *Navan Tanker Services Ltd v Meath County Council* [1998] 1 IR 166, HC; *Fairleigh Ltd v Temple Bar Renewal Ltd* [1999] 2 IR 508, HC; *DPP v Murphy* [2001] 2 ILRM 334, HC; *Gorman v Minister for the Environment* [2001] 2 IR 414, HC; *McCann v Groarke* [2001] 3 IR 431, HC; *Daly v Minister for the Marine* [2001] 3 IR 513, SC; *Kavanagh v Governor of Mountjoy Prison* [2002] 2 ILRM 81, SC and 3 IR 97. See *Delaney* in 11 ILT & SJ (1993) 192. See EQUITABLE ESTOPPEL.

legitimated. See CHILD, LEGITIMATED.

legitimus contradictor. A *devil's advocate* or *amicus curiae*; according to Kinlen J it would be desirable in nullity of marriage cases, where one or other of the parties is not before the court, to have a *legitimus contradictor* or *amicus curiae* appointed at the public's expense to argue in favour of the existence of the marriage: *per curiam* in *O'R v B* [1995] 2 ILRM 57, HC.

The court may make a declaration under the Family Law Act 1995 which is binding on the parties without the presence of the Attorney-General in the proceedings as a *legitimus contradictor*: *McG v DW* [2000] 2 ILRM 451, SC. See CONTRADICTOR.

Leopardstown Park Hospital. A house and grounds in Dublin, given in trust in 1917 for the care and treatment of persons disabled or invalided during service with the armed forces of the United Kingdom. The British Ministry of Pensions built a hospital on the grounds to provide such care. The trustees, faced with a reduction in the number of war pensioners, were given the right to admit patients other than war pensioners: Leopardstown Park Hospital (Trust Deed Amendment) Act 1974. In 1979 agreement was reached by the Irish and British authorities under which the day-to-day running of the hospital was delegated to a board of management, with two of the nine board members nominated by the British authorities: SI No 98 of 1979 as amended by SI No 443 of 2002. The hospital now comes under the general auspices of the Eastern Regional Health Authority, managed by the board of management, and with priority of admission to UK ex-servicemen and war pensioners.

lesbianism. Female homosexuality. The Defamation Act 1961, s 16 provides that words spoken and published which impute unchastity or adultery to any woman or girl does not require proof of *special* damage to render them actionable. In the UK, it has been held that an imputation of lesbianism is an imputation within the meaning of a similar section in the Slander of Women Act 1891: *Kerr v Kennedy* [1942] 1 All ER 412. See HATRED, INCITEMENT TO; SEXUAL ORIENTATION; SLANDER; VIDEO RECORDING.

lessee. A person to whom a lease (qv) is granted.

lessor. A person who grants a lease (qv).

lethal. As regards a *lethal* weapon, means capable of causing death: *Moore v Gooderham* [1960] 1 WLR 1308. See 'State obligations in respect of the use of lethal force' by Grainne Mullan BL in *Bar Review* (December 2001) 76. See FIREARM.

letter of comfort. In commercial practice, usually a letter from a parent company to the creditor of a subsidiary of the parent in respect of advances made to the subsidiary. Whether it involves an assumption of legal liability for the debts of the subsidiary will depend on the wording of the letter and the intention of the parties. In general, the effect of a letter of comfort is a matter of such uncertainty, they are inadvisable in commercial transactions, a guarantee or indemnity being much more certain. See *Kleinwort Benson Ltd v Malaysia Mining Corp* [1988] 1 All ER 714; 7 ILT & SJ (1989) 235; 8 ILT & SJ (1990) 234; *King v Aer Lingus plc* [2002] 3 IR 481, HC and [2003] ELR 173.

letter of credit. An undertaking by a banker acting on the instructions of its customer (eg the buyer of goods) to pay or to meet drafts drawn pursuant to it by the beneficiary of the credit (eg the seller of the goods) in accordance with the terms laid down in the undertaking. The sale of goods worldwide is normally arranged by means of *letters of credit* eg the buyer may instruct his bank to open a credit in favour of the seller, which is a promise by the banker to pay money to the seller in return for, say, shipping documents in respect of the goods.

Letters of credit may be revocable or irrevocable. A *revocable* credit may be amended or cancelled at any time without notice to the beneficiary. An *irrevocable* letter of credit constitutes a definite undertaking of the issuing bank, provided that the terms and conditions of the credit are complied with. See also Building Societies Act 1989, s 29(2)(q). [Bibliography: Paget UK].

letter of request. A letter (also known as a *commission rogatoire*) from a foreign court or tribunal that it is desirous of obtaining the testimony of a witness within the jurisdiction of this State; the court in this State is empowered to order the taking of such evidence. See RSC Ord 39, rr 39–44. See Foreign Tribunals Evidence Act 1856; Arbitration Act 1954, s 22(1)(d); Patents Act 1992, s 130.

Any person examined pursuant to an order made under the 1856 Act has, in effect, the same rights as he would have if he were a witness before a trial in the Irish courts, and is entitled to object or refuse to answer questions or produce documents which he would not be forced to answer or produce in an Irish court (FTEA 1856, s 5). The High Court has held that there is no power under s 1 of the 1856 Act to order discovery of documents or to order the taking of evidence which in reality solely amounted to discovery of documents: *Sabretech Inc v Shannon Aerospace Ltd* [1999] 2 IR 468, HC. The Irish court has an inherent jurisdiction to set aside an *ex parte* order pursuant to s 1 of FTEA 1856: *Voluntary Purchasing v Insurco International Ltd* [1995] 2 ILRM 145, HC.

The first time that evidence was taken under the 1856 Act on video in a criminal trial occurred in 1993; it related to a trial, alleging horse racing fraud, then taking place in Western Australia: *Irish Times*, 11 December 1993.

In a particular case the Supreme Court held that it would be oppressive to permit the applicant to examine the respondents in advance of a fraud action against them in Ireland: *Novell Inc v MCB Enterprises* [2001] 1 IR 608, SC and [2002] 1 ILRM 350, SC.

A new procedure for the taking of evidence in the State for use in proceedings outside the State is provided for in the Criminal Justice Act 1994, s 51. The Minister for Justice may, if he receives a request for assistance in obtaining evidence, nominate a judge of the District Court for the purpose of giving effect to the request. The hearing before a district judge of such evidence is the gathering of evidence and not the administration of justice and may be held *in camera*; however a *judicial review* in the High Court of a ruling of the district judge, in the gathering of such evidence, is the administration of justice and is required to be heard in open court: *de Gartori v Smithwick* [2000] 1 ILRM 463, SC. See also *Creaven v Minister for Justice* (24 February 2004, unreported) HC; *Brady v District Judge Haughton* [2004] 1 ILRM 321, HC.

Legal history was created in September 2002 when the Supreme Court of New South Wales (Australia), sat in the Four Courts in Dublin to hear the evidence of a paralysed Dublin plaintiff, Garry Mulligan, in his action for negligence against Coffs Harbour Borough Council and four New South Wales government agencies. The Australian Court, in March 2003 dismissed the plaintiff's claim, holding that the danger at the Coffs Harbour resort was, or should have been, obvious to Mr Mulligan

and that it was an inherent risk in the plaintiff's swimming activities that day.

There is also provision for obtaining evidence outside the State for use in the State by way of *letter of request* (CJA 1994, s 52). The Law Reform Commission has this whole area under review, with the intention of publishing a Consultation Paper which will examine ways to make the procedure more efficient. See website: *www.lawreform.ie*. See CLIENT ACCOUNT; COMITY.

letters missive. See SIGN MANUAL.

letters of administration. A *grant of representation* issued from the Probate Office, or from a District Probate Registry (qv), which are part of the High Court, to the effect that administration of a deceased's estate has been granted to the administrator, he having first sworn faithfully to administer same (eg RSC App Q, Form 7). The administrator undertakes to exhibit a true inventory of the estate and to render a true account thereof (RSC App Q, Form 5).

Persons who have a beneficial interest in the estate of the deceased are entitled to a grant of administration in a specified order of priority depending on whether the deceased died intestate or testate: Succession Act 1965, s 27(3); RSC Ord 79, r 5. A grant of administration cannot be made to more than three persons unless the probate officer directs otherwise: RSC Ord 79 r 5(14) and Ord 80 r 6(13).

A grant of letters of administration intestate is given where the deceased died intestate. A grant of administration with the will annexed, *cum testamento annexo*, is given where the deceased left a will, but some person other than the executor applies for a grant.

A grant may be limited as to duration, limited as to purpose, or limited to a particular part of the estate. See Succession Act 1965, s 27(1); also *Re Matthew (dec'd)* [1984] 2 All ER 396. See also Status of Children Act 1987, s 30. See ADMINISTRATION OF ESTATES; ADMINISTRATOR; INSOLVENT ESTATE.

letters of administration, priority for. Persons having a beneficial interest in the estate of another, who has died wholly intestate and domiciled in Ireland, are entitled to a grant of administration in the following order of priority: (a) the surviving spouse; (b) the surviving spouse jointly with a child of the deceased nominated by the said spouse; (c) the child or children of the deceased; (d) the issue of any child of the deceased who has died during the lifetime of the deceased; (e) the father or mother of the deceased; (f) brothers and sisters of the deceased (whether of the whole or half blood); (g) where any brother or sister survived the deceased, the children of a predeceased brother or sister; (h) nephews and nieces of the deceased (whether of the whole or half blood); (i) grandparents; (j) uncles and aunts (whether of the whole or half blood); (k) great grandparents; (l) other next-of-kin of nearest degree (whether of the whole or half blood) preferring collaterals to direct lineal ancestors; (m) the nominees of the State: RSC Ord 79, r 5(1).

letters patent. Originally, grants by the sovereign of franchises, lands or rights to another, contained in an instrument or charter, which was usually addressed to all subjects in the realm and bore the Great Seal of the Realm. The term *Letters Patent for an Invention* are no longer used; patent grants also are no longer under seal: Patents Act 1992, s 34. See PATENT; ROYAL CHARTER.

letting of goods. See HIRE; HIRER, HIRE-PURCHASE.

letting of premises. See BUSINESS TENANT; LEASE; TENANCY.

levant and couchant. [Risen and lain down].

levy. To raise money compulsorily e g by means of taxes or distress.

A planning levy is the contribution towards any public infrastructure or project, which a planning authority may require to be paid when granting planning permission: Planning and Development Act 2000, s 49. A planning authority may, when granting a permission under s 34, include conditions for requiring the payment of a contribution in respect of public infrastructure and facilities benefiting development in the area of the planning authority and that is provided, or that it is intended will be provided, by or on behalf of a local authority (regardless of other sources of funding for the infrastructure and facilities) (PDA 2000, s 48). The High Court has held that this section does not impose a requirement on the local authority to specify the public infrastructure and facilities for which a contribution is sought: *Construction Industry Federation v Dublin City Council* (2004) Irish Times, 5th March, HC.

A specific levy to raise €100m per annum over a three-year period was imposed on financial institutions by the Finance Act 2003, s 141. The *Commission for Communications Regulation* is empowered to impose a levy on electronic communication providers and on providers of postal services: Communications Regulation Act 2002, s 30. See Postal Levy Order 2003, SI No 549 of 2002; Section 30 Levy Orders, SIs Nos 346, 392 and 733 of 2003, and SI No 401 of 2004.

For the levy imposed on housing developments in respect of which planning permission would have expired under the Planning and Development Act 2000 but for the Planning and Development (Amendment) Act 2002, see PD(A)A 2002, s 4 inserting new s 96B in PDA 2000. See Companies (Auditing and Accounting) Act 2003, s 15. See also Gas (Interim) (Regulation) Act 2002, s 21; Gas Levy Order 2002, SI No 522 of 2002; Waste Management (Landfill Levy) Regulations 2002, SI No 86 of 2002.

Examples of former levies are: (a) the training levies imposed on some employers by the Industrial Training Act 1967; (b) the employment and training levy imposed on individuals by the Labour Services Act 1987 and the Youth Employment Agency Act 1981, abolished by Social Welfare Act 1999, s 34; (c) and the apprentice levy imposed on certain industry sectors by the Industrial Training (Apprenticeship Levy) Act 1994. These levies were replaced in 2000 by a new training levy; for details see TRAINING FUND. [Bibliography: Bradley]. See also BOVINE DISEASE; COMMISSION FOR AVIATION REGULATION; ELECTRICITY; FOAL; PLANNING PERMISSION, CONDITIONS ON; PLASTIC BAG; LANDFILL SITE.

lex causae. [The law governing the matter]. See *Mitchelstown Co-operative Agricultural Society v Nestlé* [1989] ILRM 582, SC.

lex domicilii. [The law of the person's domicile].

lex fori. [The law of the court in which the case is tried]. The general principle in *conflict of laws* is that procedure is governed by the *lex fori*, the domestic law of the forum: *de Gartori v Smithwick* [2000] 1 ILRM 463, SC.

lex loci celebrationis. [The law of the place where a marriage is celebrated]. A marriage abroad to be recognised by the State must have complied with the law of the place where it was celebrated. Certain marriages solemnised according to religious ceremonies abroad eg in Lourdes, but which did not comply with the local civil formalities, were regularised by the Marriage Act 1972, s 2. See also *Conlon v Mohamed* [1987] ILRM 172.

lex loci contractus. [The law of the place where the contract is made].

lex loci delicti commissi. [The law of the place where the wrong was committed]. See *Short v Ireland, A-G & British Nuclear Fuels plc* [1997] 1 ILRM 161, SC.

lex loci solutionis. [The law of the place of performance]. See *Fraser v Buckle* [1994] 1 ILRM 276, HC.

lex non cogit ad impossibilia. [The law does not compel the impossible].

lex non requirit verificari quod apparet curiae. [The law does not require that which is apparent to the court to be verified].

lex non scripta. [The unwritten law]. The common law.

lex posterior derogat priori. [A later law overrules an earlier one].

lex rei situs. [The law of the situation of the thing].

lex scripta. [The written law]. Statute law.

lex situs. [The law of the place where property is situated]. The general rule is that land and other immovables are governed by the *lex situs* eg succession to moveable property of an intestate is governed by the law of his domicile and succession to his immovables by the *lex situs*. See PRIVATE INTERNATIONAL LAW; WILL, INTERNATIONAL.

lex spectat naturae ordinem. [The law has regard to the order of nature].

lex talionis. [The law of retaliation]. Refers to primitive law embodied in the phrase 'An eye for an eye, a tooth for a tooth'.

liability. Legal obligation or duty; or the amount owed. A person who commits a wrong or breaks a contract or trust is said to be liable or responsible for it. A liability is said to be criminal or civil, depending on whether it is enforced by a criminal or civil court. A *vicarious liability* (qv) is one which falls on one person as a result of his relationship with another eg a master is generally liable for the acts of his servant performed in the course of his employment. A *contingent liability* is a future unascertained obligation. Where the justice of a case so requires it, the Supreme Court can determine the issue of liability instead of

referring the matter back to the High Court eg see *Phillips v Durgan* [1991] ILRM 321, SC. [Bibliography: Kerr (3); McAuley & McCutcheon]. See CONTINGENT LIABILITY; LIMITATION OF LIABILITY.

liability, limited. See COMPANY, LIMITED; LIMITED PARTNERSHIP; PERSONAL LIABILITY.

liability, statutory exemption from. Examples of statutory exemption from liability are in respect of: (a) loss arising from the administration of the postal services: Post Office Act 1908, s 13; (b) exemption from implied terms of carriage contracts: Sale of Goods and Supply of Service Act 1980, s 40(6); (c) terms and conditions of carriage by rail: Transport Act 1958, s 8; (d) power to cut off electricity for non-payment of account: Electricity (Supply) Act 1927, s 99; *McCord v ESB* [1980] ILRM 153. See CONTRACT OF ADHESION.

liability, strict. See STRICT LIABILITY.

liability, vicarious. See VICARIOUS LIABILITY.

liability for products. See PRODUCT LIABILITY.

libel. Defamation in writing or printing or in some other permanent form, such as a statue or film. Broadcasting words by wireless telegraphy is to be treated as publication in a permanent form: Defamation Act 1961, s 15. A court hearing a libel action must deal with the ordinary and natural meaning of the words complained of: *Bailey v Irish Mirror Group Ltd & Others* [2004] ITLR (2 February) 2004.

Libel is actionable *per se*, without proof of actual damages being suffered. In assessing the quantum of an award for libel, the jury cannot be given guidelines by the court or by counsel in relation to the appropriate level of damages and the jury's attention should not be drawn to the level of damages awarded in personal injury actions or other defamation actions; such a practice would lead to confusion, as the jury would be overwhelmed with figures: *de Rossa v Independent Newspapers plc* [1999] 4 IR 432, SC.

A libel, but not a slander, may also be a crime. *Criminal libel* is a libel which is sufficiently aggravated by its public nature (eg libel on a person in a public position). It has been held that while it is not necessary that a libel should be likely to provoke a breach of the peace in order to constitute a criminal offence, it must be a serious libel so that the public interest requires the institution of criminal proceedings: *Hilliard v Penfield Enterprises Ltd and Ors* [1990] 1 IR 138, HC. It is a good defence to show the truth of the matter charged and to show that it was for the public benefit that the matters charged were published: Defamation Act 1961, s 6. See RSC Ord 36, r 36. See Law Reform Commission, *Report on the Crime of Libel* (LRC 41, 1991). [Bibliography: McDonald; McHugh; Murphy; Duncan & O'Neill UK; Gatley UK]. See CYBER LIBEL; DEATH, EFFECT OF; DEFAMATION; LODGMENT IN COURT; MITIGATION OF DAMAGES; NAME, RIGHT TO GOOD; NEWSPAPER RULE; OFFER OF AMENDS; PUBLICATION; SLANDER.

liberty. (1) Absence of restraint. (2) A necessary condition for freedom. (3) A franchise (qv). [Bibliography: TCD].

liberty, personal. See PERSONAL LIBERTY.

liberty to apply. The right to apply to a court in respect of a judgment already entered. The circumstances or nature of a judgment sometimes necessitate subsequent applications to the court for assistance in working out the rights declared. Where the judgment is not final, there is no need to reserve expressly a liberty to apply: *Penrice v Williams* [1833] 23 Ch D 353. In the case of final judgments, where the necessity for such subsequent application is foreseen, it is usual to insert in the judgment, words expressively reserving liberty to any party to apply to the court: *Pawley v Pawley* [1905] 1 Ch 593. This does not render the judgment less final; it only permits persons having an interest under the judgment to apply to the court in relation to that interest in a summary way, without the necessity of setting the case down again. Also where parties have settled a matter, the court may stay the proceedings and give any party to the settlement *liberty to apply* to the court in the event that there is difficulty with or a breakdown in the settlement e g 'The court doth order on consent: (a) that all proceedings be stayed on the terms of said consent; and (b) liberty to apply': e g see *F v F* [1995] 2 IR 355, SC. See *McMullan v Clancy* (1999) Irish Times, 7 September 1999. Contrast with LEAVE TO APPLY; LIBERTY TO RE-ENTER.

liberty to re-enter. The permission given by a court to parties to proceedings to re-enter proceedings already commenced, where there has been no determination by the court of the issue before the court,

e g the order may be 'Adjourned generally with liberty to re-enter'. The order may be made to enable the rights of the parties to be determined at a future date, if that becomes necessary. In the District Court, such an order is sometimes used where the prosecutor does not want to have a conviction recorded for a minor offence, but wants to reserve the right to recommence the proceedings, perhaps as a deterrent to the accused offending again. Contrast with LIBERTY TO APPLY.

libraries. A county council and a city council are also a library authority: Local Government Act 2001, s 77. The functions of a library authority are to provide *library services,* which include the provision of premises and facilities for the borrowing of and reference to books and other printed matter, tapes and discs (being audio, video or both), slides and such other material, including material available by means of computers and information technologies (LGA 2001, s 78). For previous legislation, see: Local Government Act 1994, ss 32–35.

Certain copying by librarians does not infringe copyright or related rights: Copyright and Related Rights Act 2000, ss 59–70 and 227–236.

In Northern Ireland, it has been held that there is no legal duty to provide a *law library* for the use of personal litigants: *In the matter of an application by Jagat Narain* [1991] ITLR (3 June), CA in NI. Similarly, in the Republic, it has been held that there is no constitutional duty on the State to provide a law library for personal litigants: *MacGairbhit v A-G* [1991] 2 IR 412, HC. For An Chomhairle Leabharlanna (Library Council), see website: *www.librarycouncil.ie.* For composition and selection of the Council, see SI No 499 of 1997 as amended by SI No 28 of 2003. For access to the Library Catalogue of Trinity College Dublin, see website: *www.tcd.ie/Library/Catalogue.* [Bibliography: Kenny (2)]. See LAW LIBRARY.

licence. An authority to do something which would otherwise be wrongful or illegal e g to enter on land which would otherwise be a trespass. A *bare licence* (qv) can be revoked at any time. A *licence coupled with an interest* is one supported by consideration and can be revoked only in accordance with its terms. Property rights arising in licences created by law are subject to the conditions created by law and to an implied condition that the law may change those conditions; a change in the law which has the effect of reducing property values cannot of itself amount to an infringement of constitutionally protected property rights: *Hempenstall v Minister for Environment* [1993] ILRM 318, HC. See also *National Maternity Hospital v McGauran* [1994] 1 ILRM 521, HC. [Bibliography: Pearce & Mee; Power A]. See BARE LICENCE; EXCLUSIVE LICENCE.

licence, copyright. See COPYRIGHT, LICENSING OF.

licences of right, copyright. A person is entitled to play a sound recording in public or to include a sound recording in a *broadcast* or *cable programme service*, provided he gives notice to the licensing body concerned, gives the intended dates, pays the licensing body at intervals in arrears, and complies with any reasonable conditions: Copyright and Related Rights Act 2000, s 38. A person who satisfies these conditions is regarded as being the holder of a licence granted by the copyright holder (CRRA 2000, s 38(3)). There is provision for any dispute over what constitutes fair payment to be referred for determination by the Controller of Patents (CRRA 2000, s 38(4)).

In proceedings for an infringement of copyright in a *work* in which a licence is available *as of right*, if the defendant undertakes to take a licence on such terms as may be agreed or, in default of agreement, settled by the Controller of Patents, then there can be no injunction granted, no order to deliver up, and damages recoverable from the defendant are limited to three times the amount which would have been payable by the defendant as licensee (CRRA 2000, s 130). There are similar provisions in relation to proceedings for infringement of a performer's property rights (CRRA 2000, s 305).

licences of right, designs. The Controller of Patents may, on the application of any person, grant a *compulsory licence* for the use of a *registered design* on the grounds that: (a) a demand in the State for a product incorporating the design is not being met or is not being met on reasonable terms, or (b) a demand is being met by importation (other than from a member of the World Trade Organisation): Industrial Designs Act 2001, s 49. An injunction will not be granted for an infringement of a design right where a *licence of right* is available and the defendant is prepared to take such a licence (IDA 2001, s 60). See DESIGN, LICENCE OF.

licences of right, patents. A licence to a patent to which any person is entitled, as of right: Patents Act 1992, ss 68(2) and 70(1). The licence may be *voluntary* or *compulsory*. It is *voluntary* where the proprietor of the patent applies to the Controller of Patents for an entry to be made in the register to the effect that licences under the patent are to be made available as of right, in which case renewal fees will be halved and the licence terms will, in default of agreement, be settled by the Controller (PA 1992, s 68).

The licence is *compulsory* where the Controller so orders on application by any person on certain specified grounds for a licence or for an entry in the register that licences be available as of right (PA 1992, s 71). The specified grounds include: (a) that the patented invention is not being commercially worked in the State – see PA 1992, s 2(1) and *Kamborian's Patent* [1961] RPC 403; (b) that the demand in the State for the patented product is not being met on reasonable terms or is being met to a substantial extent by importation; (c) that the commercial working in the State of the patented invention is being prevented or hindered by importation of the patented product; (d) that by reason of the refusal of the proprietor to grant a licence on reasonable terms, or by reason of conditions imposed by the proprietor, the establishment or development of commercial or industrial activities in the State is unfairly prejudiced; (e) that a condition which is null and void has been included in a contract relating to the patented product or process (PA 1992, s 70(2)). A compulsory licence must be non-exclusive and non-transferable (PA 1992, s 70(3)(d)).

The Controller may grant a compulsory licence to the customers of the applicant as well as the applicant (PA 1992, s 71). See *Loewe Radio's Application* [1929] 46 RPC 479; *Hunter v Fox* [1965] RPC 416; *Allen & Hanburys v Controller of Patents* [1997] 1 ILRM 416, HC. Under draft legislation, it is proposed that a *compulsory* licence may not be granted if the demand for the product covered by the patent is met by importation from a World Trade Organisation member country: Patent (Amendment) Bill 1999. This proposed amendment to PA 1992, s 70 is necessary to comply with the *TRIPs Agreement* (qv). See PATENT; FOOD AND MEDICINES, PATENTS FOR.

licensee. (1) A person who has been granted a licence eg an intoxicating liquor licence. (2) Under common law, a person who had permission, express or implied, to enter premises for his own purposes, but not for any business of the occupier. See BARE LICENCE; OCCUPIER'S LIABILITY.

lie. An action is said to *lie* if it can be properly instituted and maintained. In relation to a client lying to the court, see BARRISTER AND CLIENT.

lien. The right to hold the property of another as security for the performance of an obligation. As regards a contract for the sale of goods, an unpaid seller's lien is the right of a seller to retain possession of goods until the payment or tender of the price: Sale of Goods Act 1893, ss 41–43. Any lien or other charge of a public limited company on its own shares is void: Companies Amendment Act 1983, s 44. Exceptions are made for charges that arise from transactions entered into in the ordinary course of business by money lending companies, and charges taken by companies on their own not fully paid shares for any amount not paid on them (SGA 1893, s 44(2)). See also Companies Act 1963, Table A, art 11; Companies Act 1990, s 125; Building Societies Act 1989, s 41(6) as amended by Central Bank and Financial Services Authority of Ireland Act 2003, s 35, Sch 1; Companies (Auditing and Accounting) Act 2003, s 36(6). In an action, a claim for a lien must be specifically and specially pleaded: *O'Keeffe v Russell & AIB plc* [1994] 1 ILRM 137, SC. See RSC Ord 22, r 10(7); Ord 45, rr 5–6; Ord 50, r 9; Ord 99, r 4. See CARRIER'S LIEN; DEPOSIT OF TITLE DEEDS; FORFEITURE; MARITIME LIEN; PRESERVED BENEFIT; SOLICITOR'S LIEN.

lien, equitable. See EQUITABLE LIEN.

lieu, in. In the place of.

life, danger to. Access to a record may be refused where the record could reasonably be expected to endanger the life or safety of any person: Freedom of Information (Amendment) Act 2003, s 18. See DIE, RIGHT TO; FREEDOM OF INFORMATION; CABINET CONFIDENTIALITY.

life, expectation of. See EXPECTATION OF LIFE, LOSS OF.

life, right to. Every individual, as an individual, has certain inherent rights of which the right to life is the most fundamental: *Conroy v Attorney-General* [1965] IR 411. The State is required by its laws to protect as best it may from unjust attack and, in the case of injustice done, to vindicate the life of every citizen: 1937 Constitution, art 40(3)(2). The right to life of the *unborn* has been expressly acknowledged by the Eighth Amendment to the 1937 Constitution, passed by referendum in 1983; the equal right of the mother is also acknowledged in that amendment (1937 Constitution, art 40(3)(3)). However, the Twelfth Amendment to the Constitution regarding the right to life was rejected by the people in 1992. See also *SPUC v Grogan* [1990] ILRM 350, SC; [1992] ILRM 461, ECJ.

The Medical Council has issued guidelines, reminding doctors of 'their obligation to preserve life and to promote health. The creation of new forms of life for experimental purposes or the deliberate and intentional destruction of in-vitro human life already formed is professional misconduct': Medical Council, *A Guide to Ethical Conduct and Behaviour* (6th edn, 2004) para 24.1. See 'The positive obligation to protect life' by Alma Clissman in *Law Society Gazette* (May 2004) 5. See ABORTION; ABORTION, MEDICAL GUIDELINES; DIE, RIGHT TO; EUROPEAN CONVENTION ON HUMAN RIGHTS; REPRODUCTIVE MEDICINE; UNBORN, RIGHT TO LIFE.

life assurance. Assurance of a class specified in the European Communities (Life Assurance) Regulations 1984, SI No 57 of 1984, as amended by Central Bank and Financial Services Authority of Ireland Act 2003, s 35, Sch 2 and by Central Bank and Financial Services Authority of Ireland Act 2004, s 10(3), Sch 2.

From 1994, EU-based life insurance companies are permitted to transact insurance business elsewhere in the EU subject to the supervision requirements of the authority where their head office is situated: EC Third Life Framework Directive; SI No 360 of 1994 as amended by CBFSAIA 2003, s 35, Sch 2. The 1994 Regulations include minimum information and disclosure requirements which insurance companies must adhere to, and include a fifteen-day 'cooling-off' period within which a policy may be cancelled.

From 2001, suppliers of life assurance are required to provide information to clients resident in Ireland: (i) before they sign a proposal or an application form in respect of life assurance, and also (ii) throughout the term of the policy: Life Assurance (Provision of Information) Regulations 2001, SI

No 15 of 2001. The information is to include: details of the policy, its appropriateness to the needs of the client, early encashment consequences, projected benefits and charges, intermediary/sales remuneration, review of premium, cancellation rights, together with other general and additional information, some of which is already subject to disclosure pursuant to SI No 360 of 1994. The 2001 Regulation was amended in 2002 by the substitution of 6% for 8% in Schedule 2, Part I, para 2: SI No 161 of 2002.

New provisions for the taxation of life assurance companies were introduced by Finance Act 2000, s 53 inserting new s 730 into the Taxes Consolidation Act 1997, as amended by Finance Act 2001, s 69 and Finance Act 2003, s 57. A new tax regime has also been introduced for the taxation of policyholders of certain foreign life assurance policies: FA 2001, s 67. The restriction on the type of investments which may be made in this scheme, has been removed: FA 2001, s 73. Group relief is also available to life assurance companies (TCA 1997, s 420 as amended by FA 2000, s 54). See also FA 2000, ss 55–56, 68, 81 and Finance Act 2002, s 48. Provision has been made to clarify that 'retirement annuity contracts' and 'personal retirement savings account contracts' are 'pension business' of a life assurance company: Finance Act 2003, s 54. See also *Re Irish Life Assurance plc* [2002] 2 IR 9, HC. See FINANCIAL COMPENSATION ORDER; INSURANCE BUSINESS; PERSONAL PORTFOLIO LIFE POLICY; UNCLAIMED LIFE ASSURANCE POLICY.

life estate. A freehold estate for the life of a person which arises by grant. The life estate may be for the life of the tenant eg *to A for life*. It may also be for the life of another, *pur autre vie* eg *to A for the life of B*. B is known as the *cestui que vie* and A the *tenant pur autre vie*; the years remaining in the estate on the death of A may be disposed of by his will or, if he dies intestate, the interest devolves on his personal representatives (qv): Statute of Frauds (Ireland) 1695; Succession Act 1965.

A life tenant is liable for waste (qv). He also has certain rights to emblements (qv) and to fixtures (qv). A life tenancy formerly could be created by operation of law eg curtesy (qv) and dower (qv), but these were abolished by the Succession Act 1965, s 11.

The relinquishing of a life interest in property by the life interest holder is a disposal for capital gains tax purposes, which may give rise to a chargeable gain: Taxes Consolidation Act 1997, ss 532, 545 and s 577A inserted by Finance Act 1998, s 69.

life imprisonment. A sentence of imprisonment for the natural life of the convicted person: *Gilligan v DPP* (12 November 2003, CCA). The Court of Criminal Appeal in this case held that a life sentence must be regarded as a sentence for the natural life of the convicted person and consequently must consider a 28-year sentence as less than the maximum life sentence. A sentence of life imprisonment is mandatory for certain offences eg non-capital murder: Criminal Justice Act 1964, s 2; *The People v Murtagh* [1966] IR 361. The court has held that a convicted murderer should serve a 15-year sentence first for attempted murder of one person, followed by a life sentence in respect of the murder of another person: *DPP v Whelan* (25 May 2003, unreported), CCA.

The Parole Board has stated that a murder conviction should result in at least twelve years of the imposed life sentence being served before a recommendation leading to a plan for early release is made: *Annual Report of the Parole Board 2002* (June 2003), available on website: *www.justice.ie*. The present Minister said in 2004 that he would not consider any recommendation for release until a minimum of 12 years had been served and 15 years in the case of gang-related murder. Higher minimum periods of imprisonment are specified for treason (qv) and for *aggravated murder*, which has replaced capital murder.

See CHILD TRAFFICKING; MURDER, AGGRAVATED; SEXUAL ASSAULT.

life in being. See PERPETUITIES, RULE AGAINST.

lifeguards. See BATHS, PUBLIC.

lifejacket. A person on a pleasure craft of less than 7 metres length overall is required to wear a *suitable flotation device or lifejacket* while on board an open craft or while on the deck of decked craft, other than when the craft is made fast to the shore or at anchor: Merchant Shipping (Pleasure Craft) (Lifejackets and Operation) (Safety) Regulations 2004, SI No 259 of 2004, reg 6(1). The master or owner must take all reasonable steps to ensure that a person who has not attained the age of 16 years complies with this requirement (reg 6(2)).

A 'suitable personal flotation device or lifejacket' means one: (a) which is sufficient to give a person using it a positive buoyancy in waters which are likely to be encountered where the vessel, on which it is required to be used or to be available for use, is reasonably likely to be, (b) which is appropriate to the body weight of the person who is to wear it, and (c) which has on it the CE conformity marking consisting of the initials 'CE' (reg 2). The regulations do not apply to certain rowing boats used in boat races (reg 3(3)).

The master or owner of a pleasure craft must ensure, that there are, at all times, on board the craft, sufficient suitable personal flotation devices for each person on board (reg 5). Every person on a personal watercraft must wear a personal flotation device or lifejacket at all times while on board, or being towed in any manner by a personal watercraft (reg 7). See FISHING VESSEL; PLEASURE CRAFT.

lifting the corporate veil. The phrase used to describe the process whereby the legislature and the court may look behind the corporate curtain and identify a company with its owners, despite being bound by the principle that a company is a separate legal person, distinct from its members. The court will look at the underlying economic reality, especially where the company has been engaged in fraudulent trading or where the company is a mere sham. See *Gilford Motor Co v Horne* [1933] Ch 935; *Powers Supermarkets Ltd v Crumlin Investments Ltd* [1981] HC; *Dublin County Council v O'Riordan* [1986] ILRM 104; *Desmond & Dedeir Ltd v Glackin* [1992] ITLR (7 December) SC.

As a general rule the corporate veil of a company should not be pierced: *Allied Irish Coal v Powell Duffryn* [1998] 2 ILRM 61, SC and 2 IR 519.

In order to lift the corporate veil and treat the acts of one corporate body as those of another: (a) there must be a factual identification of the acts of one body corporate with those of another, and (b) justice to be served must require the court to ignore the distinction between the separate corporate entities: *Lac Minerals Ltd v Chevron Mineral* [1995] 1 ILRM 161, HC.

It has been held that to ensure the full application of the 'polluter pays' principle, the domestic law of limited liability should

be suspended and the veil of incorporation lifted, so that if the company cannot comply with an order of the court, a 'fall back' order may be made against its directors and shareholders: *Wicklow County Council v Fenton* [2003] 1 ILRM 279, HC. See 'Security for Costs and the Separate Corporate Personality' by Cathal Murphy BL in *Bar Review* (April 2003) 86.

See also Merchant Shipping (Salvage and Wreck) Act 1993, s 60. See INVESTIGATION OF COMPANY BY DIRECTOR OF CORPORATE ENFORCEMENT; PERSONAL LIABILITY.

lifting weights. See WEIGHTS, MAXIMUM.

light, right to. To constitute an actionable nuisance for obstruction of ancient lights, it is not enough that the light is less than before; there must be a substantial privation of light, enough to render the occupation of a house uncomfortable according to the ordinary notions of mankind and, in the case of a business premises, to prevent the plaintiff from carrying on his business as beneficially as before: *Colls v Home & Colonial Stores* [1904] AC 179.

After the actual enjoyment of the access of light to a building has continued for 20 years without interruption, the right is deemed absolute unless enjoyed by written consent: Prescription Act 1832 (extended to Ireland in 1859 by the Prescription (Ireland) Act 1858), s 3. See also *O'Connor v Walsh* [1907] 42 ILTR 20; *Scott v Goulding Properties Ltd* [1973] IR 200; *Leech v Reilly* [1983] HC.

The Law Reform Commission has recommended that the easement of light should be capable of being acquired by *prescription* (qv) in the same manner as other easements and *profits a prendre* (qv): Law Reform Commission, *Report on the Acquisition of Easements and Profit A Prendre by Prescription* (LRC 66, 2002). The Commission recommends that it should be possible to acquire a prescriptive easement of light against the State after 30 year's user as of right. [Bibliography: Bland (1)]. See EASEMENT.

light railway. A railway (whether above, on or under the ground) whose operation is authorised by an order of the Minister, called a *light railway order*: Transport (Dublin Light Rail) (No 2) Act 1996, ss 1(1) and 9. This Act provides the necessary statutory powers to construct, maintain and operate a light rail system in Dublin, called LUAS in the Irish language meaning 'speed'. The construction is an *exempted development* (qv) as regards planning legislation; however there is provision for a public enquiry.

There is no provision for compensation for loss to business caused by disruption during the construction phase; however compensation is payable: (a) for damage to property during the surveying inspection phase (T(DLR)(No 2)A 1996, s 2); (b) for loss, injury, damage or expenditure incurred during entry on land to carry out works (T(DLR)(No 2)A 1996, s 14); and (c) as compensation for the compulsory purchase of land (T(DLR)(No 2)A 1996, s 13).

The compulsory purchase of land includes the *substratum* of land ie any sub-soil or anything beneath the surface of land required for tunnelling or for any other purpose connected with a light railway order: Road (Amendment) Act 1998, s 7. Provision has been made to enable the light railway to access a motorway; this is to enable LUAS to cross the M50 motorway at the Red Cow junction on the Naas Road intersection (R(A)A 1998, s 3).

The 1996 Act has been repealed and its provisions re-enacted in modified form, to provide a single statutory *railway order* procedure: Transport (Railway Infrastructure) Act 2001. There are similar provisions in the 2001 legislation regarding: (a) compulsory purchase of land or rights over and under land specified in a Ministerial order (T(RI)A 2001, s 45); (b) exempted development (T(RI)A 2001, s 38); (c) public inquiry (T(RI)A 2001, s 42); (d) compensation for loss, injury and damage (T(RI)A 2001, s 48(3)).

Provision has been made for the *on-street regulation* of light railways; a light railway is one designated as a light railway under a *railway order* (qv): T(RI)A 2001, ss 54–63. Matters covered include speed limits, driving under the influence of intoxicants, driver must not be disqualified from holding a driving licence, and compulsory insurance of light rail vehicles. It is an offence to use or take possession of a light rail vehicle without the consent of the relevant railway undertaking (T(RI)A 2001, s 60). Also provision has been made: (a) for new road traffic signs in connection with the on-street running of light rail vehicles: SI No 97 of 2003; and (b) for certain road facilities (eg tram only streets) and to apply certain existing regulations to light rail vehicles and their drivers: SI No 98 of 2003.

For Light Railway bye-laws on the regulation of travel and use, and works, see SIs Nos 100 and 101 of 2004. Speed limits for light rail vehicles have been set at 50 and 70 km per hour: SI No 255 of 2004. See also SIs No 403 and 404 of 2004. See RAILWAY ORDER; RAILWAY PROCUREMENT AGENCY; SUBSTRATUM OF LAND.

lighthouse. Lighthouses generally come within the ambit of the Commissioners of Irish Lights under the Merchant Shipping Act 1894. A lighthouse with a *helicopter pad* comes within the definition of an *aerodrome* (qv) but the rights, powers or privileges of a lighthouse authority is unaffected by the Irish Aviation Authority Act 1993 (IAAA 1993, s 4). See also Harbours Act 1996, s 94. See FOYLE CARLINGFORD.

lighting. See PUBLIC LIGHTING.

lighting-up hours. The period commencing one half-hour after sunset on any day and ending one half-hour before sunrise on the next day: Road Traffic General Bye-Laws 1964, SI No 294 of 1964, art 2.

like work. Two persons are regarded as employed to do *like work* in relation to entitlement to *equal pay*: (a) where both perform the *same work* under the same or similar conditions or where each is interchangeable with the other in relation to the work, or (b) where the work performed by one is of a *similar nature* to that performed by the other and any differences between the work performed or the conditions under which it is performed by each, either are of small importance in relation to the work as a whole, or occur with such irregularity as not to be significant in relation to the work as a whole, or (c) where the work performed by one is *equal in value* to that performed by the other in terms of the demands it makes in relation to such matters as skill, physical or mental effort, responsibility and working conditions: Employment Equality Act 1998, s 7(1).

It has been held that where the Labour Court had made a finding of 'like work', it must consider whether differences in pay for that work is genuinely attributable to grounds other than sex: *Irish Crown Cork Co Ltd v Desmond* [1993] ELR 180, HC. Under the previous legislation (1974) it was held that a woman could avail of equal pay legislation if doing work of greater value than a male colleague: *Murphy v Telecom Éireann* [1988] ILRM 53 at 60. Now there is statutory provision; work performed by a *primary* worker is regarded for equal pay purposes as equal in value to work performed by another (a *comparator*) where the work is of greater value but paid less (EEA 1998, s 7(3)).See also *Dept of Posts & Telegraphs v Kennefick* DEP 2/1980; *Arthur Guinness v Federated Workers' Union of Ireland* DEP 11/1983; *Comhairle Oiliuna Talmhaiochta v Doyle* [1989] IR 33; *O'Leary v Minister for Transport* [1998] 1 IR 558, SC and ELR 113; *Wilton v Steel Company of Ireland* [1999] ELR 1, HC; *Irish Times Ltd v SIPTU* [1999] ELR 35, LC. [Bibliography: Reid M]. See EQUAL PAY; RED-CIRCLING.

limitation, words of. See WORDS OF LIMITATION.

limitation of actions. The provision by which actions to enforce rights are barred if proceedings are not taken within certain periods of time: Statute of Limitations 1957. The Statute: (a) protects defendants against stale claims, (b) promotes expeditious trials with the accuracy of recent recollection and complete documentary evidence, and (c) promotes a certainty of finality of potential claims: *Tuohy v Courtney* [1994] 2 ILRM 503, SC at 506.

The Statute of Limitations has to be available on a reciprocal basis to both sides in litigation: *O'Reilly v Northern Telecom (Ireland) Ltd* [1999] 1 IR 214, HC.

The time limits prescribed include: (a) simple contract – six years from the date on which the *cause of action* accrued (SLA 1957, s 11(1)(a)); (b) quasi-contract – six years (SLA 1957, s 11(1)(b)); (c) specialty contract – twelve years (SLA 1957, s 11(5)); (d) tort (other than one causing personal injuries or slander but including breaches of community law by the State) – six years (SLA 1957, s 11(2)); (e) personal injury – two years from the cause of action or the date of knowledge if later (SLA 1957, s 11(2)(b)); Statute of Limitations (Amendment) Act 1991 as amended from 3 to 2 years by Civil Liability and Courts Act 2004, s 7); *Devlin v Roche* [2002] 2 ILRM 192, SC and 2 IR 360; (f) slander – three years (SLA 1957, s 11(2)(c)); (g) recovery of land – twelve years (SLA 1957, s 13(2)); (h) recovery of arrears of conventional rent – six years (SLA 1957, s 28); (i) redemption of mortgage – twelve years (SLA 1957, s 15); (j) judgment of court of record – twelve years (SLA 1957, s 11(6)); (k) salvage claims – two years (Civil Liability Act 1961, s 46); (l) contribution from concurrent wrongdoer – same period as the injured person is allowed by law for bringing an action against the contributor, or within the period of two years after the liability of the claimant is ascertained, or the injured person's damages are paid, whichever is the greater (Civil Liability Act 1961, s 31); (m) damages arising from breach of implied condition arising from defective motor vehicle – two years (Sale of Goods and Supply of Services Act 1980, s 13(7)); (n) damages in respect of defective products – three years (Liability for Defective Products Act 1991, s 7).

There is provision for the extension of the limitation periods in the case of disability, acknowledgment, part payment, fraud, and mistake (SLA 1957, ss 47–72; LDPA 1991, s 5; Statute of Limitations (Amendment) Act 2000). Also in relation to claims for personal injuries which come within the remit of the Personal Injuries Assessment Board, the period from the date of application to the Board and ending six months from the date of issue of authorisation from the Board to commence court proceedings, is disregarded as regards the limitation period: Personal Injuries Assessment Board Act 2003, ss 12(5) and 50.

In a particular case, the court held that the true identity of the second defendant was knowingly concealed from the plaintiff and that such concealment constituted fraud within the meaning of s 71 of the 1957 Statute: *Tierney v Midserve Ltd* [2002] 3 IR 90, HC. See DISABILITY, PERSON UNDER.

However, even where an action has been commenced within the time limit fixed by an Act of the Oireachtas, the courts have an inherent jurisdiction to dismiss a claim in the interests of justice where the lapse of time is so great that it would cause injustice to a defendant: *Toal v Duignan & Ors* [1990] ITLR (26 November) SC – a medical negligence action.

See *O'Brien v Keogh* [1972] IR 144; *Campbell v Ward* [1981] ILRM 60; *Lawless v Dublin Port and Docks Board* [1998] 2 IR 502, HC. See Merchant Shipping (Salvage and Wreck) Act 1993, s 36; British-Irish Agreement Act 1999, s 53(a); Residential Institutions Redress Act 2002, ss 7(7); 8 and 13(10).

See Law Reform Commission on Statute of Limitations: (a) *Report on Claims in respect of Latent Personal Injuries* (LRC 21, 1987); (b) *Consultation Paper on claims in Contract and Tort in respect of Latent Damage, other than Personal Injuries* (1998); (c)

Report on Claims in Contract and Tort in respect of Latent Damage (other than Personal Injury) (LRC 64, 2001). [Bibliography: Brady & Kerr]. See CAUSE OF ACTION; PRODUCT LIABILITY; STATUTE OF LIMITATIONS; SURGICAL OPERATION; TIME; TORT; UNSOUND MIND; WARSAW CONVENTION.

limitation of liability. The imposition of a ceiling or limit on liability for damage or loss by contract or by statute. See *Dún Laoghaire Corporation v Park Hill Developments Ltd* [1989] ILRM 235. See COMPANY, LIMITED; LIMITED PARTNERSHIP; PERSONAL LIABILITY.

limited administration. A grant of letters of administration of the estate of a deceased which is limited as to duration, to purpose or to a particular part of the estate. See LETTERS OF ADMINISTRATION.

limited company. See COMPANY, LIMITED.

limited owner. An owner of an interest in land which is less than a fee simple estate e g a life tenant.

limited partnership. A partnership in which there are one or more partners with unlimited liability, known as *general partners*, and other partners known as *limited partners* who contribute to the partnership assets a specified amount in money or money's worth and who enjoy immunity from liability beyond the amount so contributed, provided they take no part in the management of the business: Limited Partnership Act 1907.

A limited partner, also known as a *sleeping partner*, has no power to bind the firm. A limited partnership must be registered with the Registrar of Companies. Bankruptcy provisions apply to limited partnerships in like manner as if they were ordinary partnerships; however when all general partners are adjudicated bankrupt, the assets of the limited partnership vest in the Official Assignee (qv): Bankruptcy Act 1988, s 37. See also BA 1988, s 81(10). See Taxes Consolidation Act 1997, s 1013 as amended by Finance Act 1998, s 50. See *McCartaigh v Daly* [1986] ILRM 116. Regulations have been made which permit limited partnerships registered under the 1907 Act to have up to 50 partners, where such partnerships are formed for the purpose of, and whose main business consists of, the provision of investment and loan finance and ancillary facilities and services

to persons engaged in industrial or commercial activities: SI No 506 of 2004.

For the level of fees, in euro amounts, payable in connection with certain provisions of the Limited Partnership Act 1907, see Limited Partnership Regulations 2001, SI No 570 of 2001. Special provision has been made for the establishment, authorisation and regulation of *investment* limited partnerships. [Bibliography: Twomey]. See INVESTMENT LIMITED PARTNERSHIP; PARTNERSHIP; PARTNERSHIP AND BANKRUPTCY.

limping marriage. A marriage which is recognised in one jurisdiction but not in another, thereby deeming a party to be married in one jurisdiction and not in the other. The courts have always recognised the public policy of avoiding limping marriages: *G McG v DW & AR* [2000] 1 ILRM 107, HC.

linea recta semper praefertur transversali. [The direct line is always preferred to the collateral].

lineal consanguinity. See CONSANGUINITY.

linking services. There is a prohibition on a *building society* making it a condition of a housing loan (qv) that the borrower must take other services from the society e g financial, insurance, conveyancing, auctioneering or other services relating to land, whether provided directly by the society itself or through a subsidiary or associated body: Building Societies Act 1989, s 35(1). There is a similar prohibition on linking of services to a housing loan which applies to mortgage agents and to persons who provide auctioneering services or who construct houses who also are *mortgage intermediaries*: Consumer Credit Act 1995, s 127. See also Credit Union Act 1997, s 51.

liquid assets. Assets in readily realisable form or in cash.

liquidated. Fixed or ascertained. A company is said to be *liquidated* when it is wound up.

liquidated damages. The compensation in money for loss suffered by a person owing to breach of contract by another, which is a fixed and ascertained amount in the contract. In an action where it appears to the court that the amount of damages is substantially a matter of calculation, the court may direct that the amount for which final judgment is to be entered shall be determined by the Master of the High Court:

RSC Ord 36, r 48. See DAMAGES; PENALTY; SUMMONS, HIGH COURT; SUMMARY SUMMONS.

liquidated demand. An ascertained demand in money. The recovery of such a demand with or without interest, must be by summary summons where proceeded with in the High Court: RSC Ord 2 r 1(1). The indorsement of claim on such a summons must state the amount claimed and must state the amount claimed for costs and state that on payment of such amounts within six days after service, further proceedings will be stayed: RSC Ord 4, r 5.

Whenever a plaintiff's claim in the Circuit Court is for a debt or liquidated sum only, the endorsement of the Civil Bill, must, besides stating the nature of the claim, state that upon payment of the amount claimed and costs, within six days after service, further proceedings will be stayed: Circuit Court Rules 2001 Ord 5, r 6.

For provisions dealing with judgment by default in cases of liquidated demands, see CCR 2001, Ord 26. This also applies to claims for the delivery of specific goods or chattels.

liquidation. See WINDING UP.

liquidator. A person appointed to carry out the winding up of a company. The principal duties of the liquidator are to get in and realise the assets of the company, to pay or settle its debts, and to distribute to the members the surplus, if any, that may remain. A liquidator appointed by the court is known as an *official liquidator*. The main difference between a liquidator in a winding up by the court and in a voluntary winding up, is that the former must obtain the consent of the court or of the *committee of inspection* in order to exercise many of his powers: Companies Act 1963, s 231 as amended by the Companies Act 1990, s 124.

It has been held that if a sale by a liquidator is subject to the court's prior approval, the liquidator must accept the highest offer made, even if that offer was made subsequent to the liquidator having agreed with another party to sell the property subject to the court's consent: *Van Hool McArdle Ltd v Rohan Industrial Estates Ltd* [1980] IR 237.

A liquidator must be afforded an opportunity of making his case in respect of his fees: *Re Merchant Banking* [1987] ILRM 260. The general law of bankruptcy (qv)

must be applied by the liquidator to some aspects of winding up of insolvent companies (CA 1963, s 284; *Re Irish Attested Sales Ltd* [1962] IR 70). See also *Re GWI Ltd* [1987] HC.

Persons disqualified for appointment as a liquidator are present or recent officers or servants of the company, its auditors and close relatives of officers (CA 1990, s 146 inserting s 300A in the CA 1963) or an undischarged bankrupt (CA 1990, s 169 amending CA 1963, s 183). While there are no qualifications specified for liquidators, the Minister is empowered to add to the list of persons who are not qualified for appointment (CA 1990, s 237). See also Building Societies Act 1989, s 109. See RSC Ord 74, rr 29–48. [Bibliography: Forde (9); Robb]. See DIRECTOR OF CORPORATE ENFORCEMENT; DISQUALIFICATION ORDER; ONEROUS PROPERTY; PROVISIONAL LIQUIDATOR; WINDING UP.

liquidator, removal of. Where cause is shown, the court may remove a liquidator in a voluntary winding up and appoint another: Companies Act 1963, s 277(2). The court must be slow to dislodge a voluntary liquidator appointed with the concurrence of a majority, both numerically and in value, of its creditors: *In the matter of Gilt Construction Ltd* [1994] 2 ILRM 456, HC.

In a particular case in which the High Court disqualified a liquidator from being a liquidator, receiver or examiner of a company for seven years, and restricted him in acting as a director of a company, the court held that the liquidator had failed to act in an impartial manner, had destroyed the books and records of the company, and had failed to act in the interests of the creditors of the company: *Cahill v Grimes* (20 July 2000, unreported) HC. The Supreme Court, on appeal, upheld the disqualification and restriction, holding that while the liquidator had not been validly appointed, he could be disqualified in circumstances where he had acted as such: *Cahill v Grimes* [2002] 1 IR 372, SC.

liquidator, reports of. A liquidator is obliged to incorporate, in any returns he is required to make, a report on whether any past or present director or other officer or member of the company is subject to a *disqualification order* (qv) or has been declared personally liable for the debts of the company: Companies Act 1990, ss 144–145.

A liquidator is now required to report to the *Director of Corporate Enforcement* any matter which appears to suggest that an offence by an officer or member of a company has been committed: Companies Act 1963, s 299 as amended by Company Law Enforcement Act 2001, s 51. Also the liquidator of an *insolvent* company is required to make a report to the Director in a prescribed form and to make an application to the court for the restriction of the directors of the company, unless relieved of the obligation by the Director (CLEA 2001, s 56 and Company Law Enforcement (Section 56) Regulations 2002, SI No 324 of 2002). The liquidator may apply to the court for an extension of time in which to bring the restriction application: *Coyle v O'Brien, Hill and Hughes* [2003] 2 IR 627, HC and FL 7813.

Also the disciplinary committee or tribunal of prescribed professional bodies whose members conduct liquidations or receiverships, are required to notify the Director in certain circumstance eg where a member has not maintained proper records or is suspected of committing an indictable offence (CLEA 2001, s 58). For prescribed professional bodies, see Company Law Enforcement (Section 58) Regulations 2002, SI No 544 of 2002.

liquor. See INTOXICATING LIQUOR.

lis. An action; a suit; a dispute.

lis alibi pendens. [A suit pending elsewhere]. It may be a ground for staying an action. See LIS PENDENS.

lis inter partes. [Suit between parties]. In a *lis inter partes* the court cannot generally of its own motion seek additional information or require any particular witnesses to be called. It is not an appropriate procedure to deal with matters regarding a *ward of court* (qv): per Blayney J in *In the Matter of a Ward of Court* [1995] 2 ILRM 403, SC at 404.

lis moto. [An existing or pending action]. See ANTE LITEM MOTAM.

lis pendens. [Pending action]. The registration of an action against a landowner: Judgment (Ireland) Act 1844, s 10; *Byrne v UDT Bank Ltd* [1984] ILRM 418. A *lis pendens* does not bind or affect a purchaser or mortgagee (qv), who has no express notice of it, unless and until a memorandum containing the requisite details concerning the suit is registered in court eg the name and usual or last known abode and title, trade or profession of the person

whose estate is intended to be affected by the suit, the court, title of action, and day filed: *Re O'Byrne's Estate* [1885] 15 LR Ir 373.

A judgment mortgagee, being a volunteer, is bound by a *lis pendens* irrespective of whether or not he has notice of it and irrespective of whether or not the *lis pendens* has been registered: *AS v GS and AIB* [1994] 2 ILRM 68, HC.

A registered *lis pendens* may be *vacated* on the order of the court, even without the consent of the person who registered it: RSC Ord 63, r 1(29); *Flynn v Buckley* [1980] IR 423; Lis Pendens Act 1867.

The Brussels Convention provides that where two courts are seised of the same cause of action, the court first seised has jurisdiction: Jurisdiction of Courts and Enforcement of Judgments Act 1998, Sch 1, arts 21–23; Sch 7, arts 21–23. The *Brussels I Regulation* on the recognition and enforcement of judgments in civil and commercial matters, replaces the 1998 Act as from 1 March 2002 for all EU states except Denmark: EC (Civil and Commercial Judgments) Regulations 2002, SI No 52 of 2002. This provides clarification on the date when a court is seised. It provides that a court is seised either when the document instituting the proceedings is lodged with the court or, if the document has to be first served before being lodged, when the server receives the document for service (ie when a summons is issued) (*Regulation*, art 30). See *Dresser UK Ltd v Falcongate* [1992] 2 All ER 450. See PENDENTE LITE.

Lisbon Process. A voluntary co-ordination of a whole range of economic, social and sectoral policies amongst EU member states, with the aim of making the EU the most competitive and knowledge-based economy in the world by 2010: National Forum on Europe, *Glossary of Terms* (2003). So called as the process or strategy was launched at an EU summit in Lisbon, Portugal in 2000. The strategy covers such matters as research, education, training, Internet access and on-line business. It also deals with reform of Europe's social protection systems, which must be made sustainable so that their benefits can be enjoyed by future generations. See COPENHAGEN DECLARATION.

list for hearing. See LODGMENT IN COURT; SET DOWN.

listed building. Now, a *protected structure* (qv): Local Government (Planning and

Development) Act 1999 as replaced by Planning and Development Act 2000, ss 51–80.

listing particulars. See PROSPECTUS.

Listing Particulars Directive. The Directive (EEC) 80/390 co-ordinating the requirements for the drawing up, scrutiny and distribution of the *listing particulars* to be published for the admission of securities to the official stock exchange listing, as amended by Directives (EEC) 87/345, (EEC) 90/211, (EC) 94/18: Listing Rules 2000 (*definitions*). See LISTING RULES; PROSPECTUS.

listing requirements. The requirements which must be complied with in order to have securities of a company *listed* on a recognised stock exchange. [Bibliography: Clarke B (2)]. See LISTING RULES; PROSPECTUS.

listing rules. The rules, issued by the Irish Stock Exchange Ltd which must be complied with by companies and other issuers of securities seeking admission to, or listed on the *Official List* of the Irish Stock Exchange. The *listing rules* implement the various EC Directives relating to the admission of securities to official stock exchange listing eg the admissions directive, the interim reports directive, the listing particulars directive, the major shareholding directive, and the public offers directive (qqv).

The Irish Stock Exchange Ltd is the *competent authority* to decide on the admission of securities to the Irish stock exchange: EC (Stock Exchange) Regulations 1984, SI No 282 of 1984. In the UK, the Financial Services Authority (FSA) is the competent authority with effect from 1 May 2000: UK Financial Act 1986; Official Listing of Securities (Change of Competent Authority) Regulations 2000. The *Listing Rules* of the Irish stock exchange are those of the FSA, amended as appropriate eg references to Irish legislation, to the Irish Takeover Panel: Takeover Rules 2001 and Substantial Acquisition Rules 2001, to the Competition Authority and to requirements on director remuneration disclosure.

The *Listing Rules* (*2002*) has 27 chapters dealing with: (1) compliance with and enforcement of the listing rules, (2) sponsors, (3) conditions for listing, (4) methods of bringing securities to listing, (5) listing particulars, (6) contents of listing particulars, (7) listing application procedures, (8) publication and circulation of listing particulars, (9) continuing obligations, (10) transactions, (11) transactions with related parties, (12) financial information, (13) documents not requiring prior approval, (14) circulars, (15) purchase of own securities, (16) directors, (17) overseas companies, (18) property companies, (19) mineral companies, (20) scientific research based companies, (21) investment entities, (22) public sector issuers, (23) specialist securities including eurobonds, (24) securitised derivatives, (25) innovative high growth companies, (26) venture capital trusts, (27) strategic investment companies. Compliance with the rules is enforced by sanctions, including suspension or cancellation of listing (Listings Rules, ch 1).

It is understood that the *Listing Rules* will be changed fundamentally by the proposed EU Prospectus Directive. The Irish Stock Exchange intends to publish in 2004 new *Listing Rules* to give effect to the Prospectus Directive and other relevant EU Directives. For the *Listing Rules*, see website: *www.fsa.gov.uk/pubs/ukla/*. For notes on the present *Listing Rules*, see website: *www.ise.ie/search/frgeneral.htm*. See STOCK EXCHANGE.

lite pendente. See PENDENTE LITE.

literal rule. The rule of construction for interpreting a statute whereby the judge gives to words in the statute their natural and ordinary meaning. Effect is required to be given to a particular provision of legislation unless it would lead to a result so manifestly absurd or unjust that there is good reason to seek an alternative: *Rahinstown Estate v Hughes* [1987] ILRM 599. See also *R v Inhabitants of Ramsgate* [1827] 6 B C 712; *Inspector of Taxes v Kiernan* [1981] IR and [1982] ILRM 13; *Re Atlantic Magnetics Ltd* [1992] ITLR (16 March), SC. See INTERPRETATION OF LEGISLATION.

literary work. Means a *work*, including a computer program, but does not include a dramatic or musical work or an original database, which is written, spoken or sung: Copyright and Related Rights Act 2000, s 2(1). Copyright subsists in an *original* literary work (CRRA 2000, s 17(2)). It expires 70 years after the death of the author irrespective of the date on which the work is first lawfully made available to the public (CRRA 2000, s 24(1)). However, see PUBLISHED EDITION.

In interpreting the phrase 'literary work' the Court must take a broad view; the phrase should be taken to mean any written or printed composition which was an original composition that involved labour, time and skill in its compilation: *RTE v Magill TV Guide Ltd* [1990] ILRM 534, HC. It has been held that 'literary work' was a work which was in writing or printed and not one which was spoken or sung: *Gormley v EMI Records (Ireland) Ltd* [2000] 1 IR 74. See *Allied Discount Card Ltd v Bord Fáilte Éireann* [1990] ILRM 811, HC. Literary work includes any written table or compilation: Broadcasting and Wireless Telegraphy Act 1988, s 1. See COMPUTER PROGRAM; COPYRIGHT; COPYRIGHT, QUALIFICATION FOR; WORK.

lithograph. See ARTISTIC WORK.

litigation. Legal action by parties who are known as *litigants*. A solicitor is required to exercise due professional care and skill in the conduct of litigation in respect of a client; if he does not do so, he will be liable in tort as well as in contract: *Finlay v Murtagh* [1979] IR 249. The duty extends to the drafting of pleadings (qv): *McGrath v Kiely* [1965] IR 497.

litis aestimatio. [Measure of damages].

litter. A substance or object, whether or not intended, as waste, that, when *deposited* in a place, is likely to become unsightly, deleterious, nauseous or insanitary, whether by itself or with any other substance or object and regardless of its size or volume or the extent of the deposit: Litter Pollution Act 1997, s 2(1). *Litter* does not include: (a) waste within the meaning of the Waste Management Act 1996 which is properly confined to disposal or (b) a substance or object deposited in a litter receptacle or in a lawfully designated place for the deposit. *Deposit* means to throw, drop, dump, abandon or discard the substance or object or to allow it to escape or to be released in or into any place. It is an offence to deposit any substance or object so as to create litter in a public place or in any place that is visible to any extent from a public place: (LPA 1997, s 3(1)). There is an obligation on the occupier of a *public place* to keep it free of litter (LPA 1997, s 6).

Each local authority is required to make and implement a *litter management plan* in respect of its functional area (LPA 1997, s 3(1)). The local authority is empowered to serve a notice: (a) on an occupier of any land requiring the occupier to remove any litter which is visible from a public place (LPA 1997, s 9); and (b) on the organisers or promoters of major events requiring

them to take specified measures to prevent or limit the creation of litter and providing for its removal (LPA 1997, s 17).

The local authority also has a duty: (a) to ensure that each public road in its functional area is, as far as practicable, free of litter (LPA 1997, s 17), and (b) to take all practicable measures to prevent the creation of litter, to prevent or control its polluting effects, and to control and dispose of litter (LPA 1997, s 8).

See Litter Pollution Regulations 1999, SI No 359 of 1999. Provision has been made to increase on-the-spot fines for litter offences; also SI No 359 of 1999 has been confirmed: Waste Management (Amendment) Act 2001, s 14 amending Litter Pollution Act 1997, s 28. The Protection of the Environment Act 2003, ss 56–58, strengthens the provisions of the 1997 Act by increasing litter fines, by giving local authorities wider powers to make anti-litter bye-laws, and by imposing greater restrictions on advertising material in public places. [Bibliography: Canny (2)]. See ABANDONED VEHICLE; ADVERTISEMENT; ATM; DOG; MAJOR EVENT; MECHANICALLY PROPELLED VEHICLE; MOBILE FOOD OUTLET; MUNICIPAL WASTE; ON-THE-SPOT FINE; SKIP; VEHICLE; WASTE.

litter warden. A person authorised by a local authority to perform on behalf of the local authority, the functions of the local authority and of a litter warden under the Act: Litter Pollution Act 1997, s 2(1). It is an offence to obstruct or impede a litter warden in exercising his statutory functions (LPA 1997, s 23 (1)). A litter warden has power to issue on-the-spot fines (LPA 1997, s 28). See ON-THE-SPOT FINE.

livelihood. A right to trade and earn a livelihood is one of the unspecified personal rights guaranteed by the Constitution, art 40.3; it is not an unqualified right: *Hand & Ors v Dublin Corporation* [1991] ILRM 556, SC. The right is to earn a livelihood by lawful means; interference with that right can be protected by injunction: *Lovett v Gogan* [1995] 1 ILRM 12, SC. See PRIVATE PROPERTY, RIGHT TO; WORK, RIGHT TO.

livestock mart, business of. Means the business of selling livestock by auction or providing, for the holding of sales of livestock by auction or otherwise, a place adapted for the sale of livestock by auction: Livestock Marts Act 1967, s 1. *Livestock* means cattle, sheep or pigs (LMA 1967, s 1). It is an offence for a person to carry on the business of a livestock mart at any place unless there is for the time being a licence in force in respect of that place (LMA 1967, s 2). See Livestock Marts (Date of Test and Identification of Seller) Regulations 2002, SI No 188 of 2002.

living matter. It is now possible to patent living matter as an invention. See MICRO-ORGANISMS.

living memory. See TIME IMMEMORIAL.

living over the shop scheme. A tax incentive scheme which is aimed at providing residential accommodation in the vacant space over commercial premises in Cork, Dublin, Galway, Limerick and Waterford: Finance Act 2001, s 60. The scheme has been extended to 31 July 2006: Finance Act 2004, s 26. See also Finance Act 2003, s 27. [Bibliography: Connolly, Bradley & Purcell].

load line. Means a mark on a ship indicating the maximum depth to which a ship may be loaded: Merchant Shipping (Load Lines) Rules 2001, SI No 424 of 2001. These rules apply the provisions of the International Convention on Load Lines 1966 (as amended by a Protocol of 1988) to all Irish ships which go to sea, with certain exceptions. Provision has been made to exempt certain classes of ships under 80 tons register engaged solely in the coastal trade: Merchant Shipping (Load Lines) (Exemption) Order 2002, SI No 416 of 2002 as amended by SI No 190 of 2003.

loan. A contract whereby one person lends or agrees to lend a sum of money to another, in consideration of a promise express, or implied to repay that sum: *Chitty on Contracts*. As regards taxation, the basic principle in regard to loans is that if they are a means of fluctuating and temporary accommodation, they are to be regarded as revenue transactions and not accretions to capital: *Brosnan v Mutual Enterprises Ltd* [1997] 3 IR 257, SC and [1998] 1 ILRM 45, SC. There is now a restriction on relief to individuals in respect of loans applied in acquiring an interest in companies: Taxes Consolidation Act 1997, s 250A inserted by Finance Act 2004, s 22. [Bibliography: Burgess]. See CREDIT AGREEMENT; LOCAL LOANS FUND; MONEYLENDER.

loan to director. Formerly there was no prohibition on the making of a loan by a company to a director; however any such loan had to be disclosed in the accounts of the company: Companies Act 1963, ss 192–193. Legislation in 1990 prohibited, subject to certain limited exceptions, companies from making loans in excess of 10% of the company's assets to a director or a person *connected* to a director: Companies Act 1990, ss 31–37.

The prohibition includes the making of *quasi-loans* to a director or entering into a *credit transaction*, guarantee or security for a director; these are arrangements whereby third parties pay a director's liability in a financial transaction or provide him with goods and services on the understanding that the company will eventually pay the third party.

There are exceptions, e g inter-company loans, director's expenses, and loans entered into by the company in the ordinary course of business (CA 1990, ss 34–37).

There are civil remedies and criminal penalties for a breach of the prohibition; also the person who benefited from the arrangement can be made personally liable without limit for the debts of the company in certain circumstances (CA 1990, ss 38–40). There are disclosure requirements in the annual accounts in respect of loans in excess of £2,500 (€3,175); except in licensed banks where the total amount outstanding and the number of directors only requires disclosure (CA 1990, s 43).

In certain instances, CA 1990 provisions have frustrated *bona fide* commercial transactions between companies and their directors, including the making of loans and the granting of credit guarantees. The Company Law Enforcement Act 2001, ss 75–79 seeks to address these difficulties by amending the definitions of *credit transaction*, *connected person*, *partner*, and by other changes designed to ensure that the interests of creditors and shareholders are protected.

See also Building Societies Act 1989, s 57 as amended by Housing (Miscellaneous Provisions) Act 2002, s 23 and Sch 3. See DIRECTOR; QUASI-LOAN.

loc cit; loco citato. [At the passage quoted]. Reference to a passage in a book.

local area plan. The plan which a planning authority may at any time prepare for any particular area within its functional area or, in co-operation with another planning authority, for an area which lies within both their combined functional area: Planning and Development Act 2000, ss 2(1) and

18. The *development plan* of a planning authority may indicate that specified development in a particular area will be subject to the making of a local area plan (PDA 2000, s 10(7)). A planning authority, and An Bord Pleanála on appeal, must have regard to the local area plan in considering an application for planning permission (PDA 2000, s 18(3)).

A local area plan may be prepared in respect of any area which the planning authority considers suitable, and must be prepared in respect of an area designated as a town with a population in excess of 2,000 (PDA 2000, s 19(1)). The local area plan must be consistent with the objectives of the development plan and may include zoning (PDA 2000, s 19(2) as amended by Planning and Development (Amendment) Act 2002, s 8). Provision is made for consultation with the public before preparing, amending or revoking a local area plan (PDA 2000, s 20 as amended by Planning and Development (Amendment) Act 2002, s 9). The fact that a proposed development would materially contravene an objective in a local area plan, is sufficient reason to refuse planning permission and such refusal does not attract compensation (PDA 2000, s 192 and Sch 4, para 15). See DEVELOPMENT PLAN.

local authority. In a major reform of local government, local authorities are now either a *city council* eg Galway City Council, a *county council* eg North Tipperary County Council, a *borough council* (formerly, a corporation) eg Sligo Borough Council, or a *town council* (formerly, urban district councils or town commissioners) eg Bray Town Council: Local Government Act 2001, s 2(1) and 11.

A local authority is a body corporate with perpetual succession, with power to sue and be sued in its corporate name, and with power to acquire, hold, manage and dispose of land, and with a seal which must be judicially noticed (LGA 2001, s 11(7)).

The Act sets out the functions of a local authority as: (a) to provide a forum for the democratic representation of the local community and to provide civic leadership; (b) to carry out the functions conferred on the authority by this or any other enactment; (c) to carry out any ancillary functions; and (d) to take action to promote the community interest (LGA 2001, s 63 and Sch 12). There was provision made for the direct election of the cathaoirleach (chairman/ mayor/lord mayor) of local authorities from 2004 (LGA 2001, ss 39–40). However, this provision was repealed in 2003: Local Government (No 2) Act 2003, s 7.

Generally, members of the public and representatives of the media are entitled to be present at a meeting of a local authority: Local Government Act 2001, s 45. See Local Government (Meetings) Regulations 2002 , SI No 66 of 2002.

The general competence of local authorities has been increased considerably; provision has been made to transfer additional functions to them; and they are required to have regard to certain matters in performing their functions: Local Government Act 1991, ss 5–9.

Provision has also been made for the establishment of regional authorities for the purpose of promoting the co-ordination in different areas of the State of the provision of public services (LGA 1991, s 43). See SI No 208 of 1995. See Local Authority (Declaration of Offices) Order 2003, SI No 293 of 2003.

For employment opportunities in local authorities, see website: *www.publicjobs.ie*. [Bibliography: Canny (2); Keane (3); Maloney & Spellman]. See BOUNDARY ALTERATION; COUNTY MANAGER; LITTER; LOCAL GOVERNMENT; RESERVED FUNCTION; WASTE MANAGEMENT PLAN.

local authority, development by. Development by a local authority in its functional area is *exempted development* and normally does not require planning permission; however the local authority must not effect any development which *contravenes materially* the development plan: Planning and Development Act 2000, ss 4 and 178.

Where the development is in a class requiring an *environmental impact statement* (EIS), the approval of An Bord Pleanála is required for the development (PDA 2000, s 175). Where an EIS is not required, there is no requirement for external approval; however there is a requirement for public notification and for the submission of a planning report to the members of the authority (PDA 2000, s 179). These requirements do not apply to works of an urgent nature where the manager considers an emergency situation exists, or to works which a local authority is required to undertake by statute or by a court order (PDA 2000, s 179(6)). See *Byrne v Fingal County Council* [2002] 2 ILRM 321, HC and [2001] 4 IR 565, HC

For planning requirements in relation to specified developments by, or on behalf of, or in partnership with, local authorities, see Planning and Development Regulations 2001, SI No 600 of 2001, Pt VIII, arts 79–85.

local authority, dissolution of. The Minister is empowered in certain circumstances to remove the members of a local authority and to appoint a person or persons, commissioner(s), to carry on the business of the authority during the removal period: Local Government Act 2001, ss 215–220. The circumstances are: (i) a failure to adopt an estimate sufficient for its expenses, (ii) a failure to comply with a judgment, order, or decree of any court, (iii) a refusal or wilful neglect to comply with an express statutory requirement, (iv) the numbers of members are less than the quorum for meetings, or (v) the Minister is satisfied, after the holding of a public local inquiry, that the local authority is not duly and effectually performing its functions (LGA 2001, s 216).

For previous legislation, see Local Government Act 1941, s 48.

local authority, funding. In addition to rates, local authority funding is now provided for through two sources (a) the proceeds of motor taxation and (b) a direct exchequer contribution, both paid into a *Local Government Fund* which is managed and controlled by the Minister: Local Government Act 1998, ss 3–5.

local authority, membership of. A person who will have attained the age of 18 by polling day is eligible for election or co-option to membership of a local authority if the person is either a citizen of Ireland or is ordinarily resident in the State: Local Government Act 2001, s 12. There are provisions for disqualification from membership eg being a representative in the European Parliament, or being a Minister or Minister for State or a member of the Dáil or Seanad, or undergoing a sentence of imprisonment for a term exceeding six months, or having been convicted of corrupt practice (LGA 2001, s 13 and s 13A inserted by Local Government (No 2) Act 2003, s 2). There is also a prohibition on multiple membership of local authorities (LGA 2001, s 14). For the permitted number of members of local authorities, see LGA 2001, ss 21–22. See DUAL MANDATE.

local community. Means persons ordinarily resident in the administrative area of the local authority concerned and, where relevant as regards a function of the local authority, includes persons from outside that area who regularly use facilities of a social, economic, recreational, cultural or other nature provided by the authority: Local Government Act 2001, s 2(1).

As a forum for the democratic representation of the *local community*, a local authority may represent the interest of such community in such manner as it thinks appropriate (LGA 2001, s 64(1)). The local authority is empowered to take such steps as it considers appropriate to consult with and promote effective participation by the *local community* in local government (LGA 2001, s 127).

local election. Provision has been made for the election of members of each local authority in May or June 2004 and every fifth year thereafter: Local Government Act 2001, s 26. Local elections must be conducted in accordance with regulations made by the Minister, and the polls must be held under the proportional representation system with a single transferable vote for each elector (LGA 2001, s 27).

A person who is elected to a number of local authorities is required within three days to declare which one of those authorities the person chooses to represent: Local Elections Regulations 1995, SI No 297 of 1995 as amended by Electoral (Amendment) Act 2002, s 3 and Local Government (No 2) Act 2003, s 6. See also 1937 Constitution, art 28A(3); SI No 237 of 2004. For previous legislation, see s 81 of the Electoral Act 1963; Local Government Act 1941; Electoral Act 1992, s 2(1). See ELECTION PETITION; LOCAL AUTHORITY, MEMBERSHIP OF; VOTERS, SPECIAL.

local government. The role of local government was given constitutional recognition in 1999: Twentieth Amendment of the Constitution Act 1999. The State recognises the role of local government in providing a forum for the democratic representation of local communities, in exercising and performing at local level powers and functions conferred by law and in promoting by its initiatives the interests of such communities: 1937 Constitution, art 28A(1).

An initial reform of local government was provided for by the Local Government Act 1991. Reform of local government *funding* was provided by the Local Government (Financial Provisions) Act 1997 and Local Government Act 1998.

Following on the constitutional recognition of the role of local government in 1999, a radical reform of local government law was enacted in the Local Government Act 2001. The main aims of the Act are: (a) to enhance the role of the elected member; (b) to support community involvement in a more participative local democracy; (c) to modernise local government legislation, and to provide the framework for new financial management systems and other procedures to promote efficiency and effectiveness; and (d) to underpin the programme of local government renewal. See Local Government (Meetings) Regulations 2002, SI No 66 of 2002. For County and City Engineers Association, see website: *www.iei.ie*. [Bibliography: Butler P; Callanan; Canny (2); Collins N; Keane (3 & 4); Roche; Round Hall]. See DUAL MANDATE; LOCAL AUTHORITY; LOCAL AUTHORITY, FUNDING.

Local Government Commission. An independent body established to make recommendations on a range of local government matters eg alteration of local authority boundaries, review of local electoral areas, alteration of the number of members of a local authority, and application for the establishment or dissolution of a town council: Local Government Act 2001, ss 89–95. See BOUNDARY ALTERATION.

local loans fund. A fund which each local authority is required to maintain, into which is paid all moneys received by or on behalf of the local authority, and out of which is paid the expenses incurred by the authority in the performance of its functions, with the exception of a community fund established under s 109: Local Government Act 2001, s 97. See also Local Loans Fund Acts 1935 to 1987; Housing (Miscellaneous Provisions) Act 1992, s 15.

local road. A public road (qv) other than a national road or a regional road: Roads Act 1993, ss 2(1) and 10(1)(c). A road authority is empowered to provide assistance towards the construction or improvement of a non-public road: Local Government Act 2001, s 1. See ROAD.

locatio conductio. See BAILMENT.

locatio custodiae. See BAILMENT.

locatio operis faciendi. See BAILMENT.

lock-out. An action taken by one or more employers which consists of the exclusion of one or more employees from work or the suspension of work or the collective, simultaneous or otherwise connected termination or suspension of employment of a group of employees: Unfair Dismissals Act 1977, s 5(5). The lock-out of an employee is deemed to be a dismissal and the dismissal is deemed to be an unfair dismissal if after termination of the lock-out: (a) the employee is not permitted to resume his employment on terms at least as favourable as those specified in the Act; and (b) one or more other employees were so permitted (UDA 1977, s 5(1) as amended by Unfair Dismissals (Amendment) Act 1993, s 4).

lock-out agreement. An agreement between a vendor of property and a prospective purchaser whereby the vendor will not negotiate with other prospective purchasers for a short stipulated period; such a lock-out agreement had been held to be enforceable in UK law: *Pitt v PHH Asset Management* (1993) *Times*, 30 July; *Walford v Miles* [1992] 2 AC 128 at 139.

loco parentis. See IN LOCO PARENTIS.

locum tenens. [Holding an office]. A person who acts as lawful substitute for another. For ethical guidelines in relation to locum doctors, see Medical Council, *A Guide to Ethical Conduct and Behaviour* (6th edn, 2004) para 11.

locus in quo. [The place in which]. The scene of the event. Sometimes a judge will visit the scene: See *McAllister v Dunnes Stores* [1987] HC. For a more recent example, see JUDGES.

locus poenitentiae. [A place, or opportunity, of repentance]. A planning authority (qv) gives itself a *locus poenitentiae* by serving a notice on an applicant for planning permission, requiring further information or the production of additional evidence in respect of the application. See Local Government (Planning and Development) Regulations 1977, SI No 65 of 1977, art 26. See PLANNING PERMISSION, APPLICATION FOR.

locus regit actum. [The place governs the act].

locus sigilli; L.S. [The place of the seal].

locus standi. [A place of standing]. The right to be heard in court. The question as to whether a person has sufficient interest to maintain proceedings is a mixed question of fact and law: *The State (Lynch) v Cooney* [1982] IR 337.

A party who has a *bona fide* concern and interest in an actual or threatened infringement of the Constitution has a *locus standi* in proceedings to enforce the provisions of the Constitution: *SPUC v Coogan & Ors* [1989] ITLR (16 October), SC. Also, where the plaintiff is an aggrieved person he has, by definition, a *locus standi*: *Chambers v An Bord Pleanála & Sandoz* [1992] ILRM 296, SC.

An applicant company lacked *locus standi* where it had not established that it suffered any wrong or that any injury had been done to it or was likely to be done: *Bargaintown Ltd v Dublin Corporation* [1993] ILRM 891, HC.

Also, a company formed after a decision to grant planning permission had been made and formed primarily to challenge that decision, was held not to have *locus standi*: *Springview Ltd v Cavan Developments Ltd* [2000] 1 ILRM 437, HC. However, in another case where the plaintiff company was formed after planning permission had been granted, it was held that a liberal view should be taken in relation to *locus standi* in planning matters, as planning is a matter of general public importance: *Village Residents Association Ltd v An Bord Pleanála* [2000] 2 ILRM 59, HC. The fact that a person, seeking permission for a judicial review, did not participate in the planning process is not relevant to *locus standi* where the ground on which the court is prepared to grant leave is not one which could have been raised (*Village* case).

In criminal prosecutions commenced by the Director of Public Prosecutions (qv) at public expense, witnesses for the prosecution are not parties to the proceedings and are, accordingly, debarred from seeking to impugn any orders made, by reason of their lack of *locus standi*: *Shannon v McGuinness* [1999] 3 IR 274, HC. It has been held that the DPP has no *locus standi* to bring proceedings for recovery of a penalty imposed by the Income Tax Act 1967, s 128, now Taxes Consolidation Act 1997, s 987: *Downes v DPP* [1987] ILRM 665; Prosecution of Offences Act 1974, s 3. See also *The State (Sheehan) v Ireland* [1987] SC; *Crotty v An Taoiseach* [1987] ILRM 400; *Attorney-General v Open Door Counselling Ltd and Dublin Wellwoman Centre Ltd* [1989] ILRM

19, SC; *O'Connell v Cork Corporation* [2001] 3 IR 602, SC; *Lynch v English* [2003] FL 7771, HC; *Mulcreevy v Minister for the Environment & Dún Laoghaire – Rathdown County Council* [2004] 1 ILRM 419, SC. See also *Humphrey & O'Dowd* in 8 ILT & SJ (1990) 14; *Delaney* in 8 ILT & SJ (1990) 147.

lodged. It has been held that the expression *'shall be lodged in Court'* can only mean that the document actually reached the court in the ordinary course of its everyday business: *Hegarty & Hogan v Labour Court* [1999] ELR 198, HC.

lodger. See OCCUPATION.

lodgment in court. The payment of money into court which a defendant in an action for debt or damages or in an admiralty action, may make: RSC Ord 22 as amended by SIs Nos 229 of 1990 and 265 of 1993. In the High Court the lodgment may be: (a) a lodgment *in satisfaction* of the claim, by which the defendant is taken to admit the claim; or (b) a lodgment *with the defence denying liability*, which remains in court to await the result of the trial if the plaintiff does not accept it; in which event if he succeeds in his claim but is not awarded more than the lodgment, the defendant will be entitled to his costs against the plaintiff from the date of the lodgment; or (c) lodgment *with the defence setting up tender* which lodgment the plaintiff can accept but he is only entitled to his costs if he continues the action and disproves the tender; if he fails to disprove the tender, the defendant is entitled to his costs of the whole action.

A defendant who has made a lodgment is entitled, without court order, to *top up* the lodgment once only by lodging the additional sum in court; the second lodgment date becomes the effective date for determining costs, but only where that lodgment is made at least three months before the date on which the action is first listed for hearing (RSC Ord 22, r 1(2)); *Donohue v Dillon* [1987] HC. There is nothing in the Rules to prevent a *tender* lodgment being made after settlement negotiations have failed, even though weaknesses in the plaintiff's case may have been disclosed during the negotiations: *Kearney v Barrett and Others* [2003] FL 8772, HC and [2004] 2 ILRM 43.

A period of 14 days is allowed within which money lodged in satisfaction of a claim may be accepted by the plaintiff: RSC Ord 22, r 4(1). The court had a discretion to extend the period for acceptance because it is in the public interest to avoid the hearing of cases which do not need to be heard: *Window and Roofing Concepts Ltd v Tolmac Construction Ltd* [2004] 1 ILRM 554, HC.

There are special rules governing the lodgment of money in court in personal and fatal injury cases; the defendant may lodge money in court either at the time of delivery of the defence or within four months from the date of the Notice of Trial, or later, including topping up, by leave of the court (RSC Ord 22, rr 1(7) and 7(1) inserted by SI No 229 of 1990). See also Ord 22, rr 1(9) and 1(10) inserted by SI No 265 of 1993. The pleadings in these cases must not disclose the fact that money has been paid into court or the amount thereof and may not normally be communicated to the judge. Under recent legislation, both the plaintiff and defendant in a personal injuries action are required to serve a notice of an *offer of settlement* on the other party: Civil Liability and Courts Act 2004, s 17. After the expiration of a time period to be prescribed, such offers are to be lodged in court. The judge must not be aware of the terms of such offers until a judgment has been delivered in the action. The court must have regard to the offers and the reasonableness of the conduct of the parties in making them when considering the making of an order as to the costs in the action. This new provision is in addition to and not in substitution for existing rules (CLCA 2004, s 17(6)).

A defendant may be permitted by the court to make a late lodgment but only in special circumstances e g where the defendant discovers, as a result of settlement negotiations, that the plaintiff's injuries were more serious than originally pleaded on his behalf: *Brennan v Iarnród Éireann* [1993] ILRM 134, HC. See also *Ely v Dargan* [1967] IR 89; *Noble v Gleeson McGrath Baldwin* (19 Feb 2000, unreported) HC.

There is now provision for a 'qualified party' to make on offer of tender of payment to the other party to the cause or proceedings in the High Court in lieu of lodgment of money in court: RSC Ord 22, r 14 added by Rules of the Superior Courts (No 5) (Offer of Payment in Lieu of Lodgment) 2000, SI No 328 of 2000. *Qualified parties* include the State, the Motor Insurers' Bureau of Ireland, and any party in

respect of whom the State is providing an indemnity. See Agreement entered into by the Bureau with the Minister for Transport on 31 March 2004, clause 10. See also website: *www.mibi.ie.*

Lodgment with the defence denying liability is not permitted in actions for libel or slander or where the defence raises a question on the title to land (RSC Ord 22, r 1(3)). In defamation proceedings, a lodgment may be made by the defendant provided liability is admitted. The admission may be of part of the plaintiff's claim, provided that the defendant makes the necessary admissions in the defence and identifies in the notice of lodgment the particular allegations in respect of which payment is made; there should be a single payment rather than a separate sum in respect of each allegation: RSC Ord 22, r 1(5); *Norbrook Laboratories Ltd v Smithkline Beecham (Ireland) Ltd* [1999] 2 ILRM 391, HC and 2 IR 192. See also RSC Ord 77, r 21 as amended by SI No 344 of 1997.

In relation to claims by infants or persons of unsound mind, no settlement or compromise or payment or acceptance of money paid into court, either before or at or after trial, is valid without the approval of the court (RSC Ord 22, r 10 and Civil Liability Act 1961, s 63). See also Residential Institutions Redress Act 2002, s 25.

A plaintiff who institutes proceedings in the High Court and subsequently accepts a sum lodged which is within the jurisdiction of the Circuit Court, is still entitled to have his costs taxed on the High Court level: *Cronin v Astra Business Systems Ltd* [2003] 2 IR 603, HC. In upholding this judgment, the Supreme Court held that the value of a case cannot in all circumstances and in every case be measured by the amount of an accepted lodgment: [2004] ITLR 5 July 2004, SC. See 'The making of a lodgment at the eleventh hour' by Damien Sheridan BL in *Bar Review* (May 2001) 389. [Bibliography: Buckley, Melody]. See PAYMENT OUT OF COURT.

lodgment in court, Circuit Court. In the Circuit Court, where the defendant is *setting up tender* before action, the sum of money must be brought into Court: Circuit Court Rules 2001 Ord 15, r 8. A defendant may also lodge in court an amount which he alleges is sufficient to satisfy the plaintiff's claim, with an admission or denial of liability, at any time from *entry of appearance* to the date of *notice of trial* or to at least eight weeks before the *hearing date* (Ord 15, r 9(a) – Dublin Circuit; and Ord 15, r 9(b) – other Circuits). There is provision for making an additional lodgment (Ord 15, r 10).

Save in the case of a lodgment with a *defence of tender*, the plaintiff may, within ten days of the lodgment, serve notice on the defendant that he accepts the amount lodged; this operates as a *stay* of all further proceedings (Ord 15, r 12). As in the High Court, provision is also made for *qualified* parties (eg the State) to make an *offer of tender* of payment to the other party to the proceedings in the Circuit Court and this operates as if an actual lodgment of money had been made (Ord 15, r 21).

lodgment in court, District Court. There is provision in the District Court for: (a) a lodgment by the defendant of a sum of money *in satisfaction* of the plaintiff's claim, (b) a lodgment by the defendant as a *tender* with a notice of intention to defend, and (c) a lodgment by the plaintiff in response to a *counterclaim*: DCR 1997 Ord 41.

lodgment in court, disclosure of. In a High Court action, the fact that money has been lodged in court must be stated in the defence; however the fact that money has been lodged or the amount thereof must not be disclosed to a jury in any action tried by judge and jury, (or where the judge sits alone, the amount lodged in court must not be disclosed to him) until all questions of liability and the amount of debt and damages has been decided, except in an action to which a defence of *tender* before action is pleaded or where the plaintiff is a minor (qv) and the direction of the court is sought as to the advisability of accepting or rejecting the lodgment: RSC Ord 22, r 7.

In personal and fatal injury cases, the pleadings must not disclose the fact that money has been paid into court and this must not be communicated to the judge, except that the judge may enquire, for good or sufficient reasons, whether and in what amount, a payment has been made (RSC Ord 22, r 1(8) as inserted by SI No 229 of 1990). In relation to formal offers in personal injury cases, see Civil Liability and Courts Act 2004, s 17(4).

In a Circuit Court action, the fact that a lodgment of money in court has been made, must not be disclosed to the judge until he has decided all issues between the parties: Circuit Court Rules 2001 Ord 15, r 11. As regards disclosure to a judge in the District Court, there must be no disclosure until the judge has decided all issues between the parties: DCR Ord 41, r 2(2).

logo. See COLLECTIVE MARK.

loitering. A garda is empowered to direct a person to leave a street or public place where he has *reasonable cause* (qv) to suspect that the person is loitering in order to solicit or importune another person for the purposes of prostitution: Criminal Law (Sexual Offences) Act 1993, s 8. Evidence of the previous character and previous activity of the accused cannot be given in court to show that the garda had *reasonable cause* to so suspect: *DPP v Keogh* [1998] 1 ILRM 72, HC. See also CANVASSING.

lone parent. A widow, widower, separated or divorced spouse, unmarried person, or a person whose spouse has been committed in custody to a prison or place of detention who has at least one qualified child normally residing with that person: Social Welfare (Consolidation) Act 1993, ss 157–162; Social Welfare (No 2) Act 1995, s 8. An allowance is payable to a lone parent. Cohabitation (qv) disqualifies the person.

long occupation equity lease. The right which the tenant of a tenement has, subject to certain exceptions, to a new tenancy where the tenement was for the previous 20 years continuously in the occupation of the tenant or of his predecessors in title: Landlord and Tenant (Amendment) Act 1980, s 13(1). Provision has been made for abolition of the right to apply for a new tenancy of a dwelling under the 1980 Act, unless the tenant has served notice of intention to claim relief under s 20 of that Act before the abolition: Residential Tenancies Act 2004, s 192. The abolition takes place on and from the fifth anniversary of the commencement of Part 4 (security of tenure) of the 2004 Act. Prior to the fifth anniversary, the tenant may renounce the right to a new tenancy under the 1980 Act, whether for or without valuable consideration, having received independent legal advice in relation to the renunciation (RTA 2004, s 191). Occupation under a *Part 4 tenancy* or a *further Part 4 tenancy* is to be reckoned for the purposes of s 13(1)(b) of the LT(A)A 1980 (RTA 2004, s 55). See PART 4 TENANCY.

long possession, title by. The title which a person acquires in land by retaining adverse possession of the land for a certain period without acknowledging the true owner's title. No right of action to recover land shall be deemed to have accrued unless the land has been in the *adverse possession* of some person in whose favour the limitation period can run: Statute of Limitations Act 1957, s 18. When the true owner of land intends to use it for a particular purpose, but meanwhile has no immediate use for it, and so leaves it unoccupied, he does not lose his title to it simply because some other person enters on it and uses it for some temporary purpose: *Leigh v Jack* [1879] 5 ExD 264; *Wallis's Cayton Bay Holiday Camp Ltd v Shell-Max & BP Ltd* [1974] 3 All ER 575 at 580, both cited with approval in *Cork Corporation v Lynch* [1995] 2 ILRM 598 (1984 HC).

The appointment of a receiver to take control of a company and to arrange the sale of its assets, does not create a situation of *adverse possession* within the meaning of s 18(1) because there was no possession without right or authority, which is the essence of 'adverse possession' within the meaning of SLA 1957: *Bula Ltd and Others v Crowley and Others* [2002] FL 5044, HC and [2003] 1 ILRM 55 and 1 IR 396.

An action to recover land from a person in possession must be brought within twelve years (30 years in the case of a State authority) after the right of action accrued or from the last written acknowledgment signed by the person in possession or his agent. Time does not run against the true owner in the case of fraud, until he has discovered the fraud or could with reasonable diligence have discovered it. Time does not run also in the case of a person with a disability.

The right of action to recover land may accrue: (a) on dispossession or discontinuance; (b) on failure to take possession on death or under an assurance. See Registration of Title Act 1964, s 49. See *Maher v Maher* [1987] ILRM 582; *Durack Manufacturing v Considine* [1987] HC; *Gleeson v Feehan* [1997] 1 ILRM 522, SC; *Griffin v Bleithin* [1999] 2 ILRM 182, HC; *Battelle v Pinemeadow Ltd* [2002] FL 6825, HC. See Law Reform Commission, *Report on Title by Adverse Possession of Land* (LRC 67, 2002), which recommends the introduction by statute of a *parliamentary conveyance* (qv). [Bibliography: Pearce & Mee; Wylie (1)]. See ANIMUS POSSIDENDI; CARETAKER; LIMITATION OF ACTIONS.

long title. See INTERPRETATION OF LEGISLATION; PREAMBLE.

long vacation. The period beginning on 1 August and ending on 30 September when the Supreme and High Courts are not normally sitting: RSC Ord 118, r 2. Pleadings are not to be delivered or amended during the long vacation unless directed by the Court or on consent: RSC Ord 122, r 4. See TIME, COURT RULES; VACATION.

lord. Originally the person from whom a tenant held land.

lord chancellor. The Lord High Chancellor of Ireland for the time being, and to include or be applicable to the Lord Keeper or Lords Commissioners for the custody of the Great Seal of the Kingdom of Ireland for the time being: Lunatic Regulations (Ireland) Act 1871, s 2. The *parens patriae* jurisdiction exercised by the Lord Chancellors of Ireland prior to 1922 is now vested in the President of the High Court: Courts (Supplemental Provisions) Act 1961, s 9. See *In the matter of a Ward of Court* [1995] 2 ILRM 401, SC. In the UK, the Lord Chancellor is the chief judicial officer under the British Constitution and is President of the Supreme Court and of the House of Lords when sitting as the final Court of Appeal.

lord lieutenant. Formerly the office created for the purpose of having a representative of the Crown in an area to keep it in military order. Prior to the independence of Ireland, the Lord Lieutenant in Dublin was the Chief Governor of Ireland. The government is empowered to exercise the functions formerly exercised by the Lord Lieutenant under the Civil Bill Courts (Ireland) Act 1851. See SI No 174 of 1992. See Adaptation of Enactments Act 1922, s 11. See *Application of Gallagher* [1991] 1 IR 31. See Royal College of Surgeons in Ireland (Charter Amendment) Act 2003, s 33(2). See IRISH STOCK EXCHANGE.

lord mayor. The title given to the chairman of the borough corporation of Dublin by the Municipal Corporations (Ireland) Act 1840 and to the Chairman of the Borough Corporation of Cork (and Belfast) by letters patent. The procedure for electing a lord mayor is governed by the Electoral Act 1963, s 82; Local Elections Regulations 1965, SI No 128 of 1965.

The titles of *Mayor* and *Lord Mayor*, where previously used as the title of the chairman of an elected council, are permitted to be retained, and the council is also empowered to adopt the title *Cathaoirleach*: Local Government Act 2001, s 32. There was provision for the direct election of the Mayor/Lord Mayor/Cathaoirleach in the year 2004 and from then on (LGA 2001, s 40). However, this provision was repealed in 2003: Local Government (No 2) Act 2003, s 7. See MAYOR.

loss. Unless a policy of insurance provides otherwise, the insurer is liable for any loss proximately caused by a peril insured against. See Marine Insurance Act 1906, s 55. See TOTAL LOSS.

loss of service. See PER QUOD SERVITIUM AMISIT.

lost bill. A bill of exchange (qv) which is lost before it is overdue. The person who was the holder of the bill prior to its loss, may apply to the drawer for a duplicate which the drawer must provide, but the drawer can demand security from the applicant against the risk of the original bill being found and the drawer being liable on both bills: Bills of Exchange Act 1882, s 69. If the drawer refuses to give such a duplicate, having been requested, he can be compelled to do so.

lost modern grant. The doctrine by which a court can presume from long user, that at some time in the past an *easement* (qv) was granted by deed but that the deed has been lost and cannot be produced. The Law Reform Commission has recommended that prescription at common law and under the doctrine of *lost modern grant* should be abolished: *Report on the Acquisition of Easements and Profit A Prendre by Prescription* (LRC 66, 2002.) See PRESCRIPTION.

lost years. See EXPECTATION OF LIFE, LOSS OF.

lot. See AUCTION SALES.

lottery. Includes all competitions for money or money's worth involving guesses or estimates of future events or of past events the results of which are not yet ascertained or not yet generally known: Gaming and Lotteries Act 1956, s 21. Any kind of skill or dexterity whether bodily or mental in which persons can compete would prevent a scheme from being a lottery, if the result depended partly upon such skill or dexterity: *Scott v The Director of Public Prosecutions* [1914] 2 KB 868; *Attorney-General (McGrath) v Healy* [1972] IR 393. The law does not require every participant to be a purchaser to constitute a lottery; it is suffi-

cient that there be a substantial number: *Flynn v Denieffe & Independent Newspapers plc* [1993] ILRM 417, SC and 2 IR 28.

Generally lotteries are prohibited except where declared not to be unlawful eg private lotteries, lotteries at dances, concerts and carnivals, and lotteries conducted wholly within the State in accordance with a permit or a licence (GLA 1956, ss 23–32). For provisions regarding a court licensed lottery and appeal against a refusal to grant a Garda permit, see DCR 1997 Ord 66.

A national lottery was established by the National Lottery Act 1986 which permits the Minister to award a licence to a suitable body to operate the lottery. The surplus funds remaining, after prizes and expenses have been paid, are to be used for sport and other recreation, national culture (including the Irish language), the arts and the health of the community and such other purposes and in such amounts, as the government may determine from time to time (NLA 1986, s 5).

The playslip, completed by a person playing the National Lottery, constitutes an offer by the National Lottery Company, which offer is accepted when the player tenders the playslip and the prescribed charge to the company's representative, who, in accordance with an exception printed on the back of the playslip, is an agent of the player and not of the company, and the player is bound by this exception even if he had not read the back of the playslip: *Carroll v An Post National Lottery Company* [1996] 1 IR 443, HC.

The restriction on advertising and publicity in relation to other lotteries run under authority of a garda permit or licence has been removed (NLA 1986, s 33(1)) and the Minister may by regulation amend the value of prizes in such lotteries (NLA 1986, s 33(2)). The maximum prize money now permitted in the case of a lottery under a garda permit is €3,809 (£3,000) and it is €20,000 in the case of a District Court licensed lottery: Lottery Prizes Regulations, SI No 72 of 1987; SI No 174 of 2000; SI No 29 of 2002. The National Lottery is prohibited from imposing exclusive agency arrangements on agents who wish to act also for the REHAB and other lotteries: Restrictive Practices (National Lottery) Order 1990, SI No 130 of 1990. See also *Hall v Cox* [1899] 1 QB 198; *Barrett v*

Flynn [1916] 2 IR 1; *Camillo v O'Reilly* [1988] ILRM 738, SC; *DPP v Sports Arena & Cafolla* [1992] SC; *Jacinta Yilmaz v Kemal Yilmaz* (1993) Irish Times, 21 January 1993.

The profits of a licensed lottery are exempt from tax: Taxes Consolidation Act 1997, s 216. The European Court of Justice has held that a proposal by the Finnish state to tax a Swedish lottery prize won by a Finnish resident, when Finnish lottery prizes were not liable to tax, was incompatible with art 49 (freedom to provide services) of the *Treaty establishing the European Community*, consolidated (2002) version: *Lindman* [2003] Case C-42/02, ECJ.

An interdepartmental group has recommended the establishment of a *Gaming and Lottery Authority*, See 'Review of the Gaming and Lotteries Acts 1956–86' *Report of the Interdepartmental Group* (2000). For the National Lottery, see website: *www.lotto.ie*. See GAMING.

low-tide elevation. A naturally formed area of land which is surrounded by and above water at low water but submerged at high water: Maritime Jurisdiction Act 1959, s 1. See MARITIME JURISDICTION.

lucid interval. A temporary period of rational thought and behaviour between periods of insanity. A will made during such a period may be admitted to probate (qv) if the person had, at the time, a sound disposing mind. See *Chambers and Yatman v Queen's Proctor* [1840] 2 Curt 415; *Banks v Goodfellow* [1870] LR 5 QB 549. See SOUND DISPOSING MIND.

lucri causa. [For the purpose of gain].

Lugano Convention. The Convention on Jurisdiction and Enforcement of Judgments in civil and commercial matters in 1988 between member states of the EU and EFTA contracting states. The Convention is open to accession from non-EU and non-EFTA states. See *United Meat Packers v Nordstern* [1997] 2 ILRM 553, SC. See DCR 1997 Ord 62. See SI No 39 of 2000. See FOREIGN JUDGMENTS, ENFORCEMENT OF; JURISDICTION; MAINTENANCE ORDER.

lump. The colloquial term to describe the payment of a lump sum to self-employed persons on building contracts without deduction of tax at source. For prevention, see SUB-CONTRACTORS, PAYMENT OF. See also MAINTENANCE.

lunatic. Any person found by *inquisition* idiot, lunatic, or of unsound mind, and incapable of managing himself or his affairs: Lunatic Regulations (Ireland) Act 1871, s 2.

See CRIMINAL LUNATIC; INQUISITION; INSANE PERSON; INSANITY.

M

Maastricht Treaty. The *Treaty on European Union* signed at Maastricht on 7 February 1992 and approved by referendum in Ireland on 18 June 1992. The Treaty amends the Treaty of Rome 1957 and the Single European Act 1987. The main changes are in the areas of economic and monetary union, European citizenship, foreign and security policy, the role of the European Parliament, consumer policy, education, and health. The Maastricht Treaty includes seventeen important Protocols, including the *abortion* protocol (number 17) relating to article 40(3)(3) of the Constitution of Ireland, and the protocol on social policy (number 14) which was agreed by governments of eleven member states but not by the UK.

The Treaty also includes a number of Declarations, including one added in Portugal on 1 May 1992 relating to the 'abortion' protocol regarding the right to travel and to information. The Treaty entered into force on 1 November 1993. See 1937 Constitution, art 29(4)(4). See Government White Paper 1992 'Treaty on European Union' (Pl 8793). For the *Treaty on European Union* and the *Treaty establishing the European Community*, consolidated (2002) versions, see website: http://europa.en.int/eur-lex/en/treaties/index.html. See EUROPEAN UNION; REFERENDUM.

machinery. Apparatus, whether moving or fixed, by means of which force was applied, modified or used by mechanical means for a specific purpose: Annual Revision of Rateable Property (Ireland) Amendment Act 1860, s 7; *Irish Refining plc v Commissioner of Valuation* [1995] 2 ILRM 223, HC.

Regulations have been made to give effect in Irish law to Directive (EC) 98/37, which is a consolidating directive, replacing a number of earlier directives relating to machinery: European Communities (Machinery) Regulations 2001, SI No 518 of 2001.

Madrid Protocol. The Protocol relating to the Madrid Agreement concerning the International Registration of Marks, adopted at Madrid on 27 June 1989 and signed by Ireland in December 1989: Trade Marks Act 1996, s 58. See 'Ireland in Madrid – a new trade mark system for Ireland' by Niamh Hall in *Irish Business Law* [2001] 134. See INTERNATIONAL TRADE MARK.

maim. A bodily harm whereby a person is deprived of the use of any member of his body or of any sense which he can use in fighting, or by loss of which he is generally and permanently weakened. It is an offence to maim another: Offences Against the Person Act 1861, s 18 as amended by Criminal Law Act 1997, s 16 and Sch 3.

main road. Formerly, any road which the Minister declared by order to be a main road: Local Government Act 1925, s 1 repealed by Roads Act 1993, s 4. The words 'main road' in the Local Government (Planning and Development) Act 1963, s 89(10) have been replaced by the words 'national road or regional road' (RA 1993, s 6). See PUBLIC ROAD.

mainstreaming. (1) In the context of EU policies, mainstreaming an issue means ensuring that it is fully taken into account. Environmental considerations have been 'mainstreamed' because every EU policy decision must now take account of its environmental implications.

(2) When a special service is replaced by a service available to everyone, the service is said to be 'mainstreamed' eg when persons with a disability have equal access to the normal educational system as non-disabled. See INCLUSIVE EDUCATION.

maintenance. The supply of necessaries (qv). The financial arrangements embodied in a maintenance agreement or order. See MAINTENANCE ORDER.

maintenance and champerty. See CHAMPERTY.

maintenance agreement. An agreement for the periodic payment of sums of money by one spouse to another usually as part of a separation agreement (qv). Maintenance payments may be ordered by the court to be adjusted downwards as well as upwards: *D v D* [1990] 2 IR 361, HC. See SEPARATION AGREEMENT.

maintenance order. An order of the court which provides for the periodic payment of sums of money by one spouse to the other spouse, where it appears to the court that the spouse has failed to provide such maintenance for the applicant spouse as is proper in the circumstances: Family Law (Maintenance of Spouses and Children) Act 1976, s 5(1). A spouse when applying for a maintenance order, may join a claim in respect of her dependent children (qv).

A *periodic payment* may be required to be paid from a date before or after an order for such payment, but not before the date of application for the order (FL(MSC)A 1976, s 4 as amended by Social Welfare (Miscellaneous Provisions) Act 2002, s 16, Sch, Pt X). The applicant spouse is known as the *maintenance creditor* and the spouse ordered to pay maintenance is called the *maintenance debtor.*

The court cannot grant a maintenance order where it is proved that the applicant spouse has deserted the other spouse (FL(MSC)A 1976, s 5(2); *RK v MK* [1978] HC) unless it would otherwise be repugnant to justice: Judicial Separation & Family Law Reform Act 1989, s 38.

Also where the applicant spouse has committed adultery, the court may refuse to grant a maintenance order unless the other spouse has connived or condoned or by wilful neglect or misconduct, conduced to the adultery: FL(MSC)A 1976, s 5(3); *L v L* [1979] HC; *OC v TC* [1981] HC. In considering a maintenance order in favour of a wife, the court must ascertain the income earned or capable of being earned by the wife: *RH v NH* [1986] ILRM 352.

A maintenance order may be obtained for the support of children whose parents are not married to each other: Status of Children Act 1987, ss 15–25; *RB v HR* [1990] in 8 ILT & SJ (1990) 295, CC.

The court is empowered to make a lump sum order or periodic payments order on granting a decree of judicial separation (qv): Family Law Act 1995, s 8. It also may order *maintenance pending suit* and make retrospective payment orders (FLA 1995, ss 7 and 17; *EG v JG* [2003] 2 IR 306, HC). The court is also empowered to make a lump sum order or periodic payment order on granting a decree of divorce or at any time thereafter: Family Law (Divorce) Act 1996, s 13.

The upper age limits to which a parent is required to pay maintenance have been standardised ie up to eighteen years of age or up to 23 years of age if in full-time education or no age limit if mentally or physically disabled to the extent that it is not reasonably possible for the person to maintain himself properly: Children Act 1997, s 8.

See also *Sachs v Standard Chartered Bank* [1987] ILRM 297; *CM v TM* [1988] ILRM 262; *K v K* [1992] ITLR (4 May), SC; *McC v McC* [1994] 1 ILRM 101; *JH v RH* [1996] 3 IR 257, HC; *LM v Devally* [1997] 2 ILRM 369, HC. See also Children Act 1997, s 15. See also DCR 1997 Ord 54 as amended by SI No 42 of 1998; District Court (Maintenance) Rules 2003, SI No 614 of 2003 and DCR 1997 Ord 55, 57, and 62. [Bibliography: Duncan & Scully; Martin & McCarthy; Shannon]. See AFFILIATION ORDER; DESERTION; DIVORCE; FOREIGN JUDGMENTS, ENFORCEMENT OF; PARENTAGE, DECLARATION OF.

maintenance order, enforcement of. A maintenance order may be enforced: by seizure of the maintenance debtor's property and effecting its sale; by his imprisonment; by *attachment* of the maintenance debtor's earnings: Family Law (Maintenance of Spouses and Children) Act 1976, s 10). Such attachment requires the debtor's employer to deduct the amount of the order from his salary or wages and forward it to the District Court clerk who in turn forwards it to the maintenance creditor.

Also reciprocal enforcement of maintenance orders exists as between the State and the United Kingdom for some years: Maintenance Orders Act 1974; and more recently between the State and other *contracting* states in the EU (1988), and between EU states and EFTA countries (1993): Jurisdiction of Courts and Enforcement of Judgments (European Communities) Act 1988, ss 7, 9, and Sch 1, art 5, and Jurisdiction of Courts and Enforcement of Judgments (European Communities) Act 1993.

More simplified procedures and a more extensive international network to enforce maintenance orders across borders was introduced in 1994: Maintenance Act 1994, amending sections of the 1988 and 1993 Acts, which were consolidated in 1998: Jurisdiction of Courts and Enforcement of Judgments Act 1998.

The *Brussels I Regulation* on the recognition and enforcement of judgments in civil and commercial matters, replaces the 1998 Act as from 1 March 2002 for all EU States except Denmark: EC (Civil and Commercial Judgments) Regulations 2002, SI No 52 of 2002. An enforcement order of a maintenance order may be made by the District Court even if the amount involved exceeds that court's jurisdiction (SI No 52 of 2002, reg 6). The Master of the High Court also has jurisdiction to make such an order if he considers making the order would be more effective e g if the defendant is not resident in any District Court area but has property in the country (SI No 52 of 2002, reg 5).

maintenance pending suit. A periodic payment or lump sum payment which the court may order one spouse to pay to another, where the court has before it an application for a grant of a decree of *divorce* which the court has not yet determined: Family Law (Divorce) Act 1996, s 13. In relation to *judicial separation*, see Family Law Act 1995, ss 8, 7 and 17. The High Court has held that the court must consider all the circumstances of the parties before determining the issue of interim maintenance: *EG v JG* [2003] 2 IR 306, HC.

major accident. See DANGEROUS SUBSTANCE; EMERGENCY.

major event. (1). An event or series of events at which large numbers of persons are likely to be present; a local authority is empowered to serve a notice on the organisers or promoters of a major event which requires them to take specific measures to prevent or limit the creation of litter and to provide for its removal: Litter Pollution Act 1997, ss 17–18.

(2) An *event* designated by the Minister as an event of major importance to society for which the right of a qualifying broadcaster to provide coverage on *free* television services should be provided in the public interest: Broadcasting (Major Events Television Coverage) Act 1999, s 2(1). An *event* means an event of interest to the general public in the European Union, a member state or in the State or in a significant part of the State, that is organised by an event organiser who is legally entitled to sell the broadcasting rights of the event (B(METC)A 1999, s 1(1)).

This provision prevents major events being restricted to persons who pay by subscription or on a pay-per-view basis and implements the Television without Frontiers Directive, art 3a (Directive (EC) 89/552 as amended by Directive (EC) 97/36). Designated events are notified to the European Commission and other member states are advised; they must ensure that no broadcaster under their jurisdiction operates in a way which would frustrate the designation.

Major events which have been designated for coverage on a *live basis* on free television services include: the Irish Grand National; the Nations Cup at the Dublin Horse Show; Ireland's games in the Rugby World Cup Finals Tournament; the opening games, the semi-finals and final of the European Football Championship Finals and the FIFA World Cup Finals Tournament; Ireland's games in the European Football Championship Finals Tournament and the FIFA World Cup Finals Tournament; Ireland's home and away qualifying games in the European Football Championship and the FIFA World Cup Tournaments; the All-Ireland Senior Inter-County Football and Hurling Finals; the Summer Olympics: SI No 99 of 2003. Each of Ireland's games in the Six Nations Rugby Football Championship have been designated for coverage on a *deferred basis* on free television services.

Provision has been made: (a) for the introduction of an arbitration mechanism where the event organiser is willing to sell the broadcasting rights but is unable to agree a price with the broadcaster, (b) for an application from the broadcaster to the High Court for an order directing the event organiser to provide access to the event, subject to payment of reasonable market rates, and (c) for a not more than three-yearly review by the Minister of designation: Broadcasting (Major Events Television Coverage) (Amendment) Act 2003. See 'Pie in the Sky' by solicitor Deirdre Ní Fhloinn in *Law Society Gazette* (November 2002) 20.

major shareholding directive. Directive (EEC) 88/627 on the information to be published when a major holding in a listed company is acquired or disposed of: Listing Rules 2000 (definitions).

majority. See AGE OF MAJORITY.

majority verdict. See VERDICT; TRIAL BY JURY, CRIMINAL OFFENCES; TRIAL BY JURY, CIVIL MATTERS.

making off without payment. It is an offence for a person, knowing that payment on the spot is required or expected for goods or services, to make off dishonestly without paying for the goods or services with the intention of avoiding payment on the spot: Criminal Justice (Theft and Fraud Offences) Act 2001, s 8. [Bibliography: McGreal C].

mala fides. [Bad faith]. The court was only entitled to review a scheme (of grant payments to the owners of diseased cattle) where it was satisfied that it was being operated *mala fides*, or at least, where it involved some abuse of power: *Rooney v Minister for Agriculture* [1992] ITLR (3 February), SC. See *Foley v DPP* [1989] ITLR (25 September), HC; *Madigan v Radio Telefís Éireann* [1994] 2 ILRM 472, HC; *Fearon v DPP* [2002] FL 7329, HC. See BONA FIDES.

mala grammatica non vitiat chartam. [Bad grammar does not vitiate a deed].

mala in se. Acts which are wrong in themselves e g murder, as opposed to *mala prohibita*, which are acts which are merely prohibited e g driving a motor vehicle without insurance.

mala praxis. Failure of professional duty giving rise to a right of action for damages e g medical negligence.

maladministration. [mal: bad or badly, wrong or wrongly, imperfect or defective]. Allegations of an act of *maladministration* is a ground for the intervention of the Pensions Ombudsman; however maladministration is not defined: Pensions Act 1990, ss 126–147 as inserted by Pensions (Amendment) Act 2002, s 5. In the Statute establishing the European Ombudsman, the word 'maladministration' is also not defined. However, the types of allegations of maladministration made to the European Ombudsman have included abuse of power, avoidable delay, discrimination, failure to ensure fulfilment of obligation, lack or refusal of information, legal error, negligence, procedures, reasoning, transparency, and unfairness.

In the general Ombudsman scheme for public bodies in Ireland, the word 'maladministration' is not used. In that scheme the Ombudsman may investigate any action where it appears to him that the action may have been: taken without proper authority; taken on irrelevant grounds; the result of negligence or carelessness; based on erroneous or incomplete information; improperly discriminatory; based on an undesirable administrative practice; or otherwise contrary to sound or fair administration: Ombudsman Act 1980, s 4(2)(b).

maledicta expositio quae corrumpit textum. [It is a bad exposition which corrupts the text].

malice. Malice is a wrong or improper motive, or feeling existing in the mind of the defendant at the time of the publication of a *defamation* (qv) which actuates the publication. A defendant who acts rashly, or stupidly is protected, provided he acts in good faith but not if he uses a privileged occasion for any purpose other than that for which it was intended. A failure to retract a serious charge may constitute evidence that at the time of the original publication the defendant was actuated by malice. See *Coleman v Kearns* [1946] Ir Jur Rep 5. See PRIVILEGE.

malice aforethought. The element of *mens rea* (qv) in the crime of murder. See MURDER.

malicious damage. The offences committed by a person who unlawfully and maliciously causes damage to specified property: Malicious Damage Act 1861. A malicious intention to damage must be present in the mind of the accused; *malicious* means foresight of the consequences, or an intention to do the kind of harm which resulted from the unlawful act, or a recklessness as to whether harm would result or not. See *The People (DPP) v Walsh* [1988] ILRM 137. See also Electricity (Supply) Act 1927, s 111; Gas Works Clauses Act 1847/71.

The Law Reform Commission recommended major changes to the law on malicious damage: LRC 26 of 1988. The law was changed in 1991: Criminal Damage Act 1991 repealing the Malicious Damage Act 1861 except for ss 35–38 (interference with railways and telegraphs), ss 40–41 (killing or maiming animals), s 47 (exhibiting false signals to shipping), s 48 (cutting away buoys), s 72 (admiralty offences), s 58 (the Act to apply whether or not malice against owner of property): CDA 1991, ss 14 and 15. See also Criminal Justice Act 1993, s 13 and Criminal Law Act 1997, s 16 and Sch 3.

The description of *malicious damage* is commonly used to describe damage to property in respect of which compensation is claimed under the *malicious injuries scheme* (qv). See CRIMINAL DAMAGE TO PROPERTY; DAMAGE TO PROPERTY.

malicious falsehood. Injurious falsehood (qv).

malicious injuries scheme. Also referred to as *criminal injuries*. A scheme under which payment of compensation from public funds is made for damage occurring to property in particular instances: Malicious Injuries Act 1981. Restrictions on the scheme were introduced in 1986; compensation is now payable for damage to property: (a) caused unlawfully by one or more of a number (exceeding two) of persons riotously assembled together, or (b) caused as a result of an act committed maliciously by a person acting on behalf of or in connection with unlawful or certain other organisations: Malicious Injuries (Amendment) Act 1986, s 2.

The court has power to extend the statutory time limit for malicious injuries claims for good reasons: MIA 1981, ss 14 and 23; *Cork County Council v Whillock & Murphy* [1993] 11 ILT Dig 144, SC. See *Dublin Corporation v Murdon Ltd* [1988] ILRM 86; *Conaty v Tipperary (NR) Co Council* [1989] 7 ILT & SJ 222; *Hutch v Dublin Corporation* [1992] ILRM 596, SC and [1993] 3 IR 551, SC; *Belton v Carlow Co Council* [1997] 2 ILRM 405, SC; *Kennedy v Tipperary County Council* [1998] 1 IR 96, SC.

For the rules of procedure governing the compensation scheme, pursuant to: (a) the Malicious Injuries Act 1981 and (b) the Grand Jury (Ireland) Act 1836, s 106 amended by Local Government (Ireland) Act 1898, s 5, see RSC Ord 110; Circuit Court Rules 2001 Ord 52; DCR 1997 Ord 95. [Bibliography: Kennedy & McWilliam]. See TUMULTUOUSLY.

malicious prosecution. A tort (qv) consisting of the institution of unsuccessful criminal proceedings maliciously and without reasonable or probable cause, thereby causing actual damage to the party prosecuted. A plaintiff must prove that the criminal proceedings terminated in his favour, that the defendant instituted and/or participated in the proceedings maliciously, that there was no reasonable or probable cause for such proceedings, and that the plaintiff suffered damage: *McIntyre v Lewis & Ors* [1991] 1 IR 121, SC. Malicious prosecution also includes malicious civil proceedings involving bankruptcy (qv) or the winding up (qv) of a company. See *Brown v Hawkes* [1891] 2 QB 718; *Berry v British Transport Commission* [1962] 1 QB 306. See PRIVILEGE, LEGAL PROFESSIONAL.

malitia supplet aetatem. [Malice supplements age]. See DOLI INCAPAX.

mallard. See GAME.

man of straw. A person with little or no means and consequently not worth taking proceedings against for damages.

management buy-out; MBO. Colloquial expression meaning the obtaining of the control of a company by the executive purchasing the voting shares of the company, often with assistance of a financial or venture capital institution. The Irish Takeover Panel has emphasised in management buy-outs the particular importance of the independent board of the offeree obtaining independent advice. See also Takeover Rules 2001, Pt B, r 3.1. See IRISH TAKEOVER PANEL.

management company. (1) A company established primarily for the purpose of managing 'common areas' in apartments or other property in complexes or estates. It is usual that the 'common areas' are vested in the management company. In the initial sale of such property, it is recommended that the sale be closed on foot of (a) an undertaking by the vendor to the purchaser to furnish the vesting deed to the management company, and (b) an undertaking by the management company to the purchaser to furnish a certified copy of the vesting deed to the purchaser on request by or on behalf of the purchaser or his successor in title: 'Conveyancing Committee' in *Law Society Gazette* (December 2003) 40.

(2) In relation to an apartment complex, means the company in which functions are vested with respect to the management of the apartment complex: Residential Tenancies Act 2004, s 4(1). A tenant of a dwelling, which is one of a number of dwellings comprising an apartment complex, may request the management company to furnish in writing information on the service charges and how they have been calculated; the management company has a duty to comply with this request to the extent that the company has such a duty to the owner of the dwelling (RTA 2004, s 188). The landlord is required to forward to the management company any complaint notified in writing by the tenant to him concerning the performance by the company of its functions in relation to the complex, and the management company must have regard to the complaint and must furnish to the landlord a written statement as to the steps, if any, it has taken to deal with the matter (RTA 2004, ss 12(1)(h) and 187). See DWELLING.

manager, local authority. See COUNTY MANAGER.

managing director. The director in a company who is given responsibility for managing the everyday business affairs of the company. A board may appoint a managing director from one of its members and determine his terms of service; he may be entrusted with any of the board's powers: Companies Act 1963. Table A, arts 110–112. See also *Battle v Irish Art Promotion Centre Ltd* [1968] IR 252. See also Building Societies Act 1989, s 49(7).

mandamus. [We command]. An order of the High Court to compel a person or body to perform a legally imposed duty; it is an order directed to any person, corporation or inferior court, requiring him or them to do some particular thing, therein specified, which appertains to his or their office and for which the applicant has no other specific means of compelling performance. An order of mandamus will be granted to compel compliance with a statutory duty which is not discretionary irrespective of whether or not the person on whom the duty is placed is a public official or an official body: *Minister for Labour v Grace* [1993] ELR 50, HC.

A court will decline to exercise its discretion to grant an order of mandamus where such an order would be futile; it will not make such an order where it is clear: (a) that it would be impossible of performance by reason of the circumstances, or (b) that the doing of the act would involve a contravention of the law, or (c) that the defendants do not have the means of complying with the order: *Brady v Cavan County Council* [2000] 1 ILRM 81, SC and [1999] 4 IR 99, SC. See *The State (Reilly) v D J Clones* [1935] IR 908; *The State (Turley) v O'Floinn* [1968] IR 245. See also Justices Protection (Ireland) Act 1849, s 5. See JUDICIAL REVIEW; ROAD MAINTENANCE.

mandate. A direction, request or command. A cheque (qv) is a mandate.

mandatory injunction. See INJUNCTION.

mandatory offer. Where a person acquires securities in a company which of themselves, or when aggregated with securities already held, carry 30% or more of the voting rights, that person is generally required to make an offer to acquire all other equity shares and voting non-equity shares in the company: Irish Takeover Panel Act 1997, s 8(3); Takeover Rules 2001, Pt B, r 9. A person includes persons *acting in concert*. A mandatory bid is also generally required where a person already holding 30 to 50 per cent of the voting rights acquires further securities of such amount as will increase by more than 0.05% the aggregate percentage of voting rights conferred on him in the company in any twelve-month period (Takeover Rules, Pt B, r 9.1(b)). An offer under r 9 must generally be made unconditional when the offeror and the persons acting in concert hold securities conferring more than 50% of the voting rights (r 9.2). The principle behind the mandatory offer is that when a person obtains effective control of a company by the acquisition of shares, all shareholders should have the opportunity to obtain the price per share paid for that control; it will usually be a premium price.

The Takeover Rules were amended in 2002 to incorporate the *first* and *second* stage clearance procedure provided for in the Competition Act 2002, ss 21 and 22. The new rule 12(a)(i) requires a mandatory offeror to make his offer subject to a condition which would be satisfied on the occurrence of one of the following events: (i) clearance from the Competition Authority without a full investigation; or (ii) a default clearance where the period specified in s 21(2) of CA 2002 elapses; or (iii) clearance from the Competition Authority after a full investigation; or (iv) a determination by the Competition Authority that the merger or acquisition may be put into effect subject to conditions being complied with; or (v) a period of four months after the *appropriate date* elapsing without the Competition Authority having made a determination. [Bibliography: Lucey]. See CONCERT PARTY; TAKEOVER; IRISH TAKEOVER PANEL; SHARES, COMPULSORY PURCHASE OF.

mandatory order. An order of the court compelling compliance with its terms. Contrast with PERMISSIVE ORDER. See also INJUNCTION.

mandatum. [Mandate]. See BAILMENT.

manslaughter. An offence (formerly, a felony) involving an unlawful homicide that is not murder, or infanticide. Manslaughter may be *voluntary* and *involuntary*. A *voluntary* manslaughter is an unlawful homicide where the malice aforethought (qv) of murder may be present but because of provocation (qv), the crime is reduced from murder

to manslaughter: *The People* (*DPP*) *v MacEoin* [1978] IR 27.

An *involuntary* manslaughter arises where a person brings about the death of another by acting in some unlawful manner, but without the intention of killing or doing an act likely to kill. It may arise by the person doing an act which is intrinsically unlawful, or doing some lawful act but doing it recklessly, or culpably leaving unperformed some act which he had a legal duty to perform; the fatal negligence involved needs to be of a very high degree and such to involve a high degree of risk of substantial personal injuries to others: The *People* (*Attorney-General*) *v Dunleavy* [1948] IR 95.

The question to be considered by the jury is whether the accused was guilty of that degree of negligence which was appropriate to sustain a charge of manslaughter: *The People* (*DPP*) *v Cullagh* [1999] ITLR (31 May) CCA. See *The People* (*DPP*) *v Bambrick* [1996] 1 IR 265, CCA. For 'gross negligence manslaughter' see Law Reform Commission, 'Consultation Paper on Corporate Killing' (LRC CP 26, 2003). See HOMICIDE; PROVOCATION; SELF-DEFENCE; UNWORTHINESS TO SUCCEED; YEAR AND A DAY.

mansuetae naturae. [Tame by nature]. See ANIMALS.

manual data. See DATA.

manual handling of loads. Any transporting or supporting of a load by one or more employees, and includes lifting, putting down, pushing, pulling, carrying or moving a load, which, by reason of its characteristics or of unfavourable ergonomic conditions, involves risk, particularly of back injury, to employees: Safety Health and Welfare at Work (General Application) Regulations 1993, SI No 44 of 1993, reg 27. Every employer is required to take measures to avoid the need for the manual handling of loads by his employees; however where the need cannot be avoided, he must seek to reduce the risk involved (SI No 44 of 1993, reg 28 and Sch 8). [Bibliography: McMahon M]. See WEIGHTS.

manufactured goods. It has been held that bananas ripened in the State by a specified artificial process are *goods manufactured* within s 54 of the Corporation Tax Act 1976; *Charles McCann Ltd v O'Culachain* [1986] IR 196. This has been reversed by Finance Acts 1980, s 39(5) and 1990, s 41(1)(c); *O'Connell v Fyffes Banana*

Processing Ltd [2000] ITLR (11 September), SC. The cultivation of chrysanthemums is not a process of manufacture: *Brosnan v Leeside Nurseries Ltd* [1998] 1 ILRM 312, SC and 2 IR 304. The process of making a film is not a manufacturing process: *Saatchi & Saatchi Advertising Ltd v McGarry* [1998] 2 IR 562, SC. The process of cutting trees to specified lengths in a forest has been held to be a process for the manufacture of goods: *Longford Timber Contractors Ltd v Revenue Commissioners* [2004] Irish Times 22 July, CC.

See Finance Act 1980, s 42 and *O'Laochdha v Johnson (Ire) Ltd* [1992] 10 ILT Dig 268, HC. See also Finance Act 1993, s 44 which extends further the definition of *goods* for manufacturing relief purposes e g processing of meat, production of a newspaper. See *O'Connell v Tara Mines Ltd* [2002] 3 IR 438, SC. See now Taxes Consolidation Act 1997, s 443.

manuscript. Formerly, in relation to a work, meant the original document embodying the work, whether written by hand or not: Copyright Act 1963, s 2(1) since repealed by Copyright and Related Rights Act 2000. There is no definition of *manuscript* in the 2000 Act; however copyright protection of a literary, dramatic or musical work requires it to be recorded in *writing* or otherwise. See COPYRIGHT; PUBLISHED EDITION; WRITING.

mareva injunction. The *injunction* which the court may grant to restrain a defendant, who is not within the jurisdiction but who has assets within the jurisdiction, from removing these assets from the jurisdiction pending trial of an action for a debt due. So called after *Mareva Compania Naviera v International Bulk Carriers* [1980] 1 All ER 213.

The Courts have examined the roots of the jurisdiction to grant *Mareva* injunctions and have formally accepted that the *common law* principle has been developed and altered and applied in this country: *Criminal Assets Bureau v Sweeney* [2001] 2 ILRM 81, HC.

A Mareva injunction will be granted only if the plaintiff establishes: (a) that he has an arguable case that he will succeed in the action, and (b) the anticipated disposal of the defendant's assets is for the purpose of preventing a plaintiff from recovering damages and not merely for the purpose of carrying on a business or discharging lawful debts: *O'Mahony v Horgan* [1996] 1 ILRM 161, SC and [1995] 2 IR 411, SC.

It is not necessary for the applicant to establish as a priority that his claim would succeed; he must establish however that there is a substantial question to be tried: *Countyglen plc v Carway* [1995] 1 ILRM 481, HC. A *mareva injunction* is granted in order that a defendant does not take action designed to frustrate subsequent orders of the Court: *Deutsche Bank v Murtagh* [1995] 1 ILRM 381, HC. The Court has jurisdiction to restrain a defendant ordinarily resident in Ireland from dissipating extra-territorial assets in addition to assets within the State: *Deutche Bank* case.

In deciding whether to grant an interlocutory Mareva injunction, the court will apply the ordinary test as to whether the plaintiff had established that there was a fair question to be tried and where the balance of convenience lay as to the issuing of an injunction, taking account of the risk in the particular case of the Mareva injunction that the refusal to grant relief could involve a real risk that a judgment or award in favour of the plaintiff would remain unsatisfied: *Serge Caudron v Air Zaire* [1986] ILRM 10.

A mareva injunction to restrain a company defendant from disposing of its only asset was refused in a case where the disposal had been in contemplation prior to the plaintiff's claim: *Moloney (a minor) v Laurib Investments Ltd* [1993] ITLR (6 December).

The court is empowered by statute to make an *asset freezing order* (known as a *Mareva* injunction) against the directors of a company on the application of a person who has a civil cause of action against such directors and there is a likelihood that they will seek to evade their responsibilities by reducing their assets or by removing them from the State: Company Law Enforcement Act 2001, s 55.

A mareva injunction can be obtained by way of protective relief associated with an order for enforcement of a foreign judgment pursuant to the Brussels Convention: *Elwyn (Cottons) Ltd v Pearle Designs Ltd* [1989] ILRM 162, HC. The court will grant protective relief even though the substantive proceedings in another State have not yet been commenced. For provisional, including protective, measures under the Brussels I Regulation, see EC (Civil and

Commercial Judgments) Regulations 2002, SI No 52 of 2002, reg 10.

A failure to establish that there were any assets within the jurisdiction is not fatal to a plaintiff's application for a worldwide Mareva injunction; the fewer the assets within the jurisdiction, the greater the necessity for taking protective measures in relation to those outside it: *Bennett Enterprises Inc v Lipton & Ors* [1999 HC] 1 ILRM 81 and 2 IR 221. A worldwide interlocutory Mareva injunction may be given subject to a *Babanaft Proviso* ie that that the order is subject to a qualification that it should not affect third parties unless and to the extent that it is enforced by the courts of the States in which any of the defendants' assets are located: *Babanaft International Co S A v Bassante* [1990] 1 Ch 13 and *Bennett* case. See *Credit Suisse v Cuoghi* [1998] QB 818.

For measures to secure and preserve a *debtor's assets* in the State, see EC (Personal Insolvency) Regulations 2002, SI No 334 of 2002. See also Personal Injuries Assessment Board Act 2003, s 12(3). [Bibliography: Courtney (3); Wylie (3)]. See INJUNCTION.

marginal notes. Notes placed at the side of a part, section or provision of an Act. Such notes must not be considered or judicially noticed in relation to the construction or interpretation of the Act: Interpretation Act 1937, s 11(g). They do not form part of the Act but may be considered to ascertain the *mischief* at which the Act is aimed. See MISCHIEF OF A STATUTE.

marina. A floating marina fixed to seabed is a 'fixed mooring' and consequently a rateable hereditament: *Trustees of Kinsale Yacht Club v Commissioner of Valuations* [1994] 1 ILRM 457, SC.

marine. Of, in, near, concerned with or belonging to the sea and tidal waters, inhabiting, found or got from the sea or from non-tidal waters: Marine Institute Act 1991, s 1. The Marine Institute has functions relating to marine research and development as well as relating to shipping and shipping services (MIA 1991, s 4 as amended by Fisheries (Amendment) Act 1999, s 30). The Institute also includes the *Irish Maritime Development Office* which has the function of promoting and assisting the development of Irish shipping and Irish shipping services and seafarer training (MIA 1991, s 4A inserted by F(A)A 1999,

s 30). For the Marine Institute, see website: *www.marine.ie.*

marine adventure. There is a marine adventure where any ship, goods or other moveables are exposed to maritime perils (qv): Marine Insurance Act 1906, s 3. Every lawful marine adventure may be the subject of a contract of insurance (MIA 1906, s 3(1)).

marine casualty. (1) Means an event or process which causes or poses the threat of: (a) death or serious injury to a person; (b) the loss of a person overboard; (c) significant loss or stranding of, or damage to, a vessel or property; or (d) significant damage to the environment: Merchant Shipping (Investigation of Marine Casualties) Act 2000, s 2(1). A marine casualty is investigated either by the *Marine Casualty Investigation Board* or by a *Tribunal of Inquiry* established by the Minister (MS(IMC)A 2000, ss 26 and 38).

The marine casualty to be investigated must be in connection with the operation of: (i) a vessel in Irish waters; (ii) an Irish registered vessel, in waters anywhere; or (iii) a vessel normally located or moored in Irish waters and under the control of a resident of the State, in international waters contiguous to Irish waters. A person who is directly or indirectly involved in the operation of a vessel relevant to the investigation, may be required to submit to a physical or medical examination or to give samples to establish the presence or level of an intoxicant (MS(IMC)A 2000, s 31). The Board may also investigate an accident, after consultation with the Minister, sustained or caused by a vessel, which would have been a marine casualty if the vessel had been Irish registered (MS(IMC)A 2000, ss 2(1) and 26(1)(b)). See MARINE CASUALTY INVESTIGATION BOARD.

(2) Means a collision of ships, stranding or other incident of navigation, or other occurrence on board a ship or external to it, resulting in: (a) material damage or imminent threat of material damage to a ship or cargo, or (b) pollution: Sea Pollution Act 1991, s 3(1) as amended by Merchant Shipping (Investigation of Marine Casualties) Act 2000, s 45.

Marine Casualty Investigation Board. Provision has been made for the establishment of an independent board to investigate *marine casualties* (qv) and publish reports of such investigations: Merchant

Shipping (Investigation of Marine Casualties) Act 2000, ss 7–8. There is a requirement on every owner, charterer, master, ship's agent, ship's manager or ship's husband, to notify the Department of the Marine immediately he is aware that a marine casualty has occurred and to make a comprehensive written report to the Board, if requested (MS(IMC)A 2000, ss 23–24). The Board is empowered to carry out an investigation to establish the cause with a view to making recommendations for the avoidance of similar marine casualties; it is not the purpose of an investigation to attribute blame or fault (MS(IMC)A 2000, s 25). An investigation by the Board must cease if the Minister directs that a *Tribunal of Inquiry* be established to inquire into a marine casualty (MS(IMC)A 2000, s 39). Such an Inquiry has all the powers of a judge of the District Court and of an investigator under the 2000 Act (MS(IMC)A 2000, s 38). See SI No 252 of 2000.

marine incident. The Minister was empowered to order a formal public inquiry into a marine incident: Merchant Shipping Act 1894, s 466 (eg the inquiry into the sinking of a fishery patrol vessel near Ballycotton in 1990). The Merchant Shipping (Investigation of Marine Casualties) Act 2000, s 6 has repealed s 466 of the 1894 Act. For new provisions, see MARINE CASUALTY.

marine insurance contract. A contract whereby an insurer, in consideration of a premium (qv) paid to him, agrees to indemnify the insured against marine losses ie losses incident to *marine adventure:* Marine Insurance Act 1906, s 1. A contract of marine insurance is inadmissible in evidence unless it is embodied in a marine policy in accordance with the 1906 Act (MIA 1906, s 22). A marine policy is assigned by indorsement thereon or in other customary manner (MIA 1906, s 50). See also Finance Act 1959, ss 75 and 80. [Bibliography: Hill UK; Ivamy UK; McGuffie, Fugeman & Gray UK]. See MARINE ADVENTURE.

marital coercion. Formerly, the rebuttable presumption at common law that a married woman who committed a felony (qv), other than murder, in the presence of her husband, committed it under his coercion and was not guilty of an offence. It has been held that the defence of marital coercion did not survive the enactment of the 1937

Constitution because it offended the guarantee of equality before the law in that a similar defence was not available to a husband: *The State (DPP) v Walsh and Conneely* [1981] IR 294. See also *The People (DPP) v Murray* [1977] IR 360. [Bibliography: Charleton (4)]. See EQUALITY BEFORE THE LAW.

marital privacy. The implied constitutional right of a husband and wife to decide how many children they wish to have, if any: *McGee v Attorney-General* [1974] IR 284. In this case it was held that the prohibition of the importation of artificial contraceptives by the Criminal Law (Amendment) Act 1935, s 17 was an unjustified invasion of the plaintiff's right to privacy in her marital affairs. See *Maguire v Drury* [1995] 1 ILRM 108, HC. See WITNESS, COMPETENCE OF.

marital rape. At common law a husband could not be guilty of the rape of his wife. 'By their mutual matrimonial consent and contract the wife hath given herself ... unto her husband which she cannot retract': Hale CJ (IPC 629) [1736]. The marital exemption for rape has been abolished: Criminal Law (Rape) (Amendment) Act 1990, s 5. Criminal proceedings can only be instituted by or with the consent of the Director of Public Prosecutions. The first case alleging the rape of a wife by her husband took place in the Central Criminal Court in 1993; the husband was acquitted: *Irish Times*, 9 December 1993.

marital status. (1) Means single, married, separated, divorced or widowed: Employment Equality Act 1998, s 2(1). An employer is prohibited from discriminating against an employee or prospective employee on the grounds of marital status ie treating one person more or less favourably on the grounds of marital status (EEA 1998, ss 8(1) and 6). This does not prohibit an employer marking a change in the marital status of an employee with a benefit (EEA 1998, s 34(1)(c)). Harassment on the grounds of marital status is also prohibited (EEA 1998, s 14A inserted by Equality Act 2004, s 8). See *Eagle Star Insurance v A Worker* [1998] ELR 306, LC. See DISCRIMINATION; FAMILY STATUS; HARASSMENT; INTERVIEW BOARD.

(2) Means being single, married, separated, divorced or widowed: Equal Status Act 2000, s 2(1). A person must not discriminate on *marital status* grounds in disposing of goods or premises or in providing

a service or accommodation; treating one person less favourably than another person, in a comparable situation, because they are of different marital status is discrimination: Equal Status Act 2000, ss 5, 6 and 3, amended by Equality Act 2004, ss 48–49. Having a reasonable preferential charge for persons together with their children, or for married couples, does not constitute discrimination (ESA 2000, s 16(1)(a)). [Bibliography: Reid M].

(3) A *declaration* may be obtained from the court as to the marital status of a person eg that a marriage was valid at its inception or at a specified date or that a foreign divorce, annulment or legal separation is entitled or not entitled to recognition in the State: Family Law Act 1995, s 29. For High Court procedure, see RSC Ord 70A inserted by SI No 343 of 1997. For the rules governing a *Family Law Civil Bill* seeking a declaration of marital status, see Circuit Court Rules 2001 Ord 59, r 4(4)(e).The presence of a proper *contradictor* (qv) is not absolutely essential to the making of a declaration as to marital status: *G McG v DW & AR (No 2)* [2000] 1 ILRM 121, HC (under appeal). See PENSION SCHEME AND DISCRIMINATION.

maritime area. See DUMPING AT SEA.

maritime boundaries. The *maritime boundaries* of a county, city or town is the high water mark for the time being, unless such boundary already extends beyond that mark: Local Government Act 2001, s 227(1). Reclaimed land and structures are part of a local authority area (LGA 2001, s 227(2). See also Boundary Survey (Ireland) Act 1854. For example under that Act, see Maritime Boundaries (County of Cork) Order 1990. See also Boundary Survey (Ireland) Act 1859.

maritime claims. A shipowner and a salvor may limit their liability in respect of *maritime claims* ie claims in respect of loss of life or personal injury or loss of or damage to property occurring on board or in direct connection with the operation of the ship or with salvage operations and consequential loss: Merchant Shipping (Liability of Shipowners and Others) Act 1996, ss 6–17 and Sch 1; Convention on Liability for Maritime Claims 1976, done at London on 19 November 1976.

A person cannot limit his liability if it is proved that the loss resulted from his personal act or omission, committed with the intent to cause such loss, or recklessly and with knowledge that such loss would probably result (Convention on Liability for Maritime Claims 1976, art 4). The right to limit liability extends to *non-seagoing ships* also (MS(LSO)A 1996, s 10). However, the right to limit liability does not apply to claims in respect of the raising or removing of a ship which is sunk, wrecked, stranded or abandoned (MS(LSO)A 1996, s 11; this is in lieu of s 53 of the Merchant Shipping (Salvage and Wreck) Act 1993 which section is repealed).

A carrier is liable for the damage suffered as a result of the death of or personal injury to a passenger and the loss of or damage to baggage, if the incident which caused the damage occurred in the course of the carriage and was due to the fault or neglect of the carrier, or of his servants or agents acting within the scope of their employment: MS(LSO)A 1996, ss 18–29 and Sch 2; Convention relating to the Carriage of Passengers and their Luggage by Sea 1974, done at Athens on 13 December 1974. A carrier is not liable for certain valuables (eg moneys, gold, jewellery, works of art) unless when deposited for the agreed purpose of safekeeping (Convention relating to the Carriage of Passengers and their Luggage by Sea 1974, art 5). The 1974 Convention limits liability for damage (arts 7–8), but this limitation is without prejudice to the limits in the 1976 Convention (MS(LSO)A 1996, s 29).

The owner of a ship is not liable for any loss or damage: (a) caused by fire on board the ship, or (b) in respect of any gold, silver, watches, jewels or precious stones which were not declared in the *bill of lading* (qv) or otherwise in writing (MS(LSO)A 1996, s 38).

maritime jurisdiction. The *territorial seas* of the State is that portion of the sea which lies between the *baseline* and the *outer limit of the territorial seas*: Maritime Jurisdiction Act 1959, s 2. The seas are stated to be included in the island of Ireland (qv): 1937 Constitution, art 2. See also Criminal Justice (Illicit Traffic by Sea) Act 2003, s 28.

The outer limit of the territorial seas is the line every point of which is at a distance of three (now twelve) nautical miles (qv) from the nearest point of the baseline: (MJA 1959, s 3). The baseline is low water mark: (a) on the coast of the mainland or of any island, or (b) on any *low tide elevation* situated wholly or partly at a distance not exceeding three (now twelve) nautical miles from the mainland or an island (MJA 1959, s 4). The formerly specified three miles is now twelve miles: Maritime Jurisdiction (Amendment) Act 1988, s 2.

Every offence committed within the territorial seas or inland waters (qv) is an offence within the jurisdiction of the State (MJA 1959, ss 10–11). Control of fishing in waters in the Foyle area is vested in the Foyle Fisheries Commission by virtue of the Foyle Fisheries Act 1952 (Irish) and the Foyle Fisheries Act (NI) 1952 (UK). Subject to international law, ships of all states have the right of innocent passage through the territorial seas: United Nations Convention on the Law of the Sea 1982, art 18. See also Maritime Jurisdiction (Amendment) Act 1964; Jurisdiction of Courts (Maritime Conventions) Act 1989. See CONTINENTAL SHELF; FOYLE CARLINGFORD AND IRISH LIGHTS COMMISSION; LOW-TIDE ELEVATION; INLAND WATERS; FISHERY LIMITS, EXCLUSIVE.

maritime lien. A privileged claim upon property in respect of service done to it or injury caused by it; it is carried into effect by the process of arrest: *The Tervaete* [1922] P.259. The principal maritime liens are in respect of: salvage, seamen's wages, and damage. A maritime lien cannot be enforced by a salvor (qv) where security for the salvor's claim has been tendered or provided: Merchant Shipping (Salvage and Wreck) Act 1993, ss 33–34. It is customary for the insurers of vessels and cargo to give undertakings to pay any future salvage awards so that the salved property may be released to its owners.

maritime perils. The perils subsequent on, or incidental to, the navigation of the sea, ie *perils of the sea* (qv), fire, war perils, pirates, rovers, thieves, captures, seizures, restraints, and detainments of princes and peoples, jettisons (qv) and barratry (qv): Marine Insurance Act 1906, s 3. See MARINE INSURANCE CONTRACT.

mark. See TRADE MARK.

mark, distinctive. See DISTINCTIVE MARK.

market. At common law, a market is a franchise (qv) or privilege to establish meetings of persons to buy and sell, derived from a royal grant or from prescription (qv) which implied such a grant. Local authorities are empowered to provide market places in their area: Public Health (Ireland) Act 1878, s 103. See *Bridgeman v Limerick Corporation* [2001] 2 IR 517, SC.

market, internal. See INTERNAL MARKET.

market overt. [Open market]. An open public and legally constituted market; a market held on days prescribed by charter, statute or custom. Where goods are sold in *market overt,* according to the usage of the market, the buyer acquires a good title to the goods, provided he buys them in good faith and without notice of any defect or want of title on the part of the seller: Sale of Goods Act 1893, s 22. See RESTITUTION OF POSSESSION.

market rent. Means the rent which a willing tenant not already in occupation would give and a willing landlord would take for the dwelling, in each case on the basis of vacant possession being given, and having regard to: (a) the other terms of the tenancy, and (b) the letting values of dwellings of a similar size, type and character to the dwelling and situated in a comparable area to that in which it is situated: Residential Tenancies Act 2004, s 24. The definition is based on the definition of 'gross rent' in the Landlord and Tenant (Amendment) Act 1980, s 23(5). See RENT SETTING; RENT REVIEW.

market right. A right conferred by franchise (qv) or statute to hold a fair or market, that is to say, a concourse of buyers and sellers to dispose of commodities: Casual Trading Act 1995, s 1. A local authority may acquire any market right in its functional area by agreement or compulsorily and it may extinguish a market right owned by it (CTA 1995, ss 7–8). See also Public Health (Ireland) Act 1878. A market right is extinguished if it remains unexercised for ten years or more (CTA 1995, s 7); this provision had regard to the decision in *Skibbereen UDC v Quill* [1986] IR 123 and [1986] ILRM 170.

market value. (1) In relation to a listed security, means the last price for that security published in the Irish Stock Exchange *Daily Official List* on the relevant date: Listing Rules (*definitions,* as amended by Irish Stock Exchange Ltd).

(2) In relation to tax on gifts and inheritances, means the price the property would fetch if sold in the open market in circumstances calculated to result in the best price for the vendor: Capital Acquisitions Tax Consolidation Act 2003, s 26. An appeal in relation to the market value of real property lies to the Land Values Reference Committee under the machinery provided under the Property Values (Arbitration and Appeals) Act 1960 (CATCA 2003, s 66).

(3) In relation to land and certain proceedings relating thereto, means the price that would have been obtained in respect of the unencumbranced fee simple were the land to have been sold on the open market, in the year immediately preceding the bringing of the proceedings concerned, in such manner and subject to such conditions as might reasonably be calculated to have resulted in the vendor obtaining the best price for the land: Civil Liability and Courts Act 2004 s.45. See CIRCUIT COURT.

marketable title. As regards freehold land, a title which goes back 40 years: Vendor and Purchasers Act 1874, s 1; also known as a *good* title. A contract for the sale of land may stipulate that the title may commence at a more recent date. If the vendor shows the title which he is required to prove, he is said to show a *good* title. The conveyance or document with which the title commences is called the *root of title* (qv). See *Maconchy v Clayton* [1898] 1 IR 291. See CONVEYANCE; OPEN CONTRACT.

marking order. An order which the Minister may make to compel that goods be marked with or accompanied by any information. The Minister may also regulate or prohibit the supply of goods in relation to which the requirements are not complied with. It is an offence to contravene a *marking order*. See Consumer Information Act 1978, s 10.

marriage. The voluntary union of one man and one woman to the exclusion of all others: *Hyde v Hyde* [1868] LR 1 PD 130. The State pledges itself to guard with special care the institution of marriage, in which the family is founded, and to protect it against attack: 1937 Constitution, art 41(3)(1); *Murphy v Attorney-General* [1982] IR 241; *Muckley v Ireland* [1986] ILRM 364; *Greene v Minister for Agriculture* [1990] ILRM 364, HC.

A marriage in the State may be solemnised by, and only by, a registered solemniser: Civil Registration Act 2004, s 51. Marriages abroad must comply with the *lexi loci celebrationis* (qv). The parties to a marriage must not be within the *prohibited degrees* of relationships either by *consanguinity* (qv) or *affinity* (qv); there are twenty-eight prohibited relationships: Marriage Act 1835; Deceased Wife's Sister's Marriage Act 1907; Deceased Brother's Widow's Marriage Act 1921.

An agreement made in consideration of marriage must be evidenced in writing: Statute of Frauds (Ireland) 1695, s 2. An agreement which subverts the sanctity of marriage is void at common law eg marriage broker contracts: *Williamson v Gihan* [1805] 2 Scholes Lefroy 357. A second marriage between the same spouses is not rendered void by virtue of a first marriage between them: *B v R* [1995] 1 ILRM 491, HC.

Full age is conferred on an infant by virtue of marriage: Age of Majority Act 1985, s 2. A contract which provides that one party is to pay a certain sum to support the other in the event of future separation is void as weakening the marriage bond: *Marquess of Westmeath v Marquess of Salisbury* [1830] 5 Bli (ns). [Bibliography: Duncan & Scully; Power C; Shannon; Shatter]. See COMMON LAW MARRIAGE; CONJUGAL RIGHTS, RESTITUTION OF; CONSORTIUM; EUROPEAN CONVENTION ON HUMAN RIGHTS; JACTITATION OF MARRIAGE; MARRIAGE, NULLITY OF; MARRIAGE REGISTER; MARITAL STATUS; PRE-NUPTIAL AGREEMENT.

marriage, impediment to. There is an impediment to a marriage if: (a) the marriage would be void by virtue of the Marriage Act 1835 as amended by the Marriage (Prohibited Degrees of Relationship Acts 1907 and 1921), (b) one of the parties to the marriage is, or both are, already married, (c) one or both of the parties would be under the age of 18 years on the date of intended solemnisation and an exemption has not been granted under s 33 of the Family Law Act 1995, (d) the marriage would be void by virtue of the Marriage of Lunatics Act 1811, or (e) both parties are of the same sex: Civil Registration Act 2004, s 2(2). The persons intending to marry must attend at the office of the registrar not less than five days beforehand and make a declaration that there is no impediment to the said marriage (CRA 2004, s 46). See PROHIBITED DEGREES.

marriage, notice of. (1) A spouse may register in the Registry of Deeds pursuant to the Registration of Deeds Act, 1707 (in the case of *unregistered* property) or under the Registration of Title Act 1964 (in the case of *registered* land) a notice stating that he is married to any person, being a person having an interest in such property or land: Family Home Protection Act 1976, s 12(1). The fact that notice of a marriage has not been registered does not give rise to any inference as to the non-existence of a marriage (FHPA 1976, s 12(2)). No stamp duty, Registry of Deeds fee or land registration fee is payable in respect of any such notice (FHPA 1976, s 12(3)).

Where the notice is entered in the Land Registry, the notice may be removed subsequently when the notice no longer affects the property (eg by agreement on separation) by adapting Land Registry form 71A and lodging it along with all supporting documentation. This has been recommended as good practice: 'Conveyancing Committee' in *Law Society Gazette* (December 2003) 39. A notice of marriage registered in respect of property title which is registered in the Registry of Deeds, cannot be removed from the register.

(2) A marriage solemnised in the State between persons of any age is not valid in law unless: (a) (i) the persons concerned notify any registrar of marriages in writing of their intention to so marry not less than three months prior to the date on which the marriage is to be solemnised, or (ii) exemption from this section was granted by the court before the marriage; such a exemption will not be granted unless the applicant shows that its grant is justified by serious reasons and is in their interest, and (b) the persons concerned attend at the office of that registrar not less than five days beforehand and make a declaration that there is no impediment to the said marriage: Civil Registration Act 2004, s 46. If the registrar is satisfied that these requirements are met he will give one of the parties a *marriage registration form*, which must be given to the person solemnising the marriage (CRA 2004, s 48). When the marriage has been solemnised, this form must be signed by the parties to the marriage, by the solemniser and two witnesses to the ceremony, and submitted for registration of the marriage to the registrar (CRA 2004, s 49). For previous legislation, see Family Law Act 1995, s 32 as amended by Family Law (Miscellaneous Provisions) Act 1997, s 2.

marriage, nullity of. A matrimonial action for the purpose of obtaining a judicial decree that a purported marriage is in fact null and void. A marriage may be *void* or *voidable*. A marriage may be *void* on the grounds of: (a) lack of capacity eg where one or both of the parties is within the prohibited degree of relationships, or already married, or under the age of 18

without consent of the court; or (b) non-observance of the appropriate formalities eg previously, lack of parental consent: *Ussher v Ussher* [1912] 2 IR 445; now, non-compliance with notice requirement; or (c) lack of consent eg due to duress, parental or otherwise; *Griffith v Griffith* [1944] IR 35; *S v O'S* [1978] HC; *McK (otherwise M McC) v F McC* [1982] ILRM 277; *ACL v RL* [1982] HC; *N (Otherwise K) v K* [1986] ILRM 75; *W(C) v C* [1990] IR 696; *DB(D.O'R) v N.O'R* [1991] ILRM 160, SC.

A nullity will be granted where parental or other external pressure is exerted on one or both parties to get married, such that they were prevented from forming an independent, mature decision of their own: *DC v NM* [1997] 2 IR 218, HC. The test of whether or not a consent was an informed consent is a subjective one: *MO'M v BO'C* [1996] 1 IR 208, SC.

In deciding nullity cases based on lack of consent, the court must have regard for the condition of the parties at the time when they entered into the marriage contract: *OB v R* [2000] 1 ILRM 307, HC and [1999] 4 IR 168, HC. Failure of one party before the marriage to reveal that he had attended a psychiatrist for six years, was held in this case to render the marriage null and void. Concealment by one of the parties to a marriage of a disfigurement which is only revealed after marriage, may be grounds for a decree of nullity: *BJM v CM* [1996] 2 IR 574, HC.

A medical inspector appointed to carry out a psychiatric examination of the petitioner and respondent in marriage nullity proceedings has the authority under court order to interview the parties to the proceedings, but not non-parties: *McG v F* [2001] 2 ILRM 326, SC and 1IR 599. The court held that as nullity proceedings are judicial proceedings to determine the status of the parties, it was necessary for the nullity suit to be conducted in a court of law and not in a doctor's clinic.

The Supreme Court has held that adultery, being misconduct during the course of marriage, was a ground for judicial separation, but not for nullity; the grounds for a grant of nullity could not be extended to cover concealed misconduct and other forms of misrepresentation: *PF v GO'M* [2001] 3 IR 1, SC.

A marriage may be *voidable* if either party has not the mental capacity to marry or is impotent (qv) or the marriage is not consummated (qv): *RSJ v JSJ* [1982] ILRM 263; *D v C* [1984] ILRM 173; *MF McD (Otherwise M O'R) v W O'R* [1984] HC; *DC v DW* [1987] ILRM 58; *AMN v JPC* [1988] ILRM 170.

A *void* marriage is one which never had legal effect and consequently is void *ab initio*. Its validity may be challenged by any person with a sufficient interest, even after the death of the parties; a decree of nullity is not necessary, though desirable, and children of the marriage are illegitimate (now referred to as *children whose parents are not married to each other*: Status of Children Act 1987).

A *voidable* marriage is one which is valid until it is annulled by a *decree of nullity*; its validity may be challenged only by one of the parties to the marriage during the lifetime of both; and children of the marriage are legitimate until the marriage is annulled.

Provision has been made for the father of any child of a void or voidable marriage to be the guardian of that child, if the marriage was a voidable one which was annulled after the child's conception, or in the case of a void marriage, if the father reasonably believed at the appropriate time that it was a valid marriage: Status of Children Act 1987, s 9(3).

It has been held that a valid marriage exists between parties who had entered into the contract of marriage with the intention of divorcing at a later stage: *HS v JS* [1992] ITLR (29 June) SC.

For Rules of Court, see RSC Ord 70. The Circuit Family Court now has jurisdiction to hear and determine proceedings for a decree of nullity: Family Law Act 1995, s 38, as amended by Civil Liability and Courts Act 2004, s 51. For the rules governing a *Family Law Civil Bill* seeking a decree of nullity of marriage, see Circuit Court Rules 2001 Ord 59, r 4(4)(d). Provision has been made for the establishment and maintenance by the Courts Service of a register of all decrees of nullity of marriage: Civil Registration Act 2004, ss 13(1)(g) and 59(2). For the particulars to be entered in the register, see CRA 2004, Sch 1, Pt 7. See also *O'R v B* [1995] 2 ILRM 57, HC; *AC v PJ* [1995] 2 IR 253, HC; *JS v CS* (Nullity) [1997] 2 IR 506, HC; *C(N) v McL(K)* [2002] FL 7277, CC; *MOC v MOC* [2003] FL 7809, HC; *McG(P) v F(A)* [2003] FL 7726, HC. See LRC 9 of 1984, 20 of 1985. See also Courts and Court Officers Act 1995, s 53. [Bibliography: Shatter; Duncan & Scully; Murtagh B; Walpole; Gov Pub (3)]. See CHILD, CUSTODY OF; CHILD, ILLEGITIMATE; CHURCH ANNULMENT; GUARDIAN; HOMOSEXUAL CONDUCT; PERSONALITY DISORDER; POLYGAMOUS MARRIAGE; PREGNANCY; PSYCHIATRIC DISORDER.

marriage, objection to. A person may, at any time before the solemnisation of a marriage, lodge an objection in writing with any registrar of marriages and the objection is required to state the reasons for the objection: Civil Registration Act 2004, s 58. When the objection has been investigated and has been upheld, it can lead to the registrar taking steps to ensure that the solemnisation does not take place (CRA 2004, s 58(7)). There is provision for appeal to the Circuit Family Court against such a finding. An objection on the grounds that the marriage would be void by virtue of the Marriage of Lunatics Act 1811 must be accompanied by a certificate of a registered medical practitioner supporting the objection (CRA 2004, s 58(11)).

marriage, presumption of. There is a presumption in law that persons are married to each other, when it is proved that they cohabited and were treated as married by those who knew them. Strict proof, by evidence of an apparently valid marriage ceremony, is only required in bigamy (qv) and divorce (qv) proceedings. See *Mulhern v Clery* [1930] IR 649.

marriage, registration of. There is a requirement for the establishment and maintenance of a register of all marriages taking place in the State: Civil Registration Act 2004, s 13(1)(e). When the marriage has been solemnised, the *marriage registration form* must be signed by the parties to the marriage, by the solemniser and two witnesses to the ceremony, and submitted for registration of the marriage to the registrar (CRA 2004, s 49).

A false statement in the marriage certificate does not necessarily invalidate the marriage ceremony itself: *B v R* [1995] 1 ILRM 491, HC. See also *PL v An tArd Chláraitheoir* [1995] 2 ILRM 241, HC and 2 IR 372. See MARRIAGE, NOTICE OF.

marriage, solemnisation of. A marriage in the State may be solemnised by, and only by, a registered solemniser: Civil Registration Act 2004, s 51. An tArd-Chláraitheoir is required to establish a register of solemnisers empowered to solemnise marriages and is required to refuse to register a person if he considers that: (a) the body concerned which applies for registration of persons is not a religious body, (b) the form of marriage ceremony has not been officially approved, or (c) the person is not a fit and proper person to solemnise a marriage (CRA 2004, s 53).

A registered solemniser must not solemnise a marriage unless: (a) both parties to the marriage are present, (b) two persons professing to be 18 years or over are present as witnesses, (c) the place where the solemnisation takes place is open to the public, and (d) the solemniser is satisfied that the parties to the marriage understand the nature of the marriage ceremony and the declaration to the effect that they do not know of any impediment to the marriage and that they accept each other as husband and wife (CRA 2004, s 51). There must be provision for language interpretation where any of the key parties do not have a sufficient knowledge of the language of the ceremony to understand the ceremony and that language (CRA 2004, s 51(6)). The parties to a marriage ceremony solemnised in accordance with the 2004 Act are to be taken as married to each other when both of them have made a declaration in the presence of each other, the registered solemniser and the two witnesses that they accept each other as husband and wife (CRA 2004, s 51(7)).

There is provision for an appeal to the Minister against a refusal or cancellation of registration of solemnisers, with an onward appeal to the Circuit Court (CRA 2004, s 56).

marriage bar. Generally understood to refer to the previous requirement on women to retire from employment in the civil service on marriage: Civil Service Regulations Act 1956, s 10. The marriage bar was abolished by the Civil Service (Employment of Married Women) Act 1973, s 3. However, only widows or married women who were not supported by their husbands could apply for reinstatement to the civil service (CS(EMW)A 1973, s 4 amending s 11 of the CSRA 1956). These requirements have been held to be discriminatory: *A worker (Moran) v Department of Finance* [1993] ELR 129, LC. Section 11 of the 1956 Act has now been repealed thereby ending this rein-

statement provision: Civil Service Regulation (Amendment) Act 1996. See also *Aer Lingus Teo v Labour Court* [1990] ILRM 485, SC; *Caminity & Miley v Radio Telefís Éireann* [1994] ELR 1, EO.

marriage gratuity. Term applied to a payment made by an employer to an employee on the occasion of the latter's marriage. It has been held in a particular case and set of circumstances that the refusal to pay a marriage gratuity to a male employee was based on grounds other than sex: *Bank of Ireland v Kavanagh* [1990] 1 CMLR 88. See also *Curran v AIB* [1992] HC.

married woman. Previously married women had limited contractual and property rights. The capacity of a woman to contract is now unchanged upon marriage: Married Women Status Act 1957, s 2(1) ; Family Law Act 1995, s 36(6). See MATRIMONIAL PROPERTY; PRIVITY OF CONTRACT.

marry, breach of promise to. See BREACH OF PROMISE; ENGAGED COUPLE.

marshalling. The equitable doctrine under which if person A has claims against funds X and Y of person B, and person C has a claim only against fund X, A will be required to satisfy himself as far as possible out of fund Y. Marshalling has been given statutory recognition in the administration of estates of deceased persons; if debts are paid out of the permitted order, an adversely affected beneficiary may have recourse to property which should have been used to pay debts before his was resorted to. See Succession Act 1965, s 46(5).

The doctrine of marshalling cannot be relied upon as a defence to proceedings instituted by a creditor against one or more of several co-sureties, where they have separately mortgaged different properties as securities for their separate guarantees: *Lombard & Ulster Banking Ltd v Murray & Murray* [1987] ILRM 522.

Marsh's Library. The library formed by Narcissus Marsh (1638–1713), Church of Ireland Archbishop of Armagh, which he presented to the nation in 1701. It is the oldest public library in Ireland and one of the oldest in Europe. It contains works on medicine, religion, music, law, science and mathematics. Provision has been made for the Minister to appoint two additional 'governors and guardians' of the library: National Cultural Institutions Act 1997, s 63. See also SI No 8 of 1970; Finance

Act 2003, s 165. See website: *www. marshlibrary.ie*. See NATIONAL LIBRARY OF IRELAND.

martial law. Generally understood to mean the exercise of control and absolute power by military authorities during an emergency when the civil authority cannot function. There is no such power given to the military authorities in the 1937 Constitution. However, the government is empowered to take whatever steps it may consider necessary for the protection of the State in the case of an actual invasion and is given wide powers whenever there exists a *national emergency*. See INVASION; MILITARY TRIBUNALS; NATIONAL EMERGENCY.

masculine gender. See FEMININE GENDER.

mass balance. The *mass balance* of a specified substance is an expression of the relationship between the emissions of that substance from a specified process and its use or consumption in that process: Waste Management Act 1996, s 64. The Minister is empowered to make regulations requiring a person who carries out a process, development or operation to determine the mass balance. Section 64 has been repealed by the Protection of the Environment Act 2003, s 3 and Sch 2, Pt 1 but re-enacted as s 99D of the Environmental Agency Act 1992 by the PEA 2003, s 15. See WASTE.

master. (1) In relation to a barrister, means a barrister who is entered on the Register of Masters maintained by the Bar Council: *Code of Conduct for the Bar of Ireland* (December 2003) r 1.7(n). A barrister must not take a pupil unless his name is entered on the register; normally he must have completed seven years' practice (r 8.8).The duties of a Master include the duty of teaching the pupil the rules and customs of the Bar and ensuring that he has read and understands the *Code* and what is professional practice by a barrister (r 8.5). Masters must also familiarise themselves with any undertakings given by their pupils and must report any breach of such undertakings (r 8.9). See PUPIL; BARRISTER.

(2) In relation to a vessel (qv), means the person having, for the time being, the command or charge of the vessel: Merchant Shipping Act 1992, s 2(1). The master of a vessel must render assistance to any person in danger of being lost at sea: Merchant Shipping (Salvage and Wreck) Act 1993, ss 2(1) and 23(1). The master is required

to co-operate with a salvor during the course of a salvage operation, to exercise due care to prevent damage to the environment, and to accept re-delivery when reasonably requested by the salvor to do so (MS(SW)A 1993, s 21). However, the master may, expressly and reasonably, prohibit a salvage operation, in which event no salvage reward will be payable (MS(SW)A 1993, s 32). See also Maritime Security Act 2004, s 1(1). See EMPLOYER.

Master of High Court. An office attached to the High Court, created by the Court Officers Act 1926, s 3, the holder of which is authorised by law to exercise limited functions and powers of a judicial nature within the scope of art 37 of the 1937 Constitution: Courts and Court Officers Act 1995, s 24.

The Master has a wide jurisdiction in matters which come within that High Court's jurisdiction, eg orders made on motions of course (qv), orders for discovery (qv) of documents, orders giving liberty to serve third-party notices (qv): Courts (Supplemental Provisions) Act 1961, Sch 8; RSC Ord 63. The Master is prohibited from exercising any function, power or jurisdiction in respect of certain matters eg injunctions, bail, criminal proceedings, custody of children, ward of courts, infant settlements (CCOA 1995, s 25(2)). All orders of the Master can be appealed to the High Court (CCOA 1995, s 25(5)).

An order of *mandamus* may issue against the Master: *Elwyn (Cottons) Ltd v Master of the High Court* [1989] ITLR (22 May). The Supreme Court has held that the Master has full power to waive any technical breach of the rules as regards discovery of documents, if the object of the rule has in reality been achieved: *Taylor v Clonmel Healthcare Ltd* [2004] FL 8766, SC. See also Referendum Act 1994, s 41. [Bibliography: Barron JJ]. See FOREIGN JUDGMENTS, ENFORCEMENT OF; LIQUIDATED DAMAGES.

material change. A refusal to grant planning permission for any development which consists of or includes the making of any *material change* in the use of any structure or other land, does not attract compensation: Planning and Development Act 2000, s 191 and Sch 3, para 1. See DEVELOPMENT PLAN; HOUSE; PLANNING PERMISSION.

material contracts. In a prospectus offering shares in a company for sale to the public, all material contracts must be disclosed, including the dates, parties and general nature of the contracts. A contract is material if it has been entered into by the company within five years of the prospectus being issued, and is not a contract entered into in the ordinary course of the business carried on or intended to be carried on by the company: Companies Act 1963, Sch 3, reg 14. See *Jury v Stoker* [1882] 9 LR Ir 385. See Listing Rules 2000, para 6C.7, 6C.20, 6J.7, 6J.14. See PROSPECTUS.

material fact. A fact which a person has a duty to disclose to an insurer; it is any fact which could affect the renewal of insurance or the premium. See *Aro Road & Land Vehicles v Insurance Corporation of Ireland* [1986] IR 403, SC. See FACT; PREMIUM; UBERRIMAE FIDEI.

materials. See SERVICES, SUPPLY OF.

maternity benefit. The social welfare benefit to which a woman is entitled for a 14 (now 18) week period, provided she meets certain conditions eg certificate from a registered medical practitioner: Social Welfare (Consolidation) Act 1993, ss 37–41 as amended (eg Social Welfare Act 1997, s 10). The duration of payment of maternity benefit was increased in 2001 from 14 to 18 weeks: Social Welfare Act 2001, s 12. The woman may also be entitled to '*health and safety*' benefit (SW(C)A 1993, ss 41A–41F). See also Social Welfare (Miscellaneous Provisions) Act 2002, s 9. For changes to maternity benefit consequent on proposed amendments to 'maternity leave', eg reducing to two weeks the minimum period of benefit which must be taken before the expected date of birth, see Social Welfare (Miscellaneous Provisions) Act 2004, s 8. See also Pensions Act 1990, s 81A as amended by substitution by Social Welfare (Miscellaneous Provisions) Act 2004, s 22(1).

maternity care. 'Doctors who agree to undertake antenatal and obstetric care should keep the patient informed about the arrangements for delivery': Medical Council, *A Guide to Ethical Conduct and Behaviour* (6th edn, 2004) para 3.4.

maternity leave. The leave of at least 18 weeks to which a pregnant employee is entitled, either 18 weeks consecutively or 18 weeks, part of which is postponed: Maternity Protection Act 1994, s 8, as amended by Maternity Protection (Amendment) Act 2004, s 2. The employee is required to give written notice to the employer at least four weeks before the commencement of the leave, together with a medical certificate confirming the pregnancy and specifying the expected week of confinement (qv) (MPA 1994, s 9). The employee may choose the exact date of leave, but it must cover the two weeks before and the four weeks after the confinement (MPA 1994, s 10 amended by MP(A)A 2004, s 3). Also the employee is entitled to eight weeks *additional* unpaid maternity leave at the end of her maternity leave (MPA 1994, s 14 amended by MP(A)A 2004, s 5).

There is now provision, subject to the agreement of the employer, for: (a) the termination of *additional* maternity leave in the event of the sickness of the mother, in which case the absence from work is treated in the same way as any absence due to sickness; and (b) the postponement of maternity leave or of *additional* maternity leave in the event of the hospitalisation of the child (MPA 1994, ss 14A and 14B inserted by MP(A)A 2004, ss 6 and 7).

A pregnant employee is entitled to time off work, without loss of pay, for the purpose: (a) of receiving ante-natal or post-natal care, and (b) of attending ante-natal classes (MPA 1994, s 15, and s 15A inserted by MP(A)A 2004, s 8). The expectant father is entitled, once only, to time off from work, without loss of pay, to attend with the pregnant employee the last two ante-natal classes. An employee who is breastfeeding is entitled, without loss of pay, at the option of her employer, to either time off from work or a reduction of working hours, for the purpose of breastfeeding (MPA 1994, s 15B inserted by MP(A)A 2004, s 9).

The European Court of Justice has held that a worker should be able to take her annual leave during a period other than the period of maternity leave: *Merino Gómez v Continental Industrias del Caucho SA* [2004] Case C-342/01, 18 March 2004, ECJ. In this case the worker's maternity leave coincided with a period of annual leave in her workshop, which had been fixed in a collective agreement. The exclusion of three weeks of maternity leave from a bonus scheme, partly based on attendance at work, was held by the Labour Court not to be discriminatory: *Gallagher (Dublin) Ltd v SIPTU* [1998] ELR 98, LC.

An occupational pension scheme may make special provision in relation to maternity leave: Pensions Act 1990, s 72. A dispute in relation to maternity leave is heard by a Rights Commissioner (MPA 1994, s 31 amended by MP(A)A 2004, s 21). Where in specified proceedings, facts are established by an employee from which it may be presumed that there has been direct or indirect discrimination in relation to that person, it is a requirement for the respondent to prove the contrary (MPA 1994, s 33A inserted by MP(A)A 2004, s 22). The 2004 Act revokes the European Communities (Burden of Proof in Gender Discrimination Cases) Regulations 2001, SI No 337 of 2001, in so far as they apply to these proceedings.

See Organisation of Working Time Act 1997, s 15(4)(b). See Maternity Protection (Maximum Compensation) Regulations 1999, SI No 134 of 1999. See Maternity Protection (Extension of Periods of Leave) Order 2001, SI No 29 of 2001, revoked by MP(A)A 2004, s 26, as its provisions have been incorporated in the Act. See *Orr v Stylus Ltd* [1991] ELR 25, EAT. See *Hoffman v Barmer Ersatzkasse* [1984] ECR 3047; *Flynn v Garda Commissioner* [1995] ELR 129, EO; *Gillespie v Northern Health and Social Services Board* [1996] IRLR 214; *Coffey v Byrne* [1997] ELR 230, EAT. See JOB-SHARING; NATAL CARE ABSENCE; PARENTAL LEAVE; PROTECTIVE LEAVE; PREGNANCY.

maternity leave, returning from. An employee on maternity leave is on '*protected leave*' (qv): Maternity Protection Act 1994, s 21 amended by Maternity Protection (Amendment) Act 2004, s 13. The employee is entitled to return after the birth to her job to the same employer and on the same terms as before, provided she notifies the employer in writing at least four weeks before the date on which she expects to return to work (MPA 1994, ss 26–29 amended by MP(A)A 2004, ss 18–20). Previously, failure to comply with giving notice in writing, denied the employee of the right to return; although a contractual obligation may have been established by conduct in respect of previous maternity leave: *Scott v Yeates & Sons* [1992] ELR 83, EAT. Now, the Employment Appeals Tribunal or a Rights Commissioner may extend the time for giving notification (MPA 1994, s 28(2)).

The employer can, however, provide alternative work, provided the terms and conditions of the new contract are not less favourable to the employee than her former contract and the work is suitable in relation to the employee concerned (MPA 1994, s 27 amended by MP(A)A 2004, s 19). Prior to this amendment it was sufficient if the new contract was not '*substantially*' less favourable to the employee: *Leech v PMPA Insurance Co Ltd* P13/1982; *Tighe v Travenol Laboratories Ltd EAT* P14/1986. See also *Maguire v Aer Lingus* [2001] ELR 355, RC. The 2004 Act amendments also provide that the employee returning from protective leave is entitled to any improvements to which she would have been entitled, had she not been on protected leave. See PROTECTIVE LEAVE.

matricide. The crime of murder (qv) of one's mother.

matrimonial communications, privilege of. See PRIVILEGE, MATRIMONIAL COMMUNICATIONS.

matrimonial home. Under proposed legislation in 1993, existing and future matrimonial homes and household chattels would vest in both spouses as *joint tenants*, the surviving spouse acquiring the interest of both: Matrimonial Home Bill 1993. The Bill was found to be unconstitutional as it interfered with the constitutional family right of a married couple to make a joint decision as to the ownership of a matrimonial home: *In the matter of the Matrimonial Home Bill 1993* [1994] 1 ILRM 241, SC and 1 IR 305.

matrimonial matters. Provision has been made to give effect in Ireland to Council Regulation (EC) No 00/1347 of 29 May 2000 on the jurisdiction and the recognition and enforcement of judgments in matrimonial matters and in matters of parental responsibility for children of both spouses: European Communities (Judgments in Matrimonial Matters and Matters of Parental Responsibility) Regulations 2001, SI No 472 of 2001.

It is inappropriate for a solicitor or a firm of solicitors to represent both parties in any matrimonial/relationship dispute: *A Guide to Professional Conduct of Solicitors in Ireland* (2002) App 4, para 33.

matrimonial property. A Circuit Court judge has held that there was no concept of *matrimonial property* in Irish law as there was in other legal systems: *M v M* (18 June 2001, unreported)

Disputes between husband and wife as to the title to, or possession of, any property, may be resolved by the courts as the courts think proper and just: Family Law Act 1995, s 36; Family Law (Divorce) Act 1996, s 15(1)(b).

When a wife makes payments towards the purchase of a house which is in the sole name of the husband, or the repayment of the mortgage instalments, he becomes a trustee (qv) for her of a share in the house, the size of the share depending on the size of her contribution of which she becomes the beneficial owner: *Conway v Conway* [1976] IR 254. See also *EN v RN and MC* [1992] ITLR (27 January), SC. An extension of the circumstances in which a wife may claim a beneficial interest in the family home to include a situation where she made no direct or indirect financial contribution, was not upheld: *L v L* [1992] ILRM 115, SC.

However, on granting a decree of *judicial separation* (qv) or *divorce* (qv), the court has wide powers to make orders affecting matrimonial property, eg an order for the sale of property; a property adjustment order; an order conferring a right to occupy the family home to the exclusion of the other spouse; an order extinguishing succession rights: Family Law Act 1995, ss 5–22; Family Law (Divorce) Act 1996, ss 14–15.

Where an allowance is made by one spouse to another for the purpose of meeting household expenses, the property acquired by it belongs to the spouses as joint owners, in the absence of any agreement to the contrary: Family Law (Maintenance of Spouses and Children) Act 1976, s 21 as amended by Courts and Court Officers Act 2002, s 19. Where an agreement to marry is terminated, the rights of the previously engaged persons to any property, are governed by the rules applicable to matrimonial property: Family Law Act 1981, s 5. See *Wall v Wall* [1986] HC; *DMcC v M McC* [1986] ILRM 1. See LRC 1 of 1980. See *Leahy* in (1993) 3 ISLR 65. [Bibliography: Walpole]. See FAMILY HOME; HOUSEHOLD CHATTELS.

mature student. A person of not less than 23 years of age or such other age as may stand specified from time to time by the Minister; a local authority is empowered to make grants to mature students for the purpose of assisting them to attend

approved institutions: Local Authorities (Higher Education Grants) Act 1992, ss 2–3.

maturity. The time when a *bill of exchange* (qv) becomes due.

maxims of equity. See EQUITY, MAXIMS OF.

maximum prices order. See PRICE CONTROL.

may. Many statutes have provisions empowering a Minister to make regulations eg '*may* by regulation provide for any matter referred to in this Act as prescribed or to be prescribed': Competition Act 1991, s 23(1) (now Competition Act 2002, s 52(1)). *May* is purely permissive: *Cronin v Competition Authority* [1998] 2 ILRM 51, SC. See also *Criminal Assets Bureau v Sweeney* [2001] 2 ILRM 81. HC.

Mayor. The title given to the chairman of the borough corporations of Limerick and Waterford by the Municipal Corporations (Ireland) Act 1840, s 12 and to the chairman of the borough corporation of Galway by the Local Government (Galway) Act 1937, s 3. The procedure for electing a mayor is governed by the Electoral Act 1963, s 82; Local Elections Regulations 1965, SI No 128 of 1965.

The titles of *Mayor* and *Lord Mayor*, where previously used as the title of the chairman of an elected council, are permitted to be retained, and the council is also empowered to adopt the title *Cathaoirleach*: Local Government Act 2001, s 32. There was provision for the direct election of the Mayor/Lord Mayor/Cathaoirleach in the year 2004 and from then on (LGA 2001, s 40). However, this provision was repealed in 2003: Local Government (No 2) Act 2003, s 7. See LORD MAYOR.

McKenzie friend. The term used to denote a person who is attending court for the purposes of taking notes or of making quiet suggestions to or of assisting a lay litigant during the course of a hearing, but who is not qualified as a solicitor or barrister, and who does not act as an advocate at the hearing: *McKenzie v McKenzie* [1970] 3 All ER 1034.

In the ordinary course of events, a *McKenzie friend* may attend and assist a lay litigant but may not act as an advocate: *Quinn v Bank of Ireland* [1994], SC; *RD v McGuinness* [1999] 1 ILRM 549, HC and 2 IR 411. However, such *McKenzie friend* is present in the capacity as a member of the public and, accordingly, normally will not be permitted in proceedings required to be held 'otherwise than in public' eg in matrimonial matters. To permit a *McKenzie friend* in such circumstances, the court would require overwhelming evidence that a fair hearing could not be secured in the absence of a *McKenzie friend* (*RD* case). See *The People* (*DPP*) *v DR* [1998] 2 IR 106, CCA. However, under recent legislation, nothing contained in an enactment relating to family law, may operate to prohibit a party to proceedings to which the enactment relates from being accompanied, in such proceedings, in court by another person subject to the approval of the court and any directions it may give in that behalf: Civil Liability and Courts Act 2004, s 40. See IN CAMERA; REPRESENTATIVE.

McNaghten Rules. The rules formulated in 1843 which govern the defence of insanity: *McNaghten's Case* 10 Cl & Fin 200. The rules are: (a) every man is presumed to be sane and to possess a sufficient degree of reason to be responsible for his crime until the contrary be proved; (b) to establish the defence of insanity, it must be clearly shown that, at the time of committing the act, the accused was labouring under such a disease of mind as not to know the *nature and quality* of his act, or, if he did know this, not to know that what he was doing was wrong; (c) where a criminal act is committed by a man under some *insane delusion* as to the surrounding facts, he will be under the same degree of responsibility as if the facts had been as he imagined them.

The *McNaghten* rules do not provide the sole test for determining the issue of insanity; the rules must be read as limited to the effect of insane delusions: *Doyle v Wicklow County Council* [1974] IR 55. See also *The People* (*DPP*) *v O'Mahony* [1986] ILRM 244. [Bibliography: McAuley]. See INSANITY.

m-commerce. Mobile buying and selling. See '*Upwardly Mobile*' by solicitor Paul Lambert in *Law Society Gazette* (March 2003) 14. See ELECTRONIC COMMERCE.

me judice. [In my opinion].

means. The word *means* is a word which is *prima facie* at once explanatory and restrictive, exhaustive and exclusive: *O'Neill v Murphy* [1948] IR 72. All modern Acts have an *interpretation section* in which the principal words or phrases used in the Act are defined. Where the word *means* is used

it is usually restrictive eg in the Education (Welfare) Act 2000, s 2(1) 'the Minister' is defined as '*means* the Minister for Education and Science'. Contrast with INCLUDE.

means assessment. Improvements have been made in the *assessment of means* for the purposes of social assistance payments eg disregarded in the assessment of means are, for example: travel and meal expenses, maintenance grants received under certain schemes: Social Welfare Act 2001, s 13.

Also a new method of *assessment of capital* has been introduced, for the purposes of calculating a spouse's weekly income, in order to determine whether a qualified adult allowance is payable: Social Welfare (Capital Assessment) Regulations 2000, SI No 313 of 2000. See also SI No 314 of 2000, SI No 461 of 2002, and SI No 235 of 2003. For amendments to means assessment, see Social Welfare (Miscellaneous Provisions) Act 2003, s 8.

measure, short. See METROLOGY; SHORT WEIGHT.

measure of damages. The basis on which monetary compensation for loss is ascertained in the case of an action in tort, breach of contract or breach of statutory duty. In contract, generally, the plaintiff is to be put, as far as money can do it, in the same position as if the contract had been performed: *Robinson v Harman* [1848] 1 Exch 850. The measure of damages in a breach of contract involving failure to pay a sum of money, is limited to the sum in question and interest: *Fletcher v Tayleur* [1855] 17 CB 21. Damages are limited to those which are not remote. *Exemplary* damages (qv) may be awarded as may damages for mental distress (qv). See DAMAGES; DETERIORATION; REMOTENESS OF DAMAGES; PENALTY.

measurement, legal unit of. The legal unit of measurement is the *Systeme International d'Unites* (SI) – the metric system and other units of measurement are defined relative to that system: Metrology Act 1996, ss 18–19. See also EC (Units of Measurement) Regulations 1992, SI No 255 of 1992.

Plans, drawings and maps accompanying a planning application must be in metric scale: Planning and Development Regulations 2001, SI No 600 of 2001, art 23.

The time period during which the conversion of road speed measurement signs must be converted to the metric system has been further extended to 31 December 2004: EC (Units of Measurement)

(Amendment) Regulations 2002, SI No 619 of 2002.

mechanically propelled vehicle. A vehicle intended or adapted for propulsion by mechanical means, including: (a) a bicycle or tricycle with an attachment for propelling it by mechanical power, whether or not the attachment is being used, or (b) a vehicle the means of propulsion of which is electrical or partly electrical and partly mechanical, but not including a tramcar or other vehicle running on permanent rails: Road Traffic Act 1961, s 3(1). It does not include a disabled vehicle (qv).

It is an offence to place advertising material on a mechanically propelled vehicle in a public place, otherwise than by securing the material by some mechanical means to the body of the vehicle; 'body' does not include any windscreen wiper, wiperblade, mirror or aerial: Litter Pollution Act 1997, s 19(2) as substituted by Protection of the Environment Act 2003, s 56(b). It is permissible to paint, emboss, inscribe or apply by any method of transfer letters, figures or images on or to the body of a vehicle.

Under draft legislation, it is proposed to create a new offence of supplying a mechanically propelled vehicle to any person under the age of 16 years: Road Traffic Bill 2004, s 24. See 'Driving Force: 100 years of motoring law' by solicitor Robert Pierce in *Law Society Gazette* (December 2003) 10. See CAR TESTING; END-OF-LIFE VEHICLE; FUEL; ROAD TRAFFIC OFFENCES.

media merger. Means a merger or acquisition in which one or more of the undertakings involved carries on a *media business* in the State: Competition Act 2002, s 23(10). *Media business* means a business of providing: (a) a broadcasting service or a broadcasting services platform (eg a cable company), or (b) the publication of newspapers or periodicals consisting substantially of news and comment on current affairs (CA 2002, s 23(10)).

There are special procedures regarding media mergers including provision for the Minister, by order, to make the final decision on the matter, following consideration by the Competition Authority, having regard to the *relevant criteria*. These include the strength and competitiveness of media businesses indigenous to the State and the extent to which ownership and control of media businesses in the State is spread amongst individuals and other undertakings (CA 2002, ss 17 and 23). Such a Ministerial order must be laid before the Houses of the Oireachtas (CA 2002, s 25).

The provisions of CA 2002, Pt III have been applied to all mergers in which one or more of the undertakings involved carries on a media business in the State, *regardless of the turnover* of the undertakings involved: Competition Act (Section 18(5)) Order 2002, SI No 622 of 2002. See also Takeover Rules 2001, Pt B, r 12(a)(ii).

See prohibition by Minister in 1992 on a majority shareholding by Independent Newspapers plc in the Tribune Group: SI No 56 of 1992. For previous legislation, since repealed, see Mergers, Takeovers and Monopolies (Control) Act 1978, s 2(5) and Mergers, Takeovers and Monopolies (Newspapers) Order 1979, SI No 17 of 1979. [Bibliography: Lucey]. See IRISH TAKEOVER PANEL; MERGER/TAKE-OVER.

mediation. A voluntary process of dispute resolution whereby an independent third party assists the parties to the dispute to reach a settlement. It is a more positive form of *conciliation* (qv) in which the third party recommends solutions which the parties are free to accept or reject. In practice, the difference between *conciliation* and *mediation* may be difficult to draw. Contrast with ARBITRATION and ADJUDICATION where the parties hand over, either voluntarily or compulsorily, the determination of their dispute to a third party, generally with the understanding that they will abide by the outcome.

The *Centre for Dispute Resolution* is an independent non-profit-making organisation, supported by membership of industry and professional advisers and part financed by the EU, with the objective of settling business disputes by mediation. CDR, 79 Merrion Square, Dublin 2. Tel: (01) 661 3929; fax: (01) 661 8706; email: *cdri@indigo.ie*. See 'It's good to talk' by solicitor Evlynne Gilvarry in *Law Society Gazette* (January/February 2002) 18; 'Tough Talking' by Michael Williams in *Law Society Gazette* (July 2003) 12; 'Commercial Mediation' by Klaus Reichert BL in *Bar Review* (July 2003) 167 and (July 2004) 126; 'Recent UK caselaw on Mediation' by Mary Bunyan BL in *Bar Review* (December 2003) 266. See '*A Guide to Professional Conduct of Solicitors in Ireland*' (2002) App 4, para 6. See Education for Persons with Special Educational Needs Act 2004, s 38. See ALTERNATIVE DISPUTES RESOLUTION; CONCILIATION;

DIRECTOR OF THE EQUALITY TRIBUNAL; DISCRIMINATION; JUDICIAL SEPARATION; LABOUR COURT; PRIVATE RESIDENTIAL TENANCIES BOARD.

mediation conference. A meeting of the parties to a *personal injuries action*, ordered by the court, to discuss and attempt to settle the action: Civil Liability and Courts Act 2004, s 15. There is provision for the chairperson of the mediation conference to make a report to the court and for the court to order a party, who failed to comply with a direction to attend the mediation conference, to pay the costs of the action incurred after the giving of the direction (CLCA 2004, s 16). See PERSONAL INJURIES ACTION.

mediation in tenancy disputes. In a tenancy dispute which has been referred to the *Private Residential Tenancies Board* for resolution, if agreement is not reached as a result of initial communications by the Board with the parties, the Board will normally invite the parties to resolve the matter through mediation and if they agree the Board arranges mediation by a person appointed by it from its panel of mediators: Residential Tenancies Act 2004, ss 93 and 164(4). The objective of mediation is to have the issue or issues between the parties resolved by agreement between them without further recourse to the other dispute resolution procedures under the Act being needed (RTA 2004, s 95). The mediator is required to inquire fully into each relevant aspect of the dispute concerned, provide to, and receive from, each party such information as is appropriate and generally make such suggestions to each party and take such other actions as he considers appropriate with a view to achieving the objective.

The mediator is required to prepare a report and submit it to the Director of the Board, containing: (a) a statement of what matters, if any, relating to the dispute are agreed by the parties to be fact, (b) a summary of the matter or matters, if any, whether they go in whole or part to resolving the dispute or not, agreed to by the parties (and this summary must be contained in a document signed by each of the parties acknowledging that the matter or those matters are agreed to by them), and (c) relevant particulars in relation to the conduct of the mediation (including particulars in relation to the number and duration of sessions held by the mediator and the persons who attended any such session) and a list of any documents submitted to the mediator (but without disclosing any of their contents) (RTA 2004, s 95(4)).

The Board is required to furnish the parties with a copy of any agreement referred to in the mediator's report with a notice asking them to confirm that agreement within 21 days (RTA 2004, s 96). Unless notified during that period that the agreement no longer exists, the Board will proceed to make a determination order reflecting it within the following seven days. If an agreement no longer exists or never existed, the Board will refer the dispute to the Tenancy Tribunal for determination at the request of either or both of the parties (RTA 2004, s 96(6)).

A mediator must comply with certain requirements in relation to the disclosure of conflicts of interests, the manner in which he conducts himself and the maintenance of the absolute confidentiality of the proceedings (RTA 2004, ss 101 and 112). The Board may appoint a person as both a mediator and an adjudicator (RTA 2004, s 164(3)). A mediator is empowered to enter and inspect any dwelling to which a dispute relates by giving at least 24 hours notice of that intention (RTA 2004, s 111). See COSTS IN CIVIL PROCEEDINGS; DETERMINATION ORDER; RENT; RENT ARREARS; TENANCY DISPUTE; TENANCY TRIBUNAL; TITLE.

Medical Bureau of Road Safety. A body corporate, established for the purpose of: (a) the receipt and analysis of specimens of blood and urine, (b) the determination in respect of such specimens of the concentration of alcohol or drugs in the blood, (c) the issue of certificates, and (d) the provision of equipment for the taking or provision of specimens of blood and urine: Road Traffic Act 1968, ss 37–38; Road Traffic Act 1994, s 19. The certificate, issued by the Bureau under RTA 1994, s 19, has been amended to provide for the certification of the presence of a drug or drugs: Road Traffic Act (Pt III) (Amendment) Regulations 2001, SI No 173 of 2001. See *DPP v Mulvany* [2002] FL 7526, HC. See website: *www.ucd.ie/~legalmed/mbrs.html*. See BLOOD SPECIMEN; URINE SPECIMEN.

medical certificate. 'Strict accuracy is essential when issuing certificates, reports and other formal documents bearing the signature of a doctor': Medical Council, *A Guide to Ethical Conduct and Behaviour* (6th edn, 2004), para 9.1. Certificates should only be issued after the doctor has assessed the patient, they must be dated and be personally signed by the doctor. See APPRENTICE; MATERNITY LEAVE; REGISTER OF ELECTORS.

Medical Council. The body corporate of 25 members with main functions: (a) to prepare and establish the *General Register of Medical Practitioners*; (b) to satisfy itself as to the suitability of medical education and training, the standards of theoretical and practical knowledge for primary qualifications, the clinical training and experience required for the granting of a certificate of experience, and the adequacy and suitability of postgraduate education and training; and (c) to inquire into the conduct of registered medical practitioners for alleged professional misconduct or fitness to engage in the practice of medicine: Medical Practitioners Act 1978.

The Medical Council, following an inquiry and report by the *Fitness to Practise Committee* into the conduct of a registered medical practitioner, may if it so thinks fit, advise, admonish or censure the person in relation to his professional conduct: MPA 1978, s 48. The Council is entitled to attach conditions to the retention of a doctor's name on the register of medical practitioners (eg maintenance of clinical records, attendance at training courses) even where there is insufficient evidence to find the doctor guilty of professional misconduct: Medical Practitioners Act 1978, s 47; *Casey v Medical Council* [1999] 2 ILRM 481, HC and 2 IR 534.

The Medical Council is not obliged to provide legal aid to a doctor at an inquiry by the *Fitness to Practise Committee* into allegations regarding his conduct: *Ahmed v Medical Council* (2003) Irish Times, 3 May; [2003] FL 8471, SC and [2004] 1 ILRM 372. In relation to a doctor who had been found not guilty of an offence in the Circuit Criminal Court, the High Court held that the *Fitness to Practise Committee* was entitled to consider whether the doctor was a person who may have been guilty of inappropriate behaviour: *AA v Medical Council* [2002] 3 IR 1, HC.

See also Medical Practitioners (Amendment) Act 2002, ss 3 and 10, amending the 1978 Act. For recent rules made by the Medical Council, see SIs Nos 285 of 2003, 286 of 2003, and 287 of 2003. Under draft heads of a new Medical Practitioners Bill,

published in July 2004, it is proposed: (a) to have public hearings of the Fitness to Practise Committee and to have investigators appointed to assist their inquiries; (b) to empower the Medical Council to investigate persons posing as medical practitioners or providing services proper only to medical practitioners and to seek an injunction to prohibit such practice, (c) to provide for an appeal to the Ombudsman where complainants are dissatisfied with the way the Council has handled a complaint.

For the Medical Council, see website: *www.medicalcouncil.ie*. For guidelines issued by the Council, see ETHICAL CONDUCT. For further details on the Medical Council, see MEDICAL PRACTITIONER, REGISTERED. See also ABORTION; ABORTION, MEDICAL GUIDELINES; ADOPTION; ARTIFICIAL INSEMINATION; GENE THERAPY; IN-VITRO FERTILISATION; LIFE, RIGHT TO; REPRODUCTIVE MEDICINE; TRANSCRIPT.

medical deterioration. See DETERIORATION, MEDICAL.

medical device. An instrument, apparatus, appliance, material or other article which is intended: (a) to diagnose, prevent, monitor, treat or alleviate disease or an injury or handicap; or (b) to investigate or replace or modify the anatomy or a physiological process; or (c) to control conception; and which does not achieve its intended action by pharmacological, immunological or metabolic means: Irish Medicines Board Act 1995, s 4(5). The Irish Medicines Board has the function of advising the Minister on such matters relating to *medical devices* as may be referred to it (IMBA 1995, s 4(1)(m)). For regulations on active implantable medical devices, see SI No 253 of 1994.

See European Communities (In Vitro Diagnostic Medical Devices) Regulations 2001, SI No 304 of 2001; European Communities (Medical Devices) Regulations 1994, SI No 252 of 1994; (Amendment) Regulations 2001, SI No 444 of 2001; and Amendment Regulations 2002, SI No 576 of 2002 to give effect to Council Directives (EC) 2000/70 and (EC) 2001/104 as regards medical devices incorporating stable derivatives of human blood or human plasma. See also EC (Medical Devices) (Reclassification of Breast Implants) (Amendment) Regulations 2003, SI No 358 of 2003; EC (Medical Devices) (Tissues of Animal Origin) Regulations 2003, SI No 554 of 2003.

The 1994 Regulations prohibit the placing on the market or the putting into service of a medical device which is either custom-made or intended for clinical investigation, which does not bear the CE mark. See CE MARK.

medical ethics. See Medical Council, *A Guide to Ethical Conduct and Behaviour* (6th edn, 2004). See ETHICS COMMITTEE; TALLAGHT HOSPITAL.

medical examination. (1) 'Physical examinations should be conducted in the context of a thorough assessment of the patient, including relevant history-taking. Doctors should normally ask permission from a patient before making a physical examination. In the case of minors, the child's parent/guardian should be present or should give permission for the examination': Medical Council, *A Guide to Ethical Conduct and Behaviour* (6th edn, 2004) para 3.8. A doctor who is asked to examine or treat a violent patient, is under no obligation to put himself or other healthcare staff in danger but should attempt to persuade the person concerned to permit an assessment as to whether any therapy is required (para 18.1).

(2) In a personal injuries action, the plaintiff will normally submit to a medical examination conducted on behalf of the defendant. If a plaintiff refuses and the court considers this to be unreasonable and such as to prevent the just determination of the cause of action, the court is empowered to grant a stay of the plaintiff's action. See *Ross v Tar Upholstery Ltd* [1962] N I 3; *McGrory v Electricity Supply Board* [2003] ITLR (13 October) SC; also reported in *Law Society Gazette* (August/September 2003) 48. See Carolan in (1994) 4 ISLR 45. See INVALIDITY PENSION; INTIMATE EXAMINATION; MARINE CASUALTY; MINOR; PATIENT, CONSENT OF.

medical expenses. A claim for relief from income tax for medical expenses, may now include routine maternity care and the cost of educational psychological assessments and speech and language therapy for children: Finance Act 2001, s 8. Exempt from tax are gifts and inheritances taken exclusively for the purpose of discharging the medical expenses of a permanently incapacitated individual: Capital Acquisitions Tax Consolidation Act 2003, s 84.

medical insurance. The expenses which may be covered by a medical insurance policy qualifying for tax relief, have been widened; they are now the same as can be claimed under health expenses relief: Finance Act 2001, s 19. In addition, a system of *tax relief at source* (TRS) in respect of medical insurance relief, has been introduced from 6 April 2001. This enables tax payers to obtain tax relief immediately they pay their premiums. Tax relief is now also available in respect of premiums on qualifying insurance policies, designed to cover for future care needs of individuals who are unable to perform at least two activities of daily living or are suffering from severe cognitive impairment (FA 2001, s 20). See Medical Insurance (Relief at Source) Regulations 2001, SI No 129 of 2001; Long-Term Care Insurance (Relief at Source) Regulations 2001, SI No 130 of 2001.

medical jurisprudence. Forensic medicine (qv).

medical negligence. The test of liability in *medical negligence* cases relates to whether the practitioner is guilty of such failure that no practitioner of equal status would have been guilty of the same failure if acting with ordinary care; deviation from an accepted practice will only constitute negligence where such was one which no practitioner of equal status would have followed taking ordinary care; to follow a practice which has inherent defects constitutes negligent behaviour; the trial court is not to choose between alternative courses of treatment which it considers preferable, but to consider whether the course adopted complied with the standard of care; and in developing the principles in this area, the courts must take account, on the one hand, that doctors should not be obliged to carry out their work under frequent threat of unsustainable legal claims and, on the other, that in the view of the complete dependence on doctors, the law must not permit the development of lax or permissive standards: *Dunne v National Maternity Hospital* [1989] ILRM 735. SC; *Hughes v Staunton* [1991] 9 ILT Dig 52, HC.

In considering whether a general medical practitioner was negligent in the diagnosis of a patient, the Supreme Court has held that the proper test to be applied was whether the doctor did all that could be reasonably expected of a reasonably prudent general practitioner, exercising ordinary care and, if not, whether what he should have done would have led to a correct diagnosis either by him or by a specialist to whom he should have referred the patient: *Collins v Mid-Western Health Board* [2000] 2 IR 154, SC.

The failure by a medical practitioner in general practice to make a house visit to his patient when so requested may constitute professional negligence in a particular case e g where the patient was an ill pregnant mother whose condition had worsened and who failed to keep down prescribed medication: *O'Doherty v Whelan* [1993] ITLR (16 April) HC. Also it has been held that a gynaecologist was negligent in removing a woman's womb shortly after the birth of her first baby by Caesarian section, as it would have been unnecessary had he carried out certain procedures at the time; the plaintiff was awarded damages of €273,223: *Gough v Neary & Cronin* [2002] FL 6895, HC. The Supreme Court upheld the decision but reduced the damages by €50,000: *Law Society Gazette* (November 2003) 46 and *Gough v Neary* [2004] 1 ILRM 35, SC. A female patient, whose wrong toe was operated on in 2000, was awarded €50,000: *Counihan v Adelaide and Meath Hospital* [2004] 21 May 2004, HC. See also *Quilty v Neary & North Eastern Health Board* (12 May 2004, unreported) HC; Griffin v Patton (27 July 2004, unreported) SC.

'Junior doctors should never be asked to perform tasks for which they are not fully competent except under the direct supervision of senior colleagues who can take over should difficulty be encountered': Medical Council, *A Guide to Ethical Conduct and Behaviour* (6th edn, 2004) para 4.6. See also *Walsh v Family Planning Services Ltd* [1993] 11 ILT Dig 90, SC; *Maitland v Swan & Sligo Co Council* [1992] ITLR (6 July) HC; *Lindsay v Mid Western Health Board* [1993] 2 IR 147, SC; *Purdy v Lenihan and Others* [2003] FL 6940, SC. See 'Alternatives to Litigation in Medical Negligence Actions' by Maguire in 11 ILT & SJ (1993) 250; 'When doctors are bad for your health' by solicitor Michael Boylan in *Law Society Gazette* (November 2002) 10; 'Issues of Causation in recent Medical Negligence litigation' by John Healy BL in *Bar Review* (November 2003) 188; 'Calculating the real cost of medical negligence' by Marie O'Connor in *Law Society Gazette* (April 2004) 8. [Bibliography: Healy J; Madden; Mills; Tomkin & Hanafin]. See DIAGNOSIS, INCORRECT; DOSAGE; NO FAULT COMPENSATION; RES IPSA LOQUITUR; LIMITATION OF ACTIONS; SURGICAL OPERATION.

medical practitioner, registered. A person registered in the *General Register of Medical Practitioners* established under the Medical Practitioners Act 1978. The *Medical Council* has the responsibility for ensuring that only fully qualified and experienced persons are registered so as to enable them to engage in medical practice in the State.

The Medical Council is obliged under the 1978 Act to make rules specifying the courses of training and examinations required to qualify for registration: *Bakht v The Medical Council* [1990] ILRM 840, SC. The Council is now empowered to make rules regarding registration, education and training, but with the prior approval of the Minister; there is also provision for the laying of these rules before the Oireachtas and for the continuation of rules already made: Medical Practitioners (Amendment) Act 2002, ss 3 and 10, amending the 1978 Act. See SIs No 285 of 2003, 286 of 2003, and 287 of 2003.

There are three forms of registration – *full*, *temporary* and *internship* registration. The 2002 Act was enacted: (a) to enable account to be taken of professional experience (as well as training and qualifications) in assessing an application for full registration; (b) to provide for medical graduates of colleges in EU member states to obtain internship registration in the State; and (c) to make provision for temporary and intern registration to apply to a number of health care settings rather than solely to hospital work.

There is no right under the 1978 Act to challenge a decision of the Medical Council not to renew a doctor's temporary registration: *Anachebe v Medical Council* [2000] ITLR (23 October).

The Medical Council may extend the period of *temporary* registration for such further period or periods, provided that the aggregate of such periods does not exceed seven years (MPA 1978, s 29(2) as substituted by Medical Practitioners (Amendment) Act 2000, s 1 and confirmed by the MP(A)A 2002, s 7).

The register may be kept on computer and also a certificate signed by the Registrar is evidence of the matter stated in the certificate, unless the contrary is shown: MPA 1978, ss 26(2), (2A) and s 57 as substituted by Medical Practitioners

(Amendment) Act 1993, s 2 and s 3 respectively.

A consultant physician was awarded damages for breach by the health board of its contractual obligation to supply him with reasonable facilities for the proper discharge of his duties; it was no defence to say that its failure was due to policies imposed by the Minister for Health: *Sullivan v Southern Health Board* [1993] HC and [1997] 3 IR 123, SC.

Provision has been made for the giving of medical evidence by way of a certificate signed by a registered medical practitioner in relation to offences alleging the causing of harm or serious harm to a person: Non-Fatal Offences against the Person Act 1997, s 25.

See also *Martin v Quinn* [1980] IR 244; *DPP v O'Donoghue* [1991] 1 IR 448; *Aziz v Midland Health Board* [1995] ELR 48, HC; *Association of General Practitioners Ltd v Minister for Health* [1995] 1 IR 382, HC; *Bressan v Western Health Board* [1996] ELR 129, EO; *Barry v Medical Council* [1998] 3 IR 368, SC. See EC Treaty, art 47 of the consolidated (2002) version.

For the Medical Council, see website: *www.medicalcouncil.ie*. For the Irish Medical Organisation, see website: *www.imo.ie*. For the Irish College of General Practitioners, see website: *www.icgp.ie*. For Irish Society of Occupational Medicine, see website: *www.iol.ie/~isom*. For Medico-Legal Journal of Ireland, see website: *www.ucd.ie/~legalmed*. For independent health information in a joint Irish Medical Organisation/Department of Health project, see website: *www.myGP.ie*.

[Bibliography: Cusack; Doran & O'Driscoll; Donnelly (2); Hanafin & Tomkin; Hanafin; Madden; Mills; Sheikh]. See also BLOOD SPECIMEN; BRAIN DEATH; COMHAIRLE NA N-OSPIDÉAL; COMMON CONTRACT; DESIGNATED; ETHICAL CONDUCT; INTERNSHIP REGISTRATION; MEDICAL NEGLIGENCE; PROFESSIONAL NEGLIGENCE; SURGICAL OPERATION; UNDUE INFLUENCE.

medical practitioner and confidentiality. Medical doctors as part of their professional code undertake not to break doctor-patient confidentiality eg in the *Hippocratic Oath* they undertake, '... whatever, in connection with my professional practice, or not in connection with it, I see or hear, in the life of men, which ought not to be spoken of abroad, I will not divulge, as reckoning that all such should be kept secret'. The Irish Medical Council has stated that confidentiality is a time-honoured principle of medical ethics; while the concern of relatives and close friends is understandable, the doctor must not disclose information to any person without the consent of the patient: Medical Council, *A Guide to Ethical Conduct and Behaviour* (6th edn, 2004) para 16.1.

It provides four circumstances where exceptions may be justified in the absence of permission from the patient: (a) when ordered by a judge in a court of law or a tribunal established by law, or (b) when necessary to protect the interests of the patient, or (c) when necessary to protect the welfare of society, or (d) when necessary to safeguard the welfare of another individual or patient (para 16.3).

The normal rules on confidentiality apply to crisis pregnancy. The doctor-patient relationship between a woman seeking an abortion and her doctor supersedes marital relationships and confidentiality must be maintained regardless of requests from spouses for information: *Primary Care for the Prevention and Management of Crisis Pregnancy* (ICGP, April 2004) p 17.

A plaintiff who sues for damages for personal injuries, waives, by implication, the right of privacy which he would otherwise enjoy in relation to his medical condition: *McGrory v Electricity Supply Board* [2003] ITLR (13 October) SC; also reported in *Law Society Gazette* (August/September 2003) 48. The right of a patient to confidentiality ceased when he put his health in issue by claiming damages in a lawsuit: *Hay v University of Alberta* [1991] 2 Med L R 204, Canadian case cited with approval in the *McGrory* case. See *X v Y and Ors* [1988] 2 All ER 648; *W v Egdell & Ors* [1990] 1 All ER 835. [Bibliography: Doran & O'Driscoll; Hanafin & Tomkin]. See INFECTIOUS DISEASES; MEDICAL RECORDS; MEDICAL REPORTS.

medical preparations. A substance which is sold under a proprietary designation or any other prophylactic, diagnostic or therapeutic substance, which may be used for the prevention or treatment of any human ailment, infirmity, injury or defect: Health Acts 1947, s 65 and 1953, s 39; Misuse of Drugs Act 1977, s 36. Also included is: (a) any drug or preparation intended to prevent pregnancy resulting from sexual intercourse between human beings, and (b) other preparations which may be used for restoring, correcting or modifying physiological functions in human beings: Health (Family Planning) (Amendment) Act 1992, s 7 amending the HA 1947, s 65. Oral contraceptive pills and spermicides were controlled by the 1947 Act.

Health Act 1947, s 65 now stands repealed; however there are transitional provisions for licences granted under it: Irish Medicines Board Act 1995, s 34. The term 'medicinal products' is now generally used instead of 'medical preparations' eg see Poisons (Amendment) Regulations 2003, SI No 351 of 2003. [Bibliography: EC Pub (2)]. See CLINICAL TRIALS; MEDICINAL PRODUCT; PRESCRIPTION DRUGS.

medical records. At common law, a patient's right of access to medical records is dependant on ownership of the records, which is decided by reference to the contract between the patient and the healthcare provider. In general, a hospital or doctor, in the absence of express terms to the contrary, would be the owner of the records and consequently, in general the common law did not recognise the right of a patient to his medical records, except where such access was necessary for the continued health care of the patient. See *McInerney v MacDonald* [1991] 2 Med LR 267; *Toal v Duignan (No 1)* [1991] ILRM 135.

The common law position has been changed radically by: (a) the Data Protection Act 1988 as amended by Data Protection (Amendment) Act 2003 which gives persons access to *personal data* about themselves, with a right to rectify erroneous data, and (b) the Freedom of Information Act 1997 which gives persons a right of access to the *records* of public bodies and to *personal information* held by such bodies in respect of themselves.

The 1997 Act includes records in a variety of forms, including paper records, and includes medical records; also *public bodies* include health boards and voluntary hospitals. Access to medical records may be refused if such access might be prejudicial to the applicant's physical or mental health, well-being or emotional condition (FIA 1997, s 28(3)). There should be evidence of a real and tangible possibility of harm being caused to the general health, welfare and good of the requester as a result of direct access to the records in question: Information Commissioner in Case 99189.

Where direct access is refused, access may be permitted through a health professional with the appropriate expertise (FIA 1997, s 28(4)). In granting a separated father access to the medical records of his daughter, the High Court held that a parent enjoyed the presumption that he had the welfare of his child at heart in the absence of evidence to the contrary: *McK v The Information Commissioner* [2004] FL 8671, HC.

Hospital notes are of no evidential value if the persons who made the notes were not called to give evidence and they were not cross-examined on them: *Maloney v Jury's Hotel plc* [2000] ITLR (10 January) SC. See *Gallagher v Stanley* [1998] 2 IR 267, SC.

'It is in the interest of both doctors and patients that accurate records are always kept. These should be retained for an adequate period (this may be for periods in excess of 21 years) and eventual disposal may be subject to advice from legal and insurance bodies. Patients are entitled to receive a copy of their own medical records, provided it does not put their health (or the health of others) at risk': Medical Council, *A Guide to Ethical Conduct and Behaviour* (6th edn, 2004) para 4.10. All medical records in whatever format and wherever kept, must be safeguarded (para 16.4). Doctors should take all reasonable measures to ensure that other health professionals and ancillary staff maintain confidentiality (para 16.4). The medical records of a deceased person remain confidential and death does not absolve a doctor from the obligation of confidentiality (para 16.7).

New guidelines for family doctors and for patients, concerning the confidentiality of the medical records of general practitioners, were launched in November 2003: *Data Privacy and the Practice (2003)*. The guidelines were drawn up by the Irish College of General Practitioners, the Irish Medical Organisation, and the Department of Health. [Bibliography: Hanafin & Tomkin]. See DATA PROTECTION; FREEDOM OF INFORMATION; HEALTH PROFESSIONAL; MEDICAL PRACTITIONER AND CONFIDENTIALITY; PERSONAL DATA; PERSONAL INFORMATION.

medical reports. 'Doctors have a responsibility to supply medical reports for solicitors or insurance companies on behalf of patients they have seen or treated professionally or for whom they have been responsible. However such reports should not be given without the patient's permission': Medical Council, *A Guide to Ethical Conduct and Behaviour* (6th edn, 2004) para 8.1. A doctor who is asked by an insurance company to complete a medical report on a patient, must ensure that this is not issued without the informed consent of the patient (para 16.6). Patients should be informed that such reports may be read by non-medical personnel. A report to an insurance company on a deceased person may be issued by the doctor of the deceased, but only with the permission of the next of kin or the executors of the estate (para 16.7). Reports must be factual and true (para 8.2). Undue delay in furnishing reports may amount to professional misconduct if such a delay results in the patient being disadvantaged (para 8.3). For disclosure of medical reports in personal injuries claims, see EXPERT REPORT.

medical treatment. Treating a person differently does not constitute discrimination, where the person is so treated solely in the exercise of a clinical judgment in connection with the diagnosis of illness or the person's medical treatment: Equal Status Act 2000, s 16(2)(a).

'A competent adult patient has the right to refuse treatment. While the decision must be respected, the assessment of competence and the discussion on consent should be carried out in conjunction with a senior colleague': Medical Council, *A Guide to Ethical Conduct and Behaviour* (6th edn, 2004) para 17.1. In a particular case, the High Court admitted a patient into wardship and directed that she be given medical treatment, holding that her decision to refuse treatment stemmed from her cultural background and her desire to please her Jehovah's Witness husband and not to offend his sensibilities: *J M v St Vincent's Hospital* [2003] 1 IR 321, HC.

If a person in custody in a garda station (a) is injured, (b) is under the influence of intoxicating liquor or drugs and cannot be roused, (c) fails to respond normally to questions or conversation (otherwise than owing to the influence of intoxicating liquor alone), (d) appears to the member in charge to be suffering from a mental illness, or (e) otherwise appears to the member in charge to need medical attention, the member in charge is required to summon a doctor or cause him to be summoned, unless the person's condition appears to the member in charge to be such as to necessitate immediate removal to a hospital or other suitable place: Treatment of Persons in Custody in Garda Síochána Stations Regulations 1987, SI No 119 of 1987, reg 21.

The member in charge must ensure that any instructions given by a doctor in relation to the medical care of a person in custody are complied with. Also medical advice must be sought if the person in custody claims to need medication relating to a heart condition, diabetes, epilepsy or other potentially serious condition or the member in charge considers it necessary because the person has in his possession any such medication. See DISABLED PERSON AND MEDICAL TREATMENT.

medical treatment, consent to. See CHILD, MEDICAL TREATMENT OF; CLINICAL TRIALS, CONDUCT OF; PATIENT, CONSENT OF; SURGICAL OPERATION.

medicinal product. Any substance or combination of substances presented for treating or preventing disease in human beings or animals: Council Directive (EEC) No 65/65 of 26 January 1965. *Proprietary medicinal products* are any ready prepared medicinal product placed on the market under a special name and in a special pack. The licensing of the manufacture, preparation, importation, distribution and sale of medicinal products is the responsibility of the Irish Medicines Board: Irish Medicines Board Act 1995, ss 1(1) and 4(1)(a). The Minister is empowered to make regulations in relation to medicinal products (IMBA 1995, s 32).

The controls applicable to the prescription and supply of medicinal products to the public have been updated and consolidated in accordance with the requirements of Directive (EC) 2001/83: Medicinal Products (Prescription and Control of Supply) Regulations 200, SI No 540 of 2003. Certain exemptions are provided in respect of certain low strength homeopathic medicinal products which are available to the public without prescription. Particular restrictions are imposed on the sale of paracetamol. Restrictions are also set out relating to the dispensing of prescriptions, the requirement for the labelling of dispensed medicinal products and for pharmacy records. The supply of medicinal products by mail order is prohibited, as is supply by means of automatic vending machines. See *Genmark Pharma Ltd v Minister for Health* [1998] 3 IR 111, HC. For the *European Agency for the Evaluation of Medicinal Products* (EMEA), see website: *www.emea.eu.int*.

For former regulations, see eg SIs Nos 41, 42, 43, 256, 309 of 1996; No 142 of 1998; No 271 of 1999; SI No 116 of 2000; SI No 598 of 2002; SI No 627 of 2002; Medicinal Products (Control of Paracetamol) Regulations 2001, SI No 150 of 2001; Medicinal Products (Licencing and Sale) (Amendment) Regulations 2001, SI No 512 of 2001. See ADVERSE EVENT; ADVERSE REACTION; COSMETIC PRODUCT; CLINICAL TRIALS, CONDUCT OF; EUROPEAN AGENCY FOR THE EVALUATION OF MEDICINAL PRODUCTS; PRESCRIPTION DRUGS.

medium-sized company. A private company which satisfies at least two of the following conditions: (a) the balance sheet total does not exceed £6 million/€7.62 million, (b) turnover does not exceed £12 million/€15.24 million, (c) the average number of employees does not exceed 250: Companies Amendment Act 1986, s 8; SI No 396 of 1993. A medium-sized company may combine some of the items set out in the format specified for the profit and loss account (CAA 1986, s 11). See ACCOUNTS, COMPANY; SMALL COMPANY.

meetings. [Bibliography: Maloney & Spellman; Shaw & Smith UK]. See ASSEMBLY, RIGHT OF.

meetings of company. Meetings of a company attended by its members, comprising: (a) the *annual general meeting* held once each year; (b) an *extraordinary general meeting* which may be convened when the directors so wish, and also by requisition of a defined proportion of members: Companies Act 1963, s 132; and (c) a separate *class meeting* of members usually for the purpose of voting on proposals to vary or abrogate the rights attached to the class of shares in question. [Bibliography: Maloney & Spellman]. See ANNUAL GENERAL MEETING; CLASS RIGHTS; EXTRAORDINARY GENERAL MEETING.

melior est conditio possidentis et rei quam actoris. [The position of the possessor is the better, and that of the defendant is better than that of the plaintiff]. Possession is *prima facie* evidence of ownership and may be good against all claims except that of the true owner. The onus of proof

in an action generally rests on the claimant or plaintiff.

member in charge. The member of the Garda Síochána who is in charge of a garda station: Treatment of Persons in Custody in Garda Síochána Stations Regulations 1987, SI No 119 of 1987, reg 4. As far as practicable, the member in charge should not be the garda who was involved in the arrest of a person in custody or in the investigation of the associated offence. The member in charge is responsible for overseeing the application of the 1987 regulations in relation to persons in custody in the station and for that purpose must visit them from time to time and make any necessary enquiries (SI No 119 of 1987, reg 5). See ARRESTED PERSON, INFORMATION TO; BAIL; CHILD SUSPECT; SEARCH OF PERSON; SOLICITOR, ACCESS TO.

membership. (1) As regards a company, every person who has been allotted one or more shares in a company and has the unconditional right to be included in the company's register of members, is a member of that company. The subscribers of the memorandum and every other person who agrees to become a member of a company, and whose name is entered in its register of members, is a member of the company: Companies Act 1963, s 31.

(2) As regards a building society, every person who holds one or more shares in a building society is a member of that society; however, a society may by its rules, allow a person who does not hold a share to be a member, where that person is an applicant for or a recipient of a *housing loan* (qv): Building Societies Act 1989, ss 2(1) and 16(1).

Where two or more persons jointly hold shares in a society, the person whose name first appears in the records is the *representative joint holder* and exercises the membership rights (BSA 1989, s 16(6)). However, in the *conversion* of a building society to a public limited company, the second named person is regarded as having held the shares alone in specified circumstances eg where the first named dies (BSA 1989, s 101A inserted by Central Bank Act 1997, s 78). This provision was inserted to overcome difficulties which arose in the conversion of the Irish Permanent Building Society. Now, free shares in the successor company along with any options to purchase further shares, will in the case of joint account holders who are eligible for such shares, issue in the name of all members of the joint account (BSA 1989, s 101B inserted by Housing (Miscellaneous Provisions) Act 2002, s 23 and Sch 3).

(3) As regards a trade union, see WORK, RIGHT TO. See also OPPRESSION OF SHAREHOLDER.

memorandum. A note recording the particulars of any transaction or matter.

memorandum, sale of goods. The memorandum required in relation to a contract for the sale of goods of £10 (€12.70) or upwards, in the absence of acceptance and receipt of the goods, or part payment, or something given in earnest to bind the contract: Sale of Goods Act 1893, s 4. In the absence of such memorandum, the contract is unenforceable. The essential requirements of the memorandum are similar to those required in the Statute of Frauds, except that where the price is agreed it must be shown in the memorandum and, where not agreed, a reasonable price will be implied. See MEMORANDUM, STATUTE OF FRAUDS.

memorandum, Statute of Frauds. The memorandum required in writing in relation to certain contracts which otherwise are unenforceable: Statute of Frauds (Ireland) 1695. In relation to the memorandum: (a) it need not be made at the time of the formation of the contract, provided it is made before action is brought; (b) it must contain the names of the parties or a sufficient description of them; (c) the subject matter must be described so that it can be identified and all material terms of the contract must be stated; (d) the consideration must appear, except in contracts of guarantee where by virtue of the Mercantile Law Amendment Act 1856, consideration must be present but need not appear in the memorandum; (e) it must be signed by the party to be charged or his agent. See *Casey v Irish Intercontinental Bank* [1979] IR 364; *Tradax (Ireland) Ltd v Irish Grain Board Ltd* [1983] SC; *Morris v Barron* [1918] AC 1; *Hawkins v Price* [1947] Ch 645; *Mulhall v Haren* [1981] IR 364.

Where a memorandum or note exists which satisfies the Statute, the Court will not imply a term which would have the effect of defeating the contract: *Aga Khan v Firestone* [1992] ILRM 31, HC. A memorandum which contains any term or expression such as 'subject to contract' is not sufficient, even if it can be established by oral evidence that such a term or expression

did not form part of the originally concluded oral contract: *Boyle & Boyle v Lee & Goyns* [1992] ILRM 65, SC. Only in rare and exceptional circumstances, such as arose in *Kelly v Parkhall School* [1979] IR 349, could the words 'subject to contract' be treated as being of no effect: Egan J in *Boyle v Lee.*

If there is no memorandum, the contract cannot be enforced unless there has been *part performance* of the contract by the plaintiff; equity will then decree *specific performance.* For the acts of part performance regarded as supplanting the memorandum required by the Statute of Frauds, see *Hope v Lord Cloncurry* [1874] IR 8 Eq 555; *Lowry v Reid* [1927] NI 142; *Kennedy v Kennedy* [1984] HC. See PART-PERFORMANCE; STATUTE OF FRAUDS; UNENFORCEABLE.

memorandum of association. See ASSOCIATION, MEMORANDUM OF.

memorial. An abstract of the material parts of a deed, the enrolment of which is necessary for the registration of a deed in the Registry of Deeds: Registration of Deeds (Ireland) Act 1707, s 7. It must contain: the date of perfection of the deed; the names and addresses of all the parties and witnesses to the deed; and the lands described as in the deed itself. The memorial must be executed by one of the grantors or grantees of the deed, be attested by two witnesses (one of whom was a witness of the grantor's execution of the deed) and be proved by an affidavit made by a witness common to the memorial and the deed (RD(I)A 1707, s 6). See also DEEDS, REGISTRATION OF; SIGN MANUAL.

memory. A device in a computer where information can be stored and retrieved. The memory capacity of a computer is usually measured in *megabytes* (MB = 1,048,576 *bytes* ie 2 to the power of 20 but usually interpreted as 1 million *bytes*) or *gigabytes* (1,000 megabytes), a *byte* being a unit of data (binary term) consisting of 8 *bits* (binary digits). See COMPUTER.

memory, refreshing. See REFRESHING MEMORY.

menace. In the UK it has been held that the word *menace* must be construed literally and not limited to threats of violence but also including threats of any action detrimental to or unpleasant to the person addressed: *Thorne v Motor Trade Association* [1937] AC 797. See EXTORTION WITH MENACES.

mens rea. [Guilty mind]. To constitute a criminal offence, the offence must be accompanied by a blameworthy state of mind. What the law considers as blameworthy varies from offence to offence; *mens rea* must be considered in relation to the crime charged. It may be *intentional* e g in murder where the consequences are foreseen by the accused and desired. It may be *reckless* or be *grossly negligent* where the consequences are foreseen but not necessarily desired e g in manslaughter. It may also be *negligent*, where the consequences are not foreseen but where the law requires foresight e g dangerous driving of a motor vehicle.

Prima facie, mens rea is required for every offence, whether at common law or statutory: *Maguire v Shannon Regional Fisheries Board* [1994] 2 ILRM 253, HC. In an offence created by statute, it is a question of construction as to whether it is required; if the statute is silent on *mens rea*, there is a presumption that it is required: *The People (DPP) v Murray* [1977] IR 360 adopting *Sweet v Parsley* [1970] AC 132. *Mens rea* is not required for an offence of *strict liability* (*Maguire* case). See also *R v Tolson* [1889] 23 QBD 168. It has been held that if there is no *intention* then there is no *mens rea*: *People (DPP) v McBride* [1997] 1 ILRM 233, CCA. See *Shannon Regional Fisheries Board v Cavan County Council* [1996] 3 IR 267, SC. [Bibliography: McAuley & McCutcheon]. See INTENT; MALICE AFORETHOUGHT; STRICT LIABILITY IN CRIMINAL LAW; ACTUS NON FACIT REUM, NISI MENS SIT REA.

mensa et thoro. See DIVORCE A MENSA ET THORO.

menstruation. Failure to comply with the request for a toilet break by a female employee, who is menstruating, can amount to discrimination: *Power Supermarkets t/o Crazy Prices & Purdy* EE11/1991.

mental abnormality. See INSANITY.

mental disability. For recommendations on reform of the law relating to liability in tort of mentally disabled persons, see LRC 18 of 1985. See also *Report on Sexual Offences against the Mentally Handicapped* (LRC 33 of 1990). See also *Clery & Co v Campbell* [1994] ELR 138, LC. See MENTAL HANDICAP; SAFETY BELT.

mental disorder. (1) Under draft legislation, includes mental illness, mental handicap, dementia or any disease of the mind but does not include intoxication: Criminal Law (Insanity) Bill 2002. See DIMINISHED RESPONSIBILITY; SPECIAL VERDICT; UNFIT TO BE TRIED.

(2) Means *mental illness, severe dementia* or *significant intellectual disability* where: (a) because of the illness, disability or dementia, there is a serious likelihood of the person concerned causing immediate and serious harm to himself or to other persons, or (b) (i) because of the severity of the illness, disability or dementia, the judgment of the person concerned is so impaired that failure to admit the person to an approved centre would be likely to lead to a serious deterioration in his condition or would prevent the administration of appropriate treatment that could be given only by such admission, and (ii) the reception, detention and treatment of the person concerned in an approved centre would be likely to benefit or alleviate the condition of that person to a material extent: Mental Health Act 2001, s 3.

Mental disorder is the sole ground for *involuntary admission* of a person to an approved centre (MHA 2001, s 8(1)). The fact that a person is suffering from a personality disorder, is socially deviant, or is addicted to drugs or alcohol, is insufficient reason on its own for an involuntary admission (MHA 2001, s 8(2)).

The following may apply to a registered medical practitioner for the person to be detained – the spouse or relative of the person, a garda, an authorised officer, and with exceptions, any other person (MHA 2001, s 9).

There is provision for an automatic independent review of each decision to detain a person (MHA 2001, s 17 and ss 31–55).

Also the patient's consent must be obtained in relation to proposed treatment, and the consent must be in writing where the proposed treatment involves psycho-surgery or electro-convulsive therapy (MHA 2001, ss 56–61). In addition, psycho-surgery must be authorised by a tribunal (MHA 2001, s 58).

A garda who has reasonable grounds for believing that a person is suffering from a mental disorder and that there is a serious likelihood of the person causing immediate and serious harm to himself or others, may take the person into custody (MHA 2001, s 12).

Mental illness means a state of mind of a person which affects the person's thinking, perceiving, emotion or judgment and which seriously impairs the mental function of the person to the extent that he requires care or medical treatment in his own interest or in the interest of other persons. *Severe dementia* means a deterioration of the brain of a person which significantly impairs the intellectual function of the person thereby affecting thought, comprehension and memory and which includes severe psychiatric or behavioural symptoms such as physical aggression. *Significant intellectual disability* means a state of arrested or incomplete development of mind of a person which includes significant impairment of intelligence and social functioning and abnormally aggressive or seriously irresponsible conduct on the part of the person (MHA 2001, s 3(2)).

In making a decision under the 2001 Act, the best interest of the person must be the principal consideration, with due regard being given to the best interests of other persons who may be at risk of serious harm if the decision is not made (MHA 2001, s 4).

There are safeguards provided in relation to the use of *seclusion* and *bodily restraint* of patients – they cannot be placed in seclusion or under bodily restraint except in accordance with rules made by the Mental Health Commission (MHA 2001, s 69).

For provisions affecting a *voluntary patient*, see MHA 2001, ss 24 and 29 and DETENTION OF PATIENT. For commencement of ss 1 to 5, 7, 31 to 55 of MHA 2001, see SI No 90 of 2002. For establishment day order, see SI No 91 of 2002. See 'States of Mind' by Alma Clissmann in *Law Society Gazette* (May 2002) 20. See 'Involuntary psychiatric treatment and detention' by Simon Mills BL in *Bar Review* (February 2003) 42. For the voluntary organisation *Mental Health Ireland*, see website: *www.mensana.org*. [Bibliography: Keys; Tomkin & Hanafin; Cooney & O'Neill]. See ACCESS TO COURTS; ADMISSION ORDER; CIVIL PROCEEDINGS; CLINICAL TRIAL; PATIENT, CONSENT OF; PSYCHO-SURGERY; PSYCHIATRIC DISORDER.

mental disorder, repealed legislation. Provision has been made to repeal previous mental health legislation (eg Mental Treatment Act 1945 and Health (Mental Services) Act 1981) except eg as regards staff superannuation provisions and the power of the President of the High Court to require the Inspector of Mental Health Services to visit and examine a detained person: Mental Health Act 2001, Sch).

Under the repealed Mental Treatment Act 1945 where a person detained in a mental hospital was charged in the District Court with an indictable offence, the judge was required to certify that the person was suitable for transfer to the Central Mental Hospital if certain conditions were met eg that there was *prima facie* evidence that the person had committed the offence and would be unfit to plead if placed on trial (MTA 1945, s 207). This section was held to be unconstitutional in that the Act failed to provide adequate safeguards against abuse or error both in the making of the transfer order and in the continuance of the indefinite detention which was permitted by the section: *RT v Central Mental Hospital* [1995] 2 ILRM 354, HC. See *Bailey v Gallagher* [1996] 2 ILRM 433, SC; *Croke v Smith (No 2)* [1998] 1 IR 101, SC; *Croke v Smith* (21 December 2000, unreported) ECHR; *O'Dowd v North Western Health Board* [1983] ILRM 186; *Murphy v Greene* [1991] ILRM 404, SC; *Croke v Smith* [1994] 3 IR 525, SC.

mental distress. A ground for damages in fatal injury cases. The judge may award compensation as he considers to be reasonable for the *mental distress* resulting from the death to each dependant: Civil Liabilities Act 1961, s 49. It is subject to a maximum award of £20,000/€25,394: Civil Liability (Amendment) Act 1996, s 2. The 1996 Act extended the definition of 'dependant' to persons who, though not married, have been living as man and wife for at least three years before the date of death of one of the partners (CL(A)A 1996, s 1). A divorced spouse is not entitled to claim damages for mental distress (CL(A)A 1996, s 3). The test applied in assessing damage is one of reasonableness; this does not equate to 'moderate' or 'small': *McCarthy v Walsh* [1965] IR 246.

Damages for *mental distress* will not automatically be awarded to a plaintiff who can show it arising from breach of contract. It has been held that the *mental distress* suffered by a plaintiff on discovering that the licensed premises he had purchased had a hotel licence and not a public house licence, did not warrant damages (qv) as it was not reasonably foreseeable: *Kelly v Crowley* [1985] HC. Also mental distress will not attract damages unless it can be measured in a meaningful way: *McAnarney v Hanrahan* [1994] 1 ILRM 210, HC. Compensation of €33,260 was awarded to an employee, who was moved in breach of his contract of employment, of which €27,295 was for mental distress and emotional suffering: *O'Byrne v Dunnes Stores* [2003] ELR 297, HC. See FATAL INJURIES; NERVOUS SHOCK; WORKSTATION.

mental handicap. In all criminal proceedings, a person with a mental handicap may give unsworn evidence if the court is satisfied that he is capable of giving an intelligible account of events which are relevant to those proceedings: Criminal Evidence Act 1992, s 27. This unsworn evidence may corroborate evidence (sworn and unsworn) given by any other person (CEA 1992, s 28(3)). A person with mental handicap may also, in criminal proceedings involving physical or sexual abuse, give evidence by means of a live television link. Where the person is the alleged victim, a video recording of a statement he made to a garda may also be admissible.

The special provisions protecting young persons in custody in a garda station, apply to a person of any age whom the member in charge suspects or knows to be mentally handicapped: Treatment of Persons in Custody in Garda Síochána Stations Regulations 1987, SI No 119 of 1987, reg 22. See CHILD SUSPECT; EDUCATION; MENTALLY IMPAIRED; TELEVISION LINK.

Mental Health Commission. An independent body corporate with the following principal functions: to promote, encourage and foster the establishment and maintenance of high standards and good practices in the delivery of mental health services and to take all reasonable steps to protect the interests of persons detained in approved centres: Mental Health Act 2001, ss 32–33.

The Commission has a key function in the new mental health framework introduced by the 2001 Act. It is required: (a) to arrange for an independent review by a *mental health tribunal* of all decisions to detain a patient on an *involuntary* basis and each decision to extend the duration of such detentions, (b) to establish and administer a legal aid scheme for detained persons, (c) to maintain a register of approved centres, and (d) to appoint the Inspector of Mental Health Services. [Bibliography: Keys].

Mental Health Review Board. Under draft legislation, a proposed new body

which will have the function of reviewing at regular intervals, or on application, the cases of persons detained following verdicts of 'not guilty by reason of insanity' or findings of 'unfitness to be tried': Criminal Law (Insanity) Bill 2002, ss 10–11. The Board will determine when such persons should be released. It will replace the existing *ad hoc* Advisory Committee.

mental treatment. See MENTAL DISORDER.

mentally impaired. Suffering from a disorder of the mind, whether through mental handicap or mental illness, which is of such a nature or degree as to render a person incapable of living an independent life or guarding against serious exploitation: Criminal Law (Sexual Offences) Act 1993, s 5(5). It is an indictable offence for a person to have sexual intercourse or to commit an act of buggery with a person who is mentally impaired (CL(SO)A 1993, s 5(1)). An attempt is also an offence, as is an act of *gross indecency* by a male with a mentally impaired male. It is a defence for the accused to be able to show that he did not know and had no reason to suspect that the person was mentally impaired (CL(SO)A 1993, s 5(3)). See BUGGERY; SOLICIT.

mentor. A person, assigned by court order, to help, advise and support a child and the child's family in its efforts to prevent the child from committing further offences and to monitor the child's behaviour generally: Children Act 2001, s 131. Such an order cannot be made unless the child and the child's parents or guardian consent and agree to co-operate. Also, the court may by order assign a child to the care of a person, including a relative of the child concerned, called a 'suitable person' in the legislation (CA 2001, s 129). The court may direct a child to comply with a *suitable person* (care and supervision) order or a *mentor* (family support) order (CA 2001, ss 130 and 132).

mercantile agent. See FACTOR.

mercenary. A person recruited to fight in an armed conflict who is motivated by the desire for private gain and is promised material compensation substantially in excess of that paid or promised to combatants of similar rank and is neither a national of a party to the conflict nor a resident of the territory controlled by the party to the conflict: Geneva Convention (Amendment) Act 1998, Sch 5, art 47.

merchandise licence. A carrier's licence; a national road freight carrier's licence or an international road freight carrier's licence. See CARRIER'S LICENCE.

merchandise mark. See TRADE DESCRIPTION; FALSE TRADE DESCRIPTION.

merchant shipping. The International Convention for the Safety of Life at Sea, signed in London on 1 November 1974, has been given effect in this State by the Merchant Shipping Act 1981. For safety regulations for commercial ships and ferries, see Merchant Shipping Regulations 1988, SIs No 107, 108, 109, 110 of 1988. See also Merchant Shipping Acts 1894–1996. [Bibliography: Power UK]. See BILL OF LADING; PASSENGER BOAT; PASSENGER SHIP; MARITIME CLAIMS.

merchantable quality. Goods are of *merchantable quality* if they are fit for the purpose or purposes for which goods of that kind are commonly bought and as durable as it is reasonable to expect having regard to any description applied to them, the price (if relevant) and all the other relevant circumstances: Sale of Goods Act 1893, s 14; Sale of Goods and Supply of Services Act 1980, s 10. Where a seller sells goods (or an owner lets goods under a hire-purchase agreement) in the course of a business, there is an implied condition that the goods are of merchantable quality. See *Butterly v United Dominions Trust (Commercial) Ltd* [1963] IR 56. See also Consumer Credit Act 1995, s 76. [Bibliography: O'Reilly P]. See CONDITION; QUALITY OF GOODS.

mercy. Matters relating to mercy and leniency are best dealt with by the executive by the exercise of the prerogative of remission or commutation of sentence: *The People (DPP) v Cunningham* [2002] 2 IR 712, SC and [2003] 1 ILRM 124. See PARDON; REMISSION.

merger. The extinguishing of a right, by operation of law, by reason of its coinciding with another and greater right in the same person eg in a contract for the sale of land, the written agreement of sale becomes merged and extinguished in the subsequent conveyance under seal.

If both the benefit of a charge in property and the property subject to the charge vest in the same person, equity will treat the charge as kept alive or merged depending on the circumstances eg where there are mortgages A and B on a property with priority to A, and the owner of the *equity of redemption* (qv) redeems A, he will not be able to keep the redeemed mortgage alive

as against B if in fact he created both A and B mortgages. See *Lemon v Mark* [1899] 1 IR 416.

merger of company. The acquisition of one company by another, so that only one company remains. The most common method of merger today is where one company acquires most or all of the shares in another company so that the latter becomes a subsidiary of the former. The offer to acquire the shares may be for cash or for some of the former's own shares or a permutation of both and is usually conditional on a certain proportion being accepted.

A merger can also be accomplished by a company proposed to be, or in the course of being, wound up voluntarily by special resolution authorising the liquidator to transfer the company (the transferor) to the receiving company (the transferee) in return for stocks, shares, debentures or other interests in the transferee company: Companies Act 1963, s 260. This procedure cannot be used where the transferor company is in compulsory liquidation.

Take-overs of companies the shares of which are quoted on the Stock Exchange are subject to rules; these provide for an orderly framework for the conduct of take-overs with a view to ensuring equality of treatment of all shareholders: Irish Takeover Panel Act 1997; Takeover Rules 2001; Substantial Acquisition Rules 2001. See also Listing Rules 2000, para 4.27, 8.15–8.17.

Under recent legislation, s 77 of the Central Bank Act 1989, relating to the approval of mergers and acquisitions in the banking sector above a certain threshold, has been amended to elaborate on the criteria that the Minister will use to inform any decision made under this provision: Central Bank and Financial Services Authority of Ireland Act 2004, Sch 3.

The ability of directors to oppose take-over bids may be affected by their fiduciary duty, their power to refuse to register transfers and to issue and allot additional shares. See *Kinsella v Alliance & Dublin Consumers Gas Co* [1982] HC. See also *Hennessy v National Assn* [1947] IR 159. [Bibliography: Cahill D; Forde (5); Maher; Mason Hayes & Curran; O'Driscoll T; Power V; Weinberg & Blank (UK)]. See COMPETITION, DISTORTION OF; COVERT TAKE-OVER; IRISH TAKEOVER PANEL; TAKE-OUT MERGERS; TAKE-OVER; SHARES, DISCLOSURE OF; WHITE KNIGHT.

merger of company, EC regulations. The regulations which apply to the merger and division of plcs and certain specified unregistered companies since 1 June 1987, implementing the EC Third and Sixth Company Law Directives: European Communities (Mergers and Division of Companies) Regulations 1987, SI No 137 of 1987. The EC also has control over mergers through its competition policy e g the take-over contest for the shares of Irish Distillers plc in 1988.

The EC Commission has exclusive jurisdiction, with some rare exceptions, over very large cross-border mergers in the Community. The revised merger regulations were adopted in Council Regulation (EEC) 4064/89 whereby a merger (concentration) is defined as the merger of two or more previously independent undertakings; or where one or more persons already controlling at least one undertaking or one or more undertakings acquire, by the purchase of securities or assets, direct or indirect control of the whole or parts of one or more undertakings: OJ 1990 L 257/14.

Mergers are regulated which have a *community dimension* i e where: (a) the aggregate worldwide turnover of all the undertakings concerned is more than €5,000m and (b) the aggregate community-wide turnover of each of at least two of the undertakings concerned is more than €250m. These Regulation came into force on 21 September 1990. A proposed concentration is assessed by the EC Commission in consultation with the relevant authority in each member state. A notification from the EC Commission to the Irish Competition Authority constitutes the required notification to the Minister of the merger or acquisition concerned: Competition Act 2002, s 18(13).

For the procedures on the application of EC rules on competition relating to the control of mergers and takeovers between undertakings with an EC dimension, see EC (Rules on Competition) Regulations 1993, SI No 124 of 1993. See *Keane & Walsh* in 8 ILT & SJ (1990) 181. For tax treatment of such mergers, see EU Council Directive (EEC) 90/434 of 23 July; Taxes Consolidation Act 1997, ss 630–638.

However, new merger regulations (ECMR) came into force on 1 May 2004, implementing reforms as regards jurisdiction and procedures: Council Regulation EC 139/2004. The notifiable thresholds have not been changed but the referral process has been changed to provide a 'one-stop-shop'. See 'A new era in European merger control' by solicitor Cormac Little in *Law Society Gazette* (June 2004) 51. See 'Draft EC merger regulation published' by solicitor David Geary in *Law Society Gazette* (May 2003) 49. For the new ECMR, the implementing regulation and other related documents, including guidelines on horizontal mergers and best practices, see website: *www.europa.eu.int/comm /competition /mergers/legislation/regulation/ #implementing*.

Every offer made to acquire securities of a company to which the European Merger Regulations might be relevant, must contain a term whereby the offer will lapse if (before the first closing date or the date when an offer becomes or is declared unconditional as to acceptances) the European Commission initiates proceedings under the Merger Regulations or refers the matter back to a competent authority of a member state: Irish Takeover Panel Act 1997; Takeover Rules 2001; Substantial Acquisition Rules 2001. For previous (now repealed) legislation, see s 5 of the Merger, Takeovers and Monopolies (Control) Act 1978; Competition Act 1991, s 16. See *Airtours plc v Commission of the European Communities* (21 June 2002, unreported) CFI. [Bibliography: Lucey; Maher; Downes & Ellison UK]. See COMPETITION, DISTORTION OF; CONGLOMERATE MERGER; DIVISION OF COMPANY.

merger of company, local provision. A *merger* or *acquisition* occurs when: (a) two or more undertakings, previously independent of each other, merge; or (b) one or more individuals or other undertakings (who control an undertaking or undertakings) acquire direct or indirect control of the whole or part of one or more other undertakings, or (c) the result of an acquisition by one undertaking of another undertaking is to place the first undertaking in a position to replace the second undertaking in the business in which that undertaking was engaged immediately before its acquisition: Competition Act 2002, s 16. Also the creation of a *joint venture* to perform, on an indefinite basis, all the functions of an autonomous economic entity constitutes a merger (CA 2002, s 16(4)).

An agreed merger must be notified to the Competition Authority where each of the two or more undertakings carry on business in any part of the island of Ireland, and the turnover in the State of any *one* of the undertakings is not less than €40m, and the worldwide turnover of *each* of two or more of the undertakings is also not less than €40m (CA 2002, s 18(1)). Failure to make a notification, when so required, constitutes an offence (CA 2002, s 18(9)). There is also provision for a *voluntary notification* to the Authority where the turnover thresholds are not reached (CA 2002, s 18(3)). The Authority has indicated that it is willing to engage in pre-notification discussions of proposed mergers where it is satisfied that the parties have a *bona fide* intention of proceeding with the transaction eg a letter of intent would be evidence of such intention: 'Business Law Committee' in *Law Society Gazette* (April 2004) 36.

Also the Minister is empowered: (a) to specify, by order, a class of merger or acquisition which requires to be notified where the exigencies of the common good so warrant, and (b) to increase, by order, the turnover thresholds (CA 2002, ss 18(5) and 27)).

A merger or acquisition must not be put into effect until a determination has been made by the Authority (CA 2002, s 19). The criterion on which the Authority makes its decision is: whether the acquisition will substantially lessen competition in markets for goods and services in the State (CA 2002, s 21). There is a two-stage process of investigation. Within one month after the appropriate date, the Authority is required: (a) to give its opinion that the merger or acquisition will not substantially lessen competition and can be put into effect, or (b) to state that it intends to carry out a full investigation.

Where the Authority conducts a full investigation, it makes a determination, within four months after the *appropriate date*, that the merger or acquisition: (a) may be put into effect, or (b) may not be put into effect, or (c) may be put into effect subject to conditions specified by it being complied with (CA 2002, s 22).

Previously, the Minister made these determinations. For example, see the initial prohibition of the take over of Conoco by Statoil: SI No 45 of 1996. See also SI No 42 of 1990.

The Irish Takeover Panel is required to make rules in relation to specifying the requirement to be complied with by parties to a takeover constitutes a merger or acqui-

sition: Irish Takeover Panel Act 1997, s 8(4); Takeover Rules 2001; Substantial Acquisition Rules 2001.

There are special provisions dealing with mergers and acquisitions involving media businesses. See MEDIA MERGER.

See Competition Authority Notice N/02/003, *Notice in respect of certain terms used in section 18(1) of the Competition Act 2002*, which gives guidance on the Authority's understanding of certain terms used in connection with merger notifications. See also N/02/004, *Guidelines for Merger Analysis* which explains the Authority's position on substantive issues in merger control, and the Authority's *Procedures* for its examination of individual merger notifications. The progress of merger notifications can be followed (from initial notification, to invitations to comment, to the final determination) on the Authority's website: *www.tca.ie*.

See Solgun and USIT World plc proposed Merger or Takeover Conditional Order 2002, SI No 187 of 2002. For previous legislation, since repealed, see Restrictive Practices (Amendment) Act 1987, ss 24–25; Mergers, Takeovers and Monopolies (Control) Act 1978, s 1(3)(a); Competition Act 1991, s 15(2)). See 'New merger control regime' in *Law Society Gazette* (April 2003) 51. [Bibliography: Lucey; Maher; O'Connor T]. See COMPETITION AUTHORITY; GUN JUMPING; IRISH TAKEOVER PANEL.

merger of solicitors. The amalgamation of the professional practices of two or more solicitors by way of partnership, usually in order to widen the range of services offered and to enter new markets, while at the same time reducing overhead costs. See 'Two become one' by David Rowe in *Law Society Gazette* (June 2003) 32. See SOLE PRACTITIONER; SOLICITORLINK.

meromictic. [mero = share]. Refers to a lake which overflows, and where the water below a certain depth does not take part in the overflow due to its higher density (usually due to a higher salt or mineral concentration). A *meromictic* situation was held to exist where a provision in legislation is not assailed as itself unconstitutional, ultimately produces an unjust result: O'Flaherty J in *McMenamin v Ireland* [1997] 2 ILRM 177 at 198. It that case the judge said that the provision in legislation (dealing with the pension arrangements of district judges) had not been challenged, because that challenge if successful, would have resulted in the pension arrangements being discarded. The unjust pension arrangement was corrected by ss 24–30 of the Oireachtas (Allowances to Members) Act 1998.

mesne rates. The damage for trespass arising in an *ejectment action* for non-payment of rent or for overholding to which a plaintiff is entitled: Deasy's Act 1860, s 77. The measure of the mesne rates is the value of the premises during the period of trespass, usually but not invariably, calculated on the rent; there may also be, if the facts warrant it, damages for deterioration of the premises: *Lynham v Butler* 67 ILTR 121. See RSC Ord 41, rr 9–10. See Circuit Court Rules 2001 Ord 9, r 2. See JOINDER OF CLAIMS; RESIDENTIAL TENANCIES.

messuage. A dwellinghouse, including gardens, orchards, courtyard and outbuildings. See LAND.

metal detectors. Detection devices, the use or possession of which, is prohibited in or at a site of a registered monument or other specified monuments or in a registered archaeological area (qv) or a restricted area: National Monuments (Amendment) Act 1987, s 2. It is also an offence to use a detection device or to promote, whether by advertising or otherwise, the sale or use of detection devices, for the purpose of searching for archaeological objects. There is provision for the forfeiture of detection devices: National Monuments (Amendment) Act 1994, s 7. See ARCHAEOLOGICAL AREA; HISTORIC MONUMENT; NATIONAL MONUMENT; WRECK.

metric system. See MEASUREMENT, LEGAL UNIT OF.

metrology. The science of measurement: Explanatory Memorandum to Metrology Act 1996. *Legal metrology* is that part of metrology which is subject to regulation. The 1996 statute sets out to consolidate and update the law relating to legal metrology and to establish a re-organised legal metrology service in the State. *Legal metrology* deals with: (a) units of measurement, (b) standards through which these units are realised, (c) a system of establishing confidence in measuring instruments used in trade, and (d) control of quantities in pre-packaged goods and short measures in goods sold loose. The 1996 Act establishes control procedures to ensure measurements are accurate (MA 1996, ss 13–17) and establishes authorised units and standards

(MA 1996, ss 18–21). Prohibited under the Act are forgery, tampering with marks and instruments, removing or breaking of tags and seals, selling short measures, and misrepresentation as to quantity (MA 1996, ss 22–29). Provision has been made for the transfer of legal metrology function from Forbairt to the National Standards Authority of Ireland: Industrial Development (Enterprise Ireland) Act 1998, s 49. See website: *www.nsai.ie.* See MEASUREMENT, LEGAL UNIT OF; SHORT WEIGHT; TYPE APPROVAL.

Michaelmas. A sitting of the Court. See SITTINGS OF COURT.

micro-organisms. Micro-organisms produced by genetic engineering are not excluded from patent protection; it has been held that an application for a patent in respect of an invention entitled *Improvement in or relating to cell lines* should proceed, since the cell lines were articles for use produced from raw materials occurring in nature by giving those materials new forms, qualities and properties, they fell within the definition of an invention in the Patents Act 1964, s 2 as *manufactures*; the fact that the articles consisted of living matter was irrelevant: *National Research Development Corporation's Application* [1986] FSR 620, distinguishing *Rank Hovis McDougall Ltd v Controller of Patents* [1979] IR 142 and applying *Re Chakrabarty* 206 USPQ 193 [1980]. See *Keane* in 10 ILT & SJ (1992) 139.

The Patents Act 1992, which repeals the PA 1964, provides that rules may prescribe the 'disclosure' requirements in respect of an invention which requires for its performance the use of a micro-organism (PA 1992, s 19(2)). See O'Connor '*Of (Onco-) Mice and (Legal) Men*' in (1994) 4 ISLR 139. See European Communities (Legal Protection of Biotechnological Inventions) Regulations 2000, SI No 247 of 2000.

midnight. In relation to any particular day, the point of time at which such day ends: Interpretation Act 1937, s 12, Sch.

midwife. Originally was a woman registered in the roll of midwives in accordance with the Midwives Act 1944. The statutory bar to men becoming midwives was removed by the Employment Equality Act 1977, s 11 (now, Employment Equality Act 1998). A midwife is now a person whose name is registered in the midwives division of the register of nurses: Nurses Act 1985, s 2. It is an offence for a person to use or take the name or title of *midwife* if that person is not registered (NA 1985, s 49). See also NA 1985, s 57.

It has been held that a midwifery service can be provided by the attendance of a medical practitioner at the birth; the health board (qv) does not have to provide a midwife for a *home* delivery: Health Act 1970, s 62; *Spruyt v Southern Health Board* [1988] HC & SC. Also the High Court has held that the 1970 Act could not be read as requiring the provision of midwifery services outside a hospital or maternity home: *Lockhart, O'Brien, Clarke and Brannick v Minister for Health* (2000) Irish Times, 3 September, HC & SC. On appeal, this decision was upheld by the Supreme Court which held that while s 62 of HA 1970 required health boards to make available appropriate medical, surgical and midwifery services, that obligation would be fully complied with by providing those services within the confines of a hospital: *Irish Times*, 6 November 2003. The plaintiffs in this case had sought an order directing their local health boards to provide them with midwifery services for home births.

In a particular case, the Supreme Court has held that An Bord Altranais had not followed fair procedures in instituting inquiries of complaints against a midwife and, in particular, in not informing the midwife of the complaints and giving her an opportunity to respond: *O Ceallaigh v An Bord Altranais* [2000] 4 IR 54, SC. See also *O'Ceallaigh v An Bord Altranais* [2002] Irish Times, 5 December. See CHILD-BIRTH, ATTENDANCE AT; DOMICILIARY CHILDBIRTH; FOETAL DEATH; NURSE.

migration of company. The European Court has held that Articles 52 and 58 of the Treaty of Rome do not confer on companies the right to transfer their central management and control to another member state while retaining their status as companies incorporated under the legislation of the first member state: *R v HM Treasury and Inland Revenue Commissioners, ex parte Daily Mail and General Trust plc* [1988] STC 787 as described by *Gill* in 7ILT & SJ (1989) 59. See now EC Treaty, arts 43 and 48 of the consolidated (2002) version.

mile, nautical. See NAUTICAL MILE.

mileometer reading. A false mileometer reading has been held in the UK to be a false trade description (qv): *R v Hammerton Cars Ltd* [1976] 1 WLR 1243.

military convict. Formerly, a person under sentence of penal servitude passed by a court-martial: Defence Act 1954, s 2(1). Penal servitude was abolished and reference to a *military convict* was deleted by Criminal Law Act 1997, ss 11 and 14, Sch 2, para 1. See now DEFENCE FORCES.

military court of inquiry. An assembly of officers convened for the purpose of inquiring into any matter which may be referred to them by a convening authority, and to make such findings or declarations as may be required: Rules of Procedure (Defence Forces) 1954, r 106; Defence Act 1954. Statutory privilege extends only to the findings and recommendations of the court of inquiry: *O'Brien v Minister for Defence* [1998] 2 ILRM 156, SC. See MILITARY TRIBUNALS.

military law. The body of law dealing with the raising, maintenance and command of the defence forces; enlistment, promotion and discharge of personnel; discipline and offences in relation to persons subject to military law; courts-martial, and execution of sentences. The law is primarily contained in the principal statute: Defence Act 1954.

Subsequent legislation has provided for: (a) overseas service with the United Nations (qv) in peace keeping and enforcement: Defence (Amendment) (No 2) Act 1960 as amended and extended by Defence (Amendment) Act 1993; (b) the recruitment of women: Defence (Amendment) Act 1979; (c) appeals from courts-martial (qv): Courts-Martial Appeals Act 1983; (d) alteration in punishments in respect of offences against military law and introduction of new forms and penalties in respect of serving officers, and providing for contempt of a courts-martial: Defence (Amendment) Act 1987; (e) keeping crimes in military law in line with ordinary criminal law: Criminal Law Act 1997, s 14; (f) reorganisation of the defence forces under a single command structure: Defence (Amendment) Act 1998. [Bibliography: Humphreys & Craven]. See DEFENCE FORCES.

military prisoner. A person under sentence of imprisonment passed by a court-martial: Defence Act 1954, s 2(1). See DEFENCE FORCES AND OFFENCES.

military service pensions. Pensions payable to *veterans* of the War of Independence are exempt from income tax; the military service must have been during the pre-truce period, 1 April 1916 to 11 July 1921, or during the post-truce period 12 July 1921 to 30 September 1923: Taxes Consolidation Act 1997, s 205.

military tribunals. The tribunals which may be established for the trial of offences against military law alleged to have been committed by persons subject to military law and also to deal with a state of war or armed rebellion: 1937 Constitution, art 38(4)(1). See COURTS-MARTIAL.

milk. Means raw milk or heat-treated milk: Milk (Regulation of Supply) Act 1994, s 1(1). The Act provides for the establishment of a *National Milk Agency* to regulate the supply of milk for liquid consumption. See also Milk (Regulation of Supply) (Amendment) Acts 1995 and 1996.

It has been held that the mode of transposing the detailed *milk quota scheme*, established by community law, into domestic law is a matter of choice for Ireland: *Maher v Minister for Agriculture* [2001] 2 ILRM 481, SC and 2 IR 139. Damages were awarded against the Minister for Agriculture in relation to his mistake of law in the allocation of *milk quotas*: *Duff & Ors v Minister for Agriculture* [1997] 2 IR 22, SC and [1999] ITLR (4 October) HC. A new scheme of capital allowances has been introduced for the purchase of a *milk quota* under the proposed National Quota Restructuring Scheme: Taxes Consolidation Act 1997, ss 669A–669F inserted by Finance Act 2000, s 61 and amended by Finance Act 2002, s 30 to ensure no breach of EU rules on State aids.

The European Court of Justice has held that Italian legislation which fixed the same use-by date for high-temperature pasteurised milk and fresh pasteurised milk, while the former had a longer shelf life, prevented the former being marketed with this advantage and put a serious obstacle in the way of its free movement, and was precluded by Directive EC 92/46 and arts 28 and 30 of the Treaty establishing the European Community, the consolidated (2002) version: *Granarolo SpA v Comune di Bologna* [2003] Case C-294/01, ECJ.

See Milk Quota Regulations 2000, SI No 94 of 2000 and (Amendment) Regulations 2002, SI No 97 of 2002 to put in place arrangements for the operation of *Milk Production Partnerships* in Ireland, the functions in respect of which have been transferred from the Farm Apprenticeship Board to Teagasc: EC (Milk Quota) (Tea-gasc) Regulations 2002, SI No 496 of 2002. See also amendment Regulations 2003, SI No 123 of 2003 and 2004, SI No 208 of 2004. See *Law Society Gazette* (November 2003) 41.

millennium. A period or cycle of one thousand years. The only legislation to recognise particularly the end of the second millennium and the start of the third millennium was the Intoxicating Liquor Act 1999 which permitted all holders of *on-licences*, if they so wished, to avail of an additional two and a half hours' trading (ie to 1.30 am) on Millennium Night.

The millennium was marked officially by a £33m (€41.9m) programme of projects around the country, including: the delivery of a millennium candle and scroll to each household; the planting of 1.2 million native Irish trees, primarily oaks, in 13 forests (one tree for every household in the country); the restoration of historic Lightkeepers' houses at five headlands; the conservation and restoration of the 129-year old Gaiety Theatre; the minting of a new £1 millennium coin, the last new Irish coinage before the introduction of the euro; a new arrangement of Handel's Messiah, first performed in Dublin's Fishamble Street in 1742; the building of the Corofin Millennium Lodge and Rehabilitative Training Unit at the National Rehabilitation Hospital, Dún Laoghaire; the purchase of the Battle of the Boyne site dedicated to fostering the message of peace and reconciliation on the entire island. The millennium was also marked by a special millennium address by the President of Ireland, Mrs Mary McAleese, to a joint sitting of the Houses of the Oireachtas on 16 December 1999, the last sitting day of the century.

mine. An excavation made for the purpose of getting, wholly or substantially by means involving the employment of persons below ground, of minerals (whether in their natural state or in solution or suspension) or products of minerals: Mines and Quarries Act 1965, s 3. The exclusive right of working minerals in the State is vested in the Minister: Minerals Development Act 1979, s 12.

The 1965 Act contains provisions for protecting the lives, health and welfare of workers therein. Certain sections of the 1965 Act are repealed when particular sections of the Safety, Health and Welfare at Work Act 1989 come into force eg see SI

No 357 of 1995. Women are permitted to work in all occupations, including manual occupations below ground, in a mine: Employment Equality (Employment of Females on Underground Work in Mines) Order 1989, SI No 153 of 1991.

Relief by way of a reduction in corporation tax is not available in respect of income derived from 'mining operations': Corporation Tax Act 1976, s 58 (now replaced by Taxes Consolidation Act 1997, s 444). The term 'mining operations' is one of wide import and does not admit of precise definition; in determining whether activities were mining operations, consideration had to be given to the nature of the activity and, crucially, its relationship with the process of extraction: *O'Connell v Tara Mines Ltd* [2002] 3 IR 438, SC.

The anomaly which existed, whereby mines became rateable only seven years after opening, has been removed, with an exception for those mines already opened: Valuation Act 2001, s 59. There is now provision for the underground storage of explosives in a mine: Stores for Explosives Order 1955, SI No 42 of 1955 as amended by SI No 71 of 2003.

See *Glencar Exploration plc v Mayo County Council* [1993] 2 IR 237, HC; *Glencar Exploration plc v Mayo County Council* [2002] 1 ILRM 481, SC and 1 IR 84; *Scott and Ors v An Bord Pleanála* [1995] 1 ILRM 424, SC; *Sweeney v Duggan* [1997] 2 IR 531, SC. See QUARRY.

mineral companies. Mineral, oil and natural gas companies which wish to be listed on the stock exchange, are subject to additional disclosure requirements: Listing Rules 2000, ch 19. They may be admitted to listing without a trading record as normally required (para 3.3(a)); however, exploration companies which are not proposing to undertake extraction on a commercial scale are not suitable for listing. See LISTING RULES; STOCK EXCHANGE.

mineral rights. Minerals are either in private or State ownership. Mineral rights were often acquired by the State through dealings conducted by the Land Commission under the Land Acts 1903 and 1923. In some cases, the mineral rights vested in the Land Commission rather than in the State. The Minister is empowered to issue *State mining leases* for State minerals: Minerals Development Act 1940, s 5. Any mineral or exclusive mining rights which vested in the Land Commission are deemed to be and always to have been the property of the State and vested in the State, thus moving any doubt on licences issued by the Minister: Minerals Development Act 1999.

The Minerals Development Act 1979 established a system to regulate the working of privately owned minerals, with a right to compensation, which right could be separated from the ownership of the minerals (MDA 1979, s 20). This separation has caused complications and delays in the issuing of mining licences. In future, the right to compensation vests in the owner of the minerals at the time they are developed and there can be no separation (MDA 1999, s 3). This does not apply to situations where a sale or conveyance, separating the ownership and the right to compensation, has already taken place since 1979.

mini-prospectus. A document, not constituting *listing particulars*, which has attached to it or which contains, an application form; it must not contain any material information not contained in the listing particulars and must contain specified information: Listing Rules 2000, paras 8.12–8.13. See PROSPECTUS.

minimum age for employment. See EMPLOYMENT, MINIMUM AGE FOR.

minimum prices. See BELOW COST SELLING; PRICE CONTROL.

minimum wage. The national minimum hourly rate of *pay* which an employee is entitled to be paid by his employer in any *pay reference period*: National Minimum Wages Act 2000, s 14. The *minimum rate of pay* means the rate declared by order of the Minister (NMWA 2000, ss 2(1) and 11). *Pay* means all amounts of payment and any specified benefits-in-kind (NMWA 2000, ss 2(1) and 19 and Pt 1 of Sch eg monetary value of board with lodgings). *Pay reference period* means a period not exceeding one calendar month (NMWA 2000, s 10).

An employee who is 18 years of age or older is entitled to receive not less than the national minimum rate of pay in respect of his working hours in any pay reference period (NMWA 2000, s 14). It is an offence for an employer to refuse or fail to pay this minimum (NMWA 2000, s 35). There is a prohibition on an employer reducing the hours of work of an employee without a concomitant reduction in duties or amount of work (NMWA 2000, s 25).

There is provision for reference of a dispute on minimum pay to a Rights Commissioner, with appeal to the Labour Court, and referral or appeal to the High Court on a point of law (NMWA 2000, ss 24, 26–30).

There are special provisions for: (i) persons under 18 years of age (70% of national minimum rate of pay: NMWA 2000, s 14(b)), (ii) new entrants after, or on attaining, 18 years of age (80% first year; 90% second year: NMWA 2000, s 15); (iii) trainees (75%, 80% and 90% depending on year of study or training: NMWA 2000, s 16); and (iv) an employer in financial difficulty may be exempted by the Labour Court from the obligation for a period not exceeding one year and not less than three months: NMWA 2000, s 41.

The national minimum wage has been set at €5.97 from 1 July 2001, at €6.35 from 1 October 2002, and at €7.00 as from 1 February 2004: National Minimum Hourly Rate of Pay Orders 2000, SI No 95 of 2000; SI No 201 of 2000, and 2003 Order, SI No 250 of 2003; Prescribed Courses of Study or Training Regulations 2000, SI No 99 of 2000. The minimum rates of pay are taken into account when calculating a statutory redundancy lump sum: Redundancy Payments Act 2003, s 14. See JOINT LABOUR COMMITTEE; WAGES.

Minister. A member of the Government. The President of Ireland (qv) acting on the nomination of the Taoiseach (qv) with the previous approval of Dáil Éireann (qv), appoints members of the Government: 1937 Constitution, art 13(1)(2). The Taoiseach is empowered to assign Departments of State to members of the Government: Ministers and Secretaries (Amendment) Act 1946, s 4(1). A Minister is disqualified from being a member of a local authority: Local Government Act 1991, s 13, now Local Government Act 2001, s 13. A Minister is responsible for the performance of the functions which are assigned to his Department; he is empowered to give directions in writing to his Secretary General except as regards staff below the grade of Principal; and he may have up to two *special advisers*: Public Service Management (No 2) Act 1997, ss 3, 7, 11. See Appointment of Special Advisers Orders, SI No 344 of 1999, SIs No 100 and 176 of 2000, and SI No 331 of 2002. See CARLTONA PRINCIPLE; DELEGATION BY MINIS-

TER; GOVERNMENT; MINISTERIAL DECISIONS; MINISTERIAL RESPONSIBILITY; SEVERANCE PAY.

Minister of State. A member of either House of the Oireachtas, appointed by the government on the nomination of the Taoiseach: Ministers & Secretaries (Amendment) (No 2) Act 1977, s 1. They are not members of the government. Not more than 17 persons may be appointed: Ministers and Secretaries (Amendment) Act 1995, s 1. The government may on the recommendation of the Taoiseach remove a Minister of State. A Minister of State may resign his office by letter addressed to the Taoiseach and the resignation takes effect on and from the day it is accepted by the Taoiseach: Ministers and Secretaries (Amendment) Act 1980, s 4. A Minister of State is disqualified from being a member of a local authority: Local Government Act 1991, s 13, now Local Government Act 2001, s 13. He ceases to hold office on election to the European Parliament: European Parliament Elections Act 1997, s 11(4)(c).

A Minister of State may be entitled to one *special advisor*; however, where the Minister regularly attends meetings of the government, he may be entitled to two: Public Service Management (No 2) Act 1997, s 11(1). See Appointment of Special Advisers Orders, SI No 344 of 1999, and SIs Nos 100 and 176 of 2000. See CARLTONA PRINCIPLE; DELEGATION BY MINISTER.

Ministerial and Parliamentary offices. Provision has been made for improvement in the salary and pensions of Ministers, Ministers of State and members of the Oireachtas; the portability of pensions; the payment of long service increments for members of the Dáil and Seanad; increased remuneration for judges; linking of future salary increases of Ministers, Judges, and Oireachtas members automatically with reference to salary increases in the Civil Service; and other technical amendments: Ministerial, Parliamentary and Judicial Offices and Oireachtas Members (Miscellaneous Provisions) Act 2001.

There is also provision for a Minister or a member of the Oireachtas to decline an increase in salary or allowances (MPJOOM(MP)A 2001, ss 9, 26 and 44).

The Ministerial and Parliamentary Offices Act 1938, ss 33 and 34 are amended to provide that the Deputy Chairmen of the Dáil and Seanad continue in office (in addition to the Chairmen as heretofore) for constitutional purposes from the dissolution of each House to the day before it holds its first meeting, in order that they can exercise their constitutional role as deputy to the Chairmen who sit on the *Presidential Commission* (which exercises the functions of the President in certain circumstances) (MPJOOM(MP)A 2001, s 20). See also Public Service Superannuation (Miscellaneous Provisions) Act 2004, Sch 2.

ministerial announcement. RTÉ is required to comply with a direction from the Minister to allocate broadcasting time for any *announcements* by or on behalf of any Minister of State in connection with the functions of that Minister of State: Broadcasting Authority Act 1960, s 31(2). There is no right of reply to such a broadcast. An application to prevent the Taoiseach from making a broadcast under s 31(2) in favour of the Maastricht Treaty failed, as did the application for a right of reply: *McCann v Ireland, An Taoiseach & Ors (No 2)* 11 ILT Dig [1993] 211, HC. It was held that the word 'announcement' should be construed broadly (*McCann* case). However, see *McKenna v An Taoiseach* [1996] 1 ILRM 81, SC and [1995] 2 IR 10, SC. See also REFERENDUM.

ministerial decisions. The exercise of a Minister of a statutory power may be subject to *judicial review* and will be upheld if found to be reasonable: *The State (Crowley) v Irish Land Commission* [1951] IR 250; *Egan v Minister for Defence* [1989] 7 ILT Dig 81. Where a Minister is granted a specific duty to make decisions under a statutory code, and he makes such decisions *bona fide* having obtained and followed legal advice, he cannot be held to be negligent or to have made negligent misrepresentations, if he is found to have acted *ultra vires* (qv): *Pine Valley v Minister for the Environment* [1987] ILRM 747.

A Minister may be required to state the reasons for decisions which he makes in exercise of a statutory power e g where he refuses to grant a sea fishing boat licence to an applicant: *International Fishing Vessels Ltd v Minister for the Marine* [1989] IR 149. However, his decision made for stated valid reasons is not invalidated by unstated reasons (*International Fishing Vessels Ltd v Minister for the Marine* [1991] 2 IR 379, SC). It

has also been held that it is unconstitutional for a Minister to exercise his statutory power in such a way as to negative the expressed intention of the legislature: *Harvey v Minister for Social Welfare* [1990] ILRM 185, SC.

A Minister also is required to deal with an application under a statute (to attain a statutory right) within a reasonable time and before any critical 'cut-off' time: *Twomey v Minister for Transport & Tourism* [1993] ITLR (10 May) SC. A Minister must act reasonably: *Breen v Minister for Defence* [1990] ITLR (5 November) SC. The obligation for a Minister to act fairly in exercising his discretion includes ensuring that fair procedures are provided not only for an applicant but also for an objecting party: *Madden v Minister for the Marine* [1993] ILRM 436, HC. See STATUTORY INSTRUMENT.

ministerial directive. The Minister may, from time to time, issue policy directives to planning authorities regarding any of their functions and they must comply with such directives in the performance of their functions: Planning and Development Act 2000, s 29(1). A copy of these directives must be laid before the Houses of the Oireachtas (PDA 2000, s 29(5)). However, the Minister must not exercise any power or control in relation to any particular planning application or appeal (PDA 2000, s 30 as amended by Minister for the Environment and Local Government (Performance of Certain Functions) Act 2002). See DEVELOPMENT PLAN.

ministerial guidelines. The Minister may, at any time issue guidelines to planning authorities regarding any of their functions and they must have regard to the guidelines in the performance of their functions: Planning and Development Act 2000, s 28(1). These guidelines must be laid before the Houses of the Oireachtas (PDA 2000, s 28(5)).

ministerial order. An order made by a Minister exercising such power as is given to him under a statute e g an order to amend a schedule to an Act, viz Waste Management Act 1996, s 8. Such an order may be required under the legislation to be laid before each House of the Oireachtas before it can come into effect (WMA 1996, s 7(4)). See REGULATION; STATUTORY INSTRUMENT.

ministerial responsibility. Ministers as members of the government are *collectively* responsible to Dáil Éireann for the Departments of State administered by them: 1937 Constitution, art 28(4). See GOVERNMENT.

minor. A person under the age of eighteen years who is not or has not been married: Age of Majority Act 1985, s 2. This interpretation also applies to the terms *infancy*, *infant* and *minority*. Contracts made during infancy in respect of *necessaries* (qv) and *apprenticeship* (qv) are binding on an infant. When an infant acquires an interest in a subject of a permanent nature, which imposes a continuous liability on him, the contract cannot be enforced against him during infancy eg a lease, a partnership, a shareholding in a company or a marriage settlement.

After the infant attains full age, it will be binding on him unless he avoids it within a reasonable time eg see *Davies v Benyon-Harris* [1931] 47 TLR 424. All other contracts are unenforceable against the infant. Certain contracts entered into by infants are *absolutely void* eg a contract for repayment of money lent or to be lent; goods supplied or to be supplied (other than necessaries) and accounts stated: Infants Relief Act 1874, s 1. See *Coutts v Browne-Lecky* [1947] KB 104. See also Family Law Act 1981, s 10; Finance Act 1986, s 112, now Taxes Consolidation Act 1997, s 7; Law Reform Commission *Report on Minors' Contracts* (LRC 15, 1985).

A minor who had attained the age of sixteen can give effective consent to surgical, medical or dental treatment which, without consent, would constitute trespass to the person: Non-Fatal Offences against the Person Act 1997, s 23.

A minor is fully liable for his torts (qv) provided he has reached the age of discretion: *O'Brien v McNamee* [1953] IR 86. A minor may be made a ward of court. It is an offence for a person knowingly, with a view to financial gain, to send any document to a minor inviting him: to borrow on credit, to obtain goods or services on credit, or to hire goods, or to apply for information or advice in relation to credit: Consumer Credit Act 1995, s 139. See also Building Societies Act 1989, s 16(5). See DCR 1997 Ord 7. See LRC 17 of 1985. See CHILD, ADOPTED; DOLI INCAPAX; LODGMENT IN COURT; MARRIAGE; PAYMENT OUT OF COURT; PERSONAL INJURIES; NEXT FRIEND; RATIFICATION; SETTLEMENT; WARD OF COURT.

minor and crime. See DOLI INCAPAX; PUNISHMENT OF CHILD.

minor offence. An offence which may be tried by courts of summary jurisdiction: 1937 Constitution, art 38(2). The Constitution does not define a minor offence. It is for the Oireachtas in the first instance to determine whether an offence is a minor offence or not, though it may delegate the function to the District Court where it provides for alternative modes of trial: *DPP v Dargan* [1997] 1 ILRM 550, HC.

The main criteria for determining whether an offence is a minor one are: the severity of the penalty, the moral quality of the act, how the law stood when the statute was passed, the relationship of the offence to common law offences: *Melling v O'Mathghamhna* [1962] IR 1; *The State (Rollinson) v Kelly* [1984] ILRM 625. Secondary penalties authorised under a statute should not be taken into account: *Cartmill v Ireland* [1987] HC.

It would appear that where the punishment is less than six months' imprisonment or the fine is £500 (€635) or less, the offence is minor; whereas where the punishment is two years or more or the fine is £100,000 (€126,974) or more, the offence is non-minor. However, the Supreme Court has upheld the right of the District Court to impose consecutive sentences provided the aggregate does not exceed two years: *Meagher v O'Leary* [1998] 4 IR 33, SC. See also *Mallon v Minister for Agriculture* [1996] 1 IR 517, SC; *DPP (Travers) v Brennan* [1998] 4 IR 67, SC; *Conroy v Attorney-General* [1965] IR 411; *The State (Sheerin) v Kennedy* [1966] IR 379; *Kostan v Ireland* [1978] HC; *The State (Pheasantry) v Donnelly* [1982] ILRM 512; *The State (Wilson) v DJ Neylon* [1987] ILRM 118. See *Consultation Paper on Penalties for Minor Offences* (LRC CP 18, 2002); *Report on Penalties for Minor Offences* (LRC 69, 2003). See SUMMARY OFFENCE.

minority protection. See OPPRESSION OF SHAREHOLDER.

minutes. Notes providing a record of proceedings. A company must keep minutes of all its general meetings: Companies Act 1963, s 145. Such minutes must be signed by the chairman and when so signed are *prima facie* evidence of what occurred at the meeting. The minutes must also be open to inspection by members of the company: CA 1963, s 146 and Companies (Amendment) Act 1982, s 15.

Minutes of meetings of the board of directors and of general meetings must be produced, on request, to the *Director of Corporate Enforcement*: Companies Act 1963, s 145 as amended by Company Law Enforcement Act 2001, s 19.

Minutes contemporaneously made of the meeting of members of a board or of a tribunal are neither a necessary nor the only method of establishing the material that was before that board or tribunal: *O'Keeffe v An Bord Pleanála & Radio Tara* [1992] ILRM 237, SC.

misadventure. The killing of another while doing a lawful act with no intention of causing harm, and with no culpable negligence in the mode of doing it eg death accidentally caused in the course of a lawful game or sport. See *R v Young* 10 Cox 371; *The People (Attorney-General) v Dunleavy* [1948] IR 95. See HOMICIDE.

misappropriation. See DECEIT; FRAUDULENT CONVERSION.

miscarriage. A breach of natural justice: Finlay J in *The State (Healy) v DJ Ballagh* (22 April 1983, unreported) SC. The primary meaning of 'miscarriage of justice' is that the person is, on the balance of probability as established by relevant and admissible evidence, innocent of the offence of which he was convicted: *The People (DPP) v Pringle (No 2)* [1997] 2 IR 225, SC.

A new procedure has been established whereby a convicted person, who has exhausted the normal appeals procedure, may apply to the Court of Criminal Appeal (the Supreme Court, when the CCA is subsumed into it) for leave to appeal again where a *new* or *newly discovered* fact is alleged to show a miscarriage of justice in relation to the conviction or that the sentence imposed is excessive: Criminal Procedure Act 1993, s 2. The court is given wide powers eg to affirm or quash the conviction, to order a re-trial, to substitute another verdict, to quash or vary the sentence, to order the Garda Commissioner to have inquiries carried out, and to grant bail (CPA 1993, s 3).

A convicted person may petition the Minister for a Presidential pardon (CPA 1993, s 7). The government may establish a tribunal to inquire into an alleged miscarriage of justice in the context of advising the President on exercising the right of pardon (CPA 1993, s 8). Compensation may be payable to the convicted person

where a *newly discovered* fact shows that there had been a miscarriage (CPA 1993, s 9).

Once an applicant has satisfied one of the three conditions in CPA 1993, s 9(1)(a)(i), he is entitled to have the court enter into an inquiry whether he was entitled to a certificate that a *newly discovered* fact showed that there had been a miscarriage of justice: *The People (DPP) v Meleady (No 2)* [1997] 2 IR 249, SC. These provisions are not limited to appeals brought under s 2 of CPA 1993: *Connell v DPP* [1999] 4 IR 1, CCA. See also *The People (DPP) v Meleady (No 3)* [2001] 4 IR 16, CCA.

The court is required to carry out an objective evaluation of the *newly discovered* fact with a view to determining, in the light of it, whether the conviction was unsafe and unsatisfactory: *The People (DPP) v Gannon* [1997] 1 IR 40, SC. See *People (DPP) v McDonagh* [1996] 1 IR 305, CCA.

The court is concerned with whether the *newly discovered* facts were tantamount to providing a miscarriage of justice; it was not confined to the question of actual innocence but extended to the administration of justice itself: *The People (DPP) v Shortt (No 2)* [2002] 2 IR 696, CCA.

In relation to a claim for compensation in respect of a quashed conviction, see *Pringle v Ireland* [2000] 2 ILRM 161, HC and [1999] 4 IR 10, HC. See also International Covenant on Civil and Political Rights, UN Doc A/PV 1496 [1966]. See APPEAL; EUROPEAN CONVENTION ON HUMAN RIGHTS; PARDON.

mischief of a statute. The wrong which it is intended to redress by an enactment. The mischief is often to be found in the preamble to the Act or from the marginal notes. See MISCHIEF RULE.

mischief rule. The rule of construction for interpreting a statute whereby the judge will look at the law which existed prior to the statute, the *mischief of the statute* (qv) which it was intended to remedy and will interpret the statute in a way to suppress the mischief and advance the remedy. See *Magdalen College Case* [1616] 11 Co Rep 716; *Nestor v Murphy* [1979] IR 326; *DPP v Tivoli Cinema Ltd* [1999] 2 ILRM 153, SC and 2 IR 260.

The mischief rule has been subsumed into a more modern *purposive rule* (qv): *DPP (Ivers) v Murphy* [1999] 1 ILRM 46. See VICARIOUS LIABILITY.

mischievous propensity. See SCIENTER; ANIMALS; DOGS.

misconduct. A ground for dismissal from employment. See *Nugent v CIE* [1990] ELR 15; *Creed v KMP Co-op Society Ltd* [1990] ELR 140, EAP; *O'Connor v Brewster* [1992] ELR 10, EAT. See GROSS MISCONDUCT; HORSEPLAY; REDUNDANCY; UNFAIR DISMISSAL.

misdemeanour. Formerly, a crime which was not a felony. The word *felony* was formerly used to denote the most serious of offences, and *misdemeanour* the less serious. In the course of time, the distinction became blurred and anomalies crept in, with some very serious crimes classified as misdemeanours, while some less serious crimes were classified as felonies. In 1997, all distinctions between misdemeanours and felonies were abolished, and provision was made that the law and practice in relation to misdemeanours would apply to all offences: Criminal Law Act 1997, s 3. See FELONY.

misdescription. As regards property, an error, mistake, or mis-statement in the description of the property. If the misdescription is substantial, the purchaser will be entitled to repudiate the contract; the misdescription will be a good defence to an action for specific performance (qv). However, if the misdescription is one the only effect of which was to induce the purchaser to give a higher price than he otherwise would, and was made innocently, and compensation can be fairly assessed, the court will order specific performance subject to that compensation.

misdirection. Failure by a judge to inform the jury adequately as to the evidence or the law or as to the issues requiring a decision or a total failure so to inform. A judge sitting alone can misdirect himself e g by putting the wrong questions to himself to answer. Misdirection is a ground for appeal. For a judge to say to a jury that something is only *theoretically possible* is in effect to invite them not to consider it at all and may amount to a misdirection: *People (DPP) v Clarke* [1995] 1 ILRM 355, CCA. See *Kelly v Board of Governors of St Laurence's Hospital* [1988] IR 402 and [1989] 7 ILT Dig 23; *DPP v Kelly* [1997] 1 IR 405, HC. See RETRIAL.

misericordia. [Mercy (qv)].

misfeasance. An improper performance of an otherwise lawful act e g where there is an act of positive negligence. A *misfeasor* is a

person who is guilty of a misfeasance. Where a local authority performs its duty of repairing the highway but does so in a negligent manner, it is guilty of misfeasance; it may be sued for any resulting damage and cannot escape liability on the grounds that it employed an independent contractor to do the work: *Clements v Tyrone County Council* [1905] 2 IR 415. Damages for misfeasance will not be granted where the defendants had acted in a *bona fide* manner and had not acted maliciously: *CW Shipping Ltd v Limerick Harbour Commissioners* [1989] ILRM 416, HC.

The High Court has held that the tort of *misfeasance in public office* consists of a purported exercise of some power or authority by a public officer otherwise than in an honest attempt to perform the functions of his office resulting in loss to the claimant: *Giles Kennedy v Law Society* [2004] 1 ILRM 178, HC. To constitute the tort: (a) there must be the exercise of an otherwise legitimate public power in bad faith for an ulterior or improper motive or (b) the public officer acted in bad faith by carrying out an act in the actual knowledge that he has no legal power to do so (*Kennedy* case, following *Three Rivers District Council v Bank of England* [2003] 3 All ER 1). A high threshold exists as a precondition to the recovery of damages resulting from the *ultra vires* behaviour of public authorities.

It has been held that, in the absence of *mala fides* in the exercise by a public official of his authority, no cause of action will lie in the tort of misfeasance: *An Blascaod Mor Teo v Commissioner for Public Works* [2001] 1 ILRM 423, HC and [2000] 3 IR 565, HC. See also *Kelly v Mayo Co Co* [1964] IR 315. See NONFEASANCE; ROAD MAINTENANCE.

misfeasance suit, company. A summary procedure by which a company which is being wound up may be compensated for losses arising from various wrongs done to it (including any misfeasance or other breach of duty or trust) by its directors or other officers. The court may, on the application of the liquidator, or of a creditor or contributory, investigate the matter and order restitution and compensation. See Companies Act 1963, s 298 as amended by Companies Act 1990, s 142; RSC Ord 74, r 49. See *Re S M Barker Ltd* [1950] IR 123; *Jackson v Mortell* [1986] HC. See MacCann in 9 ILT & SJ (1991) 58.

This summary procedure may now be instituted by the *Director of Corporate*

Enforcement, in addition to a liquidator, creditor or contributory as heretofore: Companies Act 1963, s 298 as amended by Companies Act 1990, s 142 and now by Company Law Enforcement Act 2001, s 50. See also CLEA 2001, s 96. [Bibliography: Cahill N]. See WINDING UP.

misjoinder. Where a person is wrongly joined in proceedings either as plaintiff or defendant. No cause or matter may be defeated by reason of the misjoinder or non-joinder of parties; the court may order that the names of parties improperly joined be struck out, and to add parties who ought to have been joined: RSC Ord 15, r 13.

No action, cause or matter will be defeated by reason of the misjoinder or non-joinder of parties: Circuit Court Rules 2001 Ord 6, r 4.

misleading advertisement. See ADVERTISEMENT, MISLEADING.

misnomer. A mis-naming. An amendment to correct the error may be made in a suitable case. See PLEADINGS, AMENDMENT OF.

misprision of felony. Formerly, a common law misdemeanour, committed by a person who knew that a felony (qv) had been committed and could give information which might lead to the felon's arrest, but omitted to report it. The offence did not arise by the failure of a legal advisor, a doctor or a clergyman to report the matter, or where the failure was in order to avoid inviting a prosecution against oneself. See *Sykes v DPP* [1961] 3 All ER 33 at 36. There was no offence of misprision of misdemeanour.

The offence of misprision of felony has disappeared with the abolition of any distinction between a felony and a misdemeanour and the requirement that the law and practice as regards misdemeanours applies to all offences: Criminal Law Act 1997, s 3. See however CONCEALING AN OFFENCE.

misprision of treason. The offence committed by a person who fails to disclose treason (qv) which is proposed to be, or is being, or has been committed: Treason Act 1939, s 3.

misrepresentation. A statement or conduct which conveys a false or wrong impression. A misrepresentation may be *fraudulent*, *negligent* or *innocent*. As regards contract, a misrepresentation to be *operative*: must be a false representation; it must be one of fact;

it must be intended to be acted upon; and it must actually mislead and induce a contract.

A *fraudulent* misrepresentation is one made knowingly or without belief in its truth or recklessly, careless whether it be true or false: *Derry v Peek* [1889] 14 App Cas 337; *Early v Fallon* [1976] HC. The person so induced to contract may affirm or rescind the contract and sue for damages in the tort of deceit (qv), although rescission may not be allowed where the parties cannot be restored to their original position: *Northern Bank Finance Corp Ltd v Charlton* [1979] IR 149; *Carbin v Somerville* [1933] IR 276.

A *negligent* misrepresentation is one made with no reasonable grounds for believing it to be true. A special duty of care may exist between parties to a contract such as to render *negligent* the failure of one party to ascertain the falsity of a statement, which with reasonable care would have been ascertained: *Hedley Byrne & Co Ltd v Heller & Partners Ltd* [1964] AC 465; *Securities Trust Ltd v Hugh Moore & Alexander Ltd* [1964] IR 417; *Esso Petroleum Ltd v Mardon* [1975] 1 All ER 203; *Stafford v Mahoney* [1980] HC. The person induced to enter the contract may sue in the tort of negligence (qv).

An *innocent* misrepresentation is one which is not negligent or fraudulent and which may entitle the party misled to rescind the contract if the innocent misrepresentation was of a material fact: *Redgrave v Hurd* [1881] 20 Ch D 1; or to an indemnity to restore the party misled to the position he was in before he entered the contract; or to an abatement (qv).

A cause of action for misrepresentation accrues not from the date a representation was made but from the date of the alleged breaches of these assurances: *Murphy v Minister for the Marine* [1996] 2 ILRM 297, HC. See *Ennis v Butterly* [1997] 1 ILRM 28, HC and [1996] 1 IR 426, HC; *O'Donnell v Truck and Machinery Sales Ltd* [1998] 4 IR 191, SC. See INNOCENT MISREPRESENTATION; NEGLIGENT MISSTATEMENT; PATENT, REVOCATION OF; PLEADINGS.

mistake. Mistake may operate to nullify consent. However, mistake by a party to a contract cannot avoid that contract due to: (a) an error of judgement on his part, or (b) an underestimation of his own power of performance under the contract, or (c) generally an error as to the law and its effects. While a fundamental mistaken assumption can nullify consent so as to make a contract void, this rule is confined within very narrow limits: *Fitzsimons v O'Hanlon* [1999] 2 ILRM 551, HC.

Mistake may be *mutual* or *common* where the mistake is shared by both parties to the contract, or it may be *unilateral* where it is on one side only.

A *unilateral* mistake generally will not allow a party to a contract to avoid the contract unless there is a mistake as to: (a) the subject matter contracted for: *Raffles v Wichelhaus* [1864] 2 H & C 906; (b) the identity of the person with whom the contract is made: *Cundy v Lindsay* [1878] 3 App Cas 459; (c) the promise of one party which mistake is known to the other party: *Webster v Cecil* [1861] 30 Beav 62; (d) the character of a written document: See NON EST FACTUM.

A *mutual* mistake as to a fact which goes to the root of a contract will render the contract void *ab initio* e g mistake as to the fundamental subject matter of the contract or mistake as to the existence of the subject matter e g a life insurance policy taken out in the mistaken belief that the person in question is still alive, is void: *Strickland v Turner* [1852] 7 Exch 208. See also *Bell v Lever Bros* [1932] AC 161; *Cooper v Phibbs* [1867] LR 2 HL 149; *Western Potato Co-operative Ltd v Durnan* [1985] ILRM 5; *Mespil Ltd v Capaldi* [1986] ILRM 373; *Irish Life Assurance Co v Dublin Land Securities* [1986] HC.

Where mistake is *operative* i e operates to render the contract void at common law or voidable in equity, the relief available may be rescission (qv), rectification (qv) or as a defence to specific performance (qv).

Money paid under a mistake of fact is always recoverable as *money had and received* (qv) to the use of the person who has paid it; it now appears that money paid under a mistake of law is also recoverable: *Rogers v Louth County Council* [1981] ILRM 143; *Lord Mayor of Dublin v The Provost of Trinity College Dublin* [1984] HC. See *A Farewell to Equitable Mistake?* by Des Ryan in (2003) 11 ISLR 3. See COMPROMISE; ERROR; OFFER.

mistake, sale of goods. Although parties have reached agreement in the same terms and on the same subject matter, if their agreement is based on a fundamental fact, which turns out to have been mistaken, the courts may treat such a mistake as avoiding the contract which had apparently been made. See *Chartered Trust Ireland Ltd v Healy* [1985] HC.

mistake and crime. Mistake of law is no defence. A mistake of fact may be a good defence to a criminal charge where the mistake of fact, if true, would have justified the act. In a larceny case, a judge is entitled to find that there is a case to answer, even when the owners of the property have been mistaken as to the dates on which they inspected their property at the garda station: *DPP v Noonan* [2002] FL 7036, HC. For *mistake* in criminal law, see Bibliography: Charleton (4); McAuley & McCutcheon.

mistake and tort. Mistake is generally no defence in an action of tort (qv).

mistake of fact. A decision of an immigration officer to refuse a person entry into Ireland, which was based on a mistake of fact, was held to be an invalid decision: *Gulyas v Minister for Justice* [2001] 3 IR 216, HC.

misuse of drugs. See DRUGS, MISUSE OF.

mitigating factors. Factors which are considered by a court in determining sentence of an accused having established his guilt and the gravity of the offence and the nature of punishment in principle e g a plea of guilty except where caught *in flagrante delicto*, personal circumstances of the accused (including age), and the prospect of rehabilitation. A court should look at where, on the range of penalties, a particular case would lie and then make an appropriate reduction based on the mitigating circumstances: *People (DPP) v M* [1994] 2 ILRM 541, SC. When the accused is pleading guilty, a barrister should not accept instructions to tender a plea in mitigation on a basis inconsistent with the plea of guilty: *Code of Conduct for the Bar of Ireland* (December 2003) r 9.11.

mitigation of damages. Diminution of loss. In general there is a duty on a person whose legal rights have been infringed to act reasonably to mitigate his loss. The injured party can recover no more than he would have recovered if he had acted reasonably, because any further damages do not reasonably follow from the defendant's breach. Failure by a plaintiff to mitigate losses he incurred by the defendant's action, may result in a reduction in the costs awarded to the plaintiff eg in a particular case only 19 days' costs of a 22-day hearing were awarded to the plaintiff: *Deane & Ors v VHI* [1993] HC.

Damages are not restricted where the party harmed is unable to mitigate the losses due to impecuniosity: *Doran v Delaney* [1999] 1 IR 303, HC. See also *Cullen v Horgan* [1925] 2 IR 1; *Bord Iascaigh Mhara v Scallan* [1973] HC; *Malone v Malone* [1982] HC.

Where the injured party has received compensation from another source, the common law rule is that this compensation does not reduce damages to the defendant; however statute may require such a deduction. See Social Welfare (Consolidation) Act 1993, s 237; Civil Liability (Amendment) Act 1964, s 2.

In defamation (qv) actions, the following factors may be taken into account in mitigation of damages: an apology from the defendant: Defamation Act 1961, s 17; receipt by the plaintiff of compensation for the same or similar words already (DA 1961, s 26); provocation by counter-defamations; and the bad reputation of the plaintiff. Where a defendant in such an action intends to give evidence in mitigation of damages, he must furnish particulars thereof to the plaintiff not later than seven days beforehand: RSC Ord 36, r 36.

mittimus. [We send].

mixed fund. A fund consisting of the proceeds of sale of both real and personal property.

MMDS. Means a Multipoint Microwave Distribution System: Copyright and Related Rights Act 2000, s 2(1). MMDS is included in the definition of a *cable programme* (qv).

mobilia sequuntur personam. [Movables follow the person]. See FIXTURES.

mobile food outlet. A mobile outlet that is used wholly or partly for the sale of produce, food or drink: Litter Pollution Act 1997, s 15. The owner, occupier or person in charge of such an outlet must exercise litter control at all times the outlet is open to customers eg providing and maintaining adequate litter receptacles, removing litter up to one hundred metres from the outlet, and complying with any notice from the local authority.

mobile phone. Any device which is being used directly by a person for the purpose of communication by way of mobile and personal communication systems: SI No 93 of 2002. This regulation provides that the driver of a mechanically propelled vehicle that is in a public place, shall not hold or have on or about their person, a mobile phone or other similar apparatus while in the said vehicle, except when it is *parked*. 'Parked' means parked in such a location and manner that an offence under the Road Traffic Acts is not committed thereby. This statutory instrument had not been implemented in practice by 1 September 2004.

Pending a new Road Traffic Bill where such use of a mobile phone will attract one penalty point (or three if contested in court), as an interim measure, such use of a mobile phone may amount to 'careless driving' attracting five penalty points: SI No 248 of 2004. See 'The "visible hand" in the mobile telephony market' by Conleth Bradley BL in *Bar Review* (October 2000) 4; 'Upwardly Mobile' by solicitor Paul Lambert in *Law Society Gazette* (March 2003) 14. See BENEFIT-IN-KIND; COMMISSION FOR COMMUNICATIONS REGULATION; GLOBAL SYSTEM MOBILE; M-COMMERCE.

mode of address. Judges of the Superior Courts (qv) must be addressed in Irish or English by their respective titles and names, and may be referred to, in Irish, as *An Chuirt* or, in English, as *The Court*: RSC Ord 119, r 1. A judge of the Circuit Court must be addressed in Court by his title, and may be referred to in Irish as *An Chuirt* or in English as *The Court*: Circuit Court Rules 2001 Ord 3, r 2. It is customary in court to address judges of the Supreme, High and Circuit Courts as *My Lord* or *Your Lordship* or *A Thiarna Bhreithimh* and a judge of the District Court as *Judge* or *A Bhreithimh*.

In writing, it is customary to address judges of the Supreme and High Courts as *The Hon Mr/Mrs/Ms Justice* ...; of the Circuit and District Courts as *His/Her Hon Judge* .... Letters are commenced *Dear Mr/Mrs/Ms Justice* ... (Supreme and High); *Dear Judge* (Circuit and District). An arbitrator is usually addressed as *Arbitrator* or *Mr/Mrs/Ms Arbitrator*. See also DCR 1997 Ord 4.

mode of trial. The manner in which a trial is conducted eg arraignment of the accused, the selection of the jury, challenge to a juror, a trial within the trial, the closing speeches, the summing up by the judge, the verdict of the jury, and the sentence (qqv). Certain formalities in the mode of trial of felonies have been abolished e g asking the accused after conviction if he has anything to say why the court should not pass judgment according to law: Criminal Law Act 1997, s 3(2). See ALLOCUTUS; FELONY; VOIRE DIRE.

model code. The model code on director's dealings with securities: Listing Rules 2000, ch 16, App (as amended by Irish Stock Exchange Ltd). A company must require its directors and any employee likely to be in possession of unpublished *price-sensitive* information to comply with a code of dealing in terms no less exacting than those of the model code (para 16.18). See DIRECTORS AND SHARE DEALING.

model lease. A precedent for a lease of a dwelling which the *Private Residential Tenancies Board* (qv) has been given responsibility to develop and publish, and which will: (a) contain all of the provisions necessary to make the lease of the dwelling concerned an instrument which is consistent with the Residential Tenancies Act 2004 and any other relevant enactments, (b) be worded, so far as is practicable, in plain language, and (c) to the extent necessary having regard to the requirements of paragraph (a), contain provisions best calculated to ensure harmonious relations between the parties to the lease as regards their conduct towards one and another in their capacity as such parties (RTA 2004, s 152).

models. See ARTISTIC WORK.

modus et conventio vincunt legem. [Custom and agreement overrule law]. See CUSTOM AND PRACTICE.

modus legem dat donationi. [Agreement gives law to the gift].

modus operandi. [The way of performing a task].

moiety. Half; one of two equal parts. Legislation sometimes provides for payment to be made in equal moieties e g the collection of rates pursuant to the Local Government Act 1994, s 45. Samples taken from greyhounds are required to be divided into equal parts and each *moiety* placed in a separate receptacle: Public Sale of Greyhounds Regulations, SI No 76 of 1966, reg 14(2). See also *Re Rea deceased; Rea v Rea* [1902] 1 IR 451 referred to in LRC 36, 1991.

molestation. An act done by a spouse or on his authority, with the intent to annoy the other spouse and in fact be an annoyance to her. A *non-molestation clause* is generally included in a separation agreement (qv) providing that neither spouse will molest, annoy, disturb or interfere with the other. Behaviour in breach of such a clause may be restrained by injunction (qv). See ASSAULT; BARRING ORDER.

molliter manus imposit. [He laid hands on him gently]. A defence to a charge of *assault and battery* (qv).

monetary policy. One of the basic tasks of the European System of Central Banks (ESCB) is to define and implement the monetary policy of the EC: EC Treaty, art 105 of the consolidated (2002) version. The primary objective of the ESCB is to maintain price stability. Its other basic tasks are: to conduct foreign exchange operations consistent with the exchange rate policy, to hold and manage the official foreign reserves of the member States, and to promote the smooth operation of payments systems. The *European Central Bank* (qv) has the exclusive right to authorise the issue of banknotes within the Community (EC Treaty, art 106). There is provision for a Monetary Committee to be replaced by an Economic and Financial Committee (EC Treaty, art 114). See ECONOMIC AND MONETARY UNION; EURO.

monetary unit. The monetary unit of the State was the Irish pound which was issued in *legal tender* (qv) form: Central Bank Act 1989, s 24(1). From 1 January 1999, the currency unit of the State is the *euro*; the Irish pound unit was a subdivision of the euro during the transitional period: Economic and Monetary Union Act 1998, s 6. See euro.

money. The medium of exchange and measure and store of value. A *pecuniary* legacy includes any direction by a testator for the payment of money: Succession Act 1965, s 3(1). See LEGAL TENDER.

Money Advice and Budgeting Service; MABS. Under draft legislation, a service designed to target families and individuals with debt and moneylending problems and to assist them with advice: Money Advice and Budgeting Service Bill 2002. The Bill is intended to provide a statutory basis for a service currently operated by 52 local projects nationwide. Each project is incorporated as a company limited by guarantee and run by a management committee drawn from local voluntary and community groups, credit union representatives and local statutory agencies. There is provision for a *National Advisory Committee*. See

CREDIT; CONSUMER DEBT; DEBT MANAGE-
MENT SERVICE; MONEY ADVICE AND
BUDGETING SERVICE.

money bill. See BILL, MONEY.

money had and received. Money which is
paid to one person which rightfully belongs
to another eg where a person pays money
under protest he may recover the sum paid:
*Gt. Southern and Western Railway Co v Rob-
ertson* [1878] 2 LR (Ir) 548; or where
money is paid under a conditional contract
it may be recovered if the condition is not
fulfilled: *Lowis v Wilson* [1949] IR 347;
*Lord Mayor of Dublin v The Provost of Trinity
College Dublin* [1984] HC. See MISTAKE;
ULTRA VIRES.

money laundering. A person is guilty of
money laundering if he, knowing or believing
that property is or represents the proceeds
of criminal conduct, or being reckless in
that regard, without lawful authority or
excuse: (a) acquires, possesses or uses the
property, or (b) conceals or disguises its
true nature, source, location, disposition,
movement or ownership or any rights with
respect to it, or (c) converts, transfers or
handles the property, or removes it from
the State, with the intention of eg concealing its true nature: Criminal Justice
Act 1994, s 31 as amended by substitution
by Criminal Justice (Theft and Fraud
Offences) Act 2001, s 21. The proof that
the person had lawful authority or excuse
lies with that person.

Credit and financial institutions (and
persons or bodies prescribed in regulations)
are required to take measures to prevent
money laundering eg establishing the identity of customers, retention of records and
to report to the gardaí when they suspect
any offence, not just money laundering, is
being or has been committed (CJA 1994,
ss 32, 57 as amended by Disclosure of
Certain Information for Taxation and other
Purposes Act 1996, ss 2–3, and Criminal
Justice (Miscellaneous Provisions)
Act 1997, ss 14 and 15).

The following persons or bodies have
been prescribed in regulations: an accountant, an auctioneer, an estate agent, a tax
advisor, a solicitor when participating in
any of specified activities, a person who
provides money transmission services,
administration companies providing services to collective investment schemes, an
investment business firm, a trustee or custodian of a collective investment scheme,
casinos, and a dealer in high value goods,

precious metals and works of art where
payment is made in cash for a sum of
€15,000 or more: SI No 242 of 2003 as
amended by SI No 416 of 2003. The
specified activities as regards solicitors are
when they participate, whether: (a) by
assisting in the planning or execution of
transactions for their client concerning: (i)
the buying and selling of real property or
business entities; (ii) the management of
client money, securities or other assets; (iii)
the opening or management of bank, savings or securities accounts; (iv) the organisation of contributions necessary for the
creation, operation or management of companies; (v) the creation, operation or management of companies or similar structures;
(b) or by acting on behalf of and for their
client in any financial or real estate transaction: art 2a(5) of Directive (EEC) 91/308
as amended by Directive (EC) 2001/97.
See also SI No 3 of 2004.

The requirement of reporting to the
gardaí does not apply to an accountant, an
auditor, a solicitor or tax advisor in so far as
they receive or obtain information from or
relating to a client: (a) in the course of
ascertaining the legal position for that client, (b) when performing the task of
defending or representing that client in or
concerning legal proceedings, or (c) when
advising that client in relation to instituting
or avoiding judicial proceedings.

There is also a requirement on certain
designated bodies (eg banks and building
societies) to report to the gardaí any transaction connected with a State or territorial
unit, which has been designated by Ministerial order as not having in place adequate
procedures for the detection of money
laundering (CJA 1994, s 57A inserted
by CJ(TFO)A 2001, s 23) eg see SI
No 101 of 2002; SI No 52 of 2004. See SIs
Nos 104 & 105 of 1995. See 'Filthy Lucre'
by Mary Keane in *Law Society Gazette*
(October 2003) 24.

[Bibliography: Ashe & Reid; McCutch-
eon & Walsh; McGreal C]. See BUREAU DE
CHANGE; CONFISCATE; REVENUE
OFFENCE.

money lodged in court. See LODGMENT IN
COURT.

moneylender. A person who carries on the
business of moneylending or who advertises
or announces himself or holds himself out
in any way as carrying on that business; it
does not include a pawnbroker, a credit
union, a friendly society, a credit institution

(eg banks and building societies), a mortgage lender, or a person who supplies money at an APR of less than 23%: Consumer Credit Act 1995, s 2(1). A person is prohibited from engaging in the business of moneylending unless he is the holder of a *moneylender's licence*, which is issued by the Central Bank (IFSRA) and is valid for twelve months (CCA 1995, ss 98 and 93 as amended by Central Bank and Financial Services Authority of Ireland Act 2003, s 35, Sch 1 and Central Bank and Financial Services Authority of Ireland Act 2004, Sch 1).

A *moneylending agreement* is a *credit agreement* (qv) into which a moneylender enters, or offers to enter, with a *consumer* in which one or more of the following apply: APR is in excess of 23% or the agreement or negotiations or repayments were or are concluded, conducted or paid, away from the business premises of the moneylender or the supplier of goods or services (CCA 1995, s 2(1)). A person is presumed to have been engaged in moneylending if found to be in possession of a document or money in circumstances which give rise to a reasonable inference that the document or money was kept for the purpose of moneylending (CCA 1995, s 104).

There is a prohibition on increasing the charge for credit on a default (CCA 1995, s 112) and a consumer in a moneylending agreement has all the protections of a consumer to a *credit agreement*. The Central Bank is required to establish and keep a register of moneylenders; a certified copy of an entry in the register is admissible in all legal proceedings as evidence of its contents (CCA 1995, ss 151A and 151B inserted by CBFSAIA 2003, s 35, Sch 1). See *Thomas v Ashbrook* [1913] 2 IR 416. See RSC Ord 4, r 8; Ord 13 r 14; Ord 27, r 15. [Bibliography: Bird]. See COOLING-OFF PERIOD; CREDIT AGREEMENT; DEBTOR'S SUMMONS; INTEREST, EXCESSIVE; SIMPLE CONTRACT; UNCONSCIONABLE BARGAIN.

monopoly. The 1937 Constitution provides that the operation of free competition will not be allowed so to develop as to result in the concentration of the ownership or control of essential commodities in a few individuals to the common detriment: Constitution, art 45(2)(3)).

Although 'monopoly' is not defined in current competition law, the existence of a monopoly may amount to an abuse of a dominant position, which abuse is prohib-

ited: Competition Act 2002, ss 4–6. Also, there are provisions for preventing the creation of monopolies through the control of mergers and acquisitions (CA 2002, ss 16–28).

For previous legislation, since repealed, see Mergers, Takeovers and Monopolies Act 1978, ss 11–13; Competition Act 1991, s 14(7). [Bibliography: Forde (5); Mason Hayes & Curran]. See ABUSE OF MONOPOLY RIGHT; COMPETITION, DISTORTION OF; COMPETITION AUTHORITY; CONCERT PARTY; DOMINANT POSITION, ABUSE OF; MEDIA MERGER; MERGER/TAKEOVER; MONOPSONIST.

monopsonist. A person who, or entity which, has exclusive control of the market supply or purchase of a product or service. The court has held that a defendant, as a single purchaser in the relevant geographic market, was a *monopsonist* and since the defendant had the same power to control price in purchasing as a *monopsonist* had in selling, it enjoyed a dominant position: *Blemings v David Patton Ltd* [2001] 1 IR 385, HC.

month. The word *month* means a calendar month unless the contrary intention appears: Interpretation Act 1937, s 12, schedule, para 19.

Consequently where an appeal against a planning permission requires that it be made in 'the period of *one month* beginning on the day of the giving of the decision' and that day is 7 June 1995, an appeal lodged on 7 July 1995 is out of time: *McCann v An Bord Pleanála* [1997] 1 ILRM 314, HC and 1 IR 264. The *corresponding date* rule does not apply by virtue of IA 1937, s 11(h). Under the 'corresponding date' rule a one-month period would be regarded as ending on the corresponding date in the appropriate subsequent month ie 7 July 1995 in the example above. This however was rejected by the court as it would require the inclusion of two days of the same date ie 7th of both June and July (*McCann* case).

In a contract of sale *month* means *prima facie* calendar month: Sale of Goods Act 1893, s 10(2). An *income tax month* is a month beginning on the 6th day of one month and ending on the 5th day of the following month: Taxes Consolidation Act 1997, ss 525, 983, 1020(1). Where time for doing any act or taking any proceedings is limited by months, such time is to be computed by calendar months, unless otherwise expressed: RSC Ord 122, r 1.

As regards an occupational pension scheme, a 'month' means a calendar month or a period of 28 days beginning on a day to be determined by the trustees of the scheme concerned, and each consecutive period of 28 days thereafter: Pensions Act 1990 as amended by Social Welfare (Miscellaneous Provisions) Act 2003, s 24, Sch, paras 5 and 15. See TIME; COURT RULES.

Montreal Convention. An updated replacement for the *Warsaw Convention for the Unification of Certain Rules Relating to International Carriage by Air* (1929), which, together with subsequent amendments, is referred to as the 'Warsaw System'. Provision has been made for Ireland to ratify the latest Convention, which will give it the force of law in Ireland: Air Navigation and Transport (International Conventions) Act 2004.

The Warsaw System provides a worldwide system of standards and rules for carriage by air and in particular common rules in respect of liability limits for the carriage of passengers, cargo and baggage in the event of damage, delay or loss.

The Montreal Convention, done in Montreal on 28 May 1999, supersedes the Warsaw System, in every State which implements it. Where air travel takes place between Ireland and another State which has not yet ratified the Montreal Convention, the Act provides that the most recent Convention common to both Ireland and that other State will apply. While the purpose of the Act is to implement the Montreal Convention, the opportunity has been taken to restate the existing law relating to the Warsaw System so that the entire subject is covered in one piece of legislation.

The rules of the Montreal Convention are already included in European Law, for all European airlines and their passengers, through Regulations (EC) 2027/1997 and 889/2002. Ratification of the Montreal Convention extends the higher liability limits worldwide, thereby providing significant benefits for passengers travelling with non-EU airlines. The Convention also makes it easier for passengers to bring legal action, by allowing them to bring action in the State where the passenger's principal residence is. This *fifth jurisdiction* is in addition to the previous four, which are: (i) the place of business of the airline, (ii) the place of the accident, (iii) the point of origin, and (iv) the intended point of destination of the flight. The Act includes in its Schedules the full text of the Warsaw Convention with its various amendments.

monuments. See NATIONAL MONUMENT; HISTORIC MONUMENT.

moot. (1) Debate of points of law in a hypothetical case eg to give practice to student lawyers. There is an All-Ireland Moot Court competition sponsored by the Bar Council. Also Irish law students compete in the Irish heats of the American Jessop International Law Moot and in the heats of a European law moot run by the European Law Students Association. See examples in (1992) 2 ISLR 110 and (1993) 3 ISLR 147.

(2) The courts should not embark on a *moot issue* where matters of fact have not actually been established in evidence: *Brady v Donegal Co Council* [1989] ILRM 282, SC. While the court does not ordinarily give a ruling on a moot, cases concerning the care and custody of children were probably of unique character; and the court would therefore rule on the issues in order to provide guidance to those involved and in particular having regard to the absence of provision for legal assistance for children involved in such proceedings: *F v Supt of B.Garda Station* [1990] 8 ILT Dig 191. See also *Murphy v Roche* [1987] IR 106; *International Fishing Vessels Ltd v Minister for the Marine* [1991] 2 IR 379, SC; *Re Application of Tivoli Cinema Ltd* [1992] ILRM 522, HC; *DPP (Whelan) v Delaney* [1996] 1 ILRM 70, HC; *Maguire v South Eastern Health Board* [2001] 3 IR 26, HC; *The People (DPP) v D K* [2002] 3 IR 534, CCA. See HYPOTHETICAL ARGUMENTS; OBITER DICTUM.

moral right. An author has certain moral rights e g a *paternity right*, which is a right to be identified as the author, and an *integrity right*, which is a right to object to any distortion, mutilation or other modification of, or other derogatory action in relation to his *work* which would prejudice his reputation: Copyright and Related Rights Act 2000, ss 107 and 109. *Work*, in this context, means a literary, dramatic, musical or artistic work or film (CRRA 2000, s 2(1)).

There are exceptions and qualifications to these rights (CRRA 2000, ss 108, 110–111). A person also has a right not to have a work falsely attributed to him as author (CRRA 2000, s 113).

Included in moral rights, is the *right to privacy* in photographs and films, where they are commissioned by a person for private and domestic purposes (CRRA 2000, s 114). The duration of moral rights is the same as the duration of the work in which the copyright subsists, except that the right in relation to false attribution subsists for 20 years after the death of the person on whom the right is conferred (CRRA 2000, s 115). Moral rights are not assignable or alienable, but they may be transmitted on death; they may also be waived but any waiver does not affect the rights of the other joint authors, if any (CRRA 2000, ss 116–119).

An infringement of a moral right is actionable as a breach of statutory duty and reliefs include damages or other relief, including an injunction, but not an order which would prevent a building being completed or require a building to be demolished (CRRA 2000, ss 137–138).

A similar regime of protection is provided for the moral rights of *performers* which correspond to that provided for authors eg a *paternity right* (CRRA 2000, s 309) and an *integrity right* (CRRA 2000, s 311). The duration of moral rights for performers expires 50 years after the performance takes place, or where a recording is made, 50 years after it is first lawfully made available to the public (CRRA 2000, s 315). There are similar provisions for performers as are provided for authors as regards waiver of moral rights (CRRA 2000, s 316), non-assignability and non-alienability (CRRA 2000, s 317), and transmission on death (CRRA 2000, s 318) and remedies for infringement (CRRA 2000, s 319). Performance moral rights do not attach to *exclusive* recording rights. See RECORDING RIGHTS.

morality. [Bibliography: Daly CB]. See PUBLIC MORALS.

moratorium. An authorised postponement in the performance of an obligation eg on payment of a debt.

mortality cover. Means the amount payable by a life company in respect of a life policy in the event of the death of the assured: Taxes Consolidation Act 1997, s 723 as amended by Finance Act 1998, ss 49, 53. Provision has been made for the taxation at 10% of the income and capital gains of a life company investment product based on Irish equities, called a *special investment policy*. The policy holder must be entitled to, and must be paid, all benefits under the policy, other than mortality cover. See SPECIAL INVESTMENT SCHEME.

mortgage. A conveyance of an interest in land or other property as security for a loan. The mortgagor (borrower) normally remains in possession of the land until the debt is repaid. A mortgage may be *legal, equitable* or *statutory*. A *legal mortgage* is a transfer of the legal estate or interest in the land or other property; an *equitable mortgage* arises where only an equitable interest is transferred eg by deposit of title deeds (qv); a *statutory mortgage* is one arising by way of judgment mortgage (qv) under the Judgment Mortgage Act 1850.

The mortgagor has a right to redeem his mortgage on repayment of the debt; it is a legal right on the date fixed for redemption and an equitable right thereafter. The mortgagor also has an *equity of redemption*, which is the sum total of the mortgagor's rights in equity, and there must be no *clogs* (qv) on that right.

A mortgage is discharged by redemption (qv), by foreclosure (qv), or by exercise of the mortgagee's right of sale. Mortgages rank in priority according to the date of their registration.

A mortgage on registered land is created by registration of a *charge* as a burden on the land and registration of the *chargeant* as the owner of the charge. The charge operates as a mortgage by deed within the meaning of the Conveyancing Acts: Registration of Title Act 1964, s 62. See Stamp Duties Consolidation Act 1999, ss 57–58. [Bibliography: Johnston; Wylie (1); Fisher & Lightwood UK]. See CHATTEL MORTGAGE; CHARGE ON LAND; CHARGE, REGISTRATION OF; ENDOWMENT LOAN; ENDOWMENT MORTGAGE; EQUITY RELEASE SCHEMES; HOUSING LOAN; MERGER; PRIOR MORTGAGE; RECITALS; TRUSTEE INVESTMENT.

mortgage, equitable. See EQUITABLE MORTGAGE.

mortgage, judgment. See JUDGMENT MORTGAGE.

mortgage, prior. See PRIOR MORTGAGE.

mortgage agent. A mortgage lender, a mortgage intermediary, an insurer or an insurance intermediary: Consumer Credit Act 1995, s 115(2) as amended by Central Bank and Financial Services Authority of Ireland Act 2003, s 35, Sch 1.

mortgage allowance. A subsidy payable under the Housing Act 1988, s 3 towards loan charges incurred by a borrower in respect of a loan made by a specified organisation (eg assurance company, bank, building society, credit union, housing authority): Housing (Mortgage Allowance) Regulations 2001, SI No 606 of 2001. These regulations provide for a number of changes in the subsidy scheme eg increase in the allowance, increase in the minimum mortgage requirement, and appropriate euro amounts.

mortgage interest. Relief from income tax in respect of mortgage interest from 1 January 2002 is not claimable through the tax system; as from that date, tax relief is given 'at source' (TRS) ie it is given when the borrower makes a mortgage payment to the mortgage lender: Finance Act 2001, s 23. See Mortgage Interest (Relief at Source) Regulations 2001, SI No 558 of 2001.

The ceiling on *mortgage interest* which may be claimed by first-time buyers for tax relief has been increased to €4,000 (single) and €8,000 (married) and the claim period has been extended to seven years: Finance Act 2003, s 9. The *mortgage interest supplement* payable under social welfare legislation is not payable where the cohabiting spouse or partner of the claimant is in full-time employment: Social Welfare Act 2003, s 12.

mortgage intermediary. Any person who, in return for a commission, payment or consideration of any kind in relation to the credit transaction, arranges or offers to arrange the provision of a *housing loan* (qv) by a mortgage lender: Consumer Credit Act 1995, s 2(1). A mortgage intermediary must hold an authorisation from the Central Bank (IFSRA) and an appointment in writing from each undertaking for which he is an intermediary (CCA 1995, s 116 as amended by Central Bank and Financial Services Authority of Ireland Act 2003, s 35, Sch 1). Persons holding any of the following licences may be refused an authorisation as a mortgage intermediary: moneylender, bookmaker, pawnbroker, gaming, intoxicating liquor (CCA 1995, s 116(9)).

The Central Bank is required to establish and keep a register of mortgage intermediaries; a certified copy of an entry in the register is admissible in all legal proceedings as evidence of its contents (CCA 1995, ss 151A and 151B inserted by CBFSAIA 2003, s 35, Sch 1). Under recent legislation, the definition of 'mortgage intermedi-

ary' has been amended to bring 'introducers' within the scope of the 1995 Act, ie people who, although not authorised as mortgage intermediaries in their own right, introduce clients to authorised intermediaries in return for a commission: Central Bank and Financial Services Authority of Ireland Act 2004, Sch 3.

mortgage lender. A credit institution making *housing loans* (qv) or a local authority or a person whose business includes the making of housing loans as a particular percentage of his business: Consumer Credit Act 1995, s 2(1) and SI No 127 of 1996.

The Minister is empowered to require detailed information to be supplied to him by mortgage lenders in relation to the mortgage lender itself, mortgages and interest, and price, age, size and type of house: Housing (Miscellaneous Provisions) Act 2002, s 13. There is a prohibition on disclosure of this information in any way which could directly or indirectly identify a person or mortgage lender. See LEGAL INVESTIGATION OF TITLE; LINKING SERVICES; MORTGAGE PROTECTION INSURANCE; VALUATION REPORT.

mortgage of goods. See BILL OF SALE.

mortgage of leaseholds. See LEASEHOLDS, MORTGAGE OF.

mortgage of shares. See SHARES, EQUITABLE MORTGAGE OF.

mortgage protection insurance. Life insurance which provides for payment at the time of death of the insured of a sum equal to the amount of principal estimated to be outstanding on a mortgage loan at the time of death, such sum to be employed in repayment of the principal. A *building society* is required to arrange through an insurer or an intermediary nominated by it for the provision of *mortgage protection insurance* in respect of secured loans, the premium to be payable by the member in monthly instalments; there are exceptions eg in respect of loans in excess of £60,000/€76,184; and in respect of members who by reason of health would not be acceptable to an insurer.

The Central Bank is empowered to prescribe, by regulation, rules concerning: (a) removing or restricting the right of a society to require a member to effect or keep effected insurance on a housing loan with an insurer directed by the society or of any intermediary directed by the society, and (b) the arranging by a society through an insurer or intermediary nominated by it for the provision of mortgage protection insurance: Building Societies Act 1989 Act, s 11(2)(b)(iii) and (v). No such rules had been prescribed by 2002, presumably because of the Consumer Credit Act 1995, s 126.

Under the 1995 Act, a *mortgage lender* (qv), which includes a building society, is similarly required to arrange mortgage protection insurance in respect of a *housing loan* (qv). The mortgage lender is relieved of the responsibility where: (a) the house is not the principal residence of the borrower or his dependants, or (b) the borrower belongs to a class not acceptable to an insurer, or (c) the loan is to a person over fifty years of age, or (d) the borrower already has in place adequate life insurance (CCA 1995, s 126). See also Housing (Miscellaneous Provisions) Act 2002, s 6(2)(i)(ii).

mortgage suit. An action in which the plaintiff mortgagee (lender) seeks a sale by the court in lieu of foreclosure (qv). The plaintiff mortgagee usually seeks: (a) that his mortgage be declared *well charged* on the lands, (b) an order for payment of the sum due, and (c) an order that in default of payment within the specified time, the lands be sold by the court. A mortgage suit is commenced in the Circuit Court, where the rateable valuation of the land does not exceed £200 (€253.95), or otherwise in the High Court. See RSC Ord 54, r 3; Circuit Court Rules 2001 Ord 43, r 2. [Bibliography: Scanlon]. See MORTGAGEE, RIGHTS OF.

mortgagee. The person to whom property is mortgaged; the lender of the mortgage debt.

mortgagee, rights of. A mortgagee (lender) generally has the following rights where the mortgage is by deed: (a) right to possession, but only in suitable cases eg to aid a sale: *Ulster Bank Ltd v Conlon* [1957] 91 ILTR 193; (b) power of sale out of court where the redemption date has passed and there is either three months default, after notice, in payment of principal or two months arrears of interest or breach of a covenant: *Holohan v Friends Provident & Century Life Office* [1966] IR 1; (c) power to appoint a receiver, exercisable under the same conditions as a power of sale; the receiver is deemed to be an agent of the mortgagor and consequently the mortgagee is not liable for the defaults of the receiver;

(d) power to insure. See Conveyancing Act 1881, s 19.

It has been held that in the case of a default, the mortgagor should be ordered to give up possession as the property, when sold with vacant possession, would realise more: *Irish Permanent Building Society v Ryan* [1950] IR 12. See also *Irish Civil Service (Permanent) Building Society v Ingram's Representative* [1959] IR 181.

However, in the absence of a court order to repossess a *family home*, a building society may be restrained from exercising a right to possession pursuant to a clause in a mortgage deed and be ordered, by way of interlocutory relief, to deliver up possession of the house so repossessed: *McCormack v ICS Building Society* [1989] ITLR (17 April) HC.

A mortgagee may obtain an order for sale by the court of the mortgaged property by way of *mortgage suit* (qv). He also has the usual creditors' remedy against a debtor for repayment of the principal and interest due. He is entitled to retain possession of the title deeds until the mortgage is redeemed.

The court has power to adjourn proceedings by a mortgagee for possession or sale of a *family home* (qv) where it appears that the other spouse is desirous and capable of paying the arrears: Family Home Protection Act 1976, s 7. Also, the court can give permission to a mortgagee to bid and purchase at the sale of the property of a bankrupt (qv) or arranging debtor (qv): Bankruptcy Act 1988, s 53.

Where mortgaged property is sold by a building society in exercise of a power of sale, the society must ensure that the property is sold at the best price reasonably obtainable and must notify the mortgagor and any other mortgagee, with particulars of the sale within 21 days thereof: Building Societies Act 1989, s 26(1) and (5). It has been held in the UK that a building society is not bound to retain a property indefinitely until a higher price could be reached: *Reliance Permanent Building Society v Harwood-Stamper* [1944] 2 All ER 75.

A mortgagee, who sells the mortgaged property, becomes a trustee of the surplus moneys he retains and can be obliged to pay interest on those moneys to the person who is entitled to them: *Murphy v AIB* [1994] 2 ILRM 220, HC. See *Bula Ltd v Crowley* [2003] 1 ILRM 55, HC and [2002] FL 5044, HC. See RECEIVER OF

MORTGAGED PROPERTY; RETENTION OF MORTGAGED PROPERTY.

mortgages, consolidation of. See CONSOLIDATION OF MORTGAGES.

mortgagor. The person who mortgages his property as security for the mortgage debt; the borrower.

mortgagor, rights of. A mortgagor (borrower) has the following rights: (a) *equity of redemption* which he can assign, devise or mortgage again; (b) possession – he can keep all rents and profits without rendering an account; he is not liable for *waste* (qv) unless it would render the property an inadequate security; he can sue for rent or injury done to the land without joining the mortgagee; (c) leases – a mortgagor in possession may make leases which bind the mortgagor and the mortgagee; however this right is to be exercised by the mortgagee after a receiver has been appointed; Conveyancing Act 1881, s 18; Conveyancing Act 1911, s 3.

Also the right of the mortgagor in possession to grant a lease is overridden where a contrary intention is expressed in writing: CA 1881, s 18(13) and *ICC Bank plc v Verling* [1995] 1 ILRM 123, HC.

A mortgagor may also enforce his right to redeem his mortgage by a *redemption suit*. The mortgagor is entitled to possession of the title deeds on redemption of the mortgage. See EQUITY OF REDEMPTION; HOUSING LOAN; REDEMPTION; WASTE.

mortmain. [Dead hand]. Land which is inalienable. Alienation in mortmain was prohibited e g land could not be conveyed originally to a corporation except by statutory authority or by licence. There was a *mortmain* restriction on gifts of land to charities: Charitable Donations and Bequests (Ireland) Act 1844. Mortmain restrictions were repealed by the Mortmain (Repeal of Enactments) Act 1954.

mortuum vadium. [Dead pledge; a mortgage (qv)].

mother. The State must endeavour to ensure that mothers are not obliged by economic necessity to engage in labour to the neglect of their duties in the home: 1937 Constitution, art 41(2)(2). See *L v L* [1992] ILRM 115, SC.

motion. An application to a court or to a judge for an order directing something to be done in the applicant's favour. Generally, a motion may be made only after notice has been given to the parties affected but in certain cases it can be made *ex parte* (qv).

For High Court rules, see RSC Ord 52, r 2. In the Circuit Court, except where permitted by the rules, no motion may be made without notice to the parties affected thereby, and there must be at least four clear days between the service of a *notice of motion* and the day named in the motion for hearing the motion: Circuit Court Rules 2001 Ord 64. [Bibliography: Buckley, Melody]. See MOTION OF COURSE; NOTICE OF MOTION.

motion of course. A motion made *ex-parte* which an applicant is entitled to have granted as of right on his own statement and at his own risk. The Master of the High Court is empowered to make any order which may be made *as of course*: RSC Ord 63, r 1(2).

motion on notice. A motion (qv) where notice thereof is given to the other side in legal proceedings. See NOTICE OF MOTION.

motive. That which incites a person to action. Motive is generally irrelevant in the law of torts although in defamation, malice will negative the defence of qualified privilege or fair comment. See MALICE.

motor insurance, EC. EC insurance undertakings have a right to underwrite motor liability insurance risks in a member state without being established in the State where the risk is situated. This right is given effect in Ireland from 20 November 1992 by the European Communities (Non-Life Insurance) (Amendment) Regulations 1992, SI No 244 of 1992 as amended by Central Bank and Financial Services Authority of Ireland Act 2003, s 35, Sch 2. Insurers who transact third-party motor insurance business in Ireland are required to be members of the Motor Insurers' Bureau of Ireland (qv): SI No 347 of 1992.

A single authorisation system of supervision of insurance undertakings operating throughout the European Union has been established, under which insurance undertakings transacting business on either a cross-border or branch basis are subject to the overall supervisory control of the supervisory authority where their head offices are located: EC (Non-Life Insurance) Framework Regulations 1994, SI No 359 of 1994 implementing the Third Non-Life Framework Directive (EEC) 92/49 (OJ No L 228/1) as amended by CBFSAIA 2003, s 35, Sch 2.

The 1994 Regulations: (a) require non-life insurance undertakings to furnish certain information to the Minister, (b) require certain information to be disclosed to policyholders when an insurance contract is being effected, (c) incorporate a number of consumer protection measures, and (d) amend previous legislation and regulations. See also Motor Insurance (Provision of Information) (Renewal of Policy of Insurance) Regulations 2002, SI No 389 of 2002.

Provision has been made for the processing of certain claims for compensation for injury or damage arising as a result of accidents occurring in an EU member state other than the member state of residence of the injured party: EC (Fourth Motor Insurance Directive) Regulations, SI No 651 of 2003 implementing Directive (EC) 2000/26. See INSURANCE, VEHICLE.

Motor Insurers' Bureau of Ireland. A company formed by motor insurers to provide the following services by agreement with the government: (a) to pay claims for accident victims of motorists who are uninsured or untraced, (b) to act as insurer of all foreign vehicles travelling in Ireland, and (c) to act as an 'Information Centre' for foreign claimants involved in motor accidents in Ireland.

A new Agreement was entered into by the Bureau with the Minister for Transport on 31 March 2004 which applies to accidents occurring in a public place on or after 1 May 2004. The main features of this Agreement are: (a) a victim of an accident involving an uninsured vehicle must first apply directly to the Bureau for compensation; (b) redress to the Courts is available, however, where the victim is refused compensation by the Bureau or is not satisfied with the amount offered; (c) compensation for personal injuries or death is available as of right for victims of untraced 'hit and run' drivers; (d) no compensation is available in relation to: (i) drivers in a collision between two uninsured vehicles, (ii) persons who stole or obtained the vehicle by violence or threats or (iii) persons who knew, or ought reasonably to have known, that the vehicle was uninsured; and (e) compensation for property damage caused by uninsured (including stolen) vehicles is available, but not in the case of damage to a vehicle. Compensation in respect of loss of service of an injured person is specifically excluded (2004 Agreement, clause 15).

There are certain specified *conditions precedent* to the Bureau's liability eg: (a) a report of the accident must be made to the gardai within two days of the event or as soon as the claimant reasonably could, and the claimant must co-operate fully with the gardai; (b) property damage must be claimed not later than one year from the date of the accident and within the Statute of Limitations in respect of personal injuries or death; (c) all material information, including medical reports, must be furnished on demand; and (d) there are specified interview requirements in respect of the claims involving accidents caused by an untraced driver (2004 Agreement, clause 3).

Under a previous Agreement, where at the time of the accident the vehicle was being used without the consent of the owner, the Bureau would not accept liability for judgments against the owner or the driver of the vehicle in favour of persons travelling in the vehicle. The Bureau would, however, consider awarding an *ex gratia* payment if satisfied that the passenger was not aware or should not have reasonably known that the vehicle was being used without the owner's consent. It has been held that the onus is on the Bureau to prove that the passenger should have known the driver was uninsured: *Kinsella v MIBI* [1993] ITLR (19 July), SC and [1997] 3 IR 536, SC. A trial judge is entitled to reach a conclusion that if the plaintiff did not know that the car was uninsured, he ought to have known had he been approaching the matter in a responsible manner: *Ward v Ward and MIBI* [2003] FL 6995, SC.

A decision made by the MIBI can be reviewed by the court if the decision reached or the opinion formed by it was one which no reasonable body or person could form on the evidence before it: *Bowles v MIBI* [1990] ILRM 59; *Hurley v MIBI* [1993] ILRM 886, HC.

The immediately previous Agreement between the Minister and the Bureau covered road accidents occurring on or after 31 December 1988, and gave effect to the second EC Directive on Motor Insurance (EEC) 84/5 of 30 December 1983. The MIBI has been approved as the *Information Centre* and the *Compensation Body* in respect of the processing of certain claims arising from accidents arising in a member state other than that of the residence of the injured party: EC (Fourth Motor Insurance Directive) Regulations, SI No 651 of 2003. See *Ambrose v O'Regan* 10 ILT Dig [1992] 200, SC; *Bowes v Motor Insurers' Bureau of Ireland* [2000] 2 IR 81, SC; Case C 158/01 *Withers v Delaney and MIBI* [2002] ECJ. See 'Unseated Passengers and the MIBI' by Cathal Murphy BL in *Bar Review* (June 2003) 96; 'The MIBI and Co-Defendants – Recent Case Law' by William Abrahamson BL in *Bar Review* (November 2003). For the full text of the 2004 and 1988 Agreements, see website: *www.mibi.ie*. See LODGMENT IN COURT; NO CLAIMS DISCOUNT; UNTRACED DRIVER.

motor taxation. The rate of duty payable on motor vehicles is primarily contained in the Finance (Excise Duties) (Vehicles) Act 1952 as amended by Motor Vehicle (Duties and Licences) Act 2001. The 2001 Act increases the tax payable on certain vehicles from 1 April 2001. It also provides a reduced rate of motor tax on vehicles which are kept and used exclusively on an offshore island to which there is no direct road or bridge access from the mainland (MV(DL)A 2001, Schedule). It also provides an exemption from tax for vehicles used exclusively for mountain and cave rescue or for underwater search and recovery purposes (MV(DL)A 2001, s 3).

Provision is also made for a tax on bicycles which are electrically propelled (MV(DL)A 2001, Schedule). However, the Minister for the Environment has clarified that electrically-assisted bicycles, also *pedelecs*, are exempt from the requirement to pay motor tax (or to have compulsory insurance), because the electric power 'only assists the pedalling effort and is not a source of propulsion in its own right' *Irish Times*, 5 March 2002. For increases in motor tax rates and trade plate licences from 1 January 2003, see Motor Vehicles (Duties and Licences) Act 2003; and from 1 January 2004, see Motor Vehicles (Duties and Licences) Act 2004.

Motor tax receipts are paid into the *Local Government Fund*, which is also supplemented by Exchequer contributions. The Fund is ringfenced for local authority purposes, although the Minister is enabled to recoup the expenses associated with the issue of driver licences and miscellaneous fees. See INTERNET; VEHICLE, REGISTRATION OF; VINTAGE VEHICLE.

motor vehicle, abandoned. See ABANDONED VEHICLE.

motor vehicle, negligent driving of. Every person using the highway must take reasonable care in doing so, not to cause injury or damage to other users. The duty of care of the driver of a motor vehicle depends on many factors e g time, place, weather, state of light, state of the highway, speed, manner of driving, other traffic, and the state and condition of the driver. A higher standard of care is required when children are known to be present: *Brennan v Savage Smyth Co Ltd* [1982] ILRM 223. A person in control of a motor vehicle, although not driving it may be held to be negligent: *Dockery v O'Brien* [1975] 109 ILTR 127. See also *Hassett v Skehan* [1939] Ir Jur Rep 5.

It has been held that an insurer is not liable in tort or contract to a plaintiff whose claim against a deceased motorist is statute barred: *Boyce v McBride* [1987] ILRM 95. See PROPER LOOK OUT.

motor vehicle, recovery of. See RECOVERY OF MOTOR VEHICLE.

motor vehicle, sale of. There is an *implied condition* in a contract for the sale of a motor vehicle, that at the time of delivery of the vehicle, it is free from any defect which would render it a danger to the public, including persons travelling in the vehicle. There is no distinction in this regard between new and second-hand vehicles. The implied condition does not apply in the case of a sale to a dealer e g on a trade-in. See Sale of Goods and Supply of Services 1980, s 13. The protection of s 13 has been extended to the hirer of a motor vehicle by way of a hire-purchase agreement: Consumer Credit Act 1995, s 82. See *Glorney v O'Brien* [1989] 7 ILT Dig 104; *Sze Ping-Fat* in 10 ILT & SJ [1992] 192. For the Society of the Irish Motor Industry (SIMI), see website: *www.simi.ie*. See MILEOMETER READING.

motor vehicle, type approval of. See TYPE APPROVAL, MOTOR VEHICLES.

motorist, untraced. See UNTRACED DRIVER.

motorway. A public road (qv) or proposed public road specified to be a motorway in a *motorway scheme* approved by the Minister: Roads Act 1993, ss 2(1), 43, and 49. Pedestrians and pedal cyclists must not use a motorway, and persons must not permit animals to be on a motorway (RA 1993, s 43(4)). There is no right of direct access to a motorway from land adjoining it and no such right may be granted (RA 1993, s 43(2)); this includes a prohibition on the granting of planning permission which would involve direct access (RA 1993, s 46).

However, a road authority must provide such a person with an alternative means of access if the motorway deprives him of his only means of access, and he is entitled to compensation for any reduction in the value of his land which results (RA 1993, s 52(3)–(4)).

A road authority must submit a motorway scheme to An Bord Pleanála, having first notified the public and affected land owners/occupiers (RA 1993, s 48). The Board, before approving a scheme, must cause an oral hearing to be held, must consider any objections, and must consider the report and recommendations of the person conducting the inquiry (RA 1993, s 49).

The validity of an order made by the Board can only be questioned by way of a *judicial review* within eight weeks of the date of the Board's decision: Roads (Amendment) Act 1998, s 6.

Approval of the scheme by the Board has the same effect as if it were a *compulsory purchase order* (qv) made under the Local Government (No 2) Act 1960, s 10 as inserted by the Housing Act 1966, s 86 (RA 1993, s 52).

The road authority is required to prepare an environmental impact statement on the construction of a motorway (RA 1993, s 50). The National Roads Authority is empowered to direct a road authority to make a motorway scheme (RA 1993, s 20(1)(a)).

The previous functions of the Minister in relation to a scheme or proposed road development under RA 1993, ss 49–51 is now transferred to and vested in An Bord Pleanála: Planning and Development Act 2000, s 215. Also there is provision for an oral hearing instead of the previous requirement of a local inquiry or local public inquiry (PDA 2000, s 218).

The normal planning legislation does not apply to an application for permission to erect power lines on lands that are part of a motorway scheme: *Nolan v Minister for the Environment and ESB* [1991] ILRM 705, SC. See also 1998 Act, ss 2–5 and 8. See *Jackson Way Properties Ltd v Minister for the Environment* [1999] 4 IR 608, HC. See

LIGHT RAILWAY; PUBLIC ROAD; SERVICE AREA; SPEED LIMIT; SUBSTRATUM OF LAND.

movables. Personal property e g goods, as opposed to real property e g land.

mugging. The colloquial term used to describe the crime of robbery (qv) of a pedestrian.

multi-party litigation. See CLASS ACTION.

multi-storey buildings. Buildings of five storeys or more, built since 1950 or to be built. Provisions to improve and ensure the safety standards of such buildings are contained in the Local Government (Multi-Storey Buildings) Act 1988. Such buildings must be certified by a chartered engineer with experience related to either structures or gas networks, depending on the kind of appraisal required. See also Building Control Act 1990, s 23. See SIs No 285 and 286 of 1988; SI No 95 of 1990. See MANAGEMENT COMPANY.

Multilateral Investment Guarantee Agency. The Agency established in 1987 as part of the World Bank which provides insurance cover for direct foreign investment in developing countries; cover is for non-commercial risks, such as restrictions on the transfer of currency, expropriation of assets, and the risk of war or civil disturbance: Multilateral Investment Guarantee Agency Acts 1988 and 2000. The 1988 Act provided for Ireland to ratify the terms of the Convention establishing the Agency and to become a member. The 2000 Act provided for Ireland to subscribe to the 1998 capital increase of the Agency. See also Central Bank Act 1997, s 67.

multinational company. Generally understood to mean a company which is in effect a cluster of companies registered in different countries and tied together by common ownership and responding to a common management strategy. Every company which is incorporated outside the State which establishes a place of business in the State is required to make up annual accounts and to deliver certain particulars to the Registrar of Companies: Companies Act 1963, ss 351–360.

multiple defendants. The Brussels Convention permits a plaintiff to sue multiple defendants in the domestic jurisdiction of any one of them: Jurisdiction of Courts and Enforcement of Judgments Act 1998, Sch 1, art 6. The *Brussels I Regulation* on the recognition and enforcement of judgments in civil and commercial matters, replaces the 1998 Act as from 1 March 2002 for all EU States except Denmark: EC (Civil and Commercial Judgments) Regulations 2002, SI No 52 of 2002. This adds a new requirement that defendants may be sued in the domicile of any one of them, provided that the claims are so closely connected that it is expedient to hear and determine them together to avoid the risk of irreconcilable judgments resulting from separate proceedings (*Regulation* art 6(1)). See Case 198/87 *Kalfelis v Schroder* [1988] ECR 5565.

multiple tenants. Means, in relation to a dwelling, two or more persons who are tenants of the dwelling (whether as joint tenants, tenants-in-common or under any other form of co-ownership) and 'multiple tenant' means any one of them: Residential Tenancies Act 2004, s 48. The four-year security of tenure provisions of a *Part 4 tenancy* apply to a dwelling occupied by multiple tenants, and their lawful licensees, from the earliest date at which a multiple tenant has been in occupation for six months (RTA 2004, s 49). Once a *Part 4 tenancy* has come into being, each of the multiple tenants and any person subsequently accepted by the landlord as a tenant in addition to or replacement for any of those multiple tenants, benefit from the protection of that *Part 4 tenancy* without any change to its commencement date (RTA 2004, ss 50 and 53). Any licensee of a tenant or multiple tenants may apply to become a tenant on the existing tenancy terms and the landlord may not unreasonably refuse such a request (RTA 2004, s 50(7)–(8). The rights, restrictions and obligations of a tenant then apply to the former licensee.

The actions of one multiple tenant in breach of the obligations applying to the tenancy are grounds for the termination of the *Part 4 tenancy*, but only if done with the consent of the other multiple tenants (RTA 2004, s 51). A landlord may conclude that the breach was done with the consent of any tenant who does not assist the landlord in identifying the tenant responsible for the breach and any tenant who consented to it. If the landlord concludes that not all of the tenants were complicit in the breach, he may terminate the benefit of the protection of the *Part 4 tenancy* for the relevant person or persons only. A dispute in relation to this matter may be determined under the dispute resolution procedures in ss 75–126.

The death or vacating of the dwelling by the person whose occupation gave rise to the *Part 4 tenancy* does not deprive the other tenants of the benefit of that protection (RTA 2004, s 52). Where a tenancy is being terminated by all of multiple tenants, one of the tenants may sign on behalf of the others named in the notice (RTA 2004, s 73). See PART 4 TENANCY; TENANCY DISPUTE.

municipal law. The domestic or internal law of a country as opposed to international law. It may be classified as *public law* and *private law* (qqv).

municipal waste. Means household waste as well as commercial and other waste which, because of its nature or composition, is similar to household waste: Waste Management Act 1996, s 5(1). It is an offence to place municipal waste into or near a litter receptacle: Litter Pollution Act 1997, s 3(3). See WASTE; WASTE MANAGEMENT PLAN.

murder. The unlawful killing with *malice aforethought* of another human being. The killing need not be by direct violence; abandoning a child so that he dies may suffice. The human being must have had an independent existence; there can be no murder of a child before birth or even during birth. *Malice aforethought* is present where the accused intended to kill, or cause serious injury to, some person, whether it is the person who was actually killed or not: Criminal Justice Act 1964, s 4. The accused person is presumed to have intended the natural and probable consequences of his conduct, but this presumption may be rebutted (CJA 1964, s 4(2)). Evidence of remorse subsequent to the killing is not evidence of a rebuttal of the presumption in s 4: *The People (DPP) v James McDonagh* [2001] 3 IR 201, CCA.

A person convicted of murder is debarred from benefiting under his victim's will: Succession Act 1965, s 120. Also a convicted murderer whose crime accelerated succession will not be permitted to be an executor (qv): *In the Goods of Martin Glynn v Kelly & Concannon* [1992] ILRM 582, SC. A person convicted of murder must be sentenced to life imprisonment (unless the murder is an aggravated murder): Criminal Justice Act 1990, s 2.

Where the evidence does not warrant a conviction for murder, the accused may be convicted of any of the following offences if so warranted: attempted murder or man-slaughter, or causing serious harm, or offences specifically so provided for by statute (eg infanticide, concealment of birth, assisting offenders) or an attempt to commit such offences, or aiding and abetting suicide: Criminal Law Act 1997, s 9(2); Non-Fatal Offences Against the Person Act 1997, s 29. See *Attorney-General v O'Shea* [1931] IR 728. See the Law Reform Commission consultation paper on *The Mental Element in Murder* (LRC CP 17, 2001) which deals with whether some non-intentional killings deserve to be punished as murder on moral grounds, and whether this should be addressed by expanding the current *mens rea* (qv) for the offence to include reckless indifference to the value of human life. A High Court judge, Mr Justice Carney, has called for the replacement of murder and manslaughter by a single offence of 'unlawful killing', to eliminate the present contest at trial between these two offences, and to make the verdict more acceptable to the victim's family, who generally regards a manslaughter verdict as unacceptable: *Irish Times*, 30 October 2003. See 'Decriminalising Murder?' by Mr Justice Carney in *Bar Review* (December 2003) 254. See CAPITAL MURDER; CRIMINAL JURISDICTION, PLACE; DYING DECLARATION; INSANITY; MANSLAUGHTER; MURDER, AGGRAVATED; PERSUADE TO MURDER; PROVOCATION; SELF-DEFENCE; SPECIAL VERDICT; SUCCEED, UNWORTHINESS TO; UNBORN, INJURIES TO THE; YEAR AND A DAY.

murder, aggravated. Although not given the description 'aggravated' by statute, it is the murder of a member of the Garda Síochána or a prison officer acting in the course of his duty; or murder done in the course or furtherance of specified offences created by the Offences Against the State Act 1939; or murder committed within the State for a political motive of the head of a foreign state or of a member of its government or of its diplomatic officer: Criminal Justice Act 1990, s 3.

It must be proved that the accused knew of the existence of each ingredient of the offence or was reckless as to whether or not that ingredient existed eg in relation to the killing of a garda, by showing that the accused knew the deceased was a garda acting in the course of his duty or was reckless as to whether he was a garda so acting (CJA 1990, s 3(2)).

There is a minimum period of imprisonment specified for aggravated murder (40 years) and attempted aggravated murder (20 years); there are also restrictions on the power to commute or remit punishment or to grant temporary release in the case of aggravated murder (CJA 1990, ss 4–5).

Where the evidence does not warrant a conviction for aggravated murder, the accused may be convicted of murder or of the other alternative verdicts available in the case of murder. See MURDER. See also COMMUTE; RELEASE, TEMPORARY; REMISSION.

museum. The National Museum of Ireland was established by the Science and Art Museums Act 1877. Any reference in the Copyright and Related Rights Act 2000 to an archive or a prescribed archive includes a reference to a museum or prescribed museum respectively (CRRA 2000, s 2(3)–(4)). See LIBRARIES.

musical work. Means a *work* consisting of music but does not include any words, or action, intended to be sung, spoken or performed with the music: Copyright and Related Rights Act 2000, s 2(1). Copyright subsists in an *original* musical work (CRRA 2000, s 17(2)). It expires 70 years after the death of the author irrespective of the date on which the work is first lawfully made available to the public (CRRA 2000, s 24(1)). However, see PUBLISHED EDITION. See also ARTIST, TAX EXEMPTION OF; COPYRIGHT; COPYRIGHT, QUALIFICATION FOR; PERFORMING RIGHTS SOCIETY; ORIGINAL; WORK.

muster list. The master of every ship must prepare and maintain a *muster list* which must specify, *inter alia* the general emergency alarm signal and the action to be taken by crew and passengers; how the order to abandon ship is to be given; and other emergency signals: Merchant Shipping (Musters and Training) Rules 1990, SI No 85 of 1990 as amended by Merchant Shipping (Musters and Training) Rules 1993, SI No 7 of 1993.

mutatis mutandi. [The necessary changes being made].

mute. Silent. An accused person may stand mute when asked to plead, in which case the judge will decide, after hearing evidence on the matter, if: (a) he is standing *mute by malice* (ie deliberately silent) in which case he will be treated as having pleaded not guilty, or (b) he is *mute by visitation of God*, in which case he will be treated as insane and unfit to plead, unless he can be made to understand by means of signs with the aid of an interpreter (eg where he is deaf and dumb). See Juries Act 1976, s 28. See also Criminal Law Act 1997, s 9(1)(c). See PLEA; UNFIT TO PLEAD; UNFIT TO BE TRIED.

mutual insurance. Where two or more persons mutually agree to insure each other against marine losses, there is said to be mutual insurance: Marine Insurance Act 1906, s 85. See also Taxes Consolidation Act 1997, s 844. [Bibliography: Hill UK; Ivamy UK; McGuffie, Fugeman & Gray UK].

mutual recognition. (1) Where the national standard in one country is acceptable as valid in all eg regarding what specification a product must have: National Forum on Europe, *Glossary of Terms* (2003). This is an alternative approach to 'harmonisation' where standards are made fully consistent by imposing a common cross-EU law.

(2) Reciprocal recognition of qualifications by professional bodies, education or training bodies, or state institutions. In order to make it easier for persons to take up and pursue activities as self-employed persons, the Council is required to issue directives for the mutual recognition of diplomas, certificates and other evidence of qualifications: EC Treaty, art 47 of the consolidated (2002) version. The European Court of Justice has held that the Italian practice of non-recognition of degrees for a course of study, provided by a UK company in Italy, but validated and awarded by a UK university, was a breach of art 43 (freedom of establishment), as it hindered the pursuit of the company of its economic activity in Italy: *Neri v European School of Economics* [2003] Case 153/02, ECJ.

Provision has been made for appeal procedures under the EC (General System for Recognition of Higher Education Diplomas) Regulations 1991, SI No 1 of 1991 and EC (Second General System for Recognition of Professional Education and Training) Regulations1996, SI No 135 of 1996: RSC Ord 113A inserted by SI No 346 of 1997. See also EC (Second General System for Recognition of Professional Education and Training) (Amendment) Regulations 2002, SI No 434 of 2002. See also SI No 36 of 2004 which gives effect to Council Directive (EEC) 2001/19 and reaffirms decisions of the European Court of Justice. For mutual recognition of lawyers, see SI No 732 of 2003. See Case C-285/01 *Isabel Burbaud* [2003] ECJ. See 'All together now' by solicitor Wendy Hederman in *Law Society Gazette* (May 2004) 8.

(3) A document issued by an overseas company and approved by the competent authority of another member state will qualify as *listing particulars* complying with the Irish stock exchange requirements provided certain specified conditions are met: Listing Rules 2000, paras 17.68–17.79. See DRIVING LICENCE; NATIONAL STANDARDS AUTHORITY; NATIONAL QUALIFICATIONS AUTHORITY OF IRELAND; PROSPECTUS; SOLICITORS, MUTUAL RECOGNITION.

mutual society. A society which is owned and controlled generally by the persons who consume the product or service which the society provides eg a credit union, a building society. 'The term *mutual* (which does not appear in the Building Societies Act 1989 or in previous legislation) is used to indicate an organisation the ownership and ultimate control of which is vested in the members broadly on the basis of equality rather than in proportion to financial interest': Report of Registrar of Building Societies (1981) p 8.

mutuality. See SET OFF.

mutuum. A quasi-bailment of personal chattels, consisting of a loan thereof to the borrower with the intention that it will be consumed by the borrower and will be returned, not in specie, but by something similar in kind and quantity. It differs from *commodatum* (loan for use) in that in the latter, possession and not ownership vests in the borrower; in *mutuum*, the property in the chattel vests in the borrower. See PRO-MUTUUM.

N

name. See FICTITIOUS NAME.

name, change of. A change of *surname* is normally effected by formal enrolment of a deed poll (qv); it has the advantage that a record is preserved of the change for future identification. However, a name is not *ipso facto* changed by such enrolment; the change is effected by reputation and the most the deed does is assist in the establishment of that reputation. A purely informal change is just as effective as a change effected by a deed poll: *Re Talbot* [1932] IR 714. It would appear that a *Christian* name may be changed at confirmation.

Provision has been made to enable re-registration of the birth of a child for the purpose of changing the *surname* of the child to a surname jointly agreed by the mother and the father of the child, on the joint application of the mother and father of the child: Registration of Births Act 1996, s 1(4) and 1(4A) inserted by Social Welfare (Miscellaneous Provisions) Act 2002, s 16 and Sch, Pt VI.

A company may change its name by special resolution with the consent of the Minister: Companies Act 1963, s 23(1). It has been possible since 1990 to submit a change of name to the Companies Registration Office without obtaining prior approval; however no change of name will have effect until the certificate of change of name has issued. See Listing Rules 2000, para 9.40.

A building society may change its name by special resolution; however the change cannot take effect until the Central Bank is satisfied that the changed name is not undesirable: Building Societies Act 1989, s 14(3).

Provision has been made to enable a local authority to change the name of a town, townland or non-municipal town: Local Government Act 2001, ss 189–191. A *non-municipal town* means an area, not being a city or a town, which is designated a town in the report of the census of population. Before there can be a change of name, there must be consultation by the local authority, notification of prescribed bodies, consideration of submissions received, final adoption of the proposal by the elected council, and consent of the majority of the electorate of the relevant area by way of local plebiscite.

There is also provision for the change of the name of a street or of a locality; a local plebiscite is also required (LGA 2001, ss 192–195). For previous legislation, see Local Government Act 1946, ss 76–77, Local Government Act 1994, s 67. See also *Williams v Bryant* [1839] 5 M & W 447. [Bibliography: Linell (UK).] See FORE-NAME; NAME OF COMPANY; PLACENAME.

name, geographic. See GEOGRAPHICAL NAME AS TRADE MARK.

name, right to good. The State is required by its laws to protect as best as it may from unjust attack and, in the case of injustice done, vindicate the *good name* of every citizen: 1937 Constitution, art 40.3(2). The constitutional rights to life and bodily integrity take precedence over the right to the protection and vindication of one's good name: *Burke v Central Independent Television plc* [1994] 2 ILRM 161, SC.

The Supreme Court has held that a person whose good name and reputation might be affected by the outcome of a case, is not automatically entitled to be joined as a defendant, if his presence is not required by the court for the effectual and complete adjudication of the matter: *Barlow v Fanning and UCC* [2002] 2 IR 593, SC and [2003] 1 ILRM 29. See ANONYMITY; PARDON; TRIBUNALS OF INQUIRY.

name of company. The name under which a company is registered in the Registry of Companies. A name will not be accepted which in the opinion of the Minister is undesirable: Companies Act 1963, s 21. The Minister is empowered to order a change in name which in his opinion is too like the name of a company already registered (CA 1963, s 23(2)). The name of a limited company must include *limited* or *ltd* or the Irish equivalents *teoranta* or *teo* (CA 1963, s 6(1)(a)). Where the company is a public limited company, this must be included in its name or the abbreviation *plc* or the Irish equivalents *cuideachta phoible theoranta* or *cpt*: Companies Amendment Act 1983, s 4(1).

The Minister is empowered to dispense with *limited* or *teoranta* in the name of a limited company which has as its objects the promotion of commerce, art, science, religion, charity or other useful object and intends to apply profits or other income to those objects, and the payment of a dividend to its members is prohibited: Companies Act 1963, s 24.

A company which carries on business under a name other than its corporate name is required to register the former name under the Registration of Business Names Act 1963: Companies Act 1963, s 22. It is an offence to trade under a misleading name: Companies Amendment Act 1983, s 56. An unintentional mis-statement of the correct name of a company applying for planning permission will not prevent developers obtaining declarations to which they were otherwise entitled, where the mis-statement did not have the effect of misleading or disadvantaging anyone: *McDonagh v County Borough of Galway* [1993] ITLR (23 August) SC. See RSC Ord 75, r 18. See also Building Societies Act 1989, ss 13–14. See NAME, CHANGE OF; BUSINESS NAME; PASSING OFF; RECEIVER.

name of solicitor. Regulations have been made governing the name which is permitted to be used to describe the practice of a solicitor, the nameplate of the practice, and the name or names required and permitted on the professional notepaper of the practice: Solicitors (Professional Practice, Conduct and Discipline) Regulations 1996, SI No 178 of 1996. A client should not have access to the stationery of a solicitor: *A Guide to Professional Conduct of Solicitors in Ireland* (2002) ch 9.3.

name of State. See STATE.

natal care absence. A period of absence from work to which an employee is entitled for the purpose of receiving ante-natal or post-natal care or both: Maternity Protection Act 1994, ss 15, 21 and SI No 18 of 1995. See MATERNITY LEAVE; PROTECTIVE LEAVE.

nation. A body of people recognised as an entity by virtue of their historical, linguistic, or ethnic links and without regard to political or geographic boundaries. The Irish *nation* affirms its inalienable, indefeasible and sovereign right to choose its own form of government, to determine its relations with other nations and to develop its life, political, economic and cultural, in accordance with its own genius and traditions: 1937 Constitution, art 1.

It is the entitlement and birthright of every person born in the island of Ireland to be part of the Irish nation; furthermore the Irish nation cherishes its special affinity with people of Irish ancestry living abroad who share its cultural identity and heritage (1937 Constitution, new art 2 inserted by referendum: Nineteenth Amendment to the Constitution Act 1998). It is the firm will of the Irish nation, in harmony and friendship, to unite all the people who share the territory of the island of Ireland, in all the diversity of their identities and traditions (new art 3). See Declaration under Article 29.7 of the Constitution (Extension of Time) Act 1999. See NON-NATIONAL.

National Archives. The body established to preserve records and documents previously held in the Public Records Office or the State Papers Office and other public records: National Archives Act 1986, s 2(1). The Act envisages the regular transfer to the National Archives of all over-30 year old records of courts, government departments and other public bodies which are deemed worthy of permanent preservation. The public have a right of access to such records, although certain records of particular sensitivity (eg relating to security or affecting individual privacy) or which may be damaged by inspection, may have access limited (NAA 1986, ss 10–11). See National Archive Regulations 1988, SI No 385 of 1988. See Blake in 10 ILT & SJ (1992) 43. See also Copyright and Related Rights Act 2000, ss 59–70 and 227–236; Residential Institutions Redress Act 2002, s 28(3); Commissions of Investigation Act 2004 s.41. See website: *www.nationalarchives.ie*. See ARCHIVES; CENSUS.

National Council for Curriculum and Assessment. The body corporate with the object of advising the Minister on matters relating to: (a) the curriculum for early childhood education, primary and post-primary schools, and (b) the assessment procedures employed in schools and examinations on subjects which are part of the curriculum: Education Act 1998, ss 38–48 and Sch 1. For composition of the Council, see SI No 45 of 2003.

national day of mourning. A *national day of mourning* was declared for Friday 14 September 2001 in sympathy with the persons killed or injured on 11 September 2001 as a result of terrorist attacks in the USA. As there is no specific provision in Irish law for a national day of mourning, the method used was to prescribe the 14 September 2001 as a *public holiday* pursuant to the Organisation of Working Time Act 1997, Sch 2, para 1(g): Organisation of Working Time (National Day of Mourning) Regulations 2001, SI No 419 of 2001.

national debt. The debt outstanding for the time being of the Exchequer: National Treasury Management Agency Act 1990, s 1. See TREASURY MANAGEMENT, NATIONAL.

National Development Finance Agency. A body corporate with the following functions: (a) to advise any State authority of what, in the opinion of the Agency, are the optimal means of financing the cost of *public investment projects* (qv) in order to achieve value for money, (b) to advance moneys (including repayable loans and equity) and to enter into other financial arrangements in respect of projects approved by any State authority, (c) to provide advice to any State authority on all aspects of financing, refinancing and insurance of public investment projects to be duly undertaken by means of *public private partnership arrangements* (qv) or within the public sector, and (d) to form, or cause to be formed, companies for the purpose of securing finance for public investment projects: National Development Finance Agency Act 2002, s 3(1).

In carrying out its functions the Agency is required to comply with all guidelines and instructions that the Minister may, from time to time, issue to the Agency (NDFAA 2002, s 3(3)). The Agency is required to perform its functions through the National Treasury Management Agency (qv) (NDFAA 2002, s 11(1)(a)). The Agency is exempt from corporation tax and other taxes e g DIRT, capital gains tax and stamp duty: Finance Act 2003, ss 43, 72 and 139. See PUBLIC PRIVATE PARTNERSHIP ARRANGEMENT; SPECIAL PURPOSE COMPANY.

National Disability Authority. A central national body corporate with the function of: (a) assisting the Minister in the co-ordination and development of policy relating to persons with disabilities, (b) advising on appropriate standards for programmes and services provided to persons with disabilities and the monitoring of the standards and codes of practice, (c) recognising the achievement of good standards and quality, and (d) preparing strategic plans: National Disability Authority Act 1999, s 8.

The Authority is independent in the exercise of its functions (NDAA 1999, s 7). It is empowered to draft codes of practice for the purpose of achieving the aim of good standards and quality in the provision of programmes and services (NDAA 1999, s 10). The Authority is also empowered to make recommendations to the Minister for the review, reduction or withdrawal of any moneys provided by the Oireachtas for any programme or service (NDAA 1999, s 15(4)). The Minister in appointing members of the Authority, must have regard to the objective that a majority would be persons with disabilities, their representatives, families or carers (NDAA 1999, s 20(3)(a)). See also Public Service Superannuation (Miscellaneous Provisions)

Act 2004, Sch 2. See COMHAIRLE; DISABILITY.

National Economic and Social Development Office. Under draft legislation, the proposed body which will comprise three bodies to be known as the *National Economic and Social Council* (NESC), the *National Economic and Social Forum* (NESF), and the *National Council for Partnership and Performance* (NCPP): National Economic and Social Development Office Bill 2002. The Bill provides for the dissolution of the three non-statutory bodies of the same names and for the inclusion in the new body of other bodies in the future.

National Educational Welfare Board. A body corporate, consisting of a chairperson and twelve ordinary members, with the general functions to ensure that each child attends a *recognised school* or otherwise receives a *certain minimum education*, and to assist in the formulation of policies and objectives of the government, for the time being, concerning the education of children: Education (Welfare) Act 2000, ss 9–10, and Sch. The board may appoint persons as *educational welfare officers* and *liaison officers* (E(W)A 2000, ss 11–12).

The board is required to establish and maintain a register of all children in receipt of education in a place other than a recognised school (E(W)A 2000, s 14(1)). The board will register a child if it is satisfied that the child concerned is receiving a *certain minimum education* (E(W)A 2000, s 14(10)). The Minister is empowered to issue guidelines and recommendations of a general nature to the board for the purpose of assisting the board in determining whether a child is receiving a *certain minimum education* (E(W)A 2000, s 16). The board, in consultation with the parent who has applied to have their child registered, may make an assessment of the education being provided, the materials used, the time spent, and may assess the child (E(W)A 2000, s 14(5)). There is provision for an appeal from the board's decision to an Appeal Committee appointed by the Minister (E(W)A 2000, s 15). The board may, with the consent of the parent, arrange for a child to be assessed as to his intellectual, emotional and physical development (E(W)A 2000, s 10(4)). Where a parent refuses, the board may apply to the Circuit Court for an order for such an assessment; the Court will make such an order where it is satisfied that the child's behaviour, his lack of educational progress, or the regularity of his school attendance, is such that an assessment should be carried out (E(W)A 2000, s 10(5)–(6)).

The board is empowered to serve a *school attendance notice* (qv). The board is also required to establish and maintain a register of *young persons in employment* (qv). [National Educational Welfare Board, 16–22 Green Street, Dublin 7; Tel: 01 8738600; Fax: 01 8738699; email: *info@newb.ie*; website: *www.newb.ie*.] See EDUCATION; SCHOOL; SCHOOL ATTENDANCE; SCHOOL ATTENDANCE NOTICE.

national emergency. A national emergency exists when each of Houses of the Oireachtas (qv) so resolves *in time of war or armed rebellion*; nothing in the Constitution may be invoked to invalidate any law enacted by the Oireachtas which is expressed to be for the purpose of securing the State in time of war or armed rebellion or to nullify any act done or purporting to be done in time of war or armed rebellion in pursuance of such law: 1937 Constitution, art 28(3)(3).

Time of war includes a time when there is taking place an armed conflict in which the State is not a participant but in respect of which each of the Houses of the Oireachtas has resolved that arising therefrom, a *national emergency* exists affecting the vital interests of the State; a *time of war* or *armed rebellion* includes time after their termination.

The Houses of the Oireachtas resolved that a *national emergency* arising from the conflict in Europe existed on 2 September 1939 and continued to 1 September 1976 on which date the Houses of the Oireachtas resolved that a new national emergency arising from the conflict in Northern Ireland existed. See *The State (Walsh) v Lennon* [1942] IR 112; Emergency Powers Act 1976. [Bibliography: Campbell.]

National Gallery of Ireland. The institution with a board of governors and guardians statutorily constituted to dispense funds received for the purposes of the National Gallery in the improvement and enlargement of the collection of *works of art* presented to or purchased for or deposited with it: National Gallery of Ireland Acts 1854 and 1963; National Cultural Institution Act 1997, ss 60–61.

The governors and guardians are empowered to lend *works of art* for display: in the official residence of the President, in the houses of the Oireachtas, in Irish diplomatic and cultural missions, in approved premises, and in exhibitions in Ireland and abroad (NGIA 1963, s 1). The functions of the governors and guardians were further extended in 1997 to include the promotion of the *visual arts*, to permit them to engage in fundraising, and to dispose of land and property, other than cultural objects (NCIA 1997, s 60). See website: *www.nationalgallery.ie*. For requirements re liquor licences in national cultural institutions, see Finance Act 2000, ss 105, 106, 163.

national identity. The European Union (qv) is required to respect the *national identities* of its member states: Treaty on European Union, art 6 of the consolidated (2002) version. See NATION.

National Library of Ireland. The institution whose board is a body corporate with functions: to conserve, restore, maintain and enlarge the library material in its collection for the benefit of the public and to maintain a record of *library material* (including material relating to the Irish language) in relation to Ireland: National Cultural Institutions Act 1997, ss 2(1) and 12. It also has the function of contributing to the provision of access by members of the public to material relating to other countries. It is also entitled to any copyright subsisting in *coats of arms* granted or confirmed by the Chief Herald (NCIA 1997, s 13(3)). The Genealogical Office is a branch of the library (NCIA 1997, s 13). The publisher of any specified material must, within one month, deliver at his own expense, a copy of the material to the Library (NCIA 1997, ss 65–66 as amended by Copyright and Related Rights Act 2000, s 199). This includes any engraving, photograph, play script, film, microfilm, video recording, sound recording, compact disc, magnetic tape. There is separate provision for delivery to the library of books published in the State (CRRA 2000, s 198). See website: *www.nli.ie*. For requirements re liquor licences in national cultural institutions, see Finance Act 2000, ss 105, 106, 163. See BOOK AND LIBRARY; CULTURAL OBJECT; MARSH'S LIBRARY.

national lottery. See LOTTERY.

national monument. A monument or the remains of a monument the preservation of which is a matter of national importance by reason of the historical, architectural, traditional, or archaeological interest attaching thereto: National Monuments Act 1930, s 2. The constitutionality of legislation preserving national monuments has been upheld, even where a *preservation order* had the effect of sterilising part of a farmer plaintiff's land without compensation: *O'Callaghan v Commissioners of Public Works* [1985] ILRM 364.

The Commissioners may acquire by agreement or compulsorily any monument that is, in their opinion, a national monument; this includes land in the vicinity, rights, easements, interests or title: National Monuments (Amendment) Act 1994, s 11.

The Commissioners are obliged to take such reasonable steps as are necessary to avoid foreseeable risk to members of the public to whom they permitted access to a national monument: *Clancy v Commissioners of Public Works* [1991] ILRM 567, SC. It has been held that the proposed use of lands around a national monument as a refuse dump amounted to a breach of the 1930 Act, s 14: *A-G v Sligo Co Council* [1989] ITLR (20 March) SC. Also the Supreme Court granted an order halting any interference with a ditch of Carrickmines Castle without a valid consent under s 14: *Dunne & Lucas v Dún Laoghaire-Rathdown County Council* [2003] ITLR (24 March) and [2003] 2 ILRM 147; 1 IR 567.

The Supreme Court has held that the Minister was entitled to take measures such as specifying the times the national monument was open to the public, and, in particular, managing, controlling and limiting the numbers entering the site: *Casey v Minister for Arts* (24 February 2004, unreported). The site in question was Skellig Michael island which is not only a national monument but is also a World Heritage Site, having been so designated by UNESCO in 1996. See also *Mulcreevy v Minister for the Environment & Dún Laoghaire-Rathdown County Council* [2004] 1 ILRM 419, SC.

Under recent legislation – (a) discretion is given to the Minister to grant a consent or otherwise issue directions in respect of a national monument, notwithstanding the fact that such consent or directions may involve injury to, interference with, or the destruction in whole or in part, of the monument. In so doing, the Minister is not restricted to archaeological considerations alone, but can also consider the wider public interest; (b) provision is made for appropriate protection of the archaeological heritage along the routes of approved road developments including the South Eastern Route section of the M50; and (c) certain matters are clarified relating to the division of responsibilities between several Ministers concerned: National Monuments (Amendment) Act 2004.

An entrant admitted without charge to a national monument is a *recreational user* (qv): Occupiers' Liability Act 1995, s 1(1). See Planning and Development Act 2000, s 260. See HISTORIC MONUMENT; METAL DETECTOR; VALLETTA CONVENTION.

National Museum of Ireland. Institution whose board is a body corporate with functions: to maintain, manage, control, protect, preserve, record, research and enlarge the collection of *museum heritage objects* for the benefit of the public: National Cultural Institutions Act 1997, ss 2(1) and 11. It also has the function of increasing and diffusing, in and outside the State, knowledge: (a) of human life in Ireland, (b) of the natural history of Ireland, and (c) of the relations of Ireland in these respects with other countries. See CULTURAL OBJECT.

national park. National parks have been created by special legislation eg Phoenix Park Act 1925; Bourn Vincent Memorial Park Act 1932. See NATIONAL MONUMENT; NATURE RESERVE.

national parliament. The national parliament is called and known as the Oireachtas: 1937 Constitution, art 15(1)(1). See OIREACHTAS.

National Qualifications Authority of Ireland. A body corporate established with objects as follows: (a) to establish and maintain a framework of qualifications (ie a framework for the development, recognition and award of qualifications) based on standards of knowledge, skill or competence to be acquired by learners; (b) to establish and promote the maintenance and improvement of awards of two new awards councils, of any new universities, and of the Dublin Institute of Technology; and (c) to promote and facilitate *access, transfer* and *progression*: Qualifications (Education and Training) Act 1999, s 7.

The NQAI is required: (a) to establish the policies and criteria on which the framework of qualifications is based, (b) to review the operation of the framework, and (c) to determine the procedures to be implemented by providers of education and training with respect to access, transfer and progression (Q(ET)A 1999, s 8).

Access means the process by which learners may commence a programme having received recognition for knowledge, skill or competence acquired (Q(ET)A 1999, s 2(1)). *Transfer* means the process by which learners may transfer from one programme to another having received recognition for knowledge, skill or competence acquired (Q(ET)A 1999, s 2(1)). *Progression* means the process by which learners may transfer from one programme to another where each programme is at a higher level than the other (Q(ET)A 1999, s 2(1)). *Validation* means the process by which an awarding body satisfies itself that a learner may attain knowledge, skill or competence for the purpose of an award (Q(ET)A 1999, s 2(1)).

Every body and person concerned in the implementation of the 1999 Act must have regard in exercising these functions under the Act to the objects as specified in s 4(1) (Q(ET)A 1999, s 4(2)).

The NQAI was established in 2001, as were the two awards councils, the *Further Education and Training Awards Council* (FETAC) and the *Higher Education and Training Awards Council* (HETAC). See EC (Recognition of Qualifications and Experience) Regulations 2003, SI No 372 of 2003. See websites: *www.nqai.ie*; *www.fetac.ie*; and *www.hetac.ie*. See AWARD; CHARTER; COMPLETION RATE; DISABLED PERSON AND QUALIFICATION; DUBLIN INSTITUTE OF TECHNOLOGY; EDUCATION AWARD; FURTHER EDUCATION AND TRAINING AWARDS COUNCIL; HIGHER EDUCATION AND TRAINING AWARDS COUNCIL; IRISH LANGUAGE; LEARNER; NATIONAL REFERENCE POINT; STATE EXAMINATIONS COMMISSION; UNIVERSITY.

National Reference Point. An organisation in each member state of the EU which provides information on the national vocational education and training system. All the then member states established an NRP in 2002. The National Qualifications Authority of Ireland is the NRP for Ireland. See website: *www.nqai.ie*. The NRP for the UK is under the management of UK Naric at website: *www.uknrp.org.uk*. The NRPs also co-operate with each other. See NATIONAL QUALIFICATIONS AUTHORITY OF IRELAND.

national road. A public road (qv) or a proposed public road which is classified as a national road by the Minister: Roads Act 1993, ss 2(1) and 10. See MOTORWAY; WAY, PUBLIC RIGHT OF.

National Roads Authority. A body corporate with perpetual succession and with overall responsibility for the planning and supervision of works for the construction and maintenance of national roads: Roads Act 1993, ss 16–42 and Sch 3. It is required at least every five years, following public consultation, to prepare a plan for the development of national roads and to review annually implementation of the approved plan (RA 1993, s 18).

It also has the following functions (a) preparing, or arranging for the preparation of road designs, maintenance programmes, and schemes for the provision of road signs (RA 1993, s 19); (b) securing the carrying out of construction or maintenance work on national roads (RA 1993, s 19); (c) allocating and paying grants (RA 1993, s 19(f)); (d) specifying standards and carrying out research (RA 1993, s 19(g)–(h)); (e) directing road authorities to carry out certain specified functions and carrying out the function itself where the road authority fails or refuses to comply with a direction (RA 1993, s 20); (f) preparing programmes for EC financial assistance (RA 1993, s 21); (g) borrowing in respect of national roads (RA 1993, ss 25–27); (h) tolling of national roads (RA 1993, ss 56–66). See MOTORWAY; TOLL ROAD.

national school. A public elementary day school for the time being recognised by the Minister as a national school: School Attendance Act 1926, repealed by Education (Welfare) Act 2000. A national school is now, in effect, a *recognised school* providing *primary* education to its students. See CORPORAL PUNISHMENT; SCHOOL DISCIPLINE; PRE-SCHOOL SERVICE; SCHOOL AUTHORITIES DUTY.

national sporting arena. A 'designated national sporting arena' means a major arena or stadium used primarily for sport which is so designated by the Minister: Intoxicating Liquor Act 2003, s 21. The Minister is empowered to issue to the owners of such arena a certificate approving the issue of an intoxicating liquor licence. For regulations designating arenas and prescribing areas for the sale and consumption of alcohol, see SI No 271 of 2004. See INTOXICATING LIQUOR.

National Standards Authority. A body corporate with the power to declare the specification of any commodity, process or practice to be a *standard specification* (qv): National Standards Authority of Ireland Act 1996. Its functions include: (a) to encourage the use of standard specifications to improve the technical processes and methods used in industry; (b) to formulate specifications at the Minister's request; (c) to declare, with the Minister's consent, any such specifications to be standard specifications; (d) to determine, license and supervise the use of *standard marks* (qv); (e) to enter into mutual recognition agreements of *certificates of conformity* with bodies in other countries (NSAIA 1996, s 7). It is required to keep a register of standard specifications, of standard marks and of licensees; inspection of the registers is free (NSAIA 1996, s 24). See also Industrial Development (Enterprise Ireland) Act 1998, ss 49–52 as amended by Industrial Development (Science Foundation Ireland) Act 2003, s 37. See website: *www.nsai.ie*. See CE MARK; ECO-LABELLING SCHEME; STANDARD MARK; STANDARD SPECIFICATION.

National Stud. The National Stud (Amendment) Act 2000 increases further the share capital and borrowing limits of the company, established by the Minister for Agriculture to operate the National Stud Farm in County Kildare, pursuant to the National Stud Act 1945. The National Stud Farm is vested in the Minister for Agriculture. The National Stud Acts 1976 and 1993 had previously provided for increases in the share capital and borrowing limits of the company. In addition, the 2000 Act empowers the Minister to vest all or any part of the National Stud lands in the company, and empowers the company to establish subsidiaries, to acquire shares in other companies, and to enter into joint ventures. See STALLION.

national territory. Formerly, the national territory consisted of the whole island of Ireland, its islands and territorial seas: 1937 Constitution, art 2. The restriction imposed by art 3, which prohibited the enactment of laws applicable to the counties of Northern Ireland pending the re-integration of the national territory, in no way derogated from the claim in art 2 of a legal right to the entire national territory: *McGimpsey v Ireland & Ors* [1990] ILRM 440, SC.

The constitutional territorial claim to Northern Ireland was removed by referen-

dum: Nineteenth Amendment to the Constitution Act 1998, which inserted new arts 2 and 3. See Declaration under art 29.7 of the Constitution (Extension of Time) Act 1999. See GOOD FRIDAY AGREEMENT; NATION; NORTHERN IRELAND; UNITED IRELAND.

National Tourism Development Authority. A body corporate established with the general functions of encouraging, promoting and supporting (either inside or outside the State): (i) the development of tourist traffic within and to the State, and (ii) the development and marketing of tourist facilities and services in the State: National Tourism Development Authority Act 2003, ss 7–8. The Authority is required to encourage, promote and support the recruitment, education and development of persons for the purpose of employment in tourism. For operational purposes the Authority is entitled to describe itself as *Fáilte Ireland* (NTDAA 2003, s 7(5)). The Act provides for the dissolution of Bord Fáilte and of CERT Ltd (NTDAA 2003, ss 37–42). It also amends or repeals, in whole or in part, many of the Tourist Traffic Acts (NTDAA 2003, s 5 and Schs 1 and 2). See ECO-LABELLING SCHEME; TOURISM IRELAND.

national training fund. See TRAINING FUND.

National Treasury Management Agency. A body corporate established with the function of borrowing moneys for the exchequer and of managing the national debt, on behalf of and subject to the control and general superintendence of the Minister for Finance: National Treasury Management Agency Act 1990.

The role of the National Treasury Management Agency was extended in 2000: (a) to manage, through a *State Claims Agency*, personal injury and property damage compensation claims against the State and to provide risk management services, (b) to offer, through a *Central Treasury Service*, deposit and loan facilities to health boards, local authorities, vocational education committees, and designated non-commercial State bodies, and (c) to provide, through a *Fund Investment Service*, a service in respect of funds under the control of Government Ministers: National Treasury Management Agency (Amendment) Act 2000. See also Asset Covered Securities Act 2001, ss 71–80 and Sch 2, Pt IV; Housing (Miscellaneous Provisions) Act 2002, s 19;

National Development Finance Agency Act 2002, ss 11 and 24. See website: *www.ntma.ie*.

See NATIONAL DEVELOPMENT FINANCE AGENCY; STATE CLAIMS AGENCY.

National Treatment Purchase Fund Board. A corporate body with the function of making arrangements with persons, whether resident in the State or elsewhere, for the provision of hospital treatment to such classes of persons as may be determined by the Minister for Health from time to time: National Treatment Purchase Fund Board (Establishment) Order 2004, SI No 179 of 2004.

National Trust. A charity, established in the UK pursuant to their National Trust Act 1907, which has the objective of preserving places of historic interest or natural beauty. The Taoiseach announced in September 2003 that the government is to establish a National Trust in Ireland to secure the future of at least 50 great Irish houses, with tax breaks for business interests investing in them. See report *A Future for Irish Historic Houses?* (2003) by Dr Terence Dooley.

nationalisation. The bringing of the ownership of a company under the control of the State eg the acquisition of the assets of Dublin Gas by Bord Gáis Éireann: Gas (Amendment) Act 1987. See PRIVATISATION.

nationality. The legal relationship attaching to membership of a nation. The question of whether an individual possesses the nationality of a member state of the EC must be settled solely by reference to the national law of the member state concerned: Maastricht Treaty 1992, Declaration on Nationality.

An employer is prohibited from discriminating against an employee or prospective employee on the grounds of *race* ie treating persons differently on the grounds that the persons are of a different race, colour, *nationality* or ethnic or national origins: Employment Equality Act 1998, ss 8(1) and 6.

A person must not discriminate on *race grounds* in disposing of goods or premises or in providing a service or accommodation; treating one person less favourably than another because they are of different race, colour, *nationality* or ethnic or national origins, is discrimination: Equal Status Act 2000, ss 5 and 3, amended by Equality Act 2004, s 48. See 'Individual

Rights: The EC prohibition of discrimination on grounds of nationality' by solicitors Massimo De Luca and Aideen Ryan in *Bar Review* (June 2003) 128. See websites: *www.equality.ie*; *www.knowracism.ie*. [Bibliography: Reid M.] See CITIZENSHIP; EXPULSION; HATRED, INCITEMENT TO; NATURALISATION; RACE.

nations, law of. International law (qv).

natural child. Term sometimes applied to a child whose parents are not married to each other. See NATURAL PARENT.

natural family planning. See FAMILY PLANNING SERVICE.

natural gas. See BORD GÁIS; ELECTRICITY REGULATION.

natural heritage area. An area which is worthy of conservation for one or more species, communities, habitats, landforms or geological or geomorphological features, or for its diversity of natural attributes: Wildlife (Amendment) Act 2000, s 6(1)(m). For example, see Moorfield Bog/Farm Cottage Order 2003, SI No 499 of 2003. See WILDLIFE; HERITAGE.

natural justice. The rules and procedures to be followed by any person or body with the duty of adjudicating on disputes between, or the rights of, others. The main rules are that a person must not be a judge in his own cause; a person must have notice of what he is accused; and each party must be given an opportunity of adequately stating his case. See *Garvey v Ireland* [1979] 113 ILTR 61; *Gunn v National College of Art and Design* [1990] 2 IR 168, SC; *Wong v Minister for Justice* [1993] HC; *Mooney v An Post* [1994] ELR 103, HC and [1998] ELR 238, SC.

It has been held that it was fallacious to submit that a student, while well educated, did not need representation at a disciplinary hearing: *Flanagan v University College Dublin* [1989] ILRM 469, HC.

The rules of natural justice must be complied with when an employee is dismissed for misconduct: *Phelan v BIC (Ireland) Ltd* [1997] ELR 208, HC. However, the rules of natural justice do not apply in the case of the dismissal of an employee, in the absence of allegations of misconduct: *Philpott v Ogilvy & Mather Ltd* [2000] 3 IR 206, HC and ELR 225; *Sheehy v Ryan and Moriarty* [2004] ELR 87, HC. It has also been held that the application of the relevant rules of natural justice do not apply to the dismissal of a statutory board officer where the person had not been dismissed for any fault by her in the discharge of her duties: *Hickey v Eastern Health Board* [1991] 1 IR 208, SC.

To achieve natural justice in disciplinary matters, procedural requirements will vary according to the circumstances of each case; in some cases an oral hearing will be essential, in other cases not: *Sheriff v Corrigan* [2001] 1 ILRM 67, SC and [2000] ELR 233, SC. See also *A Hospital v A Worker* [1997] ELR 214, HC; *Cassidy v Shannon Castle Banquets* [2000] ELR 248, HC. See CONTRACT FOR SERVICE; FAIR PROCEDURE; NEMO JUDEX IN SUA CAUSA; AUDI ALTERAM PARTEM.

natural law. The law which is based on value judgments which emanate from some absolute source eg God's revealed word. Natural law is both anterior and superior to positive law or man-made law. There are many personal rights of the citizen which follow from the Christian and democratic nature of the State which are not mentioned in art 40 (of the 1937 Constitution) at all: *Ryan v Attorney-General* [1965] IR 294. See O'Hanlon J, Murphy T and Clarke D in 11 ILT & SJ (1993) 8, 81, 129 and 177. See NATURAL RIGHTS.

natural mineral waters. Waters derived from a natural mineral water spring, which has been extracted from the ground, and that are intended to be placed on the market in a member state in bottles or containers: EC (Natural Mineral Waters, Spring Waters and other Waters in Bottles or Containers) Regulations 2004, SI No 6 of 2004. The regulations give effect to the approximation of the laws of the member states relating to the exploitation, treatment, packaging, labelling and marketing of bottled waters.

natural parents. The parents of a child as contrasted with adopting parents. A *parent* includes the natural father of an illegitimate child: Adoption Act 1952, s 3. There is a presumption that a child's best interests would best be served in the custody of his natural parents: *MC & MC v KC & AC* [1986] ILRM 65. See PARENTAGE, DECLARATION OF.

natural person. A human being, as contrasted with an artificial person eg a company (qv).

natural rights. (1) Rights which come from the natural law (qv). 'Natural rights or human rights are not created by law but the Constitution confirms ... their existence and gives them protection. The individual has natural and human rights over which the State has no authority': *McGee v Attorney-General* [1974] IR 284. In a pluralist society the court cannot, as a matter of constitutional law, be asked to choose between differing views of experts as to the interpretation by the different religious denominations of the nature and extent of natural rights: *F v F* [1994] 2 ILRM 401, HC.

(2) The term *natural rights* also refers to rights which exist automatically with land eg the right to support, the right to water flowing in a defined channel. Such rights may also be acquired as easements (qv). [Bibliography: O'Reilly.] See FUNDAMENTAL RIGHTS; RIPARIAN; SUPPORT, RIGHT TO.

naturalisation. The process by which a person may have conferred on him *citizenship* of the State by the Minister. The applicant must be of full age; must be of good character; must have been resident in the State for a total of five out of the previous nine years, of which one year's continuous residence preceded the application; must intend to reside in the State after naturalisation; and must have made a declaration of fidelity to the nation and loyalty to the State: Irish Nationality and Citizenship Act 1956, s 15 as amended by Irish Nationality and Citizenship Act 1986, s 4. The declaration is made before a judge of the District Court: DCR 1997 Ord 94, r 2. The 1986 Act removed the previous requirement of one year's notice of intention to apply for a certificate of naturalisation.

The Minister is empowered to waive the conditions for granting a certificate in a number of instances, including where the applicant is a refugee (qv) or a stateless person (qv) (INCA 1986, s 5). The grant or refusal of a certificate of naturalisation is not subject to an order of the courts: *Osheku v Ireland* [1987] ILRM 330. However, in a particular case, a plaintiff was given a declaration of his entitlement to apply for naturalisation: *Wong v Minister for Justice* (1993) Irish Times, 10 July, HC. [Bibliography: Cubie & Ryan.] See CITIZENSHIP.

naturalisation by marriage. Significant changes have been made to the naturalisation process under which the Minister for Justice may grant citizenship in respect of non-national spouses of Irish citizens; the previous arrangement for *post-nuptial declaration of citizenship* has been abolished (with transitional arrangements) and replaced by a special system of naturalisation for such non-national spouses, with different residence conditions than apply to the normal naturalisation process: Irish Nationality and Citizenship Act 2001, ss 4 and 5.

The Minister is empowered to grant an application for naturalisation if satisfied that the applicant is of full age and good character, and is married to the Irish citizen for not less than three years, that the marriage is recognised under the laws of the State and is subsisting, that they are living together as husband and wife, that a declaration is made of fidelity to the nation and loyalty to the State: Irish Nationality and Citizenship Act 1956, s 15A inserted by INCA 2001, s 5).

There is also now a new residency requirement on the applicant – he must have one year's continuous residence in the island of Ireland immediately before the date of the application; total residence must amount to two years during the four years immediately preceding that period; and he must intend in good faith to continue to reside in the island of Ireland after naturalisation (INCA 1956, s 15A). There are also new provisions regarding the calculation of the period of residence eg non-reckonable are periods for which the non-national did not have a residence permit, or periods for which the applicant had permission to remain in the State, but the permission was for the purpose of study or to seek to be recognised as a refugee (INCA 2001, s 6 as amended by Immigration Act 2004, s 16(1)).

The Minister continues to be empowered to waive certain conditions if satisfied that the applicant would suffer serious consequences in respect of bodily integrity or liberty if not granted Irish citizenship (INCA 1956, s 15A(2)).

It has been held that citizenship acquired through marriage to an Irish citizen under the previous legislation could not be revoked by the Minister unless the Minister could establish that the marriage was a sham because the parties did not participate in the ceremony in order to become man and wife: *Kelly v Ireland* [1996] 2 ILRM 364, HC and 3 IR 537. See *Mishra v Minister for Justice* [1996] 1 IR 189, HC.

For the regulations which prescribe the procedure to be followed and the forms to be used by persons who make declarations for the purposes of the 1956 to 2001 Acts, or who apply for certificates of naturalisation, see Irish Nationality and Citizenship Regulations 2002, SI No 567 of 2002. The regulations also prescribe the form of certificates of naturalisation which the Minister may grant, and the form of notice in *Iris Oifigiúil* of the grant. See CITIZENSHIP.

nature reserve. Land, including inland water, which is by order declared to be a nature reserve: Wildlife Act 1976, s 15. The Minister may make such an order where he is satisfied that the land includes the habitat of a species or community of flora or fauna which is of scientific interest or includes an ecosystem which is of scientific interest and that the habitat or ecosystem is likely to benefit if measures are taken for its protection. For example, see Nature Reserve (Glendalough) Establishment Order 1988, SI No 68 of 1988. See REFUGE.

nautical mile. The length of one minute of an arc of a meridian of longitude: Maritime Jurisdiction Act 1959, s 1.

navigation, right of. The right of persons to use a river; it is a *right of way* and may be a private or public right. Compensation may be payable in respect of interference with a private right of navigation by agreement or in default of agreement under the Acquisition of Land (Assessment of Compensation) Act 1919. See BRIDGE; COMPENSATION AND COMPULSORY PURCHASE; SHANNON NAVIGATION; WAY, RIGHT OF.

NCT. [National Car Test.] See CAR TESTING.

ne exeat regno. [That he shall not leave the kingdom.] An injunction or order that a person not leave the jurisdiction. To obtain the writ a plaintiff must prove: (a) that there exists an equitable equivalent of an action at law which would prior to the Debtors (Ireland) Act 1872 have entitled the plaintiff to seek the arrest of the defendant; (b) that the plaintiff has a good cause of action against the defendant to the amount of £20 (€25.39) or has suffered damage to that amount; (c) that there is probable cause for believing that the defendant is about to quit Ireland; and (d) that the defendant's absence would materially prejudice the plaintiff in the prosecution of his action. See Courtney in 8 ILT & SJ (1990) 222. See also *Al Nahkel & Trading Ltd v Lowe* [1986] 1 All ER 729; *Felton* *v Callis* [1968] 3 All ER 673. See RSC Ord 40, r 21. See MAREVA INJUNCTION.

nec vi, nec dam, nec precario. [Not by violence, stealth or entreaty.] See PRESCRIPTION.

necessaries. See ALLOWANCE TO BANKRUPT; CAPACITY TO CONTRACT.

necessary. Statutes and rules of court sometimes provide for some duty or some power or privilege being 'necessary' eg providing for the discovery or inspection of documents *necessary* for the fair disposal of an action. 'Necessary' in this case means not only a case where the party applying for inspection could not possibly succeed without such inspection, but also where the party had only a slim chance of success without inspection and a very strong chance of success with inspection: *Cooper-Flynn v RTE* [2000] ITLR (5 June) HC.

In another case, where the Minister is statutorily required to be of the opinion that it is 'necessary' to examine the books or documents of a body, 'necessary' has the meaning of 'reasonably required'; Herbert J in *Dunnes Stores Ireland Company v Ryan & Minister for Enterprise* [2002] 2 IR 60, SC.

necessitas inducit privilegium quoad jura privata. [Necessity gives a privilege as to private rights.]

necessitas non habet legem. [Necessity knows no law.]

necessitas publica majorest quam privata. [Public necessity is greater than private.] See NECESSITY.

necessity. Circumstances compelling a course of action. (1) In tort (qv), *necessity* may be a good defence where the damage has been caused to prevent a greater evil and the act was reasonable. See *Leigh v Gladstone* [1909] 26 TLR 139; *Cope v Sharpe* [1912] 1 KB 496; *Lynch v Fitzgerald* [1938] IR 382; *Allman v Minister for Justice* [2002] 3 IR 540, HC and [2003] ELR 7.

(2) In crime, necessity does not excuse an offence and is not a good defence: *R v Dudley and Stephens* [1884] 14 QBD 273. See O'Hanlon J in 10 ILT & SJ (1992) 86. [Bibliography: Charleton (4); McAuley & McCutcheon.] See DURESS; OBEDIENCE TO ORDERS.

necessity, agent of. See AGENT OF NECESSITY.

neglect, wilful. See WILFUL NEGLECT.

negligence. A tort (qv) involving the breach of a legal duty of care whereby damage is caused to the party to whom the duty is owed. It is the doing by a person of some act which a reasonable and prudent man would not have done in the circumstances of the case in question, or the omission to do something which would be expected of such a man under such circumstances.

For actionable negligence there must be: (a) a duty of care between the parties; (b) a failure to observe the required duty of care; and (c) reasonably foreseeable damage suffered. The law recognises that many persons owe a duty of care to others eg occupiers, carriers, employers, bailees, highway users, possessors of skills, and producers of goods. The degree of care required is that of reasonable care.

The standard of care is the foresight and caution of the ordinary or average prudent man. But the standard of care is higher where a person puts a dangerous object attractive to children in a place where children may have access to it: *Purtill v Athlone UDC* [1968] IR 205; *Maria Rooney v The Rev Fr Connolly PP* [1987] ILRM 768. Persons professing special skills (eg a solicitor) must use such skill as is usual with persons professing such skill.

The burden of proving negligence rests with the plaintiff but where the facts speak for themselves under the doctrine of *res ipsa loquitur* (qv), the plaintiff merely proves the accident.

Where there is *contributory negligence* (qv) on the part of the plaintiff, his damages will be reduced by such amount as the court thinks just and equitable having regard to the degrees of fault of the parties: Civil Liabilities Act 1961, s 34. See *O'Toole v Heavey* [1993] 2 IR 544, SC. [Bibliography: Burke & Corbett; McMahon & Binchy; Charlesworth & Percy UK.] See CONCURRENT WRONGDOER; DUTY OF CARE; OCCUPIERS LIABILITY; INFERENCE; MEDICAL NEGLIGENCE; MITIGATION OF DAMAGES; PRIMARY FACTS; PROFESSIONAL NEGLIGENCE; SAFETY BELT.

negligence, presumption of. See RES IPSA LOQUITUR.

negligence, professional. See PROFESSIONAL NEGLIGENCE.

negligent misrepresentation. A false statement, made with no reasonable grounds for believing it to be true, which is one of fact, intended to be acted upon, and which actually misleads and induces a contract. A special *duty of care* (qv) has to exist between the parties which would render the misrepresentation a negligent one, entitling the injured party to rescind the contract and to sue for negligence: *Hedley Byrne & Co Ltd v Heller & Partners Ltd* [1964] AC 465.

Damages for negligent misrepresentation are calculated so as to put the plaintiff in the position he would have been if the representation had not been made to him: *McAnarney v Hanrahan* [1994] 1 ILRM 210, HC. See also *Donnellan v Dungoyne Ltd* [1995] 1 ILRM 389, HC.

Since 1980, a statutory liability in damages is imposed on a party to certain types of contract, who has induced another party to enter into the contract by means of a negligent misrepresentation: Sale of Goods and Supply of Services Act 1980, s 45. This provision applies to a contract of sale of goods, a hire-purchase agreement, an agreement for letting of goods, and a contract for the supply of a service. The defendant can avoid liability if he can prove that he had reasonable ground to believe and did believe up to the time the contract was made that the facts represented were true. The court may award damages instead of rescission where it would be equitable to do so (SGSSA 1980, s 45(2)).

negligent mis-statement. Where a duty of care exists between two parties, there is a general obligation not to do what foreseeably may damage another: *Donoghue v Stevenson* [1932] AC 562; and this duty of care applies to economic or financial loss as well as to physical damage caused by another's negligence: *Hedley Byrne & Co Ltd v Heller & Partners Ltd* [1964] AC 465.

The High Court has held that the following test should be applied in deciding whether or not a duty of care existed between a plaintiff and a defendant in a case where *negligent mis-statement* is alleged: (a) was the injury or damage to property reasonably foreseeable, (b) has the *proximity* or *neighbourhood* test been met, and (c) is it just and reasonable that the law should impose a duty of a given scope on the defendant for the benefit of the plaintiff: *Wildgust & Carrickowen Ltd v Bank of Ireland and Norwich Union Life Insurance Society* (1 October 2001, unreported) HC.

As regards the relationship of a company to a shareholder in respect of a negligent mis-statement, see *Securities Trust Ltd v Hugh Moore and Alexander* [1964] IR 417. See PROSPECTUS; MISREPRESENTATION; NAME OF COMPANY; NEGLIGENT MISREPRESENTATION.

negotiable instrument. An instrument, the transfer of which to the transferee (who takes it in good faith and for value) passes a good title, free from any defects affecting the title of the transferor. Notice is not required to be given to the person liable on the instrument and the transferee may sue in his own name. The most important negotiable instruments are bills of exchange, promissory notes, cheques, share and dividend warrants and debentures payable to bearer (qqv). Negotiability may be conferred by custom or statute and restricted or destroyed by the holder of the instrument. See *Bechaunaland Exploration Company v London Trading Bank Ltd* [1898] 2 QB 658. See Bills of Exchange Act 1882, ss 31–32; Consumer Credit Act 1995, s 41. [Bibliography: Richardson UK.] See NEMO DAT QUI NON HABET.

negotiation licence. The licence required for any body of persons to carry on negotiations for the fixing of wages or other conditions of employment: Trade Union Act 1941, s 7. The membership requirement for a new union seeking a negotiation licence has been doubled from 500 members to 1000: Industrial Relations Act 1990, s 21(2). See TRADE UNION, AUTHORISED.

negotiation of a bill. The transferring of a bill of exchange (qv) from one person to another so that the transferee becomes the holder of the bill: Bills of Exchange Act 1882, s 31(1).

neighbour principle. In Northern Ireland, it has been held that where farmer A renders assistance to farmer B, and sustains personal injuries in the course of that work, farmer A is in law the *neighbour* of farmer B and as such owes farmer B the duty to be reasonably careful for his safety in relation to foreseeable risks of injury: *Tanney v Shields* [1992] ITLR (19 October), HC NI. See DUTY OF CARE.

nem con; nemine contradicente. [No-one saying otherwise.]

nem dis; nemine dissentiente. [No-one dissenting.] Term used in a law report (qv) indicating that no judge dissented in the judgment given.

neminem oportet legibus esse sapientiorem. [It is not permitted to be wiser than the laws.]

nemo admittendus est inhabili tare seipsum. [Nobody is to be permitted to incapacitate himself.]

nemo agit in seipsum. [No-one can take proceedings against himself.] See CLUB.

nemo contra factum suum propriem venire potest. [No-one can go against his own deed.] See NON EST FACTUM.

nemo dat qui non habet. [No-one gives who possesses not.] A person generally cannot give a better title than he has himself: Sale of Goods Act 1893, s 21. In some instances, however, a buyer acquires a good title, notwithstanding a defect in the seller's title e g transfer of a negotiable instrument; disposition by a mercantile agent; sale under an order of the court; sale under a voidable title; sale in *market overt*; sale by a *hirer-dealer*; and under the doctrine of estoppel (qqv). See HOLDER IN DUE COURSE; NOT NEGOTIABLE.

nemo debet bis puniri pro uno delicto. [No-one should be punished twice for one fault.] See AUTREFOIS CONVICT.

nemo est haeres viventis. [No-one is heir of anyone who is alive.] See HEIR APPARENT.

nemo ex proprio dolo consequitur actionem. [No-one obtains a cause of action by his own fraud.] See EQUITY, MAXIMS OF.

nemo ex suo delicto meliorem suam conditionem facere potest. [No-one can improve his position by his own wrongdoing.] See EQUITY, MAXIMS OF.

nemo judex in sua causa. [No-one can be a judge in his own cause.] Also *nemo debet esse judex in propria causa*. One of the principles of *natural justice* (qv). The person or body making a decision must be without bias, and consequently must not have any pecuniary or personal interest in the matter to be decided unless so declared e g a judge having shares in a company which is a party to an action being heard; a foreman of a jury in a fraud case being an investor in the company defrauded: *The People (Attorney-General) v Singer* [1975] IR 408. See also *Connolly v McConnell* [1983] IR 172; *Cassidy v Shannon Castle Banquets* [2000] ELR 248, HC. Sometimes referred to as 'institutional bias' e g see *Carroll v Law Society* [2000] 1 ILRM 161, HC.

The object of the principle is to ensure that in judicial and quasi-judicial proceedings, decisions are not made by persons who could be perceived as having an interest in the decision: *Murphy v Mr Justice Flood* [2000] 2 ILRM 112, SC and [1999] 3 IR 97, SC. See AUDI ALTERAM PARTEM.

nemo plus juris ad alium transferre potest, quam ipse haberet. [The title of an assignee can be no better than that of his assignor.] See NEMO DAT QUI NON HABET.

nemo potest esse simul actor et judex. [No-one can be at once suitor and judge.] See NATURAL JUSTICE.

nemo potest facere per alium, quod per se non potest. [No-one can do through another what he cannot do himself.] See AGENT; AGENT OF NECESSITY.

nemo potest plus juris ad alium transferre quam ipse habet. [No-one can transfer a greater right to another than he himself has.]

nemo prohibetur pluribus defensionibus uti. [No-one is forbidden to use several defences.] See DEFENCE.

nemo tenetur ad impossibile. [No-one is required to do what is impossible.] See FRUSTRATION OF CONTRACT; INEVITABLE ACCIDENT.

nemo tenetur se ipsum accusare. [No-one is bound to incriminate himself.] See INCRIMINATE.

nervous shock. A person who suffers nervous shock may receive damages in tort (qv) from the person whose negligence caused the shock. In order to succeed in an action for nervous shock, a plaintiff must establish: (a) he has suffered from nervous shock in the sense of any recognisable psychiatric illness, (b) the recognisable psychiatric illness from which he is suffering was shock-induced, (c) the nervous shock was caused by the defendant's act or omission, (d) the nervous shock was suffered by reason of actual or apprehended physical injury to the plaintiff or a person other than the plaintiff, and (e) the defendant owed him a duty of care not to cause him a reasonably foreseeable injury in the form of nervous shock: *Kelly v Hennessy* [1996] 1 ILRM 321, SC and [1995] 3 IR 253, SC. It is not enough to show that there was a reasonably foreseeable risk of personal injury generally: *Jaensch v Coffey* [1984] 155 CLR 549 applied in *Kelly* case.

In the latter case, a mother who suffered nervous shock, which changed her personality and lifestyle, as a result of a road accident not involving herself but her husband and two daughters, was awarded damages.

In a particular case, involving a claim for damages for nervous shock, the court held that the plaintiff was a 'primary victim' in the sense that she was a participant in the accident and suffered injury as a direct consequence; she was not a 'secondary victim', that is a person who was not involved in the accident itself: *Curran v Cadbury*

(Ireland) Ltd [2000] 2 ILRM 343, SC. A hospital porter, who was on duty when his dead brother and seriously injured sister were admitted to hospital following a road accident, was awarded €80,000 for nervous shock: *Cuddy v Peters* (28 November 2003, unreported) HC.

In another case, the court held that while the plaintiff had suffered post-traumatic stress (PTS) on learning that a hospital had retained some of the organs of her stillborn daughter, she had failed to establish that the PTS was as a result of an actual or apprehended physical injury to herself or another person: *Devlin v National Maternity Hospital* (1 July 2004, unreported), HC. See also *Kelly v Hennessy* [1993] ILRM 530, HC. See *Byrne v Southern and Western Ry Co* [1882] discussed in *Bell v G N Ry Co* [1890] 26 LR (Ir) 428; *Hogg v Keane* [1956] IR 155. [Bibliography: McMahon & Binchy.] See POST-TRAUMATIC STRESS DISORDER; PSYCHIATRIC DAMAGE.

netting agreement. An agreement between two parties in relation to present or future financial contracts between them, providing for the determination of the *termination values* of those contracts and the *set off* (qv) of the termination values so determined as to arrive at a *net* amount due: Netting of Financial Contracts Act 1995 as amended by Central Bank and Financial Services Authority of Ireland Act 2003, s 35, Sch 1 and by Central Bank and Financial Services Authority of Ireland Act 2004, s 33, Sch 3. The 1995 Act was introduced to provide for the netting of liabilities between parties so that only the net amount is payable, hence substantially reducing risk in say, the insolvency of one party, and consequently encouraging the continued development of financial markets eg the International Financial Services Centre in Dublin.

Regulations have been made: (a) designating certain types of contracts as *financial contracts* for the purposes of the enforceability of netting, between two parties only, in relation to financial contracts in accordance with the terms of a netting agreement; (b) for the enforceability of *set off* by those parties of the amounts due under such netting agreements in accordance with the terms of a *master netting agreement*; (c) for the *set off* of money or the proceeds of collateral and for the enforceability of guarantees provided solely in relation to any netting agreement or any master netting

agreement in accordance with the terms of each; and (d) other related matters provided for under the Netting of Financial Contracts Act 1995: Netting of Financial Contracts (Designation of Financial Contracts) Regulations 2000, SI No 214 of 2000.

neutrality. A High Court judge has said that despite the great historic value attached by Ireland to the concept of neutrality, that status is nowhere reflected in the Constitution of Ireland or elsewhere in any domestic legislation. It is effectively a matter of government policy only, albeit a policy to which, traditionally at least, considerable importance was attached: Kearns J in *Horgan v An Taoiseach* [2003] 2 ILRM 357, HC at 389.

There is an identifiable rule of customary law in relation to the status of neutrality, wherein a neutral state may not permit the movement of large numbers of troops or munitions of one belligerent state through its territory en route to a theatre of war with another (*Horgan* case).

Taoiseach Eamonn de Valera said on 16 May 1945 in response to UK Prime Minister Churchill's stinging criticism of Ireland's neutrality during the Second World War: 'Mr Churchill makes it clear that in certain circumstances he would have violated our neutrality and that he would justify his action by Britain's necessity ... Could he not find in his heart the generosity to acknowledge that there is a small nation that stood alone not for one year or two, but for several hundred years against aggression?'

See SAVILLE DECLARATION; WAR.

new evidence. See FRESH EVIDENCE.

new trial. See RETRIAL.

newspaper. For statutory control of the merger and acquisition of newspapers, see MEDIA MERGER. See also BUSINESS NAME; COPYRIGHT, OWNERSHIP OF; MANUFACTURED GOODS; MERGER/TAKE-OVER; TRADING STAMP.

newspaper rule. The rule under which discovery, whether of documents or by interrogatories, will not be ordered in libel actions against newspapers so as to force them to disclose their sources of information *before* trial. The rule applies at interlocutory stages and not at the trial of the action. The status of the 'newspaper rule' has not yet been determined in the Irish courts: barrister Brendan Gogarty in 'Disclosure, Defamation and the 'Newspaper

Rule' in *Bar Review* (December 2003) 236. However, see *Kiberd v Tribunal of Inquiry* [1992] ILRM 574; *Cooper-Flynn v RTE* [2000] 3 IR 344.

next friend. The person through whom a minor (qv) brings an action, generally a close relative. On application by the defendant in an action to join the *next friend* as a third party (qv) in order to claim a contribution against the next friend as a concurrent wrongdoer (qv), the court will balance the disruption to the proceedings which would arise from such joinder, against the convenience of trying all the issues in the one action: *Michael Quirke (a minor) suing by his mother and next friend Mary Quirke v O'Shea and CRL Oil Ltd* [1992] ILRM 286, SC.

On the minor attaining full age, the next friend may apply on affidavit to the Registrar in the Central Office for a certificate that the plaintiff *lately an infant* may proceed in his own name: RSC Ord 15, rr 6 and 20.

An infant may sue by his next friend: Circuit Court Rules 2001 Ord 6, r 5. When proceedings have been brought on behalf of or against an infant, the court may appoint a next friend or a *guardian ad litem* to act for the infant (Ord 6, r 7). As regards the District Court, see DCR 1997 Ord 7. See also *D'Arcy (a minor) v Roscommon Co Council* [1992] 10 ILT Dig 56, SC; *Johnston (a minor) v Fitzpatrick* [1992] ILRM 269, SC; *Hallahan (a minor) v Keane* [1992] ILRM 595, HC. See Personal Injuries Assessment Board Act 2003, s 4(1).

next-of-kin. Those who stand nearest in blood relationship to an *intestate*. Degrees of blood relationship of a direct lineal ancestor are counted from the intestate to that ancestor. For any other relative, the degrees are counted from the intestate to the nearest ancestor, common to the intestate and the relative, and down to the relative in question. Where a direct lineal ancestor and any other relative are within the same degree of blood relationship to the intestate, the other relative is preferred to the exclusion of the direct lineal ancestor. Relatives of the *half-blood* share equally with relatives of the *whole blood* in the same degree. See Succession Act 1965, ss 71 and 72. See ANCESTOR; BLOOD RELATIONSHIP; INTESTATE SUCCESSION; RESIDUE.

nexus. Connection; bond. There is a requirement for some *nexus* between a person claiming *rectification* (qv) of a contract and the document in respect of which the reformation is sought: *Lac Minerals Ltd v Chevron Mineral* [1995] 1 ILRM 161, HC. See *Crowley v Allied Irish Banks* [1987] IR 282, SC; *Curtin v Judge Brennan* [1997] 1 IR 292, HC.

Nice Treaty. The Treaty signed at Nice, France on 26 February 2001 which came into effect when ratified by each of the 15 member states of the European Union. The Nice Treaty deals with issues left over from the negotiations which led to the Amsterdam Treaty in 1997 (sometimes referred to as the 'Amsterdam leftovers') and largely concerning significant institutional issues essential to the Union's preparations for enlargement eg: (a) the size and composition of the Commission, (b) the weighting of votes in the Council, (c) the extension of qualified majority voting, and (d) changes in other EU institutions necessitated by enlargement.

A Constitutional amendment to enable Ireland to ratify the Nice Treaty was rejected in a referendum of the people in June 2001, with 453,461 voting in favour and 529,478 voting against. Only two constituencies voted in favour – Dublin South (51.88%) and Dún Laoghaire (53.53%). Following this rejection, the government established a *National Forum on Europe* to assist the debate on the issues. In a further referendum on 19 October 2002, linked with a constitutional ban on Ireland joining an EU common defence, ratification of the Nice Treaty was approved by 906,292 votes to 534,887 votes.

Protocols adopted at Nice include: (a) Protocol on the Enlargement of the European Union; (b) Protocol on the Statute of the Court of Justice; (c) Protocol on Article 67. Provision has been made to amend the European Communities Act 1972 in order to provide that certain parts of the Treaty of Nice form part of the domestic law of the State on ratification by Ireland of the Treaty: European Communities (Amendment) Act 2002. The Nice Treaty entered into force on 1 February 2003, which is the commencement date of the 2002 Act. See also Twenty-sixth Amendment of the Constitution Act 2002. See 1937 Constitution, art 29(4)(7) and art 29(4)(8). For the White Paper on the Nice Treaty, see *www.gov.ie/iveagh/nice/*. For information on the National Forum on Europe, see *www.forumeurope.ie*. See

ENHANCED CO-OPERATION; ENLARGE-MENT OF EU; SAVILLE DECLARATION.

night. The period between 9pm in the evening and 6am in the morning of the next succeeding day: Larceny Act 1916, s 46(1). It was an offence to be found by *night* armed with any dangerous or offensive weapon or instrument with intent to commit a burglary (LA 1916, s 28; Criminal Law (Jurisdiction) Act 1976, s 21(3)), since repealed by the Criminal Justice (Theft and Fraud Offences) Act 2001, s 3 and Sch 1.

It is an offence for a person in a public place to engage in offensive conduct between the hours of 12 o'clock midnight and 7 o'clock in the morning: Criminal Justice (Public Order) Act 1994, s 5(1)(a). Any person may arrest a person found committing an indictable offence (qv) in the night and hand him over to a garda: Prevention of Offences Act 1851, s 11.

nightwork. Work carried out between midnight and 7 am on the following day: Organisation of Working Time Act 1997, s 16. An employer must ensure that an employee does not work more than an average of 8 hours per night or 48 hours per week averaged over a two-month period. This restriction does not apply to sea work or to a doctor in training (OWTA 1997, s 3(2)(a)). Also employers of persons employed in activities covered in SIs Nos 20, 21 and 52 of 1998 are exempted. There are more severe restrictions on night work by children and young persons. See CHILD, EMPLOYMENT OF; YOUNG PERSON; WORKING HOURS.

nihil facit error nominis cum de corpore constat. [A mistake as to the name has no effect when there is no mistake as to who is the person meant.] See MISNOMER.

nihil; nil. [Nothing.]

nisi. An order, rule, declaration, decree or other adjudication of a court is said to be made *nisi* when it is not final or absolute and is not to take effect until the person affected by it fails to show cause against it within a certain time eg a conditional order of garnishee (qv).

Nitrigin Éireann. Provision has been made: (a) for the transfer of the State-guaranteed debt of Nitrigin Éireann Teoranta to the Minister for Finance; and (b) for the repeal of the NET legislation by Ministerial order in the event of a future sale by NET of its 51% shareholding in Irish Fertilizer Industries and the resultant winding up of the holding company, NET: Nitrigin Éireann Teoranta Act 2001.

no claims discount. Generally understood to mean the discount on the premium in motor insurance to which the insured is entitled when there is no claim on the policy of insurance. Also called a *no claims bonus*. Where a claim is made to the Motor Insurers' Bureau of Ireland by a claimant who has his own comprehensive insurance cover (eg a claim in respect of injuries or death caused by the negligent driving of a vehicle, the owner or driver of which is unidentified or untraced) and the claimant elects to have his claim dealt with under his own comprehensive policy, his *no claims discount* will not be cancelled or reduced on account of such claim: separate protocol to Agreement between the Bureau and the Minister for Transport dated 31 March 2004 in respect of accidents occurring on or after 1 May 2004. See MOTOR INSURERS' BUREAU OF IRELAND.

no cure, no pay. Colloquial expression to describe the principle in maritime law, that a salvor is not entitled to a salvage reward unless the salvage operation succeeds in saving ship or cargo. Now, while a salvor has a right to a reward where the salvage operation has a *useful result*, the reward cannot exceed the salved value; however, as an exception, salvors are entitled to special compensation where they have been successful in preventing or minimising damage to the environment, even if no property is salved: Merchant Shipping (Salvage and Wrecks) Act 1993, ss 25–27.

no fault compensation. Colloquial expression to describe a system by which tortious causes of action are abolished and replaced by a scheme of benefits for accident victims without proof of fault. 'Of the many forms of tortious liability, it is difficult to find one more appropriate for *no fault compensation* than that of medical malpractice' McCarthy N, Supreme Court Judge 1987, and in *Hegarty v O'Loughran* [1990] ITLR (2 April), SC. No fault compensation schemes exist in Sweden, Finland and New Zealand but not in Ireland. However, no fault liability has been introduced in 1991 in respect of defective products which cause damage, irrespective of whether the producer was negligent: Liability of Defective Products Act 1991. See Murphy in 7 ILT & SJ (1989) 216. See CHILD ABUSE, REDRESS; HEPATITIS; PRODUCT LIABILITY; STRICT LIABILITY.

no foal, no fee. Colloquial expression generally understood to mean the provision of a legal service on the basis that no fee will be incurred by the client unless there is a successful outcome. A *barrister* may accept instructions from a solicitor on the basis that his ordinary fee will be paid in the event of the case being successful and that no fee will be expected if unsuccessful. This most commonly occurs with personal injuries cases but not exclusively so.

A decision of the Taxing Master has cast doubt on whether *solicitors*, who act on a *no win, no fee* basis and who are awarded their legal costs by the court, are entitled to their costs. Under his judgment, a solicitor to be entitled to his costs must be able to prove that his client had a legal responsibility for the costs: *Johnston v Church of Scientology* (2002) Irish Times, 16 November. The onus of proof in relation to the legal liability for costs was a matter for the plaintiff in this case, which the Taxing Master held she had failed to discharge.

There has been concern expressed by the Law Society that legal services advertised on a 'no foal, no fee' basis could be misinterpreted by a client that he will have no liability either to his own solicitor or to the defendant should the plaintiff client be unsuccessful.

However, the Law Society is empowered to make regulations, with the consent of the Minister, governing the form, content and size of advertisements by solicitors: Solicitors Act 1954, s 71 as amended by Solicitors (Amendment) Act 2002, s 4. Under new regulations, the following phrases are prohibited: 'no foal, no fee', 'no win, no fee', 'free first consultation', 'most cases settled out of court', 'insurance cover arranged to cover legal costs' or other words or phrases which could be construed as meaning that legal services involving contentious business would be provided by the solicitor at no cost or at reduced cost to the client: Solicitors (Advertising) Regulations 2002, SI No 518 of 2002, reg 9.

'No foal, no fee' arrangements are determined if the client moves to another solicitor, the first solicitor being then entitled to his fees on a *quantum meruit* (qv) basis: *A Guide to Professional Conduct of Solicitors in Ireland* (2002) ch 7.6. It can be implied in these contingency fee arrangements that they are conditional on the first solicitor continuing to have prosecution of the case.

See CHAMPERTY; CONTINGENCY FEE; SOLICITOR AND ADVERTISING.

nobility, title of. See TITLE OF NOBILITY.

noise. Includes vibration: Environmental Protection Agency Act 1992, s 3 as substituted by Protection of the Environment Act 2003, s 5. The Minister is empowered to make regulations for the prevention or limitation of any noise which may give rise to a nuisance or disamenity, constitute a danger to health, or damage property (EPAA 1992, s 106). A local authority or the Environmental Protection Agency may require measures to be taken to prevent or limit noise by serving a notice on the person in charge (EPAA 1992, s 107). See also SI No 179 of 1994.

Where any noise which is so loud, so continuous, so repeated, of such duration or pitch or occurring at such times as to give reasonable cause for annoyance to a person in any premises in the neighbourhood or to a person lawfully using a public place, the District Court may order the prevention or limitation of the noise (EPAA 1992, s 108). This does not apply to noise caused by aircraft or by a statutory undertaker (qv) or local authority (EPAA 1992, s 108(4)). Complaint to the District Court may be made by the person affected, the local authority, or by the Agency.

A District Court judge has said that if the plaintiffs, in a noise nuisance case against their neighbours, chose to live in a home with 'jerry-built, paper-thin walls' they would have to accept they would hear what goes on next door: Fitzpatrick J in *Walsh & Scott v Martin* (2003) Irish Times, 1 August, Dublin District Court.

All these provisions are without prejudice to the provisions of the Safety, Health and Welfare at Work Act 1989 (EPAA 1992, s 109). In addition, the Minister may make regulations requiring road authorities to carry out works or other measures to mitigate the effects of road traffic noise: Roads Act 1993, s 77.

A *noise emission* measurement of 57 specified types of equipment must be taken and indicated on a label affixed to the equipment (eg portable chain saws, hedge trimmers); in addition, *noise limits* are set for 22 of the 57 types of equipment (eg tower cranes, compressors, lawnmowers and lawn trimmers): European Communities (Noise Emission by Equipment for use Outdoors) Regulations 2001, SI No 632 of 2001. These regulations give effect to Directive (EC) 2000/14. See *Barry v Nitrogen Éireann Teo* [1994] 2 ILRM 522, HC. See also EC (Protection of Workers) (Exposure to Noise) Regulations 1990, SI No 157 of 1990. [Bibliography: Canny (2); Scannell.] See CLOSURE ORDER; DOGS; NUISANCE; VIBRATION.

nolens volens. [Unwilling or willing.]

nolle prosequi. [Unwilling to prosecute.] In criminal proceedings, the entry of a *nolle prosequi* by the prosecution before judgment, operates to stay the proceedings; it is not equivalent to an acquittal and is no bar to a new indictment (qv) at a subsequent date for the same offence. See *R v Comptroller of Patents* [1899] 1 QB 909; *Kelly v DPP* [1996] 2 IR 596 SC. See GARDA, DISCIPLINE OF.

nolo contendere. [I do not wish to contend.]

nolumus mutari. [We will not change.] Motto of the Honorable Society of King's Inns (qv).

nominal capital. See CAPITAL.

nominee. See REGISTER OF MEMBERS; THIRD-PARTY INFORMATION.

nominis umbra. [The shadow of a name.]

non aliter a significatione verborum recedi oportet quam cum manifestum est aliud sensisse testatorem. [There should be no departure from the ordinary meaning of words except in so far as it appears that the testator meant something different.] See CONSTRUCTION, RULES OF; EVIDENCE, EXTRINSIC.

non bis in idem. [Not the same in two places.] No person can be tried before a national court for acts constituting serious violations of international humanitarian law under the International War Crimes Tribunals Act 1998, for which he has already been tried by the International Tribunal for Rwanda (IWCTA 1998, Sch 4, art 9). See DOUBLE JEOPARDY.

non cepit modo et forma. [He did not take it in the manner and the form as alleged.] See REPLEVIN.

non-competition agreement. Under a new provision, capital gains tax may be payable on any amount received by a person in respect of a non-competition agreement, where such amount is not liable to income tax or not otherwise liable to capital gains tax: Finance Act 2003, s 70. See RESTRAINT OF TRADE, CONTRACT IN.

non compos mentis. [Not sound in mind.] See UNSOUND MIND; MENTAL DISORDER.

non constat. [It does not follow.]

non culpabilis. [Not guilty.]

non debet, cui plus licet, quod minus est non licere. [It is lawful for a man to do a lesser thing if he is entitled to do a greater thing.]

non-discrimination notice. A notice which the *Equality Authority* (qv) is empowered to serve on any person when it is satisfied, as a result of an inquiry it is conducting or has conducted, that the person: (a) has discriminated or is discriminating, or (b) has contravened or is contravening certain sections in the Act relating to discriminating rules or instructions or advertisements or procuring discrimination, or (c) has failed or is failing to comply with an *equality clause* or an *equal pay* term: Employment Equality Act 1998, s 62.

The notice must specify the act, omission, contravention or failure and require the person concerned to take remedial action and notify the Authority of the steps taken to comply (EEA 1998, s 62(5)).

In 2000, EEA 1998, s 62 was amended to provide for contraventions of the Equal Status Act 2000 to be also the subject of a *non-discrimination notice* served by the Equality Authority (ESA 2000, s 39 and Sch). An appeal against the notice or any of its requirements may be made to the District Court (EEA 1998, s 63 as amended by ESA 2000, s 39 and Sch). There is provision for enforcement, by injunction, of a non-discrimination notice by the High or Circuit Courts (EEA 1998, s 65). A public register of non-discrimination notices must be kept and maintained (EEA 1998, s 46). [Bibliography: Reid M.] See DISCRIMINATION.

non est factum. [It is not his deed.] The plea of a person who has executed a deed in ignorance of its character, that it is not his deed, notwithstanding its execution by him. The person who signs a contract must not have been careless at the time of signing; signing without reading a contract is carelessness. See *Bank of Ireland v McManamy* [1916] 2 IR 161; *Saunders v Anglia Building Society* [1971] AC 1004; *UDT Ltd v Westen* [1976] QB 513; *Bank of Ireland v Smyth* [1993 HC] ILRM 790.

non est inventus. [He has not been found.]

non-fatal offences. A wide range of offences against the person eg assault, assault causing harm, causing serious harm, threats to kill or cause serious harm, attacks with a syringe, coercion, harassment, poisoning, endangerment, endangering traffic, false imprisonment, abduction of child, and demanding payment of a debt causing alarm: Non-Fatal Offences against the Person Act 1997. See LRC Report on Non-Fatal Offences against the Person (LRC 45, 1994). The High Court has held that it is clear that the 1997 Act deals with offences against the person which are not only *non-fatal* but also *non-sexual*: *S O'C v Governor of Curragh Prison* [2000] 2 ILRM 76, HC. [Bibliography: Charleton (4).]

non-joinder. The omission of a person in proceedings either as plaintiff or defendant. No cause or matter may be defeated by reason of the misjoinder (qv) or non-joinder of parties; the court may order that the names of parties improperly joined, be struck out, and to add parties who ought to have been joined: RSC Ord 15, r 13.

non-life insurance. Insurance of a class specified in the European Communities (Non-Life Insurance) Regulations 1976, SI No 115 of 1976 as amended by Central Bank and Financial Services Authority of Ireland Act 2003, s 35, Sch 2 and by Central Bank and Financial Services Authority of Ireland Act 2004, s 10(3), Sch 2. A person generally may not carry on the business of non-life insurance in the State unless he is the holder of an authorisation granted by the Minister (SI No 115 of 1976, art 4). There is a requirement to establish and maintain *technical reserves* in respect of underwriting liabilities assumed (arts 14 and 27) and to establish an adequate *solvency margin* (arts 16(1) and 28). From 1994, EU-based insurance companies are permitted to transact insurance business elsewhere in the EU, subject to the supervision requirements of the authority where their head office is situated: EC Third Non-Life Insurance Framework Directive; SI No 359 of 1994 as amended by CBFSAIA 2003, s 35, Sch 2. The 1994 Regulations incorporate a number of *consumer protection measures* with which insurance companies must comply. See INSURANCE.

non liquet. [It is not clear.]

non-marital child. A child whose parents are not married to each other. See Status of Children Act 1987.

non-minor offence. See INDICTABLE OFFENCE.

non-national. (1) Means an alien within the meaning of the Aliens Act 1935, with the exception of citizens of particular countries who are exempt from the provisions of that Act eg British citizens: Immigration Act 1999, s 1(1). See also Immigration Act 2004, s 1(1). A non-national must not be in the State other than in accordance with the terms of a permission and is required to land at an approved port (IA 2004, ss 5–6). There is an obligation on a non-national to register in the district of his residence; he is given a registration certificate (IA 2004, s 9). A non-national is required to produce, on demand to a garda or immigration officer, certain specified documents eg passport, registration certificate (IA 2004, s 12). A non-national who does not have permission to be in the State, may be required to reside or remain in a particular district or place and report at specified intervals to certain officers (IA 2004, s 14). A non-national may be subjected to an *exclusion order* (qv) or *deportation order* (qv). For registration certificate, see SI No 95 of 2004.

(2) Means a person who is not a citizen of the State: Employment Permits Act 2003, s 1(1).

It has been held that a non-national has a constitutional right of access to the courts to challenge the validity of certain orders, notifications, refusals, recommendations and decisions made in respect of him and is entitled to the same degree of natural justice and fairness of procedures as a citizen of the State: *In the matter of The Illegal Immigrants (Trafficking) Bill 1999* [2000] 2 IR 360, SC.

There is a requirement on the member in charge of a garda station to inform any arrested person who is a foreign national that he may communicate with his consul and that, if he so wishes, the consul will be notified of his arrest: Treatment of Persons in Custody in Garda Síochána Stations Regulations 1987, SI No 119 of 1987, reg 14.

An obligation has been placed on carriers, bringing non-nationals to the State, to ensure compliance by their passengers with immigration requirements on arrival, contravention of which will constitute an offence by the carrier punishable by a fine, with the possibility of avoiding prosecution by payment of an 'on-the-spot' penalty: Immigration Act 2003, ss 2–3. One of the requirements is that each non-national on board has a valid passport or other equivalent document which establishes his identity and nationality, and, if required by law, a valid Irish visa (IA 2003, s 2(1)(c)). See Carrier Liability Regulations 2003, SI No 447 of 2003; Approved Ports Regulations 2003, SI No 445 of 2003; Removal Direction Regulations 2003, SI No 446 of 2003. [Bibliography: Cubie & Ryan.] See ALIEN; EMPLOYMENT PERMIT; IMMIGRATION.

non-national, exclusion on medical grounds. An immigration officer is empowered to refuse to give permission to a non-national to land or to be in the State if the officer is satisfied that the non-national suffers from a specified condition: Immigration Act 2004, s 4(3)(c)). The specified conditions are: (a) diseases subject to the International Health Regulations for the time being adopted by the World Health Assembly of the World Health Organisation; (b) tuberculosis of the respiratory system in an active state or showing a tendency to develop; (c) syphilis; (d) other infectious or contagious parasitic diseases in respect of which special provisions are in operation to prevent the spread of such diseases from abroad; (e) drug addiction; (f) profound mental disturbance, that is to say, manifest conditions of psychotic disturbance with agitation, delirium, hallucinations or confusion (IA 2004, Sch 1).

non obstante veredicto. [Notwithstanding the verdict.]

non omne quod licet honestum est. [All things that are lawful are not honourable.]

non-paternity. See PATERNITY, PRESUMPTION OF.

non placet. [It is not approved.]

non pros; non prosequitor. [He does not follow up.] See DISMISSAL FOR WANT OF PROSECUTION.

non sequitor. [It does not follow.]

non-suit. (1) Formerly, the abandonment of a case by a plaintiff; now replaced by the procedure of discontinuance (qv).

(2) An application by a defendant for a *non-suit* is an application by a defendant at the end of the plaintiff's case for a *direction* that the evidence adduced by the plaintiff is not sufficient to establish a case against the defendant. There is a different test to be applied, depending on whether the defendant intends to enter into evidence. The trial judge must inquire whether, in the event of the application being unsuccessful, the defendant would be going into evidence. If

'no', the test to be applied is whether the plaintiff had at that stage discharged the onus of proof and had satisfied the court on the balance of probability that he was entitled to judgment. If 'yes', the test to be applied is whether, treating the plaintiff's case at its highest, the tribunal of fact is entitled to arrive at the conclusion that the defendant has a case to meet. See *O'Donovan v Southern Health Board* [2001] 3 IR 385, SC which followed *O'Toole v Heavey* [1993] ILRM 343, SC and 2 IR 544.

When an application for a non-suit is made, the judge is required to rule on the arguments made in support of the application, as it is essential for the defence to know which arguments are accepted or rejected, when deciding whether or not to go into evidence: *O'Mahony v Ballagh* [2002] 2 IR 410, SC. A district judge failing to so rule fell into unconstitutionality. See DIRECTION.

non-uniformed garda. Most of the rights given by legislation to gardaí are to gardaí wearing uniform. However, some statutes give rights to gardaí, irrespective of whether they are wearing uniform or not, eg a garda, whether in uniform or not, may enter a licensed premises for the prevention or detection of offences under the liquor licensing laws: Intoxicating Liquor Act 2003, s 18. See also Licensing (Combating Drug Abuse) Act 1997, s 14.

non-user. Failure to exercise a right; it may amount to abandonment of the right eg of an easement (qv). See ABANDONMENT.

non videntur qui errant consentire. [Those who are mistaken are not deemed to consent.] See MISTAKE.

nonfeasance. The neglect or failure to perform an act which one is bound by law to perform. A local authority is not liable for injury to the user of a highway caused by its failure to repair the highway; however, s 60 of the Civil Liability Act 1961 has provided, subject to being brought into operation by order of the government, that *a road authority shall be liable for damage caused as a result of their failure to maintain adequately a public road.* It has been held that s 60(7) is merely enabling and does not impose a duty on the government to bring the section into operation and that the discretion vested in the government was not limited in any way, as to time or otherwise: *The State (Sheehan) v Ireland* [1988] ILRM 437, SC. The National Roads Authority is not liable for damage caused as a result of any failure to maintain a national road: Roads Act 1993, s 19(5). See *Harbinson v Armagh C C* [1902] 2 IR 538; *Maguire v Liverpool Corporation* [1905] 1 KB 767; *Kelly v Mayo Co Council* [1964] IR 315. See MISFEASANCE.

North-South Ministerial Council. The body established under the *Good Friday Agreement* (qv) with the function of developing consultation, co-operation and action on an all-Ireland and cross-border basis. The north-south implementation bodies operate under the Council. The British-Irish Agreement (Amendment) Act 2002 enables the work of the implementation bodies to continue, following the suspension of the Northern Ireland Assembly in October 2002. See website: *www.northsouthministerialcouncil.org.*

Northern Ireland. The territory comprising the counties of Antrim, Armagh, Down, Fermanagh, Londonderry and Tyrone: Government of Ireland Act 1920 (10 & 11 Geo 5, c 67) s 1(2). The extent of Northern Ireland is recognised by the Treaty (Confirmation of Amending Agreement) Act 1925. The courts take judicial notice of the existence of Northern Ireland and its courts: *The People v McGeough* [1978] IR 384; *MacB v MacB* [1984] HC.

The governments of Ireland and the United Kingdom have affirmed that any change in the status of Northern Ireland would only come about with the consent of a majority of the people of Northern Ireland: Anglo-Irish Agreement 1985; British-Irish Agreement 1998; *Crotty v An Taoiseach* [1987] ILRM 400. This is now enshrined in the 1937 Constitution, new art 3 inserted by referendum: Nineteenth Amendment of the Constitution Act 1998.

In relation to a *proposed road development* which is likely to have significant effects on the environment of Northern Ireland, there is a requirement on the road authority to send to the prescribed authority in Northern Ireland a copy of the environment impact statement, and the Minister, before approving the development, is required to consider any views of that prescribed authority: Roads Act 1993, ss 50(3)(c) and 51(5)(b).

A non-national who enters the State from Northern Ireland must not remain in the State for longer than a month without written Ministerial permission: Immigration Act 2004, s 4(5). A defendant in an action

is not entitled to an order for security for costs solely on the grounds that the plaintiff resides in Northern Ireland: RSC Ord 29, r 2. See also *Moyne v Londonderry Port and Harbour Commissio*ners [1986] IR 299. See Trade Union Act 1975, s 17. See also 1937 Constitution, arts 1–3. [Bibliography: Clark & McMahon; Walsh D.] For the Northern Ireland Assembly, see website: *www.ni-assembly.gov.uk.* For Co-operation Ireland, see website: *www.cooperationireland. org.* See ANGLO-IRISH AGREEMENT; BOUNDARY COMMISSION; CITIZENSHIP; EXTRADITION; FRANCHISE; GOOD FRIDAY AGREEMENT; INDEPENDENT MONITORING COMMISSION; NATION; NATIONAL EMERGENCY; NATIONAL TERRITORY; ROAD DEVELOPMENT, PROPOSED; SECURITY FOR COSTS; UNITED IRELAND; WHISKEY, IRISH.

noscitur a sociis. [Known from associates.] The meaning of a word may be determined by reference to its context.

not guilty. See ACQUITTAL.

not negotiable. The words marked on a cheque which gives the holder no better title than the previous holder: Bills of Exchange Act 1882, s 81. See *Great Western Railway Co v London & County Banking Co* [1900] 2 QB 464. See CHEQUE; NEMO DAT QUI NON HABET.

notary public. A public officer, appointed by the Chief Justice, who certifies the due execution in his presence of a deed, contract, or other writing, or verifies some act or thing done in his presence, which certification or verification he authenticates by his signature and official seal. In certain instances, his signature alone suffices. The Chief Justice may make rules, regulations or directions as to the form and mode of application to be appointed a notary public; these may include that the applicant satisfy the Chief Justice that he has, in advance of appointment, the requisite and appropriate knowledge of notarial practice and procedure: RSC Ord 127 inserted by SI No 265 of 1993, para 7.

Unless there are exceptional circumstances, a notary public must be a solicitor: *In the matter of Timothy McCarthy* [1990] ILRM 84, SC.

The main functions of a notary public include: (a) authenticating public and private documents; (b) attesting and verifying signatures to documents in order to satisfy evidential or statutory requirements of foreign governments or of overseas institutions and regulatory authorities; (c) noting and protesting bills of exchange and promissory notes for non-acceptance or non-payment; (d) drawing up ship protests; and (e) giving certificates as to the acts and instruments of persons and their identities.

A statutory declaration (qv) may be taken and received by a notary public: Statutory Declarations Act 1938, s 1(1). See Promissory Notes (Ireland) Act 1864; Courts (Supplemental Provisions) Act 1961, s 10(1)(b); Diplomatic and Consular Officers (Provision of Services) Act 1993, s 5. [Bibliography: O'Connor.] See BILL OF EXCHANGE; PROMISSORY NOTE; SHIPS PROTEST; STATUTORY DECLARATION.

notice. Knowledge or cognisance. To give *notice* is to bring matters to a person's knowledge or attention. The *doctrine of notice* is often crucial in deciding a contest for priority between competing equitable interests or between equitable and legal interests. Notice can be *actual* where a person is aware by his own knowledge of a previous claim: *Re Fuller & Co Ltd (in liquidation)* [1982] IR 161; or it can be *constructive*, where the person is not himself aware but could have been, had he made proper enquiries: *Northern Bank Ltd v Henry* [1981] IR 1; or it may be *imputed*, e g where an agent of the person has either actual or constructive notice of a previous claim: *Re Burmester* [1858] 9 Ir Ch R 41. See also Conveyancing Act 1882, s 3(1).

In the case of registered land, the register generally governs priorities, except that certain interests and rights may affect registered land without registration: Registration of Title Act 1964, s 31(1); *Tench v Molyneux* [1914] 48 ILTR 48. As regards mortgaged lands, mortgagees are under no obligation to scrutinise newspapers to see if there are any notices affecting their mortgaged property: *ICC Bank Ltd v Verling* [1995] 1 ILRM 123, HC. In relation to notice and personalty, see *Deale v Hall* [1823] 3 Russ 1; *Molloy v French* [1849] 13 Ir Eq R 216. See PRIORITY.

notice, employment. The minimum periods of notice to be given by employers and by employees when terminating a contract of employment are specified in the Minimum Notice and Terms of Employment Act 1973 and 1984. The minimum notice which an employer must give varies from one week to eight weeks depending on the length of service of the employee. There is no statutory requirement that a reason for termination be specified in the notice; however the length of notice must be specific: *Waterford Multiport Ltd v Fagan* [1999] ELR 185, HC. Minimum notice applies also to regular part-time employees: Worker Protection (Regular Part-Time Employees) Act 1991, s 1.

The minimum notice entitlement may be waived but it must be clear and unambiguous to be effective: *Industrial Yarns Ltd v Greene* [1984] ILRM 15. While the winding-up order of a company is usually notice of discharge of all its employees, the circumstances may justify the continuity of their service and the waiving of the notice: *Re Evanhenry Ltd* [1986] HC; *Dodd & Ors v Local Stores (Trading) Ltd* [1992] ELR 61, EAT.

The statutory notice must not be stringently and technically construed; the Act is not concerned with the form of notice but only with the length; the provisions of the Act are complied with once the notice conveys to the employee that he will lose his employment at the end of the period expressed or necessarily implied in the notice, once that period is not less than the statutory minimum: *Bolands Ltd (In receivership) v Ward* [1988] ILRM 383. In order to be entitled to compensation under MNTEA 1973, s 12 for failure by the employer to give the notice required under the Act, it is necessary for the employee to prove that a loss has been sustained by him by reason of the default of the employer of the duties therein: *Transaer International Airlines Ltd (In Liquidation) v Delaney and Others* [2004] ELR 1, HC.

Where a contract is for an indefinite period, then reasonable notice must be given provided that it is not less than the statutory minimum. The more important or unique the position, the longer will be the period regarded as reasonable. Even if a post is described as *permanent and pensionable*, it can be determined by reasonable notice. The reasonableness of notice has to be considered in relation to the period which would be reasonable to enable a person to find other employment: *Tierney v Irish Meat Packers* [1989] 7 ILT Dig 5, HC. Each case has to be decided on its own merits and by reference to modern standards: *Lyons v M F Kent & Co* [1996] ELR 103, HC. In this case the court decided that a 12-month notice period applied in view of the professional qualification of the employee and the status and level of responsibility of the post. See also *Bowman v Holten Press Ltd* [1952] 2 All ER, cited with approval in *Carey v Independent Newspapers (Ireland) Ltd* [2003] ITLR (3 November), HC and [2004] ELR 45, in which six months' notice was held to be the entitlement.

As regards the notice which an employee must give to an employer, this will depend on the contract of employment. The Employment Appeals Tribunal has held that the Oireachtas did not intend to give it power to make any compensatory award to an employer for a breach by an employee of the relevant notice period: *Leopard Security Ltd v Campbell* [1997] ELR 225, EAT. The remedy for a breach of the notice required in the contract lies in contract law and on the basis of compensation to the employer rather than penalty; deduction of an amount from the wages of an employee for failure to comply with notice, in the absence of an express provision for such deduction, is in contravention of the Payment of Wages Act 1991, s 5: *Curust Hardware Ltd v Dalton* [1993] ELR 10, EAT. See also *McDonnell v Minister for Education* [1940] IR 316; *Walsh v Dublin Health Authority* [1964] 98 ILTR 82; *Scott v Kelly's Express Print* [1991] ELR 160, EAT. See SI No 243 of 1973 and Protection of Employees (Employers' Insolvency) Act 1984, s 13. See also Adoption Leave Act 1995, s 30. See CONSTRUCTIVE DISMISSAL; FIXED-TERM CONTRACT; SUMMARY DISMISSAL; TRANSFER OF UNDERTAKINGS.

notice of abandonment. The notice required in marine insurance. See ABANDONMENT.

notice of attachment. The notice from the Revenue Commissioners to a debtor who owes a debt to a taxpayer by which the Revenue may collect tax owed by the taxpayer: Taxes Consolidation Act 1997, s 1002. This power is similar to a garnishee order used in civil proceedings. See ATTACHMENT; GARNISHEE.

notice of dishonour. The notice which must be given to those whom the holder of a bill of exchange (qv) wishes to hold liable. See DISHONOUR OF BILL.

notice of motion. A motion (qv) where notice thereof is given to the other side in legal proceedings. Unless the High Court gives special leave to the contrary, there must be at least two clear days between the service of a notice of motion and the day named in the notice for the hearing of the motion; however, where the notice of motion requires to be served personally out of court, it must be served not less than four clear days before the hearing of the application: RSC Ord 52, r 6.

Where a time limit is specified for the filing of a notice of motion (eg in planning appeals), the notice of motion must be filed in court and served on the mandatory parties within the time limit; it is not sufficient to file it in the court offices within the time limit: *KSK Enterprises Ltd v An Bord Pleanála* [1994] 2 ILRM 1, SC.

In the Circuit Court, except where permitted by the rules, no motion may be made without notice to the parties affected thereby, and there must be at least four clear days between the service of a *notice of motion* and the day named in the motion for hearing the motion: Circuit Court Rules 2001 Ord 64.

A civil summons in the District Court generally must be served on the defendant at least 14 days prior to the date of the sitting of the court to which it is returnable: DCR 1997 Ord 39, r 6. The period is 21 days where service is effected by registered post. See MOTION.

notice of trial. The notice which the plaintiff in a High Court action must serve within six weeks of the close of pleadings; otherwise the defendant may do so without court order; twenty-one days' notice of trial must be given: RSC Ord 36, rr 12 and 16. The actual setting down for trial must be done within fourteen days after the service of notice of trial, otherwise the notice of trial will no longer be in force (r 18). If the party who has served notice omits to set down the action for trial within seven days, the party to whom the notice has been given may set it down (r 21).

When a defence has been duly entered in Circuit Court proceedings, the plaintiff may serve notice of trial or a notice for the fixing of a date for the trial, as directed by the County Registrar: Circuit Court Rules 2001 Ord 33, r 1 and Form 15A and 15B.

notice party. A person or body who is given information, often in a specified manner, in order to ensure that they have knowledge of a particular matter. In many areas of law, the notice is mandatory eg notice must be served on the Attorney-General in any proceedings wherein any question arises as to the validity of a law, having regard to the provisions of the Constitution: RSC Ord 60, rr 1–2.

Where a defendant in an action claims to be entitled to a contribution (qv) or indemnity (qv) from a person who is not already a party to an action, the defendant may, with the leave of the court, issue and serve a *third-party notice* (qv) on that person: RSC Ord 16.

Notice parties who have joined legal proceedings on their own application and who have a *bona fide* interest in the matter, may be awarded their costs, under the general discretionary powers of the court, where the proceedings are discontinued: *Eircom plc v Director of Telecommunications Regulation* [2003] 1 ILRM 106, HC and RSC Ord 99, r 1. See JUDICIAL REVIEW; POWER OF ATTORNEY, ENDURING.

notice to admit. A party to an action may serve on the other party a *notice to admit* particular facts or documents. Unreasonable failure to admit matters may render the party in default liable to pay the costs of proving them at the trial. For the High Court, see RSC Ord 32.

Any party to proceedings in the Circuit Court may call upon any other party to admit any document or any specific fact or facts; the party refusing or neglecting to admit, may be required to pay the cost of proving the document/fact/facts unless the judge certifies that the refusal was reasonable: Circuit Court Rules 2001 Ord 31.

notice to proceed. The notice given by one party in any cause or matter to the other party of his intention to proceed, which is required where there has been no proceedings for one year from the last proceedings; one month's notice must be given: RSC Ord 122, r 11.

notice to produce. See DISCOVERY.

notice to quit. A yearly, monthly, weekly or other periodic tenancy may be determined by a *notice to quit* but not a lease or tenancy for a fixed period of time unless expressly reserved in the lease. A minimum period of notice to quit of four weeks has been provided for: Housing (Miscellaneous Provisions) Act 1992, s 16. However, for a tenancy of a dwelling, see Residential Tenancies Act 2004, s 193(d) and TENANCY, TERMINATION NOTICE. A determination of an adjudicator or the Tenancy Tribunal directing the tenant to quit a dwelling may also require any sub-tenant to quit the dwelling in the circumstances where the landlord has indicated a requirement for the termination of the sub-tenancy by the head-tenant (RTA 2004, s 116). See also EJECTMENT; LEASE, DETERMINATION OF; PART 4 TENANCY, TERMINATION OF.

notice to treat. In relation to the *compulsory purchase* (qv) of land, the notice which a local authority (qv) has power to serve stating that they are willing to *treat* for the purchase of the several interests in the land and requiring each such owner, lessee and occupier to state within a specified period (not being less than one month from the date of service of the notice to treat) the exact nature of the interest in respect of which compensation is claimed by him and details of the compensation claimed and, if the authority so require, distinguishing separate amounts of the compensation in such manner as may be specified in the notice to treat and showing how each such amount is calculated: Housing Act 1966, s 79.

The owner of land who fails to deliver to the acquiring authority a notice in writing of the amount claimed by him as compensation, can be penalised in costs: Acquisition of Land (Assessment of Compensation) Act 1919, s 5(2).

The effect of a notice to treat is to oblige the local authority to take, and the owner to surrender, the land: *Re Green Dale Building Company* [1977] IR 256. No estate passes to the acquiring local authority by virtue only of the notice to treat: *Irish Life Assurance v Dublin Land Securities* [1986] IR 332, HC.

noting a bill. A brief note or memorandum made by a notary public (qv) as an interim measure, recording that a bill of exchange has been dishonoured, as a first step to a protest (qv). The note must be made at the time of dishonour and is written into the notary's *protest register*. See Bills of Exchange Act 1882, s 51. See NOTING AND PROTESTING.

noting and protesting. The process by which formal *notice of dishonour* of a foreign bill of exchange is made: Bills of Exchange Act 1882, s 51. If a foreign bill is not so protested, the drawers and endorsers are discharged (BEA 1882, s 51(2)). A notary public (qv) must present the bill for acceptance or payment, must note the reply made on the bill, and issue a formal *certificate of dishonour* called a *protest*.

notorious facts. Matters of common knowledge of which judicial notice (qv) may be taken without formal proof.

nova causa interveniens. [New intervening cause.]

nova constitutio futuris formam imponere debet, non praeteritis. [A new law ought to regulate what is to follow, not the past.] See RETROSPECTIVE LEGISLATION.

novation. A tripartite contract whereby a contract between two parties is rescinded in consideration of a new contract being entered into between one of the parties and a third party e g where the creditor at the request of the debtor agrees to take another person as his debtor in the place of the original debtor. The effect of novation is to release the original debtor from his obligations under the contract and to impose these obligations on the new debtor. Novation frequently arises in a partnership on a change in membership of the firm, when creditors, expressly or by implication (e g by continuing to trade with the firm), accept the new firm as their debtor.

Novation of a contract may also occur when a party to the contract is adjudicated a bankrupt; the official assignee in bankruptcy becomes entitled to the contractual rights and obligations unless he expressly disclaims the contract: *Re Casey, a Bankrupt* [1991] ILRM 385, SC.

novelty. One of the requirements for an invention to be patentable: Patents Act 1992, s 9(1). The invention must be *new*; it will be considered new if it does not form part of the *state of the art* (PA 1992, s 11). Under the Patents Act 1964 (since repealed), it was held that the test of novelty should be based on what was published before the priority date (qv) and that publication outside of the State is relevant: *Wavin Pipes Ltd v Hepworth Iron Co Ltd* [1982] FRS 32.

A *novelty search report* may be requested by an applicant for a patent or, in lieu of making such request, the applicant may submit the grant of a patent obtained in a prescribed foreign State or the result of a search report associated therewith (PA 1992, ss 29–30). See also *General Tire & Rubber Co v Firestone Tyre & Rubber Co* [1975] 1 WLR 819. See PATENT CO-OPERATION TREATY; PATENTABLE INVENTION; PUBLICATION.

novus actus interveniens. [A new act intervening.] A defence in an action in tort (qv) whereby it is claimed that A is not liable for the damage done to B, if the *chain of causation* between A's act or omission is broken by the intervention of a third party, thereby rendering the damage too *remote*. There is a general duty to guard against a *novus actus interveniens* and consequently the defence will fail if the intervening act is a direct or foreseeable consequence of the defendant's act or is intentionally procured by the defendant. *Novus actus interveniens* has been pleaded as a defence to a charge of murder: *The People (Attorney-General) v McGrath* [1960] CCA.

It is of the essence of *novus actus interveniens* that the damage complained of should have resulted from the act of another person who is independent of both the plaintiff and the defendant: *Coyle v An Post* [1993] ILRM 508, SC at 526. In a particular case it was held that the fact that there were possible *concurrent wrongdoers* (qv) excluded the plea of *novus actus interveniens*: *R L v Minister for Health* [2001] 1 IR 744, HC. See *Cunningham v McGrath Bros* [1964] IR 209; *Conole v Redbank Oyster Co* [1976] IR 191; *Crowley v Allied Irish Banks* [1988] ILRM 225; *SF v DPP* [1999] 3 IR 235, SC; *Breslin v Corcoran and MIBI* [2003] 2 ILRM 189, SC and 2 IR 203, *Law Society Gazette* (July 2003) 38. See REMOTENESS OF DAMAGE.

noxious weeds. Weeds declared by the Minister to be noxious weeds e g thistle, ragworth, dock, common barberry, and the male hop plant: Noxious Weeds Act 1936, s 2. Where noxious weeds are not destroyed in accordance with a statutory notice served on a specified person (e g the owner or occupier of the land), that person commits an offence (NWA 1936, s 5).

nuclear material. It is an offence to engage in nuclear activities, or to produce, use, acquire, transfer or process nuclear equipment or nuclear material, except as authorised by regulations: Containment of Nuclear Weapons Act 2003, s 3. See RADIOACTIVE SUBSTANCE.

nuclear weapons. The Radiological Protection Institute of Ireland has been designated as the *national authority* for the implementation of a new protocol between the non-nuclear weapons States of the EU and the International Atomic Energy Agency concerning the strengthening of arrangements for the non-proliferation of nuclear weapons: Containment of Nuclear Weapons Act 2003, s 4. Provision is made for the granting of access to international inspectors to locations, facilities and sites within the State (CNWA 2003, s 5). See

Containment of Nuclear Weapons Regulations 2004, SI No 123 of 2004. See RADIOACTIVE SUBSTANCE.

nudum pactum. [A nude contract.] An agreement without consideration (qv) and which is consequently unenforceable unless it is under seal.

nuisance. A tort (qv) which involves an act or omission which amounts to an unreasonable interference with, disturbance to, or annoyance to another person in the exercise of his rights; if the rights so interfered with belong to the person as a member of the public, the act or omission is a *public nuisance*; if these rights relate to the ownership or occupation of land, or some easement (qv), profit (qv) or some other right enjoyed in connection with land, then the act or omission amounts to a *private nuisance*: *Connolly v South of Ireland Asphalt Co* [1977] IR 99. See *Daly v McMullan* [1997] 2 ILRM 232, CC. [Bibliography: Bland (2); Burke & Corbett; McMahon & Binchy.] See CLOSURE ORDER; NUISANCE, PRIVATE; NUISANCE, PUBLIC.

nuisance, private. The unlawful interference with another's servitude (easement (qv)) or the unauthorised use of a person's own property which causes damage to the property of another or interferes with the enjoyment of the property of another. The interference must be substantial to be actionable: *Mullins v Hynes* [1972] SC. The remedies are: abatement (qv); damages (which cannot include personal injuries); injunction, including a mandatory or a *quia timet* (qv) injunction to prevent a threatened nuisance: *Attorney-General (Boswell) v Rathmines & Pembroke Trust Hospital Board* [1904] 1 IR 161.

Private nuisances have been held to include interference from: smoke, heat, smell, vibrations, soil erosion, branches of trees, damage to foundations, dust, fumes, sewage, dangerous leaves and blasting operations. Defences include prescription (qv) and statutory authority. However, it is no defence to prove that the claimant came to the nuisance: *Bliss v Hall* [1838] 4 Bing NC 183; *Miller v Jackson* [1977] 3 All ER 338. See *Dewar v City and Suburban Racecourse Co* [1889] 1 IR 345; *New Imperial Windsor Hotel Co v Johnson* [1912] 1 IR 327; *Wallace v McCartan* [1917] IR 377; *Leech v Reilly* [1983] HC; *McGrane v Louth County Council* [1983] HC; *Rabette v Mayo County Council* [1984] HC; *Hanrahan v Merck Sharpe & Dohme (Ire) Ltd* [1988]

ILRM 629, SC; *Fleming, Byrne & Hayden v Rathdown School* [1993] HC. See RYLANDS V FLETCHER, RULE IN.

nuisance, public. A public nuisance consists of an act or omission which causes injury to, or materially affects the reasonable comfort and convenience of the public, or a section of the public: *Convery v Dublin County Council* [1996] 3 IR 153, SC. A public nuisance can be committed by either obstruction of a public highway or endangering it: *Cunningham v MacGrath Bros* [1964] IR 209.

A private person may bring an action for damages or an injunction for public nuisance but only if he has suffered some substantial damage to himself and different in kind from that suffered by the rest of the public: *Smith v Wilson* [1903] 2 IR 45 and *Convery* case. Public nuisance is a crime; the Attorney-General may institute criminal proceedings or he may sue for an injunction to restrain the nuisance. See BYE-LAW; SANITARY AUTHORITIES AND NUISANCE.

nul tiel. [No such.]

null and void. Having no force; invalid eg a judgment which has been *set aside* (qv).

nulla bona. [No goods.] The return made by a sheriff (qv) to an order of *fieri facias* (which authorised him to seize the goods and chattels of a person) when he has been unable to find any to seize. See BANKRUPTCY, ACT OF; FIERI FACIAS.

nulla pactione effici potest ut dolus praestetur. [By no contract may it be arranged that a man be indemnified against responsibility for his own fraud.] See INDEMNIFY.

nulla poena sine lege. [No punishment except in accordance with the law.] See PUNISHMENT.

nullity of marriage. See MARRIAGE, NULLITY OF.

nullius filius. A bastard (qv); *now a person whose parents are not married to each other*. See CHILD, ILLEGITIMATE.

nullum simile est idem. [A thing which is similar to another thing is not the same as that other thing.]

nullus videtur dolo facere qui suo jure utitur. [A malicious or improper motive cannot make wrongful in law an act which would be rightful apart from such motive.] See MOTIVE.

nunc pro tunc. [Now for then.]

nuncupative will. A privileged will involving an oral declaration before witnesses, formerly allowed as an exception for soldiers on actual military service and mariners at sea under the Wills Act 1837, s 11, as extended by the Wills (Soldiers Sailors) Act 1918, even where the testator was under 21 years of age. The exception was not re-enacted by the Succession Act 1965.

nunquam indebitatus. [Never indebted.]

nuptias non concubitus sed consensus facit. [It is consent, not habitation, which makes a marriage.] See COMMON LAW MARRIAGE; MARRIAGE.

nurse. A woman or a man whose name is entered in the register of nurses established under s 27 of the Nurses Act 1985 (NA 1985, s 2). Statutory provision for the registration, control and education of nurses is contained in the 1985 Act. It is an offence for a person to take or use the title of nurse or midwife (qv) if not registered (NA 1985, s 49). A nurse may have her name erased from the register if convicted of an indictable offence (NA 1985, s 42) or if found guilty of professional misconduct or to be unfit to practise (NA 1985, s 39). See *Kerrigan v An Bord Altranais* [1990] ITLR (30 July); *Fennessy v Minister for Health* [1991] 2 IR 361, HC.

It has been held that the Employment Equality Act 1977 was not contravened when nurses are assigned to different tasks because of their gender; it was only contravened if the assignments are less favourable treatment because of gender: *A Worker v Mid-Western Health Board* [1996] ELR 1, LC. See *Smyth v Eastern Health Board* [1996] ELR 72, EO. See Protection of Employees (Fixed-Term Work) Act 2003, s 17(c); Public Service Superannuation (Miscellaneous Provisions) Act 2004, s 7 and Sch 2. For An Bord Altranais, see website: *www.nursingboard.ie*. For the Irish Nurses' Organisation, see website: *www.ino.ie*. [Bibliography: O'Kelly & Rohan.] See DISCIPLINARY PROCEEDINGS; HOME NURSING SERVICE; MIDWIFE; VOCATIONAL TRAINING.

nursery. See PRE-SCHOOL SERVICE.

nursing home. An institution for the maintenance of more than two dependent persons: Health (Nursing Homes) Act 1990, s 2. There are certain exclusions e g state institutions, institutions for the care of physically handicapped persons which are grant aided by the State, and premises in which the majority being maintained are members of a religious order or priests. A dependent person is one who requires assistance with the activities of daily living (H(NH)A 1990, s 1). A person must not carry on a nursing home unless it is registered (H(NH)A 1990, s 3); contravention is an offence: Health (Amendment) (No 3) Act 1996, s 20. Also a person operating a nursing home must comply with regulations made in relation to standards (H(NH)A 1990, s 6).

For taxation provision, see Taxes Consolidation Act 1997, s 268 as amended. A convalescent home may be treated for tax purposes as if it were a nursing home: Finance Act 2000, s 36. Capital allowances are available for expenditure incurred on the construction or refurbishment of housing units associated with a registered nursing home, provided not less than 20% of the residential units are made available to the relevant health board at a 10% discount on the general rate charged: Finance Act 2002, s 33. In 2004, the number of beds required to qualify for capital allowances was reduced from 20 to 10, and the limitation on multistoreys was removed provided a fire safety certificate is obtained: Finance Act 2004, s 23.

The Minister for Health is empowered to make regulations which may: (a) make different provision for different classes of nursing homes, and (b) prescribe different requirements for different classes of nursing homes: Health (Miscellaneous Provisions) Act 2001, s 3 amending the Health (Nursing Homes) Act 1990. This will ensure that *convalescent homes* come within the ambit of the 1990 Act and that such homes have adequate medical, nursing and paramedical staff and facilities, consistent with the patient profile of the home. Also provision is made for the making of regulations as regards the administration of the subvention scheme.

The High Court has held that the 1990 Act entitles a health board, with the permission of the owner or following an application to the District Court, to manage a registered nursing home for a limited period, but it did not entitle the health board to obtain an interlocutory injunction to close down the registered nursing home: South Western Area Health Board v Rostrevor Nursing Home (29 August 2004, unreported) HC. If the health board had a right to require closure of a nursing home which remained on the register, the board would have had such a right conferred on it expressly or by implication by the Act.

The rates of subvention payable have been increased: SI No 227 of 1993 as amended by Nursing Homes (Subvention) (Amendment) Regulations 2001, SI No 89 of 2001. The Ombudsman and Information Commissioner has held that nursing home inspection reports should be made available to the public as a matter of routine: *Mr X v South Eastern Health Board* (2004) Irish Times, 30 March. For Irish Nursing Homes Organisation, see website: *www.carenet.ie*.

O

oath. (1) A solemn declaration by which a party calls his God to witness that what he says is true, or that what he promises to do he will do. An oath includes a solemn affirmation and statutory declaration: DCR 1997, Interpretation of Terms. See DCR 1997 Ord 8.

(2) Includes a solemn affirmation and statutory declaration: Circuit Court Rules 2001, Interpretation of Terms, para 14.

In general all evidence (qv) must be on oath. An *affirmation* may be made instead of an oath. It is a fundamental principle of the common law that *viva voce* (qv) evidence must be given on oath or affirmation; the purpose being to ensure that such evidence is true by the provision of a moral or religious and legal sanction against deliberate untruth: *Mapp v Gilhooley* [1991] ILRM 695, SC. An *appeal commissioner* may administer an oath to be taken by a person in relation to income tax or corporation tax: Taxes Consolidation Act 1997, s 860.

Solicitors continue to be prohibited from administering oaths or taking declarations from their own clients: *Law Society Gazette* (July 2004) 38. See Oaths Act 1888; Interpretation Act 1937, s 12, Sch; Diplomatic and Consular Officers (Provision of Services) Act 1993, s 5; Taxes Consolidation Act 1997, s 1096A inserted by Finance Act 1999, s 30; Children's Act 1997, s 28; Arbitration (International Commercial) Act 1998, s 8; Commissions of Investigation Act 2004, s 14(3). See Report on Oaths and Affirmations (LRC 34, 1990). See AFFIRMATION; CHILD, EVIDENCE OF;

OATH, FORM OF; PERJURY; UNLAWFUL OATH; UNSWORN STATEMENT.

oath, interpreter. An oath in the following or similar form: 'I swear by Almighty God that I will well and truly interpret and explain to the court/jury the evidence given in this case/trial/enquiry according to the best of my skill and understanding.'

oath, jury. In criminal trials the juror's oath is: 'I swear by Almighty God that I will well and truly try the issue whether the accused is (or are) guilty or not guilty of the offence (or the several offences) charged in the indictment preferred against him (or her, or them) and a true verdict give according to the evidence': Juries Act 1976, ss 18(1) and 19(1).

In relation to the issue as to whether an accused is fit to plead, the oath is: 'I swear by Almighty God that I will well and diligently inquire whether (stating the name of the accused person), the prisoner at the bar (qv) be insane or not and a true verdict give according to the best of my understanding.' (JA 1976, ss 18(1) and 19(2)).

In civil actions the juror's oath is: 'I swear by Almighty God that I will well and truly try all such issues as shall be given to me to try and true verdicts give according to the evidence.' (JA 1976, ss 18(1) and 19(3)). See UNFIT TO PLEAD.

oath, witness. An oath in the following or similar form: 'I swear by Almighty God that the evidence I shall give to this court touching this case/complaint/charge shall be the truth, and nothing but the truth.'

obedience to orders, defence of. In some circumstances, obedience to a superior's orders may be relevant in negativing the *mens rea* (qv) required to constitute an offence. As regards military forces, a soldier acting under orders of his superior officer, is justified unless the order be manifestly illegal: *Keighley v Bell* [1868] 4 F & F 773. See MARITAL COERCION.

obiter dictum. [Saying by the way.] An observation by a judge in a case on a legal question, based on facts which were not present, or not material, in the case, or which arose in such a manner as not to require a decision. The *obiter dictum* is not binding on future cases but may be persuasive. The Supreme Court may treat a decision of the High Court on the question of the constitutionality of legislation as being technically *obiter dicta* when it considers that the latter court should not have engaged in the question: *McDaid v Judge*

Sheehy [1991] ILRM 250, SC. Contrast with RATIO DECIDENDI. See MOOT; PRECEDENT.

objects clause. The clause in the *memorandum of association* of a company setting out the objects which a company has been formed to pursue: Companies Act 1963, s 6(1)(c) (as amended by Companies (Amendment) Act 1983, Sch 1, para 2). A company may by special resolution alter the provisions of its memorandum by abandoning, restricting or amending any existing object or by adopting a new object; an application to cancel the alteration may be made to the court by a minority of 15% in value of the shareholders or by 15% of the debenture holders (CA 1963, s 10 as amended by C(A)A 1983, Sch 1, para 3). The objects clause cannot be changed with retrospective effect: *Northern Bank Finance Corp v Quinn* [1979] HC. See also Building Societies Act 1989, ss 9(1) and 10(2)(a). See BELL HOUSES CLAUSE; ULTRA VIRES.

obligation. A legal duty arising out of contract (qv) or tort (qv) between two or more persons. See LIABILITY.

obligee. A person to whom a bond (qv) is made.

obligor. A person who binds himself by a bond (qv).

obliteration. See ALTERATION; ERASURE.

obscene. See CENSORSHIP OF BOOKS; DISORDERLY CONDUCT; INDECENCY; PERFORMANCE, INDECENT OR PROFANE.

obscene calls. A message by telephone which is grossly offensive or of an indecent, obscene or menacing character; the sending of such a message is an offence: Post Office (Amendment) Act 1951, s 13.

obstruction. It is an offence under many statutes for a person to obstruct another person in the exercise of a lawful function eg it is an offence for a person, by act or omission, to obstruct or hinder a person authorised by the Minister to deport a person from the State: Immigration Act 1999, s 8(1)(a). See INTIMIDATION; WILFUL OBSTRUCTION.

obstruction of government. The offence of preventing or obstructing any arm of government, whether legislative, executive, or judicial, by force of arms or other violent means, or by any form of intimidation: Offences Against the State Act 1939, s 7, as amended by the Criminal Law Act 1976, s 2. See also *The People (DPP) v Kehoe* [1983] IR 136.

obstruction of course of justice. See INTIMIDATION.

obstruction of the President. The offence of obstructing the President of Ireland (qv) in the exercise of her duties: Offences Against the State Act 1939, s 8.

obtaining credit by fraud. See CREDIT BY FRAUD, OBTAINING.

O'Byrne letter. The letter which is normally sent by a plaintiff in an action where there are two or more defendants and he wishes to have evidence to ground a subsequent application to the court, for an order that the unsuccessful defendant pay the costs of the successful defendant.

The format of the letter is typically: 'Our client cannot be expected to elect between respective defendants and unless we have an admission of liability by you within ten days, we will institute proceedings against you and Mr X. In the event that Mr X is not held liable and an order is made dismissing the claim against him with costs, application will be made to the court under the Court of Justice Act 1936, s 78 for an order that, in addition to damages and our client's costs, you should pay to our client such sum as he may have to pay for the costs of Mr X and this letter will be produced at the hearing of the said application.' The writing of an O'Byrne letter is not an essential precondition to the court exercising its discretion under CJA 1936, s 78 eg see *O'Keeffe v Russell & AIB plc* [1994] 1 ILRM 137, SC. See *Bullock v London Omnibus Co* [1907] 1 KB 264; *Rice v Toombes* [1971] IR 38. See Courts of Justice Act 1936, s 78.

occasion of qualified privilege. See PRIVILEGE.

occasional trading. Selling goods by retail at a premises or place (not being a public road or other place to which the public have access as of right) of which the person so selling has been in occupation for a continuous period of less than three months ending on the date of such selling: Occasional Trading Act 1979, s 2 as amended by Casual Trading Act 1995, s 16. It is an offence to engage in occasional trading unless the person has an *occasional trading permit* (OTA 1979, s 3). Similar exceptions apply to certain selling transactions as apply in casual trading (qv). See also Casual Trading Act 1980, s 17.

occupancy. Formerly, if an estate *pur autre vie* had been granted without any reference to the grantee's heir or successors in the conveyance, the law of occupancy applied ie the first person who entered the land after the grantee's death, succeeded to it eg where A granted land to B for the life of C and B died before C, anyone could enter and occupy the land during C's life. If the person who entered was B's heir, he was known as the *special occupant*; otherwise he was known as a *general occupant*.

The law of occupancy has been abolished; *general occupancy* was abolished by the Statute of Frauds (Ireland) 1695, s 9 and *special occupancy* was abolished by the Succession Act 1965, s 11(1). Now, on the death of a tenant *pur autre vie* intestate, his land devolves on his personal representatives for distribution with the rest of his estate, real and personal. See LIFE ESTATE; OCCUPANT.

occupant. See OCCUPANCY.

occupation. (1) A person's trade, profession or calling. See EMPLOYEE.

(2) In relation to taxation of farming and market gardening, *occupation* of land means having the right to use the land or graze livestock on the land: Taxes Consolidation Act 1997, s 654.

(3) *Occupation* is also the exercise of physical control or possession of land; having actual use of land; or taking possession of territory by armed forces.

An *occupier* of land may have: (a) a *personal right* over the land which he cannot pass on to third parties eg a caretaker or a conacre tenant, or (b) a *property right* over the possession of the land, which he can assign or sublet eg a tenant. A caretaker has a bare licence to occupy the land on the owner's behalf; he is in fact an agent of the owner and his possession is that of the owner: *Musgrave v McAvey* [1907] 41 ILTR 230. An employee generally occupies his employer's premises as a licensee only. Also as regards a lodger, it is the owner's retention of control of the premises, and the lodger's lack of possession independent of the owner, which distinguishes a lodger from a tenant. See *Waucob v Reynolds* [1850] 1 ICLR 142.

A purchaser of land is often permitted into *possession* as a caretaker, pending the closing of the sale. The effect of the caretaker agreement will depend on its terms and its proper construction eg see *Gatien Motor Co Ltd v Continental Oil* [1979] IR 406; *Corrigan v Woods* [1867] IR 1 CL 73. Contrast with POSSESSION. See also CONACRE; FORCIBLE ENTRY AND OCCUPATION;

LONG POSSESSION, TITLE BY; SHARED OWNERSHIP LEASE.

occupational injuries benefit. The injury benefit or disability benefit to which a person in insurable employment may be entitled: Social Welfare (Consolidation) Act 1993, ss 48–77. For the prescribed diseases, see SI No 392 of 1983, as amended by SI No 102 of 1985, and by SI No 234 of 2003.

occupational pension. See PENSION SCHEME.

occupiers' liability. The liability of the occupier of premises to entrants to premises as regards a danger, depends on whether the entrant is a *visitor*, a *recreational user* or a *trespasser*. Occupiers' Liability Act 1995. This legislation replaces the common law rules which differentiated liability as regards an invitee, a licensee, a contractual entrant, or a trespasser (OLA 1995, s 2). In recent years judicial decisions had tended to blur the distinctions, particularly as regards trespassers. An 'occupier' is the person exercising such control over the premises that it is reasonable to impose a duty on the person towards the entrant (OLA 1995, s 1(1)). '*Danger*' means a danger due to the state of the premises (ie not the way in which it is used); and a 'premises' includes land, water, and any fixed or moveable structures, including vessels, trains, vehicles, aircraft (OLA 1995, s 1(1)).

An occupier may by express agreement or notice extend his duty towards entrants, or in certain circumstance, restrict, modify or exclude his duty to visitors, but not below the minimum threshold set for trespassers, and such restriction cannot apply to a contract to which the entrant is a stranger (OLA 1995, ss 5 and 6).

The 1995 Act draws a distinction between visitors on the one hand and recreational users and trespassers on the other. Visitors are present by permission, by agreement or by right, and the occupier must take reasonable care of their safety under the circumstances. Recreational users and trespassers merely have a right not to be injured intentionally or by the occupier's reckless disregard for their safety. Recreational users, who are on the land for certain defined purposes, have a further protection not given to trespassers – if any 'structures' are provided on the land for their use, the occupier must keep them in a safe condition.

An occupier has no liability to a person who enters the premises to commit an offence or who commits an offence while present, unless the court determines otherwise in the interests of justice (OLA 1995, s 4(3)). [Bibliography: Burke & Corbett; McMahon & Binchy.] See INDEPENDENT CONTRACTOR.

occupiers' liability to children. Under common law, if a premises contained some *allurement*, a child who had trespassed on to the premises was converted into a *licensee* and the occupier had a duty of care to protect the child from concealed dangers. See *McNamara v ESB* [1975] IR 1; *Keane v ESB* [1981] IR 44; *Maria Rooney v The Rev Fr Connolly PP* [1987] ILRM 768. For current law, see OCCUPIERS' LIABILITY TO RECREATIONAL USERS; OCCUPIERS' LIABILITY TO TRESPASSERS.

occupiers' liability to recreational users. An occupier of premises owes a duty to a *recreational user* of the premises in respect of a danger existing on the premises: (a) not to injure the person or damage his property intentionally, and (b) not to act with reckless disregard for the person or his property: Occupiers' Liability Act 1995, s 4(1). In determining whether an occupier acted in reckless disregard, regard must be had to all the circumstances of the case (OLA 1995, s 4(2)). A list of factors are provided, including e g whether the occupier knew or had reasonable grounds for believing that a danger existed; the care which the person might reasonably be expected to take for his safety having regard to his knowledge thereof; the extent of supervision and control which an accompanying person might be expected to exercise (OLA 1995, s 4(2)). These latter two factors are important as regards the duty to children and persons with disabilities. The duty to recreational users may be extended or reduced but not below the minimum duty owed to trespassers. [Bibliography: Burke & Corbett.] See RECREATIONAL USER; RECKLESSNESS.

occupiers' liability to trespassers. An occupier of premises owes the same duty of care to a *trespasser* as to a *recreational user*, except that the duty of care which the occupier has, to take reasonable care of a structure, provided for use primarily by recreational users, does not extend to trespassers: Occupiers' Liability Act 1995, s 4(4). A *trespasser* is an entrant to the premises who is not a recreational user (qv) or a visitor (qv). See *Williams v T P Wallace Construction Ltd* [2002] 2 ILRM 63, HC (under appeal). [Bibliography: Burke & Corbett.] See OCCUPIER'S LIABILITY TO RECREATIONAL USERS.

occupiers' liability to visitors. An occupier of premises owes a duty of care ('the common duty of care') towards a visitor: Occupiers' Liability Act 1995, s 3. The *common duty of care* means a duty to take such care as is reasonable in all the circumstances to ensure that the visitor to the premises does not suffer injury or damage by reason of any danger existing thereon (OLA 1995, s 3(2)). The duty of care has to have regard to the care which a visitor may reasonably be expected to take for his own safety and the extent of supervision and control an accompanying person may reasonably be expected to exercise over the visitor's activities (OLA 1995, s 3(2)). This is an important provision as to the duty to children or persons with disabilities. The duty to visitors can be extended or reduced but not below the minimum duty owed to trespassers (OLA 1995, s 5). See *Williams v T P Wallace Construction Ltd* [2002] 2 ILRM 63, HC (under appeal). [Bibliography: Burke & Corbett.] See VISITOR.

OECD. [Organisation for Economic Co-operation and Development.] The international organisation located in Paris, with 30 member countries, which has the objective of achieving the highest sustainable economic growth, employment and living standards. See website: *www.oecd.org.*

of course. See MOTION OF COURSE.

off-licence. A licence for the sale of intoxicating liquor for consumption off the premises. See *O'Rourke v Grittar* [1995] ILRM 532, SC; *Power Supermarkets v O'Shea* [1988] IR 206. See Intoxicating Liquor Act 2003, s 17. [Bibliography: Cassidy (2).] See INTOXICATING LIQUOR.

off record. A solicitor is said to come *off record* when he obtains an order of the court declaring that he has ceased to be the solicitor acting for a party in any proceedings: RSC Ord 7, r 3. An *ex parte* application to the court is made by the solicitor; any order made by the court does not affect the rights of the solicitor and the party as between themselves (rr 4–5). The court has a wide discretion in deciding whether or not a solicitor should be permitted to come off record; to refuse an application could in certain circumstances be to insist on a forced form of liaison: *O'Fearail v Manus*

[1994] 2 ILRM 8, SC. See RETAINER; SOLICITOR, CHANGE OF; SOLICITOR, WITHDRAWAL OF.

offence. Generally, a *crime.* See OTHER OFFENCES.

offence and sentence. For comprehensive list of offences, how created, and sentences applicable, see Bibliography: Ryan & Magee.

offences against property. The group of crimes including arson, burglary, criminal damage to property, embezzlement, false pretences, forcible entry, forgery, fraudulent conversion, larceny, malicious damage, handling stolen property, and robbery (qqv).

offences against public order. The group of crimes including bigamy, blasphemy, contempt of court, indecency, obstruction of government, perjury, riot, sedition, treason, usurpation of the functions of government, and crimes involving official secrets and unlawful organisations (qqv).

offences against the person. The group of crimes including abduction, abortion, assault, assault causing harm, bestiality, causing serious harm, child abduction, coercion, endangerment, false imprisonment, harassment, incest, indecent assault, infanticide, kidnapping, manslaughter, murder, poisoning, rape, sexual assault, syringe attacks, unlawful carnal knowledge (qqv). [Bibliography: Charleton (2).]

offences against the State. Offences provided for in the Offences Against the State Acts 1939 to 1998. A garda is empowered to arrest a person in relation to specified offences where he suspects that that person has committed or is about to commit any of those offences: OASA 1939, s 30; *Trimbole v Governor of Mountjoy Prison* [1985] IR 550. Questioning of a person so detained in relation to other crimes does not necessarily affect the legality of the detention: *The People (DPP) v Quilligan* [1987] ILRM 606. A person detained under s 30 can be questioned about other offences in connection with which he had been previously detained and released on a previous occasion under s 4 of the Criminal Justice Act 1984: *Maloney v Member in Charge of Terenure Garda Station* [2002] 2 ILRM 149, HC. The constitutional guarantee on equality before the law is not breached by detention pursuant to s 30: *DPP v Quilligan & O'Reilly* [1992] ITLR (2 November) SC and [1993] 2 IR 305, SC. See also OASA 1998, ss 10 and 18.

It is an offence for a person arrested under the OASA 1939, Pt IV, to fail to respond to a demand from a garda to give a full account of his movements during a specified period in relation to the commission of an offence under investigation (OASA 1939, s 52). It has been held that there is a proper proportionality between s 52, which allows the State to protect itself, and any infringement of the citizen's rights (eg the right to silence): *Heaney v Ireland* [1997] 1 ILRM 117, SC. However, the High Court held that as this provision had been found to be in breach of the European Convention on Human Rights, a conviction under s 52 should be set aside in the interest of justice: *Quinn v Ireland* (April 2004, unreported) HC and *Law Society Gazette* (June 2004) 7.

The court may draw inferences from the failure of an accused to mention certain facts when being questioned or being charged with an offence against the State, where the accused later relies on those facts in his defence and the court considers that he reasonably should have mentioned the facts (OASA 1998, s 5). The solicitor of the accused is not entitled to access the *interview notes* of the garda who questioned the accused and, consequently, refusal of the garda to provide such notes, does not render the detention of the accused unlawful: *Lavery v Member in Charge, Carrickmacross Garda Station* [1999] 2 IR 390, SC and ITLR (24 May). See District Court Rules 2000, SI No 166 of 2000.

A government appointed committee, under the chairmanship of Mr Justice Anthony Hederman, recommended that the existing Offences against the State Acts should be repealed and replaced with one consolidated piece of legislation containing reforms of the existing statutory regime: *Report of the Committee to Review the Offences Against the State Acts 1939–1998* (2002). See Criminal Justice Bill 2004 s.32. See UNLAWFUL ORGANISATION; OBSTRUCTION OF GOVERNMENT; OBSTRUCTION OF PRESIDENT; SECRET SOCIETIES.

offences under Companies Acts, presumptions in. An officer of a company who is *in default* is liable to a fine or penalty; an officer is *in default* if he authorises or, in breach of his duty, permits the default: Companies Act 1963, s 383 as substituted by Company Law Enforcement Act 2001, s 100. An officer is *presumed* to have permitted a default unless he can establish that he took all reasonable steps to prevent it or was unable to do so (CA 1963, s 383(2)). In the former s 383, the officer had to 'knowingly and wilfully' authorise or permit the default.

It is an offence for a person (who knows or suspects that the Director of Corporate Enforcement is investigating or is likely to investigate an offence under the Companies Acts) to destroy or conceal any documentary evidence that may be relevant to the investigation (CA 1963, s 19A inserted by CLEA 2001, s 29). There is a *presumption* that the person knew or suspected that the evidence might have been relevant to an investigation of the Director, unless the court or jury is satisfied that there is reasonable doubt as to whether the person so knew or suspected.

offences under Companies Acts, trial of. Because of the potential complexity in a trial on indictment for an offence under the Companies Acts, the judge is given a wide discretion on copies of documents which he may direct be given to the jury eg: (a) any document admitted in evidence at the trial, (b) the transcript of the opening speeches of counsel, (c) any charts, diagrams, graphics, schedules or summaries of evidence produced at the trial, (d) the transcript of the whole or part of the evidence given at the trial, (e) the transcript of the judge's charge to the jury, (f) any other document that in the opinion of the judge would be of assistance to the jury in its deliberations, including, where appropriate, an affidavit by an accountant summarising, in a form which is likely to be comprehended by the jury, any transaction by the accused or other person relevant to the offence: Company Law Enforcement Act 2001, s 110.

As regards the affidavit by an accountant, such affidavit must be given in advance of the trial to the accused. Also the judge must take into account any representations made by the accused in relation to it, and may require the accountant to explain to the jury any relevant accounting procedure or principles.

offensive conduct. See DISORDERLY CONDUCT; INDECENCY.

offensive trades. Blood boiler, bone boiler, fellmonger, soap boiler, tallow melter and tripe boiler, or any other noxious or offensive trade, business or manufacture; it is an offence to carry on an offensive trade in the district of an urban sanitary authority without their approval: Public Health (Ireland) Act 1878, s 128. See EJUSDEM GENERIS.

offensive weapon. Includes a firearm that is not loaded and an imitation firearm: Firearms Act 1964, s 25(1). An *offensive weapon* now includes a wide range of knives and weapons eg flick-knives, knuckledusters, belt buckle knife; it is an offence to manufacture, sell or hire an offensive weapon: Firearms and Offensive Weapons Act 1990, s 12 and SI No 66 of 1991. It is also an offence for a person, without good reason, to have with him in a public place a knife or any article which has a blade or is sharply pointed (FAOWA 1990, s 9).

A *weapon of offence* is any article made or adapted for use for causing injury to or incapacitating a person; it is an offence for a trespasser to have with him a knife or a weapon of offence (FAOWA 1990, s 10).

A *weapon of offence* includes eg an article with a blade or sharp point, or a weapon designed to discharge noxious liquid or gas: Criminal Justice (Theft and Fraud Offences) Act 2001, s 13(2). For previous legislation, see Larceny Act 1916, s 28(1); Criminal Law (Jurisdiction) Act 1976, s 21(3). See BURGLARY, AGGRAVATED; FIREARM.

offensive words. (1) In a will it is possible for words which are offensive or defamatory and which have no testamentary value to be excluded from probate. See *In the Estate of White* [1914] P 153.

(2) A solicitor, while acting for a client or otherwise, should not use insulting language or indulge in acrimonious correspondence: *A Guide to Professional Conduct of Solicitors in Ireland* (2002) ch 6.8. A solicitor should not write offensive letters to other members of the profession (ch 7.1).

offer. A proposal to give or to do something, which when accepted constitutes an agreement. It should be distinguished from an invitation to others to make offers eg as made by an auctioneer or as made in an advertisement inviting tenders. An offer may be *express* or *implied* from conduct. The person making the offer is known as the *offeror* and the person to whom the offer is made is the *offeree*.

The general rules relating to offers are: (1) an offer may be made to a definite person, to the world at large, or to some definite class of persons; (2) an offer may be made by words or by conduct; (3) the terms of an offer must be definite; (4) the offer must be communicated to the offeree before acceptance.

An offer may be withdrawn or revoked at any time before it has been unconditionally accepted, or it may be rejected (eg by a counter-offer), or it may lapse. An offer lapses on the death of the offeror or offeree before acceptance; by non-acceptance within the time prescribed; or where no time has been prescribed, by non-acceptance within a reasonable time. An offer may be accepted by the performance of a particular condition prescribed in the offer: *Tansey v College of Occupational Therapists* [1995] 2 ILRM 601 (1986) HC.

As regards a *mistaken* offer, the offeror will be bound notwithstanding the mistake between the parties, if the offeree's interpretation of the offer is reasonable when construed objectively: *O'Neill v Ryan* [1991] ITLR (2 September) HC. See ACCEPTANCE; ELECTRONIC CONTRACT; LAPSE OF OFFER; REVOCATION OF OFFER. For formal offers in personal injuries actions, see LODGMENT IN COURT.

offer for sale. A document offering the shares of a company to the public, issued by a financial intermediary which has bought the shares outright from the company. The offer may be at fixed price or be by way of tender. An offer for sale to the public must comply with prospectus rules. See Companies Act 1963, s 51 and Companies (Amendment) Act 1983, s 21(2). See PROSPECTUS.

offer of amends. The offer made by a person in relation to an *unintentional defamation*, consisting of: (a) an offer to publish a suitable correction and a sufficient apology; and (b) an offer to take reasonable steps to notify persons, to whom the defamatory material has been distributed, that the material is alleged to be defamatory: Defamation Act 1961, s 21. An unintentional defamation is one which the person claims was published by him innocently; the offer must be accompanied by an affidavit specifying the facts relied upon to show that the words were *published innocently* in relation to the party aggrieved.

If an offer of amends is accepted, no further proceedings may follow against the person making the offer. If the offer is rejected, it is a good defence to defamation proceedings. The offer of amends may require the defamatory words to be republished; such republication is privileged: *Wil-*

lis v Irish Press Ltd [1938] 72 ILTR 238. See PUBLICATION.

offeree. See OFFER.

offeror. See OFFER.

office. A premises, room, suite of rooms or other part of premises in which more than five persons are employed in clerical work: Office Premises Act 1958, s 3. This Act provided for the protection of the health, welfare and safety of person employed in offices. It was replaced by the Safety, Health and Welfare at Work Act 1989 and now stands repealed: SI No 357 of 1995. See BUSINESS TENANT.

office copy. Attested copies of all documents filed in the High Court are admissible in evidence in all causes and matters and between all persons or parties to the same extent as the originals would be admissible: RSC Ord 39, r 3. It has been held in Northern Ireland that an office copy of an instrument deposited in the Supreme Court could not be taken as evidence of the truth of the contents or the genuineness of the execution of the instrument: *O'Kane v Mullan* [1925] NI 1. See DOCUMENTARY EVIDENCE.

office holder. It has been held that the characteristic features of an *office* are that it is created by Act of the national parliament, charter, statutory regulation, articles of association of a company or of a body corporate formed under the authority of a statute, deed of trust, grant or by prescription; and that the holder of it may be removed if the instrument creating the office authorises it: *Glover v BLN Ltd* [1973] IR 389.

An office holder is entitled to the benefit of the principles of *natural justice* (qv) before being removed from office eg where dismissed for misconduct or failing to perform the duties of the office, but not for redundancy: *Hickey v Eastern Health Board* [1990] ELR 177, SC. The rights of an employee in regard to dismissal do not depend on whether the person is a servant or an officer, but rather on the reasons for and circumstances surrounding the dismissal (*Hickey* case). The consent of an office holder may be required, in a particular case, to the abolition of his office: *Turley v Laois County Council* [1991] 9 ILT Dig 51, HC.

An office might be held for a fixed term of one year from each meeting at which the annual election of officers takes place eg in a trade union: *Kenny v Trustees of OP &*

ATS of I [1991] ELR 152, EAT. Certain office holders are excluded from the protection of the Unfair Dismissals Act 1977. As regards an officer of a local authority, see *O'Callaghan v Cork Corporation* UD 309/1978. See *Garvey v Ireland* [1981] IR 75; *Henegan v Western Regional Fisheries Board* [1986] ILRM 225. See EMPLOYEE; PROBATION IN EMPLOYMENT.

Office of Tobacco Control. A body corporate with general functions of advising and assisting the Minister in relation to the control and regulation of the manufacture, sale, marketing and smoking of tobacco products: Public Health (Tobacco) Act 2002, ss 9–32. Previously the Office operated on an administrative basis; the 2002 Act establishes the Office on a statutory basis with functions and powers.

The Office is required to establish and maintain a register of all persons who carry on the business of selling tobacco products by retail and may charge a fee for that registration (PH(T)A 2002, s 37).

A manufacturer or importer of tobacco products is required to provide the Office with information on the composition or properties of its tobacco products (PH(T)A 2002, s 40 as substituted by Public Health (Tobacco) (Amendment) Act 2004, s 11). The Office may require the carrying out of tests on the products and may, subject to certain requirements, publish such information and test results (PH(T)A 2002, s 41 as substituted by PH(T)(A)A 2004, s 12).

There is provision for the establishment of a *Tobacco Free Council*, drawn from a wide spectrum of interests, to be consulted by the office in relation to the performance of the Office of its functions (PH(T)A 2002, s 22). For the Office of Tobacco Control, see website: *www.otc.ie*. See TOBACCO PRODUCT.

officer. In relation to a body corporate, includes a director or secretary: Companies Act 1963, s 2(1). In relation to specific provisions of company law, *officer* may have a wider meaning eg as regards 'insider dealing', it includes an employee, auditor, liquidator, receiver, or examiner: Companies Act 1990, s 107. In relation to a building society, an officer means a director, chief executive or secretary of the society: Building Societies Act 1989, s 2(1).

Official Assignee. The officer of the High Court in bankruptcy matters: Courts (Supplemental Provisions) Act 1961, Sch 8, para 3. The bankrupt's property, real and personal, present and future, vested and contingent, vests in the Official Assignee, but not land which the bankrupt holds as a trustee.

The Official Assignee is empowered to perform such duties and functions as are conferred on him by statute or by rules of court; his functions are stated to be to get in and realise the property, to ascertain the debts and to distribute the assets in accordance with the Act: Bankruptcy Act 1988, ss 60–61 as amended by Courts and Court Officers Act 2002, s 34 and EC (Personal Insolvency) Regulations 2002, SI No 334 of 2002. He is empowered eg to sell the bankrupt's property by public or private auction; to make any *compromise* (qv) or *arrangement* with creditors or to *compromise* any debts or liabilities; and to mortgage or pledge any property to raise any money (BA 1988, s 61(3)).

He is also entitled to disclaim onerous property (qv), although the previous power which he had to elect not to take leasehold property has been abolished. If he does not expressly disclaim a contract to which the bankrupt was previously a party, the Official Assignee becomes entitled to the contractual rights and obligations under the contract and new terms cannot be implied or inserted by the court: *Re Casey, a Bankrupt* [1991] ILRM 385, SC. He is not a trustee for the purposes of the Statute of Limitations (BA 1988, s 133). See also Proceeds of Crime Act 1996, s 12.

The assignee in bankruptcy of a registered owner of land who has been adjudicated a bankrupt, may be registered as owner in his place: Land Registration Rules 1972, r 82 as amended by Land Registration Rules 2000, r 8 (SIs No 230 of 1972 and 175 of 2000). [Bibliography: Holohan & Sanfey.] See ARRANGING DEBTOR; BANKRUPTCY; NOVATION.

Official Journal of EU. The publication of the EU dealing with legislation and communications. See website: *www.europa.eu.int/eur-lex/html*. See COMMUNITY LAW.

official journal of patents office. See PATENTS OFFICE JOURNAL.

official language. See LANGUAGE.

official liquidator. A liquidator appointed by the court. See LIQUIDATOR; WINDING UP.

official search. A search made in the Registry of Deeds to discover the existence of all deeds and conveyances affecting unregistered land. It may be a *common* search or a *negative* search, the certificate arising from the latter being signed by the Registrar and Assistant Registrar, who are both liable to a party aggrieved in respect of any fraud, collusion or negligence in the making of such negative search. See DEEDS, REGISTRATION OF.

official secret. Information of a military nature or any other matter which prejudices the safety of the State; it is an offence to give or to get or to possess or publish any such information: Official Secrets Act 1963 as amended by Criminal Law Act 1997, s 16 and Sch 3. See also *The A-G for England and Wales v Brandon Books* [1987] ILRM 135. Evidence given to the Commission is not affected by the OSA 1963, ss 4–5: Commission to Inquire into Child Abuse Act 2000, s 32. See also Committees of the Houses of the Oireachtas (Compellability, Privileges and Immunity of Witnesses) Act 1997, s 16; Freedom of Information Act 1997, s 48. See 'The Official Secrets Act & the Irish Intelligence Services' by Niall Neligan BL in *Bar Review* (May 2001) 393. See also SPYING.

officious bystander test. The common law test which may imply a term in a contract. The test is whether the parties at the time they were making their bargain, would have agreed *of course* to a suggested express provision from an officious bystander. See *Tradax (Ireland) Ltd v Irish Grain Board Ltd* [1983] IR 1; *Sweeney v Duggan* [1997] 2 ILRM 211, SC; *Rohcon Ltd v SIAC Architectural Ltd* [2003] FL 8221, HC.

offset of repayments. An order of priority has been established for the offset of repayments against outstanding liabilities under the Taxes Consolidation Act 1997, s 1006A(4), as amended: Taxes (Offset of Payments) Regulations 2002, SI No 471 of 2002. See Finance Act 2002, s 125; Social Welfare (Miscellaneous Provisions) Act 2002, s 14(a); Social Welfare (Miscellaneous Provisions) Act 2003, s 20.

offshore fund. A unit trust fund located outside the State: Taxes Consolidation Act 1997, ss 740–747A inserted by Finance Act 1998, s 66. Prior to 1990, an offshore fund paid no tax on its income or gains; the fund rolled up its income and the investor could use the fund to convert income to capital gains at a lower tax rate. See Finance Act 2002, s 47; Finance Act 2004, s 30.

offshore installation. Any installation which is or has been maintained, or is intended to be established, for the exploration for or exploitation of minerals and includes any installation providing accommodation for persons who work on or from any such offshore installation so engaged in exploration or exploitation of minerals: Safety, Health and Welfare (Offshore Installations) Act 1987. The duty of employers to exercise reasonable care in respect of their employees under SHW(OI)A 1987, s 10(5) is a more extensive duty than the common law duty; however, as the statutory duty applied to 'every workplace' on the offshore installation, the employer was entitled to balance the greater risk, which had been removed by the installation of a mid-floor, against the lower risk which had resulted in injury to the employee: *Boyle v Marathon Petroleum (Ireland) Ltd* [1999] 2 IR 460, SC.

Previously, workers on offshore installations were protected by the terms of petroleum prospecting licences issued under the provisions of the Petroleum and Other Minerals Development Act 1960. Certain sections of SHW(OI)A 1987 are repealed when particular sections of the Safety, Health and Welfare at Work Act 1989 come into force eg see SI No 357 of 1995. See also Energy (Miscellaneous Provisions) Act 1995, s 6; Organisation of Working Time Act 1997, s 41(3).

oil pollution. Owners of ships carrying oil in bulk as cargo have *strict liability* (qv) for pollution and damage except where the discharge of oil which caused the damage resulted from an act of war or a natural phenomenon of an exceptional, inevitable or irresistible character, or was due to the act of a third party with intent to do damage, or by the failure of the authorities to maintain navigational aids: Oil Pollution of the Sea (Civil Liability and Compensation) Act 1988 as amended by the Sea Pollution Act 1991, s 37. The 1988 Act gives effect in the State to a number of International Civil Liability Conventions.

The 1988 Act was further amended in 1998 to give effect in Irish law to two Protocols, adopted by the International Maritime Organisation in 1992, which increased the maximum compensation payable in respect of any one pollution incident and also raised the ceiling payable from the International Fund: Oil Pollution of the Sea (Civil Liability and Compensation)

(Amendment) Act 1998. The 1998 Act also: (a) extended the geographical limits of Irish oil pollution jurisdiction to 200 miles offshore, (b) provided for compensation to be payable for pre-spill preventative measures, (c) included vessels previously excluded eg unladen tankers that cause damage by spillage, vessels adapted for carriage of oil in bulk.

The 1988 Act was further amended in 2003: (a) to increase the limits of liability for pollution damage, (b) to extend the liability of the Fund, (c) to establish a Supplemental Fund, and (d) to provide for recognition and enforcement of a judgment of a member state of the European Communities in relation to the Supplemental Fund: Oil Pollution of the Sea (Civil Liability and Compensation) (Amendment) Act 2003.

The Minister is required to prepare a *national plan* for preventing and minimising oil pollution damage, resulting from discharges of oil from ships, offshore units and oil handling facilities: Sea Pollution (Amendment) Act 1999, s 8. Also each harbour authority, each operator of an offshore unit or oil-handling facility and each local authority, must have in place an *oil pollution emergency plan* (SP(A)A 1999, ss 2–3). As regards a local authority, the Minister may require the plan to relate to any area of seashore which is in its functional area or contiguous thereto (SP(A)A 1999, s 2(3)). There is a duty on the master of a ship to report an oil pollution incident (SP(A)A 1999, s 7). See also SI No 44 of 1994; SI No 191 of 2003. [Bibliography: Symmons.] See SEA POLLUTION; WASTE.

Oireachtas. The expression 'the Oireachtas' means the national parliament provided for by art 5 of the Constitution: Interpretation Act 1937, s 12, Sch, para 21. The *national parliament* consists of the President (qv) and two houses, a house of representatives called *Dáil Éireann* (qv) and a senate called *Seanad Éireann* (qv); the sole and exclusive power of making laws for the State is vested in the Oireachtas: 1937 Constitution, art 15. Members of both houses are privileged from arrest in going to or coming from, and while in the precincts of either House, except in the case of treason, felony (now, an offence) or breach of the peace (qqv) (art 15(13)). Members have a right to use either of the official languages in any debates or other proceedings in either house: Official Languages Act 2003, s 6.

Certain persons are disqualified from election to either Houses of the Oireachtas eg an undischarged bankrupt: Electoral Act 1992, s 41.

Provision has been made in the Maastricht Treaty 1992, by way of Declaration, of steps to ensure that national parliaments of the EC are better informed eg by ensuring that national parliaments receive Commission proposals for legislation in good time for information or possible examination: Declaration (13) on the Role of National Parliaments in the European Union. See Oireachtas (Allowances to Members) Act 1998. The Clerk of the Dáil is designated as the Head of the Houses of the Oireachtas for the purposes of the Public Service Management Act 1997: SI No 11 of 2002. A minimum pensionable age of 65 has been set for *new entrants* to the Houses of the Oireachtas: Public Service Superannuation (Miscellaneous Provisions) Act 2004, s 11. See website: *www.irlgov.ie/oireachtas*. [Bibliography: Maloney & Spellman; McGowan Smyth.] See ACT; BILL; COMMUNITY LAW; GOVERNMENT; HOUSES OF THE OIREACHTAS COMMISSION; PRIVILEGE.

Oireachtas Committees. Certain committees of the Oireachtas are empowered to compel a person to attend before them, to respond to questioning and to produce any specified documents: Committees of the Houses of the Oireachtas (Compellability, Privileges and Immunities of Witnesses) Act 1997, s 3. Certain persons are exempt eg the President and judges (CHO(CPIW)A 1997, s 3(4)). However, notwithstanding s 3(4), a judge may be compelled to attend before an Oireachtas committee which is established for the purposes of a matter relating to that judge arising: (i) under art 35(4) of the Constitution; or (ii) pursuant to the Courts of Justice Act 1924, s 39 or Courts of Justice (District Court) Act 1946, s 20: CHO(CPIW)A 1997, s 3A inserted by Committees of the Houses of the Oireachtas (Compellability, Privileges and Immunities of Witnesses) (Amendment) Act 2004, s 1. The committee must be a committee established for the purpose of, or in connection with, the behaviour or capacity of a judge. The amendment was deemed necessary to enable the Houses of the Oireachtas to enquire into the behaviour or capacity of Circuit Court Judge Brian Curtin.

Partly exempt from being compelled to appear before an Oireachtas committee are the Attorney-General and the Director of Public Prosecutions. Certain matters are also exempt eg matters as regards Cabinet confidentiality, state security, international relations, *sub judice* matters and law enforcement (CHO(CPIW)A 1997, s 5). A person giving evidence or documents to the committee is given the same privileges and immunity as if the person were a witness before the High Court (CHO(CPIW)A 1997, s 11). For other amendments to CHO(CPIW)A 1997, see Comptroller & A-G and Committees of the Houses of the Oireachtas Act 1998, s 19.

The chief executive of the *Human Rights Commission* is required to report, when so requested to an Oireachtas committee: Human Rights Commission Act 2000, s 15. The chief executive officer of certain health bodies (eg health boards) is required when so requested to attend before an Oireachtas committee to give account for the general administration of the health body concerned: Health (Amendment) Act 2004, s 29.

In a case involving an Oireachtas Committee, which was inquiring into the circumstances of a person being shot dead by the gardaí (known as the 'Abbeylara' inquiry), the High Court held in 2001 that the Oireachtas had no power to set up inquiries which are likely to lead to findings of fact or expressions of opinion adverse to the good name of non-members of the Oireachtas. The Supreme Court subsequently held that the High Court had granted too wide a declaration. Instead it substituted for the High Court declaration a declaration 'that the conducting by the subcommittee of an inquiry into the fatal shooting at Abbeylara on 20 April 2000 capable of leading to adverse findings of fact and conclusions (including a finding of unlawful killing) as to the personal culpability of an individual not a member of the Oireachtas so as to impugn his or her good name was *ultra vires* in that the holding of such an inquiry was not within the inherent powers of the Houses of the Oireachtas': *Maguire & Ors v Ardagh & Ors* [2002] 1 IR 385, SC.

See 'Inquiries and Tribunals after Abbeylara' by Cathal Murphy BL in *Bar Review* (December 2002) 355. See Law Reform Commission, *Consultation Paper on Public Inquiries including Tribunals of Inquiry* (LRC CP 22, 2003). See also Courts Services Act 1998, s 21; Communications Regulation Act 2002, s 34; Competition Act 2002, s 38; Digital Hub Development Agency Act 2003, s 33; Taxi Regulation Act 2003, s 25; Industrial Development (Science Foundation Ireland) Act 2003, s 14; Personal Injuries Assessment Board Act 2003, s 66; Education for Persons with Special Educational Needs Act 2004, s 31; Residential Tenancies Act 2004, s 179. See also RSC Ord 131 inserted by SI No 381 of 1998. See CABINET CONFIDENTIALITY; PUBLIC ACCOUNTS, COMMITTEE OF; TRIBUNALS OF INQUIRY.

Oireachtas copyright. The copyright which subsists in any work made by or under the direction of either or both of the Houses of the Oireachtas; it expires 50 years after the work was made: Copyright and Related Rights Act 2000, s 193. The Oireachtas also holds the copyright in any Bill or enactment (CRRA 2000, s 192). The Oireachtas may give permission to copy or make available any material protected by Oireachtas copyright (CRRA 2000, s 194). See ACT; BILL.

old age. Persons who are aged 75 years or over and are permanently resident in the State are entitled to a free television licence and to an allowance for telephone and electricity/gas, irrespective of income or household composition. An application form is available from email: *freeschemes@welfare.ie*. Also, free travel on public transport is available to persons, permanently resident in the State, who are aged 66 years or older and to certain incapacitated persons under 66. These two schemes are non-statutory. The Free Telephone Allowance was extended in 2003 to persons aged 70 or over who reside in nursing homes and have their own telephone account.

Persons aged 65 or over are entitled to an age allowance (now a tax credit) when computing their income tax liability: Taxes Consolidation Act 1997, s 464 as amended by Finance Act 2000, s 8. The allowance in 2002 and 2003 is €205 for a single/widowed person and €410 for a married couple. Also persons aged 65 years or over are exempt from income tax if their total income is below the appropriate *exemption limit* (TCA 1997, s 188 as amended by FA 2000, s 2). The exemption limits were increased in 2003 to €15,000 (single) and €30,000 (married): Finance Act 2003, s 2.

For review of issues in the law as they relate to elderly persons, regarding legal capacity, capacity to make a will, enduring powers of attorney, wards of court system, protection against abuse, and protecting vulnerable adults, see Law Reform Commission, *Consultation Paper on Law and the Elderly* (LRC CP 23, 2003).

The age of an accused does not of itself, or by itself, justify a trial judge suspending a sentence: *The People* (*DPP*) *v J M* [2002] 1 IR 363, CCA. In this case however, the court held that the trial judge did not give sufficient weight to the fragile state of the 84-year old accused's mental and physical health. [Bibliography: Costello.] See AGE; PENSION, SOCIAL WELFARE.

ombudsman. The office holder, independent in the performance of his functions, appointed by the President of Ireland (qv), with power to investigate administrative actions by public bodies which adversely affect some person: Ombudsman Act 1980, ss 2–3. The ombudsman may investigate any action where it appears to him that the action may have been: taken without proper authority; taken on irrelevant grounds; the result of negligence or carelessness; based on erroneous or incomplete information; improperly discriminatory; based on an undesirable administrative practice; or otherwise contrary to sound or fair administration (OA 1980, s 4(2)(b)).

It must appear to the ombudsman that the action has or may have adversely affected some persons and if the investigation is initiated by way of complaint, rather than by the ombudsman of his own motion, the complainant must have, in the ombudsman's opinion, a sufficient interest in the matter (OA 1980, s 4(2)(a), (3), (9)).

The bodies against whom the ombudsman may hear a complaint, include local authorities and health boards, most state-sponsored bodies, all departments of State, excluding the government itself (OA 1980, s 4(2) and Sch 1; SI No 332 of 1984; SIs Nos 66 and 69 of 1985). The 1980 Act applies to the cross-border implementation bodies but only in relation to actions taken in the State by or on behalf of the bodies: British-Irish Agreement Act 1999, s 50. See also Finance Act 1981, s 52, now Taxes Consolidation Act 1997, s 1093; Ombudsman (Amendment) Act 1984; Ombudsman for Children Act 2002, s 12; Social Welfare (Miscellaneous Provisions) Act 2003, s 22; Official Languages Act 2003, s 36.

The office of the Ombudsman and that of the *Information Commissioner* (qv) are combined. The first ombudsman was a former journalist, Michael Mills. The second ombudsman was a former civil servant, Kevin Murphy, from 1994 to 1 June 2003. The third ombudsman is a former journalist, Emily O'Reilly, who took up office on the retirement of Mr Murphy. See also Public Service Superannuation (Miscellaneous Provisions) Act 2004, Sch 2. [Office of the Ombudsman, Ossory House, Lower Leeson Street, Dublin 2. Tel: 1890 22 30 30 or (01) 6785222 fax: (01) 661 0570.] See also email: *ombudsman@ombudsman. gov.ie* and website: *www.ombudsman.ie*. [Bibliography: Hogan & Morgan.] See AGRICULTURE APPEALS; GOOD FRIDAY AGREEMENT.

ombudsman, European. The independent ombudsman appointed by the European Parliament to receive complaints from any citizen of the EC, or any natural or legal person residing in a member state, concerning instances of *maladministration* in the activities of the Community institutions or bodies, with the exception of the Court of Justice and the Court of First Instance acting in their judicial role: EC Treaty, art 195 of the consolidated (2002) version. See European Parliament Elections (Amendment) Act 2004, s 2. See the *European Ombudsman Statute* and details of decisions by the Ombudsman on website: *www.euro-ombudsman.eu.int*. See MALADMINISTRATION.

ombudsman, insurance. See INSURANCE OMBUDSMAN.

Ombudsman for Children. The holder of the office of Ombudsman for Children, who is appointed by the President of Ireland, and who is independent in performing the functions of the office: Ombudsman for Children Act 2002. The Ombudsman has an examination and investigatory role in respect of complaints, regarding the performance of an administrative function of certain bodies. The complaint may be made by a child, a parent of a child, or a person who has either a personal or professional relationship to the child.

The Ombudsman must have regard for the best interest of the child, and, in so far as practicable, give due consideration to the child's wishes, having had regard to the age and understanding of the child.

The remit of the Ombudsman extends to public bodies (including health boards), schools and voluntary hospitals. In certain circumstances the Ombudsman cannot investigate certain complaints eg where civil proceedings have been instituted on behalf of the child (OCA 2002, s 11). In an unusual provision, the Ombudsman also has a promotional role in relation to the rights and welfare of children (OCA 2002, s 7). The first Ombudsman is Ms Emily Logan, whose appointment was announced on 16 December 2003. See report by Children's Rights Alliance, *The office of the Ombudsman for Children: international learning and priorities for Ireland* (2004). See also Public Service Superannuation (Miscellaneous Provisions) Act 2004, Sch 2.

Ombudsman for Credit Institutions. An independent and impartial arbitrator of unresolved disputes between a customer and his bank, or building society, or a finance house which has been prescribed as a *credit institution* under s 2 of the Consumer Credit Act 1995 (now amended by Central Bank and Financial Services Authority of Ireland Act 2003, s 35, Sch 1).

The Ombudsman is appointed by the Council of the Credit Institutions to whom he is responsible. He is empowered to deal with most complaints (eg unfair treatment, uncorrected mistake, maladministration, negligence, poor service, breach of codes of practice, breach of contract or confidentiality). He cannot deal with complaints which concern: (a) a matter where the amount in dispute is more than €100,000, (b) a limited company having an annual turnover greater than €1.5m, (c) the commercial judgement or policy of the institution or its discretion under a will or trust.

He has power to award compensation of up to €100,000 and to give such directions to a bank or building society as will do justice between the parties. Any award or direction is binding on the bank or building society but not on the customer who may pursue a legal remedy. This non-statutory scheme was established in 1990.

The Ombudsman is also designated by the Central Bank as the official arbitrator in the case of disputes arising from *cross-border credit transfers* (qv) within the EU and EFTA member states under EU Directive (EC) 97/5, art 10. [The Ombudsman for Credit Institutions, 8 Adelaide Court, Adelaide Road, Dublin 2. Tel: (01) 4783755. fax: (01) 4780157.]

Under recent legislation, provision has been made for the establishment of an independent statutory *Financial Services Ombudsman* scheme: Central Bank and Financial Services Authority of Ireland Act 2004, s 16. The Act contains an enabling provision for the existing non-statutory Ombudsman for Credit Institutions, and his staff and systems to be absorbed into the statutory scheme, with the current Ombudsman being designated by the Minister as a Deputy Ombudsman-designate under the statutory scheme. See EUROPEAN EXTRA-JUDICIAL NETWORK; FINANCIAL SERVICES OMBUDSMAN.

Ombudsman for Pensions. See PENSIONS OMBUDSMAN.

Ombudsman for the Defence Forces. Under draft legislation, it is proposed to establish the office of *Ombudsman for the Defence Forces* and to provide for the appointment, functions and staff of the Ombudsman and to amend the Defence Act 1954: Ombudsman (Defence Forces) Bill 2002.

omission. A failure to do something. It may amount to the tort of negligence (qv) where a duty existed to do that something. It may also constitute the *actus reus* (qv) in a crime. [Bibliography: McAuley & McCutcheon.] See NONFEASANCE.

omne quod solo inaedificatur solo cedit. [Everything which is built into the soil is merged therein.] See FIXTURES.

omne testamentum morte consummatum est. [Every will is completed by death.] A will is ambulatory until the death of the testator. See AMBULATORY.

omnes licentiam habent his, quae pro se indulta sunt, renunciare. [Everyone has liberty to renounce those things which are granted for his benefit.]

omnia praesumuntur legitime facta donec probetur in contrarium. [All things are presumed to have been legitimately done unless the contrary is proved.]

omnia praesumuntur rite esse acta. [All acts are presumed to have been done rightly.] 'It is a maxim of the law of England to give effect to everything to which appears to have been established for a considerable course of time, and to presume that what has been done was done of right, and not in wrong.' Pollock C B in *Gibson v Doeg* [1857] 2 H & N 615 at 623 cited with approval in *McMullen v Clancy* [2002] 3 IR 493, SC.

The maxim, however, will not be carried to such lengths as to nullify a statutory provision eg the formalities for execution of a will. The maxim cannot be relied on to dispense with formal proof that a doctor is a designated medical practitioner for the purposes of the Road Traffic Act 1978: *DPP v O'Donoghue* [1992] 10 ILT Dig 74, HC. See *Clergy v Barry* [1889] 21 LR Ir 152; *Re McLean* [1950] IR 180; *Clarke v Early* [1980] IR 223. See BEST EVIDENCE RULE; PRESUMPTION OF REGULARITY.

omnibus. A large *public service vehicle* (qv) which is for the time being used on a definite route for the carriage of passengers who are carried at separate fares and are picked up and set down along such routes whether on request or at fixed stopping places: Road Traffic Act 1961, s 3. Local authorities are now empowered to make *bye-laws* on the location and use of bus stops: RTA 1961, s 84 as substituted by Road Traffic Act 2002, s 15. See Road Traffic Bill 2004, s 22.

on approval. See APPROVAL, SALE ON.

on call. Term used to describe when an employee is on standby, available for work should the need arise. The European Court of Justice has held that the totality of time which a hospital doctor spends *on call* is 'working time' for the purposes of the Working Time Directive: Case C-151/02 *Landeshauptstadt Kiel v Norbert Jaeger* [2003] ECJ. The decisive factor was that the doctor was required to be present at a place determined by the employer and to be available to provide the employer's services immediately in case of need.

Working hours for the purposes of the national minimum wage does not include time spent on standby or *on call* at a place other than a place of work or training provided by the employer: National Minimum Wage Act 2000, s 8(2)(i). Non-reckonable pay components in calculating average hourly rate of pay include an *on-call* or standby allowance (NMWA 2000, s 19, Sch, Pt II). See also NMWA 2000, s 18(5); SI No 44 of 1998. See Maternity Protection (Health and Safety Leave Remuneration) Regulations 1995, SI No 20 of 1995, reg 4(6)(d); Nursing Homes (Care and Welfare) Regulations 1993, SI No 226 of 1993, reg 10.5; Homes for Incapacitated Persons Regulations 1985, SI No 317 of 1985, reg 12(1)(a). See WORKING HOURS.

on-the-spot fine. A monetary penalty in respect of an alleged offence, which if not paid within a specified period, will lead to a prosecution for the offence eg parking offences. Local authorities are empowered to introduce on-the-spot fines for the breach of a bye-law: Local Government Act 1994, ss 41, repealed and now Local Government Act 2001, s 206. Litter wardens, dog wardens and the gardaí are empowered to issue on-the-spot fines for litter offences: Litter Pollution Act 1997, s 28 as amended by Waste Management (Amendment) Act 2001, s 14(3). See also Road Transport Act 1986, s 13; Finance Act 1976, s 74; Road Transport Act 1999, s 16. Dublin Bus introduced on-the-spot fines in 1990 for failing to pay the appropriate fare.

On-the-spot fines may be imposed for road traffic offences which are *fixed charge offences*: Road Traffic Act 1961, s 103 as substituted by Road Traffic Act 2002, s 11(1). Notification of the alleged offence may be served by a garda or by a traffic warden; however in the case of *penalty point offences*, only by a garda (RTA 1961, s 103(3)). See Road Traffic (Offences) Regulations 2002, SI No 492 of 2002.

Provision has been made for a system of on-the-spot fines in the area of inland fisheries, to be administered by the regional fisheries boards: Fisheries Acts (Payment in Lieu of Prosecution) Regulations 2003, SI No 297 of 2003, as amended by SI No 207 of 2004. See LITTER; PENALTY POINTS.

one-man company. A company which has a sole member; it must be a private company, limited by shares or by guarantee: Directive (EEC) 98/667 (Twelfth Company Law Directive). The purpose of the Directive is to lay down uniform conditions under which single-member companies may be established throughout the European Community. See MacCann in 8 ILT & SJ (1990) 166. See SINGLE-MEMBER COMPANY.

one-parent family payment. A social welfare payment which may be payable to a widow, a widower, a separated spouse, an unmarried person, and the spouse of a prisoner, who has at least one qualified child living with the person: Social Welfare Act 1996, ss 17–21; Social Welfare Act 2003, s 3(2)(d). It replaces the deserted wife's benefit and allowance and the prisoner's wife's allowance.

onerous property. (1) Property of a company being wound up which a liquidator may disclaim with the consent of the court:

Companies Act 1963, s 290. It includes land of any tenure burdened by onerous covenants, or unprofitable contracts, property which is unsaleable or not readily saleable. A supplier is entitled to prove as a creditor for the loss sustained by the supplier by reason of the disclaimer: *Re Ranks (Ir) Ltd* [1988] ILRM 751. See *Re Farm Machinery Distributors Ltd* [1984] ILRM 273. See RSC Ord 74, rr 84–85. See also TRANSMISSION OF SHARES.

(2) The Official Assignee (qv) in bankruptcy is empowered to disclaim onerous property of the bankrupt with the leave of the court, eg land with onerous covenants, shares or stocks in companies, unprofitable contracts, property which is unsaleable or not readily saleable: Bankruptcy Act 1988, s 56. See BANKRUPTCY; OFFICIAL ASSIGNEE; REPUDIATION.

onus of proof. See BURDEN OF PROOF.

onus probandi. [The burden of proof (qv).]

op cit; opera citato. [In the work quoted.] The book previously cited.

open contract. A contract for the sale of land which is left *open* as to title (qv), in which case the law defines the extent of the vendor's duty as to the length of *title* which he must show. However, it is usual for a contract to be a *closed* one ie where the title to be shown is clearly defined. See MARKETABLE TITLE.

open court. See PUBLIC JUSTICE.

open justice. See PUBLIC JUSTICE.

open market value. The word 'value' when preceded by the word 'market' or 'open market' is generally used to convey a concept of the price that might be expected if a particular property is offered on the open market for sale by someone willing to sell at whatever price would be offered by a purchaser who is not constrained to buy the property: *Attorney-General v Shannon Foynes Port Company* (28 April 2003, unreported) HC. See COMPENSATION AND COMPULSORY PURCHASE; REVERSIONARY LEASE.

open offer. An invitation to existing holders of securities to subscribe or purchase securities in proportion to their holdings, which is not made by means of a renounceable letter (or other negotiable document): Listing Rules 2000, paras 4.22–4.26, and 8.14. Contrast with a RIGHTS ISSUE.

open season. The period during which it is lawful to hunt game (qv) with firearms, provided the person so hunting has a licence therefor. The duration of the period is specified in an order made by the Minister. See Wildlife Act 1976. See SI No 192 of 1979 as amended, eg by SI No 394 of 2003.

open space. A planning authority has the power to acquire land for open spaces, when it is a condition of the planning permission that open spaces be provided by the developer, but this has not been done: Planning and Development Act 2000, s 45. There is a limited right to compensation (PDA 2000, s 45(8)). Where the owner of the land fails to comply with a request to level, plant or otherwise adapt or maintain the land, the planning authority may publish a notice of its intention to acquire the land (an *acquisition notice*), which may be appealed to An Bord Pleanála. If there is no appeal or the notice is confirmed, the planning authority may make an order which will operate to vest the land in the planning authority (PDA 2000, s 45(5)).

See also Open Spaces Act 1906 as amended by Local Government Act 1994, Sch 1. The provisions of the 1906 Act do not apply to county and parish councils in Ireland (OSA 1906, s 21(d)). See SI No 226 of 1976. For previous legislation, see Local Government (Planning and Development) Act 1976, s 25. See *Smeltzer v Fingal County Council* [1998] 1 IR 279, HC. See JUS SPACIENDI.

opening speech. See RIGHT TO BEGIN.

operative mistake. See MISTAKE.

operative part. The part of a deed which carries out the main object as opposed to the recitals (qv). The operative part in a conveyance consists of the testatum, the consideration, the receipt clause, and the operative words.

operative words. The words which in a deed, create or transfer an estate. See WORDS OF LIMITATION.

opinion. (1) The advice given by counsel on a case submitted to him for his view on the legal issues involved. The copyright in an opinion belongs to the client: *Code of Conduct for the Bar of Ireland* (December 2003) r 3.5.

(2) The opinions of witnesses are generally irrelevant and inadmissible; a witness is required to give evidence of facts which he observed, it being left to the court to draw inferences from the facts, to form opinions and to come to conclusions. The exceptions are: opinions of experts; opinion as to the identity of a person; opinion as to handwriting by a person *acquainted* with the

handwriting; opinion of a garda as to intoxication: *A-G v Kenny* [1960] 94 ILTR 185; *DPP v Donoghue* [1987] ILRM 129. See also *The People (Attorney-General) v McGeogh* [1969] CCA. [Bibliography: Healy.] See EUROPEAN OPINION; EXPERT OPINION.

opinion, freedom to express. See EXPRESSION, FREEDOM OF.

opinions, EC. See COMMUNITY LAW.

opium poppy. A plant of the species *papaver somniferum L* or *papaver bracteatum lindl*: Misuse of Drugs Act 1984, s 2. See CANNABIS.

oppression of shareholder. Any *member* of a company who complains that the affairs of the company are being conducted or that the powers of the directors are being exercised in a manner oppressive to him or any of the members, or in disregard of his or their interests as members, may apply to the court for intervention: Companies Act 1963, s 205. *Oppression* has been defined as 'burdensome, harsh and wrongful'; the court will look at the business realities of the situation as opposed to the narrow legalistic view.

Where the court is of the opinion that there is *oppression*, it is empowered to make such order as it deems fit with a view to bringing to an end the matters complained of (CA 1963, s 205(3)) or it may order that the company be wound up (CA 1963, s 213(g)). An order under s 205(3) must be made 'with a view to bringing to an end the matters complained of'; there is no general right to compensation for loss resulting from oppression: *Irish Press plc v Ingersoll Irish Publications Ltd* [1995] 2 IR 175, SC.

A breakdown in confidence between parties does not amount to *oppression,* unless the member leaving the business is prevented by the other members from realising his investment on reasonable terms: *Horgan v Murray* [1997] 3 IR 23, SC and [1998] 1 ILRM 110, SC.

Following an investigation of a company, the Minister may apply to the court for an order against oppression (CA 1963, s 205(2)).

Only those who come within the definition of *member* in CA 1963, s 31 may present a petition under s 205(1): *O'Tuama v Allied Metropole Hotel Ltd* as reported in 7 ILT & SJ [1989] 195. In relation to whether such a petition may be held *in camera*, consideration must be given to the obligation under the Constitution, art 34(1) to administer justice in public: CA 1963, s 205(7) and *Re R Ltd* [1989] ILRM 757. An order for a hearing *in camera* will be granted only where the court is of the opinion that the hearing would involve disclosures, the publication of which would be seriously prejudicial to the legitimate interests of the company: *Irish Press plc v Ingersoll Irish Publications Ltd (No 1)* [1994] 1 IR 176.

Complaints concerning the conduct of the affairs of a company which is under the *protection of the court* cannot constitute a basis for the making of an order for relief under CA 1963, s 205: Companies (Amendment) Act 1990, s 5 as amended by Companies Act 1990, s 180(1)(b). A shareholder has no right to bring a personal action in respect of the reduced value of his shareholding resulting from damage to the company against the party who caused such damage: *O'Neill v Ryan* [1993] ILRM 557, SC. See also *Scottish Co-op Wholesale Society v Meyer* [1959] AC 324; *Re Clubman Shirts Ltd* [1983] ILRM 323; *Re Murph's Restaurants Ltd (No 2)* [1979] ILRM 141; *Re Greenore Trading Co* [1980] HC; *Re Williams Group (Tullamore) Ltd* [1985] IR 613; *McGilligan v O'Grady* [1999] 1 ILRM 303, SC; *Re Via Net Works (Ireland) Ltd* [2002] 2 IR 47, SC. See COURT PROTECTION OF COMPANY; FOSS V HARBOTTLE, RULE IN; PETITION FOR WINDING UP; SHARES, COMPULSORY PURCHASE OF; WINDING UP, COMPULSORY.

oppressive proceedings. A court has an inherent jurisdiction to *stay* oppressive proceedings which are an abuse of the process of the court e g *McGinn v Beegan* [1962] IR 364. See ABUSE OF PROCESS; MALICIOUS PROSECUTION.

ophthalmic optician. See OPTOMETRIST.

optician. See OPTOMETRIST.

optima legum interpres est consuetudo. [Custom is the best interpreter of the law.] See CUSTOM AND PRACTICE.

optimus interpres rerum usus. [The best interpreter of things is usage.] See CUSTOM AND PRACTICE.

option. A right of choice. A right conferred by agreement to buy or not any property within a certain time. A right, which may be acquired by contract, to accept or reject a present offer within a given period of time. An *option* is also a right to call for delivery or to make delivery of a specified number of shares or debentures at a specified price and within a specified time (eg *put* and *call*); it is an offence for a director of a company to deal in options to buy or sell listed shares or debentures in the company: Companies Act 1990, s 30.

As regards taxation, an *option* is an asset; the granting of an option is the disposal of an asset. A *quoted option* is an option which, at the time of its disposal, is quoted on a stock exchange. A *traded option* is an option which, at the time of its abandonment or disposal, is quoted on a stock exchange or futures exchange. Also an option includes any transaction which the grantor of a lease binds himself to enter into, including an option that binds the grantor to grant a lease for a premium. See Taxes Consolidation Act 1997, s 540. See *Kramer v Arnold* [1997] 3 IR 43, SC; *Kearns v Dillon* [1997] 3 IR 287, SC. See FIRST REFUSAL; REVOCATION OF OFFER.

optometrist. The new title for 'ophthalmic opticians': Opticians (Amendment) Act 2003, s 4 amending the Opticians Act 1956. There is provision for the registration of *optometrists* (OA 1956, ss 24, 24A and 25, as substituted or inserted by O(A)A 2003, ss 5–7). There is also provision for the registration of *dispensing opticians* (OA 1956, ss 33, 33A and 34, as substituted by O(A)A 2003, ss 8–10).

A registered optician, who is not a registered medical practitioner, is prohibited from making a medical diagnosis of a disease of the eye, but is obligated to recommend that the patient consults with a registered medical practitioner if in the course of an eye examination, the optician suspects the presence of a disease or condition of the eye (OA 1956, s 48 amended by O(A)A 2003, s 12).

It is an offence for a person to sell 'spectacles' unless the person is a registered optician or a registered medical practitioner (OA 1956, s 49).

The 2003 Act redefines *spectacles* to exclude ready-made reading spectacles, afocal sunglasses and afocal goggles, and specifies that *contact lenses*, with or without focal power, are included in the definition of spectacles (O(A)A 2003, s 2(b)). *Ready-made reading spectacles* are spectacles that have two single vision lenses each of which has the same positive spherical power not exceeding four dioptres and the purpose of which is to relieve the condition known as presbyopia (O(A)A 2003, s 2(a)). This redefinition means that the sale of ready-made reading spectacles has been deregu-

lated and that the sale of goggles with focal power will continue to be regulated.

An exemption has been provided whereby optometrists may administer, in the course of their professional practice, certain listed medicinal products that are not intended for *parenteral administration* (qv): Medicinal Products (Prescription and Control of Supply) Regulations 2003, SI No 540 of 2003, reg 20(2). See MEDICINAL PRODUCT.

or. The general and principal meaning of 'or' is 'a conjunction introducing alternatives', 'a particle co-ordinating two or more words, phrases or clauses between which there is an alternative': *In the Matter of the Estate of Clare Bernadette Doran* [2000] ITLR (9 October) HC.

oral agreement. An agreement which is not reduced to writing or evidenced in writing. Certain oral agreements are unenforceable because they are required to be by deed (qv) or are required to be evidenced in writing under the Statute of Frauds (qv).

oral agreement, modification of contract by. A contract in writing may be rescinded or varied by an oral agreement. A contract under seal may be rescinded or varied by a simple contract (qv). However, a contract which is required by the Statute of Frauds to be evidenced in writing, can be rescinded but cannot be varied by an oral agreement: *Morris v Barron* [1919] AC 1. If a contract, required by statute to be in writing, is varied by oral agreement, the contract can be enforced in its original form, the oral agreement being discarded. See VARIATION.

oral evidence. See VIVA VOCE.

oral hearing. The hearing of evidence orally. There is no authority establishing that an oral hearing is necessary in all cases; this will depend on the circumstances of the individual case: *Z v Minister for Justice* [2002] 2 ILRM 215, SC.

An employee, whose dismissal is being considered by his employer, is not entitled to an oral hearing where he makes no statement concerning the allegations of his misconduct; the purpose of the oral hearing would be to ensure that the employer did not take into account any factual material which the employee was contesting, the veracity of which could be established by cross-examination: *Mooney v An Post* [1994] ELR 103, HC and [1998] ELR 238, SC. As regards evidence before the courts, see VIVA VOCE.

oral smokeless tobacco product. It is an offence for a person to manufacture, import, supply, sell or invite an offer to purchase an oral smokeless tobacco product: Public Health (Tobacco) Act 2002, s 38(2) as substituted by Public Health (Tobacco) (Amendment) Act 2004, s 9. For previous legislation, see Tobacco (Health Promotion and Protection) Act 1988, s 6. See *United States Tobacco (Ireland) Ltd v Minister for Health* [1991] HC. See TOBACCO PRODUCT.

oral will. See NUNCUPATIVE WILL.

order. (1) A direction or command of the court. A final order of a court which has been *perfected* can be amended by the court but only in special or unusual circumstances: *Belville Holdings Ltd (in Receivership) v Revenue Commissioners* [1994] 1 ILRM 29, SC; *A-G v Open Door Counselling Ltd* [1994] 1 ILRM 256, SC. A court can only interfere after the passing and entering of a judgment where there is an accidental slip in the judgment or if the judgment as drawn up does not accurately state what the court actually decided: *Ainsworth v Wilding* [1895] 1 Ch 673. See also *Re Swire* [1885] 30 Ch D 239. However, a court may order that an order, which has been perfected, not to be communicated where counsel undertakes to enter a motion to have the order set aside: *Dorrian v Longin* (Irish Times, 14 October 1993) HC.

The court has an inherent jurisdiction to amend a judgment or order of the court where the judgment or order as drawn up does not correctly state what the court decided or intended; however this does not extend to amending an order, which has been perfected, to include an award of interest, where no argument was advanced during the action in relation to this and no award of interest was granted: *Concorde Engineering Co Ltd v Bus Atha Cliath* [1996] 1 ILRM 533, HC and [1995] 3 IR 212, HC. Regard must be had for the right of a defendant to know at the time of perfection of an order, the exact extent of the defendant's liability. See SLIP RULE.

(2) The code of procedure of the Superior Courts, the Circuit Court and the District Court consists of *orders*, subdivided into *rules*. See RSC 1986; Circuit Court Rules 2001; DCR 1997, all as amended.

order bill. A bill of exchange payable to order, or which is expressed to be payable to a particular person, or does not contain words prohibiting transfer. An *order* bill is negotiated by an endorsement coupled with delivery, whereas a *bearer* bill is negotiated by delivery alone. See Bills of Exchange Act 1882, s 8(4) and 34. See BEARER BILL; BILL OF EXCHANGE; ENDORSEMENT.

order for protection. See ARRANGING DEBTOR.

order for sale. See MORTGAGEE, RIGHTS OF.

orders, obedience to. See OBEDIENCE TO ORDERS, DEFENCE OF.

ordinary resolution. See RESOLUTION.

ordinary shares. Shares in a company which do not have any preferential rights attaching to them and which attract dividends after payments are made to the preferential shareholders and debenture-holders. The holders of ordinary shares are regarded as the owners of the equitable interest in the company, as contrasted with the secured lenders, and consequently ordinary shares are often known as *equities* and are traded on the Stock Exchange (qv). See SHARES.

ordnance map. Means a map made under the powers conferred by the Survey (Ireland) Acts 1825 to 1870 and the statutes for the time being in force amending those Acts or any of them: Interpretation Act 1937, s 12, Sch, para 22. For Ordnance Survey Ireland, see website: *www.osi.ie*.

ordnance survey. Provision has been made for the Ordnance Survey to be established as a State body (*Ordnance Survey Ireland*) outside the civil service, with considerable commercial freedom to enter into contracts and joint ventures and to sell its products and collect debts and royalties: Ordnance Survey Ireland Act 2001, as amended in respect of place names by Official Languages Act 2003, s 34. See website: *www.osi.ie*.

ordre public. [Public policy (qv).]

organisation, unlawful. See UNLAWFUL ORGANISATION.

organ transplantation. A doctor involved in organ transplantation has duties towards both donors and recipients: Medical Council, *A Guide to Ethical Conduct and Behaviour* (6th edn, 2004) para 21.1. Living donors should be counselled as to the hazards and problems involved in the proposed procedures, preferably by an independent physician. Also payment of any sort, apart from incidental expenses, should not be a factor in the ultimate decision made about organ donation (para 21.2). See BRAIN DEATH; POST-MORTEM.

organic farming. Farming in the EU which differs from other farming systems in a number of ways eg: (a) organic farming favours renewable resources and recycling, returning to the soil the nutrients found in waste products; (b) where livestock is concerned, meat and poultry production is regulated with particular concern for animal welfare and by using natural foodstuffs; and (c) organic farming respects the environment's own systems for controlling pests and disease in raising crops and livestock and avoids the use of synthetic pesticides, herbicides, chemical fertilisers, growth hormones, antibiotics or gene manipulation. Instead, organic farmers use a range of techniques that help sustain ecosystems and reduce pollution.

The EU's Agenda 2000 reform package requires member states to adopt appropriate environmental protection measures relating to all types of agriculture. Farmers are now expected to respect certain basic environmental standards without any financial compensation and the 'polluter-pays' principle is being applied. However, organic farmers are entitled to claim agri-environmental premiums since it is recognised that this particular farming system benefits the environment.

More stringent rules on organic farming have been specified for the production of livestock and livestock products, giving effect to EEC Regulation 2092/91 as amended: EC (Organic Farming) Regulations 2004, SI No 112 of 2004. See website: *www.europa.eu.int/comm/ agriculture/qual/organic/index_en.htm.*

original. For the purpose of copyright, only *original* literary, dramatic, musical and artistic work, and *original* computer programs and databases are protected: Copyright and Related Rights Act 2000, s 17(2). To be *original*, the work must be the result of at least a substantial amount of independent skill, knowledge or creative labour. If the work is partly derived from an earlier work, the later work will be entitled to copyright protection in its own right, although the author may need to obtain a licence from the earlier copyright owner.

It has been held that for copyright purposes, *originality* did not require a work to be unique, merely that there had been some original thought: *Gormley v EMI Records (Ireland) Ltd* [2000] 1 IR 74. Where there was treatment of materials already in existence, it was necessary to show some new approach. See COPYRIGHT; COMPUTER PROGRAM; DATABASE; ELECTRONIC ORIGINAL.

original jurisdiction. See JURISDICTION.

originating document. Includes every document by which proceedings in the Circuit Court are instituted: Circuit Court Rules 2001, Interpretation of Terms, para 17.

originating summons. A summons by which civil proceedings in the High Court is instituted. A *plenary* summons is an originating summons for plenary proceedings with pleadings and hearing on oral evidence. A *summary* summons (or a special summons, depending on the claim involved) is an originating summons for summary proceedings without pleadings and to be heard on affidavit with or without oral evidence. See RSC Ord 1–3. See SUMMONS, HIGH COURT.

orphan. A child whose parents are dead: Adoption Act 1952, s 3. An *orphan* also means a qualified child where: (a) both parents are dead, or (b) one parent is dead or has abandoned or failed to provide for the child and the other parent is unknown or has abandoned the child: Social Welfare Act 1995, s 20. Certain orphan allowances and pensions are no longer payable in respect of a child for whom a *Foster Care Allowance* is simultaneously being paid by a health board: Social Welfare (Miscellaneous Provisions) Act 2003, s 9. The purpose of this change is to transfer responsibility for the financial support of such children to the relevant health board. See Social Welfare Act 2003, s 2(2)(d). See FRIENDLY SOCIETY; CHILD, CARE OF; WELFARE OF CHILDREN.

orse. [Otherwise.]

ostensible authority. Apparent authority. See *Kett v Shannon* [1987] ILRM 365.

other offences. Where a person, on being convicted of an offence, admits himself guilty of any other offence and asks to have it taken into consideration in awarding punishment, the court may, if the Director of Public Prosecutions (qv) consents, take it into consideration accordingly: Criminal Justice Act 1951, s 8(1) as amended by Criminal Justice (Miscellaneous Provisions) Act 1997, s 9. See *The People (DPP) v McAuley* [2001] 4 IR 160, CCA.

oust. To bar, exclude, eject, dispossess.

ouster le main. [Out of hand.]

ouster of jurisdiction. Removal from the court of its power to hear and determine an action or case. The jurisdiction of the District Court is ousted if, in giving a decision on the case before it, it is called upon to adjudicate on a dispute of title to real property. This rule of law however, does not prevent the District Court trying offences under the Criminal Damage Act 1991 (CDA 1991, s 8).

out-patient services. Institutional services other than *in-patient services* (qv) provided at, or by persons attached to, a hospital or home and institutional services provided at a laboratory, clinic, health centre or similar premises, but does not include: (a) the giving of any drug, medicine or other preparation except where it is administered direct by the person providing the service or is for psychiatric treatment, or (b) dental, ophthalmic or aural services: Health Act 1970, s 56(1). Charges may be imposed for these services, see Health (Amendment) Acts 1986 and 1987; SI No 37 of 1994 as amended by SI No 349 of 2003. The charge is €45 from 1 January 2004 in respect of attendance at accident and emergency or casualty departments where the person concerned has not been referred by a medical practitioner: Health (Out-Patient Charges) (Amendment) Regulations 2003, SI No 653 of 2003. The charge does not apply where such attendance results in hospital admission. The usual exemptions, which include medical card holders and hardship provisions, continue to apply. See EUROPEAN HEALTH INSURANCE CARD.

out-worker. A person to whom articles or materials are given to be made up, cleaned, washed, altered, ornamented, finished or repaired or adapted for sale in his own home or on other premises not under the control or management of the person who gave out the articles or material: Social Welfare (Consolidation) Act 1993, s 2(1).

An out-worker is also defined as an employee who is employed under a *contract of service* to do work for his employer in the employee's own home or in some other place not under the control of the employer, being work that consists of the making of a product or the provision of a service specified by the employer: Organisation of Working Time Act 1997, s 2(1). An employer who employs out-workers must keep a register of them and must comply with any regulations made by the Minister in relation to conditions of their employment (OWTA 1997, s 32).

Whether an out-worker is an employee or is on a *contract for services* is a matter to be determined by the contractual terms. See *Minister for Industry v Healy* [1941] IR 545.

outdoor events. Regulations have been made setting out the type of events for which a licence is required under the Planning and Development Act 2000, Pt XVI: Planning and Development Regulations 2001, SI No 600 of 2001, Pt XVI, arts 182–199. For previous regulations, see Planning and Development (Licensing of Outdoor Events) Regulations 2001, SI No 154 of 2001. See EVENT.

outgoings. The necessary expenses and charges which the *receiver* of mortgaged property is required to discharge: Conveyancing Act 1881, s 24(8). See RECEIVER OF MORTGAGED PROPERTY.

outline permission. An application may be made to a planning authority for *outline permission* for the development of land: Planning and Development Act 2000, s 36(1). An *outline permission* does not authorise the carrying out of a development; however, the planning authority cannot refuse to grant permission on a subsequent application on the basis of any matter that was decided in the grant of outline permission (PDA 2000, s 36(4)). Outline permission ceases to have effect after three years (or such longer period, not exceeding five years, as may be specified by the authority) and consequently to gain the benefits of outline permission an application for permission must be made before the expiry of that period (PDA 2000, s 36(3)). See PLANNING PERMISSION.

over-insurance. Where the aggregate of all the insurance contracted for exceeds the total value of the insured's interests which are at risk.

overcharging. See LEGAL CHARGES; PRICE CONTROL; PRODUCT PRICES; RETAIL PRICE.

overcrowded house. A house is deemed to be *overcrowded* at any time when two or more persons of the opposite sex must sleep in the same room or where the free air space in a room used for sleeping is less than 400 cubic feet per person: Housing Act 1966, s 63. In computing the free air space, any height above 8 feet is disregarded. Also the limitation on sharing a room does not apply to children under ten years of age or to persons living together as man and wife.

It is an offence for the owner of such a house to fail to comply with a notice served on him by the housing authority requiring him to desist from causing or permitting the overcrowding (HA 1966, s 65).

overdraft. A loan from a bank to a customer effected by permitting the customer's current account to go into debit. On a current account a cause of action accrues against the debtor in respect of any sum advanced from the date of the advance: *Parr's Banking Co v Yates* [1898] 2 QB 460. A banker must make a demand before pursuing on an overdrawn current account: *Joachimson v Swiss Banking Corporation* [1921] 3 KB 112. A cause of action against the guarantor of a current account does not accrue until demand is made: *Bank of Ireland v O'Keeffe* [1987] IR 47. See also Doyle in 8 ILT & SJ [1990] 169.

A consumer must be informed of the credit limit, if any, and the annual rate of interest and the charges applicable to any advances on a current account, at the time or before an agreement of such credit is made: Consumer Credit Act 1995, s 35. Where the sum advanced is by way of overdraft *tacitly accepted* by both parties which extends beyond three months, the consumer must be *informed* of the annual rate of interest and this may be done by newspaper advertisement (CCA 1995, s 35(3)). See CHEQUE, DRAWING OF; CLAYTON'S CASE; RUNNING ACCOUNT.

overdue bill. A bill of exchange (qv) which remains in circulation when the time for its payment has passed or, if it is payable on demand, when it appears to have been in circulation for an unreasonable length of time: Bills of Exchange Act 1882, s 36(3). A person who takes an overdue bill takes it subject to the equities of prior holders (BEA 1882, s 36(2)).

overdue cheque. See CHEQUE, OVERDUE.

overhanging branches. See TREE.

overreaching conveyance. A conveyance which enables the owner of an estate to transfer it free from equitable interests or charges to which it is otherwise subject, such interests being shifted from the land to the purchase money eg on the sale of land held on trust, the equitable interest is transferred from the land to the money in the trustee's hands. Overreaching also occurs in settled land when the tenant for life transfers the *fee simple* freed and discharged from all the various estates attaching to the land by or under the settlement. See *Connolly v Keating (No 1)* [1903] 1 IR 353.

override commission. Commission paid by an insurance company to an insurance broker which is in addition to the commission which the broker keeps out of the premium paid by the client. Override commissions are paid directly by the insurance company and are generally not taken out of the funds invested by the client in the product. Brokers justify overrides on the basis that they do not come out of the pocket of the client. However, consumer groups believe that the practice encourages brokers to place higher volumes of business with particular companies, in order to achieve the override target, than they would otherwise do. The chief executive of the new Irish Financial Services Regulatory Authority, Liam O'Reilly, has said that he does not favour the practice under which insurance companies pay an override in exchange for the broker bringing in a target number of customers (March 2003).

overriding interests. The burdens which affect registered land whether they are registered or not eg rights of the public, rights acquired under the Statute of Limitations, rights of persons in actual occupation of the land. See Registration of Title Act 1964, s 72.

overseas. Outside the Republic of Ireland: Listing Rules 2000, (Definitions as amended by Irish Stock Exchange Ltd). There are special rules governing an Irish registered company having an overseas primary or secondary listing on a recognised stock exchange other than Ireland. The primary listing is in the country of first listing. See MUTUAL RECOGNITION.

overt. Open eg as in overt act and market overt (qv).

overtaking. A driver of a vehicle must not overtake, or attempt to overtake, if to do so would endanger, or cause inconvenience to, any other person: Road Traffic General Bye-Laws 1964, SI No 294 of 1964, art 19.

overtime. Hours of work in excess of normal hours for which a premium payment is usually paid by agreement. An employee cannot recover for overtime worked in excess of the limit set by legislation: *Martin v Galbraith* [1942] IR 37. Dismissal for failing to work overtime in excess of the legal limit is an unfair dismissal (qv): *Thornton v Coolock Foods Ltd* [1990] ELR 40. Requests to work overtime must be reasonable: *Holgate v Coolock Foods Ltd* [1990] ELR 91, EAT. Notice of a requirement to work overtime given at the normal finishing time is unreasonable: *Murray v Mohan* [1990] ELR 238. A refusal to work overtime in breach of a contract to do so, is a ground for dismissal: *McKenna v Farrell Bros* [1991] ELR 77, EAT. See WORKING HOURS.

overrule. To set aside eg when a higher court overrules a decision of a lower court.

ovum. See ARTIFICIAL INSEMINATION; IN-VITRO FERTILISATION.

owner. In relation to land, means a person who is entitled to receive the *rack rent* of the land or, where the land is not let at a rack rent, would be so entitled if it were so let: Planning and Development Act 2000, s 2(1). The occupier of any structure or land (or any person receiving rent out of the structure or land) is required, on being so requested by a local authority, to give information to the local authority on the ownership of the structure or land (PDA 2000, s 8).

ownership. Right to the exclusive enjoyment of something; it does not necessarily depend on possession. Ownership may be *absolute* where it is without conditions and is complete, or it may be *restricted* where it is subject to some limitation. It may be *corporeal* where it is visible or tangible, or *incorporeal* eg a right to recover a debt, or an easement (qv). It may be *legal* or *equitable* depending on the title eg in a fee simple subject to a trust, the legal fee simple is vested in the trustee, whereas the equitable fee simple resides in the beneficiary. Ownership may also be *vested* where there is a present right to the ownership, or *contingent* where ownership awaits or depends on the happening of an event. Ownership may also be *concurrent* (qv). See GOODS, PROPERTY IN; POSSESSION.

ozone layer. Provision has been made to specify target values and long-term objectives to be attained for concentrations of ozone in ambient air: Ozone in Ambient Air Regulations 2004, SI No 53 of 2004 transposing Directive (EC) 2002/3 into Irish law.

P

pace. [By permission or consent of.]

package. A bag, bottle, box, case, carton, envelope, net, sack or wrapper containing anything which is the subject of trade, manufacture or merchandise: Packaged Goods (Quality Control) Act 1980 as amended by Metrology Act 1996, Sch 1. There are provisions imposing duties on packers and importers as regards the quantity of goods included in and the marking of a package, which has been made up otherwise than in the presence of the person purchasing the package, and is a package the contents of which cannot be removed without opening it (PG(QC)A 1980, Pt II). There are also provisions regarding the marking of an *e-mark* (qv) on a package.

package holiday. A combination of at least two of the following components: (a) transport, (b) accommodation, (c) other tourist services, pre-arranged by the *organiser* when sold or offered for sale at an inclusive price and when the service covers a period of more than twenty-four hours or includes overnight accommodation: Package Holidays and Travel Trade Act 1995, s 2(1).

This legislation, which implements Directive (EC) 90/314 of 13 June 1990, greatly improves the rights of *holiday consumers*, eg by improving the right to receive information prior to the contract and prior to the holiday and by providing that the tour organiser is primarily liable for non- or defective performance by independent contractors. The European Court of Justice has held that the directive implicitly recognises the right to compensation for damage, including non-material damage eg loss of enjoyment: Case C-168/00 *Simone Leitner v TUI Deutschland GmbH & Co KG* [2002] ECJ.

The *organiser* is the person who organises packages and sells or offers them for sale to a consumer, whether directly or through a retailer (PHTTA 1995, s 3). It does not include an 'occasional' organiser (SI No 271 of 1995). There is an implied term that the consumer can transfer his booking to another person where he is prevented from proceeding with the package (PHTTA 1995, s 16).

The Circuit Court has held that due to the Brussels Convention (qv) an Irish tourist could sue a Spanish hotelier in the Irish courts for damages relating to an accident while on holidays in the hotel, as the 'event giving rise to the damage' (the reliance on the expertise of an Ireland-based tour operator in selecting the Spanish hotelier) had occurred within the jurisdiction of the court: *Re Falcon Leisure Group (Overseas) Ltd and Barbican SA* (1999) Irish Times, 19 March. See 'Damages in holiday law cases' by barrister Ann Hartnett O'Connor in *Law Society Gazette* (March 2003) 43. [Bibliography: Buttimore (1); Long; McDonald M (3).] See BROCHURE; TOUR OPERATOR; SEX TOURISM; TOUR OPERATOR; TRAVEL AGENT.

packaging waste. Regulations have been made designed to promote the recovery of packaging waste and particularly to facilitate the achievement of targets established by Directive (EC) 94/62: Waste Management (Packaging) Regulations 2003, SI No 61 of 2003. These Regulations replace SI No 242 of 1997. The new regulations will support the progress of Repak (the compliance scheme set up by industry to ensure the recovery of packaging waste) by ensuring that all producers who participate in the placing of packaging on the market, play their part in meeting the end-of-2005 targets under the Directive. All producers must segregate specified packaging waste materials arising on their own premises (eg waste aluminium, cardboard, glass, paper, plastic sheeting, steel and wood), and have it collected by authorised recovery operators for recycling.

pact. An agreement; a contract; a treaty between states.

pacta dant legem contractui. [Agreements constitute the law of contract.]

pacta sunt servanda. [Contracts are to be kept.]

pain and suffering, damages for. Compensation may be awarded for pain and suffering experienced by a person injured as a result of the tort (qv) of another. Compensation may be given for future, as well as past and present pain and suffering, including that which may accompany or result from a medical operation which is reasonably necessary to perform. See *Sexton v O'Keeffe* [1966] IR 204.

The Supreme Court has held that in assessing damages for future pain and suffering where a plaintiff has developed respiratory difficulties, the correct approach is to take this element into account as amounting to a very real possibility that the plaintiff would continue to suffer from this condition all of her life: *AN (a minor) v Bus Éireann* [2001] ITLR (24 September) SC. In a particular case the Supreme Court reduced an award in respect of pain and

suffering into the future from €70,000 to €50,000: *O'Connell v McCormaic* [2004] FL 8800, SC. See also Breen v Fagan and MIBI [2004 SC] FL 9094. See AMENITY, LOSS OF; DAMAGES; DISFIGUREMENT; GENERAL DAMAGES; NERVOUS SHOCK.

painter. See ARTIST, TAX EXEMPTION OF; HUNT.

pais. See IN PAIS.

palimony. Slang word of American origin formed by a blend of 'pal' and 'alimony' and denoting compensation claimed by the deserted party after the separation of a couple living together out of wedlock. There is no legal basis to support a claim for *palimony* in Irish law. 'The law in this country ... would lean more strongly against such a concept having regard to the special position of marriage under the constitution.' Kelly J in *Ennis v Butterly* [1997] 1 ILRM 28, HC at 38.

palm prints. Palm prints must not be taken of a person in custody except with his written consent and, where he is under the age of 17 years, the written consent of an appropriate adult: Treatment of Persons in Custody in Garda Síochána Stations Regulations 1987, SI No 119 of 1987, reg 18. Consent is not required where the garda is otherwise empowered by law. See FINGERPRINTS.

panel. The list of persons who have been summoned to serve as jurors. See JURY.

par. The par value of a company's share is the *nominal* or theoretical specific value of the share contained in its memorandum of association. The authorised or *nominal capital* of a company is the aggregate par value of the shares which its memorandum permits it to issue to subscribers. See PREMIUM; SHARES, COMPANY.

parallel trade. The trade which occurs where an entrepreneur buys goods in one country with a view to reselling them in another country where the prices are higher. Parallel trade often takes place against the wishes of the manufacturer. In order to prevent the efforts of pharmaceutical companies to limit parallel trade, the European Commission has adopted a broad interpretation of 'agreement' within the meaning of art 81(1) of the consolidated EC Treaty (2002) version eg see Case C 277/87 *Sandoz Prodotti Farmaceutici v Commission* [1990] ECR I-45. However, see 'Bayer/Adalat – a setback for parallel trade' by Cormac Little in *Law Society Gazette* (May 2004) 52.

paramount. Superior.

paraphernalia. The apparel, ornaments and gifts given by a husband to his wife. See MATRIMONIAL PROPERTY.

parcels. (1) Parts or plots of land. (2) The part of a conveyance of land, following the operative words (qv), which describes the property and often refers to a plan drawn on the deed.

parcenary. Coparcenary (qv).

pardon. The excusing of an offence or remission of a punishment. The right of pardon and the power to commute or remit punishment imposed by a court exercising criminal jurisdiction is vested in the President of Ireland: 1937 Constitution, art 13(6). This right or power may, except in capital murder (qv), also be conferred by law on other authorities; the government is given such powers which it may delegate to the Minister: Criminal Justice Act 1951, s 23; it has done so: Criminal Justice (Miscellaneous Provisions) Act 1997, s 17.

It appears that only three Presidential pardons have been granted in the history of the State to remedy miscarriages of justice: Thomas Quinn in December 1940; Walter Brady in February 1943, both granted by President Douglas Hyde; and Edward (Nicky) Kelly in April 1992 granted by President Mary Robinson. The effect of the pardon granted to Mr Kelly was 'to put him in the same position as he would have been if he had not been convicted of the charges in question': Government Statement.

A convicted person may now petition the Minister with a view to the government advising the President to grant a pardon where the person alleges that new or newly-discovered facts show that a miscarriage of justice has occurred: Criminal Procedure Act 1993, s 7. A person so pardoned may be entitled to compensation (CPA 1993, s 9).

Extradition cannot be granted where the person whose extradition is sought: (a) has been granted a pardon under art 13.6 of the Constitution of Ireland, or (b) has become immune by virtue of any amnesty or pardon in accordance with the law of the requesting country, or (c) has, by virtue of any Act of the Oireachtas, become immune from prosecution or punishment for the act for which extradition is sought: Extradition (European Union Conventions) Act 2001, s 14.

The government decided in 1999 to grant a full pension and lump sum to William Geary, a 100-year old former Garda Superintendent, who had been dismissed from the force in 1928, acknowledging that the requirements of natural justice, as currently understood, were unlikely to have been followed in his case and that he was entitled to have his good name and reputation restored: *Irish Times* 23 April 1999. See Road Traffic Act 2002, s 9(6)(b); European Arrest Warrant Act 2003, s 39. See MISCARRIAGE; REMISSION.

parens patriae. [Parent of his country.] Expression used: (a) to describe the Attorney-General (qv) when he acts on behalf of the community to ensure that the law is enforced e g to prevent an abortion taking place. See *A-G v X* [1992] ILRM 401; (b) to describe the jurisdiction exercised by the High Court in relation to a *ward of court* (qv). See *In the matter of a Ward of Court* [1995] 2 ILRM 401, SC and [1996] 2 IR 79, SC. [Bibliography: Casey J (2).]

parent. Father or mother of another. A birth certificate is admissible in criminal proceedings as evidence of the relationship of the father or mother named therein to the person to whose birth the certificate relates: Criminal Evidence Act 1992, s 5(5). See CORPORAL PUNISHMENT; LONE PARENT.

Parent/Subsidiaries Directive. The EU Directive which is concerned with the elimination of double taxation on dividends across borders within the EU from subsidiary companies to their parent company: Directive (EEC) 90/435 as amended by Directive (EC) 2003/123. The Directive, which introduces a common system of taxation to parent companies and their subsidiaries in different member states, has been given effect in Ireland by the Taxes Consolidation Act 1997, s 831, as amended by Finance Act 1999, s 29, Finance Act 2000, s 33, and Finance Act 2004, s 34. See DIVIDEND WITHHOLDING TAX.

parentage, declaration of. A declaration by the court that a named person is the parent of the applicant: Status of Children Act 1987, ss 34–36. Applications for such a declaration are confined to persons born in the State and any other person who can show good and proper reason for applying (SCA 1987, s 35). In keeping with the policy of the Adoption Acts which secures confidentiality in regard to natural parents, applications will not be accepted from adopted children.

The court will grant the declaration sought where the fact of parentage is proved on the balance of probability. See Legitimacy Declaration Act (Ireland) 1868 for similar declaration which was available to legitimate or legitimated children but not to children whose parents were not or had not been married to each other.

A child has an unenumerated right under the Constitution, deriving from art 40.3.1, to know the identity of his or her natural parent; however the right might be restricted by the constitutional right and confidentiality of the natural mother: *I O'T v B* [1998] 2 IR 321, SC.

For the rules of court governing an application for a *declaration of parentage*, see Circuit Court Rules 2001 Ord 59, r 2 and DCR 1997 Ord 61. See BLOOD TEST; BIRTH, REGISTRATION OF; GENETIC FINGERPRINTING; PATERNITY, PRESUMPTION OF.

parental duties. Means the normal day-to-day care of the child: Adoption Act 1988, s 3(1)(I)(A) and *Northern Area Health Board v An Bord Uchtála* [2003] 1 ILRM 481, SC. Adoption is permitted where the *parents* of a child, for physical or moral reasons, have failed in their *duty* towards the child and the failure is likely to continue and it constitutes an 'abandonment of their parental rights'. See ADOPTION; PHYSICAL REASONS.

parental leave. The leave from employment without pay of 14 working weeks to which an employee, who is the natural or adoptive parent of a child, is entitled to enable him or her to take care of the child: Parental Leave Act 1998, s 6. The entitlement is in respect of a child born or adopted on or after 3 December 1993. The parental leave must end before the child is five years of age. In the case of an adopted child, the leave can be taken within two years of the adoption order, where the child is between three years and eight years old at the time of adoption.

The parental leave may be taken for a continuous period of 14 weeks, or with the agreement of the employer, in separate blocks or by working reduced hours (PLA 1998, s 7). Uncontinuous leave may be taken only pursuant to an agreement between the employer and the employee: *O'Neill v Dunne Stores* [2000] ELR 306, EAT. There is provision against abuse (e g where the leave taken is not to take care of a child) (PLA 1998, s 12). Also there is

protection of employment rights during the leave (PLA 1998, s 14). The 1998 Act implements Directive (EC) 96/34 of 3 June 1996. See Parental Leave (Disputes and Appeals) Regulations 1999, SI No 6 of 1999; Parental Leave (Maximum Compensation) Regulations 1999, SI No 34 of 1999. See Circuit Court Rules (No 2) (Parental Leave Act 1998) 2000, SI No 208 of 2000.

The 1998 Act limited entitlement to parents or adoptive parents of children born or adopted on or after 3 June 1996; however, in July 2000 eligibility was extended to 3 December 1993, following a 'reasoned opinion' from the European Commission that the 1998 legislation had not fully complied with the EU Parental Leave Directive, see SI No 231 of 2000.

For the rules governing applications to the court for the enforcement of decisions of a Rights Commissioner or determinations of the Employment Appeals Tribunal, pursuant to s 22 of the Parental Leave Act 1998, see Circuit Court Rules 2001 Ord 57, r 5. See *Report of Review of Parental Leave Act* (April 2002). See ADOPTIVE LEAVE; FORCE MAJEURE LEAVE; MATERNITY LEAVE.

parental rights, abandonment of. See ADOPTION.

parental supervision order. An order made by the court for the supervision of the parents of a child found guilty of an offence, where the court is satisfied that a wilful failure of the child's parents to take care of or control the child, contributed to the child's criminal behaviour: Children Act 2001, s 111. A *parental supervision order* may order the parents: (a) to undergo treatment for alcohol or substance abuse, (b) to participate in a course in parenting skills, (c) to control and supervise the child adequately and properly, and (d) to comply with any other instructions of the court.

parenteral administration. Means administration of a medicinal product by breach of the skin or mucous membrane: Medicinal Products (Prescription and Control of Supply) Regulations 2003, SI No 540 of 2003, reg 4(1). See OPTOMETRIST.

pares. Equals; peers.

pari passu. [With equal step.] Equally; without preference. Shares in a company of a particular class rank *pari passu* for all purposes with shares of the same class: Companies Act 1963, s 80(2). The property of a company in a voluntary winding up is applied in satisfaction of its liabilities *pari passu* (CA 1963, s 275 as amended by Companies Act 1990, s 132). See CLASS RIGHTS; SUBORDINATION.

Paris Convention. The International Convention for the Protection of Industrial Property signed in Paris in 1883 and revised on a number of occasions. Ireland formally acceded to the Convention as Saorstát Éireann on 4 December 1925. The Convention provides that, as regards the protection of industrial property, every member country will afford to nationals of other member countries the same protection as it affords to its own nationals and that the filing of an application for a *patent* in one member country gives a *right of priority* to the date of that filing in respect of corresponding applications filed in other member countries within twelve months of that date. The Patents Act 1992, s 25 provides for such *convention applications* (qv).

The Paris Convention also provides for reciprocity of treatment as between proprietors of *trade marks* in the different states which have ratified the Convention. Where a person has duly filed an application for protection of a trade mark in a Convention country, the person has a right to priority for registering the same trade mark in this State for a period of six months from the date of filing of the first Convention application: Trade Marks Act 1996, s 40. There is also protection given for well known trade marks (*Marque Notoire*) in the State even if the owner does not carry on business in the State (TMA 1996, s 61). See MADRID PROTOCOL; TRADE MARK; PATENT CO-OPERATION TREATY; EUROPEAN PATENT CONVENTION; WORLD INTELLECTUAL PROPERTY ORGANISATION.

Paris Principles. The universally accepted benchmark or blueprint for national human rights institutions adopted by the 1991 International Workshop on National Institutions for the Promotion and Protection of Human Rights, subsequently adopted by the UN General Assembly in Resolution 48/134 of 20 December 1993. In establishing the Human Rights Commission (qv), the government has indicated that the objective was to take the Paris Principles as a starting point and to endeavour to set, not follow, standards of international best practice: Explanatory Memorandum to Human Rights Commission Act 2000.

parium judicium. [Judgment of one's peers.] See JURY.

park. In relation to a vehicle, means kept or leave stationary, and cognate words are construed accordingly: Road Traffic Act 1961, s 3. See *DPP v Clancy* [1986] ILRM 268. See PARKING, DANGEROUS; PARKS, PUBLIC; TRAFFIC REGULATION.

park and ride facility. A building or structure served by a bus or train service, in use for the purpose of providing, for members of the public generally, intending to continue a journey by bus or train, parking space for mechanically propelled vehicles: Taxes Consolidation Act 1997, ss 372U–372Z inserted by Finance Act 1999, s 70 and amended by Finance Act 2000, s 46. Accelerated capital allowances of up to 100% are provided to encourage the establishment of *park and ride* facilities in the larger urban areas. For amendments to capital allowances, see Finance Act 2001, s 58. The scheme has been extended to 31 July 2006: Finance Act 2004, s 26. It was previously extended to 31 December 2004: Finance Act 2002, s 23 and Finance Act 2003, s 26. [Bibliography: Connolly, Bradley & Purcell.]

parking, dangerous. It is an offence for a person to *park* (qv) a vehicle in a *public place* if, when so parked, the vehicle would be likely to cause danger to other persons using that place: Road Traffic Act 1961, s 55 as amended by the Road Traffic Act 1968, s 52. See PUBLIC PLACE.

parks, public. The development plan (qv) of a planning authority may indicate the objective of reserving, as a public park, public garden or public recreation space, land normally used as such: Local Government (Planning and Development) Act 1963, s 19(3), Sch 3, Pt IV, para 2. Conditions may be imposed on a grant of planning permission, without creating a right to compensation, which reserves as a public park, public garden or public recreation space, land normally used as such: Local Government (Planning and Development) Act 1990, s 12 and Sch 4, para 14. See also SI No 65 of 1977, class 26. See now Planning and Development Act 2000, s 10, Sch 1, Pt III, para 1(e), and s 191, Sch 5, para 25. See NATIONAL PARK.

parliament. See EUROPEAN PARLIAMENT; NATIONAL PARLIAMENT.

parliamentary conveyance. The conveyance by operation of statute of the estate or interest of a dispossessed owner of land to a person in adverse possession, beyond the limitation period, of that land. The Law Reform Commission has recommended the introduction, by statute, of a parliamentary conveyance, in order 'to further the public interest of quieting titles, thereby freeing more land for use': *Report on Title by Adverse Possession of Land* (LRC 67, 2002).

The need for a parliamentary conveyance arises from the current position whereby a person in adverse possession (squatter) of freehold land, acquires a title which is as good as a conveyance of the freehold; however in the case of leasehold land, the squatter obtains not the leasehold estate itself but the right to hold possession of the lands during the residue of the term of the lease: *Perry v Woodfarm Homes Ltd* [1975] IR 104, SC. This leaves the squatter in a precarious position as he is liable for forfeiture at any time for breach of covenant on the part of the ousted tenant, he has no right to information about the terms of the lease, and he is not in a position to satisfy a purchaser that forfeiture is not imminent. In effect this renders the title to the land unmarketable.

The practice of the Land Registry, based on the interpretation of the word 'title' in s 49 of the Registration of Title Act 1964, is that where a person has barred the right to possession of the registered owner, he will be registered with absolute title to the existing leasehold interest, thus in effect giving a squatter the advantage of a parliamentary conveyance in the case of registered land.

The Commission has recommended that the *parliamentary conveyance* should be introduced by enacting a vesting provision drafted in simple terms so as to cover all estates or interests in land, registered or unregistered. All rights appurtenant to the lands to be vested, by virtue of the parliamentary conveyance, in the squatter should also vest in him. Where the interest to be vested in the squatter is leasehold, the squatter should have the right to serve a notice on the landlord requiring that he furnish the squatter with a copy of the lease. This will give the squatter immunity from forfeiture for breach of covenant until three months from service on the tenant of a copy of the lease. See LONG POSSESSION, TITLE BY.

parliamentary franchise. See FRANCHISE.

parliamentary privilege. The rights and immunities enjoyed by members of both Houses of the Oireachtas (qv) eg privilege from arrest in going to and from and while in the precincts of either House, freedom of debate, and privilege from defamation for utterances made in either House wherever published. See 1937 Constitution, art 15. See OIREACHTAS; UTTERANCE.

parol. Verbal or oral, not in writing or under seal (qv), eg a parol contract. See ORAL AGREEMENT.

parole. Release on licence of a prisoner who is serving a sentence. The *Parole Board* was established on an administrative basis in 2001, with the function of advising the Minister for Justice on the administration of sentences, including the granting of temporary release to prisoners. Under a direction made by the Minister for Justice, the Board is to be given access to the *book of evidence* (qv) when considering parole for murderers, with a view to making it more difficult for violent killers to secure early release: *Irish Times*, 31 January 2004. The Board has no authority to make recommendations where a sentence of less than eight years is imposed, except where a specific matter is referred to the Board by the Minister. See *Annual Report of the Parole Board 2002* (June 2003), available on website: *www.justice.ie*. See RELEASE, TEMPORARY; REMISSION; PUNISHMENT.

Part A. Formerly, the part of the register kept at the Patents Office which contained registered trade marks, which, if valid, gave the registered proprietor the exclusive right to the use of the mark in relation to the goods for which it was registered: Trade Marks Act 1963, s 12(1). The original registration was after the expiration of seven years from the date of that registration, deemed to be valid in all respects unless the registration had been obtained by fraud, or the trade mark was likely to deceive or cause confusion, or was contrary to law or morality, or was of a scandalous design (TMA 1963, s 21).

In 1996, the division of the Register of Trade Marks into Parts A and B was abolished by creating a new single Register to which they are transferred; however the validity of existing Part A and Part B registrations continue to be determined by the 1963 legislation: Trade Mark Act 1996, Sch 3, paras 2 and 13. Consequently, Part A registrations will continue to be immune to an invalidity attack after seven years. Contrast with PART B. See also TRADE MARK, REGISTERED.

Part B. Formerly, the part of the register kept at the Patents Office which contained registered trade marks, which gave the registered proprietor the same rights given by registration in Part A (qv), with the exception that registration in Part B did not become immune from invalidity attack after seven years as it did in Part A: Trade Marks Act 1963, ss 13(1) and 22.

Additionally, the registered proprietor in Part B could not obtain injunction or other relief from a defendant in an infringement action, if the defendant satisfied the Court that the use of the trade mark complained of was not likely to deceive or cause confusion or to be taken as indicating a connection in the *course of trade* (qv) between the goods and the person having the right as proprietor or as registered user of the trade mark (TMA 1963, s 13(2)). See *Bismag Ltd v Ambline (Chemists) Ltd* [1940] 57 RPC 209; *Winthrop Group v Farbenfabriken Bayer AG* [1976] RPC 469; *Eurocard International v Controller of Trade Marks* [1987] HC; *Miller Brewing Co v Controller of Trade Marks* [1988] ILRM 259.

In 1996, the division of the Register of Trade Marks into Parts A and B was abolished by creating a new single Register to which they are transferred; however the validity of existing Part A and Part B registrations continue to be determined by the 1963 legislation: Trade Mark Act 1996, Sch 3, paras 2 and 13. Consequently, Part B registrations will not be immune to an invalidity attack. See TRADE MARK, REGISTERED.

Part 4 tenancy. Means a tenancy which has qualified for the statutory protection in s 28: Residential Tenancies Act 2004, s 29. Where a person has, under a tenancy, been in occupation of a dwelling for a continuous period of six months without having been served with a notice of termination, then the tenancy continues in being for the period of four years from the commencement of the tenancy, or the *relevant date*, whichever is the later (RTA 2004, s 28). 'Relevant date' means the date on which Part 4 of the 2004 Act is commenced ie 1 September 2004 (RTA 2004, s 5). '*Continuous period of six months*' means a continuous period of six months that commences on or after the relevant date and includes a continuous period of occupation under a series of two or more tenancies (RTA 2004, ss 27 and 31). The terms of a *Part 4 tenancy* are those of the tenancy it

continues, unless varied by agreement of the parties or inconsistent with the Act (RTA 2004, s 30).

A landlord is entitled to opt out of Part 4 by written notice to the tenant before the commencement of the tenancy if the dwelling concerned is one of two dwellings within a building which as originally constructed comprised a single building, and the landlord resides in the other dwelling (RTA 2004, s 25(1)–(3)). Part 4 does not apply to: (a) certain student accommodation while attracting a tax deduction for construction expenditure, or (b) a tenancy where the entitlement of the tenant to occupy the dwelling is connected with his continuance in any office, appointment or employment (RTA 2004, s 25(4)).

If a *Part 4 tenancy* continues to the expiry of the four- year period without a notice of termination being served, a new tenancy (referred to as a 'further Part 4 tenancy') comes into being, commencing on that expiry and continuing for a further four-year period (RTA 2004, s 41). The landlord may, however, serve a notice of termination in the first six months of the *further Part 4 tenancy*, without specifying a ground (RTA 2004, s 42). The period of notice given by that notice must not be less than 112 days (16 weeks). Provision is made for successive *further Part 4 tenancies* on a rolling basis, unless terminated by the landlord or the tenant (RTA 2004, ss 43–47). The terms of a *further Part 4 tenancy* are those of the tenancy it continues, unless varied by agreement of the parties or inconsistent with the Act (RTA 2004, s 46).

No provision of any lease, tenancy agreement, contract or other agreement (whether entered into before, on or after the relevant date) may operate to vary, modify or restrict in any way a provision of Part 4 of the 2004 Act, except to confer more beneficial rights for the tenant (RTA 2004, s 54). See MULTIPLE TENANTS; SUB-TENANT.

Part 4 tenancy, assignment of. If a *Part 4 tenancy* is assigned by the tenant, with the consent of the landlord, to a sub-tenant, the security of tenure protections cease for the assignor but continue for the assignee, who becomes the tenant of the landlord: Residential Tenancies Act 2004, s 38. If the assignment is to a person other than a sub-tenant, the assignment operates to convert the *Part 4 tenancy* into a periodic tenancy and the security of tenure protections in s 28 for the assignor cease accordingly (RTA 2004, s 38(1)). The assignment of a *Part 4 tenancy* with respect to only part of the dwelling is prohibited (RTA 2004, s 38(4)). See TENANCY, FIXED TERM.

Part 4 tenancy, termination of. A tenant may terminate a *Part 4 tenancy* by serving on the landlord a notice of termination giving the required period of notice: Residential Tenancies Act 2004, s 36. A *Part 4 tenancy* terminates on the death of the tenant, except where: (a) the dwelling was occupied at the time of death by the spouse, parent, child, or a person who cohabited with the tenant as husband and wife, and (b) one or more of these elects in writing to become a tenant or tenants of the dwelling (RTA 2004, s 39). A *Part 4 tenancy* is deemed to have terminated, so that the landlord can recover possession, in certain circumstances e g where the tenant is at least 28 days in arrears of rent and vacates the dwelling without notice, or is in arrears of rent and vacates without giving the required period of notice (RTA 2004, s 37).

The landlord may terminate a *Part 4 tenancy*, without grounds, by serving a notice of determination, where the period of notice terminates on or after the period of four years of the tenancy (RTA 2004, s 34(b)). The landlord may also terminate a *Part 4 tenancy* for stated reasons on one or more of the following grounds: (1) a failure by the tenant to comply with his obligations under the tenancy, (2) the dwelling being no longer suited to the accommodation needs of the occupying household by reference to the number of bedspaces, (3) the landlord intending to enter into a contract to sell the dwelling in the next three months, (4) the landlord requiring the dwelling for his own or family member occupation, (5) the landlord intending to refurbish substantially the dwelling such that vacant possession would be required, or (6) the landlord intending to change the use of the dwelling to some other use (RTA 2004, s 34(a), Table, s 35). Any of these grounds must be cited in the termination notice. Where termination is by reason of the tenant's failure to comply with the tenancy obligations, the tenant must first be notified of the failure and the intention to terminate if the failure is not remedied within a specified reasonable time. The exception to this is in the case of anti-social behaviour that falls within the definition in paragraphs (a) and (b) of s 17(1).

A tenant, whose tenancy has been terminated on the basis of one of the grounds that relates to a landlord's intentions and the ground turned out to be false, may bring a complaint to the *Private Residential Tenancies Board* (qv) that he was unjustly deprived of possession by the landlord and the Tenancies Tribunal or an adjudicator may, if appropriate, award damages up to €20,000 (RTA 2004, ss 56 and 182). For the notice periods required for termination, see TENANCY, TERMINATION NOTICE. See also REMEDIAL ACTION.

part-payment. See SALE.

part-performance. The equitable doctrine whereby a defendant will not be permitted to escape from a contract relating to land by pleading the absence of a memorandum in writing as required by the Statute of Frauds (qv), where the plaintiff has partly performed the contract in the expectation that the defendant would perform his part. The doctrine of part-performance is based on the principles of equity and is confined to contracts of a type in relation to which specific performance can be decreed.

In order to succeed under the doctrine of part-performance it must be shown that: (a) there was a concluded contract, (b) the plaintiff acted in such a way that showed an intention to perform the contract, (c) the defendant induced such acts or stood by while they were being performed, and (d) it would be unconscionable and a breach of good faith to allow the defendant to rely upon the terms of the Statute of Frauds to prevent performance of the contract: *Mackey v Wilde* [1998] 1 ILRM 449, SC and 2 IR 578. See MEMORANDUM, STATUTE OF FRAUDS; QUANTUM MERUIT; UNENFORCEABLE.

part-time worker. A *regular part-time worker* is an employee who is normally expected to work for at least eight hours a week and who has completed thirteen weeks service: Worker Protection (Regular Part-Time Employees) Act 1991. Regular part-time workers enjoyed the same protection generally as full-time workers, and employees working for at least eight hours a week were entitled to be supplied with the terms of their employment in writing: Terms of Employment (Information) Act 1994, ss 2(1) and 3.

Generally, discrimination in conditions of employment against part-time workers, has now been removed: Protection of Employees (Part-Time Work) Act 2001. The Act provides that part-time employees, generally, may not be treated less favourably than comparable full-time employees (PE(PTW)A 2001, s 9). The conditions of a part-time employee should relate to the proportion his normal hours of work bears to the normal hours of the full-time employee (PE(PTW)A 2001, s 10).

A part-time employee may be treated less favourably: (a) if the treatment is based on objective grounds (PE(PTW)A 2001, s 9(2)); (b) in relation to pensions, if the person works less than 20% of the normal hours (PE(PTW)A 2001, s 9(4)); or (c) if the person works on a casual basis and objective grounds exist (PE(PTW)A 2001, s 11). A ground is not an *objective ground* unless the treatment is appropriate and necessary to achieve a legitimate objective of the employer (PE(PTW)A 2001, s 12).

There is provision for referral of complaints to a Rights Commissioner and for an appeal to the Labour Court, but not for members of the Defence Forces (PE(PTW)A 2001, ss 16–19 as amended by Protection of Employees (Fixed-Term Work) Act 2003, s 19(3)). The 2001 Act implements the provisions of Directive (EC) 97/81 and repeals the Worker Protection (Regular Part-Time Employees) Act 1991.

The number of part-time workers is reported to have increased from 1 in 15 of the workforce in 1987 to 1 in 8 in 2000. In a particular case, the Labour Court held that requiring a female part-time worker (a lone parent with a school-going child) to work full-time, amounted *prima facie* to indirect discrimination contrary to s 22 of the Employment Equality Act 1998: *Inoue v NBK Designs Ltd* [2003] ELR 98, LC. See *Gerster v Bayern* (2 October 1997, unreported) ECJ. For discussion on the 2001 Act, see 'Part-time workers and the Law' by solicitor Michelle Ní Longain in *Law Society Gazette* (October 2002) 19. See Pensions Act 1990, s 5 as amended by Social Welfare (Miscellaneous Provisions) Act 2004, s 23 and Schedule 2. See SOCIAL POLICY; UNFAIR DISMISSAL.

particeps criminis. [A person who shares in a crime.] An accomplice (qv).

participation.   See   WORKER PARTICIPATION.

particular average. See AVERAGE.

particular estate. An estate less than the fee simple (qv) ie given for a particular length of time. It is a term used to refer to an estate granted out of a larger estate.

particulars, land. The precise physical description of a property to be sold by auction (qv) and a short statement of the nature of the title; these are usually fixed by the auctioneer (qv) following instructions by the vendor's solicitor (qv). See CONDITIONS OF SALE; SALE OF LAND.

particulars, pleadings. The details of a claim or a defence in an action which are necessary in order to enable the other side to know what case they have to meet. A party may by letter apply to the other party for a full and better statement of the nature of the claim or defence or of *further and better particulars* of any matter stated in any pleadings or notice; the court may order such statement or particulars upon such terms, including costs, as may be just and will take into consideration such letter, but will not normally order such statement or particulars to be given before defence or reply: RSC Ord 19, r 6.

The Supreme Court has held that a High Court judge was wrong in principle in requiring a party to furnish in advance to the other party, the names of the witnesses he was going to call in relation to a specific plea in the defence or in a statement of claim: *Doyle v Independent Newspapers (Ireland) Ltd* [2001] 4 IR 594, SC. While the rules do not specifically provide for the striking out of a defence for failure to comply with an order to provide further and better particulars, the court has an inherent jurisdiction to enforce orders made by it and consequently it may dismiss a claim for want of prosecution or strike out a defence: *Church & General Insurance plc v Moore* [1996] 1 ILRM 202, SC.

It has been held that the delivery of a notice for particulars does not prevent a defendant from raising the issue of jurisdiction of the court to hear the action: *Campbell International Trading House Ltd v Peter van Aart and Natur Pur Gmbh* [1992] ILRM 663.

For the rules governing a party to proceedings in the Circuit Court, obtaining further *particulars* from another party in respect of the *claim* or the *defence*, see Circuit Court Rules 2001 Ord 17. In relation to a request of a defendant for further information in a personal injuries action, see Civil Liability and Courts Act 2004, s 11. See also *Summary Procedure and the Use of Particulars*, Doyle in 7 ILT & SJ [1989] 201. See *Cooney v Browne* [1986] ILRM 444; *Brennan v Kelly* [1988] ILRM 306; *McGee v O'Reilly* [1996] 2 IR 229, SC. See PLEADINGS; TRAVERSE.

partition. (1) The division of a country into two or more separate nations. See BOUNDARY COMMISSION; NORTHERN IRELAND.

(2) The division of land owned by persons jointly among the owners in severalty (qv). Co-owners may partition by consent of the other co-owners by deed: Real Property Act 1845. A co-owner may without the consent of his co-owners apply to the court for partition: Partition Acts 1868 and 1876. The court has power to order a sale with division of the proceeds as an alternative to partition (PA 1868, ss 3 and 4 as amended). The Court also has power to order partition of property on granting a decree of *judicial separation* (qv) or *divorce* (qv): Judicial Separation and Family Law Reform Act 1989, ss 16(1) and 30; Family Law (Divorce) Act 1996, s 15(1)(e). For application for partition of a family home, see *BM v AM* [2003] FL 7913, HC. See Domestic Violence Act 1996, s 20. See *FF v CF* [1987] ILRM 1; *M(B) v M(M)* [2000] FL 6979, HC. See RSC Ord 51, r 3. See Circuit Court Rules 2001 Ord 6, r 14.

partnership. The relationship existing between two or more persons carrying on business in common with a view of profit: Partnership Act 1890, s 1. *Business* means a series of acts which, if successful, will produce profit or gain; it includes every trade, occupation or profession; *person* means a legal person and includes human and artificial or corporate persons. There are rules in Partnership Act 1890, s 2 for determining if a partnership exists.

The essential difference between a partnership and a company is that the former has no legal personality, whereas a company is a body corporate. The property of a partnership firm belongs to the individual members. They are collectively entitled to it, whereas the property of a company belongs to the company. Creditors of a partnership firm are creditors of the members of the firm and on a judgment can levy execution on the property of the partners of the firm; whereas, judgment against a company ordinarily gives no right to levy execution against the members. A partner cannot contract with his firm, whereas a member of a company can contract with the company.

There are two types of partnership: the *ordinary partnership* which is governed by the Partnership Act 1890 and the *limited partnership* formed under the Limited Partnership Act 1907. The ordinary partnership is an important feature in the State, particularly in the field of the professions; however very few limited partnerships are formed. There is now a very special type of *limited partnership*; for details, see INVESTMENT LIMITED PARTNERSHIP.

The rights of partners, between themselves, are governed by the partnership agreement or contract or the deed of partnership or partnership articles, if any. Where members of a partnership set up business under the aegis of a company, the company has its own legal personality with its own rights and duties, together with the rights and duties of shareholders: *Bayworld Investments v McMahon and Others* [2003] FL 8051, HC. However, provision has been made recently to extend employment equality legislation to partnerships: Employment Equality Act 1998, s 13A inserted by Equality Act 2004, s 7.

A formal document is not necessary to create a partnership; there may be an implied partnership from the acts of the parties thereto: see *Greenham v Gray* [1855] 4 ICLR 501. The receipt by a person of a share in the profits of a business is *prima facie* evidence that he is a partner in the business, but the receipt of a share or payment contingent on or varying with the profits does not of itself make someone a partner in a business: *O'Kelly v Darragh* [1988] ILRM 309.

As regards taxation, each partner is taxed on the profits from his share of the partnership trade. See Taxes Consolidation Act 1997, ss 1007–1013. The right of limited partners and certain general partners to set off losses, interest and capital allowances of the partnership against non-partnership interest is restricted (TCA 1997, s 1013). The restrictions now apply also to non-active partners in partnerships generally: Finance Act 2000, s 70 amending s 1013. See Companies (Amendment) Act 1986 implementing the EC 4th Directive (Annual Accounts) and the 1992 Group Account Regulations now apply to partnerships with unlimited liability in which the members are themselves limited companies: EC (Account) Regulations 1993, SI No 396 of 1993. See Copyright and Related Rights Act 2000, s 13. See Listing Rules 2000, para 6F.1(b). See Industrial Designs Act 2001, s 7. See *Macken v Revenue Commissioners* [1962] IR 302; *Meagher v Meagher* [1961] IR 96; *Williams v Harris* [1980] SC. See also RSC Ord 46, rr 3–4. See 'Equal Partners' by solicitor Ciaran O'Mara in *Law Society Gazette* (April 2004) 30. [Bibliography: Keane (1); O'Callaghan P; Twomey; Lindley (UK); Palmer (UK).] See AUDIT; BARRISTERS, PARTNERSHIP OF; FIRM; LIMITED PARTNERSHIP; PRECEDENT PARTNER; PUBLIC PRIVATE PARTNERSHIP ARRANGEMENT.

partnership, bankruptcy and. One or more partners may be adjudicated a bankrupt on the presentation of a petition by a creditor whose debt is sufficient ie £1,500/€1,905: Bankruptcy Act 1988, ss 31 and 8. An adjudication may not be made against the firm, (even though it is permissible to take proceedings or be proceeded against in the name of the firm), but such adjudication will be made against the partner(s) individually with the addition of the firm name (BA 1988, s 36).

The bankrupt partner must deliver to the Official Assignee (qv) a separate *statement of affairs* in respect of the partnership, and the other partners must also deliver such accounts and information as the Official Assignee deems necessary (BA 1988, ss 32–33).

The joint property of partners is applied in the first instance in payment of their joint debts, their separate property being applied to their separate debts. Where there is a surplus of the joint property, it is dealt with as part of the separate properties in proportion to the right and interest of each partner in the joint property. Where there is a surplus of any separate property it is dealt with as part of the joint property so far as necessary to meet any deficiency in the joint property (BA 1988, s 34). See also BA 1988, ss 74, 106, and 138. See ARRANGING DEBTOR; BANKRUPTCY; LIMITED PARTNERSHIP.

partnership, dissolution of. Dissolution of a partnership takes place, in general, by agreement, by conduct, or by bankruptcy or death of one of the partners, or by intervening illegality, or by court order on the grounds of insanity, incapacity, misconduct of a partner, or where the court considers it just and equitable: Partnership Act 1890, ss 32–35; RSC Ord 76, r 43. The court has a discretion not to award costs, arising from a dissolution, out of the partnership assets: *Baxter v Horgan* [1992] 10 ILT Dig 55, SC.

Where no time limit of a partnership is fixed, it is called a *partnership at will* and may be dissolved by any partner at any time by giving notice (PA 1890, s 26(1)). The High Court is empowered to wind up and settle the affairs of a partnership in which a bankrupt (qv) has an interest: Bankruptcy Act 1988, s 138. See *Larkin v Groeger & Eaton* 7 ILT Dig [1989] 53. See CLIENT FILE; INVESTMENT LIMITED PARTNERSHIP.

partnership, liability in. In an ordinary partnership, each partner is liable with unlimited liability for the debts of the partnership to the whole extent of his property. As between partners, each partner is bound to contribute to the debts in proportion to his share of the profits unless otherwise agreed. As regards third parties, the act of each partner, within the ordinary scope of the business, binds his co-partners whether they sanctioned it or not: Partnership Act 1890, s 5.

An act or instrument relating to the business of the firm and done or executed in the firm's name, or in any other manner showing an intention to bind the firm, by any person so authorised, whether a partner or not, is binding on the firm and on all the partners (PA 1890, s 6). See *Allied Pharmaceutical Distributors Ltd v Robert J Kidney* [1991] 2 IR 8. See FRAUD; INVESTMENT LIMITED PARTNERSHIP; LIMITED PARTNERSHIP.

partnership, number to form. The minimum number of persons who can form a partnership is two, while the maximum number of a partnership formed for the purpose of carrying on business with the object of acquisition of gain is 20. There are important exceptions in the case of partnerships involving bankers, solicitors and accountants: Companies Act 1963, ss 372 and 376; Companies (Amendment) Act 1982, s 13, as amended by Companies (Auditing and Accounting) Act 2003, s 55. See INVESTMENT LIMITED PARTNERSHIP.

partridge. See GAME.

party. A person who sues or is sued; a person who takes part in a legal transaction eg a party to a contract. A party also includes every person served with notice of or attending any proceedings, although not named on the record: RSC Ord 125, r 1.

A party includes any person entitled to appear and be heard in relation to any action, application, suit or other proceeding: Circuit Court Rules 2001, Interpretation of Terms, para 18. Persons may be joined in one action as plaintiffs and joined as defendants: Circuit Court Rules 2001 Ord 6(1) and (2).

Where a bankrupt (qv) is a party to a contract jointly with any other person, that other person may sue or be sued in respect of the contract without joining the bankrupt: Bankruptcy Act 1988, s 35.

In a particular case, it was held that the word 'parties' should be interpreted as the 'relevant parties': *McCarthy v An Bord Pleanála* [2000] 1 IR 42, HC. See DEFENDANT; PLAINTIFF.

party and party costs. The costs incurred in contentious legal matters involving two or more parties, which were necessary or proper for the attainment of justice or for enforcing or defending the rights of the party whose costs are being *taxed*; the successful litigant is generally entitled to his costs on this basis. 'Party and party costs are simply the costs that a successful party receives from the opposing party in an action': James Flynn, taxing master, High Court in 'Solicitors' Costs and the Client' *Law Society Gazette* (July/August 2002) 18. Compare with *solicitor and client costs* (qv).

As a general principle *luxury* payments are not recoverable on party and party taxation; *luxury* payments are charges merely for conducting litigation more conveniently and must be paid by the party incurring them: *Tobin & Twomey Services Ltd v Kerry Foods Ltd* [1999] 1 ILRM 428, HC. [Bibliography: Flynn & Halpin.] See RSC Ord 99, r 10. See COSTS IN CIVIL PROCEEDINGS; TAXATION OF COSTS.

party wall. The wall between adjoining properties. The general presumption at common law is that adjoining property owners are *tenants-in-common* (qv) of the party wall with mutual rights of support: *Jones v Read* [1876] IR 10 CL 315; *Miley v Hutchinson* [1940] Ir Jur Rep 37. This presumption can be rebutted e g by evidence that the wall was built entirely on one owner's land: *Barry v Dowling* [1968] HC. An owner is entitled to build a party wall (or banks, trenches, or fences) between adjoining lands and charge half the cost to his neighbour: Boundaries Act (Ireland)

1721. See also Dublin Corporation Act 1890, ss 3–5 and 9–12.

pass book. The book in which is recorded the amount invested by a saver in a bank or building society and also subsequent investments and withdrawals. Includes any type of written statement of account: Credit Union Act 1997, s 2(1). A pass book entry does not on its own, give an investor a legal entitlement to the sum entered: *Leen v Irish Permanent Building Society* [1976]; Report of Registrar of Friendly Societies (1981) p 12.

passenger. A person who is carried in a conveyance for reward. Any person carried on a vessel (qv) other than: (a) the owner, or (b) a person to whom the vessel is on hire, or (c) a person employed or engaged in any capacity on board the vessel or (d) a shipwrecked or distressed person: Merchant Shipping Act 1992, s 2(1). See also Merchant Shipping (Safety Convention) Act 1952, s 43. See MARITIME CLAIMS; PASSENGER BOAT; PASSENGER SHIP; SERVICE, SUPPLY OF.

passenger boat. A vessel carrying not more than twelve passengers for reward or on hire excluding a passenger ship (qv) with a certificate: Merchant Shipping Act 1992, s 2(1) as amended by Merchant Shipping (Investigation of Marine Casualties) Act 2000, s 44(1)(b). A vessel must not be used as a passenger boat unless a licence is in force in respect of it (MSA 1992, s 14); the licence will specify the limits (if any) beyond which the vessel shall not ply and the maximum passengers that the vessel is fit to carry (MSA 1992, s 15). Where passengers are carried on board a vessel, there is a presumption that the carriage is for reward unless the contrary is proved (MSA 1992, s 32(2)). A passenger boat must have painted on it 'licensed to carry ... passengers' (MSA 1992, s 17(2)).

The Minister may by regulation exempt from the licensing requirement specified vessels: Merchant Shipping (Miscellaneous Provisions) Act 1998, s 4. Also the 1998 Act brought 'a ferry boat working in chains' within the scope of the 1992 Act. The Minister may make regulations for the purpose of ensuring the safety of passenger boats (and unlicensed vessels) and their passengers and crew. For other amendments to 1992 Act, see MS(IMC)A 2000, s 44. For new safety requirements, see Merchant Shipping (Passenger Boat) Regulations 2002, SI No 273 of 2002, and

Amendment Regulations 2002 and 2003, SI No 555 of 2002 and SI No 648 of 2003; Licensing of Passenger Boats (Exemption) Regulations 2002, SI No 274 of 2002, and Amendment Regulations 2002, SI No 556 of 2002. See FISHING VESSEL; PASSENGER; SHIP.

passenger road service. A service provided for separate charges in respect of each passenger; it is an offence to carry on such a service without a licence: Road Transport Act 1932. To constitute an offence, the person who received the separate charges from each passenger is required to be the person who owned or otherwise controlled the vehicle: *DPP v Go-Travel Ltd* [1991] ILRM 577, SC. See also *Lovett v Gogan* [1995] 1 ILRM 12, SC and 3 IR 132.

passenger ship. A vessel carrying more than twelve passengers, excluding a vessel carrying passengers to or from the State; a vessel includes any ship or boat and any other vessel used in navigation: Merchant Shipping Act 1992, s 2(1) as amended by Merchant Shipping (Investigation of Marine Casualties) Act 2000, s 44(1)(c). A vessel must not be used as a passenger ship unless a certificate is in force in relation to it (MSA 1992, s 12) and a policy of insurance is also in force (MSA 1992, s 13). There is also a requirement for a survey at least once a year (MSA 1992, s 6). The certificate will specify the limits (if any) beyond which the vessel shall not ply and the maximum passengers that the vessel may carry (MSA 1992, s 8). A 'ferry boat working in chains' is now brought within the scope of the 1992 Act: Merchant Shipping (Miscellaneous Provisions) Act 1998, s 4. For other amendments to 1992 Act, see MS(IMC)A 2000, s 44. See EC (Passenger Ships) Regulations 2002, SI No 419 of 2002 as amended by SI No 34 of 2004 which introduce a uniform level of safety of life and property on new and existing passenger ships and high-speed craft, implementing Directives (EC) 98/18 and 2002/25. See also SIs No 636 and 637 of 2003. See MARITIME CLAIMS; PASSENGER; SHIP.

passim. [In various places; here and there.] Term used in relation to a reference appearing throughout a book.

passing of Act. The day of the *passing* of every Act is the day on which the Bill for such Act is signed by the President of Ireland: Interpretation Act 1937, s 8(1). See ACT.

passing off. A tort committed by a person who, in a manner calculated to deceive, passes off his goods or business as those of another eg by use of a similar name or trade mark (qv) or description or appearance. Passing off has evolved so that it is no longer restricted to a trader representing his own goods as the goods of somebody else: *An Post v Irish Permanent plc* [1995] 1 ILRM 336, HC and 1 IR 140. Isolated incidents of confusion of identification do not in themselves amount to passing off, as the essence of the tort is that there must be a misrepresentation which would lead a third party to believe that the defendant's business was that of the plaintiff: *Private Research Ltd v Brosnan* [1996] 1 ILRM 24, HC.

The tort includes the incorporation of a company with a name likely to give an impression to the public that it is a subsidiary or branch of another company which has established goodwill: *Guinness v Kilkenny Brewing Co Ltd* [1999] 1 ILRM 531, HC. In that case the court held that the plaintiff had an established goodwill in the name 'Kilkenny' when used in connection with beer.

A court will pay no regard to market research evidence in relation to the likelihood of confusion; the judge, as an ordinary shopper or consumer is in a position, just as well as others, to assess the likelihood of confusion: *Symonds Cider v Showerings (Ireland) Ltd* [1997] 1 ILRM 481, HC.

The remedies for a plaintiff are damages, an account, and an injunction to restrain the defendant for the future. Actual deception or an intention to deceive is not necessary to ground an action in passing off, but proof of such an intention or that a member of the consuming public has been deceived, will help the plaintiff's case. In relation to the name of goods, the test is whether the name used connotes goods manufactured or sold by another or is merely descriptive of the goods.

In relation to packaged goods, the court will consider the general *get up* of the packages; their size and shape; the material used; the combination of colours; the decoration and lettering; the arrangement of labels; the spacing of words; and the overall picture presented from the entire combination.

The law of passing off is not affected by legislation on trade marks: Trade Marks

Act 1996, s 7(2). However, a trade mark will not be registered if its use in the State is liable to be prevented by virtue of any law, including the law of passing off (TMA 1996, s 10(4)(a)).

See *Polycell Products Ltd v O'Carroll* [1959] Ir Jur Rep 34; *American Cyanamid v Ethicon Ltd* [1975] AC 396; *C & A Modes v C & A (Waterford) Ltd* [1976] IR 198; *Adidas Sportsschuhfabriken Adi Dasler K A v Charles O'Neill & Co Ltd* [1980] HC; *Three Stripes International v Charles O'Neill & Co Ltd* [1988] IR 144; *Campus Oil Ltd v Minister for Energy* [1983] IR 88; *Falcon Travel Ltd v Owners Abroad Group plc* [1991 HC] 1 IR 175 and *Coughlan* in 9 ILT & SJ [1991] 138; *Muckross Park Hotel v Randles & Dromhall Hotel Co Ltd* [1995 HC] 1 IR 130; *An Bord Trachtala v Waterford Foods plc* [1993 HC] 11 ILT Dig 212; *B & S Ltd v Irish Auto Trader Ltd* [1995] 2 ILRM 152, HC and 2 IR 142; *Local Ireland Ltd v Local Ireland-Online Ltd* [2000] 4 IR 567, HC. [Bibliography: Clark & Smyth; Wadlow UK.] See INFRINGEMENT OF TRADE MARK; NAME OF COMPANY.

passport. A document which contains particulars which enables the holder to be identified and which is intended to allow the holder to pass from one country to another without let or hindrance. Responsibility for issuing passports and visas rests with the Department of Foreign Affairs: Ministers and Secretaries Act 1924, s 1(xi).

Every person landing in the State must be in possession of a valid passport or other equivalent document which establishes his identity and nationality to the satisfaction of an immigration officer: Immigration Act 2004, s 11. There is an exemption for persons under the age of 16 years and for persons (other than non-nationals) coming from or embarking for a place in the State, Great Britain and Northern Ireland.

A citizen has a constitutional right to a passport: The State (KM RD) v The Minister for Foreign Affairs [1979] IR 73. A citizen over 18 years of age will be granted a passport who complies with the application requirements e g identity and signature certified by a garda. A child will be included on a parent's passport but only with the consent of the other parent: Cosgrove v Ireland Ors [1982] ILRM 48. From 1 October 2004, new applications for a child must be for an individual passport for that child. Children already on a parent's passport may continue to travel to most

countries until passport renewal, but there are exceptions e g USA, Czech Republic and Estonia. A child will be issued with a separate passport but only with the consent of both parents. See also *(P)I v Ireland* [1989] ILRM 810, SC.

The removal from the State of a child under seven years of age who is an Irish citizen is prohibited: (a) without the approval of parents who are married to each other, or (b) without the approval of the mother, guardian or a maternal relation of the child where the child's parents are not married to each other: Adoption Act 1952, s 40. See also Child Care Act 1991, s 18(4). The Minister must comply with the rules of *natural justice* when he intends to refuse to renew a passport: *Sohail Akram v Minister for Justice* (2000) Irish Times, 13 January, HC.

From 1 October 2003, all Irish passport holders visiting the United States require an individual machine-readable passport to avail of the US Visa Waiver Programme. See also Maritime Security Act 2004, s 8. For information on passport matters, see website: *www.irlgov.ie/iveagh*; email: *passportdublin@iveagh.irlgov.ie*; *passportcork@iveagh.irlgov.ie*. See BANGEMANN WAVE; BIOMETRICS; COMMON TRAVEL AREA; PREINSPECTION; SCHENGEN AGREEMENTS; TRAVEL, RIGHT TO.

past consideration. See CONSIDERATION.

pasturage. The right to graze animals on the lands of another. [Bibliography: Bland (1).] See COLLOP; PROFIT A PRENDRE; RUNDALE SYSTEM.

patent. An exclusive right conferred pursuant to Part II and Part III of the Patents Act 1992 (PA 1992, s 2(1)). A patent while it is in force confers on its proprietor the right to prevent all third parties from directly or indirectly using the subject matter of the patent (PA 1992, ss 40–41). It is, in effect, a bargain between the State and the inventor, whereby he is given a monopoly right in his invention for a period of time, in return for the disclosure of his invention.

There are four classes of patent: (1) a *European patent* as granted by the European Patents Office under the European Patent Convention (EPC) which when granted is, in so far as Ireland has been designated, equivalent to an Irish patent; an 'international application' under the Patent Cooperation Treaty (qv) which designates

Ireland is deemed to be an application for a European Patent (PA 1992, ss 119–132); (2) an *Irish Patent* granted by the Controller of Patents, Designs and Trade Marks and governed by Irish law which while closely modelled on the EPC is fully under the jurisdiction of the Irish Courts and Patents Office (PA 1992, ss 6–62); (3) a *short-term Irish patent* with a different standard of inventive step required; and (4) a proposed *Community Patent* applicable to member States of the EC and subject to a common system of laws (1937 Constitution, art 29(4)(11)).

Only certain inventions are patentable. Priority is given on the basis of the date of filing of an application for a patent or on a priority date arising from Ireland's membership of the Paris Convention (qv). The applicant must *disclose* the invention. The Controller of Patents publishes the notice of grant of a patent in the Patents Office Journal.

A patent may be subject to *licences of right* (qv) and there are provisions governing the issue of compulsory licences. A patent once granted can be revoked by the High Court. Renewal fees must be paid annually and there is an annual maintenance fee on pending applications. Infringement (qv) of a patent can be prevented by injunction and an action for damages.

Apart from the changes in the classes of patents, the main changes made by the 1992 legislation are: (a) longer patent life (20 years instead of 16 years) and no extensions; (b) abolition of opposition to the grant of a patent, abolition of *patents of addition* and of *provisional* patent protection; (c) minimising of responsibility of Patents Office for examination; and (d) expansion of infringement of patent to include indirect use of an invention.

Where proceedings in relation to a patent are pending before an Irish court and the European Patent Office, a stay should be granted in relation to the Irish proceedings unless there are very good reasons to the contrary: *Merck & Co v G D Searle & Co* [2001] 2 ILRM 363, HC and [2002] 3 IR 614. See *McDermott Laboratories Ltd v Controller of Patents* [1998] 2 IR 276, SC. See Patent Rules 1992, SI No 179 of 1992. See EC Treaty, art 81(1) of the consolidated (2002) version.

A number of amendments to PA 1992 are proposed in draft legislation: (a) to update the law so that it accords with the provisions of the Agreement on Trade Related Aspects of Intellectual Property Rights (*TRIPs Agreement*); and (b) to keep Irish patent law in line with recent and projected changes in the European Patent Convention and practice thereunder: Patents (Amendment) Bill 1999.

For information on over 30 million patents worldwide and advice on searching them, see website: *www.patent.gov.uk*. [Bibliography: Clark & Smyth; Murdoch (1); Terrell UK.] See COMMERCIAL PROCEEDINGS; COMMUNITY PATENT AGREEMENT; EUROPEAN PATENT CONVENTION; EXCLUSIVE JURISDICTION; FOOD AND MEDICINE; INFRINGEMENT OF PATENT; PATENTABLE INVENTION; PATENT RIGHTS; PRIORITY DATE; REGISTER OF PATENTS; ROYALTY; SIMULTANEOUS INVENTION; TRIPS AGREEMENT.

patent, application for. An application for a patent, must contain: (a) a request for a grant of a patent; (b) a specification containing a description of the invention; and (c) an abstract: Patents Act 1992, ss 15, 18, 21, 22. The application, not necessarily from the inventor, must also *disclose* the invention in a manner sufficiently clear and complete for it to be carried out by a person skilled in the art (PA 1992, s 19). The *claim* must define the matter for which protection is sought, be clear and concise and be supported by the description (PA 1992, s 20). There are special provisions governing an application for a *short-term patent* (qv).

patent, infringement of. See INFRINGEMENT OF PATENT.

patent, qualifying. See QUALIFYING PATENT.

patent, revocation of. A patent may be revoked on the application of any person on the grounds that: (a) the subject-matter of the patent is not patentable; (b) the specification of the patent does not disclose the invention sufficiently; (c) the matter disclosed in the specification extends beyond that disclosed in the application as filed; (d) the patent protection has been extended by an amendment of the application or the specification; (e) the proprietor of the patent is not entitled to the patent grant: Patents Act 1992, ss 57–58. The Controller of Patents has power to revoke a patent on his own initiative eg lack of novelty apparent after grant, or duplication of patent with European Patent already granted (PA 1992, s 60). A short-term patent (qv) may also be revoked. See *Wavin Pipes Ltd v Hepworth Iron Co Ltd* [1981] HC.

patent, surrender of. The proprietor of a patent may at any time by written notice given to the Controller of Patents offer to surrender his patent: Patents Act 1992, s 39. The patent ceases to have effect from the date when notice of acceptance is published in the Patents Office Journal (PA 1992, s 39(5)). Opposition may be made eg by a licensee. See Patent Rules 1992, SI No 179 of 1992, r 40.

patent, term of. See TERM OF PATENT.

patent agent. A person who carries on the business of acting as agent for others for the purpose, *inter alia*, of applying for patents. Any act which has to be done by or to any person in connection with a patent or any procedure relating to a patent or the obtaining thereof, the act may be done by or to an agent: Patents Act 1992, s 105(1). A person acting for gain must not, either alone or in partnership with any other person, practise, describe himself or hold himself out as a patent agent, unless he is registered as a patent agent in the register of patent agents, or as the case may be, unless he and all his partners are so registered (PA 1992, s 106(2)(a)). There are similar provisions for a company practising as a patent agent.

There are similar prohibitions in relation to European Patents unless the agent is on the list of professional representatives, called European Patent Attorneys, maintained by the European Patents Office (PA 1992, s 125).

As regards privileged communications, a patent agent is a person registered as a patent agent, a company or partnership lawfully practising as a patent agent in the State or a person or partnership which satisfies the requirements of the European Patent Convention (PA 1992, s 94(3)). See Register of Patent Agent Rules 1992, SI No 180 of 1992. A patent agent has certain privileges and immunities when appearing in proceedings before an international arbitral tribunal: Arbitration (International Commercial) Act 1998, s 12(8).

A registered *patent agent* or registered *trade mark agent* may act for applicants to register designs or for proprietors of registered designs: Industrial Designs Act 2001, s 88. The European Court of Justice has found that certain requirements regarding patent agents providing services in Italy (eg having a residence or place of business in Italy) were contrary to the provisions in the Treaty regarding freedom to provide services: Case C-131/01 *Commission v Italian Republic* [2003] ECJ. See DESIGN.

patent ambiguity. See AMBIGUITY.

Patent Co-operation Treaty; PCT. The Treaty of 1970 which has as its object to simplify and render more economical the obtaining of protection for inventions where protection is sought in several countries (art 1(2)). It is not intended to diminish rights under the Paris Convention (qv).

Under the Treaty, where patent protection is sought in a member of the contracting States, a single *international application* may be filed at one of the *receiving offices*, which will usually be the applicant's local national patent office, and the application will have a right of priority from the date of such filing.

A novelty search is carried out by an international search authority whose report is furnished to the national patent office in each country in which protection is sought and a grant of a patent is made under the authority of that national office.

Under Irish law, an international application under the PCT which designates the State is deemed to be an application for a European Patent designating the State; consequently it will only be possible to designate Ireland through a PCT application in the context of a European application: Patents Act 1992, s 127. See EUROPEAN PATENT AGREEMENT.

patent defect. See DEFECT.

patent of addition. Formerly, the patent which was granted where there had been an improvement in or modification of an invention for which a patent had been granted or applied for: Patents Act 1964, s 28. There is no provision for patents of addition in the Patents Act 1992 which repeals the 1964 Act.

patent rights. (1) The right conferred on the proprietor of a patent to prevent all third parties not having his consent from making various direct uses of the invention according as to whether the invention is a product, a process, or the product of a process: Patents Act 1992, s 40. The right is also conferred to prevent indirect use of the invention (PA 1992, s 41). The rights do not extend to acts done for non-commercial purposes, or acts done for experimental purposes, or to prevent the free circulation throughout the EC of patented products put on the market in a member state by the proprietor (PA 1992, ss 42–43). The extent of protection conferred by a patent is determined by the terms of the *claim* filed as part of the application for a patent (PA 1992, s 45).

(2) The right to do or to authorise the doing of anything which would, but for that right, be an infringement of a patent: Income Tax Act 1967, s 284, now Taxes Consolidation Act 1997, s 754. See INFRINGEMENT OF PATENT.

patent royalty. See QUALIFYING PATENT; ROYALTY.

patentable invention. An invention to be patentable must be susceptible of *industrial application*, it must be *new* and must involve an *inventive step*: Patents Act 1992, s 9(1). An invention is considered susceptible of *industrial application* if it can be made or used in any kind of industry, including agriculture (PA 1992, s 14). An invention will be considered *new* if it does not form part of the state of art, which comprises everything made available to the public (whether in the State or elsewhere) by means of a written or oral description, by use, or in any other way, before the date of filing of the patent application (PA 1992, s 11). An invention will be considered as involving an *inventive step* if, having regard to the state of art, it is not obvious to a person skilled in the art (PA 1992, s 13). There are special requirements in respect of a short-term patent (qv).

Any of the following are not to be regarded as an invention capable of being patented: (a) a discovery, a scientific theory or a mathematical method; (b) an aesthetic creation; (c) a scheme, rule or method for performing a mental act, playing a game or doing business, or a program for a computer; (d) the presentation of information; (e) a method (other than a product) for treatment of the human or animal body by surgery or therapy and a diagnostic method practised on human or animal body (PA 1992, s 9). Also a patent cannot be granted in respect of a plant or animal variety (other than a microbiological process) or an invention the publication or exploitation of which would be contrary to public order or morality (PA 1992, s 10). See SIMULTANEOUS INVENTION.

patented. The words *patent* or *patented* on a product without the number of the patent is ineffective to make a defendant in a patent infringement action aware that a patent has been obtained for the product:

Patents Act 1992, s 49(1). A person is guilty of an offence, who falsely represents that an article sold by him is patented; it is sufficient for the offence that the article has on it the words *patent* or *patented* or any words expressing or implying that the article is patented (PA 1992, s 112). See INFRINGEMENT OF PATENT.

patents, register of. The register in which is required to be entered particulars of published patent applications, of patents in force, of assignments and transmissions of, and of licences under, patents and published applications: Patents Act 1992, s 84.

patents office. The office established by statute and continued in being for the registration of patents, designs and trade marks: Patents Act 1992, s 6. It is under the control of the Controller of Patents (qv).

patents office journal. The Journal in which is published by the Controller of Patents all matters which he is directed by law to publish in the Journal and also such matters and information as appear to him to be useful or important in relation to patents or applications for patents: Patents Act 1992, s 100. The Controller is required to publish a notice of all patent grants, including a specification of the patent containing the description and claims, and drawings if any (PA 1992, s 34); and also entries in the register of licences of right (PA 1992, s 68(5)).

pater est quem nuptiae demonstrant. [He is the father whom marriage indicates.] See PATERNITY, PRESUMPTION OF.

paternity, presumption of. Where a married woman, or a woman whose marriage terminated less than ten months beforehand, gives birth to a child, her husband is presumed to be the father of the child (previously, such a child was presumed to be legitimate): Status of Children Act 1987, s 46. However, where the husband and wife are living apart under a decree of *divorce a mensa et thoro* (qv) or a judicial separation (qv) for more than ten months before the birth, the husband will be presumed not to be the child's father (formerly, such a child was presumed to be illegitimate). The person named as father in the births register kept under the Births and Deaths Registration Acts is presumed to be the father of the child.

These presumptions are rebuttable on the normal standard of proof in civil proceedings ie the balance of probability. Formerly, rebuttal of the presumption of legitimacy required to be proved beyond reasonable doubt. 'The truth should prevail over the presumption of legitimacy': *JPD v MG* [1991] ILRM 217, SC. See BIRTH, REGISTRATION OF; MARITAL STATUS; PARENTAGE, DECLARATION OF.

paternity right. See MORAL RIGHT.

patient, consent of. 'It is accepted that consent is implied in many circumstances by the very fact that the patient has come to the doctor for medical care. There are however situations where verbal and if appropriate written consent is necessary for investigation and treatment. Informed consent can only be obtained by a doctor who has sufficient training and experience to be able to explain the intervention, the risks and benefits and the alternatives. In obtaining this consent the doctor must satisfy himself/herself that the patient understands what is involved by explaining in appropriate terminology. A record of this discussion should be made in the patient's notes': Medical Council, *A Guide to Ethical Conduct and Behaviour* (6th edn, 2004) para 17.1.

In an emergency where consent cannot be obtained (eg an unconscious patient or a child not accompanied by a parent of guardian), a doctor may provide treatment that is necessary to safeguard the patient's life or health (para 18.4). Most patients with psychiatric illness are competent to give consent, and where not, the provisions of the Mental Health Act 2001 may nominate a process to give consent (para 18.2). Any decision on intervention/non-intervention in the case of a person with a disability requires his consent (para 2.2). If he lacks the capacity to give consent, a wide-ranging consultation should occur, with a second opinion considered before decisions on complex issues are raised. As regards children and consent, see CHILD, MEDICAL TREATMENT OF. See also CLINICAL TRIALS, CONDUCT OF; DYING PATIENT; MEDICAL TREATMENT; SERIOUSLY ILL PATIENT; SURGICAL OPERATION.

patient, dignity of. 'Patients must always be treated with dignity and respect. Rude and insensitive behaviour towards patients or their relatives is unacceptable': Medical Council, *A Guide to Ethical Conduct and Behaviour* (6th edn, 2004) para 3.2.

patient, information for. 'In general, doctors should ensure that a patient and family members, subject to patient consent, are as fully informed as possible about matters relating to an illness': Medical Council, *A Guide to Ethical Conduct and Behaviour* (6th edn, 2004) para 3.3. The aim is to promote understanding and compliance with recommended therapy. See SURGICAL OPERATION.

patient, photograph of. 'Identifiable audio-visual or photographic recording of a patient, or a relative of a patient, should only be taken with informed and appropriate consent': Medical Council, *A Guide to Ethical Conduct and Behaviour* (6th edn, 2004) para 16.9. The taking of photographs, digital and video recording for teaching purposes also requires the patient's informed consent (para 19.2). As far as possible these images should be taken in such a manner that a third party cannot identify the patient concerned. If the patient is identifiable, the patient should be informed about the security, storage, and eventual destruction of the record.

patient, responsibility to. 'Doctors must do their best to preserve life and promote health. Once they undertake the care of patients they should ordinarily provide continuity of care for the duration of the illness': Medical Council, *A Guide to Ethical Conduct and Behaviour* (6th edn, 2004) para 2.1. Treatment must never be refused on grounds of moral disapproval of the patient's behaviour (para 2.5).

patient charges. Statutory provision has been made to permit health boards to impose charges in respect of hospital services provided for persons entitled to recover damages or compensation for injuries sustained in a road traffic accident: Health (Amendment) Act 1986. This statutory provision reverses the effect of *Cooke v Walsh* [1984] ILRM 208. See KINLEN ORDER; ROAD TRAFFIC ACCIDENTS.

pawn. To pledge a chattel as security for a debt. The pawner parts with its possession to the pawnee (lender). The pawnee has a power of sale in default of redemption by the pawner. Any person who buys, takes in exchange, or takes in pawn a social welfare document is guilty of an offence: Social Welfare (Consolidation) Act 1993, s 227. See DURESS OF GOODS; PAWNBROKER.

pawn-ticket. A receipt in prescribed form which a pawnbroker is required to give to a pawner on taking a pledge (qv) in pawn: Pawnbrokers Act 1964, s 14 as amended by Consumer Credit Act 1995, Sch 8. A *special contract pawn-ticket* is required where the pawnbroker enters into a special contract in respect of a pledge (PA 1964, s 15 as amended by CCA 1995, Sch 8).

pawnbroker. (1) Includes any person who carries on the business of taking goods and chattels in pawn and in particular includes any person who: (a) receives or takes from any other person any goods or chattels by way of security for the repayment of any sum of money not exceeding £5,000/€6,349 advanced thereon; or (b) purchases, or receives or takes in, goods or chattels and pays or advances or lends thereon any sum of money not exceeding £5,000/€6,349 with or under an agreement or understanding expressed or implied or from the nature of the transaction to be reasonably inferred that those goods or chattels may be afterwards redeemed or purchased on any terms: Pawnbrokers Act 1964, s 2 as amended by Consumer Credit Act 1995, Part XV, and Sch 8.

(2) '*Pawnbroker*' means the holder of a licence granted under section 8 of the Pawnbrokers Act 1964 (CCA 1995, s 2(1) inserted as by Central Bank and Financial Services Authority of Ireland Act 2003, s 35, Sch 1).

It is an offence for a person to carry on the business of pawnbroker at any premises unless he holds a licence which is in force in respect of those premises; the licence is granted by the Director of Consumer Affairs (PA 1964, s 7 as amended by CCA 1995, s 153). The holder of a *pawn-ticket* (qv) is entitled to redeem the pledge (qv) to which it relates (PA 1964, s 22). The pawner (qv) is entitled to the surplus on the sale of a pledge (PA 1964, s 33 as amended by CCA 1995, Sch 8). [Bibliography: Bird.]

pawner. A person delivering an article for pawn to a pawnbroker (qv): Pawnbrokers Act 1964, s 2.

pay as you earn; PAYE. The system of collection of income tax from employees; it is deducted at source by employers by reference to tax tables so that the periodical deduction of tax keeps pace with the accruing tax liability of the employee. A person making any payment of any emolument is required to deduct or repay income tax and to account for it to the Revenue Commissioners: Income Tax Act 1967, ss 124–133, now Taxes Consolidation Act 1997, ss 983–997. See *Hearne v J A Kenny & Partners* [1989] 7 ILT Dig 24.

The PAYE tax credit for 2004 and subsequent years has been increased to €1,040 per annum: Finance Act 2004, s 3. It was €800 for 2003: Finance Act 2003, s 3. See EMOLUMENT; INCOME TAX.

pay-related benefit. The social welfare benefit to which a person may be entitled which is a percentage rate of previous earnings; the percentage rate has been progressively reduced since this measure was first introduced in 1973: Social Welfare (Consolidation) Act 1993, ss 78–82.

pay-related social insurance; PRSI. The employers' higher rate of PRSI has been reduced from 11.3% to 10.05% from 1 March 2002 and the earnings ceiling has been amended to €38,740: Social Welfare (No 2) Act 2001, s 5. Also the income ceiling for payment of optional contributions has been increased to €38,740 (SW(No 2)A 2001, s 6). See also Social Welfare (Miscellaneous Provisions) Act 2004, s 13. [Bibliography: Bradley J.] See BENEFIT-IN-KIND; SOCIAL INSURANCE FUND.

payee. The person to whom a cheque (qv) or negotiable instrument (qv) is payable.

payment. The passing of money from payer to payee in satisfaction of some debt or obligation. An unendorsed cheque which appears to have been paid by the banker on whom it is drawn is evidence of the receipt by the payee of the sum payable by the cheque: Cheques Act 1959, s 3. See PROMPT PAYMENT.

payment in due course. Discharge of a bill of exchange (qv) by payment made at or after the maturity of the bill to the holder thereof in good faith and without notice that his title to the bill is defective: Bills of Exchange Act 1882, s 59(1). See DISCHARGE OF A BILL.

payment into court. See LODGMENT IN COURT.

payment of wages. See WAGES.

payment out of court. In the High Court, money lodged in court may be paid out to the plaintiff upon receipt of a notification that the plaintiff accepts the sum lodged in satisfaction, except where the plaintiff is a minor (qv) or a person of unsound mind: RSC Ord 77, r 32; Ord 22, r 10. The Master of the High Court is empowered to make an order for the payment out of court of funds standing to the credit of a minor on attaining majority, or, if so authorised by order of a judge, for his benefit during minority: RSC Ord 63, r 1(18). An application for such an order may be made by affidavit or by letter: RSC Ord 63, r 12(4) as inserted by SI No 265 of 1993.

In the Circuit Court, money lodged in court may be paid out to the plaintiff, without the necessity for any decree or order of the court, upon lodgment with the County Registrar of a *notice of acceptance* from the plaintiff that he accepts the sum lodged in full satisfaction of his claim, except where the plaintiff is under a legal disability (eg is a minor or is of unsound mind): Circuit Court Rules 2001 Ord 15, r 13. In addition, the plaintiff is at liberty to tax his costs four days after the service of notice of acceptance (Ord 15, r 14).

For District Court, see DCR 1997 Ord 7, r 6, and Ord 41, r 2(3). See LODGMENT IN COURT.

payment to an agent. Payment of money to an agent discharges the liability of the payer to the principal, if the agent is authorised to receive the money. Such authorisation exists if: (a) the principal has expressly authorised the agent to accept payment, or (b) it is the custom of that particular type of agency, or (c) the agent had ostensible authority to accept payment. The general rule is that an agent authorised to sell is not authorised to receive payment. See PREMIUM; SECRET PROFIT; COMMISSION; AUCTIONEER.

peace, binding to. See BINDING TO PEACE.

peace commissioner. The office created by the District Justices (Temporary Provisions) Act 1923, s 4. The person appointed by the Minister with a number of duties and powers eg signing summonses and warrants, administering oaths and taking declarations, affirmations and informations: Courts of Justice Act 1924, s 88.

A search warrant issued by a peace commissioner does not speak for itself; a trial judge is entitled to rule a warrant as invalid in the absence of evidence as to the state of mind of the peace commissioner: *DPP v Owens* [1999] 2 ILRM 421, SC and 2 IR 16. It is inappropriate for a warrant issued by a peace commissioner to bear the words 'The District Court' but this did not invalidate the warrant: *DPP v Edgeworth* [2001] 2 IR 131, SC.

His former power to remand a person (in custody or in such bail as he deemed fit), who had been brought before him when a District Court judge was not immediately available, has been held to be invalid having regard to the 1937 Constitution, art 34(1), because it was a judicial and not an administrative act: *O'Mahony v Melia* [1990] ILRM 14. See Bail Act 1997, s 11. See also *Ryan v O'Callaghan* [1987] HC; *Byrne v Gray* [1988] IR 31. See COMMISSIONER FOR OATHS; JUSTICE OF THE PEACE.

peace officer. A member of the Garda Síochána, a prison officer, a member of the defence forces; it is an offence for any person to assault a peace officer acting in the execution of his duty: Criminal Justice (Public Order) Act 1994, s 19.

peat extraction. The planning threshold for peat extraction has been reduced from 50 hectares to 10 hectares: Local Government (Planning and Development) (Amendment) Regulations 2001, SI No 539 of 2001. For the Irish Peatland Conservation Council, see website: *www.ipcc.ie*. See ENVIRONMENTAL IMPACT ASSESSMENT.

pecuniary legacy. A gift of money by will. It includes an annuity (qv), a general legacy, a demonstrative legacy (qv) so far as it is not discharged out of the designated property, and any other general direction by a testator for payment of money: Succession Act 1965, s 3(1). A direction in a will to pay a successor's inheritance tax out of another fund is a *pecuniary legacy* of the amount of the tax and is taxable as such: Capital Acquisitions Tax Consolidation Act 2003, s 113(1)(c). See LEGACY.

pedestrian. Pedestrians are required to exercise care and to take all reasonable precautions to avoid causing danger or inconvenience to traffic and other pedestrians: Road Traffic General Bye-Laws 1964, SI No 294 of 1964, Pt VI. When a vehicle is approaching a zebra crossing (qv) a pedestrian must not step onto that crossing if his action is likely to cause the driver to brake suddenly or to swerve (art 38). See CYCLEWAY; FOOTWAY; MOTORWAY; PROPER LOOK OUT.

pedigree. Relationship by blood or marriage between persons. The relationship is proved by such facts as birth, marriage, death or failure of issue and may be proved by declarations made by deceased relatives. See *Berkeley Peerage Case* [1811] 4 Camp 401. See BLASKETS; DECLARATION BY DECEASED.

penal damages. Additional damages which may be awarded to a plaintiff where the court is satisfied that effective relief would not otherwise be available to a plaintiff eg where the infringement of copyright is flagrant and the defendant has benefited by reason of the infringement: *Folens v O'Dubhghaill* [1973] IR 255. A person who deals in pirate video cassettes is liable to have penal damages awarded against him: *Universal City Studios Inc v Mulligan* [1999] 3 IR 392, HC and ITLR (12 July). See EXEMPLARY DAMAGES.

penal laws. A series of statutes, commonly known as the *penal laws*, which were laws in Ireland for the suppression of popery. Religion was the gulf which divided the colonial English rulers of Ireland from the native Irish majority and these statutes were targeted against persons who were not of the protestant religion e g the 1733 Act (7 Geo II: c V) which provided that no person could be admitted as an attorney or licensed to be a solicitor in the Four Courts in Dublin 'who hath not been a Protestant from his age of 14 years'. The purpose of the 1733 Act is clear from its preamble: 'Whereas the laws now in force against popish solicitors have been found ineffectual by reason of the difficulty of convicting such solicitors, ... to the great prejudice of the protestant interest of this kingdom ... and whereas by the means of such popish solicitors, the acts against the growth of popery have been and daily are greatly eluded and evaded ... '.

For certainty, this and many old statutes were repealed by the Statute Law Revision (Pre-Union Irish Statutes) Act 1962. See 'Papists, porter and burning bricks' by Henry Murdoch BL in *Law Society Gazette* (December 2001) 10. For text of the *penal laws*, see website: *www.law.umn.edu/irishlaw/*. See SHELBOURNE LEASE.

penal servitude. Prior to 1997, imprisonment with compulsory labour; it was substituted for *transportation* (qv) by the Penal Servitude Act 1857. The last statute to prescribe penal servitude as a sentence was the Criminal Justice Act 1964, s 2. For many years, in practice, there was no distinction in the treatment of prisoners sentenced to penal servitude or imprisonment. See *Application of McLoughlin* [1970] IR 197. See also SR & O No 203 of 1937.

Now, a person cannot be sentenced to penal servitude: Criminal Law Act 1997, s 11. A court is empowered to sentence a person to imprisonment for a term not exceeding the maximum term of penal servitude specified in a statute (CLA 1997, s 11(2)). Although penal servitude as a punishment was abolished by the 1997 Act,

the features of penal servitude still apply to such a sentence imposed before the 1997 Act: *DPP v Murphy* [2001] 2 ILRM 334, HC and 1 IR 171. See also Penal Servitude Acts 1864, since repealed by Criminal Law Act 1997, s 16 and Sch 3. See PUNISHMENT.

penal statute. Legislation creating offences or providing for the recovery of penalties in civil proceedings. The Supreme Court has held that a word or expression in legislation which creates a penal or taxation liability, should be construed strictly: *Inspector of Taxes v Kiernan* [1981] IR 117.

penal sum. The amount specified in an *administration bond* to which parties thereto bind themselves. Unless otherwise directed, the sum is double the gross value of the estate of the deceased: RSC, App Q, Pt XI.

penal warrant. A warrant (qv) authorising the arrest of a specified person. See *Murphy v DJ Wallace* [1990] ITLR (24 December), HC. See REVENUE OFFENCE.

penalty. (1) A punishment. Includes any fine or other penal sum and, where a fine is ordered to be paid, any compensation, costs or expenses, in addition to such fine: DCR 1997, Interpretation of Terms. It is a matter for the Oireachtas (qv) to determine in an Act the appropriate penalty for the commission of an offence; the adequacy of the penalty cannot constitute grounds for the provision being repugnant to the Constitution: *In the matter of art 26 of the Constitution and the Regulation of Information (Services outside the State for Termination of Pregnancies) Bill 1995* [1995] 2 ILRM 81, SC. See *Consultation Paper on Penalties for Minor Offences* (LRC CP 18, 2002).

(2) The nominal sum payable on breach of contract or of a term of a contract. In a contract it is usually stipulated *in terrorem* of the other party, to compel performance of the contract by providing for a payment to be made by way of punishment if the contract is not performed.

When a contract provides that, on breach being made, a fixed sum will be payable by the party responsible, it is a question of construction whether this sum is a *penalty* or *liquidated damages*. If it is a penalty, only the actual damages suffered are recoverable; if it is liquidated damages (i e a genuine pre-estimate of damage), the sum fixed may be recovered.

The use of the words *penalty* or *liquidated damages* in a contract is not conclusive; the court will ascertain whether a sum is truly a penalty or liquidated damages. If the sum fixed is extravagant and unconscionable compared with the greatest loss which could conceivably be proved to have followed the breach, it will be held to be a penalty: *Dunlop Pneumatic Tyre Co v New Garage Motor Co* [1915] AC 79. It will be a penalty also if the breach consists only in paying a sum of money, and the sum stipulated is greater than the sum which ought to be paid: *Bradford v Lemon* [1929] NI 159.

There is a presumption that a clause is penal when a single lump sum is payable on the occurrence of one or more or all of several events, the events occasioning varying degrees of damages: *UDT Ltd v Patterson* [1975] NI 142. If the consequences of breach of contract are difficult to estimate in financial terms this, far from being an obstacle to the validity of a clause providing for damages, will point in favour of upholding it, the courts taking the view that it is better for the parties themselves to estimate the damages that will result: *Schiesser International (Ireland) v Gallagher* [1971] ILTR 22. See also *Wall v Rederiaktiebolaget Lugudde* [1915] 3 KB 66; *O'Donnell v Truck and Machinery Sales Ltd* [1998] 4 IR 191, SC. See HIRE-PURCHASE PRICE.

penalty points. A *penalty points system* for minor driving offences, which leads to automatic disqualification from driving for six months when 12 penalty points are reached: Road Traffic Act 2002, ss 2–8. This is the first legal provision which permits a person to be disqualified from driving without the direct intervention of a court.

When a person receives notice of the commission of a *penalty points offence*, the person has the option of: (a) paying a fixed charge and incurring a lower level of penalty points, or (b) allowing the matter to proceed to court. In the latter case, where the court convicts the person, the level of penalty points is increased significantly. In certain more serious offences, the option of paying a fixed charge is not available e g careless driving, using a vehicle without insurance, or driving a dangerously defective vehicle. *Penalty point offences*, and the number of points for each offence, are specified in RTA 2002, Sch 1 (as amended by Taxi Regulation Act 2003, s 57).

Penalty points are endorsed on the person's *licence record*, as distinct from their driving licence; the *licence record* is a record

jointly established and maintained by the Minister and the relevant licensing authority (RTA 2002, s 1(1)). Penalty points remain on the record for a period of three years from the 'appropriate date' (RTA 2002, s 4). The 'appropriate date' generally is 28 days from the date of notification of the endorsement of penalty points (RTA 2002, s 7).

Where the registered owner was not driving the vehicle at the time of the alleged offence, he is obligated to give the name and address of the driver; where he does not so furnish, he is presumed to have been the driver: Road Traffic Act 1961, s 130(11) as substituted by RTA 2002, s 11(1). See SI No 492 of 2002 (exceeding speed limit); and SI No 214 of 2003 (using vehicle without insurance); SI No 321 of 2003 (not wearing a seat belt); SI No 248 of 2004 (careless driving). The first person to be disqualified from driving under the penalty points system was a driver whose licence was issued in North Tipperary: statement from Minister Séamus Brennan TD on 26 March 2004. See also Road Traffic Offences Regulations 2003, SI No 322 of 2003. For proposed amendments to RTA 2002, e g to provide for the outsourcing of certain administrative functions of the gardaí, see Road Traffic Bill 2004, ss 15–18. [Bibliography: McGrath M (2).] See ELECTRONIC APPARATUS; ON-THE-SPOT FINE.

pendens lis. [A pending action.]

pendente lite. [While litigation is pending.] After an action has commenced and before it has been disposed of. A *grant pendente lite* is a grant of administration made by a court where any legal proceedings are pending, which touch upon the validity of a will or which seek to recall or revoke a grant already given: Succession Act 1965, s 27(7). See also *Re Bevan* [1948] 1 All ER 271. See also RSC Ord 47. See LIS PENDENS.

pension, social welfare. Social welfare pensions comprise old age (contributory and non-contributory pensions), widow's and widower's pension, blind pension, retirement pension, and invalidity pension: Social Welfare (Consolidation) Act 1993, ss 83–105A, 132–148, as amended. Persons who were insured prior to 1953 with at least five years' paid insurance may now qualify for a *special rate pension*: Social Welfare Act 2000, s 16. See also Social Welfare

Act 2002, s 2; Social Welfare Act 2003, ss 2(2) and 3(2).

pension adjustment order. A court order designating a portion of the retirement benefit of a spouse who is a member of a pension scheme for payment to a dependent spouse and children; such an order may be made following a decree of *judicial separation* during the lifetime of the member spouse: Family Law Act 1995, ss 12 and 18. The effect of the order is to preserve for a dependent spouse a defined interest in the member spouse's pension benefit. There is also provision for preserving of pension entitlements which would otherwise be lost as a result of a pension scheme condition requiring spouses to be residing together when the benefit is payable (FLA 1995, s 13). A similar order, in favour of a spouse and a dependent member of the family, is provided for in *divorce* proceedings: Family Law (Divorce) Act 1996, s 17.

The scope of pension adjustment orders has been extended to include *Personal Retirement Savings Accounts* (qv): Pensions (Amendment) Act 2002, s 57. For drafting a pension adjustment order, see 'Family Values' by solicitor Keith Walsh in *Law Society Gazette* (May 2004) 16.

pension fund, public. Social welfare pensions, civil service pensions, and many public sector pensions are paid for from current revenue; there is no pension fund as such. This system is unlikely to be able to cater for future public pension requirements, with the increasing old age dependency ratio, predicted by the government in 1999 to move from five workers to one person over 65 years of age, to four workers to one person over 65 by 2025. The government in recognition of this problem decided in 1999 to set aside 1% of Gross National Product each year to assist in meeting these future pension costs. £4.3 billion/€5.46 billion was set aside in 1999: see Temporary Holding Fund for Superannuation Liabilities Act 1999.

The National Pensions Reserve Fund Act 2000 provides for the establishment, financing, investment and management of a *National Pensions Reserve Fund* aimed at meeting part of the escalating Exchequer cost of social welfare and public service pensions from 2025 onwards, when according to demographic projections, the proportion of persons over 65 in the population will rise significantly. Provision is made for an independent Commission to manage the Reserve Fund and for the transfer of monies in the *Temporary Holding Fund* to the Reserve Fund and for the repeal of the Temporary Holding Fund for Superannuation Liabilities Act 1999.

pension law. For the Association of Pension Lawyers in Ireland, see website: *www.apli.ie*. See [Bibliography: Buggy & Finucane; Martin & McCarthy.]

pension scheme. An *occupational* pension scheme is any scheme or arrangement: (a) which is contained in one or more instruments or agreements, and (b) which provides benefits or is capable of providing benefits in relation to employees in any description of employment who reside within the State, and (c) which meets other requirements eg it is approved, or in the process of seeking approval, or is a statutory scheme under the appropriate provisions of the Finance Act 1972: Pensions Act 1990, s 2 as amended by Social Welfare Act 1992, s 53(b); Social Welfare Act 1993, s 42(e); Social Welfare (Miscellaneous Provisions) Act 2004, s 23, Sch 2.

The 1990 Act has four objectives: (a) the establishment of a legal framework and a supervisory system; (b) provision for compulsory preservation of pension entitlements; (c) to ensure that pension expectations in *defined benefit schemes* are backed by adequate assets; (d) progressive implementation of equal treatment of men and women.

The 1990 Act provides for the establishment of a Pensions Board to act as the regulatory body and the supervisor of the statutory requirements. It also distinguishes between a *defined contributions scheme* (one which provides benefits the rate or amount of which are determined by the amount of contributions paid by or in respect of a member) and *defined benefit schemes* (which are all others). The Pensions Board will decide whether a scheme is a defined *contributions* or a defined *benefits* scheme (PA 1990, s 81G as amended by substitution by SW(MP)A 2004, s 22(1)).

The 2002 Act: (a) provides a framework for the introduction of *Personal Retirement Savings Accounts* (PRSAs); (b) provides for the establishment of a Pensions Ombudsman; (c) amends many sections of the 1990 Act and strengthens many provisions.

The power to increase public service pensions is provided for in the Pensions (Increase) Act 1964.

The 1990 Act has been amended by the Social Welfare Act 1991, ss 60–64; Social Welfare Act 1992, ss 53–63; Social Welfare Act 1993, ss 42–52; Social Welfare (No 2) Act 1993, s 15; Social Welfare Act 1997, s 40; Social Welfare Act 1999, s 35; Social Welfare Act 2000, s 35; Pensions (Amendment) Act 1996; Family Law (Divorce) Act 1996, s 47; Pensions (Amendment) Act 2002; Social Welfare (Miscellaneous Provisions) Act 2003, s 24; Social Welfare (Miscellaneous Provisions) Act 2004, ss 22–23.

See Buckley in 9 ILT & SJ (1991) 154 for article on Pensions Act 1990. See *Turner & Ors v Hospitals Trust (1940) Ltd* [1994] ELR 35, HC. See Oireachtas (Allowances to Members) and Ministerial and Parliamentary Offices (Amendment) Act 1992. See Occupational Pension Schemes (Preservation of Benefits) Regulations 2002, SI No 279 of 2002. See also SI No 216 of 1993 (appointment of trustees); SI No 277 of 2002 (special calculations – preservation of benefits); SI No 278 of 2002 (funding standard). See Occupational Pension Schemes (Revaluation) Regulations 2000, SI No 13 of 2000; (Revaluation) Regulations 2001, SI No 23 of 2001; Revaluation Regulations 2002, SI No 18 of 2002; Revaluation Regulations 2003, SI No 77 of 2003; Revaluation Regulations 2004, SI No 49 of 2004.

For the Pensions Board, see email: *pb@pensionsboard.ie* and website: *www. pensionsboard.ie*. For the Irish Association of Pension Funds, see website: *www.iapf.ie*. [Bibliography: Buggy & Finucane; Forde (8); McLoughlin & Mooney; Martin & McCarthy; Inglis-Jones (UK).] See EQUAL PAY; INSOLVENCY OF EMPLOYER; JUDICIAL SEPARATION; MATERNITY LEAVE; MERO-MICTIC; PENSION ADJUSTMENT ORDER; PENSIONS OMBUDSMAN; PERSONAL RETIREMENT SAVINGS ACCOUNT; PREFERENTIAL PAYMENTS; PRESERVED BENEFIT; PUBLIC SERVICE PENSION SCHEME; TRUSTEE, REMOVAL OF; WHISTLE BLOWER.

pension scheme and discrimination. The principles of equal pay in the EC Treaty, art 119 and Directive (EEC) 75/117 have significant implications for occupational pension schemes eg pension benefits cannot discriminate on grounds of sex directly or indirectly: *Barber v GRE Assurance* [1990] IRLR 240 & Barry in 8 ILT & SJ (1990) 194. However the Protocol to the Maastricht Treaty 1992 (qv), limits retro-

spection to periods of employment from 17 May 1990 except where legal proceedings had been initiated: see Pensions (Amendment) Act 1996, ss 33. See also Social Welfare Act 1992, s 62.

The Pensions Act 1990, Part VII, already provides for equal treatment of men and women in occupational pension schemes. Part VII has been amended by substitution of PA 1990, ss 65 to 81J to prohibit discrimination in occupational pension schemes on additional grounds of sexual orientation, religion, age, race and disability, implementing Directives (EC) 2000/43 and (EC) 2000/78, and on grounds of marital or family status or membership of the Traveller Community, implementing commitments made in the social partnership agreement *Sustaining Progress*: Social Welfare (Miscellaneous Provisions) Act 2004, s 22. See Equality Act 2004, s 66.

pension scheme and employer. There is a statutory requirement on employers to remit employee pension contributions to the pension trustees within 21 days following the end of the month in which the deductions were made: Pensions Act 1990, s 58A inserted by the Pensions (Amendment) Act 2002, s 41.

In the UK it has been held that there is an implied limitation in pension schemes that the employer will not exercise its rights so as to destroy or seriously damage the relationship of confidence and trust between the company and its employees: *Imperial Group Pension Trust Ltd v Imperial Tobacco Ltd* [1991] IRLR and Barry in 9 ILT & SJ (1991) 150. See also *Glen Abbey Pension Trust v County Glen plc* [1992] HC.

It has been held that the Minister was entitled to abate a 'wound pension' previously granted to a member of the defence forces: *Breen v Minister for Defence* [1994] 2 IR 34, SC. See also PERSONAL RETIREMENT SAVINGS ACCOUNT.

pension scheme and forfeiture. It has been held that a provision in a teacher's pension scheme which provided for the forfeiture of pension entitlements on being convicted of an offence was *ultra vires* and was null and void and of no legal effect; the object of the Act establishing the scheme was the provision of pensions and gratuities and had nothing to do with the commission of criminal offences: *Lovett v Minister for Education* [1997] 1 ILRM 89, HC.

pension scheme and integration. The practice of *integration* has been abolished ie the practice of reducing the amount of an occupational pension scheme every time there is an increase in a social welfare pension: Social Welfare Act 1999, s 35. Where the trustees of a pension scheme increase an *integrated pension* at any time after it has commenced, they must not calculate the increase by reference to an updated State pension offset, notwithstanding the rules of the scheme: Pensions Act 1990 as amended by Social Welfare Act 2000, s 35.

pension scheme and taxation. There are various exemptions and reliefs in relation to occupational pension schemes which have been approved by the Revenue Commissioners eg employer contributions are deductible when computing the employer's profits for tax purposes, and employee contributions are deductible when computing income for the tax year: Taxes Consolidation Act 1997, ss 770–790, 836; Finance Act 2000, s 23 amending ss 770, 772 and 784; Finance Act 2002, s 10 amending ss 772, 774, 776 and 784, and Finance Act 2004, s 16 amending ss 772, 774 and 776.

In 2002, a number of changes were introduced: (a) a full pension can in future be provided for a spouse or the children of a deceased member of an occupational pension scheme; (b) the level of tax relief for contributions made by persons in occupational pension schemes has been changed to mirror the treatment of the self-employed ie a scale based on age eg 15% of remuneration up to age 30, and 30% of remuneration over 50 years of age; (c) tax on pension contribution refunds was lowered to the standard income tax rate (20% in 2002); and (d) a liberalisation of the rules governing *Retirement Annuity Contracts* (qv): Finance Act 2002, s 10.

Further changes were made in 2003 eg: (a) the circumstances in which contributions may be set back to earlier years is restricted, (b) *carry-back relief* is provided for non-ordinary annual contributions paid between the end of the tax year and the return filing date, (c) *carry-forward relief* is allowed for contributions in excess of the allowed limits, (d) the circumstances in which assets in an approved retirement fund (ARF) are treated as having been distributed are extended, (e) the scaling of maximum contributions based on age is extended to all pension products, with the 30% maximum applying to certain sportspersons who retire early, and the earnings cap for tax relief purposes is set at €254,000: Finance Act 2003, s 14.

It has been held that the children's pension payable to the widow of a garda síochána was the beneficial property of the children and was not to be aggregated with the widow's pension for income tax purposes: *O'Coindealbhain v O'Carroll* [1989] IR 229. See also Finance Act 2003, s 166.

Pensions Board. A body corporate established by the Pensions Act 1990 with main functions under that Act and amending legislation, most recently the Pensions (Amendment) Act 2002, (a) to monitor and supervise the operation of the Pensions Act and pension developments generally, including the activities of PRSA (*personal retirement savings account*) providers, the provision of these products and their operation; (b) to issue guidelines on the duties and responsibilities of trustees of schemes; and (c) to encourage the provision of appropriate training for trustees; and (d) to advise the Minister on specific matters and on pension matters generally.

Pension schemes must be registered with the Board and most schemes must pay an annual fee to meet the Board's administration costs. The Board may investigate the operation of a pension scheme and is empowered to prosecute for breaches of the legislation.

The Pensions Board provides on subscription: (a) a legislation service – a non-statutory consolidated text of the Pensions Acts and the Regulations, with regular updates, (b) guidance notes on various parts of the legislation, and (c) a Trustee Handbook and Codes of Practice on various aspects of trustee duties and responsibilities. See also Public Service Superannuation (Miscellaneous Provisions) Act 2004, Sch 2. See website: *www.pensionsboard.ie*. See PENSION SCHEME; PERSONAL RETIREMENT SAVINGS ACCOUNT.

pensions ombudsman. An independent office holder who is empowered to investigate and determine the following complaints and disputes: (a) a complaint made to him by an actual or potential beneficiary of an *occupational pension scheme* or *Personal Retirement Savings Account* (PRSA), who alleges that he has sustained financial loss occasioned by an act of *maladministration* done by or on behalf of a person responsible for the management of that scheme or, as appropriate, PRSA; (b) any dispute of fact or law that arises in relation to an act done by or on behalf of a person responsible for the management of the scheme or, as appropriate, PRSA, and that is referred to him; and (c) any other complaint or dispute which falls within a category prescribed by regulations: Pensions Act 1990, ss 126–147 inserted by Pensions (Amendment) Act 2002, s 5 and as amended by Social Welfare (Miscellaneous Provisions) Act 2004, s 23 and Sch 2.

A complaint or dispute may be referred also by a person acting for the beneficiary. The complaint must be referred to the Ombudsman within six years from the date of the act giving rise to the complaint; a three-year period applies, if later, from the date the person became aware of the act or ought to have become aware (PA 1990, s 131(4)).

The Pensions Ombudsman has all the powers, rights and privileges of a High Court judge for the purposes of his investigation (PA 1990, s 137(2)). He is empowered to order such redress, including financial redress, for the party concerned as he considers appropriate (PA 1990, s 139(3)) but any financial redress must not exceed the actual loss of benefit (PA 1990, s 139(4)). There is provision for appeal to the High Court (PA 1990, s 140) and for the enforcement of determinations of the Ombudsman by the Circuit Court (PA 1990, s 141).

Provision has been made to bring the Office of the Pensions Ombudsman within the scope of the Freedom of Information Act 1997: Social Welfare (Miscellaneous Provisions) Act 2003, s 23. However the FIA 1997 will not apply to any examination or investigation carried out by the Ombudsman. For the regulations governing his operation and jurisdiction, see Pensions Ombudsman Regulations 2003, SI No 397 of 2003.

pensions strategy. The strategy of increasing the number of persons with private or occupational pension coverage from the current (in 2004) 50% of workers to 70%. An important element in that policy is the introduction of the Personal Retirement Savings Account (PRSA). The number of persons in the EU coming to pension age is increasing rapidly and at the same time the number of persons in the active age group is decreasing, due to the baby boom generation reaching retirement age, increases in life expectancy, and a declining birth rate. 'We face the same pension challenges as other countries but in our case the full impact of the aging population will not arise until much later and this allows us more time to prepare': Minister Mary Coughlan TD on 5 March 2004. See ESRI Report, *Reforming Pensions in Europe: Evolution of Pension Financing and Sources of Retirement Income* (March 2004). See PERSONAL RETIREMENT SAVINGS ACCOUNT.

peppercorn rent. See RENT.

per. [As stated by.]

per annum. [By the year.] Annually.

per autre vie. See CESTUI QUE VIE; LIFE ESTATE.

per capita. [By heads.] Individually. Distribution per capita is where property is divided among those entitled to it in equal shares.

per cur; per curiam. [By the court.] Refers to a decision by the court. For example, see *N (Otherwise K) v K* [1986] ILRM 75; *O'Byrne v Gloucester* 7 ILT Dig [1989] 56.

per diem. [By the day.]

per incuriam. [Through want of care.] A decision of the court which is mistaken. See *Kelly v O'Sullivan* [1991] 9 ILT Dig 126, HC.

per infortunium. [By mischance.]

per mensem. [By the month.]

per minas. [By menaces (qv).] See DURESS IN CRIME.

per my et per tout. [By the half and by the whole.] Joint tenants are said to be seised *per my et per tout,* in that they have an equal right to the possession of the whole property and no one is entitled to exclusive possession of any part. See JOINT TENANCY.

per pro; per procurationem. [As an agent.] On behalf of another eg where a person signs a document for another.

per quod. [Whereby.]

per quod servitium amisit. [Whereby he lost his service.] An action by an employer for damages for the loss of service of his employee against a third party who had injured the employee. See *Bradford Corporation v Webster* [1920] 2 KB 135; *Cook v Carroll* [1945] IR 515.

A similar action is available to a parent against a third party who wrongfully deprives the parent of the legal right which he has to the services of his unmarried minor (qv) who ordinarily lives with him eg by the third party enticing, harbouring or seducing the minor. See *Barnes v Fox* [1914] 2 IR 276. See LRC Working Paper No 7, 1979. See CONSORTIUM.

per se. [By itself.] Taken alone.

per stirpes. [By stock or branches.] Distribution of the property of an intestate is *per stirpes* if it is divided amongst those entitled to it according to the number of stocks of descent ie children representing a deceased parent take in equal shares the share which would have been taken by their deceased parent had he survived, and they may in turn be represented in a similar way by their own issue through all degrees. See Succession Act 1965, s 3. See INTESTATE SUCCESSION.

per subsequens matrimonium. [By later marriage.] See CHILD, LEGITIMATED.

per totam curiam. [By the whole court.]

peremptory. An order which allows no excuse for non-compliance. An order by a judge granting an extension of time which is expressed to be 'peremptory', cannot fetter another judge from hearing an application for another extension: *Smith v Judge O'Donnell & DPP* [2004] ITLR (28 June) HC.

peremptory challenge. See JUROR, CHALLENGE TO.

perfected. Drawn up in final form eg an order of the court is said to be *perfected* when it is drawn up and approved by the judge. Every order of the High and Supreme Court must be passed and *perfected* with all convenient speed: RSC Ord 115, r 1. See *G McG v DW & AR (No 2)* [2000] 1 ILRM 121, HC (under appeal). For amendment to an order which has been perfected, see ORDER.

perfidy. [A deceitful act.] In warfare, the following acts are examples of *perfidy*: (a) feigning of an intent to negotiate under a flag of truce or of a surrender, (b) feigning of an incapacitation by wounds or sickness, (c) feigning of protected status by the use of signs, emblems or uniforms of the United Nations: Geneva Conventions (Amendment) Act 1998, Sch 5, art 37. It is prohibited to kill, injure or capture an adversary by resort to perfidy (art 37(1)).

performance. (1) The act which, being in accordance with the term or condition of a contract, discharges it eg payment or tender (qv).

(2) The equitable doctrine by which a transfer of property operates in law, whether the donee wishes it or not, as a complete or *pro tanto* discharge of a previous legal liability of the donor. It derives from the equitable doctrine that *equity imputes an intention to fulfil an obligation.* Equity presumes performance: (a) where there is a covenant to purchase and settle lands and a purchase is in fact made: *Lechmere v Earl of Carlisle* [1733] 3 P Wms 211; (b) where there is a covenant to leave personalty to another and the covenantor dies intestate and property to satisfy the covenant does in fact come to that other: *Blandy v Widmore* [1716] 1 P Wms 323; *Re Shine* [1964] IR 32. See IMPOSSIBILITY OF PERFORMANCE; PART-PERFORMANCE.

performance bond. A *guarantee* (qv) given by an agency, usually a bank, to secure the beneficiary against, for example, a seller being unable to supply goods under a contract of sale or, more commonly, to secure a beneficiary in an international construction contract against the contractor being unable to complete the project properly. Performance bonds may be: (a) *first demand* whereby the issuing agency is required to pay the beneficiary on demand; or (b) *conditional* whereby the issuing agency is only required to pay upon evidence eg that a breach of contract has actually occurred.

The Supreme Court has held that performance bonds are analogous to bills of exchange (qv) and that a bank which gives a performance guarantee must honour that guarantee according to its terms: *Celtic Insurance v Banque Nationale de Paris (Ireland) Ltd* [1995] 2 ILRM 518, SC and 2 IR 148. The only situation in which a bank may refuse to pay on demand is where it is clear that there has been fraud on the part of the person to whom the guarantee was given (*Celtic* case). See *Hibernia Meats Ltd v Ministre de L'Agriculture* [1984] HC. See Gill in 8 ILT & SJ (1990) 41.

performance, indecent or profane. It is an offence to show for gain or reward an indecent or profane performance. To constitute an offence, there must be an intention to deprave or corrupt those viewing the performance whose minds were open to such immoral influences: *Attorney-General v Simpson* [1959] 93 ILTR 33. See INDECENCY.

performers' rights. A performer has the exclusive right to authorise or prohibit: (a) the making of a recording of a performance directly from the live performance, or (b) the broadcasting live of a performance, or (c) the making of a recording directly from the broadcast of, or cable programme including, the live performance: Copyright and Related Rights Act 2000, s 203(1).

A *performance* means a performance of any actors, singers, musicians, dancers or other persons who act, sing, deliver, declaim, play in, interpret or otherwise perform literary, dramatic, musical or artistic works or expressions of works of folklore, which is a live performance given by one or more individuals and includes a performance of a variety act or any similar presentation (CRRA 2000, s 202(1)).

A person infringes the rights of a performer by undertaking, without the consent of the performer, any of the acts to which the performer has the exclusive right, or deals with or provides the means for making an illicit recording (CRRA 2000, ss 203(2) and 209–214).

The performer has an exclusive reproduction right, a right of making available copies to the public, a distribution right, and a rental and lending right (CRRA 2000, ss 204–207). These rights are *property rights*, referred to as *performers' property rights* (CRRA 2000, s 292) and are transmissible by assignment, by testamentary disposition or by operation of law, as personal or moveable property (CRRA 2000, s 293). An assignment is not effective unless it is in writing (CRRA 2000, s 293(3)). A performer who is an employee is the owner of the performer's property right, unlike the 'employee exception' provided in copyright. A performer also has *non-property rights* under ss 203, 209 and 212; these rights are not assignable or transmissible except on death (CRRA 2000, s 300).

A performer also has a right to *equitable remuneration* from the owner of the copyright in a sound recording in respect of commercial exploitation of the recording (CRRA 2000, s 208).

A number of acts are permitted in relation to performances, broadly corresponding to the exceptions permitted under copyright eg fair dealing, incidental use, copying for purpose of instruction, recordings of works of folklore, copying by librarians and archivists (CRRA 2000, s 220–254). Performers' rights extend to Ireland and member states of the European Economic Area. The government may designate other countries to enjoy protection, where it is satisfied that adequate protection is given in their law to Irish perform-

ances (CRRA 2000, s 289). See COMMERCIAL PROCEEDINGS; FAIR DEALING; EXHAUSTION PRINCIPLE; LICENCES OF RIGHT, COPYRIGHT; MORAL RIGHTS; PERFORMING RIGHTS SOCIETY; RECORDING RIGHT.

performers' rights, duration of. The performers' exclusive rights expire 50 years after the performance takes place or, in relation to the recording of a performance, 50 years after the recording is first lawfully made available to the public: Copyright and Related Rights Act 2000, s 291.

performers' rights, infringement of. An infringement of a performer's *property rights* is actionable by the rights owner: Copyright and Related Rights Act 2000, ss 303 and 209–214. The remedies are similar to those available under copyright (CRRA 2000, ss 303–305). See INFRINGEMENT OF COPYRIGHT.

An infringement of a performers' *non-property rights* is actionable as a breach of statutory duty owed to the person entitled to the right (CRRA 2000, s 308). Infringements of a performer's right may also constitute an offence eg a person commits an offence who, without the consent of the rights owner, makes for sale, rental or loan, or sells, rents or lends a recording which is, and which he knows or has reason to believe is, an illicit recording (CRRA 2000, s 258(1)). It is also an offence to make, for financial gain, a false claim to have rights in a performance (CRRA 2000, s 259).

There are provisions also for delivery up, seizure and disposal of illicit recordings, articles for making recordings, and protection-defeating devices eg unlawfully copied de-encryption devices, including 'smart cards' (CRRA 2000, ss 255–257; 261; 263–264). See DOMESTIC AND PRIVATE USE.

performers' rights, licensing of. A licence of a performer's *property rights*, granted by the owner, is binding on every successor in title to his interest in the rights, except a purchaser in good faith for valuable consideration and without notice (actual or constructive) of the licence: Copyright and Related Rights Act 2000, s 293(4).

An *exclusive licence* is a licence in writing which is signed by or on behalf of the owner, authorising the licensee, to the exclusion of all other persons, including the person granting the licence, to exercise all the rights otherwise exclusively exercisable by the rights owner (CRRA 2000, s 295(1)). An exclusive licensee has the same rights and remedies as if the licence has been an assignment, except as against the owner, and they are *concurrent* with those of the rights owner (CRRA 2000, s 306). In an action for infringement of a performer's property rights, brought by either the rights owner or exclusive licensee, the other must be joined as a plaintiff or defendant, unless the court directs otherwise (CRRA 2000, s 307).

Provision is made for the reference of proposed licensing schemes to the Controller of Patents and for the reference of disputes arising from such schemes to the Controller (CRRA 2000, ss 265–279). Provision is also made for the registration of licensing bodies (CRRA 2000, ss 280–286). There is an obligation on collecting societies (ie societies which collect royalties on behalf of performers) to register and to remain registered (CRRA 2000, s 286). See LICENCES OF RIGHT, COPYRIGHT.

Performing Rights Society Ltd; PRS. A non-profit-making company limited by guarantee and having no share capital, formed in the United Kingdom in 1914, which has the objective to protect copyright music from unauthorised exploitation and to grant permission for use on payment of a licence fee. The PRS is open to composers, authors and publishers of music and their heirs, who assign to the PRS the rights which it administers on their behalf.

These rights are the public performing rights, the broadcasting rights and the right to transmit the work to subscribers to a diffusion service, and, in the case of writer members, the film synchronisation rights composed primarily for the purpose of being included in the soundtrack of a particular cinematograph film or films in contemplation when the work was commissioned. The Society grants blanket licences which authorise the licensees to use the PRS rights referred to above. In Ireland, the PRS is now called the Irish Music Rights Organisation Ltd (IMRO).

Analogous societies are the Mechanical Copyright Protection Society Ltd which grants licences to make sound recordings, and Phonographic Performance (Ireland) Ltd which grants licences for public performances of sound recordings. See Performing Right Yearbooks. See *Performing Rights Society Ltd v Marlin Communal Aerials* [1975] SC. See Tyrrell in *Law Society Gazette* (July/August 1992) 235.

period of time. See TIME.

perils of the sea. In marine insurance, *perils of the sea* refers only to fortuitous accidents or casualties of the seas; it does not include the ordinary action of the winds and waves: Marine Insurance Act 1906, Sch 1, art 7. See MARITIME PERILS.

periodical payments. See ATTACHMENT; MAINTENANCE ORDER.

perishable goods. The court has power to order the sale of perishable goods: RSC Ord 50, r 3. See INTERNATIONAL CARRIAGE OF PERISHABLE GOODS.

perished goods. Where there is a contract for sale of specific goods and the goods without the knowledge of the seller have perished at the time when the contract is made, the contract is void: Sale of Goods Act 1893, s 6. Where there is an agreement to sell specific goods and subsequently the goods, without any fault on the part of the seller or buyer, perish before the risk passes to the buyer, the agreement is thereby avoided (SGA 1893, s 7). See SALE OF GOODS.

perjury. An offence committed by a person who asserts upon oath (qv), duly administered in a judicial proceeding before a competent court or tribunal at which evidence on oath may be heard, of the truth of some matter of fact, material to the question depending in that proceeding, which assertion the assertor does not believe to be true when he makes it, or on which he knows himself to be ignorant.

Perjury by a person before the European Court of Justice arises when he swears anything which he knows to be false or which he does not believe to be true: Courts of Justice of the European Communities (Perjury) Act 1975, s 1.

A solicitor should decline to act further in any proceedings where he has knowledge that his client has committed perjury or has mislead the court in relation to those proceedings, unless the client agrees to make a full disclosure of his conduct to the court: *A Guide to Professional Conduct of Solicitors in Ireland* (2002) ch 5.4. See also Perjury Act 1586; Short Titles Act 1962; Statute Law Revision (Pre-Union Irish Statutes) Act 1962; Arbitration Act 1954, s 7; Diplomatic and Consular Officers (Provision of Services) Act 1993, s 6; Children Act 1997, s 28(2); Residential Institutions Redress Act 2002, s 7(6). See FALSE EVIDENCE; SUBORNATION OF PERJURY.

permanent and pensionable. See NOTICE, EMPLOYMENT; ACTING CAPACITY.

permanent employee. Means an employee who is not a fixed-term employee: Protection of Employees (Fixed-Term Work) Act 2003, s 2(1). See FIXED-TERM EMPLOYEE.

permanent health insurance. The business of effecting and carrying out contracts of insurance, providing specified benefits against risks of persons becoming incapacitated in consequence of sustaining injury as a result of an accident or of an accident of a specified class or of sickness or infirmity and subject to certain provisions regarding period and termination: European Communities (Life Assurance) Regulations 1984, SI No 57 of 1984, art 8. An authorisation is required to carry on the business of permanent health insurance. Contributions to an approved permanent health insurance scheme are allowable as a tax deduction: Finance Act 1979, s 8, FA 1986, s 7, FA 1996, s 132(2), now consolidated in Taxes Consolidation Act 1997, ss 125 and 471.

There is now provision to give tax relief in respect of contributions to permanent health insurance schemes on a 'net pay' basis, similar to superannuation contributions: Finance Act 2001, s 2. See INSURANCE OMBUDSMAN; VOLUNTARY HEALTH INSURANCE.

permanent society. Originally was a building society which had not by its rules any fixed date or specified result at which it would terminate eg Irish Permanent Building Society: Building Societies Act 1874, s 5, since repealed and only of historical importance now. Contrast with TERMINATING SOCIETY.

permissive order. An order permitting, but not compelling, certain actions to take place eg permitting a health board to detain a child and to administer such medication as the psychiatrists having clinical responsibility for the child deemed appropriate but not compelling them to act contrary to their conscience or code of ethics: *DH (a minor) v Attorney-General & North Eastern Health Board* [2000] ITLR (26 June) HC. Contrast with MANDATORY ORDER.

permissive waste. See WASTE.

permit. An authority; permission; licence.

perpetua lex est, nullam legem humanam ac positivam perpetuam esse, et clausula quae abrogationem excludit, ab initio non valet. [It is an everlasting law, that no positive and human law shall be perpetual, and a clause which excludes abrogation is invalid from its commencement.]

perpetual copyright. A term of copyright which does not expire eg copyright in legal tender, notes and coins. See LEGAL TENDER.

perpetual fund. A fund which is established in connection with an undertaking mainly for one or more of a number of purposes eg the provision of superannuation allowances, pensions, periodic allowances to children, or an assurance of capital sums on death: Perpetual Funds (Registration) Act 1933, s 2. Funds registered with the Registrar of Friendly Societies pursuant to this Act are relieved from the operation of the rule of law relating to perpetuities (qv).

perpetual injunction. See INJUNCTION.

perpetuating testimony. A proceeding to place on record, evidence which is material for establishing a future claim to property: RSC Ord 39, r 35. The court may allow the deposition (qv) of a witness to be adduced in evidence on such terms as the court directs: RSC Ord 39, r 34. See also SHIP PROTEST.

perpetuities, rule against. A *limitation* of any interest in land is void if it is capable of vesting outside the perpetuity period, which consists of a life or lives in being at the time of the gift and 21 years thereafter. A *life in being* includes everyone who is alive at the time of the gift and mentioned in it either expressly or by implication. Lives must be human lives and not animals: *Re Kelly* [1932] IR 255. If there is no reference to lives in being, the period is 21 years. The perpetuity period may be extended for a *gestation period* (qv).

The rule against perpetuities does not apply to: (a) a limitation following an *estate tail*, or (b) a gift over from one charity to another, or (c) a shared ownership lease (qv): Housing (Miscellaneous Provisions) Act 1992, s 2(2), or (d) trusts governing pension schemes: Pension (Amendment) Act 1996, s 25. See also *Cadell v Palmer* [1833] 1 Cl & Fin 372; *O'Byrne v Davoren* [1994 HC] 2 ILRM 276.

In relation to the possible abolition of the rule which can block family gifts and legitimate commercial transactions, see Law Reform Commission Report, *The Rule against Perpetuities and Cognate Rules*: (LRC 62, 2000). See CHARITIES; FEE TAIL; PERPETUAL FUND; REMOTENESS; WORDS OF LIMITATION.

persistent offender. See HABITUAL CRIMINAL.

person. The object of rights and duties ie capable of having rights and being liable to duties. A *natural* person is a human being. An *artificial* person is a collection or succession of natural persons forming a corporation.

A person includes a firm and a body corporate or politic: Circuit Court Rules 2001, Interpretation of Terms, para 19. Under the Interpretation Act 1937, the word *person* is to be construed as importing a body corporate as well as an individual unless a contrary intention appears (IA 1937, ss 11(c) and 11(i)). The word *person* in s 45(1) of the Intoxicating Liquor Act 1988 must be taken to refer to an unincorporated body of persons as well as to an individual: *DPP (Barron) v Wexford Farmers' Club* [1994] 2 ILRM 295, HC. A 'person' includes a body such as a firm of solicitors: *Murphy v McNamara* [2003] 2 ILRM 333, HC and 2 IR 243. See CORPORATION; STATE; TRUE PERSON.

person in authority. See CONFESSION.

person of unsound mind. See MENTAL DISORDER; UNSOUND MIND.

persona non grata. [Unacceptable person.] A receiving State may at any time and without having to explain its decision, notify a sending State that any member of its diplomatic staff is *persona non grata,* in which case the sending State will either recall the person concerned or terminate his functions with the mission: Diplomatic Relations and Immunities Act 1967, Sch 1, art 9.

personae designatae. [Designated persons.] It has been held that the power conferred by the Firearms Act 1925, s 2 on garda superintendents was conferred *personae designatae* and accordingly it vested in them a discretion which could not be abdicated to anyone else: *Dunne v Donohoe* [2002] 2 ILRM 200, SC and 2 IR 533. See also *McLoughlin v Minister for Social Welfare* [1958] IR 1.

personal action. An action *in personam* (qv) as contrasted with an action *in rem* (qv).

personal data. Means *data* relating to a living individual who is or can be identified either from the data or from the data in conjunction with other information that is in, or is likely to come into, the possession of the *data controller* (qv): Data Protection Act 1988, s 1(1) as amended by substitu-

tion by Data Protection (Amendment) Act 2003, s 2(a)(iv).

An individual has a right to establish the existence of personal data and to be given a description of the data and the purposes for which it is kept (DPA 1988, s 3). He is also entitled to be supplied, within 40 days, with a copy of any personal data about him on making a request in writing to the data controller and on payment of any fee required (DPA 1988, s 4 as amended by DP(A)A 2003, s 5). This right of access to personal data is restricted in certain instances: (a) an *absolute restriction* eg data covered by legal professional privilege (qv); or (b) a *conditional* restriction eg where disclosure would prejudice the prevention of crime (DPA 1988, s 5 as amended by DP(A)A 2003, s 6).

A data subject is entitled to have personal data rectified or erased, as the case may be, if they have been dealt with by a data controller in contravention of the provisions of DPA 1988, s 2(1) (DP(A)A 2003, s 3(a)) eg if inaccurate, or kept for an unlawful purpose (DPA 1988, s 6 as amended by DP(A)A 2003, s 7).

Personal data must not be processed by a data controller unless, in addition to the requirements of s 2, one of the following conditions is satisfied: (a) the data subject has given consent, (b) processing is necessary for a number of reasons eg the performance of a contract to which the data subject is a party, or to prevent injury or damage to the data subject, (c) processing is necessary for the administration of justice or the performance of a function conferred on a person by an enactment, or (d) processing is necessary for the purposes of the legitimate interests pursued by the data controller or by third parties to whom the data are disclosed (DP(A)A 2003, s 4 inserting DPA 1988, s 2A).

As regards *manual* data as distinct from automated data, the provisions in s 2 dealing with the collection, processing, keeping, use and disclosure of personal data, and the additional requirements in DPA 1988, s 2A, do not come into operation until 24 October 2007 (DP(A)A 2003, s 23). However, there is a right in the meantime of access to such manual data and a right to have such manual data, which is incomplete or inaccurate, rectified erased, blocked or destroyed. The European Court of Justice has held that referring to people on a webpage and identifying them by name and giving other information about them constitutes 'processing of personal date ... by automatic means': Case C-101/01 *Bodil Lindqvist* [2003] ECJ.

For restrictions on the application of the 1988 Act to personal data provided to a Commission of Investigation, see Commissions of Investigation Act 2004, s 39. See 'FOI reloaded' by barrister Denis Kelleher in *Law Society Gazette* (August/September 2003) 22. See Practice Notes and 'Data Protection and the ECJ' in *Law Society Gazette* (January/February 2004) 54 and 67 respectively. [Bibliography: Kelleher & Murray.] See DATA PROTECTION; SENSITIVE PERSONAL DATA.

personal information. Information about an identifiable individual that: (a) would in the ordinary course of events be known only to the individual or members of the family, or friends, of the individual, or (b) is held by a public body on the understanding that it would be treated as confidential: Freedom of Information Act 1997, s 2(1). A person has a right of access to a *record* of *personal information* about himself held by a public body even if the record was created prior to the 1997 Act (FIA 1997, s 6 as amended by Freedom of Information (Amendment) Act 2003, s 4). If the record contains an express reference to the requestor, however insubstantial or trivial, it would satisfy the test for right of access: *E H v Information Commissioner (No 2)* [2002] 3 IR 600, HC. Also a person has a right to have such a record amended where the record is incomplete, incorrect or misleading (FIA 1997, s 17 as amended by FI(A)A 2003, s 12). Regulations prescribe certain classes of individuals who may apply under FIA 1997, s 17: see SI No 265 of 2003.

Access will be denied to a personal record of a person other than the requester; the denial can be accompanied by a refusal to confirm or deny the existence of a record (FIA 1997, s 28 as amended by FI(A)A 2003, s 23). A *record* is broadly defined to include records in electronic form, films, and sound recordings, as well as paper records (FIA 1997, s 2(1) as amended by FI(A)A 2003, s 2(a)). Mr Justice Quirke granted access by a separated father to his daughter's hospital medical records as there is provision under the Act to permit access where the requester is a parent or a guardian, and there is a presumption that a parent has the welfare of his child at heart, in the absence of evidence to the contrary:

McK v the Information Commissioner [2004] ITLR (16 February) HC and FL 8671.

Provision has been made for the exchange of personal information in the context of the administration of the law relating to the entry into and the removal from the State of non-nationals: Immigration Act 2003, s 8. [Bibliography: McDonagh.] See INFORMATION, ACCESS TO; FREEDOM OF INFORMATION; PERSONNEL RECORD.

personal injuries. (1) Includes any disease and any impairment of a person's physical or mental condition: Courts Act 1988, s 1(7). Actions in the High Court for recovery of damages for *personal injuries* are, since 1988, no longer tried with a jury (qv), except in the case of damages for false imprisonment or intentional trespass to the person or both. Claims for damages for personal injuries in the Circuit (qv) and District (qv) Courts are also tried without a jury.

(2) Includes any disease and any impairment of a person's physical or mental condition or death: Solicitors (Advertising) Regulations 2002, SI No 518 of 2002, reg 2. When a solicitor publishes an advertisement which contains a reference to 'personal injuries', the advertisement must include a clear reference to the prohibition on a solicitor acting for a client on the basis of a percentage or proportion of any damages that may be payable to the client (SI No 518 of 2002, reg 8). This provision extends to the use of words or phrases such as 'motor accidents', 'workplace accidents', 'public place accidents' or other words or phrases of similar nature. A solicitor instructed to make a personal injuries claim on behalf of a person who is not of full age must not settle that person's claim without first issuing proceedings in the appropriate court and having the terms of such settlement approved by that court: Solicitors (Practice, Conduct and Discipline) Regulations 1990, SI No 99 of 1990. See PERSONAL INJURIES ASSESSMENT BOARD; SOLICITOR AND ADVERTISING.

personal injuries action. Means an action for the recovery of damages, in respect of a wrong: (a) for personal injuries, (b) for both such injuries and damage to property (but only if both have been caused by the same wrong), or (c) under section 48 of the Civil Liability Act 1961 (fatal injuries), but does not include an application for compensation under the Garda Síochána

(Compensation) Acts 1941 and 1945, or an action where the damages claimed include damages for false imprisonment or trespass to the person: Civil Liability and Courts Act 2004, s 2(1).

Significant changes have been made recently in relation to personal injuries actions eg: (a) a reduction from three years to two years in which to bring a personal injuries claim, (b) a bar on bringing proceedings in court in respect of a *relevant claim* unless and until an application for assessment has been made to the Personal Injuries Assessment Board and court proceedings have been authorised, and (c) new procedures to speed up court proceedings, to facilitate transparency and settlement, and to deter bogus claimants: CLCA 2004, ss 6–32, 54; Personal Injuries Assessment Board Act 2003, ss 12, 14, 15, 17, 33, 36. See PERSONAL INJURIES ASSESSMENT BOARD.

The 2004 Act makes provision for: (a) a requirement for a *letter of claim* to be served on the alleged wrongdoer within two months of the date of cause of action, (b) stricter compliance with the rules of court to speed up actions, (c) a *personal injuries summons* which must contain specified information, (d) full and detailed particulars including previous actions or injuries which have a bearing on the current injury, (e) the defendant to specify those elements of the claim on which he requires or does not require proof, (f) the parties to swear an affidavit verifying the contents of any pleadings, (g) the creation of an offence of making a statement in such affidavit which is false or misleading and which the person knows to be false or misleading, (h) a court ordered *mediation conference*, (i) *offers of settlement* to be lodged in court which could have a bearing on the order of the court on costs, (j) *pre-trial hearings* and for the appointment by the court of approved persons to investigate and give expert evidence on any matter, (k) the court to dismiss an action where the plaintiff gives or adduces or dishonestly causes to be given or adduced evidence which is false or misleading and which the person knows is false or misleading, (l) disregard by the court in assessing damages for any income which has not been returned for taxation purposes, (m) creation of the offence of giving or adducing evidence which is false or misleading, or giving false instructions or information to a solicitor or expert; and (n) the

exclusion of certain witnesses from attending the trial until called to give evidence.

The 2004 Act also provides that where an appeal is taken to the Supreme Court, that court may, if it considers that any matter in the case, relating to either liability or damages, is of exceptional public importance and the action is one of a class of claims in which the same or similar matters arise, invite appropriate persons to make submissions to the court in relation to the matter (CLCA 2004, s 21). The Court may exercise this power on the request of a party or of a person who is not a party or of its own motion. Where a person declines an invitation from the Court to make submissions, the person must state their reasons for declining in writing. See 'Reforming Practice and Procedure' by solicitor Eamonn Hall in *Law Society Gazette* (July 2004) 20.

The Rules Committees of the Superior Courts and the Circuit Court may make rules requiring any party to a personal injuries action to disclose to the other parties, without the necessity of an application to the courts, of certain information eg the report of a medical or paramedical expert intended to be called, the names and addresses of all witnesses intended to be called, a full statement of all items of special damages: Courts and Court Officers Act 1995, s 45; SI No 391 of 1998.

See LRC Reports *Periodic Payments and Structured Settlements* (LRC 54, 1996); and *Claims in respect of Latent Personal Injuries* (LRC 21, 1987). [Bibliography: White.] See CAUSE OF ACTION; DEATH, EFFECT OF; DAMAGES; DAMAGES, PERSONAL INJURIES; DISCOVERABILITY TEST; EXPERT EVIDENCE; EXPERT REPORT; FACIAL INJURIES; FALSE EVIDENCE; INCOME TAX; JURY, ABOLITION OF; LIMITATION OF ACTIONS; LODGMENT IN COURT; MEDIATION CONFERENCE; MENTAL DISTRESS; NERVOUS SHOCK; PRIMARY FACT; PRODUCT LIABILITY, EC; REGISTER OF PERSONAL INJURIES ACTIONS; STATE CLAIMS AGENCY; SUMMONS, PERSONAL INJURIES; SURGICAL OPERATION; WITNESS, EXCLUSION OF.

Personal Injuries Assessment Board. An independent corporate body with principal functions: (a) to arrange for the making of assessments of *relevant claims*; (b) to prepare a Book of Quantum containing general guidelines as to the amounts that may be awarded or assessed in respect of specified types of injury; (c) to cause a cost-benefit analysis to be made of the legal procedures that are currently employed in the State for the purpose of awarding compensation for personal injuries; and (d) to collect and analyse relevant data: Personal Injuries Assessment Board Act 2003, ss 53–54.

A *relevant claim* is a civil action intended to be pursued for the purpose of recovering damages, in respect of a wrong, for: (a) personal injuries, or (b) both such injuries and damages to property (but only if both have been caused by the same wrong) (PIABA 2003, ss 9 and 4(1)). The Act applies to the following civil actions: (i) a civil action by an employee against his employer for negligence or breach of duty arising in the course of the employee's employment with that employer (Employer Liability claims), (ii) a civil action by a person against another arising out of that other's ownership, driving or use of a mechanically propelled vehicle (Motor Accident claims), (iii) a civil action by a person against another arising out of that other's use or occupation of land or any structure or building (Public Liability claims), (iv) a civil action not falling within any of the preceding paragraphs (PIABA 2003, s 3). Excluded is any action arising out of the provision of any health service to a person, the carrying out of a medical or surgical procedure in relation to a person or the provision of any medical advice or treatment to a person (Medical Negligence claims) (PIABA 2003, s 3(d)). Also excluded are claims in respect of an alleged breach of a provision of the Constitution or garda compensation claims (PIABA 2003, s 4(1)).

There is a bar on bringing proceedings in court in respect of a *relevant claim* unless and until an application for assessment has been made to the Board and court proceedings have been authorised e g where the respondent does not consent to an assessment being made, or the Board decides not to proceed due to the complexity of the case, or an assessment is not accepted by either party, or the court does not approve an assessment in respect of a claimant who has not full capacity (PIABA 2003, ss 12, 14, 15, 17, 33, 36).

If a claimant withdraws an application before an assessment is made, this acts as a bar against a fresh application or the bring-ing of court proceedings in respect of the *relevant claim* (PIABA 2003, s 47). The Board has a duty of care towards vulnerable parties (e g those who do not appear to have a sufficient appreciation of the legal consequences of taking a particular step) and the Board discharges this duty by providing assistance or an explanation or advising on the desirability of the person taking legal advice (PIABA 2003, s 29). The Board is empowered to make rules of procedure and has done so (PIABA 2003, s 46 and SI No 219 of 2004).

The Board is required to prepare a strategic plan for the following five-year period, comprising the key objectives, outputs and related strategies, including the use of resources (PIABA 2003, s 78). From 1 June 2004, all personal injury claims arising from workplace accidents must be referred to the Board before legal proceedings are issued: SI No 252 of 2004. From 22 July 2004, all other personal injury claims are required to be referred to the Board: SI No 438 of 2004. The Board may make a charge on the claimant of €50 and on a respondent of €850: SI No 251 of 2004. See Finance Act 2004, s 40; Civil Liability and Courts Act 2004, ss 31–32.

See 'Proposed changes to the handling of personal injuries claims' by Conor Maguire SC in *Bar Review* (October/November 2002) 331; 'Bar Council proposals for reform' in *Bar Review* (June 2003) 107; 'Solicitors have been a voice for fairness for accident victims' in *Law Society Gazette* (January/February 2004) 8; 'The Personal Injuries Assessment Board Act 2003 – a critical analysis' by David Nolan SC in *Bar Review* (February 2004) 7. See website: *www.piab.ie*. [Bibliography: Quigley & Binchy.] See ASSESSMENT, PERSONAL INJURIES; BARRISTER IN EMPLOYMENT; DAMAGES, PERSONAL INJURIES; FATAL INJURIES; INCOME TAX; INQUISITORIAL PROCEDURE; LIMITATION OF ACTIONS; SOLICITOR IN EMPLOYMENT.

personal insolvency. See BANKRUPTCY.

personal liability. Legal obligation which attaches to a person. A person may become personally liable for the debts of a limited company of which he is a member where eg: (a) the number of members is below the minimum required: Companies Act 1963, s 5; (b) where there is a failure to correctly state the company's name: CA 1963, s 114(4); (c) where the memorandum of association so provides: CA 1963, s 197(1);

(d) where he is a disqualified or restricted person: Companies Act 1990, s 162; (e) where he acts on the directions of a disqualified or restricted person: CA 1990, ss 164–165; (f) where there is a failure to meet the capital requirements imposed by CA 1990, s 150: CA 1990, s 161(4); (g) where there is a failure to keep proper books of account: CA 1990, ss 204 and 202; (h) where there is an inaccurate statutory declaration of solvency: CA 1990, s 128 inserting CA 1963, s 256(8); (i) where there has been fraudulent or reckless trading (qqv): CA 1963, s 297A as inserted by CA 1990, s 138.

Any persons who were knowingly parties to the carrying on of the business in a fraudulent manner may be made personally responsible, without any limitation of liability, for the debts or other liabilities of the company: Companies Act 1963, s 297(1). This section is constitutional and it did not create a criminal offence, although the sanction was punitive; fraud must be established on the balance of probability: *O'Keeffe v Ferris* [1997] 2 ILRM 161, SC and 3 IR 463.

Before liability can be declared under CA 1990, s 204, the following matters must be established in evidence: (a) the company in question is being wound up; (b) the company is unable to pay its debts; (c) the company has contravened CA 1990, s 202; (d) such contravention contributed to the company's inability to pay its debts or has contributed substantial uncertainty or has substantially impeded the orderly winding up of the company; (e) the *officer* (or former *officer*) of the company knowingly and wilfully authorised or permitted the contravention or the officer is a person convicted under CA 1963: *Mehigan v Duignan* [1997] 1 ILRM 171, HC and 1 IR 340. The term 'officer' of a company is not restricted solely to executives of a company (*Mehigan* case). The standard of proof required is that of a civil wrong ie on the balance of probability (*Mehigan* case).

See *Guilfoyle v Mark A Synnott* (1993) Irish Times, 10 February; *O'Keeffe v Ferris* [1994] 1 ILRM 425, HC; *Jones v Gunn* [1997] 3 IR 1, HC; *Southern Mineral Oil Ltd v Cooney* [1998] 2 ILRM 375, HC. See RSC Ord 75B inserted by SI No 278 of 1991. See also Merchant Shipping (Salvage and Wreck) Act 1993, s 60. See MacCann in 9 ILT & SJ (1991) 206 & 232. See COMPANY, LIMITED; LIFTING THE CORPO-RATE VEIL; LIMITATION OF LIABILITY; LOAN TO DIRECTOR; SURCHARGE.

personal liberty. No citizen may be deprived of his personal liberty save in accordance with law: 1937 Constitution, art 40(4)(1). See EUROPEAN CONVENTION ON HUMAN RIGHTS; HABEAS CORPUS; FALSE IMPRISONMENT; PRISON; TRESPASS TO THE PERSON.

personal portfolio life policy. A life policy under the terms of which the policyholder or a person connected with the policyholder, can select, or influence the selection of, the assets which determine the policy benefits: Finance Act 2002, s 40. Funds in such a policy can accumulate without annual taxation being imposed on income or gains (called the 'gross-roll' basis); it is only on payment to the policyholder that an *exit charge* can be made (23%) and an *addition charge* of 20%.

personal property. Goods, chattels and leaseholds; personalty. A registered trade mark is personal property: Trade Marks Act 1996, s 26. [Bibliography: Bell.] See COPYRIGHT; PERFORMERS' RIGHTS; TRADE MARK, ASSIGNMENT OF.

personal public service number (PPS Number). The Minister is empowered to introduce *personal public service numbers* by which persons will be capable of being identified in relation to their dealings with the State: Social Welfare Act 1998, s 14. The section also provides for the issue of a *public service card* which will have: (a) inscribed on it – the person's name, PPS Number, primary account number and date of issue; and (b) electronically coded – the person's date of birth, gender, primary account number, expiry date of card and the card service code. There is also provision for a *payment card* and for the sharing of information between specified bodies.

The Data Protection Commissioner has been critical of the 1996 interdepartmental report, Integrated Social Services System, that gave rise to the 1998 legislation; quoting *Marcel v Metropolitan Police Commissioner* [1992] Ch 225: 'the dossier of private information is the badge of the totalitarian State'. The government announced in March 2000 that it was intended that everyone would have a PPS Number by 2002. The issue of PPS Numbers commenced in June 2000.

Regulations have been made prescribing the information which a prescribed body may be required to share with the Department of Education and Science in relation to the use of the PPS Number as a unique student identifier at all levels of the education system: Social Welfare (Sharing of Information) Regulations 2001, SI No 242 of 2001. See also Social Welfare Act 1999, s 27; Social Welfare Act 2000, s 32; Pensions (Amendment) Act 2002, s 56; Social Welfare (Miscellaneous Provisions) Act 2004, s 11.

There is an obligation on employers, from 1 January 2003, to take reasonable steps to ensure that the PPS Number provided by an employee does, in fact, refer to that employee: Income Tax (Employment) Regulations 2002, SI No 511 of 2002. See Civil Registration Act 2004, s 2(1); Civil Liability and Courts Act 2004, ss 10(2)(b) and 12(2)(a). See also PUBLIC SERVICE IDENTITY. See BIRTH, REGISTRATION OF; DEATH, REGISTRATION OF; PRIVATE RESIDENTIAL TENANCIES REGISTER.

personal representative. An executor or administrator of the estate of a deceased person. The real and personal estate of a deceased person devolve on his death and become vested in his personal representatives, notwithstanding any testamentary disposition. The personal representatives are deemed in law to be his heirs and assigns within the meaning of all trusts and powers. See Succession Act 1965, s 10; Taxes Consolidation Act 1997, ss 799–805.

A personal representative of a divorced deceased spouse who had remarried, is under a duty to notify the previous spouse of the death and, in the event that the previous spouse makes an application to the court for a financial provision to be made out of the deceased spouse's estate, not to distribute any of the estate without leave of the court until such time as the court makes its determination: Family Law (Divorce) Act 1996, s 18(6)–(7). See also s 18(10).

The personal representative of any recipient of social welfare must deliver to the Minister a notice of intention to distribute the assets of the deceased and provide a schedule of the deceased's assets; this is to enable the Minister to obtain repayment of any moneys which were overpaid or not payable at all: Social Welfare (Consolidation) Act 1993, s 280. The personal representative must provide the Minister, on request, a copy of the Inland Revenue affidavit of the deceased: Practice Notes in

Law Society Gazette (January/February 2004) 54. [Bibliography: Keating.] See ADMINISTRATOR; DEVASTAVIT; EJECTMENT; EXECUTOR; INSOLVENT ESTATE; PROBATE TAX.

Personal Retirement Savings Account (PRSA). A contract-based product between an individual and a PRSA provider in the form of an investment account, designed as a long-term retirement account: Pensions Act 1990, ss 91–125 inserted by Pensions (Amendment) Act 2002, s 3; Taxes Consolidation Act 1997 amended by P(A)A 2002, s 4.

The objective of the PRSA framework, introduced by the 2002 Act, is to encourage pension provision by enabling persons to save for retirement in a flexible manner.

Some key aspects of PRSAs are: (a) PRSAs are regulated by the Pensions Board; (b) PRSA products must be approved by the Board and the Revenue Commissioners; (c) PRSA charges must be transparent; (d) contributions to PRSAs may be made irrespective of employment status and can be taken by the employee when changing jobs.

Contributions to PRSAs are not liable to Pay Related Social Insurance deductions or to health contribution: Social Welfare (Miscellaneous Provisions) Act 2002, ss 11 and 16, Sch, Pt III. Provision has been made to extend the PAYE 'net pay' arrangements to PRSAs; this will permit tax relief for the contributions to be allowed by the employer by operating the PAYE system on the emoluments after deducting the amount of the PRSA contributions: Income Tax (Employment) Regulations 2002, SI No 511 of 2002. A role has been given to social welfare inspectors to determine, when carrying out an examination or inquiry on PRSI, whether the employer is complying with his obligations of enabling employees to access a PRSA: Social Welfare (Miscellaneous Provisions) Act 2004, s 12.

For transfer arrangements from an occupational pension scheme to a PRSA and vice versa, see SI No 429 of 2003. See also Disclosure Regulations 2002, SI No 501 of 2002 and 2003, SI No 342 of 2003; Operational Requirements Regulations 2002, SI No 503 of 2002 and 2003, SI No 341 of 2003; Overseas Transfer Payments, SI No 716 of 2003. See Social Welfare (Miscellaneous Provisions) Act 2003, s 24, Sch, paras 9–14; Finance Act 2003, s 14;

Unclaimed Life Assurance Policies Act 2003, s 2(1); Finance Act 2004, s 86.

At end March 2004, a total of 26,899 PRSAs had been taken out with a value of €60.5m. For a detailed *Tax Guide to PRSAs*, see website: *www.revenue.ie/publications/leaflets*. For 'PRSAs: employers' obligations', and for a full listing of PRSA providers and approved products, see website: *www.pensionsboard.ie*. See 'Sunset boulevard' by solicitor Maureen Dolan in *Law Society Gazette* (August/September 2003) 26. See PENSIONS OMBUDSMAN.

personal rights. Certain *personal rights* are specifically provided for in the Constitution eg right to life, right to information, right to travel, right to a good name, right to equality before the law, right to personal liberty, right to trade and earn a livelihood; right to assembly, to form associations and to freedom of expression: 1937 Constitution, art 40. The State guarantees in its laws to respect, and, as far as practicable, by its laws to defend and vindicate the *personal rights* of the citizen (qv): 1937 Constitution, art 40(3)(1). See FUNDAMENTAL RIGHTS; CONJUGAL RIGHTS.

personal services. In relation to personal services provided in a person's home, includes but is not limited to services that are in the nature of services *in loco parentis* or involving caring for those residing in the home: Employment Equality Act 1998, s 2(1) as inserted by Equality Act 2004, s 3. As regards equality provisions on access to employment, an 'employee' does not include a person employed in another person's home for the provision of *personal services* for persons residing in that home where the services affect the private or family life of those persons. See also INJUNCTION; SPECIFIC PERFORMANCE.

personal watercraft. A craft of less than 4 metres in length which uses an internal combustion engine having a water jet pump as its primary source of propulsion and which is designed to be operated by a person or persons sitting, standing or kneeling on, rather than within the confines of, a hull: Merchant Shipping Act 1992, s 2(1) as inserted by Merchant Shipping (Investigation of Marine Casualties) Act 2000, s 44(1)(d). A personal watercraft is a '*vessel*' for the purposes of the 1992 Act. See PLEASURE CRAFT.

personality disorder. Gross personality disorder, which renders a person incapable of forming any proper marital relationship, may be a good ground for a nullity decree: *W(C) v C* [1989] IR 696. See EMOTIONAL IMMATURITY; PSYCHIATRIC DISORDER.

personalty. Personal property; includes leaseholds.

personation. The offence committed by a person who: (a) at an election applies for a ballot paper in the name of some other person, or (b) having obtained a ballot paper once at an election, applies at the same election for a ballot paper in his own name: Electoral Act 1992, s 134 and, ss 166–170. Compensation may be payable to a person arrested on a charge of personation made by a personation agent (qv) without reasonable or just cause (EA 1992, s 158). See also Local Government Act 2001, s 25 regarding local elections. See European Parliament Elections Act 1997, Sch 2, r 103; Social Welfare Act 1997, s 31; Electoral (Amendment) Act 2004, s 32.

personation agent. A person appointed in writing by a candidate in a Dáil election (or by his election agent) for the purpose of assisting in the detection of personation: Electoral Act 1992, s 60(3). One such person may be appointed as the candidate's agent in each polling station. A personation agent must not leave a polling station without the permission of the presiding officer (EA 1992, s 148). See also Presidential Elections Act 1993, s 34(4); Referendum Act 1994, s 26(3); European Parliament Elections Act 1997, Sch 2, rr 24–26.

personnel record. A record relating wholly or mainly to one or more of the following: (a) the competence or ability of an individual in his capacity as a member of the staff of a public body, or (b) his employment or employment history, or (c) an evaluation of the performance of his functions: Freedom of Information Act 1997, s 6(6) as amended by Freedom of Information (Amendment) Act 2003, s 4. A person does not have a right of access to his personnel record under the 1997 Act if it was created more than three years before commencement of that Act and provided it is not being used, or proposed to be used, in a manner to affect the person adversely. In a particular case, a civil servant was granted access to his full personnel file; the Information Commissioner had granted partial access: *Minister for Agriculture v Information Commissioner* (1999) Irish Times, 18 December, HC.

A decision to place a disputed letter or report on a person's personnel file is a mere secretarial act; it is not a decision capable of being the subject of judicial review: *Ainsworth v Minister for Defence* [2003] ITLR (21 July) HC. See FREEDOM OF INFORMATION.

persuade to murder. The offence committed by a person who persuades, or endeavours to persuade, another to commit a murder (qv): Offences Against the Person Act 1861, s 41. See AID AND ABET.

persuasive authorities. Precedents (qv) which are not binding on a court. They include *obiter dicta*, decisions of inferior courts, and decisions of the US and Canadian Supreme Courts, and of the English, Australian and New Zealand courts.

perverse verdict. A verdict altogether against the evidence. The courts will not interfere with the verdict of a jury in a case where there is evidence to support a verdict, where the trial is conducted in an exemplary manner, with express warnings given to the jury; it is for the jury to assess the evidence and to arrive at a verdict: *DPP v O'Brien* [1990] 8 ILT Dig 157. See VERDICT.

perverting the course of justice. Any act tending or intended to pervert the course of justice is an offence (formerly, a misdemeanour) at common law. Manufacturing false evidence is such an offence. *R v Vreones* [1891] 1 QB 360. See BRIBERY AND CORRUPTION.

pesticides. For the maximum residue levels for pesticides in or on: (a) foodstuffs of animal origin, see SI No 180 of 1999 as amended by SIs Nos 118 and 239 of 2004; (b) cereals, see SI No 181 of 1999 as amended by SIs Nos 119 and 240 of 2004; (c) fruit and vegetables, see SI No 105 of 1989, as amended by SIs Nos 120 and 231 of 2004. See DANGEROUS SUBSTANCE; FOOD, STANDARD OF.

pet dog and cat. Regulations have been made to enable pet dogs and cats to enter Ireland from the UK without the need for quarantine, where the pet has entered the UK from countries approved under the terms of the UK PETS (*Pet Travel Scheme*) and which are microchipped, vaccinated, blood tested and certified in accordance with the provisions of that scheme: Importation of Dogs and Cats Regulations 2003, SI No 192 of 2003. All dogs and cats entering the State must have been treated against tapeworm and ticks: SI No 193 of 2003. See also Importation of Dogs and Cats Order of 1929 (SR & O No 4 of 1929).

It is intended to permit, from early October 2004, direct travel to Ireland on approved carriers of qualifying pets from eligible countries with entry at a limited number of approved entry points, implementing Regulation (EC) 2003/998 and 2004/592. See EC (Pet Passport Regulations 2004, SI No 423 of 2004. For details of the Irish scheme, see website: *www.agriculture.gov.ie/pets*. For details on the UK PETS scheme, see website: *www.defra.gov.uk/animalh/quarantine/index*.

Petersberg tasks. The new priority humanitarian, rescue, peacekeeping and crisis management tasks incorporated in the EU Common Foreign and Security Policy as a result of the undertaking to enhance co-operation on international affairs in the Maastricht Treaty 1992: National Forum on Europe, *Glossary of Terms* (2003). So called after the place in Germany where agreement on the tasks was reached. The draft European Constitutional Treaty proposes to extend the tasks to cover joint disarmament operations, military advice and post-conflict stabilisation. See COMMON FOREIGN AND SECURITY POLICY.

petition. (1) A written application to the court for relief or remedy which is used in particular cases to commence proceedings e g in matters concerning bankruptcy, matrimonial causes, patents, wards of court and matters relating to professional disciplinary bodies and to the Companies Acts. Unless the court gives leave to the contrary, there must be at least two clear days between the service of a petition and the day for hearing it: RSC Ord 5, r 17. See also RSC Ord 5, rr 15–17; Ord 40, r 1. See also Circuit Court Rules 2001 Ord 47, r 1 and Ord 58.

A petition may be amended at any stage of proceedings: RSC Ord 28, r 1. The fact that an amendment is novel does not represent a barrier to its being permitted by the courts, where the amendment is necessary to ensure that the real questions in controversy between the parties are before the court: *Wolfe v Wolfe* [2001] 1 ILRM 389, HC and 1 IR 313.

(2) A Bill may be the subject of a joint *petition* to the President of Ireland where the majority of Seanad Éireann and not less than one-third of Dáil Éireann request the

President to decline to sign and promulgate the Bill on the ground that it contains a proposal of such national importance that the will of the people thereon ought to be ascertained: 1937 Constitution, art 27(1). If the President decides that there are such grounds, she will not sign and promulgate the Bill as law unless either the proposal is agreed: (a) by the people at a referendum (qv); or (b) by a resolution of the Dáil after a dissolution and reassembly of the Dáil (Constitution, art 27(5)).

(3) Any citizen of the European Union (qv), and any natural or legal person residing or having his registered office in a member state has the right to address, individually or in association with other citizens or persons, a *petition* to the European Parliament on a matter which comes within the Community's field of activity and which affects him directly: EC Treaty, arts 21 and 194 of the consolidated (2002) version. See ELECTION PETITION; REFERENDUM PETITION; SUMMONS.

petition for bankruptcy. See BANKRUPTCY, PETITION FOR.

petition for winding up. A petition requesting the court to wind up a company, which is presented by the company itself, or any creditor, any contributory (qv), the Minister, or in the case of oppression (qv) any person entitled by virtue of the Companies Act 1963, s 205. The right to present a petition is a statutory right which cannot be excluded by the *articles of association: Re Perevil Gold Mines Co Ltd* [1898] 1 Ch 122. See also Companies Act 1963, s 215 as amended by Companies (Amendment) Act 1983, Sch 1, para 18, and Sch 3. See WINDING UP, COMPULSORY; COURT PROTECTION OF COMPANY.

petroleum. Includes crude petroleum, oil made from petroleum or from coal, shale, peat or other bituminous substances and other fractions of petroleum: Dangerous Substances Act 1972, s 2(1). *Petroleum spirit* means petroleum which, at normal atmospheric pressure, gives off an inflammable vapour at a temperature of less than 72 degrees Fahrenheit (DSA 1972, s 20(1)).

No person may have petroleum spirit in his possession or under his control except in a store licensed by the proper local or harbour authority; this provision does not apply to a quantity not exceeding 3 gallons kept in suitable leakproof containers, securely stopped and containing not more

than one gallon each (DSA 1972, s 21). See Retail and Private Petroleum Stores (Amendment) Regulations 2002, SI No 624 of 2002. See SOLUS AGREEMENT.

petroleum, exploration for. It is unlawful for any person to search for petroleum in any area in the State unless he is the licensee under a *petroleum lease*; it is also unlawful for any person to get, raise, take or carry away petroleum unless he is the lessee under a petroleum lease: Petroleum and Other Minerals Developments Act 1960 as amended by Energy (Miscellaneous Provisions) Act 1995, s 17. All *State* petroleum vests in the Minister. See also Continental Shelf Act 1968, s 4.

A right to drill for and take away petroleum is now rateable; however there is a maximum 20-year protection period where oil was first produced before the commencement date of the Act: Valuation Act 2001, s 59(3). See COMMERCIAL PROCEEDINGS.

Petty Sessions. Originally a meeting of two or more *justices of the peace* to transact business with which it was either necessary or desirable that more than one justice would deal. Subsequently a *Petty Sessional Court* was a court of summary jurisdiction sitting in a petty sessional courthouse: Interpretation Act 1889, s 13(12). See Petty Sessions (Ireland) Act 1851. See now DISTRICT COURT.

pharmaceutical chemist, registered. A person registered in the Register of Pharmaceutical Chemists for Ireland maintained under the Pharmacy Acts 1875 to 1977. The validity of the EC Directive which placed a restriction on the recognition of pharmacy qualifications obtained in other member states, as an artificial counterbalance to the licensing system operated in certain member states, could not be challenged in a national court: *Young v Pharmaceutical Society of Ireland* [1994] 2 ILRM 262, HC; [1994] ELR 177, HC and [1995] 2 IR 91, HC.

The High Court also dismissed a challenge to the regulations, giving effect to the EC Directive, which prohibited a non-Irish EU citizen who had not graduated in Ireland as a pharmacist from running a pharmacy unless it had been in operation for not less than three years: *McCauley Chemists (Blackpool) Ltd & Sajda v Ireland* (2002) Irish Times, 1 August; EC (Recognition of Qualifications in Pharmacy) Regulations 1991, SI No 330 of 1991. The court held that the Minister in making the regulations had simply repeated what was in the Directive; the 'three-year rule' pre-dated the Directive.

See EC Treaty, art 47 of the consolidated (2002) version. For the list of qualifications in pharmacy which are recognised for the purposes of free movement within the EU, see EC (Recognition of Qualifications in Pharmacy) (Amendment) Regulations 2003, SI No 352 of 2003 and Amendment Regulations 2004 to cater for the accession States, SI No 187 of 2004.

In 2002, the regulations which restricted the opening of new pharmacies were revoked: Health (Community Pharmacy Contractor Revocation) Regulations 2002, SI No 28 of 2002. These regulations revoke the Health (Community Pharmacy Contractor Agreement) Regulations 1996, SI No 152 of 1996, which specified the criteria and procedures under which the chief executive officer of the relevant health board would determine the issue of new community pharmacy contractor agreements for the provision of community pharmacy services under the Health Act 1970.

See Regulations of the Pharmaceutical Society of Ireland 1971 to 2002; Regulation 1992: Iris Oifigiúil, 1 December 1992, and SI No 212 of 2002. See *A Worker v Pharmaceutical Society of Ireland* [1996] ELR 89, LC. See 'E-Commerce & Pharmacy Law' by Seamus Clarke BL in *Bar Review* (May 2001) 428. For the *Pharmacy Review Group Report* (2003), published in 2004, see website: *www.doh.ie*. For the Pharmaceutical Society of Ireland, see website: *www.pharmaceuticalsociety.ie*. See FAMILY PLANNING SERVICE; MEDICINAL PRODUCTS; POISON; PRESCRIPTION DRUGS.

pharmaceutical company. See SCIENTIFIC RESEARCH-BASED COMPANIES.

pheasant. An untrue allegation, made at a meeting of gun clubs in Castleisland, that two named experienced gunmen, had shot a sitting pheasant out-of-season, was held to be defamatory and they were each awarded €15,000 plus costs: *O'Sullivan & Culloty v Enright* (2004) Irish Times, 28 July, CC Killarney. See GAME.

phoenix company. The colloquial term to describe a company which is wound up having liabilities in excess of its assets and shortly thereafter reopens for business under a different name.

In order to curb this abuse of company legislation, the law was changed by widening the provisions dealing with the *disqualification* of directors and by requiring that directors of an insolvent company could only be directors of companies with a minimum share capital, fully paid up in cash: Companies Act 1990. See DIRECTORS; DISQUALIFICATION ORDER.

photograph. The *author* of a photograph includes the photographer: Copyright and Related Rights Act 2000, s 21(h). Photographs must not be taken of a person in custody in a garda station except with his written consent and, where he is under the age of 17 years, the written consent of an appropriate adult: Treatment of Persons in Custody in Garda Síochána Stations Regulations 1987, SI No 119 of 1987, reg 18. Consent is not required where the garda is otherwise empowered by law. See ARTISTIC WORK; AUTHOR; COPYRIGHT; HUNT; PATIENT, PHOTOGRAPH OF.

photographs, use of in identification. Where photographs are used for identification of the perpetrator of an offence, a series of at least twelve photographs ought always to be presented to a witness or victim for the purpose of such identification, even where the gardaí have a particular person in mind as the perpetrator; the witness or victim should be asked whether any of the persons depicted was the perpetrator: *The People v Mills* [1957] IR 106 applying *R v Dwyer* [1925] 2 KB 799.

There must be exemplary fairness in the use of photographs eg where the gardaí have a suspect, whether in custody or not, and they show a witness photographs from which the accused would be identified, prior to an identification parade, this would be unfair to the accused: *People (DPP) v Rapple* [1999] 1 ILRM 113, CCA. For preservation of photographs, see DCR 1997 Ord 31. See Criminal Justice Bill 2004, s 11. See DOCK IDENTIFICATION; FINGERPRINTS.

physical reasons. The Supreme Court has held that 'physical reasons' within the meaning of the Adoption Act 1988, s 3(1)(I)(A), includes both physical and mental disability; to hold otherwise would be gravely unjust to persons suffering from physical disability: *Northern Area Health Board v An Bord Uchtála* [2003] 1 ILRM 481, SC. Adoption is permitted where the parents of a child, for *physical* or moral *reasons*, have failed in their duty towards the child and the failure is likely to continue and it constitutes an 'abandonment of their parental rights'. See ADOPTION; PARENTAL DUTIES.

phytosanitary. Term used for the field of plant health: National Forum on Europe, *Glossary of Terms* (2003). See EUROPEAN COMMISSION FOOD AND VETERINARY OFFICE.

picketing. It is lawful to picket in contemplation or furtherance of a trade dispute. It is lawful for one or more persons, acting on their own behalf or on behalf of a trade union in contemplation or furtherance of a trade dispute, to attend at, or where that is not practicable, at the approaches to, a place where their employer works or carries on business, if they so attend merely for the purpose of peacefully obtaining or communicating information, or of peacefully persuading any person to work or abstain from working: Industrial Relations Act 1990, s 11. This protection is confined to *authorised* trade unions holding a negotiation licence and their members and officials, and only after a secret ballot has taken place (IRA 1990, ss 9 and 14). See *G T Crampton Ltd v Building & Allied Trades Union* [1998] 1 ILRM 430, SC and ELR 7 – in this case an injunction preventing picketing was granted as the plaintiff had raised a fair question to be tried and damages would be an inadequate remedy.

There is no immunity in respect of picketing of an employer's home: *Dillon v Walsh & Nolan* (1992) Irish Times, 20 December, DC. However, the High Court has held that IRA 1990, s 11(a) is not clear on whether immunity extended to a site where the employer no longer works, but did work when the trade dispute commenced: *Malincross Ltd v BATU* [2002] ELR 78, HC and 3 IR 607.

The method of picketing and the numbers picketing must be peaceful and be reasonable having regard to all the circumstances: *Brendan Dunne Ltd v Fitzpatrick* [1958] IR 29; *EI Co Ltd v Kennedy* [1968] IR 69. The legal status of *secondary picketing* (qv) was uncertain; the courts tended to regard it as unlawful; contrast *Roundabout Ltd v Beirne* [1959] IR 423 and *Ellis v Wright* [1978] IR 6. It is now lawful in certain circumstances. See SECONDARY PICKETING.

Picketing is not lawful if its purpose is unconstitutional eg if its purpose is to deprive another of their constitutional rights: *Educational Co of Ireland v Fitzpatrick* [1961] IR 323; *Murtagh Properties Ltd v Cleary* [1972] IR 330. Persons engaged in picketing may not indulge in activity which would amount to a criminal offence eg watching and besetting: Conspiracy and Protection of Property Act 1875, s 7; or threatening abusive or insulting behaviour, or disorderly conduct, in a public place, or distribution of material which is threatening: Criminal Justice (Public Order) Act 1994, ss 5–7. See IMMUNITY; SIT-IN; LABOUR INJUNCTION.

pig. A 'breeding pig' means a sow or boar kept on a holding to produce progeny: Diseases of Animals (National Pig Identification and Tracking System) Order 2002, SI No 341 of 2002. A 'production pig' means any pig over 30 kg in weight which is being fattened for slaughter; a 'sow' means a female pig after its first farrowing: Environmental Protection Agency Act 1992, Sch 1, as substituted by Protection of the Environment Act 2003, s 18 and Sch 1, para 6.2. See INTENSIVE AGRICULTURE.

pillars of the EU. The EU makes decisions in three separate 'domains' or policy areas, also known as the three 'pillars' of the EU. The three pillars are: (a) the Community domain, covering most of the common policies, where decisions are taken by the 'Community method' involving the European Commission, the Parliament and the Council; (b) the common foreign and security policy, where decisions are taken unanimously by the Council alone; and (c) the domain on police and judicial co-operation in criminal matters, where only the Council, voting unanimously, is involved in the decision making. See COMMUNITY BRIDGE.

piller, anton. See ANTON PILLER ORDER.

pilotage. A port company is under an obligation to organise and ensure the provision of pilotage services: (a) by employing pilots as members of its staff, or (b) by licensing persons to perform acts of pilotage: Harbours Act 1996, s 56. A port company may make pilotage bye-laws (HA 1996, s 71). A ship which is being navigated in a pilotage district, where pilotage is compulsory, must be under the pilotage of a licensed or employed pilot or under the pilotage of a master or first mate who is the holder of a *pilotage exemption certificate* (HA 1996, s 60). See *Turner v Pilotage Committee* [1989] 7 ILT Dig 23. See HARBOUR AUTHORITIES.

pimp. Colloquial term to describe a person who controls and directs a prostitute and lives in whole or in part on her earnings. See PROSTITUTE.

PIN. Acronym for *personal identification number,* which is a unique code to the authorised user eg in ATMs.

pinholes. Holes or similar marks on a will are deemed to be an indication that there are missing pages or that some other document was attached to the will.

piracy. (1) The infringement of copyright. See INFRINGEMENT OF COPYRIGHT; PROHIBITED GOODS.

(2) For the old crime of piracy, see Piracy Act 1837. The death penalty for piracy with violence was abolished by Criminal Justice Act 1964, s 6. The law and practice applicable to misdemeanours is that which now applies to all offences, including piracy: Criminal Law Act 1997, s 3(2).

pirated goods. See PROHIBITED GOODS.

piscary. The right to fish in the waters of another. See PROFIT A PRENDRE.

placename. Includes the name of any province, county, city, town, village, barony, parish or townland, or of any territorial feature (whether natural or artificial), district, region or place, as shown on the maps of Ordnance Survey Ireland: Official Languages Act 2003, s 31. The Minister is empowered to make a *placenames order:* (a) declaring the Irish language version of a placename specified in the order, (b) amending or revoking a placenames order (OLA 2003, s 32). Before making such an order, the Minister must have received and considered advice from *An Coimisiun Logainmneacha,* which was established by warrant dated 24 October 1946. The Minister must not make a declaration in relation to a place in a Gaeltacht area in respect of which a declaration under Part XVIII of the Local Government Act 2001 is in force (OLA 2003, s 32(2)).

In a legal document, words in the Irish language version of a *placenames order* must be construed as referring to the same place as in the English language version, unless a contrary intention appears (OLA 2003, s 33(1)). However, where the Minister has made a declaration under OLA 2003, s 32 in respect of a placename in the Gaeltacht area, the English language version of the placename will no longer have any force or effect, with exceptions (OLA 2003, s 33(2)). The 2003 Act repeals the Place

Names (Irish Forms) Act 1973. As from 1 January 2005, the Irish language version only of a Gaeltacht placename may be used on specified maps: SI No 212 of 2004. For the official Irish language version of the names of provinces and counties, see SI No 519 of 2003. See also SI No 413 of 2000; SI No 221 of 2001. See NAME, CHANGE OF.

place, dangerous. See DANGEROUS PLACE.

place of business. See FOREIGN COMPANY.

placing. (1) As regards the shares of a company, the allocation of shares by the company to a financial intermediary (an issuing house) which agrees to purchase and place them with clients.

(2) As regards stock exchange companies, a marketing of securities already in issue but not listed or not yet in issue, to specified persons or clients of the sponsor or any securities house assisting in the placing, which does not involve an offer to the public or to existing holders of the issuer's securities generally: Listing Rules 2000, paras 4.7–4.9. See FLOATATION.

plagiarism. See CHEATING.

plain language. See INTERPRETATION OF LEGISLATION, REFORM.

plaintiff. The person who brings a legal action; a plaintiff includes any person seeking relief against any other person by any form of civil proceedings: RSC Ord 125, r 1. A defendant in an action may be the plaintiff of a counterclaim (qv).

Where an action is commenced in the name of the wrong person as plaintiff, the court may, if satisfied that there was a *bona fide* mistake, order that another person be added or substituted as plaintiff: RSC Ord 15, r 2. See also Ord 15, r 13. The Court has a discretion to refuse to make the order where the action would be clearly statute barred by such a change of parties: *Kennemerland v Montgomery* [2000] 1 ILRM 370, HC. See O'BYRNE LETTER.

planning appeal. The appeal which a person may make to An Bord Pleanála against the decision of an application for planning permission: Planning and Development Act 2000, ss 37, 125–146. The only persons who can appeal are: (a) the applicant for planning permission, (b) any other person who made a submission or observation on the application in question, (c) a person with an interest in adjoining land with the permission of An Bord Pleanála; and (d) an authority or body who should have been notified of the application by the planning authority but was not (PDA 2000, ss 37(1)(a) and 37(4)). The appeal must be made within the period of four weeks from the date of the decision of the planning authority (PDA 2000, s 37(1)(d)). A person appealing to the Board is entitled to rely on the date entered in the statutory register as the date upon which planning permission was granted, even though that entry is incorrect: *Foley v Dublin Corporation* (1990) Irish Times, 26 October.

An Bord Pleanála may grant permission for a development, even if it *materially contravenes* the development plan, but only where it considers that the proposed development is of strategic or national importance, or there are conflicting objectives in the development plan, or permission should be granted having regard to regional planning guidelines or other policy directives (PDA 2000, s 37(2)). See also Planning and Development (Amendment) Act 2002, s 10.

See *Inver Resources v Limerick Corporation* [1988] ILRM 47; *Brady v Donegal Co Council* [1987] HC and [1989] 7 ILT Dig 21; *Graves v An Bord Pleanála* [1997] 2 IR 205, HC; *McAnenley v An Bord Pleanála* [2002] 2 IR 763, HC. See *Kimber* in 11 ILT & SJ (1993) 17. [Bibliography: Galligan (1); LexisNexis.] For limitations on judicial review, see JUDICIAL REVIEW, PLANNING. See also BORD PLEANÁLA, AN.

planning authority. The council of a county, the corporation of a borough, and the council of an urban district: Planning and Development Act 2000, s 2(1). A planning authority is required to carry out reviews of its organisation and systems and procedures (PDA 2000, s 255(2)). The Minister may in certain circumstances appoint a Commissioner to carry out the functions of a planning authority (PDA 2000, s 255(4)).

A planning authority in exercise of its powers (under the Local Government (Planning and Development) Act 1963) owes no duty of care at common law towards the occupiers of buildings erected in its functional area to avoid damage due to defective siting and construction: *Sunderland v Louth Co Council* [1990] ILRM 658, SC. [Bibliography: LexisNexis.] See CODE OF CONDUCT; COUNCILLOR, DISCLOSURE OF INTEREST.

planning consultations. Consultations which a planning authority has with a person who has an interest in land and who intends to make a planning application; such consultations cannot prejudice the performance by the authority of its statutory functions and cannot be relied upon in the formal planning process or in legal proceedings: Planning and Development Act 2000, s 247.

planning injunction. See INJUNCTION, PLANNING.

planning law. The body of law dealing with: (a) the permission which is required for every form of development of land, save in the case of *exempted developments* (qv); (b) the statutory duty of local planning authorities (qv) to prepare a *development plan* (qv); (c) the appeal mechanisms which exist where there is an adverse decision of the planning authority; (d) the *compensation* which is payable in respect of a refusal to grant permission or in respect of the conditions imposed; and (e) the enforcement powers of the planning authorities to ensure compliance with the terms of planning permission and to restrain unauthorised development. See Local Government (Planning and Development) Acts 1963, 1976, 1982, 1983, 1990, 1992, 1993 and 1999; and the reforming and consolidating Planning and Development Act 2000 as amended by the Planning and Development (Amendment) Act 2002.

The 1963 Act established the basic framework of planning law. The 1976 Act sought to remedy the more serious deficiencies by providing new and more extensive enforcement machinery and establishing a planning appeal board (An Bord Pleanála). The 1982 Act provided more stringent penalties for breaches. The 1983 Act altered the method of appointing the chairman and members of the planning appeal board. The 1990 Act amended and consolidated the law on planning compensation. The 1992 Act amended the law on planning appeals so that they would be dealt with expeditiously. The 1993 Act regularised the position regarding State authorities (qv) and introduced a procedure of public notice and consultation as regards development by local authorities and the 1999 Act made better provision for the protection of the architectural heritage.

The Planning and Development Act 2000 consolidated all the previous Acts and much of the regulations dealing with Environmental Assessment Regulations. It also introduced a number of significant changes and new initiatives e g the principle of sustainable development, and provision for affordable housing, architectural conservation areas, landscape conservation areas, strategic development zones, events, funfairs, and local area plans. It also provided for more delegation of decisions from the Minister to An Bord Pleanála and it also limited appeals generally to persons who made submissions or observations during the planning process.

For detailed listing of amendments to the Planning and Development Act 2000, see Local Government Act 2001, s 247 and Sch 4. Also the Planning and Development (Amendment) Act 2002 amends PDA 2000, Part V dealing with housing supply; it sets out additional ways under which an applicant for permission for development may comply with the now mandatory requirements of Part V in relation to the provision of social and affordable housing.

It has been held that planning procedures are part of the administrative systems of the State and are not part of the judicial system: *O'Flynn Construction Co Ltd v An Bord Pleanála* [2000] 1 IR 497, HC.

Consolidated regulations have been made to implement the Planning and Development Act 2000; the regulations consolidate all previous regulations made under PDA 2000 and replace the Local Government (Planning and Development) Regulations 1994 to 2001: Planning and Development Regulations 2001, SI No 600 of 2001. Parts of the consolidated regulations came into operation on 21 January 2002, with the remainder on 11 March 2002. See also Planning and Development Regulations 2002, SI No 70 of 2002 (scales of location maps and details to be indicated on location maps) and SI No 149 of 2002 (fee for licence for fingerpost signs for tourist accommodation); and Regulations 2003, SI No 90 of 2003 (amending arts 49 and 50).

Provision was made in 2000 to transfer the function of certifying *environmental impact assessments* of a local authority's own development from the Minister to An Bord Pleanála: Local Government (Planning and Development) (No 2) Regulations 2000, SI No 458 of 2000.

For the rules governing appeals and orders under the Planning Acts, see Circuit Court Rules 2001 Ord 56. For the Irish Planning Institute, see website: *www.irishplanninginstitute.ie*. See *Urban Sprawl, Once-off Housing and Planning*

Policy by James Nix in (2002) 10 ISLR 78. [Bibliography: A & L Goodbody (2); Butterworths (11); Galligan; Gore Grimes; Grist; Grist & Macken; Keane (3); Lexis-Nexis; Lyall; Nowlan; O'Donnell M; O'Sullivan & Sheppard; Simons; Walsh & Keane.] See BORD PLEANÁLA, AN; OUTDOOR EVENTS; PEAT EXTRACTION.

planning offences. A number of offences are provided for under the Planning and Development Act 2000 eg these include causing damage without lawful authority to a protected structure (PDA 2000, s 58(4)); failure to comply with a notice requiring works to be carried out in relation to endangerment of a protected structure (PDA 2000, s 63); carrying out unauthorised development (PDA 2000, s 151); failure to comply with an enforcement notice (PDA 2000, s 154); contravention of a tree preservation order or a proposed order (PDA 2000, s 205); organising an event or being in control of land on which an event is held, without a licence or in contravention of the licence (PDA 2000, s 230(3)); failure to comply with a notice in relation to a funfair (PDA 2000, s 239); taking or seeking any favour, benefit or payment by a member or official of a planning authority in connection with a consultation regarding a proposed development (PDA 2000, s 247).

A person may be prosecuted on indictment or summarily, and following conviction, commits a further offence on each day that the contravention continues (PDA 2000, s 156). Summary proceedings for a planning offence may be brought and prosecuted by a planning authority; however only the Director of Public Prosecutions may prosecute for offences involving failure to disclose certain interests under PDA 2000, ss 147 and 148 (PDA 2000, s 157). Summary proceedings may commence at any time within six months from the date the offence was committed, or at any time within six months of evidence sufficient to justify proceedings coming to the notice of the prosecutor (PDA 2000, s 157(2)). However, there is a seven-year limitation within which offences must be prosecuted (PDA 2000, s 157(4)). The onus on proving the existence of any planning permission rests with the defendant (PDA 2000, s 162).

Where a person is convicted of a planning offence, the court must order the person to pay the costs and expenses of the action, as measured by the court, to the planning authority, unless the court is satisfied that there are special and substantial reasons for not doing so (PDA 2000, s 161).

planning permission. The grant of permission which is required in respect of: (a) any *development* of land, which is not *exempted* development, and (b) the retention of an *unauthorised* development: Planning and Development Act 2000, s 32(1). *Development* means the carrying out of any *works* on, in, or over or under land or the making of any *material change* in the *use* of any structures or other land, and *develop* is to be construed accordingly: Planning and Development Act 2000, ss 2(1) and 3(1). *Land* includes any structure and any land covered with water (whether inland or coastal) (PDA 2000, s 2(1)). *Use*, in relation to land, does not include the use of the land by the carrying on of any works thereon (PDA 2000, s 2(1)); *Viscount Securities Ltd v Dublin County Council* 112 ILTR 17; *Rehabilitation Institute v Dublin Corporation* [1988] 6 ILT 198, HC. See also *Grimes v Punchestown Developments Co Ltd* [2002] 1 ILRM 409, HC.

A person who obtains planning permission is not entitled solely by reason of the permission to carry out a development e g there may be a requirement for *bye-law* approval or *licences* (PDA 2000, s 34(13)). The grant of permission to develop land or for the retention of development, enures for the benefit of the land and of all persons for the time being interested therein; consequently it can be sold and passed on with the land (PDA 2000, s 39).

A grant of permission may be subject to or without conditions. Also *outline planning* permission may be sought and obtained. Compensation may be available in limited cases where permission is refused. There are special provisions dealing with architectural conservation areas, protected structures, landscape conservation areas, special amenity areas, strategic development zones, and events and funfairs (qqv). There are also special provisions regarding the protection of the environment, with, in particular cases, the requirement for *environmental impact statements*.

The planning process is transparent, with public access to information and consultation, and provision for appeal to An Bord Pleanála and to the courts.

The concepts of *abandonment* and *intensification* are applicable to both development by material change in use and development by works. *Abandonment* is the objective sign of a decision not to continue with the development, whereas *intensification* may be the objective sign of an intention to carry out a different development: *Kildare Co Council v Goode* [2000] 1 ILRM 346, SC and [1999] 2 IR 495, SC.

The question of whether a particular activity forms part of the normal use of the land is a question of fact and degree in each particular case: *Lord Henry Mountcharles v Meath Co Council* [1997] 1 ILRM 446, HC and [1996] 3 IR 417, HC. An intensification of an existing use of land can constitute a *material change*: *Patterson v Murphy* [1978] HC; *Stafford & Son v Roadstone Ltd* [1980] HC; *Monaghan Co Council v Brogan* [1987] ILRM 564. The use of the facade of a building to display commercial advertisements unconnected with the present business user constituted a *material change*: *Dublin Corp v Regan Advertising Ltd* [1989] IR 61, SC.

The use of houses commercially for short-term lettings (e g holiday homes) was a use different from use as a private dwelling: *McMahon v Dublin Corporation* [1997] 1 ILRM 227, HC and [1996] 3 IR 509, HC.

A *use right* is capable of being abandoned, making its resumption a material change requiring authorisation: *Meath Co Council v Daly* [1988] ILRM 274. See *Palmerlane Ltd v Bord Pleanála* [1999] 2 ILRM 514, HC; *Waterford Co Co v John A Wood Ltd* [1999] 1 ILRM 217, SC; *Butler (IRFU) v Dublin Corporation* [1998] 1 ILRM 533, HC. [Bibliography: Crean; LexisNexis.] See COMPENSATION AND PLANNING PERMISSION; UNAUTHORISED DEVELOPMENT.

planning permission, application for. Means an application to a planning authority in accordance with *permission regulations* for permission for the development of land required by those regulations: Planning and Development Act 2000, s 2(1). An application may also be made for *outline permission* (PDA 2000, s 36(1)).

The Minister is required to provide, by regulation, the procedure and administration for such applications, and this can include the information required to be submitted; the publication of notices; the submission of further information; enabling third parties to make submissions or observations on an application; requiring an applicant to submit information on a previous development to assist in determining if the applicant has a history of completing developments in accordance with the permission granted (PDA 2000, s 33).

The planning authority is required to make a decision on an application within eight weeks from receipt of the application; however, where the authority seeks further information from the applicant within that eight weeks, it will have a further four weeks for consideration of the application from receipt of the information (PDA 2000, s 34(8)). Where the authority fails to make a decision within the permitted period a decision by the authority to grant the permission (known as a 'default permission') is regarded as having been given on the last day of the permitted period (PDA 2000, s 34(8)(f)). Planning applications must be available for inspection and for purchase of copies by the public (PDA 2000, s 38).

Notice to the public of intention to apply for permission must be made and this requirement is strictly interpreted by the courts: *Keleghan & Ors v Dublin Corporation and Corby* [1977] 111 ILTR 144; *Readymix (Eire) Ltd v Dublin County Council and the Minister for Local Government* [1974] SC. There must be a notice published in a newspaper and also a *site notice*: Planning and Development Regulations 2001, SI No 600 of 2001, arts 17–19. In order for an applicant to have a substantial ground for a judicial review on the basis of defects in a *site notice*, the applicant has to show that it has suffered prejudice by being misled by the defects: *Springview Ltd v Cavan Developments Ltd* [2000] 1 ILRM 437, HC. See also *Blessington & District v Wicklow County Council* [1997] 1 IR 273. For previous regulations, see Local Government (Planning and Development) Regulations 1994, SI No 86 of 1994.

An application for planning permission must be made either by or with the approval of a person who has a sufficient legal estate or interest in the property, which is the subject of the application, to carry out the proposed development: *Frescati Estates v Walker* [1975] IR 177. See also *The State (Alf-a-Bet Promotions) Ltd v Bundoran UDC* [1978] 112 ILTR 9. See SITE NOTICE; OUTLINE PERMISSION; PLANNING REGISTER.

planning permission, conditions on. A planning authority in granting permission for the development of land, is empowered to grant permission subject to a very wide range of conditions, which are not exclusive: Planning and Development Act 2000, s 34(4). Some of the specified conditions are: measures to reduce or prevent noise; development of adjoining land under the control of the applicant; provision of open spaces; planting and maintenance of shrubs and trees or landscaping; completion within time period of roads, open spaces, car parks, sewers, watermains or drains; giving adequate security for satisfactory completion; maintenance or management of the proposed development; naming and numbering and appropriate signage; preservation of drawings; conditions regulating the hours and days during which a business premises may operate.

A condition of a planning permission may state that a certain matter will be agreed between the planning authority and the developer, and, if there is no agreement, that the matter be referred to An Bord Pleanála for determination (PDA 2000, s 34(5)). The Supreme Court has specified the criteria, to which Bord Pleanála is entitled to have regard, in leaving a matter to be agreed between the developer and the planning authority e g the desirability of leaving a certain degree of flexibility in a complex enterprise, or of leaving technical matters or matters of detail to be decided later, or the impracticality of imposing detailed conditions due to the nature of the development: *Boland v An Bord Pleanála* [1996] 3 IR 435, SC.

A condition may also be specified requiring the payment of a contribution in respect of: (a) public infrastructure and facilities benefiting development in the area of the planning authority, and (b) any public infrastructure service or project (PDA 2000, ss 48–49). In a particular case, the Court held that conditions, requiring limited public access to the lands of a golf club, were invalid as unreasonable, as they had the capacity to frustrate and/or render inoperable the use of the land as a golf course: *Ashbourne Holdings Ltd v An Bord Pleanála* [2002] 1 ILRM 321, HC. In dismissing the appeal by An Bord Pleanála, the Supreme Court held that the question of public access to the Old Head of Kinsale had nothing to do with the clubhouse, the access road or the equipment shed which were the developments requiring permission or retention: [2003] 2 IR 114, SC. It held that the public access conditions, and the other conditions that assumed public access, were *ultra vires* the powers of the Board and void.

For planning conditions requiring residence or employment of the applicant in the planning authority area, see *Law Society Gazette* (November 2003) 41. For previous legislation, see Local Government (Planning and Development) Act 1963, s 26(2) and Local Government (Planning and Development) Act 1976, s 39(c). See *McDonagh & Sons Ltd v Galway Corporation* [1995] 1 IR 191, SC. See ENFORCEMENT NOTICE.

planning permission, decision on. Where: (a) an application is made to a planning authority in accordance with planning regulations for permission for the development of land, and (b) all the requirements of the regulations are complied with, the authority may decide to grant the permission, subject to or without conditions, or to refuse it: Planning and Development Act 2000, s 34(1). When making such a decision, the authority is restricted to considering the proper planning and sustainable development of the area, having regard to, *inter alia*, the development plan, any special amenity area order, any European site, and government policy (PDA 2000, s 34(2)(a)).

The authority must also have regard to: (a) the effects the development would have outside its area, and even outside the State, where appropriate (PDA 2000, s 34(2)(b)), and (b) any written submissions made by third parties (PDA 2000, s 34(3)(b)). It must also have regard to the role of the Environmental Protection Agency in relation to any *integrated pollution control licence* or *waste licence* required (PDA 2000, s 34(2)(c) as amended by Protection of the Environment Act 2003, s 61). See also Environmental Protection Agency Act 1992, s 99F inserted by PEA 2003, s 15.

A decision on an application must state the main reasons and considerations on which the decision is based (PDA 2000, s 34(10)). An appeal lies to An Bord Pleanála in relation to the decision; it must be made in the period of four weeks beginning on the day of the decision (PDA 2000, s 37 as amended by Planning and Development (Amendment) Act 2002, s 10).

Apart from the many reasons why planning permission may be refused, under a new provision, a refusal may also be made where the applicant has failed to comply with a previous permission, and the authority is of the opinion that there is a real and substantial risk that the development, in respect of which permission is sought, would not be completed in accordance with such permission if granted, and the High Court so orders, on a motion from the authority (PDA 2000, s 35).

A planning authority may grant planning permission, in relation to a development which would *contravene materially* the development plan, provided a particular procedure is complied with e g publication of notice in newspaper, service of notice on the applicant and persons who had submitted observations, consideration of further submissions, and resolution in favour passed by not less than three-quarters of the total number of members (PDA 2000, s 34(6)). Provision is also made to make a notice under section 4 of the City and County Managers (Amendment) Act 1955 (requiring a manager to grant planning permission) to be of no further effect where he, within one week of receiving the notice, by order declares his opinion that the development concerned would contravene materially the development plan (PDA 2000, s 34(6)(c)). See *Re Grange Developments Ltd* [1987] ILRM 245 and 733 and [1989] ILRM 145, SC.

planning permission, default. Planning permission is deemed to have been granted where a planning authority fails to make its decision within the appropriate period (generally eight weeks from the date of compliance by the applicant of specified requirements): Planning and Development Act 2000, s 34(8)(f).

The grant is deemed to have been given if there has been substantial compliance with the regulations by the applicant and any failure by the applicant came within the *de minimis* rule: *Molloy & Walsh v Dublin County Council* [1990] ILRM 633, HC.

The statutory right to a default permission is strictly interpreted in view of the potential consequences for any objectors to the proposed development: *McGovern v Dublin Corporation* [1999] 2 ILRM 314, HC. Also a person attempting to obtain default planning permission must himself have observed very precisely the relevant provisions of the Planning Acts: *Murray v*

Wicklow County Council [1996] 2 ILRM 411, HC and 2 IR 552.

It is not possible to obtain a valid default permission in respect of a development which constitutes a material contravention of a development plan: *Walsh v Kildare County Council* [2001] 1 IR 483, HC. See *Calor Teo v Sligo Co Council* [1991] 2 IR 267, HC; *The State (Murphy) v Dublin County Council* [1970] IR 253; *Dunne Ltd v Dublin County Council* [1974] IR 45; *Flynn v Dublin Corporation* [1997] 2 IR 558, HC.

planning permission, duration of. In general, planning permission ceases to have effect after a period of five years beginning on the date of grant of permission: Planning and Development Act 2000, s 40. A planning authority has power to *vary* this period or, in certain circumstances, to *extend* it (PDA 2000, ss 41–43).

There is provision for an extension of the time limit where *substantial* works were carried out during the relevant period or for a further extension where failure to carry out the works during the extended period was due to circumstances beyond the control of the developer (PDA 2000, s 42).

'Substantial' could be taken to mean of ample or considerable amount, quantity or dimensions; in each case, whether 'substantial works' had been carried out must be determined by the planning authority on the basis of the particular facts of the case and not by reference to any predetermined formula or 'rule of thumb': *Littondale Ltd v Wicklow Council* [1996] 2 ILRM 519, HC.

The planning authority may look only at the actual permission which they are being asked to extend and not to developments outside the relevant plot which may have benefited that plot: *Garden Village Construction Co v Wicklow Co Council* [1994] 2 ILRM 527, SC. For previous legislation, Local Government (Planning and Development) Act 1982, ss 2–3. See HOUSING STRATEGY; OUTLINE PERMISSION.

planning permission, objection to. An objector has, under the guarantees of fair procedures inherent in the 1937 Constitution, art 40(3), a right to make his case to a planning authority and, if necessary, to An Bord Pleanála, at the hearing of an appeal from the decision of the planning authority: *The State (Haverty) v An Bord Pleanála* [1987] IR 485, HC. However, see BORD PLEANÁLA, AN; PLANNING APPEAL.

planning permission, revocation of. A planning authority is empowered, where it considers it expedient, to revoke or modify a planning permission but it must not do so, unless the development to which the permission relates, no longer conforms with the *development plan*: Planning and Development Act 2000, s 44. Notice of the intention to revoke or amend a permission must be served on the person with the permission and on any other person who, in the opinion of the authority, will be materially affected, inviting them to make written submissions or observations on the proposal (PDA 2000, s 44(3)). A decision to revoke or amend is a *reserved* function (PDA 2000, s 44(11)). A person served with a notice has a right to appeal the decision of the authority to An Bord Pleanála within four weeks of the date of the decision (PDA 2000, s 44(6)).

The revocation procedure requires two essential steps: (a) a decision by the councillors that it was expedient that the particular decision be revoked, and (b) service of notice of revocation on the owner and occupier of the land affected and on any other person who, in the opinion of the council, would be affected by the revocation: *Hughes v An Bord Pleanála* [2000] 1 ILRM 452, HC.

When making a decision to revoke a planning permission, the elected members are required to act judicially in accordance with the principles of constitutional and natural justice; consequently the person, to whom planning permission had been granted, must be informed of the intention to revoke and be given an opportunity to make submissions: *Eircell Ltd v Leitrim County Council* [2000] 2 ILRM 81, HC and [2000] 1 IR 479, HC. Revocation can only take place if there has been a change in circumstance relating to the proper planning and development of the area concerned and that change has occurred since the granting of the permission (*Eircell* case).

In a particular case, the court held that work had been carried out subsequent to the planning approval and that the county council was in breach of natural justice in its revocation decision: *ESB v Cork County Council* (2000) Irish Times, 29 June, HC. See *Listowel UDC v McDonagh* [1968] IR 312; *The State (Cogley) v Dublin Corporation* [1970] IR 244. For previous legislation, see Local Government (Planning and Development) Act 1963, s 30.

planning permission, subject to. Where a contract for the sale of land is subject to planning permission being obtained, failure by the purchaser to obtain planning permission within the time limited by the contract does not entitle the vendor to treat the contract as being at an end, unless time was of the essence of the contract in relation to the closing date: *O'Connor v Coady* (2003) ITLR (15 December), HC and FL 8589.

planning register. The register which each planning authority must keep in respect of land in its functional area and which must be available for inspection during office hours: Planning and Development Act 2000, s 7. A wide variety of planning information is required to be on the register, including particulars of applications for permission, for retention and for outline permission; decisions; enforcement notices; warning letters; orders; and certificates. The register must incorporate a map for enabling a person to trace any entry in the register (PDA 2000, s 7(4)). The register may be kept in an electronic form provided it is capable of being used to make a legible copy or reproduction of any entry (PDA 2000, s 7(5)). Proof of the signature of the person purporting to certify a copy of an entry in the register is not required in any legal proceedings (PDA 2000, s 7(7)).

planning regulations. Means regulations made under : Planning and Development Act 2000, s 33 (applications for planning permission) PDA 2000, s 172(2) (planning applications to be accompanied by environmental impact statements) and PDA 2000, s 174 (planning applications to be accompanied by transboundary environmental impact statements): Planning and Development Act 2000, s 2(1). Regulations have been made dealing with the following subject matter: preliminary and general, exempted development, plans and guidelines, control of development, housing supply, architectural heritage, An Bord Pleanála, requirements in respect of specified development by local authorities, provisions with respect to certain developments by State authorities, environmental impact assessment, major accident directive, fees, compensation, strategic development zones, disclosure of interests, licensing of outdoor events, miscellaneous and transitional: Planning and Development Regulations 2001, SI No 600 of 2001, as amended by SI No 70 of 2002 (scales of location maps and details to be indicated on location maps); SI No 149 of 2002 (fee for licence for fingerpost signs for

tourist accommodation); and SI No 90 of 2003 (amending arts 49 and 50). For regulations under previous legislation, see Local Government (Planning and Development) Regulations 1994 as amended by Local Government (Planning and Development) Regulations 2000, SI No 86 of 1994 and SI No 181 of 2000.

plant. As regards Income Tax Act 1967, s 241 (as amended), includes whatever apparatus is used for carrying on a business, comprising goods, chattels, fixed or moveable, live or dead, which are kept for permanent employment in the business, but not stock in trade which is bought or made for sale: *O'Culachain v McMullan Brothers Ltd* [1995] 2 ILRM 498, SC and 2 IR 217. A canopy erected over the forecourt of petrol filling stations constitutes plant (*O'Culachain* case). Also an improved stand at a racecourse, providing shelter from the weather and greater capacity for spectators, has been held to be *plant*: *O'Grady v Roscommon Race Committee* [1996] 2 ILRM 81, SC and 1 IR 163. See *Caribmolasses Co Ltd v Commissioner of Valuation* [1994] 3 IR 189, SC. See now Taxes Consolidation Act 1997, s 284 as amended by Finance Act 2003, s 23. See BARRISTER.

plant protection products. Consolidated provisions have been put in place for the authorisation, placing on the market, use and control of plant protection products: SI No 83 of 2003. It is an offence for a person to place a plant protection product on the market except in accordance with the regulations (SI No 83 of 2003, regs 4 and 34). It is also an offence for a person to place any product on the market, containing in it or on it, a level of residue of a plant protection which exceeds the maximum specified (SI No 83 of 2003, regs 28 and 34). See also SIs No 357 and 702 of 2003; SI No 197 of 2004.

plant varieties. See VARIETAL NAMES.

plastic bag. A bag: (a) made wholly or in part of plastic, and (b) which is suitable for use by a customer at the point of sale in a supermarket, service station or other sales outlet, except exempted bags: Waste Management (Amendment) Act 2001, s 9. Regulations have been made providing for the imposition of a 15 cent *environmental levy* on plastic bags from 4 March 2002: Waste Management (Environmental Levy) (Plastic Bag) Regulations 2001, SI No 605 of 2001. The regulations provide for the arrangements for the collection of the levy and specify the times at which the levy must be paid. The levy is paid into an *Environmental Fund* (qv). The introduction of the levy is estimated to have led to a reduction of 90% in the use of plastic bags in 2002.

platinum. See GOLDSMITHS OF DUBLIN, COMPANY OF.

play group. See PRE-SCHOOL SERVICE.

plc. [Public limited company.] See COMPANY, PUBLIC LIMITED.

plea. In a criminal trial, the accused's response to the indictment (qv), which he may do by: (a) pleading guilty; or (b) pleading not guilty to the offence charged but pleading guilty to another offence of which he might be found guilty on the indictment; or (c) pleading not guilty in addition to any *demurrer* (qv) or special plea; or (d) standing mute: Criminal Law Act 1997, s 9(1). If the accused stands *mute of malice* or will not answer directly to the indictment, the court must order that a plea of *not guilty* be entered on his behalf (CLA 1997, s 9(1)(c)).

Legal objection to the indictment may be taken by: (a) a motion to quash on the ground that the indictment suffers from a defect which cannot be remedied or where the court does not have jurisdiction to try the case; or (b) a special *plea in bar* of *autrefois acquit* (qv) and *autrefois convict* (qv).

A person who pleads guilty is entitled to withdraw his plea at any time before sentence, by leave of the court: *R v Plummer* [1912] 2 KB 339. As soon as the possibility of a custodial sentence arises in a trial, whether summary or on indictment, an accused person who is not legally represented should be allowed an opportunity to retract a guilty plea, in order to ensure proper representation from the beginning of the trial: *Byrne v McDonnell* [1996] 1 ILRM 543, HC and [1997] 1 IR 392, HC. [Bibliography: Walsh D (3).] See GUILTY.

plea, fitness to. While it may be more usual for the issue of fitness to plead to be raised by the defence in criminal proceedings, a judge may raise this issue on his own motion and may have a duty so to raise: *DPP (Murphy) v PT* [1998] 1 ILRM 344, HC.

plea bargaining. An informal arrangement by which the defendant to criminal proceedings agrees to plead guilty to one or more charges in return for the prosecution extending some advantage to him eg drop-

ping another charge. There is no formal system of prosecutorial plea bargaining in the Irish criminal law system. In fact, certain communications in relation to criminal proceedings are prohibited eg see Prosecution of Offences Act 1974, s 6; Criminal Justice Act 1993, s 2(4).

In relation to a meeting in chambers between counsel and the trial judge at which an indication of sentence was given if there were a guilty plea, the Supreme Court has held that while discussions in chambers were desirable in the interests of justice, in general justice was to be administered in public pursuant to art 34(1) of the Constitution: *The People (DPP) v Heeney* [2001] 1 IR 736, SC. There was no question of any form of plea bargaining being entered into in private which would determine in advance the sentence the court would impose; the concept of plea bargaining was unacceptable in Irish law (*Heeney* case). See 'Constitutional Implications of Plea Bargaining' by Peter Charleton SC and Paul McDermott BL in *Bar Review* (October 2000) 52.

plea in bar. See AUTREFOIS ACQUIT; AUTREFOIS CONVICT.

plead. To make a plea (qv); to address the court.

pleadings. Formal written or printed statements in a civil action, usually drafted by counsel, delivered alternatively by the parties to each other, stating the allegations of fact upon which the parties to the action base their case. The purpose of pleadings is to define the issues between the parties and to ensure: (a) that the parties know the case they have to meet; and (b) that they will not be taken at a disadvantage by the introduction of matters not set out in the pleadings: *Wildgust v Bank of Ireland* [2001] 1 ILRM 24, SC. It has been held that pleadings are not required to contain matters of law: *Murphy v Times Newspapers Ltd* [2000] 1 IR 522, SC.

Pleadings in the High Court include an originating summons, statement of claim, defence, counterclaim, reply, petition or answer (qqv): RSC Ord 125, r 1.

In all cases alleging a wrong, within the meaning of the Civil Liabilities Act 1961 and 1964, particulars of such wrong, and personal injuries suffered and any items of special damage, must be set out in the statement of claim or counterclaim and particulars (qv) of any contributory negligence (qv) must be set out in the defence:

RSC Ord 19, r 5(1). In cases alleging misrepresentation, fraud, breach of trust, wilful default or undue influence, particulars with dates and items if necessary, must be set out in the pleadings (rr 5(2) and 6(1)).

It is a well-recognised principle that counsel should not sign pleadings containing an allegation of fraud unless satisfied there are substantial grounds for making such allegation: *Administralia Asigurilor de Stat v Insurance Corporation of Ireland* [1990] 2 IR 246.

For pleadings in *commercial proceedings* (qv), see RSC Ord 63A, r 6 inserted by Rules of the Superior Courts (Commercial Proceedings) 2004, SI No 2 of 2004. For pleadings in personal injuries actions, see Civil Liability and Courts Act 2004, ss 10, 12–14.

In the Circuit Court, pleadings consist of the indorsement of claim on the *civil bill*, the defence, or the defence and counterclaim: Circuit Court Rules 2001 Ord 5, Ord 10 and Ord 15. In the District Court, the pleadings (although not called as such), consist of the civil summons (which must set out concisely the nature of the plaintiff's claim and the grounds therefor), notice of intention to defend, set-off or counterclaim, interpleader, and third-party procedure: DCR 1997 Ords 39–42, and Ord 49. A person may use either of the official languages of the State in any pleadings in or document issuing from, any court: Official Languages Act 2003, s 8. [Bibliography: Buckley, Melody; Collins & O'Reilly; Gill; Blake UK; Bullen & Leak UK; Odgers UK.] See FRAUD; LITIGATION; LONG VACATION; PARTICULARS, PLEADING; PROFESSIONAL NEGLIGENCE; SPECIAL PLEADING; TRAVERSE; UNDUE INFLUENCE IN PLEADINGS.

pleadings, amendment of. There are times allowed for the amendment of pleadings without application to the court, or by consent, or by the court; however, the court may grant leave to such amendments as may be necessary for the purpose of determining the real issues in controversy between the parties: RSC Ord 28, r 1; *Krops v Irish Forestry Board Ltd* [1995] 2 ILRM 290, HC and 2 IR 113. See *Bell v Pederson* [1996] 1 ILRM 290, HC and [1995] 3 IR 511, HC; *Palamos Properties Ltd v Brooks* [1996] 3 IR 597, HC; *Wolfe v Wolfe* [2001] 1 ILRM 389, HC and 1 IR 313.

In the Circuit and District Courts, similar provisions apply: Circuit Court Rules 2001 Ord 65; DCR 1997 Ord 38, r 1. For amendment of pleadings in *commercial proceedings* (qv), see RSC Ord 63A, r 6(1)(v) inserted by Rules of the Superior Courts (Commercial Proceedings) 2004, SI No 2 of 2004. See 'Amendment of Pleadings' by Stephen Dodd BL in *Law Society Gazette* (January/February 2002) 24. See SUMMONS, AMENDMENT OF.

Pleanála, an Bord. See BORD PLEANÁLA, AN.

pleasure craft. Vessels used otherwise than for profit and used wholly or mainly for sport or recreation but includes mechanically propelled vessels that are on hire pursuant to contracts or other arrangements that do not require the owners of the vessels to provide crews or parts of crew for them: Merchant Shipping Act 1992, s 20(6). The Minister is empowered to make regulations for the purpose of ensuring the safety of pleasure craft and their occupants and that the use of pleasure craft does not create a disturbance or constitute a nuisance (MSA 1992, s 20 as amended by Merchant Shipping (Investigation of Marine Casualties) Act 2000, s 44(9)).

The Minister is also empowered to provide for the enactment by statutory and other bodies of *bye-laws* to control the use of vessels in areas under their jurisdiction (MSA 1992, s 33 as amended by MS(IMC)A 2000, s 44(11)). The *dangerous* navigation or operation or the *careless* navigation or operation of a pleasure craft is an offence (MSA 1992, ss 33–37 inserted by MS(IMC)A 2000, s 44(11)).

Regulations have been made governing the operation of pleasure craft, including personal watercraft; the regulations include provisions relating to age restrictions, the carriage and use of lifejackets, and restrictions on the use of alcohol and drugs: Merchant Shipping (Pleasure Craft) (Lifejackets and Operation) (Safety) Regulations 2004, SI No 259 of 2004. These regulations revoke SI No 284 of 2001, which in turn revoked SI No 387 of 1992 (jet skis and fast power boats). See AGE AND PLEASURE CRAFT; ALCOHOL, CONSUMPTION OF; LIFEJACKET.

plebiscite. A direct vote by the electorate. See Planning and Development Act 2000, s 180(3). See CHARGE, TAKE IN.

pledge. An article pawned with a pawnbroker: Pawnbrokers Act 1964, s 2 as amended by Consumer Credit Act 1995, Part XV and Sch 8. The transfer of the possession, but not the ownership, of a chattel as security for the payment of a debt or performance of an obligation. On default, the chattel may be sold. The Official Assignee (qv) has the right to inspect any of a bankrupt's goods which have been pledged or pawned so that he may have a reasonable opportunity of exercising the right of *redemption:* Bankruptcy Act 1988, s 68. See PAWNBROKER.

plenary. Full; conclusive; complete.

plenary summons. See SUMMONS, HIGH COURT.

plene administravit. [He has fully administered.]

plenipotentiary. A person or persons with full powers.

plover. See GAME.

plural. The use of a *plural* noun in an Act imports the singular (unless the contrary intention appears): Interpretation Act 1937, s 11(a). This interpretation also applies to nouns in instruments made wholly or partly under an Act.

point of law. Any party is entitled to raise by his pleadings any *point of law*, and any such point will be disposed of by the judge who tries the cause: RSC Ord 25. See also PRELIMINARY ISSUE.

pointsman. A garda in uniform and on traffic control duty: Road Traffic General Bye-Laws 1964, SI No 294 of 1964, art 2.

poison. It is an offence for a person, intentionally or recklessly, to administer or to cause to be taken by another person, a substance which he knows to be capable of interfering substantially with the other person's bodily functions: Non-Fatal Offences against the Person Act 1997, s 12. This includes a substance capable of inducing unconsciousness or sleep (NFOPA 1997, s 12(2)).

There are restrictions on the sale of poisons and regulations on the labelling of containers, the keeping of books and records on sales, and there are special restrictions on the sale of strychnine. See Poisons Act 1961; Irish Medicines Board Act 1995, s 35(1); Pharmacy Acts 1875 to 1977; Poisons Regulations, SI No 188 of 1982; SI No 424 of 1986; SI No 353 of 1991; SI No 351 of 2003. The National Poisons Information Centre is located at Beaumont Hospital, Dublin. Tel: (01) 8092566 and (01) 8092568. See ABORTION; ABORTION, MEDICAL GUIDELINES.

poitin. Colloquial term in the Irish language to describe an illicit spirit, the making, possession, selling or delivery of which is an offence: Illicit Distillation Act 1831. See also Spirits (Ireland) Act 1854; Illicit Distillation Act 1857; Revenue (No 2) Act 1861, s 19; Intoxicating Liquor (General) Act 1924; Intoxicating Liquor Act 1960, s 22(1); Customs and Excise (Miscellaneous Provisions) Act 1988, s 14.

police. See GARDA SÍOCHÁNA.

police co-operation. Provision has been made for co-operation between the Garda Síochána and the Police Service of Northern Ireland (PSNI): Garda Síochána (Police Co-operation) Act 2003. The Act gives effect to arts 1 and 2 of the Agreement between the governments of Ireland and the UK on police co-operation, done at Belfast on 29 April 2002. The Agreement provides for: (a) members of each police force to be eligible to apply for certain posts in the other police service, and (b) a programme for members of each police service to be seconded with full police powers to the other police service for periods not exceeding three years. The Agreement arose from the Patten Report – *Report of the Independent Commission on Policing for Northern Ireland.*

It is an objective of the European Union (qv) to provide citizens with a high level of safety by developing *common action* among the member states in the fields of police and judicial co-operation in criminal matters; this is directed at preventing and combating crime, in particular terrorism, trafficking in persons and offences against children, illicit drug trafficking and illegal arms trafficking, corruption and fraud: EC Treaty, arts 29–42 of the consolidated (2002) version. See EUROPEAN POLICE OFFICE; JOINT INVESTIGATION TEAMS.

police property. See PROPERTY IN POSSESSION OF GARDA.

policy. An instrument comprising a contract of insurance and called a life, fire, marine, accident, public liability, aviation, etc policy, according to the nature of the insurance. See INSURANCE, CONTRACT OF; ASSIGNMENT OF CONTRACT; PREMIUM.

political donation. Any contribution given for political purposes by any person whether or not a member of a political party; it includes a donation of money, or of property or goods, the supply of services without payment, or the conferring of a right to use, without payment, any property or goods: Electoral Act 1997, s 22. All donations received by a political party above a value of £4,000 (€5,079) must be disclosed, as must any donation above a value of £500 (€635) received by any member of the Houses of the Oireachtas or of the European Parliament or by any unsuccessful candidate for election to these bodies (EA 1997, s 24). There is a similar provision in relation to Presidential elections (EA 1997, ss 46–48). Particulars of all donations above a value of £4,000 (€5,079) made by companies, trade unions, friendly societies and building societies must be included in their annual report or return (EA 1997, s 26(1)). For amendments to the 1997 Act, see (a) Electoral (Amendment) Act 1998 which also introduced a new s 24A to EA 1997 and (b) Electoral (Amendment) Act 2002, s 4.

As regards local elections, a candidate must make a statement in a prescribed form of the source of income used by him to meet his election expenses with details, including the identity of the donor, of any donation over £500 (€635): Local Elections (Disclosure of Donations and Expenditure) Act 1999, s 13. For prescribed forms, see SI No 689 of 2003. *Donation statements* are available for inspection and copying by the public at the Standards in Public Office Commission, 18 Lower Leeson Street, Dublin 2. See website: *www.sipo.ie*. See ELECTION EXPENSES.

political offence. Extradition cannot be granted for an offence which is a *political offence* or an offence connected with a *political offence*: Extradition Act 1965, s 11. This envisages a political offence only in relation to the requesting State: *McGuire v Attorney-General* [1994] 2 ILRM 344. The onus of proving an offence to be a political offence or an offence connected with a political offence, lays on the person seeking the benefit of that exception: *Quinlivan v Conroy (No 2)* [2000] 3 IR 154, HC. See also *Harte v Fanning* [1988] ILRM 75.

It has been held that even if the objective of an offence is undoubtedly political, the means used must not be unacceptable in the sense that reasonable, civilised people would not regard them as political acts: *McGlinchey v Wren* [1982] IR 154. It has also been held in a particular case of murders, that they were so cowardly and callous, that it would be a distortion of language if they were accorded the status of

political offences: *Shannon v Fanning* [1984] IR 569. See also *Bourke v Attorney-General* [1972] IR 36; *Quinn v Wren* [1985] IR 322; *Finucane v McMahon* [1990] ILRM 505, SC; *Carron v McMahon* [1990] ILRM 802, SC.

A number of offences are by statute no longer regarded as political offences and criteria are laid down to be taken into account when evaluating the offences: Extradition (European Convention on Suppression of Terrorism) Act 1987, ss 3(2) and 4(1). It has been held that E(ECST)A 1987, s 3 must be strictly construed: *Sloan v Culligan* [1992] ILRM 194, SC. Further restrictions on the political offence exception have been introduced eg a political offence does not include: (a) a serious offence involving an act of violence against the life, physical integrity or liberty of a person, or (b) a serious offence involving an act against property if the act created a collective danger for persons (reversing the decision in *Magee v O'Dea* [1994] 1 ILRM 540, HC), or (c) the taking of the life of a Head of State, or (d) certain drug-related offences: Extradition (Amendment) Act 1994, ss 2–3.

Also no *international tribunal crime* may be regarded as a political offence: International War Crimes Tribunals Act 1998, s 4(2). Certain offences are not permitted to be *political offences* in relation to avoiding extradition: Extradition (European Convention on the Suppression of Terrorism) Act 1987, s 3 and Extradition (Amendment) Act 1994, Sch. Provision has been made to cater for the possibility that post-enlargement, new EU member states may become parties to the EU Convention on Extradition and not to the Convention on the Suppression on Terrorism: E(ECST)A 1987, s 3 amended by Extradition (European Union Conventions) Act 2001, s 12.

Also provision has been made to ensure that the *political offence* exception will not arise in cases involving the four Geneva Conventions of 1949: E(ECST)A 1987, s 3 further amended by the E(EUC)A 2001, s 27. The Geneva Conventions of 1949 were given effect in the State by the Geneva Conventions Act 1962 but with no specific provision for extradition.

While there is no provision for the *political offence* exemption under the *European arrest warrant*, there is a prohibition on surrendering a person where there are reasonable grounds for believing that the

European arrest warrant was issued in respect of the person for the purposes of facilitating his prosecution or punishment in the issuing State for reasons connected with his *political opinion*: European Arrest Warrant Act 2003, s 37(1)(c).

Extradition law takes precedence over refugee law: Refugee Act 1996, s 25. See also *Ellis v O'Dea* [1991] ILRM 347, SC; *Magee v Culligan* [1992] ILRM 186, SC. See EUROPEAN ARREST WARRANT, PROHIBITION ON SURRENDER; EXTRADITION; MURDER, AGGRAVATED.

political party, leader's allowance. A revision of the annual allowance payable to leaders of qualifying parties and to non-party members of the Oireachtas is provided for in the Oireachtas (Ministerial and Parliamentary Offices) (Amendment) Act 2001, s 1. The allowances, which are not subject to income tax, are however subject to a mandatory audit of expenditure from such allowances. Section 1 inserts by substitution a new s 10 in the Ministerial and Parliamentary Offices Act 1938. The 2001 Act also provides for the arrangements which come into effect on the dissolution of a parliamentary party, where another parliamentary party acquires by agreement all its members.

political party, register of. The register of political parties which meet specified criteria, eg that they are genuine political parties and are organised in the State to contest a Dáil election or a European election or a local election: Electoral Act 1992, s 25 as amended by Electoral Act 1997, s 81. Registration may be for one or more of such elections and may be for a part or the whole of the State. Registration enables a candidate in an election to add the name of his registered party to his own on the ballot paper (EA 1992, ss 25(13) and 88(2)(b)). There is provision for the public funding of political parties; this funding is in proportion to the first preference votes their candidates received at the previous general election, provided the party received more then 2% of the first preference votes: Electoral Act 1997, ss 16–20. See *Loftus v Attorney-General* [1979] IR 221. See BROADCAST.

polygamous marriage. It was held in a particular case that a South African marriage, being potentially polygamous, was not enforceable in Irish law: *Conlon v Mohamed* [1987] ILRM 172 and 7 ILT Dig [1989] 54.

poll. Taking a vote on a motion or at an election. At a general meeting of a company, questions are decided by a show of hands but there is a right to demand a poll, unless this right is expressly excluded. The right to demand a poll may be excluded only in respect of electing the chairman of the meeting or in relation to the adjournment of the meeting: Companies Act 1963, s 137. The poll involves the taking of the votes in person (or usually by proxy) by marking a voting paper *for* or *against* the motion or resolution.

A company may create different kinds of voting shares, with one carrying greater voting rights than another, although the Stock Exchange discourages the creation of non-voting shares. In the absence of provisions to the contrary, every member has one vote in respect of each share or each £10 (€12.70) of stock held by him (CA 1963, s 134(e)). See *Kinsella v Alliance Dublin Consumers Gas Co* [1982] HC. See also Building Societies Act 1989, ss 50(2), 50(13), 73(1) and Sch 2, Pt XI, para 5(q). See PROXY; CHAIRMAN; VOTING AT MEETINGS.

poll tax. A tax per person.

polling information card. The card sent to every registered elector advising the elector of the place where the elector is entitled to vote and containing a statement in relation to the identity documents required by the elector eg European Parliamentary Elections Act 1997, Sch 2, r 54; Referendum Act 1994, s 23; Electoral Act 1992, s 92. It is an offence for a person, without lawful authority: (a) to take, destroy, conceal or otherwise interfere with a *polling information card*, or (b) to present such a card at a polling station: Electoral (Amendment) Act 2004, s 35.

pollutant. Any substance so specified or any other substance (including a substance which gives rise to odour) or energy which, when emitted into the atmosphere, either by itself or in combination with any other substance, may cause air pollution: Air Pollution Act 1987, s 7(1) as amended by Environmental Protection Agency Act 1992, s 18(2) and Sch 3. Specified air pollutants are listed in the APA 1987, Sch 1. [Bibliography: LexisNexis.] See AIR POLLUTION; POLLUTING MATTER.

pollution control. See INTEGRATED POLLUTION CONTROL.

polluting matter. As regards water pollution, means any poisonous or noxious matter, and any substance (including any explosive, liquid or gas) the entry or discharge of which into any waters is liable to render those or any other waters poisonous or injurious to fish, spawning grounds or the food of any fish, or to injure fish in their value as human food, or to impair the usefulness of the bed and soil of any waters as spawning grounds or their capacity to produce the food of fish or to render such waters harmful or detrimental to public health or to domestic, commercial, industrial, agricultural or recreational uses: Local Government (Water Pollution) Act 1977, s 1. See WATER POLLUTION.

pollution, civil liability for. Liability is imposed on the occupier of premises from which effluent originates where that effluent enters waters and causes injury, loss or damage to a person or the property of a person: Local Government (Water Pollution) (Amendment) Act 1990, s 20. Liability is also imposed on the person responsible for the entry if it is a contravention of the Act. This liability is without prejudice to any other cause of action that may lie. Similar provisions apply in respect of air pollution which causes injury, loss or damage to a person or to the property of a person: Air Pollution Act 1987, ss 28A and 28B inserted by Environmental Protection Agency Act 1992, s 18(2) and Sch 3, para 4. See AIR POLLUTION; RYLANDS V FLETCHER, RULE IN; SEA POLLUTION; WATER POLLUTION.

polluter pays principle. The principle enshrined in EC environmental law, which requires that the cost of removal of damage to the environment is to be borne by the polluter and is only to be borne by the general public in exceptional circumstances. 'Environmental protection should not in principle depend of policies which rely on grants of aid and place the burden of combating pollution on the community': EC Council Recommendation 75/436 OJ 1975 No L 194/1. See EC Treaty, art 174(2) of the consolidated (2002) version; Environmental Protection Agency Act 1992, s 52(2)(d); Waste Management Act 1996, s 12.

The 'polluter pays' principle requires that the party causing pollution should pay for it in full, rather than an innocent party or the community at large, if the pollution is not remedied: WMA 1996, ss 57 and 58; *Wick-*

low County Council v Fenton [2003] 1 ILRM 279, HC. The High Court has held that the imposition by Dublin City Council of a fixed charge for the collection and disposal of domestic waste is lawful and is not in breach of the 'polluter pays' principle: *Dublin City Council v Wright* [2004] ITLR (8 February) 2004. However, the 'polluter pays' principle cannot be achieved in respect of past operations which had been permitted without conditions being imposed: *In the matter of Irish Ispat (in liquidation)* (2004) Irish Times 30 July, HC. See LIFTING THE CORPORATE VEIL.

poor box. See COURT POOR BOX.

pornography. See CHILD PORNOGRAPHY; CENSORSHIP; INDECENCY.

port, free. See FREE PORT.

portion. The provision made for a child by a parent or one *in loco parentis* so as to establish the child for life. See ADVANCEMENT; DOUBLE PORTIONS, RULE AGAINST; SATISFACTION; STRICT SETTLEMENT.

positive law. Man-made law as compared with natural law (qv).

posse comitatus. [The power of the country.] Formerly, a group of able-bodied men which the sheriff was empowered to call together to assist in keeping the peace.

possession. (1) Physical detention with the intention to hold the thing detained as one's own; continuing exercise of a claim to the exclusive use of some material object. *Possession* is *prima facie* evidence of ownership and may be good against all claims except that of the true owner. A seller in *market overt* (qv), a *factor* (qv) and the holder of a *negotiable instrument* (qv) can all give a better title than they themselves have, provided the buyer takes in good faith and for value. See NEMO DAT QUI NON HABET; OWNERSHIP.

(2) As regards land, there is a distinction between *possession* and *occupation*. A tenant has an estate or interest in land which entitles him to the *exclusive possession* of the land for the period of his tenancy, which he can assert not only against third parties, but also against the landlord. It is a *property right* which the tenant can deal with, subject to the terms of the tenancy agreement, by assignment or subletting. This is what distinguishes other *occupiers* or *users* of land, who frequently have *personal rights* over land, which they cannot pass on to third parties eg a *caretaker*, a *conacre* tenant. Contrast with OCCUPATION. Possession may develop into ownership with the efflux

of time e g *adverse possession* of land. See Statute of Limitations 1957, ss 13(2) and 45(1); *Gleeson v Feehan* [1993] 2 IR 113, SC. See also LONG POSSESSION, TITLE BY.

possession, order for. The order which a court may give to a mortgagee to aid a sale out of court, or a sale by the court in lieu of foreclosure (qv): *Ulster Bank Ltd v Conlon* [1957] 91 ILTR 193; *Irish Permanent Building Society v Ryan* [1950] IR 12; *Irish Civil Service Building Society v Ingram's Representative* [1959] IR 181.

The *Private Residential Tenancies Board* (qv) is given discretion not to allow a party wrongly deprived of possession of a dwelling to resume possession in circumstances where another party, who is not party to the dispute and was not complicit in the deprivation, is now in possession of the dwelling: Residential Tenancies Act 2004, s 118. Instead, in such circumstances, the Board may direct that damages be paid by the landlord.

possession and crime. Possession of certain objects or materials can constitute a criminal offence e g possession of a firearm with intent to endanger life, possession of drugs.

The distinctive character of *possession* is that the accused has control of the article in question and knowledge of its existence: *Minister for Posts & Telegraphs v Campbell* [1966] IR 69; he does not have to have custody. The concept of possession involves ideally that the possessor has complete physical control over the article; has knowledge of its existence, its situation and its qualities; has received it from a person who intends to confer possession of it and has himself the intention to possess it exclusively of others: *The People (DPP) v Foley* [1995] 1 IR 267, CCA.

It is an offence for a person to have in their possession, when not in their place of residence, any *article* with the intention that it be used in the course of or in connection with a wide list of crimes e g theft, burglary, deception, blackmail, extortion, demanding money with menaces, taking a vehicle without lawful authority: Criminal Justice (Theft and Fraud Offences) Act 2001, s 15. On conviction, the *article* is required to be forfeited (CJ(TFO)A 2001, s 15(3)). For previous legislation, see Larceny Act 1990, s 2. [Bibliography: McAuley & McCutcheon; McGreal C.]

possession is nine-tenths of the law. Popular paraphrase for the legal concept that possession is *prima facie* evidence of ownership and may be good against all claims except that of the true owner. See POSSESSION.

possession of drugs. A person who has possession of a controlled drug may be guilty of an offence: Misuse of Drugs Act 1977, s 3. See CONTROLLED DRUGS; DRUGS, MISUSE OF.

possession of stolen property. The offence committed by a person who, without lawful authority, possesses stolen property (otherwise than in the course of stealing), knowing that the property was stolen or being *reckless* as to whether it was stolen: Criminal Justice (Theft and Fraud Offences) Act 2001, s 18(1). A person is *reckless* if he disregards a *substantial risk* that the property handled is stolen; *substantial risk* means a risk of such a nature and degree that its disregard involves culpability of a high degree (CJ(TFO)A 2001, s 16(2)).

A person who has in his possession stolen property in such circumstances that it is reasonable to conclude that he knew it was stolen, or he was reckless as to whether it was stolen, is to be taken that he knew or was reckless (CJ(TFO)A 2001, s 18(2)). This includes circumstances where the purchase of the property was at a price below the market value. [Bibliography: McGreal C.]

possessory title. See LONG POSSESSION, TITLE BY.

possibility. A future event the happening of which is uncertain. A possibility in relation to a future interest in land is said to be *bare* or *coupled with an interest*. The possibility of reverter which exists in the grantor of a determinable fee (qv) is an example of a bare possibility; it is not transferable. A contingent remainder (qv), on the other hand, can give rise to a possibility which can be transferred.

post. [After; following.]

post, contracts by. Generally the rules governing contracts by post are: (a) an offer by post may be accepted by post, unless the offer indicates anything to the contrary; (b) an offer is only made when it actually reaches the offeree and not when it would have reached him in the ordinary course of post; (c) an acceptance is complete as soon as the letter of acceptance is posted, prepaid and properly addressed, whether it reaches the offeror or not; (d) a revocation is not complete until it actually reaches the offeree. See *Adams v Lindsell* [1818] 1 B Ald 681; *Household Fire Insurance Co v Grant* [1879] 27 WR 858; *Henthorn v Fraser* [1892] 2 Ch 27.

When a contract is made by post, the acceptance is complete as soon as the letter is put in the postbox and the location of this act, represents the place where the contract is made: *Kelly v Cruise Catering Ltd* [1994] 2 ILRM 394, SC. For An Post, see website: *www.anpost.ie*. See CONTRACT. See also FAX; LIABILITY, STATUTORY EXEMPTIONS FROM; PRESUMPTION OF REGULARITY.

post, redirection of. (1) The Employment Appeals Tribunal has held that it was not their duty to have their post redirected to their new address some ten years on, having made reasonable provision at the time: *Leonard v Willie's Restaurant* [2004] ELR 14, EAT.

(2) The existing power of the High Court to order the redirection to the Official Assignee (qv) of letters addressed to a *bankrupt,* has been extended to telegrams and postal packets: Bankruptcy Act 1988, s 72. See BANKRUPTCY.

post, service by. See SERVICE BY POST.

post diem. [After the day.]

post litem motam. [After litigation was in contemplation.]

post-date. To insert a date on a document subsequent to the date of execution thereof eg to post-date a cheque. See CHEQUE, POST-DATED.

post-mortem. [After death.] The examination of a body after death to determine the cause of death. Also referred to as an *autopsy.* The Faculty of Pathology of the Royal College of Physicians in Ireland issued new guidelines to hospitals and pathologists on post-mortem practices in February 2000, following the controversy regarding post-mortems on children and tissue and organ retention, which apparently had taken place in the past without the knowledge or consent of parents.

The guidelines include a new post-mortem consent form, which specifically addresses issues such as the retention of tissue for educational and research purposes. It also allows families to limit the extent of a non-coroner's autopsy to specific areas of the body.

Included in the guidelines is a recommendation that written information on post-mortems be made available to rela-

tives. This includes information regarding the legal and practical arrangements of both autopsy and the subsequent disposition of retained organs.

The Minister for Health established, in April 2000, a non-statutory inquiry under Ms Anne Dunne SC to inquire into the controversial post-mortems on children and tissue and organ retention. See CORONER.

post-traumatic stress disorder. A bus conductor was awarded €426,186 in damages arising from the post-traumatic stress disorder he suffered following an assault while working in 1990 on the 67A route from Maynooth: *Ledwith v Bus Átha Cliath/Dublin Bus* [2003] SC reported in *Law Society Gazette* (August/September 2003) 51. A 52-year old senior bank executive who suffered post-traumatic stress disorder after a road traffic accident was awarded €579,225 damages: *O'Connor v O'Driscoll* (23 February 2004, unreported) HC. The failure of his superiors to recognise and treat the obvious symptoms of post-traumatic stress disorder in a member of the defence forces was held to constitute negligence: *McHugh v Minister for Defence* [1999] ITLR (1 March) and [2001] 1 IR 424, HC. [Bibliography: McMahon & Binchy.] See also NERVOUS SHOCK.

postal facilities. The free telephone and postal facilities for members of the Oireachtas are no longer required to be used only on matters arising from the members' parliamentary duties: Ministerial, Parliamentary and Judicial Offices and Oireachtas Members (Miscellaneous Provisions) Act 2001, s 33.

postal packets. There are provisions regarding the interception of postal packets; they are similar to those applying to the interception of telecommunications messages ie requirements for authorisation, complaints procedure, and review by a High Court judge: Interception of Postal Packets and Telecommunications Messages (Regulation) Act 1993. See TELEPHONE TAPPING.

postal services. Provision has been made for common rules for the development of the internal market of the Community postal services and the improvement of quality of service: European Communities (Postal Service) Regulations 2002, SI No 616 of 2002. These regulations give legal effect to Directive (EC) 97/67 as amended by Directive (EC) 2002/39 which provides for the regulation of the postal service with the objective of guaranteeing the provision of a universal postal service of specified quality at affordable prices to all users. For An Post, see website: *www.anpost.ie*. For the Universal Postal Union, see website: *www.upu.int*. For postal regulator, see COMMISSION FOR COMMUNICATIONS REGULATION.

postal voter. A person whose name is entered in the postal voters list: Electoral Act 1992, s 2(1). An elector is entitled to be entered in this list if he is a member of the Garda Síochána, is a whole time member of the defence forces, or is a person deemed to be ordinarily resident in the State (ie a member of an Irish diplomatic mission resident abroad) (EA 1992, s 14). Postal voting was extended: (a) to persons with a physical illness or physical disability by the Electoral (Amendment) Act 1996, s 4 and (b) to persons whose occupation, service or employment, including full-time students, render it likely that they will be unable to go in person on polling day to vote at their appointed polling place: Electoral Act 1997, ss 63–70 and 76. Postal voting was extended to persons who were precluded by their religious beliefs from secular activities on 17 May 2002 (the date of the general election in 2002) to an extent that they would be debarred from exercising their franchise: Supplement to Postal Voters (Special Difficulty) Order 2002, SI No 186 of 2002.

A postal voter is entitled to vote by sending his ballot paper by post to the returning officer for his constituency (EA 1992, s 38(2)). See also EA 1992, ss 64–77; EA 1992, s 99 amended by Electoral (Amendment) Act 2001, s 25; Presidential Elections Act 1993, s 40; Referendum Act 1994, s 28; European Parliament Elections Act 1997, Sch 2 rr 28–40. As regards the counting of postal votes where there is a regime of electronic voting, see Electoral (Amendment) Act 2004, s 12.

Provision is also made for voting by post in the election of employees to the boards of State companies: Worker Participation (State Enterprises) (Postal Voting) Regulations 1988, SI No 171 of 1988. See also Building Societies Act 1989, s 75. See also SEANAD ÉIREANN.

posthumous child. A child born after the death of the father.

postliminium. [Beyond the threshold.] The doctrine in international law (qv) whereby persons, property and territory tend to revert to their former condition, following the withdrawal of enemy control.

potato growers. A registration scheme is imposed on all potato growers and packers by the Registration of Potato Growers and Potato Packers Act 1984 as amended by An Bord Bia (Amendment) Act 2004, ss 23–24. It is an offence to sell potatoes in a package unless: (a) such potatoes have been grown by a registered grower and packed by a registered packer, and (b) the package bears the registration number of the registered grower and registered packer.

potior est conditio defendentis. [The condition of the defendant is better.] The burden of proof is on the plaintiff. See BURDEN OF PROOF.

potior est conditio possidentis. [The condition of the possessor is the better.] The burden of proof is on the claimant to show that he has a superior title to that of the possessor.

poultrymeat. A person must not place on the market *poultrymeat* imported from a third country unless it bears an indication of the country of origin: SI No 42 of 2004 as amended by SI No 50 of 2004. This requirement is notwithstanding the European Communities (Labelling, Presentation and Advertising of Foodstuffs) Regulations 2002, SI No 483 of 2002. The 2004 regulations set out marketing standards for poultrymeat, including labelling, water content, quality grading, free range production, price per weight unit and registered number of slaughterhouse or cutting plant, and they create penalties for non-compliance. See LABELLING OF FOODSTUFFS.

pound. The *monetary unit* of the State was the Irish pound which was issued in legal tender (qv) form: Central Bank Act 1989, s 24(1). The Minister was empowered to vary the general exchange rate for the Irish Pound in respect of other monetary units (CBA 1989, s 24(2)). The one pound coin was introduced by the Coinage (Dimension and Design) (One Pound Coin) Regulations 1990, SI No 83 of 1990: Decimal Currency Act 1990, s 39(c). The £ symbol has no legal significance itself, no more than has the IR£ symbol *which appears to be a banking device*: Northern Bank v Edwards [1986] ILRM 167. However, references in contracts and other instruments to the payment of money are references to Irish pounds unless some other currency is specified: Central Bank Act 1989, s 25.

Since 1 January 1999, the Irish pound has been a subdivision of the *euro* and has been withdrawn from circulation, and no longer is legal tender, from not later than 30 June 2002 (the actual date specified was 9 February 2002): Economic and Monetary Union Act 1998, ss 6 and 9. See COINS; EURO; LEGAL TENDER.

poundage. A fee of a particular amount in each pound; a sheriff is entitled to a *poundage* in respect of that which he takes, or is deemed to have taken, upon an execution against the lands or goods of a defendant. See also Finance Act 1988, s 71, now Taxes Consolidation Act 1997, s 1006. See COUNTY REGISTRAR; SHERIFF. See also RATES.

pounds. Enclosures for the confining of animals. Pounds are either a *pound* provided under the Pounds (Provision and Maintenance) Act 1935 or a *private pound* within the meaning of the Animals Act 1985, s 5. See Control of Horses Act 1996, ss 2(1), 49–50. See DISTRESS DAMAGE FEASANT; HORSES.

poverty. A body, known as the Combat Poverty Agency, has been established to advise on all aspects of economic and social planning in relation to poverty: Combat Poverty Agency Act 1986. See also Social Welfare (Miscellaneous Provisions) Act 2002, s 16 and Sch, Pt I. See website: *www.cpa.ie*. See also SECURITY FOR COSTS.

poverty, relief of. See CHARITIES.

power. The authority conferred on a person by law to determine the legal relations of himself or others. Every *power* conferred by an Act of the Oireachtas or by an instrument made wholly or partly under any such Act, *may*, unless the contrary intention appears in such Act or instrument, be exercised from time to time as occasion requires: Interpretation Act 1937, s 15(1). Contrast with DUTY.

power boat. See JET SKIS.

power of appointment. An authority given to a person to dispose of property which is not his. The person giving the authority is called the *donor*, the person to whom it is given, is the *donee* of the power, and the persons in whose favour the donee may make an appointment are called the *objects of the power*.

A power may be *appendant*, *in gross* or *collateral*. It is *appendant* where the donee has an interest in the property and the power is to take effect wholly or in part out of that interest. The power is *in gross*, where

the donee is given an interest in the property but the exercise of it will not affect his interest. The power is *collateral* or naked where the donee is not given any interest in the property.

A power of appointment may be classified also as a *general power* which is the power to appoint property to anyone including the donee himself and is almost equivalent to ownership; and a *special power* where the power is to appoint to a special person or among a special class. Several statutes regard a donee of a special power as actual owner: Judgment Mortgage Act 1850; Succession Act 1965, ss 46 and 93. In the absence of a direction to the contrary by the donor, special powers are *exclusive* powers, by which the donee may appoint to any or all of the class: Illusory Appointments Act 1874. See Capital Acquisitions Tax Consolidation Act 2003, s 36. [Bibliography: Wylie (3).] See OFFICIAL ASSIGNEE; POWER OF ATTORNEY.

power of attorney. A formal instrument by which one person (*donor*) authorises another person (*donee*) to act for him, in relation to certain specified matters. The donor of the power is the *principal* and the donee is the *attorney*. A power of attorney is not required to be made under seal, except where otherwise required for the execution of instruments by corporate bodies: Powers of Attorney Act 1996, s 15(2). Provision is made for a simple *general power of attorney* which enables the donee to do anything the donor can lawfully do by attorney (PAA 1996, s 16 and Sch 3). The donee may execute any instrument with his own signature and, where sealing is required, with his own seal (PAA 1996, s 17).

There is protection for the donee and a third party entering into a transaction with the donee where the power of attorney is revoked and they did not know at the time that it was revoked (PAA 1996, s 18(1)–(2)). A power of attorney given by way of security and expressed to be irrevocable, cannot be revoked without the agreement of the donee and a person dealing with the donee is entitled to assume this (PAA 1996, s 18(3)). A purchaser in good faith for valuable consideration is protected in relation to revocation, if the transaction was completed within twelve months after the power came into operation (PAA 1996, ss 13(4) and 18(4)).

Where a power of attorney is expressed to be irrevocable and is given to secure: (a) a proprietary interest of the donee of the power, or (b) the performance of an obligation of the donee, then, as long as the donee has that interest, or the obligation remains undischarged, the power cannot be revoked: (i) by the donor without the consent of the donee, or (ii) by the death, incapacity or bankruptcy of the donor, or if the donor is a body corporate, by its winding up or dissolution (PAA 1996, s 20). This provision does not invalidate powers of attorney given otherwise than by way of security under the Conveyancing Act 1882, ss 8–9 (now repealed): PAA 1996, s 20(3) amended by Family Law (Miscellaneous Provisions) Act 1997, s 5.

When a solicitor holds a power of attorney from a client, he should ensure that he does not use that power of attorney to gain for himself a benefit which he would not be prepared to allow to an independent third party: *A Guide to Professional Conduct of Solicitors in Ireland* (2002) ch 2.2.

An instrument creating a power of attorney may be deposited in the Central Office (qv) of the High Court; the file of such instruments may be searched, free of charge, by any person (PAA 1996, s 22). Such filing does not afford any protection against a breach of trust or other abuses. See RSC Ord 78. Rules of the Superior Courts (No 1) (Powers of Attorney Act 1996) 2000, SI No 66 of 2000. [Bibliography: Gallagher.]

power of attorney, enduring. A power of attorney is an *enduring power* if the instrument creating the power contains a statement by the donor to the effect that the donor intends the power to be effective during any subsequent *mental incapacity* of the donor and provided it complies with this section and the regulations made thereunder: Powers of Attorney Act 1996, s 5. At common law (qv) a power of attorney was revoked automatically on the mental incapacity of the donor. *Mental incapacity* means incapacity of the donor, by reason of a mental condition, to manage his own property and his business and financial affairs (PAA 1996, s 4(1)).

The enduring power can be exercised only when the donor is or is becoming mentally incapable and has been registered in the Offices of the Wards of Court. It gives power to the donee to manage the property and affairs of the donor, to execute or exercise any of the powers or discretions vested in the donor as a *tenant*

for life within the meaning of the Settled Land Act 1882, subject to any conditions or restrictions in the instrument, and may authorise certain *personal care decisions* to be made by the donee e g where and with whom the donor should live, whom the donor should see or not see, the donor's diet and dress, and what training or rehabilitation the donor should get (PAA 1996, ss 4(1) and 6(6)). These decisions must be made in the best interest of the donor.

A number of safeguards are provided to prevent such powers of attorney being abused e g the document creating the power must include a statement from a registered medical practitioner that the donor had the mental capacity to understand the effect of creating the enduring power and a similar statement by a solicitor, after interviewing the donor, that the document was not being executed as a result of fraud or undue pressure. Additionally, specified persons must be given notice of the execution of the enduring power and subsequently of any intention to apply for registration of the power.

The court has power to register or to refuse to register the enduring power on the grounds that: (a) the enduring power was not, or is no longer valid; or (b) the donor is not or is not becoming mentally incapable; or (c) the attorney is unsuitable to be the donor's attorney; or (d) fraud or undue pressure was used to induce the donor to create the power (PAA 1996, s 10). For an objection that the attorney is *unsuitable* to be upheld by the court, a criticism far more fundamental than mere lack of management skill would have to be established; criticism of the proposed attorney must far exceed the corresponding test for the removal of a trustee: *Re Hamilton's Application* [1999] 2 ILRM 509, HC and 3 IR 310.

There is protection for the attorney and for third persons (e g a purchaser in good faith for valuable consideration) where the registered power is invalid or not in force (PAA 1996, s 13). The instrument creating an enduring power, may appoint one person as attorney or more than one person and may appoint them to act *jointly* or *jointly and severally* (qv) (PAA 1996, s 14).

An enduring power of attorney in favour of a spouse is invalidated if subsequently the marriage is annulled or dissolved, or if there is a separation, or if there are orders for protection, safety or barring: PAA 1996, s 5 as amended by Family Law (Divorce) Act 1996, s 50. See Enduring Powers of Attorney Regulations 1996, SI No 196 of 1996; Enduring Powers of Attorney (Personal Care Decisions) Regulations 1996, SI No 287 of 1996. See Rules of the Superior Courts (No 1) (Powers of Attorney Act 1996) 2000, SI No 66 of 2000. See LRC Report on *Land Law – Enduring Powers of Attorney* (LRC 31, 1989); LRC Consultation Paper on *Law and the Elderly* (LRC CP 23, 2003). [Bibliography: Gallagher.] See DISCLAIMER; GIFT; ELECTRONIC FORM; SETTLEMENT.

power of sale. See MORTGAGEE, RIGHTS OF; SETTLEMENT; TRUSTEE, POWER OF.

p.p. See PER PRO.

practicable. See AS SOON AS PRACTICABLE.

practice. The formal procedures relating to proceedings in a court, governed generally by the Rules of the Superior Courts in respect of the High and Supreme Court (RSC), the Circuit Court Rules 2001 and District Court Rules (DCR). [Bibliography: Barron; Cahill E; Collins & O'Reilly; O'Floinn; Waldron; Woods (1); Lasok UK.] See RULES OF COURT.

practice directions. The directions and notes, generally published in the Legal Diary, indicating the views of the judges, the Master of the High Court, and the registrars regarding matters of practice and procedure of the courts. The directions are issued from the Central Office (qv). Practice notes are also published by the Law Society in its monthly publication *Gazette*. The Land Registry also issues 'practice directions' and had by August 2004 issued 51 such directions, see website: *www.landregistry.ie*.

A court has held that it is not bound by a practice note: *Donohoe v Dillon* [1988] ILRM 654, HC. For example of practice direction, see SUMMONS, SERVICE OUT OF JURISDICTION.

practising certificate. The certificate awarded to a person by a body of accountants entitling that person to practise as auditor of a company or as a public auditor: Companies Act 1990, s 182, as amended by Companies (Auditing and Accounting) Act 2003, s 34. See AUDITOR, COMPANY; SOLICITOR'S PRACTISING CERTIFICATE.

praecipe. A command. A form used to secure the issue of various orders eg a *praecipe* delivered to the Central Office of the High Court for the issue of a *subpoena* (qv).

praepositus. [A person put in front.] A person in authority.

praesumitur pro negante. [It is presumed for the negative.]

praesumptio. [Presumption (qv).]

prank. In a particular case, a company has been found vicariously liable for the *prank* of a supervisor which resulted in an employee suffering personal injury: *Kennedy v Taltech Engineering Co Ltd* [1990] 8 ILT Dig 84.

pre-emption. The right of purchasing property before or in preference to other persons. As regards companies, there is no general common law principle that requires giving to existing shareholders a pre-emptive claim on new shares. Since 1983 however, pre-emption is now compulsory for every company, subject to some exceptions, and also pre-emption must apply to equity securities for which a Stock Exchange listing is sought: Companies Amendment Act 1983, s 23.

A company proposing to allot any *equity securities* must not allot any of those securities on any terms to any person unless it has made an offer to each person who holds relevant shares to allot to him on the same or more favourable terms a proportion of those securities which is as nearly as practicable equal to the proportion in nominal value held by him of the aggregate of the shares (CAA 1983, s 23).

A private company may by its memorandum or articles of association vary the right of pre-emption (CAA 1983, s 23(10)). The right does not apply to shares that have been allotted for a consideration wholly or partly other than cash (CAA 1983, s 23(4)). Waiver of the right is allowed in certain circumstances (CAA 1983, s 24).

Only *equity securities* carry the right of pre-emption; these are: (a) shares which are not subject to any ceiling on the amounts that may be distributed to their holders by way of dividends and capital, and (b) rights to subscribe for or convert into such shares (CAA 1983, s 23(13)). Consequently, they are principally *ordinary* shares and certain *preference* shares. There are special provisions for equity securities of a particular class and for shares held under an *employees' share scheme* (CAA 1983, s 23). See *Lac Minerals Ltd v Chevron Mineral* [1995] 1 ILRM 161, HC. See Listing Rules 2000, paras 9.18–9.20 and 14.8. See ANNUAL GENERAL MEETING; SHARES, COMPANY.

pre-emptive costs order. A *protective costs order* directing that the applicant will not be liable for the costs of any other party to legal proceedings, as may arise. Although the High Court has jurisdiction to make a pre-emptive costs order at an interlocutory stage in the case of a public interest challenge, such an order would not have any place in ordinary *inter partes* litigation: *R v Lord Chancellor, ex parte CPAG* [1998] 2 All ER 755; *Village Residents Association Ltd v An Bord Pleanála & McDonalds Restaurants* [2000] 4 IR 321, HC and ITLR (1 May).

The court has jurisdiction to make a *pre-emptive costs order* pursuant to Courts (Supplemental Provision] Act 1961, s 14 and Ord 99 of the Rules of the Superior Courts; however, the discretion to do so should only be exercised in the most exceptional circumstances: Village *Residents Association Ltd v An Bord Pleanála* [2001] 2 ILRM 22, HC. The court held that the making of such an order should be confined to cases involving *public interest challenges*, where: (a) the issues raised are truly ones of general public importance; and (b) the court has sufficient appreciation of the merits of the claim to conclude that it is in the public interest to make the order.

Where the judge concludes that the proceedings comprise a *bona fide* public interest, he is entitled, when exercising his discretion as to costs, to take into account findings of fact which he has made: *McEvoy & Smith v Meath County Council* [2003] ITLR (17 February).

Pre-Hospital Emergency Care Council. A body corporate with the function of recognising institutions for the education and training of emergency medical technicians and to conduct examinations leading to the *National Qualification in Emergency Medical Technology*: Pre-Hospital Emergency Care Council (Establishment) Order 2000, SI No 109 of 2000.

pre-judgment interest. Interest which a plaintiff in an action may be entitled to between the date his cause of action accrued and the date of judgment: Courts Act 1981, s 22. See INTEREST ON JUDGMENTS.

pre-nuptial agreement. An agreement between two persons, who propose to marry each other, in relation to property, maintenance and custody arrangements in the event of marriage breakdown. In the absence of legislation and case law, it would appear that pre-nuptial agreements are generally unenforceable: 'To have and to hold? – Pre-Nuptial Agreements' by solicitor Geoffrey Shannon in *Law Society Gazette* (May 2003) 12. Under the Constitution, the State pledges itself to guard with special care the institution of marriage, on which the family is founded, and to protect it against attack: 1937 Constitution, art 41(3)(1). While divorce has been provided for, it would appear that pre-nuptial agreements which might anticipate divorce, will not be recognised.

pre-retirement allowance. A scheme of a pre-retirement allowance for elderly long-term unemployed persons who have effectively retired from the labour force has been provided for in the Social Welfare Act 1988, s 28. See Social Welfare (Consolidation) Act 1993, ss 127–131. Changes have been made to the scheme to facilitate persons in receipt of a pre-retirement allowance who wish to return to the workforce, by allowing them to resume entitlement to the allowance subsequently: Social Welfare (Miscellaneous Provisions) Act 2002, s 6. See Social Welfare Act 2003, s 3(2)(a).

pre-school service. Any pre-school, play group, day nursery, creche, day-care or other similar service which caters for pre-school children including those grant-aided by health boards: Child Care Act 1991, s 49. A *pre-school child* is a child who has not attained the age of six years and who is not attending a national school (qv) or a school providing an educational programme similar to a national school (CCA 1991, s 49). A person carrying on a pre-school service must give notice to the relevant health board (CCA 1991, s 51). There is provision for supervision and inspection by the health board (CCA 1991, ss 53–55). Regulations may be made by the Minister (CCA 1991, s 50). For District Court procedure regarding obtaining a warrant to enter and inspect premises in which a pre-school service is being carried on, see DCR 1997 Ord 84, r 31.

A statutory duty is placed on persons carrying on pre-school services to take all reasonable measures to safeguard the health safety and welfare of the children concerned and to comply with the Minister's regulations (CCA 1991, s 52). These legal provisions do not apply to a person taking care of not more than three pre-school children in that person's home, or care by a relative or spouse of a relative (CCA 1991, s 58).

A new scheme of accelerated capital allowances has been introduced in respect of expenditure or extension of childcare premises that meet the required standards under CCA 1991: Taxes Consolidation Act 1997, s 843A as amended by Finance Act 2000, s 63. [Bibliography: Ward.]

pre-trial conference. The conference which takes place in *commercial proceedings* (qv) before the trial of the matter, see RSC Ord 63A, r 16 inserted by Rules of the Superior Courts (Commercial Proceedings) 2004, SI No 2 of 2004. Each party is required to complete and lodge a 'pre-trial questionnaire' in a specified form (SI No 2 of 2004, r 17 and App X, Form No 3). The judge chairing the pre-trial conference is required to establish what steps remain to be taken to prepare the case for trial, the likely length of the trial and arrangements, if any, for witnesses, information and communications technology (including video conferencing) and any other arrangements which require to be made for the trial (SI No 2 of 2004, r 19). The judge may request the parties to consult with each other with a view to agreeing the documents intended to be relied upon at the trial (SI No 2 of 2004, r 21(2)).

Where there has been a *case management conference* (qv), the judge chairing that conference will fix a date for the pre-trial conference (SI No 2 of 2004, r 16(2)). Where the proceedings are not subject to 'case management' any of the parties may apply to the registrar to fix a date for the pre-trial conference, once the exchange of pleadings, affidavits or statement of issues has been completed (r 16(1)).

When the judge chairing the pre-trial conference is satisfied that the proceedings are ready to proceed to trial, he will fix a trial date (r 20).

pre-trial discovery. See '*Pre*-trial discovery and Norwich Pharmacal Relief' by Elizabeth O'Brien BL in *Bar Review* (January 2001) 241. See also DISCOVERY; EXPERT REPORT; SOLE DISCOVERY.

pre-trial hearing. Under recent legislation, there is provision for a hearing to be held before the trial of a personal injuries action, for the purposes of determining what matters relating to the action are in dispute:

Civil Liability and Courts Act 2004, s 18. See PRE-TRIAL CONFERENCE.

pre-trial procedures. See Bibliography: Barron. See also INDICTMENT; MASTER OF HIGH COURT.

Pre-Union Irish Statute. Means an Act passed by a Parliament sitting in Ireland at any time before the coming into force of the Union with Ireland Act 1800: Interpretation Act 1937, s 12 and Sch, para 24.

preamble. The introduction to a statute which states the reason for it eg in the Succession Act 1965: 'An Act to reform the law relating to succession to the property of deceased persons and, in particular, the devolution, administration, testamentary disposition and distribution on intestacy of such property, and to provide for related matters.' It is also referred to as the 'long title' of the statute. See *Madden v Minister for the Marine* [1993] ILRM 436, HC. See INTERPRETATION OF LEGISLATION; MISCHIEF OF A STATUTE.

precatory trust. An express trust created by expressions which *prima facie* are only recommendatory; a trust which may be created by the use by the donor of *precatory words* accompanying a gift, ie words which express a wish, hope, desire or entreaty, that the donee will dispose of the property in some particular way. The Courts tend to rule against construing precatory words as trusts: *Re Adams and Kensington Vestry* [1884] 27 Ch D 394. If a gift is given absolutely, the precatory expressions attached to it are regarded as stating the motive that induced the absolute gift, rather than a fetter imposed upon it: *O'Donoghue v O'Donoghue* [1959] ILTR 56; *Chambers v Fahy* [1931] IR 17; *Re McIntosh* [1933] IR 69. See TRUST.

precautionary principle. The principle that in order to protect the environment, a precautionary approach should be widely applied, meaning that where there are threats of serious or irreversible damage to the environment, lack of full scientific certainty should not be used as a reason for postponing cost-effective measures to prevent environmental degradation: National Forum on Europe, *Glossary of Terms* (2003). The principle was adopted by the UN Convention on the Environment and Development (1992).

precedence. The ceremonial order or priority to be observed by persons on formal occasions. The President of Ireland takes precedence over all other persons in the

State: 1937 Constitution art 12(1). See JUDGES, PRECEDENCE BETWEEN.

precedent. (1) In drafting proceedings or in conveyancing, a *precedent* is a copy of an instrument used as a guide in preparing a similar instrument. [Bibliography: Buckley J F; Collins & O'Reilly; Laffoy & Wheeler; Spierin; Wylie (2); Bullen & Leak UK; Butterworths UK.]

(2) A *precedent* is also a judgment or decision of a court of law which is cited as an authority to justify a decision in a case involving a similar set of facts. A precedent may be *authoritative* where it is binding and must be followed; *persuasive* where it is worthy of consideration but need not be followed (eg based on an *obiter dictum* (qv)); *declaratory* where it merely applies an existing rule of law; and *original* where it creates and applies a new rule of law. A precedent is said to be *applied* when it is followed. It is said to be *distinguished* where a judge holds that there are important differences between the case on which the precedent was based and the case now being considered.

The Supreme Court binds all courts although it is not bound by its own decisions. The High Court binds the Circuit and District Courts; the Court of Criminal Appeal binds the Central Criminal Court, the Special Criminal Court and the Circuit and District Courts on criminal matters. The courts may adopt as *persuasive* precedents, the judgments of the US and Canadian Supreme Courts, and of the House of Lords and Australian and New Zealand courts. 'While the Irish High Court should be slow to refuse to follow a principle established since 1883 in England, it was justified in not following it where high legal authority in England had questioned it': Costello J in *Tromso Sparebank v Beirne & Ors* [1989] ILRM 257, HC. See also *Attorney-General v Ryan Car Hire Ltd* [1965] IR 642; *McDonnell v Byrne Engineering Ltd* [1978] HC. See 'Taking precedent seriously' by Mee in 11 ILT & SJ (1993) 254. See STARE DECISIS; RATIO DECIDENDI; OBITER DICTUM.

precedent, condition. See CONDITION.

precedent partner. The partner, resident in the State, first named in a partnership agreement; if there is no partner resident in the State, the precedent partner is taken as the firm's agent, factor, or manager in the State: Taxes Consolidation Act 1997, ss 880(1) and 1007(1).

precept. A command; a written order; an order or direction given by one official person or body to another requiring some act to be done. Where a person has appealed a tax assessment to the Appeal Commissioners, they may issue a *precept* to the applicant, ordering him to file with them a schedule detailing his property; his trade, profession or employment; his profits or gains from each source; and any deductions made in arriving at those profits: Taxes Consolidation Act 1997, s 935.

predecessor. A person from whom one obtains succession to property ie from a settlor (qv) or testator (qv). A *predecessor in title* is the person through whom one may trace a title in property.

preference shares. Shares in a company which carry prior or preferential rights over other shares. Usually the preference shareholders must be paid a dividend, or repaid their investment, or both as the case may be, before such payment may be made to the other shareholders.

Preference dividends are presumed to be *cumulative* ie in the absence of a contrary provision, where a preference dividend has not been paid in any year or years, then all arrears of undeclared preference dividends for those years must be paid before any other class of shareholder may get a dividend: *Webb v Earle* [1875] LR 20 Eq 556. Preference shares are usually *redeemable* at some future date although they may be irredeemable. The *articles of association* usually provide that preference shareholders have no voting rights except in exceptional circumstances.

Usually preference shares are by their terms given priority in respect of payment of capital but are excluded from participating in any surplus which may remain in a winding up. If not specifically provided for, there is doubt as to whether preference shareholders are entitled to participate rateably in a surplus: contrast *Cork Electric Supply Co v Concannon* [1932] IR 314 with *Scottish Insurance Co v Wilsons Clyde Coal Co* [1949] AC 462. See Listing Rules 2000, paras 9.45, 9.47, 13.22(h). See Building Societies Act 1989, s 10; Taxes Consolidation Act 1997, ss 131, 138. See REDEEMABLE PREFERENCE SHARES.

preferential creditor. See PREFERENTIAL PAYMENTS.

preferential debts. See PREFERENTIAL PAYMENTS.

preferential jurisdiction. Means, in relation to a flag State having concurrent jurisdiction over a relevant offence with another State, the right to exercise its jurisdiction on a priority basis, to the exclusion of the other State's jurisdiction over the offence: *Council of Europe Agreement on Illicit Traffic by Sea*, art 1, implemented by Criminal Justice (Illicit Traffic by Sea) Act 2003. The Agreement and the Act give the flag state the right to have one of its arrested ships and its crew, suspected of drug trafficking, to be surrendered to the jurisdiction of the flag state in order to be prosecuted in that flag state. This preferential jurisdiction only applies where the ship is arrested on the high seas. If the ship is in Irish territorial waters, the Irish authorities have jurisdiction. See DETENTION OF SHIP; DRUG TRAFFICKING.

preferential loan. A loan at no interest or at a preferential rate made by an employer to an employee or former employee or director; the recipient is taxed on the benefit arising from the difference between the *preferential* rate and the *specified* rate: Taxes Consolidation Act 1997, s 122 amended by Finance Act 1999, s 10; Finance Act 2002, s 8; Finance Act 2003, s 4; Finance Act 2004, s 10.

A loan is not a preferential loan if made by a financial institution at the arm's length interest rate which it charges to its customers.

The level of *specified* interest rate uses for determining the *benefit-in-kind* charge on certain preferential loans made to employees was reduced in 2003 to 4.5% in respect of mortgage loans and to 11% in respect of non-mortgage loans: Finance Act 2003, s 4. The 4.5% rate was reduced to 3.5% with effect from 1 January 2004: Finance Act 2004, s 10. See also Finance Act 2001, s 5.

preferential payments. The payment of debts in priority to others in distributing or realising an estate, as in the administration of a deceased's estate, in the distribution of a bankrupt's estate, or in the winding up of a company.

As regards a company, preferential debts include: (a) one year's rates and taxes, PAYE and social welfare contributions; (b) four months' wages or salary of any clerk, servant, workman or labourer; (c) sums due to employees for sick and holiday pay; (d) payments due for provision of superannuation benefits; (e) compensation and costs in respect of employers' liability for injuries suffered in the course of employment: Companies Act 1963, s 285, Companies Amendment Act 1982, s 10.

There is a limit of £2,500/€3,174 in each of these categories (CAA 1982, s 10(b)). These debts rank equally among themselves and abate in equal proportions if the assets are insufficient to meet them: Companies Act 1963, s 285(7). The liquidator's remuneration, together with all costs, charges and expenses in the winding up, must be paid before all preferred debts. Somewhat similar provisions regarding preferential payments apply to the distribution of the property of a bankrupt (qv): Bankruptcy Act 1988, s 81. See RSC Ord 74, rr 46 and 128(1).

In order to speed up company liquidations generally, the liquidator is entitled to advertise for preferential creditors and to exclude any creditors who do not come forward within a specified time: Companies Act 1963, s 285(14) as inserted by Companies Act 1990, s 134. See *Re Castlemahon Poultry Products* [1987] ILRM 222, SC.

As regards preferential payments in bankruptcy, see In an Arranging Debtor [1921] 2 IR 1. See also *Re United Bars* [1989] 7 ILT Dig 259; *Re H Williams (Tallaght) Ltd* [1996] 3 IR 531, HC. See Rules of Superior Courts (No 3) 1989, SI 79 of 1989, Pt XXVII. See also Social Welfare Act 1990, s 45. See CHARGE; RECEIVER.

pregnancy. The state of being with child; having conceived. The dismissal of an employee by reason of pregnancy, or matters connected therewith, is deemed to be unfair: Unfair Dismissals Act 1977, s 6(2). Dismissal is not unlawful if the employee is unable to do adequately the work for which she was employed: UDA 1977, s 6(f)(i)(I) and *McCarthy v Sunbeam Ltd* [1991] ELR 38, EAT. Where an employee is dismissed while pregnant or while on maternity leave, the employer must show that the dismissal was on exceptional grounds not associated with the pregnancy: *Mason v Winston's Jewellers* [2003] ELR 108, LC.

The mere coincidence of the date of dismissal with the ending of an employee's pregnancy is not of itself sufficient to raise an inference that the reason for the dismissal is related to the pregnancy; something else is required: *Mulcahy v Minister for Justice* [2002] ELR 12, HC. In a particular case it was held that the employer did not provide adequate assistance to a pregnant employee or take adequate account of her pregnancy, and that she had been constructively dismissed: *Mooney v International Fund Managers (Ireland) Ltd* [1999] ELR 318, EAT.

For allegation of direct discrimination under UDA 1977, s 2(a), see *Long v Power Supermarket t/a Quinnsworth* EE5/1988 in 7 ILT & SJ [1989] 86, where the Equality Officer found as a question of fact that the treatment afforded a pregnant female was the same as that afforded a sick male. See also *Maxwell v English Language Institute* [1990] ELR (226); *O'Leary v Panther Catering* [1990] ELR 157; *Webb v EMO Air Cargo (UK) Ltd* [1993] IRLR 27 and [1994] ECJ 5 CH; *McKenna v North Western Health Board* [2002] ELR 52, EO.

Employers are required to ensure that when places of work undergo modifications, extensions or conversions after 1992, or are used for the first time after 1992, pregnant women and nursing mothers must be able to lie down to rest in appropriate conditions: SI No 44 of 1993, reg 17, Sch 3, para 11 and Sch 4, para 8. This requirement also applies to other places of work whenever required by the features of the place of work, the work activity carried on and the circumstances or the hazards prevailing in relation to any such activity (reg 17(2)). See also Welfare at Work (Pregnant Employee) Regulations 2000, SI No 218 of 2000.

If an employer is required to move a pregnant employee to other work and this is not objectively feasible or the work is not suitable for her, she may be entitled to leave on health and safety grounds and to health and safety benefit: Maternity Protection Act 1994, ss 17–20; Social Welfare (Consolidation) Act 1993, s 41A, SI No 25 of 1995; Maternity Protection (Amendment) Act 2004.

Prior pregnancy can also be a ground for nullity in a subsequent marriage as affecting the true consent required for marriage: contrast *WCC v C* [1989] IR 696, HC and *DB(O'R) v N'O'R* [1988] HC as per *Woulfe* in 7 ILT & SJ (1989) 130. [Bibliography: Bolger & Kimber.] See UNFAIR DISMISSAL. See also ABORTION; CRISIS PREGNANCY; MATERNITY LEAVE; SICKNESS; UNBORN, INJURIES TO; UNBORN, RIGHT TO LIFE OF.

preinspection. The procedure by which immigration and public health requirements of United States law is completed in Ireland for passengers and crew travelling from Ireland to the US; the procedure is operated by employees of the US Immigration and Naturalisation Service (INS) who are granted certain powers and immunities under Irish law: Air Navigation and Transport (Preinspection) Act 1986. A person refused clearance to enter the USA by the INS is deemed to have arrived in the State of Ireland and to be within the jurisdiction of Irish immigration law and officials (ANT(P)A 1986, s 7 as amended by Immigration Act 2004, s 16(2)).

prejudice. Injury; pre-conceived judgment. See WITHOUT PREJUDICE.

prejudicial evidence. Evidence which invites a court to disbelieve a witness on the basis of general bad character, or to believe a witness on the basis of general good character, without being directly probative as to the issue of guilt or innocence of the crime charged. See *Newman* in (1993) 3 ISLR 96. See CHARACTER, EVIDENCE OF.

preliminary examination. Under procedures in place since 1967, where a defendant in a criminal matter was entitled to elect for trial by jury, the District Court conducted a *preliminary examination* to determine if there was sufficient evidence to return the defendant for trial by jury to a higher court: Criminal Procedure Act 1967. See *O'Shea v O'Buachalla* [2001] 3 IR 137, SC; *Hughes v Garavan* [2002] 2 ILRM 127, HC and [2003] FL 8507, SC and [2004] 1 ILRM 401; *Doyle v McDonnell* [2004] 1 ILRM 1, HC.

Preliminary examinations were abolished in 2001: Criminal Justice Act 1999, ss 8–24; Criminal Justice Act 1999 (Part III) (Commencement Order) 2001, SI No 193 of 2001. Under the new procedures, there is no testing of the evidence in the District Court, but the accused is able to apply to the trial court to have the case dismissed on the ground that there is insufficient evidence to justify putting him on trial (CPA 1967, s 4E as inserted by CJA 1999, s 9). In relation to the transitional provisions, see *Zambra v McNulty* [2002] 2 ILRM 506, SC and 2 IR 351. See also *Burns v Early* [2003] 2 ILRM 321, HC. See 'The abolition of the Preliminary Examination' by Stephen O'Sullivan BL in *Bar Review* (October/November 2001). See INDICTABLE OFFENCE.

preliminary issue. An issue which raises a question of law, which a court considers would be convenient to have decided before any evidence is given or any question or issue of fact is tried, or before any reference is made to an arbitrator; the court may order that such question of law be raised for the opinion of the court either by *special case* or in such other manner as the court deems expedient: RSC Ord 34, r 2.

If it appears to a judge that there is in a cause or matter, a question of law which it would be convenient to have decided before any evidence is given or issue of fact is tried, the judge may make an order accordingly and direct such question to be raised for the opinion of the court: Circuit Court Rules 2001 Ord 34, r 1.

A *point of law* raised in the pleadings is disposed of by the judge who tries the cause at or after the trial or may be set down for hearing before the trial RSC Ord 25, r 1. A preliminary issue of law cannot be tried *in vacuo*; it must be determined in the context of established or agreed facts: *McCabe v Ireland* [2000] 1 ILRM 410, SC and [1999] 4 IR 151, SC.

Also the court may direct a trial without a jury of any question of fact or partly of fact and partly of law: RSC Ord 36, r 7. It has been held that it is difficult to envisage situations arising in a *defamation* case where a preliminary point might be set down pursuant to Ord 36, r 7 as the establishment of defamatory meaning is based on how the words strike the ordinary person: *Duffy v News Group Newspapers Ltd* [1994] 1 ILRM 364, SC. See SPECIAL CASE.

preliminary point. A matter raised usually at the outset in a legal proceedings e g as to the jurisdiction of the court.

preliminary rulings. The rulings given by the European Court of Justice (or in certain cases, the Court of First Instance) concerning: (a) the interpretation of the Treaty; (b) the validity and interpretation of acts of the institutions of the European Community and of the European Central Bank; (c) the interpretation of the statutes of bodies established by an act of the Council, where those statutes so provide: EC Treaty, arts 225(3) and 234 of the consolidated (2002) version. The Court may not rule on the interpretation of national laws and regulations or on the conformity of such measures with Community law; it may only provide the national court with the criteria for interpretation based on Community law which will enable that court to solve the legal problem with

which it is faced: *Heineken Bronwerijen ECR* [1984] 3435.

Every member or tribunal of a member state is entitled to ask the court for a *preliminary ruling,* regardless of the stage reached in the proceedings pending before it and regardless of the nature of the decision which it is called upon to give. However, once a case has been decided in the Irish courts, a preliminary ruling cannot be sought as there is no case pending before the Irish court in respect of which a preliminary ruling could have any relevance: *McNamara v An Bord Pleanála* [1998] 2 ILRM 313, SC. An appeal does not lie against a decision to seek a preliminary ruling: *Campus Oil Co Ltd v Minister for Industry Energy* [1983] IR 82, SC.

A preliminary ruling is binding *inter partes;* it may be regarded as authoritative by all national courts where it declares a Council or Commission regulation to be void: *Societe des Produits de Mais SA* [1985] ECR 719. See also *Re Beara Fisheries and Shipping Ltd* [1988] ILRM 221; *SPUC v Grogan* [1989] IR 753; Case 377/89 *Cotter v McDermott* [1991] ECJ. See EUROPEAN COURT OF JUSTICE.

preliminary tax. The tax liability of a self-employed person, as assessed by that person, which must be paid within one month of the due date in each tax year, under the 'self-assessment' provisions introduced by the Finance Act 1988, ss 9–21 as amended, now consolidated in Taxes Consolidation Act 1997, ss 950–959. Preliminary tax includes income tax, pay related social insurance, and health contribution.

If the preliminary tax actually paid is less than 90% of the amount actually due for the year, interest will be charged on the deficiency from the due date. A 'Notice of Preliminary Tax' is the Tax Inspector's estimate of the preliminary tax due; however the taxpayer's own estimate of preliminary tax must be paid even if it is higher than that in the Notice or even if no Notice is received by the taxpayer. There is no right of appeal against the tax shown in the Notice and that amount may be pursued for collection by the Revenue Commissioners in the event that the taxpayer fails to pay his own assessment of the preliminary tax.

premature. In a particular planning case involving a Bord Pleanála decision, *development* which was stated by the Board to be *premature,* was held to mean action which can be done at a later date but that as yet it is too early to take action: *Hoburn Homes Ltd v An Bord Pleanála* [1992] ITLR (20 July) HC and [1993] ILRM 368. The decision was held to be *ultra vires* the Board's powers.

premises. [That which went before.] (1) The operative parts of a conveyance (qv) which precede the *habendum* (qv) and come after the *recitals* (qv).

(2) Popularly, land and buildings. Includes any messuage, building, vessel, structure or land or any hereditament of any tenure, together with any out-buildings and curtilage: Environmental Protection Agency Act 1992, s 3(1) as substituted by Protection of the Environment Act 2003, s 5. Includes any building, dwelling, temporary construction, vehicle, ship or aircraft: Consumer Credit Act 1995, s 2(1). A *residential premises* is a building, or part of a building, suitable for use as a dwelling together with any adjacent garden or outbuildings; a *rented residential premises* is one which has a landlord: Taxes Consolidation Act 1997, s 98(1). See also Building Societies Act 1989, s 20.

In the UK it has been held that 'premises' is an ordinary word of the English language which takes colour and content from the context in which it is used ... it has no recognised and established meaning: *Viscount Dilhorne in Maunsell v Olins* [1975] 1 All ER 16. See OCCUPIERS' LIABILITY.

premium. (1) The consideration in a contract of insurance. It is often a periodical payment; an insurer is not bound to accept a *renewal premium* except in the case of a life insurance policy. Policies usually provide that the insurer is not on risk until the premium is paid. There is a duty on the insured to disclose material facts which could affect the renewal or the renewal premium. In marine insurance, where an insurance is effected at a premium to be arranged, and no arrangement is made, a reasonable premium is payable: Marine Insurance Act 1906, s 31. See also MIA 1906, ss 52–54.

A premium paid to an insurance intermediary (qv) is treated as having been paid to the insurer when it is paid to the insurance intermediary in respect of a renewal of a policy which has been invited by the insurer, or in respect of an accepted proposal: Insurance Act 1989, s 53.

Additionally, an insurance intermediary must not accept money from a client: (a) in respect of a proposal unless it is accompanied by the completed proposal or the proposal has been accepted by the insurer, or (b) in respect of a renewal unless it has been invited by the insurer (IA 1989, s 52).

(2) The amount in excess of the par or nominal value of a share in a company which an applicant for that share is required to pay. It is for the directors to decide whether to issue shares at a premium and the size of any premium: Companies Act 1963, Table A, art 5. The aggregate amount or value of any premium received must be placed in a *share premium account*. It may not be repaid to the shareholders except by the capital reduction mechanism (CA 1963, ss 72–77 as amended). However it may be used to finance the issue to existing members of fully paid up *bonus* shares, or to pay any premium which is due when preference shares or debentures are being redeemed, or to defray the company's preliminary expenses, or the cost of issuing shares or debentures in the company, or to pay commission on such issue (CA 1963, s 62 as amended by the Companies Act 1983, Sch 1, para 11 and Companies Act 1990, s 231(1)).

(3) Includes any like sum, whether payable to the immediate or a superior lessor or to a person connected with the immediate or superior lessor: Taxes Consolidation Act 1997, s 96(1). Where a premium is payable under a short lease (a lease not longer than 50 years) part of the premium is treated as rent receivable at the time of the letting agreement (TCA 1997, s 98). See DISCOUNT, ISSUE OF SHARES AT; INSURANCE, CONTRACT OF; REDUCTION OF CAPITAL; REVERSE PREMIUM; ULTRA VIRES.

prerogative, royal. See ROYAL PREROGATIVE.

prerogative orders. Orders of *certiorari, prohibition, mandamus* and *quo warranto* (qqv). See JUDICIAL REVIEW.

prescribe. (1) To lay down with authority; to set out under a regulation. (2) To claim by prescription (qv).

prescribed limit of alcohol. See DRUNKEN DRIVING.

prescription. The vesting of a right by reason of the lapse of time eg an easement (qv). Prescription at common law required proof of user since time immemorial (qv), *nec vi, nec clam, nec precario,* ie without force, without secrecy, without permission.

The doctrine of the *lost modern grant* (qv) overcame some difficulties in establishing this proof. The Prescription Act 1832, extended to Ireland in 1859 by the Prescription (Ireland) Act 1858, lays down the periods of enjoyment required to establish title to an easement and a *profit a prendre* (qv). See *Scott v Goulding Properties Ltd* [1973] IR 200.

Twenty years' continuance of a nuisance may, by prescription, legalise the activity which constitutes the nuisance, converting it into an easement appurtenant to the land on which it exists: *Sturges v Bridgman* 11 Ch D [1879] 852 at 863. Time runs from the time the nuisance was created as regards the owner of the servient land, which may be some time after the activity, which constitutes the nuisance, commenced.

The Law Reform Commission has recommended, in order to simplify and clarify the law in this area, that the 1832 and 1858 Acts be repealed and replaced with new legislation: *Report on the Acquisition of Easements and Profit A Prendre by Prescription* (LRC 66, 2002). The Commission has recommended that there should be a statutory definition of *user as of right* in the form of a simple statement. [Bibliography: Bland (1).]

prescription drugs. The controls applicable to the prescription and supply of medicinal products to the public have been updated and consolidated in accordance with the requirements of Directive (EC) 2001/83: Medicinal Products (Prescription and Control of Supply) Regulations 2003, SI No 540 of 2003.

'A prescription must be legible, dated and signed by a registered medical practitioner. Should the need arise to prescribe a drug over the telephone, the doctor should make a record of the call and forward the appropriate prescription to the pharmacist in a reasonable time': Medical Council, *A Guide to Ethical Conduct and Behaviour* (6th edn, 2004) para 10.2. Electronic prescribing is acceptable if it meets legal and best clinical standards.

In April 2004, the Minister for Health announced that it was proposed to give nurses the power to prescribe certain drugs in a number of pilot projects in nursing homes and acute hospitals. These pilot projects would be evaluated before prescription rights were extended to nurses generally. [Bibliography: Tomkin and Hanafin.] See EDUCATIONAL GRANTS; MEDICAL PREPARATIONS; MEDICINAL PRODUCT.

present. To tender or offer eg to present a cheque (qv) for payment.

presentment. See GRAND JURY.

preservative. Any substance which is capable of inhibiting, retarding or arresting deterioration of food caused by micro-organisms and of concealing the evidence of such deterioration, but does not include some specified substances eg common salt: SI No 337 of 1981. A person may not manufacture, prepare, import, distribute or sell any food which contains any preservative other than a permitted preservative (para 11).

preserved benefit. (1) In the case of a public servant who leaves before reaching the age for receipt of a pension, means a deferred superannuation benefit which is payable at a date later than the date of the public servant's date of leaving office: Public Service Superannuation (Miscellaneous Provisions) Act 2004, s 1(1).

(2) The benefit which a member of an occupational pension scheme is entitled to, whose employment terminates (otherwise than by death) prior to normal retirement age: Pensions Act 1990, ss 28–39 as amended by Social Welfare Acts 1992, s 54 and 1993, s 45; Pensions (Amendment) Act 1996 and Pensions (Amendment) Act 2002, ss 17–26.

The qualifying service is five years, of which two years must be since 1 January 1991. The qualifying period has been reduced to two years for those leaving service after 1 June 2002 (PA 1990, s 28 amended by P(A)A 2002, s 17).

A member who is entitled to a preserved benefit is entitled to a transfer payment to another pension scheme or to a *Personal Retirement Savings Account* (PA 1990, s 34 as amended by SWA 1992, s 55 and P(A)A 2002, s 22).

A preserved benefit cannot be subject to forfeiture or a lien (qv); this now includes a minimum contributory retirement benefit (PA 1990, s 36 as amended by P(A)A 2002, s 24). See Social Welfare (Miscellaneous Provisions) Act 2003, s 24, Sch, para 16. See PENSION SCHEME AND FORFEITURE.

President of Ireland. The expression 'the President' means the President of Ireland and includes any commission or other body or authority for the time being lawfully exercising the powers and performing the duties of the President: Interpretation Act 1937, s 12, para 23. The office was established by the 1937 Constitution (arts 12–14).

The President is elected by the direct vote of the people, and may hold office for not more than two terms, each of seven years. The holder takes precedence over all other persons in the State. The President, on the nomination of Dáil Éireann, appoints the Taoiseach. She also appoints the other members of the government on the nomination of the Taoiseach and with the previous approval of the Dáil. The Dáil is summoned and dissolved by the President on the advice of the Taoiseach, although she may in her absolute *discretion* (qv) refuse to dissolve the Dáil on the advice of a Taoiseach who has ceased to retain the support of a majority in the Dáil.

Every Bill passed or deemed to have been passed by both Houses of the Oireachtas requires the signature of the President for its enactment into law. The President may, after consultation with the Council of State (qv) refer a Bill to the Supreme Court for a decision on the question as to whether it is repugnant to the Constitution. The President is also supreme commander of the defence forces and all its officers hold their commissions from her. She is responsible for the accreditation of the diplomatic representatives of the State: Republic of Ireland Act 1948.

Only *presidential electors* ie Irish citizens, 18 years and over, ordinarily resident in the constituency in which they seek to register, are entitled to vote in presidential elections: Electoral Act 1992, s 7. The law relating to presidential elections was amended and consolidated in 1993; the two principal changes introduced were: (a) the entire count to be carried out in the constituencies (as in a referendum) with the count being reported to the presidential returning officer and (b) provision for a presidential election petition to the High Court in the event of questioning of the result of the election: Presidential Elections Act 1993. See also Presidential Establishment Acts 1938, 1973 and 1991.

The Presidents of Ireland have been: Mary McAleese (1997 to present); Mary Robinson (1990–97); Patrick J Hillery (1976–90); Cearbhall O'Dálaigh (1974–76); Erskine H Childers (1973–74); Eamon de Valera (1959–73); Seán T O'Ceallaigh (1945–59); Douglas Hyde (1938–45). For the records of the office of the Secretary to the President, see website: *www.nationalarchives.ie*. For the President's Award – 'Gaisce', see website: *www.p-award.net*. See ADDRESS; ELECTION PETITION, PRESIDENTIAL; IMPEACHMENT; OBSTRUCTION OF THE PRESIDENT; PETITION.

Presidential Commission. The commission which is empowered to exercise and perform the powers and functions conferred on the President of Ireland, in her absence from the State, or incapacity, or where she has died, resigned, been removed from office or has failed to exercise and perform the powers and functions of her office: 1937 Constitution, art 14. The Commission consists of the Chief Justice, the Chairman of Dáil Éireann (An Ceann Comhairle) and the Chairman of Seanad Éireann. The first dissolution (qv) of Dáil Éireann ordered by the Presidential Commission (in the absence abroad of the President) took place in 1992: Iris Oifigiúil, 10 November 1992.

Press Council. In Ireland there is no press council to investigate complaints from members of the public about the editorial content of newspapers and magazines, as in the UK with their self-regulating *Press Complaints Commission*, which was established on a non-statutory basis in 1991. The establishment of a statutory Press Council for Ireland was recommended in 2003: *Report of the Legal Advisory Group on Defamation*. In April 2004, the Irish press industry presented a proposal to government for the establishment of a non-statutory independent Press Ombudsman and Press Council, which would be funded by the industry, and based on the system which operates in Sweden. The role of the Ombudsman would be to receive and consider individual complaints and if a resolution regarding the complaint could not be reached, to adjudicate on the issue. In May 2004, the Minister for Justice announced that proposals for the establishment of an independent Press Council would be brought before the Cabinet in the autumn. See *Regulating the Press: does Ireland need a statutory Press Council?* in *Bar Review* (December 2003) 241.

press freedom. See FAIR AND ACCURATE REPORT; FREEDOM OF PRESS; JOURNALIST, COMMUNICATIONS WITH; PUBLICATION, RIGHT OF.

presumption. A conclusion or inference as to the truth of some fact in question, drawn from other facts either proved or admitted to be true. Presumptions may be: (a) *presumptions of law* which are *irrebuttable* (*praesumptiones juris et de jure*) and evidence is not admissible to contradict them e g that a child under seven years cannot commit a crime; (b) *presumptions of law* which are *rebuttable* (*praesumptiones juris*) and which are conclusive unless disproved by evidence to the contrary e g the presumption of innocence of an accused; (c) *presumptions of fact* (*praesumptiones hominis vel facti*) which are inferences which may be drawn from other facts but not compulsorily e g that the possessor of goods recently stolen is either the thief or the receiver (now, handling stolen property (qv)). See *Maher v Attorney-General* [1973] IR 140.

presumption of constitutionality. See LEGISLATION, CONSTITUTIONALITY OF; RESOLUTION.

presumption of continuance. The presumption of fact that a proven state of affairs can be presumed to have continued in that condition for a reasonable time e g a jury is entitled to draw the inference that if a person was alive on a particular day, he was alive on a subsequent day.

presumption of death. See DEATH, PRESUMPTION OF.

presumption of good faith and value. The holder of a bill of exchange (qv) is *prima facie* presumed to be a *holder in due course* (qv): Bills of Exchange Act 1882, s 30(2).

presumption of innocence. The presumption in law, which is rebuttable, that an accused is innocent until proven guilty beyond reasonable doubt. 'The presumption of innocence is personal to the dignity and status of every citizen': Murray J in *O'C v DPP* [2000] 3 IR 87 at 103. 'The presumption of innocence is a very real thing and is not simply a procedural rule taking effect only at the trial.' Walsh J in *People (A-G) v O'Callaghan* [1966] IR 501 at 513.

The presumption of innocence in a criminal trial is implicit in the 1937 Constitution, art 38(1) that 'no person shall be tried on any criminal charge save in *due course of law*': *Rock v Ireland* [1998] 2 ILRM 35, SC and [1997] 3 IR 484, SC. A trial held otherwise than in accordance with the presumption is not one in *due course of law*; however a limitation on the presumption of innocence could be constitutionally

permissible: *O'Leary v A-G* [1991] ILRM 455, HC. See *Harvey v Ocean Accident & Guarantee Corporation* [1905] 2 IR 1; *Ryan v DPP* [1989] IR 399. See 'Presumed Guilty?' by Claire Hamilton in (2002) 10 ISLR 202. See DEFENCE BARRISTER, DUTY OF; DESERTER; UNLAWFUL ORGANISATION.

presumption of legality. See OMNIA PRAESUMUNTUR RITE ESSE ACTA.

presumption of legitimacy. See LEGITIMACY, PRESUMPTION OF.

presumption of marriage. See MARRIAGE, PRESUMPTION OF.

presumption of negligence. See RES IPSA LOQUITUR.

presumption of regularity. Where any judicial or official appointment or act is shown to have been done in a manner substantially regular, there is a presumption in law that the formal requisites for its validity were complied with. See *Re McLean* [1950] IR 180.

In a particular case concerning whether various assessments and demands had been lawfully posted by the Revenue Commissioners, it was held that the trial judge was entitled to act upon the evidence of the operation of a system and to accept it established as a matter of probability that the various documents had been posted when they were meant to have been: *Deighan v Hearne & Ors* [1990] 1 IR 499, SC. See OMNIA PRAESUMUNTUR RITE ESSE ACTA.

presumption of sanity. The presumption in law that a person is sane until the contrary is proved. See INSANITY; MCNAGHTEN RULES; UNFIT TO PLEAD.

presumption of survivorship. See DEATH, SIMULTANEOUS.

presumptions as to documents. See DOCUMENTS, PRESUMPTIONS AS TO.

pretence, false. See FALSE PRETENCE.

preventative detention. Formerly, the period of not more than ten, and not less than five years, where a person was convicted as an *habitual criminal:* Prevention of Crime Act 1908, since repealed by Criminal Law Act 1997, s 16 and Sch 3. As there were no facilities in the State for providing such detention, in practice the Act could not be applied: *The People (DPP) v Carmody* [1988] ILRM 370.

Preventative detention, by refusing bail (qv) to a person because of the likelihood of the commission of further offences, previously had no place in our legal system:

The People v O'Callaghan [1966] IR 501. A preventative sentence of a rapist to protect women from him was unknown to the State's judicial system: *DPP v Jackson* (1993) Irish Times, 27 April, CCA. See also *DPP v Ryan* [1989] 7 ILT Dig 81; *People (DPP) v Bambrick* [1996] 1 IR 265, CCA. However since 2000, see BAIL.

Preventive detention, in terms of civil confinement, is provided for under the Mental Health Act 2001. Also the Offences Against the State (Amendment) Act 1940 provides for preventative detention.

It has been held that, while there are legitimate grounds justifying preventative detention, there was no general rule relating thereto, it depended on the circumstances and nature of the detention; and in the particular form of detention contemplated in the Illegal Immigrants (Trafficking) Bill 1999, the safeguards which existed were adequate to meet the requirements of the Constitution: *In the matter of The Illegal Immigrants (Trafficking) Bill 1999* [2000] 2 IR 360, SC.

See O'Malley in 7 ILT & SJ (1989) 41. For other detention provisions which could be classed as *preventative*, see DEPORTATION ORDER AND DETENTION; SPECIAL VERDICT. See also DETENTION; INTERNMENT.

previous conduct. Evidence of previous conduct is not admissible generally as it is deemed irrelevant. However, such evidence is admissible: (a) previously, to prove guilty knowledge of a receiver of stolen goods: Larceny Act 1916, s 43, since repealed (now, handling stolen property (qv)); (b) to prove facts showing system so as to negative that an act was accidental: *Makin v A-G for New South Wales* [1894] AC 57; (c) to prove the existence of a course of business; (d) to prove a state of mind e g intention, knowledge or malice; (e) to prove the true relationship between the accused person and the prosecutrix in sexual cases, but only when the judge so allows where it would otherwise be unfair to the accused: *The People (Attorney-General) v Dempsey* [1961] IR 288; Criminal Law (Rape) Act 1981, s 3 as amended by the Criminal Law (Rape) Amendment Act 1990, s 13. See RAPE.

previous statement, inconsistent. When a witness gives evidence at a trial which is inconsistent with a previous statement of his, the trial judge should explain to the jury that in such a case, the previous statement is only evidence against the credibility of the witness and not evidence of the matters contained in it: *The People v Taylor* [1974] IR 97. See HOSTILE WITNESS.

price. The money consideration in a contract for the sale of goods: Sale of Goods Act 1893, s 1. The price may be fixed or may be left to be fixed or may be determined by the course of dealing between the parties (SGA 1893, s 8). In the absence of the foregoing, the buyer must pay a reasonable price; what is reasonable is a question of fact dependent on the circumstances of each particular case. The time of payment is not deemed to be of the essence of a contract of sale unless a different intention appears from the terms of the contract (SGA 1893, s 10(1)). See CAPACITY TO CONTRACT; PRODUCT PRICES; TRANSFER PRICING; WARRANTY, BREACH OF.

price, false or misleading indication of. It is an offence for a person offering to supply goods of any description or offering to provide any services or living accommodation to give a false or misleading indication of the price or charge for same or of the recommended price (qv) for the goods: Consumer Information Act 1978, s 7. See PRODUCT PRICES.

price, recommended. See RECOMMENDED PRICE.

price, reserve. See AUCTION SALES.

price, retail. See RETAIL PRICE.

price control. Wide statutory power is given to the Minister to make orders regulating the price of goods and services by the Prices Acts 1958, 1965 and 1972. The power extends to the interest charged and other charges made under hire-purchase and credit-sale agreements (PA 1972, s 4). Price control is achieved mainly by *maximum price orders* and *price stabilisation orders*.

These orders must not be arbitrary or unfair or otherwise they may be *ultra vires* and void: *Cassidy v Minister for Industry and Commerce* [1978] IR 297. The Minister may also make *retail price display* orders requiring retailers to display in a specified manner the prices charged by them for certain commodities, and there is a prohibition on the sale *below cost* of certain goods.

There is provision for the appointment of *advisory committees* to enquire into and report to the Minister on the pricing and marketing of goods and services; it is an offence for a person to default in attending before such a committee on being duly summoned (PA 1972, s 10). See also Restrictive Practices (Amendment)

Act 1987, ss 27–29. See Prices Stabilisation Order 2000, SI No 209 of 2000. See Retail Prices (Beverages in Licensed Premises) Order 2000, SI No 210 of 2000; SI No 222 of 2000. See BELOW COST SELLING.

price discrimination. Charging different prices for essentially the same product or service. This may amount to an *abuse of a dominant position*. As regards the take-over and merger of companies, the Listing Rules require that all shareholders of the same class be offered the same price. As far as the law is concerned, generally a shareholder is entitled to sell his shares on the best terms he can get. [Bibliography: Maher.] See DOMINANT POSITION, ABUSE OF; MERGER.

price list. See ADVERTISEMENT; PRODUCT PRICES.

price-sensitive information. See DIRECTORS AND SHARE DEALING; INSIDER TRADING.

price stabilising. The action taken in respect of non-debt securities of a company, the purpose of which is to stabilise or maintain the market price of the securities: Companies (Amendment) Act 1999. Such action does not constitute *insider trading* if it conforms to the *Stabilisation Rules* and takes place during the *stabilising period* ie from the date of the earliest public announcement of the issue or offer which states the issue or offer price and ending on the day which is 30 days after the *closing date*, or earlier if notice of termination is given to the Stock Exchange (C(A)A 1999, ss 1–2 and Sch). The *closing date* is the date on which the issuer or offeror receives the proceeds of the issue or offer. Price stabilising effected outside the State must conform with the relevant requirements of that jurisdiction (C(A)A 1999, s 2(b)). The reason for price stabilising is to foster a more orderly and controlled aftermarket for new issues and offers of securities. See COVERT TAKE-OVER; INSIDER DEALING; SHARES, DISCLOSURE OF.

price variation clause. In such a clause in a contract, effect must be given to the ordinary meaning of the words in the clause: *Marathon Petroleum v Bord Gáis Éireann* [1986] SC.

priest and privilege. See PRIVILEGE, COMMUNICATIONS TO ANOTHER; PRIVILEGE, CONFESSIONAL.

prima facie. [Of first appearance.] On the face of it; a first impression. A *prima facie* case is one in which there is sufficient evidence in support of a party's charge or allegation to call for an answer from his opponent. If a prima facie case has not been made out, the opponent may, without calling any evidence himself, submit that there is no case to answer, whereupon the case may be dismissed. See DIRECTION.

primarily. The use of the word 'primarily' in the first sentence of a definition (of a family home) meant that that it was 'in the first place' the appropriate definition: *National Irish Bank Ltd v Graham* [1994] 2 ILRM 109, SC. See FAMILY HOME.

primary facts. Basic facts determined by a trial judge; the determination of facts depending on the assessment by the judge of the credibility and quality of the witnesses. The Supreme Court will not normally reverse such findings because it has not had the advantage of seeing and hearing the witnesses as they gave their evidence: *JM and GM v An Bord Uchtála* [1988] ILRM 203. There are exceptional cases where the evidence is so clearly one way as to require the intervention of the Supreme Court: *Kennedy v Galway VEC* [1993] 11 ILT Dig 91, SC. Contrast with SECONDARY FACTS.

Findings of primary facts will not be set aside unless there is no evidence to support them; with regard to inferences drawn from primary facts which are mixed questions of fact and law, these will be set aside only if the conclusions are ones which no reasonable judge could draw: *Mara v Hummingbird Ltd* [1982] ILRM 421 cited in *Browne v Bank of Ireland Finance Ltd* [1991] ITLR (18 March), SC and *O'Culachain v McMullan Bros Ltd* [1991] 1 IR 363, HC. See also *S v S* [1992] ILRM 732, SC; *O'Keeffe v Russell & AIB plc (No 2)* [1993] ITLR (22 November) SC.

While normally bound by the findings by the trial judge of primary fact, the Supreme Court must investigate on appeal whether such findings constitute negligence, this being a matter of law in an action for damages for personal injuries: *Moore v Fulleton* [1991] ILRM 29, SC.

The Supreme Court has recommended, where judgment is not reserved in any cases tried by a judge, that the judge at the conclusion of the evidence should summarise his findings of primary fact and then invite submissions from both sides: *O'Byrne v Gloucester* [1989] 7 ILT Dig 56. See also FACT; INFERENCE.

Prime Minister. Taoiseach (qv).

primo loco. [In the first place.]

primogeniture. [Primo-genitus, first born.] The rule of inheritance according to which the eldest male in the same degree succeeded to the ancestor's land to the exclusion of others. Abolished by the Succession Act 1965, s 11 except as it applies to the descent of an *estate tail* (qv).

primus inter pares. [First among equals.] See JUDGES, PRECEDENCE BETWEEN.

principal. A person who authorises another, called an *agent*, to act on his behalf. The duty of a principal is to pay the reward or commission to the agent in accordance with the express or implied contract of agency, and to indemnify the agent against losses incurred in execution of the authority.

A principal may revoke his authority at any time except where it has been given under seal or where the authority has been *coupled with an interest*. If a principal has allowed an agent to assume authority, a revocation of authority will only be effective as against third parties, if the third parties are informed of the revocation of authority.

Where a principal represents to a third party that he has authorised an agent to act on his behalf, he may, as against the third party, not be allowed to deny the truth of the representation and be bound by the agent's act whether he in fact authorised it or not; this is known as *apparent* authority: *Kilgobbin Mink & Stud Farms Ltd v National Credit Co Ltd* [1980] IR 175. See also *Kett v Shannon* [1987] ILRM 364. See COMMISSION; SECRET PROFIT; UNDISCLOSED PRINCIPAL.

principal, undisclosed. See UNDISCLOSED PRINCIPAL.

principal in crime. Formerly, in a felony (qv), the principal *in the first degree* was the actual offender; the principal *in the second degree* was the person who aided and abetted the actual perpetrator of the felony at the time when it was committed. The aider and abetter (qv) was liable for such crimes committed by the principal in the first degree as were done in execution of their common purpose. See *The People (Attorney-General) v Ryan* [1966] Frewen 304; *The People (DPP) v Madden* [1977] IR 336.

Now, a person who aids and abets the commission of an indictable offence is dealt with as a principal offender: Criminal Law Act 1997, s 7(1). See also ACCESSORY; AID AND ABET; DURESS IN CRIME.

print. See ARTISTIC WORK.

printed document. See TYPE, SIZE OF.

prior mortgage. A building society is prohibited from making a *housing loan* (qv) on the security of any freehold or leasehold estate or interest which is subject to a *prior mortgage* unless the prior mortgage is in favour of the society: Building Societies Act 1989, s 22(4). However, the Central Bank may, by regulations, specify charges or descriptions of charges which would not materially affect the security, and a *prior mortgage* will not include any charge so specified (BSA 1989, s 22(5)). No such regulations had been made by 2003 and none were planned.

Pending such regulations, a *prior mortgage* does not include charges specified in the Building Societies (Amendment) Act 1983 or in the Land Act 1984, s 4(2), notwithstanding their repeal e g a charge on land to secure payment of the whole or part of a conventional rent, a fee farm rent or a crown rent or to secure payment of a purchase annuity, a land reclamation annuity or any other annual payment to the Land Commission. The 1983 Act was necessitated by the decision in *Rafferty v Crowley* [1984] ILRM 350.

priority. Precedence; the right to enforce a claim in preference to others. As regards *registered land,* the register is conclusive evidence of the title of the owner of the land as appearing on the register and of any right or burden, and such title, in the absence of fraud, is not affected by the owner having notice of any deed relating to the land: Registration of Title Act 1964, s 31. Registered burdens on registered land rank *inter se* according to the order in which they are registered, not according to the order in which they are created (RTA 1964, s 75).

As regards *unregistered land,* registered deeds rank *inter se* according to their date of registration, irrespective of whether the deed passes the legal or equitable estate: Registry of Deeds (Ireland) Act 1707, s 4. As between registered and unregistered deeds, the unregistered deed is deemed fraudulent and void as against the registered one; however a party claiming through a registered deed who has actual *notice* of a prior unregistered deed, cannot rely on the priority given by the 1707 Act (RD(I)A 1707, s 5). Registration gives priority but it does not amount to notice.

In the absence of registration, priority as between equitable interests or between legal and equitable interests is determined by the equitable maxims *where the equities are equal, the first in time prevails; where the equities are equal, the law prevails.* See ADMINISTRATION OF ESTATES; DEEDS, REGISTRATION OF; JUDGMENT MORTGAGE; LAND REGISTRATION; NOTICE; OVERRIDING INTEREST; WINDING UP, COMPULSORY.

priority date. As regards a patent, the *date of filing* of a patent application; this is the date that the applicant paid the filing fee and filed documents which contain: (a) an indication that a patent is sought; (b) information identifying the applicant; and (c) a description of the invention: Patents Act 1992, s 23. The date of filing is also the date which, under the law of the country where the application is made or in accordance with the terms of a treaty or convention to which the country is a party, is to be treated as the date of filing the application or is equivalent to the date of filing of an application in that country (PA 1992, s 2(1)). In the case of a *convention application* (qv), it is generally the date of application for protection in the applicant's convention country under the *right of priority* provision of the Paris Convention (qv).

A person who files an application for registration of a design in a Paris Convention country or a member country of the World Trade Organisation, has a right of priority during a period of six months from the date of the foreign application for the purpose of registering the same design in Ireland: Industrial Designs Act 2001, s 26. The foreign filing date becomes the filing date of the application in Ireland (IDA 2001, s 29). See DESIGN; HAGUE AGREEMENT; EUROPEAN PATENT TREATY; SIMULTANEOUS INVENTION; TRADE MARK, REGISTERED.

prison. A place of detention for persons committed to custody under the law: Prisons Acts 1826–1980. A place of custody administered by the Minister for Justice: Criminal Justice (Miscellaneous Provisions) Act 1997, s 19(2).

The Minister is empowered to make rules for the regulation and good government of prisons; these rules may provide for a wide range of control functions including the treatment of prisoners, the provision of educational and other services, the imposition of penalties for breaches of discipline, remission for good conduct, and photographing, measuring, fingerprinting and

palmprinting of prisoners (CJ(MP)A 1997, s 19(2)–(3)). See Rules for Government of Prisons 1947, 1983 and 1987 (SIs Nos 135 of 1983 and 90 of 1987). Provision has been made to confer on members of the Defence Forces and on the gardaí the powers and privileges of prison officers where they assist the Governor of a prison in maintaining good order and safe and secure custody: Prison Rules 2003, SI No 730 of 2003.

The prison authorities are required to take all reasonable steps and reasonable care not to expose prisoners to a risk of damage or injury, but not to guarantee that prisoners do not suffer injury during imprisonment: *Muldoon v Ireland* [1988] ILRM 367. The Safety, Health and Welfare at Work Act 1989 applies to prisons and places of detention unless its application is incompatible with safe custody, good order and security (SHWWA 1989, s 57).

Failure of the authorities to comply with the Prison Rules does not of itself entitle a prisoner to be released: *Brennan v Governor of Portlaoise Prison* [1999] 1 ILRM 190, HC. Failure to deliver correspondence to a prisoner, which is not found to be objectionable pursuant to the Rules, r 63, can constitute an unjustified breach of a prisoner's right to communicate: *Kearney v Minister for Justice* [1987] ILRM 52. See also *The State (Gallagher) v Governor of Portlaoise Prison* [1987] ILRM 45. See Prison (Disciplinary Code for Officers) Rules 1996, SI No 289 of 1996. See *Re Employment Equality Bill 1996* [1997] 2 IR 321, SC and ELR 132.

A Prisons Authority Interim Board has been established with responsibility for the general management of the prison service, pending the establishment of a statutory Prison Authority.

The Minister is empowered to direct the transfer of detainees (not under 17 years of age) from St. Patrick's Institution to prison to relieve overcrowding: Prison Act 1970, s 7 which section is continued in operation for a further 24 months from 28 June 2003 by SI No 260 of 2003. See also Public Service Superannuation (Miscellaneous Provisions) Act 2004, s 5. [Bibliography: McDermott.] See PEACE OFFICER.

prison, division of. Formerly, the division of a prison, or of prisoners, into several divisions of varying degrees of severity. Although not in practice for many years, the power of division was only abolished formally in 1997: see Criminal Justice Act 1997, s 11(4).

prison, visiting committee. A committee of independent persons appointed by the Minister, with duties to hear complaints from prisoners (in private, if so requested) and to report to the Minister on any abuses observed or found by them in such prisons: Prisons (Visiting Committees) Act 1925, s 3 as amended by Criminal Justice (Miscellaneous Provisions) Act 1997, s 19(5). See also Criminal Law Act 1997, s 16 and Sch 3.

The 1925 Act also applies to places in which persons are kept in military custody: Prisons Act 1972, s 2(8). See also Prisons Act 1970, s 4. See SIs No 138 of 1972, No 217 of 1972, No 224 of 1960, and Prison (Visiting Committees) Order 1925 (3 June1925).

prison breaking. The offence committed by a person who is in lawful custody who uses force to effect his escape (qv).

prison personnel, dismissal of. See GARDA, DISCIPLINE OF.

prisoner. Convicted prisoners have rights under the Constitution including a right of access to the courts: *Walsh v Governor of Limerick Prison* [1995] 2 ILRM 158, SC. However, where a person has been detained to serve a sentence after conviction on indictment, he is *prima facie* detained in accordance with law and it would require the most exceptional circumstances for the court to grant even a conditional order of *habeas corpus* (qv): *State (McDonagh) v Frawley* [1978] IR 131 and *Walsh* case.

An otherwise lawful imprisonment is not rendered unlawful by reason only of the conditions of detention; a prisoner who alleges that his conditions are intolerable may have many remedies to terminate the conditions: *RT v Central Mental Hospital* [1995] 2 ILRM 354, HC. The High Court has held that there is no authority for the Irish Prison Services's long-standing policy not to allow prisoners direct access to the media and that there is not any specific exclusion dealing with the media in the Prison Rules: *Holland v Governor of Portlaoise Prison* (11 June 2004, unreported) HC.

There is now provision for the transfer of a prisoner: (a) in the State to give evidence or assist in investigation outside the State, and (b) outside the State to do likewise in the State: Criminal Justice Act 1994, ss 53–54.

'Prisoners must be treated with courtesy and respect and afforded confidentiality but with due regard for security. However, doctors have a right to take appropriate precautions if they think there is a risk to themselves': Medical Council, *A Guide to Ethical Conduct and Behaviour* (6th edn, 2004) para 2.8. See VOTE, RIGHT TO.

prisoner, arrest of. A person detained in a prison may be arrested where such arrest is necessary for the proper investigation of an offence he is suspected of having committed: Criminal Justice Act 1999, s 42. The offences are confined to *arrestable offences* as defined in Criminal Law Act 1997, s 2 ie an offence which carries a punishment of five years or more. A prisoner committed to a prison cannot be removed from custody: Habeas Corpus Act 1782, s 8. There are exceptions eg: (a) a prisoner can be moved to another prison or to have a surgical operation outside the prison: Criminal Justice Act 1914, ss 17(3) and 17(6); and also (b) the 1999 Act arrest provision. See Criminal Justice Bill 2004, s 11.

prisoner, release of. The Good Friday Agreement (qv) provided that both the UK and Irish governments would put in place mechanisms for an accelerated programme for the release of 'political' prisoners, whose organisations had established and were maintaining an unequivocal ceasefire. This was given effect in the State by the Criminal Justice (Release of Prisoners) Act 1998 and in Northern Ireland by the Northern Ireland (Sentences) Act 1998, c 35.

The Minister in exercising his release powers is advised by a *Release of Prisoners Commission*. It has been held that it is for the Minister alone to decide what prisoners were 'qualifying prisoners' and whether he should request the Commission to advise him on exercising his powers of release: *Doherty v Governor of Portlaoise Prison* [2002] 2 IR 252, SC. When there was no obligation on the Minister to consider applications from prisoners, or to certify them as 'qualifying prisoners', or to seek the advice of the Commission, the Minister could not be said to have acted capriciously, arbitrarily or unjustly: *O'Neill & Quinn v Ireland* (27 March 2003, unreported) HC. On appeal, the Supreme Court held that the government was entitled to make a policy decision that persons jailed in connection with a robbery in 1996 in which Det Garda Jerry McCabe was killed, are not eligible for release under the Good Friday Agreement, and the decision which the government had made could not be characterised as capricious, arbitrary or irrational: *O'Neill & Quinn v DPP* (29 January 2004, unreported) HC. See also *O'Neill & Quinn v DPP* (1 April 2004, unreported) HC.

In a particular case, it was held that as an accused had not yet been convicted of an offence, he could not claim early release pursuant to the Good Friday Agreement 1998: *Quinlivan v Conroy (No 2)* [2000] 3 IR 154, HC and [2000] 2 ILRM 515, HC. The operation of the 1998 Act is not affected by the Criminal Justice Act 1960, s 2(9) as substituted by Criminal Justice (Temporary Release of Prisoners) Act 2003, s 1.

prisoner, transfer of. Provision is made for the transfer of prisoners between States in order that they may serve the remainder of their sentence in the country of their nationality: Council of Europe Convention on the Transfer of Sentenced Persons 1983, signed by the Irish Government on 20 August 1986 and enacted as the Transfer of Sentenced Persons Act 1995. The question of adapting the duration of sentence is now a matter for the Minister in his absolute discretion to raise in an application to the High Court: Transfer of Sentenced Persons (Amendment) Act 1997. This provision enables the Minister to negotiate transfers where countries insist on the serving of the original sentence. See *Hutchinson v Minister for Justice* [1993] ILRM 602, HC. See RSC Ord 128 inserted by SI No 347 of 1997. See SENTENCE.

prisoner of war; POW. A person who, in relation to the State and a war in which the State is a participant, is such a *prisoner of war* within the meaning of the Prisoners of War Convention 1949, art 4, para A: Prisoners of War and Enemy Aliens Act 1956, s 1(2) as amended by Geneva Conventions (Amendment) Act 1998, s 14.

Persons may also be treated as prisoners of war where the State is not a participant in a war. A prisoner of war may be interned. A captured *privileged combatant* is entitled to POW status. A *privileged combatant* is an individual who can lawfully use force in an armed conflict and cannot be held individually criminally responsible for the use of such force unless he breaches the laws of war (eg by deliberately killing pris-

oners). Originally, to qualify for privileged combatant status a person had to wear a distinctive sign or uniform and to carry their arms openly. Now, in certain circumstances, a combatant is not required to distinguish himself from the civilian population provided he carries his arms openly: Geneva Conventions (Amendment) Act 1998 incorporating Protocol 1 of the Geneva Convention (qv). A spy or a mercenary is not entitled to POW status. See 'Treatment of prisoners of war: age old problem for protagonists' by Dr Ray Murphy in *Bar Review* (March/April 2002). See INTERNMENT; MERCENARY; RED CROSS.

privacy. The right to privacy is not defined by statute or in the Constitution. 'Whilst the personal rights (of the 1937 Constitution, art 40(3)) are not described specifically, it is scarcely to be doubted in our society that the right to privacy is universally recognised and accepted with possibly the rarest of exceptions ... .' *McGee v Attorney-General* [1974] IR 284. The constitutional personal right to privacy and the right to a good name are not absolute and they must be considered in the light of art 34.1 which requires that court proceedings be held in public: *Re Ansbacher (Cayman) Ltd* [2002] 2 ILRM 491, HC.

Protection of privacy is provided by a wide range of torts eg trespass to land, goods and to the person; nuisance; and breach of confidence.

Telephone tapping of a conversation can amount to an infringement of the constitutional right to privacy: *Kennedy v Ireland* [1988] ILRM 472. An injunction may be obtained to stop the bugging of a telephone: *Mangan v McKeown & Kilsaran Concrete Products Ltd* [1991] HC. See also EC (Electronic Communications Networks and Services) (Data Protection and Privacy) Regulations 2003, SI No 535 of 2003 which revokes SI No 192 of 2002.

Certain statutes provide for the protection of privacy eg: (a) restricting the time and place of visits or telephone calls between a creditor and a consumer and also restricting written communications: Consumer Credit Act 1995, ss 45–46; (b) protecting the identity of applicants for refugee status: Refugee Act 1996, s 19 as amended by Immigration Act 2003, s 7(k); (c) protecting access to and accuracy of *personal information* (qv): Freedom of Information Act 1997, ss 6 and 17 as amended by Freedom of Information (Amendment)

Act 2003, ss 4 and 12 respectively. Under CCA 1995, a creditor must not visit or telephone a consumer without his consent between 9pm and 9am or at any time on a Sunday or public holiday (CCA 1995, s 46).

There is also a right to privacy while in police custody, but it is not breached by a medical practitioner giving evidence of his observation of the accused: *People (DPP) v Kenny* [1991] 9 ILT Dig 74, HC. In a particular case, the Supreme Court held that the facilities provided for a female driver to provide a urine sample in a cubicle in a corner of a room in which a male doctor and male garda were present, were not so deficient or did not represent such an excessive and unwarranted intrusion of her right to privacy, that she had been deprived of any real choice in opting for a urine sample, rather than a blood sample: *DPP (Traynor) v Lennon* [1999] 2 IR 402, SC.

The tort of intentional infliction of mental suffering can afford protection against improper techniques of investigation, intimidatory debt collection and harassment of tenants by landlords. See *Janvier v Sweeney* [1919] 2 KB 316. See LRC Report on *Privacy: Surveillance and the Interception of Communications* (LRC 57, 1998). See House of Lords judgment *Naomi Campbell v Daily Mirror*, discussed in 'A model decision' by solicitor Pamela Cassidy in *Law Society Gazette* (June 2004) 14.

See 'Recent developments in Privacy and Breach of Confidence' by Patrick Leonard BL in *Bar Review* (December 2001) 102; 'Family Law aspects of the European Convention on Human Rights Act 2003' by Dervla Browne BL in *Bar Review* (April 2004) 39; 'The ECHR Act 2003, a Cause Célébre for Privacy Rights in Ireland?' by Martin Canny BL and Anthony Lowry BL in *Bar Review* (April 2004) 73 and (June 2004) 114. See Law Reform Commission, *Consultation Paper on Public Inquiries including Tribunals of Inquiry* (LRC CP 22, 2003). [Bibliography: McGonagle (2).] See ANONYMITY; CONFIDENCE, BREACH OF; DATA PROTECTION; EUROPEAN CONVENTION ON HUMAN RIGHTS; HACKING; HARASSMENT; IN CAMERA; MEDICAL PRACTITIONER AND CONFIDENTIALITY; MORAL RIGHT; NATIONAL ARCHIVES; TRANSBORDER DATA FLOWS.

privacy, marital. See MARITAL PRIVACY.

privacy in telecommunications. Provision has been made in relation to the processing of personal data and the protection of privacy in the electronic communications sector: EC (Electronic Communications Networks and Services) (Data Protection and Privacy) Regulations 2003, SI No 535 of 2003, which implements Directive (EC) 2002/58. The regulations deal with security, confidentiality of communications, traffic data, itemised billing, location data, automatic call forwarding, directories of subscribers, unsolicited communications, national directory database, enforcement of and damages for contravention of the regulations. The provisions in the Directive (art 5.1) relating to confidentiality of communications are not transposed in the regulations as adequate provisions already exist by virtue of the Postal and Telecommunications Services Act 1983, s 98. The previous regulations, SI No 192 of 2002, are now revoked. See CALL FORWARDING; TELEPHONE TAPPING; UNSOLICITED CALL.

private Act. A statute concerning a particular person or town or not of general application eg The Limerick Harbour (Bridge) Act 1963, as compared with a public Act, which applies generally within the State. The cost of preparing and passing such an Act may be required to be discharged from private funds eg see The Altamont (Amendment of Deed of Trust) Act 1993. See BILL.

private bill. See BILL.

private brewer. See BREWER, PRIVATE.

private carrier. See CARRIER, PRIVATE.

private company. See COMPANY, PRIVATE; SHARE, VALUE OF.

private international law. [Conflict of laws.] That part of Irish law which deals with cases involving a *foreign element*. It deals with matters such as: (a) what system of law will be applied; (b) whether the Irish courts have jurisdiction over a case; and (c) the recognition and enforcement of judgments of foreign courts.

See Jurisdiction of Courts and Enforcement of Judgments Act 1998. The *Brussels I Regulation* on the recognition and enforcement of judgments in civil and commercial matters, replaces the 1998 Act as from 1 March 2002 for all EU states except Denmark: EC (Civil and Commercial Judgments) Regulations 2002, SI No 52 of 2002. This *Regulation* provides that the court is to apply its rules of *private international law* in determining certain matters eg the seat of a company in relation to dissolution, or whether a trust is domiciled in the member state whose courts are seised of the matter (Regulation, arts 22(2) and 60(3)). [Bibliography: Binchy (1).] See DIVORCE, FOREIGN, RECOGNITION OF; FOREIGN JUDGMENTS, ENFORCEMENT OF; INTERNATIONAL LAW; JURISDICTION; MAINTENANCE ORDER; SUMMONS, SERVICE OUT OF JURISDICTION.

private investigator. Means a person who for remuneration conducts investigations into matters on behalf of a client and includes a person who: (a) obtains or furnishes information in relation to the personal character, actions or occupation of a person or to the character or kind of business in which a person is engaged, or (b) searches for missing persons: Private Security Services Act 2004, s 2(1). See PRIVATE SECURITY AUTHORITY.

private law. The area of domestic law dealing primarily with the relations between individuals within the State, with which the State is not immediately and directly concerned, eg the law of contract and the law of torts. See PUBLIC LAW.

private member's bill. A draft legislative proposal which a member of Dáil or Seanad Éireann is entitled to initiate, other than a money bill. Private members' bills are usually rejected by government, which prefers to bring in its own legislative proposals. In recent times however, three such bills have been accepted by the government of the day, resulting in the Judicial Separation and Family Law Reform Act 1989, the Adoption Act 1991, and the Landlord and Tenant (Amendment) Act 1994, all initiated by Mr Alan Shatter TD, Solicitor. For copyright of a private member's bill, see Copyright and Related Rights Act 2000, s 192. See BILL, MONEY.

private nuisance. See NUISANCE, PRIVATE.

private papers. Each of the Houses of the Oireachtas has power to protect the 'private papers' of its members: 1937 Constitution, art 15(10). The High Court has held that documents sought by the Morris Tribunal from a Dáil deputy, regarding alleged impropriety by gardaí, were 'private papers' for the purposes of that article: *Howlin v Morris Tribunal* [2004] 2 ILRM 53. Mr Justice Kearns held that the constitutional provision was an enabling power 'whereby either House may render the private papers

of members immune from discovery and production elsewhere by declaring them to be so'.

private property. A person who enters the private property of another, without lawful authority or excuse, may commit the offence or tort of trespass (qv). A garda is entitled in the execution of his duty to go onto private property to effect an arrest, provided that he does not breach any constitutional or legal right of another: *DPP v Forbes* [1993] ILRM 817, SC. See also ENTER AND SEARCH; INVIOLABILITY OF DWELLING.

private property, right to. The State acknowledges that man, in virtue of his rational being, has the natural right, antecedent to positive law, to the private ownership of external goods; the State accordingly guarantees to pass no law attempting to abolish the right of private ownership or the general right to transfer, bequeath and inherit property: 1937 Constitution, art 43(1).

However, the Constitution recognises that the exercise of the rights to private property ought, in civil society, be regulated by the principles of social justice, and consequently provides that the State may delimit by law the exercise of these rights with a view to reconciling their exercise with the exigencies of the common good (art 43(2)).

If the means used by the State are disproportionate to the end sought, the invasion will constitute an unjust attack within the meaning of art 43(2): *Iarnród Éireann/Irish Rail v Ireland* [1995] 2 ILRM 161, HC. See also *Irish Rail v Ireland* [1996] 3 IR 321, SC and 2 ILRM 500. The Supreme Court held that the Employment Equality Bill 1996 was unconstitutional, as it imposed burdens on employers which were so onerous as to amount to a failure to protect adequately the rights of employers to earn their livelihood and also amounted to an unjust attack on their property rights: *In the matter of art 26 of the Constitution and the Employment Equality Bill 1996* [1997] 2 IR 321, SC and ELR 132.

The right to property is delimited by many statutes eg compulsory purchase of land; planning permission; succession law. Many State agencies have considerable powers to enter, use and acquire land to fulfil their statutory function. Where property is taken by the State, compensation must generally be paid. In some particular cases, social justice may not require the payment of any compensation upon a compulsory acquisition (qv) that can be justified by the State as being required by the exigencies of the common good: *Dreker v Irish Land Commission* [1984] ILRM 94.

The Supreme Court held that an unjust attack on an individual's right to private property was not envisaged by the proposal on affordable housing: *In the matter of art 26 and the Planning and Development Bill 1999* [2000] 2 IR 321, SC and [2001] 2 ILRM 81, SC. See HOUSING STRATEGY, CONSTITUTIONALITY OF. The Constitutional protection on private property is not limited to human persons; it also applies to artificial legal entities (*Iarnród Éireann* case).

The *All-Party Oireachtas Committee on the Constitution* commenced in 2003 its consideration of the articles in the Constitution dealing with private property, to ascertain the extent to which they are serving the good of individuals and the community. See also *Blake v Attorney-General* [1981] ILMR 34; *PMPS Ltd v Attorney-General* [1983] SC; *Lawlor v Minister for Agriculture* [1988] ILRM 400; *Gorman v Minister for the Environment* [2001] 2 IR 414, HC. See also *Electricity Supply Board v Gormley* [1985] SC; Electricity Supply Amendment Act 1985. See Minerals Development Act 1979. See COMPULSORY PURCHASE ORDER; DERELICT SITE; EUROPEAN CONVENTION ON HUMAN RIGHTS; FAMILY HOME AND PROPERTY RIGHTS; FORFEITURE; LICENCE; MOTORWAY; NATIONAL MONUMENT; UNFIT HOUSE; UNLAWFUL ORGANISATION.

private prosecution. Colloquial term referring to the prosecution by a member of the public as a *common informer* of another person in respect of an alleged criminal offence by that other. The right of private prosecution, both in respect of a summary offence and of an indictable offence up to the stage of an order sending the defendant forward for trial, is an important common law right which has survived the enactment of the Constitution: *Cumann Lúthchleas Gael Teo v Judge Windle* [1994] 1 IR 525, SC. See *O'Donnell v DPP* [1988] HC.

Any party with a *bona fide* concern and interest in the protection of a constitutional right (in this case the right to life of the unborn) has sufficient standing to invoke the jurisdiction of the courts to take such measures as would defend and vindicate that right: *SPUC v Coogan & Ors* [1989] IR 734. See COMMON INFORMER.

private residence. A gain accruing to an individual on the disposal of his *principal private residence* is exempt from capital gains tax, provided the individual occupied or is deemed to have occupied the residence throughout his period of ownership, with the exception of the last twelve months of ownership: Taxes Consolidation Act 1997, s 604. Up to one acre of adjoining grounds may be included as part of the residence.

private rented dwelling. See CONTROLLED DWELLING; RESIDENTIAL TENANCIES.

Private Residential Tenancies Board. An independent statutory body with functions which include the registration of tenancies, the resolution of disputes, the provision of policy advice, the development of good practice guidelines and the collection and provision of information and the carrying out of research in relation to the private rented sector: Residential Tenancies Act 2004, ss 149–181.

The Board is required to establish a *Disputes Resolution Committee* (RTA 2004 ss 157(2) and 159). The chief officer of the Board, the Director, is appointed by the Board (RTA 2004, s 160). The Board may appoint, from time to time, persons to two panels as 'mediators' and 'adjudicators' (RTA 2004, s 164). A person may be appointed as both a mediator and an adjudicator (RTA 2004, s 164(3)). The Board is required to make an annual report to the Minister not later than 30 June of each year, which report is laid before each House of the Oireachtas (RTA 2004, s 180). The Board must have regard to any guidelines issued from time to time by the Minister (RTA 2004, s 183). The Board is required to make procedural rules in relation to dispute resolution, with the consent of the Minister (RTA 2004, s 109). A member of the Board is empowered to enter and inspect any dwelling to which a dispute relates by giving at least 24 hours notice of that intention (RTA 2004, s 111).

The Board may apply to the Circuit Court on behalf of a person, who has referred or is referring a dispute to it, for such interim or interlocutory relief in the matter as the Board considers appropriate (RTA 2004, ss 189–190). This provision is to enable the Board, when requested to do so, to obtain relief in cases such as anti-social behaviour or illegal evictions.

A non-statutory Board was established in October 2001 on an *ad hoc* basis, pending legislation, to provide on a voluntary basis, a *dispute resolution service* between landlords and tenants. The establishment of the Board was a key recommendation of the *Commission on the Private Rented Residential Sector* (2000). RTA 2004, Pts 1, 4, 5, 7, 8 and 9 (other than ss 71, 72, 151(1), 182, 189, 190, 193(a) and (d), and 195(4) and (5)) came into operation on 1 September 2004: SI No 550 of 2004. It is planned to bring Pts 2, 3 and 6, and the remaining sections into operation in November/December 2004. [Private Residential Tenancies Board, Canal House, Canal Road, Dublin 6. Tel: (01) 8882960; fax: (01) 8882819; email: *Tenancies_Board@environ.ie*; website: *www.environ.ie*.] See DETERMINATION ORDER; MODEL LEASE; POSSESSION, ORDER FOR; TENANCY TRIBUNAL.

private residential tenancies register. The register of each tenancy of a dwelling in the State required to be established and maintained by the *Private Residential Tenancies Board*: Residential Tenancies Act 2004, s 127. The landlord of a dwelling is required to apply to the Board to register the tenancy (RTA 2004, s 134). It is an offence for a person to furnish false or misleading information to the Board or to fail to comply with a notice from the Board requiring the person to register a tenancy (RTA 2004, ss 143–144). The Board is empowered to carry out inspections of dwellings to ascertain the correctness of particulars specified in registration applications where it has reason to believe any of the details is false or misleading (RTA 2004, s 145). The Board by notice may require a tenant to supply the landlord's name and address or other identifying particulars in the tenant's possession (RTA 2004, s 145(4)). Failure by a tenant to comply is an offence (RTA 2004, s 145(5)).

An application for registration must contain specified particulars eg name, address and *Personal Public Service Number* (PPSN) or company registration number of the landlord or agent, the name and PPSN of each tenant, details relating to the dwelling such as address, description, number of occupants, floor area, number of bed spaces, and number of bedrooms, the tenancy commencement date, the rent and other charges, the tenancy term (if for a fixed term) and an indication if it is a sub-tenancy (RTA 2004, s 136). In any dispute referred to the Board, the tenancy commencement date stated in the register is presumed correct unless the contrary is shown (RTA 2004, s 142). A landlord or a tenant of a dwelling is entitled to a copy of the entry in respect of that dwelling in the register (RTA 2004, s 132(1)).

The Board is required to establish a *published* register consisting of an extract of data from the register, but excluding information that could lead to the disclosure of the rent or the identity of the landlord or the tenant of a dwelling, and this published register must be made available for public inspection (RTA 2004, ss 128–130). There is provision for data exchange, in relation to private residential tenancies, between the Board, local authorities, the Revenue Commissioners, and the Minister for Social and Family Affairs (RTA 2004, ss 146–148). RTA 2004, Pt 7, ss 127–148 came into operation on 1 September 2004: SI No 550 of 2004. See DWELLING.

Private Security Authority. An independent body corporate with the function of controlling and supervising persons providing *security services* and maintaining and improving standards in the provision by them of those services: Private Security Services Act 2004, ss 6, 8 and Sch 1. The Authority may: (a) grant and renew licences, (b) issue identity cards to licensees, (c) where appropriate, suspend or revoke licences, (d) establish and maintain a register of licensees, (e) specify standards to be observed in the provision of security services by licensees or particular categories of licensees, (f) specify qualifications or any other requirements (including requirements as to training) for the grant of licences, (g) undertake or commission, or collaborate or assist in, research projects and activities relating to the provision of security services, including the compilation of statistical information and other records necessary for the proper planning, development and provision of those services, (h) investigate any security services being provided by any person, (i) establish and administer a system of investigation and adjudication of complaints against licensees, (j) monitor the provision of private security services generally (PSSA 2004, s 8(2)). There is a prohibition on the provision of an unlicensed security service (PSSA 2004, s 37), and on employing an unlicensed person (PSSA 2004, s 38).

The Authority may of its own motion investigate any security services provided by any person (PSSA 2004, s 13). It is empowered to appoint an inspector (PSSA 2004, s 14). It is required to establish and maintain a register of licensees to be known as the *Private Security Register* (PSSA 2004, s 33). There is provision for an appeal from the decisions of the Authority to the *Private Security Appeal Board* and appeal to the High Court on a question of law (PSSA 2004, ss 40–41 and Sch 2). There is also provision for security services to be provided by certain persons from EU member states ie those who hold a licence from a corresponding authority (PSSA 2004, ss 42–47 and Sch 3). See DOOR SUPERVISOR; IDENTITY BADGE; IDENTITY CARD; PRIVATE INVESTIGATOR; SECURITY CONSULTANT; SECURITY EQUIPMENT, INSTALLER OF; SECURITY GUARD; SECURITY SERVICE.

private treaty. A sale of land by agreement between vendor and purchaser, as distinct from a sale by auction (qv). See SALE OF LAND.

private trust. See TRUST.

privatisation. The sales of shares in a company owned by the State to the private sector. The partial privatisation of the Irish sugar industry was provided for by the Sugar Act 1991 and of Irish Life Assurance plc by the Insurance Act 1990 (since repealed). The B & I Line was prepared for sale to the Irish Continental Group plc by the B & I Line Act 1991. See COMPANY, STATUTORY.

privatorum conventio juri publico non derogat. [An agreement between private persons does not derogate from the public right.] See ILLEGAL CONTRACTS.

privatum commodum publico cedit. [Private good yields to public good.] See PUBLIC POLICY, EVIDENCE EXCLUDED BY.

privatum in commodum publico bono pensatur. [Private loss is compensated by public good.] See PRIVATE PROPERTY, RIGHT TO.

privilege. A special right or immunity. In defamation (qv), privilege is the immunity from liability conferred by law for statements made in certain circumstances. The privilege is either *absolute* or *qualified*.

Absolute privilege, which is a complete defence to a defamation action, applies even where the words complained of are published with knowledge of their falsehood and with the intention of injuring another. It applies to: (a) judicial proceedings: *Macauley Co Ltd v Wyse Power* [1943] 77 ILTR 61; (b) parliamentary proceedings, which includes all official reports and publications of the Oireachtas and utterances made in either House wherever published: 1937 Constitution, art 15(12); (c) discussions at meetings of the government: *A-G v The Sole Member of the Beef Tribunal* [1993] ILRM 81, SC; (d) evidence before a committee of the Dáil where specifically provided for eg Select Committee (Privilege and Immunity) Act 1994; (e) oral and/or documentary evidence given to a committee of the Oireachtas: Committees of the Houses of the Oireachtas (Compellability, Privileges and Immunity of Witnesses) Act 1997, s 11; RSC Ord 131 inserted by SI No 381 of 1998; (f) reports made on the conduct and state of a pension scheme: Pensions Act 1990, s 85 inserted by Pensions (Amendment) Act 1996, s 38 and amended by Pensions (Amendment) Act 2002, s 49; (g) reports of decisions of the Director of the Equality Tribunal and determinations of the Labour Court: Employment Equality Act 1998, s 89(5); (h) utterances made in good faith by an inspector: Unclaimed Life Assurance Policies Act 2003, s 23; (i) the annual report of the Data Protection Commissioner: Data Protection Act 1988, s 14 amended by Data Protection (Amendment) Act 2003, s 15; (j) reports of the Commission on Electronic Voting: Electoral (Amendment) Act 2004, s 27; (k) reports, documents or communications in connection with dispute resolution on tenancies: Residential Tenancies Act 2004, s 114(1).

In a particular case, the Supreme Court held that privilege had been waived in a document between the DPP and the gardaí, because it had been referred to and summarised, and consequently had been 'deployed' in the proceedings: *Hannigan v DPP* [2001] 1 IR 378, SC.

Qualified privilege arises where a communication is made upon an *occasion of qualified privilege* and is fairly warranted by it; it is a good defence in the absence of malice. An *occasion of qualified privilege* arises where a person who makes a communication has a duty (legal, social or moral) or an interest to make it to the person to whom it is made, and the person to whom it is made has a corresponding duty to receive it. See *Farrelly v Arcadia Group plc* [2002] ELR 309, CC.

Privilege attaches to publication in a newspaper of a document read out in open court, but not to the publication of pleadings or other papers filed in civil proceedings, but not brought up in open court: *Stringer v Irish Times Ltd* [1995] 2 IR 108, HC.

There is no absolute privilege attaching to communications passing between sovereign states: *Walker v Ireland* [1997] 1 ILRM 363, HC and 2 IR 132, HC. See *Kirkwood Hackett v Tierney* [1952] IR 185; *Hynes-O'Sullivan v O'Driscoll* [1989] ILRM 619, SC; *Irish Press plc v Ingersoll Irish Publications Ltd (No 2)* [1994] 1 IR 208, SC. See Protection of Persons Reporting Child Abuse Act 1998, s 6; Stock Exchange Act 1995, s 68(2); Irish Takeover Panel Act 1997, s 20; Ombudsman for Children Act 2002, s 13(8); Health Insurance (Amendment) Act 2003, s 4; Containment of Nuclear Weapons Act 2003, s 11; Companies (Auditing and Accounting) Act 2003, s 58; Education for Persons with Special Educational Needs Act 2004, s 50; Commissions of Investigation Act 2004, ss 20–22 and 42. [Bibliography: Buckley, Melody; Healy.] See ADOPTION BOARD; DISCOVERY; FAIR AND ACCURATE REPORT; INFORMER'S PRIVILEGE; MALICE; UTTERANCE.

privilege, communications to another. The privilege to refrain from giving evidence which attaches to a communication made by one person to another. Four conditions must be present: (a) the communication must originate in a confidence that it would not be disclosed, (b) the element of confidentiality must be essential to the full and satisfactory maintenance of the relation between the two persons, (c) the relation must be one which, in the opinion of the community, must be sedulously fostered, and (d) the injury by the disclosure must be greater than the benefit gained: *Cook v Carroll* [1945] IR 515.

Privilege attaches to a communication by a parishioner to his parish priest in confidence in private consultation: *Cook v Carroll*; *Forristal v Forristal* [1966] 100 ILTR 182. Privilege also applies to communications from a constituent to a member of the Oireachtas (see McHugh in 11 ILT & SJ (1993) 119). It would appear that for the privilege to be waived, it must be waived clearly and unequivocally by both: *E R v J R* [1981] ILRM 125. The fact that documents are furnished in confidence to the party against whom an order of discovery is sought, does not of itself make them privileged: *Skeffington v Rooney* [1997] 2 ILRM 56, SC. See UTTERANCE.

privilege, confessional. It has been held that there is probably an unwaivable privilege attaching in the Irish common law to the seal of the confessional, but that privilege is not capable of development so as to attach to communications between a member and a counsellor of the Church of Scientology: *Johnston v Church of Scientology Mission of Dublin Ltd* [1999] ITLR (28 June) HC and [2001] 1 IR 682, HC & SC. See also *Cook v Carroll* [1945] IR 515; *E R v J R* [1981] ILRM 125.

privilege, evidential. The right or immunity conferred on a person or body which justify their refusal to produce a document or to answer a question. The following matters are generally protected from disclosure on the grounds of privilege: (a) criminating questions – a witness need not answer any question which exposes the witness to any criminal charge, penalty or forfeiture; (b) professional communications between counsel or solicitor and client; (c) matrimonial communications; (d) private consultation with parish priest; (e) title deeds of a stranger to an action.

The privilege may be waived by the person entitled to it, whereas even a willing witness will not be allowed to give evidence of a matter required to be excluded by reason of public policy. See PUBLIC POLICY, EVIDENCE EXCLUDED BY; GOVERNMENT; INCEST; INCRIMINATE; JOURNALIST, COMMUNICATIONS WITH; WITNESS, COMPETENCE OF.

privilege, legal professional. The right whereby evidence of communications between counsel or solicitor and a client may not be given without the client's consent. Legal professional privilege is a fundamental feature of the administration of justice and the rule of law; communications which qualify as privileged communications are those which contain legal advice: *A Guide to Professional Conduct of Solicitors in Ireland* (2002) ch 4.1.

The privilege applies to communications made within the ordinary scope of professional employment for contemplated or existing litigation; it extends to confidential communications only and not to, say a letter written on the client's instructions: *Bord na gCon v Murphy* [1970] IR 301. Before the privilege can be properly claimed for a particular document, the dominant purpose of its existence must be preparation for apprehended litigation: *Silver Hill Duckling v Minister for Agriculture Attorney-General* [1987] ILRM 516. The test to be applied is whether the dominant purpose for which the documents in question came into being, was in apprehension or anticipation of litigation: *Gallagher v Stanley* [1998] 2 IR 267, SC.

Communications between a lawyer and his client for the purpose of seeking or obtaining legal assistance other than legal advice are not privileged from disclosure, as they could not be said to contain any real relationship with the area of potential litigation: *Smurfit Paribas Bank Ltd v AAB Export Finance Ltd* [1990] ILRM 588, SC. However, it was held to be wrong to admit in evidence a letter handed to a person's solicitor for advice where that person had not consented to its disclosure: *Sheehan v McMahon* [1993] (29 November) SC.

Also notes made by a person to himself which were clearly made for the purpose of taking legal advice are privileged: *Horgan v Murray* [1999] 1 ILRM 257, HC. However, legal professional privilege does not extend to transcripts or solicitor's notes of evidence: *MFM v PW* [2001] 3 IR 462, HC.

Once a claim of privilege is justified, the onus moves to the challenger thereof and evidence must be adduced to challenge the claim: *The Irish Haemophilia Society Ltd v Judge Lindsay* [2001] ITLR (11 June) HC. To defeat a claim of legal professional privilege by asserting an abuse of the processes of the court, it is necessary to support the allegations to the extent that they are viable and plausible: *Corbett v DPP* [1999] 2 IR 179, HC.

Exemption from the doctrine of privilege is restricted to cases where there is an allegation against the person claiming privilege which contains a clear element of moral turpitude, as is contained in allegations of fraud, malicious prosecution, criminal conduct or conduct constituting a direct interference with the administration of justice eg abuse of the processes of the court: *Bula Ltd (in receivership) v Crowley* [1994] ILRM 495, SC and 2 IR 54; *Murphy v Kirwan* [1994] 1 ILRM 293, SC and [1993] 3 IR 501, SC. See also *Crawford v Treacy* [1999] 2 IR 171, HC.

The Flood Tribunal ordered the solicitor acting for Jackson Way Properties to produce documents relating to his dealings with the company and to identify the persons who had given him instructions on its behalf. Mr Justice Flood stated that a solicitor claiming privilege on behalf of his client must disclose the client's name; without this, how could a court or tribunal be sure that a client, in respect of which the privilege is claimed, actually existed? The solicitor sought and obtained leave to seek a judicial review of that decision: *Miley v Flood Tribunal* (2000) Irish Times, 22 June, HC. The High Court subsequently decided that a solicitor is not entitled to maintain privilege in respect of the *identity* of his client: *Miley v Mr Justice Flood, Sole Member of the Tribunal of Inquiry* [2001] 1 ILRM 489, HC and 2 IR 50. See 'Legal professional privilege and the identity of a client' by Declan McGrath BL in *Bar Review* (March 2001) 268.

See also *Tromso Sparebank v Beirne & Ors* [1989] 7 ILT Dig 83; *Duncan v Governor of Portlaoise Prison* [1997] 1 IR 558, HC; *Logue v Redmond* [1999] 2 ILRM 498, HC. See Companies Act 1990, s 23(1); Building Societies Act 1989, ss 31(5), 41(7), 46(5); Patents Act 1992, s 94; Stock Exchange Act 1995, s 68(1); Irish Takeover Panel Act 1997, s 18; Industrial Designs Act 2001, s 87; Unclaimed Life Assurance Policies Act 2003, s 24(2); Companies (Auditing and Accounting) Act 2003, s 28(3). [Bibliography: Clark (2).] See PERSONAL DATA; PUBLIC INTEREST PRIVILEGE; SOLICITOR AND CONFIDENTIALITY; WITHOUT PREJUDICE.

privilege, matrimonial communications. The right whereby evidence of communications between husband and wife during marriage may not be given. However, the privilege does not prevent evidence of such communications being given by other admissible evidence. See Criminal Justice (Evidence) Act 1924, ss 1 and 4 as amended by Criminal Evidence Act 1992. See however, INCEST. See also, however, EVIDENCE TENDING TO BASTARDISE CHILDREN; WITNESS, COMPETENCE OF.

privileged wills. Informal documents which did not require signatures or oral declarations before witnesses, previously provided for by statute, but not re-enacted by the Succession Act 1965. See NUNCUPATIVE WILL.

privilegium non valet contra rempublicam. [A privilege avails not against the state.] See PUBLIC POLICY, EVIDENCE EXCLUDED BY.

privity of contract. The relationship which exists between parties to a contract. Generally privity of contract is necessary to enable one person to sue another in contract. No one can sue on, or be sued on, a contract to which he is not a party eg a contract cannot impose liability on a stranger.

There are exceptions eg: (a) restrictive covenants running with land will bind a subsequent purchaser with notice of the covenant: *Tulk v Moxhay* [1848] 13 Jur 89; (b) transactions within the scope of the authority created by agency will bind the principal: *Pattison v Institute for Industrial Research Standards* [1979] HC; (c) inducement by a third party of a party to a contract to breach the contract will render the third party liable for damages in tort: *Lumley v Gye* [1853] 1 WR 432; (d) where a stranger acquires rights by way of a trust: *Re Schebsman* [1944] Ch; (e) statutory exceptions eg the Married Womens' Status Act 1957, ss 7–8 confer a right of action to the spouse or child of a contracting party. See also Sale of Goods and Supply of Services Act 1980, s 13(2) and (7); 14. See *Donohue v Bus Éireann* [1999] ELR 306, HC. See Quill in 9 ILT & SJ (1991) 211. See FINANCE HOUSE; NEXT FRIEND.

privy. A party is the *privy* of another by blood, title or interest where he stands in his shoes and claims through or under him: *Belton v Carlow Co Council* [1997] 2 ILRM 405, SC. See also *McCauley v McDermot* [1997] 2 ILRM 486, SC.

prize bond. A scheme whereby redeemable bonds purchased for £5 (€6.35) participate in periodic draws for prizes: Finance (Miscellaneous Provisions) Act 1956. See *Heaney v Minister for Finance* [1986] ILRM 164.

pro. [For.]

pro bono publico. [For the public good.] The entitlement of a barrister to act for a client *pro bono* is not inhibited by the rule on fees: *Code of Conduct for the Bar of Ireland* (Decembe 2003) r 11.6. See FREE LEGAL ADVICE CENTRES.

pro confesso. [As if conceded.]

pro forma. [As a matter of form.]

pro hac vice. [For this occasion.] Eg an appointment for a particular occasion.

pro indiviso. [As undivided.]

pro interesse suo. [As to his interest.]

pro-mutuum. A quasi-contract which arises when a person, acting under a mistake of fact, delivers to another a chattel which cannot be restored in specie; the recipient is required to restore its equivalent under the quasi-contract. See MUTUUM.

pro rata. [In proportion.]

pro tanto. [For so much; to that extent.]

probability. See PRESUMPTION OF REGULARITY.

probability, balance of. See BALANCE OF PROBABILITY.

probably result. In the expression 'probably result', the word 'probable' means something that is likely to happen: *APH Manufacturing BV v DHL* [2001] 1 ILRM 224, HC. On appeal, the Supreme Court held that there was no evidence to justify a finding of subjective knowledge that damage was probable: *APH Manufacturing BV v DHL* [2001] 4 IR 531, SC.

probate. A grant of representation issued from the Probate Office, or from a District Probate Registry, both of which are part of the High Court, to the effect that the will of a testator has been proved and registered in court and that administration of his effects has been granted to the executor proving the will, *he having been first sworn faithfully to administer the same* (RSC App Q, Form 6). The executor undertakes to exhibit a true inventory of the estate and to render a true account thereof (RSC App Q, Form 3). Where a grant of probate has been made and the proving executor has died and all other executors have either died or renounced, *administration with the will annexed de bonis non* will be given to the next person entitled.

An Inland Revenue Affidavit is required when applying for a grant of probate or administration with details of the assets of the deceased and all gifts made by him within two years of his death and details of all inheritances arising from his death: Finance Act 1894, s 22(1)(n); Capital Acquisitions Tax Consolidation Act 2003, ss 48 and 108. See also Status of Children Act 1987, s 30. [Bibliography: Keating; Mongey.] See ADMINISTRATION OF ESTATES; DOUBLE PROBATE; INSOLVENT ESTATE; LETTERS OF ADMINISTRATION; OFFENSIVE WORDS; SUPPLEMENTAL PROBATE; UNADMINISTERED PROBATE.

probate, revocation of. The revoking, cancelling or recalling of a grant of probate which the High Court and Circuit Court are empowered to do. See Succession Act 1965, ss 26 and 35. In the High Court, see RSC Ord 125, r 1. In proceedings for the revocation of probate or letters of administration, the person applying for such revocation is the plaintiff and the person to whom such grant was made is the defendant: Circuit Court Rules 2001 Ord 50, r 4.

probate action. Any proceedings in the High Court commenced by originating summons and seeking the grant or recall of probate, or letters of administration or similar relief: RSC Ord 125, r 1.

The Circuit Court has jurisdiction in certain specified probate matters but requires the consent of the parties in writing where the estate of the deceased includes personal estate in excess of £30,000 (€38,092) value (proposed to be increased to €100,000) or real estate with rateable valuation in excess of £200 (€253.95).

Proceedings in the Circuit Court for the purpose of obtaining a grant, or revocation of a grant, of probate or letters of administration must be initiated by the issue of a civil bill headed with the words 'Testamentary Civil Bill'. In the case of proceedings pursuant to the Succession Act 1965, the civil bill must be headed 'Succession Law Civil Bill'. See Circuit Court Rules 2001 Ord 50. See Succession Act 1965, s 6 as amended by Civil Liability and Courts Act 2004, s 47; Courts Act 1981, s 4 and Courts Act 1991, s 2. [Bibliography: Keating.]

probate office. The central probate registry located at the Four Courts in Dublin, which is attached to the High Court and which has jurisdiction for the whole State. See Court (Supplemental Provisions) Act 1961, s 55(1). See RSC Ord 79 as amended by SI No 20 of 1989. See DISTRICT PROBATE REGISTRY; SIDE BAR ORDERS.

probate tax. A tax of 2% of the taxable value of estates of persons dying on or after 18 June 1993: Finance Act 1993, ss 109–119. It was abolished in 2001 in respect of deaths occurring on or after 6 December 2000: Finance Act 2001, s 225.

There was an index-linked *threshold* before tax was payable and there was an exemption from a second charge of tax where spouses died in quick succession. No probate tax was payable in respect of any provision which a court may make in favour of a former spouse from the estate of the deceased party to a dissolved marriage: Family Law (Divorce) Act 1996, s 36. See

also Finance Act 1997, s 143 and Finance Act 2000, s 150; Finance Act 2000, s 147.

The personal representative was primarily accountable for payment of the tax, which in effect was borne proportionately by the beneficiaries, who could claim the tax as an expense in calculating any inheritance tax. [Bibliography: Boland; Connolly M.]

probation and welfare officer. An officer who carries out social inquiry and pre-sentence assessments for the courts; supervises in the community offenders who are referred by the courts; supervises offenders under community service orders or who have been conditionally released from custody; and provides a counselling service to offenders and their families. For provisions dealing with probation officer's reports involving offences committed by children, see Children Act 2001, ss 99–107. See COMMUNITY SERVICE ORDER; PROBATION OF OFFENDERS.

probation in employment. The period during which an employee is being assessed to determine his suitability for employment. The Unfair Dismissals Act 1977 does not apply to dismissal of an employee on probation where the duration of probation is one year or less (UDA 1977, s 3(1)). An office holder on probation is in an insecure position: *Hynes v Garvey* [1978] IR 174.

However, it has been held that the power of termination of employment during, or at the end of, a probationary period is not a power which can be exercised arbitrarily; a person's rights to fair procedures are not affected by being in a probationary position: *The State (Daly) v Minister for Agriculture* [1988] ILRM 173.

In a particular case it was held that termination of employment required a decision of the hospital board; they were not expected to emulate the conduct of a judge who must distance himself from any prior knowledge of the matters in issue: *O'Neill v Beaumont Hospital Board* [1990] ILRM 419, SC. As regards a civil servant, it has been held that the Minister must, during the employee's probationary period, have been satisfied that the person had failed to fulfil his conditions of probation: *Whelan v Minister for Justice* [1991] 2 IR 241, HC. The period of probation stands suspended during absence of the employee on 'protective leave' (qv): Maternity Protection Act 1994, s 25 as amended by

Maternity Protection (Amendment) Act 2004 s.17 to clarify that this applies to both female and male employees. See CIVIL SERVANT; GARDA SÍOCHÁNA.

probation of offenders. An order of the District Court releasing an offender having: (a) dismissed an information or charge or having (b) discharged the offender conditionally on his entering into a recognizance (qv), with or without securities, to be of good behaviour and to appear for conviction and sentence when called on at any time during such period, not exceeding three years, as may be specified in the order: Probation of Offenders Act 1907, s 1(1).

Such an order may be made where any person is charged before a court of summary jurisdiction (qv) with an offence punishable by that court, and the court considers that the charge is proved, but is of opinion that it is inexpedient to inflict any punishment: POA 1907, s 1(1) and Criminal Law Amendment Act 1935, s 16(2). This however does not prevent the court making a *compensation order* (qv) against the offender in favour of the injured party: Criminal Justice Act 1993, ss 6(12)(b) and 8(6). The order placing a person on probation may include requirements so as to lessen the likelihood of further involvement in crime eg avoiding certain people or places, undergoing a course of treatment (eg for alcohol or drug dependence), residing in a probation hostel, or attending a workshop or training centre.

An order of probation dismissing a charge should specify the particular ground relied upon: *Gilroy v Brennan* [1926] IR 482. Also as regards offences by an employer involving social welfare contributions, a probation order must not be made until the court is satisfied that all arrears in respect of contributions by the offending employer of an employed contributor, have been paid by the employer: Social Welfare (Consolidation) Act 1981, s 118. Similar provisions now apply to any person charged with an offence in relation to any social welfare benefit, pension, assistance or allowance: Social Welfare Act 1988, s 19. These provisions are consolidated in Social Welfare (Consolidation) Act 1993, s 217.

The Probation of Offenders Act is generally not applicable to revenue, customs or excise duty offences: see Finance Act 1984, s 78 and Taxes Consolidation Act 1997,

s 1078(8). There is provision for the finger-printing of persons dealt with under the Probation of Offenders Act in respect of indictable offences: Criminal Justice Act 1984, s 28 as proposed to be amended by Criminal Justice Bill 2004, s 12.

A district judge may issue a warrant for the arrest of a person who has failed to observe a condition of a recognisance under the 1907 Act: DCR 1997 Ord 28.

It was proposed that the Probation of Offenders Act 1907 would not apply to summary offences under the Company Law Enforcement Bill 2000, s 63. However, this provision was deleted during the passage of the Bill through the Oireachtas and was not enacted in the subsequent Company Law Enforcement Act 2001. See APOLOGY; COMMUNITY SERVICE ORDER; COSTS AND CRIMINAL PROCEEDINGS; COURT POOR BOX.

probity. Integrity and honesty, uprightness. The High Court is empowered to issue a direction to an *investment business firm* to have an officer removed or an employee dismissed on the application of the supervisory authority which considers that the *probity* of the officer or employee is liable to render him unsuitable: Investment Intermediaries Act 1995, s 36. See also Courts and Court Officers Act 1995, s 16(7) as amended by Courts and Court Officers Act 2002, s 8.

procedure. The formal manner of conducting judicial proceedings. [Bibliography: Barron; Cahill E; O'Floinn; Lasok UK.] See PRACTICE; RULES OF COURT.

proceeding. The institutions of a legal action; any step in a legal action. A proceeding may be criminal or civil. Criminal proceedings can be distinguished usually by language associated with charge and punishment (*Downes v DPP* [1987] 139 at 142); where the sanction is punitive, and where failure to pay, even where the defendant has no means, involves imprisonment. See *Melling v O'Mathgamhna* [1962] IR 1.

The word 'proceedings' in the Freedom of Information Act 1997, s 46(1) is not used in the sense of an action, but rather it means any *step* in an action; accordingly in order to fall within the exception (which would permit disclosure of a record of proceedings in a court held in public) a record must relate to a *step in an action* which is held in public: *Minister for Justice v Information Commissioner* [2001] 3 IR 43,

HC and [2002] 2 ILRM 1, HC. See CIVIL PROCEEDINGS; STAY OF PROCEEDINGS; STEP IN PROCEEDINGS; STAY OF PROCEEDINGS; SUMMARY PROCEEDINGS.

proceeds of crime. Means any property obtained or received at any time by or as a result of or in connection with the commission of an offence; *property* includes money and all other property, real or personal, heritable or moveable, including choses in action and other intangible or incorporeal property: Proceeds of Crime Act 1996, s 1(1). The word 'crime' in 'proceeds of crime' is not preceded by a definite or indefinite article, which indicates a legislative intent that the 1996 Act would have application where the plaintiff is unable to show a relationship between property alleged to be the proceeds of crime and a particular crime or crimes: *McK F and F* [2003] FL 7318, HC.

The Supreme Court has held on 17 May 2004 that PCA 1996 does not apply to the proceeds of crime committed outside the State, overturning *McK v D* [2002] FL 7125, HC.

The High Court is empowered to make, on application of an officer of the Revenue Commissioners or a member of the Garda Síochána, orders for the preservation and, where appropriate, the disposal of property: (a) which constitutes, directly or indirectly, proceeds of crime, or (b) which was acquired with property that constitutes proceeds of crime, where the property value is not less than £10,000/€12,698. There is provision for an *interim order* which prevents the property being disposed of or diminished in value for 21 days (PCA 1996, s 2), an *interlocutory order* further preserving the property (PCA 1996, s 3), and when an interlocutory order has been in force for not less than seven years, a *disposal order* directing the transfer, in whole or in part, of the property to the Minister (PCA 1996, s 4).

Despite its description as such, an order under PCA 1996, s 3 is not truly interlocutory in character in the sense of being ancillary to substantive relief; it is a free-standing substantive remedy and imposes a complete embargo on any dealing with property: *F McK v AF and JF* [2002] 2 ILRM 303, SC and 1 IR 242. An order under PCA 1996, s 3 may be appealed to the Supreme Court: *M(FM) v C(M)* [2002] FL 7041, HC. An applicant may apply for an *interim order* and for the appointment of a receiver in the one application, where a case is made for the receiver to manage the property pending the outcome of the trial: *MFM v MC (Proceeds of Crime)* [2001] 2 IR 385, HC. A constitutional challenge to HC has failed, and the court held: (a) that it had the power to appoint a receiver over property not within the jurisdiction; and (b) that the definition 'proceeds of crime' includes property obtained or received before the passing of the Act: *Murphy v G M* [2001] 4 IR 113, SC.

Where the court is satisfied that there are reasonable grounds for the stated belief of the applicant that the property constitutes the proceeds of crime and of its value, such statement is admissible evidence (PCA 1996, s 8). The owner of property, which was the subject of an interim or interlocutory order, who can show to the satisfaction of the court that he is the owner of the property and that it does not constitute proceeds of crime, may be entitled to compensation (PCA 1996, s 16).

The court may make ancillary orders in relation to anyone affected by the preservation orders eg regarding reasonable living expenses (PCA 1996, s 6). It has been held that the wording of s 6(1) places a very heavy onus on a person bringing such an application; the applicant has to satisfy the court that it is *essential* to make the order sought: *MFM v MB & Ors* [1999] 1 ILRM 540, HC and 1 IR 122. The term 'necessary expenses' in PCA 1996, s 6 is sufficiently broad to include a payment of moneys on foot of a tax return: *obiter dictum* in *Criminal Assets Bureau v Kelly* [2002] 3 IR 421, SC.

The standard of proof required to determine any question arising under the 1996 Act is that applicable to civil proceedings ie on the balance of probability (PCA 1996, s 8(2)). A number of technical amendments to PCA 1996, ss 1, 2, 3, 6, 8 and 9 are proposed in draft legislation: Proceeds of Crime (Amendment) Bill 1999. See *Gilligan v Criminal Assets Bureau* [1998] 3 IR 185, HC; *McKenna v E H* [2002] 2 ILRM 117, HC; 1 IR 72. See 'Asset Forfeiture & the European Convention on Human Rights' by Claire Hamilton BL in *Bar Review* (May 2001) 414. [Bibliography: McCutcheon & Walsh.] See BANKRUPTCY, ADJUDICATION OF; CRIMINAL ASSETS BUREAU; IMMUNITY; LAND

REGISTRATION; RECEIVER OF CRIMINAL'S PROPERTY; REGISTRAR OF COMPANIES; SEIZURE.

process. Any operation or series of operations being an activity of more than a minimal duration: SI No 283 of 1972 and *Dunleary v Glen Abbey Ltd* [1992] ILRM 1, HC. See MANUAL HANDLING OF LOADS.

process, abuse of. See ABUSE OF PROCESS.

processing. 'Processing', of or in relation to information or data, means performing any operation or set of operations on the information or data, whether or not by automatic means: Data Protection Act 1988, s 1(1) as amended by substitution by Data Protection (Amendment) Act 2003, s 2(a)(v). 'Processing' of data includes blocking the data. Compliance with specified provisions of data protection legislation is not required in respect of the processing of personal data undertaken solely with a view to *publication* of any journalistic, literary or artistic material (DP(A)A 2003, s 21). Excluded provisions include e g the right of access and the right to object. 'Publication' means the act of making the material available to the public or any section of the public in any form or by an means. See BLOCKING; DATA PROTECTION.

proclamation. A formal public announcement (e g the dissolution of the Dáil by the Presidential Commission) usually notified in Iris Oifigiúil e g see Iris Oifigiúil, 10 November 1992.

procreate. See BEGET.

procuration. Agency. See PER PRO.

procure. It is an offence for a person to *procure* another person to do anything which constitutes discrimination (qv) or victimisation (qv); an attempt to so procure is also an offence: Employment Equality Act 1998, s 14. It is also an offence for a person to procure or attempt to procure another person to engage in *prohibited conduct* (i e discrimination, sexual harassment or harassment): Equal Status Act 2000, s 13. See also See Pensions Act 1990, s 74 as amended by substitution by Social Welfare (Miscellaneous Provisions) Act 2004, s 22(1). [Bibliography: Reid M.] See AID AND ABET.

procurement. The offence committed by a person who procures any girl or woman, who is not a common prostitute or of known immoral character, to have unlawful carnal knowledge with any other person or persons. There is no offence where it is

shown that the girl needed no procuring at all and acted of her own free will: *R v Christian* 23 Cox 540. To *procure* is to obtain, cause or bring about a connection: *R v Jones* [1896] 1 QB 4. See Criminal Law Amendment Act 1885, ss 2–3 as amended by the Criminal Law Amendment Act 1935, ss 7–8. See *Attorney-General (Supt Shaughnessy) v Ryan* [1960] IR 181. *Procurement* of rape (qv) is also an offence: Criminal Law (Rape) Act 1981. See AID AND ABET.

procuring breach of contract. See INDUCING BREACH OF CONTRACT.

product authorisation. Generally understood to mean the licensing by the Irish Medicines Board (qv) of medicinal products (qv).

product liability. (1) The liability which arises by way of contract or tort for a defective product. A person who suffers loss as a result of a defective product may be able to recover damages for breach of an express or implied term of contract. In tort, the plaintiff may succeed in an action based on negligence where he is able to establish the existence of a duty of care and the breach thereof by the manufacturer, assembler, subcontractor, packager, bottler, distributor, repairer or retailer. See *Donoghue v Stevenson* [1932] AC 562; *Kirby v Burke and Holloway* [1944] IR 207; *Power v Bedford Motor Co Ltd* [1959] IR 391; *Bolands Ltd v Trouw Ireland Ltd* [1978] HC; *Cole v Webb Caravans Ltd* [1983] ILRM 595. [Bibliography: Forde (5); McMahon & Binchy.] See CONDITION; QUALITY OF GOODS; SAMPLE, SALE BY.

(2) Under the EC Products Liability Directive (85/374) a *producer* of a *product* is liable to pay compensation for death or personal injuries caused by a *defect* in his product (art 1): Liability for Defective Products Act 1991, s 2. Compensation may also be claimed in respect of loss, damage, or destruction of property used for private use or consumption. A product is said to be defective when it does not provide the safety a person is entitled to expect having regard to the presentation, expected uses and time it was put into circulation (LDPA 1991, s 5).

A *product* was defined as all movables, including electricity, with the exception of *primary agricultural products* which have not undergone initial processing (LDPA 1991, s 1(1)). A *product* is now defined to mean all moveable products, including primary agricultural products which have not undergone initial processing, and includes: (a) moveables even though incorporated into another product or into an immovable, whether by virtue of being a component part or raw material or otherwise, and (b) electricity where damage is caused as a result of a failure in the process of generation of electricity: European Communities (Liability for Defective Products) Regulations 2000, SI No 401 of 2000. These regulations give effect to Council Directive (EC) 1999/34 which amended Council Directive (EEC) 85/374.

A *producer* is defined as: (a) the manufacturer or producer of a finished product; or (b) the manufacturer or producer of any raw material or of a component part; or (c) the person who carried out processing of the products of soil, stockfarming, fisheries and game; or (d) any person who by putting his name, trade mark or other distinguishing feature on the product thereby identifies himself as its producer; or (e) the importer of goods into the EC; or (f) any person who supplied the product where the producer cannot be identified (LDPA 1991, s 2). A producer has six defences: (i) he did not put the product into circulation; or (ii) it is probable that at the time of putting the product into circulation it did not have the defect; or (iii) the product was not manufactured by him for sale or distribution for an economic purpose nor in the course of business; or (iv) the defect was due to compliance with EC law; or (v) that given the state of technical knowledge, it was not possible at the time of distribution to discover the defect; or (vi) if the product is a manufactured component the defect is the result of a design defect in the product into which the component has been fitted (LDPA 1991, s 6).

Liability is limited to the period of three years following the date the plaintiff became aware, actual or constructive, of the damage, defect or identity of the producer (LDPA 1991, s 7). A right of action expires after ten years from when the product was put into circulation, except where proceedings have already commenced (LDPA 1991, s 7(2)). No damages for property will be awarded where the damage does not exceed €444 (£350); for damage greater than €444, only the amount in excess of €444 will be awarded (LDPA 1991, s 3). See Bird in 10 ILT & SJ (1992) 188. [Bibliography: Bird; Burke & Corbett;

O'Reilly P; Schuster; Kelly & Attree UK.] See QUALITY OF GOODS.

product prices. Where traders indicate that a product is or may be for sale to consumers, they are generally required to indicate the selling price and the unit price of that product; the provisions apply to most products offered for sale by traders to consumers: European Communities (Requirement to Indicate Product Prices) Regulations 2002, SI No 639 of 2002. The indication of the selling price and of the unit price must be clearly visible. The Director of Consumer Affairs is responsible for enforcing the regulations. The regulations give effect to Directive (EC) 98/6.

production of documents. See DISCOVERY.

professional disciplinary bodies, appeals. For rules governing appeals against the decisions of disciplinary bodies dealing with nurses, dentists, medical practitioners, or veterinary surgeons, see RSC Ord 95 as amended by SI No 20 of 1989. In relation to solicitors, see RSC Ord 53 as amended by SI No 14 of 1998. See *Phillips v Medical Council* [1992] ILRM 469, HC; *Casey v Medical Council* [1999] 2 ILRM 481, HC and 2 IR 534. See DISCIPLINARY PROCEEDINGS; FITNESS TO TEACH; SOLICITOR'S DISCIPLINARY TRIBUNAL.

professional indemnity policy. A policy of insurance (qv) generally providing an indemnity to professional persons in respect of claims in negligence (qv) against them. The cover provided is often for breach of professional duty by reason of any negligent act, error or omission by the assured or any person employed by him. Generally such policies exclude any claim against the assured brought about by any dishonest, fraudulent, criminal or malicious act of the assured or of any person employed by him. Insurers are not enabled to avoid liability under a professional indemnity policy on the basis that the same act amounts to both a tort (qv) and a breach of contract (qv): *Rohan Construction v Insurance Corporation of Ireland* [1988] ILRM 373.

The Law Society is empowered to make regulations making provision for indemnity against losses arising from civil liability claims in connection with a solicitor's practice; this includes the power to require a solicitor to effect and maintain a policy of indemnity insurance: Solicitors (Amendment) Act 1994, ss 26, 54. A solicitor is required to carry run-off cover for a fixed period from the cessation of practice, currently two years: *A Guide to Professional Conduct of Solicitors in Ireland* (2002) ch 9.7 and 9.14. See Solicitors Professional Indemnity Insurance Regulations 1995, 1998, 1999, 2001 and 2004, SIs Nos 312 of 1995, 209 of 1998, 362 of 1999, 504 of 2001, and 115 of 2004. See *Law Society Gazette* (May 2004) 2.

A barrister is required to be insured for professional negligence to an extent which is reasonable having regard to his practice but not less than the minimum level of professional indemnity insurance as declared from time to time by the Bar Council: *Code of Conduct for the Bar of Ireland* (December 2003) r 2.21. A barrister may enter into an arrangement with a solicitor and/or client to limit liability but not to less than that minimum level.

Doctors must ensure that they have adequate professional indemnity for the work they perform: Medical Council, *A Guide to Ethical Conduct and Behaviour* (6th edn, 2004) para 4.15. Chartered engineers are required to arrange appropriate insurance cover in respect of professional indemnity together with statutory insurances: see *Code of Ethics – The Institution of Engineers of Ireland'* (November 2003), clause 1.4(j). See Consumer Credit Act 1995, s 144(10), as amended by Central Bank and Financial Services Authority of Ireland Act 2003, s 35, Sch 1; Investor Compensation Act 1998, s 41. See *Rafter v Solicitors' Mutual Defence Fund Ltd* [1999] 2 ILRM 305, HC. [Bibliography: O'Callaghan P.] See PROFESSIONAL NEGLIGENCE; SOLICITOR, MUTUAL RECOGNITION.

professional independence. In many professions, a core principle of conduct is independence. Solicitors are required always to retain their professional independence and not to allow their independence to be compromised: *A Guide to Professional Conduct of Solicitors in Ireland* (2002) ch 1.3. The many duties to which a barrister is subject, require his absolute independence, free from all other influence, especially such as may arise from his personal interests or external pressure: *Code of Conduct for the Bar of Ireland* (December 2003) r 2.5. A barrister is required to avoid any impairment of his independence and be careful not to compromise his professional standards in order to please his client, the court or third parties. See INSTRUCT.

professional misconduct. As regards doctors, *professional misconduct* is: (a) conduct which doctors of experience, competence and good repute consider disgraceful or dishonourable; and/or (b) conduct connected with his profession in which the doctor concerned has seriously fallen short by omission or commission of the standards of conduct expected among doctors: Medical Council, *A Guide to Ethical Conduct and Behaviour* (6th edn, 2004) para 1.5. See also BARRISTER, MISCONDUCT OF; BARRISTERS' PROFESSIONAL CONDUCT TRIBUNAL; ENGINEER, PROFESSIONAL NEGLIGENCE; FITNESS TO TEACH; MEDICAL NEGLIGENCE; NO FAULT COMPENSATION; NURSE; PROFESSIONAL INDEMNITY INSURANCE; SOLICITOR, PROFESSIONAL NEGLIGENCE; SOLICITOR, MISCONDUCT OF; PROFESSIONAL WITNESS; SURGICAL OPERATION; VETERINARY SURGERY.

professional negligence. A person who professes to exercise any profession or trade is guilty of negligence if he fails to exercise the skill and knowledge reasonably to be expected of an ordinary member of that profession or trade, as the case may be. See *Somers v Erskine* [1944] IR 368 and *Roche v Peilow* [1986] ILRM 189 (*solicitor*); *Boyle v Martin* [1932] 66 ILTR 187 (*general practitioner*); *O'Donovan v Cork County Council* [1967] IR 173 (*anaesthetist*); *Dunne v National Maternity Hospital* [1989] ITLR (24 April) (*obstetrician*); *Chariot Inns Ltd v Assicurazioni Generali SPA* [1981] ILRM 173 (*insurance broker*); *Colgan v Connolly Construction Co (Ireland) Ltd* [1980] HC (*builder*); *Western Meats Ltd v National Ice & Cold Storage Co Ltd* [1982] ILRM 99 (*meat processor*); *Crowley v Allied Irish Banks* [1988] ILRM 225 (*architect*); *Golden Vale Co-Operative v Barrett* [1987] HC (*accountant*); *Moran v Duleek Developments Ltd & Hanley* [1991] ITLR (14 October) HC (*engineer*).

A barrister must not settle a pleading claiming professional negligence without express instructions and unless he has satisfied himself that expert evidence is or will be available to support such claim: *Code of Conduct for the Bar of Ireland* (December 2003) r 5.16. The latter provision does not apply in a case of alleged professional negligence on the part of a solicitor or barrister. [Bibliography: Daly B D; McMahon & Binchy; O'Callaghan P; Jackson & Powell UK.] See BARRISTER, NEGLIGENCE OF;

ENGINEER, PROFESSIONAL NEGLIGENCE; MEDICAL NEGLIGENCE; NO FAULT COMPENSATION; PROFESSIONAL INDEMNITY INSURANCE; SOLICITOR, PROFESSIONAL NEGLIGENCE; PROFESSIONAL WITNESS; SURGICAL OPERATION.

professional privilege. See PRIVILEGE, LEGAL PROFESSIONAL.

professional services tax. See WITHHOLDING TAX.

professional witness. It is the practice of the courts to have evidence of professional witnesses, particularly medical witnesses, taken out of turn or by specially fixing a date for an action, since their inconvenience may be accompanied by hardship to other people. See *Aspell v O'Brien* [1993] 3 IR 516, HC. A High Court judge has said that when professional witnesses are called in a case of professional negligence and there is no challenge to their integrity or their professional qualifications, the practice of attacking them merely on the basis that they had appeared in similar cases is deplorable: O'Hanlon J in *Doherty v Whelan* [1993] ITLR (26 April) HC. As regards the payment of witness expenses, it has been held that a clear distinction must be drawn between the position of an ordinary witness who is called to give evidence in regard to fact and an expert witness who is called to give evidence on his opinion based on his expertise: *Staunton v Durkan* [1996] 2 ILRM 509, SC. [Bibliography: Daly B D (5); O'Flaherty; Gee Publishing.] See EXPERT OPINION; EXPERT REPORT; STANDBY FEE; WITNESS, PRIVILEGE OF.

profit a prendre. The right of a person to take the produce or part of the soil from the land of another person eg sporting and fishing rights, sand from the soil, turbary (qv), pasturage (qv). The right may be acquired by grant or by prescription. See Prescription Act 1832 (extended to Ireland in 1859 by the Prescription (Ireland) Act 1858). The Law Reform Commission has recommended that that there is no reason to distinguish between the acquisition of *profits a prendre* and easements: *Report on the Acquisition of Easements and Profit A Prendre by Prescription* (LRC 66, 2002). The Commission has recommended that it should be possible to acquire a profit a prendre in gross by prescription. [Bibliography: Bland (1); Power A.] See COMMON; EASEMENT; PISCARY; PRESCRIPTION.

profit and loss. The form of account required to be prepared by a company showing its income and expenditure during the previous accounting period: Companies Act 1963, Sch 6, regs 12–14. In a company not trading for profit, it is called an *income and expenditure* account. Banks, discount houses and assurance companies are exempted from many of the requirements (regs 23–26). The profit and loss account must give a true and fair view of the profit or loss of the company for the financial year: Companies Amendment Act 1986, s 3(1).

As regards a listed company, a *profit estimate* is for a financial period which has expired but for which the results have not yet been published: Listing Rules 2000, para 12.21. A profit estimate may be subject to assumptions only in exceptional circumstances (para 12.27). A *profit forecast* is a form of words, which expressly or by implication states a minimum or maximum for the likely level of profits for a period subsequent to that for which audited accounts have been published, even though the word 'profit' is not used (para 12.23). A *dividend forecast* must be treated as a profit forecast where there is a known policy of relating dividends to earnings. A *profit forecast* must contain the principal assumptions upon which it is based (para 12.27). See also Listing Rules 2000, paras 12.19(a), 12.20(b), 12.34, 12.35.

In a take-over situation, there is a requirement on a company to ensure that a *profit forecast* is prepared with scrupulous care, accuracy and objectivity: Takeover Rules 2001, Pt B, r 28.

As regards corporation tax, *profits* mean income and chargeable gains: Taxes Consolidation Act 1997, s 4(1). In tax law, the courts have consistently interpreted profits as being the difference between receipts in a given period and the expenditure laid out to earn those receipts in that same period, consequently the *current cost accounting* method was not an appropriate one for revenue purposes: *Carroll Industries plc v O'Culachain* [1989] ILRM 552, HC. Gains realised by a bank from compulsorily held government stocks are part of the bank's trading profits for corporation tax purposes: *Browne v Bank of Ireland Finance Ltd* [1991] ITLR (18 March) SC. See also TCA 1997, ss 79(1), 402(1) and 530(1). See ACCOUNTS, COMPANY; CURRENT COST ACCOUNTING CONVENTION.

profit-sharing scheme. See EMPLOYEES' SHARE SCHEME.

progression. See NATIONAL QUALIFICA-TIONS AUTHORITY OF IRELAND; LEARNER.

prohibited degrees. The degrees of relationship within which parties cannot marry: any such marriage is void: Marriage Act 1835. A man cannot marry his grandmother; grandfather's wife; wife's grandmother; father's sister; mother's sister; father's brother's wife; mother's brother's wife; wife's father's sister; wife's mother's sister; mother; stepmother; wife's mother; daughter; wife's daughter; son's wife; sister; son's daughter; daughter's daughter; son's son's wife; daughter's son's wife; wife's son's daughter; wife's daughter's daughter; brother's daughter; sister's daughter; brother's son's wife; sister's son's wife; wife's brother's daughter; wife's sister's daughter. Analogous prohibitions apply to a woman.

A man however is permitted to marry his deceased wife's sister and a woman may marry her deceased husband's brother: Deceased Wife's Sister's Act 1907; Deceased Brother's Widow's Act 1921. In June 2001 in the High Court, Mr Justice Smyth granted a declaration that the marriage of Mrs Winnie Kavanagh to her late aunt's husband was a valid marriage. See MARRIAGE, IMPEDIMENT TO.

prohibited goods. Counterfeit or pirated goods: European Communities (Counterfeit and Pirated Goods) Regulations 1996, SI No 48 of 1996. The purpose of these regulations is to implement Regulation (EEC) 94/3295 in relation to the interception and detention of counterfeit and pirated goods, which goods are treated as *prohibited goods* under the Customs Acts with fines for infringement. An owner of the copyright in a work may give notice to the Revenue Commissioners requesting that they treat as prohibited goods, copies of the work which are *infringing copies* (qv): Copyright and Related Rights Act 2000, s 147. These prohibited goods may be subject only to forfeiture (CRRA 2000, s 147(5)). See Industrial Designs Act 2001, ss 73–74. See COPYRIGHT; DESIGN RIGHT, INFRINGEMENT OF.

prohibited weapon. Any weapon of whatever description designed for the discharge of any noxious liquid, noxious gas, other noxious thing, and also any ammunition which contains or is designed or adapted to contain any noxious liquid, noxious gas, or other noxious thing: Firearms Act 1925, s 1(1); Firearms and Offensive Weapons Act 1990, s 4(e). See FIREARM.

prohibition. An order of the High Court preventing or prohibiting a body or person from exercising a power it does not legally possess. Relief by way of prohibition will be refused where the matter raised is properly one of defence: *Minister for Agriculture v Norgo Ltd* [1980] IR 155; *McGrail v Ruane* [1989] ILRM 498. See *R (Kelly) v Maguire* [1923] 2 IR 58; *The State (Williams) v Kelleher* [1983] ILRM 285.

Where the court grants an order of prohibition or *certiorari* (qv), the grant operates as a stay of the proceedings objected to: RSC Ord 84, r 20(7). The principles applicable to the granting or discharge of such a stay are the same as those governing the granting of interlocutory injunctions ie the balance of convenience: *McDonnell v Brady* [2001] 3 IR 588, SC.

The Supreme Court has held that an order of prohibition of the High Court had been incorrectly drawn up *by including the reasons for the prohibition*: *Carlton v DPP (No 2)* [2000] 3 IR 269, SC. See *Carlton v DPP* [1999] 2 IR 518, HC. See DUE COURSE OF LAW; JUDICIAL REVIEW; STATE SIDE ORDERS.

prohibition notice, data. The notice by which the Data Protection Commissioner (qv) may prohibit the transfer of personal data (qv) from the State to a place outside the State: Data Protection Act 1988, s 11 as substituted by Data Protection (Amendment) Act 2003, s 12. The notice is served on the person proposing to transfer the data and it must prohibit the transfer concerned either absolutely or conditionally, specifying the time when it is to take effect and the grounds for the prohibition (DPA 1988, ss 11(10) and (11) as substituted). In considering whether to issue a prohibition notice, the Commissioner must consider whether the transfer would be likely to cause damage or distress to any person. See DATA PROTECTION; TRANSBORDER DATA FLOWS.

prohibition notice, work. A notice, signed by an inspector, stating his opinion regarding an activity which involves, or is likely to involve, a risk of serious personal injury to persons at work and directing that the activity cease until the matters giving rise to the risk are rectified: Safety, Health and Welfare at Work Act 1989, s 37. A prohibition notice takes effect immediately on receipt if it so declares. There is a right of appeal against a prohibition notice to the District Court. If activities are carried on in contravention of a prohibition notice, the inspector may apply with the High Court, by motion, for an order prohibiting the continuation of the activities (SHWWA 1989, s 37(9)). Contrast with IMPROVEMENT NOTICE, WORK; WORK, PROHIBITION OF.

prohibition of trade. See TRADE, PROHIBITION OF.

prohibition of work. See WORK, PROHIBITION OF.

prohibition order. An order, served on the proprietor or person in charge of food, directing that the food not be used for human consumption, is recalled from sale or distribution and, as appropriate in the interest of public health, is detained, destroyed or rendered safe for human consumption: Food Safety Authority of Ireland Act 1998, s 54. The order must contain the opinion of an authorised officer that there is a serious risk to public health and the matters that give rise to this opinion and, if there is a contravention of food legislation, the order must specify the provision contravened. An appeal against a prohibition notice lies to the District Court within seven days of service of the order (FSAIA 1998, s 54(6)). See CLOSURE ORDER; IMPROVEMENT NOTICE, FOOD.

prolixity. Unnecessary length in summons, pleadings or affidavit, the cost of which may have to be borne by the responsible party. See RSC Ord 1, r 5; Ord 19, r 1; Ord 40, r 3. The cost of an affidavit which is prolix has to be borne by the party filing it: Circuit Court Rules 2001 Ord 25, r 16.

promise. An undertaking to do or to forbear from some act. It has no legal effect, unless it complies with the requirements of a contract or unless it is made under seal. The person making the promise is the *promisor* and to whom it is made is the *promisee*.

To claim a particular asset on the basis of a promise would require very clear evidence of the promise, of acceptance and of a detriment of such a nature, that a court would be outraged if the promise was not honoured: *Carter v Ross* (8 December 2000, unreported) HC. See BREACH OF PROMISE.

promissory estoppel. See EQUITABLE ESTOPPEL.

promissory note. An unconditional promise in writing, made by one person to another, signed by the maker, engaging to pay, on demand or at a fixed or determinable future time, a sum certain in money to,

or to the order of, a specified person or to bearer: Bills of Exchange Act 1882, s 83.

Most of the rules applicable to bills of exchange (qv) also apply to promissory notes; the main distinction between them being that a note is a *promise* to pay, whereas a bill is an *order* to pay; a promissory note must be presented for payment (BEA 1882, s 87) although it need not be presented for acceptance as must a bill. See *Creation Press Ltd v Harman* [1973] IR 313; *Tromso Sparebank v Beirne & Ors* [1990] ITLR (5 March) SC.

Where a promissory note is given to a creditor by a consumer in connection with a *credit agreement* (qv), and is negotiated to a third party, the creditor can plead against the third party, any defence available to him against the creditor, in any proceedings for enforcement of the note: Consumer Credit Act 1995, s 41(2). See also Stamp Duties Consolidation Act 1999, ss 22–28. [Bibliography: Paget UK; Richardson UK.]

promoter. A person who undertakes to form a company with reference to a given project, and to set it going, and who takes the necessary steps to accomplish that purpose: *Twycross v Grant* [1877] 36 LT 812. A promoter may incur civil and criminal liability for mis-statements in a prospectus: Companies Act 1963, ss 49–52. Rules to protect a plc from promoter fraud were introduced by Companies Amendment Act 1983, s 32. New rules have been introduced to prevent persons from being involved in the promotion or formation of a company if they have been involved previously with a company which is insolvent on its winding up or receivership, unless the first named company meets certain capital and other requirements: Companies Act 1990, ss 159. See Listing Rules 2000, paras 6C.21, 6J.15. See DIRECTOR; DISQUALIFICATION ORDER, COMPANY.

promotion. A Supreme Court judge has said that it would be wholly inappropriate to include a prospect of promotion in a contract of employment as it would not be considered as being a condition of service: Blayney J in *O'Cearbhall v Bord Telecom Éireann* [1994] ELR 54, SC.

Also the High Court has held that the decision to abandon a *promotional panel* (ie a panel of successful candidates for future promotion) was neither unreasonable nor irrational and was not *ultra vires*: *Gilheany v Revenue Commissioners* [1996] ELR 25, HC.

prompt payment. (1) Various State bodies, who obtain goods or services from a supplier, were required to pay for them by the *prescribed payment date*, in default of which they were required to pay an interest penalty which was not capable of being waived by the supplier: Prompt Payment of Accounts Act 1997, s 4.

The *prescribed payment date* was the date specified in a written contract or in the absence of such, 45 days after: (a) receipt by the purchaser of an invoice after completed delivery of the goods or services, or (b) the delivery of the goods or services, where delivery was made at the time or after receipt of the invoice (PPAA 1997, s 1(1)).

The initial interest penalty in 1997 was specified at 0.0322% per day, equivalent to 11.753% per annum: SI No 512 of 1997. The interest penalty from 6 April 1999 was 0.0274% per day: SI No 62 of 1999. The interest rate from 2 January 2001 was 0.0294% per day, equivalent to 10.74% per annum: SI No 392 of 2000. See also Prompt Payment of Accounts Act 1997 (Amendment of Schedule) Order 2000, SI No 383 of 2000.

(2) From 7 August 2002, the provisions governing *late payment* are contained in the EC (Late Payment in Commercial Transactions) Regulations 2002, SI No 388 of 2002 which repeal PPAA 1997, ss 4 to 11 and give legal effect to Directive (EC) 2000/35 of 29 June 2000.

The regulations apply, with some exceptions, to *commercial transactions* in both the public and private sector. *Commercial transactions* are transactions between undertakings or between undertakings and public authorities for the purpose of providing goods or services for remuneration (SI No 388 of 2002, reg 2(1)). It is an implied term in every contract that interest is payable if debts are not paid on time; a payment is regarded as late when 30 days have elapsed unless an alternative payment period is specified in an agreed contract. The interest rate chargeable is the European Central Bank main financing rate plus 7 percentage points unless otherwise agreed.

Also compensation may be claimed for debt recovery costs. The use of *grossly unfair terms* may be unenforceable and such terms may be challenged in court. *Grossly unfair terms* may also be challenged by organisations representing small and medium-sized enterprises (SI No 388 of 2002, reg 8). See UNFAIR TERMS.

proof. (1) The evidence by which a court is satisfied as to the truth of a fact. The *burden of proof* generally rests on the party who asserts the affirmative of the issue or question in dispute. Proof is not required for matters which are *judicially noticed*, matters which are *presumed* by law, and matters which are formally admitted. (2) The standard of strength of spirituous liquors. (3) To *prove* a will is to obtain probate of it. (4) To *prove* a debt in bankruptcy is to establish the existence of the debt. [Bibliography: Charleton (5).] See BURDEN OF PROOF; STANDARD OF PROOF; JUDICIAL NOTICE; PRESUMPTIONS; ADMIT, NOTICE TO; INTERROGATORIES; STATEMENT.

proof of will. See WILL, PROOF OF.

propensity. See *Re Employment Equality Bill 1996* [1997] 2 IR 321, SC and ELR 132. See DOGS; RECIDIVISM; SCIENTER.

proper law of a contract. The phrase used in private international law to denote the system of law by which a contract is to be interpreted. The proper law of a contract is the law which the parties intended to apply: *Vita Foods v Unus Shipping* [1939] AC 277. If there is no express choice of applicable law, the court will determine whether there is an implied choice of law in the contract. See Contractual Obligations (Applicable Law) Act 1991. See *McIlwraith v Seitz Filtration (GB) Ltd* [1998] ELR 105, LC. See Quinn in 10 ILT & SJ 244. See CONTRACT; PRIVATE INTERNATIONAL LAW.

proper look out. The failure of a driver or a pedestrian to keep a *proper look out* may amount to negligence or contributory negligence: *Stapleton v O'Regan* [1956] SC. The test is whether the area he observed was in the circumstances reasonably sufficient: *Nolan v Jennings* [1964] SC. See also *O'Connell v Shield Insurance Co Ltd* [1954] IR 286; *McEleney v McCarron* [1993] 11 ILT Dig 188, SC.

proper provision. See CHILD, PROVISION FOR; DIVORCE; JUDICIAL SEPARATION; SEPARATION AGREEMENT.

properties. Attributes, inherent qualities, characteristics, abilities; it has been held that sodium chlorate is specially dangerous by reason of its explosive *properties*: *Hardy v Special Criminal Court & A-G* [1992] ITLR (6 April) HC. See EXPLOSIVE.

property. That which can be owned; *real* property (realty) and *personal* property (personalty). As regards bankruptcy (qv), *property* includes money, goods, things in action, land and every description of property, whether real or personal and whether situate in the State or elsewhere; also obligations, easements, and every description of estate, interest, and profit, present or future, vested or contingent, arising out of or incident to property as defined: Bankruptcy Act 1988, s 3. See LICENCE; PRIVATE PROPERTY, RIGHT TO.

property, damage to. See DAMAGE TO PROPERTY; MALICIOUS INJURIES SCHEME.

property, matrimonial. See MATRIMONIAL PROPERTY.

property, right to. See EUROPEAN CONVENTION ON HUMAN RIGHTS; LICENCE; PRIVATE PROPERTY, RIGHT TO.

property, taxation of. It has been held that a taxation based on the occupation of property does not infringe any personal rights to equality: *Madigan v AG & Ors* [1986] ILRM 136. [Bibliography: Gaffney; Gannon.] See ANTI-SPECULATIVE PROPERTY TAX.

property adjustment order. An order which the court may make in respect of property on granting a decree of judicial separation (qv) eg transferring the property to the other spouse or to a child; or making a settlement of the property; or varying any ante-nuptial or post-nuptial settlement; or extinguishing or reducing the interest of either spouse under such settlement: Family Law Act 1995, s 9. Such an order may be varied subsequently (FLA 1995, s 18). A claim for a property adjustment order is a *lis pendens* (qv) registrable under the Judgment (Ireland) Act 1844, even though the claim is contingent upon the court deciding to make such an order: *AS v GS and AIB* [1994] 2 ILRM 68, HC.

A similar order may be made by the court on granting a decree of divorce or at any time thereafter: Family Law (Divorce) Act 1996, s 14. The order may restrict the extent to which it may be subsequently varied (FL(D)A 1996, s 14(2)). If after a decree of divorce is granted, either of the spouses remarries, the court will not make a property adjustment order in favour of that spouse (FL(D)A 1996, s 14(2)). Section 14 does not apply to a *family home* in which, following the decree, either of the spouses, having remarried, ordinarily resides with the new spouse (FL(D)A 1996, s 14(7)). A Supreme Court judge has said that the divorce legislation makes impossible the achievement of finality as

regards property issues: McGuinness, Mrs Justice (*Irish Times*, 23 May 2000). See MATRIMONIAL PROPERTY.

property companies. Companies listed on the stock exchange which own property (including land), carry out property-related transactions, or which are companies primarily engaged in property activities; such companies are subject to additional disclosure requirements, principally relating to *valuations*: Listing Rules 2000, ch 18.

property in goods. See GOODS, PROPERTY IN.

property in possession of garda. Property in the possession of the gardaí may by order of the court be delivered to the person appearing to the court to be the owner thereof, or, if the owner cannot be ascertained, as the court considers just; this applies to property possessed in connection with a criminal offence even though no person has been charged: Police Property Act 1897, s 1; Criminal Justice Act 1951, s 25. See also Offences Against the State Act 1939, s 29; Official Secrets Act 1963, s 16; Criminal Law Act 1976, s 9; Criminal Damage Act 1991, s 13(3); National Monuments (Amendment) Act 1994, s 7; Criminal Justice Act 1994, s 61. See *Quinn v Pratt* [1908] 2 IR 69; *Brady v District Judge Haughton* [2004] 1 ILRM 321, HC. For District Court procedure, see DCR 1997 Ord 31A. See Criminal Justice Bill 2004, s 6.

property offences. A wide range of offences involving property eg larceny, embezzlement, fraudulent conversion, obtaining by false pretences, handling stolen property, robbery, burglary, blackmail, forgery, false accounting, and bribery. [Bibliography: Charleton (4).]

proportional representation. An election system based on the principle that the distribution of seats in a representative assembly should reflect as nearly as possible the distribution of the electors' votes among the competing parties or contending candidates. Voting in the elections to Dáil Éireann, Seanad Éireann and for the President of Ireland are required to be by the system of proportional representation by means of the *single transferable vote*: 1937 Constitution, arts 12(2)(3), 16(2)(5) and 18(5). Under this system, voters number the candidates on the ballot paper in the order of their preference. A *quota* is established by dividing the total number of valid votes cast by the number of seats to be filled plus one and by adding one to this result. Candidates who reach the quota are declared elected and their surplus is divided among the other candidates in accordance with their second preferences; also candidates who are eliminated have their second preferences distributed in similar manner. A referendum to amend the Constitution to remove this voting system was defeated both in 1959 and 1968. Voting in the European Parliament and local elections is also by the system of proportional representation: European Parliament Elections Act 1997, s 7. See CONSTITUENCY; DEGRESSIVELY PROPORTIONAL; EUROPEAN PARLIAMENT; QUOTA; LOCAL ELECTION; SPOILT VOTE; TRANSFERABLE VOTE.

proportionality. (1) The principle in administrative law which requires that there be a balance between the injury to an individual's interest by an administrative measure and the consequential gain to the polity. It has been held that the principle of *proportionality*, even if it were to be adopted in this jurisdiction, could apply only to the exercise of administrative powers and not to the imposing of a sanction by the Oireachtas: *Hand v Dublin Corporation* [1991] ILRM 556, SC. The objective of a statutory provision must be of sufficient importance to warrant overriding a constitutionally protected right, otherwise it will fail the proportionality test: *Daly v Revenue Commissioners* [1996] 1 ILRM 122, HC. A Bill has been held not to constitute reasonably proportionate intervention by the State with the rights of the family: *In the matter of the Matrimonial Home Bill 1993* [1994] 1 ILRM 241, SC. See also *Balkan Tours v Minister for Communications* [1988] ILRM 101 at 108; *Enright v Ireland* [2003] 2 IR 321, HC and [2004] 1 ILRM 103.

(2) As regards EC law, in order to establish whether a provision is consonant with the principle of proportionality it is necessary to establish whether the means it employs to achieve its aim correspond to the importance of the aim and whether they are necessary for its achievement: Case 66/82 *Fromoncais SA v FORMA* [1983] ECR 395. The Amsterdam Treaty 1997 emphasised that any EC institution must, in exercising the powers conferred on it, ensure compliance with the principle of proportionality, according to which any action of the community must not go beyond what is necessary to achieve the objectives of the Treaty of Rome: Protocol on Subsidiarity and Proportionality 1997.

(3) The test applied in criminal law on the reasonableness of the relationship between the amount of force used by an accused and the provocation involved. See *The People v MacEoin* [1978] IR 27, CCA. The Supreme Court has held that it is doubtful if the *principle of proportionality* has any useful application in relation to the *conduct* of a criminal trial; such a trial is either conducted in due course of law or with due process of law in accordance with the 1937 Constitution, art 38(1) or it is not: *In the matter of National Irish Bank Ltd* [1999] 1 ILRM 321, SC and 3 IR 145. [Bibliography: O'Malley (3).] As regards sentences, see PUNISHMENT, OBJECTIVE OF. See GENEVA CONVENTIONS; SELF-DEFENCE; SUBSIDIARITY; TRIAL BY CERTIFICATION; VICARIOUS LIABILITY.

proposal form. A form completed by or for a person seeking insurance (qv). Until it is accepted by the insurer there is no contract and generally the insurer does not come on risk in respect of the event insured until the first premium has been paid. See INSURANCE, CONTRACT OF; INSURANCE AGENT; PREMIUM.

proprietary director. A director of a company who beneficially owns, or is able to control, more than 15% of the company's ordinary share capital; certain tax reliefs are not available to such a director eg in relation to a lump sum for a change in working conditions: Taxes Consolidation Act 1997, s 480. A similar definition applies to a *proprietary employee*. See also TCA 1997, ss 530 and 783.

proprietary lease. A sublease, mediate or immediate, under a building lease (qv), where the term of the former was either not less than 99 years or, if less, was equal to or greater than 20 years, or, if this was the lesser period, two thirds of the term of the building lease, and which expired at the same time as, or not more than 15 years before, the expiration of the building lease: Landlord and Tenant (Reversionary Leases) Act 1958. A proprietary lease (although not now referred to as such), entitled to acquire the fee simple, is entitled to a reversionary lease (qv): Landlord and Tenant (Amendment) Act 1980, s 30.

proprietary medicinal product. See MEDICINAL PRODUCT.

proprietary right. Rights of property; rights of ownership.

proprietor. A person who has title to property eg the proprietor of a trade mark (qv). The proprietor of a patent is the person to whom the patent was granted or the person whose title is subsequently registered: Patents Act 1992, s 2(1).

proprietor of new or original design. Formerly, either: (a) the person for whom a design is executed, where the author of the design, for good consideration executes the design for such person; (b) the person by whom the design or the right to apply the design to any article is acquired either exclusively or otherwise, or on whom it has devolved; or (c) in any other case, the author of the design: Industrial Commercial Property (Protection) Act 1927, s 3. The proprietor of such a design could apply to be registered as the registered proprietor thereof.

Now, the *author* of a design is to be treated as the proprietor of the design, unless the design is created by an employee: Industrial Designs Act 2001, s 19(1). See DESIGN.

proprietary estoppel. See EQUITABLE ESTOPPEL.

prorogation. The bringing of a session of parliament to an end by the exercise of the royal prerogative: Prorogation Act 1867 repealed by the Electoral Act 1963. In the early years of the Irish Free State (Saorstát Éireann) there was a requirement for both houses of the Oireachtas to assemble and sit, whenever the Reserve had been ordered to be called out on permanent service, if at the time the houses had stood adjourned or prorogued: Defence Forces (Temporary Provs) Act 1923, s 222. See now DISSOLUTION.

For prorogation of jurisdiction, whereby parties agree that a particular court of a member State is to have exclusive jurisdiction over any disputes in connection with a particular legal relationship, see the *Brussels I Regulation* on the recognition and enforcement of judgments in civil and commercial matters, SI No 52 of 2002, arts 23–24. See EXCLUSIVE JURISDICTION.

prosecuting barrister, duty of. It is not the duty of a prosecuting barrister to obtain a conviction by all means at his command but rather he must lay before the jury fairly and impartially the whole of the facts which comprise the case for the prosecution and must assist the court with adequate submissions of law to enable the law to be properly applied to the facts: *Code of Conduct for the*

Bar of Ireland (December 2003) r 9.19. Where a prosecuting barrister has in his possession statements from persons he does not propose to call as witnesses, or he is in possession of potentially relevant material upon which he does not propose to rely as evidence, he should show such statements and disclose such material to the defence (r 9.20). It is the duty of a prosecuting barrister to assist the court at the conclusion of the summing-up by drawing the attention of the court to any apparent error or omission of fact or law which, in his opinion, ought to be corrected (r 9.22). Prosecuting counsel ought to regard themselves as ministers of justice and not to struggle for a conviction: *obiter dictum* in *DPP v PJ* [2003] FL 8155, CCA and [2004] 1 ILRM 220, CCA. See BARRISTER, DUTY OF; DEFENCE BARRISTER, DUTY OF; SENTENCE.

prosecution. The institution of criminal proceedings in the courts. Crimes and offences are required to be prosecuted in the name of the People: 1937 Constitution, art 30(3). See DIRECTOR OF PUBLIC PROSECUTIONS; COMMON INFORMER; PROSECUTOR.

prosecutor. A person who institutes legal proceedings against another eg the Director of Public Prosecutions (DPP). A Garda Síochána may institute proceedings in courts of summary jurisdiction as a *common informer* (qv) and the DPP has no power to compel the withdrawal of the complaint: *State (Collins) v Ruane* [1984] IR 106. See also *Courtney v Well-Woman Centre* [1985] HC. Costs cannot be awarded against a garda prosecuting a case: *Dillane v Ireland* [1980] ILRM 167. A garda or private citizen can institute proceedings in the name of the DPP: *People v Roddy* [1977] IR 177; however, after a return for trial on indictment, only the DPP may prosecute.

Increasingly, persons other than the DPP and the Gardaí are given power to prosecute offences summarily eg see Consumer Credit Act 1995, s 14, as amended by Central Bank and Financial Services Authority of Ireland Act 2003, s 35, Sch 1; Mineral Development Act 1999, s 4. The Minister may prosecute summary offences under the National Beef Assurance Scheme Act 2000 (NBASA 2000, s 26). See also Equal Status Act 2000, s 44; Electronic Commerce Act 2000, s 6(1); Copyright and Related Rights Act 2000, s 11(1); Unclaimed Life Assurance Policies

Act 2003, s 5(4); Licensing of Indoor Events Act 2003, s 16. See DCR 1997 Ord 6, r 1(e).

The *Statement of General Guidelines for Prosecutors* (2001), issued by the DPP, aims to set out, in general terms, principles which should guide the initiation and conduct of prosecutions in Ireland. It is intended to give general guidance to prosecutors so that a fair, reasoned and consistent policy underlies the prosecution process. This *Statement* and the *Standards of International Association of Prosecutors* (1999) are available on website: *www.dppireland.ie*. See 'A game of high stakes' by Dr Eamonn Hall in *Law Society Gazette* (April 2002) 18. [Bibliography: Walsh D (3).] See DIRECTOR OF PUBLIC PROSECUTIONS; INDICTMENT.

prospecting licence. Legislation was introduced in 1995 to provide for the renewal of existing and future prospecting licences, and the validation of licences already renewed: Mineral Development Act 1995. See also Mineral Development Acts 1940 and 1979; Petroleum and Other Minerals Development Act 1960. See PETROLEUM, EXPLORATION FOR.

prospective damages. See GENERAL DAMAGES.

prospective owner. A person who is *prospectively* entitled to copyright by virtue of an agreement made in relation to *future copyright* ie copyright which will or may come into existence in respect of a future work or class or works or on the occurrence of a future event: Copyright and Related Rights Act 2000, s 121(4). A licence granted by a prospective owner of copyright is binding on every successor in title to his interest (CRRA 2000, s 120(5)). See COPYRIGHT.

prospectus. (1) Any document, notice, circular, advertisement or other invitation, offering to the public for subscription or purchase, any shares or debentures of a company: Companies Act 1963, s 2(1). It must specify, *inter alia*, the nominal capital of the company, the names and addresses and descriptions of the directors, the *minimum amount* required to be raised, the time of opening of the subscription lists, the amount payable on application and allotment of each share, and details of *material contracts* (CA 1963, Sch 3). The directors and promoters may incur civil and criminal liability for mis-statements in the prospectus (CA 1963, ss 49–52). See also CA 1963, ss 43–52. See Companies Act 1990,

s 238. See *Components Tube Co v Naylor* [1900] 2 IR 1; *Aarons Reefs Ltd v Twiss* [1895] 2 IR 207 and [1896] AC 273.

(2) Means a prospectus as in the *prospectus regulations* ie EC (Transferable Securities and Stock Exchange) Regulations 1992, or a *supplemental prospectus*: Listing Rules (Definitions and paras 5.14–5.16 as modified by para 5.1(e)).

For *listing particulars* requirements for stock exchange companies, eg content, financial information, procedure, publication and circulation, see Listing Rules 2000, chs 5–8, and 12. There are additional and alternative requirements relating to *listing particulars* dealing with overseas companies, property companies, mineral companies, scientific research based companies, investment entities, public sector issuers, issuers of specialised securities and miscellaneous securities, innovative high-growth companies and venture capital trusts (chs 17–26).

Under the Companies Acts 1963 to 1990, directors and proposed directors may be personally responsible for information contained in listing particulars: Listing Rules, para 16.1. See EC Directives on Listing Particulars included in the listing rules ie (EEC) 80/390, (EEC) 87/345, (EEC) 90/211 and (EC) 94/18. [Bibliography: Cahill D.] See MATERIAL CONTRACTS; LISTING RULES; MINIPROSPECTUS; PROMOTER; PUBLIC OFFERS DIRECTIVE; UNDERSUBSCRIBED.

prostitute. A woman who hires herself or is hired to a man for sexual intercourse. A reference to a prostitute now includes a reference to a male person who is a prostitute and a reference to prostitution is to be construed accordingly: Criminal Law (Sexual Offences) Act 1993, s 1(4). It is an offence for a person in a street or public place to solicit or importune another person for the purposes of prostitution (CL(SO)A 1993, s 7). A person *solicits or importunes* where the person: (a) offers his or her services as a prostitute to another person, (b) solicits or importunes another person for that other person's services as a prostitute, or (c) solicits or importunes another person on behalf of a person for the purposes of prostitution (CL(SO)A 1993, s 1(2)). This includes soliciting or importuning from or in a motor vehicle (CL(SO)A 1993, s 1(1)).

It is an offence for a person for gain to control or direct the activities of a prostitute, to organise prostitution, or to compel or coerce a person to be a prostitute (CL(SO)A 1993, s 9). It is also an offence for a person to live in whole or in part on the earnings of prostitution where the person aids and abets that prostitution (CL(SO)A 1993, s 10) or who advertises the services of a prostitute: Criminal Justice (Public Order) Act 1994, s 23. See *DPP v Keogh* [1998] 4 IR 416, HC. See also Child Trafficking and Pornography Act 1998, s 3(3). See BROTHEL; CHILD, SEXUAL EXPLOITATION OF; LOITERING; PROCUREMENT.

protected road. A public road (qv) or proposed public road specified to be a protected road in a *protected roadway scheme* approved by the Minister: Roads Act 1993, ss 2(1) and 45. A protected road is intended to be a type of road subject to some limitation of access and some limitation on traffic, somewhat between: (a) an ordinary public road to which there is widespread access and very few traffic restrictions, and (b) a motorway (qv) which is restricted to certain types of traffic and to which all access from adjoining land is prohibited. A road authority may submit a protected roadway scheme to the Minister having first notified the public and affected landowners/occupiers (RA 1993, s 48). The Minister, before approving a scheme, must cause a public local inquiry to be held, must consider any objections, and the report and recommendations of the person conducting the inquiry (RA 1993, s 49). Planning permission must not be granted which would contravene the provisions of a protected roadway scheme (RA 1993, s 46). The National Roads Authority is empowered to direct a road authority to make a protected road scheme (RA 1993, s 20(1)(c)). Similar provisions apply regarding compulsory purchase, compensation for disturbance and loss, and alternative access for adjoining landowners/occupiers as for a motorway scheme. See MOTORWAY; SERVICE AREA.

protected structure. A *structure* which is of special architectural, historical, archaeological, artistic, cultural, scientific, social or technical interest; each planning authority is required to include in its development plan (qv) a record of each such protected structure: Planning and Development Act 2000, ss 2(1) and 51. The owner or occupier of a protected structure is required to ensure that the structure, or any element of it, is not endangered (PDA 2000, s 58). *Structure* is widely defined to include the interior, all fixtures and fittings and land lying within the curtilage of the structure (PDA 2000, s 2(1)). *Endangered* means exposed to harm, decay or damage (PDA 2000, s 2(1)). The protection afforded to a protected structure includes land lying within the curtilage of the structure: *Begley v An Bord Pleanála* [2003] FL 6829, HC.

Planning permission is required for *works* carried out on a protected structure which affect its character; *works* includes the application or removal of wallpaper, plaster, paint, tiles, or other material to or from the interior or exterior (PDA 2000, ss 2(1) and 57 as amended by Planning and Development (Amendment) Act 2002, ss 6 and 13). The planning authority is empowered: (a) to serve an *endangerment notice* or *restoration notice* on the owner or occupier (PDA 2000, ss 59–60); (b) to carry out the works set out in these notices where there is non-compliance (PDA 2000, s 69); (c) to acquire the protected structure by agreement or compulsorily (PDA 2000, s 71); (d) to sell, let, transfer, exchange or use the structure so acquired (PDA 2000, s 78); (e) to issue a declaration that certain types of work would not require planning permission (PDA 2000, s 57(2)–(3)).

A refusal to grant planning permission for any development which would materially affect a protected structure or a *proposed* protected structure, does not attract compensation (PDA 2000, s 191 and Sch 3, para 3). A *proposed* protected structure means a structure in respect of which a notice is issued under PDA 2000, ss 12(3) or 55, proposing to add the structure, or a specified part of it, to the record (PDA 2000, s 2(1)). The *record* means the record included under PDA 2000, s 51 in a *development plan* (PDA 2000, s 2(1)). For previous legislation, see Local Government (Planning and Development) Act 1999, ss 1(1), 2, 8–11, 20, 22, 29.

See Planning and Development Regulations 2001, SI No 600 of 2001, arts 51–54; 18(1)(d)(iii); 21(b); 22(1)(g); 23(2); 27(2)(d)(iii); 28(1)(c)(i). These regulations revoke SI No 457 of 2000. See 'My home is my castle' by solicitor James Cahill in *Law*

Society Gazette (May 2003) 25. See GRA-NADA CONVENTION; ENDANGERMENT NOTICE; RESTORATION NOTICE; WORSHIP PUBLIC.

protected witness. See RELOCATED WITNESS.

protection. In relation to a structure or part of a structure, includes the conservation, preservation and improvement compatible with maintaining the character and interest of the `structure: Planning and Development Act 2000, s 2(1). See ENDANGERED.

protection of animals. See ANIMALS; HOUSEHOLD CHATTELS.

protection of company. See COURT PROTECTION OF COMPANY.

protection of debtor. See ARRANGING DEBTOR.

protection of employees. See eg CONTRACT OF EMPLOYMENT; EMPLOYEE; EMPLOYMENT LAW; NOTICE; EMPLOYMENT; TERMS OF EMPLOYMENT; UNFAIR DISMISSAL.

protection order. (1) An order made by a court directing the respondent to an application for a *barring order* (qv) or a *safety order* (qv): (a) not to use or threaten to use violence against, to molest or put in fear the applicant or a dependent person, and (b) if not residing where the applicant or dependent person resides, not to watch or beset that place: Domestic Violence Act 1996, s 5. A protection order may be made *ex parte* (DVA 1996, s 5(4) as substituted by Domestic Violence (Amendment) Act 2002, s 1(b)). A protection order expires on the determination of the application for the barring order. It is a criminal offence to contravene a protection order (DVA 1996, s 17). In divorce proceedings, the court may make a protection order, a safety order, or a barring order: Family Law (Divorce) Act 1996, ss 11(a), 15(1)(d). For provisions in the District Court in relation to a protection order, see DCR 1997 Ord 59, r 7.

(2) Also, a court order for the protection of goods eg see Consumer Credit Act 1995, s 66. See BARRING ORDER; SAFETY ORDER.

protective equipment, personal. All equipment designed to be worn or held by an employee for protection against one or more hazards likely to endanger the employee's safety and health at work: SI No 44 of 1993, reg 2(1). It is the duty of every employer to provide *personal protective equipment* free of charge where the use of the equipment is exclusive to the place of work (reg 7). It is the duty of every employee to make full and proper use of such equipment (reg 14(b)). The personal protective equipment must be appropriate for the risks involved (regs 21–26). See also SI No 53 of 2003.

protective leave. Means maternity leave, additional maternity leave, leave on health and safety grounds, and leave to a father of a child on the death of the child's mother: Maternity Protection Act 1994, s 21 as amended by Maternity Protection (Amendment) Act 2004, s 13. The amendment provides that (a) the period of leave taken prior to a postponement of the leave and (b) the period of resumed leave, are to be treated as separate periods of protected leave. There are various employment safeguards for employees on protective leave eg certain rights are preserved or suspended, there is voidance of certain purported terminations of employment, and there is a general right to return to work on expiry of protective leave (MPA 1994, s 22 amended by MP(A)A 2004, s 14). For general protections for employees on protective leave, including maternity leave, see MATERNITY LEAVE, RETURNING FROM.

protective trust. A trust for the life of the beneficiary, or any lesser period, which is to be determined on the occurrence of certain events eg the bankruptcy of the beneficiary, upon which the trust income is to be applied at the absolute discretion of the trustees for the benefit of the beneficiary and his family. See BANKRUPTCY, ACT OF; TRUST.

protector of the settlement. The person without whose consent a tenant in tail cannot *bar* the entail except as against his own issue. The consent of the *protector* is also required by the tenant in base fee who wishes to enlarge his estate into a fee simple. The office of protector was established by the Fines and Recoveries Act 1833. See BARRING THE ENTAIL.

protest. (1) Payment under protest is a payment of money made by a person who denies that the money is due from him, with a view to its later recovery. (2) A certificate under seal made by a notary public (qv) attesting the dishonour of a bill of exchange (qv) ie a formal written statement made and signed by the notary public that the bill was duly presented for acceptance or payment, as the case may be, and that it was refused. Such a certificate is accepted as proof that a bill has been dishonoured. See Bills of Exchange Act 1882, s 51. See NOTARY; NOTING AND PROTESTING; TENDER.

protest, right to. See ASSEMBLY, FREEDOM OF; EXPRESSION, FREEDOM OF.

protocol. (1) The minutes of a meeting setting out matters of agreement. (2) An original draft or preliminary memorandum. (3) A code of procedure. (4) A legal text, which is usually added (annexed) to a treaty and deals in a more detailed way with a certain topic e g the *Abortion Protocol* to the Maastricht Treaty.

prove. See PROOF.

provident. Providing for future needs.

provident society. See INDUSTRIAL AND PROVIDENT SOCIETY.

proving a will. Obtaining *probate* (qv) of a will.

provision. In a company's accounts, a *provision* is an amount written off or retained in order to provide for an asset's depreciation, renewal or diminution in value, or to provide for a known or unquantifiable liability: Companies Act 1963, Sch 6, reg 27(1)(a).

provision, proper. See CHILD, PROVISION FOR.

provisional arrest. An arrest of a person for the purposes of extradition; a request for such an arrest made on behalf of a requesting country must comply with certain requirements e g a statement of the offences to which the request relates, specifying the circumstances in which the offences were alleged to have been committed, and specifying the penalties to which the person would be liable if convicted: Extradition (European Union Conventions) Act 2001, s 5. See EXTRADITION.

provisional conviction. A conviction of an accused which is subject to revision at the same trial; there is no such thing in law. If a district court judge has concluded that an offence is fit to be tried summarily and the accused then pleads guilty, once the judge embarks upon an enquiry as to the penalty appropriate to the offence, he is precluded from changing his mind, there being no such thing in law as a *provisional conviction*: *Feeney v Clifford* [1990] ITLR (14 May) SC.

provisional driving licence. A licence issued to a person which permits the person to drive a vehicle, subject to certain restrictions e g the driver must display an 'L' plate and be accompanied in certain category vehicles by a *qualified* person and must not

drive a vehicle drawing a trailer. See Road Traffic (Licensing of Drivers) Regulations 1999, SI No 352 of 1999 arts 19–25. The Minister for Transport announced in December 2002 the intention of the government to introduce changes to remove anomalies regarding 'provisional licences' of which there were some 300,000 in 2002. See DRIVING LICENCE.

provisional liquidator. The liquidator appointed to a company by a court before any winding-up order is made, usually when the company's assets are in danger. He can be appointed without advertisement or notice to any party unless the court directs otherwise. See RSC Ord 74, r 14. See LIQUIDATOR; STATEMENT OF AFFAIRS; WINDING UP.

provisional specification. See COMPLETE SPECIFICATION.

proviso. A clause in a deed or statute which usually begins *provided always that.* In a deed, it usually provides a condition upon which the validity of something is based. In a statute, it usually qualifies or exempts something which, but for the proviso, would have been included.

provocation. Some act or series of acts, done by the deceased to the person accused of his killing, which would cause in any reasonable man, and certainly caused in the accused, a sudden and temporary loss of self-control, which rendered the accused so subject to passion as to make him for the moment not the master of his own mind: *The People (DPP) v MacEoin* [1978] IR 27.

However, the test now laid down in Irish law for the defence of *provocation* rejects the concept of the reasonable man (ie the *objective* test) and instead concentrates on the accused himself (ie the *subjective* test): *People (DPP) v Noonan* [1998] 1 ILRM 154, CCA and 2 IR 439. The test is whether it was *reasonably possible* (not whether it was *likely* or *probable*) that the provocation triggered the action, given the accused's state of mind and circumstances. It has been held that it is a well-settled law that the test to be applied to a plea of provocation is entirely *subjective*: *The People (DPP) v Keith Kelly* [2000] 2 IR 1, CCA and 2 ILRM 426.

In order for the defence of provocation to be left to the jury, there must be evidence of a sudden and temporary loss of control, rendering the accused so subject to passion as to make him for the moment not master of his mind: *People (DPP) v Davis* [2001] 2

ILRM 65, CCA and 1 IR 146. It is a matter for the trial judge in the first instance to decide whether there was any evidence on which such a defence could properly be allowed to be considered by the jury: *The People (DPP) v James McDonagh* [2001] 3 IR 201, CCA. The threshold is low for the defence to be allowed to be considered by the jury: *Kelly v DPP* (2004) Irish Times, 7 February, CCA.

Provocation may reduce murder to manslaughter, notwithstanding that there was intention on the part of the accused to kill or cause serious injury: *DPP v Bambrick* [1999] 2 ILRM 71, CCA.

The Law Reform Commission has provisionally recommended that the defence of provocation be retained but in a modified form: *Consultation Paper on Homicide: The Plea of Provocation* (LRC CP 27, 2003). This would involve a shift away from the current 'excuse-inspired' emphasis on the accused's loss of control, towards a focus on the conduct of the deceased which is said to have provoked the accused to the point of engaging in lethal violence. However, the courts should be in a position to take account of the accused's personal characteristics in so far as they affect the gravity of provocation. The proposed change would bring Irish law broadly in line with the law on provocation in Canada, Australia and New Zealand. [Bibliography: Charleton (4); McAuley & McCutcheon.]

proximity. There is a duty of care owed by a person to those in proximity to him. The duty is to take reasonable care that they are not injured by his acts or that they do not suffer loss as a result of his action or inaction. Racing authorities have been found to have a duty of care to persons wagering on horse races: *Madden v Irish Turf Club* [1993] ITLR (26 July) HC. See *Purtill v Athlone Urban District Council* [1968] IR 205: *McNamara v ESB* [1975] IR 1; *Nolan v Kilkenny Co Council* [1990] in 8 ILT & SJ (1990) 210., CC

proxy. A person deputed to vote for another; the instrument appointing such a person. Any member of a company who is entitled to attend and vote at a meeting of the company, may appoint someone else as his proxy to attend and vote instead of him. The proxy so appointed has the same rights as the member to speak at the meeting and to vote on a show of hands and on a poll: Companies Act 1963, s 136. A person who is both a member and a proxy can vote only

once on a show of hands: *Ernest v Loma Gold Mines* [1897] 1 Ch 1. Partial distribution of proxy invitations to some members only is prohibited (CA 1963, s 136(5)). See also RSC Ord 74, r 82 and *In the matter of Hayes Homes Ltd* (in voluntary liquidation) [2004] ITLR (26 July) HC.

A *proxy form* must be sent with the notice convening a meeting of holders of *listed* securities to each person entitled to vote at the meeting, and must conform with specified requirements eg two-way voting (ie forms which enable the shareholder to direct the proxy to vote for or against a resolution), entitlement of shareholder to appoint the proxy of his own choice: Listing Rules 2000, paras 9.26, 13.28–13.29. Similar, but more stringent, provisions regarding proxy forms apply to building societies: Building Societies Act 1989, s 72. See also Takeover Rules 2001, Part B, r 18. See POLL; VOTING AT MEETINGS.

PRSA. Personal Retirement Savings Account (qv).

PRSI. Pay related social insurance. The annual earnings ceiling up to which social insurance contributions are payable by employees was increased to €42,160 with effect from 1 January 2004: Social Welfare Act 2003, s 5. For exemption scheme for employers, see SI No 452 of 2003. [Bibliography: Bradley.] See SOCIAL INSURANCE FUND.

pseudonymous work. Means a work where the *pseudonym* adopted by the author does not reveal the identity of the author and the identity of the author is unknown: Copyright and Related Rights Act 2000, s 2(1). Copyright in a pseudonymous work expires 70 years after the date on which the work is first lawfully made available to the public, or 70 years after the death of the author where his identity becomes known during that earlier period (CRRA 2000, s 24). This applies to literary, dramatic, musical or artistic work or an original database. See also CRRA 2000, s 32. The copyright of a pseudonymous work is not infringed where it is not possible to ascertain the identity of the author by reasonable enquiry and it is reasonable to assume that the copyright has expired (CRRA 2000, s 88). See COPYRIGHT.

psychiatric damage. Under the '*aftermath doctrine*' a duty of care is imposed on a tortfeasor for psychiatric illness suffered by a person who comes upon the aftermath of an accident and is not a participant in the tort-producing event eg a person coming upon a motor accident: *McLoughlin v O'Brien* [1983] 1 AC 410. See *Fletcher v Commissioners of Public Works* (2003) Law Society Gazette, April 2003, SC and [2003] 2 ILRM 94, SC; 1 IR 465; ELR 117. See 'Psychiatric Damage in the aftermath of Fletcher' by barrister Alan Keating in *Bar Review* (December 2003) 256. See ASBESTOS; MENTAL DISTRESS; NERVOUS SHOCK.

psychiatric disorder. A mental illness; it may be a ground for the *nullity* of marriage. It has been held in a particular case that a person suffering from paranoid schizophrenia was at the time of the marriage ceremony, suffering from a psychiatric disorder of such a character that it prevented him from giving his full and informed consent to the marriage and rendered him incapable of sustaining a normal married relationship with the petitioner: *E v E* [1987] IR 147, HC. In the UK, the House of Lords has held that liability for a psychiatric illness depended on foreseeability and the relationship of proximity between the claimant and the defendant: *Alcock & Ors v Chief Constable of South Yorkshire Police* [1991] 4 All ER 907. See 'Psychiatric Injury and the Employment Appeals Tribunal: Double Bite at the Compensation Cherry?' by John Eardly BL in *Bar Review* (April 2003) 81. See MARRIAGE, NULLITY OF; MENTAL DISORDER; MENTAL TREATMENT; PERSONALITY DISORDER.

psycho-surgery. Means any surgical operation that destroys brain tissue or the functioning of brain tissue and which is performed for the purposes of ameliorating a *mental disorder* (qv): Mental Health Act 2001, s 58(6). Psycho-surgery must not be performed on a patient without the consent of the patient in writing and an authorisation of a tribunal to which the proposal has been referred by the Mental Health Commission (MHA 2001, s 58(1) and (2)). [Bibliography: Keys.]

psychotherapy. The treatment of nervous disorders by psychological methods. See *Law Society Gazette* (January/February 2004) 5.

public. The *public* means the public generally and not a particular or special class of members of the public: *Stanbridge v Healy* [1985] ILRM 290.

Public Accounts, Committee of. A committee of members of Dáil Éireann (qv)

which: (a) examines and reports to the Dáil upon the public accounts showing the appropriation of the sums granted by the Dáil to meet public expenditure; and which (b) suggests alterations and improvements in the form of the Estimates submitted to the Dáil. The committee can enquire into allegations of criminal misconduct: *Re Haughey* [1971] IR 217. Accounting officers of Departments are required to give evidence to the committee on the economy and efficiency of their Departments, and the systems, procedures and practices employed: Comptroller and Auditor General (Amendment) Act 1993, s 19.

Absolute privilege is conferred on the utterances made by members of the committee inside and outside the Houses of the Oireachtas: C & AG and Committees of the Houses of the Oireachtas (Special Provisions) Act 1998, s 11.

The chief executive of the *Human Rights Commission* is required to report, when so requested to the public accounts committee: Human Rights Commission Act 2000, s 14. The chairman of the *Dormant Accounts Fund Disbursement Board* is required, whenever required by the Public Accounts Committee, to give evidence to the PAC on any matter relating to the functions of the Board: Dormant Accounts Act 2001, s 47. See also Committees of the Houses of the Oireachtas (Compellability, Privileges and Immunity of Witnesses) Act 1997, ss 3(5) and 3(6); Ombudsman for Children Act 2002, s 18; Digital Hub Development Agency Act 2003, s 32; Personal Injuries Assessment Board Act 2003, s 65; Education for Persons with Special Educational Needs Act 2004, s 30.

public Act. A statute which has a general application as compared with a *private Act* (qv). See BILL.

public appeal, money collected in. The procedure for disposing of funds, gathered in a public appeal, which becomes impossible to apply for the purpose for which it was collected, or where a surplus remains, is provided for by the Charities Act 1961, s 48. See COLLECTION.

public auditor. Means a public auditor for the purposes of the Industrial and Provident Societies Act 1893 to 1978 and the Friendly Societies Acts 1896 to 1993: Companies Act 1990, s 182 as amended by Companies (Auditing and Accounting) Act 2003, s 34. See PRACTISING CERTIFICATE; REGISTER OF AUDITORS.

public authority. For the purposes of environmental protection, a Minister, a local authority, harbour authority, health board, a body established by statute, a company in which all the shares are held by a Minister, the Commissioners of Public Works in Ireland: Environmental Protection Agency Act 1992, s 3(1) as substituted by Protection of the Environment Act 2003, s 5. See also Local Government Act 1991, s 2(1); Heritage Act 1995, s 2(1); Local Government Act 2001, s 2(1). See ENVIRONMENTAL PROTECTION AGENCY.

public bill. See BILL.

public body. All civil service departments, health boards, local authorities, a wide-range of public offices and such other bodies as are so prescribed by regulations: Freedom of Information Act 1997, Sch 1. A public body is required to prepare and publish a reference book containing certain specified information eg: (a) a general description of its structure and organisation, functions, powers and duties, any services it provides for the public and the procedures by which any such services may be availed of by the public; (b) a general description of the records it holds and information to facilitate exercise of the right of access; (c) information on the internal rules relied upon by the body in exercising its decision-making functions (FIA 1997, ss 15–16 as amended by Freedom of Information (Amendment) Act 2003, ss 10–11). A person has a right to information regarding acts of a public body affecting him; it is a right to receive from the body a statement, in writing, giving the reason for the act and any findings on any material issues of fact made for the purposes of the act (FIA 1997, s 18 as amended by FI(A)A 2003, s 13). Regulations prescribe certain classes of individuals who may apply under s 18: see SI No 266 of 2003.

Provision has been made to impose duties on specified public bodies with regard to the official languages of the State eg duties to use the official languages on their stationery, to publish certain documents in both official languages simultaneously, and to prepare schemes to promote the use by the public body of the Irish language: Official Languages Act 2003, ss 9–19 and Sch 1. There is also provision for the establishment of a *scheme of compensation* under which a public body would be required to pay to a person a sum of money in respect of the failure of the public body to comply with the provisions of the Act (OLA 2003, s 27). See also COIMISINÉIR TEANGA, AN; PERSONAL INFORMATION; INFORMATION, ACCESS TO; DISABLED PERSON AND INFORMATION.

public company. See COMPANY, PUBLIC.

public dance licence. A licence granted under the Public Dance Halls Act 1935, s 6. In order to prevent or detect drug trafficking offences, a garda may enter, whether in uniform or not, any place in respect of which a public dancing licence is in force (PDHA 1935, s 13A as inserted by Criminal Justice (Drug Trafficking) Act 1996, s 9). There are provisions for the disqualification, suspension and revocation of a public dance licence for drug trafficking offences and for permitting premises to be used for drug-related activity: Licensing (Combating Drug Abuse) Act 1997. For District Court procedure on licensing, see DCR 1997 Ord 86. See FUNCTUS OFFICIO; RAVE DANCE.

public document. A document which is made for the purpose of the public making use of it and being able to refer to it: *Lord Blackburn in Sturla v Freccia* [1880] 5 App. Cas. 623.

public documents, evidence of. Statements appearing in public or official documents are admissible in proof of the facts recorded therein. Statements in public registers are admissible in proof of the facts recorded where the document is one required by law to be kept for public information, and the entry has been made promptly and by the proper officer. See Rules of the Superior Courts (Proof of Foreign Diplomatic, Consular and Public Documents) 1999, SI No 3 of 1999. See BANKERS' BOOKS; DOCUMENTARY EVIDENCE; NATIONAL ARCHIVES.

public execution. The carrying out in public of the court's sentence of death. Public executions were abolished by the Capital Punishment Amendment Act 1868. See DEATH PENALTY.

public exhibition of certain works. No infringement of any right created in relation to an artistic or literary work occurs by reason of the placing on display the work, or a copy thereof, in a place or premises to which members of the public have access: Copyright and Related Rights Act 2000, s 40(7A) inserted by Copyright and Related Rights (Amendment) Act 2004, s 1. The purpose of the Act is to remove any doubt as to the right of any person to place literary or artistic works protected by copyright on public exhibition without committing a breach of copyright as provided for by CRRA 2000, Pt II. The amendment was introduced to ensure that a major exhibition of James Joyce's work by the National Library in June 2004, to mark Bloomsday 1904, was not blocked by a copyright dispute.

public health. The EC is required to contribute towards ensuring a high level of human health protection by encouraging co-operation between the member states and, if necessary, lending support to their action: *Treaty establishing the European Community*, art 152 of the consolidated (2002) version. Community action must complement national policies, and be directed towards the prevention of diseases, in particular the major health scourges, including drug dependence, by promoting research into their causes and their transmission, as well as health information and education. For the *European Health Management Association*, see website: *www.ehma.org*. See CLOSURE ORDER; COMMITTEE OF THE REGIONS; IMPROVEMENT NOTICE, FOOD; PROHIBITION ORDER; WORLD HEALTH ORGANISATION.

public holidays. Days on which an employee is entitled to a paid day off work, or an extra day's annual leave (qv) or an extra day's pay, as the employer may decide. Public holidays are 1 January, St Patrick's Day, Easter Monday, Christmas Day, St Stephen's Day, the first Monday in May, June and August, the last Monday in October. The paid day off may be on the day of the public holiday or within a month of that day. The qualifying period for entitlement in respect of a public holiday is at least 40 hours work during the five weeks before the holiday. Certain *Church holidays* (qv) may be substituted for certain public holidays.

The Employment Appeals Tribunal has ruled that employees are entitled to be paid for public holidays which fall during maternity leave: *Forde v Des Gibney Ltd* P8/1985. See *Ocean Manpower Ltd v MPGWU* [1998] ELR 299, LC; *Cadbury Ireland v SIPTU* [1999] ELR 202, LC. See Organisation of Working Time Act 1997, ss 21–22 and Sch 2; SI No 475 of 1997; SI No 10 of 1999. See BANK HOLIDAYS.

public indecency. See INDECENCY.

public inquiry. See COMPULSORY PURCHASE ORDER; TRIBUNALS OF INQUIRY.

public interest. See PARENS PATRIAE; PUBLIC POLICY; RELIGIOUS FREEDOM.

public interest privilege. In a particular defamation case, the Supreme Court held that to order discovery of a garda file, assembled in an investigation of an abduction and murder which was still a live investigation, would be contrary to the public interest: *McDonald v RTE* [2001] 2 ILRM 1, SC and 1 IR 355. The High Court has held that it is a good defence to a libel action if the defendant can show that he followed good practice in publishing material which is of sufficient public interest: Sir Louis Blom-Cooper QC (2003) Irish Times, 7 August, HC. The tests to be applied include: the seriousness of the allegations, the steps taken to verify the facts, the tone of the article, whether it contained the gist of the wronged person's side of the story, the urgency of the matter, the source of the information and its status.

public international law. See INTERNATIONAL LAW.

public justice. Justice must be administered in courts in public save in such special and limited cases as may be prescribed by law: 1937 Constitution, art 34(1). The law prescribes that the general public may be excluded if a criminal offence is of an indecent or obscene nature: Criminal Justice Act 1951; or in cases involving matrimonial matters or lunacy or infancy matters; or urgent applications for *habeas corpus*, bail, injunctions; or involving the disclosure of a secret manufacturing process: Courts (Supplemental Provisions) Act 1961, s 45(1).

Provision is made for the anonymity of a child in any proceedings for an offence against a child or where a child is a witness in any such proceedings: Children Act 2001, s 252. In addition, in certain cases the press may report a case but have limitations placed on disclosure of the identity of the parties eg the identity of the complainant, and of the accused until convicted, is prohibited in rape cases: Criminal Law (Rape) Act 1980, ss 7–8; the identity of the accused and of the person against whom the offence of incest is alleged to have been committed: Criminal Law (Incest Proceedings) Act 1995, s 3. See *Beamish & Crawford Ltd v Crowley* [1969] IR 142; *Irish Times Ltd v Ireland* [1998] 1

IR 359, SC; *de Gartori v Smithwick* [2000] 1 ILRM 463, SC. See DCR 1997 Ord 14.

The President of the High Court has said that judges who privately read papers relating to public hearings of court cases were not strictly administering justice in public: *Irish Times*, 17 September 2002. He said that affidavits read in such a way and not read in open court, may in such circumstances be made available to the press. In a particular case, the allegations sought to be pleaded in a proposed amended defence, were read in private as they were were of a serious nature: *Walsh v Harrison* [2003] 2 ILRM 161, HC. See EUROPEAN CONVENTION ON HUMAN RIGHTS; IN CAMERA; MCKENZIE FRIEND.

public law. The area of domestic law dealing primarily with the relations between the State and the individual e g constitutional law and criminal law. See PRIVATE LAW.

public lighting. The maintenance of a public road (qv) includes the provision and maintenance of public lighting: Roads Act 1993, s 2(4).

public limited company. See COMPANY, PUBLIC LIMITED.

public local inquiry. The local inquiry which the Minister for the Environment and Local Government is empowered to hold, by an inspector appointed by the Minister, for the purposes of any functions conferred on the Minister or in relation to the performance of the functions of a local authority: Local Government Act 2001, ss 212–214. See LOCAL AUTHORITY, DISSOLUTION OF. See also MOTORWAY; ROAD DEVELOPMENT, PROPOSED.

public mischief. An offence committed by a person who wilfully interferes with the course of justice or with the police, by an act or attempt, which tends to the prejudice of the community e g false statements to the police with the objective of wasting their time. The common law offence still subsists despite a similar offence created by statute: *The People (DPP) v Carew* [1981] ILRM 91 and Criminal Law Act 1976, s 12. See O'Malley in 7 ILT & SJ (1989) 243.

public morals. Any practice which tends to injure public morals is a common law offence: *R v Rogier* 2 D & R 435. Conspiracy to corrupt public morals is an offence (formerly, a misdemeanour) indictable in common law: *AG (SPUC) v Open Door Counselling Ltd* [1987] ILRM 447. See O'Malley in 7 ILT & SJ (1989) 243. [Bibliography: Daly CB.] See also PATENT, REVOCATION OF.

public music licence. A licence granted under the Public Health Acts Amendment Act 1890, s 51. For District Court procedure on licensing, see DCR 1997 Ord 87. See FUNCTUS OFFICIO.

public notice. In the context of a local authority, means a notice published in at least one newspaper circulating in the local authority's administrative area: Local Government Act 2001, s 2(1).

public nuisance. See NUISANCE, PUBLIC.

Public Offers Directive. The Directive (EEC) 89/298 co-ordinating the requirements for the drawing up, scrutiny and distribution of the prospectus to be published when transferable securities are offered to the public: Listing Rules 2000 (Definitions). See PROSPECTUS.

Public Offices Commission. See ELECTION EXPENSES; POLITICAL DONATION.

public order and morality. The term used to describe an overriding condition, subject to which many rights, both constitutional and statutory, may be limited, e g see ASSEMBLY, FREEDOM OF; EXPRESSION, FREEDOM OF; PATENT, REVOCATION OF.

public order offences. A wide range of offences e g intoxication in a public place, riot, violent disorder, affray, assault, trespass on building, wilful obstruction, entering building with intention to commit an offence, failure to comply with a direction of a garda: Criminal Justice (Public Order) Act 1994. See Criminal Justice Bill 2004, s 29. See EXCLUSION ORDER.

public park. See PARKS, PUBLIC.

public place. (1) Any street, road, seashore or other place to which the public have access, whether as of right or by permission and whether subject to or free of charge: Planning and Development Act 2000, s 2(1).

(2) Any public road, and any street, road or other place to which the public have access with vehicles whether as of right or by permission and whether subject to or free of charge: Road Traffic Act 1961, s 3(1) as substituted by Road Traffic Act 1994, s 49(1)(iv) overturning *DPP v Molloy* [1994] 1 IR 583, under which it had been held that a street or place to which access with vehicles was prohibited was not a public place e g a street which has been pedestrianised and closed to traffic. A *pedestrian way* is now a public place.

It is an essential ingredient of many road traffic offences that they be committed in a *public place*. See *Stanbridge v Healy* [1985] ILRM 290; *DPP v Joyce* [1985] ILRM 206; *Montgomery v Loney* [1959] NI 171; *Lynch v Lynch* [1996] 1 ILRM 311, HC. See also Environmental Protection Act 1992, s 3(1); Criminal Law (Sexual Offences) Act 1993, s 1(1); Criminal Justice (Public Order) Act 1994, s 3; Control of Horses Act 1996, s 2(1).

public policy. The principle in law that a person will not be permitted to do that which has a tendency to be injurious to the public, or against the public good. Certain acts are said to be contrary to public policy when the law refuses to enforce or recognise them on the grounds that they are injurious to the interest of the State or the community eg the law will not enforce an illegal contract, or permit evidence to be given which would affect the security of the State. See *Egerton v Brownlow* [1853] 4HL Cas l; *Stanhope v Hospitals Trust Ltd* [1936] Ir Jur Rep 25. See also Contractual Obligations (Applicable Law) Act 1991, Sch 1, art 16; Refugee Act 1996, ss 4(2) and 17(2).

One of the defences to the recognition and enforcement of a foreign judgment is that it is contrary to public policy: Jurisdiction of Courts and Enforcement of Judgments Act 1998. The *Brussels I Regulation* on the recognition and enforcement of judgments in civil and commercial matters, replaces the 1998 Act as from 1 March 2002 for all EU States except Denmark: EC (Civil and Commercial Judgments) Regulations 2002, SI No 52 of 2002. The defence, to be successful, must now show that the judgment is 'manifestly' contrary to public policy (Regulation, art 34).

public policy, evidence excluded by. Evidence of matters which may not be given on the grounds that disclosure would affect the security of the State or the administration of justice eg:

(a) affairs of state – however, a refusal by a Minister to withhold production of a document on public interest grounds is capable of review by the courts: *Murphy v Dublin Corporation & Minister for Local Government* [1972] IR 215; *Geraghty v Minister for Local Government* [1975] IR 300; see also *Cully v NBFC Ltd* [1984] ILRM 683; *Incorporated Law Society v Minister for Justice* [1987] ILRM 42; *Director of Consumer Affairs v Sugar Distributors Ltd* [1991]

ILRM 395, HC; *Ambiorix Ltd v Minister for the Environment* [1992] ILRM 209, SC;

(b) information which would disclose channels through which information is obtained for the detection of crimes: *Attorney-General v Simpson* [1959] IR 105; but see *DPP v Holly* [1984] ILRM 149;

(c) documents specifically exempted from production by the legislature eg court of inquiry reports of the Defence Forces, board of inquiry report of UN eg see *O'Brien v Ireland* [1995] 1 ILRM 22, HC and 1 IR 568;

(d) previously at common law, statements by parents tending to bastardise their offspring, known as the rule in *Russell v Russell* [1924] AC 687, which rule no longer applies; the evidence of a husband or wife is now admissible in any proceedings to prove that marital intercourse did or did not take place between them during any period: Status of Children Act 1987, s 47; *S v S* [1983] IR 68; *AS v RB* [1984] ILRM 66;

(e) judicial disclosures eg matters which arise before judges or between jurors.

A willing witness will not be permitted to give evidence on matters if public policy requires its exclusion; also secondary evidence of the matter is not permitted.

public private partnership arrangement. An arrangement between a person (a *partner*) for the performance of the *functions* of a specified *State authority* in relation to, for example, the design and construction of an asset, together with the operation of services relating to it and the provision of finance, if required, for such design, construction and operation: State Authorities (Public Private Partnerships Arrangements) Act 2002, s 3(1)(a)(i).

The Act provides certainty as to the power of State authorities to enter into PPP arrangements with private sector partners. A number of combinations of arrangements are provided for. Also the Act applies retrospectively to PPP arrangements entered into prior to the enactment of the 2002 Act (SA(PPPA)A 2002, s 5). A PPP arrangement confers on the partner the functions of the State authority while, notwithstanding the arrangement, the functions continue also to be vested in the State authority (SA(PPPA)A 2002, s 4).

In introducing the legislation in the Dáil, the Minister of State said: 'International experience clearly shows that real benefits can be gained from PPPs. They can give better value for money compared to traditional procurement by transferring risks from the public to the private sector. PPPs can deliver improved efficiency in the adoption of whole life costing of services and innovation in the design, building and operation of assets': Dáil report, 27 November 2001. See also National Development Finance Agency Act 2002, s 1(1). See NATIONAL DEVELOPMENT FINANCE AGENCY; PUBLIC INVESTMENT PROJECT.

Public Procurement Directive. The directive which prescribes the procedures to be implemented for the award of public works contracts: Council Directive (EEC) 93/37 implemented in the State by the EC (Award of Public Works Contracts) Regulations 1992 and 1994, SIs No 36 of 1992 and 293 of 1994. Contract notices must be advertised through the EU with sufficient information to enable contractors to determine if the contract is of interest to them.

The criteria for the award of a contract must be either the lowest price or the most *economically advantageous* tender (in which case the criteria must be set out eg price, period for completion, running cost, profitability, technical merit). The procedures must be followed when the contract value exceeds the relevant thresholds in the Directive. In judicial review the courts must render effective the principles of public procurement; they are not required to apply a standard of judicial review different to that applied in a comparable situation before the European Court of Justice: *SIAC v Mayo County Council* [2002] 2 ILRM 401, SC and 3 IR 148. See also *Stewart's Foundation Ltd v Minister for Tourism* [1999] 2 ILRM 522, HC; *Whelan Group (Ennis) Ltd v Clare County Council* [2001] 1 IR 717, HC.

There is now provision for the submission of tenders for *public service contracts*, by means other than writing directly or by post, provided particular conditions are met eg the tender is opened after the time limit for its submission has expired: European Communities (Award of Public Service Contracts) (Amendment) Regulations 2001, SI No 334 of 2001. Similar provisions apply in the case of *public supply contracts* (SI No 611 of 2001) and *public work contracts* (SI No 612 of 2001). For new standard forms for mandatory use in publishing notices on public contracts,

see EC (Public Contract Notices) (Standard Forms) Regulations 2002, SI No 343 of 2002.

An application for the review by the courts of a decision to award a public contract (ie service, supply, utilities or works contracts) must be made *at the earliest opportunity* and within three months from the date when grounds for the application first arose, unless the court considers that there are good reasons for extending the period: RSC Ord 84A, r 4 as inserted by SI No 374 of 1998. The onus is on the party seeking the extension of time to demonstrate on an objective basis that there is an explanation for the delay and a justifiable reason for it: *Dekra Éireann Teo v Minister for the Environment* [2002] 2 ILRM 30, HC. The Supreme Court, in this case, held that reference under r 4 to the requirement that the application be made 'at the earliest opportunity' indicated a degree of urgency in applications of this type: [2003] 2 ILRM 210, SC and 2 IR 270; *Law Society Gazette* (October 2003) 53. The court held that Dekra had failed to explain the whole delay and had not provided the court with a 'good reason', a justifiable excuse for the delay.

public prosecutor. See DIRECTOR OF PUBLIC PROSECUTIONS.

public records. See NATIONAL ARCHIVES.

public right. A right conferred on the public eg the right of owners and occupiers of premises to cause drains to empty into a public sewer without charge: *Ballybay Meat Exports Ltd v Monaghan Co Council* [1990] ILRM 864, HC. See however SEWER.

public road. (1) A road over which a public right of way exists and the responsibility for the maintenance of which lies on a road authority: Roads Act 1993, s 2(1). A road authority may, by order, declare any road over which a public right of way exists to be a public road, having satisfied itself that the road is of general public utility, having considered the financial implications and any objections to a public advertisement of its proposed declaration (RA 1993, s 11).

A public road is a national road, regional road, or a local road; it may also be a motorway, busway, or protected road (RA 1993, ss 2(1), 10, 43, 44, 45). Only a local road requires a formal declaration (RA 1993, s 11(4)). A road constructed in future by a road authority is a public road without declaration unless the authority decides otherwise (RA 1993, s 11(7)). See

Concorde (Roadhouse) Ltd v Dublin County Council [1978] HC.

The public has the right to pass and repass on a public road, over the whole surface including the *via trita* (qv). The owner of land beside a public road is presumed to be the owner of the soil up to one-half of the road and has the right of access to and from the road: *Holland v Dublin County Council* [1979] 113 ILTR 1. This right of access is subject to the public right of passage. However, these rights are restricted in terms of access or traffic in the case of a motorway and a busway, and may be restricted on a protected road.

A person who causes damage to a public road by *excessive* weight or *extraordinary traffic* is liable to pay the extraordinary expenses incurred by the local authority in the repair thereof: Road Traffic Act 1961, s 17; *Hill v Thomas* [1893] 2 QB 333. It is an offence for any person without lawful authority or consent of a road authority to deface a public road, damage it, excavate it, permit dung or urine from an animal to be left on a public road (RA 1993, s 13(10)).

Local authorities and other public authorities are authorised by statute to interfere with public roads, but they must use reasonable care and skill eg *Johnson v Dublin Corporation* [1961] IR 24. They must also obtain the appropriate consent (RA 1993, s 53). See *Giant's Causeway Company Ltd v AG and Ors* 5 NI JR 301; *Merriman v Dublin Corporation* [1993] ILRM 58, HC. See Minister for Arts etc Act 1998, s 3(3).

(2) A *public road* as regards planning law, has the same meaning as in the Roads Act 1993: Planning and Development Act 2000, s 2(1). A licence is required for the positioning of a range of items on, under, over or along a public road eg an advertising structure, a vending machine, a telephone kiosk or pedestal, a town or landscape map, or overground electronic communications infrastructure (PDA 2000, s 254(1) and Communications Regulation Act 2002, s 54). A licence is not required if planning permission has been obtained (PDA 2000, s 254(2)). Also prior written consent from the relevant road authority is required in order for a network operator to be permitted to carry out road works for the establishment of underground electronic communications infrastructure: Communications Regulation Act 2002, s 53. See CARAVAN; CYCLEWAY; MISFEA-

SANCE; NONFEASANCE; MOTORWAY; ROAD RACE; ROAD USER'S DUTY; SIGN; TREE.

public road, abandonment of. A road authority is empowered to abandon a public road, by order, following notice to the public and consideration of objections: Roads Act 1993, s 12. Ministerial approval is required in respect of a national or regional road (RA 1993, s 12(4)). Following abandonment, the road authority ceases to be responsible for the maintenance of the road, but this does not affect any public right of way over such road (RA 1993, s 12(5)) unless that right of way is itself extinguished (RA 1993, s 73).

A public road may be extinguished by natural causes, such as the encroachment of the sea or by landslips, or if public access to it is cut off by the destruction, or lawful extinction, of the only public roads leading into it: *R v Greenhow (Inhabitants)* 1 QBD 703; *Bailey v Jamieson* 1 CPD 329. See WAY, RIGHT OF.

public sector issuer. A State or regional and local authority which wishes to issue certain debt securities must comply with specified rules: Listing Rules 2000, ch 22, as amended by Irish Stock Exchange Ltd.

public service identity. Provision has been made for the introduction of a new concept of a 'Public Service Identity' which will act as a unique and secure identifier for public service customers: Social Welfare (Consolidation) Act 1993, s 223 as amended by Social Welfare (Miscellaneous Provisions) Act 2002, s 12 and SI No 209 of 2003. The elements included in the identity are, *inter alia*, the person's name, address, date of birth, sex, nationality and the person's *Personal Public Service Number* (*PPS*), as the latter number may not be sufficient by itself to enable customers to access a particular public service. The number of agencies authorised by legislation to use the PPS as a public service identifier has been extended: Social Welfare (Miscellaneous Provisions) Act 2003, s 10; Personal Injuries Assessment Board Act 2003, s 84; Social Welfare (Miscellaneous Provisions) Act 2004, s 11. See PERSONAL PUBLIC SERVICE NUMBER.

public service obligation. As regards gas, an obligation placed on natural gas undertakings which takes account of general social, economic and environmental factors: Gas (Interim) (Regulation) Act 2002, s 21(9). This can include matters relating to security, including security of supply and technical or public safety, regularity, quality and price of supplies, and environmental protection (G(I)(R) A 2002, s 21(1)). There is provision for a possible *levy* being charged by the undertaking on customers to cover any additional costs in meeting public service obligations (G(I)(R) A 2002, s 21(2)).

public service pension scheme. Means an occupational pension scheme or pension arrangement, by whatever name called, for any part of the public service which: (a) is provided for under the Superannuation Acts 1834 to 1963 or any other enactment to like effect, or (b) is made by a relevant Minister: Public Service Superannuation (Miscellaneous Provisions) Act 2004, s 1(1). This Act removes the compulsory retirement age for *new entrants* to the public service (PSS(MP)A 2004, s 3). It also lays down a minimum age of 65 at which a pension may be paid to *new entrants* (PSS(MP)A 2004, s 10). This does not affect the payment of a death benefit or early retirement on ill health grounds.

A *new entrant* is a person who takes up appointment to a public service post on or after 1 April 2004 in the civil service, local authorities, defence forces, Garda Síochána, education and health sectors, and non-commercial State sponsored bodies, or as members of the Houses of the Oireachtas. There are exceptions for certain posts in the defence forces, Garda Síochána, prison service and the fire service. The restriction on reckoning of service for pension purposes after a person reaches a specified age is removed for *new entrants*, subject to the person not exceeding the maximum pension threshold (PSS(MP)A 2004, s 13). These pension changes have been estimated to give a savings yield of some €300m in current terms in 30–40 years time. The 2004 Act does not affect the terms of employment of those employed in the public service prior to 1 April 2004. See RETIREMENT, EARLY.

public service recruitment. Under draft legislation, it is proposed to empower government departments and other public service bodies to recruit staff directly as well as through a centralised system: Public Service (Recruitment and Appointments) Bill 2003. The purpose of the Bill is to provide a modern and efficient framework for public service recruitment which will allow for increased flexibility while maintaining the current high standards of probity.

The Bill repeals the Civil Service Commissioners Act 1956 and introduces a new framework for recruitment for the Civil Service, An Garda Síochána and other public service organisations who heretofore used the services of the *Local Appointments Commissioners* in the recruitment of their staff. The framework consists of an oversight body to be known as the *Commission for Public Service Appointments* (CPSA), a centralised recruitment body to be known as the *Public Appointments Service* (PAS), and a system of voluntary recruitment licensing. The PAS will automatically be granted a recruitment licence by the CPSA and will make its services available to government departments and offices as a centralised recruitment body in the same way as the *Civil Service Commission* has done heretofore.

Under the voluntary licensing system, Secretaries General and Heads of Office may choose to apply to the CPSA for a recruitment licence in order to recruit staff directly themselves, rather than using the PAS. The licensing system may later be extended to other public service bodies by order of the Minister for Finance, in consultation with any relevant Ministers. Eligible public service bodies will be granted licences to recruit if they can satisfy certain terms and conditions which will be specified by the CPSA under the Bill. There will be no obligation upon departments or offices to apply for recruitment licences and the services of the PAS will be made available to those who do not wish to recruit themselves.

Recruitment under licence will be subject to codes of practice which will be drawn up by the CPSA. These will prescribe the necessary standards of fairness, equality and probity for all those who recruit under the Bill and will set out requirements in relation to the conduct of candidates at competitions, in order to ensure that a standardised approach to recruitment is taken by licence holders.

public service vehicle. A mechanically propelled vehicle (qv) used for the carriage of persons for reward: Road Traffic Act 1961, s 3. A *large* public service vehicle is one having seating passenger accommodation for more than eight persons exclusive of the driver. For licensing of public service vehicles, see Road Traffic (Public Service Vehicles) (Licensing) Regulations 1978, SI No 292 of 1978 as amended by SI No 272 of 1991. Licences may be granted for wheelchair accessible public hire vehicles, SI No 172 of 1992. See also Road Traffic (Public Service Vehicles) (Amendment) Regulations 2002, SI No 411 of 2002.

Provision has been made for the regulation, including licensing, of *small* public service vehicles by the Commission for Taxi Regulation; the regulation of *large* public service vehicles continues to be the responsibility of the Minister: Taxi Regulation Act 2003, ss 33–52. [Bibliography: Pierce (2).] See COMMISSION FOR TAXI REGULATION.

public trust. A charitable trust. See CHARITIES.

public waste collector. A local or other sanitary authority (qv) for the purposes of the Local Government (Sanitary Services) Acts 1878 to 1964. See WASTE OPERATION.

public works. See COMMISSIONERS OF PUBLIC WORKS; PUBLIC PROCUREMENT DIRECTIVE; STATE AUTHORITY.

public worship, disturbance of. The offence of disturbing public worship in a riotous, violent, or indecent manner which is being held in any church, churchyard or burial ground. See Ecclesiastic Courts Jurisdiction Act 1860, s 2; Offences Against the Person Act 1861, s 36. See WORSHIP, PUBLIC.

publication. (1) In relation to defamation (qv), *publication* is the making known of the defamatory matter to some person other than the person of whom it is made. Any person who makes the defamatory words, who repeats them, who distributes them, or who disseminates them, publishes them. An *innocent publication*, which is a ground for making an *offer of amends* (qv), means: (a) that the publisher did not intend to publish the words about the party aggrieved, and that he did not know of circumstances under which they might be understood to refer to the party aggrieved; or (b) that the words were not defamatory on the face of them and the publisher did not know of circumstances under which the words might be understood to be defamatory of the party aggrieved: Defamation Act 1961, s 21(5). In either case the publisher must have exercised all reasonable

care in relation to the publication. See RSC Ord 36, r 36.

(2) As regard inventions, prior publication can destroy the *novelty* required for the grant of a patent. An invention must be new ie not forming part of the *state of the art*: Patents Act 1992, s 11. *State of the art* comprises everything made available to the public (whether in the State or elsewhere) by means of a written or oral description, by use or in any other way, before the date of filing of the patent application.

(3) In relation to copyright, see PUBLISHED EDITION.

publication, right of. There is a constitutional right to publish information which is not a breach of copyright: *The A-G for England and Wales v Brandon Books* [1987] ILRM 135. However, certain statutes prohibit publication or broadcast of certain matters eg matters likely to lead members of the public to identify: (a) the complainant (or the accused until convicted) in rape cases: Criminal Law (Rape) Act 1981, ss 7–8 and Criminal Law (Rape) Amendment Act 1990, s 14; or (b) a child in care proceedings: Child Care Act 1991, s 31(1). Additionally, no person may publish any information about a proceedings in the District Court in relation to the sending forward for trial of an accused, other than that proceedings in relation to a specified charge have been brought against the named person and the decision resulting: Criminal Procedure Act 1967, s 4J inserted by Criminal Justice Act 1999, s 9. See also IN CAMERA; PUBLIC JUSTICE.

public contract. See PUBLIC PROCUREMENT DIRECTIVE.

public investment project. Includes projects involving *public private partnership arrangements* (qv): National Development Finance Agency Act 2002, s 1(1). See NATIONAL DEVELOPMENT FINANCE AGENCY; SPECIAL PURPOSE COMPANY.

publicci juris. [Of public right.]

publicity. Improper publicity of a trial in the media, or even pre-trial publicity, may interfere with the constitutional right of an accused to a fair trial. The accused, however, would have to establish that it is not possible to avoid such unfairness by the trial judge giving appropriate directions and rulings to the jury: *Z v DPP* [1994] 2 ILRM 481, SC.

In a similar judgment, the High Court refused to prevent the trial of Mr George Redmond, former Dublin assistant county manager, on corruption charges; the judge said that it had been conceded on behalf of Mr Redmond, that it would be possible for the trial judge, before empanelling any jury, to warn that no person should serve who, because of the publicity, felt they could not deal fairly or in an unbiased way with the case: *Irish Times*, 31 October 2002.

The Court of Criminal Appeal has held that the perception that the courts never stop a trial on the grounds of adverse media publicity was wrong: *DPP v Nevin* (14 March 2003, unreported) CCA. The trial judge has a discretion in the matter and the appeal court should not interfere with that discretion unless it was exercised wrongly. There was a big difference between a one-day trial taking place immediately after adverse publicity and a 40-day trial.

Prejudicial publicity of an accused (eg repeated photographs of the accused wearing handcuffs and chained to a prison officer) may be capable of amounting to contempt of court: *People (DPP) v Davis* [2001] 2 ILRM 65, CCA and 1 IR 146. See *D v DPP* [1994] 2 IR 465, SC. See Law Reform Commission *Consultation Paper on Public Inquiries including Tribunals of Inquiry* (LRC CP 22, 2003). See CORRUPTION; FAIR TRIAL; STAY OF PROCEEDINGS.

publish. See PUBLICATION.

published edition. In relation to the copyright in the *typographical arrangement of a published edition*, means a published edition of the whole or any part of one or more literary, dramatic or musical works or original databases: Copyright and Related Rights Act 2000, s 2(1). The author of a typographical arrangement of a published edition includes the publisher (CRRA 2000, s 21(e)). Copyright subsists in the typographical arrangement of published editions (CRRA 2000, s 17(2)(c)). The copyright expires 50 years after the date on which it is first lawfully made available to the public (CRRA 2000, s 29). See BOOK AND LIBRARY; COPYRIGHT, QUALIFICATION FOR.

puffer. See AUCTION SALES.

puisne. [Later born; younger.]

puisne mortgage. An equitable mortgage created out of the mortgagor's equity of redemption (qv): *Antrim County Land, Building and Investment Co Ltd v Stewart* [1904] 2 IR 357. Where a redemption suit is brought by a *puisne* mortgagee, the costs

of each prior mortgage are added to his security, and the total is paid, with interest, according to the respective priority of each mortgage. See *Hilliard v Moriarty* [1894] 1 IR 316. See REDEMPTION.

punctuation. The division of words in a document by stops and commas etc. The sense of a document is to be collected from the words and the context and not from the punctuation: *Sandford v Raikes* [1916] 1 Mer 646.

punishment. Sentence; the penalty inflicted by a court on a convicted offender. It is the primary sanction of the criminal law. The penalty may be: (a) formerly, the death penalty for capital murder or treason; now, imprisonment for life, of not less than 40 years, for aggravated murder and treason: Criminal Justice Act 1990, s 4; (b) simple imprisonment without hard labour; (c) a money fine; (d) an order to pay compensation; (e) a community service order (qv); (f) a probation order; (g) formerly, imprisonment with hard labour (*The People v Giles* [1974] IR 422); (h) formerly, penal servitude (*The State (Jones) v O'Donovan* [1973] IR 329).

Unless a sentence is *fixed by law*, a court is empowered to impose a fine in lieu of or in addition to dealing with the offender in any other way: Criminal Law Act 1997, s 10(3). A person convicted on indictment of an *attempt* to commit an offence cannot have a penalty imposed greater than that for the completed offence (CLA 1997, s 10(2)). Also where no specified maximum sentence is provided for in any enactment for an offence, the maximum sentence is two years' imprisonment (CLA 1997, s 10)).

A person must not be punished twice for what is essentially a single incident; this however does not prevent *alternative* charges being brought against an accused: Interpretation Act 1937, s 14; *O'Brien v District Judge Pattwell* [1994] 2 ILRM 465, SC. In relation to *parole*, a sentence of imprisonment may be reactivated after its original currency has expired, but there must be fairness of procedure in relation to such re-activation: *Cunningham v Governor of Mountjoy Prison* [1987] ILRM 34.

A District Court is empowered to impose consecutive sentences up to a maximum of two years' imprisonment: Criminal Justice Act 1984, s 12. The Court of Criminal Appeal is empowered to review unduly lenient sentences: Criminal Justice Act 1993, s 2. See REVIEW OF SENTENCE. See Law Reform Commission *Report on Sentencing* (LRC 53, 1996) and Consultation Paper (C-1993). See Ní Raifeartaigh in 11 ILT & SJ (1993) 101; O'Malley in 11 ILT & SJ (1993) 201. [Bibliography: Canny (5); O'Mahony; O'Malley (3).] See CHARACTER; CONCURRENT SENTENCES; COMPENSATION ORDER; CONSECUTIVE SENTENCES; CONVICTION, EVIDENCE OF; GUILTY; HANGING; LIFE IMPRISONMENT; PARDON; PRISONER, TRANSFER OF; PREVENTATIVE DETENTION; PROBATION OF OFFENDERS; MITIGATING FACTORS; RAPE; RELEASE, TEMPORARY; REMISSION; SENTENCE; SUCCEED, UNWORTHINESS TO; VICTIM IMPACT REPORT.

punishment, objective of. The object of passing sentence is not merely to deter the criminal from committing a crime again but to induce the criminal, in so far as possible, to turn to an honest life: *The People v O'Driscoll* [1972] Frewen 351, CCA. The particular punishment is subject to the principle of proportionality; the sentence must match the circumstances of the offence and the relevant personal circumstances of the defendant, the likelihood of a reoccurrence of misconduct on release, and the prospect of rehabilitation: *DPP v WC* [1994] 1 ILRM 321, CCC; *People (DPP) v M* [1994] 2 ILRM 541, SC and 3 IR 306.

The general impact of a crime on a victim is a factor in sentencing, but the key issues are as stated, as criminal law is an action between the State and the offender, rather than between the offender and the victim (*DPP v M* case). However, a court is required to take into account in determining the sentence, the effect of certain offences on the victim; the offences concerned are sexual offences and offences involving violence or threat of violence to the person: Criminal Justice Act 1993, s 5.

In Northern Ireland it has been held that if the existing level of sentences for a particular offence is failing to deter, then the level of sentencing may well have to rise: *Queen v Gregory & Carroll* [1993] ITLR (10 May) CA of NI.

punishment of child. Where a court is satisfied of the guilt of a child charged with an offence, it may reprimand the child or deal with the case by making one or more of these orders: (a) a conditional discharge order, (b) an order that the child pay a fine or costs, (c) an order that the parent or guardian be bound over, (d) a compensa-

tion order, (e) a parental supervision order, (f) an order that the parent or guardian pay compensation, (g) an order imposing a community sanction, (h) an order that the child be detained in a children detention school, including an order under Children Act 2001, s 155, (i) a detention and supervision order: Children Act 2001, s 98. A court is not empowered to pass a sentence of imprisonment on a child or commit a child to prison (CA 2001, s 156). See CHILD, CRIME AND; CORPORAL PUNISHMENT; DETENTION OF CHILD; WHIPPING.

punitive damages. Synonymous with *exemplary damages* (qv): *McIntyre v Lewis & Dolan* [1991] ITLR (22 April) SC. See also Civil Liability Act 1961, ss 7(2) and 14(4); Landlord and Tenant (Amendment) Act 1980, s 17(4). See EXEMPLARY DAMAGES.

pupil. Means a barrister in his first year of practice who is required by the Code of Conduct to be a pupil of a Master: *Code of Conduct for the Bar of Ireland* (December 2003) r 1.7(m). Any person intending to practise as a barrister must complete a continuous period of not less than 12 months' pupillage with a Master who is registered as such with the Bar Council (r 8.7). A pupil is under a duty not to communicate to any third party, information entrusted to his Master and coming to the pupil's knowledge in the course of his pupillage (r 3.3(b)). See BARRISTER; MASTER. In relation to other pupils, see CORPORAL PUNISHMENT; LEARNER; SCHOOL AUTHORITY'S DUTY; SCHOOL DISCIPLINE; SUSPENSION.

pur autre vie. [For the life of another.] See LIFE ESTATE.

purchase. To acquire land by a lawful act eg by a conveyance, as opposed to a title acquired by act of law.

purchase, compulsory. See COMPULSORY PURCHASE ORDER.

purchase, words of. See WORDS OF PURCHASE.

purchase notice. Formerly, the notice whereby the owner of land could require the planning authority to purchase his interest in the land; it arose only where planning permission was refused on an appeal to An Bord Pleanála (qv) and where as a result of that decision, the land had become *incapable of reasonably beneficial use in its existing state*: Local Government (Planning and Development) Act 1963, s 29. It has been held in England that this did not mean merely that the land had become less valuable: *R v Minister of Housing and Local Government, ex parte Chichester RDC* [1960] 2 All ER 407. An appeal to confirm or annul a purchase notice lay to An Bord Pleanála. See also *Portland Estates Ltd v Limerick Corporation* [1980] SC. See Local Government (Planning and Development) Act 1990, s 12(4).

The consolidating legislation Planning and Development Act 2000 does not provide for such notices and the 2000 Act has repealed the 1963 and 1990 Acts. See COMPENSATION AND PLANNING PERMISSION.

purchaser. (1) A person who acquires land by purchase (qv).

(2) In a transaction of sale, the opposite party to the vendor. A purchaser of any estate or interest in land is entitled to have any instrument creating a *power of attorney* (qv) which affects title thereto, or a certified or attested copy, furnished by the vendor to the purchaser free of expense: Powers of Attorney Act 1996, s 23.

(3) A grantee, lessee, assignee, mortgagee, chargeant or other person who *in good faith* acquires an estate or interest in property for valuable consideration: Succession Act 1965, s 3. The inclusion of the words 'in good faith' puts the purchaser on an obligation to make all reasonable enquiries when buying either from the personal representative of a deceased owner or from a person who has acquired the property from the personal representative by an assent. The Law Reform Commission has recommended that the definition of *'purchaser'* should be amended by the deletion of the words 'in good faith', as the personal representative should have power to dispose of any part of the deceased's estate in due course of administration, with minimal restrictions: Report on *Positive Covenants over freehold land and other proposals* (LRC 70, 2003). According to the Commission, the drafters of the 1965 Act had the intention that the words 'in good faith' would have had a meaning equivalent to 'at arm's length'.

purchaser for value without notice. A person who purchases property *bona fides* for valuable consideration without notice of any prior right or title; he is generally entitled to priority. See NOTICE; POWER OF ATTORNEY.

purchaser's equity. The equitable interest which the purchaser of land acquires; he acquires an *equity* proportionate to the amount of the purchase price paid: *Tempany v Hynes* [1976] IR 101. See Lyall in 7 ILT & SJ 270.

purpose. A warrant for the arrest of a person convicted of an offence (eg in Northern Ireland) must not be endorsed unless the *purpose* of the arrest is to enable him to be taken to a place where he is to undergo imprisonment on foot of a sentence which has been passed: Extradition Act 1965, s 43(3). The word *purpose* in this context must be given a subjective meaning in the sense of what one knows will probably be achieved by an act: *Lloyd v Hogan* [1996] 2 ILRM 313, HC. The European Arrest Warrant Act 2003, s 50 repeals EA 1965, ss 41–55. See EUROPEAN ARREST WARRANT.

purposive rule The rule of interpretation of legislation which is more concerned with the overall result which the legislature wishes to achieve, rather than the meaning of particular words and phrases. The Supreme Court has held that the Adoption Act 1988 is a remedial, social statute designed to permit the adoption of children who had previously been denied the benefits of adoption, and a purposive approach should be applied to its interpretation: *Northern Area Health Board v An Bord Uchtála* [2003] 1 ILRM 481, SC. See *Bank of Ireland v Purcell* [1989] IR 327 and [1990] ILRM 106; *DPP (Ivers) v Murphy* [1999] 1 ILRM 46. See INTERPRETATION OF LEGISLATION; MISCHIEF RULE; PHYSICAL REASONS.

putative. Commonly regarded as being eg the *putative father* (qv).

putative father. Formerly the person alleged to be the father of an illegitimate child in proceedings for an affiliation order (qv). See PARENTAGE, DECLARATION OF; PATERNITY, PRESUMPTION OF.

pyramid of titles. The series of titles which may exist, particularly in respect of urban land, where a particular piece of land may have been the subject of a series of successive fee farm grants (qv), long leases and subleases. See TITLE.

pyramid selling. A trading scheme under which goods and services are to be provided by a promoter to be supplied to or for others under transactions effected by participants, where the prospect is held out to participants of receiving payments or other benefits in respect of persons who become participants and which provides for payments by a participant to the promoter: Pyramid Selling Act 1980. It is an offence to induce or attempt to induce a person to become a participant in a pyramid selling scheme (PSA 1980, s 2). There is a prohibition on certain payments to promoters of such schemes and provision is made for the return to participants of payments for goods in certain instances (PSA 1980, ss 3–4).

The Dublin District Court has held that an investment scheme known as 'Women Empowering Women' did not come within the scope of the 1980 Act and that the plaintiffs had failed to show the ingredients necessary to establish that there was a contractual relationship between them and the defendant: *Snedker v Laird* (2002) Irish Times, 5 December.

Q

qua. [In the capacity of; as.]

quae non valeant singula, juncta juvant. [Words which are of no effect by themselves are effective when combined.]

quaelibet concessio fortissime contra donatorem interpretanda est. [Every grant is to be construed as strongly as possible against the grantor.]

quaere. [Question.] See SED QUAERE.

qualification. See NATIONAL QUALIFICATIONS AUTHORITY OF IRELAND.

qualification shares. The specified number of shares required by the articles of association (qv) of a company to be held by a director; in which event the director must obtain the specified shares within two months of his appointment or within such shorter time as the articles provide: Companies Act 1963, s 180. If the articles do not provide for qualifying shares, a director does not have to own shares in the company.

qualified acceptance. The acceptance of an offer to create a contract must generally be unqualified. There can be a conditional acceptance of a bill of exchange. See ACCEPTANCE OF BILL.

qualified child. Certain short-term social welfare benefits (e g Unemployment Benefit and Disability Benefit) provide for increases where there is a *qualified child*; the increase previously ceased when the child attained

18 years of age. However, now the increase will continue to be payable where the child is in full-time education up to the end of June following the child's 18th birthday: Social Welfare (Miscellaneous Provisions) Act 2002, s 7.

qualified majority voting. See COUNCIL OF MINISTERS.

qualified privilege. See PRIVILEGE.

qualified property. A limited right to property eg the right of a bailee to possession. See BAILMENT.

qualified title. The registration of an interest in land in the Land Registry where the title can be established only for a limited period or only subject to specified reservations: Registration of Title Act 1964, ss 33, 39, 40, 48. Registration with a *qualified title* has the same effect as if the registration were absolute, save that it will not prejudice the enforcement of any right appearing on the register as excepted.

qualifying patent. A patent in relation to which the research, planning, processing, experimenting, testing, devising, designing, developing or similar activity leading to the invention, that is the subject of the patent, was carried out in the State: Finance Act 1973, s 34 as amended by Finance Act 1992, s 19, now consolidated in Taxes Consolidation Act 1997, ss 141 and 234. There is an exemption from tax for income from *qualifying patents* when earned by any person who is resident in the State and not resident in any other country. Income means a royalty or sum paid to use the patented invention; any royalty paid after 22 April 1996 must not be in excess of an arm's length royalty.

quality of goods. Includes their state or condition: Sale of Goods Act 1893, s 62. Where a seller sells goods in the course of a business, there is an implied condition that the goods supplied are of *merchantable quality* (qv), except that there is no such condition: (a) as regards defects specifically drawn to the buyer's attention before the contract is made, or (b) if the buyer examines the goods before the contract is made, as regards defects which that examination ought to have revealed.

Where a seller sells goods in the *course of a business* and the buyer, expressly or by implication, makes known to the seller any particular purpose for which the goods are being bought, there is an implied condition that the goods are reasonably fit for that purpose, whether or not that is a purpose for which such goods are commonly supplied, except where the circumstances show that the buyer does not rely, or that it is unreasonable for him to rely, on the seller's skill or judgement. See Sale of Goods Act 1893, s 14; Sale of Goods and Supply of Services Act 1980, s 10.

Any term in a contract which exempts a seller from these implied conditions is void where the buyer *deals as a consumer* (qv) and in any other case, is not enforceable unless it is shown to be fair and reasonable (SGA 1893, s 55; SGSSA 1980, s 22).

The existence of a *credit agreement* (qv) does not in any way affect the rights of a consumer against the supplier of the goods or services; if the credit agreement is with someone other than the supplier, the consumer can in certain instances take proceedings against the creditor e g where he has failed to obtain the satisfaction against the supplier to which he is entitled: Consumer Credit Act 1995, s 42. See *Draper v Rubenstein* [1925] 87 ILTR 198; *Egan v McSweeney* [1956] 90 ILTR 40; *T O'Regan Sons Ltd v Micro-Bio (Ireland) Ltd* [1980] HC; *McCullagh Sales Ltd v Chetham Timber Co (Ireland) Ltd* [1983] HC. [Bibliography: Bird; O'Reilly P.] See FAIR AND REASONABLE TERMS; PRODUCT LIABILITY.

quality service statement. The statement which solicitors are encouraged by the Law Society to display in the reception, or other suitable area, to provide assurances to clients on the legal services they can expect to receive as consumers of those services. A sample 'quality service statement' is available to solicitors on the Society's website under *Guidance and Ethics Committee*: *www.lawsociety.ie.*

quamdiu se bene gesserit. [During good behaviour.]

quando acciderint. [When it happens.]

quando aliquid mandatur, mandatur et omne per quod perrenitur ad illud. [When anything is commanded, everything by which it can be accomplished is also commanded.]

quando aliquid prohibetur fieri, prohibetur ex directo et per obliquum. [When the doing of anything is forbidden, then the doing of it either directly or indirectly is forbidden.]

quando lex aliquid alicui concedit, concedere videtur id sine quo res ipsa esse non potest. [When the law gives anything to anyone, it gives also all those things without which the thing itself could not exist.] Eg the right of way to a *close*, see WAY, RIGHT OF.

quando plus fit quam fieri debet, videtur etiam illud fieri quod faciendum est. [When more is done than ought to be done, then that is considered to have been done which ought to have been done.]

quantity, wrong. See WRONG QUANTITY.

quantum. [How much; amount.] A *book of quantum* is a legal publication with details of damages awarded in legal actions. [Bibliography: Pierce; White.] See DAMAGES; JURY, ABOLITION OF; PERSONAL INJURIES ASSESSMENT BOARD.

quantum meruit. [As much as he has earned.] Where work is done or services performed by one person for another in circumstances which imply that the work done or services performed will be paid for, there is an implied promise to pay *quantum meruit*, i e as much as he deserves.

A claim for *quantum meruit* may arise from contract e g from an implied agreement to pay a reasonable sum or where there is acceptance of partial performance of a contract: *Planche v Colburn* [1831] 8 Bing 14. It can also arise from quasi-contract eg: (a) for work done where a contract has been discharged by the breach of the defendant; or (b) in respect of work done under a void contract, believed to be valid: *O'Connor v Listowel UDC* [1957] Ir Jur Rep 43 applying *Craven-Ellis v Canons Ltd* [1936] 2 KB 403; or (c) for preparatory work requested by the defendant who received no benefit: *Folens & Co v Minister for Education* [1984] ILRM 265 applying *Brewer Street Investments Ltd v Barclay's Woolen Co* [1953] 3 WLR 869; or (d) as a result of agency: *Chaieb v Carter* [1987] SC.

An action in *quantum meruit* may be brought to recover the value of benefits conferred on a defendant on foot of an unenforceable contract e g where there is a failure to satisfy the writing requirement of the Statute of Frauds (Ireland) 1695. [Bibliography: Goff & Barron UK; Tettenborn UK.] See KINLEN ORDER; PART-PERFORMANCE; RETAINER.

quantum ramifactus. [The amount of damage suffered.]

quantum valebrant. [As much as they were worth.] An action for payment for goods supplied, similar to *quantum meruit* (qv), but in respect of goods.

quarantine. See PET DOG AND CAT.

quarry. Means an excavation, or system of excavations, made for the purpose of, or in connection with, the getting of minerals (whether in their natural state or in solution or suspension) or products of minerals, being neither a mine nor merely a well or bore-hole or a well or bore-hole combined: Mines and Quarries Act 1965, s 3. A quarry has the meaning assigned to it by MQA 1965, s 3: Planning and Development Act 2000, s 261(13). Provision has been made for the control of quarries, their registration, the conditions under which they operate, including the control of emissions, including polluting matter, waste and noise. Under the registration system, quarry owners/operators must supply full details of their operations to the relevant planning authority by 27 April 2005 – the area of the quarry, the material being extracted, the hours of operation and the traffic, noise and dust generated by the quarry. For amendments to 1965 Act, see SI No 357 of 1995. For Guidelines to planning authorities on Quarries and Ancillary Activities, see website: *www.environ.ie*. See MINE.

quash. To discharge; to annul; to set aside; to make void. The quashing of a conviction is strictly confined to circumstances in which there is a breach of the fundamental tenets of constitutional justice: *McNally v District Judge Martin* [1995] 1 ILRM 350, SC.

quasi. [As if it were.]

quasi-easement. Description sometimes given to rights exercised by a landowner over his own land which, if he did not own that land, could exist as easements. It has been held that upon the grant of part of a tenement, there would pass to the grantee as easements, all quasi-easements over the land retained which: (i) were continuous and apparent, (ii) were necessary to the reasonable enjoyment of the land granted, and (iii) had been, and were at the time of the grant, used by the grantor for the benefit of the part granted: rule under *Wheeldon v Burrows* [1879] 12 Ch D 31. A right of way does not generally fall within the rule but a worn track may well pass under the rule. See Conveyancing Act 1881, s 6(1). See also *Clancy v Byrne* [1877] IR 11 CL 355; *Head v Meara* [1912] 1 IR 262. [Bibliography: Bland (1); Lyall; Walsh E S.] See APPURTENANT; EASEMENT; LOST MODERN GRANT.

quasi ex contractu. [As if arising out of contract.]

quasi-estoppel. A voluntary promise to forego a right (ie a promise without *consideration*) does not give a cause of action but may operate as a quasi-estoppel as the court will not allow a promisor to act inconsistently with a promise. See *Central London Property Trust v High Trees House* [1946] KB 130; *Cullen v Cullen* [1962] IR 268.

quasi-contracts. Contracts implied by law, giving a right to a person to recover money from another: *Moses v Macferlan* [1760] 1 W Bl 219. These can arise by: (a) *money had and received* (qv) by the defendant to the use of the plaintiff; (b) money paid by the plaintiff to the defendant's use: *Brewer St Investments v Barclay's Woolen Co* [1954] 2 All ER 1330; (c) *quantum meruit* (qv); (d) contribution from a *concurrent wrongdoer* (qv): Civil Liability Act 1961, s 30.

quasi-judicial. Having a character which is partly judicial eg where there is an exercise of discretion following the hearing of evidence, as in the case of proceedings before an arbitrator. See ARBITRATION.

quasi-loan. A transaction under which one party (the creditor) agrees to pay, or pays otherwise than in pursuance of an agreement, a sum for another (the borrower) or agrees to reimburse, or reimburses otherwise than in pursuance of an agreement, expenditure incurred by another party for another (the borrower): (i) on terms that the borrower (or a person on his behalf) will reimburse the creditor or (ii) in circumstances giving rise to a liability on the borrower to reimburse the creditor: Companies Act 1990, s 25(2). For amendment to CA 1990 s 25, see Company Law Enforcement Act 2001, s 75. See LOAN TO DIRECTOR.

quasi-tail. An estate *pur autre vie* which is limited to a person and the heirs of his body eg *to B and the heirs of his body for the life of A*. See *Ex p Sterne* [1801] 6 Ves 156. See FEE TAIL; LIFE ESTATE.

question, leading. See LEADING QUESTION.

questioning. See INTERROGATION; JUDGES' RULES.

qui approbat non reprobat. [He who accepts cannot reject.] See ELECTION.

qui facit per alium facit per se. [He who does something through another does it through himself.] A principal is liable for the acts of his agent. Generally an employer is liable for the acts of his employee. See AGENT; EMPLOYER, DUTY OF; VICARIOUS LIABILITY.

qui jure suo utitur neminem laedit. [He who exercises his legal right inflicts upon no-one any injury.]

qui omne dicit nihil excludit. [He who says everything excludes nothing.]

qui prior est temptore potier est jure. [He who is first in time has the strongest claim in law.] The equitable maxim that where there are two equal equitable claims made to the same property, the first in time prevails. See EQUITY, MAXIMS OF; NOTICE; PRIORITY.

qui sentit commodum sentire debet et onus; et e contra. [He who enjoys the benefit ought also to bear the burden.] See ELECTION.

qui tacet consentire videtur. [He who is silent is deemed to consent.] See SILENCE, RIGHT TO.

quia timet. [Because he fears.] An action by a person for an *injunction* to prevent or restrain some act, feared or threatened, which if done, would cause the person substantial damage, for which money would be no adequate or sufficient remedy. The plaintiff must show a very strong possibility of grave damage; the cost to the defendant must also be considered. There must be a proven substantial risk of danger: *Szabo v Esat Digiphone Ltd* [1998] 2 ILRM 102, HC. Also the principles to be applied to an *interlocutory quia timet* injunction are the same as apply to any interlocutory injunction (*Szabo* case). See *Attorney-General v Rathmines and Pembroke Hospital Board* [1904] 1 IR 161; *Independent Newspapers v Irish Press* [1932] IR 615; *C & A Modes v C & A (Waterford) Ltd* [1976] IR 148. See INJUNCTION.

quicquid plantatur solo, solo cedit. [Whatever is fixed to the soil, belongs to the soil.] See FIXTURES.

quid pro quo. [Something for something.] An essential of a valid contract ie consideration (qv).

quiet enjoyment, covenant for. The usual covenant (qv) in a lease (qv) that the lessee will have quiet enjoyment eg: 'And the Lessor doth hereby covenant with the Lessee that the Lessee performing and observing his covenants may quietly hold and enjoy the said premises during the said term without interruption by the Lessor or any person claiming through him.' A cov-

enant for quiet enjoyment is implied in every lease on behalf of the landlord: Deasy's Act 1860, s 41. However, a lessee who has not paid rent or performed other covenants is not able to invoke the implied covenant for quiet enjoyment arising under s 41: *Riordan v Carroll t/a Wyvern Gallery* [1996] 2 ILRM 263, HC. For proposed amendments to s 41, see *Consultation Paper on General Law of Landlord and Tenant Law* (LRC CP 28, 2003) paras 18.42–18.44. See DEASY'S ACT; LANDLORD, OBLIGATIONS OF.

quit, notice to. See NOTICE TO QUIT.

quit rent. Perpetual rents on land reserved to the Crown (now the State) under the Settlement of Ireland Acts 1662 and 1665. They have largely disappeared as the Land Purchase Acts provided that if land was subject to a quit rent, the rent could be redeemed by the tenant purchasing the land. Where not redeemed and where the land is registered, a quit rent remains a burden which affects the land without registration: Registration of Title Act 1964, s 72(1)(a). See also Statute of Limitations 1957, s 2(1).

quittance. A discharge from an obligation.

quo ligatur, eo dissolvitur. [Whatsoever binds can also release.]

quo warranto. [By what authority.] A proceeding by which inquiry is made as to the authority of a person who has claimed or usurped any office or franchise. The proceeding is now by way of judicial review (qv). See RSC Ord 84, r 18.

quoad hoc. [As to this.]

quod ab initio non valet, in tractu temporis non convalescit. [That which is bad from the beginning does not improve by length of time.] For example, see 'void marriage' under MARRIAGE, NULLITY OF.

quod aedificatur in area legata cedit legato. [That which is built on ground that is devised passes to the devisee.]

quod per me non possum, nec per alium. [What I cannot do in person, I cannot do by proxy.] See PROXY.

quorum. [Of whom.] The minimum number of persons who constitute a valid formal meeting. Unless the articles of association provide otherwise, the quorum for a private company is two and for a public company is three members present in person: Companies Act 1963, s 134(c).

quota. The number of votes sufficient to secure the election of a candidate: the number is obtained by dividing the number of all valid ballot papers by a number exceeding by one the number of vacancies to be filled, and by adding one to the result, any fractional remainder being disregarded: Electoral Act 1992, s 120. Where at the end of any count the number of votes credited to a candidate is greater than the quota, the surplus is transferred to the continuing candidate or candidates (EA 1992, s 121). A candidate may be deemed to be elected without reaching the quota (EA 1992, s 124). See also Presidential Elections Act 1993, s 50; European Parliament Elections Act 1997, Sch 2, r 84. For quotas in agricultural law, see Bibliography: Walsh ES.

quota hopping. Colloquial expression to describe the practice whereby fishing boats from one State are registered under the flag of another State in order to avail of the fishing quota of the country of registration. Provisions to prevent this practice are contained in the Fisheries (Amendment) Act 1994, s 5. The Minister is empowered, in deciding on an application for a fishing boat licence, to take account of economic linkage criteria with Ireland eg volume of landings at Irish ports.

quoties in verbis nulla est ambiguitas ibi nulla expositio contra verba expressa fienda est. [When in the words there is no ambiguity then no interpretation contrary to the actual words is to be adopted.]

quousque. [Until.]

qv, quod vide. [Which see.]

R

race. A dismissal from employment is deemed to be unfair where it results wholly or mainly from the race or colour of the employee: Unfair Dismissals Act 1977, s 6(2), as amended by Unfair Dismissals (Amendment) Act 1993, s 5(a). An employer is prohibited from discriminating against an employee or prospective employee on the grounds of *race* ie treating persons differently on the grounds that the persons are of a different race, colour, nationality or ethnic or national origins: Employment Equality Act 1998, ss 8(1) and 6. See *Kennedy v Kellor Services (Ireland) Ltd* [2000] ELR 137, EAT; *Martinez v Network Catering* [2001] ELR 144, EO;

Eng v St James's Hospital [2002] ELR 143, EO; *Ntoko v Citibank* [2004] ELR 116, LC.

A person must not discriminate on *race grounds* in disposing of goods or premises or in providing a service or accommodation; treating one person less favourably than another, in a comparable situation, because they are of different race, colour, nationality or ethnic or national origins, is discrimination: Equal Status Act 2000, ss 5 and 3, amended by Equality Act 2004, ss 48–49. See websites: *www.equality.ie*; *www.knowracism.ie*.

In 1997, the EU established an independent body to contribute to the fight against racism, xenophobia and antisemitism throughout Europe, the *European Monitoring Centre on Racism and Xenophobia* (EUMC); see website: *www.eumc.eu.int*. For the First National Report by Ireland under the UN International Convention on the Elimination of all forms of Racial Discrimination (April 2004), see website: *www.justice.ie*. See Case 224/00 *Commission v Italy* [2002] 19 March, ECJ. [Bibliography: Reid M.] See HATRED, INCITEMENT TO; PENSION SCHEME AND DISCRIMINATION; ROAD RACE; VIDEO RECORDING.

rack rent. A rent which represents the full annual value of a holding: *Ex p Connolly to Sheridan* [1900] LR 6.

racketeering. See EXTORTION WITH MENACES.

radio and television commission. See BROADCASTING COMMISSION OF IRELAND.

radio frequency plan. A set of tables indicating frequency allocations in the radio spectrum; responsibility for revising and republishing the plan, from time to time, rests with the *Commission for Communications Regulation* (qv): Communications Regulation Act 2002, ss 10 and 35.

radioactive substance. Any substance capable of emitting *ionising radiation* (qv) and includes any radio-nuclide, whether natural or artificial: Radiological Protection Act 1991 as amended by Energy (Miscellaneous Provisions) Act 1995, s 26; Food Safety Authority of Ireland Act 1998, s 65 and Radiological Protection (Amendment) Act 2002. These Acts give effect to the 1986 Convention on Assistance in the Case of a Nuclear Accident or Radiological Emergency, and the 1979 Convention on the Physical Protection of Nuclear Material. They also provide for the establishment of the *Radiological Protection Institute* *of Ireland* and for radiological protection measures generally.

The 2002 Act: (a) strengthens the Institute's licensing powers by requiring a person to whom a licence has been granted, to comply with any condition attached to the licence; (b) introduces a grant scheme for radon gas remediation works; and (c) clarifies the summary prosecution powers of the relevant Minister, the Institute and the Food Safety Authority of Ireland. See Ionising Radiation Order 2000, SI No 125 of 2000. For the Radiological Protection Institute of Ireland, see website: *www.rpii.ie.* See IONISING RADIATION; NUCLEAR WEAPONS; RADON; SELLAFIELD MOX PLANT.

radon. Means *radon-222* gas in air: SI No 125 of 2000. Radon is a naturally occurring odourless radioactive gas found in soil and rocks. Radon gas can access buildings and domestic dwellings and it has been linked as a contributing factor to increasing the risk of lung cancer. Grants (*remediation works grants*) may be payable by the Radiological Protection Institute of Ireland to assist persons to reduce the level of radon gas in a house where the level is greater than 200 becquerels per cubic metre: Radiological Protection (Amendment) Act 2002, s 5. See RADIOACTIVE SUBSTANCE.

railway and EU. For licensing of railway undertakings, see SI No 537 of 2003, implementing Directive (EC) 2001/13. For access to railway infrastructure, see SI No 536 of 2003, implementing Directive (EC) 2001/12.

railway order. An order made by the Minister which authorises the applicant to construct, maintain, improve and operate the railway or the railway works specified in the order, subject to such conditions, restrictions and requirements as the Minister thinks proper and specifies in the order: Transport (Railway Infrastructure) Act 2001, s 43. The *Railway Procurement Agency*, CIE or any person with the consent of the Agency can apply for a railway order (T(RI)A 2001, s 37). The application process is specified, including an *environmental impact statement*, application available for public inspection, public inquiry, and order by the Minister (T(RI)A 2001, ss 36–43).

Any application for a *judicial review* of a railway order must be made within eight weeks from the date the order was made (T(RI)A 2001, s 47). The carrying out of works authorised under a railway order, is

exempted development for the purposes of the Planning and Development Act 2000 (T(RI)A 2001, s 38). The Agency or CIE are authorised to acquire compulsorily land or rights under or over land or any substratum of land, specified in the railway order (T(RI)A 2001, s 45). See LIGHT RAILWAY; SUBSTRATUM OF LAND.

Railway Procurement Agency. A new independent, commercial, statutory public body whose main function is the procurement of new railway infrastructure: Transport (Railway Infrastructure) Act 2001, ss 8–35. The functions of the agency are to secure the provision of, or to provide, new railway infrastructure as determined by the Minister, to enter into agreements with other persons to provide such railway infrastructure, and to acquire and facilitate the development of land adjacent to such railway infrastructure (T(RI)A 2001, s 11). This will permit private sector participation in the construction, operation and maintenance of new railways.

Provision has been made for the transfer of property, rights and liabilities from CIE to the Agency in respect of the Dublin light railway project (T(RI)A 2001, ss 33–35). Also the Transport (Dublin Light Rail) Act 1996 is repealed (T(RI)A 2001, s 3). See BYE-LAW; INTEGRATED TICKETING SYSTEM.

railway safety. Under draft legislation, it is proposed to introduce a new regulatory framework for railway safety, which will apply to all railways to which the public have access and to those parts of industrial railways which have a connection to the public railway network or which cross a public road: Railway Safety Bill 2001. An independent *Railway Safety Commission* is to be established with powers to inspect railway infrastructure, to investigate and publish reports on *railway incidents*, and with wide-ranging enforcement powers. The safety regulatory functions of the Minister for Public Enterprise will be transferred to the Commission. There is also provision for a *Railway Safety Advisory Council.*

For regulations governing the *interoperability* of the trans-European high-speed railway system, which gives effect to Directive (EC) 96/48, see SI No 118 of 2002. By 'interoperability' is meant the ability of the high-speed rail system to allow the safe and uninterrupted movement of high-speed trains which accomplish the specified levels of performance. See also EC (Interoperability of the Trans-European conventional rail system) Regulations 2004, SI No 61 of 2004. See LIGHT RAILWAY; SUBSTRATUM OF LAND.

RAM. [Random access memory.] Generally understood to mean the volatile memory of a computer which can be written to as well as read. DRAM is dynamic RAM and SDRAM is synchronous DRAM. See COMPUTER.

ramp. Means an artificial lump in or on the surface of a roadway: Road Traffic Act 1961, s 101A inserted by Dublin Transport Authority (Dissolution) Act 1987, s 9. A ramp must not exceed a height of 10cms above the road surface: SIs No 32 and 291 of 1988.

random crime check. See ROAD TRAFFIC CHECK.

random roadside inspections. Provision has been made for random roadside vehicle inspections of commercial vehicles weighing over 3.5 tonnes, mini-buses, other buses and coaches over one year old by the gardaí or persons appointed by the Minister: EC (Random Roadside Vehicle Inspection) Regulations 2003, SI No 227 of 2003 as amended by SI No 98 of 2004. These regulations implement Directive (EC) 2000/30 as amended by Directive (EC) 2003/26.

rape. The offence committed by a man if he has unlawful sexual intercourse with a woman who at the time of the intercourse does not consent to it, and at that time he *knows* that she does not consent to the intercourse or he is *reckless* as to whether she does or does not consent to it: Criminal Law (Rape) Act 1981, s 2. The jury must be told not only that it must be satisfied beyond reasonable doubt that the complainant had not consented to sexual intercourse, but also that the accused *knew* that the complainant had not consented or was *reckless* as to whether or not she had consented: People (*DPP*) v McDonagh [1996] 2 ILRM 468, SC and 1 IR 565. *Knowledge* and *recklessness* are two distinct issues.

At a trial of a rape offence, no evidence may be adduced and no question may be asked in cross-examination about any sexual experience of the complainant with any person, including the accused, unless the judge so allows where he is satisfied it would otherwise be unfair to the accused (CL(R)A 1981, s 3(1) as amended by the Criminal Law (Rape) Amendment

Act 1990, s 13). An application to so question should be made as early as possible in a trial and if unsuccessful may be repeated at further stages of the trial: *DPP v McDonagh & Cawley* [1991] 9 ILT Dig 171, CCA.

There is now provision for separate legal representation for complainants in rape and serious sexual assault cases when application is made to the court by the defence, seeking leave to adduce evidence or cross-examine about the complainant's past sexual experience with any person: Sex Offenders Act 2001, s 34 (inserting Criminal Law (Rape) Act 1981, s 4A).

There are provisions governing the anonymity of the complainant and of the accused, by restricting publication and broadcasts which could lead members of the public to identify them (CL(R)A 1981, ss 7–8). The restriction on the identity of the accused does not apply after he has been convicted of the offence; except where it might lead to the identification of the complainant (CL(R)AA 1990, s 14).

It has been held that, except in wholly exceptional circumstances, the appropriate sentence for rape is immediate and substantial terms of imprisonment or detention; a plea of guilty is a relevant factor to be considered in the imposition of sentence and may constitute a mitigating circumstance: *The People (DPP) v Tiernan* [1988] IR 250, SC. However, the category of case where a judge may consider imposing a non-custodial sentence where the accused has pleaded guilty, is very rare: *DPP v WC* [1994] 1 ILRM 321, CCC. The Court of Criminal Appeal has held that judges in rape cases must start from the basis that a custodial sentence is the norm: *DPP v Davis* [13 July 2004, unreported] CCA.

The trial of a person indicted for a rape offence is by the Central Criminal Court (CL(R)AA 1990, s 10). See also *The People (Attorney-General) v Dermody* [1956] IR 307; *People (DPP) v Creighton* [1994] 2 IR 570, CCA; *DPP v G* [1994] 1 IR 587, SC; *People (DPP) v LG* [2003] 2 IR 517, CCA. See LRC 24 of 1988.

For the crime of rape under CL(R)AA 1990, s 4, see SEXUAL ASSAULT.

In an armed conflict, there is a requirement that women be the object of special respect and be protected in particular against rape, forced prostitution, and any other form of indecent assault: Geneva Conventions (Amendment) Act 1998, Sch 5, art 76. For the Rape Crisis Centre, see website: *www.drcc.ie*. [Bibliography: O'Malley (2).] See CARNAL KNOWLEDGE, UNLAWFUL; CONSENT; COMPLAINT; CORROBORATION; MARITAL RAPE; PROCUREMENT; PUNISHMENT; SEXUAL ASSAULT; SEXUAL OFFENCES.

rate of exchange. The numerical proportion between the currencies of two states in relation to an exchange of one currency for the other. The Minister is empowered to vary the general exchange rate for the Irish pound in respect of other monetary units: Central Bank Act 1989, s 24(2). The Minister exercised this power to widen the permitted fluctuation of the Irish pound in the Exchange Rate Mechanism from 2 August 1993.

As regards VAT payable on intra-Community acquisitions, the VAT rate is the rate applicable to the supply of similar goods in the State and where the invoice is in a foreign currency, the *rate of exchange* is the latest selling rate recorded by the Central Bank for the currency at the time the tax becomes due, unless an alternative arrangement is agreed with the Revenue Commissioners. As regards taxation, a rate of exchange is an arm's length rate of exchange between different currencies: Taxes Consolidation Act 1997, ss 79, 402. In relation to legal proceedings, and the rate of exchange to be used to determine the Irish currency equivalent of amounts expressed in foreign currencies, see CURRENCY, FOREIGN. For *euro*, see CONVERSION RATE.

rateable hereditament. All land, buildings and opened mines; all commons (qv), and rights of common, and all other profits (qv) to be had, received or taken out of land; all rights of fishery; and canals, navigations and rights of navigations, and rights of way (qv) and other tolls levied in respect of such rights and easements, and all other tolls: Poor Relief (Ireland) Act 1838, s 63. See also Valuation (Ireland) Act 1852, s 12; Valuation Act 1986.

It has been held that the words *incorporeal hereditaments* cannot be safely confined to such incorporeal rights in land as might, in former times, have passed to the heir: *Telecom Éireann v Commissioner of Valuation* [1998] 1 ILRM 64, SC and [1997] 2 IR 575 SC.

If a particular property falls within any one of the categories of fixed property which are deemed to be a rateable hereditament, no further enquiry has to be made as to whether it falls within any other category: *Kinsale Yacht Club v Commission of Valuation* [1994] 1 ILRM 457, SC.

Parts of a building held under separate titles are properly regarded as separate rating units; structural severance of the parts is not essential: *Carlile Trust Ltd v Dublin Corporation* [1965] IR 456. See also *International Mushrooms Ltd v Commissioner of Valuations* [1994] 2 ILRM 121, HC. See RATES.

rateable occupier. The occupier who must pay the rate levied on the property occupied: Poor Relief (Ireland) Act 1838, s 71. To be such an occupier: (a) the occupation must be exclusive: *Carroll v Mayo County Council* [1967] IR 364; (b) the occupation must be of value or benefit to the occupier: *Sinnott v Neale* [1948] Ir Jur Rep 10; and (c) the occupation must not be for too transient a period: *Dublin Corporation v Dublin Port and Docks Board* [1978] IR 266. See RATES.

rateable valuation. Means the valuation under the Valuation Acts of the property in relation to which the expression is used: Interpretation Act 1937, s 12, para 25. *Rateable valuation* has now been replaced by *market value* in many statutes. See Civil Liability and Courts Act 2004, ss 45–48, 50–53. See CIRCUIT COURT; MARKET VALUE.

rates. A form of taxation on property based on a valuation (qv) which is used to finance expenditure by local authorities: Poor Relief (Ireland) Act 1838. The making and levying of such rates as may be necessary is provided for (PR(I)A 1838, s 61) and must be paid *by the person in the actual occupation of the rateable property at the time of the rate made* (s 71). An occupier includes every person in the immediate use of any hereditament rateable under the Act, whether corporeal or incorporeal.

A local authority has a duty to make one rate for the whole financial year: Local Government Act 1946, s 29 as substituted by Local Government Act 1994, s 45.

Where a hereditament is unoccupied at the making of the rate, the rate is made on the owner, who is defined as the person for the time being entitled to occupy the hereditament: Local Government Act 1946, ss 14 and 23. Rates levied by county councils are known as the *county* rate and by urban authorities as the *municipal* rate.

Each year the local authority determines the rate having received the final lists of valuations for its area; the *rate book* is then compiled in the light of the appropriate poundage and valuations, is signed and sealed and demand notes are issued to the rate collectors: Public Bodies Order 1946, arts 61–63, 68, form RA1. See *Butterly v Corporation of Dublin* [1986] HC.

An appeal against the rate may be brought on the ground: (a) that the rate as determined is wholly illegal: *Kettle v Dublin County Council* 57 ILTR 113 or (b) the ratepayer is aggrieved by the rate, or has material objection to any persons being included or excluded from the rate or has material objection to the sum charged on any person: PR(I)A 1838, ss 106–112 as modified by the Valuation (Ireland) Act 1852, s 28; Poor Relief (Ireland) Act 1849, ss 22–23 and 29–30. See also Local Government (Financial Provisions) Act 1983. See also *Stevenson v Orr* [1916] 2 IR 619. Rates on domestic dwellings were abolished in 1979: Local Government (Financial Provisions] Act 1978.

A rating authority is required to send an inspector of taxes a copy of the last county or municipal rate made by the authority; this measure enables the Revenue to trace landlords of properties which are let: Taxes Consolidation Act 1997, s 898. See *Coakley & Co Ltd v Commissioners of Valuations* [1996] 2 ILRM 90, SC. See also Valuation (Ireland) Act 1852; Valuation Act 1986.

The valuation code has been amended and the law has been largely consolidated to facilitate a *revaluation* of all rateable property in the State and to make new provision in relation to categories of properties in respect of which rates may not be made: Valuation Act 2001. If a local authority is a rating authority, it is required at its *budget meeting* to determine by resolution the annual rate on valuation to be levied: Local Government Act 2001, s 103. See *Slatterys Ltd v Commissioner of Valuations* [2001] 4 IR 92, SC.

[Bibliography: Canny (2).] See DOMESTIC HEREDITAMENT; ESTIMATES MEETING; MARINA; RATES, RECOVERY OF; RATEABLE HEREDITAMENT; RATEABLE OCCUPIER; RATES, EXEMPTION FROM; RECLAIMED LAND; TOLL; VALUATION.

rates, exemption from. Relief from rates has been provided in respect of dwellings: Local Government (Financial Provisions) Act 1978, s 3. It has been held that, apart from specific exceptions to be found in other statutes, the grounds for exemption from rates are to be found in the proviso to Poor Relief (Ireland) Act 1838, s 63 dealing with churches, chapels, burial grounds, infirmaries, hospitals, charity schools and buildings exclusively used for charitable purposes or for the education of the poor and buildings dedicated to or *used for public purposes*: *McGahon and Ryan v Commissioner of Valuations* [1934] IR 736; *Barrington's Hospital v Commissioner of Valuations* [1957] IR 299.

Property is *used for public purposes* where, and only where it belongs to the government or each member of the public has an interest in the property: *Guardians of the Londonderry Union v Londonderry Bridge Commissioners* IR 2 CL 577; *Maynooth College v Commissioner of Valuations* [1958] IR 189. See also *St Macartan's Diocesan Trust v Commissioner of Valuations* [1990] 1 IR 508; *Dublin Co Council v West Link Bridge Ltd* [1994] 2 ILRM 204, HC and [1996] 1 IR 487, SC; *Port of Cork Company v Commissioner of Valuations* [2003] 1 ILRM 389, HC and [2004] 1 ILRM 151, SC.

Societies established exclusively for the purpose of science, literature or fine arts may be entitled to exemption from local rates: Scientific Societies Act 1843; Valuation (Ireland) Amendment Act 1854. See Quinn in 8 ILT & SJ (1990) 286.

Now, all *relevant property* is rateable, except as specified, rather than 'hereditaments' or 'tenements': Valuation Act 2001, Pt IV and Sch 4. See SCIENTIFIC SOCIETIES.

rates, mesne. See MESNE RATES.

rates, recovery of. The payment of arrears of county or municipal rates is normally enforced by summons in the District Court, on failure to pay on foot of a notice in the name of the rate collector demanding payment within six days thereof: Poor Relief (Ireland) Act 1838, s 73.

The court may order the payment of the sum found due with costs, and in default, may issue a warrant to levy the sum by distress (qv) and sale of the goods and chattels of the defendant. There is no monetary limit on the jurisdiction of the District Court in respect of summary proceedings by summons for recovery of arrears of rates. See also *County Council of Clare v McInerney* [1902] 2 IR 536.

ratification. The act of adopting a contract or other transaction by a person who was not bound by it originally. The ratification of a contract by a minor on reaching *full age* (qv) is itself void: Infants Relief Act 1874, s 2. A minor may enter into a fresh contract on reaching full age: *Holmes v Brierley* [1888] 4 TLR. However, a new contract to pay a *debt* contracted during infancy is unenforceable (IRA 1874, s 2). See *Leslie v Sheill* [1914] 3 KB 607.

A contract made by an agent with no or insufficient authority may be ratified by his principal only if: (a) the agent expressly contracted as agent; (b) the principal was named or ascertained when the contract was made; (c) the principal had contractual capacity at the date of the contract and at the date of ratification; and (d) the principal at the time of ratification has full knowledge of the material facts or intends to ratify the contract whatever the facts may be. Ratification dates back to the original making of the contract. See *Barclay's Bank v Breen* [1962] 96 ILTR 179; *Brennan v O'Connell* [1980] IR 13. See AGENT.

ratification of treaty. The formal approval of a treaty after it has been signed. See CHARGE ON PUBLIC FUNDS.

rating authority. Means a county council, a city council, or a town council for the boroughs of Clonmel, Drogheda, Kilkenny, Sligo and Wexford: Local Government Act 2001, s 2(1).

ratio decidendi. The reason for a judicial decision. It is the *ratio decidendi* which forms the precedent for other similar cases. Contrast with *obiter dictum*. See PRECEDENT.

ratio legis. [The reason for the law.] The underlying principle or objective of the law, particularly of legislation. See INTERPRETATION OF LEGISLATION.

ratione soli. [By reason only.]

rationes. The pleadings in a suit. See PLEADINGS.

rave dance. Popularly understood to mean wild and uninhibited dancing induced by music and drugs. The gardaí are given significant powers in respect of an 'unlicensed dance'; this means a gathering of persons at any place, which is open to the public, and the purpose of which, a Garda Superintendent (or higher rank) reasonably believes, is to entitle persons to dance and at which music is played and which will be an occasion for the sale, supply or distribution of drugs: Licensing (Combating Drug Abuse) Act 1997, s 1(1). The gardaí in such a circumstance have power to remove

persons preparing for or at such a dance, to stop persons proceeding to such a dance, and to enter and to seize equipment (L(CDA)A 1997, ss 12–15).

re. [In the matter of.]

re-arrest. A person who has been released from custody, does not have to be brought into a public street before his re-arrest: *Quinlivan v Governor of Portlaoise Prison* [1998] 1 ILRM 294, SC. See DETENTION.

re-engagement. The redress which may be available to a successful applicant in a claim alleging unfair dismissal from employment. The *re-engagement* can be to his former position or to another reasonably suitable position (*Holden v Bank of Ireland* (1993) Irish Times, 6 July) and it may be awarded from the date of dismissal (*Harrison v Gateau Ltd* UD 158/1981) or can be subject to a prior period of suspension (*Healy v O'Neill* UD 82/1982). See Unfair Dismissals Act 1977, s 7(1)(b). See also *The State (IPU) v EAT* [1987] ILRM 36. Contrast with RE-INSTATEMENT. See also EMPLOYMENT APPEALS TRIBUNAL; VICTIMISATION.

re-entry, proviso for. See LEASE, DETERMINATION OF.

re-examination. See EXAMINATION.

re-instatement. (1) The redress which may be available to a successful applicant in a claim alleging unfair dismissal from employment. The re-instated employee is treated in all respects as if he had not been dismissed and he returns to his former position on the terms and conditions on which he was employed immediately before the dismissal: Unfair Dismissals Act 1977, s 7(1)(a). Re-instatement entitles the employee to benefit from any improvement in terms and conditions which may have occurred between the dates of dismissal and re-instatement (UDA 1977, s 1 as amended by Unfair Dismissals (Amendment) Act 1993, s 2(b)). In a particular case involving a yacht club, re-instatement was ordered as it was considered that with committee members changing every year, the personal difficulties associated with resuming work would not be as great as with an unchanging board of directors: *Hurley v Royal Cork Yacht Club* [1999] ELR 7, EAT. In another case in which a bus driver was dismissed for failure to collect three fares from passengers (involving amounts of €0.70 and €1.10), the Employment Appeals Tribunal held that the appropriate sanction was unpaid suspension and that he should be re-instated: *Wallace v Bus Eireann* (2004) Irish Times, 3 September, EAT. See *Groves v Aer Lingus Teo* UD 265/79; *Lundy v Airmotive Ireland Ltd* [1992] ELR 211, CC. Contrast with RE-ENGAGEMENT. See also EMPLOYMENT APPEALS TRIBUNAL; VICTIMISATION.

(2) Replacement or repair of damaged property under an insurance policy; many such policies have a *re-instatement clause* therein giving to the insurer the right to re-instate the property, at the option of the insurer, rather than paying an amount in respect of damage to the property. If the insurer chooses this option, he has a duty to replace it substantially to the same condition prior to the damage and may be liable in negligence if he fails to do so properly. See *St. Alban's Investments Co v Sun Alliance & London Insurance Co Ltd* [1984] ILRM 50l. See STRIKE OUT.

re-instatement notice. See HABITABLE HOUSE.

re-insurance. The act of an insurer in relieving himself of part or of the whole of the liability he has undertaken, by insuring the subject matter himself with other insurers. Re-insurance was formerly illegal. Re-insurance can take the form of *facultative re-insurance* ie re-insurance against liability on a stated policy, or *treaty re-insurance* ie re-insurance against liabilities on policies in general.

Direct insurers authorised in the State are not permitted to accept re-insurance business in classes of insurance for which they do not hold a direct authorisation: Insurance Act 1989, s 22 as amended by Central Bank and Financial Services Authority of Ireland Act 2003, s 35, Sch 1.

Where an insurance company agrees to re-insure a secured risk which turns out to be unsecured, then the re-insurer is not bound to indemnify the insurer for any loss incurred on such risk: *International Commercial Bank plc v Insurance Corp of Ireland* [1990] ITLR (3 December) HC and [1992] ITLR (9 November) SC. See *Winterthur Swiss Insurance v Insurance Corporation of Ireland* [1989] ILRM 13. See also Marine Insurance Act 1906, s 9.

The existing system of notification by re-insurance undertakings has been strengthened and the Minister has been empowered to make regulations for the authorisation and supervision of re-insurance undertakings: Insurance Act 2000. See Reinsurance (Form of Notification) Regulations 1999, SI No 437 of 1999.

The form of notice to be given to the Minister by companies wishing to carry on re-insurance in the State is prescribed in SI No 473 of 2000. See COMMERCIAL PROCEEDINGS.

reading the Riot Act. See RIOTOUS ASSEMBLY.

real estate. Real property; realty; land, tenements, and hereditaments. Where real estate is included (either by a specific or a general description) in a residuary gift made by the will of a testator, it is deemed to be a part of the residue of the testator's estate and not to be the subject of a specific disposition: Taxes Consolidation Act 1997, s 799(2)(c). See ELECTRONIC FORM.

real security. A security charged on land.

realty. Real property; generally freehold interest in land. See ELECTRONIC FORM.

reason, rule of. The method used in the USA to determine whether a restraint of trade was illegal pursuant to the wide-sweeping Sherman Act 1890; only undue and unreasonable restraints would be condemned: *Standard Oil v US* [1911] 221 US 1. The *rule of reason* approach was adopted in *Master Foods Ltd t/a Mars v HB Ice Cream* [1992] ITLR (5 October) HC and has been adopted in judgments of the European Court of Justice eg *Procureur du Roi v Dassonville* [1974] ECR 852(6). The *rule of reason* is also applied by the Competition Authority in interpreting agreements which appear to prevent, restrict or distort competition in trade: see Iris Oifigiúil p 665 on 10 September 1993.

reasonable cause. Expression sometimes used in a statute where a garda or an authorised officer is empowered to stop a vehicle or enter any land or premises, if necessary by force, where that person has *reasonable cause* to suspect that an offence has been committed eg Animal Remedies Act 1993, s 11. A 'hunch' is not sufficient; some basis for the suspicion must be shown. The test is an objective one ie whether a reasonable man, would believe that there was a reasonable cause: *Dallison v Caffery* [1965] 1 QB 348. Nothing in the nature of a *prima facie* case is required: *Dumbell v Roberts* [1944] 1 All ER 326. See ENTER AND SEARCH.

reasonable doubt. See BEYOND REASONABLE DOUBT.

reasonable expectation. See LEGITIMATE EXPECTATION.

reasonable man. A careful man; a man of ordinary prudence: *Murphy v Hurley* [1929] SC; *Curry v Foster* [1960] Ir Jur Rep 33. The law of negligence lays down that the standard of care is that which is expected from a reasonably careful man in the circumstances: *McComiskey v McDermott* [1974] IR 75.

reasonable time. A *reasonable time* is a question of fact: Sale of Goods Act 1893, s 56. An authorised officer may enter premises at all *reasonable times*: Consumer Credit Act 1995, s 8B(1)(a) as inserted by Central Bank and Financial Services Authority of Ireland Act 2003, s 35, Sch 1. Entry to a butcher's shop on a Sunday afternoon has been held as reasonable: *Small v Bickley* [1875] 40 JP 119. See OFFER.

reasonableness. The test applied in assessing damages for mental distress is one of *reasonableness*; this does not mean 'moderate' or 'small', but it does rule out compensation being measured by reference to an 'imagined worst case': *McCarty v Walsh* [1965] IR 246. In a particular case it was held that when forming a decision to dismiss an employee, the effect of the dismissal on the employee is relevant to its reasonableness: *Lundy v Airmotive Ireland Ltd* [1992] ELR 211, CC. See also *Orange v Director of Telecommunications* [2000] 4 IR 159, SC.

reasonably practicable. Phrase used in some statutory provisions which impose a duty e g *so far as is reasonably practicable* in relation to safety at work legislation: Safety, Health and Welfare at Work Act 1989, s 6. *Practicable* has been interpreted to mean, in effect, technologically possible; *reasonably practicable* has been interpreted to mean a level of precaution which takes account of the balance between the risk involved in a particular hazard and the cost involved in remedying it. See *Edwards v National Coal Board* [1949] 1 KB 704; *Kirwan v Bray UDC* [1969] SC; *Bradley v CIE* [1976] IR 217; *Brady v Beckmann Instruments Inc* [1986] ILRM 361; *Keane v ESB* [1981] IR 44. See 'Building Confidence' by solicitor Geoffrey Shannon in *Law Society Gazette* (September 2002) 24.

reasoned opinion. (1) An opinion with reasons issued by the European Commission to the government of a member state, outlining the steps that need to be taken for the member state to fully implement EU law. It is an 'early warning system' as part of the scrutiny by the Commission of the actions by member states to implement EU law. If the Commission is dissatisfied with the steps taken, it may refer the matter to the European Court of Justice. See EC Treaty, arts 226–228 of the consolidated (2002) version.

(2) An opinion with reasons issued by the parliament of a member state that a proposal for a law, made by the European Commission, is in breach of the principle of subsidiarity: National Forum on Europe, *Summary of the Draft Constitutional Treaty for the European Union – Glossary of Terms* (2003).

rebate. A refund; a credit; a discount.

rebus sic stantibus. [In these circumstances.]

rebut. To contradict; to disprove; to oppose; e g to disprove a presumption.

rebuttal, evidence in. Evidence to answer or defeat his opponent's evidence which the party *beginning* in the trial of an action may be allowed to adduce. Generally rebuttal evidence is not allowed, as the party beginning is normally expected to anticipate his opponent's evidence. However, in criminal trials, the trial judge has a discretion to allow the prosecution to call evidence in relation to some new matter introduced by the defence, which the prosecution could not have foreseen.

In civil cases, the party beginning may be allowed to call rebuttal evidence to answer evidence on a matter the proof of which lay with his opponents, and also where he has been taken by surprise. See *Riordan v O'Shea* [1926] 60 ILTR 61; *Attorney-General v Gleeson* [1930] 64 ILTR 225.

recall of witness. See WITNESS, RECALL OF.

recaption. The lawful retaking by a person, without causing a breach of the peace, of his chattels from another, which other had wrongfully taken and detained them.

receipt. Written acknowledgment of money paid or of goods received. A receipt under seal is conclusive whereas a receipt under hand is but *prima facie* evidence of same which can be rebutted. A receipt is not a written offer; hence its acceptance does not make its terms binding on the person who receives it. See *Chapelton v Barry RDC* [1940] 1 KB 532. See PAYMENT; VOUCHER.

receiver, company. A person appointed by the court or by creditors of a company to manage the company's business until satisfaction of a debt. Often a debenture will authorise the appointment of a receiver on certain conditions being satisfied. The court has an inherent jurisdiction to appoint a receiver over charged assets. A body corporate cannot be a receiver of the property of a company, nor may an undischarged bankrupt or an officer, or servant, or auditor of a company, or their close relatives: Companies Act 1963, ss 314 and 315 as amended by the Companies Act 1990, s 170.

The appointment of a receiver operates to *crystallise* floating charges which then become fixed; it also operates to suspend the company's powers and the directors' authority in relation to the assets covered by the receivership. However, this does not interfere with the power of the directors to institute proceedings in the name of the company in the interest of the company or its creditors: *Lascomme Ltd v UDT (Ireland) Ltd* [1994] 1 ILRM 227, HC.

Appointment of a receiver by the court operates to dismiss the company's existing employees, although they may become employed by the receiver. The appointment of a receiver out of court, however, does not of itself automatically terminate employment contracts with the company.

The receiver has power to do everything necessary to realise the security and he may apply to the court for directions: CA 1963, s 316(1), as amended by the CA 1990, s 171; *Industrial Development Authority v Moran* [1978] IR 159. The following may also apply to the court for directions in connection with the performance by the receiver of his functions: an officer, member, contributory, liquidator or employees. A receiver is not bound by the company's contractual obligations: *Airlines Airspares v Handley Page* [1970] 1 Ch 193; *Ardmore Studios (Ireland) Ltd v Lynch* [1965] IR 1.

Receivers are *fiduciaries* for those who appointed them and owe those persons duties of good faith, including a duty of care to the company: *McGowan v Gannon* [1983] ILRM 516. A receiver, in selling property of a company, must exercise all reasonable care to obtain the best price reasonably obtainable for the property as at the time of sale: CA 1963, s 316A as inserted by CA 1990, s 172. He must give notice to the creditors if he intends to sell by private contract a non-cash asset of *requisite value* to an officer of the company (CA 1963, s 316A(3)). Section 316A referred not to value nor cost but to price: *In the matter of Bula Ltd* [2002] 2 ILRM 513, HC and [2003] FL 7793, SC and 2 IR 430. See also *McCarter v Roughan and McLaughlin* [1984] ILRM 447.

Every business letter, order for goods or invoices issued by or for the company or the receiver, must state that a receiver has been appointed (CA 1963, s 317). The directors and secretary and such other officers and employees of the company as the receiver directs, must draw up a statement of the company's affairs at the date of the receiver's appointment (CA 1963, s 320 as amended by CA 1990, ss 173–174). The receiver must make certain information and accounts available to the company and to the Registrar of Companies (CA 1963, ss 319(1) and 321).

The court may, on cause shown, remove a receiver and appoint another (CA 1963, s 322A as inserted by CA 1990, s 175) and may determine or limit a receivership on the application of a receiver (CA 1963, s 322B as inserted by CA 1990, s 176). The court may also order the return of assets of a company in receivership which have been improperly transferred (CA 1990, s 178).

A receiver has an obligation to pay preferential creditors (CA 1963, s 98). However, the court may order that s 98 is not to apply to a company where an examiner has been or is about to be appointed: Companies (Amendment) (No 2) Act 1999, s 17.

While there are no qualifications specified for receivers, the Minister is empowered to add to the list of persons who are not qualified for appointment (CA 1990, s 237). See also Building Societies Act 1989, s 40(5).

A receiver appointed by the court over any property is chargeable to income tax, corporation tax and to capital gains tax as if the property were not under the control of the court: Taxes Consolidation Act 1997, ss 1049 and 1051(f).

A receiver of a company is now required to send a statement to the *Director of Corporate Enforcement* as to whether, in his opinion, the company is solvent at the end of the receivership: Company Law Enforcement Act 2001, s 52. Also the disciplinary committee or tribunal of prescribed professional bodies whose members conduct liquidations or receiverships, are required to notify the Director in certain circumstance eg where a member has not maintained proper records or is suspected of committing an indictable offence (CLEA 2001, s 58). For prescribed professional bodies, see Company Law Enforcement (Section 58) Regulations 2002, SI No 544 of 2002. See *Re Manning Furniture Ltd* [1996] 1 ILRM 13, HC; *Bula Ltd and Others v Crowley and Others* [2002] FL 5044, HC and [2003] 1 ILRM 55. See Land Registration Rules 1986, SI No 310 of 1986, r 4. [Bibliography: Forde (1) and (9); McGrath S; Keane (1); Ussher; Kerr (UK); Picardu (UK).] See DIRECTOR OF CORPORATE ENFORCEMENT; DISQUALIFICATION ORDER.

receiver by way of equitable execution. Where an application is made to the Circuit Court for the appointment of a *receiver by way of equitable execution*, the judge is required to have regard to the amount of the judgment held by the applicant, to the amount which may probably be obtained by the receiver, and to the probable costs and expenses of and incidental to his appointment: Circuit Court Rules 2001 Ord 39. See EQUITABLE EXECUTION.

receiver of bankrupt's property. The receiver or manager of a bankrupt's property, or of the property of an *arranging debtor* (qv), who the High Court is empowered to appoint; the court may direct the receiver to take immediate possession of such property or any part thereof: Bankruptcy Act 1988, s 73. See BANKRUPTCY.

receiver of criminal's property. The receiver appointed by the court to take possession of property, which constitutes the *proceeds of crime*, and in accordance with the court's directions, to manage, keep possession or dispose of or otherwise deal with it: Proceeds of Crime Act 1996, s 7. The receiver may only be appointed while an *interim* or *interlocutory* order in respect of the property is in force. A receiver is not liable to any person in respect of loss or damage except as caused by his negligence (PCA 1996, s 7(2)). See PROCEEDS OF CRIME.

receiver of mortgaged property. A receiver appointed by the mortgagee (lender) under an express power in the mortgage deed or under statutory power given by the Conveyancing Act 1881, s 19.

The statutory power arises when the mortgage is by deed and after the redemption date has passed; it becomes exercisable where there is default of three months after notice is given to the mortgagor demanding payment of the principal outstanding, or interest is in arrears for two months, or there has been a breach of covenant, other than for payment of money.

The receiver is deemed in law to be the *agent of the mortgagor* and consequently the mortgagee is not liable to the mortgagor for the receiver's default. Moneys received by the receiver must be applied: to discharge the outgoings; to meet annual payments which have priority to the mortgage; to discharge his commission, insurance and repairs; to discharge interest on the mortgage and, if directed by the mortgagee in writing, to discharge the principal; and to pay the residue to the mortgagor. The receiver is entitled to commission at the rate of up to 5% or such higher rate as the court thinks fit to allow: CA 1881, s 24(6) and *In the matter of City Car Sales Ltd* [1995] 1 ILRM 221, HC.

It has been held that the powers of CA 1881, s 24(3) do not entitle the receiver to appropriate any part of the proceeds of sale of the dairy produce or the cattle on land subject to a mortgage: *Donohue v Agricultural Credit Corporation* [1986] IR 165. See *Re Edenfell Holdings Ltd* [1999] 1 IR 443, SC; *Bula Ltd v Crowley* [2003] 1 ILRM 55, HC and [2002] FL 5044, HC. [Bibliography: Wylie (3).]

receiver of wreck. A person appointed by the Minister to be a *receiver of wreck* in respect of any specified area of the State: Merchant Shipping (Salvage and Wreck) Act 1993, s 41. Anyone, other than the owner, who finds or recovers a wreck must deliver it into the possession of the receiver (MS(SW)A 1993, s 44). The receiver must give notice of taking possession of a wreck with a view to establishing ownership, must hand it over to the rightful owner, and if unclaimed, notify the Director of the National Museum who may take possession of the wreck if it is of archaeological, historical or artistic merit (MS(SW)A 1993, ss 45–50). See WRECK.

receiving stolen goods. Formerly, the offence committed by a person who received stolen goods knowing them, at the time he received them, to have been stolen: Larceny Act 1916, s 33. The offence has now been abolished and replaced by the wider offence of *handling stolen property* (qv), which includes receiving: Larceny Act 1990, s 3 which substitutes a new LA 1916, s 33.

In the former offence of receiving, the original act of dishonesty included not only a stealing of the goods but also the obtaining of them in circumstances which amounted to a felony or misdemeanour. It had to be shown that the accused took the goods into his possession, actual or constructive. The goods had also to be stolen by a person other than the accused. It had to be shown that the accused at the time he received them, knew they were stolen; this guilty knowledge could be shown by *inference* eg the price, place or time when he received them.

In the absence of a reasonable explanation from the possessor of recently stolen goods, a jury was entitled to conclude that he was either the thief or the guilty receiver. Evidence that: (a) other property, stolen within one year previously, has been found in the accused's possession, or that (b) the accused was convicted, within five years previously, of any offence involving fraud or dishonesty, was admissible to prove guilty knowledge on the part of the accused (LA 1916, s 43 repealed by LA 1990). See *Attorney-General v Farnan* [1933] 67 ILTR 208; *The People (Attorney-General) v Berber and Levey* [1944] IR 405; *The People v Carney and Mulcahy* [1955] IR 324. See also LRC 23 of 1987. See HANDLING STOLEN PROPERTY; UNLAWFUL POSSESSION OF GOODS.

recidivism. Habitual relapse into crime. It has been held that the Oireachtas was entitled to enact a provision which had regard to the danger of *recidivism* with regard to sexual crime, as well as the addictive character of certain sexual offences involving minors, and the need to avoid a situation where persons convicted of such offences or with a clear propensity to engage in such behaviour, could secure access to employment on an equal footing with other employees: *Re Employment Equality Bill 1996* [1997] 2 IR 321, SC and ELR 132.

reciprocity. The term used in international law to describe the agreement of states to bestow privileges on each others' subjects. See *Government of Canada v Employment Appeals Tribunal* [1992] ELR 29. See FRANCHISE.

recitals. Statements in an instrument, commencing *whereas* ... , which explain or lead up to the operative part of the instrument. In a conveyance (qv), they may be *narrative recitals* which set out the facts and instruments necessary to show title, or *introductory recitals* which explain the motive for the execution of the deed. They are not necessary to the validity of the deed (qv), but they are useful from the purchaser's standpoint because: they may act as an estoppel (qv) against the vendor; they explain the operative part of the deed; they are evidence of their truth after 20 years: Vendor and Purchaser Act 1874, s 2(2). An erroneous and unnecessary reference to a repealed statute in a recital to a mortgage deed will not invalidate the mortgage: *Bray UDC v Coughlan* [1989] ITLR (24 July).

reckless trading. Includes: (a) the carrying on of a business by an officer of a company who ought to have known that his actions or those of the company would cause loss to the creditors of the company or (b) being a party to the contracting of a debt by the company where the officer did not honestly believe on reasonable grounds that the company would be able to pay the debt as it fell due for payment: Companies Act 1963, s 297A(2) as inserted by s 138 of the Companies Act 1990.

If in the course of the winding up of a company or in the course of examinership (under the Companies Amendment Act 1990), it appears that any person was, while an officer of the company, knowingly a party to the carrying on of any business of the company, in a reckless manner, he can be declared by the court to be personally responsible for all or any part of the debts or other liabilities of the company, without limitation (CA 1963, s 297A(1)(a)). There is not a collective responsibility on the board of directors of a company as regards reckless trading; reckless trading must be proved against each individual defendant officer of the company ie that his conduct fell within the ambit of conduct prohibited or liable to be penalised: *Re Hefferon Kearns Ltd (No 2), Dublin Heating Co Ltd v Hefferon & Ors* [1993] HC as reported by MacCann in 11 ILT & SJ (1993) 31.

If the court considers that the person has acted honestly and responsibly, it may relieve him wholly or partly from personal liability, on whatever terms it deems fit (CA 1963, s 297A(6)). See Flynn in 9 ILT & SJ (1991) 186 and MacCann in 10 ILT & SJ (1991) 31 and 61. See FRAUDULENT TRADING.

recklessness. Intentional creation of unjustifiable risk. Under common law, an occupier was required not do an act which was intended to injure a trespasser, or was so *reckless* as to be likely to injure the trespasser, whose presence was known or ought to have been known: *Coffey v McEvoy* [1912] 2 IR 95. The higher the likelihood of trespassers being present, the greater the likelihood that the conduct of the occupier was reckless: *Donovan v Landy's Ltd* [1963] IR 441. It was also held that *recklessness* is found if a person consciously disregards a substantial and unjustifiable risk which involves culpability to a high degree: *People v Murray* [1977] IR 360, 403.

An occupier now owes a duty of care not to act with *reckless disregard* for an entrant to his premises, be they a recreational user (qv) or trespasser (qv).

The test for *recklessness* is an objective one: *APH Manufacturing BV v DHL* [2001] 1 ILRM 224, HC. On appeal, the Supreme Court held that while the test for recklessness was an objective one, *recklessness* was the commission of an act, conscious of the danger of damage but not caring whether damage would occur; the court would not lightly infer recklessness from the sort of evidence which would merely justify a finding of negligence: *APH Manufacturing BV v DHL* [2001] 4 IR 531, SC. See also *Tiernan v O'Callaghan* [1944] 78 ILTR 36. See also Mary McAleese (now, President of Ireland), 'Just What is Recklessness?' [1981] 5 DULJ 29. See CAUSING SERIOUS HARM; CRIMINAL DAMAGE TO PROPERTY; OCCUPIER'S LIABILITY TO TRESPASSERS.

reclaimed land. Newly reclaimed land is capable of being valued for rates: Valuation (Ireland) Act 1854, s 4; *Coal Distributors Ltd v Commissioner of Valuation* [1990] ILRM 172.

reclamation. Clearly means that land, which was otherwise not going to be available for significant agricultural use, was being put in a condition where it would be so available, by the carrying out of whatever works were necessary: *Dolan v Cooke* [2001] ITLR (25 June) SC. In this case it was held that the making of a road could not be regarded as field drainage or reclamation of land.

recognisance. An obligation or bond made before a court of record (qv) binding a person (called the *recognisor*) to perform some act eg to appear before a court or to keep the peace or to be of good behaviour, or to ensure the attendance of an accused at his trial. For High Court, see RSC Ord 84, rr 16–17.

Where a *bond* or *recognisance* is required from any person, the judge may authorise the acceptance of an instrument executed by a solvent person or corporation (including an insurance company) approved by him: Circuit Court Rules 2001 Ord 44.

For the District Court, see DCR 1997 Ord 12, rr 19–20; Ord 18; Ord 25, r 8; Ord 101, r 4; Estreatment of Recognisances Rules 2003, SI No 411 of 2003. See BAIL, CONDITIONS OF; BAILSPERSON; ESTREAT.

recommendations of EC. See COMMUNITY LAW; EUROPEAN RECOMMENDATION.

recommended price. The price of goods recommended by the manufacturer, producer or other supplier and the recommended price generally for supply by retail in the area where the goods are offered: Consumer Information Act 1978, s 7(2)(b). See PRICE, FALSE OR MISLEADING INDICATION OF; PRODUCT PRICES; RESALE PRICE MAINTENANCE.

reconciliation. The act of settling disputes and harmonising differences. See INDUSTRIAL RELATIONS OFFICER; JUDICIAL SEPARATION; LABOUR COURT.

reconstruction of company. A capital reorganisation of a company arising from a *compromise* or *arrangement* between shareholders or creditors, or between any class of them: Companies Act 1963, ss 201–203. On application, the court will stay or restrain all further proceedings against the company, thereby allowing it to continue in business.

The court will summon meetings of each class of shareholder and creditor affected to consider the arrangement, which will be sanctioned by the court only if the scheme is supported by at least three-fourths in value of each class affected by it who vote, either in person or by proxy. If the scheme involves *reconstruction* of one or more companies or an *amalgamation* of two or more companies, the court possesses extensive powers that facilitate making the scheme effective.

A 'scheme of arrangement' is the preferred route for the take-over of a company having a very large retail shareholding base eg in the case of a demutualised former building society, as the take-over is effective and binding on all shareholders, when a 75% majority of shareholders actually voting, vote in favour of the scheme. This compares with the requirement under a 'tender offer' of acceptance by 80% of shareholders *by value* to allow compulsory acquisition of the minority shareholders. The take-over of First Active plc by the Royal Bank of Scotland in 2004 was effected by way of a scheme of arrangement.

There is provision for a compromise or a scheme of arrangement in respect of a company which is subject to the protection of the court: Companies (Amendment) Act 1990, ss 17(4)(e) and 24 and Companies (Amendment) (No 2) Act 1999, ss 22–24, 26. Also reconstruction orders made by courts outside the State may be enforced by the High Court (C(A)A 1990, s 36). There is provision for exemption from stamp duty in relation to the transfer of property on the reconstruction or amalgamation of companies: Stamp Duties Consolidation Act 1999, s 80 as amended by Finance Act 2004, s 68.

It has been clarified, for the avoidance of doubt, that the High Court in exercise of its powers under the Companies Act 1963, ss 203 and 204 as regards a *compromise* or *arrangement* between shareholders and creditors, has to have regard to the Irish Takeover Panel and its powers under the Irish Takeover Panel Act 1997, and that nothing in CA 1963, ss 201, 203 or 204 prejudices the jurisdiction of the Takeover Panel with respect to a compromise or arrangement which constitutes a *take-over* within the meaning of ITPA 1997: CA 1963, s 201 as amended by Company Law Enforcement Act 2001, s 92. See Takeover Rules 2001, Pt B, r 41. See also Credit Union Act 1997, s 161 as amended by Central Bank and Financial Services Authority of Ireland Act 2003, s 35, Sch 1. See *Re Pye (Ireland) Ltd* [1985] HC; *Re John Power Son Ltd* [1934] IR 412; *Re Van Dyk Models Ltd* 100 ILTR 177 [1966.] [Bibliography: Forde (7); O'Driscoll T.] See MERGER; COURT PROTECTION OF COMPANY; TENDER OFFER.

reconversion. The notional restoration of previously notionally converted property to its original character in contemplation of equity. Reconversion may take place by act of the party for whose benefit the conversion was directed or by operation of law. An absolute owner who is *sui juris* may elect to take the property in whatever form he chooses; if he wishes to take it in its unconverted form, a reconversion takes place.

Reconversion also takes place by law in certain conditions where property, though subject to an inoperative trust for conversion, has not actually been converted, and the property is *at home*. See *McDonagh v Nolan* [1882] 9 LR IR 262. [Bibliography: Wylie (3).] See CONVERSION IN EQUITY.

reconveyance. The revesting in the mortgagor of the legal estate on redemption of the mortgage. A reconveyance is not necessary in specified circumstances. See REDEMPTION.

record. (1) A memorial of an action in a court of record (qv). (2) An authentic account of some event. (3) To make a written account.

(4) Any disc, tape, perforated roll or other device in which sounds are embodied so as to be capable of being automatically reproduced therefrom: Broadcasting and Wireless Telegraphy Act 1988, s 1(1). It is an offence to supply a record with the intent that it may be comprised in an illegal broadcast (BWTA 1988, s 5(2)(a)). It was held that, under the previous copyright legislation, power CDs on which sounds, text, graphics and visual images are recorded, constitute records: Copyright Act 1963, s 2(1); *Mandarin Ltd v Mechanical Copyright Protection Society Ltd* [1999] 1 ILRM 154, HC. See now SOUND RECORDING.

(5) Any memorandum, book, plan, map, drawing, diagram, pictorial or graphic work or other document: Freedom of Information Act 1997, s 2(1). A copy, in any form, of a record is deemed, for the purposes of the Act, to have been created at the same time as the record: Freedom of Information (Amendment) Act 2003, s 2(a). See INFORMATION, ACCESS TO; PERSONAL INFORMATION; PERSONNEL RECORD. See also COURT OF RECORD; TAPE RECORDING.

recording conversations. A solicitor may make an electronic recording of a conversation with a colleague, client or third party: *A Guide to Professional Conduct of Solicitors in Ireland* (2002) ch 6.10. If a solicitor proposes to record a conversation, he should warn the party to be recorded that the conversation will be recorded. There may be exceptional circumstances where such warning need not be given. See TAPE RECORDING; TELEPHONE TAPPING.

recording right. The exclusive right of a performer to authorise or prohibit the making of a recording of a performance directly from the live performance: Copyright and

Related Rights Act 2000, s 203(1)(a). An infringement of a recording right is actionable as a breach of *statutory duty* owed to the person entitled to the right (CRRA 2000, s 308(1)(b)).

An 'exclusive recording contract' is a contract between a performer and another person under which that person is entitled to the exclusion of all other persons (including the performer) to make recordings of one or more of that performer's performances with a view to their commercial exploitation (CRRA 2000, s 215(1)). Provision has been made to deal with infringement of rights deriving from these contracts eg *primary* infringement through copying, making use of or dealing in illicit recordings and *secondary* infringement through providing means for making illicit recordings (CRRA 2000, s 216–219). Recording rights in relation to a performance, other than exclusive recording rights, are not assignable or transmissible (CRRA 2000, s 301). See COMMERCIAL PROCEEDINGS; PERFORMERS' RIGHTS; SOUND RECORDING.

recount. In an election, the returning officer (qv) must re-examine and recount ballot papers at the conclusion of any count at the request of any candidate or his election agent; he is not required to do so more than once: Electoral Act 1992, s 125(1). Each candidate has a right to demand one complete re-examination and recount (EA 1992, s 125(3)). See also Presidential Elections Act 1993, s 52; Referendum Act 1994, s 36; European Parliament Elections Act 1997, Sch 2, r 89. See ELECTION AGENT; SPOILT VOTE.

recourse, right of. The right which the *holder in due course* (qv) has as against every person who signed a negotiable instrument (qv), if the party primarily liable on it fails to meet his obligation.

recovered memory. Where a person is charged with very old offences on the basis of alleged recovered memory, the person is entitled to seek to inform himself about every aspect of the therapy associated with the recovery: *NC v DPP* [2001] ITLR (3 September) SC. In this case the therapist had since died and consequently the prosecution of the accused was prevented by the court from proceeding.

recovery. A collusive action, called *common recovery,* first recognised in *Taltarum's case* 1472, which was used to *bar an entail* until its abolition by the Fines and Recoveries Act 1833, which substituted a simple disentailing assurance. See BARRING THE ENTAIL.

recovery of goods. As regards goods the subject of a hire-purchase agreement, the owner has no authority, without the hirer's consent, to enter on the hirer's premises for the purpose of taking back the goods: Consumer Credit Act 1995, s 64 and Sch 5. Where one-third of the *hire-purchase price* (qv) has been paid or tendered, the owner cannot enforce any right to recover possession of the goods otherwise than by legal proceedings. There are special provisions governing motor vehicles. See *Capital Finance Co Ltd v Bray* [1963] 1 All ER 604; *Mercantile Credit Company of Ireland Ltd v O'Malley* [1957] IR 22; *Irish Buyway Ltd v Ivory* 86 ILTR 83; *United Dominions Trust (Commercial) Ltd v Jeremiah Byrne* [1957] IR 77; *McDonald v Bowmaker (Ireland) Ltd* [1949] IR 317. See RSC Ord 27, rr 2 and 16. See RECOVERY OF MOTOR VEHICLE.

recovery of land. See EJECTMENT; MORTGAGEE, RIGHTS OF.

recovery of motor vehicle. As regards a motor vehicle the subject of a hire-purchase agreement, the owner is entitled to enforce any right he may have to enter any land of the hirer for the purpose of taking back the vehicle; this does not include, however, the hirer's home or any building attached thereto: Consumer Credit Act 1995, Sch 5.

Where one-third of the *hire-purchase price* (qv) has been paid, the owner cannot enforce any right to recover possession of the vehicle otherwise than by legal proceedings (CCA 1995, s 64).

However, where the owner has commenced legal proceedings to recover possession of the vehicle and the vehicle has been abandoned or has been left unattended in circumstances likely to result in damage to the vehicle, the owner is entitled to enforce a right to recover possession of the vehicle (CCA 1995, s 64(3) and Sch 5). *Motor vehicle* means a vehicle intended or adapted for propulsion by mechanical means (CCA 1995, s 2(1)). See *McDonald v Bowmaker (Ireland) Ltd* [1949] IR 317. See RSC Ord 27, rr 2 and 16.

recreational user. As regards occupiers' liability to entrants on premises, means an entrant who, with or without the occupier's permission or at the occupier's implied invitation, is present on premises without a *charge* being imposed for the purpose of engaging in a recreational activity: Occupiers' Liability Act 1995, s 1(1). *Recreational activity* means any recreational activity conducted in the open air (including any sporting activity), scientific research and nature study so conducted, exploring caves and visiting sites and buildings of historical, architectural, traditional, artistic, archaeological or scientific importance (OLA 1995, s 1(1)). An entrant is not a recreational user if he comes within the definition of a *visitor* (qv). A 'charge' does not include a reasonable charge for vehicle parking facilities. See NATIONAL MONUMENT; OCCUPIERS' LIABILITY TO RECREATIONAL USERS.

recrimination. Formerly, a defence plea in a suit for *divorce a mensa et thoro* (qv) by the respondent, whereby in answer to the petitioner's allegations of adultery (qv) on the part of the respondent, the respondent alleged that the petitioner had also committed adultery. It could be a complete defence to such a petition. However, recrimination on the part of an applicant is not now a bar to the grant of a decree of judicial separation (qv): Judicial Separation and Family Law Reform Act 1989, s 44. See *Chettle v Chettle* [1821] 161 ER 1399. See CONDONATION; CONNIVANCE.

recruitment. See EMPLOYMENT AGENCY; EMPLOYMENT PERMIT; PUBLIC SERVICE RECRUITMENT; WORK IN EU.

rectification. (1) The correction of an error in a register, or instrument or judgment eg due to a clerical error or an error of draftsmanship.

(2) Where parties have reduced a contract between them to writing which does not accurately express their agreement, it may be rectified under the *doctrine of rectification*. The doctrine is invoked where the consent of the parties is real and undoubted, but it has by mistake been inaccurately expressed in a later written agreement. The onus of proof on the plaintiff is heavy; oral evidence to justify rectification must be conclusive rather than on the balance of probability.

It has been held that rectification can be granted where there was prior accord on a term of the proposed agreement, outwardly expressed and communicated between the parties; the common intention of the parties must be continuous and must have the necessary precision; the onus of proof on the plaintiff is heavy: *Irish Life Assurance Co Ltd v Dublin Land Securities Ltd* [1989] IR 253, SC. See *Ferguson v Merchant Banking Ltd* [1993] ILRM 136, HC; *R McD v V McD* [1993] ILRM 717, HC; *Lac Minerals Ltd v Chevron Mineral* [1995] 1 ILRM 161, HC. See O'Ceidigh in 8 ILT & SJ (1990) 186. [Bibliography: Delaney H (2); Wylie (3).] See DATA PROTECTION; MISTAKE; REGISTER OF TRADE MARKS; SLIP RULE.

recycling. In relation to waste, the subjection of waste to any process or treatment to make it re-usable in whole or in part: Waste Management Act 1996, s 5(1). There are a wide range of provisions intended to support measures to reduce the production of waste and to promote its recovery, including mandatory 'deposit and refund' schemes, 'take back' schemes, charges by retailers for items of packaging, and 'recycling credit schemes' (WMA 1996, ss 27–31 as amended by Protection of the Environment Act 2003, s 28). See WASTE MANAGEMENT PLAN.

red-circling. Phrase used in employment law to describe a special agreement to protect the pay of a comparator for reasons personal to the comparator eg that the employee is unfit to do the duties of a higher grade. It has been held that there can be no requirement that a 'red-circling' situation be recognised, factual and acknowledged in order to constitute a defence against a claim of discrimination in pay; it is sufficient if the differential in pay between the claimants and the comparators is in fact based on grounds other than sex: *Minister for Transport v Campbell* [1996] ELR 106, HC.

The High Court has held that 'red-circling' involved an imprecise negotiation term that did not occur in legislation and such phrases should not be construed as if they appeared in statutes: *Fitzgerald v South Eastern Health Board* [2002] 2 IR 674, HC and [2003] ELR 257. See also *Department of Tourism v Four Workers* [1998] ELR 1, LC; *42 Named Male Employees v University College Cork* [1999] ELR 337, EO. See EQUAL PAY; LIKE WORK.

Red Cross. The Irish Red Cross Society established in 1938 with the primary objective of furnishing volunteer aid to the sick, wounded and shipwrecked at sea and armed forces in time of war and to furnish relief to prisoners of war and to such citizens as are *protected persons*: Red Cross Acts 1938 and 1954; Geneva Conventions (Amendment) Act 1998, s 13. It is an offence to use the Red Cross emblem without Ministerial consent. See *Walsh v Irish Red Cross Society* [1997] 2 IR 479, SC. See WAR.

reddendo singula singulis. [Giving each to each.]

reddendum. That which is to be paid; the clause in a lease which specifies the rent which is payable and the time when payable eg: 'Yielding therefor during the said term, the yearly rent of € ... clear of all deductions by equal half yearly payments on ... , the first payment to be made on ... .'

redeemable shares. Includes shares which are liable at the option of the company or the shareholder to be redeemed: Companies Act 1990, s 206. A company may now issue redeemable shares and redeem them, except where the nominal value of the issued share capital which is not redeemable is less than one-tenth of the nominal value of the total issued share capital of the company; also no such shares can be redeemed unless they are fully paid (CA 1990, s 207). There is provision for cancelling of shares on redemption or for holding them as *treasury shares* (qv) instead of cancellation (CA 1990, ss 208–209). Previously, a limited company could, if authorised by its articles of association, issue preference shares which could be redeemed at the option of the company, without going through the cumbersome capital reduction procedure: Companies Act 1963, ss 64–65 as amended by Companies Act 1983, Sch 1, para 12. See also CA 1990, ss 220–221. See RSC Ord 75, r 19. See Nolan in 9 ILT & SJ (1991) 9. See PREFERENCE SHARES.

redemption. The repayment of a mortgage debt whereby the equitable and legal estates merge in the mortgagor (qv). A mortgagor may bring a *redemption suit* to compel the mortgagee to reconvey the land on payment of debt and interest and to return his title deeds: RSC Ord 18, r 2; Ord 54 r 3. See also Circuit Court Rules 2001 Ord 9, r 2.

The rules of a building society must provide for the conditions on which a borrower of a housing loan (qv) can redeem the amount due from him before the end of the period for which such a loan was made: Building Societies Act 1989, Sch 2, Pt II, para 5(e).

Where all moneys secured by a mortgage have been fully paid or discharged, a building society may issue a receipt under the seal of the society; this receipt operates to vacate the mortgage and, without any reconveyance or re-surrender, vests the estate or interest in the property in the person for the time being entitled to the *equity of redemption* (qv) (BSA 1989, s 27).

A simplified procedure for discharging mortgages of housing authorities and other specified cases is provided for in the Housing Act 1988, s 18. See also PAWN.

redemption, equity of. See EQUITY OF REDEMPTION.

redemption fee. In relation to a loan, any sum in addition to principal and any interest due on such principal (without regard to the fact of the redemption of the loan) at the time of redemption of the whole or part of the loan: Building Societies Act 1986, s 6; SI No 27 of 1987, Sch 1; SI No 339 of 1987; Consumer Credit Act 1995, s 121(6). A member of a building society may at any time before the time agreed, repay the society the whole or any part of a loan, and is not liable to pay any redemption fee in relation to the loan or any part of the loan.

Notwithstanding the repeal of BSA 1986, this provision is continued in force as regards existing and future housing loans; however the ban on redemption fees does not apply to fixed-rate interest loans as it restricts the making of such loans: Building Societies Act 1989, s 6. The 1989 Act provides that the ban does not apply to a *housing loan* (qv) in respect of which the mortgage or loan agreement provides that the rate of interest may not be changed or may only be changed at intervals of not less than one year (BSA 1989, s 6(3)).

Similar exemptions to the ban on redemption fees were introduced by CCA 1995 in respect of *housing loans* (qv). Additionally, redemption fees may be applied to a housing loan where the interest rate cannot be increased for five years by more than 2% above the rate at the making of the agreement (CCA 1995, s 121(2)). For amendment to CCA 1995, s 121(4), see Central Bank and Financial Services Authority of Ireland Act 2003, s 35, Sch 1.

redenomination. See Economic and Monetary Union Act 1998 (Redenomination of Negotiable Debt Instruments) Order 1998, SI No 424 of 1998. See CAPITAL.

redress. See RELIEF; REMEDY.

reduction of capital. The reduction of capital of a company which must be approved by special resolution of the members, by creditors and by the court e g reduction in share capital of the exploration company Oliver Resources plc approved by the High Court (*Irish Times*, 17 November 1992). See Companies Act 1963, ss 72–77 as amended. See RSC Ord 75, r 17. See Listing Rules 2000, para 14.10. See CAPITAL RECONSTRUCTION.

redundancy. Includes dismissal of an employee where the dismissal is due to the complete or partial closing down of his place of employment or due to a decrease in his employer's requirements for employees of his kind and qualifications: Redundancy Payments Act 1967, s 7(2) as amended by Redundancy Payments Act 1971 and Redundancy Payments Act 2003.

The two important characteristics of redundancy are 'impersonality' and 'change': *St Ledger v Frontline Distributors Ltd* [1995] ELR 160, EAT; *Moloney v W Deacon & Sons Ltd* [1996] ELR 230, EAT. This view of the Employment Appeals Tribunal is confirmed by the insertion into the definition of a redundancy situation, in RPA 1967, s 7(2) of the words 'for one or more reasons not related to the employee concerned' (RPA 2003, s 5).

Redundancy is a substantial ground justifying dismissal; however, selection for dismissal in contravention of an agreed or established procedure is an unfair dismissal: Unfair Dismissals Act 1977, s 6. An employer is required to act fairly in relation to the criteria to be applied in making a selection for redundancy, including the procedural and substantive aspect of the employer's decision: *Boucher v Irish Productivity Centre* [1994] ELR 205, EAT. See also *Kelly v Aer Rianta International* [1998] ELR 170, EAT.

An employee who is dismissed by his employer is presumed to have been dismissed by reason of redundancy, unless the contrary is proved (RPA 1971, s 10(b)). An employer has an obligation to look at alternatives to redundancy and to consider all employees as candidates for redundancy: *Mulcahy v Kelly & Barry, Architects* [1993] ELR 35, EAT.

Reorganisation of a company by replacement of an employee by an outside contract worker comes within the definition of a redundancy situation: *McCafferty v Nostex Properties Ltd* [1990] ELR 87, EAT. There is no general right to a hearing prior to dismissal involving redundancy even for an officer: *Hickey v Eastern Health Board* [1991] 9 ILT Dig 24, SC. In a particular case, an employer was estopped from using alleged misconduct as a reason for selection for redundancy, since the employment of the employee continued after the alleged misconduct: *Fox v Des Kelly Carpets Ltd* [1992] ELR 182, EAT.

An employee is entitled to a redundancy lump-sum payment provided he has had 104 weeks' continuous employment with the dismissing employer (RPA 1967, s 7(5) as amended by the RPA 1971). The lump sum was related to the employee's age, length of service and his normal earnings. In 2003: (a) the age differentiation was repealed, (b) provision was made to preserve continuity of service for certain 'breaks' in employment and to protect employees who commence their employment abroad, and (c) provision was made for enhanced redundancy payments of two weeks' pay per year of service, plus one extra week's pay (RPA 2003, ss 8, 11, 12 and 16). Calculation of redundancy payment may be made by double-clicking on the Redundancy Calculator icon on the home page of website: *www.entemp.ie*.

There are safeguards where there are changes in the ownership of the company or business (RPA 1967, s 20). Acceptance and retention by an employee of a redundancy payment, where a business is transferred to another owner, breaks that employee's continuity of service: Minimum Notice and Terms of Employment Act 1973, Sch 1, para 7, as amended by Unfair Dismissals (Amendment) Act 1993, s 15.

Redundancy now applies to regular part-time workers: Worker Protection (Regular Part-time Employees) Act 1991, s 1.

See also *Kelly v Tokus Grass Products* 196/1981; *McSorely v Mogul of Ireland Ltd* 992/1982; *Irish Shipping v Adams* [1987] HC; *Bates v Model Bakery Ltd* [1993] 1 IR 359, SC; *O'Brien v Smurfit (Ireland) Ltd* [1997] ELR 74, EAT. See also Adoptive Leave Act 1995, ss 27–29. See SI No 197 of 2003. See 'Redundancy & Fair Procedures' by Barry in 11 ILT & SJ (1993) 190; 'Beyond what is deemed Unfair Redundancy' by Forde in (1994) ELR. [Bibliography: Barrett; Barry J; Forde (8); Redmond (1).] See ACQUIRED RIGHTS; ALTERNATIVE EMPLOYMENT; EMPLOYMENT AWARDS;

INSOLVENCY OF EMPLOYER; REDUN-
DANCY, COLLECTIVE; TIME OFF; UNFAIR
DISMISSAL; WORK.

redundancy, collective. Occurs where in
the same establishment a number of
employees are dismissed for redundancy in
a period of 30 days. The number varies
with the size of the workforce. Where an
employer proposes to create *collective redun-
dancies,* he has a statutory obligation to
notify the Minister before the first dismissal
takes effect and to enter into consultation
with employees' representatives with a view
to reaching an agreement: Protection of
Employment Act 1977.

**redundancy and employers' insolvency
fund.** See REDUNDANCY; INSOLVENCY OF
EMPLOYER.

redundancy payment. The ceiling on the
annual reckonable earnings to be taken into
account in the calculation of a *statutory*
redundancy lump sum payment has been
increased from IR£15,600 to £20,800
(€26,411): Redundancy Payments (Lump
Sum) Regulations 2001, SI No 41 of 2001.

Since 1999, the first £8,000 (€10,160) of
non-statutory redundancy payment,
increased by £600 (€765) for each complete year of service, is exempt from tax;
this may be increased by up to £4,000
(€5,080) as an additional amount in certain
circumstances; as an alternative the taxpayer may claim an amount known as
SCSB – *standard capital superannuation benefit*: Finance Act 1993, s 8, now Taxes
Consolidation Act 1997, ss 123, 201 and
Sch 3.

In 2002, the additional amount limit was
increased from €5,080 to €10,000 and it
may be availed of by an individual every ten
years: Finance Act 2002, s 15.

refer to drawer. The words written on a
cheque by a banker which indicate that the
cheque is being dishonoured for want of
funds. It has been held that the return of
cheques by a bank marked 'refer to drawer
– present again' and 'return to drawer' are
reasonably capable of a defamatory meaning: *Pyke v Hibernian Bank* [1950] IR 105.
See also *Grealy v Bank of Nova Scotia*
[1975] HC. See DEFAMATION.

referee. (1) A person to whom a question is
referred for an opinion; an arbitrator. (2) A
person who provides a character reference
for another. See ARBITRATION;
REFERENCE.

reference. (1) The submission of a matter
to an arbitrator for his decision. (2) The

submission of a Bill by the President of
Ireland to the Supreme Court for a decision as to its constitutionality. (3) As
regards employment, a statement made
concerning an employee usually made by
his employer or former employer. It has
been held that no action lies against an
employer for refusing to furnish a certificate
of character in respect of an employee
leaving the employment: *Lint v Johnston*
[1894] 28 ILTR 16. An employer who
gives a reference which he knows to be
untrue to a prospective employer, may be
liable in deceit (qv) or in negligence for a
mis-statement (qv) or in defamation (qv).
See also BORD PLEANÁLA, AN; EUROPEAN
COURT OF JUSTICE. See ARBITRATION;
PRESIDENT OF IRELAND.

referendum. The submission to the decision of the people of the State:(a) of an
amendment of the Constitution, a *constitutional* referendum; or (b) of a Bill which is
the subject of a petition to the President of
Ireland, an *ordinary* referendum: 1937
Constitution, arts 27 and 47; Referendum
Act 1994, s 2.

A statement in relation to the proposal
which is the subject of the referendum may
be prescribed for the information of voters
by resolution of each House of the Oireachtas (RA 1994, s 23). Provision has been
made for the inclusion of a descriptive
heading on the ballot paper, where two or
more referenda are taking place on the
same polling day (RA 1994, s 24(3)).

It has been held that the use by the
government of public funds to finance a
campaign designed to influence voters in
favour of an affirmative vote in a referendum, amounted to an interference with the
democratic and constitutional process for
the amendment of the Constitution: *McK-
enna v An Taoiseach* [1996] 1 ILRM 81, SC
and [1995] 2 IR 10, SC. Information on a
referendum is now prepared and distributed by the Referendum Commission (qv):
Referendum Act 1998.

It has also been held that RTÉ's allocation of uncontested broadcasting time
(political broadcasts) did not hold the balance equally between those for and against
the divorce referendum in 1995 and the
allocation was unconstitutional: *Coughlan v
RTÉ and Attorney-General* [2000] SC.

Every citizen who has the right to vote at
an election for members of Dáil Éireann
has the right to vote at a referendum:
Constitution, art 47(3). Applications to the

courts failed to stop the referendum on the Maastricht Treaty 1992 eg *Slattery & Ors v An Taoiseach* [1993] 1 IR 286, SC; *Price v An Taoiseach* [1992] SC; *McKenna v An Taoiseach* [1993] 11 ILT Dig 67, HC. See CONSTITUTION; PETITION; PROPORTIONAL REPRESENTATION; TRANSFERABLE VOTE.

Referendum Commission. The independent commission which has two functions: (a) to promote public awareness of the subject matter of a referendum in a way which is fair to all, and (b) adjudicating on the application of bodies who wish to appoint agents to oversee the voting process: Referendum Act 1998. See *McKenna v An Taoiseach (No 2)* [1995] 2 IR 10; *Sherwin v Minister for the Environment* [1998] HC.

The previous requirement on the Referendum Commission to prepare, publish and distribute a statement setting out the arguments *for* and *against* a proposal to amend the Constitution of Ireland has been repealed: Referendum Act 2001.

The Commission is now required to prepare, publish and distribute a statement containing a general explanation of the subject matter of the proposal, to promote public awareness of the referendum and to encourage the electorate to vote at the poll (RA 2001, s 1). The previous provision was criticised by some politicians, on the ground that it inevitably leads to the arguments against a referendum proposal being given the same coverage and weight as those in favour, when this was not the outcome wished by those in favour. See website: *www.refcom.ie.*

referendum petition. A petition to the High Court which questions the validity of a referendum result; leave to present a referendum petition must be sought within seven days of publication of the provisional referendum certificate: Referendum Act 1994, ss 2 and 42. The only way in which the result of a referendum may be challenged is by a petition based on the grounds set out in RA 1994, s 43(1); the standard of proof which lay on the petitioner was the normal civil standard of proof on the *balance of probabilities*: *Hanafin v Minister for the Environment* [1996] 2 ILRM 161, SC and 2 IR 321.

In spending public money on an advertising campaign for an affirmative vote in the divorce referendum in 1995, the government acted in breach of its obligations under the Constitution. However, the Supreme Court decided that there was no basis to interfere with the Divisional Court's finding of fact that the advertising campaign had not materially affected the result of the referendum (*Hanafin* case).

referral. Means a referral to An Bord Pleanála: (a) under Planning and Development Act 2000, s 5 – decision on what is development and what is exempted development, (b) under PDA 2000, s 34(5) – determination on disagreement relating to conditions under which planning permission has been granted, (c) under PDA 2000, s 37(5) – declaration on a protected structure, (d) under PDA 2000, s 96(5) – determination in relation to a matter in dispute re provision on affordable housing, and (e) under PDA 2000, s 193(2) – determination of dispute in relation to whether a new structure substantially replaces a demolished or destroyed structure: Planning and Development Act 2000, s 2(1) as amended by Planning and Development (Amendment) Act 2002, s 6. The 2002 Act added (c). See also BORD PLEANÁLA, AN; CONSULTANT REFERRAL; TENANCY DISPUTE.

reformatory schools. Institutions for young offenders which had as their objective the teaching of a trade and the imparting of the principles of good citizenship. Under previous legislation, schools for the industrial training of youthful offenders in which youthful offenders were lodged, clothed and fed, as well as taught: Children's Act 1908, s 44 (since repealed). See *Jenkins v Delap* [1989] 7 ILT Dig 259.

There were three forms of school provided for by law: (a) *industrial schools* for persons up to 12 years of age and in certain circumstances up to 15 years of age; (b) *reformatory schools* for persons between 12 and 17 years of age; and (c) *St Patrick's Institution* (formerly known as borstal institutions) for persons between 16 and 19 years of age. In essence, detention in a reformatory school was similar to that encountered in an industrial school, although a detainee in a reformatory school was likely to be held in the company of older and more delinquent detainees and under a stricter regime: *McM v Manager of Trinity House* [1995] 2 ILRM 546, HC and 1 IR 595.

The District Court is not prohibited by statute from imposing consecutive periods of detention in St Patrick's Institution exceeding twelve months: *The State (Clinch) v D J Connellan* [1986] ILRM 455.

Provision has been made for the abolition of reformatory and industrial schools and their replacement by *children detention schools*, managed by boards of management appointed by the Minister for Education: Children Act 2001, ss 157–224. See Criminal Justice Administration Act 1914, s 11(1); Criminal Justice Act 1960, ss 12–13; Child Care Act 1991, s 79. For previous legislation, see Children Act 1908, ss 57–58; Children Act 1941, ss 9–10, 12; Children (Amendment) Act 1949, s 4. See *DPP (Houlihan) v Gencer* [1997] 1 ILRM 57, SC and [1996] 1 IR 281, SC. [Bibliography: Barnes; Osborough (3).] See CHILDREN'S RESIDENTIAL CENTRE; PUNISHMENT OF CHILD.

refoulement. Expulsion or return or a refugee. See Criminal Justice (United Nations Convention against Torture) Act 2000, s 4. See REFUGEE, NON-REFOULEMENT.

refresher fee. A fee per day in addition to the *brief fee*. As the length of High Court proceedings is often underestimated by everyone concerned, the *refresher fee* is stipulated to ensure that counsel is reasonably paid for the work he does and the fact that he will have to forego other work: *Commissioner of Irish Lights v Maxwell* [1998] 1 ILRM 421, SC. See BRIEF FEE.

refreshing memory. A witness in court may refresh his memory while under examination about an event, by referring to a writing made by himself at the time of the event or so soon after that the judge considers it likely that the event was fixed in his memory. A witness may also refresh his memory from a writing made by another person, if when the witness read it, he knew it to be correct. The writing does not itself become evidence although it must be handed to the opposite party who may cross-examine on it. An expert may refresh his memory by reference to professional treatises. See *Jones v Stroud* [1825] 2 C P 196; *Talbot de Malahide (lord) v Cusack* [1864] 17 ICLR 213; *Northern Bank Company v Carpenter* [1931] IR 268.

refuge. Land which is designated by the Minister by order that it be a refuge for fauna, where the Minister considers that a particular species of fauna should be specially protected: Wildlife Act 1976, s 17. For example, see Refuge for Fauna (Cliffs of Moher) Designation Order 1988, SI No 98 of 1988. See NATURE RESERVE.

refugee. A person, who owing to a well-founded fear of being persecuted for reasons of race, religion, nationality, *membership of a particular social group* or political opinion, is outside the country of his nationality and is unable, or owing to such fear, is unwilling to avail himself of the protection of that country; or who, not having a nationality and being outside the country of his former habitual residence is unable or, owing to such fear, is unwilling to return to it: United Nations Convention relating to the Status of Refugees of 28 July 1951, art 1, as amended by the Protocol of 31 January 1967 art 1: Refugee Act 1996, s 2.

Prior to the commencement of the 1996 Act, the UN Convention had not been incorporated into domestic law, but the Minister had undertaken to apply the principles of the convention in deciding applications for refugee status and the Minister was bound by that undertaking: *Gutrani v Governor of Mountjoy Prison* [1993] 2 IR 427, SC.

The burden of proof of establishing that an applicant for refugee status has a well-founded fear of persecution rests with the applicant: *Z v Minister for Justice* [2002] 2 ILRM 215, SC. For a critical appraisal of this case, see Siobhan Stack BL in *Bar Review* (June/July 2002) 287.

An applicant for refugee status is an *asylum-seeker*, becoming a *refugee* on being so declared. There are two categories of refugee: (1) a *Convention refugee* being a person who comes within the UN Convention requirements and who applies for refugee status (RA 1996, ss 2 and 5, as amended by Immigration Act 2003, s 7(a)); and (2) a *programme refugee* being a person as part of a group of persons who are granted temporary protection or resettlement in the State on foot of a government decision and whose status on arrival is automatically registered eg Bosnian refugees (RA 1996, s 24 as amended by IA 2003, s 7(m)).

In the definition of a refugee, *membership of a particular social group* includes membership of a trade union and includes membership of a group of persons whose defining characteristic is their belonging to the female or male sex or having a particular sexual orientation (RA 1996, s 1(1)).

On being granted refugee status, the refugee has statutory rights, including the right to reside and travel freely, health, social welfare and property rights, education, employment benefits, religious freedom and access to the courts (RA 1996, s 3).

Asylum-seekers whose application for refugee status has been rejected may be required to leave the State; the Minister may permit them to remain in the State on humanitarian grounds on a temporary basis or they may be given *residency status*, renewable annually, if they have a child born in the State. Regulations have been made: (a) setting out where persons detained under RA 1996, s 9(8) or s 9(13) may be detained; and (b) providing for their treatment while in detention: Refugee (Places and Conditions of Detention) Regulations 2000, SI No 344 of 2000.

For amendments to 1996 Act, see Immigration Act 1999, s 11; Immigration Act 2003, s 7; Immigration Act 2004, s 16(4). See UNHCR Handbook on Procedures and Criteria for Determining Refugee States (Geneva 1989); the Law of Refugee Status (Hathaway, Toronto 1991). See *Ji Yoa Lau v Minister for Justice* [1993] ILRM 64, HC; *Fakih v Minister for Justice* [1993] ILRM 274, HC; *KA v Minister for Justice* [2003] 2 IR 93, HC. See Irish Nationality and Citizenship Act 1986, s 5. See Civil Legal Aid (Refugee Legal Service) Orders 1999, SIs No 74 and 262 of 1999; Refugee Act (Appeals) Regulations 2002, SI No 571 of 2002; Safe Countries of Origin Order 2003, SI No 422 of 2003. See website: *www.justice.ie*. [Bibliography: Cubie & Ryan; Wallace UK.] See ASYLUM, CLAIM FOR; BIOMETRICS; COUNCIL OF EUROPE DEVELOPMENT BANK; ILLEGAL IMMIGRANT; INTERNAL PROTECTION ALTERNATIVE; NATURALISATION; NON-NATIONAL; STATELESS PERSON; TRANSLATION; UNHCR.

refugee, application procedure. The Refugee Act 1996 (as amended by Immigration Act 1999, s 11 and Immigration Act 2003, s 7) sets out the application procedure for refugee status, including interview by an immigration officer, application to Minister, reference of application to the independent *Refugee Applications Commissioner*, investigation by the Commissioner, recommendation and reports by the Commissioner, appeal to *Refugee Appeal Tribunal*.

It has been held that the absence of an *oral hearing* at the hearing of an appeal for an application for refugee status did not infringe the right of an applicant to natural and constitutional justice: *Zgnat'ev v Minister for Justice* (17 July 2001, unreported) HC.

The Minister is obliged to grant a declaration that a person is a refugee, where the Commissioner or Appeal Board so recommends (RA 1996, s 17 as amended by IA 2003, s 7(j)); in any other case he has a discretion. The Minister is also empowered to withhold the rights and privileges of refugee status on grounds of national security or public policy.

The 1999 Act provides for: (a) the Commissioner to be responsible for applications from initiation to final recommendation and to be empowered to delegate functions, (b) the Appeals Tribunal to sit in single-person divisions, (c) a right to fingerprint applicants over 14 years of age, and (d) the establishment of a Refugee Advisory Board on which there is representation of refugee and asylum organisations and observer status for the United Nations High Commissioner for Refugees (UNHCR).

Detailed procedures have been specified in relation to the determination by the *Refugee Appeals Tribunal* of appeals against recommendations of the *Refugee Applications Commissioner* on applications for recognition as a refugee: Refugee (Appeals) Regulations 2002, SI No 571 of 2002, now replaced by Refugee (Appeals) Regulations 2003, SI No 424 of 2003. See also SI No 345 of 2000 (application form); SI No 346 of 2000 and SI No 426 of 2002 (temporary residence certificate); SI No 347 of 2000 (travel document).

See also *Ulhaq v Minister for Justice* [2001] ITLR (27 August); *Sarfaraz v Minister for Justice* [2001] 3 IR 224, HC; *B v Governor of Training Unit* [2002] 2 ILRM 161, SC; *VZ v Minister for Justice* [2002] 2 IR 135, SC; *VR v Refugee Appeals Tribunal* [2003] 2 IR 63, HC. See 'Manifestly unfounded procedures and the fear of persecution' by Sunniva McDonagh BL in *Bar Review* (June/July 2002) 284. See 'Refugee Law & Procedure' by Wesley Farrell BL and Conor Gallagher BL in *Bar Review* (May 2001) 431 and (June/July 2001) 488. In 2003, refugee status was granted to 345 (4%) out of over 8,600 applicants at initial application stage and to 825 (17%) out of over 5,000 applicants on appeal. See NON-NATIONAL.

refugee, non-refoulement. Under the principle of *non-refoulement*, a person must not be expelled from the State to the frontiers of territories where, in the opinion of the Minister, the life or freedom of that person would be threatened on account of his race, religion, nationality, membership of a particular social group or political opinion: Refugee Act 1996, s 5; Geneva Convention, art 33. This provision applies to all persons, not just to persons who comply with the definition of a refugee. The principle of *non-refoulement* must be met as a precondition to the making of a deportation order (qv): Immigration Act 1999, s 3(1). See *Baby O v Minister for Justice* [2002] 2 IR 169, SC and [2003] 1 ILRM 241.

refuse disposal. See HOUSEHOLD REFUSE; NATIONAL MONUMENT; TRADE REFUSE; WASTE.

regional authority. A body established in accordance with s 43 of the Local Government Act 1991: Planning and Development Act 2000, s 2(1). Provision has been made for the making by regional authorities of *regional planning guidelines,* which will provide a long-term strategic planning framework for the development of their region, dealing with issues such as population trends, transport and waste, which are better dealt with in a regional context, and within a longer time-frame than the *development plan* (qv) of a planning authority (PDA 2000, ss 21–27).

The planning guideline for a region is for a period not less than 12 years and not more then 20 years (PDA 2000, s 23(1)(b)) and must take into account the proper planning and sustainable development of the whole region and of government policy (PDA 2000, s 23(4)(a)). Procedures are set out for public notification and consultation in relation to regional planning guidelines and their review (PDA 2000, ss 24–26). A planning authority is required to have regard to the regional planning guidelines in force for its area when making or adopting a *development plan* (PDA 2000, s 27(1)). See also Local Government Act 2001, s 237. See LOCAL AUTHORITY.

regional fisheries board. A corporate body with functions which include the management, protection, conservation and development of fisheries in its region, the promotion of angling, and the management of any fisheries under its own possession: Fisheries Act 1980, s 11 and Sch 2. The Minister is empowered to appoint a commission to perform the functions of the central or of a regional fisheries board: Fisheries (Amendment) Act 1995, s 3. For example, see SI No 51 of 1996. Provision has been made to revise the board structures of the *central* and *regional* fisheries boards and to provide for the acquisition and management by regional fisheries boards of State-owned fisheries and fisheries properties where appropriate: Fisheries (Amendment) Act 1999, ss 3–21. [Bibliography: Comerford (2).] See ON-THE-SPOT FINE.

regional road. A public road or a proposed public road which is classified as a regional road: Roads Act 1993, s 2(1) and 10. See PUBLIC ROAD; WAY, RIGHT OF.

regional technical college. See EDUCATION; EDUCATIONAL AWARDS; INSTITUTE OF TECHNOLOGY.

register. Formal written record.

register of auditors. The register which the registrar of companies is required to maintain of the names of persons or firms that have been notified to him as qualified for appointment as auditor of a company or as public auditor: Companies Act 1990, s 198 as substituted by Companies (Auditing and Accounting) Act 2003, s 38. It is an offence for a person to act as an auditor or to describe himself as an auditor or to hold himself out to be an auditor unless his name is on the register. See also C(AA)A 2003, ss 39–40. See AUDITOR, COMPANY.

register of companies. When a company has been struck off the register, the court may, if satisfied that is just, order that the name of the company be restored to the register; the company is deemed to have continued in existence as if its name had not been struck off: Companies (Amendment) Act 1982, s 12(6). This has the automatic effect of validating retrospectively all acts done in the name or on behalf of the company during the period between its dissolution and the restoration of its name to the register: *Re Amantiss Enterprises Ltd* [2000] 2 ILRM 177, HC.

An application for the restoration of a company to the register of companies is made to the court by originating *Notice of Motion* grounded upon an affidavit: Circuit Court Rules 2001 Ord 53 as amended by SI No 615 of 2003.

In holding that C(A)A 1982, s 12B(9), inserted by Companies (Amendment) (No 2) Act 1999, s 46 is ambiguous, the Supreme Court held that there was no convincing reason why the legislature would choose to deny the Registrar of Companies or creditors of a company access to the High Court in relation to an application to restore a company to the register: *In the matter of Deauville Communications Worldwide Ltd* [2002] 2 ILRM 388, SC and 2 IR 32. However, the High Court in ordering the restoration cannot impose a penalty: *Goode v Philips Electrical (Ireland) Ltd* [2002] 2 IR 613, SC.

Certain information, such as company name, registered office, address and Annual Return Date may be accessed free of charge on the Companies Registration Office website: *www.cro.ie*. See CREDITOR.

register of electors. The register, which is required to be published in each year, of persons who were entitled to be registered as electors on the *qualifying date* (ie 1 September in the year in which the register comes into force): Electoral Act 1992, ss 13 and 20, and Sch 2, r 1. Persons may be entitled to be registered as presidential electors, Dáil electors, European electors and/or local government electors (qqv).

The register must be prepared by reference to registration areas and a person must not be registered more than once or in more than one such area (EA 1992, ss 11(1) and 13(1)). A *special voters list* must also be prepared without removing the names of these voters from the register (EA 1992, s 17). Also certain electors are entitled to have their names entered in a *postal voters* list (EA 1992, s 14). See also Local Government Act 2001, ss 2(1) and 24(1).

An applicant to be entered on the supplement to the register, must sign an application form in the presence of a garda or in the presence of an official of the registration authority (EA 1992, Sch 2, Pt 11 (14A) inserted by Electoral (Amendment) Act 2002, s 1(i)). If the applicant is unable to go to a garda station due to physical illness or disability, the application form must be accompanied by a medical certificate.

register of members. Every company must keep a register of its members, which must not be kept outside the State: Companies Act 1963, s 116. It must be open to the inspection of any member (CA 1963, s 119). Often the real ownership of shares is disguised by having them registered in the names of *nominees*. A company may by its articles of association require that infor-

mation be furnished to it as to the beneficial ownership of its shares.

The beneficial ownership of a notifiable percentage (5%) of shares in a public limited company must be declared; and in the case of a private company, a person with a financial interest in the company may obtain a *disclosure order* from the court in relation to share ownership: Companies Act 1990, ss 67–88 and 97–104.

A building society is required to keep a register of its members; unlike a company however, there is no requirement to make the register available to be consulted by other members or by the public: Building Societies Act 1989, s 65. See DISCLOSURE ORDER; SHARES, DISCLOSURE OF.

register of patents. The register kept at the Patents Office in which is entered particulars of published patent applications, of patents in force, of assignments and transmission of patents and of licences: Patents Act 1992, s 84. It is open to inspection by the public and certified copies, sealed with the seal of the Controller of Patents, must be given to any person requiring them, on payment of the prescribed fee. Notice of a trust must not be entered in the register but an equitable interest can be recorded: PA 1992, s 84(5); *Kakkar v Szelke* [1989] FSR 225. See PATENT.

register of personal injuries actions. The register of personal injuries actions which the Courts Service is required to establish and maintain, and which is to be made available to such persons as establish, to the satisfaction of the Courts Service, a sufficient interest in seeking access to it: Civil Liability and Courts Act 2004, s 30. See PERSONAL INJURIES.

register of trade marks. The register which is required to be kept by the Controller of Trade Marks, open to inspection by the public, in which is entered all registered trade marks (qv), particulars of registrable transactions affecting a registered trade mark (eg an assignment thereof), and such other matters as may be prescribed: Trade Marks Act 1996, s 66. There are provisions governing the rectification of any entry made in the register (TMA 1996, s 67).

The Controller is required to state in writing the reasons for his decision to refuse an application for the removal of a mark from the register: *Anheuser Busch v Controller of Trade Marks* [1988] ILRM 247, HC. See TRADE MARK, REGISTERED.

registered agreement. See EMPLOYMENT AGREEMENT.

registered charge. See CHARGE, REGISTERED.

registered company. See COMPANY, REGISTERED.

registered design. See DESIGN.

registered employment agreement. See EMPLOYMENT AGREEMENT.

registered land. See LAND REGISTRATION.

registered office. A company must have a registered office in the State to which all communications and notices may be addressed; notice of any change in its situation must be given to the Registrar of Companies within 14 days of the change: Companies (Amendment) Act 1982, s 4. The company's name must be displayed outside its registered office conspicuously and legibly: Companies Act 1963, s 114(a). See Listing Rules 2000, paras 6C.1 and 6J.1.

The registered office of a building society is known as its *Chief Office*: Building Societies Act 1989, s 15. See FOREIGN COMPANY; SEAT OF CORPORATION.

registered trade mark. See TRADE MARK, REGISTERED.

registered trade union. See TRADE UNION, REGISTERED.

registrar. An official responsible for compiling and keeping records. In many cases, he is also empowered with important decision-making functions eg Registrar of Companies, Registrar of Friendly Societies.

registrar of companies. The officer, appointed by the Minister, with responsibility for administering the Companies Registration Office (CRO), which is located at Parnell House, 14 Parnell Square, Dublin 1: Companies Act 1963, s 368. The Registrar must be satisfied that all statutory prerequisites have been met before he issues the certificate of incorporation (CA 1963, ss 17–18 and 20; Companies Amendment Act 1983, Pt II). The Registrar may refuse to register a company where the objects are unlawful: *R v Registrar of Companies* [1931] 2 KB 197.

Every registered company must deliver an annual return to the Registrar each year and he can strike off the register companies which are no longer carrying on business or who fail to make returns: CA 1963, ss 125–129 as amended by Companies Act 1990, s 244; Companies Amendment Act 1982, ss 11–12 as amended by CA 1990, s 245

and Companies (Amendment) (No 2) Act 1999, s 46.

If a company fails to make good any *default* under the Companies Act 1963, within 14 days of notice requiring it to do so, the court may make an order directing the company to make good the default within such time as may be specified in the order (CA 1963, s 371). A company was ordered by the High Court to file *annual returns* for the years 1998 and 1999 by 31 August 2000: *Registrar of Companies v Celtic Helicopters Ltd* (2000) Irish Times, 1 August. This is understood to be the first time that CA 1963, s 371 has been used in legal proceedings.

The Registrar has authority to institute prosecutions in respect of numerous provisions of the Companies Acts eg concerning annual accounts and returns, and liquidations and receiverships (CAA 1982, s 16).

The Registrar is required to keep a register of persons subject to *disqualification orders* (CA 1990, s 168), a register of *restricted persons* (CA 1990, s 153) and a register of auditors (CA 1990, s 198). Where property, which is the subject of an *interim* or *interlocutory* order for its preservation, is an interest in a company, notice of the order must be entered in the register of companies by the Registrar: Proceeds of Crime Act 1996, s 10(7)–(9). The Registrar is also required to register a building society as a public limited company following a *conversion* procedure completed by the society: Building Societies Act 1989, s 106(1)–(2). The duties of the Registrar may be performed by an assistant registrar or by any other person employed in the office of the Registrar: C(A)(No 2)A 1999, s 52.

Any person is entitled to inspect the documents kept at the registry and to have certified copies made of them (CA 1963, s 370). Provision has been made for evidence to be delivered in court on behalf of the Registrar by way of written certificate; there is no longer a requirement to subpoena or serve a witness summons on the Registrar (CA 1963, s 370(4) inserted by Company Law Enforcement Act 2001, s 62).

Provision has been made to improve compliance by companies of their obligation to file returns, including empowering the Registrar to levy fines without the need to institute court proceedings (CLEA 2001, ss 59–66). See also Companies

(Auditing and Accounting) Act 2003, ss 46–47. Under the 2001 Act, the Registrar takes over some of the Minister's former functions eg in relation to approval for the name of a company to be registered, approval for a change of name, and approval to dispense with 'limited' in the name (CLEA 2001, ss 85–88 and 95).

Certain information on every company registered in the CRO is available on the CRO website: website: *www.cro.ie*. For the CRO, see email: *info@cro.ie*. For a subscription service with detailed information on companies, see website: *www.vision-NET.ie*. See also COMPANY; COMPANY, REGISTERED; STRIKE OFF.

registrar of credit unions The person, appointed by the Irish Financial Services Regulatory Authority, as the delegate of that Authority for managing the performance and exercise of the powers and functions of the Central Bank under the Credit Union Act 1997: Central Bank Act 1942, s 33W to AF, inserted by Central Bank and Financial Services Authority of Ireland Act 2003, s 26. The Registrar must administer the system of regulation and supervision of credit unions with a view to the protection of members' funds and the maintenance of the financial stability and well-being of credit unions generally: Credit Union Act 1997, s 84 as amended by the CBFSAIA 2003, s 35, Sch 1. The supervision of credit unions was previously the responsibility of the Registrar of Friendly Societies. See CREDIT UNION.

registrar of friendly societies. The officer with powers and functions mainly relating to the registration, regulation and supervision of friendly societies, trade unions, industrial and provident societies and formerly of credit unions (qqv). See Friendly Societies Act 1896, Registrar of Friendly Societies (Adaptation) Order 1926; Registry of Friendly Societies Act 1936; Friendly Societies (Amendment) Act 1977.

The Registrar is obliged to consider whether the rules proposed for registration of an industrial and provident society conflict with Industrial and Provident Societies Act 1893; even when they do so conflict, the registrar does not commit an actionable wrong in registering them: *Kerry Co-operative Creameries Ltd v An Bord Bainne* [1990] ILRM 664, HC. See also *McMahon v Ireland* [1988] ILRM 610; *The State (Plunkett) v Registrar of Friendly Societies* [1998] 4 IR 1, SC. See CREDIT UNION;

FRIENDLY SOCIETY; INDUSTRIAL AND PROVIDENT SOCIETY; PERPETUAL FUND; SCIENTIFIC SOCIETIES.

registration of births. See BIRTH, REGISTRATION OF.

registration of business names. See BUSINESS NAME.

registration of charge. See CHARGE, REGISTRATION OF.

registration of deeds. See DEEDS, REGISTRATION OF.

registration of electors. See REGISTER OF ELECTORS.

registration of judgment. See JUDGMENT.

registration of land. See LAND REGISTRATION.

registration of marriage. See MARRIAGE, REGISTRATION OF

registration of title. See LAND REGISTRATION.

registry of deeds. See DEEDS, REGISTRATION OF.

regularity, presumption of. See PRESUMPTION OF REGULARITY.

regulation. A formal order made by a designated Minister exercising his power to make subordinate legislation, usually in the form of a statutory instrument (qv). Ministers have been given a general power to implement EC law by regulation, including provisions repealing, amending or applying, with or without modification, other law: European Communities Act 1972, s 3. This has been found to be constitutional as, having regard to the number of Community laws, the obligations of membership would necessitate in some instances the making of Ministerial regulations rather than legislation of the Oireachtas (qv): *Meagher v Minister for Agriculture* [1994] 1 ILRM 1, SC and 1 IR 329.

The court will not accept a submission that regulations, which were made for the purpose of giving effect to EC Directives, did not include every requirement of the relevant directive: *Mallon v Minister for Agriculture* [1996] 1 IR 517, SC.

The test is whether the repeal or amendment of a statute did not amount to a determination of principles and policies by the Minister. Where power to make regulations or orders is more than a mere giving effect to principles and policies which are contained in the statute itself, this is an unconstitutional delegation of legislative power: *Laurentiu v Minister for Justice* [2000] 1 ILRM 1, SC. See also *Leontjava & Chang v Minister for Justice* (22 January

2004, unreported) HC and (23 June 2004, unreported) SC.

To remove any doubt regarding existing regulations implementing EC law, and to ensure that the State could comply with its obligations to EFTA contracting states under the European Economic Area Agreement, these regulations have been confirmed with retrospective effect: European Communities (Amendment) Act 1993, s 5.

The Minister was held to have acted *ultra vires* the powers given to him by the Livestock (Artificial Insemination) Act 1947 in establishing and enforcing an exclusivity scheme by dividing the State into nine areas and awarding an exclusive licence for each area: *O'Neill v Minister for Agriculture* [1997] 2 ILRM 435, SC. See *Purcell v Attorney-General* [1996] 2 ILRM 153, SC. See AMENDMENT OF LEGISLATION; BETTER REGULATION; EEA AGREEMENT; IRRATIONALITY, TEST OF; STATUTORY INSTRUMENT.

regulation of EC. Legislation of the European Community which has a general application and is binding in its entirety and *directly applicable* in all member states: EC Treaty, art 249 of the consolidated (2002) version. It has been held that the fact that an EC regulation is directly applicable does not prevent the provisions of that regulation from empowering a Community institution or a member state to take implementation measures: *Maher v Minister for Agriculture* [2001] 2 ILRM 481, SC and 2 IR 139 applying Case 230/78 *Eridania v Minister for Agriculture and Forestry* [1979] ECR 2749. There is no obligation on a body charged with the introduction of regulations to consult with those affected in advance: *Ryanair v Aer Rianta* [2003] 2 IR 143, SC.

For the definition of a Regulation under the proposed *Treaty establishing a Constitution for Europe*, see EUROPEAN REGULATION. See also DELEGATED REGULATION; DIRECT APPLICABILITY; COMMUNITY LAW; INTERPRETATION OF LEGISLATION, EUROPEAN.

regulator. A person who, or body which, is empowered to influence the market for the provision of a product or service eg by establishing standards, by controlling prices, by issuing licences to be in the market, by promoting competition, by requiring bonding schemes to protect consumers, by approving providers, by promoting security and continuation of supply, by ensuring compliance with obligations, and by the investigation of complaints. In recent times the liberalisation of the market in relation to a number of areas (eg aviation, electricity, gas, communications, and transport) has been matched by the appointment of *regulators* with statutory powers to assist the attainment of the objectives of the liberalisation. See BETTER REGULATION; COMMISSION FOR AVIATION REGULATION; COMMISSION FOR COMMUNICATIONS REGULATION; COMMISSION FOR ENERGY REGULATION; CONSUMER AFFAIRS, DIRECTOR OF; TAXI.

rehabilitation. Health boards are required to make available a service for the training of disabled persons (whether mentally or physically handicapped) for employment and for making arrangements with employers for placing disabled persons in suitable employment: Health Act 1970, s 68. The National Rehabilitation Board, established under the Health (Corporate Bodies) Act 1961, advised the Minister on rehabilitation services, co-ordinated the work of other bodies engaged in rehabilitation and provided direct services itself eg vocational assessment. The National Rehabilitation Board was dissolved in 2000 and its functions taken over by Comhairle, FÁS, the health boards, and the National Disability Authority (qqv). See *O'Briain v National Rehabilitation Board* [2002] ELR 210, EAT. For the Rehab Group, see website: *www.rehab.ie*. For National Rehabilitation Hospital, see *www.nrh.ie*. For an international perspective, see *www.rehab-international.org* and *www.disabilityworld.org*. See DISABLED DRIVER.

rehearing. A re-arguing of a case which has already been adjudicated upon eg an appeal from conviction in the District Court results in a complete rehearing in the Circuit Court. Also an appeal lies to the High Court from an order of the Circuit Court in a civil action by way of rehearing: Courts of Justice Act 1936, s 38. While appeals to the Supreme Court are by way of rehearing, this is interpreted as involving a rehearing of the legal issues arising in the court of trial and not a rehearing of the oral evidence: RSC Ord 58 and *Hay v O'Grady* [1993] 11 ILT Dig 27, SC. See DE NOVO; FRESH EVIDENCE.

rejected goods. Unless otherwise agreed, where goods are delivered to a buyer and he refuses to accept them having the right so to do, he is not bound to return them to the seller, but it is sufficient if he intimates to the seller that he refuses to accept them: Sale of Goods Act 1893, s 36.

rejection of offer. An offer is rejected if the rejection is communicated to the offeror, or if the offer is accepted subject to conditions, or if the offeree makes a counter-offer. See *Hyde v Wrench* [1840] 3 Beav 334. See OFFER.

rejoinder. (1) Answer in pleadings made by a defendant to a plaintiff's reply.

(2) In the sale of land, the response of the purchaser to replies of the vendor to requisitions on title raised by the purchaser. The general rule is that the vendor must answer satisfactorily all proper requisitions. Where the purchaser is not satisfied with the replies given by the vendor, he will send rejoinders or answers. See Law Society's *Conditions of Sale* (2001).

related company. A company related to another company. There are a number of definitions of what constitutes a *related* company for the purposes of the Companies Acts eg where the other company is its holding company or subsidiary: Companies Act 1990, s 140. There are provisions whereby: (a) the assets of related companies can be ordered to be pooled in the case of the winding up of both; or (b) one can be required to contribute to the debts of the other where only one is being wound up (CA 1990, ss 140–141). A related company does not include a company registered outside the State: *Re Tuskar Resources plc* [2001] 1 IR 668, HC.

relation back. The doctrine whereby an act is referred back to an earlier date and made effective from that date eg a person who enters land with lawful authority but who, by a wrongful act, becomes a trespasser *ab initio*, his wrongful act relates back to his initial entry. Probate when granted relates back to the testator's death. An adjudication of bankruptcy is no longer related back to the act of bankruptcy; the vesting of the bankrupt's property in the Official Assignee (qv), does not now, subject to some exceptions, commence at an earlier date than the date of adjudication: Bankruptcy Act 1988, s 44(2). See BANKRUPTCY, ADJUDICATION OF.

relations. Next-of-kin (qv).

relations, prohibited degrees of. See PROHIBITED DEGREES; MARRIAGE.

relatives. Relations (qv). The term includes those connected to a person by marriage.

As regards adoption, relatives mean a grandparent, brother, sister, uncle or aunt, whether of the whole blood, of the half-blood or by affinity: Adoption Act 1952, s 3. See ADOPTION, APPLICATION FOR.

relator. A person at whose suggestion or information an action is instituted by the Attorney-General (qv) in a matter of public interest eg in the case of an act which is unlawful having regard to the Constitution. See RSC Ord 15, r 20. It has been held in England that if the Attorney-General does not consent to relator proceedings, his decision is final and is not subject to review: *Gouriet v Union of Post Office Workers* [1977] 3 WLR 300. See also *Attorney-General at the Relation of the Society for the Protection of Unborn Children (Ireland) Ltd v Open Door Counselling Ltd and Dublin Wellwoman Centre Ltd* [1989] ILRM 19, SC. For details on *relator action*, see website: *www.attorneygeneral.ie*. [Bibliography: Collins & O'Reilly.] See RIGHT OF WAY.

release. The renunciation, discharge or giving up of rights or claims against another. A release of an obligation under a contract may be obtained by a deed, whether or not the release is based on consideration. As regards the administration of estates, the executors normally require a release from those beneficially entitled before handing over the property eg in the form of a covenant not to sue.

A mortgagee is not entitled to refuse to release his security in the sale by a liquidator of mortgaged land, merely because the liquidator is disputing his claim and the matter is awaiting adjudication: *McCairns (PMPA) (In Liquidation)* [1989] ILRM 501, HC. See ACCORD AND SATISFACTION.

release, temporary. The Minister for Justice is empowered to direct the temporary release of a person serving a sentence of imprisonment: Criminal Justice Act 1960, s 2 as substituted by Criminal Justice (Temporary Release of Prisoners) Act 2003, s 1. The 2003 Act was necessitated by the need to provide a clearer legislative basis for the power of the Minister, by setting down the principles which apply to the exercise of this power.

The Minister may order the temporary release for the purpose of: (i) assessing the person's ability to reintegrate into society upon such release, (ii) preparing him for release, or (iii) assisting the gardaí in the prevention, detection or investigation of an offence. The person may be released also where there exists circumstance that, in the opinion of the Minister, justify the prisoner's temporary release on grounds of health, or on other humanitarian grounds. Release may also be directed in order to: (i) ensure the good government of the prison concerned, or (ii) to maintain good order in, and humane and just management of, the prison concerned. Finally, release may be ordered where the Minister is of the opinion that the person has been rehabilitated and would, upon being released, be capable of reintegrating into society. The granting of a period of temporary release does not create an entitlement to further periods of temporary release.

The Minister must not give a direction for temporary release of a person where the release is prohibited by another enactment e g persons convicted of treason and aggravated murder: Criminal Justice Act 1990, s 5; or persons convicted of drug trafficking offences under the Misuse of Drugs Act 1977, s 27 as amended by Criminal Justice Act 1999, s 5.

The temporary release of a person in custody is a privilege or concession to which the person has no right: *Ryan v Governor of Limerick Prison* [1989] 7 ILT Dig 84. However, a prisoner who has been granted regular periods of temporary release is entitled to be given an explanation if his temporary release is not renewed: *Sherlock v Governor of Mountjoy Prison* [1991] 1 IR 451, HC.

Temporary release is quite distinct from the general executive power of remission: *Kinahan v Minister for Justice* [2001] 4 IR 454, SC. The Minister is not permitted to categorise or classify prisoners for temporary release under the 1960 Act (i e prior to the amendment in 2003): *Corish v Minister for Justice* [2000] ITLR (20 March) HC.

While a convicted person may be allowed temporary release from prison, there is no similar provision in relation to remand prisoners: *DPP v Goulding* [2000] 1 ILRM 147, SC and [1999] 2 IR 398, SC. There is no distinction between temporary release and any form of release under escort, and both are a matter exclusively within the discretion of the Minister: *McHugh v Minister for Justice* [1997] 1 IR 245, SC. See *McCabe v Ireland* [2000] 1 ILRM 410, SC.

A prisoner on 'temporary release renewable monthly' does not have his release reconsidered every month; provided he complies with the conditions of his release, he is entitled to continue his release: *Dowling v Minister for Justice* [2003] 2 IR 535, SC. See *McAlister v Minister for Justice* [2003] 1 ILRM 161, HC. See also Criminal Law (Insanity) Bill 2002, s 13. [Bibliography: McDermott.] See PAROLE.

relevancy test. The test which must be complied with in order to support an application for the discovery of documents (qv); discovery may be ordered of any documents which might reasonably be supposed to contain information which would advance the case of one party or damage that of the other: *Sterling Winthrop v Farbenfabriken Bayer AG* [1967] IR 97 as cited in *Dunne v National Maternity Hospital* [1989] ITLR (27 November) SC. See RETRIAL.

relevant. A fact which is so connected directly or indirectly with a *fact in issue* in a case that it tends to prove or disprove the fact in issue. Only *relevant* evidence is admissible in any proceedings. See ADMISSIBILITY OF EVIDENCE; FACT IN ISSUE.

relief. The remedy which a plaintiff seeks or obtains in an action.

relief of poverty. See CHARITIES.

religion. See RELIGIOUS BELIEF; RELIGIOUS FREEDOM.

religion, advancement of. A trust which has as its object the advancement of religion may meet the legal requirements of a charity. See CHARITIES; RELIGIOUS FREEDOM.

religious association. The European Union respects and does not prejudice the status under national law of churches and religions and religious associations and communities in the member states; the EU equally respects the status of philosophical and non-confessional organisations: Amsterdam Treaty 1997, Declaration 11, p 133.

religious belief. Includes religious background or outlook: Employment Equality Act 1998, s 2(1); Equal Status Act 2000, s 2(1). An employer is prohibited from discriminating against an employee or prospective employee on the grounds of religious belief i e treating people differently on the grounds that one person has a different religious belief from the other or no religious belief (EEA 1998, ss 8(1) and 6). *Harassment* on the grounds of religious belief is also prohibited (EEA 1998, s 14A inserted by Equality Act 2004, s 8).

However a religious, educational or medical institution is not taken to discriminate against a person if: (a) it gives more favourable treatment on the grounds of religious belief where it does so reasonably to maintain the *religious ethos* of the institution or (b) it takes action reasonably necessary to prevent a person from undermining the *religious ethos* of the institution (EEA 1998, s 37(1)). See *Greally v Minister for Education & Ors* [1999] 2 ILRM 297, HC and ELR 106.

A person must not discriminate on *religion grounds* in disposing of goods or premises or in providing a service or accommodation; treating one person less favourably than another person, in a comparable situation, because one has a different *religious belief* from the other (or that one has a religious belief and the other has not) is discriminatory: Equal Status Act 2000, ss 5, 6 and 3, amended by EA 2004, ss 48–49.

There is no discrimination where the goods or services are provided for a religious purpose (ESA 2000, s 5(2)(e)). See *Re Employment Equality Bill 1996* [1997] 2 IR 321, SC and ELR 132. [Bibliography: Reid M.] See DISCRIMINATION; EDUCATIONAL ESTABLISHMENT; EUROPEAN CONVENTION ON HUMAN RIGHTS; PENSION SCHEME AND DISCRIMINATION; VOCATIONAL TRAINING.

religious employer. The nature of the relationship between a religious superior and a subordinate is unlikely to be that of an employer/employee. See *Reverend Fr Buckley v Bishop Cathal Daly* 112/85 UD (Northern Ireland). See Barry in 10 ILT & SJ (1992) 222. The High Court has held that a change of bishops is more akin to a change in the managing director and cannot be construed as a transfer of undertaking: *Sheehy v Ryan and Moriarty* [2004] ELR 87, HC. See INCARDINATION; VOW.

religious ethos. A religious denomination is not required to change the general atmosphere or ethos of its school merely to accommodate a child of a different religious persuasion who wishes to attend that school: Barrington J in *Campaign to Separate Church and State Ltd v Minister for Education* [1998] 2 ILRM 81, SC and 3 IR 321. However, it is constitutionally impermissible for a school chaplain to instruct a child in a religion which is not the child's religion, without the knowledge and consent of the child's parents (*Campaign* case).

See also DISCRIMINATION; ETHOS; RELIGIOUS BELIEF; VOCATIONAL TRAINING.

religious freedom. Freedom of conscience and the free profession and practice of religion are, subject to public order and morality, guaranteed to every citizen: 1937 Constitution, art 44(2)(1). The State is required to respect and honour religion and further guarantees not to *endow* any religion or to impose any disability or make any discrimination on the ground of religious profession, belief or status (arts 44(1), 44(2)(2) and 44(2)(3)).

Although the Constitution places a duty on the State to respect and honour religion, the State is not placed in the position of an arbiter of religious truth; its only function is to protect public order and morality: *Corway v Independent Newspapers Ltd* [2000] 1 ILRM 426, SC at 430.

State aid to a denominational school for education purposes and the payment of chaplains' salaries is not 'endowment' of religion; the effect of art 44(2) is to outlaw the 'establishment' by the State of any religion: *Campaign to Separate Church and State Ltd v Minister for Education* [1998] 2 ILRM 81, SC.

The recognition by the State of the special position of the Roman Catholic Church and the recognition of other specified churches in arts 44(1)(2) and 44(1)(3) was deleted by referendum (qv) of the people in 1972: Fifth Amendment to the Constitution.

Parents have a constitutional right to decide the religion of their children and the State cannot interfere with this right; in the case of disagreement between parents, the courts will endeavour to supply the place of the parents: *Re Tilson infants* [1951] IR 1; Guardianship of Infants Act 1964. A Minister who prohibits activities, which he concludes are offensive on religious grounds to many members of the Irish public, is not acting *ultra vires* in his exercise of a statutory authority, requiring him to have regard for the *public interest*: *Tara Prospecting Ltd v Minister for Energy* [1993] ILRM 771, HC.

See also *Quinn's Supermarket Ltd v Attorney-General* [1972] IR 1; *McGee v Attorney-General* [1974] IR 284; *Mulloy v Minister for Education* [1975] IR 88. See ADOPTION, CONSENT TO; EUROPEAN CONVENTION ON HUMAN RIGHTS; FOSTER-PARENTS; HATRED, INCITEMENT TO; WORSHIP, PUBLIC; VOW.

religious observance. The director of a *children detention school* (qv) is required to ensure that each child is given the opportunity, as far as practicable, to receive religious assistance and instruction and the opportunity of practising his religion: Children Act 2001, s 199.

relocated witness. Any person who intends to give or has given evidence in proceedings for an offence and who as a consequence has moved residence, under any programme operated by the Garda Síochána for the protection of witnesses, to any place, whether within or outside the State: Criminal Justice Act 1999, s 40. It is an offence to attempt to ascertain the whereabouts, or new name, of a relocated witness (CJA 1999, s 40(1)). It is also an offence to disclose this information without lawful authority (CJA 1999, s 40(2)).

The Supreme Court, overturning a High Court decision, granted an order directing the Garda Commissioner to be orally examined in order to ascertain what debts, if any, are owed by the State to a person under the witness protection programme: *Foley v Bowden & Garda Commissioner* [2003] 2 IR 607, SC and [2004] 1 ILRM 22, SC. In this case the plaintiff was seeking an order to assist him in formulating a *garnishee* (qv) order to attach any sum due to the person under the programme.

The Court of Criminal Appeal has held that if there was an agreement between a witness and the Gardaí, or the prosecution authorities, that he would give certain specific evidence and in return would be paid a specific amount of money, that evidence would be unlawfully obtained and could be excluded: *DPP v Gilligan* [2003] FL 8123, CCA. See also *Re Quigley* [1983] NI 245.

The Court has referred two points of law to the Supreme Court in relation to the witness protection programme: (a) the circumstances under which evidence from witnesses involved in the programme is admissible in a criminal trial, and (b) the nature of corroborative evidence required from accomplice witnesses who have participated in the programme: *Gilligan v DPP* (27 January 2004) CCA.

remainder. A grant to take effect in possession on the natural determination of a *particular* (qv) estate of freehold created by the same instrument eg *to A for life, remainder to B for life, remainder to C in tail*; B and C take remainders and the grantor retain the reversion (qv) in fee simple. See CONTINGENT REMAINDER; TENANT FOR LIFE.

remand. The sending back of a person charged with a crime, pending the hearing of the charge at a future date. The court is empowered to remand an accused from time to time as the occasion requires: Criminal Procedure Act 1967, ss 21–33. An order remanding an accused for a period longer than eight days can only be made with the consent of both the prosecutor and the accused: CPA 1967, s 24; *Barry v Fitzpatrick* [1996] 1 ILRM 512, SC.

Where the District Court remands a person or sends him forward for trial or sentence, the court may either: (a) commit him to prison or other lawful custody; or (b) release him conditionally on his entering into a recognisance (qv) with or without security (CPA 1967, s 22). See also CPA 1967, ss 4Q, 24 and 27 as amended by Criminal Justice (Miscellaneous Provisions) Act 1997, ss 4–5 and Criminal Justice Act 1999, ss 9 and 21. See European Arrest Warrant Act 2003, s 27. See *Maguire v O'Hanrahan* [1988] ILRM 243. See DCR 1997 Ord 19. See BAIL; RELEASE, TEMPORARY.

remanent pro defectu emptorum. [They are left in my hands for want of buyers.]

remarriage. A party to a marriage, which has been dissolved by a decree of divorce, may marry again: Family Law (Divorce) Act 1996, s 10(1). A person who remarries is not entitled to a provision out of the estate of their deceased former spouse (FL(D)A 1996, s 18(2)) or to have a *property adjustment order* made in their favour (FL(D)A 1996, s 14(3)). Also on remarriage, entitlement to any periodic payments from their former spouse ceases (FL(D)A 1996, ss 13(5) and 19(4)), as also does entitlement to any pension contingent benefit (FL(D)A 1996, ss 17(3), 17(19)). See DIVORCE; FATAL INJURIES.

remedial action. If a dispute referred to the *Private Residential Tenancies Board* (qv) relates to the termination of a tenancy for failure by the landlord or tenant to fulfil his obligations relating to the tenancy, any remedial action taken by the other party subsequent to the receipt of the notice of termination must not be taken into consideration by the Board, a mediator, an adjudicator or the Tenancies Tribunal in dealing with the dispute: Residential Tenancies Act 2004, s 87. See PART 4 TENANCY, TERMINATION OF; TENANCY, TERMINATION NOTICE; TENANCY DISPUTE.

remedial statute. Legislation which is intended to remedy a defect in existing law.

remedy. The means provided by the law whereby the violation of a right is prevented, redressed or compensated. A remedy may be provided by: (a) a judicial or quasi-judicial process eg by court action or arbitration; (b) by agreement between the parties eg accord and satisfaction; or (c) by the act of the injured party eg abatement or distress (qv). A plaintiff is entitled to take advantage of the remedy which is most advantageous to her: *Kennedy v Allied Irish Banks Ltd* [1998] 2 IR 48, SC. See ACCORD AND SATISFACTION; EUROPEAN CONVENTION ON HUMAN RIGHTS.

Remembrance Fund. A fund of €9m established by the government to address the needs of the victims of the conflict in Northern Ireland and their families in this jurisdiction. A Commission to administer the fund was announced in November 2003. Payments of up to €15,000 may be payable to bereaved families, to spouses and to dependent children. Also a grant may be paid to the Northern Ireland Memorial Fund. Closing date for applications is 1 November 2006. For details of the scheme, application forms and guidance notes, see website: *www.justice.ie.*

remise. To release or surrender.

remission. The pardoning of an offence or the cancelling in whole or in part of an obligation. The Minister for Justice has power to commute or remit, in whole or in part, any punishment imposed by a court exercising criminal jurisdiction; this power is not unconstitutional but it must be exercised sparingly and for special reasons with the proper maintenance of records: 1937 Constitution, art 13.6; Criminal Justice Act 1951, s 23; *Brennan v Minister for Justice* [1995] 2 ILRM 206, HC and 1 IR 612. This power of the Minister is delegated to him by order of the government: CJA 1951, s 23A inserted by Criminal Justice (Miscellaneous Provisions) Act 1997, s 17.

The sentencing of a person by a court to a term of imprisonment, with a direction that he be brought back to the court subsequently, in order for the court to consider suspending the balance of his sentence, did not involve an encroachment by the judicial arm of government upon the executive's power to commute a sentence: *People (DPP) v Aylmer* [1995] 2 ILRM 624, SC.

The *prison rules* made by the Minister may provide for remission for good conduct of a portion of a convicted person's sentence (CJ(MP)A 1997, s 19(3)(f)). A prisoner may obtain a remission of up to one-quarter of the total sentence on account of good behaviour during imprisonment; the remission may be lost in whole or in part. See Rules for the Government of Prisons 1947, r 38(1) (S R & O No 320 of 1947). For an example of a sentence which could not be reconciled with the remission rules, see *O'Brien v Governor of Limerick Prison* [1997] 2 ILRM 349, SC.

In relation to restrictions on the power to remit punishment for treason and aggravated murder, see Criminal Justice Act 1990, s 5. See *Dempsey v Minister for Justice* [1994] 1 ILRM 401. [Bibliography: McDermott.] See PARDON; PAROLE.

remittal of action. Transfer of an action from one level of court to another. Any action which is pending in the High or Circuit Court may be remitted or transferred to a lower court, on application to the court in which it is pending by any party to the action before commencement of the trial, if the court so orders: Courts Act 1991, s 15; Courts of Justice Act 1924, s 25. See also Courts and Court Officers Act 2002, s 18. Where an action claiming *unliquidated* damages is remitted from the High Court to the Circuit Court, the latter court has jurisdiction to award damages without limit: Courts of Justice Act 1936, s 20 as amended by the Courts Act 1991, s 2(3)(a).

Where the High Court remits an action to the Circuit Court, it does not necessarily follow that it was unreasonable to have commenced the proceedings in the High Court: *O'Shea v Mallow Urban Council* [1993] ILRM 884, HC. Where an action is remitted to the District Court, that court is limited to awarding between £5,000 (€6,349) and £10,000 (€12,698) in an action for unliquidated damages (CA 1991, s 15(2)).

A *family law action* which might have been commenced in the Circuit or District Court, may be remitted by the High Court to either of those courts on the application of any party: RSC Ord 70A, r 15(1) as inserted by SI No 343 of 1997. The court has a discretion whether to remit a case under r 15 and the onus is on the person seeking to have the case remitted to convince the court that it is in the interests of justice to do so: *MW v DW* [2000] 1 ILRM 416, SC.

Whenever the High Court transfers any action or proceeding to the Circuit Court, the plaintiff is required to lodge with the County Registrar, within 14 days from the date of the order for transfer, the summons and all pleadings, orders and all documents: Circuit Court Rules 2001 Ord 35. The action or proceeding is taken and heard in the Circuit Court as if it had originally commenced in that court.

For rules of the High and District Courts in relation to remittals, see RSC Ord 49, r 7; DCR 1997 Ord 39, r 15.

remoteness. A disposition of a future interest in property is void for *remoteness* where it is not to take effect within the period allowed by the rule against perpetuities (qv), or where it offends against the rules against inalienability (qv) or accumulations (qv) or the rule in *Whitby v Mitchell*. This latter rule states that if an interest in realty is given to an unborn person, any remainder (qv) to that unborn person's issue is void together with all subsequent limitations.

remoteness of damage. (1) In contract (qv), the general rule is that damages for breach of contract will apply only to the loss flowing naturally from the breach, such that a reasonable man could foresee, or such as may reasonably be supposed to have been in the contemplation of the parties, at the time they made the contract, as the probable result of the breach of it; otherwise, the loss will be too remote: *Hadley v Baxendale* [1854] 9 Exch 341; *French v West Clare Railway Co* [1897] 31 ILT & SJ 140; *Victoria Laundry v Newman Industries* [1949] 2 KB 528; *Stock v Urey* [1955] NI 71; *Wagon Mound Case* [1961] AC 388; *McGrath v Kiely* [1965] IR 497; *Lee Donoghue v Rowan* [1981] HC.

Where it is reasonably foreseeable that a person may be unable to mitigate or remedy the consequences of another person's breach of duty by reason of impecuniosity, such additional losses which may arise in this manner are recoverable and are not to be regarded as being too remote: *Doran v Delaney* [1999] 1 ILRM 225, HC.

(2) In tort (qv), a defendant is liable only for the damage of such a kind as a reasonable man would have foreseen: *Burke v John Paul Ltd* [1967] IR 277. The owner of a car who left it unattended and unlocked on a public street with the keys in the ignition, was held not to be liable for the injuries caused to the plaintiff by the negligent driving of the thief who stole the car: *Breslin v Corcoran and MIBI* [2003] 2 ILRM 189, SC and 2 IR 203: *Law Society Gazette* (July 2003) 38. The court held that there was nothing to suggest in the case that the owner should have anticipated that there was a reasonable probability that the car, if stolen, would be driven so carelessly as to cause injury to another user of the road such as the plaintiff. See DAMAGES; ECONOMIC LOSS; NOVUS ACTUS INTERVENIENS.

remuneration. 'Remuneration is not mere payment for work done but is what the doer expects to get as a result of the work he does in so far as what he expects to get is quantified in terms of money': *S & U Stores Ltd v Lee* [1969] 2 All ER 419 approved of in *McGivern v Irish National Insurance Co Ltd* PS/1982 (EAT).

There is a presumption of transfer of the rental right in the case of a *film* production agreement; the author and the performer, however, are entitled to *equitable remuneration* in such circumstances: Copyright and Related Rights Act 2000, ss 125–126 and 298–299. An agreement is void in so far as it purports to restrict the right to equitable remuneration (CRRA 2000, ss 125(6) and 298(6)).

Remuneration is not to be considered inequitable because it is paid by way of a single payment or at the time of the transfer of the rental right (CRRA 2000, ss 126(6) and 299(6)) reversing, as regards *films*, *Phonographic Performance (Ireland) Ltd v Controller of Industrial and Commercial Property* [1996] 1 ILRM 1, SC and 2 IR 560 in which it had been held that the use of the word *remuneration* in the Copyright Act 1963, s 17(5) (since repealed) implied that the payment was to be made after and not before the event, and that the basic meaning of the term 'to remunerate' was 'to pay for a service rendered' and so 'remuneration' was a payment for a service which has been rendered in the past.

A performer also has a right to *equitable remuneration* in a *sound recording* when it is played in public or included in a broadcast or cable programme service (CRRA 2000, s 208). See Protection of Employees (Fixed-Term Work) Act 2003, s 2(1). See

EQUAL PAY; FILM; PERFORMERS' RIGHTS; SOUND RECORDING; WAGE.

remuneration of directors. A director of a company is not entitled to remuneration for acting as a director except by express agreement; the *articles of association* usually provide for such remuneration to be determined by the company in a general meeting. Remuneration of directors and loans to them must be disclosed in the company's accounts: Companies Act 1963, ss 191; Companies Act 1986, Sch, para 49(a).

The annual report and accounts of a *listed* company must contain a statement of the company's policy on executive directors' remuneration and of the amount of each element in the remuneration package of each director by name, together with a total for each director, both for the current and previous financial period: Listing Rules 2000, para 12.43A(c) as amended in 1999 by the Irish Stock Exchange Ltd. Previously, the amount could be reported as an aggregate figure for all executive directors. See DIRECTORS' SERVICE CONTRACT; GOLDEN UMBRELLA; LOAN TO DIRECTOR.

remuneration of trustees. Generally, a trustee is not entitled to remuneration for his work as a trustee no matter how onerous it may be: *Re Ormsby* [1809] 1 Ball & B 189. This is based on the principle that a trustee should not obtain a material benefit from his position. There are exceptions e g where remuneration is provided for expressly in the trust instrument; or where so ordered by the court; or where the trustee's work has generated a profit for the beneficiary which the trustee is not allowed to retain. See *Boardman v Phipps* [1967] 2 AC 46. See TRUSTEE, DUTY OF.

render. To yield or to pay.

rendez-vous clause. A clause in an important legal document (such as a new treaty) which the heads of the governments of the EU have not yet agreed, but which they have decided to revisit at a later date.

rendition. The backing of warrants; the term *extradition* is often used to embrace the term *rendition*. It is similar to extradition except that the handing over of fugitives is not based on a formal agreement between States but on the enactment by these States of virtually identical legislation which provides for the handing over of fugitives to each other State eg Extradition Act 1965, Part III in this State and the

Backing of Warrants (Ireland) Act 1965 in the UK. The European Arrest Warrant Act 2003, s 50 repeals Part III of the 1965 Act. [Bibliography: Forde (3).] See EUROPEAN ARREST WARRANT; EXTRADITION; JUDICIAL AUTHORITY.

renewable energy project. A project in one of the technology categories of: solar power, wind power, water power or biomass: Taxes Consolidation Act 1997, s 486B as inserted by Finance Act 1998, s 62. An investor company may obtain tax relief in respect of its investment in such a project. Provision has been made to extend the qualifying period to 31 December 2006: Finance Act 2004, s 39. *Biomass* means the biodegradable fraction of products, waste and residues from agriculture, forestry and related industries, as well as the biodegradable fraction of industrial and municipal waste (FA 2004, s 49). See BIOFUEL.

renewable fine. See LEASE FOR LIVES RENEWABLE FOR EVER.

renewal. Includes 'extension' and cognate words must be read accordingly: Protection of Employees (Fixed-Term Work) Act 2003, s 2(1).

renewal of insurance. See PREMIUM.

renewal of summons. See SUMMONS, RENEWAL OF.

renominalisation. See CAPITAL.

renouncing probate. See RENUNCIATION.

rent. (1) A periodic payment payable by a tenant to the landlord for the possession and use of land. It includes any *sum or return* and consequently may include money or services and goods: Deasy's Act 1860, s 1. In the absence of any provision in a lease for the payment of rent, a covenant to pay rent is implied (DA 1860, s 42). A *peppercorn* rent is a nominal rent which serves as an acknowledgement of the tenancy. A landlord may bring an action for *ejectment* for non-payment of rent. See *McQuaid v Lynam* [1965] IR 564. Under recent legislation, s 42 of the 1860 Act and court proceedings for ejectment for non-payment of rent do not apply to certain dwellings: Residential Tenancies Act 2004 s.193(a).

(2) A tenant of a dwelling is required to pay to the landlord the rent on the day it falls due for payment and other charges and taxes in accordance with the lease or tenancy agreement: Residential Tenancies Act 2004, s 16(a). Where a dispute over the rent in a tenancy of a dwelling has been

referred to the *Private Residential Tenancies Board*, the rent must continue to be paid, there must be no increase in rent if the dispute concerns the amount of rent payable, and there must not be a termination of the tenancy until a determination in relation to the dispute has been made (RTA 2004, s 86). The circumstances, financial or otherwise, of the landlord or tenant must not be taken into consideration by a mediator, adjudicator or the Tenancy Tribunal in dealing with a dispute about a rent (RTA 2004, s 120). A landlord is required within one month of a change in the rent applicable to a tenancy, to notify the Board of the revised rent together with any other change in particulars that may have occurred by that time. No fee may be imposed in respect of such notification. See MARKET RENT; TENANT, OBLIGATIONS OF; PART 4 TENANCY, TERMINATION OF.

(3) As regards taxation, rent includes any payment in the nature of rent e g work done by the tenant on the leased premises: Taxes Consolidation Act 1997, s 96(1). There is an allowance against tax for rent paid by certain tenants (TCA 1997, s 473 as amended by Finance Act 2000, s 13). A tenant paying rent to a non-resident landlord is required to treat the rent as an annual payment from which standard rate income tax must be deducted and paid over to the Revenue Commissioners (TCA 1997, ss 238, 1041). Provision has been made to ensure that asylum seekers are not entitled to *rent supplement*: Social Welfare (Miscellaneous Provisions) Act 2003, s 13. See also Finance Act 2003, s 16. See DISTRESS; EJECTMENT; LEASE; SET OFF.

rent-a-room relief. Under a new scheme, from 6 April 2001 when a person rents out a room or rooms in their principal private residence, no tax is payable on the rent received, up a limit of £6,000 (€7,618). The rent does not affect the person's entitlement to mortgage interest relief, to capital gains exemption, and does not have stamp duty implications.

rent allowance. An allowance payable to a person who is entitled to retain possession as the tenant of a dwelling under s 9 of the Housing (Private Rented Dwellings) Act 1982 in certain circumstances and where the person satisfies the 'means' test: SI No 188 of 1998. Provision has been made to increase the minimum rent for the purposes of the scheme for persons affected by the decontrol of rents: SI No 121 of

2002. Also provision has been made to continue entitlement to rent allowance to successor tenants for whom the protection of the 1982 Act ceased on 26 July 2002: SI No 354 of 2002. The amount of 'means' was also increased. See also SI No 729 of 2003.

As regards the *rent supplement* under the supplementary welfare allowance scheme, this is payable only where the applicant is lawfully within the State: SI No 210 of 2003. Under this regulation, the *rent supplement* is not payable where the applicant has made an application for asylum and such application is awaiting final decision by the Minister. Also the rent supplement is not payable where the cohabiting spouse or partner of the claimant is in full-time employment: Social Welfare Act 2003, s 12.

rent arrears. Provision has been made for arrears of rent or other charges under a tenancy of certain dwellings to be recovered using the dispute resolution procedures of the *Private Residential Tenancies Board* (qv): Residential Tenancies Act 2004, ss 23 and 75–126. The amount of rent arrears stipulated to be payable in a *determination* is required to be the gross amount of the arrears as reduced by: (a) any amounts due in respect of debts due by the landlord to the tenant under s 48 of Deasy's Act 1860, (b) any set off for expenditure on repairs by the tenant under s 87 of the Landlord and Tenant (Amendment) Act 1980, (c) any compensation due by the landlord to the tenant under s 61 of the 1980 Act, or (d) as warranted in the opinion of the adjudicator or the Tenancy Tribunal and as increased by any amount considered appropriate by the adjudicator or Tribunal in respect of costs incurred in pursuing the arrears, damages or the cost of repairs caused by the tenant's failure to comply with the obligations of the tenancy (RTA 2004, s 119). The breakdown of the calculation must be included in the determination. See DETERMINATION ORDER; DWELLING; PART 4 TENANCY, TERMINATION OF.

rent book. The Minister is empowered to make regulations requiring the landlord of a rented *house* to provide the tenant with a rent book or other document that would serve the same purpose: Housing (Miscellaneous Provisions) Act 1992, s 17. *House* includes any building or part of a building used as a dwelling e g house, flat or maisonette (H(MP)A 1992, s 1(1)). There is provision for inspection by a person authorised by the housing authority (H(MP)A 1992, s 17(3)).

Under the regulations, the rent book must contain, *inter alia*, the address of the rented dwelling, name and address of landlord or agent, tenant's name, term of tenancy, amount of rent and when and how to be paid, particulars of any payments other than rent, amount of deposit and conditions for refund, an inventory of furnishings and appliances supplied by the landlord for the tenant's exclusive use, and statement of tenant's basic statutory rights: SI No 146 of 1993. Tenants of controlled dwellings (qv) are already entitled to rent books.

The establishment of the *Private Residential Tenancies Board* (qv) has changed substantially the regulation of tenancies; however, local authorities continue to be responsible for the enforcement of rent book regulations.

rent control. The control of rents in respect of *controlled dwellings*: Housing (Private Rented Dwellings) Act 1982 as amended by Housing Act 1992. The terms of the tenancy of a controlled dwelling are fixed by a Rent Tribunal: Housing (Private Rented Dwellings) (Amendment) Act 1983. The Rent Tribunal must take into account the effect its decisions will have on the parties: *Beatty & Beatty v Rent Tribunal* [2003] ITLR (2 June) HC. [Bibliography: de Blacam (1).] See CONTROLLED DWELLING.

rent deposit. A landlord is required to return or repay promptly any deposit paid by the tenant to the landlord on entering into the agreement for the tenancy or lease of a dwelling: Residential Tenancies Act 2004, s 12(1)(d). There is no such requirement when at the date of the request for the return or repayment there is a default: (a) in payment of rent equal to or greater than the deposit or (b) in the tenant's obligation not to cause deterioration in the condition of the dwelling, the cost of restoration of which is equal to or greater than the deposit (RTA 2004, s 12(4)). Where not equal or greater but there is a default, there is provision for a proportionate return or repayment. See DWELLING; LANDLORD, OBLIGATIONS OF.

rent relief. A person living in rented residential accommodation may be entitled to rent relief as regards his income tax liability: Taxes Consolidation Act 1997, s 473 amended by Finance Act 2001, s 9.

rent review. A review of the rent under the tenancies of certain dwellings must not take place more frequently than once in every period of 12 months, nor in the period of 12 months beginning on the commencement of the tenancy, unless there has been substantial change in the nature of the accommodation in the interim: Residential Tenancies Act 2004, s 20. Either the landlord or the tenant may require a review to be carried out, despite the absence of provision for such a review in the lease or tenancy agreement (RTA 2004, s 21). Under the review, a rent above the *market rent* must not be set (RTA 2004, s 19(2)(b)). The tenant must be given written notice of the new rent at least 28 days before the date from which it is to have effect (RTA 2004, s 22(2)). The tenant may refer a dispute concerning the new rent to the *Private Residential Tenancies Board* (qv) before the effective date of the new rent or the expiry of 28 days from receipt by the tenant of the notice, whichever is the later (RTA 2004, s 22(3)). See DWELLING; MARKET RENT; TENANCY DISPUTE.

rent review clause. A clause in a lease which provides for a periodic review of the rent payable under the lease, provided the property is not subject to some statutory rent control. The clause may provide for a predetermined increase, or an increase based on an escalator clause, or it may be subject to agreement or arbitration. For review of rents payable under sporting leases and reversionary leases (qv), see Landlord and Tenant (Amendment) Act 1984, ss 3 and 5. See also Landlord and Tenant (Amendment) Act 1980, s 24. See *Hynes v O'Malley Property Ltd* [1989] ILT Dig 204; *Erin Executor and Trustee Co v Farmer* [1987] HC. See DISREGARD CLAUSE; TENANT STATUTORY.

rent seck. [Dry rent] A rent payable in respect of land to a person who has no reversion in it (eg a fee farm grant) and with no power of distress. Distress and other remedies, however, are provided by Deasy's Act 1860 and the Conveyancing Act 1881, s 44. See FEE FARM GRANT.

rent setting. In setting the rent under the tenancy of certain dwellings, there is a prohibition on setting the rent above the *market rent* for that tenancy at that time:

Residential Tenancies Act 2004, s 19. See DWELLING; MARKET RENT; RENT REVIEW.

rent tribunal. See RENT CONTROL; TENANCY DISPUTE.

rentcharges. Charges relating to land which do not arise from the relationship of landlord and tenant eg tithe rentcharges (qv); perpetual rentcharges sometimes created by a fee farm grant (qv); payment of advances under the Landed Property Improvement (Ireland) Act 1847; and an annuity charged on land: *Revenue Commissioners v Malone* [1951] IR 269. See also the definition of rentcharges in the Statute of Limitations 1957, s 2(1).

rented house, registration of. The Minister is empowered to make regulations requiring a landlord of a house let for rent or other valuable consideration to register the tenancy with the housing authority and to furnish such particulars as the regulations require: Housing (Miscellaneous Provisions) Act 1992, s 20. There is provision for a register to be kept by the housing authority, for inspection of the register by any person, and for inspection of the house by a person authorised by the housing authority. See Registration of Rented Houses Regulations 1996, SI No 30 of 1996. Provision has been made under the Residential Tenancies Act 2004 for the repeal of these regulations, which are now replaced by the registration requirements in Part 7 (ss 127–145) of the 2004 Act (RTA 2004, s 10(2)). See PRIVATE RESIDENTIAL TENANCIES REGISTER.

rented house, standard of. The Minister is empowered to prescribe standards for houses let for rent or other valuable consideration and it is the duty of the landlord of such house to ensure that the house complies with the standards prescribed: Housing (Miscellaneous Provisions) Act 1992, s 18. The regulations may make provision for such matters as, classes of houses or tenancies, maintenance, quality and condition of accommodation, ventilation and lighting, facilities for heating, cooking and storage of food, water supplies, sanitary facilities and drainage (H(MP)A 1992, s 18(7)). There is provision for inspection by a person authorised by the housing authority (H(MP)A 1992, s 18(2)). The standards are specified in SI No 147 of 1993.

The establishment of the *Private Residential Tenancies Board* (qv) has changed substantially the regulation of tenancies; however, local authorities continue to be responsible for the enforcement of standards regulations.

rented residential accommodation. Under a new measure, the capital expenditure incurred in the refurbishment of rental residential property is allowed to be set off against rental income over a seven-year period: Finance Act 2001, s 63. The cost of interest has been restored as a deductible expense in calculating tax on rental income from residential property; this is the interest on borrowed moneys employed in the purchase, improvement or repair of such property by an individual, partnership or company and which accrues on or after 1 January 2002: Finance Act 2002, s 17. See PRIVATE RESIDENTIAL TENANCIES BOARD; SECTION 23 RELIEF.

renunciation. A disclaimer. A renunciation by a person appointed by a testator as his executor, giving up his right to extract probate, must be in writing; the person is known as a *renunciant*. A renunciation by a spouse to her legal right (qv) in an estate must be in writing: Succession Act 1965, s 113. See RSC Ord 79, r 38; Ord 80, r 43.

A bill of exchange is discharged where the holder of the bill, at or after its maturity, absolutely and unconditionally renounces his rights against the acceptor; such renunciation must be in writing unless the bill is delivered up to the acceptor: Bills of Exchange Act 1882, s 62(1); *Terex Equipment Ltd v Irish and Machinery Sales Ltd* [1994] 1 ILRM 557, HC. See also Stamp Duties Consolidation Act 1999, s 63.

renvoi. [To send back.] The doctrine in private international law (qv) regarding the choice of law where the law of more than one country may be applicable. See *Re Adams deceased* [1967] IR 424; *Re Interview Ltd* [1975] IR 382; *Kutchera v Buckingman International Holdings Ltd* [1988] IR 61. See Contractual Obligations (Applicable Law) Act 1991, Sch 1, art 15. [Bibliography: Binchy.] See CONTRACT.

reopen case. See FRESH EVIDENCE.

reorganisation of company. See RECONSTRUCTION OF COMPANY; COURT PROTECTION OF COMPANY.

repackaging of goods. The European Court of Justice has confirmed the right of a trade mark owner to prevent the use of its trade mark on repackaged goods unless the repackaging is necessary in order to enable the marketing of the product and provided that the interests of the trademark owner are safeguarded: *Boehringer* (Case C-143/00) and *Merck, Sharp & Dohme* (Case C-443/99). See also *Hoffmann-La Roche v Centrafarm* (Case C-102/77) [1978] ECR 1139. See 'Parallel Universe' by solicitor Dorit McCann in *Law Society Gazette* (June 2002) 24.

repair. The landlord of a dwelling is required: (a) to carry out repairs to the structure and to the interior of the dwelling, and (b) to reimburse the tenant in certain circumstances for vouched expenses incurred by the tenant on repairs for which the landlord is responsible: Residential Tenancies Act 2004, s 12. A tenant of a dwelling is required: (a) not to do anything which causes the dwelling to deteriorate beyond reasonable wear and tear, and (b) to restore the dwelling, as the landlord may reasonably require, if it has deteriorated beyond reasonable wear and tear, or to defray the costs incurred by the landlord in so doing (RTA 2004, s 16).

A covenant (qv) in a lease will generally require the tenant to be responsible for the repair of the interior and the landlord to be responsible for the repair of the exterior, the common areas and the structural integrity of the premises. If there is no repairing covenant in the lease, the tenant is required by statute to 'keep the premises in good and substantial repair and condition' and to 'give peaceable possession of the premises in good and substantial repair and condition' on determination of the lease: Deasy's Act 1860, s 42 which no longer applies to dwellings under the 2004 Act (RTA 2004, s 193(a)). The words *'good and substantial repair and condition'* have been interpreted as imposing on the tenant a duty to put the premises into a state of repair at the beginning of the term if it is out of repair, and to keep it in good and substantial repair thereafter until the end of the term. See *Whelan v Maddigan* [1978] ILRM 136.

Certain minimum standards are imposed on landlords in relation to any class of dwelling let for rent: Housing (Miscellaneous Provisions) Act 1992, s 18 and Housing (Standard of Rented Houses) Regulations 1993, SI No 147 of 1993. A housing authority is empowered to serve a *repairs notice* on the owner of premises which it considers unfit for human habitation: Housing Act 1966, s 66. See also Public Health (Ireland) Act 1878. See LANDLORD, OBLIGATIONS OF; RENTED HOUSE, STANDARD OF; UNFIT HOUSE.

repair, breach of covenant to. A landlord's remedies for a breach by a tenant of a covenant to repair are: (a) *damages for breach of contract*. The damages cannot exceed the amount by which the reversion (ie the value of the property to the landlord) is diminished: Landlord and Tenant (Amendment) Act 1980, s 65; (b) *specific performance* under which the court will order the tenant to carry out the repairs; this remedy is seldom used; (c) *entry of premises* with the landlord carrying out the repairs and recovering the costs thereof from the tenant, but only if there is specific provision for this in the lease; (d) *forfeiture* under which the lease is terminated by the landlord before the term ends, provided there is specific provision for this in the lease.

The tenant's remedies for breach by a landlord of a covenant to repair are: (a) *damages for breach of contract*; and (b) *set off against the rent* in respect of the reasonable expenditure incurred by the tenant in effecting the repairs himself, provided there is no prohibition on set off in the lease. A statutory right to set off may apply notwithstanding anything to the contrary in the lease. For detail, see SET OFF.

A breach of an obligation to repair in a tenancy of a dwelling may lead to termination of the tenancy or be resolved through the dispute resolution procedures of the *Private Residential Tenancies Board* (qv). See LEASE, DETERMINATION OF; PART 4 TENANCY, TERMINATION OF; TENANCY, TERMINATION NOTICE.

repatriation. Resumption by a person of his former nationality; sending back a person to his own country. See ALIEN; DEPORTATION; NATIONALITY; REFUGEE.

repeal. The cancellation or annulment of a statute or part of a statute. It may be express eg 'the enactments mentioned in the Sch 2 are hereby repealed to the extent specified in the third column'. It may be implied ie the necessary result of the subsequent enactment. The repeal of a repealing enactment does not revive the enactment originally repealed.

Where an Act repeals in whole or in part a previous statute, then, unless the contrary intention appears, such repeal does not prejudice any legal proceedings pending at the time of such repeal, or affect any right acquired under the portion so repealed:

Interpretation Act 1937, s 21; *Wood v Wicklow Co Council* [1995] ILRM 51, HC; *McKone Estates Ltd v Dublin Co Council* [1995] 2 ILRM 283, SC.

Where an Act repeals the whole or a portion of a previous statute and substitutes other provisions for the statute or portion repealed, the statute or portion so repealed shall, unless the contrary is expressly provided in the repealing Act, continue in force until the substituted provisions come into operation (IA 1937, s 19(1)).

Where an Act repeals a common law offence, the repeal does not apply retrospectively, unless a contrary intention appears, and any prosecution in respect of such offence may be instituted, continued, or enforced: Interpretation (Amendment) Act 1997 which was intended to cure a possible defect in the Non-Fatal Offences Against the Person Act 1997. The Supreme Court has held that common-sense dictated that where a common law offence was repealed by statute, in the absence of any saving provision, it ceased to exist for all purposes and no prosecution could take place after the repealing statute had taken effect: *Grealis & Corbett v DPP* [2001] 3 IR 144, SC and [2002] 1 ILRM 241, SC. It also held that the 1997 Act must be interpreted as having prospective effect in order for it not to offend against the constitutional prohibition on retroactive penal legislation. See *Quinlivan v Governor of Portlaoise Prison* [1997] HC; *Mullins v Harnett* [1998] 2 ILRM 304; *Doolan v DPP* [1992] IR 399.

The substitution of one section in an Act by another may have the effect of the repeal of the previous section and its replacement by the new section eg section 3 of the Larceny Act 1990 amends s 33 of the Larceny Act 1916 by substitution: *People (DPP) v Gilligan* [1992] ILRM 769, CCA.

It would appear that an enactment may be *de facto* repealed without any legislation having been adopted for the purposes of such repeal: Farm Tax Act 1985 and *Purcell v A-G* [1989] ITLR (18 December) HC. What remains of such legislation is unenforceable both retrospectively and prospectively. See GENERALIA SPECIALIBUS NON DEROGANT; INTERPRETATION OF LEGISLATION; REPLACE.

repetitive legal work. A solicitor's remuneration should reflect the amount of work performed by him; regard should be had for the repetitive nature of work where it involves the preparation of instructions in respect of second and subsequent motions involving identical factors: *Ormond v Ireland* [1988] ILRM 490, HC.

replace. Where a Statutory Instrument is stated to *replace* another earlier statutory instrument, the earlier SI is revoked when the later SI comes into force: *O'Flynn Construction Co Ltd v An Bord Pleanála* [2000] 1 IR 497, HC.

replevin. A means whereby a person from whom goods or chattels have been allegedly unlawfully taken can have them judicially restored to him pending an action for their return, upon giving security to prosecute the action and return the goods if so directed by the court. See RSC, App B, Pt II. [Bibliography: Dixon & Gilliland.] See CONVERSION.

replication. Reply (qv).

reply. The answer of a plaintiff to a defence or counterclaim; in High Court proceedings a reply must be delivered within fourteen days from delivery of the defence; a reply is not necessary in any case where all the material statements of fact in the relevant pleading are merely to be denied and put in issue: RSC Ord 23. In the Circuit Court, no pleadings subsequent to defence, or defence and counterclaim, are allowed: Circuit Court Rules 2001 Ord 15, r 18.

reply, right of. The right of a party or his legal representatives to re-address the Court.

report. See Rules of the Superior Courts (Disclosure of Reports and Statements) 1998, SI No 391 of 1998. See EXPERT REPORT; LAW REPORT.

representation. (1) Taking the place of another eg an agent for his principal. (2) Being represented in a legislative body eg the Houses of the Oireachtas. (3) A statement or assertion of fact made by one party to another which induces a course of action eg entering into a contract. A representation may amount to a condition (qv) or a warranty (qv); it may create an estoppel (qv) or it may be an expression of opinion or mere *puffing* and thereby have no legal effect. See MISREPRESENTATION.

representational payment. Members of local authorities are now entitled to a payment, called a *representational payment,* from 1 January 2002: Local Government Act 2001, s 142; Local Government (Representational Payment to Members) Regulations 2001, SI No 552 of 2001. The annual rate of payment for a member of a county or city council is €11,000.

representative. A person who stands in the place of another eg an agent for his principal; a personal representative for a testator.

The dismissal of an employee may be unfair where the employee is not offered the opportunity to have a representative present at any meeting which led to his dismissal: *McEvoy v Avery Dennison Ltd* [1992] ELR 172, EAT. An employee is entitled to be legally represented at a hearing to consider his dismissal: *Maher v Irish Permanent plc (No 1)* [1998] ELR 77, HC. In an employment dismissal case, the court held that while the plaintiff was represented by his solicitor, her efficacy was nullified because the defendant denied her the complainant's statement and the opportunity to make representations and submissions: *Cassidy v Shannon Castle Banquets* [2000] ELR 248, HC.

In an inquiry into a person's professional conduct, the person is entitled to have present at the inquiry, any person who might assist in the person's defence; the fact that the inquiry is held in private is not made public just because persons are present who have a proper interest in the hearing: *O Ceallaigh v Fitness to Practice Committee of An Bord Altranais* [1999] 2 IR 552, SC. 'Person representing' in the Nurses Act 1985, s 38(4) means any person whom it could reasonably be submitted was assisting in the preparation and presentation of the case; it was a subjective test and any application to allow persons to remain in the hearing should be granted unless unreasonable (*O Ceallaigh* case).

However, there is no general right at common law or under the 1937 Constitution to be represented by an organisation of one's choice in the negotiation of terms and conditions of employment; an employer has freedom of choice as to whether he will negotiate or consult with any organisation on such matters: *Association of GPs v Minister for Health* [1995] 2 ILRM 481. See LEGAL REPRESENTATION; MCKENZIE FRIEND; TRANSCRIPT.

representative action. See CLASS ACTION.

reprieve. The formal suspension of the execution of a sentence. See PARDON.

reproductive medicine. The Medical Council has issued guidelines on genetic testing and reproductive medicine: 'In a rapidly evolving and complex area, doctors are reminded of their obligation to preserve life and to promote health. The creation of new forms of life for experimental purposes or the deliberate and intentional destruction of in-vitro human life already formed is professional misconduct': *A Guide to Ethical Conduct and Behaviour* (6th edn, 2004), para 24.1. The areas covered in the guidelines are abortion, adoption, artificial insemination, gene therapy, genetic testing, and in-vitro fertilisation (qqv). See 'Human genetics and the need for regulation' by Stephen Dodd BL in *Bar Review* (May 2001) 418. See ABORTION, MEDICAL GUIDELINES; CLONE; HUMAN REPRODUCTION.

Republic of Ireland. The description of the State: Republic of Ireland Act 1948. See STATE.

republication of defamation. The original publisher of a defamatory statement is liable for its republication by another person where the repetition or republication of the words to a third party is the natural and probable result of the original publication: *Speight v Gosnay* [1891] 60 LJ QB 231. This common law rule survives today: *Ewins v Carlton* [1997] 2 ILRM 223. Republication of a libel in Ireland, as a natural result of a UK publication, gives an Irish court jurisdiction as regards the libel: *Hunter & Callaghan v Duckworth and Blom-Cooper* [2000] ITLR (17 January) HC.

republication of will. The re-execution by a testator of a will or codicil previously revoked: Succession Act 1965, s 87. See WILL.

repudiation. Words or conduct indicating that a person does not intend to be or does not regard himself as being bound by an obligation eg repudiation of a contract. An *examiner* of a company, under the protection of the court, may not repudiate a contract entered into by the company prior to the protection period, except in relation to a contract with a negative pledge (eg not to borrow money except from the person to whom the pledge had been given) which would prejudice the survival of the company: Companies (Amendment) Act 1990, s 7 as amended by Companies (Amendment) (No 2) Act 1999, s 18. However, the company, with the permission of the court, may repudiate certain contracts made by it where proposals for a *compromise* or a *scheme of arrangement* are to be formulated (C(A)A 1990, s 20). See BREACH OF CONTRACT; COURT PROTECTION OF COMPANY; ONEROUS PROPERTY; REPUDIATORY BREACH; STRIKE.

repudiatory breach. The decision by a party to a contract not to perform his contractual obligations. The other party may treat the contract as terminated and sue for damages. See *Athlone Rural District Council v A-G Campbell Son (No 2)* 1912 47 ILTR 142; *Woodar Investments v Wimpey Construction* [1980] 1 All ER 571; *House of Spring Gardens Ltd v Point Blank* [1985] FSR 327.

repugnant. Contrary to, or inconsistent with. The Oireachtas (qv) must not enact any law which is in any respect repugnant to the Constitution and any law which is so repugnant is invalid to the extent of the repugnancy: 1937 Constitution, art 15(4).

reputation. The estimation in which a person is generally held. Disparagement of a person's reputation may constitute the tort of defamation. See *Hill v Cork Examiner Publications Ltd* [2001] 4 IR 219, SC. See CHARACTER, EVIDENCE OF; DEFAMATION.

reputed ownership, doctrine of. The doctrine whereby a bankrupt trader was deemed to be the reputed owner, with the true owner's consent, of goods which at the time the trader became bankrupt were in his possession, order or disposition; under the doctrine these goods became available for distribution to his creditors. The doctrine has not been re-enacted in the consolidating Bankruptcy Act 1988 which repeals the Hire-Purchase Act 1946, s 17(1) and Agricultural Credit Act 1947, s 32(3).

request, letter of. See LETTER OF REQUEST.

requisition. A request to a judge in a criminal trial, when the jury has retired, to correct matters in the judge's summing up and charge to the jury. The judge may, if he thinks fit, recall the jury and direct them further.

requisitions on title. The questions in writing which are put by the purchaser to the vendor of real property, having received from the vendor the *abstract of title* (qv). The vendor is bound to answer all relevant questions put to him. Compliance with the questions usually requires the production of originals of documents, the furnishing of searches (qv) and statutory declarations (qv), the proving of performance of covenants (qv) and of compliance with planning permission (qv). See *Hanafin v Gaynor* [1991] 9 ILT Dig 76, HC.

res. [Things.]

res accessoria sequitur rem principalem. [Accessory things follow principal things.]

res extincta. [Things extinct.] There can be no contract in relation to a matter which is non-existent. See *Couturier v Hastie* [1856] 5 HL Cas 673. See FRUSTRATION.

res furtivae. [Stolen goods.]

res gestae. [Things done; the events which happened.] Facts which are parts of the same *transaction* as the fact in issue are admissible as forming parts of the res gestae. A transaction is any physical act, or series of connected acts, together with the accompanying words. See *The People (Attorney-General) v Crosbie & Meehan* [1966] IR 490; *People (DPP) v O'Callaghan* [2004] FL 8706, SC and 1 ILRM 438. See FACT IN ISSUE.

res integra. [A whole thing; an unopened thing.] Refers to where a point has to be decided on principle as there is no rule or decision of court governing it. See *Re United Bars Ltd* [1989] 7 ILT Dig 259.

res inter alios acta alteri nocere non debet. [A transaction between others does not prejudice a person who was not a party to it.] An admission generally is admissible only against the party making it. See ADMISSION.

res ipsa loquitur. [The thing speaks for itself.] In negligence actions, the plaintiff must prove negligence (qv) on the part of the defendant. However, under the maxim *res ipsa loquitur*, there is a presumption of negligence on the part of the defendant where: (a) the cause of an accident is shown to have been under the control of the defendant or his servants at the time of the accident, and (b) the accident is such as in the ordinary course of events would not have happened, if those in control of the cause of the damage had used proper care: *Maitland v Swan & Sligo Co Council* [1992] ITLR (6 July) SC.

When the maxim is properly invoked, the onus will be on the defendant to show that he was not negligent. However, the burden of proving causation still lays with the plaintiff; the courts treat separately the question of causation and the issue of the absence or otherwise of reasonable care: *Cosgrove v Ryan and ESB* [2003] 1 ILRM 544, HC.

In a *medical negligence* (qv) action where no evidence of the defendant's lack of care is adduced by the plaintiff then, before the principle of *res ipsa loquitur* becomes applicable, the onus is on the plaintiff to establish that the accident was such that, in the ordinary course of things, did not happen with the use of care: *Duffy v North Eastern Health Board* [1989] ITLR (13 February). In a particular case it was held that there was clear evidence that damage of the sort the plaintiff suffered could occur in cases of hip replacement with no negligence: *Callaghan v Gleeson and Lavelle* [2002] FL 7554, HC. A court is entitled to conclude that the hospital was responsible without being able to say precisely how the injury to the plaintiff was caused: Doherty v Reynolds [2004] FL 8899, HC.

Res ipsa loquitur does not have to be specifically pleaded before a plaintiff may rely on it, if the facts pleaded and proved show that the doctrine is applicable to the case: *O'Reilly v Lavelle* [1990] 2 IR 372; *Mullen v Quinnsworth Ltd* [1990] ITLR (28 May) SC. See also *Scott v London & St Katherine Docks Co* [1865] 3 H & C 596; *Collen Bros v Scaffolding Ltd* [1959] IR 245; *Merriman v Greenhill Foods Ltd* [1997] 1 ILRM 46, SC and [1996] 3 IR 73, SC. See BURDEN OF PROOF; SURGICAL OPERATION.

res judicata pro veritate acciptur. [A thing adjudicated is received as the truth.] Parties and their privies are estopped from denying not only the state of affairs established by a judgment but also the grounds upon which that judgment was based.

Such estoppel may be: (a) *cause of action estoppel* e g where one party brings an action against another and judgment is given on it, there is a strict rule of law that he cannot bring another action against the same party for the same cause or (b) *issue estoppel* e g where the degree or proportion of liability in a negligence action has already been fixed by a court in a separate action between the parties: *Murphy v Hennessy* [1985] ILRM 100.

The doctrine of *res judicata* reflected the maxim *interest rei publicae ut sit finis litium* (qv) and ensured that a litigant could not engage in an abuse of process by challenging in other proceedings, a final decision against him made by a court of competent jurisdiction in previous proceedings in which he had a full opportunity of contesting that decision: *Belton v Carlow Co Council* [1997] 2 ILRM 405, SC.

It has been held that the doctrine *res judicata* applied only where the issues in the later action were substantially the same as those in the earlier litigation or where it was appropriate to seek all the reliefs in the earlier litigation: *Ulster Bank Ltd v Lyons* [2000] 3 IR 337, HC. An order made on consent striking out proceedings, although final, cannot satisfy an essential requirement in order to invoke the doctrine of *res judicata*; such an order is not a judicial determination of the claim: *Sweeney v Bus Atha Cliath/Dublin Bus* [2004] ITLR (23 February).

The doctrine of *res judicata* applies to certificates issued by a local government auditor: *The State (Dowling) v Leonard* [1960] IR 381. The doctrine of *res judicata* does not restrain the Commissioner of Valuations from using a statutory system to re-open the issue of the exemption from liability for rates: *Gael Linn Teo v Commissioner of Valuation* [1999] 3 IR 296, SC. See also *Cassidy v O'Rourke* [1983] ILRM 332; *McCarthy Construction v Waterford County Council* [1987] HC; *Dublin Co Council v Taylor* [1989] 7 ILT Dig 150; *Breathnach v Ireland* [1989] IR 489, (No 4) 11 ILT Dig [1993] 212, HC; *Dublin Corporation v Building & Allied Trade Union* [1996] 2 ILRM 547, SC; *McGuinness v Motor Distributers Ltd* [1997] 2 IR 171, HC; *In the matter of NIB (No 2)* [1999] 2 ILRM 443, HC; *Limerick VEC v Carr* [2001] 3 IR 480, HC; *AA v Medical Council* [2002] 3 IR 1, HC; *People (DPP) v O'Callaghan* [2004] FL 8706, SC and 1 ILRM 438. [Bibliography: McDermott P A (2).] See ISSUE ESTOPPEL; FINALITY IN LITIGATION.

res nova. [A new thing.] A matter which has not yet been decided.

res nullius. [A thing belonging to no one.] See BONO VACANTIA.

res perit domino. [The loss falls on the owner.]

res sic stantibus. [Things standing so or remaining the same.]

res sua. [A person's own goods.]

res sua nemini servit. [No one can have an easement over his own property.] See EASEMENT.

resale price maintenance. An agreement for the maintenance of minimum prices at which goods are to be resold. Such an agreement (eg between producers and retailers) is not invalid at common law, unless the person challenging the agreement is able to show that the price level maintained is unreasonable or is designed to produce a monopoly: *Cade v Daly*

[1910] 1 IR 306. Some prices are now controlled by the Prices Acts 1958, 1965 and 1972 and regulations thereunder. Also, such *resale price maintenance* agreements may amount to a distortion of competition and be prohibited and void: Competition Act 2002, s 4(1). For previous legislation, since repealed, see Competition Act 1991, s 4(1). See also COMPETITION, DISTORTION OF; PRICE CONTROL; RESTRICTIVE PRACTICES.

rescission. Abrogation or revocation, particularly of a contract. A contract may be rescinded where there has been some mistake, mutual or unilateral. Where *mutual,* the mistake must have been fundamental; where *unilateral* there must have been some element of unfairness or sharp practice involved to justify the equitable remedy: *Cooper v Phibbs* [1867] 2 HL 149; *Solle v Butcher* [1950] 1 KB 671.

The court will not grant an order rescinding a contract where the mistake by one of the parties is not shared or contributed to by the other party who is unaware that the contract does not give effect to the intention of that party: *Ferguson v Merchant Banking Ltd* [1993] ILRM 136, HC.

A contract to subscribe for shares may be rescinded if it is induced by a material allegation which was not true, even if there was no fraud in the matter: *Components Tube Co v Naylor* [1900] 2 IR 1. Rescission will not be ordered where *restitutio in integrum* (qv) is no longer possible or where it would disrupt third-party rights: *Northern Bank Finance Corp v Charlton* [1979] IR 149. See *McCormick v Collinstown Stud Ltd* [1993] HC; *Browne v Mariena Properties Ltd* [1998] 1 IR 568, SC; *Hade v Meehan* [2002] FL 6862, HC. See 'A Farewell to Equitable Mistake?' by Des Ryan in (2003) 11 ISLR 3. [Bibliography: Delaney H (2); Wylie (3).] See MISTAKE; ORAL AGREEMENT, MODIFICATION OF CONTRACT BY.

rescous. Rescue of distrained goods which are being taken to the pound (qv).

rescue of company. See COURT PROTECTION OF COMPANY.

rescuer. A person who sustains injuries during rescue operations arising from the negligence of another, may have a good cause of action, provided that that other by his negligence brought about the peril situation which prompted the rescue. The principle of rescue is essentially a doctrine of foreseeability and it cannot come into operation without an initial negligence; where a person by his fault creates a situation of peril, he must answer for it to any person who attempts to rescue the person who was thereby placed in danger: *Phillips v Durgan* [1991] ILRM 321, SC. See also *Wagner v International Railroad Company* [1921] 133 NE 437; *Chadwick v British Transport Commission* [1963] 2 QB 650; *Alcock v Chief Constable of South Yorkshire Police* [1992] 1 AC 310; *White v Chief Constable of South Yorkshire Police* [1999] 2 AC 455. See Delaney: *The Duty of Care to Rescuers* (1959) 25 Ir Jur 7. See Keating and Lowry: *The Aftermath Doctrine* in (2002) 10 ISLR 141. See also CRIMINAL INJURIES COMPENSATION TRIBUNAL.

research. (1) One barrister cannot hand over papers to another barrister for drafting or research unless such other barrister is briefed with him or his pupil: *Code of Conduct for the Bar of Ireland* (December 2003) r 7.6. See BRIEF; INSTRUCT.

(2) A trader or a professional person, who makes a donation to an Irish university or an *approved body* (eg National College of Ireland) to teach or undertake research in an *approved subject*, may deduct the cost of the donation as a business expense when computing his profits for tax purposes: Taxes Consolidation Act 1997, s 767 as amended by Finance Act 2000, s 22.

(3) A tax credit is available for research and development (R&D) expenditure carried out by a company: Taxes Consolidation Act 1997, ss 766 and 766A, inserted by Finance Act 2004, s 33. The new s 766 deals with R&D expenditure other than on buildings and the new s 766A contains rules for the treatment of expenditure on buildings. A credit of 20% of the 'incremental' spend on R&D over a defined base, can be offset against the company's corporation tax liability for the current year. For years 2004, 2005 and 2006 the base will be the R&D expenditure incurred in 2003; for year 2007 the base will be expenditure in 2004, for year 2008 the base will be 2005 and so on. Relevant expenditure on a building or structure which is to be used for carrying out R&D also attracts a 20% tax credit but allowed over a four year period. For the categories of activities which are research and development activities for the purpose of TCA 1997, s 766, see SI No 434 of 2004.

reservation. A clause in a deed whereby the donor, lessor or grantor reserves to himself some new thing out of that which he has granted eg a rent in a lease, a wayleave (qv).

reservation of title. See RETENTION OF TITLE.

reserve. In a company's accounts, a *reserve* must not normally include amounts written off or retained in order to provide for an asset's depreciation, renewal or diminution in value or to provide for a known and unquantifiable liability: Companies Act 1963, Sch 6, reg 27(1)(b). A *revenue reserve* is an amount regarded as free for distribution through the profit and loss account; a *capital reserve* must not include any amount so regarded (reg 27(1)(c)). See CAPITAL.

reserve member. One or more persons may be appointed to a *tribunal of inquiry* to be a *reserve member*: Tribunals of Inquiry (Evidence) (Amendment) Act 2002, s 5. The role of the reserve member is to sit with the tribunal and hear evidence, examine documents and be present at deliberations of the tribunal. The person must not otherwise participate in the deliberations or proceedings or seek to influence the decisions of the tribunal. The rationale for the reserve member provision, is that the person will be fully *au fait* with the tribunal's work and be in a position to replace a full member if that should become necessary.

reserve price. See AUCTION SALES.

reserved functions. The functions of a local authority which are exercisable and performed only by resolution of the elected council of the local authority at a meeting of the authority: Local Government Act 2001, s 131. Certain functions are designated as *reserved functions* (LGA 2001, s 131(2)). The Minister may by order designate a specified function to be a reserved function (s 131(3)). These provisions apply also to joint bodies of local authorities. However, *function* does not include a function relating to employees of the authority, other than the appointment or suspension or removal of the manager (LGA 2001, ss 131(5) and 145(1)). It is the duty of the manager to carry into effect all lawful directions of the elected council in relation to its exercise of the reserved functions (LGA 2001, s 132).

For previous legislation, see County Management Act 1940, s 16 and Sch 2; Local Government Act 1991, s 41; Local Government Act 1991 (Reserved Functions) Order 1993, SI No 37 of 1993). See

also Environmental Protection Agency Act 1992, s 45(5). See COUNTY MANAGER; HEALTH BOARD.

reserved judgment. (1) The formal decision of a court made following consideration by the judge or judges, at a date subsequent to the otherwise conclusion of the trial of an action. Contrast with EXTEMPORE JUDGMENT.

(2) In relation to a judgment in court proceedings, means where a decision in the proceedings or the reasons for those decisions, or both, are not announced by the court upon the conclusion of the hearing of the proceedings, but instead are postponed: (a) without a date for such announcement being specified at the time, or (b) for a period of not less than 14 days after such conclusion: Courts and Court Officers Act 2002, s 46(11). Provision has been made for the establishment and maintenance by the Courts Service (qv) of a *register of reserved judgments* of civil proceedings in the Supreme, High, Circuit and District Courts which will be accessible to members of the public. In introducing the provision in the Dáil, the Minister said that the register would be a 'monitoring provision' and that he hoped it would secure the legitimate expectation that judgments would be delivered in a reasonable timeframe. See also Civil Liability and Courts Act 2004, s 55. See 'No Reservations' by Conor O'Mahony in *Law Society Gazette* (July/August 2002) 33. See JUDGMENT.

residence. The place of a person's home; the place where he abides. Formerly, a person could be *ordinarily resident* in more than one electoral constituency: *Quinn v Mayor of City of Waterford* [1991] ILRM 433, SC; now, a person is deemed not to have given up ordinary residence if he intends to resume residence within 18 months after giving it up: Electoral Act 1992, s 11(3).

There are provisions for determining the residence of members of the defence forces, prisoners, patients or inmates in hospitals or homes (EA 1992, s 11(4)–(6)). Also certain persons are deemed to be resident in the State eg civil servant members of missions abroad (EA 1992, s 12). See EC (Right of Residence for Non-Economically Active Persons) Regulations 1993, SI No 109 of 1993.

As regards taxation, an individual is *resident* in the State for a tax year if he is *present* in the State: (a) for an aggregate of 183 days in the current year, or (b) for an aggregate of 280 days or more in the current and preceding tax year: Taxes Consolidation Act 1997, s 819. *Present* means personally present. An individual who spends less than 30 days, in aggregate, of a tax year in the State is not regarded as resident for that tax year; such a period is disregarded when performing the 280-day test for the tax year and the next tax year. A resident is taxed on his worldwide income. A non-resident is taxed on income arising in the State. See TCA 1997, ss 818–825 and 825A inserted by Finance Act 1998, s 13.

Where an Irish resident employee works outside the State, other than the UK, he may be entitled to income tax relief: Taxes Consolidation Act 1997, s 823. The definition of a *qualifying day* is amended to put beyond doubt that such a day is a day on which the individual is absent from the State and not just at midnight: Finance Act 2001, s 31. Also a termination date of 31 December 2003 is now specified.

The tax credit, to which an individual is entitled, in respect of interest paid on a home loan is limited to buying or improving a *qualifying residence* i e his sole or main residence, the home of his former or legally separated spouse, or the home of his dependent relative (TCA 1997, s 244). For definition of *resident* in relation to the requirement for a director of a company, registered in the State, to be resident in the State, see Companies (Amendment) (No 2) Act 1999, s 44(8).

Where the words *ordinarily resident* appear in a statute but are not defined, the court is required to interpret them in accordance with their ordinary meaning in the light of the general intention of the statute: *Deutsche Bank AG v Murtagh* [1995] 2 IR 122, HC.

As regards corporate residence for taxation purposes, see *Corporate Residence, Taxation and E-Commerce* by Cian Carroll in (2002) 10 ISLR 32. For residence requirements for many social welfare allowances and benefits, see SOCIAL WELFARE LAW. See also ABODE; DOMICILE; HABITUAL RESIDENCE.

residence, right of. (1) A right given to a person to live on property and, in some cases, to receive support in the form of food, fuel and other material benefits. The right is often created where land is conveyed *inter vivos* or devised to another subject to the right e g where a farmer devises the farm to his children with a *right of residence* reserved for his widow. The right is registrable as a *burden* on registered land and is a lien for money's worth: Registration of Title Act 1964, ss 69(1) and 81. Of less importance now due to the legal right of spouses: Succession Act 1965, s 111–115. See *National Bank v Keegan* [1931] IR 344; *Johnston v Horrace* [1993] ILRM 594, HC.

(2) A right of residence for one spouse in a *family home* may, to the exclusion of the other, be ordered by the court arising from a *judicial separation* (qv). Such an order does not amount to an unjust attack on the property rights of either spouse and may be balanced by a reduction in the maintenance (qv) otherwise payable: *F v F* [1994] 2 ILRM 401, HC. See PROPERTY ADJUSTMENT ORDER.

(3) The right of entry to the State and right of residence is governed by: (a) European Communities (Aliens) Regulations 1977, SI No 393 of 1977 in respect of certain categories of persons; and (b) EC (Right of Residence for Non-Economically Active Persons) Regulations 1997, SI No 57 of 1997 in respect of non-economically active EU nationals, other than the UK. For deportation powers in relation to such persons, see Immigration Act 1999, s 3(2)(c)–(d). See also Immigration Act 2004, s 2(2).

A national of a member state of the European Union who is a student, retired person or other economically non-active person, and their accompanying dependants, may not be refused leave to land in the State unless the person is suffering from a specified disease or disability (e g tuberculosis, syphilis, profound mental disturbance), or his personal conduct is such that it would be contrary to public policy or would endanger public security to grant him leave to land: SI No 57 of 1997 (regs 3, 4). A *residence permit* is required for a national of an EU member state to take up residence in the State and it may only be issued where the Minister is assured that the applicant has sufficient resources to support himself and to provide full medical and health insurance for himself, his spouse and dependants (regs 5–7). These restrictions do not apply to a person born in the UK.

A deportation order from another member state cannot deprive a person of his

European Union right to reside with his spouse, unless evidence establishes that there is no genuine intention to reside in the State or that the marriage is a sham: *Kweder v Minister for Justice* [1996] 1 IR 381, HC. The European Court of Justice has held that member states may limit rights of residence for EU citizens, where those citizens pose a serious threat to public order or public security: Case C-100/01 *Ministre de l'Intérieur v Olazabal* [2002] ECJ. See also Case C-413/99 *Baumbast, R v Secretary of State for the Home Department* [2002] ECJ ; Case C-138/02 *Collins v Secretary of State for Work and Pensions* [2004] ECJ (23 March). See NON-NATIONAL.

residential property tax. Formerly, the tax charged in respect of all *relevant residential property* owned by an assessable person where the *market value* exceeded an exemption limit and the income of the assessable person exceeded an income limit: Finance Act 1983, s 96. *Relevant residential property* was any residential property to which the assessable person was the owner and which was occupied by him as a dwelling or dwellings (FA 1983, s 97). *Market value* was the price which the unencumbered fee simple (qv) of the property would fetch on the open market (FA 1983, s 98).

There was inflation relief in respect of the income limit and exemption limit (FA 1983, ss 100–101). There was also relief in respect of qualifying children residing with the taxpayer and simplification in respect of the inflation relief: Finance Act 1990, ss 121–125. See also Finance Acts 1991, s 112, 1992, ss 218–221; 1994, ss 113–123; 1995, ss 151–155. An assessable person who did not lodge a return or failed to comply with a notice was liable to penalty (FA 1983, s 112). See *Madigan v Attorney-General Ors* [1986] ILRM 136.

With effect from 1 August 1993, any person selling a residential property valued in excess of the *market value threshold* must provide the purchaser with a certificate from the Revenue Commissioners (*clearance certificate*) indicating that all residential property tax has been paid: Finance Act 1993, s 107. If such certificate is not forthcoming, the purchaser is required to deduct an amount from the purchase price and remit it to the Revenue. The amount is 1.5% of the difference between the sale price and the market value exemption limit, multiplied by the number of years that the vendor has owned the property, up to a maximum of five years.

Residential property tax was abolished in 1997 by Finance Act 1997, s 131. The *market value threshold* was increased to £200,000 (€253,948) by Finance Act 1999, s 198 and to £300,000 (€380,921) by Finance Act 2000, s 134. Consequently for sales below the threshold, a residential property clearance certificate is not required. Also for sales of an estate or interest completed after 10 February 2000 there is no requirement to obtain a clearance certificate, where the estate or interest had been previously acquired after 5 April 1996 by a *bona fide* purchaser for full consideration. In relation to sales occurring on or after 5 April 2003, the threshold is €1,000,000: Finance Act 2003, s 154. [Bibliography: Boland; Connolly M; Keegan B.] See ANTI-SPECULATIVE PROPERTY TAX.

residential tenancies. Under recent legislation, provision has been made to implement the reforms of the private rented sector recommended by the *Commission on the Private Rented Residential Sector* (2000): Residential Tenancies Act 2004. The Act introduces a measure of security of tenure for tenants, specifies minimum obligations applying to landlords and tenants and provides for the establishment of a *Private Residential Tenancies Board* to resolve disputes arising in the sector, to operate a system of tenancy registration and to provide information and policy advice. The Act also contains provisions relating to rent setting and reviews and procedures for the termination of tenancies, including gradated notice periods linked to the duration of a tenancy.

There are some consequential amendments to the existing landlord and tenant code. The Act provides for repeals, including the Housing (Registration of Rented Houses) Regulations 1996 (SI No 30 of 1996) which are replaced by the registration requirements in Part 7 (ss 127–145) of the Act (RTA 2004, s 10(2)). RTA 2004, Pts 1, 4, 5, 7, 8 and 9 (other than ss 71, 72, 151(1), 182, 189, 190, 193(a) and (d), and 195(4) and (5)) came into operation on 1 September 2004: SI No 550 of 2004. It is planned to bring Pts 2, 3 and 6, and the remaining sections into operation in November/December 2004. See PRIVATE RESIDENTIAL TENANCIES BOARD; PRIVATE RESIDENTIAL TENANCIES REGISTER.

residential unit. Means a house or apartment intended for use as a residence: SI No 85 of 1997.

A solicitor is prohibited from acting for both vendor and purchaser in the sale and purchase for value of a newly constructed residential unit or a residential unit in course of construction, where the vendor is the builder of that residential unit or is associated with the builder of that residential unit. See also *A Guide to Professional Conduct of Solicitors in Ireland* (2002) ch 3.3.

residuary devisee. The person named in a will who is to take the *real* property remaining after satisfying specific gifts of real property in the will. The residuary devise includes any lapsed or void devises: Succession Act 1965, s 91.

residuary legatee. The person entitled under a will to the balance of the *personal* estate remaining after paying the debts, expenses and legacies bequeathed by the will. The residuary legacy includes any lapsed or void legacies.

residue. That which remains of a deceased's estate after payment of debts, funeral and testamentary expenses, legacies and annuities. Where a testator does not effectually dispose of the residue of his property, he dies intestate as to it e g if a share of residue lapses, it does not fall into residue, but goes to the next-of-kin (qv) on intestate succession (qv).

resignation, employment. Termination by an employee of a contract of employment in accordance with its terms. Failure by an employer to accept the withdrawal of a letter of resignation, where the resignation has been made in ignorance of a grievance procedure, amounts to a *constructive dismissal* (qv): *Keane v Western Health Board* [1990] ELR 108, EAT. Also an employer was not permitted to rely on a letter of resignation which arose from a misstatement by the employer e g that the employee was required to retire and that he had no choice in the matter: *O'Reilly v Minister for Industry and Commerce* [1997] ELR 48, HC.

resile. To withdraw from.

resisting arrest. See ARREST, RESISTING.

resolution. A formal expression of opinion or intention by a meeting.

Decisions of a company are made by the resolution of its members. The articles of association provide who is entitled to vote and in what circumstances. Resolutions are either *ordinary* or *special*. An *ordinary* resolution is one which needs a simple majority of the votes cast to pass. A *special resolution* is one which has been passed by not less than three-fourths of the votes cast by such members as being entitled so to do, vote in person or (where proxies are allowed) by proxy at a general meeting of which at least 21 days' notice has been given specifying the intention to propose the resolution as a special resolution has been duly given: Companies Act 1963, s 141.

All *special business* must be transacted by special resolution. *Special business* is defined as all business transacted at an extraordinary general meeting and also at an annual general meeting other than the principal business of an agm: CA 1963, Table A, art 53.

Notices of ordinary and special resolutions must sufficiently describe what is being proposed so as to permit shareholders to form a reasoned judgement, and in particular, must not be misleading: *Kaye v Croydon Tramways Co* [1898] 1 Ch 358; *Jackson v Munster Bank* [1884] 13 LR Ir 118.

As regards resolutions of the Houses of the Oireachtas, they enjoy the presumption of constitutional validity: *Goodman International v Mr Justice Hamilton* [1992] ILRM 145, HC & SC. The passing of such resolutions may be evidenced by producing a copy of the Journal of the relevant House: Criminal Evidence Act 1992, s 11. As regards a *rescinding resolution* of a local authority, see *Cartmill v Donegal County Council* [1987] IR 192, HC. See also Building Societies Act 1989, ss 50(17), 74, and Sch 2, Pt XI, para 5(n). See INDUSTRIAL AND PROVIDENT SOCIETY; PROXY; STATUTORY INSTRUMENT; VOTING AT MEETINGS.

resoluto jure concedentis resolvitur jus concessum. [The grant of a right comes to an end on the termination of the right of the grantor.]

respite. To discharge or dispense with.

respite care grant. See CARER.

respondeat superior. [Let the principal answer.] Refers to the liability of an employer generally for the acts of an employee. See VICARIOUS LIABILITY.

respondent. A person against whom a petition is sought, a summons issued, or an appeal brought.

respondentia. The securing of repayment of a loan by cargo on board a ship. See BOTTOMRY.

responsibility. Care and consideration for the outcome of one's own actions. See DUTY OF CARE; COLLECTIVE RESPONSIBILITY; MINISTERIAL RESPONSIBILITY.

rest period. Any period which is not working time: Protection of Young Persons (Employment) Act 1996, s 1(1); Organisation of Working Time Act 1997, s 2(1). An employee is entitled to a rest period of not less than 11 consecutive hours in each period of 24 hours (OWTA 1997, s 11). He is entitled to a break of at least 15 minutes after 4 hours 30 minutes work and at least 30 minutes break after 6 hours of work (OWTA 1997, s 12). He is also entitled to a rest period of 24 consecutive hours every week in addition to his daily rest period (OWTA 1997, s 13). A *collective agreement* approved by the Labour Court, a *registered employment agreement* or an *employment regulation order* may exempt affected employers and employees from compliance with the rest period provisions, provided that the employees benefit from *compensatory rest* (OWTA 1997, ss 4(5), 4(6) and 6). See *Coastal Line Container Terminal Ltd v SIPTU* [1999] ELR 205, LC, and on appeal see [2000] 1 IR 549, HC, and ELR 1. For special rest periods for young persons, see YOUNG PERSON. See also WORKING HOURS.

restatement of statute. A statute in the form of a single text, certified by the Attorney-General to be a statement of the law contained in the provisions of the statutes to which it relates: Statute Law (Restatement) Act 2002, s 2(1). The continued amendments to Acts often makes them difficult to follow eg it is often necessary to consult several Acts to identify a particular point of law. The purpose of the 2002 Act is to empower the Attorney-General to publish a certified version of the text of an Act incorporating any amendments made by subsequent Acts into one up-to-date statement of the Act (to be known as a *restatement*).

A restatement does not alter the substance or operation of the law and, consequently, does not require the approval of the Houses of the Oireachtas, although it must be laid before each House before being published (SL(R)A 2002, ss 4 and 8). A restatement of the law, which is so certified by the Attorney-General, is *prima*

facie evidence of the law and must be judicially noticed (SL(R)A 2002, s 5). A restatement may be made available in printed or electronic form, it may include a statutory instrument, it may include annotations eg showing the derivation of its provisions, and it may exclude spent, repealed or otherwise surplus provisions (SL(R)A 2002, ss 2 and 3). See 'As clear as mud?' by barrister Edward Donelan in *Law Society Gazette* (May 2003) 28. Contrast with CODE; CONSOLIDATION ACT.

restaurant. See INTOXICATING LIQUOR.

restitutio in integrum. [Restoration to the original position.] The remedy by which a court orders that a contract be rescinded or otherwise that the parties be placed in the position they occupied before entering into a transaction. See LRC Consultation Paper on *Aggravated, Exemplary and Restitutionary Damages* (1998). See DAMAGES.

restitution of possession. Restoration of possession to the rightful owner. Where a person is convicted of an offence related to the theft of property, the court may order: (a) restoration of the stolen property to the rightful owner; or (b) the delivery to the person of property representing the proceeds of the stolen property; or (c) the payment of a sum representing the value of the stolen property, but so that the person does not recover more than the value of the stolen property: Criminal Justice (Theft and Fraud Offences) Act 2001, s 56.

Where a person has bought the stolen property in good faith, or has lent money on the security of it in good faith, the court may order that the purchaser or lender shall be entitled to recover the sums paid or lent (CJ(TFO)A 2001, s 56(3)). An order under this section will only be made where the court is of the opinion that the evidence at the trial warrants it. [Bibliography: McGreal C.] See MONEY HAD AND RECEIVED; PROPERTY IN POSSESSION OF GARDA; UNJUST ENRICHMENT.

restoration notice. The notice which a planning authority is empowered to serve on the owner or occupier of a *protected structure* (qv) requiring the person served to carry out works to restore the character of the structure: Planning and Development Act 2000, s 60. The planning authority is empowered to carry out the restoration itself in the event of a default (PDA 2000, s 69). An appeal lies to the District Court against a restoration notice (PDA 2000, s 61). For previous legislation, see Local

Government (Planning and Development) Act 1999, ss 11, 12 and 20. See PROTECTED STRUCTURE; ENDANGERMENT NOTICE.

restorative justice. According to the Law Reform Commission, *restorative justice*: (a) is effectively a problem solving approach to crime, involving the parties themselves and the community generally, (b) views crime as a breakdown in relationships which causes harm to the victim and the community, and (c) seeks to repair this harm by attending to the needs of the victim and by trying to reintegrate the offender into the community and thus prevent reoffending. The Commission plans to publish a Consultation Paper on the subject of *restorative justice*, and will be looking at the developments in other jurisdictions, such as New Zealand and Australia where restorative justice is already an integral part of the criminal justice system. See website: *www.lawreform.ie*. See CAUTION; DIVERSION PROGRAMME; VICTIM SUPPORT.

restraint of trade, contract in. Contractual interference with individual liberty of action in trading, which as a general rule is void as being contrary to public policy. A contract in which a party (*the covenantor*) agrees with any other party (*the covenantee*) to restrict his liberty in the future to carry on trade with other persons not parties to the contract in such manner as he chooses: *Esso Petroleum Co Ltd v Harpers Garage (Stourport) Ltd* [1968] AC 269.

The tests to be applied to determine whether the contract is void are: (a) does the restraint go further than to afford adequate protection to the party in whose favour it has been granted; if so, the covenant is *prima facie* void; (b) can the covenant be justified as being in the interests of the party restrained; (c) is the covenant contrary to the public interest.

The onus of showing that the restraint is reasonable rests with the party seeking to uphold the transaction. See *House of Spring Gardens Ltd v Point Blank Ltd* [1985] FSR 327; *Macken v O'Reilly* [1978] SC.

Covenants in employment contracts that restrict or deter an employee from freely exercising his trade, profession or calling are generally void. Any payment made to a prospective, former or current employee in respect of a restrictive covenant is taxable: Taxes Consolidation Act 1997, s 127.

An employee who solicits orders from his employer's customers, intending to meet the orders personally rather than *qua* employee, breaches an implied term in an employment contract.

The Competition Authority does not consider employees to be *undertakings* within the meaning of the Competition Act 1991; however, if an employee leaves his employment, and the former employer seeks to enforce a non-competition clause in the employment contract, the Authority would regard this as a restriction on competition within the meaning of CA 1991, s 4(1): (now Competition Act 2002, s 4(1)): Iris Oifigiúil (18 September 1992). See Notification No CA/1011/92E – Peter Mark/Majella Stapleton in Iris Oifigiúil (26 February 1993); Notification No CA/1130/92 *Apex Fire Protection Ltd v Murtagh* [1993] ELR 201.

See also *Stanford Supply Co Ltd v O'Toole* [1972] HC; *Faccenda Chicken Ltd v Fowler* [1985] ICR 589; *ECI European Chemical Industries Ltd v Bell* [1981] ILRM 345; *Orr Ltd v Orr* [1987] ILRM 702; *Time Manager International v O'Donovan & McCabe* [1990] in 8 ILT & SJ (1990) 164; *RGDATA Ltd v Tara Publishing Co Ltd* [1995] 1 IR 89, HC; *Premier Dairies Ltd v Doyle* [1996] 1 ILRM 363, SC. See *Post-Employment Restraints and Competition Law* by Forde in 11 ILT & SJ (1993) 214. See COMPETITION, DISTORTION OF; INJUNCTION; NON-COMPETITION AGREEMENT; SEVERANCE; TRADE UNION; UNFAIR PRACTICES.

restraint order. An order which the court may make prohibiting a person from dealing with *realisable property* eg property held by a defendant in drug trafficking offences: Criminal Justice Act 1994, s 24. See *Re Peters* [1988] 3 WLR 182.

restricted user clause. A clause usually found in a shopping centre lease which obliges the tenant to engage only in a specified line or lines of business; it may also grant a tenant the sole right to engage in the specified activity and state that no other tenant will have such a right. Also called an *exclusive user* or *permitted user* clause. The Competition Authority has held that such clauses do not generally offend against the Competition Act 1991, s 4(1) (now Competition Act 2002, s 4(1)) as they do not generally have as an object or effect, the prevention, restriction or distortion of trade: Iris Oifigiúil, p 665 on 10 September 1993.

restriction order. The order which a court may make restricting a person from acting as a director of a company: Companies Act 1990, ss 150–158. A register of such persons must be kept by the Registrar of Companies (CA 1990, s 153). See DIRECTORS' RESTRICTION ORDER; DISQUALIFICATION ORDER, COMPANY.

restrictive covenant. See COVENANT; RESTRAINT OF TRADE.

Restrictive Practices Commission. Originally known as the Fair Trade Commission (qv), a name to which it reverted as a result of the Restrictive Practices (Amendment) Act 1987, s 5(1); SI No 2 of 1988. It no longer exists: Competition Act 1991, s 22. See COMPETITION AUTHORITY.

restrictive practice, orders relating to. The orders which the Minister could make, if he considered that the exigencies of the common good warranted, prohibiting restrictive practices, unfair practices or unfair methods of competition: Restrictive Practices Acts 1972 and 1987, s 8, since repealed. See Competition Act 2002, ss 4–6. See also Competition Act 1991, s 2(2) and 22, since repealed. See *Director of Fair Trade and Consumer Affairs v Sugar Distributors Ltd* [1991] ILRM 395, HC. See BELOW COST SELLING; BOYCOTT; COMPETITION, DISTORTION OF; HELLO MONEY; LOTTERY.

restructure of pay. See WAGES.

resulting trust. A trust (qv) which arises in circumstances where the beneficial interest comes back to the settlor/transferor or to the person who provided the purchase money. A resulting trust arises where: (a) the trust fails, or does not exhaust the whole of the fund, in which case the whole fund or the residue, as the case may be, results back to the settlor; or (b) where a purchase is made in the name of a stranger who provides no consideration, he holds in trust for the provider of the purchase money, unless there is clear evidence of intention to bestow the beneficial interest or the presumption of *advancement* arises: *Heavey v Heavey* [1977] ILTR 1; *Baines v McLean* [1934] ILTR 197; or (c) where a voluntary transfer of property is made but no intention of a gift can be inferred: *Owens v Green* [1932] IR 225. See also *Daniels & O'Shea v Dunne* [1990] 8 ILT & SJ 35. The concept of an implied or resulting trust was devised by equity in order to defeat the misappropriation of property as a consequence of potentially fraudulent or

improvident transactions: *Lynch v Burke* [1996] 1 ILRM 114, SC. See *Fitzpatrick v Criminal Assets Bureau* [2000] 1 ILRM 299, SC. See Leahy on *Indirect contributions and the law of trusts* in (1993) 3 ISLR 65. [Bibliography: Delaney H (2); Wylie (3).] See JOINT ACCOUNT.

resuscitate. See SERIOUSLY ILL PATIENT.

retail planning guidelines. The planning guidelines, issued by the Minister under the Planning and Development Act 2000, s 28, which came into effect from 1 January 2001, and which the planning authorities and An Bord Pleanála must have regard to when exercising their planning functions: Retail Planning Guidelines for Planning Authorities (December 2000). The guidelines are intended to ensure: (a) that the principles of sustainable land use development would apply to the future development of the retail sector in Ireland, and (b) that a competitive retail sector benefiting the consumer would be facilitated.

The guidelines prescribe a maximum floor area of 6,000 square metres gross for large-scale single retail warehouse developments. A review on this cap commenced in 2003, taking into account of: (a) the need to ensure effective competition in this sector of retailing, and (b) ongoing developments in retail formats (eg the IKEA type store), while ensuring proper planning and sustainable development. The review was nearing completion on 1 September 2004. The guidelines also prescribe a maximum area of 3,000 square metres net retail floorspace for foodstore development, except in the Greater Dublin Area, where the cap is 3,500 square metres. It was not proposed to review these latter floorspace caps. See website: *www.environ.ie*. See also Planning and Development Regulations 2001, SI No 600 of 2001, art 10(2)(b)(vii) and (viii).

retail price. All retail prices must be stated as tax-inclusive: Prices and Charges Order 1973, SI No 9 of 1973. It is an offence to prevent, without reasonable cause, a person from reading retail prices of goods or to interfere or obstruct that person. See Consumer Information Act 1978, s 15. See Retail Price (Beverages in Licensed Premises) Display Order 1999, SI No 263 of 1999. [Bibliography: Maher.] See PRODUCT PRICES.

retail price display order. See PRICE CONTROL; PRODUCT PRICES.

retainer. (1) The right of the personal representative of a deceased person to retain out of the assets sufficient to pay any debt due to him from the deceased in priority to other creditors whose debts are of equal degree. It is restricted where the estate is insolvent or where the personal representative is not entitled to the debt in his own right: Succession Act 1965, s 46. See also Bankruptcy Act 1988, s 122.

(2) The retainer of a solicitor is a contract whereby, in return for the offer of a client to employ him, a solicitor, expressly or by implication, undertakes to fulfil certain obligations: *A Guide to Professional Conduct of Solicitors in Ireland* (2002) ch 2.2. Where a client determines the retainer, there is no objection to the solicitor seeking an explanation for the determination (ch 7.6). A solicitor cannot terminate a retainer without good cause and without reasonable notice where the retainer is for work from which the client will derive no benefit until the work is completed (ch 2.3). If a solicitor terminates his retainer for good cause, he is entitled to be paid on a *quantum meruit* (qv) basis.

A barrister may not have a retainer or enter into any agreement to do all the work of a solicitor's office, whether advisory or contentious, but he may have a retainer to do all the work of a particular client and be paid an individual fee for each piece of work: *Code of Conduct for the Bar of Ireland* (December 2003) r 4.15. See OFF RECORD; RETAINER; SOLICITOR, CHANGE OF; SOLICITOR, WITHDRAWAL OF.

retention of mortgaged property. A building society may retain a mortgaged property on the default of the mortgagor (borrower), in exercise of a power given by the mortgage and in exercise of an *adopted* power to develop land which it may also have: Building Societies Act 1989, ss 26(2) and 21.

The *value* of the mortgaged property must be determined by an independent competent person, appointed by the society and agreed to by the mortgagor and any other mortgagee, and the value so determined is to be treated as if it were money received by the mortgagee (BSA 1989, s 26(2)). Particulars of the value must be sent by registered post to the mortgagor and any other mortgagee (BSA 1989, s 26(5)). In the event of failure to agree a valuer, there is provision for the court to appoint one (BSA 1989, s 26(3)).

retention of title clause. Also known as a *reservation of title* clause. A term in a contract for sale of goods by which title in the goods remains with the seller until the goods are paid for; if the original buyer sells the goods, he holds the proceeds of that sale as fiduciary for the original seller and the latter is entitled to trace the proceeds of that sale. Difficulties concerning the effectiveness of a retention of title clause often arise where the goods sold are altered physically or are admixed with other goods.

It has been held that a retention of title clause which gave the buyer an express right to sell the goods and to hold in trust all moneys so received, created a *charge* on the proceeds of sale which required registration under the Companies Act 1963, s 99: *Carroll Group Distributors Ltd v J F Bourke Ltd* [1990] ILRM 285, HC. See *Re Interview Ltd* [1975] IR 382; *Aluminium Industrie Vaassen BV v Romalpa Aluminium Ltd* [1976] 2 All ER 552; *Re Stokes McKiernan Ltd* [1978] HC; *Frigosccondia (Contracting) Ltd v Continental Irish Meats Ltd* [1982] ILRM 396; *Sugar Distribution Ltd v Monaghan Cash & Carry Ltd* [1982] ILRM 399; *Re Galway Concrete Ltd* [1983] ILRM 493; *Somers v Allen* [1984] ILRM 437; *Uniake v Cassidy Electrical Supply Co Ltd* [1987] HC. See Report on *Debt Collection: (2) Retention of Title* (LRC 28, 1989). See McCormack in 8 ILT & SJ (1990) 248; de Lacy in 8 ILT & SJ (1990) 279. [Bibliography: Forde (5); Maguire; Parris UK.] See CHARGE, REGISTRATION OF.

retention permission. See UNAUTHORISED DEVELOPMENT.

retention tax. See DEPOSIT INTEREST RETENTION TAX; WITHHOLDING TAX.

retirement, early. It has been held that early retirement by an officer of the Defence Forces is not a right, but a statutory concession; the Minister has a right to refuse an application for such early retirement: Defence Act 1954, ss 42 and 47; *Egan v Minister for Defence and Ors* [1989] 7 ILT Dig 81. In a particular case, an employee, who applied for early retirement and then endeavoured to retract his application, was ordered to be reinstated to his job: *Griffin v Telecom Éireann* (1992) Irish Times, 4 May, CC.

When an employer relies on the normal retirement age provisions of the Unfair Dismissals Act 1977, s 2(1)(b), the employer must ensure that the precise age of retirement is given to the employee in writing: *Kieran v Iarnród Éireann* [1996] ELR 12, EAT. See also *Tipperary North Riding Co Council v Treacy* [1996] ELR 4, EAT; *Tipperary North Riding Co Council v Doyle* [1996] ELR 93, EAT; *Scally v Westmeath County Council* [1996] ELR 96, EAT. See PUBLIC SERVICE PENSION SCHEME.

retirement annuity contracts; (RACs). The new retirement options introduced by the Finance Act 1999 have been extended to cover separated or divorced spouses of proprietary directors who benefit from pension provision made by a *pension adjustment order*: Finance Act 2001, s 18. Also: (a) payments made under a retirement annuity are now subject to tax under the PAYE system, and (b) the special limit of 5% of net relevant earnings that applied to RACs is abolished.

In 2002, the rules governing RACs for the self-employed were liberalised; it is no longer a requirement for the person to terminate his RAC on becoming an employee and joining an occupational pension scheme: Finance Act 2002, s 10. See also Finance Act 2003, s 14.

retirement relief. Generally understood to mean the relief from capital gains tax when an individual, aged over 55, disposes of business assets, or farm, or shares in a family company, as defined, by way of sale or gift: Capital Gains Tax 1975, s 26 as amended. See now Taxes Consolidation Act 1997, s 598 as amended by Finance Act 1998, s 72; Finance Act 2002, s 59 and Finance Act 2003, s 68. See FAMILY COMPANY.

retours sans protet. [Return without protest.] A direction by the drawer that a bill of exchange (qv) should not be protested. See PROTEST.

retraction. The withdrawal of a renunciation (qv).

retreat. See FORCE.

retrial. A new trial.

The various aspects of a criminal trial are not severable; where there is to be a retrial, the High Court has no jurisdiction to issue an order of prohibition in respect of a matter which may or may not arise in the retrial: *Ryan v DPP* [1989] 7 ILT Dig 104. The Court of Criminal Appeal in quashing a conviction is entitled to exercise its discretion and refuse to order a retrial: *DPP v Brophy* [1992] ITLR (9 March) CCA. It may also authorise a retrial but this is not a

mandatory order on the prosecution to retrial the accused: *McCowan v DPP* [2004] FL 8912, SC.

In civil matters, documents created after a trial may be relevant at a retrial where they contain matters which would advance the case of one party or damage that of the other: *Dunne v National Maternity Hospital* [1989] ITLR (27 November) SC. Where the Supreme Court on appeal finds for a plaintiff on the issue of liability, it may order that a retrial be on the issue of damages only: *Mullen v Quinnsworth Ltd* [1991] ITLR (17 June) SC. In a defamation action, the judge will order a retrial where the jury is inconclusive as to whether the words complained of were defamatory, even where they assessed the damages as zero: *Kenna v McKinney* [1992] HC.

In an appeal to the Supreme Court of a trial by jury, a new trial will not be granted on the ground of misdirection or of the improper admission or rejection of evidence, or because the verdict of the jury was not taken upon a question which the Judge at the trial was not asked to leave to them, unless in the opinion of the Supreme Court some substantial wrong or miscarriage has been thereby occasioned *in the trial*: see RSC Ord 58, r 7(2). The rule applies where there has been a wrong or miscarriage *in the trial*, as distinct from the *result of the trial*: *Kelly v Board of Governors of St Laurence's Hospital* [1988] IR 402. See also *Cooper-Flynn v RTE & Bird* (28 April 2004, unreported) SC. See DNA; GUILTY; ISSUE ESTOPPEL; JURY; MISCARRIAGE; TRIAL BY JURY, CIVIL MATTERS.

retransmission. Copyright does not subsist in an immediate retransmission, without alteration of a cable programme or a broadcast: Copyright and Related Rights Act 2000, s 20. See BROADCAST AND COPYRIGHT.

retroactive legislation. See RETROSPECTIVE LEGISLATION.

retrospective legislation. Legislation which takes away or impairs any vested right acquired under existing laws or creates a new obligation, or imposes a new duty, or attaches a new disability in respect to transactions or considerations already past: *Craies on Statute Law* cited with approval in many Irish cases eg *Dublin Heating Co Ltd v Heffernan Kearns Ltd* [1992] ILRM 51 at 56; *Alba Radio Ltd v Haltone (Cork) Ltd* [1995] 2 ILRM 466, HC at 469.

The Oireachtas (qv) cannot declare acts to be infringements of the law, which were not so at the date of their commission: 1937 Constitution, art 15(5). The Supreme Court has held that the Interpretation Act 1997 must be interpreted as having *prospective* effect in order for it not to offend against the constitutional prohibition on retroactive penal legislation: *Grealis & Corbett v DPP* [2001] 3 IR 144, SC.

However, the retrospective operation of criminal *procedural rules* is not an infringement of the Constitution: *Re McGrath and Harte* [1941] IR 68; nor is the retrospective application of the Garda Síochána (Discipline) Regulations 1989: *McGrath v Commissioner of Garda Síochána* [1993] ILRM 38, HC. However, see *Healy v Garda Commissioner* (1993) Irish Times, 14 July, HC. See GARDA, DISCIPLINE OF.

The constitutional prohibition does not affect legislation which gives a right retrospectively to recover disability benefit payments wrongly paid in the first place: *Minister for Social Welfare v Scanlon* [2001] 2 ILRM 342, SC and 1 IR 64. The words in the legislation giving retrospective effect must lead clearly and unambiguously or by necessary implication to that effect.

The European Court of Human Rights has held that the provision under which a confiscation order could be imposed in respect of drug trafficking carried on before the commencement of the legislation, breaches the retroactive imposition of criminal penalties: *Welsh v UK* [1995] ECHR; Criminal Justice Act 1994, s 4(5).

It has been held that the Constitution did not contain any general prohibition on retrospection of legislation, nor could it be interpreted as a general prohibition: *Magee v Culligan* [1992] ILRM 186, SC. However, unless a contrary intention appears, a statute is presumed to be prospective and not retrospective: *Hamilton v Hamilton* [1982] IR 471.

Whether a statute is to have retrospective affect or not is a matter of construction of the provision concerned; there is a presumption against retrospective construction: *O'H v O'H* [1990] 2 IR 558, HC reported in 9 ILT & SJ (1991) 28 and 50. An inspector appointed under the Companies Act 1990 can procure documents predating the commencement of the Act: *Chestvale Properties Ltd & Hoddle Investments Ltd v Glackin & Ors* [1992] ILRM 221, HC.

Generally the courts lean against injurious retrospection of legislation, holding that the position in which a person already finds himself at the time when the new law is actually passed should not be affected for the worse: *Fitzpatrick v Minister for Industry and Commerce* [1931] IR 457. However, see *M v D* [1998] 3 IR 175, HC.

It has been held that the Employment Equality Act 1977 does not have retrospective effect: *Aer Lingus Teo v Labour Court* [1990] ILRM 485, SC. It has also been held that the invalidity of conviction by an improperly re-appointed District Court judge is not cured by retrospective legislation: *Shelly v DJ Mahon & DPP* [1990] ITLR (23 July); Courts (No 2) Act 1988.

Retrospective legislation may be drafted in such a manner as to help prevent it being found to be unconstitutional by providing that in so far as any provisions in the legislation conflict with the constitutional right of any person, the provisions will be subject to such limitations as are necessary to secure that they do not so conflict – eg legislation giving the Commissioners of Public Works retrospective power to carry out developments on in or under land, has such a provision: State Authorities (Development and Management) Act 1993, s 2(3).

See *Condon v Minister for Labour* [1980] HC; *Doyle v An Taoiseach* [1986] ILRM 693; *Lawlor v Minister for Agriculture* [1988] ILRM 400. See EUROPEAN CONVENTION ON HUMAN RIGHTS; EUROPEAN COURT; ULTRA VIRES.

retrospective legislation, example of. Examples of other legislation intended to have retrospective effect: Income Tax (Amendment) Act 1986 retrospectively to 1973 to close a loophole in the law of taxation on the grounds that otherwise the loss of income to the Exchequer would be considerable; Mental Treatment Act 1961 to validate detentions for which no lawful authority existed; Garda Síochána Act 1979 to validate the appointment of the then Garda Commissioner when the previous occupant had been found to have been unfairly dismissed (*Garvey v Ireland* [1980] IR 75); Local Government (Planning and Development) Act 1982, s 6 to validate planning permissions following the decision in *The State (Pine Valley) v Dublin Co Co* [1984] IR 407; the abolition of the death penalty: Criminal Justice Act 1990; judges' pensions: Courts (Supplemental Provisions) (Amendment) Act 1991; the Presidential Establishment (Amendment) Act 1991; the Statute of Limitations (Amendment) Act 1991; validation of certain payments already made: Housing (Miscellaneous Provisions) Act 1992, s 35; planning permission deemed not to have been required for certain developments commenced or completed: Local Government (Planning and Development) Act 1993, s 4(1); and validation of regulations already made to implement EC law: European Communities (Amendment) Act 1993, s 5.

For other examples of retrospective legislation, see Greyhound Industry (Amendment) Act 1993, s 4(2); Commissioners of Public Works (Functions and Powers) Act 1996; Merchant Shipping (Commissioners of Irish Lights) Act 1997, s 3; Minister for Arts etc Act 1998, ss 3(1) and 6(2); Civil Liability (Assessment of Hearing Injury) Act 1998, s 2; Family Law (Miscellaneous Provisions) Act 1997, s 5(2); Immigration Act 1999, s 2; State Authorities (Public Private Partnerships Arrangements) Act 2002, s 5; Minister for the Environment and Local Government (Performance of Certain Functions) Act 2002; Courts and Court Officers Act 2002, s 1(5); Minister for Community, Rural and Gaeltacht Affairs (Powers and Functions) Act 2003, ss 2 and 3.

return. A report. Execution orders (qv) and other orders are returnable ie the person to whom they are directed is bound or may be required to make a return or report on them. The term *return* is mostly used with reference to the time when an order is returnable. Some orders are returnable on the date named in them; others are returnable as soon as they are executed. A summons is said to be returnable on the day appointed for hearing it.

return for trial. Formerly, the order returning an accused for trial. *A-G v Sheehy* [1990] 2 IR 434. An accused is now *sent forward for trial* to the trial court. See INDICTABLE OFFENCE; PRELIMINARY EXAMINATION.

returning officer. The officer with the general duty to do such acts and things as may be necessary for effectually conducting an election, to ascertain and declare the results and to furnish a return of the persons elected: Electoral Act 1992, s 31. In Cork and Dublin, the sheriffs are the returning officers for their areas while in the rest of the country, county registrars are the returning officers (EA 1992, s 30).

The decision of the returning officer is final subject only to reversal on a petition questioning the election (EA 1992, s 128). There is provision for the appointment of deputy returning officers in Dáil elections (EA 1992, s 30(3)) and for the appointment of a presidential returning officer and local returning officers for presidential elections: Presidential Elections Act 1993, ss 9–10. See also European Parliament Elections Act 1997, ss 16–18. See COUNTY REGISTRAR; ISLAND, POLLING ON; SHERIFF.

revaluation. See ASSET VALUATION; PENSION SCHEME; VALUATION.

revenue. Income; yield of taxes. It is a principle and practice that the Irish Courts do not aid the collection by another country of its revenue; a passport fee is not capable of being a revenue raising device: *McDonald v McMahon* [1990] 8 ILT Dig 60.

If the purpose of the action by the foreign state is the enforcement of a sanction, power or right at the instance of the state in its sovereign capacity, it will not be entertained by an Irish court: *Bank of Ireland v Meenegan & UK Commissioners of Customs and Excise* [1995] 1 ILRM 96, HC.

revenue audit. A cross-check by the Revenue Commissioners of the information and figures shown by a taxpayer in his tax returns against those shown in the business records: *Revenue Booklet IT 32, Revenue audit guide for small business*. An authorised officer of the Revenue Commissioners has wide powers in conducting the audit eg requiring any persons on the premises to produce any records or property for inspection, searching the premises for records and property, taking copies of or extracts from the records, but may not breach professional client confidentiality: Taxes Consolidation Act 1997, s 905.

The Revenue uses three methods for selecting a taxpayer for audit: (a) general screening of tax returns for trends and patterns, (b) screening of a particular sector from time to time for tax compliance, and (c) a random selection. Full disclosure of any inaccuracy in tax returns made *before the audit starts*, prevents a defaulting taxpayer having his name published (TCA 1997, s 1086).

When a solicitor is the subject of a Revenue audit, all necessary steps should be taken by the solicitor to ensure that there is no breach of confidentiality as regards his clients: *A Guide to Professional Conduct of Solicitors in Ireland* (2002) ch 4.2. For the memorandum of understanding between the Revenue Commissioners and the Law Society of Ireland concerning the audit of the tax returns of solicitors and solicitors' practices, see App 6.

Revenue Commissioners, Office of. The office with responsibility for the collection and administration of most taxes and duties in the State, VIES (Vat Information Exchange System), Intrastat (the collection system for Intra-Community Statistics). The Revenue Commissioners are empowered to give information to the Gardaí or to the Criminal Assets Bureau where they have reasonable grounds for suspecting that the information relates to a person who has derived profits from unlawful activity and that the information will assist in an investigation into drug trafficking or money laundering: Criminal Justice Act 1964, s 63A as inserted by Disclosure of Certain Information for Taxation and Other Purposes Act 1996, s 1. A *Revenue Powers Group* was established in 2003 to enquire into the main statutory powers of the Revenue Commissioners to establish tax liabilities, including investigation with a view to prosecution of Revenue offences. The Group reported in February 2004, concluding that the Revenue's powers are characteristic of those of other administrations and are needed, provided that adequate statutory safeguards are introduced for the taxpayer, including additional appeal provisions. See 'An Inspector calls' by solicitor Julie Burke (a member of the Group) in *Law Society Gazette* (April 2004) 22. See website: *www.revenue.ie*. [Bibliography: Corrigan K.]

Revenue Court. A court which specialises in offences relating to taxes, duties, customs or exchange control. The Law Reform Commission does not recommend the establishment of a specialised criminal revenue court, but it does recommend that judges with particular qualifications or experience in revenue law should be assigned to complex revenue trials. See LRC Consultation Paper, *A Fiscal Prosecutor and a Revenue Court* (LRC CP 24, 2003).

revenue investigations. See Bibliography: Donnelly & Walsh.

revenue offence. In relation to extradition (qv), a *revenue offence* is an offence in connection with taxes, duties, customs or exchange control: Extradition (European Union Conventions) Act 2001, s 13(a); European Arrest Warrant Act 2003, s 38(3). Formerly, there was an absolute bar on extradition for a revenue offence: Extradition Act 1965, s 13. This absolute bar has now been removed: E(EUC)A 2001, s 13 and EAWA 2003, s 38(2)).

In addition to these statutory provisions, extradition for revenue offences will apply where such is provided for in bilateral extradition agreements or by the *backing of warrant* arrangements ie there must be a specific provision.

Also extradition for fraud against the European Communities' *financial interests* or *money laundering* will not be refused solely on the grounds that the offence constitutes a *revenue offence* as defined in the Extradition Act 1965: Criminal Justice (Theft and Fraud Offences) Act 2001, s 47. See Extradition Act 1965, ss 3 and 50; Extradition (Amendment) Act 1994, s 3. The relevant part of EA 1965, s 50 and the definition of 'revenue offence' must be construed in a strict and literal manner: *Newell v O'Toole* [2003] 1 ILRM 1, HC. An applicant seeking to resist extradition on the grounds that the offence is a revenue offence must satisfy the court that it is a revenue offence as a matter of Irish law; the relevance or weight value of the opinion of foreign experts is highly problematic (*Newell* case). EAWA 2003, s 50 repeals EA 1965, ss 41–55.

In relation to betting offences, the power of the Revenue Commissioners to arrest and imprison a person for failure to pay fines for revenue offences is unconstitutional: *Murphy v DJ Wallace* [1990] ITLR (24 December) HC.

It was held that there was an absence of due process of law in the trial and sentencing to prison of a person who had failed to make a return of income: Finance Act 1983, s 94(2), now Taxes Consolidation Act 1997, s 1078(2); *O'Callaghan v DJ Clifford* (1993) Irish Times, 3 April, SC; *Byrne v Conroy* [1998] 2 ILRM 113, SC and [1998] 3 IR 1, SC. However, the Finance Act 2002, s 133 makes it an offence to fail to comply with an order to make a tax return. Also the *revenue offence* of 'knowingly or wilfully' failing to comply with obligations regarding the furnishing of tax returns or the keeping of records has been amended to make this failure an offence unless there is a reasonable excuse (FA 2002, s 133).

A new criminal offence has been created, that of falsifying, concealing, destroying or otherwise disposing of material by a person where the person knows, suspects, is or would be, relevant to the investigation of a *revenue offence*: Finance Act 2003, s 161.

For application procedure for an order for the Revenue Commissioners to inspect and take copies of entries in bank books or records pursuant to Taxes Consolidation Act 1997, s 908A (as inserted by Finance Act 1999, s 207 and amended by Finance Act 2000, s 68; Finance Act 2002, s 132 and Finance Act 2004, s 88), see District Court (Taxes Consolidation Act 1997) Rules 1999, SI No 234 of 1999 as amended by SI No 283 of 2003. See PROBATION OF OFFENDERS.

revenue penalty. A penalty which the Revenue is entitled to impose for failure by a taxpayer to comply with some statutory requirement; it does not amount to a criminal penalty requiring a trial: *McLoughlin v Tuite* [1989] 7 ILT Dig 321. The Revenue previously had power, at their discretion, to abate a penalty in its entirety; in general, fines or penalties can now only be reduced by 50%: Waiver of Certain Tax, Interest and Penalties Act 1993, s 10. See TAX, FALSE STATEMENT.

revenue statute. Legislation dealing with the raising of revenue eg taxation. Words or expressions which create a taxation liability should be construed strictly: *Inspector of Taxes v Kiernan* [1981] IR 117. Also in legislation dealing with rates, any ambiguity in relation to the granting of relief against rates, must be construed against the ratepayer: *Slattery v Flynn* [2003] 1 ILRM 450, HC.

reversal. The setting aside of a judgment on appeal. See APPEAL; SET ASIDE.

reverse premium. A payment made or benefit granted to a lessee as an inducement to enter into a lease. A reverse premium is assessed for taxation purposes as a rent unless it is assessed as a receipt of a trade or of a profession: Finance Act 2002, s 18 inserting Taxes Consolidation Act 1997, s 98A.

reverse take-over transaction. Means a transaction entered into by a relevant company whereby it acquires securities of another company, a business or assets of any kind and pursuant to which the relevant company will or may be obliged to increase by more than 100% its existing issued share capital that confers voting rights: Takeover Rules 2001, Pt A, r 2.1(a). A company which proposes to enter into a reverse take-over transaction is required to notify the Irish Takeover Panel promptly; the Panel may specify requirements which it deems appropriate (Pt B, r 40). See IRISH TAKE-OVER PANEL; TAKEOVER.

reversing. Before reversing, a driver of a vehicle is required to ensure that he can do so without endangering other traffic or pedestrians: Road Traffic General Bye-Laws 1964, SI No 294 of 1964, art 25.

reversion. The residue of ownership which continues in the person who makes a grant of an estate eg when a fee simple owner makes a grant of a life estate, the fee simple (qv) which he retains is a reversion. See LEASEHOLD, MORTGAGE OF.

reversionary lease. The lease to which *building lessees* and *proprietary lessees* were entitled to on termination of their leases: Landlord and Tenant (Reversionary Leases) Act 1958. The right to a reversionary lease is now linked to the right to purchase the fee simple under the Landlord and Tenant (Ground Rents) (No 2) Act 1978: Landlord and Tenant (Amendment) Act 1980, s 30.

In the absence of agreement, the court will fix the terms of the reversionary lease according to the provisions LT(A)A 1980, s 34 ie for a term of 99 years at a rent not lower than the old rent, unless a new covenant or condition is included, with the rent being calculated at one-eighth of the open market value of the land. The reversionary lease is deemed to be a *graft* on the previous lease. See *Bargaintown Ltd v Dublin Corporation* [1993] ILRM 890, HC. See OPEN MARKET VALUE.

revesting. The vesting of property again in its original owner eg stolen property. See Criminal Justice (Theft and Fraud Offences) Act 2001, s 56. For previous legislation, see Sale of Goods Act 1893, s 24, repealed by CJ(TFO)A 2001, s 3 and Sch 1. See PROPERTY IN POSSESSION OF GARDA; RESTITUTION OF POSSESSION.

review. See APPEAL; JUDICIAL REVIEW.

review of sentence. There are three permissible reviews of a sentence: (a) by the trial judge where he reserves to himself a power to consider suspending a sentence, having regard to the behaviour of the accused, at a later date; the decision by the judge at that later date is not a sentence but a carrying into effect of a sentence already imposed; (b) on appeal by the accused against the severity of the sentence; and (c) by the Court of Criminal Appeal on the application of the Director of Public Prosecutions for a review on the basis that the sentence was unduly lenient, pursuant to the Criminal Justice Act 1993, s 2(1).

If it appears to the Director of Public Prosecutions that a sentence imposed by a court on conviction of a person on indictment was *unduly lenient*, he may apply to the Court of Criminal Appeal (qv) to review the sentence (CJA 1993, s 2(1)). An application by the DPP must be made within 28 days from the day on which the sentence was imposed; this time runs from the imposition of sentence by the trial judge and not from the date of the review, if any, by the trial judge: *People (DPP) v Finn* [2001] 2 ILRM 211, SC and 2 IR 25. In calculating the 28 days, the date on which the sentence was imposed is excluded: *The People (DPP) v McKenna* [2002] 1 IR 347, CCA.

That Court may refuse the application or it may impose such sentence as could have been imposed on the convicted person by the sentencing court concerned (CJA 1993, s 2(3)). The onus of proof is on the prosecutor to show by specific submission of law or fact, rather than by simple assertion, that the sentence was unduly lenient: *The People (DPP) v Redmond* [2001] 3 IR 390, CCA. The Court should not impose a more severe sentence on review unless an error in principle is shown in the trial judge's decision: *DPP v Egan* [2001] 2 ILRM 299, SC. In a particular case involving an insurance fraud, the Court of Criminal Appeal increased from three to five years a prison sentence imposed on a company director, the court describing the fraud as 'calculated, deliberate and sophisticated': *DPP v Byrne* (2003) Irish Times, 21 October, CCA. See also *The People (DPP) v McAuley* [2001] 4 IR 160, CCA.

There is an appeal to the Supreme Court on a point of law of exceptional public importance (CJA 1993, s 3). Provision is made for legal aid to be granted to a person whose sentence is the subject of an application or appeal (CJA 1993, s 4).

The DPP bears the onus of proving that the sentence was 'unduly lenient'; the reviewing court will only intervene where there is a substantial departure from what would be regarded as the appropriate sentence: *DPP v Byrne* [1995] 1 ILRM 279, CCA. Unless imposed by statute, there is no principle that a court should apply a minimum sentence: *People (DPP) v Clarkin* [2003] ITLR (19 May) CCA and FL 7070. See also *DPP v Alexion* (2003, unreported).

In February 2003, the Attorney-General requested the Law Reform Commission to consider, as a matter of urgency, a reform of the law to empower the DPP to appeal 'unduly lenient' sentences imposed in the District Court; this followed the controversy concerning the sentence imposed by the District Court on celebrity chef Tim Allen for the possession of child pornography. In June 2004, the Commission published a Consultation Paper on *Prosecution Appeals from Unduly Lenient Sentences in the District Court* (LRC CP 33, 2004), in which it recommended that there should be a change in the law, because it is in the public interest that offenders should be sentenced appropriately, and that there should be a procedure in place for rectifying inordinately undue leniency in the sentencing outcome. The Commission distinguishes between *inconsistency* and *disparity* in sentences, stating that real or perceived inconsistency ie failure to apply appropriate sentencing principles, should be capable of being remedied by way of appeal. On the other hand, *disparity* of sentences can be justified on the basis of sentencing principles as applied to the variation of the circumstances of the crime and of the defendant.

Where an accused appeals against the severity of his sentence to the Court of Criminal Appeal, that court is strictly limited to considering the state of facts existing at the date when the sentence was imposed: *The People (DPP) v Cunningham* [2002] 2 IR 712, SC and [2003] 1 ILRM 124. It cannot receive evidence in relation to events or facts subsequently occurring relating to the behaviour of the accused, his state of health or otherwise. See MISCARRIAGE; REMISSION.

revival. The renewal of rights which were at an end or in abeyance by subsequent acts or events eg a will once revoked may be revived by republication (qv).

revocation. Recalling, revoking or cancelling.

(1) Revocation by act of a party is an intentional or voluntary revocation e g revocation of a will: Succession Act 1965, s 85. There is no general presumption that a subsequent will revokes a former one.

(2) Revocation can operate by a rule of law irrespective of the intention of the parties e g the power of attorney or authority of an agent is generally revoked by the death of the principal.

(3) Many statutes provide for the revocation of a right already bestowed e g the revocation of a patent (qv) or of planning permission (qv).

(4) A person who takes property under a disposition which can be revoked, will not be taxed on the gift or inheritance, unless and until the power to revoke it is released or is no longer exercisable e g when the disponer dies without revoking the disposition: Capital Acquisitions Tax Consolidation Act 2003, s 39. See DEPENDENT RELATIVE REVOCATION; TRADE MARK, REVOCATION OF; WILL, REVOCATION OF.

revocation of offer. An offer may be revoked at any time before acceptance; once accepted an offer is irrevocable. Revocation does not take effect until it is actually communicated to the offeree. If the offeree agrees to keep his offer open for a specified time, he may nevertheless revoke it before the expiration of that time, unless it has been accepted before notice of revocation has reached the offeree, or there is consideration for keeping the offer open. See *Dickinson v Dodds* [1876] 2 Ch D 463; *Byrne v Van Tienhoven* [1880] 5 CPD 349. See OFFER; OPTION.

reward. It was an offence to advertise publicly a reward, with or without an offer to pay compensation, for the return of any property which has been stolen or lost, *no questions asked* or enquiry made: Larceny Act 1861, s 102, since repealed by the Criminal Justice (Theft and Fraud Offences) Act 2001, s 3 and Sch 1. See ADOPTION, FOREIGN; ARCHAEOLOGICAL OBJECT; BRIBERY AND CORRUPTION; SALVAGE; SURROGATE MOTHER.

RIAI contract. The standard form of building contracts of the Royal Institute of the Architects of Ireland. [Bibliography: Keane D.] See FINAL CERTIFICATE.

rider. A statement e g added to a jury's verdict. See INQUEST.

right. An interest recognised and protected by the law, respect for which is a duty, and disregard for which is a wrong.

right not to give evidence. A trial judge must expressly instruct the jury not to draw any inference from the exercise by the accused of his right not to give evidence: *The People* (*DPP*) *v Coddington* (2001) ITLR (6 August) CCA.

right of entry. See ENTRY, RIGHT OF.

right of establishment. Every citizen of the European Union has the freedom to seek employment, to work, to exercise the right of establishment and to provide services in any member state: *Charter of Fundamental Rights of the European Union* OJ C 364/1 of 18 December 2000.

Under art 43 of the EC Treaty, consolidated (2002) version, restrictions on the freedom of establishment of nationals of a member state in the territory of another member state shall be prohibited. Such prohibition also applies to restrictions on the setting-up of agencies, branches or subsidiaries by nationals of any member state established in the territory of any member state. Freedom of establishment shall include the right to take up and pursue activities as self-employed persons and to set up and manage undertakings, in particular companies or firms within the meaning of the second paragraph of art 48, under the conditions laid down for its own nationals by the law of the country where such establishment is effected.

In the case of the medical and allied and pharmaceutical professions, the progressive abolition of restrictions will be dependent upon co-ordination of the conditions for their exercise in the various member states (art 47(3)). See Case C-168/01 *Bosal Holding BV v Staatssecretaris van Financien* [2003] ECJ; Case C-243/01 *Criminal Proceedings against Piergiorgio Gambelli* [2003] ECJ. See EUROPEAN CONVENTION ON HUMAN RIGHTS; FREEDOM OF ESTABLISHMENT; INTERNAL MARKET; SOLICITOR, INTERNATIONAL PRACTICE; SOLICITOR, MUTUAL RECOGNITION; WORKERS, FREEDOM OF MOVEMENT.

right of first refusal. See FIRST REFUSAL.

right of way. See WAY, RIGHT OF.

right to begin. The right to begin in the trial of an issue generally belongs to the party on whom the burden of proof (qv) rests. In criminal cases, the prosecution begins except if the accused raises some special *plea in bar* e g *autrefois acquit* (qv). In civil cases, where the onus of proving at least one of the issues rests with the plaintiff or if he claims unliquidated damages, he is entitled to begin.

right to bodily integrity. See BODILY INTEGRITY, RIGHT TO.

right to die. See DIE, RIGHT TO.

right to emblements. See EMBLEMENTS.

right to fixtures. See FIXTURES.

right to life. See LIFE, RIGHT TO.

right to light. See LIGHT, RIGHT TO.

right to private property. See PRIVATE PROPERTY, RIGHT TO.

right of representation. See REPRESENTATIVE; NATURAL JUSTICE; SOLICITOR, ACCESS TO.

right to silence. See SILENCE, RIGHT TO.

right to support. See SUPPORT, RIGHT TO.

right to work. See WORK, RIGHT TO.

rights, natural. See NATURAL RIGHTS.

Rights Commissioner. A person appointed by the Minister under the Industrial Relations Act 1969 to investigate and issue recommendations to resolve certain types of trade disputes, usually relating to individual grievances, and to make recommendations on disputes under the Unfair Dismissals Act 1977, Maternity Protection Act 1994, and Adoptive Leave Act 1995, which either party may appeal to the Employment Appeals Tribunal (qv).

The Rights Commissioner is independent in the performance of his function, while also operating as a service of the Labour Relations Commission: Industrial Relations Act 1990, s 35. He cannot investigate a dispute if a party to the dispute objects (IRA 1969, s 13(3)(b)(ii) and IRA 1990, s 36). A Rights Commissioner is an office holder and is not employed under a contract of service: *Walker v Department of Social, Community and Family Affairs* [1999] ELR 260.

A Rights Commissioner is precluded from dealing with a dispute in relation to unfair dismissal if brought in reliance on s 13(2) of the Industrial Relations Act 1969: Unfair Dismissals Act 1977, s 8(10); *Sutcliffe v McCarthy & Ors* [1993] ELR 53, HC. He can only deal with such a claim under UDA 1977, s 8(1) using the procedure prescribed by s 8(2). See now Unfair Dismissals (Amendment) Act 1993, s 7 amending UDA 1977, s 8.

The High Court has declared a Rights Commissioner's recommendation to be without efficacy and *ultra vires* even though the recommendation was not binding on the parties: *An Taoiseach v Colin Walker*

[1992] HC reported by Barry in 11 ILT & SJ (1993) 30. See Walker in (1986) 5 JISLL 67. See also Protection of Young Persons (Employment) Act 1996, ss 18–19; Organisation of Working Time Act 1997, ss 27–28, 31. See National Minimum Wages Act 2000, ss 24 and 26.

rights issue. An offer to existing holders of securities to subscribe or purchase further securities in proportion to their holdings, made by means of a *renounceable* letter (or other negotiable document) which may be traded (as a 'nil paid' rights) for a period before payment for the securities is due: Listing Rules 2000, paras 4.16–4.21 and 8.14.

While there may be an element of *bonus* in a rights issue, they are not bonus shares. In a rights issue, new funds are raised whereas an issue of bonus shares involves a distribution of profits hitherto undistributed. See *Re Afric Sive* [1988] HC. Contrast with OPEN OFFER. See also BONUS SHARES.

rights management information. Information which identifies the owner of rights in copyright works, recordings of performances or databases: Copyright and Related Rights Act 2000, ss 375–376. Provision has been made in these sections for rights, remedies and penalties in respect of unlawful acts which interfere with *rights management information*.

rights protection measure. Means any process, treatment, mechanism or system which is designed to prevent or inhibit the unauthorised exercise of any of the rights conferred by the Copyright and Related Rights Act 2000 (CRRA 2000, s 2(1)). There are provisions designed to combat the use of protection-defeating devices, or information which would enable or assist persons to circumvent *rights protection measures* (CRRA 2000, s 370).

These rights protection measures do not interfere with a person undertaking acts which are permitted in relation to works protected by copyright or performances and databases also protected (CRRA 2000, s 374).

There is also a provision to combat unauthorised reception of transmissions (CRRA 2000, s 372). It is an offence to receive a broadcast or cable programme to which a rights protection measure is applied, knowing or having reason to believe that it is being received unlawfully with the intention to avoid payment (CRRA 2000, s 371).

The Minister may restrict the application of these provisions to countries which do not offer adequate protection to Irish encrypted transmissions in their territory (CRRA 2000, s 373).

riot. The offence of *riot* is committed where: (a) 12 or more persons who are present together at any place, use or threaten to use unlawful violence for a common purpose, and (b) the conduct of those persons, taken together, is such as would cause a person of reasonable firmness present at that place to fear for his or another person's safety; each of the persons using unlawful violence for the common purpose commit the offence of riot: Criminal Justice (Public Order) Act 1994, s 14. The place may be a public place, a private place or both.

The common law offence of riot has been abolished (CJ(PO)A 1994, s 14(4)). Every reference to the common law offences of 'riot' or 'riot and to tumult' in previous enactments is to be construed as a reference to the new offence of 'violent disorder' (CJ(PO)A 1994, s 15(5)). See MALICIOUS INJURIES SCHEME; RIOTOUS ASSEMBLY; UNLAWFUL ASSEMBLY; VIOLENT DISORDER.

riotous assembly. The statutory offence committed whenever an unlawful assembly (qv) of twelve or more persons did not disperse within an hour after a justice of the peace (qv) has read, or attempted to read, them a proclamation as prescribed, calling on them to disperse: Riot Act 1787, s 1 since repealed by Criminal Law Act 1997, s 16 and Sch 3. From this comes the popular expression *reading the Riot Act*. Force could be used to quell a riotous assembly but only so much force as was reasonable to protect lives and property. See *Lynch v Fitzgerald* [1938] IR 382. For modern offences, see RIOT; VIOLENT DISORDER.

riparian. Property bounded by a river or stream. Riparian owners, or owners of land on the banks of a river or stream, have a right to water flowing in a defined channel; they may sue to protect their natural rights if the river or stream is dammed or diverted: *McClone v Smith* [1888] 22 LR Ir 559. The owners of the bed and soil of waters, and the corporeal fishing rights in them, are entitled to an order restraining interference with the said waters: *Tennant v Clancy* [1988] ILRM 214. See also *Uyettewaal v Commissioners of Public Works* [1987] IR 439, HC.

ripping off. In a libel action, the sentence in a newspaper article, 'the inspectors were *ripping off* the State' implied that the inspectors (appointed by the Minister to investigate a company) were stealing in the moral sense; it should not be interpreted as meaning merely 'charging too much': Geoghegan J in *Foley v Independent Newspapers (Ireland) Ltd* (1993) Irish Times, 22 December, HC, holding that the article was libellous.

risk, transfer of. As regards the sale of goods, the principle by which risk generally passes with the property, unless the parties agree otherwise: Sale of Goods Act 1893, ss 20 and 33. See GOODS, PROPERTY IN; HEALTH INSURANCE.

river basin district. Seven districts, namely Eastern, Western, South Eastern, South Western, North Western, Neagh Bann, and Shannon: EC (Water Policy) Regulations 2003, SI No 722 of 2003, implementing Directive (EC) 2000/60. Three of the river basin districts (RBDs) relate to river basins shared with Northern Ireland. The regulations require local authorities, acting jointly with each RBD, to establish environmental objectives, to establish programmes of measures for the achievement of these objectives, to make river basin management plans, and to establish RBD advisory councils. Co-ordination and guidance at national level is the responsibility of the Minister and the Environmental Protection Agency.

road. Includes: (a) any street, lane, footpath, square, court, alley or passage, (b) any bridge, viaduct, underpass, subway, tunnel, overpass, flyover, carriageway (whether single or multiple), pavement or footway, (c) any weighbridge, toll plaza, service area, emergency telephone, margin, hard shoulder, island, roundabout, and (d) any other necessary or prescribed structure or thing forming part of the road: Roads Act 1993, s 2(1). In planning law, a *road* has the same meaning as in the Roads Act 1993: Planning and Development Act 2000, s 2(1).

A *public road* is a road over which a public right of way exists and the responsibility for the maintenance of which lies on a road authority (RA 1993, s 2(1)). A public road may be classified by Ministerial order as a *national* road, a *regional* road, or a *local* road (RA 1993, s 10). A public road is a *motorway* when so specified in a motorway scheme (RA 1993, s 43) or a *busway* when so specified in a busway scheme (RA 1993, s 44), or a *protected road* when so specified in a protected road scheme (RA 1993, s 45).

Forms have been prescribed to be used by local authorities in connection with the preparation and submission to An Bord Pleanála of schemes for the provision of motorways, busways and protected roads: Roads Regulations 2000, SI No 453 of 2000. See HIGHWAY; MOTORWAY; PUBLIC ROAD.

road, closure of. A road authority is empowered to close a public road (qv) to traffic, by order, for a specified period to facilitate a road race or any other event, for carrying out works, or for any other purpose, as it thinks fit: Roads Act 1993, s 75.

road authority. The council of a county, the corporation of a county or other borough, or the council of an urban district: Roads Act 1993, s 2(1). As regards toll roads, a road authority means: (a) in the case of the national road, the National Roads Authority, (b) in the case of a regional road or a local road, a road authority as defined above (RA 1993, s 56). A county council may provide assistance towards the improvement of non-public roads: Local Government Act 2001, s 81. See *Finlay v Laois County Council* [2002] FL 7173, HC. See DANGEROUS STRUCTURE; DRAIN; ROAD, CLOSURE OF; SIGN; SKIP; TOLL ROAD.

road development, proposed. Any *proposed road development* in respect of which an environmental impact statement is required: Roads Act 1993, s 2(1). It is such a development if it consists of the construction of a motorway or busway, or any prescribed type of development consisting of the construction of a proposed public road or the improvement of an existing public road (RA 1993, s 50(1)). A proposed road development must not be carried out unless An Bord Pleanála has approved it or approved it with modifications (RA 1993, s 51(1)). The Board must, prior to such approval, consider the environmental impact statement submitted by the road authority, and consider the report and any recommendation of the person who conducted an oral hearing in relation to the proposed development (RA 1993, s 51(5)). See Directive (EEC) 85/337.

The previous functions of the Minister in relation to a scheme or proposed road development under RA 1993, ss 49–51 is now transferred to and vested in An Bord Pleanála: Planning and Development Act 2000, s 215. Also there is provision for an oral hearing instead of a local inquiry or local public inquiry (PDA 2000, s 218). See NORTHERN IRELAND.

road freight licence. See CARRIER'S LICENCE.

road haulage. See [Bibliography: Canny (1).] See CARRIER'S LICENCE.

road maintenance. Local authorities have a statutory duty to repair and maintain roads within their areas: Local Government (Ireland) Act 1898, s 82(1); Roads Act 1993, s 13(1)–(2). The statutory duty is to keep the roads in their county in good condition and repair: *Brady v Cavan County Council* [2000] 1 ILRM 81, SC and [1999] 4 IR 99, SC. An order for *mandamus* is not the appropriate remedy for non-performance of this statutory duty (*Brady* case).

A local authority has been held to be equally responsible with the driver for an accident on a road which had been recently resurfaced with tar and loose chippings: *Tobin v Tipperary (NR) County Council* [1992] CC reported in 11 ILT & SJ (1993) 139. A local authority has been found to be in breach of duty, which constituted negligence, in failing to construct a drain in a road: *McEneaney v Monaghan County Council* (26 July 2001, unreported) HC. See MISFEASANCE; NONFEASANCE; PUBLIC ROAD.

road race. A prescribed class of race, time trial or speed trial on a public road (qv) involving persons, vehicles or animals: Roads Act 1993, s 74(1). A person who intends to hold a road race must give notice in writing to the road authority and to the Superintendent of the Garda Síochána and must comply with the written notice from the road authority (RA 1993, s 74(2) and (3)). See ROAD, CLOSURE OF.

road traffic accidents. Accidents which often have legal consequences, whether in respect of prosecution for a road traffic offence or an action for damages arising from e g negligence (qv) or breach of statutory duty. Such an action for damages for *personal injuries* is no longer heard by a jury, as formerly in the High Court.

There is provision for the payment of damages by the Motor Insurer's Bureau of Ireland in the case of an uninsured driver. Damages may also be recoverable by dependants in respect of a death from fatal injuries. See ACCIDENT, REPORTING OF; FATAL INJURIES; JURY, ABOLITION OF;

MOTOR INSURERS' BUREAU OF IRELAND; MOTOR VEHICLE, NEGLIGENT DRIVING OF; PATIENT CHARGES.

road traffic check. The Gardaí have a common law power to require motorists to stop, as part of their common law power to detect and prevent crime; this includes the widespread operation of random check-points and in the vicinity of licensed premises: *DPP (Stratford) v Fagan* [1994] 2 ILRM 349, SC. This power to stop a vehicle must however be exercised in a *bona fide* manner, not capricious, arbitrary or improper; it includes saturation road blocks mounted by the Gardaí especially at Christmas time: *DPP v Fagan* [1993] ITLR (8 March) HC and [1994] 3 IR 265, SC. See STOP, OBLIGATION TO.

road traffic offences. The wide range of offences connected with the ownership, driving or control of mechanically propelled vehicles in public places, including drunken, dangerous, and careless driving (qqv): Road Traffic Acts 1961 to 2002. The first ever reported road traffic case is believed to be *Gibbons v Pepper* [1695] 2 Ld Raym 38. Over 90% of prosecutions in District Courts are road related: Dáil Debates, vol 347, vol 2680.

The Road Traffic Act 2002 provided for: (a) introduction of a system of *penalty points* for road traffic offences; (b) the increase of certain financial penalties for road traffic offences; (c) the introduction of a revised system of fixed charges to replace the previous on-the-spot fine system; (d) the extension of the use of cameras for the establishment of a constituent of a road traffic offence; (e) the preliminary breath testing of drivers where they are involved in a road accident or a breach of road traffic law, in addition to the existing provision regarding alcohol consumption; (f) a framework for implementing the EU sponsored *European Convention on Driving Disqualifications*, which permits the imposition by member states of driving disqualifications for offences committed in another state; (g) the use of contractors for certain services; (h) the control of traffic by local authorities for reasons of environmental protection; and (i) the assignment of the responsibility for the control of taxi stands and bus stops from the Gardaí to local authorities. For amendments to RTA 2002 as regards penalties and penalty points, see Taxi Regulation Act 2003, ss 56–57. See Road Traffic (Offences) Regulations 2002, SI No 492 of 2002. See 'Driving Force: 100 years of motoring law' by solicitor Robert Pierce in *Law Society Gazette* (December 2003) 10. [Bibliography: McGrath M (2); Pierce; Woods (3); Round Hall.] See CARELESS DRIVING; ELECTRONIC APPARATUS; DISQUALIFICATION ORDER, DRIVING; DRIVING INSTRUCTION; PENALTY POINTS; TRAFFIC WARDENS.

road user's duty. A person using a public road (qv) has a duty to take reasonable care for his own safety and for that of any other person using the public road: Roads Act 1993, s 67.

roadway. That portion of a road which is provided primarily for the use of vehicles: Roads Act 1993, s 2(1). See FOOTWAY.

roadworthiness of vehicles. Provision has been made for the testing for roadworthiness of commercial vehicles (every year, after transition period) and private vehicles (cars – on fourth anniversary and every two years thereafter). For *light goods vehicles*, see SI No 243 of 2004. For *national car test*, see CAR TESTING.

rob. The word 'rob' used in a UK extradition warrant (qv) has been held to convey a meaning that the accused deprived a person of property unjustifiably by force and that this constituted an adequate description of the *corresponding offence* (qv) in Ireland of robbery with violence: *O'Shea v Conroy* [1995] 2 ILRM 527, HC.

robbery. A person who steals is guilty of robbery if, at the time or immediately before the stealing and in order to do so, he uses force or threatens force on any person: Criminal Justice (Theft and Fraud Offences) Act 2001, s 14.

The previous *statutory* provision for the offence of robbery under the Larceny Act 1916, s 23 (as amended by Criminal Law (Jurisdiction) Act 1976, s 5) has been repealed, and any *common law* offence of robbery is abolished (CJ(TFO)A 2001, s 3 and Sch 1). [Bibliography: McGreal C.] See also THEFT.

robes. See DRESS IN COURT.

rod licence. See FISHING LICENCE.

rogatory letter. See LETTER OF REQUEST.

rolled-up plea. The plea used in the defence of fair comment in an action for defamation (qv) which usually states: 'in so far as the words complained of consist of facts, they are true in substance and in fact, and in so far as they consist of expressions of opinion they are fair comment made in good faith and without malice upon the said facts which are a matter of public interest'. The court will not order the defendant to specify which words are statement of facts and which are statements of opinions, this being a question to be decided by the jury. See also Defamation Act 1961, s 23.

rollover relief. The entitlement to defer tax on the *capital gain* of a former asset until the new asset, which replaced it, was disposed of; the deferral also applied to the disposal of the new asset, if it in turn was replaced by a further asset: Taxes Consolidation Act 1997, s 597. Rollover relief was generally not available where only part of the proceeds of the former asset disposal was used to acquire the new asset. Rollover relief is no longer available in respect of disposals made on and from 4 December 2002. See CAPITAL GAINS TAX.

room ownership scheme. A scheme where by agreement, whether legally enforceable or not, a member who participates in, or contributes capital to, a *hotel partnership*, may acquire on preferential terms, or obtain the use of a room in the hotel building in which the investment is made: Taxes Consolidation Act 1997, s 409. Where such a room ownership exists, no industrial building allowance is allowable in respect of hotel investments for which capital expenditure is incurred after 26 March 1997. This is a tax anti-avoidance measure.

root of title. The conveyance or other document with which the title to land commences. A *good root* of title is some instrument dealing with the ownership of the whole legal and equitable estate, containing a description by which the property can be identified and showing nothing to cast any doubt on the title eg a conveyance for value, a settlement for value, a legal mortgage of a fee simple.

The conditions of sale of land may provide for any document to be a satisfactory root of title; in the absence of such a provision the purchaser can ask for: (a) 40 years' title where the freehold is being sold; (b) in the case of the sale of leasehold, the lease itself, however old, in addition to assignments during the forty years prior to the purchase date; (c) in the sale of a reversionary interest, the document creating the reversionary interest, however old, in addition to the 40 years prior to the purchase date. See ABSTRACT OF TITLE; MARKETABLE TITLE.

roundabout. A road junction so constructed that traffic which enters it must proceed slowly in a circular direction: Road Traffic (Signs) Regulations 1962, SI No 171 of 1962, art 2.

rout. See UNLAWFUL ASSEMBLY.

royal charter. A grant by the Crown, in the form of letters patent under the Great Seal, to persons therein designated, of specified rights and privileges. Royal charters and letters patent relating to local authorities continue to apply for ceremonial and related purposes in accordance with local civic tradition but otherwise cease to have effect: Local Government Act 2001, s 11(16).

Royal College of Surgeons in Ireland. The body in Dublin which was initially incorporated by charter or letters patent dated 11 February 1784 for the training of surgeons. There followed charters in 1828, 1844, 1883 and 1885. Provision has been made to update the charters eg in relation to membership, governance, administration, discipline and other matters necessary for the efficient management of the body: Royal College of Surgeons in Ireland (Charter Amendment) Acts 1965 and 2003. The RCSI became a recognised college of the National University of Ireland in 1977. See website: *www.rcsi.ie*.

Royal Irish Academy. An independent all-Ireland body of 299 members elected in recognition of their distinction as scholars. The Academy promotes study and excellence in the sciences, humanities and social sciences. See website: *www.ria.ie*. See BIOETHICS, IRISH COUNCIL FOR.

Royal Irish Constabulary. Every mention of or reference to the Royal Irish Constabulary contained in any statute or statutory rule, order, or regulation in force in Saorstát Éireann (qv) is to be construed and take effect as a mention of or reference to the Garda Síochána (qv): Garda Síochána Act 1924, s 19.

royal prerogative. *The residue of discretionary or arbitrary authority which at any given time is legally left in the hands of the Crown*: Dicey on the Law of the Constitution. It has been held that no royal prerogative in existence prior to the 1922 Constitution was vested in the State by virtue of that Constitution: *Byrne v Ireland* [1972] IR 241; *Webb & Webb v Ireland Attorney-General* [1988] IR 353, SC. See TREASURE TROVE.

royalty. Share of the sales or profits arising from a product paid to the owner thereof eg payments to an author by a publisher, or by a licensee to a patentee. The person making a payment in respect of any royalty, or other sum, paid in respect of a patent, is entitled to deduct income tax at source: Income Tax Act 1967, s 433, now Taxes Consolidation Act 1997, s 237(2). The recipient of such income is entitled to have his tax liability computed as if such royalty income had been spread over a number of years (ITA 1967, s 291, now TCA 1997, s 759). Advance royalties may qualify as income from a *qualifying patent* (qv): Finance Act 1973, s 34, now Taxes Consolidation Act 1997, s 234; *Pandion Haliaetus v Revenue Commissioners* [1988] ILRM 419.

Where a bankrupt's property includes the copyright in any work and he is liable to pay royalties to the author, the author will be entitled to receive royalties in full where the Official Assignee (qv) sells any copies of the work or authorises it to be performed: Bankruptcy Act 1988, s 48. See COPYRIGHT, LICENSING OF; DATABASE RIGHT; PERFORMERS' RIGHTS, LICENSING OF; SOUND RECORDING.

rule against perpetuities. See PERPETUITIES, RULE AGAINST.

rule of law. (1) A legal rule. (2) The government of the State based on the general acceptance of the law.

rule of reason. See REASON, RULE OF.

rule of 78. The formula often used for spreading charges in relation to *credit agreements* (qv) where payments are made by instalments. The rule assumes that charges are spread in the ratio in which the number of instalments remaining, bears to the total number of instalments in the contract. For example, in a 12-month contract of equal monthly instalments, 12/78 of the charge is attributable to the first month, 11/78 in the second month etc. The method is known as the *rule of 78* because the sum of the numbers 1 to 12 is 78. See Consumer Credit Act 1995, ss 52–53 as amended by Central Bank and Financial Services Authority of Ireland Act 2003, s 35, Sch 1.

rules of court. (1) Means rules made by the authority for the time being having power to make rules regulating the practice and procedure of the court in relation to which the expression is used: Interpretation Act 1937, s 12, para 26. See Rules of the Superior Courts 1986, SI No 15 of 1986

(RSC) as amended; new consolidated Circuit Court Rules 2001, SI No 510 of 2001; District Court Rules 1997, SI No 93 of 1997 (DCR) as amended.

Where a statute confers a new statutory jurisdiction on the High Court, the Rules of the Superior Courts apply in the absence of any indication to the contrary: *F McK v AF and JF* [2002] 2 ILRM 303, SC and 1 IR 242. Also where additional jurisdiction is conferred by statute on the Circuit Court, the Circuit Court Rules are applicable to the additional jurisdiction, unless expressly provided otherwise by the statute: *Inspector of Taxes v Arida Ltd* [1995] 2 IR 230, SC.

Where there is no rule provided to govern practice and procedure in the Circuit Court, the practice and procedure of the High Court may be followed: Circuit Court Rules 2001 Ord 67, r 16. For example, of a refusal by the Circuit Court to import a High Court rule, see *Aerospan Board Centre (Dublin) Ltd v Dean Furniture Ltd* [1987] CC as reported in 7 ILT & SJ (1989) 79.

Any conflict between the provisions of a statute and the rules of procedural law, including the Rules of the Superior Courts, must be resolved in favour of the former: *McKenna v E H* [2002] 2 ILRM 117, HC; 1 IR 72. 'Rules of procedure should always be regarded as the servants and not the masters of justice': Flood J in *County Meath VEC v Joyce* [1994] 2 ILRM 210, HC.

Provision has been made: (a) for the Attorney-General to be a member of the *rules of court* committees; and (b) for certain members of these committees to delegate their membership to other persons: Courts and Court Officers Act 2002, ss 35 and 36.

Provision has been made to replace the amounts specified in Irish pounds in the Rules of the Superior Courts (SI No 15 of 1986 as amended) by convenient euro amounts: Rules of the Superior Courts (No 4) (Euro Changeover) 2001, SI No 585 of 2001. See also Civil Liability and Courts Act 2004 s.9. [Bibliography: Buckley, Melody; Cordial; De Blacam (3); Deale; Delaney (4); Delaney & McGrath; Gill; Goldberg; O'Floinn; Round Hall; Waldron; Wood.]

(2) A *rule of court* is also an order or direction of the court, giving effect to a private agreement, a breach of which may result in a sanction or punishment eg an agreement in relation to the custody of children or access to children, entered into

voluntarily by the father and mother, may be made a *rule of court* if the court is satisfied that the agreement is fair and reasonable: Guardianship of Infants Act 1964, s 24 as inserted by Children Act 1997, s 11. The agreement is given the effect of a court order eg in this case, the agreement becomes an order of the court pursuant to GIA 1964, ss 11(1)(2)(a) or 11B, the breach of which attracts a fine and/or a term of imprisonment. See Courts Service Act 1998, s 30. See LANGUAGE; PERSONAL INJURIES ACTION; PRACTICE DIRECTIONS; SEPARATION AGREEMENT.

rules of the road. The publication issued under that title by the Minister, being the edition thereof which at the relevant time, is the latest edition: Road Traffic Act 1961, s 3(4). Failure to observe the Rules of the Road is only evidential in its effect.

rules of trade. See WORLD TRADE ORGANISATION.

run with the land. See COVENANT.

rundale system. A system of frequent redistribution of land, prevalent in the western counties of Ireland, whereby rights of pasturage continue to be owned in common by many landowners, particularly of mountain land, and whereby rights to arable land are periodically redistributed amongst the farmers of a neighbourhood. The Land Commission is empowered to purchase land where it requires it to facilitate rearrangement of lands held in rundale or intermixed plots: Land Act 1950, s 27(1)(c). For arrangements following the dissolution of the Land Commission in 1999, see LAND COMMISSION.

running account. A facility under a *credit agreement* (qv) whereby the consumer is enabled to receive cash, goods or services to an amount or value such that, taking into account payments made, the credit limit (if any) is not at any time exceeded: Consumer Credit Act 1995, s 2(1). Examples of running accounts are overdrafts, credit card accounts, shop budget accounts; contrast with fixed sum credit such as term loans or personal loans. A credit agreement which operates by way of a running account must contain certain specified information eg credit limit if any, and interest charged and the APR (CCA 1995, s 31(2)).

rural district councils. Formerly, the bodies established to exercise the functions previously exercised by the boards of guardians (qv): Local Government (Ireland) Act 1898. These councils were later abolished and their functions transferred to the county councils. See Local Government Act 1925, ss 3 and 9; Local Government (Dublin) Act 1930, s 82; County Management Act 1940, s 36; Local Government Act 2001, s 5(1), Sch 3, Pt I. See COUNTY COUNCIL.

rural renewal scheme. For amendment to the tax treatment of this scheme, see Finance Act 2001, s 59. The scheme has been extended to 31 July 2006: Finance Act 2004, s 26. It had previously been extended to 31 December 2004: Finance Act 2002, s 23. See also Finance Act 2003, s 28. See URBAN RENEWAL.

Rylands v Fletcher, Rule in. An occupier of land or buildings, who brings or keeps on it anything which, though perhaps harmless while it remains there, will do damage if it escapes, is bound to prevent its escape and is liable for all the damage if it does escape. The rule is one of strict liability independent of wrongful intent or negligence.

Defences include: Act of God; act of a stranger; consent or default of the plaintiff; statutory authority; and accidental fire which occurs on land or in buildings and escapes without negligence (Accidental Fires Act 1943). There is no Irish precedent to indicate that the burden of proving that there was no negligence lay on the defendant where the defendant had a statutory authority to carry out the act complained of: *Cosgrove v Ryan and ESB* [2003] 1 ILRM 544, HC. See *Noonan v Hartnett* [1950] 84 ILTR 41; *McKenzie v O'Neill & Roe Ltd* [1977] HC. See also *Healy v Bray UDC* [1962] Ir Jur Rep 9; *Berkery v Flynn* [1982] HC; *Daly v McMullan* [1997] 2 ILRM 232, CC; *Superquinn Ltd v Bray UDC* [1998] 3 IR 542, HC. See FIRE, LIABILITY FOR; POLLUTION, CIVIL LIABILITY FOR.

S

S. R. & Ord Statutory Rules and Orders (qv).

sacerdotal privilege. See PRIVILEGE, CONFESSIONAL.

sacrilege. The offence which consisted of breaking and entering and committing a felony in, or entering, committing a felony in and then breaking out of, any place of divine worship: Larceny Act 1916, s 24 repealed by the Criminal Law (Jurisdiction) Act 1976, s 21. The offence remains as the statutory offence of burglary (qv): Criminal Justice (Theft and Fraud) Offences Act 2001, s 12.

safety at work. At common law, an employer is under a duty to provide a safe system of work for his employees. By statute, a general duty is placed on all employers to ensure so far as is *reasonably practicable*, the safety, health and welfare at work of all their employees, which includes those undergoing training for employment or receiving work experience: Safety, Health and Welfare at Work Act 1989, s 6. There is also a general duty in respect of persons who are not employees to ensure that they are not exposed to risks to their safety and health (SHWWA 1989, s 7). At European level, the EC is required to support and complement the activities of the member states in improving in particular of the working environment to protect workers' health and safety: EC Treaty, art 137(1)(a) of the consolidated (2002) version.

Every place at which any person has at any time to work must be kept in a safe condition: Safety in Industry Act 1980, s 12(1). Every dangerous part of any machinery, other than prime movers and transmission machinery, must be securely fenced: Factories Act 1955, s 23(1). The Mines and Quarries Act 1965 contains specific provisions regarding safety at places of work to which it relates. For amendments to the 1955 and 1965 Acts, see SI No 357 of 1995.

An employee has a duty to take reasonable care for his own safety and health and that of any other persons who might be affected by his acts or omissions at work: Safety in Industry Act 1980, s 8(1)(a); *Kennedy v East Cork Foods Ltd* [1973] IR 244; SHWWA 1989, s 9. Once an employer is aware that the work an employee is required to do could damage the employee's health, the employer has a responsibility to investigate the matter before exposing the employee to risk: *Nolan v Ryans Hotels plc* [1999] ELR 215, EAT. See also *Williams v T P Wallace Construction Ltd* [2002] 2 ILRM 63, HC (under appeal); *McGann v Manning Construction Ltd* (2003) ITLR (5 May) HC.

The first comprehensive reform of occupational safety and health law since the

foundation of the State culminated in the 1989 Act which extended protection legislation to all employers and employees; it also provided for the establishment of the National Authority for Occupational Safety and Health (styled *Health and Safety Authority* or HEA). It imposed general duties on designers and manufacturers regarding articles and substances for use at work, and on persons who design or construct places of work (SHWWA 1989, ss 10–11). The HEA has extensive enforcement powers through: improvement plans (qv), improvement notices (qv), prohibition notices (qv), and in extreme cases *ex parte* applications to the High Court.

The period within which the HEA can bring a prosecution has been extended in circumstances where proceedings are delayed by an inquest (SHWWA 1989, s 51 amended by Organisation of Working Time Act 1997, s 38). This addresses the difficulties highlighted in *National Authority for Occupational Safety and Health v Fingal Co Council* [1997] ILRM 128, HC and 2 IR 547. See also OWTA 1997, s 41.

See also *Close v Steel Company of Wales* [1962] AC 367; *Daly v Avonmore Creameries Ltd* [1984] IR 131; *Johnson v Gresham Hotel Company* [1986] HC; *Hetherington v Ultra Tyre Service Ltd* [1993] 2 IR 535, SC; *National Authority v O'K Tools* [1997] 1 IR 534, HC; *National Authority v O'Brien* [1997] 1 IR 543, HC; *Barclay v An Post* [1998] 2 ILRM 385, HC; *DPP v Roseberry Construction Ltd* (November 2001, unreported), Naas Circuit Court; *DPP v O'Flynn Construction Ltd* (20 February 2003, unreported), Cork Circuit Criminal Court. See SI No 279 of 1960 (docks) as amended by SI No 357 of 1995; SI No 423 of 1981 (unfenced machinery); Safety, Health and Welfare at Work (General Application) Regulations 1993, SI No 44 of 1993. See Exposure to Asbestos (Amendment) Regulations 2000, SI No 74 of 2000. See also SI No 357 of 1995.

Under draft legislation, it is proposed to consolidate and update the 1989 Act, and to provide for new penalties for serious health and safety breaches, on-the-spot fines for employers and employees (e g failure to wear appropriate safety equipment), and testing of employees for the presence of an intoxicant: Safety, Health and Welfare at Work Bill 2004. See 'Risky Business' by solicitor Barrett Chapman in *Law Society Gazette* (June 2003) 26. See 'Toeing the

Line' by solicitor Geoffrey Shannon in *Law Society Gazette* (July 2004) 24. For *Health and Safety Authority,* see website: *www.hsa.ie/osh*. For *National Safety Council,* see website: *www.nsi.ie*. For the *European Agency for Safety and Health at Work*, see website: *www.agency.osha.eu.int*. [Bibliography: Byrne R (2); Greer & Nicholson; McMahon & Binchy; Shannon; White.] See ACCESS; CARCINOGENS; CONFINED SPACE; CONSTRUCTION SAFETY; PREGNANCY; OFFSHORE INSTALLATION; REASONABLY PRACTICABLE; SAFETY STATEMENT; WORK ACTIVITY; WORK, PROHIBITION OF.

safety at work, equipment. Regulations have been made concerning the minimum health and safety requirement for the use of *work equipment* by workers at work: Safety, Health and Welfare at Work (General Application) (Amendment) Regulations 2001, SI No 188 of 2001. These regulations amend SI No 44 of 1993 to give effect to Council Directive (EC) 95/63 amending Directive 89/655/EC. The 1993 regulations have been amended to strengthen the existing provisions dealing with protective and preventative services concerning competency and also to introduce requirements for the provision of measures relating to fire-fighting: SI No 53 of 2003.

It has been held that breach of work safety legislation which resulted in an employee being injured by using *defective equipment*, constituted a breach of the employers' statutory duty, for which the employer may seek indemnity from the third party who supplied the equipment: *Everett v Thorsman Ireland Ltd* [2000] 1 IR 256, HC. See DISPLAY SCREEN EQUIPMENT.

safety belt. A person driving and a person occupying a front seat of passenger vehicles and station wagons, having passenger accommodation of not more than eight persons exclusive of the driver, must wear a safety belt, unless the person is exempted, or produces a certificate of a registered medical practitioner that because of physical or mental disability or for medical or psychological reasons, it was undesirable or inadvisable for the person to wear a safety belt on the occasion in question: Road Traffic (Construction, Equipment and Use of Vehicles) Amendment No 2 Regulations 1978, SI No 360 of 1978.

In a negligence action involving the collision of motor vehicles, failure of a plaintiff to wear a safety belt has been held to amount to *contributory negligence* (qv), resulting in a reduction of 15% in the damages which would otherwise have been awarded: *Sinnott v Quinnsworth Ltd* [1984] ILRM 523. A reduction of 14% was made in *Conley v Strain* [1989] 7 ILT Dig 149, HC and 20% in *Ward v Walsh* [1992] 10 ILT Dig 74, SC.

Penalty points apply for the offence of not wearing a safety belt or permitting a person under 17 years of age to occupy a front seat or rear seat when not wearing a safety belt or appropriate child restraint: SIs No 321 and 322 of 2003. For the removal of the exemption from wearing seat belts by taxi drivers, see SI No 402 of 2004. See PENALTY POINTS.

safety order. An order made by a court directing the respondent to an application: (a) not to use or threaten to use violence against, not to molest or put in fear the applicant or a dependent person, and (b) if the respondent is not residing at the place where the applicant or the dependent person resides, not to watch or beset that place: Domestic Violence Act 1996, s 2.

Such an order, which can last for up to five years where granted by the District Court, is intended to provide protection for spouses, cohabitants and their children. For procedure in District Court, see DCR 1997 Ord 59, r 4.

Where the court is of opinion that the safety or welfare of the applicant or dependent person so requires, it may make a *protection order* (qv) until determination of the safety order application (DVA 1996, s 5). It is a criminal offence to contravene any such orders (DVA 1996, s 17). Neither of these orders, bar the respondent from residing at the place where the applicant or dependent person resides, whereas a *barring order* does.

In divorce proceedings, the court may make a safety order, barring order or protection order: Family Law (Divorce) Act 1996, ss 11(a), 15(1)(d). A divorced person may apply for a safety order against a former spouse (FL(D)A 1996, s 51).

An application for the making, varying or discharging of a safety order in the Circuit Court is instituted by the issuing of a *Domestic Violence Civil Bill*: Circuit Court Rules 2001 Ord 59, r 5.

safety representative. The person whom employees have a right to appoint to represent them in relation to consultations with their employer regarding the development and promotion of measures for their safety, health and welfare at work and the ascertaining of the effectiveness of such measures: Safety, Health and Welfare at Work Act 1989, s 13. [Bibliography: Byrne R (2)].

safety statement. The statement which must be prepared by every employer specifying: (i) the arrangements made for safeguarding safety, health and welfare at work; (ii) the resources provided for this; (iii) the co-operation required from employees; (iv) the names of persons responsible for performance of the tasks in the statement: Safety, Health and Welfare at Work Act 1989, s 12. In preparing the safety statement, the employer must be in possession of an assessment in writing of the risks to safety and health at the place of work: SI No 44 of 1993, reg 10. A guide to drafting a safety statement is available to solicitors on the Law Society website under *Precedents for practice*: *www.lawsociety.ie*. [Bibliography: Byrne R (2)].

salary. Generally understood to mean a fixed regular payment, often monthly, made by an employer for professional or office work as opposed to manual work. A practising barrister may not undertake work at a salary: *Code of Conduct for the Bar of Ireland* (December 2003) r 11.1(b). See BARRISTER IN EMPLOYMENT.

sale. (1) The act of selling. (2) A contract for a sale of goods. See SALE OF GOODS.

sale, bill of. See BILL OF SALE.

sale by court. When any property is ordered by the Court to be sold, the order must direct who is to have carriage of sale, and where same shall be held, and by whom the conditions and contracts of sale and abstract of title will be prepared: Circuit Court Rules 2001 Ord 43, r 3.

Where the court orders and agrees a sale of property, on the application of a party seeking partition and sale, the court is not the vendor; the vendor comprises all the parties to the suit, and the solicitor having carriage of sale is their agent for whose acts the parties are liable: *Blackall v Blackall* [2000] 3 IR 456, HC.

sale and return. See APPROVAL, SALE ON.

sale of goods. A contract for the sale of goods is a contract whereby the seller transfers or agrees to transfer the property in the goods to the buyer for a money consideration called the price: Sale of Goods Act 1893, s 1. A contract of sale may be made in writing, or by word of mouth, or partly in writing and partly by word of mouth, or may be implied by the conduct of the parties (SGA 1893, s 3). However the Minister may by order require certain contracts to be in writing: Sale of Goods and Supply of Services 1980, s 54.

Where under a contract of sale, the property in the goods is transferred from the seller to the buyer, the contract is called a *sale*. But where the transfer of the property is to take place at a future time or subject to some condition thereafter to be fulfilled, the contract is called an *agreement to sell* (SGA 1893, s 1(3)). An agreement to sell becomes a sale when the time elapses or the conditions are fulfilled subject to which the property in the goods is to be transferred (SGA 1893, s 1(4)).

A contract for the sale of any goods of the value of £10 (€12.70) or upwards is not enforceable by action unless the buyer accepts part of the goods so sold, and actually receives the same, or gives something in earnest to bind the contract, or in part payment, or unless some note or memorandum in writing of the contract be made and signed by the party to be charged or his agent in that behalf (SGA 1893, s 4).

If a person sells goods but remains in possession of the goods and subsequently disposes of them to another person who receives them in good faith and without notice of the previous sale, the subsequent disposition has the same effect as if the true owner of the goods had authorised the disposition: Sale of Goods Act 1893, s 25(1); *Hanley v ICC Finance Ltd* [1996] 1 ILRM 463, HC.

See *Uniacke v Cassidy Electrical Supply Company* [1987] HC. The Law Reform Commission has recommended that the State should ratify the United Nations Vienna Convention for the International Sale of Goods: see *Kaczorowska* in 9 ILT & SJ (1991) 281 and LRC 42 of 1992. [Bibliography: Bird; Forde (5); Grogan, King & Donelan; O'Reilly P; Benjamin UK.] See CONTRACT; PRICE.

sale of land. The usual practice in the sale of land by *private treaty* (qv) is for the purchaser to sign the contract for the sale of land which is then returned to the vendor for his acceptance and signing, whereupon a binding agreement is in force. There is no provision, as in the UK, for an exchange of contracts with the contract being binding only on such exchange. See *Embourg Ltd v Tyler Group Ltd* [1996] 3 IR 480, SC.

Where the parties have used the *general conditions* in a standard contract of sale, approved by the Law Society, the court will interpret any ambiguities therein in an open manner without favouring either side; this is in contrast to the norm where the court usually interprets a clause against the party who had inserted it: *Browne v Mariena Properties Ltd* [1998] 1 IR 568, SC.

In a sale by *auction* (qv) of land, an agreement is in force when the property is knocked down to the highest bidder, the necessary memorandum to that agreement being signed by the bidder while still in the auctioneer's premises and signed by the auctioneer on behalf of the vendor. See Law Reform Commission Report on *Interest of Vendor and Purchaser in Land during the period between Contract and Completion* (LRC 49, 1995).

Certain restrictions are imposed on local authorities wishing to dispose of land, including the requirement for Ministerial consent: Local Government Act 2001, ss 183–184. [Bibliography: Wylie (2).] See CONVEYANCE; CONDITION; CONDITIONS OF SALE; EJECTMENT; ELECTRONIC FORM; MORTGAGEE, RIGHT OF; SETTLEMENT; STATUTE OF FRAUDS; TRUSTEE, POWER OF.

salmon. Provision has been made for the establishment of a *National Salmon Commission* with the function of assisting and advising the Minister in relation to the conservation, management, protection and development of the national salmon resource and for making recommendations on quotas for the taking of salmon: Fisheries Act 1980, ss 55A–55D as inserted by Fisheries (Amendment) Act 1999, s 22. Provision has also been made for a tagging scheme for wild salmon and sea trout: F(A)A 1999, ss 24–26; SI No 174 of 2003.

salmon dealer's licence. It is not lawful for any person, other than the Electricity Supply Board, to sell, expose for sale or keep for sale at any place salmon or trout unless such person is the holder of a *salmon dealer's licence,* and such place is a place at which he is authorised by that licence to sell salmon or trout: Fisheries Act 1959, Part X as amended by Fisheries (Amendment) Act 1994, s 20. It is an offence for any person to buy salmon or trout from a person whom he knows or has reason to believe is selling in breach of the licensing

provision. A licence is similarly required for the export for sale of salmon or trout. Similar provisions apply to eels and molluscan shellfish. See *Tiernan v North Western Regional Fisheries Board* [1997] 2 IR 104, HC. [Bibliography: Comerford (1)].

salmon rod licence. A licence which authorises the person named therein to use during the period and in the fishing district specified therein, a salmon rod: Fisheries (Amendment) Act 1991, s 16. For licence fees, see SIs No 687 and 688 of 2003.

salus populi est suprema lex. [The welfare of the people is the paramount law].

salvage. (1) The voluntary saving of maritime property from danger at sea.

(2) The compensation allowed to salvors by whose assistance a ship or cargo or the lives of persons belonging to her are saved from danger or loss at sea. See Jurisdiction of Courts (Maritime Conventions) Act 1989, s 2. See SALVAGE OPERATION; SALVOR.

(3) The damaged property to which a marine insurer is entitled, where the cost of repairs will exceed the repaired value, and where the doctrine of *constructive total loss* (qv) comes into play; in which event, the insured is entitled to give notice of abandonment and the insurer is bound to pay the full value as for a total loss and becomes entitled to the subject matter insured. There is no such doctrine in non-marine insurance law and the insured is, strictly speaking, only entitled to the difference between the value of the undamaged property and the value of what remains. In practice, however, insurers often pay as for a total loss of goods which are seriously damaged and when they do so they are entitled to the damaged goods as salvage, or their value. [Bibliography: Hill UK.] See INEQUALITY OF POSITION; RE-INSTATEMENT.

salvage contracts. The master of a vessel has the authority to bind both the ship and cargo owners to a salvage contract in all circumstances; he does not have to seek their authorisation: Merchant Shipping (Salvage and Wreck) Act 1993, s 18.

salvage operation. Means any act or activity undertaken to assist a *vessel* (qv) or any other *property* in danger in navigable *tidal waters* (qv) or in any harbour; *property* in this context means any property not permanently and intentionally attached to the shoreline and includes *freight at risk*: Merchant Shipping (Salvage and Wreck) Act 1993, s 12.

A reward for undertaking the salvage operation is payable where the operation had a *useful result* (MS(SW)A 1993, s 25). Certain criteria for fixing the award are specified eg including the salved value, the skill of the salvors, the nature and degree of danger; but the award, while fixed with a view to encouraging salvage operations, must not exceed the salved value, except that special compensation is payable where the salvor has been successful in preventing or minimising damage to the environment (MS(SW)A 1993, ss 25–27). See MASTER; NO CURE, NO PAY.

salvage payments. Payments made in respect of property which will be repaid before all other prior charges on the property, provided: (a) the payments had the effect of saving the property from loss, (b) the payments were made by a person with an interest in the property, and (c) the payments were made voluntarily and not under any duty or obligation, or as agent for someone else: *Re Powers' Policies* [1899] 2 IR 6; *Re Kavanagh* [1952] Ir Jur Rep 38.

salvo jure. [Without prejudice].

salvor. 'A person who, without any particular relation to a ship in distress, proffers useful service, and gives it as a volunteer adventurer without any pre-existing covenant that connected him with the duty of employing himself for the preservation of the ship': *Lord Stowell in the Neptune* [1824] 1 Hag Adm 227. A salvor may have a *maritime lien* (qv). No remuneration is due to a salvor from shipwrecked persons whose lives are saved by a salvor: Merchant Shipping (Salvage and Wreck) Act 1993, s 29(1). A salvor has a duty to carry out *salvage operations* (qv) with due care, to prevent or minimise damage to the environment, to seek assistance or the intervention of other salvors when reasonable (MS(SW)A 1993, s 20). However, a salvor of human life, is entitled to a fair share of the salvage reward in respect of the salvor of the vessel or cargo or in respect of environmental protection (MS(SW)A 1993, s 29). See MASTER; MARITIME CLAIM.

sample. Specimen presented for examination as evidence of the composition or quality of the whole. See Food Safety Authority of Ireland Act 1998, s 51. See

Murdoch: [1981] 44 MLR 388. See BODILY SAMPLE; SAMPLE, SALE BY.

sample, sale by. In a contract for sale by sample there is an implied condition that the bulk will correspond with the sample in quality, that the buyer will have a reasonable opportunity of comparing the bulk with the sample, and that the goods will be free from any defect rendering them unmerchantable, which would not be apparent on reasonable examination of the sample: Sale of Goods and Supply of Services 1980, s 10. There are similar provisions governing goods which are let under a hire-purchase agreement: Consumer Credit Act 1995, s 77. See MERCHANTABLE QUALITY.

sanction. (1) A penalty or punishment as a means of enforcing obedience to the law. (2) A measure taken by one or more states against another state which is violating international law eg by the prohibition of trade and impounding of assets eg see SI No 144 of 1993 in relation to the Federal Republic of Yugoslavia (Serbia and Montenegro). See also EC (Zimbabwe) (Sanctions) Regulations 2002, SI No 282 of 2002; EC (Counter Terrorism Financial Sanctions) Regulations 2004, SI No 459 of 2004; EC (Usama Bin Laden, Al-Qaida and Taliban of Afghanistan) (Sanctions) Regulations 2004, SI No 457 of 2004. See TRADE, PROHIBITION OF.

sanctuary. Formerly, consecrated places where execution of the law could not take place. It has been held that there was no form of sanctuary which could be availed of by a person who had been requested to submit to a breath test, on the basis that at the time of the request, his vehicle was in the car park of a hotel: *Dougal v Mahon* [1989] 7 ILT Dig 229.

sanitary authorities. Sanitary authorities comprise all the country boroughs and borough corporations, county councils and urban district councils (qqv). See Public Health Act 1878. However, provision has been made for the *water functions* of a town sanitary authority to be transferred to and be the functions of the relevant county council to form a single sanitary district: Local Government Act 2001, ss 83–84. Under proposed legislation 'sanitary authorities' will become 'water services authorities' in so far as delivery of water services is concerned: see WATER SERVICES. See LOCAL AUTHORITY; SANITARY SERVICES.

sanitary authorities and nuisances. Sanitary authorities (qv) have a duty to inspect their districts from time to time and take steps to abate nuisances (qv): Public Health (Ireland) Act 1878. Nuisances include any accumulation or deposit which is a *nuisance or injurious to health*. A *summary* (qv) procedure is provided for, which involves serving a notice on the person by whose act, default or sufferance the nuisance arises or continues (PH(I)A 1878, s 110).

Nuisance or injurious to health include not only things which are injurious to health, but also anything which, though not injurious to health, really diminishes the comfort of life: *Bishop Auckland Local Board v Bishop Auckland Iron Co* [1882] 20 QBD 138. See also BYE-LAW.

sanitary conveniences. Urinals, water closets, privies and ashpits and other similar conveniences for public accommodation which a local authority is empowered to provide: Public Health (Ireland) Act 1878, s 49. A local authority is not authorised to construct such a convenience in such a location as to be a nuisance (qv): *Sellors v Matlock Bath Local Board* [1884–85] 24 QBD 928. See also Public Health Acts Amendment Act 1890, ss 20–21; Public Health Acts Amendment Act 1907, ss 39 and 47.

sanitary facilities. Every employer is required to provide and maintain suitable and sufficient sanitary and washing facilities available for the use of employees; more stringent requirements are laid down for places of work which are used for the first time after 1992 or which undergo modification after 1992 or where required by the features of the place of work: SI No 44 of 1993, reg 17, Schs 2–4.

sanitary services. The services which *sanitary authorities* have a duty or are empowered to provide eg the provision and maintenance of sewers and of water supplies, the abatement of nuisances, the control of building standards, the prevention of buildings becoming dangerous, refuse collection, street cleaning and lighting, and the provision of burial grounds: Local Government (Sanitary Services) Act 1878 to 1964.

sanity, presumption of. See INSANITY; MCNAGHTEN RULES.

sans frais. [Without expense.] An endorsement of a bill of exchange *sans frais* indicates that the endorser accepts liability for the value of the bill but not for the expenses involved in enforcing it. See Bills of Exchange Act 1882, s 16. See ENDORSEMENT.

sans recours. [Without recourse (to me).] An endorsement on a bill of exchange such that the endorser (eg an agent endorsing for his principal) is not personally liable: Bills of Exchange Act 1882, s 16.

Saorstát Éireann. The Irish Free State; the previous name of the territory of Ireland: Constitution of the Irish Free State (Saorstát Éireann) 1922; Articles of Agreement for a Treaty between Great Britain and Ireland (6 December 1921). The laws in force in Saorstát Éireann continue to have full force and effect until repealed or amended, provided they are not repugnant to the 1937 Constitution, art 50). See BOUNDARY COMMISSION; LEGISLATION, CONSTITUTIONALITY OF.

Saorstát Éireann statute. Means an Act of the Oireachtas of Saorstát Éireann: Interpretation Act 1937, s 12, para 27.

SARS. [Severe Acute Respiratory Syndrome.] SARS was designated as an infectious disease in 2003: Infectious Diseases (Amendment) Regulations 2003, SI No 115 of 2003 and SI No 180 of 2003. See INFECTIOUS DISEASES.

satellite dish. Planning permission is not required for the erection of one satellite dish, up to one metre in diameter, to the side or rear of a house, except a building listed for preservation in the development plan: Planning and Development Regulations 2001, SI No 600 of 2001, Sch 2, class 4. A satellite dish must not be erected on, or forward of, the front wall of a house. For previous regulations, see Local Government (Planning and Development) Regulations 1994, SI No 86 of 1994.

satisfaction. (1) The extinguishment of an obligation or a claim by performance. See *Murphy & Murphy (infants) v O'Donohue Ltd & Ors* [1992] ILRM 378, SC.

(2) The equitable doctrine by which the donation of property, if accepted by the donee, operates as a complete or *pro tanto* discharge of a prior claim of the donee: *Lord Chichester v Coventry* [1867] 36 LJ Ch 673. A prior debt may be satisfied by a legacy, where the legacy is a sum of money equal to or greater than the debt: *Talbot v Duke of Shrewsbury* [1714] Prec Ch 394. Equity presumes a person is just before he is generous. A portion (qv) may be satisfied by a legacy eg where a father or person *in loco parentis* covenants to provide a portion

and subsequently gives a legacy, the court will presume that the covenant is satisfied by the legacy *in toto* or *pro tanto* depending on the amount of the legacy. See *Ellard v Phelan* [1914] 2 IR 76. [Bibliography: Wylie (3)].

satisfaction, certificate of. The certificate which issues from the judgments office of the courts to authenticate that a judgment has been paid. Lodgement of this certificate: (a) in the Registry of Deeds will operate as a reconveyance of the land so as to vacate a judgment mortgage in the case of unregistered land; or (b) to cancel a judgment mortgage as a burden on registered land: Judgment Mortgage Act 1850, s 9; Judgment Mortgage Act 1858; Registration of Title Act 1964.

satisfaction piece. A creditor's document which shows that a debt has been paid.

satisfied. The use of the word *satisfied* in the Mental Treatment Act 1945, s 260 indicates that the Oireachtas had in mind a higher standard of proof than that which a plaintiff ordinarily would be required to discharge in a civil case: *O'Dowd v North Western Health Board* [1983] ILRM 186, SC.

saving certificate. A security issued by the Minister for Finance under which the purchaser thereof, by virtue of an immediate payment of a specified sum, becomes entitled after a specified period to receive a larger sum consisting of the said sum so originally paid and accumulated interest thereon: Finance Act 1929, s 34(5). An Post was granted an *interlocutory* injunction in 1994 preventing Irish Permanent plc from offering financial products to the public called 'savings certificates': *An Post v Irish Permanent plc* [1995] 1 ILRM 336, HC and 1 IR 140. The case was subsequently settled with the defendant giving an undertaking not to sell, advertise or otherwise deal in products bearing the name 'saving certificates'.

savings directive. The EU directive under which interest paid on savings in one member state to 'beneficial owners' who are resident for tax purposes in another member state, will be made subject to taxation in the State of residence: Savings Directive (EC) 2003/48. A 'beneficial owner' is any individual who receives an interest payment for his personal benefit. It excludes companies or other legal persons, as the evasion of interest taxation is seen as a problem associated primarily with individuals. For implementing provision in Ireland, see Taxes Consolidation Act 1997, Chapter 3A, ss 898B–898O initially inserted by SI No 717 of 2003, and subsequently inserted by Finance Act 2004, s 90 and Sch 4, which also revokes the SI.

A return of interest payments made to or secured for beneficial owners must be made by the paying agent to the Revenue Commissioners within three months of the end of the tax year, commencing with the tax year 2005 (TCA 1997, s 898H inserted by FA 2004). See 'Long arm of the law' by solicitor Max Barrett in *Law Society Gazette* (January/February 2004) 42. See FINANCIAL SERVICES ACTION PLAN; TIN.

savings protection scheme. A scheme of protection for depositors with credit institutions under which a depositor may be compensated for 90% of a deposit up to a maximum compensation of €15,000: EC (Deposit Guarantee Schemes) Regulations 1995, SI No 168 of 1995 as amended by Central Bank Act 1997, s 81, and as amended by Central Bank and Financial Services Authority of Ireland Act 2003, s 35, Sch 2; EC (Deposit Guarantee Schemes) Regulations 2002, SI No 104 of 2002 and 2003, SI No 85 of 2003. See also Credit Union Act 1997, ss 6(1)(f) and 46, as amended by CBFSAIA 2003, s 35, Sch 1.

For previous legislation, see Central Bank Act 1989, Ch V, ss 53–73; Building Societies Act 1989, s 94; Building Societies (Savings Protection) Regulations 1990, SI No 108 of 1990. See INVESTOR COMPENSATION.

SC. Senior counsel (qv).

sc; scil; scilicet. [That is to say].

scandalising the court. The offence of contempt of court which arises when what is said or done by the accused is of such a nature as to be calculated to endanger public confidence in the court and thereby interfere with the administration of justice: *State (DPP) v Walsh* [1981] IR 412 cited in *Desmond & Dedeir v Glackin & Minister for Industry & Commerce* [1992] ILRM 489, HC.

scandalous matter. The court may at any stage of proceedings, order to be struck out or amended any matter in any endorsement or pleading which is scandalous or which may tend to prejudice, embarrass or delay the fair trial of the action: RSC Ord 19, r 27. See OFFENSIVE WORDS.

Sch. An appendix to an Act of the Oireachtas or to a Statutory Instrument (qv).

scheduled offence. An offence declared to be a *scheduled offence* by order of the government when Part V of the Offences Against the State Act 1939 is in force. Part V provides for the establishment of *Special Criminal Courts* and is brought into force by proclamation whenever the government is satisfied that the ordinary courts are inadequate to secure the effective administration of justice and the preservation of public peace and order: SI No 142 of 1972.

Conviction of a scheduled offence in a Special Criminal Court previously resulted in forfeiture of any office or employment which was remunerated out of public funds: OASA 1939, s 34; this section however has been found to be unconstitutional as it amounted to an unreasonable and unjustified interference with personal rights: *Cox v Ireland* [1991] 9 ILT Dig 170, HC; the section was impermissibly wide and discriminate: *Cox v Ireland* [1992] 2 IR 503, SC. See also *McDonnell v Ireland* [1996] 2 ILRM 222, HC; *Murphy v Ireland* [1996] 2 ILRM 461, HC and 3 IR 307.

There is no requirement that an arrest under the OASA 1939, s 30 must be predominantly motivated by a desire to investigate a scheduled offence: *The People (DPP) v Howley* [1989] ILRM 629, SC. Scheduled offences are heard by the Special Criminal Court (qv). Scheduled offences have been declared to be offences under the Malicious Damage Act 1861 (now largely repealed), Explosive Substances Act 1883, Firearms Act 1925 to 1971, Offences Against the State Act 1939 and the Conspiracy and Protection of Property Act 1875, SI No 282 of 1972.

The expression 'scheduled offences' as used in OASA 1939 can include 'ordinary' as well as 'subversive' offences: *Kavanagh v Government of Ireland* [1996] 1 ILRM 133, HC. A scheduled offence may be tried summarily by the District Court if the DPP consents: *Kershaw v DPP* [2003] FL 7030, HC. See *DPP v Sweeney* [1996] 2 IR 313, HC. See also Offences against the State (Amendment) Act 1998, s 14 and 18.

scheme of arrangement. (1) An agreement between a debtor and his creditors allowing his debts to be paid in accordance with that agreement, rather than by his being adjudged a bankrupt. In bankruptcy, the court has power to approve a *scheme of arrangement*. For provisions regarding an arrangement with creditors, see ARRANGING DEBTOR. See also COMPOSITION; BANKRUPTCY.

(2) For *scheme of arrangement* whereby a company proposes to enter into a compromise or arrangement with its creditors or its members, which requires the sanction of the court, see RECONSTRUCTION OF COMPANY. See also Credit Union Act 1997, s 161 as amended by Central Bank and Financial Services Authority of Ireland Act 2003, s 35, Sch 1.

(3) For provisions regarding a company which is subject to court protection of examinership, see COURT PROTECTION OF COMPANY, SCHEME OF ARRANGEMENT.

Schengen Agreements. The agreements, signed by some member states of the EU in Schengen on 14 June 1985 and 19 June 1990, on the gradual abolition of checks at common borders, aimed at enhancing European integration. The Schengen area also includes Iceland and Norway. While the UK and Ireland are not signatories to the Schengen agreements, recognition has been given to the continuing *common travel area* between the UK and Ireland, and to the right of each to opt into the agreements in the future: Amsterdam Treaty 1997 and *second protocol* on *Schengen acquis*. Ireland's wish to maintain its common travel area with the UK in order to maximise freedom of movement into and out of Ireland, was noted in a *Declaration* to the Amsterdam Treaty. See *Kweeder v Minister for Justice* [1996] 1 IR 381, HC; *DL, JL and Others v Minister for Justice* (23 January 2003, unreported) Case ref 109/02 and 108/02. See SOCIAL WELFARE LAW.

Schengen alert. A document that indicates that: (a) a European arrest warrant has been issued in respect of the person and, where appropriate, that the undertaking required by section 11(3) has been given, (b) has been transmitted electronically by or on behalf of the judicial authority concerned to the Garda Síochána using equipment designed, or intended for use, for the purposes of the Schengen Information System (SIS), and (c) is capable of being viewed by the garda by means of equipment designed or intended for use for those purposes. The SIS means the system referred to in Title IV of the Convention implementing the Schengen Agreement of 14 June 1985 between certain EU member states on the gradual abolition of border checks: European Arrest Warrant Act 2003, s 14(10). When a Schengen alert has been issued, a garda may arrest the person named in the warrant before the warrant is received in the State in certain circumstances. See EUROPEAN ARREST WARRANT.

school. An establishment which: (a) provides *primary* education to its students and which may also provide early childhood education, or (b) provides *post-primary* education to its students and which may also provide courses in adult, continuing or vocational education or vocational training: Education Act 1998, s 2(1). A *recognised* school is one which is so designated by the Minister (EA 1998, s 10). See also Education for Persons with Special Educational Needs Act 2004, s 1(1).

Recognised schools must provide education to students which is appropriate to their abilities and needs, including those with a disability or other special educational needs (EA 1998, s 9). They must also have a board of management which, *inter alia*, must publish the policy of the school regarding admission, suspension and expulsion (EA 1998, s 15). There is a right of appeal to the Secretary General of the Department of Education (EA 1998, s 29). Recognised schools are entitled to State funding (EA 1998, s 12). The Minister has wide powers to prescribe curricula for recognised schools i e subjects offered, syllabus, amount of instruction (EA 1998, s 30).

Recognised schools are required to use their available resources, *inter alia*, to comply with any regulations made by the Minister (EA 1998, ss 9(i) and 33). The *ethos* of a school is guarded by the requirement on the school to promote the moral, spiritual, social and personal development of students, having regard to the *characteristic spirit* of the school (EA 1998, s 9(d)). See also EA 1998, ss 15(2)(b) and 30(2)(b).

The duty of a school master is to take care of his pupils as a careful parent would of his children; it is not necessary that the children should be under constant supervision: *Flynn v O'Reilly* [1999] 1 ILRM 458, SC. See *McCann v Minister for Education* [1997] 1 ILRM 1, HC.

An application for the admission of a child to a *recognised school* can be refused only where such refusal is in accordance with the policy of the school published under EA 1998, s 15(2)(d): Education (Welfare) Act 2000, s 19(1). Also the board

of management of a recognised school is required to prepare and submit to the National Educational Welfare Board a statement of the school's *attendance strategy*, including the identification at an early stage of students who are at risk of developing school attendance problems (E(W)A 2000, s 22). See EDUCATIONAL ESTABLISHMENT; NATIONAL EDUCATIONAL WELFARE BOARD; PRE-SCHOOL SERVICE; SCHOOL YEAR; SCHOOL DISCIPLINE, SPECIAL EDUCATIONAL NEEDS; STATE EXAMINATIONS COMMISSION.

school attendance. It is an offence for a parent not to comply with a warning issued to him for failing to send a child below the school leaving age (qv), to school: School Attendance Act 1926, s 17; School Attendance (Amendment) Act 1967; SI No 105 of 1972.

The onus of proof, on the balance of probabilities, that a child is receiving 'suitable elementary education' at home, rests on the parents; 'suitable elementary education' is not to be interpreted so as to require the giving of an education which exceeds the 'certain minimum education, moral, intellectual and social' as required by the Constitution: *DPP v Best* [2000] 2 ILRM 1, SC. In this case, the court held that a 'suitable elementary education' was a question of fact to be determined by the district judge on the evidence presented; it held that the fact that the legislature had not defined what constituted a 'certain minimum' *education* did not prevent a district judge from pronouncing a formal order of conviction or acquittal as the case may be. However, see NATIONAL EDUCATIONAL WELFARE BOARD.

Where a parent fails to send a child to school, a *care order* may be made, committing the child to the care of the health board (qv): Child Care Act 1991, s 75 amending SAA 1926, s 17. See DCR 1997 Ord 84, r 33.

Under legislation enacted in 2000, a parent of a child is required to cause the child concerned to attend a *recognised school* on each school day: Education (Welfare) Act 2000, ss 8 and 17 repealing the SAA 1926 and S(A)A 1967. There are exceptions e g where the child is on a register of children who are in receipt of education in a place that is not a recognised school but the National Educational Welfare Board has satisfied itself that the child concerned is receiving a *certain minimum education*

(E(W)A 2000, ss 14 and 17(2)). When a child is absent from school, the parent is required to notify the principal of the school of the reasons for the child's absence (E(W)A 2000, s 18). The principal of a recognised school is also required to establish and maintain a register of all students attending that school (E(W)A 2000, s 20(1)) and a record of attendance or non-attendance on each school day (E(W)A 2000, s 21(1)). See 'School Attendance, the Common Good' by Dympna Glendenning BL in *Bar Review* (May 2001) 381. See EDUCATION.

school attendance notice. A notice served on a parent by the National Educational Welfare Board, where it is of opinion that a parent is failing or neglecting to cause his child to attend a *recognised school*: Education (Welfare) Act 2000, s 25. The notice will: (a) require the parent to cause the child to attend a specified school; and (b) inform the parent that failure to comply with the notice constitutes an offence (E(W)A 2000, s 25(1)). It will be a good defence for the parent to show that he has made all reasonable efforts to cause the child to attend (E(W)A 2000, s 25(6)).

school authority's duty. The duty of care owed by a school authority to pupils while on its premises in course of normal school activities is to take reasonable care to protect them from foreseeable risks of personal injury or harm: *Mapp (an infant) v Gilhooley* [1990] ITLR (5 March) HC. In measuring that duty, the court must take into account all relevant factors, including the age of the children, the activities in which they may be engaged, the degree of supervision and the opportunity which those in charge had to prevent or minimise the mischief complained of.

A school was held liable for injuries sustained in a fall by a six-year-old pupil while her class was being supervised by two 11-year-old pupils: *Motyer v Whitechurch National School* (2003) Irish Times, 23 May, CC. A school was also held liable for serious injuries sustained by a student in horseplay during an unsupervised school lunchbreak: *Murphy v Co Wexford Vocational Education Committee* [2004] Irish Times, 30 July, SC. The school authority's duty to supervise pupils does not extend to pupils waiting to be collected outside school grounds after school hours: *Dolan v Keo-*

hane [1992] ITLR (27 April) HC. See CORPORAL PUNISHMENT; PRE-SCHOOL SERVICE.

school discipline. Teachers in schools are required to have a lively regard for the improvement and general welfare of their pupils, to treat them with kindness combined with firmness and to aim at governing them through their affections and reason and not by harshness and severity; ridicule, sarcasm or remarks likely to undermine a pupil's self-confidence are prohibited: Department of Education Circular 9/82, January 1982. The enforcement of discipline in a national school has been held to be a matter for the teachers and the board of management; 'it is not a matter for the courts, whose function, at most, is to ensure that the disciplinary complaint was dealt with fairly': *Murtagh & Murtagh v Board of Management of St Emer's National School* [1991] ILRM 549, SC.

The courts will be slow in intervening in the decision-making authority of an *unrecognised* school regarding suspension or expulsion unless there appears to be a want of any reasonable basis for the decision: *Students A & B v A Secondary School* [2000] ITLR (31 January) HC. In *recognised* schools 'expulsion should be resorted to only in the most extreme of indiscipline and only after every effort at rehabilitation has failed and every other sanction has been exhausted': Education Departmental Circular M33/91. See also *Fitzgerald v Northcote* [1865] F & F 656; *The State (Smullen) v Duffy & Others* [1980] ILRM 46.

The board of management of a *recognised school* is required to prepare, in accordance with guidelines which may be issued by the National Educational Welfare Board a *code of behaviour* specifying: (a) the standard of behaviour to be observed by students, (b) the measures to be taken when a student fails or refuses to observe those standards, (c) the procedures to be followed before a student may be suspended or expelled, (d) the grounds for removing a suspension imposed, and (e) the procedure to be followed relating to notification of a child's absence from school: Education (Welfare) Act 2000, s 23. Where a recognised school is of the opinion that a student should be expelled from the school, the *educational welfare officer* must first be notified in writing of the opinion and the reasons therefor

(E(W)A 2000, s 24(1)). Normally, the student should not be expelled until 20 school days have elapsed, to enable the officer to ensure that provision is made for the continued education of the student concerned (E(W)A 2000, s 24(2)–(5)).

The Board, in addition to the parent or the student, may appeal the suspension of a student or the refusal to enrol a student at a school: Education Act 1998, s 29(1)(a)–(c) as amended by E(W)A 2000, s 26. [Bibliography: Glendenning.] See CORPORAL PUNISHMENT; SCHOOL; SUSPENSION.

school leaving age. Provision has been made for the *school leaving age* to be 16 years of age or the completion of three years of post-primary education, whichever occurs later: Education (Welfare) Act 2000, s 2(1) and 17. When a person has reached 18, there is no longer a requirement on the parent to cause the person to attend school. See *Green Paper on Education* 1992. The school leaving age previously was 15 years of age: School Attendance Act 1926 (Extension of Application) Order 1972, SI No 105 of 1972. See SCHOOL ATTENDANCE; YOUNG PERSONS IN EMPLOYMENT REGISTER.

school year. The 12-month period commencing on a day that falls between the first day of July and the first day of October in any year as prescribed by the Minister: Education Act 1998, s 2(1). The Minister may prescribe the minimum number of days in a school year that a school be open and any matters relating to the length of the school year, school week or school day (EA 1998, s 25).

Science Foundation Ireland. A corporate body with functions of promoting, developing and assisting the carrying out of *oriented basic research* in *strategic areas of scientific endeavour* that concerns the future development and competitiveness of industry and enterprise in the State: Industrial Development (Science Foundation Ireland) Act 2003, ss 6–7. 'Strategic areas of scientific endeavour' include information and communications technologies (ICTs) and biotechnology (ID(SFI)A 2003, s 7(3)). 'Oriented basic research' means research that is carried out with the expectation that it will produce a broad base of knowledge that is likely to form the background to the solution of recognised or expected current or future problems or possibilities (ID(S-FI)A 2003, s 2(1)). The Foundation is an agency of Forfás (qv). See INFORMATION SOCIETY COMMISSION.

scienter. Knowledge. The common law rule that an animal must be kept securely by its owner from causing damage where he knows or is presumed to know of its mischievous disposition. The requirement of *scienter* is not that the dog *will* bite somebody but that, having displayed a vicious propensity, it *may* do so: *McCarthy N in Duggan v Armstrong* [1993] ILRM 222, SC. The owner of a dog is now liable for damage caused in an attack on any person by the dog and for injury done by it to any livestock; it is no longer necessary to show a previous mischievous propensity in the dog: Control of Dogs Act 1986, s 21. The *scienter* action however has not been abolished; there is now a statutory remedy under s 21 and the common law remedy. A circuit court judge is reported as having said 'the days when a dog is entitled to a first bite are gone': *Martin F in O'Sullivan v Delahunty* (1988) Irish Times, 19 September, CC. See also *Kavanagh v Centreline Ltd* [1987] IRLM 306. See ANIMALS; DOGS.

scientific evidence. The courts must not take on the role of a determining scientific authority resolving disputes between scientists; the court should apply common sense and an understanding of the logic and likelihood of events to conflicting opinions and theories: *Best v Wellcome Foundation Ltd* [1992] ILRM 609, SC. See FORENSIC EVIDENCE.

scientific research based companies. Companies which are primarily involved in the laboratory research and development of chemical or biological products or processes and may include other similar innovative science based companies: Listing Rules 2000, ch 20. The rules set out the criteria which must be met by such companies to obtain a listing on the stock exchange. The rules are intended to enable such companies without an adequate trading record to raise finance by listing their securities. For the European Federation of Pharmaceutical Industries Associations, see website: *www.efpia.org*. See STOCK EXCHANGE.

scientific societies. Societies established exclusively for the promotion of science, literature or the fine arts may under a certificate granted by the Registrar of Friendly Societies, obtain an exemption from local rates in respect of lands and buildings occupied by them: Scientific Societies Act 1843. The fact that an institute is a teaching institution does not of itself prevent it from being *instituted for the purposes of science exclusively*: *Gurteen Agricultural College v Registrar of Friendly Societies* [1999 HC] 2 ILRM 535. Also the word 'science' is to be given a broad interpretation and includes not only pure or abstract science, but also applied sciences such as electricity and engineering; also the word 'exclusively' must be given its ordinary meaning and not given a literal meaning that would be contrary to the intentions of the legislature: *Transport Museum Society of Ireland Ltd v Registrar of Friendly Societies* [2000] 1 ILRM 264, HC.

scintilla juris. [A spark or fragment of a right].

scribere est agere. [To write is to act].

scrip. A memorandum or certificate of shares (qv) in a company; it is generally a negotiable instrument (qv).

scrip dividend. The allocation to a member of a company of ordinary shares in the company in lieu of a cash dividend; the shares are treated as fully paid up. Often called *bonus shares* or *scrip issue*. A scrip issue enables a company to increase its equity while avoiding the transaction costs normally associated with share issues. Formerly, a scrip issue was treated for tax purposes as income to the value of the cash dividend foregone: Finance Act 1974, s 56.

As from 1993, no tax charge arose from the acquisition; in the event of a subsequent disposal, the additional shares were treated as acquired, at no additional cost, at the same time as the earlier shareholding was acquired by the shareholder: Finance Act 1993, s 36. However, since 3 December 1997, a shareholder who exercises an option to receive additional shares in a company instead of a cash dividend is taxed as if he had received the cash dividend: Taxes Consolidation Act 1997, s 816 as amended by Finance Act 1998, s 43. See Listing Rules 2000, paras 14.12–14.15A. See BONUS SHARES.

script. A draft of a *will* (qv) or *codicil* (qv) or written instructions relating thereto. In probate actions, every *script* in the custody or under the control of a party making an affidavit, is required to be annexed thereto: Circuit Court Rules 2001 Ord 50, r 10.

scrutiny. An inquiry into the validity of votes recorded in an election.

scrutiny of laws. See COMMUNITY LAW.

sculpture. See ARTISTIC WORK; ARTIST, TAX EXEMPTION OF.

scuttling. The deliberate sinking of a ship for the purpose of recovering insurance money.

SE. [*Societas Europaea.*] See EUROPEAN COMPANY.

se defendendo. [In self-defence (qv)].

sea, carriage by. See CARRIAGE BY SEA.

sea-fishing boat licence. A licence granted by the *Registrar General of Fishing Boats* pursuant to the Fisheries (Consolidation) Act 1959, s 222B inserted by Fisheries (Amendment) Act 2003, s 4. Provision has been made for an independent statutory appeal process for such licensing (F(A)A 2003, ss 6–21 and Sch 1). It is an offence for a person on board a sea-fishing boat to fish or attempt to fish, save under and in accordance with the licence. See CONSERVATION OF FISH STOCKS.

sea pollution. Local authorities have responsibility for the protection of the coastline from pollution arising from an incident at sea. Ships are required to have certain oil pollution equipment on board and to follow specified procedures to reduce the discharge of oil into the sea; similar requirements apply to chemical tankers to prevent pollutant discharges: Sea Pollution Act 1991 (Annexes I & II of MARPOL). There is provision for regulations to be made to prevent pollution by sewage, garbage or by harmful substances (Annexes III, IV and V).

Under draft legislation, it is proposed to give legal effect to a number of instruments which have been agreed at the International Maritime Organisation relating to the protection of the marine environment: Sea Pollution (Miscellaneous Provisions) Bill 2003. These are: (a) the Protocol to the International Convention on Oil Pollution Preparedness, Response and Co-operation 1990 (OPRC); (b) the International Convention on the control of Harmful Anti-Fouling Systems 2001 (AFS Convention); (c) Annex VI as added to the International Convention on the Prevention of Pollution from Ships (MARPOL) by the Protocol of 1997; and (d) the International Convention on Civil Liability for Bunker Oil Pollution Damage 2001 (Bunkers Convention). The Bill also proposes to amend Part III of the Merchant Shipping Act 1992. See also BURIAL AT SEA; DUMPING AT SEA; OIL POLLUTION.

seafarer. Means any person, including a master, who is employed or engaged in any capacity on board a ship: EC (Merchant Shipping) (Organisation of Working Time) Regulations 2003, SI No 532 of 2003. These regulations provide seafarers with an entitlement to specified minimum hours of rest and require records to be kept of seafarers' daily hours of rest. For regulations governing working time of workers on board sea-going vessels, see SI No 709 of 2003.

seafarer allowance. The number of days required to be at sea to qualify for the *seafarer allowance* has been reduced from 169 to 161: Finance Act 2001, s 30.

seaground. See SHORE.

seal. Wax impressed and attached to a document so as to authenticate it. Sealing is a solemn mode of expressing consent to a written instrument. 'To constitute a sealing neither wax nor wafer nor a piece of paper, not even an impression is necessary': *Re Sandilands* [1871] LR 6CP 411. Every company must have a seal with its name engraved on it: Companies Act 1963, s 114(b). Contracts which require the company seal for their execution include conveyancing of property, granting a power of attorney, issuing share certificates and warrants (CA 1963, ss 40 and 87 as amended by Companies Amendment Act 1977, s 5). See *Re Hussey* [1987] HC. See also Presidential Seal Act 1937. See RSC Ord 116. There is now provision by which a contract may be sealed *electronically*, see ELECTRONIC CONTRACT. See DEED.

seaman. See ABSENT WITHOUT LEAVE; DESERTION; TRADE DISPUTE.

Seanad Éireann. The upper house of the Oireachtas, established by the 1937 Constitution, composed of sixty members, of whom eleven are *nominated* members and forty-nine are *elected* members (1937 Constriction, art 18). The nominated members, are nominated, with their prior consent, by the Taoiseach. Six of the forty-nine elected members are elected by university graduates who have reached the age of eighteen years and are Irish citizens; at present Dublin University graduates elect three members, and the National University of Ireland graduates also elect three members: Seanad Electoral (University Members) Act 1937 as amended by Electoral Act 1992, s 166. In 1979, the seventh amendment to the Constitution was passed which permitted a redistribution by law of these six seats among the existing universities and other institutions of higher education; no such legislation has been enacted as of May 2002.

The remaining forty-three members are elected from panels: 1937 Constitution, art 18(7). The electorate is confined to members of the new Dáil, members of the outgoing Seanad, and the elected members of the county and borough councils. Voting is by secret postal ballot. See Seanad Electoral (Panel Members) Acts 1947 and 1954; Iris Oifigiúil, 19 March 1993. See DISSOLUTION; UTTERANCE.

search engine. On the Internet, a programme which searches for keywords in files and documents found on the *worldwide web*, and other networks. A search engine may be a dedicated one for a *website* or it may search across many sites. For example, see website: *www.google.com*. See INTERNET; WORLDWIDE WEB.

search of person. A garda, who has effected a lawful arrest, has the power to conduct a search of the arrested person's body and retain objects found in the course of the search, even without a search warrant: *The People (DPP) v McFadden* [2003] 2 ILRM 201, CCA and 2 IR 105. Where such a search yields evidence in favour of any other criminal charge, it may be retained by the gardaí to prevent it being removed or destroyed.

A garda conducting a search of a person in custody must ensure, so far as practicable, that the person understands the reason for the search and that it is conducted with due respect for the person being searched: Treatment of Persons in Custody in Garda Siochána Stations Regulations 1987, SI No 119 of 1987, reg 17(1). A failure on the part of the garda to observe any provision of the 1987 Regulations does not of itself render that person liable to any criminal or civil proceedings, or of itself affect the lawfulness of the custody of the detained person, or the admissibility in evidence of any statement made by him: Criminal Justice Act 1984, s 73.

However, the lawful exercise of the power to search a person *without* their consent, and to retain articles found thereby, is subject to the precondition that the person is informed of the reason for the search (*McFadden* case). A search of a person in custody involving removal of underclothing must, where practicable, be carried out by a

doctor (1987 Regulations, reg 17(4)). See
DRUGS, MISUSE OF; STOP AND SEARCH.

search warrant. A written order giving
authority to the person named therein to
enter specified premises and to search for
and seize specified property. Certain statutes empower the issuing of a warrant
which permits not only the searching of
premises but also any persons found on the
premises e g Offences Against the State
Act 1939, s 29 and Misuse of Drugs
Act 1977, s 26(2). The Gardaí have wide
powers of search and seizure for which they
do not require the protection of a search
warrant: *Jennings v Quinn* [1968] IR 305.

Some statutes require that the information grounding an application for a search
warrant is to be laid by a particular person
e g a member of the Garda Síochána not
below the rank of inspector.

A search warrant is not invalidated by the
inclusion of an error which was not calculated to mislead and which did not in fact
mislead: *DPP v Edgeworth* [2001] 2 IR 131,
SC. However, the Supreme Court has held
that where a search warrant, obtained pursuant to customs law, carries on its face a
statement that it has been issued on a basis
which is not authorised by statute, the
warrant is invalid and must be quashed:
Single Imports Ltd v Revenue Commissioners
[2000] 2 IR 243, SC.

A search warrant may be issued by someone who is not a judge e g a peace commissioner (qv): *Ryan v O'Callaghan* [1987]
HC; Larceny Act 1916, s 42, since
repealed. There is provision for the issue by
the District Court of a warrant for the
search of any place and the persons found
there, when the court is satisfied that there
are reasonable grounds for suspecting that
evidence of an offence under this Act is to
be found in the place: Criminal Justice
(Theft and Fraud Offences) Act 2001,
ss 48–49.

For power of a garda to seize any property during a search which he believes to be
evidence of an offence, see Criminal Law
Act 1976, s 9. For power to search for
material relevant to an investigation outside
the State, see Criminal Justice Act 1994,
s 55 and SI No 179 of 2003 (designating
the State of Israel, the Rwandese Republic,
and the Kingdom of Thailand). However, a
search warrant, issued pursuant to a 'letter
of request' from another jurisdiction under
s 55, is invalid if the 'letter of request' is
sent via a route contrary to that specified in

the legislation: *Creaven v Minister for Justice*
(24 February 2004, unreported). For application procedure and forms relating to
search warrants under various statutes, see
DCR 1997 Ord 34 as amended by District
Court (Company Law Enforcement)
Rules 2002, SI No 207 of 2002 and District Court (Theft and Fraud Offences)
Rules 2003, SI No 412 of 2003.

See *The People (DPP) v Balfe* [1998] 4 IR
50, CCA. See also Criminal Justice
Act 1984, s 6; Criminal Damage Act 1991,
s 13; Child Care Act 1991, s 35; Criminal
Justice (Sexual Offences) Act 1993,
ss 10(1) and 12; Regulation of Information
Act 1995, s 9; Stock Exchange Act 1995,
s 66 as amended by Investor Compensation
Act 1998, s 82; Criminal Assets Bureau
Act 1996, s 14; Criminal Justice (Miscella-
neous Provisions) Act 1997, s 10; Road
Transport Act 1999, s 16; Copyright and
Related Rights Act 2000, ss 137 and 245;
Communications Regulation Act 2002,
s 40; Competition Act 2002, s 45(4);
Employment Permits Act 2003, s 2(5);
Immigration Act 2004, s 15; Criminal Jus-
tice Bill 2004, ss 5, 10, 12 and 34–36. See
ENTRY AND SEARCH; FORCIBLE ENTRY;
STOP AND SEARCH; WARRANT.

searches. Investigations made by or on
behalf of a purchaser for the purpose of
finding any incumbrances affecting the title
to property. Searches in the Registry of
Deeds comprise: (a) *hand search* which may
be made by any member of the public; (b)
official search with the issue of an official
certificate of the result.

Official searches comprise a *common
search* and a *negative search*, the latter rendering the officials, signing the certificate
issued therein, liable to damages to the
party aggrieved by any fraud, collusion or
neglect in making the search. The search is
directed at ascertaining whether any acts
are disclosed by the Registry which are
inconsistent with the title as disclosed by
the *abstract of title* (qv).

It may be necessary to conduct a search
in the Companies Office in respect of
charges registered pursuant to the Companies Act 1963: *Roche v Peilow* [1986]
ILRM 189. The Controller of Patents will
on request cause a search to be made as
regards any product, process or apparatus:
Patents Act 1992, s 89. A search report is
an essential prerequisite to any action for
infringement of a *short-term* patent (qv) (PA
1992, s 66). Where there is provision for a

search of an employee's property contained in the contract of employment, failure to comply with a search request, can be sufficient ground for dismissal: *Donohoe v Professional Contract Services Ltd* [1997] ELR 35, EAT. For search of a non-national or his luggage, see Immigration Act 2004, s 7(3). For search of ship or fixed platform, see Maritime Security Act 2004, s 6. See CHARGE, REGISTRATION OF; LAND REGISTRATION.

seashore. The foreshore (qv) and every beach, bank, and cliff contiguous thereto and includes all sands and rocks contiguous to the foreshore; the removal of beach material (qv) from the seashore in contravention of a *prohibitory order* is an offence: Foreshore Act 1933, ss 1 and 6.

A *seashore* has the same meaning as in the Foreshore Act 1933: Planning and Development Act 2000, s 2(1). Preserving any existing *right of way*, in particular rights of way which give access to the seashore, is an objective which may be indicated in the *development plan* of a planning authority (PDA 2000, s 10, Sch 1, Pt IV, para 8). See FORESHORE; SHORE.

season, open. See OPEN SEASON.

seat. It is not permissible for a person to be admitted to a theatre after 9.30pm unless he has previously engaged or paid for a *seat* in that theatre: Intoxicating Liquor Act 1927, s 20. *Seat* must be interpreted as including a place of standing: *DPP v Tivoli Cinema Ltd* [1999] 2 ILRM 153, SC and 2 IR 260.

seat belt. See SAFETY BELT.

seat of corporation. The domicile of a corporation; a corporation has its seat in the State if, but only if: (a) it was incorporated or formed under the law of the State, or (b) its central management and control is exercised in the State: Jurisdiction of Courts and Enforcement of Judgments Act 1998, s 15(2) and Sch 9, Pt III. The *Brussels I Regulation* on the recognition and enforcement of judgments in civil and commercial matters, replaces the 1998 Act as from 1 March 2002 for all EU States except Denmark: EC (Civil and Commercial Judgments) Regulations 2002, SI No 52 of 2002. Under this *Regulation*, a company or other legal person is domiciled at the place where it has its *statutory seat*, central administration, or principal place of business; for the UK and Ireland *statutory seat* means the registered office or, where there is no such office anywhere, the place

of incorporation or, where there is no such place anywhere, the place under the law of which the formation took place (*Regulation* art 60).

seaweed. It has been held that the general public has no right to enter on the foreshore (qv) to take away seaweed: *Mahoney v Neenan* [1966] IR 559. However, seaweed driven above high water mark belongs to the owner of the land upon which it is driven and seaweed floating in the sea may be recovered by the general public in exercise of the public right to fish in the sea: *Brew v Haren* [1877] IR 11 CL 198.

seaworthiness of ship. In a voyage policy (qv) of insurance there is an implied warranty that at the commencement of the voyage the ship shall be seaworthy for the purposes of the particular adventure insured: Marine Insurance Act 1906, s 39(1). See PASSENGER BOAT; PASSENGER SHIP.

second mortgage. A mortgage subsequent to a prior mortgage. See PRIOR MORTGAGE.

second opinion. 'Patients are entitled to a second or further medical opinion about their illness. Doctors must either initiate or facilitate a request for this and provide the information necessary for an appropriate referral': Medical Council, *A Guide to Ethical Conduct and Behaviour* (6th edn, 2004) para 3.7. Even if a general practitioner is not convinced that a referral to a consultant is necessary, he is required to accept and facilitate a request for such referral (para 12.1).

secondary facts. Inferred facts; facts which do not follow directly from an assessment or evaluation of the credibility of the witnesses by the trial judge, or the weight to be attached to their evidence, but derive from inferences drawn from the *primary* facts. The Supreme Court will draw its own inferences on an appeal where it considers that the inferences drawn by the trial judge were not correct: *JM and GM v An Bord Uchtála* [1988] ILRM 203; *Hanrahan v Merck Sharpe & Dohme (Irl) Ltd* [1988] ILRM 629, SC. See also *Pernod Ricard v FII (Fyffes)* 7 ILT Dig [1989] 53. Contrast with PRIMARY FACT. See FACT.

secondary picketing. Picketing of an employer who is not a party to a trade dispute. It is lawful if it is reasonable for the picketers to believe at the commencement of their attendance and throughout the continuance of their attendance that the employer being picketed has directly *assisted* the employer in dispute for the purposes of frustrating the strike or other industrial action: Industrial Relations Act 1990, s 11. Any action taken by an employer in the health services to maintain life-preserving services, during the strike or industrial action, does not constitute assistance (IRA 1990, s 11(3)). See PICKETING; STRIKE.

secondment. Temporary removal from employment. There is generally a provision in legislation establishing state-sponsored organisations that an employee stands *seconded* from employment with the organisation immediately upon election to either House of the Oireachtas or of the Assembly of the European Communities until he ceases to be a member eg see Industrial Development Act 1986, s 40(2); Environmental Protection Agency Act 1992, s 35(2).

During the period of *secondment* of a garda to the Police Service of Northern Ireland, the garda continues to be paid as a member of the Garda Síochána but is not subject to the direction or control of the Commissioner: Garda Síochána (Police Co-operation) Act 2003, s 4.

secret, official. See OFFICIAL SECRET.

secret ballot. See BALLOT; STRIKE.

secret manufacturing process. See PUBLIC JUSTICE.

secret prior use. Acts carried out before the date of filing or priority of a patent by a person in the State which would have constituted an infringement of the patent if it were in force: Patents Act 1992, s 55(1). Such a person is allowed to continue to carry out such acts and to assign his rights without infringing the patent (PA 1992, s 55(2)).

secret profit. It is a breach of duty for an agent to make a secret profit, or accept a bribe, beyond the commission agreed with the principal, in which event the principal: may recover the amount of the secret profit from the agent; may refuse to pay the agent commission; may dismiss the agent without notice; may repudiate the contract the subject of the secret payment whether or not the secret payment had had any effect on the contract; and may sue the agent receiving and the third party giving the secret payment for any loss he may have sustained by entering the contract. An agent receiving and a person paying a bribe commit a criminal offence: Prevention of Corruption Act 1906. See BRIBERY AND CORRUPTION.

secret societies. The promotion of secret societies within the army or Garda Síochána is an offence: Offences Against the State Act 1939, s 16.

secret trust. An express trust (qv) based on the expressed intention of the settlor communicated to and acquiesced in by the secret trustee. A secret trust may be a *fully secret* one where the existence of the trust or its terms are not disclosed in the will or other instrument creating it: *Revenue Commissioners v Stapleton* [1937] IR 225; or a *half secret* trust where property is given on trust to trustees but the particulars of the trust are not disclosed in the will or instrument itself: *Re Browne* [1944] IR 90.

A secret trust by will must be communicated to the legatee in the testator's lifetime before or after the execution of the will; the legatee must accept the trust, or at least must not object; the terms of the trust must not be vague or uncertain; and the trust must not be illegal: *Re Kings Estate* [1888] 21 LR Ir 273.

The principles of law applicable to *half secret* trusts and *fully secret* trusts are the same; the only difference between these trusts is that the person named in the will is an express trustee in the case of a half secret trust and a beneficiary in the case of a fully secret trust: *Re Prendiville* [1995] 2 ILRM 578, HC.

secret voting. See BALLOT.

secretary. The person in a company whose principal function is regarded as being to ensure that the company's affairs are conducted in accordance with the law and with its own regulations. Every company must have a secretary, who may be one of the directors: Companies Act 1963, s 175.

There are no professional qualifications required of a secretary; the position may be occupied by a body corporate. However, the directors of a *public limited company* must take all reasonable steps to ensure that the secretary is a person who appears to them to have the requisite knowledge and experience to discharge the functions of secretary: Companies Act 1990, s 236. A register must be kept by a company of the name and address of its secretary: CA 1963, s 195 as substituted by the CA 1990, s 51. The secretary must also be named in the statement required to be delivered to the Registrar of Companies: Companies Amendment Act 1982, s 3.

It is the duty of each director and secretary of a company to ensure that the requirements of the Companies Acts are complied with by the company: Companies Act 1963, s 383(3) as substituted by Company Law Enforcement Act 2001, s 100. In addition, the duties of the secretary are, *inter alia*, to sign the annual return which is made to the Registrar; to issue share and debenture certificates; to deliver to the Registrar a return of all allotments of shares; to keep and make available for inspection the minutes of general meetings and the various registers concerning shareholders, debenture holders, charges, director and secretaries; to send out copies of the balance sheet and the auditors' and directors' reports; and to ensure that the company's name is published on its business letters.

Every company must, within 30 days of beginning its trade, profession or business, deliver a written statement to the Revenue Commissioners which gives specified information, including the company's name and address, and the name of the company secretary, or in the case of a non-resident company, the name of the company's agent or representative in the State: Taxes Consolidation Act 1997, s 882. For secretary of building society, see Building Societies Act 1989, ss 14(2) and 49. [Bibliography: Doyle.] See REGISTRAR OF COMPANIES.

section 3 resolution. Generally understood to mean a resolution of the elected members of a local authority directing that certain works, of which they have been informed, not be proceeded with: City and County Management (Amendment) Act 1955, s 3. It does not apply to works which the authority is required by statute or court order to undertake; this includes works which the authority is under a statutory duty to perform, even though it may have an administrative discretion as to the location in which the works are carried out: *East Wicklow Conservation Community Ltd v Wicklow Co Council* [1997] 2 ILRM 72, SC.

A *section 3 resolution* is now a *section 139 resolution* of the Local Government Act 2001, which also repeals the 1955 Act. The manager is required to comply with such a resolution duly and lawfully passed (LGA 2001, s 139(2)).

section 4 resolution. Generally understood to mean a resolution of the elected members of a local authority requiring the manager to do any particular act, matter or thing: City and County Management (Amendment) Act 1955, s 4. Under the section, a local authority may by resolution

require any particular act, matter or thing specifically mentioned in the resolution and which the local authority or the manager can lawfully do or effect, to be done or effected in performance of the executive functions of the local authority.

A *section 4 resolution* is now a *section 140 resolution* of the Local Government Act 2001, which also repeals the 1955 Act.

The intention to propose such a resolution must be given in writing to the manager and, except for planning matters, must be signed by at least three members of the council; the resolution must be passed by a majority of members present but in circumstances where at least one-third of the total number of the members of the local authority vote in favour.

There are limitations, however, in that such a resolution does not apply or extend to the performance of any function of a local authority *generally*, or to the *executive* functions of the manager in relation to employees of the local authority, or so as to prevent the performance of a function required by law or court order (LGA 2001, s 140(11)).

In addition such a resolution can only be put into effect if and when and so far as money for the purpose is or has been provided. Once such a resolution is validly passed, the elected members are *functus officii* and it is likely that it cannot be rescinded, revoked or varied: Interpretation Act 1937, s 15(3). A council resolution which is not in exercise of a reserved function of a power derived from (the former) s 4 is not binding on the manager; he is free to act on it as he thinks fit: *Browne v Dundalk UDC* [1993] ILRM 328, HC.

Section 4 resolutions have been frequently used to require the manager to decide an application for planning permission (qv) in a particular manner. Since 1991, the notice required for a section 4 resolution in planning matters must be signed by not less than three-quarters of the total members and the resolution requires not less than three-quarters of the total members voting in favour to be passed: Local Government Act 1991, ss 44–45. See now Planning and Development Act 2000, s 34(7) and Local Government Act 2001, s 140(11).

It has been held that a planning authority exercising its powers under (the former) s 4 of the 1955 Act must do so in a judicial manner, without taking into consideration irrelevant considerations, and that once such a resolution is made the Manager was bound to carry out the decision as a mere executive duty: *Sharpe Ltd v Dublin City & County Manager* [1989] ILRM 545; *Flanagan v Galway City & County Manager* [1990] 2 IR 66. It has been held that (the former) s 4 motions are more suited to executive functions which do not have to be exercised in a judicial manner: *Kenny Homes & Co v Galway County Manager* [1995] 2 ILRM 586, HC and 1 IR 178. See also *Griffin v Galway City & Co Mgr* [1991] 9 ILT Dig 226, HC. In a particular case, the High Court held that the County Manager was entitled to conclude that the section 4 motion was invalid and thus not binding on him: *Wicklow County Council v Wicklow County Manager, An Bord Pleanála, and Byrne* [2003] ITLR (31 March) HC and FL 9024. The Supreme Court has held that a s 4 resolution in favour of a planning application does not constitute a decision to grant permission: *Kerry Co Council v Lovett* [2003] 2 IR 589, SC and ITLR (6 October). See COUNTY MANAGER; PLANNING PERMISSION, DECISION ON; SURCHARGE.

section 23 relief. Generally understood to mean the tax relief obtained by a person incurring expenditure on the construction of certain residential premises for letting, whereby he can deduct the qualifying expenditure from the resulting rental income: Finance Act 1981, s 23 and 24. The qualifying period of this scheme was originally extended to 31 March 1987: Finance Act 1983, s 29–30. The qualifying period of the restored scheme was 27 January 1988 to 31 March 1991: Finance Act 1988, s 27. There was also a scheme of tax relief applicable to expenditure incurred on the *refurbishment* of *specified buildings*: Finance Act 1985, s 21 which was similarly restored: Finance Act 1988, s 28. There was a further extension of the time limits in areas designated under the urban renewal scheme ie to end November 1993 in respect of laying foundations for new-building developments, while the final deadline for relief was extended to 31 July 1994: Finance Act 1993, s 32. Certain tax reliefs are now provided for in the Taxes Consolidation Act 1997 as amended for specified areas eg Custom House Docks Area; Temple Bar Area; qualifying resort areas; designated islands; Dublin Dockland Area; designated areas, streets, enterprise areas, multi-storey car parks in certain urban areas; and qualifying areas including rural areas (TCA 1997, ss 322–372T).

In 2002, the various 'section 23' type reliefs were codified and consolidated: Finance Act 2002, s 24 and Sch 2. See also Finance Act 2004, s 26. See Practice Note in *Law Society Gazette* (June 2004) 44. [Bibliography: Connolly, Bradley & Purcell; Judge].

section 31. Popularly understood to refer to the power given to the Minister to direct Radio Telefis Éireann by order to refrain from broadcasting any matter or any matter of a particular class, where the Minister is of the opinion that the broadcast of such matter would be likely to promote, or incite to, crime or would tend to undermine the authority of the State: Broadcasting Authority Act 1960, s 31(1) as amended by the Broadcasting Authority Act 1976, s 16. Any such order may remain in force for not greater than twelve months, which period may be extended (BAA 1960, s 31(1)A and (1)B). Any such order also applies to independent radio and television broadcasts: Radio and Television Act 1988, ss 12 and 18.

The European Commission of Human Rights has held that the restrictions imposed by Section 31 were legitimate: *Purcell, O'Cuaig & Ors v Ireland* (1991) Irish Times, 11 June. The Supreme Court has held that while RTÉ has a legal duty to obey a ministerial order made pursuant to section 31 prohibiting the broadcast of reports of interviews with spokesmen for Sinn Féin, such a duty did not extend to prohibiting the broadcasting on any subject or under any circumstances of a person who was a member of Sinn Féin: *O'Toole v RTÉ (No 2)* [1993] ILRM 458, SC. See also *The State (Lynch) v Cooney* [1983] ILRM 89; *O'Toole v RTÉ* [1993] ILRM 454; *Brandon Book Publishers Ltd v RTÉ* [1993 HC] ILRM 806.

The last order under s 31 was SI No 1 of 1993 as, in January 1994, the government decided not to renew the order.

secundum legem. [According to law].

secured creditor. See CREDITOR.

securities. (1) Things deposited or pledged to ensure the fulfilling of an obligation. (2) Written evidence of ownership eg certificates. (3) *Securities* are also defined as shares in the share capital of any body corporate or stock of any body corporate, or debentures, debenture stock or bonds of any body corporate: Central Bank Act 1971, s 2 as amended by Central Bank and Financial Services Authority of Ireland Act 2003, s 35, Sch 1. Certain designated securities may be transferred by electronic means: Central Bank Act 1989, s 139 as amended by Central Bank Act 1997, s 63. See also Taxes Consolidation Act 1997, s 749 as amended by Finance Act 2003, s 31; Building Societies Act 1989, s 29(2)(c).

(4) Shares, debt securities, collective investment schemes, miscellaneous warrants, certificates representing debt securities, warrants or options to subscribe or purchase securities and other securities of any description: Listing Rules 2000 (Definitions, as amended by Irish Stock Exchange Ltd). [Bibliography: Johnston.] See CREST; DEBENTURE; MARKET VALUE; PRE-EMPTION; PRICE STABILISING; STOCK EXCHANGE; UNIT TRUST SCHEME.

securitisation of mortgage. The transfer, sale or assignment of mortgages to a company or body, usually referred to as a *special purpose vehicle* (SPV). Securitisations are often very complex transactions, the purpose of which is to enable funds of a financial mortgage institution (bank or building society or lender) tied up in existing mortgages, to be used to create new funds so that the institution can lend to new customers. Typically the institution assigns equitably to the SPV, which issues interest bearing bonds to investors, which interest is funded by the mortgage loan portfolio, the proceeds of the bond issue going to the institution. Often the mortgagor (borrower) is unaware of the underlying funding arrangement as his relationship with the institution is unchanged.

The Minister is empowered to make regulations governing the securitisation of mortgages of residential property: Housing (Miscellaneous Provisions) Act 1992, s 13. These regulations may deal generally with the protection of the interests of mortgagors and may prescribe such matters as e g information to be given to mortgagors, the obtaining of their consent to the disposal, and undertakings to be given by the body acquiring the mortgage.

The management of these *qualifying assets*, which the body acquires from the original lender, is subject to tax on the profit or gains: Finance Acts 1991, s 31 and 1996, s 55. Interest paid by a securitisation vehicle in respect of a subordinated debt,

subject to a limit of 25% of subordinated debt carried, is not treated as a distribution and a tax deduction is allowable for the interest paid: Taxes Consolidation Act 1997, s 110 as substituted by Finance Act 2003, s 48. The 2003 Act provision broadens the nature of the assets which may be securitised and the type of persons from whom they may be acquired, as well as relaxing the rules relating to the tax deductions available to a securitisation vehicle.

Provision has been made for the securitisation of local authority housing loans, primarily to finance payments by the State in respect of adopting EU equality provisions for social security payments: Securitisation (Proceeds of Certain Mortgages) Act 1995. See also Stamp Duties Consolidation Act 1999, s 105. See ASSET COVERED SECURITIES; SYNTHETIC SECURITISATION.

security consultant. Means a person who for remuneration advises on methods of protecting property, including information recorded in non-legible form, from vandalism, intrusion, trespass, theft or from being otherwise damaged or interfered with but does not include: (a) a person who advises on such methods in the ordinary course of carrying out an audit, or (b) an installer of security equipment: Private Security Services Act 2004, s 2(1). See PRIVATE SECURITY AUTHORITY.

security equipment, installer of. Means a person: (a) who for remuneration installs, maintains, repairs or services electronic or other devices designed, constructed or adapted to give warning of or monitor or record unauthorised entry or misconduct on or in the vicinity of premises, and (b) who may in that connection, as necessary, advise on methods of protecting the devices from damage or interference: Private Security Services Act 2004, s 2(1). See PRIVATE SECURITY AUTHORITY.

security guard. Means a person who for remuneration guards or patrols or provides any other protective services in relation to persons or property and includes a person who for those purposes: (a) provides those services exclusively for an employer who is not a private security employer, (b) monitors security equipment, (c) supervises and inspects security guards while they are guarding or patrolling, (d) accompanies a guard dog while the dog is guarding or patrolling, or (e) controls, supervises, regulates, restricts or directs the movements of persons, whether in vehicles or otherwise, in relation to any premises or any other place where a public or private event or function is taking place or about to take place: Private Security Services Act 2004, s 2(1). See PRIVATE SECURITY AUTHORITY.

security for costs. The security, by way of lodgment into court of money or by a bond, which the court may order the plaintiff in an action to provide, on the application of the defendant: RSC Ord 29. Security may be ordered eg: (a) where the plaintiff resides outside the European Union and the defendant has a defence upon the merits; (b) where an insolvent person sues as nominal plaintiff for another; (c) where the plaintiff is a company without realisable assets. See *Thalle v Soares* [1957] IR 182.

The right to security for costs is not an absolute one; the court has to exercise a discretion based on the facts of the individual case: *Fares v Wiles* [1994] ILRM 465, SC. No unnecessary monetary obstacle should be placed in the path of those who seek access to the courts: *Malone v Brown Thomas & Co Ltd* [1995] 1 ILRM 369, SC.

The court has a discretion as regards a company's security for costs pursuant to an application under the Companies Act 1963, s 390 (ie where there is reason to believe that the company will be unable to pay the defendant's costs if successful in his defence): *SPUC v Grogan* [1990] ITLR (12 February) HC. The court will dismiss an appeal by a company where the company fails to provide security for costs in the amount fixed: *Superwood Holdings plc v Sun Alliance and London Insurance plc* (15 March 2004, unreported) SC. See 'Security for Costs and the Separate Corporate Personality' by Cathal Murphy BL in *Bar Review* (April 2003) 86.

Where the defendants establish that they appear to have a *prima facie* defence, the onus passes to the plaintiff company to satisfy the court that it should exercise its discretion: *Wexford Rope and Twine Co Ltd v Gaynor & Modler* [2000] ITLR (17 April) HC. Security for costs will not be ordered where a plaintiff insolvent company has sufficient funds available to pay the costs, as these costs would rank in priority to all other claims: Companies Act 1963, ss 281

and 285; *Comhlucht Paipéar Riomhaireachta Teo v Údarás na Gaeltachta* [1990] ILRM 266, SC.

A *statutory regulator* is not prevented from obtaining an order for security for costs in judicial review proceedings: *Broadnet Ireland Ltd v Office of the Director of Telecommunications Regulation* [2000] 3 IR 281, HC and [2000] 2 ILRM 241, HC.

Security for costs of a *respondent* (qv) will be ordered only in special circumstances.

For provisions governing a party to proceedings in the Circuit Court seeking security for costs from another party, see Circuit Court Rules 2001 Ord 16. For provisions dealing with security for costs in the District Court, see DCR 1997 Ord 43. See *SEE Co Ltd v Public Lighting Services* [1987] ILRM 255; *Salih v General Accident Fire Life Assurance Corporation* [1987] IR 628, HC; *Irish Commercial Society v Plunkett* [1987] ILRM 504; *Performing Rights Society Ltd v Casey* [1990] 8 ILT Dig 105; *Irish Press plc v Ingersoll Irish Publications Ltd* [1995] 1 ILRM 117, SC; *Pitt v Bolger* [1996] 2 ILRM 68, HC and [1996] 1 IR 108, HC; *Lancefort Ltd v An Bord Pleanála* [1998] 2 IR 511, HC; *Lismore Homes Ltd (in receivership) v Bank of Ireland Finance Ltd* [1999] 1 IR 501, SC and [2001] 3 IR 536, SC and [2002] 1 ILRM 541, SC. See also Arbitration Act 1954, s 22(1)(a); Building Societies Act 1989, s 64(6); Patents Act 1992, s 91; Residential Tenancies Act 2004, s 124(4). [Bibliography: Buckley, Melody; Buttimore (2).] See COURT PROTECTION OF COMPANY, PETITION FOR; NORTHERN IRELAND; SUFFICIENT.

security for costs, amount. The amount of security for costs and the time and manner in which it is given is determined by the Master of the High Court; the court must bear in mind that no litigant should be denied access to the courts because of poverty: RSC Ord 29, rr 6–7 and *Fallon v An Bord Pleanála* [1991] ILRM 799, SC. There is no fixed or invariable practice that an order for security of costs is confined to one third of the costs: *Village Residents Association v An Bord Pleanála* [2000] 2 ILRM 59, HC.

Where security for costs of discovery is ordered, the amount of the security will be calculated on the basis of such a substantial proportion of the total costs of discovery as appears to be justified from the evidence before the court: *Framus Ltd v CRH plc*

[2003] 1 ILRM 462, HC. In determining the ability of the plaintiff to pay the costs of a successful defendant, the cost of the High Court only should be considered and not the costs of a possible appeal to the Supreme Court: *Irish Press Ltd v Warburg Pincus & Co Ltd* [1997] 2 ILRM 263, HC.

security for costs, failure to comply. The High Court has a general discretion to strike out a plaintiff's action for failure to comply with an order for security for costs: *Lough Neagh Explorations Ltd v Morrice & Minister for Transport* [1999] 1 ILRM 62, HC. The Supreme Court, in upholding the High Court decision, held that this discretion was the ultimate sanction to be used sparingly and only in extreme cases to secure compliance with the rules, rather than to punish the defaulter: *Lough Neagh Explorations Ltd v Morrice* [1999] 4 IR 515, SC

security for costs, non-resident plaintiff. Neither mere residence outside the jurisdiction nor the poverty of the appellant is a sufficient justification for compelling an appellant to lodge security for costs: *Malone v Brown Thomas & Co Ltd* [1995] 1 ILRM 369, SC. In a particular case, it was held that as an individual litigant, who was a plaintiff resident in Ireland, could not be ordered to give security for costs, a plaintiff who was resident outside Ireland, but within the European Union, should not be so ordered: *Maher v Phelan* [1996] 1 ILRM 359, HC and [1996] 1 IR 95, HC; Treaty of Rome 1957, art 7; now EC Treaty, art 14 of the consolidated (2002) version. See also *Proetta v Neil* [1996] 1 ILRM 457, HC and [1996] 1 IR 100, HC.

As regards international commercial arbitration, a non-resident person or company cannot be ordered to provide security for costs solely on the grounds of their non-residence: Arbitration (International Commercial) Act 1998, s 7(2).

security for costs, refusal of. The court may refuse to order security if a *prima facie* case has been made by the plaintiff that his inability to give security flows from the wrong committed by the defendant: *Collins v Doyle* [1982] ILRM 495; *Jack O'Toole Ltd v MacEoin Kelly* [1987] ILRM 269. The onus of proof rests with the plaintiff to adduce *prima facie* evidence of the alleged causal connection: *Framus Ltd v CRH plc* [2003] 1 ILRM 462, HC. Where the financial status of the plaintiff is inextricably linked to the outcome of the proceedings,

the court will exercise its discretion against ordering security for costs: *Ochre Ridge Ltd v Cork Bonded Warehouses Ltd* [2001] ITLR (5 February).

security of tenure. See TENURE, SECURITY OF.

security service. Means a service provided by a private security employer or by any one of the following persons in the course of an employment or as an independent contractor: (a) door supervisor, (b) supplier or installer of security equipment, (c) private investigator, (d) security consultant, (e) security guard, (f) provider of protected forms of transport, (g) locksmith, (h) supplier or installer of safes: Private Security Services Act 2004, s 2(1). However, except in the case of a door supervisor or security guard, a *security service* does not include a service provided by a person whose principal function is to provide it only for the person's employer. There is a prohibition on the provision of an unlicensed *security service* (PSSA 2004, s 37), and on employing an unlicensed person (PSSA 2004, s 38). See PRIVATE SECURITY AUTHORITY.

secus. [Otherwise].

sed quaere. [But question.] Enquire further.

sedition. The publication, orally or in writing, of words intended to bring into hatred or contempt, or to excite disaffection against the government and parliament, or to raise discontent or disaffection among the people of the State or to promote ill will and hostility between different classes of people: *R v Burns* [1886] 26 Cox CC 335. *Sedition* must be punishable in accordance with law: 1937 Constitution, art 40(6)(1)(1). [Bibliography: Larkin.] See also LIBEL.

sed quis custodiet ipsos custodies. [But who will police the police.] See Caroline Carney SC in *Bar Review* (October/November 2002) 335.

seduction. The tort of undue persuasion of a person whereby the services of the party seduced are lost to another, where the relationship of master and servant existed between the party seduced and that other. No action now lies for inducing a spouse to leave or remain apart from the other spouse: Family Law Act 1981, s 1(1).

A parent, however, continues to have a right of action against a person who entices, harbours or seduces his child. The action is now regarded as anachronistic. See *Hamilton v Long* [1903] 2 IR 407;

Murray v Fitzgerald [1906] 2 IR 254; *Brennan v Kearns* [1943] 77 ILTR 194. See also LRC Working Paper 6 and Report No 1 of 1981. See PER QUOD SERVITIUM AMISIT.

Seed Capital Relief. See BUSINESS DEVELOPMENT SCHEME.

segregation. A housing authority is required to draw up and adopt a written statement of its policy to counteract undue segregation in housing between people of different social backgrounds: Housing Act 1988, s 20(1A) as inserted by Housing (Miscellaneous Provisions) Act 1992, s 28. This is a *reserved function* (qv) of the authority. See also HOUSING STRATEGY.

seised. Feudal term referring to one possessed of a freehold (qv).

seisin. Feudal concept of possession.

seizure. Property which is the subject of an *interim, interlocutory* or *disposal* order, may be seized by a member of the Garda Síochána or an officer of customs and excise, to prevent it being removed from the State: Proceeds of Crime Act 1996, s 15.

See also Copyright and Related Rights Act 2000, ss 127, 137 and 241. See Criminal Justice Bill 2004, s 6. See PROCEEDS OF CRIME.

self-assessment. Provision for the assessment and collection of income tax from the self-employed and certain other persons is provided for by the Finance Act 1988, ss 9–21. Self-assessment in respect of gifts and inheritance taxes was introduced by the Finance Act 1989, s 74. Companies were brought within the self-assessment procedure by the Taxation of Companies (Self-Assessment) Regulations 1989, SI 178 of 1989. See now Taxes Consolidation Act 1997, ss 950–959. 31 October has now been specified as the latest date under self-assessment for filing a tax return and payment of tax due: Finance Act 2001, s 80. [Bibliography: Cassells, Clayton & Moore.] See PRELIMINARY TAX.

self-defence. Acting so as to defend one's person, the person of another, or one's own or another's property against felonious attack. A person so acting may be excused from doing an act which would otherwise be an offence.

In relation to a charge of murder (qv), if the accused used more force than may objectively be considered to be necessary for his own protection, then the killing is unlawful; in such circumstances, the act will be murder if the accused has *malice aforethought* (qv). If the accused used more force than was reasonably necessary but no more than he honestly believed to be necessary in the circumstances, then there is no malice aforethought and the unlawful act is manslaughter: *The People (Attorney-General) v Dwyer* [1972] IR 416.

Where a judge permits the issue of self-defence to go to the jury, he is obliged in his charge to the jury to tell them what matters they should consider in relation to that defence: *Dunne v DPP* (2002) Irish Times, 26 November.

Under common law, a person who is attacked is entitled to use *proportionate* force in retaliation to protect himself; he is entitled to defend not only himself and his family but anyone else who is attacked in his presence: *People v Keatley* [1954] IR 12. The killing of a trespasser of property will only be justified where the interference involves an offence (formerly, a felony) of violence (eg robbery, arson or burglary) and only where the interference is used so as to endanger life. See also *The People (Attorney-General) v Commane* [1975] CCA; *People (DPP) v Clarke* [1995] 1 ILRM 355, CCA and [1994] 3 IR 289, CCA. See Occupiers' Liability Act 1995, s 8(a). For statutory provision on the use of force, see FORCE.

As regards international law, the International Court of Justice has held that the right of self-defence exists as an inherent right under customary international law as well as under the UN Charter: ICJ Reports 1986, para 176. See 'Self Defence – A legal basis for the attacks on Afghanistan?' by Conor Keogh BL in *Bar Review* (October/November 2001) 3.

self-employed. Safety, health and welfare at work regulations apply to a self-employed person as they apply to an employer and as if that self-employed person was an employer and his own employee: SI No 44 of 1993, reg 4(1). See also SELF-ASSESSMENT.

self-help. An extra-judicial remedy eg in the case of trespass where the person in possession may eject the trespasser using no more force than is necessary: *Green v Goddard* [1798] 2 Salk 641. The removal of persons from an aircraft who have committed or are about to commit an offence is authorised: Air Navigation and Transport Act 1975, s 4(4)(a). See DISTRESS.

self-service. Commonly understood to mean where a buyer selects goods which are exposed for sale. A sale of goods in this manner does not prevent the sale from being a sale by description: Sale of Goods Act 1893, s 13; Sale of Goods and Supply of Services Act 1980, s 10. See DESCRIPTION, SALE BY.

Sellafield MOX Plant. The Irish government in 2001 initiated legal action against the United Kingdom on two separate fronts in relation to the Mixed Oxide (MOX) plant at Sellafield in Cumbria, because of concerns about a potential nuclear accident or incident or about radioactive discharges into the Irish Sea. The first proceedings were under the OSPAR Convention, where Ireland was seeking the release of information, withheld by the UK, relating to the economic justification of the MOX plant which involves an expansion of Sellafield's radioactive operations. The Tribunal held that Ireland could not gain access to confidential information as it was not environmental information (22 July 2003). However, the Tribunal held that: (a) Ireland has a right under the OSPAR Convention to access to information on the marine environment, (b) the UK has an obligation to make such information available, and (c) Ireland has a right to redress under the Convention to vindicate its rights to such information.

The second proceedings are under the *UN Convention on the Law of the Sea 1982* (UNCLOS) in which Ireland claims that the UK has violated numerous provisions of the Convention concerning pollution, environmental impact assessments and failure to co-operate. These latter proceedings commenced in June 2003 before the Permanent Court of Arbitration in The Hague. See RADIOACTIVE SUBSTANCE.

seller. A person who sells or agrees to sell goods: Sale of Goods Act 1893, s 62. A seller may maintain an action against the buyer for the price of the goods, where the property in the goods has passed to the buyer, and the buyer wrongfully neglects and refuses to pay for the goods (SGA 1893, s 49). A seller also may maintain an action for non-acceptance of goods by the buyer (SGA 1893, s 50). See RSC Ord 4, r 13; Ord 13, r 15; Ord 27, rr 2 and 16. See *Spicer-Cowan Ireland Ltd v Play Print Ltd* [1980] HC. See UNPAID SELLER.

semble. [It appears.] Term used in law reports and text books where a proposition of law is introduced which cannot be stated too definitely as there may be doubt about

it. For example, see *Murphy v Asahi Synthetic Fibres* [1986] ILRM 24.

semi-state company. See COMPANY, STATUTORY.

semper in dubiis benigniora praeferenda. [In doubtful matters the more liberal construction should always be preferred].

semper praesumitur pro legitimatione puerorum. [It is always to be presumed that children are legitimate.] See LEGITIMACY, PRESUMPTION OF.

senator. A member of Seanad Éireann (qv). See SEVERANCE PAY; UTTERANCE.

senior counsel; SC. A senior barrister of professional eminence, called to the Inner Bar by the Chief Justice in the Supreme Court, on the approval of the government. A Senior Counsel (equivalent to a Queen's Counsel or QC in England) takes precedence over junior counsel in court and wears a silk gown (hence the phrase *to take silk*). It is unprofessional conduct for a barrister to apply to the government for admission to the Inner Bar unless that barrister has a *bona fide* intention to conduct his practice as a member of the Inner Bar and enjoys a status of professional eminence by virtue of his practice at the Bar: *Code of Conduct for the Bar of Ireland* (December 2003) r 10.2. Admission to the Inner Bar is confined to practising barristers (r 10.1). A client is never required to retain the services of a Senior Counsel (r 10.3). See BARRISTER.

sensitive personal data. Means *personal data* as to (a) the racial or ethnic origin, the political opinions or the religious or philosophical beliefs of the data subject, (b) whether the data subject is a member of a trade union, (c) the physical or mental health or condition or sexual life of the data subject, (d) the commission or alleged commission of any offence by the data subject, or (e) any proceedings for an offence committed or alleged to have been committed by the data subject: Data Protection Act 1988, s 1(1) as inserted by Data Protection (Amendment) Act 2003, s 2(a)(i).

There is a prohibition on the processing by a data controller of *sensitive personal information* unless certain conditions are met, in addition to the conditions applying to personal data. At least one of the following conditions must be met: (a) the consent of the data subject has been explicitly given, (b) processing is necessary to comply with a right or obligation on the data controller under employment law, (c) processing is necessary to protect the vital interests of the data subject eg to prevent injury or damage, (d) processing is carried out by a not-for-profit body which exists for political, philosophical or trade union purposes and does not involve disclosure to a third party, (e) the information contained in the data has been made public as a result of the deliberate steps of the data subject, (f) processing is necessary for the administration of justice, (g) processing is necessary for establishing, exercising or defending legal rights, (h) processing is necessary for medical purposes and is undertaken by a health professional or another person subject to a duty of confidentiality, (i) other conditions relating to statistical purposes, electoral activity and people's political opinions, reasons of substantial public interest, collection of taxes, entitlement to benefits eg social welfare benefits (DP(A)A 2003, s 4 inserting new DPA 1998, s 2B).

As regards manual data, the provisions in DPA 1998, s 2 dealing with the collection, processing, keeping, use and disclosure of personal data, and the additional requirements of DPA 1998, s 2B, do not come into operation until 24 October 2007 (DP(A)A 2003, s 23). However, there is a right in the meantime of access to manual data and a right to have such manual data, which is incomplete or inaccurate, rectified, erased, blocked or destroyed. See PERSONAL DATA.

sent. Under Immigration Act 1999, s 6(B) there is a requirement that a person, the subject of a deportation order, be 'sent' notification of the making of the deportation order; 'sent' means sent and not necessarily received: *DP v Governor of the Training Unit* [2001] 1 Ir 492, HC. For amendment to s 6, see Illegal Immigrants (Trafficking) Act 2000, s 10(c); Immigration Act 2004, s 16(5).

sentence. Any punishment or measure involving deprivation of liberty ordered by a court or tribunal on account of the commission of an offence: Transfer of Sentenced Persons Act 1995, s 1. This legislation makes provision for the transfer between the State and places outside the State of persons detained in prisons, hospitals or other institutions under court or tribunal orders.

Sentencing has been held to involve aspects of retribution, deterrence, protection of society, reparation and rehabilita-

tion; where a sentence incorporated elements of retribution only, it might run its course and not be varied: *The People (DPP) v MS* [2000] 2 IR 592, CCA and [2000] 2 ILRM 311, CCA. In this case the court also held that in cases relating to sexual offences, there were important aspects relating to the protection of society and rehabilitation of the defendant. A trial judge must have regard to the extent to which the accused has redeemed and rehabilitated himself into society: *DPP v B(R)* [2003] FL 7216, CCA.

Sentences are required to be proportionate to the crime and also to the personal circumstances of the accused: *The People (DPP) v Sheedy* [2000] 2 IR 184, CCA. A custodial sentence is never mandatory in the absence of statutory direction to that effect: *The People (DPP) v McCormack* [2000] 4 IR 356, CCA; *The People (DPP) v R O'D* [2000] 4 IR 361, CCA. The court, on appeal, will have regard to any unjustified disparity of sentences between a number of participants in the same crime: *DPP v Duffy and O'Toole* [2003] 2 IR 192, CCA and FL 7296.

A prosecuting barrister should not attempt by advocacy to influence the court in regard to sentence: *Code of Conduct for the Bar of Ireland* (December 2003) r 9.23. If, however, an accused person is unrepresented it is proper for a prosecuting barrister to inform the court of any mitigating circumstances. See Law Reform Commission *Consultation Paper on Sentencing* (1993) and Report (LRC 53, 1996). The Minister for Justice has stated that, in order to achieve more uniformity in sentencing, he is considering the possibility of providing a statutory basis for sentencing principles and guidelines: Minister Michael McDowell TD on 19 June 2002. See also 'Principled Discretion: Towards the development of a sentencing canon' by Tom O'Malley BL in *Bar Review* (January/February 2002) 135. See *Consultation Paper on Penalties for Minor Offences* (LRC CP 18, 2002). [Bibliography: Canny (5); O'Mahony; O'Malley (3).] See also GUILTY; OTHER OFFENCES; PUNISHMENT; REVIEW OF SENTENCE; VICTIM IMPACT REPORT.

sentence, transfer of execution of. Under draft legislation, it is proposed that: (a) in the case of a person sentenced by an Irish court who has fled from this State to his state of nationality without either commencing or completing the sentence, the

Minister for Justice may request the authorities in that state to enforce the Irish sentence; (b) in the case of Irish nationals who have fled back to this State from a sentencing state prior to the commencement or completion of a sentence, the Minister must give his consent to a request from the sentencing state before an application can be made to the High Court for a warrant for the person's arrest. The Minister will be required to satisfy himself as to certain matters before the application is made to the High Court. The criteria include a discretionary provision whereby the Minister may, having regard to all the circumstances, decide not to make an application. Following arrest, the High Court may make orders for the carrying out of the foreign sentence in Ireland: Transfer of Execution of Sentences Bill 2003.

The Bill gives effect to: (a) the provisions in *Article 2* of the Additional Protocol to the 1983 Council of Europe Convention on the Transfer of Sentenced Persons; and (b) *Articles 6–69* of the Schengen Convention (ie Chapter 5 of Title III of the Convention) dealing with transfer of enforcement of criminal judgments.

Sentence Review Group. A group established to advise the government on the administration of long-term prison sentences and to make recommendations in respect thereof to the Minister for Justice. A prisoner is not entitled to legal representation at a hearing before the Group but may be entitled to have documents disclosed to him: *Barry v Sentence Review Group* [2001] 4 IR 167, HC.

separation, judicial. See JUDICIAL SEPARATION; DIVORCE A MENSA ET THORO.

separation agreement. An agreement made between a husband and wife which usually contains terms relating to: the living apart of the parties; the custody of any children; the maintenance by one spouse of the other; the manner in which the family property is to be dealt with; an undertaking by each not to molest the other; an indemnification clause; and a covenant not to bring *judicial separation* proceedings for matrimonial misbehaviour prior to the agreement (see *Courtney v Courtney* [1923] 2 IR 31).

Such an agreement is void if it excludes or limits the operation of the Family Law (Maintenance of Spouses and Children) Act 1976 which has as its objective the protection of economically vulnerable spouses.

A separation agreement may be made a *rule of court* if the court is satisfied that it is fair and reasonable and protects the interests of both spouses and dependent children (FL(MSC)A 1976, s 8). Having the agreement a rule of court enables a spouse to have *maintenance* paid through the District Court and to have it enforced by an *attachment* (qv) of *earnings order*.

In granting a decree of *divorce*, the court may make certain orders (eg periodic payments order) to protect a dependent spouse, and dependent members of the family; in considering such orders the court is required to *have regard to* the terms of any separation agreement which had been entered into by the spouses and which is still in force: Family Law (Divorce) Act 1996, s 20(4). The court will be slow to interfere with the terms of such agreement where the parties are well-educated intelligent persons who had the benefit of competent legal advice: *MG v MG* [2000] ITLR (2 October) CFC. However, where the separation agreement has been entered into many years ago, the courts will not uphold its terms if it does not provide proper provision for the dependent spouse: *K v K* [2003] ITLR (24 February), HC and FL 6866. Various relief orders may be made by the court where spouses are legally separated outside the State and the separation is recognised as valid in the State: Family Law Act 1995, ss 23–28.

Persons who have entered into a separation agreement are barred from obtaining a decree of judicial separation under the Judicial Separation and Family Law Reform Act 1989 and consequently, the ancillary reliefs under that Act (eg property transfer order) are not available to them: *PO'D v AO'D* [1998] 1 ILRM 543, SC. See *Dalton v Dalton* [1982] ILRM 418; *PJ v JJ* [1992] ILRM 273, HC. The Dublin Solicitors' Bar Association relaunched its family law separation agreement in 2003. It is available on disc from DSBA Secretary at email: *info@dsba.ie*. [Bibliography: Kennedy & Maguire; Murtagh B; Shannon; Walpole.] See DIVORCE; DIVORCE A MENSA ET THORO; DUM CASTA CLAUSE; JUDICIAL SEPARATION; MAINTENANCE AGREEMENT; MOLESTATION; PRE-NUPTIAL AGREEMENT.

separation of powers. The division of the functions of government ie legislative, executive, and judicial, between independent separate institutions. The *legislative* power, which is the power to make laws for the State, is reserved to the Oireachtas: 1937 Constitution, art 15(2)(1). The *executive* power, which is the power to carry laws into effect, is vested in the Government (art 28(2)). The *judicial* power, which is the power to administer justice, is reserved to the Courts (art 34(1)).

The Supreme Court has held that the doctrine of the *separation of powers* required that no-one of the three institutions of government be paramount; all three institutions exercised their powers for the benefit of the State and it was for the benefit of the State that they were independent in the exercise of their respective functions: *TD (a minor) v Minister for Education* [2001] 4 IR 259, SC.

The Courts have no power to interfere with the exercise by the government of its executive functions; however, if it is clearly established that the government has acted otherwise than in accordance with the provisions of the Constitution, the Courts are obliged to intervene: *McKenna v An Taoiseach* [1996] 1 ILRM 81, SC. See also *Kavanagh v Government of Ireland* [1996] 1 ILRM 132, HC. The Oireachtas cannot alter or reverse the finding of a court because this would amount to trespass by the legislature on the judicial domain and thus contravene the constitutional separation of powers between the various organs of the State: *Howard v Commissioners of Public Works* [1994] 2 ILRM 301, HC.

See *Buckley v Attorney-General* [1950] IR 67; *Re Haughey* [1971] IR 217; *Murphy v Dublin Corporation* [1972] IR 215; *Boland v An Taoiseach* [1974] IR 338; *Crotty v An Taoiseach* [1987] ILRM 400; *The State (Calcul International) v Appeal Commissioners* [1987] HC. See 'The separation of powers and the granting of mandatory orders to enforce constitutional rights' by Blathna Ruane BL in *Bar Review* (March/April 2002). [Bibliography: Morgan.] See BYE-ELECTION; COMMUNITY LAW; COURTS; GOVERNMENT; OIREACHTAS.

sequestration. The legal process whereby a person is temporarily deprived of his property until he clears his contempt, arising from his refusal or his neglect to obey a direction to pay money into court or do any other act in a limited time, after due service of such judgment or order: RSC Ord 43, rr 2–4; App F, form 17. See also RSC Ord 42, rr 4 and 6. See Building Societies Act 1989, s 40(5).

In a particular case, the court ordered *sequestration* against directors of a company, which the court held had been operated as a vehicle to avoid liability without the essential requirements of company law being observed by the directors: *Sligo Corporation v Cartron Bay Construction* (25 May 2001, unreported).

seriatim. [In order.] Serially.

series trade mark. The proprietor of a *series* of trade marks may apply for their registration as a series in a single registration: Trade Mark Rules 1996, SI No 199 of 1996, r 30.

serious loss of capital. See CAPITAL, SERIOUS LOSS OF.

seriously ill patient. 'For the seriously ill patient who is unable to communicate or understand, it is desirable that the doctor discusses management with the next of kin or the legal guardians prior to the doctor reaching a decision particularly about the use or non-use of treatments which will not contribute to recovery from the primary illness': Medical Council, *A Guide to Ethical Conduct and Behaviour* (6th edn, 2004) para 22.1. In the event of a dispute between the doctor and relatives, a second opinion should be sought from a suitably qualified and independent medical practitioner. The Council has reiterated its view that access to nutrition and hydration remain one of the basic needs of human beings, and all reasonable and practical efforts should be made to maintain both. See DYING PATIENT; EUTHANASIA; HUNGER STRIKE.

serjeants-at-law. Formerly senior barristers of the Order of the Coif who had an exclusive audience in the Court of Common Pleas. Judges were chosen from their ranks but the order died out with the abolition of this rule by the Judicature Act 1873, s 8. The last serjeant-at-law was AM Sullivan (1871–1959) who was called to the Irish Bar in 1892 and retained the courtesy title after the establishment of the Irish Free State (qv). For recently reported case involving Sergeant Sullivan, see *Frost v R (Lord Chancellor) – House of Lords 1920* [2000] 1 ILRM 479. [Bibliography: Hart A R; Hogan & Osborough; Sullivan].

servant. See EMPLOYEE; OFFICE HOLDER.

service. The relationship of a servant to his master. See EMPLOYEE.

service, aftersale. See SPARE PARTS.

service, contract for and of. See CONTRACT FOR SERVICES; CONTRACT OF SERVICES.

service, supply of. Includes the rendering or provision of a service or facility and an offer to supply: Sale of Goods and Supply of Services Act 1980, s 2.

In every contract for the supply of a service where the supplier is acting *in the course of a business*, the following terms are implied: (a) that the supplier has the necessary skill to render the service; (b) that he will supply the service with due skill, care and diligence; (c) that where materials are used, they will be sound and reasonably fit for the purpose for which they are required; and (d) that where goods are supplied under the contract, they will be of *merchantable quality* (qv): SGSSA 1980, s 39. *In the course of a business* includes the professions and the activities of any State authority or local authority (SGSSA 1980, s 2).

The implied terms may be excluded by agreement between the parties but where the recipient of the service *deals as consumer* (qv), the exclusion must be shown to be *fair and reasonable* (qv) and that it has been specifically brought to his attention (SGSSA 1980, s 40). There is provision for exclusions in respect of the supply of electricity and the international carriage of passengers or goods by land, sea or air.

Certain statements purporting to restrict the rights of recipients of a service can amount to an offence (SGSSA 1980, s 41). See *Brown v Norton* [1954] IR 34; *Hollier v Rambler Motors* [1972] 2 All ER 399; *Thornton v Shoe Lane Parking Ltd* [1971] 1 All ER 686. [Bibliography: Grogan, King & Donelan.] See CONTRACT; VALUE ADDED TAX.

service area. A motorway scheme or a protected road scheme may include provision for a service area; facilities or services may be provided in a service area for persons and vehicles using the motorway (qv) or protected road (qv), either directly by the road authority or by agreement with the authority or jointly: Roads Act 1993, s 54.

service by post. Where a document is required to be served by post, then, unless a contrary intention appears, it is deemed to have been effected at the time such letter would be delivered in the ordinary course of post, unless the contrary is proved: Interpretation Act 1937, s 18. See Personal Injuries Assessment Board Act 2003, s 79(1)(c). See FAX; PRESUMPTION OF REGULARITY.

service charge. A charge made by a local authority in relation to a domestic water supply or a domestic refuse collection or disposal: Local Government (Financial Proviaions) Acts 1983 and 2000. A person who pays such a charge may claim tax relief: Taxes Consolidation Act 1997, s 477 as amended by Finance Act 2002, s 6, which abolishes the ceiling on the amount claimable for services provided by local authorities and private operators, other than refuse collection services based on a 'tag' system. The maximum tax relief in respect of service charges previously was €195: Finance Act 2001, s 10.

Provision was made in 2000 to validate retrospectively service charges made by local authorities: Local Government (Financial Provisions) Act 2000. Any service charge made before the passing of this Act is deemed to have been validly made and, if not recovered, can be recovered as if the 2000 Act had been in force at the time of making of the service charge (LG(FP)A 2000, s 3(2)). This does not apply to any court proceedings concerning the validity of a charge commencing before 18 April 2000 (LG(FP)A 2000, s 4). See also *O'Connell v Cork Corporation* [2001] 3 IR 602, SC.

service industry. Any undertaking engaged in the provision of a specified service e g software development, training services, intellectual property services: Industrial Development (Services Industries) Order 2003, SI No 458 of 2003. The Order sets out the service industries which are eligible for assistance under the Industrial Development Acts. See INDUSTRIAL DEVELOPMENT.

service of civil bill. For rules governing the service of a *civil bill* within the jurisdiction of the Circuit Court, see Circuit Court Rules 2001 Ord 11, r 10 and Ord 14, r 3(vi). For service of a *domestic violence civil bill*, see Ord 59, r 5. See CIVIL BILL.

service of summons. See CASE STATED; FAX; SUMMONS, SERVICE OF; SUMMONS, SERVICE OUT OF JURISDICTION.

service out of jurisdiction. For provisions governing the service out of the jurisdiction of a *civil bill* of the Circuit Court, see Circuit Court Rules 2001 Ord 13 and Ord 14. See SUMMONS, SERVICE OUT OF JURISDICTION.

services, false or misleading statement as to. It is an offence for a person in the course or for the purposes of a trade, business or profession, to make a statement which he knows to be false or to make recklessly a statement which is false to a material degree as to a number of matters relating to a service, e g provision, nature, effect, fitness, time, manner, examination, approval, use, evaluation, or place: Consumer Information Act 1978, s 6. See *Director of Consumer Affairs v Sunshine Holidays Ltd* [1984] ILRM 551.

services, loss of. See PER QUOD SERVITIUM AMISIT.

services, provision of. Natural and legal persons in the EC have the freedom to provide services within the EC: EC Treaty, arts 45–55 of the consolidated (2002) version. 'Services' include, in particular, activities of the professions, of craftsmen, or of a commercial or industrial character (art 50). Freedom to *provide* services implies the right to *receive* services: *Luisi & Carbone v Ministero del Tesoro* [1984] ECR 377. Medical termination of pregnancy, performed in accordance with the law of the state in which it is carried out, constitutes a service: *SPUC v Grogan* 3 CMLR 1991, 849. See Council Directive (EEC) 73/148. See *A-G v X* [1992] ILRM 401. See COMMERCIAL PROCEEDINGS; DISCRIMINATION, GOODS AND SERVICES.

servient tenement. A tenement subject to a servitude or easement (qv).

servitium. Services.

servitude. An easement (qv). [Bibliography: Pearce & Mee.] See also EUROPEAN CONVENTION ON HUMAN RIGHTS; PENAL SERVITUDE.

session. The period when the Houses of the Oireachtas are sitting.

set aside. To cancel; to make void. The courts have wide powers to *set aside* previous decisions on appeal e g where judgment has been entered in default of appearance of the defendant, the court is empowered to set aside or vary the judgment upon such terms as may be just: RSC Ord 13, r 11.

A judgment of a court may be *set aside* on the grounds of fraud; the complainant is required to produce evidence of new facts discovered since the judgment which would in all probability have had a significant effect on the judgment: *Dennis v Leinster Paper Co* [1901] 2 IR 337. Fraud must be pleaded with particularity and established on the balance of probability: *Tassan Din v*

Banco Ambrosiano SPA [1991] 1 IR 569, HC. See also *Waite v House of Spring Gardens* [1985] HC; *Albans Investment Company v Sun Alliance* [1990] HC.

A grant of leave to apply for a judicial review may be *set aside* by the High Court but only in exceptional cases: *Adam v Minister for Justice* [2001] 3 IR 54, SC; *Gordon v DPP* [2002] 2 IR 369, SC and [2003] 1 ILRM 81; *Ainsworth v Minister for Defence* [2003] ITLR (21 July) HC.

A foreign judgment may not in general be re-examined on the merits: *La Societe Anonyme La Chemo-Serotherapie Belge v Dolan & Co Ltd* [1961] IR 281. For discussion on whether fraud could be a ground for setting aside a foreign judgment, see Gill in 7 ILT & SJ (1989) 29.

In the Circuit Court, an application to set aside any court proceeding for irregularity will not be allowed unless made within a reasonable time: Circuit Court Rules 2001 Ord 67, r 7. As regards the District Court and *set aside*, see DCR 1997 Ord 10, r 23. See AQUACULTURE; CANCELLATION; FINALITY IN LITIGATION; RES JUDICATA; THIRD-PARTY NOTICE.

set down. The request that a case be listed for hearing. See RSC Ord 36, r 18; RSC Ord 30, rr 1–4. See NOTICE OF TRIAL.

set off. (1) Counterbalancing of mutual debts between parties; where there is mutuality there can be set off e g *Freaney v Bank of Ireland* [1975] IR 376. See *Barrington v Bank of Ireland* [1993] ITLR (19 April) HC; *Re Frederick Inns Ltd* [1994] 1 ILRM 387, SC.

(2) A lease will generally provide that rent must be paid without any deduction or set off. However, if the lease does not so provide, a right of set off may be exercised by the tenant in respect of all just debts due by the landlord to the tenant: Deasy's Act 1860, s 48. Also a right of set off exists in respect of the reasonable cost of repairs carried out by a tenant which the landlord has failed to carry out, irrespective of a prohibition on set off contained in the lease: Landlord and Tenant (Amendment) Act 1980, s 87. This applies to certain premises; the repairs must be ones which the landlord is liable for and he must have been given a reasonable opportunity to carry them out. See also 1980 Act, s 61. For set off in relation to tenancies of dwellings, see RENT ARREARS; RENT DEPOSIT.

(3) A pleading by way of defence to the whole or part of a plaintiff's claim, whereby

the defendant claims a liquidated amount; it has the same effect as a cross action and may be used as a shield as well as a sword: RSC Ord 19, r 2. A defendant in an action may set off or set up by way of counterclaim against the claims of the plaintiff, any right or claim, and such set off has the same effect as a cross action, so as to enable the judge to pronounce a final judgment in the same action, both on the original and on the counterclaim: Circuit Court Rules 2001 Ord 15, r 7.

A counterclaim or set off in respect of a claim for unliquidated damages cannot be maintained in proceedings to recover possession brought by a lessor: *Riordan v Carroll t/a Wyvern Gallery* [1996] 2 ILRM 263, HC.

(3) Statutory arrangements are sometimes made to *set off* payments due by a party to an authority or person (e g a Minister) against payments due to that party from the authority or person e g Housing Acts 1966, s 10 and 1988, s 19. The Revenue Commissioners may set any claim for a repayment of tax against outstanding tax liabilities before making any repayment to the taxpayer: Taxes Consolidation Act 1997, s 1006A inserted by Finance Act 2000, s 164. There is also provision for appropriation of payments (TCA 1997, s 1006B). See also RSC Ord 21, r 16; Ord 99, r 37(14); DCR 1997 Ord 41, r 5. See COUNTERCLAIM; NETTING AGREEMENT.

settle. (1) To compromise (qv) a case. (2) To create a settlement (qv). (3) To draw up a document and decide upon its terms e g where counsel *settles* a document.

settled account. See ACCOUNT SETTLED.

settled land. Land which is the subject of a settlement (qv). See also Bibliography: Arnold; Pearce & Mee; Wylie (2).

settlement. (1) A compromise of a case. An agreement between parties to a dispute to settle it out of court. See Personal Injuries Assessment Board Act 2003, s 6(3)–(4). See COMPROMISE; PERSONAL INJURIES; WITHOUT PREJUDICE.

(2) A deed, will or other instrument under which any land stands for the time being limited to, or in trust for, any persons by way of succession: Settled Land Acts 1882 and 1890. Extensive powers are given by these Acts to the *tenant for life* or other limited owner in possession of the settled land, including the power of sale at the best price; the power to lease the land, or to exchange settled land for other land and take money for equality of exchange; the power to concur in partition of the land and to raise money by mortgage of the land.

Capital money, which is money raised by a tenant for life through the exercise of the powers under the Acts, must be paid to *trustees of the settlement* or into the court to be invested in authorised securities or to be applied for specified purposes, the object being the benefit of the tenant for life and all others who would have been entitled to the property in succession.

A *tenant for life* cannot delegate his functions by a *general* power of attorney: Powers of Attorney Act 1996, s 16(2). An attorney appointed under an *enduring* power of attorney has all the powers and discretions of a tenant for life within the meaning of the Settled Land Acts 1882 (SLA 1882, s 6(3)). See *Landy v Power* [1962–63] Ir Jur Rep 45; *Northern Bank Ltd v Allen* [1984] HC. See also Conveyancing Act 1881, s 60; Landlord and Tenant (Reversionary Leases) Act 1958.

(3) Any trust, disposition, covenant, agreement or arrangement, and any transfer of money or other property: Taxes Consolidation Act 1997, s 10(1). See also TCA 1997, ss 794, 808, 909. See COMPOUND SETTLEMENT; PROPERTY ADJUSTMENT ORDER; STRICT SETTLEMENT; TRUST FOR SALE.

settlement, EU. A settlement which has been approved by a court of a *contracting* state in the EU in the course of proceedings and which is enforceable in the State in which it was concluded, is enforceable in the State in which enforcement is sought under the same conditions as *authentic instruments* (qv): Jurisdiction of Courts and Enforcement of Judgments Act 1998, Sch 1, art 51. For enforcement of settlements in EU and EFTA countries, see JCEJA 1998, Sch 7, art 51.

The *Brussels I Regulation* on the recognition and enforcement of judgments in civil and commercial matters, replaces JCEJA 1998 as from 1 March 2002 for all EU states except Denmark, and provides similar arrangements for the enforcement of court approved settlements: EC (Civil and Commercial Judgments) Regulations 2002, SI No 52 of 2002 and *Regulation* art 58. See COMPROMISE.

settlor. A person who makes a settlement (qv) of his property.

several. Separate, in contrast to *joint*. See JOINT AND SEVERAL OBLIGATION.

severalty. Separate and exclusive possession. Property is said to belong to persons in *severalty* when the share of each is sole and exclusive, as contrasted with concurrent or co-ownership. See JOINT TENANCY.

severance. Where a contract is made up of several parts, and it is possible to divide it up so as to preserve some part and to disregard the other part, the contract is said to be severable. There can be no severance where the contract is illegal involving immoral or prohibited acts or otherwise against public policy: *Miller v Karlinski* [1945] TLR 85. However, severance may be possible where the illegal promise forms a collateral or incidental part of the transaction and no compelling social, economic or moral imperative would be subverted by enforcement of the rest of the transaction: *Carney v Herbert* [1985] AC 301.

Where any provisions of an Act (eg section, subsection or part thereof) is found to be unconstitutional, the remaining provisions in the Act may continue with full effect, if found by the court to be severable from the repugnant provisions; the court may hold that consequential deletions be made to other provisions of the Act: 1937 Constitution, art 15(4)(2); Companies Act 1990; *Desmond & Dedeir Ltd v Minister for Industry and Commerce* [1992] ITLR (7 December) SC.

Severance may also be possible in relation to a *covenant* in restraint of trade which is too wide, if severance leaves a covenant remaining which is not too wide: *Mulligan v Corr* [1925] IR 169: *European Chemical Industries Ltd v Bell* [1981] ILRM 345. See also *Lewis v Squash (Ireland) Ltd* [1983] ILRM 363; *Greene v Minister for Agriculture* [1990] ILRM 364, HC; *Mallon v Minister for Agriculture* [1996] 1 IR 517, SC; *Bank of Ireland v Smyth* [1996] 1 ILRM 241, SC and [1995] 2 IR 459, SC.

severance, words of. Words in a grant which denote that tenants are to take a distinct share in a property eg *in equal shares* or *equally*. See JOINT TENANCY; TENANCY IN COMMON.

severance and injurious affection. In assessing compensation to an owner of land in respect of its compulsory purchase (qv) by a local authority, regard must be had not only to the value of the land, but also to the damage, if any, to be sustained by the owner of the land by reason of the *severing* of the land taken from other land of such owner or otherwise *injuriously affecting* that other land by the exercise of the statutory power of acquisition: Land Clauses Consolidation Act 1845, s 63. It has been held that under s 63, compensation for the *injurious affection* of land retained by the owner is limited to that caused by works and user on the land which has been taken, thereby excluding injury due to user on other lands: *Chadwick & Goff v Fingal County Council* [2003] ITLR (10 November) HC, FL 8809 and [2004] 1 ILRM 521. See COMPENSATION AND COMPULSORY PURCHASE.

severance pay. Payment to an employee whose contract of employment is terminated. A scheme of *severance payments* for former holders of ministerial office and a scheme of *termination allowances* for defeated members of both Houses of the Oireachtas, has been provided for: Ministerial and Parliamentary Offices (Amendment) Act 1992, ss 5 and 10; Finance Act 1993, s 7, now Taxes Consolidation Act 1997, ss 124 and 201. See DISABILITY AND SEVERANCE.

Seville Declaration. The national declaration made by Ireland at the European Council at Seville on 21 June 2002 which stated that Ireland's policy of military neutrality is not affected by the Treaty of Nice. It also made a commitment that a referendum would have to be held before Ireland could become involved in an EU common defence. The national declaration was accompanied by a declaration by the European Council which confirmed that the EU Treaties, including the Nice Treaty, do not involve a mutual defence commitment, nor do they compromise the specific character of the security and defence policy of certain member states. It notes that Ireland has drawn attention, in this regard, to its traditional policy of military neutrality.

There is now a constitutional ban on Ireland joining an EU common defence. This was inserted by referendum on 19 October 2002, linked to a provision to enable the Nice Treaty to be ratified. See Twenty-sixth Amendment of the Constitution Act 2002. See 1937 Constitution, art 29(4)(9). For *White Paper* on Seville Declaration. see *www.irlgov.ie/iveagh*.

sewage charges. A sanitary authority is not empowered to make a charge for the disposal of domestic sewage from 31 December 1996: Local Government (Financial Provisions) Act 1997, s 12(3).

sewage effluent. As regards water pollution (qv), means effluent from any works, apparatus, plant or drainage pipe used for the disposal to waters of sewage, whether treated or untreated: Local Government (Water Pollution) Act 1977, s 1.

The Minister is empowered to make regulations for the collection, treatment, discharge or disposal of sewage or other effluents from: (a) any plant or drainage pipe vested in or controlled or used by a sanitary authority for the treatment of drinking water, or (b) any plant, sewer or drainage pipe vested in or controlled or used by a sanitary authority for the treatment and disposal of sewage or other effluents: Environmental Protection Agency Act 1992, s 59. This is to enable implementation of Council Directive on urban waste water treatment ((EC) 91/271). See also AGRICULTURAL WASTE; INTEGRATED POLLUTION CONTROL.

sewer. As regards water pollution legislation, means a sewer within the meaning of the Local Government (Sanitary Services) Acts 1878 to 1964 that is vested in or controlled by a sanitary authority, and includes a sewage treatment works, and a sewage disposal works, that is vested in or controlled by a sanitary authority: Local Government (Water Pollution) Act 1990, s 2.

There is an obligation on sanitary authorities to cause to be made and to maintain such sewers as may be necessary for effectually draining their district: Public Health (Ireland) Act 1878, s 17. Sewer includes sewers and drains of every description, except drains serving one premises only or *combined drains* (PH(I)A 1878, s 2; Local Government (Sanitary Services) Act 1948, ss 10–11).

A *combined drain* is deemed to be a drain and not a sewer and comprises a single private drain used for the drainage of two or more separate premises (LG(SS)A 1948, ss 10–11). It is not necessary for a pipe to carry sewage in order for it to be a sewer: *Ferrand v Halles Land and Building Company* [1893] 2 QB 135. A grid or grating to drain off surface water is a sewer within the meaning of PH(I)A 1878, s 2: *Merriman v Dublin Corporation* [1993] ILRM 58, HC.

Machinery exists to compel a sanitary authority to provide sewers for its district: Public Health (Ireland) Act 1896, s 15. Owners and occupiers are entitled to connect their drains to existing sewers (PH(I)A 1878, s 23 and *Ballybay Meat Exports Ltd v*

Monaghan Co Council [1990] ILRM 864, HC) and can be compelled so to connect: Local Government (Sanitary Services) Act 1962, s 8. However, the consent of the sanitary authority to such a connection is required: Planning and Development Act 2000, s 258(3). That consent is deemed to have been given where planning permission or building bye-law approval has been granted in relation to a structure (PDA 2000, s 258(7)).

Where the Environmental Protection Agency proposes to grant a waste licence for an activity which involves the discharge of a trade effluent into a sewer, it must obtain the consent of the sanitary authority: Waste Management Act 1996, s 52. See also *St Annes Estate Ltd v Dublin County Council* [1978] HC; *Merriman v Dublin Corporation* [1992] 10 ILT Dig 200, HC; *Carty v Fingal County Council* [2000] 1 ILRM 64, SC and [1999] 3 IR 577, SC. See Planning and Development Act 2000, ss 182(1), 258 and 259. See COMBINED DRAIN; INTEGRATED POLLUTION CONTROL; PUBLIC RIGHT; TRADE EFFLUENT; WAYLEAVE.

sex discrimination. Discrimination on gender grounds; it is prohibited. [Bibliography: Eardly (2).] See DISCRIMINATION; EQUAL PAY; GENDER GROUND.

sex offender. A person convicted of a *qualifying sexual offence* is required to notify the Gardaí of his name and home address within seven days of being subject to the requirement, and similarly if the person changes his name or address, or leaves the State: Sex Offenders Act 2001, s 10. The High Court has held that this requirement does not constitute a penalty and does not conflict with the Constitutional ban on retrospective offences when applied to a person convicted prior to SOA 2001: *Enright v Ireland* [2003] 2 IR 321, HC and [2004] 1 ILRM 103. The requirements however constitute a real and substantive punitive element: *DPP v Y(N)* [2002] FL 6838, CCA.

It is an offence not to comply with the notification requirement (SOA 2001, s 12). A *qualifying sexual offence* is one listed in the Schedule to the Act; the emphasis is on targeting child sex abusers and the serious sex offender (SOA 2001, s 3).

A garda, not below the rank of Chief Superintendent, may apply to the Circuit Court for a *sex offender order* against a sex offender, prohibiting the sex offender from doing one or more things specified in the order, on evidence that an order is necessary to protect the public from serious harm (SOA 2001, s 16). It is an offence to contravene such an order (SOA 2001, s 22).

It is also an offence for a sex offender to apply for or to accept work or to offer services, a necessary or regular part of which consists mainly of unsupervised access to, or contact with children or mentally impaired persons, without informing the employer/organisation of his conviction (SOA 2001, s 26).

There is now an obligation on the court, in sentencing a sex offender, to consider whether or not to impose a sentence involving *post-release supervision* (SOA 2001, ss 26–31). Non-compliance with a post-release supervision condition is an offence (SOA 2001, s 33). It has been held that a certificate for post-release supervision can be issued in respect of a crime which pre-dated SOA 2001: *DPP v Cawley* (2002) Irish Times, 15 June, CCC.

For procedures in respect of applications under SOA 2001, s 11 (discharge from obligation to notify certain information), SOA 2001, s 16 (sex offender order) and SOA 2001, s 19 (discharge or variation of sex offender order), see Circuit Court Rules (No 1) (Sex Offenders Act) 2001, SI No 433 of 2001, now incorporated in the consolidated Circuit Court Rules 2001, SI No 510 of 2001, Ord 68. See also District Court (Sex Offenders) Rules 2002, SI No 206 of 2002 for amendment to the District Court Rules 1997, SI No 93 of 1997, Ord 38 and to provide for the notification of convictions of sex offenders.

sex shop. A retail unit which *inter alia* rents or presents for viewing sexually explicit printed material or films (including videos), clothing, sex aids and toys: proposed *special planning control scheme* of Dublin City Council for O'Connell Street in March 2003. Under the scheme, planning permission will be required to open a sex shop on O'Connell Street. The scheme proposes restrictions on other developments eg newsagents, convenience store, fast food outlets, ATM lobbies, Internet cafes, phone call centres and amusement arcades. See website: *www.dublincity.ie*. See ARCHITECTURAL CONSERVATION AREA.

sex tourism. Popularly understood to mean tourist travel with the object of sexual activity. It is an offence for a citizen of the State

to do an act in a place outside the State, against or involving a child, if the act constitutes an offence under the law of the place, and if it would constitute an offence in the State if done in the State: Sexual Offences (Jurisdiction) Act 1996, s 2(1). The jurisdiction not only applies to citizens of the State, but also to persons ordinarily resident in the State. The Supreme Court has held that SO(J)A 1996, s 2(1) does not create a new offence but merely extends the jurisdiction to try existing offences: *BH v DPP* [2003] 2 IR 43, SC and FL 6873.

It is also an offence to promote information likely to promote the commission of such sexual offences or to transport a person for the purpose of enabling the offence to be committed (SO(J)A 1996, ss 3 and 4). The offences now extend to trafficking in or taking or detaining a child for sexual exploitation, or allowing a child to be used for child pornography: Child Trafficking and Pornography Act 1998, s 11. See CHILD PORNOGRAPHY.

sexual abuse. An act of sexual abuse includes: (a) any act causing, inducing or coercing a person: (i) to participate in any sexual activity, or (ii) to observe any other person engaging in any sexual activity, or (b) any act committed against, or in the presence of, a person that any reasonable person would regard as misconduct of a sexual nature: Statute of Limitations 1957, s 48A(7) inserted by Statute of Limitations (Amendment) Act 2000, s 2. If such an act is recognised by law as giving rise to a cause of action, it may place the person under a legal disability such that time does not run as regards the Statute of Limitations. See also DELAY AND SEXUAL ABUSE; DISABILITY, PERSON UNDER; CHILD ABUSE; CHILD, EMERGENCY CARE OF.

sexual advance. 'A doctor's professional position must never be used to pursue a relationship of an emotional, sexual or exploitative nature with a patient, the patient's spouse, or a near relative of a patient. The practice of medicine involves a complex affinity between doctors and their patients with the latter sometimes becoming emotionally dependent. Doctors should be aware of this and are urged to take special care and prudence in circumstances which could leave them open to an allegation of abuse of their position': Medical Council, *A Guide to Ethical Conduct and Behaviour* (6th edn, 2004) para 3.11.

sexual assault. The offence of *indecent assault* is now known as *sexual assault*: Criminal Law (Rape) (Amendment) Act 1990, s 2. The offence had its origin as and remained a common law offence; it had not been abolished with the introduction of the Non-Fatal Offences against the Person Act 1997: *Hamilton v DPP* (2000) Irish Times, 29 April, HC.

The offence of *aggravated sexual assault* is a sexual assault that involves serious violence or the threat of serious violence or is such as to cause injury, humiliation or degradation of a grave nature to the person assaulted (CL(R)(A)A 1990, s 3). It is an offence (formerly, a felony) carrying a sentence of imprisonment for life.

A sexual assault that includes: (a) penetration (however slight) of the anus or mouth by the penis, or (b) penetration (however slight) of the vagina by any object held or manipulated by another person is the offence of *rape under section 4* (CL(R)(A)A 1990, s 4). It is also an offence (formerly, a felony) carrying a sentence of life imprisonment.

The punishment on indictment for the crime of sexual assault has been increased from a maximum term of imprisonment of five years: (a) to 14 years where the victim is a person under 17 years of age; and (b) to 10 years in any other case: Sex Offenders Act 2001, s 37.

There is also provision for separate legal representation for complainants in rape and serious sexual assault cases when application is made to the court by the defence, seeking leave to adduce evidence or cross-examine about the complainant's past sexual experience with any person SOA 2001, s 34 inserting new Criminal Law (Rape) Act 1981, s 4A. [Bibliography: O'Malley T (2).] See ASSAULT, INDECENT; DOLI INCAPAX; SEX OFFENDER; SEXUAL OFFENCES.

sexual exploitation. See CHILD, SEXUAL EXPLOITATION OF; CHILD PORNOGRAPHY, CHILD TRAFFICKING; SEX TOURISM.

sexual harassment. (1) Any form of unwanted verbal, non-verbal or physical conduct of a sexual nature, being conduct which has the purpose or effect of violating a person's dignity and creating an intimidating, hostile, degrading, humiliating or offensive environment for the person: Employment Equality Act 1998, s 14A inserted by Equality Act 2004, s 8. Such unwanted conduct may consist of acts, requests, spoken words, gestures or the production, display or circulation of written words, pictures or other material. Sexual harassment constitutes discrimination by the victim's employer in relation to the victim's conditions of employment. For previous legislation, see EEA 1998, s 23 repealed by EA 2004, s 14.

'Unsolicited, unreciprocated behaviour of a sexual nature, to which the recipient objects or could not reasonably be expected to consent and may include: (a) unwanted physical conduct; (b) lewd or suggestive behaviour whether verbal or physical; (c) sexually derogative statements or sexually discriminatory remarks; (d) the display of pornographic or sexually explicit material in the workplace': definition noted with approval by Costello J in *The Health Board v BC and the Labour Court* [1994] ELR 27, HC.

The Labour Court has held that freedom from sexual harassment is a condition of work which an employee of either sex is entitled to expect and that the Court would treat any denial of that freedom as discrimination within the terms of the Employment Equality Act 1977 (repealed by EEA 1998): *A Worker v A Garage Proprietor* EE02/1985. There is an onus on an employer to inform, educate and instruct its employees on sexual harassment: *Allen v Dunnes Stores Ltd* [1996] ELR 203, EAT. An employer is only vicariously liable for the sexual harassment or assault of an employee by other employees where the employees were acting in the scope of their employment when the harassment or assault took place: *The Health Board v BC and the Labour Court* [1994] ELR 24, HC.

The Labour Court has also held that the initiating, pursuit and fulfilment by an employer of a sexual interest in a female employee without or outside that employee's consent is a breach of the 1977 Act; in considering consent the Court must have regard for the employer's dominant position in the employment relationship: *A Worker v A Company* EEO2/90 in 8 ILT & SJ [1990] 244 & [1990] ELR 187.

The Labour Court has found that a school failed in its duty to act reasonably so as to protect two female teachers from further incidents of sexual harassment by male pupils: *Murray v De La Salle School* (2002) Irish Times, 1 February. See *Two Female Teachers v Board of Management* [2001] ELR 159, EO.

Where two persons of the same sex are involved, particular circumstances must be established to justify the claim that the conduct of one constitutes sexual harassment of the other: *A Worker v A Company* [1992] ELR 40, LC. It is irrelevant that the perpetrator of the harassment is not an employee of the company if the employer was in a position to protect the worker. An employee is entitled to a work environment which is free from the fear of sexual harassment: *An Employee v An Employer* [1993] ELR 76.

In the UK it has been held that sexual harassment is a particularly degrading and unacceptable form of treatment which it must have been the intention of parliament to restrain: *Strathclyde Regional Council v Porcelli* [1986] IRLR 134 as considered in *A Limited Company v One Female Employee* EE10/1988. See also *A Worker v A Company* [1992] ELR 73, LC; *A Worker v A Company* [1993] ELR 6, LC; A *Company v A Worker* [1994] ELR 202, LC; *Williams v St James Hospital Board* [1995] ELR 180, EAT; A *Worker v An Employer* [1996] ELR 65, EO; *A Worker v A Company* [1996] ELR 85, LC; *Martin v Blooms Hotel* [1999] ELR 116, EAT; *A Female Employee v A Company* [2000] ELR 147, EO; *New Era Packaging v A Worker* [2001] ELR 122, LC. See Barry in 10 ILT & SJ (1992) 102; Flynn in 10 ILT & SJ (1992) 205; *Codd* in (1994) ELR xxxi.

(2) Sexual harassment is any form of unwanted verbal, non-verbal or physical conduct of a sexual nature, being conduct which has the purpose or effect of violating a person's dignity and creating an intimidating, hostile, degrading, humiliating or offensive environment for the person: Equal Status Act 2000, s 11(4) amended by substitution by Equality Act 2004, s 51. Such unwanted conduct may consist of acts, requests, spoken words, gestures or the production, display or circulation of written words, pictures or other material.

A person in authority in an educational establishment, a person providing services or accommodation or disposing of goods or premises, is prohibited from sexually harassing another person (ESA 2000, s 11(1)). See 'Sex equality and the Equal Status Act' by Cliona Kimber BL and Marguerite Bolger BL in *Bar Review* (January 2001) 198. [Bibliography: Bolger & Kimber; Harvey and Twomey; Reid M.] See CON-STRUCTIVE DISMISSAL; DISCRIMINATION; HARASSMENT.

sexual intercourse. Sexual intercourse is proven in cases of sexual offences (qv) by proof of *penetration*. It has been held that if the male organ entered the opening of the vagina, this amounts to penetration even if there is no emission: *The People (Attorney-General) v Dermody* [1956] IR 307. References to *sexual intercourse* in the Criminal Law (Sexual Offences) Act 1993 must be construed as references to *carnal knowledge* as defined in section 63 of the Offences against the Person Act 1861: CL(SO)A 1993, s 1(3). See BUGGERY; CARNAL KNOWLEDGE; EVIDENCE TENDING TO BASTARDISE CHILDREN.

sexual offences. These offences include: (a) *bestiality* (qv): Offences against the Person Act 1861, ss 61–62; (b) *buggery* (qv) with a person under 17 years of age or a mentally impaired person of any age: Criminal Law (Sexual Offences) Act 1993, ss 3 and 5; (c) *gross indecency* by a male with a male under 17 years of age (CL(SO)A 1993, s 4); (d) *soliciting* or *importuning* for the purposes of commission of a sexual offence (CL(SO)A 1993, s 6); (e) *unlawful carnal knowledge* of a girl under 15 years: Criminal Law Amendment Act 1935, s 1; (f) *unlawful carnal knowledge* of a girl under 17 years (CLAA 1935, ss 2–3); (g) *rape* (qv): Criminal Law (Rape) Act 1981, s 2 and Criminal Law (Rape) Act 1990; (h) indecent assault of a female (CL(R)A 1981, s 10) now called *sexual assault* (qv); (i) *aggravated sexual assault*: Criminal Law (Rape) (Amendment) Act 1990, s 3; (j) *rape* under section 4 (CL(R)(A)A 1990, s 4); (k) *sexual offences* against a child outside the State: Sexual Offences (Jurisdiction) Act 1996.

A person may be charged with more than one of these offences arising out of the same act: *O'B v Pattwell* [1994] 2 ILRM 465, SC. It has been held that SO(J)A 1996, s 2(1) is unambiguous and did not create a new offence but rather extended the jurisdiction to try certain existing offences: *BH v DPP* [2003] 2 IR 43, SC and FL 6873.

It is also an offence for a person, who has custody, charge or care of a child: (a) to cause or encourage unlawful sexual intercourse or buggery with the child; or (b) to cause or encourage the seduction or prostitution of, or sexual assault on, the child: Children Act 2001, s 249. See also Mental

Treatment Act 1945, s 254; Criminal Evidence Act 1992, s 2(1) as amended by Criminal Justice (Miscellaneous Provisions) Act 1997, s 16. See Criminal Law Act 1997, Sch 1, paras 5, 7, 10. [Bibliography: O'Malley (2); Charleton (4).] See COMPLAINT; CONSENT; PROCUREMENT; SOLICIT; TELEVISION LINK; VICTIM IMPACT STATEMENT.

sexual orientation. Means heterosexual, homosexual or bisexual orientation: Employment Equality Act 1998, s 2(1); Equal Status Act 2000, s 2(1). An employer is prohibited from discriminating against an employee or a prospective employee on the grounds of *sexual orientation* (EEA 1998, ss 6 and 8(1)). *Harassment* on the grounds of sexual orientation is also prohibited (EEA 1998, s 14A inserted by Equality Act 2004, s 8).

A dismissal from employment of a lesbian for *behaviour* arising from her sexual orientation was not discriminatory, as a man would have suffered the same treatment for a similar display of his sexual orientation: *A Worker v Brookfield Leisure Ltd* [1994] ELR 79, LC.

A person must not discriminate on *sexual orientation* grounds in disposing of goods or premises or in providing a service or accommodation; treating one person less favourably than another person, in a comparable situation, because they are of different sexual orientation is discriminatory: Equal Status Act 2000, ss 5, 6 and 3, amended by EA 2004, ss 48–49. See Flynn, *Discrimination on Grounds of Sexual Orientation* in (1993) ELR Vol 4 No 4. See O'Connor, 'Sexual Orientation and Asylum Cases' in (2003) 11 ISLR 130. [Bibliography: Reid M.] See DISCRIMINATION. See also HARASSMENT; HATRED, INCITEMENT TO; HOMOSEXUAL CONDUCT; LESBIANISM; PENSION SCHEME AND DISCRIMINATION; UNFAIR DISMISSAL; VIDEO RECORDING.

shadow director. A person in accordance with whose directions or instructions the directors of a company are accustomed to act; he is deemed generally to be a director. There is an exemption for persons who give advice in a professional capacity. The invariable characteristic of a shadow director was that his role was hidden behind that of the validly appointed or indeed *de facto* directors, through whom, in a concealed way, the shadow director directed the affairs of the company: *Re Lynrowan Enterprises Ltd* [2002] FL 8565, HC. See Companies Act 1990, s 27; Companies (Auditing and Accounting) Act 2003, s 54. See DE FACTO; DIRECTORS.

shadow licence holder. A person who is not the *relevant* licence holder but who controls the business the subject of the licence or who enjoys or is entitled to the profits: Licensing (Combating Drug Abuse) Act 1997, s 21(6). *Relevant* licence means an intoxication liquor, public dancing and public music and singing licence. A person who is disqualified from holding a relevant licence, is also disqualified from being a shadow licence holder (L(CDA)A 1997, s 21(1)).

Shannon Navigation. The river Shannon, the lakes from or through which it flows and certain other rivers which flow into it or into those lakes: Shannon Navigation Act 1990, s 1. This Act enabled the Commissioners of Public Works to undertake the care, management, control and improvement of the Shannon navigation. It also extended the powers of the Commissioners to the Ballinamore and Ballyconnell navigation and the section of the River Erne navigation which is within the State. The Commissioners had power to acquire land compulsorily (SNA 1990, Sch). See also Act for the Improvement of the Navigation of the River Shannon 1839 (2 & 3 Vict, c.61) and also 5 & 6 Vict, c.89.

Responsibility for the Shannon Navigation was vested in 1998 in the Minister for Arts, Heritage, Gaeltacht and the Islands: Minister for Arts Act 1998. Provision has been made for the responsibility to be transferred to the cross-border implementation body *Waterways Ireland*: British-Irish Agreement Act 1999, ss 8–13. See NAVIGATION, RIGHT OF; WATERWAYS.

share, value of. The High Court has held that there is no acceptable scientific way of approaching the task of valuing a private company and the undertaking could not be carried out as a matter of art: *BD v JD* [2003] FL 8851, HC. For valuation of shares in private companies, see [Bibliography: Giblin].

share capital. See CAPITAL; CAPITAL, SERIOUS LOSS OF; SHARES, COMPANY.

share certificate. An instrument under the seal of a company, which certifies that the person named therein is entitled to a stated number of shares. It is not a negotiable instrument nor a document of title and it is only *prima facie* evidence of its contents: Companies Act 1963, ss 80–87; Companies

Amendment Act 1977, s 5. The true evidence of title is the holder's name registered in the register of members.

A *share warrant to bearer* is a certificate under the seal of a company stating that the bearer of the warrant is entitled to the shares therein specified; it is a negotiable instrument in that the shares can be transferred by delivery of the warrant: Companies Act 1963, ss 88 and 118. Provision is often made in such warrants for detaching coupons in order to claim future dividends. See Listing Rules 2000, paras 13.20–13.27A. See CREST SYSTEM; SHARES, COMPANY; SHARES, EQUITABLE MORTGAGE OF.

share fisherman. A self-employed person who is the member of the crew of a fishing vessel and whose principal means of livelihood is derived from a share in the profits or gross earnings of the working of the vessel: Social Welfare (No 2) Act 1993, Pt II. An optional scheme of social insurance for *share fishermen* was introduced to overcome the difficulties caused by the decisions in *DPP v McLoughlin* [1986] ILRM 493 and *Minister for Social Welfare v Griffiths* [1992] ILRM 667, which held that the share fishermen were not employees. See also *Doherty v Kincasslagh Trawlers* [1999] ELR 251, EAT.

share option scheme. A share option granted on or after 6 April 1986 to an employee or a director, was chargeable to tax under Schedule E in the tax year in which the option is exercised or sold: Taxes Consolidation Act 1997, s 128. A taxpayer in an *unapproved* share option scheme could elect to defer the income tax charge on the gain arising on the exercise of a share option, until the shares were sold, or for seven years, whichever was the earlier (TCA 1997, s 128 amended and s 128A inserted by Finance Act 2000, s 27). The option to defer payment of tax for share options exercised after 28 March 2003 has been abolished: Finance Act 2003, s 7. An employee includes a prospective or former employee; this is to ensure that a share option is taxable even if granted before an employee takes up employment, or after he has ceased to hold an employment. Share options exercised on or after 30 June 2003 are taxable at the higher rate of income tax in force in the tax year in which the option is exercised (FA 2003, s 8).

A person who is a member of an *approved* share option scheme is no longer chargeable to income tax on the exercise of the option, but is chargeable to capital gains tax on the full gain (ie the difference between the amount paid for the shares and the amount received): Finance Act 2001, s 15. However, the scheme must be open to all employees and on similar terms, and there must a minimum three-year period between the date of the grant of the option and any subsequent sale of the shares. The scheme, however, can contain a *key employee* element where options can be granted without the similar terms and conditions. Shares used in the scheme must form part of the ordinary share capital of the company. See also Finance Act 2002, s 11. For *Corporate Governance, Share Option and other Incentive Schemes*, Irish Association of Investment Managers (1999), see website: *www.iaim.ie*.

share premium account. The account in which is placed the aggregate amount or value of the premium received on the issue of shares of a company. A reduction of the share premium account requires approval by special resolution of the members of a company and by the High Court eg cancellation of £40m of the share premium account of Aran Energy plc in 1993 by effectively setting against it the debit balance of £40m in the company's profit and loss account: Iris Oifigiúil, 9 July 1993, p 518. See PREMIUM.

share price, movement of. A company with a quotation on the Stock Exchange is obliged to make a public announcement as soon as possible regarding any major new developments in its sphere of activity which may have the effect of moving the share price: Companies Act 1990, s 119. The objective is to prevent *insider dealing* (qv) from taking place. See WARNING ANNOUNCEMENT.

share transfer. See TRANSFER OF SHARES.

share warrant. See SHARE CERTIFICATE.

shared ownership lease. A lease granted for a term of between 20 and 100 years on payment to the lessor of between 25% and 75% of the market value of the house and which gives to the lessee the right to buy out the interest of the lessor, in one or more transactions and on the terms specified in the lease: Housing (Miscellaneous Provisions) Act 1992, s 2(1). Shared ownership is a means of enabling a person to purchase a portion of the equity in a house and to pay a rent to the owner of the remaining equity for the right of occupation. A housing authority may grant shared ownership leases and charge rent for occupation of the leased house, the maintenance of which is the responsibility of the lessee (H(MP)A 1992, s 3).

Approved housing bodies may provide houses under the shared ownership scheme under amended terms (H(MP)A 1992, ss 2 and 3 as amended by Planning and Development (Amendment) Act 2002, ss 16 and 17). Persons granted a shared ownership lease by an approved body are eligible for subsidy on their rent on the same terms as are applicable to a lessee under a lease granted under the scheme by a housing authority (H(MP)A 1992, s 4 as amended by PDA 2000, s 18).

There is control on the first resale of houses purchased under the shared ownership scheme within 20 years from the date of the lease, including a formula-based clawback on any profits; also controlled is the purchase of the interest of the housing authority in the house: Housing (Miscellaneous Provisions) Act 2002, s 10. See also Stamp Duties Consolidation Act 1999, s 103; Residential Tenancies Act 2004, ss 3(2)(e) and 200. See GROUND RENT; PERPETUITIES, RULE AGAINST.

shareholder. One who owns shares as a member of a company. See DERIVATIVE ACTION; SHARES, COMPANY; VOTING AT MEETINGS.

shareholder, oppression of. See OPPRESSION OF SHAREHOLDER.

shareholding, building society. The value of a person's shares in a building society is taken as the amount standing to his credit in respect of the payments made by him on the shares and interest credited to the shares by way of capitalisation: Building Societies Act 1989, s 2(2). Where a society becomes converted into a public limited company, every shareholding in the society becomes a deposit of the same amount with the successor company (BSA 1989, s 107(1)(a)).

shares, building society. A share in a building society is entirely different from a share in a limited liability company. 'A share in a limited liability company is part of the capital and is something which cannot be got rid of. It may be transferred to someone else, but it cannot be put out of existence. A share in this building society represented no proportionate quota of the company's capital. There might be as many shares in this society as people like to apply

for ...': *Irvine & Fullarton Building Society v Cuthbertson* [1905] 45 SLR 17.

A building society with an *authorisation* may raise funds to be used for the objects of the society, by the issue of shares of one or more than one denomination, either with or without accumulating interest, and may repay such funds: Building Societies Act 1989, s 18(1). A repayment of such funds to a shareholder, however, is not permitted, other than at the shareholder's request, at particular times e g between the date the member indicated his intention to propose a resolution at a meeting and the date of the meeting (BSA 1989, s 18(2)). Also shares must not be issued without voting rights (BSA 1989, s 18(4)).

A society is required to keep at least 50% of its funding liabilities in the form of members' shareholdings, although the Central Bank may grant a dispensation from this requirement (BSA 1989, s 18(3)).

The rules of a society must state the manner of determination of the terms on which shares are to be issued and repaid, and the manner in which shareholders are to be informed of changes in the terms on which their shares are held (BSA 1989, s 10(2)(b), and Sch 2, Pt II, para 5(c)). The rules must also state whether any preferential or deferred shares (qv) are to be issued and, if so, within what limits and on what terms.

Every person holding one or more shares in a society is a *member* (qv) of the society (BSA 1989, s 16(1)) and two or more persons may jointly hold shares in a society (BSA 1989, s 16(3)). The Central Bank may impose as a condition to an *authorisation* granted to a society, limitations on the issue of shares or debt instruments (BSA 1989, s 17(6)(a)).

The rights of share account holders in building societies are unaffected by the transfer of moneys in their accounts to the care of the State, pursuant to the Dormant Accounts Act 2001 (BSA 1989, s 16).

shares, company. A definite portion of the capital of a company. A share in a company is, in effect, a bundle of proprietary rights which can be sold or exchanged for money or other consideration: *In the matter of Sugar Distributors Ltd* [1996] 1 ILRM 345, HC. A share means a share in the share capital of a company and includes *stock* except where a distinction between stock and shares is expressed or implied: Companies Act 1963, s 2(1). A share is *personal* property (CA 1963, s 79).

Shares may be divided into different classes e g *preference, ordinary, deferred,* or *founders'* shares. The ownership of a share entitles the owner to receive a proportionate part of the profits of the company and to take part in the control of the company in accordance with the *articles of association,* which also regulate the mode in which the shares may be transferred.

Most articles of association give the board the exclusive power and a wide discretion over allocating further shares. Existing shareholders are not in common law entitled to be given the opportunity to subscribe for additional shares before those shares are offered to others; however a proposed allotment can be enjoined which has as its purpose to convert a minority into a majority: *Nash v Lancegage Safety Glass (Ireland) Ltd* [1958] 90 ILTR 11. However, since 1983 *pre-emption* (qv) is now compulsory for every company with certain exceptions.

Shares may not be issued at a discount (qv). However, shares may be allotted for a consideration other than cash. Shares allotted by a company and any premium (qv) payable on them may be paid up in money or in money's worth, including goodwill and expertise: Companies Amendment Act 1983, s 26(1). However, in a public limited company (plc), every subscriber to its memorandum of association must pay for his shares in cash (CAA 1983, s 35). A plc is prohibited from accepting as payment for shares an undertaking to do work or perform services (CAA 1983, s 26(2)), or to an undertaking which is to be or may be performed more than five years after the date of the allotment (CAA 1983, s 29).

Where a plc proposes to allot shares in exchange wholly or partly for something other than cash, the consideration must be valued by someone who would be eligible to be the company's auditor (CAA 1983, s 30).

Where a company has created and issued shares and there is reason to apprehend that such shares were invalidly created or issued, the court may declare that such creation or issue is valid for all purposes, if the court is satisfied that it would be just and equitable to do so: CA 1963, s 89(1) as amended by CA 1990, s 227. The court should only do so where the objective is to validate the defective title to shares, so as to protect innocent persons who subscribed for the shares in good faith (*Sugar Distributors* case).

A majority shareholder in a company is not entitled to recover any loss incurred by the alleged wrongdoing of a defendant, given that the loss was suffered by the company and not by the individual shareholder, see *Heaphy v Heaphy* [2004] FL 8986, HC.

Contrast *shares* with *debentures* which can resemble shares in various respects but are fundamentally different. See *Eddison v Allied Irish Banks* [1987] HC; *Lombard Ulster Banking v Bank of Ireland* [1987] HC; *Re PMPS* [1988] HC; *Pernod Ricard and Comrie plc v FII (Fyffes) plc* 7 ILT Dig [1989] 53; *Re Sugar Distributers Ltd* [1995] 2 IR 194, HC. See Powers of Attorney Act 1996, s 19. [Bibliography: Forde (1); Foy.] See CAPITAL; CAPITAL RECONSTRUCTION; COMMERCIAL PROCEEDINGS; CONTRACTS FOR DIFFERENCES; DEBENTURES; DISTRINGAS NOTICE; DIVIDEND; EMPLOYEES' SHARE SCHEME; FORFEITURE OF SHARES; FRAUD; MATERIAL CONTRACTS; OFFER FOR SALE; OPTION; PROSPECTUS; SURRENDER OF SHARES; TAKE OUT MERGER; TRANSFER OF SHARES.

shares, compulsory purchase of. Where a company makes a take-over bid for all the shares of another company, and the offer is accepted by the holders of 80% in value of the shares, the offeror can upon the same terms acquire the shares of the members who had not accepted the offer, unless such persons obtain an order of the court preventing this compulsory acquisition: Companies Act 1963, s 204. However, see European Communities (Mergers and Divisions) Regulations 1987, SI No 137 of 1987 in respect of relevant mergers and divisions.

Also, the court can order the purchase of the shares of a minority shareholder in proceedings alleging *oppression of the shareholder* (qv); the court has a wide discretion in valuing these shares: CA 1963, s 205(3) and *Re Clubman Shirts Ltd* [1991] ILRM 43, HC. Where a shareholder is opposing the compulsory purchase of his shares and seeks an order of the court to prevent such acquisition, the onus is on the dissenting shareholder to show that the court should exercise its discretion in his favour: *Duggan v Stoneworth Investment Ltd* [2000] 1 IR 563, SC and [2000] 2 ILRM 263, SC. The

High Court has held that the principle of compulsory acquisition of minority shareholders was justified by reference to the public interest in the pursuit of corporate acquisitions and takeovers: *Moran v Valentia Communications* [2001] FL 4911, HC. See Linnane in 8 ILT & SJ (1990) 253. See GOING CONCERN; MERGER OF COMPANY; DIVISION OF COMPANY; TENDER OFFER.

shares, disclosure of. The Minister was empowered to obtain information on the ownership of shares and debentures of a company and to impose restrictions on them: Companies Act 1990, ss 15–16 e g restriction imposed by the Minister on the shares in UPH Ltd registered in the name of Aurum Nominees (Iris Oifigiúil, 18 August 1992). This power now rests with the *Director of Corporate Enforcement* rather than the Minister (CA 1990, ss 14–16 as amended by Company Law Enforcement Act 2001, ss 26–27 and Sch).

A director or secretary of a company (public and private) is required to notify the company of the extent of his interest in shares or debentures of the company or another *related* company and of any changes; the company must keep a register of these interests and disclose them in the directors' report and report them to the Stock Exchange where dealing facilities are provided for such shares or debentures (CA 1990, ss 53–65). See Listing Rules 2000, para 16.13.

The beneficial owner of a notifiable percentage (5%) of the issued share capital of a public limited company (plc) is required to declare that fact to the company and this information must be available to directors, shareholders, employees and creditors of the company (CA 1990, ss 67–88). There is provision for dealing with *concert parties* (qv): CA 1990, ss 73–75.

A person who fails to make the required notification loses the power to enforce any rights or interest in the shares by action or legal proceedings (CA 1990, s 79(3)). In what is believed to be the first use of this section, the property company Dunloe Ewart plc advised a shareholder, Mr Liam Carroll, on 17 September 2002 that he had lost the power over any shares held by him in the company: *Irish Times*, 18 September 2002. The High Court subsequently, on 3 October 2002, restored his rights to 110.5 million votes.

There is an exemption from the disclosure requirements in respect of shareholdings as a result of *price stabilising* until the end of the *stabilising period*: Companies (Amendment) Act 1999, s 3(1). There are also disclosure requirements in respect of large acquisitions or disposals of shares in plcs: see COVERT TAKE-OVER.

A *listed* company is required to notify the Stock Exchange when it becomes aware that a person has 3% or more of the nominal value of capital, carrying voting rights: Listing Rules 2000, para 9.11 as amended by Irish Stock Exchange Ltd.

A general regime of disclosure of share ownership for private companies is not provided for, but a person with a financial interest in such a company may be able to obtain a *disclosure order* from the court, compelling disclosure in certain circumstances (CA 1990, ss 97–104). See CONCERT PARTY; DISCLOSURE ORDER; IRISH TAKEOVER PANEL; PRICE STABILISING; REGISTER OF MEMBERS.

shares, disposal of. The disposal of shares may give rise to a tax liability involving a capital gain. There is an exemption from capital gains tax for certain disposals by an investor company of shares held by it in an investee company in certain specified circumstances: Taxes Consolidation Act 1997, ss 626B and 626C, and Sch 25A, inserted by Finance Act 2004, ss 40–42. See BED AND BREAKFAST; CAPITAL GAINS TAX.

shares, equitable mortgage of. An equitable mortgage of shares in a company is normally created by the deposit of the share certificate, with or without delivery of a *blank transfer* to the lender. The borrower remains on the register of members and retains all the rights of a member unless other arrangements are made as between himself and the lender. It is common practice for the transferor to sign and hand over a blank transfer i e a transfer signed by the transferor, but with a blank for the name of the transferee. An equitable mortgage of shares can be defeated if the transferor obtains a second share certificate from the company and sells the shares to a *bona fide* purchaser.

shares, investigation of. The Minister is empowered to appoint inspectors to investigate suspected contraventions of the requirements to disclose ownership of shares by directors or secretaries of companies or of their spouses or children or of the prohibition on the dealing in options (qv) by a director: Companies Act 1990, s 64.

shares, purchase of own. Subject to certain exceptions, a company is not permitted to give, whether directly or indirectly, any financial assistance for the acquisition of its own shares: Companies Act 1963, s 60; *CH (Ireland) Inc (in liquidation) v Credit Suisse Canada* [1999] 4 IR 542, HC. However, a company may, if so authorised by its articles, purchase its own shares, including any redeemable shares (qv): Companies Act 1990, s 211. Such a purchase cannot be made if as a result the nominal value of the issued share capital which is not redeemable would be less than one-tenth of the nominal value of the total issued share capital of the company.

There are many advantages eg: (a) the purchase of shares of employees, acquired through an employee share scheme, on their ceasing to be employed by the company; (b) buying out a dissident shareholder; and (c) providing a market for unlisted shares. There are provisions to prevent abuse eg market rigging of listed shares (CA 1990, s 215). The Stock Exchange is given a role in effecting compliance (CA 1990, s 230).

Purchases or early redemption by a *listed* company of its own securities must not be made at a time when, under the provisions of the *model code*, a director of the company would be prohibited from dealing in its securities, unless certain requirements are met eg the price or value of the securities would not likely be substantially affected by the publication of the information: Listing Rules 2000, ch 15. The rules deal with purchases which are *market purchases* or *off-market purchases* and with notification requirements. See also Listing Rules 2000, paras 12.43(n) and 14.16.

The Stock Exchange is now required to report to the *Director of Corporate Enforcement* apparent breaches of the legal provisions regarding the purchase by a company of its own shares (CA 1990, s 230 as amended by Company Law Enforcement Act 2001, s 39). See also CLEA 2001, s 89.

The Minister is empowered to make regulations governing the purchase by companies of their own shares (CA 1990, s 228). No such regulations had been made by 2003 and there were no definite plans to make them. For taxation of the acquisition by a company of its own shares, see Finance Act 1991, ss 59–72, now Taxes Consolidation Act 1997, ss 173–186. See *McGill v Bogue* [2000] FL 4911, SC. See

Linnane in 11 ILT & SJ (1993) 216. See DIRECTORS AND SHARE DEALING; MODEL CODE.

sheep. Animals of the ovine species. A *national identification system* for sheep was introduced in 2001 in the aftermath of the foot and mouth disease crisis: Diseases of Animals (National Sheep Identification System) Order 2001, SI No 281 of 2001. See also Diseases of Animals (Importation of Sheep) Order 2004, SI No 503 of 2004.

Shelbourne lease. A lease for 20 to 30 years, determinable on the expiration of three lives, once common in parts of Ireland, due to the *penal laws* which debarred Catholics from purchasing land and limited the length of leases that could be granted to them to 31 years: Statute of 1703, 2 Ann, c.6(Ir). See PENAL LAWS.

Shelley's case, rule in. It is a rule of law that when a person by any deed or will takes an estate of freehold (qv) and by the same deed or will an estate is limited either mediately or immediately *to his heirs* or *to the heirs of his body,* these words are words of limitation and confer no estate to his heirs: *Shelley's Case* 1581. See *Finch v Foley* [1949] Ir Jur Rep 30. See WORDS OF LIMITATION.

shellfish. See AQUACULTURE; SALMON DEALER'S LICENCE.

sheriff. The office holder with wide powers, eg to execute an order of *fieri facias* (qv), originally appointed by the Lord Lieutenant, whose appointment is now governed by the Court Officers Act 1945, s 12; Court Officers Act 1951, s 6; Electoral Act 1963, s 3, Sch 1; Juries Act 1976, s 33. Special tax collection sheriffs were appointed in 1986; legislation was introduced to ensure that they would not be required by virtue of their office to act as returning officers at elections or referenda: Electoral (Amendment) Act 1986, ss 1–2. The certificate from the Collector-General to the sheriff, certifying the amount of outstanding tax liability in default, may now be issued in an electronic format: Taxes Consolidation Act 1997, s 962 as amended by Finance Act 2004, s 84.

An *order for protection* issued by the court will protect a debtor against execution unless the sheriff has made a seizure or has gone into possession: Bankruptcy Act 1988, s 89. See Capital Acquisitions Tax Consolidation Act 2003, s 64. See *Kennedy v Hearne* [1988] ILRM 52 and [1988] SC. See DCR 1997 Ord 48. See

Report on Debt Collection: (i) The Law relating to Sheriffs (LRC 27, 1988). [Bibliography: Dixon & Gilliland; Glanville.] See COUNTY REGISTRAR; ENTRY, RIGHT OF; PEACE OFFICER; POUNDAGE; RETURNING OFFICER.

sheriff's interpleader. See INTERPLEADER.

shift work. See WORKING HOURS.

ship. (1) Includes every description of vessel used in navigation not propelled by oars: Merchant Shipping Act 1894, s 742. A *seagoing ship* means a ship which in fact goes to sea, and not merely one which could go to sea: *Salt Union v Wood* [1893] 1 QB 370. In marine insurance, a ship includes the hull, materials and outfit, stores and provisions for the officers and crew and, in the case of vessels engaged in a special trade, the ordinary fittings requisite for the trade: Marine Insurance Act 1906, Sch 1, art 15.

(2) 'Ship' includes a hovercraft or submersible craft, any vessel used in navigation and any other floating craft of any description: Criminal Justice Act 1994, s 3(1) as amended by Criminal Justice (Illicit Traffic by Sea) Act 2003, s 28(a)(ii).

Previously, the only persons who could own a ship in the Irish Ship Register was an Irish national or a body corporate incorporated under the laws of Ireland: Mercantile Marine Act 1955, s 16. Now, any national of an EU member state or a body corporate of an EU member state can own or own shares in a ship registered in Ireland: Merchant Shipping (Miscellaneous Provisions) Act 1998, s 3; *EC Commission v Ireland* [1998] 1 CMLR 806. There are restrictions placed on ships anchoring in Irish coastal waters outside of a harbour e g the transfer of cargo, oil or stores can only take place with a *permit*.

See Merchant Shipping (Safe Manning, Hours of Work and Watchkeeping) Regulations 1998, SI No 551 of 1998, as amended by (Amendment) Regulations 2002, SI No 425 of 2002 to include a definition of 'international voyage' and to extend the application of reg 5 (safe manning document) to passenger ships on international voyages and by SI No 532 of 2003. See *Doran v Power* [1995] 2 IR 402, SC; *The Marshall Gelovani* [1995] 1 IR 159, HC; *The Kapitan Labunets* [1995] 1 IR 164, HC; *Re the Von Rocks* [1998] 3 IR 41, SC. See Equal Status Act 2000, s 46; Copyright and Related Rights Act 2000, s 185(b); Industrial Designs Act 2001, s 48(2). See

the *Brussels I Regulation* (arts 7, 14, 64 re ships) on the recognition and enforcement of judgments in civil and commercial matters, as implemented by EC (Civil and Commercial Judgments) Regulations 2002, SI No 52 of 2002. For provisions to reduce the discharges of ship-generated waste and cargo residues, see SIs No 117 and 659 of 2003. See Sea Pollution (Amendment) Act 1999, s 12; Maritime Security Act 2004, s 1(1). [Bibliography: Power UK.] See ADMIRALTY ACTION; BILL OF LADING; CHARGE ON SHIP; DETENTION OF SHIP; MARITIME CLAIMS; PASSENGER SHIP; SEAFARER; TERRORISM; VESSEL.

ship, arrest of. See DETENTION OF SHIP.

ship protest. A formal declaration, made by a ship's master or a member of its crew, before a notary public or other competent person, describing some event or happening relating to a ship, its cargo or crew, which the declarant desires to be formally recorded for subsequent evidential use. See DEPOSITION; NOTARY PUBLIC.

shipping grants. Grants up to 25% of approved capital expenditure on certain new or second-hand ships may be made by the Minister: Shipping Investment Grants Act 1987.

shock, nervous. See NERVOUS SHOCK.

shop. See RESTRICTED USER CLAUSE; SAFE SYSTEM OF WORK; WORKING HOURS.

shore. It has been held that the words 'shores', 'strands' and 'seagrounds' are synonymous; they denote the land lying between the high and low water marks at ordinary tides: *O'Sullivan v Aquaculture Licences Appeal Board* [2001] 1 IR 646, HC. The high and low water marks are determined by the ordinary or neap tides and the land affected belongs to the State in the normal course, whereas land covered by the spring tides and high spring tides do not belong to the State (*O'Sullivan* case). See FORESHORE.

short-term patent. A patent for a term of ten years which is less costly and simpler to obtain; it is intended to be more appropriate for less technologically complex inventions which do not have a long life cycle. An invention is patentable as a *short-term* patent if it is new and susceptible of industrial application provided it is not clearly lacking an inventive step: Patents Act 1992, s 63. An application for a short-term patent must contain: (a) a request for a grant of a short-term patent; (b) a specification: (i) which describes the invention and the best method of performing it known to the applicant, (ii) incorporates one or more claims, not exceeding five, (iii) accompanied by drawings and an abstract (PA 1992, s 63(7)).

As short-term patent applications are not subject to a novelty check or to detailed examination, an action for infringement of a short-term patent must not be instituted by the proprietor unless he has requested and obtained a *Search Report* from the Controller of Patents, which report will be published and made available to the Court and to the party against whom proceedings are contemplated (PA 1992, s 66).

In addition to the normal grounds for revocation of a patent, a further special ground is provided in the case of short-term patents ie that the claims of the specification of the short-term patent are not supported by the description (PA 1992, s 67). A short-term patent and a normal patent cannot co-exist in respect of the same invention (PA 1992, s 64). See PATENT.

short-time. A reduction in remuneration or hours of work by 50% in any week caused by diminished requirements for the work the employee performs under his contract of employment, provided that this is temporary and the employer gives notice to that effect prior to the reduction: Redundancy Payments Act 1967, s 11(2) as amended by the Redundancy Payments Act 1979. The special exemption from taxation of the *unemployment benefit* payable to certain systematic short time workers is continued to December 2004: Finance Act 2003, s 5. See LAY-OFF.

short title. The title by which an Act may be cited eg Succession Act 1965. See PREAMBLE.

short weight and measure. A person who sells or exposes for sale or offers for sale any product by weight, measure or number, is guilty of an offence if the quantity of goods is less than that purported or less than corresponds with the price charged on the basis of the total price to be paid for the goods or the stated price per number or unit of measurement used to determine the total price: Metrology Act 1996, s 28. See METROLOGY.

shorthand reporting. See TRANSCRIPT.

show cause. See NISI.

SI Statutory Instrument (qv).

sic. [So; thus.] Used to indicate that a word or statement is intended as written, despite the fact that there is an obvious error or it results in an absurdity.

sic utere tuo ut alienum non laedas. [So use your own property as not to injure your neighbours.] See NUISANCE.

sick pay. Payment to an employee during periods of sickness may arise as a result of the employment contract or as a result of the State welfare insurance schemes. *Disability benefit* from the State scheme is payable to insured workers during periods of incapacity for work. To be eligible, the person must be unfit for work due to illness and must satisfy the contribution conditions. In addition *pay related benefit* may be payable. However where the incapacity is the result of a prescribed industrial disease, *injury benefit* may be payable instead. An *invalidity pension* is payable, instead of disability benefit, to insured persons who are permanently incapable of working and who satisfy the contribution conditions. See DISABILITY BENEFIT; INVALIDITY PENSION; SOCIAL WELFARE LAW.

sickness. The ill-health of an employee may render him incapable of performing his duties; this incapacity may be a good cause to justify dismissal: Unfair Dismissals Act 1977, s 6(4). A single medical report is not sufficient: *Lawless v Dublin Co Council* [1990] ELR 101, EAT.

For a dismissal on grounds of incapacity to be deemed fair, the onus is on the employer to show that: (a) it was the incapacity which was the reason for the dismissal; (b) the reason was substantial; (c) the employee received fair notice that the question of his dismissal for incapacity was being considered; and (d) the employee was afforded an opportunity of being heard: *Bolger v Showerings (Ireland) Ltd* [1990] ELR 184, HC. The court has refused to intervene in a decision to place a civil servant on compulsory sick leave with pay: *Ahern v Minister for Industry & Commerce* 9 ILT Dig [1991] 127, HC.

The exploiting of the sick leave system by a civil servant leading to persistent absenteeism may provide sufficient grounds for his dismissal: *Lang v Government of Ireland* [1993] ELR 234, HC.

The Advocate-General of the European Court has given an opinion that the dismissal of a female worker outside her periods of maternity leave because of absence due to illness originating in pregnancy or childbirth does not constitute discrimination based on sex: see 8 ILT & SJ (1990)

279. However, an Equality Officer has found that the treatment as normal illness of pregnancy-related illness during pregnancy and resulting in an incapacity to work, is direct discrimination: *McKenna v North Western Health Board* [2002] ELR 52, EO. See also *Duff v Dún Laoghaire Corp* [1991] ELR 82, EAT; *Gavin v Bus Éireann* [1990] ELR 103, EAT; *Mulhern v An Post* [1990] ELR 131, CC; *Molloy v Irish Glass Bottle Co Ltd* UD 693/1983. See UNFAIR DISMISSAL.

side-bar orders. Particular types of order made by a court: RSC Ord 30. Known as a *side-bar* due to their origin in Westminster Hall where at a bar or partition, which came to be known as the side-bar, attorneys would move judges on their way to their respective courts. An example of a side-bar order is an order to proceed, notwithstanding the death of a party, his right surviving, which order is made in the High Court by the Master and in the Circuit Court by the County Registrar: RSC Ord 30; Ord 63, r 1(1); Circuit Court Rules 2001 Ord 19.

A side-bar order may also be made by a Probate Officer directing a party cited to extract a grant of probate or to renounce his rights: RSC Ord 79, rr 57–58. See also RSC Ord 63, r 1(1). A wide range of side-bar orders may now be made by the County Registrar: Courts and Court Officers Act 1995, s 34 and Sch 2.

sight lines. Vision lines at the entrance to a site, which may be a condition of a planning permission, to ensure that a vehicle exiting the site has sight of oncoming traffic and vice versa. The planning permission may require documentary evidence from the applicant, before the commencement of development, of consent for location of vision lines over third-party lands. See *Law Society Gazette* (November 2003) 42.

sign. Any sign, hoarding or other structure used for the purpose of advertising: Roads Act 1993, s 71(8). It is an offence to erect, place or retain a sign on a public road (qv) without lawful authority or the consent of the road authority; the sign may be removed by an authorised person (RA 1993, s 71(1)(a)). This provision does not apply to a sign which relates to an election or referendum unless it is in place for seven days or longer after the poll (RA 1993, s 71(10)). The National Roads Authority is empowered to prepare, or arrange the preparation of, schemes for the provision of traffic signs (RA 1993, s 19(1)(c)). See

Road Traffic (Signs) Regulations 1997, SI No 181 of 1997 as amended by SI No 273 of 1998, SI No 97 of 2003, and by SI No 403 of 2004. See ADVERTISEMENT; TRADE MARK.

sign manual. Formerly a document signed at the head by the Sovereign in his own hand. Where the cy-pres (qv) doctrine is applied by the government and where there are no trustees, it is done by *letters missive* under the present sign manual procedure; in the procedure the plaintiff submits a memorial to the government, which replies with the letters missive to the Attorney-General to be issued to the court which makes the appropriate order: *Merrins v A-G* [1945] 79 ILTR 121.

signals. It is an offence to signal smuggling vessels; proof that such signal was not for the purpose of giving notice to the vessel, lies on the defendant: Customs Consolidation Act 1876, ss 190–191. See also MALICIOUS DAMAGE.

signature. A person's name written in his own hand or a sign or other such mark to signify his name. A person signs a document as a token of his intention to be bound by its contents. Illiterate persons commonly sign by making a cross; companies sign by their corporate seal. A rubber stamp or typed words may be interpreted as a signature.

At common law, a person sufficiently signed a document if it was signed in his name and with his authority by someone else, and in such a case the agent's signature was treated as being that of his principal: *Dundalk AFC v FAI National League* [2001] 1 IR 434, HC. See *Casey v Irish Intercontinental Bank* [1979] IR 364; *Kelly v Ross & Ross* [1980] HC. There is now provision for an *electronic signature* (qv) e g see Civil Registration Act 2004, s 2(1). See ACKNOWLEDGMENT; NON EST FACTUM; TRADE MARK, REGISTERED.

significant. See CAUSE OF ACTION.

silence, right to. The right in general which a suspect or an accused person has to remain silent. It is an immunity conferred by the common law against self-incrimination both before and during a trial. The common law right of suspects in custody to remain silent is also a constitutional right: *People (DPP) v Finnerty* [2000] 1 ILRM 191, SC and [1999] 4 IR 364, SC. However, the common law right dated from a time when an accused was not competent to give evidence in his defence in a criminal trial: *Heaney v Ireland* [1996] 1 IR 580, SC.

No inference can be drawn from the silence of a suspect detained pursuant to the Criminal Justice Act 1984, s 4; also the judge, at his subsequent trial before a jury, should make no reference to the fact that he refused to answer questions during his detention (*Finnerty* case). However, there is no prohibition on the trial judge commenting on the accused's failure to give evidence, as long as it was fair: *The People (DPP) v Connolly* [2003] 2 IR 1, CCA.

The State is entitled to encroach on the right to silence where reasonably necessary to maintain public peace and order, although the right must be affected as little as possible: *Rock v Ireland* [1998] 2 ILRM 35, SC. There are some occasions where the right to silence is excluded by statute e g it is an offence for a person to fail to give an account of his movement and actions during a specified period when so demanded by a garda: Offences Against the State Act 1939, s 52. This restriction on the right to silence is not regarded as excessive and is proportionate to the objective it was designed to achieve: *Heaney v Ireland* [1994] 2 ILRM 420, HC and [1996] 1 IR 580, SC. The 1939 Act was amended in 1998 to require the garda to inform the person in ordinary language of the consequences provided in s 52 in respect of a failure to comply with the demand: Offences Against the State Act 1998, s 13.

A government appointed committee, under the chairmanship of Mr Justice Anthony Hederman, recommended that, s 52 should be repealed, and that inferences should only be drawn from a person's silence during interrogation if the accused has had access to legal advice: *Report of the Committee to Review the Offences Against the State Acts 1939–1998* (2002).

Also an inference may be drawn in the trial of an arrested person if he fails (a) to account to the garda for marks on clothing or footwear; or (b) to explain his presence at the scene of a crime: Criminal Justice Act 1984, s 18–19. These sections have been found to be constitutional: *Rock v Ireland* [1998] 2 ILRM 35, SC.

Also in any proceedings against a person for a drug trafficking offence, the court may draw inferences from the failure of the accused to mention certain facts when being questioned or on being charged, where the accused later relies on those facts in his defence, and where the court considers that he could reasonably have been expected to mention those facts previously: Criminal Justice (Drug Trafficking) Act 1996, s 7.

Any confession admitted against an accused person in a criminal trial should be a voluntary confession; it is immaterial whether the compulsion or inducement used to extract an involuntary confession comes from the executive or from the legislature: *In the matter of National Irish Bank Ltd* [1999] 1 ILRM 321, SC and 3 IR 145.

A witness called to court to give evidence in Ireland for use in criminal proceedings in another jurisdiction, pursuant to the Criminal Justice Act 1994, s 51, is compellable both in the sense of attending the proceedings and in the sense of answering the questions put, unless he can establish that there are reasonable grounds to fear that the answer will tend to incriminate him: *de Gortari v District Judge Smithwick* [2001] 1 ILRM 354, HC and [2000] 2 IR 553, HC.

The Companies Act 1990, s 19(6) provides that a statement made by a person in compliance with the section may be used in evidence against him. This provision has been held to be unconstitutional as it constituted more than a minimum invasion of the person's constitutional rights, in not immunising answers given under compulsion for later use in criminal proceedings: *Dunnes Stores Ireland Company v Ryan & Minister for Enterprise* [2002] 2 IR 60, HC. The Company Law Enforcement Act 2001, s 29 repealed CA 1990, s 19 and substituted a new s 19 and s 19A. [Bibliography: Charleton (5).] See ADMISSION; CONFESSION; INCRIMINATE; INVESTIGATOR, TRIBUNAL; OFFENCES AGAINST THE STATE; RIGHT NOT TO GIVE EVIDENCE; UNLAWFUL ORGANISATION; UNLAWFUL POSSESSION OF GOODS.

silk, to take. See SENIOR COUNSEL.

silver. See GOLDSMITHS OF DUBLIN, COMPANY OF.

similiter. [In like manner].

simple contracts. All contracts which are not under seal; they require consideration (qv) to support them. Some simple contracts are required to be in writing e g bills of exchange and promissory notes: Bills of Exchange Act 1882, s 3(1); contracts of marine insurance: Marine Insurance Act 1906, s 22; hire-purchase agreements: Consumer Credit Act 1995, s 58.

Certain other contracts are unenforceable unless they are *evidenced* by some memorandum in writing signed by the party to be charged or his agent: (a) contracts specified in the Statute of Frauds 1695, s 2 and (b) contracts specified in the Sale of Goods Act 1893, s 4 ie in the absence of acceptance and receipt of the goods or of part payment. See STATUTE OF FRAUDS; SALE OF GOODS; SALE OF LAND.

simplex commendatio non obligat. [A mere recommendation does not impose a liability.] See PRECATORY TRUST.

simpliciter. [Simply.] Absolutely; without qualification.

Simpson's Hospital. The hospital in Dundrum in County Dublin which has its origins in the last will of George Simpson dated 11 December 1778 whereby he bequeathed the residue of his estate to trustees in trust 'to erect, support and maintain an Hospital for the reception of such poor, decayed, blind and gouty men, as they shall think worthy of such a charity'. The charity was established by the Simpson's Hospital Estates Act 1779 as amended by the Simpson's Hospital Act 1861. The 1779 Act was further amended in 2003 to broaden the objects of the charity to include women: SI No 516 of 2003 and Health Act 1970, s 76.

simultaneous death. See DEATH, SIMULTANEOUS.

simultaneous invention. Understood to be where two or more persons have made the same invention independently of each other at or about the same time. The right to a patent belongs to the person whose patent application has the earlier or earliest date: Patents Act 1992, s 16(2). See PRIORITY DATE.

simultaneously. May not mean existing or taking place at exactly the same time eg in relation to determining the place where copyright protection subsists, *simultaneously*, in relation to making the work first available to the public, means within the previous 30 days. See COPYRIGHT, QUALIFICATION FOR.

sine die. [Without a day.] Indefinitely. See ADJOURNMENT.

sine qua non. [Without which not.] An indispensable condition.

Single European Act; SEA. The Act done at Luxembourg on the 17 February 1986 and at The Hague on the 28 February 1986 which brought about many amendments to the constitutional treaties of the European Community. Its most important provision is in relation to the establishment of an *internal market* (qv) by 31 December 1992. Its other provisions are: (a) to establish a tribunal to hear certain classes of action, (b) to extend the role of the European Parliament in the decision-making process, (c) to permit further delegations of power from the Council to the Commission; and (d) various measures on monetary capacity, social policy, economic and social cohesion, research and development, the environment and European political co-operation.

Certain portions of the SEA were incorporated into Irish domestic law by the European Communities (Amendment) Act 1986; however it was held that it would be unconstitutional for the State to ratify the SEA: *Crotty v An Taoiseach* [1987] ILRM 400. This Supreme Court decision necessitated an amendment to the Constitution which was carried by a substantial majority. See Tenth Amendment to the Constitution Act 1987; Referendum (Amendment) Act 1987. The government ratified the SEA on 25 June 1987 by depositing the instrument of ratification with the government of the Italian Republic and it came into force on 1 July 1987. See 1937 Constitution, art 29(4)(3). [Bibliography: EC Pub (1).] See BORDER; COMMUNITY LAW; FIRST INSTANCE, COURT OF; MAASTRICHT TREATY.

single member company. A private company limited by shares or by guarantee may now be formed by one person and may have one member: European Communities (Single-Member Private Limited Companies) Regulations 1994, SI No 275 of 1994, as amended by European Communities (Single-Member Private Limited Companies) Regulations 2001, SI No 437 of 2001, which deletes reg 12 (connected person).

The provisions of the Companies Acts which apply to private companies limited by shares or by guarantee apply also to a single member, with modifications. The sole member may dispense with the holding of an AGM, although the accounts and reports which would normally be laid before the AGM must still be prepared and forwarded to the member. See also Companies (Amendment) (No 2) Act 1999, s 32.

single trader. See ONE MAN COMPANY; SOLE TRADER.

singular. The use of a singular noun in an Act imports the plural (unless the contrary intention appears): Interpretation Act 1937, s 11(a). This interpretation also applies to nouns in instruments made wholly or partly under an Act. See *The People v Kelly (No 2)* [1983] IR 1.

sit-in. Occupation of premises usually in pursuance of a trade dispute. There is no immunity to a union or its members for unlawful occupation of premises despite the existence of a *bona fide* trade dispute. The occupation may amount to trespass (qv) or to a criminal offence under the Prohibition of Forcible Entry and Occupation Act 1971, the Conspiracy and Protection of Property Act 1875 or the Criminal Law (Jurisdiction) Act 1976. See *F W Woolworth Ltd v Haynes* [1984] HC; *Galt v Philp* [1982] SLT 28. See FORCIBLE ENTRY AND OCCUPATION.

site exclusion order. See ANTI-SOCIAL BEHAVIOUR.

site notice. An applicant for planning permission is required to give notice of the intention to make the application by the erection or fixing of a *site notice* which complies with specified requirements: Planning and Development Regulations 2001, SI No 600 of 2001, arts 17, 19, 20 and 22. Where a *site notice*, because of its content or for any other reason, is misleading or inadequate for the information of the public, the planning application is invalid (art 26(3)(b)). For prescribed notice, see SI No 600 of 2001, Sch 3, Form No 1. For site notices for developments by local authorities and State authorities, see arts 81 and 87 respectively.

The omission from a *site notice* that the planning application could be inspected in the offices of the planning authority, could in certain circumstances amount to a substantial ground to justify a judicial review, but only if the person seeking the judicial review had been misled or did not realise that the planning application could be inspected: *Village Residents Association Ltd v An Bord Pleanála* [2000] 2 ILRM 59, HC. See *Ardoyne House Management Co Ltd v Bardas Átha Cliath* [1998] 2 IR 147, HC. For previous regulations, see Local Government (Planning and Development) Regulations 1994, SI No 86 of 1994, art 16. See PLANNING PERMISSION, APPLICATION FOR.

site value, cleared. See CLEARED SITE VALUE.

sitting. There is a duty on employers to provide any employee with suitable facilities for sitting, where the employee has reasonable opportunities for sitting without detriment to his work or where a substantial proportion of any work done by the employee can properly be done sitting: Safety, Health and Welfare at Work Regulations 1995, SI No 358 of 1995.

sittings of court. The sittings of the Supreme Court and in Dublin of the High Court are four in every year: the *Michaelmas* sittings begin on the first Monday of October and end on 21 December; the *Hilary* sittings begin on 11 January and end on the Friday of the week preceding the Easter vacation; the *Easter* sittings begin on the Monday of the week following Easter vacation and end on the Thursday preceding Whit Sunday; and the *Trinity* sittings begin on the Wednesday following Whitsun week and end on the 31 July: RSC Ord 118, r 1. If 11 January is a Saturday or Sunday, the *Hilary* sittings begin on the following Monday. See also DCR 1997 Ord 1. See STATUTORY SITTING; VACATION.

Skillnets. A company limited by guarantee and not having a share capital, incorporated in December 1998, with the objective of demonstrating the effectiveness of an enterprise-led network approach to training. Skillnets launched the *Training Networks Programme* in 1999 to give enterprises an opportunity to collaborate in addressing shared training needs. Skillnets is funded by the Irish exchequer and by the EU. Enterprises contribute financially by their participation in the training networks. The programme finished its pilot phase in 2002 and has been extended for a second phase to 2005. See email: *info@skillnets.co* and website: *www.skillnets.com*. See TRAINING.

skip. A container used for the storage or removal of builder's materials, rubble, waste, rubbish or other materials and which is designed to be transported by means of a mechanically propelled vehicle: Roads Act 1993, s 72(13). A road authority (qv) may, after consultation with the Garda Commissioner, make bye-laws to regulate and control skips on public roads (RA 1993, s 72(1)). A person who contravenes a bye-law is guilty of an offence (RA 1993, s 72(6)). It is an offence if the person who owns or is in charge of a skip (which is parked or situated in a public place) does not take measures to prevent the creation of litter in the vicinity of the skip: Litter Pollution Act 1997, s 4(2). See ABANDONED VEHICLE; WASTE.

skipper. In relation to a fishing vessel (qv), means the person having for the time being the command or charge of the vessel: Merchant Shipping Act 1992, s 2(1).

slander. Defamation by means of spoken words. *Words* include visual images, gestures and other methods of signifying meaning: Defamation Act 1961, s 14(2). Slander is a tort and not a crime and is not actionable without proof of *special damage* (ie some real or actual loss, such as the loss of friendship, or the loss of a contractual or other tangible business advantage) and the damage must flow directly from the words complained of. See *Dinnegan v Ryan* [2002] 3 IR 178, HC.

However, slander is actionable without proof of special damage in the case of words imputing: (a) a criminal offence punishable by imprisonment; (b) a contagious venereal disease; (c) unfitness of the plaintiff for his office or business: *McMullan v Mulhall* [1929] IR 420; *Bennett v Quane* [1948] Ir Jur Rep 28; (d) unchastity or adultery of a woman: Defamation Act 1961, s 16. See RSC Ord 36, r 36. [Bibliography: McDonald; Duncan & O'Neill UK; Gatley UK.] See DEFAMATION; LESBIANISM; LODGMENT IN COURT; MITIGATION OF DAMAGES; NAME, RIGHT TO GOOD; OFFER OF AMENDS; PUBLICATION; VULGAR ABUSE.

slander of goods. A tort (qv) consisting of a false and malicious statement on merchandise sold. See *White v Mellin* [1895] AC 154; *Norbrook Laboratories Ltd v Smithkline Beecham (Ireland) Ltd* [1999 HC] 2 ILRM 391. See Civil Liability Act 1961, s 20(1). See INJURIOUS FALSEHOOD.

slander of title. A tort (qv) consisting of a false and malicious statement of fact, written or spoken, which denies or casts doubts over the plaintiff's title to property, thereby causing damage to him. See *Riding v Smith* [1876] 2 Ex D 91. See Civil Liability Act 1961, s 20(1). See INJURIOUS FALSEHOOD.

slaughter. A person is not permitted to slaughter an animal in a *slaughter-house*, unless he is a registered veterinary surgeon or the holder of a slaughter licence for the time being in force: Slaughter of Animals Act 1935, s 19. See also Abattoirs Act 1988, s 47. See ABATTOIR.

slavery. Condition of an unfree person who has no rights and who is in the ownership of his master: *Sommerset's Case* [1772] 20 St Tr 1. No-one shall be held in slavery or servitude; slavery and the slave trade shall be prohibited in all their forms: Universal Declaration of Human Rights 1948 art 4. See also Slave Trade Act 1824, as amended by Slave Trade Act 1843, and as subsequently amended in 1997 to delete references to 'felony' and to apply the provisions of *slave-trading abroad* by British citizens to Irish citizens: Criminal Law Act 1997, s 13 and Sch 1, para 1. See EUROPEAN CONVENTION ON HUMAN RIGHTS.

sleeping partner. See LIMITED PARTNERSHIP.

slip rule. The rule which provides that clerical mistakes in judgments or orders, or errors arising therein from any accidental slip or omission, may be corrected at any time by the court on motion without appeal: RSC Ord 28, r 11. Undue delay is not a bar to making an order, unless it would be inequitable to make the order because it would prejudice the rights of other parties to the proceedings or right acquired by third parties: *McMullen v Clancy* [2002] 3 IR 493, SC. The application should be made to the judge who made the original order, even where that judge has, in the meantime, been appointed to the Supreme Court (*McMullen* case).

In a particular case, the High Court has held that it could not correct an error in an order drawn up by a district court clerk and subsequently signed by the district court judge: *DPP v Anthony Coyne* [1991] HC. See *G McG v DW & AR (No 2)* [2000] 1 ILRM 121, HC (under appeal); *Limerick VEC v Carr* [2001] 3 IR 480, HC. See also Arbitration Act 1954, s 28; Patents Act 1992, s 110. See also DCR 1997 Ord 12, r 17. See CLERICAL ERROR; ORDER; SUMMONS, AMENDMENT OF; TYPOGRAPHICAL ERROR.

slot machine. 'A machine which is operated by the insertion of a coin in a slot': *Oxford English Dictionary* as quoted in *DPP v Cafolla* [1992] ITLR (22 June), SC. See GAMING.

small claims. An alternative method of commencing and dealing with civil proceedings in respect of small claims, not exceeding € 1,269.74 (£1,000), instituted under the District Court (Small Claims Procedure) Rules 1999 (SI No 191 of

1999) inserting Ord 53A in the DCR 1997, and as amended by SI No 410 of 2003.

The *small claims procedure* applies to claims: (a) in relation to *consumer* contracts, by a consumer against a vendor in respect of goods or services purchased, or (b) in relation to *tort*, by the claimant against the respondent in respect of minor damage caused to the claimant's property (but excluding personal injuries), or (c) prior to the establishment of the *Private Residential Tenancies Board* (qv), in relation to *tenancy*, by a tenant against the landlord in respect of the non-return of any sum paid by the tenant as rent deposit or any such sum known as 'key money'.

A *consumer* means a purchaser of goods or a service of a type ordinarily supplied for private use or consumption, where the purchaser does not make the contract in the course of a business and the vendor does make the contract in the course of a business. The small claims procedure does not apply to claims for debts, or for personal injuries, or arising from a hire-purchase agreement, or arising from an alleged breach of a leasing agreement. Also the claimant cannot be a body corporate. The Small Claims Registrar will endeavour to settle the dispute between the parties; if he fails he refers the matter to the District Court for hearing.

The scheme was initially introduced as a pilot scheme in Dublin, Cork and Sligo in December 1991 as an alternative, simpler and less expensive method of dealing with small claims. Due to the success of the scheme it was subsequently extended to all District Court areas in 1993. The 2003 regulations substitute a euro amount for the Irish pound and add a rule to provide for service by email. See Bird in 10 ILT & SJ (1992) 35. For details on Small Claims procedure, see website: *www.courts.ie*. [Bibliography: European Consumer Centre; McHugh.] See EUROPEAN CONSUMER CENTRE; RENT DEPOSIT.

small company. A private company which satisfies at least two of the following conditions: (a) balance sheet total does not exceed £1.5 million/€1.9million, (b) turnover does not exceed £3 million/€3.81m, (c) the average number of employees does not exceed 50: Companies Amendment Act 1986, s 8; SI No 396 of 1993. A small company is exempted from the necessity of preparing and publishing a full set of accounts (CAA 1986, s 10). It need only draw up an abridged balance sheet and is not obliged to annex the profit and loss account or the report of the directors to the Registrar of Companies. It must, however, satisfy the overriding requirement that the accounts give a *true and fair view* of the company's affairs.

As regards the payment of *preliminary tax*, a 'small company' is a company whose corporation tax liability does not exceed €50,000: Finance Act 2002, s 58. A small company can base its preliminary tax on 100% of its liability for the previous year. See ACCOUNTS, COMPANY; MEDIUM-SIZED COMPANY.

smoke. Includes soot, ash, grit and any other particle emitted in smoke: Air Pollution Act 1987, s 7(1).

smoking. 'Smoke' in relation to a tobacco product, includes sniffing, chewing or sucking such a product: Public Health (Tobacco) Act 2002, s 2(1). The smoking of a tobacco product in a *specified place* has been prohibited since 29 March 2004 (PH(T)A 2002, s 47 as substituted by Public Health (Tobacco) (Amendment) Act 2004, s 16). A *specified place* means: (a) a place of work, and the following in so far as they are *places of work*, (b) an aircraft, train, ship or other vessel, public service vehicle, or other vehicles used for the carriage of members of the public for reward, (c) a health premises, (d) a hospital that is not a health premises, (e) a school or college, (f) a public building, (g) a cinema, theatre, concert hall or other place normally used for indoor public entertainment, (h) a licensed premises, or (i) a registered club.

The smoking ban does not apply to a dwelling, a prison, a nursing home, a hospice, a psychiatric hospital, the Central Mental Hospital, a place which is wholly uncovered by any roof, an outdoor part of a premises provided not more than 50% is surrounded by walls, a bedroom in an hotel or 'bed and breakfast', or living accommodation provided: (a) for charitable purposes (ie hostels for the homeless) or (b) for educational objectives above secondary level (ie student residences). However this does not give rise to a right to smoke in these premises and it does not relieve employers of the need to exercise a duty of care to protect their employees.

There are provisions governing the display of signs to indicate where smoking is or is not permitted (PH(T)A 2002, s 46 as substituted by PH(T)(A)A 2004, s 15). The Department of Health has confirmed that a plenary summons has been served on the Minister for Health by Liam O'Riordan, claiming that the smoking ban has infringed his civil liberties and constitutional rights: *Irish Times*, 16 June 2004.

Regulations have also been made to simplify the procedure for the sale of nicotine replacement medicinal products in pharmacies eg nicotine chewing gum and other like products, widely used to assist persons to stop smoking: Poisons (Amendment) Regulations 2003, SI No 351 of 2003. Smoking at work, where prohibited, may be a good ground for the dismissal of an employee: *Byrne v Readibake Ltd* [1993] ELR 136, EAT. Norway became, on 1 June 2004, the second country in the world to introduce a ban on smoking in the workplace; there have been similar bans in some regions in the USA, but not nationwide. See 'Up in smoke' by solicitor Maura Connolly in *Law Society Gazette* (July 2004) 12. See websites: *www.otc.ie* and *www.smokefreeatwork.ie*. See EUROPEAN TRANSPARENCY DIRECTIVE; TOBACCO PRODUCT.

smuggling. A variety of offences created by the Customs Consolidation Act 1876 as amended. See SIGNALS.

snuff. See SMOKING; TOBACCO PRODUCT.

social employment scheme. A scheme designed to provide unemployed persons with work for an average of 2 1/2 days per week for up to one year on projects intended to benefit the community. The eligibility requirements that a person must be receiving either unemployment benefit or unemployment assistance did not discriminate against a married woman ineligible for either: *Vavasour v Northside Centre for the Unemployed & FÁS* [1993] ELR 112, HC and [1995] 1 IR 450, HC. These schemes are now known as 'Community Employment': Social Welfare Act 1995, s 18. See *Lefever v Irish Wheelchair Association* [1996] ELR, EAT; *Morley v Rock Foundation* [1997] ELR 236, EAT; *Hyde v Kelleher & FAS* [2004] ELR 145, EAT.

social housing. Housing assessed by a *housing authority* as needed to house people who are: homeless, living in overcrowded accommodation, living in housing that is unfit for human habitation, elderly, disabled or handicapped, or young persons leaving institutional care: Housing Act 1988, s 9(2). The housing strategy of a *planning authority* must

estimate the amount of housing required and must provide that up to 20% of land to be used for residential purposes is provided for *social* and *affordable* housing: Planning and Development Act 2000, s 94(4). See Residential Tenancies Act 2004, s 3(2)(c). See 'Social and Affordable' by James Macken SC in *Bar Review* (October 2000) 41. [Irish Council for Social Housing, 50 Merrion Square, Dublin 2. See website: *www.icsh.ie*.] See AFFORDABLE HOUSING; HOUSING STRATEGY.

social insurance fund. A fund established for the purpose of providing moneys for meeting the expenditure on benefits and making payments under the Social Welfare Acts, the Redundancy Payments Acts 1967 to 1991 and the Protection of Employees (Employer's Solvency) Acts 1984 and 1990: Social Welfare (Consolidation) Act 1993, ss 6–8 as amended eg by Social Welfare Act 2000, s 29. It is funded by *employment contributions* (including PRSI), self-employment contributions (including PRSI), optional contributions, voluntary contributions and moneys provided by the Oireachtas (SW(C)A 1993, s 6). See *Re Coombe Importers Ltd* [1999] 1 IR 492, HC.

The Minister for Finance in his Budget 2002 speech in December 2001 said that the social insurance fund would have a €1.4 billion surplus at the end of 2001 and that he intended to have the fund make a contribution to the Exchequer in 2002 of €635m. This payment to the Exchequer was subsequently given legal effect by the Social Welfare (No 2) Act 2001, s 7. See also Social Welfare (Miscellaneous Provisions) Act 2002, s 13; Redundancy Payments Act 2003, s 2. [Bibliography: Bradley].

social market economy. The type of economic model which has characterised the countries in the European Union since reconstruction after the Second World War, in which the economy is primarily based on the competitive operation of the market but with significant regulation in the public interest and in addition, in most cases, a significant consultative role for the social partners in the management of the economy, and in some countries, also at firm level: National Forum on Europe, *Glossary of Terms* (2003).

social policy. The policy of the EC whereby the member states agree to promote employment, improved living and working conditions, proper social protection, dialogue between management and labour, the development of human resources with a view to lasting high employment and the combating of exclusion: EC Treaty, arts 136–145 of the consolidated (2002) version.

Important changes to increase the Community's capacity to act on social matters were agreed by eleven of the then twelve EC member states (excluding the UK): Maastricht Treaty 1992; Protocol and Annexed Agreement. The main changes are: (a) revised policy objectives including the promotion of employment and the integration of persons excluded from the labour market; (b) qualified majority voting procedures in relation to decisions on working conditions, information and consultation of workers, and on equality between men and women; (c) unanimous decision in the area of social security, and representation and collective defence of the interests of workers and employers; and (d) increased role for the social partners.

The Protocol reconfirms the commitment to *equal pay* and extends it to include piece rate and part-time pay. Also member states are permitted to maintain or bring in measures to make it easier for women to pursue a vocational activity or to prevent or compensate for disadvantages in their professional careers.

social welfare law. The body of law dealing with financial and other support from the State to a wide range of persons e g the sick, disabled persons, unemployed, the elderly and the family. About one million persons are in receipt of social welfare payments from the State. The law is contained in the Social Welfare (Consolidation) Act 1993 together with amending statutes.

Decisions relating to entitlement to social welfare payments and to insurability of employment are made by *deciding officers* appointed by the Minister (SW(C)A 1993, ss 246–250). These decisions may be appealed to an *Appeals Officer*. The *Appeals Officer* is empowered to award costs; where it was reasonable to expect legal representation, then it would *prima facie* be unfair to refuse costs to a successful applicant: *O'Sullivan v Minister for Social Welfare* [1997] 1 IR 464, HC. A further appeal on a point of law lies to the High Court: *Kingham v Minister for Social Welfare* [1985] HC (SW(C)A 1993, s 271). See also *Denny & Sons v Minister for Social Welfare* [1998]

ELR 36, SC. See RSC Ord 90 as amended by SI No 67 of 1991.

Whenever a person has appealed a decision of a deciding officer, and the Chief Appeals Officer certifies that the ordinary appeals procedures are inadequate to secure the effective processing of the appeal, he can direct the appellant to submit the appeal to the Circuit Court: Social Welfare Act 1997, s 34, as amended by SWA 1999, s 29. This provision is intended to deal with cases where there are threats against Social Welfare staff. See Cousins in 10 ILT & SJ (1992) 114 & 159.

In the High Court it was held that social welfare legislation is not taxing legislation in its origin or intent; therefore, it is not to be interpreted strictly but rather it is to be construed purposefully: Ó *Síocháin v Neenan* [1997 HC] 2 ILRM 451, SC. However, on appeal to the Supreme Court, see Ó *Síocháin v Neenan* [1997] 2 ILRM 444, SC.

Certain benefits payable under the Social Welfare Acts are treated as emoluments and are subject to PAYE e g unemployment benefit: Taxes Consolidation Act 1997, s 126 as amended by Finance Act 2000, s 16 and by Finance Act 2002, s 7. Social welfare revised payments have been brought forward to be paid at the start of the year (2002); this ties in with the change of the tax year to the calendar year: Social Welfare (No 2) Act 2001, ss 2, 3, 4.

A person to be entitled to many social welfare allowances or benefits must have been 'habitually resident in the State' at the date of making of an application therefor: Social Welfare (Miscellaneous Provisions) Act 2004, s 17 and Schedule 1. A person is presumed not to have been 'habitually resident in the State' unless the contrary is shown (SW(MP)A 2004, Sch 1). 'Habitually resident in the State' means being present in the State or any other part of the *Common Travel Area* (ie the United Kingdom of Great Britain and Northern Ireland, the Channel Islands and the Isle of Man) for a continuous period of two years ending on the date of the application (Sch 1). See *Robinson v Minister for Social Welfare* [1995] ELR 86, HC. See website: *www.welfare.ie*. [Bibliography: Clarke R (3); Whyte; White UK.] See CONSOLIDATION ACT; EURO-JUS; INFLATION.

social welfare tribunal. A tribunal, consisting of a chairman and four ordinary members, which hears and decides applications for adjudication in relation to whether social welfare should be available to persons engaged in an industrial dispute, notwithstanding the trade dispute disqualification in SW(C)A 1993, s 47 (unemployment benefit) and s 125 (unemployment assistance): Social Welfare (Consolidation) Act 1993, ss 274–276. A party to the application may make an opening statement, call witnesses, cross-examine, give evidence on his own behalf and make a final address to the tribunal. The decision of the tribunal, which may be by a majority, is recorded and a copy sent to the applicant, and any interested party. See also Social Welfare Act 1996, s 33. See *Re Roderick O'Connor* [1995] ELR 152. See STRIKE.

societas Europaea, SE. [European Company (qv)].

societies, secret. See SECRET SOCIETIES.

society, friendly. See FRIENDLY SOCIETY.

sodomy. Anal intercourse between a man and another man or a woman. See BUGGERY.

software. (1) Computer program; instructions which make hardware work. There are two main types of software: (a) *system software* (operating systems) which controls the working of the computer, and (b) *applications software* such as word processing, spreadsheets, and databases, which perform the tasks required by users of computers. Compare with HARDWARE.

(2) Means a sequence of instructions used to control data equipment or used by *data equipment* to process data: Taxes Consolidation Act 1997, s 912(1). *Data equipment* means any equipment which uses electronic, magnetic, optical or photographic means for *processing* information that is in a form that can be processed (data). *Processing* means performing logical or arithmetical operations on data, or storing, reproducing or communicating data. The powers conferred on the Revenue Commissioners in relation to the keeping, production, inspection, checking or removal of records also apply to the data equipment and the software used to process the records (TCA 1997, s 912(2)). A person using data equipment is required to give a Revenue officer reasonable assistance in the course of his inspection (TCA 1997, s 912(3)).

Provision has been made to treat the grant of a licence of or a right to use software and the computer software itself as two separate assets for capital allowances purposes, and to have apportionment of the allowances: TCA 1997, s 288 as amended by Finance Act 2000, s 41. See COMPUTER PROGRAM; TRADE SECRET.

soil. Means the top layer of the land surface of the earth that is composed of disintegrated rock particles, humus, water and air: Environmental Protection Agency Act 1992, s 3 as substituted by Protection of the Environment Act 2003, s 5.

solatium. An additional amount awarded by a court for injured feeling or mental distress. See FATAL INJURIES; MENTAL DISTRESS.

sole. Single, unmarried; separate.

sole, corporation. See CORPORATION SOLE.

sole agent. See COMMISSION; AGENT.

sole discovery. An action where the sole object is the discovery of documents and is not part of other proceedings. The High Court has jurisdiction at common law to entertain an action for sole discovery. However, the court must exercise self-restraint in exercising this jurisdiction and should only exercise it where the plaintiff is in a position to prove that he has suffered a wrong, but is not in a position to identify the wrongdoer, whereas the defendant is: *Doyle v Commissioner of Garda Síochána* [1998] 2 ILRM 523, SC. The plaintiff in this case unsuccessfully sought discovery of all documentation in the possession of the Gardaí concerning their investigation of the bomb explosions which occurred in Dublin and Monaghan on 17 May 1974. See DISCOVERY.

sole licence. See EXCLUSIVE LICENCE.

sole practitioner. A solicitor who is practising as a sole principal in a solicitor's practice: Solicitors (Amendment) Act 1994, s 2. A solicitor is not permitted to practise as a sole practitioner or as a partner for a period of up to three years after admission as a solicitor, without the consent of the Law Society (S(A)A 1994, s 37).

The Society is empowered to require a sole practitioner who has abandoned his practice or has ceased to practise to produce any documents relating to the practice; it may also seek a High Court order to control his bank accounts (S(A)A 1994, ss 27–28). Arrangements are provided for the continuation of the practice of a sole practitioner who has died, is incapacitated, bankrupt or who has abandoned his practice; the Society may apply to the High Court to sell his practice in circumstances where it is likely there will be a claim from clients on the *Compensation Fund* (S(A)A 1994, ss 31–33).

A solicitor who is a sole practitioner or the sole principal of a firm should endeavour to have arrangements in place so that in the event of accident or illness, the practice may be carried on with the minimum of interruption of the clients' affairs: *A Guide to Professional Conduct of Solicitors in Ireland* (2002) ch 9.15. Approximately 47% of solicitors in the Republic of Ireland are sole practitioners, while 75% of solicitors are in practices of three or fewer solicitors. See 'Two become one' by David Rowe in *Law Society Gazette* (June 2003) 32. See EXECUTOR; SOLICITOR.

sole trader. A person carrying on business in his own name. A sole trader's business is part of his property and its obligation and debts are the trader's own personal liability. Contrast with a registered company which exists in law entirely separate from its owners; its business is not necessarily disrupted with the death of the principal owner; and ownership is easily transferred by selling of shares. See PARTNERSHIP; COMPANY; ONE MAN COMPANY.

solemn declaration. A declaration made by each member state of the EC. It may clarify the intention of a Treaty entered into by the members but it is not legally binding, although it would be taken into account by the EC Court of Justice. For example, see solemn declaration on the Abortion Protocol in the Maastricht Treaty.

solemn form. See WILL, PROOF OF.

solicit. It is an offence to solicit or importune another person (whether or not for the purposes of prostitution) for the purposes of the commission of an act which would be an offence under the Criminal Law (Sexual Offences) Act 1993, s 3 (buggery of persons under 17 years of age), or s 4 (gross indecency with males under 17 years of age), or, s 5 (mentally impaired persons) or under the Criminal Law Amendment Act 1935, s 1 (defilement of girl under 15 years of age) or s 2 (defilement of girl between 15 and 17 years of age): Criminal Law (Sexual Offences) Act 1993, s 6 as amended by substitution by Children Act 2001, s 250.

Soliciting or importuning by a prostitute, or by a client or by a third party on behalf of a prostitute or client is an offence (CL(SO)A 1993, s 7). See AID AND ABET; BUGGERY; GROSS INDECENCY; LOITERING; MENTALLY IMPAIRED; PROCURE; PROSTITUTE.

solicitor. (1) Includes a firm of solicitors or any partner therein: Circuit Court Rules 2001, Interpretation of Terms, para 21.

(2) A person who has been admitted as a solicitor and whose name is on the roll of solicitors; included is a firm of solicitors or a former or deceased solicitor unless the context otherwise requires: Solicitors (Amendment) Act 1994, s 2, and Solicitor Act 1954, s 54 as substituted by S(A)A 1994, s 62. To be admitted as a solicitor, the person must have attained the age of 21, must have complied with the prescribed requirements as regards being bound by indentures of apprenticeship, attendance at courses, passing of examinations, and satisfying the Law Society that he is a fit and proper person to be a solicitor (SA 1954, s 24 as substituted by S(A)A 1994, s 40).

A solicitor must not practise as a solicitor unless a *practising certificate* in respect of him is in force (S(A)A 1994, s 56). It is an offence for an unqualified person to act as a solicitor or for a person to pretend to be or to imply by certain actions to be a solicitor: Solicitors Act 1954, ss 55, 56 as amended by S(A)A 1994, ss 63, 64. A certificate issued by the Society to the effect that an unqualified person was acting as a solicitor must be admitted as *prima facie* evidence of the facts therein stated (S(A)A 1994, s 60).

It is an offence for a solicitor to fail to maintain accounting records in accordance with regulations made by the Society (SA 1954, s 66 as substituted by S(A)A 1994, s 76 and amended by Solicitors (Amendment) Act 2002, s 3). See ACCOUNTS, SOLICITOR.

A solicitor must not: (a) act as an agent for an unqualified person, or (b) reward, or agree to reward, an unqualified person for legal business introduced by such person to the solicitor (SA 1954, ss 59 and 62). See Employment Equality Act 1998, s 67 amended by Equality Act 2004, s 28; and Equal Status Act 2000, s 23(6) inserted by EA 2004, s 57.

However, provision may be made by regulation for the incorporation of solicitors practices (*incorporated practices*), and for fee-sharing between solicitors and non-solicitors (*multi-disciplinary arrangements*) (S(A)A 1994, ss 70–71). The European Court of Justice has held that a national regulation which prohibits any multi-disciplinary partnerships between members of the Bar and accountants is not contrary to the Treaty of the European Community, since that regulation could reasonably be considered to be necessary for the proper practice of the legal profession, as organised in the country concerned: Case C-309/99 *Wouters, Savelbergh, Price Water-house Belastingadviseurs BV v Algemene Raad van de Nederlandse Orde van Advocaten* [2002] ECJ .

A solicitor who provides *investment business services* or *investment advice* in a manner which is not incidental to the provision of legal services, is deemed to be an investment business firm requiring authorisation under the Investment Intermediaries Act 1995: Investor Compensation Act 1998, s 47.

A solicitor has a right of audience before all courts: Courts Act 1971, s 17. He is an officer of the court. The jurisdiction of the High Court to discipline solicitors as officers of the court continues to exist: Judicature (Ireland) Act 1877, s 78; *Re IPLG Ltd* (1992) Law Society Gazette (October 1992) HC. Solicitors are now eligible for appointment as judges to all the courts; see JUDGES, QUALIFICATION OF. In 2002, a solicitor was appointed as a High Court judge for the first time, Mr Justice Michael Peart. See 'His Highness' by Conal O'Boyle in *Law Society Gazette* (July/August 2002) 14.

A solicitor owes a duty of care to his client and he also is in a fiduciary relationship to him: *A Guide to Professional Conduct of Solicitors in Ireland* (2002) ch 2.2.

The Solicitors Acts 1954 to 2002 provide for the regulation of the profession, the protection of clients and the investigation of complaints. The maximum fines which may be imposed for offences under these Acts have been amended (S(A)A 2002, s 22). Also the High Court is empowered to make an order prohibiting a solicitor, or any other person concerned, from contravening any provision of the Solicitors Acts 1954 to 2002 or any provision of regulations made under those Acts, notwithstanding that such contravention may constitute an offence (S(A)A 2002, s 18). The order is made on the application of the Law Society.

For the Indecon Report for the Competition Authority on competition in the legal profession, see 'The Competition Authority review of professions' by Paul McGarry BL

in *Bar Review* (April 2003) 51. See also *Law Society Gazette* (April 2003) 5. The report is available on website: *www.tca.ie.* [Bibliography: Hogan; O'Callaghan P; Adamson UK; Cordery UK.] See BARRISTER; DISBARRED; BILL OF COSTS; CLIENT ACCOUNT; CLIENT'S MONEY; CONTENTIOUS BUSINESS; COMPANY, REGISTERED; COMPENSATION FUND; CONSULTANCY REFERRAL SCHEME; INJUNCTION, CRIMINAL; LAW AGENT; LAW SOCIETY OF IRELAND; LEGAL SERVICES; MERGER OF SOLICITORS; NAME OF SOLICITOR; PARTNERSHIP, NUMBER TO FORM; SOLE PRACTITIONER; STATE SOLICITOR; UNCONSCIONABLE BARGAIN; UNDUE INFLUENCE.

solicitor, access to. The right of reasonable access to a solicitor of a detained person is constitutional in origin; it is directed towards the vital function of ensuring that the detained person is aware of his rights and has independent advice to permit him to reach a truly free decision as to his attitude to interrogation or to making any statement, whether exculpatory or inculpatory, and must be seen as a contribution towards a measure of equality in the position of him and his interrogators: *DPP v Healy* [1990] ILRM 313, SC; 1937 Constitution, art 40(3). An incriminating statement will be inadmissible if obtained when the accused's constitutional right is being deliberately and consciously violated (*Healy* case). See also *People v Buck* [2002] 2 ILRM 454, SC and 2 IR 268. See also Criminal Justice Act 1984, s 5.

Although there is no general right to be informed of the right of access to a solicitor, an arrested person is entitled to be informed without delay by the Gardaí that he is entitled to consult a solicitor; however, a failure to so inform him does not affect the lawfulness of the custody or the admissibility of statements made by him (CJA 1984, s 73(3)); Treatment of Persons in Custody in Garda Síochána Stations Regulations 1987, SI No 119 of 1987, reg 8; *DPP v Spratt* [1995] 2 ILRM 117, HC. See *People (DPP) v Connell* [1995] 1 IR 244, CCA. See 'The right to a Solicitor – Recent Developments' by Niall McFadden BL in *Bar Review* (December 2002) 390. See ARRESTED PERSON, COMMUNICATIONS FROM; BLOOD SPECIMEN; COURTS MARTIAL; LEGAL ADVICE; LEGAL AID; LEGAL REPRESENTATION; REPRESENTATIVE.

solicitor, change of. A client may change his solicitor whenever he wishes to do so: *A Guide to Professional Conduct of Solicitors in Ireland* (2002) ch 2.3. The client however must pay the fees and outlays of the first solicitor, in which event the client's file belongs to the client and should be transferred to the new solicitor (ch 7.6). The file transferred should include instructions, briefs, copies of correspondence written to third parties and documents prepared by third parties for the benefit of the client. Any item which deals with the substance of the matter and which would assist the new solicitor should be included. The new solicitor should endeavour to ensure that the first solicitor's costs are discharged by the client.

A party suing or defending by a solicitor in the High Court is entitled, without the order of the court except in matrimonial matters, to change or discharge his solicitor, provided notice is given to the other side and the change or discharge is filed in the Central Office (qv): RSC Ord 7, r 2. For a solicitor to cease acting for a client, see OFF RECORD; RETAINER; SOLICITOR, WITHDRAWAL OF.

solicitor, complaint against. The Law Society is required to investigate any complaint received from a client of a solicitor alleging that the services provided by the solicitor were inadequate in any material respect and were not of the quality that could reasonably be expected from him as a solicitor: Solicitors (Amendment) Act 1994, s 8. The Society is required, unless the claim is frivolous or vexatious, to investigate the matter and to take appropriate steps to resolve the matter by agreement between the parties, and may make a determination or a direction in the matter eg to direct the solicitor to take particular actions. The Society is also empowered to impose sanctions on a solicitor where it finds that the solicitor has issued a bill of costs which is excessive (S(A)A 1994, s 9).

The Society may direct that all documents in connection with the complaint, in the possession or under the control or within the procurement of a solicitor, be produced (S(A)A 1994, s 10). If it appears to the Society that a solicitor is obstructing the investigation of the complaint, the Society may apply to the High Court for an order compelling the solicitor to respond appropriately (S(A)A 1994, s 10A inserted by Solicitors (Amendment) 2002, s 13).

This order may provide for censoring the solicitor and may require the payment of a money penalty.

Also a person authorised by the Society is empowered to attend at the place of business of a solicitor without notice to inspect documents where it appears to the Society that this is necessary for the purpose of investigating a complaint against a solicitor or an allegation of misconduct or the capacity of the solicitor (S(A)A 1994, s 14 as amended by S(A)A 2002, s 15).

The Society is empowered to require a solicitor to make a contribution of up to €3,000 towards the cost of an investigation (S(A)A 1994, s 12 as substituted by S(A)A 2002, s 14). If the Society is of the opinion that the complaint is justified but is not of sufficient seriousness to warrant an application being made to the Disciplinary Tribunal, the Society may reprimand the solicitor in writing.

The Supreme Court has held that the investigation of fraudulent claims is not an authorised purpose under the Solicitors' Accounts Regulations: *Kennedy v Law Society of Ireland (No 3)* [2002] 2 IR 458, SC. However, the High Court subsequently rejected the plaintiff's claim for damages, holding that the plaintiff had fallen short, on the balance of probabilities, of establishing a case that the Society had actual knowledge of or was recklessly indifferent to the possibility that it lacked the appropriate statutory powers: *Giles Kennedy v Law Society* [2004] 1 ILRM 178, HC and *Law Society Gazette* (August/September 2003) 51. See also LAW SOCIETY OF IRELAND; SOLICITOR'S DISCIPLINARY TRIBUNAL.

solicitor, continuing professional development of. As from 2003, solicitors are required to undertake *continuing professional development* (CPD) ie a course or courses of further education or training (or both), whether relating to law or to management, intended to develop a solicitor in his professional knowledge, skills and abilities: Solicitors (Continuing Professional Development) Regulations 2003, SI No 37 of 2003. This also includes a course specifically approved by the education committee of the Law Society. Solicitors are required to undertake 20 hours of continuing professional development during the relevant period. The initial cycle is two-and-a-half years, running from 1 July 2003 to 31 December 2005. Thereafter, the cycles consist of two-year periods. A minimum of

15 hours is required to be in group study and up to five hours may be by way of private study. At least five hours of the total cycle must be spent on training in management and professional development skills. See 'Learning Curve' in *Law Society Gazette* (June 2003) 22; 'CPD – a review' in *Law Society Gazette* (January/February 2004) 25.

solicitor in employment. An in-house solicitor who generally has only one client, his employer, to whom he owes a duty of loyalty. Where the employer instructs the solicitor to act in a way which, in the opinion of the solicitor, would amount to unprofessional conduct or which may even be illegal, the solicitor should advise the employer that those instructions cannot be acted upon: *A Guide to Professional Conduct of Solicitors in Ireland* (2002) ch 1.3. In-house solicitors who hold 'practising certificates' are subject to the statutory regulation of the Law Society in the same way as solicitors in private practice. Their advice is privileged in the same way as the advice of colleagues in private practice; however, employed practising solicitors should have systems in place to assist identification of privileged communications between themselves and their employers, where acting as such and not merely administratively (ch 4.1).

An employed solicitor may receive his instructions from one or more employees in an organisation (ch 2.1). As regards undertakings, an employed solicitor should not give a professional undertaking to do something which is outside his control (ch 6.5). If it has not been delegated to him, it is outside his control.

An employed solicitor may practise: (a) in the solicitor's own name, in which case a clear indication should be given on his notepaper that the letter has emanated from the legal department of his employer's organisation; (b) in the name of the employer, in which case an indication should be given on the notepaper that the letter emanated from the solicitor's practice within the organisation; or (c) under a business name (ch 9.3).

A solicitor in the employment of the Personal Injuries Assessment Board may appear on behalf of the Board in an application to the courts to secure information which a party, not involved in a claim for personal injuries, is failing to supply to support the claimant's case: Personal Inju-

ries Assessment Board Act 2003, ss 27 and 82. This provision applies notwithstanding: (a) any rule of law relating to the representation of bodies corporate, or (b) that the solicitor would be prohibited from doing so by virtue of any rule of law or provision of any enactment or code of conduct imposing restrictions on employed solicitors in relation to engaging in activity of that kind.

See also Law Society, *Information Booklet for Solicitors commencing Employment in the Corporate and Public Services Sector* (February 2002).

solicitor, international practice. A lawyer's practice in a member state, other than the state in which his qualification was obtained, is facilitated by the EU Directive on Establishment (EC) 98/5, implemented in Ireland by Solicitors (Amendment) Act 2002, s 20. Under the Directive the immigrant lawyer is subject to the rules of professional conduct which apply to lawyers in the host state. This Directive applies to the *European Economic Area* (qv) and the *Swiss Confederation* (qv).

Where a lawyer with an office established in a member state provides legal services in another member state, without actually establishing an office there, his practice is governed by the EU Directive on Services (EEC) 77/249 (SI No 58 of 1979, SI No 197 of 1981, and SI No 226 of 1986). The lawyer remains subject to the rules of the state in which he has an office, but without prejudice to respect for the rules of the host state.

The relationship between lawyers in international practice is also governed by the codes adopted by the International Bar Association and by CCBE, the association of Bars and Law Societies of Europe. Both codes have as their basis the principles of good conduct common to all lawyers: *A Guide to Professional Conduct of Solicitors in Ireland* (2002) ch 11.1. See International Bar Association 1988, 'International Code of Ethics' and 'Code of Conduct for Lawyers in the European Community, CCBE 1999 (*Guide to Professional Conduct of Solicitors*, Apps 3 and 2 respectively).

A solicitor should not commence any form of proceedings against any lawyer in another jurisdiction concerning a matter of professional conduct without first informing the Bar or Law Society to which the other lawyer belongs, for the purpose of allowing that body an opportunity to assist in reaching a settlement of the matter (ch

11.3). A solicitor who instructs a solicitor outside the jurisdiction is personally liable to pay all fees reasonably and properly incurred by that lawyer, unless there has been an express agreement that the solicitor is not to be made personally liable (ch 11.4). The alternative is for the solicitor to advise the client to employ a foreign lawyer directly and to give assistance to the client in locating a lawyer. For CCBE see website: *www.ccbe.org*. See BARRISTER, INTERNATIONAL PRACTICE; SOLICITOR, MUTUAL RECOGNITION.

solicitorlink. The confidential service provided by the Law Society of Ireland to solicitors wishing to buy, sell or merge their practices. Identities are not revealed until the parties agree. The Society is not involved in any negotiations. See *Law Society Gazette* (November 2003) 4. See MERGER OF SOLICITORS.

solicitor, misconduct of. *Misconduct* of a solicitor is widely defined to include: the commission of treason or of an offence, the contravention of a provision of the Solicitors Acts 1954 to 2002 or any order or regulation made thereunder, or having direct or indirect connection with a person who has contravened specified provisions (eg an unqualified person drawing up certain legal documents or advertising legal services), or any other conduct tending to bring the solicitors' profession into dispute: Solicitors (Amendment) Act 1960, s 3 as amended by Solicitors (Amendment) Act 2002, s 7. See also *A Guide to Professional Conduct of Solicitors in Ireland* (2002) ch 1.4. See SOLICITOR'S DISCIPLINARY TRIBUNAL; WHISTLE BLOWER.

solicitor, mutual recognition. The Law Society is empowered to grant exemptions from its examinations to persons from jurisdictions outside the EU who are qualified to practise in a *corresponding* profession to the profession of solicitor: Solicitors Act 1954, s 44 as substituted by Solicitors (Amendment) Act 1994, s 52. This power can only come into effect by Ministerial order when *reciprocal provisions* are in operation in the other jurisdiction in respect of Irish solicitors. Provisions are in place in respect of the following lawyers, subject to sitting the Qualified Lawyers Transfer Test (QLTT), New York Bar attorneys and Pennsylvanian attorneys having five years' practising experience (SI No 241 of 1997), and New Zealand qualified solicitors (SI No 133 of 1999), and attorneys or counsel-

lors at law in the State of California, USA (SI No 459 of 2003).

Lawyers from EU states are entitled to practise in this jurisdiction by virtue of Council Directive (EEC) 77/249 of 22 March 1977 (implemented by SI No 58 of 1979, SI No 197 of 1981, and SI No 226 of 1986); by Directive (EEC) 89/48 (implemented by EC (General System for the Recognition of Higher Education Diplomas) Regulations 1991, SI No 1 of 1991 and Qualified Lawyers (European Community) Regulations 1991, SI No 85 of 1991.

Provision was made in 2002 to facilitate the practice of the profession of lawyer throughout the *European Economic Area* (qv) and the *Swiss Confederation* (qv): Solicitors (Amendment) Act 2002, s 20. This provides for the implementation of the EU Directive (EC) 98/5 and any corresponding measure. Regulations may be made which will provide that rules of a competent authority governing professional practice, conduct and discipline, shall have effect in relation: (a) to member state *lawyers* who are pursuing their professional activities in Ireland using their home-country professional title; and (b) to other lawyers who have acquired the right to practise the profession of lawyer in Ireland. The regulations may authorise the competent authority to require professional indemnity insurance and, in relation to professional activities which are those of a solicitor, contributions to the *Compensation Fund* (qv).

Further provision was made in 2003 to provide for the registration of such lawyers, their professional activities, conduct and discipline and, subject to certain conditions, their admission into the professions of barrister and solicitor: SI No 732 of 2003. See 'The Free Movement of Lawyers' by Colm Hagan in (2003) 11 ISLR 149. See *'One to Watch: New Legislation'* by Alma Clissmann in *Law Society Gazette* (March 2004) 4. See 'All together now' by solicitor Wendy Hederman in *Law Society Gazette* (May 2004) 8. [Bibliography: O'Callaghan P.] See SOLICITOR, INTERNATIONAL PRACTICE.

solicitor, professional negligence. The standard of care expected of a solicitor is that of a reasonably careful and skilful solicitor and should take into account that the relationship of a solicitor and client is a fiduciary relationship: *A Guide to Professional Conduct of Solicitors in Ireland* (2002) ch 2.2. Where a solicitor is guilty of such failure as no other solicitor of equal status and skill would be guilty of if acting with ordinary care; this does not mean that a solicitor following a practice which was general and which was approved of by colleagues of similar skill would escape liability, if it were established that such practice had inherent defects which ought to be obvious to any person giving the matter due consideration: *Hanafin v Gaynor* [1991] 9 ILT Dig 76 applying *Dunne v National Maternity Hospital* [1989] ILRM 735.

Generally, a solicitor will not be held liable in negligence if he properly presents all aspects of his client's claim to appropriate and competent counsel and he acts on the advice received: *Millard v McMahon* (1968, unreported) HC. However, he cannot rely blindly on counsel's advice. He must exercise his own professional skill, judgement and experience, and satisfy himself that the advice received is correct.

A solicitor has a *prima facie* duty to advise a purchaser of a house to have an independent inspection by a suitably qualified person: *O'Connor v First National Building Society* [1991] ILRM 208, HC.

The primary duty of a solicitor acting for a vendor is to protect his client; that obligation is perfectly consistent also with the duty of care to the purchaser in certain circumstances: *Doran v Delaney* [1998] 2 ILRM 1, SC and [1998] 2 IR 61, SC. The factors which determine whether a solicitor while acting for a client, also owes a duty of care to a third party are: (a) the solicitor must assume responsibility for advice or information furnished to the third party; (b) the solicitor must let it be known to the third party expressly or impliedly that he claims, by reason of his calling, to have the requisite skill or knowledge to give the advice or furnish the information; (c) the third party must have relied on that information as a matter for which the solicitor has assumed personal responsibility; (d) the solicitor must have been aware that the third party was likely so to rely (*Doran* case). See also *Roche v Peilow* [1986] ILRM 189; *Kehoe v CJ Louth & Son* [1992] ILRM 283, SC. See Solicitors (Amendment) 1994, s 8. See 'Practice Pitfalls: professional negligence and the solicitor' by solicitor Patrick Groarke in *Law Society*

Gazette (July 2003) 12. See LITIGATION; PROFESSIONAL NEGLIGENCE.

solicitor, restoration to roll. Where a solicitor has been struck off the roll of solicitors for, *inter alia*, dishonest conduct, he may apply to the High Court for a conditional or full restoration to the roll: Solicitors (Amendment) Act 1960 as amended by Solicitors (Amendment) Act 1994, s 19. The applicant must satisfy the court that he is a fit and proper person to be allowed to practise and that his restoration would not adversely affect public confidence in the solicitors' profession and the administration of justice, irrespective of whether he is seeking a conditional or full restoration: *Re Burke* [2001] 4 IR 445, SC.

solicitor, retainer of. Where a solicitor's retainer by a client is not in writing and the client disputes the terms of the retainer, there is no principle in law that the client's evidence must automatically be accepted by the court in preference to that of the solicitor: *Mackie v Wilde* [1995] 1 ILRM 468, HC and [1998] 2 IR 570, HC disapproving of UK case *Griffith v Evans* [1993] 2 All ER 1364. See however CONTENTIOUS BUSINESS.

solicitor, struck off. A former solicitor whose name has been struck off the roll of solicitors. A former solicitor who has been struck off, or has been suspended, or has had a practising certificate refused or suspended, or who has given an undertaking not to practise as a solicitor, is prohibited from seeking or accepting employment in connection with the provision of *legal services* (qv) without disclosing that he is an unqualified person: Solicitors Act 1954, s 63 as substituted by Solicitors (Amendment) Act 1994, s 21. There is a similar restriction on anyone employing such a person (SA 1954, s 60 as substituted by S(A)A 1994, s 20). When a solicitor is struck off or suspended, there is a requirement on the Law Society to publish the order of the Court in Iris Oifigiúil and in the *Gazette* of the Society (S(A)A 1994, s 23(3)).

solicitor, withdrawal of. A solicitor who has accepted instructions to appear in court for a client who is in custody may not withdraw from the client's case without obtaining permission from the court before which that client is next scheduled to appear: Solicitors (Amendment) Act 1994, s 74. See also *A Guide to Professional Conduct of Solicitors in Ireland* (2002) ch 2.3.

See BARRISTER, WITHDRAWAL OF; OFF RECORD; RETAINER.

solicitor and advertising. A solicitor is prohibited from publishing an *advertisement* which: (a) is likely to bring the solicitor's profession into disrepute, or (b) is in bad taste, or (c) reflects unfavourably on other solicitors, or (d) asserts that the solicitor has specialist knowledge superior to that of other solicitors, or (e) is false or misleading in any respect, or (f) is published in an *inappropriate location*, or (g) does not comply with regulations made by the Law Society: Solicitors Act 1954, s 71 as inserted by Solicitors (Amendment) Act 2002, s 4. *Advertisement* means any communication (whether oral or in writing or other visual form and whether produced by electronic or other means) which is intended to publicise or otherwise promote a solicitor in relation to the solicitor's practice (SA 1954, s 71(10) as inserted). *Inappropriate location* means a hospital, clinic, doctor's surgery, funeral home, cemetery, crematorium or other location of a similar character (SA 1954, s 71(10) as inserted).

There are prohibitions on advertisements which expressly or impliedly: (a) refer to claims for personal injuries, the possible outcome of such claims or the provision of legal services in connection with such claims; or (b) encourage or offer any inducement to any person or group or class of persons to make such claims (SA 1954, s 71(2)(h) and (i) as inserted). Breach by a solicitor of the provisions on advertising amounts to misconduct: Solicitors (Amendment) Act 1960, s 3 as amended by S(A)A 2002, s 7.

For provisions prohibiting unqualified persons publishing advertisements offering services of a legal nature, see S(A)A 2002, s 5.

See Solicitors (Advertising) Regulations 2002, SI No 518 of 2002. See *A Guide to Professional Conduct of Solicitors in Ireland* (2002) ch 9.5. See *Law Society Gazette* (December 2002) 2 and (January/February 2004) 54. For previous regulations, see Solicitors (Advertising) Regulations 1996, SI No 351 of 1996. See NO FOAL, NO FEE; PERSONAL INJURIES; UNSOLICITED APPROACH.

solicitor and client costs. The costs incurred in non-contentious legal matters which a solicitor claims from a client; they also include costs incurred in contentious matters which a party to an action is not entitled to recover from the other party; they are only *taxed* when the client so requests. 'On a taxation as between solicitor and own client, all cost incurred with the express or implied approval of the client evidenced in writing shall be conclusively presumed to have been reasonably incurred, and where the amount thereof has been so expressly or impliedly approved by the client, to have been reasonable in amount': RSC Ord 99, r 11(3).

'The solicitor-and-client fee is the amount that a client owes to his solicitor in respect of work undertaken on his behalf ... The practice of routinely charging a solicitor-and-client fee must cease. The fee is only chargeable if costs are incurred and approved by the client': James Flynn, taxing master High Court in 'Solicitors' Costs and the Client' *Law Society Gazette* (July/August 2002) 18.

A solicitor cannot lawfully sue for his costs for one month after delivery of the costs; a client has twelve months within which to demand and obtain taxation of the costs: Attorney and Solicitors (Ireland) Act 1849, ss 2 and 6; *The State (Gallagher Shatter & Co) v de Valera* [1986] ILRM 3. Compare with *party and party costs* (qv). See *A Guide to Professional Conduct of Solicitors in Ireland* (2002) ch 10.1. [Bibliography: Flynn & Halpin.] See BARRISTER AND FEES; BRIEF FEE; COSTS IN CIVIL PROCEEDINGS; CONTENTIOUS BUSINESS; LEGAL CHARGES; LEGAL COSTS ACCOUNTANT; LEGAL SERVICES; TAXATION OF COSTS.

solicitor and confidentiality. A solicitor has a professional duty to keep confidential all matters coming within the solicitor/client relationship, including the existence of that relationship: *A Guide to Professional Conduct of Solicitors in Ireland* (2002) ch 4.2. These matters can only be disclosed with the consent of the client or by direction of the court. Particular care is required with office systems and also where solicitors share accommodation or staff with non-solicitors (chs 9.1 and 9.12).

A lawyer, whether solicitor or barrister, is under a duty not to communicate to any third party, information entrusted to him by or on behalf of his lay client: *McMullen v Carty* (1998, unreported), SC. 'This privilege of confidentiality belongs to the client, not the lawyer. It may be waived by the client, not the lawyer, but such waiver may be implied in certain circumstances as well as being express': Lynch J in *McMullen* case.

Where a solicitor believes on reasonable grounds that there is a real risk of death or serious injury to his client or to a third party, confidentiality may be waived to the extent necessary (*Guide* ch 4.2). Where a solicitor enters into a settlement, the details of which are to be kept confidential, the solicitor is not precluded from representing a future client against the same defendant, provided that the terms of the first settlement are kept confidential: Law Society, *Guidance and Ethics Committee* in *Law Society Gazette* (June 2003) 41. See 'Practice Pitfalls: professional negligence and the solicitor' by solicitor Patrick Groarke in *Law Society Gazette* (July 2003) 12. See CHILD ABUSE, REPORTING; DOCUMENTS INTENDED FOR ANOTHER; EXECUTOR; PRIVILEGE, LEGAL PROFESSIONAL; REVENUE AUDIT; SOLICITOR AND DISCLOSURE; WILL, SUPPLY OF COPY.

solicitor and counsel. Where counsel is instructed, it is the duty of a solicitor to ensure that counsel has all the instructions and information which the solicitor has and which are or may be necessary for counsel to properly represent the client's interest within a reasonable time: *A Guide to Professional Conduct of Solicitors in Ireland* (2002) ch 8.2. In general, a barrister must be attended in court by his instructing solicitor or his clerk or assistant but it is not necessary that he be so attended when moving an application for an adjournment: *Code of Conduct for the Bar of Ireland* (December 2003) r 5.15.

It has been held that the duty of a solicitor with regard to the conduct of a case in court where counsel has been briefed is firstly, to brief appropriate and competent counsel and secondly, to instruct them properly in relation to the facts of the case which he has obtained from his client, and to make provision for the attendance of appropriate witnesses and other proofs; a solicitor has not got any vicarious liability for the individual conduct of counsel: *Fallon v Gannon* [1988] ILRM 193.

It is the duty of the solicitor to ensure that counsel is adequately attended on in court (*Guide* ch 8.3). A solicitor acting on a general retainer from a client is not entitled, without instructions from the client, to seek the advice of or instruct counsel (ch 8.1). A

spirit of co-operation and trust should always exist between solicitor and counsel (ch 8.4).

It is undesirable for a barrister to consult with a client in any matter unless the solicitor instructing him is present or has instructed him to do so (*Bar Code* r 4.11). If a barrister has accepted a brief in a case, he may not, without the consent of the solicitor who has briefed him, accept a further brief in any other case which is likely to reduce to a serious degree the time and attention that he should properly give to the case in which he had first accepted a brief (r 4.6). A barrister may not hand over his brief to another barrister to conduct a case unless his instructing solicitor so directs (r 4.8). See BRIEF; INSTRUCT; COMPROMISE; RETAINER; SOLICITOR'S OFFICE.

solicitor and court. A solicitor has an overriding duty to the court to ensure in the public interest that the proper and efficient administration of justice is achieved and should assist the court in the administration of justice and should not deceive or knowingly or recklessly mislead the court: *A Guide to Professional Conduct of Solicitors in Ireland* (2002) ch 5.1. A solicitor should not assert what he knows to be untrue or substantiate a fraud, as that would amount to a positive deception of the court. A solicitor advocate has a duty to assist the court in reaching a just decision and in furtherance of that aim, he must advise the court of all relevant cases and statutory provisions. See BARRISTER AND COURT.

solicitor and disclosure. A Supreme Court judge has said that solicitors in matrimonial proceedings should advise their clients as to their obligations in relation to making full disclosure and, if necessary, the court should not be slow to make a solicitor personally liable for costs wasted by unnecessary and unreasonable recalcitrant behaviour on behalf of their clients: Barron J in *MS v DW* [2000] 1 ILRM 416, SC. See also PRIVILEGE, LEGAL PROFESSIONAL; SOLICITOR AND CONFIDENTIALITY.

solicitor and divorce proceedings. A solicitor acting for a party in *divorce* proceedings, is required prior to instituting the proceedings, to discuss reconciliation possibilities with his client and supply the names and addresses of persons who are qualified to effect a reconciliation between estranged spouses, to discuss the possibility of engaging in mediation to help effect a separation or a divorce on an agreed basis, to discuss the possibility of effecting a separation by deed or in writing, and to ensure that the client is aware of *judicial separation* as an alternative to divorce: Family Law (Divorce) Act 1996, ss 6–7. The originating documents by which the divorce proceedings are instituted must be accompanied by a *certificate* from the solicitor that he has complied with this requirement.

solicitor and documents. With certain exceptions, only a solicitor is permitted to draw up or prepare certain legal *documents* for fee, gain or reward e g documents relating to real or personal estate or any legal proceedings, applications to the Land Registry, and documents relating to probate or letters of administration. There are exceptions e g acts done: (a) by a person for no fee, gain or reward, (b) by a practising barrister or by a barrister in the full-time services of the State for conveyancing services, (c) by EU lawyers. Certain documents are excluded e g a purely banking or commercial or mercantile document, a transfer of stocks, shares, bonds, debentures or other stock exchange securities, including a letter or power of attorney exclusively for their sale or transfer. See Solicitors Act 1954, s 58 as amended by Solicitors (Amendment) Act 1994, s 77. For further possible exceptions, see CONVEYANCING SERVICES; CREDIT UNIONS. See DOCUMENTS INTENDED FOR ANOTHER.

solicitor's accounts. See ACCOUNTS, SOLICITOR.

solicitor's apprentice. Includes a person who has completed the term of his indentures of apprenticeship but who has not yet been admitted as a solicitor: Solicitors (Amendment) Act 1994, s 2. A person is not capable of being bound by indentures of apprenticeship unless he has attained the age of 17 years and has attended such courses and passed such examinations as are prescribed: Solicitors Act 1954, s 25 as substituted by S(A)A 1994, s 41. The term of service under an indenture must not exceed two years (SA 1954, s 26 substituted by S(A)A 1994, s 42). Only a solicitor in practice for at least five years may take on an apprentice without the prior approval of the Law Society and he is limited to two apprentices at the one time (SA 1954, ss 29 and 36 as substituted by S(A)A 1994, ss 44 and 47 respectively).

The Law Society may prescribe the conditions under which a person may serve their apprenticeship in Northern Ireland, England or Wales (S(A)A 1994, s 53).

It has been held that the Law Society, through its Education Committee, has jurisdiction to enquire into allegations of misconduct of an apprentice and matters of discipline outside the educational sphere: *Carroll v Law Society* [2000] 1 ILRM 161, HC and (*No 2*) [2003] 1 IR 284. However, provision has now been made to enable the Society to make an application to the *Solicitor's Disciplinary Tribunal* to hold an inquiry into alleged *misconduct* of the apprentice: Solicitors (Amendment) Act 2002, s 19. Where the Tribunal finds that there has been misconduct, it is required to make a report to the High Court; the apprentice may appeal to the High Court. *Misconduct* means the commission of specified offences (e g pretending to be a solicitor, or drawing up legal documents), or the commission of an *arrestable offence* (within or outside the State), or any other conduct which, if engaged in by a solicitor, would tend to bring the solicitors' profession into disrepute (S(A)A 2002, s 19(7)). See also *Abrahamson v Law Society of Ireland* [1996] 2 ILRM 481, HC; *Bloomer v Law Society of Ireland* [1995] 3 IR 14, HC and ELR 220.

See the Solicitors Acts (Apprentice Fees) Regulations 2001, SI No 331 of 2001, Regulations 2002, SI No 377 of 2002, Regulations 2003, SI No 262 of 2003; Regulations 2004, SI No 405 of 2004; the Solicitors Acts (Apprenticeship and Education) Regulations 2001, SI No 546 of 2001. For *Solicitors' Apprentices Debating Society of Ireland*, see website: *www.sadsi.ie*. See INDENTURE OF APPRENTICE.

solicitor's client. Includes the personal representative of a client and any person on whose behalf the instructing person was acting, and includes a beneficiary under a will, intestacy or trust: Solicitors (Amendment) Act 1994, s 2. See CLIENT ACCOUNT; CLIENT FILE; CLIENTS' MONEY.

Solicitor's Disciplinary Tribunal. The disciplinary tribunal established by the Solicitors (Amendment) Act 1960, s 6 as substituted by Solicitors (Amendment) Act 1994, s 16 and amended by Solicitors (Amendment) Act 2002, s 8. The maximum number of solicitor and lay members of the Tribunal was increased by the 2002 Act to 30 and provision was made for *gender balance* (qv).

The Tribunal is empowered to hold an inquiry into the conduct of a solicitor on the ground of alleged *misconduct* (S(A)A 1994, s 17 as amended by S(A)A 2002, s 9). The Tribunal has all the powers of the High Court in enforcing the attendance of witnesses, compelling the production of documents, and compelling discovery; it may require the applicant and respondent solicitor to submit an outline of the evidence to be given by each of their witnesses and to decide on its relevance (S(A)A 1994, s 25 as amended by S(A)A 2002, s 11).

Provision has been made by the 2002 Act for an appeal to the High Court against a finding of the Tribunal that there is no *prima facie* case for inquiry or that there has been no misconduct on the part of the solicitor (S(A)A 2002, s 9).

The Tribunal is empowered, where it finds misconduct, either: (a) to advise, admonish or censure the solicitor; and/or to direct him to pay a sum of up to €15,000 to the aggrieved party and/or to the Compensation Fund; or (b) to make a report to the High Court with their opinion as to the fitness or otherwise of the solicitor to be a member of the solicitor's profession and their recommended sanction. There is provision for the publication of an order, or notice of an order and its effect, made by the Tribunal (S(A)A 1994, s 23 as amended by S(A)A 2002, s 17).

The High Court, after consideration of the report from the Tribunal, may impose a variety of sanctions, taking account of any previous findings of misconduct, eg to strike the name of the solicitor off the roll; to suspend for a period; to prohibit from practising as a sole practitioner or in a particular area of work; to censure or to censure and require him to pay a money penalty (S(A)A 1994, s 18 as amended by S(A)A 2002, s 10).

The High Court has wide powers eg: (a) requiring a bank to furnish information relating to the financial affairs of the solicitor's practice; (b) requiring the solicitor to swear an affidavit disclosing information relating to bank accounts; (c) requiring the solicitor not to reduce his assets below a specified value in cases where there is likely to be a drain on the Compensation Fund; (d) directing a bank or any bank not to make payments out of the solicitor's account.

The Supreme Court has held that where a complaint has been made against a solicitor, the following procedures are required by the principles of natural justice: (a) the solicitor should be notified of the complaint and given an opportunity to respond to it; and (b) the notification of the complaint and any response thereto should be before the tribunal before it makes its decision as to whether there is a *prima facie* case for inquiry: *O'Callaghan v Disciplinary Tribunal* [2002] 1 ILRM 89, SC. The High Court has held that in the absence of any statutory basis, there is no general duty imposed on the State to provide legal aid to a solicitor appearing before the tribunal on a complaint of alleged misconduct: *Malocco v Disciplinary Tribunal* [2002] ITLR (17 February). See *Carroll v Disciplinary Tribunal* [2003] 1 IR 278, HC. See RSC Ord 53 as amended by SI No 14 of 1998. See 'New Disciplinary Tribunal chairman lays down the law' in *Law Society Gazette* (March 2004) 4. See SOLICITOR, MISCONDUCT OF.

solicitor's lien. A lien (qv) may be exercised by a solicitor on all the files of a particular client if there are costs outstanding on one of those files: *Audley Hall Cotton Spinning Co* [1886] LR 6EQ 245 and *A Guide to Professional Conduct of Solicitors in Ireland* (2002) ch 2.4. The solicitor's lien arises by operation of law and not by unilateral act of the solicitor: *Re Galdan Properties Ltd* [1988] IR 213, SC. A solicitor's lien does not exist: (a) over a will, or (b) over documents or papers held on trust or on accountable receipt, or (c) over a debt which has become statute barred. A solicitor when exercising a lien must ensure that it does not reflect badly on the solicitor or on the legal profession in general.

When a solicitor hands over files to a new solicitor acting for his former client, subject to and without prejudice to the first solicitor's lien for costs, the new solicitor must return them on demand to the first solicitor, as long as the lien subsists.

A solicitor has a common law right to exercise a lien on monies held (*Guide* ch 9.11). If a solicitor holds moneys in the client account which are greater than due to the solicitor, the exercise of the lien should be limited to the amount due. A solicitor cannot exercise a lien on moneys coming into the solicitor's control if the monies were sent to him for a specific purpose eg for the payment of stamp duty.

A solicitor's lien extends only to costs incurred by the client against whom it is claimed: *Ring v Kennedy* [1999] 3 IR 316, HC. A solicitor's lien is overridden by the right of a liquidator of an insolvent company to all documents belonging to the company: *Re Macks Bakeries (in liquidation) and Luby v O'Connor* [2003] ITLR (5 May); [2003] 2 ILRM 75 and 2 IR 396. See also *Park Hall School v Overend* [1987] ILRM 345. See ENDORSEMENT; LAND CERTIFICATE.

solicitor's office. A barrister must not have a room in a solicitor's office: *Code of Conduct for the Bar of Ireland* (December 2003) r 4.14. Also a barrister may not work in or be an employee of a solicitor's office (r 4.16). See RETAINER.

solicitor's practising certificate. The certificate issued by Law Society of Ireland (qv) certifying that the solicitor (qv) named therein is entitled to practise as a solicitor: Solicitors Act 1954, ss 46–53 as amended. A solicitor must not practise as a solicitor unless a *practising certificate* in respect of him is in force; this does not apply to a solicitor in the full-time service of the State, or to a solicitor whose name is on the roll and who is employed full time to provide conveyancing services for his employer: Solicitors (Amendment) Act 1994, s 56. A solicitor who acts without a practising certificate is guilty of misconduct (S(A)A 1994, s 57).

A practising certificate may be issued subject to conditions (SA 1954, s 49 as substituted by S(A)A 1994, s 61 and amended by Solicitors (Amendment) Act 2002, s 2). The 2002 Act extends the circumstances under which the Law Society may refuse a practising certificate or issue it subject to conditions, to include, as well as the financial state of the practice, the number and nature of complaints made against a solicitor and the need adequately to protect the solicitor's clients.

Conditions may be imposed even while the certificate is in force (S(A)A 1994, s 59). The Law Society may apply to the High Court to have a practising certificate suspended (S(A)A 1994, s 58). The Supreme Court has held that where a judgment against a solicitor remains unsatisfied, even without an indemnity, this does not in itself justify a decision to refuse a practising certificate: *Kennedy v Law Society* [1999] 2 IR 583, SC.

It is a matter of contract between the principal or partners of a firm and the solicitor employees of that firm whereby the practising certificates of assistant solicitors are paid for by the firm: 'A Guide to Professional Conduct of Solicitors in Ireland' (2002) ch 7.7.

The Law Society prepares two statutory instruments each year in relation to practising certificates, one setting out the application form (eg SI No 467 of 1999, Practising Certificate 2000 Regulations) and the other the fees payable (eg SI No 472 of 1999, Practising Certificate 2000 Fees). For the year 2003, see SIs No 604 and 605 of 2002. For the year 2004, see SIs No 673 and 674 of 2003. [Bibliography: O'Callaghan P].

solus agreement. Generally a promise given by a petrol wholesaler who undertakes to keep a retailer supplied with petrol if the retailer in turn agrees to take all the petrol he will require only from that wholesaler; the retailer may also undertake to keep the petrol station open at all reasonable hours and to take a minimum quantity.

Solus agreements have been restricted so that they could run for a maximum period of ten years only; a wholesaler has been prohibited from discriminating between *solus* and *non-solus* retailers, although the wholesaler could charge a lower price to solus retailers provided the differential was *reasonable and justifiable*; there was a restriction on wholesaler-owned retail outlets: SI No 294 of 1961; SI No 70 of 1981. See also *Continental Oil Company of Ireland Ltd v Moynihan* [1977] 111 ILTR 5; *Irish Shell Ltd v Dan Ryan Ltd* [1985] HC.

In 1993, the Competition Authority granted a *category licence* under the Competitions Act 1991, s 4(2) in respect of certain motor fuel agreements ie agreements whereby one party, the reseller, agrees with the other party, the supplier, in consideration for the according of special commercial or financial advantages, to purchase only from the supplier: Iris Oifigiúil, 9 July 1993, p 513. See COMPETITION, DISTORTION OF; EXCLUSIVE DISTRIBUTION AGREEMENT.

solvency, declaration of. A statutory declaration made by the directors of a company in a *voluntary winding up* that they are of the opinion that the company will be able to pay its debts in full within a period not exceeding 12 months from when the winding up commences: Companies Act 1963, s 256 as amended by the Companies Act 1990, s 128. The declaration of solvency must be accompanied by a report by an independent person ie a person qualified to be the company's auditor: CA 1963, s 256(2)(c).

If a declaration of solvency is made and shortly afterwards the company is wound up and cannot pay its debts in full, then any director who made the declaration is deemed not to have had reasonable grounds for his opinion until the contrary is shown: CA 1963, s 256(9). As regards the position where a declaration of solvency has not been made by the directors, see *Walsh v Registrar of Companies* [1987] HC. See PERSONAL LIABILITY; WINDING UP.

solvency margin. In life insurance, the solvency margins which are required are specified in arts 17–18 of the European Communities (Life Assurance) Regulations 1984, SI No 57 of 1984 as amended by Central Bank and Financial Services Authority of Ireland Act 2003, s 35, Schedule 2.

solvent. In a position to pay debts as they fall due. See FLOATING CHARGE; INSOLVENT.

solvents, sale of. It is an offence for a person to sell, offer or make available a substance to a person under the age of 18 years, or to a person acting on behalf of that person, if he knows or has reasonable cause to believe that the substance is, or its fumes are, likely to be inhaled by the person under the age of 18 years for the purpose of causing intoxication: Child Care Act 1991, s 74. This offence is intended to tackle the problem of *glue-sniffing* among children.

solvitur in modum solventis. [Money paid is to be applied according to the wish of the person paying it].

sound. The European Court of Justice has held that for a 'sound' to be registered as a trade mark, the sound must be capable of distinguishing the goods or services of one undertaking from another, and the sound must be capable of graphical representation by means of figures, lines or characters that are clear, precise, self-contained, easily accessible, intelligible, durable and objective: Case C-283/01 *Shield Mark BV v Joost Kist hodn MEMEX* [2003] ECJ.

sound broadcasting service. A broadcasting service which transmits, relays or distributes by wireless telegraphy, communications, sounds, signs, or signals intended for direct reception by the general public whether such communications, sounds, signs or signals are received or not: Radio and Television Act 1988, s 2(1).

This Act provides for the Independent Radio and Television Commission (now called the *Broadcasting Commission of Ireland*) to arrange for the provision of sound broadcasting services additional to those provided by RTÉ (RTA 1988, s 4). The Minister is empowered, following a report from the Commission, to specify the areas in relation to which applications for a sound broadcasting contract are to be invited by the Commission; the Minister is required to have regard to the availability of radio frequencies for sound broadcasting (RTA 1988, s 5).

The Commission in awarding contracts is required to have regard to a wide range of specified matters eg the quality, range and type of programmes proposed to be provided; the extent to which the proposed service serves recognisable local communities and is supported by various interests in the community, or serves communities of interest (RTA 1988, s 6). See ADVERTISEMENT, RADIO; BROADCASTING; BROADCASTING COMMISSION OF IRELAND.

sound disposing mind. An essential requirement for a valid will: Succession Act 1965, s 77. It is essential that the testator shall understand the nature of the act and its effect; shall understand the extent of the property of which he is disposing, and shall be able to comprehend and appreciate the claims to which he ought to give effect, and with a view to the latter object, that no disorder of the mind shall poison his affections; pervert his sense of right; or prevent the exercise of his natural faculties; that no insane delusions shall influence his will in disposing of his property and bring about a disposal of it which, if the mind had been sound, would not have been made: *Banks v Goodfellow* [1870] LR 5 QB 549. See also *Parker v Felgate* [1883] 8 PD 171; *In bonis Glynn dec'd* [1990] 2 IR 326. See TESTAMENTARY CAPACITY.

sound recording. Means a *fixation* of sounds, or of the representations thereof, from which the sounds are capable of being reproduced, regardless of the medium on which the recording is being made, or the method by which the sounds are being reproduced: Copyright and Related Rights Act 2000, s 2(1). *Fixation* means the embodiment of sounds or images from which they can be perceived, reproduced or communicated through a device (CRRA 2000, s 2(1)). Copyright subsists in a sound recording (CRRA 2000, s 17(2)). The *author* of a sound recording includes the producer (CRRA 2000, s 21(a)). The copyright in a sound recording expires 50 years after the sound recording is made, or where it is first lawfully made public during this period, 50 years after that date (CRRA 2000, s 26).

A performer has a right to *equitable remuneration* from the copyright owner in a sound recording when it is played in public, or included in a broadcast or cable programme service (CRRA 2000, s 208(1)). The right is not assignable, except to a collecting society to collect on behalf of the performer; the right can be transmitted by testamentary disposition or by operation of law, and is assignable by anyone who legally acquires the right (CRRA 2000, s 208(2)–(3)).

A body which has gathered copyrights in sound recordings for the purpose of exploitation, is supplying a service within the meaning of Value Added Tax Act 1972: *Phonographic Performance (Ireland) Ltd v Somers, Inspector of Taxes* [1992] ILRM 657, HC. See Coughlan in 10 ILT & SJ (1992) 180. See COPYRIGHT; COPYRIGHT, QUALIFICATION FOR; DOCUMENTARY EVIDENCE; LICENCES OF RIGHT, COPYRIGHT; RECORDING RIGHTS.

soundtrack. See FILM.

sources of law. The *primary sources* of Irish law include the Constitution, legislation, delegated legislation, statutory instruments, bye-laws, judgments of courts and tribunals, law reports and digests. *Secondary sources* of law include books, reference books, periodicals, Law Reform Commission reports and consultation papers, dictionaries, and parliamentary debates. See websites: *www.bailii.org* and *www.irish-law.org*. [Bibliography: O'Malley (1); Osborough WN.] See REPORTS; PRECEDENT; APPENDICES.

sovereign immunity. The exemption from liability given to foreign diplomats: Diplomatic Relations and Immunities Acts 1967 and 1976; *Saorstát & Continental Steamship Co v de las Morenas* [1945] IR 291; *McMahon v McDonald* [1988] SC. It has been held that while the doctrine of absolute *sovereign immunity* no longer exists, immunity will be accorded to an activity which touches the actual business of the foreign government; consequently, persons employed by embassies who are involved in the employing government's business organisation and interest, do not have access to the Employment Appeals Tribunal: *Government of Canada v EAT* [1992] 2 IR 484, SC.

The doctrine of sovereign immunity does not apply in respect of commercial or trading activities in which a foreign government participates: *McElhinney v Williams* [1996] 1 ILRM 276, SC and [1995] 3 IR 382, SC. There is no principle whereby sovereign immunity should be granted only where the country claiming it grants reciprocal immunity to other nations (*McElhinney* case). Also, there is no principle of public international law, whereby the immunity granted to a foreign state should be restricted by making it liable in respect of tortious acts committed on its behalf by its servants or agents which cause personal injuries to a person affected by an act or omission, when such act or omission is committed *jure imperii* (*McIlhinney* case). See *Schmidt v Home Secretary* [1995] 1 ILRM 301, HC and [1997] 2 IR 121, SC; *Geraghty v Embassy of Mexico* [1998] ELR 310, EAT; *O'Shea v The Italian Embassy* [2002] ELR 276, EO. See IMMUNITY.

sovereign state. Ireland is declared to be a *sovereign* independent, democratic state: 1937 Constitution, art 5. This declaration of sovereignty means that the State is not subject to any power of government save those designated by the People in the Constitution itself, and the State is not amenable to any external authority: *Byrne v Ireland* [1972] IR 241. See, however, COMMUNITY LAW. See *The changing face of State Sovereignty* by Trevor Redmond in (2002) 10 ISLR 50. See also PRIVILEGE.

spam. An unsolicited email or text message sent to many recipients at one time; it is the electronic equivalent of junk mail and is an abuse of the Internet. Concern was expressed in the Dáil that the Electronic Commerce Act 2000 did not deal with this problem. However, provision was made in 2003 to make illegal the sending of spam, originating in the EU, to the general public: EC (Electronic Communications Networks and Services) (Data Protection and Privacy) Regulations 2003, SI No 535 of 2003. The regulations place restrictions on unsolicited direct marketing by telephone, fax, automated calling systems, email, SMS and MMS. The use of 'cookies' and other devices such as 'Spyware' is subject to regulation and require the consent of users. The regulations give a right to subscribers to determine which of their personal data are included in a publicly available directory of subscribers. A breach of the 2003 Regulations can attract a fine on summary conviction of up to €3,000 (reg 17).

spare parts. In a contract for the sale of goods there is an implied warranty that spare parts and an adequate aftersale service will be made available by the seller for a reasonable period. The Minister may by order define, in relation to any class of goods, what shall be a reasonable period. See Sale of Goods and Supply of Services Act 1980, s 12.

special agent. See AGENT.

special amenity order. The order which a planning authority (qv) has power to make (on its own initiative or on direction by the Minister) which declares any particular area to be an area of *special amenity* by reason of its outstanding natural beauty or its special recreational value: Planning and Development Act 2000, s 202. The order must state the objective of the planning authority in relation to the preservation or enhancement of the character or special features of the area, including objectives for the prevention or limitation of development in the area.

The making of such an order must be confirmed by An Bord Pleanála to be effective; there are also provisions regarding public notice of such an order, objections thereto, and an oral hearing. Compensation is not payable in respect of a refusal of permission for development in such an area (PDA 2000, s 191(1)(a), Sch 3, para 6). For an example of a special amenity order, see Fingal County Council (Howth) Special Amenity Area (Confirmation) Order 2000, SI No 133 of 2000.

For previous legislation, see Local Government (Planning and Development) Act 1963, s 42(1) as substituted by the Local Government (Planning and Development) Act 1976, s 40(a); Local Government (Planning and Development) Act 1990, s 12(1)(a), Sch 2, para 6. [Bibliography: Galligan (1)].

special care order. An order which the court is empowered to make which commits a child to the care of the health board concerned and which authorises the health board to provide appropriate care, education and treatment for the child, and for that purpose to place, and detain the child in a *special care unit*: Child Care Act 1991, s 23B inserted by the Children Act 2001, s 16.

The court will only make such an order where it is satisfied that: (a) the behaviour of the child is such that it poses a real and substantive risk to his health, safety, development or welfare, and (b) the child requires special care or protection. Before applying for a special care order, the health board is required to convene a *family welfare conference* (qv).

There is provision for an *interim special care order* and also for a garda to deliver a child to the custody of the health board where the behaviour of the child is such that there is not sufficient time to await an interim order.

Health boards are empowered to provide *special care units* or to have others provided them on behalf of the health board (CCA 1991, s 23K as inserted by CA 2001, s 16). A child on being found guilty of an offence cannot be ordered to be placed or detained in a special care unit (CCA 1991, s 23N as inserted by CA 2001, s 16). See 'Babes in the hood' by solicitor Geoffrey Shannon in *Law Society Gazette* (November 2003) 12. See CHILDREN DETENTION SCHOOLS.

special case. The stating by the parties to any cause or matter, of questions of law arising therein, for the opinion of the court: RSC Ord 34, rr 1–8. See also RSC Ord 56, r 4(d). See PRELIMINARY ISSUE.

special control area. An area in relation to which a *special control area order* is in operation: Air Pollution Act 1987, ss 7(1) and 39.

special courts. The courts which may be established by law for the trial of offences in cases where it may be determined in accordance with such law that the ordinary courts are inadequate to secure the effective administration of justice, and the preservation of public peace and order: 1937 Constitution, art 38(3)(l).

The Special Criminal Court was established under the Offences Against the State Act 1939, Part V. It is a matter for the government to decide whether Part V should be brought into force or should cease to be in force; this was essentially a political decision, and was entitled to the presumption of constitutionality: *Kavanagh v Government of Ireland* [1996] 1 IR 321, SC and [1997] 1 ILRM 321, SC. The court which was established pursuant to a government proclamation on 26 May 1972, has jurisdiction extending to crimes in addition to those committed by subversives: *Gilligan v Ireland* [2001] 1 ILRM 473, SC.

Members of the Special Criminal Court must be either a judge of the High, Circuit or District Court, a barrister or solicitor of not less than seven years' standing, or an army officer not below the rank of commandant; they are appointed and removable at the will of the government (OASA 1939, s 39). The court consists of three persons without a jury and its decision is that of the majority. An appeal by the defence lies to the Court of Criminal Appeal; there is no prosecution avenue of appeal from an acquittal by the Special Criminal Court.

A person may be sent for trial to the Special Criminal Court if charged with a *scheduled offence* (qv), which is a list of particular offences (OASA 1939, s 45), or if charged with a non-scheduled offence where the Director of Public Prosecutions (qv) so requests and certifies as required (OASA 1939, s 46). Such certification by the DPP is not reviewable by the Courts unless the applicant can establish: (a) a *prima facie* case of some irregularity of a serious nature such as to amount to some impropriety: *Foley v DPP* [1989] ITLR (25 September) HC, or (b) evidence of *mala fides* on the part of the DPP or evidence that the DPP was influenced by an improper motive or improper policy: *Kavanagh v Government of Ireland* [1996] 1 ILRM 132, HC.

Also a person lawfully before the Special Criminal Court in respect of a scheduled offence, may be tried by the court in respect of a non-scheduled offence: *McElhinney v Special Criminal Court* [1989] ILRM 411, SC. See also Criminal Justice (Verdicts) Act 1976. See *Eccles v Ireland* [1986] ILRM 343. See also Offences Against the State Act (Special Criminal Court Rules) 1975, SI No 234 of 1975 as amended by SI No 536 of 2001. See 'Constitutional aspects of non-jury courts' by Peter Charleton SC and Paul McDermott BL in *Bar Review* (November 2000) 66 and (December 2000) 141. See 'Time to decommission the Special Criminal Court?' by solicitor Pat Igoe in *Law Society Gazette* (April 2002) 5.

A government appointed committee, under the chairmanship of Mr Justice Anthony Hederman, recommended that the Special Criminal Court should be retained, subject to keeping it under regular review: *Report of the Committee to Review the Offences Against the State Acts 1939–1998* (2002). See also *Consultation Paper on Prosecution Appeals in cases brought on Indictment* (LRC CP 19, 2002). [Bibliography: Walsh D (3)].

Special Criminal Court. See SPECIAL COURTS.

special damages. The damages which the law does not presume to flow from the defendant's act and which must be expressly pleaded and proved eg loss of earnings, medical expenses. Slander is not actionable without proof of *special damage,* although there are some exceptions. The term *special damages* is also used to denote damages which are capable of substantially exact calculation, as distinct from those not capable of such calculation which are known as *general damages.* See *Doran v Dublin Plant Hire Ltd* [1990] 2 IR 488; *Hogan v Steele & Co Ltd & ESB* [2000] 1 ILRM 330, HC; [2001] 2 ILRM 321, SC and [2000] 4 IR 587, SC. See DAMAGES; GENERAL DAMAGES; KINLEN ORDER; PLEADINGS; SLANDER.

special educational needs. The educational needs of students who have a disability and the educational needs of exceptionally able students: Education Act 1998, s 2(1). It is a requirement for *recognised* schools to use their available resources to ensure that the educational needs of all students, including those with a disability or other special educational needs, are identified and provided for (EA 1998, s 9(a)). See also EA 1998, s 7(1)(a).

Under recent legislation, *disability* in the 1998 Act and *special educational needs* means, in relation to a person, a restriction in the capacity of the person to participate in and benefit from education on account of an enduring physical, sensory, mental health or learning disability, or any other condition which results in a person learning differently from a person without that condition and cognate words must be construed accordingly: Education for Persons with Special Educational Needs Act 2004, ss 1(1) and 52. There is provision in the Act for the appointment by the *National Council for Special Education* of special educational needs organisers (EPSENA 2004, s 26). [Bibliography: Glendenning.] See

DISABLED PERSON AND EDUCATION; EDUCATION PLAN; INCLUSIVE EDUCATION; INTEGRATED EDUCATION.

special exemption order. An order of the District Court exempting the holder of an *on-licence* from the legal provisions relating to prohibited hours in respect of licensed premises, during the hours and on the occasion specified in the order: Intoxicating Liquor Act 1927, s 5 substituted by Intoxicating Liquor Act 2003, s 11. A special exemption order expires at the latest at 2.30 am, or where it extends to any Monday which is not a public holiday, at 1 am. A local authority for the licensing area concerned, may adopt a resolution in respect of these expiry times and the court, while exercising its discretion, must have regard to the terms of such resolution.

special investment scheme. An authorised unit trust scheme where a substantial part of the investment is in Irish equities; the effective rate of tax charged is 10% on the income and capital gains accruing to the scheme, no tax being payable by the holder: Finance Act 1993, s 13, now Taxes Consolidation Act 1997, ss 737 and 839. These schemes are now in the process of being wound up; provision has been made to facilitate the use of any unused capital losses in the final year to be set-off against capital gains that were taxed in any of the previous three years: Finance Act 2003, s 50.

special plea. See AUTREFOIS ACQUIT; AUTREFOIS CONVICT; PLEA.

special pleading. Sometimes refers to the essential requirement in pleadings (qv) which if not raised would likely take the opposite party by surprise or would raise issues of fact not arising out of the pleadings eg fraud, release, payment, performance, Statute of Limitations, Statute of Frauds, or facts showing illegality, either by statute or at common law: RSC Ord 19, r 15.

special portfolio investment accounts. These accounts cannot be commenced after 5 April 2001; accounts existing at that date have removed from them the requirement that the investment be focused on Irish equities and bonds: Finance Act 2001, s 56. To facilitate the phasing out of SPIAs, any unrelieved losses at the time of closing of these accounts can be offset by the holder against gains: Finance Act 2002, s 50

special purpose company. Companies which the *National Development Finance Agency* (qv) may form with the prior consent of the Minister, for the purpose of financing a *public investment project* (qv) where, in its opinion, it is necessary or expedient to do so: National Development Finance Agency Act 2002, s 5. See SECURITISATION OF MORTGAGE.

special resolution. See RESOLUTION.

special savings account. An account in which a relevant deposit made by an individual is held, which meets certain conditions and in respect of which a declaration has been made; the interest on such a deposit is taxed at 20%. This retention tax deducted at source satisfies the income tax liability of the account holder on the interest. The balance on the account (including interest) must not exceed £50,000/€63,487. No withdrawals may be made from the account for the first three months; for later withdrawals, the account holder must give 30 days' notice. See Taxes Consolidation Act 1997, ss 256, 264, 839 as amended by Finance Act 1998, s 131(1).

special savings incentive account; (SSIA). The SSIA is a new savings initiative, which commenced on 1 May 2001, and under which the Exchequer will contribute 25p for every £1 saved in the account: Finance Act 2001, s 33. The main features are: (a) every resident person who is 18 years old or over can open one account only during the 12-month period from 1 May 2001; (b) in the first year, the saver must save an agreed amount not less than £10 (€12.70) and not more than £200 (€253.95) in any one month; (c) after the first year there is no obligation to save a fixed amount, but the amount saved in any one month must not exceed £200; (d) if the savings account is allowed to run to full term of five years, only the investment return will suffer tax at 23% ie the amount saved and the Exchequer contribution goes to the saver untaxed; (e) however, any withdrawals before the full term will attract taxation at 23% on the withdrawal. It is an offence for a person to open more than one account (FA 2001, s 33 inserting new Taxes Consolidation Act 1997, s 848T). See Special Savings Incentive Accounts Regulations 2001, SI No 176 of 2001.

The closing date of an SSIA is the fifth anniversary of the end of the month in which a subscription was first made; the holder has three months ending on that date to make the required *closing declaration*: Finance Act 2002, s 49. See CREDIT UNION.

special summons. Procedure in the superior courts by special summons may be adopted where there is no other procedure prescribed by the Rules of the Superior Courts and the proceeding is one: (a) which is required or authorised by law to be brought in a summary manner, or (b) which is required or authorised by law: RSC Ord 3, r (21) as substituted by Rules of the Superior Courts (No 2) (Amendment to Order 3) 2001, SI No 269 of 2001. See SUMMONS, HIGH COURT.

special term account. See CREDIT UNION.

special trading house. See TRADING HOUSE, SPECIAL.

special verdict. (1) A verdict by which the facts alone of the case are found by the jury and the legal inferences therefrom are drawn by the court; such verdicts are exceptionally rare eg *R v Dudley and Stevens* 14 QBD 273; Defamation Act 1961, s 3.

(2) A verdict of *guilty but insane* which is brought in when the accused at the time of commission of the alleged crime was insane in the legal sense: Trial of Lunatics Act 1883. The special verdict is a verdict of acquittal; the only order which the court can make is an order that the accused person be kept in custody as a criminal lunatic; it is a matter for the Executive (the government or the Minister, as the case may be) to order the accused person's release when it is satisfied, having regard to his mental health, that it is safe to release him: *DPP v John Gallagher* [1991] ILRM 339, SC and 1 IR 31.

The Minister is advised by an *advisory committee* on whether it is safe to release such a person. In a particular case, it was held that as the findings of the advisory committee were consistent with the evidence before it, it was not open to the applicant to challenge the Minister's decision to accept those findings: *Application of Gallagher (No 2)* [1996] 3 IR 10, HC.

A person found *guilty but insane* must be kept at the Central Mental Hospital; however the Minister has the power to sanction his temporary release to another psychiatric hospital: *O'Halloran v Minister for Justice* [2000] 1 ILRM 234, HC and [1999] 4 IR 287, HC. See also *Application of Maguire* [1996] 3 IR 1, HC.

Under a major reform of the law dealing with insanity, it is proposed that the special verdict of 'not guilty by reason of insanity' will in future be returned where the accused person is found to have committed the alleged act, but where it is also found, having heard evidence relating to the mental condition of the accused given by a consultant psychiatrist, that: (a) the accused person was suffering *at the time* from a *mental disorder* (qv), and (b) the mental disorder was such that the accused person ought not to be held responsible for the act alleged by reason of the fact that he: (i) did not know the nature or quality of the act, or (ii) did not know that what he was doing was wrong, or (iii) was unable to refrain from committing the act: Criminal Law (Insanity) Bill 2002, s 4. The test relates to the time of the alleged commission of the offence and not to the time of trial. See INSANITY; LEGAL AID; MENTAL HEALTH REVIEW BOARD; VERDICT.

special voter. See VOTERS, SPECIAL.

special waste. See TOXIC AND DANGEROUS WASTE.

specialia generalibus derogant. [Special words derogate from general ones.] See GENERALIA SPECIALIBUS NON DEROGANT.

specialist securities. Issuers of specialist securities, including eurobonds, and special securities representing shares, must comply with certain listing requirements. See Irish Stock Exchange publications, *Listing Rules for Specialist Securities – (a) Asset Backed Debt, (b) Bonds and (c) Warrants*. See LISTING RULES.

specialist tribunals. It has been held that the courts should be slow to interfere with the decision of a specialist statutory tribunal by means of a judicial review on grounds of irrationality: *Camara v Minister for Justice* [2001] ITLR (7 May).

specialty contract. A contract under seal; a deed. See DEED.

specialty debt. A debt due under a deed. See DEED.

specialty rule. The rule in international law which requires that a person who has been extradited will not be proceeded against, sentenced or detained for any offence committed prior to his surrender other than that for which he was extradited: European Convention on Extradition 1957, art 14; Extradition Act 1965, s 20. See *The State (Jennings) v Furlong* [1966] IR 183; *Shannon v Fanning* [1985] ILRM 385; *Ellis v O'Dea & Shields* [1990] 8 ILT Dig 159.

A person who has consented to being surrendered to a Convention country, may waive his rights to the specialty rule; the renunciation must be recorded before the High Court, and the consent of the Minister for Justice is also required: Extradition (European Union Conventions) Act 2001, s 7. Also a person, extradited for one offence may be tried or prosecuted for other offences committed before extradition: (a) if the offences do not give rise to imprisonment or detention or (b) if imprisonment is involved, if certain other provisions apply (E(EUC)A 2001, s 15). Analogous provisions apply as regards the specialty rule in the case of persons extradited to Ireland (E(EUC)A 2001, s 16). See *Adams v DPP* [2001] 2 ILRM 401, HC and [2001] 1 IR 47, SC.

A person will be surrendered on foot of a European Arrest Warrant when the law of the issuing state provides that the person will only be proceeded against in respect of the offence specified in the warrant, or an undertaking in writing is given to the High Court by the issuing judicial authority in that regard: European Arrest Warrant Act 2003, s 22(1). However, there are circumstances where the specialty rule is disapplied and the person may be surrendered even if it is intended to proceed against him for other offences e g where a restriction on his liberty is not involved, or if it is involved, it is in respect of an offence for which he has been convicted before surrender (EAWA 2003, s 22(2)–(6)).

specific goods. See GOODS.

specific performance. The equitable discretionary remedy by which a party to an agreement is compelled by order of the court to perform his obligations according to the terms of that agreement e g in contracts for the sale, purchase or lease of land, or the sale of unique chattels not readily available on the market. Specific performance of the sale of land may be ordered with an abatement of the purchase price to compensate for loss incurred as a result of an error: *O'Brien v Kearney* [1995] 2 ILRM 232, HC. See also *O'Dwyer v Boyd* [2003] 1 ILRM 112, SC.

In any action for breach of contract to deliver specific or ascertained goods, the court may, if it thinks fit, on the application of the plaintiff, direct that the contract be performed specifically, without giving the defendant the option of retaining the goods on payment of damages: Sale of Goods Act 1893, s 52.

Specific performance will not be granted: (a) where damages are an adequate remedy; or (b) where the court cannot supervise the execution of the contract (eg a building contract); or (c) where one of the parties is a minor (qv); or (d) where the contract is for personal services, although express negative stipulations therein may be enforced by injunction (qv).

However, an interim injunction was ordered by the High Court restraining the purported termination of a plaintiff's service: *McCann v Irish Medical Organisation* [1990] 8 ILT & SJ 67. The courts traditionally have been loath to grant specific performance of a contract of employment although there are exceptions and the well established practice is to continue payment of salary pending trial: *Gee v Irish Times Ltd* [2001] ELR 249, HC. In recent years *Fennelly Orders* have become more usual, at least at the interlocutory stage. See also *Robb v London Borough of Hammersmith & Fulham* [1991] IRLR 72.

The High Court has recently held that before an order for specific performance of an employment contract could be granted, there must exist sufficient confidence on the part of the employer in the servant's ability and other necessary attributes for it to be reasonable for the court to make the order: *Keane v Swim Ireland* [2004] ELR 6, HC.

Specific performance may be refused also where the party against whom it is sought would not have entered the contract but for a misrepresentation (qv). It may also be refused where there has been delay in seeking the remedy. See *Murphy v Harrington* [1927] IR 339; *Smelter Corporation of Ireland v O'Driscoll* [1977] IR 305; *McCarter v Roughan and McLaughlin* [1986] ILRM 447; *O'Neill v Ryan* [1991] ITLR (2 September) HC; *Higgins v Argent Development Ltd* [2002] FL 4998, HC. See Companies Act 1963, s 97; Arbitration Act 1954, s 26. [Bibliography: Delaney H (2); Farrell J; Wylie (3).] See FENNELLY ORDER; INTERLOCUTORY INJUNCTION.

specificatio. The making of a new article out of the chattel of one person by the work of another.

specification. The form of information required to be supplied in the application for a patent (qv). See PATENT, APPLICATION FOR; COMPLETE SPECIFICATION.

speech, freedom of. See EXPRESSION, FREEDOM OF.

speed detector. A *speed meter detector* means any device which is capable of being used to indicate the existence of, or to frustrate the operation of, electronic or other apparatus being used to give indications from which the speed at which a person was driving can be inferred: Road Traffic (Speed Meter Detectors) Regulations 1991, SI No 50 of 1991. It is an offence to have such a detector in a mechanically propelled vehicle, whether or not the device is actually in use. The supply or fitting of such detectors is also an offence. See also Road Traffic Act 1968, s 9.

speed limit. The *general* speed limit for motor vehicles is 60mph, the *motorway* speed limit is 70mph, and the *ordinary* speed limit (applying to all goods vehicles with a gross design vehicle weight in excess of 3,500 kilograms and to all vehicles drawing a trailer) is 50mph. The speed limit for single deck buses/coaches is 50mph and the limit for double deck buses and single deck buses with standing passengers is 40mph. Special speed limits apply to built-up areas e g 30mph. See Road Traffic Act 1961, ss 5, 45 and 46 as amended by Road Traffic Act 1968, s 25. See Road Traffic (General & Ordinary Speed Limits) Regulations 1992; SIs No 194, 195, 196 and 197 of 1992.

Under more recent legislation, speed limits are classified as ordinary, general, built-up area, special and motorway (RTA 1961, s 47(3) as amended by Road Traffic Act 1994, s 34). Responsibility for certain speed limits is transferred to local authorities (RTA 1994, s 33), and the motorway speed limit is given a specific statutory basis in primary legislation (RTA 1994, s 31).

Under draft legislation, it is proposed to change speed limits from 'miles per hour' to 'kilometres per hour' and to have: (a) an *ordinary* speed limit, prescribed by the Minister in respect of all public roads, with the possibility of different limits depending on the class of vehicle or category of road, (b) a *built-up area* speed limit of 50kph, (c) a non-urban *regional and local roads* speed limit of 80kph, (d) a *national* roads speed limit of 100kph, (e) a *motorway* speed limit of 120kph; (f) *special* speed limits made by a major local authority through bye-laws, which can range from 30 to 120kph; (g) a *speed limit at road works,* made by order of a

county or city manager: Road Traffic Bill 2004, ss 4–14. It will be an offence to exceed any of these speed limits (s 11). There are approximately 50,000 speed limit signs throughout the State which have to be changed and consequently there are transitional provisions. The Minister for Transport announced on 10 September 2004 the establishment of a Metric Changeover Board and 20 January 2005 as the changeover date from miles to kilometres. See PENALTY POINTS.

sperm. See ARTIFICIAL INSEMINATION.

spes successionis. A mere hope of succeeding to property. *Administration with will annexed* under *spes successionis* may be granted to the child of a universal legatee or devisee on such person's renunciation and consent. *Administration intestate* may be granted to the child of a person who is entitled to all the estate on the renunciation and consent of such person. See RSC Ord 79, rr 5(12) and 5(13); Ord 80 rr 6(11) and 6(12). See *Re Simpson* [1904] 2 Ch 1.

spit. It is an offence for a taxi passenger to spit in or on or to deliberately soil any part of the vehicle: Taxi Regulation Act 2003, s 40(2)(b). A similar offence is provided for in respect of large public service vehicles: SI No 191 of 1963. A person must not spit on the platform of any railway station or on the permanent way: SI No 109 of 1984. Spitting is also prohibited in many instances e g in rooms where raw materials and products are worked on or stored: SI No 126 of 1995.

It has been held that spitting at the back of a uniformed police sergeant, the spittle landing on his raincoat and leaving a faint mark when removed later with a tissue, did not support a conviction for criminal damage: *A (a juvenile) v The Queen* [1978] Crim. L. Rev 689. See also LRC 45, 1994, paras 1.20 and 1.49.

splitting of action. The division of an action to be made the ground of two or more different proceedings in order to bring the cases within the jurisdiction of a court. Such splitting in the District Court will lead to a dismissal of such proceedings with costs: DCR 1997 Ord 39, r 12. A plaintiff is similarly prohibited from dividing his cause of action into two or more different actions to bring them within the jurisdiction of the Circuit Court: Courts Act 1991, s 2(3)(b) amending the Courts of Justice Act 1936, s 23.

spoilt vote. A ballot paper in an election which is deemed to be invalid and is not to be counted eg where it does not bear the official stamp, or where (under proportional representation) the number one preference is not indicated definitely, or where there is included some writing calculated to identify the elector: Electoral Act 1992, s 118(2). It is normal practice for a returning officer to discuss with all candidates, or their agents, in relation to ballot papers whose validity is in doubt before deciding on their validity.

He must endorse *rejected* on any ballot paper which is not to be counted (EA 1992, s 118(3)). Where he adjudicates on a doubtful ballot paper and rules it valid, he may record on the paper an indication of his decision, thus ensuring that the same paper will not come up again for adjudication later in the count or on a recount (EA 1992, s 118(4)). A voter who inadvertently spoils his ballot paper may be given another ballot paper (EA 1992, s 102). See also Presidential Elections Act 1993, s 48; Referendum Act 1994, s 34; European Parliament Elections Act 1997, Sch 2, r 63.

sponsalia per verba de praesenti. The declaration by parties in the present tense, agreeing to take each other as husband or wife, which previously constituted a valid marriage under common law. *Sponsillia per verba de futuro et copula* was a promise to marry in the future, the parties becoming husband and wife on a subsequent consummation. See MARRIAGE.

sponsors' mark. The distinctive mark of a maker, worker of, or dealer in, an article of precious metal struck on such article, a register of which must be kept by the Company of Goldsmiths of Dublin, which registration is valid for a period of ten years and may be renewed every ten years: Hallmarking Act 1981, ss 1 and 9. See GOLDSMITHS OF DUBLIN, COMPANY OF.

sport. (1) All forms of physical activity which aim at expressing or improving physical fitness; it is: (a) *competitive* sport if it is through organised participation and aimed at obtaining improved results in competitions, or (b) *recreational* sport if it is through casual or regular participation and aimed at improving mental well-being and forming social relationships: Irish Sports Council Act 1999, s 2(1). The *Irish Sports Council* is a corporate body with functions which include: (a) to encourage the promotion, development and co-ordination of

competitive sport and the achievement of excellence therein, (b) to develop strategies for increasing participation in recreational sport and for co-ordinating their implementation, and (c) to take appropriate action to combat doping in sport (ISCA 1999, s 6). The Council must comply with any general policy directives given by the Minister (ISCA 1999, s 9) and must submit to the Minister a strategy statement for each ensuing three-year period (ISCA 1999, s 25). See *Vowles v Evans* [2003] EWCA Civ 318 discussed in *Sports Injuries and the Law of Negligence* by Ray Ryan in (2003) 11 ISLR 60. For news and views on GAA, see website *www.anfearrua.com*. See SPORTS BODY.

(2) European Union law applies to sport in so far as it constitutes an economic activity: *Walgrave v Union Cycliste Internationale* [1974] ECR 1405, ECJ. The payment of a fee on the transfer of *out of contract* football players was abolished: Case C-415/93 *Union Royale Belge des Societes de Football Association ASBL v Bosman* [1995] ECR I-4921. Under the current football transfer system, a player *under contract* is entitled to move to another club only with the consent of his present club. See 'EU Law and the Rules of Sporting Organisations' by Brian Kennedy BL in *Bar Review* (November 2000) 80. For *US National Sports Law Institute* see website: *www.mu.edu/law/sports/nsli.html*. For *Sports Law Programme of Marquette University Law School* see website: *www.mu.edu/la/sports/sports.html*. [Bibliography: Blanpain & Inston UK.] See GOLF; NATIONAL SPORTING ARENA.

sporting lease. A lease to which a sports club is entitled which carries on some outdoor sport, game or recreation and which holds land in accordance with specified conditions: Landlord and Tenant (Amendment) Act 1971, s 2(1). This legislation was introduced to ameliorate the position of sporting or recreational clubs (such as, for example, golf clubs and football clubs) which held land under leases, under which they had no right to obtain reversionary leases or to acquire the fee simple in the property which they held. They had no such rights because the land which they held was not subsidiary and ancillary to any buildings which they might occupy under the lease. The effect of the 1971 Act was to give such clubs a right to a new lease for 99 years, subject to paying a 'fair rent'. There is provision for review of the rent every five years where the terms of the lease have been settled by the court.

A claim to enlarge an interest in property from a *sporting lease* to a *fee simple* may only be made in respect of land comprising permanent buildings and such ground as is ancillary and subsidiary thereto: *Fitzgerald (Trustees of Castleknock Tennis Club) v Corcoran* [1991] ILRM 545, SC. The Supreme Court held in this case that the trustees were entitled to invoke the provisions of Landlord and Tenant (Ground Rents) (No 2) Act 1978, s 14 so as to entitle them to acquire the fee simple in the clubhouse and such ground as was subsidiary and ancillary thereto, The Law Reform Commission has recommended that the lessee of a sporting or recreational club should not have the right to buy out the fee simple: *Report on Land Law and Conveyancing Law* (LRC 44, 1992). [Bibliography: Bland (1).] See GROUND RENT; RENT REVIEW CLAUSE.

sports body. The income of an amateur sports body, established for and existing for the *sole purpose* of promoting athletic or amateur games or sports, is exempt from *income tax:* Taxes Consolidation Act 1997, s 235. The exemption is only in respect of so much of the income of the body as is shown to the satisfaction of the Revenue Commissioners to be income which has been or will be applied to that sole purpose. A withdrawal of exemption can be made retrospective only to the tax year 1984–85, as the withdrawal measure was introduced in response to the decision in *O'Reilly and Ors v Revenue Commissioners* [1984] ILRM 406.

Income tax relief is now available to individual taxpayers who make a donation to a sports body, which is certified by the Revenue Commissioners as complying with s 235, for the funding of a capital project, costing up to €40 million, which has been approved by the Minister: TCA 1997, s 847A inserted by Finance Act 2002, s 41. The relief applies at the taxpayer's marginal rate. The minimum qualifying donation is €250. The scheme is operational from 1 May 2002.

Rollover relief in relation to *capital gains tax* is available to a 'disposal made by a body of persons established for the *sole purpose* of promoting athletic or amateur games or sports, being a disposal which is made in relation to such of the activities of that body as are directed to that purpose.' (TCA 1997, s 652).

sports injury clinic. Capital allowances are available in respect of capital expenditure incurred on the construction or refurbishment of buildings used as *private sports injury clinics*: Finance Act 2002, s 34. The sole or main purpose of the clinic must be the diagnosis, alleviation and treatment of sports-related injuries. The clinic must provide day-patient, in-patient and out-patient medical and surgical services and in-patient accommodation of at least 20 beds. Not less than 20% of the capacity of the clinic must be available for public patients at a minimum 10% fee discount to the State. Previously, where an investor fell into any of the excluded categories, all the investors were denied relief; now relief will be denied only to the excluded investor: Finance Act 2004, s 24. See SPORT.

sportspersons' tax relief. Provision has been made for income tax relief on retirement to be given in respect of certain income of specified sportspersons: Finance Act 2002, s 12 inserting a new Taxes Consolidation Act 1997, s 480A. The sportspersons specified are athlete, badminton player, boxer, cyclist, footballer, golfer, jockey, motor racing driver, rugby player, squash player, swimmer and tennis player.

The income to which the relief applies are earnings deriving directly from actual participation in the sport concerned such as prize money and performance fees, but not sponsorship, advertising or endorsement fees. The tax relief, which is given by way of a repayment of tax when the sportsperson ceases permanently to be engaged in the sport, takes the form of a deduction from earnings of 40% of those earnings for up to any ten years of assessment back to and including the tax year 1990/91 for which the sportsperson was resident in the State.

spot check. See ROAD TRAFFIC CHECK.

spouse. Husband or wife. In respect of certain social welfare provisions and higher education grants, a spouse means each person of a married couple who are living together or a man and a woman who are not married to each other but are cohabiting as man and wife: Social Welfare Act 1992, s 17(a); Local Authorities (Higher Education Grants) Act 1992, s 2. See EVIDENCE TENDING TO BASTARDISE CHILDREN; EUROPEAN CONVENTION ON

HUMAN RIGHTS; PRIVILEGE, MATRIMO-
NIAL COMMUNICATIONS; MATRIMONIAL
PROPERTY.

spouse, legal right of. Prior to the Succession Act 1965, a testator could disinherit
his spouse. However this Act introduced an
important new provision which gives the
surviving spouse a *legal right* to a share in
his estate; to one-third of the estate where
the testator leaves a spouse and children; to
one-half of the estate where there are no
children. This legal right has priority over
devises, bequests and shares on intestacy; it
may be renounced by a spouse in writing by
ante-nuptial contract or during marriage.

The surviving spouse's legal right vests in
that spouse on the death of the other
spouse and has the same quality as an
interest arising under a will or a share
arising on intestacy: *O'Dwyer v Keegan*
[1997] 2 ILRM 401, SC and 2 IR 585. In
this case, the surviving spouse was coma-
tose and died 12 hours after her husband;
her estate automatically included her legal
right immediately on her husband's death.

A devise or bequest to a spouse is
deemed to have been intended to be in
satisfaction of the spouse's legal right, unless
it is expressed in the will to be in addition
to the legal right. The spouse may *elect*
between her legal rights and rights under
the will. See Succession Act 1965,
ss 111–115.

Following grant of a decree of *judicial
separation*, the court may make an order
extinguishing the share that either spouse
would otherwise be entitled to in the estate
of the other spouse as a legal right or on an
intestacy under the Succession Act 1965
where it is satisfied eg that adequate and
reasonable financial provision has been
made for that spouse: Family Law
Act 1995, s 14. See also *Bank of Ireland v
Caffin* [1971] IR 123; *Reilly v McEntee*
[1984] ILRM 572. See ELECTION; DISIN-
HERITANCE; JUDICIAL SEPARATION;
RENUNCIATION; SUCCEED, UNWORTHI-
NESS TO.

spouses, transactions between. The law
often treats transactions between spouses or
former spouses in a different way than
transactions between other parties, particularly in relation to taxation eg capital acquisitions tax on gifts and stamp duty on the
transfer of property between spouses.
There is also an exemption from stamp
duty on certain transfers between spouses
following court orders under the Family

Law Act 1995 and the Family Law
(Divorce) Act 1996: Stamp Duties Consolidation Act 1999, s 97. This exemption is
extended to include transfers between
spouse executed on foot of a foreign court
order to like effect, made under or in consequence of the dissolution of marriage,
where the dissolution is entitled to be recognised as valid in the State (SDCA 1999,
s 97 as amended by Finance Act 2000,
s 131). See also Capital Acquisitions Tax
Consolidation Act 2003, ss 70–71.

spring board. A person who has obtained
information in confidence is not allowed to
use it as a *spring board* for activities detrimental to the person who has made the
confidential information, and spring board
it remains even when all the features have
been published or can be ascertained by
actual inspection by members of the public:
*Terrapin Builders Ltd v Builders Sup-
ply Co Ltd* [1960] RPC 128 as adopted by
House of Spring Gardens v Point Blank
[1984] IR 611. See CONFIDENCE, BREACH
OF.

spying. Colloquial term to describe the
offence committed by a person who, in any
manner prejudicial to the safety or preservation of the State, obtains, records, communicates or publishes certain specified
information: Official Secrets Act 1963,
s 9(1). The fact that a person charged had
been in communication with or attempted
to communicate with a foreign agent or
with a member of an unlawful organisation
is evidence that the act in respect of which
he is charged has been done in a manner
prejudicial to the safety or preservation of
the State (OSA 1963, s 10).

The specified information includes information relating to: (a) the number, description, armament, equipment, disposition,
movement or condition of the Defence
Forces or of any vessel or aircraft belonging
to the State; (b) any operation of any of the
Defence Forces or of the Garda Síochána;
(c) any measures for the defence or fortifi-
cation of any place on behalf of the State;
or (d) munitions of war. A member of an
armed force, engaged in espionage during a
conflict, who is captured, has no right to
the status of prisoner of war and may be
treated as a spy: Geneva Conventions
(Amendment) Act 1998, Sch 5, art 46. See
also OFFICIAL SECRET.

squatter. A person who wrongfully enters
upon land; he may acquire a title to it by
adverse or *long possession*. Where a squatter

bars the right of action and title of the dispossessed owner of land, he acquires a title good against anyone other than a person with a better title to the land. See *O'Connor v Foley* [1906] 2 IR 20; *Perry v Woodfarm Homes Ltd* [1975] IR 104.

The deliberate 'taking' of land is rare. Squatter usually fall into one of the following categories: (a) a family member holding adverse to the interest of other family members, often under an intestacy; (b) a person who has encroached on neighbouring land, due to inadequacy of maps; (c) a person who has a defective paper title which is impossible or impracticable to rectify, and (d) a person who has taken possession of land which has been effectively abandoned: *Report on Title by Adverse Possession of Land* (LRC 67, 2002).

A garda is empowered to direct a squatter to leave a house immediately in a peaceful manner and the squatter must comply with the direction: Housing (Miscellaneous Provisions) Act 1997, s 20. This power arises where the garda has received notice from the housing authority that the squatter is or has been engaged in *anti-social behaviour* and that it is necessary in the interest of *good estate management* that the squatter be required to leave. [Bibliography: Wylie (1).] See ESTATE MANAGEMENT; LONG POSSESSION, TITLE BY; PARLIAMENTARY CONVEYANCE.

stabit praesumptio donec probetur in contrarium. [A presumption will stand good until the contrary is proved.] See PRESUMPTION.

staff. 'A member of a body of persons employed in a business': *An Foras Áiseanna Saothair v Minister for Social Welfare & Ryan* [1991] No 653 Sp, HC. Many state-sponsored bodies have power to appoint such staff as they may determine but with the consent of the Minister eg Labour Services Act 1987, s 7(1)(a).

stag. A person who subscribes to an issue of shares with no intention of keeping those allotted to him, but in the speculative hope that he can sell them at a profit. The process is called *stagging*. See *R v Greenstein* [1975] 2 WLR 1353.

stake. Any payment for the right to take part in a game and any other form of payment required to be made as a condition of taking part in a game: Gaming and Lotteries Act 1956, s 2. See GAMING; STAKEHOLDER.

stakeholder. (1) A person with whom money is deposited pending the decision of a bet or wager. Money paid to a stakeholder to abide the result of a wager can be recovered from him at any time before it has been paid away; this applies even if the person demanding the return of his stake has lost the wager, as in effect he is revoking the stakeholders' authority as an agent for him: *Grehane v Thompson* [1867] IR 2 CL 64.

(2) A stakeholder may also be a person who holds money or property which is claimed by rival claimants but in which he himself claims no interest eg an auctioneer in relation to a deposit in the sale of land by auction. See *Desmond v Brophy* [1986] ILRM 547 See DEPOSIT; INTERPLEADER.

stakeholder's interpleader. See INTERPLEADER.

stale. Ineffective, usually because of lapse of time. See CHEQUE, STALE; LACHES; LIMITATION OF ACTIONS.

stalking. Popular expression for the offence of harassment. See HARASSMENT.

stallion. The profits or gains arising from the sale of services of mares within the State by stallions are exempt from income tax and corporation tax: Taxes Consolidation Act 1997, s 231. However, profits or gains or losses must be included in the annual return of income: Finance Act 2003, s 35. The same applies to stud greyhound service fees and profits from the occupation of certain woodlands (TCA 1997, ss 232–233).

stamp duties. Revenue raised by means of stamps affixed to written instruments eg to conveyances and leases: Stamp Duties Management Act 1891 and Stamp Act 1891 as amended and now repealed and consolidated in the Stamp Duties Consolidation Act 1999 and since amended by Finance Act 2000, ss 125–133 and Finance Act 2004, ss 66–75, 89 and Sch 3, para 3. Stamp duties are either fixed in amount or *ad valorem* ie proportionate to the value of the property on which the instrument is based.

Stamp duty was a voluntary tax; however unstamped documents could not be used as evidence in court proceedings and were ineffective for such purposes as registration of title; the tax, has been since 1991, a compulsory tax: Finance Act 1991, ss 94 and 96–110.

No stamp duty is payable on any instrument whereby property is transferred between spouses or former spouses: Family Home Protection Act 1976, s 14, Finance Act 1990, s 114; Family Law (Divorce) Act 1996, s 33. See SDCA 1999, ss 96–97.

Substantial changes to the rates applying to covenants, mortgages, stock transfers, leases, conveyances, collateral and counterpart instruments were made in the Finance Act 1990. The government is empowered to impose, vary or terminate stamp duties by order: Imposition of Duties Act 1957; *McDaid v Judge Sheehy* [1991] ILRM 250, SC. See also Building Societies Act 1989, s 118 as amended by SDCA 1999, Sch 4.

The Revenue Commissioners may be required to express their opinion as to whether any executed instrument is chargeable with any stamp duty and with what amount (SDCA 1999, s 20). Any person dissatisfied with an assessment, may appeal to the Appeal Commissioners (SDCA 1999, s 21).

A rate of stamp duty of 9% on conveyances, transfers and leases of residential property applied to instruments executed on or after 15 June 2000: Finance (No 2) Act 2000, ss 1– 4. There were reliefs in respect of first-time purchasers and other owner-occupiers. A person whose marriage has been dissolved or is the subject of a judicial separation may be treated as a first-time purchaser.

For changes to stamp duty law and rates applicable, see Finance Act 2001, ss 201– 214. The threshold below which stamp duty is not payable on mortgages has been increased to €254,000 (FA 2001, s 213). The rate of stamp duty for investors in residential property has been reduced to the same level as owner-occupiers, who are not first-time buyers; this has effect on transfers of property executed on or after 6 December 2001: Finance Act 2002, ss 113–114.

The stamp duty on *non-residential property* was increased and the valuation bands were changed as from 4 December 2004 eg a 9% rate applies to transactions of €150,000 and over: Finance Act 2003, ss 143. See *Cherry Court v Revenue Commissioners* [1995] 2 IR 212, HC; *Kenny v Revenue Commissioners* [1996] 3 IR 315, HC. See Stamp Duty (Particulars to be Delivered) Regulations 1995, SI No 144 of 1995 as amended by SI No 542 of 2003. [Bibliography: Connelly M; Donegan & Friel; Goodman; O'Connor & Cahill.] See UNSTAMPED INSTRUMENT.

stamps. Fees payable in any public office must be collected in money or by means of stamps: Public Offices (Fees) Act 1879. Increasingly this provision is being excluded in new statutes eg Irish Aviation Authority Act 1993, s 43(7); Radiological Protection (Amendment) Act 2002, s 2(e). Excise duty payable on certain excise licences and on certification on registration of a club, is no longer payable by means of affixing stamps to the application notice: Finance Act 2000, ss 103–104. See also Industrial Designs Act 2001, s 9(4); Communications Regulation Act 2002, s 30(1); Competition Act 2002, s 54; Residential Tenancies Act 2004, s 176(6).

standard form of contract. It has been held that where the terms of a contract have been completely agreed between the parties thereto, a jurisdiction clause in a subsequent standard form of order is not part of the contract: *Unidare plc v James Scott Ltd* [1991] 2 IR 88, SC. The Minister may by order require a person who uses a standard form of contract in the course of a business to give notice to the public whether he is or is not willing to contract on other terms: Sale of Goods and Supply of Services Act, s 52. See CONTRACT OF ADHESION; INVOICE.

standard mark. A mark prescribed, or deemed to have been prescribed, for use in connection with a commodity, process or practice to indicate that it conforms to a particular *standard specification*: National Standards Authority of Ireland Act 1996, ss 3(1) and 20. A standard mark includes the words 'Caighdean Eireannach' or the initials 'CE' and may include the words 'Irish Standard' or the initials 'IS' or any other mark (NSAIA 1996, s 20(3)). The NSAI may grant a person a licence to use a standard mark (NSAIA 1996, s 21). It is an offence for a person to use a standard mark without a licence or to make a false representation that he is licensed or entitled to use the mark (NSAIA 1996, s 22). See STANDARD SPECIFICATION; NATIONAL STANDARDS AUTHORITY.

standard of care. The standard established or imputed by law as regards the *duty of care*, owed by one person to another person, the breach of which may constitute the tort of *negligence* or *breach of statutory duty* eg between a doctor and a patient, or between an occupier of premises and an entrant, or between an employer and an employee. An adult standard of care is not usually imputed to a child. However in the USA, it has been held that where an infant participates with adults in a sport ordinarily played by adults, on a course or field used by adults for that sport, and commits a primary tortuous act, he should be held to the same standard of care as the adult participants: *Neumann v Shlansky* 318 NYS 2d 925 (1971); 312 NYS 2d at 951. In this case the plaintiff was struck by a golf ball driven by the defendant, an 11 year-old boy. See BREACH OF DUTY; DEFENCE FORCES; DUTY OF CARE; MEDICAL NEGLIGENCE; NEGLIGENCE; NEIGHBOUR PRINCIPLE; ROAD USER'S DUTY; SCHOOL AUTHORITY'S DUTY; STATUTORY DUTY.

standard of proof. In civil cases, the standard of proof normally required is proof on the *balance of probability* (qv). However, see RECTIFICATION. The Employment Appeals Tribunal has held that the standard of proof on matters before it is proof on the balance of probabilities: *Casey v Dunnes Stores* [2003] ELR 313.

In criminal cases, where the burden of proof (qv) rests with the prosecution, the guilt of the accused must be proved *beyond reasonable doubt*; the accused is entitled to acquittal if his evidence does no more than raise a doubt in the jury's mind. However, see Proceeds of Crime Act 1996, s 8(2) where the standard of proof is that applicable to civil cases. In criminal cases, where the burden of proof on any issue rests with the accused, the standard of proof is on the balance of probability. See *The People (Attorney-General) v Byrne* [1974] IR 1. [Bibliography: Charleton (5); Healy.] See INFERENCE; PROCEEDS OF CRIME.

standard specification. A *specification* declared to be a standard specification for the commodity, process or practice to which it relates: National Standards Authority of Ireland Act 1996, ss 3(1) and 16. It includes a specification deemed to have been so declared.

A *specification* includes description of any commodity, process or practice by reference to any one or more of the following namely: nature, quality, strength, purity, composition, quantity, dimensions, weight, grade, durability, origin, age and any other characteristic (NSAIA 1996, s 3(1)). It is an offence to make a false representation that a commodity, process or practice is of standard specification (NSAIA 1996, s 19).

As regards EC law, a *standard* is a *technical specification* approved by a recognised standardising body for repeated or continuous application, with which compliance is not compulsory: Council Directive (EEC) 83/189 art 1. In recognition that technical regulations may act as barriers to the free movement of goods, there is provision for: (a) standards institutions in member states to keep each other advised on national standards; and (b) the drawing up of European standards (art 6(3)). See Travers in 11 ILT & SJ (1993) 35. See STANDARD MARK.

standard time. The time for general purposes in the State which is one hour in advance of Greenwich mean time throughout the year (Standard Time Act 1968, s 1(1)) and which during a period of winter time is Greenwich mean time (Standard Time (Amendment) Act 1971, s 1(1)(a)). Any reference to a specified point in time in any enactment or any legal document shall be construed accordingly. See WINTER TIME.

Standards in Public Office Commission. A Commission consisting of six members with wide investigative powers in relation to complaints about acts or omissions of persons in public life: Standards in Public Office Act 2001. The chairperson must be a judge, or former judge, of the Supreme or High Court, and the ordinary members are the Comptroller and Auditor General, the Ombudsman, the Clerk of both the Dáil and the Seanad, and a person who is a former member of the Houses of the Oireachtas (SPOA 2001, s 2).

The complaints which the Commission investigates are those which concern matters which would be inconsistent with the proper performance of the functions of the office concerned or with the maintenance of confidence in such performance by the general public, where the matter is of significant public importance.

The Commission takes on the functions of the *Public Offices Commission* under the Public Office Act 1995 and the Electoral Act 1997. See website: *www.sipo.ie*. Email is: *sipo@ombudsman.gov.ie*. See ETHICS IN PUBLIC OFFICE; TAX CLEARANCE CERTIFICATE.

standby fee. A fee paid to a witness, usually a professional witness, for being available to testify in legal proceedings, in addition to a fee paid for actual attendance. A standby fee will be allowed in taxation of costs to secure the attendance of witnesses: *Aspell v O'Brien* [1993] ILRM 590, SC and 3 IR 516. See also RSC Ord 99, r 37(18).

standing mute. See MUTE.

standing orders. The rules governing the formal manner of proceedings of a body. The Houses of the Oireachtas (qv) have the power to make their own rules and standing orders, with power to attach penalties for their infringement: 1937 Constitution, art 15(10). For standing orders of a local authority, see Local Government Act 2001, s 2(1) and Sch 10, para 16(1).

stare decisis. The doctrine by which previous judicial decisions must be followed. It is a policy and not a binding, unalterable rule: *The State (Quinn) v Ryan* [1965] IR 70. The circumstances in which a court may depart from the principle of *stare decisis* are extremely rare: *JD v Connellan* [2004] 1 ILRM 202, HC. The Supreme Court has refused to follow its own previous decisions but will only do so for the most compelling reasons. See also *McNamara v ESB* [1975] IR 1; *Costello v Director of Public Prosecutions* [1984] ILRM 413; *Doyle v Hearne* [1988] ILRM 318; *DH v Groarke* [2002] 3 IR 522, SC. See PRECEDENT.

state. A self-governing political community; the central political authority. Ireland is declared to be a sovereign, independent state: 1937 Constitution, art 5. The name of the State is *Eire*, or in the English language, *Ireland* (art 4). The description of the State is the *Republic of Ireland*: Republic of Ireland Act 1948. It is impermissible for requesting courts to refer to the State as anything other than 'Ireland' when referring to it in the English language: per Walsh J and McCarthy J in *Ellis v O'Dea & Shields* [1990] 8 ILT Dig 159. The State, like any individual, is a juristic person and is capable of holding property and being sued for the wrongful acts of its servants: *Byrne v Ireland* [1972] IR 241. See also *Crotty v An Taoiseach* [1987] ILRM 400. For practice and procedure where the State is a party, see Bibliography: Collins & O'Reilly.

state aid. Any aid granted by a member state, or through State resources in any form whatsoever, which distorts or threatens to distort competition by favouring certain undertakings or the production of certain goods, is incompatible with the common market, in so far as it affects trade between member states: *EC Treaty*, art 87 of the consolidated (2002) version. There are exceptions eg aid which has a social character and aid to make good damage caused by natural disasters or exceptional circumstances. There may be other exceptions eg aid to promote the economic development of areas with an abnormally low standard of living or serious underemployment.

The European Commission is empowered to decide that a state aid be abolished or altered, and may refer the matter to the Court of Justice if the State does not comply (art 88). See Case C-36/00 *Kingdom of Spain v Commission of the European Communities* [2002] ECJ. Regulations have been made to enable on-site monitoring visits to be carried out to review the compatibility of state aid with the common market with respect to arts 87 and 88: EC (On-Site Monitoring) Regulations 2002, SI No 444 of 2002. [Bibliography: Quigley & Collins UK].

State authority. (1) As regards planning matters, means a Minister of the government or the Commissioners of Public Works: Planning and Development Act 2000, s 2(1). The Minister is empowered to provide, by regulation, that planning permission will not be required in respect of specified classes of *development* by, or on behalf of, a State authority, where the development is, in the opinion of the Minister, in connection with or for the purposes of public safety or order, the administration of justice or national security or defence (PDA 2000, s 181(1)). Regulations may provide for a public consultation and information process. For previous legislation, see Local Government (Planning and Development) Act 1993, ss 1–2.

Previously, a State authority was held to be exempted from the necessity of applying for planning permission; the State authority was required however to consult with the planning authority to such extent as determined by the Minister: Local Government (Planning and Development) Act 1963, s 84; *Byrne & Ors v Commissioners of Public Works* [1992] HC – 'Luggala' interpretive centre case. However, in a later case, it was held that section 84 did not exempt a State authority from the necessity to apply for planning permission: *Howard & Ors v Commissioners of Public Works* [1993] – 'Mullaghmore' interpretive centre case. In 1993, on appeal of both these cases, the Supreme Court held that a State authority was required to apply for planning permission: *Howard v Commissioners for Public Works* [1993] ILRM 665, SC hence necessitating the 1993 Act which repealed LG(PD)A 1963, s 84 (LG(PD)A 1993, s 5). The 2000 Act now consolidates the law.

A State authority is also any authority being: (a) a Minister of the Government, or (b) the Commissioners of Public Works; such a State authority has, and is deemed always to have had, power to carry out, or procure the carrying out of any *development* ie the carrying out of any works on, in or under land or the making of any material change in the use of any structures or land: State Authorities (Development and Management) Act 1993. See also *Howard v Commissioners of Public Works* [1994] 2 ILRM 301, HC. See Commissioners of Public Works (Functions and Powers) Act 1996, s 5. See also Courts Service Act 1998, s 33. For planning regulations governing development by or on behalf of State Authorities, see Planning and Development Regulations 2001, Pt IX, arts 86–91: SI No 600 of 2001.

(2) As regards the limitation of actions, a *State authority* means any authority being: (a) a Minister of State, or (b) the Commissioners of Public Works in Ireland, or (c) the Irish Land Commission, or (d) the Revenue Commissioners, or (e) the Attorney-General: Statute of Limitations 1957, s 2(1).

(3) As regards roads, a *State authority* means any authority being a Minister of the Government or the Commissioners of Public Works: Roads Act 1993, s 2(1).

(4) See also National Development Finance Agency Act 2002, s 1(1) and 22. See PLANNING PERMISSION; PUBLIC PRIVATE PARTNERSHIP ARRANGEMENT.

State Claims Agency. The service, under the remit of the National Treasury Management Agency (NTMA), with responsibility for managing personal injury and property damage compensation claims against the State: National Treasury Management Agency (Amendment) Act 2000.

Managing a claim means taking all steps necessary to dispose of a claim, whether by agreement or otherwise (NTMA(A)A 2000, s 6). A *claim* is defined as a claim which is wholly or mainly one for compensation or damages for loss of life or personal injury or loss of, or damage to, property, occasioned by an act, omission or other matter constituting a cause of action against one or more State authorities (NTMA(A)A 2000, s 7).

The Attorney-General in his role as legal advisor to the government is empowered to give directions to the Agency in its claims management function, where the interest of the State so requires (NTMA(A)A 2000, s 10).

The NTMA is known as the State Claims Agency when it is performing these functions. The objective in the new service is to manage claims and counterclaims so as to ensure that the State's liability and associated legal and other expenses are contained at the lowest achievable level. The State Claims Agency is responsible for the management of clinical claims. See CLINICAL CLAIM; NATIONAL TREASURY MANAGEMENT AGENCY.

State emblems. Any emblem of Ireland notified as a State emblem under art 6ter of the Paris Convention 1887: Trade Marks Act 1996, s 2(1). Such State emblems and official signs or hallmarks are protected under the Convention (TMA 1996, ss 62–63). A trade mark which consists of or contains any State emblem of Ireland requires Ministerial consent for its registration (TMA 1996, s 9(1)).

State Examinations Commission. A body corporate of five members, appointed by the government, with the following functions: (a) to organise the holding of examinations, (b) to ensure the preparation of examination papers and other examination materials, (c) to determine procedures in places where examinations are conducted including the supervision of examinations, (d) to make arrangements for the marking of work presented for examination, (e) to issue results of examinations, (f) to determine procedures to enable the review and appeal of results of examinations at the request of candidates, (g) to charge and collect fees for examinations and apply such moneys to the carrying out of its functions, and (h) to designate where examinations may be held: Education Act 1998, s 54; State Examination Commission (Establishment) Order 2003, SI No 373 of 2003. These functions were previously the responsibility of the Department of Education and Science.

Examinations which come within the remit of the Commission are any of those standing specified for the time being in Schedule 2 to the 1998 Act ie Leaving Certificate, Junior Certificate, Technological Certificate, Trade Certificate, Certificate in Commerce, Ceardteastas Gaeilge,

Teastas i dTeagasc na Gaeilge, Typewriting Teachers Certificate, Commercial Instructors Certificate. See NATIONAL QUALIFICATIONS AUTHORITY OF IRELAND.

State guarantee. See GUARANTEE.

State Laboratory. The central laboratory which provides a comprehensive analytical and advisory service to government departments and offices. It may be designated by the State Chemist or the Revenue Commissioners to analyse, test or examine a sample: Finance Act 1998, s 101. A document which purports to be a certificate from the State Laboratory is sufficient evidence of the facts stated therein without proof of any signature or seal on it. See also Customs and Excise (Miscellaneous Provisions) Act 1988, s 4; Protection of Animals Kept for Farming Purposes Act 1984, s 10(3)); EC (Export and Import of Certain Dangerous Chemicals) Regulations 2002, SI No 395 of 2002; EC (Certain Contaminants in Foodstuffs) Regulations 2001, SI No 400 of 2001. See also SI No 267 of 2003. See FORENSIC SCIENCE LABORATORY; MEDICAL BUREAU OF ROAD SAFETY.

State land. Land which belongs to the State, the Nation, the People or a State Authority: State Property Act 1954. See also Energy (Miscellaneous Provisions) Act 1995, s 17; State Property Act 1998. See BONA VACANTIA; ESCHEAT.

state of emergency. See NATIONAL EMERGENCY.

state of the art See PUBLICATION.

state side orders. The orders of the High Court by which it exercises supervisory jurisdiction over inferior courts, administrative bodies and individuals. The orders are of *certiorari, prohibition, mandamus* and *habeas corpus* (qqv). These orders are now obtained by the procedure of *judicial review*. The orders are used to check bodies or persons who have exceeded their legal powers; or to prevent bodies or persons from exercising a power which they do not possess; or to compel bodies or persons to perform a legally imposed duty; or to compel a person in whose custody another person is detained to produce the body of that other person before the court and certify in writing the grounds of his detention and if not satisfied to order his release. See JUDICIAL REVIEW.

State solicitor. Solicitors who undertake State work on a contract basis for areas outside of Dublin. There are 32 local State solicitors, the bulk of whose work relates to criminal matters for which the Office of the *Chief Prosecution Solicitor* (qv) is responsible. A State solicitor should not appear for a defendant in any criminal proceedings within the State solicitors area, where a summons is issued by the Garda Síochána, the Director of Public Prosecutions, the Attorney-General or any government department: *A Guide to Professional Conduct of Solicitors in Ireland* (2002) ch 3.4. This restriction applies also to the partner or qualified assistant of the State solicitor. See CHIEF STATE SOLICITOR.

state-sponsored company. See COMPANY, STATUTORY; EQUALITY BEFORE THE LAW.

stateless person. A person who is not considered as a national by any state under the operation of its law: United Nations Convention relating to the Status of Stateless Persons of September 28, 1954, art 1. See NATURALISATION; REFUGEE.

statement. When a statement of an accused is put in evidence, it becomes evidence in the real sense of the word, not only against the person who made it but also for him; it is not permissible for the trial judge to draw a distinction between the incriminating facts and the exculpatory parts: *People (DPP) v Clarke* [1995] 355, CCA. Provision has been made for the admission in criminal proceedings of written statements of matters which are not in dispute between the parties; previously such statements had to be proved by oral evidence: Criminal Justice Act 1984, s 21. See also Rules of the Superior Courts (Disclosure of Reports and Statements) 1998, SI No 391 of 1998. For proposed admissibility of previous inconsistent witness statements, see Criminal Justice Bill 2004, part 3, ss 14–19. See CONFESSION; EXPERT REPORT; JUDGES' RULES; PREVIOUS STATEMENT, INCONSISTENT; SOLICITOR, ACCESS TO; UNSWORN STATEMENT.

statement, liability for false. See DECEIT.

statement of affairs. (1) The statement required to be filed in court of a company's affairs following a winding up order or the appointment of a provisional liquidator by the court. It must be in a prescribed form and verified by affidavit. See Companies Act 1963, s 224; RSC Ord 74, rr 24–28. The statement may be used in evidence against any person making or concurring in making it: Companies Act 1990, s 18. While directors have a duty to be careful and prudent in the preparation of a statement of affairs, they are not bound to use outside experts to ascertain valuations: *Somers v Kennedy* [1998] 1 IR 1, SC.

(2) The statement required to be made by a bankrupt and by an arranging debtor (qv): Bankruptcy Act 1988, ss 19 and 91. See BANKRUPT, DUTIES OF.

statement of claim. A written or printed statement by a plaintiff in an action by *plenary* summons in the High Court, stating the facts on which he relies to support his claim against the defendant, and the relief which he claims: RSC Ord 20. The plaintiff may amend his statement of claim once without leave (Ord 28, r 2). The statement of claim must be served within 21 days after service of the summons (Ord 20, r 2) in default of which the defendant may apply to dismiss the action for want of prosecution (Ord 27, r 1, as amended by SI No 63 of 2004; *McGowan v Doherty* [1986] HC). See Practice Notes in *Law Society Gazette* (May 2004) 39.

When a plaintiff has obtained an interlocutory injunction on foot of a plenary summons, it is wholly inappropriate that the plaintiff should delay in serving a statement of claim having already obtained the benefit of the court's equitable jurisdiction: *IFPA v Youth Defence* [2004] 2 ILRM 21, SC.

The court may, at any stage in the proceedings, allow a plaintiff to alter or amend his pleadings for the purpose of determining the real questions in controversy between the parties (RSC Ord 28, r 1; *O'Leary v Minister for Transport* [2000] ITLR (20 January) HC). The statement of claim may be amended to introduce a new and hitherto unpleaded claim (Ord 28, r 6 and *Rubotham v M & B Bakeries Ltd and Irish National Insurance Co plc* [1993] ILRM 219, HC). A late amendment to the statement of claim will be allowed if there is no real injustice to the other party: *O'Neill v Canada Life Assurance* [1999] ITLR (29 March). The Supreme Court has held that that the court had jurisdiction to strike out an entire statement of claim but not a portion of it: *Aer Rianta v Ryanair* (2004) Irish Times, 3 April 2004. See *Murphy v Minister for the Marine* [1996] 2 ILRM 297, HC; *Wolfe v Wolfe* [2001] 1 ILRM 389, HC and 1 IR 313; *F McK v AF and JF* [2002] 2 ILRM 303, SC and 1 IR 242.

In arbitration, *points of claim* are the equivalent to the statement of claim. See INDORSEMENT OF CLAIM; PLEADINGS.

station bail. The setting at liberty of a person on a recognisance (qv), the person having been charged with an offence in a garda station: Criminal Procedure Act 1967, s 31(1) as amended by Criminal Justice (Miscellaneous Provisions) Act 1997, s 3 and by Maritime Security Act 2004, s 10(a). The District Court does not receive seisin of the matter until the charge is laid before a judge: *The State (Lynch) v Ballagh* [1987] ILRM 65. See also *The State (DPP) v Ruane* [1987] HC. See DCR 1997 Ord 17, r 4. See BAIL.

statistics. Includes, in addition to numerical data, information not expressible numerically which is necessary for the collection, compilation, analysis or interpretation of data: Statistics Act 1993, s 3(1). This Act: (a) establishes the Central Statistics Office (CSO) as a statutory body with responsibility for the compilation of official statistics, (b) establishes a National Statistics Board to guide the strategic direction of the CSO, (c) provides for the confidentiality of all information collected by the CSO and for its use for statistical purposes only, (d) provides that the Taoiseach may prescribe by order a statutory requirement on persons and undertakings to provide statistical information.

Statistics are collected on many matters e g population; vital, social and educational matters; local government; employment and unemployment; emigration and immigration; agriculture; sea and inland fisheries; industry; commerce; banking, insurance and finance; transport; and ancient monuments. See, for example, Statistics (Census of Population) Order 1996, SI No 91 of 1996.

The Labour Court has held that it would be alien to the ethos of the court to oblige parties to undertake the inconvenience and expense involved in producing elaborate statistical evidence to prove matters which are obvious to the members of the court by drawing on their own knowledge and experience: *Inoue v NBK Designs Ltd* [2003] ELR 98, LC.

A CSO publication or a document signed by the Director General of the CSO must be accepted in legal proceedings as *prima facie* evidence of any official statistic (SA 1993, s 45). See also EC (Intrastat) Regulations 1993, SI No 136 of 1993, and

(Amendment) Regulations 2002, SI No 466 of 2002. See also SI No 465 of 2002 (road freight); SI No 9 of 2003 (industrial production); SI No 39 of 2003 (national employment survey); SI No 40 of 2003 (service inquiries); SI No 118 of 2003 (retail sales); SI No 122 of 2003 (industrial commodities production); SI No 715 of 2003 (carriage of passengers, freight and mail by air). For Central Statistics Office, see email: *information@cso.ie* and website: *www.cso.ie*. See CENSUS; CONSUMER PRICE INDEX; VITAL STATISTICS.

status. The legal position or condition of a person eg a minor, a married woman, a dependent child, a child whose parents are not married to each other, an adopted child, a person of full age, an alien (now, a non-national), an Irish citizen, a citizen of the EC, a bankrupt, a person of unsound mind, a ward of court (qv). The legal rights and duties, powers and disabilities, of a person depend on the legal status of that person. See CHILD, STATUS OF.

status quo. The state in which things are, or were. The Supreme Court has held that where the relief sought by a plaintiff is the preservation of the *status quo*, this is considered to be an important aspect of the *balance of convenience* (qv): *Dunne & Lucas v Dún Laoghaire-Rathdown County Council* [2003] ITLR (24 March) SC. Where a large civil engineering project is involved, the mere mention of an enormous sum of money as the total costs of the scheme does not in any way constitute evidence as to the balance of convenience. The purported damage and expense must be established and not simply invoked.

status quo ante. [The same state as before.] See *Curust Financial Services Ltd v Loewe-Lack-Werk Otto Loewe GmbH & Co KG* [1994] 1 IR 450, SC.

statute, interpretation of. See INTERPRETATION OF LEGISLATION.

statute-barred. Term used to indicate that proceedings in a cause of action have not been commenced within the time allowed by statute. See *Sheehan v Amond* [1982] IR 235; *Byrne v PJ Quigley Ltd* [1995] ELR 205, EAT; *Behan v Bank of Ireland* [1998] 2 ILRM 507, SC; *Lawless v Port & Docks Board* [1998] 1 ILRM 514, HC. See CAUSE OF ACTION; LIMITATION OF ACTIONS; STATUTE OF LIMITATIONS.

statute law. The body of law enacted by the parliamentary process. A *statute* includes, in addition to Acts of the Oireachtas (qv),

Acts of the Oireachtas of Saorstát Éireann (qv), Acts of the Parliament of the former United Kingdom of Great Britain and Ireland, and Acts of a Parliament sitting in Ireland at any time before the coming into force of the Union with Ireland Act 1800: Interpretation Act 1937, s 3. The text of Irish Statutes are also available from website: *www.attorneygeneral.ie* and *www.irlgov.ie/oireachtas*. See ACT; BILL; STATUTORY INSTRUMENT.

Statute of Frauds (Ireland). The Statute passed in 1695 to prevent fraud and perjury. It required certain contracts to be *evidenced* by some memorandum in writing signed by the party to be charged or his agent. These contracts are: (a) any special promise by an executor to answer damages out of his own estate; (b) any special promise to answer for the debt, default or miscarriage of another person (a *contract of guarantee*): *Dunville & Co v Quinn* [1908] 42 ILTR 49; (c) an agreement in consideration of marriage: *Saunders v Cramer* [1842] 5 I Eq 12; (d) any contract for the sale of land or any interest in land; (e) any agreement not to be performed within the space of one year from the making thereof: *Naughton v Limestone Land Co Ltd* [1952] Ir Jur Rep 19; *Hynes v Hynes* [1984] HC.

In a particular case, the Supreme Court held that proceedings should not be dismissed due to the absence of a note or memorandum for the purpose of the Statute of Frauds: *Supermac's v Katesan (Naas) Ltd* [2001] 1 ILRM 145, SC and [2000] 4 IR 273, SC. See also *Guardian Builders v Sleecon & Berville* [1989] 7 ILT Dig 22; *Riordan v Carroll t/a Wyvern Gallery* [1996] 2 ILRM 263, HC; *Higgins v Argent Development Ltd* [2002] FL 4998, HC. See AUCTIONEER; ELECTRONIC FORM; MEMORANDUM, STATUTE OF FRAUDS; ORAL AGREEMENT, MODIFICATION OF CONTRACT BY; PART-PERFORMANCE; QUANTUM MERUIT; TRUST, EXPRESS.

Statute of Limitations. The 1957 Statute which specifies time limits within which legal proceedings are to be taken: Statute of Limitations 1957 to 2000. A claim brought after the expiration of the limitation period is only disbarred if a defendant pleads the Statute in his defence; consequently, the Statute does not affect a plaintiff's right to sue but affects his right to succeed and consequently is not an invasion on his constitutional right of access to the courts: *Tuohy v Courtney* [1994] 3 IR 1.

See Law Reform Commission reports, *Statute of Limitations*: (a) *Claims in respect of Latent Personal Injuries* (LRC 21, 1987) (b) *Claims in Contract and Tort in respect of Latent Damage* (*other than Personal Injury*) (LRC 64, 2001). See LIMITATION OF ACTIONS; TIME.

statutory company. See COMPANY, STATUTORY.

statutory declaration. A written statement of facts which the person making it, the *declarant*, signs and solemnly declares conscientiously believing it to be true, before a notary public (qv), a commissioner for oaths (qv), or a peace commissioner (qv): Statutory Declarations Act 1938. A statutory declaration in connection with an application for a grant, loan, subsidy, or assistance under the Housing Acts, may be made by a person before a clergyman or a member of the Garda Síochána: Housing (Miscellaneous Provisions) Act 1992, s 21.

It is an offence for a person to make a statutory declaration knowing it to be false or misleading in any material respect (SDA 1938, s 6). Declarations were substituted for oaths in many cases by the Statutory Declarations Act 1835 and are now required by many statutes eg Companies (Amendment) Act 1983, s 5(5). See Interpretation Act 1937, s 12, Sch.

statutory duty. A duty or liability, imposed by some statutes. A failure to carry out a statutory duty may amount to a tort (qv) depending on the construction of the statute. A breach of a statutory duty may give rise to a private right of action where the absence of such a right would infringe the constitutional right of the plaintiff eg the right to earns one's livelihood: *Parsons v Kavanagh* [1990] ILRM 560.

Failure to comply with the provisions of the Building Control Act 1990 does not entitle a person to bring any civil proceedings by reason only of that contravention (BCA 1990, s 21). Failure to comply with general statutory duties imposed on employers, employees, designers and manufacturers in relation to safety, health and welfare at work cannot confer a right of action in civil proceedings; however breach of a duty imposed by regulations may do so: Safety, Health and Welfare at Work Act 1989, s 60. See Companies (Auditing and Accounting) Act 2003, s 33. See also *Dunleary v Glen Abbey Ltd* [1992] ILRM 1, HC; *HMIL Ltd v Minister for Agriculture* [2002] FL 4937, SC. See MORAL RIGHT;

PERFORMERS' RIGHTS, INFRINGEMENT OF; RECORDING RIGHT; TORT.

statutory functions. Powers and duties conferred on a body or person by legislation. A common law duty of care is owed by a body exercising statutory functions, where a relationship of proximity exists between the statutory body and the person or body affected by its decision, where there is foreseeability of damage, and in the absence of any compelling reason based on public policy: *Beatty & Beatty v Rent Tribunal* [2003] ITLR (2 June) HC. See STATUTORY DUTY.

statutory instrument. (1) An order, regulation, rule, scheme or bye-law made in exercise of a power conferred by statute: Statutory Instruments Act 1947. They are often formal documents by which designated Ministers exercise their power to make subordinate legislation, which power is given to them by various statutes. A regulation made by a Statutory Instrument enjoys a presumption of constitutionality: *Minister for Agriculture v Brennan* [1999] 3 IR 228, HC.

Statutory instruments may be cited by number and year and also by their title eg SI No 46 of 1987; Courts Martial (Legal Aid) Regulations 1987. Many statutory instruments are required to be placed before the Houses of the Oireachtas (qv) and only become effective after a specified period if they are not annulled by a resolution of either House.

The granting of leave to seek a judicial review of the making of a statutory instrument does not in any way hinder, impede or prevent the continued operation of the statutory instrument: *Gorman v Minister for the Environment* [2001] 1 IR 306, HC. A statutory instrument made pursuant to the European Communities Act 1972 has the status of a statute and could effectively amend an earlier statutory provision: *O'Connell v EPA* [2003] 1 IR 532, SC. [Bibliography: Humphreys].

(2) An instrument made, issued or granted under a power or authority conferred by statute: Statute Law (Restatement) Act 2002, s 1(1). A *restatement Act* may include a statutory instrument (SL(R)A 2002, s 2(3)). See AMENDMENT OF LEGISLATION; BYE-LAW; REGULATION; RESTATEMENT OF STATUTE; STATUTORY RULES AND ORDERS.

statutory interpretation. The interpretation of statutes is said to be by the *mischief* approach and the *literal* approach. Under the former, the judge is concerned primarily with ascertaining the policy or goals which the provision in question was adopted to promote, and the provision will be applied in the light of that purpose.

Under the *literal* approach, the judge will give effect to the literal meaning of the provision even if that is inconsistent with what the legislature was endeavouring to achieve. Words in a statute are to be considered in their context and surrounding circumstances: *Dillon v Minister for Posts Telegraphs* [1981] ILRM 477. See INTERPRETATION OF LEGISLATION.

statutory power, restraint of. No special principle governs the grant of an interlocutory injunction restraining the exercise of a statutory power: *Pesca Valentia Ltd v Minister for Fisheries* [1986] ILRM 68. See INJUNCTION.

statutory rape. See CARNAL KNOWLEDGE, UNLAWFUL; SEXUAL ASSAULT; RAPE.

statutory rules and orders. [SR & O.] The former name given to statutory instruments (qv) in the period 1922–1947. [Bibliography: Humphreys].

statutory sitting. The sitting of the court at which a bankrupt must make a full disclosure of his property and at which the creditors may prove their debts and choose and appoint a *creditors' assignee*: Bankruptcy Act 1988, s 17. A statutory sitting is held within three weeks of the publication of the notice of the adjudication of the debtor as a bankrupt in Iris Oifigiúil (qv) and in at least one daily newspaper in circulation in the area where the bankrupt resides. For procedure, see SI No 79 of 1989, Part VII. The second sitting, formerly held, was abolished by the 1988 Act. See BANKRUPTCY.

statutory tenant. See TENANT, STATUTORY.

statutory undertaker. Means a person authorised by or under any enactment or order having statutory force to construct, work, or carry on a railway, canal, inland navigation, dock, harbour, gas, electricity, telecommunications or other public undertaking: Planning and Development Act 2000, s 2(1). A statutory undertaker does not require planning permission when doing work to repair or replace its infrastructure; however it does require permission when proposing to erect new infrastructure, unless specifically exempted (PDA 2000, s 4). A statutory undertaker who wishes to carry out works on roads must obtain consent: Roads Act 1993, s 53. See also Environmental Protection Agency Act 1992, s 3 as substituted by Protection of the Environment Act 2003, s 5. See PLANNING PERMISSION.

stay of execution. The suspension of the operation of a judgment or order of a court. The court may, at or after the time of giving judgment or making an order, stay execution until such time as it thinks fit; also any party against whom judgment has been given, may apply to the court for a stay of execution or other relief against the judgment, upon the grounds of facts which have arisen too late to be pleaded: RSC Ord 42, rr 17 and 28.

While the Court has discretion to grant a stay, special reasons must exist to enable that discretion to be exercised: *Rohan Construction Ltd v Antigen Ltd* [1989] ITLR (8 May). An appeal of a judgment does not automatically operate as a stay on execution: RSC Ord 58, r 18; Ord 61, r 6. In order to be entitled to a stay, a defendant raising the issue of liability on appeal does not have to prove a probability that his appeal on that issue will succeed: *Irish Press plc v Ingersoll Irish Publications Ltd* [1995] 1 ILRM 117, SC, disapproving of *Corish v Hogan* [1990] ITLR (21 May) SC.

When deciding whether to grant a stay of execution on an award of damages (qv), the Court must balance conflicting considerations so that the justice will not be denied to either party: *Redmond v Ireland and A-G* [1992] ILRM 291, SC. A stay which has been granted without objection from the plaintiff may be later removed where the justice of the case lay in such removal: *Emerald Meats Ltd v Minister for Agriculture (No 2)* [1993] 11 ILT Dig 116, SC. A stay will be granted on an order of discovery (qv) where a refusal to grant the stay would determine the action: *Magaleasing UK Ltd v Barrett* [1991] ITLR (29 July) SC.

It has been held that the Supreme Court has not the power to grant a stay of execution of an order of the High Court to release a person: *The State (Trimbole) v Governor of Mountjoy Prison* [1985] IR 567.

A judge in the Circuit Court is empowered on pronouncing any judgment or making any order to *stay execution* of the judgment or order for such period and on such terms as he thinks just: Circuit Court Rules 2001 Ord 33, r 13. For the District Court, see DCR 1997 Ord 46, r 7; Ord 48, r 3(2); Ord 101, rr 5–6 as amended by

District Court (Appeals to the Circuit Court) Rules 2003, SI No 484 of 2003. See also Enforcement of Court Orders Act 1926, ss 21 and 51. See *O'Toole v RTE* [1993] ILRM 454, SC; *Darby v Anderson* [2003] 1 ILRM 420, HC. See EXECUTION OF JUDGMENT; INSTALMENT DECREE; STOP ORDER.

stay of proceedings. The suspension of proceedings by a court eg: (a) where the proceedings are vexatious or frivolous, (b) where there is a risk of an unfair trial due to prejudicial pre-trial publicity, or (c) where legal proceedings are instituted contrary to an arbitration agreement, or (d) where no reasonable cause of action is shown; or (e) on acceptance of a lodgment, or (f) where a preliminary issue of law is to be decided.

As regards a company, when a winding-up order has been made or a provisional liquidator appointed, no action or proceeding may be proceeded with or commenced against the company except by leave of the court and subject to such terms as the court may impose: Companies Act 1963, s 222. This does not apply to proceedings before the Employment Appeals Tribunal: Companies (Amendment) Act 1986, s 23. The court may allow secured creditors to proceed to enforce their security in such company cases and also proceedings in respect of fatal accidents under the Civil Liabilities Act 1961. See *Doyle v Irish National Insurance Co plc* [1998] 1 ILRM 502, HC.

Where money is lodged in the Circuit Court by the defendant, the plaintiff may within ten days of the lodgment, serve notice on the defendant that he accepts the amount lodged, which notice operates as a *stay* of all further proceedings, except as to costs: Circuit Court Rules 2001 Ord 15, r 12. This does not apply in the case of a lodgment with a *defence of tender*. See also Ord 5, r 6. As regards stay of proceedings in the High Court, see RSC Ord 19, r 28; Ord 22, r 4(2); Ord 34, r 2; Ord 56, r 2; and in the District Court, see DCR 1997 Ord 39, r 8. See also *Murphy v Hennessy* [1985] ILRM 100; *Parkarran Ltd v M & P Construction Ltd* [1996] 1 IR 83, HC.

The DPP was given leave in the High Court to challenge the decision of the Circuit Criminal Court to *stay indefinitely* the trial of former Taoiseach Charles Haughey on charges of obstructing the McCracken Tribunal, the latter court finding that there was a real and substantial risk that the defendant would not receive a fair trial, due particularly to: (a) remarks regarding the matter made by the Tánaiste; and (b) a leaflet which had been circulated: *DPP v Haughey* (2000) Irish Times, 1 July 2000, HC. Subsequently, the High Court held that the order of the Circuit Court judge was not final in the nature of an order of prohibition or permanent stay; it was for the judge to decide whether there was unavoidable unfairness of trial and there was no requirement of law that an attempt to empanel an unbiased jury must first be made: *DPP v Haugh and Haughey (No 2)* [2001] 1 IR 162, HC. See also Pensions Act 1990, s 136 inserted by Pensions (Amendment) Act 2002, s 5. See ABUSE OF PROCESS; ARBITRATION; FORUM NON CONVENIENS; LIQUIDATED DEMAND; LODGMENT IN COURT; OPPRESSIVE PROCEEDINGS; PATENT; PAYMENT OUT OF COURT; PROHIBITION; STEP IN PROCEEDINGS.

stealing. Means committing the offence of theft: Criminal Justice (Theft and Fraud) Offences Act 2001, ss 2(1) and 4. See LARCENY; ROBBERY; STOLE; THEFT.

stenographer, official. Means the person appointed to attend the trial and, where necessary, to make a report: RSC Ord 86, r 1. The official stenographer is required at the conclusion of the trial to sign the shorthand note taken by him and certify the same to be complete and correct (Ord 86, r 14). The statutory requirement for a record and transcript of criminal proceedings arises under the Courts of Justice Act 1924, s 33 as substituted by the Criminal Justice (Miscellaneous Provisions) Act 1997, s 7. See also RSC Ord 123. The shorthand note of the official stenographer, and the transcript which may be produced from it, are a record created by the court, and therefore fall outside the exceptions at s 46(1)(a)(I) of the Freedom of Information Act 1997, irrespective of whether the stenographer is employed by or is an independent contractor to the Court Service: *Minister for Justice v Information Commissioner* [2001] 3 IR 43, HC and [2002] 2 ILRM 1, HC. See TRANSCRIPT.

step-child. A child of one's spouse by a former union. Usually in legislation, the term 'member of the family' includes a step-child eg Criminal Justice Act 1999, s 41(4)(b); Non-Fatal Offences Against the Person Act 1997, s 1. A 'dependant' in legislation may also include a step-child eg Civil Liability (Amendment) Act 1996, ss 1 and 4; Air Navigation and Transport (International Conventions) Act 2004, s 7. An 'orphan' for social welfare purposes includes a step-child: Social Welfare (Consolidation) Act 1993, s 62(1). A 'child' usually includes a step-child eg Irish Takeover Rules 2001, r 2.1(a); Ombudsman Contributory Pension Scheme 1991, SI No 269 of 1989.

The term 'step-child' is usually referred to as 'stepchild' in taxation legislation eg Taxes Consolidation Act 1997, s 6; Capital Acquisitions Tax Consolidation Act 2003, s 2. See also Criminal Assets Bureau Act 1996, s 1; Health (Nursing Homes) Act 1990, s 2; Companies Act 1990, s 3(1); Building Societies Act 1989, s 52(3); Married Women's Status Act 1957, s 8(5). See CHILD; FATAL INJURIES.

step in proceedings. Delivery of pleadings or taking any other steps in court proceedings is fatal to an application by a party to an arbitration agreement to have the court proceedings *stayed* in respect of any matter agreed to be referred to arbitration: Arbitration Act 1980, s 5 as amended by Arbitration Act 1998, s 18.

The court will only refuse to *stay* proceedings if satisfied that the party seeking such order has instituted some process in the action which involves costs which are lost when the matter is referred to arbitration; seeking an extension of time from the other party within which to lodge a defence is not a step in the proceedings: *O'Flynn v An Bord Gáis Éireann* [1982] ILRM 324. See also *MacCormack Products Ltd v Town of Monaghan Co-op Ltd* [1988] IR 304.

In a particular case, the Supreme Court has held that orders extending the time for the service of the book of evidence were 'steps' taken under the Criminal Procedure Act 1967: *DPP v Zambra* [2002] 2 IR 351, SC. However, even though an application for an adjournment is the invoking of the court's jurisdiction, it is not sufficient to constitute a 'step' as it is a totally neutral act: *O'Dwyer v Boyd* [2003] 1 ILRM 112, SC.

The Supreme Court also held that the word 'step' as used in s 28 of the Refugee Act 1996 envisaged a stage in the procedure by which a significant and discernible movement was taken towards the determination of the status of the applicant: *IU v*

Minister for Justice [2002] 2 IR 125, SC. See ARBITRATION, DOMESTIC.

sterile transaction. In a company, a transaction which has no tangible economic benefit to the company. Sterile transactions which fall within the terms of a particular object's clause of a company's memorandum of association are not *ultra vires*. See *Parke v Daily News Ltd* [1962] Ch 927; *Re Horsley Weight Ltd* [1982] 2 Ch 442.

stet. [Let it stand].

stet processus. [Stay of proceedings].

stillborn child. Means a child who, at birth, weighs not less than 500 grammes or has a gestational age of not less than 24 weeks and shows no sign of life: Civil Registration Act 2004, s 2(1). 'Stillbirth' must be construed accordingly. Provision has been made for the registration of stillbirths occurring in the State (CRA 2004, ss 13(1)(b), 28–30). Also there is provision for recording the father's name similarly as pertains where a live birth occurs and the parents are not married (CRA 2004, s 22(6)). A coroner is required to notify a registrar if in the course of his duties, he ascertains that a body is that of a stillborn child (CRA 2004, s 28(7)). No person other than an tArd-Chláraitheoir or his staff may search the register of stillbirths (CRA 2004, s 62). For the particulars to be entered in the register of stillbirths, see CRA 2004, Sch 1, Pt II. There are about 300 stillbirths each year. The legislation is intended to assist the parents of stillborn children to cope with their loss by providing tangible evidence of the existence of their child. See also Vital Statistics (Stillbirths) Regulations 1994, SI No 427 of 1994. For previous legislation, see Stillbirths Registration Act 1994, s 1.

stirpes. Stocks or families. See PER STIRPES.

stock. (1) A family or line of descent. (2) The capital of a company consisting of fully paid shares which have been converted and combined into one unit eg 1000 shares of €1 each becoming stock of €1,000; formerly called its joint-stock, signifying that it was a common or joint fund contributed by its members. See COMMERCIAL PROCEEDINGS; SUCCESSION; COMPANY; SHARES, COMPANY.

stock exchange. An organised financial market, whose members provide an *investment service* in respect of *investment instruments*: Stock Exchange Act 1995, s 3(1) as amended by Central Bank and Financial Services Authority of Ireland Act 2003, s 35, Schedule 1. An *investment service* includes execution of orders, managing portfolios, and underwriting or placing issues. *Investment instruments* include transferable securities, stocks, bonds, government and public securities, interest rate and exchange rate swaps. The approval of the Central Bank is required for a person to operate a stock exchange established in the State (SEA 1995, ss 8–9). The Irish Stock Exchange (qv) is deemed to be an approved stock exchange (SEA 1995, s 10). The Central Bank is required to exercise its regulatory and supervisory functions in order to promote the proper and orderly regulation and supervision of stock exchanges and their member firms and the protection of investors (SEA 1995, s 28). For amendments to the 1995 Act, see Investor Compensation Act 1998, ss 70–83, and Central Bank and Financial Services Authority of Ireland Act 2004, Sch 1 and 3.

The practice of an exchange may amount to a custom which is incorporated as an implied term into contracts between buyers and sellers of securities. Companies which seek a stock exchange quotation for their securities must satisfy the rules for admission of securities for listing. Electronic trading commenced on the Dublin Stock Exchange on 6 June 2000. See Prescribed Stock Exchange Regulations 1997, SI No 256 of 1997. For Irish Stock Exchange, see website: *www.ise.ie*. For London Stock Exchange, see website: *www.londonstockexchange.com*. [Bibliography: Cahill D; Clarke B (2); Forde (5).] See IRISH FINANCIAL SERVICES REGULATORY AUTHORITY; LISTING RULES; STOCKBROKER.

stock repo transaction. A transaction in which a *repo* seller agrees to sell stock to a *repo* buyer for a cash price on the basis that at the end of the fixed financing period, the *repo* seller will buy back equivalent stock at a price equal to the original price plus interest. Such a transaction is exempt from stamp duty: Stamp Duties Consolidation Act 1999, s 87A inserted by Finance Act 2000, s 129.

stock transfer. The Stock Transfer Act 1963 provides for a simplified transfer of securities. See TRANSFER OF SHARES.

stockbroker. In effect a person who is a member of an approved stock exchange and whose regular occupation or business is the provision of *investment services*: Stock Exchange Act 1995, s 3(1). A register of members must be kept by the exchange and be open for inspection to the public (SEA 1995, s 25). The acquisition of shares in a member firm of a stock exchange at certain thresholds (20%, 33% or 50%) must be notified to the Central Bank and requires its approval (SEA 1995, ss 39–49). A member firm, as a precondition to business, previously was required to inform clients and investors of the existence and the extent of any compensation or protection schemes (SEA 1995, s 51), now repealed by the Investor Compensation Act 1998, s 7. See also ICA 1998, s 38. See also Investment Intermediaries Act 1995, s 50. For examples of stockbrokers, see websites: *www.davy.ie* and *www.ncb.ie*.

Moneys transferred by a client to the bank account of an authorised member of the Irish Stock Exchange must be returned to the client where the purpose for which the moneys have been transferred cannot be completed e g where the moneys are to purchase shares and prior to the settlement date the member is suspended from the exchange: *In the Matter of Money Markets International Stockbrokers Ltd (in liquidation)* [1999] ITLR (23 August), HC. See also *Re Money Markets International Ltd (No 2)* [2001] 2 IR 17, HC. See INVESTOR COMPENSATION.

stole. The word 'stole' used in a UK extradition warrant (qv) has been held to convey that the accused took another person's property without right or permission with the intention of not returning it and this constituted an adequate description of the *corresponding* offence (qv) in Ireland of simple larceny (qv) under s 2 of the Larceny Act 1916: *O'Shea v Conroy* [1995] 2 ILRM 527, HC and 1 IR 295.

stolen property. A garda is entitled to require a person to give an account of how that person came by property in their possession, where the garda has reasonable grounds for believing that the property was stolen: Criminal Justice (Theft and Fraud Offences) Act 2001, s 19(1). It is an offence not to give such account (CJ(TFO)A 2001, s 19(2)). See also s 20. [Bibliography: McGreal C.] See HANDLING STOLEN PROPERTY; POSSESSION OF STOLEN PROPERTY; RESTITUTION OF POSSESSION; REVESTING; WITHHOLDING INFORMATION.

stop, obligation to. The obligation of a person driving a vehicle in a public place to stop the vehicle on being so required by a garda: Road Traffic Act 1961, s 109. The Gardaí have a common law power to require a motorist to stop: *DPP (Stratford) v Fagan* [1994] 2 ILRM 349, SC.

stop and search. A garda has power to stop and search a person where he suspects that the person has *anything stolen or unlawfully obtained*: Dublin Police Act 1842, s 29. The suspect may be stopped for the purpose of exercising the power of search and need not be formally placed under arrest prior to the search; the garda must tell the suspect of his suspicion and his power under s 29: *DPP v Rooney* [1993] ILRM 61, HC. See SEARCH OF PERSON.

stop order. An order of the court made on the application of a person having any derivative interest in any funds or securities standing in court, to stay the transfer, sale, payment out or other disposition of the funds or securities, without notice to the applicant, which application is made *ex parte* and grounded on an affidavit of facts: RSC Ord 46, rr 14–18. The derivative interest which the applicant must have, may be by way of assignment, or charge or lien or otherwise eg a judgment creditor. [Bibliography: Glanville.] See CHARGING ORDER; DISTRINGAS NOTICE.

stoppage in transitu. The right which an unpaid seller has to resume possession of goods and to retain them until payment or tender of the price, where the buyer has become insolvent. The right exists only as long as the goods are in transit; if the buyer or his agent obtains delivery of the goods before their arrival at the appointed destination, the transit is at an end. The seller's right is not affected by any sale or disposition of the goods by the buyer, unless the seller has assented thereto, or unless the documents of title to the goods have been transferred to a person who takes them in good faith and for valuable consideration. See Sale of Goods Act 1893, ss 44–48.

stopping of cheque. See CHEQUE, COUNTERMAND OF PAYMENT.

strand. See SHORE.

stranger. One who is not privy or party to an act or transaction.

stranger to the consideration. A phrase used where a person may be a party to a contract, but cannot sue for its performance because he is a *stranger to the consideration* eg A, B and C enter into a contract under which A promises both B and C that if B will perform an act, A will give €200 to C; B can compel A to pay C, but C cannot sue as he is a stranger to the consideration.

There is an exception as regards a bill of exchange where an antecedent debt or liability suffices as consideration (ie *past consideration*), in addition to consideration sufficient to support a simple contract: Bills of Exchange Act 1882, s 27. See *Roscorla v Thomas* [1842] 3 QB 234: *Dunlop Tyre Co v Selfridge & Co* [1915] AC 847; *Shadwell v Shadwell* [1860] 9 CB(NS) 159. See CONSIDERATION; PRIVITY OF CONTRACT.

strategic development zone. Where, in the opinion of the government, specified development is of economic or social importance to the State, the government may by *order*, designate one or more sites for the establishment of a *strategic development zone* to facilitate such development: Planning and Development Act 2000, s 166. The *order* must specify the type of development that may be established in the zone and state the reasons for specifying the development and for designating the site or sites (PDA 2000, s 166(3)).

Where a site is designated, a draft planning scheme may be prepared by the relevant development agency (eg IDA Ireland) and submitted to the planning authority (PDA 2000, ss 168–169). There is provision for public display and consultation, for the making of the scheme and for the decision of the planning authority to be appealed to An Bord Pleanála, for stated reasons, within four weeks of the date of the decision (PDA 2000, s 169). The appeal may be made by the development agency or by any person who had made submissions or observations in respect of the draft scheme (PDA 2000, s 169(6)).

A planning scheme made for a strategic development zone is deemed to form part of any development plan in force (PDA 2000, s 169(9)).

Also, a planning authority must grant permission in respect of an application for a development in such a zone, where it is satisfied that the development would be consistent with the planning scheme; such a grant cannot be subject to an appeal to An Bord Pleanála, as the primary planning issues will already have been settled when the planning scheme was adopted (PDA 2000, s 170).

For an example of a *strategic development zone* designated by government order, see Planning and Development (Designation of Strategic Development Zone – Hansfield,

Blanchardstown) Order 2001, SI No 273 of 2001. See also Planning and Development Regulations 2001, Part 14, art 179: SI No 600 of 2001. See PLANNING PERMISSION.

stray dog. Includes any dog which appears to be unaccompanied by a person unless such dog is in the premises of its owner or of some other person who has the dog in his charge or of any other person with that person's consent: Control of Dogs Act 1986, s 11(11). Stray dogs may be seized by dog wardens or the garda and disposed of or destroyed. A person claiming a stray dog must produce a current dog licence in respect of that dog (CDA 1986, s 11(5)(b) as substituted by Control of Dogs (Amendment) Act 1992, s 5).

stray horse. A horse apparently wandering at large, lost, abandoned or unaccompanied (whether tethered or untethered) by any person apparently in charge of it in a public place or on any premises without the owner's or occupier's consent: Control of Horses Act 1996, s 2(1). A stray horse may be seized and detained by an authorised person or a garda (CHA 1996, s 37).

street. See NAME, CHANGE OF.

street collection. See COLLECTION.

street trading. Selling of goods by retail in a street to passers-by which was regulated by the Street Trading Act 1926, which now stands repealed as it applies to casual trading (qv) or occasional trading (qv). See CASUAL TRADING.

strict liability. Legal obligation or duty which is independent of wrongful intent or negligence. See *Mullen v Quinnsworth Ltd* [1991] ITLR (17 June) SC. See also O'Higgins in 9 ILT & SJ (1991) 134. Contrast with *fault liability* which is dependent on proof of negligence. See ACT OF GOD; OIL POLLUTION; PRODUCT LIABILITY; RYLANDS V FLETCHER, RULE IN.

strict liability in criminal law. 'If a matter is made a criminal offence, it is essential that there should be something in the nature of *mens rea* ... . But there are exceptions to this rule ... and the reason for this is, that the legislature has thought it so important to prevent the particular act from being committed that it absolutely forbids it to be done; and if it is done the offender is liable to a penalty whether he has any mens rea or not, and whether or not he intended to commit a breach of the law': *Pearks, Gunston & Tee Ltd v Ward*

[1902] 2 KB 1. *Mens rea* is not a requirement for an offence of *strict liability* e g the pollution of rivers and streams: *Maguire v Shannon Regional Fisheries Board* [1994] 2 ILRM 253, HC. [Bibliography: McAuley & McCutcheon.] See MENS REA.

strict settlement. A settlement which was designed to keep land in the family. The usual settlement gave a life interest to the husband and a fee tail (qv) to the children. Provision was made for the wife by giving her a *jointure* (qv) and for the children, who did not obtain the land under the entails, by giving them *portions* (qv). The difficulties which such a settlement created were overcome by the Settled Land Acts 1882 and 1890, which gave extensive powers to the *tenant for life* and protected the interests of those entitled in succession. See SETTLEMENT.

stress in employment. See HARASSMENT IN EMPLOYMENT.

stricti juris. [According to strict right or law].

strike. Cessation of work by any number or body of workers acting in combination, or a concerted refusal or a refusal under common understanding of any number of workers to continue to work for their employer, done as a means of compelling their employer, or to aid other workers in compelling their employer, to accept or not to accept terms or conditions of or affecting employment: Industrial Relations Act 1990, s 8. See also Unfair Dismissals Act 1977, s 1; Redundancy Payments Act 1967, s 6. Such action can expose the participants to liability unless it is *in contemplation or furtherance of a trade dispute* (qv).

As from 18 July 1992 the rules of every trade union must contain certain provisions relating to the holding of a *secret ballot* in respect of strikes and other industrial action (IRA 1990, s 14). Evidence of compliance with s 14 of sufficient weight must be produced; a bald assertion that a ballot had been carried out in accordance with the rules of the union and the provisions of the 1990 Act is insufficient: *Daru Bricklaying Ltd v BATU* [2002] 2 IR 619, HC; [2003] 1 ILRM 227 and ELR 244. Action taken in disregard of or contrary to the outcome of a secret ballot does not enjoy the immunity conferred on members and trade unions by IRA 1990, ss 10–12 (IRA 1990, s 17). The failure by a trade union to hold a secret ballot in accordance with s 14 of the Act of 1990 does not affect its immunity from suit in tort: *Nolan Transport (Oaklands) Ltd v Halligan* [1999] 1 IR 128, SC and [1998] ELR 177, SC.

Supportive action by another trade union must not be taken without the approval of the Irish Congress of Trade Unions (IRA 1990, s 14(3)).

An employee going on strike does not necessarily frustrate or repudiate his contract of employment: *Becton Dickinson Ltd v Lee* [1973] IR 1; *Bates v Model Bakery Ltd* [1992] ELR 193, SC.

Dismissal of an employee for taking part in a strike will be deemed an unfair dismissal if one or more of the striking employees were not dismissed, or were dismissed but subsequently permitted to resume employment: Unfair Dismissals Act 1977, s 5(2) as amended by Unfair Dismissals (Amendment) Act 1993, s 4.

'If doctors decide to participate in an organised collective or individual withdrawal of services, they are not released from their ethical responsibilities to patients': Medical Council, *A Guide to Ethical Conduct and Behaviour* (6th edn, 2004) para 1.7. The doctors must guarantee emergency services and also such care as may be required for those for whom they hold clinical responsibility.

Unemployment resulting directly from a trade dispute in which the claimant is involved, disqualifies him from receiving social welfare benefit or assistance: Social Welfare (Consolidation) Act 1993, ss 47(1) and 125(3). However, unemployment benefit or assistance may be paid to a person on strike if the Social Welfare Tribunal considers that the person was unreasonably deprived of his employment (SW(C)A 1993, s 274 as amended by Social Welfare Act 1996, s 33). Workers in Irish Press Newspapers who were involved in a trade dispute over the dismissal of the group business editor, Colm Rapple, were held by the Social Welfare Tribunal to have been unreasonably deprived of their employment and consequently entitled to social welfare: *Re Roderick O'Connor* [1995] ELR 152. See *Twomey* in (1993) 3 ISLR 131. See LABOUR INJUNCTION; TRADE DISPUTE; PICKETING; SOCIAL WELFARE TRIBUNAL; UNLAWFUL INTERFERENCE WITH CONSTITUTIONAL RIGHTS.

strike off. The Registrar of Companies is empowered to strike defunct companies off the register: Companies Act 1963, s 311 as amended by Companies (Amendment)

(No 2) Act 1999, s 49. Provision is also made to *strike off* a company which has failed to file its annual returns on time; failure for one year can result in the company being struck off: Companies (Amendment) Act 1982, s 12, 12A–12D, as inserted by C(A)(No 2)A 1999, s 46. The Registrar may restore a company to the register, in which case the company is deemed to have continued in existence as if its name had not been struck off: CA 1963, s 311A as amended by C(A)(No 2)A 1999, s 50. See also C(A)(No 2)A 1999, s 48. A creditor may apply to the courts to have a company restored to the register, so that the creditor will not be inhibited in pursuit of its claim by the dissolution of the company: *Re Haltone (Cork) Ltd* [1996] 1 IR 32, HC. See website: *www.cro.ie*. See 'Restoring companies to the Register' by Patrick Leonard BL in *Bar Review* (December 2000) 182.

strike out. (1) An order of a court to withdraw an action or a claim or a defence eg a defence may be struck out where a defendant fails to comply with an order of discovery (qv): RSC Ord 31, r 21, *Murphy v O'Donohue Ltd* [1995] 2 ILRM 519, HC. The High Court, on appeal, may order the reinstatement of the defence on such terms as to security, time and mode of trial or otherwise as the court thinks fit; this includes the lodgment of a sum in court as an earnest of *bona fides* or security: RSC Ord 37, r 10 and *Decospan NV v Benhouse Ltd* [1995] 2 ILRM 620, HC.

(2) An order for the dismissal of an action for want of prosecution or the striking out of a defence, which may be made where a party to proceedings fails to comply with an order for discovery or inspection of documents: Circuit Court Rules 2001 Ord 32, r 6. The Circuit Court is required to strike out an action, cause or matter with costs, which the court has not the jurisdiction to try and determine: Circuit Court Rules 2001 Ord 5, r 9.

(3) Where the District Court is of opinion that the complaint before it discloses no offence at law, it may *strike out* the complaint with or without awarding costs: DCR 1997 Ord 38, r 1(4). It may also strike out the action if neither the prosecutor nor accused appears. A district court judge may also strike out any case brought in his court which the court has not jurisdiction to hear: DCR 1997 Ord 51, r 8. The district court may also strike out a case where there

is excessive delay in bringing a case (the onus being on the State to justify the delay) or where the defendant would be prejudiced by the delay (the onus being on the defendant to prove prejudice): *DPP v Carlton* [1992] 10 ILT Dig 73, HC.

The court may order any pleading to be struck out on the ground that it discloses no reasonable cause of action or where it appears from the pleadings that the action is frivolous or vexatious, the court may order the action to be stayed or to be dismissed: RSC Ord 19, r 28. However, a claim which rests on matters which might be proved at a trial, should not be struck out: *Leinster Leader Ltd v Williams Group Tullamore Ltd* [1999] ITLR (30 August) HC.

A court has jurisdiction to strike out any claim which is an *abuse of process* of court: *Kelly v Ireland* [1986] ILRM 318. However, it should only exercise this inherent jurisdiction where it is clearly established that the plaintiff's claim is unsustainable; where there are questions of fact and of controversial legal arguments to be resolved, the matter cannot be said to be so clear and unassailable that the plaintiff's claim should be struck out: *DK v AK and Governors of Rotunda Hospital* [1993] ILRM 710, HC. See also *Olympia Productions Ltd v Cameron Mackintosh* [1992] ITLR (3 February) HC; *Conlon v Times Newspapers Ltd* [1995] 2 ILRM 76, HC; *Murphy v J. Donohoe Ltd* [1996] 1 IR 123, SC; *Murray v Times Newspapers Ltd* [1997] 3 IR 97, SC; *Mercantile Credit Company of Ireland Ltd v Heelan* [1998] 1 IR 81, SC; *Jestdale Ltd v Millennium Theatre Co Ltd* [2001] 3 IR 337, HC.

The essence of a strike out of proceedings by consent of the parties is to terminate the proceedings without any recourse to a judicial decision on the claims made in the proceedings: *Sweeney v Bus Átha Cliath/Dublin Bus* [2004] ITLR (23 February) HC. In a particular case, an action was struck out as the judge was satisfied that the sole purpose of the proceedings was to inflict damage on the plaintiff's competitor and this was an improper use of the process of the courts: *Seán Quinn Group v An Bord Pleanála* [2001] 2 ILRM 94, HC and 1 IR 505.

The Labour Court and the Director of the Equality Tribunal are both empowered to strike out cases before them which are not being pursued: Employment Equality

Act 1998, s 102 amended by Equality Act 2004, s 44. The Director of the Equality Tribunal may dismiss a case referred to the Director where it appears, at any time after the expiry of one year from the date of reference, that the complainant has ceased to pursue the reference: Equal Status Act 2000, s 38. See ENLARGEMENT OF JURISDICTION; STATEMENT OF CLAIM.

strokehaul. Means any weighted instrument or device which may be used, whether with a rod and line or otherwise, to foul-hook fish: Fisheries Act 1980, s 2(1). It is an offence to strokehaul a fish.

structure. Means any building, structure, excavation, or other thing constructed or made on, in or under any land, or any part of a structure so defined: Planning and Development Act 2000, s 2(1). A planning authority has the power, in exceptional circumstances, to serve a notice requiring the removal or alteration of a structure or the discontinuance in use, subject to a right of appeal and a limited right to compensation (PDA 2000, s 46). An *unauthorised structure* is in effect any structure which is erected without permission or which is not an exempted development; any structure erected before 1 October 1964, which is the date the Local Government (Planning and Development) Act 1963 commenced, is lawful (LG(PD)A 1963, s 2(1)). See also Local Government Act 2001, s 2(1).

stuffers and swallowers. Colloquial expression to describe a person who attempts to avoid detection for a drug trafficking offence. Where a garda suspects that an arrested person has concealed a controlled drug in his body, the person may be brought to and detained in a place designated by the Minister: Criminal Justice (Drug Trafficking) Act 1996, s 2. See DETENTION; DRUG TRAFFICKING.

sub colore juris. [Under colour of the law].

sub-contractors, payment of. Any person who receives from a *principal contractor* any payment in relation to the performance of the whole or any part of a *relevant contract* ie construction, forestry or meat processing: Finance Act 1970, s 17 as amended, now Taxes Consolidation Act 1997, ss 530–531 as amended by Finance Acts 1998, ss 37 and 133(1)(a); and Finance Act 1999, s 18. Every principal contractor is required to deduct *relevant contracts withholding tax* (*RCWT or RCT*) from that payment. No such deduction of tax is required where a sub-contractor has a *certificate of authorisation* from the Revenue Commissioners.

For the regulatory provisions governing the scheme for deduction of taxes from payments to sub-contractors, see Income Tax (Relevant Contract) Regulation 2000 and 2001, SI No 71 of 2000 and SI No 131 of 2001.

Certain sectors have been added to the specified industries eg rendering of the carcasses of slaughtered animals: Finance Act 2002, s 51. Provision has been made to combat deliberate late payment of *relevant contract tax*: Finance Act 2003, s 33. Also the Revenue Commissioners are empowered to set up and maintain a register of principal contractors and to require all new principal contractors to register formally with the Commissioners: Finance Act 2004, s 20.

sub judice. [In course of trial.] Not yet decided; under judicial consideration. When a matter is before a court and is *sub judice*, any words or action which have a tendency to interfere with the fair administration of justice may amount to a *contempt of court*. See *Desmond v Minister for Industry & Commerce* [1992] ILRM 489, HC. The courts may act to prevent the publication in the media of anything which may prejudice the fair trial of an action and impose a punishment for such publication. The rules of the Houses of the Oireachtas prohibit debate on a matter which is *sub judice*. See *Farrell* in (1994) 4 ISLR 85. See CONTEMPT OF COURT.

sub modo. [Under consideration or restriction].

sub nom; sub monine. [Under the name].

sub rosa. [Under the rose.] Confidentially.

sub silentio. [Under silence].

sub-tenant. Means the person in whose favour the sub-tenancy concerned of a dwelling has been created: Residential Tenancies Act 2004, Sch, para 1. Protection is afforded to a sub-tenancy created, with the written consent of the landlord, out of a *Part 4 tenancy* or a *further Part 4 tenancy* (RTA 2004, s 32(1)). The creation of a sub-tenancy in respect of a part only of such a dwelling is prohibited and any such sub-tenancy purported to be created is void (RTA 2004, s 32(2)–(3)).

A tenant of a dwelling who proposes to create a sub-tenancy out of the tenancy is required, before he creates the sub-tenancy, to inform the person of the fact that it is a sub-tenancy which will be created in the person's favour (RTA 2004, s 185). A tenant who fails to comply with this requirement is guilty of an offence.

The protection afforded to a *Part 4 tenancy* applies to a sub-tenancy as long as the head-tenancy continues to exist. If a head-tenancy is terminated by the head-landlord in circumstances where no requirement to terminate the sub-tenancy is notified or if the head-tenancy is terminated by the head-tenant, the sub-tenant becomes the tenant of the head-landlord but the tenancy is deemed to have commenced on the commencement date of the head-tenancy. The Schedule to the 2004 Act adapts ss 34 to 39 (dealing with terminations) for application to sub-tenancies and makes provision for former sub-tenants to refer complaints to the *Private Residential Tenancies Board* (qv) that a termination ground cited by a head-tenant turned out to be false. The Tenancy Tribunal or an adjudicator, on the hearing of such a complaint, may make a determination, if the adjudicator or the Tribunal considers it proper to do so, that the head-tenant pay to the complainant an amount by way of damages for the deprivation of possession (RTA 2004, Sch, para 8(3)). 'Head-landlord' and 'head-tenant' mean respectively, the landlord and the tenant, under the *Part 4 tenancy* concerned.

Where the landlord under the head-tenancy proposes to terminate the head-tenancy, he must indicate in the notice of termination served in respect of the head-tenancy whether or not he requires the sub-tenancy to be terminated (RTA 2004, s 70). If the sub-tenancy is required to be terminated, a copy of the notice of termination must be served on the sub-tenant. Where the head-tenant is disputing the termination notice, he must require the sub-tenant to advise him within ten days of receipt of the notice whether or not he also is to refer a dispute to the Board (RTA 2004, s 81). Where the head-tenant, is not disputing the validity of a termination notice served on him, he must serve a notice of termination on the sub-tenant within 28 days (RTA 2004 s 71).

Where the head-tenant has received a notice of termination indicating that termination of the sub-tenancy is not required, he is required to notify the sub-tenant within 28 days: (a) of the contents of the termination notice; and (b) of the fact that a dispute in relation to the termination of the head-tenancy has been referred to the Board where that be the case (RTA 2004, s 72). Where a dispute referral results in a *determination order* of the Board, the head-tenant must notify the sub-tenant of the particulars of the order within 14 days of receipt (RTA 2004, s 72(3)). See DETERMI-NATION ORDER; PART 4 TENANCY; TEN-ANCY; TENANCY, FIXED TERM; TENANCY DISPUTE.

sub tit; sub titulo. [Under the title of].

sub voce. [Under the title].

subinfeudation. See FEUDAL SYSTEM.

subject to contract. Generally, an offer or acceptance made *subject to contract* means that no legally binding agreement or contract will exist until the formal contract has been completed by the parties. There may be a binding contract if the court can conclude that all the terms of a bargain have been agreed and set down in writing and signed.

The Supreme Court has held that when the term 'subject to contract' was placed at the head of a document so as to govern the whole document, it could be understood to mean that there was not as yet any con-cluded agreement; however, where it appeared in the body of the document, whether there was a concluded agreement was a matter of construction: *Jodifern Ltd v Fitzgerald* [2000] 3 IR 321, SC.

See *Lowis v Wilson* [1949] IR 347; *O'Flaherty v Arran Property* [1976] SC; *Kelly v Park Hall Schools* [1979] 213 ILTR 9 ; *Casey v Irish Intercontinental Bank* [1979] IR 364; *Mulhall v Haren* [1981] IR 364; *Carthy v O'Neill* [1981] ILRM 443; *Cunningham v Maher* 9 ILT & SJ [1991 CC] 168; *Boyle & Boyle v Lee & Goyns* [1992] ILRM 65, SC; *Embourg Ltd v Tyler Group Ltd* [1996] 3 IR 480, SC. See ACCEPTANCE; GAZUMPING; MEMORAN-DUM, STATUTE OF FRAUDS; PLANNING PERMISSION, SUBJECT TO.

subletting. A grant to another by a *lessee* of a letting for a period less than the period held by the lessee under his lease. The lessee retains a reversion (qv) on the subletting or sublease and remains subject to all the rights and liabilities under the lease. See LEASE; LEASE, CREATION OF; SUB-TENANT; TENANCY, FIXED TERM.

submission. (1) The instrument by which a dispute or question is referred to arbitration pursuant to an agreement between the parties.

(2) A district judge is entitled to invite submissions on the issues raised before him and to direct that the submissions be in writing and exchanged between the parties: *per curiam* in *DPP v Maughan* [2003] 1 ILRM 155, HC. In this case the High Court held that the decision of the district judge to dismiss the case on the basis of the failure of the prosecution to submit written submissions was unreasonable and irrational.

subordinate legislation. See DELEGATED LEGISLATION.

subordination of debt. A process whereby one creditor, secured or unsecured, agrees to rank after another eg subordinated bond issues, particularly by banks and other financial institutions. There is statutory rec-ognition of *subordination of debts* in the winding up of a company: Companies Act 1963, s 275 as amended by Companies Act 1990, s 132. [Bibliography: Cahill D; Wood (UK)].

subornation of perjury. The offence of procuring a person to commit a perjury (qv) which he actually commits in conse-quence of such procurement.

subpoena. [Under penalty.] An order issued in an action or arbitration requiring the person to whom it is directed to be present at a specified place and time and for a specified purpose under penalty. A *subpoena ad testificandum* commands a witness to attend and give evidence. A *subpoena duces tecum* commands a witness to attend and give evidence and to bring with him and to produce certain documents specified in the subpoena. Before a court grants a *subpoena duces tecum* it should have material before it showing that the documents sought to be produced are relevant to the claim being made and in any event, should await the outcome of discovery: *McConnell v Commis-sioner of An Garda Síochána* [2003] 2 IR 19, HC.

In High Court proceedings a *praecipe* in a particular form is delivered and filed at the Central Office when it is intended to apply for the issue of a subpoena; in Circuit Court proceedings, a *witness summons* is issued by the county registrar or by the court (in case of difficulty); and in the District Court it is issued by the judge or by the clerk of the court: RSC Ord 61, rr 18–19; RSC Ord 39, r 25–34, Appendix D, and as amended by SI No 166 of 1997; Circuit Court Rules 2001 Ord 24; DCR 1997 Ord 21. An order of the Master of the

High Court must be obtained before a *subpoena duces tecum* may be served on a public official to produce any record in his custody: RSC Ord 39, rr 30–31.

A District Court judge may issue a warrant for the arrest of a person who fails to appear to a witness summons and no just excuse is offered for such failure: DCR 1997 Ord 21, rr 5–7; Ord 44. In civil proceedings in the District Court, but not criminal, where it appears that reasonable expenses have not been paid or offered, the court may set aside or disregard the witness summons: DCR 1997 Ord 44, r 1(5). See also Circuit Court Rules 2001 Ord 24, r 3.

A Circuit Court judge may attach a witness who fails without lawful excuse to attend or he may impose a fine: Circuit Court Rules 2001 Ord 24, r 3. In the High Court, any person wilfully disobeying an order requiring his attendance will be deemed guilty of *contempt of court* (qv) and may be dealt with accordingly: RSC Ord 39, r 7. If he attends but refuses to be sworn, or to answer any lawful question, he may be ordered to pay any costs occasioned by his refusal or objection (rr 12–14).

A subpoena may be issued against a person having custody of a will in order to compel lodgment of the will in the probate office: RSC Ord 79, r 59. See ADOPTION BOARD; WITNESS SUMMONS; WITNESS SUMMONS.

subrogation. Substitution. Subrogation is a convenient way of describing a transfer of rights from one person to another, without assignment or assent of the person from whom the rights are transferred and which takes place by operation of law in a whole variety of circumstances eg arising from contract as in insurance or to prevent an unjust enrichment (qv): *Orakpo v Manson Investments Ltd* [1977] 3 WLR 229 cited in *Highland Finance v Sacred Heart College* [1993] ILRM 263, HC. See also *Highland Finance v Sacred Heart College* [1998] 2 IR 180, SC.

In subrogation, a person or thing is substituted for another, so that the same rights and duties which attach to the original person or thing, attach to the substituted one. If one person is substituted for another, he is said *to stand in the other's shoes*.

In insurance, the insurer can be subrogated to the rights of the insured and can maintain an action against a third party who caused the loss suffered by the insured, but only when the insured has been paid. The insurer can enforce a remedy which the insured could have enforced against a third party. Also, a person paying the premium on a policy of insurance belonging to another may be subrogated to that other. See *Driscoll v Driscoll* [1918] 2 IR 152; *Orakpo v Manson Investments* [1978] AC 95; *Hibernian Insurance v Eagle Star Insurance* [1987] HC; *Zurich Insurance v Shield Insurance* [1988] IR 174, SC; *Incorporated Law Society v Owens* [1990] 8 ILT Dig 64.

Where moneys are advanced for the purchase of property by the borrower, the lender is entitled to be subrogated to the rights of the vendor unless the bargain between the lender and the borrower is inconsistent with the retention of a right of subrogation: *Bank of Ireland Finance Ltd v Daly* [1978] IR 79. The equitable doctrine of subrogation will not be applied if its application would product an unjust result; subrogation may lead to an unjust result if the lender obtains all he bargained for: *Highland Finance v College of Agriculture* [1997] 2 ILRM 89, SC.

See also Marine Insurance Act 1906, s 79. For subrogation in international contract law, see Contractual Obligations (Applicable Law) Act 1991, Sch 1, art 13. [Bibliography: Corrigan & Campbell; O'Regan Cazabon].

subscribe. To sign or attest; to write under. To apply for shares in a company.

subscribing witness. A person who signs a document as an attesting witness. See ATTESTATION.

subscription. An application for shares. See PROSPECTUS.

subsequent bankruptcy. Where an *undischarged bankrupt* (qv) is again adjudicated a bankrupt. Formerly, the Official Assignee (qv) claimed the assets of the second bankruptcy for the benefit of the first bankruptcy. Now, creditors of second and subsequent bankruptcies have priority in those bankruptcies: Bankruptcy Act 1988, s 43.

All *after-acquired property* (qv) in the possession of or unclaimed by the Official Assignee at the date of the subsequent bankruptcy transfers or vests to the credit of the subsequent bankruptcy. Any surplus arising on a subsequent bankruptcy is transferred to the credit of the former bankruptcy.

subsidiarity, principle of. The principle enshrined in European Community law whereby in areas which do not fall within its exclusive competence, the Community is to take action only if and in so far as the objectives of the proposed action cannot be sufficiently achieved by the member states and can, therefore, by reason of the scale or effects of the proposed action, be better achieved by the Community: EC Treaty, art 5 of the consolidated (2002) version. Also any action by the Community must not go beyond what is necessary to achieve the objectives of the Treaty. The Edinburgh European Council (December 1992) agreed guidelines to be used in examining whether a proposal for a Community measure conforms with the article.

An example of subsidiarity is the new EC policy on *education*, wherein national governments are fully responsible for the content of education and the organisation of educational systems and the EC role is to support and supplement the actions of the member states (EC Treaty, art 149). The Amsterdam Treaty 1997 emphasised that the institutions of the EU must, in exercising the powers conferred on them, ensure that the principle of subsidiarity is complied with: Protocol on Subsidiarity and Proportionality. See Walker CF, *Subsidiarity: Its Application in Practice* (Institute of European Affairs, Dublin, 1994). See 'Subsidiarity, Federalism and the Internal Market' by Mr Justice Nial Fennelly in *Bar Review* (November 2000) 75. See PROPORTIONALITY.

subsidiary company. See HOLDING COMPANY.

subsidy. A subvention.

substantial. It has been held that for a ground to be *substantial* (e g to obtain leave to apply for a judicial review of a planning decision), the ground had to be reasonable, arguable and weighty: *Village Residents Association Ltd v An Bord Pleanála* [2000] 1 IR 65, HC. See also *Village Residents Association Ltd v An Bord Pleanála* [2000] 4 IR 321, HC. See JUDICIAL REVIEW, PLANNING.

substantial acquisition. An acquisition is regarded as a *substantial acquisition* where a person acquires in aggregate 10% or more of the voting rights of a company and when aggregated with securities already held, confers 15% or more, but less than 30% of the voting rights of the company, and such acquisitions are made within a seven-day period: Irish Takeover Panel Act 1997, s 8(2) and Substantial Acquisitions Rules 2001, r 3(a).

A substantial acquisition of securities, whether in one or a series of transactions, must take place at an acceptable speed: General Principles: ITPA 1997, Sch. The purpose of the Rules are: (a) to slow down the rate at which a stake can be built up in a company, so that small shareholders can participate in any premium which may be payable in the build-up of a larger holding; and (b) to give the management time to consider the acquisition and to take whatever steps are necessary to protect the interests of the shareholders.

The Substantial Acquisition Rules (SARs) do not apply to an acquisition of securities by a person: (a) who has announced a firm intention to make an offer under the Takeover Rules 2001, in which case he is subject to those latter Rules; or (b) which results in his holding of 30% or more of the voting rights of the company, in which case he is subject to the Takeover Rules 2001, Part B, r 5, and may, if appropriate be obliged to make a mandatory offer under r 9 of these latter Rules. Certain 'tender offers' are subject to the SARs (r 7). See IRISH TAKEOVER PANEL; MANDATORY OFFER; SHARES, COMPULSORY PURCHASE OF; TENDER OFFER.

substantial grounds. Where the court is required by statute to be satisfied that there are *substantial grounds* for a particular view, substantial means something more than *reasonable grounds*: *Richardson v London County Council* [1957] 2 WLR 751 cited with approval in *O'Dowd v North Western Health Board* [1983] ILRM 186, SC. Substantial grounds has also been held to mean more than probable or *prima facie* grounds: *Murphy v Greene* [1991] ILRM 404, SC.

In order to obtain leave to apply for a judicial review of a planning decision, there must be *substantial grounds* for contending that the decision is invalid; it has been held that substantial grounds means that the grounds: (a) must be reasonable: *Scott & Ors v An Bord Pleanála* [1995] 1 ILRM 424, SC at 429, (b) must be reasonable, arguable and weighty and not be trivial or tenuous: *McNamara v An Bord Pleanála* [1995] 2 ILRM 125, HC. It would appear that as regards factual matters, substantial grounds means something more than reasonable, whereas on matters of contention of law, reasonable grounds will suffice. See JUDICIAL REVIEW, PLANNING; SATISFIED.

substantive law. The actual law, as opposed to adjectival or procedural law. See ADJECTIVE LAW.

substantive notice. A notice which the Equality Authority (qv) is empowered to serve on a person, if it appears to the Authority that there is a failure in a business to implement any provision of an *equality action plan* (qv): Employment Equality Act 1998, s 70(2). The notice may require the person to take such act as is specified in the notice, is reasonably required for the implementation of the plan, and is within the person's power to take. An appeal against a substantive notice lies to the Labour Court (EEA 1998, s 71). The High or Circuit Courts may make an order directing the person to comply with the notice (EEA 1998, s 72).

Where a *substantive notice* concerns an *equality review* or *equality action plan* which relates to matters governed by the Equal Status Act 2000, the person on whom the notice has been served may appeal to the District Court against the notice (EEA 1998, s 71 as amended by Equal Status Act 2000, s 39 and Schedule). [Bibliography: Reid M.] See EQUALITY REVIEW.

substitute. See REPEAL.

substituted service. See SUMMONS, SERVICE OF.

substratum. [Bottom or basis].

substratum of land. (1) Means any subsoil or anything beneath the surface of land required: (a) for the purpose of a tunnel or tunnelling or anything connected therewith, or (b) for any other purpose connected with a motorway, busway or protected road scheme or a light railway order: Roads (Amendment) Act 1998, ss 2, 5 and 7. This clarifies the power of the local authority (and the Board of CIE) to acquire compulsorily the substratum necessary for a tunnel without having to acquire all the land above or below it or any buildings located on the land. See now Transport (Railway Infrastructure) Act 2001, ss 2(1) and 45.

(2) Means any subsoil or anything underneath the surface of land required: (a) for the purposes of a tunnel or tunnelling or anything connected therewith, or (b) for any other purpose connected with a scheme within the meaning of the Roads Act 1993: Planning and Development Act 2000, s 2(1). See COMPULSORY PURCHASE ORDER; LAND.

subversive offence. See SCHEDULED OFFENCE.

succeed, unworthiness to. The preclusion of certain specified persons from taking any share in the estate of another eg a sane person who has been guilty of the murder, attempted murder or manslaughter of another; a spouse against whom the deceased obtained a decree of divorce a *mensa et thoro;* a spouse guilty of desertion for at least two years; a person found guilty of an offence against the deceased (or against his spouse or child) punishable by imprisonment for at least two years: Succession Act 1965, s 120. See also Judicial Separation and Family Law Reform Act 1989, s 17. See SPOUSE, LEGAL RIGHT OF.

succession. The devolution of property on the death of its owner; where property passes on the death of a corporation sole to his successor. [Bibliography: Keating].

succession, law of. The branch of law governing the devolution of property on the death of its owner. Property devolves on death to *personal representatives,* known as *executors* where the deceased left a will (testate succession) and *administrators* where there is no will (intestate succession). Executors are usually appointed by the will and administrators by the court. The personal representatives transfer the property to the *beneficiaries.*

The State guarantees to pass no law attempting to abolish the general right to bequeath or inherit property, subject to regulation of that right by the principles of social justice: 1937 Constitution, art 43. The Succession Act 1965 changed the previous law significantly; *inter alia,* it gives the surviving spouse a *legal right* to a share in the estate and provides protection for the interest of children. There is provision for the extinguishing of succession rights where a decree of *judicial separation* has been granted: Family Law Act 1995, s 14. See also Family Law (Divorce) Act 1996, s 18. See *Report on the Hague Convention on Succession to the Estates of Deceased Persons* (LRC 36, 1991). [Bibliography: Brady; Corrigan & Williams; Keating; Lyall; Maguire; Maxwell; Mongey; O'Callaghan J M (1); Pearce & Mee; Spierin & Fallon; Theobald UK.] See DIVORCE; WILL; INTESTATE SUCCESSION; PROBATE; LETTERS OF ADMINISTRATION; ADMINISTRATION OF ESTATES.

succession rights. The surviving spouse is entitled to the whole of the other spouse's estate on an intestacy (ie where there is no will) and where there are no children; where there are issue, the surviving spouse takes two-thirds and the issue take one-third: Succession Act 1965, ss 66–73. Where there is a will, the spouse is entitled as per the terms of the will, but cannot obtain less than the *legal right* ie one-half of the estate where there are no children and one-third of the estate where there are children (SA 1965, ss 111–115). See however DIVORCE; INTESTATE SUCCESSION; JUDICIAL SEPARATION; REMARRIAGE; SPOUSE, LEGAL RIGHT OF; SUCCEED, UNWORTHINESS TO.

successor. For capital acquisitions tax purposes, a person who takes an inheritance: Capital Acquisitions Tax Consolidation Act 2003, s 2.

successor company. The public company, limited by shares, into which a building society converts itself: Building Societies Act 1989, s 100. Such a company's independence is protected for a period of five years after conversion against any one person gaining control. See CONVERSION.

successor in title. The person entitled to succeed to property or property rights. The person may be subject to commitments entered into by the previous owner eg a licence granted by a copyright holder is binding on the successor in title to his interest. The Law Reform Commission has recommended that the duplicate statutory provisions governing successors in title to land (Deasy's Act 1860, ss 12–13 and Conveyancing Act 1881, ss 10–11) should be amalgamated into a single provision, or set of provisions, which should remove the inconsistencies and uncertainties which exist in the current statutory provisions: *Consultation Paper on General Law of Landlord and Tenant Law* (LRC CP 28, 2003) paras 18.25 to 18.39. See COPYRIGHT, LICENSING OF; INVENTOR; MANAGEMENT COMPANY; PERFORMERS' RIGHTS, LICENSING OF; PROSPECTIVE OWNER.

sue. To bring an action against a person.

sufferance, tenancy by. See TENANCY BY SUFFERANCE.

sufficient. The word 'sufficient' in its plain meaning signifies adequate or enough: Companies Act 1963, s 390 (sufficient security for costs); *Lismore Homes Ltd (in receivership) v Bank of Ireland Finance Ltd* [2001] 3 IR 536, SC and [2002] 1 ILRM 541, SC. In this case it was held that it is directly related to the defendant's costs and is not a sufficient sum to meet the justice of the case. The term 'sufficient' in s 390 involves making an assessment of the actual costs that a defendant would incur: *Superwood Holdings plc v Sun Alliance and London Insurance plc* [2003] FL 7321, HC. See 'Security for Costs and the Separate Corporate Personality' by Cathal Murphy BL in *Bar Review* (April 2003) 86. See SECURITY FOR COSTS.

suffrage. Right to vote in an election. See DIRECT UNIVERSAL SUFFRAGE; ELECTION; FRANCHISE.

suggestio falsi. [Suggestion of falsehood.] An active misrepresentation (qv) as opposed to a *suppressio veri* (qv) or passive misrepresentation.

sui generis. [Of its own right.] Constituting a class of its own; the only one of its kind.

sui juris. [Of one's own right.] A person of full legal capacity. A person who can validly contract and bind himself by legal obligation uncontrolled by any other person.

suicide. Formerly, the common law felony (qv) of self-murder, the death taking place within a year and a day. The crime of suicide or attempted suicide has been abolished: Criminal Law (Suicide) Act 1993, s 2(1). However, a person who aids, abets, counsels or procures the suicide of another, or an attempt by another to commit suicide is guilty of an offence (CL(S)A 1993, s 2(2)). A person who assists another in suicide by killing that other is guilty of murder. A *suicide pact* survivor may be guilty of an offence as encouraging the suicide of another (CL(S)A 1993, s 2(3)).

The *year and a day rule* has been abolished for all purposes including for the purpose of determining whether a person committed suicide; consequently a coroner is no longer prevented from returning a verdict in respect of a self-inflicted injury in excess of a year and a day before death: Criminal Justice Act 1999, s 38. See *Verrier v DPP* [1966] 3 All ER 568.

The Minister for Health and Children is now required to make an annual report to each House of the Oireachtas on the measures taken by health boards to prevent suicides: Health (Miscellaneous Provisions) Act 2001, s 4. The report must be made not later than nine months after the end of the year, beginning with 2002.

In insurance law, there is a rebuttable presumption against suicide and in favour of an accident: *Harvey v Ocean Accident & Guarantee Corporation* [1905] 2 IR 1; *The State (McKeown) v Scully* [1986] ILRM 133; *Kelleher v Irish Life Assurance Co Ltd* [1989] 7 ILT Dig 229. See *Report of the Department of Justice's Advisory Group on Prison Deaths* (1991). See O'Mahony in 10 ILT & SJ (1992) 258. See INQUEST.

suit. A legal proceeding; an action.

suitor. A person who is a party to a suit.

suitors, funds of. The cash and securities belonging to suitors and other persons which have been transferred to or paid into and deposited with the High Court. In the ordinary way these funds may be used only for the benefit of those entitled to them. A small proportion of the funds is represented by unclaimed balances and dividends which have accumulated over a long period, as long as two centuries, and these funds have been used principally for renovation work on the *King's Inns* (qv) building. See Funds of Suitors Act 1984. See also Iris Oifigiúil, 10 November 1992 and 7 May 1999. See RSC Ord 77.

Under recent legislation, provision has been made for the realisation of the dormant funds of suitors for the purpose defraying the costs of providing, managing and maintaining court buildings of the Courts Service: Civil Liability and Courts Act 2004, ss 33–38.

sum assured. Often refers to the maximum sum which is payable under a policy of insurance. The sum payable may be less if there is an average clause (qv). Where a fixed sum is payable irrespective of loss the policy, is called a *valued policy*. The sum payable may also be affected by the operation of a *reinstatement clause* (qv).

In marine insurance (qv) a valued policy is one which specifies the agreed value of the subject matter insured; in the absence of fraud, the value fixed by the policy is, as between the insurer and the assured, conclusive of the insurable value whether the loss be total or partial: Marine Insurance Act 1906, s 27. See INSURANCE, CONTRACT OF.

summary conviction. See SUMMARY OFFENCE; SUMMARY PROCEEDINGS.

summary dismissal. Dismissal of an employee without the notice to which the employee is entitled by statute or by virtue of his contract of employment. It may be justified by reason of the employee's misconduct eg theft, fighting. See *McCarthy v O'Sullivan Brothers Ltd* [1991] ELR

44, EAT; *Caffrey v Avonmore Creameries Ltd* [1991] ELR 51, EAT; *O'Mahony v Whelan* [1992] ELR 117, EAT. See NOTICE, EMPLOYMENT; UNFAIR DISMISSAL.

summary judgment. The judgment which may be given where the plaintiff's claim in a Circuit Court *civil bill* is: (a) for a debt or liquidated demand in money, or (b) for the delivery of a chattel or specific goods in an action for *detinue*, or (c) for the enforcement, performance or carrying out of a trust, or (d) for ejectment, with or without a claim for rent or *mesne profits*: Circuit Court Rules 2001 Ord 28, r 5.

The plaintiff may apply to the court for summary judgment where the defendant has entered an appearance or has delivered a defence. Summary judgment will be ordered unless the defendant: (a) satisfies the judge that *prima facie* he has a good defence to the plaintiff's claim; or (b) pays into court, to abide the result, such sum as may be deemed sufficient to entitle him to defend (Ord 28, r 5). For summary judgment procedure in the District Court, see DCR 1997 Ord 46. As regards the High Court, see SUMMARY SUMMONS.

summary offence. An offence heard by the District Court (qv), without a jury and for which the maximum punishment is generally six months imprisonment and/or a fine. An accused is not entitled to trial by jury in such cases either because the offence is *minor* (qv) or because the accused has waived his right to a jury trial, which he can do in certain cases. Research conducted in 2002 shows that even where a defendant has a right to trial by jury, very few opt for it: Prof John Jackson and Prof Seán Doran, Queen's University Belfast. For trial of summary offences, see DCR 1997 Ord 23. See ELECTION; INDICTABLE OFFENCE.

summary proceedings. Proceedings, without a jury, in the District Court of summary offences (qv) and those indictable offences (qv) which may be heard by the District Court on the consent of the accused and the agreement of the Director of Public Prosecutions (qv): Criminal Justice Act 1951, s 2.

Summary proceedings for an offence must be instituted within six months of the offence unless otherwise provided for by statute: Petty Sessions (Ireland) Act 1851, s 10(4). Many statutes permit (a) *one year* from the offence eg Industrial Relations Act 1990, s 5 and Residential Tenancies Act 2004 s.9(4); or (b) *two years* eg Irish

Medicines Board Act 1995, s 32(6), Competition Act 2002, s 8(11), and Unclaimed Life Assurance Policies Act 2003, s 5(3); Commissions of Investigation Act 2004, s 49(2); or (c) *three years* from the date an offence under the Companies Acts was committed or discovered: Companies Act 1990, s 240 as amended by Companies (Amendment) (No 2) Act 1999, s 41.

The Electronic Commerce Act 2000 provides that summary proceedings may be commenced at any time within twelve months from the date on which evidence sufficient to justify bringing proceedings comes to knowledge (ECA 2000, s 6(2)). The time limits specified in the Safety, Health and Welfare at Work Act, s 51(3) apply only to offences being prosecuted summarily and not to those being prosecuted on indictment: *DPP v BJN Construction Ltd* [2003] FL 7818, HC.

Minor offences may be tried by courts of summary jurisdiction: 1937 Constitution, art 38(2). There is specific provision for the summary trial of indictable offences under the Criminal Justice (Theft and Fraud Offences) Act 2001, where the court is of the opinion that the facts proved or alleged constitute a *minor offence* fit to be tried summarily and the accused does not object and the Director of Public Prosecutions consents (CJ(TFO)A 2001, s 53). See also Criminal Justice (Safety of United Nations Workers) Act 2000, s 7; Copyright and Related Rights Act 2000, s 11(2); Local Government Act 2001, s 235; Communications Regulation Act 2002, s 43; Public Health (Tobacco) Act 2002, s 6; Competition Act 2002, s 8(9); Taxi Regulation Act 2003, s 45; Containment of Nuclear Weapons Act 2003, s 16; Civil Registration Act 2004, ss 8(1)(i) and 71.

It has been held that a planning authority can prosecute minor indictable offences clearly thought to be fit to be tried summarily; there is no reason to give the expression 'prosecuted summarily' a narrow interpretation to confine it to prosecutions for summary offences, as a failure to obtain planning permission can often be a very minor matter: *TDI Metro Ltd & Halligan v Delap & Fingal Co Council* [2000] 4 IR 520, SC; ITLR (17 July) and [2001] 1 ILRM 338, SC, overturning the High Court decision. In this case the court held that it would be strange if the Oireachtas intended that, although a planning authority would be the normal prosecuting

authority for summary offences, it could not deal with minor instances of indictable offences, clearly thought fit to be tried summarily. See DIRECTOR OF CORPORATE ENFORCEMENT; MINOR OFFENCE.

summary proceedings and witnesses. There is no general obligation to furnish the accused with statements of the proposed prosecution witnesses; the district judge should decide, in the interest of justice, whether such statements are furnished or not, and should take into account such matters as the seriousness of the charge and the importance of the statements or documents: *DPP v Doyle* [1994] 1 ILRM 529, SC.

An accused is entitled to apply for statements of evidence before he has made his election as between summary trial or trial on indictment; there is no general obligation to furnish these statements, but they may be obtained in a suitable case: *O'Driscoll v Judge Wallace* [1995] 1 IR 237, HC.

The prosecution is also not obliged to call as witnesses those persons who made statements: *O'Regan v DPP* [2000] 2 ILRM 68, SC. There is no requirement on the prosecution in *summary proceedings*, to procure the attendance of witnesses or tender them for examination: *Geaney v DPP* [2000] 1 IR 412, HC. The practice in *indictable proceedings* is for the prosecution to call or tender for cross-examination all witnesses whose names are included in the book of evidence.

summary summons. A summons by which specified civil proceedings are commenced in the High Court and where the proceedings are heard on affidavit (qv) without pleadings and with or without oral evidence: RSC Ord 1, r 3; Ord 2.

A summary summons indorsed with a claim, other than for an account, is set down before the Master by the plaintiff, following entrance of an appearance by the defendant, on motion for *liberty to enter final judgment* for the amount claimed (or for the recovery of land) supported by an affidavit showing that the plaintiff is entitled to the relief claimed and stating that in the belief of the deponent, there is no defence to the action: RSC Ord 37. The very presence of a factual dispute does not preclude the summary disposal of the matter; the provision for notice to cross-examine indicates that the court may resolve issues of fact in summary proceedings: *Criminal Assets Bureau v Kelly* [2000] 1 ILRM 271, HC.

In uncontested actions, the Master may deal with the matter summarily; in contested actions, or where *pre-judgment interest* (qv) is claimed, the Master must transfer the case, when in order, to the court (Ord 37, rr 4–6). An action should be remitted for *plenary hearing* where a closer and fuller examination is required to determine the issue of law: RSC Ord 37, r 7; *Bank of Ireland v EBS* [1998] 2 ILRM 451, SC.

The test to be applied in deciding whether *leave to defend* should be granted is whether, looking at the whole situation, the defendant has satisfied the court that there is a fair and reasonable probability that he has a real and *bona fide* defence: *Aer Rianta cpt v Ryanair Ltd* [2002] 1 ILRM 381, SC and [2001] 4 IR 607, SC. The hurdle faced by a defendant in seeking leave to defend is a low one: Hardiman J in *Aer Rianta* case. It has been held also that where the court decides that the defendant has an arguable case, he is entitled to exercise his right to defend and it cannot be a condition precedent to his defence that he should lodge a particular sum of money in court: *Calor Teoranta v Colgan* [1990] SC: see Doyle in 8 ILT & SJ (1990) 255. See also Criminal Procedure Act 1993, s 5. See *First National Commercial Bank plc v Anglin* [1996] 1 IR 75, SC.

summary trial. See SUMMARY OFFENCE; SUMMARY PROCEEDINGS.

summer time. The period which was prescribed by the Summer Time Act 1925 and the Summer Time Order 1926, which now stand repealed. Any enactment expressed to apply or operate during a period of summer time shall be construed as operating or applying during the period previously prescribed: Standard Time Act 1968, s 1(2). See STANDARD TIME.

summing-up. The address by a judge to a jury after the closing speeches by the parties in which he summarises the evidence and gives directions in relation to the law eg burden and onus of proof, effect of presumptions of law. A defective summing-up or charge to the jury can be a good ground for an appeal. See *People v Byrne* [1974] IR 1; *People (DPP) v LG* [2003] 2 IR 517, CCA. See ACCOMPLICE; CHILD, EVIDENCE OF; CLOSING SPEECHES; CORROBORATION; PREVIOUS STATEMENT,

INCONSISTENT; REQUISITION; VISUAL IDENTIFICATION.

summons. A written command issued to a defendant for the purpose of getting him to attend court on a specified date to answer a specified complaint (qv): *DPP v Clein* [1983] ILRM 76. A summons does not confer jurisdiction; it is merely a process to compel the attendance of a person accused of an offence; the jurisdiction to enter upon the hearing of the charge derives from the making of the complaint stated on the summons and not deriving from the existence of the summons: *Finnegan v Clifford* [1996] 1 ILRM 446, HC.

There are two procedures for the issue of a summons in *criminal proceedings*: (a) a summons issued pursuant to s 10 of the Petty Sessions (Ireland) Act 1851 by a District Court judge; and (b) a summons issued by a District Court clerk *as a matter of administrative procedure*: Courts (No 3) Act 1986 as amended by Civil Liability and Courts Act 2004, s 49. The 1986 provision was designed to overcome the objection in *The State (Clarke) v D J Roche and Senezio* [1987] ILRM 309 by creating a new method of issuing a summons which does not involve the administration of justice in criminal matters by non-judicial personages.

The time limit for summary proceedings commenced under s 1 of the Courts (No 3) Act 1986 is six months from the date of the alleged offence to the date of application for the issue of a summons. There is no bar to the prosecution if the date upon which the summons is returned before a district judge and the case is first brought before him is more than six months from the date of the alleged offence: *Murray v McArdle* [2000] 1 ILRM 540, HC.

No other time limit arises except in the case of certain statutory offences where other time limits may apply: *DPP v D J Roche and Paul Kelly and DPP v Arthur Nolan* [1988] SC. See also *DPP v Logan* [1994] 2 ILRM 229, SC; *DPP v Howard* [1990] ITLR (26 February) HC.

Where a special time limit applies under statute, a failure to recite the relevant statutory provision on the face of the summons does not invalidate the summons: *DPP v Fox* [1997] 1 ILRM 440, HC.

The issue of a summons need not be based on a complaint; it can be issued on a simple application by a person designated in C(No 3)A 1986, s 1(4): *Murray v McArdle* [1999] 2 ILRM 283, HC. A defect of form in a summons issued pursuant to the 1986 Act will not invalidate the proceedings: *DPP v Ballagh & Mahon* [1999] 2 ILRM 223, HC. The procedure under the 1986 Act for the issue of Summons does not replace Petty Sessions (Ireland) Act 1851, ss 10 and 11.

The actual attendance of an accused in court can cure a defect in a summons where the defect related to the process for procuring such attendance: *Joyce v CC Judge for Western Circuit* [1987] ILRM 316. For the procedure in the District Court regarding the issue of summonses, see DCR 1997 Ord 15 (in respect of offences) and Ord 99 (in respect of other matters). The issuing of a summons in summary proceedings of a *civil nature* is an administrative procedure only; the issuing of such a summons by a District Court clerk does not impinge on the judicial role of the district court judge: *Kerry Co Council v McCarthy* [1997] 2 ILRM 481, SC.

See also *The State (Attorney-General) v Judge Roe* [1951] IR 172; *DPP v Hennessy* [1990] 8 ILT & SJ 102; *DPP v O'Donnell* [1995] 2 IR 294, HC. *Killeen v DPP* [1997] 3 IR 218, SC.

summons, amendment of. The district court has a discretion to amend a summons on application to it (eg amending the date of the alleged offence), provided that this is not prejudicial to the defendant: District Court Rules 1997 Ord 12, r 2. See County Officers and Courts (Ireland) Act 1877, s 76. See *DPP v Corbett* [1992] ILRM 674, HC; *People (DPP) v Doyle* [1997] 1 IR 422, HC; *DPP v Canniffe* [2002] 3 IR 554, SC and [2003] 1 ILRM 410.

summons, Dáil Éireann. The Dáil is summoned and dissolved by the President of Ireland on the advice of the Taoiseach: 1937 Constitution, art 13(2)(1).

summons, High Court. Civil proceedings are commenced in the High Court (qv) by originating summons, except those cases commenced by petition (qv). A summons may be plenary, summary or special.

A *plenary* summons (form 1) is used for cases requiring pleadings (qv) and oral evidence; it must be used for some claims eg for unliquidated damages: RSC Ord 1, r 2. The primary manner of proving disputed facts in plenary proceedings is by oral evidence: *Bula Ltd v Tara Mines Ltd* [1995] 1 ILRM 401, HC.

A *summary* summons (form 2) is used for proceedings to be heard on affidavit (qv) without pleadings eg for liquidated sums or for the recovery of possession of land; it may be supplemented by oral evidence in certain circumstances: RSC Ord 1, r 3; Ord 2; Ord 37; *RG v BG* [1993] ITLR (1 February), HC; *National Irish Bank Ltd v Graham* [1994] 2 ILRM 109.

A *special* summons (form 3) is used mainly for equity claims eg in relation to probate matters or the administration of trusts: RSC Ord 1, r 4; Ord 3; Ord 38. See *United Meat Packers v Nordstern* [1997] 2 ILRM 553, SC. [Bibliography: Barron.] See APPEARANCE; CIVIL PROCEEDINGS.

summons, personal injuries. The summons required to commence proceedings in respect of a personal injuries action in the High, Circuit or District Courts: Civil Liability and Courts Act 2004, s 10. It must specify: (a) the plaintiff's name, the address at which he ordinarily resides and his occupation, (b) the personal public service number allocated and issued to the plaintiff, (c) the defendant's name, the address at which he ordinarily resides (if known to the plaintiff) and his occupation (if known to the plaintiff), (d) the injuries to the plaintiff alleged to have been occasioned by the wrong of the defendant, (e) full particulars of all items of special damage in respect of which the plaintiff is making a claim, (f) full particulars of the acts of the defendant constituting the said wrong and the circumstances relating to the commission of the said wrong, (g) full particulars of each instance of negligence by the defendant. See PERSONAL INJURIES ACTION.

summons, renewal of. A High Court summons remains in full force and effect for twelve months from the date of issue: RSC Ord 8. A summons may be renewed by order of the court after the expiration of twelve months (or by the Master before such expiration) on showing by affidavit that the summons has not been served and the reasons therefor, showing that reasonable efforts have been made to serve it, and that the claim is still unsatisfied. In determining whether to grant a renewal, the court will regard the prejudice to the dependant equally with that of prejudice to the plaintiff: *Prior v Independent Television News Ltd* [1993] ILRM 638, HC.

An important factor in deciding whether to renew a summons is the lapse of time between the date of the alleged event and the first notification of the claim to the defendant: *O'Reilly v Northern Telecom Ltd* [1999] 1 ILRM 371, HC and 1 IR 214. It is not a good reason to renew a summons, simply to prevent a defendant availing of the Statute of Limitations: *Roche v Clayton* [1998] 1 IR 596, SC.

The renewal may be for a period of six months from the date of renewal and from time to time during the currency of the renewed summons. A defendant is at liberty before entering an appearance to serve a *notice of motion* to set aside such an order, where it has been obtained on an *ex parte* application.

In the District Court a second summons may be issued, on application to the court (eg due to difficulty in serving the first summons within the time limit): Petty Sessions (Ireland) Act 1851, s 10; Courts (No 3) Act 1986, s 1 as amended by Civil Liability and Courts Act 2004, s 49; *DPP v McKillen* [1992] 10 ILT Dig 73, HC.

summons, service of. A High Court summons may be served: (a) by *personal service* by delivery to the defendant in person of a copy, showing him the original or duplicate original at the same time; (b) by *non-personal service* by delivery of a copy summons to the spouse, child, parent, brother, sister, or to any clerk or servant (over 16 years of age) of the defendant, and, at the same time showing the original or duplicate original summons; (c) by *service on a solicitor* who accepts service on behalf of the defendant and undertakes in writing to enter an appearance; (d) by *service deemed good* by the court where the service actually effected does not comply with all the requirements but does so substantially; (e) by *substituted service* by order of the court in particular cases eg by post, by advertisement, by delivery to an agent, or otherwise as the court deems fit; (f) by *service out of the jurisdiction*. See RSC Ord 9.

For rules governing the service of a *civil bill* within the jurisdiction of the Circuit Court, see Circuit Court Rules 2001 Ord 11, r 10 and Ord 14, r 3(vi). For service of a *domestic violence civil bill*, see Ord 59, r 5. Service of a *civil summons* in District Court proceedings is effected by summons server or by registered post: DCR 1997 Ord 10; Courts Act 1964, s 7 as amended by Courts Act 1971, s 22.

Provision has been made for the service of summonses in summary criminal proceedings also by registered pre-paid post to the last known residence or most usual place of abode or last place of business of the person to whom it is addressed: Courts Act 1991, s 22. In considering s 22, the Supreme Court has held that the section does not require personal service in the sense that that expression is normally understood ie service on the accused himself: *Brennan v Judge Windle* [2003] ITLR (27 October) SC and FL 7856, and 2 ILRM 520.

Provision has also been made for service of a summons, issued outside the State, on a person in the State, requiring the person to appear as a defendant or a witness in criminal proceedings outside the State: Criminal Justice Act 1994, s 49. See AFFIDAVIT OF SERVICE; SUMMONS SERVER.

summons, service out of jurisdiction. Subject to the exceptions below, a summons may be served out of the jurisdiction *with the leave of the court*, which will be given only in particular circumstances eg if the action is in respect of land within the jurisdiction; or to enforce foreign arbitration awards under the Arbitration Act 1980; or in respect of a contract which is to be governed by Irish law; or in respect of a tort committed within the jurisdiction. See RSC Ord 9; Ord 11, r 1 as amended by SI No 243 of 1995; Ord 11B inserted by SI No 101 of 1994; Circuit Court Rules 2001 Ord 13 and Ord 14; DCR 1997 Ord 11.

However, a summons may be served out of the jurisdiction *without the leave of the court*, if the summons complies with the following conditions: (a) each claim made by the summons is one which by virtue of the Jurisdiction of Courts and Enforcement of Judgments Act 1988 (now 1998 Act), the court has power to hear and determine; and (b) the summons is endorsed before it is issued with a statement that the court has power to hear and determine the claim and that no proceedings involving the same cause of action are pending in another *contracting* state: Practice Direction from the President of the High Court, 1 June 1988.

The test to be applied when deciding to allow service out of the jurisdiction under RSC Ord 11, r 1(h) is whether the person out of the jurisdiction would, if he were within the jurisdiction, be a proper person to be joined in the action against the other defendants: *Short v Ireland, A-G & British Nuclear Fuels plc* [1997] 1 ILRM 161, SC;

Analog Devices BV v Zurich Insurance [2002] 2 ILRM 366, SC and 1 IR 272.

Service of a summons on a limited liability company incorporated in Belgium at its place of business is not service effected in accordance with the Rules and is bad: *O'Connor v Commercial General and Marine Ltd* [1996] 2 ILRM 291, HC and 1 IR 68. *Notice* of the summons must be served; it is an essential requirement that a copy of the full endorsement of the summons is given, and not just the summons itself.

Service of a summons on a person outside the State, may also be served in accordance with arrangements made by the Minister where: (a) the summons requires the person charged with an offence to appear before a court in the State, or (b) the summons requires the person to attend as a witness in a criminal proceeding: Criminal Justice Act 1994, s 50. Compliance with this type of summons is entirely voluntary (CJA 1994, s 50(2)).

See *Grehan v Medical Incorporated* [1986] ILRM 627; *Kutchera v Buckingham International Holdings* [1988] ILRM 1 and 501; *Mitchelstown Co-op Ltd v Nestle* [1989] ILRM 582, SC; *Campbell v Holland Dredging Co (Ire) Ltd* [1990] 8 ILT Dig 63; *McKenna v EH* [2002] 2 ILRM 117, HC. See SERVICE OUT OF JURISDICTION.

summons server. Means a person appointed by a County Registrar under the provisions of the Court Officers Act 1926, s 44: District Court Rules 1997, Interpretation of Terms. See also RSC Ord 9.

A summons server of a *civil bill* in the Circuit Court is required to compare the copies of the bill with the original, prior to service: Circuit Court Rules 2001 Ord 11, rr 7 and 16.

summum jus summa injuria. [Extreme law is extreme injury.] See EQUITY.

Sunday trading. Prohibition on Sunday trading was repealed by the Statute Law Revision (Pre-Union Irish Statutes) Act 1962. Intoxicating liquor may be sold on a Sunday between the hours of 12.30pm and 11.00pm; the permitted hours are different where the Sunday is on the eve of a bank holiday or is St Patrick's Day or is the 23 December: Intoxicating Liquor Act 2000, s 3.

Sunday work. Where an employee is required to work on a Sunday, and this has not already been taken into account in relation to his pay, he is entitled to compensation by way of a payment or time off work in lieu or a combination of both: Organisation of Working Time Act 1997, s 14. See Code of Practice on Sunday Working in the Retail Trade 1998 (SI No 444 of 1998).

super altum mare. [Upon the high seas].

super visum corporis. [Upon view of the body.] See CORONER; INQUEST.

superficies solo cedit. [Whatever is attached to the land forms part of it.] See FIXTURES.

Superintendent Registrar. The officer appointed by a local registration authority (ie a health board) after consultation with an tArd-Chláraitheoir, with responsibility for managing, controlling and administering the Civil Registration Service on behalf of the authority: Civil Registration Act 2004, s 17. The Registrar is responsible for the registration of births, stillbirths, marriages and deaths within the functional area of the authority. See CIVIL REGISTRATION.

superior courts. The courts above the inferior courts (qv) in the hierarchy of courts eg High Court, Central Criminal Court, Court of Criminal Appeal, Supreme Court. [Bibliography: Goldberg].

superior orders, obedience to. See OBEDIENCE TO ORDERS, DEFENCE OF.

supermarket. See OCCUPIERS' LIABILITY TO VISITORS.

supermarket trolley. A local authority is empowered to make bye-laws for the regulation of the provision and use of supermarket trolleys, including the imposition of duties on the owners or managers of retail outlets in cases where supermarket trolleys from these outlets are abandoned: Litter Pollution Act 1997, s 21(2)(f) substituted by Protection of the Environment Act 2003, s 57.

supervision order. An order which the District Court is empowered to make, authorising a health board (qv) to have a child visited on such periodic occasions as the board may consider necessary to satisfy itself as to the welfare of the child and to give to his parents, or to a person acting *in loco parentis*, any necessary advice as to the care of the child: Child Care Act 1991, s 19(2).

The court may make a supervision order on being satisfied on similar grounds as apply to a *care order* (qv) but not so serious as would justify the latter order but yet desirable that the child be visited periodically (CCA 1991, s 19(1)). A supervision order remains in force for not more than twelve months but a further order may be made with effect from the expiration of the previous order (CCA 1991, s 19(5) and (6)).

The court may give directions for the care of the child eg to attend medical or psychiatric examination, treatment or assessment at a hospital, clinic or other place specified by the court (CCA 1991, s 19(4)). A health board has a duty to apply for a care order or a supervision order in respect of a child who requires care or protection (CCA 1991, s 16). For District Court procedure in relation to supervision orders, see DCR 1997 Ord 84, r 16. See also Domestic Violence Act 1996, s 7. See CARE ORDER.

supplemental probate, grant of. A grant of representation given to a proving executor where subsequently a codicil (qv) is discovered.

supply of services. See SERVICES, SUPPLY OF.

support, right to. The natural right of support is a right not to have support removed by a neighbour, and is confined to support for land in its natural state: *Latimer v Official Co-operative Society* [1885] 26 LR Ir 305. No natural right to support exists in respect of buildings on land although such a right may be acquired by easement (qv): *Gatelly v Martin* [1900] 2 IR 269. The demolition of one of two semi-detached houses which had been built together as one, was a breach of the easement of support: *Todd v Cinelli* [1999] ITLR (12 April) HC.

A local authority which exercises its power to demolish a dangerous building must protect an existing easement of support enjoyed by an adjoining terraced building and its weather-proofing: *Treacy v Dublin Corporation* [1992] ILRM 650, SC. See *Report on the Acquisition of Easements and Profit A Prendre by Prescription* (LRC 66, 2002). [Bibliography: Bland (1).] See FLAT.

suppressio veri, suggestio falsi. [The suppression of truth is the suggestion of falsehood.] Misrepresentation (qv). See *Delaney v Keogh* [1905] 2 IR 267.

suppression of documents. It is an offence for a person dishonestly to destroy, deface or conceal certain *documents*, with the intention of making a gain for himself or another or of causing a loss to another: Criminal Justice (Theft and Fraud Offences) Act 2001, s 11. *Documents* include valuable securities, wills, testamentary documents, or original documents in a court or government department or office. Also it is an offence to falsify, conceal, destroy or otherwise dispose of a document or record which a person knows or suspects would be relevant to an investigation by the Gardaí of an offence, which the person knows or suspects is being or will be carried out (CJ(TFO)A 2001, s 51).

It is sufficient to prove that the accused did the act charged dishonestly with the intention of causing loss or making a gain; it is not necessary to prove an intention dishonestly to cause such loss or gain at the expense of a particular person (CJ(TFO)A 2001, s 54 (1)). [Bibliography: McGreal C].

suppression order. See UNLAWFUL ORGANISATION.

supra. [Above].

supra protest. See ACCEPTANCE OF BILL.

supranational. Transcending national limits or boundaries: National Forum on Europe, *Glossary of Terms* (2003). In the context of the EU, the term usually refers to the institutions which exist to pursue the common EU interests shared by the member states. It also refers to the discharge of functions and exercise of powers by these institutions, transcending national boundaries, in the domain where the member states have conferred those functions and powers on them in the treaties.

Supreme Court. The court of final appeal in the State: 1937 Constitution, art 34(4)(1). It consists of the Chief Justice (qv) and not more than seven other judges: Courts and Court Officers Act 1995, s 6. The court may sit in two or more divisions and they may sit at the same time with three or five judges, except that constitutional cases require five judges (CCOA 1995, s 7). The Supreme Court can set aside its own decisions in rare and exceptional cases as an exercise of its inherent jurisdiction to protect constitutional rights and justice: *Bula Ltd v Tara Mines (No 6)* [2000] 4 IR 412, SC.

The decision of the court is that of the majority although each judge may deliver a separate judgment except in a decision on a question as to the validity of a law having regard to the Constitution, when one decision only may be delivered (Constitution, arts 26(2)(2) and 34(4)(5)). Separate judgments may be given when the constitutionality of a pre-1937 law is in issue eg see *A-G v X* [1992] ILRM 401, SC.

The Supreme Court hears appeals from the High Court and from the *Court of Criminal Appeal* (qv) on points of law of exceptional public importance, and in certain circumstances from the *Central Criminal Court* (qv); it considers references to it from the President of Ireland on the constitutionality of certain Bills (Constitution, art 26(1)); it is consulted by the *Circuit Court* and the *High Court* by way of *case stated* (qv); it considers questions of law referred to it by the Director of Public Prosecutions, without prejudice to a verdict by a trial judge in favour of a defendant, on a point of law. An appeal lies also to the Supreme Court from an *acquittal by direction* of a trial judge in the Central Criminal Court: *The People (DPP) v O'Shea* [1982] IR 384; Criminal Procedure Act 1967, s 34; Criminal Procedure Act 1993, s 11.

The Supreme Court is a court of appeal and has no originating jurisdiction except as outlined above; it cannot therefore consider a question of the interpretation of the Constitution which had never arisen in or been decided in the High Court: *A-G v Open Door Counselling Ltd* [1994] 1 ILRM 256, SC and 2 IR 333. It also cannot determine on appeal any issue which was not tried in the High Court: *O'Cearbhaill v Bord Telecom Éireann* [1993] ELR 253, SC.

The grounds for an appeal to the Supreme Court from an order of the High Court under the Solicitors Acts 1954–1994 is no longer limited to points of law: Solicitors (Amendment) Act 1994, s 39.

See *Riordan v Ireland (No 4)* [2001] 3 IR 365, SC. In relation to the jurisdiction of the Supreme Court to review the findings of a trial judge on facts rather than on law, see FACT; SECONDARY FACTS. See Supreme Court and High Court (Fees) Order 2003, SI No 89 of 2003. See 'Supreme Courts – what are they for' by Conor Maguire SC in *Bar Review* (June 2004) 112. [Bibliography: Goldberg; O'Floinn.] See also APPEAL; CHIEF JUSTICE; EUROPEAN COURT OF JUSTICE; LEGISLATION, CONSTITUTIONALITY OF; REVIEW OF SENTENCE.

sur. [Upon].

surcharge. The function of a local authority auditor in *charging* or *surcharging:* (a) the person who has made, or authorised the making of an illegal payment by the local authority; or (b) any member or officer of a local authority in respect of the amount of any deficiency or loss incurred by his negligence or misconduct: Local Government (Ireland) Act 1871, ss 12 and 20. The ordinary principles of the law of negligence apply to the making of a charge under s 20; there does not have to be any element of moral culpability or gross negligence on the part of the person against whom the charge is made: *Downey v O'Brien* [1994] 2 ILRM 130, HC.

The members of a local authority who vote for a proposal in consequence of which an illegal payment is made out of the funds of the local authority, must be surcharged on any surcharge which may be subsequently made as a result of the decision: Local Government Act 2001, s 112. For previous legislation, now repealed, see City and County Management (Amendment) Act 1955, s 16(1). Surcharging also applied to health boards (qv): Health Act 1970, s 28(2), now repealed by Comptroller and Auditor General (Amendment) Act 1993, s 20, Sch 4. A *surcharge* may also be imposed on a person who fails to file a return of income by the return filing date: Taxes Consolidation Act 1997, s 1084, as amended to cover genuine mistakes, by Finance Act 2004, s 86(3). See also TCA 1997, ss 440 and 441 See AUDITOR, LOCAL GOVERNMENT.

surcharge, classification of. Surcharges have been judicially classified in respect of payments which are: (a) unfounded in whole or in part: *The State (Raftis) v Leonard* [1960] IR 408; (b) illegal eg where *ultra vires* (qv): *R (Jephson) v Roscommon JJ* 12 LR (Ir) 331; (c) incurred through negligence or misconduct: *R (Kennedy) v Browne* [1907] 2 IR 505; and (d) sums which ought to have been, but were not brought into the accounts by accounting persons. See *R (Drury) v Dublin Corporation and Campbell* 41 ILTR 97.

surety. A guarantor; a person who binds himself, usually by deed, to satisfy the obligations of another person, if the latter fails to do so. A surety to an *administration bond* must swear he is worth at least half of the penal sum (qv) in the bond. See also DCR 1997 Ord 18, rr 3, 6 and 14; Ord 17, r 4(2); Ord 20; Ord 101, r 4. See BAIL; BAIL, INDEMNIFICATION OF SURETY; BAILPERSON; GUARANTEE; MARSHALLING; RECOGNISANCE; STATUTE OF FRAUDS.

surgical operation. A medical practitioner is under a greater duty of care to explain the consequences of *elective* surgery than would be the case in *non-elective* surgery, so that the patient can give an informed consent to the medical procedure; the mere following of an accepted practice could not be regarded as meeting the standard of care required: *Walsh v Family Planning Services Ltd* [1993] 11 ILT Dig 90, SC.

When deciding what risks ought to be disclosed to a patient before a surgical operation, the test to be adopted by the courts was the test of the reasonable patient; by adopting that test it was the patient thus informed, rather than the doctor, who made the real choice as to whether the treatment was carried out: *Geoghegan v Harris* [2000] 3 IR 536, HC. See 'Consent to treatment by Patients – Disclosure Revisited' by Ciaran Craven BL in *Bar Review* (October 2000) 56 and (November 2000) 111.

The Supreme Court has held that there may be all sorts of circumstances where an unnecessary medical procedure is carried out but where there is no actionable negligence; negligence and unnecessariness are not synonyms: *Gough v Neary* [2004] 1 ILRM 35, SC.

In a case concerning a surgical operation, prior to the Statute of Limitations (Amendment) Act 1991, it had been held that the then three-year period of limitation began to run when a provable personal injury, capable of attracting compensation, occurred to a person; it did not begin to run from the date of the occurrence of the wrongful act nor could it be postponed until the time when the person could have discovered, by reasonable diligence, that such damage was caused by the wrongful act complained of: *Hegarty v O'Loughran & Edwards* [1990] ITLR (2 April) SC. The limitation period now runs from the date of accrual of the cause of action or from the date of knowledge, if later (SL(A)A 1991). Under recent legislation, provision has been made to reduce the three year limitation period to two years: Civil Liability and Courts Act 2004, s 7.

In a particular case involving a person who went into a coma after an appendix operation, it was held that it would be an unjustifiable extension of the law to say that negligence on the part of the defendants must be inferred in the absence of an explanation that must be proved on the balance of probability; the defendants had established that there was no negligence in the anaesthetic procedure and thus rebutted the burden of proof that rested on them: *Lindsay v Mid-Western Health Board* [1993] ILRM 550, SC. See also *Callaghan v Gleeson and Lavelle* [2002] FL 7554, HC.

The Supreme Court has held that a finding by a trial judge that a surgeon deliberately falsified his record of an operation with a view to misleading the court was clearly of the utmost seriousness: *Carroll v Lynch* (2003) Irish Times, 16 May. In this case, the Chief Justice held that there was no evidence whatsoever to justify such a finding. See also *Dunleavy v McDevitt & North Western Health Board* 10 ILT Dig [1992 SC] 296. [Bibliography: Donnelly (2); Tomkin & Hanafin.] See CAUSE OF ACTION; LIMITATION OF ACTIONS; MEDICAL NEGLIGENCE; MINOR; PATIENT, CONSENT OF; PSYCHO-SURGERY; RES IPSA LOQUITUR.

surname. Family as distinct from Christian or first name. The surname of a child entered on the register of births is required to be, subject to any linguistic modifications, (a) that of the mother or father or of both or (b) such other name requested by the mother and father as the registrar permits: Civil Registration Act 2004, s 19 and *First Schedule*. See also Registration of Business Names Act 1963, s 2; Companies Act 1963, s 195(15) as substituted by Companies Act 1990, s 51. See FORENAME; NAME, CHANGE OF.

surplus assets. The assets remaining on the winding-up (qv) of a company after its debts have been paid and capital returned to ordinary and preference shareholders. The question as to whether preference shareholders have a right to participate in the distribution of these surplus assets is a question of construction of any clause in the *articles of association* delimiting their rights exhaustively and exclusively: *Cork Electric Supply Co Ltd v Concannon and Others* [1932] IR 314.

surplus in bankruptcy. Any surplus remaining in a bankrupt's estate after the payment of one pound in the pound, with interest at the rate currently paid on judgment debts. The High Court will order the surplus to be paid or delivered to or vested in the bankrupt, his personal representatives (qv) or assigns, which order is deemed to be a conveyance, assignment or transfer of the property: Bankruptcy Act 1988, s 86. See also BA 1988, ss 102 and 121. See BANKRUPTCY.

surprise. The Circuit Court may review a judgment made in default of appearance of the defendant, or in default of defence, where the defendant has been taken by surprise: Circuit Court Rules 2001 Ord 30. For High Court provision, see SET ASIDE.

Under draft legislation, notice must be given to the prosecution by the defence if the defence intends to adduce evidence, during the course of a trial for an offence, as to the mental condition of the accused: Criminal Law (Insanity) Bill 2002, s 14. See also ALIBI; REBUTTAL, EVIDENCE IN; SPECIAL PLEADING.

surrender. (1) The yielding up of the residue of a term of interest in land: *Wallis v Heads* [1893] 2 Ch 75. See Deasy's Act 1860, s 7. See *Consultation Paper on General Law of Landlord and Tenant Law* (LRC CP 28, 2003) paras 18.19 and 18.20. See also Criminal Justice (Illicit Traffic by Sea) Act 2003, ss 7, 8, 17, 18. See LEASE, DETERMINATION OF; TENANCY, TERMINATION NOTICE. See also ABANDONMENT.

(2) The giving up to the appropriate authority of a fugitive from justice. See EUROPEAN ARREST WARRANT, PROHIBITION ON SURRENDER.

surrender of shares. The yielding up of the shares of a company where the *articles of association* so permit and the circumstances are such as to justify their forfeiture: *Bellerby v Rowland Marwood's SS Co Ltd* [1902] 2 Ch 14. Where a valid surrender of shares in a plc brings the allotted share capital below the authorised minimum, the company is required to re-register as another form of company: Companies (Amendment) Act 1983, ss 19 and 43 (as amended by Companies Act 1990, s 232(b)). See FORFEITURE OF SHARES.

surrender value. (1) The amount which an insurer will pay to an insured on termination before the maturity date of a policy of insurance.

(2) The monetary value of a policy where it is surrendered by the policy holder to the insurance undertaking: Unclaimed Life Assurance Policies Act 2003, s 2(1).

surrogate. A person appointed to act in the place of another.

surrogate mother. A woman who agrees with another to conceive and give birth to a child for that other by means of artificial insemination by the semen of that other.

Payment to a surrogate mother could be in contravention of the prohibition of any payment or other reward in consideration of the adoption (qv) of a child: Adoption Act 1952, s 42(1). See ARTIFICIAL INSEMINATION; HUMAN REPRODUCTION.

surveillance. A watch kept on a suspected offender. Surveillance of a suspect can be justified and may not be illegal: *The State (Kane) v Governor of Mountjoy Prison* [1987] HC. Where a person who is entitled to liberty is placed under continuous garda surveillance and challenges that surveillance, the onus is on the garda authorities to provide adequate justification for the surveillance: *DPP v Kane, McCaughey and Carlin* [1988] HC & SC. See LRC Report on *Privacy: Surveillance and the Interception of Communications* (LRC 57, 1998). [Bibliography: Walsh D (3)].

survival of causes of action. See DEATH, EFFECT OF.

survivorship, presumption of. See DEATH, SIMULTANEOUS.

survivorship, right of. The right of a person to property by reason of his having survived another person, who had an interest in it eg on the death of one of two joint tenants, his interest passes to the survivor. See JOINT ACCOUNT; JOINT TENANCY.

survivor's pension. The social welfare pension to which a widow or widower may be entitled; entitlement ceases on remarriage or cohabitation: Social Welfare (Consolidation) Act 1993, ss 100–105A as amended (eg Social Welfare Act 1994, s 11 and Social Welfare (No 2) Act 1995, s 3); *Foley v Moulton* [1989] ILRM 169. Renamed a *widow* or *widower's pension* in 1996: Social Welfare Act 1996, s 27. See *Ó Síocháin v Neenan* [1997] 2 ILRM 451, HC and [1998] 2 ILRM 444, SC.

sus per coll; suspendatur per collum. [Let him be hanged by the neck.] See DEATH PENALTY; HANGING.

suspended sentence. A sentence which is ordered not to take place immediately, usually on conditions eg upon the offender entering into a recognisance (qv) with or without securities, to keep the peace and be of good behaviour for a specified period. See *R v Spratling* [1911] 2 KB 77; *The State (Woods) v Governor of Portlaoise Prison* 108 ILTR 54.

suspension. To debar temporarily from the exercise of an office or occupation. An employee may be suspended from employment pending investigation of allegations of irregularities or misconduct where the employee has been made aware of the allegations and the suspension is for reasons of good administration; suspension, which can constitute a form of disciplinary action, is not permitted in order that an inquiry can be carried out in the absence of the employee being made aware of the allegations: *Gavin, Lynch & Deegan v Minister for Finance* [2000] ITLR (12 June) SC and ELR 190.

Whether a suspension invokes fair procedures, or not, hinges on: (a) the gravity of the reasons for the suspension; (b) the implications for the person concerned; and (c) the likely consequences for that person following suspension: *McNamara v South Western Area Health Board* [2001] ELR 317, HC. In this case it was held that the suspension of a senior consultant without pay is more than a mere 'holding operation' pending a full review of whether to dismiss that person; it is a sanction which will have damaging implications for any professional person.

Under fair procedures guaranteed under the Constitution, the employee should be given some form of advance warning as there is always a possibility that some simple explanation would obviate the necessity for suspension: *Deegan v Minister for Finance* [1998] ELR 280, HC.

A suspension should continue only for such period of time as is necessary or reasonably practicable to have a full hearing into the matter to determine whether the employee should be dismissed, reinstated or dealt with in some other way: *Allman v Minister for Justice* [2002] 3 IR 540, HC and [2003] ELR 7. The suspension of a person can be rendered invalid by an unjustified delay in holding an enquiry into matters alleged against the person: *Flynn v An Post* [1987] IR 68, SC. Whether a suspension is for too long a period is a question of fact and judgment: *Martin v Nationwide Building Society* [2001] 1 IR 228, HC. See also *Shortt v Datapackaging Ltd* [1994] ELR 251, HC; *Phelan v BIC Ireland Ltd* [1997] ELR 208, HC.

Where a party who initiates an inquiry is ultimately found to have erred in law, that does not *of itself* render invalid a continuation of a suspension imposed pending the completion of the inquiry: *McGrath v Minister for Justice* [2003] ITLR (7 July) SC and 1 IR 622. Damages will be awarded only where the person suspended can establish negligence ie a failure to exercise reasonable care by reference to a recognised duty.

An injunction to lift the suspension of a person will not be granted, even if a strong *prima facie* case has been made, where damages would be an adequate remedy and where the balance of convenience does not warrant the lifting of the suspension: *Sweeney v Sligo Vocational Educational Committee* [1988] HC.

A three-day suspension of a pupil from a national school was not a matter for judicial review: *Murtagh v St Emer's National School* [1991] ILRM 549, SC. However, suspension of a pupil in a school under the Vocational Education Act 1930 was held to be vested in the Vocational Education Committee, and not in the Principal or the Board of Management: *McKenna v Ó Ciarán* [2002] 3 IR 35, HC.

An injunction to lift the suspension of a GAA chairman was granted because the management committee had acted contrary to natural justice: *O'Murchu v Waterford Gaelic Athletic Association County Board* [1991] HC. Indefinite suspension of an employee may amount to a dismissal: *Deegan & Ors v Dunnes Stores* [1992] ELR 184, EAT. Suspension of a garda was held not to be punishment in nature and did not in any way prejudice a disciplinary process which was underway: *Fowley v Garda Commissioner* (2002) Irish Times, 23 November, HC. See also *The State (Co Donegal VEC) v Minister for Education* [1986] ILRM 399; *Maher v Allied Irish Banks plc* [1998] ELR 204, DC; *O'Donovan v Allied Irish Banks Ltd* [1998] ELR 209, DC. See INTERLOCUTORY INJUNCTION.

sustainable development. (1) 'Development which is capable of being maintained at a steady level without exhausting natural resources or causing severe ecological damage': *Collins English Dictionary*.

(2) 'Sustainable development is about achieving environmental, economic and social objectives in an integrated way. It is all about balance – between human activity and the natural resource base upon which it depends, and between the needs of the people today and those of future generations': Comhar, the National Sustainable Development Partnership, which was established by the government in 1999 as a forum for consultation and dialogue on issues related to sustainable development. For Comhar, see website: *www.comhar-nsdp.ie*.

Although not legally defined, 'sustainable development' is of significance in some statutes and treaties. One of the tasks of the EC is to promote throughout the Community a harmonious and *sustained development* of economic activities: EC Treaty, arts 2 and 6 of the consolidated (2002) version. The term also appears in the Treaty on European Union, art 2 and Preamble of the consolidated (2002) version. Also in planning law, the proper planning and *sustainable development* of an area is a regular requirement. Chartered engineers are required to promote the principles of sustainable development and the needs of present and future generations: *Code of Ethics – The Institution of Engineers of Ireland* (November 2003) clause 2.2.

See also European Bank for Reconstruction and Development Act 1991, Schedule, art 2(1)(vii); Fisheries (Amendment) Act 1999, s 5. For the Commission on Sustainable Development, see website: *www.un.org/esa/sustdev*. For the International Institute for Sustainable Development, see website: *www.iisd.org*. For planning guidelines on sustainable rural housing, see website: *www.irishspatialstrategy.ie*. For World Resources Institute, see website: *www.wri.org*. See DEVELOPMENT PLAN; HOUSING STRATEGY; PLANNING LAW; REGIONAL AUTHORITY;TOWN RENEWAL PLAN.

Sustainable Energy Ireland. The body corporate, replacing the Irish Energy Centre, with wide functions relating to the promotion and assistance of environmentally and economically sustainable production, supply and use of energy: Sustainable Energy Act 2002. The body also has the function of promoting and assisting the reduction of greenhouse gas emissions and transboundary air pollutants. See website: *www.sei.ie*.

swabs. Swabs must not be taken from a person in custody in a garda station except with his written consent and, where he is under the age of 17 years, the written consent of an appropriate adult: Treatment of Persons in Custody in Garda Síochána Stations Regulations 1987, SI No 119 of 1987, reg 18. Consent is not required where the garda is otherwise empowered by law. A garda was empowered to take swabs from an arrested person's skin or samples of his hair for the purpose of making any test designed to see if the person had been in contact with firearms or explosives:

Criminal Law Act 1976, s 7. See also Criminal Justice Act 1984, s 6. This power has been repealed and replaced by a wider power to take bodily samples, which includes swabs. See Criminal Justice (Forensic Evidence) Act 1990. See Criminal Justice Bill 2004, ss 12–13. See BODILY SAMPLE.

swap transaction. Generally understood to mean the exchange of debt with fixed interest rates for debt with floating rates, or in one currency for another. Swap transactions enable a borrower to convert a floating interest loan into a fixed rate loan, or in the case of a foreign currency loan to purchase the foreign currency on a forward-contract basis. Swaps are a common method of hedging against movement in interest and exchange rates.

Power has been given to certain State companies to effect such transactions: Financial Transactions of Certain Companies and Other Bodies Act 1992. The legislation was introduced because the UK House of Lords had held that such transactions entered into by a UK local authority was *ultra vires* its powers (*Hazell v Hammersmith and Fulham London Borough Council* [1991] 2 WLR 372) and there was concern that this decision might lead to doubt as to the legality of such transactions by Irish bodies which did not have express statutory power to enter into them. See also Finance Act 1993, s 137 See BORROWING.

swear. The word 'swear', in the case of persons for the time being allowed by law to affirm or declare instead of swearing, includes *affirm* and *declare*: Interpretation Act 1937, s 12, para 31. See AFFIRMATION; OATH; DECLARATION.

sweepstake. Formerly was a drawing or distribution of prizes by lot or chance whether with or without reference to the result of a future uncertain event: Public Charitable Hospitals (Temporary Provisions) Act 1930, s 1(1). The famous Irish Hospital Sweepstakes ran its last sweepstake in January 1986. Provision has been made for the disposal of prize moneys left unclaimed: Public Hospitals (Amendment) Act 1990.

A mechanism was provided in 2000 by which an *ex-gratia* payment of £20,000 (€25,395) could be paid to former employees of the sweepstake, or in the case of deceased employees, to their personal representative: Hospitals' Trust (1940) Limited (Payment to Former Employees)

Act 2000. It was estimated that there could be 147 beneficiaries.

Swiss Confederation. Provision has been made to give the force of law, once they are ratified, to seven *sectoral agreements* which have been signed between the European Union and Switzerland: European Communities and Swiss Confederation Act 2001. The seven agreements cover the following areas: free movement of persons; air transport; rail and road transport; trade in agricultural products; mutual recognition in relation to conformity assessment (ie mutual recognition of the results of tests of conformity to standards for most industrial products); government procurement (ie right of access to government contracts); and scientific and technological co-operation.

The seven agreements were signed in Luxembourg on 21 June 1999 and will enter into force after ratification by each EU member state; Switzerland ratified the agreements on 16 October 2000 following approval by the Swiss people in a referendum. The agreement of the *free movement of people*: (a) affords Switzerland a transition period to facilitate the liberalisation of its labour market and (b) lasts for seven years at which time Switzerland is required to renew it indefinitely or repudiate it. See SI No 195 of 2002. See SOLICITOR, MUTUAL RECOGNITION.

symbols of the European Union. Under the proposed *Treaty establishing a Constitution for Europe*, agreed but not yet ratified, the symbols of the European Union will be: (a) the flag, which is a circle of twelve golden stars on a blue background; (b) the anthem, which is based on the Ode to Joy from the Ninth Symphony by Ludwig van Beethoven; (c) the motto which is 'Unity in diversity'; (d) the currency which is the 'euro'; and (e) Europe Day which is to be celebrated on 9 May throughout the Union. See EUROPE DAY; EUROPEAN UNION.

syndicate. A type of association which is neither a partnership nor an unincorporated company, sometimes found in insurance and banking. Syndicates of underwriters at and outside Lloyd's and banks providing finance by means of *syndicated loans* fall into this category. A member of a syndicate is not liable to a party contracting with the syndicate for a defaulting member's share. A syndicate which has the object of *acquisition of gain* must be registered as a company if the number of its members exceeds 20 persons; or in the case of a bank if its members exceeds ten persons: Companies Act 1963, ss 372 and 376.

synthetic securitisation. A securitisation which involves the transfer of the risk rather than the transfer of an asset eg the risk of default on a loan rather than the loan itself. See SECURITISATION OF MORTGAGE.

syringe. Includes any part of a syringe or a needle or any sharp instrument capable of piercing skin and passing onto or into a person, blood or any fluid or substance resembling blood: Non-Fatal Offence against the Person Act 1997, s 1(1). A variety of offences involving syringes are created by the 1997 Act, including: (a) injuring or threatening to injure another with a syringe, (b) possessing a syringe, (c) placing or abandoning a syringe (NFOPA 1997, ss 6–8). It is an offence for a taxi passenger, deliberately, to leave a syringe or sharp instrument in any part of the vehicle: Taxi Regulation Act 2003, s 40(2)(c). See also ASSAULT.

T

tabula in naufragio. [Plank in the shipwreck.]

tacking. The equitable doctrine by which a third mortgagee, with no notice of a second mortgage at the time his mortgage was made, can squeeze out the second mortgage, by acquiring the first mortgage and the legal estate therein. He could tack on his third mortgage to the legal estate; the doctrine is based on the maxim of *where the equities are equal, the law prevails*. However the doctrine of tacking has no application to registered instruments, where the priority of mortgages is based on their time of registration: Registration of Deeds (Ireland) Act 1707 and Registration of Title Act 1964.

tail. See FEE TAIL.

tail docking. The removal or mutilation of the tail or part of the tail of an animal. It is an offence in the case of a bovine animal, except in certain limited circumstances eg where performed under anaesthetic by a registered veterinary surgeon where necessary for the proper treatment of disease or injury in a single animal: Prohibition on Tail Docking Regulations 2003, SI No 263 of 2003.

take-out merger. The provision by which a company, which acquires at least 80% in value of another company's shares, is entitled to acquire for itself the remaining 20% or less, on the same terms: Companies Act 1963, s 204. Because of the significance of this power, the court must be satisfied that the requirements of CA 1963, s 204 have been strictly complied with. A take-out of dissident shareholders is possible also using powers to change a company's constitution or capital structures, provided 75% in value of each class affected who vote agree and the court consents (CA 1963, ss 201–204). See *Re National Bank Ltd* [1966] 2 All ER 1006. See MANDATORY OFFER; MERGER.

take-over. Any agreement or transaction which leads to the acquisition of *control* of a *relevant* company or any invitation, offer or proposal made or intended to be made with a view to concluding such an agreement: Irish Takeover Panel Act 1997, s 1(1). *Control* means the holding, whether directly or indirectly, of securities carrying not less than 30% of the voting rights of the company. A *relevant* company is a public limited company (plc) or other bodies corporate incorporated in Ireland whose securities are currently being traded, on a market regulated by a recognised stock exchange, or were so traded within the previous five years (ITPA 1997, s 2). Exempted are UCITS and investment companies.

The definition of a 'relevant company' which brings it subject to the jurisdiction of the Irish Takeover Panel has been expanded: Irish Takeover Panel (Relevant Company) Regulations 2001, SI No 87 of 2001. Now, public limited companies incorporated in the State and authorised to trade on the London Stock Exchange, the New York Stock Exchange, Nasdaq, EAS-DAQ and the Neuer Markt come within the Panel's remit. Companies which are currently not authorised to trade on these exchanges, but were so authorised in the previous five years, also come within the jurisdiction of the Panel. See also Proposed Merger or Takeover Prohibition Order 1998, SI No 102 of 1998. See Takeover Rules 2001; Substantial Acquisition Rules 2001. See Listing Rules 2000, para 10.45. [Bibliography: Clarke B.] See ACQUISITIONS; CONCERT PARTY; COVERT

TAKE-OVER; DISPOSALS; IRISH TAKEOVER PANEL; JUDICIAL REVIEW, TAKE-OVER; MANDATORY OFFER; MERGER; REVERSE TAKE-OVER TRANSACTION; SCHEME OF ARRANGEMENT; SUBSTANTIAL ACQUISITION.

Tallaght hospital. A new voluntary hospital in Tallaght, being a merger of the Adelaide, Meath and National Children's Hospitals, necessitated the Health (Amendment) (No 2) Act 1996 which confers on the Minister additional statutory powers in relation to amending a hospital charter by order. The Charter for Tallaght hospital is set out in SI No 228 of 1996; it deals, *inter alia*, with the ethical status of the hospital as being to promote and secure the availability, between doctor and patient, of medical and surgical procedures as are lawfully provided in the State.

Tánaiste. A member of the government nominated by the Taoiseach; she acts for all purposes for the Taoiseach if the Taoiseach should be temporarily absent or if the Taoiseach should die or become permanently incapacitated: 1937 Constitution, art 28(6). 'Absent' means being temporarily unable to fulfil his functions through illness, incapacity or being incommunicado whether at home or abroad; the Tánaiste is not required to remain within the geographical confines of the State when the Taoiseach is absent; the Tánaiste complies with her constitutional duty provided she is not herself absent in this specific sense: *Riordan v Ireland* [1996] 2 ILRM 107, HC and [1995] 3 IR 62, HC.

The Supreme Court has held that the Tánaiste was a constitutional officer and that, although the powers and duties of the Tánaiste were not fully described in the Constitution, as our system of government was a cabinet system, the manner in which the Tánaiste and the Taoiseach shared the burdens of office was a matter for arrangement among themselves: *Riordan v Taoiseach (No 1)* [1999] 4 IR 321, SC. See TAOISEACH.

tangible property. *Corporeal* property eg goods, compared with intangible property eg choses in action (qv).

Taoiseach. [Prime Minister.] The head of government appointed by the President of Ireland, on the nomination of Dáil Éireann: 1937 Constitution, art 13(1)(1). The Taoiseach is required to resign from office on ceasing to retain the support of a majority in Dáil Éireann, unless on his advice the

President dissolves the Dáil and on the reassembly after the dissolution the Taoiseach secures the support of a majority in the Dáil (art 28(10)).

The Constitution does not require the presence of either the Taoiseach or Tánaiste in the State at all times, but if a duty or function falls to be performed by the Taoiseach within the State on any given occasion, then it will be necessary for either the Taoiseach or the Tánaiste to be in the State or to return to the State to perform that duty or function: *Riordan v An Tánaiste* [1998] 1 ILRM 494, SC.

Any reference in a pre-1922 statute to the 'President of the Executive Council' is deemed to be a reference to the Taoiseach: *Haughey v Moriarty* [1999] 3 IR 1, SC.

The office of Taoiseach has been held by: Bertie Ahern (1997 to present); John Bruton (1994–97); Albert Reynolds (1992–94); Charles J Haughey (1979–81; 1982–82; 1987–1992); Garrett Fitzgerald (1981–82; 1982–87); John M Lynch (1966–73; 1977–79); Liam Cosgrave (1973–77); Seán F Lemass (1959–66); John A Costello (1948–51; 1954–57); Eamon de Valera (1932–48; 1951–54; 1957–59); W T Cosgrove (1922–32). See website: *www.taoiseach.ie*. See also TÁNAISTE.

tape recording. In a District Court case in which chief executive of Ryanair, Mr Michael O'Leary was fined for dangerous driving, Judge John Brophy said that the use by an Irish Times reporter of a tape recorder during the court hearing was illegal and he confiscated the machine: *Irish Times*, 29 March 2003. See HEARSAY.

Target. Trans-European Automated Real-time Gross Settlement Express Transfer system: Central Bank Act 1989, s 135 inserted by substitution by Euro Changeover (Amounts) Act 2001, s 5. A person is not compellable to make any payment or do any act: (a) on a public holiday; or (b) on a day on which the TARGET system is closed, which that person would not be compellable to do on Christmas Day or on Good Friday by virtue of any rule of law relating to banking.

tax. See TAXATION LAW.

tax, appeal. A person aggrieved by the tax assessment made by an Inspector of Taxes may appeal to the Appeal Commissioners: Taxes Consolidation Act 1997, ss 932–949. The Appeal Commissioners have no power to award costs. There is a right to have the appeal reheard by a judge of the Circuit Court (TCA 1997, s 942). However, the Circuit Court judge has power to award costs: Circuit Court Rules 2001 Ord 66 and *Inspector of Taxes v Arida Ltd* [1996] 1 ILRM 74, HC. There is provision also for the statement of a case to the High Court where the appellant or the inspector of taxes is dissatisfied on legal grounds with the determination of the appeal either before the Appeal Commissioners (TCA 1997, s 941) or the Circuit Court (TCA 1997, s 943).

In a particular case, the Supreme Court held that the Criminal Assets Bureau had left a person 'in the dark' over his right to appeal tax assessments and had failed to act in accordance with fair procedures: *Keogh v Criminal Assets Bureau* (17 May, unreported) SC. For a step-by-step guide to hearings before the Appeal Commissioners, see 'Tax Appeal Hearings' by Aoife Goodman BL in *Bar Review* (December 2001) 63. See also Capital Acquisitions Tax Consolidation Act 2003, ss 66–68.

tax, false statement. A taxpayer who knowingly makes a false statement or representation in relation to his tax return, to obtain an allowance or reduction of tax to which he is not entitled (or a person who assists him to do so) is liable to specified penalties (financial or at the discretion of the court, imprisonment or both) on a graduated scale: Income Tax Act 1967, s 516 as amended by Waiver of Certain Tax, Interest and Penalties Act 1993, s 11. See now Taxes Consolidation Act 1997, s 1056. See REVENUE PENALTY.

tax, prior opinion. An inspector of taxes is not bound by a prior opinion of the Revenue Commissioners on the prospective liability of a taxpayer: *Pandion Haliaetus v Revenue Commissioners* [1988] ILRM 419.

tax, repayment of. A general right to repayment of tax overpaid has been provided for: Finance Act 2003, s 17. This section deals with income tax, corporation tax and capital gains tax. The repayment is made irrespective of whether the tax was overpaid under an assessment or otherwise and irrespective of the presence or absence of any mistake on the part of the taxpayer. Subject to certain transitional arrangements, a claim for repayment of tax has to be made within four years from the end of the period to which it relates. As regards repayment of excise duty, VAT, stamp duty and residential property tax, see Finance Act 2003, ss 98, 124/125, 142 and 155 respectively.

As regards repayment of 'capital acquisitions tax', see Capital Acquisitions Tax Consolidation Act 2003, ss 51 and 57, as amended by Finance Act 2003, s 145. See INTEREST AND TAX; OFFSET OF REPAYMENTS.

tax, time limits. The inability of a person to comply with tax time limits because his assets have been frozen is a statable defence to proceedings by the inspector of taxes seeking entry of final judgment against the person: *CAB v Byrne* [2001] ITLR (2 July) HC.

tax and patents. See QUALIFYING PATENT.

tax and the courts. The traditional approach to tax liability is that the courts do not look at the substance or financial results of a transaction, but rather at the legal effects and legal rights of the parties according to legal ideas and concepts; and an exemption from tax is governed by the same considerations as a liability to tax: *McGrath v McDermott (Inspector of Taxes)* [1988] ILRM 181. It is an established rule of law that a citizen is not to be taxed unless the language of the relevant section of the taxing statute clearly imposes an obligation: *Texaco (Ireland) Ltd v Murphy, Inspector of Taxes* [1992] ILRM 304, SC. Also any relief from taxation must also be given in clear and unambiguous terms: *O'Connell v Fyffes Banana Processing Ltd* [2000] ITLR (11 September) SC. See DOUBLE TAXATION AGREEMENT; TAX AVOIDANCE.

tax assessment. The assessment of tax made by an inspector of taxes or revenue officer: Taxes Consolidation Act 1997, ss 918–922. Where a tax payer fails to file a return, or files an unsatisfactory return, the inspector is entitled to make an assessment to the best of his judgement. The assessment made by the inspector must state the amount of the assessment and the time limit within which it may be appealed. The function of an inspector in making an assessment of tax is purely administrative and therefore constitutional: *Deighan v Hearne* [1990] 1 IR 499; *Criminal Assets Bureau v Hutch* [1999] ITLR (21 June) HC. See also Capital Acquisitions Tax Consolidation Act 2003, s 49. See *Criminal Assets Bureau v Kelly* [2002] 3 IR 421, SC.

There is effectively a maximum four-year limit on which an assessment to tax can be made on a deceased person (TCA 1997, s 1048). See 'Bogus Foreign Deposit Accounts: Time Limits on Revenue Claims

against the Estates of Deceased Persons' by Joseph Hogan SC in *Bar Review* (February 2004) 11 and (April 2004) 46.

tax avoidance. Formerly, where a transaction resulted in the avoidance of a tax liability, the taxpayer was entitled to the benefit of the relevant statutory provision: *McGrath v McDermott (Inspector of Taxes)* [1988] ILRM 181; it was not for the courts to intervene; taxation should be according to the strict wording of the legislation: *McDermott v McGrath* [1989] IR 258. However, since 1989, if a transaction is a *tax avoidance transaction* as defined, it is ineffective to avoid tax: Finance Act 1989, s 86. It is such a transaction if it gives rise to a tax advantage and was not undertaken primarily for purposes other than to give rise to the tax advantage.

For a transaction to be struck down, the Revenue Commissioners must first form an opinion that it is such a transaction and notify the taxpayer, who may appeal to the Appeal Commissioners. See now Taxes Consolidation Act 1997, ss 806–817 as amended by Finance Act 1998, ss 12 and 43. Interest will not qualify for tax relief under TCA 1997, Pt VIII if a scheme has been put in place and the sole or main benefit of the scheme is to obtain a reduction in tax liability (TCA 1997, s 817A inserted by Finance Act 2000, s 73(1)). See also Finance Act 2004, s 32. See BOND WASHING; FISCAL NULLITY, DOCTRINE OF.

tax clearance certificate. A certificate issued by the Collector-General to a person where that person has complied with all the obligations imposed on him in relation to the payment of taxes, interest and penalties, and the delivery of returns: Finance Act 1992, s 242(2). A tax clearance certificate is required in many cases eg before a person can obtain a grant from many State schemes or as a precondition for the issue of a liquor licence (FA 1992, s 156).

The requirement of a tax clearance certificate was extended: (a) in 1993 as a precondition to the granting of an excise licence for a wholesale dealer in spirits, beer or wine, a bookmaker's licence, a gaming licence, an auctioneer's licence, or a licence for a vendor of hydrocarbon oil or liquid petroleum gas: Finance Act 1993, ss 79 and 140; (b) in 1995 as a precondition to undertaking contract work for a government department or a government funded body: Finance Act 1995, s 177; and (c) in 1997 as a precondition to obtaining or renewing a moneylender's licence, a mortgage intermediary's licence, or a credit intermediary's licence: Finance Act 1997, s 160. See now Taxes Consolidation Act 1997, ss 1094–1095 as amended by Finance Act 1999, s 212 and Finance Act, s 127. See also Prompt Payment of Accounts Act 1997, s 14; Finance Act 2002, s 86; Taxi Regulation Act 2003, s 37; Private Security Services Act 2004, s 24.

There is now a requirement for members of the Oireachtas and the Attorney-General to provide to the *Standards in Public Office Commission* a tax clearance certificate within nine months of election or appointment: Standards in Public Office Act 2001, ss 21 and 25. There are other provisions dealing with evidence of compliance by persons to be appointed as judges or to a senior office (SPOA 2001, ss 22–23).

tax defaulters. The Revenue Commissioners are required to publish, on a quarterly basis, the names of tax defaulters ie those on whom fines or penalties were imposed by the courts in relation to tax offences or those who have made settlements with the Revenue. A settlement will not be published if: (a) before the Revenue investigation, the taxpayer made a complete voluntary disclosure, or (b) the total of tax, interest and penalties comprised in the settlement is less than £10,000 (€12,700), or (c) the settlement was made under the 1988 or 1993 tax amnesty. If no penalty is imposed, there will not be publication.

Provision was made: (a) in 2000 for publication of a brief summary of the nature and circumstances of the default; and (b) in 2002: (i) to bring customs and excise duties within the scope of the provision; (ii) to confirm that the Revenue Commissioners may publicise or reproduce the list of tax defaulters in any other manner (eg on their website) after publication in Iris Oifigiúil; (iii) to provide that there will not be publication of a settlement where the degree of neglect on the part of the taxpayer is relatively minor, specifically where the penalty involved is less than 15% of the tax. See Taxes Consolidation Act 1997, s 1086 as amended by Finance Act 2000, s 162 and by Finance Act 2002, s 126.

The powers of the Revenue Commissioners to publish details of tax defaulters have been extended to cover self-employed defaulters in relation to PRSI and levies:

Social Welfare (Consolidation) Act 1993, s 20(3) as substituted by Social Welfare (Miscellaneous Provisions) Act 2002, s 14(b). See also Social Welfare (Miscellaneous Provisions) Act 2003, s 20. See AMNESTY.

tax-geared penalty. A penalty under the tax system which represents a proportion of the tax undercharge rather than being a fixed penalty. Tax-geared penalties generally apply where there is fraud or negligence in making an incorrect return. They now also apply where there is a tax undercharge and no return has been made eg see Taxes Consolidation Act 1997, ss 1053 and 1072 as amended by Finance Act 2002, ss 130–131 respectively. For tax-geared penalties in relation to VAT and capital acquisitions tax, see Finance Act 2003, ss 127 and 146 respectively. See DEPOSIT INTEREST RETENTION TAX; DIVIDEND WITHHOLDING TAX.

tax information exchange agreement. An agreement entered into by the government with the government of another State which provides for the exchange of information between the tax authorities on a reciprocal basis: Finance Act 2003, s 38. *Double Taxation Treaties* already provide for the exchange of information; however, the 2003 Act gives the government a general power to exchange information. This power has been extended to include gift tax and inheritance tax: Finance Act 2004, s 82. See also Capital Acquisitions Tax Consolidation Act 2003, s 106 as amended by FA 2004, s 79.

tax liability in EU. It would appear that a tax liability in any EU member state is enforceable in Ireland: SI No 462 of 2002 as amended by SI No 344 of 2003 and implementing Directive (EC) 2001/44 and (EC) 2002/94. The Directives allow for the principle of direct enforcement of the penal statutes of other EU member states, including income and capital taxes and VAT, by means of the mechanism and procedures laid down. See 'Enforcement of Foreign Tax Liabilities – All's changed utterly?' by Patrick Hunt SC in *Bar Review* (April 2003) 60.

tax penalty. A civil penalty imposed under tax legislation may now be pursued in the District, Circuit or High Courts depending on the level of penalty being imposed; previously such penalty could only be pursued in the High Court: Taxes Consolidation

Act 1997, s 1061 as amended by Finance Act 2003, s 162.

tax return. Penalties apply where a person fails to make the relevant tax returns or where he fraudulently or negligently makes an incorrect return: Taxes Consolidation Act 1997, ss 1052–1053. The penalty for failure to make a return does not apply to a failure to provide on the prescribed form the detail required by the form, unless, following delivery of the return, the failure is brought to the person's attention and the person fails to remedy matters without unreasonable delay (TCA 1997, s 1052 as amended by Finance Act 2004, s 86(2)). See *Lennon v Judge Clifford* [1996] 2 IR 590, SC. See ELECTRONIC TAX RETURN.

tax year. The tax year has been changed to align it with the calendar year as from 1 January 2002: Finance Act 2001, s 77. It formerly was the twelve months beginning on the 6 April. Consequently, the tax year for 2002 was from 1 January to 31 December. The previous tax year was from 6 April 2001 to 31 December 2001, a period of nine months with an appropriate adjustment in allowances.

taxation law. The body of law dealing with the raising of revenue by the State by compulsory contribution by individuals and by companies, levied on goods and services, income and wealth. *Direct* taxes are those imposed on the individual, usually in accordance with his ability to pay e g income tax. *Indirect* taxes are those applied to goods and services e g value added taxes. Local taxes which are imposed by local authorities include rates (qv).

Other taxes include: anti-speculation property tax, capital gains tax, corporation tax, capital acquisitions tax on gifts and inheritances, probate tax, pay related social insurance contributions, customs and excise duties, capital duty on the contribution of assets to companies, stamp duty on conveyances and other documents for the transfer or assignment of property and for certain other purposes, and residential property tax.

Taxation statutes enjoy an especially strong presumption of constitutionality: *Madigan v Attorney-General & Ors* [1986] ILRM 136. The enactment of legislation providing for the nation's finances, including the kind of taxes which should be imposed, what rates should apply and what allowances should be given, is the duty of the Oireachtas and not a function of the courts: *MhicMhathuna v Ireland* [1995] 1 ILRM 69, SC. However, the method of collection of a tax can be struck down as unconstitutional if it fails to pass the *proportionality* test i e the objective of the provision must be of sufficient importance to warrant overriding a constitutionally protected right: *Daly v Revenue Commissioners* [1996] 1 ILRM 122, HC. See also Electronic Commerce Act 2000, s 11. See Taxes Consolidation Act 1997 as amended; District Court (Taxes Consolidation Act 1997) Rules 2000, SI No 238 of 2000 as amended by SI No 283 of 2003.

A member state of the European Community must not impose, directly or indirectly, on the products of other member states any internal taxes of any kind in excess of that imposed directly or indirectly on similar domestic products: EC Treaty, art 90 of the consolidated (2002) version. The Council, acting unanimously, has harmonising powers in the field of turnover taxes, excise duties and other forms of indirect taxation, to the extent necessary to ensure the establishment and functioning of the internal market (EC Treaty, art 93). See 'The European Court of Justice and Domestic Tax Legislation' by Patrick Hunt SC in *Bar Review* (June/July 2002) 291.

For the Irish Taxation Institute, see website: *www.taxireland.ie.* [Bibliography: Bohan; Boland; Brennan P; Brennan & Howley; Bristow; Burke, O'Driscoll & Giblin; Butterworths; Cooney, Martyn & Reck; Cremin; Hennessy & Keegan; Hennessy & Moore; Judge; Irish Taxation Institute; Keegan; Keegan & Murray; Lenahan; Moore; O'Cuinneagain; O'Halloran M; O'Reilly & Carroll; Scully, Judge & Lynch; Gov Pub (1).] See DOUBLE TAXATION AGREEMENT; REVENUE PENALTY; SELF-ASSESSMENT; TAX AND THE COURTS; TAX AVOIDANCE; TAX, PRIOR OPINION; THIRD-PARTY INFORMATION; UNLAWFUL ORGANISATION.

taxation of awards. The practice has been that awards made by the courts are not taxable in the hands of the recipient, although the income thereby arising (e g investment income, capital gains) is taxable. It is understood that the Revenue Commissioners believe that awards made under 'social legislation' (e g maternity protection, employment equality, parental leave, adoptive leave) should be taxed. See 'Is the Revenue jumping on the Compo Bandwagon' by solicitor Richard Grogan in

Law Society Gazette (October 2002) 14. It is now clear that there is an obligation on an employer to deduct income tax at source from any awards or settlements made in respect of an employment dispute. See EMPLOYMENT AWARDS.

taxation of costs. The procedure whereby a solicitor's bill of costs is examined by a Taxing Master and allowed or reduced. It 'is an important means of protecting the public in a situation where the client is almost invariably in a dependent position in relation to his solicitor': Lynch J in *Agritex Ltd v O'Driscoll* [1995] 2 ILRM 23, HC. A solicitor who has delivered a bill of costs cannot deliver a higher bill when taxation of those costs is sought (*Agritex* case).

Where *party and party costs* (qv) are awarded by a court, the court also orders that they be taxed: RSC Ord 99 as amended by SI No 265 of 1993. In the case of *solicitor and client costs* (qv), they are not taxed unless the client demands that they be taxed; in such taxation, all costs are allowed except in so far as they are of an unreasonable amount or have been unreasonably incurred; all amounts incurred with the express or implied approval of the client are conclusively presumed to have been reasonably incurred (r 11). If these costs are reduced by one-sixth or more, the solicitor claiming the costs, must pay for the costs of taxation (r 29(13)).

A notice to tax may be restricted so as to seek the taxation of only one or more items in the bill of costs: RSC Ord 99, r 28(2) inserted by SI No 265 of 1993, para 6.

It has been held that the Courts and Court Officers Act 1995, ss 27(6) and 27(7) were intended to be complementary and to apply to all *three stages* of taxation of costs under RSC Ord 99 ie: (i) the initial adjudication on or taxation of the bill of costs, (ii) the review of taxation of items objected to by a party, and (iii) the review by the court: *Gannon v Flynn* [2000] 3 IR 306, HC and 2 ILRM 551. The Court held that since the 1995 Act, a taxing master has no power or discretion to award costs for professional services in relation to the taxation of costs; this particular view was upheld by the Supreme Court: *Gannon v Flynn* [2001] 3 IR 531, SC.

See *O'Sullivan v Hughes* [1986] ILRM 555; *The State (Shatter & Co) v de Valera* [1987] ILRM 599 & [1990] 8 ILT Dig 240, SC; *Staunton v Durkan* [1996] 2

ILRM 509, SC; *Gaspari v Iarnród Éireann* [1997] 1 ILRM 207, HC; *Tobin & Twomey Services Ltd v Kerry Foods Ltd* [1999] 1 ILRM 428, HC; *Minister for Finance v Goodman* [2000] 1 ILRM 278, HC and [1999] 3 IR 321 and 333, HC.

All costs directed to be taxed in the Circuit Court are taxed by the County Registrar (who for this purpose has all the powers of the Taxing Master of the High Court): Circuit Court Rules 2001 Ord 66, r 6. A *scale of costs* is provided for in District Court proceedings; where the court is of opinion that there is no scale provided, it may measure the costs: DCR 1997 Ord 51. See also Residential Institutions Redress Act 2002, s 27; Civil Liability and Courts Act 2004. s 43. [Bibliography: Flynn & Halpin.] See also BARRISTER; BRIEF FEE; CONTENTIOUS BUSINESS; COSTS IN CIVIL PROCEEDINGS; INSTRUCTION FEE; STANDBY FEE.

taxation of costs, recovery of. Costs which have been taxed and a certificate therefor issued by the taxing master for the amount due, may be recovered: (a) in the case of party and party costs by having the amount entered in the judgment and by executing the judgment; and (b) in the case of solicitor and client costs, by issuing separate proceedings for their recovery.

taxation of costs, review of. An application may be made to the High Court for an order requiring the Taxing Master to review the taxation and the court may give directions to the Taxing Master or it may itself settle the matter. The court has jurisdiction to determine appropriate fees on an appeal from a ruling of the Taxing Master: *Best v Wellcome Foundation* [1996] 1 ILRM 34, HC and [1996] 3 IR 378, HC.

A party seeking a review of the taxation of costs must produce for the Court duly certified copies of the original bill of costs, notice of objections and submissions in support of same and any replying submissions and any other material documents: RSC Ord 99, r 38(5) as amended by Rules of the Superior Courts (No 3) (Documentation for Review of Taxation) 2000, SI No 329 of 2000. This change in rule removes the previous requirement on the Taxing Master to transmit this material to the High Court.

The High Court has held that the Courts and Court Officers Act 1995, s 27 imposed a heavier burden than heretofore on any party challenging a ruling of the Taxing

Master; the Court should not intervene unless an error of the order of 25% or more had been established in relation to an item under challenge: *Superquinn Ltd v Bray UDC (No 2)* [2001] 1 IR 459, HC. This is the standard to be adopted in determining whether an error as to amount became 'unjust'.

The Supreme Court has held that the onus is on the applicant to show that the Taxing Master not only erred in principle but also that the decision was unjust: *Cronin v Astra Business Systems* [2004] ITLR 5 July, SC. Comparator cases have been held to be a valuable guide to the assessment of costs; the taxing master was in error in rejecting comparisons: *Doyle v Deasy & Guinness* [2003] FL 7909, HC.

taxi. Means a *street service vehicle* ie a *small public service vehicle* the driver of which offers on a public road himself and the vehicle for hire and for that purpose stands or drives the vehicle on a public road: Taxi Regulation Act 2003, s 2(1). It is an offence for a person to drive or use a mechanically propelled vehicle in a public place for the carriage of persons for reward unless both the driver and the vehicle are licensed (TRA 2003, s 43). A person who hires a taxi and who, without reasonable excuse, does not pay the fare, is guilty of an offence (TRA 2003, s 40(5)).

In a landmark decision, which led to the deregulation of the taxi sector and then to the 2003 Act, it was held that the Minister, in restricting the number of taxi licences for reasons unrelated to qualitative standards concerning the vehicles and their drivers, had affected not only the right of citizens to work in the industry for which they may be qualified, but also the right of the public to the services of taxis and had restricted the development of the taxi industry: *Humphrey v Minister for the Environment* [2001] 1 ILRM 241, HC and 1 IR 263.

Regulations were subsequently made providing for the revocation of regulatory provisions involving quantitative restrictions on the licensing of taxis and hackneys: Road Traffic (Public Service Vehicles) (Amendment) (No 3) Regulations 2000, SI No 367 of 2000. Also provision was made to enable the capital cost of a taxi acquired on or before 21 November 2000 to be written off over five years at the rate of 20% per annum against the trading income of the licence owner: Finance Act 2001, s 51. See also SI No 534 of 2001.

In addition, the government in 2002 established a *Taxi Hardship Panel* to consider the nature and extent of extreme personal financial hardship arising directly from the liberalisation of the taxi licensing regime. The *Panel* recommended in December 2002 a sliding scale of payments, ranging from €15,000 for surviving spouses of drivers with dependants and no other income, to €3,000 for operators of wheelchair-accessible taxis who can demonstrate a reduction in income, to nothing for those whose only claim is the loss of the capital value of their licence. Applicants to the *Taxi Hardship Payments Scheme* must be tax compliant and fall into one of six specified categories. The Scheme is administered by ADM Ltd on behalf of the government. See website: *www.adm.ie*.

There are new requirements in relation to taximeters and the fitting of a device capable of printing automatic receipts for taxi fares: Road Traffic (Public Service Vehicles) (Amendment) Regulations 2002, SI No 411 of 2002. Also, local authorities are empowered to make *bye-laws* on the number, location and operation of taxi stands: Road Traffic Act 1961, s 84 as substituted by Road Traffic Act 2002, s 15, and as proposed to be amended by Road Traffic Bill 2004, s 22. A taxi sign may now be in English or in the Irish language (TACSAÍ): SI No 157 of 2004. [Bibliography: Pierce (2).] See CAR TESTING; COMMISSION FOR TAXI REGULATION; HACKNEY.

taxidermy. See WILDLIFE DEALING.

taxing master. See TAXATION OF COSTS.

TD. [Teachta Dála.] A member of Dáil Éireann (qv). A TD who is returned in an election as a member for two or more constituencies, must declare for one: Electoral Act 1992, s 35. A TD may voluntarily resign his membership by notice in writing to the Chairman of the Dáil; it takes effect on receipt by the Chairman (EA 1992, s 34). A person is disqualified from membership of the Dáil unless he is a citizen and has reached 21 years of age, or where he is of unsound mind or an undischarged bankrupt or where he is undergoing a sentence of imprisonment as specified (EA 1992, s 41). See DUAL MANDATE; ELECTION EXPENSES; POLITICAL DONATION; SEVERANCE PAY; UTTERANCE.

teacher. Means: (a) a person who has achieved, before a particular date, the qualifications required by the Minister for employment as a teacher in a recognised school, or (b) a person who is eligible for registration under regulations made by the Teaching Council: Teaching Council Act 2001. The general aim of the legislation is: (a) to promote teaching as a profession and the professional development of teachers; (b) to maintain and improve the quality of teaching in the State; (c) to provide for the establishment of standards for education and training of teachers; (d) to provide for the registration and regulation of teachers; (e) to enhance professional standards and competence; and (f) to establish a *Teaching Council* which has a major role in achieving these aims.

In a particular case, the court held that the Vocational Education (Amendment) Act 1944, s 7 did not give the Minister power to suspend payment of the salary of a teacher on the grounds of unreasonable behaviour or otherwise: *Carr v Minister for Education* [2001] 2 ILRM 272, SC and [2000] ELR 57 and 78, SC. Also it has been held that there are sufficiently close ties and controls exercised by the Department of Education in relation to individual teachers that the Department is the 'employer' for the purposes of the Payment of Wages Act 1991: *Sullivan v Department of Education* [1998] ELR 217, EAT.

An interactive website for students, teachers and parents was launched in February 2002 which provides online tuition in science and business studies: see *www.skoool.ie*. See also *Greally v Minister for Education* [1995] 3 IR 481, HC; [1999] 1 IR 1 and ELR 106, HC; *Loscher v Mount Temple Comprehensive School* [1996] ELR 98, CC; *Hanrahan v St Vincent's College* [1996] ELR 138, EO; *Hanly v Mayo VEC* [1999] ELR 10, EAT; *Moore v Board of Management* [2001] ELR 209, EAT; *Moore v Holy Child National School* [2003] ELR 82, CC. See FITNESS TO TEACH; SCHOOL.

teacher, language qualification. The compulsory requirement of an Irish language qualification for a vocational teacher was upheld by the European Court of Justice, which decided that the nature of the post justified a linguistic requirement and consequently there was no discrimination: *Groeher v Minister for Education (ECJ)* [1990] ILRM 335. Any requirement for teachers in primary and post-primary schools to have proficiency in the Irish language, does not infringe equality legislation: Employment Equality Act 1998,

s 36(3). See ACADEMIC STAFF; CORPORAL PUNISHMENT; SCHOOL AUTHORITY'S DUTY.

technology fund. A fund established to provide further financial resources for education and training, particularly in the fields of science and technology: Scientific and Technological Education (Investment) Fund Acts 1997 and 1998. See also Finance Act 1999, s 37.

teeming and lading. Term used to describe the irregular interference by a person with the moneys of another. It come in many forms, some of which may amount to improper professional behaviour and others may constitute an offence eg: (a) using moneys from a client account in an accounting period and refunding the money to the account before the end of the accounting period, or (b) misappropriation of cash remittances from customers and using amounts from later customers to fill the gap left by the earlier misappropriation. In the commercial area, the risk signs for *teeming and lading* include: one person handling cash and cheques and also entering details in the accounts, this person not taking holidays and never sick, being secretive about their work, having more money than might be expected, and the existence of timing differences between when a company says it paid and when it gets entered in the records. See *Thoroughbred Breeders' Association of South Africa v Price Waterhouse* 416/99 ZASCA 66 (1 June 2001), Supreme Court of SA. In the discipline of a solicitor, the Law Society reported that he had systematically falsified the book of accounts by means of 'teeming and lading' of clients' moneys: *Law Society Gazette* (December 2003) 44. See ACCOUNTS, SOLICITOR.

telecommunications regulator. Formerly, the Director of Telecommunications Regulation, established by the Telecommunications (Miscellaneous Provisions) Act 1996. The creation of the office was and is part of the liberalisation of the rapidly changing telecommunications industry. EU Commission Directives have accelerated the process. The office of Director of Telecommunications Regulation was abolished in 2002 and replaced by the Commission for Communications Regulation: Communications Regulation Act 2002.

The Minister may designate a company to be licensed by the Commission to construct and operate the *digital* terrestrial television infrastructure: Broadcasting

Act 2001, ss 7–8. See BROADCASTING COMMISSION OF IRELAND.

The once state-owned 'Telecom Éireann' became a plc as 'Eircom' in 1999, the privatisation and floatation having been made possible under the Postal and Telecommunications Services (Amendment) Act 1999.

The High Court has ruled that there is no obligation to supply air time to unlicensed mobile telephone service operators: *Meridian Communications Ltd v Eircell Ltd* [1999] ITLR (18th October) HC. See *Orange v Director of Telecommunications* [1999] 2 ILRM 81, HC; [2000] 4 IR 136, HC and [2000] 4 IR 159, SC; *Zockoll Group Ltd v Telecom Éireann* [1998] 3 IR 287, HC. See website: *www.odtr.ie*. [Bibliography: Corbet & Hederman.] See COMMISSION FOR COMMUNICATIONS REGULATION; PRIVACY IN TELECOMMUNICATIONS.

telegraph. It is an offence to damage telegraphs or prevent or obstruct telegraphic communications: Malicious Damage Act 1861, s 37 as amended by Criminal Damage Act 1991, s 14(2)(a). [Bibliography: Hall.]

telemedicine. The use of technology to practise medicine where the doctor and patient are not physically present together. 'Telemedicine allows doctors to practise medicine from a distance even across national boundaries using telecommunication systems such as telephone, internet and video link. Doctors providing telemedicine services to patients in Ireland must be registered with the Medical Council. In certain circumstances, doctors in Ireland will consult with colleagues abroad; this is acceptable provided the overseas doctor is licensed in the jurisdiction in which he or she practises and is currently in good standing. When providing telemedicine services, doctors must pay attention to issues such as record keeping and confidentiality as well as the training, competence, authorisation, legislation and indemnity required to practise telemedicine in any jurisdiction.': Medical Council, *A Guide to Ethical Conduct and Behaviour* (6th edn, 2004) para 10.6.

telephone services. See LIABILITY, STATUTORY EXEMPTIONS FROM; OLD AGE; PRIVACY IN TELECOMMUNICATIONS; THIRD GENERATION; UNSOLICITED CALL.

telephone tapping. It is an offence without lawful authority to intercept a telephone message, or to disclose the substance of a message which has been intercepted: Postal and Telecommunications Act 1983, s 98 as amended by Interception of Postal Packets and Telecommunications Messages (Regulations) Act 1993, s 13. *Intercept* means listen to, or record by any means, in the course of its transmission, a telecommunications message; it does not include listening or recording which is consented to by either the person making the telephone call or by the person intended to receive the message (PTA 1983, s 98(5) as amended by IPPTM(R)A 1993, s 13(3); see also IPPTM(R)A 1993, s 1).

The Minister may give an authorisation of interceptions but only for the purpose of criminal investigation or in the interests of the security of the State (IPPTM(R)A 1993, ss 2, 4 and 5) and only in response to an application for an authorisation from the Commissioner of the Garda Síochána or the Chief of Staff of the Defence Forces, as appropriate (IPPTM(R)A 1993, s 6).

There is provision for a Complaints Referee to investigate an alleged interception and to quash an authorisation, to direct the destruction of any copy of the communication intercepted, and/or to make a recommendation on compensation (IPPTM(R)A 1993, s 9). There is provision also for a review from time to time of the operation of the 1993 Act by a judge of the High Court (IPPTM(R)A 1993, s 8). It has been held that an interception of a telephone call which is unlawful cannot become lawful on the basis of what is heard during it: *DPP v Dillon* [2002] FL 6920, CCA and [2003] 1 ILRM 531. See also ARRESTED PERSON, COMMUNICATIONS FROM; HARASSMENT; PRIVACY.

television broadcast. [Bibliography: Hall.] See BROADCAST; MAJOR EVENT; TELEVISION PROGRAMME SERVICE.

television dealer. A person who by trade or business, sells television sets by wholesale or retail, or lets such sets on hire or hire-purchase: Wireless Telegraphy Act 1972, s 1(1). Such dealers are required to make returns to the Minister on sales and lettings: Broadcasting and Wireless Telegraphy Act 1988, s 10.

television licence. A licence granted by the Minister to a person to keep and have possession of a television set in any specified place in the State or in any specified vehicle, ship or aircraft: Wireless Telegraphy Act 1926, s 5. It is an offence for a person to have an unlicensed television set: Broadcasting and Wireless Telegraphy Act 1988, s 12. The television licence fee is €152 per annum from 1 January 2004, payable to An Post: Television Licences Regulations 2002, SI No 608 of 2002, as amended by SI No 720 of 2003. See OLD AGE.

television link. Provision has been made to enable witnesses to give evidence by live television link in *criminal cases* involving physical or sexual abuse: Criminal Evidence Act 1992, ss 12–13 as amended by Child Trafficking and Pornography Act 1998, s 10. A witness may give evidence in this manner if the court permits; however, if the witness is under 17 years of age (or is mentally handicapped) the witness is entitled to give such evidence unless the court sees good reason to the contrary (CEA 1992, s 13(1)). The jurisdiction of the court to allow evidence to be given by way of television link does not require a prior finding that the person involved had a mental handicap: *O'Sullivan v Hamill* [1999] 2 IR 9, HC. An intermediary may be used to convey questions to the witness (CEA 1992, s 14). There is also provision in any criminal proceeding for the giving of evidence by a person who is outside the State through a live television link with the permission of the court (CEA 1992, s 29).

Evidence was given for the first time in the Central Criminal Court, by a doctor in a rape case, via a live satellite television link from Australia: *Irish Times*, 27 July 2000.

Apart from overseas witnesses, the purpose of the 1992 Act is to make it easier for victims and vulnerable witnesses to give evidence. The witness gives evidence from a witness room and does not have to be in the presence of the accused when recounting the facts of the offence. Wigs and gowns are not worn by judges and lawyers when the TV link is being used.

In *criminal* proceedings on indictment, the court may now permit a person to give evidence through a live television link where it is satisfied that the person is likely to be in fear or subject to intimidation otherwise: Criminal Justice Act 1999, s 39. For amendments to CEA 1992, ss 5, 7, 13, 15, 16, see CJA 1999, ss 18–20.

Evidence in extradition proceedings may be given by a person outside the State through a live television link, with the permission of the court: Criminal Evidence Act 1992, s 29 as amended by Extradition (European Union Conventions) Act 2001, s 24.

In *civil* proceedings concerning the welfare of a child, the court may hear evidence from a child through a live television link; questions to the child may be put through an intermediary: Children Act 1997, ss 19–22. The evidence must be video-recorded and the evidence may be given within or outside the State. The proceedings may also be concerning the welfare of a person who is of full age but who has a mental disability to such an extent that it is not reasonably possible for the person to live independently (CA 1997, s 20(b)).

There is no constitutional right to 'confrontation' as would require in all circumstances that the evidence of a witness be given in the physical presence of an accused; the giving of evidence through a live television link is not unfair and does not amount to an interference with an accused's right to a fair trial: *Donnelly v Ireland* [1998] 1 ILRM 401, SC and [1998] 1 IR 321, SC.

In *commercial proceedings* (qv) the judge may allow a witness to give evidence, whether within or outside the State, through a live video link or by other means: RSC Ord 63A, r 23 inserted by Rules of the Superior Courts (Commercial Proceedings) 2004, SI No 2 of 2004. Evidence so given is to be recorded by video or otherwise as the judge may direct. See *White v Ireland* [1995] 2 IR 268, HC. See DCR 1997 Ord 62, r 22. [Bibliography: Healy.] See CHILD, EVIDENCE OF; LEGAL AID; IDENTIFICATION PARADE; VIDEO RECORDING; VIDEO-CONFERENCE; VISUAL IDENTIFICATION.

television programme service. A service which comprises a compilation of audio-visual programme material of any description and is transmitted or relayed by means of wireless telegraphy directly or indirectly for reception by the general public: Radio and Television Act 1988, s 2(1). This Act provides for the Independent Radio and Television Commission (now called the *Broadcasting Commission of Ireland*) to arrange for the provision of one television programme service additional to that provided by RTÉ (RTA 1988, s 4).

The Commission is required to ensure that the service in its programming is responsive to the interests and concerns of the whole community; upholds the democratic values enshrined in the 1937 Constitution; includes a reasonable proportion of news and current affairs programmes; and has regard to the formation of public awareness and understanding of the values and traditions of other countries, particularly those of the EC (RTA 1988, s 18(3)). See also Broadcasting Act 1990, s 6. For licensing provision for the purposes of retransmission of programme services in the UHF television bands, see SI No 675 of 2003. See BROADCASTING COMMISSION OF IRELAND; MAJOR EVENT.

temperamental incompatibility. Not a ground for granting a nullity decree in marriage; however a purported marriage may be null and void from the outset by reason of elements of immaturity in the character and temperament of both parties and an inability to form and sustain a normal marriage relationship: *PC v VC* [1990] 2 IR 91.

Temple Bar. Provision has been made for the transfer of the Minister's shareholding in Temple Bar Properties Ltd to Dublin City Council: Local Government Act 2001, ss 238–242. See website: *www.templebar.ie*.

temporary dwellings. A temporary dwelling means any: (a) tent, or (b) van or other conveyance, or (c) shed, hut or similar structure, or vessel on inland waters used for human habitation or constructed or adapted for such use: Local Government (Sanitary Services) Act 1948, s 2(1). A sanitary authority may by order prohibit the erection or retention of temporary dwellings on any land or water (LG(SS)A 1948, s 31). See *Listowel UDC v McDonagh* 105 ILTR 99; *Gammell v Dublin Co Council* [1983] ILRM 413.

It is an offence to erect, place, or retain, without lawful authority a temporary dwelling on a national road, motorway, busway or protected road: Roads Act 1993, s 69. See TRAVELLER; TRESPASS, OFFENCE OF.

temporary event. See EVENT.

temporary release. See RELEASE, TEMPORARY.

tenancy. The relationship of a *tenant* (qv) to that land which he holds from another. A 'tenancy' includes a periodic tenancy and a tenancy for a fixed term, whether oral or in writing or implied, and, where the context so admits, includes a sub-tenancy and a tenancy or sub-tenancy that has been terminated: Residential Tenancies Act 2004, s 5(1). A 'tenancy agreement' includes an

oral tenancy agreement (RTA 2004, s 4(1)). A 'contract of tenancy' does not include an agreement to create a tenancy (RTA 2004, s 4(1). [Bibliography: Bland (2).] See LEASE; PART 4 TENANCY; SUB-TENANT.

tenancy, controlled. See CONTROLLED DWELLING.

tenancy, fixed term. A tenant of a *fixed term tenancy* is entitled to terminate the tenancy where the landlord has refused consent to an assignment or sub-letting, despite anything to the contrary in the lease or tenancy agreement: Residential Tenancies Act 2004, s 186. The notice period required is that specified in the Act even if the lease or tenancy agreement provides for a greater notice period. A tenant of a *fixed term tenancy* with a period of at least six months, who intends to remain in occupation after the expiry of the period, must give notice to the landlord between three months and one month before the expiry of the period (RTA 2004, s 195). If the tenant fails to give notice, the landlord may be awarded damages for any loss or damage suffered. See PART 4 TENANCY.

tenancy, termination notice. Under recent legislation, a tenancy of a dwelling may not be terminated by the landlord or the tenant by means of a notice of forfeiture, a re-entry or any other process or procedure not provided by Part 5 (notice periods and other procedural requirements): Residential Tenancies Act 2004, s 58. A notice of termination to be valid must: (a) be in writing, (b) be signed by the landlord or his authorised agent or, as appropriate, the tenant, (c) specify the date of service of it, (d) be in such form (if any) as may be prescribed, (e) if the duration of the tenancy is a period of more than six months, state (where the termination is by the landlord) the reason for the termination, (f) specify the termination date, that is to say, the day (stating the month and year in which it falls): (i) on which the tenancy will terminate, and (ii) on or before which (in the case of a termination by the landlord) the tenant must vacate possession of the dwelling concerned, (and indicating that the tenant has the whole of the 24 hours of the termination date to vacate possession), and (g) state that any issue as to the validity of the notice or the right of the landlord or tenant, as appropriate, to serve it must be referred to the *Private Residential Tenancies Board* under Part 6 (dispute resolution) of the Act within 28 days from the date of receipt of it (RTA 2004, s 62).

Gradated minimum notice periods are specified, linked to the duration of the tenancy eg: (a) where termination is by the landlord – duration of tenancy of less than six months (notice period of 28 days); six or more months (35 days); one year or more (42 days); two years or more (56 days); three years or more (84 days); four years or more years (112 days); and (b) termination by the tenant – duration of tenancy of less than six months (notice period of 28 days); six or more months (35 days); one year or more (42 days); two or more years (56 days) (RTA 2004, s 66).

Shorter notice periods apply where the termination of the tenancy by the landlord is due to the tenant's failure to comply with the tenancy obligations (RTA 2004, s 67). In the case of anti-social behaviour falling within the definition in s 17(1)(a) and (b), or behaviour that is threatening to the dwelling or property containing the dwelling, the notice period is seven days. For other unremedied breaches of the tenant's obligations, the notice period is 28 days and where termination is for the non-payment of rent, the notice can be served once 14 days have elapsed from the service of notice to the tenant seeking the rent due.

Shorter notice periods also apply where the termination of the tenancy by the tenant is due to the landlord's failure to comply with the tenancy obligations (RTA 2004, s 68). Where the landlord has been notified of the breach and has failed to remedy it within a reasonable time, the notice to be given by the tenant is 28 days. Where a breach by the landlord of a tenant's right to peaceful occupation involves behaviour that poses an imminent danger of death or serious injury or danger to the fabric of the dwelling, the notice period is seven days.

It is an offence for a person who serves an invalid termination notice to do any act, in reliance on the notice, that affects adversely, or is calculated to affect adversely, any interest of the person on whom the notice is served (RTA 2004, s 74). It is a defence to show that the defendant neither knew nor could reasonably be expected to have known of the existence of any fact that gave rise to the invalidity of the notice concerned.

A provision of a lease or tenancy agreement is void where it could be reasonably inferred that the purpose of the provision is to facilitate a party being at all times in a position to terminate the lease or tenancy on the grounds of non-compliance by the other party with the provision in question (RTA 2004, s 184). For a deemed termination of a tenancy, see RTA 2004, s 194.

Previously, many tenancies could, under common law, be terminated on one week's notice ie by a *notice to quit* served on a tenant by a landlord, or a *notice of surrender* served on a landlord by a tenant. Now a notice terminating certain tenancies outside the remit of the 2004 Act, must be in writing and served not less than four weeks before the date on which the notice is to take effect: Housing (Miscellaneous Provisions) Act 1992, s 16. The s 16 requirement applies to lettings of residential accommodation; it does not apply to holiday lettings, tenancies tied to employment, or tenancies made *bona fide* for the temporary convenience of a landlord or tenant. The parties may agree a longer period of notice; in the absence of such agreement, the minimum notice periods (subject to H(MP)A 1992, s 16) are provided by common law as follows: (a) *tenancy from year to year* – half a year's notice (183 days) expiring on the anniversary of the commencement of the tenancy; (b) *monthly tenancy* – one month's notice expiring on a gale day; (c) *quarterly tenancy* – three months' notice expiring on a gale day. RTA 2004, s 193(e) provides that H(MP)A 1992, s 16 does not apply to a dwelling to which the RTA 2004 applies. See DWELLING; LEASE, DETERMINATION OF; PART 4 TENANCY, TERMINATION OF; SUB-TENANT; TENANCY TRIBUNAL.

tenancy at will. A lease where the lessor lets land to another to hold at the will of the lessor; the lessee is known as a *tenant at will*. Either party may terminate the tenancy at any time. See *Bellew v Bellew* [1982] IR 447. The Law Reform Commission has recommended that a *tenancy at will* should not be regarded as creating the relationship of landlord and tenant and that arrangements involving the occupation of land, free from rent for indefinite periods, should be regarded as a form of licence: *Consultation Paper on General Law of Landlord and Tenant Law* (LRC CP 28, 2003) para 18.07. [Bibliography: Wylie (4).] See LEASE.

tenancy by sufferance. Arises where a tenant holds on after the lawful title under which he previously held the tenancy has expired; he has no estate in the land and is just not a trespasser. The Law Reform Commission has reached the preliminary conclusion that a *tenancy by sufferance* does not create the relationship of landlord and tenant: *Consultation Paper on General Law of Landlord and Tenant Law* (LRC CP 28, 2003) para 18.08. See LEASE.

tenancy dispute. Includes references to a *disagreement* and, unless the context does not admit of such a construction, a *complaint*: Residential Tenancies Act 2004, s 75. A *'disagreement'* is deemed to include: (a) any issue arising between the parties with regard to the compliance by either with his obligations as landlord or tenant under the tenancy, (b) any matter with regard to the legal relations between the parties that either or both of them requires to be determined (for example, whether the tenancy has been validly terminated), and, without prejudice to the generality of the foregoing, is deemed to include a claim by the landlord for arrears of rent to which the tenant has not indicated he disputes the landlord's entitlement but which it is alleged the tenant has failed to pay.

Proceedings may not be instituted in any court in respect of a dispute that may be referred to the *Private Residential Tenancies Board* for resolution, unless: (a) damages of more than €20,000 is being claimed, or (b) recovery of arrears of rent or other charges of more than €60,000 (or such lesser amount of €20,000 as is applicable under certain circumstances) is being claimed (RTA 2004, s 182). Reference of disputes to the Board may be for the purposes of mediation, determination by an adjudicator, or determination by the Tenancy Tribunal.

Parties to a tenancy of a dwelling are entitled to refer a dispute between them to the Board, as is a licensee who has been refused consent to become a tenant, and as is a third party affected by a landlord's failure to enforce the obligations of a tenancy (RTA 2004, ss 76–77). For a non-exhaustive list of the types of disputes and complaints which may be referred to the Board, see RTA 2004, s 78. A dispute relating to the validity of a termination notice must be referred to the Board within 28 days of the receipt of the notice (RTA 2004, s 80). The Board may extend the time for referral of a dispute to it for resolution where the applicant shows good

cause for the extension (RTA 2004, s 88). An appeal lies to the Circuit Court against a refusal to extend the time.

The referring party may withdraw the matter referred to the Board at any time, but may have costs and expenses awarded against him, if the other party objects to the withdrawal (RTA 2004, s 82). The Board has a right not to deal with certain references eg where statute-barred or trivial or vexatious (RTA 2004, s 84).

When a dispute is referred to the Board, it initially communicates with the parties with a view to having the matter resolved by agreement; the Board may include an indication of the typical outcome of issues of the kind concerned (RTA 2004, s 92). If agreement is not reached, the Board invites the parties to resolve the matter through mediation and if they agree the Board arranges mediation by a person from its panel of mediators (RTA 2004, s 93). If any party rejects the offer of mediation or fails to respond to the invitation, the Board arranges for the matter to be the subject of adjudication by a person from its panel of adjudicators (RTA 2004, s 93(3)). If the Board considers that mediation is not appropriate, it may arrange adjudication or refer the dispute to the Tenancy Tribunal (RTA 2004, s 94). See ADJUDICATORS IN TENANCY DISPUTES; ARBITRATION AGREEMENT; DETERMINATION ORDER; MEDIATION IN TENANCY DISPUTES; TENANCY TRIBUNAL; TITLE.

tenancy in common. The ownership of land by two or more persons where they have undivided possession but where there is no right of survivorship; the interest of a tenant in common passes on death as part of his estate. Tenants in common need not have an equal share; they need not claim under the same interest, and their interests need not have been created at the same time. Equity favoured tenancy in common as it regarded the right of survivorship of *joint tenancies* to be unfair.

In a *court sale* of land, subject to a *tenancy in common*, the court is not the vendor; the solicitor having carriage of sale is agent for the parties to the suit and all the parties are bound by the sale: *Bank of Ireland v Smith* [1966] IR 646; *Re Bannister, Broad v Munton* [1879] 12 Ch D 131. Notice to terminate such a court sale cannot be given without the authority of all the parties or the approval of the court, as the parties are the vendors: *Blackall v Blackall* [2000]

ITLR (24 July) HC. See DEATH, SIMULTA-
NEOUS; JOINT TENANCY.

Tenancy Tribunal. One or more independent tribunals, each with three members
from the *Disputes Resolution Committee* of
the *Private Residential Tenancies Board* and
appointed by the Board: Residential Tenancies Act 2004, ss 102–103. The Tribunal
makes determinations on disputes: (a)
which have been referred to it directly by
the Board without prior mediation or adjudication, (b) which have been referred to it
by the Board following mediation which
has not resolved the matter, and (c) by way
of an appeal from the determination of an
adjudicator (RTA 2004, s 104).

Each of the parties is entitled to be heard
at the hearing and to be represented and to
present evidence and witnesses before the
Tribunal (RTA 2004, s 104(6)). The Tribunal may require that the evidence of a
witness before it be given on oath (RTA
2004, s 105). There is provision for cross-
examination of witnesses and they enjoy the
same immunities and privileges as witnesses in the High Court. Proceedings
before the Tribunal must be in public, but
it may direct that the identity of the parties
not be disclosed (RTA 2004, s 106).

In the case of an appeal from the determination of an adjudicator, the Tribunal
may have regard to the adjudicator's report
(RTA 2004, s 104(7)). Unless it decides
not to deal with a reference to it, the
Tribunal is required to make a determination in relation to the dispute and to notify
the Board of that determination (RTA
2004, ss 85 and 108). A member of the
Tribunal is empowered to enter and inspect
any dwelling to which a dispute relates by
giving at least 24 hours' notice of that
intention (RTA 2004, s 111).

The Tribunal is empowered to make one
or more of the following declarations or
directions: (a) a direction that a specified
amount of rent or other charge be paid on,
or on and from, or by a specified date, (b) a
declaration as to whether or not an amount
of rent set under a tenancy of a dwelling
complies with s 19(1) (*market rent* – and if
the declaration is that that amount does not
so comply, the declaration must be accompanied by an indication by the Tribunal as
to what amount, in its opinion, would comply), (c) a direction as to the return or
payment, in whole or in part, of the
amount of a deposit, (d) a direction that a
specified amount of damages or costs or

both be paid, (e) a direction that a dwelling
be quitted by a specified date, (f) a declaration as to the validity or otherwise of a
notice of termination of a tenancy, (g) a
declaration with regard to the right to
return to, or continue in, occupation of a
dwelling (and such a declaration may
include provision to the effect that any
period of interruption in possession that
has occurred is to be disregarded for one or
more purposes), (h) a declaration that a
term of a lease or tenancy agreement is
void by reason of s 184 (voidance provisions to facilitate terminations), (i) in the
special circumstances of a dispute heard, a
direction that the whole or part of the costs
or expenses incurred by the Tribunal in
dealing with the dispute be paid by one or
more of the parties (RTA 2004, s 115).

The amount, other than costs or
expenses of whatsoever kind, that the Tribunal may direct to be paid to a party must
not exceed: (a) if solely of damages –
€20,000, (b) if solely by way of arrears of
rent or other charges €20,000 or an amount
equal to twice the annual rent of the dwelling concerned, whichever is the higher, but
subject to a maximum of €60,000 (RTA
2004, s 115(3)).

The Tribunal may also give such directions as it thinks appropriate for the purpose of providing relief of an interim
nature, while making clear that that relief
may not necessarily be the relief provided
for by the final determination (RTA 2004,
s 117). See ADJUDICATORS IN TENANCY
DISPUTES; ARBITRATION AGREEMENT;
DETERMINATION ORDER; MEDIATION IN
TENANCY DISPUTES; NOTICE TO QUIT;
POSSESSION, ORDER FOR; RENT; RENT
ARREARS; SUB-TENANT; TENANCY DIS-
PUTE; TITLE.

tenant. Means the person for the time being
entitled to the occupation of a dwelling
under a tenancy and, where the context so
admits, includes a person who has ceased
to be entitled to that occupation by reason
of the termination of the tenancy: Residential Tenancies Act 2004, s 5(1). [Bibliogra-
phy: Deale.] See LEASE; COVENANT;
MULTIPLE TENANTS; RENT BOOK; RENTED
HOUSE, STANDARD OF; SMALL CLAIM;
TENANCY, TERMINATION NOTICE.

tenant, business. See BUSINESS TENANT.

tenant, obligations of. A tenant of a dwelling is required: (a) to pay to the landlord
the rent on the day it falls due for payment
and other charges and taxes in accordance

with the lease or tenancy agreement, (b) to ensure that no act or omission by the tenant results in there being non-compliance by the landlord with relevant obligations (including SI No 147 of 1993), (c) to allow the landlord access to the dwelling, at reasonable intervals, for the purpose of inspection, (d) to notify the landlord of any defect in the dwelling that requires to be repaired; (e) to allow access for repairs to be carried out, (f) not to do anything which causes the dwelling to deteriorate beyond reasonable wear and tear, (g) to restore the dwelling, as the landlord may reasonably require, if it has deteriorated beyond reasonable wear and tear, or to defray the costs incurred by the landlord in so doing, (h) not to behave or allow others *behave in a way which is anti-social*, (i) not to act or allow others to act in a way which would invalidate or increase the premium on the landlord's insurance, and to pay to the landlord any such premium increase, (j) not to assign or sub-let the tenancy without the written consent of the landlord, (k) not to *alter or improve* the dwelling without the written consent of the landlord, (l) not to use the dwelling, or cause it to be used, for any purpose other than as a dwelling without the written consent of the landlord, (m) to notify the landlord of the identity of each person who resides ordinarily in the dwelling: Residential Tenancies Act 2004, s 16.

No provision of any lease, tenancy agreement, contract or other agreement may operate to vary, modify or restrict in any way the obligations under s 16 (RTA 2004, s 18(1)). However, obligations additional to those specified in s 16 may be imposed on the tenant but only if consistent with the 2004 Act (RTA 2004, s 18(3)).

The landlord has a discretion to withhold consent in relation to change of use, assignment or sub-letting, but must not unreasonably withhold consent in relation to repairing, painting and decorating. The landlord is entitled to be reimbursed by the tenant for any costs or expenses reasonably incurred by him in deciding upon a request for consent (RTA 2004, s 17(3)).

'Alter or improve' includes altering a locking system on a door giving entry to the dwelling (RTA 2004, s 17(1)). 'Behave in a way which is anti-social' means: (a) engage in behaviour that constitutes the commission of an offence, being an offence the commission of which is reasonably likely to affect directly the well-being or welfare of

others, (b) engage in behaviour that causes or could cause fear, danger, injury, damage or loss to any person living, working or otherwise lawfully in the dwelling concerned or its vicinity and includes violence, intimidation, coercion, harassment or obstruction of, or threats to, any such person, or (c) engage, persistently, in behaviour that prevents or interferes with the peaceful occupation of that or a neighbourhood dwelling (RTA 2004, s 17(1)). See MANAGEMENT COMPANY; PRIVATE RESIDENTIAL TENANCIES BOARD; RENT DEPOSIT; RENT REVIEW; LANDLORD, OBLIGATIONS OF.

tenant, statutory. A tenant who is given statutory protection eg security of tenure is given in business leases by providing for a renewal of such a lease at a marketable rent: Landlord and Tenant (Amendment) Act 1980. In a particular case, the use of a multiplier rent review clause was held to be invalid as it was designed as an ingenious method of circumventing the right of a tenant to a renewal of the lease: *Bank of Ireland v Fitzmaurice* [1989] ILRM 452. The statutory protection given to certain tenants by the Rent Restrictions Act 1960 was declared unconstitutional as an unjust attack on the landlord's property rights: *Blake v Attorney-General* [1982] IR 117. See CONTROLLED DWELLING.

tenant for life. A tenant for life is a trustee for the remainderman pursuant to Settled Land Act 1882, s 53; this trust arises by operation of Statute and cannot be removed by will: *Roberts v Kenny* [2000] 1 IR 33, HC. See SETTLEMENT.

tenant in tail. See FEE TAIL.

tenant pur autre vie. [Tenant for the life of another.] See LIFE ESTATE.

tenant purchase scheme. A scheme since 1966 whereby the tenant of a dwelling could purchase the dwelling from a local authority; the sale is effected by a *transfer order*, which may be subject to *special conditions*, and since 1978 was required to vest in the tenant the fee simple: Housing Act 1966, s 90; Landlord and Tenant (Ground Rents) Acts 1978, s 4 and 1987.

A *transfer order* normally provides for payment of the purchase money by instalments and may be secured by way of mortgage (qv) or charge (qv). The *special conditions* may include: (a) a requirement that the dwelling be occupied as a normal place of residence by the purchaser; and (b) a prohibition on the sale of the dwelling without the consent of the housing authority (HA 1966, s 89). Since 1988, tenant purchase schemes did not require a housing authority to put the dwelling into good structural condition before selling it to a tenant: Housing Act 1988, s 23.

From 1992, where a dwelling is occupied by a tenant, the housing authority may sell it, in the state of repair and condition existing at the date of sale, to: (a) the tenant in accordance with a *purchase scheme*, or (b) to another housing authority, or (c) to a voluntary housing body: Housing (Miscellaneous Provisions) Act 1992, s 26(1) substituting a new s 90 in the Housing Act 1966. Where the dwelling is not occupied by a tenant, the housing authority may sell the dwelling to any person (HA 1966, s 90(1)(b) as inserted). There is no warranty given as the state of repair or condition or its fitness for human habitation (HA 1966, s 90(8) as inserted). Also the housing authority has no liability after the date of the sale for any charges relating to the dwelling eg provision of services or insurance (HA 1966, s 90(6A) inserted by Housing (Miscellaneous Provisions) Act 2002, s 15).

Generally the sale of a house to tenants must continue to grant freehold title but, where appropriate, a leasehold interest may be conveyed in the case of a transfer to an approved voluntary body or a disposal by means of a *shared ownership lease*. Special conditions may be attached by the housing authority on the sale of a house including restrictions on resale or mortgaging. See FLAT.

tender. (1) An offer of performance in accordance with the terms of a contract eg an offer by a debtor to his creditor of the exact amount of the debt. If such a tender is made but the other party refuses to accept it, the party tendering is freed from liability under the contract if the tender was made under such circumstances that the other party had a reasonable opportunity of examining the goods or the money tendered. However, a tender of money does not discharge the debt unless it is followed by payment of the sum tendered into court on action being brought. A tender of money must be unconditional although it may be made *under protest* (qv) so as to reserve the right of the payer to dispute the amount. The debtor must meet any contractual terms set as to the place, time and manner of payment: *Morrow v Carty* [1957] NI 174. See LEGAL TENDER.

(2) An offer for sale by tender eg where a manufacturer or local authority issues advertisements soliciting tenders for the supply of goods, the advertisement is an *invitation to treat*, and the tender, setting out the terms upon which the supplier is prepared to contract, constitutes an offer. Usually the tender document sets out the terms of the contract. There is no obligation on the manufacturer or local authority to accept any of the tenders unless it has undertaken in the statement inviting tenders to accept the lowest.

(3) Payment into court of a sum of money, offered before action, in satisfaction of a claim, which acts as a defence to the action. See RSC Ord 27, rr 3 and 9, as amended by SI No 63 of 2004. See LODGMENT IN COURT.

tender offer. Means an invitation made by a person by public advertisement to holders of a class of securities of a relevant company to tender securities of that company, up to a stated number, for purchase by that person, on terms stipulated in the advertisement: Takeover Rules 2001, Part A, r 2.1(a). Certain tender offers are subject to the Substantial Acquisition Rules 2001 (r 7).

Generally, 50% of shareholders by value must accept for the offeror to gain control, and 80% of shareholders by value must accept to allow the offeror to acquire compulsorily the minority shareholders pursuant to the Companies Act 1963, s 204. See SHARES, COMPULSORY PURCHASE OF; RECONSTRUCTION OF COMPANY; SUBSTANTIAL ACQUISITION.

tenement. A thing which could be held by common law tenure, ie land. For the purposes of statutory protection of business tenants (qv), a *tenement* means a premises consisting of a defined portion of a building, or of land covered wholly or partly by buildings where the land not covered by buildings is subsidiary and ancillary to the buildings; such premises must be held by the occupier on a tenancy and the letting must not have been made either for the temporary convenience of either party or be dependent on the continuance in any office, or employment, or appointment of the tenant: Landlord and Tenant (Amendment) Act 1980, s 5. A tenement in this context, excludes agricultural lettings.

tenendum. [To be held.]

tenor. The general import of a document or submission; the substance of some matter.

tenor, executor according to. See EXECUTOR ACCORDING TO THE TENOR.

tenure. The relationship between a tenant and his reversioner or landlord. The possession or holding of an office or position. The term or length of time an office or position lasts.

tenure, security of. A landlord cannot recover possession of a *controlled dwelling* without a court order; such an order will not be made unless the court considers it reasonable and one of the specified grounds for such an order is proved by the landlord: Housing (Private Rented Dwellings) Act 1982, s 16. These restrictions do not apply to service or employment lettings, or to lettings *bona fide* for the temporary convenience or to meet a temporary necessity of the landlord or the tenant, or to recovery by a local authority in exercise of their statutory powers (H(PRD)A 1982, ss 9 and 16; Housing Act 1966, ss 62(6), 66(17) and 118(1)). For recent security of tenure provisions in relation to tenancies of dwellings, see PART 4 TENANCY; MULTIPLE TENANTS; SUB-TENANTS. [Bibliography: Pearce & Mee.] See also BUSINESS TENANT; CONTROLLED DWELLING; LEASE, DETERMINATION OF; TENANCY, TERMINATION NOTICE.

teoranta, teo. [Limited.] See COMPANY, LIMITED.

term. (1) A fixed period of time for which a right is to be enjoyed or an obligation borne. (2) The period for which an estate is granted. (3) A provision, condition or limitation. (4) A provision in a contract which creates legal obligations.

term of patent. Formerly, the term of a patent ran for 16 years from the date of filing of a complete specification: Patents Act 1964, s 26. The term could be extended on the application of the patentee for a further term of five, or in exceptional cases ten years, on the grounds that the patentee has been inadequately remunerated for his patent (PA 1964, s 27). See *John Hilton v Controller of Patents* [1932] HC; *Re Smithkline Beckman Corp* [1984] HC; *Re Fisons Pharmaceuticals Ltd* [1984] ILRM 393; *Re Technobiotic Ltd* [1990] 2 IR 499, HC; *Re Sandoz Ltd* [1990] HC & [1991] HC. See RSC Ord 94, rr 26–44.

Since 1992, a patent takes effect from the date on which notice of its grant is published in the Patents Office Journal and,

subject to renewal fees being paid, remains in force for a period of 20 years beginning with the date of filing of the patent application: Patents Act 1992, s 36. There is no provision for an extension of the term. The term of a *short-term patent* (qv) is ten years. Patents granted under the 1964 Act are extended to 20 years unless they have already been extended pursuant to s 27 (PA 1992, s 5, Sch 1 para 2(2)). See Patent Rules 1992, SI No 179 of 1992, r 34.

terminally ill patient. See EUTHANASIA; DYING PATIENT; SERIOUSLY ILL PATIENT.

terminating society. Originally was a building society which by its rules was to terminate at a fixed date or when a result specified in its rules was attained e g Cork Mutual Benefit Terminating Society (1893): Building Societies Act 1874, s 5; since repealed and only of historical importance now. [Bibliography: Murdoch (2).] Contrast with PERMANENT SOCIETY.

termination of employment. In a particular case it was held that the date of termination of employment was the date the employee received his last pay package: *Reilly v An Post* [1992] ELR 129, CC. [Bibliography: Barry J.] See DISMISSAL OF EMPLOYEE; INJUNCTION.

termination of pregnancy. See ABORTION; ABORTION, MEDICAL GUIDELINES.

termination of tenancy. See PART 4 TENANCY, TERMINATION OF; TENANCY, TERMINATION NOTICE.

terminus a quo. [The starting point.] See *Barnaby (London) Ltd v Mullen* [1997] 2 ILRM 341, SC.

terminus ad quem. [The finishing point.]

terms of employment. The written statement which an employer is required to give to an employee, setting out the conditions under which he is employed e g name of employer, place of work, nature of work, duration, method of calculation of remuneration, hours of work, paid leave, sick leave, pension scheme, period of notice, reference to collective agreements, and the *pay reference period* selected by his employer: Terms of Employment (Information) Act 1994, s 3 as amended by National Minimum Wages Act 2000, s 44. A change in the terms of employment may only be achieved by *consensus ad idem*: *Brennan v Religious of the Sacred Heart* [2000] ELR 297, EAT.

The 1994 Act applies not only to contracts of service and of apprenticeship but also to contracts under which workers are supplied by employment agencies (TE(I)A 1994, s 1(1)). There is provision: (a) for complaints by an employee to a Rights Commissioner that the employer has contravened the 1994 Act, (b) for an appeal to the Employment Appeals Tribunal, and (c) for enforcement by the District Court of the determination of the Tribunal (TE(I)A 1994, ss 8–9). See DCR 1997 Ord 99B as amended by District Court (Terms of Employment Information) Rules 2003, SI No 409 of 2003.

A contract of employment is deemed to include a term giving a right to non-discriminatory *equal pay* for like work, and a gender and non-gender *equality clause*: Employment Equality Act 1998, ss 20–21, 30. See CONTRACT OF EMPLOYMENT; EQUALITY CLAUSE.

terra. [Land.]

territorial jurisdiction. See JURISDICTION.

territorial sea. The government may by order prescribe the charts which may be used for establishing the *territorial seas* of the State: Maritime Jurisdiction Act 1959, s 13; Maritime Jurisdiction Charts Order 1959, SI No 174 of 1959. See *People (DPP) v Van Onzen* [1996] 2 ILRM 387, CCA. See MARITIME JURISDICTION.

territorial waters. See MARITIME JURISDICTION.

terrorism. There is currently no definition of terrorism in Irish law. In the UK, 'terrorism' is defined as 'use of violence for political ends and includes the use of violence for the purpose of putting the public or any section of the public in fear': Emergency Provisions (Northern Ireland) Act 1978. The word 'terrorism' owes its origins to the Reign of Terror during the French Revolution and the use of the guillotine by the French revolutionaries.

Under draft legislation, provision is made to enhance the capacity of the State to address the problem of *international terrorism* following the events of 11 September, 2001: Criminal Justice (Terrorist Offences) Bill 2002. The Bill is intended to give effect to: (a) international conventions relating to the taking of hostages, the suppression of terrorist bombings, and the suppression of the financing of terrorism; (b) the EU framework decision on combating terrorism; and (c) the convention on the prevention and punishment of crimes against internationally protected persons, including diplomats. See 'Criminalising International Terrorism: The Criminal Justice (Terrorist

Offences) Bill 2002' by Niall Neligan BL in *Bar Review* (July 2004) 152.

Also under recent legislation, effect is given to the United Nations Convention for the Suppression of Unlawful Acts against the Safety of Maritime Navigation (1988) and the Protocol to that Convention for the Suppression of Unlawful Acts against the Safety of Fixed Platforms on the Continental Shelf (1988), the text of which was laid before the Dáil and Seanad on 11 November 2003: Maritime Security Act 2004. The Convention and Protocol are among a suite of international instruments against terrorism which member states of the United Nations are enjoined to implement as soon as possible. The Act creates specific offences against the safety of Irish ships and other ships which are in Irish territorial waters and against fixed platforms on the Continental Shelf (subject to imprisonment for life on conviction on indictment), and consequentially provides, on standard lines, for extra-territorial jurisdiction to cover offences committed outside the State in breach of the Convention or Protocol, the apprehension and detention of alleged offenders and handing them over to the appropriate authorities, extradition, bail, avoidance of double jeopardy and other necessary matters, on the model of provisions of the Criminal Justice (Terrorist Offences) Bill 2002, which Bill had not been enacted by 1 September 2004.

See Extradition (European Convention on Suppression of Terrorism) Act 1987 as amended by European Arrest Warrant Act 2003, s 51 and Sch, Pt B, art 2(2). See Financial Transfers (Counter Terrorism) Order 2003, SI No 134 of 2003; EC (Counter Terrorism Financial Sanctions) Regulations 2003, SI No 135 of 2003. See 'The Gunpowder Plot – the first act of modern terrorism' by Niall Neligan BL in *Bar Review* (March/April 2002). For prevention of terrorism in the UK, see Bibliography: Donohue L K; Walker UK. See EXTRADITION; JOINT INVESTIGATION TEAMS; POLICE CO-OPERATION; UNLAWFUL ORGANISATION.

test case. An action, the result of which will affect other similar cases which are not litigated. Contrast with REPRESENTATIVE ACTION.

test tube fertilisation. See EMBRYO IMPLANTATION.

testament. A will. A distinction is sometimes drawn between a *will* (a disposition of real property) and a *testament* (relating to personal property).

testamentary capacity. The ability in law to make a valid will e g having attained 18 years of age or having been married, being of *sound disposing mind* and having the *animus testandi* (qv): Succession Act 1965, s 77. In legal proceedings where it is alleged that a testator was not of sound mind, it is necessary to give particulars of any specific instance of delusion or mental incapacity: RSC Ord 19, r 6(1). As a matter of public policy there is a presumption of testamentary capacity: *In bonis Glynn dec'd* [1990] 2 IR 326.

A person who has been diagnosed as a paranoid schizophrenic can have testamentary capacity if he meets the test of a 'sound disposing mind' as defined in *Banks v Goodfellow* [1870] LR5 QB 549: *O'Donnell v O'Donnell* [1999] ITLR (3 May) HC. See Law Reform Commission, *Consultation Paper on Law and the Elderly* (LRC CP 23, 2003). [Bibliography: Keating.] See MINOR; SOUND DISPOSING MIND.

testamentary disposition. See DISPOSITION.

testamentary expenses. The expenses incurred in the proper performance of an executor's duties. Priority in payment out of a deceased's estate is given to funeral and testamentary expenses. See ADMINISTRATION OF ESTATES; EXECUTOR; INSOLVENT ESTATE.

testamentary freedom. The right of a person to dispose of his property by will according to his wishes. The State guarantees to pass no law attempting to abolish the general right to transfer, bequeath and inherit property: 1937 Constitution, art 43(1)(2). Testamentary freedom is now limited by the Succession Act 1965. See SPOUSE, LEGAL RIGHT OF; CHILD, PROVISION FOR.

testamentary guardian. A guardian appointed by a deed or will: Status of Children Act 1987, s 9. A person who is entitled to appoint a guardian of an infant may make the appointment by will notwithstanding that he has not the capacity to make a will i e notwithstanding that he has not attained the age of eighteen years or is or has not been married: Succession Act 1965, s 77(2).

testate. Having made a will. Contrast with INTESTACY.

testate succession. Devolution of property where the deceased left a will. [Bibliography: Keating.] See WILL; PROBATE.

testator/testatrix. A person, male/female, who makes a will. A person may be a testator notwithstanding that he might fall within the statutory definition of an intestate: *G(R) v PSG* [1981] HC. See EXECUTOR; INTESTACY.

testatum. The start of the operative part of a deed which usually begins: Now this Indenture witnesseth that, in pursuance of said Agreement, and in consideration of the sum of € ... .

teste meipso. [Witness myself.]

testimonium. The concluding clause in a deed or will by which the parties have signed their names in witness of what it contains eg: In witness whereof the parties hereto have hereunto set their respective hands and seals the day and year first above written.

testimony. The evidence of a witness given *viva voce* in court and offered as evidence of the truth of that which he asserts. There is provision for *perpetuating* testimony (qv). See OATH.

thatched roof. A grant is available for the renewal or repair of thatched roofs of houses; a higher level of grant is available for applicants who have a medical card: Housing (Improvement Grants) (Thatched Roofs) Regulations 2001, SI No 610 of 2001.

theatre. The King was empowered to grant *letters patent* to theatres in the city and county of Dublin: Dublin Stage Regulation Act 1786, s 1. Liquor licences to sell beer spirits and wine could be granted to such theatres established under a royal patent, or to any licensed theatre or other licensed *place of public entertainment*: Excise Act 1835, s 7. The Point Theatre in Dublin has been held to be a place of public entertainment within the meaning of s 7 and entitled to a liquor licence: *Point Exhibition v Revenue Commissioners* [1993] ILRM 621, HC. A *place of entertainment* need not afford seating to its patrons for a particular event: *Royal Dublin Society v Revenue Commissioners* [2000] 1 IR 270, SC. See *DPP v Tivoli Cinema Ltd* [1999] 2 ILRM 153, SC and 2 IR 260. See SEAT.

theft. It is an offence to *appropriate* property dishonestly without the consent of its owner and with the intention of *depriving* its owner of it: Criminal Justice (Theft and

Fraud Offences) Act 2001, s 4. 'Appropriate' in relation to property, means usurps, or adversely interferes with the proprietary rights of the owner of the property (CJ(TFO)A 2001, s 4(5)). 'Depriving' means temporarily or permanently depriving (CJ(TFO)A 2001, s 4(5)). 'Dishonestly' means without a claim of right made in good faith (CJ(TFO)A 2001, s 2(1)). 'Property' means money and all other property, real or personal, including things in action and other intangible property (CJ(TFO)A 2001, s 2(1)). A person is regarded as the *owner* of property if he has possession or control of it, or has in it any proprietary right or interest (CJ(TFO)A 2001, s 2(4)). *Consent* obtained by deception or intimidation is not consent (CJ(TFO)A 2001, s 4(2)).

There are exceptions e g generally a person cannot steal land, or things forming part of the land; also a person who picks mushrooms or flowers or fruit growing wild on land, does not steal what is picked, unless done for reward (CJ(TFO)A 2001, s 5).

Criminal proceedings of theft by one spouse from another can only be taken by or with the consent of the Director of Public Prosecutions (CJ(TFO)A 2001, s 62 amending the Married Women's Status Act 1957, s 9 which previously restricted such offences to where the spouses were living apart or where property was taken wrongly when one spouse was leaving or deserting).

In the trial of a person for theft, the court (or jury, as the case may be) has to consider whether the person believed: (a) that he had acted dishonestly, or (b) that the owner of the property had consented or would have consented to its appropriation, or (c) that the owner could not be discovered by taking reasonable steps (CJ(TFO)A 2001, s 4(4)). See District Court (Theft and Fraud Offences) Rules 2003, SI No 412 of 2003. [Bibliography: McGreal C.] See ALTERNATIVE VERDICTS; DISHONESTY; LARCENY; POSSESSION OF STOLEN PROPERTY; RESTITUTION OF POSSESSION; ROBBERY.

thick capitalisation. Term used to describe the practice of capitalising a 'tonnage tax' company or a 'tonnage tax' trade through a preponderance of equity, rather than debt, and capitalising other activities of the company by means of tax deductible borrowings. In the new tonnage tax regime introduced by s 53 of the Finance Act 2002, the practice of 'thick capitalisation' is countered: Finance Act 2003, s 62. See TONNAGE TAX.

Third Generation. In relation to mobile telephony services, means a mobile and wireless communications system capable of supporting innovative multimedia services beyond the capability of second generation systems such as GSM (global system mobile): Wireless Telegraphy (Third Generation and GSM Mobile Telephony Licence) Regulations 2002, SI No 345 of 2002, reg 2. These regulations provide for the issue of licences under the Wireless Telegraphy Act 1926 for apparatus for wireless telegraphy used solely for the purpose of providing Third Generation and GSM mobile telephony services. See also SI 340 of 2003. See GLOBAL SYSTEM MOBILE.

third-party information. Persons, companies and government departments are required to make a return to the Revenue Commissioners of payments made to third parties for services rendered, including payments for copyright: Finance Act 1992, s 226. Particulars must also be given where payment is given in a form other than money. Returns must also be made by persons or companies who receive income belonging to others, by persons who are nominee holders of securities, by persons who act as intermediaries in relation to UCITS or who, as agents, receive rents or other payments arising from premises. Excluded are payments from which income tax has been deducted, payments which do not exceed £3,000/€3,809 in a year, and payments where the value of goods provided as part of the service exceeds two thirds of the total charge. Any statutory or other body which pays a rent subsidy must also make a return, giving the name and address of the person to whom paid and the premises in respect of which it was paid: Finance Act 1995, s 14. See now Taxes Consolidation Act 1997, s 894.

Officers of the Revenue Commissioners are empowered to make enquiries in relation to certain third-party returns e g returns made by financial institutions in relation to those to whom they pay interest gross: Finance Act 2003, s 158.

third-party notice. A notice issued and served in an action, by leave of the court, on a person who is not already a party to the action, following an application by a defendant, where he claims to be entitled to contribution (qv) or indemnity (qv) from that person: RSC Ord 16. The application is made by motion on notice to the plaintiff made within 28 days from the time limited for delivery of the defence (Ord 16, rr 1(2) and 1(3)). See also Civil Liability Act 1961, s 27(1)(b).

When considering the joinder of a third-party, the court is entitled to balance the disruption to the existing proceedings, which could arise from such joinder, against the convenience of trying all the issues in one action: *Wicklow County Council v Fenton* [2002] 2 ILRM 469, HC and 2 IR 583.

As regards a claim for personal injuries arising from an accident, facts must be alleged by the defendant which would support his claim that the proposed third-party had contributed to the accident: *Johnston (a minor) v Fitzpatrick* [1991] ILRM 269, SC. There is no inflexible rule that an application for liberty to issue and serve a third-party notice must be based on a *direct* affidavit (qv) of the facts, rather than on an *information and belief* affidavit, although in certain circumstances, the former will be necessary (*Johnston* case).

Although there is no statutory provision or rule limiting the time for making an application to *set aside* a third-party notice, a cut-off point is necessary in the interest of orderly litigation and it must be not later than the entry of the defence of the third-party: *Grogan v Ferrum Trading Co Ltd* [1996] 2 ILRM 216, HC. The mere fact that the third party has not yet delivered a defence, does not mean that the application to set aside has been brought *'as soon as is reasonably possible'*: *Boland v Dublin Corporation* [2003] 1 ILRM 172, SC.

In considering whether a third-party notice was served *'as soon as is reasonably possible'*, the whole circumstances of the case and its general progress must be considered: *Connolly v Casey* [2000] 1 IR 345, SC and [2000] 2 ILRM 226, SC, applied by *Molloy v Dublin Corporation* [2002] 2 ILRM 22, SC and [2001] 4 IR 52, SC.

The Supreme Court has held that there is no reason to make any distinction between a third party out of the jurisdiction and a domestic third party on the question of the propriety of its joinder: *McCarthy v Pillay* [2003] 2 ILRM 284, SC and 1 IR 592. The third-party procedure was held to be an adequate vehicle to bring the issue before the court, as to whether the county

council owed a statutory duty to provide the respondents with a serviced halting camp site: *County Meath VEC v Joyce and Meath Co Co* [1994] 2 ILRM 210, HC and [1997] 3 IR 402, HC.

When the third party is served with the notice he becomes a party to the action and has the same rights in respect of defence as if he had been duly sued in the ordinary way by the defendant (RSC Ord 16, r 3).

For the procedure in the Circuit Court for permission to issue a notice on a person, not already a party to an action, to appear at the trial (eg where a defendant claims an indemnity from the third party), see Circuit Court Rules 2001 Ord 7. The *third-party notice* must be served within 21 days of the making of the order joining the third party. Where the third party enters an appearance, he is required to deliver his defence within ten days from the date thereof.

The third-party procedure in the District Court is governed by DCR 1997 Ord 42. See *International Commercial Bank plc v Insurance Corp of Ireland plc* [1989] 7 ILT Dig 326; *Dowling Armour Pharmaceutical Co Inc* [1996] 2 ILRM 417, HC; *Golden Vale plc v Food Industries plc* [1996] 2 IR 221, HC. See NEXT FRIEND; O'BYRNE LETTER.

threat. A mere oral threat to commit a crime generally does not constitute a crime. However, a *threat* to kill or murder any person which is contained in any letter or writing, maliciously sent, with knowledge of its contents, is an offence (formerly, a felony); Offences Against the Person Act 1861, s 16. It is also an offence to make a *threat*: (a) to damage property of another; or (b) to damage one's own property in a way likely to endanger the life of another: Criminal Damage Act 1991, s 3. Formerly, when the threat was in language which causes or might cause a *breach of the peace* (qv) or was in threatening or abusive language within the provisions of the Dublin Police Act 1842, s 14(13), it was a crime, since repealed by the Criminal Justice (Public Order) Act 1994, Sch. See CONFESSION; DURESS; EXTORTION BY MENACES; TRESPASS TO PERSON.

threatening. The offence committed by an accused who threatens to commit any act which is an offence against a UN worker, premises or vehicle and intends that the person to whom he makes the threat, shall fear that it will be carried out: Criminal

Justice (Safety of United Nations Workers) Act 2000, s 4. The offence is committed where the accused makes the threat, in or outside the State, in order to compel the person to do or refrain from doing such an act. See UNITED NATIONS WORKER, OFFENCES AGAINST.

ticket. Where a ticket contains a written offer subject to printed conditions, those conditions are incorporated into the contract formed by acceptance of the offer, if adequate *notice* of the conditions are given to the offeree. See *Richardson v Rowntree* [1894] AC 217.

tidal water. Any part of the sea and any part of a river within the ebb and flow of the tide at the ordinary spring tides and not being part of a harbour: Merchant Shipping (Salvage and Wreck) Act 1993, s 2(1). See SALVAGE OPERATION.

tied insurance agent. A person who enters into an agreement or arrangement with an insurer, whereby he undertakes to refer all proposals of insurance to such insurer, or which restricts his freedom to refer proposals of insurance to other insurers: Insurance Act 1989, s 51(3). An insurer is responsible for any act or omission of its tied insurance agent in respect of contracts of insurance offered or issued by the insurer, as if the tied insurance agent was an employee of the insurer (IA 1989, s 51(2)). See INSURANCE OMBUDSMAN.

tiered interest rate. The rate of interest on a loan where the rate: (a) is determined by reference to the amount of the loan made, or to the amount outstanding at any time on foot of the loan, or to the income of the member to whom the loan is made, as the case may be, and (b) is greater than the lowest rate of interest applicable at the time to loans of the same type made by a building society to members generally: Building Societies Act 1989, s 24(2).

Under the Building Societies (Amendment) Act 1986 it was prohibited to charge tiered interest rates on loans made by a society on or after 23 October 1986 or on loans made before 1 August 1986 on which a tiered rate was not being charged on that date (BS(A)A 1986, ss 4(1) and 4(2)).

Notwithstanding the repeal of the 1986 Act by the 1989 Act, a society must not charge a tiered interest rate on a loan made under the *repealed enactments* in respect of a *house*, unless a tiered rate was lawfully charged on the date of the repeal: BSA 1989, ss 24(1)(a) and 24(2)(b). Further-

more, a society must not charge a tiered interest rate on a *housing loan* (qv), unless the tiered rate is charged from the day on which the mortgage securing the loan is created, and the charging of a tiered rate is specifically mentioned in the mortgage, and is acknowledged in writing by the member in a form to be specified by the Central Bank (BSA 1989, s 24(1)(b)).

A member who is wrongly charged a tiered interest rate is not in breach of his mortgage agreement if he does not pay the additional sum involved (BS(A)A 1986, s 5).

timber. See ESTOVERS.

time. In statutory provisions, where a period of time is expressed to begin on or to be reckoned from a particular day that day shall, unless the contrary intention appears, be deemed to be included in such period: Interpretation Act 1937, s 11(h). Time limits up to six days do not include a Saturday, Sunday or public holiday (qv) and where the time expires on any such day, the time is extended to the first following day which is not a Saturday, Sunday or public holiday: Companies Act 1990, s 4. See also Waste Management Act 1996, s 17.

As regards planning legislation, in calculating time periods or other time limits, the period between 24 December and 1 January (both days inclusive) is to be disregarded, except in relation to plans and guidelines (Pt II): Planning and Development Act 2000, s 251.

As regards the Statute of Limitations 1957, the statutory period of time is construed as ending on the last day of the period; however, if the act required (eg issuing a summons) is impossible to do on the last day because the offices of the court are closed, the period will be construed as ending on the next day the offices are open: *Poole v O'Sullivan* [1993] ILRM 55, HC. In personal injuries actions arising from an accident, the date on which the accident occurs is deemed to be included in the limitation period: *McGuinness v Armstrong Patents Ltd* [1980] IR 289.

Time limits in statutory provisions may be either mandatory or discretionary; in deciding into which category a provision falls, the court must seek to interpret the meaning, intention and objective of the legislation at issue: *Irish Refining plc v Commissioner of Valuation* [1990] 1 IR 568, SC. The High Court has held that that the legislative intention for the imposition of a time limit in the Consumer Credit Act 1995, s 149(6), was that a failure by the Director of Consumer Affairs to comply with the time stipulation would render her exercise of the powers in the section *voidable* rather than *void*: *Director of Consumer Affairs v Bank of Ireland* [2003] 2 IR 217, HC. See also *Cork County Council v Whillock* [1993] 11 ILT Dig 144, SC.

Many statutes place a time limit on appealing from the date of a decision, determination or recommendation. The words 'the date of the Equality Officer's recommendation' means the date appearing on the recommendation and not the date of receipt by a party: *Hegarty v Labour Court* [1999] 2 ILRM 177, HC and 3 IR 603 (under appeal).

Universal Co-ordinated Time replaced Greenwich Mean Time for navigational warnings from 1 February 1993: Merchant Shipping (Navigation Warnings) (Amendment) Rules 1992. See STANDARD TIME; MONTH; WEEK; YEAR.

time, court rules. The court has power to enlarge or abridge the time for doing any act or taking any proceedings. The time for delivering amending or filing any pleadings, answer or other document may be enlarged by consent. Where time is limited by months, such time is to be computed by calendar months.

Where any limited time less than six days is allowed, certain days are not reckoned in the computation of such limited time (Saturday, Sunday, Christmas Day, Good Friday). Where any particular number of days is not expressed to be *clear days,* the same is reckoned exclusively of the first day and inclusive of the last day. The time of the *long vacation* (qv) is not to be reckoned in computing time. In relation to personal injuries proceedings, see Civil Liability and Courts Act 2004, s 9.

It has been held that a plaintiff seeking an extension of time within which to appeal would need to establish: (a) that she had formed an intention to appeal within the limited time; (b) that failure to file a notice of appeal within time was due to mistake on her part or on the part of her legal advisors; and (c) that she had an arguable case on appeal: *Clonmel Foods Ltd v Eire Continental Trading Co Ltd* [1955] IR 170 considered in *Dalton v Minister for Finance* [1989] ILRM 519, SC. Prejudice to the other party is a relevant factor and conse-

quently, the extension of time may be limited to a particular ground of appeal: *Brewer v Commissioners of Public Works in Ireland* [2004] 1 ILRM 286, SC. There is a desirability of adhering to time limits prescribed by court rules: *Bord na Móna v Sisk* [1990] 1 IR 85, SC. See RSC Ord 122.

The Circuit Court may enlarge or abridge any of the times fixed in the rules for taking any steps or doing any acts in any proceedings: Circuit Court Rules 2001 Ord 67, r 6. A District Court judge may abridge or extend the time for service or lodgment of any summons or civil summons: DCR 1997 Ord 12, r 1. See DAY; PEREMPTORY; VACATION.

time sharing. Protection is given to purchasers who enter into contracts for the *time sharing* of immovable property: European Communities (Contracts for Time Sharing of Immovable Property – Protection of Purchasers) Regulations 1997, SI No 204 of 1997.

These regulations provide that consumers may withdraw from the contract within a ten-day cooling-off period or, in the absence or non-provision of certain information, within three months. Also the vendor is prohibited from seeking *deposits* and must supply a *brochure* with specific information about the property e g description, current status (e g under completion), associated services and facilities, the price and the right to cancellation. The *contract* must contain the foregoing and other information e g right or otherwise of resale or exchange for another property.

These regulations have been strengthened to copper fasten the purchaser's option to obtain a time-share contract in the *purchaser's language* and to introduce penalties for non-compliance with the regulations: SI No 144 of 2000.

time-shifting. Term used in relation to copyright and performers' rights where a *fixation* (e g recording) of a broadcast or cable programme is made solely to enable it to be viewed or listened to at another time or place; where this is done for private and domestic use, it does not infringe a right: Copyright and Related Rights Act 2000, ss 101 and 250.

time limits, statutory. See TIME.

time immemorial. A term used to denote a time before legal memory. Fixed by the Statute of Westminster 1275 as 1189, the first year of the reign of Richard 1.

time of essence of a contract. Time is of the essence of a contract when the parties have expressly provided for it to be so in the contract or when the circumstances show that the parties intended it to be so. Where a conditional contract of sale fixes the date by which a condition must be met, the date so fixed must be strictly adhered to: *Aberfoyle Plantations v Cheng* [1960] AC 115: *Crean v Drinan* [1983] ILRM 82; *Hynes v Independent Newspapers* [1980] IR 204.

If a contract does not originally make time of the essence, one party may subsequently serve notice that from a stated date, time will be of the essence: *Nolan v Driscoll* [1978] HC. See *Kramer v Arnold* [1997] 3 IR 43, SC. See also Sale of Goods Act 1893, s 10(1) and Judicature Act 1877, s 28(7). See also PLANNING PERMISSION; PRICE; VOIDABLE.

time off. An employee who has been given notice of dismissal for redundancy may take reasonable time off during working hours on full pay to seek or be trained for future employment: Redundancy Payments Act 1967, s 7. See REDUNDANCY.

time policy. A contract of insurance to insure the subject-matter for a definite period of time: Marine Insurance Act 1906, s 25(1).

TIN. [Taxation Identification Number.] In the context of the EU Savings Directive, means a unique identification number allocated by the relevant territory to an individual for the purposes of taxation and, in relation to the State, means an individual's PPS (Personal Public Service) number: Taxes Consolidation Act 1997, s 898B inserted by Finance Act 2004, s 90 and Sch 4. See SAVINGS DIRECTIVE.

tipping of waste. See WASTE.

tithe rentcharges. Originally a rentcharge on land, payable previously in kind, and later in money. Any such tithe rentcharges which subsisted on 28 September 1975 were extinguished by the Land Act 1984, s 7(3).

title. (1) An appellation of office or distinction eg lord mayor (qv). (2) A description or heading eg of an action at law or the description of an Act of parliament: *Vacher v London Society of Compositors* [1913] AC 107. (3) The right to ownership of property or evidence of such right. Such a title may be: (a) *original,* where the person entitled does not take from any predecessor eg in the case of copyright, and (b) *derivative,* where the person takes the place of a pred-

ecessor, by act of parties or by operation of law. For a checklist on title-parties relating to estates, see *Stynes* in 7 ILT & SJ (1989) 92. See Criminal Damage Act 1991, s 8.

The title to any lands or property must not be drawn into question in any dispute resolution proceedings before a mediator, an adjudicator or the Tenancies Tribunal: Residential Tenancies Act 2004, s 110. See also Deasy's Act 1860, s 101.

A certificate of title given to a lending institution in relation to a client's mortgage transaction should be dated as of the date of parting with the loan funds: Practice Note in *Law Society Gazette* (July 2004) 39. A working group has been established to explore the possibility of drafting a standard *certificate of title* for use in commercial conveyancing: *Law Society Gazette* (January/February 2004) 55. See ABSTRACT OF TITLE; LEGAL COSTS, INVESTIGATION OF TITLE; LODGMENT IN COURT; LONG POSSESSION, TITLE BY; MARKETABLE TITLE; ROOT OF TITLE; TITLE OF NOBILITY.

title, long. See PREAMBLE.

title, short. See SHORT TITLE.

title by long possession. See LONG POSSESSION, TITLE BY.

title deeds. The documents and instruments conferring or evidencing the title to land. In the case of *unregistered* land, they consist of deeds and conveyances, eg conveyances of freehold, fee farm grants and sub-grants, leases and subleases and mortgages. In the case of *registered* land, they consist of the entries in the Land Registry on the folio relating to the land, the charges registered thereon, the land certificate and charge certificates.

Failure of the vendor to produce the title deeds, which were specified in the contract for the sale of a premises, entitled the purchaser to rescind the contract and to have his deposit returned with the accrued interest: *Tyndarius Ltd v O'Mahony & others* [2003] FL 7239, SC. In this case the vendor had mislaid some of the deeds and had offered statutory declarations in lieu thereof, which was not acceptable to the purchaser. See Building Societies Act 1989, s 76(11). See DEPOSIT OF TITLE DEEDS; DOCUMENTARY, EVIDENCE.

title of nobility. A title of nobility cannot be conferred by the State and government approval is required prior to any citizen accepting a title of nobility or honour: 1937

Constitution, art 40(2). See CIVIC HON-
OUR; HONOUR.

title to goods. In contracts for the sale of
goods and hire-purchase of goods there are
implied terms as to title: Sale of Goods and
Supply of Services Act 1980, s 10 and
Consumer Credit Act 1995, s 74. Where
goods are sold by a person who is not the
owner thereof, and who does not sell them
under the authority or with the consent of
the owner, the buyer acquires no better title
to the goods than the seller had, unless the
owner of the goods is by his conduct precluded from denying the seller's authority
to sell: Sale of Goods Act 1893, s 21. See
FACTOR; MARKET OVERT; NEMO DAT QUI
NON HABET; RETENTION OF TITLE; VOID-
ABLE TITLE, SALE UNDER.

tobacco product. Means: (a) any product
consisting, in whole or in part, of tobacco,
that is intended to be smoked, (b) a
tobacco product within the meaning of the
Finance (Excise Duty on Tobacco Products) Act, 1977 (inserted by section 86(1)
of the Finance Act, 1997), or (c) any ciga-
rette paper, tube or filter manufactured for
use in the smoking of tobacco, other than a
medicinal product within the meaning of
the Irish Medicines Board Act, 1995: Public Health (Tobacco) Act 2002, s 2(1) as
substituted by Public Health (Tobacco)
(Amendment) Act 2004, s 2.

The 2002 Act provides a more comprehensive and strengthened legislative basis
for regulating and controlling the sale, marketing and smoking of tobacco products
and for enforcing such controls. The 2004
Act gives effect to Directive (EC) 2003/33
and re-enacts and amends the 2002 Act. In
the High Court, counsel for the Minister
for Health advised the court that the Minister accepted that various sections of the
2002 Act which had a 'cross-European
impact', should have been notified under
the EU Transparency Directive and that
this had not been done: *Gallagher (Ireland) Ltd v Minister for Health* (2002) Irish
Times, 28 January, SC. This necessitated
the 2004 Act, the Bill of which was notified
to the European Commission in accordance with the Directive.

There is a comprehensive ban on tobacco
advertising and all forms of sponsorship by
the tobacco industry (PH(T)A 2002, s 36
as substituted by PH(T)(A)A 2004, s 7).
There is also a prohibition on certain marketing practices e g sale by retail of cigarettes in packets of less than 20 cigarettes;

sale of oral smokeless tobacco products;
sale of confectioneries which resemble
tobacco products; sale or supply of tobacco
products which do not bear a prescribed
warning; and certain sales promotion
devices (PH(T)A 2002, s 38 as substituted
by PH(T)(A)A 2004, s 9).

There is a prohibition on certain assertions in relation to tobacco products e g that
smoking does not cause life threatening
diseases (PH(T)A 2002, s 42 as substituted
by PH(T)(A)A 2004, s 12). It is also an
offence to sell a tobacco product by retail to
persons under 18 years of age; it is a good
defence for the seller to prove that he made
all reasonable efforts to satisfy himself that
the person had attained 18 years of age
(PH(T)A 2002, s 45).

There is a prohibition on the sale of
tobacco products by means of self-service,
except in licensed premises or in a registered club in accordance with regulations
(PH(T)A 2002, s 43 as substituted by
PH(T)(A)A 2004, s 14). The Minister is
empowered to prescribe standards and
requirements to be complied with in the
manufacture and sale of tobacco products
(PH(T)A 2002, s 39 as amended by
PH(T)(A)A 2004, s 10).

It is also an offence if a person offers
cigarettes for sale or delivery without a tax
stamp: Finance Act 1994, s 74.

Following publication in 2003 of a scientific report on the adverse effects of passive
smoking, *The Health Effects of Environmental
Tobacco Smoke in the Workplace*, the Minister
introduced regulations to ban smoking in
places of work. See SMOKING.

The Minister may impose, by order,
quantitative restrictions on personal impor-
tations of tobacco products from an accession state, where that state has been
allowed to apply a rate of duty which is less
than the minimum specified in EU law:
Finance Act 2004, s 46. For regulations
dealing with health-warning labelling, new
maximum yields of tar, nicotine and carbon
monoxide in cigarettes, product description
and further product information, see EC
(Manufacture, Presentation and Sale of
Tobacco Products) Regulations 2003, SI
No 425 of 2003. For previous legislation,
see also Tobacco Products (Control of
Advertising, Sponsorship and Sales Promotion) Act 1978 and see Tobacco (Health
Promotion and Protection) Act 1988,
which Acts are repealed by the 2002 Act.
See ADVERTISEMENT; EXCISE LAW; OFFICE

OF TOBACCO CONTROL; ORAL SMOKELESS TOBACCO PRODUCT.

toll. A tax paid for some privilege or compensation paid for some service provided eg a payment for passing over a road, bridge or ferry. The right to demand a toll may arise by way of franchise (qv) or by statute. See TOLL ROAD.

toll road. A public road or proposed public road in respect of which a *toll scheme* is in force: Roads Act 1993, s 56. A toll scheme, the decision on which is a reserved function (qv) of a road authority, must be approved by the Minister (RA 1993, s 57). Road authorities are empowered to charge and collect tolls in respect of toll roads (RA 1993, s 59) and to enter into agreements with other persons in relation to the financing, maintenance, construction and operation of toll roads (RA 1993, s 63). A road authority as regards tolls on regional and local roads is the local authority, and on national roads is the National Roads Authority (RA 1993, s 56).

A person who is given the use or enjoyment of a *hereditament* and the power to manage it, including the power to collect tolls in respect of that hereditament, is an occupier of the hereditament and liable to pay rates thereon: *Dublin County Council v Westlink Toll Bridge Ltd* [1996] 2 ILRM 232, SC and 1 IR 487. For amendments to Roads Act 1993, ss 58, 60, 61, 63, 65 and 66, see Planning and Development Act 2000, ss 272–277.

Tolls charged for the use of toll roads and toll bridges are subject to value added tax: European Court of Justice Case C-358/97. This was implemented in Ireland by the Finance Act 2001, s 199(b).

tonnage tax. An alternative method of calculating the profits of shipping companies, for the purposes of corporation tax; the profits are calculated by reference to the tonnage of the ships used in the shipping trade: Finance Act 2002, s 53. It is optional; if a shipping company does not wish to elect for the tonnage method and wishes to remain subject to the normal corporation tax rules, it may do so. The tonnage tax scheme has been amended to conform more fully with EU requirements eg the tonnage tax regime is confined to profits derived from shipping activities: Finance Act 2003, s 62. See THICK CAPITALISATION.

tontine. An insurance scheme whereby contributors to the scheme pay into a fund which is divided at the end of a specified period among the survivors by way of repayment of capital or by annuity.

topography right. A right which exists in its creator where the topography of a semiconductor product is the result of the creator's own intellectual effort: European Communities (Protection of Topographics of Semiconductor Products) Regulations 1988, SI No 101 of 1988 as amended eg SI No 113 of 1999. Protection is given which consists of the exclusive right to reproduce and commercially exploit the topographics; the right commences at the time of creation and lasts for ten years from first commercial exploitation or fifteen years after creation. The Regulations implement Council Directive (EEC) 87/54 and Council Decisions (EEC) 90/510–511. See INTELLECTUAL PROPERTY.

tort. [Crooked; twisted; distorted; a wrong.] A civil wrong, independent of contract, which arises from a breach of a duty imposed by law, the main remedy for which is an action for unliquidated damages (qv). The principal torts are trespass, nuisance, defamation and negligence (qqv).

The remedies for tort are either *extra-judicial* or *judicial*. The *extra-judicial* remedies are: distress damage feasant; re-entry on land; expulsion of a trespasser; abatement of nuisance (qqv). The *judicial* remedies are: damages, injunction; restitution of property (qqv). The defences in tort include: necessity; statutory authority; *volenti non fit injuria*; inevitable accident; statute-barred (qqv).

Action for damages in tort is commenced, in the Circuit Court by *civil bill*, and in the High Court and District Court by *summons*. See also SMALL CLAIMS.

In the District Court, proceedings founded on tort may be taken, brought, heard and determined at a sitting of the court: (a) wherein the defendant resides or carries on any profession, business or occupation, or (b) at the election of the plaintiff, wherein the tort is alleged to have been committed: DCR 1997 Ord 39, r 1.

As regards the Statute of Limitations 1957, the word 'tort' is sufficiently wide to embrace a breach of statutory duty and breaches of community law by the State: SL 1957, s 11(2) and *Tate v Minister for Social Welfare* [1995] 1 ILRM 507, HC. See *Murphy v Minister for the Marine* [1996] 3 IR 517, HC.

Formerly, an action in tort in respect of a felony (qv) could not be brought unless the offender had first been prosecuted or a reasonable cause had been shown as to why this had not been done; this requirement no longer applies, due to the abolition of any distinction between a felony and a misdemeanour and the requirement that the applicable law and practice regarding all offences is that relating to misdemeanours: Criminal Law Act 1997, s 3. See Law Reform Commission report, *Statute of Limitations: Claims in Contract and Tort in respect of Latent Damage* (*other than Personal Injury*) (LRC 64, 2001). [Bibliography: Burke & Corbett; Corbett V; McMahon & Binchy; Clerk & Lindsell UK; Salmond UK; Street UK.] See IMMUNITY; VICISSITUDES PRINCIPLE.

tort, EU jurisdiction. A person domiciled in a *contracting* state of the EU may, in another contracting state, be sued in matters relating to tort, delict or quasi-delict, in the courts for the place where the harmful event occurred or in the place of domicile of the defendant: Jurisdiction of Courts and Enforcement of Judgments Act 1998, Sch 1, art 5. However, from 2002 see below. It has been held that jurisdiction lies in either the courts for the place: (a) where the event ultimately causing the harm occurred; or (b) where the actual harm occurred: Case 21/76 *Bier v Mines de Potasse* [1976] ECR 1735. See *Casey v Ingersoll-Rand Sales Co Ltd* [1996] 2 ILRM 456, HC and [1997] 2 IR 115, HC.

It has also been held that the phrase '*tort, delict or quasi-delict*' must be independently interpreted and not by reference to national law: Case 189/87 ECR *Kalfelis v Banque Schroder*, see 7 ILT & SJ [1989] 2. As regards tort and EFTA States, see JCEJA 1998, Sch 7, art 5.

The *Brussels I Regulation* on the recognition and enforcement of judgments in civil and commercial matters, replaces JCEJA 1998 as from 1 March 2002 for all EU States except Denmark: EC (Civil and Commercial Judgments) Regulations 2002, SI No 52 of 2002. Jurisdiction is now given not only to the court of the place where the harmful event occurred, but also to the place where it may occur (*Regulation*, art 5(3)).

tortfeasor. A person who commits a tort. See JOINT TORTFEASORS.

tortious. Wrongful.

torture. An act or omission by which severe pain or suffering, whether physical or mental, is intentionally inflicted on a person: Criminal Justice (United Nations Convention against Torture) Act 2000, s 1(1). A *public official* who carries out an act of torture on a person, whether within or outside the State, is guilty of the offence of torture (CJ(UNCT)A 2000, s 2(1)). A *public official* includes a person acting in an official capacity (CJ(UNCT)A 2000, s 1(1)).

Also a person who carries out an act of torture at the instigation of, or with the consent or acquiescence of a public official, is guilty of the offence of torture (CJ(UNCT)A 2000, s 2(2)). It is also an offence to attempt to or conspire to commit the offence of torture or to impede or obstruct the arrest or prosecution of a person in relation to the offence of torture (CJ(UNCT)A 2000, s 3).

A person so charged must be tried in the Central Criminal Court and is liable on conviction on indictment to imprisonment for life (CJ(UNCT)A 2000, ss 3 and 5(4)).

The 2000 Act gives effect in the State to the Convention against Torture and Other Cruel, Inhumane or Degrading Treatment or Punishment, adopted by resolution 39/46 of the General Assembly of the United Nations on 10 December 1984 as set out in CJ(UNCT)A 2000, Sch.

The *Committee against Torture* and a *conciliation commission* set up under the Convention (arts 17 and 21(1)(e)) must be accorded such privileges and immunities as are necessary for the independent exercise of their functions (CJ(UNCT)A 2000, s 11).

'No one shall be subject to torture or to inhuman or degrading treatment or punishment': European Convention on Human Rights. Torture includes the infliction of mental suffering by creating a state of anguish and stress by means other than bodily assault: Greek Case, Yearbook of European Convention on Human Rights Vol XII, 1986, p 461.

Provision for the establishment of a European Committee for the prevention of torture is made by the European Convention for the prevention of Torture and Inhuman or Degrading Treatment or Punishment which came into force as regards Ireland on 1 February 1989. See also *Ireland v United Kingdom* in 8 ILT & SJ [1990] 216.

A doctor must not countenance, condone or participate in the practice of torture or other forms of cruel, inhuman or degrading procedures, whatever the offence of which the victim of such procedures is suspected, accused or guilty, and whatever the victim's beliefs or motives, and in all situations, including armed conflict and civil strife: Declaration of Tokyo, October 1975. The Medical Council supports this Declaration: *A Guide to Ethical Conduct and Behaviour* (6th edn, 2004), para 2.8. See also 'Family Law aspects of the European Convention on Human Rights Act 2003' by Dervla Browne BL in *Bar Review* (April 2004) 39. See EUROPEAN CONVENTION ON HUMAN RIGHTS; VIDEO RECORDING.

total loss. In marine insurance, the total loss of the subject matter insured may be either actual or constructive. Actual loss arises where the ship or cargo is totally destroyed or so damaged that it can never arrive *in specie* (qv) at its destination. See Marine Insurance Act 1906, s 60. See CONSTRUCTIVE TOTAL LOSS.

totalisator. An apparatus or organisation by means of which an unlimited number of persons can each stake money in respect of a future event on the terms that the amount to be won by the successful stakers is dependent on or to be calculated with reference to the total amount staked by means of the apparatus in relation to that event but not necessarily on the same contingency: Totalisator Act 1929, s 1. The 1929 Act made provision for the regulation and control of totalisators and for the setting up and working of totalisators. See also Irish Horseracing Industry Act 1994, s 63. See *Madden v Irish Turf Club* [1997] 2 ILRM 148, SC.

Horse Racing Ireland and Bord na gCon are now empowered: (a) to enter into contracts with off-course bookmaker shops to operate a Tote betting service on their behalf; and (b) to enter into reciprocal arrangements with foreign Tote operators to facilitate punters from different jurisdictions to bet into the Tote pools of the other: Horse and Greyhound Racing Act 2001, ss 17 and 18. See Totalisator (Horse Racing) Regulations 2002, SI No 72 of 2002; Greyhound Race Track (Superfecta) Regulations 2003, SI No 663 of 2003. See BET; WAGERING CONTRACT.

tote. The popular name for the *totalisator* (qv).

toties quoties. [As often as something happens.] Repeatedly.

Tourism Ireland. A publicly owned limited company established by Bord Fáilte and the Northern Ireland Tourist Board with the approval of the North/South Ministerial Conference and incorporated on 11 December 2000. Its remit is to promote the island of Ireland as a tourist destination, which it does via international tourism marketing programmes, and publication of information on tourism and market research. See website: *www.tourismireland.com*. See ECO-LABELLING SCHEME; NATIONAL TOURISM DEVELOPMENT AUTHORITY.

tour operator. A person other than a carrier who arranges for the purpose of selling or offering for sale to the public, accommodation for travel by air, sea or land transport to destinations outside Ireland, or who holds himself out by advertising or otherwise as one who may make available such accommodation, either solely or in association with other accommodation, facilities or services: Transport (Tour Operators and Travel Agents) Act 1982, s 2.

A person may not carry on business as a tour operator without a licence granted by the Minister. A *bond* is a prerequisite to the granting of a licence, being an arrangement for the protection of persons, during the validity of the licence, who enter into contracts with tour operators relating to overseas travel. See SI No 175 of 1987; RSC Ord 102. See *Balkan Tours Ltd v Minister for Communications* [1988] ILRM 101. See also Package Holidays and Travel Trade Act 1995. [Bibliography: Buttimore (1); McDonald M (3).] See EUROPEAN EXTRA-JUDICIAL NETWORK; PACKAGE HOLIDAY; SEX TOURISM; TRANSPORT AUXILIARY; TRAVEL AGENT; TRAVELLERS' PROTECTION FUND.

town. The area comprised in a town (not being an urban district) in which the Towns Improvement (Ireland) Act 1854, is in operation: Interpretation Act 1937, Sch, para 32. The 1854 Act has been repealed by the Local Government Act 2001, s 5(1) and Sch 3, Pt 1. For a list of *towns* (local government areas) see LGA 2001, Sch 6.

As there is no definition of *town* in the Judgments (Ireland) Act 1850, its meaning must be ascertained by reference to the law as it was and the English language as used in 1850: *Irish Bank of Commerce v O'Hara*

[1992] ITLR (10 August) SC. See BOUND-
ARY ALTERATION; LOCAL AREA PLAN;
NAME, CHANGE OF.

town commissioners. Formerly, the bodies
which, as corporations aggregate, exercised
functions in relation to the paving, lighting,
draining, cleansing and supplying with
water of a number of towns: Town
Improvements (Ireland) Act 1854; Lighting
of Towns (Ireland) Act 1828. Some towns
became urban district councils: Public
Health (Ireland) Act 1878, s 4; Local Government (Ireland) Act 1898, s 22. Town
commissioners were not sanitary, planning
or fire authorities, but they were housing
authorities, except in respect of grants
under the Housing Act 1966 and of certain
functions (eg the homeless) under the
Housing Act 1988, s 21. A county council
is deemed to have, and always to have had,
a power to provide dwellings or building
sites in a town commissioners' area without
withdrawing that power from the commissioners: Housing Act 1988, s 20(2).

Town Commissioners are now *Town
Councils* under the Local Government
Act 2001, s 11. The 2001 Act repealed the
1854 Act and s 22 of the 1898 Act (LGA
2001, s 5(1) and Sch 3, Pt I). See COUNTY
MANAGER; LOCAL GOVERNMENT; TOWN
COUNCILS.

town councils. A local authority: Local
Government Act 2001, s 2. A town council
is a body corporate with perpetual succession, with power to sue and be sued in its
corporate name, and with a seal which
must be judicially noticed (LGA 2001,
s 11(7)).

As from 1 January 2002 all Urban District councils and Town Commissioners
became *Town Councils* eg Bray UDC
became Bray Town Council. Provision has
been made to enable towns with a population of at least 7,500 to have a town council, following a procedure involving a
proposal to the county council signed by at
least 100 qualified electors or 10% of qualified electors, whichever is the greater (LGA
2001, s 185). See COUNTY MANAGER;
LOCAL AUTHORITY.

town renewal. A scheme of tax reliefs has
been introduced to foster renewal and
improvement in certain towns by providing
accelerated capital allowances in respect of
the construction or refurbishment of industrial buildings and commercial premises:
Taxes Consolidation Act 1997,
ss 372AA–AJ as inserted by Finance

Act 2000, s 89. Certain amendments have
been made to this scheme eg increasing the
qualifying floor area limits: Finance
Act 2001, s 80. The scheme has been
extended to 31 July 2006: Finance
Act 2004, s 26. The scheme previously had
a three-year life span from 1 April 2000 to
31 March 2003 and was extended to
31 December 2004 by the Finance
Act 2003, ss 26 and 29, before being further extended by the 2004 Act. [Bibliogra-
phy: Connolly, Bradley & Purcell.]

town renewal plan. A written statement
and a plan indicating the objectives for: (a)
the renewal on a sustainable basis, of an
area comprising the whole or part of the
eligible town to which the town renewal plan
relates, and (b) improvements in the physical environment of the area to which the
plan relates: Town Renewal Act 2000,
s 3(6). A county council may prepare and
submit one or more such plans to the
Minister for the Environment and Local
Government, who may recommend to the
Minister for Finance that he make an order
which would grant relief from income tax
and corporation tax in relation to construction, refurbishment or conversion of buildings, structures or houses which are
consistent with the plan (TRA 2000, ss 3,
5–7).

An *eligible town* means a town, the population of which exceeded 500 persons but
did not exceed 6,000 persons in the most
recent census, and which is not in the
administrative counties of Fingal, South
Dublin, Dún Laoghaire-Rathdown, and
which does not already come within the
existing renewal schemes of TCA 1997,
ss 351 (qualifying resort), 372B (qualifying
area), or 372L (qualifying rural area) (TRA
2000, s 1(1)).

The county council in selecting an eligible town, must have regard to any criteria
which the Minister specifies in writing;
such criteria may only have regard to the
need for: (a) the promotion of the physical
renewal and revitalisation of towns, (b) the
promotion of towns as cultural, commercial, social and residential centres, (c) the
promotion of sustainable development patterns, and (d) the enhancement of the
amenities, heritage, and environment of
towns (TRA 2000, s 3(3)).

The county council has a statutory duty
to monitor the implementation of the *town*

renewal plan for the area which has been approved as a qualifying area (TRA 2000, s 8).

toxic and dangerous waste. Hazardous waste. See Basel Convention on the control of transboundary movements of hazardous waste and their disposal, ratified by Ireland on 7 February 1994. See WASTE MANAGEMENT PLAN.

tracing. The equitable right of beneficiaries or creditors to follow assets to which they are entitled (or other assets into which they have been converted) into the hands of those who hold them. Thus beneficiaries and creditors have the right to follow the property of a deceased person into the hands of anybody other than a purchaser. Also where money which has been borrowed can be traced, the lender may be entitled to a *tracing order*. The right to trace ends with a purchaser for value who has no notice of the circumstances which have given rise to the right to trace: *Incorporated Law Society v Owens* [1990] 8 ILT Dig 64. See *Shanahan's Stamp Auctions v Farrelly* [1962] IR 386; *Re Irish Shipping Ltd* [1986] ILRM 518. See Succession Act 1965, s 59. [Bibliography: Delaney H (2).]

trade. For the purpose of taxation, means every trade, manufacture, adventure or concern in the nature of trade: Income Tax Act 1967, s 1(1), now Taxes Consolidation Act 1997, s 3(1). Since 1983, the profits of any trade consisting of or involving illegal activities are taxable, reversing the decision in *Collins v Mulvey* 31 TC 151, and since 1996, where the Criminal Assets Bureau has carried out an investigation, identified suspected criminal assets and has taken action to recover those assets, the estimated illegal earnings are assessed to tax: Finance Act 1983, s 19 as amended by Disclosure of Certain Information for Taxation and Other Purposes Act, s 11, now consolidated as Taxes Consolidation Act 1997, s 58. See *Airspace Investments Ltd v Moore* [1994] 2 ILRM 151, HC. See LIVELIHOOD.

trade, course of. See COURSE OF TRADE.

trade, prohibition of. The Minister may by regulation prohibit trade with other States eg the prohibition imposed in 1990, with penalties for infringement, of trade with Iraq pursuant to Regulation (EEC) 90/2340 of 8 August 1990: SI No 215 of 1990. See *Bosphorus Hava v Minister for Transport* [1994] 2 ILRM 551, HC. See also

SI No 66 of 2003 which gives effect to Regulation (EC) 2003/208 of 3 February 2003.

trade, right to. See LIVELIHOOD.

Trade and Business Body. The cross-border corporate body established with the function of developing co-operation on business development opportunities, North and South: British-Irish Agreement Act 1999, ss 18–20. It operates under the name Inter*Trade*Ireland. See website: *www.intertradeireland.com*. See GOOD FRIDAY AGREEMENT.

trade associations. Trade unions, employer organisations and professional organisations must not discriminate as regards admission to membership or benefits: Employment Equality Act 1998, s 13. It has been held that as persons, who are unable to join professional and trade associations, may be placed at a serious competitive disadvantage relative to members of the association, it is well established under EC law that rules of admission to such associations must be based on objective criteria with a proper appeal procedure: *Donovan v Electricity Supply Board* [1994] 2 ILRM 325, HC; *Re Sarabex Ltd* [1979] ICMLR 262. [Bibliography: Power V; Reid M.]

trade description. Any description, statement or other indication, direct or indirect, concerning goods, as to their number, quantity, measure, gauge, capacity, weight; mode of manufacturing or producing, etc; material composition; person by whom manufactured; place and time of manufacture; fitness for purpose and physical characteristics; other history etc. See Consumer Information Act 1978, s 2(1); Merchandise Marks Act 1887, s 3(1) for full definition.

A trade description also concerns the contents of books and their authors, films and producers, and recordings and performers. [Bibliography: Grogan, King & Donelan; O'Keeffe UK.] FALSE TRADE DESCRIPTION; DEFINITION ORDER; MILEOMETER READING; TRADE MARK.

trade dispute. Any dispute between employers and workers which is connected with the employment or non-employment, or the terms or conditions of or affecting the employment, of any person: Industrial Relations Act 1990, s 8. *Worker* in this context means a person who is or was employed whether or not in the employment of the employer with whom a trade dispute arises (IRA 1990, s 8). The term *non-employment* cannot have an unrestricted meaning: *Bradbury Ltd v Duffy* [1984] 3 JISLL 86.

The Supreme Court has held that a *bona fide* trade dispute may exist where one party denied that there was a dispute and the other believed that he had been wronged and was in dispute as a result or, that there was more than one dispute between the parties: *Nolan Transport (Oaklands) Ltd v Halligan* [1999] 1 IR 128, SC and [1998] ELR 177, SC.

There is statutory protection to *authorised* trade unions, their members and officials, in respect of acts done in contemplation or furtherance of a trade dispute: Industrial Relations Act 1990, ss 9–13. For example, actions in respect of tortious acts cannot be entertained by any court (IRA 1990, s 13), or acts by a person which induce or threaten to induce another person to break a contract of employment, or a threat to break his own contract of employment (IRA 1990, s 12), or acts which are an interference with the trade, business or employment of some other person (IRA 1990, s 12). There is no immunity for a trade union in respect of actions taken against them for restitution, for breach of constitutional rights or for breach of contract.

Seamen can no longer be indicted for conspiracy in furtherance of a trade dispute by taking industrial action: Merchant Shipping (Miscellaneous Provisions) Act 1998, s 1 repealing s 16 of the Conspiracy and Protection of Property Act 1875. See *Universe Tankships v ITWF* [1989] IRLR 363; *Hayes v Ireland* [1987] ILRM 651. See also *Esplanade Pharmacy Ltd v Larkin* [1957] IR 285; *Becton Dickinson & Co Ltd v Lee* [1973] IR 1. For fines, see IRA 1990, Sch 1, as amended by Industrial Relations (Miscellaneous Provisions) Act 2004, s 14. See CONSPIRACY; INDUSTRIAL ACTION; IMMUNITY; LABOUR INJUNCTION; LABOUR RELATIONS COMMISSION; PICKETING; SECRET BALLOT; STRIKE; TRADE UNION.

trade dispute, new resolution procedure. A new procedure has been provided for the processing of claims on behalf of employees where their employer has refused to follow the voluntary procedure outlined in the *Code of Practice on Voluntary Dispute Resolution*: Industrial Relations (Amendment) Act 2001 as amended by Industrial Relations (Miscellaneous Provisions) Act 2004.

The new procedure provides an avenue for the processing of claims without the need of recourse to industrial action. Under the new procedure, an authorised trade union (or an excepted body) may in certain circumstances make a unilateral referral to the Labour Court and the Court will make a recommendation which is not legally binding at that stage. If the recommendation does not resolve the dispute, the Court is empowered at the request of the trade union to issue a binding determination (IR(A)A 2001, s 6) which must be in writing, including a statement of the reasons for the determination (IR(A)A 2001, s 7). This determination may be enforced (where the employer fails to comply with it within the period specified, or if no time is specified, as soon as may be after the determination is communicated to the parties) by way of an 'enforcement order' of the Circuit Court (IR(A)A 2001, s 10 as substituted by the IR(MP)A 2004, s 4). There is provision for an appeal on a point of law only to the High Court (IR(A)A 2001, s 11).

The circumstances under which a trade union (or excepted body) may refer the dispute to the Labour Court are: (a) it is not the practice of the employer to engage in collective bargaining negotiations, and any internal dispute resolution procedures have failed, (b) the employer has failed to observe a provision of the Code of Practice or where the dispute has been referred to the Labour Relations Commission, the Commission is of the opinion that no further effort on its part will advance the resolution of the dispute, (c) the trade union, excepted body or employees have not acted in a manner to frustrate the employer in observing the Code, and (d) the trade union, excepted body or employees, have not had recourse to industrial action after the dispute was referred to the Labour Relations Commission in accordance with the Code (IR(A)A 2001, s 2 as amended by IR(MP)A 2004, s 2). Any question as to whether the requirements of s 2 have been met may be determined by the Labour Court by way of a preliminary hearing or as part of its investigation of the dispute (IR(A)A 2001, s 3 as substituted by IR(MP)A 2004, s 3).

The previous provision, under which a review by the Labour Court of its determination could be sought after a period of time, has been repealed (IR(A)A 2001, s 9 repealed by IR(MP)A 2004, s 16). See VICTIMISATION.

trade effluent. As regards *water pollution* (qv), means effluent from any works, apparatus, plant or drainage pipe used for the disposal of waters or to a sewer of any liquid (whether treated or untreated), either with or without particles of matter in suspension therein, which is discharged from premises used for carrying on any trade or industry, including mining, but does not include domestic sewage or storm water: Local Government (Water Pollution) Act 1977, s 1. The powers of local authorities to carry out reviews of trade effluent discharge licences have been extended: Local Government (Water Pollution) (Amendment) Act 1990, s 5. A person who contributes towards capital expenditure of a local authority on an approved scheme for the treatment of trade effluents, is entitled to a capital allowance as if his contribution had bought an asset for use in his trade: Taxes Consolidation Act 1997, s 310. See INTEGRATED POLLUTION CONTROL.

trade-in. Generally understood to mean a part payment by way of exchange in a contract for the sale of goods where the consideration (qv) is partly goods and partly money. See *Clarke v Reilly* [1962] 96 ILTR 96. See HIRE-PURCHASE PRICE; MOTOR VEHICLE, SALE OF.

trade mark. Any sign capable of being represented graphically which is capable of distinguishing goods or services of one undertaking from those of another undertaking: Trade Marks Act 1996, s 6(1). A trade mark may, in particular, consist of words (including personal names), designs, letters, numerals or the shape of goods or of their packaging (TMA 1996, s 6(2)). Particular types of trade marks are 'collective marks' (qv) and 'certification marks' (qv).

The law was updated in 1996 to give effect to Directive (EEC) 89/104 and to provide for securing trade marks in respect of services. Infringement of an *unregistered* trade mark gives no cause of action, except in relation to an action for *passing off* (qv). A *registered* trade mark however is personal property and is a property right, the proprietor of which has all the statutory rights and remedies of the 1996 Act (TMA 1996, s 7 and 26).

The vendor of goods to which a trade mark, or mark, or trade description has been applied, is deemed to warrant that the mark is a genuine trade mark and that the trade description is not a false trade description: Merchandise Marks Act 1887, s 17.

The test of ownership of a trade mark is that ownership vests in the party using it first in a jurisdiction: *Montex Holdings Ltd v Controller of Patents* [2000] 1 ILRM 481, HC and [2000] 1 IR 577, HC. The Supreme Court held that there was ample evidence before the High Court to justify a finding of the likelihood of confusion: *Montex Holdings Ltd v Controller of Patents* [2001] 3 IR 85, SC and [2002] 1 ILRM 208, SC.

The fact that a trade description is a trade mark, or part of a trade mark, within the meaning of the Trade Marks Act 1996, does not prevent it from being a false trade description when applied to goods; there is an exception however for some previous trade marks: Consumer Information Act 1978, s 24. See Trade Mark Rules 1996, SI No 199 of 1996. See 'The protection of trade marks against cybersquatters' by Anne Bateman BL in *Bar Review* (March 2001) 298. [Bibliography: Clark & Smyth; Forde (13); Tierney; Kerly (UK).] See COMMERCIAL PROCEEDINGS; COMMUNITY TRADE MARK; SOUND; TRADE MARK, REGISTERED.

trade mark, assignment of. At common law, trade marks could only be assigned with the *goodwill* of the business in the goods in relation to which they were used. *Registered* trade marks (qv) are transmissible by assignment, testamentary disposition or operation of law in the same way as other personal property; they are transmissible either in connection with the goodwill of a business or independently: Trade Marks Act 1996, s 28(1). The assignment is not effective unless it is in writing (TMA 1996, s 28(3)). The assignment may also be partial ie limited to some but not all of the goods or services or limited to use (TMA 1996, s 28(2)). An assignment is a registrable transaction (TMA 1996, s 29(2)).

An application for registration is assignable, reversing the previous law which required the assignee to await the registration of the mark in the assignor's name before the assignee could have his title recorded (TMA 1996, s 31). *Unregistered* trade marks can be assigned with the goodwill of the business and nothing in the 1996

Act is to be construed as affecting such assignment (TMA 1996, s 28(6)).

trade mark, associated. See ASSOCIATED TRADE MARK.

trade mark, certification. See CERTIFICATION TRADE MARK.

trade mark, community. See COMMUNITY TRADE MARK.

trade mark, infringement of. See INFRINGEMENT OF TRADE MARK.

trade mark, international. See INTERNATIONAL TRADE MARK.

trade mark, licence of. A licence of a registered trade mark, which is a registrable transaction, and is required to be in writing, may be: (a) *exclusive*, authorising the licensee to use the mark to the exclusion of all others, including the grantor, and (b) *limited* in relation to use, locality or to some but not all the goods or services: Trade Marks Act 1996, ss 32–35.

trade mark, registered. A trade mark registered in the register of trade marks: Trade Marks Act 1996, s 45. Registration is in respect of particular goods or services or in respect of classes of goods or services (TMA 1996, s 39). There are *absolute* and *relative* grounds for refusal of registration.

The *absolute* grounds include: (a) a sign which is not a trade mark; (b) a trade mark which is devoid of any distinctive character; (c) a trade mark which consists exclusively of signs or indications which may serve, in trade, to designate the kind, quality, quantity, intended purpose, value, geographical origin, the time of production of goods or of rendering of services, or other characteristics; (d) a trade mark which consists exclusively of signs or indications which have become customary in the current language of the trade; (e) a sign which consists of specified shapes; (f) a trade mark which is contrary to public policy or accepted principles of morality or its use is prohibited in the State (TMA 1996, s 8).

The term 'bubble wrap' was denied registration in Ireland as a trade mark as it was held to be a generic term in this country for this type of material; the Patent Office claimed that the term was devoid of any distinctive character: *Sealed Air Corporation v Patent Office* (2003) Irish Times, 3 August, HC. A Community trade mark was granted for 'Doublemint' as a chewing gum as the word had numerous meanings, it was deprived of any descriptive function: Case C-191.01P *Office for Harmonisation in the Internal Market v Wm Wrigley Jr Company* [2003] ECJ.

The *relative* grounds for refusal include that: (a) the trade mark is *identical* with an earlier trade mark and the goods or services for which the trade mark is applied for are *identical* with the goods and services for which the earlier trade mark is protected, (b) the trade mark is *similar* to an earlier trade mark and there exists a *likelihood of confusion*; which includes the *likelihood of association* of the later trade mark with the earlier trade mark (TMA 1996, s 10). The proprietor of a registered trade mark has exclusive rights in the trade mark; any use in the State without the proprietor's consent, constitutes an infringement of his rights (TMA 1996, s 13).

There is provision for appeal to the court against a refusal to register a trade mark within three months of the decision of the Controller of Patents (TMA 1996, s 79). The court is not empowered to enlarge the time, as a rule of court cannot amend a statutory provision without statutory authority: *Proctor and Gamble v Controller of Patents* [2003] 2 IR 580, SC, overturning the High Court decision in [2001] 2 IR 443, HC.

Registered trade marks include *collective marks* and *certification marks*. Registration of trade marks in other countries is facilitated by the priority obtainable via the Paris Convention (qv) and by single applications for a *Community trade mark* (qv) and an *international trade mark* (qv). See also Trade Mark Rules 1996, SI No 199 of 1996. See *Anheuser-Busch Inc v Controller of Patents* [1996] 2 IR 242, HC.

Provision has been made to enable certain details regarding the seniority of *community trade marks* to be recorded in the Register of Trade Marks: Trade Marks (Section 66) Regulations 2001, SI No 9 of 2001.

The cost of registering, or renewing the registration of, a trade mark is deductible in a trader's tax computation as a trading expense: Taxes Consolidation Act 1997, s 86. [Bibliography: Tierney; Kerly (UK).] See COURSE OF TRADE; EXCLUSIVE JURISDICTION; INFRINGEMENT OF TRADE MARK; PART A; PART B; REGISTER OF TRADE MARKS; SOUND; TRAFFICKING IN TRADE MARKS; TRADING STAMP; VARIETAL NAMES.

trade mark, registration period. The registration of a trade mark is for a period of ten years; it may be renewed from time to time for successive periods of ten years thereafter, subject to payment of prescribed renewal fees: Trade Marks Act 1996, ss 47–48.

trade mark, revocation of. The registration of a trade mark may be revoked on any of the following grounds: (a) it has not been put to genuine use in the five-year period since registration, or (b) such use has been suspended for an uninterrupted five-year period, or (c) it has become a common name in the trade for a product or service, or (d) it is liable to mislead the public: Trade Marks Act 1996, s 51. The burden of proving *use* is on the proprietor of the trade mark and not on the applicant: TMA 1996, s 99 and Trade Mark Rules 1996, SI No 199 of 1996, r 41(3).

trade mark agent. It is an offence for an individual who is not a registered trade mark agent to carry on business under any name or description which contain the words 'registered trade mark agent': Trade Marks Act 1996, s 85. Similar provisions apply to a partnership and a company where all the partners or directors must be registered trade mark agents. Registered trade mark agents who are registered to act before the Community trade mark office in Alicante, Spain, may use the title 'Community Trade Mark Attorney' (TMA 1996, s 85(9)).

A trade mark agent has certain privileges and immunities when appearing in proceedings before an international arbitral tribunal: Arbitration (International Commercial) Act 1998, s 12(8). See Residence of Trade Mark Agents Regulations 2000, SI No 34 of 2000. A registered *patent agent* or registered trade mark agent may act for applicants to register designs or for proprietors of registered designs: Industrial Designs Act 2001, s 88. See DESIGN.

trade mark at common law. A mark used so widely in connection with a group or class of goods that the public recognise goods carrying that mark as associated with the owner of the mark. Use of that mark by another could be grounds for an action of *passing-off* (qv).

trade refuse. See WASTE.

trade regulation. See BELOW COST SELLING; COMPETITION AUTHORITY; COMPETITION, DISTORTION OF; HELLO MONEY; MERGER OF COMPANY; PRICE CONTROL; WITHHOLDING OF SUPPLIES.

trade secret. Information concerning commercial, manufacturing or production processes of a firm where the disclosure of such information would be a breach of confidence or breach of contract. Such disclosure can be prevented by injunction (qv).

Breach of confidence can arise: (a) where the information has the necessary confidence about it ie it must not be something which is public knowledge; (b) the information must have been imparted to the defendant in circumstances imposing an obligation of confidence; (c) the unauthorised use of the information would be to the detriment of the plaintiff. Breach of contract could arise in the case of the relationship of employer and employee. See *Cranleigh Precision Engineering v Bryant* [1965] I WLR 1293; *Aksjeselskapet Jutul v Waterford Iron Founders Ltd* [1977] HC.

In data protection legislation, there is an obligation on a data controller to inform an individual who is a data subject, the logic involved in the automatic processing of data, where this is the sole basis for any decision significantly affecting the individual: Data Protection Act 1988, ss 4(1)(a)(iv) and 4(12) inserted by Data Protection (Amendment) Act 2003, s 5. This obligation to inform does not apply, where to do so would adversely affect trade secrets or intellectual property (in particular any copyright protecting computer software). See CONFIDENCE, BREACH OF; EMPLOYEE; PUBLIC JUSTICE.

trade union. Any combination, whether temporary or permanent, the principal objects of which are under its constitution the regulation of the relations between workmen and masters, or between workmen and workmen, or between masters and masters, or the imposing of restrictive conditions on the conduct of any trade or business, and also the provision of benefits to members: Trade Union Act 1913, s 2; *National Union of Journalists (NUJ) and IPU v Sisk* [1992] ILRM 96, SC; Barry in 9 ILT & SJ (1991) 271.

A trade union may be *unregistered* (qv), *certified* (qv), *registered* (qv) or *authorised* (qv). The statutory immunities conferred on trade unions by the Industrial Relations Act 1990 are restricted to *authorised* trade unions only (IRA 1990, ss 9–13).

The rules of a club, association or union, form the contract between the officers and the members and set down how the affairs of the body should be conducted; consequently, its affairs are not in general susceptible to judicial review in the absence of *mala fides* or disregard of the rules: *McEvoy v Prison Officers Association* [1999] 1 ILRM 445, SC. See *Riordan v Butler* [1940] IR 347; *Sheriff v McMullen* [1952] IR 236. For Irish Congress of Trade Unions, see website: *www.ictu.ie*. For the European Trade Union Confederation, see website: *www.etuc.org*. [Bibliography: Kerr; Kerr & Whyte; Maguire C (1).] See IMMUNITY; TRADE DISPUTE; PICKETING; UNFAIR DISMISSAL; UNLAWFUL INTERFERENCE WITH CONSTITUTIONAL RIGHTS; WORK, RIGHT TO.

trade union, authorised. A body of persons entitled to be granted or to hold a *negotiation licence:* Trade Union Act 1941, s 7 as amended by the Trade Union Acts of 1971 and 1975. It is an offence for any body of persons to carry on negotiations for the fixing of wages or other conditions of employment unless such body is the holder of a negotiation licence or is an *excepted body*: Trade Union Act 1941, s 6.

Excepted bodies include teachers' organisations, civil service staff associations, bodies exempted by the Minister and a body carrying on negotiations with its own employees: TUA 1941, s 6(3). An *excepted body* includes a body, all the members of which are employed by the same employer, and which carries on negotiations for the fixing of the wages or other conditions of employment of its own members (but of no other employees): Trade Union Act 1942, s 2. The object of s 2 has been held to be to relieve the hardship that would arise if employees of small firms, choosing not to join a large outside trade union, were deprived of the benefit of trade union representation in carrying on negotiations in-house: *Iarnród Éireann v Holbrooke* [2001] 1 IR 237, SC and ELR 65.

Generally, to obtain a negotiation licence, a union must be registered with the Registrar of Friendly Societies, have not less than 500 members, and maintain a deposit in the High Court depending on the size of the union. For new trade unions, the minimum number of members must be 1,000: Industrial Relations Act 1990, s 21(2).

Authorised trade unions, their members and officials are entitled to the protection of the Industrial Relations Act 1990, ss 9–13. This protection, originally confined to those in trade and industry by the Trade Disputes Act 1906, was extended to all employees, except members of the Defence Forces and the Gardaí by the Trade Disputes (Amendment) Act 1982.

Certain advantages under employment protection legislation accrue to authorised trade unions and their members eg dismissal for trade union membership or activity is deemed to be unfair only if the union is an authorised or excepted one. See *Irish Aviation Executive Staff Association v Minister for Labour* [1981] ILRM 350; *Post Office Workers Union v Minister for Labour* [1981] ILRM 355; *O'Riordan v Clune* [1991] ELR 89, EAT. See RSC Ord 107. See TRADE UNION.

trade union, certified. A body which has been certified by the Registrar of Friendly Societies that it is a union within the meaning of the Trade Union Acts 1871–1982. A body must apply to the Registrar in compliance with the Trade Union Act 1913, s 2(3). The only advantage of being a certified trade union is that the certificate issued is conclusive evidence that the body is a trade union. The immunities conferred by the Industrial Relations Act 1990 and the advantages conferred by the employment legislation of the 1970s do not apply to a certified trade union. See TRADE UNION.

trade union, registered. A body of seven or more members of a trade union which has been registered with the Registrar of Friendly Societies in accordance with the Trade Union Act 1871. The certificate of registration is conclusive evidence that the holder is a trade union within the meaning of the Trade Union Acts.

There are a number of advantages in registration eg: (a) exemption from income tax on investments (Income Tax Act 1967, s 336, now Taxes Consolidation Act 1997, s 213), and (b) property vesting in succeeding trustees without need of conveyance or assignment.

The exemption of registered trade unions from income tax in respect of interest and dividends which are applied for the purposes of *provident* benefits, has been extended to income which is applied to the education or training of the trade union's members and dependent children of members: Taxes Consolidation Act 1997, s 213 amended by Finance Act 2000, s 74.

However, the immunities conferred by the Industrial Relations Act 1990 are restricted to *authorised* trade unions only as are the advantages conferred by the employment legislation of the 1970s.

It has been held that an Irish registered trade union is entitled to transfer its engagements to a UK registered trade union which has members within the State and an Irish negotiation licence: Trade Union Act 1975; *National Union of Journalists (NUJ) & Irish Print Union v Sisk* [1992] ILRM 96, SC. See NEGOTIATION LICENCE; TRADE UNION.

trade union, unregistered. A trade union which is an unincorporated voluntary association of individuals similar in legal status to a social club. It has no legal personality itself and consequently any action concerning the union, its property or activities, must be brought or defended by way of *representative action* (qv). See *Nolan v Fagan* [1985] HC; RSC Ord 15, r 9.

trade union subscriptions. A new tax allowance of €130, at the standard rate, in respect of trade union subscriptions was introduced by the Finance Act 2001, s 11. It was increased to €200 for 2004 and subsequent years: Finance Act 2004, s 4.

trading house, special. A company which exists solely for the purpose of carrying on a trade which consists solely of the selling of export goods manufactured by a firm which employs less than 200 persons: Finance Act 1987, s 29 as amended by SI No 61 of 1988. A special trading house, to benefit from the special 10% rate of corporation tax (FA 1987, s 29) must have a licence which may be granted by the Minister: Export Promotion (Amendment) Act 1987, s 2. An appeal against a refusal to grant such a licence lies to the Circuit Court (EP(A)A 1987, s 2).

The requirements to qualify as a special trading house have been set out by the Minister: it must be a registered company; its business must be solely the sale abroad of Irish *goods* to which it has title; it must not be the manufacturer of those goods or of any other goods; it must *sell only by wholesale*. *Goods* means goods manufactured in Ireland, and includes data processing equipment and computer software services. *Selling by wholesale* means selling to a person who carries on a business of selling such goods or who uses the goods for the purpose of a trade or undertaking. See now Taxes Consolidation Act 1997, s 443(12).

trading stamp. Any stamp, coupon, voucher, token or similar device which is, or is intended to be, delivered to any person upon, or in connection with, the purchase of goods or the provision of services and is, or is intended to be, *redeemable* by that or some other person: Trading Stamps Act 1980, s 1. *Redeemable* means exchanged for money, goods or services. It does not include a newspaper or periodical of which the stamp forms part or in which it is contained. It also excludes a stamp which is redeemable only from the seller of the goods, or his supplier, or the person who provides the service.

A trading stamp must bear on its face in clear and legible characters a value expressed in the currency of the State and the name or registered trade mark (qv) of the issuing company (TSA 1980, s 4). See TRADING STAMP SCHEME.

trading stamp scheme. Any arrangement for making trading stamps (qv) available for use in shops or elsewhere, including arrangements for their redemption: Trading Stamps Act 1980, s 1. There are restrictions on persons who may carry on business as promoters of trading stamps (TSA 1980, s 2) and provision for the redemption of trading stamps for cash (TSA 1980, s 5). An exchange of goods or services for trading stamps is to be regarded as a monetary consideration for the purposes of the Sale of Goods Act 1893 and the Sale of Goods and Supply of Services Act 1980 (TSA 1980, s 8).

traffic calming measures. Means measures which restrict and control the speed or movement of mechanically propelled vehicles; a road authority is empowered to provide traffic calming measures: Road Traffic Act 1994, s 38.

traffic management. The Commissioner of the Garda Síochána is empowered to carry out various functions regarding the management of road traffic pursuant to the Road Traffic Acts 1961 to 1987. The Commissioner is required to have regard to any recommendations made to him by the National Roads Authority in relation to the performance of his function: Roads Act 1993, s 23(1). See CROWD CONTROL; TRAFFIC REGULATION.

traffic refuge. A refuge for pedestrians on a roadway provided by a raised pavement, guard posts or similar means: Road Traffic (Signs) Regulations 1962, SI No 171 of 1962, art 2.

traffic regulation. The Minister is empowered to make traffic and parking regulations in a single code to replace: (a) the existing general regulations made by the Minister (Road Traffic Act 1968, s 60); and (b) the local traffic and parking bye-laws or temporary rules on a county basis made by the Garda Commissioner (Road Traffic Act 1961, ss 89–90): Road Traffic Act 1994, s 35, as proposed to be amended by Road Traffic Bill 2004, s 23.

Road authorities are given power to make bye-laws governing the type of parking controls in their area and to apply traffic management measures eg traffic signs (RTA 1994, ss 36–37). See Road Traffic (Traffic and Parking) Regulations 1997, SI No 182 of 1997 as amended by SI No 274 of 1998, SI No 98 of 2003 and SI No 404 of 2004. See Road Traffic (Signs) Regulations 1997, SI No 181 of 1997 as amended by SI No 273 of 1998, and by SI No 97 of 2003.

traffic sign. See TRAFFIC REGULATION; SIGN.

traffic wardens. (1) Persons employed by a local authority (qv) to carry out functions in respect of certain road traffic or related offences: Local Authorities (Traffic Wardens) Act 1975, s 2. Offences which come within the remit of traffic wardens are: (a) offences under the Road Traffic Acts which relate to the prohibition or restriction of the stopping or parking of mechanically propelled vehicles; (b) the offence of using a vehicle not displaying a valid test disc; (c) the offence of failing to display a current licence disc (Finance Act 1976, s 73); (d) the offence of using a vehicle for which a licence under the Finance (Excise Duties) (Vehicle) Act 1952 is not in force, or for not affixing and exhibiting such a licence (LA(TW)A 1975, s 3 as substituted by Road Traffic Act 2002, s 12). See Road Traffic Bill 2004, s 25.

The duties and powers of traffic wardens have been changed to reflect the new on-the-spot arrangements for road traffic offences with the introduction of the *penalty points* system; they do not have the power to issue such fines for *penalty point offences*.

(2) Traffic wardens are also persons authorised by the Minister to carry out functions (eg on-the-spot fines) as specified in the Road Traffic Act 1961, s 130(19) as substituted by Road Traffic Act 2002, s 11(1). Such persons are not civil servants (RTA 1961, s 130(19)(d)). [Bibliography: Pierce (2).] See PENALTY POINTS.

trafficking. See CHILD TRAFFICKING; DRUG TRAFFICKING.

trafficking in illegal immigrants. See ILLEGAL IMMIGRANT; JOINT INVESTIGATION TEAMS.

trafficking in trade marks. It has been held that *trafficking* in a trade mark conveyed the notion of dealing in a trade mark primarily as a commodity in its own right and not for the purpose of identifying or promoting merchandise with which the proprietor of the mark was connected: *Holly Hobbie trade mark* [1984] RPC 329.

trailer. There is a general prohibition on the towing of a trailer by a motorcycle; this prohibition is relaxed under specified conditions relating to the motorcycle and the trailer: Road Traffic (Construction and Use of Vehicles) Regulations 2003, SI No 5 of 2003 as amended by SI No 99 of 2004.

train pass. See BENEFIT IN KIND.

trainee garda. See GARDA SÍOCHÁNA.

training. The imparting of skill, knowledge and ability to another. An employer has a duty at common law to provide adequate training and instruction to his employee. There is a statutory duty on all employers in providing training to ensure that his employees receive, during time off from their duties and without loss of remuneration, adequate safety and health training: SI No 44 of 1993, regs 13 and 26(d). There is also a statutory duty on every employee, taking into account training and instructions, given by his employer, to make correct use of machinery, apparatus, tools, dangerous substances, transport equipment and other means of production (SI No 44 of 1993, reg 14). See also SI No 53 of 2003.

The Unfair Dismissals Act 1977 does not apply to dismissal of an employee while undergoing training which is one year or less from commencement of employment. The Act does not apply also to dismissals during training for specified qualifications eg nurse, health inspector, social worker (UDA 1977, s 3).

Formerly, training levies were imposed on employers in designated industrial activities by way of *levy orders* and could be appealed to a Levy Appeals Tribunal: Industrial Training Act 1967, ss 21–22. Also an apprentice training levy was imposed on certain industry sectors: Industrial Training (Apprentice Levy) Act 1994. All these levies were replaced by a single levy to create a *training fund* (qv): National

Training Fund Act 2000. Rules may be made on the employment and training of certain industrial apprentices (ITA 1967, ss 27–36).

An Foras Áiseanna Saothair (FÁS), took over the functions and powers of An Chomhairle Oiliuna (AnCO), the National Manpower Service and the Youth Employment Agency on 1 January 1988: Labour Services Act 1987.

Refusal or failure to avail of any reasonable opportunity of receiving training provided by or approved of by FÁS, without just cause, can lead to disqualification of unemployment assistance: Social Welfare (Consolidation) Act 1993, s 47(4)(c). A person who has paid fees in respect of an approved training course in information technology or language skills may qualify for tax relief: Taxes Consolidation Act 1997, s 476 as amended by Finance Act 2000, s 21(e).

See Protection of Employees (Fixed-Term Work) Act 2003, ss 2(1) and 10(3). See *Cityview Press Ltd v An Chomhairle Oiliuna* [1980] IR 381; Fox *v National Council of the Blind* [1995] ELR 74, EO. The Royal College of Surgeons in Ireland launched in 2000 the world's first *online* training programme for surgeons – BEST or electronic Basic Surgery Training. For *FÁS*, see website: *www.fas.ie*. For the *Irish Institute for Training and Development*, see website: *www.iitd.ie*. For *European Training Foundation*, see website: *www.etf.eu.int*. See APPRENTICESHIP; CONTINUING PROFESSIONAL DEVELOPMENT; COPENHAGEN DECLARATION; EUROPEAN CENTRE FOR THE DEVELOPMENT OF VOCATIONAL TRAINING; SAFETY AT WORK; SKILLNETS; VOCATIONAL EDUCATION COMMITTEE; VOCATIONAL TRAINING; WEIGHTS MAXIMUM; WITHHOLDING TAX.

training fund. A new *national training fund* and an associated levy on employers, established to finance a range of schemes aimed at: (a) raising the skills of persons in employment, and (b) providing training to persons who wish to acquire skills for the purpose of taking up employment: National Training Fund Act 2000. The levy is set at 0.7% of the reckonable earnings of employees, insured for the purposes of social welfare legislation, and is payable by employers.

The cost of the levy is offset by a comparable reduction in the employers' PRSI contributions. The 2000 Act also provides for the abolition of the former *sectoral levies* and the *apprenticeship levies*, by repealing certain sections of the Industrial Training Act 1967 and repealing the entire Industrial Training (Apprenticeship Levy) Act 1994. See also Social Welfare (Miscellaneous Provisions) Act 2003, s 21; Social Welfare Act 2003, s 15; Social Welfare (Miscellaneous Provisions) Act 2004, s 21.

training grants. Training grants may be made by An Foras Áiseanna Saothair (FÁS) or by Enterprise Ireland or by IDA Ireland: Industrial Training Act 1967, ss 19–20; Labour Services Act 1987; Industrial Development Act 1986, s 28 as amended by Industrial Development (Enterprise Ireland) Act 1998, s 43 and Industrial Development (Science Foundation Ireland) Act 2003, s 30. Certain training and employment grants are exempt from income or corporation tax: Taxes Consolidation Act 1997, ss 225–226, overturning *Jacobs International v O'Cleirigh v Jacobs International* 2 ITR 165.

tram. See LIGHT RAILWAY.

trans-European networks. The EC is required to contribute to the establishment and development of trans-European networks in the areas of transport, telecommunications and energy infrastructures; there is a requirement to take account in particular of the need to link island, landlocked and peripheral regions with the central regions of the Community: EC Treaty, art 154 of the consolidated (2002) version. The funding of such infrastructures in the less prosperous regions of the EC is provided for, as is the financing of specific projects through the Cohesion Fund (qv). See COMMITTEE OF THE REGIONS.

transactions of company. There are rules governing transactions of *listed* companies (e g acquisitions, disposals, take-overs and mergers) and also of transactions between listed companies and *related parties*, to prevent current or recent directors or substantial shareholders taking advantage of their position: Listing Rules 2000, chs 10 and 11. See ACQUISITIONS; DISPOSALS; TAKE-OVERS.

transborder data flows. The transfer across national borders, by whatever medium, of *personal data* undergoing automatic processing or collected with a view to being automatically processed: Data Protection Convention 1981, art 12(1). A party to the Convention may not, for the sole purpose of privacy, prohibit or subject to special authorisation transborder flows of personal data going to the territory of another party (art 12(2)). Nevertheless, a party may derogate from this requirement in specific circumstances. See Data Protection Act 1988, s 11 as substituted by Data Protection (Amendment) Act 2003, s 12. See PROHIBITION NOTICE, DATA.

Transboundary Convention. Means the *United Nations Economic Commission for Europe Convention on Environmental Impact Assessment in a Transboundary Context*, done at Espoo (Finland) on 25 February 1991. The Minister is empowered to make regulations requiring the submission of an *environmental impact statement* (EIS) in respect of an application for development of land, where the development is likely to have significant effects on the environment in another member state of the European Community or of a state which is a party to the Transboundary Convention: Planning and Development Act 2000, s 174(1).

This provision governs the situation where the planning authority, or An Bord Pleanála on appeal, is aware that the development is likely to have such effects or also where the other state concerned considers that the development would be likely to have such effects. The planning authority, or An Bord Pleanála, may impose conditions on a grant of planning permission in order to reduce or eliminate potential transboundary effects of any proposed development (PDA 2000, s 174(3)). The Minister may request information from another state in respect of any development which is likely to have significant environmental effects in Ireland and may forward submissions or observations, or enter into discussions with, the other state on these effects and measure envisaged to reduce or eliminate those effects (PDA 2000, s 174(4)–(5)).

Provision has been made for the Environmental Protection Agency (qv) to consider and address the impact of *transboundary emissions* in administering Integrated Pollution Prevention and Control licensing: Environmental Protection Agency Act 1992, s 85 inserted by Protection of the Environment Act 2003, s 15. See ENVIRONMENTAL IMPACT STATEMENT.

transcript. The reproduction in longhand of the notes taken, usually in shorthand, of the proceedings at a hearing. The transcript must be certified by the trial judge; the report of the official stenographer includes the original shorthand notes and the transcript thereof. While no transcript is ever perfect, in the absence of mistakes or defect being established, the Court of Criminal Appeal will hear and determine an appeal on the report of the official stenographer pursuant to the provisions of the Courts of Justice Act 1924, s 33: *DPP v McKeever* [1994] 2 ILRM 186, Section 33 is now substituted by Criminal Justice (Miscellaneous Provisions) Act 1997, s 7.

The court disapproves of trawling through the transcript of a trial for errors and omissions and including as a ground of appeal such errors or omissions not thought worthy of mention or objection during the course of the trial: *People (DPP) v James Ryan* [1993] ITLR (19 April) CCA and 11 ILT Dig [1993] 285.

In a personal injuries action, it was held that the defendant should not be required to bear the cost of a daily transcript of the evidence, as there were instructing solicitor, one junior and two senior counsel, and there was no detailed scientific evidence in the case: *Ward v Walsh* [1992] 10 ILT Dig 74, SC. See RSC Ord 123; Ord 86, r 14; Ord 96, r 36. A shorthand writer will no longer be provided at the public expense at the trial or hearing of chancery and family law proceedings begun after 30 April 2004: Rules of the Superior Courts (Shorthand Reporting) 2004, SI No 137 of 2004 amending RSC Ord 123.

In a criminal trial, a transcript of counsel's speeches ought to be made as a matter of routine: *obiter dictum* in *The People (DPP) v Connolly* [2003] 2 IR 1, CCA. Access was denied to a person, under 'freedom of information', to the shorthand note and transcript in a criminal prosecution of his wife, on the basis that these documents were created by the court and on the basis that disclosure of the contents was regulated by the rules of court: *Minister for Justice v The Information Commissioner* [2001] 3 IR 43, HC.

In a case regarding an inquiry into the fitness of a midwife to practice, it was held that the provision of transcripts would prolong the hearing; there was considerable difference between hearing the evidence and reading it: *O Ceallaigh v Fitness to Practice Committee of An Bord Altranais* [1999] 2 IR 552, SC.

In an inquiry by the Irish Medical Council into the conduct of a doctor who had

been struck off the British register for professional misconduct, the High Court held
that the Council must call oral evidence
from complainants; it could not prove such
evidence by reference to transcript evidence
from the British General Medical Council
inquiry as this would deny the doctor the
opportunity of confronting his accusers:
Dr Sebastian Borges v Medical Council
(2003) Irish Times, 6 March, HC. This
decision was upheld by the Supreme Court:
Irish Times, 31 January 2004.

An employee of long-standing with an
otherwise unblemished record, the subject
of a disciplinary hearing in relation to an
alleged sexual assault, is entitled at the very
least to have access to the recorded words
of his accuser where such record is in
existence; a reasonable and fair employer
would have made the transcript available to
the employee's representative: *C v Mid-
Western Health Board* [2000] ELR 38, EAT,
distinguishing *State (D & D) v Groark*
[1990] 1 IR 305. See STENOGRAPHER,
OFFICIAL.

transfer. The passage of a right from one
person to another either: (a) by act of the
parties eg in a conveyance of land, or (b)
by operation of law eg forfeiture, bankruptcy, succession (qqv). See also
NATIONAL QUALIFICATIONS AUTHORITY
OF IRELAND.

transfer of action. See REMITTAL OF
ACTION.

transfer of employment. See ACQUIRED
RIGHTS, EMPLOYEES; TRANSFER OF
UNDERTAKINGS.

transfer of engagements. A building society may transfer its engagements to another
society to any extent, and that other society
may undertake to fulfil the engagements,
provided each resolves to do so by special
resolution, or, if the Central Bank consents,
by resolution of the board of directors:
Building Societies Act 1989, ss 96(1)–(2)
and 99(2). See also Credit Union
Act 1997, s 129 as amended by Central
Bank and Financial Services Authority of
Ireland Act 2003, s 35, Schedule 1.

transfer of prisoners. See PRISONER,
TRANSFER OF.

transfer of sentence. See SENTENCE,
TRANSFER OF EXECUTION OF.

transfer of shares. The change in ownership of shares which takes place when they
are transferred under a proper instrument
of transfer, or when vested in another person by operation of law, the name of the

new owner being entered in the register of
members: Companies Act 1963, ss 81 and
31(2). The standard form of transfer for
fully paid transferable shares in most limited companies is set out in the Stock
Transfer Act 1963, Sch 1. *Share warrants* to
bearer are transferred by mere delivery (CA
1963, s 88). A stamp duty of 1% applies to
the transfer on sale of shares: Stamp Duties
Consolidation Act 1999, Sch 1, as
amended by Finance Act 2003,
s 143(1)(b).

In a private company, its *articles of association* must impose restrictions on the
transferability of its shares, whereas in
other companies a member has an unfet-
tered right to transfer shares unless the
articles provide otherwise. Some articles
give directors the right to decline to register
a transfer, but such a refusal must be exercised *bona fide* and in the best interest of
the company. See also *Casey v Bentley*
[1902] 2 IR 376; *Lee & Co (Dublin) Ltd v
Egan (Wholesale) Ltd* [1978] HC; *Pernod
Ricard and Comrie plc v FII Fyffes plc* [1989]
7 ILT Dig 53, HC.

The Official Assignee (qv) in bankruptcy,
is empowered, without court order, to
transfer stocks and shares of the bankrupt
(qv) to the same extent as the bankrupt
could have: Bankruptcy Act 1988, s 67. See
Stock Transfer (Forms) Regulations 1998,
SI No 546 of 1998. See Stamp Duties
Consolidation Act 1999, ss 64–66. See
CAPITAL GAINS TAX; DISTRINGAS NOTICE;
SHARES, COMPANY; SHARES, EQUITABLE
MORTGAGE OF; SHARES, COMPULSORY
PURCHASE; TRANSMISSION OF SHARES.

transfer of trial. A Circuit Court judge is
empowered to transfer by order the trial of
a person charged with an indictable offence
to the Circuit Court within the Dublin
Circuit: Courts Act 1981, s 31; Circuit
Court Rules 2001 Ord 63.

transfer of undertakings. Any transfer of
an undertaking, business, or part of an
undertaking or business from one employer
to another employer as a result of a legal
transfer (including the assignment or forfeiture of a lease) or merger: EC (Protection
of Employees on Transfer of Undertakings)
Regulations 2003, SI No 131 of 2003,
reg 3(1). The regulations give effect to
Directive (EC) 2001/23 and revoke SI
No 306 of 1980 and SI No 487 of 2000.

'Transfer' means the transfer of an economic entity which retains its identity (SI
No 131 of 2003, reg 3(2)). The regulations

apply to public and private undertakings engaged in economic activities whether or not they are operating for gain (reg 3(3)). However, an administrative reorganisation of public administrative authorities is not a transfer (reg 3(4)).

The *transferor's* rights and obligations arising from a contract of employment, existing on the date of a transfer, are transferred to the *transferee* (SI No 131 of 2003, reg 4(1) and *Brett v Niall Collins Ltd* [1995] ELR 69, EAT). It is prohibited to dismiss an employee on the grounds of the transfer of the undertaking, unless the dismissal is attributable to economic, technical or organisational reasons which entail changes to the workforce after the transfer (SI No 131 of 2003, reg 5 and *Cunningham v Oasis Stores Ltd* [1995] ELR 183, EAT). If a contract of employment is terminated because the transfer involves a substantial change in working conditions to the detriment of the employee, the employer will be regarded as having been responsible for the termination (reg 5(3)).

In determining whether in fact a transfer of an undertaking has taken place, all the circumstances of the case must be considered and it is the substance and not the form of the transfer which will be looked at (*Brett* case).

Regulations 3 and 4 do not apply where the transferor is the subject of bankruptcy or insolvency proceedings (SI No 131 of 2003, reg 6 and *Blaney v Willis* [2002] ELR 193, EAT). Protection is not lost by the transfer of the undertaking to a paying agent: *O'Beirne v Fox* [1990] ELR 151. Protection is not lost either in the contracting out of a business if the business retains its identity or if there is a change in the legal or natural person who is responsible for carrying on the business regardless of whether or not ownership of the business is transferred: *Bannon v Employment Appeals Tribunal* [1992] ELR 203, HC reported by Barry in 10 ILT & SJ (1992) 242.

However, transfer of a contract alone does not constitute a transfer of undertakings: *Cannon v Noonan Cleaning Co Ltd* [1998] ELR 153, EAT applying *Suzen v Zernacher Gebaudereinigung GmbH* [1997] ECR I-467. Reversion of the lease of a business premises to the original lessor constitutes a transfer of undertakings: *Guidon v Farrington* [1992] ELR 146, EAT. Acceptance of a redundancy payment in respect of employment with the first employer does

not break continuity of service: *Yorke & Tuite v Teenoso Ltd* [1992] ELR 161, EAT; it now does – see REDUNDANCY.

There is an obligation on the transferor and the transferee concerned to inform and consult with their respective employees' representatives (SI No 131 of 2003, reg 8). An employer has a duty of care to his employees to ensure that statements made to the employees, regarding the transfer, are true: *King v Aer Lingus plc* [2002] 3 IR 481, HC and [2003] ELR 173. However, an employer is not obligated to inform an employee that the business is being taken over or transferred where the employee has already before this given notice of his resignation: *Cave v Vehicle Maintenance (Dublin) Ltd* [1998] ELR 319, EAT.

There is provision for complaints to be heard by a Rights Commissioner, with provision for an appeal to the Employment Appeals Tribunal, and to the High Court on a point of law (SI No 131 of 2003, regs 10–11).

See National Minimum Wages Act 2000, s 46. See also *Nova Colour Graphic Supplies v Employment Appeals Tribunal* [1987] IR 426, HC; *Ennis & Bonney v Coffey & Ryan* UD 132/88 and 133/88, 7 ILT & SJ [1989] 5; *Westman Holdings Ltd v McCormack & Ors* [1991] ILRM 833, SC; *Mythan v Employment Appeals Tribunal* [1990] ELR 1, HC; *Purcell & McHugh v Bewley's Manufacturing Ltd* [1990] ELR 68, CC; *Sweeney v Deantus Alfa Teo* [1993] ELR 22, EAT; *Guidon v Farrington* [1993] ELR 98, EAT; *Mulqueen v Verit Hotel* [1993] ELR 162, EAT; *Gray v ISPCA* [1994] ELR 225, EAT; *Roche v Salthill Hotel Ltd* [1996] ELR, EAT 15; *Power v St Paul's Nursing Home* [1998] ELR 212, EAT; *Walsh v Denford Taverns Ltd* [1998] ELR 315, EAT; *Re Irish Life Assurance plc* [2002] 2 IR 9, HC; *Abler and Others v Sodexho Catering Gesellschaft mbH* [2003] Case C-340/01, ECJ. See Barry in 7 ILT & SJ (1989) 262 & 294 and in 11 ILT & SJ (1993) 166. See 'All the right moves' by solicitor Ciaran O'Meara in *Law Society Gazette* (August/September 2003) 32. [Bibliography: Byrne G; Redmond (1).]

transfer order. See TENANT PURCHASE SCHEME.

transfer pricing. The term used to describe the arrangement by a company, with operations in different countries with different tax rates, by which the profits are maximised in the country with the lower tax rates, by artificially inflating or reducing prices or costs of goods or services between the different parts of the enterprise in the different countries, including the cost of funding. Such arrangements are given no protection in double tax agreements between Ireland and other states, as all such agreements have included article 9 of the OECD Model Convention which provides for the tax-deprived state to adjust the profits of the company in its jurisdiction so as to capture any profits transferred to the lower tax state. See DOUBLE TAXATION AGREEMENT.

transferable vote. A vote in an election which is: (a) capable of being given so as to indicate the voter's preference for the candidates in order, and (b) capable of being transferred to the next choice when the vote is not required to give a prior choice the necessary quota of votes, or when, owing to the deficiency in the number of votes given for a prior choice, that choice is excluded from the list of candidates: Electoral Act 1992, s 37. A *transferable paper* is a ballot paper on which, following a first preference, a second or subsequent preference is recorded in consecutive numerical order for a continuing candidate (EA 1992, s 118(1)). See also Presidential Elections Act 1993, s 45; European Parliament Elections Act 1997, s 7(3). See PROPORTIONAL REPRESENTATION; QUOTA.

transit in rem judicatem. [It passes into a *res judicata* (qv).] A cause of action is merged into a judgment; further proceedings cannot be taken on the same cause of action other than to enforce the judgment already obtained.

transitu, stoppage in. See STOPPAGE IN TRANSITU.

translation. As regards the recognition and enforcement of judgments or settlements of other EU contracting states, a document will be admissible as evidence of a *translation* if: (a) it purports to be a translation of certain matters (eg a court judgment or a settlement); and (b) it is certified as correct by a person competent to do so: Jurisdiction of Courts and Enforcement of Judgments Act 1998, s 12. The *Brussels I Regulation* on the recognition and enforcement of judgments in civil and commercial matters, replaces the 1998 Act as from 1 March 2002 for all EU States except Denmark: EC (Civil and Commercial Judgments) Regulations 2002, SI No 52 of 2002. It contains a similar provision on the admissibility of a translation (reg 9(3)).

In an application for refugee status, failure to translate into English the applicant's answers in full to an official questionnaire, may amount to a breach of fair procedures: *Stefan v Minister for Justice* [2002] 2 ILRM 134, SC and [2001] 4 IR 203, SC. For *Translation Centre for the Bodies of the European Union*, see website: *www.cdt.eu.int*. For a commercial translation service into and from many languages, see website: *www.legaltranslations.ie*. See LANGUAGE.

transmission capacity right. A right to use wired, radio or optical transmission paths for the transfer of voice, data or information: Taxes Consolidation Act 1997, s 769A inserted by Finance Act 2000, s 64 and amended by Finance Act 2003, s 20 – an anti-avoidance measure. The expenditure incurred by a company on such rights may be written off over the life of the agreement relating to the use of the rights, subject to a maximum write-off period of seven years.

transmission of shares. The automatic vesting of shares of a company in another person by operation of law eg on the death of a shareholder, the automatic vesting in favour of the personal representative takes place. The personal representative may be entitled to be registered as shareholder himself; in any event, he has power to transfer the shares even though he is not registered as a member of the company. In the case of bankruptcy of a shareholder, the Official Assignee (qv) is entitled to disclaim the bankrupt's shares within twelve months of the date of adjudication of bankruptcy. See Companies Act 1963, ss 81(2), 82, and 87 as amended by Companies Act 1977, s 5(1); Bankruptcy Act 1988, s 56.

transparency. Making it possible to see clearly and to follow from outside the way in which decisions are reached: National Forum on Europe, *Glossary of Terms* (2003). The European Council at Edinburgh (December 1992) decided that *transparency* would be improved by: (a) improving access to the work of the Council (eg by open debates and publication of voting records); (b) by improved information on the role of the Council (eg better information on the decisions of Council); (c) simplification of and easier access to Community legislation (eg unofficial and official codification of Community legislation). See EUROPEAN TRANSPARENCY DIRECTIVE.

transport accessibility. The Minister is empowered to make regulations requiring road or rail passenger vehicles and bus and rail stations to be readily accessible and usable by persons with a disability: Equal Status Act 2000, ss 17–18.

transport auxiliary. Self-employed persons or employees who are either a forwarding agent, freight agent, airfreight agent, road haulage broker, tour operator (qv), travel agent (qv), air broker, air travel organiser: (all category A); a shipping and forwarding agent, shipping agent, shipbroker: (category B); a market or lairage operator: (category C): European Communities (Transport Auxiliaries) Regulations 1988, SI No 18 of 1988. These Regulations provide for a grant of a *certificate of experience* to any appropriately experienced person who wishes to operate as a transport auxiliary in any other EC member state, implementing Directive (EEC) 82/470.

transport policy. The EC Council is empowered to lay down: (a) common rules applicable to international transport to and from the territory of a member state or passing across the territory of one or more member states; (b) the conditions under which non-resident carriers may operate transport services within a member state; (c) measures to improve transport safety; and (d) any other appropriate provisions: EC Treaty, arts 70–71 and arts 72–80 of the consolidated (2002) version. For the European Conference of Ministers of Transport, see website: *www.oecd.org/cem*.

transportation. Formerly, the penalty for felons who were transported overseas to a penal colony; it was abolished and replaced by *penal servitude* (qv) under the Penal Servitude Act 1857. Penal servitude was abolished in 1997 and the 1857 Act was repealed: Criminal Law Act 1997, s 16 and Sch 3.

transposing of words. The alteration of the order of words in a document which the court may make in order to give effect to the intention of the parties. See *Parkhurst v Smith* [1742] Willes 327.

transsexual. 'A person who has undergone medical and surgical procedures to alter external sexual characteristics to those of the opposite sex': *Collins English Dictionary*. Transsexualism is 'an established and recognised condition'; gender identity disorder

(GID) has been recognised for at least 25 years as a 'genuine psychiatric medical condition' which is irreversible and incurable: McKechnie J in *Foy v Registrar of Births* (2002) Irish Times, 10 July, HC. In this case the court rejected the application of a transsexual to have her male birth certificate altered to record her gender as female; the court upheld the practice of the Registrar of Births of registering a child's sex in accordance with the child's external genitalia at birth.

The European Court of Justice has held that it is for member states to determine the conditions under which legal recognition is given for change of gender: Case C-117/01 *KB v National Health Service Pensions Agency* [2004] 7 January 2004, ECJ.

travel, right to. There is a constitutional right to travel outside the State: *The State (KM) v Minister for Foreign Affairs* [1979] IR 73; *Lennon v Ganley* [1981] ILRM 84. It is an unenumerated right under the Constitution. In 1992, an amendment to the Constitution provided that art 40(3)(3) – the right to life of the unborn – shall not limit freedom to travel between the State and another state: Thirteenth Amendment to the Constitution Act 1992. The amended Constitution does not now confer a right to an abortion outside Ireland; it merely prevents injunctions against travelling for that purpose: *A & B v Eastern Health Board & C* [1998] 1 ILRM 460, HC.

In a particular case, two persons from Northern Ireland were banned from travelling south of the border during the period of a three-year suspended sentence: *DPP v Warnock & Morton* (1993) Irish Times, 24 March, CCC. See also *A-G v X* [1992] ILRM 401, SC; *Kingston & Whelan* in 10 ILT & SJ [1992] 95. See ABORTION; ABORTION, MEDICAL GUIDELINES; BAYER INJUNCTION; COMMON TRAVEL AREA; NE EXEAT REGNO; PASSPORT; SCHENGEN AGREEMENTS.

travel agent. A person other than a carrier who, as agent, sells or offers to sell to, or purchases or offers to purchase on behalf of the public, accommodation on air, sea or land transport to destinations outside Ireland or who holds himself out by advertising or otherwise as one who may make available such accommodation, either solely or in association with other accommodation, facilities or services: Transport (Tour Operators and Travel Agents) Act 1982, s 2. Similar requirements concerning a *bond* and a *licence* apply as in the case of a tour operator (qv). See *Balkan Tours v Minister for Communications* [1988] ILRM 101; *Minister for Tourism Transport v Grimes* [1988] HC. See SI No 176 of 1987; RSC Ord 102. See also Package Holiday and Travel Trade Act 1995. [Bibliography: Buttimore (1); McDonald M (3).] See PACKAGE HOLIDAY; SEX TOURISM; TOUR OPERATOR; TRANSPORT AUXILIARY; TRAVELLERS' PROTECTION FUND.

travel tax. The foreign travel excise duty of £5 on passenger tickets was abolished for tickets issued on or after 1 January 2000: Finance Act 2000, s 102.

traveller. A person belonging to the class of persons who traditionally pursue or have pursued a nomadic way of life: Housing (Traveller Accommodation) Act 1998, ss 2(1) and 29. In planning law, a *traveller* means a traveller within the meaning of s 2 of the 1998 Act: Planning and Development Act 2000, s 2(1). Provision is made for a housing authority to provide, improve, manage and control *halting sites* for travellers: Housing Act 1988, s 13 as amended by H(TA)A 1998, s 29.

A halting site may be a site for *permanent* residence (a normal place of residence) or may be a site for *temporary* residence (ie with limited facilities for travellers otherwise than as their normal place of residence or pending the provision of temporary accommodation). Under H(TA)A 1998, a housing authority must carry out regular assessments on the need for *traveller accommodation* and must adopt and implement five-year accommodation programmes to meet the needs identified (H(TA)A 1998, ss 5–23).

The incorporation of a residence or indigenous policy in a traveller accommodation programme is within the statutory power of a housing authority: *McDonagh v Clare County Council* [2002] 2 IR 634, HC and [2003] 1 ILRM 36. A housing authority was held to have failed to discharge its statutory obligation to provide a site for the applicant's caravan: *O'Donoghue v City of Limerick* [2003] FL 6943, HC.

The adoption of the accommodation programme is a *semi-reserved function* in that if the elected members fail to adopt the programme within a specific time, the manager is obliged to adopt it (H(TA)A 1998, s 14). Planning permission is not required for the provision of a halting site; however:

(a) the objectives in relation to traveller accommodation must now be included in the *development plan* (qv) the adoption of which involves a public process (H(TA)A 1998, s 26), (b) the drawing up of a *traveller accommodation programme* involves a public process (H(TA)A 1998, ss 8–10), and (c) the actual works to be carried out at a particular site is now subject to a public consultation process (Local Government (Planning and Development) Regulations 1998, SI No 124 of 1998). The annual report of a local authority must record the steps taken to secure the implementation of the *traveller accommodation programme*: Local Government Act 2001, s 244.

In a particular case it was held that the nature and size of a proposed halting site for travellers was one which no reasonable planning authority could consider was consistent with proper planning and development of an area: *Wilkinson v Dublin County Council* [1991] ILRM 605, HC.

Where a temporary dwelling (eg a caravan) is in a public place within five miles of a halting site in which the dwelling could be appropriately accommodated, the housing authority may require it to be removed to the site: Housing (Miscellaneous Provisions) Act 1992, s 10 as amended by H(TA)A 1998, s 32.

A similar provision is also available in respect of a temporary dwelling which is unfit for human habitation or which is likely to obstruct the use of public or private amenities; there is no mileage limit on the alternative site (H(MP)A 1992, s 10(1)(b)). Also a temporary dwelling, which is within one mile of a halting site, can be moved outside the one mile radius, without the need for an alternative site, if the dwelling is causing a nuisance or obstruction, or is creating a risk to certain services, or obstructs or interferes with the use or enjoyment of an amenity by any person (H(MP)A 1992, s 10(1)(c) as amended by Housing (Miscellaneous Provisions) Act 2002, s 21). See *Ward v South Dublin Co Council* [1996] HC; *Keogh v Galway Corporation* [1995] 3 IR 457, HC; *Roughan v Clare County Council* [1998] HC; *Jeffers v Louth County Council* [2003] FL 8804, HC. [Bibliography: Binchy (3); Canny (2).] See CARAVAN; DEVELOPMENT PLAN; HATRED, INCITEMENT TO; HOUSING; TEMPORARY DWELLING; UNFAIR DISMISSAL; VIDEO RECORDING.

Traveller community. Means the community of people who are commonly called Travellers and who are identified (both by themselves and others) as people with a shared history, culture and traditions including, historically, a nomadic way of life on the island of Ireland: Equal Status Act 2000, s 2(1) and Employment Equality Act 1998, s 2(1) as inserted by ESA 2000, s 39 and Sch.

An employer is prohibited from discriminating against an employee, or a prospective employee, on the grounds that he is a member of the Traveller community (EEA 1998, ss 8(1) and 6). *Harassment* on the grounds of being a member of the Traveller community is also prohibited (EEA 1998, s 14A inserted by Equality Act 2004, s 8).

A person must not discriminate on 'Traveller community' grounds in disposing of goods or premises or in providing a service or accommodation; treating one person less favourably than another person, in a comparable situation, because one is a member of the Traveller community and the other is not, is discriminatory: Equal Status Act 2000, ss 5, 6 and 3, amended by EA 2004, ss 48–49.

A Dublin hotel, which had refused to take a booking for a Traveller's wedding, was held by the Equality Tribunal to have discriminated against the persons seeking the booking on the grounds that they were Travellers and was ordered to pay €4,000 in compensation: *Maughan & McDonagh v Spa Hotel, Lucan* (2004) Irish Times, 16 April, ET. See *Collins v Kyle* [2002] ELR 129, EO; *Nevin v The Plaza Hotel* [2002] ELR 177, EO; *McDonagh v The Castle Inn* [2002] ELR 355, EO; *Burke v Ned Kelly's Tavern* [2003] ELR 28, EO; *Maguire v North Eastern Health Board* [2003] ELR 340, EO. The *Irish Traveller Movement's Legal Unit* can be contacted at email: *itmlu1@hotmail.com*. See 'Last chance saloon' by barrister Cliona Kimber in *Law Society Gazette* (August/September 2003) 12. [Bibliography: Reid M.] See DISCRIMINATION; HARASSMENT; PENSION SCHEME AND DISCRIMINATION.

travellers' protection fund. A fund established by the Minister from which payments may be made in respect of losses or liabilities incurred by customers of tour operators (qv) or travel agents (qv) in consequence of the inability or failure of the tour operators or travel agents to meet their financial or contractual obligations in respect of overseas travel contracts. A tour operator is obligated to make contributions to the fund as specified. See Transport (Tour Operators and Travel Agents) Act 1982, ss 15–19.

traverse. An express and specific denial of a fact in pleadings (qv). Where a defence traverses the plaintiff's claim and the plaintiff has sufficient information of all matters arising out of the defence, the court will not order the defendant to furnish particulars of his traverse: *Behan v Medical Council* [1993] ILRM 240, HC. See PARTICULARS, PLEADINGS.

treason. 'Treason shall consist only in levying war against the State, or assisting any State or person or inciting or conspiring with any person to levy war against the State, or attempting by force of arms or other violent means to overthrow the organs of government established by this Constitution, or taking part or being concerned in or inciting or conspiring with any person to make or to take part or be concerned in any such attempt.': 1937 Constitution, art 39.

Treason may be committed by every person within the State and by Irish citizens (or persons ordinarily resident within the State) outside the State: Treason Act 1939, s 1. There can be no conviction for treason on the uncorroborated evidence of one witness. A person convicted of treason must be sentenced to imprisonment for life (of not less than 40 years); previously the mandatory sentence was death: Criminal Justice Act 1990, ss 2–5. See also COMMUTE; MISPRISION OF TREASON; RELEASE, TEMPORARY; REMISSION; UNLAWFUL ORGANISATION.

treasure trove. Any money, coin, gold, silver, plate or bullion found in the earth, or other private place, which contains a substantial amount of gold or silver. If the owner is unknown, it belongs to the State. It was held in *Webb & Webb v Ireland & Attorney-General* [1988] ILRM 565, SC that treasure trove is a royalty or franchise vested in the State by virtue of its sovereign nature and not by royal prerogative, as no royal prerogative in existence prior to the 1922 Constitution was vested in the State by virtue of that Constitution (*Byrne v Ireland* [1972] IR 241 approved). The right of the State to treasure trove has the characteristics of the prerogative at common law, which included the practice of rewarding a diligent and honest finder. A coroner (qv) has jurisdiction to inquire into the finding of treasure trove: Coroners Act 1962, s 49. Treasure trove is now an archaeological object: National Monuments (Amendment) Act 1994, s 14. See *Re 'La Lavia'* [1996] 1 ILRM 194, SC and [1999] 3 IR 413, SC. See ARCHAEOLOGICAL OBJECT.

treasury management, national. The borrowing of moneys for the Exchequer and the management of the national debt. An agency to which is delegated the functions in this regard of the Minister for Finance has been established: National Treasury Management Agency Act 1990. See EXCHEQUER BILLS.

treasury shares. When a company acquires its own shares, it may cancel them or hold them; those held by the company are known as *treasury shares*: Companies Act 1990, s 209. See also Finance Act 1991, s 70, now Taxes Consolidation Act 1997, s 184. See Nolan in 9 ILT & SJ (1991) 9. See Listing Rules 2000, para 15.19 as inserted by the Irish Stock Exchange Ltd. See ANNUAL GENERAL MEETING.

treat, notice to. See NOTICE TO TREAT.

treaty. An agreement between the governments of two or more states. A treaty usually requires to be ratified by a state before it comes into force in respect of that state. As a matter of international law, the decision to ratify a treaty is purely a matter for the discretion of the State: *Hutchinson v Minister for Justice* [1993] ILRM 602, HC. Approval by the Dáil may be required before this State is bound by any such agreement: 1937 Constitution, art 29(5)(1). The treaty-making powers of the government are judicially reviewable: *McGimpsey v Attorney-General and Ireland* [1989] ILRM 209 and [1990] ILRM 440. See also 1937 Constitution, art 29(5)(2). See CONVENTION; CHARGE ON PUBLIC FUNDS; INTERNATIONAL AGREEMENTS.

Treaty, the. Popularly refers to the Articles for a Treaty between Great Britain and Ireland, signed in London on 6 December 1921, under which Ireland was to have Dominion status within the British Empire and was to be styled and known as the *Irish Free State*.

Treaty establishing a Constitution for Europe. See EUROPEAN UNION CONSTITUTION.

Treaty establishing the European Community. See EUROPEAN COMMUNITY.

Treaty of Rome 1957. The European Economic Community Treaty signed in Rome in 1957 which established a common market between six countries: France, Germany, the Netherlands, Belgium, Luxembourg and Italy. It was the foundation block upon which was subsequently built the *Treaty establishing the European Community*, and the *Treaty on European Union*. See EUROPEAN COMMUNITY; EUROPEAN UNION.

Treaty of European Union. See MAASTRICHT TREATY; EUROPEAN UNION.

treaty shopping. The term used in tax law to describe the process by which a person resident in a third country seeks to obtain the benefit of a tax treaty between two other countries. A double tax treaty is intended to be used by the residents of the two contracting states; it normally confers substantial benefits on these residents through the reduction or elimination of tax on interest, royalties and dividends. A treaty shopper endeavours to obtain these benefits eg if Ireland does not have a double tax agreement with country 'A', but the UK has, then if income from country 'A' can be routed through a UK resident company, it is subject to the 'A'-UK double tax treaty, and the income can then be routed to Ireland under the UK-Ireland double tax treaty. See DOUBLE TAXATION AGREEMENT.

tree. The encroachment of trees on an adjoining property may constitute a *nuisance* (qv). Where the encroachment of tree roots causes damage to the property of a neighbouring occupier, he may seek damages, an injunction or abate the nuisance himself; he may even cut the roots as soon as they project into his property: *Lemmon v Webb* [1894] 3 Ch 1. Similar provisions apply to overhanging branches.

An occupier of land must take reasonable and prudent care that a tree is not a danger to persons using an adjoining public highway: *Lynch v Hetherton* [1990] ILRM 857, HC. The owner or occupier of land must take all reasonable steps to ensure that a tree, shrub, hedge or other vegetation on land is not a hazard or potential hazard to persons using a public road (qv): Roads Act 1993, s 70(2)(a). Where there is such a hazard, a road authority is empowered to serve notice on the owner or occupier of the land requiring corrective action; the authority may take immediate action itself to reduce or remove the hazard where it presents an immediate and serious hazard (RA 1993, s 70(2)(b) and (9)).

It is an offence to uproot any tree over ten years old or to cut down trees other than specified ones, without first giving notice to the Gardaí: Forestry Act 1946, s 37. It is often a condition of a planning permission (qv) that specified trees on the site are preserved.

A number of bodies are given power by statute to lop, cut or remove trees or shrubs or plant without payment of compensation e g in the vicinity of a service aerodrome: Defence (Amendment) Act 1987, s 7 or in the vicinity of a State airport: Air Navigation and Transport (Amendment) Act 1998, s 46. This has been held not to be unconstitutional: Electricity Supply Act 1927, s 98; *ESB v Gormley* [1985] IR 129. The 1927 Act, s 98 has been amended by Electricity Regulation Act 1999, s 45.

The *Railway Procurement Agency*, CIÉ or a railway undertaking may lop, remove or cut any tree, shrub or hedge which obstructs or interferes with the exercise of their functions e g surveys, inspections, or the maintenance or operation of a railway: Transport (Railway Infrastructure) Act 2001, s 49. See also Communications Regulation Act 2002, s 58.

For the Tree Council of Ireland, see website: *www.treecouncil.ie*. For Crann, an organisation founded in 1986 to increase broadleaf tree cover in Ireland, see website: *www.crann.ie*. See ESTOVERS; FORESTRY.

tree preservation order. An order which a planning authority may make, in the interests of amenity or the environment, to preserve a tree, trees, groups of trees or woodlands: Planning and Development Act 2000, s 205(1). The order may: (a) prohibit the cutting down, topping, lopping or wilful destruction of trees, and (b) require the owner or occupier to enter into an agreement with the planning authority to ensure the proper management of the trees, subject to the authority providing assistance as may be agreed (PDA 2000, s 205(2)). There is provision for notice of the intention to make an order to be served on the owner and occupier and to be published, for the submission of observations on the proposal, and for an order to be made. There is no provision for an appeal of an order. It is an offence to contravene a *tree preservation order* or a proposed order (PDA 2000, s 205(10)). See *Wicklow Co Council v An Bord Pleanála* [1990] 8 ILT

Dig 107. See Air Navigation and Transport (Amendment) Act 1998, s 46(2).

trespass. [To pass beyond.] A tort (qv) consisting of the unlawful direct interference with the person, land or goods of another. It is actionable *per se* without proof of actual damage. Trespass may also amount to a crime. [Bibliography: Burke & Corbett.]

See MESNE RATES; PRIVATE PROPERTY; TRESPASS AB INITIO; TRESPASS TO GOODS; TRESPASS TO LAND; TRESPASS TO THE PERSON.

trespass, offence of. (1) The offence which is committed by a person who wilfully trespasses on land and refuses to leave after a warning to leave is given: Summary Jurisdiction (Ireland) Act 1851, s 8. A warning given by posting a *warning off* notice is not sufficient.

(2) It is an offence for a person without lawful excuse, to trespass on any building or the curtilage thereof in such a manner as causes or is likely to cause fear in another person: Criminal Justice (Public Order) Act 1994, s 13. It is also an offence to enter a building as a trespasser, or to be in the *vicinity* (qv) of such building, with intent to commit an offence (CJ(PO)A 1994, s 11).

(3) It is an offence to trespass: (a) on a railway, which has been built pursuant to a *railway order* (qv), which is not a public road, or (b) on any land, machinery or equipment used for the railway: Transport (Railway Infrastructure) Act 2001, s 64. There must be a prominent notice in legible characters at the nearest railway station warning persons not to trespass.

(4) It is an offence for a person, without the duly given consent of the owner, to enter and occupy *land*, or to bring onto or place on any land any *object*, where this is likely to: (i) substantially damage the land, (ii) substantially and prejudicially affect any amenity, (iii) prevent persons entitled to use the land from making reasonable use of it, (iv) otherwise render the land or its lawful use, unsanitary or unsafe, (v) substantially interfere with the land or its lawful use: Criminal Justice (Public Order) Act 1994, s 19C inserted by Housing (Miscellaneous Provisions) Act 2002, s 24.

An 'object' includes any temporary dwelling and an animal of any kind or description (CJ(PO)A 1994, s 19A as inserted). Also 'land' is widely defined to include car parks, open spaces, playing fields, or land covered with water.

A garda is empowered to direct a person whom he suspects of committing such an offence to leave the land concerned and to remove any such objects; failure to comply with such a direction is an offence (CJ(PO)A 1994, s 19D as inserted). The gardaí are empowered to remove such objects from the land, to store them and to dispose of them (CJ(PO)A 1994, s 19F as inserted).

See also ASSAULT; FORCIBLE ENTRY AND OCCUPATION.

trespass to goods. The direct unlawful interference with the goods of another. It can consist of: (a) the *trespass* to goods *per se: ESB v Hastings Co* [1965] Ir Jur Rep 51; (b) *conversion* (qv) and (c) *detinue* (qv). The defences include: consent of the owner, lawful justification and self-defence.

trespass to land. A *tort* (qv) consisting of, intentionally or negligently, entering or remaining on, or directly causing anything to come into contact with, land in the possession of another, without lawful justification. Trespass is actionable *per se* ie the plaintiff does not have to show damage to succeed. The owner of premises may re-enter his own property and expel a trespasser using reasonable force: *Beattie v Mair* [1882] 20 Lr Ir 208; however the use of *ejectment proceedings* is preferable. Defences to trespass include: consent (eg licence (qv)), legal authority, and necessity (qv). See *O'Brien v McNamee* [1953] IR 86; *Keating & Co Ltd v Jervis Shopping Centre Ltd* [1997] 1 IR 512, HC; *Giles Kennedy v Law Society* [2004] 1 ILRM 178, HC. [Bibliography: Burke & Corbett.] See EJECTMENT; JUS TERTII; MESNE RATES; OCCUPIERS' LIABILITY TO TRESPASSERS; TRESPASS, OFFENCE OF.

trespass to the person. The tort of unlawful direct interference with a person, being either *assault, battery* or *false imprisonment. Assault* is the threat of, or attempt to apply, force to another which puts that other in reasonable apprehension that immediate violence will befall him: *Dullaghan v Hillen* [1957] Ir Jur Rep 10.

Battery is the touching of the person of another, either directly or indirectly, however slightly, with either hostile intention or against the other person's will: *R v Day* [1845] 9 JP 212.

False imprisonment is the unlawful and total restraint of the personal liberty of another whether by constraining him or compelling him to a particular place or

confining him to a prison or police station or private place or by detaining him against his will in a public place: *Dullaghan v Hillen* [1957] Ir Jur Rep 10.

The defences to the tort of trespass to the person include: consent; self-defence; lawful authority; reasonable chastisement by a parent or some other in *loco parentis*. See *Ross v Curtis* [1990] 8 ILT Dig 64. [Bibliography: Burke & Corbett.] See CORPORAL PUNISHMENT; JURY, ABOLITION OF.

trespasser ab initio. A person who abuses a right, authority or licence which he has to enter the land or premises of another; he becomes a trespasser *ab initio*, and becomes liable for trespass from the time of entry and not from the time he abused the right.

trial. The formal examination and determination of a matter of law or fact by a court of law. In civil actions, such trial is by a judge sitting alone, except in the High Court where, since the abolition of juries for *personal injury* actions, a trial is with a judge and jury only in a limited number of actions. In criminal matters, the trial is before a judge and jury, except in the District Court, the Special Criminal Court, and military courts. The essential ingredient of a trial of a criminal offence is that it is before a court or judge which has the power to punish in the event of a verdict of guilty: *Goodman International v Mr Justice Hamilton* [1992] ILRM 145, HC & SC.

Where a barrister accepts a brief he has an obligation to attend the trial or hearing: *Code of Conduct for the Bar of Ireland* (December 2003) r 4.12. If a barrister subsequently finds that he is unable to attend, he must return the brief to his solicitor as soon as possible. For the right to trial by jury in criminal matters, see TRIAL BY JURY, CRIMINAL OFFENCES. See also DUE COURSE OF LAW; TRIAL BY JURY, CIVIL MATTERS; JURY, ABOLITION OF; NOTICE OF TRIAL.

trial, separate. See DEFENDANT, JOINT.

trial booklet. In *commercial proceedings* (qv), the booklet, indexed and in chronological sequence, and containing copies of any pleadings, affidavits, statements of issues, documents or extracts therefrom in respect of which agreement has been reached between the parties, statements provided for in rule 22 (essential elements of oral evidence to be given at the trial by witnesses), correspondence and any other documents intended to be relied upon at the trial: RSC Ord 63A, r 21(1)(a) inserted by Rules of the Superior Courts (Commercial Proceedings) 2004, SI No 2 of 2004. Unless otherwise directed by the judge chairing the pre-trial conference, the plaintiff is required, in consultation with the other parties, to prepare and lodge with the registrar, not less than four days prior to the date fixed for the trial, a trial booklet and a *case summary* (qv). The trial booklet may be produced, lodged and served by electronic means, as directed by the judge (r 21(3)).

trial by certification. The Supreme Court has held that a provision which provided for a process of *trial by certification* was unconstitutional, where the certificate purported to prove the entire case; such a process was an intrusion into the rights of the accused to a trial in due court of law, and there was no proportionality between the process of trial by certification, the objective of the proposed legislation, and the limitation of the constitutional right: *Re Employment Equality Bill 1966* [1997] 2 IR 321, SC and ELR 132. *See O'Callaghan v DJ Clifford* [1993] 3 IR 603, SC.

trial by jury, civil matters. Trial by jury in civil matters is now restricted to certain causes of action within the jurisdiction of the High Court, since the abolition of juries in respect of actions for the recovery of damages for *personal injuries*: Courts Act 1988, s 2(1). A person is still entitled to a jury trial in certain actions e g defamation, false imprisonment. In such actions, a majority verdict of the nine of twelve members of the jury is necessary and sufficient to determine the verdict; the verdict of such nine members or upwards must be taken and recorded as the verdict of the jury, without disclosure of the dissentients, if any: Courts of Justice Act 1924, s 95. Also the *same* nine must concur in the answer to be given to each question and the judge must so direct the jury: *Arnott v O'Keefe* [1977] IR 1, SC. The failure of a judge to give this direction in its full form will not lead to an order for a retrial unless the court is satisfied that a substantial wrong or miscarriage resulted from the directions given: *Cooper-Flynn v RTE & Bird* (28 April 2004, unreported) SC. In this case the directions given by the judge in the High Court had been acquiesced in without reservation by the party who was now arguing that they were incorrect. The function of the judge is similar to that of a judge in a criminal trial e g deciding questions of law

and directing the jury accordingly. See TRIAL BY JURY, CRIMINAL OFFENCES; SUMMING UP.

trial by jury, criminal offences. No person may be tried on any criminal charge without a jury, except for minor offences (qv) or in the case of trial in special courts (qv) or by military courts: 1937 Constitution, art 38. It is a personal right under the Constitution: *People (DPP) v O'Shea* [1982] IR 384. In a trial by jury, the functions of the judge are to decide questions of law and to direct the jury accordingly, to ensure that the rules of evidence are observed in the conduct of the case, and in cases of conviction to impose punishment (qv). The role of the jury is to decide on the guilt or innocence of the accused.

A *majority verdict* of ten from a minimum of eleven jurors is now sufficient for a conviction; formerly the jury had to be unanimous in its verdict: Criminal Justice Act 1984, s 25. Where there is a majority verdict, the foreman must state the number of jurors who agreed and disagreed; failure to comply with this requirement will lead to a reversal of the conviction on appeal: CJA 1984, s 18(2); *DPP v Ryan* (1999) Irish Times, 13 July 1999, CCA.

Also, before the court may accept a majority verdict, the jury must have had at least two hours for deliberation; and where the accused is acquitted, the fact that it was a majority verdict, cannot be disclosed. Before the two hours has expired the trial judge may inform the jury that he will accept a majority verdict after two hours: *DPP v O'Callaghan* 9 ILT Dig [1991] 270, CCA; *DPP v Brophy* [1992] ILRM 709, CCA. During the two-hour period, the jury must be able to talk to one another when deliberating and the deliberations must be in secret; the period does not include any time the jury spend in the courtroom: *DPP v Jackie Kelly* [1988] CCA. These provisions regarding majority verdicts are not unconstitutional: *O'Callaghan v A-G & DPP* [1993] ILRM 764, SC and 2 IR 17. See RSC Ord 36, rr 5, 10, 34. See also *DPP v McKeever* [1994] 2 ILRM 186, CCA. See JURY; MILITARY TRIBUNAL; SUMMARY OFFENCE; SUMMING UP; VERDICT.

trial within a trial. See VOIRE DIRE.

tribunal and arbitration centre. The centre, with a tribunal room and public gallery, and six consultation rooms, and state-of-the-art recording system, located in Bow Street Friary, near the Four Courts in Dublin, offered as a new service by the Law Society of Ireland. Bookings phone: (01) 804 4150.

tribunals. Bodies with quasi-judicial or administrative functions established by statute and being outside the hierarchy of the court system eg the Employment Appeals Tribunal (qv) established by the Redundancy Payments Act 1967. Such bodies must comply with the principles of natural justice (qv); they are subject to judicial review (qv), and where provided for, an appeal may lie from the findings of these bodies to the courts. It appears that tribunals should furnish unequivocal findings of fact referable to the evidence which supports their findings: *semble* in *North Western Health Board v Martyn* [1987] IR 565, SC.

In reviewing the decision of an expert tribunal (eg the Competition Authority), a court should exhibit curial deference; the greater the level of expertise and specialised knowledge which a particular tribunal has, the greater reluctance there should be on the part of the court to substitute its own view for that of the tribunal: *M & J Gleeson v Competition Authority* [1999] 1 ILRM 401, HC.

For procedure where the approval of the High Court is required in respect of an award by a tribunal to a minor, see RSC Ord 22, r 10(10) inserted by SI No 52 of 1997. A barrister may be a member or chairman of any panel or tribunal or investigating body which does not involve him in direct contact or negotiation with the public and he may be remunerated for such offices: *Code of Conduct for the Bar of Ireland* (December 2003) r 2.9. See ADMINISTRATIVE TRIBUNAL; TRIBUNALS OF INQUIRY.

tribunals of inquiry. Tribunals established for inquiring into a definite matter of urgent public importance and with power to enforce the attendance and examination of witnesses and the production of documents: Tribunal of Inquiry (Evidence) Act 1921. The *separation of powers* (qv) prevent the courts from reviewing a decision of the Oireachtas establishing an inquiry under the 1921 Act: *Haughey v Moriarty* [1999] 3 IR 1, SC.

The instrument by which a tribunal is appointed may be amended either: (a) at the request of the tribunal or (b) with the consent of the tribunal following consulta-

tion between the tribunal and the Attorney-General; the tribunal must not request or consent to such amendment unless it satisfies itself that the amendment will not prejudice the legal rights of any person who has co-operated with or provided information to the tribunal: Tribunals of Inquiry (Evidence) (Amendment) (No 2) Act 1998. This Act followed an earlier Act in 1998 which only permitted an amendment at the request of the tribunal; the amendments were required in the context of the Flood Tribunal.

A tribunal of inquiry may consist of one or more persons, sitting with or without an assessor or assessors; an assessor is not a *member* of the tribunal: Tribunals of Inquiry (Evidence) (Amendment) Act 1979, s 2.

A tribunal may make such orders as it considers necessary for the purpose of its functions and in that respect has the powers, rights and privileges which are vested in the High Court (TI(E)(A)A 1979, s 4). A tribunal, however, does not have powers in excess of those vested in the High Court; consequently it does not have the power to order a person to appear before the tribunal's lawyers in private session and to answer questions: *Lawlor v Mr Justice Flood* [1999] 3 IR 107, SC.

A statement or admission by a person before a tribunal of inquiry is not admissible as evidence against that person in any criminal proceedings (TI(E)(A)A 1979, s 5).

The powers of tribunals were strengthened in 1997: (a) by giving them additional powers in relation to orders for costs, (b) by providing immunity for persons supplying written statements or documents to tribunals, and (c) by providing a mechanism whereby orders of tribunals may be enforced by the High Court: Tribunals of Inquiry (Evidence) (Amendment) Act 1997.

In 2002, provision was made: (a) to prevent a risk of prejudice in respect of any pending criminal trial arising from a tribunal's proceedings eg by providing for exclusion of the public and for prohibiting publication of a tribunal's report if required; (b) to provide a clear legal basis for the appointment of additional and *reserve members* of tribunals; (c) to empower a tribunal to appoint *investigators* to assist it in carrying out its functions; and (d) to increase fines for offences relating to non-co-operation with and obstruction of a tribunal: Tribunals of Inquiry (Evidence) (Amendment) Act 2002. However, the court has held that it is a misconception to perceive a lawyer representing a party before a tribunal as having some particular function of assisting the tribunal in carrying out its remit: *Minister for Finance v Goodman (No 2)* [1999] 3 IR 333, HC.

A tribunal which has been appointed to enquire into matters of public interest pursuant to resolutions of the Oireachtas, may enquire into all matters within its terms of reference, including matters which are the subject of current civil proceedings or allegations of breaches of the criminal law or matters which involve allegations attacking the good name of a citizen: *Goodman International v Mr Justice Hamilton* [1992] ILRM 145, HC & SC. The introduction by a tribunal of public documents, containing findings adverse to a person, without notice to that person, is not a breach of fair procedures: *Desmond v Mr Justice Moriarty* (2004) ITLR (8 March) SC.

A tribunal established by a resolution of both Houses of the Oireachtas pursuant to the 1921–1998 Acts is not conducting a trial; it is merely conducting an inquiry and, consequently, findings, rulings and decisions made by it do not constitute the administration of justice: *Murphy v Mr Justice Flood* [2000] 2 ILRM 112, SC and [1999] 3 IR 97, SC. Where a person, who is required to produce documents, claims privilege, the tribunal is empowered to adjudicate on such claim (*Murphy*). The findings and recommendations of a tribunal could be accepted or rejected by the Dáil and therefore the tribunal is not administering justice or exercising a legislative or executive function: *Haughey v Moriarty* [1999] 3 IR 1, SC.

The High Court has held that it would be very damaging to the public interest if a tribunal withheld disclosure of relevant material when the person affected by the allegations in the inquiry might need that material to establish the truth and vindicate his good name: *O'Callaghan v Flood (now Mahon) Tribunal* [7 July 2004, unreported] HC. See also *Boyhan & Ors v Tribunal of Inquiry into the Beef Industry* [1992] ILRM 545, HC; *Kiberd v Tribunal of Inquiry into the Beef Industry* [1992] ILRM 574, HC; *A-G v Hamilton (No 2)* [1993] 3 IR 227, SC; *Finnegan v Flood* [2002] 3 IR 47, HC.

See *O'Doherty* (1997) ICLSA pp 42–01. See also Freedom of Information Act 1988, s 22 as amended by Freedom of Information (Amendment) Act 2003, s 17. See SI No 175 of 2002. See also ADMINISTRATIVE TRIBUNAL; ACCIDENT; CASTING VOTE; COMMISSION OF INQUIRY; COMMISSION OF INVESTIGATION; MARINE CASUALTY INVESTIGATION BOARD; HEPATITIS; INVESTIGATOR, TRIBUNAL; RESERVE MEMBER; SPECIALIST TRIBUNALS; UTTERANCE.

tribunals of inquiry, findings of. The *Flood* (now *Mahon*) Tribunal: (a) in its *Second* Interim Report on 26 September 2002, found that certain payments made to Mr Ray Burke, former Minister for Foreign Affairs, amounted to corrupt payments; it also held that certain named witnesses obstructed and hindered the tribunal; (b) in its *Third* Interim Report on 30 September 2002 (but not published until January 2004) found that certain payments made to Mr George Redmond gave 'rise to a reasonable inference that the payments were made in order to influence him in the performance of his duties as an Assistant City and County Manager for Dublin and that they amounted to corrupt payments'. It also found that certain named persons, including Mr Redmond, hindered and obstructed the tribunal.

tribunals of inquiry, law reform. Certainty has been expressly provided to the current chairperson of the *Flood* (now *Mahon*) Tribunal to deal with issues relating to the award of costs: Tribunals of Inquiry (Evidence) (Amendment) Act 2004. To avoid any ambiguity and out of an abundance of caution in the situation which has arisen with the change of chairperson, a new subsection to s 6 of the Tribunals of Inquiry (Evidence) (Amendment) Act 1979 (as amended by the Tribunals of Inquiry (Evidence) (Amendment) Act 1997) has been inserted, to the effect that the person who is the sole member of a tribunal or is the chairperson may make an order in relation to any costs that were incurred before his appointment and that have not already been determined (TI(E)(A)A 2004, s 2). In exercising this power, the sole member or chairperson must have regard to any report of the tribunal relating to its proceedings in the period before his appointment. These new provisions apply to tribunals appointed and costs incurred before or after the passing of the Act.

The Act also provides for an express power for a tribunal, on its own volition, to seek the direction of the High Court relating to the performance of the functions of the tribunal, including relating to costs (TI(E)(A)A 2004, s 3). Similar provision is provided for inspectors appointed under the Companies Act 1990 and, a somewhat similar provision is also contained in s 25 of the Commission to Inquire into Child Abuse Act 2000, setting up the *Laffoy* Commission. The 2004 Act also provides an express statutory power for the chairperson, if the tribunal has more than one member, to direct other members of a tribunal to sit as separate divisions and to determine the conditions that will apply, including the preparation of reports (TI(E)(A)A 2004, s 3).

See also Law Reform Commission, *Consultation Paper on Public Inquiries including Tribunals of Inquiry* (LRC CP 22, 2003). The Paper deals with: public inquiries in general, company inspectors, commission to inquire into child abuse, parliamentary inquiries, tribunal of inquiry, powers of the tribunal, constitutional justice, publicity and privacy, the information gathering stage, alternatives to public inquiries, downstream proceedings, and costs. See COMMISSION OF INVESTIGATION.

tribunals of inquiry, other. The government is empowered to establish a committee to inquire into matters dealt with in a petition for a grant of a *pardon* by the President; the committee is a tribunal within the meaning of the Tribunals of Inquiry (Evidence) Act 1921 and the Tribunals of Inquiry (Evidence) (Amendment) Act 1979: Criminal Procedure Act 1993, s 8. The National Authority for Occupational Safety and Health is empowered, with Ministerial consent, to direct that an inquiry be held into any accident, disease or occurrence: Safety, Health and Welfare Act 1989, s 47. See ADMINISTRATIVE TRIBUNAL; ACCIDENT; COMMISSION OF INQUIRY; MARINE CASUALTY INVESTIGATION BOARD.

tribunals of inquiry, public. The Supreme Court has held that, normally, hearings before a tribunal must be held in public: *J Murphy v Flood* [2000] 2 IR 298, SC. It held that s 2(a) of the Tribunals of Inquiry (Evidence) Act 1921 was couched in the negative (eg 'A tribunal ... shall not refuse to allow the public ... to be present ... unless ... .' etc) and a private session was

an exception to the general mode of procedure contemplated for hearings. It is of the essence of tribunals of inquiries that they be held in public for the purpose of allaying the public disquiet that led to their appointment: *George Redmond v Flood Tribunal of Inquiry* [1999] 1 ILRM 241, SC and 3 IR 79. A tribunal is now also empowered to exclude the public from its proceedings 'where there is a risk of prejudice to criminal proceedings': Tribunals of Inquiry (Evidence) (Amendment) Act 2002, s 2 amending TI(E)A 1921, s 2(a).

tribunals of inquiry, recent types of. Tribunals of inquiry have been held in recent times into *moneylending* in Dublin (1970); the *Betelguese* tanker disaster in Bantry Bay, Whiddy inquiry (1979); the *Stardust fire* (1981); the *Kerry Babies* inquiry (1985); the *Hamilton* inquiry into the Beef Processing Industry (1991–93); the *Finlay* inquiry into the Blood Transfusion Service Board (1996–97); the *McCracken* Tribunal into payments to politicians by Dunnes Stores (1997); the *Moriarty* Tribunal into the financial affairs of Michael Lowry and former Taoiseach Charles Haughey and the so-called Ansbacher Accounts (1997–present), the *Flood* (now the *Mahon*) Tribunal into planning permissions (1997–present) – for decisions, rulings and reports, see *www.flood-tribunal.ie*; the *Lindsay* Tribunal into the infection with HIV and Hepatitis C of Persons with Haemophilia and Related Matters (1999–September 2002) – for report see website: *www.doh.ie*; the *Barr* inquiry into the fatal shooting of John Carty by Garda marksmen in Abbeylara, Co Longford (2002–present); the *Morris* Tribunal into Complaints concerning some Gardaí in the Donegal Division (2002–present), the interim report of which was published on 15 July 2004; the *Harding Clark* inquiry into the medical practice of obstetrician Dr Michael Neary (2003–present).

trick, larceny by. See LARCENY BY TRICK.

Trinity. A sitting of the court. See SITTINGS OF COURT.

Trinity College. The College of the Holy and Undivided Trinity of Queen Elizabeth near Dublin established by charter dated 3rd day of March 1592; the 'University of Dublin' means the university established by the charter and letters patent incorporating Trinity College: Universities Act 1997, s 3(1). The 1997 Act provides a common constitution for all universities operating in the State.

The charters and letters patent of Trinity College have been amended by a private Act to provide for an amended composition of the Body Corporate and the Board of Trinity: The Trinity College, Dublin (Charter and Letters Patent Amendment) Act 2000. Trinity College is described in the Act as called and known as the 'Provost, Fellows and Scholars of the College of the Holy and Undivided Trinity of Queen Elizabeth near Dublin'. See website: *www.tcd.ie.* [Bibliography: Parkes S M.]

tripartite contract. A contract to which there are three parties. It is a matter of construction as to whether such a transaction binds all the parties equally or whether the relationship subsists in a series of separate transactions. See *Fox v Higgins* [1912] 46 ILTR 22; *Henley Forklift (Ireland) Ltd v Lansing Bagnall & Co Ltd* [1979] SC. See also FINANCE HOUSES; NOVATION.

TRIPs Agreement. The Agreement on Trade Related Aspects of Intellectual Property annexed to the Agreement establishing the World Trade Organisation (WTO). Ireland ratified the WTO Agreement, with the TRIPs Agreement annexed, on 30 December 1994. The TRIPs Agreement covers a wide range of *intellectual property* issues, including patents, and includes minimum provisions to be included in the patent law of member countries of the WTO. In general, Irish patent law is compatible with the TRIPs Agreement, the main exception being the provisions governing compulsory licences. See *Allen and Hanburys Ltd v Controller of Patents* [1996] 3 IR 401, HC. See LICENCES OF RIGHT, PATENTS.

trout. A licence is not required for angling for trout and coarse fish: Fisheries (Amendment) Act 1991, s 3. Provision has been made for the establishment of Fisheries Co-Operative Societies to raise and disburse for the public benefit funds for the development of trout and coarse fisheries in specified areas (F(A)A 1991, s 4). A person may not be entitled to angle for trout or coarse fish unless he is the holder of a share certificate in such a society (F(A)A 1991, s 9). Exempted are persons 66 years of age and over or under 18, or unemployed, or in receipt of an invalidity pension. See FISHERY SOCIETY; SALMON; SALMON DEALER'S LICENCE.

truck system. The practice by which employers paid their employees in tokens exchangeable for goods, which was prohibited by the Truck Acts 1831, 1887 and 1896. These Acts were repealed by the Payment of Wages Act 1991. See WAGES.

true person. The expression 'true person' in the Companies Act 1990, s 14(1) means the real individuals who are financially interested in the success or failure of a company; if an inspector appointed by the Minister to determine the true persons so interested finds a company as a shareholder of the company he is investigating, he must go further and seek to determine the persons who are the beneficial owners of the company: *Lyons v Curran* [1993] ILRM 375, HC. See INVESTIGATION OF COMPANY BY DIRECTOR OF CORPORATE ENFORCEMENT.

trust. An equitable obligation binding a person (called the *trustee*) to deal with property over which he has control (called the *trust property*) for the benefit of persons (called *beneficiaries* or *cestuis que trust*) of whom he may himself be one, and any one of whom may enforce the obligation. The person creating the trust is called the *settlor* or *donor*. A trust is either a *private* trust, for the benefit of an individual or class but not for the benefit of the public at large; or a *public* or *charitable* trust for the benefit of the public at large, although it may confer a benefit on an individual or class.

A trust may be either an express, an implied, a resulting, or a constructive trust (qqv). In a will, an *executed* trust is one which is finally declared by the instrument creating it, where the executor may be said to be his own conveyancer. An *executory* trust is one created by a direction to make a settlement upon trusts which are indicated in, but are not finally declared by, the instrument containing the direction; some further act is required to give effect to it.

No special form of words are necessary to create a trust, but the words must be imperative, the subject-matter of the trust must be certain, and the objects or persons intended to benefit under the trust must be certain: *Chambers v Fahy* [1931] IR 17. *Perpetual* trusts are prohibited: *O'Byrne v Davoren* [1994] 2 ILRM 276, HC.

See Listing Rules 2000, paras 13.10–13.12 and App 2. See also *Brown v Gregg* [1945] IR 224.

In relation to practical problems where trustees' powers are outdated, overly restricted or inadequate, see Law Reform Commission Report, *Variation of Trusts* (LRC 63, 2000). [Bibliography: Corrigan & Williams; Delaney H (2); Keane (2); Keogan, Mee & Wylie; Kiely; O'Callaghan J M (2); Wylie (3); Snell UK.] See ELECTRONIC FORM; FOREIGN TRUST; TRUSTEE; TRUSTEE INVESTMENTS; USE.

trust, breach of. See BREACH OF TRUST.

trust, charitable. See CHARITABLE TRUST.

trust, discretionary. See DISCRETIONARY TRUST.

trust, express. A trust in which the settlor has declared the terms of the trust. A trust to take effect on the death of the settlor must be created by WILL (qv) duly executed by the settlor. A trust to take effect in the lifetime of the settlor must comply with the evidence requirements of the Statute of Frauds (Ireland) 1695 and the Statute of Uses 1634 in respect of freehold land. The courts however never allowed these statutes to be used as *engines of fraud* and have recognised trusts, not created in accordance with the statutes, called *secret* trusts (qv). A *resulting* trust (qv) arises when an express trust fails, the trustee holding the property in trust for the donor. See FRAUDULENT CONVERSION.

trust, future. See FUTURE TRUST.

trust, illusory. See ILLUSORY TRUST.

trust, implied. A trust which the court infers from the presumed intention of the parties eg where property is held in the name of a person, an *implied trust* will be implied in favour of the person who supplied the purchase money. See RESULTING TRUST.

trust, protective. See PROTECTIVE TRUST.

trust, resulting. See RESULTING TRUST.

trust, secret. See SECRET TRUST.

trust, void. A trust which, because it is illegal, unconstitutional or contrary to public policy, will not be enforced eg a trust which is to take effect on the future separation of husband and wife: *Westmeath v Westmeath* [1831] 2 Dow & Cl 519; a trust conditional on children being reared as Roman Catholics: *Re Blake* [1955] IR 89. [Bibliography: Delaney H (2).]

trust, voidable. A trust, the creation of which was induced by mistake, fraud, or duress, and which may be set aside or rectified by the court. The assignment of property to trustees with the intention of defeating creditors is voidable at the instance of the party prejudiced, although there is protection for the *bona fide* purchaser for value with no notice of the intention to defraud: Conveyancing (Ireland) Act 1634; Bankruptcy Act 1988, ss 7(1)(a) and 57. [Bibliography: Delaney H (2).] See ILLUSORY TRUST.

trust corporation. A corporation to which the High Court may grant *probate* or *administration* which: (a) is appointed by the court; or (b) is empowered by its constitution to undertake trust business (being established by Act or Charter or a Bank under the Central Bank Act 1942 or a company having an issued capital of at least £250,000 (€317,434) of which at least £100,000 (€126,974) has been paid up in cash); or (c) satisfies the President of the High Court that it undertakes the administration of any charitable, ecclesiastical or public trust without remuneration: Succession Act 1965, s 30. See RSC Ord 79, rr 17–19; Ord 80, rr 21–23.

trust for sale. A trust created by the vesting of the legal estate of land in trustees on trust to sell the land and to hold the income until sale and the proceeds thereafter for the beneficiaries. Under the doctrine of conversion (qv), the rights of the beneficiaries are deemed to be rights in personalty. In a trust for sale, the trustees have an obligation to sell the land although they have a discretion to postpone the sale.

Land which is held on trust for sale, where the proceeds are to be applied for any person for life or other limited period, is deemed to be *settled land;* the *tenant for life* in such case cannot exercise the statutory powers without the consent of the court: Settled Land Acts 1882 and 1890. See SETTLED LAND.

trust property. All property, realty or personalty, whether a legal estate or an equitable one, or whether in possession, reversion (qv) or remainder (qv), can be made the object of a trust. On the death of one trustee the trust property devolves on the other trustees as they hold as joint tenants (qv); on the death of a sole or surviving trustee, the legal estate, still subject to the trust, vests on his personal representative (qv): Succession Act 1965, s 10.

The usual way of vesting trust property in new trustees is by a *vesting declaration* in a deed appointing new trustees: Trustee Act 1893, s 12. In any case of difficulty the court will make a vesting order. For proposals on the power of the gardai to investigate property held in trust, see Criminal Justice Bill 2004, s 28.

trustee. A person who holds property on trust (qv) for another. A sane adult person who is capable of taking and holding property is capable of being a trustee; a registered company may be a trustee. The trust instrument usually appoints the original trustees, and when they die, or refuse to accept trusteeship, new ones are appointed either by a person nominated to so appoint, or by the surviving trustee, or by the personal representative (qv) of the last trustee, or by the court, or by the Commissioners of Charitable Donations and Bequests (qv): Trustee Act 1893, ss 10 and 25; Trustee Act 1931; Charities Act 1961, s 43; Charities Act 1973, s 2; Succession Act 1965, s 57. If an incapacitated person is chargeable to income tax, that person's representative (eg his trustee, guardian or committee) is assessable and chargeable to tax on his behalf: Taxes Consolidation Act 1997, ss 1045, 1046. [Bibliography: Corrigan & Williams; Wylie (3).] See BENEFICIARY, REMEDIES OF; BREACH OF TRUST; MONEY LAUNDERING.

trustee, bankrupt. The court is empowered to substitute a new trustee in place of one who becomes bankrupt: Trustee Act 1893, s 25(1). See *Re Barker's Trusts* [1875] 2 Ch D 43. A sole trustee who is bankrupt or an *arranging debtor* (qv), will be permitted, without the leave of the court, to prove in his own bankruptcy or arrangement for a debt due from him to the trust estate: Bankruptcy Act 1988, Sch 1, para 12, reversing *Re Howard and Gibbs, ex p Shaw* [1822] 2 Gl and J 127. See BANKRUPTCY.

trustee, duty of. The primary duty of a trustee is to get in and preserve the property subject to the trust. He must administer the trust in accordance with the trust instrument. He must keep accounts and produce them to any beneficiary when required. He must pay over the trust property and income to the parties entitled. Unless the trust instrument directs the trustee to retain the trust in its present state, he must invest it in securities named by law: Trustee (Authorised Investments) Act 1958. See TRUSTEE INVESTMENTS.

A trustee must not make a profit for himself; he is not allowed to put himself in a position where his interest and his duty conflict: *Bray v Ford* [1896] AC 44. However, the trust instrument may provide for remuneration of a trustee and the court has an inherent jurisdiction so to do. A trustee cannot purchase the trust property from himself and his co-trustees, unless there is an express power in the trust instrument or the court orders such a sale. Also a trustee cannot delegate his powers – the maxim *delegatus non potest delegare* (qv) – unless expressly authorised or delegation is usual in the ordinary course of the business; a trustee however may appoint a solicitor to be his agent to receive and give a discharge for any money receivable under the trust: Trustee Act 1893, s 17. A court cannot give directions to a trustee while an issue with a non-party remains undetermined: *Bank of Ireland v Gleeson* [2000] ITLR (15 May) SC.

The trustees of an occupational pension scheme are required to provide for the proper investment of the resources of the scheme: Pensions Act 1990, s 59 as substituted by Pensions (Amendment) Act 2002, s 42. See ABSOLUTE DISCRETION; REMUNERATION OF TRUSTEE; UNDUE INFLUENCE.

trustee, power of. A trustee has a wide range of powers, unless prohibited in the trust instrument eg power of sale, power to insure, to renew leaseholds, to give receipts, to compromise, to use income for a minor's maintenance: Trustee Act 1893, ss 13–14 and 18–21; Conveyancing Act 1911, ss 9–10 and 43; Succession Act 1965, s 58.

trustee, removal of. A trustee may be removed by a power in the trust instrument, or by the court, or by the provisions of the Trustee Act 1893, ss 10 and 25 where a trustee is unfit or incapable of acting or remains outside the jurisdiction for more than twelve months, or becomes a bankrupt (qv) or is guilty of an offence (formerly, a felony). The court places the welfare of the beneficiaries above all else. See *Arnott v Arnott* [1924] 58 ILTR 145.

Before determining whether a trustee should be removed from office, it is necessary to determine whether such removal would be detrimental to the welfare of the beneficiaries of the trust: *Spencer v Kinsella* [1996] 2 ILRM 401, HC. See also Pensions Act 1990, s 63 as amended by Social Welfare Act 1993, s 49 and Pensions (Amendment) Act 1996, ss 26–27. See BREACH OF TRUST.

trustee, retirement of. A trustee may retire in accordance with a provision in the trust instrument, or with the consent of the beneficiaries who are entitled to the whole beneficial interest, or when new trustees are lawfully appointed to replace him. He may also retire by *deed of retirement* or exceptionally, by payment of the trust money into court: Trustee Act 1893, ss 11 and 42.

trustee de son tort. [Trustee of his own wrongdoing.] A person who intermeddles in a trust without authority; he is held liable to account as a trustee. See *Re Barney* [1891] 2 Ch 265.

trustee in bankruptcy. See WINDING UP BY TRUSTEE.

trustee of debenture stock. See DEBENTURE.

trustee investments. Investment of trust property which is permitted by law. These include securities of the government, of the ESB, ACC, Bord na Móna, and county councils, county borough corporations; debentures (qv) of any industrial or commercial company registered in the State, provided a dividend of not less than 5% has been paid on the ordinary shares in each of the five previous years; securities guaranteed by the Minister for Finance; loan stock of the Bank of Ireland and Allied Irish Banks; bank deposit accounts including the Post Office Savings Bank and the Trustee Savings Banks; real securities in the State: Trustee (Authorised Investments) Act 1958, s 1.

The Minister may vary the list of investments by order, which he has done on a number of occasions eg to include building societies (qv) (T(AI)A 1958, s 2 as amended by Central Bank Act 1997, s 80). A simpler method of amending the list of authorised trustee investments has been provided for: Central Bank Act 1989, s 138. Also, interest bearing deposits with the Central Bank have been made authorised investments for trustees (CBA 1989, s 137). See Trustee (Authorised Investments) Order 1998, SI No 28 of 1998 as amended by SI No 595 of 2002.

In relation to the power to invest in real securities in the State, this does not entitle the trustee to buy land, but merely empowers him to invest funds in mortgages of realty: see Trustee Act 1893, ss 3, 5, 8, 9.

trustee savings bank; TSB. A society formed for the purpose of establishing and maintaining an institution in the nature of a bank, whose business is under the supervision of trustees: Trustee Savings Banks Act 1989, s 9(1). A trustee savings bank requires a licence to operate and may operate abroad with the consent of the Central Bank (qv) which is the supervisory and licensing authority. Such banks are required

to invest a proportion of their funds with the Exchequer and are paid interest thereon (TSBA 1989, s 32). There is also provision to convert from trustee to company status (TSBA 1989, s 57) and to amalgamate with another TSB (TSBA 1989, ss 47–48). See also SI No 133 of 1992.

The assets of a bankrupt officer of a trustee savings bank must be charged with all moneys received by him by virtue of his office and remaining due by him to the bank: Bankruptcy Act 1988, s 81(10).

Provision has been made to facilitate the sale of TSB Bank by its Trustees, by amending and extending sections 57 and 64 of the Trustee Savings Banks Act 1989 and Sch 12 of the Taxes Consolidation Act 1997: Trustee Savings Bank (Amendment) Act 2001. The acquisition of TSB Bank by Irish Life & Permanent plc was completed in April 2001. See also Finance Acts 1990, ss 59–61; 1993, ss 42–43, now consolidated into Taxes Consolidation Act 1997, ss 4(1) and 704–705. See also Finance Act 2001, s 17; Central Bank and Financial Services Authority of Ireland Act 2003, s 35, Sch 1. See CREDIT INSTITUTION.

Tulk & Moxhay, Rule in. The rule under which a head-landlord may enforce a restrictive covenant against a sub-tenant eg as to user of the premises: *Tulk v Moxhay* [1848] 2 Ph 774. A sub-sub-lessee was restrained by the assignee of a lease from breaching a covenant in the sublease in *Craig v Greer* [1899] 1 IR 258. See also *Northern Ireland Carriers Ltd v Larne Harbour Ltd* [1981] NI 171; *Williams & Co Ltd v LSD* [1970] No 1665p, HC. See FREEHOLD COVENANT.

tumultuously. Involving a type of mob out of control, agitated and heavily imbued with some emotion, whether of wantonness, anger, indignation or some other strong motivating force: Malicious Injuries Act 1981, s 6(1); *Duggan v Dublin Corporation* [1991] ILRM 330, SC. There is a right to compensation for the unlawful taking of property during a riot ie where more than two persons are tumultuously and riotously assembled together (MIA 1981, s 6(1) and 6(2) as amended by Malicious Injuries (Amendment) Act 1986, s 4). See MALICIOUS INJURIES SCHEME.

tunnel. See SUBSTRATUM OF LAND.

turbary, common of. The right of digging and taking away of turf as fuel from the land of another. [Bibliography: Bland (1).] See BORD NA MÓNA; PROFIT A PRENDRE.

turf. See BORD NA MÓNA; TURBARY.

turpi causa. [Bad cause.] See EX TURPI CAUSA.

twinning. The linking for social and cultural reasons of two areas, usually between two towns or cities in different countries. Local authorities are empowered to enter into arrangements for twinning: Local Government Act 1991, s 49.

A local authority is empowered to enter into arrangements for the *twinning* of its administrative area, or part of it, with any other area: Local Government Act 2001, s 75. The authority must be satisfied that the arrangement is justified as regards: (a) the benefits likely to accrue; (b) the social, cultural and general interest, and (c) the cost involved. The expenditure incurred and other particulars on *twinning* must be recorded in the annual report of the authority (LGA 2001, s 75(5)).

two-speed Europe. Colloquial expression to describe a possible future situation when a group of EU member states decide to move faster than others along the road of European integration. For example of a mechanism for this to happen, see ENHANCED CO-OPERATION. See also EURO; SCHENGEN AGREEMENTS.

type, size of. The Minister may by order prohibit the seller of goods or supplier of services from making use of any printed contract, guarantee, or other specified class of document unless it is printed in type of at least such size as the order prescribes: Sale of Goods and Supply of Services Act 1980, s 53.

type approval. The examination, including testing in accordance with international practices, and approval of a particular design of instrument to show that it is suitable for use for a prescribed purpose and is capable of achieving the accuracies required: Metrology Act 1996, ss 2(1) and 14.

type approval, motor vehicles. Application may be made by manufacturers who wish to have their products type-approved under the relevant EC Directives: SIs No 13 of 1990, 35 of 1989; 305 of 1978. The Framework Directive (EEC) 92/53 which puts in place the European Whole Vehicle Type Approval System (ECWVTA) for motor vehicles, is given effect in Irish law by SI No 345 of 1992. See also SI No 183 of 1999; SI No 261 of 2002; SI No 570 of 2002; SI No 421 of 2003; SI No 244 of 2004.

typeface. Where copyright subsists in articles for producing materials in particular typefaces, the copyright expires 25 years from the end of the calendar year in which the articles were marketed for the first time: the period previously was 15 years: Industrial Designs Act 2001, s 89(f) amending the Copyright and Related Rights Act 2000, s 85(2).

typographical arrangement of a published edition. See PUBLISHED EDITION.

typographical error. An obvious typographical error does not affect a certificate, where there is no inherent defect in the certificate: *DPP v Flahive* [1988] ILRM 133.

A clerical mistake or omission in a decision of the *Hepatitis C and HIV Tribunal* may be corrected by the Tribunal: Hepatitis C Compensation Tribunal (Amendment) Act 2002, s 5(d).

Occasionally, a typographical or drafting error occurs in the drafting of a statute eg see typographical error in Criminal Law (Rape) (Amendment) Act 1990, s 19(a) subsequently corrected by Criminal Law Act 1997, Sch 1, para 9. See also Finance Act 2000, ss 46(b) and 160. See Employment Equality Act 1998, s 70(1)(a) as amended by Equal Status Act 2000, s 39 and Sch – insertion of 'is' before 'required'. See Planning and Development Act 2000, s 37(6) as amended by Planning and Development (Amendment) Act 2002, s 10. See Capital Acquisitions Tax Consolidation Act 2003, ss 74, 75 and 100 amended by Finance Act 2003, ss 151 and 152. See also Social Welfare (Miscellaneous Provisions) Act 2003, s 22. See *Paper Properties Ltd v Power Corporation plc* [1996] 1 ILRM 475, HC. See SLIP RULE.

U

Uachtarán na hÉireann. [President of Ireland (qv)].

uberrimae fidei. [Of the utmost good faith]. A contract is said to be *uberrimae fidei* when the promisee is under an obligation to inform the promisor of all those facts and surrounding circumstances which may influence the promisor in deciding whether or not to enter the contract. All contracts of insurance fall into this class. In insurance contracts, the insured must also disclose those *material facts* which would affect the premium the insurer should impose, if he does accept the risk.

The consequence of non-disclosure is to allow the insurer to avoid the policy. Before renewing a policy of insurance, it is necessary for the insured to disclose material facts which could affect the renewal or the premium. Also a fraudulent claim by an insured may allow an insurer to avoid liability even though he was on risk when the loss occurred.

Where an insurance company significantly limits the disclosure required (eg in a special promotion offer), subsequent non-disclosure by the insured may not entitle the insurer to repudiate liability: *Kelleher v Irish Life Assurance Co Ltd* [1993] ILRM 643, SC and 3 IR 393. The appropriate test is whether a reasonable person reading the proposal form could conclude that information over and above that sought in the form was not required (*Kelleher* case). Also non-disclosure can only be relevant to some fact of which the person has knowledge at the relevant time: *Keating v New Ireland Assurance Co plc* [1989] 7 ILT Dig 321 and [1990] ILRM 110, SC. See Ellis in 8 ILT & SJ (1990) 45. See also *Furey v Eagle, Star & British Dominions Insurance Co* [1922] 56 ILTR l09; *Irish National Assurance v O'Callaghan* [1934] 68 ILTR 248; *Griffin v Royal Liver Friendly Society* [1942] Ir Jur Rep 29; *Chariot Inns Ltd v Assicurazioni Generali SPA* [1981] ILRM 173; *Harney v Century Insurance Co Ltd* [1983] HC; *Aro Road & Land Vehicles v Insurance Corporation of Ireland* [1986] SC; *Keenan v Shield Insurance Co Ltd* [1987] IR 113, HC; *Curran v Norwich Union Life Insurance Society* [1987] HC.

See also Marine Insurance Act 1906, s 17. See CONTRA PROFERENTEM; INSURANCE; PROSPECTUS.

ubi aliquid, conceditur, conceditur et id sine quo res ipsa esse non potest. [Where anything is granted, that is also granted without which the thing itself is not able to exist] eg the right of way presumed to be given by the grantor of land to a *close* surrounded by the grantor's land. See WAY, RIGHT OF.

ubi easem ratio ibi idem jus. [Like reasons make like law].

ubi jus ibi remedium. [Where there is a right, there is a remedy]. [Bibliography: O'Flaherty]. See EQUITY, MAXIMS OF.

ubi remedium ibi jus. [Where there is a remedy, there is a right].

ubi supra. [At the place above].

UCITS. See UNDERTAKINGS FOR COLLECTIVE INVESTMENT IN TRANSFERABLE SECURITIES.

Ullans. The variety of the Scots language traditionally found in parts of Northern Ireland and Donegal. The new cross-border corporate body, *An Foras Teanga*, has the function of promoting greater awareness and use of Ullans and of Ulster Scots cultural issues, both within Northern Ireland and throughout the island: British-Irish Agreement Act 1999, ss 24–30 and Annex 1 and 2. The cultural issues relate to the cultural traditions of the population of Northern Ireland and the border counties which are of Scottish ancestry and the influence of their cultural traditions on others, both within the island of Ireland and the rest of the world (Annex 2, part 5, para 1.7). See GOOD FRIDAY AGREEMENT; FORAS TEANGA.

ultima voluntas testatoris est perimplenda secundum veram intentionem suam. [Effect is to be given to the last will of a testator according to his true intention]. See ARMCHAIR PRINCIPLE.

ultra. [Beyond].

ultra vires. [Beyond the power]. An act in excess of the authority conferred by law and therefore invalid. A company's powers are limited to carrying out of its objects as set out in its *memorandum of association;* an act in excess of that power, eg in a contract, is *ultra vires* and void. It has been held that an ultra vires transaction cannot be rendered effective by all the company's members attempting to ratify it or by extending the objects clause with retrospective effect: *Ashbury Railway Carriage Co v Riche* [1875] LR 7 HL 653.

However, *ultra vires* acts are effective in favour of a person relying on such acts, if he was not aware at the time that the company was acting beyond its powers: Companies Act 1963, s 8(1). In addition, any transaction entered into by the board of directors of a company is deemed to be within the capacity of the company in favour of a person dealing with the company in good faith and any limitation imposed by the company's articles or memorandum of association cannot be relied upon by the company against such person: European Communities (Companies) Regulations 1973, SI No 163 of 1973. These provisions do not apply to statutory companies unless they are incorporated under the Companies Acts.

A member or debenture holder may on application to the court restrain a company from acting beyond its power: Companies Act 1963, s 8(2).

The general competence of local authorities has been widened considerably thereby reducing the possibility that they will engage in activities which are *ultra vires* their powers: Local Government Act 1991, s 6. Damages will not be awarded for an *ultra vires* action or decision, unless it involved the commission of a tort, or was activated by malice, or was carried out in the knowledge that it was *ultra vires*: *O'Donnell v Corp of Dún Laoghaire* [1991] ILRM 301, HC; *Pine Valley Developments Ltd v Minister for the Environment* [1987] IR 23; *Glencar Exploration plc v Mayo County Council* [2002] 1 ILRM 481, SC and 1 IR 84.

Premiums paid to an insurance company on *ultra vires* policies are recoverable as money paid without consideration: *Flood v Irish Provident Assur Co* [1912] 2 Ch 597n. See *Re Bansha Woolen Mill Co* [1887] 21 LR Ir 181; *Re Cummins* [1939] IR 60; *Hennessy v National Agricultural Industrial Development Association* [1947] IR 159; *Northern Bank Finance Corporation v Quinn* [1979] HC. See also Building Societies Act 1989, s 12(1), 12(2) and 18(7). See CERTIORARI; STERILE TRANSACTIONS.

umbrella fund. Means a UCITS which is divided into a number of sub-funds: EC (Undertakings for Collective Investment in Transferable Securities) Regulations 2003, SI No 211 of 2003, reg 2(1) as amended by Central Bank and Financial Services Authority of Ireland Act 2004, s 10(3), Sch 2 and s 34, Sch 4. Where a UCITS is constituted as an umbrella fund, the assets belong exclusively to the relevant sub-fund and must not be used to discharge the liabilities of or claims against any other sub-fund (reg. 23(2)). See UNDERTAKINGS FOR COLLECTIVE INVESTMENT IN TRANSFERABLE SECURITIES.

umpire. See ARBITRATION.

UN. United Nations (qv).

unadministered probate, grant of. A grant of representation to another executor, whose rights had been reserved by the first executor who had extracted a grant but has since died.

unambiguous. It has been held that if a term in a lease has an *unambiguous* meaning, that meaning ought to be given full effect: *Hynes Ltd v O'Malley Property Ltd* [1989] ITLR (27 February) SC.

unascertained goods. Goods defined by description only eg 5 kilos of coal. Property in unascertained goods is not transferred to the buyer until the goods are ascertained: Sale of Goods Act 1893, s 16. See GOODS, PROPERTY IN.

unauthorised development. Means, in relation to land, the carrying out of any unauthorised *works* (including the construction, erection or making of any unauthorised *structure*) or the making of any unauthorised *use*: Planning and Development Act 2000, s 2(1). Permission for the retention of an *unauthorised development* may be obtained by applying for permission; the application may be granted with or without conditions, or may be refused (PDA 2000, ss 32(1)(b), 34(1) and 34(12)). Any person who has carried out or is carrying out unauthorised development is guilty of an offence (PDA 2000, s 151).

In a particular case, the court in ordering the removal of an antennae and support structure, held that the right to the enforcement of the law by an adjoining landowner, whose property was devalued by the existence of an unauthorised development, outweighed any 'public interest' which was asserted by the other party: *Dublin City Council v Eircom plc* [2002] 3 IR 327, HC. See *McGoldrick v An Bord Pleanála* [1997] 1 IR 497, HC. See PLANNING PERMISSION.

unauthorised use. Means, in relation to land, *use* commenced after 1 October 1964, being use which is a *material change* in use of any structure or other land: Planning and Development Act 2000, s 2(1). Use does not include the use of the land by the carrying out of any works thereon (PDA 2000, s 2(1)). See PLANNING PERMISSION.

unborn, injuries to the. The laws relating to wrongs apply to an unborn child for his protection in like manner as if the child were born, provided that the child is subsequently born alive: Civil Liability Act 1961, s 58. Consequently, a child may sue for all injuries sustained before birth as a result of another person's tort (qv). See *Dunne v National Maternity Hospital* [1989] ILRM 735.

unborn, right to life of the. The State acknowledges the right to life of the unborn and, with due regard to the equal right to life of the mother, guarantees in its laws to respect, and, as far as practicable, by its laws to defend and vindicate that right: 1937 Constitution, art 40.3.3, inserted by referendum. See *A-G v X* [1992] ILRM 401.

The Maastricht Treaty 1992 provides that 'Nothing in the *Treaty on European Union*, or in the *Treaties establishing the European Communities*, or in the Treaties or Acts modifying or supplementing those Treaties, shall affect the application in Ireland of Article 40.3.3 of the Constitution of Ireland': Protocol No 17.

The member states, by Solemn Declaration, have agreed that this Protocol shall not limit freedom either to travel between member states or to obtain or make available in Ireland, information relating to services lawfully available in member states. They also declared that they will be favourably disposed to amending the Protocol so as to extend its application to a future constitutional amendment concerning the subject matter of art 40.3.3 if Ireland so requests.

The European Court of Human Rights has ruled that it is for national authorities to determine when the right to life begins: *Thi-Nho Vo v Government of France* (8 July 2004, unreported) ECHR. See *SPUC v Grogan (No 5)* [1998] 4 IR 343, SC; *Baby O v Minister for Justice* [2002] 2 IR 169, SC and [2003] 1 ILRM 241. See Kingston & Whelan in 10 ILT & SJ (1992) 93, 104, 166 and 279. See ABORTION; ABORTION, MEDICAL GUIDELINES; LIFE, RIGHT TO; TRAVEL, RIGHT TO.

uncalled capital. The amount remaining unpaid on partly paid shares in a company. See CAPITAL.

uncertainty. Failure to define or limit with sufficient exactitude. A gift by will or trust may be void for uncertainty. However a disposition will not be void for uncertainty simply because it is difficult to interpret; the court should endeavour to give effect to the expressed or implied wishes of the testator: *O'Byrne v Davoren* [1994] 2 ILRM 276, HC. There is a presumption of simultaneous death in cases of uncertainty: Succession Act 1965, s 5. 'Uncertainty' can only be displaced by 'certainty': *Re Kennedy* [2000] 2 IR 571, HC. See also AMBIGUITY; DEATH, SIMULTANEOUS.

unchastity. Words spoken and published which impute unchastity to any woman or girl do not require proof of *special damage* to render them actionable. See SLANDER; LESBIANISM.

unclaimed funds in court. See SUITORS, FUNDS OF.

unclaimed life assurance policy. The proceeds of *unclaimed life assurance policies* taken out by Irish residents are required to be paid to the State; this does not apply to occupational pension schemes, group health insurance or disability benefit schemes and sponsored superannuation schemes: Unclaimed Life Assurance Policies Act 2003.

A policy is deemed to be unclaimed when: (a) in the case where the policy has a specified term which has expired, the insurance undertaking has received no communication from the policy holder for a period of five years or more, or (b) in the case where the policy does not have a specified term, the undertaking has received no communication from the policy holder for 15 years or more (ULAPA 2003, s 6(2)). There is an obligation on insurance undertakings to notify holders of unclaimed policies (ULAPA 2003, s 8). Publication of a notice satisfies the notification requirements in certain instance eg where the value of the policy is less than €500, or such other amount as specified by order of the Minister (ULAPA 2003, s 9). For the form of prescribed notice, see Unclaimed Life Assurance Policies (Section 9) Regulations 2003, SI No 93 of 2003.

The *net encashment value* of the policy in respect of policy holders who cannot be traced is required to be transferred to the *Dormant Accounts Fund* established under the Dormant Accounts Act 2001 (DAA 2001, s 10). The rights of policy holders are not affected by the transfer (ULAPA 2003, s 14). A procedure is provided for the policy holder to make a claim on moneys which have been transferred to the Fund (ULAPA 2003, s 15).

The new legislation in many ways mirrors that provided for dormant accounts. In May 2004, the National Treasury Management Agency announced that €22.4m had been transferred to the Agency from insurance firms, far less than the earlier estimates of €45 to €60m. See website: *www.dormantaccounts.ie*. See CONTINUING RISK POLICY; DORMANT ACCOUNT.

unconscionable bargain. A contract which is harsh in its terms and where one party is clearly in a stronger bargaining position or where the bargain is so improvident that no reasonable man would enter it. In a suitable case, the court will intervene and set aside the transaction or amend the terms in order to produce what the court sees as a fairer transaction. It is an exception to the general rule that consideration need not be adequate to the promise.

In cases where a sale is at gross under-value and between persons not on an equal footing, and the transaction is thus improvident, it is not necessary to show improper behaviour. See *Slator v Nolan* [1876] IR 11 Eq 367; *Grealish v Murphy* [1946] IR 35; *Smyth v Smyth* [1978] HC; *JH v WJH* [1979] HC; *Rooney v Conway* [1982] NI Ch; *McCoy v Greene Cole* [1984] HC. See INEQUALITY OF POSITION; MONEYLENDER; PENALTY; UNFAIR TERMS.

unconscionable use. See WASTE.

unconstitutional Act. The High Court has held that the only damages that can be awarded in relation to an invalid Act, are those damages which can be shown to have flowed directly from the effects of the invalid Act, without any intervening imponderables and events: *An Blascaod Mór Teo v Commissioner for Public Works* [2001] 1 ILRM 423, HC and [2000] 3 IR 565, HC. In this case, it was held that the plaintiffs had not been dispossessed of their property on the Great Blasket and had not established a sufficient direct causal link between the heads of damage and the passing of the invalid Act. See LEGISLATION, CONSTITUTIONALITY OF.

unconstitutional contract. A contract the formation or performance of which is in breach of the Constitution of the State. The question as to whether a person can contract out of a constitutional right was raised but no opinion was given in *Becton Dickinson Ltd v Lee* [1973] IR 1.

uncontrollable impulse. See IRRESISTIBLE IMPULSE.

uncultivated foods. Foods which are not commercially produced or harvested, including wild mushrooms, fruit and berries and fish and game harvested through recreational activities: Food Safety Authority of Ireland Act 1998, s 2(1). The Authority is required to give advice, on request, to a Minister in relation to food production, including the harvest of uncultivated foods (FSAIA 1998, s 15(f)).

undefended case. Where a defendant to a proceedings fails to enter an appearance (qv) or a defence (qv), the plaintiff may obtain judgment. See JUDGMENT IN DEFAULT OF APPEARANCE; JUDGMENT IN DEFAULT OF DEFENCE.

under lease. A sublease. See LEASE.

undersubscribed. Where shares in a company are offered for subscription but the entire offer is not taken up. In the case of shares offered to the public for the first time, no allotment may be made until at least the *minimum amount* is raised: Companies Act 1963, s 53(1). By minimum amount is meant the sum stated in the prospectus and which in the directors' opinion it is necessary to raise in order to pay for the company's preliminary expenses, any commissions, the purchase price to be paid for any property it is intended to buy with the proceeds of the issue, and any working capital.

Where a public limited company (plc) offers its shares and the offer is undersubscribed, it is prohibited to allot the shares which are subscribed unless the offer stated that the allotments would be made in such circumstances: Companies (Amendment) Act 1983, s 22. See also C(A)A 1983, Sch 1, para 7. See PROSPECTUS; UNDERWRITER.

undertaking. (1) A promise which involves an obligation to act in accordance with the promise, which obligation may be enforced in law eg an undertaking by a defendant to a court. Undertakings given by a foreign state in relation to extradition (qv) matters cannot be relied upon: *Sloan v Culligan* [1992] ILRM 194, SC.

(2) An undertaking given by a solicitor is any unequivocal declaration of intention, addressed to someone who reasonably places reliance on it, which is made by a solicitor in the course of his practice, whereby the solicitor becomes personally bound: *A Guide to Professional Conduct of Solicitors in Ireland* (2002) ch 6.5. A solicitor is required to honour the terms of a professional undertaking as a matter of conduct (ch 6.5.2). Where a client changes solicitor, the first solicitor should be released from undertakings to third parties; no solicitor should co-operate with a client who seeks to leave his former solicitor with an outstanding undertaking (ch 7.6). The Law Society has power to enforce undertakings as a matter of conduct, and the court, similarly, by virtue of its inherent

jurisdiction over its own officers (ch 6.5.11). An undertaking should not be given in relation to funds to be recovered on behalf of children, as the court has exclusive jurisdiction, see COMPROMISE. [Bibliography: O'Callaghan P].

(3) A person being an individual, a body corporate or an unincorporated body of persons engaged for gain in the production, supply or distribution of goods or the provision of a service: Competition Act 2002, s 3(1). For previous legislation, since repealed, see Competition Act 1991, s 3(1). See *Greally v Minister for Education* [1995] 3 IR 481, HC.

(4) A body corporate, a partnership, an unincorporated body of persons or a sole trader: Stock Exchange Act 1995, s 3(1) as amended by Central Bank and Financial Services Authority of Ireland Act 2003, s 35, Sch 1. See Listing Rules 2000 (Definitions, as amended by Irish Stock Exchange Ltd). See GAIN.

Undertakings for Collective Investment in Transferable Securities; UCITS. An undertaking, whether established as a company or as a unit trust, the sole object of which is the collective investment in transferable securities of capital raised from the public and which operates on the principle of risk spreading, and the units of which are, at the request of the holders, repurchased or redeemed, directly or indirectly out of those undertaking's assets: EC (Undertakings for Collective Investment in Transferable Securities) Regulations 2003, SI No 211 of 2003, reg 3(2), revoking SI No 78 of 1989 as amended by Central Bank and Financial Services Authority of Ireland Act 2003, s 35, Sch 2.

Under the regulations, UCITS may be constituted as unit trusts, or investment companies with fixed capital, or investment companies with variable capital, or common contractual funds. These regulations were amended by SI No 212 of 2003 to give effect to the 'Product Directive' (Directive (EC) 2001/108) which expands the product range for UCITS. The definition of UCITS is expanded to include investment in other liquid financial assets. A separate amending SI was necessary to set out the transitional and grandfathering provisions required for the implementation of the Product Directive. See SI No 497 of 2003 amended by SI No 737 of 2003.

The Central Bank (qv) is the supervisory authority for entities establishing in Ireland as UCITS. The provisions of the Unit Trusts Act 1990 do not apply to a UCITS that is authorised under the UCITS Regulations (UTA 1990, s 2). See amending regulations SI No 497 of 2003. See Company Law Enforcement Act 2001, s 108 amending Companies Act 1990, s 258. For taxation of UCITS, see Taxes Consolidation Act 1997, ss 734, 737, 738, 739, 739A as amended or inserted by Finance Act 1998, ss 42 and 49, FA 1999, s 64; FA 2000, s 57. See 'Split Capital Collective Investment Schemes' by Barry Mansfield BL in (2002) 10 ISLR 187. See INVESTMENT LIMITED PARTNERSHIP; INVESTMENT COMPANY; TAKE-OVER; THIRD-PARTY INFORMATION; UMBRELLA FUND.

underwater heritage order. See WRECK.

underwriter. (1) A person, as insurer, who joins with others in entering into a policy of insurance; he subscribes his name to the policy against the sum for which he accepts liability.

(2) In a public issue of shares in a company, a person who offers to take up shares and debentures not taken up by the public, in consideration of a commission at a rate disclosed in the prospectus. A *sub-underwriting agreement* is a contract between an underwriter and another person which, in exchange for a commission, relieves the underwriter of liability. See also Competition Act 2002, s 16(6)(a). See FLOATATION; SHARES, COMPANY.

undesirable administrative practice. See OMBUDSMAN.

undischarged bankrupt. A bankrupt who has not obtained a discharge by way of a *certificate of conformity* (prior to 1989); or an order or certificate of *discharge* (since 1989): Bankruptcy Act 1988, s 85. An undischarged bankrupt cannot own property, be a director of a company, be a member of the Oireachtas, a county councillor or a member of a local authority or be a solicitor or auctioneer. See Electoral Act 1992, s 41; Debtors Ireland Act 1872, s 20; Local Government (Ireland) Act 1898, s 104(1); Local Government (Application of Enactments) Order 1898; Companies Act 1990, s 169 amending Companies Act 1963, s 183; Building Societies Act 1989, s 64(1).

An insurance agent (qv) and insurance broker (qv) are disqualified from acting as such if adjudged bankrupt: Insurance Act 1989, s 55. Where the *Director of Corporate Enforcement* has reason to believe that an undischarged bankrupt is acting as a company director, he may require the person to furnish by a specified date, a sworn statement setting out the facts of his financial position: Companies Act 1963, s 183A inserted by Company Law Enforcement Act 2001, s 40. The Director may apply to the court for a *disqualification order* against a director of a company on the grounds that he is an undischarged bankrupt. See BANKRUPTCY; BANKRUPTCY, DISCHARGE FROM; DISQUALIFICATION ORDER, COMPANY.

undisclosed principal. A principal whose existence and identity is not disclosed at the time of making a contract. When an agent (qv) conceals the fact that he is merely the agent of another (the principal) and has authority at the time of the contract to act on behalf of that other, either the agent or the principal (when discovered) can be sued by the third party and the third party may be sued by either.

The option of the third party is subject to two considerations: (a) the option is alternative, so that if the third party unequivocally indicates either principal or agent as liable to him, he cannot afterwards sue the other; (b) if the third party by his words or conduct induces the principal to believe that a settlement has been agreed between the third party and his agent, in consequence of which the principal settles with his agent, the third party cannot sue the principal on the contract.

The undisclosed principal's right to sue is limited where the agent has contracted in terms which import that the agent was the real and only principal. Also the third party may use any defence or counter claim against a suit by the principal, which he would have in relation to the agent. See *O'Keefe v Horgan* [1897] ILT 429; *Keighley Maxsted & Co v Durant* [1901] AC 240. See AGENT.

undue influence. The equitable doctrine under which a court will set aside an agreement or a disposition of property made by a person under circumstances which show, or give rise to the presumption, that the person has not been allowed to exercise a free and deliberate judgement in the matter.

A presumption of undue influence arises in transactions between parent and child, solicitor and client, trustee and beneficiary, guardian and ward, physician and patient, but not husband and wife.

Where the relationship between the donor and the donee is such as to give rise to the presumption of undue influence and it is shown that a *substantial benefit* has been obtained, the onus lies on the donee to establish that the gift or transaction resulted from the *free exercise of the donor's will*: *Carroll v Carroll* [2000] 1 ILRM 210, SC and [1999] 4 IR 241, SC. The court interferes not on the ground that any wrongful act has been committed by the donee, but on public policy grounds, and to prevent the relations which existed between the parties and the influence arising therefrom, from being abused (*Carroll* case).

The presumption may be rebutted by evidence eg that the other party had independent legal advice and took it; it may also be rebutted by proof that the transaction was the result of the free exercise of independent will by the other party: *Provincial Bank v McKeever* [1941] IR 471.

A contract induced by undue influence is voidable at the option of the party influenced; however, conduct by that person after the undue influence has ceased may amount to an *affirmation* of the contract: *Allcard v Skinner* [1887] 36 Ch D 145.

A person dealing with his own property is not entitled to the same amount of protection as a person called upon to give a consent in relation to a dealing with other property eg under the Family Home Protection Act 1976 where there is another's interest: *Bank of Nova Scotia v Hogan* [1997] 1 ILRM 407, SC and [1996] 3 IR 239, SC. See also *Morley v Loughnan* [1893] Ch 736; *Leonard v Leonard* [1988] ILRM 245; *McGonigle v Black* [1989] 7 ILT Dig 103. The Law Society has recommended that to overcome any challenge to a voluntary transaction where a solicitor acts for the transferor and transferee, he should ensure: (a) that independent advise, based on the full facts, is obtained, (b) that that advice is stored on the main transfer file, and (c) that the transferee is not present when the transferor is instructing the solicitor in relation to the proposed transaction: practice note in *Law Society Gazette* (November 2003) 43. See also Electoral Act 1992, s 136; Merchant Shipping (Salvage and Wreck) Act 1993, s 19. See DURESS; INEQUALITY OF POSITION; INSTRUCT.

undue influence in pleadings. In any legal proceedings where undue influence is pleaded, the party making the plea, before the case is set down for trial, must give particulars of the persons against whom the charge of undue influence is preferred, the nature of the conduct alleged to constitute the undue influence and the dates upon which the acts alleged to constitute undue influence were exercised: RSC Ord 19, rr 5(2) and 6(1). See PLEADINGS.

unemployment benefit. The social welfare benefit to which a person may be entitled in respect of any day of unemployment; the person must generally be capable of work, be available for employment, and genuinely be seeking employment: Social Welfare (Consolidation) Act 1993, ss 42–47 as amended. Alternatively, means tested, *unemployment assistance* may be available (SW(C)A 1993, ss 119–126). See Social Welfare Act 2003, ss 2(2)(a), 8 and 11; Social Welfare (Miscellaneous Provisions) Act 2004, s 7.

unenforceable. That which cannot be proceeded for, or sued upon, in the courts. An unenforceable contract is a contact which cannot be enforced by action because of some technical defect e g where there is an absence of writing as required by the Statute of Frauds in the case of a contract for the sale of land. However, under the doctrine of *part performance,* an otherwise unenforceable contract may be enforceable e g in the sale of land where there is entry into possession of land with the agreement or acquiescence of the defendant: *Kennedy v Kennedy* [1983] HC. See also *Hope v Lord Cloncurry* [1874] IR 8 Eq 555; *Lowry v Reid* [1927] NI 142. See MEMORANDUM, STATUTE OF FRAUDS; PART PERFORMANCE; QUANTUM MERUIT.

UNESCO. [United Nations Educational, Scientific and Cultural Organisation]. A specialised agency of the United Nations. Its main objective is to contribute to peace and security in the world by promoting collaboration among nations through education, science, culture and communication in order to further universal respect for justice, for the rule of law and for human rights and fundamental freedom which are affirmed by the peoples of the world, without distinction of race, sex, language or religion, by the Charter of the UN. UNESCO has 188 member countries and was founded in 1945. See website: *www.unesco.org.*

unfair and oppressive procedure. See FAIR PROCEDURES.

unfair contract terms. See UNFAIR TERMS.

unfair dismissal. The dismissal of an employee is deemed to be an unfair dismissal unless, having regard for all the circumstances, there were substantial grounds justifying the dismissal: Unfair Dismissals Act 1977, s 6. The onus of proof is on the employer to show that there were substantial grounds, which include: the capability, competence or qualifications of the employee for the work he was employed to do; the employee's conduct; redundancy; or the fact that continuation of the employment would contravene another statutory requirement; however, regard must be had to the reasonableness or otherwise of the conduct of the employer and to compliance with dismissal procedures and codes of practice (UDA 1977, ss 6(6) and 6(7) as amended by Unfair Dismissals (Amendment) Act 1993, s 5(b)).

A dismissal is deemed to be an unfair dismissal if it results wholly or mainly from trade union membership; or religious or political opinions; or race, colour or sexual orientation; or age; or the employee's membership of the travelling community; or legal proceedings against the employer where the employee is a party or a witness; or unfair selection for redundancy; or pregnancy, attendance at ante-natal classes, giving birth or breastfeeding, or exercising rights to protective leave or natal care absence or adoptive leave (UDA 1977, s 6(2) as amended by UD(A)A 1993, s 5(a); Maternity Protection Act 1994, s 38; Maternity Protection (Amendment) Act 2004, s 23). See Adoptive Leave Act 1995, ss 22–27. See *White v Betson* [1992] ELR 120, EAT.

A dismissal is deemed to have taken place: (a) if the employer terminates the contract of employment with or without notice; or (b) if the contract is for a *fixed term* (qv) and is not renewed; or (c) if the employee, with or without notice, terminates the employment because of the conduct of the employer (known as *constructive dismissal*) (UDA 1977, s 1). An employee may request from the employer a written statement of the reasons for the dismissal, which must be supplied within fourteen days (UDA 1977, s 14(4) as amended by UD(A)A 1993, s 9).

The *unfair dismissal* protection applies to employees who have at least one year's continuous service with the same employer.

See *McGowan v McLaughlin* [2000] ELR 106, EAT. One year's service is not required where dismissal is for pregnancy, giving birth or breastfeeding, or trade union membership or activity (UD(A)A 1993, s 14 and MPA 1994, s 38). Employees who have reached normal retirement age or who work for close relatives in a private house or farm (except in the case of pregnancy) or who work in specified employments are not covered by this dismissal legislation, nor are parties to an illegal contract.

Where a term or condition of the employment contract contravened the Income Tax Acts or the Social Welfare Acts, the employee, notwithstanding the contravention, is entitled to redress for unfair dismissal (UDA 1977, ss 8(11) and 8(12) inserted by UD(A)A 1993, s 7(d)) overturning *Lewis v Squash Ireland Ltd* [1983] ILRM 363. However, this exception regarding the enforcement of an illegal contract does not apply to an action for *wrongful dismissal* (qv): *Hayden v Seán Quinn Properties Ltd* [1994] ELR 45, HC.

The unfair dismissal legislation now applies to all local authority employees, with the exception of the manager: Local Government Act 2001, s 164.

The conduct of an employee is a material consideration in determining the employee's right of redress for unfair dismissal: *Carney v Balkan Tours Ltd* [1997] 1 IR 153, SC and ELR 102. See *Locke v Southern Health Board* [1987] HC; *Loftus v Bord Telecom* [1987] HC; *O'Riordan Jnr & Ors v Clune* [1991] ELR 89, EAT; *Cavanagh v Dunnes Stores Ltd* [1995] ELR 164, EAT; *Shortt v Data Packaging Ltd* [1996] ELR 7, EAT; *Kileen v ISS Ireland Ltd* [1998] ELR 103, LC; *Central Bank of Ireland v Gildea* [1997] 2 ILRM 391, SC and ELR 238; *Zimmerman v Der Deutsche Schuliverein Ltd* [1999] ELR 211, EAT; *Preston v Standard Piping Ltd* [1999] ELR 233, EAT; *McCormack v Manufacturing Services* [2000] ELR 86, EAT; *A Worker v Nypro Ltd* [2003] ELR 114, LC. [Bibliography: Madden & Kerr; Redmond (1)]. See BALANCE OF PROBABILITY; EMPLOYMENT AGENCY; FIXED-TERM CONTRACT; MISCONDUCT; PART-TIME WORKER; PREGNANCY; SICKNESS; WRONGFUL DISMISSAL; RE-INSTATEMENT; RE-ENGAGEMENT.

unfair dismissal, redress for. Redress for an employee for unfair dismissal includes: (a) *re-instatement* to his former position, or (b) *re-engagement* in the former or a suitable alternative position, or (c) *financial compensation* not exceeding 104 weeks remuneration; compensation may be paid even if no financial loss has been incurred by the employee; also payments under the social welfare and income tax codes are to be disregarded: Unfair Dismissals Act 1977, s 7 as amended by Unfair Dismissals Act 1993, s 6. The cap of 104 weeks is required to be removed by Directive (EC) 2002/73 of 23 September 2000, which must be implemented in Ireland by 5 October 2005.

A claim for redress is heard by a Rights Commissioner (qv) or the Employment Appeals Tribunal (qv); notice of the claim with a copy to the employer must be given within six months of the dismissal or within twelve months in *exceptional circumstances* (UDA 1977, s 8(2) as amended by UD(A)A 1993, s 7(a); *Devereux v McInerney & Co Ltd* UD 39/89; *Kavanagh v PARK* UD 1130/88 as reported in 7 ILT & SJ [1989] 279). *Exceptional circumstances* means something at least unusual, probably quite unusual, but not necessarily highly unusual: *O'Briain v National Rehabilitation Board* [2002] ELR 210, EAT. Prolonged illness may constitute exceptional circumstances: *McDonagh v Dell Computer Corporation* [2003] ELR 233, EAT.

The Unfair Dismissals Act gives a worker who feels he was unfairly dismissed an additional remedy and does not limit the worker's rights to proceed for relief through the courts if he so elects: *Parsons v Iarnród Éireann* [1997] 2 IR 523, SC and ELR 203.

For rules governing applications to the court for redress under s 10 of the Unfair Dismissals Act 1977 and s 11 of the Unfair Dismissals Act 1993 (e g appeals from and enforcement of determinations of the Employment Appeals Tribunal), see Circuit Court Rules 2001 Ord 57, r 1. See RE-INSTATEMENT; RE-ENGAGEMENT.

unfair practices. Formerly, practices so defined in the Sch 3 to the Restrictive Practices Act 1972, since repealed. See Competition Act 1991, s 22. See COMPETITION, DISTORTION OF.

unfair terms. (1) A contractual term is regarded as *unfair* if, contrary to the requirements of *good faith*, it causes a significant imbalance in the parties' rights and obligations under the contract to the detriment of the consumer, taking into account the nature of the goods or services for which the contract was concluded and all the circumstances attending the conclusion of the contract: European Communities (Unfair Terms in Consumer Contracts) Regulations 1995, SI No 27 of 1995. An *unfair term* in a contract concluded with a consumer (*consumer contract* (qv)) by a seller or supplier is not binding on the consumer.

Examples of *unfair terms* include terms which have the object or effect of: (a) requiring the consumer who fails to fulfil his obligation to pay a disproportionately high sum in compensation; (b) authorising the seller or supplier to dissolve the contract on a discretionary basis where the same facility is not granted to the consumer; (c) allowing the seller or supplier to increase their price without giving the consumer the corresponding right to cancel the contract; (d) obliging the consumer to fulfil all his obligations where the seller or supplier does not perform his: non-exhaustive list included in Sch 3.

In making an assessment of *good faith*, particular regard must be had to: (a) the strength of the bargaining position of the parties, (b) whether the consumer had an inducement to agree to the term, (c) whether the goods or services were sold or supplied to the special order of the consumer, and (d) the extent to which the seller or supplier has dealt fairly and equitably with the consumer whose legitimate interests he has to take into account: SI No 27 of 1995, Sch 2. See Directive (EEC) 93/13 of 5 April 1993.

The High Court has held that 15 terms, which had been added to standard building contracts, were *unfair* and consequently were prohibited in future contracts: *Director of Consumer Affairs* [2001] High Court Record No 229SP/2001. The court also ordered that as regards *stage payments* or interim payments, such payments must not exceed the percentages specified in the Irish Homebuilders Association Code of Practice, or exceed the extent and value of the works carried out at the date specified for such payments. For the full text of the High Court order and the percentages specified in the IHA Code of Practice, see *www.odca.ie*. See also 'Safe as Houses' by solicitor Patrick Dorgan in *Law Society Gazette* (January/February 2002) 12. The government has indicated its intention to introduce legislation which would prohibit stage payments in house-building contracts, except in the case of once-off properties.

Regulations have been made to provide that *consumer organisations*, set up for the purpose of protecting consumer rights, be allowed to bring an injunction to prohibit the use or, as may be appropriate, the continued use of any term in contracts concluded by sellers or suppliers, adjudged by the court to be an *unfair term*: European Communities (Unfair Terms in Consumer Contracts) (Amendment) Regulations, SI No 307 of 2000. Consequently, in this respect, consumer organisations now have the same power as the Director of Consumer Affairs. See 'What makes a term in a standard form contract unfair?' by John Breslin BL in *Bar Review* (January/February 2002) 131.

(2) Where a contract between a purchaser and a supplier purports to waive or vary: (a) the relevant payment date where the contract does not specify the date or period for payment, or (b) the implied term that interest is payable if payment is not on time, the supplier may apply to the Circuit Court for an order that the term is *grossly unfair* and that the term is unenforceable, varying the term, and directing the purchaser to pay compensation: EC (Late Payment in Commercial Transactions) Regulations 2002, SI No 388 of 2002, reg 6. *Grossly unfair terms* may also be challenged by organisations representing small and medium sized enterprises (reg 8). See INTEREST, EXCESSIVE; PROMPT PAYMENT.

unfit. Has a more limited meaning than 'incapable': *DPP v Fanagan* [1991] HC. See INCAPABLE.

unfit food. See FOOD UNFIT FOR HUMAN CONSUMPTION; FOOD BUSINESS, SUSPENSION OF.

unfit house. A house which a housing authority is of opinion is unfit for human habitation in any respect: Housing Act 1966, s 66. The housing authority must serve on the owner a *repairs notice* giving particulars of the unfitness and requiring the owner to execute the works specified in the notice; or if the housing authority is of opinion that the house is not capable of being rendered fit at a reasonable expense, they must give the owner the opportunity of making an offer to carry out works or to use the house in a particular manner. If an undertaking is not accepted or accepted and contravened, the authority must make a *closing order* or a *demolition order*. It is an offence to make use of a house for human habitation where a repairs notice, closing order or a demolition order has not been complied with or which is contrary to an undertaking (HA 1966, s 68).

It has been held that lettings by a housing authority under the provisions of the 1966 Act are subject to an implied warranty that the premises let are fit for human habitation: *Siney v Dublin Corporation* [1979] SC. See CLEARED SITE VALUE; RENTED HOUSE, STANDARD OF.

unfit to be tried. Under draft legislation an accused person will be deemed to be *unfit to be tried* if the person is unable by reason of *mental disorder* (qv) to understand the nature or course of the proceedings so as to: (a) plead to the charge, (b) instruct a legal representative, (c) make a proper defence, (d) in the case of a trial by jury, challenge a juror to whom the person might wish to object, or (e) understand the evidence: Criminal Law (Insanity) Bill 2002. The decision on fitness to be tried will be decided by the court and not by a jury, as heretofore. See also 'Crazy Situation' by solicitor Dara Robinson in *Law Society Gazette* (January/February 2003) 12. See MENTAL HEALTH REVIEW BOARD.

unfit to plead. The question as to whether a person is fit to plead is determined by a jury specially empanelled for the purpose. The test is whether the person is of sufficient intellect to comprehend the course of the proceedings so as to make a proper defence, to challenge a juror to whom he might wish to object, and to understand the detail of the evidence. If the jury find the accused unfit to plead, he must be detained in the Central Mental Hospital at the pleasure of the government.

See *The State (Coughlan) v Minister for Justice* [1968] ILTR 177; *O'C v Judges of the Dublin Metropolitan District* [1994] 3 IR 246, SC; *RT v Director of Central Mental Hospital* [1995] 2 IR 65, HC. See *Robertson* [1968] 3 All ER 557; *People v O'Donnell* [1996] CCC; *DPP (Murphy) v PT* [1999] 3 IR 254, HC. See also Lunatic (Ireland) Act 1821 s 17; Lunatic Asylums (Ireland) Acts 1845, s 8 and 1875, s 13; Mental Treatment Act 1961, s 39.

Under draft legislation, the concept of 'unfit to plead' is to be replaced by the concept of 'unfit to be tried': Criminal Law (Insanity) Bill 2002. See INSANITY; OATH, JURY; UNFIT TO BE TRIED.

unfitness for office. Words spoken and published which impute that a person is unfit for his office or business do not require proof of *special damage* to render them actionable. See SLANDER.

UNHCR. [United Nations High Commissioner for Refugees]. The UN refugee organisation which is mandated to lead and co-ordinate international action for the worldwide protection of refugees and the resolution of refugee problems. In Ireland the UNHCR liaises with government departments on refugee matters, promotes international refugee law, undertakes refugee law training and initiatives to raise awareness of refugee issues. The High Court has held that s 16(4) of the Refugee Act 1996 obliges the Irish authorities to give the High Commissioner certain minimal information concerning appeals: *VR v Refugee Appeals Tribunal* [2003] 2 IR 63, HC. [UNHCR Liaison Office for Ireland, 27 Fitzwilliam Street Upper, Dublin 2. Tel: (01) 632 8675. Fax: (01) 632 8676. email: *iredu@unhcr.ch.*] See website: *www.unhcr.ch.* See INTERNAL PROTECTION ALTERNATIVE; REFUGEE; ASYLUM, CLAIM FOR.

uniform, wearing of. It is an offence to put on or wear the uniform of the Garda Síochána: Garda Síochána Act 1924, s 15; Police Force Amalgamation Act 1925, s 19. It is also an offence to wear without permission the uniform of the Defence Forces: Defence Act 1954, s 264 as amended by Defence (Amendment) Act 1987, s 14. A member of the Garda Síochána or of the defence forces is not permitted to wear his uniform in a civil court when he is a defendant in a criminal matter.

An Equality Officer has found that a requirement that all female trainees, other than chefs, should wear a standard female trainee dress uniform, was based on the conventional view that women should wear skirts, and amounted to direct discrimination on gender grounds: *Keane v CERT* [2002] ELR 135, EO. See DRESS CODE.

unilateral. One-sided. See MISTAKE.

unincorporated association. (1) An association of persons bound together by identifiable rules and having an identifiable membership eg a golf club.

(2) Two or more persons bound together for one or more common purposes, not being business purposes, by mutual undertakings each having mutual duties and obligations, in an organisation which has rules which identify in whom control of it and its

funds rests and on what terms and which can be joined or left at will: *Conservative and Unionist Central Office v Burrell* [1982] 1 WLR 522 at 525. [Bibliography: Warburton UK]. See CLUB.

unincorporated body. A body which has no legal existence separate from its members, who are individually liable for its debts without limit eg a partnership. See INCORPORATION; COMPANY.

uninsured driver. See MOTOR INSURER'S BUREAU OF IRELAND.

unintentional defamation. See OFFER OF AMENDS.

union, trade. See TRADE UNION.

unit trust scheme. Any arrangement made for the purpose, or having the effect, of providing facilities for the participation by the public, as beneficiaries under a trust, in profits or income arising from the acquisition, holding, management or disposal of securities or any other property whatsoever: Unit Trusts Act 1990, s 1 as amended by Central Bank and Financial Services Authority of Ireland Act 2003, s 35, Sch 1.

The 1990 Act provides, in the public interest and in the interests of holders of units of unit trust schemes, for the control and regulation of such schemes, and to prohibit in certain circumstances, the advertising of, and the purchase or sale of units of such schemes. The Act also provides for developments in accepted international practice with regard to the supervision and operation of unit trusts, repealing the initial Unit Trusts Act 1972. The Central Bank (qv) is given statutory responsibility for the supervision of unit trust schemes eg the authorisation of schemes and the establishment and maintenance of a register of authorised schemes. [Bibliography: Clarke B (2)]. See UNDERTAKINGS FOR COLLECTIVE INVESTMENT.

United Ireland. The governments of Ireland and the United Kingdom have declared that, if in the future a majority of the people of Northern Ireland (qv) clearly wish for and formally consent to the establishment of a United Ireland, they will introduce and support in their respective parliaments, legislation to give effect to that wish: Anglo-Irish Agreement 1985; *Crotty v An Taoiseach* [1987] ILRM 400. See also 1937 Constitution, arts 1–3; *McGimpsey v Attorney-General Ireland* [1989] ILRM 209, HC; [1990] ILRM 440, SC.

The Irish government has accepted that the democratic right of self-determination

by the people of Ireland as a whole must be achieved and exercised with, and subject to the agreement and consent of a majority of the people of Northern Ireland: Joint Declaration of British and Irish Governments (5 December 1993) para 5. Both governments accept that Irish unity would be achieved only by those who favour this outcome persuading those who do not, peacefully and without coercion or violence, and that if, in the future, a majority of the people of Northern Ireland are so persuaded, both governments will support and give legislative effect to their wish (para 7).

The Anglo-Irish Agreement has been replaced by the British-Irish Agreement done at Belfast on 10 April 1998. Under this latter Agreement, both governments recognise that it is for the people of the island of Ireland alone to exercise their right to self-determination, that it would be wrong to change the status of Northern Ireland save with the consent of a majority of its people, and that if the people of the island of Ireland so determine, it will be a binding obligation on both governments to introduce and support in their respective parliaments, legislation to give effect to that wish.

As part of that Agreement, the people agreed by referendum in 1998 to give up the constitutional territorial claim to Northern Ireland (1937 Constitution, arts 2 and 3), which came into effect in 1999 when the conditions were satisfied for the entry into force of the Agreement: Nineteenth Amendment of the Constitution Act 1998. In the new art 3 it is recognised 'that a united Ireland shall be brought about only by peaceful means with the consent of a majority of the people, democratically expressed, in both jurisdictions in the island'. See ANGLO-IRISH AGREEMENT; GOOD FRIDAY AGREEMENT; NATION.

United Nations. The international organisation established by Charter at San Francisco on 26 June 1945 with the objective of helping to secure international peace and to encourage international co-operation in the solution of economic, social and humanitarian problems. Ireland became a member in 1955. Service with the United Nations does not equate with war: Defence Act 1960, s 4 and *Ryan v Ireland* [1989] 7 ILT & SJ 118. See website: *www.un.org*. For the UN Charter, see *www.un.org/aboutun/charter/index.html*. See DEFENCE

FORCES AND UN; GARDA SÍOCHÁNA; HUMAN RIGHTS COVENANTS; INTERNATIONAL COURT OF JUSTICE; INTERNATIONAL LABOUR ORGANISATION; INTERNATIONAL MARITIME ORGANISATION; INTERNATIONAL MONETARY FUND; MILITARY LAW; PUBLIC POLICY, EVIDENCE EXCLUDED BY. UNESCO; WORLD BANK; WORLD HEALTH ORGANISATION; WORLD TRADE ORGANISATION.

United Nations workers, offences against. Where a person does outside the State an act to a United Nations worker, that if done in the State, would constitute an offence, he is guilty of an offence and liable as if the offence had been committed in the State: Criminal Justice (Safety of United Nations Workers) Act 2000, s 2. A similar provision exists in relation to offences in connection with premises or vehicles of UN workers (CJ(SUNW)A 2000, s 3). The offences are deemed to have been committed in the Dublin Metropolitan District and are prosecuted by the Director of Public Prosecutions (CJ(SUNW)A 2000, s 5). The Act allows Ireland to accede to the Convention on the Safety of United Nations and Associated Personnel, adopted by the UN General Assembly on 9 December 1994 and which entered into force on 15 January 1999.

United States. See PREINSPECTION; PRECEDENT; RULE OF REASON; UTTERANCE.

unities, four. See JOINT TENANCY.

universal agent. See AGENT.

Universal Copyright Convention. This Convention was signed in Geneva on 6 September 1952 and revised in Paris in 1971. Each contracting state undertakes to give the published or unpublished works of all other contracting states the same protection as it gives to similar works of its own nationals, as well as the protection specially granted by the Convention. The Convention provides for a minimum term of protection of the life of the author and 25 years after his death.

Under the UCC the only formality to secure protection is the use of the symbol © on all published copies of the work, accompanied by the name of the copyright owner and the year of first publication, placed in such a manner and such location as to give reasonable notice of the claim to protection. Ireland is a member of the Convention. Works published in any country of the Convention or of the Berne Copyright Union are given the same protection in Ireland as if the works were first published within the State: Copyright (Foreign Countries) Order 1978. [Bibliography: Copinger UK; Laddie UK]. See BERNE COPYRIGHT CONVENTION.

Universal Declaration of Human Rights; UDHR. The catalogue of fundamental human rights, adopted by the United Nations General Assembly on 10 December 1948, which is a common standard of achievement for all societies to aspire to and which promises an era of 'universal respect for and observance of human rights and fundamental freedoms': Preamble to UDHR. For the Declaration, see website: *www.un.org*. See HUMAN RIGHTS COVENANTS.

universal succession. Succession to the property of another in its entirety. See SPES SUCCESSIONIS.

university. An educational establishment with *objects* (e g to advance knowledge through teaching, scholarly research and scientific investigation) and *functions* (e g to provide courses of study, conduct examinations and award degrees and other qualifications): Universities Act 1997, ss 12–13. A person must not use the word 'university' to describe an educational establishment or facility, without the approval of the Minister, except where it was so described before the 30th day of July 1996 (UA 1997, s 52).

The 1997 Act provides a common constitution for all universities operating in the State e g executive power is entrusted to a governing authority to which both the chief officer and the academic council are subordinate. Universities must draw up a strategic development plan, establish procedures for the resolution of disputes, carry out quality assurance, and prepare and implement an *equality* policy. Academics are granted *academic freedom* (UA 1997, s 14).

A university is required to operate with and give all reasonable assistance to the National Qualifications Authority of Ireland in carrying out its functions and provide such information as the Authority requires: Qualifications (Education and Training) Act 1999, s 40. A university may apply to the new awards councils to have one or more of their programmes validated (Q(ET)A 1999, s 40(5)) See also Q(ET)A 1999, s 41 re new universities.

The European Court of Justice has held that a long-service increment for university professors in Austria, which was confined to those whose experience was gained solely in Austrian universities, was an obstacle to the free movement of workers and was incompatible with EC law: Case C-224/01 *Gerhard Kobler v Republic of Austria* [2003] ECJ. See ACADEMIC FREEDOM; COMPLETION RATE; EDUCATIONAL ESTABLISHMENT; HIGHER EDUCATION AUTHORITY; NATIONAL QUALIFICATIONS AUTHORITY OF IRELAND; TRINITY COLLEGE; VISITOR.

unjust. See TAXATION OF COSTS.

unjust enrichment. The profit or gain unjustly obtained. A person who deliberately breaks a contract because he calculates that he will make a profit from so doing, even after calculating damages payable for loss suffered by the other party, will have the profit or gain unjustly obtained by him considered by the court, in addition to the injury suffered by his victim: *Hickey & Co Ltd v Roches Stores (Dublin) Ltd (No 1)* [1976] HC and *(No 2)* [1980] ILRM 107.

Where a creditor or owner is compensated or recovers goods by virtue of the Consumer Credit Act 1995, the court is required to ensure that he does not obtain any unjustified enrichment (CCA 1995, s 55).

As regards taxation, unjust enrichment occurs where a trader would obtain a windfall gain if refunded tax which was paid in error. The unjust enrichment provisions in relation to VAT, which already apply to repayments, have been extended to interest payments: Finance Act 2003, s 124. See also *Thurstan v Nottingham Permanent Benefit Building Society* [1903] AC 6 cited in *Highland Finance v Sacred Heart College* [1993] ILRM 263, HC; *Dublin Corporation v The Ancient Guild of Bricklayers* [1991] HC; *O'Rourke v Revenue Commissioners* [1996] 2 IR 1, HC. [Bibliography: Goff & Barron UK; Tettenborn UK]. See CONSTRUCTIVE TRUST; SUBROGATION.

unjustified recovery. See EXAGGERATED CLAIM.

unlawful arrest. An arrest which does not comply with the law. If an arresting garda is in a person's dwelling unlawfully as a trespasser, the arrest of the person by the garda is unlawful: *DPP v Gaffney* [1988] ILRM 39 applying *Morris v Beardmore* [1981] AC 446. See also *The People (DPP) v Coffey* [1987] ILRM 727.

Where proof of a valid arrest is not an essential ingredient to ground a charge, the jurisdiction of the District Court to embark on any criminal proceedings is not affected by the fact that the accused has been brought to the court by an illegal process: *DPP (McTiernan) v Bradley* [2000] 1 IR 420, HC.

A jury awarded two persons damages of €175,000 and €100,000 respectively for their unlawful arrest and detention for three days in 1991: *Walshe & Bedford v Fennessy, Minister for Justice, & A-G* (2003) Irish Times, 22 May, HC. See ARREST WITHOUT WARRANT.

unlawful assembly. The common law misdemeanour which consisted of the assembly of three or more persons: (a) with intent to commit a crime by open force; or (b) in such a manner as to give ground in the mind of their neighbours any reasonable apprehension of violence: *Barrett v Tipperary County Council* [1964] IR 22.

An unlawful assembly became a *rout* as soon as the assembled persons did any act towards carrying out their illegal purpose. It became a *riot* (qv) as soon as the illegal purpose was put into effect by persons mutually intending to resist any opposition. An unlawful assembly could be dispersed forcibly, even by private persons acting on their own initiative, but only with so much force as was reasonable to protect lives and property. See *Lynch v Fitzgerald* [1938] IR 382. The common law offences of 'rout' and of 'unlawful assembly' have been abolished: Criminal Law (Public Order) Act 1994, s 15(6). New offences of 'riot' and 'violent disorder' have been created. See RIOT; VIOLENT DISORDER.

unlawful carnal knowledge. See CARNAL KNOWLEDGE, UNLAWFUL.

unlawful interference in economic relations. The tort of interference by unlawful means in the trade or activities or economic, commercial activities of another. It is necessary for the plaintiff to prove, conjunctively, that the defendant: (a) used unlawful means to interfere in the plaintiff's business interest, (b) that the unlawful means were used with the intention of injuring the plaintiff, and (c) that the plaintiff suffered actual damage: *O'Neill & Co Ltd v Adidas Sportschuhfabriken & Ors* [1992] ITLR (17 August) SC. The tort is not established where the defendant used unlawful means with the sole intention of promoting his own economic interests in contrast to intending to injure those of the plaintiff (*O'Neill* case).

unlawful interference with constitutional rights. An action lies for damages for unlawful interference by a person with the constitutional rights of another; a trade union does not have immunity under the Trade Disputes Act 1906, s 4 (now, the Industrial Relations Act 1990, ss 9–13) in respect of such action: *Hayes v Ireland & INTO & Ors* [1987] ILRM 651.

It has been held that *exemplary damages* (qv) are properly awardable in the case of a breach of a constitutional right even where the defendants are neither servants nor agents of the government or the executive: *Conway v INTO* [1991 SC] ILRM 497. Also a person may be entitled to an *injunction* to protect the invasion of his constitutional rights; the test is whether the plaintiff has a constitutional right and if that right is being threatened and not the usual tests for the equitable remedy of an injunction: *Lovet v Grogan* [1995] 1 ILRM 12. See CONSTITUTIONAL RIGHT; EVIDENCE AND CONSTITUTIONAL RIGHTS; PRIVATE PROSECUTION; SOLICITOR, ACCESS TO.

unlawful oath. It is an offence to administer an unlawful oath: Offences Against the State Act 1939, s 17(1). See also Riot Act 1787, s 6, since repealed by Criminal Law Act 1997, s 16 and Sch 3. See OATH.

unlawful organisation. An organisation which: encourages treason; or advocates by force an alteration of the Constitution; or raises an armed force without lawful authority; or encourages the commission of crimes; or encourages the attainment of any object, lawful or unlawful, by unlawful means; or encourages the non-payment of taxes: Offences Against the State Act 1939, s 18.

It is an offence to be a member of an unlawful organisation (OASA 1939, s 21). Evidence of the belief of a Chief Superintendent of the Garda Síochána that the accused was a member on the date specified in the indictment (qv) is evidence that the accused was then such a member; however this does not require the court to convict on the evidence of that belief (OASA 1939, s 3(2) and *O'Leary v A-G* [1991] ILRM 455, HC). Additionally, proof that the person possessed incriminating documents relating to the unlawful organisation is also evidence, unless the contrary is proved, that he was a member (OASA 1939, s 24). Such possession is evidence only; it is not proof and the probative value of such possession might be shaken in many ways: *O'Leary v A-G* [1995] 2 ILRM 259, SC and 1 IR 254.

Also inferences may be drawn by the court in relation to: (a) a failure by the accused to answer any material question (which includes failure to give a full account of his movements or actions), or (b) the giving of false or misleading information or the silence of the accused: Offences against the State (Amendment) Act 1998, ss 2 and 18. An accused must give the prosecution prior notice of any witnesses he intends to call (OS(A)A 1998, s 3 as amended by Criminal Justice Act 1999, s 24).

It is an offence for a person to collect, record or possess information which is likely to be useful to an unlawful organisation in the commission of a serious offence (OS(A)A 1998, ss 8 and 18). It is also an offence to direct the activities of an unlawful organisation (OS(A)A 1998, ss 6 and 18). See also OS(A)A 1998, ss 4 and 18. The first person to be convicted in the State of 'directing' an unlawful organisation was Michael McKevitt, the leader of the 'Real IRA': *DPP v McKevitt* (2003) Irish Times, 7 August, SCC.

The government (qv) may make a *suppression order* against an unlawful organisation and thereby all the property of the organisation becomes forfeited to the Minister (OASA 1939, s 19).

The Minister is empowered to require any bank to pay into the High Court moneys which in his opinion stand forfeited under expanded forfeiture powers in respect of the property of organisations in respect of which a *suppression order* has been issued: Offences Against the State (Amendment) Act 1985; *Clancy v Ireland* [1989] ILRM 670, HC. See *People (DPP) v McGurk* [1994] 2 IR 579, CCA.

A government appointed committee, under the chairmanship of Mr Justice Anthony Hederman, recommended that membership of an unlawful organisation should be retained as an offence, as should rendering assistance to such an organisation, but that the opinion of a Garda Superintendent alone should not be sufficient to convict a person: *Report of the Committee to Review the Offences Against the State Acts 1939–1998* (2002). See MALICIOUS INJURIES SCHEME; SPYING.

unlawful possession of goods. Formerly, the summary offence committed by a person who is charged with having in his possession or conveying anything which may be reasonably suspected of being stolen or unlawfully obtained and who does not give an account to the satisfaction of the court how he came by it: Criminal Justice Act 1951, s 13, since repealed by the Criminal Justice (Theft and Fraud Offences) Act 2001, s 3 and Sch 1. See now, POSSESSION OF STOLEN PROPERTY. See also HANDLING STOLEN PROPERTY; RECEIVING STOLEN GOODS.

unlimited company. See COMPANY, UNLIMITED.

unliquidated damages. Unascertained damages to be determined by the court. The Circuit Court has jurisdiction to award unlimited damages where an action for unliquidated damages is remitted to it by the High Court: Courts Act 1991, s 2(3)(a). See DAMAGES; PENALTY; REMITTAL OF ACTION.

unnamed persons, insurance of. There is a general requirement in insurance law that each individual be named on a policy of insurance. In order to remove any obstacles that may have existed in relation to the issue of certain *group insurance* policies, the law was amended to provide that nothing in the Life Assurance Act 1774, s 2 (as applied by the Life Assurance (Ireland) Act 1866), shall invalidate a policy of insurance for the benefit of *unnamed persons* from time to time falling within a specified class or description, if the class or description is stated in the policy with sufficient particularity, to make it possible to establish the identity of all persons who, at any given time, are entitled to benefit under the policy: Insurance Act 1989, s 26.

unnatural offence. Buggery (qv).

uno flato. [With one breath]. On a single occasion; in a short space of time.

unofficial action. Commonly means industrial action taken or a strike by members of a trade union which is contrary to union policy or union rules. A strike or industrial action which is contrary to the outcome of a secret ballot does not enjoy the immunity conferred by ss 10–12 of the Industrial Relations Act 1990 (IRA 1990, s 17). Also, unofficial work stoppages can justify the dismissal of the employees involved: *Barry & Ors v Gardeur (Ireland) Ltd* [1991] ELR 31, EAT. See STRIKE.

unpaid seller. A seller of goods in circumstances in which the whole of the price has not been paid or tendered, or, in which a negotiable instrument (qv) received as a conditional payment has been dishonoured: Sale of Goods Act 1893, s 38. An unpaid seller, notwithstanding that the property in the goods may have passed to the buyer, has: (1) a lien on the goods or right to retain them for the price while he is in possession of them; (2) a right of stopping the goods *in transitu* if the buyer is insolvent; (3) a right of resale (SGA 1893, ss 39–48). See LIEN.

unreasonableness. See IRRATIONALITY, TEST OF; WEDNESBURY TEST.

unregistered company. A company which has not been registered under the Companies Acts. It has no legal existence separate from its members, who are individually liable for its debts without limit. Certain provisions of the Companies Acts, however, apply to unregistered companies eg see Companies Act 1963, s 377 as amended by Companies Act 1990, s 250, Ninth Schedule to 1963 Act Regulations 1999, SI No 63 of 1999 and SI No 64 of 1999. Provision has been made for the winding up of unregistered companies (CA 1963, Pt X). [Bibliography: Keane R (1)].

unregistered rights. See BURDENS; INHIBITIONS.

unreported judgments. The written judgments of the Superior Courts which have not been published in the law reports. They may be and are frequently cited in court.

unsafe premises. See OCCUPIER'S LIABILITY.

unsecured loans. A building society may provide unsecured or partly secured loans, provided it has *adopted* the power so to do: Building Societies Act 1989, s 23 as amended by Housing (Miscellaneous Provisions) Act 2002, s 23 and Sch 3. See BRIDGING LOAN.

unsolicited approach. A solicitor is prohibited from making a direct approach to any person who is not an existing client with a view to being instructed to provide legal services, where such direct unsolicited approach is likely to bring the solicitors' profession into disrepute: Solicitors (Advertising) Regulations 2002, SI No 518 of 2002, reg 13(a). There is a direct prohibition on making an unsolicited approach to a non-client: (i) at an inappropriate location; (ii) at or adjacent to the scene of a calamitous event or situation affecting that person; or (iii) in, at, or adjacent to, a garda station, prison or courthouse (reg 13(b)).

unsolicited call. Means a call that is not requested by the called party: EC (Electronic Communications Networks and Services) (Data Protection and Privacy) Regulations 2003, SI No 535 of 2003, reg 2(1). A person must not use any publicly available telecommunications service to make an *unsolicited call* for the purpose of direct marketing to the line of a subscriber where the subscriber has notified the person that he does not consent to the receipt of such a call (reg 13(4)). There is a similar prohibition on unsolicited *communications* by means of an automatic calling machine, a facsimile machine or by email unless the person has been notified by the subscriber that he consents to the receipt of the communication (reg 13(1)). The previous regulations, SI No 192 of 2002, are now revoked. See PRIVACY IN TELECOMMUNICATIONS.

unsolicited goods. Goods sent to a person that are sent without any prior request by him or on his behalf: Sale of Goods and Supply of Services Act 1980, s 47. Where *unsolicited goods* are sent to a person with a view to his acquiring them and are received by him and the recipient has neither agreed to acquire nor agreed to return them, the recipient may treat the goods as if they were an unconditional gift to him and any right of the sender to the goods is extinguished, provided the sender does not take possession of them within six months of their receipt, or earlier if the recipient gives notice to the sender.

It is an offence to demand payment for unsolicited goods where the person making the demand has no reasonable cause to believe that there is a right to payment. In relation to *invoices* see SGSSA 1980, s 49.

It is now an offence for a person, acting in the course of trade, to demand payment, without reasonable cause, for what he knows to be unsolicited *goods* or *services*: European Commission (Protection of Consumers in respect of Contracts made by means of Distance Communications) Regulations 2001, SI No 207 of 2001, reg 11.

unsound mind. A grant of administration of an estate may be made to the *committee* of a person of unsound mind: RSC Ord 79, rr 26–27. For provisions governing the appointment of a guardian to a person of unsound mind, see RSC Ord 67.

An application to the Circuit Court to have a person declared to be of unsound mind must be commenced by *civil bill* together with two affidavits – one made by a person having an interest in the wellbeing of the person alleged to be of unsound mind, and the other by a medical practitioner: Circuit Court Rules 2001 Ord 47. A person of unsound mind may sue by his *committee* or *next friend,* and may defend by the committee or by the *guardian ad litem* appointed for that purpose in accordance with Order 19 (side bar applications) of these rules, or by the Court: Circuit Court Rules 2001 Ord 6, r 8.

An extension of the limitation period within which an action must be commenced is permitted where the claimant is of unsound mind at any time on the date the cause of action accrued: *Rohan v Bord na Móna* [1991] ILRM 123, HC. See Personal Injuries Assessment Board Act 2003, ss 18, 35 and 36. See also LIMITATION OF ACTIONS; WARD OF COURT; INQUISITION; INSANITY; MENTAL DISORDER; TESTAMENTARY CAPACITY; UNFIT TO PLEAD.

unstamped instrument. An unstamped or insufficiently stamped instrument, which by law is required to be stamped, will not be admitted as evidence in any civil proceedings: Stamp Duties Consolidation Act 1999, s 127(4). If the instrument is one which may be legally stamped after execution, it may be admitted in evidence when the unpaid duty and penalty is paid (SDCA 1999, s 127(1)). An unstamped instrument is admissible in criminal proceedings (SDCA 1999, s 127(4)). See STAMP DUTIES.

unsworn statement. (1) The statement which an accused formerly had a right to make in criminal proceedings without being sworn; the right has been abolished: Criminal Justice Act 1984, s 23. An accused, if giving evidence, must now do so on oath and be liable to cross-examination. However, this provision does not affect the right of an accused: (a) to make an unsworn statement if he makes it by way of mitigation before the court passes sentence on him, or (b) if unrepresented, to address the court or jury in like manner as his counsel or solicitor would have been so entitled if he has been represented.

(2) As regards the unsworn evidence of a child or of a person with a mental handicap, see CHILD, EVIDENCE OF; MENTAL HANDICAP.

untraced driver. Compensation for the personal injury or death of any person caused by the negligent use of a vehicle in a public place, where the vehicle remains *unidentified* or *untraced*, is the liability of the Motor Insurers' Bureau of Ireland (qv): Agreement between the Bureau and the Minister for Transport dated 31 March 2004 in respect of accidents occurring on or after 1 May 2004 (clause 6.1). There are certain *conditions precedent* to the Bureau's liability, including notification to the Gardaí or the accident within two days of the event or as soon as the claimant reasonably could, and full co-operation by the claimant with the Gardaí (clause 3). In addition the claimant must make himself available for interview by the authorised agents of the Bureau and must answer all reasonable questions relating to the circumstances of the accident, the answers to which may not be used in any criminal proceedings (clause 3.3). The liability of the Bureau does not extend to damage to property caused by an unidentified vehicle (clause 7.1).

Under the previous 1988 Agreement, negligence in the driving of an unknown vehicle by an unknown driver was a condition precedent to the liability of the Bureau; in the absence of proved causative negligence on the part of that person, the Bureau had no liability: *Rothwell v MIBI* [2003] 1 ILRM 521, SC and 1 IR 268. The Circuit Court held that the 1988 Agreement had not correctly transposed the relevant EC Directive into Irish law, as the Directive permitted national schemes to restrict liability to a limited extent when 'the vehicle' remained unidentified, not the 'driver': *Dublin Bus v MIBI* (1999) Irish Times, 2 November 1999. The Supreme Court however has held that the 1988 Agreement between the Bureau and the Minister gave full effect to the Second Council Directive (EEC) 84/5 in the results to be achieved by that Directive: *Bowes v Motor Insurers' Bureau of Ireland* [2000] 2 IR 81, SC. The 2004 Agreement now removes any ambiguity.

For the full text of the 2004 and 1988 Agreements, see website: *www.mibi.ie*. See also MOTOR INSURERS' BUREAU OF IRELAND; NO CLAIMS DISCOUNT.

unvalued policy. A policy of insurance which does not specify the value of the subject-matter insured, but, subject to the limit of the sum insured, leaves the insurable value to be subsequently ascertained: Marine Insurance Act 1906, s 28.

unworthiness to succeed. See SUCCEED, UNWORTHINESS TO.

upset price. See AUCTION SALES.

urban district councils. The bodies which were formerly *urban sanitary authorities*: Local Government (Ireland) Act 1898, s 22; Public Health (Ireland) Act 1878, ss 4–7. Urban district councils are now *Town Councils*: Local Government Act 2001, s 11. See BOUNDARY ALTERATION; TOWN COUNCILS.

urban renewal. Statutory provision for the designation by the Minister of *urban renewal areas* and for the remission of rates in such areas, is contained in the Urban Renewal Act 1986. This Act also provided for the establishment of the Custom House Docks Development Authority (URA 1986, ss 8–22). This Authority was given the power to acquire land compulsorily within a specified area and to have the same authority as a housing authority under the Housing Act 1966 Part V: Urban Renewal (Amendment) Act 1987. The Authority was dissolved on the establishment of the Dublin Docklands Development Authority: Dublin Docklands Development Authority Act 1997 as amended by Housing (Miscellaneous Provisions) Act 2002, s 22.

Tax incentives to promote the redevelopment of certain inner city *designated areas* is provided for: Finance Act 1986, ss 41–45; FA 1987, s 27; FA 1991, s 54; FA 1992, ss 29–30; FA 1993, ss 30–32 as amended. See consolidation of provisions in Taxes Consolidation Act 1997, ss 322–329 (Custom House Docks), ss 330–338 (Temple Bar Area), ss 339–350A (designated areas, streets, enterprise area and multi-storey car parks in certain urban areas), ss 351–359 (qualifying resort areas), ss 360–365 (designated islands), ss 372A–372K (qualifying areas), ss 372L–372T (qualifying rural areas) as amended by Finance Acts 1998, 1999 and 2000. The tax incentives may include capital allowances in respect of construction; deduction from rental income of construction expenditure and from the income of the individual owner occupier; and *double rent* deduction where occupied for the purpose of trade or profession. See also Temple Bar Area (Renewal and Development) Act 1991.

A new urban renewal scheme was introduced in 1998, under which the Minister makes recommendations to the Minister for Finance on which areas should qualify for relief, following consideration of *integrated area plans* (IAP) submitted to him by a local authority or an authorised company (eg Ballymun Development Company): Urban Renewal Act 1998. The IAP must consist of a written statement and a plan indicating the objectives for the social and economic renewal of the area and improvements in the area's physical environment (URA 1998, s 7). There is provision for a reduction in rates levied on premises in the area (URA 1998, s 10). Relief from income tax or corporation tax is dependent on certification that the development is consistent with the objectives of the IAP (URA 1998, s 11). In the Dublin Docklands area, there is provision for the Authority to recommend to the Minister for Finance that certain tax incentives may be applied to qualifying areas (URA 1998, ss 13–16).

Restrictions on the schemes in TCA 1997, ss 372A–H and ss 372L–T to meet EU requirements were provided for and the termination of the scheme was extended to 31 December 2000: Finance Act 2000, ss 44–45. Provision was made: (a) for the extension of *Urban Renewal Schemes* to 31 December 2004; (b) for the recommendation from the Minister to be deemed to be consistent with the *integrated area plan* or *town renewal plan*, even though not contained in that plan; and (c) capital allowances not to apply where there is State aid: Finance Act 2002, ss 23–25. A final expiry date of 31 December 2004 was set for various incentive schemes eg Town Renewal Scheme, Park and Ride Scheme, and Student Accommodation Scheme: Finance Act 2003, s 26. However these schemes have now been extended to 31 July 2006: Finance Act 2004, s 26. Provision has also been made to facilitate the making of orders in line with the recommendations of the *Expert Advisory Panel on Urban Renewal* (FA 2003, s 27). See also FA 2003, ss 30 and 32.

For Dublin Docklands Development Authority, see website: *www.ddda.ie*. [Bibliography: Connolly, Bradley & Purcell; Judge]. See CONSERVATION.

urine specimen. The specimen of urine which a garda may require certain persons at a garda station to provide for a designated doctor; it is an offence to *refuse* or *fail* to comply with the requirement: Road Traffic Act 1994, ss 13(1), 14(1). The omission of '1994' after 'Road Traffic Act' by the garda making the requirement of the person is immaterial: *DPP v Mangan*

[2001] 1 IR 373, SC and [2002] 1 ILRM 417, SC. When such a person is required to provide a blood specimen, he has the *option* to provide a urine specimen instead (RTA 1994, s 13(1)(b)). Only one offence is created by the words 'refuses or fails'; evidence of refusal and non-compliance is sufficient to establish 'failure': *DPP v Doyle* [1997] 1 ILRM 379, HC.

To escape the obligation of permitting a blood specimen to be taken, the person concerned must actually provide such a specimen of urine, not simply agree to provide such a specimen within a limited or reasonable time: *DPP (O'Driscoll) v O'Connor* [2000] 1 ILRM 61, SC. If the circumstances in which a urine sample was to be provided involved an excessive or unnecessary intrusion on the dignity of the person concerned by reasonable standards of modesty, it would amount to a deprivation of the option to which the person was entitled: *DPP (Traynor) v Lennon* [1999] 2 IR 402, SC.

Where a person declares that he wishes to avail of the option to provide a urine sample and is unable to do so, the obligation to provide a blood specimen is revived and any refusal to permit the taking of blood is the offence with which the person should be charged: *DPP v Swan* [1994] 1 ILRM 314, SC; *DPP v Mangan* [2001] 1 IR 373, SC. A quantity of the urine specimen must be offered to the person (RTA 1994, s 18(2)).

Under certain circumstances, a person may be required to provide a blood or urine specimen in a hospital eg where the driver or person in charge of the vehicle has been admitted to hospital (RTA 1994, s 15). See *Connolly v Salinger* [1982] ILRM 482; *DPP v Regan* [1993] ILRM 336, HC.

For power of garda to have a urine sample taken in relation to other offences, see BODILY SAMPLE. [Bibliography: McGrath M (2)]. See BLOOD SPECIMEN; DESIGNATED; DRUNKEN DRIVING; IN CHARGE; MEDICAL BUREAU OF ROAD SAFETY.

usage. See CUSTOM AND PRACTICE.

use. Before the Statute of Uses (1634), if A conveyed land to B with the intention that B was to hold it for the benefit of C, B was said to hold the land *to the use* of C. At common law B, as the *feoffee to uses*, was the legal owner of the land while in the Court of Chancery he was regarded as the nominal owner, bound to allow C, the *cestui que use*, to have the profits and benefit of the land.

The Statute of Uses 1634 (1536 in England) sought to abolish *uses* by providing that where a person was seized of an estate of freehold to the use of another, the *use* should be converted to a legal estate and the *cestui que use* should become the legal owner. The Statute failed to abolish uses, as in *Jane Tyrrel's Case* [1557] Dyer 155a, it was held that if there was a *use* upon a *use*, the Statute executed the first *use* and was then exhausted, so that the first *cestui que use* held on behalf of the second *cestui que use*, who still had an equitable estate. The second *use* became known as a trust (qv). The formula developed to *unto and to the use of B and his heirs in trust for C and his heirs* which vests the legal estate in B and the equitable estate in C. [Bibliography: Wylie (2)]. See also PLANNING PERMISSION.

user. The enjoyment, benefit or use of a thing. See CUSTOM AND PRACTICE.

usque ad medium filum aquae (viae). [As far as the middle of the stream (road)]. See PUBLIC ROAD; RIPARIAN.

usurpation. Unauthorised or illegal assumption of rights.

usurpation of government. The offence which may be committed by: (a) setting up, maintaining, or taking part in any body purporting to be a government or legislature not authorised by the Constitution; or (b) establishing, maintaining or taking part in any court or tribunal not constitutionally based; or (c) partaking in any army or police force not authorised by law: Offences Against the State Act 1939, s 6 as amended by the Criminal Law Act 1976, s 2.

usury. Illegal or excessive interest; under the Usury Laws, repealed in 1854, interest above certain rates was prohibited. Protection is now given to borrowers and consumers by the Consumer Credit Act 1995 as amended by Central Bank and Financial Services Authority of Ireland Act 2003, s 35, Schedule 1. See INTEREST, EXCESSIVE; MONEYLENDERS.

ut infra. [As (mentioned) below].

ut res magis valeat quam pereat. [It is better for a thing to have effect than to be made void]. See *Curtis v Stovin* [1889] 22 QBD 512; *An Foras Áiseanna Saothair v Minister for Social Welfare & Ryan* [1991] No 653 Sp, HC.

ut supra. [As (mentioned) above].

uterine. Born of the same mother but not of the same father.

utter. The offence committed by a person who uses, offers, publishes, delivers, disposes of, tenders or puts off a *forgery* (qv) knowing it to be forged and having the same intent (whether to defraud or deceive) that the law requires for the corresponding forgery.

utterance. Utterances made in either House of the Oireachtas are privileged; members of each House are not, in respect of any such utterances, amenable to any court or any authority other than the House itself: 1937 Constitution, art 15(12) and (13). They cannot be forced, either directly or indirectly, to give evidence at any tribunal in relation to such utterances; this includes any questions relating to the disclosure of the sources of information on foot of which the utterances were based: *Attorney-General v Mr Justice Hamilton, Sole Member of the Beef Tribunal (No 2)* [1993] ILRM 821, SC.

The word 'privileged' does not have the same connotation as in the law of defamation; it means that an utterance made in either House cannot attract or be the subject matter of any form of legal proceedings, wherever it may be published (*A-G v Hamilton* case). See also *Re Haughey* [1971] IR 216. See *McHugh* in 11 ILT & SJ (1993) 119. See Residential Institutions Redress Act 2002, s 18. See EXPRESSION, FREEDOM OF; PRIVILEGE, COMMUNICATION TO ANOTHER.

v. versus (qv).

vacantia bona. See BONA VACANTIA.

vacate. To cancel or rescind; to make void or of no effect; to annul.

vacation. The periods in the year during which the Supreme and High Courts are not normally sitting. There are four vacations in every year: (a) *Christmas* – which begins on 24 December and ends on 6 January; (b) *Easter* – which begins on the Monday of the week before Easter week and ends on the Saturday of Easter week; (c) *Whitsun* – which begins on the Friday of the week preceding Whitsun and ends on the Saturday of Whitsun week; and (d) *Long* – which begins on 1 August and ends on 30 September: RSC Ord 118, r 2 as amended by SI No 253 of 2004. One of the judges of the High Court is selected to hear in Dublin all such applications as may require to be heard immediately or promptly during vacations eg injunctions, habeas corpus.

The months of August and September are the vacation months for the Circuit Court; however the court sits in Dublin during these months to hear urgent applications or cases from the District Court: Circuit Court Rules 2001 Ord 1, rr 5 and 6. See LONG VACATION; SITTINGS OF COURT.

vaccine, care involving. The Supreme Court has held that the legal duty of the manufacturer of a vaccine to exercise sufficient care is not discharged by merely complying with mandatory or minimum requirements imposed by national health authorities where the vaccine was manufactured or by merely relying on one particular point of view concerning the risks involved: *Kenneth Best v Wellcome Foundation Ltd* [1992] ITLR (28 September) SC and [1993] 3 IR 421, SC. See IMMUNISATION SCHEMES.

vadium. See BAILMENT; PAWNBROKER; PLEDGE.

vagrancy. The Vagrancy Act 1824, s 4 (as applied to Ireland by the Prevention of Crimes Act 1871, s 15) created a wide range of offences eg professing to tell fortunes, exposing obscene pictures, exposure of wounds to obtain alms. Parts of s 4 have been: (a) repealed with the creation of modern offences eg entering a building with intent to commit an offence: Criminal Justice (Public Order) Act 1994, ss 11–12, or (b) amended eg by removal of the homelessness offence: Housing Act 1988, s 28, or (c) declared unconstitutional eg *King v Attorney-General* [1981] IR 233. See also Firearms and Offensive Weapons Act 1990, s 18. The Vagrancy Act 1898 has been repealed in its entirety: Criminal Law (Sexual Offences) Act 1993, s 14. See also Criminal Law Act 1997, s 16 and Sch 3. See WANDERING ABROAD.

validation. See NATIONAL QUALIFICATIONS AUTHORITY OF IRELAND.

Valletta Convention. The European Convention for the Protection of the Archaeological Heritage revised at Valletta on 16 January 1993 and ratified by Dáil Éireann on 13 February 1997. See ARCHAEOLOGICAL OBJECT; ARCHAEOLOGICAL AREA.

valuable consideration. Money or money's worth. Consideration in money or money's worth: Succession Act 1965, s 3(1).

The title of a purchaser of land for valuable consideration in good faith and without notice of an adjudication of bankruptcy, whereby the land became vested in the Official Assignee (qv), will not be affected by the adjudication, provided the purchaser has registered his conveyance before registration of the Official Assignee's vesting certificate (if according to law any conveyance of the land is required to be registered), unless the vesting certificate is registered within two months after the adjudication: Bankruptcy Act 1988, s 46. See also Taxes Consolidation Act 1997, s 127(3). See CONSIDERATION; GOOD CONSIDERATION; HOLDER FOR VALUE; NOTICE; PRIORITY; INTERPRETATION CLAUSE.

valuable security. Means a document: (a) creating, transferring, surrendering or releasing any right to, in or over property, (b) authorising the payment of money or delivery of any property, or (c) evidencing the creation, transfer, surrender or release of any such right, the payment of money or delivery of any property or the satisfaction of any obligation: Criminal Justice (Theft and Fraud Offences) Act 2001, s 11(3). It is an offence for a person dishonestly to procure by any deception the execution of a *valuable security*, with the intention of making a gain for himself or causing loss to another (CJ(TFO)A 2001, s 11(2)). [Bibliography: McGreal C.]

valuation. (1) The estimate of the net annual value of every *tenement* or rateable *hereditament* which formerly had to be made annually: Valuation (Ireland) Act 1852. The Commissioner of Valuations sent a list of valuations in each area to the local authorities, which lists were published, and any person aggrieved by reason of the valuation was entitled to complain by notice in writing (V(I)A 1852, ss 17–18) and the hereditament was then valued again by a different valuer: *Armstrong v Commissioner of Valuations* [1905] 2 IR 448. An appeal lay to the Circuit Court and on a point of law to the High Court: Courts of Justice Act 1936, s 31(3). See also *Davey v Commissioner of Valuations* [1956] IR 295. For revaluation see V(I)A 1852, s 34 and Local Government (Ireland) Act 1898, s 65.

The annual revision was abolished in 1988 and new proceedings were adopted for the continuous revision of rateable properties: Valuation Act 1988, s 3. Revisions may be requested by the local authority, the ratepayer or an officer of the Commissioner. Section 3 gives the facility to reopen the issue of the exemption status of a premises at any time, notwithstanding a prior determination on the issue of law by a competent tribunal: *Gael Linn Teo v Commissioner of Valuation* [1999] 3 IR 296, SC.

Provision was also made for global valuation (qv) of public utilities. A Valuation Tribunal to hear valuation appeals was established; the decision of the tribunal is final, subject to the right of appeal to the High Court on a point of law (VA 1988, ss 2 and 5). The form of *case stated* by the Tribunal to the Court was specified in *Mitchelstown Co-Op Society Ltd v Commissioner of Valuation* [1989] ILRM 582, SC The members of the tribunal are appointed by the Minister (VA 1988, Sch 1).

The application of the poor law valuation system to agricultural land has been held to be unconstitutional: *Brennan v Attorney-General* [1984] ILRM 355. It has also been held that the profit-earning ability of a business is an essential element in determining the net annual value of a hereditament: *Rosses Point Hotel v Commissioner of Valuation* [1987] ILRM 512. The courts have wide powers when dealing with valuation matters: *Siuicre Éireann v Commissioner of Valuation* [1992] ITLR (27 July) SC. See *Caribmolasses Company Ltd v Commissioner of Valuation* [1993] ITLR (30 August) SC.

The valuation code has been amended and the law has been largely consolidated to facilitate a *revaluation* of all rateable property in the State and to make new provision in relation to categories of properties in respect of which rates may not be made: Valuation Act 2001. Under the new provisions, all *relevant* property is rateable, except as specified, rather than *hereditaments* or *tenements* (VA 2001, Pt IV and Sch 4). For Valuation Office, see email: *info@valoff.ie* and website: *www.valoff.ie*. [Bibliography: Killen & Williams.] See ASSET VALUATION; GRIFFITH'S VALUATION; RATES.

(2) Where there is agreement to sell goods on terms that the price is to be fixed by the valuation of a third party, and such third party cannot or does not make such valuation, the agreement is avoided: Sale of Goods Act 1893, s 9.

(3) As regards capital gains tax (qv), it has been held that the High Court was entitled, on a case stated, to examine whether there was evidence to support a valuation decision made in the Circuit Court: *McMahon v Murphy* [1989] 7 ILT Dig 151. See also Capital Acquisitions Tax Consolidation Act 2003, s 30.

valuation, industrial plant. Statutory provision has been made to continue the rating of industrial plant which had traditionally been considered rateable, prior to court decisions which had decided otherwise: Valuation Act 1986.

Valuation Acts. Means the Acts for the time being in force relating to the value of rateable property: Interpretation Act 1937, s 12, para 33.

valuation report. (1) As regards a building society, the written report which must be available, dealing with the adequacy of the security to be taken by a building society in respect of a loan to be made by the society: Building Society Act 1976, s 79. The report must be furnished to the member of the society at the same time as he is notified of the society's approval of the loan: Building Societies Act 1986, s 6(1)(b); SI No 27 of 1987, Sch 1; SI No 339 of 1987, art 6. Notwithstanding the repeal of the 1976 and 1986 Acts, this provision, that the valuation report must be furnished to the member, continues in force as if made by the Central Bank: Building Societies Act 1989, s 6(2). See also Housing Act 1966, s 90(10) as inserted by Housing (Miscellaneous Provisions) Act 1992, s 26(1).

(2) As regards a *mortgage lender* (qv), there is a similar provision requiring the lender to give to the applicant a copy of the valuation report when the lender either approves the making of a *housing loan* (qv) or refuses to make the loan: Consumer Credit Act 1995, s 123. The lender may not charge the applicant for the report, if the loan application is refused.

(3) As regards a public limited company, the report which the company must have prepared by an independent person whenever it proposes to allot fully or partly paid-up shares on a non-cash consideration: Companies (Amendment) Act 1983, ss 30–33. The report must be sent to the proposed allottee. The report must contain a note that the assets valued, together with any cash that is being paid, are worth not less than the nominal value of the shares to be allotted plus any premium on them

(C(A)A 1983, s 30(8)(d)). See ALLOT-
MENT, SHARES; ASSET VALUATION; HOUS-
ING; PREMIUM.

value. Valuable consideration, as in *purchaser for value.*

value added tax. A tax charged, levied and
paid: (a) on the supply of goods and services effected within the State for consideration by a *taxable person* in the course or
furtherance of any business carried on by
him, and (b) on goods imported into the
State: Value Added Tax 1972, s 2(1) as
amended by Value Added Tax (Amendment) Act 1978, s 30 and annual Finance
Acts eg Finance Act 2000, ss 107–124.

The 21% rate of tax on the supply of
certain goods and services was reduced to
20% from 1 January 2001, and increased
from 4.2% to 4.3% on the supply of livestock, live greyhounds and the hire of
horses: Finance Act 2001, s 187. The 20%
rate was increased back to 21% from
1 March 2002: Appropriation Act 2001,
s 2(2)(e); Finance Act 2002, s 103. The
12.5% rate was increased to 13.5% with
effect from 1 January 2003: Finance
Act 2003, s 119. The 4.3% rate on the
supply of livestock, live greyhounds and the
hire of horses was increased to 4.4% with
effect from 1 January 2004: Finance
Act 2004, s 59.

The Supreme Court has held that taxable as separate services are: (a) the supply
of a cable link signal and (b) the connection
of the viewer to the cable link: *Mac
Carthaigh v Cablelink Ltd* [2004] ITLR
(19 January) SC and 1 ILRM 359. See
'Single or Multiple Supplies for VAT –
Mystic Twilight gives way to Morning Mist'
by Niall O'Hanlon BL in *Bar Review* (April
2004) 67.

A legal mechanism has been provided for
a supplier who has invoiced out VAT at a
higher rate than should have applied, to
give a refund and issue a new invoice:
Finance Act 1993, s 91(b). VAT is now
applicable to tolls (FA 2001, s 199(b)). For
other amendments to VAT legislation, see
Finance Act 2001, ss 181–200 and Finance
Act 2002, ss 98–110; Finance Act 2003,
ss 112–131.

Records are normally required to be
retained by taxable persons for six years
from the date of the last transaction; however in relation to immovable property
transactions, records for the VAT life of the
property must be retained from beginning

to end, plus a further period of six years
(FA 2003, s 121).

The Revenue Commissioners have no
discretion to refuse to register a company
for VAT if that company had entered into a
transaction which was, on its face, a *bona
fide* trading transaction: *WLD Ltd v Revenue Commissioners* [1995] 1 IR 99, HC.

With the completion of the Single Market, significant changes have been made in
respect of VAT on goods purchased from
other EC member states from 1 January
1993. Generally goods supplied by a VAT
registered trader in Ireland to a VAT registered trader in other EC states are zero-
rated. Also VAT is not payable at the point
of entry in Ireland in respect of goods
purchased from other member states.

However, private individuals buying
goods in another member state for their
own personal use, pay VAT in that member
state and there is no Irish VAT liability,
except: (a) in respect of new motor vehicles, boats and airplanes, which are subject
to Irish VAT when brought into Ireland by
traders or private individuals; and (b) goods
purchased through 'distance selling'
arrangements (eg mail order sales and tele-
shopping) in excess of £27,565/€35,000
annual value.

It is the duty of a barrister to register for
VAT on reaching the appropriate income
level: *Code of Conduct for the Bar of Ireland*
(December 2003) r 7.12. See *Erin Executors
v Revenue Commissioners* [1995] 1 ILRM
289, HC and [1998] 2 IR 287, SC. See
Appropriation Act 2003, s 2(2)(b); Finance
Act 2004, ss 54–65. See also Value Added
Tax Regulations 1979, SI No 63 of 1979 as
amended by SI No 219 of 2002; Value
Added Tax (Returns) Regulations 2002, SI
No 267 of 2002; Value Added Tax (Elec-
tronic Invoicing and Storage) Regula-
tions 2002, SI No 504 of 2002; Value
Added Tax (Waiver of Exemption) (Letting
of Immovable Goods) Regulations 2003, SI
No 504 of 2003. See also Circuit Court
Rules 2001, SI No 510 of 2001, Ord 66,
rr 2, 8, 9, 30; Ord 26, r 9; Ord 27, r 5;
Ord 28, r 10. [Bibliography: Gov Pub (1);
Butler B; Cassidy & Somers; Cremins &
O'Brien; Gannon; Moore; O'Reilly & Car-
roll; Somers and Cassidy; Hoskins UK.]
See ELECTRONICALLY SUPPLIED SERVICES;
INTEREST AND TAX; RATE OF EXCHANGE;
SOUND RECORDING; TOLL ROAD.

value added tax, country prefix. The
identifying prefix which traders in member

states are required to place before their VAT number e g EI in respect of Ireland. The identifying prefixes for other member states are: AT – Austria, BE – Belgium, DE – Germany, DK – Denmark, EL – Greece, ES – Spain, FI – Finland, FR – France, GB – United Kingdom, IT – Italy, LU – Luxembourg, NL – Netherlands, PT – Portugal and SE – Sweden. The identifying prefixes for the ten States which joined the EU on 1 May 2004 are: CY – Cyprus, CZ – Czech Republic, EE – Estonia, LV – Latvia, LT – Lithuania, HU – Hungary, MT – Malta, PL – Poland, SI – Slovenia, and SK – Slovakia.

value for money audits. See AUDITOR, LOCAL GOVERNMENT; COMPTROLLER AND AUDITOR GENERAL.

valued policy. See SUM ASSURED.

variation. Change in a contractual term. Consideration must be present if a contractual term is deleted or altered, leaving the rest of the contract untouched, unless the change is by deed: *Fenner v Blake* [1900] 2 QB 427. A variation may require to be evidenced in writing: *McQuaid v Lynam* [1965] IR 564. See MEMORANDUM, STATUTE OF FRAUDS; MEMORANDUM, SALE OF GOODS; ORAL AGREEMENT, MODIFICATION OF CONTRACT BY; WAIVER.

varietal names. The names for plant varieties which are the subject of applications for *plant breeders' rights* under the Plant Varieties (Proprietary Rights) Act 1980 as amended by the Plant Varieties (Proprietary Rights) (Amendment) Act 1998. A *plant breeder's right* means all proprietary rights in relation to any variety of any plant genus or species which has been independently bred or discovered and developed (PV(PR)(A)A 1998, s 5).

The Minister may by regulation provide for the selection of names and for the entry in a register of the names so selected. See SI No 369 of 1992 and SI No 332 of 1993. Where a plant variety is entered in the register every person who sells the reproductive material of that plant variety is required to use that name as the name of the variety. Failure to do so constitutes an actionable wrong in proceedings at the suit of the relevant holder of the plant breeders' rights. It is not permitted to register varietal names under the Trade Marks Act 1996. See *Wheatcroft Bros TMs* 71 RPC 43. For the *Community Plant Variety Office*, see website: *www.cpvo.fr.*

vastum. [Waste.]

VAT. Value added tax (qv).

VEC. See VOCATIONAL EDUCATION COMMITTEE.

vehicle. Ordinarily means a carriage or other conveyance on land. The term *vehicle* is not defined per se in the Road Traffic Acts. A person commits an offence if he does not take measures to prevent the creation of litter from a vehicle of which he is the registered owner, or the person in control, on a public road or in a public place: Litter Pollution Act 1997, s 4. See Road Traffic (Construction and Use of Vehicles) Regulations 2003, SI No 5 of 2003 as amended by SI No 99 of 2004. See ABANDONED VEHICLE; MECHANICALLY PROPELLED VEHICLE; PUBLIC SERVICE VEHICLE; INSURANCE, VEHICLE; FUEL; TYPE APPROVAL, MOTOR VEHICLES.

vehicle, registration of. Only *authorised* dealers are permitted to hold unregistered vehicles on their premises as from 1 January 1993. Such vehicles must be registered before the dealer releases them to unauthorised traders or to retail customers. A private individual or an unauthorised trader who imports a vehicle must register the vehicle and pay the *Vehicle Registration Tax* by the next working day. Authorisation of dealers is by the Revenue Commissioners. See Finance Act 1992, ss 130–144; Finance (No 2) Act 1992, ss 4–23; Finance Act 1993, ss 52–56 as amended e g by Local Government (Financial Provisions) Act 1997, s 17 and Finance Act 2004, s 52. See also Taxes (Electronic Transmission of Vehicle Registration Returns) Order 2002, SI No 464 of 2002.

There is now a right of appeal to the Appeal Commissioners: Finance Act 1995, s 104(2A) as inserted by Finance Act 2000, s 98. See also Finance Act 1992, ss 131 and 133 as amended by Finance Act 2000, ss 100 and 101.

Under an experimental scheme to encourage the purchase of new technology vehicles, the Revenue will repay or remit 50% of the vehicle registration tax in respect of series-production hybrid electric vehicles: Finance Act 2001, s 168. The scheme operates from 1 January 2001 to 31 December 2004: Finance Act 2003, s 101. There is also provision for the issue of a single vehicle registration certificate, called a *registration certificate*, which replaces the *vehicle registration certificate* and the *vehicle licensing certificate,* implementing

Directive (EC) 1999/37: FA 2003, s 102; SI No 213 0f 2004.

The European Court of Justice has held that in the absence of harmonisation, member states are free to prescribe the conditions for the registration of vehicles in their territory, but they must also comply with the Treaty rules on the free movement of workers: Case C-232/01 *Criminal Proceedings against Hans Van Lent* [2003] ECJ.

vehicle insurer, proceedings against. For leave of the court to institute and prosecute proceedings or to execute judgment against a vehicle insurer, see Road Traffic Act 1961, s 76. See *Stanbridge v Healy* [1985] ILRM 290; *Boyce v McBride* [1987] ILRM 95. See RSC Ord 91.

vehicle testing. See CAR TESTING; ROADWORTHINESS OF VEHICLES.

veil, lifting the. See LIFTING THE CORPORATE VEIL.

vendee. A purchaser, usually of land.

venditioni exponas. [That you expose for sale.] When an order of *fieri facias* (qv) has been issued and the sheriff returns that he has taken goods but that they remain in his hands unsold, this order may be sued out to compel a sale of goods for any price they may fetch. See RSC Ord 43, r 1; Ord 42, r 35.

vendor. A seller, usually of land.

vendor's rights. Until completion of the sale of land, the vendor has a lien on the property for the unpaid purchase money; if he is still in possession and still unpaid he can refuse to give up possession. A vendor has a right to keep the rent and profits accruing before the time fixed for completion. See *Re Aluminium Shopfronts* [1987] IR 419, HC.

venereal disease. There is a prohibition on the advertisement of cures for venereal disease: Venereal Diseases Act 1917.

venia aetatis. [Privilege of age.]

venue of trial. The location of the proceedings. The venue of the Circuit Court for proceedings depends on the matter to be tried and heard e g where the matter relates to the *title of land*, the venue is in the county in which the land is situate; in *probate matters*, the venue is in the county where the testator or intestate at the time of his death ordinarily resided: Circuit Court Rules 2001 Ord 2.

For venue of the District Court for civil proceedings, see DCR 1997 Ord 39, r 1. For the High Court, see RSC Ord 36, rr 1–2.

It has been held that while the summonsing procedure existed purely to bring an accused before the court, the assumption had to remain that the *court venue* was then one where the court had jurisdiction to amend or otherwise deal with the case: *O'Brien v O'Halloran* [2000] 1 IR 330, HC. Failure to exercise jurisdiction in a prescribed area was at most an irregularity and not a jurisdictional error, which a district judge had full power to waive if it appeared reasonable and appropriate to do so: *O'Brien v O'Halloran* [2001] 1 IR 556, SC.

verba accipienda sunt secundum subjectam materiem. [Words are to be interpreted in accordance with the subject matter.]

verba chartarum fortuis accipiuntur contra proferentem. [The words of a deed are to be interpreted most strongly against him who uses them.] This maxim is to be interpreted in the context that the interpretation works no wrong. See CONTRA PROFERENTEM.

verba cum effectu accipienda sunt. [Words are to be interpreted in such a way as to give them some effect.]

verba intentioni, non e contra, debent inservire. [Words ought to be made subservient to the intent, and not the other way about.]

verba ita sunt intelligenda ut res magis valeat quam pereat. [Words are to be understood that the object may be carried out and not fail.]

verba relata hoc maxime operantur per referentiam ut in eis inesse videntur. [Words to which reference is made in an instrument have the same operation as if they were inserted in the instrument referring to them.]

verbatim. Exactly; word for word; precisely.

verdict. The answer of a jury (qv) to a question put to them for their decision. The verdict is usually announced by the foreman, who is chosen by the jurors to speak for them.

Where the jury disagree and are unable to agree, they are discharged and a new jury is called to try the case. It is more desirable that a jury be urged to agree if possible rather than that they be told that they are entitled to disagree: *McIntyre v Lewis & Dolan* [1991] 1 IR 121, SC. In civil cases, a majority verdict of nine of twelve members is required: Courts of Justice Act 1924 s.95. In criminal cases, a majority verdict of ten from a minimum of eleven jurors is sufficient: Criminal Justice Act 1984, s 25. Such a majority verdict is not repugnant to the Constitution: *O'Callaghan v A-G & DPP* [1993] 2 IR 17, SC.

It has been held that the introduction of further issues by a judge to a jury after the jury has delivered its verdict, is of doubtful propriety: *The People (DPP) v Mulvey* [1987] IR 502, CCA. In general a person who is charged with an offence, may be convicted of a lesser offence whose ingredients are included in the offence charged; there is special provision in relation to murder: see ALTERNATIVE VERDICT. The finding of a coroner's jury is also called a verdict. See also INQUEST; JURY; SPECIAL VERDICT; TRIAL BY JURY, CRIMINAL OFFENCES; TRIAL BY JURY, CIVIL MATTERS.

versus. Against, abbreviated to *v* eg *Attorney-General v O'Reilly.*

vertical agreements. Agreements or concerted practices entered into between two or more undertakings that operate, for the purposes of the agreement, at a different level of the production or distribution chain, and relate to the conditions under which the parties may purchase, sell or resell certain goods or services: Notice of Competition Authority 5 December 2003. Vertical agreements may amount to a distortion of competition and be unlawful. See also EU 'Guidelines on vertical restraints' (OJ 2000 C291/1). See 'Competition Authority issues new notice and declaration on Vertical Restraints' by solicitor Marco Hickey in *Law Society Gazette* (March 2004) 47.

vessel. (1) Includes any ship or boat and any other vessel used in navigation and *personal watercraft*: Merchant Shipping Act 1992, s 2(1) as amended by Merchant Shipping (Investigation of Marine Casualties) Act 2000, s 44(1)(e).

(2) A waterborne craft of any type, whether self-propelled or not, and includes an air cushion craft and any structure in or on water: Environmental Protection Agency Act 1992, s 3(1) as substituted by Protection of the Environment Act 2003, s 5.

(3) Any ship or other waterborne craft, whether self-propelled or not, or any structure capable of navigation: Merchant Shipping (Salvage and Wreck) Act 1993, s 2(1).

(4) Means a ship or other floating craft of any description and includes a hovercraft or submersible craft: Criminal Justice (Illicit Traffic by Sea) Act 2003, s 1(1).

The limitation period for the commencement of an action as between vessels founded on negligence is two years from the date of damage or loss: Civil Liability Act 1961, s 46(2). The court has a discretion to extend the time subject to such conditions as it deems fit (CLA 1961, s 46(3)). The fact that the parties are negotiating to achieve a settlement is not of itself a good reason for extending the normal period of limitation: *Carlton v O'Regan* [1997] 1 ILRM 370, HC. See *Southport Corporation v Morris* [1893] 1 QB 359; *The MV 'Turquoise Bleu'* [1996] 1 ILRM 406, HC and [1995] 3 IR 437, HC. See COMMERCIAL PROCEEDINGS; FISHING VESSEL; PASSENGER BOAT; PASSENGER SHIP; PERSONAL WATERCRAFT; PLEASURE CRAFT; SHIP.

vessel in distress. The master of a ship registered in the State has a duty to assist vessels in distress: Merchant Shipping (Safety Convention) Act 1952. Wide powers are given to an authorised officer (or a harbour master in a harbour) to save a *vessel in distress* or its cargo and apparel and shipwrecked persons: Merchant Shipping (Salvage and Wreck) Act 1993, ss 7–11. A vessel in distress includes a wrecked or stranded vessel (MS(SW)A 1993, s 2(1)). The power includes requiring the master of any vessel near at hand to give aid, or demanding the use of a vehicle, vessel or aircraft that may be near at hand (MS(SW)A 1993, s 7(1)). Foreign commercial vessels in serious distress have a *prima facie* right under customary international law to the benefit of a port or anchorage of refuge in the nearest maritime state in which such facilities are available, but the state may refuse refuge where there is a significant risk of substantial harm to the state or its citizens: *ACT Shipping Ltd v Minister for the Marine* [1995] 2 ILRM 30, HC and 3 IR 406.

vessel monitoring. Provision has been made to establish a vessel traffic monitoring and information system with a view to enhancing the safety and efficiency of maritime traffic, improving the response of the authorities to incidents, accidents or potentially dangerous situations at sea, and contributing to a better prevention and detection of pollution by ships: EC (Vessel Traffic Monitoring and Information System) Regulations 2004, SI No 81 of 2004.

The regulations give effect to Directive (EC) 2002/59.

vest. To clothe with legal rights.

vested. An estate is said to be vested when there is a present right to its ownership. See OWNERSHIP.

vesting before completion. The right of a local authority to vest the title in lands, the subject of a compulsory purchase order (qv), in the authority before the assessment or payment of compensation: Housing Act 1966, s 81. As regards the compulsory acquisition of a *protected structure* (qv), and the vesting of the title, see Planning and Development Act 2000, ss 74–76. See NOTICE TO TREAT; OPEN SPACE.

vesting by deed poll. The right of a local authority to vest the title in lands, the subject of a compulsory purchase order (qv), in themselves, by deed poll in specified circumstances by paying the purchase money agreed or assessed into court e g where the owner refuses to convey the land: Land Clauses Act 1845, ss 69–70.

vesting declaration. See TRUST PROPERTY.

vesting order. The order which a local authority has power to make to acquire a derelict site (qv), having followed a specified procedure of giving notice to the occupier and the owner, publishing a notice in a newspaper circulating in the area, obtaining the consent of the Minister if any objection is not withdrawn: Derelict Sites Act 1990, s 17.

Any person who had an estate or interest in the land immediately prior to the making of the vesting order is entitled to obtain compensation (DSA 1990, s 19). Vesting orders may also be obtained under the Planning and Development Act 2000, s 45 in relation to open spaces and under the Forestry Act 1946. The Minister may revoke any vesting order made under the Land Purchase Acts where the Land Commission has not entered into actual possession of the land: Irish Land Commission (Dissolution) Act 1992, s 7.

veterinary surgery. The art and science of veterinary surgery and medicine: Veterinary Surgeons Act 1881, s 2. It is an offence for a person to practise or to hold himself out as practising veterinary surgery or veterinary medicine unless he is a registered veterinary surgeon: Veterinary Surgeons Act 1931, s 46.

The register of veterinary surgeons is maintained by the Veterinary Council which has the responsibility also of inquiring into the conduct of registered veterinary surgeons for alleged professional misconduct (VSA 1931). It also is required to satisfy itself as to the adequacy of veterinary education and training in Ireland. See also Veterinary Surgeons Acts 1900, 1920, 1952, 1960; SIs No 85 of 1954 and 66 of 1988.

Consolidated regulations have been made to provide for the mutual recognition of qualifications in veterinary medicine across the EU: EC (Recognition of Qualifications in Veterinary Medicine) Regulations 2003, SI No 288 of 2003. The regulations also require the Veterinary Council to examine applications for registration from persons with a relevant Third Country qualification, where such qualification has already been recognised by another member state. For regulations extending the circumstances under which this examination is to take place, and to amend the mutual recognition arrangements to take account of the enlargement of the EU from 1 May 2004, see SI No 265 of 2004.

For the principles governing the organisation of veterinary checks on products entering the EC from third countries, see SI No 292 of 2000. Local authorities are given greater flexibility in the appointment of veterinary staff by the Local Government Act 2001, s 246. See Control of Horses Act 1996, s 2(1). For *Veterinary Council,* see *www.vci.ie.* See ABATTOIR; EUROPEAN COMMISSION FOOD AND VETERINARY OFFICE; IRISH MEDICINES BOARD; SLAUGHTER.

vexata quaestio. [A vexed question.] A problem which has not been settled despite having been discussed repeatedly.

vexatious proceedings. See ABUSE OF PROCESS; GARDA, COMPLAINTS AGAINST.

vi et armis. [With force and arms.] See TRESPASS.

via trita. The strips of land alongside the metalled tracks of a *public road* (qv). The public has the right to pass and repass on the *via trita,* in the absence of clear evidence to the contrary. See *Attorney-General (Cork County Council) v Perry* [1904] 2 IR 247.

vibration. Formerly, it was an offence to create noise or vibration in an area which was so loud, so continuous or so repeated or of such duration or pitch as to give reasonable cause for annoyance to persons in any premises in the neighbourhood or to persons lawfully using any public place: Local Government (Planning and Development) Act 1963, s 51, repealed by Environmental Protection Agency Act 1992, s 18(1) and largely replaced by EPAA 1992, s 108. See NOISE; NUISANCE.

vicarious liability. The liability which falls on one person as a result of an action of another eg the liability generally of an employer for the acts and omissions of his employees. In order for there to be vicarious liability, there firstly has to be primary liability: *Deighan v Ireland* [1995] 1 ILRM 88, HC. An employer is vicariously liable for wrongful acts done by a servant in the course of his employment: *Poland v Parr* [1927] 2 KB 240. However, the means employed by an employee may be so unreasonable and excessive as to take the act of the employee out of the class of acts which are impliedly authorised by the employer eg using a customer as a shield against an intruder: *Reilly v Ryan* [1991] ILRM 449, HC

An employer may be found to be vicariously liable for a person who is not an employee but is an independent contractor (contract for services) where in practical terms the degree of control exercised by the employer was the same as one would expect a master to have over a servant: *Phelan v Coillte Teo* [1993] ELR 57, HC; see Barry in 11 ILT & SJ (1993) 2.

Anything done by a person in the course of his employment is treated for the purposes of the Employment Equality Act 1998, in any proceedings thereunder, as done also by the person's employer, whether or not it was done with the employer's knowledge or approval (EEA 1998, s 15).

The Supreme Court has held that provisions which made employers vicariously liable in relation to criminal offences were far from being regulatory in nature, would attract a substantial measure of opprobrium, and were disproportionate to the mischief sought to be awarded and consequently were unconstitutional: *Re Employment Equality Bill 1996* [1997] 2 IR 321, SC and ELR 132.

The State is vicariously liable for the negligence of its servants; the common law rule that the State was immune from action did not survive the enactment of the 1922 Constitution: *Byrne v Ireland* [1972] IR 241. See also *Doyle v Fleming's Coal Mine Ltd* [1953] 87 ILTR 198. See Equal Status Act 2000, s 42. For vicarious liability in respect of an agent, see 'Special Agents' by barrister Murray Smith in *Law Society Gazette* (April 2003) 31. See PRANK; SEXUAL HARASSMENT; TIED INSURANCE AGENT.

vicinity. It has been held in the UK that the natural meaning of *vicinity* is 'the state of being near in space': *Adler v George* [1994] 1 All ER 628. See CLOSURE ORDER; EXCLUSION ORDER; TRESPASS, OFFENCE OF.

vicious propensity. See ANIMALS; SCIENTER.

vicissitudes principle. The principle in common law that a court, in assessing damages for loss of income into the future, must have regard to the vicissitudes which can in the normal course of life befall a person, resulting in a diminution of their earning capacity or the duration of their working life: *Phillips v London and South Western Railway Co* [1879] 5 CPD 280. The matters to which regard must be had are 'unemployment, redundancy, illness, accident and the like': *Reddy v Bates* [1983] IR 141, SC. The occurrence of a natural illness is one of the vicissitudes of life to be considered in the assessment of future loss; however, tortiously caused accidents are not to be regarded in the same way as other vicissitudes of life: *R L v Minister for Health* [2001] 1 IR 744, HC.

victim impact statement. A statement, prepared by the Gardaí, on the physical or emotional harm, or any loss or damage to property, suffered by the victim of a crime through or by means of the offence, and any other effects of the offence on the victim. The statement is put before the judge after the accused has been found guilty but before sentencing.

Judges have generally requested such information before passing sentence, but in 1992 the formal practice was initiated in the Central Criminal Court by Mr Justice Declan Budd of requesting a Victim Impact Statement in *DPP v Kiernan* (a case involving the rape of a mentally retarded woman) and the practice has been followed in other courts since.

In New Zealand there is a statutory requirement for a Victim Impact Statement: Victim of Offences Act 1987. The Victim Impact Statement is usually in narrative form and covers: (a) details on the victim eg age, occupation, relationship with offender; (b) physical injuries eg long/

short-term effects, medical/dental reports; (c) property damage or loss; (d) financial costs e g loss of wages; (e) emotional/psychological effects; (f) other effects on victim or victim's lifestyle.

In Ireland, there is now a statutory requirement on courts, in determining the sentence to be imposed on a person for certain offences, to take into account any effect (whether long-term or otherwise) of the offence on the victim: Criminal Justice Act 1993, s 5. The court may where necessary receive evidence or submissions concerning the effects on the victim, and must receive evidence of the victim when the victim so requests. The offences concerned are sexual offences and offences involving violence or the threat of violence to the person.

As a general principle, a potential victim or alleged potential victim, can never be heard by a court determining a matter related to the criminal process: *Application of Maguire* [1996] 3 IR 1, HC. In another case, the court held that while the court was obliged to take into account the effect of a crime on a victim pursuant to Criminal Justice Act 1993, s 5, that did not amount to allowing the victim to express their own view as to what the appropriate sentence should be: *The People (DPP) v R O'D* [2000] 4 IR 361, CCA. See Law Reform Commission Consultation Paper on *Sentencing* (LRC 45, 1993). See COMPENSATION ORDER.

victim support. The voluntary organisation established in 1985 which offers emotional support and practical help to victims of crime. Help is offered through a network of branches throughout the country and also by the *Victim Witness Programme* based in the Four Courts, *Families of Murder Victims Programme*, the *Tourist Victim Support* and a national 24 hour helpline service. See Victim Support Charter, Department of Justice, Equality and Law Reform 1999. See Victim Support, 32 Arran Quay, Dublin 7. Tel: (01) 8780870; fax: (01) 8780944. See also email: *info@victimsupport.ie* and website: *www.victimsupport.ie*. See CAUTION; RESTORATIVE JUSTICE.

victim of violence. A person killed before 10 April 1998 as a result of acts committed on behalf of, or in connection with, an unlawful organisation: Criminal Justice (Location of Victims' Remains) Act 1999, Sch, art 3(3)(a). An unlawful organisation in this regard is: (i) an unlawful organisa-

tion in respect of which a suppression order has been made pursuant to the Offences against the State Act 1939, or (ii) an organisation proscribed pursuant to the UK Northern Ireland (Emergency Provisions) Act 1996 (CJ(LVR)A 1999, Sch, art 3(3)(b)).

An Independent Commission has been established to facilitate the location of the remains of victims of violence. There is a prohibition on the use of evidence obtained in the process in any criminal proceedings (CJ(LVR)A 1999, s 5). The Commission was established in the context of the *Good Friday Agreement* (qv) and the recognition that the location of the remains of the victims of violence was essential to reconciliation. See REMEMBRANCE FUND.

victim's charter. See DIRECTOR OF PUBLIC PROSECUTIONS.

victimisation. (1) Victimisation occurs where dismissal or other adverse treatment of an employee by his employer occurs: as a reaction to a complaint of discrimination, any proceedings by a complainant, an employee having represented or otherwise supported a complainant, the work of an employee (a comparator) having been compared with the work of another employee, an employee having been a witness under equality legislation, an employee having opposed by lawful means an act which is unlawful under equality legislation, or an employee having given notice of an intention to do any of these things: Employment Equality Act 1998, s 74(2) amended by substitution by Equality Act 2004, s 29.

The dismissal of an employee in circumstances amounting to victimisation is an offence (EEA 1998, s 98 amended by EA 2004, s 40). On conviction, the court may order reinstatement or re-engagement of the employee, if the employee consents or alternatively, may order compensation to be paid to the employee, in addition to a fine for the offence.

Where the employer: (a) delays implementing re-instatement or re-engagement, the Circuit Court may order compensation in respect of the delay; or (b) fails to implement re-instatement or re-engagement, the court may order compensation in lieu of up to two years' pay (EEA 1998, ss 92–93). See *SIPTU v Dunne* [1993] ELR 65; *Kirwan v PWA International Ltd* [1996] ELR 193, EO; *A Female Employee v A Hospital* [2001] ELR 79, EO; *McCarthy v Dublin Corporation* [2001] ELR

255, EO; *Daniels v Irish Blood Transfusion Service* [2003] LC. See also Pensions Act 1990, ss 65(1), 75 and 81H (7) as amended by substitution by Social Welfare (Miscellaneous Provisions) Act 2004, s 22(1).

(2) There is a prohibition on victimisation arising from an employee's membership or activity on behalf of a trade union, a manager discharging his managerial duties, or other employees arising from trade disputes in which the *Code of Practice on Voluntary Dispute Resolution* has been invoked or is intended to be invoked: Industrial Relations (Miscellaneous Provisions) Act 2004, s 8. 'Victimise' in this context, means to do any act (whether of commission or omission) that, on objective grounds, adversely affects the interests of the employee or his well-being and includes any act specified in the *Code of Practice*, but does not include any act constituting a dismissal of the employee within the meaning of the Unfair Dismissals Acts 1977 to 2001 (IR(MP)A 2004, s 8(4)). There is provision for a complaint of victimisation to be heard by a Rights Commissioner (IR(MP)A 2004, s 9), with a right of appeal to the Labour Court (IR(MP)A 2004, s 10), a right of appeal on a point of law to the High Court (IR(MP)A 2004, s 12), and enforcement by the Circuit Court of a decision of the Rights Commissioner or of a determination of the Labour Court (IR(MP)A 2004, s 13). For *Code of Practice on Victimisation,* see SI No 139 of 2004. See TRADE DISPUTE, NEW RESOLUTION PROCEDURE.

(3) A person must not discriminate on *victimisation grounds* in disposing of goods or premises, or in providing a service or accommodation: Equal Status Act 2000, ss 5, 6 and 3, amended by Equality Act 2004, ss 48–49. It is discrimination to treat one person less favourably than the other person because one has sought redress under the Act, or has given evidence in criminal proceedings under the Act, or has appeared as a witness before the Equality Authority, or has opposed by lawful means an act which is unlawful under the Act, and the other has not (ESA 2000, s 3(2)(j)).

(4) There is also a prohibition on victimisation of an employee who exercises his rights to receive the national minimum rate of pay: National Minimum Wages Act 2000, s 36. [Bibliography: Reid M.] See DISCRIMINATION; PROCURE.

videlicet; viz. [Namely; that is to say.]

video. A video comes within the definition of *film* for copyright and related rights purposes: Copyright and Related Rights Act 2000, s 2(1). See FILM; TELEVISION LINK.

video-conference. 'A facility enabling participants in distant locations to take part in a conference by means of electronic sound and video communication': *Collins English Dictionary.* In February 2003, the Minister for Justice established a committee to examine the possible use of video-conferencing in criminal and civil trials. The committee, chaired by Mrs Susan Denham of the Supreme Court, will consider the use of video-conferencing in relation to a number of areas, including bail applications, remand hearings, and the taking of evidence in civil litigation. See PATIENT, PHOTOGRAPH OF; TELEVISION LINK.

video recording. (1) Evidence by means of a video recording may be admissible in court proceedings eg *DPP v McElhinney* [1988] SCC. Evidence of a video film is admissible; however the usual and proper warnings required in relation to identification evidence, must be given to the jury: *People (DPP) v Maguire* [1995] 2 IR 286, CCA.

Also a video recording may be admissible in proceedings relating to sexual offences and offences involving violence of evidence of any fact stated therein: (a) of any evidence given by a person under 17 years of age through a *live television link* (qv), and (b) of any statement made by a victim under 14 years of age during an interview with a garda: Criminal Evidence Act 1992, s 16.

If, on the balance of probabilities, video evidence was likely to have been available in relation to an alleged crime, there is an onus on the Gardaí or the Director of Public Prosecutions to give some explanation as to why it was not sought or obtained: Hardiman J in *Dunne v DPP* [2002] 2 ILRM 241, SC and 2 IR 305. Mr Justice Kearns has said in the High Court that where video evidence was not obtained or was lost, the courts should not yield too quickly to applications to prevent trials if there was an explanation for the absence of the evidence, and where this explanation satisfied the court that the evidence could have no possible bearing on the guilt or innocence of the accused: *Irish*

Times, 21 May 2004. See *Southern Health Board v CH and CJ* [1996] 2 ILRM 142, SC and 1 IR 219; *Braddish v DPP* [2001] 3 IR 127, SC and [2002] 1 ILRM 151, SC. For video recording of an accused, see INTERROGATION.

(2) Any disc or magnetic tape containing information by the use of which the whole or part of a *video work* may be produced; a *video work* means any series of visual images (whether with or without sound), (a) produced, whether electronically or by other means, by the use of information contained on any disc or magnetic tape, and (b) showing a moving picture: Video Recordings Act 1989, s 1(1). A licence is required by persons who wish to sell or let on hire video recordings either by wholesale or by retail (VRA 1989, s 18).

The *supply* of video recordings requires the authorisation of the Official Censor of Films in the form of a *supply certificate* in respect of the video work contained in a video recording (VRA 1989, s 3). *Supply* includes supply in any manner, whether or not for reward and includes supply by way of sale, letting on hire, exchange or loan (VRA 1989, s 1(1)). A supply certificate contains a classification as to the suitability of the video work for different age groups (VRA 1989, s 4).

The Censor may refuse a certificate if he is of opinion that the video work is unfit for viewing on specified grounds eg: (a) the viewing of the work would be likely to cause or encourage persons to commit crimes or would tend to deprave or corrupt persons, or would be likely to stir up hatred against a group of persons on account of their race, colour, nationality, religion, ethnic or national origins, membership of the Travelling community, or sexual orientation, or (b) the work depicts acts of gross violence or cruelty towards humans or animals, including mutilation and torture (VRA 1989, s 3).

The Censor may issue *prohibition orders* in respect of video works (VRA 1989, ss 3(3) and 7); an appeal lies to the Censorship of Films Appeal Board (VRA 1989, s 10). Provision has been made for the appointment of assistant censors and for the refund of fees in the event of a successful appeal: Censorship of Films (Amendment) Act 1992. For the reasons behind the official classifications by the censor for new film, video and DVD releases, see website: *www.ifco.ie* which went live on 2 September

2004. See DOCUMENTARY EVIDENCE; INFRINGEMENT OF COPYRIGHT; PATIENT, PHOTOGRAPH OF; TELEVISION LINK; WITHHOLDING TAX.

viduity. Widowhood.

Vienna Convention. The United Nations (Vienna) Convention on Contracts for the International Sale of Goods 1980. See LRC 42, 1992. See Manning in (1994) 4 ISLR 99.

view, right to. An owner of property has no right to a view from the property. However, an adjacent building constructed in such a manner as interferes with a view, may interfere with a right to light. See LIGHT, RIGHT TO.

vigilantibus non dormientibus, jura subveniunt. [The laws give help to those who are watchful and not to those who sleep.] Equitable maxim that delay defeats equity. See LACHES; LIMITATIONS OF ACTIONS.

village renewal. See CONSERVATION.

vinculo matrimonii. See DIVORCE A VINCULO MATRIMONII.

vindictive damages. Punitive or exemplary damages (qv).

vintage vehicle. A vehicle which is over 30 years old. Also sometimes referred to as a *veteran* or *listed* vehicle. Special provisions apply to such vehicles, eg reduced motor tax and vehicle registration tax. For examples, see Finance (Excise Duties) (Vehicles) Act 1952, Sch, Pt II, para 5, as amended by Motor Vehicles (Duties and Licences) Act 2003, s 5; Finance Act 1992, s 130. See CAR TESTING.

violent disorder. The offence committed where: (a) three or more persons who are present together at any place, use or threaten to use unlawful violence, and (b) the conduct of those persons, taken together, is such as would cause a person of reasonable firmness present at that place to fear for his or another person's safety; each of the persons using or threatening to use unlawful violence commits the offence of violent disorder: Criminal Justice (Public Order) Act 1994, s 15. The place may be a public place, a private place or both. The common law offence of *riot* has been abolished (CJ(PO)A 1994, s 14(4)), and every reference to the common law offences of 'riot' or 'riot and to tumult' in previous enactments is to be construed as a reference to the offence of 'violent disorder' (CJ(PO)A 1994, s 15(5)). See AFFRAY; RIOT.

vir et uxor consentur in lege una persona. [Husband and wife are considered one person in law.] See HUSBAND AND WIFE.

virgo intacta. [Untouched virgin.] A female whose hymen has not been broken. Evidence that a spouse is *virgo intacta* may be sufficient to obtain a decree of nullity of marriage on the grounds that the marriage has not been consummated: *AMN v JPC* [1988] ILRM 170. See MARRIAGE, NULLITY OF.

virus. An intrusive programme which infects computer files by inserting in those files, a copy of itself. The copies are usually executed when the file is loaded into memory, enabling the virus to infect other files. Some viruses take up memory space or destroy the computer's hard disc. See COMPUTER; CYBERCRIME.

vis et metus. [Force and fear.]

vis major. [Greater force.] Insuperable accident; irresistible force eg a storm; unforeseeable conditions beyond the charterer's control. [Bibliography: Tiberg UK.] See ACT OF GOD; FORCE MAJEURE.

visa. An 'Irish visa' means an endorsement made on a passport or travel document for the purposes of indicating that the holder thereof is authorised to land in the State subject to any other conditions of landing being fulfilled: Immigration Act 2003 Act, s 1(1). An 'Irish transit visa' means an endorsement made on a passport or travel document for the purposes of indicating that the holder thereof is authorised to arrive at a port in the State for purposes of passing through the port in order to travel to another state subject to any other conditions of arrival being fulfilled (IA 2003, s 1(1)).

The Minister may by order declare the members of the class of non-nationals who are not required to have a valid *Irish visa* when landing in the State, or who require a valid *Irish transit visa*: Immigration Act 2004, s 17. Such orders may be made for the purposes of: (a) ensuring the integrity of the immigration system, (b) the maintenance of national security, (c) public order or public health, or the orderly regulation of the labour market, or (d) for the purposes of reciprocal immigration arrangements with other states or the promotion of tourism. For the approved ports for entry into the State for the purposes of the 2004 Act, see SI No 57 of 2004. For the classes of persons who are required to have a transit visa and the classes of persons exempt from Irish visa requirements, see SI No 56 of 2004.

An immigration officer is empowered to refuse to give permission to a non-national, who is not the holder of a valid Irish visa, to land or to be in the State (IA 2004, s 4(3)(e)). See *The State (Kugan) v Fitzgibbon St Garda Station* [1986] ILRM 95; *The State (Bouzagon) v Fitzgibbon St Garda Station* [1986] ILRM 98.

The Council of Ministers is required to adopt measures on the crossing of the external boundaries of the member states which will establish rules on visas, including a uniform format for visas: EC Treaty, art 62(2) of the consolidated (2002) version. See also AMSTERDAM TREATY; IMMIGRATION; LAISSEZ-PASSER; PASSPORT.

visitor. (1) As regards *occupiers' liability* to entrants on premises, means: (a) an entrant as of right, (b) an entrant who is present at the invitation, or with the permission, of the occupier, (c) an entrant who is present at the express invitation (or with the permission for social reasons) of a resident member of the occupier's family, (d) an entrant who is a member of the occupier's family and ordinarily resident on the premises, (e) an entrant who is present by virtue of an express or implied term of a contract: Occupiers' Liability Act 1995, s 1(1). A visitor also includes any such entrant whose presence has become unlawful after entry and who is taking reasonable steps to leave. Visitors exclude entrants who are *recreational users* (qv). The circuit court has held that a person who entered under a contract was definitely in the category of a 'visitor', and by paying a charge he was outside the category of 'recreational user': *Heaves v Westmeath County Council* [2002] *Law Society Gazette* (May 2002) 38. See OCCUPIERS' LIABILITY TO VISITORS.

(2) As regards institutions, a person appointed to make a *visitation* ie a visit to the institution for the purpose of investigating an allegation that some internal rule or statute or ordinance of the institution has been maladministered. The Minister is empowered to request the *Visitor* to a university to inquire into any matter which gave rise to his opinion that the functions of the university were being performed in a manner which, *prima facie*, constituted a breach of the laws, statutes or ordinances applicable to the university: Universities Act 1997, ss 19–20. See *Patel v Bradford University* [1978] 1 WLR 1488; *Cassin v*

Aston University [1983] 1 All ER 88. See Costello: *The University Visitor: A Local Employment Court* 10 JISLL 12; Kenny, '*The Visitation in University College, Dublin* (1961)' 11 *University Review* 19.

visual identification. In cases where a verdict depends substantially on the correctness of the visual identification of an accused, the attention of the jury should be drawn in general terms to the fact that in a number of instances, visual identification of an accused person had been shown subsequently to be erroneous, and for the necessity to treat such evidence with caution: *The People (Attorney-General) v Casey* [1963] IR 33. The trial judge must also relate the general warning to the particular facts in which the witness observed the accused: *DPP v O'Reilly* [1990] ITLR (9 July). See also *DPP v McCarthy* [1993] 21 ILT Dig 186, CCA.

There is a distinction in degree between recognition and mere visual identification of a person not previously known to the witness; however, this distinction does not justify abandoning or neglecting the warning rules in relation to identification evidence as set out in *People (A-G) v Casey (No 2)* [1963] IR 33: *People (DPP) v Smith* [1999] 2 ILRM 161, CCA.

Witnesses may be asked to identify persons in court: *The State (Daly) v Ruane* [1988] ILRM 117. However, where a witness gives evidence through a live *television link* (qv) in criminal cases of physical or sexual abuse, the witness may not be required to identify the accused at the trial, if evidence is given that the accused was known to the witness before the offence is alleged to have been committed: Criminal Evidence Act 1992, s 18.

The Court of Criminal Appeal has found that a purported identification of an accused *at court* was of negligible value: *DPP v Cahill and Costello* [2001] 3 IR 494, CCA. See DOCK IDENTIFICATION; IDENTIFICATION PARADE.

vital statistics. Means statistics in relation to births, stillbirths, deaths, marriages, decrees of divorce, decrees of nullity, adoptions, or any other prescribed matter: Civil Registration Act 2004, s 73(1). The Minister is empowered to collect, compile, abstract and publish vital statistics (CRA 2004, s 73(2)). There is a prohibition on the publication of vital statistics in a manner which identifies a person to whom the statistics relate (CRA 2004, s 73(4)). See STATISTICS.

viva voce. [By word of mouth.] Generally the evidence of witnesses at the trial of an action must be made *viva voce*, ie orally, in open court and subject to examination, although the court has power, for sufficient reason, to order that any particular fact may be proved by affidavit (qv). In *commercial proceedings* (qv), a party intending to rely upon the oral evidence of a witness, including an expert witness must, prior to the date of the trial, serve upon the other party or parties a written statement outlining the essential elements of that evidence signed and dated by the witness: RSC Ord 63A, r 22 inserted by Rules of the Superior Courts (Commercial Proceedings) 2004, SI No 2 of 2004. See also Circuit Court Rules 2001 Ord 23. See DECLARATION BY DECEASED; DEPOSITION; DOCUMENTARY EVIDENCE; OATH.

viz. Videlicet (qv).

vocational education committees. A body corporate with perpetual succession which has a duty to supply or aid the supply of technical education in its area and to establish and maintain a suitable system of continuing education in its area. In 1993, the Dublin Institute of Technology and the Regional Technical Colleges (now, Institutes of Technology) became independent from the VEC.

There are new structures and procedures provided for, to enable vocational education committees (VECs) to meet, in as efficient and effective a manner as possible, the needs of vocational education in their area: Vocational Education (Amendment) Act 2001.

Provision has been made for: (a) revised composition of membership of committees, including representation for staff of the VEC and parents of students, (b) clarification of the functions of VECs into *reserved* and *executive* functions, (c) additional functions eg the planning and co-ordination of the provision of education and ancillary services in educational institutions established or maintained by a VEC, and (d) revised reporting, accounting and financial procedures. See COMPTROLLER AND AUDITOR GENERAL; EDUCATION; INSTITUTE OF TECHNOLOGY; SUSPENSION; TEACHER; YOUTH WORK.

vocational training. Any system of instruction which enables a person being instructed to acquire, maintain, bring up to date or perfect the knowledge or technical capacity required for the carrying on of an occupational activity: Employment Equality Act 1998, s 12(2). *Discrimination* (qv) in relation to vocational training is prohibited (EEA 1998, s 12(1)). There is an exemption in respect of the training of nurses and primary teachers on the grounds of religion, in order to maintain the *religious ethos* of a hospital or primary school (EEA 1998, s 12(4)).

Where an educational or training body applies to the appropriate Minister for an order permitting the body concerned to reserve places in a vocational training course offered by the body, the Minister may by order allow the body to reserve places in such numbers as seem reasonably necessary to the Minister to meet the purposes set out in s 12(4) (EEA 1998, s 12(5)). The Minister in 2003 permitted the Church of Ireland College of Education in Rathmines to reserve 32 places in its vocational education courses leading to a B.Ed degree from UCD: SI No 319 of 2003. For deletion of s 12(3) of the EEA 1998, see Equality Act 2004, s 6.

The EC is required to implement a vocational training policy which supports and supplements the actions of the member states, while fully respecting the responsibility of the member States for the content and organisation of vocational training: EC Treaty, art 150 of the consolidated (2002) version. See *EEA v Football Association of Ireland* [1991] ELR 12 and [1992] ELR 57, LC. See FÁS; SKILLNETS; TRAINING.

void. Empty; destitute of legal effect; of no force eg a contract which is contrary to public policy. See VOID CONTRACTS.

void contracts. A contract which is destitute of legal effect. A contract may be void on the face of it or evidence may be required to show that it is void. Property generally does not pass under a void contract, although it has been held in England that property in goods delivered in pursuance of an illegal contract may pass to the purchaser: *Singh v Ali* [1960] AC 167.

Some contracts are declared void by statute, eg wagering contracts. Contracts which are void at common law include: (a) contracts to oust the jurisdiction of the courts: *Scott v Avery* [1856] 5 HL Cas 811; (b) contracts which subvert the sanctity of marriage, eg marriage broker contracts, contracts for future separation: *Williamson v Gihan* [1805] 2 S & L 357; *Marquess of*

Westmeath v Marquess of Salisbury [1830] 5 Bli (ns) 339; and (c) contracts in restraint of trade: *Nordenfelt v Maxim Nordenfelt* [1894] AC 535. See QUANTUM MERUIT.

void marriage. See MARRIAGE, NULLITY OF.

voidable. Capable of being voided or set aside eg a voidable contract is one which one of the parties can put an end to at his option, without reference to the other party, so that the contract is binding if he elects to treat it as binding and void if he elects to treat it as void eg in the case of a contract induced by fraud: *Phillips v Brooks* [1919] 2 KB 243.

If, however, the party entitled to rescind the contract affirms it, or fails to exercise his right within a reasonable time, so that the position of the parties becomes altered, or if he takes a benefit under the contract, or if third parties acquire rights under it, he will be bound by it.

voidable marriage. See MARRIAGE, NULLITY OF.

voidable title, sale under. When the seller of goods has a voidable title thereto, but his title has not been avoided at the time of sale, the buyer acquires a good title to the goods, provided he buys them *in good faith* and without notice of the seller's defect of title: Sale of Goods Act 1893, s 23. *In good faith* means done honestly, whether done negligently or not (SGA 1893, s 62(2)). See NEMO DAT QUI NON HABET.

voire dire. [To speak the truth.] A *trial within a trial* which is resorted to whenever before, or in the course of, a trial an issue arises involving a decision of law by the judge without the presence of the jury eg whether a child witness is capable of understanding an oath; whether a confession is voluntary; whether a witness is privileged from answering a specific question; or whether some point of law be argued, at the request of the defence, in the absence of the jury. See *The People (Attorney-General) v Ainscough* [1960] IR 136; *The People v O'Brien* [1969] CCA; *The People (DPP) v Conroy* [1988] ILRM 4.

volenti non fit injuria. [That to which a man consents cannot be considered an injury.] The defence to an action in tort, that the plaintiff with full knowledge and appreciation of the danger, voluntarily accepted the risk and exposed himself to the danger eg by taking part in a boxing match. Mere knowledge of the risk, or *sciens*, is not sufficient. *Volenti non fit injuria* is a partial defence: Civil Liability Act 1961, s 34. See *Flynn v Irish Sugar Mfg Co Ltd* [1928] IR 525; *Judge v Reape* [1968] IR 226. See GOLF.

voluntary. (1) Free exercise of will involving an act of choice. (2) Without valuable consideration (qv).

voluntary care. See welfare of children.

voluntary conveyance. A disposition of an interest in land without valuable consideration or marriage to support it; it may be void if the grantor becomes bankrupt. Land conveyed to others by way of a *voluntary conveyance* can be recaptured by the Official Assignee; the conveyance is void if the grantor becomes bankrupt within two years of the conveyance, and it is voidable within five years unless it can be shown that at the time the conveyance was made, the bankrupt was solvent without the aid of the lands conveyed: Bankruptcy Act 1988, s 59. See OFFICIAL ASSIGNEE.

voluntary discovery. See DISCOVERY.

voluntary health insurance. A voluntary scheme of insurance for defraying the cost to persons, paying subscriptions to the Voluntary Health Insurance Board, of medical, surgical, hospital and other health services: Voluntary Health Insurance Act 1957, s 4(1). The Minister is empowered to specify the extent of the scheme and he also appoints the members of the board, which is a body corporate with perpetual succession with power to sue and to be sued in its corporate name and to acquire, hold and dispose of land.

The VHI is an *undertaking* within the meaning of the Competition Act 1991 (now, Competition Act 2002) while it is a non-profit-making body, it still operates *for gain*: *Deane & Ors v VHI* [1992] ITLR (31 August), SC. The VHI was held to have acted unreasonably and unfairly in deciding to withdraw all cover from the plaintiff's hospital: *Deane & Ors v VHI* [1993] HC. See also *Ormiston v Gypsum Industries Ltd* EE16/1992 [1993] ELR and as reported by Barry in 11 ILT & SJ (1993) 94.

The *de facto* monopoly of the VHI ended with the enactment of the Health Insurance Act 1994. In 1996, the 1957 Act was further amended to restructure the Board of the VHI, to permit it to develop new types of health insurance products and activities; the board is now obliged to notify premium increases to the Minister, which he is empowered to disallow: Voluntary

Health Insurance (Amendment) Act 1996. In 1998, the power was given to the VHI to offer health insurance to its customers in respect of medical, surgical or other related services (as an agent for an international healthcare plan) where the customer wishes to reside outside the State for a temporary period: Voluntary Health Insurance (Amendment) Act 1998. For VHI and BUPA respectively, see websites: *www.vhi.ie* and *www.bupa.ie* [Bibliography: Tomkin & Hanafin.] See HEALTH INSURANCE; WITHHOLDING TAX.

voluntary trust. A trust in favour of a volunteer (qv).

voluntary waste. See WASTE.

voluntary winding up. See WINDING UP, VOLUNTARY.

voluntas in delictis non exitus spectatur. [In crimes, the intention, and not the result, is looked at.] See MENS REA.

volunteer. (1) A person who takes under a disposition for which he, or anyone on his behalf, has not given valuable consideration (qv). Equity will not assist a volunteer; consequently an incompleted trust for the benefit of a volunteer will be unenforceable. See *Plumptre's Marriage Settlement* [1910] 2 Ch 609. See TRUST.

(2) A person who gives his services without any express or implied promise of remuneration. He may be liable in damages if he performs a voluntary act negligently, but not if he fails to perform it at all. See AGENT, GRATUITOUS; EQUITY, MAXIMS OF; NEIGHBOUR PRINCIPLE.

volunteer development worker. A person who is employed temporarily outside the State in a developing country under conditions of remuneration similar to local conditions; such persons on return to Ireland may be given credit for social welfare contributions for the period spent abroad, for up to five years, the credits being referable to the contributions paid during the last period of insurable employment in Ireland: Social Welfare (Consolidation) Act 1993, s 27. See also Social Welfare (No 2) Act 1993, ss 11–13; Social Welfare Act 1999, s 24.

vote, right to. A person does not have an absolute right to vote under the Constitution; a person in lawful detention has some of his rights suspended, which could include the lack of facilities to vote: *Breathnach v Ireland* [2001] 3 IR 230, SC. A lack of facilities to vote is not arbitrary, unreasonable or unjust and is not in breach of a prisoner's constitutional rights. However, the European Court of Human Rights has ruled that prisoners should not automatically lose the right to vote, holding that legislatures should strike a fair balance by tailoring the restriction on the right to vote to sentences of particular gravity, or leave the issue to be decided by judges: *Hirst v Government of the United Kingdom* (2004) Irish Times, 5 April, ECHR. See FRANCHISE; PERSONATION; SPOILT VOTE.

voters, special. Persons whose names are included in the special voters list: Electoral Act 1992, s 2(1). An elector is entitled to be entered in this list if he satisfies the registration authority that he is unable to go in person to vote by reason of his physical illness or physical disability (EA 1992, s 27 and Sch 2, rr 19–23). A first application must be accompanied by a certificate from a medical practitioner (r 19(c)).

Special voters are entitled to cast their vote on a ballot paper delivered to the special voter by a special presiding officer accompanied by a member of the Garda Síochána (EA 1992, ss 81–82, Dáil elections); European Parliament Election Act 1997, Sch 2, rr 41–47, European elections. See also Presidential Elections Act 1993, s 41; Referendum Act 1994, s 29; Electoral Act 1997, s 76. As regards the counting of special voter ballot papers where there is electronic voting, see Electoral (Amendment) Act 2004, s 12. See *Draper v Ireland* [1984] IR 277. See DISABLED VOTER.

voting at elections. Voting in presidential, European, and Dáil elections must be by the elector in person at the polling station allotted to him, except where permitted either at another polling station, or by postal vote, or in another manner for special voters eg see Electoral Act 1992, s 38. For rules governing the counting of votes, see 1992 Act, ss 118–128. See POSTAL VOTER; SPOILT VOTE.

voting at meetings. All questions arising at a meeting of a company must be decided in the first place by a show of hands; however members are empowered to demand a poll except in respect of the election of chairman and voting on adjournments: Companies Act 1963, s 137; *Re Horburg Co* [1879] 21 Ch D 109.

When voting is by show of hand, each member has one vote only irrespective of the number of shares he holds; when voting is on a poll, every member has a vote for every share he has, which he can use to vote some for and some against a resolution as he so wishes (CA 1963, s 138). A member can appoint another person, a *proxy*, who need not be a member, to attend, speak and vote for the member (CA 1963, s 136). See ARM'S LENGTH, AT; CHAIRMAN; COUNCILLOR, DISCLOSURE OF INTEREST; POLL; PROXY; RESOLUTION.

voting by post. See POSTAL VOTER.

vouch. To bear witness; to summon; to answer for.

voucher. A document which evidences a transaction eg a receipt for money.

vow. Solemn promise. Members of religious communities usually bind themselves by agreement to vows eg vow of celibacy, vow of obedience. The power of a religious superior appears to be absolute or virtually absolute, the vow of obedience being a converse of that power; the making of an order by a religious superior is unlikely to be intended to be subject to review by any other tribunal: *Sister O'Dea v O'Briain & Ors* [1992 HC] ILRM 364. See Barry in 10 ILT & SJ (1992) 222. See FAIR PROCEDURE.

voyage policy. A contract of insurance to insure the subject matter at and from or from one place to another or others: Marine Insurance Act 1906, s 25(1).

vulgar abuse. The use of words in an abusive way or in anger about a person so that they injure only the pride of the person rather than his reputation, is unlikely to be defamatory. To call someone a 'shithead' or a 'gobshite' was vulgar abuse: Lardner J in *Kenna v McKinney* (1992) Irish Times, 11 December 1992. See ABUSE; ARSEHOLE; DEFAMATION.

wagering contract. An agreement between two parties that upon the happening of some uncertain event, one party will pay a sum of money to the other, which party is to pay depending on the issue of the event. Neither party must have any other interest in the contract other than the sum he will win or lose. If either of the parties may win but cannot lose, or may lose but cannot win, it is not a wagering contract. Wagering contracts are not illegal but the courts will give no assistance in enforcing them; every contract by way of gaming (qv) or wagering is void and no action may lie for the recovery of any money won thereon: Gaming and Lotteries Act 1956, s 36(1) and (2).

A bet placed with *the Tote* is not a wager as the Racing Board is legally bound to pay the money received to successful ticket holders and consequently cannot win or lose: *Duff v Racing Board* [1971] HC. It was held that the defendants owed a duty of care, as regards the eligibility of a horse to take part in a race, to the holder of a jackpot ticket affected by that race at Punchestown: *Madden v Irish Turf Club & Ors* [1993] ITLR (26 July) HC.

A promise express, or implied: (a) to pay any person any sum of money paid by him in respect of a gaming or wagering contract; or (b) to pay any money by way of commission, fee, reward or otherwise, in respect of such contracts, is null and void and no action can be brought to recover any such money (GLA 1956, s 36(3)). This is an exception to the usual rule that an agent is liable to be indemnified for all lawful acts by his principal.

A contract of insurance is not a wager if the assured has an insurable interest (qv) in the subject matter insured. See *Pujolus v Heaps* [1938] 72 ILTR 96; *McElwain v Mercer* [1859] 9 ICLR 13. See GAMING; TOTALISATOR.

wages. Any sums payable by an employer to his employee in connection with his employment, including: any fee, bonus or commission, or any holiday, sick or maternity pay: Payment of Wages Act 1991, s 1. Wages must be paid by one or more of specified modes eg cash, cheque, draft or other bill of exchange; a postal, money or paying order; a credit transfer to an account specified by the employee (PWA 1991, s 2).

Employees paid in cash before commencement of the 1991 Act (or who entered an agreement to be paid other than in cash under the Payment of Wages Act 1979) continue to be entitled to be paid in cash until another mode of payment is agreed with the employer (PWA 1991, s 3).

An employer must give each employee a written statement of wages and deductions (PWA 1991, s 4). Deductions must not be made unless required by statute, or authorised by the contract of employment, or authorised by the employee in writing (PWA 1991, s 5). The Employment Appeals Tribunal has held that the deduc-

tion of pay of a suspended employee in particular circumstances was not in accordance with the 1991 Act: *Murphy v Ryanair plc* [1993] ELR 215, EAT. It also held that the non-payment of a qualification allowance to a teacher constituted an unlawful deduction within the meaning of the 1991 Act: *Sullivan v Department of Education* [1998] ELR 217, EAT.

See Payment of Wages (Appeals) Regulations 1991, SI No 351 of 1991.

An employee is entitled to be paid his salary or wage during his absence in order to comply with a jury summons: Juries Act 1976, s 29. Employees may also be entitled to a mandatory injunction (qv) compelling their employer to pay their wages and salaries: *Boyle & Ors v An Post* [1992] ELR 65, HC. See *Glasgow v Independent Printing* [1901] 2 IR 278.

There are exemptions from income tax of certain *lump sums* paid to employees in respect of pay reductions under agreed pay restructuring schemes. The maximum tax free lump sum is now £20,000 (€25,395) in respect of a reduction in pay of more than 20%: Taxes Consolidation Act 1997, s 202 as amended by Finance Act 2000, s 18.

For rules governing applications to the court for the enforcement of decisions of a Rights Commissioner or determinations of the Employment Appeals Tribunal, pursuant to s 8 of the Payment of Wages Act 1991, see Circuit Court Rules 2001 Ord 57, r 2. See ATTACHMENT; CASH; EMOLUMENTS; MAINTENANCE ORDER; MINIMUM WAGE; NOTICE, EMPLOYMENT.

wages, minimum. See JOINT LABOUR COMMITTEE; MINIMUM WAGE.

waiver. The relinquishing, renouncing, disclaiming, forbearance or abandonment of a claim to a right or benefit. A waiver may be express or implied. Waiver of a contractual right does not have to be evidenced in writing because, the right continues, although it may be unenforceable, unlike the case of a *variation* (qv) where the contractual right is extinguished.

Waiver may have the effect of affecting the range of remedies available to the party forbearing: *Car & General Insurance Corporation v Munden* [1936] IR 584. It is not an act of waiver to intimate that one may be prepared to waive some contractual right in certain circumstances: *SA. Fonderes Lion MV v International Factors (Ireland) Ltd* [1984] ILRM 66. As regards waiver of constitutional rights, see *Murphy v Stewart* [1975] IR 97. See AMNESTY.

wall. See PARTY WALL.

wandering abroad. The homelessness offence contained in the Vagrancy Act 1824 (as applied in Ireland by the Prevention of Crimes Act 1871, s 15) which has been repealed: Housing Act 1988, s 28. See LRC 11 of 1985.

want of prosecution. See DISMISSAL FOR WANT OF PROSECUTION.

war. War must not be declared and the State must not *participate* in any war save with the assent of Dáil Éireann: 1937 Constitution, art 28(3)(1). Some quite egregious disregard of constitutional duties and obligations would have to take place before the courts could intervene as regards art 28: *Horgan v Ireland* [2003] 2 ILRM 357, HC at 400. What constitutes *participation* is a matter for the government and the Dáil and not for the courts.

In the case of actual invasion, however, the government may take whatever steps they consider necessary for the protection of the State. The rights of the parties to an armed conflict to choose the methods and means of warfare are not limited eg it is prohibited to employ weapons, projectiles and materials and methods of warfare of a nature to cause superfluous injury or unnecessary suffering: Geneva Conventions (Amendment) Act 1998, Sch 5, art 35. See GENEVA CONVENTION; NATIONAL EMERGENCY; NEUTRALITY; PRISONER OF WAR.

war, time of. See NATIONAL EMERGENCY.

war crimes. Offences created by the law governing the conduct of combatants during warfare. See Geneva Conventions Acts 1962 and 1998. Provision has been made for Ireland to co-operate with the International Criminal Tribunals for the former Yugoslavia and for Rwanda and, by regulation, with any other war crime tribunal or court that may be established by the United Nations in the future: International War Crimes Tribunals Act 1998, s 37.

A judge of an international war crimes tribunal who was a practising barrister or practising solicitor prior to their appointment, is qualified for appointment as a judge of the Superior Courts of Ireland: Courts (Supplementary Provisions) Act 1961, s 5(2) as substituted by Courts and Court Officers Act 2002, s 4. See *The Prosecution of Gender Crimes in the International Criminal Tribunal for the former Yugoslavia* by Michelle Breslin in (2003) 11

ISLR 82. See ASYLUM; EXTRADITION; GENEVA CONVENTION; HORS DE COMBAT; PERFIDY; POLITICAL OFFENCE.

War of Independence. See MILITARY SERVICE PENSIONS.

ward. (1) A person under the care and protection of another; a person under the care of a guardian (qv) appointed by the court or a minor (qv) or person of unsound mind brought under the authority of the protection of the court.

(2) A district electoral area, now known as an *electoral division*: Local Government Act 2001, s 223. Any reference in any enactment to a *district electoral division* or a *ward* is to be read as a reference to an electoral division (LGA 2001, s 223(2)). The Minister may by order divide a county, city or town also into local electoral areas and fix the number of local authority members to be elected from such areas (LGA 2001, s 223(1)). The electoral divisions are the building blocks used to form local electoral areas.

ward of court. The protection by the court of persons, and their property, who are unable to look after themselves eg minors (qv): RSC Ord 65. A ward includes a person who has been declared to be of unsound mind and incapable of managing his person or property and includes, where the context so admits, a person in respect of whom or whose property an order has been made under the Lunacy Regulations (Ireland) Act 1871, ss 68 or 70: RSC Ord 67, r 1. The High Court refused an injunction sought by parents to restrain the medical examination of their 22-year-old disabled son as part of the procedures which could result in his being made a ward of court: *Dolan v Registrar of High Court* (19 March 2004, unreported) HC.

In wardship proceedings, the trial judge is placed in the position of a good parent who must decide prudently on issues relating to the welfare of the child; the proceedings however must be fair and in accordance with constitutional justice: *In the matter of MK, SK and WK* [1999, SC] 2 ILRM 321 and 2 IR 99.

The most usual circumstance in which a minor is made a ward of court is where it is thought desirable to obtain independent protection of the minor's property interests. See *In the Matter of JS, an Infant* [1977] 211 ILTR 146; Guardianship of Infants Act 1964, s 11(1). A minor may be made a ward of court by proceedings commenced by originating summons: RSC Ord 65, App K, form no 19.

However, it has been held that the court has jurisdiction to take a minor into wardship when no property matter is involved, if to do so is in the minor's welfare: *The State (Bruton) v Judge of Circuit Court and Bruton* [1984] HC. The jurisdiction of the High Court to take persons of unsound mind into wardship whether they have property or not *is and must always remain a discretionary jurisdiction*: *Re Midland Health Board* [1988] ILRM 251.

A ward of court may make a representation, regarding his land, amounting to a *promissory estoppel*, which will preclude the ward from enforcing his title to the land: *In the matter of JR, a ward of Court* [1993] ILRM 657, HC. A health board is not obliged to provide in the home of a ward of court, the equivalent care and maintenance service, both medical and practical, that he would receive as an in-patient in a hospital: *K(C) v Northern Area Health Board* [2003] 2 IR 544, SC and FL 7622.

When a person is made a ward of court, all matters affecting the ward's welfare become the responsibility of the court; failure to comply with an order of the court constitutes a contempt (qv) and may result in imprisonment of the person in contempt: *Re McLorinan, a Minor* [1935] IR 373.

The *committee of the person* of the ward has rights and duties in relation to the care of the ward which includes taking litigation on behalf of the ward: *Re K (Ward of Court) (Committee of Person)* [2001] 1 IR 338, SC. For general guidelines on procedure, see Costello in *Law Society Gazette* (May 1993) 143. See *In the Matter of a Ward of Court* [1995] 2 ILRM 401, SC. See RSC Ord 67 as amended by SI No 20 of 1989. For rules of court governing the remuneration of *committees of wards of court*, see SI No 208 of 2002. There is no longer a requirement for special circumstances or special cause to exist before remuneration would be allowed. See Law Reform Commission, *Consultation Paper on Law and the Elderly* (LRC CP 23, 2003). See DIE, RIGHT TO; INQUISITION; LEGAL AID; POWER OF ATTORNEY, ENDURING; UNSOUND MIND.

warehouse. It has been held that if a person through his negligence injures property in a warehouse, he must take responsibility for damaging whatever goods are there; because a warehouse is part of the world of commerce, it is foreseeable that there will be economic loss and possible loss of profits: *Egan v Sisk* [1986] ILRM 283.

warning. In relation to the administration of estates, a direction to a *caveator* to enter an appearance setting forth his interest and that in default of so doing, the caveat will cease to have effect: RSC Ord 79, rr 47–51; Ord 80, rr 48–55. See CAUTION; CAVEAT; CORROBORATION; FIRE WARNING LABEL; INCRIMINATE.

warning, employment. It has been held in a particular case that a written warning by an employer to an employee that failure to follow a set procedure would lead to dismissal is necessary to justify a dismissal of the employee: *Carroll v Foxrock Inn* [1990] ELR 236.

warning announcement. Where a *listed* company is aware that knowledge of impending developments has occurred, or is likely to occur, and this is likely to lead to a substantial movement in the price of its listed securities, it must without delay notify the stock exchange with at least a *warning announcement* that it expects shortly to release information which may lead to such a movement: Listing Rules 2000, para 9.4.

warning letter. Means a notification in writing from a planning authority to the owner, occupier or any other person carrying out a *development*, stating that it has come to the attention of the authority that *unauthorised development* may have been, is being or may be carried out, and advising the person of the possible penalties and costs involved, and inviting the person to make submissions or observations: Planning and Development Act 2000, ss 2(1) and 152. The planning authority is required to conduct an investigation to enable it to make a decision on whether it should issue an *enforcement notice* (PDA 2000, s 153). Under previous legislation a *warning notice* was issued instead of a warning letter. See ENFORCEMENT NOTICE.

warning notice. The notice which a planning authority had power to serve where it appeared to them that land was being or was likely to be developed without permission or any unauthorised use was being or was likely to be made of land: Local Government (Planning and Development) Act 1976, s 26 as amended by Local Government (Planning and Development) Act 1992, s 19(4). See *Dublin Co Council v Taylor* [1989] 7 ILT Dig 150; *Mountcharles* *v Meath County Council* [1996] 3 IR 417, HC and [1997] 1 ILRM 446, HC. The *warning notice* has been replaced by a *warning letter* under the consolidating Planning and Development Act 2000. See FIRE WARNING LABEL; INJUNCTION, PLANNING; WARNING LETTER.

warrant. (1) A document authorising some action eg a dividend warrant authorising the payment of money.

(2) An order in writing authorising the arrest of a specified person; arrest warrants are issued pursuant to the District Court Rules. A garda properly executing a warrant is protected against any irregularity or want of jurisdiction which may have occurred in the issue of the warrant: Constabulary (Ireland) Act 1836, s 50; Public Officers Protection (Ireland) Act 1803, s 6.

A *spent* warrant cannot be lawfully executed; however a re-issued warrant has exactly the same function as a warrant issued *de novo*: *Healy v Governor of Cork Prison* [1997] 2 ILRM 357, SC and [1998] 2 IR 93, SC. See *Lloyd v Judge Hogan* [1996] 2 IR 581, HC. See DCR 1997 Ord 26, r 11. See also DCR 1997 Ord 16; Ord 21, rr 5–6; Ord 25. See Criminal Justice Act 1984, s 13(4) and (5). See *McGirl v McArdle* [1989] ILRM 495. See Criminal Justice Bill 2004, ss 37–38. See COMMITTAL WARRANT; DISTRESS; EXTRADITION; IDENTIFICATION; PENAL WARRANT; SEARCH WARRANT; ARREST WITHOUT WARRANT.

warrant, search. See SEARCH WARRANT.

warrant, share. See SHARE CERTIFICATE.

warrantor. A person who gives a warranty (qv).

warranty. (1) A term in a contract which gives rise to a right to recover damages in the event that it is breached but which does not entitle the injured party to repudiate the contract. Where a representation is made in the course of dealings for a contract for the very purpose of inducing the other party to act on it, and it actually induces him to act on it by entering into the contract, there is *prima facie* ground for inferring that the representation was intended as a warranty: *Carey v Independent Newspapers (Ireland) Ltd* [2003] ITLR (3 November) HC; FL 8229; [2004] ELR 45.

(2) An agreement with reference to goods which are the subject of a contract of sale, but collateral to the main purpose of such contract, the breach of which gives rise to a claim for damages, but not a right to reject the goods and treat the contract as repudiated: Sale of Goods Act 1893, s 62. See CONDITION; GUARANTEE; SERVICE, SUPPLY OF; SPARE PARTS; WARRANTY, BREACH OF.

warranty, breach of. Where there is a breach of warranty by a seller of goods, the buyer is not entitled to reject the goods, but he may maintain an action for damages for the breach, or set up the breach in diminution or extinction of the price. The measure of damages for breach of warranty is the estimated loss directly and naturally resulting, in the ordinary course of events, from the breach.

As regards quality, such loss is *prima facie* the difference between the value of the goods at delivery to the buyer and the value they would have had if they had answered the warranty on quality. The fact that the buyer has set up the breach in diminution or extinction of the price or that the seller has replaced goods or remedied a breach, does not of itself prevent the buyer from maintaining an action for the same breach if he has suffered further damage. A breach of warranty can amount to a total failure of consideration: *Yeoman Credit Ltd v Apps* [1962] QB 508.

See *McAuley v Horgan* [1925] IR 1; *Egan v McSweeney* [1956] 90 ILTR 40. See Sale of Goods Act 1893, s 53; Sale of Goods and Supply of Services Act 1980, s 21. See CONDITION.

warranty of authority, breach of. A person who professes to act as an agent, where in fact he has no authority from the alleged principal or has exceeded his authority, is liable to an action for a *breach of warranty of authority* at the suit of the party with whom he professed to contract. The action is based, not on the original contract, but on an implied promise by the agent that he had authority to make the original contract.

The action can be brought only by the third party and not by the principal. The agent is liable whether he acted fraudulently or innocently and even if his authority has been terminated without his knowledge, by the death, lunacy or bankruptcy of the principal: *Yonge v Townbee* [1910] 2 KB 215. However, the agent is not liable if his lack of authority was known to the third party or if the contract excludes his liability. See also DECEIT; ULTRA VIRES.

Warsaw Convention. The *International Convention for the Unification of Certain*

Rules relating to International Carriage by Air done at Warsaw on 12 October 1929 and given the force of law in the State by the Air Navigation and Transport Act 1936, s 17(1). The Convention has provisions in relation to the documents of carriage (passenger and luggage tickets, air consignment notes), the liability of the carrier, and the limitation of that liability (ANTA 1936, Sch 1).

A carrier is liable for damage sustained by a passenger if the accident took place on board the aircraft or in the course of any of the operations of embarking or disembarking (ANTA 1936, Sch 1, art 17). The meanings of *embarking* and *disembarking* have a wider connotation than their ordinary meaning in common parlance; they include a passenger's journey by shuttle bus between the terminal building and the aircraft: *Burke v Aer Lingus plc* [1997] 1 ILRM 148, HC.

The Supreme Court has held that there are two distinct, but closely related, elements of art 25 of the Convention – the test for recklessness is an objective one, while the test for knowledge that damage would probably result is subjective; *APH Manufacturing BV v DHL* [2001] 4 IR 531, SC. A claim for damages under the Convention is barred if not brought within two years, reckoned from the date of arrival at the destination, or from the date the aircraft should have arrived, or from the date on which the carriage stopped (ANTA 1936, Sch 1, art 29(1) and *Burke* case). See *Galvin v Aer Rianta* [1995] 3 IR 486, HC; *APH Manufacturing v DHL* [2001] 1 ILRM 224, HC. For the replacement of the Warsaw Convention, see MONTREAL CONVENTION. See also AIR LAW; INTERNATIONAL AGREEMENTS.

waste. (1) Acts or omissions of a tenant which does lasting damage to property or which alters the nature of the property. Waste may be voluntary, permissive, equitable or ameliorating. *Voluntary* waste is the doing of positive acts which makes the property less valuable to the person entitled after the life tenant e g opening mines or cutting the timber more than 20 years old; it is forbidden unless the life estate is made *without impeachment of waste*: *Templemore v Moore* [1862] 25 ICLR 14.

Permissive waste is omitting to do what ought to be done e g allowing buildings to go into disrepair; the life tenant is only liable if the grantor expressly put a duty to repair on him. *Equitable* waste is the doing of wanton acts by a life tenant who makes unconscionable use of his right to commit voluntary waste. *Ameliorating* waste is the doing of acts which, though nominally waste, are really for the benefit of the property: *Craig v Greer* [1899] 2 IR 258.

The remedy for waste is by way of an *injunction* (qv) and *damages* (qv).

(2) *Waste* also means any substance or object belonging to a category of waste specified in Waste Management Act 1996, Sch 1 or for the time being included in the European Waste Catalogue (WMA 1996, s 4(1)).

Hazardous waste means hazardous waste for the time being mentioned in the list prepared pursuant to art 1(4) of Directive (EEC) 91/689 of 12 December 1991, being either *Category I* waste (e g mineral oils) or *Category II* waste (e g pcbs). Wastes are also categorised as: (a) *commercial* – waste from premises used wholly or mainly for the purpose of trade or business or for the purposes of sport, recreation, education or entertainment; (b) *household* – waste produced within the curtilage of a building used for the purposes of living accommodation; (c) *industrial* – includes waste produced or arising from manufacturing or industrial activities or processes; (d) *municipal* – household waste as well as commercial and other waste which, because of its nature or composition, is similar to household waste; (e) *agricultural* waste (qv) (WMA 1996, s 5(1)).

It is an offence for a person to hold, transport, recover or dispose of waste in a manner that causes or is likely to cause environmental pollution (qv) (WMA 1996, s 32(1)). It is also an offence to transfer the control of waste to any person who is not properly authorised to deal with such waste (WMA 1996, s 32(2)). A local authority is empowered to serve a notice in respect of waste, requiring specific action to be taken to prevent or limit environmental pollution (WMA 1996, s 55). See SIs Nos 146, 147, 162, 163, 165 of 1998.

See Waste Management (Licensing) Regulations 2004, SI No 395 of 2004, replacing previous regulations: SI No 185 of 2000 (save for arts 3 and 4 and First Schedule), SI No 397 of 2001, and SIs Nos 336 and 337 of 2002. See also Waste Management Act 1996, s 54 amended by Planning and Development Act 2000, s 257 and Protection of the Environment

Act 2003, s 45. Provision has been made to introduce new powers for local authorities to make charges for *waste services*, as an *executive* (ie managerial) function (PEA 2003, s 52). For information on the Race against Waste Campaign, see website: *www.raceagainstwaste.com*. [Bibliography: LexisNexis; Maguire, O'Reilly & Roche.] See DANGEROUS GOODS; DEVASTAVIT; LIFE TENANT; PLANNING PERMISSION, DECISION ON.

waste collection. Each local authority is required to collect, or arrange for the collection of, *household* waste within its functional area, except where: (a) an *adequate* collection service is available, or (b) the estimated cost of collection would be unreasonably high, or (c) *adequate* arrangements for disposal can reasonably be made by the holder of the waste: Waste Management Act 1996, s 33 as amended by Protection of the Environment Act 2003, s 30. In holding that the county council was not under a statutory duty to collect household waste where an adequate service already exists, the court held that the term 'adequate' may not be interpreted broadly, where it is divorced from a factual matrix: *O'Connell v Cork County Council* [2003] FL 7278, HC. See also *de Burca v Wicklow County Council* [2002] 2 IR 196, HC.

A local authority is empowered to make bye-laws requiring the holder of waste to present the waste in a manner specified (WMA 1996, s 35). This clearly envisaged the requirement for separating waste into separate containers or for using wheelie-bins, but not for the fitting of prepaid stickers on bins to permit their collection: *O'Connell v Cork Corporation* [2001] 3 IR 602, SC. However the 2003 Act provides that waste placed for collection must bear evidence, in such manner as is provided in the bye-laws, of the payment of any charge in respect of the collection of the waste (WMA 1996, s 35(3)(gg) inserted by PEA 2003, s 32).

A local authority is under no duty to collect household waste from a person if that person has failed to pay the relevant waste charge or has failed to present the waste in the manner specified in WMA 1996, s 35(3)(gg): WMA 1996, s 33(6) amended by PEA 2003, s 30.

A person, other than a local authority, requires a *waste collection permit* to collect waste for profit: (WMA 1996, s 34 as amended by Waste Management (Amend-

ment) Act 2001, s 6 and PEA 2003, s 31). For the procedures for making an application for a permit, the public consultation, the consideration by the local authority, and the grant, refusal and review by the local authority, see Waste Management (Collection Permit) Regulations 2001, SIs No 402 and 540 of 2001. See BYE-LAW; POLLUTER PAYS PRINCIPLE; SERVICE CHARGE; WASTE SERVICE.

waste disposal. Provision has been made to allow for the *intensification of use* of a waste disposal facility operated by a local authority: Waste Management (Amendment) Act 2001, s 7. Clarification is also provided on the licensing requirements for certain waste recovery and disposal facilities by eliminating a duplication of the requirements under the Environmental Protection Agency Act 1992 (as amended by Protection of the Environment Act 2003) and the Waste Management Act 1996 (WM(A)A 2001, s 13). For list of '*waste disposal activities*' see WMA 1996, Sch 3, as substituted by PEA 2003, s 54 and Sch 3. See LANDFILL SITE.

waste disposal/recovery. A local authority is required to provide and operate, or arrange for the provision and operation of, such facilities as may be necessary for the recovery and disposal of *household* waste arising within its functional area: Waste Management Act 1996, s 38. A *waste licence* for the facility (ie landfill site or premises) from the Environmental Protection Agency is required (WMA 1996, s 39 as amended by Protection of the Environment Act 2003, s 33). For a *single licence* provision, see WMA 1996, s 39A inserted by PEA 2003, s 34.

The EPA in considering an application for or a review of a waste licence must have consideration for the relevant air and water quality and waste management plans, and an environmental impact statement, and that *best available techniques* will be used to limit any emission from the activity (WMA 1996, s 40 as amended by PEA 2003, s 35). No appeal lies from a decision by the EPA on a waste licence except by way of judicial review to the High Court within two months from the date the decision is given (WMA 1996, s 43 and RSC Ord 84).

No appeal lies to the Supreme Court except with the leave of the High Court, where it certifies that its decision involved a point of law of exceptional public importance and that it is desirable in the public interest that an appeal be taken to the Supreme Court (WMA 1996, s 43(5)(c)). Strict adherence to the two month time limit for application to the court and notification of all mandatory notice parties is essential eg see in planning law: *KSK Enterprises Ltd v An Bord Pleanála* [1994] 2 ILRM 1.

The EPA was granted an order by the High Court requiring a waste disposal company to cease accepting waste at its premises at Upper Sheriff Street, Dublin, because of non-compliance with its licence: *EPA v Swalcliffe Ltd (t/a Dublin Waste)* [2003] HC. See *Wicklow County Council v Fenton* [2002] 2 ILRM 469, HC and 2 IR 583; *Wicklow County Council v Fenton* [2003] 1 ILRM 279, HC.

There is a presumption, in certain circumstances, that recovery or disposal of waste on, in or over land, was carried on with the consent of the owner of the land eg the length of time it was carried on (WMA 1996, s 11A inserted by PEA 2003, s 23). There is provision for the review, and revocation or suspension of waste licences (WMA 1996, ss 46 and 48A inserted by PEA 2003, ss 40–41). For list of 'waste recovery activities' see WMA 1996, Sch 4, as substituted by PEA 2003, s 55 and Sch 4. See BEST AVAILABLE TECHNIQUES; END-OF-LIFE VEHICLE; LANDFILL SITE.

waste management plan. The plan which each local authority is required to make, dealing with: (a) the prevention, minimisation, collection, recovery and disposal of *non-hazardous waste* in its functional area; and (b) information on the implementation of measures pertaining to the *hazardous waste management plan* (qv) and any recommendations of the Environmental Protection Agency (qv): Waste Management Act 1996, s 22 as amended by Protection of the Environment Act 2003, ss 26–27.

The public must be invited to comment prior to the drafting of the plan. Also the plan must include: (a) reference to the measures to be taken to prevent or minimise the production of waste; and also (b) information on the type, quantity and origin of waste. Each local authority is required to ensure that the necessary steps are taken to attain the objectives set out in the plan (WMA 1996, s 22(12)).

The review, variation or replacement of a waste management plan is an *executive* (ie managerial) rather than a *reserved* function (WMA 1996, s 22(10) as amended by PEA 2003, s 26(2)(b)).

See Waste Management (Licensing) Regulations 2004, SI No 395 of 2004, replacing previous regulations: SI No 185 of 2000 (save for arts.3 and 4 and First Schedule), SI No 397 of 2001, and SIs Nos 336 and 337 of 2002. See Waste Management (Farm Plastics) Regulations 200, SI No 341 of 2001. [Bibliography: O Laoire; Scannell.] See DISPOSAL; DUMPING AT SEA; ENVIRONMENT ASSESSMENT DIRECTIVE; TOXIC AND DANGEROUS WASTE; LITTER; HOUSEHOLD REFUSE; TRADE REFUSE.

waste service. Means any service, facility, approval or other thing which a local authority may or is required to render, supply, grant, issue or otherwise provide in the performance of any of its functions under this Act: Waste Management Act 1996, s 5(1) inserted by Protection of the Environment Act 2003, s 20(1)(c).

A local authority may make a charge in respect of the provision of any *waste service* by, or on behalf of, that authority (WMA 1996, s 75 inserted by PEA 2003, s 52). The local authority may waive all or a portion of the charge on grounds of personal hardship. The making of a charge and the exercise of the power of waiver is an *executive* (ie managerial) function of the local authority (WMA 1996, s 75(8)). See WASTE COLLECTION.

waste water. For the regulations which prescribe the requirements as regards *collecting systems* and *treatment standards* for urban waste water treatment plants, see Urban Waste Water Treatment Regulations 2001, SI No 254 of 2001. See COMMA.

wasted management time. The losses which arise when management time of a plaintiff company is wasted in remedying the failure of a defendant has been held in the UK to be recoverable from the defendant: *Tate & Lyle v GLC* [1982] 1 WLR 149. The bases of a claim for wasted management time are: (a) the plaintiff's management, in order to keep damage within reasonable bounds, performed remedial work to correct the defendant's failure; (b) the plaintiff lost the benefit of this management time, which would have been spent on other activities, but for the acts of the defendant; and (c) the plaintiff may have suffered additional financial costs as a result of the management time wasted. See 'Counting the Days' by Paul Jacobs in *Law Society Gazette* (March 2003) 20.

wasting asset. An asset with a predictable useful life of 50 years or less: Taxes Consolidation Act 1997, s 560(1). The *residual* or *scrap value* of an asset is its value at the end of its predictable useful life. Freehold land is not a wasting asset. Plant and machinery are wasting assets. A life interest in trust property is not a wasting asset unless the life expectancy of the life tenant is 50 years or less; life expectancy is calculated using Revenue approved actuarial tables. In calculating a chargeable gain on the disposal of a wasting asset, the person disposing of the asset is not allowed to deduct the full cost of the asset. He is required to eliminate the cost relating to the part of the asset that has expired or wasted while he held the asset. The disposal of a *chattel wasting asset* is exempt and does not give rise to a chargeable gain; however this exemption does not apply to trade assets on which capital allowances were claimable (TCA 1997, s 603).

watching and besetting. Formerly, an offence under the Conspiracy and Protection of Property Act 1875, s 7, now repealed and replaced by a wider offence of coercion, which includes watching and besetting: Non-Fatal Offences against the Person Act 1997, ss 9 and 31. See *Barton v Harten* [1925] 2 IR 37. See BARRING ORDER; COERCION; HARASSMENT; PICKETING; SAFETY ORDER; SIT-IN.

water, drinking. See DRINKING WATER.

water, right to. A right exists to a supply of water for domestic purposes: Waterworks Clauses Act 1847, s 53. This right does not apply in relation to a dwelling house which contravenes planning law: Local Government (Planning and Development) Act 1990, s 26. A sanitary authority is empowered to serve notice requiring connection to a public water supply system: Local Government (Sanitary Services) Act 1962, s 8(2). [Bibliography: Bland (1).] See DRINKING WATER; RIPARIAN; WATER SUPPLY.

water charges. A sanitary authority is empowered to make charges for water supplied by it; the power became a *reserved function* (qv) exercisable by elected members from 1 January 1985: SI No 341 of 1985; Public Health (Ireland) Act 1878, s 65A inserted by Local Government Financial Provisions (No 2) Act 1983. Disconnection can be made by the sanitary authority where the water charges remain wholly or partly unpaid and if disconnection has been authorised by the District Court: Local Government (Delimitation of Water Supply Disconnection Powers) Act 1995, s 3.

However, after 31 December 1996 a sanitary authority is not empowered to make a charge for a supply by them of water for *domestic purposes*: Local Government (Financial Provisions) Act 1997, s 12. See *O'Donnell v Corp of Dún Laoghaire* [1991] ILRM 301; *Fingal County Council v Lynch* [1997] 2 IR 569, HC. For water disconnection rules in the District Court, see DCR 1997 Ord 85. See INCONVENIENCE; SERVICE CHARGE.

Water Framework Directive. The EU Directive which sets a framework for comprehensive management of water resources in the European Community, within a common approach and with common objectives, principles and basic measures: Directive (EC) 2000/60. It addresses inland surface waters, estuarine and coastal waters and groundwater. The fundamental objective of the Water Framework Directive aims at maintaining 'high status' of waters where it exists, preventing any deterioration in the existing status of waters and achieving at least 'good status' in relation to all waters by 2015. Member states have to ensure that a co-ordinated approach is adopted for the achievement of the objectives of the WFD and for the implementation of programmes of measures for this purpose.

The objectives of the WFD are: (a) to protect and enhance the status of aquatic ecosystems (and terrestrial ecosystems and wetlands directly dependent on aquatic ecosystems); (b) to promote sustainable water use based on long-term protection of available water resources; (c) to provide for sufficient supply of good quality surface water and groundwater as needed for sustainable, balanced and equitable water use; (d) to provide for enhanced protection and improvement of the aquatic environment by reducing/phasing out of discharges, emissions and losses of priority substances; (e) to contribute to mitigating the effects of floods and droughts; (f) to protect territorial and marine waters; (g) to establish a register of 'protected areas' eg areas designated for protection of habitats or species.

The Directive is very broad in its scope and relates to water quality in rivers, lakes, canals, groundwater, transitional (estuarine) waters and coastal waters out a distance of at least one nautical mile. See website: *www.wfdireland.ie*. See DRINKING WATER.

water pollution. It is an offence for a person to cause or permit any *polluting matter* (qv) to enter waters: Local Government (Water Pollution) Act 1977, s 3(1). It is also an offence for a person to discharge or cause or permit the discharge of any *trade effluent* (qv) or *sewage effluent* (qv) to any waters except under and in accordance with a licence (LG(WP)A 1977, s 4(1) and SI No 16 of 1978).

Any person may apply to the appropriate court for an order directing the party responsible to mitigate or remedy any effects of such contraventions within such period and in such manner as may be specified in the order (LG(WP)A 1977, s 10 as substituted by the LG (Water Pollution) (Amendment) Act 1990, s 7). An appeal in relation to the granting or refusal of a licence lies to An Bord Pleanála (qv) (LG(WP)A 1977, s 21 as substituted by the LG(WP)(A)A 1990, s 16). More extensive powers are given to local authorities to prevent and abate pollution: LG(WP)(A)A 1990, s 10. See DCR 1997 Ord 96, rr 4–6. See *Ballybay Meat Exports Ltd v Monaghan Co Co* [1990] ILRM 864; *Clarke v Brady* [1991] 9 ILT Dig 226, HC; *Maguire v Shannon Regional Fisheries Board* [1994] 2 ILRM 253, HC. See also LG(WP)(A)A 1990, s 6 and SI No 96 of 1978 and Control of EDC, TRI, PER and TCB Discharges Regulation 1994; also SI No 419 of 1994 and SI No 42 of 1999. See Protection of Groundwater Regulations 1999, SI No 41 of 1999. See EC (Protection of Waters against Pollution from Agricultural Sources) Regulations 2003, SI No 213 of 2003. See Courts Act 1991, s 10. See RSC Ord 108. [Bibliography: Canny (2); Maguire, O'Reilly & Roche; Scannell.] See GROUNDWATER.

water services. Under draft legislation, it is proposed that the present 'sanitary authorities' will become 'water services authorities' (defined in terms of county and city councils) in so far as delivery of water services is concerned: Water Services Bill 2003. The central aims of the Bill are: (a) to facilitate a more coherent expression of the law as it relates to water services by means of a single enactment which would represent a comprehensive legal framework; (b) to develop a modern and progressive approach in relation to the sustainable management of water services; (c) to strengthen administrative arrangements for planning the delivery of water services at local and national level; and (d) to introduce a new licensing system and regulatory framework for group water services schemes, to assist in their development, and to address water quality problems in the sector.

Each water services authority is enabled to provide water services within its functional area, and with the consent of the relevant authority, outside its functional boundaries. Such services must be in accordance with prescribed standards. Water services authorities will also be responsible for the supervision of water services provision in their areas, through a new system of licensing. Complementary provisions enable a water services authority to intervene directly to assist with the development or delivery of services (eg to facilitate the acquisition of land, provide technical assistance, or take over on a temporary basis while operational problems are resolved). The activities of water services authorities will, in turn, be supervised by the Minister, who is provided with new powers of supervision and intervention for this purpose.

Provision is included for a broad range of powers to enable water services authorities to carry out their functions, both operational and supervisory. Exercise of these powers will generally be at the discretion of a particular authority, but the Minister will have powers to prescribe performance standards, and to direct water services authorities to provide specific services.

The Bill provides for a strategic planning process, to facilitate sustained improvement in the management and operation of water services infrastructure. Each water services authority will be required to make a six-year strategic plan for this purpose, which will be subject to the approval of the Minister. New 'duty of care' provisions place specific responsibilities on owners and occupiers of premises in relation to the conservation of water supplies, avoidance of risk to public health or the environment, and protection of water services infrastructure.

water supply. Sanitary authorities are under a statutory duty to supply their districts with a supply of suitable water, proper and sufficient for public and private purposes: Public Health (Ireland) Act 1878, ss 61 and 65; Housing of the Working Classes Act 1885, s 7. Machinery exists to compel a sanitary authority to comply with this duty:

Public Health (Ireland) Act 1896, s 15. A sanitary authority can require the owner of premises to connect the premises to the public water supply: Local Government (Sanitary Services) Act 1962, s 8. As regards water charges, see *Athlone UDC v Gavin* [1986] ILRM 277 and water charges. See WATER SERVICES; WAYLEAVE.

watercourse. A watercourse, even an artificial one, may be acquired as an easement (qv). See *Hanna v Pollock* [1900] 2 IR 644; *Kelly v Dea* [1966] 200 ILTR 1. See RIPARIAN.

waterways. Provision has been made for the establishment of Waterways Ireland, a corporate body with immediate responsibility for the management, maintenance and development of the Shannon-Erne Waterway, and from 1 April 2000 of the Erne System, the Grand Canal (including the Barrow Navigation) the lower Bann Navigation, the Royal Canal and the Shannon Navigation: British-Irish Agreement Act 1999, ss 8–13. For Inland Waterways Association of Ireland, see website: *www. iwai.ie*. [Bibliography: O'Laoghaire.] See GOOD FRIDAY AGREEMENT.

way, right of. The right to pass over the lands of another. A right of way is either public or *private*. In order to establish that a *public* right of way has been created, it has to be proved that there was an intention by the owner to dedicate his land to the public, that there was an actual dedication, and that the public accepted the dedication: *Smeltzer v Fingal County Council* [1999] 1 ILRM 24, HC. A public right of way may be more readily inferred when it leads to a place of public interest rather than when it simply peters out: *Murphy v Wicklow Co Council* [1999] IEHC 225, the Glen of the Downs case. There is a *public* right of way on a highway (qv).

A *private* right of way may arise by way of easement (qv) or by necessity e g the right of way presumed to be given by the grantor of land to a *close* surrounded by the grantor's lands. A private right of way may be lost by abandonment: *O'Gara v Murray* [1989] 7 ILT Dig 82.

A planning authority may create a public right of way over land by agreement with any person having power to create, by dedication, such a right: Planning and Development Act 2000, s 206. A planning authority also has power by order to create a public right of way without agreement (PDA 2000, s 207). In exercising this compulsory

power, the authority must first: (i) serve notice of its intention on the owner and occupier and on any person who will be affected by the creation of right of way; and (ii) advertise the proposed order in a newspaper circulating in its functional area (PDA 2000, s 207(2)). A person served with the notice can appeal the order of the planning authority to An Bord Pleanála (PDA 2000, s 207(5)). The authority has a duty to preserve a right of way created under PDA 2000, ss 206 and 207 (PDA 2000, s 208).

Where a planning authority intends to include, for the first time, the preservation of a specific public right of way in its *development plan*, it must first notify the owner and occupier of the land, and they have a right to object (PDA 2000, s 14). If the members of the authority decide to include the right of way in the plan, the owner and occupier may appeal the decision to the Circuit Court on the basis that no public right of way exists (PDA 2000, s 14(4)).

The preservation of such a right of way, included in a development plan after commencement of this section, will be the responsibility of the landowner and not the planning authority (PDA 2000, s 208(1)). Where land is acquired compulsorily, provision has been made which permits the extinguishment of public rights of way, whether over lands the subject of the acquisition or over land adjacent to or associated with such land (PDA 2000, s 222).

It is the function of a local authority to protect the right of the public to use public rights of way in its administrative area: Roads Act 1993, s 73(11). A public right of way, once created, lasts indefinitely unless it is extinguished by an appropriate procedure e g under the 1993 Act; it cannot be extinguished by abandonment (*Murphy* case). A road authority is empowered to extinguish a public right of way over a public road by following a specified procedure; Ministerial approval is required where the order relates to a national or regional road (RA 1993, s 73). In cases other than public roads, the planning authority is similarly empowered (RA 1993, s 73(13)). Where the authority extinguishes the right of way to facilitate the development of land, reasonable costs can be recovered from the developer (RA 1993, s 73(12)). See also Fisheries Act 1980, s 39.

Only the Attorney-General or a person specifically injured can sue in respect of an *obstruction* of a public right of way; a person who has not been injured can bring proceedings in the name of the Attorney-General, with his leave in a *relator* action (*Smeltzer* case). See *Ashbourne Holdings Ltd v An Bord Pleanála* [2002] 1 ILRM 321, HC and (10 March 2003, unreported) SC. See 'Why the farmer and the hill walker should be friends' by solicitor Pat Igoe in *Law Society Gazette* (August/September 2003) 8. [Bibliography: Bland (1).] See EASEMENT; JUS SPACIENDI; PUBLIC ROAD; RELATOR; ZEBRA CROSSING.

wayleave. A right of way over or through land (eg for the carriage of goods, to carry gas in pipes; to carry wires on pylons, etc), created by express grant, by reservation (qv) or by statute. A sanitary authority is empowered to carry any sewer (qv) into, through, or under any lands whatsoever within their district after giving reasonable notice to the owner or occupier: Public Health (Ireland) Act 1878, s 18. Similar power is given in respect of the laying of pipes for the supply of water (PH(I)A 1878, s 64). Compensation is payable for any damage sustained by the exercise of this power (PH(I)A 1878, s 274).

weapon, offensive. See OFFENSIVE WEAPON.

wear and tear. 'Damage, depreciation, or loss resulting from ordinary use': *Collins English Dictionary*. The write off period for annual *wear and tear* allowances in respect of capital expenditure incurred on or after 4 December 2002 on plant and machinery has been increased from five years to eight years: Finance Act 2003, s 23. There are exceptions e g taxis and certain fishing boats. The annual rate for write-off for capital expenditure on hotel buildings and holiday camps has been reduced to 4% ie giving a 25-year tax life (FA 2003, s 25). See BARRISTER; TENANT.

web page. A document on the *worldwide web* (qv). A web page consists of an HTML (*hypertext markup language*) file, with associate files for graphics and scripts, in a particular directory on a particular machine. Usually a web page contains links to other web pages. See WORLDWIDE WEB.

webmaster. A person responsible for creating and maintaining a *world wide web* site. The person will normally respond to emails, ensure the site is operating properly, create and update web pages, and maintain the overall structure and design of the site (for example, see *webmaster@taoiseach.irlgov.ie*). See WORLDWIDE WEB.

website. A group of related HTML (*hypertext markup language*) documents and associated files, scripts and data bases. Most web sites have a *home page* as their starting point, which frequently functions as a table of contents for the site. A user needs a *web browser* and an *Internet* connection to access a website. See WORLDWIDE WEB.

wedding presents. See ENGAGED COUPLE.

Wednesbury test. The test applied by the courts in reviewing the action taken by a local authority where, despite the local authority having taken into account matters it ought to have taken into account, the authority has nevertheless come to a conclusion so unreasonable that no reasonable authority could ever come to it: *Associated Provincial Picture Houses Ltd v Wednesbury Corporation* [1948] 1 KB 223, cited with approval in *O'Keeffe v An Bord Pleanála* [1993] 1 IR 39 and [1992] ILRM 237, but ruled as inappropriate in *SIAC v Mayo County Council* [2002] 2 ILRM 401, SC at 416. See 'If not O'Keefe, Then What?' by Imelda Higgins BL in *Bar Review* (June 2003) 123. See IRRATIONALITY, TEST OF.

week. When used without qualification, a *week* means the period between midnight on any Saturday and midnight on the next following Saturday: Interpretation Act 1937, s 12, Sch.

The *income tax week* means one of the successive periods of seven days in a year of assessment beginning on the first day of that year: Taxes Consolidation Act 1997, s 126(4). This is now 1 January to 7 January for the first week and 8 to 14 January for the second week: Finance Act 2001, s 77. The definition of income tax week is of relevance in relation to the tax treatment of certain benefits payable under the Social Welfare Acts.

A '*week*' means a period of five consecutive weekdays and, in determining such a period, a Saturday or a public holiday must be disregarded and 'weeks' must be construed accordingly: Freedom of Information (Amendment) Act 2003, s 2(c). See MIDNIGHT; TIME.

weekday. A day which is not a Sunday: Interpretation Act 1937, s 12, Sch.

weighbridge. A machine for weighing vehicles. A road authority may (and, if required by the Minister, must) provide on or adjacent to any public road a *weighbridge* of such dimensions, power, design and construction as may be approved by the Minister: Road Traffic Act 1961, s 15(2). The distance a driver may be directed to a weighbridge to have his vehicle weighed has been increased from 5 miles to 25 kilometres (RTA 1961, s 16 as amended by Road Transport Act 1999, s 17).

It is an offence for a person to use on a public road a laden vehicle which exceeds the maximum permitted weight; the offence is committed by the driver, the owner and the *consignor* (RTA 1961, s 12 as amended by RTA 1999, s 17). A *consignor* means a person who engages the services of another person for the carriage by road of merchandise in a vehicle (RTA 1961, s 12(4C)).

weighing facility. The weighing scales or weighing machine which is required to be provided in a prominent position by any person who offers food for sale by retail by weight. See Consumer Information Act 1978, s 14.

weight, short. See SHORT WEIGHT.

weights, maximum. The statutory maximum weights which were prohibited from being lifted or carried by employed persons eg not more than 55 kilograms in the case of adult males, 16 kilograms in the case of males between 16 and 18 years of age and adult females, 11 kilogrammes in the case of females between 16 and 18 years of age, and 8 kilogrammes in the case of 14 to 16 year olds: Factories Act 1955 (Manual Labour) (Maximum Weights and Transport) Regulations 1972, SI No 283 of 1972; *Dunleavy v Glen Abbey Ltd* [1990] ELR 121. These 1972 Regulations were repealed in 1995 (SI No 357 of 1995) following the more general but comprehensive 1993 Regulations (SI No 44 of 1993). See MANUAL HANDLING OF LOADS. See also PROCESS.

weights and measures. See METROLOGY.

welfare. In relation to a minor, comprises the religious and moral, intellectual, physical and social welfare of the minor: Status of Children Act 1987, s 9. In relation to protecting the *welfare* of persons in the context of domestic violence, means the physical and psychological welfare of the person: Domestic Violence Act 1996, s 1(1). See BARRING ORDER; CHILD, CUSTODY OF; GUARDIAN; SAFETY AT WORK; SAFETY ORDER.

welfare of children. There is a constitutional presumption that the welfare of children is found within the family; the parents of children have the primary responsibility for their upbringing and welfare: *North Western Health Board v H W* [2001] 3 IR 622, SC. By welfare is meant their religious, moral, intellectual, physical and social welfare. The Constitution has relegated the State to a subordinate and subsidiary role; however the State can intervene to supply the place of the parents in exceptional circumstances, in the interest of the common good or where parents, for physical or moral reasons, have failed in their duty: 1937 Constitution, art 42.5 and *NWHB* case. In this case the Supreme Court refused to order a PKU screening test on an infant child to which the parents objected.

It is the function of health boards to promote the *welfare of children* up to 18 years of age who are not receiving adequate care and protection and to provide child care and family support services: Child Care Act 1991, s 3.

It is the duty of a health board to take into its care any child in its area who requires care or protection provided this is not against the wishes of a parent having custody (*voluntary care*) and where the child appears to be lost or deserted or abandoned, to endeavour to reunite him with his parent (CCA 1991, s 4). A health board may also take a child into care with a view to his adoption (CCA 1991, s 6). Child care advisory committees must be established and the health board must have regard to their advice (CCA 1991, s 7). A health board also has power to take a child into care against the wishes of his parents: see CARE ORDER.

A health board may also make an application to the courts for a *safety order* (qv) or *barring order* (qv) to protect a child or a person of full age who has a physical or mental disability; the court will make such an order if it is of the opinion that the person has been or is being assaulted, illtreated, sexually abused or seriously neglected or the person's health, development or welfare has been, is being or is likely to be avoidably impaired or seriously neglected: Domestic Violence Act 1996, s 6. When a court grants a decree of divorce, it may give such directions regarding access to, custody of, and welfare of any dependent member of the family concerned who is a child: Family Law (Divorce) Act 1996, ss 5(2)and 15(1)(f). See also AFTERCARE; CHILD, EMERGENCY CARE OF; HEARSAY; JUDICIAL SEPARATION; LEGAL AID.

well charging order. See MORTGAGE SUIT.

welsh mortgage. A mortgage whereby the mortgagor (qv) is under no obligation to repay the principal and whereby the mortgagee (qv) takes possession of the land and takes the rents and profits in lieu of interest or until payment of interest and principal; the mortgagee has no right to call in the principal whereas the mortgagor is entitled to redeem at any time on its payment. See *Cassidy v Cassidy* [1889] 24 LR Ir 577. See Statute of Limitations 1957, s 34.

Western Development Commission. A body corporate with the general function to promote, and procure the promotion of, and assist in, foster and encourage economic and social development in the western region, which comprises the counties of Clare, Donegal, Galway, Leitrim, Mayo, Roscommon and Sligo: Western Development Commission Act 1998. It is empowered to provide loans to business and social enterprises and projects and to purchase shares in share capital, but it is prohibited from distributing grant aid (WDCA 1998, s 8).

wet time. Generally means hours of intermittent employment in respect of which supplementary benefit is payable under s 28 of the Insurance (Intermittent Employment) Act 1942. See ANNUAL LEAVE.

whiplash. An injury to the soft tissues of the neck due to an acceleration-deceleration collision type force, commonly due to a head-on or rear-end collision motor accident. See 'A Pain in the Neck' by consultant orthopaedic physician Dr Aideen Henry in *Law Society Gazette* (September 2002) 8.

whipping. The infliction of corporal punishment as a punishment has been obsolete in practice for many years; however it was, until 1997, still authorised in some statutes e g Offences Against the Persons Act 1861, s 21; Whipping Act 1820 and 1862. The punishment of whipping whether under the sentence of a court or for offences against prison discipline is abolished: Criminal Law Act 1997, s 12. The European Court of Human Rights (qv) has ruled that whipping of a 15-year old boy with birch twigs,

ordered by an Isle of Man court, constituted degrading punishment under the European Convention on Human Rights (qv); it did not amount to torture or inhuman punishment: *Tyrer v UK* Judgment of the Court, Series A, No 26. For repeal of 1820 and 1862 Acts, see Criminal Law Act 1997, s 16 and Sch 3. See CORPORAL PUNISHMENT; PUNISHMENT.

whiskey, Irish. Spirits which have been distilled in the State or Northern Ireland from a mash of cereals which has been saccharified by the diastase of malt contained therein, with or without other natural diastases, fermented by the action of yeast, and distilled at an alcoholic strength of less than 94.8% by volume, in such a way that the distillate has an aroma and flavour derived from the materials used, and the spirits have been matured in wooden casks in a warehouse in the State or in Northern Ireland for not less than three years: Irish Whiskey Act 1980. Irish whiskey is not to be regarded as corresponding to that description unless it complies with this definition. See *Scotch Whisky Association v Cooley Distillery plc* [1991] HC. See DESCRIPTION, SALE BY.

whistle blower. Colloquial expression to describe a person who reports suspicions in respect of some wrongdoing.

(1) Certain persons are required to report to the Pensions Board where they have reasonable cause to believe that a material misappropriation or a fraudulent conversion of the resources of a pension scheme is occurring or is to be attempted, e g an auditor, actuary, trustee, insurance intermediary, or investment business firm to the scheme: Pensions Act 1990, s 83 as inserted by Pensions (Amendment) Act 1996, s 38. Where a person makes a report to the Board in good faith, concerning the state and conduct of a pension scheme, whether or not such a report is required under s 83, no liability or action will lie against the person in any court for so doing (PA 1990, s 84 as inserted by P(A)A 1996, s 38). This includes an employee. An employer who dismisses an employee for making such a report is guilty of an offence (PA 1990, s 80 amended by P(A)A 1996, s 37). Any such report is *absolutely privileged* (PA 1990, s 85 as inserted by P(A)A 1996, s 38). In 2002, the provisions regarding whistle blowing were

extended to cover *Personal Retirement Savings Accounts* (PRSAs): Pensions (Amendment) Act 2002, ss 46–49. The Pensions Board have introduced a low-cost telephone number for whistle blowers making reports: Tel: 1890 – 656565.

(2) Protection is given to persons who report to the Competition Authority that in their opinion an offence under competition law has been committed; they are not liable for damages in respect of their communication to the Authority unless it is proved that they had not acted reasonably and in good faith in forming that opinion and in communicating it to the Authority: Competition Act 2002, s 50. An employer is prohibited from penalising an employee in such circumstances; in any proceedings before a Rights Commissioner or the Employment Appeals Tribunal it is presumed, unless the contrary is proved, that the employee acted in good faith (CA 2002, s 50(3) and Sch 3). It is an offence to make a statement to the Authority knowing that it is false (CA 2002, s 50(5)). [Bibliography: Lucey.]

(3) As regards whistle blowing in the professions, other than the accountancy profession, this has been largely left to each profession to regulate itself, sometimes within a statutory framework e g the Medical Council has within its remit to inquire into the conduct of registered medical practitioners for alleged professional misconduct or fitness to engage in the practice of medicine: Medical Practitioners Act 1978. 'Where risk to a patient exists in relation to a colleague's conduct or competence, doctors should express their concern initially to the colleague concerned and advise remedial action. Where local systems of support or remediation are available they should be availed of as the next step. Should the colleague's response be unsatisfactory, then the doctor should refer the matter to the Medical Council': Medical Council, *A Guide to Ethical Conduct and Behaviour* (6th edn, 2004) para 4.3. Also where a doctor becomes aware that the use of alcohol or other drugs is affecting the competence of a colleague, the doctor is required to express their anxiety directly to the colleague concerned and advise that expert professional help be obtained or that the colleague be referred to the Medical Council's Health Committee (para 5.1). If such approaches fail or where the interests of patients are or may be at risk, the facts must be given promptly to the Fitness to Practice Committee of the Medical Council. The same guideline applies 'when other forms of physical or psychological disorder or the ageing process appear to seriously affect a doctor's professional competence' (para 5.2).

(4) As regards nurses, 'Any circumstances which could place patients/clients in jeopardy or which militate against safe standards of practice should be made known to appropriate persons or authorities': *Code of Professional Conduct of each Nurse and Midwife* (2000).

(5) In the legal professions, the system of control of professional misbehaviour or misconduct is based primarily on acting on complaints from clients rather than on whistle blowing by colleagues from the same profession. However, the Bar Council has in place a process to consider complaints of misconduct by a barrister against another barrister. The Law Society will act on a complaint from a client or from any person on behalf of the client (which might be another solicitor) in relation to alleged misconduct, inadequate professional services, or excessive fees. Also, if a solicitor is of the opinion that another solicitor is engaged in serious misconduct, this should be brought to the attention of the Law Society: *A Guide to Professional Conduct of Solicitors in Ireland* (2002) ch 7.8. See BARRISTERS, DISPUTES BETWEEN; BARRISTERS' PROFESSIONAL CONDUCT TRIBUNAL.

(6) The Institute of Accountants in Ireland has a system in place to deal with complaints from members of the public (who are usually clients of accountants), but also from the Institute's own regulatory committees, and also importantly in relation to reports in the media which relate to its members.

(7) If a chartered engineer becomes aware, or has reasonable grounds for believing, that another chartered engineer is engaging in conduct or has engaged in conduct which is in breach of the Code of Ethics and is likely to result in a serious detriment to any person or persons, the chartered engineer must inform the Institution of Engineers: 'Code of Ethics – The Institution of Engineers of Ireland' (November 2003) clause 1.11.

See 'Touting for Business: the rise of the Whistle Blower' by Henry Murdoch BL in *Law Society Gazette* (October 2003) 8. See also AUDITOR, COMPANY; CHILD ABUSE, REPORTING; CONCEALING AN OFFENCE; MONEY LAUNDERING; VICTIMISATION.

whistle blowing campaigns. The Gardaí conduct campaigns to encourage the public to provide information on crime. These campaigns range from the low profile one of having a free phone 'Garda Confidential Line' (Tel: 1800 666 111) in which confidentiality is guaranteed, to 'Crimestoppers' (Free phone: 1800 250 025), which is a partnership between private industry and the Gardaí, aimed at persons who have information on crime, who are guaranteed anonymity and cash awards in appropriate cases. The Gardaí, like most police forces, have an official fund available to pay for information from informers. The fund comes from the 'Secret Service Account' and appears in the list of allocations in the Minister for Finance annual budget statements.

The Revenue Commissioners conduct high-visibility campaigns to deter revenue fraud, including the publication of the names of tax cheats. In its war against illegal drugs, the Revenue operates its *Drugs Watch Scheme*, where there is a Customs and Excise confidential reporting telephone number (1800 295 295). The Revenue are empowered under the Inland Revenue Regulation Act 1890 to make ex-gratia awards to whistle blowers whose information leads to the recovery of unpaid taxes or excise duty. 'The Commissioners may at their discretion reward any person who informs them of any offence against any Act relating to inland revenue or assists in the recovery of any fine or penalty' (IRRA 1890, s 32). In 1890 a reward exceeding £50 required the consent of the Treasury; now such payments are subject to a maximum award of €5,000 other than in the most exceptional of cases.

In recent times there have been very high profile campaigns by the software industry to stamp out software piracy, and by the insurance industry to combat fraudulent and inflated insurance claims. The Business Software Alliance encourages persons who have information to disclose it on a confidential basis either by email to *infoireland@bsa.org* or by calling an international hotline (1890 510 010). The BSA offer a reward of 10% of any recovery value up to an award of €10,000 for information which leads to a successful prosecution or settlement.

The Irish Insurance Federation (IIF) estimates that fraud costs Irish insurers €100m annually and that the most common frauds are: (a) staging accidents in order to make a claim; (b) inflating a claim following a genuine accident; (c) making false declarations or failing to disclose information in order to get insurance; (d) inflating the value of insured property or getting cover for items which do not exist; and (e) taking out multiple policies to cover the same risk in order to make multiple claims. To counter this, the industry has established a Locall telephone facility, *Insurance Confidential* (1890 333 333), in order that concerned members of the public can report suspect claims. The IIF stated in April 2004 that more than 3,000 calls had been received in the first year of operation of the hotline, resulting in 1,500 new cases of alleged fraud coming to light. Almost one in four of the calls related to exaggeration of personal injuries and car repair costs.

white knight. Popularly understood to mean a corporate hero of sorts which comes to the rescue of a company besieged by a take-over bid which it regards as unfriendly; the white knight makes an alternative take-over bid for the shares of the company at a price sufficient to stave off the unfriendly take-over. The white knight is initially regarded as friendly; whether this remains the case after the take-over battle is another matter. See IRISH TAKEOVER PANEL; MERGER.

whole blood. See BLOOD RELATIONSHIP.

wholesale debt instrument. Means a certificate of deposit or commercial paper, as appropriate: Taxes Consolidation Act 1997, s 246A inserted by Finance Act 2003, s 49. The section details rules for the tax treatment of such instruments.

widow. The words '*widow, widower, married woman, married man, spinster or bachelor*' indicate marital status and where a person holds an occupation, these words are not a title trade or profession as required by the Judgment Mortgage Act 1850; that Act requires that the title trade or profession of the plaintiff and the defendant be inserted in the affidavit registering a mortgage: *AIB v Griffin* [1992] ILRM 590, HC. See JUDGMENT MORTGAGE; SURVIVOR'S PENSION.

widowed parent grant. A grant of €2,500 (in 2002), or such higher amount as may be prescribed, paid to a widowed parent on the death of the other spouse: Social Welfare Act 2000, ss 13–15; Social Welfare

(Miscellaneous Provisions) Act 2002, s 4. A widowed parent may also be entitled to an additional allowance in computing income tax liability following the death of a spouse: Taxes Consolidation Act 1997, s 463 as amended by Finance Act 2000, s 7. The grant was increased to €2,700 from 3 December 2003: Social Welfare Act 2003, s 7.

widower. A man who has lost his wife by death and has not married again. Restrictions are placed on the adoption of children by a widower which do not apply to a widow: Adoption Act 1974, s 5. However, a widower may now complete the adoption process and have an adoption order made in his favour, if he and his wife had applied for an adoption order but she had died before the adoption order had been made: *T O'G v Attorney-General* [1985] ILRM 61. See also PROHIBITED DEGREES; SURVIVOR'S PENSION; WIDOW.

wife. See FAMILY HOME; HUSBAND AND WIFE; MATRIMONIAL PROPERTY; SPOUSE, LEGAL RIGHT OF.

wig and gown. See DRESS IN COURT.

wild animal. See ANIMALS.

wild animals, protected. Animals which are statutorily protected and listed: Wildlife Act 1976, Sch 5. Hares and deer are listed as game which may be hunted with firearms during *open season* (qv).

wild birds, protected. All wild birds are statutorily protected, including game (qv), except species which are commonly regarded as pests and are listed: Wildlife Act 1976, Sch 3. See SI No 254 of 1986. See *Devlin v Minister for Arts* [1999] 1 ILRM 462, SC.

wildlife. In 2000, the Wildlife Act 1976 was substantially amended to bring the law into line with the conservation of wildlife and wildlife habitats as required by various EU Directives and changes in the international scientific approach to conservation: Wildlife (Amendment) Act 2000. There has been a move away from the protection of individual species towards the protection of ecosystems.

The 2000 Act improves existing measures to enhance conservation and protection of wildlife species and their habitats. It gives new powers to the Minister to acquire lands and rights over land, and to create *Natural Heritage Areas*. The Act also deals with the licensing and regulation of commercial shoot operators, and the regulation and control of wildlife dealing. [Bibliography: Comerford (1).]

wildlife dealing. It is an offence for a person to carry on *business as a wildlife dealer* except under and in accordance with a wildlife dealer's licence: Wildlife Act 1976, s 47. Wildlife dealing means buying for resale any protected wild birds or protected wild animals and includes engaging in taxidermy in respect of such birds or animals (WA 1976, s 2(3)). Records must be kept in a form prescribed by the Minister: Wildlife Act 1976 (Wildlife Dealing) Regulations 1977, SI No 253 of 1977.

It is an offence for a person who is the owner, manager or person otherwise in charge of any hotel, guest house, inn, restaurant, public eating house, registered club, or any other premises in which meals are provided for reward to purchase a protected wild bird (qv) or protected wild animal (qv) from anybody except a licensed wildlife dealer (WA 1976, s 45(4)). See also Wildlife (Amendment) Act 2000.

wilful neglect. The common law misdemeanour (qv) (now, offence) to refuse or neglect to provide sufficient food or other necessaries to life to any person, such as a child, apprentice, servant or aged or sick person unable to provide or take care of himself, or for the provision of which there is an obligation by duty or contract. See Offences Against the Person Act 1861, s 26; Conspiracy and Protection of Property Act 1875, s 6. See PLEADINGS.

wilful obstruction. The offence committed by any person who, without lawful authority or reasonable excuse, wilfully prevents or interrupts the free passage of any person or vehicle in any public place: Criminal Justice (Public Order) Act 1994, s 9.

will. A disposition by which the person making it (the *testator/testatrix*) provides for the distribution or administration of property after his/her death. A will is *ambulatory* in that it remains revocable until death.

Formerly the law did not allow land to be devised. However, the Wills Act 1837 allowed all land to be disposed of by a written will witnessed by two credible witnesses. This Act was repealed by the Succession Act 1965. Under the 1965 Act, which amended and consolidated the law of succession, *realty* and *personalty* devolve in the same way under new rules as to intestate succession (qv). Primogeniture and canons of descent were abolished except in so far as they apply to the descent of an *estate tail.* The Act also made new provision: (a) to give the surviving spouse a legal right (qv) to a share of the estate; and (b) to allow the children of a testator to apply to the court to have just provision made for them out of the estate.

A valid will can be made by a person who has attained 18 years or has been married and is of sound disposing mind (SA 1965, s 77). The will must be in writing; there is no longer any provision for privileged wills (qv). No particular form of words are required so long as the testator's intention can be ascertained. Extrinsic evidence (qv) is admissible to show the intention of the testator and to assist in the construction of or to explain any contradiction in a will (SA 1965, s 90). A will is construed to speak and take effect as if it had been executed immediately before the testator's death, unless a contrary intention appears (SA 1965, s 89). In construing a will, the court will presume that the testator did not intend to die intestate: *Mulhern v Brennan* [1999] 3 IR 528, HC. See *Re Mitten* [1934] 68 ILTR 38; *Re Farrell* [1954] 88 ILTR 57; *In b Corboy* [1969] IR 148.

A will must be signed at the foot or end thereof by the testator or by some person in his presence and by his direction and the signature must be made or acknowledged by the testator in the presence of at least two witnesses present at the same time and each witness must attest by his signature the signature of the testator in the presence of the testator (SA 1965, s 78). No form of attestation (qv) is necessary and witnesses do not have to sign in each other's presence. They do not need to know that they are witnessing a will; they only need to know that they are witnessing a signature. See *Re Dowling* [1933] IR 150; *Re Kiernan* [1933] IR 222; *Clarke v Early* [1980] IR 223.

A devise or bequest to an attesting witness or to the spouse of a witness is void but does not affect the validity of the will (SA 1965, s 82). An executor may be a witness but then cannot benefit under the will. If a parent asks a son or a daughter who is a solicitor to make a will, there is potential for conflict of interest if the solicitor is to benefit: *A Guide to Professional Conduct of Solicitors in Ireland* (2002) ch 3.6. For standard and non-standard wills, see website: *www.wills.ie.* [Bibliography: Brady; Corrigan & Williams; Keating; McGuire, Maxwell; Mongey; Spierin;

Spierin & Fallon; Theobald UK.] See ADMINISTRATION OF ESTATES; CHILD, PROVISION FOR; CONSTRUCTION SUIT; DYING; GIFT; LEGACY; LUCID INTERVAL; OFFENSIVE WORDS; PINHOLES; PROBATE; SUBPOENA; SUCCEED, UNWORTHINESS TO; SUCCESSION, LAW OF; TESTAMENTARY CAPACITY; WORDS OF LIMITATION.

will, drafting of. A solicitor in drafting a will, owes a duty of care not only to the testator but also to potential beneficiaries under the will: *Wall v Hegarty* [1980] ILRM 124. In the UK it has been held that a solicitor, having received instructions from his client, is under an obligation to reduce those instructions to proper form: *Glynn v Frearsons* [1999] Ch 326. Also a solicitor is under an obligation to ensure that a will he has drafted is executed effectively. It has been held that a solicitor was negligent in providing a draft will to the testator with written instructions on how it might be effectively executed: *Esterhuizen v Allied Dunbar Assurance plc* [1998] 2 FLR 668.

Also delay by a solicitor in drafting a will may amount to negligence: *White v Jones* [2001] Lloyd's Rep PN 274. In this case the solicitor was held to be negligent in not drafting a will for a 78-year old client, apparently in good health, who died a month after he had given the solicitor instructions. For solicitor's mistake in drawing up a will, see *Kelly v Cahill* [2001] HC discussed in *Law Society Gazette* (May 2001) 33.

A barrister may draft a will without a fee and without the instructions of a solicitor, but he should not do so unless it is a matter of urgency or is done for a friend or for charitable reasons: *Code of Conduct for the Bar of Ireland* (December 2003) r 4.3. [Bibliography: Spierin.]

will, international. A will made in accordance with the Hague Convention on the Conflict of Laws relating to the form of Testamentary Dispositions 1961. Such a disposition will be valid as regards form if it complies with the internal law: (a) of the place where it was made, or (b) of the place of the testator's domicile or nationality or habitual residence or (c) in so far as immovable property is concerned, of the place where the property is situated: Succession Act 1965, s 102. See LEX SITUS.

will, limited. A will which deals with the estate of a testator in this country when another will exists which deals with his estate abroad. Only the will specifically limited to property in this State will be admitted to proof although all other wills must be produced to the Probate Officer.

will, proof of. A will is proved in *solemn form* when it is declared valid following court proceedings; it is proved in *common form* when it is admitted to proof in the Probate Office or District Probate Registry without litigation. Where a will is in any language other than Irish or English, it may be admitted to proof by the probate officer in terms of a translation in Irish or English: RSC Ord 79, r 5(10); Ord 80, r 6(9). See *Re Corboy* [1969] IR 148.

will, reading of. The reading of a will to a testator who nods and makes an 'X' at the foot of a will may be sufficient to have the will admitted to probate, if it involves a testator whose mind has deteriorated sharply between the time he formulated the contents of a will and the date of its execution: *Re Glynn (deceased)* [1990] 2 IR 326 at 331.

Up to 50 years ago it used to be the custom that following the death of the testator, the next-of-kin and the beneficiaries would be assembled and the solicitor would read out the will to the group. At one such reading in Cork in 1769, Hanna, housekeeper to the testator Dennis Tolam, on hearing that she had been left his broken water jug, kicked out in rage and smashed the jug and to her delight out flowed a stack of coins. Other beneficiaries who had been left old socks and old boots were similarly rewarded: see Eamonn G Mongey, *The Weird and Wonderful World of Wills*, p 26. The custom has died out, with restrictions placed on solicitors on disclosing the testator's affairs except to the executor, and even on giving a copy of the will to a beneficiary: see EXECUTOR; WILL, SUPPLY OF COPY. See also TESTAMENTARY CAPACITY.

will, revocation of. A will may be revoked by: (a) another will or codicil duly executed; or (b) by some writing executed like a will declaring an intention to revoke the will; or (c) tearing or destruction by the testator or by someone in his presence and by his direction, with intent to revoke; or (d) by subsequent marriage of the testator, except a will made in contemplation of that marriage.

Revocation may be conditional in which case the will remains unrevoked until the condition is fulfilled. Also deletions made

after execution of a will, initialled by a testatrix but not signed by witnesses in the manner required, do not effect revocation of a will or any part thereof: *In the matter of the Estate of Margaret Ismay Myles, deceased* [1993] ILRM 34, HC. See also *In the Goods of Keenan* [1946] 80 ILTR; *Re Millar* [1931] IR 364; *Re Bentley* [1930] IR 455; *Re Fleming, deceased* [1987] ILRM 638. Succession Act 1965, s 85. See ALTERATION; DEPENDENT RELATIVE REVOCATION.

will, supply of copy. A solicitor acting for the executor should not supply a copy of, or extract from, a will to a beneficiary unless directed by the executor: *A Guide to Professional Conduct of Solicitors in Ireland* (2002) ch 4.2. The executor should be advised, however, that it is recommended and normal practice to supply an extract of the relevant part of the will to an interested legatee. See EXECUTOR.

winding up. The process whereby the end is put to the carrying on of the business of a company or partnership. The assets are collected and realised, the resulting proceeds are applied in discharge of all its debts and liabilities, and any balance (surplus) which remains after paying the costs and expenses of winding up is distributed among the members according to their rights and interests, or otherwise dealt with as the constitution of the company or partnership directs. Also called *liquidation*. A liquidator is appointed by the members or by the creditors or by the court to carry out the winding up.

The winding up of a partnership is either voluntary (ie by agreement between the partners) or by order of a court made in an action for the dissolution of the partnership.

Companies are wound up in three different ways: (a) compulsory winding up by the court, (b) voluntary winding up by the members, or (c) voluntary winding up by the creditors: Companies Act 1963 Part IV, ss 206–313 as amended eg Companies (Amendment) (No 2) Act 1999, ss 49–50. Certain provisions of the Companies Acts also apply to insolvent companies which go out of business without formally going into liquidation: Companies Act 1990, s 251. Also a building society may, subject to certain modifications, be wound up under the Companies Acts as if the society were a company: Building Societies Act 1989, s 109. See *In the matter of CHA Ltd* [1999] 2 ILRM 76, HC and 1 IR 437.

A winding up petition is not a legitimate means of seeking to enforce payment of a debt which is *bona fide* disputed by the company: *Re WMG (Toughening) Ltd (No 2)* [2003, SC] 1 IR 389, cited *in In the matter of ICT International Cotton and Textile Trading Company Ltd* [2004] ITLR (14 June) HC. See also Adoptive Leave Act 1995, s 38; Credit Union Act 1997, s 133 as amended by Central Bank and Financial Services Authority of Ireland Act 2003, s 35, Sch 1; Proceeds of Crime Act 1996, s 13; Employment Equality Act 1998, s 103(1); National Minimum Wages Act 2000, s 49. See EC (Corporate Insolvency) Regulations 2002, SI No 333 of 2002. For winding up of Insurance Undertakings, see SI No 168 of 2003 as amended by SI No 360 of 2003. See website: *www.liquidations.ie*. [Bibliography: Forde (9).] See LIQUIDATOR; PREFERENTIAL PAYMENTS; MALICIOUS PROSECUTION; ONEROUS PROPERTY; PHOENIX COMPANY.

winding up, compulsory. A compulsory winding up by the court may be imposed on a company at the instigation of any member, or contributory (qv), or creditor, or the Minister in particular circumstances. The court appoints the liquidator (known as the *official liquidator*) and determines his remuneration. The liquidator is an officer of the court and works under its supervision.

The grounds under which the court may order a company to be wound up are set out in Companies Act 1963, s 213. These include where the company has passed a special resolution for compulsory liquidation; or the company does not commence its business within a year of its incorporation, or suspends its business for a whole year; or the number of members is reduced below the minimum allowable; or the company is unable to pay its debts; or the court is of the opinion that it is just and equitable that the company should be wound up; or the court is satisfied that the affairs of the company are being conducted, or the powers of the directors are being exercised, in a manner oppressive to any member of the company.

The most frequent ground on which orders for a winding up are sought is that the company is unable to pay its debts (CA 1963, s 213(e)). A company is deemed to be unable to pay its debts if either: (a) a creditor proves that the company owes that creditor more than £1,000 (€1,269.74), that the demand for payment was made in writing and that the company has for three weeks failed to comply; or (b) a judgment creditor of the company has levied execution and has remained unsatisfied: CA 1963, ss 214 and 345 as amended by Companies Act 1990, s 123.

The procedure governing compulsory winding-up is contained in the CA 1963, ss 216–250; it involves the presentation of a petition to the High Court for a *winding up order*: RSC Ord 74, rr 7–23. The principles applicable to restrain the presentation of a winding-up petition are specified in *Truck & Machinery Sales Ltd v Marabeni Komatsu Ltd* [1996] 1 IR 12, HC.

The winding-up dates from the presentation of the petition and not from the date of the winding up order: CA 1963, s 220(2). Any disposition of property made after commencement of the winding up is void, unless the court otherwise orders: CA 1963, s 218 and *Re Ashmark Ltd* [1990 HC] ILRM 330. A liquidator is prohibited from selling non-cash assets of a requisite value to an officer or former officer of the company unless he gives notice to the creditors of the company: CA 1990, s 124 amending the CA 1963, s 231.

The petition of a creditor of an alleged debt will be dismissed where the company disputes liability in good faith and on substantial grounds: *Clandown Ltd v Davis* [1994] 2 ILRM 536, HC. The court will look at the justification presented in the petition to wind up a company in receivership; it may amount to an abuse of court: *Re Bula Ltd (in receivership)* [1988] SC.

The court has a discretion to replace a voluntary liquidation with a compulsory liquidation in certain circumstances eg where the assets of the company have gone to an associated company without payment, the liquidation is in the hands of the nominee of the persons who had control of the company, and the nominee of the majority creditors has been rejected: *In the matter of Hayes Homes Ltd (in voluntary liquidation)* [2004] ITLR 26 July, HC.

A company which is under the protection of the court, can be wound up by order of the court, following receipt of the *examiner's* report: Companies (Amendment) Act 1990, s 17. The winding up is deemed to have commenced on the date of the making of the order (C(A)A 1990, s 17(6)). See also *Re Frederick Inns Ltd* [1994] 1 ILRM 387, SC; *Re Greendale Developments Ltd (No 2)* [1998] 1 IR 8, SC.

A significant role has been given to the *Director of Corporate Enforcement* in relation to a company which is in official liquidation eg to apply to the court for: (a) an order which would permit him to examine the books and documents of the company; (b) an order to determine what part, if any, the directors and officers of the failed company played in its failure and whether there are grounds for seeking to have such persons restricted or disqualified; (c) an order for payment or delivery of company property and an order to enter premises and seize any money, property, books or papers of the company; and (d) an order to have an expanded list of persons (eg contributory, director, secretary) arrested on probable cause that they are about to quit the State: Companies Act 1963, ss 243, 245, 245A and 247 as amended by Company Law Enforcement Act 2001, ss 43, 44, 45 and 46 respectively. See also CLEA, ss 93 and 94.

For winding-up rules for companies, see SI No 28 of 1966. See 'Recovery of post-petition cheque payments' by Micheal O'Connell BL in *Bar Review* (June/July 2001) 441. See also COURT PROTECTION OF COMPANY; COSTS IN CIVIL PROCEEDINGS; LIQUIDATOR; PETITION FOR WINDING UP; STATEMENT OF AFFAIRS; STAY OF PROCEEDINGS.

winding up, voluntary. A voluntary winding up *by members* is accomplished by special resolution of the company to wind itself up and by preparation by the directors of a *declaration of solvency* ie a statutory declaration that they are of the opinion that the company will be able to pay its debts in full within a period not exceeding twelve months from when the winding up commences: Companies Act 1963, s 256 as amended by Companies Act 1990, s 128; RSC Ord 74, r 139 as amended by SI No 265 of 1993, para 4.

A liquidator may be appointed by the shareholders who may fix his remuneration (CA 1963, s 258(1)). A voluntary winding up dates from the passing of the special resolution (CA 1963, s 220(1)).

A voluntary winding up *by creditors* is accomplished at a publicly advertised meeting of creditors, following the members' meeting at which the proposal to wind up the company has been put (CA 1963, s 266

as amended by CA 1990, s 130). While the creditors may accept the liquidator nominated by the shareholders, they may appoint their own nominee to the office (CA 1963, s 267). However, before the resolution is put, the fact that any creditor has a connection with the proposed liquidator must be disclosed to the meeting (CA 1990, s 147 inserting new CA 1963, s 301A). The Court may also, on application, appoint some other person as liquidator.

The creditors can appoint a *committee of inspection* whose function is to determine the liquidator's remuneration and monitor the winding up (CA 1963, ss 268–269).

Where the liquidator forms the opinion that the company will not be able to pay its debts, the creditors may substitute their own liquidator and the winding up becomes a creditors' winding up (CA 1963, s 261 as substituted by CA 1990, s 129). Also a failure to make a statutory declaration of solvency strictly in compliance with s 256 results in the ensuing liquidation being a creditors' winding up; the court cannot cure a defective declaration: *Re Favon Investments Co Ltd (in liquidation)* [1992] ITLR (21 December) HC.

A creditor of the company may bring an application to examine persons under CA 1963, s 245 provided he can show that such examination would probably result in some benefit to him: *In the Matter of Comet Food Machinery Ltd (in voluntary liquidation)* [1999] 1 ILRM 475, SC.

In a creditors' voluntary winding up of a company, the creditors' nominee for liquidator is now selected on the basis of a *majority in value* only of the creditors, as opposed to a *majority in number and value* as previously: CA 1963, s 267 as amended by Company Law Enforcement Act 2001, s 47.

Similar powers are given to the *Director of Corporate Enforcement* to seek the assistance of the court in a voluntary winding up as in an official liquidation eg power to examine books, to summon persons before the court for examination, to order payment or delivery of company property, and to order the arrest of persons about to abscond (CA 1963, ss 282A–282D inserted by CLEA 2001, s 49). See CREDITORS' MEETING; LIQUIDATOR; SOLVENCY, DECLARATION OF.

winding up by trustee. A bankrupt's estate may be wound up by a trustee and *committee of inspection* as an alternative to its being administered by the Official Assignee (qv): Bankruptcy Act 1988, ss 110–114. The trustee and committee are appointed by the creditors following a resolution by them that the bankruptcy be wound up in that way. The trustee, who is subject to the control of the court, will in general have the same power and functions as are conferred on the Official Assignee (qv). See BANKRUPTCY.

winter time. The period during which for general purposes in the State the time is Greenwich meantime: Standard Time (Amendment) Act 1971. The period begins at two o'clock GMT in the morning of the Sunday following the fourth Saturday in October and ending either at two o'clock GMT in the morning of the Sunday following the third Saturday in the month of March in the following year or, if the last-mentioned Sunday is Easter Day, at two o'clock GMT in the morning of the Sunday following the second Saturday in the month of March in that year (ST(A)A 1971, s 1(1)(c)). The Minister may vary by order the period of winter time (ST(A)A 1971, s 2). See SI No 395 of 1994. See SUMMER TIME.

WIPO. [World Intellectual Property Organisation (qv).]

withdrawal from jury. The procedure by which a judge withdraws an issue or a case from the jury eg when he decides that the plaintiff or the prosecution has failed to discharge the appropriate onus of proof. See *Hynes-O'Sullivan v O'Driscoll* [1989] ILRM 619, SC. See DIRECTION.

withdrawal of food products. See PROHIBITION ORDER.

withering permission. See HOUSING STRATEGY.

withholding information. It is an offence to withhold information concerning firearms and stolen goods: Criminal Justice Act 1984, ss 15–16. It is also an offence if a person fails, without reasonable excuse, to disclose information to a garda where he has information which he knows or believes might be of material assistance in: (a) preventing the commission of a serious offence; or (b) securing the apprehension, prosecution or conviction for a serious offence: Offences against the State Act 1998, ss 9 and 18.

withholding of supplies. The withholding of grocery goods from a person by a supplier or wholesaler is prohibited in specified circumstances eg on the grounds that a person is or is not a member of a trade association: Restrictive Practices (Groceries) Order 1987, SI No 142 of 1987. The Minister is empowered to amend or revoke the order: Competition Act 2002, s 49. [Bibliography: Lucey; O'Reilly M.]

withholding tax. A tax called *professional services withholding tax (PSWT)* which must be deducted at source by *accountable persons* from payments for professional services: Taxes Consolidation Act 1997, s 520. Accountable persons include government departments, local authorities, health boards, and state-sponsored bodies (TCA 1997, Sch 13). The list of accountable persons, who must deduct withholding tax at the standard rate when making payments for professional services to individuals and companies, has been updated: Finance Act 2001, s 14; Finance Act 2003, s 10; Personal Injuries Assessment Board Act 2003, s 85; Finance Act 2004, s 5. For previous list, see Finance Act 2000, s 20.

Professional services include services of doctors, dentists, pharmacists, opticians, veterinary surgeons, architects, engineers, quantity surveyors, accountants, auditors, consultants (economic, marketing, or business), solicitors, barristers, other legal agents, geologists, and providers of training services on behalf of An Foras Áiseanna Saothair. *Professional services* do not include the work of a film or video maker: *Iskra Productions Ltd v An Foras Áiseanna Saothair* (1992) Irish Times, 22 October, CC. The change in the method of collection of withholding tax effected by Finance Act 1990, s 26(1) has been held to be unconstitutional having failed to pass the test of proportionality: *Daly v Revenue Commissioners* [1996] 1 ILRM 122, HC and [1995] 3 IR 1, HC.

There is also an obligation on the purchaser of certain specified assets to withhold 15% of the consideration representing an amount of *capital gains tax* and paying it over to the Revenue Commissioners eg on the sale of land, minerals in the State or mining exploration rights, exploration or exploitation rights, and certain share transactions: Taxes Consolidation Act 1997, s 980. The threshold was initially increased to £300,000 (€380,921); also the production of certain Revenue certificates by the vendor will be sufficient authority for the purchaser not to withhold tax (TCA 1997, s 980 amended by Finance Act 2000, s 87). The threshold has been further increased to €500,000: Finance Act 2002, s 63. An agent of the vendor may now sign the application for the Revenue certificate (CG50A): Finance Act 2003, s 71.

The Revenue Commissioners are empowered to carry out an on site audit of accountable persons in relation to PSWT (FA 2003, s 159). For the abolition of withholding tax on certain interest and royalties made between associated companies of different member states, see SI No 721 of 2003, implementing Directive (EC) 2003/49. Two companies are associated if one owns at least 25% of the other, or at least 25% of each company is owned by a third company. This SI has now been revoked and its provisions re-enacted by the Finance Act 2004, s 41 and Sch 1, inserting new TCA 1997, s 267G. See also DIVIDEND WITHHOLDING TAX; SUB CONTRACTORS, PAYMENT TO.

without prejudice. Where communications, written or oral, made by a party to a civil action, are stated to be *without prejudice*, they cannot be given in evidence against the party making them. A letter headed *without prejudice* protects from disclosure the whole of the correspondence of which it forms part. However, such correspondence may be produced in evidence where: (a) the parties consent, or (b) the letter cloaks an illegality eg a threat, or (c) an offer to settle is accepted and the letters are proved to show the terms of the settlement.

Letters written and oral communications made during a dispute between parties, which are made or written for the purpose of settling the dispute, and which are expressed or otherwise proved to have been made 'without prejudice', cannot generally be admitted in evidence. Where the privilege is challenged, the court is entitled to examine the communications to determine whether they are of such a nature as to attract privilege: *Ryan v Connolly* [2001] 2 ILRM 174, SC and 1 IR 627.

It is a well established rule that offers made in the course of settlement negotiations are not normally admissible in evidence; this is usually achieved by marking the relevant correspondence or documents 'without prejudice'. The rule is founded on the public policy that parties are to be encouraged as far as possible to settle their disputes without recourse to litigation. However, statements in documents marked 'without prejudice' which relate solely to a party's future conduct and which could not be regarded as admissions made as part of an offer of settlement, would not necessarily be protected from disclosure: *Greencore Group plc v Murphy* [1996] 1 ILRM 210, HC. See *A Guide to Professional Conduct of Solicitors in Ireland* (2002) ch 7.3.

without recourse to me. See SANS RECOURS.

without reserve. The phrase used in an *auction* (qv) where there is no reserve price.

witness. (1) To attest by signature. (2) A person who gives evidence, usually on oath (qv). The normal meaning of 'witness' is one who is a spectator of an incident or one who is present at an incident: *Re Gibson, decd* [1949] cited in *Dundalk AFC v FAI National League* [2001] 1 IR 434, HC.

The death of an alibi witness before a criminal trial takes place may unfairly prejudice an accused: *People (DPP) v Quilligan & O'Reilly (No 3)* [1993] 11 ILT Dig 88, SC. A solicitor should not call a witness whose evidence is untrue to the solicitor's knowledge, as opposed to his belief: *A Guide to Professional Conduct of Solicitors in Ireland* (2002) ch 5.1. The names of all witnesses and all material facts must be disclosed to the court in a criminal trial, irrespective of whether the witnesses and facts are detrimental to the prosecution case. If the prosecutor knows of a credible witness who can give evidence concerning material facts which tend to show the accused to be innocent, he must either call that witness or make the witness statement available to the defence.

A barrister must not appear in any case in which he is likely to be a witness: *Code of Conduct for the Bar of Ireland* (December 2003) r 3.13. If being engaged in a case it becomes apparent that he is likely to be a witness on a question of fact, he should not continue to appear as a barrister if he can retire without jeopardising his client's interest. A barrister may not coach a witness in his evidence (r 5.18). A barrister must not confer with a witness whom he called, while such witness is under cross-examination, without prior leave of the other parties or the court (r 5.20). Also when conducting a case, a barrister must not make statements or ask questions which are merely scandalous or are intended only for the purpose of vilifying, insulting or annoying a witness or some other person (r 5.22). [Bibliography: Healy.] See ATTEST; INTIMIDATION; PROFESSIONAL WITNESS; STANDBY FEE; UNFAIR DISMISSAL; VIVA VOCE.

witness, advertising for. It is permissible for a solicitor, acting on the instructions of his client, to advertise for witnesses to come forward to give evidence as to a particular occurrence but the advertisement should not invite persons to testify as to particular facts: *A Guide to Professional Conduct of Solicitors in Ireland* (2002) ch 5.6.

witness, competence of. In general, all persons are *competent* to give evidence and may be *compelled* to attend to give evidence by subpoena (qv). Exceptions include any person who is prevented by disease of mind or by extreme youth or other cause from understanding the questions put to him. A spouse of a party to a civil action is competent to give evidence but is not compellable to disclose communications made one to the other during marriage.

In criminal proceedings, the spouse (or *former spouse*) of an accused is *competent* to give evidence at the instance of: (a) the accused or any person charged with him, and (b) the prosecution except where the accused and spouse are charged in the same proceedings: Criminal Evidence Act 1992, ss 21 and 25. A spouse (or *former spouse*) of an accused is *compellable* to give evidence at the instance of the accused (CEA 1992, s 23). Also a spouse of an accused is *compellable* to give evidence at the instance of the prosecution where the offence: (a) involves violence to the spouse, a child of either spouse, or any person under 17; or (b) is a sexual offence against a child of either spouse or against any person under 17 (CEA 1992, s 22). None of these provisions however affect any right of a spouse or former spouse in respect of marital privacy (qv) (CEA 1992, s 26). A *former spouse* includes, in relation to the accused, a person who has been granted a decree of divorce or of judicial separation or has entered into a separation agreement (CEA 1992, s 20 amended by Family Law (Divorce) Act 1996, s 49). See *DPP v T* [1988] CCA. See O'Connor in 7 ILT & SJ (1989) 95. See INCEST.

An accomplice is not a competent witness for the prosecution if he is jointly indicted and jointly tried. See *Attorney-General v O'Sullivan* [1930] 552. See Criminal Justice (Evidence) Act 1924, ss 1

and 4 as amended by CEA 1992; Committees of the Houses of the Oireachtas (Compellability, Privileges and Immunity of Witnesses) Act 1997, s 3. See LRC 13, 1985. See INCRIMINATE; PRIVILEGE, MATRIMONIAL COMMUNICATIONS.

witness, credibility of. See CREDIBILITY.

witness, exclusion of. The court in a personal injuries action is empowered to direct that certain witnesses not attend the trial until called to give evidence: Civil Liability and Courts Act 2004, s 54. The court may also give other directions to secure that a witness does not communicate with other witnesses or receive information which might influence him. See PERSONAL INJURIES ACTION.

witness, expenses of. The District Court has the power to order a party to summary proceedings to pay to the other party such costs and witnesses' expenses as it thinks fit to award: DCR 1997 Ord 36. There is no objection to the payment by a solicitor to any witness of reasonable expenses or reasonable compensation for loss of time for attending court or the payment of a reasonable fee for the services of an expert witness: *A Guide to Professional Conduct of Solicitors in Ireland* (2002) ch 5.6. However, a solicitor should not make payments or offer to make payments to a witness, contingent upon the nature of the evidence given or the outcome of a case. See SUBPOENA.

witness, hostile. See HOSTILE WITNESS.

witness, interview of. A solicitor is entitled to interview a witness and to take statements from him in any civil or criminal proceedings, whether that witness has been interviewed or called as a witness by the other party, provided there is no question of tampering with the evidence of a witness or suborning him to change his story: *A Guide to Professional Conduct of Solicitors in Ireland* (2002) ch 5.6. However, where a witness is in the course of being cross-examined, a solicitor should not discuss the case with the witness, whether or not that witness is the client, without the leave of the court or without the consent of counsel or the solicitor for the other side.

witness, privilege of. A witness enjoys *absolute privilege* in judicial proceedings in respect of his evidence. He is immune from suit in respect of oral evidence and with regard to documents produced in the course of a hearing; this includes an expert witness also: *E O'K v D K* [2001] 1 IR 636,

HC and [2001] 3 IR 568, SC. However, if a witness abuses his absolute privilege by making an unwarranted and irrelevant attack on another citizen unconnected with the proceedings, his action would constitute an abuse of the legal process and be punishable as a contempt of court: *Looney v Bank of Ireland* [1996] 1 IR 157, HC and [1997] (unreported) SC. See also *Fagan v Burgess* [1999] 3 IR 306, HC. See Companies (Auditing and Accounting) Act 2003, s 28; Commissions of Investigation Act 2004, s 20; Residential Tenancies Act 2004, s 105(4). See CONTEMPT OF COURT; PRIVILEGE.

witness, recall of. A witness may be recalled in a criminal trial at the discretion of the judge, on request of the jury: *The People v O'Brien* [1963] IR 65. When deciding, on an application by counsel for the accused in a sexual assault case, to recall the complainant to be cross-examined, the trial judge has to balance the rights and justice of the situation: *The People (DPP) v J E M* [2001] 4 IR 385, CCA.

A district judge has a right to recall a witness on his own motion, but this practice should be used sparingly in criminal cases as otherwise the judge may appear partisan: *Magee v O'Dea* [1994] 1 ILRM 540, HC. The judge may recall a witness to give evidence of a formal or technical nature, after the prosecution have closed their case, but that power must be used sparingly: *Bates v Judge Brady* [2003] FL 7817, HC. A barrister who has asked for leave to recall a witness after a recess, should not, without notice to the court and the other parties, confer with that witness during the recess: *Code of Conduct for the Bar of Ireland* (Dec 2003) r 5.19.

witness order. An order made by a trial court requiring a person whose statement of evidence was served on the accused or whose *deposition* (qv) was taken to: (a) attend before the court and give evidence, and (b) produce to that court any document or thing specified in the order: Criminal Procedure Act 1967, s 4K as inserted by Criminal Justice Act 1999, s 9. A person who disobeys a witness order is guilty of contempt of court. If a trial court is satisfied that a person is unlikely to comply with a witness order, the court may commit him to custody until the trial. See SUBPOENA.

witness protection programme. See RELOCATED WITNESS.

witness summons. The summons issued out of a trial court, requiring the person to whom the summons is directed to: (a) attend before the court and give evidence; and (b) produce to that court any document or thing specified in the summons: Criminal Procedure Act 1967, s 4L inserted by Criminal Justice Act 1999, s 9. The summons may be issued at the request of the prosecutor or the accused. A person who disobeys a witness summons is guilty of contempt of court. See also Competition Authority (Witness Summons) Regulations 1999, SI No 137 of 1999.

A witness summons is one issued by the County Registrar requiring the person to whom the summons is directed to comply with the requirements thereof at the time and place stated therein: Circuit Court Rules 2001 Ord 24. See also INQUEST AND WITNESSES; SUBPOENA.

witnessing part. See TESTATUM.

woodcock. See GAME.

woodcut. See ARTISTIC WORK.

word, invented. See INVENTED WORD; CHARACTER OR QUALITY OF GOODS.

words, meaning of. See DEFINITION ORDER; DICTIONARY, USE OF; INTERPRETATION OF LEGISLATION; LITERAL RULE; STATUTORY INTERPRETATION; VERBA CHARTARUM.

words, operative. See OPERATIVE WORDS.

words, precatory. See PRECATORY TRUST.

words of limitation. The words in a conveyance (qv) or a will (qv) which have the effect of marking out the duration of the estate eg in a grant *to A and his heirs*, the words *and his heirs* are words of limitation and confer no estate on his heirs (Shelley's Case 1581) but create a *fee simple* in A. A fee simple may also be created by the words *to A in fee simple*: Conveyancing Act 1881, s 51.

A *fee tail* (qv) may be created by the words *to A and the heirs of his body* and a *life estate* (qv) by *to A for life* or by the use of expressions insufficient to create a fee simple or fee tail eg *to A* or *to A for ever*.

A devise of real estate in a will without words of limitation, is to be construed as passing the whole estate which the testator had power to dispose of, unless a contrary intention appears from the will: Succession Act 1965, s 94. See *Re McIntyre, Crawford v Ruttledge* [1970] HC. See WORDS OF PURCHASE; REMOTENESS; SHELLEY'S CASE, RULE IN.

words of purchase. The words in a conveyance (qv) or a will (qv) which denote the person who is to take an estate or interest in land eg in a grant *to A and his heirs*, the words *to A* are words of purchase and *and his heirs* are words of limitation. The words *heirs* when used as words of purchase are to be construed to mean those entitled under Part VI of the Succession Act 1965 (SA 1965, s 15). See WORDS OF LIMITATION.

words of severance. See SEVERANCE, WORDS OF.

work. (1) Means a literary, dramatic, musical or artistic work, sound recording, film, broadcast, cable programme, typographical arrangement of a published edition or an original database and includes a computer program: Copyright and Related Rights Act 2000, s 2(1). A *copyright work* means a work in which copyright subsists (CRRA 2000, s 2(1)). *Work* as regards *moral rights*, means literary, dramatic, musical or artistic work or film (CRRA 2000, s 2(1)). See ARTISTIC WORK; COPYRIGHT; COMPUTER-GENERATED; DRAMATIC WORK; LIKE WORK; MUSICAL WORK; LITERARY WORK.

(2) An employee is deemed to have been dismissed by reason of redundancy if the dismissal is attributable wholly or mainly to the fact that his employer has decided that the *work* for which the employee had been employed should henceforth be done: (a) in a different manner for which the employee is not sufficiently qualified or trained; or (b) by a person who is also capable of doing *other work* for which the employee is not sufficiently trained: Redundancy Payments Act 1967, s 7(2)(d) and (e) as amended by Redundancy Payments Act 1971, s 4. It has been held that this section means that there had to be a change in the way the work is done or some other form of change in the nature of the job; the definition of *other work* in RPA 1967, s 7(2)(e) must involve, partly at least, work of a different kind: *St Ledger v Frontline Distribution Ltd* [1995] ELR 160, EAT. More work or less work of the same kind does not mean *other work*. See REDUNDANCY.

work, prohibition of. The High Court is empowered to order that the use of a place of work, or part thereof, be restricted or prohibited on an *ex parte* application by the National Authority for Occupational Safety and Health; the Authority may apply to the court when it considers that the risk to the safety and health of persons is so serious that the restriction or prohibition is neces-

sary until specified measures have been taken to reduce the risk to a reasonable level: Safety, Health and Welfare at Work Act 1989, s 39. 'An employer is entitled to make money on the sweat of his employees, but not on their blood.' Kelly J in *HSA v Zoe Developments* (1997) Irish Times, 18 November, HC. See *also HSA v Kilkishen Homes* (November 2002, unreported) HC. See PROHIBITION NOTICE.

work, right to. The Constitution recognises the right to work in that it requires that the State shall, in particular, direct its policy towards securing that the citizens (all of whom, men and women equally, have an adequate means of livelihood) may through their occupations find the means of making reasonable provision for their domestic needs: art 45(2)(1).

It has been held that a compulsory retirement scheme does not infringe the right to work: *Rodgers v ITGWU* [1978] HC. However a union may not be able to refuse membership to a person if the refusal is to prevent that person exercising the right to work: *Murphy v Stewart* [1973] IR 97. See also *Scally v Minister for the Environment* [1988] HC. See LIVELIHOOD.

work activity. A work activity may be prescribed by the Minister, for the purpose of protecting the safety, health or welfare of persons at work, which may then not be carried on except in accordance with the terms and conditions of a licence: Safety, Health and Welfare at Work Act 1989, s 59.

work equipment. Any machine, apparatus, tool or installation used at work: Safety Health and Welfare at Work (General Application) Regulations 1993, SI No 44 of 1993, reg 2(1). Every employer has a duty to ensure that work equipment is suitable for the work to be carried out (reg 19).

work experience. See SAFETY AT WORK.

work in EU. Each member state is required to provide a service for those seeking work in another member state: EC Treaty, art 40 of the consolidated (2002) version. A network of offices has been established throughout the EU; the offices in this State are the FÁS Employment Services Offices which operate the *EURES* placement service.

work permit. An alien (now, a *non-national*) was not allowed to enter into the service of an employer in the State save in accordance with a permit issued to the employer by the Minister: Aliens Order 1946, art 4 (SR & O No 395 of 1946) as inserted by Aliens

(Amendment) Order 1975, SI No 128 of 1975, art 3. See Aliens Act 1935, s 6. It was held that 'enter into the service of' does not equate with 'being in the service of' and that there was nothing in the article to indicate a continuing obligation: *Gleeson v Chi Ho Cheung* [1997] 1 IR 521, HC. 'Work permits' are now called 'employment permits' and art 4 of SR & O No 395 of 1946 is revoked: Employment Permits Act 2003, s 2(12). A Rights Commissioner has held that deductions from employee wages in respect of work permit fees, should not have been made by the company: *Goral and Others v Nolan Transport* (2003) Irish Times, 13 December, RC. See EMPLOYMENT PERMIT; ENLARGEMENT OF EU.

work to rule. A form of industrial action by employees which takes the form of working slower than usual and reducing output, by paying exaggerated attention to rules relating to that work. Also known as *go-slow*. See *Secretary of State for Employment v ASLEF* [1972] 2 QB 455.

worker. Any person aged 15 years or more who has entered into or works under a contract with an employer: Industrial Relations Act 1990, s 23. The definition has been amended to give officers of local authorities and health boards access to the Labour Relations Commission, Labour Court and Rights Commissioner: Industrial Relations Act 1990 (Definition of 'Worker') Order 1998, SI No 264 of 1998. However, a person employed by an Irish embassy abroad who is not a civil servant, but whose salary is paid by the State and who is subject to the control of the State, does not fall within the definition of a worker in IRA 1990, s 23: *A Worker v Department of Foreign Affairs* [2001] ELR 141, LC. See INDUSTRIAL ACTION; TRADE DISPUTE.

worker democracy. See EUROPEAN EMPLOYEES' FORUM; WORKER PARTICIPATION.

worker participation. The involvement of employees at board level in the company of their employment which is provided for by statute e g Worker Participation (State Enterprises) Act 1977 which provides for the election of worker representatives to one-third of board places in single-tier boards of specified state enterprises. A lower percentage of worker directors is provided for in individual statutes e g Labour Services Act 1987 establishing FÁS; also see National Disability Authority Act 1999,

s 20(4)(b). The 1977 Act specifically does not apply to certain State companies e g Irish Aviation Authority Act 1993, s 71.

Worker participation at board level has been extended to further state enterprises and provision has been made to enable sub-board participative arrangements to be set up in a wide range of such organisations: Worker Participation (State Enterprises) Act 1988. A number of amendments to the 1977 Act are provided for, including giving power to the Minister to provide for worker representation less than one-third of board size in certain State enterprises, subject to a minimum of two worker directors (WP(SE)A 1988, ss 9–23). See also Worker Participation (State Enterprises) Regulations 1988, SIs No 170, 171 and 172 of 1988).

Worker participation now extends to regular part-time workers: Worker Protection (Regular Part-time Employees) Act 1991, s 1. See Code of Practice on Employee Representatives (Declaration) Order 1993, SI No 169 of 1993. See also Air Companies (Amendment) Act 1993, s 13; Telecommunications (Miscellaneous Provisions) Act 1996, s 10. See EUROPEAN EMPLOYEES' FORUM; POSTAL VOTING RULES.

workers, freedom of movement of. There is a right to freedom of movement for workers within the EC under the EC Treaty, art 39 of the consolidated (2002) version. Member states are required to abolish any discrimination based on nationality between workers of these states as regards employment, remuneration and other conditions of work and employment. See *Scally v Minister for the Environment* [1996] 1 IR 367, HC; Case C-138/02 *Collins v Secretary of State for Work and Pensions* [2004] 23 March, ECJ. See Cousins in 8 ILT & SJ (1990) 258. See EURO-JUS; FREE MOVEMENT; SOLICITOR, INTERNATIONAL PRACTICE; SOLICITOR; MUTUAL RECOGNITION; RIGHT OF ESTABLISHMENT.

working at home. See HOME CARER'S ALLOWANCE.

working capital. See CAPITAL; UNDERSUBSCRIBED.

working days. Days other than Saturdays, Sundays or public holidays: Domestic Violence Act 1996, s 4(3)(f) as substituted by Domestic Violence (Amendment) Act 2002, s 1(a). See also Dormant Accounts Act 2001, s 12(9); Planning and

Development Act 2000, s 146(4); Immigration Act 1999, s 3(12); Organisation of Working Time Act 1997, s 12(4); Prompt Payment of Accounts Act 1997, s 5(3).

working hours. Generally, an employer must not permit an employee to work, in each period of seven days, more than an *average* of 48 hours: Organisation of Working Time Act 1997, s 15. The averaging is permitted: (a) over two months for nightworkers, (b) over four months for most employees, (c) over six months for certain categories of employment e g agriculture and tourism, and (d) over up to twelve months for employees covered by a collective agreement approved by the Labour Court (OWTA 1997, ss 15, 16, 24).

The restriction on working hours do not apply to: (a) a person engaged in sea fishing, other work at sea, or the activities of a doctor in training, (b) a person who is employed by a relative in a private dwelling house or a farm, (c) a person whose working time is determined by himself (OWTA 1997, s 3(2)). See also National Minimum Wages Act 2000, s 45.

It has been contended that an employer has a duty to exercise reasonable care not to occasion injury to his employee by overworking him: *Johnstone v Blomsbury Health Authority* [1991] 2 All ER 293 (CA) as reported by White in 9 ILT & SJ (1991) 240. See Night Work and Shift Work Regulations 2000, SI No 11 of 2000.

Employers are required to keep: (a) a record of the number of hours worked by employees on a daily and weekly basis, (b) a record of leave granted to employees in each week, (c) a weekly record of the notification of starting and finishing times of employees, and (d) a copy of the statement provided to each employee under the provisions of the Terms of Employment (Information) Act 1994: Organisation of Working Hours (Records) (Prescribed Form and Exemptions) Regulations 2001, SI No 473 of 2001. See *Ocean Manpower Ltd v MPGWU* [1998] ELR 299, LC.

For the rules governing applications to the Circuit Court for the enforcement of determinations of the Labour Court, pursuant to Organisation of Working Time Act 1997, s 29, see Circuit Court Rules 2001 Ord 57, r 4. For amendments to OWTA 1997, ss 28(8) and 39, see Protection of Employees (Fixed-Term Work) Act 2003, s 19(2). See CHILD, EMPLOYMENT OF; OVERTIME; NIGHTWORK; ON CALL; OVERTIME; REST PERIOD; SUNDAY WORK; WORKING TIME DIRECTIVE; YOUNG PERSON; ZERO HOUR CONTRACT.

working-men's club. See FRIENDLY SOCIETY.

Working Time Directive. Directive (EC) 93/104 of 23 November 1993 which is implemented in the State by the Organisation of Working Time Act 1997. The legal basis for the Directive was Article 118a of the Treaty of Rome which allows for qualified majority voting on proposals concerning the health and safety of workers; now, EC Treaty, art 137 of the consolidated (2002) version. The UK challenge on this was rejected by the European Court of Justice: *United Kingdom v Council of the European Union* [1996] ECR 1–5755. See ON CALL; WORKING HOURS.

works. Includes any act or operation of construction, excavation, demolition, extension, alteration, repair or renewal: Planning and Development Act 2000, s 2(1). *Unauthorised works* means any works on, in, over or under land commenced on or after 1 October 1964, being *development*; excluded are *exempted development* or development for which there is permission (PDA 2000, s 2(1)). In relation to a *protected structure* or proposed protected structure, 'works' includes any act or operation involving the application or removal of plaster, paint, wall paper, tiles or other material to or from the surfaces of the interior or exterior of the structure (PDA 2000, s 2(1)). It has been held that 'works' of themselves, and without more, cannot be treated as a 'change of use' so as to deprive a developer of an exemption to which, as works alone, he would be entitled: *Esat Digiphone v South Dublin County Council* [2002] 2 ILRM 547, HC and 3 IR 585. See PLANNING PERMISSION.

workstation. An assembly comprising *display screen equipment* (qv) which may be provided with a keyboard or input device and/or software determining the operator and machine interface, and includes optional accessories: SI No 44 of 1993, reg 29. Every employer is required to evaluate the health and safety conditions to which workstations give rise for his employees, particularly as regards possible risks to eyesight, physical problems and problems of mental distress (SI No 44 of 1993, reg 31). Minimum requirements for display screen equipment and workstations have been specified (SI No 44 of 1993, Schs 10, 11).

World Bank. The specialised agency of the United Nations, founded in 1944, which works with over 100 developing economies, with the primary focus of helping the poorest people and the poorest countries. In 2002 it provided more than US$19.5 billion in loans to its client countries. The bank is owned by more than 184 member countries. See website: *www.worldbank.org*. See MULTILATERAL INVESTMENT GUARANTEE AGENCY; INTERNATIONAL DEVELOPMENT ASSOCIATION.

World Court. Term sometimes used to describe the International Court of Justice (qv) of the United Nations.

World Health Organisation; WHO. The specialised agency of the United Nations dealing with health matters. Its objective is the attainment by all peoples of the highest possible level of health. 'Health' is defined in the WHO Constitution as a state of complete physical, mental and social well-being and not merely the absence of disease or infirmity. The WHO has 192 member countries and was established in 1945. See website: *www.who.int*.

World Intellectual Property Organisation; WIPO. An inter-governmental organisation and successor since 1970 of the United International Bureaux for the Protection of Intellectual Property (BIRPI) which had been in existence for over 80 years. WIPO administers the Paris Convention (qv), which is an open convention, open to all states who have but to inform WIPO of their accession; WIPO then informs all other member states of that accession. WIPO is now an agency of the United Nations. See website: *www.wipo.int*. [Bibliography: von Lewinski.] See DOMAIN NAME; HAGUE AGREEMENT; INTERNATIONAL TRADE MARK.

World Trade Organisation; WTO. A specialised agency of the United Nations. It is the only global organisation dealing with the *rules of trade* between nations. At its core are the WTO agreements, negotiated and signed by the vast majority of the world's trading partners and ratified by their governments or parliaments. The goal of the WTO is to assist producers of goods and services, exporters and importers conduct their business. It has 144 member countries. See website: *www.wto.org*.

worldwide injunction. See MAREVA INJUNCTION.

worldwide web. [www.] The total set of hypertext documents residing on HTTP (*hypertext transfer protocol*) servers all around the world. Documents on the *worldwide web* are called *pages* or *web pages*. Files may contain text, graphic images, movie files and sounds. The *worldwide web* was developed by Timothy Berners-Lee in 1989 for the European Laboratory for Particle Physics (CERN).

A website offering a database of British and Irish law, organised by the British and Irish Legal Information Institute (BAILII) was launched in 2000. Free web access is afforded to primary legal materials from Ireland, Northern Ireland, England, Scotland and Wales. See *www.bailii.org*. In relation to consumers being misled by online advertising, see 'Caught in the Web' by solicitor Sinead Morgan in *Law Society Gazette* (January/February 2004) 38. [Bibliography: Butterworths (2).] See INTERNET.

worship, public. The State acknowledges that the homage of public worship is due to Almighty God: 1937 Constitution, art 44(1). In considering what type of works to a *protected structure* (qv), which is regularly used as a place of *public worship*, would not require planning permission, the planning authority is required to respect liturgical requirements: Planning and Development Act 2000, s 57(5). See PUBLIC WORSHIP, DISTURBANCE OF; RELIGIOUS FREEDOM.

worts. The liquid which is fermented to produce beer: Finance Act 1992, s 89.

wounding. See BODILY HARM, GRIEVOUS.

wound pension. See PENSION.

wreck. (1) A vessel, or part of a vessel, lying wrecked on, in or under the seabed or on or in land covered by water, and any objects contained in or on the vessel and any objects that were formerly contained in or on a vessel and are lying on, in or under the sea bed or on or in land covered by water: National Monuments (Amendment) Act 1987, s 1(1). The Commissioners for Public Works may make an *underwater heritage order* designating as a restricted area, an area of the sea bed, or land covered by water, around and including a site where a wreck or an archaeological object lies or formerly lay (NM(A)A 1987, s 3). There are further provisions to protect such sites. The finder of a wreck or an *archaeological object* (qv) must report it within four days:

National Monument (Amendment) Act 1994, s 18. Also there is provision for the forfeiture of prohibited detection devices (NM(A)A 1994, s 7). See VALLETTA CONVENTION.

(2) A *wreck* includes a wrecked or stranded vessel, which includes: (a) a vessel which is sunk, partially sunk, wrecked, grounded, stranded or abandoned, (b) any part of such a vessel, and (c) any article, thing or collection of things, being or forming part of the tackle, equipment, cargo, stores, bunkers, oil or ballast of a wrecked vessel: Merchant Shipping (Salvage and Wreck) Act 1993, ss 2(1) and 39. The Minister has the general superintendence throughout the State of all matters relating to wrecks (MS(SW)A 1993, s 40).

The owners of a wreck have a duty to remove it if it constitutes a hindrance to navigation, a threat to coastal communities or the marine environment (MS(SW)A 1993, s 51). It is an offence for an unauthorised person to board a wreck without the permission of the owner (MS(SW)A 1993, s 56). See HERITAGE; RECEIVER OF WRECK; MARITIME CLAIMS.

writ. (1) A document issued in the name of a court, or a duly appointed person, commanding the person to whom it is addressed to do or to forebear from doing some act eg a summons (qv); or a direction to hold an election: Electoral Act 1992, Sch 4.

(2) In the UK, a process issued in the High Court at the instance of the plaintiff for the purpose of giving the defendant notice of the claim made against him. The practice in England as regards 'the dropping of the distinction' between *service* of a writ and *notice* of it, is of no relevance in Ireland: *O'Connor v Commercial General and Marine Ltd* [1996] 2 ILRM 293, HC and 1 IR 68. See BYE-ELECTION; DISSOLUTION; SUMMONS, SERVICE OUT OF JURISDICTION.

writ of restitution. The district court may award a *writ of restitution* to a tenant against whom a decree for possession for non payment of rent has been executed, provided the tenant pays the arrears of rent, rent due and costs within six months of the execution: DCR 1997 Ord 47, r 12; Landlord and Tenant Law Amendment Act Ireland 1860, ss 70–71.

writer. See ARTIST, TAX EXEMPTION OF; AUTHOR.

writing. (1) The word 'writing' includes printing, typewriting, lithography, photography, and other modes of representing or reproducing words in visible form, and cognate words shall be construed accordingly: Interpretation Act 1937, s 12, para 36.

(2) 'Writing' is required to be construed as including electronic modes of representing or reproducing words in visible form: Electronic Commerce Act 2000, s 2(2). Where a person by law or otherwise is required or permitted to *give information* in writing, the person may give the information in electronic form, whether as an electronic communication or otherwise (ECA 2000, s 12(1)). *Give information* includes: make an application, make or lodge a claim or a return, make a request, make an unsworn statement, lodge or issue a certificate, lodge an objection, record and disseminate a court order, and serve a notification (ECA 2000, s 12(5)). Information may be given electronically only: (a) where the information is reasonably accessible for subsequent reference ie readable and interpretable, (b) where, in the case of a public body, its information technology and procedural requirements are met, and (c) where, in other cases, there is consent to the information being given in that form (ECA 2000, s 12(2)).

(3) Includes any form of notation or code whether by hand or otherwise, and regardless of the method by which, or medium in or on which, it is recorded, and references to *'written'* are to be construed accordingly: Copyright and Related Rights Act 2000, s 2(1). See COPYRIGHT; ELECTRONIC COMMERCE; ELECTRONIC TAX RETURN.

writing, contracts requiring. Some contracts are required to be in writing eg contracts without consideration (qv); and some contracts are required to be evidenced in writing eg contracts for the sale of land. See DEED; ELECTRONIC COMMERCE; ORAL AGREEMENT, MODIFICATION OF CONTRACT BY; SALE OF GOODS; SIMPLE CONTRACTS; STATUTE OF FRAUDS; TRADE MARK, LICENCE OF.

wrong. (1) An act contrary to law. (2) A tort (qv) involving the breach of a duty imposed by law or the violation of a right. (3) A tort, breach of contract or breach of trust whether the act is committed by the person to whom the wrong is attributed or by one for whose acts he is responsible, and whether or not the act is also a crime, and whether or not the wrong is intentional:

Civil Liability Act 1961, s 2(1). See *O'Donnell v Truck & Machinery Sales Ltd* [1997] 1 ILRM 466, HC. See CONTRIBUTORY NEGLIGENCE; PLEADINGS.

wrong baby. See BABY, WRONG.

wrong quantity. Where a seller delivers to a buyer a quantity of goods less than he contracted to sell, the buyer may reject them, but if the buyer accepts the goods so delivered, he must pay for them at the contract rate: Sale of Goods Act 1893, s 30. See *Wilkinson v McCann Verdon Co* [1901] 35 ILTR 115; *Norwell v Black* [1931] 65 ILTR 104.

wrongdoer. A person who commits or is otherwise responsible for a wrong: Civil Liability Act 1961, s 2(1). See CONCURRENT WRONGDOER; UNJUST ENRICHMENT.

wrongful dismissal. An employee has a claim for damages at common law for *wrongful* dismissal. Apart from loss of pension rights, a wrongfully dismissed employee is entitled to damages representing loss of earnings in kind, but bonus payments, overtime, incentive payments, or commission may be recovered only if the employee can show that the employer was contractually bound to allow him earn them.

The relief at common law for *wrongful dismissal* is damages; in the absence of such a claim, interlocutory relief (eg an injunction) is not available as equitable relief has no independent existence: *Philpot v Ogilvy & Mather Ltd* [2000] 3 IR 206, HC.

An employee also has a statutory right of redress if he is *unfairly* dismissed. Formerly, in seeking redress he had to choose between an action at common law for wrongful dismissal or the statutory procedure under the Unfair Dismissals Act 1977 (UDA 1977, s 15). However, he now may pursue both the common law and statutory remedies at the same time, up until the point where a hearing in the courts under the common law has commenced, on the one hand, or a recommendation of a rights commissioner has issued (or a hearing of the Employment Appeals Tribunal has commenced) on the other hand (UDA 1977, s 15 as amended by Unfair Dismissals (Amendment) Act 1993, s 10).

The High Court has held that a statutory claim for unfair dismissal and the common law claim for wrongful dismissal are mutually exclusive: *Orr v Zomax Ltd* [2004] ITLR (21 June) HC and FL 8944. An employee who alleges unfair dismissal and institutes proceedings at common law is not entitled to argue that the principles applicable under the statutory scheme for unfair dismissal should be imported into the common law.

In a wrongful dismissal action, an employee will not be able to enforce a contract which contravenes the Income Tax Acts or Social Welfare Acts, whereas he may do so under an unfair dismissal action: Unfair Dismissals Act 1977, ss 8(11) and 8(12) inserted by the Unfair Dismissals Act 1993, s 7(d); *Hayden v Seán Quinn Properties Ltd* [1994] ELR 45. See *Meskell v CIE* [1973] IR 121; *Carvill v Irish Industrial Bank Ltd* [1968] IR 325; *Parsons v Iarnród Éireann* [1997] 2 IR 523, SC; *Dooley v Great Southern Hotels Ltd* [2001] ELR 340, HC; *Sheehy v Ryan and Moriarty* [2004] ELR 87, HC. See 'Wrongful Dismissal – A right to general damages?' by Tom Mallon BL and Patrick Millen BL in *Bar Review* (October/November 2002) 307. [Bibliography: Redmond (1).] See NATURAL JUSTICE; UNFAIR DISMISSAL.

wrongful interference with goods. See CONVERSION; DETINUE; TRESPASS TO GOODS.

www. See INTERNET.

X

xenophobia. See RACE.

x-ray. See IONISING RADIATION.

Y

yacht. See CHARGE ON SHIP; VALUE ADDED TAX.

year. When used without qualification, means a period of twelve months beginning on the 1st day of the month of January in any year: Interpretation Act 1937, s 12, Sch. The exchequer and local financial year is the calendar year: Exchequer and Local Financial Years Act 1974.

The *income tax* year previously commenced on the 6th day of April in one calendar year and ended on the 5th day of April in the following calendar year. From 2002 the income tax year commences on

1st January: Finance Act 2001, s 77. It is also referred to as the *year of assessment*. The *practice year* of a solicitor means any year ending on 31 December: Solicitors (Amendment) Act 1994, s 3(1)(b). The *licensing year* means a period of twelve months ending on the 30th day of September in any year: DCR 1997, Interpretation of Terms.

In employment, the *annual leave* (qv) year begins on 1 April. A year as regards the Unfair Dismissals Act 1977 means a calendar year (ie a year beginning on 1 January and ending on 31 December) or a period ending on the day before the date of the anniversary: *McGowan v McLaughlin* [2000] ELR 106, EAT. For fixed-term employees, a year means any period of 52 weeks: Protection of Employees (Fixed-Term Work) Act 2003, s 2(1). See SCHOOL YEAR.

year, executor's. See EXECUTOR'S YEAR.

year-and-a-day rule. The rule of law that an act or omission is conclusively presumed not to have caused a person's death if more than a year and a day elapsed between the act or omission and the death; this rule has been abolished: Criminal Justice Act 1999, s 38.

young offender. See REFORMATORY SCHOOLS.

young person. For the purposes of employment, a person who has reached the age of 16 years but has not reached the age of 18 years: Protection of Young Persons (Employment) Act 1996, s 1 as amended by Education (Welfare) Act 2000, s 31.

It is an offence for an employer to employ a young person: (a) without first requiring production of a birth certificate or other satisfactory evidence of age; or (b) without first obtaining written consent of the parent or guardian; or (c) to require or permit the young person to work: (i) for more than eight hours in any day or 40 hours in any week, or (ii) between 10pm and 6am; or (iii) between 11pm and 7am where the Minister is satisfied that exceptional circumstances exist (PYP(E)A 1996, s 6).

The employer must ensure that a young person receives: (a) a minimum rest period of 12 consecutive hours in each period of 24 hours, and (b) two days rest period in any seven days; this provision does not apply to the shipping or fishing sectors. A young person must also have a break of at least half an hour after a maximum of four

and a half hours' work. There are provisions to exclude the operation of the 1996 Act by regulations in the case of the employment of close relatives (PYP(E)A 1996, s 9). See also Organisation of Working Time Act 1997, s 36. A person under the age of 18 cannot be employed on or in an offshore installation: Safety, Health and Welfare (Offshore Installations) Act 1987, s 14.

The employer of young persons (16 and 17 year olds) employed to carry out general duties in a licensed premises must have regard to a specified *Code of Practice*: Protection of Young Persons (Employment in Licenced Premises) Regulations 2001, SI No 350 of 2001. There are also restrictions on the hours of work e g starting and finishing times. See CHILD, EMPLOYMENT OF; DOUBLE EMPLOYMENT; IDENTITY CARD.

young persons in employment register. The register required to be established and maintained by the National Educational Welfare Board: Education (Welfare) Act 2000, s 29. Any *young person* (or a child who will cease to be a child for the purposes of the Act) may apply to the board to be registered (E(W)A 2000, s 29(2)–(3)). *Young person* means a person who is of an age prescribed by the Minister but does not include a person who has reached the age of 18 years (E(W)A 2000, s 29(17)). The board is required to prepare a plan to assist such persons to avail of educational and training opportunities and to issue a certificate of registration (E(W)A 2000, s 29(5)–(6)).

An employer must not employ a young person on any work unless the young person is the holder of a valid certificate (E(W)A 2000, s 29(9)). An *educational welfare officer* has a variety of functions in relation to young persons in employment e g to enter premises where he has reasonable grounds for believing that a young person is employed in work (E(W)A 2000, s 30).

youth work. Means a planned programme of education designed for the purpose of aiding and enhancing the personal and social development of young persons through their voluntary participation, and which is: (a) complementary to their formal, academic or vocational education and training; and (b) provided primarily by vocational youth work organisations: Youth Work Act 2001, s 3. *Young person*, in this context, means a person who has not attained the age of 25 years (YWA 2001, s 2).

The Act provides a legal framework for the provision of youth work programmes and services by the Minister for Education and Science and the vocational education committees (VECs).

The Minister is responsible for the development and co-ordination of youth work programmes and services, research, and monitoring and assessment of programmes and services (YWA 2001, s 8). The VECs for their areas are responsible for: (a) ensuring the provision of youth work programmes or youth work services or both, by co-ordinating its plans, and by providing assistance to others, including financial assistance, and (b) the preparation and implementation of development plans (YWA 2001, s 9).

There is provision for the appointment by the Minister of an *assessor of youth work* (YWA 2001, s 16), the establishment of a *national youth work advisory committee* (YWA 2001, ss 17–18), a local *youth work committee* (YWA 2001, ss 19–20) and a local *voluntary youth council* (YWA 2001, ss 21–23) in each VEC area. The original youth work legislation, Youth Work Act 1997 is repealed (YWA 2001, s 7).

Z

zebra crossing. A portion of a roadway on which roadway markings have been provided and at which beacons have been provided: Road Traffic (Signs) Regulations 1962, SI No 171 of 1962, art 9. A driver approaching a zebra crossing must yield the right of way to a pedestrian on the crossing (SI No 171 of 1962, art 22(9)). See PEDESTRIAN.

zero hour contract. A contract of employment which requires the employee to make himself available to work in a week ie a certain number of hours, or as and when the employer requires, or a combination of both: Organisation of Working Time Act 1997, s 18. Where the employer fails to require the employee to work at least 25% of the time the employee is required to be available, the employee is entitled to payment for 25% of the contract hours or 15 hours whichever is less. See also National Minimum Wages

Act 2000, s 19 and Sch, Pt I, para 6. See *Ocean Manpower Ltd v MPGWU* [1998] ELR 299, LC.

zero interest. There is a prohibition on the advertising of credit as being without charge (eg zero interest) if the availability of the credit is dependent on certain conditions (eg insurance or maintenance) which could result in the consumer paying more than a cash customer: Consumer Credit Act 1995, s 25.

zillmerizing. The method of modifying the *net premium reserve method* of valuing a long-term insurance policy, by increasing the part of the future premiums for which credit is taken so as to allow for initial expenses: European Communities (Life Assurance) Regulations 1984, SI No 57 of 1984, arts 2(1) and 17(2)(e)(ii), as amended by Central Bank and Financial Services Authority of Ireland Act 2003, s 35, Sch 2.

zoning. The designation by a planning authority in its *development plan* of permitted uses of the land. A development plan is required to have objectives for the *zoning* of land for use solely or primarily of particular areas for particular purposes, whether residential, commercial, industrial, agricultural, recreational, as open space or otherwise, or a mixture of those uses: Planning and Development Act 2000, s 10(2)(a). There is no presumption in law that any land zoned in a particular development plan will remain so zoned in any subsequent development plan (PDA 2000, s 10(8)).

It is permissible for a planning authority to grant permission for the development of a hotel on land zoned for agriculture: *Schwestermann v An Bord Pleanála* [1995] 1 ILRM 269, HC. A planning authority is entitled to act upon legal advice it has received, when it takes a decision on a *rezoning* application: *Costigan v Laois County Council* [2000] ITLR (22 May) SC. See COMPENSATION AND PLANNING PERMISSION; DEVELOPMENT PLAN.

zoo. The Dublin Zoo is under the control and management of the Zoological Society of Ireland. Its objectives are the maintenance, exhibition, study for educational purposes, breeding and conservation of all species of living animals; the promotion of the study and knowledge of zoology, and the cultivation of an interest in the conservation of animals. The Commissioners of

Public Works have responsibility for advising the government in relation to Dublin Zoo. Regulations have been made relating to the keeping of wild animals in zoos, giving effect to Directive (EC) 1999/22: EC (Licensing and Inspection of Zoos) Regulations 2003, SI No 440 of 2003. See website: *www.dublinzoo.ie*.

zoonoses. A wide variety of diseases e g salmonellosis, listeriosis, tuberculosis, brucellosis: European Communities (Zoonoses) Regulations 1996, SI No 2 of 1996. The regulations provide for the taking of samples for bacteriological testing and for the slaughter of breeding domestic fowl confirmed as infected with salmonella. For monitoring of zoonoses and zoonotic agents, see SI No 154 of 2004 which implements Directive (EC) 2003/99 and revokes Part III of the 1996 regulations. The 2004 regulations also provides for the authorisation of officers to investigate food-borne outbreaks of illness and for the approval of laboratories to conduct tests.

Appendix 1

LAW REPORT ABBREVIATIONS

Law Reports

Note
Reference to Irish Labour Court and other employment determinations are listed at the end of this Appendix. See also ELR.

Abbreviation	Report	Period
AC	Appeal Cases	1891–present
A & E	Adolphus & Ellis	1834–1840
Aleyn	Aleyn	1646–1648
All ER	All England Law Reports	1936–present
Amb	Ambler	1737–1784
App Cas	Appeal Cases	1875–1890
Ball & B	Ball and Beatty, Chancery	1807–1814
B & Ad	Barnewall & Adolphus	1830–1834
B & Ald	Barnewall & Alderson	1817–1822
B & C	Barnewall & Cresswell	1822–1830
B & S	Best & Smith	1861–1870
Beav	Beaven	1838–1866
Bing	Bingham	1822–1834
Bli (ns)	Bligh, New Series	1826–1837
Burr	Burrow	1756–1772
Casey	Judgments of the Court of Criminal Appeal–Ireland (See Frewen for 1924–1983)	1984–1989
Camp	Campbell	1807–1816
CB (NS)	Common Bench, New Series	1856–1865
CC	Circuit Court–Ireland unreported	-
CCA	Court of Criminal Appeal Ireland–unreported	-
Ch D	Chancery Division	1875–1890
Ch	Chancery (UK)	1891–present
Cl & Fin	Clark & Finnelly	1831–1846
Co Rep	Coke	1572–1616
Cox	Cox's Equity	1783–1796
Cox CC	Cox's Criminal Cases	1843–1941
C & P	Carrington & Payne	1823–1841
CMLR	Common Market Law Reports	1962–present

CPD	Common Pleas Division	1875–1880
Cr App R	Criminal Appeal Reports	1908–present
Curt	Curteis	1834–1844
D & R	Dowling & Ryland	1821–1827
DC	District Court–Ireland unreported	-
Dow & Cl	Dow & Clark's Appeals	1827–1832
Dyer	Dyer	1513–1582
E & B	Ellis & Blackburn	1851–1858
ECR	European Court Reports	1954–present
EEC OJ	EEC Official Journal	1952–present
EHRR	European Court of Human Rights	1979–present
ELR	Employment Law Reports – Ireland	1990–present
ER	English Reports	1220–1865
Ex	Exchequer Reports	1847–1856
Ex	Exchequer Cases	1865–1875
Exch	Exchequer Reports	1847–1856
Ex D	Exchequer Division	1875–1880
F & F	Foster & Finlayson	1856–1867
Fed Cas	Federal Cases (USA)	1789–1880
Frewen	Judgments of the Court of Criminal Appeal–Ireland (Casey)	1924–1983 1984–1989
FSR	Fleet Street Reports	1963–present
Gl and J	Glyn and Jameson	1819–1828
Hag	Haggard	1789–1838
Hare	Hare	1841–1853
H & C	Hurlstone & Coltman	1862–1866
HC	High Court–Ireland unreported	
HL	House of Lords Appeals	1866–1875
HL Cass	House of Lords Cases or HLC	1847–1866
IBL	Irish Business Law	1998–
ICJ	International Court of Justice	-
ICLJ	Irish Criminal Law Journal	1991–present
ICLR	Irish Common Law Reports	1849–1866
I Eq R	Irish Equity Reports or Ir Eq	1838–1850
IJEL	Irish Journal of European Law	1992–present
ILRM	Irish Law Reports Monthly Index 1976–90 (1992)	1976–present

ILSI	Incorporated Law Society of	1971–present
Or ILSI Gazette	Ireland Gazette	
ILTR	Irish Law Times Reports	1867–1980
ILT & SJ	Irish Law Times and	1980–present
	Solicitor's Journal	
ILT Dig	Irish Law Times Digest	1980–present
	(incorporated in ILT & SJ)	
IR	Irish Reports	1838–present
Ir Ch R	Irish Chancery Reports	1850–1856
IR CL	Irish Reports Common Law	1867–1877
IR Eq R	Irish Reports, Equity	1866–1878
Irish Digests	Maxwell	1894–1918
	Ryland	1919–1928
	Ryland	1929–1938
	Harrison	1939–1948
	Harrison	1949–1958
	Ryan	1959–1970
	De Blaghd	1971–1983
	–	1984–1988
Ir Jur Rep	Irish Jurist Reports	1935–1965
	(New Series)	1966–1985
IRLR	Industrial Relations Law	1972–present
	Reports (UK)	
ISLR	Irish Student Law Review	1991–present
ITLR	Irish Times Law Reports	1989–2001
		2003–present
JP	Justice of the Peace & Local	1837–present
	Government Review	
Jur	Jurist Reports	1837–1854
KB (or QB)	King's or Queen's Bench	1841–present
Ld Ray	Raymond	1694–1732
Leach	Leach	1730–1815
LJ Ch	Law Journal Chancery	1831–1949
LJ KB(QB)	Law Journal Reports	1831–1949
	King's (Queen's)	
LJ CP	Law Journal Reports,	1822–1880
	Common Pleas	
LRC	Law Reform Commission Reports	1981–present
LR CP	Law Reports, Common Pleas	1865–1875
LR Ex	Law Reports, Exchequer Cases	1865–1875
LR Eq	Law Reports, Equity Cases	1865–1875
LR HL	Law Reports, House of Lords	1865–1875
LR (Ir)	Law Reports (Ireland)	1878–1893

or Lr Ir

LR P & D	Law Reports, Probate & Divorce	1865–1875
LR QB	Law Reports, Queen's Bench	1865–1875
LT	Law Times Reports	1859–1947
Mac & G	Macnaghten & Gorden	1849–1851
Madd	Maddock	1815–1822
Mer	Merivale	1815–1817
MLR	Modern Law Review	1937–present
M & W	Meeson & Welsby	1836–1847
NE	North Eastern Reporter (USA)	-
NI	Northern Ireland Law Reports	1925–present
NI JR	New Irish Jurist	1900–1905
NLJ	New Law Journal	1965–present
NSWSR	New South Wales Law Reports	1901–present
OJ	Official Journal of the European Communities	1952–present
P	Law Journal Reports (Probate)	1831–1949
PD	Probate Division	1875–1890
Peake	Peake	1790–1794
Prec Ch	Precedents in Chancery	1689–1722
P Wms	Peere Williams	1695–1735
QBD	Queen's Bench Division	1875–1890
QB	Queen's Bench	1841–present
RPC	Reports on Patent Cases	1884–present
RR	Russell & Ryan	1799–1824
RTR	Road Traffic Reports	1970–present
Russ	Russell	1823–1829
SC	Supreme Court–Ireland unreported	-
SCC	Special Criminal Court Ireland–unreported	-
Sel Cas Ch	Select Cases in Chancery	1724–1733
S & L	Schoales & Lefroy (Ir)	1802–1806
SLT	Scots Law Times	1893–present
Sm & Bat	Smith & Batty (Ir)	1824–1825
Stark	Starkie	1814–1823
Supp OJ	Supplement to the Official Journal of Industrial and Commercial Property (Irish)	1928–present
Taunt	Taunton	1807–1819
TR	Taxation Reports	1939–present
TR	Term Reports	1785–1800
TLR	Times Law Reports	1884–1952

USPQ	U S	Patents Quarterly
Ves	Vesey	1789–1817
W Bl	Blackstone	1746–1780
Willes	Willes	1737–1760
WLR	Weekly Law Reports	1953–present
WR	Weekly Reporter	1853–1906

Irish Labour Court and
other employment
determinations:

(See also ELR)

DEE	Labour Court determination under the Employment Equality Act 1977
DEP	Labour Court determination under the Anti-Discrimination (Pay) Act 1974
EE or EP or EO	Equality Officer determination
M	Employment Appeals Tribunal determination under the Minimum Notice & Terms of Employment Act 1973
P	Employment Appeals Tribunal determination under the Maternity Protection of Employment Act 1981
UD	Employment Appeals Tribunal determination under the Unfair Dismissals Act 1977

Appendix 2

LISTING OF LAW REFORM COMMISSION'S REPORTS

LAW REFORM COMMISSION'S REPORTS
The following are the publications of the Law Reform Commission in the period to 1 September 2004 listed by subject area.

LRC	Report of the Commission
WP	Working Paper
C	Consultation Paper
LRC-CP	Consultation Paper

Conflict of laws

Domicile and Habitual Residence as connecting factors in the Conflict of Laws	– Working Paper – Report	WP 10, 1981 LRC 7, 1983
Private International Law aspects of Capacity to Marry and choice of law in proceedings for Nullity of Marriage		LRC 19, 1985

Contract

Minors' Contracts		LRC 15, 1985
United Nations (Vienna) Convention on Contracts for the International Sale of Goods 1980		LRC 42, 1992
Research Paper on Retention of Title (Barbara Maguire)		1989
Claims in Contract and Tort in respect of Latent Damage (other than personal injury)–Report on Statutes of Limitation		LRC 64, 2001

Crime

Child Sexual Abuse	– Consultation Paper – Report	LRC CP2, 1989 LRC 32, 1990
Confiscation of the Proceeds of Crime		LRC 35, 1991
The Law relating to Dishonesty		LRC 43, 1992
Corporate Killing	– Consultation Paper	LRC CP 26, 2003
Crime of Libel	– Consultation Paper – Report	LRC CP5, 1991 LRC 41, 1991
Cultural Objects – Unidroit Convention on Stolen or Illegally Exported Objects		LRC 55, 1997
DNA Database, Establishment of	– Consultation Paper	LRC CP 29, 2004
Homicide: The Mental Element in Murder (main proposal is to widen the definition of the mental element in murder to include reckless indifference to the value of human life).	– Consultation Paper	LRC CP17, 2001

Cohabitees, Rights and Duties of	– Consultation Paper	LRC CP 32, 2004
Criminal Conversation and the Enticement and Harbouring of a Spouse		WP 5, 1978
Divorce a Mensa et Thoro and related matters		LRC 8, 1983
Family Courts		LRC 52, 1996
First Report on Family Law – criminal conversation – enticement of spouse or child – loss of consortium – personal injury to a child – seduction of a child – matrimonial property – breach of promise of marriage		LRC 1, 1980
Illegitimacy		LRC 4, 1982
Jurisdiction in Proceedings for Nullity of Marriage, Recognition of Foreign Nullity Decrees, and the Hague Convention on the Celebration and Recognition of the Validity of Marriages		LRC 20, 1985
Loss of Consortium and Loss of Services of a Child		WP 7, 1979
Nullity of Marriage		LRC 9, 1984
Recognition of Foreign Adoption Decrees		LRC 29, 1989
Recognition of Foreign Divorces and Legal Separations	– Working Paper	WP 11, 1984
	– Report	LRC 10, 1985
Restitution of Conjugal Rights, Jactitation of Marriage and related matters		LRC 6, 1983
Seduction and Enticement and Harbouring of a Child		WP 6, 1979

General

Annual Reports of Commission		1977 to date
Law and the Elderly	– Consultation Paper	LRC CP 23, 2003
Second Programme for examination of certain branches of the law with a view to their reform: 2000–2007 (Includes – tribunal of inquiry, homicide, including corporate homicide, penalties for minor offences, compensation for personal injuries, trusts including charities, succession and the protection of the elderly).	Twenty-second Annual Report 2000	December 2001
Statutory Drafting and Interpretation: Plain Language and the Law	– Consultation Paper	LRC-CP14, 1999
	– Report	LRC 61, 2000
Twenty-fourth Annual Report 2002		2003

Land

Defective Premises		LRC 3, 1982
Gazumping		LRC 59, 1999
Interest of Vendor and Purchaser in Land during the period between Contract and Completion		LRC 49, 1995
Land Law and Conveyancing Law		
(1) General Proposals		LRC 30, 1989
(2) Enduring Powers of Attorney		LRC 31, 1989
(3) Passing of Risk from Vendor to Purchaser		LRC 39, 1991
(4) Service of Completion Notices		LRC 40, 1991
(5) Further General Proposals		LRC 44, 1992
(6) Further General Proposals including the execution of deeds		LRC 56, 1998
(8) Business Tenancies		LRC CP21, 2003
Judgment Mortgages	– Consultation Paper	LRC CP 30, 2004
Liability of Builders, Vendors and Lessors for the Quality and Fitness of Premises		WP 1, 1977
The Rule against Perpetuities and Cognate Rules (abolition of the rule which can block family gifts and legitimate commercial transactions).		LRC 62, 2000
Report on the Acquisition of Easements and Profits A Prendre by Prescription.		LRC 66, 2002
Report on Title by Adverse Possession of Land		LRC 67, 2002
General Law of Landlord and Tenant	– Consultation Paper	LRC CP 28, 2003

Personal injuries

Periodic Payments and Structured Settlements		LRC 54, 1996

Practice and procedure

Aggravated, Exemplary and Restitutionary Damages (Control of Excessive Damage Awards)	– Consultation Paper	LRC CP12, 1998
	– Report	LRC 60, 2000
Bail – Examination of Law		LRC 50, 1995
Contempt of Court	– Consultation Paper	LRC CP4, 1991
	– Report	LRC 47, 1994
Court Poor Box	– Consultation Paper	LRC CP 31, 2004
Class Actions – Consultation Paper on Multi-Party Litigation		LRC CP 25, 2003
The Deductibility of Collateral Benefits from Awards of Damages: Civil Liability (Amendment) Act 1964, s 2		LRC CP15, 1999

Debt Collection

    (1) The Law Relating to Sheriffs   LRC 27, 1988

    (2) Retention of Title   LRC 28, 1989

Family Courts	– Consultation Paper	LRC CP8, 1994
	– Report	LRC 52, 1996
Fiscal Prosecutor and a Revenue Court	– Consultation Paper	LRC CP 24, 2003
Foreign Public Documents – Abolishing the Requirement of Legislation for (Hague Convention)		LRC 48, 1995
Indexation of Fines		LRC 37, 1991
Indexation of Fines – A Review of Developments		LRC 65, 2002
Judgment Mortgages	– Consultation Paper	LRC CP 30, 2004
Judicial Review of Administrative Action: The Problem of Remedies		WP 8, 1979
Judicial Review Procedure	– Consultation Paper	LRC CP 20, 2003
Judicial Review Procedure	– Report	LRC 71, 2004
Prosecution Appeals in Cases brought on Indictment	– Consultation Paper	LRC CP 19, 2002
Prosecution Appeals from Unduly Lenient Sentences in the District Court	– Consultation Paper	LRC CP 33, 2004
Public Inquiries including Tribunals of Inquiry		LRC CP 22, 2003
Sentencing		LRC CP6, 1993
		LRC 53, 1996
Service of Documents Abroad re Civil Proceedings (the Hague Convention)		LRC 22, 1987
Statute of Limitations:		
– Claims in respect of Latent Personal Injuries		LRC 21, 1987
– Claims in Contract and Tort in respect of Latent Damages (other than Personal Injuries)	– Consultation Paper	LRC CP13, 1998
	– Report	LRC 64, 2001

Succession

Hague Convention on Succession to the Estates of Deceased Persons		LRC 36, 1991

Tort

Civil Law of Defamation	– Consultation Paper	LRC CP3, 1991
	– Report	LRC 38, 1991
Civil Liability for Animals	– Working Paper	WP 3, 1977
	– Report	LRC 2, 1982

Claims in Contract and Tort in respect of Latent Damage (other than personal injury) – Report on the Statutes of Limitation		LRC 64, 2001
Liability in Tort of Mentally Disabled Persons		LRC 18, 1985
Liability in Tort of Minors and the Liability of Parents for Damage caused by Minors		LRC 17, 1985
Occupier's Liability	– Consultation Paper	LRC CP 7, 1993
	– Report	LRC 46, 1994
Privacy: Surveillance and the Interception of Communications	– Consultation Paper	LRC CP10, 1996
	– Report	LRC 57, 1998

Trusts

Variation of Trusts (Practical Problems where Trustees' Powers are Outdated, Overly Restricted or Inadequate)		LRC 63, 2000

Law under Review by the Law Reform Commission on 1 September 2004

- Class actions
- Cohabitee, rights and duties
- Corporate homicide
- Court poor box
- Criminal law and procedure
- DNA databank, establishment of a
- e-Conveyancing
- Elderly, law and the elderly
- Judicial Review
- Landlord and Tenant law
- Lenient Sentences in the District Court, appeal by the DPP
- Prosecution appeals
- Public Inquiries
- Revenue court and Fiscal prosecutor.

Appendix 3

AMENDMENTS TO THE CONSTITUTION OF IRELAND 1937 (INCLUDING DEFEATED AMENDMENTS)

Number	Subject	Objective and Reference in Dictionary	Year*
1st	Time of War	Art 51 empowered the Oireachtas to amend the Constitution, without a referendum, for a limited period. During that period, the 1st Amendment (1939) defined 'time of war' (Art 28.3.3) and the 2nd Amendment (1941) contained a large number of minor amendments, including a wider definition of 'time of war'.	1939
2nd	General	See CONSTITUTION OF IRELAND; NATIONAL EMERGENCY.	1941
(3rd)	Proportional Representation	To substitute for proportional representation, the 'straight vote' system in single-member constituencies. See PROPORTIONAL REPRESENTATION.	1959 (defeated)
(3rd)	Dáil Constituencies	To provide that in forming Dáil constituencies, the population per deputy in any case may not be greater or less than the national average by more than one sixth. See CONSTITUENCY.	1968 (defeated)
(4th)	Proportional Representation	To substitute for proportional representation, the 'straight vote' system in single-member constituencies. See PROPORTIONAL REPRESENTATION.	1968 (defeated)
3rd	Treaty of Rome	To enable the State to ratify the Treaty of Rome 1957 and other treaties of the European Community. See EUROPEAN COMMUNITY.	1972
4th	Voting Age	To lower the voting age from 21 to 18; amendment to art 16. See FRANCHISE.	1972
5th	Catholic Church	To remove from the Constitution the special recognition give to the Holy Catholic Apostolic Church as guardian of the Faith professed by the great majority of the citizens. See RELIGIOUS FREEDOM.	1972
6th	Adoption	To remove any doubt about the legality of adoptions made by a person or body, not a judge or court appointed or established under the Constitution. Art.37(2) inserted. See ADOPTION.	1979
7th	Seanad Representation	To permit Seanad representation to be given to new universities or other institutes of higher education. See SEANAD ÉIREANN.	1979
8th	Right to Life	To give constitutional recognition to the right to life of the unborn. See UNBORN, RIGHT TO LIFE OF THE.	1983

9th	Right to Vote	To enable the State to extend the right to vote in Dáil elections to non-nationals. See FRANCHISE.	1984
(10th)	Divorce	To remove the constitutional prohibition on divorce.	1986 (defeated)
10th	Single European Act	To enable the State to ratify the Single European Act which amended the Treaty of Rome. See SINGLE EUROPEAN ACT.	1987
11th	Maastricht Treaty	To enable the State to ratify the Treaty on European Union, signed at Maastricht, which amended the Treaty of Rome. See MAASTRICHT TREATY.	1992
	and		
	Community Patent Agreement	To enable the State to ratify the Agreement relating to Community Patents. See COMMUNITY PATENT AGREEMENT.	
(12th)	Abortion	To provide a constitutional exception to allow abortion in limited circumstances. See ABORTION.	1992 (defeated)
13th	Right to Travel	To provide that the right to life of the unborn would not limit freedom to travel between the State and another state. See TRAVEL, RIGHT TO.	1992
14th	Right to Information	To provide that the right to life of the unborn would not limit freedom to obtain information on services lawfully available in another state. See ABORTION.	1992
15th	Divorce	To enable courts designated by law to grant a dissolution of marriage under specified conditions. See DIVORCE.	1995
16th	Bail	To enable that provision be made by law for the refusal of bail to a person charged with a serious offence where considered necessary to prevent the commission of a serious offence by that person. See BAIL.	1996
17th	Cabinet Confidentiality	To provide for the confidentiality of discussions at meetings of the government, except where the High Court determines otherwise. See CABINET CONFIDENTIALITY.	1997
18th	Amsterdam Treaty	To enable the State to ratify the Amsterdam Treaty, which amended the Treaty of Rome. See AMSTERDAM TREATY.	1998
19th	British-Irish Agreement	To enable the State to be bound by the British-Irish Agreement; to enable the institutions established under that Agreement to exercise powers; to enable the State to exercise extra-territorial jurisdiction; and to amend Arts 2 and 3 in relation to the constitutional claim to Northern Ireland. See GOOD FRIDAY AGREEMENT.	1998

20th	Local Government	To give constitutional recognition to the role of local government in providing a forum for the democratic representation of local communities. See LOCAL GOVERNMENT.	1999
21st	Death Penalty	To provide a Constitutional ban on the death penalty. See DEATH PENALTY.	2001
23rd	International Criminal Court	To enable the State to ratify the Statute of the International Criminal Court done at Rome on the 17 July 1998 and signed by Ireland on 7 October 1998, subject to ratification. See INTERNATIONAL CRIMINAL COURT.	2001
(24th)	Treaty of Nice	To enable the State to ratify the Nice Treaty and to exercise the options or discretions provided by the Treaty should it so decide. See NICE TREATY.	2001 (defeated)
(25th)	Abortion	To provide that the life of the unborn in the womb be protected in accordance with a proposed statute See ABORTION	2002 (defeated)
26th	Treaty of Nice	To enable the State to ratify the Nice Treaty and to exercise the options or discretions provided by the Treaty, subject to Oireachtas approval, and to provide a constitutional ban on Ireland joining an EU common defence. See COMMON DEFENCE; NICE TREATY.	2002
27th	Citizenship	To restrict the right to Irish citizenship, unless otherwise provided for by law, to persons born in the island of Ireland with at least one parent who is an Irish citizen or entitled to be an Irish citizen. See CITIZENSHIP.	2004

* year of referendum

Note

(a) There is no 12th amendment to the Constitution. The 12th proposed amendment was defeated in 1992 while, on the same day, the 13th and 14th amendments were approved. There was no attempt to fill the 12th vacant number as happened in the case of the defeated 3rd proposed amendment in 1959 and again in 1968 and the defeated 4th proposed amendment in 1968, these numbers re-appearing in 1972 in approved amendments to the Constitution.

(b) There is no 22nd amendment to the Constitution. In 2001 a Bill was withdrawn, which would have provided for the 22nd amendment to the Constitution to provide for the establishment by law of a body to investigate whether a judge engaged in conduct constituting misbehaviour or was affected by incapacity: Twenty–second Amendment to the Constitution Bill 2001. There is no 24th or 25th amendment to the Constitution as the proposed amendments were defeated.

Appendix 4

THE IRISH JUSTICE SYSTEM (AS AT 1 SEPTEMBER 2004)

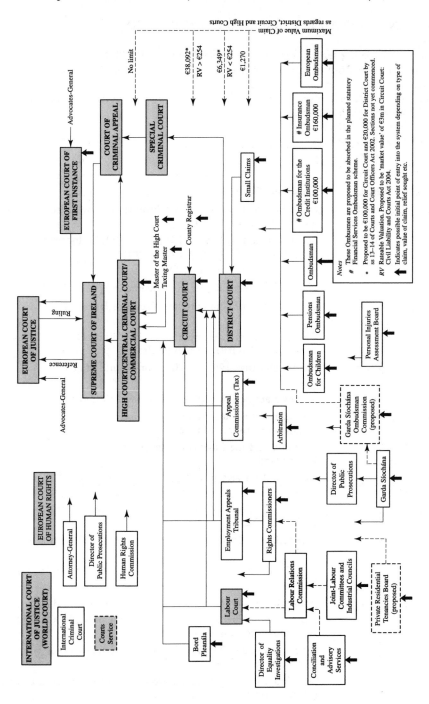

Appendix 5

BIBLIOGRAPHY

BOOKS ON IRISH LAW REFERRED TO IN DICTIONARY

Notes
* * Regular updating service; may also be available on CD-ROM and the Internet.
* \+ Not a legal text but of historical interest or helpful in understanding the law
* F Forthcoming publication

The year in brackets is the year of publication, followed by the publisher in most instances. Relevant website addresses are:

* www.butterworths.ie
* www.lexisnexis.ie
* www.roundhall.ie
* www.taxireland.ie

Author or Editor	Title and Edition
A and L Goodbody	(1) A Practical Guide to Data Protection Law in Ireland (2003) – Thomson Round Hall
	(2) Irish Planning Law and Practice (1990) – looseleaf – Supplement 2001 (2001) – LexisNexis
AIB	A Guide to Franchising (2000)⁺
Amory Solicitors	Divorce: A practical guide to Divorce in Ireland (1997)
Appleby T and O'Hanlon F	The Taxation of Capital Gains (2003) – Irish Taxation Institute*
Arnold L J	The Restoration Land Settlement in County Dublin (1660 – 1688) (1993) – Irish Academic Press
Ashe M and Murphy Y	Insider Dealing (1992) – Thomson Round Hall
Ashe M and Reid P	Money Laundering (2000) – Thomson Round Hall
Babington A B	The Jurisdiction and Practice of County Courts in Ireland On Equity and Probate Matters (1916)
Bacik I, Kingston J, and Whelan A	Abortion and the Law: An Irish Perspective (1997) – Thomson Round Hall
Bacik I and O'Connell M	Crime and Poverty in Ireland (1998) – Thomson Round Hall
Bacik I and Livingstone	Towards a culture of Human Rights in Ireland (2001) – Cork University Press
Ball F E	The Judges in Ireland 1221 – 1921 (1993) – Thomson Round Hall
Barnes J	Irish Industrial Schools 1868–1908 (1989)⁺ – Irish Academic Press
Barrett G	Redundancy Law and Practice (2000) – LexisNexis
Barron J	Practice and Procedure in the Master's Court (2000 – 2nd edn) – Thomson Round Hall
Barry J et al	What is the Law? Termination and Redundancy (2002) – Thomson Round Hall
Bell L	(1) Modern Law of Personal Property in England and Ireland (1991) – Butterworths (LexisNexis)
	(2) Equity and Trusts (2004) – Thomson Round Hall

Berger V	The Case Law of the European Court of Human Rights: A Practical Guide – Thomson Round Hall
	Vol 1 1960–87 (1989)
	Vol 2 1988–90 (1992)
	Vol 3 1991–93 (1995)
Beytagh F X	Constitutionalism in Contemporary Ireland: An American Perspective (1996) – Thomson Round Hall
Binchy W	(1) Irish Conflict of Laws (1988); (2005– 2nd edn)[F] – LexisNexis
	(2) A Casebook of Irish Family Law (1984) – Professional Books
	(3) Travellers – equality and the Constitution (1997) – Trinity College Dublin
Binchy W and Byrne R	Annual Review of Irish Law (annual volume for each year from 1987 to 2002) – edn 2002 – (2003)[F] – Thomson Round Hall
Binchy W and Sarkin J	Human Rights, the Citizen and the State: South African and Irish Approaches (2001) – Thomson Round Hall
Bird T	Consumer Credit Law (1998) – Thomson Round Hall
de Blacam M	(1) The Control of Private Rented Dwellings (1992) Thomson Round Hall
	(2) Drunken Driving and the Law (3rd edn, 2003) Thomson Round Hall
	(3) Judicial Review (2001) Butterworths (LexisNexis)
Bland P	(1) The Law of Easements and Profit A Prendre (1997) – Thomson Round Hall
	(2) Conveyancing and Property Law Journal (4 issues annually) – Thomson Round Hall (Sweet and Maxwell)
Bohan B and McCarthy F	Bohan: Capital Acquisitions Tax (2002 – 2nd edn)
Boland T	Capital Taxes Acts 1995 – 96
Bolger M and Kimber C	Sex Discrimination Law (2000) – Thomson Round Hall
Boyle D	Irish Law Times (20 issues annually) – Thomson Round Hall
Bradley C	Judicial Review (1999) – Thomson Round Hall
Bradley J	PRSI and Levy Contributions (2001) – Irish Taxation Institute *
Bradley J et al	Finax 2001 (reference guide to Finance Act 2001 and Finance (No 2) Act 2000 (2001) – Irish Taxation Institute.* For Finax 2003, see Irish Taxation Institute
Brady J C	Succession Law in Ireland (1995 – 2nd edn) – LexisNexis
Brady J C and Kerr T	The Limitation of Actions in the Republic of Ireland (1994) – Law Society of Ireland
Breen, Casey and Kerr	Liber Memorialis: Professor James C Brady (2001) – Thomson Round Hall
Brennan E	Bar Review – 6 issues per annum – Thomson Round Hall
Brennan F	A Company purchasing its own Shares (1992)
Brennan F and Howley S	(1) Tax Acts Commentary 1999 – 2000 (1999) – Butterworths (LexisNexis)

	(2) Tax Acts Commentary 2000 – 2001 (2000) – Butterworths (LexisNexis)
	(3) Tax Acts Commentary 2001–2002 (2001) – Butterworths (LexisNexis)
Brennan F, Moore P, O'Sullivan H and Clarke A	Corporation Tax (2003) – Irish Taxation Institute *
Brennan N and Hennessy J	Forensic Accounting (2001) – Thomson Round Hall
Brennan O	Laying down the Law (1991) – Oak Tree Press
Brennan P	Tax Acts 2001–02 (2001) – Butterworths (LexisNexis)
Breslin J	Banking Law (2004 – 2nd edn) – Thomson Round Hall
Bristow J	Taxation in Ireland – An Economist's Perspective (2004)+ – Institute of Public Administration
Browne D	Separation and Divorce Matters for Women (1989) – Attic Press Dublin
Brown J	Competition Law and Regulation in Ireland: the New Business Requirements (1992) – Competition Press
Buckley J F (was Laffoy and Wheeler)	Irish Conveyancing Precedents (1991) – LexisNexis
Buckley M	Capital Tax Acts 2001–02 (2001) – Butterworths (LexisNexis)
Buckley Melody	Civil Procedure and Practice: An Introduction (2004) – Thomson Round Hall
Buggy B and Finucane K	Irish Pension Law and Practice (1996) – Oak Tree Press
Burke P and Corbett V	The Law of Torts (2003) – Thomson Round Hall
Burke J, O'Driscoll T and Giblin B H	Case Law (2003) – Irish Taxation Institute*
Butler B	VAT Acts 2001–02 (2001) – Butterworths (LexisNexis)
Butler J, Glynn D and Judge N E	Finax 1996 – Commentary on the Finance Act 1996
Butler P	Keane on Local Government (2003 – 2nd edn) – First Law and Law Society of Ireland
Butterworths (now LexisNexis)	(1) Guide to the European Communities (1989)
	(2) Researching the Legal Web (1999)
	(3) Irish Tax Library on CD-ROM (2001)
	(4) Irish Reports 1838 – 1998
	(5) The Irish Digests 1894 – 1999
	(6) Irish Tax Reports 1922–2000 (2001)
	(7) Irish Property Law Direct – new electronic service (2000) – CD
	(8) Tax Guide 2001–02 (2001)
	(9) Irish Planning Law Direct (2003) – online
	(10) Irish Annotated Statutes (2002)

	(11) Irish Annotated Statutes: The Planning and Development Acts Set 1963 to 2000 (2002)
Buttimore J	(1) Holiday Law in Ireland (1999) – Blackhall
	(2) Security for Costs (1999) – Blackhall
Byrne G	Transfer of Undertakings: employment aspects of business transfers in Irish and European law (1999) – Blackhall
Byrne P	The EEC Convention on Jurisdiction and the Enforcement of Judgments (1990) – Thomson Round Hall
Byrne R	(1) Irish Commercial Law (1988 – 2nd Edition) – Thomson Round Hall
	(2) Safety, Health and Welfare at Work Law in Ireland: A Guide (1995 – 3 rd edn) – Nifast Publications
	(3) Irish Law Times (20 issues annually), edited in 2004 by David Boyle – Thomson Round Hall
Byrne R and Binchy W	Annual Review of Irish Law – annual volume for each year from 1987 to 2002 – latest edition 2002 (2003) – Thomson Round Hall
Byrne R and McCutcheon P	The Irish Legal System (4th edn – 2001) – Butterworths (LexisNexis)
Cahill D	Corporate Finance Law (1999) – Thomson Round Hall
Cahill E	(1) Discovery and Disclosure in Ireland (2002)
	(2) Practice and Procedure (4 issues annually)
Cahill N	Enforcement of Company Law (2004) – LexisNexis
Callanan M	Local Government Act 2001 (2002) – Thomson Round Hall
Campbell C	Emergency Law in Ireland 1918 – 1925 (1994) – Clarendon Press (Oxford University Press)
Cannon R	Land Law (2001) – Thomson Round Hall Nutshells
Cannon R and Neligan N	Evidence Law (2002) – Thomson Round Hall
Canny J	(1) The Law of Road Transport and Haulage (1999) – Thomson Round Hall
	(2) The Law of Local Government (2000) – Thomson Round Hall
	(3) Construction and Building Law (2001) – Thomson Round Hall
	(4) What is the law? Buying and Selling a House (2002) – Thomson Round Hall
	(5) Sentencing Penalties (2003) – Thomson Round Hall
Carroll P	The Garda Siochana Guide (1991) – Law Society of Ireland
Casey E	Judgments of the Court of Criminal Appeal 1984 – 1989 (1991) – Incorporated Council of Law Reporting in Ireland
Casey J	(1) Constitutional Law in Ireland (2000 – 3rd edn) – Thomson Round Hall
	(2) The Irish Law Officers (Roles and Responsibilities of the Attorney General and Director of Public Prosecutions) (1996) – Thomson Round Hall – Sweet and Maxwell
Cassells F, Clayton C, and Moore P	Self Assessment (1988)

Cassidy B and Somers J	Law of Value Added Tax (2003) – Irish Taxation Institute
Cassidy C	(1) The Licensing Acts 1833–1995 (1996) – Thomson Round Hall
	(2) The Licensing Handbook (2002) – Thomson Round Hall
	(3) Cassidy on the Licensing Acts (2002 – 2nd edn), updated annually – Thomson Round Hall
Cazabon A O'R	Irish Insurance Law (1999) – Thomson Round Hall
Central Bank of Ireland	Exchange Control Manual (1979)*
Charleton P	(1) Controlled Drugs and the Criminal Law (1986) – An Clo Liuir
	(2) Offences against the Person (1992) – Thomson Round Hall
	(3) Criminal Law – Cases and Materials (1992) – for update see (4)
	(4) Criminal Law (1999) – with McDermott P A and Bolger M – LexisNexis
	(5) The Irish Law of Evidence (2005)^F – with McDermott P A – LexisNexis
Clark R	(1) Contract Law in Ireland (1998 – 4th edn); (2004 – 5th edn) – Thomson Round Hall
	(2) Data Protection Law in Ireland (1990) – Thomson Round Hall
	(3) Annotated Guide to Social Welfare Law (1995) – Thomson Round Hall (Sweet and Maxwell – London)
	(4) Irish Current Law Statutes Annotated (1984 –)* – Thomson Round Hall
	(5) Irish Copyright and Design Law (looseleaf – 2001) – Butterworths (LexisNexis)
Clark R and McMahon J	Contemporary Issues in Law and Politics (1998) – Thomson Round Hall
Clark R and Smyth S	(1) Intellectual Property Law in Ireland (1997) – LexisNexis
	(2) Intellectual Property Law in Ireland (2004 – 2nd edn) – LexisNexis
Clarke B	(1) Takeovers and Mergers Law in Ireland (1999) – Thomson Round Hall
	(2) Irish Investment and Listing Regulation (1998 –)* – Thomson Round Hall
Coggans S and Jackson N	The Family Law (Divorce) Act 1996 (1998) – Thomson Round Hall
Cole J S R	Irish Cases on Evidence (1982) – Law Society of Ireland
Collins A M and O'Reilly J	(1) Civil Proceedings and the State in Ireland: A Practitioner's Guide (1990) – (2nd edn – 2003) – Thomson Round Hall
	(2) Irish Journal of European Law (1 or 2 issues annually – 1992) – Irish Society for European Law
Collins N	Local Government Managers at Work (1987)$^+$ – Institute of Public Administration

Comerford H	(1) Wildlife Legislation 1976 – 2000 (2001) – Thomson Round Hall
	(2) Inland Fisheries Legislation (2004) – Thomson Round Hall
Comerford H and Fogarty A	Environmental Law, A Glossary and Handbook (2000) – Thomson Round Hall
Competition Authority	A Guide to Irish Legislation on Competition (1992)
Comyn Sir J	(1) Summing it up – Memoirs of an Irishman at Law in England (1991)[+] – Thomson Round Hall
	(2) Watching Brief – Further memoirs of an Irishman at Law in England (1993)[+] – Thomson Round Hall
	(3) Leave to Appeal (1994)[+] – Thomson Round Hall
	(4) If Your Lordship Pleases (1996)[+] – Thomson Round Hall
Condon J and Muddiman J	Capital Acquisition Tax (2003) – Irish Taxation Institute [*]
Conlan P	EC Labour Legislation in Ireland (1997) – Gill and Macmillan
Connolly A	Gender and the Law in Ireland (1993) – Oak Tree Press
Connolly M	(1) Capital Tax Acts 2000 – 2001 (2000)
	(2) Stamp Duties Consolidation Act 1999 (2000) – Butterworths (LexisNexis)
Connolly M, Bradley M and Purcell B	Capital Allowances (2003) – Irish Taxation Institute [*]
Conway H	Co-ownership of Land (2000) – Butterworths (LexisNexis)
Cooney T, Martyn J and Reck P	Taxation Summary (2003) – Irish Taxation Institute [*]
Cooney T and O'Neill	Psychiatric Detention – Civil Commitment in Ireland (1996)
Corbet R and Hederman W	Telecommunications Law in Ireland (1999) – Mason Hayes and Curran
Corbett V	Tort Nutcases (2004) – Thomson Round Hall
Cordial M	Consolidated Circuit Court Rules (2001 – updated annually) – Thomson Round Hall
Corrigan A and Williams A	Trust and Succession Law (2003) – Irish Taxation Institute[*]
Corrigan K	Revenue Law (2000) – Thomson Round Hall
Corrigan M and Campbell J A	A Casebook of Irish Insurance Law (1993) – Oak Tree Press
Costello J	(1) Older People: law and finance (1999)
	(2) Law and Finance in Retirement (2nd edn – 2002) – Blackhall
Coughlan P	Property Law (2nd edn – 1998) – Gill and Macmillan
Courtney T B	(1) The Law of Private Companies (2nd edn – 2002) – LexisNexis
	(2) Commercial Law Practitioner (11 issues annually- 1994) – Brehon Publishing
	(3) Mareva Injunctions and Related Interlocutory Orders (1998) – LexisNexis
Cousins M	The Irish Social Welfare System: Law and Social Policy (2002 – 2nd edn) – Thomson Round Hall

Cox N and Heffernan L	Dublin University Law Journal (Vol 25 – 2004) – Thomson Round Hall
Craven C and Humphreys G	Military Law in Ireland (1997) – Thomson Round Hall
Crawford J	Anglicising the Government of Ireland 1556 – 78 (1993)[+] – Irish Academic Press
Crean J	Do you require planning permission? (2002 – 2nd edn) – Thomson Round Hall
Cremins D and O'Brien D	Value Added Tax (2001) – Irish Taxation Institute [*]
Crossman V	Politics, Law and Order in 19th Century Ireland (1996) – Gill and Macmillan
Cubie D and Ryan F	Immigration, Asylum and Citizenship Law (2004) – Thomson Round Hall
Curtin D	Irish Employment Equality Law (1990) – Thomson Round Hall
Curtin D and O'Keeffe D	Constitutional Adjudication in European Community and National Law (1992) – Butterworths (LexisNexis)
Cusack D A	Medico-Legal Journal of Ireland (2 issues annually), edited in 2004 by Asim Sheikh – Thomson Round Hall
Daly B D	(1) Handbook of Irish Case Law (1989)
	(2) Company Law Reports 1963 – 1993 (1995) – Thomson Round Hall (Sweet and Maxwell)
	(3) Professional Negligence Law Reports 1968 – 1993 (1995) – Brehon Dublin
	(4) The Irish Courts Guide (1998) – Inns Quay
	(5) The Role of the Expert Witness (1999) – Inns Quay
Daly C B	Law and Morals (1993) – Four Courts Press
Dawson N, Greer D, Ingram P	One Hundred and Fifty Years of Irish Law (1996) – Thomson Round Hall
De Blacam	See de Blacam
Deale K E L	The Law of Landlord and Tenant in the Republic of Ireland (1968)
Dee E	Discovery (2004) – Thomson Round Hall
Delaney and McGrath	Civil Procedure in the Superior Courts (2001) – Thomson Round Hall
Delaney H	(1) The Courts Acts (Annotated) 1924 – 1997 including the Courts Service Act 1998 (1999) – Thomson Round Hall
	(2) Equity and the Law of Trusts in Ireland (3rd edn – 2003) – Thomson Round Hall
	(3) Irish Law Reports Monthly (14 issues annually) – Thomson Round Hall
	(4) Judicial Review of Administrative Action (2001) – Thomson Round Hall
	(5) Equity and the Law of Trusts in Ireland: cases and materials (2002) – Thomson Round Hall
Delany V T H	The Law relating to Charities in Ireland (1962)
Dempsey B	Company Law on Computer (1992)

Dempsey F J	Handbook of Essential Law for the Irish Hotel and Catering Industry (2nd edn – 1994) – CERT
Dixon G Y and Gilliland W L	The Law relating to Sheriffs in Ireland (1888)
Donegan D and Friel R	Irish Stamp Duty Law (3rd edn – 2001) – Butterworths (LexisNexis)
Donnelly A and Walsh M	Revenue Investigations and Enforcement (2002) – Butterworths (LexisNexis)
Donnelly M	(1) The Law of Banks and Credit Institutions (1999) – Thomson Round Hall
	(2) Consent: bridging the gap between doctor and patient (2002) – Cork University Press
Donohue L K	Counter-terrorist law and Emergency Powers in the United Kingdom 1922 – 2000 (2000) – Irish Academic Press
Doolan B	(1) Principles of Irish Law (1999 – 5th edn) – Gill and Macmillan
	(2) A Casebook on Irish Company Law (1987) – Gill and Macmillan
	(3) Constitutional Law and Constitutional Rights in Ireland (3rd edn – 1994) – Gill and Macmillan
	(4) Casebook of Irish Contract Law (1989) – Gill and Macmillan
	(5) Casebook of Irish Business Law (1989) – Gill and Macmillan
Doran K, O'Driscoll A et al	Risk Manager for GPs (2002) – Thomson Round Hall
Doyle C	(1) Company Directors and the Law in Ireland (1992)
	(2) The Company Secretary (2nd edn – 2002) – Thomson Round Hall
Driscoll D	Irish Human Rights Review 2000 (2001) – Thomson Round Hall
Duggan F	EC Environment Legislation – A Handbook for Local Authorities (1992) – Environmental Research Unit
Duncan W and Scully P	Marriage Breakdown in Ireland: Law and Practice (1990) – Butterworths (LexisNexis)
Eardly J	(1) Bullying and Stress in the Workplace: employers and employees – a guide (2002) – First Law
	(2) Sex Discrimination at Work: A Practical Guide to the Law in Ireland (2004) – First Law
EC Publications	(1) Treaties Establishing the European Communities (1987)
	(2) The Rules Governing Medicaments in the European Community (1984)
Egan P	Irish Corporate Procedures (1996) – Jordan, Bristol
Ellis E and Eustace PB	Registry of Deeds Dublin – Abstract of Wills – Vol III 1785 – 1832 (1984) – Stationery Office
Ellis H	Insurance Brokers – Their Role and Regulation in the Republic of Ireland (1987)
European Consumer Centre	The Small Claims Court (2000)

Farrell B	Coroners: Practice and Procedure (2000) – Thomson Round Hall
Farrell J	Irish Law of Specific Performance (1995) – LexisNexis
Farry M	(1) Education and the Constitution (1996) – Thomson Round Hall (Sweet and Maxwell)
	(2) Irish Education Manual – Post Primary Schools (2001 – updated annually)* – Thomson Round Hall
	(3) Primary Education Management Manual (2002 – updated annually)* – Thomson Round Hall
Feeney M	Taxation of Companies 2000 – 2001 (2000) – Butterworths (LexisNexis)
Fennell C	(1) The Law of Evidence in Ireland (2nd edn – 2003) – Butterworths (LexisNexis)
	(2) Crime and Crisis in Ireland: justice by illusion (1993) – Cork University Press
Ferguson G, Gilvarry E and Langford K	Employee Share Schemes in Ireland (2000)
FIE (IBEC)	Guide to Employment Legislation (1991)
Finlay T A	(1) The Constitution fifty years on (1988) – Thomson Round Hall
	(2) Advocacy: has it a future (1986) – Thomson Round Hall
Fitsimons J and Mulcahy R	Contract Law – Round Hall Nutshell (2000)
Fitzgerald J B	Land Registry Practice (2nd edn – 1995) – Thomson Round Hall
Fitzpatrick T	Law of Capital Acquisitions Tax (2003) – Irish Taxation Institute *
Flynn J and Halpin T	Taxation of Costs (1999) – Thomson Round Hall
Fogarty A and Comerford H	Environment Law, A Glossary and Handbook (2000) – Thomson Round Hall (Sweet and Maxwell)
Forde M	(1) Company Law in Ireland (3rd edn – 1999) – Thomson Round Hall
	(2) Constitutional Law of Ireland (1987) – Mercier Press
	(3) Extradition Law in Ireland (2nd edn – 1995) – Thomson Round Hall
	(4) Bankruptcy Law in Ireland (1990) – Mercier Press
	(5) Commercial Law in Ireland (2nd edn – 1997); (3rd edn – 2004) – LexisNexis
	(6) Industrial Relations Law (1991) – Thomson Round Hall
	(7) Reorganising Failing Business (The Legal Framework) (1991) – Mercier Press
	(8) Employment Law (2nd edn – 2001) – Thomson Round Hall
	(9) The Law of Company Insolvency (1993) – Thomson Round Hall
	(10) Arbitration – Law and Procedure (1994) – Thomson Round Hall
	(11) Cases and Materials on Irish Company Law (2nd edn – 1998) – Thomson Round Hall

	(12) The Law of Extradition in the United Kingdom (1995) – Thomson Round Hall
	(13) Commercial Legislation (1998) – Thomson Round Hall
Foy A	The Capital Markets – Irish and International Laws and Regulations (1998) – Thomson Round Hall
Fraser U and Harvey C	Sanctuary in Ireland: perspectives on asylum law and policy (2004) – Institute of Public Administration
Friel R	(1) The Law of Contract (2000 – 2nd edn) – Thomson Round Hall
	(2) The Law of Contract – Cases and Materials (2002) – Thomson Round Hall
Fullerton J and Kandola R	Managing Diversity in Ireland – Implementing the Employment Equality Act 1998 (1999) – Oak Tree Press
Gaffney M	Taxation of Property Transactions (2003) – Irish Taxation Institute *
Gallagher B	Powers of Attorney Act 1996 (2001) – Thomson Round Hall
Gallagher, Ellard and Langan	Food Safety: Essential Facts (2001) – Thomson Round Hall and Food Safety Authority
Galligan E	(1) Irish Planning Law and Procedure (2004 – 2nd edn) – Thomson Round Hall
	(2) Irish Planning and Environmental Law Journal (4 issues annually) – Thomson Round Hall
Gannon F	VAT on Property (2003) – Irish Taxation Institute *
Garvey H and Macaulay D	The Blackhall Guide to Employment Law in Ireland (1999)
Gee Publishing	(1) Expert Witness Directory No 3
	(2) Committee on the Financial Aspects of Corporate Governance – Cadbury Report – 1992
Giblin B H	Irish Tax Reports 1922–2000 (2001) – Butterworths (LexisNexis)
	Irish Tax Reports 2000, Cases etc (2001) – Butterworths (LexisNexis)
Giblin H	(1) Valuation of Shares in Private Companies (1999 – 4th edn)
	(2) Irish Tax Reports 1922 – 1998 (1994)*
Gill S	Draft Order Precedents in the Circuit Court (2001) – on CD-ROM from Sam Gill, Knockanes, Adare, Co Limerick
Ginnel L	The Brehon Laws (1894)
Glanville S	The Enforcement of Judgments (1999) – Thomson Round Hall
Glendenning D	Education and the Law (1999) – LexisNexis
Goldberg D	(1) Consolidated Criminal Legislation (2002)* – Thomson Round Hall
	(2) Consolidated Superior Court Rules (2002) – Thomson Round Hall
Goodman A	Stamp Acts (2003) – Irish Taxation Institute *
Gore Grimes J	Key Issues in Planning and Environmental Law (2002) – Butterworths (LexisNexis)
Government Publications	(1) Law of Value-Added Tax (1987)*

(2) Bankruptcy Law Committee Report (1972)

(3) The Law of Nullity in Ireland (1976)

(4) Report on the Criminal Legal Aid Review Committee (1981)

(5) Scheme of Civil Legal Aid and Advice (1986)

Greer D and Dawson N	Mysteries and Solutions in Irish legal history (2001) – Four Courts
Greer D, Dawson N and Ingram P	One Hundred and Fifty Years of Irish Law (1996) – Thomson Round Hall
Greer D and Nicholson JW	The Factory Acts in Ireland 1802–1914 (2002) – Four Courts
Griffin P	European Financial Law (2000)
Grist B	An Introduction to Irish Planning Law (1999) – Institute of Public Administration
Grist B and Macken J	Irish Planning Law Factbook (2003 – updated annually) – looseleaf and CD-ROM – Thomson Round Hall
Grogan V King T, Donelan E J	Sale of Goods and Supply of Services (1983) – Law Society of Ireland
Gwynn Morgan D	A Judgement too far? Judicial activism and the Constitution (2003) – Cork University Press
Haccius C and O'Brien P	Double Taxation Agreements (Sept 2004) – Irish Taxation Institute*
Hadden T and Boyle K	The Anglo-Irish Agreement – Commentary Text and Official Review (1989) – Sweet and Maxwell, London
Hadfield B	Judicial Review: a thematic approach (1995) – Gill and Macmillan
Haigh S P	Contract Law in an E-Commerce Age (2001) – Thomson Round Hall
Hall EG	The Electronic Age: telecommunications in Ireland (1993) – Oak Tree Press
Hanafin P	Last Rights: Death, dying and the Law in Ireland (1997) – Cork University Press
Hanafin P and Tomkin D	Irish Medical Law (1995) – Thomson Round Hall
Hart A R	A history of the King's Serjeants at Law in Ireland: honour rather than advantage? (2000) – Four Courts
Harvey N and Twomey A F	Sexual Harassment in the Workplace (1995) – Oak Tree Press
Healy J	Irish Laws of Evidence (2004) – Thomson Round Hall
Healy J	Medical Negligence: Common Law Perspectives (1999) – Sweet and Maxwell
Healy M	The Old Munster Circuit (1939)[+] – M Joseph Ltd, London
Heffernan L	Human Rights: A European Perspective (1994) – Thomson Round Hall in association with the Irish Centre for European Law
Heney M	The Tallaght Two: justice delayed (1995)[+] – Gill and Macmillan
Hennessy L and Keegan B	Direct Tax Acts (2001) – Irish Taxation Institute *

Hennessy L and Moore P	Taxes Consolidation Act 1997 (1998)
Henry B	Dublin Hanged (1994)+ – Irish Academic Press
Hensey B	The Health Services of Ireland (1988)+ – Institute of Public Administration
Hickey E	Irish law and lawyers in modern folk tradition (1999) – Four Courts
Higgins E and Keher N	Your Rights at Work (1996 – 2nd edn) – Institute of Public Administration
Hill N and O'Keeffe G	Dangerous Driving Cases (1999) – Thomson Round Hall
Hogan D	The Legal Profession in Ireland 1789–1922 (1986)+ – Law Society of Ireland
Hogan D and Hall E	History of the Law Society of Ireland 1851 – 2001 (2002) – Four Courts
Hogan D and Osborough W N	Brehons, Sergeants and Attorneys (1990)+ – Irish Academic Press
Hogan G and Morgan D	Administrative Law in Ireland (1998 – 3rd edn) – Thomson Round Hall (Sweet and Maxwell)
Hogan G and Whyte G	The Irish Constitution (4th edn – 2003) – Butterworths (LexisNexis)
Holohan B and Sanfey M	Bankruptcy Law and Practice in Ireland (1992) – Thomson Round Hall
Humphreys G and Craven C	Military Law in Ireland (1997) – Thomson Round Hall
Humphreys R F	Index to Irish Statutory Instruments (1988); Supplement (1990) – Butterworths (LexisNexis)
Hutchinson B	(1A) Consolidated Company Legislation (2003) – Thomson Round Hall
	(1B) Company Law Practitioner (2004) – monthly journal – Thomson Round Hall
	(2) Arbitration Law and Practice (2004) – LexisNexis
ICEL	(1) Insider Dealing – Papers from Irish Centre for European Law Conference (1990)
	(2) The New Competition Legislation (1991)
	(3) The New Product Liability Regime (1992)
	(4) Legal Aspects of Commercial Sea-Fishing in the EC (1992)
	(5) European Initiatives in Intellectual Property (1993)
	(6) Irish Competition Law and Practice in Ireland (1993)
	(7) Legal Aspects of Doing Business in the EC (1993)
Immigrant Council	Handbook on Immigrants' Rights and Entitlements in Ireland (2003) – Immigrant Council of Ireland
Ingram P, Greer D and Dawson N	One Hundred and Fifty Years of Irish Law (1996) – Thomson Round Hall
Irish Taxation Institute	(1) Taxing Financial Transactions (2004)
	(2) Electronic Publishing – TaxFind on CD-ROM (2003)*- TaxFind on Line (2003)*
	(3) FINAK 2003

Jackson N and Coggans S	The Family Law (Divorce) Act 1996 (1998) – Thomson Round Hall
Johnston W	Banking and Security Law in Ireland (1998) – LexisNexis
Johnston W and O'Conor O	Arthur Cox Banking Law Handbook (2004) – LexisNexis
Judge N E	Irish Income Tax 1999- 2000 (1999) – Butterworths (LexisNexis) Judge Irish Income Tax 2002 by Prof John Ward (2002) – Butterworths (LexisNexis)
Keane D	(1) The RIAI Contracts – A Working Guide (2001) – Royal Institute of the Architects of Ireland (RIAI) (2) Building and the Law (2002 – 4th edn) – RIAI
Keane R Chief Justice	(1) Company Law (2000 – 3rd edn) – LexisNexis (2) Equity and the Laws of Trusts in the Republic of Ireland (1988) – Butterworths (LexisNexis) (3) The Law of Local Government in the Republic of Ireland (1982) – Law Society of Ireland (4) Keane on Local Government (2003) – 2nd edn by Patrick Butler SC – First Law and Law Society of Ireland
Keating A	(1) Probate Law and Practice (1999) – Thomson Round Hall (Sweet and Maxwell) (2) Probate Law and Practice Case Book (1999) – Thomson Round Hall (3) Probate Causes and related matters (2000) – Thomson Round Hall (4) The Construction of Wills (2001) – Thomson Round Hall (5) Keating on Probate (2nd edn – 2002) – Thomson Round Hall (6) The Law of Wills (2002) – Thomson Round Hall (7) The Law and Practice of Personal Representatives (2004) – Thomson Round Hall
Keegan B	Residential Property Tax Legislation (2002) – Irish Taxation Institute
Keegan B and Murray C	Direct Tax Acts 2003 – Irish Taxation Institute
Keegan S	Tax Guide 1995 – 96
Kelleher D and Murray K	(1) Information Technology Law in Ireland (1997, 1st edn); (2004, 2nd edn)[F] – LexisNexis (2) Information Technology Law in the European Union (1999) – Sweet and Maxwell, London
Kelleher S	Companies (Amendment) Act 1986. A Guide to the Accounting Reporting and Filing Requirements (1987) – Institute of Chartered Accountants in Ireland
Kelly A	Compulsory Irish – The Language and the Education System 1870's – 1970's (2000)[+] – Irish Academic Press
Kelly C and Murphy A	Copyright and Related Rights Act 2000 (2002) – Thomson Round Hall

Kelly F	A Guide to Early Irish Law (1989) – Dublin Institute for Advanced Studies
Kelly J M	The Irish Constitution (2003 – 4th edn) – by Hogan G and Whyte G – LexisNexis
Kennedy D and Maguire E	Irish Family Law Handbook (1999 – 1st edn); (2004 – 2nd edn) – LexisNexis
Kennedy and McWilliams	The Law on Compensation for Criminal Injuries in the Republic of Ireland (1977)
Kenny C	(1) King's Inns and the Kingdom of Ireland: The Irish 'inn of court' 1541 – 1800 (1991) – Irish Academic Press in association with the Irish Legal History Society
	(2) King's Inns and the Battle of the Books 1972: cultural controversy at a Dublin library (2002)+ – Four Courts in association with the Irish Legal History Society
Keoghan A, Mee J, and Wylie JCW	The Law and Taxation of Trusts (2004) – LexisNexis
Kerr A	(1) Trade Union and Industrial Relations Acts of Ireland, Commentary (1991)
	(2) Civil Liability Acts (Annotated) (1999 – 2nd edn) – Thomson Round Hall
	(3) Irish Employment Legislation (1999 –)* – looseleaf service
	(4) Employment Equality Legislation (2001) – Thomson Round Hall
	(5) Trade Union Law (2nd edn – 2001) – Thomson Round Hall
	(6) Employment Rights Legislation (2002) – Thomson Round Hall
	(7) Termination of Employment Statutes (2000) – Thomson Round Hall
Kerr A and Hogan G	Dublin University Law Journal (1 volume per annum); editors in 2004 – Neville Cox and Liz Heffernan
Kerr A and Whyte G	Irish Trade Union Law (1985) – Professional Books
Keys M	Mental Health Act 2001 (2002) – Thomson Round Hall
Keville C and Lucey M C	Irish Perspectives on European Law (2003) – Thomson Round Hall
Kiely T O'Neill	The Principles of Equity as applied in Ireland (1936)
Kilkelly U	(1) Child Law (2005)F – LexisNexis
	(2) ECHR and Irish Law (2004) – Jordan Publishing
Killen D M and Williams B	Journal of Valuation Tribunal Judgments
	(Vol 1 – Sept 1988 to June 1994) (1996) includes CD-ROM – Institute of Public Administration
	(Vol 2 – July 1994 to Dec 1998) (1999) includes CD-ROM – Institute of Public Administration
Kimber C	(1) Irish Employment Law Journal (2004) – Thomson Round Hall
	(2) Employment Law Reports (6 issues annually) – Thomson Round Hall

Kingston J, Whelan A and Bacik I	Abortion and the Law: An Irish Perspective (1997) Thomson Round Hall (Sweet and Maxwell)
Kotsonouris M	(1) Talking to your Solicitor (1992) – Gill and Macmillan
	(2) Retreat from Revolution – The Dail Courts 1920 – 1924 (1994) – Irish Academic Press
Laffoy M and Wheeler D (now Buckley J F)	Irish Conveyancing Precedents (1991) – looseleaf – LexisNexis
Larkin J	The Trial of William Drennan (1991) – Irish Academic Press
Larragy P	The Guide to Company Law (2003) – Institute of Chartered Secretaries and Administrators
Lavery P	Commercial Secrets: The Action for Breach of Confidence in Ireland (1996) – Thomson Round Hall (Sweet and Maxwell)
Lee G	A Memoir of the South Western Circuit (1990)[+] – Moytura, Dublin
Lenahan O	Tolley's Taxation in the Republic of Ireland (2003) and (2004) – LexisNexis
LexisNexis (see also Butterworths)	Irish Planning Law Direct (launched 2003) – online
Linehan D M	Irish Land and Conveyancing Law (1989) – Legis Publications
Litton F	The Constitution of Ireland 1937 – 1987 (1988)[+] – Institute of Public Administration
Long I	What is the Law? Consumer Rights (2004) – Thomson Round Hall
Lucey M C	The Competition Act 2002 (2003) – Thomson Round Hall
Lyall A	Land Law in Ireland (2000 – 2nd edn) – Thomson Round Hall
Lyden J and MacGrath M	Irish Building and Engineering Case Law (1989) – Society of Chartered Surveyors in the Republic of Ireland
Lynch I et al	Corporate Insolvency and Rescue (1996) – LexisNexis
McAllister D L	Registration of Title (1973) – Incorporated Council of Law Reporting for Ireland
McArdle J	Irish Legal Anecdotes (1995) – Gill and Macmillan
McAteer W, Reddin G and Deegan G	Income Tax (2003) – Irish Taxation Institute*
McAuley F	(1) Insanity, Psychiatry and Criminal Responsibility (1993) – Thomson Round Hall
	(2) Irish Jurist (1848 – present) – Thomson Round Hall
McAuley F and McCutcheon J P	Criminal Liability (2000) – Thomson Round Hall
MacCann L et al	Butterworths (LexisNexis) Irish Companies Acts (looseleaf – 2004)
MacCann L	(1) A Casebook on Company Law (1991) – Butterworths (LexisNexis)
	(2) Companies Acts 1963 – 1990 (1993) – LexisNexis
McCarthy A and Power V JG	Irish Competition Law: The Competition Act 2002 (2003) – Butterworths (LexisNexis)
McConville C	Company Law (2001) – Nutshell Series – Thomson Round Hall
McCormack G	The New Companies Legislation (1991) – Thomson Round Hall

McCormack M	DIY Divorce: divorce on a shoestring (2002) – Merlin
McCullagh C	Crime in Ireland: a sociological introduction (1996)[+] – Cork University Press
McCutcheon J P	The Larceny Act 1916 (1988)
McCutcheon J P and Walsh DPJ	The Confiscation of Criminal Assets: law and procedure (1999)
McDermott PA	(1) Prison Law (2000) – Thomson Round Hall
	(2) The Law on Res Judicata and Double Jeopardy (1999) – LexisNexis
	(3) Contract Law (2001) – Butterworths (LexisNexis)
	(4) Irish Criminal Law Journal (4 issues annually) – Thomson Round Hall
McDermott and Robinson	The Children Act 2001 (2003) – Thomson Round Hall
McDermott S and Woulfe R	Compulsory Purchase and Compensation in Ireland: Law and Practice (1992) – LexisNexis
McDonagh M	Freedom of Information Law in Ireland (1998) – Thomson Round Hall
MacDonagh S	How free are you? (2002) – Brandon
McDonald M	(1) Irish Law of Defamation (1991 – 2nd edn) – Thomson Round Hall
	(2) Hotel, Restaurant and Public House Law (1992) – LexisNexis
	(3) European Community Tourism Law and Policy
	(2003) – Blackhall
McDonald T	Buying a House in Ireland (2002) – Blackhall
McGahon D	Irish Company Law Index (1991) – Gill and Macmillan
McGann J R	Cheques: The Paying and Collecting Banker (1973) – Institute of Bankers in Ireland
McGarry S	Franchising in Ireland (1996) – McGarry Consulting
McGonagle M	(1) Media Law (2nd edn – 2003) – Thomson Round Hall
	(2) Journalists and the Law (2000) – Thomson Round Hall
McGowan Smyth J	The Houses of the Oireachtas (1979 – 4th edn) – Institute of Public Administration
McGrath S	Company Law – Essential Law Text (2003) – Thomson Round Hall
McGrath M	(1) Liquor Licensing Law (2001) – Butterworths (LexisNexis)
	(2) Irish Road Traffic Law Service (2004) – looseleaf – LexisNexis
McGreal C	Criminal Justice (Theft and Fraud Offences) Act 2001 – Thomson Round Hall
McGuire W J	The Succession Act 1965; A Commentary (Second Edition by Robert A Pearce) (1983) – Law Society of Ireland
McHugh D	(1) Libel Law: a journalist's handbook (2001) – Four Courts
	(2) Going to Court – A Consumer's Guide (2003) – First Law
	(3) The Small Claims Court in Ireland (2003)

McIntyre TJ and McMullin S	Criminal Law: Essential Law Text (2001) – Thomson Round Hall
McLoughlin A MacKenzie P	Surviving: a personal guide to judicial separation in Ireland (2004) – TownHouse Lawful Occasions: the Old Eastern Circuit (1991)+ – Mercier Press Cork
Mackey N	Constitutional Rights: a practical guide for the layperson (1992)
Mackey R	Windward of the Law (1991)+ – W H Allen, UK
McLoughlin A and Mooney J	(1) Pensions: Revenue and Practice (2000 – 4th edn) (2) Persons, Revenue Law and Practice (2001) – Irish Taxation Institute *
McMahon BME and Binchy W	(1) Law of Torts (2000 – 3rd edn) – LexisNexis (2) Casebook on the Irish Law of Torts (2004 – 3rd edn) – LexisNexis
McMahon BME and Murphy F	European Community Law in Ireland (1989) – Butterworths (LexisNexis)
McMahon J and Clark R	Contemporary Issues in Law and Politics (1998 –) – Thomson Round Hall (Sweet and Maxwell)
McMahon M	(1)What is the Law? Construction Health and Safety (2002) – Thomson Round Hall (2) What is the Law? Fire Safety (2001) – Thomson Round Hall (3) What is the Law? Manual Handling (2002) – Thomson Round Hall (4) A–Z of Health and Safety Risk Assessment in Ireland (1998), with Geoffrey Shannon – Thomson Round Hall (5) A–Z of Health and Safety for High Risk Environments (2001), with Gerry O'Sullivan and Nevan Mulrooney – Thomson Round Hall
Mac Unfraidh G	Athbhreithniu Breithiunach (2002) – CoiscÚim
Madden D	Medicine, Law and Ethics in Ireland (2002) – Butterworths (LexisNexis)
Madden D and Kerr T	Unfair Dismissal (1990 and 1996) – cases and commentary – IBEC
Madden D H	Deeds, Conveyances and Judgment Mortgages (1901)
Maguire B	Research Paper on Retention of Title (for Law Reform Commission) (1989)
Maguire B, O'Reilly M and Roche M	Irish Environmental Legislation (1999) – Thomson Round Hall (Sweet and Maxwell)
Maguire C	(1) Trade Union Membership and the Law (1999) – Thomson Round Hall (2) Employment Law Report (6 issues annually) – Thomson Round Hall (3) ELR Index 1990 – 1999 (2000) – Thomson Round Hall
Maher I	Competition Law – Alignment and Reform (1999) – Thomson Round Hall (Sweet and Maxwell)
Mahon A P	Auctioneering and Estate Agency Law in Ireland (1990)

Maloney M and Spellman J	The Law of Meetings (1999) – Thomson Round Hall
Martin M, McCarthy et al	Family Law Practitioner: Maintenance, Pensions and Taxation in Family Law Proceedings (2001) – Thomson Round Hall
Massey P and O'Hare P	Competition Law and Policy in Ireland (1996) – Oak Tree Press
Mason Hayes and Curran	The Irish Mergers Act (A Guide) (1992)
Matheson Ormsby Prentice	A Guide for Business and Industry to Environmental Law in Ireland (1991)
Maxwell T H	Miller's Probate Practice (1900)
Mee J and Pearce R	Land Law (2000, 2nd edn) – Thomson Round Hall
Meenan F	Working within the Law: a practical guide for employers and employees (1999 – 2nd edn) – Oak Tree Press
Microsoft Press	Computer Dictionary (1997 – 3rd edn)
Mills S	Irish Medical Law and Ethics (2004) – bimonthly electronic bulletin – contact email: *imle@medicalimi.com*
Mills S and Spence R	Irish Clinical Practice and the Law (2002) – Butterworths (LexisNexis)
Mongey E G	(1) Probate Practice in a Nutshell (1998)
	(2) The Weird and Wonderful World of Wills (1997)[+] – Fort Publications
	(3) How to succeed in probate practice by trying (1987) – Society of Young Solicitors
Morgan A	The Belfast Agreement: A practical legal analysis (1999) – Belfast Press, London
Morgan D G	(1) Constitutional Law of Ireland (1990 – 2nd edn) – Thomson Round Hall in association with Irish Academic Press
	(2) The Separation of Powers in the Irish Constitution (1997) – Thomson Round Hall
	(3) A Judgment too Far? – Judicial Activism and the Constitution (2002) – Cork University Press
Morgan DG and Hogan G	Administrative Law in Ireland (1998 – 3rd edn) – Thomson Round Hall (Sweet and Maxwell)
Moore A	(1) Tax Acts 1991–92 (1992)
	(2) Tax Acts 1995–96
	(3) VAT Acts 1995–96
	(4) The Tax Book 98
Mulcahy R and Fitsimmons J	Contract Law – Round Hall Nutshell (2000)
Murdoch H	(1) Invention and the Irish Patent System (1971)[+] – Trinity College Administration Bureau
	(2) Building Society Law in Ireland – A Guide (1989) – Topaz Publications
	(3) Murdoch's Dictionary of Irish Law (2004 – 4th edn) – LexisNexis
	(4) Murdoch's Irish Legal Companion (2004) – online and on CD-ROM – Lendac Data Systems and Topaz Publications

Murphy T	(1) Rethinking the War on Drugs in Ireland (1996) – Cork University Press
	(2) Western Jurisprudence (2004), with a team of contributors – Thomson Round Hall
Murphy Y	Journalists and the Law (2000 – 2nd edn) – Thomson Round Hall
Murphy Y and Ashe M	Insider Dealing in Ireland (1992) – Thomson Round Hall
Murtagh B	Tax Implications of Marriage Breakdown (2003) – Irish Taxation Institute
Nestor J	Law of Child Care (2004) – Blackhall Publishing
Nolan S and Hollingsworth G	Buying and Selling a Business (2003) – Irish Taxation Institute
Norfolk D and Bannister F	IT Policies and Procedures in Ireland (1999) – Thomson Round Hall
Nowlan K I	(1) A Guide to the Planning Acts (1978) – Law Society of Ireland
	(2) A Guide to Planning Legislation in the Republic of Ireland (1988)
O'Brien K and Trueick J	Payroll and Taxation for Employers (2000 – updated annually) – Thomson Round Hall
O'Brien M A	Irish Law for the Layperson (1996) – author
O'Callaghan J M	(1) Taxation of Estates: The Law in Ireland (1993) – Butterworths (LexisNexis)
	(2) Taxation of Trusts (1994) – Butterworths (LexisNexis)
O'Callaghan P	The Law on Solicitors in Ireland (2000) – LexisNexis
O'Cearuil M	(1) Bunreacht na hEireann. A Study of the Irish Text (1999) – Stationery Office
	(2) Bunreacht na hEireann: two texts or two constitutions (2002) – The Ireland Institute (CoiscÚim)
	(3) Bunreacht na hEireann: an teacs Gaeilge aran chaighdeanu (2003) – CoiscÚim
O'Cofaigh E	The Building Regulations Explained (1993) – Royal Institute of the Architects of Ireland
O'Connell M	(1) Corporate Governance – Guidelines for Small Business (2001) – Small Firms Association
	(2) Who'd want to be a company director? A guide to the Enforcement of Irish Company Law (2003) – First Law
O'Connell M and Bacik I	Crime and Poverty in Ireland (1998) – Thomson Round Hall
O'Connor R	The Law and Practice in Ireland Relating to Cheques and Analogous Instruments (1993) – Institute of Bankers in Ireland
O'Connor E R	The Irish Notary (1987) – Professional Books
O'Connor K	Thou Shalt Not Kill (1995)[+] – Gill and Macmillan
O'Connor M and Cahill P	The Law of Stamp Duties (2001) – Irish Taxation Institute
O'Connor P (editor)	A plain English guide to legal terms (2003) – National Adult Literacy Agency

O'Connor P A	Key Issues in Irish Family Law (1988) – Thomson Round Hall
O'Connor T	Competition Law Source Book (1996) – Thomson Round Hall (Sweet and Maxwell)
O'Cuinneagain M, et al	Tax Guide 2000 – 2001 (1999)
O'Dell E	(1) Dublin University Law Journal – Trinity College Dublin
	(2) Leading Cases of the Twentieth Century (2000) – Thomson Round Hall
O'Donnell I and McAuley F	Criminal Justice History: Themes and Controversies (2003) – Four Courts Press
O'Donnell J L	Examinerships – The Companies (Amendment) Act 1990 (1993) – Oak Tree Press
O'Donnell M	Planning Law (1999) – LexisNexis
O'Driscoll T	Company Reorganisations and Amalgamations (2004) – Irish Taxation Institute
O'Flaherty H	Justice, Liberty and the Courts (1998) – Thomson Round Hall
O'Floinn B	Practice and Procedure in the Superior Courts (1996) – Butterworths (LexisNexis)
O'Halloran K	(1) Adoption Law and Practice (1993) – LexisNexis
	(2) Charity Law (2000) – Thomson Round Hall
	(3) Child Care Law: a comparative review of new legislation in Northern Ireland and the Republic of Ireland (1996) – Thomson Round Hall
O'Halloran K and Cormacain R	Charity Law in Northern Ireland (2001) – Thomson Round Hall
O'Halloran M	Irish Taxation – Law and Practice (2004) – Irish Taxation Institute
O'Higgins P	A Bibliography of Irish Trials and other Legal Proceedings (1986) – Professional Books
O'Higgins P and McEldowney J	The Common Law Tradition (1990) – Irish Academic Press
O'Kane B	How to form a limited company (1999 – 3rd edn) – Oak Tree Press
O'Keeffe G and Hill N	Dangerous Driving Cases (1999) – Thomson Round Hall
O'Kelly S and Rohan J	Nursing Law (1994) – Butterworths (LexisNexis)
O'Laoghaire D	Inland Waters (1995) – Butterworths (LexisNexis)
O'Laoire D	Waste Management Legislation (2001) – Thomson Round Hall
O'Mahony P	(1) Crime and Punishment in Ireland (1993) – Thomson Round Hall
	(2) Criminal Chaos: Seven Crises in Irish Criminal Justice (1996) – Thomson Round Hall
	(3) Criminal Justice in Ireland (2002) – Institute of Public Administration
O'Malley L	Business Law (1986) – Sweet and Maxwell
O'Malley T	(1) Sources of Law (2nd edn – 2001) – Thomson Round Hall
	(2) Sexual Offences: Law, Policy and Punishment (1996) – Thomson Round Hall (Sweet and Maxwell)

	(3) Sentencing Law and Practice (1999) – Thomson Round Hall
O'Mara C et al	Practical Employment Law – updated annually* – Thomson Round Hall
O'Morain P	Access to Justice: the history of the Free Legal Advice Centres 1969–2003 (2003) – Free Legal Advice Centres
O'Regan Cazabon A	Irish Insurance Law (1999) – Thomson Round Hall
O'Reilly and Redmond	Cases and Materials on the Irish Constitution (1980) – Law Society of Ireland
O'Reilly J	Human Rights and Constitutional Law (1992) – Thomson Round Hall
O'Reilly J and Collins A M	(1) Civil Proceedings and the State in Ireland: A Practitioners Guide (1990); (2nd edn – 2003) – Thomson Round Hall
	(2) Irish Journal of European Law (1 or 2 issues annually)
O'Reilly M	The Grocery Trade: A Guide to the Restrictive Practices Grocery Order 1997 (2003) – Blackhall
O'Reilly M F and Carroll B A	Carrolls' Tax Planning in Ireland (1986)
O'Reilly M, Maguire B and Roche M	Irish Environmental Legislation (1999) – Thomson Round Hall (Sweet and Maxwell)
O'Reilly P	Commercial and Consumer Law (2000) – LexisNexis
Osborough W N	(1) The Irish Statutes Revisited 1310 – 1800 (1995) – Thomson Round Hall
	(2) Studies in Irish Legal History (1999) – Four Courts Press
	(3) Borstal in Ireland: Custodial Provision for the Young Adult Offender 1906–1974 (1975) – Institute of Public Administration
O Siochain P A	(1) The Criminal Law of Ireland (1988 – 8th edn) – Kells Publishing Company
	(2) Outline of Evidence, Practice and Procedure in Ireland (1952)
O'Sullivan D J	The Irish Constabularies 1822 – 1922 (1999) – Brandon Press
O'Sullivan P A and Shepherd K	Source Book on Planning Law in Ireland (1987); Planning Law and Practice (looseleaf) – LexisNexis
O'Tuathail S and Ni Chulachain	Tuairisci Speisialta 1980 – 1998 (2000) (Irish Reports as gaeilge)
Parkes S M	A Danger to Men? A History of Women in Trinity College 1904 to 2004 (2004)+ – Lilliput Press, Dublin
Pearce R and Mee J	Land Law (2000 – 2nd edn) – Thomson Round Hall
Phelan D R	(1) It's God we ought to crucify: validity and authority in law (2000) – Four Courts
	(2) Revolt or Revolution: The Constitutional Boundaries of the European Communities (1997) – Thomson Round Hall (Sweet and Maxwell)
Phelan M B	Guide to the Companies Act 1990 (1991) – Gill and Macmillan
Pierse R	(1) Quantum of Damages for Personal Injuries (1997 and 1999) – Thomson Round Hall
	(2) Road Traffic Law (1995 – 2nd edn) – Butterworths (LexisNexis); (2003 – 3rd edn) – First Law
Power A	Intangible Property Rights in Ireland (2003) – LexisNexis

Power B J	Accountancy Law and Practice for Limited Companies (1987) – Gill and Macmillan
Power C	(1) Family Legislation Service (2000 – updated annually)* – Thompson Round Hall
	(2) Child Law Legislation (2001) – Thomson Round Hall
	(3) Marital Breakdown Legislation – Thomson Round Hall
Power V J G	Competition Law and Practice (2001) – Butterworth (LexisNexis)
von Prondzynski F and McCarthy C	Employment Law (1989) – Sweet and Maxwell, London
Quigley P and Binchy W	Personal Injuries Assessment Board Act 2003: Implications for the Legal Practice (2004) – First Law
Quinn A P	Credit Unions in Ireland (1999) – Oak Tree Press
Quinn G, McDonagh M, and Kimber C	Disability Discrimination Law in the United States, Australia and Canada (1993) – Oak Tree Press
Redmond M	(1) Dismissal Law in Ireland (1999) – LexisNexis
	(2) Guide to Irish Labour Law (1984)
Reid M	Equality Law in Ireland (2004) – LexisNexis
Reid P and Ashe M	Money Laundering (2000) – Thomson Round Hall
Robb J H	The Law and Practice of Bankruptcy and Arrangements in Ireland (1907)
Robbins J	Fools and Mad: A history of the Insane in Ireland (1986)[+] – Institute of Public Administration
Roche D	Local Government in Ireland (1982)[+] – Institute of Public Administration
Roche M, Maguire B and O'Reilly M	Irish Environmental Legislation (1999) – Thomson Round Hall (Sweet and Maxwell)
Rose D	The Final Decision on Adoption Recognition in Europe (2002)[+] – RD Publications
Round Hall (now Thomson Round Hall)	Westlaw IE Current Awareness On Line – (2003)
	Consolidated Superior Court Rules (2002 – updated annually)*
	Consolidated Road Traffic Legislation (2003)
	Consolidated Company Legislation – Brian Hutchinson (Consultant Editor) (2003)
	Consolidated Local Government Legislation (2002 – updated annually)
	The Business Administration Service (2000) – online and CD-ROM
	What is the Law? Company Directors (2003)
	Irish Current Law Monthly Digest – 11 issues annually.
Ryan E F and Magee P P	The Irish Criminal Process (1983) – Mercier Press
Ryan F	(1) Constitutional Law – Nutshell Series (2002) – Thomson Round Hall
	(2) Constitutional Law – Essential Law Text Series (2001) – Thomson Round Hall

Scannell Y	Environmental and Planning Law (2004 – 2nd edn) – Thomson Round Hall
Scanlon J W	Practice and Procedure in Administration and Mortgage Suits in Ireland (1963) – Incorporated Council of Law Reporting for Ireland
Schuster A	The New Products Liability Regime and Annotation of the Liability for Defective Products Act 1991 (1992) – Irish Centre for European Law
Scully M, Judge N E, Lynch O F	Finak 2000 – Commentary on Finance Act 2000 (2000)
Shannon G	(1) Divorce Act in Practice (1999) – Thomson Round Hall
	(2) Family Law Practitioner – updated annually* – Thomson Round Hall
	(3) Irish Journal of Family Law (4 issues annually) – Thomson Round Hall
	(4) Health and Safety: Law and Practice (2002) – Thomson Round Hall
	(5) Child Law (2004) – Thomson Round Hall
	(6) Divorce: The Changing Landscape in Ireland (2001) – Thomson Round Hall
Shatter A J	Family Law in the Republic of Ireland (1997 – 4th edn) – LexisNexis
Sheeran N	Irish Business Law (1991) – Gill and Macmillan
Sheikh A	Medico-Legal Journal of Ireland (2 issues annually) – Thomson Round Hall
Shiels D	Abuse of Process: Unjust and Improper Conduct of Civil Litigation in Ireland (2002) – First Law
Simons G	Planning and Development Law (2003) – Thomson Round Hall
Smyth P and Brady R	Democracy Blindfolded; the case for a freedom of information Act in Ireland (1994) – Cork University Club
Somers J and Cassidy B	Law of Value Added Tax (2001) – Irish Taxation Institute *
Somers J and Cassidy B	Law of Value Added Tax (2003) – Irish Taxation Institute
Spellman J and Maloney M	The Law of Meetings (1999) – Thomson Round Hall
Spierin B	Wills – Irish Precedents and Drafting (1999) – DAP Press
Spierin B and Fallon P	The Succession Act 1965 and Related Legislation: A Commentary (2003) – LexisNexis Butterworths
Spollen A L	Corporate Fraud – The dangers from within (1997)[+] – Oak Tree Press
Stewart E	Arbitration: commentary and sources (2003) – First Law
Stout R	Administrative Law in Ireland (1985) – Institute of Public Administration
Sullivan A M	The Last Serjeant (1952)[+] – Macdonald, London
Sweet and Maxwell (now Thomson Round Hall)	Irish Current Law Statutes Annotated (1984)*

Symmons C	Ireland and the Law of the Sea (2000 – 2nd edn) – Thomson Round Hall
TCD	Law and Liberty in Ireland (1993) – Oak Tree Press in association with Trinity College Dublin Law School
Tierney M	Irish Trade Marks Law and Practice (1987) – Gill and Macmillan
Tomkin D and Hanafin P	Irish Medical Law (1995) – Thomson Round Hall
Travers N J and Byrne P	Irish Competition Law Reports (1996)* – Baikonur, Delgany
Twomey M J	Partnership Law (2000) – LexisNexis
Ussher P	Company Law in Ireland (1986) – Sweet and Maxwell, London
Vanston G T B	The Law relating to Local Government in Ireland (1915)
Veritas Publications	The Canon Law – Letter and Spirit – a practical guide to the code of Canon Law (1995)
Waldron J K	Rules of the Superior Courts 1986. Guide to Changes from the former Rules (Government Publications 1986)
Walls M and Bergin D	The Law of Divorce in Ireland (1997) – Jordans, Bristol
Walpole H	Tax Implications of Marital Breakdown (2000 – 4th edn) – Taxation Institute of Ireland
Walsh D	(1) Bloody Sunday and the rule of law in Northern Ireland (2000) – Macmillan, Basingstoke
	(2) The Irish Police (1998) – Thomson Round Hall
	(3) Criminal Procedure (2002) – Thomson Round Hall
Walsh D and McCutcheon J P	The Confiscation of Criminal Assets: Law and Procedure (1999)
Walsh E M and Keane R	Planning and Development Law (1984) – Law Society of Ireland
Walsh E S	Agriculture and the Law (1996) – Thomson Round Hall (Sweet and Maxwell)
Walsh M	Irish Tax Treaties 2001 (2001) – Butterworths (LexisNexis)
Walsh T and McCarthy D	Customs Code of the European Union (1996) – Butterworths (LexisNexis)
Ward A J	The Irish Constitutional Tradition 1782 – 1992 (1994)+ – Irish Academic Press
Ward J W	Judge Irish Income Tax 2001–02 (2001) – Butterworths (LexisNexis)
Ward P	The Child Care Act (2004 – 2nd edn) – Thomson Round Hall
Ward P and Byrne P	Irish Family Law Reports (1996) – Baikonur, Delgany
Watson D	Victims of Recorded Crime in Ireland (2000) – Oak Tree Press in association with the Economic and Social Research Institute
Whelan A	Law and Liberty in Ireland (1993) – Oak Tree Press in association with Trinity College Dublin Law School
Whelan A, Kingston J and Bacik I	Abortion and the Law (1997) – Thomson Round Hall (Sweet and Maxwell)
White F	Commercial Law (2003) – Thomson Round Hall
White J P M	(1) The Irish Law of Damages for Personal Injuries and Death (1989) – Butterworths (LexisNexis)

Vol 1 Law and Practice

Vol 2 Quantum for Non-pecuniary Loss

(2) Civil Liability for Industrial Accidents (1994)

Vol 3 (2000) – Oak Tree Press

Whyte G · (1) Social Welfare Law in Ireland (1987) – Thomson Round Hall

(2) Social Inclusion and the Legal System: Public Interest Law in Ireland (2002) – Institute of Public Administration

William Fry · The Company's Act 1990, A Commentary (1993)

Williams A G · Principles of Corporation Tax in the Republic of Ireland (1981) – Law Society of Ireland

Wood K · The High Court: a user's guide (2nd edn – 2002) – Four Courts

Wood K and O'Shea · Divorce in Ireland: marital breakdown, answers and alternatives (2002) – First Law

Woods J V · (1) The District Court Practitioner, – Practice and Procedure in civil, licensing and family law proceedings (1997) – author

(2) Liquor Licensing Laws of Ireland (1992) – author

(3) A Guide to Road Traffic Offences (1990) – author

Wylie J C W · (1) Irish Land Law (1997) – 3rd edn – LexisNexis

(2) Conveyancing Law (1999) – part of Butterworths Irish Annotated Statutes Library; Irish Conveyancing Law (1996, 2nd edn); (2005, 3rd edn)[F] – LexisNexis

(3) A Casebook on Equity and Trusts in Ireland (1998 – 2nd edn) – LexisNexis

(4) Irish Landlord and Tenant Law (1998 – 2nd edn) – with J Farrell – LexisNexis

(5) Casebook on Irish Land Law (1987) – LexisNexis

Zuckerman A · Civil Procedure (2003) – LexisNexis Butterworths

BOOKS ON UK LAW

The following are books published in the United Kingdom on UK or EU law, referred to in Dictionary, and of varying relevance to Irish law.

Author	Title and Edition
Abrahamson M W	Engineering Law and the Institution of Civil Engineers Contract (1979 UK) – 4th edn
Adamson H	Free Movement of Lawyers (1998 UK)
Anderson M	European Economic Interest Groupings (1990 UK)
Archbold	Pleadings, Evidence and Practice in Criminal Cases (1979 UK)*
Bean D	Injunctions (1984 UK) – 3rd edn
Benjamin	Sale of Goods (1987 UK)
Bennion F A R	Statutory Interpretation (1999 UK) – 3rd edn – supplement
Bercusson B	European Labour Law (2000 UK) – 2nd edn
Bernstein R	Handbook of Arbitration Practice (1987 UK)
Blackstone	Criminal Practice (1993 UK)
Blake S	A practical approach to legal advice and drafting (1993 UK)
Blanpain R and Inston R	The Bosman Case – The end of the Transfer System? – Sweet and Maxwell (1997)

Bowstead	Bowstead on Agency (1985 UK)
Bullen Leak and Jacob	Precedents of Pleadings (1975 UK)
Burgess R A	The Law of Borrowing (1990 UK)
Burke J	Jowitt's Dictionary of English Law (1977 UK) – 2nd edn
Butterworths	Encyclopaedia of Forms and Precedents (1966 UK)
Byles	Bills of Exchange (1983 UK)
Byrne W J	A Dictionary of English Law (1993 UK)
Cameron Markby Hewitt	EC Insurance Law (1991 UK)
Chalmers	See Ivamy
Charlesworth and Percy	Charlesworth and Percy on Negligence (1990 UK)
Cheshire, Fifoot and Furmston	Law of Contract (1996 UK) – 13th edn
Chitty	Chitty on Contracts (1989 UK)
Clarke L	Confidentiality and the Law (1990 UK)
Clarke M A	International Carriage of Goods by Road CMR (1982 UK)
Clerk and Lindsell	Clerk and Lindsell on Torts (1989 UK)
Copinger and Skone James	Copyright (1980 UK)
Cordery	Cordery on Solicitors (2000 UK) – looseleaf
Cross Sir Rupert	Cross and Tapper on Evidence (1999 UK) – 9th edn
Dicey A V	Law of the Constitution (1962 UK)
Dine J	EC Company Law (1991 UK)
Dowling J A	Northern Ireland Planning Law (1995 UK)
Downes T A and Ellison J	The Legal Control of Mergers in the European Communities (1990 UK)
Duncan and Neill	Defamation (1983 UK)
Fisher and Lightwood	Law of Mortgage (1988 UK)
Ford HAJ and Lee WA	Principles of the Law of Trusts (1998 UK)
Forde M	The Law of Extradition in the United Kingdom (1995 UK)
Gatley	Gatley on Libel and Slander (2003 UK) – 10th edn
Goff and Barron	The Law of Restitution (1993 UK) – 4th edn
Goode R M	Commercial Law (1995 UK) – 2nd edn
Gough W J	Company Charges (1996 UK) – 2nd edn
Groves P, et al	Intellectual Property and the Internal Market of the European Community (1993 UK)
Gurry F	Breach of Confidence (1984 UK)
Harris, O'Boyle and Warbrick	Law of the Convention on Human Rights (2000 UK) – 2nd edn
Hill C	Maritime Law (1995 UK) – 4th edn
Holden J	Law and Practice of Banking (1990 UK) – 5th edn
Hoskin, E	VAT Case Digest – UK and Community Law (1991 UK)
Inglis-Jones N	The Law and Occupational Pension Schemes (1989 UK)

Ivamy H	Chalmer's Marine Insurance (1993 UK) – 10th edn
Jackson R M and Powell J L	Professional Negligence (1992 UK) – 3rd edn
Jones C, van der Wonde M, Lewis X	EEC Competition Law Handbook (1990 – 1993 UK)
Kelly P and Attree R	European Product Liability (1997 UK)
Kerly	Kerly's Law of Trade Marks and Trade Names (2001 UK) – 13th edn
Kerr	Kerr on the Law and Practice as to Receivers (1989 UK) – 17th edn
Laddie H, Prescott P and Victoria M	The Modern Law of Copyright and Designs (2000 UK)
Lasok K	European Court of Justice – Practice and Procedure (1994 UK) – 2nd edn
Lester and Pannick	Human Rights and Practice (2004 UK)
von Lewinski S	WIPO Treaties 1996 (2000 UK)
Lindley	Lindley on the Law of Partnership (1984 UK)
	Lindley and Banks on Partnership (1990 UK)
Linell A	The Law of Names (1938 UK)
MacGillivray and Parkington	Insurance Law (1988 UK)
McGregor H	Damages (1988 UK)
McGuffie K C, Fugeman P A and Gray P V	British Shipping Laws (1964/70 UK)
Margo R D	Aviation Insurance (2000 UK) – 3rd edn
Milson S F	Historical Foundations of the Common Law (1981 UK)
Murdoch J R	Law of Estate Agency and Auctions (1994 UK) – 3rd edn
Moore M	Managing Lawyers (1991 UK)
Napley, Sir D	The Technique of Persuasion (1991 UK) – 4th edn
Newbold W	Organising Lawyers (1991 UK)
Odgers	Principles of Pleading and Practice (1975 UK)
Ogus A I	The Law of Damages (1973 UK)
O'Keeffe	Law Relating to Trade Descriptions (1980 UK)
Oppenheim C	The Legal and Regulatory Environment for Electronic Information (1999 UK) – 3rd edn
Ovey E and Waters M	Building Societies Act 1986 (1987)
Paget	Law of Banking (1996 UK) – 11th edn
Palmer	Palmer's Company Law (1987 UK)
Parris J	Retention of Title (1982 UK);
	Effective Retention of Title Clauses (1986 UK)
Parry and Clark	Law of Succession (1996 UK) 10th edn
Phibson	Evidence (1982 UK)
Picarda	The Law relating to Receivers, Managers and Administrators (2000 UK) – 3rd edn
Powell-Smith V	Problems in Construction Claims (1990 UK)

Power V J G	European Shipping Law (1993 UK)
Quigley C and Collins A	EC State Aid: law and policy (2003 UK) – Hart Publishing
Reed C	Internet Law – Text and Materials (2000 UK)
Richardson D	Negotiable Instruments (1983 UK)
Rowlatt, Marks and Moss	Law of Principal and Surety (1982 UK)
Russell	The Law of Arbitration (1982 UK)
Salmond and Heuston	The Law of Torts (1996 UK) – 21st edn
Salter R	The Modern Law of Guarantees (2000 UK)
Shaw Sir S and Smith E D	Law of Meetings (1979 UK)
Shawcross and Beaumont	Air Law (2000 UK) – 4th edn – looseleaf
Snell	Snell's Principles of Equity (1990 UK) – 29th edn
Spenser J R and Flin R	The Evidence of Children: the law and the psychology (1993 UK) – 2nd edn
Stone M	Cross-Examination in Criminal Trials (1995 UK)
Street	Street on Torts (1999 UK) – 10th edn
Stroud	Stroud's Judicial Dictionary of words and phrases (2000 UK) – 6th edn
Terrell	Law of Patents (1982 UK)
Tettenborn A M	Law of Restitution in England and Ireland (1996 UK) – 2nd edn
Theobald	Theobald on Wills (2001 UK) – 16th edn
Tiberg H	The Law of Demurrage (1995 UK) – 4th edn
Wadlow C	The Law of Passing off (1995 UK) – 2nd edn
Walker C	The Prevention of Terrorism in British Law (1992 UK) – 2nd edn
Wallace R	Refugees and Asylum – A Community Perspective (1996 UK)
Warburton J	Unincorporated Associations (1992 UK) – Sweet and Maxwell
Weinberg and Blank	Take-overs and Mergers (1989 UK)*
Wharton	Whartons Law Lexicon (1938 UK) – 14th edn
Whish R	Competition Law (2000 UK) – 4th edn
White C	Law for Northern Ireland Social Workers (1995 UK)
Williams and Muirhunter	The Law and Practice in Bankruptcy (1979 UK)
Wood P	The Law of Subordinated Debt (1990 UK)
Wurtzburg and Mills	Building Society Law (1989 UK)